JOSEPHUS

COMPLETE WORKS

Includes:

LIFE OF FLAVIUS JOSEPHUS
THE ANTIQUITIES OF THE JEWS
THE WARS OF THE JEWS
DISCOURSE CONCERNING HADES
SEVEN DISSERTATIONS
TABLES OF JEWISH WEIGHTS AND MEASURES
LIST OF ANCIENT TESTIMONIES AND RECORDS CITED BY JOSEPHUS
TEXTS OF THE OLD TESTAMENT PARALLEL TO JOSEPHUS' HISTORIES

20 FULL-PAGE ILLUSTRATIONS

TRANSLATED BY WILLIAM WHISTON, A.M.
Foreword by William Sanford LaSor, Ph.D., Th.D.

KREGEL PUBLICATIONS
GRAND RAPIDS, MICHIGAN 49501

This new popularly priced edition of the
COMPLETE WORKS OF FLAVIUS
JOSEPHUS is a combination of the William
Whiston translation published by William P.
Nimmo, Edinburgh, Scotland in 1867 and the
Standard Edition published by Porter and
Coates, Philadelphia, Pennsylvania.

Library of Congress Catalog Card Number 60-15405
ISBN 0-8254-2951-X (cl)
ISBN 0-8254-2952-8 (pb)

First Kregel Publications edition 1960.
Reprinted in 1963, 1964, 1966, 1967, 1969,
1970, 1971, 1972, 1973, 1974, 1976, 1977,
1978, 1980, 1981, 1982.

Printed in The United States of America

CONTENTS

CONTENTS

LIST OF ILLUSTRATIONS

FOREWORD

William Sanford LaSor

Josephus, or more accurately Joseph ben Matthias, was born the year Gaius (better known as Caligula) acceded to the throne of the Roman Empire, A.D. 37, and died sometime after A.D. 100. He was the son of a priestly family and through his Hasmonean mother could boast of royal blood. For the biographical details we are completely dependent on his own works, specifically his *Life* and *Wars of the Jews*. In brief we can divide his life into two parts, each about thirty-three years in length: the first half could be described as the life of Joseph ben Matthias and Jewish priest, general, and prisoner; the second half, with some reservations, as the life of Flavius Josephus the Roman citizen and author. In all fairness we must add that even the Roman Josephus was a Jew and was doubtless writing to honor his fellow countrymen and to defend Judaism. He never regained the confidence of his own people, however, and even down to modern times has been looked upon as a renegade.

The young Joseph was precocious, and when he was only fourteen rabbis came to him for advice. At the age of sixteen, he set himself to learn at first hand the tenets of the three major sects of Judaism, proposing to spend some time as a member of each group. He began by adopting the ascetic life under the influence of Banus — it would seem from the description that Banus was an Essene — and he continued for three years. At the age of nineteen, Josephus joined the Pharisees, and remained in that sect for the rest of his life. Obviously, this does not allow time for a careful consideration of the Sadducees, nor, for that matter, for any personal experience of the Pharisees — unless, of course, we deduct time spent on studying the Pharisees from the three years under Banus. It is possible that Josephus means for us to understand that he spent a year on each of three sects, and then made his decision. He tells us little about the Sadducees, and his information on the Essenes seems to be dependent on others, particularly Philo; we are forced to conclude, therefore, that however good were his intentions, he failed to realize them fully.

In A.D. 64, when he was about twenty-six, Josephus went to Rome to obtain the release of certain priests who had been sent there by Felix to be tried by Nero. On the way, like Paul, Josephus was ship-wrecked. His goal was achieved with the aid of the Jewish actor Aliturus and the Emperor's wife Poppaea whom Josephus calls "God-fearing" (perhaps indicating that she was a proselyte to Judaism). That was the year of the burning of Rome.

Josephus' visit to Rome apparently opened his eyes to the fact that Rome could be neither defeated nor defied, and he returned to his own land determined to work for peace. The Roman governor of Syria, Florus, was more interested in fanning the embers of hatred into a blazing war. The two hot spots were Jerusalem and Caesarea — the latter being the seat of the governor. In A.D. 66, Cestius Gallus, who had meantime become governor, led a Roman force against Jerusalem, but for some reason that cannot be fully understood, he decided to retreat; the Jewish forces pursued the Romans, and in the pass at Beth-horon the Roman Twelfth Legion was put to rout. It never recovered from the disgrace.

Josephus seems to have been convinced against his earlier judgment and cast his lot with the Jewish revolt. The rout of the Twelfth Legion took place in the autumn of A.D. 66, and Vespasian's forces arrived in the spring of the following year. It is not clear what Josephus' office and mission were, but he was in Galilee, either as general in charge of the Jewish forces (*Wars of the Jews*, II, xx, 4) or as an arbitrator to pacify those who were agitating for war (*Life* 28-29). Perhaps he was playing a double rôle. When the forces of Vespasian advanced, Josephus was deserted by most of his army, and he withdrew to the fortress of Jotapata where he withstood a siege for six weeks. At last he was forced to surrender to the Romans (July A.D. 67).

Josephus made a remarkable prophecy — some would say he was "inspired" — that Vespasian would one day become Emperor. In itself, this was almost unthinkable, since the Julian (or Caesarean) line was still occupying the throne and no Emperor had yet been created outside of Rome. Who would have thought that less than a year later, Nero's suicide would bring the family of the Caesars to an end, or that two years later Vespasian would be named Emperor by his legions? The prophecy seems to have given Josephus a place of privilege from the start, for he was more of a reporter, interpreter, and go-between than a prisoner.

With the death of Nero and the hectic period that followed, during which time there were three emperors and constant rebellion in Rome, the war with the Jews was suspended. When Vespasian was named Emperor, Josephus was freed and accompanied him to Alexandria, taking the name Flavius, the family name of Vespasian. With the resumption of the Jewish War, Josephus returned to Jerusalem with Titus the son of the Emperor and witnessed the destruction of Jerusalem. Because of his activities he earned the bitter hatred of the Jews, for he continuously went around the walls of the city advocating surrender; at the same time, he was suspected of treachery by the Romans. It can be said with reasonable certainty, I think, that he was acting in the interest of his people, for it was obvious that their stubborn refusal to surrender could only result in the complete destruction of the city (which Rome apparently did not desire) and even of the entire population.

After the destruction of Jerusalem, Josephus was given a tract of land near Jerusalem, a number of books, and the chance to retire to a life of quiet contemplation. He chose, however, to return to Rome with Titus, where he became a client of the Flavian family, received Roman citizenship, and was commissioned to write a history of the Jewish people. Josephus maintained his position under succeeding emperors, but with the death of Titus he seems to have shifted his purpose slightly, becoming an apologist for the Jewish people rather than an impartial historian. In his *Life* he mentions King Agrippa II as already dead, which requires a date later than A.D. 100, but of the date or the circumstances of the end of his life we have no record.

Josephus can be characterized as an egotist and opportunist who was not also without redeeming qualities. If there was an unexplained survival in a death pact with his colleagues that may sound as though he used marked sticks when the lots were drawn, if there was collaboration with Rome in the war against his own people, there is also a reasonableness in his view that Rome could not be defeated, and there is likewise the sobering truth that no one, even the greatest of patriots, could have persuaded the Jewish fanatics to give up their hopeless revolt. His domestic life reflects something of his nature, for he was married three times, perhaps four; he was deserted by one wife and divorced another.

Josephus' first literary work was the *Wars of the Jews,* published in the closing years of the reign of Vespasian. Since at that time Josephus was not confident of his ability to write in good Greek style, he composed the work first in Aramaic. According to his own word, he translated it into Greek; scholars, however, can find little trace of translation style, and are inclined to the view that Josephus rewrote the book (or probably had other writers work on it) in Greek. The *Wars of the Jews* was written under the commission of the Emperor, and can be looked upon as a bit of propaganda, designed to deter others who might have been tempted to revolt (*Wars of the Jews* III, v, 8). The title, on the analogy of Caesar's *Gallic War,* is probably to be understood from the Roman viewpoint: the war against the Jews, rather than the Jewish War against Rome. It is Josephus' most carefully written work.

His *Antiquities of the Jews* was published about fifteen years later (A.D. 93 or 94). It is obviously patterned after the *Roman Antiquities* of Dionysius of Halicarnassus published a century earlier (the titles are markedly similar: *Romaic Archaeology* and *Judaic Archeology;* likewise the division of each work into twenty books). Josephus is no longer writing by commission of the Emperor, for the Emperor's name occurs only once (to date the work), and the dedication is to Epaphroditus. The author's purpose is no longer to exalt Rome or to warn those who would rebel; he is now seeking to exalt the Jewish people in the eyes of the Greco-Roman world. For the most part, Josephus has drawn his material from the Bible (the Greek version, or Septuagint), to which he has added some legendary material and some details from secular historians. Except for the period of Josephus' own life, however, the work offers little of historical value beyond that which is already recorded in the Scriptures of his people.

The *Life* was written, as we have mentioned, shortly after A.D. 100, principally as an apology for his own life, to defend himself against charges made by Justus of Tiberias concerning Josephus' conduct during the war in Galilee.

Against Apion is an apology for Judaism in which Josephus evaluates the ideals of Hellenism and shows its deficiencies, while at the same time showing the excellencies of the Jewish religion.

The relationship of Josephus to the New Testament documents has been frequently discussed, and this brief foreword is not the place to enter into the discussion. We can only point out the principal passages and the attitudes toward them. Josephus' reference to Jesus Christ is found in *Antiquities of the Jews* XVIII, iii, 3. Most modern scholars would deny the authenticity of the passage, claiming either (a) that it was wholly a Christian interpolation or (b) that it was worked over by Christian hands. The passage concerning John the Baptist occurs in *Antiquities of the Jews* XVIII, v, 2, and that concerning James the brother of Jesus in the same book XX, ix, 1. Scholars are generally convinced that editors have worked over these passages. In my opinion, a reasonable position is taken by the great translator of Josephus, H. St. John Thackeray,[1] who holds that the passages are the work of Josephus, and that a Christian censor or copyist has made slight omissions and alterations which have distorted the original account, giving it "a wholly different complexion." Josephus' account of the death of Herod Agrippa I is found in *Antiquities of the Jews* XIX, viii, 2, and has often been quoted in connection with Luke's description in Acts 12:20-23. The two records supplement each other nicely, and can only by distorted interpretation be taken as contradictory. The whole problem of Luke's dependence on Josephus can not be discussed here. The most critical passage is Acts 5:36-37 compared with *Antiquities of the Jews* XX, v, 1-2. The two accounts are so different that we would be forced to suppose that Luke was careless to the point of stupidity if he had made use of Josephus and garbled the account so completely. It seems more reasonable to suppose that the two passages refer to different events.[2] The ability of Josephus as a historian, in my opinion, does not compare favorably with Luke's ability as a historian, wherever we can check their works — a point which we ought to keep in mind when discussing the relationship between Luke and Josephus.

With the discovery of the *Dead Sea Scrolls* in 1947 and the following years, Josephus has become once more the focus of scholarly attention. Most scholars will agree that the community that produced the Dead Sea Scrolls, located in what is now known as *Qumran,* was in some way closely related to the Essenes. It is well known that one of our principal sources of information concerning this sect is Josephus. Accordingly, Josephus has been studied in fine detail for any clues that might shed further light on the Qumran community. Now I would not want to deprecate the work that scholars have done in this area; certainly I myself have combed Josephus for light on the Dead Sea sect. Yet it would be generally admitted, I believe, that in spite of his claim that he studied the Jewish sects at first hand, Josephus made use of other sources when he wrote about the Essenes. He does not exhibit the first-hand knowledge in this area that he does, for example, in describing the Jewish wars. This has therefore forced all of us who have worked in the subject to handle Josephus with great caution. In general we can say

---

[1] *Josephus the Man and the Historian* (New York: Jewish Institute of Religion Press, 1929), pp. 125-153.

[2] Cf. E. von Dobschütz, "Josephus," Hastings' *Dictionary of the Apostolic Church* (New York: Charles Scribner's Sons, 1922), vol. 1, p. 653.

that the Qumran fellowship as portrayed in its own literature is not exactly the same as the Essenes as pictured in Josephus.[3] There are several possible explanations of the differences: (1) the two groups may have been entirely distinct, which seems unlikely in the geographical location involved; (2) there may have been considerable development of the Qumran group between the time of the writing of its documents (let us say, mid-first century B.C.) and the time of Josephus' experience (c. A.D. 50); this is highly probable; (3) there may have been different sects within the Essenes, since Josephus suggests that they were located in various parts of the land, and the group described by Josephus could have differed in various ways from the group at Qumran; this too is quite probable; or (4) Josephus may have given us a distorted picture of the Essenes, reflecting inaccuracies which he found in Philo. Perhaps a combination of these factors should be considered. It seems reasonable to conclude that the continuing study of Josephus and the Dead Sea Scrolls will clarify many points in both bodies of writing.[4]

A word about the translator of this edition of Josephus is in order. *William Whiston,* mathematician and theologian, was born at Norton, Leicestershire, December 9, 1667, and died August 22, 1752. He received the B.A. degree from Cambridge in 1690, was appointed deputy to Newton's professorship in 1701, and succeeded Newton at Cambridge in 1703. His lectures on mathematics and natural philosophy, together with his scientific experiments, led him to be the first to popularize the theories of Newton. In the course of his theological investigations he became a convinced Arian, and set forth his views in an essay which led to the loss of his professorship in 1710. From that time, he lived in London, lecturing, writing, and receiving gifts from his friends. He remained in the Church of England until 1747, when he joined the Baptists so he would not have to hear the Athanasian Creed repeated in the service. Some idea of the breadth of his interests can be gained from the fact that he published works on science, fulfilled prophecy, theology, and ordination to the clergy. He held that the Tatars were the lost tribes and believed that the millennium would begin in 1766.

His translation of Josephus appeared in 1737, and has been reprinted many times. The text on which it was based is no longer accepted as the best text, and Whiston was not the best-equipped translator for the task. Accordingly, the work has many deficiencies. However, it remains to the present the *best complete English translation of Josephus.* The work of H. St. John Thackeray, for the *Loeb Classical Library,* was interrupted by his death in 1930, when he had completed the *Life,* the *Wars of the Jews,* and the first five books and part of the sixth of the *Antiquities.* The work was carried on by the brilliant American scholar Ralph Marcus, whose untimely death on Christmas day 1956 once again interrupted the work. The Loeb edition

[3] Cf. W. S. LaSor, *Amazing Dead Sea Scrolls and the Christian Faith* (revised edition; Chicago: Moody Press, 1959), pp. 177-189; Millar Burrows, *More Light on the Dead Sea Scrolls* (New York: Viking Press, 1958), pp. 273-274.

[4] For a bibliography of works in this area, see W. S. LaSor, *Bibliography of the Dead Sea Scrolls 1948-1957* (Pasadena, Calif.: The Library, Fuller Theological Seminary, 1958), §§ 2763, 3101-3109, 3801. It is my privilege to continue to publish Qumran bibliography in *Revue de Qumrân,* subject indices for which will be found in the last issue of each year's volume.

of Josephus, excellent as it is, remains therefore incomplete. Moreover, because of the fact that it contains the Greek text on alternate pages facing the translation the Loeb edition is much more expensive than the average reader, who perhaps cannot handle the Greek text anyway, either can afford or is willing to pay. We are therefore grateful to *Kregel Publications* for making available to the English-speaking world an inexpensive edition of the Complete Works of Josephus.

WILLIAM SANFORD LASOR, PH.D., TH.D.
FULLER THEOLOGICAL SEMINARY
PASADENA, CALIFORNIA

8 October 1960

INTRODUCTORY ESSAY

BY THE

REV. HENRY STEBBING, D.D.

VALUABLE as are the remains of classical antiquity, the Works of Josephus may be placed, at least, on a level with the most esteemed monuments of ancient learning. While the historians of Greece and Rome inform us of events connected with perishable states and polities, the annals of the Jewish people enable us to trace the progress of dispensations, the importance and stability of which, instead of diminishing, are perpetually on the increase.

The writings of Josephus may be classed under the two heads of historical and controversial; the former comprehending the Antiquities, and the Wars of the Jews; and the latter, his treatise against Apion, and some essays of minor character. His earliest production was the history of the memorable and terrific war which ended in the downfal of his nation. This work seems to have been commenced with no higher view than that of giving a general and popular account of the scenes in which he had been engaged. It was, therefore, originally written in Syro-chaldaic, or in the common language of the Jews inhabiting Palestine. When Josephus arrived at Rome, he found numerous accounts of the war in circulation. Some of these narratives were by persons who had but limited means of learning the truth. Others were the production of men who wrote in a spirit of bitter prejudice. Even among those who had some portion of the ability and information necessary to such an undertaking, none, perhaps, could be found so thoroughly well prepared for the undertaking as Josephus. Greatly to the benefit of posterity, therefore, he employed his first days of repose in the preparation of his work for a more extended circulation. The Greek language was, at that time, understood by most persons of even an ordinary degree of intelligence. It was read and spoken commonly among a large portion of his own people. The Septuagint translation of the Bible had rendered it venerable in their eyes, and must have obliged the priestly order, to which Josephus belonged, to cultivate it with more than ordinary diligence. In this popular and elegant language, therefore, he put forth his work, and the admiration with which it was received confirmed, at once, the opinion of his genius and merit entertained by the greatest men of his time. His qualifications were the better estimated from the candour which circumstances, as well as nature, taught him to cultivate. Faithful to the duties of patriotism, he was yet sufficiently awake to the vices, to the folly and obstinacy, of his countrymen. This enabled him to view and speak of things with a liberal mind. He manifested a tender regret for the fall of his nation, well calculated to conciliate the affections of the people whose sufferings he shared; but he had too much gratitude not to refrain from violating the dignity of those by whom they had been conquered, for he was in the daily habit of experiencing their bounty and their tolerance. The real defects of his work, moreover, were not such as could be readily detected by popular readers. They consisted chiefly of errors in the early part of the narrative, and were confined to a period of Jewish history, the interest of which would be greatly diminished by the awful grandeur of that which described the fall of the commonwealth.

The second great work of Josephus occupies the first place in the modern editions of his writings, but was not composed till about eighteen years after the History of the Jewish Wars. This interesting production of his matured mind was undertaken with the desire of giving to the world a narrative which might remove the prejudices entertained against his nation. He was evidently ambitious of imitating the celebrated classical historians, and of relating the events, so dear to the memory of his people, in a style which might render the subject acceptable to the learned and accomplished of all nations. This feeling was natural, and in many respects laudable. But it exposed him to dangers peculiar to the matters of which he had to treat. There was one grand and authoritative source of information. It bore the seal of Divine inspiration, and had been received, from generation to generation, as the sublime record of God's dealings with his people. To this primary fountain of information an honest historian must necessarily have turned with profound reverence. From this he must have felt it his duty to draw the most important parts of his narrative; nor could he regard it as allowable, we should have supposed, to place any other source of intelligence in competition with one so superior to the ordinary foundations of historical truth.

But Josephus had designed his work for the use of Gentile readers. He was anxious to inspire them with respect for a faith hitherto despised. In order to effect this, he deemed it necessary to modify certain parts of his narrative, lest the naked facts might strengthen, rather than allay, the prejudices which it was his object to overcome. Such, at least, is one of the supposed reasons of those discrepancies which exist between the history of Josephus and that of Scripture. That he was justified in even the minutest departure from the plain statements of the Bible, few believers in revelation would venture to assert. But he has had many apologists; and it has been suggested that, in his time, there were other sacred books existing, besides those received into the canon of Scripture, and which, though not of equal authority, were notwithstanding held in great reverence by the Jewish people. It is also observed, that the Rabbinical traditions were regarded, at this period, as of indisputable weight; and, still further, that it is not known whether he took as his authority the original text of the Hebrew Bible, or a version, or paraphrase.*

These suggestions are worthy of attention, but they do not completely exonerate the historian from the charge of having either weakly yielded too much to the desire of conciliating his readers, or made a bad estimate of the value of the materials before him. It has been thought by some that he might frequently write from mere memory. This could only be excused on the supposition that he could

---

* De ipso Josepho non est prætereundem quod ex sacris Hebræorum litteris origines suas translaturum se est pollicitus, neque subtrahendo quicquam, neque addendo, id eum pari fide non præstitisse. Eodem consilio, quo Persis nuper Hieronymus Xaverius, Jesuita, interpolatam a se evangelicam dedit historiam, etiam Græcis ille rerum in V. Testamento gestarum transmisit memoriam. Nonnulla, quæ erant in Canone, supprimens, alia (ut quum Salomoni verba gratia pro XL. regni anni) LXXX. tribuit, et in numero talentorum argenti, ad templi usum a Davide relicto, 1 Chron. xxii. 14, centum millia pro mille millibus substituit. Minuitans, atque de Scriptis Apocryphis non pauca adjiciens, uti in ejus de Moyse trienni, de eodem juvene cum Æthiopibus bellum gerente, de Tharbi, regis Æthiopum filia, connubium ejus expetente, et aliis ejusdem farinæ narrationibus licet perspicere. Jacobus Usserius, in Epis. ad Lud. Capellum, p. 42.

not, at times, get access to the necessary documents, a notion which seems plainly contradicted by the fact, that he was the keeper of the sacred books, the possession of which must have enabled him readily to correct any error admitted into the first impression of his work.

It would be difficult, indeed, to advance an argument sufficiently strong to clear him from the charge of not having given that constant attention to the simple narrative of the Bible, which might have prevented those discrepancies, and therefore errors, to be found in his Antiquities. But while it must be acknowledged that his apologists have scarcely succeeded in their plea, it is almost equally clear that he has been criticised by others with too great strictness and asperity. " Baronius," says Casaubon, " never omits any opportunity of abusing Josephus. But if all his errors, I do not speak of those in which he departs from Scripture, and for which he cannot be excused, were put together, they would scarcely amount to a hundredth part of those admitted by Eusebius alone, either into his Chronicle, or other portions of his works."† Whatever construction, however, may be put upon the fact, that the uninspired writer is wanting in a close adherence to the Bible narrative, there is this valuable lesson to be drawn from such discrepancies, Scripture remains alone, in its separate and sublime authority. Apart from, and infinitely exalted above, all other sources of information, the very pride and imperfections of those who would imitate or rival it, serve but the more to prove its Divine excellence. But for the variations in Josephus, he might imperceptibly have been set up as equal to writers chosen by God to describe his ways and doings. The Antiquities would have become a substitute for the Bible ; and some men would probably have rejoiced to exchange the plain and succinct account, the exquisite beauty of which is only completely visible to spiritual understandings, for the classical and brightly-coloured style of the mere historian. It is, perhaps, in the simple circumstance, that he aimed only at being an historian, that he sought to imitate models framed in a spirit, and fitted for materials, wholly different to those peculiar to his subject, that we may most readily find the cause of the errors with which his work may be fairly charged. He paraphrased and adorned the general statement of facts, not with the desire of falsifying, but by yielding to his literary tastes, and to those of the people for whom he wrote. The temptation under which a writer labours, when detailing sublime and mysterious occurrences, and which, though convinced of their truth himself, he trembles lest others may doubt, is of no ordinary kind. He fears lest the mode of his relating the facts should be wanting in earnestness and dignity. They have appeared to him bright and noble under the shining light of his own imagination ; and he easily yields to the flattering suggestion, that by its use he may make the record, in this its somewhat modified structure, more acceptable than it was likely to be in its simpler form.

So far was Josephus from being regarded by ancient Christian writers as a wilful offender against the veracity of history, that he is commonly honoured in their treatises with the name of Philalethes, or, the lover of truth.* That he was not ignorant of the importance of fidelity, as the first characteristic of a good historian, is evident from his own remarks. Speaking, in his Life, of one who had violated

† Fabricii Bibliotheca Græca, Art. Jos.

* Fabricii Bibliotheca Græca, Art. Jos. Eusebius, the ecclesiastical historian, speaks of him as worthy of all credit, lib. iii. c. 9. Sozomen names him as equally celebrated among the Romans and the Jews, Hist. Eccles. lib. i. c. 1. And Evagrius speaks of his history as copious, and highly valuable, lib. v. c. 24.

the truth, he says, "I have a mind to say a few things to Justus, who hath himself written a history concerning these affairs; as also to others who profess to write history, but have little regard to truth, and are not afraid, either out of ill-will or good-will to some persons, to relate falsehoods. These men do like those who compose forged deeds and conveyances, and because they are not brought to the like punishment with them, care not for the truth." At the conclusion of the eleventh chapter of the tenth book of the Antiquities, he says, "Now as to myself, I have so described these matters as I have found them and read them. But if any one is inclined to another opinion about them, let him enjoy his different sentiments without any blame from me." But the personal character of a writer must not be passed over·in the estimate taken of the honesty of his narrative. In this respect Josephus may claim honourable attention. The predominant sentiment of his writings is veneration for God and his providence, nor does he omit any opportunity of showing the value of integrity, or the supreme beauty of holiness. His faults may, therefore, fairly be ascribed to somewhat of timidity on the one side, and of literary vanity on the other. Most of the errors with which he has been charged are clearly referable to these sources. Of the others, which cannot be so accounted for, there are some that appear to have originated in the different opinions which prevailed among the Jews of his time, and threw no small obscurity over portions of the Scripture narrative; while the remainder, whether omissions, or statements plainly opposed to the inspired history, must be left without conjecture, and are better disposed of by the acknowledgment that such discrepancies cannot be accounted for, unless by suppositions which involve us in new difficulties.

It is somewhat curious that the two severest critics of Josephus should be the Romanist historian Baronius, and the sceptic Bayle; the one little attentive to the rules of historical evidence, and readily admitting into his work whatever the flood of common tradition cast up; the other anxious only to discover differences in the language of those who acknowledged the divinity of revelation, that he might, by attacking them separately, destroy the treasure equally dear to both. The latter, in a pretended fit of zeal, observes, "I have been long indignant against Josephus, and those who spare him on this subject. A man who made open profession of Judaism, the law of which was founded on the divinity of Scripture, dares to recount things otherwise than he read of them in the book of Genesis. He changes, he adds, he suppresses circumstances; in a word, he puts himself in opposition to Moses in such a manner that one of them must be a false historian." This statement involves a gross injustice, and is as illogical as it is unjust. Two writers may assuredly disagree in some points, without exposing themselves to the sweeping charge of falsehood as their general character. If disagreement in a few instances should oblige us to consider, that of the writers so differing only one can be worthy of credit, and that, consequently, the rest ought to be regarded as undeserving of any attention, the number of historical references would soon be diminished to such a degree, that the next step would be the annihilation of history altogether. The fact is, that wherever human inquiry begins, human error will be introduced, in greater or less proportion. There will, accordingly, be discrepancies in the statement of witnesses; but, except in the points where they precisely differ, they may be in such general harmony, that each may strengthen the cause of each, and neither the one nor the other, notwithstanding their occasional contradictions, merit the charge of injustice or dishonesty. A very slight comparison of the most esteemed historians will afford ample illustrations of this fact. The experience gathered in the collection of evidence of any kind tends to the same purpose, and plainly shows that several witnesses to a narrative may differ in many minor points, yet be highly deserving of credit as to the main and more important facts.

Such are the two great historical works of Josephus. They are followed by his celebrated treatise on the Antiquities of the Jews, a production not less admired than his former volumes for elegance of style and copiousness of learning.* Jerome speaks of it with astonishment, and declares himself unable to tell how a Jew, confined as the learned of his nation were to the study of their own books, should have become so extensively acquainted with Grecian literature. The object of the work was to defend the Jews against the scorn of Gentile philosophers and infidels. Apion, and others, had attempted to throw ridicule on their high pretensions to antiquity. Their history, it was said, occupied no place in the records of those great writers to whom the world looked for information. It was almost unknown; while that of the Egyptians, Carthaginians, Greeks, and others, filled the volumes of authors read and admired in every corner of the earth. Josephus produced facts, as well as arguments, in confutation of this species of attack. The nations, he contended, to whose writers the appeal had been made against his own, were indebted for all their learning to those more ancient countries with which the Jews had early intercourse. They were known, moreover, to have been singularly inattentive to the careful chronicling of events. This is abundantly proved by the contradictions existing in the works of their most popular authors; while, on the contrary, in regard to the Jews, there were but twenty-two books acknowledged by the nation, and these had the seal of remote antiquity, and the authority of works written by men in high public offices, and endowed with the richest gifts of Divine wisdom. The whole argument is worked out in a masterly and lucid style; nor could even the modern reader find a more powerful statement in favour of the authenticity of the ancient Scriptures, or of the great truths of Jewish history.

In the second part of the treatise, the writer enters upon the task of answering those more general accusations against the Jews, which contributed so greatly to render them objects of hatred among the proud and ignorant Gentiles. Their laws and customs, the ordinary conduct of their affairs, the most conspicuous features of their personal character, had all afforded topics of insulting comment. Josephus answers his assailants with a keen and comprehensive view of the odious follies of which they were themselves guilty, and then shows that the customs which had provoked their scorn rested upon principles which merited the most profound respect.

The writings of which we have given this brief account must have exercised, in ancient times, no slight degree of influence on the minds of inquiring men. This is sufficiently evidenced by the high position which their author continued to hold, for many years, in the court of the most accomplished of Roman emperors.† The style again in which he writes shows not only his confidence in the importance of the subjects handled, but his expectation of the most profitable results from

* Eusebius speaks of this work as worthy of great esteem, and as containing answers to the calumnies of Apion, the grammarian, and others who had endeavoured to cast doubts upon the origin of the Jews. Eccles. Hist. lib. iii. c. 9.

† He was, says Sozomen, as highly honoured, ἐπιδοξότατος, by the Romans as the Jews. Hist. Eccles. lib. i. c. 1.

his labours. Rome, at the period when he wrote, was filled with men deeply engaged in religious speculation. The spirit of the ancient times, when war only furnished employment for active minds, was rapidly departing, or submitting itself to the influence of a change destined to present every principle of society under a new form. Superstition and philosophy had joined hands. Hosts of theories, of creeds, and rites, from the farthest corners of the earth, had begun to establish themselves in the midst of cities and provinces celebrated for their refinement. It was no longer beneath the dignity of the sternest man to inquire, if not openly, yet secretly, into the pretensions of these novel systems, and to try whether they might not present some hitherto neglected means of warding off approaching ills.

In such a state of the public mind, the common rumours afloat respecting the religion of the Jews could scarcely fail to attract attention. However despised the people, and despised especially they were at this period, so ancient a faith, and one the fundamental doctrine of which was in accordance with the most approved philosophers, must still have claimed at least a share of the awakened curiosity. But as yet no work existed from which information might be gained as to the real origin and institutions of this remarkable nation. The notions commonly entertained respecting them were derived from sources utterly undeserving of credit. Some portions of the Scriptures had been brought before the notice of a few diligent students; but they were altogether a sealed volume to the great mass of those who might, notwithstanding, have a very sincere desire to become acquainted with Jewish antiquities. There were, moreover, floating traditions which had no small weight with the mass of the people, and the origin of which could easily be traced to Palestine, and the mysterious oracles of its inhabitants. This would furnish still stronger motives for inquiry into their real doctrines and history. That a mighty Deliverer, a lofty Renovator of the human race, was to arise out of the East, had long been a well-known report among heathen nations. The boastful claims of the Jews, whose devotion and patriotism would never allow them to keep silence on this point; the increasing importance of the Christians, speaking a similar language, and referring their own hopes and triumphs to a Leader sprung from this race; would yet further increase the curiosity of mankind respecting the Jews, and render the want of some work of authority every day more perceptibly understood.

Josephus had thus an open field for literary exertion. There was scarcely a subject in that age better calculated to excite attention, or reward the writer for his labour. It is not, therefore, as an obscure author, known only to his own people, and owing his limited success to the accidental interest taken in his work by Christians, that Josephus is to be viewed; but as a writer highly esteemed and popular in his age through a vast portion of the civilized world, and most probably, therefore, exercising considerable influence on religious opinion. It is almost impossible for us in these days to estimate the value or assign the rank of such a writer in times and countries like those in which he lived. Our Bibles make us intimate from childhood with the sublimest passages of ancient lore, with the most wonderful manifestations of Divine power and grace. We become familiar with the possession of this wealth, and can scarcely persuade ourselves to think of periods when the smallest portion of such spiritual treasures would have been viewed as a benefaction of marvellous worth. The information supplied by Josephus is now, as far as his Antiquities are concerned, already given to the most unlearned from the first and purest source of sacred erudition; but when no such means of instruction were open, and men had been left for ages in the dark perplexities of heathen fable, the publication of a work like his on the origin of the only religious system that could secure the admiration of thoughtful men, must have tended materially to stimulate, while it in part satisfied, the new desire of intelligence.

The tone in which such of the early Christian writers as speak of Josephus allude to his works, afford fair reason to conjecture that their circulation had been found useful to the general cause of religion. It must indeed have been difficult for a Gentile reader, of an active and honest mind, to have studied his pages, and not felt disposed to inquire for the sequel of the history. The Jew had his fatal prejudices to combat, his present, literal, earthly patriotism, pointing to the soil where his beloved city lately stood, and bounding even the farthest future with visions of its recovered glory. The Gentile, on the other hand, as he read Josephus, was free to inquire, whether the sublime plans of Jehovah might not contemplate an end commensurate with the happiness of universal man. His ignorance of conventional interpretations was an advantage to him; and learning from the uninspired historian the simple facts connected with the mightiest dispensations of Providence, he had new motives for searching the original records, and for employing his best efforts in securing to himself a name among the people of God.

But the writings of Josephus have not lost their use, notwithstanding the vast advantages now enjoyed in the general circulation of the Bible. They may still be read with profit by the careful inquirer. Little need be said respecting that portion which refers to the period subsequent to the destruction of Jerusalem. In regard to this, it is evidently of great importance to possess the account given by a contemporary and credible witness. The knowledge of what took place in an age succeeding that in the events of which we are more particularly interested, is often powerfully illustrative of the earlier epoch. Thus what Josephus tells us in the narrative of the Wars throws no small degree of light upon the character of his countrymen, not only of the period when he wrote, but of that also when every mode of thought, every custom and passion, derived unspeakable importance from its connexions, near or remote, with the awful complication of influences that brought the Redeemer to the cross. The mind of the people is exhibited in many parts of the history with a terrible distinctness of delineation. Its most striking features at that time were evidently not impressed by any sudden convulsion. The lines which an age of suffering and remorse had more deeply furrowed had been traced long before by struggles of heart and spirit, by pride and fear, by mysterious hopes and apprehensions, the fruit of those inwardly understood warnings which, finally despised, left them to unutterable misery.

The account which Josephus gives of the Jewish wars has, therefore, a manifest use beyond that of merely satisfying our curiosity as to facts. It opens the path to inquiries closely connected with the history of our religion, and brings to light many of the secret causes which operated most powerfully to the degradation and ruin of God's ancient people.

Nor has time diminished the interest attached to other parts of this author's writings. "The Antiquities," though of little value as history, when compared with the authoritative accounts of Scripture, is a work eminently calculated to assist an inquiring mind in the general investigation of ancient mysteries. Traditional evidence, traditional interpretations, and the new facts which may be supplied from the full storehouses of national memory, will never be despised by those who know how often an obscure point is cleared up when it is discovered what were the ruling sentiments of the period when the narrative was written. While, therefore, it is utterly subversive of the authority of the Bible to place tradition upon the same level, nor less inconsistent with sound reason to modify plain declarations, clearly stated doctrines, according to the uncertain temper of human wisdom, it is surely unwise to reject those helps for the confirmation or illustration of sacred history which are known to be profitably used in the study of records of every other species. Hence the value of Josephus. He was intimately acquainted with whatever had been taught by the learned of his nation. He had been familiarized in childhood to its superstitions. The spirit of popular Judaism was the chief instructor of his later years ; and as a man of education, he knew well through what revolutions and by what various trials his countrymen had been proved, instructed, and warned of God. Though from his pages, therefore, it is not often that we can add to our stock of positive knowledge, we may in many cases trace by their help the progress of error, discover its origin, and estimate the relative force of those deplorable corruptions whereby it became at last so indissolubly bound up with the national constitution.

However cautiously, moreover, we receive information from sources not of the highest authority, where our doing so may modify our notions in respect to the surer communications, it would be unreasonable to reject the knowledge which, not coming within the intention of a divine witness to render, may have been fairly the subject of interest to a human observer. It is evident that there must have been numberless very curious circumstances perpetually occurring in the period alluded to, but which were not essential to the completeness of that succinct narrative of God's proceedings which the Bible gives. From these the uninspired historian might readily gather an abundant store of remarkable incidents, and such as would confer no slight value on his work in those distant ages when it would be impossible to recover, through other means, any fragment of the past.

We cannot now tell whether Josephus employed to the best purpose the advantages which his position afforded. It is fair to presume that his good sense and ability led him to such an examination of evidence as prevented the introduction of any thing into his narrative which had not the best support that tradition could bestow. If in any case, therefore, we can consult an ancient historian with respect and confidence, Josephus will be read as a valuable guide to a most important branch of knowledge. Separating him from the inspired writers by that impassable barrier which a true reverence for Scripture will infallibly create, we may yet refresh ourselves with his vivid descriptions, his often eloquent harangues, and his not unfrequent detail of affecting incidents, which almost make us feel and hear the strong pulsations of Israel's proud and breaking heart.

The Memoir of this eminent writer, as given by himself, leaves us nothing to desire in respect to his biography, but some authentic account of his latter days. There is only a very vague tradition that he died in the reign of Domitian, and shared the fate of his beloved friend and patron Epaphroditus. But of Epaphroditus himself too little is known to give any certainty to this report. It is possible, therefore, that Josephus was allowed to spend the close of his life in some safe retreat, and in the enjoyment of that ample provision for his wants supplied him by the liberality of his earlier patrons.

Josephus, we have already seen, was esteemed in the first ages of Christianity as an author deserving a high degree of respect for research and integrity. Pious

and learned men of later ages have continued to view him in the same light. The
care bestowed upon numerous editions of his works in the original Greek proves
that they have been deemed worthy of the attention of the most erudite of modern
scholars.   Some passages in his writings have engaged the attention of several
acute critics, especially that in which he distinctly refers to the actions and character of Jesus Christ.   The controversy thence excited is one of more than ordinary interest, but, like many others of a similar character, it is so intimately connected with questions of history and opinion, that few persons are competent to
form a judgment of the relative worth of the arguments employed.

The works of Josephus were early translated into English. Thomas Lodge, who
combined in himself the several characters of poet and physician, was the first who
attempted the task.   His version was published about the year 1602, and another
in the year 1609 and 1620.   He died of the plague in 1625, and appears to have
enjoyed among his contemporaries some reputation both for talent and learning.
His translation, however, did not, it appears, satisfy the next generation, as at the
beginning of the following century Sir Roger L'Estrange, a name better known by
its connexion with that of Seneca, published a new translation, which obtained sufficient favour to secure the circulation of five editions in less than forty years.
The first of these was published at Oxford in 1700, and the second at London in
1702. The last edition of this version appeared in 1733; but was followed in the
space of four years by the first edition of Whiston's translation, a work which
speedily set aside the former versions, and obtained for its author not only the
approbation of mere general readers, but the praise of the learned as well on the
continent as in England.*

That this translation is free from errors, or the best which could be made, few
competent judges will venture to affirm.   But it would be an equal violation of
fair criticism to deny that it has great merits, or that it is equal, on the whole, to
any of the translations from ancient authors which are most popular among us.   It
has been well observed by an elegant and acute scholar, that, whatever may be the
faults of Whiston, he has in most cases caught the tone and feeling of his author,
and that the want of this merit would be but badly atoned for by a much superior
degree of grace and smoothness.

Readily allowing, however, that an improvement might be made in some parts
of Whiston's translation, he richly deserves the gratitude of the English reader
for having put him in possession of an author so valuable as Josephus, and with
so little loss as to the more important objects of such a writer.   Through his version Josephus has been made familiar to tens of thousands, who would otherwise
have remained ignorant of some of the most awful and edifying portions of Jewish history.   The fulfilment of our Lord's prophecy respecting Jerusalem, and of
earlier predictions setting forth the lamentable events which would attend the final
apostacy of Israel, is portrayed in the pages of Josephus with terrible exactness.
We may, perhaps, without presumption ascribe the existence of his works to Divine
Providence; for there are few persons who have read his narrative that have not
felt themselves more deeply impressed than ever with the solemn truths of Scripture, and the tremendous certainty of the Divine judgments.

* Nihilo tamen minus ea Whistono laus debetur, inter omnes fere omnium gentium Josephi interpretes
nullum tantâ ingenii et judicii acie, tantoque studio in vertendis hujus scriptoris operibus versatum esse.
Fabricii Bibliotheca Græca, T. V. lib. iv. c. 8, p. 47.

FLAVIUS JOSEPHUS.

THE

LIFE OF FLAVIUS JOSEPHUS

1. THE family from which I am derived is not an ignoble one, but hath descended all along from the priests; and as nobility among several people is of a different origin, so with us to be of the sacerdotal dignity, is an indication of the splendour of a family. Now, I am not only sprung from a sacerdotal family in general, but from the first of the twenty-four* courses; and as among us there is not only a considerable difference between one family of each course and another, I am of the chief family of that first course also; nay, further, by my mother I am of the royal blood; for the children of Asmoneus, from whom that family was derived, had both the office of the high priesthood and the dignity of a king for a long time together. I will accordingly set down my progenitors in order. My grandfather's father was named Simon, with the addition of Psellus: he lived at the same time with that son of Simon the high priest, who first of all the high priests was named Hyrcanus. This Simon Psellus had nine sons, one of whom was Matthias, called Ephlias: he married the daughter of Jonathan the high priest; which Jonathan was the first of the sons of Asmoneus, who was high priest, and was the brother of Simon the high priest also. This Matthias had a son called Matthias Curtus, and that in the first year of the government of Hyrcanus: his son's name was Joseph, born in the ninth year of the reign of Alexandra: his son Matthias was born in the tenth year of the reign of Archelaus; as was I born to Matthias in the first year of the reign of Caius Cæsar. I have three sons: Hyrcanus, the eldest, was born in the fourth year of the reign of Vespasian, as was Justus born in the seventh, and Agrippa in the ninth. Thus have I set down the genealogy of my family as I have found it described† in the public records, and so bid adieu to those who calumniate me, [as of a lower original.]

2. Now, my father Matthias was not only eminent on account of his nobility, but had a higher commendation on account of his righteousness; and was in great reputation in Jerusalem, the greatest city we have. I was myself brought up with my brother, whose name was Matthias, for he was my own brother, by both father and mother; and I made mighty proficiency in the improvements of my learning, and appeared to have both a great memory and understanding. Moreover, when I was a child, and about fourteen years of age, I was commended by all for the love I had to learning; on which account the high priests and principal men of the city came then frequently to me together, in order to know my opinion about the accurate understanding of points of the law; and when I was about sixteen years old, I had a mind to make trial of the several sects that were among us. These sects are three:—The first is that of the Pharisees, the second that of the Sadducees, and the third that of the Essens, as we have frequently told you; for I thought that by this means I might choose the best, if I were once acquainted with them all; so I contented myself with hard fare, and underwent great difficulties, and went through them all. Nor did I content myself with these trials only; but when I was informed that one, whose name was Banus, lived in the desert, and used no other clothing than grew upon trees, and had no other food than what grew of its own accord, and bathed himself in cold water frequently, both night and day, in order to preserve his chastity, I imitated him in those things, and continued with him three years.‡ So when I had accomplished my desires, I returned back to the city, being now nineteen years old, and began to conduct myself according to the rules of the sect of the Pharisees, which is of kin to the sect of the Stoics, as the Greeks call them.

---

* We may hence correct the error of the Latin copy of the second book Against Apion, sect. 8, (for the Greek is there lost,) which says there were then only four tribes or courses of the priests, instead of twenty-four. Nor is this testimony to be disregarded, as if Josephus there contradicted what he had affirmed here; because even the account there given better agrees to twenty-four than to four courses, while he says that each of those courses contained above 5000 men, which, multiplied by only four, will make not more than 20,000 priests; whereas the number 120,000, as multiplied by 24, seems much the most probable, they being about one-tenth of the whole people, even after the captivity, (See Ezra ii. 36-39; Neh. vii. 39-42; 1 Esd. v. 24, 25; with Ezra ii. 64; Neh. vii. 66; 1 Esd. v. 41.) Nor will this common reading or notion of but four courses of priests agree with Josephus's own further assertion elsewhere, (Antiq. b. vii. ch. xiv. sect. 7,) that David's partition of the priests into twenty-four courses had continued to that day.

† An eminent example of the care of the Jews about their genealogies, especially as to the priests, (See Against Apion, b. i. sect. 7.)

‡ When Josephus here says that from sixteen to nineteen, or for three years, he made trial of the three Jewish sects, the Pharisees, the Sadducees, and the Essens, and yet says presently, in all our copies, that he stayed besides with one particular ascetic, called *Banus*, παρ' αὐτω, *with him*, and this still before he was nineteen, there is little room left for his trial of the three other sects. I suppose, therefore, that for παρ' αὐτω, *with him*, the old reading might be παρ' αὐτοις, *with them*; which is a very small emendation, and takes away the difficulty before us. Nor is Dr Hudson's conjecture, hinted at by Mr Hall in his preface to the Doctor's edition of Josephus, at all improbable, that this Banus, by this his description, might well be a follower of John the Baptist, and that from him Josephus might easily imbibe such notions as afterwards prepared him to have a favourable opinion of Jesus Christ himself, who was attested to by John the Baptist.

3. But when I was in the twenty-sixth year of my age, it happened that I took a voyage to Rome; and this on the occasion which I shall now describe. At the time when Felix was procurator of Judea, there were certain priests of my acquaintance, and very excellent persons they were, whom on a small and trifling occasion he had put into bonds, and sent to Rome to plead their cause before Cæsar. These I was desirous to procure deliverance for; and that especially because I was informed that they were not unmindful of piety towards God, even under their afflictions, but supported themselves with figs and nuts.* Accordingly, I came to Rome, though it were through a great number of hazards, by sea; for, as our ship was drowned in the Adriatic Sea, we that were in it, being about six hundred in number,† swam for our lives all the night; when, upon the first appearance of the day, and upon our sight of a ship of Cyrene, I and some others, eighty in all, by God's providence, prevented the rest, and were taken up into the other ship: and when I had thus escaped, and was come to Dicearchia, which the Italians call Puteoli, I became acquainted with Aliturius, an actor of plays, and much beloved by Nero, but a Jew by birth; and through his interest became known to Poppea, Cæsar's wife; and took care, as soon as possible, to entreat her to procure that the priests might be set at liberty; and when, besides this favour, I had obtained many presents from Poppea, I returned home again.

4. And now I perceived innovations were already begun, and that there were a great many very much elevated in hopes of a revolt from the Romans. I therefore endeavoured to put a stop to these tumultuous persons, and persuaded them to change their minds; and laid before their eyes against whom it was that they were going to fight, and told them that they were inferior to the Romans not only in martial skill but also in good fortune, and desired them not rashly, and after the most foolish manner, to bring on the dangers of the most terrible mischiefs upon their country, upon their families, and upon themselves. And this I said with vehement exhortation, because I foresaw that the end of such a war would be most unfortunate to us. But I could not persuade them; for the madness of desperate men was quite too hard for me.

5. I was then afraid, lest, by inculcating these things so often, I should incur their hatred and their suspicions, as if I were of our enemies' party, and should run into the danger of being seized by them and slain since they were already possessed of Antonia, which was the citadel: so I retired into the inner court of the temple; yet did I go out of the temple again after Manahem and the principal of the band of robbers were put to death, when I abode among the high priests and the chief of the Pharisees; but no small fear seized upon us when we saw the people in arms, while we ourselves knew not what we should do, and were not able to restrain the seditious. However, as the danger was directly upon us, we pretended that we were of the same opinion with them; but only advised them to be quiet for the present and to let the enemy go away, still hoping that Gessius [Florus] would not be long ere he came, and that with great forces, and so put an end to these seditious proceedings.

6. But, upon his coming and fighting, he was beaten, and a great many of those that were with him fell; and this disgrace which Gessius [with Cestius] received, became the calamity of our whole nation; for those that were fond of the war were so far elevated with this success that they had hopes of finally conquering the Romans. Of which war another occasion was ministered; which was this:—Those that dwelt in the neighbouring cities of Syria seized upon such Jews as dwelt among them, with their wives and children, and slew them, when they had not the least occasion of complaint against them; for they did neither attempt any innovation or revolt from the Romans, nor had they given any marks of hatred or treacherous designs towards the Syrians; but what was done by the inhabitants of Scythopolis was the most impious and the most highly criminal of all; ‡ for when the Jews, their enemies, came upon them from without, they forced the Jews that were among them to bear arms against their own countrymen, which it is unlawful for us to do; § and when, by their assistance, they had joined battle with those who attacked them, and had beaten them, after that victory they forgot the assurances they had given these their fellow-citizens and confederates, and slew them all, being in number many ten thousands, [13,000.] The like miseries were undergone by those Jews that were the inhabitants of Damascus; but we have given a more accurate account of these things in the books of the Jewish war. I only mention them now, because I would demonstrate to my readers that the Jews' war with the Romans was not voluntary, but that, for the main, they were forced by necessity to enter into it.

7. So when Gessius had been beaten, as we have said already, the principal men of Jerusalem, seeing that the robbers and innovators had arms in great plenty, and fearing lest they, while they were unprovided with arms, should be in subjection to their enemies—which also came to be the case afterward—and, being informed that all Galilee had not yet revolted from the Romans, but that some part of it was still quiet, they sent me and two others of the priests, who were men of excellent characters, Joazar and Judas, in order to persuade the ill men there to lay down their arms, and to teach them this lesson,—That it were better to have those arms reserved for the most courageous men that the nation had, [than to be kept there,] for that it had been resolved, That those our best men should always have their arms ready against futurity, but still so that they should wait to see what the Romans would do.

8. When I had therefore received these instructions, I came into Galilee, and found the people of Sepphoris in no small agony about

---

* We may note here that religious men among the Jews, or at least those that were priests, were sometimes ascetics also, and like Daniel and his companions in Babylon, (Dan. i. 8-16,) ate no flesh, but *figs and nuts*, &c., only. This was like the ξηροφαγια, or austere diet of the Christian ascetics in Passion-Week. Constitut. v. 18.

† It has been thought the number of Paul and his companions on ship-board, (Acts xxvii. 38,) which are 276 in our copies, are too many; whereas we find here that Josephus and his companions, a very few years after the other, were about 600.

‡ See Jewish War, b. ii. ch. xviii. sect. 3.
§ The Jews might collect this unlawfulness of fighting against their brethren from that law of Moses, (Lev. xix. 16,) "Thou shalt not stand against the blood of thy neighbour;" and that, (ver. 17,) "Thou shalt not avenge, nor bear any grudge against the children of thy people, but thou shalt love thy neighbour as thyself;" as well as from many other places in the Pentateuch and Prophets. (See Antiq. b. viii. ch. viii. sect. 8.)

their country, by reason that the Galileans had resolved to plunder it, on account of the friendship they had with the Romans; and because they had given their right hand, and made a league with Cestius Gallus, the president of Syria: but I delivered them all out of the fear they were in, and persuaded the multitude to deal kindly with them, and permitted them to send to those that were their own hostages with Gessius to Dora, which is a city of Phœnicia, as often as they pleased; though I still found the inhabitants of Tiberias ready to take arms, and that on the occasion following:—

9. There were three factions in this city. The first was composed of men of worth and gravity; of these Julius Capellus was the head. Now he, as well as all his companions, Herod, the son of Miarus, and Herod, the son of Gamalus, and Compsus, the son of Compsus, (for as to Compsus's brother Crispus, who had once been governor of the city under the great king* [Agrippa], he was beyond Jordan in his own possessions;) all these persons before named gave their advice that the city should then continue in their allegiance to the Romans and to the king; but Pistus, who was guided by his son Justus, did not acquiesce in that resolution, otherwise he was himself naturally of a good and virtuous character: but the second faction was composed of the most ignoble persons, and was determined for war. But as for Justus, the son of Pistus, who was the head of the third faction, although he pretended to be doubtful about going to war, yet was he really desirous of innovation, as supposing that he should gain power to himself by the change of affairs. He therefore came into the midst of them, and endeavoured to inform the multitude that "the city Tiberias had ever been a city of Galilee; and that in the days of Herod the tetrarch, who had built it, it had obtained the principal place; and that he had ordered that the city Sepphoris should be subordinate to the city Tiberias; that they had not lost this pre-eminence even under Agrippa the father, but had retained it until Felix was procurator of Judea; but he told them, that now they had been so unfortunate as to be made a present by Nero to Agrippa, junior; and that, upon Sepphoris's submission of itself to the Romans, that was become the capital city of Galilee, and that the royal treasury and the archives were now removed from them." When he had spoken these things, and a great many more, against king Agrippa, in order to provoke the people to a revolt, he added that "this was the time for them to take arms, and join with the Galileans as their confederates, (whom they might command, and who would now willingly assist them, out of the hatred they bare to the people of Sepphoris; because they preserved their fidelity to the Romans,) and to gather a great number of forces, in order to punish them." And, as he said this, he exhorted the multitude, [to go to war;] for his abilities lay in making harangues to the people, and in being too hard in his speeches for such as opposed him, though they advised what was more to their advantage, and this by his craftiness and his fallacies, for he was not unskilful in the learning of the Greeks; and in dependence on that skill it was that he undertook to write a history of these affairs, as aiming, by this way of haranguing, to disguise the truth; but as to this man, and how ill were his character and conduct of life, and how he and his

brother were, in great measure, the authors of our destruction, I shall give the reader an account in the progress of my narration. So when Justus had, by his persuasions, prevailed with the citizens of Tiberias to take arms, nay, and had forced a great many so to do against their wills, he went out, and set the villages that belonged to Gadara and Hippos on fire; which villages were situated on the borders of Tiberias, and of the region of Scythopolis.

10. And this was the state Tiberias was now in; but as for Gischala, its affairs were thus:— When John, the son of Levi, saw some of the citizens much elevated upon their revolt from the Romans, he laboured to restrain them; and entreated them that they would keep their allegiance to them; but he could not gain his purpose, although he did his endeavours to the utmost; for the neighbouring people of Gadara, Gabara, and Sogana, with the Tyrians, got together a great army, and fell upon Gischala, and took Gischala by force, and set it on fire; and when they had entirely demolished it, they returned home. Upon which John was so enraged, that he armed all his men, and joined battle with the people forementioned; and rebuilt Gischala after a manner better than before, and fortified it with walls for its future security.

11. But Gamala persevered in its allegiance to the Romans for the reason following:—Philip, the son of Jacimus, who was their governor under king Agrippa, had been unexpectedly preserved when the royal palace at Jerusalem had been besieged; but, as he fled away, had fallen into another danger; and that was of being killed by Manahem, and the robbers that were with him; but certain Babylonians, who were of his kindred, and were then in Jerusalem, hindered the robbers from executing their design. So Philip stayed there four days, and fled away on the fifth, having disguised himself with fictitious hair, that he might not be discovered; and when he was come to one of the villages to him belonging, but one that was situated at the borders of the citadel of Gamala, he sent to some of those that were under him, and commanded them to come to him; but God hindered that his intention, and this for his own advantage also; for had it not so happened, he had certainly perished; for a fever having seized upon him immediately, he wrote to Agrippa and Bernice, and gave them to one of his freedmen to carry them to Varus, who at this time was procurator of the kingdom, which the king and his sister had intrusted him withal, while they were gone to Berytus with an intention of meeting Gessius. When Varus had received these letters of Philip, and had learned that he was preserved, he was very uneasy at it, as supposing that he should appear useless to the king and his sister, now Philip was come. He therefore produced the carrier of the letters before the multitude, and accused him of forging the same; and said, that he spake falsely when he related that Philip was at Jerusalem fighting amongst the Jews against the Romans. So he slew him. And when this freedman of Philip did not return again, Philip was doubtful what should be the occasion of his stay, and sent a second messenger with letters, that he might, upon his return, inform him what had befallen the other that had been sent before, and why he tarried so long. Varus accused this messenger also, when he came, of telling a falsehood, and slew him; for he was puffed up by the Syrians that were at Cæsarea, and had great expectations; for they said that Agrippa would be slain by the Romans for the crimes which the Jews had committed, and that he should himself take

---

* That this Herod Agrippa, the father, was of old called a *Great King*, as here appears by his coins still remaining; to which Havercamp refers us.

the government, as derived from their kings; for Varus was, by the confession of all, of the royal family, as being a descendant of Sohemus, who had enjoyed a tetrarchy about Libanus; for which reason it was that he was puffed up, and kept the letters to himself. He contrived also that the king should not meet with those writings, by guarding all the passes, lest any one should escape, and inform the king what had been done. He moreover slew many of the Jews, in order to gratify the Syrians of Cæsarea. He had a mind also to join with the Trachonites in Batanea, and to take up arms and make an assault upon the Babylonian Jews that were at Ecbatana; for that was the name they went by. He therefore called to him twelve of the Jews of Cæsarea, of the best character, and ordered them to go to Ecbatana, and inform their countrymen who dwelt there that Varus hath heard that "you intend to march against the king; but, not believing that report, he hath sent us to persuade you to lay down your arms; and that this compliance will be a sign that he did well not to give credit to those that raised the report concerning you." He also enjoined them to send seventy of their principal men to make a defence for them as to the accusation laid against them. So when the twelve messengers came to their countrymen at Ecbatana, and found that they had no designs of innovation at all, they persuaded them to send the seventy men also; who, not at all suspecting what would come, sent them accordingly. So these seventy went down to Cæsarea, together with the twelve ambassadors; where Varus met them with the king's forces, and slew them all together, with the [twelve] ambassadors, and made an expedition against the Jews of Ecbatana. But one there was of the seventy who escaped, and made haste to inform the Jews of their coming; upon which they took their arms, with their wives and children, and retired to the citadel at Gamala, leaving their own villages full of all sorts of good things, and having many ten thousands of cattle therein. When Philip was informed of these things, he also came to the citadel of Gamala; and when he was come, the multitude cried aloud, and desired him to resume the government, and to make an expedition against Varus and the Syrians of Cæsarea; for it was reported that they had slain the king. But Philip restrained their zeal, and put them in mind of the benefits the king had bestowed upon them, and told them how powerful the Romans were, and said it was not for their advantage to make war with them; and at length he prevailed with them. But now, when the king was acquainted with Varus's design, which was to cut off the Jews of Cæsarea, being many ten thousands, with their wives and children, and all in one day, he called to him Equiculus Modius, and sent him to be Varus's successor, as we have elsewhere related. But still Philip kept possession of the citadel of Gamala, and of the country adjoining to it, which thereby continued in their allegiance to the Romans.

12. Now, as soon as I was come into Galilee, and had learned this state of things by the information of such as told me of them, I wrote to the sanhedrim at Jerusalem about them, and required their direction what I should do. Their direction was, that I should continue there, and that, if my fellow-legates were willing, I should join with them in the care of Galilee. But those my fellow-legates, having gotten great riches from those tithes which as priests were their dues, and were given to them, determined to return to their own country. Yet when I desired them to stay so long, that we might first settle

the public affairs, they complied with me. So I removed, together with them, from the city of Sepphoris, and came to a certain village called Bethmaus, four furlongs distant from Tiberias; and thence I sent messengers to the senate of Tiberias, and desired that the principal men of the city would come to me: and when they were come, Justus himself being also with them, I told them that I was sent to them by the people of Jerusalem as a legate, together with these other priests, in order to persuade them to demolish that house which Herod the tetrarch had built there, and which had the figures of living creatures in it, although our laws have forbidden us to make any such figures; and I desired that they would give us leave so to do immediately. But for a good while Capellus and the principal men belonging to the city would not give us leave, but were at length entirely overcome by us, and were induced to be of our opinion. So Jesus, the son of Sapphias, one of those whom we have already mentioned as the leader of a seditious tumult of mariners and poor people, prevented us, and took with him certain Galileans, and set the entire palace on fire, and thought he should get a great deal of money thereby, because he saw some of the roofs gilt with gold. They also plundered a great deal of the furniture, which was done without our approbation; for, after we had discoursed with Capellus and the principal men of the city, we departed from Bethmaus, and went into Upper Galilee. But Jesus and his party slew all the Greeks that were inhabitants of Tiberias, and as many others as were their enemies before the war began.

13. When I understood this state of things, I was greatly provoked, and went down to Tiberias, and took all the care I could of the royal furniture, to recover all that could be recovered from such as had plundered it. They consisted of candlesticks made of Corinthian brass, and of royal tables, and of a great quantity of uncoined silver; and I resolved to preserve whatsoever came to my hand for the king. So I sent for ten of the principal men of the senate, and for Capellus, the son of Antyllus, and committed the furniture to them, with this charge, that they should part with it to nobody else but to myself. From thence, I and my fellow-legates went to Gischala, to John, as desirous to know his intentions, and soon saw that he was for innovations, and had a mind to the principality, for he desired me to give him authority to carry off that corn which belonged to Cæsar, and lay in the villages of Upper Galilee; and he pretended that he would expend what it came to in building the walls of his own city. But when I perceived what he endeavoured at, and what he had in his mind, I said I would not permit him so to do; for that I thought either to keep it for the Romans or for myself, now I was intrusted with the public affairs there by the people of Jerusalem: but, when he was not able to prevail with me, he betook himself to my fellow-legates; for they had no sagacity in providing for futurity, and were very ready to take bribes: so he corrupted them with money to decree that all that corn which was within his province should be delivered to him; while I, who was but one, was outvoted by two, and held my tongue. Then did John introduce another cunning contrivance of his; for he said that those Jews who inhabited Cæsarea Philippi, and were shut up by the order of the king's deputy there, had sent to him to desire him that, since they had no oil that was pure for their use, he would provide a sufficient quantity of such oil for them, lest they should be forced to make use of oil that

came from the Greeks, and thereby transgress their own laws. Now this was said by John, not out of his regard to religion, but out of his most flagrant desire of gain; for he knew that two sectaries were sold with them of Cæsarea for one drachma; but that at Gischala fourscore sectaries were sold for four sectaries: so he gave order that all the oil which was there should be carried away, as having my permission for so doing; which yet I did not grant him voluntarily, but only out of fear of the multitude, since, if I had forbidden him, I should have been stoned by them. When I had therefore permitted this to be done by John, he gained vast sums of money by this his knavery.

14. But when I had dismissed my fellow-legates, and sent them back to Jerusalem, I took care to have arms provided, and the cities fortified; and when I had sent for the most hardy among the robbers, I saw that it was not in my power to take their arms from them; but I persuaded the multitude to allow them money as pay, and told them it was better for them to give them a little willingly rather than to [be forced to] overlook them when they plundered their goods from them. And when I had obliged them to take an oath not to come into that country, unless they were invited to come, or else when they had not their pay given them, I dismissed them, and charged them neither to make an expedition against the Romans, nor against those their neighbours that lay round about them; for my first care was to keep Galilee in peace. So I was willing to have the principal of the Galileans, in all seventy, as hostages for their fidelity, but still under the notion of friendship. Accordingly, I made them my friends and companions as I journeyed, and set them to judge causes; and with their approbation it was that I gave my sentences, while I endeavoured not to mistake what justice required, and to keep my hands clear of all bribery in those determinations.

15. I was now about the thirtieth year of my age; in which time of life it is a hard thing for any one to escape the calumnies of the envious, although he restrain himself from fulfilling any unlawful desires, especially where a person is in great authority. Yet did I preserve every woman free from injuries; and as to what presents were offered me, I despised them, as not standing in need of them; nor indeed would I take those tithes, which were due to me as a priest, from those that brought them. Yet do I confess, that I took part of the spoils of those Syrians which inhabited the cities that adjoined to us, when I had conquered them, and that I sent them to my kindred at Jerusalem; although, when I twice took Sepphoris by force, and Tiberias four times, and Gadara once, and when I had subdued and taken John, who often laid treacherous snares for me, I did not punish [with death] either him or any of the people fore-named, as the progress of this discourse will shew. And on this account, I suppose, it was that God,* who is never unacquainted with those that do as they ought to do, delivered me still out of the hands of these my enemies, and afterwards preserved me when I fell into those many dangers which I shall relate hereafter.

16. Now the multitude of the Galileans had

* Our Josephus shews, both here and everywhere, that he was a most religious person, and one that had a deep sense of God and His providence upon his mind; and ascribed all his numerous and wonderful escapes and preservations, in times of danger, to God's blessing him, and taking care of him; and this on account of his acts of piety, justice, humanity, and charity, to the Jews his brethren.

that great kindness for me, and fidelity to me, that when their cities were taken by force, and their wives and children carried into slavery, they did not so deeply lament for their own calamities, as they were solicitous for my preservation. But when John saw this, he envied me, and wrote to me, desiring that I would give him leave to come down, and make use of the hot baths of Tiberias for the recovery of the health of his body. Accordingly, I did not hinder him, as having no suspicion of any wicked designs of his; and I wrote to those to whom I had committed the administration of the affairs of Tiberias by name, that they should provide a lodging for John, and for such as should come with him, and should procure him what necessaries soever he should stand in need of. Now at this time my abode was in a village of Galilee, which is named Cana.

17. But when John was come to the city of Tiberias, he persuaded the men to revolt from their fidelity to me, and to adhere to him; and many of them gladly received that invitation of his, as ever fond of innovations, and by nature disposed to changes, and delighting in seditions; but they were chiefly Justus and his father Pistus that were earnest for their revolt from me, and their adherence to John. But I came upon them, and prevented them; for a messenger had come to me from Silas, whom I had made governor of Tiberias, as I have said already, and had told me of the inclinations of the people of Tiberias, and advised me to make haste thither; for that if I made any delay, the city would come under another jurisdiction. Upon the receipt of this letter of Silas, I took two hundred men along with me, and travelled all night, having sent before a messenger to let the people of Tiberias know that I was coming to them. When I came near to the city, which was early in the morning, the multitude came out to meet me, and John came with them, and saluted me, but in a most disturbed manner, as being afraid that my coming was to call him to an account for what I was now sensible he was doing. So he, in great haste, went to his lodging. But when I was in the open place of the city, having dismissed the guards I had about me, excepting one, and ten armed men that were with him, I attempted to make a speech to the multitude of the people of Tiberias; and standing on a certain elevated place, I entreated them not to be so hasty in their revolt; for that such a change in their behaviour would be to their reproach, and that they would then justly be suspected by those that should be their governors hereafter, as if they were not likely to be faithful to them neither.

18. But before I had spoken all I designed, I heard one of my own domestics bidding me come down; for that it was not a proper time to take care of retaining the good-will of the people of Tiberias, but to provide for my own safety, and escape my enemies there; for John had chosen the most trusty of those armed men that were about him out of those thousand that he had with him, and had given them orders, when he sent them to kill me, having learned that I was alone, excepting some of my domestics. So those that were sent came, as they were ordered, and they had executed what they came about, had I not leaped down from the elevation I stood on, and with one of my guards, whose name was James, been carried [out of the crowd] upon the back of one Herod of Tiberias, and guided by him down to the lake, where I seized a ship, and got into it, and escaped my enemies unexpectedly, and came to Taricheæ.

19. Now, as soon as the inhabitants of that city understood the perfidiousness of the people of Tiberias, they were greatly provoked at them. So they snatched up their arms, and desired me to be their leader against them; for they said they would avenge their commander's cause upon them. They also carried the report of what had been done to me to all the Galileans, and eagerly endeavoured to irritate them against the people of Tiberias, and desired that vast numbers of them would get together, and come to them, that they might act in concert with their commander, what should be determined as fit to be done. Accordingly, the Galileans came to me in great numbers, from all parts, with their weapons, and besought me to assault Tiberias, to take it by force, and to demolish it, till it lay even with the ground, and then to make slaves of its inhabitants, with their wives and children. Those that were Josephus's friends also, and had escaped out of Tiberias, gave him the same advice. But I did not comply with them, thinking it a terrible thing to begin a civil war among them; for I thought that this contention ought not to proceed further than words; nay, I told them that it was not for their own advantage to do what they would have me to do, while the Romans expected no other than that we should destroy one another by our mutual seditions; and by saying this, I put a stop to the anger of the Galileans.

20. But now John was afraid for himself, since his treachery had proved unsuccessful; so he took the armed men that were about him, and removed from Tiberias to Gischala, and wrote to me to apologise for himself concerning what had been done, as if it had been done without his approbation; and desired me to have no suspicion of him to his disadvantage. He also added oaths and certain horrible curses upon himself, and supposed he should be thereby believed in the points he wrote about to me.

21. But now another great number of the Galileans came together again with their weapons, as knowing the man, how wicked and how sadly perjured he was, and desired me to lead them against him, and promised me that they would utterly destroy both him and Gischala. Hereupon I professed that I was obliged to them for their readiness to serve me; and that I would more than requite their good-will to me. However, I entreated them to restrain themselves; and begged of them to give me leave to do what I intended, which was to put an end to these troubles without bloodshed; and when I had prevailed with the multitude of the Galileans to let me do so, I came to Sepphoris.

22. But the inhabitants of this city having determined to continue in their allegiance to the Romans, were afraid of my coming to them; and tried, by putting me upon another action, to divert me, that they might be freed from the terror they were in. Accordingly they sent to Jesus, the captain of those robbers who were in the confines of Ptolemais, and promised to give him a great deal of money, if he would come with those forces he had with him, which were in number eight hundred, and fight with us. Accordingly he complied with what they desired, upon the promises they had made him, and was desirous to fall upon us when we were unprepared for him, and knew nothing of his coming beforehand: so he sent to me, and desired that I would give him leave to come and salute me. When I had given him that leave, which I did without the least knowledge of his treacherous intentions beforehand, he took his band of robbers, and made haste to come to me.

Yet did not this knavery succeed well at last: for, as he was already nearly approaching, one of those with him deserted him, and came to me, and told me what he had undertaken to do. When I was informed of this, I went into the market-place, and pretended to know nothing of his treacherous purpose. I took with me many Galileans that were armed, as also some of those of Tiberias; and when I had given orders that all the roads should be carefully guarded, I charged the keepers of the gates, to give admittance to none but Jesus, when he came, with the principal of his men, and to exclude the rest; and in case they aimed to force themselves in, to use stripes [in order to repel them.] Accordingly, those that had received such a charge did as they were bidden, and Jesus came in with a few others; and when I had ordered him to throw down his arms immediately, and told him, that if he refused so to do, he was a dead man, he seeing armed men standing all round about him, was terrified, and complied; and as for those of his followers that were excluded, when they were informed that he was seized, they ran away. I then called Jesus to me by himself, and told him, that "I was not a stranger to that treacherous design he had against me, nor was I ignorant by whom he was sent for; that, however, I would forgive him what he had done already, if he would repent of it, and be faithful to me hereafter." And thus, upon his promise to do all that I desired, I let him go, and gave him leave to get those whom he had formerly had with him, together again. But I threatened the inhabitants of Sepphoris, that, if they would not leave off their ungrateful treatment of me, I would punish them sufficiently.

23. At this time it was that two great men, who were under the jurisdiction of the king [Agrippa,] came to me out of the region of Trachonitis, bringing their horses and their arms, and carrying with them their money also; and when the Jews would force them to be circumcised, if they would stay among them, I would not permit them to have any force put upon them,[*] but said to them, "Every one ought to worship God according to his own inclinations, and not to be constrained by force; and that these men, who had fled to us for protection, ought not to be so treated as to repent of their coming hither." And when I had pacified the multitude, I provided for the men that were come to us whatsoever it was they wanted, according to their usual way of living, and that in great plenty also.

24. Now King Agrippa sent an army to make themselves masters of the citadel of Gamala, and over it Equiculus Modius; but the forces that were sent were not enow to encompass the citadel quite round, but lay before it in the open places, and besieged it. But when Ebutius the decurion, who was intrusted with the government of the great plain, heard that I was at Simonias, a village situated in the confines of Galilee, and was distant from him sixty furlongs, he took a hundred horsemen that were with him by night, and a certain number of footmen, about two hundred, and brought the inhabitants of the city

---

[*] Josephus's opinion is here well worth noting:— That every one is to be permitted to worship God according to his own conscience, and is not to be compelled in matters of religion; as one may here observe, on the contrary, that the rest of the Jews were still for obliging all those who married Jewesses to be circumcised, and become Jews; and were ready to destroy all that would not submit to do so. See sect. 31, and Luke ix. 54.

Gibea along with him as auxiliaries, and marched in the night, and came to the village where I abode. Upon this I pitched my camp over against him, which had a great number of forces in it; but Ebutius tried to draw us down into the plain, as greatly depending upon his horsemen; but we would not come down; for when I was satisfied of the advantage that his horse would have if we came down into the plain, while we were all footmen, I resolved to join battle with the enemy where I was. Now Ebutius and his party made a courageous opposition for some time: but when he saw that his horse were useless to him in that place, he retired back to the city Gibea, having lost three of his men in the fight. So I followed him directly with two thousand armed men; and when I was at the city Besara, that lay in the confines of Ptolemais, but twenty furlongs from Gibea, where Ebutius abode, I placed my armed men on the outside of the village, and gave orders that they should guard the passes with great care, that the enemy might not disturb us until we should have carried off the corn, a great quantity of which lay there: it belonged to Bernice the queen, and had been gathered together out of the neighbouring villages into Besara: so I loaded my camels and asses, a great number of which I had brought along with me, and sent the corn into Galilee. When I had done this, I offered Ebutius battle; but when he would not accept of the offer, for he was terrified at our readiness and courage, I altered my route, and marched towards Neopolitanus, because I had heard that the country about Tiberias was laid waste by him. This Neopolitanus was captain of a troop of horse, and had the custody of Scythopolis intrusted to his care by the enemy; and when I had hindered him from doing any further mischief to Tiberias, I set myself to make provision for the affairs of Galilee.

25. But when John, the son of Levi, who, as we before told you, abode at Gischala, was informed how all things had succeded to my mind, and that I was much in favour with those that were under me, as also that the enemy were greatly afraid of me, he was not pleased with it, as thinking my prosperity tended to his ruin. So he took up a bitter envy and enmity against me; and hoping that, if he could inflame those that were under me to hate me, he should put an end to the prosperity I was in, he tried to persuade the inhabitants of Tiberias and of Sepphoris, (and for those of Gabara he supposed they would be also of the same mind as the others,) which were the greatest cities of Galilee, to revolt from their subjection to me, and to be of his party; and told them that he would command them better than I did. As for the people of Sepphoris, who belonged to neither of us, because they had chosen to be in subjection to the Romans, they did not comply with his proposal; and for those of Tiberias, they did not indeed so far comply as to make a revolt from under me, but they agreed to be his friends, while the inhabitants of Gabara did go over to John; and it was Simon that persuaded them so to do, one who was both the principal man in the city, and a particular friend and companion of John. It is true, these did not openly own the making a revolt, because they were in great fear of the Galileans, and had frequent experience of the good-will they bore to me; yet did they privately watch for a proper opportunity to lay snares for me; and indeed I thereby came into the greatest danger on the occasion following.

26. There were some bold young men of the village of Dabaritta, who observed that the wife of Ptolemy, the king's procurator, was to make a progress over the great plain with a mighty attendance, and with some horsemen that followed as a guard to them, and this out of a country that was subject to the king and queen, into the jurisdiction of the Romans; and fell upon them on a sudden, and obliged the wife of Ptolemy to fly away, and plundered all the carriages. They also came to me to Taricneæ, with four mules' loading of garments, and other furniture; and the weight of the silver they brought was not small; and there were five hundred pieces of gold also. Now I had a mind to preserve these spoils for Ptolemy, who was my countryman; and it is prohibited * by our laws even to spoil our enemies; so I said to those that brought these spoils, that they ought to be kept, in order to rebuild the walls of Jerusalem with them when they came to be sold; but the young men took it very ill that they did not receive a part of those spoils for themselves, as they expected to have done; so they went among the villages in the neighbourhood of Tiberias, and told the people that I was going to betray their country to the Romans, and that I used deceitful language to them when I said that what had been thus gotten by rapine should be kept for the rebuilding of the walls of the city of Jerusalem; although I had resolved to restore these spoils again to their former owner; and indeed they were herein not mistaken as to my intentions; and when I had gotten clear of them, I sent for two of the principal men, Dassion, and Janneus the son of Levi, persons that were among the chief friends of the king, and commanded them to take the furniture that had been plundered, and to send it to him; and I threatened that I would order them to be put to death by way of punishment, if they discovered this my command to any other person.

27. Now, when all Galilee was filled with this rumour, that their country was about to be betrayed by me to the Romans, and when all men were exasperated against me, and ready to bring me to punishment, the inhabitants of Taricheæ did also themselves suppose that what the young men said was true, and persuaded my guards and armed men to leave me when I was asleep, and to come presently to the hippodrome, in order there to take counsel against me their commander; and when they had prevailed with them, and they were gotten together, they found there a great company assembled already, who all joined in one clamour, to bring the man who was so wicked to them as to betray them, to his due punishment; and it was Jesus, the son of Sapphias, who principally set them on. He was ruler in Tiberias, a wicked man, and naturally disposed to make disturbances in matters of consequence; a seditious person he was indeed, and an innovator beyond everybody else. He then took the laws of Moses into his hands, and came

* How Josephus could say here that the Jewish laws forbade them to "spoil even their enemies," while yet a little before his time our Saviour had mentioned it as then a current maxim with them, "Thou shalt love thy neighbour, and hate thine enemy," (Matt. v. 43,) is worth our inquiry. I take it that Josephus, having been now for many years an Ebionite Christian, had learned this interpretation of the law of Moses from Christ, whom he owned for the true Messiah, as it follows in the succeeding verses, which, though he might not read in St Matthew's Gospel, yet he might have read much the same exposition in their own Ebionite or Nazarene Gospel itself; of which improvements made by Josephus, after he was become a Christian, we have already had several examples in this his Life, sect. 3, 13, 15, 19, 21, 23, and shall have many more therein before its conclusion, as well as we have them elsewhere in all his later writings.

into the midst of the people, and said, "O my fellow-citizens! if you are not disposed to hate Josephus on your own account, have regard, however, to these laws of your country, which your commander-in-chief is going to betray; hate him therefore on both these accounts, and bring the man who hath acted thus insolently to his deserved punishment."

28. When he had said this, and the multitude had openly applauded him for what he had said, he took some of the armed men, and made haste away to the house in which I lodged, as if he would kill me immediately, while I was wholly insensible of all till this disturbance happened; and by reason of the pains I had been taking, was fallen fast asleep; but Simon, who was intrusted with the care of my body, and was the only person that stayed with me, and saw the violent incursion the citizens made upon me, awaked me, and told me of the danger I was in, and desired me to let him kill me, that I might die bravely and like a general, before my enemies came in and forced me [to kill myself,] or killed me themselves. Thus did he discourse to me; but I committed the care of my life to God, and made haste to go out to the multitude. Accordingly, I put on a black garment, and hung my sword at my neck, and went by such a different way to the hippodrome, wherein I thought none of my adversaries would meet me; so I appeared among them on the sudden, and fell down flat on the earth, and bedewed the ground with my tears: then I seemed to them an object of compassion; and when I perceived the change that was made in the multitude, I tried to divide their opinions before the armed men should return from my house; so I granted them that I had been as wicked as they supposed me to be; but still I entreated them to let me first inform them for what use I had kept that money which arose from the plunder, and that they might then kill me, if they pleased: and, upon the multitude's ordering me to speak, the armed men came upon me, and when they saw me, they ran to kill me; but when the multitude bade them hold their hands, they complied; and expected that as soon as I should own to them that I kept the money for the king, it would be looked on as a confession of my treason, and they should then be allowed to kill me.

29. When, therefore, silence was made by the whole multitude, I spake thus to them:—"O my countrymen! I refuse not to die, if justice so require. However, I am desirous to tell you the truth of this matter before I die; for as I know that this city of yours [Tarichææ] was a city of great hospitality, and filled with abundance of such men as have left their own countries, and are come hither to be partakers of your fortune, whatever it be, I had a mind to build walls about it, out of this money, for which you are so angry with me, while yet it was to be expended in building your own walls." Upon my saying this, the people of Tarichææ and the strangers cried out, that "they gave me thanks; and desired me to be of good courage," although the Galileans and the people of Tiberias continued in their wrath against me, insomuch that there arose a tumult among them, while some threatened to kill me, and some bade me not to regard them: but when I promised them that I would build them walls at Tiberias, and at other cities that wanted them, they gave credit to what I promised, and returned every one to his own home. So I escaped the forementioned danger, beyond all my hopes, and returned to my own house, accompanied with my friends, and twenty armed men also.

30. However, these robbers and other authors of this tumult, who were afraid on their own account, lest I should punish them for what they had done, took six hundred armed men, and came to the house where I abode, in order to set it on fire. When this their insult was told me, I thought it indecent for me to run away, and I resolved to expose myself to danger, and to act with some boldness; so I gave order to shut the doors, and went up into an upper room, and desired that they would send in some of their men to receive the money, [from the spoils;] for I told them they would then have no occasion to be angry with me; and when they had sent in one of the boldest of them all, I had him whipped severely; and I commanded that one of his hands should be cut off and hung about his neck; and in this case was he put out to those that sent him. At which procedure of mine they were greatly affrighted, and in no small consternation, and were afraid that they should themselves be served in like manner if they stayed there; for they supposed that I had in the house more armed men than they had themselves: so they ran away immediately, while I, by the use of this stratagem, escaped this their second treacherous design against me.

31. But there were still some that irritated the multitude against me, and said that those great men that belonged to the king ought not to be suffered to live, if they would not change their religion to the religion of those to whom they fled for safety; they spake reproachfully of them also, and said that they were wizards, and such as called in the Romans upon them. So the multitude was soon deluded by such plausible pretences as were agreeable to their own inclinations, and were prevailed on by them: but when I was informed of this, I instructed the multitude again, that those who fled to them for refuge ought not to be persecuted. I also laughed at the allegation about witchcraft,* and told them that the Romans would not maintain so many ten thousand soldiers, if they could overcome their enemies by wizards. Upon my saying this, the people assented for a while; but they returned again afterwards, as irritated by some ill people against the great men; nay, they once made an assault upon the house in which they dwelt at Tarichææ, in order to kill them; which, when I was informed of, I was afraid lest so horrid a crime should take effect, and nobody else would make that city their refuge any more. I therefore came myself, and some others with me, to the house where these great men lived, and locked the doors, and had a trench drawn from their house leading to the lake, and sent for a ship, and embarked therein with them, and sailed to the confines of Hippos: I also paid them the value of their horses; nor in such a flight could I have their horses brought to them. I then dismissed them, and begged of them earnestly that they would courageously bear this distress which befell them. I was also myself greatly displeased that I was compelled to expose those that had fled to me, to go again into an enemy's country; yet did I think it more eligible that they should perish among the Romans, if it should so happen, than in the country that was under my jurisdiction. However, they escaped at length, and King Agrippa forgave them their offences; and this was the conclusion of what concerned these men.

32. But as for the inhabitants of the city of

---

* Here we may observe the vulgar Jewish notion of witchcraft, but that our Josephus was too wise to give any countenance to it.

Tiberias, they wrote to the king, and desired him to send them forces sufficient to be a guard to their country; for that they were desirous to come over to him. This was what they wrote to him; but when I came to them, they desired me to build their walls, as I had promised them to do; for they had heard that the walls of Taricheæ were already built. I agreed to their proposal accordingly; and when I had made preparation for the entire building, I gave order to the architects to go to work; but on the third day, when I was gone to Taricheæ, which was thirty furlongs distant from Tiberias, it so fell out, that some Roman horsemen were discovered on their march, not far from the city, which made it to be supposed that the forces were come from the king; upon which they shouted, and lifted up their voices in commendations of the king, and in reproaches against me. Hereupon one came running to me, and told me what their dispositions were; and that they had resolved to revolt from me;—upon hearing which news I was very much alarmed; for I had already sent away my armed men from Taricheæ to their own homes, because the next day was our Sabbath; for I would not have the people of Taricheæ disturbed [on that day] by a multitude of soldiers; and, indeed, whenever I sojourned at that city, I never took any particular care for a guard about my own body, because I had had frequent instances of the fidelity its inhabitants bore to me. I had now about me no more than seven armed men, besides some friends, and was doubtful what to do; for to send to recall my own forces I did not think proper, because the present day was almost over; and had those forces been with me, I could not take up arms on the next day, because our laws forbade us so to do, even though our necessity should be very great; and if I should permit the people of Taricheæ, and the strangers with them, to guard the city, I saw that they would not be sufficient for that purpose, and I perceived that I should be obliged to delay my assistance a great while; for I thought with myself that the forces that came from the king would prevent me, and that I should be driven out of the city. I considered, therefore, how to get clear of these forces by a stratagem; so I immediately placed those my friends of Taricheæ, on whom I could best confide, at the gates, to watch those very carefully who went out at those gates; I also called to me the heads of families, and bade every one of them seize upon a ship,* to go on board it, and to take a master with them, and follow him to the city of Tiberias. I also myself went on board one of those ships, with my friends, and the seven armed men already mentioned, and sailed for Tiberias.

33. But now, when the people of Tiberias perceived that there were no forces come from the king, and yet saw the whole lake full of ships, they were in fear what would become of their city, and were greatly terrified, as supposing that the ships were full of men on board; so they then changed their minds, and threw down their weapons, and met me with their wives and children, and made acclamations to me with great commendations; for they imagined that I did not know their former inclinations [to have been

against me,] so they persuaded me to spare the city; but when I was come near enough, I gave order to the masters of the ships to cast anchor a good way off the land, that the people of Tiberias might not perceive that the ships had no men on board; but I went nearer to the people in one of the ships, and rebuked them for their folly, and that they were so fickle as, without any just occasion in the world, to revolt from their fidelity to me. However, I assured them that I would entirely forgive them for the time to come, if they would send ten of the ringleaders of the multitude to me; and when they complied readily with this proposal, and sent me the men forementioned, I put them on board a ship, and sent them away to Taricheæ, and ordered them to be kept in prison.

34. And by this stratagem it was that I gradually got all the senate of Tiberias into my power, and sent them to the city forementioned, with many of the principal men among the populace; and those not fewer in number than the other; but, when the multitude saw into what great miseries they had brought themselves, they desired me to punish the author of this sedition: his name was Clitus, a young man, bold and rash in his undertakings. Now, since I thought it not agreeable to piety to put one of my own people to death, and yet found it necessary to punish him, I ordered Levi, one of my own guards, to go to him, and cut off one of Clitus's hands; but as he that was ordered to do this was afraid to go out of the ship alone among so great a multitude, I was not willing that the timorousness of the soldier should appear to the people of Tiberias;—so I called to Clitus himself, and said to him, "Since thou deservest to lose both thine hands for thy ingratitude to me, be thou thine own executioner, lest if thou refusest so to be, thou undergo a worse punishment." And when he earnestly begged of me to spare him one of his hands, it was with difficulty that I granted it. So, in order to prevent the loss of both his hands, he willingly took his sword, and cut off his own left hand; and this put an end to the sedition.

35. Now the men of Tiberias, after I was gone to Taricheæ, perceived what stratagem I had used against them, and they admired how I had put an end to their foolish sedition without shedding of blood. But now, when I had sent for some of those multitudes of the people of Tiberias out of prison, among whom were Justus and his father Pistus, I made them to sup with me; and during our supper time I said to them, that I knew the power of the Romans was superior to all others; but did not say so [publicly,] because of the robbers. So I advised them to do as I did, and to wait for a proper opportunity, and not to be uneasy at my being their commander; for that they could not expect to have another who would use the like moderation that I had done. I also put Justus in mind how the Galileans had cut off his brother's hands before ever I came to Jerusalem, upon an accusation laid against him, as if he had been a rogue, and had forged some letters; as also how the people of Gamala, in a sedition they raised against the Babylonians, after the departure of Philip, slew Chares, who was a kinsman of Philip, and withal how they had wisely punished Jesus, his brother Justus's sister's husband, [with death.] When I had said this to them during supper-time, I in the morning ordered Justus, and all the rest that were in prison, to be loosed out of it, and sent away.

36. But before this, it happened that Philip, the son of Jacimus, went out of the citadel of

* In this section, as well as in the 18th and 33d, those small vessels that sailed on the sea of Galilee, are called by Josephus Νηες, and Πλοια, and Σκαφαι; i. e., plainly ships; so that we need not wonder at our evangelists, who still call them ships; nor ought we to render them boats, as some do. Their number was in all 230, as we learn from our author elsewhere. (Jewish War, b. ii. ch. xxi. sect 8.)

Gamala upon the following occasion: When Philip had been informed that Varus was put out of his government by King Agrippa, and that Equiculus Modius, a man that was of old his friend and companion, was come to succeed him, he wrote to him, and related what turns of fortune he had had, and desired him to forward the letters he sent to the king and queen. Now, when Modius had received these letters, he was exceedingly glad, and sent the letters to the king and queen, who were then about Berytus. But when king Agrippa knew that the story about Philip was false, (for it had been given out, that the Jews had begun a war with the Romans, and that this Philip had been their commander in that war,) he sent some horsemen to conduct Philip to him; and when he was come, he saluted him very obligingly, and shewed him to the Roman commanders, and told them that this was the man of whom the report had gone about as if he had revolted from the Romans. He also bid him to take some horsemen with him, and to go quickly to the citadel of Gamala, and to bring out thence all his domestics, and to restore the Babylonians to Batanea again. He also gave it him in charge to take all possible care that none of his subjects should be guilty of making any innovation. Accordingly, upon these directions from the king, he made haste to do what he was commanded.

37. Now there was one Joseph, the son of a female physician, who excited a great many young men to join with him. He also insolently addressed himself to the principal persons at Gamala, and persuaded them to revolt from the king, and take up arms, and gave them hopes that they should, by his means, recover their liberty: and some they forced into the service; and those that would not acquiesce in what they had resolved on, they slew. They also slew Chares, and with him Jesus, one of his kinsmen, and a brother of Justus of Tiberias, as we have already said. Those of Gamala also wrote to me, desiring me to send them an armed force, and workmen to raise up the walls of their city; nor did I reject either of their requests. The region of Gaulanitis did also revolt from the king, as far as the village Solyma. I also built a wall about Seleucia and Soganni, which are villages naturally of very great strength. Moreover, I, in like manner, walled several villages of Upper Galilee, though they were very rocky of themselves. Their names are Jamnia, and Meroth, and Achabare. I also fortified, in the Lower Galilee, the cities Taricheæ, Tiberias, Sepphoris, and the villages, the cave of Arbela, Bersobe, Selamin, Jotapata, Capharecho, and Sigo, and Japha, and Mount Tabor.* I also laid up a great quantity of corn in these places, and arms withal, that might be for their security afterward.

38. But the hatred that John, the son of Levi, bore to me, grew now more violent, while he could not bear my prosperity with patience. So he proposed to himself, by all means possible, to make away with me; and built the walls of Gischala, which was the place of his nativity. He then sent his brother Simon, and Jonathan, the son of Sisenna, and about a hundred armed men, to Jerusalem, to Simon, the son of Gamaliel,†

in order to persuade him to induce the commonalty of Jerusalem to take from me the government over the Galileans, and to give their suffrages for conferring that authority upon him. This Simon was of the city of Jerusalem, and of a very noble family, of the sect of the Pharisees, which are supposed to excel others in the accurate knowledge of the laws of their country. He was a man of great wisdom and reason, and capable of restoring public affairs by his prudence, when they were in an ill posture. He was also an old friend and companion of John; but at that time he had a difference with me. When therefore he had received such an exhortation, he persuaded the high priests, Ananus, and Jesus the son of Gamala, and some others of the same seditious faction, to cut me down, now I was growing so great, and not to overlook me while I was aggrandising myself to the height of glory; and he said that it would be for the advantage of the Galileans if I were deprived of my government there. Ananus also, and his friends, desired them to make no delay about the matter, lest I should get the knowledge of what was doing too soon, and should come and make an assault upon the city with a great army. This was the counsel of Simon: but Ananus the high priest demonstrated to them that this was not an easy thing to be done, because many of the high priests and of the rulers of the people, bore witness that I had acted like an excellent general, and that it was the work of ill men to accuse one against whom they had nothing to say.

39. When Simon heard Ananus say this, he desired that the messengers would conceal the thing, and not let it come among many: for that he would take care to have Josephus removed out of Galilee very quickly. So he called for John's brother, [Simon,] and charged him that they should send presents to Ananus and his friends: for, as he said, they might probably by that means persuade them to change their minds. And indeed Simon did at length thus compass what he aimed at; for Ananus, and those with him, being corrupted by bribes, agreed to expel me out of Galilee, without making the rest of the citizens acquainted with what they were doing. Accordingly, they resolved to send men of distinction as to their families, and of distinction as to their learning also. Two of these were of the populace, Jonathan ‡ and Ananias, by sect Pharisees; while the third, Jozar, was of the stock of the priests, and a Pharisee also; and Simon, the last of them, was of the youngest of the high priests. These had it given them in charge, that, when they were come to the multitude of the Galileans, they should ask them what was the reason of their love to me? and if they said that it was because I was born at Jerusalem, that they should reply, that they four were all born at the same place; and if they should say, it was because I was well versed in their law, they should reply, that neither were they unacquainted with the practices of their country; but if, besides these, they should say they loved me because I was a priest, they should reply, that two of these were priests also.

40. Now, when they had given Jonathan and his companions these instructions, they gave them forty thousand [drachmæ] out of the public

* Part of these fortifications on Mount Tabor may be those still remaining. and which were seen lately by Mr Maundrel. See his Travels, p. 112.

† This Gamaliel may be the very same that is mentioned by the rabbins in the Mishna, in Juchasin, and in Porta Mosis, as is observed in the Latin notes. He might be also that Gamaliel II., whose grandfather was Gamaliel I., who is mentioned in Acts v. 34; and at whose feet

St Paul *was brought up*, Acts xxii. 3. See Prid. at the year 449.

‡ This Jonathan is also taken notice of in the Latin notes, as the same that is mentioned by the rabbins in Porta Mosis.

money: but when they heard that there was a certain Galilean that then sojourned at Jerusalem, whose name was Jesus, who had about him a band of six hundred armed men, they sent for him, and gave him three months' pay, and gave him orders to follow Jonathan and his companions, and be obedient to them. They also gave money to three hundred men that were citizens of Jerusalem to maintain them all, and ordered them also to follow the ambassadors; and when they had complied, and were gotten ready for the march, Jonathan and his companions went out with them, having along with them John's brother and a hundred armed men. The charge that was given them by those that sent them was this: That if I would voluntarily lay down my arms, they should send me alive to the city of Jerusalem; but that, in case I opposed them, they should kill me, and fear nothing; for that it was their command for them so to do. They also wrote to John to make all ready for fighting me, and gave orders to the inhabitants of Sepphoris, and Gabara, and Tiberias, to send auxiliaries to John.

41. Now, as my father wrote me an account of this, (for Jesus the son of Gamala, who was present in that council, a friend and companion of mine, told him of it,) I was very much troubled, as discovering thereby that my fellow-citizens proved so ungrateful to me, as, out of envy, to give order that I should be slain; my father earnestly pressed me also in his letter to come to him, for that he longed to see his son before he died. I informed my friends of these things, and that in three days' time I should leave the country and go home. Upon hearing this, they were all very sorry, and desired me, with tears in their eyes, not to leave them to be destroyed; for so they thought they should be, if I were deprived of the command over them: but as I did not grant their request, but was taking care of my own safety, the Galileans, out of their dread of the consequence of my departure, that they should then be at the mercy of the robbers, sent messengers over all Galilee to inform them of my resolution to leave them. Whereupon, as soon as they heard it, they got together in great numbers, from all parts, with their wives and children; and this they did, as it appeared to me, not more out of their affection to me, than out of their fear on their own account; for, while I staid with them, they supposed that they should suffer no harm. So they all came into the great plain, wherein I lived, the name of which was Asochis.

42. But wonderful it was what a dream I saw that very night; for when I had betaken myself to my bed, as grieved and disturbed at the news that had been written to me, it seemed to me, that a certain person stood by me,* and said, "O Josephus! leave off to afflict thy soul, and put away all fear; for what now grieves thee will render thee very considerable, and in all respects most happy; for thou shalt get over not only these difficulties, but many others, with great success. However, be not cast down, but remember that thou art to fight with the Romans." When I had seen this dream, I got up with an intention of going down to the plain. Now, when the whole multitude of the Galileans, among whom were the women and children, saw me, they threw themselves down upon their

faces, and, with tears in their eyes, besought me not to leave them exposed to their enemies, nor to go away and permit their country to be injured by them; but, when I did not comply with their entreaties, they compelled me to take an oath, that I would stay with them: they also cast abundance of reproaches upon the people of Jerusalem, that they would not let their country enjoy peace.

43. When I heard this, and saw what sorrow the people were in, I was moved with compassion to them, and thought it became me to undergo the most manifest hazards for the sake of so great a multitude; so I let them know I would stay with them; and when I had given order that five thousand of them should come to me armed, and with provisions for their maintenance, I sent the rest away to their own homes; and, when those five thousand were come, I took them, together with three thousand of the soldiers that were with me before, and eighty horsemen, and marched to the village of Chabolo, situated in the confines of Ptolemais, and there kept my forces together, pretending to get ready to fight with Placidus, who was come with two cohorts of footmen, and one troop of horsemen; and was sent thither by Cestius Gallus to burn those villages of Galilee that were near Ptolemais. Upon whose casting up a bank before the city Ptolemais, I also pitched my camp at about the distance of sixty furlongs from that village; and now we frequently brought out our forces as if we would fight, but proceeded no further than skirmishes at a distance; for when Placidus perceived that I was earnest to come to a battle, he was afraid, and avoided it; yet did he not remove from the neighbourhood of Ptolemais.

44. About this time it was that Jonathan and his fellow-legates came. They were sent, as we have said already, by Simon, and Ananus the high priest; and Jonathan contrived how he might catch me by treachery, for he durst not make any attempt upon me openly. So he wrote me the following epistle:—"Jonathan and those that are with him, and are sent by the people of Jerusalem to Josephus, send greeting. We are sent by the principal men of Jerusalem, who have heard that John of Gischala hath laid many snares for thee, to rebuke him, and to exhort him to be subject to thee hereafter. We are also desirous to consult with thee about our common concerns, and what is fit to be done. We, therefore, desire thee to come to us quickly, and to bring only a few men with thee; for this village will not contain a great number of soldiers." Thus it was that they wrote, as expecting one of these two things; either that I should come without armed men, and then they should have me wholly in their power: or if I came with a great number, they should judge me to be a public enemy. Now it was a horseman who brought the letter, a man at other times bold, and one that had served in the army under the king. It was the second hour of the night that he came, when I was feasting with my friends and the principal of the Galileans. This man, upon my servant's telling me that a certain horseman of the Jewish nation was come, was called in at my command, but did not so much as salute me at all, but held out a letter, and said, "This letter is sent thee by those that are come from Jerusalem; do thou write an answer to it quickly, for I am obliged to return to them very soon." Now my guests could not but wonder at the boldness of the soldier; but I desired him to sit down and sup with us; but when he refused so to do, I held the letter in my hands

---

* This I take to be the first of Josephus's remarkable or divine dreams, which were predictive of the great things that afterwards came to pass; of which see more in the note on Antiq. b. iii. chap. viii. sect. 9. The other is in the War, b. iii. chap. viii. sect. 3, 9.

as I received it, and fell a-talking with my guests about other matters; but a few hours afterwards, I got up, and when I had dismissed the rest to go to their beds, I bid only four of my intimate friends to stay; and ordered my servant to get some wine ready. I also opened the letter so, that nobody could perceive it; and understanding thereby presently the purport of the writing, I sealed it up again, and appeared as if I had not yet read it, but only held it in my hands. I ordered twenty drachmæ should be given to the soldier for the charges of his journey; and when he took the money, and said that he thanked me for it, I perceived that he loved money, and that he was to be caught chiefly by that means; and I said to him, "If thou wilt but drink with us, thou shalt have a drachma for every glass thou drinkest." So he gladly embraced this proposal, and drank a great deal of wine, in order to get the more money, and was so drunk, that at last he could not keep the secrets he was intrusted with, but discovered them without my putting questions to him,—viz., That a treacherous design was contrived against me; and that I was doomed to die by those that sent him. When I heard this, I wrote back this answer:—"Josephus to Jonathan, and those that are with him, sendeth greeting. Upon the information that you are come in health into Galilee, I rejoice, and this especially, because I can now resign the care of public affairs here into your hands, and return into my native country,—which is what I have desired to do a great while; and I confess I ought not only to come to you as far as Xaloth, but further, and this without your commands: but I desire you to excuse me, because I cannot do it now, since I watch the motions of Placidus, who hath a mind to go up into Galilee; and this I do here at Chabolo. Do you, therefore, on the receipt of this epistle, come hither to me. Fare you well."

45. When I had written thus, and given the letter to be carried by the soldier, I sent along with him thirty of the Galileans of the best characters, and gave them instructions to salute those ambassadors, but to say nothing else to them. I also gave orders to as many of those armed men, whom I esteemed most faithful to me, to go along with the others, every one with him whom he was to guard, lest some conversation might pass between those whom I sent and those who were with Jonathan. So those men went [to Jonathan.] But, when Jonathan and his partners had failed in this their first attempt, they sent me another letter, the contents whereof were as follows:—"Jonathan, and those with him, to Josephus, send greeting. We require thee to come to us to the village Gabaroth, on the third day, without any armed men, that we may hear what thou hast to lay to the charge of John [of Gischala.]" When they had written this letter, they saluted the Galileans whom I sent; and came to Japha, which was the largest village of all Galilee, and encompassed with very strong walls, and had a great number of inhabitants in it. There the multitude of men, with their wives and children, met them, and exclaimed loudly against them; and desired them to be gone, and not to envy them the advantage of an excellent commander. With these clamours Jonathan and his partners were greatly provoked, although they durst not shew their anger openly; so they made them no answer, but went to other villages. But still the same clamours met them from all the people, who said, "Nobody should persuade them to have any other commander besides Josephus." So Jonathan and his partners went away from them

without success, and came to Sepphoris, the greatest city of all Galilee. Now the men of that city, who inclined to the Romans in their sentiments, met them indeed, but neither praised nor reproached me; and when they were gone down from Sepphoris to Asochis, the people of that place made a clamour against them, as those of Japha had done; whereupon they were able to contain themselves no longer, but ordered the armed men that were with them to beat those that made the clamour with their clubs; and when they came to Gabara, John met them with three thousand armed men; but, as I understood by their letter that they had resolved to fight against me, I arose from Chabolo, with three thousand armed men also, but left in my camp one of my fastest friends, and came to Jotapata, as desirous to be near them, the distance being no more than forty furlongs. Whence I wrote thus to them:—"If you are very desirous that I should come to you, you know there are two hundred and forty cities and villages in Galilee: I will come to any of them which you please, excepting Gabara and Gischala,—the one of which is John's native city, and the other in confederacy and friendship with him."

46. When Jonathan and his partners had received this letter, they wrote me no more answers, but called a council of their friends together; and taking John into their consultation, they took counsel together by what means they might attack me. John's opinion was, that they should write to all the cities and villages that were in Galilee; for that there must be certainly one or two persons in every one of them that were at variance with me; and that they should be invited to come, to oppose me as an enemy. He would also have them send this resolution of theirs to the city of Jerusalem, that its citizens, upon the knowledge of my being adjudged to be an enemy by the Galileans, might themselves also confirm that determination. He said also, that when this was done, even those Galileans who were well affected to me, would desert me out of fear. When John had given them this counsel, what he had said was very agreeable to the rest of them. I was also made acquainted with these affairs about the third hour of the night, by the means of one Saccheus who had belonged to them, but now deserted them and came over to me, and told me what they were about; so I perceived that no time was to be lost. Accordingly I gave command to Jacob, an armed man of my guard, whom I esteemed faithful to me, to take two hundred men, and to guard the passages that led from Gabara to Galilee, and to seize upon the passengers, and send them to me, especially such as were caught with letters about them: I also sent Jeremias himself, one of my friends, with six hundred armed men, to the borders of Galilee, in order to watch the roads that led from this country to the city Jerusalem; and gave him charge to lay hold of such as travelled with letters about them, to keep the men in bonds upon the place, but to send me the letters.

47. When I had laid these commands upon them, I gave them orders, and bid them take their arms, and bring three days' provision with them, and be with me the next day. I also parted those that were about me into four parts, and ordained those of them that were most faithful to me to be a guard to my body. I also set over them centurions; and commanded them to take care that not a soldier which they did not know, should mingle himself among them. Now, on the fifth day following, when I was at

Gabaroth, I found the entire plain that was before the village full of armed men, who were come out of Galilee to assist me; many others of the multitude, also out of the village, ran along with me : but as soon as I had taken my place, and began to speak to them, they all made an acclamation, and called me the benefactor and saviour of the country; and when I had made them my acknowledgments, and thanked them, [for their affection to me,] I also advised them to fight with nobody,* nor to spoil the country, but to pitch their tents in the plain, and be content with their sustenance they had brought with them; for I told them that I had a mind to compose these troubles without shedding any blood. Now it came to pass, that on the very same day those who were sent by John with letters, fell among the guards whom I had appointed to watch the roads; so the men were themselves kept upon the place, as my orders were; but I got the letters, which were full of reproaches and lies ; and I intended to fall upon these men, without saying a word of these matters to any body.

48. Now, as soon as Jonathan and his companions heard of my coming, they took all their own friends, and John with them, and retired to the house of Jesus, which indeed was a large castle, and no way unlike a citadel; so they privately led a band of armed men therein, and shut all the other doors but one, which they kept open, and they expected that I should come out of the road to them, to salute them; and indeed they had given orders to the armed men, that when I came they should let nobody besides me come in, but should exclude others; as supposing that, by this means, they should easily get me under their power: but they were deceived in their expectation, for I perceived what snares they had laid for me. Now, as soon as I was got off my journey, I took up my lodgings over against them, and pretended to be asleep; so Jonathan and his party, thinking that I was really asleep and at rest, made haste to go down into the plain to persuade the people that I was an ill governor: but the matter proved otherwise; for, upon their appearance, there was a cry made by the Galileans immediately, declaring their good opinion of me as their governor; and they made a clamour against Jonathan and his partners for coming to them when they had suffered no harm, and as though they would overturn their happy settlement; and desired them by all means to go back again, for that they would never be persuaded to have any other to rule over them but myself. When I heard of this, I did not fear to go down into the midst of them ; I went therefore myself down presently, to hear what Jonathan and his companions said. As soon as I appeared, there was immediately an acclamation made to me by the whole multitude, and a cry in my commendation by them, who confessed their thanks was owing to me for my good government of them.

49. When Jonathan and his companions heard this, they were in fear of their own lives, and in danger lest they should be assaulted by the Galileans on my account; so they contrived how they might run away; but as they were not able to get off, for I desired them to stay, they looked down with concern at my words to them. I ordered, therefore, the multitude to restrain entirely their acclamations, and placed the most faithful of my armed men upon the avenues, to be a guard to us, lest John should unexpectedly fall upon us; and I encouraged the Galileans to take their weapons, lest they should be disturbed at their enemies, if any sudden assault should be made upon them; and then, in the first place, I put Jonathan and his partners in mind of their [former] letter, and after what manner they had written to me, and declared they were sent by the common consent of the people of Jerusalem to make up the differences I had with John, and how they had desired me to come to them; and as I spake thus, I publicly shewed that letter they had written, till they could not at all deny what they had done, the letter itself convicting them. I then said, " O Jonathan! and you that are sent with him as his colleagues, if I were to be judged as to my behaviour, compared with that of John's, and had brought no more than two or three witnesses,† good men and true, it is plain you had been forced, upon the examination of their characters beforehand, to discharge the accusations: that, wherefore, you may be informed that I have acted well in the affairs of Galilee, I think three witnesses too few to be brought by a man that hath done as he ought to do ; so I gave you all these for witnesses. Inquire of them ‡ how I have lived, and whether I have not behaved myself with all decency, and after a virtuous manner among them. And I further conjure you, O Galileans! to hide no part of the truth, but to speak before these men as before judges, whether I have in anything acted otherwise than well."

50. While I was thus speaking, the united voices of all the people joined together, and called me their benefactor and saviour, and attested to my former behaviour, and exhorted me to continue so to do hereafter; and they all said, upon their oaths, that their wives had been preserved free from injuries, and that no one had ever been aggrieved by me. After this, I read to the Galileans two of those epistles which had been sent by Jonathan and his colleagues, and which those whom I had appointed to guard the road had taken, and sent to me. These were full of reproaches and of lies, as if I had acted more like a tyrant than a governor against them; with many other things besides therein contained, which were no better indeed than impudent falsities. I also informed the multitude how I came by these letters, and that those who carried them delivered them up voluntarily; for I was not willing that my enemies should know anything of the guards I had set, lest they should be afraid, and leave off writing hereafter.

51. When the multitude heard these things, they were greatly provoked at Jonathan and his colleagues that were with him, and were going to attack them, and kill them; and this they had certainly done, unless I had restrained the anger of the Galileans, and said, that " I forgave Jonathan and his colleagues what was past, if they

---

* Josephus's directions to his soldiers here are much the same that John the Baptist gave (Luke iii. 14 :)—" Do violence to no man, neither accuse any falsely, and be content with your wages." Whence Dr Hudson confirms this conjecture, that Josephus, in some things, was, even now, a follower of John the Baptist, which is no way improbable. See the note on sect 2.

† We here learn the practice of the Jews in the days of Josephus, to inquire into the characters of witnesses before they were admitted ; and that their number ought to be three, or two at the least, also exactly as in the law of Moses, and in the Apostolical Constitutions, b. ii. ch. xxxvii. See Horeb Covenant Revived, pp 97, 98.

‡ This appeal to the whole body of the Galileans by Josephus, and the testimony they gave him of integrity in his conduct as their governor, is very like that appeal and testimony in the case of the prophet Samuel, (1 Samuel xii. 1-5,) and perhaps was done by Josephus in imitation of him.

would repent, and go to their own country, and tell those who sent them the truth as to my conduct." When I had said this, I let them go, although I knew they would do nothing of what they had promised. But the multitude were very much enraged against them, and entreated me to give them leave to punish them for their insolence; yet did I try all methods to persuade them to spare the men; for I knew that every instance of sedition was pernicious to the public welfare. But the multitude was too angry with them to be dissuaded; and all of them went immediately to the house in which Jonathan and his colleagues abode. However, when I perceived that their rage could not be restrained, I got on horseback, and ordered the multitude to follow me to the village Sogane, which was twenty furlongs off Gabara; and by using this stratagem, I so managed myself as not to appear to begin a civil war amongst them.

52. But when I was come near Sogane, I caused the multitude to make a halt, and exhorted them not to be so easily provoked to anger, and to the inflicting such punishments as could not be afterwards recalled: I also gave order, that a hundred men, who were already in years, and were principal men among them, should get themselves ready to go to the city of Jerusalem, and should make a complaint before the people, of such as raised seditions in the country. And I said to them, that "in case they be moved with what you say, you shall desire the community to write to me, and to enjoin me to continue in Galilee, and to order Jonathan and his colleagues to depart out of it." When I had suggested these instructions to them, and while they were getting themselves ready as fast as they could, I sent them on this errand the third day after they had been assembled: I also sent five hundred armed men with them [as a guard.] I then wrote to my friends in Samaria, to take care that they might safely pass through the country; for Samaria was already under the Romans, and it was absolutely necessary for those that go quickly [to Jerusalem] to pass through that country; for in that road you may, in three days' time, go from Galilee to Jerusalem. I also went myself, and conducted the old men as far as the bounds of Galilee, and set guards in the roads, that it might not be easily known by any one that these men were gone. And when I had thus done, I went and abode at Japha.

53. Now Jonathan and his colleagues, having failed of accomplishing what they would have done against me, sent John back to Gischala, but went themselves to the city of Tiberias, expecting it would submit itself to them; and this was founded on a letter which Jesus, their then governor, had written them, promising that, if they came, the multitude would receive them, and choose to be under their government; so they went their ways with this expectation. But Silas, who, as I said, had been left curator of Tiberias by me, informed me of this, and desired me to make haste thither. Accordingly, I complied with his advice immediately, and came thither; but found myself in danger of my life, from the following occasion: Jonathan and his colleagues had been at Tiberias, and had persuaded a great many of such as had a quarrel with me to desert me; but when they heard of my coming, they were in fear for themselves, and came to me; and when they had saluted me, they said that I was a happy man in having behaved myself so well in the government of Galilee; and they congratulated me upon the honours that were paid me: for they said that my glory was a credit to them, since they had been my teachers

and fellow-citizens; and they said further, that it was but just that they should prefer my friendship to them rather than John's, and that they would have immediately gone home, but that they staid that they might deliver up John into my power; and when they said this, they took their oaths of it, and those such as are most tremendous amongst us, and such as I did not think fit to disbelieve. However, they desired me to lodge somewhere else, because the next day was the Sabbath; and that it was not fit the city of Tiberias should be disturbed [on that day.]

54. So I suspected nothing, and went away to Taricheæ; yet did withal leave some to make inquiry in the city how matters went, and whether anything was said about me: I also set many persons all the way that led from Taricheæ to Tiberias, that they might communicate from one to another, if they learned any news from those that were left in the city. On the next day, therefore, they all came into the Proseucha;* it was a large edifice, and capable of receiving a great number of people; thither Jonathan went in, and though he durst not openly speak of a revolt, yet did he say that their city stood in need of a better governor than it then had. But Jesus, who was the ruler, made no scruple to speak out, and said openly, "O fellow-citizens! it is better for you to be in subjection to four than to one; and those such as are of high birth, and not without reputation for their wisdom;" and pointed to Jonathan and his colleagues. Upon his saying this, Justus came in and commended him for what he had said, and persuaded some of the people to be of his mind also. But the multitude were not pleased with what was said, and had certainly gone into a tumult, unless the sixth hour, which was now come, had not dissolved the assembly, at which hour our laws require us to go to dinner on Sabbath-days; so Jonathan and his colleagues put off their council till the next day, and went off without success. When I was informed of these affairs, I determined to go to the city of Tiberias in the morning. Accordingly, on the next day, about the first hour of the day, I came from Taricheæ, and found the multitude already assembled in the Proseucha; but on what account they were gotten together, those that were assembled did not know. But when Jonathan and his colleagues saw me there unexpectedly, they were in disorder; after which they raised a report of their own contrivance, that Roman horsemen were seen at a place called Union, in the borders of Galilee, thirty furlongs distant from the city. Upon which report, Jonathan and his colleagues cunningly exhorted me not to neglect this matter, nor to suffer the land to be spoiled by the enemy. And this they said with a design to remove me out of the city, under the pretence of the want of extraordinary assistance, while they might dispose the city to be my enemy.

55. As for myself, although I knew of their design, yet did I comply with what they proposed, lest the people of Tiberias should have occasion to suppose that I was not careful of their security. I therefore went out; but, when I was at the place, I found not the least footsteps of any enemy; so I returned as fast as ever I could, and found the whole council assembled,

* It is worth noting here, that there was now a great Proseucha, or place of prayer, in the city of Tiberias itself, though such Proseucha used to be out of cities, as the synagogues were within them. Of them, see Le Moyne on Polycarp's Epistle, page 76. It is also worth our remark, that the Jews, in the days of Josephus, used to dine at the sixth hour, or noon; and that, in obedience to their notions of the law of Moses also.

and the body of the people gotten together, and Jonathan and his colleagues bringing vehement accusations against me, as one who had no concern to ease them of the burdens of war, and as one that lived luxuriously. And as they were discoursing thus, they produced four letters as written to them, from some people that lived at the borders of Galilee, imploring that they would come to their assistance, for that there was an army of Romans, both horsemen and footmen, who would come and lay waste the country on the third day; they desired them also to make haste, and not to overlook them. When the people of Tiberias heard this, they thought they spake truth, and made a clamour against me, and said I ought not to sit still, but to go away to the assistance of their countrymen. Hereupon I said (for I understood the meaning of Jonathan and his colleagues) that I was ready to comply with what they proposed, and without delay to march to the war which they spake of, yet did I advise them, at the same time, that since these letters declared that the Romans would make their assault in four several places, they should part their forces into five bodies, and make Jonathan and his colleagues generals of each body of them, because it was fit for brave men not only to give counsel, but to take the place of leaders, and assist their countrymen when such a necessity pressed them; for, said I, it is not possible for me to lead more than one party. This advice of mine greatly pleased the multitude; so they compelled them to go forth to the war. But their designs were put into very much disorder, because they had not done what they had designed to do, on account of my stratagem, which was opposite to their undertakings.

56. Now there was one whose name was Ananias, (a wicked man he was, and very mischievous;) he proposed that a general religious fast * should be appointed the next day for all the people, and gave order that at the same hour they should come to the same place, without any weapons, to make it manifest before God, that while they obtained His assistance, they thought all these weapons useless. This he said, not out of piety, but that they might catch me and my friends unarmed. Now, I was hereupon forced to comply, lest I should appear to despise a proposal that tended to piety. As soon, therefore, as we were gone home, Jonathan and his colleagues wrote to John to come to them in the morning, and desiring him to come with as many soldiers as he possibly could, for that they should then be able easily to get me into their hands, and to do all they desired to do. When John had received this letter, he resolved to comply with it. As for myself, on the next day, I ordered two of the guards of my body, whom I esteemed the most courageous and the most faithful, to hide daggers under their garments, and go along with me, that we might defend ourselves, if any attack should be made upon us by our enemies. I also myself took my breastplate, and girded on my sword, so that it might be, as far as it was possible, concealed, and came into the Proseucha.

57. Now Jesus, who was the ruler, commanded that they should exclude all that came with me, for he kept the door himself, and suffered none but his friends to go in. And while we were

engaged in the duties of the day, and had betaken ourselves to our prayers, Jesus got up, and inquired of me what was become of the vessels that were taken out of the king's palace when it was burnt down, [and] of the uncoined silver: and in whose possession they now were? This he said, in order to drive away time till John should come. I said that Capellus, and the ten principal men of Tiberias, had them all; and I told him that they might ask them whether I told a lie or not. And when they said they had them, he asked me, What is become of those twenty pieces of gold which thou didst receive upon the sale of a certain weight of uncoined money? I replied, that I had given them to those ambassadors of theirs, as a maintenance for them, when they were sent by them to Jerusalem. So Jonathan and his colleagues said that I had not done well to pay the ambassadors out of the public money. And when the multitude were very angry at them for this, for they perceived the wickedness of the men, I understood that a tumult was going to arise; and being desirous to provoke the people to a greater rage against the men, I said, "But if I have not done well in paying our ambassadors out of the public stock, leave off your anger at me, for I will repay the twenty pieces of gold myself."

58. When I had said this, Jonathan and his colleagues held their peace; but the people were still more irritated against them, upon their openly shewing their unjust ill-will to me. When Jesus saw this change in the people, he ordered them to depart, but desired the senate to stay, for that they could not examine things of such a nature in a tumult; and as the people were crying out that they would not leave me alone, there came one and told Jesus and his friends privately, that John and his armed men were at hand: whereupon Jonathan and his colleagues, being able to contain themselves no longer, (and perhaps the providence of God hereby procuring my deliverance, for, had not this been so, I had certainly been destroyed by John,) said, "O you people of Tiberias! leave off this inquiry about the twenty pieces of gold; for Josephus hath not deserved to die for them; but he hath deserved it by his desire of tyrannising, and by cheating the multitude of the Galileans with his speeches, in order to gain the dominion over them." When he had said this, they presently laid hands upon me, and endeavoured to kill me: but as soon as those that were with me saw what they did, they drew their swords, and threatened to smite them, if they offered any violence to me. The people also took up stones, and were about to throw them at Jonathan; and so they snatched me from the violence of my enemies.

59. But as I was gone out a little way, I was just upon meeting John, who was marching with his armed men. So I was afraid of him, and turned aside, and escaped by a narrow passage to the lake, and seized on a ship, and embarked in it, and sailed over to Taricheæ. So, beyond my expectation, I escaped this danger. Whereupon I presently sent for the chief of the Galileans, and told them after what manner, against all faith given, I had been very near to destruction from Jonathan and his colleagues, and the people of Tiberias. Upon which the multitude of the Galileans were very angry, and encouraged me to delay no longer to make war upon them, but to permit them to go against John, and utterly to destroy him, as well as Jonathan and his colleagues. However, I restrained them, though they were in such a rage, and desired them to tarry a while, till we should be informed

---

* One may observe here, that this lay-Pharisee, Ananias, as we have seen he was, (sect. 39,) took upon him to appoint a fast at Tiberias, and was obeyed; though indeed it was not out of religion, but knavish policy.

what orders those ambassadors that were sent by them to the city of Jerusalem should bring thence; for I told them that it was best to act according to their determination; whereupon they were prevailed on. At which time also, John, when the snares he had laid did not take effect, returned back to Gischala.

60. Now, in a few days, those ambassadors whom we had sent came back again, and informed us that the people were greatly provoked at Ananus, and Simon the son of Gamaliel, and their friends; that, without any public determination, they had sent to Galilee, and had done their endeavours that I might be turned out of the government. The ambassadors said further, that the people were ready to burn their houses. They also brought letters, whereby the chief men of Jerusalem, at the earnest petition of the people, confirmed me in the government of Galilee, and enjoined Jonathan and his colleagues to return home quickly. When I had gotten these letters, I came to the village Arbela, where I procured an assembly of the Galileans to meet, and bid the ambassadors declare to them the anger of the people of Jerusalem at what had been done by Jonathan and his colleagues, and how much they hated their wicked doings, and how they had confirmed me in the government of their country, as also what related to the order they had in writing for Jonathan and his colleagues to return home. So I immediately sent them the letter, and bid him that carried it to inquire, as well as he could, how they intended to act [on this occasion.]

61. Now when they had received that letter, and were thereby greatly disturbed, they sent for John, and for the senators of Tiberias, and for the principal men of the Gabarens, and proposed to hold a council, and desired them to consider what was to be done by them. However, the governors of Tiberias were greatly disposed to keep the government to themselves; for they said it was not fit to desert their city, now it was committed to their trust, and that otherwise I should not delay to fall upon them; for they pretended falsely that so I had threatened to do. Now John was not only of their opinion, but advised them, that two of them should go to accuse me before the multitude [at Jerusalem,] that I do not manage the affairs of Galilee as I ought to do; and that they would easily persuade the people, because of their dignity, and because the whole multitude are very mutable. When, therefore, it appeared that John had suggested the wisest advice to them, they resolved that two of them, Jonathan and Ananias, should go to the people of Jerusalem, and the other two [Simon and Joazar] should be left behind to tarry at Tiberias. They also took along with them a hundred soldiers for their guard.

62. However, the governors of Tiberias took care to have their city secured with walls, and commanded their inhabitants to take their arms. They also sent for a great many soldiers from John, to assist them against me, if there should be occasion for them. Now John was at Gischala. Jonathan, therefore, and those that were with him, when they were departed from Tiberias, and as soon as they were come to Dabaritta, a village that lay in the utmost parts of Galilee, in the great plain, they, about midnight, fell among the guards I had set, who both commanded them to lay aside their weapons, and kept them in bonds upon the place, as I had charged them to do. This news was written to me by Levi, who had the command of that guard committed to him by me. Hereupon I

said nothing of it for two days; and, pretending to know nothing about it, I sent a message to the people of Tiberias, and advised them to lay their arms aside, and to dismiss their men, that they might go home; but supposing that Jonathan, and those that were with him, were already arrived at Jerusalem, they made reproachful answers to me; yet was I not terrified thereby, but contrived another stratagem against them; for I did not think it agreeable with piety to kindle the fire of war against the citizens. As I was desirous to draw those men away from Tiberias, I chose out ten thousand of the best of my armed men, and divided them into three bodies, and ordered them to go privately, and lie still as an ambush, in the villages. I also led a thousand into another village, which lay indeed in the mountains, as did the others, but only four furlongs distant from Tiberias; and gave orders that, when they saw my signal, they should come down immediately, while I myself lay with my soldiers in the sight of everybody. Hereupon the people of Tiberias, at the sight of me, came running out of the city perpetually, and abused me greatly. Nay, their madness was come to that height, that they made a decent bier for me, and, standing about it, they mourned over me in the way of jest and sport; and I could not but be myself in a pleasant humour upon the sight of this madness of theirs.

63. And now, being desirous to catch Simon by a wile, and Joazar with him, I sent a message to them, and desired them to come a little way out of the city, and many of their friends to guard them; for I said I would come down to them, and make a league with them, and divide the government of Galilee with them. Accordingly Simon was deluded, on account of his imprudence, and out of the hopes of gain, and did not delay to come; but Joazar, suspecting snares were laid for him, staid behind. So when Simon was come out, and his friends with him for his guard, I met him, and saluted him with great civility, and professed that I was obliged to him for his coming up to me; but a little while afterward I walked along with him, as though I would say something to him by himself; but when I had drawn him a good way from his friends, I took him about the middle, and gave him to my friends that were with me, to carry him into a village; and commanding my armed men to come down, I with them made an assault upon Tiberias. Now, as the fight grew hot on both sides, and the soldiers belonging to Tiberias were in a fair way to conquer me, (for my armed men were already fled away,) I saw the posture of my affairs; and encouraging those that were with me, I pursued those of Tiberias, even when they were already conquerors, into the city. I also sent another band of soldiers into the city by the lake, and gave them orders to set on fire the first house they could seize upon. When this was done, the people of Tiberias thought that their city was taken by force, and so threw down their arms for fear; and implored, they, their wives, and children, that I would spare their city. So I was over-persuaded by their entreaties, and restrained the soldiers from the vehemency with which they pursued them; while I myself, upon the coming on of the evening, returned back with my soldiers, and went to refresh myself. I also invited Simon to sup with me, and comforted him on occasion of what had happened; and I promised that I would send him safe and secure to Jerusalem, and withal would give him provisions for his journey thither.

64. But on the next day, I brought ten thousand armed men with me, and came to Tiberias. I

then sent for the principal men of the multitude into the public place, and enjoined them to tell me who were the authors of the revolt; and when they told me who the men were, I sent them bound to the city Jotapata; but, as to Jonathan and Ananias, I freed them from their bonds, and gave them provisions for their journey, together with Simon and Joasar, and five hundred armed men who should guard them; and so I sent them to Jerusalem. The people of Tiberias also came to me again, and desired that I would forgive them for what they had done; and they said they would amend what they had done amiss with regard to me, by their fidelity for the time to come; and they besought me to preserve what spoils remained upon the plunder of the city, for those that had lost them. Accordingly, I enjoined those that had got them to bring them all before us; and when they did not comply for a great while, and I saw one of the soldiers that were about me with a garment on that was more splendid than ordinary, I asked him whence he had it; and when he replied that he had it out of the plunder of the city, I had him punished with stripes; and I threatened all the rest to inflict a severer punishment upon them, unless they produced before us whatsoever they had plundered; and when a great many spoils were brought together, I restored to every one of Tiberias what they claimed to be their own.

65. And now I am come to this part of my narration, I have a mind to say a few things to Justus, who hath himself written a history concerning these affairs; as also to others who profess to write history, but have little regard to truth, and are not afraid, either out of ill-will or good-will to some persons, to relate falsehoods. These men do like those who compose forged deeds and conveyances; and because they are not brought to the like punishment with them, they have no regard to truth. When, therefore, Justus undertook to write about these facts, and about the Jewish war, that he might appear to have been an industrious man, he falsified in what he related about me, and could not speak truth even about his own country; whence it is that, being belied by him, I am under a necessity to make my defence; and so I shall say what I have concealed till now; and let no one wonder that I have not told the world these things a great while ago; for although it be necessary for a historian to write the truth, yet is such a one not bound severely to animadvert on the wickedness of certain men,—not out of any favour to them, but out of an author's own moderation. How then comes it to pass, O Justus! thou most sagacious of writers, (that I may address myself to him as if he were here present,) for so thou boastest of thyself, that I and the Galileans have been the authors of that sedition which thy country engaged in, both against the Romans and against the king [Agrippa, junior]—for before ever I was appointed governor of Galilee by the community of Jerusalem, both thou and all the people of Tiberias had not only taken up arms, but had made war with Decapolis of Syria. Accordingly, thou hadst ordered their villages to be burnt, and a domestic servant of thine fell in the battle. Nor is it I only who say this; but so it is written in the Commentaries of Vespasian, the emperor; as also how the inhabitants of Decapolis came clamouring to Vespasian at Ptolemais, and desired that thou, who wast the author, [of that war,] mightst be brought to punishment; and thou hadst certainly been punished at the command of Vespasian, had not King Agrippa, who had power given him to have thee put to death, at the earnest entreaty of his sister Ber-

nice, changed the punishment from death into a long imprisonment. Thy political administration of affairs afterward doth also clearly discover both thy other behaviour in life, and that thou wast the occasion of thy country's revolt from the Romans; plain signs of which I shall produce presently. I have also a mind to say a few things to the rest of the people of Tiberias on thy account; and to demonstrate to those that light upon this history, that you bare no good-will, neither to the Romans nor to the king. To be sure, the greatest cities of Galilee, O Justus! were Sepphoris and thy country Tiberias; but Sepphoris, situated in the very midst of Galilee, and having many villages about it, and able with ease to have been bold and troublesome to the Romans, if they had so pleased,—yet did it resolve to continue faithful to those their masters, and at the same time excluded me out of their city, and prohibited all their citizens from joining with the Jews in the war; and, that they might be out of danger from me, they, by a wile, got leave of me to fortify their city with walls: they also, of their own accord, admitted of a garrison of Roman legions, sent them by Cestius Gallus, who was then president of Syria, and so had me in contempt, though I was then very powerful, and all were greatly afraid of me; and at the same time that the greatest of our cities, Jerusalem, was besieged, and that temple of ours, which belonged to us all, was in danger of falling under the enemy's power, they sent no assistance thither, as not willing to have it thought they would bear arms against the Romans; but as for thy country, O Justus! situated upon the lake of Genesareth, and distant from Hippos thirty furlongs, from Gadara sixty, and from Scythopolis, which was under the king's jurisdiction, a hundred and twenty; when there was no Jewish city near, it might easily have preserved its fidelity [to the Romans] if it had so pleased them to do; for the city and its people had plenty of weapons; but, as thou sayest, I was *then* the author [of their revolt;] and pray, O Justus! who was that author *afterwards?*—for thou knowest that I was in the power of the Romans before Jerusalem was besieged, and before the same time Jotapata was taken by force, as well as many other fortresses, and a great many of the Galileans fell in the war. It was therefore then a proper time, when you were certainly freed from any fear on my account, to throw away your weapons, and to demonstrate to the king and to the Romans that it was not of choice, but as forced by necessity, that you fell into the war against them; but you staid till Vespasian came himself as far as your walls, with his whole army; and then you did indeed lay aside your weapons out of fear, and your city had for certain been taken by force, unless Vespasian had complied with the king's supplication for you, and had excused your madness. It was not I, therefore, who was the author of this, but your own inclinations to war. Do not you remember how often I got you under my power, and yet put none of you to death? Nay, you once fell into a tumult one against another, and slew one hundred and eighty-five of your citizens, not on account of your good-will to the king and the Romans, but on account of your own wickedness, and this while I was besieged by the Romans in Jotapata. Nay, indeed, were there not reckoned up two thousand of the people of Tiberias during the siege of Jerusalem, some of whom were slain, and the rest caught and carried captives? But thou wilt pretend that thou didst not engage in the war, since thou didst flee to the king! Yes, indeed, thou didst flee to him; but I say it was out of fear of me. Thou sayest, indeed, that it is I who am a wicked man. But then, for what reason was it that King Agrippa, who procured thee thy life when thou wast condemned to die by Vespasian, and who bestowed so much riches upon thee, did twice afterward put thee in bonds, and as often obliged thee to run away from thy country, and, when he had once ordered thee to be put to death, he granted thee a pardon at the earnest desire of Bernice? And when (after so many of thy wicked pranks) he had made thee his secretary, he caught thee falsifying his epistles, and drove thee away from his sight. But I shall not inquire accurately into these matters of scandal against thee. Yet cannot I but wonder at thy impudence, when thou hast the assurance to say, that thou hast better related these affairs [of the war] than have all the others that have written about them, whilst thou didst not know what was done in Galilee; for thou wast then at Berytus with the king; nor didst thou know how much the Romans suffered at the siege of Jotapata, or what miseries they brought upon us; nor couldst thou learn by inquiry what I did during that siege myself; for all those that might afford such information were quite destroyed in that siege. But perhaps thou wilt say, thou hast written of what was done against the people of Jerusalem exactly. But how should that be? for neither wast thou concerned in that war, nor hast thou read the commentaries of Cæsar; of which we have evident proof, because thou hast contradicted those commentaries of Cæsar in thy history. But if thou art so hardy as to affirm that thou hast written that history better than all the rest, why didst thou not publish thy history while the Emperors Vespasian and Titus, the generals in that war, as well as King Agrippa and his family, who were men very well skilled in the learning of the Greeks, were all alive? for thou hast had it written these twenty years, and then mightst thou have had the testimony of thy accuracy. But now, when these men are no longer with us, and thou thinkest thou canst not be contradicted, thou venturest to publish it. But then I was not in like manner afraid of my own writing, but I offered my books to the emperors themselves, when the facts were almost under men's eyes; for I was conscious to myself that I had observed the truth of the facts; and as I expected to have their attestation to them, so I was not deceived in such expectation. Moreover, I immediately presented my history to many other persons, some of whom were concerned in the war, as was King Agrippa and some of his kindred. Now the Emperor Titus was so desirous that the knowledge of these affairs should be taken from these books alone, that he subscribed his own hand to them, and ordered that they should be published; and for King Agrippa, he wrote me sixty-two letters, and attested to the truth of what I had therein delivered; two of which letters I have here subjoined, and thou mayst thereby know their contents :—" King Agrippa to Josephus, his dear friend, sendeth greeting. I have read over thy book with great pleasure, and it appears to me that thou hast done it much more accurately, and with greater care, than have the other writers. Send me the rest of these books. Farewell, my dear friend." " King Agrippa to Josephus, his dear friend, sendeth greeting. It seems by what thou hast written, that thou standest in need of no instruction, in order to our information from the beginning. However, when thou comest to me, I will inform thee of a great many things which thou dost not know." So when this history was perfected, Agrippa, neither by way of flattery, which was not agreeable to him, nor by way of

irony, as thou wilt say, for he was entirely a stranger to such an evil disposition of mind, but he wrote this by way of attestation to what was true, as all that read histories may do. And so much shall be said concerning Justus,* which I am obliged to add by way of digression.

66. Now, when I had settled the affairs of Tiberias, and had assembled my friends as a sanhedrim, I consulted what I should do as to John: whereupon it appeared to be the opinion of all the Galileans that I should arm them all, and march against John, and punish him as the author of all the disorders that had happened. Yet was not I pleased with their determination; as purposing to compose these troubles without bloodshed. Upon this I exhorted them to use the utmost care to learn the names of all that were under John; which, when they had done, and I thereby was apprised who the men were, I published an edict, wherein I offered security and my right hand to such of John's party as had a mind to repent; and I allowed twenty days' time to such as would take this most advantageous course for themselves. I also threatened that, unless they threw down their arms, I would burn their houses, and expose their goods to public sale. When the men heard of this, they were in no small disorder, and deserted John; and to the number of four thousand threw down their arms, and came to me. So that no others staid with John but his own citizens, and about fifteen hundred strangers that came from the metropolis of Tyre; and when John saw that he had been outwitted by my stratagem, he continued afterward in his own country, and was in great fear of me.

67. But about this time it was that the people of Sepphoris grew insolent, and took up arms, out of a confidence they had in the strength of their walls, and because they saw me engaged in other affairs also. So they sent to Cestius Gallus, who was president of Syria, and desired that he would either come quickly to them, and take their city under his protection, or send them a garrison. Accordingly Gallus promised them to come, but did not send word when he would come: and when I had learned so much, I took the soldiers that were with me, and made an assault upon the people of Sepphoris, and took

* The character of this history of Justus of Tiberias, the rival of our Josephus, which is now lost, with its only remaining fragment, are given us by a very able critic, Photius, who read that history. It is in the 33d code of his Bibliotheca, and runs thus :—" I have read" (says Photius) " the chronology of Justus of Tiberias, whose title is this, [The Chronology of] the Kings of Judah, which succeeded one another. This [Justus] came out of the city of Tiberias in Galilee. He begins his history from Moses, and ends it not till the death of Agrippa, the seventh [ruler] of the family of Herod, and the last king of the Jews; who took the government under Claudius, had it augmented under Nero, and still more augmented by Vespasian. He died in the third year of Trajan, where also his history ends. He is very concise in his language, and slightly passes over those affairs that were most necessary to be insisted on; and being under the Jewish prejudices, as indeed he was himself also a Jew by birth, he makes not the least mention of the appearance of Christ, or what things happened to Him, or of the wonderful works that He did. He was the son of a certain Jew, whose name was Pistus. He was a man, as he is described by Josephus, of a most profligate character; a slave both to money and to pleasures. In public affairs he was opposite to Josephus; and it is related, that he laid many plots against him; but that Josephus, though he had his enemy frequently under his power, did only reproach him in words, and so let him go without further punishment. He says also that the history which this man wrote is for the main fabulous, and chiefly as to those parts where he describes the Roman war with the Jews, and the taking of Jerusalem."

the city by force. The Galileans took this opportunity, as thinking they had now a proper time for shewing their hatred to them, since they bore ill-will to that city also. They then exerted themselves as if they would destroy them all utterly, with those that sojourned there also. So they ran upon them, and set their houses on fire, as finding them without inhabitants; for the men, out of fear, ran together to the citadel. So the Galileans carried off everything, and omitted no kind of desolation which they could bring upon their countrymen. When I saw this, I was exceedingly troubled at it, and commanded them to leave off, and put them in mind that it was not agreeable to piety to do such things to their countrymen: but since they neither would hearken to what I exhorted, nor to what I commanded them to do, (for the hatred they bore to the people there was too hard for my exhortations to them,) I bade those my friends, who were most faithful to me, and were about me, to give out reports, as if the Romans were falling upon the other part of the city with a great army; and this I did, that, by such a report being spread abroad, I might restrain the violence of the Galileans, and preserve the city of Sepphoris. And at length this stratagem had its effect; for, upon hearing this report, they were in fear for themselves, and so they left off plundering, and ran away; and this more especially, because they saw me, their general, do the same also; for, that I might cause this report to be believed, I pretended to be in fear as well as they. Thus were the inhabitants of Sepphoris unexpectedly preserved by this contrivance of mine.

68. Nay, indeed, Tiberias had like to have been plundered by the Galileans also upon the following occasion:—The chief men of the senate wrote to the king, and desired that he would come to them, and take possession of their city. The king promised to come, and wrote a letter in answer to theirs, and gave it to one of his bed-chamber, whose name was Crispus, and who was by birth a Jew, to carry it to Tiberias. When the Galileans knew that this man carried such a letter, they caught him and brought him to me; but as soon as the whole multitude heard of it, they were enraged, and betook themselves to their arms. So a great many of them got together from all quarters the next day, and came to the city Asochis, where I then lodged, and made heavy clamours, and called the city of Tiberias a traitor to them, and a friend to the king; and desired leave of me to go down and utterly destroy it; for they bore the like ill-will to the people of Tiberias as they did to those of Sepphoris.

69. When I heard this, I was in doubt what to do, and hesitated by what means I might deliver Tiberias from the rage of the Galileans; for I could not deny that those of Tiberias had written to the king, and invited him to come to them; for his letters to them, in answer thereto, would fully prove the truth of that. So I sat a long time musing with myself, and then said to them, "I know well enough that the people of Tiberias have offended; nor shall I forbid you to plunder the city. However, such things ought to be done with discretion; for they of Tiberias have not been the only betrayers of our liberty, but many of the most eminent patriots of the Galileans, as they pretended to be, have done the same. Tarry, therefore, till I shall thoroughly find out those authors of our danger, and then you shall have them all at once under your power, with all such as you shall yourselves bring in also." Upon my saying this, I pacified the multitude, and they left off their anger, and went their ways; and I gave orders that he who brought the king's letters should be put into bonds; but in a few days I pretended that I was obliged, by a necessary affair of my own, to go out of the kingdom. I then called Crispus privately, and ordered him to make the soldier that kept him drunk, and to run away to the king. So when Tiberias was in danger of being utterly destroyed a second time, it escaped the danger by my skilful management, and the care that I had for its preservation.

70. About this time it was that Justus, the son of Pistus, without my knowledge, ran away to the king; the occasion of which I will here relate. Upon the beginning of the war between the Jews and the Romans, the people of Tiberias resolved to submit to the king, and not to revolt from the Romans; while Justus tried to persuade them to betake themselves to their arms, as being himself desirous of innovations, and having hopes of obtaining the government of Galilee, as well as of his own country [Tiberias] also. Yet did he not obtain what he hoped for, because the Galileans bore ill-will to those of Tiberias, and this on account of their anger at what miseries they had suffered from them before the war; thence it was that they would not endure that Justus should be their governor. I myself also, who had been intrusted by the community of Jerusalem with the government of Galilee, did frequently come to that degree of rage at Justus, that I had almost resolved to kill him, as not able to bear his mischievous disposition. He was therefore much afraid of me, lest at length my passion should come to extremity; so he went to the king, as supposing that he would dwell better and more safely with him.

71. Now when the people of Sepphoris had, in so surprising a manner, escaped their first danger, they sent to Cestius Gallus, and desired him to come to them immediately, and take possession of their city, or else to send forces sufficient to repress all their enemies' incursions upon them; and at the last they did prevail with Gallus to send them a considerable army, both of horse and foot, which came in the night-time, and which they admitted into the city. But when the country round about it was harassed by the Roman army, I took those soldiers that were about me, and came to Garisme, where I cast up a bank, a good way off the city Sepphoris; and when I was at twenty furlongs' distance, I came upon it by night, and made an assault upon its walls with my forces: and when I had ordered a considerable number of my soldiers to scale them with ladders, I became master of the greatest part of the city. But soon after, our unacquaintedness with the places forced us to retire, after we had killed twelve of the Roman footmen, and two horsemen, and a few of the people of Sepphoris, with the loss of only a single man of our own. And when it afterwards came to a battle in the plain against the horsemen, and we had undergone the dangers of it courageously for a long time, we were beaten; for upon the Romans encompassing me about, my soldiers were afraid, and fell back. There fell in that battle one of those that had been intrusted to guard my body; his name was Justus, who at this time had the same post with the king. At the same time also there came forces, both horsemen and footmen, from the king, and Sylla their commander, who was the captain of his guard; this Sylla pitched his camp at five furlongs' distance from Julias, and set a guard upon the roads, both that which led to Cana, and that which led to the fortress Gamala, that he might

hinder their inhabitants from getting provisions out of Galilee.

72. As soon as I had got intelligence of this, I sent two thousand armed men, and a captain over them, whose name was Jeremiah, who raised a bank a furlong off Julias, near to the river Jordan, and did no more than skirmish with the enemy; till I took three thousand soldiers myself, and came to them. But on the next day, when I had laid an ambush in a certain valley, not far from the banks, I provoked those that belonged to the king to come to a battle, and gave orders to my own soldiers to turn their backs upon them, until they should have drawn the enemy away from their camp, and brought them out into the field, which was done accordingly; for Sylla, supposing that our party did really run away, was ready to pursue them, when our soldiers that lay in ambush took them on their backs, and put them all into great disorder. I also immediately made a sudden turn with my own forces, and met those of the king's party, and put them to flight. And I had performed great things that day, if a certain fate had not been my hindrance; for the horse on which I rode, and upon whose back I fought, fell into a quagmire, and threw me on the ground; and I was bruised on my wrist, and carried into a village named Cepharnome, or Capernaum. When my soldiers heard of this, they were afraid I had been worse hurt than I was; and so they did not go on with their pursuit any further, but returned in very great concern for me. I therefore sent for the physicians, and while I was under their hands, I continued feverish that day; and, as the physicians directed, I was that night removed to Taricheæ.

73. When Sylla and his party were informed what happened to me, they took courage again; and understanding that the watch was negligently kept in our camp, they by night placed a body of horsemen in ambush beyond Jordan, and when it was day they provoked us to fight; and as we did not refuse it, but came into the plain, their horsemen appeared out of that ambush in which they had lain, and put our men into disorder, and made them run away; so they slew six men of our side. Yet did they not go off with the victory at last; for when they heard that some armed men were sailed from Taricheæ to Julias, they were afraid, and retired.

74. It was not now long before Vespasian came to Tyre, and King Agrippa with him: but the Tyrians began to speak reproachfully of the king, and called him an enemy to the Romans; for they said that Philip, the general of his army, had betrayed the royal palace and the Roman forces that were in Jerusalem, and that it was done by his command. When Vespasian heard of this report, he rebuked the Tyrians for abusing a man who was both a king and a friend to the Romans; but he exhorted the king to send Philip to Rome, to answer for what he had done before Nero. But when Philip was sent thither, he did not come into the sight of Nero, for he found him very near death, on account of the troubles that then happened, and a civil war; and so he returned to the king. But when Vespasian was come to Ptolemais, the chief men of Decapolis of Syria made a clamour against Justus of Tiberias, because he had set their villages on fire: so Vespasian delivered him to the king, to be put to death by those under the king's jurisdiction; yet did the king only put him into bonds, and concealed what he had done from Vespasian, as I have before related. But the people of Sepphoris met Vespasian, and saluted him, and had forces sent him, with Placidus their commander:

he also went up with them, as I also followed them, till Vespasian came into Galilee. As to which coming of his, and after what manner it was ordered, and how he fought his first battle with me near the village Taricheæ, and how from thence they went to Jotapata, and how I was taken alive, and bound, and how I was afterward loosed, with all that was done by me in the Jewish war, and during the siege of Jerusalem, I have accurately related them in the books concerning the war of the Jews. However, it will, I think, be fit for me to add now an account of those actions of my life which I have not related in that book of the Jewish war.

75. For, when the siege of Jotapata was over, and I was among the Romans, I was kept with much care, by means of the great respect that Vespasian shewed me. Moreover, at his command, I married a virgin, who was from among the captives of that country :* yet did she not live with me long, but was divorced, upon my being freed from my bonds, and my going to Alexandria. However, I married another wife at Alexandria, and was thence sent, together with Titus, to the siege of Jerusalem, and was frequently in danger of being put to death,— while both the Jews were very desirous to get me under their power, in order to have me punished; and the Romans also, whenever they were beaten, supposed that it was occasioned by my treachery, and made continual clamours to the emperors, and desired that they would bring me to punishment, as a traitor to them: but Titus Cæsar was well acquainted with the uncertain fortune of war, and returned no answer to the soldiers' vehement solicitations against me. Moreover, when the city of Jerusalem was taken by force, Titus Cæsar persuaded me frequently to take whatsoever I would of the ruins of my country, and said that he gave me leave so to do; but when my country was destroyed, I thought nothing else to be of any value which I could take and keep as a comfort under my calamities; so I made this request to Titus, that my family might have their liberty: I had also the holy books † by Titus's concession: nor was it long after, that I asked of him the life of my brother, and of fifty friends with him; and was not denied. When I also went once to the temple, by the permission of Titus, where there were a great multitude of captive women and children, I got all those that I remembered, as among my own friends and acquaintances, to be set free, being in number about one hundred and ninety; and so I delivered them, without their paying any price of redemption, and restored them to their former fortune; and when I was sent by Titus Cæsar with Cerealius, and a thousand horsemen, to a certain village called Thecoa, in order to know whether it were a place fit for a camp, as I came back, I saw many captives crucified; and remembered three of them as my former acquaintance. I was very sorry at this in my mind, and went with tears in my eyes to Titus, and told him of them; so he immediately commanded them to be taken down, and to have the greatest care taken of them, in order to their recovery;

---

* Here Josephus, a priest, honestly confesses that he did that at the command of Vespasian, which he had before told us was not lawful for a priest to do by the law of Moses, (Antiq. b. iii. ch. xii. sect. 2.) I mean, the taking a captive woman to wife. See also Against Appion, b. i. sect. 7. But he seems to have been quickly sensible that his compliance with the commands of an emperor would not excuse him, for he soon put her away, as Reland justly observes here.

† Of this most remarkable clause, and its most important consequences, see Essay on the Old Testament, pp. 193-195.

yet two of them died under the physician's hands, while the third recovered.

76. But when Titus had composed the troubles in Judea, and conjectured that the lands which I had in Judea would bring me no profit, because a garrison to guard the country was afterward to pitch there, he gave me another country in the plains, and, when he was going away to Rome, he made choice of me to sail along with him, and paid me great respect; and when we were come to Rome, I had great care taken of me by Vespasian; for he gave me an apartment in his own house, which he lived in before he came to the empire. He also honoured me with the privilege of a Roman citizen, and gave me an annual pension; and continued to respect me to the end of his life, without any abatement of his kindness to me; which very thing made me envied, and brought me into danger; for a certain Jew, whose name was Jonathan, who had raised a tumult in Cyrene, and had persuaded two thousand men of that country to join with him, was the occasion of their ruin; but when he was bound by the governor of that country, and sent to the emperor, he told him that I had sent him both weapons and money. However, he could not conceal his being a liar from Vespasian, who condemned him to die; according to which sentence he was put to death. Nay, after that, when those that envied my good fortune did frequently bring accusations against me, by God's providence I escaped them all. I also received from Vespasian no small quantity of land, as a free gift, in Judea; about which time I divorced my wife also, as not pleased with her behaviour, though not till she had been the mother of three children; two of whom are dead, and one, whom I had named Hyrcanus, is alive. After this I married a wife who had lived at Crete, but a Jewess by birth: a woman she was of eminent parents, and such as were the most illustrious in all the country, and whose character was beyond that of most other women, as her future life did demonstrate. By her I had two sons; the elder's name was Justus, and the next Simonides, who was also named Agrippa: and these were the circumstances of my domestic affairs. However, the kindness of the emperor to me continued still the same; for when Vespasian was dead, Titus, who succeeded him in the government, kept up the same respect for me which I had from his father; and when I had frequent accusations laid against me, he would not believe them: and Domitian, who succeeded, still augmented his respects to me; for he punished those Jews that were my accusers; and gave command that a servant of mine, who was a eunuch, and my accuser, should be punished. He also made that country I had in Judea tax-free, which is a mark of the greatest honour to him who hath it; nay, Domitia, the wife of Cæsar, continued to do me kindnesses. And this is the account of my whole life; and let others judge of my character by them as they please; but to thee, O Epaphroditus,* thou most excellent of men! do I dedicate all this treatise of our Antiquities; and so, for the present, I here conclude the whole.

---

* Of this Epaphroditus, see the note on the Preface to the Antiquities.

THE

ANTIQUITIES OF THE JEWS

PREFACE

1. THOSE who undertake to write histories, do not, I perceive, take that trouble on one and the same account, but for many reasons, and those such as are very different one from another, for some of them apply themselves to this part of learning to shew their skill in composition, and that they may therein acquire a reputation for speaking finely; others of them there are who write histories, in order to gratify those that happened to be concerned in them, and on that account have spared no pains, but rather gone beyond their own abilities in the performance; but others there are who, of necessity and by force, are driven to write history, because they are concerned in the facts, and so cannot excuse themselves from committing them to writing, for the advantage of posterity: nay, there are not a few who are induced to draw their historical facts out of darkness into light, and to produce them for the benefit of the public, on account of the great importance of the facts themselves with which they have been concerned. Now of these several reasons for writing history, I must profess the two last were my own reasons also; for since I was myself interested in that war which we Jews had with the Romans, and knew myself its particular actions, and what conclusion it had, I was forced to give the history of it, because I saw that others perverted the truth of those actions in their writings.

2. Now I have undertaken the present work, as thinking it will appear to all the Greeks† worthy of their study; for it will contain all our antiquities, and the constitution of our government, as interpreted out of the Hebrew Scriptures; and indeed I did formerly intend, when I wrote of the war,‡ to explain who the Jews originally were,—what fortunes they had been subject to,—and by what legislator they had been instructed in piety, and the exercise of other virtues,—what wars also they had made in remote ages, till they were unwillingly engaged in this last with the Romans; but because this work would take up a great compass, I separated it into a set treatise by itself, with a beginning of its own, and its own conclusion; but in process of time, as usually happens to

such as undertake great things, I grew weary, and went on slowly, it being a large subject, and a difficult thing to translate our history into a foreign, and to us unaccustomed language. However, some persons there were who desired to know our history, and so exhorted me to go on with it; and above all the rest, Epaphroditus,§ a man who is a lover of all kind of learning, but is principally delighted with the knowledge of history; and this on account of his having been himself concerned in great affairs, and many turns of fortune, and having shewn a wonderful vigour of an excellent nature, and an immovable virtuous resolution in them all. I yielded to this man's persuasions, who always excites such as have abilities in what is useful and acceptable, to join their endeavours with his. I was also ashamed myself to permit any laziness of disposition to have a greater influence upon me than the delight of taking pains in such studies as were very useful: I thereupon stirred up myself, and went on with my work more cheerfully. Besides the foregoing motives, I had others which I greatly reflected on; and these were, that our forefathers were willing to communicate such things to others; and that some of the Greeks took considerable pains to know the affairs of our nation.

3. I found, therefore, that the second of the Ptolemies was a king who was extraordinarily diligent in what concerned learning and the collection of books; that he was also peculiarly ambitious to procure a translation of our law, and of the constitution of our government therein contained, into the Greek tongue. Now Eleazar, the high priest, one not inferior to any other of that dignity among us, did not envy the forenamed king the participation of that advantage, which otherwise he would for certain have denied him, but that he knew the custom of our nation was, to hinder nothing of what we esteemed ourselves from being communicated to others. Accordingly, I thought it became me both to imitate the generosity of our high priest, and to suppose there might even now be many lovers of learning like the king; for he did not obtain all our writings at that time; but those who were sent to Alexandria as interpreters gave him only the books of the law, while there were a vast number of other matters in our

---

* This preface of Josephus is excellent in its kind, and highly worthy the repeated perusal of the reader, before he set about the perusal of the work itself.

† That is, all the Gentiles, both Greeks and Romans.

‡ We may seasonably note here, that Josephus wrote his Seven Books of the Jewish War long before he wrote these his Antiquities. Those books of the War were published about A.D. 75; and these Antiquities, A.D. 93, about eighteen years later.

§ This Epaphroditus was certainly alive in the third year of Trajan, A.D. 100. See the note on the first book Against Apion, sect. 1. Who he was we do not know; for as to Epaphroditus, the freed-man of Nero, and afterwards Domitian's secretary, who was put to death by Domitian, in the 14th or 15th year of his reign, he could not be alive in the third of Trajan.

sacred books. They indeed contain in them the history of five thousand years; in which time happened many strange accidents, many chances of war, and great actions of the commanders, and mutations of the form of our government. Upon the whole, a man that will peruse this history may principally learn from it that all events succeed well, even to an incredible degree, and the reward of felicity is proposed by God; but then it is to those that follow His will, and do not venture to break His excellent laws;— and that so far as men any way apostatise from the accurate observation of them, what was practicable before becomes impracticable;* and whatsoever they set about as a good thing is converted into an incurable calamity. And now I exhort all those that peruse these books to apply their minds to God; and to examine the mind of our legislator, whether he hath not understood his nature in a manner worthy of him; and hath not ever ascribed to him such operations as become his power, and hath not preserved his writings from those indecent fables which others have framed, although, by the great distance of time when he lived, he might have securely forged such lies; for he lived two thousand years ago; at which vast distance of ages the poets themselves have not been so hardy as to fix even the generations of their gods, much less the actions of their men, or their own laws. As I proceed, therefore, I shall accurately describe what is contained in our records, in the order of time that belongs to them; for I have already promised so to do throughout this undertaking, and this without adding anything to what is therein contained, or taking away anything therefrom.

4. But because almost all our constitution depends on the wisdom of Moses, our legislator, I cannot avoid saying somewhat concerning him beforehand, though I shall do it briefly: I mean, because otherwise those that read my book may wonder how it comes to pass that my discourse, which promises an account of laws and historical facts, contains so much of philosophy. The reader is therefore to know, that Moses deemed it exceeding necessary that he who would conduct his own life well, and give laws to others, in the first place should consider the divine nature, and upon the contemplation of God's operations should thereby imitate the best of all patterns, so far as it is possible for human nature to do, and to endeavour to follow after it; neither could the legislator himself have a right mind without such a contemplation; nor would anything he should write tend to the promotion of virtue in his readers: I mean, unless they be taught first of all, that God is the Father and Lord of all things, and sees all things, and that thence he bestows a happy life upon those that follow him; but plunges such as do not walk in the paths of virtue into inevitable miseries. Now when Moses was desirous to teach this lesson to his countrymen, he did not begin the establishment of his laws after the same manner that other legislators did: I mean, upon contracts and other rites between one man and another, but by raising their minds upwards to regard God, and his creation of the world; and by persuading them, that we men are the most excellent of the creatures of God upon earth. Now when once he had brought them to submit to religion, he easily persuaded them to submit in all other things; for, as to other legislators, they followed fables, and, by their discourses, transferred the most reproachful of human vices unto the gods, and so afforded wicked men the most plausible excuses for their crimes; but, as for our legislator, when he had once demonstrated that God was possessed of perfect virtue, he supposed that men also ought to strive after the participation of it; and on those who did not so think and so believe, he inflicted the severest punishments. I exhort, therefore, my readers to examine this whole undertaking in that view; for thereby it will appear to them that there is nothing therein disagreeable. either to the majesty of God, or to his love to mankind; for all things have here a reference to the nature of the universe; while our legislator speaks some things wisely, but enigmatically, and others under a decent allegory, but still explains such things as required a direct explication plainly and expressly. However, those that have a mind to know the reasons of everything, may find here a very curious philosophical theory, which I now indeed shall wave the explication of; but if God afford me time for it, I will set about writing it,† after I have finished the present work. I shall now betake myself to the history before me, after I have first mentioned what Moses says of the creation of the world, which I find described in the sacred books after the manner following.

---

* Josephus here plainly alludes to the famous Greek proverb: If God be with us, every thing that is impossible becomes possible.

† As to this intended work of Josephus, concerning the reasons of many of the Jewish laws, and what philosophical or allegorical sense they would bear, the loss of which work is by some of the learned not much regretted, I am inclinable in part to Fabricius's opinion, ap. Havercamp, pp. 63, 64, that "we need not doubt but, among some vain and frigid conjectures derived from Jewish imaginations, Josephus would have taught us a greater number of excellent and useful things, which perhaps nobody, neither among the Jews nor among the Christians, can now inform us of; so that I would give a great deal to find it still extant."

CHAPTER I

THE CONSTITUTION OF THE WORLD, AND THE DISPOSITION OF THE ELEMENTS

1. IN the beginning God created the heaven and the earth; but when the earth did not come into sight, but was covered with thick darkness, and a wind moved upon its surface, God commanded that there should be light; and when that was made he considered the whole mass, and separated the light and the darkness; and the name he gave to one was *Night*, and the other he called *Day;* and he named the beginning of light and the time of rest, *The Evening* and *The Morning;* and this was ind~ed the first day: but Moses said it was one day,—the cause of which I am able to give even now; but because I have promised to give such reasons for all things in a treatise by itself, I shall put off its exposition till that time. After this, on the second day, he placed the heaven over the whole world, and separated it from the other parts; and he determined it should stand by itself. He also placed a crystalline [firmament] round it, and put together in a manner agreeable to the earth, and fitted it for giving moisture and rain, and for affording the advantage of dews. On the third day he appointed the dry land to appear, with the sea itself round about it; and on the very same day he made the plants and the seeds to spring out of the earth. On the fourth day he adorned the heavens with the sun, the moon, and the other stars; and appointed them their motions and courses, that the vicissitudes of the seasons might be clearly signified. And on the fifth day he produced the living creatures, both those that swim and those that fly; the former in the sea, the latter in the air: he also sorted them as to society and mixture, for procreation, and that their kinds might increase and multiply. On the sixth day he created the four-footed beasts, and made them male and female: on the same day he also formed man. Accordingly Moses says that in just six days the world and all that is therein was made; and that the seventh day was a rest, and a release from the labour of such operations;—whence it is that we celebrate a rest from our labours on that day, and call it the Sabbath; which word denotes *rest* in the Hebrew tongue.

2. Moreover, Moses, after the seventh day was over,* begins to talk philosophically; and concerning the formation of man, says thus:—That God took dust from the ground, and formed man, and inserted in him a spirit and a soul.† This man was called Adam, which in the Hebrew tongue signifies *one that is red*, because he was formed out of red earth, compounded together; for of that kind is virgin and true earth. God also presented the living creatures, when he had made them, according to their kinds, both male and female, to Adam, who gave them those names by which they are still called. But when he saw that Adam had no female companion, no society, for there was no such created, and that he wondered at the other animals which were male and female, he laid him asleep, and took away one of his ribs, and out of it formed the woman; whereupon Adam knew her when she was brought to him, and acknowledged that she was made out of himself. Now a woman is called in the Hebrew tongue *Issa;* but the name of this woman was Eve, which signifies *the mother of all living.*

3. Moses says further, that God planted a paradise in the east, flourishing with all sorts of trees; and that among them was the tree of life, and another of knowledge, whereby was to be known what was good and evil; and that when he brought Adam and his wife into this garden, he commanded them to take care of the plants. Now the garden was watered by one river,‡ which ran round about the whole earth, and was parted into four parts. And Phison, which denotes a multitude, running into India, makes its exit into the sea, and is by the Greeks called Ganges. Euphrates also, as well as Tigris, goes down into

---

* Since Josephus, in his Preface, sect. 4, says that Moses wrote some things enigmatically, some allegorically, and the rest in plain words, since in his account of the first chapter of Genesis, and the first three verses of the second, he gives us no hints of any mystery at all; but when he here comes to ver. 4, &c., he says that Moses, after the seventh day was over, began to talk philosophically, it is not very improbable that he understood the rest of the second and the third chapters in some enigmatical, or allegorical, or philosophical sense. The change of the name of God, just at this place, from Elohim to Jehovah Elohim, from God to Lord God in the Hebrew, Samaritan, and Septuagint, does also not a little favour some such change in the narration or construction.

† We may observe here that Josephus supposed man to be compounded of spirit, soul, and body, with St Paul (1 Thess. v. 23) and the rest of the ancients: he elsewhere says also, that the blood of animals was forbidden to be eaten, as having in it soul and spirit.—Antiq., b. iii. chap. xi. sect. 2.

‡ Whence this strange notion came, which yet is not peculiar to Josephus, but, as Dr Hudson says here, is derived from older authors, as if four of the greatest rivers in the world, running two of them at vast distances from the other two, by some means or other watered paradise, is hard to say. Only, since Josephus has already appeared to allegorise this history, and take notice that these four names had a particular signification: Phison for Ganges, *a multitude;* Phrath for Euphrates, either *a dispersion* or *a flower;* Diglath for Tigris, *what is swift* with *narrowness;* and Geon for Nile, *what arises from the east,*—we perhaps mistake him when we suppose he literally means those for rivers; especially as to Geon or Nile, which arises from the east, while he very well knew the literal Nile arises from the south; though what further allegorical sense he had in view is now, I fear, impossible to be determined.

the Red Sea.* Now the name Euphrates, or Phrath, denotes either a dispersion, or a flower: by Tigris, or Diglath, is signified what is swift, with narrowness; and Geon runs through Egypt, and denotes what arises from the east, which the Greeks call Nile.

4. God therefore commanded that Adam and his wife should eat of all the rest of the plants, but to abstain from the tree of knowledge; and foretold to them that, if they touched it, it would prove their destruction. But while all the living creatures had one language,† at that time the serpent, which then lived together with Adam and his wife, shewed an envious disposition, at his supposal of their living happily, and in obedience to the commands of God; and imagining that, when they disobeyed them, they would fall into calamities, he persuaded the woman, out of a malicious intention, to taste of the tree of knowledge, telling them that in that tree was the knowledge of good and evil; which knowledge when they should obtain, they would lead a happy life, nay, a life not inferior to that of a god: by which means he overcame the woman, and persuaded her to despise the command of God. Now when she had tasted of that tree, and was pleased with its fruit, she persuaded Adam to make use of it also. Upon this they perceived that they were become naked to one another; and being ashamed thus to appear abroad, they invented somewhat to cover them; for the tree sharpened their understanding; and they covered themselves with fig-leaves; and tying these before them, out of modesty, they thought they were happier than they were before, as they had discovered what they were in want of. But when God came into the garden, Adam, who was wont before to come and converse with him, being conscious of his wicked behaviour, went out of the way. This behaviour surprised God, and he asked what was the cause of this his procedure, and why he, that before delighted in that conversation, did now fly from it, and avoid it. When he made no reply, as conscious to himself that he had transgressed the command of God, God said, "I had before determined about you both, how you might lead a happy life, without any affliction, and care, and vexation of soul; and that all things which might contribute to your enjoyment and pleasure should grow up by my providence, of their own accord, without your own labour and painstaking; which state of labour and painstaking would soon bring on old age, and death would not be at any remote distance; but now thou

hast abused this my good-will, and hast disobeyed my commands; for thy silence is not the sign of thy virtue, but of thy evil conscience." However, Adam excused his sin, and entreated God not to be angry at him, and laid the blame of what was done upon his wife, and said that he was deceived by her, and thence became an offender, while she again accused the serpent. But God allotted him punishment, because he weakly submitted to the counsel of his wife, and said, the ground should not henceforth yield its fruits of its own accord, but that when it should be harassed by their labour it should bring forth some of its fruits, and refuse to bring forth others. He also made Eve liable to the inconveniency of breeding, and the sharp pains of bringing forth children, and this because she persuaded Adam with the same arguments wherewith the serpent had persuaded her, and had thereby brought him into a calamitous condition. He also deprived the serpent of speech, out of indignation at his malicious disposition towards Adam. Besides this, he inserted poison under his tongue, and made him an enemy to men; and suggested to them that they should direct their strokes against his head, that being the place wherein lay his mischievous designs towards men, and it being easiest to take vengeance on him that way; and when he had deprived him of the use of his feet, he made him to go rolling all along, and dragging himself upon the ground. And when God had appointed these penalties for them, he removed Adam and Eve out of the garden into another place.

CHAPTER II

CONCERNING THE POSTERITY OF ADAM, AND THE TEN GENERATIONS FROM HIM TO THE DELUGE

1. ADAM and Eve had two sons. The elder of them was named Cain, which name, when it is interpreted, signifies *a possession;* the younger was Abel, which signifies *sorrow.* They had also daughters. Now, the two brethren were pleased with different courses of life; for Abel, the younger, was a lover of righteousness, and, believing that God was present at all his actions, he excelled in virtue, and his employment was that of a shepherd. But Cain was not only very wicked in other respects, but was wholly intent upon getting, and he first contrived to plough the ground. He slew his brother on the occasion following:—They had resolved to sacrifice to God. Now Cain brought the fruits of the earth, and of his husbandry; but Abel brought milk, and the first-fruits of his flocks; but God was more delighted with the latter oblation,‡ when he was honoured with what grew naturally of its own accord, than he was with what was the invention of a covetous man, and gotten by forcing the ground; whence it was that Cain was very angry that Abel was preferred by God before him; and he slew his brother, and hid his dead body, thinking to escape discovery. But God, knowing what had been done, came to Cain, and asked him what was become of his

* By the Red Sea is not here meant the Arabian Gulf, which alone we now call by that name, but all that South Sea, which included the Red Sea and the Persian Gulf, as far as the East Indies; as Reland and Hudson here truly note, from the old geographers.

† Hence it appears that Josephus thought several, at least, of the brute animals, particularly the serpent, could speak before the Fall. And I think few of the more perfect kinds of those animals want the organs of speech at this day. Many inducements there are also to a notion that the present state they are in is not their original state; and that their capacities have been once much greater than we now see them, and are capable of being restored to their former condition. But as to this most ancient, and authentic, and probably allegorical account of that grand affair of the fall of our first parents, I have somewhat more to say in way of conjecture, but, being only a conjecture, I omit it: only thus far, that the imputation of the sin of our first parents to their posterity, any further than as some way the cause or occasion of man's mortality, seems almost entirely groundless; and that both man, and the other subordinate creatures, are hereafter to be delivered from the curse then brought upon them, and at last to be delivered from that bondage of corruption, (Rom. viii. 19–22.)

‡ St John's account of the reason why God accepted the sacrifice of Abel, and rejected that of Cain, as also why Cain slew Abel, on account of that his acceptance with God, is much better than this of Josephus: I mean, because "Cain was of the evil one, and slew his brother. And wherefore slew he him? Because his own works were evil, and his brother's righteous," (1 John iii. 12.) Josephus's reason seems to be no better than a pharisaical notion or tradition.

brother, because he had not seen him of many days, whereas he used to observe them conversing together at other times. But Cain was in doubt with himself, and knew not what answer to give to God. At first he said that he was himself at a loss about his brother's disappearing; but when he was provoked by God, who pressed him vehemently, as resolving to know what the matter was, he replied he was not his brother's guardian or keeper, nor was he an observer of what he did. But in return, God convicted Cain as having been the murderer of his brother; and said, "I wonder at thee, that thou knowest not what is become of a man whom thou thyself hast destroyed." God therefore did not inflict the punishment [of death] upon him, on account of his offering sacrifice, and thereby making supplication to Him not to be extreme in his wrath to him; but He made him accursed, and threatened his posterity in the seventh generation. He also cast him, together with his wife, out of that land. And when he was afraid that in wandering about he should fall among wild beasts, and by that means perish, God bid him not to entertain such a melancholy suspicion, and to go over all the earth without fear of what mischief he might suffer from wild beasts; and setting a mark upon him that he might be known, he commanded him to depart.

2. And when Cain had travelled over many countries, he, with his wife, built a city, named Nod, which is a place so called, and there he settled his abode; where also he had children. However, he did not accept of his punishment in order to amendment, but to increase his wickedness; for he only aimed to procure every thing that was for his own bodily pleasure, though it obliged him to be injurious to his neighbours. He augmented his household substance with much wealth, by rapine and violence; he excited his acquaintance to procure pleasures and spoils by robbery, and became a great leader of men into wicked courses. He also introduced a change in that way of simplicity wherein men lived before; and was the author of measures and weights. And whereas they lived innocently and generously while they knew nothing of such arts, he changed the world into cunning craftiness. He first of all set boundaries about lands; he built a city, and fortified it with walls, and he compelled his family to come together to it; and called that city Enoch, after the name of his eldest son Enoch. Now Jared was the son of Enoch; whose son was Malaleel; whose son was Mathusela; whose son was Lamech; who had seventy-seven children by two wives, Silla and Ada. Of those children by Ada, one was Jabal; he erected tents, and loved the life of a shepherd. But Jubal, who was born of the same mother with him, exercised himself in music;[*] and invented the psaltery and the harp. But Tubal, one of his children by the other wife, exceeded all men in strength, and was very expert and famous in martial performances. He procured what tended to the pleasures of the body by that method; and first of all invented the art of making brass. Lamech was also the father of a daughter, whose name was Naamah; and because he was so skilful in matters of divine revelation, that he knew he was to be punished for Cain's murder of his brother, he made that known to his wives. Nay, even while Adam was alive, it came to pass that the posterity of Cain became exceedingly wicked, every one successively dying

* From this Jubal, not improbably, came Jobel, the trumpet of jobel or jubilee; that large and loud musical instrument used in proclaiming the liberty at the year of jubilee.

one after another, more wicked than the former. They were intolerable in war, and vehement in robberies; and if any one were slow to murder people, yet was he bold in his profligate behaviour, in acting unjustly, and doing injury for gain.

3. Now, Adam, who was the first man, and made out of the earth, (for our discourse must now be about him,) after Abel was slain, and Cain fled away on account of his murder, was solicitous for posterity, and had a vehement desire of children, he being two hundred and thirty years old; after which time he lived other seven hundred, and then died. He had indeed many other children,[†] but Seth in particular. As for the rest, it would be tedious to name them; I will therefore only endeavour to give an account of those that proceeded from Seth. Now this Seth, when he was brought up, and came to those years in which he could discern what was good, became a virtuous man; and as he was himself of an excellent character, so did he leave children behind him who imitated his virtues.[‡] All these proved to be of good dispositions. They also inhabited the same country without dissensions, and in a happy condition, without any misfortunes falling upon them, till they died. They also were the inventors of that peculiar sort of wisdom which is concerned with the heavenly bodies, and their order. And that their inventions might not be lost before they were sufficiently known, upon Adam's prediction that the world was to be destroyed at one time by the force of fire, and at another time by the violence and quantity of water, they made two pillars;[§] the one of brick, the other of stone: they inscribed their discoveries on them both, that in case the pillar of brick should be destroyed by the flood, the pillar of stone might remain, and exhibit those discoveries to mankind; and also inform them that there was another pillar of brick erected by them. Now this remains in the land of Siriad to this day.

CHAPTER III

CONCERNING THE FLOOD; AND AFTER WHAT MANNER NOAH WAS SAVED IN AN ARK, WITH HIS KINDRED, AND AFTERWARDS DWELT IN THE PLAIN OF SHINAR

1. Now this posterity of Seth continued to esteem God as the Lord of the universe, and to

† The number of Adam's children, as says the old tradition, was thirty-three sons and twenty-three daughters.

‡ What is here said of Seth and his posterity, that they were very good and virtuous, and at the same time very happy, without any considerable misfortunes. for seven generations, [see ch. ii. sect. 1, before; and ch. iii. sec. 1, hereafter,] is exactly agreeable to the state of the world and the conduct of Providence in all the first ages.

§ Of Josephus's mistake here, when he took Seth the son of Adam for Seth or Sesostris, king of Egypt, the erecter of this pillar in the land of Siriad, see Essay on the Old Testament, Appendix, pp. 159, 160. Although the main of this relation might be true, and Adam might foretell a conflagration and a deluge, which all antiquity witnesses to be an ancient tradition; nay, Seth's posterity might engrave their inventions in astronomy on two such pillars, yet it is no way credible that they could survive the deluge, which has buried all such pillars and edifices far under ground, in the sediment of its waters; especially since the like pillars of the Egyptian Seth or Sesostris were extant after the flood, in the land of Siriad, and perhaps in the days of Josephus also, as is shewn in the place here referred to.

have an entire regard to virtue, for seven generations; but in process of time they were perverted, and forsook the practices of their forefathers, and did neither pay those honours to God which were appointed them, nor had they any concern to do justice towards men. But for what degree of zeal they had formerly shewn for virtue, they now shewed by their actions a double degree of wickedness, whereby they made God to be their enemy; for many angels* of God accompanied with women, and begat sons that proved unjust, and despisers of all that was good, on account of the confidence they had in their own strength, for the tradition is that these men did what resembled the acts of those whom the Grecians call giants. But Noah was very uneasy at what they did; and, being displeased at their conduct, persuaded them to change their dispositions and their acts for the better;—but, seeing that they did not yield to him, but were slaves to their wicked pleasures, he was afraid they would kill him, together with his wife and children, and those they had married; so he departed out of that land.

2. Now God loved this man for his righteousness; yet he not only condemned those other men for their wickedness, but determined to destroy the whole race of mankind, and to make, another race that should be pure from wickedness; and cutting short their lives, and making their years not so many as they formerly lived, but one hundred and twenty only,† he turned the dry land into sea; and thus were all these men destroyed: but Noah alone was saved; for God suggested to him the following contrivances and way of escape:—That he should make an ark of four stories high, three hundred cubits‡ long, fifty cubits broad, and thirty cubits high. Accordingly he entered into that ark, and his wife and sons, and their wives; and put into it not only other provisions, to support their wants there, but also sent in with the rest all sorts of living creatures, the male and his female, for the preservation of their kinds; and others of them by sevens. Now this ark had firm walls, and a roof, and was braced with cross beams, so that it could not be any way drowned or overborne by the violence of the water; and thus was Noah, with his family, preserved. Now he was the tenth from Adam, as being the son of Lamech, whose father was Mathusela. He was the son of Enoch, the son of Jared; and Jared was the son of Malaleel, who, with many of his sisters, were the children of Cainan, the son of Enos. Now Enos was the son of Seth, the son of Adam.

3. This calamity happened in the six hundredth year of Noah's government, [age,] in the second month,§ called by the Macedonians Dius,

but by the Hebrews Marchesuan; for so did they order their year in Egypt; but Moses appointed that Nisan, which is the same with Xanthicus, should be the first month for their festivals, because he brought them out of Egypt in that month: so that this month began the year as to all the solemnities they observed to the honour of God, although he preserved the original order of the months as to selling and buying, and other ordinary affairs. Now he says that this flood began on the twenty-seventh [seventeenth] day of the forementioned month; and this was two thousand six hundred and fifty-six [one thousand six hundred and fifty-six] years from Adam, the first man; and the time is written down in our sacred books, those who then lived having noted down,‖ with great accuracy, both the births and deaths of illustrious men.

4. For indeed Seth was born when Adam was in his two hundred and thirtieth year, who lived nine hundred and thirty years. Seth begat Enos in his two hundred and fifth year; who, when he had lived nine hundred and twelve years, delivered the government to Cainan his son, whom he had in his hundred and ninetieth year; he lived nine hundred and five years. Cainan, when he had lived nine hundred and ten years, had his son Malaleel, who was born in his hundred and seventieth year. This Malaleel, having lived eight hundred and ninety-five years, died, leaving his son Jared, whom he begat when he was in his hundred and sixty-fifth year. He lived nine hundred and sixty-two years; and then his son Enoch succeeded him, who was born when his father was one hundred and sixty-two years old. Now he, when he had lived three hundred and sixty-five years, departed, and went to God; whence it is that they have not written down his death. Now Mathusela, the son of Enoch, who was born to him when he was one hundred and sixty-five years old, had Lamech for his son when he was one hundred and eighty-seven years of age, to whom he delivered the government, when he had retained it nine hundred and sixty-nine years. Now Lamech, when he had governed seven hundred and seventy-seven years, appointed Noah his son to be ruler of the people, who was born to Lamech when he was one hundred and eighty-two years old, and retained the government nine hundred and fifty years. These years collected together make up the sum before set down; but let no one inquire into the deaths of these men, for they extended their lives along together with their children and grandchildren; but let him have regard to their births only.

5. When God gave the signal, and it began to rain, the water poured down forty entire days, till it became fifteen cubits higher than the earth, which was the reason why there was no greater number preserved, since they had no

---

* This notion, that the fallen angels were, in some sense, the fathers of the old giants, was the constant opinion of antiquity.

† Josephus here supposes that the life of these giants, for of them only do I understand him, was now reduced to 120 years; which is confirmed by the fragment of Enoch, sect. 10, in Authent. Rec., Part I. p. 268. For as to the rest of mankind, Josephus himself confesses their lives were much longer than 120 years, for many generations after the Flood, as we shall see presently; and he says they were gradually shortened till the days of Moses, and then fixed [for some time] at 120, (chap. vi. sect. 5.) Nor indeed need we suppose that either Enoch or Josephus meant to interpret these 120 years for the life of men before the Flood, to be different from the 120 years of God's patience [perhaps while the ark was preparing] till the Deluge; which I take to be the meaning of God when he threatened this wicked world, that if they so long continued impenitent, their days should be no more than 120 years.

‡ A cubit is about twenty-one English inches.

§ Josephus here truly determines, that the year at

the Flood began about the autumnal equinox. As to what day of the month the Flood began, our Hebrew and Samaritan, and perhaps Josephus's own copy, more rightly placed it on the 17th day, instead of the 27th, as here; for Josephus agrees with them as to the distance of 150 days, to the 17th day of the 7th month; as Gen. vii. ult. with viii. 3.

‖ Josephus here takes notice, that these ancient genealogies were first set down by those that then lived, and from them were transmitted down to posterity; which I suppose to be the true account of that matter. For there is no reason to imagine that men were not taught to read and write soon after they were taught to speak; and perhaps all by the Messiah himself, who, under the Father, was the Creator or Governor of mankind, and who frequently, in those early days, appeared to them.

place to fly to. When the rain ceased, the water did but just begin to abate, after one hundred and fifty days (that is, on the seventeenth day of the seventh month) it then ceasing to subside for a little while. After this the ark rested on the top of a certain mountain in Armenia; which, when Noah understood, he opened it; and seeing a small piece of land about it, he continued quiet, and conceived some cheerful hopes of deliverance; but a few days afterward, when the water was decreased to a greater degree, he sent out a raven, as desirous to learn whether any other part of the earth were left dry by the water, and whether he might go out of the ark with safety; but the raven, finding all the land still overflowed, returned to Noah again. And after seven days he sent out a dove, to know the state of the ground; which came back to him covered with mud, and bringing an olive-branch. Hereby Noah learned that the earth was become clear of the flood. So after he had stayed seven more days, he sent the living creatures out of the ark; and both he and his family went out, when he also sacrificed to God, and feasted with his companions. However, the Armenians call this place (Αποβατήριον*) The Place of Descent; for the ark being saved in that place, its remains are shewn there by the inhabitants to this day.

6. Now all the writers of barbarian histories make mention of this flood and of this ark; among whom is Berosus the Chaldean; for when he is describing the circumstances of the flood, he goes on thus:—"It is said there is still some part of this ship in Armenia, at the mountain of the Cordyæans; and that some people carry off pieces of the bitumen, which they take away, and use chiefly as amulets for the averting of mischiefs." Hieronymus the Egyptian, also, who wrote the Phœnician Antiquities, and Mnaseas, and a great many more, make mention of the same. Nay, Nicolaus of Damascus, in his ninety-sixth book, hath a particular relation about them, where he speaks thus:—"There is a great mountain in Armenia, over Minyas, called Baris, upon which it is reported that many who fled at the time of the Deluge were saved; and that one who was carried in an ark came on shore upon the top of it; and that the remains of the timber were a great while preserved. This might be the man about whom Moses, the legislator of the Jews wrote."

7. But as for Noah, he was afraid, since God had determined to destroy mankind, lest he should drown the earth every year; so he offered burnt-offerings, and besought God that Nature might hereafter go on in its former orderly course, and that he would not bring on so great a judgment any more, by which the whole race of creatures might be in danger of destruction; but that, having now punished the wicked, he would of his goodness spare the re-

mainder, and such as he had hitherto judged fit to be delivered from so severe a calamity; for that otherwise these last must be more miserable than the first, and that they must be condemned to a worse condition than the others, unless they be suffered to escape entirely; that is, if they be reserved for another deluge, while they must be afflicted with the terror and sight of the first deluge, and must also be destroyed by a second. He also entreated God to accept of his sacrifice, and to grant that the earth might never again undergo the like effects of his wrath; that men might be permitted to go on cheerfully in cultivating the same—to build cities, and live happily in them; and that they might not be deprived of any of those good things which they enjoyed before the Flood; but might attain to the like length of days and old age which the ancient people had arrived at before.

8. When Noah had made these supplications, God, who loved the man for his righteousness, granted entire success to his prayers, and said that it was not he who brought the destruction on a polluted world, but that they underwent that vengeance on account of their own wickedness; and that he had not brought men into the world if he had himself determined to destroy them, it being an instance of greater wisdom not to have granted them life at all, than, after it was granted, to procure their destruction; "but the injuries," said he, "they offered to my holiness and virtue, forced me to bring this punishment upon them; but I will leave off for the time to come to require such punishments, the effects of so great wrath, for their future wicked actions, and especially on account of thy prayers; but if I shall at any time send tempests of rain in an extraordinary manner, be not affrighted at the largeness of the showers, for the waters shall no more overspread the earth. However, I require you to abstain from shedding the blood of men, and to keep yourselves pure from murder; and to punish those that commit any such thing. I permit you to make use of all the other living creatures at your pleasure, and as your appetites lead you; for I have made you lords of them all, both of those that walk on the land, and those that swim in the waters, and of those that fly in the regions of the air on high—excepting their blood, for therein is the life: but I will give you a sign that I have left off my anger, by my bow," [whereby is meant the rainbow, for they determined that the rainbow was the bow of God;] and when God had said and promised thus, he went away.

9. Now when Noah had lived three hundred and fifty years after the Flood, and that all that time happily, he died, having the number of nine hundred and fifty years: but let no one, upon comparing the lives of the ancients with our lives, and with the few years which we now live, think that what we have said of them is false; or make the shortness of our lives at present an argument that neither did they attain to so long a duration of life; for those ancients were beloved of God, and [lately] made by God himself; and because their food was then fitter for the prolongation of life, might well live so great a number of years; and besides, God afforded them a longer time of life on account of their virtue, and the good use they made of it in astronomical and geometrical discoveries, which would not have afforded the time of foretelling [the periods of the stars] unless they had lived six hundred years; for the Great Year is completed in that interval. Now I have for witnesses to what I have said all those that have written Antiquities, both among the Greeks and barbar-

---

* This Αποβατήριον, or Place of Descent, is the proper rendering of the Armenian name of this very city. It is called in Ptolemy Naxuana, and by Moses Chorenensis, the Armenian historian, Idsheuan; but at the place itself, Nachidsheuan, which signifies The first place of descent, and is a lasting monument of the preservation of Noah in the ark, upon the top of that mountain, at whose foot it was built, as the first city or town after the Flood. See Antiq. b. xx. ch. ii. sect. 3; and Moses Chorenensis, who also says elsewhere that another town was related by tradition to have been called Seron, or The Place of Dispersion, on account of the dispersion of Xisuthrus's or Noah's sons, from thence first made. Whether any remains of this ark be still preserved, as the people of the country suppose, I cannot certainly tell. Mons. Tournefort had, not very long since, a mind to see the place himself, but met with too great dangers and difficulties to venture through them.

ians; for even Manetho, who wrote the Egyptian History, and Berosus, who collected the Chaldean Monuments, and Mochus, and Hestiæus, and besides these, Hieronymus the Egyptian, and those who composed the Phœnician History, agree to what I here say: Hesiod also, and Hecatæus, Hellanicus, and Acusilaus; and besides, Ephorus and Nicolaus relate that the ancients lived a thousand years: but as to these matters, let every one look upon them as he thinks fit.

CHAPTER IV

CONCERNING THE TOWER OF BABYLON, AND THE CONFUSION OF TONGUES

1. Now the sons of Noah were three,—Shem, Japhet, and Ham, born one hundred years before the Deluge. These first of all descended from the mountains into the plains, and fixed their habitation there; and persuaded others who were greatly afraid of the lower grounds on account of the flood, and so were very loath to come down from the higher places, to venture to follow their examples. Now the plain in which they first dwelt was called Shinar. God also commanded them to send colonies abroad, for the thorough peopling of the earth,—that they might not raise seditions among themselves, but might cultivate a great part of the earth, and enjoy its fruits after a plentiful manner: but they were so ill instructed, that they did not obey God; for which reason they fell into calamities, and were made sensible, by experience, of what sin they had been guilty; for when they flourished with a numerous youth, God admonished them again to send out colonies; but they, imagining the prosperity they enjoyed was not derived from the favour of God, but supposing that their own power was the proper cause of the plentiful condition they were in, did not obey him. Nay, they added to this their disobedience to the Divine will, the suspicion that they were therefore ordered to send out separate colonies, that, being divided asunder, they might the more easily be oppressed.

2. Now it was Nimrod who excited them to such an affront and contempt of God. He was the grandson of Ham, the son of Noah,—a bold man, and of great strength of hand. He persuaded them not to ascribe it to God, as if it was through his means they were happy, but to believe that it was their own courage which procured that happiness. He also gradually changed the government into tyranny,—seeing no other way of turning men from the fear of God, but to bring them into a constant dependence upon his power. He also said he would be revenged on God, if he should have a mind to drown the world again; for that he would build a tower too high for the waters to be able to reach! and that he would avenge himself on God for destroying their forefathers!

3. Now the multitude were very ready to follow the determination of Nimrod, and to esteem it a piece of cowardice to submit to God; and they built a tower, neither sparing any pains, nor being in any degree negligent about the work; and, by reason of the multitude of hands employed in it, it grew very high, sooner than any one could expect; but the thickness of it was so great, and it was so strongly built, that thereby its great height seemed, upon the view, to be less than it really was. It was built of burnt brick, cemented together with mortar,

made of bitumen, that it might not be liable to admit water. When God saw that they acted so madly, he did not resolve to destroy them utterly, since they were not grown wiser by the destruction of the former sinners; but he caused a tumult among them, by producing in them divers languages; and causing that, through the multitude of those languages, they should not be able to understand one another. The place wherein they built the tower is now called *Babylon;* because of the confusion of that language which they readily understood before; for the Hebrews mean by the word *Babel,* Confusion. The Sibyl also makes mention of this tower, and of the confusion of the language, when she says thus:—"When all men were of one language, some of them built a high tower, as if they would thereby ascend up to heaven; but the gods sent storms of wind and overthrew the tower, and gave every one his peculiar language; and for this reason it was that the city was called *Babylon.*" But as to the plain of Shinar, in the country of Babylonia, Hestiæus mentions it, when he says thus:—"Such of the priests as were saved, took the sacred vessels of Jupiter Enyalius, and came to Shinar of Babylonia."

CHAPTER V

AFTER WHAT MANNER THE POSTERITY OF NOAH SENT OUT COLONIES, AND INHABITED THE WHOLE EARTH

AFTER this they were dispersed abroad, on account of their languages, and went out by colonies everywhere; and each colony took possession of that land which they light upon, and unto which God led them; so that the whole continent was filled with them, both the inland and maritime countries. There were some also who passed over the sea in ships, and inhabited the islands : and some of those nations do still retain the denominations which were given them by their first founders; but some have lost them also; and some have only admitted certain changes in them, that they might be the more intelligible to the inhabitants; and they were the Greeks who became the authors of such mutations; for when, in after ages, they grew potent, they claimed to themselves the glory of antiquity,—giving names to the nations that sounded well (in Greek) that they might be better understood among themselves; and setting agreeable forms of government over them, as if they were a people derived from themselves.

CHAPTER VI

HOW EVERY NATION WAS DENOMINATED FROM THEIR FIRST INHABITANTS

1. Now they were the grand-children of Noah, in honour of whom names were imposed on the nations by those that first seized upon them. Japhet, the son of Noah, had seven sons: they inhabited so, that, beginning at the mountains Taurus and Amanus, they proceeded along Asia, as far as the river Tanais, and along Europe to Cadiz; and settling themselves on the lands which they light upon, which none had inhabited before, they called the nations by their own names; for Gomer founded those whom the Greeks now call Galatians, [Galls,] but were then called Gomerites. Magog founded those that

TOWER OF BABEL

from him were named Magogites, but who are by the Greeks called Scythians. Now as to Javan and Madai, the sons of Japhet; from Madai came the Madeans, who are called Medes by the Greeks; but from Javan, Ionia and all the Grecians are derived. Thobel founded the Thobelites, who are now called Iberes; and the Mosocheni were founded by Mosoch; now they are Cappadocians. There is also a mark of their ancient denomination still to be shewn; for there is even now among them a city called Mazaca, which may inform those that are able to understand, that so was the entire nation once called. Thiras also called those whom he ruled over, Thirasians; but the Greeks changed the name into Thracians. And so many were the countries that had the children of Japhet for their inhabitants. Of the three sons of Gomer, Aschanax founded the Aschanaxians, who are now called by the Greeks Rheginians. So did Riphath found the Ripheans, now called Paphlagonians; and Thrugramma the Thrugram-means, who, as the Greeks resolved, were named Phrygians. Of the three sons of Javan also, the son of Japhet, Elisa gave name to the Eliseans, who were his subjects; they are now the Æolians. Tharsus to the Tharsians; for so was Cilicia of old called; the sign of which is this, that the noblest city they have, and a metropolis also, is Tarsus, the *tau* being by change put for the *theta*. Cethimus possessed the island Cethima; it is now called Cyprus: and from that it is that all islands, and the greatest part of the sea-coasts, are named Cethim by the Hebrews: and one city there is in Cyprus that has been able to preserve its denomination; it is called Citius by those who use the language of the Greeks, and has not, by the use of that dialect, escaped the name of Cethim. And so many nations have the children and grand-children of Japhet possessed. Now when I have premised somewhat, which perhaps the Greeks do not know, I will return and explain what I have omitted; for such names are pronounced here after the manner of the Greeks, to please my readers; for our own country language does not so pronounce them: but the names in all cases are of one and the same ending; for the name we here pronounce Noeas, is there Noah, and in every case retains the same termination.

2. The children of Ham possessed the land from Syria and Amanus, and the mountains of Libanus, seizing upon all that was on its sea-coasts and as far as the ocean, and keeping it as their own. Some, indeed, of its names are utterly vanished away; others of them being changed, and another sound given them, are hardly to be discovered; yet a few there are which have kept their denominations entire: for of the four sons of Ham, time has not at all hurt the name of Chus; for the Ethiopians, over whom he reigned, are even at this day, both by themselves and by all men in Asia, called Chusites. The memory also of the Mesraites is preserved in their name; for all we who inhabit this country [of Judea] call Egypt Mestre, and the Egyptians Mestreans. Phut also was the founder of Libyia, and called the inhabitants Phutites, from himself: there is also a river in the country of the Moors which bears that name; whence it is that we may see the greatest part of the Grecian historiographers mention that river and the adjoining country by the appellation of Phut: but the name it has now has been by change given it from one of the sons of Mesraim, who was called Lybyos. We will inform you presently what has been the occasion why it has been called Africa also.

Canaan, the fourth son of Ham, inhabited the country now called Judea, and called it from his own name Canaan. The children of these [four] were these: Sabas, who founded the Sabeans; Evilas, who founded the Evileans, who are called Getuli; Sabathes founded the Sabathens; they are now called by the Greeks, Astaborans; Sabactas settled the Sabactens; and Ragmus the Ragmeans; and he had two sons, the one of whom, Judadas, settled the Judadeans, a nation of the western Ethiopians, and left them his name; as did Sabas to the Sabeans. But Nimrod, the son of Chus, stayed and tyrannised at Babylon, as we have already informed you. Now all the children of Mesraim, being eight in number, possessed the country from Gaza to Egypt, though it retained the name of one only, the Philistim; for the Greeks call that part of that country Palestine. As for the rest, Ludieim, and Enemim, and Labim, who alone inhabited in Libya, and called the country from himself, Nedim, and Phethrosim, and Chesloim, and Cepthorim, we know nothing of them besides their names; for the Ethiopic war,* which we shall describe hereafter, was the cause that those cities were overthrown. The sons of Canaan were these: Sidonius, who also built a city of the same name; it is called by the Greeks, Sidon; Amathus inhabited in Amathine, which is even now called Amathe by the inhabitants, although the Macedonians named it Epiphania, from one of his posterity; Arudeus possessed the island Aradus: Arucas possessed Arce, which is in Libanus;—but for the seven others, [Eueus,] Chetteus, Jebuseus, Amorreus, Gergesus, Eudeus, Sineus, Samareus, we have nothing in the sacred books but their names, for the Hebrews overthrew their cities; and their calamities came upon them on the occasion following:—

3. Noah, when, after the Deluge, the earth was re-settled in its former condition, set about its cultivation; and when he had planted it with vines, and when the fruit was ripe, and he had gathered the grapes in their season, and the wine was ready for use, he offered sacrifice, and feasted, and, being drunk, he fell asleep, and lay naked in an unseemly manner. When his youngest son saw this, he came laughing, and shewed him to his brethren; but they covered their father's nakedness. And when Noah was made sensible of what had been done, he prayed for prosperity to his other sons; but for Ham, he did not curse him, by reason of his nearness in blood, but cursed his posterity. And when the rest of them escaped that curse, God inflicted it on the children of Canaan. But as to these matters, we shall speak more hereafter.

4. Shem, the third son of Noah, had five sons, who inhabited the land that began at Euphrates, and reached to the Indian Ocean; for Elam left behind him the Elamites, the ancestors of the Persians. Ashur lived at the city Nineve; and named his subjects Assyrians, who became the most fortunate nation, beyond others. Arphaxad named the Arphaxadites, who are now called Chaldeans. Aram had the Aramites, which the Greeks call Syrians; as Laud founded

* One observation ought not here to be neglected, with regard to that Ethiopic war, which Moses, as general of the Egyptians, put an end to, Antiq. b. ii. chap. x., and about which our late writers seem very much unconcerned—viz., That it was a war of that consequence, as to occasion the removal or destruction of six or seven nations of the posterity of Mitzraim, with their cities: which Josephus would not have said, if he had not had ancient records to justify those his assertions, though those records be now all lost.

the Laudites, which are now called Lydians. Of the four sons of Aram, Uz founded Trachonitis and Damascus; this country lies between Palestine and Celesyria; Ul founded Armenia; and Gather the Bactrians; and Mesa the Mesaneans; it is now called Charax Spasini. Sala was the son of Arphaxad; and his son was Heber, from whom they originally called the Jews, Hebrews.* Heber begat Joctan and Phaleg: he was called Phaleg, because he was born at the dispersion of the nations to their several countries; for Phaleg, among the Hebrews, signifies *division*. Now Joctan, one of the sons of Heber, had these sons, Elmodad, Saleph, Asermoth, Jera, Adoram, Aizel, Decla, Ebal, Abimael, Sabeus, Ophir, Euilat, and Jobab. These inhabited from Cophen, an Indian river, and in part of Asia adjoining to it. And this shall suffice concerning the sons of Shem.

5. I will now treat of the Hebrews. The son of Phaleg, whose father was Heber, was Ragau; whose son was Serug, to whom was born Nahor; his son was Terah, who was the father of Abraham, who accordingly was the tenth from Noah, and was born in the two hundred and ninety-second year after the Deluge; for Terah begat Abram in his seventieth year. Mahor begat Haran when he was one hundred and twenty years old; Nahor was born to Serug in his hundred and thirty-second year; Ragau had Serug at one hundred and thirty; at the same age also Phaleg had Ragau; Heber begat Phaleg in his hundred and thirty-fourth year; he himself being begotten by Sala when he was an hundred and thirty years old, whom Arphaxad had for his son at the hundred and thirty-fifth year of his age. Arphaxad was the son of Shem, and born twelve years after the Deluge. Now Abram had two brethren, Nahor and Haran: of these Haran left a son, Lot; as also Sarai and Milcha his daughters, and died among the Chaldeans, in a city of the Chaldeans, called Ur; and his monument is shewn to this day. These married their nieces. Nahor married Milcha, and Abram married Sarai. Now Terah, hating Chaldea, on account of his mourning for Haran, they all removed to Haran of Mesopotamia, where Terah died, and was buried, when he had lived to be two hundred and five years old; for the life of man was already by degrees diminished, and became shorter than before, till the birth of Moses; after whom the term of human life was one hundred and twenty years, God determining it to the length that Moses happened to live. Now Nahor had eight sons by Milcha: Uz and Buz, Kemuel, Chesed, Azau, Pheldas, Jadelph, and Bethuel. These were all the genuine sons of Nahor; for Teba and Gaam, and Tachas, and Maaca, were born of Reuma his concubine; but Bethuel had a daughter, Rebecca,—and a son, Laban.

CHAPTER VII

HOW ABRAM, OUR FOREFATHER, WENT OUT OF THE LAND OF THE CHALDEANS, AND LIVED IN THE LAND THEN CALLED CANAAN, BUT NOW JUDEA

1. Now Abram, having no son of his own, adopted Lot, his brother Haran's son, and his wife Sarai's brother; and he left the land of Chaldea when he was seventy-five years old, and at the command of God went into Canaan, and therein he dwelt himself, and left it to his posterity. He was a person of great sagacity, both for understanding all things and persuading his hearers, and not mistaken in his opinions; for which reason he began to have higher notions of virtue than others had, and he determined to renew and to change the opinion all men happened then to have concerning God; for he was the first that ventured to publish this notion, that there was but one God, the Creator of the universe; and that, as to other [gods,] if they contributed anything to the happiness of men, that each of them afforded it only according to his appointment, and not by their own power. This his opinion was derived from the irregular phenomena that were visible both at land and sea, as well as those that happen to the sun and moon, and all the heavenly bodies, thus:—"If [said he] these bodies had power of their own, they would certainly take care of their own regular motions; but since they do not preserve such regularity, they make it plain, that in so far as they co-operate to our advantage, they do it not of their own abilities, but as they are subservient to Him that commands them; to whom alone we ought justly to offer our honour and thanksgiving." For which doctrines, when the Chaldeans and other people of Mesopotamia raised a tumult against him, he thought fit to leave that country; and at the command, and by the assistance of God, he came and lived in the land of Canaan. And when he was there settled, he built an altar, and performed a sacrifice to God.

2. Berosus mentions our father Abram without naming him, when he says thus:—"In the tenth generation after the Flood, there was among the Chaldeans a man righteous and great, and skilful in the celestial science." But Hecatæus does more than barely mention him; for he composed and left behind him a book concerning him. And Nicolaus of Damascus, in the fourth book of his history, says thus:—"Abram reigned at Damascus, being a foreigner, who came with an army out of the land above Babylon, called the land of the Chaldeans. But after a long time he got him up, and removed from that country also with his people, and went into the land then called the land of Canaan, but now the land of Judea, and this when his posterity were become a multitude; as to which posterity of his we relate their history in another work." Now the name of Abram is even still famous in the country of Damascus; and there is shewn a village named from him, *The Habitation of Abram*.

CHAPTER VIII

THAT WHEN THERE WAS A FAMINE IN CANAAN, ABRAM WENT THENCE INTO EGYPT; AND AFTER HE HAD CONTINUED THERE A WHILE, HE RETURNED BACK AGAIN

1. Now, after this, when a famine had in-

---

* That the Jews were called Hebrews, from this their progenitor Heber, our author Josephus here rightly affirms; and not from Abram the Hebrew, or *passenger* over Euphrates, as many of the moderns suppose. Shem is also called the father of all the children of Heber, or of all the Hebrews, in a history long before Abram passed over Euphrates, (Gen. x. 21,) though it must be confessed that (Gen. xiv. 13) where the original says they told *Abram the Hebrew*, the Septuagint renders it the *passenger*, περάτης. But this is spoken only of Abram himself, who had then lately passed over Euphrates: and is another signification of the Hebrew word, taken as an appellative, and not as a proper name.

vaded the land of Canaan, and Abram had discovered that the Egyptians were in a flourishing condition, he was disposed to go down to them, both to partake of the plenty they enjoyed, and to become an auditor of their priests, and to know what they said concerning the gods; designing either to follow them, if they had better notions than he, or to convert them into a better way, if his own notions proved the truest. Now, seeing he was to take Sarai with him, and was afraid of the madness of the Egyptians with regard to women, lest the king should kill him on occasion of his wife's great beauty, he contrived this device:—he pretended to be her brother, and directed her in a dissembling way to pretend the same, for he said it would be for their benefit. Now, as soon as he came into Egypt, it happened to Abram as he supposed it would; for the fame of his wife's beauty was greatly talked of; for which reason Pharaoh, the king of Egypt, would not be satisfied with what was reported of her, but would needs see her himself, and was preparing to enjoy her; but God put a stop to his unjust inclinations, by sending upon him a distemper, and a sedition against his government. And when he inquired of the priests how he might be freed from these calamities, they told him that this his miserable condition was derived from the wrath of God, upon account of his inclinations to abuse the stranger's wife. He then out of fear asked Sarai who she was, and who it was that she brought along with her. And when he had found out the truth, he excused himself to Abram, that supposing the woman to be his sister, and not his wife, he set his affections on her, as desiring an affinity with him by marrying her, but not as incited by lust to abuse her. He also made him a large present in money, and gave him leave to enter into conversation with the most learned among the Egyptians; from which conversation, his virtue and his reputation became more conspicuous than they had been before.

2. For whereas the Egyptians were formerly addicted to different customs, and despised one another's sacred and accustomed rites, and were very angry one with another on that account, Abram conferred with each of them, and confuting the reasonings they made use of every one for their own practices, demonstrated that such reasonings were vain and void of truth; whereupon he was admired by them in those conferences as a very wise man, and one of great sagacity, when he discoursed on any subject he undertook; and this not only in understanding it, but in persuading other men also to assent to him. He communicated to them arithmetic, and delivered to them the science of astronomy; for, before Abram came into Egypt, they were unacquainted with those parts of learning; for that science came from the Chaldeans into Egypt, and from thence to the Greeks also.

3. As soon as Abram was come back into Canaan, he parted the land between him and Lot, upon account of the tumultuous behaviour of their shepherds, concerning the pastures wherein they should feed their flocks. However, he gave Lot his option, or leave, to choose which lands he would take; and he took himself what the other left, which were the lower grounds at the foot of the mountains; and he himself dwelt in Hebron, which is a city seven years more ancient than Tanis of Egypt. But Lot possessed the land of the plain, and the river Jordan, not far from the city of Sodom, which was then a fine city; but is now destroyed by the will and wrath of God;—the cause of which I shall shew in its proper place hereafter.

CHAPTER IX

THE DESTRUCTION OF THE SODOMITES BY THE ASSYRIAN WAR

At this time, when the Assyrians had the dominion over Asia, the people of Sodom were in a flourishing condition, both as to riches and the number of their youth. There were five kings that managed the affairs of this country: Ballas, Barsas, Senabar, and Sumobor, with the king of Bela; and each king led on his own troops; and the Assyrians made war upon them; and, dividing their army into four parts, fought against them. Now every part of the army had its own commander; and when the battle was joined, the Assyrians were conquerors; and imposed a tribute on the kings of the Sodomites, who submitted to this slavery twelve years; and so long they continued to pay their tribute: but on the thirteenth year they rebelled, and then the army of the Assyrians came upon them, under their commanders Amraphel, Arioch, Chodorlaomer, and Tidal. These kings had laid waste all Syria, and overthrown the offspring of the giants; and when they were come over against Sodom, they pitched their camp at the vale called the Slime Pits, for at that time there were pits in that place; but now, upon the destruction of the city of Sodom, that vale became the Lake Asphaltites, as it is called. However, concerning this lake we shall speak more presently. Now when the Sodomites joined battle with the Assyrians, and the fight was very obstinate, many of them were killed, and the rest were carried captive; among which captives was Lot, who had come to assist the Sodomites.

CHAPTER X

HOW ABRAM FOUGHT WITH THE ASSYRIANS, AND OVERCAME THEM, AND SAVED THE SODOMITE PRISONERS, AND TOOK FROM THE ASSYRIANS THE PREY THEY HAD GOTTEN

1. When Abram heard of their calamity, he was at once afraid for Lot his kinsman, and pitied the Sodomites his friends and neighbours; and thinking it proper to afford them assistance, he did not delay it, but marched hastily, and the fifth night fell upon the Assyrians, near Dan, for that is the name of the other spring of Jordan; and before they could arm themselves, he slew some as they were in their beds, before they could suspect any harm; and others, who were not yet gone to sleep, but were so drunk they could not fight, ran away. Abram pursued after them, till on the second day he drove them in a body unto Hoba, a place belonging to Damascus; and thereby demonstrated that victory does not depend on multitude and the number of hands, but the alacrity and courage of soldiers overcome the most numerous bodies of men, while he got the victory over so great an army with no more than three hundred and eighteen of his servants, and three of his friends: but all those that fled returned home ingloriously.

2. So Abram, when he had saved the captive Sodomites who had been taken by the Assyrians, and Lot also, his kinsman, returned home in peace. Now the king of Sodom met him at a certain place, which they called The King's Dale, where Melchisedec, king of the city Salem, received him. That name signifies *the righteous king;* and such he was without dispute, inso-

much that, on this account, he was made the priest of God: however, they afterward called Salem *Jerusalem.* Now this Melchisedec supplied Abram's army in an hospitable manner, and gave them provisions in abundance; and as they were feasting, he began to praise him, and to bless God for subduing his enemies under him. And when Abram gave him the tenth part of his prey, he accepted of the gift: but the king of Sodom desired Abram to take the prey, but entreated that he might have those men restored to him whom Abram had saved from the Assyrians, because they belong to him; but Abram would not do so; nor would make any other advantage of that prey than what his servants had eaten; but still insisted that he should afford a part to his friends that had assisted him in the battle. The first of them was called Eschol, and then Enner, and Mambre.

3. And God commended his virtue, and said, Thou shalt not, however, lose the rewards thou hast deserved to receive by such thy glorious actions. He answered, And what advantage will it be to me to have such rewards, when I have none to enjoy them after me?—for he was hitherto childless. And God promised that he should have a son, and that his posterity should be very numerous, insomuch that their number should be like the stars. When he heard that, he offered a sacrifice to God, as he commanded him. The manner of the sacrifice was this:— He took an heifer of three years old, and a she-goat of three years old, and a ram in like manner of three years old, and a turtle dove and a pigeon;* and as he was enjoined, he divided the three former; but the birds he did not divide. After which, before he built his altar, where the birds of prey flew about, as desirous of blood, a divine voice came to him, declaring that their neighbours would be grievous to his posterity when they should be in Egypt, for four hundred years,† during which time they should be afflicted; but afterwards should overcome their enemies, should conquer the Canaanites in war, and possess themselves of their land, and of their cities.

4. Now Abram dwelt near the oak called Ogyges,—the place belongs to Canaan, not far from the city of Hebron: but being uneasy at his wife's barrenness, he entreated God to grant that he might have male issue; and God required of him to be of good courage; and said that he would add to all the rest of the benefits that he had bestowed on him ever since he led him out of Mesopotamia, the gift of children. Accordingly Sarai, at God's command, brought to his bed one of her handmaidens, a woman of Egyptian descent, in order to obtain children by her; and when this handmaid was with child, she triumphed, and ventured to affront Sarai, as if the dominion were to come to a son to be born of her: but when Abram resigned her into the hand of Sarai, to punish her, she contrived to fly away, as not able to bear the instances of Sarai's severity to her; and she entreated God to have compassion on her. Now a divine angel met her, as she was going forward in the wilderness, and bid her return to her master and mistress; for, if she would submit to that wise advice, she would live better hereafter; for that

the reason of her being in such a miserable case was this, that she had been ungrateful and arrogant towards her mistress. He also told her, that if she disobeyed God, and went on still in her way, she should perish · but if she would return back, she should become the mother of a son who should reign over that country. These admonitions she obeyed, and returned to her master and mistress, and obtained forgiveness. A little while afterwards, she bare Ismael, which may be interpreted *Heard of God,* because God had heard his mother's prayer.

5. The forementioned son was born to Abram when he was eighty-six years old: but when he was ninety-nine, God appeared to him, and promised him that he should have a son by Sarai, and commanded that his name should be Isaac; and shewed him, that from this son should spring great nations and kings, and that they should obtain all the land of Canaan by war, from Sidon to Egypt. But he charged him, in order to keep his posterity unmixed with others, that they should be circumcised in the flesh of their foreskin, and that this should be done on the eighth day after they were born: the reason of which circumcision I will explain in another place. And Abram inquiring also concerning Ismael, whether he should live or not, God signified to him that he should live to be very old, and should be the father of great nations. Abram, therefore, gave thanks to God for these blessings; and then he, and all his family, and his son Ismael were circumcised immediately, the son being that day thirteen years of age, and he ninety-nine.

CHAPTER XI

HOW GOD OVERTHREW THE NATION OF THE SODOMITES, OUT OF HIS WRATH AGAINST THEM FOR THEIR SINS

1. ABOUT this time the Sodomites grew proud, on account of their riches and great wealth: they became unjust towards men, and impious towards God, insomuch that they did not call to mind the advantages they received from him: they hated strangers, and abused themselves with Sodomitical practices. God was therefore much displeased at them, and determined to punish them for their pride, and to overthrow their city, and to lay waste their country, until there should neither plant nor fruit grow out of it.

2. When God had thus resolved concerning the Sodomites, Abraham, as he sat by the oak of Mambre, at the door of his tent, saw three angels; and, thinking them to be strangers, he rose up and saluted them, and desired they would accept of an entertainment, and abide with him; to which when they agreed, he ordered cakes of meal to be made presently: and when he had slain a calf, he roasted it, and brought it to them, as they sat under the oak. Now they made a show of eating; and besides, they asked him about his wife Sarah, where she was; and when he said she was within, they said they would come again hereafter, and find her become a mother. Upon which the woman laughed and said that it was impossible she should bear children, since she was ninety years of age, and her husband was a hundred. Then they concealed themselves no longer, but declared that they were angels of God; and that one of them was sent to inform them about the child, and two of the overthrow of Sodom.

---

* It is worth noting here, that God required no other sacrifices under the law of Moses, than what were taken from these five kinds of animals which he here required of Abram. Nor did the Jews feed upon any other domestic animals than the three here named, as Reland observes on Antiq. b. iv. ch. v. sect. 4.

† As to this affliction of Abram's posterity for 400 years, see Antiq. b. ii. ch. ix. sect. 1.

3. When Abraham heard this, he was grieved for the Sodomites; and he rose up, and besought God for them, and entreated him that he would not destroy the righteous with the wicked. And when God had replied that there was no good man among the Sodomites; for if there were but ten such men among them, he would not punish any of them for their sins, Abraham held his peace. And the angels came to the city of the Sodomites, and Lot entreated them to accept of a lodging with him; for he was a very generous and hospitable man, and one that had learned to imitate the goodness of Abraham. Now when the Sodomites saw the young men to be of beautiful countenances, and this to an extraordinary degree, and that they took up their lodgings with Lot, they resolved themselves to enjoy these beautiful boys by force and violence; and when Lot exhorted them to sobriety, and not to offer any thing immodest to the strangers, but to have regard to their lodging in his house; and promised, that if their inclinations could not be governed, he would expose his daughters to their lust, instead of these strangers—neither thus were they made ashamed.

4. But God was much displeased at their impudent behaviour, so that he both smote those men with blindness, and condemned the Sodomites to universal destruction. But Lot, upon God's informing him of the future destruction of the Sodomites, went away, taking with him his wife and daughters, who were two, and still virgins; for those that were betrothed * to them were above the thoughts of going, and deemed that Lot's words were trifling. God then cast a thunderbolt upon the city, and set it on fire with its inhabitants; and laid waste the country with the like burning, as I formerly said when I wrote the Jewish war.† But Lot's wife continually turning back to view the city as she went from it, and being too nicely inquisitive what would become of it, although God had forbidden her so to do, was changed into a pillar of salt;‡ for I have seen it, and it remains at this day. Now he and his daughters fled to a certain small place, encompassed with the fire, and settled in it. It is to this day called *Zoar*, for that is the word which the Hebrews use for a small thing. There it was that he lived a miserable life, on account of his having no company, and his want of provisions.

5. But his daughters, thinking that all man-

kind were destroyed, approached to their father,§ though taking care not to be perceived. This they did, that human kind might not utterly fail. And they bare sons: the son of the elder was named Moab, which denotes one derived from his father. The younger bare Ammon, which name denotes one derived from a kinsman. The former of whom was the father of the Moabites, which is even still a great nation; the latter was the father of the Ammonites: and both of them are inhabitants of Celesyria. And such was the departure of Lot from among the Sodomites.

CHAPTER XII

CONCERNING ABIMELECH; AND CONCERNING ISMAEL, THE SON OF ABRAHAM; AND CONCERNING THE ARABIANS, WHO WERE HIS POSTERITY

1. ABRAHAM now removed to Gerar of Palestine, leading Sarah along with him, under the notion of his sister, using the like dissimulation that he had used before, and this out of fear; for he was afraid of Abimelech, the king of that country, who did also himself fall in love with Sarah, and was disposed to corrupt her; but he was restrained from satisfying his lust, by a dangerous distemper which befell him from God. Now when his physicians despaired of curing him, he fell asleep, and saw a dream, warning him not to abuse the stranger's wife; and when he recovered, he told his friends that God had inflicted that disease upon him, by way of punishment, for his injury to the stranger, and in order to preserve the chastity of his wife; for that she did not accompany him as his sister, but as his legitimate wife; and that God had promised to be gracious to him for the time to come, if this person be once secure of his wife's chastity. When he had said this, by the advice of his friends, he sent for Abraham, and bid him not be concerned about his wife, or fear the corruption of her chastity; for that God took care of him, and that it was by His providence that he received his wife again, without her suffering any abuse; and he appealed to God, and to his wife's conscience, and said that he had not any inclination at first to enjoy her, if he had known she was his wife: but since, said he, thou leddest her about as thy sister, I was guilty of no offence. He also entreated him to be at peace with him, and to make God propitious to him; and that, if he thought fit to continue with him, he should have what he wanted in abundance; but that if he designed to go away, he should be honourably conducted, and have whatsoever supply he wanted when he came thither. Upon his saying this, Abraham told him that his pretence of kindred to his wife was no lie, because she was his brother's daughter; and that he did not think himself safe in his travels abroad, without this sort of dissimulation; and that he

---

* These sons-in-law to Lot, as they are called, (Gen. xix. 12-14,) might be so styled because they were betrothed to Lot's daughters, though not yet married to them. See the note on Antiq. b. xiv. ch. xiii. sect. 1.

† Of the War, b. iv. ch. viii. sect. 4.

‡ This pillar of salt was, we see here, standing in the days of Josephus; and he had seen it. That it was standing then, is also attested by Clement of Rome, contemporary with Josephus; as also that it was so in the next century, is attested by Irenæus, with the addition of an hypothesis, how it came to last so long, with all its members entire.—Whether the account that some modern travellers give be true, that it is still standing, I do not know. Its remote situation, at the utmost southern point of the Sea of Sodom, in the wild and dangerous deserts of Arabia, makes it exceedingly difficult for inquisitive travellers to examine the place; and for common reports of country people, at a distance, they are not very satisfactory. In the meantime, I have no opinion of Le Clerc's dissertation or hypothesis about this question, which can only be determined by eye-witnesses. When Christian princes, so called, lay aside their foolish and unchristian wars and quarrels, and send a body of fit persons to travel over the East, and bring us faithful accounts of all ancient monuments, and procure us copies of all ancient records, at present lost among us, we may hope for full satisfaction in such inquiries, but hardly before.

§ I see no proper wicked intention in these daughters of Lot, when in a case which appeared to them of unavoidable necessity, they procured themselves to be with child by their father. Without such an unavoidable necessity, incest is a horrid crime; but whether in such a case of necessity as they apprehended this to be, according to Josephus, it was any such crime, I am not satisfied. In the meantime, their making their father drunk, and their solicitous concealment of what they did from him, shews that they despaired of persuading him to an action which, at the best, could not but be very suspicious and shocking to so good a man.

was not the cause of his distemper, but was only solicitous for his own safety. He said also, that he was ready to stay with him. Whereupon Abimelech assigned him land and money; and they covenanted to live together without guile, and took an oath at a certain well called Beersheba, which may be interpreted *The Well of the Oath*. And so it is named by the people of the country unto this day.

2. Now in a little time Abraham had a son by Sarah, as God had foretold to him, whom he named Isaac, which signifies *Laughter;* and indeed they so called him, because Sarah laughed when God * said that she should bear a son, she not expecting such a thing, as being past the age of child-bearing, for she was ninety years old, and Abraham an hundred; so that this son was born to them both in the last year of each of those decimal numbers. And they circumcised him upon the eighth day. And from that time the Jews continue the custom of circumcising their sons within that number of days. But as for the Arabians, they circumcise after the thirteenth year, because Ismael, the founder of their nation, who was born to Abraham of the concubine, was circumcised at that age; concerning whom I will presently give a particular account, with great exactness.

3. As for Sarah, she at first loved Ismael, who was born of her own handmaid Hagar, with an affection not inferior to that of her own son, for he was brought up in order to succeed in the government; but when she herself had born Isaac, she was not willing that Ismael should be brought up with him, as being too old for him, and able to do him injuries when their father should be dead; she therefore persuaded Abraham to send him and his mother to some distant country. Now, at the first he did not agree to what Sarah was so zealous for, and thought it an instance of the greatest barbarity to send away a young child† and a woman unprovided of necessaries; but at length he agreed to it, because God was pleased with what Sarah had determined; so he delivered Ismael to his mother, as not yet able to go by himself; and commanded her to take a bottle of water, and a loaf of bread, and so to depart, and to take Necessity for her guide. But as soon as her necessary provisions failed, she found herself in an evil case; and when the water was almost spent, she laid the young child, who was ready to expire, under a fig-tree, and went on further, that so he might die while she was absent.

But a divine angel came to her, and told her of a fountain hard by, and bid her take care and bring up the child, because she should be very happy by the preservation of Ismael. She then took courage, upon the prospect of what was promised her, and, meeting with some shepherds, by their care she got clear of the distresses she had been in.

4. When the lad was grown up, he married a wife, by birth an Egyptian, from whence the mother was herself derived originally. Of this wife were born to Ismael twelve sons: Nabaioth, Kedar, Abdeel, Mabsam, Idumas, Masmaos, Masaos, Chodad, Theman, Jetur, Naphesus, Cadmas. These inhabited all the country from Euphrates to the Red Sea, and called it Nabatene. They are an Arabian nation, and name their tribes from these, both because of their own virtue, and because of the dignity of Abraham their father.

CHAPTER XIII

CONCERNING ISAAC, THE LEGITIMATE SON OF ABRAHAM

1. Now Abraham greatly loved Isaac, as being his only begotten,‡ and given to him at the borders of old age by the favour of God. The child also endeared himself to his parents still more, by the exercise of every virtue, and adhering to his duty to his parents, and being zealous in the worship of God. Abraham also placed his own happiness in this prospect, that, when he should die, he should leave this his son in a safe and secure condition; which, accordingly, he obtained by the will of God; who, being desirous to make an experiment of Abraham's religious disposition towards himself, appeared to him, and enumerated all the blessings he had bestowed on him; how he had made him superior to his enemies; and that his son Isaac, who was the principal part of his present happiness, was derived from him; and he said that he required this son of his as a sacrifice and holy oblation. Accordingly, he commanded him to carry him to the mountain Moriah, and to build an altar, and offer him for a burnt-offering upon it; for that this would best manifest his religious disposition towards him, if he preferred what was pleasing to God before the preservation of his own son.

2. Now Abraham thought that it was not right to disobey God in anything, but that he was obliged to serve him in every circumstance of life, since all creatures that live enjoy their life by his providence, and the kindness he bestows on them. Accordingly, he concealed this command of God, and his own intentions about the slaughter of his son, from his wife, as also from every one of his servants, otherwise he should have been hindered from his obedience to God; and he took Isaac, together with two of his servants, and laying whatever things were necessary for a sacrifice upon an ass, he went away to the mountain. Now the two servants went along with him two days; but on the third day, as soon as he saw the mountain, he left those servants that were with him till then in the plain, and, having his son alone with him, he

---

* It is well worth observation, that Josephus here calls that principal angel, who appeared to Abraham and foretold the birth of Isaac, directly *God;* which language of Josephus here, prepares us to believe those other expressions of his, that *Jesus was a wise man, if it be lawful to call him a man*, Antiq. b. xviii. chap. iii. sect. 3; and of *God the Word*, in his homily concerning Hades, may be both genuine. Nor is the other expression of *divine angel*, used presently, and before, also of any other signification.

† Josephus here calls Ismael a young child, or infant, though he was about 13 years of age; as Judas calls himself and his brethren young men, when he was 47, and had two children, Antiq. b. ii. chap. vi. sect. 8, and they were of much the same age as is a damsel of 12 years old called a little child, Mark v. 39–42, five several times. Herod also is said by Josephus to be a very young man at 25. See the note on Antiq. b. xiv. chap. ix. sect. 2, and of the War, b. i. chap. x. And Aristobulus is styled a very little child at 16 years of age, Antiq. b. xv. chap. ii. sect. 6, 7. Domitian is also called by him a very young child, when he went on his German expedition at about 18 years of age, of the War, b. vii. chap. iv. sect. 2. Samson's wife, and Ruth, when they were widows, are called children, Antiq. b. v. chap. viii. sect. 6, and chap. ix. sect. 2, 3.

‡ Note that both here and Heb. xi. 17, Isaac is called Abraham's only-begotten son, though he at the same time had another son, Ismael. The Septuagint expresses the true meaning, by rendering the text *the beloved son*.

came to the mountain. It was that mountain upon which king David afterwards built the temple.* Now they had brought with them every thing necessary for a sacrifice excepting the animal that was to be offered only. Now Isaac was twenty-five years old. And as he was building the altar, he asked his father what he was about to offer, since there was no animal there for an oblation :—to which it was answered, "That God would provide himself an oblation, he being able to make a plentiful provision for men out of what they have not, and to deprive others of what they already have, when they put too much trust therein; that therefore, if God pleased to be present and propitious at this sacrifice, he would provide himself an oblation."

3. As soon as the altar was prepared, and Abraham had laid on the wood, and all things were entirely ready, he said to his son, "O son! I poured out a vast number of prayers that I might have thee for my son; when thou wast come into the world, there was nothing that could contribute to thy support for which I was not greatly solicitous, nor anything wherein I thought myself happier than to see thee grown up to man's estate, and that I might leave thee at my death the successor to my dominion; but since it was by God's will that I became thy father, and it is now his will that I relinquish thee, bear this consecration to God with a generous mind; for I resign thee up to God, who has thought fit now to require this testimony of honour to himself, on account of the favours he hath conferred on me, in being to me a supporter and defender. Accordingly thou, my son, wilt now die, not in any common way of going out of the world, but sent to God, the Father of all men, beforehand, by thy own father, in the nature of a sacrifice. I suppose he thinks thee worthy to get clear of this world neither by disease, neither by war, nor by any other severe way, by which death usually comes upon men, but so that he will receive thy soul with prayers and holy offices of religion, and will place thee near to himself, and thou wilt there be to me a succourer and supporter in my old age; on which account I principally brought thee up, and thou wilt thereby procure me God for my Comforter instead of thyself."

4. Now Isaac was of such a generous disposition, as became the son of such a father, and was pleased with this discourse, and said, "That he was not worthy to be born at first, if he should reject the determination of God and of his father, and should not resign himself up readily to both their pleasures; since it would have been unjust if he had not obeyed, even if his father alone had so resolved." So he went immediately to the altar to be sacrificed. And the deed had been done if God had not opposed it; for he called loudly to Abraham by his name, and forbade him to slay his son; and said, "It was not out of a desire of human blood that he was commanded to slay his son, nor was he willing that he should be taken away from him whom he had made his father, but to try the temper of his mind, whether he would be obedient to such a command. Since, therefore, he now was satisfied as to that his alacrity, and the surprising

readiness he shewed in this his piety, he was delighted in having bestowed such blessings upon him; and that he would not be wanting in all sort of concern about him, and in bestowing other children upon him; and that his son should live to a very great age; that he should live a happy life, and bequeath a large principality to his children, who should be good and legitimate." He foretold also that his family should increase into many nations,† and that those patriarchs should leave behind them an everlasting name, that they should obtain the possession of the land of Canaan, and be envied by all men. When God had said this, he produced to them a ram, which did not appear before, for the sacrifice. So Abraham and Isaac, receiving each other unexpectedly, and having obtained the promises of such great blessings, embraced one another; and when they had sacrificed, they returned to Sarah, and lived happily together, God affording them his assistance in all things they desired.

CHAPTER XIV

CONCERNING SARAH, ABRAHAM'S WIFE; AND HOW SHE ENDED HER DAYS

Now Sarah died a little while after, having lived one hundred and twenty-seven years. They buried her in Hebron, the Canaanites publicly allowing them a burying-place; which piece of ground Abraham bought, for four hundred shekels, of Ephron, an inhabitant of Hebron; and both Abraham and his descendants built themselves sepulchres in that place.

CHAPTER XV

HOW THE NATION OF THE TROGLODYTES WERE DERIVED FROM ABRAHAM BY KETURAH

ABRAHAM after this married Keturah, by whom six sons were born to him; men of courage and of sagacious minds:—Zambran, and Jazar, and Madan, and Madian, and Josabak, and Sous. Now the sons of Sous were Sabathan and Dadan: the sons of Dadan were Latusim, and Assur, and Luom: the sons of Madian were Ephas, and Ophren, and Anoch, and Ebidas, and Eldas. Now, for all these sons and grandsons, Abraham

---

* Here is a plain error in the copies, which say that King David afterwards built the temple on this mount Moriah, while it was certainly no other than King Solomon who built that temple, as, indeed Procopius cites it from Josephus. For it was for certain David, and not Solomon, who built the first altar there, as we learn, 2 Sam. xxiv. 18, &c., 1 Chron. xxi. 22, &c., and Antiq. b. vii. chap. xiii. sect 4.

† It seems both here and in God's parallel blessing to Jacob, (chap. xix. sect. 1,) that Josephus had yet no notion of the hidden meaning of that most important and most eminent promise, "In thy seed shall all the families of the earth be blessed! He saith not, And to seeds, as of many, but as of one; and to thy seed, which is Christ," (Gal. iii. 16.) Nor is it any wonder, he being, I think, as yet not a Christian; and had he been a Christian,—yet since he was, to be sure, till the latter part of his life, no more than an Ebionite Christian, who, above all the apostles, rejected and despised St Paul,—it would be no great wonder if he did not now follow his interpretation. In the meantime, we have in effect St Paul's exposition in the Testament of Reuben, sect. 6, in Authent. Rec. Part i. p. 302, who charges his sons "to worship the seed of Judah, who should die for them in visible and invisible wars, and should be among them an eternal king." Nor is that observation of a learned foreigner of my acquaintance to be despised, who takes notice that, as *seeds*, in the plural, must signify *posterity*, so *seed*, in the singular, may signify either *posterity*, or *a single person*; and that in this promise of all nations being happy in the seed of Abraham, or Isaac, or Jacob, &c., it is always used in the singular. To which I shall add, that it is sometimes, as it were, paraphrased by the son of Abraham, the son of David, &c., which is capable of no such ambiguity.

contrived to settle them in colonies; and they took possession of Troglodytis, and the country of Arabia the Happy, as far as it reaches to the Red Sea. It is related of this Ophren, that he made war against Libya and took it; and that his grandchildren, when they inhabited it, called it (from his name) Africa: and, indeed, Alexander Polyhistor gives his attestation to what I here say, who speaks thus:—"Cleodemus the prophet, who was also called Malchus, who wrote a history of the Jews, in agreement with the history of Moses, their legislator, relates that there were many sons born to Abraham by Keturah; nay, he names three of them, Apher, and Surim, and Japhran: that from Surim was the land of Assyria denominated; and that from the other two (Apher and Japhran) the country of Africa took its name, because these men were auxiliaries to Hercules, when he fought against Libya and Antæus; and that Hercules married Aphra's daughter, and of her he begat a son, Diodorus; and that Sophon was his son; from whom that barbarous people called Sophacians were denominated."

CHAPTER XVI

HOW ISAAC TOOK REBEKA TO WIFE

1. Now when Abraham, the father of Isaac, had resolved to take Rebeka, who was granddaughter to his brother Nahor, for a wife to his son Isaac, who was then about forty years old, he sent the ancientest of his servants to betroth her, after he had obliged him to give him the strongest assurances of his fidelity; which assurances were given after the manner following:—They put each other's hands under each other's thighs; then they called upon God as the witness of what was to be done. He also sent such presents to those that were there as were in esteem, on account that they either rarely or never were seen in that country. The servant got thither not under a considerable time; for it requires much time to pass through Mesopotamia, in which it is tedious travelling, both in winter for the depth of the clay, and in summer for want of water; and, besides this, for the robberies there committed, which are not to be avoided by travellers but by caution beforehand. However, the servant came to Haran; and when he was in the suburbs, he met a considerable number of maidens going to the water; he therefore prayed to God that Rebeka might be found among them, or her whom Abraham sent him as his servant to espouse to his son, in case his will were that this marriage should be consummated, and that she might be made known to him by the sign, That while others denied him water to drink, she might give it him.

2. With this intention he went to the well, and desired the maidens to give him some water to drink: but while the others refused, on pretence that they wanted it all at home, and could spare none for him, one only of the company rebuked them for their peevish behaviour towards the stranger, and said, What is there that you will ever communicate to any body, who have not so much as given the man some water? She then offered him water in an obliging manner; and now he began to hope that his grand affair would succeed; but desiring still to know the truth, he commended her for her generosity and good-nature, that she did not scruple to afford a sufficiency of water to those that wanted it, though it cost her some pains to draw it; and asked who were her parents, and wished them

joy of such a daughter. "And mayest thou be espoused," said he, "to their satisfaction, into the family of an agreeable husband, and bring him legitimate children!" Nor did she disdain to satisfy his inquiries, but told him her family. "They," says she, "call me Rebeka; my father was Bethuel, but he is dead; and Laban is my brother; and, together with my mother, takes care of all our family affairs, and is the guardian of my virginity." When the servant heard this, he was very glad at what had happened, and at what was told him, as perceiving that God had thus plainly directed his journey: and producing his bracelets, and some other ornaments which it was esteemed decent for virgins to wear, he gave them to the damsel, by way of acknowledgment, and as a reward for her kindness in giving him water to drink; saying, it was but just that she should have them, because she was so much more obliging than any of the rest. She desired also that he would come and lodge with them, since the approach of the night gave him not time to proceed further; and producing his precious ornaments for women, he said he desired to trust them to none more safely than to such as she had shewn herself to be; and that he believed he might guess at the humanity of her mother and brother, that they would not be displeased, from the virtue he found in her; for he would not be burdensome, but would pay the hire for his entertainment, and spend his own money. To which she replied, that he guessed right as to the humanity of her parents; but complained that he should think them so parsimonious as to take money, for that he should have all on free cost: but she said she would first inform her brother Laban, and, if he gave her leave, she would conduct him in.

3. As soon then as this was over, she introduced the stranger; and for the camels, the servants of Laban brought them in, and took care of them; and he was himself brought into supper by Laban. And, after supper, he says to him, and to the mother of the damsel, addressing himself to her, "Abraham is the son of Terah, and a kinsman of yours; for Nahor, the grandfather of these children, was the brother of Abraham, by both father and mother; upon which account he hath sent me to you, being desirous to take this damsel for his son to wife. He is his legitimate son, and is brought up as his only heir. He could indeed have had the most happy of all the women in that country for him, but he would not have his son marry any of them; but, out of regard to his own relations, he desired him to match here, whose affection and inclination I would not have you despise, for it was by the good pleasure of God that other accidents fell out in my journey, and that thereby I lighted upon your daughter and your house; for when I was near to the city, I saw a great many maidens coming to a well, and I prayed that I might meet with this damsel, which has come to pass accordingly. Do you, therefore, confirm that marriage, whose espousals have been already made by a divine appearance; and shew the respect you have for Abraham, who hath sent me with so much solicitude, in giving your consent to the marriage of this damsel." Upon this they understood it to be the will of God, and greatly approved of the offer, and sent their daughter, as was desired. Accordingly Isaac married her, the inheritance being now come to him; for the children by Keturah were gone to their own remote habitations.

CHAPTER XVII

CONCERNING THE DEATH OF ABRAHAM

A LITTLE while after this, Abraham died. He was a man of incomparable virtue, and honoured by God in a manner agreeable to his piety towards him. The whole time of his life was one hundred seventy and five years; and he was buried in Hebron, with his wife Sarah, by their sons Isaac and Ismael.

CHAPTER XVIII

CONCERNING THE SONS OF ISAAC, ESAU AND JACOB; OF THEIR NATIVITY AND EDUCATION

1. Now Isaac's wife proved with child, after the death of Abraham;* and when her belly was greatly burdened, Isaac was very anxious, and inquired of God; who answered that Rebeka should bear twins, and that two nations should take the names of those sons; and that he who appeared the second should excel the elder. Accordingly she, in a little time, as God had foretold, bare twins; the elder of whom, from his head to his feet, was very rough and hairy, but the younger took hold of his heel as they were in the birth. Now the father loved the elder, who was called Esau, a name agreeable to his roughness, for the Hebrews call such a hairy roughness [Esau,† or] Seir; but Jacob, the younger, was best beloved by his mother.

2. When there was a famine in the land, Isaac resolved to go into Egypt, the land there being good; but he went to Gerar, as God commanded him. Here Abimelech the king received him, because Abraham had formerly lived with him, and had been his friend; and as in the beginning he treated him exceeding kindly, so he was hindered from continuing in the same disposition to the end, by his envy at him; for when he saw that God was with Isaac, and took such great care of him, he drove him away from him. But Isaac, when he saw how envy had changed the temper of Abimelech, retired to a place called the Valley, not far from Gerar; and as he was digging a well, the shepherds fell upon him, and began to fight, in order to hinder the work; and because he did not desire to contend, the shepherds seemed to get the better of him; so he still retired, and dug another well: and when certain other shepherds of Abimelech's began to offer him violence, he left that also, and still retired; thus purchasing security to himself by a rational and prudent conduct. At length the king gave him leave to dig a well without disturbance. He named this well Rehoboth, which denotes *a large space;* but of the former wells, one was called Escon, which denotes *strife;* the other Sitenna, which name signifies *enmity.*

3. It was now that Isaac's affairs increased, and his power was in a flourishing condition; and this from his great riches. But Abimelech, thinking Isaac throve in opposition to him, while their living together made them suspicious of each other, and Isaac's retiring shewing a secret enmity also, he was afraid that his former friendship with Isaac would not secure him, if Isaac should endeavour to revenge the injuries he had formerly offered him; he therefore renewed his friendship with him, and brought with him Philoc, one of his generals. And when he had obtained every thing he desired, by reason of Isaac's good nature, who preferred the earlier friendship Abimelech had shewn to himself and his father to his later wrath against him, he returned home.

4. Now when Esau, one of the sons of Isaac, whom the father principally loved, was now come to the age of forty years, he married Adah, the daughter of Helon, and Aholibamah, the daughter of Esebeon; which Helon and Esebeon were great lords among the Canaanites, thereby taking upon himself the authority, and pretending to have dominion over his own marriages, without so much as asking the advice of his father; for had Isaac been the arbitrator, he had not given him leave to marry thus, for he was not pleased with contracting any alliance with the people of that country; but not caring to be uneasy to his son, by commanding him to put away these wives, he resolved to be silent.

5. But when he was old, and could not see at all, he called Esau to him, and told him, that besides his blindness and the disorder of his eyes, his very old age hindered him from his worship of God, [by sacrifice;] he bid him therefore to go out a hunting, and when he had caught as much venison as he could, to prepare him a supper,‡ that after this he might make supplication to God, to be to him a supporter and an assister during the whole time of his life; saying, that it was uncertain when he should die, and that he was desirous, by prayers for him, to procure, beforehand, God to be merciful to him.

6. Accordingly Esau went out a hunting; but Rebeka§ thinking it proper to have the supplication made for obtaining the favour of God to Jacob, and that without the consent of Isaac, bid him kill kids of the goats, and prepare a supper. So Jacob obeyed his mother, according to all her instructions. Now when the supper was got ready, he took a goat's skin, and put it about his arm, that by reason of its hairy roughness, he might by his father be believed to be Esau; for they being twins, and in all things else alike, differed only in this thing. This was done out

---

* The birth of Jacob and Esau is here said to be after Abraham's death: it should have been after Sarah's death. The order of the narration in Genesis, not always exactly according to the order of time, seems to have led Josephus into this error, as Dr Bernard observes here.

† For Seir in Josephus, the coherence requires that we read *Esau* or *Seir,* which signify the same thing.

‡ The supper of savoury meat, as we call it, (Gen. xxvii. 4,) to be caught by hunting, was intended plainly for a festival or a sacrifice; and upon the prayers that were frequent at sacrifices, Isaac expected, as was then usual in such eminent cases, that a divine impulse would come upon him, in order to the solemn blessing of his son there present, and his foretelling his future behaviour and fortune. Whence it must be, that when Isaac had unwittingly blessed Jacob, and was afterwards made sensible of his mistake, yet did he not attempt to alter it, how earnestly soever his affection for Esau might incline him to wish it might be altered, because he knew that this blessing came not from himself, but from God, and that an alteration was out of his power. A second afflatus then came upon him, and enabled him to foretell Esau's future behaviour and fortune also.

§ Whether Jacob or his mother Rebeka were most blameable in this imposition upon Isaac in his old age, I cannot determine. However, the blessing being delivered as a prediction of future events, by a divine impulse, and foretelling things to befall to the posterity of Jacob and Esau in future ages, was for certain providential; and according to what Rebeka knew to be the purpose of God, when he answered her inquiry, "before the children were born," (Gen. xxv. 23,) "that one people should be stronger than the other people; and the elder, Esau, should serve the younger, Jacob." Whether Isaac knew or remembered this old oracle, delivered in our copies only to Rebeka; or whether, if he knew and remembered it, he did not endeavour to

of his fear, that before his father had made his supplications, he should be caught in his evil practice; and lest he should, on the contrary, provoke his father to curse him. So he brought in the supper to his father. Isaac perceiving, by the peculiarity of his voice, who he was, called his son to him, who gave him his hand, which was covered with the goat's skin. When Isaac felt that, he said, "Thy voice is like the voice of Jacob, yet, because of the thickness of thy hair, thou seemest to be Esau." So suspecting no deceit, he ate the supper, and betook himself to his prayers and intercessions with God: and said, "O Lord of all ages, and Creator of all substance; for it was thou that didst propose to my father great plenty of good things, and hast vouchsafed to bestow on me what I have; and hast promised to my posterity to be their kind supporter, and to bestow on them still greater blessings,—do thou, therefore, confirm these thy promises, and do not overlook me, because of my present weak condition, on account of which I most earnestly pray to thee. Be gracious to this my son; and preserve him, and keep him from every thing that is evil. Give him a happy life, and the possession of as many good things as thy power is able to bestow. Make him terrible to his enemies, and honourable and beloved among his friends!"

7. Thus did Isaac pray to God, thinking his prayers had been made for Esau. He had but just finished them, when Esau came in from hunting; and when Isaac perceived his mistake, he was silent: but Esau required that he might be made partaker of the like blessing from his father that his brother had partook of: but his father refused it, because all his prayers had been spent upon Jacob; so Esau lamented the mistake. However, his father being grieved at his weeping, said, that "he should excel in hunting and strength of body, in arms, and all such sorts of work; and should obtain glory for ever on those accounts, he and his posterity after him; but still should serve his brother."

8. Now the mother delivered Jacob, when she was afraid that his brother would inflict some punishment upon him, because of the mistake about the prayers of Isaac; for she persuaded her husband to take a wife for Jacob out of Mesopotamia, of her own kindred, Esau having married already Basemmath, the daughter of Ismael, without his father's consent; for Isaac did not like the Canaanites, so that he disapproved of Esau's former marriages, which made him take Basemmath to wife, in order to please him; and indeed he had a great affection for her.

CHAPTER XIX.

CONCERNING JACOB'S FLIGHT INTO MESOPOTAMIA, BY REASON OF THE FEAR HE WAS IN OF HIS BROTHER.

1. Now Jacob was sent by his mother to Meso-

alter the divine determination, out of his fondness for his elder and worser son Esau, to the damage of his younger and better son Jacob; as Josephus elsewhere supposes, Antiq. b. ii. ch. vii. sect. 3, I cannot certainly say. If so, this might tempt Rebeka to contrive, and Jacob to put this imposition upon him. However, Josephus says here, that it was Isaac, and not Rebeka, who inquired of God at first, and received the forementioned oracle, (sect. 1;) which, if it be the true reading, renders Isaac's procedure more inexcusable. Nor was it probably any thing else that so much encouraged Esau formerly to marry two Canaanitish wives, without his parents' consent, as Isaac's unhappy fondness for him.

potamia, in order to marry Laban her brother's daughter, (which marriage was permitted by Isaac, on account of his obsequiousness to the desires of his wife;) and he accordingly journeyed through the land of Canaan; and because he hated the people of that country, he would not lodge with any of them, but took up his lodging in the open air, and laid his head on a heap of stones that he had gathered together. At which time he saw in his sleep such a vision standing by him;—he seemed to see a ladder, that reached from the earth unto heaven, and persons descending upon the ladder that seemed more excellent than human; and at last God himself stood above it, and was plainly visible to him; who, calling him by his name, spake to him these words:—

2. "O Jacob, it is not fit for thee, who art the son of a good father, and grandson of one who had obtained a great reputation for his eminent virtue, to be dejected at thy present circumstances, but to hope for better times, for thou shalt have great abundance of all good things by my assistance; for I brought Abraham hither, out of Mesopotamia, when he was driven away by his kinsmen, and I made thy father a happy man; nor will I bestow a lesser degree of happiness on thyself; be of good courage, therefore, and under my conduct proceed on this thy journey, for the marriage thou goest so zealously about shall be consummated; and thou shalt have children of good characters, but their multitude shall be innumerable; and they shall leave what they have to a still more numerous posterity, to whom, and to whose posterity, I give the dominion of all the land, and their posterity shall fill the entire earth and sea, so far as the sun beholds them; but do not thou fear any danger, nor be afraid of the many labours thou must undergo, for by my providence I will direct thee what thou art to do in the time present, and still much more in the time to come."

3. Such were the predictions which God made to Jacob; whereupon he became very joyful at what he had seen and heard; and he poured oil on the stones, because on them the prediction of such great benefits was made. He also vowed a vow, that he would offer sacrifices upon them, if he lived and returned safe: and if he came again in such a condition, he would give the tithe of what he had gotten to God. He also judged the place to be honourable, and gave it the name of Bethel, which, in the Greek, is interpreted, *The House of God*.

4. So he proceeded on his journey to Mesopotamia, and at length came to Haran; and meeting with shepherds in the suburbs, with boys grown up, and maidens sitting about a certain well, he stayed with them, as wanting water to drink; and beginning to discourse with them, he asked them whether they knew such a one as Laban, and whether he was still alive. Now they all said they knew him, for he was not so inconsiderable a person as to be unknown to any of them; and that his daughter fed her father's flock together with them; and that indeed they wondered that she was not yet come, for by her means thou mightest learn more exactly whatever thou desirest to know about that family. While they were saying this the damsel came, and the other shepherds that came down along with her. Then they shewed her Jacob, and told her that he was a stranger, who came to inquire about her father's affairs. But she, as pleased, after the custom of children, with Jacob's coming, asked him who he was, and whence he came to them, and what it was he lacked that he came hither. She also wished it might be in their power to supply the wants he came about.

5. But Jacob was quite overcome, not so much by their kindred, nor by that affection which might arise thence, as by his love to the damsel, and his surprise at her beauty, which was so flourishing, as few of the women of that age could vie with. He said then, "There is a relation between thee and me, elder than either thy or my birth, if thou be the daughter of Laban; for Abraham was the son of Terah, as well as Haran and Nahor. Of the last of whom (Nahor) Bethuel thy grandfather was the son. Isaac my father was the son of Abraham and of Sarah, who was the daughter of Haran. But there is a nearer and later cement of mutual kindred which we bear to one another, for my mother Rebeka was sister to Laban thy father, both by the same father and mother; I therefore and thou are cousin-germans; and I am now come to salute you, and to renew that affinity which is proper between us. Upon this the damsel, at the mention of Rebeka, as usually happens to young persons, wept, and that out of the kindness she had for her father, and embraced Jacob, she having learned an account of Rebeka from her father, and knew that her parents loved to hear her named; and when she had saluted him, she said that "he brought the most desirable and greatest pleasures to her father, with all their family, who was always mentioning his mother, and always thinking of her, and her alone; and that this will make thee equal in his eyes to any advantageous circumstances whatsoever." Then she bid him go to her father, and follow her while she conducted him to him; and not to deprive him of such a pleasure, by staying any longer away from him.

6. When she had said thus, she brought him to Laban; and being owned by his uncle, he was secure himself, as being among his friends; and he brought a great deal of pleasure to them by his unexpected coming. But a little while afterward, Laban told him that he could not express in words the joy he had at his coming; but still he inquired of him the occasion of his coming, and why he left his aged mother and father, when they wanted to be taken care of by him; and that he would afford him all the assistance he wanted. Then Jacob gave him an account of the whole occasion of his journey, and told him, "that Isaac had two sons that were twins, himself and Esau; who, because he failed of his father's prayers, which by his mother's wisdom were put up for him, sought to kill him, as deprived of the kingdom* which was to be given him of God, and of the blessings for which their father prayed; and that this was the occasion of his coming hither, as his mother had commanded him to do: for we are all (says he) brethren one to another; but our mother esteems an alliance with your family more than she does one with the families of the country; so I look upon yourself and God to be the supporters of my travels, and think myself safe in my present circumstances."

7. Now Laban promised to treat him with great humanity, both on account of his ancestors, and particularly for the sake of his mother, towards whom, he said, he would shew his kindness, even though she were absent, by taking care of him; for he assured him he would make him the head shepherd of his flock, and give him authority sufficient for that purpose; and when he should have a mind to return to his parents, he would send him back with presents, and this in as honourable a manner as the nearness of their relation should require. This Jacob heard gladly; and said he would willingly, and with pleasure, undergo any sort of pains while he tarried with him, but desired Rachel to wife, as the reward of those pains, who was not only on other accounts esteemed by him, but also because she was the means of his coming to him; for he said he was forced by the love of the damsel to make this proposal. Laban was well pleased with this agreement, and consented to give the damsel to him, as not desirous to meet with any better son-in-law; and said he would do this, if he would stay with him some time, for he was not willing to send his daughter to be among the Canaanites, for he repented of the alliance he had made already by marrying his sister there. And when Jacob had given his consent to this, he agreed to stay seven years; for so many years he had resolved to serve his father-in-law, that, having given a specimen of his virtue, it might be better known what sort of a man he was: and Jacob accepting of his terms, after the time was over, he made the wedding-feast; and when it was night, without Jacob's perceiving it, he put his other daughter into bed to him, who was both elder than Rachel, and of no comely countenance: Jacob lay with her that night, as being both in drink and in the dark. However, when it was day he knew what had been done to him; and he reproached Laban for his unfair proceeding with him; who asked pardon for that necessity which forced him to do what he did; for he did not give him Lea out of any ill design, but as overcome by another greater necessity that, notwithstanding this, nothing should hinder him from marrying Rachel; but that when he had served another seven years, he would give him her whom he loved. Jacob submitted to this condition, for his love to the damsel did not permit him to do otherwise; and when another seven years were gone, he took Rachel to wife.

8. Now each of these had handmaids, by their father's donation. Zilpha was handmaid to Lea, and Bilha to Rachel; by no means slaves,† but, however, subject to their mistresses. Now Lea was sorely troubled at her husband's love to her sister; and she expected she should be better esteemed if she bare him children: so she entreated God perpetually; and when she had born a son, and her husband was on that account better reconciled to her, she named her son Reubel, because *God had had mercy upon her, in giving her a son;* for that is the signification of this name. After some time she bare

---

* By this "deprivation of the kingdom that was to be given Esau of God," as the first-born, it appears that Josephus thought that a "kingdom to be derived from God" was due to him whom Isaac should bless as his first-born; which I take to be that kingdom which was expected under the Messiah, who therefore was to be born of his posterity whom Isaac should so bless. Jacob, therefore, by obtaining this blessing of the first-born, became the genuine heir of that kingdom, in opposition to Esau.

† Here we have the difference between slaves for life and servants, such as we now hire for a time agreed upon on both sides, and dismiss again after the time contracted for is over, which are no slaves, but free men and free women. Accordingly, when the apostolical constitutions forbid a clergyman to marry perpetual servants or slaves, b. vi. ch. xvii., it is meant only of the former sort; as we learn elsewhere from the same constitutions, ch. xlvii. Can. lxxxii. But concerning these twelve sons of Jacob; the reasons of their several names, and the times of their several births in the intervals here assigned,—their several excellent characters, their several faults and repentance, the several accidents of their lives, with their several prophecies at their deaths, see the Testaments of these twelve patriarchs, still preserved at large in Authent. Rec. part i. pp. 294-443.

three more sons; Simeon, which name signifies *that God had hearkened to her prayer*. Then she bare Levi, *the confirmer of their friendship*. After him was born Judah, which denotes *thanksgiving*. But Rachel, fearing lest the fruitfulness of her sister should make herself enjoy a lesser share of Jacob's affections, put to bed to him her handmaid Bilha; by whom Jacob had Dan: one may interpret that name into the Greek tongue, *a divine judgment*. And after him Nepthalim, as it were, *unconquerable in stratagems*, since Rachel tried to conquer the fruitfulness of her sister by this stratagem. Accordingly, Lea took the same method, and used a counter-stratagem to that of her sister; for she put to bed to him her own handmaid. Jacob therefore had by Zilpha a son whose name was Gad, which may be interpreted *fortune;* and after him Asher, which may be called *a happy man*, because he added glory to Lea. Now Reubel, the eldest son of Lea, brought apples of mandrakes* to his mother. When Rachel saw them, she desired that she would give her the apples, for she longed to eat them; but when she refused, and bid her be content that she had deprived her of the benevolence she ought to have had from her husband, Rachel, in order to mitigate her sister's anger, said she would yield her husband to her; and he should lie with her that evening. She accepted of the favour; and Jacob slept with Lea by the favour of Rachel. She bare then these sons: Issachar, denoting *one born by hire;* and Zabulon, *one born as a pledge of benevolence towards her:* and a daughter, Dina. After some time Rachel had a son, named Joseph, which signified *there should be another added to him*.

9. Now Jacob fed the flocks of Laban, his father-in-law, all this time, being twenty years; after which he desired leave of his father-in-law, to take his wives and go home; but when his father-in-law would not give him leave, he contrived to do it secretly. He made trial, therefore, of the disposition of his wives, what they thought of this journey;—when they appeared glad, and approved of it. Rachel took along with her the images of the gods which, according to their laws, they used to worship in their own country, and ran away together with her sister. The children also of them both, and the handmaids, and what possessions they had, went along with him. Jacob also drove away half the cattle, without letting Laban know of it beforehand; but the reason why Rachel took the images of the gods, although Jacob had taught her to despise such worship of those gods, was this, That in case they were pursued, and taken by her father, she might have recourse to these images, in order to obtain his pardon.

10. But Laban, after one day's time, being acquainted with Jacob's and his daughters' departure, was much troubled, and pursued after them, leading a band of men with him; and on the seventh day overtook them, and found them resting on a certain hill; and then indeed he did not meddle with them, for it was even-tide; but God stood by him in a dream, and warned him to receive his son-in-law and his daughters in a peaceable manner; and not to venture upon any

---

* I formerly explained these mandrakes, as we, with the Septuagint and Josephus, render the Hebrew word *Dudaim*, of the Syrian Maux, with Ludolphus, Authent. Rec. part i. p. 420; but have since seen such a very probable account in MS. of my learned friend, Mr Samuel Barker, of what we still call *Mandrakes*, and their description by the ancient naturalists and physicians, as inclines me to think these here mentioned were really mandrakes, and no other.

thing rashly, or in wrath to them, but to make a league with Jacob; and he told him, that if he despised their small number, and attacked them in a hostile manner, he would himself assist them. When Laban had been thus forewarned by God, he called Jacob to him the next day, in order to treat with him, and shewed him what dream he had; in dependence whereupon he came confidently to him, and began to accuse him; alleging him that he had entertained him when he was poor, and in want of all things, and had given him plenty of all things which he had; "For," said he, "I have joined my daughters to thee in marriage, and supposed that thy kindness to me would be greater than before; but thou hast had no regard to either thy mother's relation to me, nor to the affinity now newly contracted between us; nor to those wives whom thou hast married; nor to those children, of whom I am the grandfather. Thou hast treated me as an enemy, by driving away my cattle; and by persuading my daughters to run away from their father; and by carrying home those sacred paternal images which were worshipped by my forefathers, and have been honoured with the like worship which they paid them, by myself. In short, thou hast done this whilst thou art my kinsman, and my sister's son, and the husband of my daughters, and was hospitably treated by me, and didst eat at my table." When Laban had said this, Jacob made his defence:—That he was not the only person in whom God had implanted the love of his native country, but that he had made it natural to all men; and that therefore it was but reasonable that, after so long time, he should go back to it. "But as to the prey, of whose driving away thou accusest me, if any other person were the arbitrator, thou wouldst be found in the wrong; for, instead of those thanks I ought to have had from thee, for both keeping thy cattle and increasing them, how is it that thou art unjustly angry at me because I have taken, and have with me a small portion of them? But then, as to thy daughters, take notice, that it is not through any evil practices of mine that they follow me in my return home, but from that just affection which wives naturally have to their husbands. They follow, therefore, not so properly myself as their own children." And thus far of his apology was made, in order to clear himself of having acted unjustly. To which he added his own complaint and accusation of Laban; saying, "While I was thy sister's son, and thou hadst given me thy daughters in marriage, thou hast worn me out with thy harsh commands, and detained me twenty years under them. That, indeed, which was required in order to my marrying thy daughters, hard as it was, I own to have been tolerable; but as to those that were put upon me after those marriages, they were worse, and such indeed as an enemy would have avoided." For certainly Laban had used Jacob very ill; for when he saw that God was assisting to Jacob in all that he desired, he promised him, that of the young cattle which should be born, he should have sometimes what was of a white colour, and sometimes what should be of a black colour; but when those that came to Jacob's share proved numerous, he did not keep his faith with him, but said he would give them to him the next year, because of his envying him the multitude of his possessions. He promised him as before, because he thought such an increase was not to be expected; but when it appeared to be fact, he deceived him.

11. But then, as to the sacred images, he bid him search for them; and when Laban accepted

of the offer, Rachel, being informed of it, put those images into that camel's saddle on which she rode, and sat upon it; and said, that her natural purgation hindered her rising up: so Laban left off searching any further, not supposing that his daughter in such circumstances would approach to those images. So he made a league with Jacob, and bound it by oaths, that he would not bear him any malice on account of what had happened; and Jacob made the like league, and promised to love Laban's daughters. And these leagues they confirmed with oaths also, which they made upon certain mountains, whereon they erected a pillar, in the form of an altar: whence that hill is called Gilead; and from thence they call that land the Land of Gilead at this day. Now when they had feasted after the making of the league, Laban returned home.

CHAPTER XX

CONCERNING THE MEETING OF JACOB AND ESAU

1. Now as Jacob was proceeding on his journey to the land of Canaan, angels appeared to him, and suggested to him good hope of his future condition; and that place he named the Camp of God. And being desirous of knowing what his brother's intentions were to him, he sent messengers to give him an exact account of every thing, as being afraid, on account of the enmities between them. He charged those that were sent to say to Esau, "Jacob had thought it wrong to live together with him, while he was in anger against him, and so had gone out of the country; and that he now, thinking the length of time of his absence must have made up their differences, was returning; that he brought with him his wives, and his children, with what possessions he had gotten, and delivered himself, with what was most dear to him, into his hands; and should think it his greatest happiness to partake together with his brother of what God had bestowed upon him." So these messengers told him this message. Upon which Esau was very glad, and met his brother with four hundred men. And Jacob, when he heard that he was coming to meet him with such a number of men, was greatly afraid: however, he committed his hope of deliverance to God; and considered how, in his present circumstances, he might preserve himself and those that were with him, and overcome his enemies if they attacked him injuriously. He therefore distributed his company into parts; some he sent before the rest, and the others he ordered to come close behind, that so, if the first were overpowered when his brother attacked them, they might have those that followed as a refuge to fly unto. And when he had put his company in this order, he sent some of them to carry presents to his brother. The presents were made up of cattle, and a great number of four-footed beasts of many kinds, such as would be very acceptable to those that received them, on account of their rarity. Those who were sent went at certain intervals of space asunder, that by following thick, one after another, they might appear to be more numerous, that Esau might remit of his anger on account of these presents, if he were still in a passion. Instructions were also given to those that were sent to speak gently to him.

2. When Jacob had made these appointments all the day, and night came on, he moved on with his company; and, as they were gone over

a certain river called Jabboc. Jacob was left behind; and meeting with an angel, he wrestled with him, the angel beginning the struggle; but he prevailed over the angel, who used a voice, and spake to him in words, exhorting him to be pleased with what had happened to him, and not to suppose that his victory was a small one, but that he had overcome a divine angel, and to esteem the victory as a sign of great blessings that should come to him; and that his offspring should never fail; and that no man should be too hard for his power. He also commanded him to be called Israel, which in the Hebrew tongue signifies *one that struggled with the divine angel.*[*] These promises were made at the prayer of Jacob; for when he perceived him to be the angel of God, he desired he would signify to him what should befall him hereafter. And when the angel had said what is before related, he disappeared; but Jacob was pleased with these things, and named the place Phanuel, which signifies *the face of God.* Now when he felt pain by this struggling upon his broad sinew, he abstained from eating that sinew himself afterward; and for his sake it is still not eaten by us.

3. When Jacob understood that his brother was near, he ordered his wives to go before, each by herself, with the handmaids, that they might see the actions of the men as they were fighting, if Esau were so disposed. He then went up to his brother Esau, and bowed down to him, who had no evil design upon him, but saluted him, and asked him about the company of the children and of the women; and desired, when he had understood all he wanted to know about them, that he would go along with him to their father; but Jacob pretending that the cattle were weary, Esau returned to Seir, for there was his place of habitation; he having named the place Roughness, from his own hairy roughness.

CHAPTER XXI

CONCERNING THE VIOLATION OF DINA'S CHASTITY

1. Hereupon Jacob came to the place till this day called Tents, (Succoth;) from whence he went to Shechem, which is a city of the Canaanites. Now as the Shechemites were keeping a festival, Dina, who was the only daughter of Jacob, went into the city to see the finery of the women of that country. But when Shechem, the son of Hamor the king, saw her, he defiled her by violence; and, being greatly in love with her, desired of his father that he would procure the damsel to him for a wife:—to which desire he condescended, and came to Jacob, desiring him to give leave that his son Shechem might, according to law, marry Dina. But Jacob, not knowing how to deny the desire of one of such great dignity, and yet not thinking it lawful to marry his daughter to a stranger, entreated him to give him leave to have a consultation about what he desired him to do. So the king went away, in hopes that Jacob would grant him this marriage. But Jacob informed his sons of the defilement of their sister, and of the address of Hamor, and desired them to give their advice what they should do. Upon this the greatest part said nothing, not knowing what advice to

---

[*] Perhaps this may be the proper meaning of the word Israel by the present and the old Jerusalem analogy of the Hebrew tongue. In the meantime, it is certain that the Hellenists of the first century, in Egypt and elsewhere, interpreted *Israel* to be *a man seeing God,* as is evident from the argument fore cited.

give. But Simeon and Levi, the brethren of the damsel by the same mother, agreed between themselves upon the action following:—It being now the time of a festival, when the Shechemites were employed in ease and feasting, they fell upon the watch when they were asleep, and, coming into the city, slew all the males,* as also the king and his son with them, but spared the women; and when they had done this without their father's consent, they brought away their sister.

2. Now while Jacob was astonished at the greatness of this act, and was severely blaming his sons for it, God stood by him, and bid him be of good courage; but to purify his tents, and to offer those sacrifices which he had vowed to offer when he went first into Mesopotamia, and saw his vision. As he was therefore purifying his followers, he lighted upon the gods of Laban, (for he did not before know they were stolen by Rachel,) and he hid them in the earth, under an oak, in Shechem; and departing thence, he offered sacrifice at Bethel, the place where he saw his dream, when he went first into Mesopotamia.

3. And when he was gone thence, and was come over against Ephrata, he there buried Rachel, who died in child-bed: she was the only one of Jacob's kindred that had not the honour of burial at Hebron; and when he had mourned for her a great while, he called the son that was born of her Benjamin,† because of the sorrow

the mother had with him. These are all the children of Jacob, twelve males and one female;—of them eight were legitimate—viz., six of Lea, and two of Rachel; and four were of the handmaids, two of each; all whose names have been set down already.

CHAPTER XXII

HOW ISAAC DIED, AND WAS BURIED IN HEBRON

FROM thence Jacob came to Hebron, a city situate among the Canaanites; and there it was that Isaac lived: and so they lived together for a little while; for as to Rebeka, Jacob did not find her alive. Isaac also died not long after the coming of his son, and was buried by his sons, with his wife, in Hebron, where they had a monument belonging to them from their forefathers. Now Isaac was a man who was beloved of God, and was vouchsafed great instances of providence by God, after Abraham his father, and lived to be exceeding old, for when he had lived virtuously one hundred and eighty-five years, he then died.

---

* Of this slaughter of the Shechemites by Simeon and Levi, see Authent. Rec., part i. pp. 309, 418, 432-439. But why Josephus has omitted the circumcision of these Shechemites, as the occasion of their death; and of Jacob's great grief, as in the Testament of Levi, § 5, I cannot tell.

† Since Benoni signifies *the son of my sorrow*, and Benjamin, *the son of days*, or *one born in the father's old age*, (Gen. xliv. 20,) I suspect Josephus's present

copies to be here imperfect; and suppose that, in correspondence to other copies, he wrote that Rachel called her son's name Benoni; but his father called him Benjamin, (Gen. xxxv. 18.) As for Benjamin, as commonly explained, *the son of the right hand*, it makes no sense at all, and seems to be a gross modern error only. The Samaritan always writes this name truly Benjamin, which probably here is of the same signification, only with the Chaldee termination *in*, instead of *im* in the Hebrew, as we pronounce Cherubin or Cherubim indifferently. Accordingly, both the Testament of Benjamin, (sect. 2, p. 401,) and *Philo de Nominum Mutatione*, (p. 1059,) write the name Benjamin; but explain it not *the son of the right hand*, but *the son of days*.

BOOK II

CONTAINING THE INTERVAL OF TWO HUNDRED AND TWENTY YEARS

FROM THE DEATH OF ISAAC TO THE EXODUS OUT OF EGYPT

CHAPTER I

HOW ESAU AND JACOB, ISAAC'S SONS, DIVIDED THEIR HABITATION; AND ESAU POSSESSED IDUMEA, AND JACOB CANAAN

1. AFTER the death of Isaac, his sons divided their habitations respectively, nor did they retain what they had before; but Esau departed from the city of Hebron, and left it to his brother, and dwelt in Seir, and ruled over Idumea. He called the country by that name from himself, for he was named Adom; which appellation he got on the following occasion:—One day returning from the toil of hunting very hungry, (it was when he was a child in age,) he lighted on his brother when he was getting ready lentil-pottage for his dinner, which was of a very red colour, on which account he the more earnestly longed for it, and desired him to give him some of it to eat; but he made advantage of his

brother's hunger, and forced him to resign up to him his birthright; and he, being pinched with famine, resigned it up to him, under an oath. Whence it came that, on account of the redness of this pottage, he was, in way of jest, by his contemporaries, called *Adom*, for the Hebrews call what is red *Adom*, and this was the name given to this country; but the Greeks gave it a more agreeable pronunciation, and named it *Idumea*.

2. He became the father of five sons, of whom Jaus, and Jalomus, and Coreus, were by one wife, whose name was Alibama; but of the rest, Aliphaz was born to him by Ada, and Raguel by Basemmath: and these were the sons of Esau. Aliphaz had five legitimate sons—Theman, Omer, Saphus, Gotham, and Kanaz; for Amalek was not legitimate, but by a concubine, whose name was Thamna. These dwelt in that part of Idumea which is called Gebalitis, and that denominated from Amalek, Amalekitis; for Idumea

was a large country, and did then preserve the name of the whole, while in its several parts it kept the names of its peculiar inhabitants.

CHAPTER II

HOW JOSEPH, THE YOUNGEST OF JACOB'S SONS, WAS ENVIED BY HIS BRETHREN, WHEN CERTAIN DREAMS HAD FORESHEWN HIS FUTURE HAPPINESS

1. IT happened that Jacob came to so great happiness as rarely any other person had arrived at. He was richer than the rest of the inhabitants of that country; and was at once envied and admired for such virtuous sons, for they were deficient in nothing, but were of great souls, both for labouring with their hands and enduring of toil, and shrewd also in understanding; and God exercised such a providence over him, and such a care of his happiness, as to bring him the greatest blessings, even out of what appeared to be the most sorrowful condition, and to make him the cause of our forefathers' departure out of Egypt, him and his posterity. The occasion was this:—When Jacob had his son Joseph born to him by Rachel, his father loved him above the rest of his sons, both because of the beauty of his body, and the virtues of his mind, for he excelled the rest in prudence. This affection of his father excited the envy and the hatred of his brethren; as did also his dreams which he saw, and related to his father and to them, which foretold his future happiness, it being usual with mankind to envy their very nearest relations such their prosperity. Now the visions which Joseph saw in his sleep were these:—

2. When they were in the middle of harvest, and Joseph was sent by his father, with his brethren, to gather the fruits of the earth, he saw a vision in a dream, but greatly exceeding the accustomary appearances that come when we are asleep; which, when he was got up, he told his brethren, that they might judge what it portended. He said, he saw the last night, that his wheat-sheaf stood still in the place where he set it, but that their sheaves ran to bow down to it, as servants bow down to their masters; but as soon as they perceived the vision foretold that he should obtain power and great wealth, and that his power should be in opposition to them, they gave no interpretation of it to Joseph, as if the dream were not by them understood: but they prayed that no part of what they suspected to be its meaning might come to pass; and they bare a still greater hatred to him on that account.

3. But God, in opposition to their envy, sent a second vision to Joseph, which was much more wonderful than the former; for it seemed to him that the sun took with him the moon and the rest of the stars, and came down to the earth, and bowed down to him. He told the vision to his father, and that, as suspecting nothing of ill-will from his brethren, when they were there also, and desired him to interpret what it should signify. Now Jacob was pleased with the dream; for, considering the prediction in his mind, and shrewdly and wisely guessing at its meaning, he rejoiced at the great things thereby signified, because it declared the future happiness of his son; and that, by the blessing of God, the time would come when he should be honoured, and thought worthy of worship by his parents and brethren, as guessing that the moon and sun

were like his mother and father; the former, as she that gave increase and nourishment to all things, and the latter, he that gave form and other powers to them; and that the stars were like his brethren, since they were eleven in number, as were the stars that receive their power from the sun and moon.

4. And thus did Jacob make a judgment of this vision, and that a shrewd one also; but these interpretations caused very great grief to Joseph's brethren; and they were affected to him hereupon as if he were a certain stranger that was to have those good things which were signified by the dreams, and not as one that was a brother, with whom it was probable they should be joint partakers; and as they had been partners in the same parentage, so should they be of the same happiness. They also resolved to kill the lad; and having fully ratified that intention of theirs, as soon as their collection of the fruits was over, they went to Shechem, which is a country good for feeding of cattle, and for pasturage; there they fed their flocks, without acquainting their father with their removal thither; whereupon he had melancholy suspicions about them, as being ignorant of his sons' condition, and receiving no messenger from the flocks that could inform him of the true state they were in; so, because he was in great fear about them, he sent Joseph to the flocks, to learn the circumstances his brethren were in, and to bring him word how they did.

CHAPTER III

HOW JOSEPH WAS THUS SOLD BY HIS BRETHREN INTO EGYPT, BY REASON OF THEIR HATRED TO HIM; AND HOW HE THERE GREW FAMOUS AND ILLUSTRIOUS, AND HAD HIS BRETHREN UNDER HIS POWER

1. Now these brethren rejoiced as soon as they saw their brother coming to them, not indeed as at the presence of a near relation, or as at the presence of one sent by their father, but as at the presence of an enemy, and one that by divine providence was delivered into their hands; and they already resolved to kill him, and not let slip the opportunity that lay before them; but when Reubel, the eldest of them, saw them thus disposed, and that they had agreed together to execute their purpose, he tried to restrain them, shewing them the heinous enterprise they were going about, and the horrid nature of it; that this action would appear wicked in the sight of God, and impious before men, even though they should kill one not related to them, but much more flagitious and detestable to appear to have slain their own brother; by which act the father must be treated unjustly in the son's slaughter, and the mother* also be in perplexity while she laments that her son is taken away from her, and this not in a natural way neither. So he entreated them to have a regard to their own consciences, and wisely to consider what mischief would betide them upon the death of so good a child and their youngest brother; that they would also fear God, who was already both a spectator and a witness of

---

* We may here observe, that in correspondence to Joseph's second dream, which implied that his mother, who was then alive, as well as his father, should come and bow down to him, Josephus represents her here as still alive after she was dead, for the decorum of the dream that foretold it; as the interpretation of the dream does also in all our copies, Gen. xxxvii. 10

the designs they had against their brother; that he would love them if they abstained from this act, and yielded to repentance and amendment; but in case they proceeded to do the fact, all sorts of punishment would overtake them from God for this murder of their brother, since they polluted his providence, which was everywhere present, and which did not overlook what was done, either in deserts or in cities; for wheresoever a man is, there ought he to suppose that God is also. He told them further, that their consciences would be their enemies, if they attempted to go through so wicked an enterprise, which they can never avoid, whether it be a good conscience, or whether it be such a one as they will have within them when once they have killed their brother. He also added this besides to what he had before said, that it was not a righteous thing to kill a brother, though he had injured them; that it is a good thing to forget the actions of such near friends, even in things wherein they might seem to have offended; but that they were going to kill Joseph, who had been guilty of nothing that was ill towards them, in whose case the infirmity of his small age should rather procure him mercy, and move them to unite together in the care of his preservation: that the cause of killing him made the act itself much worse, while they determined to take him off out of envy at his future prosperity, an equal share of which they would naturally partake while he enjoyed it, since they were to him not strangers, but the nearest relations, for they might reckon upon what God bestowed upon Joseph as their own; and that it was fit for them to believe, that the anger of God would for this cause be more severe upon them, if they slew him who was judged by God to be worthy of that prosperity which he hoped for; and, while by murdering him, they made it impossible for God to bestow it upon him.

2. Reubel said these, and many other things, and used entreaties to them, and thereby endeavoured to divert them from the murder of their brother; but when he saw that his discourse had not mollified them at all, and that they made haste to do the fact, he advised them to alleviate the wickedness they were going about, in the manner of taking Joseph off; for as he had exhorted them first, when they were going to revenge themselves, to be dissuaded from doing it, so, since the sentence for killing their brother had prevailed, he said that they would not, however, be so grossly guilty, if they would be persuaded to follow his present advice, which would include what they were so eager about, but was not so very bad, but, in the distress they were in, of a lighter nature. He begged of them, therefore, not to kill their brother with their own hands, but to cast him into the pit that was hard by, and so let him die; by which they would gain so much, that they would not defile their own hands with his blood. To this the young men readily agreed; so Reubel took the lad, and tied him to a cord, and let him down gently into the pit, for it had no water at all in it; who, when he had done this, went his way to seek for such pasturage as was fit for feeding his flocks.

3. But Judas, being one of Jacob's sons also, seeing some Arabians, of the posterity of Ismael, carrying spices and Syrian wares out of the land of Gilead to the Egyptians, after Reubel was gone, advised his brethren to draw Joseph out of the pit, and sell him to the Arabians; for if he should die among strangers a great way off, they should be freed from this barbarous action. This, therefore, was resolved on; so they drew Joseph up out of the pit, and sold him to the merchants for twenty pounds.* He was now seventeen years old; but Reubel, coming in the night-time to the pit, resolved to save Joseph, without the privity of his brethren; and when, upon his calling to him, he made no answer, he was afraid that they had destroyed him after he was gone; of which he complained to his brethren; but when they had told him what they had done, Reubel left off his mourning.

4. When Joseph's brethren had done thus to him, they considered what they should do to escape the suspicions of their father. Now they had taken away from Joseph the coat which he had on when he came to them at the time they let him down into the pit; so they thought proper to tear that coat to pieces, and to dip it into goat's blood, and then to carry it and shew it to their father, that he might believe he was destroyed by wild beasts; and when they had so done, they came to the old man, but this not till what had happened to his son had already come to his knowledge. Then they said that they had not seen Joseph, nor knew what mishap had befallen him; but that they had found his coat bloody and torn to pieces, whence they had a suspicion that he had fallen among wild beasts, and so perished, if that was the coat he had on when he came from home. Now Jacob had before some better hopes that his son was only made a captive; but now he laid aside that notion, and supposed that this coat was an evident argument that he was dead, for he well remembered that this was the coat he had on when he sent him to his brethren; so he hereafter lamented the lad as now dead, and as if he had been the father of no more than one, without taking any comfort in the rest; and so he was also affected with his misfortune before he met with Joseph's brethren, when he also conjectured that Joseph was destroyed by wild beasts. He sat down also clothed in sackcloth and in heavy affliction, insomuch that he found no ease when his sons comforted him, neither did his pains remit by length of time.

CHAPTER IV

CONCERNING THE SIGNAL CHASTITY OF JOSEPH.

1. Now Potiphar, an Egyptian, who was chief cook to king Pharaoh, bought Joseph of the merchants, who sold him to him. He had him in the greatest honour, and taught him the learning that became a free man, and gave him leave to make use of a diet better than was allotted to slaves. He intrusted also the care of his house to him. So he enjoyed these advantages, yet did not he leave that virtue which he had before, upon such a change of his condition; but he demonstrated that wisdom was able to govern the uneasy passions of life, in such as have it in reality, and do not only put it on for a show, under a present state of prosperity.

2. For when his master's wife was fallen in love with him, both on account of his beauty of body and his dexterous management of affairs; and supposed that, if she should make it known to him, she could easily persuade him to come and lie with her, and that he would look upon it

---

* The Septuagint have twenty pieces of gold; the Testament of Gad thirty; the Hebrew and Samaritan twenty of silver; and the vulgar Latin thirty. What was the true number and true sum cannot, therefore, now be known.

as a piece of happy fortune that his mistress should entreat him, as regarding that state of slavery he was in, and not his moral character, which continued after his condition was changed; so she made known her naughty inclinations, and spake to him about lying with her. However, he rejected her entreaties, not thinking it agreeable to religion to yield so far to her, as to do what would tend to the affront and injury of him that purchased him, and had vouchsafed him so great honours. He, on the contrary, exhorted her to govern that passion; and laid before her the impossibility of her obtaining her desires, which he thought might be conquered, if she had no hope of succeeding: and he said, that as to himself, he would endure anything whatever before he would be persuaded to it; for although it was fit for a slave, as he was, to do nothing contrary to his mistress, he might well be excused in a case where the contradiction was to such sort of commands only. But this opposition of Joseph, when she did not expect it, made her still more violent in her love to him; and as she was sorely beset with this naughty passion, so she resolved to compass her design by a second attempt.

3. When, therefore, there was a public festival coming on, in which it was the custom for women to come to the public solemnity, she pretended to her husband that she was sick, as contriving an opportunity for solitude and leisure, that she might entreat Joseph again; which opportunity being obtained, she used more kind words to him than before, and said that it had been good for him to have yielded to her first solicitation, and to have given her no repulse, both because of the reverence he ought to bear to her dignity who solicited him, and because of the vehemence of her passion by which she was forced, though she were his mistress, to condescend beneath her dignity; but that he may now, by taking more prudent advice, wipe off the imputation of his former folly: for, whether it were that he expected the repetition of her solicitations she had now made, and that with greater earnestness than before, for that she had pretended sickness on this very account, and had preferred his conversation before the festival and its solemnity; or whether he opposed her former discourses, as not believing she could be in earnest, she now gave him sufficient security, by thus repeating her application, that she meant not in the least by fraud to impose upon him; and assured him that, if he complied with her affections, he might expect the enjoyment of the advantages she already had; and if he were submissive to her, he should have still greater advantages; but that he must look for revenge and hatred from her, in case he rejected her desires, and preferred the reputation of chastity before his mistress; for that he would gain nothing by such procedure, because she would then become his accuser, and would falsely pretend to her husband that he had attempted her chastity; and that Potiphar would hearken to her words rather than to his, let his be ever so agreeable to the truth.

4. When the woman had said thus, and even with tears in her eyes, neither did pity dissuade Joseph from his chastity, nor did fear compel him to a compliance with her; but he opposed her solicitations, and did not yield to her threatenings, and was afraid to do an ill thing, and chose to undergo the sharpest punishment rather than to enjoy his present advantages by doing what his own conscience knew would justly deserve that he should die for it. He also put her in mind that she was a married woman, and that she ought to cohabit with her husband only; and

desired her to suffer these considerations to have more weight with her than the short pleasure of lustful dalliance, which would bring her to repentance afterwards, would cause trouble to her, and yet would not amend what had been done amiss. He also suggested to her the fear she would be in lest they should be caught, and that the advantage of concealment was uncertain, and that only while the wickedness was not known, [would there be any quiet for them;] but that she might have the enjoyment of her husband's company without any danger: and he told her that in the company of her husband she might have great boldness from a good conscience, both before God and before men: nay, that she would act better like his mistress, and make use of her authority over him better while she persisted in her chastity, than when they were both ashamed for what wickedness they had been guilty of; and that it is much better to depend on a good life, well acted, and known to have been so, than upon the hopes of the concealment of evil practices.

5. Joseph, by saying this, and more, tried to restrain the violent passion of the woman, and to reduce her affections within the rules of reason; but she grew more ungovernable and earnest in the matter; and since she despaired of persuading him, she laid her hands upon him, and had a mind to force him. But as soon as Joseph had got away from her anger, leaving also his garment with her, for he left that to her, and leaped out of her chamber, she was greatly afraid lest he should discover her lewdness to her husband, and greatly troubled at the affront he had offered her; so she resolved to be beforehand with him, and to accuse Joseph falsely to Potiphar, and by that means to revenge herself on him for his pride and contempt of her; and she thought it a wise thing in itself, and also becoming a woman, thus to prevent his accusation. Accordingly she sat sorrowful and in confusion, framing herself so hypocritically and angrily, that the sorrow, which was really for her being disappointed of her lust, might appear to be for the attempt upon her chastity; so that when her husband came home, and was disturbed at the sight of her, and inquired what was the cause of the disorder she was in, she began to accuse Joseph: and, "O husband," said she, "mayest thou not live a day longer if thou dost not punish the wicked slave who has desired to defile thy bed; who has neither minded who he was when he came to our house, so as to behave himself with modesty; nor has he been mindful of what favours he had received from thy bounty, (as he must be an ungrateful man, indeed, unless he, in every respect, carry himself in a manner agreeable to us:) this man, I say, laid a private design to abuse thy wife, and this at a time of a festival, observing when thou wouldst be absent. So that it now is clear that his modesty, as it appeared to be formerly, was only because of the restraint he was in out of fear of thee, but that he was not really of a good disposition. This has been occasioned by his being advanced to honour beyond what he deserved and what he hoped for; insomuch that he concluded, that he who was deemed fit to be trusted with thy estate and the government of thy family, and was preferred above thy eldest servants, might be allowed to touch thy wife also." Thus, when she had ended her discourse, she shewed him his garment, as if he had then left it when he attempted to force her. But Potiphar not being able to disbelieve what his wife's tears shewed, and what his wife said, and what he saw himself, and being seduced by his love to his wife, did not set himself about the

examination of the truth; but, taking it for granted that his wife was a modest woman, and condemning Joseph as a wicked man, he threw him into the malefactors' prison, and had a still higher opinion of his wife, and bare her witness that she was a woman of a becoming modesty and chastity.

CHAPTER V

WHAT THINGS BEFELL JOSEPH IN PRISON

1. Now Joseph, commending all his affairs to God, did not betake himself to make his defence, nor to give an account of the exact circumstances of the fact, but silently underwent the bonds and the distress he was in, firmly believing that God, who knew the cause of his affliction and the truth of the fact, would be more powerful than those that inflicted the punishments upon him:—a proof of whose providence he quickly received; for the keeper of the prison taking notice of his care and fidelity in the affairs he had set him about, and the dignity of his countenance, relaxed his bonds, and thereby made his heavy calamity lighter and more supportable to him: he also permitted him to make use of a diet better than that of the rest of the prisoners. Now, as his fellow-prisoners, when their hard labours were over, fell to discoursing one among another, as is usual in such as are equal sufferers, and to inquire one of another what were the occasions of their being condemned to a prison: among them the king's cupbearer, and one that had been respected by him, was put in bonds, on the king's anger at him. This man was under the same bonds with Joseph, and grew more familiar with him; and upon his observing that Joseph had a better understanding than the rest had, he told him of a dream he had, and desired he would interpret its meaning, complaining that, besides the afflictions he underwent from the king, God did also add to him trouble from his dreams.

2. He therefore said that in his sleep he saw three clusters of grapes hanging upon three branches of a vine, large already, and ripe for gathering; and that he squeezed them into a cup which the king held in his hand; and when he had strained the wine, he gave it to the king to drink, and that he received it from him with a pleasant countenance. This, he said, was what he saw; and he desired Joseph, that if he had any portion of understanding in such matters, he would tell him what this vision foretold:—who bid him be of good cheer, and expect to be loosed from his bonds in three days' time, because the king desired his service, and was about to restore him to it again; for he let him know that God bestows the fruit of the vine upon men for good; which wine is poured out to him, and is the pledge of fidelity and mutual confidence among men, and puts an end to their quarrels, takes away passion and grief out of the minds of them that use it, and makes them cheerful. "Thou sayest that thou didst squeeze this wine from three clusters of grapes with thine hands, and that the king received it: know, therefore, that this vision is for thy good, and foretells a release from thy present distress within the same number of days as the branches had whence thou gatheredst thy grapes in thy sleep. However, remember what prosperity I have foretold thee when thou hast found it true by experience; and when thou art in authority, do not overlook us in this prison, wherein thou wilt leave us when thou art gone to the place we have fore-told; for we are not in prison for any crime, but for the sake of our virtue and sobriety are we condemned to suffer the penalty of malefactors, and because we are not willing to injure him that has thus distressed us, though it were for our own pleasure." The cupbearer, therefore, as was natural to do, rejoiced to hear such an interpretation of his dream, and waited the completion of what had been thus shewn him before-hand.

3. But another servant there was of the king, who had been chief baker, and was now bound in prison with the cupbearer; he also was in good hope, upon Joseph's interpretation of the other's vision, for he had seen a dream also; so he desired that Joseph would tell him what the visions he had seen the night before might mean. They were these that follow:—"Methought," says he, "I carried three baskets upon my head; two were full of loaves, and the third full of sweetmeats and other eatables, such as are prepared for kings; but that the fowls came flying, and ate them all up, and had no regard to my attempt to drive them away;"—and he expected a prediction like to that of the cupbearer. But Joseph, considering and reasoning about the dream, said to him that he would willingly be an interpreter of good events to him, and not of such as his dream denounced to him; but he told him that he had only three days in all to live, for that the [three] baskets signify that on the third day he should be crucified, and devoured by fowls, while he was not able to help himself. Now both these dreams had the same several events that Joseph foretold they should have, and this to both the parties; for on the third day before-mentioned, when the king solemnised his birthday, he crucified the chief baker, but set the butler free from his bonds, and restored him to his former ministration.

4. But God freed Joseph from his confinement, after he had endured his bonds two years, and had received no assistance from the cupbearer, who did not remember what he had said to him formerly; and God contrived this method of deliverance for him. Pharaoh the king had seen in his sleep the same evening two visions; and after them had the interpretations of them both given him. He had forgotten the latter, but retained the dreams themselves. Being therefore troubled at what he had seen, for it seemed to him to be all of a melancholy nature, the next day he called together the wisest men among the Egyptians, desiring to learn from them the interpretation of his dreams. But when they hesitated about them, the king was so much the more disturbed. And now it was that the memory of Joseph, and his skill in dreams, came into the mind of the king's cupbearer, when he saw the confusion that Pharaoh was in; so he came and mentioned Joseph to him, as also the vision he had seen in prison, and how the event proved as he had said; as also that the chief baker was crucified on the very same day; and that this also happened to him according to the interpretation of Joseph. That Joseph himself was laid in bonds by Potiphar, who was his head cook, as a slave; but, he said, he was one of the noblest of the stock of the Hebrews; and said further, his father lived in great splendour. "If, therefore, thou wilt send for him, and not despise him on the score of his misfortunes, thou wilt learn what thy dreams signify." So the king commanded that they should bring Joseph into his presence; and those who received the command came and brought him with them, having taken care of his habit, that it might be decent, as the king had enjoined them to do.

5. But the king took him by the hand; and, "O young man," says he, "for my servant bears witness that thou art at present the best and most skilful person I can consult with; vouchsafe me the same favours which thou bestowedst on this servant of mine, and tell me what events they are which the visions of my dreams foreshew; and I desire thee to suppress nothing out of fear, nor to flatter me with lying words, or with what may please me, although the truth should be of a melancholy nature. For it seemed to me that, as I walked by the river, I saw kine fat and very large, seven in number, going from the river to the marshes; and other kine of the same number like them, met them out of the marshes, exceeding lean and ill-favoured, which ate up the fat and the large kine, and yet were no better than before, and not less miserably pinched with famine. After I had seen this vision, I awaked out of my sleep; and, being in disorder, and considering with myself what this appearance should be, I fell asleep again, and saw another dream, much more wonderful than the foregoing, which still did more affright and disturb me:—I saw seven ears of corn growing out of one root, having their heads borne down by the weight of the grains, and bending down with the fruit, which was now ripe and fit for reaping; and near these I saw seven other ears of corn, meagre and weak for want of rain, which fell to eating and consuming those that were fit for reaping, and put me into great astonishment."

6. To which Joseph replied:—"This dream," said he, "O king, although seen under two forms, signifies one and the same event of things; for when thou sawest the fat kine, which is an animal made for the plough and for labour, devoured by the worser kine, and the ears of corn eaten up by the smaller ears, they foretell a famine, and want of the fruits of the earth for the same number of years, and equal with those when Egypt was in a happy state; and this so far that the plenty of these years will be spent in the same number of years of scarcity, and that scarcity of necessary provisions will be very difficult to be corrected; as a sign whereof, the ill-favoured kine, when they had devoured the better sort, could not be satisfied. But still God foreshews what is to come upon men, not to grieve them, but that, when they know it beforehand, they may by prudence make the actual experience of what is foretold the more tolerable. If thou, therefore, carefully dispose of the plentiful crops which will come in the former years, thou wilt procure that the future calamity will not be felt by the Egyptians."

7. Hereupon the king wondered at the discretion and wisdom of Joseph; and asked him by what means he might so dispense the foregoing plentiful crops, in the happy years, as to make the miserable crops more tolerable. Joseph then added this his advice: To spare the good crops, and not permit the Egyptians to spend them luxuriously; but to reserve what they would have spent in luxury beyond their necessity, against the time of want. He also exhorted him to take the corn of the husbandmen, and give them only so much as will be sufficient for their food. Accordingly Pharaoh being surprised at Joseph, not only for his interpretation of the dream, but for the counsel he had given him, intrusted him with dispensing the corn; with power to do what he thought would be for the benefit of the people of Egypt, and for the benefit of the king, as believing that he who first discovered this method of acting would prove the best overseer of it. But Joseph having this power given him by the king, with leave to make use of his seal, and to wear purple, drove in his cha-

riot through all the land of Egypt, and took the corn of the husbandmen,* allotting as much to every one as would be sufficient for seed and for food, but without discovering to any one the reason why he did so.

CHAPTER VI

HOW JOSEPH, WHEN HE WAS BECOME FAMOUS IN EGYPT, HAD HIS BRETHREN IN SUBJECTION

1. JOSEPH was now grown up to thirty years of age, and enjoyed great honours from the king, who called him Psothom Phanech, out of regard to his prodigious degree of wisdom; for that name denotes *the revealer of secrets*. He also married a wife of very high quality; for he married the daughter of Petephres,† one of the priests of Heliopolis: she was a virgin, and her name was Asenath. By her he had children before the scarcity came on; Manasseh, the elder, which signifies *forgetful*, because his present happiness made him forget his former misfortunes; and Ephraim, the younger, which signifies *restored*, because he was restored to the freedom of his forefathers. Now after Egypt had happily passed over seven years, according to Joseph's interpretation of the dreams, the famine came upon them in the eighth year; and because this misfortune fell upon them when they had no sense of it beforehand,‡ they were all sorely afflicted by it, and came running to the king's gates; and he called upon Joseph, who sold the corn to them, being become confessedly a saviour to the whole multitude of the Egyptians. Nor did he open this market of corn for the people of that country only, but strangers had liberty to buy also; Joseph being willing that all men, who are naturally akin to one another, should have assistance from those that lived in happiness.

2. Now Jacob also, when he understood that foreigners might come, sent all his sons into Egypt to buy corn; for the land of Canaan was grievously afflicted with the famine, and this great misery touched the whole continent. He only retained Benjamin, who was born to him by Rachel, and was of the same mother with Joseph. These sons of Jacob then came into Egypt, and applied themselves to Joseph, wanting to buy corn; for nothing of this kind was done without his approbation, since even then only was the honour that was paid the king himself advantageous to the persons that paid it, when they took care to honour Joseph also. Now, when he well knew his brethren, they thought nothing of him; for he was but a youth when he left them, and was now come to an age so much greater, that the lineaments of his face were changed, and he was not known by them: besides this, the greatness of the dignity wherein he appeared, suffered them not so much as to suspect it was he. He now made trial what sentiments they

---

* That is, bought it for Pharaoh at a very low price.

† This Petephres, who was now a priest of On, is the same name with him who is before called head cook or captain of the guard, and to whom Joseph was sold. See Gen. xxxvii. 36, xxxix. 1, with xli. 50. They are also affirmed to be one and the same person in the Testament of Joseph, (sect. 18,) for he is there said to have married the daughter of his master and mistress. Nor is this a notion peculiar to that testament, but, as Dr Bernard confesses, (note on Antiq. b. ii. chap. iv. sect. 1,) common to Josephus, to the Septuagint interpreters, and to other learned Jews of old time.

‡ This entire ignorance of the Egyptians of these years of famine before they came, seems to me almost incredible.

had about affairs of the greatest consequence; for he refused to sell them corn, and said they were come as spies of the king's affairs; and that they came from several countries, and joined themselves together, and pretended that they were of kin, it not being possible that a private man should breed up so many sons, and those of so great beauty of countenance as they were, such an education of so many children being not easily obtained by kings themselves. Now, this he did in order to discover what concerned his father, and what happened to him after his own departure from him, and as desiring to know what was become of Benjamin his brother; for he was afraid that they had ventured on the like wicked enterprise against him that they had done to himself, and had taken him off also.

3. Now, these brethren of his were under distraction and terror, and thought that very great danger hung over them; yet not at all reflecting upon their brother Joseph, and standing firm under the accusations laid against them, they made their defence by Reubel, the eldest of them, who now became their spokesman: "We come not hither," said he, "with any unjust design, nor in order to bring any harm to the king's affairs; we only want to be preserved, as supposing your humanity might be a refuge for us from the miseries which our country labours under, we having heard that you proposed to sell corn not only to your own countrymen, but to strangers also, and that you determined to allow that corn, in order to preserve all that want it; but that we are brethren, and of the same common blood, the peculiar lineaments of our faces, and those not so much different from one another, plainly shew. Our father's name is Jacob, a Hebrew man, who had twelve of us for his sons by four wives; which twelve of us, while we were all alive, were a happy family; but when one of our brethren, whose name was Joseph, died, our affairs changed for the worse; for our father could not forbear to make a long lamentation for him; and we are in affliction, both by the calamity of the death of our brother and the miserable state of our aged father. We are now, therefore, come to buy corn, having intrusted the care of our father, and the provision for our family to Benjamin, our youngest brother; and if thou sendest to our house, thou mayest learn whether we are guilty of the least falsehoods in what we say."

4. And thus did Reubel endeavour to persuade Joseph to have a better opinion of them. But when he had learned from them that Jacob was alive, and that his brother was not destroyed by them, he for the present put them in prison, as intending to examine more into their affairs when he should be at leisure. But on the third day he brought them out, and said to them, "Since you constantly affirm that you are not come to do any harm to the king's affairs; that you are brethren, and the sons of the father whom you named, you will satisfy me of the truth of what you say, if you leave one of your company with me, who shall suffer no injury here; and if, when ye have carried corn to your father, you will come to me again, and bring your brother, whom you say you left there, along with you, for this shall be by me esteemed an assurance of the truth of what you have told me." Hereupon they were in greater grief than before; they wept, and perpetually deplored one among another the calamity of Joseph; and said, "They were fallen into this misery as a punishment inflicted by God for what evil contrivances they had against him." And Reubel was large in his reproaches of them for their too late repentance, whence no profit arose to Joseph, and earnestly exhorted them to bear

with patience whatever they suffered, since it was done by God in way of punishment, on his account. Thus they spake to one another, not imagining that Joseph understood their language. A general sadness also seized on them at Reubel's words, and a repentance for what they had done; and they condemned the wickedness they had perpetrated, for which they judged they were justly punished by God. Now, when Joseph saw that they were in this distress, he was so affected at it that he fell into tears, and, not being willing that they should take notice of him, he retired; and after a while came to them again, and taking Symeon,* in order to his being a pledge for his brethren's return, he bid them take the corn they had bought, and go their way. He also commanded his steward privily to put the money which they had brought with them for the purchase of corn into their sacks, and to dismiss them therewith; who did what he was commanded to do.

5. Now, when Jacob's sons were come into the land of Canaan, they told their father what had happened to them in Egypt, and that they were taken to have come thither as spies upon the king; and how they said they were brethren, and had left their eleventh brother with their father, but were not believed; and how they had left Symeon with the governor, until Benjamin should go thither, and be a testimonial of the truth of what they had said: and they begged of their father to fear nothing, but to send the lad along with them. But Jacob was not pleased with anything his sons had done; and he took the detention of Symeon heinously, and thence thought it a foolish thing to give up Benjamin also. Neither did he yield to Reubel's persuasion, though he begged it of him; and gave leave that the grandfather might, in way of requital, kill his own sons, in case any harm came to Benjamin in the journey. So they were distressed, and knew not what to do: nay, there was another accident that still disturbed them more,—the money that was found hidden in their sacks of corn. Yet, when the corn they had brought failed them, and when the famine still afflicted them, and necessity forced them, Jacob did† [not] still resolve to send Benjamin with his brethren, although there was no returning into Egypt unless they came with what they had promised. Now, the misery growing every day worse, and his sons begging it of him, he had no other course to take in his present circumstances. And Judas, who was of a bold temper on other occasions, spake his mind very freely to him: "That it did not become him to be afraid on account of his son, nor to suspect the worst, as he did; for nothing could be done to his son but by the appointment of God, which must also for certain come to pass, though he were at home with him; that he ought not to condemn them to such manifest destruction; nor deprive them of that plenty of food they might have from Pharaoh, by his unreasonable fear about his son Benjamin, but ought to take care of the preservation of Symeon, lest, by attempting to hinder Benjamin's journey, Symeon should perish. He exhorted him to trust God for him; and said he would either bring his son back to him safe, or together with his, lose his own life." So that Jacob was at length per-

---

* The reason why Symeon might be selected out of the rest for Joseph's prisoner, is plain in the Testament of Symeon—viz., that he was one of the bitterest of all Joseph's brethren against him, sect. 2; which appears also in part by the Testament of Zabulon, sect. 3.

† The coherence seems to shew that the negative particle is here wanting, which I have supplied in brackets; and I wonder none have hitherto suspected that it ought to be supplied.

suaded, and delivered Benjamin to them, with the price of the corn doubled; he also sent presents to Joseph of the fruits of the land of Canaan; balsam and rosin, as also turpentine and honey.[*] Now, their father shed many tears at the departure of his sons, as well as themselves. His concern was, that he might receive them back again safe after their journey; and their concern was, that they might find their father well, and no way afflicted with grief for them. And this lamentation lasted a whole day; so that the old man was at last tired with grief, and stayed behind; but they went on their way for Egypt, endeavouring to mitigate their grief for their present misfortunes, with the hopes of better success hereafter.

6. As soon as they came into Egypt, they were brought down to Joseph: but here no small fear disturbed them, lest they should be accused about the price of the corn, as if they had cheated Joseph. They then made a long apology to Joseph's steward; and told him, that when they came home they found the money in their sacks, and that they had now brought it along with them. He said he did not know what they meant: so they were delivered from that fear. And when he had loosed Symeon, and put him into a handsome habit, he suffered him to be with his brethren; at which time Joseph came from his attendance on the king. So they offered him their presents; and upon his putting the question to them about their father, they answered, that they found him well. He also, upon his discovery that Benjamin was alive, asked whether this was their younger brother? for he had seen him. Whereupon they said he was: he replied, that the God over all was his protector. But when his affection to him made him shed tears, he retired, desiring he might not be seen in that plight by his brethren. Then Joseph took them to supper, and they were set down in the same order as they used to sit at their father's table. And although Joseph treated them all kindly, yet did he send a mess to Benjamin that was double to what the rest of the guests had for their shares.

7. Now, when after supper they had composed themselves to sleep, Joseph commanded his steward both to give them their measures of corn, and to hide its price again in their sacks; and that withal they should put into Benjamin's sack the golden cup, out of which he loved himself to drink:—which things he did, in order to make trial of his brethren, whether they would stand by Benjamin when he should be accused of having stolen the cup, and should appear to be in danger; or whether they would leave him, and, depending on their own innocency, go to their father without him.—When the servant had done as he was bidden, the sons of Jacob, knowing nothing of all this, went their way, and took Symeon along with them, and had a double cause of joy, both because they had received him again, and because they took back Benjamin to their father, as they had promised. But presently a troop of horsemen encompassed them, and brought with them Joseph's servant, who had put the cup into Benjamin's sack. Upon which unexpected attack of the horsemen they were much disturbed, and asked what the reason was that they came thus upon men, who a little before had been by their lord thought worthy of an honourable and hospitable reception! They replied, by calling them wicked wretches, who had forgot that very hospitable and kind treatment which Joseph had given

them, and did not scruple to be injurious to him, and to carry off that cup out of which he had, in so friendly a manner, drank to them, and not regarding their friendship with Joseph, no more than the danger they should be in if they were taken, in comparison of the unjust gain. Hereupon he threatened that they should be punished; for though they had escaped the knowledge of him who was but a servant, yet had they not escaped the knowledge of God, nor had gone off with what they had stolen; and, after all, asked why we come upon them? as if they knew nothing of the matter: and he told them that they should immediately know it by their punishment. This, and more of the same nature, did the servant say, in way of reproach to them: but they being wholly ignorant of anything here that concerned them, laughed at what he said; and wondered at the abusive language which the servant gave them, when he was so hardy as to accuse those who did not before so much as retain the price of their corn, which was found in their sacks, but brought it again, though nobody else knew of any such thing,—so far were they from offering any injury to Joseph voluntarily. But still, supposing that a search would be a more sure justification of themselves than their own denial of the fact, they bid him search them, and that if any of them had been guilty of the theft, to punish them all; for being no way conscious to themselves of any crime, they spake with assurance, and, as they thought, without any danger to themselves also. The servants desired there might be a search made; but they said the punishment should extend to him alone who should be found guilty of the theft. So they made the search; and, having searched all the rest, they came last of all to Benjamin, as knowing it was Benjamin's sack in which they had hidden the cup, they having indeed searched the rest only for a show of accuracy: so the rest were out of fear for themselves, and were now only concerned about Benjamin, but still were well assured that he would also be found innocent; and they reproached those that came after them for their hindering them, while they might, in the meanwhile, have gotten a good way on their journey. But as soon as they had searched Benjamin's sack, they found the cup, and took it from him; and all was changed into mourning and lamentation. They rent their garments, and wept for the punishment which their brother was to undergo for his theft, and for the delusion they had put on their father, when they promised they would bring Benjamin safe to him. What added to their misery was, that this melancholy accident came unfortunately at a time when they thought they had been gotten off clear: but they confessed that this misfortune of their brother, as well as the grief of their father for him, was owing to themselves, since it was they that forced their father to send him with them, when he was averse to it.

8. The horsemen therefore took Benjamin and brought him to Joseph, his brethren also following him; who, when he saw him in custody, and them in the habit of mourners, said, "How came you, vile wretches as you are, to have such a strange notion of my kindness to you, and of God's providence, as impudently to do thus to your benefactor, who in such an hospitable manner had entertained you?"—Whereupon they gave up themselves to be punished, in order to save Benjamin; and called to mind what a wicked enterprise they had been guilty of against Joseph. They also pronounced him more happy than themselves, if he were dead,

---

[*] Of the precious balsam of Judea, and the turpentine, see the note on Antiq. b. viii. ch. vi. sect. 6.

in being freed from the miseries of this life; and if he were alive, that he enjoyed the pleasure of seeing God's vengeance upon them. They said further, that they were the plague of their father, since they should now add to his former affliction for Joseph, this other affliction for Benjamin. Reubel also was large in cutting them upon this occasion. But Joseph dismissed them; for he said they had been guilty of no offence, and that he would content himself with the lad's punishment; for he said it was not a fit thing to let him go free for the sake of those who had not offended; nor was it a fit thing to punish them together with him who had been guilty of stealing. And when he had promised to give them leave to go away in safety, the rest of them were under great consternation, and were able to say nothing on this sad occasion. But Judas, who had persuaded their father to send the lad from him, being otherwise also a very bold and active man, determined to hazard himself for the preservation of his brother. "It is true," * said he, "O governor, that we have been very wicked with regard to thee, and on that account deserve punishment; even all of us may justly be punished, although the theft were not committed by all, but only by one of us, and he the youngest also: but yet there remains some hope for us, who otherwise must be under despair on his account, and this from thy goodness, which promises us a deliverance out of our present danger. And now I beg thou wilt not look at us, or at that great crime we have been guilty of, but at thy own excellent nature, and take advice of thine own virtue, instead of that wrath thou hast against us; which passion those that otherwise are of lower character indulge, as they do their strength, and that not only on great, but also on very trifling occasions. Overcome, Sir, that passion, and be not subdued by it, nor suffer it to slay those that do not otherwise presume upon their own safety, but are desirous to accept of it from thee; for this is not the first time that thou wilt bestow it on us, but before, when we came to buy corn, thou affordedst us great plenty of food, and gavest us leave to carry so much home to our family as has preserved them from perishing by famine. Nor is there any difference between not overlooking men that were perishing for want of necessaries, and not punishing those that seem to be offenders, and have been so unfortunate as to lose the advantage of that glorious benefaction which they received from thee. This will be an instance of equal favour, though bestowed after a different manner; for thou wilt save those this way whom thou didst feed the other; and thou wilt hereby preserve alive, by thy own bounty, those souls which thou didst not suffer to be distressed by famine, it being indeed at once a wonderful and a great thing to sustain our lives by corn, and to bestow on us that pardon, whereby, now we are distressed, we may continue those lives. And I am ready to suppose, that God is willing to afford thee this opportunity of shewing thy virtuous disposition, by bringing us into this calamity, that it may appear thou canst forgive the injuries that are done to thyself, and mayest be esteemed kind to others, besides those who, on other accounts,

stand in need of thy assistance; since it is indeed a right thing to do well to those who are in distress for want of food, but still a more glorious thing to save those who deserve to be punished, when it is on account of heinous offences against thyself; for if it be a thing deserving commendation to forgive such as have been guilty of small offences, that tend to a person's loss, and this be praiseworthy in him that overlooks such offences, to restrain a man's passion as to crimes which are capital to the guilty, is to be like the most excellent nature of God himself:—and truly, as for myself, had it not been that we had a father, who had discovered, on occasion of the death of Joseph, how miserably he is always afflicted at the loss of his sons, I had not made any words on account of the saving of our own lives; I mean, any further than as that would be an excellent character for thyself, to preserve even those that would have nobody to lament them when they were dead, but we would have yielded ourselves up to suffer whatsoever thou pleasedst; but now (for we do not plead for mercy to ourselves, though indeed, if we die, it will be while we are young, and before we have had the enjoyment of life) have regard to our father, and take pity of his old age, on whose account it is that we make these supplications to thee. We beg thou wilt give us those lives which this wickedness of ours has rendered obnoxious to thy punishment; and this for his sake who is not himself wicked, nor does his being our father make us wicked. He is a good man, and not worthy to have such trials of his patience; and now we are absent, he is afflicted with care for us: but if he hear of our deaths, and what was the cause of it, he will on that account die an immature death; and the reproachful manner of our ruin will hasten his end, and will directly kill him, nay, will bring him to a miserable death, while he will make haste to rid himself out of the world, and bring himself to a state of insensibility, before the sad story of our end come abroad into the rest of the world. Consider these things in this manner, although our wickedness does now provoke thee with a just desire of punishing that wickedness, and forgive it for our father's sake; and let thy commiseration of him weigh more with thee than our wickedness. Have regard to the old age of our father, who, if we perish, will be very lonely while he lives, and will soon die himself also. Grant this boon to the name of Fathers, for thereby thou wilt honour him that begat thee, and will grant it to thyself also, who enjoyest already that denomination; thou wilt then, by that denomination, be preserved of God, the Father of all,—by shewing a pious regard to which, in the case of our father, thou wilt appear to honour him who is styled by the same name; I mean, if thou wilt have this pity on our father, upon this consideration, how miserable he will be if he be deprived of his sons! It is thy part therefore to bestow on us what God has given us, when it is in thy power to take it away, and so to resemble him entirely in charity; for it is good to use that power, which can either give or take away, on the merciful side; and when it is in thy power to destroy, to forget that thou ever hadst that power, and to look on thyself as only allowed power for preservation; and that the more any one extends this power, the greater reputation does he gain to himself. Now, by forgiving our brother what he has unhappily committed, thou wilt preserve us all; for we cannot think of living if he be put to death, since we dare not shew ourselves alive to our father without our brother,

* This oration seems to me too large, and too unusual a digression, to have been composed by Judas on this occasion. It seems to me a speech or declamation composed formerly, in the person of Judas, and in the way of oratory, that lay by him, and which he thought fit to insert on this occasion. See two more such speeches or declamations, Antiq b. vi. ch. xiv. sect. 4.

but here must we partake of one and the same catastrophe of his life; and so far we beg of thee, O governor, that if thou condemnest our brother to die, thou wilt punish us together with him, as partners of his crime,—for we shall not think it reasonable to be reserved to kill ourselves for grief of our brother's death, but so to die rather as equally guilty with him of this crime! I will only leave with thee this one consideration, and then will say no more—viz., that our brother committed his fault when he was young, and not yet of confirmed wisdom in his conduct; and that men naturally forgive such young persons. I end here, without adding what more I have to say, that in case thou condemnest us, that omission may be supposed to have hurt us, and permitted thee to take the severer side; but in case thou settest us free, that this may be ascribed to thy own goodness, of which thou art inwardly conscious, that thou freest us from condemnation: and that not by barely preserving us, but by granting us such a favour as will make us appear more righteous than we really are, and by representing to thyself more motives for our deliverance than we are able to produce ourselves. If, therefore, thou resolvest to slay him, I desire thou wilt slay me in his stead, and send him back to his father; or if thou pleasest to retain him with thee as a slave, I am fitter to labour for thy advantage in that capacity, and, as thou seest, am better prepared for either of those sufferings." * So Judas, being very willing to undergo anything whatever for the deliverance of his brother, cast himself down at Joseph's feet, and earnestly laboured to assuage and pacify his anger. All his brethren also fell down before him, weeping and delivering themselves up to destruction for the preservation of the life of Benjamin.

10. But Joseph, as overcome now with his affections, and no longer able to personate an angry man, commanded all that were present to depart, that he might make himself known to his brethren when they were alone; and when the rest were gone out he made himself known to his brethren, and said, " I commend you for your virtue, and your kindness to our brother: I find you better men than I could have expected from what you contrived about me. Indeed, I did all this to try your love to your brother; so I believe you were not wicked by nature in what you did in my case, but that all has happened according to God's will, who has hereby procured our enjoyment of what good things we have; and, if he continue in a favourable disposition, of what we hope for hereafter. Since, therefore, I know that our father is safe and well, beyond expectation, and I see you so well disposed to your brother, I will no longer remember what guilt you seem to have had about me, but will leave off to hate you for that your wickedness; and do rather return you my thanks, that you have concurred with the intentions of God to bring things to their present state. I would have you also rather to forget the same, since that imprudence of yours is come to such a happy conclusion, than to be uneasy and blush at those your offences. Do not, therefore, let your evil intentions, when you condemned me, and that bitter remorse which might follow, be a grief to you now, because those intentions were frustrated. Go, therefore, your way, rejoicing in what has happened by the Divine Providence, and inform your father of it, lest he

should be spent with cares for you, and deprive me of the most agreeable part of my felicity; I mean, lest he should die before he comes into my sight, and enjoy the good things that we now have. Bring, therefore, with you our father, and your wives and children, and all your kindred, and remove your habitations hither; for it is not proper that the persons dearest to me should live remote from me, now my affairs are so prosperous, especially when they must endure five more years of famine." When Joseph had said this, he embraced his brethren, who were in tears and sorrow; but the generous kindness of their brother seemed to leave among them no room for fear, lest they should be punished on account of what they had consulted and acted against him; and they were then feasting. Now the king, as soon as he heard that Joseph's brethren were come to him, was exceeding glad of it, as if it had been a part of his own good fortune; and gave them waggons full of corn, and gold and silver, to be conveyed to his father. Now when they had received more of their brother, part to be carried to their father, and part as free gifts to every one of themselves, Benjamin having still more than the rest, they departed.

CHAPTER VII

THE REMOVAL OF JOSEPH'S FATHER, WITH ALL HIS FAMILY TO HIM, ON ACCOUNT OF THE FAMINE

1. As soon as Jacob came to know, by his sons returning home, in what state Joseph was, that he had not only escaped death, for which yet he lived all along in mourning, but that he lived in splendour and happiness, and ruled over Egypt, jointly with the king, and had intrusted to his care almost all his affairs, he did not think any thing he was told to be incredible, considering the greatness of the works of God, and his kindness to him, although that kindness had, for some late times, been intermitted; so he immediately and zealously set out upon his journey to him.

2. When he came to the Well of the Oath, (Beersheba,) he offered sacrifice to God; and being afraid that the happiness there was in Egypt might tempt his posterity to fall in love with it, and settle in it, and no more think of removing into the land of Canaan, and possessing it, as God had promised them; as also being afraid, lest, if this descent into Egypt were made without the will of God, his family might be destroyed there; out of fear, withal, lest he should depart this life before he came to the sight of Joseph, he fell asleep, revolving these doubts in his mind.

3. But God stood by him, and called to him twice by his name; and when he asked who he was, God said, " No, sure; it is not just that thou, Jacob, shouldst be unacquainted with that God who has been ever a protector and a helper to thy forefathers, and after them to thyself: for when thy father would have deprived thee of the dominion, I gave it thee; and by my kindness it was that, when thou wast sent into Mesopotamia all alone, thou obtainedst good wives, and returnedst with many children, and much wealth. Thy whole family also has been preserved by my providence; and it was I who conducted Joseph, thy son, whom thou gavest up for lost, to the enjoyment of great prosperity. I also made him lord of Egypt, so that he differs but little from a king. Accordingly, I come now as a guide to thee in this journey; and fore-

---

* In all this speech of Judas we may observe, that Josephus still supposed that death was the punishment of theft in Egypt, in the days of Joseph, though it never was so among the Jews, by the law of Moses.

tell to thee, that thou shalt die in the arms of Joseph; and I inform thee that thy posterity shall be many ages in authority and glory, and that I will settle them in the land which I have promised them."

4. Jacob, encouraged by this dream, went on more cheerfully for Egypt with his sons, and all belonging to them. Now they were in all seventy. I once, indeed, thought it best not to set down the names of this family, especially because of their difficult pronunciation, [by the Greeks;] but, upon the whole, I think it necessary to mention those names, that I may disprove such as believe that we came not originally from Mesopotamia, but are Egyptians. Now Jacob had twelve sons; of these Joseph was come thither before. We still, therefore, set down the names of Jacob's children and grandchildren. Reuben had four sons—Anoch, Phallu, Assaron, Charmi; Simeon had six—Jamuel, Jamin, Avod, Jachin, Soar, Saul; Levi had three sons—Gersom, Caath, Merari; Judas had three sons—Sala, Phares, Zerah; and by Phares two grandchildren—Esrom and Amar; Issachar had four sons—Thola, Phua, Jasob, Samaron; Zabulon had with him three sons—Sarad, Helon, Jalel. So far is the posterity of Lea, with whom went her daughter Dinah. These are thirty-three. Rachel had two sons, the one of whom, Joseph, had two sons also, Manasses and Ephraim. The other, Benjamin, had ten sons—Bolau, Bacchar, Asabel, Geras, Naaman, Jes, Ros, Momphis, Opphis, Arad. These fourteen added to the thirty-three before enumerated, amount to the number forty-seven; and this was the legitimate posterity of Jacob. He had besides, by Bilhah, the handmaid of Rachael, Dan and Nephthali; which last had four sons that followed him—Jesel, Guni, Issari, and Sellim. Dan had an only-begotten son, Usi. If these be added to those before-mentioned, they complete the number fifty-four. Gad and Aser were the sons of Zilpha, who was the handmaid of Lea. These had with them, Gad seven—Saphoniah, Augis, Sunis, Azabon, Aerin, Eroed, Ariel. Aser had a daughter, Sarah, and six male children, whose names were Jomne, Isus, Isoui, Baris, Abar, and Melchiel. If we add these, which are sixteen, to the fifty-four, the forementioned number [70] is completed,* Jacob not being himself included in that number.

5. When Joseph understood that his father was coming, for Judas his brother was come before him, and informed him of his approach, he went out to meet him, and they met together at Heroopolis. But Jacob almost fainted away at this unexpected and great joy; however, Joseph revived him, being yet not himself able to contain from being affected in the same manner, at the pleasure he now had; yet was he not wholly overcome with his passion, as his father was. After this he desired Jacob to travel on slowly; but he himself took five of his brethren with him, and made haste to the king, to tell him that Jacob and his family were come, which was a joyful hearing to him. He also bid Joseph tell him what sort of life his brethren loved to lead, that he might give them leave to follow the same; who told him they were good shep-

herds, and had been used to follow no other employment but this alone. Whereby he provided for them, that they should not be separated, but live in the same place, and take care of their father; as also hereby he provided, that they might be acceptable to the Egyptians, by doing nothing that would be common to them with the Egyptians; for the Egyptians are prohibited to meddle with feeding of sheep.†

6. When Jacob was come to the king, and saluted him, and wished all prosperity to his government, Pharaoh asked him how old he now was; upon whose answer, that he was an hundred and thirty years old, he admired Jacob on account of the length of his life. And when he had added, that still he had not lived so long as his forefathers, he gave him leave to live with his children in Heliopolis; for in that city the king's shepherds had their pasturage.

7. However, the famine increased among the Egyptians; and this heavy judgment grew more oppressive to them, because neither did the river overflow the ground, for it did not rise to its former height, nor did God send rain upon it;‡ nor did they indeed make the least provision for themselves, so ignorant were they what was to be done; but Joseph sold them corn for their money. But when their money failed them, they bought corn with their cattle and their slaves; and if any of them had a small piece of land, they gave up that to purchase them food, by which means the king became the owner of all their substance; and they were removed, some to one place and some to another, that so the possession of their country might be firmly assured to the king, excepting the lands of the priests, for their country continued still in their own possession. And indeed this sore famine made their minds as well as their bodies slaves, and at length compelled them to procure a sufficiency of food by such dishonourable means. But when this misery ceased, and the river overflowed the ground, and the ground brought forth its fruits plentifully, Joseph came to every city, and gathered the people thereto belonging together, and gave them back entirely the land which, by their own consent, the king might have possessed alone, and alone enjoyed the fruits of it. He also exhorted them to look on it as every one's own possession, and to fall to their husbandry with cheerfulness; and to pay, as a tribute to the king, the fifth part§ of the fruits for the land which the king, when it was his own, restored to them. These men rejoiced upon their becoming unexpectedly owners

---

† Josephus thought that the Egyptians hated or despised the employment of a shepherd in the days of Joseph; whereas Bishop Cumberland has shewn that they rather hated such Phœnician or Canaanite shepherds that had long enslaved the Egyptians of old time. See his Sanchoniatho, pp. 361, 362.

‡ Reland here puts the question, how Josephus could complain of its not raining in Egypt during this famine, while the ancients affirm that it never does naturally rain there? His answer is, that when the ancients deny that it rains in Egypt, they only mean the Upper Egypt above the Delta, which is called Egypt in the strictest sense; but that in the Delta, [and by consequence in the Lower Egypt adjoining to it,] it did of old, and still does, rain sometimes. See the Note on Antiq. b. iii. ch. i. sect. 6.

§ Josephus supposes that Joseph now restored the Egyptians their lands again, upon the payment of a fifth part as tribute. It seems to me rather that the land was now considered as Pharaoh's land, and this fifth part as its rent, to be paid to him, as he was their landlord, and they his tenants; and that the lands were not properly restored, and this fifth part reserved as tribute only, till the days of Sesostris. See Essay on the Old Testament, Append. 148, 149.

---

* All the Greek copies of Josephus have the negative particle here, that Jacob himself was not reckoned one of the seventy souls that came into Egypt; but the old Latin copies want it, and directly assure us he was one of them. It is therefore hardly certain which of these was Josephus's true reading, since the number seventy is made up without him, if we reckon Leah for one; but if she be not reckoned, Jacob must himself be one, to complete the number.

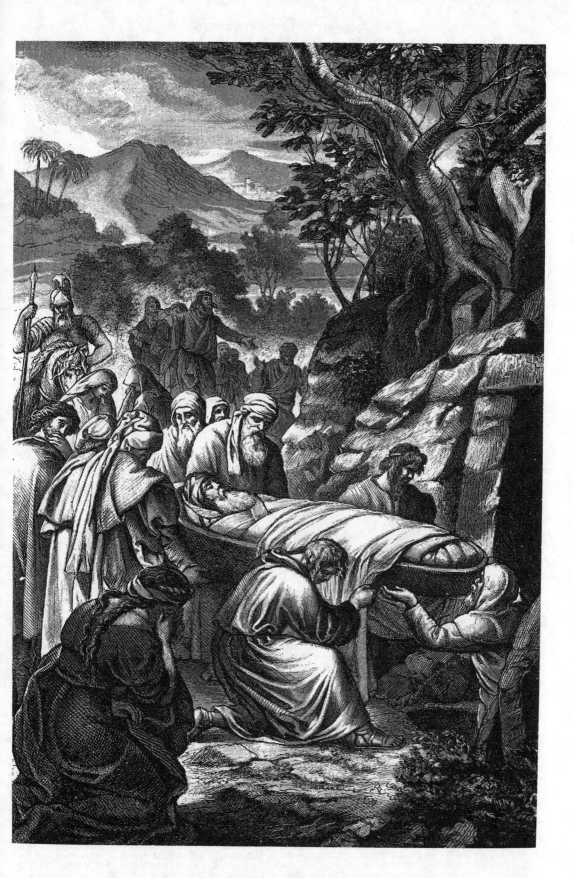

BURIAL OF JACOB AT HEBRON

of their lands, and diligently observed what was enjoined them; and by this means Joseph procured to himself a greater authority among the Egyptians, and a greater love to the king from them. Now this law, that they should pay the fifth part of their fruits as tribute, continued until their later kings.

CHAPTER VIII

OF THE DEATH OF JACOB AND JOSEPH

1. Now when Jacob had lived seventeen years in Egypt, he fell into a disease, and died in the presence of his sons; but not till he made his prayers for their enjoying prosperity, and till he had foretold to them prophetically how every one of them was to dwell in the land of Canaan. But this happened many years afterward. He also enlarged upon the praises of Joseph;* how he had not remembered the evil doings of his brethren to their disadvantage; nay, on the contrary, was kind to them, bestowing upon them so many benefits, as seldom are bestowed on men's own benefactors. He then commanded his own sons that they should admit Joseph's sons, Ephraim and Manasses, into their number, and divide the land of Canaan in common with them; concerning whom we shall treat hereafter. However, he made it his request that he might be buried at Hebron. So he died, when he had lived full a hundred and fifty years, three only abated, having not been behind any of his ancestors in piety towards God, and having such a recompense for it, as it was fit those should have who were so good as these were. But Joseph, by the king's permission, carried his father's dead body to Hebron, and there buried it at a great expense. Now his brethren were at first unwilling to return back with him, because they were afraid lest, now their father was dead, he should punish them for their secret practices against him; since he was now gone, for whose sake he had been so gracious to them. But he persuaded them to fear no harm, and to entertain no suspicions of him: so he brought them along with him, and gave them great possessions, and never left off his particular concern for them.

2. Joseph also died when he had lived a hundred and ten years; having been a man of admirable virtue, and conducting all his affairs by the rules of reason; and used his authority with moderation, which was the cause of his so great felicity among the Egyptians, even when he came from another country, and that in such ill circumstances also, as we have already described. At length his brethren died, after they had lived happily in Egypt. Now the posterity and sons of these men, after some time, carried their bodies, and buried them at Hebron: but as to the bones of Joseph, they carried them into the land of Canaan afterward, when the Hebrews went out of Egypt, for so had Joseph made them promise him upon oath; but what became of every one of these men, and by what toils they got the possession of the land of Canaan, shall be shewn hereafter, when I have first explained upon what account it was that they left Egypt.

---

* As to this encomium upon Joseph, as preparatory to Jacob's adopting Ephraim and Manasses into his own family, and to be admitted for two tribes, which Josephus here mentions, all our copies of Genesis omit it, (ch. xlviii.;) nor do we know whence he took it, or whether it be not his own embellishment only.

CHAPTER IX

CONCERNING THE AFFLICTIONS THAT BEFELL THE HEBREWS IN EGYPT, DURING FOUR HUNDRED YEARS.†

1. Now it happened that the Egyptians grew delicate and lazy, as to painstaking; and gave themselves up to other pleasures, and in particular to the love of gain. They also became very ill affected towards the Hebrews, as touched with envy at their prosperity; for when they saw how the nation of the Israelites flourished, and were become eminent already in plenty of wealth, which they had acquired by their virtue and natural love of labour, they thought their increase was to their own detriment; and having, in length of time, forgotten the benefits they had received from Joseph, particularly the crown being now come into another family, they became very abusive to the Israelites, and contrived many ways of afflicting them; for they enjoined them to cut a great number of channels for the river, and to build walls for their cities and ramparts, that they might restrain the river, and hinder its waters from stagnating, upon its running over its own banks: they set them also to build pyramids,‡ and by all this wore them out; and forced them to learn all sorts of mechanical arts, and to accustom themselves to hard labour. And four hundred years did they spend under these afflictions; for they strove one against the other which should get the mastery, the Egyptians desiring to destroy the Israelites by these labours, and the Israelites desiring to hold out to the end under them.

2. While the affairs of the Hebrews were in this condition, there was this occasion offered itself to the Egyptians, which made them more solicitous for the extinction of our nation. One of those sacred scribes,§ who are very sagacious in foretelling future events truly, told the king, that about this time there would be a child born to the Israelites, who, if he were reared, would bring the Egyptian dominion low, and would raise the Israelites; that he would excel all men in virtue, and obtain a glory that would be remembered through all ages. Which thing was so feared by the king, that, according to this man's opinion, he commanded that they should cast every male child, which was born to the Israelites, into the river, and destroy it; that besides this, the Egyptian midwives‖ should

---

† As to the affliction of Abraham's posterity for 400 years, see Antiq. book i. chap. x. sect. 3; and as to what cities they built in Egypt, under Pharaoh Sesostris, and of Pharaoh Sesostris's drowning in the Red Sea, see Essay on the Old Testament, Append. pp. 132-162.

‡ Of this building of the pyramids of Egypt by the Israelites, see Perizonius Orig. Ægyptiac. chap. xxi. It is not impossible they might build one or more of the small ones; but the large ones seem much later. Only, if they be all built of stone, this does not so well agree with the Israelites' labours, which are said to have been in brick, and not in stone, as Mr Sandys observes in his Travels, pp. 127, 128.

§ Dr Bernard informs us here, that instead of this single priest or prophet of the Egyptians, without a name in Josephus, the Targum of Jonathan names the two famous antagonists of Moses, Jannes and Jambres. Nor is it at all unlikely that it might be one of these who foreboded so much misery to the Egyptians, and so much happiness to the Israelites, from the rearing of Moses.

‖ Josephus is clear that these midwives were Egyptians, and not Israelites, as in our other copies: which is very probable, it being not easily to be supposed that Pharaoh could trust the Israelite midwives to execute so barbarous a command against their own nation. (Consult, therefore, and correct, hence, our ordinary

watch the labours of the Hebrew women, and observe what is born, for those were the women who were enjoined to do the office of midwives to them; and by reason of their relation to the king, would not transgress his commands. He enjoined also, That if any parents should disobey him, and venture to save their male children alive,* they and their families should be destroyed. This was a severe affliction indeed to those that suffered it, not only as they were deprived of their sons, and, while they were the parents themselves, they were obliged to be subservient to the destruction of their own children, but as it was to be supposed to the extirpation of their nation, while upon the destruction of their children, and their own gradual dissolution, the calamity would become very hard and inconsolable to them: and this was the ill state they were in. But no one can be too hard for the purpose of God, though he contrive ten thousand subtle devices for that end; for this child, whom the sacred scribe foretold, was brought up and concealed from the observers appointed by the king; and he that foretold him did not mistake in the consequences of his preservation, which were brought to pass after the manner following:—

3. A man, whose name was Amram, one of the nobler sort of the Hebrews, was afraid for his whole nation, lest it should fail, by the want of young men to be brought up hereafter, and was very uneasy at it, his wife being then with child, and he knew not what to do. Hereupon he betook himself to prayer to God; and entreated him to have compassion on those men who had nowise transgressed the laws of his worship, and to afford them deliverance from the miseries they at that time endured, and to render abortive their enemies' hopes of the destruction of their nation. Accordingly God had mercy on him, and was moved by his supplication. He stood by him in his sleep, and exhorted him not to despair of his future favours. He said further, that he did not forget their piety towards him, and would always reward them for it, as he had formerly granted his favour to their forefathers, and made them increase from a few to so great a multitude. He put him in mind, that when Abraham was come alone out of Mesopotamia into Canaan, he had been made happy, not only in other respects, but that when his wife was at first barren, she was afterwards by him enabled to conceive seed, and bear him sons. That he left to Ismael and to his posterity the country of Arabia; as also to his sons by Ketura, Troglodytis: and to Isaac, Canaan. That by my assistance, said he, he did great exploits in war, which, unless you be yourselves impious, you must still remember. As for Jacob, he became well known to strangers also, by the greatness of that prosperity in which he lived, and left to his sons, who came into Egypt with no more than seventy souls, while you are now become above six hundred thousand. Know, therefore, that I shall provide for you all in common what is for your good, and particularly for thyself what shall make thee famous; for

that child, out of dread of whose nativity the Egyptians have doomed the Israelite children to destruction, shall be this child of thine, and shall be concealed from those who watch to destroy him: and when he is brought up in a surprising way, he shall deliver the Hebrew nation from the distress they are under from the Egyptians. His memory shall be famous while the world lasts; and this not only among the Hebrews, but foreigners also:—all which shall be the effect of my favour to thee, and to thy posterity. He shall also have such a brother, that he shall himself obtain my priesthood, and his posterity shall have it after him to the end of the world.

4. When the vision had informed him of these things, Amram awaked and told it to Jochebed, who was his wife. And now the fear increased upon them on account of the prediction in Amram's dream; for they were under concern, not only for the child, but on account of the great happiness that was to come to him also. However, the mother's labour was such as afforded a confirmation to what was foretold by God; for it was not known to those that watched her, by the easiness of her pains, and because the throes of her delivery did not fall upon her with violence. And now they nourished the child at home privately for three months; but after that time Amram, fearing he should be discovered, and by falling under the king's displeasure, both he and his child should perish, and so he should make the promise of God of none effect, he determined rather to intrust the safety and care of the child to God, than to depend on his own concealment of him, which he looked upon as a thing uncertain, and whereby both the child, so privately to be nourished, and himself, should be in imminent danger; but he believed that God would some way for certain procure the safety of the child, in order to secure the truth of his own predictions. When they had thus determined, they made an ark of bulrushes, after the manner of a cradle, and of a bigness sufficient for an infant to be laid in, without being too straitened: they then daubed it over with slime, which would naturally keep out the water from entering between the bulrushes, and put the infant into it, and setting it afloat upon the river, they left its preservation to God; so the river received the child, and carried him along. But Miriam, the child's sister, passed along upon the bank over against him, as her mother had bid her, to see whither the ark would be carried; where God demonstrated that human wisdom was nothing, but that the Supreme Being is able to do whatsoever he pleases: that those who, in order to their own security, condemn others to destruction, and use great endeavours about it, fail of their purpose; but that others are in a surprising manner preserved, and obtain a prosperous condition almost from the very midst of their calamities; those, I mean, whose dangers arise by the appointment of God. And, indeed, such a providence was exercised in the case of this child, as shewed the power of God.

5. Thermuthis was the king's daughter. She was now diverting herself by the banks of the river; and seeing a cradle borne along by the current, she sent some that could swim, and bid them bring the cradle to her. When those that were sent on this errand, came to her with the cradle, and she saw the little child, she was greatly in love with it, on account of its largeness and beauty; for God had taken such great care in the formation of Moses, that he caused him to be thought worthy of bringing up, and providing for, by all those that had taken the

---

copies, Exod. i. 15, 22. And, indeed, Josephus seems to have had much completer copies of the Pentateuch, or other authentic records now lost, about the birth and actions of Moses, than either our Hebrew, Samaritan, or Greek Bibles afford us, which enabled him to be so large and particular about him.

* Of this grandfather of Sesostris, Ramestes the Great, who slew the Israelite infants, and of the inscription on his obelisk, containing, in my opinion, one of the oldest records of mankind, see Essay on the Old Test. Append. pp. 139, 145, 147, 217-220.

most fatal resolutions, on account of the dread of his nativity, for the destruction of the rest of the Hebrew nation. Thermuthis bid them bring her a woman that might afford her breast to the child; yet would not the child admit of her breast, but turned away from it, and did the like to many other women. Now Miriam was by when this happened, not to appear to be there on purpose, but only as staying to see the child; and she said, "It is in vain that thou, O queen, callest for these women for the nourishing of the child, who are no way of kin to it; but still, if thou wilt order one of the Hebrew women to be brought, perhaps it may admit the breast of one of its own nation." Now since she seemed to speak well, Thermuthis bid her procure such a one, and to bring one of those Hebrew women that gave suck. So when she had such authority given her, she came back and brought the mother, who was known to nobody there. And now the child gladly admitted the breast, and seemed to stick close to it; and so it was, that, at the queen's desire, the nursing of the child was entirely intrusted to the mother.

6. Hereupon it was that Thermuthis imposed this name *Mouses* upon him, from what had happened when he was put into the river; for the Egyptians call water by the name of *Mo*, and such as are saved out of it by the name of *Uses;* so by putting these two words together, they imposed this name upon him; and he was, by the confession of all, according to God's prediction, as well for his greatness of mind as for his contempt of difficulties, the best of all the Hebrews; for Abraham was his ancestor, of the seventh generation. For Moses was the son of Amram, who was the son of Caath, whose father, Levi, was the son of Jacob, who was the son of Isaac, who was the son of Abraham. Now Moses's understanding became superior to his age, nay, far beyond that standard; and when he was taught, he discovered greater quickness of apprehension than was usual at his age; and his actions at that time promised greater, when he should come to the age of a man. God did also give him that tallness, when he was but three years old, as was wonderful; and for his beauty, there was nobody so unpolite as, when they saw Moses, they were not greatly surprised at the beauty of his countenance: nay, it happened frequently, that those that met him as he was carried along the road, were obliged to turn again upon seeing the child, that they left what they were about, and stood still a great while to look on him; for the beauty of the child was so remarkable and natural to him on many accounts, that it detained the spectators, and made them stay longer to look upon him.

7. Thermuthis, therefore, perceiving him to be so remarkable a child, adopted him for her son, having no child of her own. And when one time she had carried Moses to her father, she shewed him to him, and said she thought to make him her father's successor, if it should please God she should have no legitimate child of her own; and said to him, "I have brought up a child who is of a divine form,* and of a generous mind; and as I have received him from the bounty of the river, in a wonderful manner, I thought proper to adopt him for my son, and the heir of thy kingdom." And when she had said this, she put the infant into her father's hands: so he took him, and hugged him close to his breast;

and on his daughter's account, in a pleasant way, put his diadem upon his head; but Moses threw it down to the ground, and, in a puerile mood, he wreathed it round, and trod upon it with his feet; which seemed to bring along with it an evil presage concerning the kingdom of Egypt. But when the sacred scribe saw this, (he was the same person who foretold that his nativity would bring the dominion of that kingdom low,) he made a violent attempt to kill him: and crying out in a frightful manner, he said, "This, O king! this child is he of whom God foretold, that if we kill him we shall be in no danger; he himself affords an attestation to the prediction of the same thing, by his trampling upon thy government, and treading upon thy diadem. Take him, therefore, out of the way, and deliver the Egyptians from the fear they are in about him; and deprive the Hebrews of the hope they have of being encouraged by him." But Thermuthis prevented him, and snatched the child away. And the king was not hasty to slay him, God himself, whose providence protected Moses, inclining the king to spare him. He was, therefore, educated with great care. So the Hebrews depended on him, and were of good hopes that great things would be done by him; but the Egyptians were suspicious of what would follow such his education. Yet because, if Moses had been slain, there was no one, either akin or adopted, that had any oracle on his side for pretending to the crown of Egypt, and likely to be of greater advantage to them, they abstained from killing him.

CHAPTER X

HOW MOSES MADE WAR WITH THE ETHIOPIANS

1. Moses, therefore, when he was born, and brought up in the foregoing manner, and came to the age of maturity, made his virtue manifest to the Egyptians; and shewed that he was born for the bringing them down, and raising the Israe-ites; and the occasion he laid hold of was this:— The Ethiopians, who are next neighbours to the Egyptians, made an inroad into their country, which they seized upon, and carried off the effects of the Egyptians, who, in their rage, fought against them, and revenged the affronts they had received from them; but, being over-come in battle, some of them were slain, and the rest ran away in a shameful manner, and by that means saved themselves; whereupon the Ethiopians followed after them in the pursuit; and thinking that it would be a mark of coward-ice if they did not subdue all Egypt, they went on to subdue the rest with greater vehemence; and when they had tasted the sweets of the country, they never left off the prosecution of the war; and as the nearest parts had not courage enough at first to fight with them, they proceeded as far as Memphis, and the sea itself; while not one of the cities was able to oppose them. The Egyptians, under this sad oppression, betook themselves to their oracles and prophecies: and when God had given them this counsel, to make use of Moses the Hebrew and take his assistance, the king commanded his daughter to produce him, that he might be the general† of their army. Upon which, when she

---

* What Josephus here says of the beauty of Moses, that he was of a fair form, is very like what St Stephen says of the same beauty; that he was beautiful in the sight of God, Acts vii. 20.

† This history of Moses, as general of the Egyptians against the Ethiopians, is wholly omitted in our Bibles; but is thus cited by Irenæus, from Josephus, and that

had made him swear he would do him no harm, she delivered him to the king, and supposed his assistance would be of great advantage to them. She withal reproached the priest, who, when they had before admonished the Egyptians to kill him, was not ashamed now to own their want of his help.

2. So Moses, at the persuasion both of Thermuthis and the king himself, cheerfully undertook the business: and the sacred scribes of both nations were glad; those of the Egyptians, that they should at once overcome their enemies by his valour, and that by the same piece of management Moses would be slain; but those of the Hebrews, that they should escape from the Egyptians, because Moses was to be their general; but Moses prevented the enemies, and took and led his army before those enemies were apprised of his attacking them; for he did not march by the river, but by land, where he gave a wonderful demonstration of his sagacity; for when the ground was difficult to be passed over, because of the multitude of serpents, (which it produces in vast numbers, and indeed is singular in some of those productions, which other countries do not breed, and yet such as are worse than others in power and mischief, and an unusual fierceness of sight, some of which ascend out of the ground unseen, and also fly in the air, and so come upon men at unawares, and do them a mischief,) Moses invented a wonderful stratagem to preserve the army safe, and without hurt; for he made baskets, like unto arks, of sedge, and filled them with ibes,* and carried them along with them; which animal is the greatest enemy to serpents imaginable, for they fly from them when they come near them; and as they fly they are caught and devoured by them, as if it were done by the harts; but the ibes are tame creatures, and only enemies to the serpentine kind: but about these I say no more at present, since the Greeks themselves are not unacquainted with this sort of bird. As soon, therefore, as Moses was come to the land which was the breeder of these serpents, he let loose the ibes, and by their means repelled the serpentine kind, and used them for his assistants before the army came upon that ground. When he had therefore proceeded thus on his journey, he came upon the Ethiopians before they expected him; and, joining battle with them, he beat them, and deprived them of the hopes they had of success against the Egyptians, and went on in overthrowing their cities, and indeed made a great slaughter of these Ethiopians. Now when the Egyptian army had once tasted of this prosperous success, by the means of Moses, they did not slacken their diligence, insomuch that the Ethiopians were in danger of being reduced to slavery, and all sorts of destruction; and at length they retired to Saba, which was a royal city of Ethiopia, which Cambyses afterwards named Meroë, after the name of his own sister.

---

soon after his own age:—"Josephus says, that when Moses was nourished in the king's palace, he was appointed general of the army against the Ethiopians, and conquered them, when he married that king's daughter; because out of her affection for him, she delivered the city up to him." See the fragments of Irenæus, ap. edit. Grab. p. 472. Nor perhaps did St Stephen refer to any thing else when he said of Moses, before he was sent by God to the Israelites, that he was not only learned in all the wisdom of the Egyptians, but was also mighty in words and in deeds, (Acts vii. 22.)

* Pliny speaks of these birds called Ibes; and says, "The Egyptians invoked them against the serpents." Hist. Nat. book x. chap. 28. Strabo speaks of this island Meroë, and these rivers Astapus and Astaboras, book xvi. pp. 771, 786; and book xvii. p. 821.

The place was to be besieged with very great difficulty, since it was both encompassed by the Nile quite round, and the other rivers, Astapus and Astaboras, made it a very difficult thing for such as attempted to pass over them; for the city was situate in a retired place, and was inhabited after the manner of an island, being encompassed with a strong wall, and having the rivers to guard them from their enemies, and having great ramparts between the wall and the rivers, insomuch, that when the waters come with the greatest violence it can never be drowned; which ramparts make it next to impossible for even such as are gotten over the rivers to take the city. However, while Moses was uneasy at the army's lying idle, (for the enemies durst not come to battle,) this accident happened:—Tharbis was the daughter of the king of the Ethiopians: she happened to see Moses as he led the army near the walls, and fought with great courage; and admiring the subtlety of his undertakings, and believing him to be the author of the Egyptians' success, when they had before despaired of recovering their liberty, and to be the occasion of the great danger the Ethiopians were in, when they had before boasted of their great achievements, she fell deeply in love with him; and upon the prevalency of that passion, sent to him the most faithful of all her servants to discourse with him about their marriage. He thereupon accepted the offer, on condition she would procure the delivering up of the city; and gave her the assurance of an oath to take her to his wife; and that when he had once taken possession of the city, he would not break his oath to her. No sooner was the agreement made, but it took effect immediately; and when Moses had cut off the Ethiopians, he gave thanks to God, and consummated his marriage, and led the Egyptians back to their own land.

CHAPTER XI

HOW MOSES FLED OUT OF EGYPT INTO MIDIAN

1. Now the Egyptians, after they had been preserved by Moses, entertained a hatred to him, and were very eager in compassing their designs against him, as suspecting that he would take occasion, from his good success, to raise a sedition, and bring innovations into Egypt; and told the king he ought to be slain. The king had also some intentions of himself to the same purpose, and this as well out of envy at his glorious expedition at the head of his army, as out of fear of being brought low by him; and being instigated by the sacred scribes, he was ready to undertake to kill Moses; but when he had learned beforehand what plots there were against him, he went away privately; and because the public roads were watched, he took his flight through the deserts, and where his enemies could not suspect he would travel, and, though he was destitute of food, he went on, and despised that difficulty courageously; and when he came to the city Midian, which lay upon the Red Sea, and was so denominated from one of Abraham's sons by Keturah, he sat upon a certain well, and rested himself there after his laborious journey, and the affliction he had been in. It was not far from the city, and the time of the day was noon, where he had an occasion offered him by the custom of the country of doing what recommended his virtue, and afforded him an opportunity of bettering his circumstances.

2. For that country having but little water, the shepherds used to seize on the wells before others came, lest their flocks should want water, and lest it should be spent by others before they came. There were now come, therefore, to this well seven sisters that were virgins, the daughters of Raguel, a priest, and one thought worthy by the people of the country of great honour. These virgins, who took care of their father's flocks, which sort of work it was customary and very familiar for women to do in the country of the Troglodytes, they came first of all, and drew water out of the well in a quantity sufficient for their flocks, into troughs, which were made for the reception of that water; but when the shepherds came upon the maidens, and drove them away, that they might have the command of the water themselves, Moses, thinking it would be a terrible reproach upon him if he overlooked the young women under unjust oppression, and should suffer the violence of the men to prevail over the right of the maidens, he drove away the men, who had a mind to more than their share, and afforded a proper assistance to the women; who, when they had received such a benefit from him, came to their father, and told him how they had been affronted by the shepherds, and assisted by a stranger, and entreated that he would not let this generous action be done in vain, nor go without a reward. Now the father took it well from his daughters that they were so desirous to reward their benefactor; and bid them bring Moses into his presence, that he might be rewarded as he deserved; and when Moses came, he told him what testimony his daughters bare to him, that he had assisted them; and that, as he admired him for his virtue, he said that Moses had bestowed such his assistance on persons not insensible of benefits, but where they were both able and willing to return the kindness, and even to exceed the measure of his generosity. So he made him his son, and gave him one of his daughters in marriage; and appointed him to be the guardian and superintendent over his cattle; for of old, all the wealth of the barbarians was in those cattle.

CHAPTER XII

CONCERNING THE BURNING BUSH, AND THE ROD OF MOSES

1. Now Moses, when he had obtained the favour of Jethro, for that was one of the names of Raguel, stayed there and fed his flock; but some time afterward, taking his station at the mountain called Sinai, he drove his flocks thither to feed them. Now this is the highest of all the mountains thereabout, and the best for pasturage, the herbage being there good; and it had not been before fed upon, because of the opinion men had that God dwelt there, the shepherds not daring to ascend up to it; and here it was that a wonderful prodigy happened to Moses; for a fire fed upon a thorn-bush, yet did the green leaves and the flowers continue untouched, and the fire did not at all consume the fruit-branches, although the flame was great and fierce. Moses was affrighted at this strange sight, as it was to him; but he was still more astonished when the fire uttered a voice, and called to him by name, and spake words to him, by which it signified how bold he had been in venturing to come into a place whither no man had ever come before, because the place was divine; and advised him

to remove a great way off from the flame, and to be contented with what he had seen; and though he were himself a good man, and the offspring of great men, yet that he should not pry any further: and he foretold to him, that he should have glory and honour among men, by the blessing of God upon him. He also commanded him to go away thence with confidence to Egypt, in order to his being the commander and conductor of the body of the Hebrews, and to his delivering his own people from the injuries they suffered there: "For," said God, "they shall inhabit this happy land which your forefather Abraham inhabited, and shall have the enjoyment of all sorts of good things; and thou, by thy prudence, shalt guide them to those good things." But still he enjoined him, when he had brought the Hebrews out of the land of Egypt, to come to that place, and to offer sacrifices of thanksgiving there. Such were the divine oracles which were delivered out of the fire.

2. But Moses was astonished at what he saw, and much more at what he heard; and he said, "I think it would be an instance of too great madness, O Lord, for one of that regard I bear to thee, to distrust thy power, since I myself adore it, and know that it has been made manifest to my progenitors: but I am still in doubt how I, who am a private man, and one of no abilities, should either persuade my own countrymen to leave the country they now inhabit, and to follow me to a land whither I lead them; or, if they should be persuaded, how can I force Pharaoh to permit them to depart, since they augment their own wealth and prosperity by the labours and works they put upon them!"

3. But God persuaded him to be courageous on all occasions, and promised to be with him, and to assist him in his words, when he was to persuade men; and in his deeds, when he was to perform wonders. He bid him also to take a signal of the truth of what he said, by throwing his rod upon the ground; which when he had done, it crept along, and was become a serpent, and rolled itself round in its folds, and erected its head, as ready to revenge itself on such as should assault it; after which it became a rod again as before. After this God bid Moses to put his right hand into his bosom: he obeyed, and when he took it out it was white, and in colour like to chalk, but afterward it returned to its wonted colour again. He also, upon God's command, took some of the water that was near him, and poured it upon the ground, and saw the colour was that of blood. Upon the wonder that Moses shewed at these signs, God exhorted him to be of good courage, and to be assured that he would be the greatest support to him; and bid him make use of those signs, in order to obtain belief among all men, that "thou art sent by me, and dost all things according to my commands. Accordingly I enjoin thee to make no more delays, but to make haste to Egypt, and to travel night and day, and not to draw out the time, and so make the slavery of the Hebrews and their sufferings to last the longer."

4. Moses having now seen and heard these wonders that assured him of the truth of these promises of God, had no room left him to disbelieve them: he entreated him to grant him that power when he should be in Egypt; and besought him to vouchsafe him the knowledge of his own name; and, since he had heard and seen him, that he would also tell him his name, that when he offered sacrifice he might invoke him by such his name in his oblations. Whereupon God declared to him his holy name, which had

never been discovered to men before; concerning which it is not lawful for me to say any more.* Now these signs accompanied Moses, not then only, but always when he prayed for them: of all which signs he attributed the firmest assent to the fire in the bush; and believing that God would be a gracious supporter to him, he hoped he should be able to deliver his own nation, and bring calamities on the Egyptians.

CHAPTER XIII

HOW MOSES AND AARON RETURNED INTO EGYPT TO PHARAOH

1. So Moses, when he understood that the Pharaoh, in whose reign he fled away, was dead, asked leave of Raguel to go to Egypt, for the benefit of his own people: and he took with him Zipporah, the daughter of Raguel, whom he had married, and the children he had by her, Gersom and Eleazer, and made haste into Egypt. Now the former of those names, Gersom, in the Hebrew tongue, signifies *that he was in a strange land;* and Eleazer, *that, by the assistance of the God of his fathers, he had escaped from the Egyptians.* Now when they were near the borders, Aaron his brother, by the command of God, met him, to whom he declared what had befallen him at the mountain, and the commands that God had given him. But as they were going forward, the chief men among the Hebrews, having learned that they were coming, met them; to whom Moses declared the signs he had seen; and while they could not believe them, he made them see them. So they took courage at these surprising and unexpected sights, and hoped well of their entire deliverance, as believing now that God took care of their preservation.

2. Since then Moses found that the Hebrews would be obedient to whatsoever he should direct, as they promised to be, and were in love with liberty, he came to the king, who had indeed but lately received the government, and told him how much he had done for the good of the Egyptians, when they were despised by the Ethiopians, and their country laid waste by them; and how he had been the commander of their forces, and had laboured for them, as if they had been his own people; and he informed him in what danger he had been during that expedition, without having any proper returns made him as he had deserved. He also informed him distinctly what things happened to him at mount Sinai; and what God said to him; and the signs that were done by God, in order to assure him of the authority of those commands which he had given him. He also exhorted him not to disbelieve what he told him, nor to oppose the will of God.

---

* This superstitious fear of discovering the name with four letters, which of late we have been used falsely to pronounce Jehovah, but seems to have been originally pronounced Jahoh, or Jao, is never, I think, heard of till this passage of Josephus; and this superstition, in not pronouncing that name, has continued among the Rabbinical Jews to this day, (though whether the Samaritans and Caraites observed it so early, does not appear.) Josephus also durst not set down the very words of the ten commandments, as we shall see hereafter, Antiq. book iii. ch. v. sect. 4; which superstitious silence, I think, has yet not been continued even by the Rabbins. It is however no doubt but both these cautious concealments were taught Josephus by the Pharisees; a body of men at once very wicked and very superstitious.

3. But when the king derided Moses, he made him in earnest see the signs that were done at mount Sinai. Yet was the king very angry with him, and called him an ill man, who had formerly run away from his Egyptian slavery, and came now back with deceitful tricks, and wonders and magical arts, to astonish him. And when he had said this, he commanded the priests to let him see the same wonderful sights; as knowing that the Egyptians were skilful in this kind of learning, and that he was not the only person who knew them, and pretended them to be divine; as also he told him, that when he brought such wonderful sights before him, he would only be believed by the unlearned. Now when the priests threw down their rods, they became serpents. But Moses was not daunted at it; and said, "O king, I do not myself despise the wisdom of the Egyptians, but I say that what I do is so much superior to what these do by magic arts and tricks, as divine power exceeds the power of man: but I will demonstrate that what I do is not done by craft, or counterfeiting what is not really true, but that they appear by the providence and power of God." And when he had said this, he cast his rod down upon the ground, and commanded it to turn itself into a serpent. It obeyed him, and went all round, and devoured the rods of the Egyptians, which seemed to be dragons, until it had consumed them all. It then returned to its own form, and Moses took it into his hand again.

4. However, the king was no more moved when this was done than before; and being very angry, he said that he should gain nothing by this his cunning and shrewdness against the Egyptians;—and he commanded him that was the chief taskmaster over the Hebrews, to give them no relaxation from their labours, but to compel them to submit to greater oppressions than before; and though he allowed them chaff before for making their bricks, he would allow it them no longer; but he made them to work hard at brick-making in the daytime, and to gather chaff in the night. Now when their labour was thus doubled upon them, they laid the blame upon Moses, because their labour and their misery were on his account become more severe to them; but Moses did not let his courage sink for the king's threatenings; nor did he abate of his zeal on account of the Hebrews' complaints; but he supported himself, and set his soul resolutely against them both, and used his own utmost diligence to procure liberty to his countrymen. So he went to the king, and persuaded him to let the Hebrews go to mount Sinai, and there to sacrifice to God, because God had enjoined them so to do. He persuaded him also not to counterwork the designs of God, but to esteem his favour above all things, and to permit them to depart, lest, before he be aware, he lay an obstruction in the way of the divine commands, and so, occasion his own suffering such punishments as it was probable any one that counterworked the divine commands should undergo, since the severest afflictions arise from every object to those that provoke the divine wrath against them; for such as these have neither the earth nor the air for their friends; nor are the fruits of the womb according to nature, but everything is unfriendly and adverse towards them. He said further, that the Egyptians should know this by sad experience; and that besides, the Hebrew people should go out of their country without their consent.

CHAPTER XIV

CONCERNING THE TEN PLAGUES WHICH CAME UPON THE EGYPTIANS

1. BUT when the king despised the words of Moses, and had no regard at all to them, grievous plagues seized the Egyptians; every one of which I will describe, both because no such plagues did ever happen to any other nation as the Egyptians now felt,—and because I would demonstrate that Moses did not fail in any one thing that he foretold them; and because it is for the good of mankind, that they may learn this caution:—Not to do any thing that may displease God, lest he be provoked to wrath, and avenge their iniquities upon them. For the Egyptian river ran with bloody water at the command of God, insomuch that it could not be drunk, and they had no other spring of water neither; for the water was not only of the colour of blood, but it brought upon those that ventured to drink of it, great pains and bitter torment. Such was the river to the Egyptians; but it was sweet and fit for drinking to the Hebrews, and no way different from what it naturally used to be. As the king therefore knew not what to do in these surprising circumstances, and was in fear for the Egyptians, he gave the Hebrews leave to go away; but when the plague ceased, he changed his mind again, and would not suffer them to go.

2. But when God saw that he was ungrateful, and upon the ceasing of this calamity would not grow wiser, he sent another plague upon the Egyptians:—An innumerable multitude of frogs consumed the fruit of the ground; the river was also full of them, insomuch that those who drew water had it spoiled by the blood of these animals, as they died in, and were destroyed by, the water; and the country was full of filthy slime, as they were borne and as they died: they also spoiled their vessels in their houses, which they used, and were found among what they ate and what they drank, and came in great numbers upon their beds. There was also an ungrateful smell, and a stink arose from them, as they were born, and as they died therein. Now, when the Egyptians were under the oppression of these miseries, the king ordered Moses to take the Hebrews with him, and be gone. Upon which the whole multitude of the frogs vanished away; and both the land and the river returned to their former natures. But as soon as Pharaoh saw the land freed from this plague, he forgot the cause of it, and retained the Hebrews; and, as though he had a mind to try the nature of more such judgments, he would not yet suffer Moses and his people to depart, having granted that liberty rather out of fear than any good consideration.[*]

3. Accordingly God punished his falseness with another plague, added to the former; for there arose out of the bodies of the Egyptians an innumerable quantity of lice, by which, wicked as they were, they miserably perished, as not able to destroy this sort of vermin either with washes or with ointments. At which terrible judgment the king of Egypt was in disorder, upon the fear into which he reasoned himself, lest his people should be destroyed, and that the manner of this death was also re-

proachful, so that he was forced in part to recover himself from his wicked temper to a sounder mind, for he gave leave for the Hebrews themselves to depart. But when the plague thereupon ceased, he thought it proper to require that they should leave their children and wives behind them, as pledges of their return; whereby he provoked God to be more vehemently angry at him, as if he thought to impose on his providence, and as if it were only Moses, and not God, who punished the Egyptians for the sake of the Hebrews: for he filled that country full of various sorts of pestilential creatures, with their various properties, such indeed, as had never come into the sight of men before, by whose means the men perished themselves, and the land was destitute of husbandmen for its cultivation; but if any thing escaped destruction from them, it was killed by a distemper which the men underwent also.

4. But when Pharaoh did not even then yield to the will of God, but, while he gave leave to the husbands to take their wives with them, yet insisted that the children should be left behind, God presently resolved to punish his wickedness with several sorts of calamities, and those worse than the foregoing, which yet had so generally afflicted them; for their bodies had terrible boils, breaking forth with blains, while they were already inwardly consumed; and a great part of the Egyptians perished in this manner. But when the king was not brought to reason by this plague, hail was sent down from heaven; and such hail it was, as the climate of Egypt had never suffered before, nor was it like to that which falls in other climates in winter time,[†] but was larger than that which falls in the middle of spring to those that dwell in the northern and north-western regions. This hail broke down their boughs laden with fruit. After this a tribe of locusts consumed the seed which was not hurt by the hail: so that to the Egyptians all hopes of the future fruits of the ground were entirely lost.

5. One would think the forementioned calamities might have been sufficient for one that was only foolish, without wickedness, to make him wise, and to make him sensible what was for his advantage. But Pharaoh, led not so much by his folly as by his wickedness, even when he saw the cause of his miseries, he still contested with God, and wilfully deserted the cause of virtue; so he bid Moses take the Hebrews away, with their wives and children, but to leave their cattle behind, since their own cattle were destroyed. But when Moses said that what he desired was unjust, since they were obliged to offer sacrifices to God of those cattle; and the time being prolonged on this account, a thick darkness, without the least light, spread itself over the Egyptians, whereby their sight being obstructed, and their breathing hindered by the thickness of the air, they died miserably, and under a terror lest they should be swallowed up by the dark cloud. Besides this, when the darkness, after three days and as many nights, was dissipated, and when Pharaoh did not still repent and let the Hebrews go, Moses came to him and said, "How long wilt thou be disobedient to the command of God? for he enjoins thee to let the Hebrews go; nor is there any other way of being freed from the calamities you are under, unless you do so." But the king was angry at what he said, and threatened to

---

[*] Of this judicial hardening the hearts, and blinding the eyes of wicked men, or infatuating them, as a just punishment for their other wilful sins, to their own destruction, see the note on Antiq. b. vii. ch. ix. sect. 6.

[†] As to this winter or spring hail near Egypt and Judea, see the like on thunder and lightning there, in the note on Antiq. b. vi. ch. v. sect. 6.

cut off his head if he came any more to trouble him about these matters. Hereupon Moses said he would not speak to him any more about them, for that he himself, together with the principal men among the Egyptians, should desire the Hebrews to go away. So when Moses had said this, he went his way.

6. But when God had signified, that with one more plague he would compel the Egyptians to let the Hebrews go, he commanded Moses to tell the people that they should have a sacrifice ready, and that they should prepare themselves on the tenth day of the month Xanthicus, against the fourteenth, (which month is called by the Egyptians, Pharmuth, and Nisan by the Hebrews; but the Macedonians call it Xanthicus,) and that he should carry away the Hebrews with all they had. Accordingly, he having got the Hebrews ready for their departure, and having sorted the people into tribes, he kept them together in one place: but when the fourteenth day was come, and all were ready to depart, they offered the sacrifice, and purified their houses with the blood, using bunches of hyssop for that purpose; and when they had supped, they burnt the remainder of the flesh, as just ready to depart. Whence it is that we do still offer this sacrifice in like manner to this day, and call this festival *Pascha*, which signifies *the feast of the passover;* because on that day God passed us over, and sent the plague upon the Egyptians; for the destruction of the first-born came upon the Egyptians that night, so that many of the Egyptians who lived near the king's palace persuaded Pharaoh to let the Hebrews go. Accordingly he called for Moses, and bid them begone; as supposing, that if once the Hebrews were gone out of the country, Egypt should be freed from its miseries. They also honoured the Hebrews with gifts;[*] some in order to get them to depart quickly, and others on account of their neighbourhood, and the friendship they had with them.

CHAPTER XV

HOW THE HEBREWS, UNDER THE CONDUCT OF MOSES, LEFT EGYPT

1. So the Hebrews went out of Egypt, while the Egyptians wept, and repented that they had treated them so hardly.—Now they took their journey by Letopolis, a place at that time deserted, but where Babylon was built afterwards, when Cambyses laid Egypt waste; but as they went away hastily, on the third day they came to a place called Beelzephon, on the Red Sea; and when they had no food out of the land, because it was a desert, they eat of loaves kneaded of flour, only warmed by a gentle heat; and this

food they made use of for thirty days; for what they brought with them out of Egypt would not suffice them any longer time; and this only while they dispensed it to each person, to use so much only as would serve for necessity, but not for satiety. Whence it is that, in memory of the want we were then in, we keep a feast for eight days, which is called *the feast of unleavened bread.* Now the entire multitude of those that went out, including the women and children, was not easy to be numbered; but those that were of an age fit for war, were six hundred thousand.

2. They left Egypt in the month Xanthicus, on the fifteenth day of the lunar month; four hundred and thirty years after our forefather Abraham came into Canaan, but two hundred and fifteen years only after Jacob removed into Egypt.† It was the eightieth year of the age of Moses, and of that of Aaron three more. They also carried out the bones of Joseph with them, as he had charged his sons to do.

3. But the Egyptians soon repented that the Hebrews were gone; and the king also was mightily concerned that this had been procured by the magic arts of Moses; so they resolved to go after them. Accordingly they took their weapons, and other warlike furniture, and pursued after them, in order to bring them back, if once they overtook them, because they would now have no pretence to pray to God against them, since they had already been permitted to go out; and they thought they should easily overcome them, as they had no armour, and would be weary with their journey; so they made haste in their pursuit, and asked of every one they met which way they were gone. And indeed that land was difficult to be travelled over, not only by armies, but by single persons. Now Moses led the Hebrews this way, that in case the Egyptians should repent and be desirous to pursue after them, they might undergo the punishment of their wickedness, and of the breach of those promises they had made to them. As also he led them this way on account of the Philistines, who had quarrelled with them, and hated them of old, that by all means they might not know of their departure, for their country is near to that of Egypt; and thence it was that Moses led them not along the road that tended to the land of the Philistines, but he was desirous that they should go through the desert, that so after a long journey, and after many afflictions, they might enter upon the land of Canaan. Another reason of this was, that God commanded him to bring the people to mount Sinai, that there they might offer him sacrifices. Now when the Egyptians had overtaken the Hebrews, they prepared to fight them, and by their multitude they drove them into a narrow place; for the number that pursued after them was six hundred chariots, with fifty thousand horsemen, and two hundred thousand footmen, all armed. They also seized on the passages by which they imagined the Hebrews might fly, shutting them up‡ between inaccessible precipices and the sea;

---

[*] These large presents made to the Israelites, of vessels of silver, and vessels of gold, and raiment, were, as Josephus truly calls them, gifts really given them; not lent them, as our English falsely renders them. They were spoils required, not borrowed of them, (Gen. xv. 14; Exod. iii. 22, xi. 2; Ps. cv. 37,) as the same version falsely renders the Hebrew word here used, (Exod. xii. 33, 36.) God had ordered the Jews to demand these as their pay and reward, during their long and bitter slavery in Egypt, as atonements for the lives of the Egyptians, and as the condition of the Jews' departure, and of the Egyptians' deliverance from these terrible judgments, which had they not now ceased, they had soon been all dead men, as they themselves confess, (ch. xii. 33.) Nor was there any sense in borrowing or lending, when the Israelites were finally departing out of the land for ever.

† Why our Masorete copy so groundlessly abridges this account in Exod. xii. 40, as to ascribe 430 years to the sole peregrination of the Israelites in Egypt, when it is clear even by that Masorete chronology elsewhere, as well as from the express text itself, in the Samaritan, Septuagint, and Josephus, that they sojourned in Egypt but half that time,—and that by consequence, the other half of their peregrination was in the land of Canaan, before they came into Egypt,—is hard to say. See Essay on the Old Testament, pp. 62, 63.

‡ Take the main part of Reland's excellent note here, which greatly illustrates Josephus, and the Scripture, in this history, as follows: "[A traveller, says Reland, whose name was] Eneman, when he returned out o.

for there was [on each side] a [ridge of] mountains that terminated at the sea, which were impassable by reason of their roughness, and obstructed their flight; wherefore they there pressed upon the Hebrews with their army, where [the ridges of] the mountains were closed with the sea; which army they placed at the chops of the mountains, that so they might deprive them of any passage into the plain.

4. When the Hebrews, therefore, were neither able to bear up, being thus, as it were, besieged, because they wanted provisions, nor saw any possible way of escaping; and if they should have thought of fighting, they had no weapons; they expected a universal destruction, unless they delivered themselves up to the Egyptians. So they laid the blame on Moses, and forgot all the signs that had been wrought by God for the recovery of their freedom; and this so far, that their incredulity prompted them to throw stones at the prophet, while he encouraged them and promised them deliverance; and they resolved that they would deliver themselves up to the Egyptians. So there was sorrow and lamentation among the women and children, who had nothing but destruction before their eyes, while they were encompassed with mountains, the sea, and their enemies, and discerned no way of flying from them.

5. But Moses, though the multitude looked fiercely at him, did not, however, give over the care of them, but despised all dangers, out of his trust in God, who, as he had afforded them the several steps already taken for the recovery of their liberty, which he had foretold them, would not now suffer them to be subdued by their enemies, to be either made slaves or be slain by them; and, standing in the midst of them, he said, "It is not just of us to distrust even men, when they have hitherto well managed our affairs, as if they would not be the same men hereafter; but it is no better than madness, at this time, to despair of the providence of God, by whose power all those things have been performed which he promised, when you expected no such things: I mean all that I have been concerned in for your deliverance and escape from slavery. Nay, when we are in the utmost distress, as you see we are, we ought rather to hope that God will succour us, by whose operation it is that we are now encompassed within this narrow place, that he may deliver us out of such difficulties as are otherwise insurmountable, and out of which neither you nor your enemies expect you can be delivered, and may at once demonstrate his own power and his providence over us. Nor does God use to give his help in small difficulties to those whom he favours, but in such cases where no one can see how any hope in man can better their condition. Depend, therefore, upon such a protector as is able to make small things great, and to shew that this mighty force against you is nothing but weakness, and be not affrighted at the Egyptian army, nor do you despair of being preserved, because the sea before and the mountains behind afford you no opportunity for flying; for even these mountains, if God so please, may be made plain ground for you, and the sea become dry land."

CHAPTER XVI

HOW THE SEA WAS DIVIDED ASUNDER FOR THE HEBREWS, WHEN THEY WERE PURSUED BY THE EGYPTIANS, AND SO GAVE THEM AN OPPORTUNITY OF·ESCAPING FROM THEM

1. WHEN Moses had said this, he led them to the sea, while the Egyptians looked on, for they were within sight. Now these were so distressed by the toil of their pursuit that they thought proper to put off fighting till the next day. But when Moses was come to the sea-shore, he took his rod, and made supplication to God, and called upon him to be their helper and assistant; and said, "Thou art not ignorant, O Lord, that it is beyond human strength and human contrivance to avoid the difficulties we are now under; but it must be thy work altogether to procure deliverance to this army, which has left Egypt at thy appointment. We despair of any other assistance or contrivance, and have recourse only to that hope we have in thee; and if there be any method that can promise us an escape by thy providence, we look up to thee for it. And let it come quickly, and manifest thy power to us; and do thou raise up this people unto good courage and hope of deliverance, who are deeply sunk into a disconsolate state of mind. We are in a helpless place, but still it is a place that thou possessest; still the sea is thine, the mountains also that enclose us are thine; so that these mountains will open themselves if thou commandest them, and the sea also, if thou commandest it, will become dry land. Nay, we might escape by a flight through the air, if thou shouldst determine we should have that way of salvation."

2. When Moses had thus addressed himself to God, he smote the sea with his rod, which parted asunder at the stroke, and receiving those waters into itself, left the ground dry, as a road and a place of flight for the Hebrews. Now when Moses saw this appearance of God, and that the sea went out of its own place and left dry land, he went first of all into it, and bid the Hebrews to follow him along that divine road, and to rejoice at the danger their enemies that followed them were in: and gave thanks to God for this so surprising a deliverance which appeared from him.

3. Now, while these Hebrews made no stay, but went on earnestly, as led by God's presence with them, the Egyptians supposed at first that they were distracted, and were going rashly upon manifest destruction. But when they saw that they were going a great way without any harm, and that no obstacle or difficulty fell in their journey, they made haste to pursue them, hoping that the sea would be calm for them also.

Egypt, told me that he went the same way from Egypt to mount Sinai, which he supposed the Israelites of old travelled; and that he found several mountainous tracks that ran down towards the Red Sea. He thought the Israelites had proceeded as far as the desert of Etham, (Exod. xiii. 20,) when they were commanded by God to return back, (Exod. xiv. 2,) and to pitch their camp between Migdol and the sea; and that when they were not able to fly, unless by sea, they were shut in on each side by mountains. He also thought we might evidently learn hence, how it might be said that the Israelites were in Etham before they went over the sea, and yet might be said to have come into Etham after they had passed over the sea also. Besides, he gave me an account how he passed over a river in a boat near the city Suez, which he says must needs be the Heroopolis of the ancients, since that city could not be situate anywhere else in that neighbourhood."

As to the famous passage produced here by Dr Bernard, out of Herodotus, as the most ancient heathen testimony of the Israelites coming from the Red Sea into Palestine, Bishop Cumberland has shewn that it belongs to the old Canaanite or Phœnician shepherds, and their retiring out of Egypt into Canaan or Phœnicia, long before the days of Moses. Sanchoniatho, p. 374, &c.

They put their horse foremost, and went down themselves into the sea. Now the Hebrews, while these were putting on their armour, and therein spending their time, were beforehand with them, and escaped them, and got first over to the land on the other side without any hurt. Whence the others were encouraged, and more courageously pursued them, as hoping no harm would come to them neither: but the Egyptians were not aware that they went into a road made for the Hebrews, and not for others; that this road was made for the deliverance of those in danger, but not for those that were earnest to make use of it for the others' destruction. As soon, therefore, as ever the whole Egyptian army was within it, the sea flowed to its own place, and came down with a torrent raised by storms of wind,* and encompassed the Egyptians. Showers of rain also came down from the sky, and dreadful thunders and lightning, with flashes of fire. Thunderbolts also were darted upon them; nor was there anything which used to be sent by God upon men as indications of his wrath which did not happen at this time, for a dark and dismal night oppressed them. And thus did all these men perish, so that there was not one man left to be a messenger of this calamity to the rest of the Egyptians.

4. But the Hebrews were not able to contain themselves for joy at their wonderful deliverance, and destruction of their enemies. Now, indeed, supposing themselves firmly delivered, when those that would have forced them into slavery were destroyed, and when they found they had God so evidently for their protector; and now these Hebrews having escaped the danger they were in, after this manner, and besides that, seeing their enemies punished in such a way as is never recorded of any other men whomsoever, were all the night employed in singing of hymns, and in mirth.† Moses also composed a song

---

* Of these storms of wind, thunder, and lightning, at this drowning of Pharaoh's army, almost wanting in our copies of Exodus, but fully extant in that of David, (Ps. lxxvii. 16, 17, 18,) and in that of Josephus here, see Essay on the Old Test., Append. pp. 154, 155.

† What some have here objected against this passage of the Israelites over the Red Sea, in this one night, from the common maps—viz., that this sea being here about thirty miles broad, so great an army could not pass over it in so short a time, is a great mistake. Mons. Thevenot, an authentic eye-witness, informs us that this sea, for about five days' journey, is nowhere more than about eight miles over-cross, and in one place but four or five miles, according to De Lisle's map, which is made from the best travellers themselves, and not copied from others. What has been further objected against this passage of the Israelites and drowning of the Egyptians, being miraculous also—viz., that Moses might carry the Israelites over at a low tide without any miracle, while yet the Egyptians, not knowing the tide so well as he, might be drowned upon the return of the tide, is a strange story indeed! That Moses, who never had lived here, should know the quantity and time of the flux and reflux of the Red Sea better than the Egyptians themselves in its neighbourhood! Yet does Artapanus, an ancient heathen historian, inform us that this was what the more ignorant Memphites, who lived at a great distance, pretended, though he confesses that the more learned Heliopolitans, who lived much nearer, owned the destruction of the Egyptians and the deliverance of the Israelites to have been miraculous; and De Castro, a mathematician, who surveyed this sea with great exactness, informs us that there is no great flux or reflux in this part of the Red Sea, to give a colour to this hypothesis; nay, that at the elevation of the tide there is little above half the height of a man. See Essay on the Old Test., Append. pp. 239, 240. So vain and groundless are these and the like evasions and subterfuges of our modern sceptics and unbelievers, and so certainly do thorough inquiries and authentic evidence disprove and confute such evasions and subterfuges upon all occasions!

---

unto God, containing his praises, and a thanksgiving for his kindness, in hexameter verse.‡

5. As for myself, I have delivered every part of this history as I found it in the sacred books; nor let any one wonder at the strangeness of the narration, if a way were discovered to those men of old time, who were free from the wickedness of the modern ages, whether it happened by the will of God, or whether it happened of its own accord,—while, for the sake of those that accompanied Alexander, king of Macedonia, who yet lived, comparatively, but a little while ago, the Pamphylian Sea retired and afforded them a passage § through itself, when they had no other

---

‡ What that hexameter verse in which Moses's triumphant song is here said to be written distinctly means, our present ignorance of the old Hebrew metre or measure will not let us determine. Nor does it appear to me certain that even Josephus himself had a distinct notion of it, though he speaks of several sorts of that metre or measure both here and elsewhere. Antiq. book iv. ch. viii. sect. 44, and book vii. ch. xii. sect 3.

§ Take here the original passages of the four old authors that still remain as to this transit of Alexander the Great over the Pamphylian Sea; I mean, of Callisthenes, Strabo, Arrian, and Appian. As to Callisthenes, who himself accompanied Alexander in this expedition, Eustathius, in his Notes on the third Iliad of Homer, (as Dr Bernard here informs us,) says, that "this Callisthenes wrote how the Pamphylian Sea did not only open a passage for Alexander, but, by rising and elevating its waters, did pay him homage as its king." Strabo's account is this, (Geog. book xiv. p. 666:) "Now about Phaselis is that narrow passage, by the sea-side, through which Alexander led his army. There is a mountain called Climax, which adjoins to the Sea of Pamphylia, leaving a narrow passage on the shore, which in calm weather is bare, so as to be passable by travellers; but when the sea overflows it is covered to a great degree by the waves. Now then, the ascent by the mountains being round about and steep, in still weather they make use of the road along the coast; but Alexander fell into the winter season, and committing himself chiefly to fortune, he marched on before the waves retired; and so it happened that they were a whole day in journeying over it, and were under water up to the navel." Arrian's account is this, (book i. pp. 72, 73:) "When Alexander removed from Phaselis, he sent some part of his army over the mountains to Perga, which road the Thracians shewed him. A difficult way it was, but short. However, he himself conducted those that were with him by the sea-shore. This road is impassable at any other time than when the north wind blows; but if the south wind prevail there is no passing by the shore. Now at this time, after strong south winds, a north wind blew, and that not without the Divine Providence, (as both he and they that were with him supposed,) and afforded him an easy and quick passage." Appian, when he compares Cæsar and Alexander together (De Bel. Civil. book ii. p. 522) says, "That they both depended on their boldness and fortune, as much as on their skill in war. As an instance of which, Alexander journeyed over a country without water, in the heat of summer, to the oracle of [Jupiter] Hammon, and quickly passed over the Bay of Pamphylia, when, by Divine Providence, the sea was cut off—thus Providence restraining the sea on his account, as it had sent him rain when he travelled [over the desert.]"

N.B.—Since, in the days of Josephus, as he assures us, all the more numerous original historians of Alexander gave the account he has here set down as to the providential going back of the waters of the Pamphylian Sea, when he was going with his army to destroy the Persian monarchy, which the forenamed authors now remaining fully confirm, it is without all just foundation that Josephus is here blamed by some late writers for quoting those ancient authors upon the present occasion; nor can the reflections of Plutarch, or any other author later than Josephus, be in the least here alleged to contradict him. Josephus went by all the evidence he then had, and that evidence of the most authentic sort also. So that, whatever the moderns may think of the thing itself, there is hence not the least colour for finding fault with Josephus: he would rather have been much to blame had he omitted these quotations.

way to go; I mean, when it was the will of God to destroy the monarchy of the Persians: and this is confessed to be true by all that have written about the actions of Alexander; but as to these events, let every one determine as he pleases.

6. On the next day Moses gathered together the weapons of the Egyptians, which were brought to the camp of the Hebrews by the current of the sea, and the force of the winds assisting it; and he conjectured that this also happened by Divine Providence, that so they might not be destitute of weapons. So when he had ordered the Hebrews to arm themselves with them, he led them to mount Sinai, in order to offer sacrifice to God, and to render oblations for the salvation of the multitude, as he was charged to do beforehand.

BOOK III

CONTAINING THE INTERVAL OF TWO YEARS,

FROM THE EXODUS OUT OF EGYPT TO THE REJECTION OF THAT GENERATION

CHAPTER I

HOW MOSES, WHEN HE HAD BROUGHT THE PEOPLE OUT OF EGYPT, LED THEM TO MOUNT SINAI; BUT NOT TILL THEY HAD SUFFERED MUCH IN THEIR JOURNEY

1. WHEN the Hebrews had obtained such a wonderful deliverance, the country was a great trouble to them, for it was entirely a desert, and without all sustenance for them; and also had exceeding little water, so that it not only was not at all sufficient for the men, but not enough to feed any of the cattle; for it was parched up, and had no moisture that might afford nutriment to the vegetables; so they were forced to travel over this country, as having no other country but this to travel in. They had indeed carried water along with them, from the land over which they had travelled before, as their conductor had bidden them: but when that was spent, they were obliged to draw water out of wells, with pain, by reason of the hardness of the soil. Moreover, what water they found was bitter, and not fit for drinking, and this in small quantities also; and as they thus travelled, they came late in the evening to a place called Marah,* which had that name from the badness of its water, for *Mar* denotes *bitterness.* Thither they came afflicted both by the tediousness of their journey, and by their want of food, for it entirely failed them at that time. Now here was a well, which made them choose to stay in the place, which, although it were not sufficient to satisfy so great an army, did yet afford them some comfort, as found in such desert places; for they heard from those who had been to search that there was nothing to be found if they travelled on further. Yet was this water bitter, and not fit for men to drink; and not only so, but it was intolerable even to the cattle themselves.

2. When Moses saw how much the people were cast down, and that the occasion of it could not be contradicted, for the people were not in the nature of a complete army of men, who might oppose a manly fortitude to the necessity that distressed them; the multitude of the children, and of the women also, being of too weak capacities to be persuaded by reason, blunted the courage of the men themselves,—he was therefore in great difficulties, and made everybody's calamity his own; for they ran all of them to him, and begged of him; the women begged for their infants, and the men for the women, that he would not overlook them, but procure some way or other for their deliverance. He therefore betook himself to prayer to God that he would change the water from its present badness and make it fit for drinking. And when God had granted him that favour, he took the top of a stick that lay down at his feet, and divided it in the middle, and made the section lengthways. He then let it down into the well, and persuaded the Hebrews that God had hearkened to his prayers, and had promised to render the water such as they desired it to be, in case they would be subservient to him in what he should enjoin them to do, and this not after a remiss or negligent manner. And when they asked what they were to do in order to have the water changed for the better, he bid the strongest men among them that stood there, to draw up water,† and told them that, when the greatest part was

---

* Dr Bernard takes notice here that this place *Mar*, where the waters were bitter, is called by the Syrians and Arabians *Mariri*, and by the Syrians sometimes *Morath*, all derived from the Hebrew *Mar.* He also takes notice that it is called The Bitter Fountain by Pliny himself; which waters remain there to this day, and are still bitter, as Thevenot assures us; and that there are also abundance of palm-trees. See his Travels, part i. chap. xxvi. p. 166.

† The additions here to Moses's account of the sweetening of the waters at Marah, seems derived from some ancient profane author, and he such an author also as looks less authentic than are usually followed by Josephus. Philo has not a syllable of these additions, nor any other ancienter writer that we know of. Had Josephus written these his Antiquities for the use of Jews, he would hardly have given them these very improbable circumstances; but writing to Gentiles, that they might not complain of his omission of any accounts of such miracles derived from Gentiles, he did not think proper to conceal what he had met with there about this matter; which procedure is perfectly agreeable to the character and usage of Josephus upon many occasions. This note is, I confess, barely conjectural; and since Josephus never tells us when his own copy, taken out of the temple, had such additions, or when any ancient notes supplied them; or indeed when they are derived from Jewish, and when from Gentile antiquity,—we can go no further than bare conjectures in such cases; only the notions of Jews were generally so different from those of Gentiles, that we may sometimes make no improbable conjectures to which sort such ad-

drawn up, the remainder would be fit to drink: so they laboured at it till the water was so agitated and purged as to be fit to drink.

3. And now removing from thence, they came to Elim; which place looked well at a distance, for there was a grove of palm-trees; but when they came near to it, it appeared to be a bad place, for the palm-trees were no more than seventy; and they were ill-grown and creeping trees by the want of water, for the country about was all parched, and no moisture sufficient to water them, and make them hopeful and useful, was derived to them from the fountains, which were in number twelve: they were rather a few moist places than springs, which not breaking out of the ground, nor running over, could not sufficiently water the trees. And when they dug into the sand they met with no water; and if they took a few drops of it into their hands, they found it to be useless, on account of its mud. The trees also were too weak to bear fruit, for want of being sufficiently cherished and enlivened by the water. So they laid the blame on their conductor, and made heavy complaints against him, and said that this their miserable state, and the experience they had of adversity, were owing to him; for that they had then journeyed an entire thirty days, and had spent all the provisions they had brought with them, and meeting with no relief, they were in a very desponding condition. And by fixing their attention upon nothing but their present misfortunes, they were hindered from remembering what deliverances they had received from God, and those by the virtue and wisdom of Moses also; so they were very angry at their conductor, and were zealous in their attempt to stone him, as the direct occasion of their present miseries.

4. But as for Moses himself, while the multitude were irritated and bitterly set against him, he cheerfully relied upon God, and upon his consciousness of the care he had taken of these his own people: and he came into the midst of them, even while they clamoured against him, and had stones in their hands in order to despatch him. Now he was of an agreeable presence, and very able to persuade the people by his speeches; accordingly he began to mitigate their anger, and exhort them not to be overmindful of their present adversities, lest they should thereby suffer the benefits that had formerly been bestowed on them to slip out of their memories; and he desired them by no means, on account of their present uneasiness, to cast those great and wonderful favours and gifts, which they had obtained of God, out of their minds, but to expect deliverance out of those their present troubles which they could not free themselves from, and this by the means of that Divine Providence which watched over them; seeing it is probable that God tries their virtue, and exercises their patience by these adversities, that it may appear what fortitude they have, and what memory they retain of his former wonderful works in their favour, and whether they will not think of them upon occasion of the miseries they now feel. He told them it appeared they were not really good men, either in patience, or in remembering what had been successfully done for them, sometimes by contemning God and his commands, when by those commands they left the land of Egypt; and

sometimes by behaving themselves ill towards him who was the servant of God, and this when he had never deceived them, either in what he said, or had ordered them to do by God's command. He also put them in mind of all that had passed: how the Egyptians were destroyed when they attempted to detain them, contrary to the command of God; and after what manner the very same rivers was to the others bloody, and not fit for drinking, but was to them sweet and fit for drinking; and how they went a new road through the sea, which fled a long way from them, by which very means they were themselves preserved, but saw their enemies destroyed; and that when they were in want of weapons, God gave them plenty of them:—and so he recounted all the particular instances, how when they were, in appearance, just going to be destroyed, God had saved them in a surprising manner; that he had still the same power, and that they ought not even now to despair of his providence over them; and accordingly he exhorted them to continue quiet, and to consider that help would not come too late, though it come not immediately, if it be present with them before they suffer any great misfortune; that they ought to reason thus: that God delays to assist them, not because he has no regard to them, but because he will first try their fortitude, and the pleasure they take in their freedom, that he may learn whether you have souls great enough to bear want of food, and scarcity of water, on its account; or whether you rather love to be slaves, as cattle are slaves to such as own them, and feed them liberally, but only in order to make them more useful in their service. That as for himself, he shall not be so much concerned for his own preservation; for if he die unjustly, he shall not reckon it any affliction; but that he is concerned for them, lest, by casting stones at him, they should be thought to condemn God himself.

5. By this means Moses pacified the people, and restrained them from stoning him, and brought them to repent of what they were going to do; and because he thought the necessity they were under made their passion less unjustifiable, he thought he ought to apply himself to God by prayer and supplication; and going up to an eminence, he requested of God for some succour for the people, and some way of deliverance from the want they were in, because in him, and in him alone, was their hope of salvation; and he desired that he would forgive what necessity had forced the people to do, since such was the nature of mankind, hard to please, and very complaining under adversities. Accordingly God promised he would take care of them, and afford them the succour they were desirous of. Now when Moses had heard this from God, he came down to the multitude; but as soon as they saw him joyful at the promises he had received from God, they changed their sad countenances into gladness. So he placed himself in the midst of them, and told them he came to bring them from God a deliverance from their present distresses. Accordingly a little after came a vast number of quails, which is a bird more plentiful in this Arabian gulf than anywhere else, flying over the sea, and hovered over them, till wearied with their laborious flight, and, indeed, as usual, flying very near to the earth, they fell down upon the Hebrews, who caught them and satisfied their hunger with them, and supposed that this was the method whereby God meant to supply them with food. Upon which Moses returned thanks to God for affording them his assistance so suddenly, and sooner than he had promised them.

6. But presently after this first supply of food,

---

ditions belong. See also somewhat like these additions in Josephus's account of Elisha's making sweet the bitter and barren spring near Jericho, (War, b. iv. ch. viii. sect. 3.)

ISRAEL DRINKING FROM THE ROCK

he sent them a second; for as Moses was lifting up his hands in prayer, a dew fell down; and Moses, when he found it stick to his hands, supposed this was also come for food from God to them; he tasted it, and perceiving that the people knew not what it was, and thought it snowed, and that it was what usually fell at that time of the year, he informed them that this dew did not fall from heaven after the manner they imagined, but came for their preservation and sustenance. So he tasted it, and gave them some of it, that they might be satisfied about what he had told them. They also imitated their conductor, and were pleased with the food, for it was like honey in sweetness and pleasant taste, but like in its body to bdellium, one of the sweet spices, and in bigness equal to coriander seed. And very earnest they were in gathering it; but they were enjoined to gather it equally*—the measure of an omer for each one every day—because this food should not come in too small a quantity, lest the weaker might not be able to get their share, by reason of the overbearing of the strong in collecting it. However, these strong men, when they had gathered more than the measure appointed for them, had no more than others, but only tired themselves more in gathering it, for they found no more than an omer a-piece; and the advantage they got by what was superfluous was none at all, it corrupting, both by the worms breeding in it, and by its bitterness. So divine and wonderful a food was this! It also supplied the want of other sorts of food to those that fed on it; and even now, in all that place, this manna comes down in rain,† according to what Moses then obtained of God, to send it to the people for their sustenance. Now the Hebrews call this food *manna;* for the particle *man,* in our language, is the asking of a question, *What is this?* So the Hebrews were very joyful at what was sent them from heaven. Now they made use of this food for forty years, or as long as they were in the wilderness.

7. As soon as they were removed thence, they came to Rephidim, being distressed to the last degree by thirst; and while in the foregoing days they had lit on a few small fountains, but now found the earth entirely destitute of water, they were in an evil case. They again turned their anger against Moses; but he at first avoided the fury of the multitude, and then betook himself to prayer to God, beseeching him, that as he had

given them food when they were in the greatest want of it, so he would give them drink, since the favour of giving them food was of no value to them while they had nothing to drink: and God did not long delay to give it them, but promised Moses that he would procure them a fountain, and plenty of water from a place they did not expect any; so he commanded him to smite the rock which they saw lying there,‡ with his rod, and out of it to receive plenty of what they wanted; for he had taken care that drink should come to them without any labour or painstaking. When Moses had received this command from God, he came to the people, who waited for him, and looked upon him; for they saw already that he was coming apace from his eminence. As soon as he was come, he told them that God would deliver them from their present distress, and had granted them an unexpected favour; and informed them, that a river should run for their sakes out of the rock; but they were amazed at that hearing, supposing they were of necessity to cut the rock in pieces, now they were distressed by their thirst, and by their journey—while Moses, only smiting the rock with his rod, opened a passage, and out of it burst water, and that in great abundance, and very clear; but they were astonished at this wonderful effect, and, as it were, quenched their thirst by the very sight of it. So they drank this pleasant, this sweet water; and such it seemed to be, as might well be expected where God was the donor. They were also in admiration how Moses was honoured by God; and they made grateful returns of sacrifices to God for his providence towards them. Now that Scripture which is laid up in the temple, § informs us, how God foretold to Moses, that water should in this manner be derived out of the rock.

CHAPTER II

HOW THE AMALEKITES, AND THE NEIGHBOURING NATIONS, MADE WAR WITH THE HEBREWS, AND WERE BEATEN, AND LOST A GREAT PART OF THEIR ARMY

1. THE name of the Hebrews began already to be everywhere renowned, and rumours about them ran abroad. This made the inhabitants of those countries to be in no small fear. Accordingly they sent ambassadors to one another, and exhorted one another to defend themselves, and to endeavour to destroy these men. Those that induced the rest to do so, were such as inhabited Gobolitis and Petra. They were called *Amalekites,* and were the most warlike of the nations that lived thereabout; and whose kings exhorted one another and their neighbours to go to this war against the Hebrews; telling them that an army of strangers, and such a one as had run away from slavery under the Egyptians, lay in wait to ruin them; which army they were not, in common prudence and regard to their own safety, to overlook, but to crush them before they gather strength, and come to be in prosperity; and perhaps attack them first in a hostile

---

* It seems to me, from what Moses, (Ex. xvi. 18,) St Paul, (2 Cor. viii. 15,) and Josephus here say, compared together, that the quantity of manna that fell daily and did not putrify, was just so much as came to an omer a-piece, through the whole host of Israel, and no more.

† This supposal that the sweet honey-dew or manna, so celebrated in ancient and modern authors, as falling usually in Arabia, was of the very same sort with this manna sent to the Israelites, savours more of Gentilism than of Judaism or Christianity. It is not improbable that some ancient Gentile author, read by Josephus, so thought, nor would he here contradict him; though just before, and (Antiq. b. iv. ch. iii. sect. 2) he seems directly to allow that it had not been seen before. However, this food from heaven is here described to be like snow, and in Artapanus, a heathen writer, it is compared to meal, "like to oatmeal, in colour like to snow, rained down by God," (Essay on the Old Test. Append. p. 239;) but as to the derivation of the word *manna,* whether from *man,* which Josephus says then signified *What is it?* or from *mannah, to divide, i.e.,* a *dividend* or *portion* allotted to every one, it is uncertain: I incline to the latter derivation. This manna is called *angels' food,* (Ps. lxxviii. 26,) and by our Saviour, (John vi. 31, &c.,) as well as by Josephus here and elsewhere, (Antiq. b. iii. ch. v. sect. 3,) said to be sent the Jews from heaven.

‡ This rock is there at this day, as the travellers agree, and must be the same that was there in the days of Moses, as being too large to be brought thither by our modern carriages.

§ Note here that the small book of the principal laws of Moses is ever said to be laid up in the holy house itself; but the larger Pentateuch, as here, somewhere within the limits of the temple and its courts only. See Antiq. b. v. ch. i. sect. 17.

manner, as presuming upon our indolence in not attacking them before; and that we ought to avenge ourselves of them for what they have done in the wilderness, but that this cannot be so well done when they have once laid their hands on our cities and our goods: that those who endeavour to crush a power in its first rise, are wiser than those that endeavour to put a stop to its progress when it is become formidable; for these last seem to be angry only at the flourishing of others, but the former do not leave any room for their enemies to become troublesome to them. After they had sent such embassages to the neighbouring nations, and among one another, they resolved to attack the Hebrews in battle.

2. These proceedings of the people of those countries occasioned perplexity and trouble to Moses, who expected no such warlike preparations; and when these nations were ready to fight, and the multitude of the Hebrews were obliged to try the fortune of war, they were in a mighty disorder, and in want of all necessaries, and yet were to make war with men who were thoroughly well prepared for it. Then, therefore, it was that Moses began to encourage them, to exhort them to have a good heart, and rely on God's assistance, by which they had been advanced into a state of freedom, and to hope for victory over those who were ready to fight with them, in order to deprive them of that blessing: that they were to suppose their own army to be numerous, wanting nothing, neither weapons, nor money, nor provisions, nor such other conveniences as, when men are in possession of, they fight undauntedly; and that they are to judge themselves to have all these advantages in the divine assistance. They are also to suppose the enemy's army to be small, unarmed, weak, and such as want those conveniences which they know must be wanted, when it is God's will that they shall be beaten; and how valuable God's assistance is, they had experienced in abundance of trials; and those such as were more terrible than war, for that is only against men; but these were against famine and thirst, things indeed that are in their own nature insuperable; as also against mountains, and that sea which afforded them no way for escaping; yet had all these difficulties been conquered by God's gracious kindness to them. So he exhorted them to be courageous at this time, and to look upon their entire prosperity to depend on the present conquest of their enemies.

3. And with these words did Moses encourage the multitude, who then called together the princes of their tribes and their chief men; both separately and conjointly. The young men he charged to obey their elders, and the elders to hearken to their leader. So the people were elevated in their minds, and ready to try their fortune in battle, and hoped to be thereby at length delivered from all their miseries: nay, they desired that Moses would immediately lead them against their enemies without the least delay, that no backwardness might be a hindrance to their present resolution. So Moses sorted all that were fit for war into different troops, and set Joshua, the son of Nun, of the tribe of Ephraim, over them; one that was of great courage, and patient to undergo labours; of great abilities to understand, and to speak what was proper; and very serious in the worship of God; and indeed made, like another Moses, a teacher of piety towards God. He also appointed a small party of the armed men to be near the water, and to take care of the children, and the women, and of the entire camp. So that whole

night they prepared themselves for the battle; they took their weapons, if any of them had such as were well made, and attended to their commanders as ready to rush forth to the battle as soon as Moses should give the word of command. Moses also kept awake, teaching Joshua after what manner he should order his camp. But when the day began, Moses called for Joshua again, and exhorted him to approve himself in deeds such a one as his reputation made men expect from him; and to gain glory by the present expedition, in the opinion of those under him, for his exploits in this battle. He also gave a particular exhortation to the principal men of the Hebrews, and encouraged the whole army as it stood armed before him. And when he had thus animated the army, both by his words and works, and prepared everything, he retired to a mountain, and committed the army to God and to Joshua.

4. So the armies joined battle; and it came to a close fight, hand to hand, both sides shewing great alacrity, and encouraging one another. And indeed, while Moses stretched out his hand towards heaven,[*] the Hebrews were too hard for the Amalekites; but Moses not being able to sustain his hands, thus stretched out, (for as often as he let down his hands, so often were his own people worsted,) he bade his brother Aaron, and Hur, their sister Miriam's husband, to stand on each side of him, and take hold of his hands, and not permit his weariness to prevent it, but to assist him in the extension of his hands. When this was done, the Hebrews conquered the Amalekites by main force; and indeed they had all perished, unless the approach of the night had not obliged the Hebrews to desist from killing any more. So our forefathers obtained a most signal and most seasonable victory; for they not only overcame those that fought against them, but terrified also the neighbouring nations, and got great and splendid advantages, which they obtained of their enemies by their hard pains in this battle: for when they had taken the enemy's camp, they got ready booty for the public, and for their own private families, whereas till then they had not any sort of plenty of even necessary food. The forementioned battle, when they had once got it, was also the occasion of their prosperity, not only for the present, but for the future ages also; for they not only made slaves of the bodies of their enemies, but subdued their minds also, and after this battle, became terrible to all that dwelt round about them. Moreover, they acquired a vast quantity of riches; for a great deal of silver and gold was left in the enemy's camp; as also brazen vessels, which they made common use of in their families; many utensils also that were embroidered, there were of both sorts, that is of what were weaved, and what were the ornaments of their armour, and other things that served for use in the family, and for the furniture of their rooms; they got also the prey of their cattle, and of whatsoever uses to follow camps, when they remove from one place to

---

[*] This eminent circumstance seems to me the earliest intimation we have of the proper posture used of old in solemn prayer, which was the stretching out of the hands [and eyes] towards heaven, as other passages of the Old and New Testament inform us. Nay, by the way, this posture seems to have continued in the Christian Church, till the clergy, instead of learning their prayers by heart, read them out of a book, which is in a great measure inconsistent with such an elevated posture, and which seems to me to have been only a later practice, introduced under the corrupt state of the Church.

another. So the Hebrews now valued themselves upon their courage, and claimed great merit for their valour; and they perpetually inured themselves to take pains, by which they deemed every difficulty might be surmounted. Such were the consequences of this battle.

5. On the next day, Moses stripped the dead bodies of their enemies, and gathered together the armour of those that were fled, and gave rewards to such as had signalised themselves in the action; and highly commended Joshua, their general, who was attested to by all the army, on account of the great actions he had done. Nor was any one of the Hebrews slain; but the slain of the enemy's army were too many to be enumerated. So Moses offered sacrifices of thanksgiving to God, and built an altar, which he named *The Lord the Conqueror.* He also foretold that the Amalekites should utterly be destroyed, and that hereafter none of them should remain, because they fought against the Hebrews, and this when they were in the wilderness, and in their distress also. Moreover, he refreshed the army with feasting. And thus did they fight this first battle with those that ventured to oppose them, after they were gone out of Egypt. But when Moses had celebrated this festival for the victory, he permitted the Hebrews to rest for a few days, and then he brought them out after the fight, in order of battle; for they had now many soldiers in light armour. And going gradually on, he came to mount Sinai, in three months' time after they were removed out of Egypt; at which mountain, as we have before related, the vision of the Bush, and the other wonderful appearances, had happened.

CHAPTER III

THAT MOSES KINDLY RECEIVED HIS FATHER-IN-LAW, JETHRO, WHEN HE CAME TO HIM TO MOUNT SINAI

Now when Raguel, Moses's father-in-law, understood in what a prosperous condition his affairs were, he willingly came to meet him. And Moses took Zipporah, his wife, and his children, and pleased himself with his coming. And when he had offered sacrifice, he made a feast for the multitude, near the Bush he had formerly seen; which multitude, every one, according to their families, partook of the feast. But Aaron and his family took Raguel, and sung hymns to God, as to him who had been the author and procurer of their deliverance, and their freedom. They also praised their conductor, as him by whose virtue it was that all things had succeeded so well with them. Raguel also, in his eucharistical oration to Moses, made great encomiums upon the whole multitude: and he could not but admire Moses for his fortitude, and that humanity he had shewn in the delivery of his friends.

CHAPTER IV

HOW RAGUEL SUGGESTED TO MOSES TO SET HIS PEOPLE IN ORDER, UNDER THEIR RULERS OF THOUSANDS, AND RULERS OF HUNDREDS, WHO LIVED WITHOUT ORDER BEFORE; AND HOW MOSES COMPLIED IN ALL THINGS WITH HIS FATHER-IN-LAW'S ADMONITION

1. THE next day, Raguel saw Moses in the midst of a crowd of business, for he determined the differences of those that referred them to him, every one still going to him, and supposing

that they should then only obtain justice, if he were the arbitrator; and those that lost their causes thought it no harm while they thought they lost them justly and not by partiality. Raguel, however, said nothing to him at that time, as not desirous to be any hindrance to such as had a mind to make use of the virtue of their conductor. But afterward he took him to himself, and when he had him alone, he instructed him in what he ought to do; and advised him to leave the trouble of lesser causes to others, but himself to take care of the greater, and of the people's safety; for that certain others of the Hebrews might be found that were fit to determine causes, but that nobody but a Moses could take care of the safety of so many ten thousands. "Be not, therefore," says he, "insensible of thine own virtue, and what thou hast done by ministering under God to the people's preservation. Permit, therefore, the determination of common causes to be done by others, but do thou reserve thyself to the attendance on God only, and look out for methods of preserving the multitude from their present distress. Make use of the method I suggest to you, as to human affairs; and take a review of the army, and appoint chosen rulers over tens of thousands, and then over thousands; then divide them into five hundreds, and again into hundreds, and into fifties; and set rulers over each of them, who may distinguish them into thirties, and keep them in order; and at last number them by twenties and by tens: and let there be one commander over each number, to be denominated from the number of those over whom they are rulers, but such as the whole multitude have tried, and do approve of, as being good and righteous men;[*] and let those rulers decide the controversies they have one with another. But if any great cause arise, let them bring the cognisance of it before the rulers of a higher dignity; but if any great difficulty arise that is too hard for even their determination, let them send it to thee. By these means two advantages will be gained; the Hebrews will have justice done them, and thou wilt be able to attend constantly on God, and procure him to be more favourable to the people."

2. This was the admonition of Raguel; and Moses received his advice very kindly, and acted according to his suggestion. Nor did he conceal the invention of this method, nor pretend to it himself, but informed the multitude who it was that invented it: nay, he has named Raguel in the books he wrote, as the person who invented this ordering of the people, as thinking it right to give a true testimony to worthy persons, although he might have gotten reputation by ascribing to himself the inventions of other men; whence we may learn the virtuous disposition of Moses: but of such his disposition, we shall have proper occasion to speak in other places of these books.

CHAPTER V

HOW MOSES ASCENDED UP TO MOUNT SINAI, AND RECEIVED LAWS FROM GOD, AND DELIVERED THEM TO THE HEBREWS

1. Now Moses called the multitude together,

---

[*] This manner of electing the judges and officers of the Israelites by the testimonies and suffrages of the people, before they were ordained by God, or by Moses, deserves to be carefully noted, because it was the pattern of the like manner of the choice and ordination of Bishops, Presbyters. and Deacons. in the Christian Church.

and told them that he was going from them unto mount Sinai to converse with God; to receive from him, and to bring back with him, a certain oracle; but he enjoined them to pitch their tents near the mountain, and prefer the habitation that was nearest to God, before one more remote. When he had said this, he ascended up to mount Sinai, which is the highest of all the mountains that are in that country,* and is not only very difficult to be ascended by men, on account of its vast altitude, but because of the sharpness of its precipices also; nay, indeed, it cannot be looked at without pain of the eyes: and besides this, it was terrible and inaccessible, on account of the rumour that passed about, that God dwelt there. But the Hebrews removed their tents as Moses had bidden them, and took possession of the lowest parts of the mountain; and were elevated in their minds, in expectation that Moses would return from God with promises of the good things he had proposed to them. So they feasted and waited for their conductor, and kept themselves pure as in other respects, and not accompanying with their wives for three days, as he had before ordered them to do. And they prayed to God that he would favourably receive Moses in his conversing with him, and bestow some such gift upon them by which they might live well. They also lived more plentifully as to their diet; and put on their wives and children more ornamental and decent clothing than they usually wore.

2. So they passed two days in this way of feasting; but on the third day, before the sun was up, a cloud spread itself over the whole camp of the Hebrews, such a one as none had before seen, and encompassed the place where they had pitched their tents; and while all the rest of the air was clear, there came strong winds, that raised up large showers of rain, which became a mighty tempest. There was also such lightning, as was terrible to those that saw it; and thunder with its thunderbolts, were sent down, and declared God to be there present in a gracious way to such as Moses desired he should be gracious. Now, as to these matters, every one of my readers may think as he pleases; but I am under a necessity of relating this history as it is described in the sacred books. This sight, and the amazing sound that came to their ears, disturbed the Hebrews to a prodigious degree, for they were not such as they were accustomed to; and then the rumour that was spread abroad, how God frequented that mountain, greatly astonished their minds, so they sorrowfully contained themselves within their tents, as both supposing Moses to be destroyed by the divine wrath, and expecting the like destruction for themselves.

3. When they were under these apprehensions, Moses appeared as joyful and greatly exalted. When they saw him, they were freed from their fear, and admitted of more comfortable hopes as to what was to come. The air also was become clear and pure of its former disorders, upon the appearance of Moses; whereupon he called together the people to a congregation, in order to their hearing what God would say to them: and when they were gathered together, he stood on an eminence whence they might all hear him, and said, "God has received me graciously, O Hebrews, as he has formerly done, and has suggested a happy method of living for you, and an order of political government, and is now present in the camp: I therefore charge you, for his sake and the sake of his works, and what we have done by his means, that you do not put a low value on what I am going to say, because the commands have been given by me that now deliver them to you, nor because it is the tongue of a man that delivers them to you; but if you have a due regard to the great importance of the things themselves, you will understand the greatness of him whose institutions they are, and who has not disdained to communicate them to me for our common advantage; for it is not to be supposed that the author of these institutions is barely Moses, the son of Amram and Jochebed, but he who obliged the Nile to run bloody for your sakes, and tamed the haughtiness of the Egyptians by various sorts of judgments; he who provided a way through the sea for us; he who contrived a method of sending us food from heaven, when we were distressed for want of it; he who made the water to issue out of a rock, when we had very little of it before; he by whose means Adam was made to partake of the fruits both of the land and of the sea; he by whose means Noah escaped the deluge; he by whose means our forefather Abraham, of a wandering pilgrim, was made the heir of the land of Canaan; he by whose means Isaac was born of parents that were very old; he by whose means Jacob was adorned with twelve virtuous sons; he by whose means Joseph became a potent lord over the Egyptians: he it is who conveys these instructions to you by me as his interpreter. And let them be to you venerable, and contended for more earnestly by you than your own children and your own wives; for if you will follow them, you will lead a happy life; you will enjoy the land fruitful, the sea calm, and the fruit of the womb born complete, as nature requires; you will be also terrible to your enemies: for I have been admitted into the presence of God, and been made a hearer of his incorruptible voice; so great is his concern for your nation, and its duration."

4. When he had said this, he brought the people, with their wives and children, so near the mountain, that they might hear God himself speaking to them about the precepts which they were to practise; that the energy of what should be spoken might not be hurt by its utterance by that tongue of a man, which could but imperfectly deliver it to their understanding. And they all heard a voice that came to all of them from above, insomuch that no one of these words escaped them, which Moses wrote on two tables; which it is not lawful for us to set down directly, but their import we will declare.†

5. The first commandment teaches us, That there is but one God, and that we ought to worship him only;—the second commands us not to make the image of any living creature to worship it;—the third, That we must not swear by God in a false matter;—the fourth, That we

---

* Since this mountain, Sinai, is here said to be the highest of all the mountains that are in that country it must be that now called St Katherine's, which is on third higher than that within a mile of it, now called Sinai, as Mons. Thevenot informs us, Travels. part i. chap. xxiii. p. 168. The other name of it, Horeb, is never used by Josephus, and perhaps was its name among the Egyptians only, whence the Israelites were lately come, as Sinai was its name among the Arabians, Canaanites, and other nations. Accordingly, when (1 Kings ix. 8) the Scripture says that Elijah came to Horeb, the mount of God, Josephus justly says, (Antiq. b. viii. chap. xiii. sect. 7,) that he came to the mountain called Sinai: and Jerome, here cited by Dr Hudson, says, that he took this mountain to have two names, Sinai and Choreb. De Nomin. Heb. p. 427.

† Of this and another like superstitious notion of the Pharisees, which Josephus complied with, see the note on Antiq. b. ii. chap. xii. sect. 4.

must keep the seventh day, by resting from all sorts of work;—the fifth, That we must honour our parents;—the sixth, That we must abstain from murder;—the seventh, That we must not commit adultery;—the eighth, That we must not be guilty of theft;—the ninth, That we must not bear false witness;—the tenth, That we must not admit of the desire of any thing that is another's.

6. Now when the multitude had heard God himself giving those precepts which Moses had discoursed of, they rejoiced at what was said; and the congregation was dissolved: but on the following days they came to his tent, and desired him to bring them, besides, other laws from God. Accordingly he appointed such laws, and afterwards informed them in what manner they should act in all cases; which laws I shall make mention of in their proper time; but I shall reserve most of those laws for another work,* and make there a distinct explication of them.

7. When matters were brought to this state, Moses went up again to mount Sinai, of which he had told them beforehand. He made his ascent in their sight; and while he stayed there so long a time, (for he was absent from them forty days,) fear seized upon the Hebrews, lest Moses should have come to any harm: nor was there any thing else so sad, and that so much troubled them, as this supposal that Moses was perished. Now there was a variety in their sentiments about it; some saying that he was fallen among wild beasts; and those that were of this opinion were chiefly such as were ill-disposed to him; but others said that he was departed, and gone to God; but the wiser sort were led by their reason to embrace neither of those opinions, with any satisfaction, thinking, that as it was a thing that sometimes happens to men to fall among wild beasts, and perish that way, so it was probable enough that he might depart and go to God, on account of his virtue; they therefore were quiet, and expected the event: yet were they exceeding sorry upon the supposal that they were deprived of a governor and a protector, such a one indeed as they could never recover again; nor would this suspicion give them leave to expect any comfortable event about this man, nor could they prevent their trouble and melancholy upon this occasion. However, the camp durst not remove all this while, because Moses had bidden them afore to stay there.

8. But when the forty days, and as many nights, were over, Moses came down, having tasted nothing of food usually appointed for the nourishment of men. His appearance filled the army with gladness, and he declared to them what care God had of them, and by what manner of conduct of their lives they might live happily; telling them, that during these days of his absence he had suggested to him also that he would have a tabernacle built for him, into which he would descend when he came to them; and how we should carry it about with us when we remove from this place; and that there would be no longer any occasion for going up to mount Sinai, but that he would himself come and pitch his tabernacle amongst us, and be present at our prayers; as also, that the tabernacle should be of such measures and construction as he had shewn him; and that you are to fall to the work,

* This other work of Josephus, here referred to, seems to be that which does not appear to have been ever published, which yet he intended to publish, about the reasons of many of the laws of Moses; of which see the note on the Preface, sect. 4.

and prosecute it diligently. When he had said this, he shewed them the two tables, with the ten commandments engraven upon them, five upon each table: and the writing was by the hand of God.

CHAPTER VI

CONCERNING THE TABERNACLE WHICH MOSES BUILT IN THE WILDERNESS FOR THE HONOUR OF GOD, AND WHICH SEEMED TO BE A TEMPLE

1. HEREUPON the Israelites rejoiced at what they had seen and heard of their conductor, and were not wanting in diligence according to their ability; for they brought silver, and gold, and brass, and of the best sorts of wood, and such as would not at all decay by putrefaction; camels' hair also, and sheep-skins, some of them dyed of a blue colour, and some of a scarlet; some brought the flower for the purple colour, and others for white, with wool dyed by the flowers aforementioned; and fine linen and precious stones, which those that use costly ornaments set in ouches of gold; they brought also a great quantity of spices; for of these materials did Moses build the tabernacle, which did not at all differ from a movable and ambulatory temple. Now when these things were brought together with great diligence, (for every one was ambitious to further the work even beyond their ability,) he set architects over the works, and this by the command of God; and indeed the very same which the people themselves would have chosen, had the election been allowed to them. Now their names are set down in writing in the sacred books; and they were these: Besaleel the son of Uri, of the tribe of Judah, the grandson of Miriam, the sister of their conductor; and Aholiab, the son of Ahisamach, of the tribe of Dan. Now the people went on with what they had undertaken with so great alacrity, that Moses was obliged to restrain them, by making proclamation, that what had been brought was sufficient, as the artificers had informed him; so they fell to work upon the building of the tabernacle. Moses also informed them, according to the direction of God, both what the measures were to be, and its largeness; and how many vessels it ought to contain for the use of the sacrifices. The women also were ambitious to do their parts, about the garments of the priests, and about other things that would be wanted in this work, both for ornament and for the divine service itself.

2. Now when all things were prepared, the gold, and the silver, and the brass, and what was woven, Moses, when he had appointed beforehand that there should be a festival, and that sacrifices should be offered according to every one's ability, reared up the tabernacle;† and when he had measured the open court, fifty cubits broad and a hundred long, he set up brazen pillars, five cubits high, twenty on each of the longer sides, and ten pillars for the breadth behind; every one of the pillars also had a ring. Their chapiters were of silver, but their bases were of brass: they resembled the sharp ends of spears, and were of brass, fixed into the ground. Cords were also put through the rings, and were tied at their further ends to brass nails of a cubit long, which, at every pillar, were driven into the

† Of this tabernacle of Moses, with its several parts and furniture, see my description at large, (chap. vi., vii., viii., ix., x., xi., xii., herein belonging.)

floor, and would keep the tabernacle from being shaken by the violence of winds; but a curtain of fine soft linen went round all the pillars, and hung down in a flowing and loose manner from their chapiters, and enclosed the whole space, and seemed not at all unlike to a wall about it. And this was the structure of three of the sides of this inclosure; but as for the fourth side, which was fifty cubits in extent, and was the front of the whole, twenty cubits of it were for the opening of the gates, wherein stood two pillars on each side, after the resemblance of open gates. These were made wholly of silver, and polished, and that all over, excepting the bases, which were of brass. Now on each side of the gates there stood three pillars, which were inserted into the concave bases of the gates, and were suited to them; and round them was drawn a curtain of fine linen; but to the gates themselves, which were twenty cubits in extent, and five in height, the curtain was composed of purple, and scarlet, and blue, and fine linen, and embroidered with many and divers sorts of figures, excepting the figures of animals. Within these gates was the brazen laver for purification, having a basin beneath of the like matter, whence the priests might wash their hands and sprinkle their feet; and this was the ornamental construction of the inclosure about the court of the tabernacle, which was exposed to the open air.

3. As to the tabernacle itself, Moses placed it in the middle of that court, with its front to the east, that, when the sun arose, it might send its first rays upon it. Its length, when it was set up, was thirty cubits, and its breadth was twelve [ten] cubits. The one of its walls was on the south, and the other was exposed to the north, and on the back part of it remained the west. It was necessary that its height should be equal to its breadth, [ten cubits.] There were also pillars made of wood, twenty on each side; they were wrought into a quadrangular figure, in breadth a cubit and a half, but the thickness was four fingers: they had thin plates of gold affixed to them on both sides, inwardly and outwardly: they had each of them two tenons belonging to them, inserted into their bases, and these were of silver, in each of which bases there was a socket to receive the tenon; but the pillars on the west wall were six. Now all these tenons and sockets accurately fitted one another, insomuch that the joints were invisible, and both seemed to be one entire and united wall. It was also covered with gold, both within and without. The number of pillars was equal on the opposite sides, and there were on each part twenty, and every one of them had the third part of a span in thickness; so that the number of thirty cubits were fully made up between them; but as to the wall behind, where the six pillars made up together only nine cubits, they made two other pillars, and cut them out of one cubit, which they placed in the corners, and made them equally fine with the other. Now every one of the pillars had rings of gold affixed to their fronts outward, as if they had taken root in the pillars, and stood one row over against another round about, through which were inserted bars gilt over with gold, each of them five cubits long, and these bound together the pillars, the head of one bar running into another, after the nature of one tenon inserted into another; but for the wall behind, there was but one row of bars that went through all the pillars, into which row ran the ends of the bars on each side of the longer walls; the male with its female being so fastened in their joints, that they held the whole firmly together; and for this reason was all this joined so fast together, that the tabernacle might not be shaken, either by the winds, or by any other means, but that it might preserve itself quiet and immovable continually.

4. As for the inside, Moses parted its length into three partitions. At the distance of ten cubits from the most secret end, Moses placed four pillars, the workmanship of which was the very same with that of the rest; and they stood upon the like bases with them, each a small matter distant from his fellow. Now the room within those pillars was the most holy place; but the rest of the room was the tabernacle, which was open for the priests. However, this proportion of the measures of the tabernacle proved to be an imitation of the system of the world: for that third part thereof which was within the four pillars, to which the priests were not admitted, is, as it were, a Heaven peculiar to God; but the space of the twenty cubits, is, as it were, sea and land, on which men live, and so this part is peculiar to the priests only: but at the front, where the entrance was made, they placed pillars of gold, that stood on bases of brass, in number seven; but then they spread over the tabernacle veils of fine linen and purple, and blue, and scarlet colours, embroidered. The first veil was ten cubits every way, and this they spread over the pillars which parted the temple, and kept the most holy place concealed within; and this veil was that which made this part not visible to any. Now the whole temple was called *The Holy Place;* but that part which was within the four pillars, and to which none were admitted, was called *The Holy of Holies.* This veil was very ornamental, and embroidered with all sorts of flowers which the earth produces; and there were interwoven into it all sorts of variety that might be an ornament, excepting the forms of animals. Another veil there was which covered the five pillars that were at the entrance. It was like the former in its magnitude, and texture, and colour; and at the corner of every pillar a ring retained it from the top downwards half the depth of the pillars, the other half affording an entrance for the priests, who crept under it. Over this there was a veil of linen, of the same largeness with the former: it was to be drawn this way or that way by cords, the rings of which, fixed to the texture of the veil, and to the cords also, were subservient to the drawing and undrawing of the veil, and to the fastening it at the corner, that then it might be no hindrance to the view of the sanctuary, especially on solemn days; but that on other days, and especially when the weather was inclined to snow, it might be expanded, and afford a covering to the veil of divers colours; whence that custom of ours is derived, of having a fine linen veil, after the temple has been built, to be drawn over the entrances; but the ten other curtains were four cubits in breadth, and twenty-eight in length; and had golden clasps, in order to join the one curtain to the other, which was done so exactly that they seemed to be one entire curtain. These were spread over the temple, and covered all the top and parts of the walls, on the sides and behind, so far as within one cubit of the ground. There were other curtains of the same breadth with these, but one more in number, and longer, for they were thirty cubits long; but these were woven with hair, with the like subtlety as those of wool were made, and were extended loosely down to the ground, appearing like a triangular front and elevation at the gates, the eleventh curtain being used for this very purpose. There were also other curtains made of skins above these, which

afforded covering and protection to those that were woven, both in hot weather, and when it rained; and great was the surprise of those who viewed these curtains at a distance, for they seemed not at all to differ from the colour of the sky; but those that were made of hair and of skins, reached down in the same manner as did the veil at the gates, and kept off the heat of the sun, and what injury the rains might do; and after this manner was the tabernacle reared.

5. There was also an ark made, sacred to God, of wood that was naturally strong, and could not be corrupted. This was called *Eron*, in our own language. Its construction was thus: Its length was five spans, but its breadth and height was each of them three spans. It was covered all over with gold, both within and without, so that the wooden part was not seen. It had also a cover united to it, by golden hinges, after a wonderful manner; which cover was every way evenly fitted to it, and had no eminences to hinder its exact conjunction. There were also two golden rings belonging to each of the longer boards, and passing through the entire wood, and through them gilt bars passed along each board, that it might thereby be moved and carried about, as occasion should require; for it was not drawn in a cart by beasts of burden, but borne on the shoulders of the priests. Upon this its cover were two images, which the Hebrews call *Cherubims;* they are flying creatures, but their form is not like to that of any of the creatures which men have seen, though Moses said he had seen such beings near the throne of God. In this ark he put the two tables whereon the ten commandments were written, five upon each table, and two and a half upon each side of them; and this ark he placed in the most holy place.

6. But in the holy place he placed a table, like those at Delphi: its length was two cubits, and its breadth one cubit, and its height three spans. It had feet also, the lower half of which were complete feet, resembling those which the Dorians put to their bedsteads; but the upper parts towards the table were wrought into a square form. The table had a hollow towards every side, having a ledge of four fingers' depth, that went round about like a spiral, both on the upper and lower part of the body of the work. Upon every one of the feet was there also inserted a ring, not far from the cover, through which went bars of wood beneath, but gilded, to be taken out upon occasion, there being a cavity where it was joined to the rings; for they were not entire rings; but before they came quite round, they ended in acute points, the one of which was inserted into the prominent part of the table, and the other into the foot; and by these it was carried when they journeyed. Upon this table, which was placed on the north side of the temple, not far from the most holy place, were laid twelve unleavened loaves of bread, six upon each heap, one above another: they were made of two tenth-deals of the purest flour, which tenth deal [an omer] is a measure of the Hebrews, containing seven Athenian *cotylæ;* and above these loaves were put two vials full of frankincense. Now after seven days other loaves were brought in their stead, on the day which is by us called the *Sabbath;* for we call the seventh day the *Sabbath.* But for the occasion of this invention of placing loaves here we will speak to in another place.

7. Over against this table, near the southern wall, was set a candlestick of cast gold, hollow within, being of the weight of one hundred pounds, which the Hebrews call *Chinchares;* if it be turned into the Greek language, it denotes a *talent.* It was made with its knops, and lilies, and pomegranates, and bowls, (which ornaments amounted to seventy in all;) by which means the shaft elevated itself on high from a single base, and spread itself into as many branches as there are planets, including the sun among them. It terminated in seven heads, in one row, all standing parallel to one another; and these branches carried seven lamps, one by one, in imitation of the number of the planets. These lamps looked to the east and to the south, the candlestick being situate obliquely.

8. Now between this candlestick and the table, which, as we said, were within the sanctuary, was the altar of incense, made of wood indeed, but of the same wood of which the foregoing vessels were made, such as was not liable to corruption; it was entirely crusted over with a golden plate. Its breadth on each side was a cubit, but the altitude double. Upon it was a grate of gold, that was extant above the altar, which had a golden crown encompassing it round about, whereto belonged rings and bars, by which the priests carried it when they journeyed. Before this tabernacle there was reared a brazen altar, but it was within made of wood, five cubits by measure on each side, but its height was but three, in like manner adorned with brass plates, as bright as gold. It had also a brazen hearth of net-work; for the ground underneath received the fire from the hearth, because it had no basis to receive it. Hard by this altar lay the basins, and the vials, and the censers, and the caldrons, made of gold; but the other vessels, made for the use of the sacrifices, were all of brass. And such was the construction of the tabernacle; and these were the vessels thereto belonging.

CHAPTER VII

CONCERNING THE GARMENTS OF THE PRIESTS, AND OF THE HIGH PRIEST

1. THERE were peculiar garments appointed for the priests, and for all the rest, which they call *Cohanææ* [priestly] garments, as also for the high priests, which they call *Cahanææ Rabbæ,* and denote the high priest's garments. Such was therefore the habit of the rest; but when the priest approaches the sacrifices, he purifies himself with the purification which the law prescribes; and, in the first place, he puts on that which is called *Machanase,* which means somewhat that is fast tied. It is a girdle, composed of fine twined linen, and is put about the privy parts, the feet being to be inserted into them, in the nature of breeches; but above half of it is cut off, and it ends at the thighs and is there tied fast.

2. Over this he wore a linen vestment, made of fine flax doubled: it is called *Chethone,* and denotes *linen,* for we call linen by the name of *Chethone.* This vestment reaches down to the feet, and sits close to the body; and has sleeves that are tied fast to the arms: it is girded to the breast a little above the elbows, by a girdle often going round, four fingers broad, but so loosely woven that you would think it were the skin of a serpent. It is embroidered with flowers of scarlet, and purple, and blue, and fine twined linen; but the warp was nothing but fine linen. The beginning of its circumvolution is at the breast; and when it has gone often round, it is there tied, and hangs loosely there down to the ankles: I mean this all the time the priest is not

about any laborious service, for in this position it appears in the most agreeable manner to the spectators; but when he is obliged to assist at the offering sacrifices, and to do the appointed service, that he may not be hindered in his operations by its motion, he throws it to the left, and bears it on his shoulder. Moses indeed calls this belt *Abaneth;* but we have learned from the Babylonians to call it *Emia,* for so it is by them called. This vestment has no loose or hollow parts anywhere in it, but only a narrow aperture about the neck; and it is tied with certain strings hanging down from the edge over the breast and back, and is fastened above each shoulder: it is called *Massabazanes.*

3. Upon his head he wears a cap, not brought to a conic form, nor encircling the whole head, but still covering more than the half of it, which is called *Masnaemphthes;* and its make is such, that it seems to be a crown, being made of thick swathes, but the contexture is of linen; and it is doubled round many times, and sewed together: besides which, a piece of fine linen covers the whole cap from the upper part, and reaches down to the forehead, and hides the seams of the swathes, which would otherwise appear indecently: this adheres closely upon the solid part of the head, and is thereto so firmly fixed, that it may not fall off during the sacred service about the sacrifices. So we have now shewn you what is the habit of the generality of the priests.

4. The high priest is indeed adorned with the same garments that we have described, without abating one; only over this he puts on a vestment of a blue colour. This also is a long robe, reaching to his feet, [in our language it is called *Meeir,*] and is tied round with a girdle, embroidered with the same colours and flowers as the former, with a mixture of gold interwoven. To the bottom of which garment are hung fringes, in colour like pomegranates, with golden bells,* by a curious and beautiful contrivance; so that between two bells hangs a pomegranate, and between two pomegranates a bell. Now this vesture was not composed of two pieces, nor was it sewed together upon the shoulders and the sides, but it was one long vestment so woven as to have an aperture for the neck; not an oblique one, but parted all along the breast and the back. A border also was sewed to it, lest the aperture should look too indecently: it was also parted where the hands were to come out.

5. Besides these the high priest put on a third garment, which is called the *Ephod,* which resembles the Epomis of the Greeks. Its make was after this manner: it was woven to the depth of a cubit, of several colours, with gold intermixed, and embroidered, but it left the middle of the breast uncovered: it was made with sleeves also; nor did it appear to be at all differently made from a short coat. But in the void place of this

garment there was inserted a piece of the bigness of a span, embroidered with gold, and the other colours of the ephod, and was called *Essen,* [the breastplate,] which in the Greek language signifies the *Oracle.* This piece exactly filled up the void space in the ephod. It was united to it by golden rings at every corner, the like rings being annexed to the ephod, and a blue riband was made use of to tie them together by those rings: and that the space between the rings might not appear empty, they contrived to fill it up with stitches of blue ribands. There were also two sardonyxes upon the ephod, at the shoulders to fasten it, in the nature of buttons, having each end running to the sardonyxes of gold, that they might be buttoned by them. On these were engraven the names of the sons of Jacob, in our own country letters, and in our own tongue, six on each of the stones, on either side; and the elder sons' names were on the right shoulder. Twelve stones also there were upon the breastplate, extraordinary in largeness and beauty; and they were an ornament not to be purchased by men, because of their immense value. These stones, however, stood in three rows, by four in a row, and were inserted into the breastplate itself, and they were set in ouches of gold, that were themselves inserted in the breastplate, and were so made that they might not fall out. Now the first three stones were a sardonyx, a topaz, and an emerald. The second row contained a carbuncle, a jasper, and a sapphire. The first of the third row was a ligure, then an amethyst, and the third an agate being the ninth of the whole number. The first of the fourth row was a chrysolite, the next was an onyx, and then a beryl, which was the last of all. Now the names of all those sons of Jacob were engraven in these stones, whom we esteem the heads of our tribes, each stone having the honour of a name, in the order according to which they were born. And whereas the rings were too weak of themselves to bear the weight of the stones, they made two other rings of a larger size, at the edge of that part of the breastplate, which reached to the neck, and inserted into the very texture of the breastplate, to receive chains finery wrought, which connected them with golden bands to the tops of the shoulders, whose extremity turned backwards, and went into the ring on the prominent back part of the ephod; and this was for the security of the breastplate, that it might not fall out of its place. There was also a girdle sewed to the breastplate, which was of the forementioned colours, with gold intermixed, which, when it had gone once round, was tied again upon the seam, and hung down. There were also golden loops that admitted its fringes at each extremity of the girdle, and included them entirely.

6. The high priest's mitre was the same that we described before, and was wrought like that of all the other priests; above which there was another, with swathes of blue embroidered, and round it was a golden crown polished, of three rows, one above another; out of which arose a cup of gold, which resembled the herb which we call *Saccharus;* but those Greeks that are skilful in botany call it *Hyoscyamus.* Now, lest any one that has seen this herb, but has not been taught its name, and is unacquainted with its nature, or, having known its name, knows not the herb when he sees it, I shall give such as these are a description of it. This herb is oftentimes in tallness above three spans, but its root is like that of a turnip, (for he that should compare it thereto would not be mistaken;) but its leaves are like the leaves of mint. Out of its branches it sends

---

* The use of these golden bells at the bottom of the high priest's long garment seems to have been this: That by shaking his garment at the time of his offering incense in the temple, on the great day of expiation, or at other proper periods of his sacred ministrations there, on the great festivals, the people might have notice of it, and might fall to their own prayers at the time of incense, or other proper periods; and so the whole congregation might at once offer those common prayers jointly with the high priest himself to the Almighty. See Luke i. 10; Rev. viii. 3, 4. Nor probably is the son of Sirach to be otherwise understood, when he says of Aaron, the first high priest, Ecclus. xlv. 9. "And God encompassed Aaron with pomegranates, and with many golden bells round about, that as he went there might be a sound, and a noise made that might be heard in the temple, for a memorial to the children of his people."

out a calyx, cleaving to the branch; and a coat encompasses it, which it naturally puts off when it is changing, in order to produce its fruit. This calyx is of the bigness of the bone of the little finger, but in the compass of its aperture is like a cup. This I will further describe for the use of those who are unacquainted with it. Suppose a sphere be divided into two parts, round at the bottom, but having another segment that grows up to a circumference from that bottom; suppose it become narrower by degrees, and that the cavity of that part grow decently smaller, and then gradually grow wider again at the brim, such as we see in the navel of a pomegranate, with its notches. And indeed such a coat grows over this plant as renders it a hemisphere, and that, as one may say, turned accurately in a lathe, and having its notches extant above it, which, as I said, grow like a pomegranate, only that they are sharp, and end in nothing but prickles. Now the fruit is preserved by this coat of the calyx, which fruit is like the seed of the herb Sideritis: it sends out a flower that may seem to resemble that of poppy. Of this was a crown made, as far as from the hinder part of the head to each of the temples; but this *Ephielis*, for so this calyx may be called, did not cover the forehead, but it was covered with a golden plate,* which had inscribed upon it the name of God in sacred characters. And such were the ornaments of the high priest.

7. Now here one may wonder at the ill-will which men bear to us, and which they profess to bear on account of our despising that Deity which they pretend to honour; for if any one do but consider the fabric of the tabernacle, and take a view of the garments of the high priest, and of those vessels which we make use of in our sacred ministration, he will find that our legislator was a divine man, and that we are unjustly reproached by others: for if any one do without prejudice, and with judgment, look upon these things, he will find they were every one made in way of imitation and representation of the universe. When Moses distinguished the tabernacle into three parts,† and allowed two of them to the priests, as a place accessible and common, he denoted the land and the sea, these being of general access to all; but he set apart the third division for God, because heaven is inaccessible to men. And when he ordered twelve loaves to be set on the table, he denoted the year, as distinguished into so many months. By branching out the candlestick into seventy parts, he secretly intimated the *Decani*, or seventy divisions of the planets; and as to the seven lamps upon the candlesticks, they referred to the course of the planets, of which that is the number. The veils, too, which were composed of four things, they declared the four elements; for the fine linen was proper to signify

the earth, because the flax grows out of the earth; the purple signified the sea, because that colour is dyed by the blood of a sea shell-fish; the blue is to signify the air; and the scarlet will naturally be an indication of fire. Now the vestment of the high priest being made of linen, signified the earth; the blue denoted the sky, being like lightning in its pomegranates, and in the noise of the bells resembling thunder. And for the ephod, it shewed that God had made the universe of four [elements;] and as for the gold interwoven, I suppose it related to the splendour by which all things are enlightened. He also appointed the breastplate to be placed in the middle of the ephod, to resemble the earth, for that has the very middle place of the world. And the girdle which encompassed the high priest round, signified the ocean, for that goes round about and includes the universe. Each of the sardonyxes declares to us the sun and the moon; those, I mean, that were in the nature of buttons on the high priest's shoulders. And for the twelve stones, whether we understand by them the months, or whether we understand the like number of the signs of that circle which the Greeks call the *Zodiac*, we shall not be mistaken in their meaning. And for the mitre, which was of a blue colour, it seems to me to mean heaven; for how otherwise could the name of God be inscribed upon it? That it was also illustrated with a crown, and that of gold also, is because of that splendour with which God is pleased. Let this explication ‡ suffice at present, since the course of my narration will often, and on many occasions, afford me the opportunity of enlarging upon the virtue of our legislator.

CHAPTER VIII

OF THE PRIESTHOOD OF AARON

1. WHEN what has been described was brought to a conclusion, gifts not being yet presented, God appeared to Moses, and enjoined him to bestow the high priesthood upon Aaron his brother, as upon him that best of them all deserved to obtain that honour, on account of his virtue. And when he had gathered the multitude together, he gave them an account of Aaron's virtues, and of his good-will to them, and of the dangers he had undergone for their sakes. Upon which, when they had given testimony to him in all respects, and shewed their readiness to receive him, Moses said to them, "O you Israelites, this work is already brought to a conclusion in a

---

* The reader ought to take notice here, that the very Mosaic Petalon, or golden plate, for the forehead of the Jewish high priest, was itself preserved, not only till the days of Josephus, but of Origen; and that its inscription, *Holiness to the Lord*, was in the Samaritan characters. See Antiq. b. viii. ch. iii. sect. 8; Essay on the Old Test. p. 154; and Reland, De Spol. Templi, p. 132.

† When Josephus, both here and chap. vi. sect. 4, supposes the tabernacle to have been parted into three parts, he seems to esteem the bare entrance to be a third division, distinct from the holy and the most holy places; and this the rather, because in the temple afterward there was a real distinct third part, which was called the Porch; otherwise Josephus would contradict his own description of the tabernacle, which gives us a particular account of no more than two parts.

‡ This explication of the mystical meaning of the Jewish tabernacle and its vessels, with the garments of the high priest, is taken out of Philo, and fitted to Gentile philosophical notions. This may possibly be forgiven in Jews greatly versed in heathen learning and philosophy, as Philo had ever been, and as Josephus had long been when he wrote these Antiquities. In the meantime, it is not to be doubted, but in their education they must both have learned more Jewish interpretations, such as we meet with in the epistle of Barnabas, in that to the Hebrews, and elsewhere among the old Jews. Accordingly, when Josephus wrote his books of the Jewish War, for the use of the Jews, at which time he was comparatively young, and less used to Gentile books, we find one specimen of such a Jewish interpretation; for there (b. vii. ch. v. sect. 5) he makes the seven branches of the temple candlestick, with their seven lamps, an emblem of the seven days of creation and rest, which are here emblems of the seven planets. Nor certainly ought ancient Jewish emblems be explained any other way than according to ancient Jewish, and not Gentile, notions. See the War, b. i. ch. xxxiii. sect. 2.

manner most acceptable to God, and according to our abilities. And now since you see that he is received into this tabernacle, we shall first of all stand in need of one that may officiate for us, and may minister to the sacrifices and to the prayers that are to be put up for us; and, indeed, had the inquiry after such a person been left to me, I should have thought myself worthy of this honour, both because men are naturally fond of themselves, and because I am conscious to myself that I have taken a great deal of pains for your deliverance; but now God himself has determined that Aaron is worthy of this honour, and has chosen him for his priest, as knowing him to be the most righteous person among you. So that he is to put on the vestments which are consecrated to God; he is to have the care of the altars, and to make provision for the sacrifices; and he it is that must put up prayers for you to God, who will readily hear them, not only because he is himself solicitous for your nation, but also because he will receive them as offered by one whom he hath himself chosen to this office."* The Hebrews were pleased with what was said, and they gave their approbation to him whom God had ordained; for Aaron was, of them all, the most deserving of this honour, on account of his own stock and gift of prophecy, and his brother's virtue. He had at that time four sons, Nadab, Abihu, Eleazer, and Ithamar.

2. Now Moses commanded them to make use of all the utensils which were more than were necessary to the structure of the tabernacle, for covering the tabernacle itself, the candlestick, and altar of incense, and the other vessels, that they might not be at all hurt when they journeyed, either by the rain or by the rising of the dust. And when he had gathered the multitude together again, he ordained that they should offer half a shekel for every man, as an oblation to God; which shekel is a piece among the Hebrews, and is equal to four Athenian drachmæ.† Whereupon they readily obeyed what Moses had commanded; and the number of the offerers was six hundred and five thousand five hundred and fifty. Now this money that was brought by the men that were free, was given by such as were above twenty years old, but under fifty; and what was collected was spent in the uses of the tabernacle.

3. Moses now purified the tabernacle and the priests; which purification was performed after the following manner:—He commanded them to take five hundred shekels of choice myrrh, an equal quantity of cassia, and half the foregoing weight of cinnamon and calamus, (this last is a sort of sweet spice;) to beat them small, and wet them with a hin of oil of olives, (a *hin* is our

own country measure, and contains two Athenian *choas*, or *congiuses ;*) then mix them together and boil them, and prepare them after the art of the apothecary, and make them into a very sweet ointment; and afterward to take it to anoint and purify the priests themselves, and all the tabernacle, as also the sacrifices. There were also many, and those of various kinds of sweet spices that belonged to the tabernacle, and such as were of very great price, and were brought to the golden altar of incense, the nature of which I do not now describe, lest it should be troublesome to my readers; but incense‡ was to be offered twice a day, both before sun-rising and at sun-setting. They were also to keep oil already purified for the lamps; three of which were to give light all day long,§ upon the sacred candlestick, before God, and the rest were to be lighted at the evening.

4. Now all was finished. Besaleel and Aholiab appeared to be the most skilful of the workmen, for they invented finer works than what others had done before them, and were of great abilities to gain notions of what they were formerly ignorant of; and of these, Besaleel was judged to be the best. Now the whole time they were about this work, was the interval of seven months; and after this it was that was ended the first year since their departure out of Egypt. But at the beginning of the second year, on the month *Xanthicus*, as the Macedonians call it, but on the month *Nisan*, as the Hebrews call it, on the new moon, they consecrated the tabernacle, and all its vessels, which I have already described.

5. Now God shewed himself pleased with the work of the Hebrews, and did not permit their labours to be in vain; nor did he disdain to make use of what they had made, but he came and sojourned with them, and pitched his tabernacle in the holy house. And in the following manner did he come to it:—The sky was clear, but there was a mist over the tabernacle only, encompassing it, but not with such a very deep and thick cloud as is seen in the winter season, nor yet in so thin a one as men might be able to discern any thing through it; but from it there dropped a sweet dew, and such a one as shewed the presence of God to those that desired and believed it.

6. Now when Moses had bestowed such honorary presents on the workmen as it was fit they should receive who had wrought so well, he offered sacrifices in the open court of the tabernacle, as God commanded him, a bull, a ram, and a kid of the goats for a sin-offering. Now I shall speak of what we do in our sacred offices in my discourse about sacrifices, and therein shall inform men in what cases Moses bid us offer a whole burnt-offering, and in what cases the law permits us to partake of them as of food. And when Moses had sprinkled Aaron's vestments, himself and his sons, with the blood of the beasts that were slain, and had purified them with spring waters and ointment, they became God's priests. After this manner did he consecrate them and their garments for seven days together. The same he did to the tabernacle, and the vessels thereto belonging, both with oil first incensed, as I said, and with the

---

* It is well worth our observation that the two principal qualifications required in this section for the constitution of the first high priest, (viz., that he should have an excellent character for virtuous and good actions, as also that he should have the approbation of the people,) are here noted by Josephus, even where the nomination belonged to God himself, which are the very same qualifications which the Christian religion requires in the choice of Christian bishops, priests, and deacons : as the Apostolical Constitutions inform us, b. ii. ch. iii.

† This weight and value of the Jewish shekel, in the days of Josephus, equal to about 2s. 10d. sterling, is, by the learned Jews, owned to be one-fifth larger than were their old shekels ; which determination agrees perfectly with the remaining shekels that have Samaritan inscriptions, coined generally by Simon the Maccabee, about 230 years before Josephus published his Antiquities, which never weigh more than two shillings and fourpence halfpenny, and commonly but two shillings and fourpence farthing. See Reland, De Nummis Samaritanorum, p. 188.

‡ The incense was here offered, according to Josephus's opinion, before sun-rising, and at sun-setting; but in the days of Pompey, according to the same Josephus, the sacrifices were offered in the morning, and at the ninth hour. Antiq. b. xiv. ch. iv. sect. 3.

§ Hence we may correct the opinions of the modern Rabbins, who say that only one of the seven lamps burned in the day-time ; whereas, our Josephus, an eye-witness, says there were three.

blood of bulls and of rams, slain day by day one, according to its kind. But on the eighth day he appointed a feast for the people, and commanded them to offer sacrifice according to their ability. Accordingly they contended one with another, and were ambitious to exceed each other in the sacrifices which they brought, and so fulfilled Moses's injunctions. But as the sacrifices lay upon the altar, a sudden fire was kindled from among them of its own accord, and appeared to the sight like fire from a flash of lightning, and consumed whatsoever was upon the altar.

7. Hereupon an affliction befell Aaron, considered as a man and a father, but was undergone by him with true fortitude—for he had indeed a firmness of soul in such accidents, and he thought this calamity came upon him according to God's will—for whereas he had four sons, as I said before, the two eldest of them, Nadab and Abihu, did not bring those sacrifices which Moses bade them bring, but which they used to offer formerly, and were burnt to death. Now when the fire rushed upon them, and began to burn them, nobody could quench it. Accordingly they died in this manner. And Moses bid their father and their brethren to take up their bodies, to carry them out of the camp, and to bury them magnificently. Now the multitude lamented them, and were deeply affected at this their death, which so unexpectedly befell them. But Moses entreated their brethren and their father not to be troubled for them, and to prefer the honour of God before their grief about them; for Aaron had already put on his sacred garments.

8. But Moses refused all that honour which he saw the multitude ready to bestow upon him, and attended to nothing else but the service of God. He went no more up to Mount Sinai; but he went into the tabernacle, and brought back answers from God for what he prayed for. His habit was also that of a private man; and in all other circumstances he behaved himself like one of the common people, and was desirous to appear without distinguishing himself from the multitude, but would have it known that he did nothing else but take care of them. He also set down in writing the form of their government, and those laws, by obedience whereto, they would lead their lives so as to please God, and so as to have no quarrels one among another. However, the laws he ordained were such as God suggested to him; so I shall now discourse concerning that form of government, and those laws.

9. I will now treat of what I before omitted, the garment of the high priest: for he [Moses] left no room for the evil practices of [false] prophets; but if some of that sort should attempt to abuse the divine authority, he left it to God to be present at his sacrifices when he pleased, and when he pleased to be absent.* And he was willing this should be known, not to the Hebrews only, but to those foreigners also who were there. For as to those stones,† which we

told you before, the high priest bare on his shoulders, which were sardonyxes, (and I think it needless to describe their nature, they being known to everybody,) the one of them shined out when God was present at their sacrifices; I mean that which was in the nature of a button on his right shoulder, bright rays darting out thence, and being seen even by those that were most remote; which splendour yet was not before natural to the stone. This has appeared a wonderful thing to such as have not so far indulged themselves in philosophy, as to despise Divine Revelation. Yet will I mention what is still more wonderful than this: for God declared beforehand, by those twelve stones which the high priest bare on his breast, and which were inserted into his breastplate, when they should be victorious in battle; for so great a splendour shone forth from them before the army began to march, that all the people were sensible of God's being present for their assistance. Whence it came to pass that those Greeks, who had a veneration for our laws, because they could not possibly contradict this, called that breastplate *the Oracle.* Now this breastplate, and this sardonyx, left off shining two hundred years before I composed this book, God having been displeased at the transgressions of his laws. Of which things we shall further discourse on a fitter opportunity; but I will now go on with my proposed narration.

---

* Of this strange expression, that Moses "left it to God to be present at his sacrifices when he pleased, and when he pleased to be absent," see the note on b. ii. Against Apion, sect. 16.

† These answers by the oracle of Urim and Thummim, which words signify *light* and *perfection*, or, as the Septuagint render them, *revelation* and *truth*, and denote nothing further, that I see, but the shining stones themselves, which were used, in this method of illumination, in revealing the will of God, after a perfect, and true manner, to his people Israel: I say, these answers were not made by the shining of the precious stones, after an awkward manner, in the high priest's breastplate, as the modern Rabbins vainly suppose, for certainly the shining of the **stones** might precede

or accompany the oracle, without itself delivering that oracle, (see Antiq. b. vi. chap. vi. sect. 4,) but rather by an audible voice from the mercy-seat between the cherubims. See Prideaux's Connect. at the year 534. This oracle had been silent, as Josephus here informs us, two hundred years before he wrote his Antiquities, or ever since the days of the last good high priest of the family of the Maccabees, John Hyrcanus. Now it is here very well worth our observation, that the oracle before us was that by which God appeared to be present with, and gave directions to, his people Israel as their king, all the while they submitted to him in that capacity; and did not set over them such independent kings as governed according to their own wills and political maxims, instead of divine directions. Accordingly, we meet with this oracle (besides angelic and prophetic admonitions) all along from the days of Moses and Joshua to the anointing of Saul, the first of the succession of the kings, (Num. xxvii. 21; Josh. vi. 6, &c.; xix. 50; Judges i. 1; xviii. 4, 5, 6, 30, 31; xx. 18, 23, 26, 27, 28; xxi. 1, &c.; 1 Sam. i. 17, 18; iii. *per tot.* iv. *per tot.*;) nay, till Saul's rejection of the divine commands in the war with Amalek, when he took upon him to act as he thought fit, (1 Sam. xiv. 3, 18, 19, 36, 37;) then this oracle left Saul entirely, (which indeed he had seldom consulted before, 1 Sam. xiv. 35; 1 Chron. x. 14; xiii. 3; Antiq. b. vii. chap. iv. sect. 2,) and accompanied David, who was anointed to succeed him, and who consulted God by it frequently, and complied with its directions constantly, (1 Sam. xiv. 37, 41; xv. 26; xxii. 13, 15; xxiii. 9, 10; xxx. 7, 8, 18; 2 Sam. ii. 1; v. 19, 23; xxi. 1; xxiii. 14; 1 Chron. xiv. 10, 14; Antiq. b. vi. chap. xii. sect. 5.) Saul, indeed, long after his rejection by God, and when God had given him up to destruction for his disobedience, did once afterwards endeavour to consult God when it was too late; but God would not then answer him, neither by dreams, nor by Urim, nor by prophets, (1 Sam. xxviii. 6.) Nor did any of David's successors, the kings of Judah, that we know of, consult God by this oracle, till the very Babylonish captivity itself, when those kings were at an end; they taking upon them, I suppose, too much of despotic power and royalty, and too little owning the God of Israel for the supreme King of Israel, though a few of them consulted the prophets sometimes, and were answered by them. At the return of the two tribes, without the return of the kingly government, the restoration of this oracle was expected, (Neh. vii. 63; 1 Esd. v. 40; 1 Macc. iv. 46; xiv. 41.) And indeed it may seem to have been restored for some time after the Babylonish captivity, at least in the days of that excellent high priest, John Hyrcanus, whom Josephus esteemed as a king, a priest, and a prophet; and who, he says, foretold several things that came to

10. The tabernacle being now consecrated, and a regular order being settled for the priests, the multitude judged that God now dwelt among them, and betook themselves to sacrifices and praises to God, as being now delivered from all expectation of evils, and as entertaining a hopeful prospect of better times hereafter. They offered also gifts to God, some as common to the whole nation, and others as peculiar to themselves, and these tribe by tribe; for the heads of the tribes combined together, two by two, and brought a waggon and a yoke of oxen. These amounted to six, and they carried the tabernacle when they journeyed. Besides which, each head of a tribe brought a bowl, and a charger, and a spoon, of ten darics, full of incense. Now the charger and the bowl were of silver, and together they weighed two hundred shekels, but the bowl cost no more than seventy shekels; and these were full of fine flour mingled with oil, such as they used on the altar about the sacrifices. They brought also a young bullock, and a ram, with a lamb of a year old, for a whole burnt-offering; as also a goat for the forgiveness of sins. Every one of the heads of the tribes brought also other sacrifices, called *peace-offerings*, for every day two bulls, and five rams, with lambs of a year old, and kids of the goats. These heads of tribes were twelve days in sacrificing, one sacrificing every day. Now Moses went no longer up to mount Sinai, but went into the tabernacle, and learned of God what they were to do, and what laws should be made; which laws were preferable to what have been devised by human understanding, and proved to be firmly observed for all time to come, as being believed to be the gift of God, insomuch that the Hebrews did not transgress any of those laws, either as tempted in times of peace by luxury, or in times of war by distress of affairs. But I say no more here concerning them, because I have resolved to compose another work concerning our laws.

CHAPTER IX

THE MANNER OF OUR OFFERING SACRIFICES

1. I WILL now, however, make mention of a few of our laws which belong to purifications,

and the like sacred offices, since I am accidentally come to this matter of sacrifices. These sacrifices were of two sorts; of those sorts one was offered for private persons, and the other for the people in general; and they are done in two different ways: in the one case, what is slain is burnt, as a whole burnt-offering, whence that name is given to it; but the other is a thank-offering, and is designed for feasting those that sacrifice. I will speak of the former. Suppose a private man offer a burnt-offering, he must slay either a bull, a lamb, or a kid of the goats, and the two latter of the first year, though of bulls he is permitted to sacrifice those of a greater age; but all burnt-offerings are to be of males. When they are slain, the priests sprinkle the blood round about the altar: they then cleanse the bodies, and divide them into parts, and salt them with salt, and lay them upon the altar, while the pieces of wood are piled one upon another, and the fire is burning; they next cleanse the feet of the sacrifices and the inwards in an accurate manner, and so lay them to the rest to be purged by the fire, while the priests receive the hides. This is the way of offering a burnt-offering.

2. But those that offer thank-offerings do indeed sacrifice the same creatures, but such as are unblemished, and above a year old; however, they may take either males or females. They also sprinkle the altar with their blood: but they lay upon the altar the kidneys and the caul, and all the fat, and the lobe of the liver, together with the rump of the lamb; then, giving the breast and the right shoulder to the priests, the offerers feast upon the remainder of the flesh for two days; and what remains they burn.

3. The sacrifices for sins are offered in the same manner as is the thank-offering. But those who are unable to purchase complete sacrifices, offer two pigeons, or turtle-doves; the one of which is made a burnt-offering to God, the other they give as food to the priests. But we shall treat more accurately about the oblation of these creatures in our discourse concerning sacrifices. But if a person fall into sin by ignorance, he offers a ewe lamb, or a female kid of the goats, of the same age; and the priests sprinkle the blood at the altar, not after the former manner, but at the corners of it. They also bring the kidneys and the rest of the fat, together with the lobe of the liver, to the altar, while the priests bear away the hides and the flesh, and spend it in the holy place, on the same day;*

pass accordingly; but about the time of his death, he here implies, that this oracle quite ceased, and not before. The following high priests now putting diadems on their heads, and ruling according to their own will, and by their own authority, like the other kings of the Pagan countries about them; so that while the God of Israel was allowed to be the supreme King of Israel, and his directions to be their authentic guides, God gave them such directions as their supreme king and governor; and they were properly under a theocracy, by this oracle of Urim, but no longer, (see Dr Bernard's notes here;) though I confess I cannot but esteem the high priest Jaddus's divine dream, (Antiq. b. xi. chap. viii. sect. 4,) and the high priest Caiphas's most remarkable prophecy, (John xi. 47-52,) as two small remains or specimens of this ancient oracle, which properly belonged to the Jewish high priests: nor perhaps ought we entirely to forget that eminent prophetic dream of our Josephus himself, (one next to a high priest, as of the family of the Asamoneans or Maccabees,) as to the succession of Vespasian and Titus to the Roman empire, and that in the days of Nero, and before either Galba, Otho, or Vitellius were thought of to succeed him. (Of the War, b. iii. chap. viii. sect. 9.) This, I think, may be well looked on as the very last instance of any thing like the prophetic Urim among the Jewish nation, and just preceded their fatal desolation: but how could it possibly come to pass that such great men as Sir John Marsham and Dr Spenser,

should imagine that this oracle of Urim and Thummim, with other practices as old or older than the law of Moses, should have been ordained in imitation of somewhat like them among the Egyptians, which we never hear of till the days of Diodorus Siculus, Ælian, and Maimonides, or little earlier than the Christian era at the highest, is almost unaccountable; while the main business of the law of Moses was evidently to preserve the Israelites from the idolatrous and superstitious practices of the neighbouring Pagan nations; and while it is so undeniable, that the evidence for the great antiquity of Moses's law is incomparably beyond that for the like or greater antiquity of such customs in Egypt or other nations, which indeed is generally none at all, it is most absurd to derive any of Moses's laws from the imitation of those heathen practices. Such hypotheses demonstrate to us how far inclination can prevail over evidence, in even some of the most learned part of mankind.
* What Reland well observes here, out of Josephus, as compared with the law of Moses, Lev. vii. 15, (that the eating of the sacrifice the same day it was offered, seems to mean only before the morning of the next, although the latter part, i.e., the night, be in strictness part of the next day, according to the Jewish reckoning,) is greatly to be observed upon other occasions also. The Jewish maxim in such cases, it seems, is this: That

for the law does not permit them to leave of it until the morning. But if any one sin, and is conscious of it himself, but hath nobody that can prove it upon him, he offers a ram, the law enjoining him so to do; the flesh of which the priests eat, as before, in the holy place, on the same day. And if the rulers offer sacrifices for their sins, they bring the same oblations that private men do; only they so far differ, that they are to bring for sacrifices a bull or a kid of the goats, both males.

4. Now the law requires, both in private and public sacrifices, that the finest flour be also brought; for a lamb the measure of one-tenth deal,—for a ram two,—and for a bull three. This they consecrate upon the altar, when it is mingled with oil; for oil is also brought by those that sacrifice; for a bull the half of a hin, and for a ram the third part of the same measure, and one quarter of it for a lamb. This hin is an ancient Hebrew measure, and is equivalent to two Athenian choas, (or congiuses.) They bring the same quantity of oil which they do of wine, and they pour the wine about the altar; but if any one does not offer a complete sacrifice of animals, but brings fine flour only for a vow, he throws a handful upon the altar as its first fruits, while the priests take the rest for their food, either boiled or mingled with oil, but made into cakes of bread. But whatsoever it be that a priest himself offers, it must of necessity be all burnt. Now the law forbids us to sacrifice any animal at the same time with its dam: and, in other cases, not till the eighth day after its birth. Other sacrifices there are also appointed for escaping distempers, or for other occasions, in which meat-offerings are consumed, together with the animals that are sacrificed; of which it is not lawful to leave any part till the next day, only the priests are to take their own share.

CHAPTER X

CONCERNING THE FESTIVALS; AND HOW EACH DAY OF SUCH FESTIVAL IS TO BE OBSERVED

1. THE law requires, that out of the public expenses a lamb of the first year be killed every day, at the beginning and at the ending of the day; but on the seventh day, which is called the *Sabbath*, they kill two, and sacrifice them in the same manner. At the new moon, they both perform the daily sacrifices, and slay two bulls, with seven lambs of the first year, and a kid of the goats also, for the expiation of sins; that is, if they have sinned through ignorance.

2. But on the seventh month, which the Macedonians call *Hyperberetæus*, they make an addition to those already mentioned, and sacrifice a bull, a ram, and seven lambs, and a kid of the goats, for sins.

3. On the tenth day of the same lunar month, they fast till the evening; and this day they sacrifice a bull, and two rams, and seven lambs, and a kid of the goats for sins. And besides these, they bring two kids of the goats; the one of which is sent alive out of the limits of the camp into the wilderness for the scapegoat, and to be an expiation for the sins of the whole multitude; but the other is brought into a place of great cleanness within the limits of the camp,

and is there burnt, with its skin, without any sort of cleansing. With this goat was burnt a bull, not brought by the people, but by the high priest, at his own charges; which, when it was slain, he brought of the blood into the holy place, together with the blood of the kid of the goats, and sprinkled the ceiling with his finger seven times, as also its pavement, and again as often toward the most holy place, and about the golden altar: he also at last brings it into the open court, and sprinkles it about the great altar. Besides this, they set the extremities, and the kidneys, and the fat, with the lobe of the liver, upon the altar. The high priest likewise presents a ram to God as a burnt-offering.

4. Upon the fifteenth day of the same month, when the season of the year is changing for winter, the law enjoins us to pitch tabernacles in every one of our houses, so that we preserve ourselves from the cold of that time of the year; as also that when we should arrive at our own country, and come to that city which we should have then for our metropolis, because of the temple therein to be built, and keep a festival for eight days, and offer burnt-offerings, and sacrifice thank-offerings, that we should then carry in our hands a branch of myrtle, and willow, and a bough of the palm-tree, with the addition of the pome citron. That the burnt-offering on the first of those days was to be a sacrifice of thirteen bulls, and fourteen lambs, and fifteen rams, with the addition of a kid of the goats, as an expiation for sins : and on the following days the same number of lambs, and of rams, with the kids of the goats; but abating one of the bulls every day till they amounted to seven only. On the eighth day all work was laid aside, and then, as we said before, they sacrificed to God a bullock, a ram, and seven lambs, with a kid of the goats, for an expiation of sins. And this is the accustomed solemnity of the Hebrews, when they pitch their tabernacles.

5. In the month of Xanthicus, which is by us called *Nisan*, and is the beginning of our year, on the fourteenth day of the lunar month, when the sun is in Aries, (for in this month it was that we were delivered from bondage under the Egyptians,) the law ordained that we should every year slay that sacrifice which I before told you we slew when we came out of Egypt, and which was called the *Passover;* and so do we celebrate this passover in companies, leaving nothing of what we sacrifice till the day following. The feast of unleavened bread succeeds that of the passover, and falls on the fifteenth day of the month, and continues seven days, wherein they feed on unleavened bread; on every one of which days two bulls are killed, and one ram, and seven lambs. Now these lambs are entirely burnt, beside the kid of the goats which is added to all the rest, for sins; for it is intended as a feast for the priest on every one of those days. But on the second day of unleavened bread, which is the sixteenth day of the month, they first partake of the fruits of the earth, for before that day they do not touch them. And while they suppose it proper to honour God, from whom they obtain this plentiful provision, in the first place, they offer the first-fruits of their barley, and that in the manner following: They take a handful of the ears, and dry them, then beat them small, and purge the barley from the bran; they then bring one tenth deal to the altar, to God: and, casting one handful of it upon the fire, they leave the rest for the use of the priest; and after this it is that they may publicly or privately reap their harvest. They also at this

---

the day goes before the night; and this appears to me to be the language both of the Old and New Testament. See also the note on Antiq. b. iv. ch. iv. sect. 4, and Reland's note on b. iv. chap. viii. sect. 28.

participation of the first-fruits of the earth, sacrifice a lamb, as a burnt-offering to God.

6. When a week of weeks has passed over after this sacrifice, (which weeks contain forty and nine days,) on the fiftieth day, which is Pentecost, but is called by the Hebrews *Asartha*, which signifies *Pentecost*, they bring to God a loaf, made of wheat flour, of two tenth deals, with leaven; and for sacrifices, they bring two lambs; and when they have only presented them to God, they are made ready for supper for the priests; nor is it permitted to leave anything of them till the day following. They also slay three bullocks for a burnt-offering, and two rams; and fourteen lambs, with two kids of the goats, for sins; nor is there any one of the festivals but in it they offer burnt-offerings; they also allow themselves to rest on every one of them. Accordingly, the law prescribes in them all what kinds they are to sacrifice, and how they are to rest entirely, and must slay sacrifices, in order to feast upon them.

7. However, out of the common charges, baked bread, [was set on the table of shewbread,] without leaven, of twenty-four tenth deals of flour, for so much is spent upon this bread; two heaps of these were baked; they were baked the day before the Sabbath, but were brought into the holy place on the morning of the Sabbath, and set upon the holy table, six on a heap, one loaf still standing over-against another; where two golden cups full of frankincense were also set upon them, and there they remained till another Sabbath, and then other loaves were brought in their stead, while the loaves were given to the priests for their food, and the frankincense was burnt in that sacred fire wherein all their offerings were burnt also; and so other frankincense was set upon the loaves instead of what was there before. The [high] priest also, of his own charges, offered a sacrifice, and that twice every day. It was made of flour mingled with oil, and gently baked by the fire; the quantity was one tenth deal of flour; he brought the half of it to the fire in the morning, and the other half at night. The account of these sacrifices I shall give more accurately hereafter; but I think I have premised what for the present may be sufficient concerning them.

CHAPTER XI

OF THE PURIFICATIONS

1. MOSES took out the tribe of Levi from communicating with the rest of the people, and set them apart to be a holy tribe; and purified them by water taken from perpetual springs, and with such sacrifices as were usually offered to God on the like occasions. He delivered to them also the tabernacle, and the sacred vessels, and the other curtains, which were made for covering the tabernacle, that they might minister under the conduct of the priests, who had been already consecrated to God.

2. He also determined concerning animals; which of them might be used for food, and which they were obliged to abstain from; which matters, when this work shall give me occasion, shall be further explained; and the causes shall be added, by which he was moved to allot some of them to be our food, and enjoined us to abstain from others. However, he entirely forbade us the use of blood for food, and esteemed it to contain the soul and spirit. He also for-

bade us to eat the flesh of an animal that died of itself, as also the caul, and the fat of goats, and sheep, and bulls.

3. He also ordered, that those whose bodies were afflicted with leprosy, and who had a gonorrhœa, should not come into the city;[*] nay, he removed the women, when they had their natural purgations, till the seventh day; after which he looked on them as pure, and permitted them to come in again. The law permits those who have taken care of funerals to come in after the same manner, when this number of days is over; but if any continued longer than that number of days in a state of pollution, the law appointed the offering two lambs for a sacrifice; the one of which they are to purge by fire, and for the other, the priests take it for themselves. In the same manner do those sacrifice who have had the gonorrhœa. But he that sheds his seed in his sleep, if he go down into cold water, has the same privilege with those who have lawfully accompanied with their wives. And for the lepers, he suffered them not to come into the city at all, nor to live with any others, as if they were in effect, dead persons: but if any one had obtained, by prayer to God, the recovery from that distemper, and had gained a healthful complexion again, such a one returned thanks to God, with several sorts of sacrifices, concerning which we will speak hereafter.

4. Whence one cannot but smile at those who say that Moses was himself afflicted with the leprosy when he fled out of Egypt, and that he became the conductor of those who on that account left that country, and led them into the land of Canaan; for, had this been true, Moses would not have made these laws to his own dishonour, which indeed it was more likely he would have opposed, if others had endeavoured to introduce them; and this the rather, because there are lepers in many nations, who are yet in honour, and not only free from reproach and avoidance, but who have been great captains of armies, and been intrusted with high offices in the commonwealth, and have had the privilege of entering into holy places and temples; so that nothing hindered, but if either Moses himself, or the multitude that was with him, had been liable to such a misfortune in the colour of his skin, he might have made laws about them for their credit and advantage, and have laid no manner of difficulty upon them. Accordingly, it is a plain case, that it is out of violent prejudice only, that they report these things about us; but Moses was pure from any such distemper, and lived with countrymen who were pure of it also, and thence made the laws which concerned others that had the distemper. He did this for the honour of God; but as to these matters, let every one consider them after what manner he pleases.

5. As to the women, when they have born a child, Moses forbade them to come into the temple, or touch the sacrifices, before forty days were over, supposing it to be a boy; but if she has born a girl, the law is that she cannot be admitted before twice that number of days be over; and when after the before-mentioned time appointed for them, they perform their sacrifices, the priests distribute them before God.

---

[*] We may also here note, that Josephus frequently calls the camp *the city*, and the court of the Mosaic tabernacle *a temple*, and the tabernacle itself *a holy house*, with allusion to the latter city, temple, and holy house, which he knew so well long afterwards.

6. But if any one suspect that his wife has been guilty of adultery, he was to bring a tenth deal of barley flour; they then cast one handful to God, and gave the rest of it to the priests for food. One of the priests set the woman at the gates that are turned towards the temple, and took the veil from her head, and wrote the name of GOD on parchment, and enjoined her to swear that she had not at all injured her husband; and to wish that, if she had violated her chastity, her right thigh might be put out of joint; that her belly might swell, and that she might die thus: but that if her husband, by the violence of his affection, and of the jealousy which arose from it, had been rashly moved to this suspicion, that she might bear a male child in the tenth month. Now when these oaths were over, the priest wiped the name of GOD out of the parchment, and wrung the water into a vial. He also took some dust out of the temple, (if any happened to be there,) and put a little of it into the vial, and gave it her to drink; whereupon the woman, if she were unjustly accused, conceived with child, and brought it to perfection in her womb: but if she had broken her faith of wedlock to her husband, and had sworn falsely before God, she died in a reproachful manner: her thigh fell off from her, and her belly swelled with a dropsy. And these are the ceremonies about sacrifices, and about the purifications thereto belonging, which Moses provided for his countrymen. He also prescribed the following laws to them:—

CHAPTER XII

SEVERAL LAWS

1. As for adultery, Moses forbade it entirely, as esteeming it a happy thing that men should be wise in the affairs of wedlock; and that it was profitable both to cities and families that children should be known to be genuine. He also abhorred men's lying with their mothers, as one of the greatest crimes; and the like for lying with their father's wife, and with aunts, and sisters, and sons' wives, as all instances of abominable wickedness. He also forbade a man to lie with his wife when she was defiled by her natural purgation: and not to come near brute beasts; nor to approve of the lying with a male, which was to hunt after unlawful pleasures on account of beauty. To those who were guilty of such insolent behaviour, he ordained death for their punishment.

2. As for the priests, he prescribed to them a double degree of purity:* for he restrained them in the instances above, and moreover forbade them to marry harlots. He also forbade them to marry a slave, or a captive, and such as got their living by cheating trades, and by keeping inns: as also a woman parted from her husband, on any account whatsoever. Nay, he did not think it proper for the high priest to marry even the widow of one that was dead, though he allowed that to the priests; but he permitted him only to marry a virgin, and to retain her. Whence it is that the high priest is not to come

near to one that is dead, although the rest are not prohibited from coming near to their brethren, or parents, or children, when they are dead; but they are to be unblemished in all respects. He ordered that the priest, who had any blemish, should have his portion indeed among the priests; but he forbade him to ascend the altar, or to enter into the holy house. He also enjoined them, not only to observe purity in their sacred ministrations, but in their daily conversation, that it might be unblameable also; and on this account it is that those who wear the sacerdotal garments are without spot, and eminent for their purity and sobriety: nor are they permitted to drink wine so long as they wear those garments.† Moreover, they offer sacrifices that are entire, and have no defect whatsoever.

3. And truly Moses gave them all these precepts, being such as were observed during his own lifetime; but though he lived now in the wilderness, yet did he make provision how they might observe the same laws when they should have taken the land of Canaan. He gave them rest to the land from ploughing and planting every seventh year, as he had prescribed to them to rest from working every seventh day; and ordered, that then what grew of its own accord out of the earth, should in common belong to all that pleased to use it, making no distinction in that respect between their own countrymen and foreigners: and he ordained, that they should do the same after seven times seven years, which in all are fifty years; and that fiftieth year is called by the Hebrews *The Jubilee*, wherein debtors are freed from their debts, and slaves are set at liberty; which slaves became such, though they were of the same stock, by transgressing some of those laws the punishment of which was not capital, but they were punished by this method of slavery. This year also restores the land to its former possessors in the manner following:— When the Jubilee is come, which name denotes *liberty*, he that sold the land, and he that bought it, meet together, and make an estimate, on one hand, of the fruits gathered; and, on the other hand, of the expenses laid out upon it. If the fruits gathered come to more than the expenses laid out, he that sold it takes the land again; but if the expenses prove more than the fruits, the present possessor receives of the former owner the difference that was wanting, and leaves the land to him; and if the fruits received, and the expenses laid out, prove equal to one another, the present possessor relinquishes it to the former owners. Moses would have the same law obtain as to those houses also which were sold in villages; but he made a different law for such as were sold in a city; for if he that sold it tendered the purchaser his money again within a year, he was forced to restore it; but in case a whole year had intervened, the purchaser was to enjoy what he had bought. This was the constitution of the laws which Moses learned of God when the camp lay under mount Sinai; and this he delivered in writing to the Hebrews.

4. Now when this settlement of laws seemed to be well over, Moses thought fit at length to take a review of the host, as thinking it proper to settle the affairs of war. So he charged the heads of the tribes, excepting the tribe of Levi,

---

* These words of Josephus are remarkable, that the lawgiver of the Jews required of the priests a double degree of purity, in comparison of that required of the people, of which he gives several instances immediately. It was for certain the case also among the first Christians, of the clergy, in comparison of the laity, as the Apostolical Constitutions and Canons everywhere inform us.

† We must here note with Reland, that the precept given to the priests of not drinking wine while they wore the sacred garments, is equivalent to their abstinence from it all the while they ministered in the temple; because they then alway, and then only, wore those sacred garments, which were laid up there from one time of ministration to another.

to take an exact account of the number of those that were able to go to war; for as to the Levites, they were holy, and free from all such burdens. Now when the people had been numbered, there were found six hundred thousand that were able to go to war, from twenty to fifty years of age, besides three thousand six hundred and fifty. Instead of Levi, Moses took Manasseh, the son of Joseph, among the heads of tribes; and Ephraim instead of Joseph. It was indeed the desire of Jacob himself to Joseph, that he would give him his sons to be his own by adoption, as I have before related.

5. When they set up the tabernacle, they received it into the midst of their camp, three of the tribes pitching their tents on each side of it; and roads were cut through the midst of these tents. It was like a well-appointed market; and everything was there ready for sale in due order; and all sorts of artificers were in the shops; and it resembled nothing so much as a city that sometimes was movable, and sometimes fixed. The priests had the first places about the tabernacle; then the Levites, who, because their whole multitude was reckoned from thirty days old, were twenty-three thousand eight hundred and eighty males; and, during the time that the cloud stood over the tabernacle, they thought proper to stay in the same place, as supposing that God there inhabited among them; but when that removed, they journeyed also.

6. Moreover, Moses was the inventor of the form of their trumpet, which was made of silver. Its description is this:—In length it was little less than a cubit. It was composed of a narrow tube, somewhat thicker than a flute, but with so much breadth as was sufficient for admission of the breath of a man's mouth: it ended in the form of a bell, like common trumpets. Its sound was called in the Hebrew tongue *Asosra*. Two of these being made, one of them was sounded when they required the multitude to come together to congregations. When the first of them gave a signal, the heads of the tribes were to assemble, and consult about the affairs to them properly belonging; but when they gave the signal by both of them, they called the multitude together. Whenever the tabernacle was removed, it was done in this solemn order:—At the first alarm of the trumpet, those whose tents were on the east quarter prepared to remove; when the second signal was given, those that were on the south quarter did the like; in the next place, the tabernacle was taken to pieces, and was carried in the midst of six tribes that went before, and of six that followed, all the Levites assisting about the tabernacle; when the third signal was given, that part which had their tents towards the west, put themselves in motion; and at the fourth signal, those on the north did so likewise. They also made use of these trumpets in their sacred ministrations, when they were bringing their sacrifices to the altar, as well on the Sabbaths as on the rest of the [festival] days; and now it was that Moses offered that sacrifice which was called the *Passover in the Wilderness*, as the first he had offered after the departure out of Egypt.

CHAPTER XIII

HOW MOSES REMOVED FROM MOUNT SINAI, AND CONDUCTED THE PEOPLE TO THE BORDERS OF THE CANAANITES

A LITTLE while afterwards he rose up, and went from mount Sinai; and, having passed through several mansions, of which we will speak anon, he came to a place called *Hazeroth*, where the multitude began again to be mutinous, and to blame Moses for the misfortunes they had suffered in their travels; and that when he had persuaded them to leave a good land, they at once had lost that land, and instead of that happy state he had promised them, they were still wandering in their present miserable condition, being already in want of water; and if the manna should happen to fail, they must then utterly perish. Yet while they generally spake many and sore things against the man, there was one of them who exhorted them not to be unmindful of Moses, and of what great pains he had been at about their common safety; and not to despair of assistance from God. The multitude thereupon became still more unruly, and more mutinous against Moses than before. Hereupon Moses, although he was so basely abused by them, encouraged them in their despairing condition, and promised that he would procure them a great quantity of flesh meat, and that not for a few days only, but for many days. This they were not willing to believe; and when one of them asked, whence he could obtain such vast plenty of what he promised, he replied, "Neither God nor I, although we hear such opprobrious language from you, will leave off our labours for you; and this shall soon appear also." As soon as ever he had said this, the whole camp was filled with quails, and they stood round about them, and gathered them in great numbers. However, it was not long ere God punished the Hebrews for their insolence, and those reproaches they had used towards him; for no small number of them died; and still to this day the place retains the memory of this destruction, and is named *Kibroth-hattaavah*, which is, *The Graves of Lust*.

CHAPTER XIV

HOW MOSES SENT SOME PERSONS TO SEARCH OUT THE LAND OF THE CANAANITES, AND THE LARGENESS OF THEIR CITIES; AND FURTHER, THAT WHEN THOSE WHO WERE SENT WERE RETURNED, AFTER FORTY DAYS, AND REPORTED THAT THEY SHOULD NOT BE A MATCH FOR THEM, AND EXTOLLED THE STRENGTH OF THE CANAANITES, THE MULTITUDE WERE DISTURBED, AND FELL INTO DESPAIR; AND WERE RESOLVED TO STONE MOSES, AND TO RETURN BACK AGAIN INTO EGYPT, AND SERVE THE EGYPTIANS

1. WHEN Moses had led the Hebrews away from thence to a place called *Paran*, which was near to the borders of the Canaanites, and a place difficult to be continued in, he gathered the multitude together to a congregation; and standing in the midst of them, he said, "Of the two things that God determined to bestow upon us, Liberty, and the Possession of a Happy Country, the one of them ye already are partakers of, by the gift of God, and the other you will quickly obtain; for we now have our abode near the borders of the Canaanites, and nothing can hinder the acquisition of it, when we now at last are fallen upon it: I say, not only no king nor city, but neither the whole race of mankind, if they were all gathered together, could do it. Let us therefore prepare ourselves for the work, for the Canaanites will not resign up their land to us without fighting, but it must be wrested from them by great struggles in war. Let us then send spies, who may take a view of the goodness of the land, and what strength it is of; but,

above all things, let us be of one mind, and let us honour God, who above all is our helper and assister."

2. When Moses had said thus, the multitude requited him with marks of respect; and chose twelve spies, of the most eminent men, one out of each tribe, who, passing over all the land of Canaan, from the borders of Egypt, came to the city Hamath, and to mount Lebanon; and having learned the nature of the land, and of its inhabitants, they came home, having spent forty days in the whole work. They also brought with them of the fruits which the land bare; they also shewed them the excellency of those fruits, and gave an account of the great quantity of the good things that land afforded, which were motives to the multitude to go to war. But then they terrified them again with the great difficulty there was in obtaining it; that the rivers were so large and deep that they could not be passed over; and that the hills were so high that they could not travel along for them; that the cities were strong with walls, and their firm fortifications round about them. They told them also, that they found at Hebron, the posterity of the giants. Accordingly these spies, who had seen the land of Canaan, when they perceived that all these difficulties were greater there than they had met with since they came out of Egypt, they were affrighted at them themselves, and endeavoured to affright the multitude also.

3. So they supposed, from what they had heard, that it was impossible to get the possession of the country. And when the congregation was dissolved, they, their wives and children, continued their lamentation, as if God would not indeed assist them, but only promised them fair. They also again blamed Moses, and made a clamour against him and his brother Aaron, the high priest. Accordingly they passed that night very ill, and with contumelious language against them; but in the morning they ran to a congregation, intending to stone Moses and Aaron, and so to return back into Egypt.

4. But of the spies, there were Joshua, the son of Nun, of the tribe of Ephraim, and Caleb, of the tribe of Judah, that were afraid of the consequence, and came into the midst of them, and stilled the multitude, and desired them to be of good courage; and neither to condemn God, as having told them lies, nor to hearken to those who had affrighted them, by telling them what was not true concerning the Canaanites, but to those that encouraged them to hope for good success; and that they should gain possession of the happiness promised them, because neither the height of mountains nor the depth of rivers could hinder men of true courage from attempting them, especially while God would take care of them beforehand, and be assistant to them. "Let us then go," said they, "against our enemies, and have no suspicion of ill success, trusting in God to conduct us, and following those that are to be our leaders." Thus did these two exhort them, and endeavour to pacify the rage they were in. But Moses and Aaron fell on the ground, and besought God, not for their own deliverance, but that he would put a stop to what the people were unwarily doing, and would bring their minds to a quiet temper, which were now disordered by their present passion. The cloud also did now appear, and stood over the tabernacle, and declared to them the presence of God to be there.

CHAPTER XV

HOW MOSES WAS DISPLEASED AT THIS, AND FORETOLD THAT GOD WAS ANGRY, AND THAT THEY SHOULD CONTINUE IN THE WILDERNESS FOR FORTY YEARS, AND NOT, DURING THAT TIME, EITHER RETURN INTO EGYPT, OR TAKE POSSESSION OF CANAAN

1. MOSES came now boldly to the multitude, and informed them that God was moved at their abuse of him, and would inflict punishment upon them, not indeed such as they deserved for their sins, but such as parents inflicted on their children, in order to their correction: For, he said, that when he was in the tabernacle, and was bewailing with tears that destruction which was coming upon them, God put him in mind what things he had done for them, and what benefits they had received from him, and yet how ungrateful they had been to him; that just now they had been induced, through the timorousness of the spies, to think that their words were truer than his own promise to them; and that on this account, though he would not indeed destroy them all, nor utterly extirpate their nation, which he had honoured more than any other part of mankind, yet he would not permit them to take possession of the land of Canaan, nor enjoy its happiness; but would make them wander in the wilderness, and live without a fixed habitation, and without a city, for forty years together, as a punishment for this their transgression; but that he hath promised to give that land to our children, and that he would make them the possessors of those good things which, by your ungoverned passions, you have deprived yourselves of.

2. When Moses had discoursed thus to them, according to the direction of God, the multitude grieved, and were in affliction, and entreated Moses to procure their reconciliation to God, and to permit them no longer to wander in the wilderness, but to bestow cities upon them; but he replied, that God would not permit of any such trial, for that God was not moved to this determination from any human levity or anger, but that he had judicially condemned them to that punishment. Now we are not to disbelieve that Moses, who was but a single person, pacified so many ten thousands when they were in anger, and converted them to a mildness of temper; for God was with him, and prepared the way to his persuasions of the multitude; and as they had often been disobedient, they were now sensible that such disobedience was disadvantageous to them, and that they had still thereby fallen into calamities.

3. But this man was admirable for his virtue, and powerful in making men give credit to what he delivered, not only during the time of his natural life, but even there is still no one of the Hebrews, who does not act even now as if Moses were present, and ready to punish him if he should do any thing that is indecent; nay, there is no one but is obedient to what laws he ordained, although they might be concealed in their transgressions. There are also many other demonstrations that his power was more than human, for still some there have been, who have come from the parts beyond Euphrates, a journey of four months, through many dangers, and at great expenses, in honour of our temple; and yet, when they had offered their oblations, could not partake of their own sacrifices, because Moses had forbidden it, by somewhat in the law that did not permit them, or somewhat that had be-

fallen them, which our ancient customs made inconsistent therewith; some of these did not sacrifice at all, and others left their sacrifices in an imperfect condition; nay, many were not able, even at first, so much as to enter into the temple, but went their ways in this state, as preferring a submission to the laws of Moses before the fulfilling of their own inclinations, even when they had no fear upon them that anybody could convict them, but only out of a reverence to their own conscience. Thus this legislation, which appeared to be divine, made this man to be esteemed as one superior to his own nature. Nay, further, a little before the beginning of this war, when Claudius was emperor of the Romans, and Ismael was our high priest, and when so great a famine * was come upon us, that one

* See Antiq. b. xx. chap. ii. sect. 6; and Acts xi. 28.

tenth deal [of wheat] was sold for four drachmæ, and when no less than seventy cori of flour were brought into the temple, at the feast of unleavened bread, (these cori are thirty-one Sicilian, but forty-one Athenian medimni,) not one of the priests was so hardy as to eat one crumb of it, even while so great a distress was upon the land; and this out of a dread of the law, and of that wrath which God retains against acts of wickedness, even when no one can accuse the actors. Whence we are not to wonder at what was then done, while to this very day the writings left by Moses have so great a force, that even those that hate us do confess, that he who established this settlement was God, and that it was by the means of Moses, and of his virtue: but as to these matters, let every one take them as he thinks fit.

BOOK IV

CONTAINING THE INTERVAL OF THIRTY-EIGHT YEARS,

FROM THE REJECTION OF THAT GENERATION TO THE DEATH OF MOSES

CHAPTER I

THE FIGHT OF THE HEBREWS WITH THE CANAANITES, WITHOUT THE CONSENT OF MOSES; AND THEIR DEFEAT

1. Now this life of the Hebrews in the wilderness was so disagreeable and troublesome to them, and they were so uneasy at it, that although God had forbidden them to meddle with the Canaanites, yet could they not be persuaded to be obedient to the words of Moses, and to be quiet; but supposing they should be able to beat their enemies, even without his approbation, they accused him, and suspected that he made it his business to keep them in a distressed condition, that they might always stand in need of his assistance. Accordingly they resolved to fight with the Canaanites, and said that God gave them his assistance,—not out of regard to Moses's intercessions, but because he took care of their entire nation, on account of their forefathers, whose affairs he took under his own conduct; as also, that it was on account of their own virtue, that he had formerly procured them their liberty, and would be assisting to them, now they were willing to take pains for it. They also said that they were possessed of abilities sufficient for the conquest of their enemies, although Moses should have a mind to alienate God from them; that, however, it was for their advantage to be their own masters, and not so far to rejoice in their deliverance from the indignities they endured under the Egyptians, as to bear the tyranny of Moses over them, and to suffer themselves to be deluded, and live according to his pleasure, as though God did only foretell what concerns us out of his kindness to him, as if they were not all the posterity of Abraham; that God made him alone the author of all the knowledge we have, and we must still

learn it from him; that it would be a piece of prudence to oppose his arrogant pretences, and to put their confidence in God, and to resolve to take possession of that land which he had promised them, and not to give ear to him, who, on this account, and under the pretence of divine authority, forbade them so to do. Considering, therefore, the distressed state they were in at present, and that in those desert places they were still to expect things would be worse with them, they resolved to fight with the Canaanites, as submitting only to God, their supreme commander, and not waiting for any assistance from their legislator.

2. When, therefore, they had come to this resolution, as being best for them, they went against their enemies; but those enemies were not dismayed, either at the attack itself, or at the great multitude that made it, and received them with great courage. Many of the Hebrews were slain: and the remainder of the army, upon the disorder of their troops, were pursued, and fled, after a shameful manner, to their camp. Whereupon this unexpected misfortune made them quite despond; and they hoped for nothing that was good; as gathering from it, that this affliction came from the wrath of God, because they rashly went out to war without his approbation.

3. But when Moses saw how deeply they were affected with this defeat, and being afraid lest the enemies should grow insolent upon this victory, and should be desirous of gaining still greater glory, and should attack them, he resolved that it was proper to withdraw the army into the wilderness to a further distance from the Canaanites: so the multitude gave themselves up again to his conduct; for they were sensible that, without his care for them, their affairs would not be in a good condition; and he caused the host to remove, and he went further

into the wilderness, as intending there to let them rest, and not to permit them to fight the Canaanites before God should afford them a more favourable opportunity.

CHAPTER II

THE SEDITION OF CORAH AND OF THE MULTITUDE AGAINST MOSES, AND AGAINST HIS BROTHER, CONCERNING THE PRIESTHOOD

1. THAT which is usually the case of great armies, and especially upon ill success, to be hard to be pleased, and governed with difficulty, did now befall the Jews; for they being in number six hundred thousand, and, by reason of their great multitude, not readily subject to their governors, even in prosperity, they at this time were more than usually angry, both against one another and against their leader, because of the distress they were in, and the calamities they then endured. Such a sedition overtook them, as we have not the like example either among the Greeks or the Barbarians, by which they were in danger of being all destroyed, but were notwithstanding saved by Moses, who would not remember that he had been almost stoned to death by them. Nor did God neglect to prevent their ruin; but, notwithstanding the indignities they had offered their legislator and the laws, and their disobedience to the commandments which he had sent them by Moses, he delivered them from those terrible calamities, which, without his providential care, had been brought upon them by this sedition. So I will first explain the cause whence this sedition arose, and then will give an account of the sedition itself; as also of what settlements Moses made for their government, after it was over.

2. Corah, a Hebrew of principal account, both by his family and by his wealth, one that was also able to speak well, and one that could easily persuade the people by his speeches, saw that Moses was in an exceeding great dignity, and was uneasy at it, and envied him on that account, (he was of the same tribe with Moses, and of kin to him,) was particularly grieved, because he thought he better deserved that honourable post on account of his great riches, and not inferior to him in his birth. So he raised a clamour against him among the Levites, who were of the same tribe, and especially among his kindred, saying, "That it was a very sad thing that they should overlook Moses, while he hunted after, and paved the way to glory for himself, and by ill arts should obtain it, under the pretence of God's command, while, contrary to the laws, he had given the priesthood to Aaron, not by the common suffrage of the multitude, but by his own vote, as bestowing dignities in a tyrannical way on whom he pleased." He added, "That this concealed way of imposing on them was harder to be borne than if it had been done by an open force upon them, because he did now not only take away their power without their consent, but even while they were unapprised of his contrivances against them; for whosoever is conscious to himself that he deserves any dignity, aims to get it by persuasion, and not by an arrogant method of violence; but those that believe it impossible to obtain those honours justly, make a show of goodness, and do not introduce force, but by cunning tricks grow wickedly powerful: that it was proper for the multitude to punish such men, even while they think themselves

concealed in their designs, and not suffer them to gain strength, till they have them for their open enemies. For what account," added he, "is Moses able to give, why he has bestowed the priesthood on Aaron and his sons? for if God had determined to bestow that honour on one of the tribe of Levi, I am more worthy of it than he is; I myself being equal to Moses by my family, and superior to him both in riches and in age: but if God had determined to bestow it on the eldest tribe, that of Reuben might have it most justly; and then Dathan, and Abiram, and [On, the son of] Peleth, would have it; for these are the oldest men of that tribe, and potent on account of their great wealth also."

3. Now Corah, when he said this, had a mind to appear to take care of the public welfare; but in reality he was endeavouring to procure to have that dignity transferred by the multitude to himself. Thus did he, out of a malignant design, but with plausible words, discourse to those of his own tribe; and when these words did gradually spread to more of the people, and when the hearers still added to what tended to the scandals that were cast upon Aaron, the whole army was full of them. Now of those that conspired with Corah, there were two hundred and fifty, and those of the principal men also, who were eager to have the priesthood taken away from Moses's brother, and to bring him into disgrace: nay, the multitude themselves were provoked to be seditious, and attempted to stone Moses, and gathered themselves together after an indecent manner, with confusion and disorder. And now they all were, in a tumultuous manner, raising a clamour before the tabernacle of God, to prosecute the tyrant, and to relieve the multitude from their slavery under him who, under colour of the divine commands, laid violent injunctions upon them; for that had it been God who chose one that was to perform the office of a priest, he would have raised a worthy person to that dignity, and would not have produced such a one as was inferior to many others, nor have given him that office; and that in case he had judged it fit to bestow it on Aaron, he would have permitted it to the multitude to bestow it, and not have left it to be bestowed by his own brother.

4. Now although Moses had a great while ago foreseen this calumny of Corah, and had seen that the people were irritated, yet was he not affrighted at it; but being of good courage, because he had given them right advice about their affairs, and knowing that his brother had been made partaker of the priesthood at the command of God, and not by his own favour to him, he came to the assembly: and, as for the multitude, he said not a word to them, but spake as loud to Corah as he could; and being very skilful in making speeches, and having this natural talent among others, that he could greatly move the multitude with his discourses, he said, "O Corah, both thou and all these with thee (pointing to the two hundred and fifty men) seem to be worthy of this honour; nor do I pretend but that this whole company may be worthy of the like dignity, although they may not be so rich, or so great as you are: nor have I taken and given this office to my brother, because he excelled others in riches, for thou exceedest us both in the greatness of thy wealth;* nor indeed because he was of an eminent family, for God, by giving us the same common ancestor,

---

* Reland here takes notice, that although our Bibles say little or nothing of these riches of Corah, yet that both the Jews and Mohammedans, as well as Josephus, are full of it.

has made our families equal: nay, nor was it out of brotherly affection, which another might yet have justly done; for certainly unless I had bestowed this honour out of regard to God, and to his laws, I had not passed by myself and given it to another, as being nearer of kin to myself than to my brother, and having a closer intimacy with myself than I have with him; for surely it would not be a wise thing for me to expose myself to the dangers of offending, and to bestow the happy employment on this account upon another. But I am above such base practices: nor would God have overlooked this matter, and seen himself thus despised; nor would he have suffered you to be ignorant of what you were to do in order to please him; but he hath himself chosen one that is to perform that sacred office to him, and thereby freed us from that care. So that it was not a thing that I pretend to give, but only according to the determination of God; I therefore propose it still to be contended for by such as please to put in for it, only desiring, that he who has been already preferred, and has already obtained it, may be allowed now also to offer himself for a candidate. He prefers your peace, and your living without sedition, to this honourable employment, although in truth it was with your approbation that he obtained it: for though God were the donor, yet do we not offend when we think fit to accept it with your goodwill; yet would it have been an instance of impiety not to have taken that honourable employment when he offered it; nay, it had been exceedingly unreasonable, when God had thought fit any one should have it for all time to come, and had made it secure and firm to him, to have refused it. However, he himself will judge again who it shall be whom he would have to offer sacrifices to him, and to have the direction of matters of religion; for it is absurd that Corah, who is ambitious of this honour, should deprive God of the power of giving it to whom he pleases. Put an end, therefore, to your sedition and disturbance on this account; and to-morrow morning do every one of you that desire the priesthood bring a censer from home, and come hither with incense and fire: and do thou, O Corah, leave the judgment to God, and await to see on which side he will give his determination upon this occasion, but do not thou make thyself greater than God. Do thou also come, that this contest about this honourable employment may receive determination. And I suppose we may admit Aaron without offence to offer himself to this scrutiny, since he is of the same lineage with thyself, and has done nothing in his priesthood that can be liable to exception. Come ye therefore together, and offer your incense in public before all the people; and when you offer it, he whose sacrifice God shall accept shall be ordained to the priesthood, and shall be clear of the present calumny on Aaron, as if I had granted him that favour because he was my brother."

CHAPTER III

HOW THOSE THAT STIRRED UP THIS SEDITION WERE DESTROYED, ACCORDING TO THE WILL OF GOD; AND HOW AARON, MOSES'S BROTHER, BOTH HE AND HIS POSTERITY, RETAINED THE PRIESTHOOD

1. WHEN Moses had said this, the multitude left off the turbulent behaviour they had indulged, and the suspicion they had of Moses, and commended what he had said; for those proposals were good, and were so esteemed of the people. At that time, therefore, they dissolved the assembly; but on the next day they came to the congregation, in order to be present at the sacrifice, and at the determination that was to be made between the candidates for the priesthood. Now this congregation proved a turbulent one, and the multitude were in great suspense in expectation of what was to be done; for some of them would have been pleased if Moses had been convicted of evil practices; but the wiser sort desired that they might be delivered from the present disorder and disturbance, for they were afraid that if this sedition went on, the good order of their settlement would rather be destroyed; but the whole body of the people do naturally delight in clamours against their governors, and, by changing their opinions upon the harangues of every speaker, disturb the public tranquillity. And now Moses sent messengers for Abiram and Dathan, and ordered them to come to the assembly, and wait there for the holy offices that were to be performed. But they answered the messenger that they would not obey his summons; nay, would not overlook Moses's behaviour, who was growing too great for them by evil practices. Now when Moses heard of this their answer, he desired the heads of the people to follow him, and he went to the faction of Dathan, not thinking it any frightful thing at all to go to these insolent people; so they made no opposition, but went along with him. But Dathan and his associates, when they understood that Moses and the principal of the people were coming to them, came out, with their wives and children, and stood before their tents, and looked to see what Moses would do. They had also their servants about them to defend themselves, in case Moses should use force against them.

2. But he came near, and lifted up his hands to heaven, and cried out with a loud voice, in order to be heard by the whole multitude, and said, "O Lord of the creatures that are in heaven, in the earth, and in the sea; for thou art the most authentic witness to what I have done, that it has all been done by thy appointment, and that it was thou that affordest us assistance when we attempted anything, and shewedst mercy on the Hebrews in all their distresses, do thou come now, and hear all that I say, for no action or thought escapes thy knowledge; so that thou wilt not disdain to speak what is true for my vindication without any regard to the ungrateful imputations of these men. As for what was done before I was born, thou knowest best, as not learning them by report, but seeing them, and being present with them when they were done; but for what has been done of late, and which these men, although they know them well enough, unjustly pretend to suspect, be thou my witness. When I lived a private quiet life, I left those good things, which by my own diligence, and by thy counsel, I enjoyed with Raguel my father-in-law; and I gave myself up to this people, and underwent many miseries on their account. I also bore great labours at first, in order to obtain liberty for them, and now in order to their preservation; and have always shewed myself ready to assist them in every distress of theirs. Now, therefore, since I am suspected by those very men whose being is owing to my labours, come thou, as it is reasonable to hope thou wilt; thou, I say, who shewedst me that fire at mount Sinai, and madest me to hear its voice, and to see the several wonders which that place afforded me; thou who commandedst me to go to Egypt,

and declare thy will to this people; thou who disturbedst the happy estate of the Egyptians, and gavest us the opportunity of flying away from our slavery under them, and madest the dominion of Pharaoh inferior to my dominion; thou who didst make the sea dry land for us, when we knew not whither to go, and didst overwhelm the Egyptians with those destructive waves which had been divided for us; thou who didst bestow upon us the security of weapons when we were naked; thou who didst make the fountains that were corrupted to flow, so as to be fit for drinking, and didst furnish us with water that came out of the rocks, when we were in the greatest want of it; thou who didst preserve our lives with [quails, which was] food from the sea, when the fruits of the ground failed us; thou who didst send us such food from heaven as had never been seen before; thou who didst suggest to us the knowledge of thy laws, and appoint to us a form of government,—come thou, I say, O Lord of the whole world, and that as such a Judge and a Witness to me as cannot be bribed, and shew how I have never admitted of any gift against justice, from any of the Hebrews, and have never condemned a poor man that ought to have been acquitted, on account of one that was rich; and have never attempted to hurt this commonwealth. I am now here present, and am suspected of a thing the remotest from my intentions, as if I had given the priesthood to Aaron, not at thy command, but out of my own favour to him; do thou at this time demonstrate that all things are administered by thy providence, and that nothing happens by chance, but is governed by thy will, and thereby attains its end: as also demonstrate that thou takest care of those that have done good to the Hebrews; demonstrate this, I say, by the punishment of Abiram and Dathan, who condemn thee as an insensible Being, and one overcome by my contrivances. This wilt thou do by inflicting such an open punishment on these men who so madly fly in the face of thy glory, as will take them out of the world, not in an ordinary manner, but so that it may appear they do not die after the manner of other men: let that ground which they tread upon, open about them and consume them, with their families and goods. This will be a demonstration of thy power to all men: and this method of their sufferings will be an instruction of wisdom for those that entertain profane sentiments of thee. By this means I shall be found a good servant in the precepts thou hast given by me. But if the calumnies they have raised against me be true, mayest thou preserve these men from every evil accident, and bring all that destruction on me which I have imprecated upon them. And when thou hast inflicted punishment on those that have endeavoured to deal unjustly with this people, bestow upon them concord and peace. Save this multitude that follow thy commandments, and preserve them free from harm, and let them not partake of the punishment of those that have sinned; for thou knowest thyself it is not just, that for the wickedness of those men the whole body of the Israelites should suffer punishment."

3. When Moses had said this, with tears in his eyes, the ground was moved on a sudden; and the agitation that set it in motion was like that which the wind produces in waves of the sea. The people were all affrighted; and the ground that was about their tents sunk down at the great noise, with a terrible sound, and carried whatsoever was dear to the seditious, into itself, who so entirely perished, that there was not the least appearance that any man had ever been seen there, the earth that had opened itself about them closing again, and becoming entire as it was before, insomuch that such as saw it afterward did not perceive that any such accident had happened to it. Thus did these men perish, and become a demonstration of the power of God. And truly, any one would lament them, not only on account of this calamity that befell them, which yet deserves our commiseration, but also because their kindred were pleased with their sufferings; for they forgot the relation they bare to them, and at the sight of this sad accident approved of the judgment given against them; and because they looked upon the people about Dathan as pestilent men, they thought they perished as such, and did not grieve for them.

4. And now Moses called for those that contended about the priesthood, that trial might be made who should be priest, and that he whose sacrifice God was best pleased with, might be ordained to that function. There attended two hundred and fifty men, who indeed were honoured by the people, not only on account of the power of their ancestors, but also on account of their own, in which they excelled the others: Aaron also and Corah came forth, and they all offered incense, in those censers of theirs which they brought with them before the tabernacle. Hereupon so great a fire shone out as no one ever saw in any that is made by the hand of man, neither in those eruptions out of the earth that are caused by subterraneous burnings, nor in such fires as arise of their own accord in the woods, when the agitation is caused by the trees rubbing one against another: but this fire was very bright, and had a terrible flame, such as is kindled at the command of God; by whose eruption on them, all the company, and Corah himself, were destroyed,* and this so entirely, that their very bodies left no remains behind them. Aaron alone was preserved, and not at all hurt by the fire, because it was God that sent the fire, to burn those only who ought to be burned. Hereupon Moses, after these men were destroyed, was desirous that the memory of this judgment might be delivered down to posterity, and that future ages might be acquainted with it; and so he commanded Eleazar, the son of Aaron, to put their censers near the brazen altar, that they might be a memorial to posterity of what these men suffered, for supposing that the power of God might be eluded. And thus Aaron was now no longer esteemed to have the priesthood by the favour of Moses, but by the public judgment of God; and thus he and his children peaceably enjoyed that honour afterward.

CHAPTER IV

WHAT HAPPENED TO THE HEBREWS DURING THIRTY-EIGHT YEARS IN THE WILDERNESS

1. HOWEVER, this sedition was so far from ceasing upon this destruction, that it grew much stronger, and became more intolerable. And the occasion of its growing worse was of that nature, as made it likely the calamity would never cease,

* It appears here, and from the Samaritan Pentateuch, and in effect, from the psalmist, as also from the Apostolical Constitutions, from Clement's first epistle to the Corinthians, from Ignatius's epistle to the Magnesians, and from Eusebius, that Corah was not swallowed up with the Reubenites, but burned with the Levites of his own tribe. See Essay on the Old Testament, pp. 64,

but last for a long time; for the men, believing already that nothing is done without the providence of God, would have it that these things came thus to pass, not without God's favour to Moses; they therefore laid the blame upon him, that God was so angry, and that this happened not so much because of the wickedness of those that were punished, as because Moses procured the punishment; and that these men had been destroyed without any sin of theirs, only because they were zealous about the divine worship; as also, that he who had been the cause of this diminution of the people, by destroying so many men, and those the most excellent of them all, besides his escaping any punishment himself, had now given the priesthood to his brother so firmly, that nobody could any longer dispute it with him; for no one else, to be sure, could now put in for it, since he must have seen those that first did so, to have miserably perished. Nay, besides this, the kindred of those that were destroyed made great entreaties to the multitude to abate the arrogance of Moses, because it would be safest for them so to do.

2. Now Moses, upon his hearing for a good while that the people were tumultuous, was afraid that they would attempt some other innovation, and that some great and sad calamity would be the consequence. He called the multitude to a congregation, and patiently heard what apology they had to make for themselves, without opposing them, and this lest he should imbitter the multitude: he only desired the heads of the tribes to bring their rods,* with the names of their tribes inscribed upon them, and that he should receive the priesthood in whose rod God should give a sign. This was agreed to. So the rest brought their rods, as did Aaron also, who had written the tribe of Levi on his rod. These rods Moses laid up in the tabernacle of God. On the next day he brought out the rods, which were known from one another by those who brought them, they having distinctly noted them, as had the multitude also; and as to the rest, in the same form Moses had received them, in that they saw them still; but they also saw buds and branches grown out of Aaron's rod, with ripe fruits upon them: they were almonds, the rod having been cut out of that tree. The people were so amazed at this strange sight, that though Moses and Aaron were before under some degree of hatred, they now laid that hatred aside, and began to admire the judgment of God concerning them; so that hereafter they applauded what God had decreed, and permitted Aaron to enjoy the priesthood peaceably. And thus God ordained him priest, three several times, and he retained that honour without further disturbance. And hereby this sedition of the Hebrews, which had been a great one, and had lasted a great while, was at last composed.

3. And now Moses, because the tribe of Levi was made free from war and warlike expeditions, and was set apart for the divine worship, lest they should want and seek after the necessaries of life, and so neglect the temple, commanded the Hebrews, according to the will of God, that when they should gain the possession of the land of Canaan, they should assign forty-eight good and fair cities to the Levites; and permit them to enjoy their suburbs, as far as the limit of two thousand cubits would extend from the walls of the city. And besides this, he appointed that the people should pay the tithe of their annual fruits of the earth, both to the Levites and to the priests. And this is what that tribe receives of the multitude; but I think it necessary to set down what is paid by all, peculiarly to the priests.

4. Accordingly he commanded the Levites to yield up to the priests thirteen of their forty-eight cities, and to set apart for them the tenth part of the tithes which they every year receive of the people; as also, that it was but just to offer to God the first-fruits of the entire product of the ground; and that they should offer the first-born of those four-footed beasts that are appointed for sacrifices, if it be a male, to the priests, to be slain, that they and their entire families may eat them in the holy city; but that the owners of those first-born which are not appointed for sacrifices in the laws of our country, should bring a shekel and a half in their stead: but for the first-born of a man, five shekels: that they should also have the first-fruits out of the shearing of the sheep; and that when any baked bread-corn, and made loaves of it, they should give somewhat of what they had baked to them. Moreover, when any have made a sacred vow, I mean those that are called *Nazarites*, that suffer their hair to grow long, and use no wine, when they consecrate their hair,† and offer it for a sacrifice, they are to allot that hair for the priests, [to be thrown into the fire.] Such also as dedicate themselves to God, as a corban, which denotes what the Greeks call a *gift*, when they are desirous of being freed from that ministration, are to lay down money for the priests: thirty shekels if it be a woman, and fifty if it be a man; but if any be too poor to pay the appointed sum, it shall be lawful for the priests to determine that sum as they think fit. And if any slay beasts at home for a private festival, but not for a religious one, they are obliged to bring the maw and the cheek, [or breast,] and the right shoulder of the sacrifice to the priests. With these, Moses contrived that the priests should be plentifully maintained, besides what they had out of those offerings for sins, which the people gave them, as I have set it down in the foregoing book. He also ordered, that out of every thing allotted for the priests, their servants, [their sons,] their daughters, and their wives, should partake, as well as themselves, excepting what came to them out of the sacrifices that were offered for sins; for of those none but the males of the family of the priests might eat, and this in the temple also, and that the same day they were offered.

5. When Moses had made these constitutions, after the sedition was over, he removed, together with the whole army, and came to the borders of Idumea. He then sent ambassadors to the king of the Idumeans, and desired him to give him a passage through his country; and agreed to send him what hostages he should desire, to secure him from an injury. He desired him also, that he would allow his army liberty to buy provisions; and, if he insisted upon it, he would pay down a price for the very water they should drink. But the king was not pleased with this embassage from Moses: nor did he allow a passage for the army, but brought his people armed to meet Moses, and to hinder them, in case they should endeavour to force their passage. Upon which Moses consulted God by the oracle, who would not have him begin the war first; and so

---

* Concerning these twelve rods of the twelve tribes of Israel, see St Clement's account, much larger than that in our Bibles, 1 Epist. sect. 45; as is Josephus's present account in some measure larger also.

† Grotius, on Numb. vi. 18, takes notice that the Greeks also, as well as the Jews, sometimes consecrated the hair of their heads to the gods.

BLOOMING ROD OF AARON

he withdrew his forces, and travelled round about through the wilderness.

6. Then it was that Miriam, the sister of Moses, came to her end, having completed her fortieth year * since she left Egypt, on the first † day of the lunar month Xanthicus. They then made a public funeral for her, at a great expense. She was buried upon a certain mountain, which they called *Sin ;* and when they had mourned for her thirty days, Moses purified the people after this manner: He brought a heifer that had never been used to the plough or to husbandry, that was complete in all its parts, and entirely of a red colour, at a little distance from the camp, into a place perfectly clean. This heifer was slain by the high priest, and her blood sprinkled with his finger seven times before the tabernacle of God; after this, the entire heifer was burnt in that state, together with its skin and entrails; and they threw cedar-wood, and hyssop, and scarlet wool, into the midst of the fire; then a clean man gathered all her ashes together, and laid them in a place perfectly clean. When therefore any persons were defiled by a dead body, they put a little of these ashes into spring water, with hyssop, and, dipping part of these ashes in it, they sprinkled them with it, both on the third day, and on the seventh, and after that they were clean. This he enjoined them to do also when the tribes should come into their own land.

7. Now when this purification, which their leader made upon the mourning for his sister, as it has been now described, was over, he caused the army to remove, and to march through the wilderness and through Arabia; and when he came to a place which the Arabians esteem their metropolis, which was formerly called *Arce,* but has now the name of *Petra,* at this place, which was encompassed with high mountains, Aaron went up one of them in the sight of the whole army, Moses having before told him that he was to die, for this place was over against them. He put off his pontifical garments, and delivered them to Eleazar his son, to whom the high priesthood belonged, because he was the elder brother; and died while the multitude looked upon him. He died in the same year wherein he lost his sister, having lived in all a hundred twenty and three years. He died on the first day of that lunar month which is called by the Athenians *Hecatombæon,* by the Macedonians *Lous,* but by the Hebrews *Abba.*

CHAPTER V

HOW MOSES CONQUERED SIHON AND OG, KINGS OF THE AMORITES, AND DESTROYED THEIR WHOLE ARMY, AND THEN DIVIDED THEIR LAND BY LOT TO TWO TRIBES AND A HALF OF THE HEBREWS

1. THE people mourned for Aaron thirty days, and when this mourning was over, Moses removed the army from that place, and came to the river Arnon, which, issuing out of the moun-

* Josephus here uses this phrase "when the fortieth year was completed," for when it was begun; as does St Luke, "when the day of Pentecost was completed," Acts ii. 1.

† Whether Miriam died, as Josephus's Greek copies imply, on the first day of the month, may be doubted, because the Latin copies say it was on the tenth, and so say the Jewish calendars also, as Dr Bernard assures us. It is said her sepulchre is still extant near Petra, the old capital city of Arabia Petræa, at this day, as also that of Aaron not far off.

tains of Arabia, and running through all that wilderness, falls into the lake Asphaltitis, and becomes the limit between the land of the Moabites and the land of the Amorites. This land is fruitful, and sufficient to maintain a great number of men with the good things it produces. Moses therefore sent messengers to Sihon, the king of this country, desiring that he would grant his army a passage, upon what security he should please to require; he promised that he should be in no way injured, neither as to that country which Sihon governed, nor as to its inhabitants; and that he would buy his provisions at such a price as should be to their advantage, even though he should desire to sell them their very water. But Sihon refused his offer, and put his army into battle array, and was preparing everything in order to hinder their passing over Arnon.

2. When Moses saw that the Amorite king was disposed to enter upon hostilities with them, he thought he ought not to bear that insult; and, determining to wean the Hebrews from their indolent temper, and prevent the disorders which arose thence, which had been the occasion of their former sedition, (nor indeed were they now thoroughly easy in their minds,) he inquired of God, whether he would give him leave to fight? which, when he had done, and God also promised him the victory, he was himself very courageous, and ready to proceed to fighting. Accordingly, he encouraged the soldiers; and he desired of them that they would take the pleasure of fighting, now God gave them leave so to do. They then upon the receipt of this permission, which they so much longed for, put on their whole armour, and set about the work without delay. But the Amorite king was not now like to himself, when the Hebrews were ready to attack him; but both he himself was affrighted at the Hebrews, and his army, which before had shewed themselves to be of good courage, were then found to be timorous: so they could not sustain the first onset, nor bear up against the Hebrews, but fled away, as thinking this would afford them a more likely way for their escape than fighting; for they depended upon their cities, which were strong, from which yet they reaped no advantage when they were forced to fly to them; for as soon as the Hebrews saw them giving ground, they immediately pursued them close; and when they had broken their ranks, they greatly terrified them, and some of them broke off from the rest, and ran away to the cities. Now the Hebrews pursued them briskly, and obstinately persevered in the labours they had already undergone; and being very skilful in slinging, and very dexterous in throwing of darts, or any thing else of that kind; and also having nothing but light armour, which made them quick in the pursuit, they overtook their enemies; and for those that were most remote, and could not be overtaken, they reached them by their slings and their bows, so that many were slain; and those that escaped the slaughter were sorely wounded, and these were more distressed with thirst than with any of those that fought against them, for it was the summer season; and when the greatest number of them were brought down to the river out of a desire to drink, as also when others fled away by troops, the Hebrews came round them, and shot at them; so that, what with darts and what with arrows, they made a slaughter of them all. Sihon their king was also slain. So the Hebrews spoiled the dead bodies, and took their prey. The land also which they took was full of abundance of fruits, and the army went all

over it without fear, and fed their cattle upon it; and they took the enemies prisoners, for they could no way put a stop to them, since all the fighting men were destroyed. Such was the destruction which overtook the Amorites, who were neither sagacious in counsel nor courageous in action. Hereupon the Hebrews took possession of their land, which is a country situate between three rivers, and naturally resembling an island: the river Arnon being its southern limit; the river Jabbok determining its northern side, which, running into Jordan, loses its own name, and takes the other: while Jordan itself runs along by it, on its western coast.

3. When matters were come to this state, Og, the king of Gilead and Gaulanitis, fell upon the Israelites. He brought an army with him, and came in haste to the assistance of his friend Sihon; but though he found him already slain, yet did he resolve still to come and fight the Hebrews, supposing he should be too hard for them, and being desirous to try their valour; but failing of his hope, he was both himself slain in the battle, and all his army was destroyed. So Moses passed over the river Jabbok, and overran the kingdom of Og. He overthrew their cities, and slew all their inhabitants, who yet exceeded in riches all the men in that part of the continent, on account of the goodness of the soil, and the great quantity of their wealth. Now Og had very few equals, either in the largeness of his body or handsomeness of his appearance. He was also a man of great activity in the use of his hands, so that his actions were not unequal to the vast largeness and handsome appearance of his body; and men could easily guess at his strength and magnitude when they took his bed at Rabbath, the royal city of the Ammonites; its structure was of iron, its breadth four cubits, and its length a cubit more than double thereto. However, his fall did not only improve the circumstances of the Hebrews for the present, but by his death he was the occasion of further good success to them; for they presently took those sixty cities which were encompassed with excellent walls, and had been subject to him; and all got both in general and in particular a great prey.

CHAPTER VI

CONCERNING BALAAM THE PROPHET, AND WHAT KIND OF MAN HE WAS

1. Now Moses, when he had brought his army to Jordan, pitched his camp in the great plain over against Jericho. This city is a very happy situation, and very fit for producing palm-trees and balsam; and now the Israelites began to be very proud of themselves, and very eager for fighting. Moses then, after he had offered for a few days sacrifices of thanksgiving to God, and feasted the people, sent a party of armed men to lay waste the country of the Midianites, and to take their cities. Now the occasion which he took for making war upon them was this that follows:—

2. When Balak, the king of the Moabites, who had from his ancestors a friendship and league with the Midianites, saw how great the Israelites were grown, he was much affrighted on account of his own and his kingdom's danger; for he was not acquainted with this, that the Hebrews would not meddle with any other country, but were to be contented with the possession of the land of Canaan, God having forbidden them

to go any further.* So he, with more haste than wisdom, resolved to make an attempt upon them by words: but he did not judge it prudent to fight against them, after they had such prosperous successes, and even became out of ill successes more happy than before; but he thought to hinder them, if he could, from growing greater, and so he resolved to send ambassadors to the Midianites about them. Now these Midianites, knowing there was one Balaam, who lived by Euphrates, and was the greatest of the prophets at that time, and one that was in friendship with them, sent some of their honourable princes along with the ambassadors of Balak, to entreat the prophet to come to them, that he might imprecate curses to the destruction of the Israelites. So Balaam received the ambassadors, and treated them very kindly; and when he had supped, he inquired what was God's will, and what this matter was for which the Midianites entreated him to come to them. But when God opposed his going, he came to the ambassadors, and told them that he was himself very willing and desirous to comply with their request, but informed them that God was opposite to his intentions, even that God who had raised him to great reputation on account of the truth of his predictions; for that this army, which they entreated him to come and curse, was in the favour of God; on which account he advised them to go home again, and not to persist in their enmity against the Israelites: and when he had given them that answer, he dismissed the ambassadors.

3. Now the Midianites, at the earnest request and fervent entreaties of Balak, sent other ambassadors to Balaam, who, desiring to gratify the men, inquired again of God; but he was displeased at this [second] trial,† and bid him by no means to contradict the ambassadors. Now Balaam did not imagine that God gave this injunction in order to deceive him, so he went along with the ambassadors; but when the divine angel met him in the way, when he was in a narrow passage, and hedged in with a wall on both sides, the ass on which Balaam rode under-

---

* What Josephus here remarks is well worth our remark in this place also—viz., That the Israelites were never to meddle with the Moabites or Ammonites, or any other people, but those belonging to the land of Canaan, and the countries of Sihon and Og beyond Jordan, as far as the desert and Euphrates; and that therefore no other people had reason to fear the conquests of the Israelites; but that those countries given them by God were their proper and peculiar portion among the nations, and that all who endeavoured to dispossess them might ever be justly destroyed by them.

† Note that Josephus never supposes Balaam to be an idolater, nor to seek idolatrous enchantments, or to prophesy falsely, but to be no other than an ill-disposed prophet of the true God; and intimates that God's answer the second time, permitting him to go, was ironical and on design that he should be deceived, (which sort of deception, by way of punishment for former crimes, Josephus never scruples to admit, as ever esteeming such wicked men justly and providentially deceived.) But perhaps we had better keep here close to the text, which says (Numb. xxiii. 20, 21) that God only permitted Balaam to go along with the ambassadors, in case they came and called him, or positively insisted on his going along with them on any terms; whereas Balaam seems out of impatience to have risen up in the morning, and saddled his ass, and rather to have called them, than stayed for their calling him; so zealous does he seem to have been for his reward of divination, his wages of unrighteousness, (Numb. xxii. 7, 17, 18, 37; 2 Pet. ii. 15; Jude 5, 11;) which reward or wages the truly religious prophets of God never required nor accepted, as our Josephus justly takes notice in the cases of Samuel, (Antiq. b. v. chap. iv. sect. 1,) and Daniel, (Antiq. b. x. chap. xi. sect. 8.) See also Gen. xiv. 22, 23; 2 Kings v. 15, 16, 26, 27; and Acts viii. 17.

stood that it was a divine spirit that met him, and thrust Balaam to one of the walls, without regard to the stripes which Balaam, when he was hurt by the wall, gave her; but when the ass, upon the angel's continuing to distress her, and upon the stripes which were given her, fell down, by the will of God, she made use of the voice of a man, and complained of Balaam as acting unjustly to her; that whereas he had no fault to find with her in her former service to him, he now inflicted stripes upon her, as not understanding that she was hindered from serving him in what he was now going about, by the providence of God. And when he was disturbed by reason of the voice of the ass, which was that of a man, the angel plainly appeared to him, and blamed him for the stripes he had given his ass; and informed him that the brute creature was not in fault, but that he was himself come to obstruct his journey, as being contrary to the will of God. Upon which Balaam was afraid, and was preparing to return back again: yet did God excite him to go on his intended journey, but added this injunction, that he should declare nothing but what he himself should suggest to his mind.

4. When God had given him this charge, he came to Balak; and when the king had entertained him in a magnificent manner, he desired him to go to one of the mountains to take a view of the state of the camp of the Hebrews. Balak himself also came to the mountain, and brought the prophet along with him, with a royal attendance. This mountain lay over their heads, and was distant sixty furlongs from the camp. Now when he saw them, he desired the king to build him seven altars, and to bring him as many bulls and rams; to which desire the king did presently conform. He then slew the sacrifices, and offered them as burnt-offerings, that he might observe some signal of the flight of the Hebrews. Then said he, "Happy is this people, on whom God bestows the possession of innumerable good things, and grants them his own providence to be their assistant and their guide; so that there is not any nation among mankind but you will be esteemed superior to them in virtue, and in the earnest prosecution of the best rules of life, and of such as are pure from wickedness, and will leave those rules to your excellent children, and this out of the regard that God bears to you, and the provision of such things for you as may render you happier than any other people under the sun. You shall retain that land to which he hath sent you, and it shall ever be under the command of your children; and both all the earth, as well as the sea, shall be filled with your glory: and you shall be sufficiently numerous to supply the world in general, and every region of it in particular, with inhabitants out of your stock. However, O blessed army! wonder that you are become so many from one father: and truly, the land of Canaan can now hold you, as being yet comparatively few; but know ye that the whole world is proposed to be your place of habitation for ever. The multitude of your posterity also shall live as well in the islands as on the continent, and that more in number than are the stars of heaven. And when you are become so many, God will not relinquish the care of you, but will afford you an abundance of all good things in times of peace, with victory and dominion in times of war. May the children of your enemies have an inclination to fight against you, and may they be so hardy as to come to arms, and to assault you in battle, for they will not return with victory, nor will their return be agreeable to their children and wives. To so great a degree of valour will you be raised by the providence of God, who is able to diminish the affluence of some, and to supply the wants of others."

5. Thus did Balaam speak by inspiration, as not being in his own power, but moved to say what he did by the Divine Spirit. But then Balak was displeased, and said he had broken the contract he had made, whereby he was to come, as he and his confederates had invited him, by the promise of great presents: for whereas he came to curse their enemies, he had made an encomium upon them, and had declared that they were the happiest of men. To which Balaam replied, "O Balak, if thou rightly considerest this whole matter, canst thou suppose that it is in our power to be silent, or to say anything, when the Spirit of God seizes upon us?—for he puts such words as he pleases in our mouths, and such discourses as we are not ourselves conscious of. I well remember by what entreaties both you and the Midianites so joyfully brought me hither, and on that account I took this journey. It was my prayer, that I might not put any affront upon you, as to what you desired of me; but God is more powerful than the purposes I had made to serve you; for those that take upon them to foretell the affairs of mankind, as from their own abilities, are entirely unable to do it, or to forbear to utter what God suggests to them, or to offer violence to his will; for when he prevents us, and enters into us, nothing that we say is our own. I then did not intend to praise this army, nor to go over the several good things which God intended to do to their race; but since he was so favourable to them, and so ready to bestow upon them a happy life and eternal glory, he suggested the declaration of those things to me: but now, because it is my desire to oblige thee thyself, as well as the Midianites, whose entreaties it is not decent for me to reject, go to, let us again rear other altars, and offer the like sacrifices that we did before, that I may see whether I can persuade God to permit me to bind these men with curses." Which, when Balak had agreed to, God would not, even upon second sacrifices, consent to his cursing the Israelites.* Then fell Balaam upon his face, and foretold what calamities would befall the several kings of the nations, and the most eminent cities, some of which of old were not so much as inhabited; which events have come to pass among the several people concerned, both in the foregoing ages, and in this, till my own memory, both by sea and by land. From which completion of all these predictions that he made, one may easily guess that the rest will have their completion in time to come.

6. But Balak being very angry that the Israelites were not cursed, sent away Balaam without thinking him worthy of any honour. Whereupon, when he was just upon his journey, in order to pass the Euphrates, he sent for Balak, and for the princes of the Midianites, and spake thus to them:—"O Balak, and you Midianites that are here present, (for I am obliged even without the will of God to gratify you,) it is true no entire destruction can seize upon the nation of the Hebrews, neither by war, nor by plague, nor by scarcity of the fruits of the earth, nor can any other unexpected accident be their entire

* Whether Josephus had in his copy but two attempts of Balaam in all to curse Israel; or whether by this his twice offering sacrifice, he meant twice besides that first time already mentioned, which yet is not very probable, cannot now be certainly determined. In the meantime, all other copies have three such attempts of Balaam to curse them in the present history.

ruin; for the providence of God is concerned to preserve them from such a misfortune; nor will it permit any such calamity to come upon them whereby they may all perish; but some small misfortunes, and those for a short time, whereby they may appear to be brought low, may still befall them; but after that they will flourish again, to the terror of those that brought those mischiefs upon them. So that if you have a mind to gain a victory over them for a short space of time, you will obtain it by following my directions:—Do you therefore set out the handsomest of such of your daughters as are most eminent for beauty,* and proper to force and conquer the modesty of those that behold them, and these decked and trimmed to the highest degree you are able. Then do you send them to be near the Israelites' camp, and give them in charge, that when the young men of the Hebrews desire their company, they allow it them; and when they see that they are enamoured of them, let them take their leaves; and if they entreat them to stay, let them not give their consent till they have persuaded them to leave off their obedience to their own laws and the worship of that God who established them, and to worship the gods of the Midianites and Moabites; for by this means God will be angry at them."† Accordingly, when Balaam had suggested this counsel to them, he went his way.

7. So when the Midianites had sent their daughters, as Balaam had exhorted them, the Hebrew young men were allured by their beauty, and came to discourse with them, and besought them not to grudge them the enjoyment of their beauty, nor to deny them their conversation. These daughters of the Midianites received their words gladly, and consented to it, and stayed with them; but when they had brought them to be enamoured of them, and their inclinations to them were grown to ripeness, they began to think of departing from them: then it was that these men became greatly disconsolate at the women's departure, and they were urgent with them not to leave them, but begged they would continue there, and become their wives; and they promised them they should be owned as mistresses of all they had. This they said with an oath, and called God for the arbitrator of what they promised; and this with tears in their eyes, and all other such marks of concern, as might shew how miserable they thought themselves without them, and so might move their compassion for them. So the women, as soon as they perceived they had made them their slaves, and had caught them with their conversation, began to speak thus to them:—

8. "O you illustrious young men! we have houses of our own at home, and great plenty of good things there, together with the natural affectionate love of our parents and friends; nor is it out of our want of any such things that we came to discourse with you: nor did we admit of your invitation with design to prostitute the beauty of our bodies for gain; but taking you

for brave and worthy men, we agreed to your request, that we might treat you with such honours as hospitality required: and now seeing you say that you have a great affection for us, and are troubled when you think we are departing, we are not averse to your entreaties; and if we may receive such assurance of your good-will as we think can alone be sufficient, we will be glad to lead our lives with you as your wives; but we are afraid that you will in time be weary of our company, and will then abuse us, and send us back to our parents, after an ignominious manner." And they desired that they would excuse them in their guarding against that danger. But the young men professed they would give them any assurance they should desire; nor did they at all contradict what they requested, so great was the passion they had for them. "If then," said they, "this be your resolution; since you make use of such customs and conduct of life as are entirely different from all other men,‡ insomuch that your kinds of food are peculiar to yourselves, and your kinds of drink not common to others, it will be absolutely necessary, if you would have us for your wives, that you do withal worship our gods; nor can there be any other demonstration of the kindness which you say you already have, and promise to have hereafter to us, than this, that you worship the same gods that we do. For has any one reason to complain, that now you are come into this country, you should worship the proper gods of the same country? especially while our gods are common to all men, and yours such as belong to nobody else but yourselves." So they said they must either come into such methods of divine worship as all others came into, or else they must look out for another world, wherein they may live by themselves, according to their own laws.

9. Now the young men were induced by the fondness they had for these women, to think they spake very well; so they gave themselves up to what they persuaded them, and transgressed their own laws; and supposing there were many gods, and resolving that they would sacrifice to them according to the laws of that country which ordained them, they both were delighted with their strange food, and went on to do every thing that the women would have them do, though in contradiction to their own laws; so far, indeed, that this transgression was already gone through the whole army of the young men, and they fell into a sedition that was much worse than the former, and into danger of the entire abolition of their own institutions; for when once the youth had tasted of these strange customs, they went with insatiable inclinations into them; and even where some of the principal men were illustrious on account of the virtues of their fathers, they also were corrupted together with the rest.

10. Even Zimri, the head of the tribe of Simeon, accompanied with Cozbi, a Midianitish woman, who was the daughter of Sur, a man of authority

---

* Such a large and distinct account of this perversion of the Israelites by the Midianite women, of which our other copies give us but short intimations, (Numb. xxxi. 16; 2 Pet. ii. 15; Jude 11; Rev. ii. 14,) is preserved, as Reland informs us, in the Samaritan Chronicle, in Philo, and in other writings of the Jews, as well as here by Josephus.

† This grand maxim, That God's people of Israel could never be hurt nor destroyed, but by drawing them to sin against God, appears to be true, by the entire history of that people, both in the Bible and in Josephus; and is often taken notice of in them both. See in particular a most remarkable Ammonite testimony to this purpose, (Judith v. 5-21.)

‡ What Josephus here puts into the mouths of these Midianite women, who came to entice the Israelites to lewdness and idolatry—viz., that their worship of the God of Israel, in opposition to their idol gods, implied their living according to the holy laws which the true God had given them by Moses, in opposition to those impure laws which were observed under their false gods, well deserves our consideration; and gives us a substantial reason for the great concern that was ever shewn, under the law of Moses, to preserve the Israelites from idolatry, and in the worship of the true God; it being of no less consequence than, Whether God's people should be governed by the holy laws of the true God, or by the impure laws derived from Demons, under the Pagan idolatry.

in that country; and being desired by her to disregard the laws of Moses, and to follow those she was used to, he complied with her; and this both by sacrificing after a manner different from his own, and by taking a stranger to wife. When things were thus, Moses was afraid that matters should grow worse, and called the people to a congregation, but then accused nobody by name, as unwilling to drive those into despair, who, by lying concealed, might come to repentance; but he said that they did not do what was either worthy of themselves, or of their fathers, by preferring pleasure to God, and to the living according to his will; that it was fit they should change their courses while their affairs were still in a good state: and think that to be true fortitude which offers not violence to their laws, but that which resists their lusts. And besides that, he said it was not a reasonable thing, when they had lived soberly in the wilderness, to act madly now when they were in prosperity; and that they ought not to lose, now they have abundance, what they had gained when they had little:— and so did he endeavour, by saying this to correct the young men, and to bring them to repentance for what they had done.

11. But Zimri arose up after him, and said, "Yes, indeed, Moses, thou art at liberty to make use of such laws as thou art so fond of, and hast, by accustoming thyself to them, made them firm; otherwise, if things had not been thus, thou hadst often been punished before now, and hadst known that the Hebrews are not easily put upon; but thou shalt not have me one of thy followers in thy tyrannical commands, for thou dost nothing else hitherto, but, under pretence of laws, and of God, wickedly impose on us slavery, and gain dominion to thyself, while thou deprivest us of the sweetness of life, which consists in acting according to our own wills, and is the right of free men, and of those that have no lord over them. Nay, indeed, this man is harder upon the Hebrews than were the Egyptians themselves, as pretending to punish, according to his laws, every one's acting what is most agreeable to himself; but thou thyself better deservest to suffer punishment, who presumest to abolish what every one acknowledges to be what is good for him, and aimest to make thy single opinion to have more force than that of all the rest: and what I now do, and think to be right, I shall not hereafter deny to be according to my own sentiments. I have married, as thou sayest rightly, a strange woman, and thou hearest what I do from myself as from one that is free; for truly I did not intend to conceal myself. I also own that I sacrificed to those gods to whom you did not think it fit to sacrifice; and I think it right to come at truth by inquiring of many people, and not like one that lives under tyranny, to suffer the whole hope of my life to depend upon one man; nor shall any one find cause to rejoice who declares himself to have more authority over my actions than myself."

12. Now when Zimri had said these things, about what he and some others had wickedly done, the people held their peace, both out of fear of what might come upon them, and because they saw that their legislator was not willing to bring his insolence before the public any further, or openly to contend with him; for he avoided that, lest many should imitate the impudence of his language, and thereby disturb the multitude. Upon this the assembly was dissolved. However, the mischievous attempt had proceeded further, if Zimri had not been first slain, which came to pass on the following

occasion :—Phineas, a man in other respects better than the rest of the young men, and also one that surpassed his contemporaries in the dignity of his father, (for he was the son of Eleazar the high priest, and the grandson of [Aaron] Moses's brother,) who was greatly troubled at what was done by Zimri, he resolved in earnest to inflict punishment on him, before his unworthy behaviour should grow stronger by impunity, and in order to prevent this transgression from proceeding further, which would happen if the ringleaders were not punished. He was of so great magnanimity, both in strength of mind and body, that when he undertook any very dangerous attempt, he did not leave it off till he overcame it, and got an entire victory. So he came into Zimri's tent, and slew him with his javelin, and with it he slew Cozbi also. Upon which, all those young men that had a regard to virtue, and aimed to do a glorious action, imitated Phineas's boldness, and slew those that were found to be guilty of the same crime with Zimri. Accordingly, many of those that had transgressed, perished by the magnanimous valour of these young men, and the rest all perished by a plague, which distemper God himself inflicted upon them. So that all those their kindred, who, instead of hindering them from such wicked actions, as they ought to have done, had persuaded them to go on, were esteemed by God as partners in their wickedness, and died. Accordingly, there perished out of the army, no fewer than fourteen* [twenty-four] thousand at this time.

13. This was the cause why Moses was provoked to send an army to destroy the Midianites, concerning which expedition we shall speak presently, when we have first related what we have omitted; for it is but just not to pass over our legislator's due encomium, on account of his conduct here, because, although this Balaam, who was sent for by the Midianites to curse the Hebrews, and when he was hindered from doing it by divine providence, did still suggest that advice to them, by making use of which, our enemies had well-nigh corrupted the whole multitude of the Hebrews with their wiles, till some of them were deeply infected with their opinions; yet did he also do him great honour, by setting down his prophecies in writing. And while it was in his power to claim this glory to himself, and make men believe they were his own predictions, there being no one that could be a witness against him, and accuse him for so doing, he still gave his attestation to him, and did him the honour to make mention of him on this account. But let every one think of these matters as he pleases.

CHAPTER VII

HOW THE HEBREWS FOUGHT WITH THE MIDIANITES, AND OVERCAME THEM

1. Now Moses sent an army against the land of Midian, for the causes forementioned, in all twelve thousand, taking an equal number out of every tribe, and appointed Phineas for their commander; of which Phineas we made mention a little before, as he that had guarded the laws

---

* The mistake in all Josephus's copies, Greek and Latin, which have here fourteen thousand, instead of twenty-four thousand, is so flagrant, that our very learned editors, Bernard and Hudson, have put the latter number directly in the text. I choose rather to put it in brackets.

of the Hebrews, and had inflicted punishment on Zimri when he had transgressed them. Now the Midianites perceived beforehand how the Hebrews were coming, and would suddenly be upon them: so they assembled their army together, and fortified the entrances into their country, and there awaited the enemy's coming. When they were come, and they had joined battle with them, an immense number of the Midianites fell; nor could they be numbered, they were so very many: and among them fell all their kings, five in number—viz., Evi, Zur, Reba, Hur, and Rekem, who was of the same name with a city, the chief and capital of all Arabia, which is still now so called by the whole Arabian nation, *Arecem*, from the name of the king that built it; but is by the Greeks called *Petra*. Now when the enemies were discomfited, the Hebrews spoiled their country, and took a great prey, and destroyed the men that were its inhabitants, together with the women; only they let the virgins alone, as Moses had commanded Phineas to do, who indeed came back, bringing with him an army that had received no harm, and a great deal of prey; fifty-two thousand beeves, seventy-five thousand six hundred sheep, sixty thousand asses, with an immense quantity of gold and silver furniture, which the Midianites made use of in their houses; for they were so wealthy that they were very luxurious. There were also led captive about thirty-two thousand virgins.* So Moses parted the prey into parts, and gave one fiftieth part to Eleazar and the two priests, and another fiftieth part to the Levites; and distributed the rest of the prey among the people. After which they lived happily, as having obtained an abundance of good things by their valour, and there being no misfortune that attended them or hindered their enjoyment of that happiness.

2. But Moses was now grown old, and appointed Joshua for his successor, both to receive directions from God as a prophet, and for a commander of the army, if they should at any time stand in need of such a one; and this was done by the command of God, that to him the care of the public should be committed. Now Joshua had been instructed in all those kinds of

---

* The slaughter of the Midianite women that had prostituted themselves to the lewd Israelites, and the preservation of those that had not been guilty therein; the last of which were no fewer than thirty-two thousand, both here and Numb. xxxi. 15, 16, 17, 35, 40, 46, and both by the particular command of God, are highly remarkable, and shew that, even in nations otherwise for their wickedness doomed to destruction, the innocent were sometimes providentially taken care of, and delivered from that destruction; which directly implies, that it was the wickedness of the nations of Canaan, and nothing else, that occasioned their excision. See Gen. xv. 16; 1 Sam. xv. 18, 33. Apost. Constit. b. viii. ch. xii. p. 402. In the first of which places, the reason of the delay of the punishment of the Amorites is given, because "their iniquity was not yet full." In the second, Saul is ordered to go and destroy the sinners, "the Amalekites;" plainly implying that they were therefore to be destroyed, because they were sinners, and not otherwise. In the third, the reason is given why king Agag was not to be spared—viz., because of his former cruelty: "As thy sword hath made the (Hebrew) women childless, so shall thy mother be made childless among women by the Hebrews." In the last place, the apostles, or their *amanuensis* Clement, gave this reason for the necessity of the coming of Christ, that "men had formerly perverted both the positive law and that of nature; and had cast out of their mind the memory of the Flood, the burning of Sodom, the plagues of the Egyptians, and the slaughter of the inhabitants of Palestine," as signs of the most amazing impenitence and insensibility under the punishments of horrid wickedness.

---

learning which concerned the laws and God himself, and Moses had been his instructor.

3. At this time it was that the two tribes of Gad and Reuben, and the half tribe of Manasseh, abounded in a multitude of cattle, as well as in all other kinds of prosperity; whence they had a meeting, and in a body came and besought Moses to give them, as their peculiar portion, that land of the Amorites which they had taken by right of war, because it was fruitful and good for feeding of cattle; but Moses, supposing that they were afraid of fighting with the Canaanites, and invented this provision for their cattle as a handsome excuse for avoiding that war, he called them *arrant cowards*, and said they had only contrived a decent excuse for that cowardice; and that they had a mind to live in luxury and ease, while all the rest were labouring with great pains to obtain the land they were desirous to have; and that they were not willing to march along and undergo the remaining hard service, whereby they were, under the divine promise, to pass over Jordan and overcome those our enemies which God had shewn them, and so obtain their land. But these tribes, when they saw that Moses was angry with them, and when they could not deny but he had a just cause to be displeased at their petition, made an apology for themselves, and said that it was not on account of their fear of dangers, nor on account of their laziness, that they made this request to him, but that they might leave the prey they had gotten in places of safety, and thereby might be more expedite, and ready to undergo difficulties, and to fight battles. They added this also, that when they had built cities, wherein they might preserve their children, and wives, and possessions, if he would bestow them upon them, they would go along with the rest of the army. Hereupon Moses was pleased with what they said; so he called for Eleazar, the high priest, and Joshua, and the chief of the tribes, and permitted these tribes to possess the land of the Amorites; but upon this condition, that they should join with their kinsmen in the war until all things were settled. Upon which condition they took possession of the country, and built them strong cities, and put into them their children, and their wives, and whatsoever else they had that might be an impediment to the labours of their future marches.

4. Moses also now built those ten cities which were to be of the number of the forty-eight, [for the Levites;] three of which he allotted to those that slew any person involuntarily, and fled to them; and he assigned the same time for their banishment with that of the life of that high priest under whom the slaughter and flight happened; after which death of the high priest he permitted the slayer to return home. During the time of his exile, the relations of him that was slain may, by this law, kill the manslayer if they caught him without the bounds of the city to which he fled, though this permission was not granted to any other person. Now the cities which were set apart for this flight were these: Bezer, at the borders of Arabia; Ramoth, of the land of Gilead; and Golan, in the land of Bashan. There were to be also, by Moses's command, three other cities allotted for the habitation of these fugitives out of the cities of the Levites, but not till after they should be in possession of the land of Canaan.

5. At this time the chief men of the tribe of Manasseh came to Moses, and informed him that there was an eminent man of their tribe dead, whose name was Zelophehad, who left no male children, but left daughters; and asked

him whether these daughters might inherit his land or not. He made this answer, that if they shall marry into their own tribe, they shall carry their estate along with them; but if they dispose of themselves in marriage to men of another tribe, they shall leave their inheritance in their father's tribe. And then it was that Moses ordained that every one's inheritance should continue in his own tribe.

CHAPTER VIII

THE POLITY SETTLED BY MOSES; AND HOW HE DISAPPEARED FROM AMONG MANKIND

1. WHEN forty years were completed, within thirty days Moses gathered the congregation together near Jordan, where the city Abila now stands, a place full of palm-trees; and all the people being come together, he spake thus to them:—

2. "O you Israelites and fellow-soldiers, who have been partners with me in this long and uneasy journey; since it is now the will of God, and the course of old age, at a hundred and twenty, requires it that I should depart out of this life; and since God has forbidden me to be a patron or an assistant to you in what remains to be done beyond Jordan, I thought it reasonable not to leave off my endeavours even now for your happiness, but to do my utmost to procure for you the eternal enjoyment of good things, and a memorial for myself, when you shall be in the fruition of great plenty and prosperity: come, therefore, let me suggest to you by what means you may be happy, and may leave an eternal prosperous possession thereof to your children after you, and then let me thus go out of the world; and I cannot but deserve to be believed by you, both on account of the great things I have already done for you, and because, when souls are about to leave the body, they speak with the sincerest freedom. O children of Israel! there is but one source of happiness for all mankind, the favour of God;* for he alone is able to give good things to those that deserve them, and to deprive those of them that sin against him; towards whom, if you behave yourselves according to his will, and according to what I, who well understand his mind, do exhort you to, you will both be esteemed blessed, and will be admired by all men; and will never come into misfortunes, nor cease to be happy: you will then preserve the possession of the good things you already have, and will quickly obtain those that you are at present in want of,—only do you be obedient to those whom God would have you to follow:—nor do you prefer any other constitution of government before the laws now given you; neither do you disregard that way of divine worship which you now have, nor change it for any other form: and if you do this, you will be the most courageous of all men, in undergoing the fatigues of war, and will not be easily conquered by any of your enemies; for while God is present with you to assist you, it is to be expected that you will be able to despise the opposition of all mankind; and great rewards of virtue are proposed for you, if you preserve that virtue through your whole lives. Virtue itself is indeed the principal and the first reward, and after that it bestows abundance of others; so that your exercise of virtue towards other men

will make your own lives happy, and render you more glorious than foreigners can be, and procure you an undisputed reputation with posterity. These blessings you will be able to obtain, in case you hearken to and observe those laws which, by divine revelation, I have ordained for you; that is, in case you withal meditate upon the wisdom that is in them. I am going from you myself, rejoicing in the good things you enjoy; and I recommend you to the wise conduct of your law, to the becoming order of your polity, and to the virtues of your commanders, who will take care of what is for your advantage; and that God, who has been till now your leader, and by whose good-will I have myself been useful to you, will not put a period now to his providence over you, but, as long as you desire to have him your Protector in your pursuits after virtue, so long will you enjoy his care over you. Your high priest also, Eleazar, as well as Joshua, with the senate, and chief of your tribes, will go before you, and suggest the best advices to you; by following which advices you will continue to be happy: to whom do you give ear without reluctance, as sensible that all such as know well how to be governed, will also know how to govern, if they be promoted to that authority themselves; and do not you esteem liberty to consist in opposing such directions as your governors think fit to give you for your practice,—as at present indeed you place your liberty in nothing else but abusing your benefactors; which error, if you can avoid for the time to come, your affairs will be in a better condition than they have hitherto been; nor do you ever indulge such a degree of passion in these matters as you have oftentimes done when you have been very angry at me; for you know that I have been oftener in danger of death from you than from our enemies. What I now put you in mind of, is not done in order to reproach you; for I do not think it proper, now I am going out of the world, to bring this to your remembrance, in order to leave you offended at me, since, at the time I underwent those hardships from you, I was not angry at you; but I do it in order to make you wiser hereafter, and to teach you that this will be for your security: I mean, that you never be injurious to those that preside over you, even when you are become rich, as you will be to a great degree when you have passed over Jordan, and are in possession of the land of Canaan. Since, when you shall have once proceeded so far by your wealth, as to a contempt and disregard of virtue, you will also forfeit the favour of God; and when you have made him your enemy, you will be beaten in war, and will have the land which you possess taken away again from you by your enemies, and this with great reproaches upon your conduct. You will be scattered over the whole world, and will, as slaves, entirely fill both sea and land; and when once you have had the experience of what I now say, you will repent and remember the laws you have broken when it is too late. Whence I would advise you, if you intend to preserve these laws, to leave none of your enemies alive when you have conquered them, but to look upon it as for your advantage to destroy them all, lest, if you permit them to live, you taste of their manners, and thereby corrupt your own proper institutions. I also do further exhort you to overthrow their altars, and their groves, and whatsoever temples they have among them, and to burn all such, their nation, and their very memory with fire; for by this means alone the safety of your own happy constitution can be firmly secured to you. And in order to prevent your ignorance of virtue, and the de-

---

* These words of Josephus are so true, that they deserve to be had in constant remembrance.

generacy of your nature into vice, I have also ordained you laws, by divine suggestion, and a form of government, which are so good, that if you regularly observe them you will be esteemed of all men the most happy."

3. When he had spoken thus, he gave them the laws and the constitution of government written in a book. Upon which the people fell into tears, and appeared already touched with the sense that they should have a great want of their conductor, because they remembered what a number of dangers he had passed through, and what care he had taken of their preservation: they desponded about what would come upon them after he was dead, and thought they should never have another governor like him; and feared that God would then take less care of them when Moses was gone, who used to intercede for them. They also repented of what they had said to him in the wilderness when they were angry; and were in grief on those accounts, insomuch that the whole body of the people fell into tears with such bitterness, that it was past the power of words to comfort them in their affliction. However, Moses gave them some consolation; and by calling them off the thought, how worthy he was of their weeping for him, he exhorted them to keep to that form of government he had given them; and then the congregation was dissolved at this time.

4. Accordingly, I shall now first describe this form of government which was agreeable to the dignity and virtue of Moses; and shall thereby inform those that read these Antiquities, what our original settlements were, and shall then proceed to the remaining histories. Now those settlements are all still in writing, as he left them; and we shall add nothing by way of ornament, nor anything besides what Moses left us; only we shall so far innovate as to digest the several kinds of laws into a regular system: for they were by him left in writing as they were accidentally scattered in their delivery, and as he upon inquiry had learned them of God. On which account I have thought it necessary to premise this observation beforehand, lest any of my own countrymen should blame me, as having been guilty of an offence herein. Now part of our constitution will include the laws that belong to our political state. As for those laws which Moses left concerning our common conversation and intercourse one with another, I have reserved that for a discourse concerning our manner of life, and the occasions of those laws; which I propose to myself, with God's assistance, to write, after I have finished the work I am now upon.

5. When you have possessed yourselves of the land of Canaan, and have leisure to enjoy the good things of it, and when you have afterward determined to build cities, if you will do what is pleasing to God, you will have a secure state of happiness. Let there be then one city of the land of Canaan, and this situate in the most agreeable place for its goodness, and very eminent in itself, and let it be that which God shall choose for himself by prophetic revelation. Let there also be one temple therein, and one altar, not reared of hewn stones, but of such as you gather together at random; which stones, when they are whited over with mortar, will have a handsome appearance, and be beautiful to the sight. Let the ascent to it be not by steps,* but

by an acclivity of raised earth. And let there be neither an altar nor a temple in any other city; for God is but one, and the nation of the Hebrews is but one.

6. He that blasphemeth God let him be stoned, and let him hang upon a tree all that day, and then let him be buried in an ignominious and obscure manner.

7. Let those that live as remote as the bounds of the land which the Hebrews shall possess, come to that city where the temple shall be, and this three times in a year, that they may give thanks to God for his former benefits, and may entreat him for those they shall want hereafter; and let them, by this means, maintain a friendly correspondence with one another by such meetings and feastings together—for it is a good thing for those that are of the same stock, and under the same institution of laws, not to be unacquainted with each other; which acquaintance will be maintained by thus conversing together, and by seeing and talking with one another, and so renewing the memorials of this union; for if they do not thus converse together continually, they will appear like mere strangers to one another.

8. Let there be taken out of your fruits a tenth, besides that which you have allotted to give to the priests and Levites. This you may indeed sell in the country, but it is to be used in those feasts and sacrifices that are to be celebrated in the holy city: for it is fit you should enjoy those fruits of the earth which God gives you to possess, so as may be to the honour of the donor.

9. You are not to offer sacrifices out of the hire of a woman who is a harlot,† for the Deity is not pleased with any thing that arises from such abuses of nature; of which sort none can be worse than this prostitution of the body. In like manner no one may take the price of the covering of a bitch, either of the one that is used in hunting, or in keeping of sheep, and thence sacrifice to God.

10. Let no one blaspheme those gods which other cities esteem such;‡ nor may any one steal what belongs to strange temples; nor take away the gifts that are dedicated to any god.

11. Let not any one of you wear a garment made of woollen and linen, for that is appointed to be for the priests alone.

12. When the multitude are assembled together unto the holy city for sacrificing every seventh year, at the Feast of Tabernacles, let the high priest stand upon a high desk, whence he may be heard, and let him read the laws to all the people; and let neither the women nor the children be hindered from hearing, no, nor the servants neither; for it is a good thing that those laws should be engraven in their souls, and preserved in their memories, that so it may not be possible to blot them out; for by this means they will not be guilty of sin, when they cannot plead ignorance of what the laws have enjoined them. The laws also will have a greater authority among them, as foretelling what they will suffer if they break them: and imprinting in their souls by this hearing what they command them to do, that so there may always be within their minds that intention of the laws which they have de-

* This law seems not to have belonged to the altar of the tabernacle, (Exod. xxvii. 4,) nor to that of Ezekiel, (chap. xliii. 17;) but rather to occasional altars of any considerable altitude and largeness; as also probably to

Solomon's altar. The reason of the law is obvious: that before the invention of stairs, decency could not be otherwise provided for in the loose garments which the priests wore.

† The hire of harlots was given to Venus in Syria, and against some such practice this law seems to have been made.

‡ The Apostolical Constitutions expound this law of Moses, of magistrates.

spised and broken, and have thereby been the causes of their own mischief. Let the children also learn the laws, as the first thing they are taught, which will be the best thing they can be taught, and will be the cause of their future felicity.

13. Let every one commemorate before God the benefits which he bestowed upon them at their deliverance out of the land of Egypt, and this twice every day, both when the day begins and when the hour of sleep comes on, gratitude being in its own nature a just thing, and serving not only by way of return for past, but also by way of invitation of future favours. They are also to inscribe the principal blessings they have received from God upon their doors, and shew the same remembrance of them upon their arms; as also they are to bear on their forehead and their arm those wonders which declare the power of God, and his good-will towards them, that God's readiness to bless them may appear everywhere conspicuous about them.*

14. Let there be seven men to judge in every city,† and these such as have been before most zealous in the exercise of virtue and righteousness. Let every judge have two officers allotted him out of the tribe of Levi. Let those that are chosen to judge in the several cities be had in great honour; and let none be permitted to revile any others when these are present, nor to carry themselves in an insolent manner to them; it being natural that reverence towards those in high offices among men should procure men's fear and reverence towards God. Let those that judge be permitted to determine according as they think to be right, unless any one can shew that they have taken bribes, to the perversion of justice, or can allege any other accusation against them, whereby it may appear that they have passed an unjust sentence; for it is not fit that causes should be openly determined out of regard to gain, or to the dignity of the suitors, but that the judges should esteem what is right before all other things, otherwise God will by that means be despised, and esteemed inferior to those, the dread of whose power has occasioned the unjust sentence; for justice is the power of God. He, therefore, that gratifies those in great dignity, supposes them more potent than God himself. But if these judges be unable to give a just sentence about the causes that come before them, (which case is not unfrequent in human affairs,) let them send the causes undetermined to the holy city, and there let the high priest, the prophet, and the sanhedrim, determine as it shall seem good to them.

15. But let not a single witness be credited; but three, or two at the least, and those such whose testimony is confirmed by their good lives. But let not the testimony of women be admitted, on account of the levity and boldness of their sex:‡ nor let servants be admitted to give testimony, on account of the ignobility of their soul; since it is probable that they may not speak truth, either out of hope of gain, or

fear of punishment. But if any one be believed to have borne false witness, let him, when he is convicted, suffer all the very same punishments which he against whom he bore witness was to have suffered.

16. If a murder be committed in any place, and he that did it be not found, nor is there any suspicion upon one as if he had hated the man, and so had killed him, let there be a very diligent inquiry made after the man, and rewards proposed to any one who will discover him: but if still no information can be procured, let the magistrates and senate of those cities that lie near the place in which the murder was committed, assemble together, and measure the distance from the place where the dead body lies; then let the magistrates of the nearest city thereto purchase a heifer, and bring it to a valley, and to a place therein where there is no land ploughed or trees planted, and let them cut the sinews of the heifer; then the priests and Levites, and the senate of that city, shall take water and wash their hands over the head of the heifer; and they shall openly declare that their hands are innocent of this murder, and that they have neither done it themselves, nor been assisting to any that did it. They shall also beseech God to be merciful to them, that no such horrid act may any more be done in that land.

17. Aristocracy, and the way of living under it, is the best constitution: and may you never have any inclination to any other form of government; and may you always love that form, and have the laws for your governors, and govern all your actions according to them; for you need no supreme governor but God. But if you shall desire a king let him be one of your own nation; let him be always careful of justice and other virtues perpetually; let him submit to the laws, and esteem God's commands to be his highest wisdom; but let him do nothing without the high priest and the votes of the senators; let him not have a great number of wives, nor pursue after abundance of riches, nor a multitude of horses, whereby he may grow too proud to submit to the laws. And if he affect any such things, let him be restrained, lest he become so potent that his state be inconsistent with your welfare.

18. Let it not be esteemed lawful to remove boundaries, neither our own, nor of those with whom we are at peace. Have a care you do not take those land-marks away which are, as it were, a divine and unshaken limitation of rights made by God himself, to last for ever; since this going beyond limits and gaining ground upon others, is the occasion of wars and seditions; for those that remove boundaries are not far off an attempt to subvert the laws.

19. He that plants a piece of land, the trees of which produce fruits before the fourth year, is not to bring thence any first-fruits to God, nor is he to make use of that fruit himself, for it is not produced in its proper season; for when nature has a force put upon her at an unseasonable time, the fruit is not proper for God nor for the master's use; but let the owner gather all that is grown on the fourth year, for then it is in its proper season; and let him that has gathered it carry it to the holy city, and spend that, together with the tithe of his other fruits, in feasting with his friends, with the orphans, and the widows. But on the fifth year the fruit is his own, and he may use it as he pleases.

20. You are not to sow with seed a piece of land which is planted with vines; for it is enough that it supply nourishment to that plant, and be

---

* Whether these phylacteries, and other Jewish memorials of the law here mentioned by Josephus, were literally meant by God I much question. The Karaites, who keep close to the written law, think they were not literally to be understood.

† Here, as well as elsewhere, are but *seven* judges appointed for small cities, instead of *twenty-three* in the modern rabbins.

‡ The Pentateuch says not a word about the exclusion of women as witnesses in courts of justice. It is very probable, however, that this was the practice of the Jews in the days of Josephus.

not harassed by ploughing also. You are to plough your land with oxen, and not to oblige other animals to come under the same yoke with them, but to till your land with those beasts that are of the same kind with each other. The seeds are also to be pure, and without mixture, and not to be compounded of two or three sorts, since Nature does not rejoice in the union of things that are not in their own nature alike: nor are you to permit beasts of different kinds to gender together, for there is reason to fear that this unnatural abuse may extend from beasts of different kinds to men, though it takes its first rise from evil practices about such smaller things. Nor is any thing to be allowed, by imitation whereof any degree of subversion may creep into the constitution; nor do the laws neglect small matters, but provide that even those may be managed after an unblameable manner.

21. Let not those that reap and gather in the corn that is reaped, gather in the gleanings also, but let them rather leave some handfuls for those that are in want of the necessaries of life, that it may be a support and a supply to them, in order to their subsistence. In like manner when they gather their grapes, let them leave some smaller bunches for the poor, and let them pass over some of the fruits of the olive trees, when they gather them, and leave them to be partaken of by those that have none of their own; for the advantage arising from the exact collection of all, will not be so considerable to the owners as will arise from the gratitude of the poor; and God will provide that the land shall more willingly produce what shall be for the nourishment of its fruits, in case you do not merely take care of your own advantage, but have regard to the support of others also: nor are you to muzzle the mouths of the oxen when they tread the ears of corn in the thrashing-floor; for it is not just to restrain our fellow-labouring animals, and those that work in order to its production, of this fruit of their labours: nor are you to prohibit those that pass by at the time when your fruits are ripe to touch them, but to give them leave to fill themselves full of what you have; and this whether they be of your own country or strangers,—as being glad of the opportunity of giving them some part of your fruits when they are ripe; but let it not be esteemed lawful for them to carry any away: nor let those that gather the grapes, and carry them to the wine-presses, restrain those whom they meet from eating of them; for it is unjust, out of envy, to hinder those that desire it, to partake of the good things that come into the world according to God's will, and this while the season is at the height, and is hastening away as it pleases God. Nay, if some, out of bashfulness, are unwilling to touch these fruits, let them be encouraged to take of them (I mean, those that are Israelites) as if they were themselves the owners and lords, on account of the kindred there is between them: nay, let them desire men that come from other countries, to partake of these tokens of friendship which God has given in their proper season; for that is not to be deemed as idly spent, which any one out of kindness communicates to another, since God bestows plenty of good things on men, not only for themselves to reap the advantage, but also to give to others in a way of generosity; and he is desirous, by this means, to make known to others his peculiar kindness to the people of Israel, and how freely he communicates happiness to them, while they abundantly communicate out of their great superfluities to even these

foreigners also. But for him that acts contrary to this law, let him be beaten with forty stripes, save one,* by the public executioner; let him undergo this punishment, which is a most ignominious one for a free man, and this because he was such a slave to gain as to lay a blot upon his own dignity; for it is proper for you who have had the experience of the afflictions in Egypt, and of those in the wilderness, to make provision for those that are in the like circumstances; and while you have now obtained plenty yourselves, through the mercy and providence of God, to distribute of the same plenty, by the like sympathy, to such as stand in need of it.

22. Besides those two tithes, which I have already said you are to pay every year, the one for the Levites, the other for the festivals, you are to bring every third year a third tithe to be distributed to those that want;† to women also that are widows, and to children that are orphans. But as to the ripe fruits, let them carry that which is ripe first of all into the temple; and when they have blessed God for that land which bare them, and which he had given them for a possession, when they have also offered those sacrifices which the law has commanded them to bring, let them give the first-fruits to the priests. But when any one hath done this, and hath brought the tithe of all that he hath, together with those first-fruits that are for the Levites, and for the festivals, and when he is about to go home, let him stand before the holy house, and return thanks to God, that he hath delivered them from the injurious treatment they had in Egypt, and hath given them a good land and a large, and lets them enjoy the fruit thereof; and when he hath openly testified that he hath fully paid the tithes [and other dues] according to the laws of Moses, let him entreat God that he will be ever merciful and gracious to him; and continue so to be to all the Hebrews, both by preserving the good things which he hath already given them, and by adding what it is still in his power to bestow upon them.

23. Let the Hebrews marry, at the age fit for it, virgins that are free, and born of good parents. And he that does not marry a virgin, let him not corrupt another man's wife, and marry her, nor grieve her former husband: nor let free men marry slaves, although their affections should strongly bias any of them so to do; for it is decent, and for the dignity of the persons themselves, to govern those their affections. And further, no one ought to marry a harlot, whose matrimonial oblations, arising from the prostitution of her body, God will not receive; for by these means the dispositions of the children will be liberal and virtuous; I mean when they are not born of base parents, and of the lustful conjunction of such as marry women that are not free. If any one has been espoused to a woman as to a virgin, and does not afterward find her so to be, let him bring his action, and accuse her, and let him make use of such indications,‡

---

* This penalty was five times inflicted on St Paul himself by the Jews, (2 Cor. xi. 24.)

† Josephus's plain and express interpretation of this law of Moses, that the Jews were bound every third year to pay three tithes—that to the Levites, that for sacrifices at Jerusalem, and this for the indigent, the widow, and the orphans—is fully confirmed by the practice of good old Tobit, against the opinions of the rabbins, (Tobit, i. 6, 7, 8.)

‡ Josephus here determines nothing what were these particular tokens of virginity or of corruption : perhaps he thought he could not easily describe them to the heathens, without saying what they might have

to prove his accusation, as he is furnished withal; and let the father or the brother of the damsel, or some one that is after them nearest of kin to her, defend her. If the damsel obtain a sentence in her favour, that she had not been guilty, let her live with her husband that accused her: and let him not have any further power at all to put her away, unless she give him very great occasions of suspicion, and such as can be no way contradicted: but for him that brings an accusation and calumny against his wife in an impudent and rash manner, let him be punished by receiving forty stripes save one, and let him pay fifty shekels to her father: but if the damsel be convicted, as having been corrupted, and is one of the common people, let her be stoned, because she did not preserve her virginity till she were lawfully married; but if she were the daughter of a priest, let her be burnt alive. If any one has two wives, and if he greatly respect and be kind to one of them, either out of his affection to her, or for her beauty, or for some other reason, while the other is of less esteem with him; and if the son of her that is beloved be the younger by birth than another born of the other wife, but endeavours to obtain the right of primogeniture from his father's kindness to his mother, and would thereby obtain a double portion of his father's substance, for that double portion is what I have allotted him in the laws,—let not this be permitted; for it is unjust that he who is the elder by birth should be deprived of what is due to him, on the father's disposition of his estate, because his mother was not equally regarded by him. He that hath corrupted a damsel espoused to another man, in case he had her consent, let both him and her be put to death, for they are both equally guilty; the man, because he persuaded the woman willingly to submit to a most impure action, and to prefer it to lawful wedlock; the woman, because she was persuaded to yield herself to be corrupted, either for pleasure or for gain. However, if a man light on a woman when she is alone, and forces her, where nobody was present to come to her assistance, let him only be put to death. Let him that hath corrupted a virgin not yet espoused, marry her; but if the father of the damsel be not willing that she should be his wife, let him pay fifty shekels as the price of her prostitution. He that desires to be divorced from his wife for any cause* whatsoever, (and many such causes happen among men,) let him in writing give assurance that he will never use her as his wife any more; for by this means she may be at liberty to marry another husband, although before this bill of divorce be given, she is not to be permitted so to do: but if she be misused by him also, or if, when he is dead, her first husband would marry her again, it shall not be lawful for her to return to him. If a woman's husband die, and leave her without children, let his brother marry her; and let him call the son that is born to him by his brother's name, and educate him as the heir of his inheritance; for this procedure will be for the benefit of the public, because thereby families will not fail, and the estate will continue among the kindred: and this will be for the solace of wives under their affliction, that they are to be married to the next relation of their former husbands; but if the brother will not marry her, let the woman come before

the senate, and protest openly that this brother will not admit her for his wife, but will injure the memory of his deceased brother, while she is willing to continue in the family, and to bear him children; and when the senate have inquired of him for what reason it is that he is averse to this marriage, whether he gives a bad or a good reason, the matter must come to this issue, That the woman shall lose the sandals of the brother, and shall spit in his face, and say, He deserves this reproachful treatment from her, as having injured the memory of the deceased;—and then let him go away out of the senate, and bear this reproach upon him all his life long; and let her marry to whom she pleases, of such as seek her in marriage. But now, if any man take captive, either a virgin, or one that hath been married,† and has a mind to marry her, let him not be allowed to bring her to bed to him, or to live with her as his wife, before she hath her head shaven, and hath put on her mourning habit, and lamented her relations and friends that were slain in the battle, that by this means she may give vent to her sorrow for them, and after that may betake herself to feasting and matrimony; for it is good for him that takes a woman, in order to have children by her, to be complaisant to her inclinations, and not merely to pursue his own pleasure, while he hath no regard to what is agreeable to her; but when thirty days are past, as the time of mourning, for so many are sufficient to prudent persons for lamenting the dearest friends, then let them proceed to the marriage; but in case, when he hath satisfied his lust, he be too proud to retain her for his wife, let him not have it in his power to make her a slave, but let her go away whither she pleases, and have that privilege of a free woman.

24. As to those young men that despise their parents, and do not pay them honour, but offer them affronts, either because they are ashamed of them, or think themselves wiser than they,—in the first place let their parents admonish them in words, (for they are by nature of authority sufficient for becoming their judges,) and let them say thus to them:—That they cohabited together, not for the sake of pleasure, nor for the augmentation of their riches, by joining both their stocks together, but that they might have children, to take care of them in their old age, and might by them have what they then should want;—and say further to him, "That when thou wast born we took thee up with gladness, and gave God the greatest thanks for thee, and brought thee up with great care, and spared for nothing that appeared useful for thy preservation, and for thy instruction in what was most excellent; and now, since it is reasonable to forgive the sins of those that are young, let it suffice thee to have given so many indications of thy contempt of us;—reform thyself, and act more wisely for the time to come; considering that God is displeased with those that are insolent towards their parents, because he is himself the Father of the whole race of mankind, and seems to bear part of that dishonour which falls upon those that have the same name, when they do not meet with due returns from their children; and on such the law inflicts inexorable punishment; of which punishment mayest thou never have experience!" Now if the insolence of young men be thus

---

thought a breach of modesty; which seeming breach of modesty laws cannot always avoid.

* See our Saviour's words upon this very subject, (Matt. xix. 3.)

† Here it is supposed that this captive's husband was dead before, or rather was slain in this very battle, otherwise it would have been adultery in him that married her.

cured, let them escape the reproach which their former errors deserved; for by this means the lawgiver will appear to be good, and parents happy, while they never behold either a son or a daughter brought to punishment; but if it happen that these words and instructions, conveyed by them in order to reclaim the man, appear to be useless, then the offender renders the laws implacable enemies to the insolence he has offered his parents; let him therefore be brought forth* by these very parents, out of the city, with a multitude following him, and there let him be stoned; and when he has continued there for one whole day, that all the people may see him, let him be buried in the night; and thus it is that we bury all whom the laws condemn to die, upon any account whatsoever. Let our enemies that fall in battle be also buried; nor let any one dead body lie above the ground, or suffer a punishment beyond what justice requires.

25. Let no one lend to any one of the Hebrews upon usury, neither usury of what is eaten or what is drunken; for it is not just to make advantage of the misfortunes of one of thy own countrymen: but when thou hast been assistant to his necessities, think it thy gain, if thou obtainest their gratitude to thee; and withal that reward which will come to thee from God, for thy humanity towards him.

26. Those who have borrowed either silver or any sorts of fruits, whether dry or wet, (I mean this when the Jewish affairs shall, by the blessing of God, be to their own mind,) let the borrowers bring them again, and restore them with pleasure to those who lent them; laying them up, as it were, in their own treasuries, and justly expecting to receive them thence, if they shall want them again; but if they be without shame, and do not restore it, let not the lender go to the borrower's house, and take a pledge himself, before judgment be given concerning it: but let him require the pledge, and let the debtor bring it of himself, without the least opposition to him that comes upon him under the protection of the law; and if he that gave the pledge be rich, let the creditor retain it till what he lent be paid him again; but if he be poor, let him that takes it return it before the going down of the sun, especially if the pledge be a garment, that the debtor may have it for a covering in his sleep, God himself naturally shewing mercy to the poor. It is also not lawful to take a mill-stone, nor any utensil thereto belonging, for a pledge, that the debtors may not be deprived of instruments to get their food withal, and lest they be undone by their necessity.

27. Let death be the punishment for stealing a man; but he that hath purloined gold or silver, let him pay double. If any one kill a man that is stealing something out of his house, let him be esteemed guiltless, although the man were only breaking in at the wall. Let him that hath stolen cattle pay fourfold what is lost, excepting the case of an ox, for which let the thief pay fivefold. Let him that is so poor that he cannot pay what mulct is laid upon him, be his servant to whom he was adjudged to pay it.

28. If any one be sold to one of his own nation, let him serve him six years, and on the seventh let him go free. But if he have a son by a woman-servant in his purchaser's house, and if, on account of his good-will to his master,

and his natural affection to his wife and children, he will be his servant still, let him be set free only at the coming of the year of jubilee, which is the fiftieth year, and let him then take away with him his children and wife, and let them be free also.

29. If any one find gold or silver on the road, let him inquire after him that lost it, and make proclamation of the place where he found it, and then restore it to him again, as not thinking it right to make his own profit by the loss of another. And the same rule is to be observed in cattle found to have wandered away into a lonely place. If the owner be not presently discovered, let him that is the finder keep it with himself, and appeal to God that he has not purloined what belongs to another.

30. It is not lawful to pass by any beast that is in distress, when in a storm it is fallen down in the mire, but to endeavour to preserve it, as having a sympathy with it in its pain.

31. It is also a duty to shew the roads to those who do not know them, and not to esteem it a matter for sport, when we hinder others' advantages, by setting them in a wrong way.

32. In like manner, let no one revile a person blind or dumb.

33. If men strive together, and there be no instrument of iron, let him that is smitten be avenged immediately, by inflicting the same punishment on him that smote him: but if when he is carried home he lie sick many days, and then die, let him that smote him escape punishment; but if he that is smitten escape death, and yet be at great expense for his cure, the smiter shall pay for all that has been expended during the time of his sickness, and for all that he has paid the physician. He that kicks a woman with child, so that the woman miscarry,† let him pay a fine in money, as the judges shall determine, as having diminished the multitude by the destruction of what was in her womb; and let money also be given to the woman's husband by him that kicked her; but if she die of the stroke, let him also be put to death, the law judging it equitable that life should go for life.

34. Let no one of the Israelites keep any poison ‡ that may cause death, or any other harm: but if he be caught with it, let him be put to death, and suffer the very same mischief that he would have brought upon them for whom the poison was prepared.

35. He that maimeth any one, let him undergo the like himself, and be deprived of the same member of which he hath deprived the other, unless he that is maimed will accept of money instead of it; § for the law makes the sufferer the judge of the value of what he hath suffered, and permits him to estimate it, unless he will be more severe.

36. Let him that is the owner of an ox which pusheth with his horn, kill him: but if he pushes and gores any one in the thrashing-floor, let him be put to death by stoning, and let him not be thought fit for food: but if his owner be convicted as having known what his nature was, and hath not kept him up, let him also be put to death, as being the occasion of the ox's having killed a man. But if the ox have killed a man-

---

* See Herod the Great insisting on the execution of this law, (Antiq. b. xvi. ch. xi. sect. 2.)

† The law seems rather to mean, that if the infant be killed, though the mother escape, the offender must be put to death; and not only when the mother is killed, as Josephus understood it.

‡ What we render a *witch*, Philo and Josephus understood of a poisoner.

§ This permission of redeeming this penalty with money is not in our copies.

servant, or a maid-servant, let him be stoned; and let the owner of the ox pay thirty shekels * to the master of him that was slain : but if it be an ox that is thus smitten and killed, let both the oxen, that which smote the other and that which was killed, be sold, and let the owners of them divide their price between them.

37. Let those that dig a well or a pit, be careful to lay planks over them, and so keep them shut up, not in order to hinder any person from drawing water, but that there may be no danger of falling into them : but if any one's beast fall into such a well or pit thus digged and not shut up, and perish, let the owner pay its price to the owner of the beast. Let there be a battlement round the tops of your houses instead of a wall, that may prevent any persons from rolling down and perishing.

38. Let him that hath received any thing in trust for another, take care to keep it as a sacred and divine thing; and let no one invent any contrivance, whereby to deprive him that hath intrusted it with him of the same, and this whether he be a man or a woman; no, not although he or she were to gain an immense sum of gold, and this where he cannot be convicted of it by any body; for it is fit that a man's own conscience, which knows what he hath, should, in all cases, oblige him to do well. Let this conscience be his witness, and make him always act so as may procure him commendation from others; but let him chiefly have regard to God, from whom no wicked man can lie concealed: but if he in whom the trust was reposed, without any deceit of his own, lose what he was intrusted withal, let him come before the seven judges, and swear by God that nothing hath been lost willingly, or with a wicked intention, and that he hath not made use of any part thereof, and so let him depart without blame; but if he hath made use of the least part of what was committed to him, and it be lost, let him be condemned to repay all that he had received. After the same manner as in these trusts, it is to be, if any one defraud those that undergo bodily labour for him. And let it be always remembered, that we are not to defraud a poor man of his wages; as being sensible that God has allotted these wages to him instead of land and other possessions; nay, this payment is not at all to be delayed, but to be made that very day, since God is not willing to deprive the labourer of the immediate use of what he hath laboured for.

39. You are not to punish children for the faults of their parents, but on account of their own virtue rather to vouchsafe them commiseration, because they were born of wicked parents, than hatred, because they were born of bad ones: nor indeed ought we to impute the sin of children to their fathers, while young persons indulge themselves in many practices different from what they have been instructed in, and this by their proud refusal of such instruction.

40. Let those that have made themselves eunuchs be had in detestation; and do you avoid any conversation with them who have deprived themselves of their manhood, and of that fruit of generation which God has given to men for the increase of their kind: let such be driven away, as if they had killed their children, since they beforehand have lost what should procure them; for evident it is, that while their soul is become effeminate, they have withal transfused that effeminacy to their body also. In like manner do you treat all that is of a monstrous nature when it is looked on; nor is it lawful to geld men or any other animals.†

41. Let this be the constitution of your political laws in time of peace, and God will be so merciful as to preserve this excellent settlement free from disturbance: and may that time never come which may innovate anything, and change it for the contrary. But since it must needs happen that mankind fall into troubles and dangers, either undesignedly or intentionally, come let us make a few constitutions concerning them, that so being apprised beforehand what ought to be done, you may have salutary counsels ready when you want them, and may not then be obliged to go to seek what is to be done, and so be unprovided, and fall into dangerous circumstances. May you be a laborious people, and exercise your souls in virtuous actions, and thereby possess and inherit the land without wars; while neither any foreigners make war upon it, and so afflict you, nor any internal sedition seize upon it, whereby you may do things that are contrary to your fathers, and so lose the laws which they have established: and may you continue in the observation of those laws which God hath approved of, and hath delivered to you. Let all sort of warlike operations, whether they befall you now in your own time, or hereafter in the times of your posterity, be done out of your own borders; but when you are about to go to war, send embassages and heralds to those who are your voluntary enemies, for it is a right thing to make use of words to them before you come to your weapons of war; and assure them thereby, that although you have a numerous army, with horses and weapons, and, above these, a God merciful to you, and ready to assist you, you do however desire them not compel you to fight against them, nor to take from them what they have, which will indeed be our gain, but what they will have no reason to wish we should take to ourselves; and if they hearken to you, it will be proper for you to keep peace with them; but if they trust in their own strength as superior to yours, and will not do you justice, lead your army against them, making use of God as your supreme commander, but ordaining for a lieutenant under him, one that is of the greatest courage among you; for these different commanders, besides their being an obstacle to actions that are to be done on the sudden, are a disadvantage to those that make use of them. Lead an army pure, and of chosen men, composed of all such as have extraordinary strength of body and hardiness of soul; but do you send away the timorous part, lest they run away in the time of action, and so afford an advantage to your enemies. Do you also give leave to those that have lately built them houses, and have not yet lived in them a year's time; and to those that have planted them vineyards, and have not yet been partakers of their fruits,—to continue in their own country; as well as those also who have betrothed, or lately married them wives, lest they have such an affection for these things that they be too sparing of their lives, and, by reserving themselves for these enjoyments, they become voluntary cowards, on account of their wives.

42. When you have pitched your camp, take

---

† This law is said to be so rigorous elsewhere, as to inflict death on him that does it; which seems only a Pharisaical interpretation : only we may hence observe, that the Jews could then have no oxen, but only bulls and cows.

care that you do nothing that is cruel; and when you are engaged in a siege, and want timber for the making of warlike engines, do not you render the land naked by cutting down trees that bear fruit, but spare them, as considering that they were made for the benefit of men; and that if they could speak they would have a just plea against you, because, though they are not occasions of the war, they are unjustly treated, and suffer in it; and would, if they were able, remove themselves into another land. When you have beaten your enemies in battle, slay those that have fought against you; but preserve the others alive, that they may pay you tribute, excepting the nation of the Canaanites; for as to that people, you must entirely destroy them.

43. Take care, especially in your battles, that no woman use the habit of a man, nor man the garment of a woman.

44. This was the form of political government which was left us by Moses. Moreover, he had already delivered laws in writing,* in the fortieth year, [after they came out of Egypt,] concerning which we will discourse in another book. But now on the following days (for he called them to assemble continually) he delivered blessings to them, and curses upon those that should not live according to the laws, but should transgress the duties that were determined for them to observe. After this, he read to them a poetic song, which was composed in hexameter verse; and left it to them in the holy book: it contained a prediction of what was to come to pass afterward; agreeably whereto all things have happened all along, and do still happen to us; and wherein he has not at all deviated from the truth. Accordingly, he delivered these books† with the ark: into which he also put the Ten Commandments, written on two tables. He delivered to them the tabernacle also; and exhorted the people, that when they had conquered the land, and were settled in it, they should not forget the injuries of the Amalekites, but make war against them, and inflict punishment upon them for what mischief they did them when they were in the wilderness; and that, when they had got possession of the land of the Canaanites, and when they had destroyed the whole multitude of its inhabitants, as they ought to do, they should erect an altar that should face the rising sun, not far from the city of Shechem, between the two mountains, that of Gerizzim, situate on the right hand, and that called Ebal, on the left; and that the army should be so divided, that six tribes should stand upon each of the two mountains, and with them the Levites and the priests. And that first, those that were upon mount Gerizzim should pray for the best blessings upon those who were diligent about the worship of God, and the observation of his laws, and who did not reject what Moses had said to them; while the other wished them all manner of happiness also; and when these last put up the like prayers, the former praised them. After this, curses were denounced upon those that should transgress those laws, they answering one another alternately, by way of confirmation of what had been said. Moses also wrote their blessings and their curses, that they might learn them so thoroughly, that they might never be forgotten by length of time. And when he was ready to die, he wrote these blessings and curses

upon the altar, on each side of it; where he says also the people stood, and then sacrificed and offered burnt-offerings; though after that day they never offered upon it any other sacrifice, for it was not lawful so to do. These are the constitutions of Moses; and the Hebrew nation still live according to them.

45. On the next day, Moses called the people together, with the women and children, to a congregation, so as the very slaves were present also, that they might engage themselves to the observation of these laws by oath; and that, duly considering the meaning of God in them, they might not, either for favour of their kindred, or out of fear of any one, or indeed for any motive whatsoever, think anything ought to be preferred to these laws, and so might transgress them; that in case any one of their own blood, or any city, should attempt to confound or dissolve their constitution of government, they should take vengeance upon them, both all in general, and each person in particular; and when they had conquered them, should overturn their city to the very foundations, and, if possible, should not leave the least footsteps of such madness: but that if they were not able to take such vengeance, they should still demonstrate that what was done was contrary to their wills. So the multitude bound themselves by oath so to do.

46. Moses taught them also by what means their sacrifices might be the most acceptable to God; and how they should go forth to war, making use of the stones (in the high priest's breastplate) for their direction, ‡ as I have before signified. Joshua also prophesied while Moses was present. And when Moses had recapitulated whatsoever he had done for the preservation of the people, both in their wars and in peace, and had composed them a body of laws, and procured them an excellent form of government, he foretold, as God had declared to him, "That if they transgressed that institution for the worship of God, they should experience the following miseries:—Their land should be full of weapons of war from their enemies, and their cities should be overthrown, and their temple should be burnt; that they should be sold for slaves, to such men as would have no pity on them in their afflictions; that they would then repent, when that repentance would no way profit them under their sufferings. Yet," said he, "will that God who founded your nation, restore your cities to your citizens, with their temple also; and you shall lose these advantages, not once only, but often."

47. Now when Joshua had encouraged Joshua to lead out the army against the Canaanites, by telling him that God would assist him in all his undertakings, and had blessed the whole multitude, he said, "Since I am going to my fore-fathers, and God has determined that this should be the day of my departure to them, I return him thanks while I am still alive and present with you, for that providence he hath exercised over you, which hath not only delivered us from the miseries we lay under, but hath bestowed a state of prosperity upon us; as also, that he hath assisted me in the pains I took, and in all the contrivances I had in my care about you, in order to better your condition, and hath on all occasions shewed himself favourable

---

* These laws seem to be those above mentioned, sect. 4 of this chapter.

† See the note on Antiq. b. iii. chap. i. sect. 7.

‡ Dr Bernard well observes here, how unfortunate this neglect of consulting the Urim was to Joshua himself in the case of the Gibeonites; who put a trick upon him and ensnared him, with a solemn oath to preserve them, contrary to his commission to extirpate all the Canaanites, root and branch.

to us: or rather he it was who first conducted our affairs, and brought them to a happy conclusion, by making use of me as a vicarious general under him, and as a minister in those matters wherein he was willing to do you good: on which account I think it proper to bless that Divine Power which will take care of you for the time to come, and this in order to repay that debt which I owe him, and to leave behind me a memorial that we are obliged to worship and honour him, and to keep those laws which are the most excellent gift of all those he hath already bestowed upon us, or which, if he continue favourable to us, he will bestow upon us hereafter. Certainly a human legislator is a terrible enemy when his laws are affronted, and are made to no purpose. And may you never experience that displeasure of God which will be the consequence of the neglect of these his laws, which he, who is your Creator, hath given you!"

48. When Moses had spoken thus at the end of his life, and had foretold what would befall to every one of their tribes* afterward, with the addition of a blessing to them, the multitude fell into tears, insomuch that even the women, by beating their breasts, made manifest the deep concern they had when he was about to die. The children also lamented still more, as not able to contain their grief; and thereby declared, that even at their age they were sensible of his virtue and mighty deeds; and truly there seemed to be a strife betwixt the young and the old, who should most grieve for him. The old grieved, because they knew what a careful protector they were to be deprived of, and so lamented their future state; but the young grieved, not only for that, but also because it so happened that they were to be left by him before they had well tasted of his virtue. Now one may make a guess at the excess of this sorrow and lamentation of the multitude, from what happened to the legislator himself; for although he was always persuaded that he ought not to be cast down at the approach of death, since the undergoing it was agreeable to the will of God and the law of nature, yet what the people did so overbore him that he wept himself. Now as he went thence to the place where he was to vanish out of their sight, they all followed after him

---

* Since Josephus assures us here that Moses blessed every one of the tribes of Israel, it is evident that Simeon was not omitted in his copy, as it now is, both in our Hebrew and Samaritan copies.

weeping; but Moses beckoned with his hand to those that were remote from him, and bade them stay behind in quiet, while he exhorted those that were near to him that they would not render his departure so lamentable. Whereupon they thought they ought to grant him that favour, to let him depart according as he himself desired; so they restrained themselves, though weeping still towards one another. All those who accompanied him were the senate, and Eleazar the high priest, and Joshua their commander. Now as soon as they were come to the mountain called *Abarim*, (which is a very high mountain, situate over against Jericho, and one that affords, to such as are upon it, a prospect of the greatest part of the excellent land of Canaan,) he dismissed the senate; and as he was going to embrace Eleazar and Joshua, and was still discoursing with them, a cloud stood over him on the sudden, and he disappeared in a certain valley, although he wrote in the holy books that he died, which was done out of fear, lest they should venture to say that, because of his extraordinary virtue, he went to God.

49. Now Moses lived in all one hundred and twenty years; a third part of which time, abating one month, he was the people's ruler; and he died on the last month of the year, which is called by the Macedonians *Dystrus*, but by us *Adar*, on the first day of the month. He was one that exceeded all men that ever were in understanding, and made the best use of what that understanding suggested to him. He had a very graceful way of speaking and addressing himself to the multitude: and as to his other qualifications, he had such a full command of his passions, as if he had hardly any such in his soul, and only knew them by their names, as rather perceiving them in other men than in himself. He was also such a general of an army as is seldom seen, as well as such a prophet as was never known, and this to such a degree, that whatsoever he pronounced, you would think you heard the voice of God himself. So the people mourned for him thirty days; nor did any grief so deeply affect the Hebrews as did this upon the death of Moses; nor were those that had experienced his conduct the only persons that desired him, but those also that perused the laws he left behind him had a strong desire after him, and by them gathered the extraordinary virtue he was master of. And this shall suffice for the declaration of the manner of the death of Moses.

BOOK V

FROM THE DEATH OF MOSES TO THE DEATH OF ELI

CHAPTER I

HOW JOSHUA, THE COMMANDER OF THE HEBREWS, MADE WAR WITH THE CANAANITES, AND OVERCAME THEM, AND DESTROYED THEM, AND DIVIDED THEIR LAND BY LOT TO THE TRIBES OF ISRAEL

1. WHEN Moses was taken away from among men, in the manner already described, and when all the solemnities belonging to the mourning for him were finished, and the sorrow for him was over, Joshua commanded the multitude to get themselves ready for an expedition. He also sent spies to Jericho to discover what forces they had, and what were their intentions; but he put his camp in order, as intending soon to pass over Jordan at a proper season. And calling to him the rulers of the tribe of Reuben, and the governors of the tribe of Gad, and [the half tribe of] Manasseh, (for half of this tribe had been permitted to have their habitation in the country of the Amorites, which was the seventh part of the land of Canaan,*) he put them in mind what they had promised Moses; and he exhorted them that, for the sake of the care that Moses had taken of them, who had never been weary of taking pains for them, no not when he was dying, and for the sake of the public welfare, they would prepare themselves, and readily perform what they had promised; so he took fifty thousand of them who followed him, and he marched from Abila to Jordan, sixty furlongs.

2. Now when he had pitched his camp, the spies came to him immediately, well acquainted with the whole state of the Canaanites; for at first, before they were all discovered, they took a full view of the city of Jericho without disturbance, and saw which parts of the walls were strong, and which parts were otherwise, and indeed insecure, and which of the gates were so weak as might afford an entrance to their army. Now those that met them took no notice of them when they saw them, and supposed they were only strangers, who used to be very curious in observing everything in the city, and did not take them for enemies; but at even they retired to a certain inn that was near to the wall, whither they went to eat their supper; which supper, when they had done, and were considering how to get away, information was given to the king as he was at supper that there were some persons come from the Hebrews' camp to view the city as spies, and that they were in the inn kept by Rahab, and were very solicitous that they might not be discovered. So he sent immediately some to them, and commanded to catch them, and bring them to him, that he might examine them by torture, and learn what their business was there. As soon as Rahab understood that these messen-

gers were coming, she hid the spies under stalks of flax, which were laid dried on the top of her house; and said to the messengers that were sent by the king, that certain unknown strangers had supped with her a little before sunsetting, and were gone away, who might easily be taken, if they were any terror to the city, or likely to bring any danger to the king. So these messengers being thus deluded by the woman,† and suspecting no imposition, went their ways without so much as searching the inn; but they immediately pursued them along those roads which they most probably supposed them to have gone, and those particularly which led to the river, but could hear no tidings of them; so they left off the pains of any further pursuit. But when the tumult was over, Rahab brought the men down, and desired them as soon as they should have obtained possession of the land of Canaan, when it would be in their power to make her amends for her preservation of them, to remember what danger she had undergone for their sakes: for that if she had been caught concealing them, she could not have escaped a terrible destruction, she and all her family with her, and so she bid them go home; and desired them to swear to her to preserve her and her family when they should take the city and destroy all its inhabitants, as they had decreed to do; for so far she said she had been assured by those divine miracles of which she had been informed. So these spies acknowledged that they owed her thanks for what she had done already, and withal swore to requite her kindness, not only in words, but in deeds; but they gave her this advice, that when she should perceive that the city was about to be taken, she should put her goods, and all her family, by way of security, in her inn, and to hang out scarlet threads before her doors [or windows] that the commander of the Hebrews might know her house, and take care to do her no harm; for said they, we will inform him of this matter, because of the concern thou hast had to preserve us; but if any one of thy family fall in the battle, do not thou blame us; and we beseech that God, by whom we have sworn, not then to be displeased with us, as though we had broken our oaths. So these men, when they had made this agreement, went away, letting themselves down by a rope from the wall, and escaped, and came and told their own people whatsoever they had done in their journey to this city. Joshua also told Eleazar the high priest, and the senate, what the spies had sworn to Rahab; who confirmed what had been sworn.

---

* The Amorites were one of the seven nations of Canaan. Hence Reland is willing to suppose that Josephus did not here mean that their land beyond Jordan was a seventh part of the whole of Canaan, but meant the Amorites as a seventh nation.

† It plainly appears, by the history of these spies and the innkeeper Rahab's deception of the king of Jericho's messengers, and yet the great commendation of her faith and good works in the New Testament, (Heb. xi. 31; James ii. 25,) that the best men did not then scruple to deceive those public enemies who might justly be destroyed, and this by telling direct falsehoods; I mean all this where no oath was demanded of them, otherwise they never durst venture on such a procedure

3. Now while Joshua, the commander, was in fear about their passing over Jordan, for the river ran with a strong current, and could not be passed over with bridges, for there never had been bridges laid over it hitherto; and while he suspected, that if he should attempt to make a bridge, that their enemies would not afford him time to perfect it, and for ferry-boats they had none,—God promised so to dispose of the river, that they might pass over it, and that by taking away the main part of its waters. So Joshua, after two days, caused the army, and the whole multitude, to pass over in the manner following:—The priests went first of all, having the ark with them; then went the Levites bearing the tabernacle and the vessels which belonged to the sacrifices; after which the entire multitude followed, according to their tribes, having their children and their wives in the midst of them, as being afraid for them, lest they should be borne away by the stream. But as soon as the priests had entered the river first, it appeared fordable, the depth of the water being restrained, and the sand appearing at the bottom, because the current was neither so strong nor so swift as to carry it away by its force; so they all passed over the river without fear, finding it to be in the very same state as God had foretold he would put it in; but the priests stood still in the midst of the river till the multitude should be passed over, and should get to the shore in safety; and when all were gone over, the priests came out also, and permitted the current to run freely as it used to do before. Accordingly the river, as soon as the Hebrews were come out of it, arose again presently, and came to its own proper magnitude as before.

4. So the Hebrews went on further fifty furlongs, and pitched their camp at the distance of ten furlongs from Jericho: but Joshua built an altar of those stones which all the heads of the tribes, at the command of the prophets, had taken out of the deep, to be afterwards a memorial of the division of the stream of this river, and upon it offered sacrifice to God; and in that place celebrated the passover, and had great plenty of all the things which they wanted hitherto; for they reaped the corn of the Canaanites, which was now ripe, and took other things as prey; for then it was that their former food, which was manna, and of which they had eaten forty years, failed them.

5. Now while the Israelites did this, and the Canaanites did not attack them, but kept themselves quiet within their own walls, Joshua resolved to besiege them; so on the first day of the feast [of the passover] the priests carried the ark round about, with some part of the armed men to be a guard to it. These priests went forward, blowing with their seven trumpets, and exhorted the army to be of good courage, and went round about the city, with the senate following them; and when the priests had only blown with the trumpets, for they did nothing more at all, they returned to the camp; and when they had done this for six days, on the seventh Joshua gathered the armed men, and all people together, and told them these good tidings, that the city should now be taken, since God would on that day give it them, by the falling down of the walls, and this of their own accord, and without their labour. However, he charged them to kill every one they should take, and not to abstain from the slaughter of their enemies, either for weariness or for pity, and not to fall on the spoil, and be thereby diverted from pursuing their enemies as they ran away; but to destroy all the animals, and to take nothing for their peculiar advantage. He commanded them also to bring together all the silver and gold, that it might be set apart as first-fruits unto God out of this glorious exploit, as having gotten them from the city they first took; only that they should save Rahab and her kindred alive, because of the oath which the spies had sworn to her.

6. When he had said this, and had set his army in order, he brought it against the city: so they went round the city again, the ark going before them, and the priests encouraging the people to be zealous in the work; and when they had gone round it seven times, and had stood still a little, the wall fell down, while no instrument of war, nor any other force, was applied to it by the Hebrews.

7. So they entered into Jericho, and slew all the men that were therein, while they were affrighted at the surprising overthrow of the walls, and their courage was become useless, and they were not able to defend themselves; so they were slain, and their throats cut, some in the ways, and others as caught in their houses,—nothing afforded them assistance, but they all perished, even to the women and the children; and the city was filled with dead bodies, and not one person escaped. They also burnt the whole city, and the country about it; but they saved alive Rahab, with her family, who had fled to her inn; and when she was brought to him, Joshua owned to her that he owed her thanks for her preservation of the spies: so he said he would not appear to be behind her in her benefaction to her; whereupon he gave her certain lands immediately, and had her in great esteem ever afterwards.

8. And if any part of the city escaped the fire, he overthrew it from the foundation; and he denounced a curse* against its inhabitants, if any should desire to rebuild it: how, upon his laying the foundation of the walls he should be deprived of his eldest son; and upon finishing it he should lose his youngest son. But what happened hereupon, we shall speak hereafter.

9. Now there was an immense quantity of silver and gold, and besides those of brass also, that was heaped together out of the city when it was taken, no one transgressing the decree, nor purloining for their own peculiar advantage; which spoils Joshua delivered to the priests, to be laid up among their treasures. And thus did Jericho perish.

10. But there was one Achar,† the son [of Charmi, the son] of Zebedias, of the tribe of Judah, who, finding a royal garment woven entirely of gold, and a piece of gold that weighed two hundred shekels;‡ and thinking it a very hard case, that what spoils he, by run-

---

* Upon occasion of this devoting of Jericho to destruction, and the exemplary punishment of Achar, and of the punishment of the future breaker of it, Hiel, (1 Kings xvi. 34,) as also of the punishment of Saul, (1 Sam. xv.,) we may observe what was the true meaning of that law, (Lev. xxvii. 28:) "None devoted, which shall be devoted of men, shall be redeemed; but shall surely be put to death;" i.e. whenever any of the Jews' public enemies had been solemnly devoted to destruction, it was utterly unlawful to permit those enemies to be redeemed.

† That the name of this chief was not Achan, as in the common copies, but Achar, is evident by the allusion to that name in the curse of Joshua, "Why hast thou troubled us?—the Lord shall trouble thee;" where the Hebrew word alludes only to the name Achar, but not to Achan. Accordingly, this Valley of Achar, or Achor, is a known place, a little north of Gilgal.

‡ This passage ought to be read thus:—"A piece of gold that weighed fifty shekels, and one of silver that weighed two hundred shekels."

ning some hazard, had found, he must give away, and offer it to God, who stood in no need of it, while he that wanted it must go without it,—made a deep ditch in his own tent, and laid them up therein, as supposing he should not only be concealed from his fellow-soldiers, but from God himself also.

11. Now the place where Joshua pitched his camp was called Gilgal, which denotes *liberty;* for since now they had passed over Jordan, they looked on themselves as freed from the miseries which they had undergone from the Egyptians, and in the wilderness.

12. Now, a few days after the calamity that befell Jericho, Joshua sent three thousand armed men to take Ai, a city situate above Jericho; but, upon the sight of the people of Ai, with them they were driven back, and lost thirty-six of their men. When this was told the Israelites, it made them very sad, and exceedingly disconsolate, not so much because of the relation the men that were destroyed bare to them, though those that were destroyed were all good men, and deserved their esteem, as by the despair it occasioned; for while they believed that they were already, in effect, in possession of the land, and should bring back the army out of the battles without loss, as God had promised beforehand, they now saw unexpectedly their enemies bold with success; so they put sackcloth on their garments, and continued in tears and lamentation all the day, without the least inquiry after food, but laid what had happened greatly to heart.

13. When Joshua saw the army so much afflicted, and possessed with forebodings of evil as to their whole expedition, he used freedom with God, and said, "We are not come thus far out of any rashness of our own, as though we thought ourselves able to subdue this land with our own weapons, but at the instigation of Moses, thy servant, for this purpose, because thou hast promised us, by many signs, that thou wouldst give us this land for a possession, and that thou wouldst make our army always superior in war to our enemies, and accordingly some success has already attended upon us agreeably to thy promises; but because we have now unexpectedly been foiled, and have lost some men out of our army, we are grieved at it, as fearing what thou hast promised us; and what Moses foretold us cannot be depended on by us; and our future expectation troubles us the more, because we have met with such a disaster in this our first attempt; but do thou, O Lord, free us from these suspicions, for thou art able to find a cure for these disorders, by giving us victory, which will both take away the grief we are in at present, and prevent our distrust as to what is to come."

14. These intercessions Joshua put up to God, as he lay prostrate on his face: whereupon God answered him, That he should rise up, and purify his host from the pollution that had got into it; that "things consecrated to me have been impudently stolen from me," and that "this has been the occasion why this defeat had happened to them;" and that when they should search out and punish the offender, he would ever take care they should have the victory over their enemies. This Joshua told the people; and calling for Eleazar the high priest and the men in authority, he cast lots, tribe by tribe; and when the lot shewed that this wicked action was done by one of the tribe of Judah, he then again proposed the lot to the several families thereto belonging; so the truth of this wicked action was found to belong to the family of Zachar; and when the inquiry was made man by man, they took Achar, who, upon God's reducing him to a terrible extremity, could not deny the fact: so he confessed the theft, and produced what he had taken in the midst of them, whereupon he was immediately put to death; and attained no more than to be buried in the night in a disgraceful manner, and such as was suitable to a condemned malefactor.

15. When Joshua had thus purified the host, he led them against Ai: and having by night laid an ambush round about the city, he attacked the enemies as soon as it was day; but as they advanced boldly against the Israelites, because of their former victory, he made them believe he retired, and by that means drew them a great way from the city, they still supposing that they were pursuing their enemies, and despised them, as though the case had been the same with that in the former battle; after which Joshua ordered his forces to turn about, and placed them against their front: he then made the signals agreed upon to those that lay in ambush, and so excited them to fight; so they ran suddenly into the city, the inhabitants being upon the walls, nay, others of them being in perplexity, and coming to see those that were without the gates. Accordingly, these men took the city, and slew all that they met with; but Joshua forced those that came against him to come to a close fight, and discomfited them, and made them run away; and when they were driven towards the city, and thought it had not been touched, as soon as they saw it was taken, and perceived it was burnt, with their wives and children, they wandered about the fields in a scattered condition, and were no way able to defend themselves, because they had none to support them. Now when this calamity was come upon the men of Ai, there were a great number of children, and women, and servants, and an immense quantity of other furniture. The Hebrews also took herds of cattle, and a great deal of money, for this was a rich country. So when Joshua came to Gilgal, he divided all these spoils among the soldiers.

16. But the Gibeonites, who inhabited very near to Jerusalem, when they saw what miseries had happened to the inhabitants of Jericho, and to those of Ai, and suspected that the like sore calamity would come as far as themselves, they did not think fit to ask for mercy of Joshua; for they supposed they should find little mercy from him, who made war that he might entirely destroy the nation of the Canaanites; but they invited the people of Cephirah and Kiriathjearim, who were their neighbours, to join in league with them; and told them, that neither could they themselves avoid the danger they were all in, if the Israelites should prevent them, and seize upon them; so when they had persuaded them, they resolved to endeavour to escape the forces of the Israelites. Accordingly, upon their agreement to what they proposed, they sent ambassadors to Joshua to make a league of friendship with him, and those such of the citizens as were best approved of, and most capable of doing what was most advantageous to the multitude. Now these ambassadors thought it dangerous to confess themselves to be Canaanites, but thought they might, by this contrivance, avoid the danger, namely, by saying that they bare no relation to the Canaanites at all, but dwelt at a very great distance from them: and they said further, that they came a long way, on account of the reputation he had gained for his virtue; and as a mark of the truth of what they said they shewed him the habit they were in, for that

their clothes were new when they came out, but were greatly worn by the length of time they had been on their journey; for indeed they took torn garments, on purpose that they might make him believe so. So they stood in the midst of the people, and said that they were sent by the people of Gibeon, and of the circumjacent cities, which were very remote from the land where they now were, to make such a league of friendship with them, and this on such conditions as were customary among their forefathers: for when they understood that, by the favour of God, and his gift to them, they were to have the possession of the land of Canaan bestowed upon them, they said that they were very glad to hear it, and desired to be admitted into the number of their citizens. Thus did these ambassadors speak; and shewing them the marks of their long journey, they entreated the Hebrews to make a league of friendship with them. Accordingly Joshua, believing what they said, that they were not of the nation of the Canaanites, entered into friendship with them; and Eleazar the high priest, with the senate, sware to them that they would esteem them their friends and associates, and would attempt nothing that should be unfair against them, the multitude also assenting to the oaths that were made to them. So these men having obtained what they desired, by deceiving the Israelites, went home: but when Joshua led his army to the country at the bottom of the mountains of this part of Canaan, he understood that the Gibeonites dwelt not far from Jerusalem, and that they were of the stock of the Canaanites; so he sent for their governors, and reproached them with the cheat they had put upon him; but they alleged, on their own behalf, that they had no other way to save themselves but that, and were therefore forced to have recourse to it. So he called for Eleazar the high priest, and for the senate, who thought it right to make them public servants, that they might not break the oath they had made to them; and they ordained them to be so;—and this was the method by which these men found safety and security under the calamity that was ready to overtake them.

17. But the king of Jerusalem took it to heart that the Gibeonites had gone over to Joshua; so he called upon the kings of the neighbouring nations to join together, and make war against them. Now when the Gibeonites saw these kings, which were four, besides the king of Jerusalem, and perceived that they had pitched their camp at a certain fountain not far from their city, and were getting ready for the siege of it, they called upon Joshua to assist them; for such was their case, as to expect to be destroyed by these Canaanites, but to suppose they should be saved by those that came for the destruction of the Canaanites, because of the league of friendship that was between them. Accordingly, Joshua made haste with his whole army to assist them, and marching day and night, in the morning he fell upon the enemies as they were going up to the siege; and when he had discomfited them he followed them, and pursued them down the descent of the hills. The place is called Bethhoron; where he also understood that God assisted him, which he declared by thunder and thunderbolts, as also by the falling of hail larger than usual. Moreover, it happened that the day was lengthened,* that the night might

not come on too soon, and be an obstruction to the zeal of the Hebrews in pursuing their enemies: insomuch, that Joshua took the kings, who were hidden in a certain cave at Makkedah, and put them to death. Now, that the day was lengthened at this time, and was longer than ordinary, is expressed in the books laid up in the temple.†

18. These kings which made war with, and were ready to fight the Gibeonites, being thus overthrown, Joshua returned again to the mountainous parts of Canaan; and when he had made a great slaughter of the people there, and took their prey, he came to the camp at Gilgal. And now there went a great fame abroad among the neighbouring people of the courage of the Hebrews; and those that heard what a number of men were destroyed were greatly affrighted at it: so the kings that lived about mount Libanus, who were Canaanites, and those Canaanites that dwelt in the plain country, with auxiliaries out of the land of the Philistines, pitched their camp at Beroth, a city of the Upper Galilee, not far from Cadesh, which is itself also a place in Galilee. Now the number of the whole army was three hundred thousand armed footmen, and ten thousand horsemen, and twenty thousand chariots; so that the multitude of the enemies affrighted both Joshua himself and the Israelites; and they, instead of being full of hopes of good success, were superstitiously timorous, with the great terror with which they were stricken. Whereupon God upbraided them with the fear they were in, and asked them, whether they desired a greater help than he could afford them; and promised them that they should overcome their enemies; and withal charged them to make their enemies' horses useless, and to burn their chariots. So Joshua became full of courage upon these promises of God, and went out suddenly against the enemies; and after five days' march he came upon them, and joined battle with them, and there was a terrible fight, and such a number were slain as could not be believed by those that heard it. He also went on in the pursuit a great way, and destroyed the entire army of the enemies, few only excepted, and all the kings fell in the battle; insomuch, that when there wanted men to be killed, Joshua slew their horses, and burnt their chariots, and passed all over their country without opposition, no one daring to meet him in battle; but he still went on, taking their cities by siege, and again killing whatever he took.

19. The fifth year was now past, and there was not one of the Canaanites remained any longer, excepting some that had retired to places of great strength. So Joshua removed his camp to the mountainous country, and placed the tabernacle in the city of Shiloh, for that seemed a fit place for it, because of the beauty of its situation, until such time as their affairs would permit them to build a temple; and from thence he went to Shechem, together with all the people, and raised an altar where Moses had beforehand directed; then did he divide the army, and placed one half of them on mount Gerizzim, and the other half on mount Ebal, on which mountain the altar was; he also placed there the tribe of Levi, and the priests. And when they had sacrificed, and denounced the [blessings and the] curses, and had left them engraven upon the altar, they returned to Shiloh.

---

* Whether this lengthening of the day were physical and real, or whether only apparent, cannot now be determined; philosophers and astronomers will naturally incline to this latter opinion. The fact itself was mentioned in the book of Jasher, now lost, (Josh. x. 13.) and is confirmed by Isaiah, (xxviii. 21,) Habakuk, (iii. 11,) and by the son of Sirach, (Ecclus. xlvi. 4.)

† See the note on Antiq. b. iii. chap. ii. sect. 7.

20. And now Joshua was old, and saw that the cities of the Canaanites were not easily to be taken, not only because they were situate in such strong places, but because of the strength of the walls themselves, which being built round about, the natural strength of the places on which the cities stood seemed capable of repelling their enemies from besieging them, and of making those enemies despair of taking them ; for when the Canaanites had learned that the Israelites came out of Egypt in order to destroy them, they were busy all that time in making their cities strong. So he gathered the people together to a congregation at Shiloh ; and when they, with great zeal and haste, were come thither, he observed to them what prosperous successes they had already had, and what glorious things had been done, and those such as were worthy of that God who enabled them to do those things, and worthy of the virtue of those laws which they followed. He took notice also, that thirty-one of those kings that ventured to give them battle were overcome, and every army, how great soever it were, that confided in their own power, and fought with them, was utterly destroyed ; so that not so much as any of their posterity remained ; and as for the cities, since some of them were taken, but the others must be taken in length of time, by long sieges, both on account of the strength of the walls, and of the confidence the inhabitants had in them thereby, he thought it reasonable that those tribes that came along with them from beyond Jordan, and had partaken of the dangers they had undergone, being their own kindred, should now be dismissed and sent home, and should have thanks for the pains they had taken together with them. As also, he thought it reasonable that they should send one man out of every tribe, and he such as had the testimony of extraordinary virtue, who should measure the land faithfully, and without any fallacy or deceit should inform them of its real magnitude.

21. Now Joshua, when he had thus spoken to them, found that the multitude approved of his proposal. So he sent men to measure their country, and sent with them some geometricians, who could not easily fail of knowing the truth, on account of their skill in that art. He also gave them a charge to estimate the measure of that part of the land that was most fruitful, and what was not so good ; for such is the nature of the land of Canaan, that one may see large plains, and such as are exceeding fit to produce fruit, which yet, if they were compared to other parts of the country, might be reckoned exceedingly fruitful ; yet if it be compared with the fields about Jericho, and to those that belong to Jerusalem, will appear to be of no account at all ; and although it so falls out that these people have but a very little of this sort of land, and that it is, for the main, mountainous also, yet does it not come behind other parts, on account of its exceeding goodness and beauty ; for which reason Joshua thought the land for the tribes should be divided by estimation of its goodness, rather than the largeness of its measure, it often happening, that one acre of some sort of land was equivalent to a thousand other acres. Now the men that were sent, which were in number ten, travelled all about, and made an estimation of the land, and in the seventh month came to him to the city of Shiloh, where they had set up the tabernacle.

22. So Joshua took both Eleazar and the senate, and with them the heads of the tribes, and distributed the land to the nine tribes, and to the half-tribe of Manasseh, appointing the dimensions to be according to the largeness of each tribe. So when he had cast lots, Judah had assigned him by lot the upper part of Judea, reaching as far as Jerusalem, and its breadth extended to the Lake of Sodom. Now in the lot of this tribe there were the cities of Askelon and Gaza. The lot of Simeon, which was the second, included that part of Idumea which bordered upon Egypt and Arabia. As to the Benjamites, their lot fell so, that its length reached from the river Jordan to the sea ; but in breadth it was bounded by Jerusalem and Bethel ; and this lot was the narrowest of all, by reason of the goodness of the land ; for it included Jericho and the city of Jerusalem. The tribe of Ephraïm had by lot the land that extended in length from the river Jordan to Gezer ; but in breadth as far as from Bethel, till it ended at the Great Plain. The half-tribe of Manasseh had the land from Jordan to the city Dora ; but its breadth was at Bethshan, which is now called Scythopolis ; and after these was Issachar, which had its limits in length, mount Carmel and the river, but its limit in breadth was mount Tabor. The tribe of Zebulon's lot included the land which lay as far as the Lake of Genesareth, and that which belonged to Carmel and the sea. The tribe of Aser had that part which was called the *Valley*, for such it was, and all that part which lay over against Sidon. The city Arce belonged to their share, which is also named Actipus. The Naphthalites received the eastern parts, as far as the city of Damascus and the Upper Galilee, unto mount Libanus, and the Fountains of Jordan, which rise out of that mountain ; that is, out of that part of it whose limits belong to the neighbouring city of Arce. The Danites' lot included all that part of the valley which respects the sun-setting, and were bounded by Azotus and Dora ; as also they had all Jamnia and Gath, from Ekron to that mountain where the tribe of Judah begins.

23. After this manner did Joshua divide the six nations that bear the name of the Sons of Canaan, with their land, to be possessed by the nine tribes and a half ; for Moses had prevented him, and had already distributed the land of the Amorites, which itself was so called also from one of the sons of Canaan, to the two tribes and a half, as we have shewn already. But the parts about Sidon, as also those that belonged to the Arkites, and the Amathites, and the Aradians, were not yet regularly disposed of.

24. But now was Joshua hindered by his age from executing what he intended to do, (as did those that succeeded him in the government, take little care of what was for the advantage of the public :) so he gave it in charge to every tribe to leave no remainder of the race of the Canaanites in the land that had been divided to them by lot ; that Moses had assured them beforehand, and they might rest fully satisfied about it, that their own security and their observation of their own laws depended wholly upon it. Moreover, he enjoined them to give thirty-eight cities to the Levites, for they had already received ten in the country of the Amorites ; and three of these he assigned to those that fled from the man-slayers, who were to inhabit there ; for he was very solicitous that nothing should be neglected which Moses had ordained. These cities were of the tribe of Judah, Hebron ; of that of Ephraim, Shechem ; and of that of Naphthali, Cadesh, which is a place of Upper Galilee. He also distributed among them the rest of the prey not yet distributed, which was very great ; whereby they had an affluence of great riches, both all in general, and every one in particular : and this of

gold and of vestments, and of other furniture, besides a multitude of cattle, whose number could not be told.

25. After this was over, he gathered the army together to a congregation, and spake thus to those tribes that had their settlement in the land of the Amorites, beyond Jordan,—for fifty thousand of them had armed themselves, and had gone to the war along with them :—"Since that God, who is the Father and Lord of the Hebrew nation, has now given us this land for a possession, and promised to preserve us in the enjoyment of it as our own for ever ; and since you have with alacrity offered yourselves to assist us when we wanted that assistance on all occasions, according to his command, it is but just, now all our difficulties are over, that you should be permitted to enjoy rest, and that we should trespass on your alacrity to help us no longer; that so, if we should again stand in need of it, we may readily have it on any future emergency, and not tire you out so much now as may make you slower in assisting us another time. We, therefore, return you our thanks for the dangers you have undergone with us, and we do it not at this time only, but we shall always be thus disposed; and be so good as to remember our friends, and to preserve in mind what advantages we have had from them ; and how you have put off the enjoyments of your own happiness for our sakes, and have laboured for what we have now, by the good-will of God obtained, and resolved not to enjoy your own prosperity till you have afforded us that assistance. However, you have, by joining your labour with ours, gotten great plenty of riches, and will carry home with you much prey, with gold and silver, and, what is more than all these, our good-will towards you, and a mind willingly disposed to make a requital of your kindness to us, in what case soever you shall desire it, for you have not omitted anything which Moses beforehand required of you, nor have you despised him because he was dead and gone from you, so that there is nothing to diminish that gratitude which we owe to you. We therefore dismiss you joyful to your own inheritances; and we entreat you to suppose, that there is no limit to be set to the intimate relation that is between us ; and that you will not imagine, because this river is interposed between us, that you are of a different race from us, and not Hebrews ; for we are all the posterity of Abraham, both we that inhabit here, and you that inhabit there ; and it is the same God that brought our forefathers and yours into the world, whose worship and form of government we are to take care of, which he has ordained, and are most carefully to observe ; because, while you continue in those laws, God will also shew himself merciful and assisting to you ; but if you imitate the other nations, and forsake those laws, he will reject your nation." When Joshua had spoken thus, and saluted them all, both those in authority one by one, and the whole multitude in common, he himself stayed where he was ; but the people conducted those tribes on their journey, and that not without tears in their eyes; and indeed they hardly knew how to part one from the other.

26. Now when the tribe of Reuben, and that of Gad, and as many of the Manassites as followed them, were passed over the river, they built an altar on the banks of Jordan, as a monument to posterity, and a sign of their relation to those that should inhabit on the other side. But when those on the other side heard that those who had been dismissed had built an altar, but did not hear with what intention they built it, but supposed it to be by way of innovation,

and for the introduction of strange gods, they did not incline to disbelieve it; but thinking this defamatory report, as if it were built for divine worship, was credible, they appeared in arms, as though they would avenge themselves on those that built the altar ; and they were about to pass over the river, and to punish them for their subversion of the laws of their country ; for they did not think it fit to regard them on account of their kindred, or the dignity of those that had given the occasion, but to regard the will of God, and the manner wherein he desired to be worshipped ; so these men put themselves in array for war. But Joshua, and Eleazar the high priest, and the senate, restrained them ; and persuaded them first to make trial by words of their intention, and afterwards, if they found that their intention was evil, then only to proceed to make war upon them. Accordingly, they sent as ambassadors to them Phineas the son of Eleazar, and ten more persons that were in esteem among the Hebrews, to learn of them what was in their mind when, upon passing over the river, they had built an altar upon its banks ; and as soon as these ambassadors were passed over, and were come to them, and a congregation was assembled, Phineas stood up and said, That the offence they had been guilty of was of too heinous a nature to be punished by words alone, or by them only to be amended for the future, yet that they did not so look at the heinousness of their transgression as to have recourse to arms, and to a battle for their punishment immediately ; but that, on account of their kindred, and the probability there was that they might be reclaimed, they took this method of sending an embassage to them : "That when we have learned the true reasons by which you have been moved to build this altar, we may neither seem to have been too rash in assaulting you by our weapons of war, if it prove that you made the altar for justifiable reasons, and may then justly punish you if the accusation prove true ; for we can hardly suppose that you, who have been acquainted with the will of God, and have been hearers of those laws which he himself hath given us, now you are separated from us, and gone to that patrimony of yours, which you, through the grace of God, and that providence which he exercises over you, have obtained by lot, can forget him, and can leave that ark and that altar which is peculiar to us, and can introduce strange gods and imitate the wicked practices of the Canaanites. Now this will appear to have been a small crime if you repent now, and proceed no further in your madness, but pay a due reverence to, and keep in mind the laws of your country ; but if you persist in your sins, we will not grudge our pains to preserve our laws ; but we will pass over Jordan and defend them, and defend God also, and shall esteem of you as of men no way differing from the Canaanites, but shall destroy you in the like manner as we destroyed them ; for do not you imagine that, because you are got over the river, you are got out of the reach of God's power ; you are everywhere in places that belong to him, and impossible it is to overrun his power, and the punishment he will bring on men thereby ; but if you think that your settlement here will be any obstruction to your conversion to what is good, nothing need hinder us from dividing the land anew, and leaving this old land to be for the feeding of sheep ; but you will do well to return to your duty, and to leave off these new crimes ; and we beseech you, by your children and wives, not to force us to punish you. Take therefore such measures in this assembly, as supposing that your own safety, and the safety of those that are dearest to you, is therein concerned, and believe that it is better for you to be conquered by words, than to continue in your purpose, and to experience deeds and war therefore."

27. When Phineas had discoursed thus, the governors of the assembly, and the whole multitude, began to make an apology for themselves, concerning what they were accused of; and they said, That they neither would depart from the relation they bare to them, nor had they built the altar by way of innovation; that they owned one and the same common God with all the Hebrews, and that brazen altar which was before the tabernacle, on which they would offer their sacrifices; that as to the altar they had raised, on account of which they were thus suspected, it was not built for worship, "but that it might be a sign and a monument of our relation to you for ever, and a necessary caution to us to act wisely, and to continue in the laws of our country, but not a handle for transgressing them, as you suspect : and let God be our authentic witness, that this was the occasion of our building this altar; whence we beg you will have a better opinion of us, and do not impute such a thing to us as would render any of the posterity of Abraham well worthy of perdition, in case they attempt to bring in new rites, and such as are different from our usual practices."

28. When they had made this answer, and Phineas had commended them for it, he came to Joshua and explained before the people what answer they had received. Now Joshua was glad that he was under no necessity of setting them in array, or of leading them to shed blood, and make war against men of their own kindred : and accordingly he offered sacrifices of thanksgiving to God for the same. So Joshua after that dissolved this great assembly of the people, and sent them to their own inheritances, while he himself lived in Shechem. But in the twentieth year after this when he was very old, he sent for those of the greatest dignity in the several cities, with those in authority, and the senate, and as many of the common people as could be present; and when they were come he put them in mind of all the benefits God had bestowed on them, which could not but be a great many, since from a low estate they were advanced to so great a degree of glory and plenty; and exhorted them to take notice of the intentions of God, which had been so gracious towards them; and told them that the Deity would continue their friend by nothing else but their piety; and that it was proper for him, now that he was about to depart out of this life, to leave such an admonition to them; and he desired that they would keep in memory this his exhortation to them.

29. So Joshua, when he had thus discoursed to them, died, having lived a hundred and ten years; forty of which he lived with Moses, in order to learn what might be for his advantage afterwards. He also became their commander after his death for twenty-five years. He was a man that wanted not wisdom nor eloquence to declare his intentions to the people, but very eminent on both accounts. He was of great courage and magnanimity in action and in dangers, and very sagacious in procuring the peace of the people, and of great virtue at all proper seasons. He was buried in the city of Timnah, of the tribe of Ephraim.* About the same time

died Eleazar the high priest, leaving the high priesthood to his son Phineas. His monument also, and sepulchre, are in the city of Gabatha.

CHAPTER II

HOW, AFTER THE DEATH OF JOSHUA THEIR COMMANDER, THE ISRAELITES TRANSGRESSED THE LAWS OF THEIR COUNTRY, AND EXPERIENCED GREAT AFFLICTIONS; AND WHEN THERE WAS A SEDITION ARISEN, THE TRIBE OF BENJAMIN WAS DESTROYED, EXCEPTING ONLY SIX HUNDRED MEN

1. AFTER the death of Joshua and Eleazar, Phineas prophesied,† that according to God's will they should commit the government to the tribe of Judah, and that this tribe should destroy the race of the Canaanites; for then the people were concerned to learn what was the will of God. They also took to their assistance the tribe of Simeon : but upon this condition, that when those that had been tributary to the tribe of Judah should be slain, they should do the like for the tribe of Simeon.

2. But the affairs of the Canaanites were at this time in a flourishing condition, and they expected the Israelites with a great army at the city Bezek, having put the government into the hands of Adonibezek, which name denotes the *Lord of Bezek*, for *Adoni* in the Hebrew tongue signifies *Lord*. Now they hoped to have been too hard for the Israelites because Joshua was dead ; but when the Israelites had joined battle with them, I mean the two tribes before mentioned, they fought gloriously, and slew above ten thousand of them, and put the rest to flight; and in the pursuit they took Adonibezek, who, when his fingers and toes were cut off by them, said, "Nay, indeed, I was not always to lie concealed from God, as I find by what I now endure, while I have not been ashamed to do the same to seventy-two kings."‡ So they carried him alive as far as Jerusalem; and when he was dead, they buried him in the earth, and went on still in taking the cities; and when they had taken the lower city, which was not under a considerable time, they slew all the inhabitants; but the upper city was not to be taken without great difficulty, through the strength of its walls, and the nature of the place.

3. For which reason they removed their camp to Hebron; and when they had taken it, they slew all the inhabitants. There were till then left the race of giants, who had bodies so large, and countenances so entirely different from

---

* Moses Chorenensis sets down the famous inscription at Tangier concerning the old Canaanites driven out of Palestine by Joshua thus : "We are those exiles that were governors of the Canaanites, but have been driven

away by Joshua the robber, and are come to inhabit here."

† By *prophesying*, when spoken of a high priest, Josephus means no more than consulting God by Urim. If St John, who was contemporary with Josephus, made use of this style, when he says that "Caiaphas being high priest that year, prophesied that Jesus should die for that nation, and not for that nation only, but that also he should gather together in one the children of God that were scattered abroad," (xi. 51, 52,) he may possibly mean, that this was revealed to the high priest by an extraordinary voice from between the cherubims, when he had his breastplate, or Urim and Thummim, on before.

‡ This great number of seventy-two *reguli*, or small kings, as well as the thirty-one kings of Canaan subdued by Joshua, and thirty-two kings, or royal auxiliaries to Benhadad king of Syria, (1 Kings xx. 1,) intimate to us what was the ancient form of government among several nations before the monarchies began— viz., that every city or large town, with its neighbouring villages, was a distinct government by itself.

PHINEAS INQUIRES CONCERNING THE ALTAR

other men, that they were surprising to the sight, and terrible to the hearing. The bones of these men are still shewn to this very day, unlike to any credible relations of other men. Now they gave this city to the Levites as an extraordinary reward, with the suburbs of two thousand cities; but the land thereto belonging they gave as a free gift to Caleb, according to the injunctions of Moses. This Caleb was one of the spies which Moses sent into the land of Canaan. They also gave land for habitation to the posterity of Jethro, the Midianite, who was the father-in-law to Moses; for they had left their own country, and followed them, and accompanied them in the wilderness.

4. Now the tribes of Judah and Simeon took the cities which were in the mountainous part of Canaan, as also Askelon and Ashdod, of those that lay near the sea; but Gaza and Ekron escaped them, for they, lying in a flat country, and having a great number of chariots, sorely galled those that attacked them: so these tribes, when they were grown very rich by this war, retired to their own cities, and laid aside their weapons of war.

5. But the Benjamites, to whom belonged Jerusalem, permitted its inhabitants to pay tribute. So they all left off, the one to kill, and the other to expose themselves to danger, and had time to cultivate the ground. The rest of the tribes imitated that of Benjamin, and did the same; and, contenting themselves with the tributes that were paid them, permitted the Canaanites to live in peace.

6. However, the tribe of Ephraim, when they besieged Bethel, made no advance, nor performed anything worthy of the time they spent, and of the pains they took about that siege; yet did they persist in it, still sitting down before the city, though they endured great trouble thereby: but, after some time, they caught one of the citizens that came to them to get necessaries, and they gave him some assurances, that if he would deliver up the city to them, they would preserve him and his kindred; so he sware that, upon those terms, he would put the city into their hands. Accordingly, he that thus betrayed the city was preserved with his family; and the Israelites slew all the inhabitants, and retained the city for themselves.

7. After this, the Israelites grew effeminate as to fighting any more against their enemies, but applied themselves to the cultivation of the land, which producing them great plenty and riches, they neglected the regular disposition of their settlement, and indulged themselves in luxury and pleasures; nor were they any longer careful to hear the laws that belonged to their political government: whereupon God was provoked to anger, and put them in mind, first, how, contrary to his directions, they had spared the Canaanites: and, after that, how those Canaanites, as opportunity served, used them very barbarously. But the Israelites, though they were in heaviness at these admonitions from God, yet were they still very unwilling to go to war; and since they got large tributes from the Canaanites, and were indisposed for taking pains by their luxury, they suffered their aristocracy to be corrupted also, and did not ordain themselves a senate, nor any other such magistrates as their laws had formerly required, but they were very much given to cultivating their fields, in order to get wealth; which great indolence of theirs brought a terrible sedition upon them, and they proceeded so far as to fight one against another, from the following occasion:—

8. There was a Levite,* a man of a vulgar family, that belonged to the tribe of Ephraim, and dwelt therein: this man married a wife from Bethlehem, which is a place belonging to the tribe of Judah. Now he was very fond of his wife, and overcome with her beauty; but he was unhappy in this, that he did not meet with the like return of affection from her, for she was averse to him, which did more inflame his passion for her, so that they quarrelled one with another perpetually; and at last the woman was so disgusted at these quarrels, that she left her husband, and went to her parents in the fourth month. The husband being very uneasy at this her departure, and that out of his fondness for her, came to his father and mother-in-law, and made up their quarrels, and was reconciled to her, and lived with them there four days, as being kindly treated by her parents. On the fifth day he resolved to go home, and went away in the evening; for his wife's parents were loath to part with their daughter, and delayed the time till the day was gone. Now they had one servant that followed them, and an ass on which the woman rode; and when they were near Jerusalem, having gone already thirty furlongs, the servant advised them to take up their lodgings somewhere, lest some misfortune should befall them if they travelled in the night, especially since they were not far off enemies, that season often giving reason for suspicion of dangers from even such as are friends; but the husband was not pleased with this advice, nor was he willing to take up his lodging among strangers, for the city belonged to the Canaanites, but desired rather to go twenty furlongs further, and so to take their lodgings in some Israelite city. Accordingly, he obtained his purpose, and came to Gibeah, a city of the tribe of Benjamin, when it was just dark; and while no one that lived in the market-place invited him to lodge with him, there came an old man out of the field, one that was indeed of the tribe of Ephraim, but resided in Gibeah, and met him, and asked him who he was, and for what reason he came thither so late, and why he was looking out for provisions for supper when it was dark? To which he replied, that he was a Levite, and was bringing his wife from her parents, and was going home; but he told him his habitation was in the tribe of Ephraim: so the old man, as well because of their kindred as because they lived in the same tribe, and also because they had thus accidentally met together, took him in to lodge with him. Now certain young men of the inhabitants of Gibeah, having seen the woman in the market-place, and admiring her beauty, when they understood that she lodged with the old man, came to the doors, as contemning the weakness and fewness of the old man's family; and when the old man desired them to go away, and not to offer any violence or abuse there, they desired him to yield them up the strange woman, and then he should have no harm done to him: and when the old man alleged that the Levite was of his kindred, and that they would be guilty of horrid wickedness if they suffered themselves to be overcome by their pleasures, and so offend against their laws, they despised his righteous admonition, and laughed him to scorn. They also threatened to kill him if he

---

* Josephus's early date of this history, before the beginning of the Judges, or when there was no king in Israel, (Judges xix. 1,) is strongly confirmed by the large number of Benjamites, both in the days of Asa and Jehoshaphat, (2 Chron. xiv. 8, and xvi. 17,) who yet were here reduced to six hundred men.

became an obstacle to their inclinations; whereupon, when he found himself in great distress, and yet was not willing to overlook his guests, and see them abused, he produced his own daughter to them; and told them that it was a smaller breach of the law to satisfy their lust upon her, than to abuse his guests, supposing that he himself should by this means prevent any injury to be done to those guests. When they no way abated of their earnestness for the strange woman, but insisted absolutely on their desires to have her, he entreated them not to perpetrate any such act of injustice; but they proceeded to take her away by force, and indulging still more the violence of their inclinations, they took the woman away to their house, and when they had satisfied their lust upon her the whole night, they let her go about daybreak. So she came to the place where she had been entertained, under great affliction at what had happened; and was very sorrowful upon occasion of what she had suffered, and durst not look her husband in the face for shame, for she concluded that he would never forgive her for what she had done; so she fell down, and gave up the ghost: but her husband supposed that his wife was only fast asleep, and, thinking nothing of a more melancholy nature had happened, endeavoured to raise her up, resolving to speak comfortably to her, since she did not voluntarily expose herself to these men's lust, but was forced away to their house; but as soon as he perceived she was dead, he acted as prudently as the greatness of his misfortunes would admit, and laid his dead wife upon the beast, and carried her home; and cutting her, limb by limb, into twelve pieces, he sent them to every tribe, and gave it in charge to those that carried them, to inform the tribes of those that were the cause of his wife's death, and of the violence they had offered to her.

9. Upon this the people were greatly disturbed at what they saw, and at what they heard, as never having had the experience of such a thing before; so they gathered themselves to Shiloh, out of a prodigious and a just anger, and assembling in a great congregation before the tabernacle, they immediately resolved to take arms, and to treat the inhabitants of Gibeah as enemies; but the senate restrained them from doing so, and persuaded them, that they ought not so hastily to make war upon people of the same nation with them, before they discoursed with them by words concerning the accusation laid against them; it being part of their law, that they should not bring an army against foreigners themselves, when they appear to have been injurious, without sending an embassage first, and trying whereby whether they will repent or not: and accordingly they exhorted them to do what they ought to do in obedience to their laws, that is, to send to the inhabitants of Gibeah, to know whether they would deliver up the offenders to them, and, if they deliver them up, to rest satisfied with the punishment of those offenders; but if they despised the message that was sent them, to punish them, by taking up arms against them. Accordingly they sent to the inhabitants of Gibeah, and accused the young men of the crimes committed in the affair of the Levite's wife, and required of them those that had done what was contrary to the law, that they might be punished, as having justly deserved to die for what they had done; but the inhabitants of Gibeah would not deliver up the young men, and thought it too reproachful to them, out of fear of war, to submit to other men's demands upon

them; vaunting themselves to be no way inferior to any in war, neither in their number nor in courage. The rest of their tribe were also making great preparation for war, for they were so insolently mad as also to resolve to repel force by force.

10. When it was related to the Israelites what the inhabitants of Gibeah had resolved upon, they took their oath that no one of them would give his daughter in marriage to a Benjamite, but make war with greater fury against them than we have learned our forefathers made war against the Canaanites; and sent out presently an army of four hundred thousand against them, while the Benjamites' army was twenty-five thousand and six hundred; five hundred of whom were excellent at slinging stones with their left hands, insomuch that when the battle was joined at Gibeah the Benjamites beat the Israelites, and of them there fell two thousand men; and probably more had been destroyed had not the night come on and prevented it, and broken off the fight; so the Benjamites returned to the city with joy, and the Israelites returned to their camp in a great fright at what had happened. On the next day, when they fought again, the Benjamites beat them; and eighteen thousand of the Israelites were slain, and the rest deserted their camp out of fear of a greater slaughter. So they came to Bethel, a city that was near their camp, and fasted on the next day; and besought God, by Phineas the high priest, that his wrath against them might cease, and that he would be satisfied with these two defeats, and give them the victory and power over their enemies. Accordingly God promised them so to do, by the prophesying of Phineas.

11. When therefore they had divided the army into two parts, they laid the one half of them in ambush about the city Gibeah, by night, while the other half attacked the Benjamites, who retiring upon the assault, the Benjamites pursued them, while the Hebrews retired by slow degrees, as very desirous to draw them entirely from the city; and the other followed them as they retired, till both the old men and the young men that were left in the city, as too weak to fight, came running out together with them, as willing to bring their enemies under. However, when they were a great way from the city, the Hebrews ran away no longer, but turned back to fight them, and lifted up the signal they had agreed on to those that lay in ambush, who rose up, and with a great noise fell upon the enemy. Now, as soon as ever they perceived themselves to be deceived, they knew not what to do; and when they were driven into a certain hollow place which was in a valley, they were shot at by those that encompassed them, till they were all destroyed, excepting six hundred, which formed themselves into a close body of men, and forced their passage through the midst of their enemies, and fled to the neighbouring mountains, and, seizing upon them, remained there; but the rest of them, being about twenty-five thousand, were slain. Then did the Israelites burn Gibeah, and slew the women, and the males that were under age; and did the same also to the other cities of the Benjamites;—and, indeed, they were enraged to that degree, that they sent twelve thousand men out of the army, and gave them orders to destroy Jabesh Gilead, because it did not join with them in fighting against the Benjamites. Accordingly, those that were sent slew the men of war, with their children and wives, excepting four hundred virgins. To such a degree had they proceeded in their anger, because they not only had the suffering of the Levite's

wife to avenge, but the slaughter of their own soldiers.

12. However, they afterward were sorry for the calamity they had brought upon the Benjamites, and appointed a fast on that account, although they supposed those men had suffered justly for their offence against the laws; so they recalled by their ambassadors those six hundred which had escaped. These had seated themselves on a certain rock called *Rimmon*, which was in the wilderness. So the ambassadors lamented not only the disaster that had befallen the Benjamites, but themselves also, by this destruction of their kindred; and persuaded them to take it patiently, and to come and unite with them, and not, so far as in them lay, to give their suffrage to the utter destruction of the tribe of Benjamin; and said to them, "We give you leave to take the whole land of Benjamin to yourselves, and as much prey as you are able to carry away with you." So these men with sorrow confessed, that what had been done was according to the decree of God, and had happened for their own wickedness; and assented to those that invited them, and came down to their own tribe. The Israelites also gave them the four hundred virgins of Jabesh Gilead for wives; but as to the remaining two hundred, they deliberated about it how they might compass wives enough for them, and that they might have children by them; and whereas they had, before the war began, taken an oath, that no one would give his daughter to wife to a Benjamite; some advised them to have no regard to what they had sworn, because the oath had not been taken advisedly and judiciously, but in a passion, and thought that they should do nothing against God, if they were able to save a whole tribe which was in danger of perishing; and that perjury was then a sad and dangerous thing, not when it is done out of necessity, but when it is done with a wicked intention. But when the senate were affrighted at the very name of perjury, a certain person told them that he could shew them a way whereby they might procure the Benjamites wives enough, and yet keep their oath. They asked him what his proposal was. He said, "That three times in a year, when we meet in Shiloh, our wives and our daughters accompany us: let then the Benjamites be allowed to steal away, and marry such women as they can catch, while we will neither incite them nor forbid them; and when their parents take it ill, and desire us to inflict punishment upon them, we will tell them, that they were themselves the cause of what had happened, by neglecting to guard their daughters, and that they ought not to be over angry at the Benjamites, since that anger was permitted to rise too high already." So the Israelites were persuaded to follow this advice, and decreed, That the Benjamites should be allowed thus to steal themselves wives. So when the festival was coming on, these two hundred Benjamites lay in ambush before the city, by two and three together, and waited for the coming of the virgins, in the vineyards and other places where they could lie concealed. Accordingly the virgins came along playing, and suspected nothing of what was coming upon them, and walked after an unguarded manner, so those that lay scattered in the road rose up, and caught hold of them: by this means these Benjamites got them wives, and fell to agriculture, and took good care to recover their former happy state. And thus was this tribe of the Benjamites, after they had been in danger of entirely perishing, saved in the manner fore-mentioned, by the wisdom of the Israelites: and accordingly it presently flourished, and soon increased to be a multitude, and came to enjoy all other degrees of happiness. And such was the conclusion of this war.

CHAPTER III

HOW THE ISRAELITES AFTER THIS MISFORTUNE, GREW WICKED, AND SERVED THE ASSYRIANS; AND HOW GOD DELIVERED THEM BY OTHNIEL, WHO RULED OVER THEM FORTY YEARS

1. Now it happened that the tribe of Dan suffered in like manner with the tribe of Benjamin; and it came to do so on the occasion following:—When the Israelites had already left off the exercise of their arms for war, and were intent upon their husbandry, the Canaanites despised them, and brought together an army, not because they expected to suffer by them, but because they had a mind to have a sure prospect of treating the Hebrews ill when they pleased, and might thereby for the time to come dwell in their own cities the more securely; they prepared therefore their chariots, and gathered their soldiery together; their cities also combined together, and drew over to them Askelon and Ekron, which were within the tribe of Judah, and many more of those that lay in the plain. They also forced the Danites to fly into the mountainous country, and left them not the least portion of the plain country to set their foot on. Since then these Danites were not able to fight them, and had not land enough to sustain them, they sent five of their men into the midland country, to seek for a land to which they might remove their habitation. So these men went as far as the neighbourhood of mount Libanus, and the fountains of the Lesser Jordan, at the great plain of Sidon, a day's journey from the city; and when they had taken a view of the land, and found it to be good and exceeding fruitful, they acquainted their tribe with it, whereupon they made an expedition with the army, and built there the city Dan, of the same name with the son of Jacob, and of the same name with their own tribe.

2. The Israelites grew so indolent, and unready of taking pains, that misfortunes came heavier upon them, which also proceeded in part from their contempt of the divine worship; for when they had once fallen off from the regularity of their political government, they indulged themselves further in living according to their own pleasure, and according to their own will, till they were full of the evil doings that were common among the Canaanites. God therefore was angry with them, and they lost that their happy state which they had obtained by innumerable labours, by their luxury; for when Chusan, king of the Assyrians, had made war against them, they lost many of their soldiers in the battle, and when they were besieged, they were taken by force; nay, there was some, who, out of fear, voluntarily submitted to him, and though the tribute laid upon them was more than they could bear, yet did they pay it, and underwent all sort of oppression for eight years; after which time they were freed from them in the following manner:—

3. There was one whose name was Othniel, the son of Kenaz, of the tribe of Judah, an active man, and of great courage. He had an admonition from God, not to overlook the Israelites in such a distress as they were now in, but to endeavour boldly to gain them their liberty; so when he had procured some to assist him in this dangerous undertaking, (and few they

were, who, either out of shame at their present circumstances, or out of a desire of changing them, could be prevailed on to asssist him,) he first of all destroyed that garrison which Chusan had set over them ; but when it was perceived that he had not failed in his first attempt, more of the people came to his assistance ; so they joined battle with the Assyrians, and drove them entirely before them, and compelled them to pass over Euphrates. Hereupon Othniel, who had given such proofs of his valour, received from the multitude authority to judge the people : and when he had ruled over them forty years, he died.

CHAPTER IV

HOW OUR PEOPLE SERVED THE MOABITES EIGHT-TEEN YEARS, AND WERE THEN DELIVERED FROM SLAVERY BY ONE EHUD, WHO RETAINED THE DOMINION EIGHTY YEARS

1. WHEN Othniel was dead, the affairs of the Israelites fell again into disorder ; and while they neither paid to God the honour due to him, nor were obedient to the laws, their afflictions increased, till Eglon, king of the Moabites, did so greatly despise them on account of the disorders of their political government, that he made war upon them, and overcame them in several battles, and made the most courageous to·submit, and entirely subdued their army, and ordered them to pay him tribute. And when he had built him a royal palace at Jericho,* he omitted no method whereby he might distress them ; and indeed he reduced them to poverty for eighteen years. But when God had once taken pity of the Israelites, on account of their afflictions, and was moved to compassion by their supplications put up to him, he freed them from the hard usage they had met with under the Moabites. This liberty he procured for them in the following manner :—

2. There was a young man of the tribe of Benjamin, whose name was Ehud, the son of Gera, a man of very great courage in bold undertakings, and of a very strong body, fit for hard labour, but best skilled in using his left hand, in which was his whole strength ; and he also dwelt at Jericho. Now this man became familiar with Eglon, and that by means of presents, with which he obtained his favour, and insinuated himself into his good opinion ; whereby he was also beloved of those that were about the king. Now, when on a time, he was bringing presents to the king, and had two servants with him, he put a dagger on his right thigh secretly, and went in to him : it was then summer time, and the middle of the day, when the guards were not strictly on their watch, both because of the heat, and because they were gone to dinner. So the young man, when he had offered his presents to the king, who then resided in a small parlour that stood conveniently to avoid the heat, fell into discourse with him, for they were now alone, the king having bid his servants that attended him to go their ways, because he had a mind to talk with Ehud. He was now sitting on his throne ; and fear seized upon Ehud lest he should miss his stroke, and

not give him a deadly wound ; so he raised himself up, and said he had a dream to impart to him by the command of God ; upon which the king leaped out of his throne for joy of the dream ; so Ehud smote him to the heart, and, leaving his dagger in his body, he went out, and shut the door after him. Now the king's servants were very still, as supposing that the king had composed himself to sleep.

3. Hereupon Ehud informed the people of Jericho privately of what he had done, and exhorted them to recover their liberty ; who heard him gladly, and went to their arms, and sent messengers over the country, that should sound trumpets of rams' horns ; for it was our custom to call the people together by them. Now the attendants of Eglon were ignorant of what misfortune had befallen him for a great while ; but, towards the evening, fearing some uncommon accident had happened, they entered into his parlour, and when they found him dead, they were in great disorder, and knew not what to do ; and before the guards could be got together, the multitude of the Israelites came upon them, so that some of them were slain immediately, and some of them were put to flight, and ran away toward the country of Moab, in order to save themselves. Their number was above ten thousand. The Israelites seized upon the ford of Jordan, and pursued them, and slew them, and many of them they killed at the ford, nor did one of them escape out of their hands ; and by this means it was that the Hebrews freed themselves from slavery under the Moabites. Ehud was also on this account dignified with the government over all the multitude, and died after he had held the government eighty years.† He was a man worthy of commendation, even besides what he deserved for the forementioned act of his. After him Shamgar, the son of Anath, was elected for their governor, but died in the first year of his government.

CHAPTER V

HOW THE CANAANITES BROUGHT THE ISRAELITES UNDER SLAVERY FOR TWENTY YEARS ; AFTER WHICH THEY WERE DELIVERED BY BARAK AND DEBORAH, WHO RULED OVER THEM FOR FORTY YEARS

1. AND now it was that the Israelites, taking no warning by the former misfortunes to amend their manners, and neither worshipping God nor submitting to the laws, were brought under slavery by Jabin, the king of the Canaanites, and that before they had a short breathing time after the slavery under the Moabites ; for this Jabin came out of Hazor, a city that was situate over the lake Semechonitis, and had in pay three hundred thousand footmen, and ten thousand horsemen, with no fewer than three thousand chariots. Sisera was the commander of all his army, and was the principal person in the king's favour. He so sorely beat the Israelites when they fought with him, that he ordered them to pay tribute.

2. So they continued to undergo that hardship for twenty years, as not good enough of themselves to grow wise by their misfortunes. God was willing also hereby the more to subdue their

---

* It appears by Judges i. 16, iii. 13, that Eglon's pavilion was at the city of Palm-Trees, as the place where Jericho had stood is called after its destruction by Joshua, that is, at or near the demolished city. Accordingly, Josephus says it was at Jericho, or near to the same spot of ground on which Jericho had formerly stood.

† These eighty years are necessary to Josephus's usual large numbers between the exodus and the building of the temple, of 592, or 612 years, but not to the smallest number of 480 years, which lesser number Josephus seems sometimes to have followed.

obstinacy and ingratitude towards himself: so when at length they were become penitent, and were so wise as to learn that their calamities arose from their contempt of the laws, they besought Deborah, a certain prophetess among them (which name in the Hebrew tongue signifies a *Bee*) to pray to God to take pity on them, and not to overlook them, now they were ruined by the Canaanites. So God granted them deliverance, and chose them a general, Barak, one that was of the tribe of Naphtali. Now Barak, in the Hebrew tongue, signifies *Lightning*.

3. So Deborah sent for Barak, and bade him choose out ten thousand young men to go against the enemy, because God had said that number was sufficient, and promised them victory. But when Barak said that he would not be the general unless she would also go as a general with him, she had indignation at what he said, and replied, "Thou, O Barak, deliverest up meanly that authority which God hath given thee into the hand of a woman, and I do not reject it!" So they collected ten thousand men, and pitched their camp at mount Tabor, where, at the king's command, Sisera met them, and pitched his camp not far from the enemy; whereupon the Israelites, and Barak himself, were so affrighted at the multitude of those enemies, that they were resolved to march off, had not Deborah retained them, and commanded them to fight the enemy that very day, for that they should conquer them, and God would be their assistance.

4. So the battle began; and when they were come to close fight, there came down from heaven a great storm, with a vast quantity of rain and hail, and the wind blew the rain in the face of the Canaanites, and so darkened their eyes, that their arrows and slings were of no advantage to them, nor would the coldness of the air permit the soldiers to make use of their swords; while this storm did not so much incommode the Israelites, because it came in their backs. They also took such courage, upon the apprehension that God was assisting them, that they fell upon the very midst of their enemies, and slew a great number of them; so that some of them fell by the Israelites, some fell by their own horses, which were put into disorder, and not a few were killed by their own chariots. At last Sisera, as soon as he saw himself beaten, fled away, and came to a woman whose name was Jael, a Kenite, who received him, when he desired to be concealed; and when he asked for somewhat to drink, she gave him sour milk, of which he drank so unmeasurably that he fell asleep; but when he was asleep, Jael took an iron nail, and with a hammer drove it through his temples into the floor; and when Barak came a little afterward, she shewed Sisera nailed to the ground: and thus was this victory gained by a woman, as Deborah had foretold. Barak also fought with Jabin at Hazor; and when he met with him, he slew him: and when the general was fallen, Barak overthrew the city to the foundation, and was the commander of the Israelites for forty years.

CHAPTER VI

HOW THE MIDIANITES AND OTHER NATIONS FOUGHT AGAINST THE ISRAELITES, AND BEAT THEM, AND AFFLICTED THEIR COUNTRY FOR SEVEN YEARS; HOW THEY WERE DELIVERED BY GIDEON, WHO RULED OVER THE MULTITUDE FOR FORTY YEARS

1. Now when Barak and Deborah were dead, whose deaths happened about the same time, afterwards the Midianites called the Amalekites and Arabians to their assistance, and made war against the Israelites, and were too hard for those that fought against them; and when they had burnt the fruits of the earth, they carried off the prey. Now when they had done this for three years, the multitude of the Israelites retired to the mountains, and forsook the plain country. They also made themselves hollows under ground, and caverns, and preserved therein whatever had escaped their enemies; for the Midianites made expeditions in harvest-time, but permitted them to plough the land in winter, that so, when the others had taken the pains, they might have fruits for them to carry away. Indeed, there ensued a famine and a scarcity of food; upon which they betook themselves to their supplications to God, and besought him to save them.

2. Gideon also, the son of Joash, one of the principal persons of the tribe of Manasseh, brought his sheaves of corn privately, and thrashed them at the wine-press; for he was too fearful of their enemies to thrash them openly in the thrashing-floor. At this time somewhat appeared to him in the shape of a young man, and told him that he was a happy man, and beloved of God. To which he immediately replied, "A mighty indication of God's favour to me, that I am forced to use this wine-press, instead of a thrashing-floor!" But the appearance exhorted him to be of good courage, and to make an attempt for the recovery of their liberty. He answered, that it was impossible for him to recover it, because the tribe to which he belonged was by no means numerous; and because he was but young himself, and too inconsiderable to think of such great actions; but the other promised him that God would supply what he was defective in, and would afford the Israelites victory under his conduct.

3. Now, therefore, as Gideon was relating this to some young men, they believed him, and immediately there was an army of ten thousand men got ready for fighting. But God stood by Gideon in his sleep, and told him, that mankind were too fond of themselves, and were enemies to such as excelled in virtue. Now, that they might not pass God over, but ascribe the victory to him, and might not fancy it obtained by their own power, because they were a great army, and able of themselves to fight their enemies, but might confess that it was owing to his assistance, he advised him to bring his army about noon, in the violence of the heat, to the river, and to esteem those that bent down on their knees and so drank, to be men of courage; but for all those that drank tumultuously, that he should esteem them to do it out of fear, and as in dread of their enemies. And when Gideon had done as God had suggested to him, there were found three hundred men that took water with their hands tumultuously; so God bid him take these men, and attack the enemy. Accordingly, they pitched their camp at the river Jordan, as ready the next day to pass over it.

4. But Gideon was in great fear, for God had told him beforehand that he should set upon his enemies in the night-time; but God, being willing to free him from his fear, bid him take one of his soldiers, and go near to the Midianites' tents, for that he should from that very place have his courage raised, and grow bold. So he obeyed, and went and took his servant Phurah with him; and as he came near to one of the tents, he discovered that those that were in it

were awake, and that one of them was telling to his fellow-soldier a dream of his own, and that so plainly, that Gideon could hear him. The dream was this:—He thought he saw a barley-cake, such a one as could hardly be eaten by men, it was so vile, rolling through the camp, and overthrowing the royal tent, and the tents of all the soldiers. Now the other soldier explained this vision to mean the destruction of the army; and told him what his reason was which made him so conjecture—viz., That the seed called *barley* was all of it allowed to be of the vilest sort of seed, and that the Israelites were known to be the vilest of all the people of Asia, agreeably to the seed of barley, and that what seemed to look big among the Israelites was this Gideon and the army that was with him; "and since thou sayest thou didst see the cake overturning our tents, I am afraid lest God hath granted the victory over us to Gideon."

5. When Gideon had heard this dream, good hope and courage came upon him; and he commanded his soldiers to arm themselves, and told them of this vision of their enemies. They also took courage at what was told them, and were ready to perform what he should enjoin them; so Gideon divided his army into three parts, and brought it out about the fourth watch of the night, each watch containing a hundred men: they all bare empty pitchers and lighted lamps in their hands, that their onset might not be discovered by their enemies. They had also each of them a ram's horn in his right hand, which he used instead of a trumpet. The enemy's camp took up a large space of ground, for it happened that they had a great many camels; and as they were divided into different nations, so they were all contained in one circle. Now when the Hebrews did as they were ordered beforehand, upon their approach to their enemies, and, on the signal given, sounded with their rams' horns, and brake their pitchers, and set upon their enemies with their lamps, and a great shout, and cried, "Victory to Gideon, by God's assistance," a disorder and a fright seized upon the other men while they were half asleep, for it was night-time, as God would have it; so that a few of them were slain by their enemies, but the greatest part by their own soldiers, on account of the diversity of their language; and when they were once put into disorder, they killed all that they met with, as thinking them to be enemies also. Thus there was a great slaughter made; and as the report of Gideon's victory came to the Israelites, they took their weapons and pursued their enemies, and overtook them in a certain valley encompassed with torrents, in a place which these could not get over; so they encompassed them, and slew them all, with their kings, Oreb and Zeeb; but the remaining captains led those soldiers that were left, which were about eighteen thousand, and pitched their camp a great way off the Israelites. However, Gideon did not grudge his pains, but pursued them with all his army, and joining battle with them, cut off the whole enemies' army, and took the other leaders, Zebah and Zalmuna, and made them captives. Now there were slain in this battle of the Midianites, and of their auxiliaries the Arabians, about a hundred and twenty thousand; and the Hebrews took a great prey, gold, and silver, and garments, and camels, and asses; and when Gideon was come to his own country of Ophrah, he slew the kings of the Midianites.

6. However, the tribe of Ephraim was so displeased at the good success of Gideon, that they resolved to make war against him, accusing him because he did not tell them of his expedition against their enemies: but Gideon, as a man of temper, and that excelled in every virtue, pleaded, that it was not the result of his own authority or reasoning that made him attack the enemy without them, but that it was the command of God, and still the victory belonged to them as well as those in the army;—and by this method of cooling their passions he brought more advantage to the Hebrews than by the success he had gained against these enemies, for he thereby delivered them from a sedition which was arising among them; yet did this tribe afterwards suffer the punishment of this their injurious treatment of Gideon, of which we will give an account in due time.

7. Hereupon Gideon would have laid down the government, but was over-persuaded to take it, which he enjoyed forty years, and distributed justice to them, as the people came to him in their differences; and what he determined was esteemed valid by all; and when he died, he was buried in his own country of Ophrah.

CHAPTER VII

THAT THE JUDGES WHO SUCCEEDED GIDEON MADE WAR WITH THE ADJOINING NATIONS FOR A LONG TIME

1. Now Gideon had seventy sons that were legitimate, for he had many wives; but he had also one that was spurious, by his concubine Drumah, whose name was Abimelech, who, after his father's death, retired to Shechem, to his mother's relations, for they were of that place; and when he had got money of such of them as were eminent for many instances of injustice, he came with them to his father's house, and slew all his brethren, except Jotham, for he had the good fortune to escape and be preserved; but Abimelech made the government tyrannical, and constituted himself a lord, to do what he pleased, instead of obeying the laws; and he acted more rigidly against those that were the patrons of justice.

2. Now when, on a certain time, there was a public festival at Shechem, and all the multitude was there gathered together, Jotham his brother, whose escape we before related, went up to mount Gerizzim, which hangs over the city Shechem, and cried out so as to be heard by the multitude, who were attentive to him. He desired they would consider what he was going to say to them; so when silence was made, he said, That when the trees had a human voice, and there was an assembly of them gathered together, they desired that the fig-tree would rule over them; but when that tree refused so to do, because he was contented to enjoy that honour which belonged peculiarly to the fruit it bare, and not that which should be derived to it from abroad, the trees did not leave off their intentions to have a ruler, so they thought proper to make the offer of that honour to the vine; but when the vine was chosen, it made use of the same words which the fig-tree had used before, and excused itself from accepting the government; and when the olive-tree had done the same, the brier, whom the trees had desired to take the kingdom, (it is a sort of wood good for firing,) it promised to take the government, and to be zealous in the exercise of it; but that then they must sit down under its shadow, and if they should plot against it to destroy it, the principle of fire that was in it should destroy

them. He told them that what he had said was no laughing matter; for that when they had experienced many blessings from Gideon, they overlooked Abimelech, when he overruled all, and had joined with him in slaying his brethren; and that he was no better than a fire himself. So when he had said this, he went away, and lived privately in the mountains for three years, out of fear of Abimelech.

3. A little while after this festival, the Shechemites, who had now repented themselves of having slain the sons of Gideon, drove Abimelech away both from their city and their tribe; whereupon he contrived how he might distress their city. Now at the season of vintage the people were afraid to go out and gather their fruits, for fear Abimelech should do them some mischief. Now it happened that there had come to them a man of authority, one Gaal, that sojourned with them, having his armed men and his kinsmen with him; so the Shechemites desired that he would allow them a guard during their vintage; whereupon he accepted of their desires, and so the people went out, and Gaal with them at the head of his soldiery; so they gathered their fruit with safety; and when they were at supper in several companies, they then ventured to curse Abimelech openly; and the magistrates laid ambushes in places about the city, and caught many of Abimelech's followers, and destroyed them.

4. Now there was one Zebul, a magistrate of the Shechemites, that had entertained Abimelech. He sent messengers, and informed him how much Gaal had irritated the people against him, and excited him to lay ambushes before the city, for that he would persuade Gaal to go out against him, which would leave it in his power to be revenged on him; and when that was once done, he would bring him to be reconciled to the city. So Abimelech laid ambushes, and himself lay with them. Now Gaal abode in the suburbs, taking little care of himself; and Zebul was with him. Now as Gaal saw the armed men coming on, he said to Zebul, That some armed men were coming; but the other replied, They were only shadows of huge stones: and when they were come nearer, Gaal perceived what was the reality, and said, They were not shadows, but men lying in ambush. Then said Zebul, "Didst not thou reproach Abimelech for cowardice? why dost thou not then shew how very courageous thou art thyself, and go and fight him?" So Gaal, being in disorder, joined battle with Abimelech, and some of his men fell; whereupon he fled into the city, and took his men with him. But Zebul managed his matters so in the city, that he procured them to expel Gaal out of the city, and this by accusing him of cowardice in this action with the soldiers of Abimelech. But Abimelech, when he had learned that the Shechemites were again coming out to gather their grapes, placed ambushes before the city, and when they were coming out, the third part of his army took possession of the gates, to hinder the citizens from returning in again, while the rest pursued those that were scattered abroad, and so there was slaughter everywhere; and when he had overthrown the city to the very foundations, for it was not able to bear a siege, and had sown its ruins with salt, he proceeded on with his army till all the Shechemites were slain. As for those that were scattered about the country, and so escaped the danger, they were gathered together unto a certain strong rock, and settled themselves upon it, and prepared to build a wall about it: and when Abimelech knew their intentions, he prevented

them, and came upon them with his forces, and laid faggots of dry wood round the place, he himself bringing some of them, and by his example encouraging the soldiers to do the same. And when the rock was encompassed round about with these faggots, they set them on fire, and threw in whatsoever by nature caught fire the most easily: so a mighty flame was raised, and nobody could fly away from the rock, but every man perished, with their wives and children, in all about fifteen hundred men, and the rest were a great number also. And such was the calamity which fell upon the Shechemites; and men's grief on their account had been greater than it was, had they not brought so much mischief on a person who had so well deserved of them, and had they not themselves esteemed this as a punishment for the same.

5. Now Abimelech, when he had affrighted the Israelites with the miseries he had brought upon the Shechemites, seemed openly to affect greater authority than he now had, and appeared to set no bounds to his violence, unless it were with the destruction of all. Accordingly he marched to Thebes, and took the city on the sudden; and there being a great tower therein, whereunto the whole multitude fled, he made preparation to besiege it. Now as he was rushing with violence through the gates, a woman threw a piece of a mill-stone upon his head, upon which Abimelech fell down, and desired his armour-bearer to kill him, lest his death should be thought to be the work of a woman; —who did what he was bid to do. So he underwent this death as a punishment for the wickedness he had perpetrated against his brethren, and his insolent barbarity to the Shechemites. Now the calamity that happened to these Shechemites was according to the prediction of Jotham. However, the army that was with Abimelech, upon his fall, was scattered abroad, and went to their own homes.

6. Now it was that Jair the Gileadite,[*] of the tribe of Manasseh, took the government. He was a man happy in other respects also, but particularly in his children, who were of a good character. They were thirty in number, and very skilful in riding on horses, and were intrusted with the government of the cities of Gilead. He kept the government twenty-two years, and died an old man; and he was buried in Camon, a city of Gilead.

7. And now all the affairs of the Hebrews were managed uncertainly, and tended to disorder, and to the contempt of God and of the laws. So the Ammonites and Philistines had them in contempt, and laid waste the country with a great army; and when they had taken all Perea, they were so insolent as to attempt to gain the possession of all the rest: but the Hebrews, being now amended by the calamities they had undergone, betook themselves to supplications to God; and brought sacrifices to him, beseeching him not to be too severe upon them, but to be moved by their prayers to leave off his anger against them. So God became more merciful to them, and was ready to assist them.

8. When the Ammonites had made an expedition into the land of Gilead, the inhabitants of the country met them at a certain mountain, but wanted a commander. Now there was one whose name was Jephtha, who, both on account of his father's virtue, and on account of that army which he maintained at his own expenses, was a

---

[*] Josephus omits Tola among the judges, yet all his commentators conclude, that in his sum of the years of the judges, Tola's twenty-three years are included.

potent man: the Israelites therefore sent to him, and entreated him to come to their assistance, and promised him the dominion over them all his lifetime. But he did not admit of their entreaty; and accused them, that they did not come to his assistance when he was unjustly treated, and this in an open manner by his brethren; for they cast him off, as not having the same mother with the rest, but born of a strange mother, that was introduced among them by his father's fondness; and this they did out of a contempt of his inability [to vindicate himself.] So he dwelt in the country of Gilead, as it is called, and received all that came to him, let them come from what place soever, and paid them wages. However, when they pressed him to accept the dominion, and sware they would grant him the government over them all his life, he led them to the war.

9. And when Jephtha had taken immediate care of their affairs, he placed his army at the city Miseph, and sent a message to the Ammonite [king,] complaining of his unjust possession of their land. But that king sent a contrary message: and complained of the exodus of the Israelites out of Egypt, and desired him to go out of the land of the Amorites, and yield it up to him, as at first his paternal inheritance. But Jephtha returned this answer: That he did not justly complain of his ancestors about the land of the Amorites, and ought rather to thank them that they left the land of the Ammonites to them, since Moses could have taken it also; and that neither would he recede from that land of their own, which God had obtained for them, and they had now inhabited [above] three hundred years, but would fight with them about it.

10. And when he had given them this answer, he sent the ambassadors away. And when he had prayed for victory and had vowed to perform sacred offices, and if he came home in safety, to offer in sacrifice what living creature soever should first meet him: * he joined battle with the enemy, and gained a great victory, and in his pursuit slew the enemies all along as far as the city Minnith. He then passed over to the land of the Ammonites, and overthrew many of their cities, and took their prey, and freed his own people from that slavery which they had undergone for eighteen years. But as he came back, he fell into a calamity no way correspondent to the great actions he had done; for it was his daughter that came to meet him; she was also an only child and a virgin: upon this Jephtha heavily lamented the greatness of his affliction, and blamed his daughter for being so forward in meeting him, for he had vowed to sacrifice her to God. However, this action that was to befall her was not ungrateful to her, since she should die upon occasion of her father's victory, and the liberty of her fellow-citizens: she only desired her father to give her leave, for two months, to bewail her youth with her fellow-citizens; and then she agreed, that at the fore-mentioned time he might do with her according to his vow. Accordingly, when that time was over, he sacrificed his daughter as a burnt-offering, offering such an oblation as was neither conformable to the law, nor acceptable to God, not weighing with himself what opinion the hearers would have of such a practice.

11. Now the tribe of Ephraim fought against him, because he did not take them along with him in his expedition against the Ammonites, but because he alone had the prey, and the glory of what was done, to himself. As to which he said, first, that they were not ignorant how his kindred had fought against him, and that when they were invited, they did not come to his assistance, whereas they ought to have come quickly, even before they were invited. And in the next place, that they were going to act unjustly; for while they had not courage enough to fight their enemies, they came hastily against their own kindred: and he threatened them that, with God's assistance, he would inflict a punishment upon them, unless they would grow wiser. But when he could not persuade them, he fought with them with those forces which he sent for out of Gilead, and he made a great slaughter among them; and when they were beaten, he pursued them, and seized on the passages of Jordan by a part of his army which he had sent before, and slew about forty-two thousand of them.

12. So when Jephtha had ruled six years, he died, and was buried in his own country, Sebee, which is a place in the land of Gilead.

13. Now, when Jephtha was dead, Ibzam took the government, being of the tribe of Judah, and of the city of Bethlehem. He had sixty children, thirty of them sons, and the rest daughters; all whom he left alive behind him, giving the daughters in marriage to husbands, and taking wives for his sons. He did nothing in the seven years of his administration that was worth recording, or deserved a memorial. So he died an old man, and was buried in his own country.

14. When Ibzan was dead after this manner, neither did Helon, who succeeded him in the government, and kept it ten years, do anything remarkable: he was of the tribe of Zebulon.

15. Abdon also, the son of Hilel, of the tribe of Ephraim, and born at the city Pyrathon, was ordained their supreme governor after Helon. He is only recorded to have been happy in his children; for the public affairs were then so peaceable, and in such security, that neither did he perform any glorious action. He had forty sons, and by them left thirty grandchildren; and he marched in state with these seventy, who were all very skilful in riding horses; and he left them all alive after him. He died an old man, and obtained a magnificent burial in Pyrathon.

CHAPTER VIII

CONCERNING THE FORTITUDE OF SAMSON, AND WHAT MISCHIEFS HE BROUGHT UPON THE PHILISTINES

1. AFTER Abdon was dead, the Philistines overcame the Israelites, and received tribute of them for forty years; from which distress they were delivered after this manner:—

2. There was one Manoah, a person of such great virtue, that he had few men his equals, and without dispute the principal person of his country. He had a wife celebrated for her beauty, and excelling her contemporaries. He had no children; and, being uneasy at his want of posterity, he entreated God to give them seed of their own bodies to succeed them; and with that intent he came constantly into the suburbs, † together with his wife; which suburbs were in the Great Plain. Now, he was fond of his wife

* Josephus justly condemns Jephtha for his rash vow, whether it were for sacrificing his daughter, or for dedicating her to perpetual virginity. If he had vowed her for a sacrifice, she ought to have been redeemed, (Lev. xxvii. 1-8.)

† Probably there was a synagogue or place of devotion in those suburbs.

to a degree of madness, and on that account was unmeasurably jealous of her. Now, when his wife was once alone, an apparition was seen by her: it was an angel of God, and resembled a young man, beautiful and tall, and brought her the good news, that she should have a son, born by God's providence, that should be a goodly child, of great strength; by whom, when he was grown up to man's estate, the Philistines should be afflicted. He exhorted her also not to poll his hair, and that he should avoid all other kinds of drink, (for so had God commanded,) and be entirely contented with water. So the angel, when he had delivered that message, went his way, his coming having been by the will of God.

3. Now the wife informed her husband when he came home, of what the angel had said, who shewed so great an admiration of the beauty and tallness of the young man that had appeared to her, that her husband was astonished, and out of himself for jealousy, and such suspicions as are excited by that passion; but she was desirous of having her husband's unreasonable sorrow taken away; accordingly she entreated God to send the angel again, that he might be seen by her husband. So the angel came again by the favour of God, while they were in the suburbs, and appeared to her when she was alone without her husband. She desired the angel to stay so long till she might bring her husband; and that request being granted, she goes to call Manoah. When he saw the angel he was not yet free from suspicion, and he desired him to inform him of all that he had told his wife; but when he said it was sufficient that she alone knew what he had said, he then requested of him to tell who he was, that when the child was born, they might return him thanks, and give him a present. He replied that he did not want any present, for that he did not bring them the good news of the birth of a son out of the want of anything; and when Manoah had entreated him to stay, and partake of his hospitality, he did not give his consent. However, he was persuaded, at the earnest request of Manoah, to stay so long as while he brought him one mark of his hospitality;—so he slew a kid of the goats, and bid his wife boil it. When all was ready, the angel enjoined him to set the loaves and the flesh, but without the vessels, upon the rock; which when they had done, he touched the flesh with the rod which he had in his hand, which, upon the breaking out of a flame, was consumed, together with the loaves; and the angel ascended openly, in their sight, up to heaven, by means of the smoke, as by a vehicle. Now Manoah was afraid that some danger would come to them from this sight of God; but his wife bade him be of good courage, for that God appeared to them for their benefit.

4. So the woman proved with child, and was careful to observe the injunctions that were given her; and they called the child, when he was born, Samson, which name signifies one that is *strong*. So the child grew apace; and it appeared evidently that he would be a prophet,[*] both by the moderation of his diet, and the permission of his hair to grow.

5. Now when he once came with his parents to Timnath, a city of the Philistines, when there was a great festival, he fell in love with a maid of that country, and he desired of his parents

that they would procure him the damsel for his wife; but they refused so to do, because she was not of the stock of Israel; yet because this marriage was of God, who intended to convert it to the benefit of the Hebrews, he over-persuaded them to procure her to be espoused to him; and as he was continually coming to her parents, he met a lion, and, though he was naked, he received his onset, and strangled him with his hands, and cast the wild beast into a woody piece of ground on the inside of the road.

6. And when he was going another time to the damsel, he lit upon a swarm of bees making their combs in the breast of that lion; and taking three honeycombs away, he gave them, together with the rest of his presents, to the damsel. Now the people of Timnath, out of a dread of the young man's strength, gave him during the time of the wedding-feast (for he then feasted them all) thirty of the most stout of their youth, in pretence to be his companions, but in reality to be a guard upon him, that he might not attempt to give them any disturbance. Now as they were drinking merrily and playing, Samson said, as was usual at such times, "Come, if I propose you a riddle, and you can expound it in these seven days' time, I will give you every one a linen shirt and a garment, as the reward of your wisdom." So they being very ambitious to obtain the glory of wisdom, together with the gains, desired him to propose his riddle: he said, "That a devourer produced sweet food out of itself, though itself were very disagreeable:"— and when they were not able, in three days' time, to find out the meaning of the riddle, they desired the damsel to discover it by the means of her husband, and tell it them; and they threatened to burn her if she did not tell it them. So when the damsel entreated Samson to tell it her, he at first refused to do it; but when she lay hard at him, and fell into tears, and made his refusal to tell it a sign of his unkindness to her, he informed her of his slaughter of a lion, and how he found bees in his breast, and carried away three honeycombs, and brought them to her. Thus he, suspecting nothing of deceit, informed her of all, and she revealed it to those that desired to know it. Then on the seventh day, whereon they were to expound the riddle proposed to them, they met together before sunsetting, and said, "Nothing is more disagreeable than a lion to those that light on it; and nothing is sweeter than honey to those that make use of it." To which Samson made this rejoinder: "Nothing is more deceitful than a woman, for such was the person that discovered my interpretation to you." Accordingly he gave them the presents he had promised them, making such Askelonites as met him upon the road his prey, who were themselves Philistines also. But he divorced this his wife; and the girl despised his anger, and was married to his companion, who had made the former match between them.

7. At this injurious treatment Samson was so provoked, that he resolved to punish all the Philistines, as well as her: so it being then summer-time, and the fruits of the land being almost ripe enough for reaping, he caught three hundred foxes, and joining lighted torches to their tails, he sent them into the fields of the Philistines, by which means the fruits of the fields perished. Now when the Philistines knew that this was Samson's doing, and knew also for what cause he did it, they sent their rulers to Timnath, and burnt his former wife, and her relations, who had been the occasion of their misfortunes.

8. Now when Samson had slain many of the

---

[*] Here, by a *prophet*, Josephus seems only to mean one that was born by a particular providence, lived after the manner of a Nazarite, and was to have an extraordinary commission and strength from God for the judging and avenging his people Israel, without any prophetic revelations at all.

Philistines in the plain country, he dwelt at Etam, which is a strong rock of the tribe of Judah; for the Philistines at that time made an expedition against that tribe: but the people of Judah said that they did not act justly with them, in inflicting punishments upon them while they paid their tribute, and this only on account of Samson's offences. They answered, that in case they would not be blamed themselves, they must deliver up Samson, and put him into their power. So they being desirous not to be blamed themselves, came to the rock with three thousand armed men, and complained to Samson of the bold insults he had made upon the Philistines, who were men able to bring calamity upon the whole nation of the Hebrews; and they told him they were come to take him, and to deliver him up to them, and put him into their power; so they desired him to bear this willingly. Accordingly, when he had received assurance from them upon oath, that they would do him no other harm than only to deliver him into his enemies' hands, he came down from the rock, and put himself into the power of his countrymen. Then did they bind him with two cords, and lead him on, in order to deliver him to the Philistines; and when they came to a certain place, which is now called the *Jaw-bone*, on account of the great action there performed by Samson, though of old it had no particular name at all, the Philistines, who had pitched their camp not far off, came to meet them with joy and shouting, as having done a great thing, and gained what they desired; but Samson broke his bonds asunder, and catching up the jaw-bone of an ass that lay down at his feet, fell upon his enemies, and smiting them with his jaw-bone, slew a thousand of them, and put the rest to flight, and into great disorder.

9. Upon this slaughter, Samson was too proud of what he had performed, and said that this did not come to pass by the assistance of God, but that his success was to be ascribed to his own courage; and vaunted himself, that it was out of a dread of him that some of his enemies fell, and the rest ran away upon his use of the jaw-bone; but when a great thirst came upon him, he considered that human courage is nothing, and bare his testimony that all is to be ascribed to God, and besought him that he would not be angry at anything he had said, nor give him up into the hands of his enemies, but afford him help under his affliction, and deliver him from the misfortune he was under. Accordingly God was moved with his entreaties, and raised him up a plentiful fountain of sweet water at a certain rock; whence it was that Samson called the place the *Jaw-bone*,* and so it is called to this day.

10. After this fight Samson held the Philistines in contempt, and came to Gaza, and took up his lodgings in a certain inn. When the rulers of Gaza were informed of his coming hither, they seized upon the gates, and placed men in ambush about them, that he might not escape without being perceived; but Samson, who was acquainted with their contrivances against him, arose about midnight, and ran by force upon the gates, with their posts and beams, and the rest of their wooden furniture, and carried them away on his shoulders, and bare them to the mountain that is over Hebron, and there laid them down.

11. However, he at length† transgressed the laws of his country, and altered his own regular way of living, and imitated the strange customs of foreigners, which thing was the beginning of his miseries; for he fell in love with a woman that was a harlot among the Philistines; her name was Delilah, and he lived with her. So those that administered the public affairs of the Philistines came to her, and, with promises, induced her to get out of Samson what was the cause of that his strength, by which he became unconquerable to his enemies. Accordingly, when they were drinking, and had the like conversations together, she pretended to admire the actions he had done, and contrived to get out of him by subtlety, by what means he so much excelled others in strength. Samson, in order to delude Delilah, for he had not yet lost his senses, replied, that if he were bound with seven such green withs of a vine as might still be wreathed, he should be weaker than any other man. The woman said no more then, but told this to the rulers of the Philistines, and hid certain of the soldiers in ambush within the house; and when he was disordered in drink and asleep, she bound him as fast as possible with the withs; and then, upon her awakening him, she told him some of the people were upon him; but he broke the withs, and endeavoured to defend himself, as though some of the people were upon him. Now this woman, in the constant conversation Samson had with her, pretended that she took it very ill that he had such little confidence in her affections to him, that he would not tell her what she had desired, as if she would not conceal what she knew it was for his interest to have concealed. However, he deluded her again, and told her, that if they bound him with seven cords, he should lose his strength. And when upon doing this, she gained nothing, he told her the third time, that his hair should be woven into a web; but when, upon doing this, the truth was not yet discovered, at length Samson, upon Delilah's prayer, (for he was doomed to fall into some affliction,) was desirous to please her, and told her that God took care of him, and that he was born by his providence, and that "thence it is that I suffer my hair to grow, God having charged me never to poll my head, and thence my strength is according to the increase and continuance of my hair." When she had learned thus much, and had deprived him of his hair, she delivered him up to his enemies, when he was not strong enough to defend himself from their attempts upon him; so they put out his eyes, and bound him, and had him led about among them.

12. But in process of time Samson's hair grew again. And there was a public festival among the Philistines, when the rulers and those of the most eminent character were feasting together, (now the room wherein they were, had its roof supported by two pillars;) so they sent for Samson, and he was brought to their feast, that they might insult him in their cups. Hereupon he, thinking it one of the greatest misfortunes, if he should not be able to revenge himself when he was thus insulted, persuaded the boy that led him by the hand, that he was weary and wanted to rest himself, and desired he would bring him near the pillars; and as soon as he came to them, he rushed with force against them, and overthrew the house, by overthrowing its pillars, with three thousand men in it, who were all slain, and Samson with them. And such was the end of this man, when he had ruled over the Israelites twenty years. And indeed, this man deserves to be admired for his courage and strength, and magnanimity at his death, and

---

* This fountain, called Lehi, or the *Jaw-bone*, is still in being, travellers assure us.

† Samson's prayer was heard, but it was before this his transgression.

that his wrath against his enemies went so far as to die himself with them. But as for his being ensnared by a woman, that is to be ascribed to human nature, which is too weak to resist the temptations to that sin; but we ought to bear him witness, that in all other respects, he was one of extraordinary virtue. But his kindred took away his body, and buried it in Sarasat, his own country, with the rest of his family.

CHAPTER IX

HOW UNDER ELI'S GOVERNMENT OF THE ISRAEL-ITES, BOOZ MARRIED RUTH, FROM WHOM CAME OBED, THE GRANDFATHER OF DAVID

1. Now after the death of Samson, Eli the high priest was governor of the Israelites. Under him, when the country was afflicted with a famine, Elimelech of Bethlehem, which is a city of the tribe of Judah, being not able to support his family under so sore a distress, took with him Naomi his wife, and the children that were born to him by her, Chilion and Mahlon; and removed his habitation into the land of Moab; and upon the happy prosperity of his affairs there, he took for his sons wives of the Moabites, Orpah for Chilion, and Ruth for Mahlon. But in the compass of ten years both Elimelech, and a little while after him, the sons died; and Naomi being very uneasy at these accidents, and not being able to bear her lonesome condition, now those that were dearest to her were dead, on whose account it was that she had gone away from her own country, she returned to it again, for she had been informed it was now in a flourishing condition. However, her daughters-in-law were not able to think of parting with her; and when they had a mind to go out of the country with her, she could not dissuade them from it; but when they insisted upon it, she wished them a more happy wedlock than they had with her sons, and that they might have prosperity in other respects also; and seeing her own affairs were so low, she exhorted them to stay where they were, and not to think of leaving their own country, and partaking with her of that uncertainty under which she must return. Accordingly, Orpah stayed behind; but she took Ruth along with her, as not to be persuaded to stay behind her, but would take her fortune with her, whatsoever it should prove.

2. When Ruth was come with her mother-in-law to Bethlehem, Booz, who was near of kin to Elimelech, entertained her; and when Naomi was so called by her fellow-citizens, according to her true name, she said, "You might more truly call me *Mara.*" Now Naomi signifies in the Hebrew tongue, *happiness*, and Mara, *sorrow.* It was now reaping time; and Ruth, by the leave of her mother-in-law, went out to glean, that they might get a stock of corn for their food. Now it happened that she came into Booz's field; and after some time Booz came thither, and when he saw the damsel he inquired of his servant that was set over the reapers concerning the girl. The servant had a little before inquired about all her circumstances, and told them to his master, who kindly embraced her, both on account of her affection to her mother-in-law, and her remembrance of that son of hers to whom she had been married, and wished that she might experience a prosperous condition; so he desired her not to glean, but to reap what she was able, and gave her leave to carry it home. He also gave it in charge to that servant who was over the reapers, not to hinder her when she took it away, and bade him give her her dinner, and make her drink when he did the like to the reapers. Now what corn Ruth received of him, she kept for her mother-in-law, and came to her in the evening, and brought the ears of corn with her; and Naomi had kept for her a part of such food as her neighbours had plentifully bestowed upon her. Ruth also told her mother-in-law what Booz had said to her; and when the other had informed her that he was near of kin to them, and perhaps was so pious a man as to make some provision for them, she went out again on the days following, to gather the gleanings with Booz's maid-servants.

3. It was not many days before Booz, after the barley was winnowed, slept in his thrashing-floor. When Naomi was informed of this circumstance, she contrived it so that Ruth should lie down by him, for she thought it might be for their advantage that he should discourse with the girl. Accordingly, she sent the damsel to sleep at his feet; who went as she bade her, for she did not think it consistent with her duty to contradict any command of her mother-in-law. And at first she lay concealed from Booz, as he was fast asleep; but when he awaked about midnight, and perceived a woman lying by him, he asked who she was;—and when she told him her name, and desired that he whom she owned for her lord would excuse her, he then said no more; but in the morning, before the servants began to set about their work, he awaked her, and bid her take as much barley as she was able to carry, and go to her mother-in-law before any body there should see that she had lain down by him, because it was but prudent to avoid any reproach that might arise on that account, especially when there had been nothing done that was ill. But as to the main point she aimed at, the matter should rest here,—"He that is nearer of kin than I am, shall be asked whether he wants to take thee to wife: if he says he does, thou shalt follow him; but if he refuse it, I will marry thee, according to the law."

4. When she had informed her mother-in-law of this, they were very glad of it, out of the hope they had that Booz would make provision for them. Now about noon Booz went down into the city, and gathered the senate together, and when he had sent for Ruth, he called for her kinsman also; and when he was come, he said, "Dost thou not retain the inheritance of Elimelech and his sons?" He confessed that he did retain it, and that he did as he was permitted to do by the laws, because he was their nearest kinsman. Then said Booz, "Thou must not remember the laws by halves, but do everything according to them; for the wife of Mahlon is come hither, whom thou must marry, according to the law, in case thou wilt retain their fields." So the man yielded up both the field and the wife to Booz, who was himself of kin to those that were dead, as alleging that he had a wife already, and children also; so Booz called the senate to witness, and bid the woman to loose his shoe and spit in his face, according to the law; and when this was done Booz married Ruth, and they had a son within a year's time. Naomi was herself a nurse to this child; and by the advice of the women called him *Obed*, as being to be brought up in order to be subservient to her in her old age, for Obed in the Hebrew dialect signifies a *servant*. The son of Obed was Jesse, and David was his son, who was king, and left his dominions to his sons for one-and-twenty generations. I was therefore obliged to relate this history of Ruth, because I

had a mind to demonstrate the power of God, who, without difficulty, can raise those that are of ordinary parentage to dignity and splendour, to which he advanced David, though he were born of such mean parents.

CHAPTER X

CONCERNING THE BIRTH OF SAMUEL; AND HOW HE FORETOLD THE CALAMITY THAT BEFELL HE SONS OF ELI

1. AND now upon the ill state of the affairs of the Hebrews, they made war again upon the Philistines. The occasion was this: Eli, the high priest, had two sons, Hophni and Phineas. These sons of Eli were guilty of injustice towards men, and of impiety towards God, and abstained from no sort of wickedness. Some of their gifts they carried off, as belonging to the honourable employment they had; others of them they took away by violence. They also were guilty of impurity with the women that came to worship God, [at the tabernacle,] obliging some to submit to their lust by force, and enticing others by bribes; nay, the whole course of their lives was no better than tyranny. Their father therefore was angry at them for such their wickedness, and expected that God would suddenly inflict His punishments upon them for what they had done. The multitude took it heinously also: and as soon as God had foretold what calamity would befall Eli's sons, which He did both to Eli himself, and to Samuel the prophet, who was yet but a child, he openly shewed his sorrow for his sons' destruction.

2. I will first despatch what I have to say about the prophet Samuel, and after that will proceed to speak of the sons of Eli, and the miseries they brought on the whole people of the Hebrews. Elcanah, a Levite, one of a middle condition among his fellow-citizens, and one that dwelt at Ramathaim, a city of the tribe of Ephraim, married two wives, Hannah and Peninnah. He had children by the latter; but he loved the other best, although she was barren. Now Elcanah came with his wives to the city Shiloh to sacrifice, for there it was that the tabernacle of God was fixed, as we have formerly said. Now when, after he had sacrificed, he distributed at that festival portions of the flesh to his wives and children, and when Hannah saw the other wife's children sitting round about their mother, she fell into tears, and lamented herself on account of her barrenness and lonesomeness; and suffering her grief to prevail over her husband's consolations to her, she went to the tabernacle to beseech God to give her seed, and to make her a mother; and to vow to consecrate the first son she should bear to the service of God, and this in such a way, that his manner of living should not be like that of ordinary men. And as she continued at her prayers a long time, Eli, the high priest, for he sat there before the tabernacle, bid her go away, thinking she had been disordered with wine; but when she said she had drank water, but was in sorrow for want of children, and was beseeching God for them, he bid her be of good cheer, and told her that God would send her children.

3. So she came to her husband full of hope, and ate her meal with gladness. And when they had returned to their own country, she found herself with child, and they had a son born to them, to whom they gave the name of Samuel, which may be styled one that was *asked*

of God. They therefore came to the tabernacle to offer sacrifice for the birth of the child, and brought their tithes with them; but the woman remembered the vow she had made concerning her son, and delivered him to Eli, dédicating him to God, that he might become a prophet. Accordingly his hair was suffered to grow long, and his drink was water. So Samuel dwelt and was brought up in the temple. But Elcanah had other sons by Hannah, and three daughters.

4. Now when Samuel was twelve years old, he began to prophesy: and once when he was asleep God called to him by his name; and he, supposing he had been called by the high priest, came to him; but when the high priest said he did not call him, God did so thrice. Eli was then so far illuminated, that he said to him, "Indeed, Samuel, I was silent now as well as before: it is God that calls thee; do thou therefore signify it to him, and say, I am here ready." So when he heard God speak again, he desired him to speak, and to deliver what oracles he pleased to him, for he would not fail to perform any ministration whatsoever he should make use of him in;—to which God replied, "Since thou art here ready, learn what miseries are coming upon the Israelites,—such indeed as words cannot declare, nor faith believe; for the sons of Eli shall die on one day, and the priesthood shall be transferred into the family of Eleazar; for Eli hath loved his sons more than he hath loved my worship, and to such a degree as is not for their advantage." Which message Eli obliged the prophet by oath to tell him, for otherwise he had no inclination to afflict him by telling it. And now Eli had a far more sure expectation of the perdition of his sons; but the glory of Samuel increased more and more, it being found by experience that whatsoever he prophesied came to pass accordingly.*

CHAPTER XI

HEREIN IS DECLARED WHAT BEFELL THE SONS OF ELI, THE ARK, AND THE PEOPLE; AND HOW ELI HIMSELF DIED MISERABLY

1. ABOUT this time it was that the Philistines made war against the Israelites, and pitched their camp at the city Aphek. Now when the Israelites had expected them a little while, the very next day they joined battle, and the Philistines were conquerors, and slew above four thousand of the Hebrews, and pursued the rest of their multitude to their camp.

2. So the Hebrews being afraid of the worst, sent to the senate, and to the high priest, and desired that they would bring the ark of God, that by putting themselves in array, when it was present with them, they might be too hard for their enemies, as not reflecting that he who had condemned them to endure these calamities was greater than the ark, and for whose sake it was that this ark came to be honoured. So the ark came, and the sons of the high priest with it, having received a charge from their father, that if they pretended to survive the taking of the ark, they should come no more into his presence; for Phineas officiated already as high priest, his father having resigned his office to him, by reason

* Although there had been a few occasional prophets before, yet was Samuel the first of a constant succession of prophets in the Jewish nation, (see Acts iii. 24.) The others were rather sometimes called righteous men, (Matt. x. 41; xiii. 17.)

of his great age. So the Hebrews were full of courage, as supposing that, by the coming of the ark, they should be too hard for their enemies : their enemies also were greatly concerned, and were afraid of the ark's coming to the Israelites; however, the upshot did not prove agreeable to the expectation of both sides, but when the battle was joined, that victory which the Hebrews expected, was gained by the Philistines, and that defeat the Philistines were afraid of, fell to the lot of the Israelites, and thereby they found that they had put their trust in the ark in vain, for they were presently beaten as soon as they came to a close fight with their enemies, and lost about thirty thousand men, among whom were the sons of the high priest; but the ark was carried away by their enemies.

3. When the news of this defeat came to Shiloh, with that of the captivity of the ark, (for a certain young man, a Benjamite, who was in the action, came as a messenger thither,) the whole city was full of lamentations. And Eli the high priest, who sat upon a high throne at one of the gates, heard their mournful cries, and supposed that some strange thing had befallen his family. So he sent for the young man; and when he understood what had happened in the battle, he was not much uneasy as to his sons, or what was told him withal about the army, as having beforehand known by divine revelation that those things would happen, and having himself declared them beforehand,—for what sad things come unexpectedly, they distress men the most; but as soon as [he heard] the ark was carried captive by their enemies, he was very much grieved at it, because it fell out quite differently from what he expected; so he fell down from his throne and died, having in all lived ninety-eight years, and of them retained the government forty.

4. On the same day his son Phineas's wife died also, as not able to survive the misfortune of her husband; for they told her of her husband's death as she was in labour. However, she bare a son at seven months, who lived, and to whom they gave the name of Icabod, which signifies *disgrace*,—and this because the army received a disgrace at this time.

5. Now Eli was the first of the family of Ithamar, the other son of Aaron that had the government; for the family of Eleazar officiated as high priest at first, the son still receiving that honour from the father which Eleazar bequeathed to his son Phineas; after whom Abiezer his son took the honour, and delivered it to his son, whose name was Bukki, from whom his son Ozi received it; after whom, Eli, of whom we have been speaking, had the priesthood, and so he and his posterity until the time of Solomon's reign; but then the posterity of Eleazar reassumed it.

BOOK VI

CONTAINING THE INTERVAL OF THIRTY-TWO YEARS

FROM THE DEATH OF ELI TO THE DEATH OF SAUL

CHAPTER I

THE DESTRUCTION THAT CAME UPON THE PHILISTINES, AND UPON THEIR LAND, BY THE WRATH OF GOD, ON ACCOUNT OF THEIR HAVING CARRIED THE ARK AWAY CAPTIVE ; AND AFTER WHAT MANNER THEY SENT IT BACK TO THE HEBREWS

1. WHEN the Philistines had taken the ark of the Hebrews captive, as I said a little before, they carried it to the city of Ashdod, and put it by their own god, who was called Dagon, * as one of their spoils; but when they went into his temple the next morning to worship their god, they found him paying the same worship to the ark, for he lay along, as having fallen down from the basis whereon he had stood : so they took him up and set him on his basis again, and were much troubled at what had happened; and as they frequently came to Dagon and found him still lying along, in a posture of adoration to the ark, they were in very great distress and confusion. At length God sent a very destructive disease upon the city and country of Ashdod, for they died of the dysentery and flux, a sore distemper, that brought death upon them very suddenly; for before the soul could, as usual in easy deaths, be well loosed from the body, they brought up their entrails, and vomited up what they had eaten, and what was entirely corrupted by the disease. And as to the fruits of their country, a great multitude of mice arose out of the earth, and hurt them, and spared neither the plants nor the fruits. Now while the people of Ashdod were under these misfortunes, and were not able to support themselves under their calamities, they perceived that they suffered thus because of the ark, and that the victory they had gotten, and their having taken the ark captive, had not happened for their good; they therefore sent to the people of Askelon, and desired that they would receive the ark among them. This desire of the people of Ashdod was not disagreeable to those of Askelon, so they granted them that favour. But when they had gotten the ark, they were in the same miserable condition; for the ark carried along with it the disasters that the people of Ashdod had suffered, to those who received it from them. Those of Askelon also sent it away from themselves to others; nor did it stay among those others neither; for since they were pursued by the same disasters, they still sent it to the neighbouring cities; so that the ark went round, after this manner, to the five cities of the Philistines, as though it exacted these disasters as a tribute to be paid for its coming among them.

2. When those that had experienced these miseries were tired out with them, and when those that heard of them were taught thereby not to admit the ark among them, since they

---

* Dagon is generally supposed to have been like a man above the navel and like a fish beneath it.

paid so dear a tribute for it, at length they sought for some contrivance and method how they might get free from it : so the governors of the five cities, Gath, and Ekron, and Askelon, as also of Gaza, and Ashdod, met together, and considered what was fit to be done ; and at first they thought proper to send the ark back to its own people, as allowing that God had avenged its cause ; that the miseries they had undergone came along with it, and that these were sent on their cities upon its account, and together with it. However, there were those that said, they should not do so, nor suffer themselves to be deluded, as ascribing the cause of their miseries to it, because it could not have such power and force upon them ; for, had God had such a regard to it, it would not have been delivered into the hands of men : so they exhorted them to be quiet, and to take patiently what had befallen them, and to suppose there was no other cause of it but nature, which, at certain revolutions of time, produces such mutations in the bodies of men, in the earth, in plants, and in all things that grow out of the earth. But the counsel that prevailed over those already described, was that of certain men, who were believed to have distinguished themselves in former times for their understanding and prudence, and who, in their present circumstances, seemed above all the rest to speak properly. These men said, it was not right either to send the ark away, or to retain it, but to dedicate five golden images, one for every city, as a thank-offering to God, on account of his having taken care of their preservation, and having kept them alive when their lives were likely to be taken away by such distempers as they were not able to bear up against. They also would have them make five golden mice like to those that devoured and destroyed their country,* to put them in a bag, and lay them upon the ark ; to make them a new cart also for it, and to yoke milch kine to it ; † but to shut up their calves, and keep them from them, lest, by following after them, they should prove a hindrance to their dams, and that the dams might return the faster out of a desire of those calves ; then to drive these milch kine that carried the ark, and leave it at a place where three ways met, and to leave it to the kine to go along which of those ways they pleased ; that in case they went the way to the Hebrews, and ascended to their country, they should suppose that the ark was the cause of their misfortunes ; but if they turned into another road, they said, " We will pursue after it, and conclude that it has no such force in it."

3. So they determined that these men spake well ; and they immediately confirmed their opinion by doing accordingly. And when they had done as has been already described, they brought the cart to a place where three ways met, and left it there, and went their ways ; but the kine went the right way, and as if some persons had driven them, while the rulers of the Philistines followed after them, as desirous to know where they would stand still, and to whom

they would go. Now there was a certain village of the tribe of Judah, the name of which was Bethshemesh, and to that village did the kine go ; and though there was a great and good plain before them to proceed in, they went no further, but stopped the cart there. This was a sight to those of that village, and they were very glad ; for it being then summer-time, and all the inhabitants being then in the fields gathering in their fruits, they left off the labours of their hands for joy, as soon as they saw the ark, and ran to the cart, and taking the ark down, and the vessel that had the images in it, and the mice, they set them upon a certain rock which was in the plain ; and when they had offered a splendid sacrifice to God, and feasted, they offered the cart and the kine as a burnt-offering : and when the lords of the Philistines saw this, they returned back.

4. But now it was that the wrath of God overtook them, and struck seventy persons‡ of the village of Bethshemesh dead, who, not being priests, and so not worthy to touch the ark, had approached to it. Those of that village wept for these that had thus suffered, and made such a lamentation as was naturally to be expected on so great a misfortune that was sent from God ; and every one mourned for his own relations. And since they acknowledged themselves unworthy of the ark's abode with them, they sent to the public senate of the Israelites, and informed them that the ark was restored by the Philistines ; which when they knew, they brought it away to Kirjathjearim, a city in the neighbourhood of Bethshemesh. In this city lived one Abinadab, by birth a Levite, and who was greatly commended for his righteous and religious course of life ; so they brought the ark to his house, as to a place fit for God himself to abide in, since therein did inhabit a righteous man. His sons also ministered to the divine service at the ark, and were the principal curators of it for twenty years ; for so many years it continued in Kirjathjearim. having been but four months with the Philistines.

CHAPTER II

THE EXPEDITION OF THE PHILISTINES AGAINST THE HEBREWS, AND THE HEBREWS' VICTORY UNDER THE CONDUCT OF SAMUEL THE PROPHET, WHO WAS THEIR GENERAL

1. Now while the city of Kirjathjearim had the ark with them, the whole body of the people betook themselves all that time to offer prayers and sacrifices to God, and appeared greatly concerned and zealous about his worship. So Samuel the prophet, seeing how ready they were to do their duty, thought this a proper time to speak to them, while they were in this good disposition, about the recovery of their liberty, and of the blessings that accompanied the same. Accordingly he used such words as he thought were most likely to excite that inclination, and to persuade them to attempt it : " O you Israelites," said he, " to whom the Philistines are still grievous enemies, but to whom God begins to be gracious, it behoves you not only to be desirous of liberty, but to take the proper methods to obtain it. Nor are you to be contented with an inclination to get clear of

---

* Upon the coins of Tenedos and other cities, a field-mouse is engraven, together with Apollo Smintheus, or *Apollo, the driver away of field-mice,* on account of his being supposed to have freed certain tracts of ground from those mice ; which coins shew how great a judgment such mice have sometimes been, and how the deliverance from them was then esteemed the effect of a divine power.

† This device of the Philistines, illustrated by the fact that Agrouerus, or Agrotes, the *husbandman,* had a statue and temple, carried about by one or more yoke of oxen in Phœnicia.

‡ These seventy men, being not so much as Levites, touched the ark in a rash or profane manner, and were slain by the hand of God for their rashness and profaneness.

your lords and masters, while you still do what will procure your continuance under them. Be righteous, then, and cast wickedness out of your souls, and by your worship supplicate the Divine Majesty with all your hearts, and persevere in the honour you pay to him; for if you act thus, you will enjoy prosperity; you will be freed from your slavery, and will get the victory over your enemies: which blessings it is not possible you should attain, either by weapons of war, or by the strength of your bodies, or by the multitude of your assistants; for God has not promised to grant these blessings by those means, but by being good and righteous men; and if you will be such, I will be security to you for the performance of God's promises." When Samuel had said thus, the multitude applauded his discourse, and were pleased with his exhortation to them, and gave their consent to resign themselves up to do what was pleasing to God. So Samuel gathered them together to a certain city called Mizpeh, which, in the Hebrew tongue, signifies a *watch-tower;* there they drew water, and poured it out to God, and fasted all day, and betook themselves to their prayers.

2. This their assembly did not escape the notice of the Philistines: so when they had learned that so large a company had met together, they fell upon the Hebrews with a great army and mighty forces, as hoping to assault them when they did not expect it, nor were prepared for it. This thing affrighted the Hebrews, and put them into disorder and terror; so they came running to Samuel, and said that their souls were sunk by their fears, and by the former defeat they had received, and "that thence it was that we lay still, lest we should excite the power of our enemies against us. Now while thou hast brought us hither to offer up our prayers and sacrifices, and take oaths [to be obedient], our enemies are making an expedition against us, while we are naked and unarmed; wherefore we have no other hope of deliverance but that by thy means, and by the assistance God shall afford us upon thy prayers to him, we shall obtain deliverance from the Philistines." Hereupon Samuel bade them be of good cheer, and promised them that God would assist them; and taking a sucking lamb, he sacrificed it for the multitude, and besought God to hold His protecting hand over them when they should fight with the Philistines, and not to overlook them, nor suffer them to come under a second misfortune. Accordingly, God hearkened to his prayers, and accepting their sacrifice with a gracious intention, and such as was disposed to assist them, he granted them victory and power over their enemies. Now while the altar had the sacrifice of God upon it, and had not yet consumed it wholly by its sacred fire, the enemy's army marched out of their camp, and was put in order of battle, and this in hope that they should be conquerors, since the Jews* were caught in distressed circumstances, as neither having their weapons with them, nor being assembled there in order to fight. But things so fell out, that they would hardly have been credited, though they had been foretold by anybody: for, in the first place, God disturbed their enemies with an earthquake, and moved the ground under them to such a degree, that he caused it to tremble, and made them to shake, insomuch that by its trembling, he made some unable to keep their feet,

and made them fall down, and, by opening its chasms, he caused that others should be hurried down into them; after which he caused such a noise of thunder to come among them, and made fiery lightning shine so terribly round about them, that it was ready to burn their faces; and he so suddenly shook their weapons out of their hands, that he made them fly and return home naked. So Samuel with the multitude pursued them to Bethcar, a place so called; and there he set up a stone as a boundary of their victory and their enemy's flight, and called it the *Stone of Power*, as a signal of that power God had given them against their enemies.

3. So the Philistines, after this stroke, made no more expeditions against the Israelites, but lay still out of fear, and out of remembrance of what had befallen them: and what courage the Philistines had formerly against the Hebrews, that, after this victory, was transferred to the Hebrews. Samuel also made an expedition against the Philistines, and slew many of them, and entirely humbled their proud hearts, and took from them that country, which, when they were formerly conquerors in battle, they had cut off from the Jews, which was the country that extended from the borders of Gath to the city of Ekron: but the remains of the Canaanites were at this time in friendship with the Israelites.

CHAPTER III

HOW SAMUEL, WHEN HE WAS SO INFIRM WITH OLD AGE THAT HE COULD NOT TAKE CARE OF THE PUBLIC AFFAIRS, INTRUSTED THEM TO HIS SONS; AND HOW, UPON THE EVIL ADMINISTRATION OF THE GOVERNMENT BY THEM, THE MULTITUDE WERE SO ANGRY, THAT THEY REQUIRED TO HAVE A KING TO GOVERN THEM, ALTHOUGH SAMUEL WAS MUCH DISPLEASED THEREAT

1. BUT Samuel the prophet, when he had ordered the affairs of the people after a convenient manner, and had appointed a city for every district of them, he commanded them to come to such cities, to have the controversies that they had one with another determined in them, he himself going over those cities twice in a year, and doing them justice; and by that means he kept them in very good order for a long time.

2. But afterwards he found himself oppressed with old age, and not able to do what he used to do, so he committed the government and the care of the multitude to his sons,—the elder of whom was called Joel, and the name of the younger was Abiah. He also enjoined them to reside and judge the people, the one at the city of Bethel, and the other at Beersheba, and divided the people into districts that should be under the jurisdiction of each of them. Now these men afford us an evident example and demonstration how some children are not of the like dispositions with their parents; but sometimes perhaps good and moderate, though born of wicked parents; and sometimes shewing themselves to be wicked, though born of good parents: for these men, turning aside from their father's good courses, and taking a course that was contrary to them, perverted justice for the filthy lucre of gifts and bribes, and made their determinations not according to truth, but according to bribery, and turned aside to luxury, and a costly way of living; so that as, in the first place, they practised what was contrary to the will of God, so did they, in the second place, what was contrary to the will of the prophet their father, who had taken a great deal of care, and made a very careful provision that the multitude should be righteous.

---

* This is the first place in these Antiquities, where Josephus begins to call his nation Jews, he having hitherto usually, if not constantly, called them either Hebrews or Israelites.

3. But the people, upon these injuries offered to their former constitution and government by the prophet's sons, were very uneasy at their actions, and came running to the prophet, who then lived at the city Ramah, and informed him of the transgressions of his sons; and said, that as he was himself old already, and too infirm by that age of his to oversee their affairs in the manner he used to do, so they begged of him, and entreated him to appoint some person to be king over them, who might rule over the nation, and avenge them of the Philistines, who ought to be punished for their former oppressions. These words greatly afflicted Samuel, on account of his innate love of justice, and his hatred to kingly government, for he was very fond of an aristocracy, as what made the men that used it of a divine and happy disposition; nor could he either think of eating or sleeping, out of his concern and torment of mind at what they had said, but all the night long did he continue awake, and revolved these notions in his mind.

4. While he was thus disposed, God appeared to him, and comforted him, saying, that he ought not to be uneasy at what the multitude desired, because it was not he, but Himself whom they so insolently despised, and would not have to be alone their king: that they had been contriving these things from the very day that they came out of Egypt; that, however, in no long time they would sorely repent of what they did, which repentance yet could not undo what was thus done for futurity: that they would be sufficiently rebuked for their contempt, and the ungrateful conduct they have used towards me, and towards thy prophetic office. "So I command thee to ordain them such a one as I shall name beforehand to be their king, when thou hast first described what mischiefs kingly government will bring upon them, and openly testified before them into what a great change of affairs they are hasting."

5. When Samuel had heard this, he called the Jews early in the morning, and confessed to them that he was to ordain them a king; but he said that he was first to describe to them what would follow, what treatment they would receive from their kings, and with how many mischiefs they must struggle. "For know ye," said he, "that, in the first place, they will take your sons away from you, and they will command some of them to be drivers of their chariots, and some to be their horsemen, and the guards of their body, and others of them to be runners before them, and captains of thousands, and captains of hundreds; they will also make them their artificers, makers of armour, and of chariots, and of instruments; they will make them their husbandmen also, and the curators of their own fields, and the diggers of their own vineyards; nor will there be anything which they will not do at their commands, as if they were slaves bought with money. They will also appoint your daughters to be confectioners, and cooks, and bakers; and these will be obliged to do all sorts of work which women slaves that are in fear of stripes and torments submit to. They will, besides this, take away your possessions, and bestow them upon their eunuchs, and the guards of their bodies, and will give the herds of your cattle to their own servants: and to say briefly all at once, you, and all that is yours, will be servants to your king, and will become no way superior to his slaves; and when you suffer thus, you will thereby be put in mind of what I now say; and when you repent of what you have done, you will beseech God to have mercy upon you, and to grant you a quick de-

liverance from your kings; but he will not accept your prayers, but will neglect you, and permit you to suffer the punishment your evil conduct has deserved."

6. But the multitude was still so foolish as to be deaf to these predictions of what would befall them; and too peevish to suffer a determination which they had injudiciously once made, to be taken out of their mind; for they could not be turned from their purpose, nor did they regard the words of Samuel, but peremptorily insisted on their resolution, and desired him to ordain them a king immediately, and not to trouble himself with fears of what would happen hereafter, for that it was necessary they should have with them one to fight their battles, and to avenge them of their enemies, and that it was no way absurd, when their neighbours were under kingly government, that they should have the same form of government also. So when Samuel saw that what he had said had not diverted them from their purpose, but that they continued resolute, he said, "Go you every one home for the present; when it is fit I will send for you, as soon as I shall have learned from God who it is that he will give you for your king."

CHAPTER IV

THE APPOINTMENT OF A KING OVER THE ISRAELITES, WHOSE NAME WAS SAUL; AND THIS BY THE COMMAND OF GOD

1. THERE was one of the tribe of Benjamin, a man of a good family, and of a virtuous disposition: his name was Kish. He had a son, a young man of a comely countenance, and of a tall body, but his understanding and his mind were preferable to what was visible in him: they called him Saul. Now this Kish had some fine she-asses that were wandered out of the pasture wherein they fed, for he was more delighted with these than with any other cattle he had, so he sent out his son, and one servant with him, to search for the beasts; but when he had gone over his own tribe in search after the asses, he went to other tribes; and when he found them not there neither, he determined to go his way home, lest he should occasion any concern to his father about himself; but when his servant that followed him told him, as they were near the city Ramah, that there was a true prophet in that city, and advised him to go to him, for that by him they should know the upshot of the affair of their asses, he replied, that if they should go to him, they had nothing to give him as a reward for his prophecy, for their subsistence-money was spent. The servant answered, that he had still the fourth part of a shekel, and he would present him with that; for they were mistaken out of ignorance, as not knowing that the prophet received no such reward.* So they went to him; and when they were before the gates, they lit upon certain maidens that were going to fetch water; and they asked them which was the prophet's house. They shewed them which it was; and bid them make haste before he sat down to supper, for he had invited many guests to a feast, and that he used to sit down before those that were invited. Now Samuel had then gathered many together to feast with him on this very account; for while he every day prayed to God to tell him beforehand whom he would make king, he had informed

---

* See the note on b. iv. ch. vi. sect. 3.

him of this man the day before, for that he would send him a certain young man out of the tribe of Benjamin about this hour of the day; and he sat on the top of the house in expectation of that time's being come. And when the time was completed, he came down and went to supper; so he met with Saul, and God discovered to him that this was he who should rule over them. Then Saul went up to Samuel and saluted him, and desired him to inform him which was the prophet's house; for he said he was a stranger, and did not know it. When Samuel had told him that he himself was the person, he led him in to supper, and assured him that the asses were found which he had been to seek, and that the greatest of good things were assured to him: he replied, "I am too inconsiderable to hope for any such thing, and of a tribe too small to have kings made out of it, and of a family smaller than several other families; but thou tellest me this in jest, and makest me an object of laughter, when thou discoursest with me of greater matters than what I stand in need of." However, the prophet led him in to the feast, and made him sit down, him and his servant that followed him, above the other guests that were invited, which were seventy in number; * and he gave orders to the servants to set the royal portion before Saul. And when the time of going to bed was come, the rest rose up, and every one of them went home; but Saul stayed with the prophet, he and his servant, and slept with him.

2. Now as soon as it was day, Samuel raised up Saul out of his bed, and conducted him homeward; and when he was out of the city, he desired him to cause his servant to go before, but to stay behind himself, for that he had somewhat to say to him, when nobody else was present. Accordingly, Saul sent away his servant that followed him; then did the prophet take a vessel of oil, and poured it upon the head of the young man, and kissed him, and said, "Be thou a king, by the ordination of God, against the Philistines, and for avenging the Hebrews for what they have suffered by them; of this thou shalt have a sign, which I would have thee take notice of:—As soon as thou art departed hence, thou wilt find three men upon the road, going to worship God at Bethel; the first of whom thou wilt see carrying three loaves of bread, the second carrying a kid of the goats, and the third will follow them carrying a bottle of wine. These three men will salute thee, and speak kindly to thee, and will give thee two of their loaves, which thou shalt accept of. And thence thou shalt come to a place called *Rachel's Monument*, where thou shalt meet with those that will tell thee thy asses are found; after this, when thou comest to Gabatha, thou shalt overtake a company of prophets, and thou shalt be seized with the divine spirit,† and prophesy along with them, till every one that sees thee shall be astonished, and wonder, and say, Whence is it that the son of Kish has arrived at this degree of happiness? And when these signs have happened to thee, know that God is with thee; then do thou salute thy father and thy kindred. Thou shalt also come when I send for thee to Gilgal, that we may offer thank-offerings to God for these blessings." When Samuel had said

this, and foretold these things, he sent the young man away. Now all things fell out to Saul according to the prophecy of Samuel.

3. But as soon as Saul came into the house of his kinsman Abner, whom indeed he loved better than the rest of his relations, he was asked by him concerning his journey, and what accidents happened to him therein; and he concealed none of the other things from him, no, not his coming to Samuel the prophet, nor how he told him the asses were found, but he said nothing to him about the kingdom, and what belonged thereto, which he thought would procure him envy, and when such things are heard, they are not easily believed; nor did he think it prudent to tell those things to him, although he appeared very friendly to him, and one whom he loved above the rest of his relations, considering, I suppose, what human nature really is, that no one is a firm friend, neither among our intimates nor of our kindred; nor do they preserve that kind disposition when God advances men to great prosperity, but they are still ill-natured and envious at those that are in eminent stations.

4. Then Samuel called the people together to the city Mizpeh, and spake to them in the words following, which he said he was to speak by the command of God:—That when he had granted them a state of liberty, and brought their enemies into subjection, they were become unmindful of his benefits, and rejected God that he should not be their king, as not considering that it would be most for their advantage to be presided over by the best of beings, for God is the best of beings, and they chose to have a man for their king, while kings will use their subjects as beasts, according to the violence of their own wills and inclinations, and other passions, as wholly carried away with the lust of power, but will not endeavour so to preserve the race of mankind, as his own workmanship and creation, which, for that very reason, God would take care of. "But since you have come to a fixed resolution, and this injurious treatment of God has quite prevailed over you, dispose yourselves by your tribes and sceptres, and cast lots."

5. When the Hebrews had so done, the lot fell upon the tribe of Benjamin; and when the lot was cast for the families of this tribe, that which was called *Matri* was taken; and when the lot was cast for the single persons of the family, Saul, the son of Kish, was taken for their king. When the young man knew this, he prevented [their sending for him,] and immediately went away and hid himself. I suppose that it was because he would not have it thought that he willingly took the government upon him; nay, he shewed such a degree of command over himself, and of modesty, that while the greatest part are not able to contain their joy, even in the gaining of small advantages, but presently shew themselves publicly to all men, this man did not only shew nothing of that nature, when he was appointed to be the lord of so many and so great tribes, but crept away and concealed himself out of the sight of those he was to reign over, and made them seek him, and that with a good deal of trouble. So when the people were at a loss, and solicitous, because Saul disappeared, the prophet besought God to shew where the young man was, and to produce him before them. So when they had learned of God the place where Saul was hidden, they sent a man to bring him; and when he was come, they set him in the midst of the multitude. Now he was taller than any of them, and his stature was very majestic.

---

* It seems not improbable that these seventy guests of Samuel, with himself at the head of them, were a Jewish sanhedrim, and that hereby Samuel intimated to Saul that these seventy-one were to be his constant counsellors.

† An instance of this divine fury we have after this in Saul, chap. v. sect 2, 3; 1 Sam. xi. 6.

6. Then said the prophet, "God gives you this man to be your king: see how he is higher than any of the people, and worthy of this dominion." So as soon as the people had made acclamation, *God save the king*, the prophet wrote down what would come to pass in a book, and read it in the hearing of the king, and laid up the book in the tabernacle of God, to be a witness to future generations of what he had foretold. So when Samuel had finished this matter, he dismissed the multitude, and came himself to the city Ramah, for it was his own country. Saul also went away to Gibeah, where he was born; and many good men there were who paid him the respect that was due to him; but the greater part were ill men, who despised him and derided the others, who neither did bring him presents, nor did they in affection, or even in words, regard to please him.

CHAPTER V

SAUL'S EXPEDITION AGAINST THE NATION OF THE AMMONITES, AND VICTORY OVER THEM, AND THE SPOILS HE TOOK FROM THEM

1. AFTER one month, the war which Saul had with Nahash, the king of the Ammonites, obtained him respect from all the people; for this Nahash had done a great deal of mischief to the Jews that lived beyond Jordan by the expedition he had made against them with a great and warlike army. He also reduced their cities into slavery, and that not only by subduing them for the present, which he did by force and violence, but by weakening them by subtlety and cunning, that they might not be able afterward to get clear of the slavery they were under to him: for he put out the right eyes * of those that either delivered themselves to him upon terms, or were taken by him in war; and this he did, that when their left eyes were covered by their shields, they might be wholly useless in war. Now when the king of the Ammonites had served those beyond Jordan in this manner, he led his army against those that were called *Gileadites;* and having pitched his camp at the metropolis of his enemies, which was the city of Jabesh, he sent ambassadors to them, commanding them either to deliver themselves up, on condition to have their right eyes plucked out, or to undergo a siege, and to have their cities overthrown. He gave them their choice, Whether they would cut off a small member of their body, or universally perish. However, the Gileadites were so affrighted at these offers, that they had not courage to say anything to either of them, neither that they would deliver themselves up, nor that they would fight him; but they desired that he would give them seven days' respite, that they might send ambassadors to their countrymen, and entreat their assistance; and if they came to assist them they would fight; but if that assistance were impossible to be obtained from them, they said they would deliver themselves up to suffer whatever he pleased to inflict upon them.

2. So Nahash, contemning the multitude of the Gileadites, and the answer they gave, allowed them a respite, and gave them leave to send to whomsoever they pleased for assistance.

So they immediately sent to the Israelites, city by city, and informed them what Nahash had threatened to do to them, and what great distress they were in. Now the people fell into tears and grief at the hearing of what the ambassadors from Jabesh said; and the terror they were in permitted them to do nothing more; but when the messengers were come to the city of king Saul, and declared the danger in which the inhabitants of Jabesh were, the people were in the same affliction as those in the other cities, for they lamented the calamity of those related to them; and when Saul was returned from his husbandry into the city, he found his fellow-citizens weeping; and when, upon inquiry, he had learned the cause of the confusion and sadness they were in, he was seized with a divine fury, and sent away the ambassadors from the inhabitants of Jabesh, and promised them to come to their assistance on the third day, and to beat their enemies before sun-rising, that the sun upon its rising might see that they had already conquered, and were freed from the fears they were under; but he bid some of them stay to conduct them the right way to Jabesh.

3. So being desirous to turn the people to this war against the Ammonites by fear of the losses they should otherwise undergo, and that they might the more suddenly be gathered together, he cut the sinews of his oxen, and threatened to do the same to all such as did not come with their armour to Jordan the next day, and follow him and Samuel the prophet whithersoever they should lead them. So they came together, out of fear of the losses they were threatened with, at the appointed time; and the multitude were numbered at the city Bezek; and he found the number of those that were gathered together, besides that of the tribe of Judah, to be seven hundred thousand, while those of that tribe were seventy thousand. So he passed over Jordan, and proceeded in marching all that night, thirty furlongs, and came to Jabesh before sunrising. So he divided the army into three companies; and fell upon their enemies on every side on the sudden, and when they expected no such thing; and joining battle with them, they slew a great many of the Ammonites, as also their king Nahash. This glorious action was done by Saul, and was related with great commendation of him to all the Hebrews: and he thence gained a wonderful reputation for his valour; for although there were some of them that contemned him before, they now changed their minds, and honoured him, and esteemed him as the best of men: for he did not content himself with having saved the inhabitants of Jabesh only, but he made an expedition into the country of the Ammonites, and laid it all waste, and took a large prey, and so returned to his own country most gloriously: so the people were greatly pleased at these excellent performances of Saul, and rejoiced that they had constituted him their king. They also made a clamour against those that pretended he would be of no advantage to their affairs; and they said, Where now are these men?—let them be brought to punishment, with all the like things that multitudes usually say when they are elevated with prosperity, against those that lately had despised the authors of it; but Saul, although he took the good-will and the affection of these men very kindly, yet did he swear that he would not see any of his countrymen slain that day, since it was absurd to mix this victory, which God had given them, with the blood and slaughter of those that were of the same lineage with themselves; and that it was more agreeable to be

---

* "He that exposes his shield to the enemy with his left hand, thereby hides his left eye, and looks at the enemy with his right eye: he, therefore, that plucks out that eye, makes men useless in war."—*Theodoret.*

men of a friendly disposition, and so to betake themselves to feasting.

4. And when Samuel had told them that he ought to confirm the kingdom to Saul by a second ordination of him, they all came together to the city of Gilgal, for thither did he command them to come. So the prophet anointed Saul with the holy oil in the sight of the multitude, and declared him to be king the second time; and so the government of the Hebrews was changed into a regal government; for in the days of Moses and his disciple Joshua, who was their general, they continued under an aristocracy; but after the death of Joshua, for eighteen years in all, the multitude had no settled form of government, but were in an anarchy; after which they returned to their former government, they then permitting themselves to be judged by him who appeared to be the best warrior, and most courageous, whence it was that they called this interval of their government, the *Judges*.

5. Then did Samuel the prophet call another assembly also, and said to them, "I solemnly adjure you, by God Almighty, who brought those excellent brethren, I mean Moses and Aaron, into the world, and delivered our fathers from the Egyptians, and from the slavery they endured under them, that you will not speak what you say to gratify me, nor suppress any thing out of fear of me, nor be overborne by any other passion, but say, What have I ever done that was cruel or unjust? or what have I done out of lucre or covetousness, or to gratify others? Bear witness against me, if I have taken an ox or a sheep, or any such thing. which yet when they are taken to support men it is esteemed blameless; or have I taken an ass for mine own use of any one to his grief?—lay some one such crime to my charge, now we are in your king's presence." But they cried out, that no such thing had been done by him, but that he had presided over the nation after a holy and righteous manner.

6. Hereupon Samuel, when such a testimony had been given him by them all, said, "Since you grant that you are not able to lay any ill thing to my charge hitherto, come on now, and do you hearken while I speak with great freedom to you. You have been guilty of great impiety against God, in asking you a king. It behoves you to remember, that our grandfather Jacob came down into Egypt, by reason of a famine, with seventy souls only of our family, and that their posterity multiplied there to many ten thousands, whom the Egyptians brought into slavery and hard oppression; that God himself, upon the prayers of our fathers, sent Moses and Aaron, who were brethren, and gave them power to deliver the multitude out of their distress, and this without a king. These brought us into this very land which you now possess; and when you enjoyed these advantages from God, you betrayed his worship and religion; nay, moreover, when you were brought under the hands of your enemies, he delivered you,—first by rendering you superior to the Assyrians and their forces; he then made you to overcome the Ammonites, and the Moabites, and last of all the Philistines; and these things have been achieved under the conduct of Jephtha and Gideon. What madness therefore possessed you to fly from God, and to desire to be under a king?—yet have I ordained him for king whom he chose for you. However, that I may make it plain to you that God is angry and displeased at your choice of kingly government, I will so dispose him that he shall declare this very plainly to you by strange signals; for what none of you ever saw here before, I mean

a winter storm in the midst of harvest,* I will entreat of God, and will make it visible to you." Now, as soon as he had said this, God gave such great signals by thunder and lightning, and the descent of hail, as attested the truth of all that the prophet had said, insomuch that they were amazed and terrified, and confessed they had sinned, and had fallen into that sin through ignorance; and besought the prophet, as one that was a tender and gentle father to them, to render God so merciful as to forgive this their sin, which they had added to those other offences whereby they had affronted him and transgressed against him. So he promised them that he would beseech God, and persuade him to forgive them these their sins. However, he advised them to be righteous, and to be good, and ever to remember the miseries that had befallen them on account of their departure from virtue : as also to remember the strange signs God had shewn them, and the body of laws that Moses had given them, if they had any desire of being preserved and made happy with their king; but he said, that if they should grow careless of these things, great judgments would come from God upon them, and upon their king: and when Samuel had thus prophesied to the Hebrews, he dismissed them to their own homes, having confirmed the kingdom to Saul the second time.

CHAPTER VI

HOW THE PHILISTINES MADE ANOTHER EXPEDITION AGAINST THE HEBREWS, AND WERE BEATEN

1. Now Saul chose out of the multitude about three thousand men, and he took two thousand of them to be the guards of his own body, and abode in the city Bethel, but he gave the rest of them to Jonathan his son, to be the guards of his body; and sent him to Gibeah, where he besieged and took a certain garrison of the Philistines, not far from Gilgal; for the Philistines of Gibeah had beaten the Jews, and taken their weapons away, and had put garrisons into the strongest places of the country, and had forbidden them to carry any instrument of iron, or at all to make use of any iron in any case whatsoever; and on account of this prohibition it was that the husbandmen, if they had occasion to sharpen any of their tools, whether it were the coulter or the spade, or any instrument of husbandry, they came to the Philistines to do it. Now as soon as the Philistines heard of this slaughter of their garrison, they were in a rage about it, and, looking on this contempt as a terrible affront offered them, they made war against the Jews, with three hundred thousand footmen, and thirty thousand chariots, and six thousand horses; and they pitched their camp at the city Michmash. When Saul, the king of the Hebrews, was informed of this, he went down to the city Gilgal, and made proclamation over all the country, that they should try to regain their liberty; and called them to the war against the Philistines, diminishing their forces, and despising them as not very considerable, and as not so great but they might hazard a battle with them But when the people about Saul observed how numerous the Philistines were, they were under a great consternation; and some of them hid them-

---

* Reland observes, that although thunder and lightning with us usually happen in summer, yet in Palestine and Syria they are chiefly confined to winter.

selves in caves, and in dens under ground, but the greater part fled into the land beyond Jordan, which belonged to Gad and Reuben.

2. But Saul sent to the prophet, and called him to consult with him about the war and the public affairs; so he commanded him to stay there for him, and to prepare sacrifices, for he would come to him within seven days, that they might offer sacrifices on the seventh day, and might then join battle with their enemies. So he waited,* as the prophet sent to him to do; yet did not he, however, observe the command that was given him, but when he saw that the prophet tarried longer than he expected, and that he was deserted by the soldiers, he took the sacrifices and offered them; and when he heard that Samuel was come, he went out to meet him. But the prophet said he had not done well in disobeying the injunctions he had sent to him, and had not stayed till his coming, which being appointed according to the will of God, he had prevented him in offering up those prayers and those sacrifices that he should have made for the multitude, and that he therefore had performed divine offices in an ill manner, and had been rash in performing them. Hereupon Saul made an apology for himself, and said that he had waited as many days as Samuel had appointed him; that he had been so quick in offering his sacrifices, upon account of the necessity he was in, and because his soldiers were departing from him, out of their fear of the enemy's camp at Michmash, the report being gone abroad that they were coming down upon him to Gilgal. To which Samuel replied, "Nay, certainly, if thou hadst been a righteous man,† and hadst not disobeyed me, nor slighted the commands which God suggested to me concerning the present state of affairs, and hadst not acted more hastily than the present circumstances required, thou wouldst have been permitted to reign a long time, and thy posterity after thee." So Samuel being grieved at what happened, returned home; but Saul came to the city Gibeah, with his son Jonathan, having only six hundred men with him; and of these the greater part had no weapons, because of the scarcity of iron in that country, as well as of those that could make such weapons; for, as we shewed a little before, the Philistines had not suffered them to have such

* Saul seems to have stayed till near the time of the evening sacrifice, on the seventh day, which Samuel the prophet of God had appointed him. but not till the end of that day, as he ought to have done; and Samuel appears, by delaying to come till the full time of the evening sacrifice on that seventh day, to have tried him, (who seems to have been already for sometime declining from his strict and bounden subordination to God and his prophet,) whether he would stay till the priest came, who alone could lawfully offer the sacrifices, or would boldly and profanely usurp the priest's office, which he venturing upon, was justly rejected for his profaneness. And, indeed, since Saul had accepted kingly power, the divine settlement by Moses had soon been laid aside under the kings, had not God restrained Saul and other kings in some degree of obedience to himself; nor was even this severity sufficient to restrain most of the future kings of Israel and Judah from the greatest idolatry and impiety.

† By this answer of Samuel, and that from a divine commission, which is fuller in 1 Sam. xiii. 14, concerning the great wickedness of Saul in venturing, even under a seeming necessity of affairs, to usurp the priest's office, we are in some degree able to answer the question, Whether, if there were a city or country of lay Christians without any clergyman, it were lawful for the laity alone to baptize, or celebrate the eucharist; or whether they ought not rather, till they procure clergymen to come among them, to confine themselves within those bounds of piety and Christianity which belong alone to the laity. To which latter opinion I incline.

iron or such workmen. Now the Philistines divided their army into three companies, and took as many roads, and laid waste the country of the Hebrews, while king Saul, and his son Jonathan saw what was done, but were not able to defend the land, having no more than six hundred men with them; but as he, and his son, and Abiah the high priest, who was of the posterity of Eli the high priest, were sitting upon a pretty high hill, and seeing the land laid waste, they were mightily disturbed at it. Now Saul's son agreed with his armour-bearer, that they would go privately to the enemy's camp, and make a tumult and a disturbance among them; and when the armour-bearer had readily promised to follow him whithersoever he should lead him, though he should be obliged to die in the attempt, Jonathan made use of the young man's assistance, and descended from the hill, and went to their enemies. Now the enemy's camp was upon a precipice which had three tops, that ended in a small, but sharp and long extremity, while there was a rock that surrounded them, like lines made to prevent the attacks of an enemy. There it so happened, that the out-guards of the camp were neglected, because of the security that here arose from the situation of the place, and because they thought it altogether impossible, not only to ascend up to the camp on that quarter, but so much as to come near it. As soon, therefore, as they came to the camp, Jonathan encouraged his armour-bearer, and said to him, "Let us attack our enemies; and if, when they see us, they bid us come up to them, take that for a signal of victory; but if they say nothing, as not intending to invite us to come up, let us return back again." So when they were approaching to the enemy's camp, just after break of day, and the Philistines saw them, they said one to another, "The Hebrews come out of their dens and caves;" and they said to Jonathan and to his armour-bearer, "Come on, ascend up to us, that we may inflict a just punishment upon you, for your rash attempt upon us." So Saul's son accepted of that invitation, as what signified to him victory, and he immediately came out of the place whence they were seen by their enemies: so he changed his place, and came to the rock which had none to guard it, because of its own strength; from thence they crept up with great labour and difficulty, and so far overcame by force the nature of the place, till they were able to fight with their enemies. So they fell upon them as they were asleep, and slew about twenty of them, and thereby filled them with disorder and surprise, insomuch that some of them threw away their entire armour, and fled; but the greatest part, not knowing one another, because they were of different nations, suspected one another to be enemies, (for they did not imagine there were only two of the Hebrews that came up,) and so they fought one against another; and some of them died in the battle, and some, as they were flying away, were thrown down from the rock headlong.

3. Now Saul's watchmen told the king that the camp of the Philistines was in confusion; then he inquired whether anybody was gone away from the army; and when he heard that his son, and with him his armour-bearer, were absent, he bade the high priest take the garments of his high priesthood, and prophesy to him what success they should have; who said that they should get the victory, and prevail against their enemies. So he went out after the Philistines, and set upon them as they were slaying one another. Those also who had fled to dens and caves, upon hearing that Saul was gaining a

victory, came running to him. When, therefore, the number of the Hebrews that came to Saul amounted to about ten thousand, he pursued the enemy, who were scattered all over the country; but then he fell into an action, which was a very unhappy one, and liable to be very much blamed; for, whether out of ignorance, or whether out of joy for a victory gained so strangely, (for it frequently happens that persons so fortunate are not then able to use their reason consistently,) as he was desirous to avenge himself, and to exact a due punishment of the Philistines, he denounced a curse * upon the Hebrews : That if any one put a stop to his slaughter of the enemy, and fell on eating, and left off the slaughter or the pursuit before the night came on, and obliged them so to do, he should be accursed. Now after Saul had denounced this curse, since they were now in a wood belonging to the tribe of Ephraim, which was thick and full of bees, Saul's son, who did not hear his father denounce that curse, nor hear of the approbation the multitude gave to it, broke off a piece of a honeycomb, and ate part of it. But, in the meantime, he was informed with what a curse his father had forbidden them to taste any thing before sun-setting : so he left off eating, and said his father had not done well in this prohibition, because, had they taken some food, they had pursued the enemy with greater vigour and alacrity, and had both taken and slain many more of their enemies.

4. When therefore they had slain many ten thousands of the Philistines, they fell upon spoiling the camp of the Philistines, but not till late in the evening. They also took a great deal of prey and cattle, and killed them, and ate them with their blood. This was told to the king by the scribes, that the multitude were sinning against God as they sacrificed, and were eating before the blood was well washed away, and the flesh was made clean. Then did Saul give order that a great stone should be rolled into the midst of them, and he made proclamation that they should kill their sacrifices upon it, and not feed upon the flesh with the blood, for that was not acceptable to God. And when all the people did as the king commanded them, Saul erected an altar there, and offered burnt-offerings upon it to God.† This was the first altar that Saul built.

5. So when Saul was desirous of leading his men to the enemy's camp before it was day, in order to plunder it, and when the soldiers were not unwilling to follow him, but indeed shewed great readiness to do as he commanded them, the king called Ahitub the high priest, and enjoined him to know of God whether he would grant them the favour and permission to go against the enemy's camp, in order to destroy those that were in it; and when the priest said that God did not give any answer, Saul replied, "And not without some cause does God refuse to answer what we inquire of him, while yet a little while ago he declared to us all that we desired beforehand, and even prevented us in his

answer. To be sure, there is some sin against him that is concealed from us, which is the occasion of his silence. Now I swear by him himself, that though he that hath committed this sin should prove to be my own son Jonathan, I will slay him, and by that means will appease the anger of God against us, and that in the very same manner as if I were to punish a stranger, and one not at all related to me, for the same offence." So when the multitude cried out to him so to do, he presently set all the rest on one side, and he and his son stood on the other side, and he sought to discover the offender by lot. Now the lot appeared to fall upon Jonathan himself. So when he was asked by his father what sin he had been guilty of, and what he was conscious of in the course of his life that might be esteemed instances of guilt or profaneness, his answer was this : "O father, I have done nothing more than that yesterday, without knowing of the curse and oath thou hadst denounced, while I was in pursuit of the enemy, I tasted of a honeycomb." But Saul sware that he would slay him, and prefer the observation of his oath, before all the ties of birth and nature; and Jonathan was not dismayed at this threatening of death, but, offering himself to it generously and undauntedly, he said, "Nor do I desire you, father, to spare me : death will be to me very acceptable, when it proceeds from thy piety, and after a glorious victory; for it is the greatest consolation to me that I leave the Hebrews victorious over the Philistines." Hereupon all the people were very sorry, and greatly afflicted for Jonathan; and they sware that they would not overlook Jonathan, and see him die, who was the author of their victory. By which means they snatched him out of the danger he was in from his father's curse, while they made their prayers to God also for the young man, that he would remit his sin.

6. So Saul, having slain about sixty thousand of the enemy, returned home to his own city, and reigned happily : and he also fought against the neighbouring nations, and subdued the Ammonites, and Moabites, and Philistines, and Edomites, and Amalekites, as also the king of Zobah. He had three male children, Jonathan, and Isui, and Melchishua : with Merab and Michal his daughters. He had also Abner, his uncle's son, for the captain of his host : that uncle's name was Ner. Now Ner and Kish, the father of Saul, were brothers. Saul had also a great many chariots and horsemen, and against whomsoever he made war he returned conqueror, and advanced the affairs of the Hebrews to a great degree of success and prosperity, and made them superior to other nations; and he made such of the young men as were remarkable for tallness and comeliness, the guards of his body.

CHAPTER VII

SAUL'S WAR WITH THE AMALEKITES, AND CONQUEST OF THEM

1. Now Samuel came unto Saul, and said to him, that he was sent by God to put him in mind that God had preferred him before all others, and ordained him king; that he therefore ought to be obedient to him, and to submit to his authority, as considering, that though he had the dominion over the other tribes, yet that God had the dominion over him, and over all things; that accordingly God said to him, that "because the Amalekites did the Hebrews a

---

* This rash vow or curse of Saul, which was not executed, I suppose, principally because Jonathan did not know of it, is very remarkable; it being of the essence of the obligation of all laws, that they be sufficiently known and promulgated, otherwise the conduct of Providence, in God's refusing to answer by Urim till this breach of Saul's vow or curse was understood and set right, is very remarkable.

† Here we have still more indications of Saul's affectation of despotic power, and of his entrenching upon the priesthood, and making and endeavouring to execute a rash vow or curse, without consulting Samuel or the Sanhedrim.

great deal of mischief while they were in the wilderness, and when, upon their coming out of Egypt, they were making their way to that country which is now their own, I enjoin thee to punish the Amalekites, by making war upon them, and when thou hast subdued them, to leave none of them alive, but to pursue them through every age, and to slay them, beginning with the women and the infants, and to require this as a punishment to be inflicted upon them for the mischief they did to our forefathers : to spare nothing, neither asses nor other beasts ; nor to reserve any of them for your own advantage and possession, but to devote them universally to God, and, in obedience to the commands of Moses, to blot out the name of Amalek entirely." *

2. So Saul promised to do what he was commanded ; and supposing that his obedience to God would be shewn, not only in making war against the Amalekites, but more fully in the readiness and quickness of his proceedings, he made no delay, but immediately gathered together all his forces ; and when he had numbered them in Gilgal, he found them to be about four hundred thousand of the Israelites, besides the tribe of Judah, for that tribe contained by itself thirty thousand. Accordingly, Saul made an irruption into the country of the Amalekites, and set many men in several parties in ambush at the river, that so he might not only do them a mischief by open fighting, but might fall upon them unexpectedly in the ways, and might thereby compass them round about, and kill them. And when he had joined battle with the enemy, he beat them ; and pursuing them as they fled, he destroyed them all. And when that undertaking had succeeded, according as God had foretold, he set upon the cities of the Amalekites ; he besieged them, and took them by force, partly by warlike machines, partly by mines dug under ground, and partly by building walls on the outsides. Some they starved out with famine, and some they gained by other methods ; and after all, he betook himself to slay the women and the children, and thought he did not act therein either barbarously or inhumanly ; first, because they were enemies whom he thus treated, and, in the next place, because it was done by the command of God, whom it was dangerous not to obey. He also took Agag, the enemy's king, captive ;—the beauty and tallness of whose body he admired so much that he thought him worthy of preservation : yet was not this done, however, according to the will of God, but by giving way to human passions, and suffering himself to be moved with an unseasonable commiseration, in a point where it was not safe for him to indulge it ; for God hated the nation of the Amalekites to such a degree, that he commanded Saul to have no pity on even those infants which we by nature chiefly compassionate ; but Saul preserved their king and governor from the miseries which the Hebrews brought on the people, as if he preferred the fine appearance of the enemy to the memory of what God had sent him about. The multitude were also guilty, together with Saul; for they spared the herds, and the flocks, and took them for a prey, when God had commanded they should not spare them. They also carried

off with them the rest of their wealth and riches ; but if there were anything that was not worthy of regard, that they destroyed.

3. But when Saul had conquered all these Amalekites that reached from Pelusium of Egypt to the Red Sea, he laid waste all the rest of the enemy's country : but for the nation of the Shechemites, he did not touch them, although they dwelt in the very middle of the country of Midian ; for, before the battle, Saul had sent to them, and charged them to depart thence, lest they should be partakers of the miseries of the Amalekites ; for he had a just occasion for saving them, since they were of the kindred of Raguel, Moses's father-in-law.

4. Hereupon Saul returned home with joy, for the glorious things he had done, and for the conquest of his enemies, as though he had not neglected anything which the prophet had enjoined him to do when he was going to make war with the Amalekites, and as though he had exactly observed all that he ought to have done. But God was grieved that the king of the Amalekites was preserved alive, and that the multitude had seized on the cattle for a prey, because these things were done without his permission ; for he thought it an intolerable thing that they should conquer and overcome their enemies by that power which he gave them, and then that he himself should be so grossly despised and disobeyed by them, that a mere man that was a king would not bear it. He therefore told Samuel the prophet, that he repented that he had made Saul king, while he did nothing that he had commanded him, but indulged his own inclinations.' When Samuel heard that, he was in confusion ; and began to beseech God all that night to be reconciled to Saul, and not to be angry with him ; but he did not grant that forgiveness to Saul which the prophet asked for, as not deeming it a fit thing to grant forgiveness of [such] sins at his entreaties, since injuries do not otherwise grow so great as by the easy tempers of those that are injured ; for while they hunt after the glory of being thought gentle and good-natured, before they are aware, they produce other sins. As soon, therefore, as God had rejected the intercession of the prophet, and it plainly appeared he would not change his mind, at break of day Samuel came to Saul at Gilgal. When the king saw him, he ran to him, and embraced him, and said, "I return thanks to God, who hath given me the victory, for I have performed everything that he hath commanded me." To which Samuel replied, "How is it, then, that I hear the bleating of the sheep, and the lowing of the greater cattle in the camp ?" Saul made answer that the people had reserved them for sacrifices ; but that, as to the nation of the Amalekites, it was entirely destroyed, as he had received it in command to see done, and that no man was left ; but that he had saved alive the king alone, and brought him to him, concerning whom, he said they would advise together what should be done with him. But the prophet said, "God is not delighted with sacrifices, but with good and with righteous men, who are such as follow his will and his laws, and never think that anything is well done by them but when they do it as God had commanded them : that he then looks upon himself as affronted, not when any one does not sacrifice, but when any one appears to be disobedient to him. But that from those who do not obey him, nor pay him that duty which is the alone true and acceptable worship, 'he will not kindly accept their oblations, be those they offer ever so many and so fat, and be the presents they make

---

* The reason of this severity is distinctly given, (1 Sam. xv. 18 :) "Go, and utterly destroy the sinners, the Amalekites ;" nor indeed do we ever meet with these Amalekites but as very cruel and bloody people. See that most barbarous of all cruelties, that of Haman the Agagite, or one of the posterity of Agag, the old king of the Amalekites, (Esth. iii. 1-15.)

him ever so ornamental, nay, though they were made of gold and silver themselves; but he will reject them, and esteem them instances of wickedness, and not of piety. And that he is delighted with those that still bear in mind this one thing, and this only, how to do that, whatsoever it be, which God pronounces or commands for them to do, and to choose rather to die than to transgress any of those commands; nor does he require so much as a sacrifice from them. And when these do sacrifice, though it be a mean oblation, he better accepts of it as the honour of poverty, than such oblations as come from the richest men that offer them to him. Wherefore, take notice that thou art under the wrath of God, for thou hast despised and neglected what he commanded thee. How dost thou then suppose that he will respect a sacrifice out of such things as he hath doomed to destruction? unless perhaps thou dost imagine that it is almost all one to offer it in sacrifice to God as to destroy it. Do thou therefore expect that thy kingdom will be taken from thee, and that authority which thou hast abused by such insolent behaviour as to neglect that God who bestowed it upon thee." Then did Saul confess that he had acted unjustly, and did not deny that he had sinned, because he had transgressed the injunctions of the prophet; but he said that it was out of a dread and fear of the soldiers that he did not prohibit and restrain them when they seized on the prey. "But forgive me," said he, "and be merciful to me, for I will be cautious how I offend for the time to come." He also entreated the prophet to go back with him, that he might offer his thank-offerings to God; but Samuel went home, because he saw that God would not be reconciled to him.

5. But then Saul was so desirous to retain Samuel, that he took hold of his cloak, and because the vehemence of Samuel's departure made the motion to be violent, the cloak was rent. Upon which the prophet said, that after the same manner should the kingdom be rent from him, and that a good and a just man should take it; that God persevered in what he had decreed about him; that to be mutable and changeable in what is determined, is agreeable to human passions only, but is not agreeable to the Divine Power. Hereupon Saul said that he had been wicked; but that what was done, could not be undone: he therefore desired him to honour him so far, that the multitude might see that he would accompany him in worshipping God. So Samuel granted him that favour, and went with him and worshipped God. Agag also, the king of the Amalekites, was brought to him; and when the king asked, How bitter death was? Samuel said, "As thou hast made many of the Hebrew mothers to lament and bewail the loss of their children, so shalt thou, by thy death, cause thy mother to lament thee also." Accordingly he gave order to slay him immediately at Gilgal, and then went away to the city Ramah.

CHAPTER VIII

HOW, UPON SAUL'S TRANSGRESSION OF THE PROPHET'S COMMANDS, SAMUEL ORDAINED ANOTHER PERSON TO BE KING PRIVATELY, WHOSE NAME WAS DAVID, AS GOD COMMANDED HIM

1. Now Saul being sensible of the miserable condition he had brought himself into, and that he had made God to be his enemy, he went up to his royal palace at Gibeah, which name de-

notes a *hill*, and after that day he came no more into the presence of the prophet. And when Samuel mourned for him, God bid him leave off his concern for him, and to take the holy oil, and go to Bethlehem to Jesse the son of Obed, and to anoint such of his sons as he should shew him for their future king. But Samuel said, he was afraid lest Saul, when he came to know of it, should kill him, either by some private method, or even openly. But upon God's suggesting to him a safe way of going thither, he came to the forementioned city; and when they all saluted him, and asked what was the occasion of his coming, he told them, he came to sacrifice to God. When, therefore, he had gotten the sacrifice ready, he called Jesse and his sons to partake of those sacrifices; and when he saw his eldest son to be a tall and handsome man, he guessed by his comeliness that he was the person who was to be their future king. But he was mistaken in judging about God's providence; for when Samuel inquired of God whether he should anoint this youth whom he so admired, and esteemed worthy of the kingdom, God said, "Men do not see as God seeth. Thou indeed hast respect to the fine appearance of this youth, and thence esteemest him worthy of the kingdom, while I propose the kingdom as a reward, not of the beauty of bodies, but of the virtue of souls, and I inquire after one that is perfectly comely in that respect; I mean one who is beautiful in piety, and righteousness, and fortitude and obedience; for in them consists the comeliness of the soul." When God had said this, Samuel bade Jesse to shew him all his sons. So he made five others of his sons to come to him: of all of whom, Eliab was the eldest, Aminadab the second, Shammah the third, Nathaniel the fourth, Rael the fifth, and Asam the sixth. And when the prophet saw that these were no way inferior to the eldest in their countenances, he inquired of God which of them it was that he chose for their king; and when God said it was none of them, he asked Jesse whether he had not some other sons besides these; and when he said that he had one more, named David, but that he was a shepherd, and took care of the flocks, Samuel bade them call him immediately, for that till he was come they could not possibly sit down to the feast. Now, as soon as his father had sent for David, and he was come, he appeared to be of a yellow complexion, of a sharp sight, and a comely person in other respects also. This is he, said Samuel privately to himself, whom it pleases God to make our king. So he sat down to the feast, and placed the youth under him, and Jesse also, with his other sons; after which he took oil in the presence of David, and anointed him, and whispered him in the ear, and acquainted him that God chose him to be their king; and exhorted him to be righteous, and obedient to his commands, for that by this means his kingdom would continue for a long time, and that his house should be of great splendour, and celebrated in the world; that he should overthrow the Philistines; and that against what nations soever he should make war, he should be the conqueror, and survive the fight; and that while he lived he should enjoy a glorious name, and leave such a name to his posterity also.

2. So Samuel, when he had given him these admonitions, went away. But the Divine Power departed from Saul, and removed to David, who, upon this removal of the Divine Spirit to him, began to prophesy; but as for Saul, some strange and demoniacal disorders came upon him, and brought upon him such suffocations as were ready to choke him; for which the physicians could

find no other remedy but this, That if any person could charm those passions by singing, and playing upon the harp, they advised them to inquire for such a one, and to observe when these demons came upon him and disturbed him, and to take care that such a person might stand over him, and play upon the harp, and recite hymns to him.* Accordingly Saul did not delay, but commanded them to seek out such a man; and when a certain stander-by said he had seen in the city of Bethlehem a son of Jesse, who was yet no more than a child in age, but comely and beautiful, and in other respects one that was deserving of great regard, who was skilful in playing on the harp, and in singing of hymns, [and an excellent soldier in war,] he sent to Jesse, and desired him to take David away from the flocks, and send him to him, for he had a mind to see him, as having heard an advantageous character of his comeliness and his valour. So Jesse sent his son, and gave him presents to carry to Saul; and when he was come, Saul was pleased with him, and made him his armour-bearer, and had him in very great esteem; for he charmed his passion, and was the only physician against the trouble he had from the demons, whensoever it was that it came upon him, and this by reciting of hymns, and playing upon the harp, and bringing Saul to his right mind again. However, he sent to Jesse, the father of the child, and desired him to permit David to stay with him, for that he was delighted with his sight and company, which stay, that he might not contradict Saul, he granted.

CHAPTER IX

HOW THE PHILISTINES MADE ANOTHER EXPEDITION AGAINST THE HEBREWS, UNDER THE REIGN OF SAUL; AND HOW THEY WERE OVERCOME BY DAVID'S SLAYING GOLIATH IN SINGLE COMBAT

1. Now the Philistines gathered themselves together again, no very long time afterward: and having gotten together a great army, they made war against the Israelites; and having seized a place between Shochoh and Azekah, they there pitched their camp. Saul also drew out his army to oppose them; and by pitching his own camp on a certain hill, he forced the Philistines to leave their former camp, and to encamp themselves upon such another hill, over against that on which Saul's army lay, so that a valley, which was between the two hills on which they lay, divided their camps asunder. Now there came down a man out of the camp of the Philistines, whose name was Goliath, of the city of Gath, a man of vast bulk, for he was of four cubits and a span in tallness, and had about him weapons suitable to the largeness of his body, for he had a breastplate on that weighed five thousand shekels: he had also a helmet and greaves of brass, as large as you would naturally suppose might cover the limbs of so vast a body. His spear was also such as was not carried like a light thing in his right hand, but he carried it as lying on his shoulders. He had also a lance of six hundred shekels; and many followed him to carry his armour. Wherefore this Goliath stood between the two armies, as they were in battle-array, and sent out a loud voice, and said to Saul and the Hebrews, "I will free you from fighting and from dangers; for what necessity is there that your army should fall and be afflicted? Give me a man of you that will fight with me, and he that conquers shall have the reward of the conqueror, and determine the war; for these shall serve those others to whom the conqueror shall belong; and certainly it is much better and more prudent to gain what you desire by the hazard of one man than of all." When he had said this, he retired to his own camp; but the next day he came again, and used the same words, and did not leave off for forty days together, to challenge the enemy in the same words, till Saul and his army were therewith terrified, while they put themselves in array as if they would fight, but did not come to a close battle.

2. Now while this war between the Hebrews and the Philistines was going on, Saul sent away David to his father Jesse, and contented himself with those three sons of his whom he had sent to his assistance, and to be partners in the dangers of the war: and at first David returned to feed his sheep and his flocks; but after no long time he came to the camp of the Hebrews, as sent by his father, to carry provisions to his brethren, and to know what they were doing; while Goliath came again, and challenged them and reproached them, that they had no man of valour among them that durst come down to fight him; and as David was talking with his brethren about the business for which his father had sent him, he heard the Philistine reproaching and abusing the army, and had indignation at it, and said to his brethren, "I am ready to fight a single combat with this adversary." Whereupon Eliab, his eldest brother, reproved him, and said that he spake too rashly and improperly for one of his age, and bid him go to his flocks and to his father. So he was abashed at his brother's words, and went away, but still he spake to some of the soldiers that he was willing to fight with him that challenged them. And when they had informed Saul what was the resolution of the young man, the king sent for him to come to him: and when the king asked what he had to say, he replied, "O king, be not cast down, nor afraid, for I will depress the insolence of this adversary, and will go down and fight with him, and will bring him under me, as tall and as great as he is, till he shall be sufficiently laughed at, and thy army shall get great glory when he shall be slain by one that is not yet of man's estate, neither fit for fighting, nor capable of being intrusted with the marshalling an army, or ordering a battle, but by one that looks like a child, and is really no older in age than a child."

3. Now Saul wondered at the boldness and alacrity of David, but durst not presume on his ability, by reason of his age; but said, he must on that account be too weak to fight with one that was skilled in the art of war, "I undertake this enterprise," said David, "in dependence on God's being with me, for I have had experience already of his assistance; for I once pursued after and caught a lion that assaulted my flocks, and took away a lamb from them, and I snatched the lamb from out of the wild beast's mouth, and when he leaped upon me with violence, I took him by the tail, and dashed him against the ground. In the same manner did I avenge myself on a bear also; and let this adversary of ours be esteemed like one of these wild beasts, since he has a long while reproached our army and blasphemed our God, who yet will reduce him under my power."

---

* The Greeks had such singers of hymns; and usually children or youths were picked out for that service. Those called *singers to the harp*, did the same that David did here, *i.e.* join their own vocal and instrumental music together.

4. However, Saul prayed that the end might be, by God's assistance, not disagreeable to the alacrity and boldness of the child; and said, "Go thy way to the fight." So he put about him his breastplate, and girded on his sword, and fitted the helmet to his head, and sent him away. But David was burdened with his armour, for he had not been exercised to it, nor had he learned to walk with it; so he said, "Let this armour be thine, O king, who art able to bear it; but give me leave to fight as thy servant, and as I myself desire." Accordingly he laid by the armour, and taking his staff with him, and putting five stones out of the brook into a shepherd's bag, and having a sling in his right hand, he went towards Goliath. But the adversary seeing him come in such a manner, disdained him, and jested upon him, as if ne had not such weapons with him as are usual when one man fights against another, but such as are used in driving away and avoiding of dogs; and said, "Dost thou take me not for a man, but a dog?" To which he replied, "No, not for a dog, but for a creature worse than a dog." This provoked Goliath to anger, who thereupon cursed him by the name of God, and threatened to give his flesh to the beasts of the earth, and to the fowls of the air, to be torn in pieces by them. To whom David answered, "Thou comest to me with a sword, and with a spear, and with a breastplate; but I have God for my armour in coming against thee, who will destroy thee and all thy army by my hands; for I will this day cut off thy head, and cast the other parts of thy body to the dogs; and all men shall learn that God is the protector of the Hebrews, and that our armour and our strength is in his providence; and that without God's assistance, all other warlike preparations and power are useless." So the Philistine being retarded by the weight of his armour, when he attempted to meet David in haste, came on but slowly, as despising him, and depending upon it that he should slay him who was both unarmed and a child also, without any trouble at all.

5. But the youth met his antagonist, being accompanied with an invisible assistant, who was no other than God himself. And taking one of the stones that he had out of the brook, and had put into his shepherd's bag, and fitting it to his sling, he slang it against the Philistine. This stone fell upon his forehead, and sank into his brain, insomuch that Goliath was stunned, and fell upon his face. So David ran, and stood upon his adversary as he lay down, and cut off his head with his own sword; for he had no sword himself. And upon the fall of Goliath, the Philistines were beaten, and fled; for when they saw their champion prostrate on the ground, they were afraid of the entire issue of their affairs, and resolved not to stay any longer, but committed themselves to an ignominious and indecent flight, and thereby endeavoured to save themselves from the dangers they were in. But Saul and the entire army of the Hebrews made a shout and rushed upon them, and slew a great number of them, and pursued the rest to the borders of Gath, and to the gates of Ekron; so that there were slain of the Philistines thirty thousand, and twice as many wounded. But Saul returned to their camp, and pulled their fortifications to pieces, and burnt it; but David carried the head of Goliath into his own tent, but dedicated his sword to God, [at the tabernacle.]

CHAPTER X

SAUL ENVIES DAVID FOR HIS GLORIOUS SUCCESS, AND TAKES AN OCCASION OF ENTRAPPING HIM, FROM THE PROMISE HE MADE HIM OF GIVING HIM HIS DAUGHTER IN MARRIAGE; BUT THIS UPON CONDITION OF BRINGING HIM SIX HUNDRED HEADS OF THE PHILISTINES

1. Now the women were an occasion of Saul's envy and hatred to David; for they came to meet their victorious army with cymbals and drums, and all demonstrations of joy, and sang thus: the wives said, that "Saul had slain his many thousands of the Philistines:" the virgins replied, that "David has slain his ten thousands." Now, when the king heard them singing thus, and that he had himself the smallest share in their commendations, and the greater number, the ten thousands, were ascribed to the young man; and when he considered with himself that there was nothing more wanting to David, after such a mighty applause, but the kingdom, he began to be afraid and suspicious of David. Accordingly, he removed him from the station he was in before, for he was his armour-bearer, which, out of fear, seemed to him much too near a station for him; and so he made him captain over a thousand, and bestowed on him a post better indeed in itself, but, as he thought, more for his own security; for he had a mind to send him against the enemy, and into battles, as hoping he would be slain in such dangerous conflicts.

2. But David had God going along with him whithersoever he went, and accordingly he greatly prospered in his undertakings, and it was visible that he had mighty success, insomuch that Saul's daughter, who was still a virgin, fell in love with him; and her affection so far prevailed over her, that it could not be concealed, and her father became acquainted with it. Now Saul heard this gladly, as intending to make use of it for a snare against David, and he hoped that it would prove the cause of destruction and of hazard to him; so he told those that informed him of his daughter's affection, that he would willingly give David the virgin in marriage, and said, "I engage myself to marry my daughter to him if he will bring me six hundred heads of my enemies,* supposing that when a reward so ample was proposed to him, and when he should aim to get him great glory, by undertaking a thing so dangerous and incredible, he would immediately set about it, and so perish by the Philistines; and my designs about him will succeed finely to my mind, for I shall be freed from him, and get him slain, not by myself, but by another man." So he gave order to his servants, to try how David would relish this proposal of marrying the damsel. Accordingly, they began to speak thus to him: That king Saul loved him, as well as did all the people, and that he was desirous of his affinity by the marriage of this damsel. To which he gave this answer:— "Seemeth it to you a light thing to be made the king's son-in-law? It does not seem so to me, especially when I am one of a family that is low, and without any glory or honour." Now when

---

* Josephus says thrice in this chapter, and twice afterwards, that Saul required not a bare hundred of the foreskins of the Philistines, but six hundred of their heads. The Septuagint have 100 foreskins, but the Syriac and Arabic 200. Now that these were not *foreskins*, with our other copies, but *heads*, with Josephus's copy, seems somewhat probable, from 1 Sam. xxix. 4.

Saul was informed by his servants what answer David had made, he said,—"Tell him that I do not want any money or dowry from him, which would be rather to set my daughter to sale than to give her in marriage; but I desire only such a son-in-law as hath in him fortitude, and all other kinds of virtue," of which he saw David was possessed, and that his desire was to receive of him, on account of marrying his daughter, neither gold nor silver, nor that he should bring such wealth out of his father's house, but only some revenge on the Philistines, and, indeed, six hundred of their heads, than which a more desirable or a more glorious present could not be brought him; and that he had much rather obtain this than any of the accustomed dowries for his daughter—viz., that she should be married to a man of that character, and to one who had a testimony as having conquered his enemies.

3. When these words of Saul were brought to David, he was pleased with them, and supposed that Saul was really desirous of this affinity with him; so that, without bearing to deliberate any longer, or casting about in his mind whether what was proposed was possible, or was difficult or not, he and his companions immediately set upon the enemy, and went about doing what was proposed as the condition of the marriage. Accordingly, because it was God who made all things easy and possible to David, he slew many [of the Philistines,] and cut off the heads of six hundred of them, and came to the king, and by shewing him these heads of the Philistines, required that he might have his daughter in marriage. Accordingly Saul, having no way of getting off his engagements, as thinking it a base thing either to seem a liar when he promised him this marriage, or to appear to have acted treacherously by him, in putting him upon what was in a manner impossible, in order to have him slain, he gave him his daughter in marriage: her name was Michal.

CHAPTER XI

HOW DAVID, UPON SAUL'S LAYING SNARES FOR HIM, DID YET ESCAPE THE DANGERS HE WAS IN, BY THE AFFECTION AND CARE OF JONATHAN, AND THE CONTRIVANCES OF HIS WIFE MICHAL; AND HOW HE CAME TO SAMUEL THE PROPHET

1. HOWEVER, Saul was not disposed to persevere long in the state wherein he was; for when he saw that David was in great esteem both with God and with the multitude, he was afraid; and being not able to conceal his fear as concerning great things, his kingdom and his life, to be deprived of either of which was a very great calamity, he resolved to have David slain; and commanded his son Jonathan and his most faithful servants to kill him: but Jonathan wondered at his father's change with relation to David, that it should be made to so great a degree, from shewing him no small goodwill, to contrive how to have him killed. Now, because he loved the young man, and reverenced him for his virtue, he informed him of the secret charge his father had given him, and what his intentions were concerning him. However, he advised him to take care and be absent the next day, for that he would salute his father, and, if he met with a favourable opportunity, he would discourse with him about him, and learn the cause of his disgust, and shew how little ground there was for it, and that for it he ought not to kill a

man that had done so many good things to the multitude, and had been a benefactor to himself, on account of which he ought in reason to obtain pardon, had he been guilty of the greatest crimes: and "I will then inform thee of my father's resolution." Accordingly, David complied with such an advantageous advice, and kept himself then out of the king's sight.

2. On the next day Jonathan came to Saul, as soon as he saw him in a cheerful and joyful disposition, and began to introduce a discourse about David: "What unjust action, O father, either little or great, hast thou found so exceptionable in David, as to induce thee to order us to slay a man who hath been of great advantage to thy own preservation, and of still greater to the punishment of the Philistines? A man who hath delivered the people of the Hebrews from reproach and derision, which they underwent for forty days together, when he alone had courage enough to sustain the challenge of the adversary, and after that brought as many heads of our enemies as he was appointed to bring, and had, as a reward for the same, my sister in marriage: insomuch that his death would be very sorrowful to us, not only on account of his virtue, but on account of the nearness of our relation; for thy daughter must be injured at the same time that he is slain, and must be obliged to experience widowhood before she can come to enjoy any advantage from their mutual conversation. Consider these things, and change your mind to a more merciful temper, and do no mischief to a man who, in the first place, hath done us the greatest kindness of preserving thee; for when an evil spirit and demons had seized upon thee, he cast them out, and procured rest to thy soul from their incursions: and, in the second place, hath avenged us of our enemies; for it is a base thing to forget such benefits." So Saul was pacified with these words; and sware to his son that he would do David no harm; for a righteous discourse proved too hard for the king's anger and fear. So Jonathan sent for David, and brought him good news from his father, that he was to be preserved. He also brought him to his father; and David continued with the king, as formerly.

3. About this time it was that, upon the Philistines making a new expedition against the Hebrews, Saul sent David with an army to fight with them; and joining battle with them he slew many of them, and after his victory he returned to the king. But his reception by Saul was not as he expected upon such success, for he was grieved at his prosperity, because he thought he would be more dangerous to him by having acted so gloriously: but when the demoniacal spirit came upon him, and put him into disorder, and disturbed him, he called for David into his bed-chamber wherein he lay, and having a spear in his hand, he ordered him to charm him with playing on his harp, and with singing hymns; which when David did at his command, he with great force threw the spear at him; but David was aware of it before it came, and avoided it, and fled to his house, and abode there all that day.

4. But at night the king sent officers, and commanded that he should be watched till the morning, lest he should get quite away, that he might come into the judgment-hall, and so might be delivered up, and condemned and slain. But when Michal, David's wife, the king's daughter, understood what her father designed, she came to her husband, as having small hopes of his deliverance, and as greatly concerned about her own life also, for she could not bear to live in

case she were deprived of him; and she said,—"Let not the sun find thee here when it rises, for if it do, that will be the last time it will see thee: fly away then while the night may afford the opportunity, and may God lengthen it for thy sake! for know this, that if my father find thee, thou art a dead man." So she let him down by a cord out of the window, and saved him: and after she had done so, she fitted up a bed for him as if he were sick, and put under the bed-clothes a goat's liver;* and when her father, as soon as it was day, sent to seize David, she said to those that were there, that he had not been well that night, and shewed them the bed covered, and made them believe, by the leaping of the liver, which caused the bed-clothes to move also, that David breathed like one that was asthmatic. So when those that were sent told Saul that David had not been well in the night, he ordered him to be brought in that condition, for he intended to kill him. Now when they came, and uncovered the bed, and found out the woman's contrivance, they told it to the king; and when her father complained of her that she had saved his enemy, and had put a trick upon himself, she invented this plausible defence for herself, and said, That when he threatened to kill her, she lent him her assistance for his preservation, out of fear; for which her assistance she ought to be forgiven, because it was not done of her own free choice, but out of necessity: "For," said she, "I do not suppose that thou wast so zealous to kill thy enemy, as thou wast that I should be saved." Accordingly Saul forgave the damsel; but David, when he had escaped this danger, came to the prophet Samuel to Ramah, and told him what snare the king had laid for him, and how he was very near to death by Saul's throwing a spear at him, although he had been no way guilty with relation to him, nor had he been cowardly in his battles with his enemies, but had succeeded well in them all, by God's assistance; which thing was indeed the cause of Saul's hatred to David.

5. When the prophet was made acquainted with the unjust proceedings of the king, he left the city Ramah, and took David with him, to a certain place called Naioth, and there he abode with him. But when it was told Saul that David was with the prophet, he sent soldiers to him, and ordered them to take him and bring him to him; and when they came to Samuel, and found there a congregation of prophets, they became partakers of the Divine Spirit, and began to prophesy, which when Saul heard of, he sent others to David, who prophesying in like manner as did the first, he again sent others; which third sort prophesying also, at last he was angry, and went thither in great haste himself; and when he was just by the place, Samuel, before he saw him, made him prophesy also. And when Saul came to him, he was disordered in mind,† and under the vehement agitation of a spirit; and, putting off his garments,‡ he fell down, and lay on the ground all that day and night, in the presence of Samuel and David.

6. And David went thence, and came to Jonathan, the son of Saul, and lamented to him what snares were laid for him by his father; and said, that though he had been guilty of no evil, nor had offended against him, yet he was very zealous to get him killed. Hereupon Jonathan exhorted him not to give credit to such his own suspicions, nor to the calumnies of those that raised those reports, if there were any that did so, but to depend on him, and take courage; for that his father had no such intentions, since he would have acquainted him with that matter, and have taken his advice, had it been so, as he used to consult with him in common when he acted in other affairs. But David sware to him that so it was; and he desired him rather to believe him, and to provide for his safety, than to despise what he, with great sincerity, told him: that he would believe what he said, when he should either see him killed himself, or learn it upon inquiry from others: and that the reason why his father did not tell him of these things was this, that he knew of the friendship and affection that he bore towards him.

7. Hereupon, when Jonathan found that this intention of Saul was so well attested, he asked him what he would have him do for him? To which David replied, "I am sensible that thou art willing to gratify me in everything, and procure me what I desire. Now, to-morrow is the new moon, and I was accustomed to sit down then with the king at supper: now, if it seem good to thee, I will go out of the city, and conceal myself privately there; and if Saul inquire why I am absent, tell him that I am gone to my own city Bethlehem, to keep a festival with my own tribe; and add this also, that thou gavest me leave so to do. And if he say, as is usually said in the case of friends that are gone abroad, It is well that he went, then assure thyself that no latent mischief or enmity may be feared at his hand; but if he answer otherwise, that will be a sure sign that he has some designs against me. Accordingly thou shalt inform me of thy father's inclinations; and that, out of pity to my case and out of thy friendship for me, as instances of which friendship thou hast vouchsafed to accept of the assurances of my love to thee, and to give the like assurances to me, that is, those of a master to his servant; but if thou discoverest any wickedness in me, do thou prevent thy father, and kill me thyself."

8. But Jonathan heard these last words with indignation, and promised to do what he desired of him, and to inform him if his father's answers implied any thing of a melancholy nature, and any enmity against him. And that he might the more firmly depend upon him, he took him out into the open field, into the pure air, and sware that he would neglect nothing that might tend to the preservation of David; and he said, "I appeal to that God, who, as thou seest, is diffused everywhere, and knoweth this intention of mine, before I explain it in words, as the witness of this my covenant with thee, that I will not leave off to make frequent trials of the purpose of my father till I learn whether there be any lurking distemper in the most secret parts of his soul; and when I have learnt it, I will not conceal it from thee, but will discover it to thee, whether he be gently or peevishly disposed; for this God himself knows, that I pray he may always be with thee, for he is with thee now, and will not forsake thee, and will make thee superior to thine enemies, whether my father be one of them or whether I myself be such. Do thou only re-

---

* Since the Septuagint, as well as Josephus, render the word here used the liver of the goat; and since this rendering is so clear and probable, it is almost unaccountable that our commentators should so much as hesitate about its true interpretation.

† These agitations of Saul seem to me to have been no other than demoniacal; and that the same demon which used to seize him, since he was forsaken of God, was now in a judicial way brought upon him not only in order to disappoint his intentions against David, but to expose him to the contempt of all that saw him.

‡ What is meant by Saul's lying down naked all that day, and all that night, and whether any more than laying aside his royal apparel, or upper garments, is by no means certain.

member what we now do; and if it fall out that
I die, preserve my children alive, and requite
what kindness thou hast now received to them."
When he had thus sworn, he dismissed David,
bidding him go to a certain place of that plain
wherein he used to perform his exercises; for
that, as soon as he knew the mind of his father,
he would come thither to him with one servant
only; "and if," says he, "I shoot three darts
at the mark, and then bid my servant to carry
these three darts away, for they are before him,
—know thou that there is no mischief to be
feared from my father; but if thou hearest me
say the contrary, expect the contrary from the
king. However, thou shalt gain security by my
means, and shalt by no means suffer any harm;
but see thou dost not forget what I have desired
of thee in the time of thy prosperity, and be
serviceable to my children." Now David, when
he had received these assurances from Jonathan,
went his way to the place appointed.

9. But on the next day, which was the new
moon, the king, when he had purified himself, as
the custom was, came to supper; and when there
sat by him his son Jonathan on his right hand,
and Abner, the captain of his host, on the other
hand, he saw David's seat was empty, but said
nothing, supposing that he had not purified himself since he had accompanied with his wife, and
so could not be present; but when he saw that
he was not there the second day of the month
neither, he inquired of his son Jonathan why the
son of Jesse did not come to the supper and the
feast, neither the day before nor that day. So
Jonathan said that he was gone, according to the
agreement between them, to his own city, where
his tribe kept a festival, and that by his permission: that he also invited him to come to
their sacrifice; "and," says Jonathan, "if thou
wilt give me leave, I will go thither, for thou
knowest the good-will that I bear him;" and
then it was that Jonathan understood his father's
hatred to David, and plainly saw his entire disposition; for Saul could not restrain his anger,
but reproached Jonathan, and called him the son
of a runagate, and an enemy; and said he was a
partner with David, and his assistant, and that
by his behaviour he shewed he had no regard to
himself, or to his mother, and would not be persuaded of this—that while David is alive, their
kingdom was not secure to them; yet did he
bid him send for him, that he might be punished;
and when Jonathan said, in answer, "What
hath he done that thou wilt punish him?" Saul
no longer contented himself to express his anger
in bare words, but snatched up his spear, and
leaped upon him, and was desirous to kill him.
He did not indeed do what he intended, because
he was hindered by his friends; but it appeared
plainly to his son that he hated David, and
greatly desired to despatch him, insomuch that
he had almost slain his son with his own hands
on his account.

10. And then it was that the king's son rose
hastily from supper; and being unable to admit
anything into his mouth for grief, he wept all
night, both because he had himself been near
destruction, and because the death of David was
determined; but as soon as it was day, he went
out into the plain that was before the city, as
going to perform his exercises, but in reality to
inform his friend what disposition his father was
in towards him, as he had agreed with him to
do; and when Jonathan had done what had been
thus agreed, he dismissed his servant that followed him, to return to the city; but he himself
went into the desert, and came into his presence,
and communed with him. So David appeared,

and fell at Jonathan's feet, and bowed down to
him, and called him the preserver of his soul;
but he lifted him up from the earth, and they
mutually embraced one another, and made a
long greeting, and that not without tears. They
also lamented their age, and that familiarity
which envy would deprive them of, and that
separation which must now be expected, which
seemed to them no better than death itself. So
recollecting themselves at length from their
lamentation, and exhorting one another to be
mindful of the oaths they had sworn to each
other, they parted asunder.

CHAPTER XII

HOW DAVID FLED TO AHIMELECH, AND AFTER-
WARDS TO THE KINGS OF THE PHILISTINES
AND OF THE MOABITES; AND HOW SAUL SLEW
AHIMELECH AND HIS FAMILY

1. BUT David fled from the king, and that
death he was in danger of by him, and came to
the city Nob, to Ahimelech the priest, who,
when he saw him coming all alone, and neither
friend nor a servant with him, he wondered at
it, and desired to learn of him the cause why
there was nobody with him. To which David
answered, That the king had commanded him
to do a certain thing that was to be kept secret,
to which, if he had a mind to know so much, he
had no occasion for any one to accompany him;
"however, I have ordered my servants to meet
me at such and such a place." So he desired
him to let him have somewhat to eat; and that
in case he would supply him, he would act the
part of a friend, and be assisting to the business
he was now about: and when he had obtained
what he desired, he also asked him whether he
had any weapons with him, either sword or
spear. Now there was at Nob a servant of Saul,
by birth a Syrian, whose name was Doeg, one
that kept the king's mules. The high priest
said that he had no such weapons; but he added,
"Here is the sword of Goliath, which, when
thou hadst slain the Philistine, thou didst
dedicate to God."

2. When David had received the sword, he
fled out of the country of the Hebrews into that
of the Philistines, over which Achish reigned;
and when the king's servants knew him, and he
was made known to the king himself, the servants informing him that he was that David who
had killed many ten thousands of the Philistines, David was afraid lest the king should put
him to death, and that he should experience
that danger from him which he had escaped
from Saul; so he pretended to be distracted and
mad, so that his spittle ran out of his mouth;
and he did other the like actions before the king
of Gath, which might make him believe that
they proceeded from such a distemper. Accordingly the king was very angry at his servants
that they had brought him a madman, and he
gave orders that they should eject David immediately [out of the city.]

3. So when David had escaped in this manner
out of Gath, he came to the tribe of Judah, and
abode in a cave by the city of Adullam. Then
it was that he sent to his brethren, and informed
them where he was, who then came to him with
all their kindred, and as many others as were
either in want or in fear of king Saul, came and
made a body together, and told him they were
ready to obey his orders; they were in all about
four hundred. Whereupon he took courage,

now such a force and assistance was come to him; so he removed thence, and came to the king of the Moabites, and desired him to entertain his parents in his country while the issue of his affairs were in such an uncertain condition. The king granted him this favour, and paid great respect to David's parents all the time they were with him.

4. As for himself, upon the prophet's commanding him to leave the desert, and to go into the portion of the tribe of Judah, and abide there; he complied therewith; and coming to the city Hareth, which was in that tribe, he remained there. Now when Saul heard that David had been seen with a multitude about him, he fell into no small disturbance and trouble; but as he knew that David was a bold and courageous man, he suspected that somewhat extraordinary would appear from him, and that openly also, which would make him weep and put him into distress; so he called together to him his friends, and his commanders, and the tribe from which he was himself derived, to the hill where his palace was; and sitting upon a place called Aroura, his courtiers that were in dignities, and the guards of his body, being with him, he spake thus to them:—"You that are men of my own tribe, I conclude that you remember the benefits that I have bestowed upon you, and that I have made some of you owners of land, and made you commanders, and bestowed posts of honour upon you, and set some of you over the common people, and others over the soldiers; I ask you, therefore, Whether you expect greater and more donations from the son of Jesse? for I know that you are all inclinable to him, (even my own son Jonathan himself is of that opinion, and persuades you to be of the same;) for I am not unacquainted with the oaths and the covenants that are between him and David, and that Jonathan is a counsellor and an assistant to those that conspire against me, and none of you are concerned about these things, but you keep silence and watch, to see what will be the upshot of these things." When the king had made this speech, not one of the rest of those that were present made any answer; but Doeg the Syrian, who fed his mules, said, that he saw David when he came to the city Nob to Ahimelech the high priest, and that he learned future events by his prophesying; that he received food from him, and the sword of Goliath, and was conducted by him with security to such as he desired to go to.

5. Saul, therefore, sent for the high priest, and for all his kindred, and said to them, "What terrible or ungrateful thing hast thou suffered from me, that thou hast received the son of Jesse, and hast bestowed on him both food and weapons, when he was contriving to get the kingdom?—and further, Why didst thou deliver oracles to him concerning futurities? for thou couldst not be unacquainted that he was fled away from me, and that he hated my family." But the high priest did not betake himself to deny what he had done, but confessed boldly that he had supplied him with these things not to gratify David, but Saul himself: and he said, "I did not know that he was thy adversary, but a servant of thine, who was very faithful to thee, and a captain over a thousand of thy soldiers, and, what is more than these, thy son-in-law, and kinsman. Men do not choose to confer such favours on their adversaries, but on those who are esteemed to bear the highest good-will and respect to them. Nor is this the first time that I prophesied for him, but I have done it often, and at other times, as

well as now. And when he told me that he was sent by thee in great haste to do somewhat, if I had furnished him with nothing that he desired, I should have thought that it was rather in contradiction to thee than to him; wherefore do not thou entertain any ill opinion of me, nor do thou have a suspicion of what I then thought an act of humanity, from what is now told thee of David's attempts against thee, for I did then to him as to thy friend and son-in-law, and captain of a thousand, and not as to thine adversary."

6. When the high priest had spoken thus, he did not persuade Saul, his fear was so prevalent, that he could not give credit to an apology that was very just. So he commanded his armed men that stood about him to kill him, and all his kindred; but as they durst not touch the high priest, but were more afraid of disobeying God than the king, he ordered Doeg the Syrian to kill them. Accordingly, he took to his assistance such wicked men as were like himself, and slew Ahimelech and all his family, who were in all three hundred and eighty-five. Saul also sent to Nob,[*] the city of the priests, and slew all that were there, without sparing either women or children, or any other age, and burnt it; only there was one son of Ahimelech, whose name was Abiathar, who escaped. However, these things came to pass as God had foretold to Eli the high priest, when he said that his posterity should be destroyed, on account of the transgressions of his two sons.

7. [†] Now this king Saul, by perpetrating so barbarous a crime, and murdering the whole family of the high priestly dignity, by having no pity of the infants, nor reverence for the aged, and by overthrowing the city which God had chosen for the property, and for the support of the priests and prophets which were there, and had ordained as the only city allotted for the education of such men, gives all to understand and consider the disposition of men, that while they are private persons, and in a low condition, because it is not in their power to indulge nature, nor to venture upon what they wish for, they are equitable and moderate, and pursue nothing but what is just, and bend their whole minds and labours that way; then it is that they have this belief about God, that he is present to all the actions of their lives, and that he does not only see the actions that are done, but clearly knows those their thoughts also, whence those actions do arise; but when once they are advanced into power and authority, then they put off all such notions and, as if they were no other than actors upon a theatre, their disguised parts and manners, and take up boldness, insolence, and a contempt of both human and divine laws, and this at a time when they especially stand in need of piety and righteousness, because they are then most of all exposed to envy, and all they think and all they

---

* Nob was not a city allotted to the priests, nor had the prophets any particular cities allotted them. It seems the tabernacle was now at Nob, and probably a school of the prophets was here also. It was full two days' journey on foot from Jerusalem, (1 Sam. xxi. 5.) This city seems to have been the chief seat of the family of Ithamar, which here perished, according to God's former terrible threatenings to Eli, (1 Sam. ii. 27-36; iii. 11-18.)

† This section contains an admirable reflection of Josephus concerning the wickedness of men in great authority, and the danger they are in of rejecting that regard to justice and humanity, to Divine Providence and the fear of God, which they either really had, or pretended to have, while they were in a lower condition. It is to the like purport with one branch of Agur's prayer: "Give me not riches, lest I be full, and deny thee, and say, Who is the Lord?" (Prov. xxx. 8, 9)

say are in the view of all men; then it is that they become so insolent in their actions, as though God saw them no longer, or were afraid of them because of their power: and whatsoever it is that they either are afraid of by the rumours they hear, or they hate by inclination, or they love without reason, these seem to them to be authentic, and firm, and true, and pleasing both to men and to God; but as to what will come hereafter, they have not the least regard to it. They raise those to honour indeed who have been at a great deal of pains for them, and after that honour they envy them; and when they have brought them into high dignity, they do not only deprive them of what they had obtained, but also on that very account of their lives also, and that on wicked accusations, and such as on account of their extravagant nature are incredible. They also punish men for their actions, not such as deserve condemnation, but from calumnies and accusations without examination; and this extends not only to such as deserve to be punished, but to as many as they are able to kill. This reflection is openly confirmed to us from the example of Saul, the son of Kish, who was the first king who reigned after our aristocracy and government under the judges were over; and that by his slaughter of three hundred priests and prophets, on occasion of his suspicion about Ahimelech, and by the additional wickedness of the overthrow of their city, and this as if he were endeavouring in some sort to render the temple [tabernacle] destitute both of priests and prophets; which endeavour he shewed by slaying so many of them, and not suffering the very city belonging to them to remain, that so others might succeed them.

8. But Abiathar, the son of Ahimelech, who alone could be saved out of the family of priests slain by Saul, fled to David, and informed him of the calamity that had befallen their family, and of the slaughter of his father: who hereupon said, He was not unapprised of what would follow with relation to them when he saw Doeg there; for he had then a suspicion that the high priest would be falsely accused by him to the king; and he blamed himself as having been the cause of this misfortune. But he desired him to stay there, and abide with him, as in a place where he might be better concealed than anywhere else.

CHAPTER XIII

HOW DAVID, WHEN HE HAD TWICE THE OPPORTUNITY OF KILLING SAUL, DID NOT KILL HIM; ALSO, CONCERNING THE DEATH OF SAMUEL AND NABAL

1. ABOUT this time it was that David heard how the Philistines had made an inroad into the country of Keilah, and robbed it; so he offered himself to fight against them, if God, when he should be consulted by the prophet, would grant him the victory. And when the prophet said that God gave a signal of victory, he made a sudden onset upon the Philistines with his companions, and he shed a great deal of their blood, and carried off their prey, and stayed with the inhabitants of Keilah till they had securely gathered in their corn and their fruits. However, it was told Saul the king that David was with the men of Keilah; for what had been done, and the great success that had attended him, were not confined among the people where the things were done, but the fame of it went all abroad, and came to the hearing of others, and both the fact

as it stood and the author of the fact, were carried to the king's ears. Then was Saul glad when he heard David was in Keilah: and he said, "God hath now put him into my hands, since he hath obliged him to come into a city that hath walls, and gates, and bars;" so he commanded all the people suddenly, and when they had besieged and taken it to kill David. But when David perceived this, and learned of God that if he stayed there the men of Keilah would deliver him up to Saul, he took his four hundred men and retired into a desert that was over-against a city called Engedi. So that when the king heard that he was fled away from the men of Keilah, he left off his expedition against him.

2. Then David removed thence, and came to a certain place called the New Place, belonging to Ziph; where Jonathan, the son of Saul, came to him, and saluted him, and exhorted him to be of good courage, and to hope well as to his condition hereafter, and not to despond at his present circumstances, for that he should be king, and have all the forces of the Hebrews under him: he told him that such happiness uses to come with great labour and pains: they also took oaths that they would, all their lives long, continue in good-will and fidelity one to another; and he called God to witness as to what execrations he had made upon himself if he should transgress his covenant, and should change to a contrary behaviour. So Jonathan left him there, having rendered his cares and fears somewhat lighter, and returned home. Now the men of Ziph, to gratify Saul, informed him that David abode with them, and [assured him] that if he would come to them, they would deliver him up, for that if the king would seize on the straits of Ziph, David would not escape to any other people. So the king commended them, and confessed that he had reason to thank them, because they had given him information of his enemy; and he promised them, that it should not be long ere he would requite their kindness. He also sent men to seek for David, and to search the wilderness wherein he was; and he promised that he himself would follow them. Accordingly they went before the king, to hunt for and to catch David, and used endeavours not only to shew their good-will to Saul, by informing him where his enemy was, but to evidence the same more plainly by delivering him up into his power. But these men failed of those their unjust and wicked desires, who, while they underwent no hazard by not discovering such an ambition of revealing this to Saul, yet did they falsely accuse and promised to deliver up a man beloved by God, and one that was unjustly sought after to be put to death, and one that might otherwise have lain concealed, and this out of flattery, and expectation of gain from the king; for when David was apprised of the malignant intentions of the men of Ziph, and the approach of Saul, he left the Straits of that country and fled to the great rock that was in the wilderness of Maon.

3. Hereupon Saul made haste to pursue him thither; for, as he was marching, he learned that David was gone away from the Straits of Ziph, and Saul removed to the other side of the rock. But the report that the Philistines had again made an incursion into the country of the Hebrews, called Saul another way from the pursuit of David, when he was ready to be caught; for he returned back again to oppose those Philistines, who were naturally their enemies, as judging it more necessary to avenge himself of them than to take a great deal of pains to catch an enemy of his own, and to overlook the ravage that was made in the land.

4. And by this means David unexpectedly es-

caped out of the danger he was in, and came to the Straits of Engedi; and when Saul had driven the Philistines out of the land, there came some messengers, who told him that David abode within the bounds of Engedi; so he took three thousand chosen men that were armed, and made haste to him; and when he was not far from those places, he saw a deep and hollow cave by the wayside; it was open to a great length and breadth, and there it was that David with his four hundred men were concealed. When, therefore, he had occasion to ease nature, he entered into it by himself alone; and being seen by one of David's companions, and he that saw him saying to him that he had now, by God's providence, an opportunity of avenging himself of his adversary; and advising him to cut off his head, and so deliver himself out of that tedious wandering condition, and the distress he was in, he rose up and only cut off the skirt of that garment which Saul had on; but he soon repented of what he had done; and said it was not right to kill him that was his master, and one whom God had thought worthy of the kingdom: "for that although he were wickedly disposed towards us, yet does it not behove me to be so disposed towards him." But when Saul had left the cave, David came near and cried out aloud, and desired Saul to hear him; whereupon the king turned his face back, and David, according to custom, fell down on his face before the king, and bowed to him; and said, "O king, thou oughtest not to hearken to wicked men, nor to such as forge calumnies, nor to gratify them so far as to believe what they say, nor to entertain suspicions of such as are your best friends, but to judge of the dispositions of all men by their actions; for calumny deludes men, but men's own actions are a clear demonstration of their kindness. Words, indeed, in their own nature, may be either true or false, but men's actions expose their intentions nakedly to our view. By these, therefore, it will be well for thee to believe me, as to my regard to thee and to thy house, and not to believe those that frame such accusations against me as never came into my mind, nor are possible to be executed, and do this further by pursuing after my life, and have no concern either day or night, but how to compass my life and to murder me, which thing I think thou dost unjustly prosecute; for how comes it about that thou hast embraced this false opinion about me, as if I had a desire to kill thee?—or how canst thou escape the crime of impiety towards God, when thou wishest thou couldst kill, and deemest thine adversary a man who had it in his power this day to avenge himself, and to punish thee, but would not do it?— nor make use of such an opportunity, which, if it had fallen out to thee against me, thou hadst not let it slip, for when I cut off the skirt of thy garment, I could have done the same to thy head." So he shewed him the piece of his garment, and thereby made him agree to what he had said to be true; and added, "I, for certain, have abstained from taking a just revenge upon thee, yet art thou not ashamed to prosecute me with unjust hatred.* May God do justice and determine about each of our dispositions!"—But Saul was amazed at the strange delivery he had received; and, being greatly affected with the moderation and the disposition of the young man, he groaned; and when David had done the same, the king an-

swered that he had the justest occasion to groan, "for thou hast been the author of good to me, as I have been the author of calamity to thee; and thou hast demonstrated this day, that thou possessest the righteousness of the ancients, who determined that men ought to save their enemies, though they caught them in a desert place. I am now persuaded that God reserves the kingdom for thee, and that thou wilt obtain the dominion over all the Hebrews. Give me then assurances upon oath, That thou wilt not root out my family, nor, out of remembrance of what evil I have done thee, destroy my posterity, but save and preserve my house." So David sware as he desired, and sent back Saul to his own kingdom; but he, and those that were with him, went up the Straits of Mastheroth.

5. About this time Samuel the prophet died. He was a man whom the Hebrews honoured in an extraordinary degree; for that lamentation which the people made for him, and this during a long time, manifested his virtue, and the affection which the people bore for him; as also did the solemnity and concern that appeared about his funeral, and about the complete observation of all his funeral rites. They buried him in his own city of Ramah; and wept for him a very great number of days, not looking on it as a sorrow for the death of another man, but as that in which they were every one themselves concerned. He was a righteous man, and gentle in his nature; and on that account he was very dear to God. Now he governed and presided over the people alone, after the death of Eli the high priest, twelve years, and eighteen years together with Saul the king. And thus we have finished the history of Samuel.

6. There was a man that was a Ziphite, of the city of Maon, who was rich, and had a vast number of cattle; for he fed a flock of three thousand sheep, and another flock of a thousand goats. Now David had charged his associates to keep these flocks without hurt and without damage, and to do them no mischief, neither out of covetousness, nor because they were in want, nor because they were in the wilderness, and so could not easily be discovered, but to esteem freedom from injustice above all other motives, and to look upon the touching of what belonged to another man as a horrible crime, and contrary to the will of God. These were the instructions he gave, thinking that the favours he granted this man were granted to a good man, and one that deserved to have such care taken of his affairs. This man was Nabal, for that was his name—a harsh man, and of a very wicked life; being like a cynic in the course of his behaviour, but still had obtained for his wife a woman of a good character, wise and handsome. To this Nabal, therefore, David sent ten men of his attendants at the time when he sheared his sheep, and by them saluted him; and also wished he might do what he now did for many years to come, but desired him to make him a present of what he was able to give him, since he had, to be sure, learned from his shepherds that we had done them no injury, but had been their guardians a long time together, while we continued in the wilderness; and he assured him he should never repent of giving anything to David. When the messengers had carried this message to Nabal, he accosted them after an inhuman and rough manner; for he asked them who David was? and when he heard that he was the son of Jesse, he said, "Now is the time that fugitives grow insolent, and make a figure, and leave their masters." When they told David this, he was wroth, and commanded four hundred armed men

---

to follow him, and left two hundred to take care of the stuff, (for he had already six hundred,) and went against Nabal : he also swore that he would that night utterly destroy the whole house and possessions of Nabal ; for that he was grieved, not only that he had proved ungrateful to them, without making any return for the humanity they had shewn him, but that he had also reproached them, and used ill language to them, when he had received no cause of disgust from them.

7. Hereupon one of those that kept the flocks of Nabal, said to his mistress, Nabal's wife, that when David sent to her husband he had received no civil answer at all from him ; but that her husband had moreover added very reproachful language, while yet David had taken extraordinary care to keep his flocks from harm, and that what had passed would prove very pernicious to his master.   When the servant had said this, Abigail, for that was his wife's name, saddled her asses, and loaded them with all sorts of presents ; and, without telling her husband anything of what she was about (for he was not sensible on account of his drunkenness) she went to David.   She was then met by David as she was descending a hill, who was coming against Nabal with four hundred men.   When the woman saw David, she leaped down from her ass, and fell on her face, and bowed down to the ground ; and entreated him not to bear in mind the words of Nabal, since he knew that he resembled his name.   Now Nabal, in the Hebrew tongue, signifies *folly.*   So she made her apology, that she did not see the messengers whom he sent.   "Forgive me, therefore," said she, "and thank God, who hath hindered thee from shedding human blood ; for so long as thou keepest thyself innocent, he will avenge thee of wicked men,* for what miseries await Nabal, they will fall upon the heads of thine enemies.   Be thou gracious to me, and think me so far worthy as to accept of these presents from me ; and, out of regard to me, remit that wrath and that anger which thou hast against my husband and his house, for mildness and humanity become thee, especially as thou art to be our king."   Accordingly David accepted her presents, and said, "Nay, but, O woman, it was no other than God's mercy which brought thee to us to-day ; for, otherwise, thou hadst never seen another day, I having sworn to destroy Nabal's house this very night,† and to leave alive not one of you who belonged to a man that was wicked and ungrateful to me and my companions ; but now hast thou prevented me, and seasonably mollified my anger, as being thyself under the care of God's providence : but as for Nabal, although for thy sake he now escape punishment, he will not always avoid justice ; for his evil conduct, on some other occasion, will be his ruin."

8. When David had said this, he dismissed the woman.   But when she came home and found her husband feasting with a great company, and oppressed with wine, she said nothing to him then about what had happened ; but on the next day, when he was sober, she told him all the particulars, and made his whole body to appear like that of a dead man by her words, and by that grief which arose from them ; so Nabal survived ten days, and no more, and then died. And when David heard of his death, he said that God had justly avenged him of this man, for that Nabal had died by his own wickedness, and had suffered punishment on his account, while he had kept his own hands clean.   At which time he understood that the wicked are prosecuted by God ; that he does not overlook any man, but bestows on the good what is suitable to them, and inflicts a deserved punishment on the wicked.   So he sent to Nabal's wife, and invited her to come to him, to live with him, and to be his wife.   Whereupon she replied to those that came, that she was not worthy to touch his feet ; however, she came, with all her servants, and became his wife, having received that honour on account of her wise and righteous course of life.   She also obtained the same honour partly on account of her beauty.   Now David had a wife before, whom he married from the city Abesar ; for as to Michal, the daughter of king Saul, who had been David's wife, her father had given her in marriage to Phalti, the son of Laish, who was of the city of Gallim.

9. After this came certain of the Ziphites, and told Saul that David was come again into their country, and, if he would afford them his assistance, they could catch him.   So he came to them with three thousand armed men ; and upon the approach of night, he pitched his camp at a certain place called Hachilah.   But when David heard that Saul was coming against him, he sent spies, and bid them let him know to what place of the country Saul was already come ; and when they told him that he was at Hachilah, he concealed his going away from his companions, and came to Saul's camp, having taken with him Abishai, his sister Zeruiah's son, and Ahimelech the Hittite.   Now Saul was asleep, and the armed men, with Abner their commander, lay round about him in a circle. Hereupon David entered the king's tent ; but he did neither kill Saul, though he knew where he lay, by the spear that was stuck down by him, nor did he give leave to Abishai, who would have killed him, and was earnestly bent upon it so to do ; for he said it was a horrid crime to kill one that was ordained king by God, although he was a wicked man ; for that he who gave him the dominion would in time inflict punishment upon him.   So he restrained his eagerness ; but that it might appear to have been in his power to have killed him when he refrained from it, he took his spear, and the cruse of water which stood by Saul as he lay asleep, without being perceived by any in the camp, who were all asleep, and went securely away, having performed everything among the king's attendants that the opportunity afforded, and his boldness encouraged him to do.   So when he had passed over a brook, and was gotten up to the top of a hill, whence he might be sufficiently heard, he cried aloud to Saul's soldiers, and to Abner their commander, and awaked them out of their sleep, and called both to him and to the people. Hereupon the commander heard him, and asked who it was that called him.   To whom David replied,—"It is I, the son of Jesse, whom you make a vagabond.   But what is the matter? Dost thou, that art a man of so great dignity, and of the first rank in the king's court, take so

---

* In this and the two next sections, we may perceive how Abigail would understand the "not avenging ourselves, but heaping up coals of fire on the head of the injurious," (Prov. xxv. 22 ; Rom. xii. 20 ;) not as we commonly do now, of melting them into kindness, but of leaving them to the judgment of God, "to whom vengeance belongeth," (Deut. xxxii. 35 ; Ps. xciv. 1 ; Heb. x. 30,) and who will take vengeance on the wicked.

† How sacred soever an oath was esteemed among the people of God in old times, they did not think it obligatory where the action was plainly unlawful.   It was so in this case of David, who, although he had sworn to destroy Nabal and his family, yet does he bless God for preventing his keeping his oath, and from shedding blood, as he had sworn to do.

little care of thy master's body? and is sleep of more consequence to thee than his preservation and thy care of him? This negligence of yours deserves death, and punishment to be inflicted on you, who never perceived when, a little while ago, some of us entered into your camp, nay, as far as to the king himself, and to all the rest of you. If thou look for the king's spear and his cruse of water, thou wilt learn what a mighty misfortune was ready to overtake you in your very camp without your knowing it." Now when Saul knew David's voice, and understood that when he had him in his power while he was asleep, and his guards took no care of him, yet did not he kill him, but spared him, when he might have cut him off, he said that he owed him thanks for his preservation; and exhorted him to be of good courage, and not be afraid of suffering any mischief from him any more, and to return to his own home, for he was now persuaded that he did not love himself so well as he was loved by him: that he had driven away him that could guard him, and had given many demonstrations of his good-will to him: that he had forced him to live so long in a state of banishment, and in great fears of his life, destitute of his friends and his kindred, while still he was often saved by him, and frequently received his life again when it was evidently in danger of perishing. So David bade them send for the spear and the cruse of water, and take them back; adding this withal, That God would be the judge of both their dispositions, and of the actions that flowed from the same, "who knows that when it was this day in my power to have killed thee, I abstained from it."

10. Thus Saul having escaped the hands of David twice, he went his way to his royal palace, and his own city: but David was afraid, that if he stayed there he should be caught by Saul; so he thought it better to go up into the land of the Philistines and abide there. Accordingly, he came with the six hundred men that were with him to Achish, the king of Gath, which was one of their five cities. Now the king received both him and his men, and gave them a place to inhabit in. He had with him also his two wives, Ahinoam and Abigail; and he dwelt in Gath. But when Saul heard this, he took no further care about sending to him, or going after him, because he had been twice in a manner caught by him, while he was himself endeavouring to catch him. However, David had no mind to continue in the city of Gath, but desired the king, that since he had received him with such humanity, that he would grant him another favour, and bestow upon him some place of that country for his habitation, for he was ashamed, by living in the city, to be grievous and burdensome to him. So Achish gave him a certain village called Ziklag; which place David and his sons were fond of when he was king, and reckoned it to be their peculiar inheritance. But about those matters we shall give the reader further information elsewhere. Now the time that David dwelt in Ziklag, in the land of the Philistines, was four months and twenty days. And now he privately attacked those Geshurites and Amalekites that were neighbours to the Philistines, and laid waste their country, and took much prey of their beasts and camels, and then returned home; but David abstained from the men, as fearing they should discover him to king Achish; yet did he send part of the prey to him as a free gift. And when the king inquired whom they had attacked when they brought away the prey, he said, those that lay to the south of the Jews, and inhabited

in the plain; whereby he persuaded Achish to approve of what he had done, for he hoped that David had fought against his own nation, and that now he should have him for his servant all his life long, and that he would stay in his country.

CHAPTER XIV

HOW SAUL, UPON GOD'S NOT ANSWERING HIM CONCERNING THE FIGHT WITH THE PHILISTINES, DESIRED A NECROMANTIC WOMAN TO RAISE UP THE SOUL OF SAMUEL TO HIM; AND HOW HE DIED, WITH HIS SONS, UPON THE OVERTHROW OF THE HEBREWS IN BATTLE

1. ABOUT the same time the Philistines resolved to make war against the Israelites, and sent to all their confederates that they would go along with them to the war to Reggan, [near the city Shunem,] whence they might gather themselves together and suddenly attack the Hebrews. Then did Achish, the king of Gath, desire David to assist them with his armed men against the Hebrews. This he readily promised; and said that the time was now come wherein he might requite him for his kindness and hospitality; so the king promised to make him the keeper of his body after the victory, supposing that the battle with the enemy succeeded to their mind; which promise of honour and confidence he made on purpose to increase his zeal for his service.

2. Now Saul, the king of the Hebrews, had cast out of the country the fortune-tellers, and the necromancers, and all such as exercised the like arts, excepting the prophets; but when he heard that the Philistines were already come, and had pitched their camp near the city Shunem, situate in the plain, he made haste to oppose them with his forces; and when he was come to a certain mountain called Gilboa, he pitched his camp over against the enemy; but when he saw the enemy's army he was greatly troubled, because it appeared to him to be numerous, and superior to his own; and he inquired of God by the prophets concerning the battle, that he might know beforehand what would be the event of it; and when God did not answer him, Saul was under a still greater dread, and his courage fell, foreseeing, as was but reasonable to suppose, that mischief would befall him, now God was not there to assist him; yet did he bid his servants to inquire out for him some woman that was a necromancer, and called up the souls of the dead, that so he might know whether his affairs would succeed to his mind; for this sort of necromantic women that bring up the souls of the dead, do by them foretell future events to such as desire them. And one of his servants told him that there was such a woman in the city Endor, but was known to nobody in the camp; hereupon Saul put off his royal apparel, and took two of those his servants with him, whom he knew to be most faithful to him, and came to Endor to the woman, and entreated her to act the part of a fortune-teller, and to bring up such a soul to him as he should name to her. But when the woman opposed his motion, and said, She did not despise the king who had banished this sort of fortune-tellers, and that he did not do well himself, when she had done him no harm, to endeavour to lay a snare for her, and to discover that she exercised a forbidden art, in order to procure her to be punished,—he sware that nobody should know what she did; and that he would not tell any

one else what she foretold, but that she should incur no danger. As soon as he had induced her by this oath to fear no harm, he bade her bring up to him the soul of Samuel. She not knowing who Samuel was, called him out of Hades. When he appeared, and the woman saw one that was venerable, and of a divine form, she was in disorder, and, being astonished at the sight, she said,—"Art not thou king Saul?" for Samuel had informed her who he was. When he had owned that to be true, and had asked her whence her disorder arose, she said, that she saw a certain person ascend, who in his form was like to a god. And when he bid her tell him what he resembled, in what habit he appeared, and of what age he was, she told him he was an old man already, and of a glorious personage, and had on a sacerdotal mantle. So the king discovered by these signs that he was Samuel; and he fell down upon the ground and saluted and worshipped him. And when the soul of Samuel asked him why he had disturbed him, and caused him to be brought up, he lamented the necessity he was under; for he said, that his enemies pressed heavily upon him; that he was in distress what to do in his present circumstances; that he was forsaken of God, and could obtain no prediction of what was coming, neither by prophets nor by dreams: and that "these were the reasons why I have recourse to thee, who always tookest care of me." But * Samuel, seeing that the end of Saul's life was come, said,—"It is in vain for thee to desire to learn of me anything further, when God has forsaken thee: however, hear what I say, that David is to be king, and to finish this war with good success: and thou art to lose thy dominion and thy life, because thou didst not obey God in the war with the Amalekites, and hast not kept his commandments, as I foretold thee while I was alive. Know, therefore, that the people shall be made subject to their enemies, and that thou, with thy sons, shall fall in the battle to-morrow, and thou shalt then be with me [in Hades.]"

3. When Saul heard this, he could not speak for grief, and fell down on the floor, whether it were from the sorrow that arose upon what Samuel had said, or from his emptiness, for he had taken no food the foregoing day nor night, he easily fell quite down: and when with difficulty he had recovered himself, the woman would force him to eat, begging this of him as a favour on account of her concern in that dangerous instance of fortune-telling, which it was not lawful for her to have done, because of the fear she was under of the king, while she knew not who he was, yet did she undertake it, and go through with it; on which account she entreated him to admit that a table and food might be set before him, that he might recover his strength, and so get safe to his own camp. And when he opposed her motion, and entirely rejected it, by reason of his anxiety, she forced him, and at last persuaded him to it. Now she had one calf that she was very fond of, and one that she took a great deal of care of, and fed it herself, for she was a woman that got her living by the labour of her own hands, and had no other possession

but that one calf; this she killed, and made ready its flesh, and set it before his servants and himself. So Saul came to the camp while it was yet night.

4. Now it is but just to recommend the generosity of this woman,† because when the king had forbidden her to use that art whence her circumstances were bettered and improved, and when she had never seen the king before, she still did not remember to his disadvantage that he had condemned her sort of learning, and did not refuse him as a stranger, and one that she had had no acquaintance with; but she had compassion upon him, and comforted him, and exhorted him to do what he was greatly averse to, and offered him the only creature she had, as a poor woman, and that earnestly, and with great humanity, while she had no requital made her for her kindness, nor hunted after any future favour from him, for she knew he was to die; whereas men are naturally either ambitious to please those that bestow benefits upon them, or are very ready to serve those from whom they may receive some advantage. It would be well therefore to imitate the example of this woman, and to do kindnesses to all such as are in want; and to think that nothing is better, nor more becoming mankind, than such a general beneficence, nor what sooner will render God favourable, and ready to bestow good things upon us. And so far may suffice to have spoken concerning this woman. But I shall speak further upon another subject, which will afford me an opportunity of discoursing on what is for the advantage of cities, and people, and nations, and suited to the taste of good men, and will encourage them all in the prosecution of virtue, and is capable of shewing them the method of acquiring glory, and an everlasting fame; and of imprinting in the kings of nations, and the rulers of cities, great inclination and diligence of doing well; as also of encouraging them to undergo dangers, and to die for their countries, and of instructing them how to despise all the most terrible adversities; and I have a fair occasion offered me to enter on such a discourse by Saul king of the Hebrews; for although he knew what was coming upon him, and that he was to die immediately by the prediction of the prophet, he did not resolve to fly from death, nor so far to indulge the love of life as to betray his own people to the enemy, or to bring a disgrace on his royal dignity; but, exposing himself, as well as all his family and children to dangers, he thought it a brave thing to fall together with them, as he was fighting for his subjects, and that it was better his sons should die thus, shewing their courage, than to leave them to their uncertain conduct afterward, while, instead of succession and posterity, they gained commendation and a lasting name. Such a one alone seems to me to be a just, a courageous, and a prudent man; and when any one has arrived at these dispositions, or shall hereafter arrive at them, he is the man that ought to be by all honoured with the testimony of a virtuous or courageous man; for as to those who go out to war with hopes of success, and that they shall return safe, supposing they should have performed some glorious action, I think those do not do well who call those valiant men, as so many historians, and other writers who treat of them are wont to do, although I confess those do justly deserve some

---

* This history of Saul's consultation with a necromancer is easily understood, especially if we consult Ecclus. xlvi. 20. "Samuel prophesied after his death, and shewed the king his end, and lift up his voice from the earth in prophecy," to blot out "the wickedness of the people." Nor does the exactness of the accomplishment of this prediction, the very next day, permit us to suppose any imposition upon Saul in the present history.

† These commendations of this woman of Endor, and of Saul's courage, when yet he knew he should die in the battle, are somewhat unusual digressions in Josephus. They seem extracted from some declamations composed formerly, in the way of oratory, that lay by him, and which he thought fit to insert upon this occasion.

commendation also; but those only may be styled courageous and bold in great undertakings, and despisers of adversities, who imitate Saul; for as for those that do not know what the event of war will be as to themselves, and though they do not faint in it, but deliver themselves up to uncertain futurity, and are tossed this way and that way, this is not so very eminent an instance of a generous mind, although they happen to perform many great exploits: but when men's minds expect no good event, but they know beforehand they must die, and that they must undergo that death in the battle also, after this, neither to be affrighted nor to be astonished at the terrible fate that is coming, but to go directly upon it when they know it beforehand,—this it is that I esteem the character of a man truly courageous. Accordingly this Saul did, and thereby demonstrated, that all men who desire fame after they are dead, are so to act as they may obtain the same: this especially concerns kings, who ought not to think it enough in their high stations that they are not wicked in the government of their subjects, but to be no more than moderately good to them. I could say more than this about Saul and his courage, the subject affording matter sufficient; but that I may not appear to run out improperly in his commendation, I return again to that history from which I made this digression.

5. Now when the Philistines, as I said before, had pitched their camp, and had taken an account of their forces, according to their nations, and kingdoms, and governments, king Achish came last of all with his own army; after whom came David with his six hundred armed men. And when the commanders of the Philistines saw him, they asked the king whence these Hebrews came, and at whose invitation. He answered, That it was David, who who was fled away from his master Saul, and that he had entertained him when he came to him, and that now he was willing to make him this requital for his favours, and to avenge himself upon Saul, and so was become his confederate. The commanders complained of this, that he had taken him for a confederate who was an enemy; and gave him counsel to send him away, lest he should unawares do his friends a great deal of mischief, by entertaining him, for that he afforded him an opportunity of being reconciled to his master, by doing a mischief to our army. They thereupon desired him, out of a prudent foresight of this, to send him away with his six hundred armed men, to the place he had given him for his habitation; for that this was that David whom the virgins celebrated in their hymns, as having destroyed many ten thousands of the Philistines. When the king of Gath heard this, he thought they spake well; so he called David, and said to him, "As for myself, I can bear witness that thou hast shewn great diligence and kindness about me, and on that account it was that I took thee for my confederate; however, what I have done does not please the commanders of the Philistines, go therefore within a day's time to the place I have given thee, without suspecting any harm, and there keep my country, lest any of our enemies should make an incursion upon it, which will be one part of that assistance which I expect from thee." So David came to Ziklag, as the king of Gath bade him; but it happened, that while he was gone to the assistance of the Philistines, the Amalekites had made an incursion, and taken Ziklag before, and had burnt it; and when they had taken a great deal of other prey out of that place, and out of the other parts of the Philistines' country, they departed.

6. Now when David found that Ziklag was laid waste, and that it was all spoiled, and that as well as his own wives, who were two, as the wives of his companions, with their children, were made captives, he presently rent his clothes, weeping and lamenting, together with his friends; and indeed he was so cast down with these misfortunes, that at length tears themselves failed him. He was also in danger of being stoned to death by his companions, who were greatly afflicted at the captivity of their wives and children, for they laid the blame upon him of what had happened; but when he had recovered himself out of his grief, and had raised up his mind to God, he desired the high priest Abiathar to put on his sacerdotal garments, and to inquire of God, and to prophecy to him, Whether God would grant, that if he pursued after the Amalekites, he should overtake them, and save their wives and their children, and avenge himself on the enemies?—and when the high priest bade him to pursue after them, he marched apace, with his four hundred men, after the enemy; and when he was come to a certain brook called Besor, and had lighted upon one that was wandering about, an Egyptian by birth, who was almost dead with want and famine, (for he had continued wandering about without food in the wilderness three days,) he first of all gave him sustenance, both meat and drink, and thereby refreshed him. He then asked him to whom he belonged, and whence he came. Whereupon the man told him he was an Egyptian by birth, and was left behind by his master, because he was so sick and weak that he could not follow him. He also informed him that he was one of those who had burnt and plundered, not only other parts of Judea, but Ziklag itself also. So David made use of him as a guide to find out the Amalekites; and when he had overtaken them, as they lay scattered about on the ground, some at dinner, some disordered, and entirely drunk with wine, and in the fruition of their spoils and their prey, he fell upon them on the sudden, and made a great slaughter among them, for they were naked, and expected no such thing, but had betaken themselves to drinking and feasting, and so they were all easily destroyed. Now some of them that were overtaken as they lay at the table, were slain in that posture; and their blood brought up with it their meat and drink. They slew others of them as they were drinking to one another in their cups; and some of them when their full bellies had made them fall asleep; and for so many as had time to put on their armour, they slew them with the sword, with no less ease than they did those that were naked; and for the partisans of David, they continued also the slaughter from the first hour of the day to the evening, so that there were not above four hundred of the Amalekites left; and they only escaped by getting upon their dromedaries and camels. Accordingly David recovered not only all the other spoils which the enemy had carried away, but his wives also, and the wives of his companions; but when they were come to the place where they had left the two hundred men, which were not able to follow them, but were left to take care of the stuff, the four hundred men did not think fit to divide among them any other parts of what they had gotten, or of the prey, since they did not accompany them, but pretended to be feeble, and did not follow them in the pursuit of the enemy, but said they should be contented to have safely recovered their wives; yet did David pronounce that this opinion of theirs was evil and unjust, and that when God had granted them such a favour, that they had

avenged themselves on their enemies, and had recovered all that belonged to themselves, they should make an equal distribution of what they had gotten to all, because the rest had tarried behind to guard their stuff; and from that time this law obtained among them, that those who guarded the stuff should receive an equal share with those that had fought in the battle. Now when David was come to Ziklag, he sent portions of the spoils to all that had been familiar with him, and to his friends in the tribe of Judah; and thus ended the affairs of the plundering of Ziklag, and of the slaughter of the Amalekites.

7. Now upon the Philistines joining battle, there followed a sharp engagement, and the Philistines became the conquerors, and slew a great number of their enemies; but Saul the king of Israel, and his sons, fought courageously, and with the utmost alacrity, as knowing that their entire glory lay in nothing else but dying honourably, and exposing themselves to the utmost danger from the enemy, (for they had nothing else to hope for;) so they brought upon themselves the whole power of the enemy, till they were encompassed round and slain, but not before they had killed many of the Philistines. Now the sons of Saul were Jonathan, Abinadab, and Malchisua; and when these were slain, the multitude of the Hebrews were put to flight, and all was disorder and confusion, and slaughter, upon the Philistines pressing in upon them. But Saul himself fled, having a strong body of soldiers about him; and upon the Philistines sending after him those that threw javelins and shot arrows, he lost all his company except a few. As for himself, he fought with great bravery; and when he had received so many wounds that he was not able to bear up, nor to oppose any longer, and yet was not able to kill himself, he bid his armour-bearer to draw his sword and run him through, before the enemy should take him alive. But his armour-bearer not daring to kill his master, he drew his own sword, and placing himself over-against its point, he threw himself upon it; and when he could neither run it through him, nor, by leaning against it, make the sword pass through him, he turned him round, and asked a certain young man that stood by, who he was; and when he understood that he was an Amalekite, he desired him to force the sword through him, because he was not able to do it with his own hands, and thereby to procure him such a death as he desired. This the young man did accordingly; and he took the golden bracelet that was on Saul's arm, and his royal crown that was on his head, and ran away. And when Saul's armour-bearer saw that he was slain,

he killed himself; nor did any of the king's guards escape, but they all fell upon the mountain called Gilboa. But when those Hebrews that dwelt in the valley beyond Jordan, and those who had their cities in the plain, heard that Saul and his sons were fallen, and that the multitude about them were destroyed, they left their own cities, and fled to such as were the best fortified and fenced; and the Philistines finding those cities deserted, came and dwelt in them.

8. On the next day, when the Philistines came to strip their enemies that were slain, they got the bodies of Saul and of his sons and stripped them, and cut off their heads. And they sent messengers all about their country to acquaint them that their enemies were fallen; and they dedicated their armour in the temple of Astarte, but hung their bodies on crosses at the walls of the city Bethshan, which is now called Scythopolis. But when the inhabitants of Jabesh-Gilead heard that they had dismembered the dead bodies of Saul and of his sons, they deemed it so horrid a thing to overlook this barbarity, and to suffer them to be without funeral rites, that the most courageous and hardy among them (and indeed that city had in it men that were very stout both in body and mind) journeyed all night, and came to Bethshan, and approached to the enemy's wall, and taking down the bodies of Saul and of his sons, they carried them to Jabesh, while the enemy were not able enough, nor bold enough, to hinder them, because of their great courage; so the people of Jabesh wept all in general, and buried their bodies in the best place of their country, which was called Aroura; and they observed a public mourning for them seven days, with their wives and children, beating their breasts, and lamenting the king and his sons, without tasting either meat or drink* [till the evening.]

9. To this his sad end did Saul come, according to the prophecy of Samuel, because he disobeyed the commands of God about the Amalekites, and on the account of his destroying the family of Ahimelech, the high priest, with Ahimelech himself, and the city of the high priests. Now Saul, when he had reigned eighteen years while Samuel was alive, and after his death two [and twenty,] ended his life in this manner.

---

* This way of speaking in Josephus is almost like that of St Paul, (Acts xxvii. 33;) and as the nature of the thing, and the impossibility of strictly fasting so long, require us here to understand Josephus of only fasting till the evening; so must we understand St Paul, that they kept all those days entirely as fasts till the evening, but not longer.

BOOK VII

FROM THE DEATH OF SAUL TO THE DEATH OF DAVID

CHAPTER I

HOW DAVID REIGNED OVER ONE TRIBE AT HEBRON, WHILE THE SON OF SAUL REIGNED OVER THE REST OF THE MULTITUDE; AND HOW, IN THE CIVIL WAR WHICH THEN AROSE, ASAHEL AND ABNER WERE SLAIN

1. THIS fight proved to be on the same day whereon David was come back to Ziklag, after he had overcome the Amalekites. Now when he had been already two days at Ziklag, there came to him the man who slew Saul, which was the third day after the fight. He had escaped out of the battle which the Israelites had with the Philistines, and had his clothes rent, and ashes upon his head. And when he had made his obeisance to David, he inquired of him whence he came. He replied, from the battle of the Israelites: and he informed him that the end of it was unfortunate, many ten thousands of the Israelites having been cut off, and Saul, together with his sons, slain. He also said that he could well give him this information, because he was present at the victory gained over the Hebrews, and was with the king when he fled. Nor did he deny that he had himself slain the king, when he was ready to be taken by the enemy, and he himself exhorted him to do it, because, when he was fallen on his sword, his great wounds had made him so weak that he was not able to kill himself. He also produced demonstrations that the king was slain, which were the golden bracelets that had been on the king's arms, and his crown, which he had taken away from Saul's dead body, and had brought them to him. So David having no longer room to call in question the truth of what he said, but seeing most evident marks that Saul was dead, he rent his garments, and continued all that day, with his companions, in weeping and lamentation. This grief was augmented by the consideration of Jonathan, the son of Saul, who had been his most faithful friend, and the occasion of his own deliverance. He also demonstrated himself to have such great virtue, and such great kindness for Saul, as not only to take his death to heart, though he had been frequently in danger of losing his life by his means, but to punish him that slew him: for when David had said to him, that he was become his own accuser, as the very man who had slain the king, and when he understood that he was the son of an Amalekite, he commanded him to be slain. He also committed to writing some lamentations and funeral commendations of Saul and Jonathan, which have continued to my own age.

2. Now when David had paid these honours to the king, he left off his mourning, and inquired of God, by the prophet, which of the cities of the tribe of Judah he would bestow upon him to dwell in; who answered that he bestowed upon him Hebron. So he left Ziklag and came to Hebron, and took with him his wives, who were in number two, and his armed men: whereupon all the people of the forementioned tribe came to him, and ordained him their king. But when he heard that the inhabitants of Jabesh-Gilead had buried Saul and his sons [honourably,] he sent to them and commended them, and took what they had done kindly, and promised to make them amends for their care of those that were dead; and at the same time he informed them that the tribe of Judah had chosen him for their king.

3. But as soon as Abner, the son of Ner, who was general of Saul's army, and a very active man, and good-natured, knew that the king and Jonathan, and his two other sons, were fallen in the battle, he made haste into the camp; and, taking away with him the remaining son of Saul, whose name was Ishbosheth, he passed over to the land beyond Jordan, and ordained him the king of the whole multitude, excepting the tribe of Judah; and made his royal seat in a place called in our language *Mahanaim*, but in the language of the Grecians, *The Camps;* from whence Abner made haste with a select body of soldiers, to fight with such of the tribe of Judah as were disposed to it, for he was angry that this tribe had set up David for their king; but Joab, whose father was Suri, and his mother Zeruiah, David's sister, who was general of David's army, met him, according to David's appointment. He had with him his brethren, Abishai and Asahel, as also all David's armed men. Now when he met Abner at a certain fountain, in the city of Gibeon, he prepared to fight; and when Abner said to him that he had a mind to know which of them had the more valiant soldiers, it was agreed between them that twelve soldiers of each side should fight together. So those that were chosen out by both the generals for this fight, came between the two armies, and throwing their lances one against the other, they drew their swords, and catching one another by the head, they held one another fast, and ran each other's swords into their sides and groins, until they all, as it were by mutual agreement, perished together. When these were fallen down dead, the rest of the army came to a sore battle, and Abner's men were beaten; and when they were beaten, Joab did not leave off pursuing them, but he pressed upon them, and excited the soldiers to follow them close, and not to grow weary of killing them. His brethren also pursued them with great alacrity, especially the younger Asahel, who was the most eminent of them. He was very famous for his swiftness of foot, for he could not only be too hard for men, but is reported to have out-run a horse, when they had a race together. This Asahel ran violently after Abner, and would not turn in the least out of the straight way, either to the one side or to the other. Hereupon Abner turned back, and attempted artfully to avoid his violence. Sometimes he bade him leave off the pursuit, and take the armour of one of his soldiers; and sometimes, when he could not persuade him so

to do, he exhorted him to restrain himself, and not to pursue him any longer, lest he should force him to kill him, and he should then not be able to look his brother in the face; but when Asahel would not admit of any persuasions, but still continued to pursue him, Abner smote him with his spear, as he held it in his flight, and that by a back-stroke, and gave him a deadly wound, so that he died immediately; but those that were with him pursuing Abner, when they came to the place where Asahel lay, they stood round about the dead body, and left off the pursuit of the enemy. However, both Joab * himself, and his brother Abishai, ran past the dead corpse, and making their anger at the death of Asahel an occasion of greater zeal against Abner, they went on with incredible haste and alacrity, and pursued Abner to a certain place called Ammah: it was about sunset. Then did Joab ascend a certain hill, as he stood at that place, having the tribe of Benjamin with him, whence he took a view of them, and of Abner also. Hereupon Abner cried aloud, and said that it was not fit that they should irritate men of the same nation to fight so bitterly one against another; that as for Asahel his brother, he was himself in the wrong, when he would not be advised by him not to pursue him any further, which was the occasion of his wounding and death. So Joab consented to what he said, and accepted these words as an excuse, [about Asahel,] and called the soldiers back with the sound of the trumpet, as a signal for their retreat, and thereby put a stop to any further pursuit. After which Joab pitched his camp there that night; but Abner marched all that night, and passed over the river Jordan, and came to Ishbosheth, Saul's son, to Mahanaim. On the next day, Joab counted the dead men, and took care of all their funerals. Now there were slain of Abner's soldiers about three hundred and sixty; but those of David nineteen, and Asahel, whose body Joab and Abishai carried to Bethlehem; and when they had buried him in the sepulchre of their fathers, they came to David to Hebron. From this time, therefore, they began an intestine war, which lasted a great while, in which the followers of David grew stronger in the dangers they underwent; and the servants and subjects of Saul's sons did almost every day become weaker.

4. About this time David was become the father of six sons, born of as many mothers. The eldest was by Ahinoam, and he was called Ammon; the second was Daniel, by his wife Abigail; the name of the third was Absalom, by Maacah, the daughter of Talmai, king of Geshur; the fourth he named Adonijah, by his wife Haggith; the fifth was Shephatiah, by Abitail; the sixth he called Ithream, by Eglah. Now while this intestine war went on, and the subjects of the two kings came frequently to action and to fighting, it was Abner, the general of the host of Saul's son, who, by his prudence, and the great interest he had among the multitude, made them all continue with Ishbosheth; and indeed, it was a considerable time that they continued of his party; but afterwards Abner was blamed, and an accusation was laid against him, that he went in unto Saul's concubine : her name was Rispah, the daughter of Aiah. So when he was complained of by Ishbosheth, he was very uneasy and angry at it, because he had

not justice done him by Ishbosheth, to whom he had shewn the greatest kindness; whereupon he threatened to transfer the kingdom to David, and demonstrate that he did not rule over the people beyond Jordan by his own abilities and wisdom, but by his warlike conduct and fidelity in leading his army. So he sent ambassadors to Hebron to David, and desired that he would give him security upon oath that he would esteem his companion and his friend, upon condition that he should persuade the people to leave Saul's son, and choose him king of the whole country; and when David had made that league with Abner, for he was pleased with his message to him, he desired that he would give this as the first mark of performance of the present league, that he might have his wife Michal restored to him, as her whom he had purchased with great hazards, and with those six hundred heads of the Philistines which he had brought to Saul her father. So Abner took Michal from Phaltiel, who was then her husband, and sent her to David, Ishbosheth himself affording him his assistance; for David had written to him that of right he ought to have this his wife restored to him. Abner also called together the elders of the multitude, the commanders and captains of thousands, and spake thus to them : That he had formerly dissuaded them from their own resolution, when they were ready to forsake Ishbosheth, and to join themselves to David; that, however, he now gave them leave so to do, if they had a mind to it, for they knew that God had appointed David to be king of all the Hebrews, by Samuel the prophet; and had foretold that he should punish the Philistines, and overcome them, and bring them under. Now, when the elders and rulers heard this, and understood that Abner was come over to those sentiments about the public affairs which they were of before, they changed their measures, and came into David. When these men had agreed to Abner's proposal, he called together the tribe of Benjamin, for all of that tribe were the guards of Ishbosheth's body, and he spake to them to the same purpose; and when he saw that they did not in the least oppose what he said, but resigned themselves up to his opinion, he took about twenty of his friends and came to David, in order to receive himself security upon oath from him; for we may justly esteem those things to be firmer which every one of us do by ourselves, than those which we do by another. He also gave him an account of what he had said to the rulers, and to the whole tribe of Benjamin; and when David had received him in a courteous manner, and had treated him with great hospitality for many days, Abner, when he was dismissed, desired him to permit him to bring the multitude with him, that he might deliver up the government to him when David himself was present, and a spectator of what was done.

5. When David had sent Abner away, Joab, the general of his army, came immediately to Hebron: and when he had understood that Abner had been with David, and had parted with him a little before, under leagues and agreements that the government should be delivered up to David, he feared lest David should place Abner, who had assisted him to gain the kingdom, in the first rank of dignity, especially since he was a shrewd man in other respects, in understanding affairs, and in managing them artfully, as proper seasons should require, and that he should himself be put lower, and deprived of the command of the army; so he took a knavish and a wicked course. In the first place, he endeavoured to calumniate Abner to the king, exhorting him to have a care of him,

---

* Joab, Abishai, and Asahel, were David's nephews, the sons of his sister Zeruiah, as 1 Chron. ii. 16; and Amasa was also his nephew by his other sister Abigail, ver. 17.

and not to give attention to what he had engaged to do for him, because all he did tended to confirm the government to Saul's son: that he came to him deceitfully, and with guile, and was gone away in hopes of gaining his purpose by this management; but when he could not thus persuade David, nor saw him at all exasperated, he betook himself to a project bolder than the former:—he determined to kill Abner; and in order thereto, he sent some messengers after him, to whom he gave in charge, that when they should overtake him they should recall him in David's name, and tell him that he had somewhat to say to him about his affairs, which he had not remembered to speak of when he was with him. Now when Abner heard what the messenger said, (for they overtook him in a certain place called *Besira*, which was distant from Hebron twenty furlongs,) he suspected none of the mischief which was befalling him, and came back. Hereupon Joab met him in the gate, and received him in the kindest manner, as if he were Abner's most benevolent acquaintance and friend; for such as undertake the vilest actions, in order to prevent the suspicion of any private mischief intended, do frequently make the greatest pretences to what really good men sincerely do. So he took him aside from his own followers, as if he would speak with him in private, and brought him into a void place of the gate, having himself nobody with him but his brother Abishai; then he drew his sword, and smote him in the groin; upon which Abner died by this treachery of Joab, which, as he said himself, was in the way of punishment for his brother Asahel, whom Abner smote and slew as he was pursuing after him in the battle of Hebron, but as the truth was, out of his fear of losing his command of the army, and his dignity with the king, and lest he should be deprived of those advantages, and Abner should obtain the first rank in David's court. By these examples any one may learn how many and how great instances of wickedness men will venture upon for the sake of getting money and authority, and that they may not fail of either of them; for as when they are desirous of obtaining the same, they acquire them by ten thousand evil practices; so when they are afraid of losing them, they get them confirmed to them by practices much worse than the former, as if [no] other calamity so terrible could befall them as the failure of acquiring so exalted an authority; and when they have acquired it, and by long custom found the sweetness of it, the losing it again: and since this last would be the heaviest of all afflictions, they all of them contrive and venture upon the most difficult actions, out of the fear of losing the same. But let it suffice, that I have made these short reflections upon that subject.

6. When David heard that Abner was slain, it grieved his soul: and he called all men to witness, with stretching out his hands to God, and crying out that he was not a partaker in the murder of Abner, and that his death was not procured by his command or approbation. He also wished the heaviest curses might light upon him that slew him, and upon his whole house; and he devoted those that had assisted him in this murder to the same penalties on its account; for he took care not to appear to have had any hand in this murder, contrary to the assurances he had given, and the oaths he had taken to Abner. However, he commanded all the people to weep and lament this man, and to honour his dead body with the usual solemnities; that is, by rending their garments, and putting on sackcloth, and that this should be the habit in which they should go before the bier; after which he followed it himself, with the elders and those that were rulers, lamenting Abner, and by his tears demonstrating his good-will towards him while he was alive, and his sorrow for him now he was dead, and that he was not taken off with his consent. So he buried him at Hebron in a magnificent manner, and indited funeral elegies for him; he also stood first over the monument weeping, and caused others to do the same; nay, so deeply did the death of Abner disorder him, that his companions could by no means force him to take any food, for he affirmed with an oath that he would taste nothing till the sun was set. This procedure gained him the good-will of the multitude; for such as had an affection for Abner were mightily satisfied with the respect he paid him when he was dead, and the observation of that faith he had plighted to him, which was shewn in his vouchsafing him all the usual ceremonies, as if he had been his kinsman and his friend, and not suffering him to be neglected and injured with a dishonourable burial, as if he had been his enemy; insomuch that the entire nation rejoiced at the king's gentleness and mildness of disposition, every one being ready to suppose that the king would have taken the same care of them in the like circumstances, which they saw he shewed in the burial of the dead body of Abner. And indeed David principally intended to gain a good reputation, and therefore he took care to do what was proper in this case, whence none had any suspicion that he was the author of Abner's death. He also said this to the multitude, That he was greatly troubled at the death of so good a man; and that the affairs of the Hebrews had suffered great detriment by being deprived of him, who was of so great abilities to preserve them by his excellent advice, and by the strength of his hands in war. But he added, that " God, who hath a regard to all men's actions, will not suffer this man [Joab] to go off unrevenged; but know ye, that I am not able to do anything to these sons of Zeruiah, Joab, and Abishai, who have more power than I have; but God will requite their insolent attempts upon their own heads." And this was the fatal conclusion of the life of Abner.

CHAPTER II

THAT UPON THE SLAUGHTER OF ISHBOSHETH, BY THE TREACHERY OF HIS FRIENDS, DAVID RECEIVED THE WHOLE KINGDOM.

1. WHEN Ishbosheth, the son of Saul, had heard of the death of Abner, he took it to heart to be deprived of a man that was of his kindred, and had indeed given him the kingdom, but was greatly afflicted, and Abner's death very much troubled him; nor did he himself outlive any long time, but was treacherously set upon by the sons of Rimmon, (Baanah and Rechab were their names,) and was slain by them; for these being of a family of the Benjamites, and of the first rank among them, thought that if they should slay Ishbosheth, they should obtain large presents from David, and be made commanders by him, or, however, should have some other trust committed to them. So when they once found him alone, and asleep at noon, in an upper room, when none of his guards were there, and when the woman that kept the door was not watching, but was fallen asleep also, partly on account of the labour she had undergone, and partly on account of the heat of the day, these men went into the room in which Ishbosheth, Saul's son,

lay asleep, and slew him; they also cut off his head, and took their journey all that night and the next day, as supposing themselves flying away from those they had injured, to one that would accept of this action as a favour, and would afford them security. So they came to Hebron, and shewed David the head of Ish-bosheth, and presented themselves to him as his well-wishers, and such as had killed one that was his enemy and antagonist. Yet David did not relish what they had done as they expected, but said to them, "You vile wretches, you shall immediately receive the punishment you deserve. Did not you know what vengeance I executed on him that murdered Saul, and brought me his crown of gold, and this while he who made this slaughter did it as a favour to him, that he might not be caught by his enemies? Or do you imagine that I am altered in my disposition, and suppose that I am not the same man I then was, but am pleased with men that are wicked doers, and esteem your vile actions, when you are become murderers of your master, as grateful to me, when you have slain a righteous man upon his bed, who never did evil to anybody, and treated you with great good-will and respect? Wherefore you shall suffer the punishment due on his account, and the vengeance I ought to inflict upon you for killing Ishbosheth, and for supposing that I should take his death kindly at your hands; for you could not lay a greater blot on my honour than by making such a supposal." When David had said this, he tormented them with all sorts of torments, and then put them to death: and he bestowed all accustomed rites on the burial of the head of Ishbosheth, and laid it in the grave of Abner.

2. When these things were brought to a conclusion, all the principal men of the Hebrew people came to David to Hebron, with the heads of thousands, and other rulers, and delivered themselves up to him, putting him in mind of the good-will they had borne to him in Saul's lifetime, and the respect they then had not ceased to pay him when he was captain of a thousand, as also that he was chosen of God by Samuel the prophet, he and his sons: * and declaring besides, how God had given him power to save the land of the Hebrews, and overcome the Philistines. Whereupon he received kindly this their alacrity on his account; and exhorted them to continue in it, for that they should have no reason to repent of being thus disposed to him. So when he had feasted them, and treated them kindly, he sent them out to bring all the people to him; upon which there came to him about six thousand and eight hundred armed men of the tribe of Judah, who bare shields and spears for their weapons, for these had [till now] continued with Saul's son, when the rest of the tribe of Judah had ordained David for their king. There came also seven thousand and one hundred out of the tribe of Simeon. Out of the tribe of Levi came four thousand and seven hundred, having Jehoiada for their leader. After these came Zadok the high priest, with twenty-two captains of his kindred. Out of the tribe of Benjamin the armed men were four thousand; but the rest of the tribe continued, still expecting that some one of the house of Saul should reign over them. Those of the

tribe of Ephraim were twenty thousand and eight hundred; and these mighty of valour, and eminent for their strength. Out of the half-tribe of Manasseh came eighteen thousand of the most potent men. Out of the tribe of Issachar came two hundred, who foreknew what was to come hereafter,† but of armed men twenty thousand. Of the tribe of Zebulon fifty thousand chosen men. This was the only tribe that came universally in to David; and all these had the same weapons with the tribe of Gad. Out of the tribe of Naphthali the eminent men and rulers were one thousand, whose weapons were shields and spears; and the tribe itself followed after, being (in a manner) innumerable [thirty-seven thousand.] Out of the tribe of Dan there were of chosen men twenty-seven thousand and six hundred. Out of the tribe of Asher were forty thousand. Out of the two tribes that were beyond Jordan, and the rest of the tribe of Manasseh, such as used shields, and spears, and head-pieces, and swords, were an hundred and twenty thousand. The rest of the tribes also made use of swords. This multitude came together to Hebron to David, with a great quantity of corn and wine, and all other sorts of food, and established David in his kingdom with one consent; and when the people had rejoiced for three days in Hebron, David and all the people removed and came to Jerusalem.

CHAPTER III

HOW DAVID LAID SIEGE TO JERUSALEM; AND WHEN HE HAD TAKEN THE CITY, HE CAST THE CANAANITES OUT OF IT, AND BROUGHT IN THE JEWS TO INHABIT THEREIN

1. Now the Jebusites, who were the inhabitants of Jerusalem, and were by extraction Canaanites, shut their gates, and placed the blind, and the lame, and all their maimed persons, upon the wall, in way of derision of the king; and said, that the very lame themselves would hinder his entrance into it. This they did out of contempt of his power, and as depending on the strength of their walls. David was hereby enraged, and began the siege of Jerusalem, and employed his utmost diligence and alacrity therein, as intending, by the taking of this place, to demonstrate his power, and to intimidate all others that might be of the like [evil] disposition towards him: so he took the lower city by force, but the citadel held out still; ‡ whence it was that the king, knowing that the proposal of dignities and rewards would encourage the soldiers to greater actions, promised that he who should first go over the ditches that were beneath the citadel, and should ascend to the citadel itself and take it, should have the command of the entire people conferred upon him. So they all were ambitious to ascend, and thought no pains too great in order to ascend thither, out of their desire of the chief

---

* This may be a true observation of Josephus, that Samuel, by command from God, entailed the crown on David and his posterity; for no further did that entail ever reach,—Solomon himself having never had any promise made him that his posterity should always have the right to it.

† These words of Josephus, "who foreknew what was to come hereafter," are best paraphrased by the parallel text, (1 Chron. xii. 32,)—"Who had understanding of the times, to know what Israel ought to do;" that is, Who had so much knowledge in astronomy as to make calendars for the Israelites.

‡ What our other copies say of Mount Sion, as alone properly called the City of David, (2 Sam. v. 6-9,) and of this its siege and conquest now by David, Josephus applies to the whole city Jerusalem; perhaps, after David had united them together, or joined the citadel to the lower city, Josephus esteemed them as one city.

command. However, Joab, the son of Zeruiah, prevented the rest, and as soon as he was got up to the citadel, cried out to the king, and claimed the chief command.

2. When David had cast the Jebusites out of the citadel, he also rebuilt Jerusalem, and named it, *The City of David*, and abode there all the time of his reign: but for the time that he reigned over the tribe of Judah only in Hebron, it was seven years and six months. Now when he had chosen Jerusalem to be his royal city, his affairs did more and more prosper, by the providence of God, who took care that they should improve and be augmented. Hiram, also, the king of the Tyrians, sent ambassadors to him, and made a league of mutual friendship and assistance with him. He also sent him presents, cedar-trees, and mechanics, and men skilful in building and architecture, that they might build him a royal palace at Jerusalem. Now David made buildings round about the lower city: he also joined the citadel to it, and made it one body; and when he had encompassed all with walls, he appointed Joab to take care of them. It was David, therefore, who first cast the Jebusites out of Jerusalem, and called it by its own name, *The City of David*; for under our forefather Abraham it was called (Salem or) Solyma;[*] but after that time, some say that Homer mentions it by that name of Solyma, [for he named the temple Solyma, according to the Hebrew language, which denotes *security*.] Now the whole time from the warfare under Joshua our general against the Canaanites, and from that war in which he overcame them, and distributed the land among the Hebrews, (nor could the Israelites ever cast the Canaanites out of Jerusalem until this time, when David took it by siege,) this whole time was five hundred and fifteen years.

3. I shall now make mention of Araunah, who was a wealthy man among the Jebusites, but was not slain by David in the siege of Jerusalem, because of the good-will he bore to the Hebrews, and a particular benignity and affection which he had to the king himself; which I shall take a more seasonable opportunity to speak of a little afterwards. Now David married other wives over and above those which he had before: he had also concubines. The sons whom he had were in number eleven, whose names were Ammon, Emnos, Eban, Nathan, Solomon, Jeban, Elien, Phalna, Ennaphen, Jenae, Eliphale; and a daughter, Tamar. Nine of these were born of legitimate wives, but the two last-named of concubines; and Tamar had the same mother with Absalom.

CHAPTER IV

THAT WHEN DAVID HAD CONQUERED THE PHILISTINES, WHO MADE WAR AGAINST HIM AT JERUSALEM, HE REMOVED THE ARK TO JERUSALEM, AND HAD A MIND TO BUILD A TEMPLE

1. WHEN the Philistines understood that David was made king of the Hebrews, they made war against him at Jerusalem; and when they had seized upon that valley which is called *The Valley of the Giants*, and is a place not far from the city, they pitched their camp therein: but the king of the Jews, who never permitted himself to do anything without prophecy,[†] and the command of God, and without depending on Him as a security for the time to come, bade the high priest to foretell to him what was the will of God, and what would be the event of this battle. And when he foretold that he should gain the victory and the dominion, he led out his army against the Philistines; and when the battle was joined, he came himself behind, and fell upon the enemy on the sudden, and slew some of them, and put the rest to flight. And let no one suppose that it was a small army of the Philistines that came against the Hebrews, as guessing so from the suddenness of their defeat, and from their having performed no great action, or that was worth recording, from the slowness of their march and want of courage; but let him know that all Syria and Phœnicia, with many other nations besides them, and those warlike nations also, came to their assistance, and had a share in this war:—which thing was the only cause why, when they had been so often conquered, and had lost so many ten thousands of their men, they still came upon the Hebrews with greater armies; nay, indeed, when they had so often failed of their purpose in these battles, they came upon David with an army three times as numerous as before, and pitched their camp on the same spot of ground as before. The king of Israel therefore inquired of God again concerning the event of the battle; and the high priest prophesied to him, that he should keep his army in the groves, called the *Groves of Weeping*, which were not far from the enemy's camp, and that he should not move, nor begin to fight, till the trees of the grove should be in motion without the winds blowing; but as soon as these trees moved, and the time foretold to him by God was come, he should without delay go out to gain what was an already prepared and evident victory; for the several ranks of the enemy's army did not sustain him, but retreated at the first onset, whom he closely followed, and slew them as he went along, and pursued them to the city of Gaza, (which is the limit of their country:) after this he spoiled their camp, in which he found great riches; and he destroyed their gods.

2. When this had proved the event of the battle, David thought it proper, upon a consultation with the elders and rulers, and captains of thousands, to send for those that were in the flower of their age out of all his countrymen, and out of the whole land, and withal for the priests and the Levites, in order to their going to Kirjathjearim, to bring up the ark of God out of that city, and to carry it to Jerusalem, and there to keep it, and offer before it those sacrifices and those honours with which God used to be well pleased; for had they done thus in the reign of Saul, they had not undergone any great misfortunes at all. So when the whole body of the people were come together, as they had resolved to do, the king came to the ark, which the priests brought out of the house of Aminadab, and laid it upon a new cart, and permitted their brethren and their children to draw it, together with the

---

[*] Some copies of Josephus have here Solyma, or Salem; and others Hierosolyma, or Jerusalem. The latter best agree to what Josephus says elsewhere, that this city was called Solyma or Salem, before the days of Melchisedec; but was by him called Hierosolyma or Jerusalem. I rather suppose it to have been so called after Abraham had received that oracle *Jehovah Jirah*.

[†] Saul very rarely, but David very frequently, consulted God by Urim; and David aimed always to depend, not on his own prudence or abilities, but on the Divine direction, contrary to Saul's practice. When Michal laughed at David's dancing before the ark, it is probable she did so because her father Saul did not use to pay such a regard to the ark, and because she thought it beneath the dignity of a king to be so religious.

oxen. Before it went the king, and the whole multitude of the people with him, singing hymns to God, and making use of all sorts of songs usual among them, with variety of the sounds of musical instruments, and with dancing and singing of psalms, as also with the sounds of trumpets and of cymbals, and so brought the ark to Jerusalem. But as they were come to the threshing-floor of Chidon, a place so called, Uzzah was slain by the anger of God; for as the oxen shook the ark, he stretched out his hand, and would needs take hold of it. Now because he was not a priest,* and yet touched the ark, God struck him dead. Hereupon both the king and the people were displeased at the death of Uzzah; and the place where he died is still called the *Breach of Uzzah* unto this day. So David was afraid; and supposing that if he received the ark to himself into the city, he might suffer in the like manner as Uzzah had suffered, who, upon his bare putting out his hand to the ark, died in the manner already mentioned, he did not receive it to himself into the city, but he took it aside unto a certain place belonging to a righteous man, whose name was Obededom, who was by his family a Levite, and deposited the ark with him; and it remained there three entire months. This augmented the house of Obededom, and conferred many blessings upon it; and when the king heard what had befallen Obededom, how he was become, of a poor man, in a low estate, exceedingly happy, and the object of envy to all those that saw or inquired after his house, he took courage, and hoping that he should meet with no misfortune thereby, he transferred the ark to his own house, the priests carrying it, while seven companies of singers, who were set in that order by the king, went before it, and while he himself played upon the harp, and joined in the music, insomuch that when his wife Michal, the daughter of Saul, who was our first king, saw him so doing, she laughed at him; but when they had brought in the ark, they placed it under the tabernacle which David had pitched for it, and he offered costly sacrifices and peace-offerings, and treated the whole multitude, and dealt both to the women, and the men, and the infants, a loaf of bread and a cake, and another cake baked in a pan, with a portion of the sacrifice. So when he had thus feasted the people, he sent them away, and he himself returned to his own house.

3. But when Michal his wife, the daughter of Saul, came and stood by him, she wished him all other happiness; and entreated that whatsoever he should further desire, to the utmost possibility, might be given him by God, and that he might be favourable to him; yet did she blame him, that so great a king as he was should dance after an unseemly manner, and in his dancing uncover himself among the servants and the handmaidens: but he replied, that he was not ashamed to do what was acceptable to God, who had preferred him before her father, and before all others; that he would play frequently, and dance, without any regard to what the handmaidens and she herself thought of it. So this Michal had no children; however, when she was afterward married to him to whom Saul her father had given her, (for at this time David had taken her away from him, and had her himself,)

she bare five children. But concerning those matters I shall discourse in a proper place.

4. Now when the king saw that his affairs grew better almost every day, by the will of God, he thought he should offend him, if, while he himself continued in houses made of cedar, such as were of a great height, and had the most curious works of architecture in them, he should overlook the ark while it was laid in a tabernacle, and was desirous to build a temple to God, as Moses had predicted such a temple should be built.† And when he had discoursed with Nathan the prophet about these things, and had been encouraged by him to do whatsoever he had a mind to do, as having God with him and his helper in all things, he was thereupon the more ready to set about that building. But God appeared to Nathan that very night, and commanded him to say to David,‡ that he took his purpose and his desires kindly, since nobody had before now taken it into their head to build him a temple, although upon his having such a notion he would not permit him to build him that temple, because he had made many wars, and was defiled with the slaughter of his enemies; that, however, after his death, in his old age, and when he had lived a long life, there should be a temple built by a son of his, who should take the kingdom after him, and should be called Solomon, whom he promised to provide for, as a father provides for his son, by preserving the kingdom for his son's posterity, and delivering it to them; but that he would still punish him if he sinned, with diseases and barrenness of land. When David understood this from the prophet, and was overjoyful at this knowledge of the sure continuance of the dominion to his posterity, and that his house should be splendid, and very famous, he came to the ark, and fell down on his face, and began to adore God, and to return thanks to him for all his benefits, as well for those that he had already bestowed upon him, in raising him from a low state, and from the employment of a shepherd, to so great dignity of dominion and glory, as for those also which he had promised to his posterity; and, besides, for that providence which he had exercised over the Hebrews, in procuring them the liberty they enjoyed. And when he had said thus, and had sung a hymn of praise to God, he went his way.

CHAPTER V

HOW DAVID BROUGHT UNDER THE PHILISTINES, AND THE MOABITES, AND THE KINGS OF SOPHENE, AND OF DAMASCUS, AND OF THE SYRIANS, AS ALSO THE IDUMEANS, IN WAR; AND HOW HE MADE A LEAGUE WITH THE KING OF HAMATH; AND WAS MINDFUL OF THE FRIENDSHIP THAT JONATHAN, THE SON OF SAUL, HAD BORNE TO HIM

1. A LITTLE while after this, he considered that he ought to make war against the Philistines, and not to see any idleness or laziness permitted in his management, that so it might prove, as God had foretold to him, that, when he had over-

---

* Josephus seems to be right, when he observes that Uzzah was no priest, and was therefore struck dead for touching the ark, contrary to the law. It is not improbable that the putting this ark in a cart, when it ought to have been carried by the priests or Levites, might be also an occasion of the anger of God on that breach of his law.

† Josephus here informs us, that, according to his understanding of the sense of his copy of the Pentateuch, Moses had himself foretold the building of the temple, which yet is nowhere in our present copies.

‡ Josephus seems to confound the two distinct predictions which God made to David and to Nathan, concerning the building him a temple by one of David's posterity: the one belongeth to Solomon, the other to the Messiah.

thrown his enemies, he should leave his posterity to reign in peace afterward : so he called together his army again, and when he had charged them to be ready and prepared for war, and when he thought that all things in his army were in a good state, he removed from Jerusalem, and came against the Philistines ; and when he had overcome them in battle, and had cut off a great part of their country, and adjoined it to the country of the Hebrews, he transferred the war to the Moabites ; and when he had overcome two parts of their army in battle, he took the remaining part captive, and imposed tribute upon them, to be paid annually. He then made war against Hadadezer, the son of Rehob, king of Sophene ; and when he had joined battle with him at the river Euphrates, he destroyed twenty thousand of his footmen, and about seven thousand of his horsemen ; he also took a thousand of his chariots, and destroyed the greatest part of them, and ordered that no more than one hundred should be kept.*

2. Now when Hadad, king of Damascus and of Syria, heard that David fought against Hadadezer, who was his friend, he came to his assistance with a powerful army, in hopes to rescue him ; and when he had joined battle with David at the river Euphrates, he failed of his purpose, and lost in the battle a great number of his soldiers ; for there were slain of the army of Hadad twenty thousand, and all the rest fled. Nicolaus [of Damascus] also makes mention of this king in the fourth book of his histories ; where he speaks thus : "A great while after these things had happened, there was one of that country whose name was Hadad, who was become very potent : he reigned over Damascus and the other parts of Syria, excepting Phœnicia. He made war against David, the king of Judea, and tried his fortune in many battles, and particularly in the last battle at Euphrates, wherein he was beaten. He seemed to be the most excellent of all their kings in strength and manhood." Nay, besides this, he says of his posterity, that "they succeeded one another in his kingdom, and in his name ;" where he thus speaks : "When Hadad was dead, his posterity reigned for ten generations, each of his successors receiving from his father *that* his dominion, and *this* his name : as did the Ptolemies in Egypt. But the third was the most powerful of them all, and was willing to avenge the defeat his forefather had received : so he made an expedition against the Jews, and laid waste the city which is now called Samaria." Nor did he err from the truth ; for this is that Hadad who made the expedition against Samaria, in the reign of Ahab, king of Israel ; concerning whom we shall speak in due place hereafter.

3. Now when David had made an expedition against Damascus and the other parts of Syria, and had brought it all into subjection, and had placed garrisons in the country, and appointed that they should pay tribute, he returned home. He also dedicated to God at Jerusalem the golden quivers, the entire armour which the guards of Hadad used to wear : which Shishak, the king of Egypt, took away when he fought with David's grandson, Rehoboam, with a great deal of other wealth which he carried out of Jerusalem. However, these things will come to be explained in their proper places hereafter. Now as for the king of the Hebrews, he was assisted by God, who gave him great success in his wars ; and he made

an expedition against the best cities of Hadadezer, Betah, and Machon ; so he took them by force, and laid them waste. Therein was found a very great quantity of gold and silver, besides that sort of brass which is said to be more valuable than gold ; of which brass Solomon made that large vessel which was called The [Brazen] Sea, and those most curious lavers, when he built the temple for God.

4. But when the king of Hamath was informed of the ill success of Hadadezer, and had heard of the ruin of his army, he was afraid on his own account, and resolved to make a league of friendship and fidelity with David, before he should come against him ; so he sent to him his son Joram, and professed that he owed him thanks for fighting against Hadadezer, who was his enemy, and made a league with him of mutual assistance and friendship. He also sent him presents, vessels of ancient workmanship, both of gold, of silver, and of brass. So when David had made this league of mutual assistance with Toi, (for that was the name of the king of Hamath,) and had received the presents he sent him, he dismissed his son with that respect which was due on both sides ; but then David brought those presents that were sent him, as also the rest of the gold and silver which he had taken of the cities which he had conquered, and dedicated them to God. Nor did God give victory and success to him only when he went to the battle himself, and led his own army, but he gave victory to Abishai, the brother of Joab, general of his forces, over the Idumeans,† and by him to David, when he sent him with an army into Idumea ; for Abishai destroyed eighteen thousand of them in the battle ; whereupon the king [of Israel] placed garrisons through all Idumea, and received the tribute of the country, and of every head among them. Now David was in his nature just, and made his determination with regard to truth. He had for the general of his whole army Joab ; and he made Jehoshaphat, the son of Ahilud, recorder : he also appointed Zadok, of the family of Phineas, to be high priest, together with Abiathar, for he was his friend : he also made Seisan the scribe ; and committed the command over the guards of his body to Benaiah, the son of Jehoiada. His elder sons were near his body, and had the care of it also.

5. He also called to mind the covenants and the oaths he had made with Jonathan, the son of Saul, and the friendship and affection Jonathan had for him ; for besides all the rest of the excellent qualities with which he was endowed, he was also exceeding mindful of such as had at other times bestowed benefits upon him. He therefore gave order that inquiry should be made, whether any of Jonathan's lineage were living, to whom he might make return of that familiar acquaintance which Jonathan had had with him, and for which he was still debtor. And when one of Saul's freed men was brought to him, who was acquainted with those of his family that were still living, he asked him whether he could tell him of any one belonging to Jonathan that was now alive, and capable of a requital of the benefits which he had received from Jonathan. And when he said that a son of his was remaining, whose name was Mephibosheth, but that he was lame of his feet ; for when his nurse heard that the father and grandfather of the child

---

* David's reserving only one hundred chariots for himself, was most probably done in compliance with the law of Moses, (Deut. xvii. 16.)

† By this great victory over the posterity of Esau, and by the consequent tribute paid by them to the Jews, were the prophecies delivered to Rebekah before Jacob and Esau were born, and by old Isaac before his death, that the elder should serve the younger, and that Jacob should be Esau's lord, remarkably fulfilled.

were fallen in the battle, she snatched him up, and fled away, and let him fall from her shoulders, and his feet were lamed. So when he had learned where and by whom he was brought up, he sent messengers to Machir, to the city of Lodebar, for with him was the son of Jonathan brought up, and sent for him to come to him. So when Mephibosheth came to the king, he fell on his face and worshipped him, but David encouraged him, and bade him be of good cheer, and expect better times. So he gave him his father's house, and all the estate which his grandfather Saul was in possession of, and bade him come and diet with him at his own table, and never to be absent one day from that table. And when the youth had worshipped him, on account of his words and gifts given to him, he called for Ziba, and told him that he had given the youth his father's house, and all Saul's estate. He also ordered that Ziba should cultivate his land, and take care of it, and bring him the profits of all to Jerusalem. Accordingly David brought him to his table every day; and bestowed upon the youth, Ziba and his sons, who were in number fifteen, and his servants, who were in number twenty. When the king had made these appointments, and Ziba had worshipped him, and promised to do all that he had bidden him, he went his way; so that this son of Jonathan dwelt at Jerusalem, and dieted at the king's table, and had the same care that a son could claim taken of him. He also had himself a son, whom he named Micha.

CHAPTER VI

HOW THE WAR WAS WAGED AGAINST THE AMMON-ITES, AND HAPPILY CONCLUDED

1. THESE were the honours that such as were left of Saul's and Jonathan's lineage received from David. About this time died Nahash, the king of the Ammonites, who was a friend of David's; and when his son had succeeded his father in the kingdom, David sent ambassadors to him to comfort him; and exhorted him to take his father's death patiently, and to expect that he would continue the same kindness to himself which he had shewn to his father. But the princes of the Ammonites took this message in evil part, and not as David's kind dispositions gave reason to take it; and they excited the king to resent it; and said that David had sent men to spy out the country, and what strength it had, under the pretence of humanity and kindness. They further advised him to have a care, and not to give heed to David's words, lest he should be deluded by him, and so fall into an inconsolable calamity. Accordingly, Nahash's [son,] the king of the Ammonites, thought these princes spake what was more probable than the truth would admit, and so abused the ambassadors after a very harsh manner; for he shaved the one half of their beards, and cut off one half of their garments, and sent his answer not in words but in deeds. When the king of Israel saw this, he had indignation at it, and shewed openly that he would not overlook this injurious and contumelious treatment, but would make war with the Ammonites, and would avenge this wicked treatment of his ambassadors on their king. So that the king's intimate friends and commanders, understanding that they had violated their league, and were liable to be punished for the same, made preparations for war; they also sent a thousand talents to the Syrian king of Mesopotamia, and endeavoured to prevail with him to assist them for that pay, and Shobach. Now these kings had twenty thousand footmen. They also hired the king of the country called Maacah, and a fourth king, by name Ishtob; which last had twelve thousand armed men.

2. But David was under no consternation at this confederacy, nor at the forces of the Ammonites; and putting his trust in God, because he was going to war in a just cause, on account of the injurious treatment he had met with, he immediately sent Joab, the captain of his host, against them, and gave him the flower of his army, who pitched his camp by Rabbath, the metropolis of the Ammonites; whereupon the enemy came out, and set themselves in array, not all of them together, but in two bodies; for the auxiliaries were set in array in the plain by themselves, but the army of the Ammonites at the gate over-against the Hebrews. When Joab saw this, he opposed one stratagem against another, and chose out the most hardy part of his men, and set them in opposition to the king of Syria, and the kings that were with him, and gave the other part to his brother Abishai, and bid him set them in opposition to the Ammonites; and said to him, That in case he should see that the Syrians distressed him, and were too hard for him, he should order his troops to turn about, and assist him: and he said, That he himself would do the same to him, if he saw him in the like distress from the Ammonites. So he sent his brother before, and encouraged him to do everything courageously and with alacrity, which would teach them to be afraid of disgrace, and to fight manfully; and so he dismissed him to fight with the Ammonites, while he fell upon the Syrians. And though they made a strong opposition for a while, Joab slew many of them, but compelled the rest to betake themselves to flight; which, when the Ammonites saw, and were withal afraid of Abishai and his army, they stayed no longer, but imitated their auxiliaries, and fled to the city. So Joab, who had thus overcome the enemy, returned with great joy to Jerusalem to the king.

3. This defeat did not still induce the Ammonites to be quiet, nor to own those that were superior to them to be so, and be still, but they sent to Chalaman, the king of the Syrians, beyond Euphrates, and hired him for an auxiliary. He had Shobach for the captain of his host, with eighty thousand footmen, and ten thousand horsemen. Now when the king of the Hebrews understood that the Ammonites had again gathered so great an army together, he determined to make war with them no longer by his generals, but he passed over the river Jordan himself with all his army; and when he met them he joined battle with them, and overcame them, and slew forty thousand of their footmen, and seven thousand of their horsemen. He also wounded Shobach, the general of Chalaman's forces, who died of that stroke; but the people of Mesopotamia, upon such a conclusion of the battle, delivered themselves up to David, and sent him presents, who at winter-time returned to Jerusalem. But at the beginning of the spring, he sent Joab, the captain of his host, to fight against the Ammonites, who overran all their country, and laid it waste, and shut them up in their metropolis, Rabbath, and besieged them therein.

CHAPTER VII

HOW DAVID FELL IN LOVE WITH BATHSHEBA, AND
SLEW HER HUSBAND URIAH, FOR WHICH HE IS
REPROVED BY NATHAN

1. BUT David fell now into a very grievous sin, though he was otherwise naturally a righteous and a religious man, and one that firmly observed the laws of our fathers; for when late in an evening he took a view round him from the roof of his royal palace, where he used to walk at that hour, he saw a woman washing herself in her own house: she was one of extraordinary beauty, and therein surpassed all other women; her name was Bathsheba. So he was overcome by that woman's beauty, and was not able to restrain his desires, but sent for her, and lay with her. Hereupon she conceived with child, and sent to the king, that he should contrive some way of concealing her sin, (for, according to the laws of their fathers, she who had been guilty of adultery ought to be put to death.) So the king sent for Joab's armour-bearer from the siege, who was the woman's husband, and his name was Uriah; and when he was come, the king inquired of him about the army, and about the siege; and when he had made answer, that all their affairs went according to their wishes, the king took some portions of meat from his supper, and gave them to him, and bade him go home to his wife, and take his rest with her. Uriah did not do so, but slept near the king with the rest of his armour-bearers. When the king was informed of this, he asked him why he did not go home to his house, and to his wife, after so long an absence; which is the natural custom of all men, when they come from a long journey. He replied, that it was not right, while his fellow-soldiers, and the general of the army, slept upon the ground, in the camp, and in an enemy's country, that he should go and take his rest, and solace himself with his wife. So when he had thus replied, the king ordered him to stay there that night, that he might dismiss him the next day to the general. So the king invited Uriah to supper, and after a cunning and dexterous manner plied him with drink at supper till he was thereby disordered; yet did he nevertheless sleep at the king's gates, without any inclination to go to his wife. Upon this the king was very angry at him; and wrote to Joab, and commanded him to punish Uriah, for he told him that he had offended him; and he suggested to him the manner in which he would have him punished, that it might not be discovered that he was himself the author of this his punishment; for he charged him to set him over against that part of the enemy's army where the attack would be most hazardous, and where he might be deserted, and be in the greatest jeopardy; for he bade him order his fellow-soldiers to retire out of the fight. When he had written thus to him, and sealed the letter with his own seal, he gave it to Uriah to carry to Joab. When Joab had received it, and upon reading it understood the king's purpose, he set Uriah in that place where he knew the enemy would be most troublesome to them; and gave him for his partners some of the best soldiers in the army; and said that he would also come to their assistance with the whole army, that if possible they might break down some part of the wall, and enter the city. And he desired him to be glad of the opportunity of exposing himself to such great pains, and not to be displeased at it,

since he was a valiant soldier, and had a great reputation for his valour, both with the king and with his countrymen. And when Uriah undertook the work he was set upon with alacrity, he gave private orders to those who were to be his companions, that when they saw the enemy make a sally, they should leave him. When, therefore, the Hebrews made an attack upon the city, the Ammonites were afraid that the enemy might prevent them, and get up into the city, and this at the very place whither Uriah was ordered; so they exposed their best soldiers to be in the fore-front, and opened their gates suddenly, and fell upon the enemy with great vehemence, and ran violently upon them. When those that were with Uriah saw this, they all retreated backward, as Joab had directed them beforehand; but Uriah, as ashamed to run away and leave his post, sustained the enemy, and receiving the violence of their onset, he slew many of them; but being encompassed round, and caught in the midst of them, he was slain, and some other of his companions were slain with him.

2. When this was done, Joab sent messengers to the king, and ordered them to tell him that he did what he could to take the city soon; but that as they made an assault on the wall, they had been forced to retire with great loss; and bade them, if they saw the king angry at it, to add this, that Uriah was slain also. When the king had heard this of the messengers, he took it heinously, and said that they did wrong when they assaulted the wall, whereas they ought, by undermining and other stratagems of war, to endeavour the taking of the city, especially when they had before their eyes the example of Abimelech, the son of Gideon, who would needs take the tower in Thebes by force, and was killed by a large stone thrown at him by an old woman; and, although he was a man of great prowess, he died ignominiously by the dangerous manner of his assault. That they should remember this accident, and not come near the enemy's wall, for that the best method of making war with success was to call to mind the accidents of former wars, and what good or bad success had attended them in the like dangerous cases, that so they might imitate the one, and avoid the other. But when the king was in this disposition, the messengers told him that Uriah was slain also; whereupon he was pacified. So he bade the messengers go back to Joab and tell him, that this misfortune is no other than what is common among mankind; and that such is the nature, and such the accidents of war, insomuch that sometimes the enemy will have success therein, and sometimes others; but that he ordered him to go on still in his care about the siege, that no ill accident might befall him in it hereafter: that they should raise bulwarks and use machines in besieging the city; and when they have gotten it, to overturn its very foundations, and to destroy all those that are in it. Accordingly, the messengers carried the king's message with which they were charged, and made haste to Joab. But Bathsheba, the wife of Uriah, when she was informed of the death of her husband, mourned for his death many days; and when her mourning was over, and the tears which she shed for Uriah were dried up, the king took her to wife presently; and a son was born to him by her.

3. With this marriage God was not well pleased, but was thereupon angry at David; and he appeared to Nathan the prophet in his sleep, and complained of the king. Now Nathan was a fair and prudent man; and considering

that kings, when they fall into a passion, are guided more by that passion than they are by justice, he resolved to conceal the threatenings that proceeded from God, and made a good-natured discourse to him, and this after the manner following:—He desired that the king would give him his opinion in the following case : —"There were," said he, "two men inhabiting the same city, the one of them was rich and [the other poor.] The rich man had a great many flocks of cattle, of sheep, and of kine; but the poor man had but one ewe-lamb. This he brought up with his children, and let her eat her food with them; and he had the same natural affection for her which any one might have for a daughter. Now upon the coming of a stranger to the rich man, he would not vouchsafe to kill any of his own flocks, and thence feast his friend; but he sent for the poor man's lamb, and took her away from him, and made her ready for food, and thence feasted the stranger." This discourse troubled the king exceedingly; and he denounced to Nathan, that "this man was a wicked man, who could dare to do such a thing; and that it was but just that he should restore the lamb fourfold, and be punished with death for it also." Upon this, Nathan immediately said, that he was himself the man who ought to suffer those punishments, and that by his own sentence; and that it was he who had perpetrated this great and horrid crime. He also revealed to him, and laid before him, the anger of God against him, who had made him king over the army of the Hebrews, and lord of all the nations, and these many and great nations round about him; who had formerly delivered him out of the hands of Saul, and had given him such wives as he had justly and legally married; and now this God was despised by him, and affronted by his impiety, when he had married, and now had another man's wife; and by exposing her husband to the enemy, had really slain him; that God would inflict punishments upon him on account of those instances of wickedness; that his own wives should be forced by one of his sons; and that he should be treacherously supplanted by the same son; and that although he had perpetrated his wickedness secretly, yet should that punishment which he was to undergo be inflicted publicly upon him; "that, moreover," said he, "the child who was born to thee of her, shall soon die." When the king was troubled at these messages, and sufficiently confounded, and said, with tears and sorrow, that he had sinned, (for he was without controversy a pious man, and guilty of no sin at all in his whole life, excepting those in the matter of Uriah,) God had compassion on him, and was reconciled to him, and promised that he would preserve to him both his life and his kingdom; for he said, that seeing he repented of the things he had done, he was no longer displeased with him. So Nathan, when he had delivered this prophecy to the king, returned home.

4. However, God sent a dangerous distemper upon the child that was born to David of the wife of Uriah; at which the king was troubled, and did not take any food for seven days, although his servants almost forced him to take it; but he clothed himself in a black garment, and fell down, and lay upon the ground in sackcloth, entreating God for the recovery of the child, for he vehemently loved the child's mother; but when, on the seventh day, the child was dead, the king's servants durst not tell him of it, as supposing that when he knew it, he would still less admit of food and other care

of himself, by reason of his grief at the death of his son, since when the child was only sick, he so greatly afflicted himself, and grieved for him; but when the king perceived that his servants were in disorder, and seemed to be affected as those are who are very desirous to conceal something, he understood that the child was dead; and when he had called one of his servants to him, and discovered that so it was, he arose up and washed himself, and took a white garment, and came into the tabernacle of God. He also commanded them to set supper before him, and thereby greatly surprised his kindred and servants, while he did nothing of this when the child was sick, but did it all when he was dead. Whereupon, having first begged leave to ask him a question, they besought him to tell them the reason of this his conduct; he then called them unskilful people, and instructed them how he had hopes of the recovery of the child while it was alive, and accordingly did all that was proper for him to do, as thinking by such means to render God propitious to him; but that when the child was dead, there was no longer any occasion for grief, which was then to no purpose. When he had said this, they commended the king's wisdom and understanding. He then went in unto Bathsheba his wife, and she conceived and bare a son; and by the command of Nathan the prophet, called his name Solomon.

5. But Joab sorely distressed the Ammonites in the siege, by cutting off their water, and depriving them of other means of subsistence, till they were in the greatest want of meat and drink, for they depended only on one small well of water, and this they durst not drink of too freely, lest the fountain should entirely fail them. So he wrote to the king, and informed him thereof; and persuaded him to come himself to take the city, that he might have the honour of the victory. Upon this letter of Joab's, the king accepted of his good-will and fidelity, and took with him his army, and came to the destruction of Rabbath; and when he had taken it by force, he gave it to his soldiers to plunder it; but he himself took the king of the Ammonites' crown, the weight of which was a talent of gold; * and it had in its middle a precious stone called a sardonyx; which crown David ever after wore on his own head. He also found many other vessels in the city, and those both splendid and of great price; but as for the men, he tormented them,† and then destroyed them: and when he had taken the other cities of the Ammonites by force, he treated them after the same manner.

CHAPTER VIII

HOW ABSALOM MURDERED AMNON, WHO HAD FORCED HIS OWN SISTER ; AND HOW HE WAS BANISHED, AND AFTERWARDS RECALLED BY DAVID

1. WHEN the king was returned to Jerusalem,

---

* A talent of gold was about seven pounds weight.
† I am inclined to think that the meaning of this passage, at least as the words are in Samuel, might only be this : That they were made the lowest slaves, to work in timber or stone, in harrowing the fields, in hewing timber, in making and burning bricks, and the like hard services, but without taking away their lives. We never elsewhere meet with such methods of cruelty in putting men to death in all the Bible, nor do the words in Samuel seem naturally to refer to any such thing.

a sad misfortune befell his house, on the occasion following : He had a daughter who was yet a virgin, and very handsome, insomuch that she surpassed all the most beautiful women ; her name was Tamar ; she had the same mother with Absalom. Now Amnon, David's eldest son, fell in love with her, and being not able to obtain his desires, on account of her virginity, and the custody she was under, was so much out of order, nay, his grief so ate up his body, that he grew lean, and his colour was changed. Now there was one Jonadab, a kinsman and friend of his, who discovered this his passion, for he was an extraordinary wise man, and of great sagacity of mind. When, therefore, he saw that every morning Amnon was not in body as he ought to be, he came to him, and desired him to tell him what was the cause of it : however, he said that he guessed that it arose from the passion of love. Amnon confessed his passion, that he was in love with a sister of his, who had the same father with himself. So Jonadab suggested to him by what method and contrivance he might obtain his desires ; for he persuaded him to pretend sickness, and bade him, when his father should come to him, to beg of him that his sister might come and minister to him ; for, if that were done, he should be better, and should quickly recover from his distemper. So Amnon lay down on his bed, and pretended to be sick, as Jonadab had suggested. When his father came, and inquired how he did, he begged of him to send his sister to him. Accordingly, he presently ordered her to be brought to him ; and when she was come, Amnon bade her make cakes for him, and fry them in a pan, and do it all with her own hands, because he should take them better from her hand [than from any one's else.] So she kneaded the flower in the sight of her brother, and made him cakes, and baked them in a pan, and brought them to him ; but at that time he would not taste them, but gave order to his servants to send all that were there out of his chamber, because he had a mind to repose himself, free from tumult and disturbance. As soon as what he had commanded was done, he desired his sister to bring his supper to him into the inner parlour ; which, when the damsel had done, he took hold of her, and endeavoured to persuade her to lie with him. Whereupon the damsel cried out, and said, " Nay, brother, do not force me, nor be so wicked as to transgress the laws, and bring upon thyself the utmost confusion. Curb this thy unrighteous and impure lust, from which our house will get nothing but reproach and disgrace." She also advised him to speak to his father about this affair ; for he would permit him [to marry her.] This she said, as desirous to avoid her brother's violent passion at present. But he would not yield to her ; but, inflamed with love and blinded with the vehemency of his passion, he forced his sister ; but as soon as Amnon had satisfied his lust, he hated her immediately, and giving her reproachful words, bade her rise up and be gone. And when she said that this was a more injurious treatment than the former, if, now he had forced her, he would not let her stay with him till the evening, but bid her go away in the daytime, and while it was light, that she might meet with people that would be witness of her shame,—he commanded his servant to turn her out of his house. Whereupon she was sorely grieved at the injury and violence that had been offered to her, and rent her loose coat, (for the virgins of old time wore such loose coats tied at the hands, and let down to the ankles, that the inner coats might not be seen,) and sprinkled ashes on her

head ; and went up the middle of the city, crying out and lamenting for the violence that had been offered her. Now Absalom, her brother, happened to meet her, and asked her what sad thing had befallen her, that she was in that plight ; and when she had told him what injury had been offered her, he comforted her, and desired her to be quiet, and take all patiently, and not to esteem her being corrupted by her brother as an injury. So she yielded to his advice, and left off her crying out, and discovering the force offered her to the multitude : and she continued as a widow with her brother Absalom a long time.

2. When David his father knew this, he was grieved at the actions of Amnon ; but because he had an extraordinary affection for him, for he was his eldest son, he was compelled not to afflict him ; but Absalom watched for a fit opportunity of revenging this crime upon him, for he thoroughly hated him. Now the second year after this wicked affair about his sister was over, and Absalom was about to go to shear his own sheep at Baalhazor, which is a city in the portion of Ephraim, he besought his father, as well as his brethren, to come and feast with him : but when David excused himself, as not being willing to be burdensome to him, Absalom desired he would however send his brethren ; whom he did send accordingly. Then Absalom charged his own servants, that when they should see Amnon disordered and drowsy with wine, and he should give them a signal, they should fear nobody, but kill him.

3. When they had done as they were commanded, the rest of his brethren were astonished and disturbed, and were afraid for themselves, so they immediately got on horseback, and rode away to their father : but somebody there was who prevented them, and told their father they were all slain by Absalom ; whereupon he was overcome with sorrow, as for so many of his sons that were destroyed at once, and that by their brother also ; and by this consideration, that it was their brother that appeared to have slain them, he aggravated his sorrow for them. So he neither inquired what was the cause of this slaughter, nor stayed to hear anything else, which yet it was but reasonable to have done, when so very great, and by that greatness so incredible a misfortune was related to him, he rent his clothes, and threw himself upon the ground, and there lay lamenting the loss of all his sons, both those who, as he was informed, were slain, and of him who slew them. But Jonadab, the son of his brother Shemeah, entreated him not to indulge his sorrow so far, for as to the rest of his sons he did not believe that they were slain, for he found no cause for such a suspicion ; but he said it might deserve inquiry as to Amnon, for it was not unlikely that Absalom might venture to kill him on account of the injury he had offered to Tamar. In the meantime, a great noise of horses, and a tumult of some people that were coming, turned their attention to them ; they were the king's sons, who were fled away from the feast. So their father met them as they were in their grief, and he himself grieved with them ; but it was more than he expected to see those his sons again, whom he had a little before heard to have perished. However, there were tears on both sides ; they lamenting their brother who was killed, and the king lamenting his son, who was killed also ; but Absalom fled to Geshur, to his grandfather by his mother's side, who was king of that country, and he remained with him three whole years.

4. Now David had a design to send to Absalom,

not to come that he should to be punished, but that he might be with him, for the effects of his anger were abated by length of time. It was Joab, the captain of his host, that chiefly persuaded him so to do; for he suborned an ordinary woman, that was stricken in age, to go to the king in mourning apparel, who said thus to him:—That two of her sons, in a coarse way, had some difference between them, and that in the progress of that difference they came to an open quarrel, and that one was smitten by the other, and was dead; and she desired him to interpose in this case, and to do her the favour to save this her son from her kindred, who were very zealous to have him that had slain his brother put to death, that so she might not be further deprived of the hopes she had of being taken care of in her old age by him; and that if he would hinder this slaughter of her son by those that wished for it, he would do her a great favour, because the kindred would not be restrained from their purpose by anything else than by the fear of him:—and when the king had given his consent to what the woman had begged of him, she made this reply to him:—"I owe thee thanks for thy benignity to me in pitying my old age, and preventing the loss of my only remaining child; but in order to assure me of this thy kindness, be first reconciled to thine own son, and cease to be angry with him; for how shall I persuade myself that thou hast really bestowed this favour upon me, while thou thyself continuest after the like manner in thy wrath to thine own son? for it is a foolish thing to add wilfully another to thy dead son, while the death of the other was brought about without thy consent:"—and now the king perceived that this pretended story was a subornation derived from Joab, and was of his contrivance; and when, upon inquiry of the old woman, he understood it to be so in reality, he called for Joab, and told him he had obtained what he requested according to his own mind; and he bid him bring Absalom back, for he was now displeased, but had already ceased to be angry with him. So Joab bowed himself down to the king, and took his words kindly, and went immediately to Geshur, and took Absalom with him, and came to Jerusalem.

5. However, the king sent a message to his son beforehand, as he was coming, and commanded him to retire to his own house, for he was not yet in such a disposition as to think fit at present to see him. Accordingly, upon the father's command, he avoided coming into his presence, and contented himself with the respects paid him by his own family only. Now his beauty was not impaired, either by the grief he had been under, or by the want of such care as was proper to be taken of a king's son, for he still surpassed and excelled all men in the tallness of his body, and was more eminent [in a fine appearance] than those that dieted the most luxuriously; and indeed such was the thickness of the hair of his head, that it was with difficulty he was polled every eighth day; and his hair weighed two hundred shekels,* which are five pounds. However, he dwelt in Jerusalem two years, and became the father of three sons and one daughter; which daughter was of very great beauty, and which Rehoboam, the son of Solomon, took to wife afterward, and had by her a son named Abijah; but Absalom sent to Joab, and desired him to pacify his father entirely towards him; and to beseech him to give him leave

to come to him to see him, and speak with him; but when Joab neglected so to do, he sent some of his own servants, and set fire to the field adjoining to him; which, when Joab understood, he came to Absalom, and accused him of what he had done; and asked him the reason why he did so? To which Absalom replied, that "I have found out this stratagem that might bring thee to us, while thou hast taken no care to perform the injunction I laid upon thee, which was this, to reconcile my father to me; and I really beg it of thee, now thou art here, to pacify my father as to me, since I esteem my coming hither to be more grievous than my banishment, while my father's wrath against me continues." Hereby Joab was persuaded, and pitied the distress that Absalom was in, and became an intercessor with the king for him; and when he had discoursed with his father, he soon brought him to that amicable disposition towards Absalom, that he presently sent for him to come to him; and when he had cast himself down upon the ground, and had begged for the forgiveness of his offences, the king raised him up, and promised him to forget what he had formerly done.

CHAPTER IX

CONCERNING THE INSURRECTION OF ABSALOM AGAINST DAVID; AND CONCERNING AHITHOPHEL AND HUSHAI; AND CONCERNING ZIBA AND SHIMEI; AND HOW AHITHOPHEL HANGED HIMSELF

1. Now Absalom, upon this his success with the king, procured to himself a great many horses, and many chariots, and that in a little time also. He had moreover fifty armourbearers that were about him, and he came early every day to the king's palace, and spake what was agreeable to such as came for justice and lost their causes, as if that happened for want of good counsellors about the king, or perhaps because the judges mistook in that unjust sentence they gave; whereby he gained the good-will of them all. He told them, that had he but such authority committed to him, he would distribute justice to them in a most equitable manner. When he had made himself so popular among the multitude, he thought he had already the good-will of the people secured to him; but when four years* had passed since his father's reconciliation to him, he came to him, and besought him to give him leave to go to Hebron, and pay a sacrifice to God, because he vowed it to him when he fled out of the country. So when David had granted his request, he went thither, and great multitudes came running together to him, for he had sent to a great number so to do.

2. Among them came Ahithophel the Gilonite, a counsellor of David's, and two hundred men out of Jerusalem itself, who knew not his intentions, but were sent for as to a sacrifice. So he was appointed king by all of them, which he obtained by this stratagem. As soon as this news was brought to David, and he was informed of what he did not expect from his son, he was affrighted at this his impious and bold under-

---

* Dr Wall thinks that the LXX meant not its weight, but its value was twenty shekels.

* This is one of the best corrections that Josephus's copy affords us of a text that, in our ordinary copies, is grossly corrupted. They say that this rebellion of Absalom was forty years after what went before, (of his reconciliation to his father,) whereas the series of the history shews it could not be more than four years after it.

taking, and wondered that he was so far from re-membering how his offence had been so lately forgiven him, that he undertook much worse and more wicked enterprises; first, to deprive him of that kingdom which was given him of God; and, secondly, to take away his own father's life. He therefore resolved to fly to the parts beyond Jordan; so he called his most intimate friends together, and communicated to them all that he had heard of his son's madness. He committed himself to God, to judge between them about all their actions; and left the care of his royal palace to his ten concubines, and went away from Jerusalem, being willingly accompanied by the rest of the multitude, who went hastily away with him, and particularly by those six hundred armed men, who had been with him from his first flight in the days of Saul. But he persuaded Abiathar and Zadok, the high priests, who had determined to go away with him, as also all the Levites, who were with the ark, to stay behind, as hoping that God would deliver him without its removal; but he charged them to let him know privately how all things went on; and he had their sons, Ahimaaz the son of Zadok, and Jonathan the son of Abiathar, for faithful ministers in all things; but Ittai the Gittite went out with him whether David would let him or not, for he would have persuaded him to stay, and on that account he appeared the more friendly to him; but as he was ascending the mount of Olives barefooted, and all his company were in tears, it was told him that Ahithophel was with Absalom, and was of his side. This hearing augmented his grief; and he besought God earnestly to alienate the mind of Absalom from Ahithophel, for he was afraid that he should persuade him to follow his pernicious counsel, for he was a prudent man, and very sharp in seeing what was advantageous. When David was gotten upon the top of the mountain, he took a view of the city; and prayed to God with abundance of tears, as having already lost his kingdom; and here it was that a faithful friend of his, whose name was Hushai, met him. When David saw him with his clothes rent, and having ashes all over his head, and in lamentation for the great change of affairs, he comforted him, and exhorted him to leave off grieving; nay, at length he besought him to go back to Absalom, and appear as one of his party, and to fish out the secretest counsels of his mind, and to contradict the counsels of Ahithophel, for that he could not do him so much good by being with him as he might by being with Absalom. So he was prevailed on by David, and left him, and came to Jerusalem, whither Absalom himself came also a little while afterward.

3. When David was gone a little further, there met him Ziba, the servant of Mephibosheth (whom he had sent to take care of the possessions which had been given him, as the son of Jonathan, the son of Saul) with a couple of asses, loaden with provisions, and desired him to take as much of them as he and his followers stood in need of. And when the king asked him where he had left Mephibosheth, he said he had left him in Jerusalem, expecting to be chosen king in the present confusions, in remembrance of the benefits Saul had conferred upon them. At this the king had great indignation, and gave to Ziba all that he had formerly bestowed on Mephibosheth, for he determined that it was much fitter that he should have them than the other; at which Ziba greatly rejoiced.

4. When David was at Bahurim, a place so called, there came out a kinsman of Saul's, whose name was Shimei, and threw stones at him, and gave him reproachful words; and as his friends stood about the king and protected him, he persevered still more in his reproaches, and called him a bloody man, and the author of all sorts of mischief. He bade him also go out of the land as an impure and accursed wretch; and he thanked God for depriving him of his kingdom, and causing him to be punished for what injuries he had done to his master [Saul,] and this by the means of his own son. Now when they were all provoked against him, and angry at him, and particularly Abishai, who had a mind to kill Shimei, David restrained his anger. "Let us not," said he, "bring upon ourselves another fresh misfortune to those we have already, for truly I have not the least regard nor concern for this dog that ravest at me: I submit myself to God, by whose permission this man treats me in such a wild manner; nor is it any wonder that I am obliged to undergo these abuses from him, while I experience the like from an impious son of my own; but perhaps God will have some commiseration upon us; if it be his will we shall overcome them." So he went on his way without troubling himself with Shimei, who ran along the other side of the mountain, and threw out his abusive language plentifully. But when David was come to Jordan, he allowed those that were with him to refresh themselves; for they were weary.

5. But when Absalom, and Ahithophel his counsellor, were come to Jerusalem, with all the people, David's friend, Hushai, came to them; and when he had worshipped Absalom, he withal wished that his kingdom might last a long time, and continue for all ages. But when Absalom said to him, "How comes this, that he who was so intimate a friend of my father's, and appeared faithful to him in all things, is not with him now, but hath left him, and is come over to me?" Hushai's answer was very pertinent and prudent; for he said, "We ought to follow God and the multitude of the people; while these, therefore, my lord and master, are with thee, it is fit that I should follow them, for thou hast received the kingdom from God. I will therefore, if thou believest me to be thy friend, shew the same fidelity and kindness to thee which thou knowest I have shewn to thy father: nor is there any reason to be in the least dissatisfied with the present state of affairs, for the kingdom is not transferred into another, but remains still in the same family, by the son's receiving it after his father." This speech persuaded Absalom, who before suspected Hushai. And now he called Ahithophel, and consulted with him what he ought to do; he persuaded him to go in unto his father's concubines; for he said, that "by this action the people would believe that thy difference with thy father is irreconcilable, and will thence fight with great alacrity against thy father, for hitherto they are afraid of taking up open enmity against him, out of an expectation that you will be reconciled again." Accordingly, Absalom was prevailed on by this advice, and commanded his servants to pitch him a tent upon the top of the royal palace, in the sight of the multitude; and he went in and lay with his father's concubines. Now this came to pass according to the prediction of Nathan, when he prophesied and signified to him that his son would rise up in rebellion against him.

6. And when Absalom had done what he was advised to by Ahithophel, he desired his advice, in the second place, about the war against his father. Now Ahithophel only asked him to let him have ten thousand chosen men, and he promised he would slay his father, and bring the soldiers back again in safety; and he said, that

then the kingdom would be firm to him when David was dead, [but not otherwise.] Absalom was pleased with this advice, and called for Hushai, David's friend, (for so did he style him,) and informed him of the opinion of Ahithophel: he asked, further, what was his opinion concerning that matter. Now he was sensible that if Ahithophel's counsel were followed, David would be in danger of being seized on, and slain; so he attempted to introduce a contrary opinion, and said, "Thou art not unacquainted, O king, with the valour of thy father, and of those that are now with him; that he hath made many wars, and hath always come off with victory, though probably he now abides in the camp, for he is very skilful in stratagems, and in foreseeing the deceitful tricks of his enemies; yet will he not leave his own soldiers in the evening, and will either hide himself in some valley, or will place an ambush at some rock; so that, when our army joins battle with him, his soldiers will retire for a little while, but will come upon us again, as encouraged by the king's being near them; and in the meantime your father will shew himself suddenly in the time of the battle, and will infuse courage into his own people when they are in danger, but bring consternation to thine. Consider therefore, my advice, and reason upon it, and if thou canst not but acknowledge it to be the best, reject the opinion of Ahithophel. Send to the entire country of the Hebrews, and order them to come and fight with thy father; and do thou thyself take the army, and be thine own general in this war, and do not trust its management to another; then expect to conquer him with ease, when thou overtakest him openly with his few partizans, but hast thyself many ten thousands, who will be desirous to demonstrate to thee their diligence and alacrity. And if thy father shall shut himself up in some city, and bear a siege, we will overthrow that city with machines of war, and by undermining it." When Hushai had said this, he obtained his point against Ahithophel, for his opinion was preferred by Absalom before the other's: however, it was no other than God * who made the counsel of Hushai appear best to the mind of Absalom.

7. So Hushai made haste to the high priests, Zadok and Abiathar, and told them the opinion of Ahithophel, and his own, and that the resolution was taken to follow this latter advice. He therefore bade them send to David, and tell him of it, and to inform him of the counsels that had been taken; and to desire him further to pass quickly over Jordan, lest his son should change his mind, and make haste to pursue him, and so prevent him, and seize upon him before he be in safety. Now the high priests had their sons concealed in a proper place out of the city, that they might carry news to David of what was transacted. Accordingly, they sent a maid-servant, whom they could trust, to them, to carry the news of Absalom's counsels, and ordered them to signify the same to David with all speed.

So they made no excuse nor delay, but taking along with them their father's injunctions, because pious and faithful ministers; and, judging that quickness and suddenness was the best mark of faithful service, they made haste to meet with David. But certain horsemen saw them when they were two furlongs from the city, and informed Absalom of them, who immediately sent some to take them; but when the sons of the high priests perceived this, they went out of the road, and betook themselves to a certain village, (that village was called Bahurim;) there they desired a certain woman to hide them, and afford them security. Accordingly she let the young men down by a rope into a well, and laid fleeces of wool over them; and when those that pursued them came to her, and asked her whether she saw them, she did not deny that she had seen them, for that they stayed with her some time, but she said they then went their ways; and she foretold, that, however, if they would follow them directly, they would catch them; but when, after a long pursuit, they could not catch them, they came back again; and when the woman saw those men were returned, and that there was no longer any fear of the young men's being caught by them, she drew them up by the rope, and bade them go on their journey. Accordingly they used great diligence in the prosecution of that journey, and came to David and informed him accurately of all the counsels of Absalom. So he commanded those that were with him to pass over Jordan while it was night, and not to delay at all on that account.

8. But Ahithophel, on rejection of his advice, got upon his ass and rode away to his own country, Gilon; and calling his family together, he told them distinctly what advice he had given Absalom; and since he had not been persuaded by it, he said he would evidently perish, and this in no long time, and that David would overcome him, and return to his kingdom again; so he said it was better that he should take his own life away with freedom and magnanimity, than expose himself to be punished by David, in opposition to whom he had acted entirely for Absalom. When he had discoursed thus to them, he went into the inmost room of his house, and hanged himself; and thus was the death of Ahithophel, who was self-condemned; and when his relations had taken him down from the halter, they took care of his funeral. Now, as for David, he passed over Jordan, as we have said already, and came to Mahanaim, a very fine and very strong city; and all the chief men of the country received him with great pleasure, both out of the shame they had that he should be forced to flee away, [from Jerusalem,] and out of the respect they bare him while he was in his former prosperity. These were Barzillai the Gileadite, and Siphar the ruler among the Ammonites, and Machir the principal man of Gilead; and these furnished him with plentiful provisions for himself and his followers, insomuch that they wanted no beds nor blankets for them, nor loaves of bread, nor wine; nay, they brought them a great many cattle for slaughter, and afforded them what furniture they wanted for their refreshment when they were weary, and for food, with plenty of other necessaries.

* This reflection of Josephus's, that God brought to naught the dangerous counsel of Ahithophel, and directly infatuated wicked Absalom to reject it, is a very just one, and in him not unfrequent. Nor does Josephus ever puzzle himself, or perplex his readers, with subtle hypotheses as to the manner of such judicial infatuations by God, while the justice of them is generally so obvious. That peculiar manner of the divine operations, or permissions, or the means God makes use of in such cases, is often impenetrable by us. "Secret things belong to the Lord our God; but those things that are revealed belong to us, and to our children for ever, that we may do all the words of this law," (Deut. xxix. 29.)

CHAPTER X

HOW, WHEN ABSALOM WAS BEATEN, HE WAS CAUGHT IN A TREE BY HIS HAIR, AND WAS SLAIN

1. AND this was the state of David and his

followers: but Absalom got together a vast army of the Hebrews to oppose his father, and passed therewith over the river Jordan, and sat down not far off Mahanaim, in the country of Gilead. He appointed Amasa to be captain of all his host, instead of Joab his kinsman: his father was Ithra, and his mother Abigail: now she and Zeruiah, the mother of Joab, were David's sisters; but when David had numbered his followers, and found them to be about four thousand, he resolved not to tarry till Absalom attacked him, but set over his men captains of thousands, and captains of hundreds, and divided his army into three parts; the one part he committed to Joab, the next to Abishai, Joab's brother, and the third to Ittai, David's companion and friend, but one that came from the city Gath: and when he was desirous of fighting himself among them, his friends would not let him: and this refusal of theirs was founded upon very wise reasons:—"For," said they, "if we be conquered when he is with us, we have lost all good hopes of recovering ourselves; but if we should be beaten in one part of our army, the other parts may retire to him, and may thereby prepare a greater force, while the enemy will naturally suppose that he hath another army with him." So David was pleased with this their advice, and resolved himself to tarry at Mahanaim; and as he sent his friends and commanders to the battle, he desired them to shew all possible alacrity and fidelity, and to bear in mind what advantages they had received from him, which, though they had not been very great, yet had they not been quite inconsiderable; and he begged of them to spare the young man Absalom, lest some mischief should befall himself, if he should be killed; and thus did he send out his army to the battle, and wished them victory therein.

2. Then did Joab put his army in battle array over-against the enemy in the Great Plain, where he had a wood behind him. Absalom also brought his army into the field to oppose him. Upon the joining of the battle, both sides shewed great actions with their hands and their boldness; the one side exposing themselves to the greatest hazards, and using their utmost alacrity, that David might recover his kingdom; and the other being no way deficient, either in doing or suffering, that Absalom might not be deprived of that kingdom, and be brought to punishment by his father, for his impudent attempt against him. Those also that were the most numerous were solicitous that they might not be conquered by those few that were with Joab, and with the other commanders, because that would be the greatest disgrace to them; while David's soldiers strove greatly to overcome so many ten thousands as the enemy had with them. Now David's men were conquerors, as superior in strength and skill in war; so they followed the others as they fled away through the forests and valleys; some they took prisoners, and many they slew, and more in the flight than in the battle, for there fell about twenty thousand that day. But all David's men ran violently upon Absalom, for he was easily known by his beauty and tallness. He was himself also afraid lest his enemies should seize on him, so he got upon the king's mule and fled; but as he was carried with violence, and noise, and a great motion, as being himself light, he entangled his hair greatly in the large boughs of a knotty tree, that spread a great way, and there he hung after a surprising manner; and as for the beast, it went on further, and that swiftly, as if his master had been still upon his back;

but he hanging in the air upon the boughs, was taken by his enemies. Now when one of David's soldiers saw this, he informed Joab of it; and when the general said, That if he had shot at and killed Absalom, he would have given him fifty shekels,—he replied, "I would not have killed my master's son if thou wouldst have given me a thousand shekels, especially when he desired that the young man might be spared, in the hearing of us all." But Joab bade him shew him where it was that he saw Absalom hang; whereupon he shot him to the heart, and slew him, and Joab's armour-bearers stood round the tree, and pulled down his dead body, and cast it into a great chasm that was out of sight, and laid a heap of stones upon him, till the cavity was filled up, and had both the appearance and the bigness of a grave. Then Joab sounded a retreat, and recalled his own soldiers from pursuing the enemy's army, in order to spare their countrymen.

3. Now Absalom had erected for himself a marble pillar in the king's dale, two furlongs distant from Jerusalem, which he named Absalom's Hand, saying, that if his children were killed, his name would remain by that pillar; for he had three sons and one daughter, named Tamar, as we said before, who, when she was married to David's grandson, Rehoboam, bare a son, Abijah by name, who succeeded his father in the kingdom; but of these we shall speak in a part of our history which will be more proper. After the death of Absalom, they returned every one to their own homes respectively.

4. But now Ahimaaz, the son of Zadok the high priest, went to Joab, and desired he would permit him to go and tell David of this victory, and to bring him the good news that God had afforded his assistance and his providence to him. However, he did not grant his request, but said to him, "Wilt thou, who hast always been the messenger of good news, now go and acquaint the king that his son is dead?" So he desired him to desist. He then called Cushi, and committed the business to him, that he should tell the king what he had seen. But when Ahimaaz again desired him to let him go as a messenger, and assured him that he would only relate what concerned the victory, but not concerning the death of Absalom, he gave him leave to go to David. Now he took a nearer road than the former did, for nobody knew it but himself, and he came before Cushi. Now as David was sitting between the gates,* and waiting to see when somebody would come to him from the battle, and tell him how it went, one of the watchmen saw Ahimaaz running, and before he could discern who he was, he told David that he saw somebody coming to him, who said, he was a good messenger. A little while after, he informed him, that another messenger followed him; whereupon the king said, that he also was a good messenger: but when the watchman saw Ahimaaz, and that he was already very near, he gave the king notice, that it was the son of Zadok the high priest, who came running. So David was very glad, and said he was a messenger of good tidings, and brought him some such news from the battle as he desired to hear.

5. While the king was saying thus, Ahimaaz appeared, and worshipped the king. And when

---

* The reader need not be surprised at this account of David's throne, that it was between two gates; gates being in cities, as well as at the temple, large open places, with a portal at the entrance, and another at the exit, between which judicial causes were heard, and public consultations taken.

the king inquired of him about the battle, he said he brought him the good news of victory and dominion. And when he inquired what he had to say concerning his son, he said that he came away on the sudden as soon as the enemy was defeated, but that he heard a great noise of those that pursued Absalom, and that he could learn no more, because of the haste he made when Joab sent him to inform him of the victory. But when Cushi was come, and had worshipped him, and informed him of the victory, he asked him about his son, who replied, "May the like misfortune befall thine enemies as hath befallen Absalom." That word did not permit either himself or his soldiers to rejoice at the victory, though it was a very great one; but David went up to the highest part of the city,* and wept for his son, and beat his breast, tearing [the hair of] his head, tormenting himself all manner of ways, and crying out, "O my son! I wish that I had died myself, and ended my days with thee!" for he was of a tender natural affection, and had extraordinary compassion for this son in particular. But when the army and Joab heard that the king mourned for his son, they were ashamed to enter the city in the habit of conquerors, but they all came in as cast down, and in tears, as if they had been beaten. Now while the king covered himself, and grievously lamented his son, Joab went in to him, and said, "O my lord the king, thou art not aware that thou layest a blot on thyself by what thou now doest; for thou now seemest to hate those that love thee, and undergo dangers for thee; nay, to hate thyself and thy family, and to love those that are thy bitter enemies, and to desire the company of those that are no more, and who have been justly slain; for had Absalom gotten the victory, and firmly settled himself in the kingdom, there had been none of us left alive, but all of us, beginning with thyself and thy children, had miserably perished, while our enemies had not wept for us, but rejoiced over us, and punished even those that pitied us in our misfortunes; and thou art not ashamed to do this in the case of one that has been thy bitter enemy, who, while he was thine own son, hath proved so wicked to thee. Leave off, therefore, thy unreasonable grief, and come abroad, and be seen by thy soldiers, and return them thanks for the alacrity they shewed in the fight; for I myself will this day persuade the people to leave thee, and to give the kingdom to another, if thou continuest to do thus: and then I shall make thee to grieve bitterly and in earnest." Upon Joab's speaking thus to him, he made the king leave off his sorrow, and brought him to the consideration of his affairs. So David changed his habit, and exposed himself in a manner fit to be seen by the multitude, and sat in the gates; whereupon all the people heard of it, and ran together to him, and saluted him. And this was the present state of David's affairs.

CHAPTER XI

HOW DAVID, WHEN HE HAD RECOVERED HIS KINGDOM, WAS RECONCILED TO SHIMEI, AND

TO ZIBA; AND SHEWED A GREAT AFFECTION TO BARZILLAI; AND HOW, UPON THE RISE OF A SEDITION, HE MADE AMASA CAPTAIN OF HIS HOST, IN ORDER TO PURSUE SHEBA; WHICH AMASA WAS SLAIN BY JOAB

1. Now those Hebrews that had been with Absalom, and had retired out of the battle, when they were all returned home, sent messengers to every city to put them in mind of what benefits David had bestowed upon them, and of that liberty which he had procured them, by delivering them from many and great wars. But they complained, that whereas they had ejected him out of his kingdom, and committed it to another governor, which other governor, whom they had set up, was already dead; they did now beseech David to leave off his anger at them, and to become friends with them, and, as he used to do, to resume the care of their affairs, and to take the kingdom again. This was often told to David. And, this notwithstanding, David sent to Zadok and Abiathar the high priests, that they should speak to the rulers of the tribe of Judah after the manner following:— That it would be a reproach upon them to permit the other tribes to choose David for their king, before their tribe, and this, said he, while you are akin to him, and of the same common blood. He commended them also to say the same to Amasa, the captain of their forces, That whereas he was his sister's son, he had not persuaded the multitude to restore the kingdom of David; that he might expect from him not only a reconciliation, for that was already granted, but that supreme command of the army also which Absalom had bestowed upon him. Accordingly, the high priests, when they had discoursed with the rulers of the tribe, and said what the king had ordered them, persuaded Amasa to undertake the care of his affairs. So he persuaded that tribe to send immediately ambassadors to him, to beseech him to return to his own kingdom. The same did all the Israelites, at the like persuasion of Amasa.

2. When the ambassadors came to him, he came to Jerusalem; and the tribe of Judah was the first that came to meet the king at the river Jordan; and Shimei, the son of Gera, came with a thousand men, which he brought with him out of the tribe of Benjamin; and Ziba, the freedman of Saul, with his sons, fifteen in number, and with his twenty servants. All these, as well as the tribe of Judah, laid a bridge [of boats] over the river, that the king, and those that were with him, might with ease pass over it. Now as soon as he was come to Jordan, the tribe of Judah saluted him. Shimei also came upon the bridge, took hold of his feet, and prayed him to forgive him what he had offended, and not to be too bitter against him, nor to think fit to make him the first example of severity under his new authority; but to consider that he had repented of his failure of duty, and had taken care to come first of all to him. While he was thus entreating the king, and moving him to compassion, Abishai, Joab's brother, said, And shall not this man die for this, that he hath cursed that king whom God hath appointed to reign over us? But David turned himself to him, and said, "Will you never leave off, ye sons of Zeruiah? Do not you, I pray, raise new troubles and seditions among us, now the former are over; for I would not have you ignorant, that I this day begin my reign, and therefore swear to remit to all offenders their punishments, and not to animadvert on any one that has sinned. Be thou, therefore," said he, "O Shimei, of good courage, and

---

* Since David was now in Mahanaim, and in the open place of that city-gate, and since our other copies say he went up to the chamber over the gate. (2 Sam. xviii. 33,) I think we ought to correct our present reading in Josephus, and for *city*, should read *gate*. Accordingly we find David presently, (2 Sam. xix. 8,) sitting as before, in the *gate* of the city.

do not at all fear being put to death." So he worshipped him, and went on before him.

3. Mephibosheth also, Saul's grandson, met David, clothed in a sordid garment, and having his hair thick and neglected; for after David was fled away, he was in such grief that he had not polled his head, nor had he washed his clothes, as dooming himself to undergo such hardships upon occasion of the change of the king's affairs. Now he had been unjustly calumniated to the king by Ziba, his steward. When he had saluted the king, and worshipped him, the king began to ask him why he did not go out of Jerusalem with him, and accompany him during his flight? He replied, that this piece of injustice was owing to Ziba; because, when he was ordered to get things ready for his going out with him, he took no care of it, but regarded him no more than if he had been a slave; "and, indeed, had I had my feet sound and strong, I had not deserted thee, for I could then have made use of them in my flight: but this is not all the injury that Ziba has done to me, as to my duty to thee, my lord and master, but he hath calumniated me besides, and told lies about me of his own invention; but I know thy mind will not admit of such calumnies, but is righteously disposed, and a lover of truth, which it is also the will of God should prevail. For when thou wast in the greatest danger of suffering by my grandfather, and when, on that account, our whole family might justly have been destroyed, thou wast moderate and merciful, and didst then especially forget all those injuries, when, if thou hadst remembered them, thou hadst the power of punishing us for them; but thou hast judged me to be thy friend, and hast set me every day at thine own table; nor have I wanted anything which one of thine own kinsmen, of greatest esteem with thee, could have expected." When he had said this, David resolved neither to punish Mephibosheth, nor to condemn Ziba, as having belied his master; but said to him, that as he had [before] granted all his estate to Ziba, because he did not come along with him, so he [now] promised to forgive him, and ordered that the one half of his estate should be restored to him.* Whereupon Mephibosheth said, "Nay, let Ziba take all; it suffices me that thou hast recovered thy kingdom."

4. But David desired Barzillai the Gileadite, that great and good man, and one that had made a plentiful provision for him at Mahanaim, and had conducted him as far as Jordan, to accompany him to Jerusalem, for he promised to treat him in his old age with all manner of respect—to take care of him, and provide for him. But Barzillai was so desirous to live at home, that he entreated him to excuse him from attendance on him; and said, that his age was too great to enjoy the pleasures [of a court,] since he was fourscore years old, and was therefore making provision for his death and burial; so he desired him to gratify him in this request, and dismiss him; for he had no relish of his meat or his drink, by reason of his age; and that his ears were too much shut up to hear the sound of pipes, or the melody of other musical instruments, such as all those that live with kings delight in. When he entreated for this so earnestly, the king said, "I dismiss thee; but thou shalt grant me thy son Chimham, and upon him will I bestow all sorts

of good things." So Barzillai left his son with him, and worshipped the king, and wished him a prosperous conclusion of all his affairs according to his own mind, and then returned home: but David came to Gilgal, having about him half the people [of Israel,] and the [whole] tribe of Judah.

5. Now the principal men of the country came to Gilgal to him with a great multitude, and complained of the tribe of Judah, that they had come to him in a private manner, whereas they ought all conjointly, and with one and the same intention, to have given him the meeting. But the rulers of the tribe of Judah desired them not to be displeased if they had been prevented by them: for, said they, "We are David's kinsmen, and on that account we the rather took care of him, and loved him, and so came first to him;" yet had they not, by their early coming, received any gifts from him, which might give them who came last any uneasiness. When the rulers of the tribe of Judah had said this, the rulers of the other tribe were not quiet, but said further, "O brethren, we cannot but wonder at you when you call the king your kinsman alone, whereas he that hath received from God the power over all of us in common, ought to be esteemed a kinsman to us all; for which reason the whole people have eleven parts in him, and you but one part:† we are also elder than you; wherefore you have not done justly in coming to the king in this private and concealed manner."

6. While these rulers were thus disputing one with another, a certain wicked man, who took a pleasure in seditious practices (his name was Sheba, the son of Bichri, of the tribe of Benjamin) stood up in the midst of the multitude, and cried aloud, and spake thus to them:—"We have no part in David, nor inheritance in the son of Jesse." And when he had used those words, he blew with a trumpet, and declared war against the king; and they all left David, and followed him; the tribe of Judah alone stayed with him, and settled him at his royal palace at Jerusalem. But as for his concubines, with whom Absalom his son had accompanied, truly he removed them to another house; and ordered those that had the care of them to make a plentiful provision for them; but he came not near them any more. He also appointed Amasa for the captain of his forces, and gave him the same high office which Joab before had; and he commanded him to gather together, out of the tribe of Judah, as great an army as he could, and come to him within three days, that he might deliver to him his entire army, and might send him to fight against [Sheba] the son of Bichri. Now while Amasa was gone out, and made some delay in gathering the army together, and so was not yet returned, on the third day the king said to Joab, —"It is not fit we should make any delay in this affair of Sheba, lest he should get a numerous army about him, and be the occasion of greater mischief, and hurt our affairs more than did Absalom himself; do not thou therefore wait any longer, but take such forces as thou hast at hand, and that [old] body of six hundred men and thy brother Abishai with thee, and pursue after our enemy, and endeavour to fight him wheresoever thou canst overtake him. Make haste to prevent him, lest he seize upon some fenced cities, and cause us great labour and pains before we take him."

7. So Joab resolved to make no delay, but tak-

---

* By David's disposal of half Mephibosheth's estate to Ziba, one would imagine that he was doubtful whether Mephibosheth's story were entirely true or not. Nor is this odd way of mourning that Mephibosheth made use of here wholly free from suspicion of hypocrisy.

† I prefer Josephus's reading here, when it supposes eleven tribes, including Benjamin, to be on the one side, and the tribe of Judah alone on the other.

ing with him his brother, and those six hundred men, and giving orders that the rest of the army which was at Jerusalem should follow him, he marched with great speed against Sheba; and when he was come to Gibeon, which is a village forty furlongs distant from Jerusalem, Amasa brought a great army with him, and met Joab. Now Joab was girded with a sword, and his breastplate on; and when Amasa came near him to salute him, he took particular care that his sword should fall out, as it were, of its own accord; so he took it up from the ground, and while he approached Amasa, who was then near him, as though he would kiss him, he took hold of Amasa's beard with his other hand, and he smote him in his belly when he did not foresee it, and slew him. This impious and altogether profane action, Joab did to a young man, and his kinsman, and one that had done him no injury, and this out of jealousy that he would obtain the chief command of the army, and be in equal dignity with himself about the king: and for the same cause it was that he killed Abner; but as to that former wicked action, the death of his brother Asahel, which he seemed to revenge, afforded him a decent pretence, and made that crime a pardonable one; but in this murder of Amasa there was no such covering for it. Now when Joab had killed this general, he pursued after Sheba, having left a man with the dead body, who was ordered to proclaim aloud to the army that Amasa was justly slain, and deservedly punished. "But," said he, "if you be for the king, follow Joab his general, and Abishai, Joab's brother:" but because the body lay on the road, and all the multitude came running to it, and, as is usual with the multitude, stood wondering a great while at it, he that guarded it removed it thence, and carried it to a certain place that was very remote from the road, and there laid it, and covered it with his garment. When this was done, all the people followed Joab. Now as he pursued Sheba through all the country of Israel, one told him that he was in a strong city, called Abelbethmaachah. Hereupon Joab went thither, and set about it with his army, and cast up a bank round it, and ordered his soldiers to undermine the walls, and to overthrow them; and since the people in the city did not admit him, he was greatly displeased at them.

8. Now there was a woman of small account, and yet both wise and intelligent, who seeing her native city lying at the last extremity, ascended upon the wall, and, by means of the armed men, called for Joab; and when he came to her, she began to say, that "God ordained kings and generals of armies, that they might cut off the enemies of the Hebrews, and introduce a universal peace among them; but thou art endeavouring to overthrow and depopulate a metropolis of the Israelites, which hath been guilty of no offence." But he replied, "God continue to be merciful unto me: I am disposed to avoid killing any one of the people, much less would I destroy such a city as this; and if they will deliver me up Sheba, the son of Bichri, who hath rebelled against the king, I will leave off the siege, and withdraw the army from the place." Now as soon as the woman heard what Joab said, she desired him to intermit the siege for a little while, for that he should have the head of his enemy thrown out to him presently. So she went down to the citizens, and said to them, "Will ye be so wicked as to perish miserably, with your children and wives, for the sake of a vile fellow, and one whom nobody knows who he is? And will you have him for your king instead of David, who hath been so great a benefactor to

you, and oppose your city alone to such a mighty and strong army?" So she prevailed with them, and they cut off the head of Sheba, and threw it into Joab's army. When this was done, the king's general sounded a retreat, and raised the siege. And when he was come to Jerusalem, he was again appointed to be general of all the people. The king also constituted Benaiah captain of the guards, and of the six hundred men. He also set Adoram over the tribute, and Sabathes and Achilaus over the records. He made Sheva the scribe; and appointed Zadok and Abiathar the high priests.

CHAPTER XII

HOW THE HEBREWS WERE DELIVERED FROM A FAMINE WHEN THE GIBEONITES HAD CAUSED PUNISHMENT TO BE INFLICTED FOR THOSE OF THEM THAT HAD BEEN SLAIN: AS ALSO WHAT GREAT ACTIONS WERE PERFORMED AGAINST THE PHILISTINES BY DAVID, AND THE MEN OF VALOUR ABOUT HIM

1. AFTER this, when the country was greatly afflicted with a famine, David besought God to have mercy on the people, and to discover to him what was the cause of it, and how a remedy might be found for that distemper. And when the prophets answered, that God would have the Gibeonites avenged, whom Saul the king was so wicked as to betray to slaughter, and had not observed the oath which Joshua the general and the senate had sworn to them. If, therefore, said God, the king would permit such vengeance to be taken for those that were slain as the Gibeonites should desire, he promised that he would be reconciled to them, and free the multitude from their miseries. As soon therefore as the king understood that this it was which God sought, he sent for the Gibeonites, and asked them what it was they would have; —and when they desired to have seven sons of Saul delivered to them to be punished, he delivered them up, but spared Mephibosheth, the son of Jonathan. So when the Gibeonites had received the men, they punished them as they pleased; upon which God began to send rain, and to recover the earth to bring forth its fruits as usual, and to free it from the foregoing drought; so that the country of the Hebrews flourished again. A little afterward the king made war against the Philistines; and when he had joined battle with them, and put them to flight, he was left alone, as he was in pursuit of them; and when he was quite tired down, he was seen by one of the enemy, whose name was Achmon, the son of Araph; he was one of the sons of the giants. He had a spear, the handle of which weighed three hundred shekels, and a breastplate of chain-work, and a sword. He turned back, and ran violently to slay [David] their enemy's king, for he was quite tired out with labour; but Abishai, Joab's brother, appeared on the sudden, and protected the king with his shield, as he lay down, and slew the enemy. Now the multitude were very uneasy at these dangers of the king, and that he was very near to be slain; and the rulers made him swear that he would no more go out with them to battle, lest he should come to some great misfortune by his courage and boldness, and thereby deprive the people of the benefits they now enjoyed by his means, and of those that they might hereafter enjoy by his living a long time among them.

2. When the king heard that the Philistines

were gathered together at the city Gazara, he sent an army against them, when Sibbechai the Hittite, one of David's most courageous men, behaved himself so as to deserve great commendation, for he slew many of those that bragged, they were of the posterity of the giants, and vaunted themselves highly on that account, and thereby was the occasion of victory to the Hebrews. After which defeat, the Philistines made war again; and when David had sent an army against them, Nephan his kinsman fought in a single combat with the stoutest of all the Philistines, and slew him, and put the rest to flight. Many of them also were slain in the fight. Now a little while after this, the Philistines pitched their camp at a city which lay not far off the bounds of the country of the Hebrews. They had a man who was six cubits tall, and had on each of his feet and hands one more toe and finger than men naturally have. Now the person who was sent against them by David out of his army was Jonathan, the son of Shimea, who fought this man in a single combat, and slew him; and as he was the person who gave the turn to the battle, he gained the greatest reputation for courage therein. This man also vaunted himself to be of the sons of the giants. But after this fight, the Philistines made war no more against the Israelites.

3. And now David being freed from wars and dangers, and enjoying for the future a profound peace,* composed songs and hymns to God, of several sorts of metre; some of those which he made were *trimeters*, and some were *pentameters*. He also made instruments of music, and taught the Levites to sing hymns to God, both on that called the Sabbath-day, and on other festivals. Now the construction of the instruments was thus: The viol was an instrument of ten strings; it was played upon with a bow; the psaltery had twelve musical notes, and was played upon by the fingers; the cymbals were broad and large instruments, and were made of brass. And so much shall suffice to be spoken by us about these instruments, that the readers may not be wholly unacquainted with their nature.

4. Now all the men that were about David were men of courage. Those that were most illustrious and famous of them for their actions,

* This section shews that, in the opinion of Josephus, David composed the Book of Psalms, not at several times before, as their present inscriptions frequently imply, but generally at the latter end of his life. Nor does Josephus seem to have ascribed any of them to any other author than to David himself. However, we must observe here, that as Josephus says that the song at the Red Sea was composed by Moses in the *hexameter tune*, or *metre ;* as also, that the Song of Moses was an *hexameter poem ;* so does he say that the *Psalms of David* were of *various kinds of metre*, and particularly that they contained *trimeters* and *pentameters ;* all which implies that he thought these Hebrew poems might be best described to the Greeks and Romans under those names and characters of *Hexameters, Trimeters,* and *Pentameters.* Now, it appears that the instruments of music that were originally used, by the command of king David and Solomon, and were carried to Babylon at the captivity of the two tribes, were brought back after that captivity; as also, that the singers and musicians, who outlived that captivity, came back with those instruments; and that this music, and these instruments at the temple, could not but be well known to Josephus, who accordingly gives us a short description of three of the instruments, and gives us a distinct account, that such psalms and hymns were sung in his days at that temple, so that Josephus's authority is beyond exception in these matters. That the ancient music of the Hebrews was very complete also, and had in it great variety of tunes, is evident by the number of their musical instruments, and by the testimony of Jesus, the son of Sirach, (Ecclus. i. 18.)

were thirty-eight; of five of whom I will only relate the performances, for these will suffice to make manifest the virtues of the others also; for these were powerful enough to subdue countries, and conquer great nations. First, therefore, was Jessai, the son of Achimaas, who frequently leaped upon the troops of the enemy, and did not leave off fighting, till he overthrew nine hundred of them. After him was Eleazar, the son of Dodo, who was with the king at Arasam. This man, when once the Israelites were under a consternation at the multitude of the Philistines, and were running away, stood alone, and fell upon the enemy, and slew many of them, till his sword clung to his hand by the blood he had shed, and till the Israelites, seeing the Philistines retire by his means, came down from the mountains and pursued them, and at that time won a surprising and a famous victory, while Eleazar slew the men, and the multitude followed and spoiled their dead bodies. The third was Sheba, the son of Ilus. Now this man, when, in the wars against the Philistines, they pitched their camp at a place called Lehi, and when the Hebrews were again afraid of their army, and did not stay, he stood still alone, as an army and a body of men; and some of them he overthrew, and some who were not able to abide his strength and force, he pursued. These are the works of the hands, and of fighting, which these three performed. Now at the time when the king was once at Jerusalem, and the army of the Philistines came upon him to fight him, David went up to the top of the citadel, as we have already said, to inquire of God concerning the battle, while the enemy's camp lay in the valley that extends to the city Bethlehem, which is twenty furlongs distant from Jerusalem. Now David said to his companions,—" We have excellent water in my own city, especially that which is in the pit near the gate," wondering if any one would bring him some of it to drink; but he said that he would rather have it than a great deal of money. When these three men heard what he said, they ran away immediately, and burst through the midst of their enemy's camp, and came to Bethlehem; and when they had drawn the water, they returned again through the enemy's camp to the king, insomuch that the Philistines were so surprised at their boldness and alacrity, that they were quiet, and did nothing against them, as if they despised their small number. But when the water was brought to the king, he would not drink it, saying, that it was brought by the danger and the blood of men, and that it was not proper on that account to drink it. But he poured it out to God, and gave him thanks for the salvation of the men. Next to these was Abishai, Joab's brother; for he in one day slew six hundred. The fifth of these was Benaiah, by lineage a priest; for being challenged by [two] eminent men in the country of Moab, he overcame them by his valour. Moreover, there was a man, by nation an Egyptian, who was of a vast bulk, and challenged him, yet did he, when he was unarmed, kill him with his own spear, which he threw at him, for he caught him by force, and took away his weapons while he was alive and fighting, and slew him with his own weapons. One may also add this to the forementioned actions of the same man, either as the principal of them in alacrity, or as resembling the rest. When God sent a snow, there was a lion who slipped and fell into a certain pit, and because the pit's mouth was narrow, it was evident he would perish, being enclosed with the snow; so when he saw no way to get out and save himself, he roared. When Benaiah heard the wild beast, he went towards him, and coming at the noise he made, he went down into the mouth of the pit, and smote him, as he struggled, with a stake that lay there, and immediately slew him. The other thirty-three were like these in valour also.

CHAPTER XIII

THAT WHEN DAVID HAD NUMBERED THE PEOPLE, THEY WERE PUNISHED; AND HOW THE DIVINE COMPASSION RESTRAINED THAT PUNISHMENT

1. Now king David was desirous to know how many ten thousands there were of the people, but forgot the commands of Moses,* who told them beforehand, that if the multitude were numbered, they should pay half a shekel to God for every head. Accordingly the king commanded Joab, the captain of his host, to go and number the whole multitude; but when he said there was no necessity for such a numeration, he was not persuaded [to countermand it,] but he enjoined him to make no delay, but to go about the numbering of the Hebrews immediately. So Joab took with him the heads of the tribes, and the scribes, and went over the country of the Israelites, and took notice how numerous the multitude were, and returned to Jerusalem to the king, after nine months and twenty days; and he gave in to the king the number of the people, without the tribe of Benjamin, for he had not yet numbered that tribe, no more than the tribe of Levi, for the king repented of his having sinned against God. Now the number of the rest of the Israelites was nine hundred thousand men, who were able to bear arms and go to war; but the tribe of Judah, by itself, was four hundred thousand men.

2. Now when the prophets had signified to David that God was angry at him, he began to entreat him, and to desire he would be merciful to him, and forgive him his sin. But God sent Nathan the prophet to him, to propose to him the election of three things, that he might choose which he liked best: Whether he would have a famine come upon the country for seven years, or would have a war, and be subdued three months by his enemies? or, whether God should send a pestilence and a distemper upon the Hebrews for three days? But as he was fallen to a fatal choice of great miseries, he was in trouble, and sorely confounded; and when the prophet had said that he must of necessity make his choice, and had ordered him to answer quickly, that he might declare what he had chosen to God, the king reasoned with himself, that in case he should ask for famine, he would appear to do it for others, and without danger to himself, since he had a great deal of corn hoarded up, but to the harm of others; that in case he should choose to be overcome [by his enemies] for three months, he would appear to have chosen war because he had valiant men about him, and strongholds, and that therefore he feared nothing therefrom: so he chose that affliction which is common to kings and to their subjects, and in which the fear was equal on all sides; and said this beforehand, that it was much better to fall into the hands of God, than into those of his enemies.

3. When the prophet had heard this, he declared it to God; who thereupon sent a pestilence and a mortality upon the Hebrews; nor did they die after one and the same manner, nor so that it was easy to know what the distemper was. Now, the miserable disease was one indeed, but it carried them off by ten thousand causes and occasions, which those that were afflicted could not understand; for one died upon the neck of another, and the terrible malady seized them before they were aware, and brought them to their end suddenly, some giving up the ghost immediately with very great pains and bitter grief; and some were worn away by their distempers, and had nothing remaining to be buried, but as soon as ever they fell were entirely macerated; some were choked, and greatly lamented their case, as being also stricken with a sudden darkness; some there were who, as they were burying a relation, fell down dead, without finishing the rites of the funeral. Now there perished of this disease, which began with the morning, and lasted till the hour of dinner, seventy thousand. Nay, the angel stretched out his hand over Jerusalem, as sending this terrible judgment upon it; but David had put on sackcloth, and lay upon the ground, entreating God, and begging that the distemper might now cease, and that he would be satisfied with those that had already perished; and when the king looked up into the air, and saw the angel carried along thereby into Jerusalem, with his sword drawn, he said to God, that he might justly be punished, who was their shepherd; but that the sheep ought to be preserved, as not having sinned at all; and he implored God that he would send his wrath upon him, and upon all his family, but to spare the people.

4. When God heard his supplication, he caused the pestilence to cease; and sent Gad the prophet to him, and commanded him to go up immediately to the thrashing-floor of Araunah the Jebusite, and build an altar there to God, and offer sacrifices. When David heard that, he did not neglect his duty, but made haste to the place appointed him. Now Araunah was thrashing wheat; and when he saw the king and all his servants coming to him, he ran before, and came to him, and worshipped him: he was by his lineage a Jebusite, but a particular friend of David's; and for that cause it was that, when he overthrew the city, he did him no harm, as we informed the reader a little before. Now Araunah inquired, wherefore is my lord come to his servant? He answered, to buy of him the thrashing-floor, that he might therein build an altar to God, and offer a sacrifice. He replied, that he freely gave him both the thrashing-floor, and the ploughs and the oxen for a burnt-offer-

---

* The words of God by Moses (Exod. xxx. 12) sufficiently justify the reason here given by Josephus for the great plague mentioned in this chapter. Nor indeed could David's neglect of executing this law excuse the people, who ought still to have brought half a shekel a-piece with them, when they came to be numbered. The great reason why nations are punished by and with their wicked governors is this, that they almost constantly comply with them in their neglect of or disobedience to the divine laws, and that they submit to several wicked political laws and commands of those governors, instead of the righteous laws of God. Accordingly Josephus well observes, that it was the duty of the people of Israel to take care that their kings, when they should have them, did not exceed their proper limits of power, and prove ungovernable by the laws of God. Nor do I think that negligence peculiar to the Jews: those nations which are called *Christians* are sometimes indeed solicitous to restrain their governors from breaking the human laws of their several kingdoms, but without the like care for restraining them from breaking the laws of God. "Whether it be right in the sight of God, to hearken unto men more than to God, judge ye," (Acts v. 19.) "We ought to obey God rather than men," (v. 29.)

ing; and he besought God graciously to accept his sacrifice. But the king made answer, that he took his generosity and magnanimity kindly, and accepted his good-will; but he desired him to take the price of them all, for that it was not just to offer a sacrifice that cost nothing. And when Araunah said he would do as he pleased, he bought the thrashing-floor of him for fifty shekels; and when he had built an altar, he performed divine service, and brought a burnt-offering, and. offered peace-offerings also. With these God was pacified, and became gracious to them again. Now it happened that Abraham * came and offered his son Isaac for a burnt-offering at that very place; and when the youth was ready to have his throat cut, a ram appeared on a sudden, standing by the altar, which Abraham sacrificed in the stead of his son, as we have before related. Now when king David saw that God had heard his prayer, and had graciously accepted of his sacrifice, he resolved to call that entire place *The Altar of the People*, and to build a temple to God there; which words he uttered very appositely to what was to be done afterward; for God sent the prophet to him, and told him that there should his son build him an altar,—that son who was to take the kingdom after him.

CHAPTER XIV

THAT DAVID MADE GREAT PREPARATIONS FOR THE HOUSE OF GOD; AND THAT UPON ADONIJAH'S ATTEMPT TO GAIN THE KINGDOM, HE APPOINTED SOLOMON TO REIGN

1. AFTER the delivery of this prophecy, the king commanded the strangers to be numbered, and they were found to be one hundred and eighty thousand; of these he appointed fourscore to be hewers of stone, and the rest of the multitude to carry the stones, and of them he set over the workmen three thousand and five hundred. He also prepared a great quantity of iron and brass for the work, with many (and those exceedingly large) cedar-trees, the Tyrians and Sidonians sending them to him, for he had sent to them for a supply of those trees; and he told his friends that these things were now prepared, that he might leave materials ready for the building of the temple to his son, who was to reign after him, and that he might not have them to seek then, when he was very young, and by reason of his age, unskilful in such matters, but might have them lying by him, and so might the more readily complete the work.

2. So David called his son Solomon, and charged him, when he had received the kingdom, to build a temple to God; and said, "I am willing to build God a temple myself, but he prohibited me, because I was polluted with blood and wars; but he hath foretold that Solomon, my youngest son, should build him a temple, and should be called by that name; over whom he hath promised to take the like care as a father takes over his son; and that he would make the country of the Hebrews happy under him, and that not only in other respects, but by giving it peace, and freedom from wars, and from internal seditions, which are the greatest of all blessings.

Since, therefore," says he, "thou wast ordained king by God himself before thou wast born, endeavour to render thyself worthy of this his providence, as in other instances, so particularly in being religious, and righteous, and courageous. Keep thou also his commands, and his laws, which he hath given us by Moses, and do not permit others to break them. Be zealous also to dedicate to God a temple which he hath chosen to be built under thy reign; nor be thou affrighted by the vastness of the work, nor set about it timorously, for I will make all things ready before I die: and take notice, that there are already ten thousand talents of gold, and a hundred thousand talents of silver collected together. I have also laid together brass and iron without number, and an immense quantity of timber, and of stones. Moreover, thou hast many ten thousand stone-cutters, and carpenters; and if thou shalt want anything further, do thou add somewhat of thine own. Wherefore, if thou performest this work, thou wilt be acceptable to God, and have him for thy patron." David also further exhorted the rulers of the people to assist his son in this building, and to attend to the divine service, when they should be free from all their misfortunes, for that they by this means should enjoy, instead of them, peace and a happy settlement; with which blessings God rewards such men as are religious and righteous. He also gave orders, that when the temple should be once built, they should put the ark therein, with the holy vessels; and he assured them, that they ought to have had a temple long ago, if their fathers had not been negligent of God's commands, who had given it in charge, that when they had got the possession of this land they should build him a temple. Thus did David discourse to the governors, and to his son.

3. David was now in years, and his body, by length of time, was become cold and benumbed, insomuch that he could get no heat by covering himself with many clothes; and when the physicians came together, they agreed to this advice, that a beautiful virgin, chosen out of the whole country, should sleep by the king's side, and that this damsel would communicate heat to him, and be a remedy against his numbness. Now there was found in the city one woman, of a superior beauty to all other women, (her name was Abishag,) who, sleeping with the king, did no more than communicate warmth to him, for he was so old that he could not know her as a husband knows his wife; but of this woman we shall know more presently.

4. Now the fourth son of David was a beautiful young man, and tall, born to him of Haggith his wife. He was named Adonijah, and was in his disposition like to Absalom: and exalted himself, as hoping to be king, and told his friends that he ought to take the government upon him. He also prepared many chariots and horses, and fifty men to run before him. When his father saw this, he did not reprove him, nor restrain him from his purpose, nor did he go so far as to ask wherefore he did so. Now Adonijah had for his assistants, Joab, the captain of the army, and Abiathar the high priest; and the only persons that opposed him were Zadok the high priest, and the prophet Nathan, and Benaiah, who was captain of the guards, and Shimei, David's friend, and all the other most mighty men. Now Adonijah had prepared a supper out of the city, near the fountain that was in the king's paradise, and had invited all his brethren, except Solomon, and had taken with him Joab, the captain of the army, and Abiathar, and the rulers of the tribe of Judah; but had not invited to this feast either

---

* What Josephus adds here is very remarkable, that this mount Moriah was not only the very place where Abraham offered up Isaac long ago, but that God had foretold to David by a prophet, that here his son should build him a temple.

Zadok the high priest, or Nathan the prophet, or Benaiah, the captain of the guards, nor any of those of the contrary party. This matter was told by Nathan the prophet to Bathsheba, Solomon's mother, that Adonijah was king, and that David knew nothing of it; and he advised her to save herself and her son Solomon, and to go by herself to David, and say to him, that he had indeed sworn that Solomon should reign after him; but that, in the meantime, Adonijah had already taken the kingdom. He said that he, the prophet himself, would come after her, and when she had spoken thus to the king, would confirm what she had said. Accordingly Bathsheba agreed with Nathan, and went into the king, and worshipped him; and when she had desired leave to speak with him, she told him all things in the manner that Nathan had suggested to her; and related what a supper Adonijah had made, and who they were whom he had invited,—Abiathar the high priest, and Joab the general, and David's sons, excepting Solomon and his intimate friends. She also said that all the people had their eyes upon him, to know whom he would choose for their king. She desired him also to consider, how, after his departure, Adonijah, if he were king, would slay her, and her son Solomon.

5. Now, as Bathsheba was speaking, the keeper of the king's chambers told him that Nathan desired to see him; and when the king had commanded that he should be admitted, he came in, and asked him whether he had ordained Adonijah to be king, and delivered the government to him, or not; for that he had made a splendid supper and invited all his sons, except Solomon; as also that he had invited Joab, the captain of his host, [and Abiathar the high priest,] who are feasting with applauses, and many joyful sounds of instruments, and wish that his kingdom may last for ever; but he hath not invited me, nor Zadok the high priest, nor Benaiah the captain of the guards; and it is but fit that all should know whether this be done by thy approbation or not. When Nathan had said thus, the king commanded that they should call Bathsheba to him, for she had gone out of the room when the prophet came; and when Bathsheba was come, David said, "I swear by Almighty God, that thy son Solomon shall certainly be king, as I formerly swore; and that he shall sit upon my throne, and that this very day also." So Bathsheba worshipped him, and wished him a long life; and the king sent for Zadok the high priest, and Benaiah the captain of the guards; and when they were come, he ordered them to take with them Nathan the prophet, and all the armed men about the palace, and to set his son Solomon upon the king's mule, and to carry him out of the city to the fountain called Gihon, and to anoint him there with the holy oil, and to make him king. This he charged Zadok the high priest, and Nathan the prophet, to do; and commanded them to follow Solomon through the midst of the city, and to sound the trumpets, and to wish aloud that Solomon the king may sit upon the royal throne for ever, that so all the people may know that he is ordained king by his father. He also gave Solomon a charge concerning his government, to rule the whole nation of the Hebrews, and particularly the tribe of Judah, religiously and righteously. And when Benaiah had prayed to God to be favourable to Solomon,—without any delay they set Solomon upon the mule, and brought him out of the city to the fountain, and anointed him with oil, and brought him into the city again, with acclamations and wishes that his kingdom might con-

tinue a long time: and when they had introduced him into the king's house, they set him upon the throne :—whereupon all the people betook themselves to make merry, and to celebrate a festival, dancing and delighting themselves with musical pipes, till both the earth and the air echoed with the multitude of the instruments of music.

6. Now when Adonijah and his guests perceived this noise, they were in disorder: and Joab, the captain of the host, said he was not pleased with these echoes and the sound of these trumpets. And when supper was set before them, nobody tasted of it; but they were all very thoughtful what would be the matter. Then Jonathan the son of Abiathar the high priest, came running to them; and when Adonijah saw the young man gladly, and said to him that he was a good messenger, he declared to them the whole matter about Solomon, and the determination of king David; hereupon both Adonijah and all his guests rose hastily from the feast, and every one fled to their own homes. Adonijah also, as afraid of the king for what he had done, became a supplicant to God, and took hold of the horns of the altar, which were prominent. It was also told Solomon that he had so done; and that he desired to receive assurances from him that he would not remember the injury he had done, and not inflict any severe punishment for it. Solomon answered very mildly and prudently that he forgave him this his offence; but said withal, that if he were found out in any attempt for new innovations, that he would be the author of his own punishment. So he sent to him, and raised him up from the place of his supplication. And when he was come to the king, and had worshipped him, the king bid him go away to his own house, and have no suspicion of any harm; and desired him to shew himself a worthy man, as what would tend to his own advantage.

7. But David being desirous of ordaining his son king of all the people, called together their rulers to Jerusalem, with the priests and the Levites; and having first numbered the Levites, he found them to be thirty-eight thousand, from thirty years old to fifty; out of which he appointed twenty-three thousand to take care of the building of the temple, and out of the same, six thousand to be judges of the people and scribes; four thousand for porters to the house of God, and as many for singers to sing to the instruments which David had prepared, as we have said already. He divided them also into courses; and when he had separated the priests from them, he found of these priests twenty-four courses, sixteen of the house of Eleazar, and eight of that of Ithamar; and he ordained that one course should minister to God eight days, from Sabbath to Sabbath. And thus were the courses distributed by lot, in the presence of David, and Zadok, and Abiathar the high priests, and of all the rulers: and that course which came up first, was written down as first, and accordingly the second, and so on to the twenty-fourth; and this partition hath remained to this day. He also made twenty-four parts of the tribe of Levi; and when they cast lots, they came up in the same manner for their courses of eight days: he also honoured the posterity of Moses, and made them the keepers of the treasures of God, and of the donations which the king dedicated: he also ordained that all the tribe of Levi, as well as the priests, should serve God night and day, as Moses had enjoined them.

8. After this he parted the entire army into

twelve parts, with their leaders [and captains of hundreds] and commanders. Now every part had twenty-four thousand, which were ordered to wait on Solomon, by thirty days at a time, from the first day to the last, with the captains of thousands and captains of hundreds : he also set rulers over every part, such as he knew to be good and courageous men ; he set others also to take charge of the treasures, and of the villages, and of the fields, and of the beasts, whose names I do not think it necessary to mention. When David had ordered all these offices after the manner before mentioned, he called the rulers of the Hebrews, and their heads of tribes, and the officers over the several divisions, and those that were appointed over every work and every possession ; and standing upon a high pulpit, he said to the multitude as follows :—"My brethren and my people, I would have you know that I intended to build a house for God, and prepared a large quantity of gold, and a hundred thousand talents of silver; but God prohibited me by the prophet Nathan, because of the wars I had on your account, and because my right hand was polluted with the slaughter of our enemies ; but he commanded that my son, who was to succeed me in the kingdom, should build a temple for him. Now, therefore, since you know that of the twelve sons whom Jacob our forefather had, Judah was appointed to be king, and that I was preferred before my six brethren, and received the government from God, and that none of them were uneasy at it, so do I also desire that my sons be not seditious one against another, now Solomon has received the kingdom, but to bear him cheerfully for their lord, as knowing that God hath chosen him; for it is not a grievous thing to obey even a foreigner as a ruler if it be God's will, but it is fit to rejoice when a brother hath obtained that dignity, since the rest partake of it with him. And I pray that the promises of God may be fulfilled ; and that this happiness which he hath promised to bestow upon king Solomon, over all the country, may continue therein for all time to come. And these promises, O son, will be firm, and come to a happy end, if thou shewest thyself to be a religious and a righteous man, and an observer of the laws of thy country ; but if not, expect adversity upon thy disobedience to them."

9. Now when the king had said this, he left off ; but gave the description and pattern of the building of the temple in the sight of them all, to Solomon; of the foundations and of the chambers, inferior and superior; how many they were to be, and how large in height and in breadth ; as also he determined the weight of the golden and silver vessels; moreover he earnestly excited them with his words, to use the utmost alacrity about the work: he exhorted the rulers also, and particularly the tribe of Levi, to assist him, both because of his youth, and because God had chosen him to take care of the building of the temple, and of the government of the kingdom. He also declared to them that the work would be easy, and not very laborious to them, because he had prepared for it many talents of gold, and more of silver, with timber, and a great many carpenters and stonecutters, and a large quantity of emeralds, and all sorts of precious stones :—and he said, that even now he would give of the proper goods of his own dominion, two hundred talents, and three hundred other talents of pure gold, for the most holy place ; and for the chariot of God, the cherubim, which are to stand over and cover the ark. Now, when David had done speaking,

there appeared great alacrity among the rulers, and the priests, and the Levites, who now contributed and made great and splendid promises for a future contribution ; for they undertook to bring of gold five thousand talents, and ten thousand drachms, and of silver ten thousand talents, and many ten thousand talents of iron : and if any one had a precious stone he brought it, and bequeathed it to be put among the treasures ; of which Jachiel, one of the posterity of Moses, had the care.

10. Upon this occasion all the people rejoiced, as in particular did David, when he saw the zeal and forward ambition of the rulers, and the priests, and of all the rest; and he began to bless God with a loud voice, calling him the Father and Parent of the universe, and the Author of human and divine things, with which he had adorned Solomon, the patron and guardian of the Hebrew nation, and of its happiness, and of that kingdom which he hath given his Son. Besides this, he prayed for happiness to all the people ; and to Solomon his son, a sound and a righteous mind, and confirmed in all sorts of virtue; and then he commanded the multitude to bless God. Upon which they all fell down upon the ground and worshipped him. They also gave thanks to David, on account of all the blessings which they had received ever since he had taken the kingdom. On the next day he presented sacrifices to God, a thousand bullocks, and as many lambs, which they offered for burnt-offerings. They also offered peace-offerings; and slew many ten thousand sacrifices ; and the king feasted all day, together with all the people; and they anointed Solomon a second time with the oil, and appointed him to be king ; and Zadok to be the high priest of the whole multitude. And when they had brought Solomon to the royal palace, and had set him upon his father's throne, they were obedient to him from that day.

CHAPTER XV

WHAT CHARGE DAVID GAVE TO HIS SON SOLOMON AT THE APPROACH OF HIS DEATH; AND HOW MANY THINGS HE LEFT HIM FOR THE BUILDING OF THE TEMPLE

1. A LITTLE afterward, David also fell into a distemper, by reason of his age; and perceiving that he was near to death, he called his son Solomon, and discoursed to him thus:—" I am now, O my son, going to my grave, and to my fathers, which is the common way which all men that now are, or shall be hereafter, must go; from which way it is no longer possible to return, and to know anything that is done in this world. On which account I exhort thee, while I am still alive, though already very near to death, in the same manner as I have formerly said in my advice to thee, to be righteous towards thy subjects, and religious towards God, that hath given thee thy kingdom ; to observe his commands, and his laws, which he hath sent us by Moses; and neither do thou, out of favour or flattery, allow any lust or other passion to weigh with thee to disregard them; for if thou transgressest his laws, thou wilt lose the favour of God, and thou wilt turn away his providence from thee in all things; but if thou behave thyself so as it behoves thee, and as I exhort thee, thou wilt preserve our kingdom to our family, and no other house will bear rule over the Hebrews, but we ourselves for all ages. Be thou also mindful of the transgressions

of Joab,* the captain of the host, who hath slain two generals out of envy, and those righteous and good men, Abner the son of Ner, and Amasa the son of Jether; whose death do thou avenge as shall seem good to thee, since Joab hath been too hard for me, and more potent than myself, and so hath escaped punishment hitherto. I also commit to thee the son of Barzillai, the Gileadite, whom, in order to gratify me, thou shalt have in great honour, and take great care of; for we have not done good to him first, but we only repay that debt which we owe to his father, for what he did to me in my flight. There is also Shimei, the son of Gera, of the tribe of Benjamin, who, after he had cast many reproaches upon me, when, in my flight, I was going to Mahanaim, met me at Jordan, and received assurances that he should then suffer nothing. Do thou now seek out for some just occasion, and punish him."

2. When David had given these admonitions to his son about public affairs, and about his friends, and about those whom he knew to deserve punishment, he died, having lived seventy years, and reigned seven years and six months in Hebron, over the tribe of Judah, and thirty-three years in Jerusalem, over all the country. This man was of an excellent character, and was endowed with all the virtues that were desirable in

a king, and in one that had the preservation of so many tribes committed to him; for he was a man of valour in a very extraordinary degree, and went readily and first of all into dangers, when he was to fight for his subjects, as exciting the soldiers to action by his own labours, and fighting for them, and not by commanding them in a despotic way. He was also of very great abilities in understanding, and apprehension of present and future circumstances, when he was to manage any affairs. He was prudent and moderate, and kind to such as were under any calamities; he was righteous and humane, which are good qualities peculiarly fit for kings; nor was he guilty of any offence in the exercise of so great an authority, but in the business of the wife of Uriah. He also left behind him greater wealth than any other king, either of the Hebrews or of other nations, ever did.

3. He was buried by his son Solomon, in Jerusalem, with great magnificence, and with all the other funeral pomp which kings use to be buried with; moreover, he had great and immense wealth buried with him, the vastness of which may be easily conjectured at by what I shall now say; for a thousand and three hundred years afterwards, Hyrcanus the high priest, when he was besieged by Antiochus, that was called the Pious, the son of Demetrius, and was desirous of giving him money to get him to raise the siege, and draw off his army; and having no other method of compassing the money, opened one room of David's sepulchre, and took out three thousand talents, and gave part of that sum to Antiochus, and by this means caused the siege to be raised, as we have informed the reader elsewhere. Nay, after him, and that many years, Herod the king opened another room, and took away a great deal of money, and yet neither of them came at the coffins of the kings themselves, for their bodies were buried under the earth so artfully, that they did not appear even to those that entered into their monuments;—but so much shall suffice us to have said concerning these matters.

---

* David is blamed by some for recommending Joab and Shimei to be punished by Solomon, if he could find a proper occasion, after he had borne with the first a long while, and seemed to have pardoned the other entirely; yet I cannot discern any fault in David in these cases. Joab's murder of Abner and Amasa was very barbarous, and could not properly be forgiven, for a dispensing power in kings for the crime of wilful murder is warranted by no law of God, Shimei's cursing the Lord's anointed, and this without any just cause, was the highest act of treason against God and his anointed king, and justly deserved death; and though David could forgive treason against himself, yet he had done no more in the case of Shimei than promised him that he would not *then*, on the day of his return and re-inauguration, or upon that occasion, himself put him to death.

BOOK VIII

CONTAINING THE INTERVAL OF ONE HUNDRED AND SIXTY-THREE YEARS

FROM THE DEATH OF DAVID TO THE DEATH OF AHAB

CHAPTER I

HOW SOLOMON, WHEN HE HAD RECEIVED THE KINGDOM, TOOK OFF HIS ENEMIES

1. WE have already treated of David and his virtue, and of the benefits he was the author of to his countrymen; of his wars also and battles, which he managed with success, and then died an old man, in the foregoing book. And when Solomon his son, who was but a youth in age, had taken the kingdom, and whom David had declared, while he was alive, the lord of that people, according to God's will; when he sat upon the throne, the whole body of the people made joyful acclamation to him, as is usual at the beginning of a reign; and wished that all

his affairs might come to a blessed conclusion; and that he might arrive at a great age, and at the most happy state of affairs possible.

2. But Adonijah, who, while his father was living, attempted to gain possession of the government, came to the king's mother Bathsheba, and saluted her with great civility; and when she asked him, whether he came to her as desiring her assistance in any thing or not; and bade him tell her if that were the case, for that she would cheerfully afford it him; he began to say, that she knew herself that the kingdom was his, both on account of his elder age, and of the disposition of the multitude; and that yet it was transferred to Solomon her son, according to the will of God. He also said that he was contented to be a servant under him, and was pleased with

the present settlement; but he desired her to be a means of obtaining a favour from his brother to him, and to persuade him to bestow on him in marriage Abishag, who had indeed slept by his father, but, because his father was too old, he did not lie with her, and she was still a virgin. So Bathsheba promised him to afford him her assistance very earnestly, and to bring this marriage about, because the king would be willing to gratify him in such a thing, and because she would press it to him very earnestly. Accordingly he went away, in hopes of succeeding in this match. So Solomon's mother went presently to her son, to speak to him about what she had promised, upon Adonijah's supplication to her. And when her son came forward to meet her, and embraced her, and when he had brought her into the house where his royal throne was set, he sat thereon, and bid them set another throne on the right hand for his mother. When Bathsheba was sat down, she said, "O my son, grant me one request that I make of thee, and do not anything to me that is disagreeable or ungrateful, which thou wilt do if thou deniest me." And when Solomon bid her to lay her commands upon him, because it was agreeable to his duty to grant her everything she should ask, and complained that she did not begin her discourse with a firm expectation of obtaining what she desired, but had some suspicion of a denial,— she entreated him to grant, that his brother Adonijah might marry Abishag.

3. But the king was greatly offended at these words, and sent away his mother, and said that Adonijah aimed at great things; and that he wondered that she did not desire him to yield up the kingdom to him, as to his elder brother, since she desired that he might marry Abishag; and that he had potent friends, Joab the captain of the host, and Abiathar the priest. So he called for Benaiah, the captain of the guards, and ordered him to slay his brother Adonijah; he also called for Abiathar, the priest, and said to him, "I will not put thee to death, because of those other hardships which thou hast endured with my father, and because of the ark which thou hast borne along with him; but I inflict this following punishment upon thee, because thou wast among Adonijah's followers, and wast of his party. Do not thou continue here, nor come any more into my sight, but go to thine own town, and live on thine own fields, and there abide all thy life; for thou hast offended so greatly, that it is not just that thou shouldest retain thy dignity any longer." For the forementioned cause, therefore, that the house of Ithamar was deprived of the sacerdotal dignity, as God had foretold to Eli, the grandfather of Abiathar. So it was transferred to the family of Phineas, to Zadok. Now those that were of the family of Phineas, but lived privately during the time that the high priesthood was transferred to the house of Ithamar (of which family Eli was the first that received it) were these that follow: Bukki, the son of Abishua the high priest; his son was Joatham; Joatham's son was Meraioth; Meraioth's son was Arophæus; Arophæus's son was Ahitub; and Ahitub's son was Zadok, who was first made high priest in the reign of David.

4. Now when Joab the captain of the host heard of the slaughter of Adonijah, he was greatly afraid, for he was a greater friend to him than to Solomon; and suspecting, not without reason, that he was in danger, on account of his favour to Adonijah, he fled to the altar, and supposed he might procure safety thereby to himself, because of the king's piety towards God.

But when some told the king what Joab's supposal was, he sent Benaiah, and commanded him to raise him up from the altar, and bring him to the judgment-seat, in order to make his defence. However, Joab said he would not leave the altar, but would die there rather than in another place. And when Benaiah had reported his answer to the king, Solomon commanded him to cut off his head there,* and let him take that as a punishment for those two captains of the host whom he had wickedly slain, and to bury his body, that his sins might never leave his family, but that himself and his father, by Joab's death, might be guiltless; and when Benaiah had done what he was commanded to do, he was himself appointed to be captain of the whole army. The king also made Zadok to be alone the high priest, in the room of Abiathar, whom he had removed.

5. But as to Shimei, Solomon commanded that he should build him a house, and stay at Jerusalem, and attend upon him, and should not have authority to go over the brook Cedron: and that if he disobeyed that command, death should be his punishment. He also threatened him so terribly, that he compelled him to take an oath that he would obey. Accordingly, Shimei said that he had reason to thank Solomon for giving him such an injunction; and added an oath, that he would do as he bade him; and, leaving his own country, he made his abode in Jerusalem: but three years afterwards, when he heard that two of his servants were run away from him, and were in Gath, he went for his servants in haste; and when he was come back with them, the king perceived it, and was much displeased that he had contemned his commands, and, what was more, had no regard to the oaths he had sworn to God; so he called him, and said to him, "Didst not thou swear never to leave me, nor to go out of this city to another? Thou shalt not therefore escape punishment for thy perjury; but I will punish thee, thou wicked wretch, both for this crime, and for those wherewith thou didst abuse my father when he was in his flight, that thou mayest know that wicked men gain nothing at last, although they be not punished immediately upon their unjust practices; but that in all the time wherein they think themselves secure, because they have yet suffered nothing, their punishment increases, and is heavier upon them, and that to a greater degree than if they had been punished immediately upon the commission of their crimes." So Benaiah, on the king's command, slew Shimei.

CHAPTER II

CONCERNING THE WIFE OF SOLOMON; CONCERNING HIS WISDOM AND RICHES; AND CONCERNING WHAT HE OBTAINED OF HIRAM FOR THE BUILDING OF THE TEMPLE

1. SOLOMON having already settled himself firmly in his kingdom, and having brought his enemies to punishment, he married the daughter of Pharaoh, king of Egypt, and built the walls of Jerusalem much larger and stronger than those that had been before,† and thenceforward

---

* This execution upon Joab, as a murderer, even when he had taken sanctuary at God's altar, is perfectly agreeable to the law of Moses, (Exod. xxi. 14.)

† This building of the walls of Jerusalem, soon after David's death, illustrates the conclusion of the 51st Psalm, where David prays, "Build thou the walls of Jerusalem;"—they being, it seems, unfinished or imperfect at that time.

he managed public affairs very peaceably : nor was his youth any hindrance in the exercise of justice, or in the observation of the laws, or in the remembrance of what charges his father had given him at his death; but he discharged every duty with great accuracy, that might have been expected from such as are aged, and of the greatest prudence. He now resolved to go to Hebron, and sacrifice to God upon the brazen altar that was built by Moses. Accordingly, he offered there burnt-offerings, in number a thousand; and when he had done this, he thought he had paid great honour to God; for, as he was asleep that very night, God appeared to him, and commanded him to ask of him some gifts which he was ready to give him as a reward for his piety. So Solomon asked of God what was most excellent, and of the greatest worth in itself, what God would bestow with the greatest joy, and what it was most profitable for man to receive; for he did not desire to have bestowed upon him either gold or silver, or any other riches, as a man and a youth might naturally have done, for these are the things that generally are esteemed by most men, as alone of the greatest worth, and the best gifts of God; but, said he, "Give me, O Lord, a sound mind and a good understanding, whereby I may speak and judge the people according to truth and right-eousness." With these petitions, God was well pleased; and promised to give him all those things that he had not mentioned in his option, riches, glory, victory over his enemies; and, in the first place, understanding and wisdom, and this in such a degree, as no other mortal man, neither kings nor ordinary persons, ever had. He also promised to preserve the kingdom to his posterity for a very long time, if he con-tinued righteous and obedient to him, and imi-tated his father in those things wherein he excelled. When Solomon heard this from God, he presently leaped out of his bed; and when he had worshipped him, he returned to Jerusa-lem; and after he had offered great sacrifices before the tabernacle, he feasted all his own family.

2. In these days a hard cause came before him in judgment, which it was very difficult to find any end of; and I think it necessary to explain the fact about which the contest was, that such as light upon my writings may know what a difficult cause Solomon was to determine; and those that are concerned in such matters may take this sagacity of the king for a pattern, that they may the more easily give sentence about such questions. There were two women, who were harlots in the course of their lives, that came to him, of whom she that seemed to be injured began to speak first, and said, "O king, I and this other woman dwell together in one room. Now it came to pass that we both bore a son at the same hour of the day; and on the third day this woman overlaid her son, and killed it, and then took my son out of my bosom, and removed him to herself; and as I was asleep she laid her dead son in my arms. Now, when in the morning I was desirous to give the breast to the child, I did not find my own, but saw the woman's dead child lying by me; for I considered it exactly, and found it so to be. Hence it was that I demanded my son, and when I could not obtain him, I have recourse, my lord, to thy assistance; for since we were alone, and there was nobody there that could convict her, she cares for nothing, but perseveres in the stout denial of the fact." When this woman had told this her story, the king asked the other woman what she had to say in contradiction to that

story. But when she denied that she had done what was charged upon her, and said that it was her child that was living, and that it was her antagonist's child that was dead, and when no one could devise what judgment could be given, and the whole court were blind in their understanding, and could not tell how to find out this riddle, the king alone invented the fol-lowing way how to discover it: He bade them bring in both the dead child and the living child; and sent one of his guards, and com-manded him to fetch a sword, and draw it, and to cut both the children into two pieces, that each of the women might have half the living and half the dead child. Hereupon all the people privately laughed at the king, as no more than a youth. But, in the meantime, she that was the real mother of the living child cried out, that he should not do so, but deliver that child to the other woman, as her own, for she would be satisfied with the life of the child, and with the sight of it, although it were esteemed the other's child; but the other woman was ready to see the child divided, and was desirous, moreover, that the first woman should be tor-mented. When the king understood that both their words proceeded from the truth of their passions, he adjudged the child to her that cried out to save it, for that she was the real mother of it; and he condemned the other as a wicked woman, who had not only killed her own child, but was endeavouring to see her friend's child destroyed also. Now the multitude looked on this determination as a great sign and demon-stration of the king's sagacity and wisdom; and, after that day, attended to him as to one that had a divine mind.

3. Now the captains of his armies, and officers appointed over the whole country, were these :— Over the lot of Ephraim was Ures; over the toparchy of Bethlehem was Dioclerus; Abina-dab, who married Solomon's daughter, had the region of Dora and the sea-coast under him; the Great Plain was under Benaiah, the son of Achilus; he also governed all the country as far as Jordan; Gabaris ruled over Gilead and Gaulanitis, and had under him the sixty great and fenced cities [of Og;] Achinadab managed the affairs of all Galilee, as far as Sidon, and had himself also married a daughter of Solomon's, whose name was Basima; Banacates had the sea-coast about Arce; as had Shaphot Mount Tabor, and Carmel, and [the lower] Galilee as far as the river Jordan; one man was appointed over all this country; Shimei was intrusted with the lot of Benjamin; and Gabares had the coun-try beyond Jordan, over whom there was again one governor appointed. Now the people of the Hebrews, and particularly the tribe of Judah, received a wonderful increase when they betook themselves to husbandry and the cultivation of their grounds; for as they enjoyed peace, and were not distracted with wars and troubles, and having besides an abundant fruition of the most desirable liberty, every one was busy in aug-menting the product of their own lands, and making them worth more than they had for-merly been.

4. The king had also other rulers, who were over the land of Syria and the Philistines, which reached from the river Euphrates to Egypt, and these collected his tributes of the nations. Now these contributed to the king's table, and to his supper every day,* thirty cori of fine flour, and

---

* Compare the daily furniture of king Solomon's table, here set down, and 1 Kings iv. 22, 23, with the like daily furniture of Nehemiah the governor's table, after the

sixty of meal; as also ten fat oxen, and twenty oxen out of the pastures, and a hundred fat lambs; all these were besides what were taken by hunting harts and buffaloes, and birds and fishes, which were brought to the king by foreigners day by day. Solomon had also so great a number of chariots, that the stalls of his horses for those chariots were forty thousand; and besides these, he had twelve thousand horsemen, the one half of whom waited upon the king in Jerusalem, and the rest were dispersed abroad, and dwelt in the royal villages; but the same officer who provided for the king's expenses supplied also the fodder for the horses, and still carried it to the place where the king abode at that time.

5. Now the sagacity and wisdom which God had bestowed upon Solomon was so great, that he exceeded the ancients, insomuch that he was no way inferior to the Egyptians, who are said to have been beyond all men in understanding; nay, indeed, it is evident that their sagacity was very much inferior to that of the king's. He also excelled and distinguished himself in wisdom above those who were most eminent among the Hebrews at that time for shrewdness: those I mean were Ethan, and Heman, and Chalcol, and Darda, the sons of Mahol. He also composed books of odes and songs, a thousand and five; of parables and similitudes, three thousand; for he spake a parable upon every sort of tree, from the hyssop to the cedar; and in like manner also about beasts, about all sorts of living creatures, whether upon the earth, or in the seas, or in the air; for he was not unacquainted with any of their natures, nor omitted inquiries about them, but described them all like a philosopher, and demonstrated his exquisite knowledge of their several properties. God also enabled him to learn that skill which expels demons,* which is a science useful and sanative to men. He composed such incantations also by which distempers are alleviated. And he left behind him the manner of using exorcisms, by which they drive away demons, so that they never return, and this method of cure is of great force unto this day; for I have seen a certain man of my own country whose name was Eleazar, releasing people that were demoniacal in the presence of Vespasian, and his sons, and his captains, and the whole multitude of his soldiers. The manner of the cure was this:—He put a ring that had a root of one of those sorts mentioned by Solomon to the nostrils of the demoniac, after which he drew out the demon through his nostrils; and when the man fell down immediately, he abjured him to return into him no more, making still mention of Solomon, and reciting the incantations which he composed. And when Eleazar would persuade and demonstrate to the spectators that he had such a power, he set a little way off a cup or basin full of water, and commanded the demon as he went

out of the man to overturn it, and thereby to let the spectators know that he had left the man; and when this was done the skill and wisdom of Solomon was shewn very manifestly: for which reason it is, that all men may know the vastness of Solomon's abilities, and how he was beloved of God, and that the extraordinary virtues of every kind with which this king was endowed, may not be unknown to any people under the sun; for this reason, I say, it is that we have proceeded to speak so largely of these matters.

6. Moreover Hiram, king of Tyre, when he had heard that Solomon succeeded to his father's kingdom, was very glad of it, for he was a friend of David's. So he sent ambassadors to him, and saluted him, and congratulated him on the present happy state of his affairs. Upon which Solomon sent him an epistle, the contents of which here follow:

SOLOMON TO KING HIRAM

"†Know thou that my father would have built a temple to God, but was hindered by wars, and continual expeditions; for he did not leave off to overthrow his enemies till he made them all subject to tribute. But I give thanks to God for the peace I at present enjoy, and on that account I am at leisure, and design to build a house to God, for God foretold to my father that such a house should be built by me; wherefore I desire thee to send some of thy subjects with mine to Mount Lebanon, to cut down timber; for the Sidonians are more skilful than our people in cutting of wood. As for wages to the hewers of wood, I will pay whatsoever price thou shalt determine."

7. When Hiram had read this epistle, he was pleased with it, and wrote back this answer to Solomon:

HIRAM TO KING SOLOMON

" It is fit to bless God that he hath committed thy father's government to thee, who art a wise man, and endowed with all virtues. As for myself, I rejoice at the condition thou art in, and will be subservient to thee in all that thou sendest to me about; for when by my subjects I have cut down many and large trees of cedar and cypress wood, I will send them to sea, and will order my subjects to make floats of them, and to sail to what place soever of thy country thou shalt desire, and leave them there, after which thy subjects may carry them to Jerusalem: but do thou take care to procure us corn for this timber, which we stand in need of, because we inhabit an island."‡

The copies of these epistles remain at this day, and are preserved not only in our books, but among the Tyrians also; insomuch that if any one would know the certainty about them, he may desire of the keepers of the public records of Tyre to shew him them, and he will find what is there set down to agree with what we have said. I have said so much out of a desire that my readers may know that we speak nothing but the truth, and do not compose a history out of some plausible relations, which deceive men and please them at the same time, nor attempt to avoid examination, nor desire men to believe us immediately; nor are we at liberty to depart

---

Jews were come back from Babylon; and to remember withal, that Nehemiah was now building the walls of Jerusalem, and maintained, more than usual, above 150 considerable men every day; and that, because the nation was then very poor, at his own charges also, without laying any burden upon the people at all, (Neh. v. 18, 19.)

* I entirely differ from Josephus in this, that such books and arts of Solomon were parts of that wisdom which was imparted to him by God in his younger days; they must rather have belonged to such profane but curious arts as we find mentioned, (Acts xix. 13-20,) and had been derived from his heathen wives and concubines in his old age, when he had forsaken God, and God had forsaken him, and given him up to demoniacal delusions.

† These epistles of Solomon and Hiram are those in 1 Kings v. 3-9, and, as enlarged, in 2 Chron. ii. 3-16; but here given us by Josephus in his own words.

‡ What Josephus here puts into his copy of Hiram's epistle to Solomon, that Tyre was now an *island*, is, I suppose, his own conjectural paraphrase.

from speaking truth, which is the proper commendation of a historian, and yet to be blameless. But we insist upon no admission of what we say, unless we be able to manifest its truth, by demonstration and the strongest vouchers.

9. Now king Solomon, as soon as this epistle of the king of Tyre was brought him, commended the readiness and good-will he declared therein, and repaid him in what he desired, and sent him yearly twenty thousand cori of wheat, and as many baths of oil: now the bath is able to contain seventy-two sextaries. He also sent him the same measure of wine. So the friendship between Hiram and Solomon hereby increased more and more; and they swore to continue it for ever. And the king appointed a tribute to be laid on all the people, of thirty thousand labourers, whose work he rendered easy to them, by prudently dividing it among them; for he made ten thousand cut timber in mount Lebanon for one month, and then to come home; and the rest two months, until the time when the other twenty thousand had finished their task at the appointed time; and so afterward it came to pass, that the first ten thousand returned to their work every fourth month: and it was Adoram who was over this tribute. There were also of the strangers who were left by David, who were to carry the stones and other materials, seventy thousand; and of those that cut the stones, eighty thousand. Of these three thousand and three hundred were rulers over the rest. He also enjoined them to cut out large stones for the foundations of the temple, and that they should fit them and unite them together in the mountain, and so bring them to the city. This was done, not only by our own country workmen, but by those workmen whom Hiram sent also.

CHAPTER III

OF THE BUILDING OF THE TEMPLE

1. SOLOMON began to build the temple in the fourth year of his reign, on the second month, which the Macedonians call *Artemisius*, and the Hebrews *Jar;* five hundred and ninety-two years after the exodus out of Egypt, but one thousand and twenty years from Abraham's coming out of Mesopotamia into Canaan; and after the Deluge one thousand four hundred and forty years; and from Adam, the first man who was created, until Solomon built the temple, there had passed in all three thousand one hundred and two years. Now that year on which the temple began to be built, was already the eleventh year of the reign of Hiram; but from the building of Tyre to the building of the temple, there had passed two hundred and forty years.

2. Now, therefore, the king laid the foundations of the temple very deep in the ground, and the materials were strong stones, and such as would resist the force of time: these were to unite themselves with the earth, and become a basis and a sure foundation for that superstructure which was to be erected over it: they were to be so strong, in order to sustain with ease those vast superstructures, and precious ornaments, whose own weight was to be not less than the weight of those other high and heavy buildings which the king designed to be very ornamental and magnificent. They erected its entire body, quite up to the roof, of white stone: its height was sixty cubits, and its length was the same, and its breadth twenty. There was another building erected over it, equal to it in its

measures; so that the entire altitude of the temple was a hundred and twenty cubits. Its front was to the east. As to the porch, they built it before the temple: its length was twenty cubits, and it was so ordered that it might agree with the breadth of the house; and it had twelve cubits in latitude, and its height was raised as high as a hundred and twenty cubits. He also built round about the temple, thirty small rooms, which might include the whole temple, by their closeness one to another, and by their number and outward position round it. He also made passages through them, that they might come into one through another. Every one of these rooms had five cubits in breadth,* and the same in length, but in height twenty. Above these were other rooms, and others above them, equal, both in their measures and number; so that these reached to a height equal to the lower part of the house; for the upper part had no buildings about it. The roof that was over the house was of cedar; and truly every one of these rooms had a roof of their own, that was connected with the other rooms; but for the other parts, there was a covered roof common to them all, and built with very long beams, that passed through the rest, and through the whole building, that so the middle walls, being strengthened by the same beams of timber, might be thereby made firmer; but as for that part of the roof that was under the beams, it was made of the same materials, and was all made smooth, and had ornaments proper for roofs, and had plates of gold nailed upon them; and as he enclosed the walls with boards of cedar, so he fixed on them plates of gold, which had sculptures upon them; so that the whole temple shined, and dazzled the eyes of such as entered, by the splendour of the gold that was on every side of them. Now the whole structure of the temple was made, with great skill, of polished stones, and those laid together so very harmoniously and smoothly, that there appeared to the spectators no signs of any hammer, or other instrument of architecture, but as if, without any use of them, the entire materials had naturally united themselves together, that the agreement of one part with another seemed rather to have been natural, than to have arisen from the force of tools upon them. The king also had a fine contrivance for an ascent to the upper room over the temple, and that was by steps in the thickness of its wall; for it had no large door on the east end, as the lower house had, but the entrances were by the sides, through very small doors. He also overlaid the temple, both within and without, with boards of cedar, that were kept close together by thick chains, so that this contrivance was in the nature of a support and a strength to the building.

3. Now when the king had divided the temple into two parts, he made the inner house of twenty cubits, [every way,] to be the most secret chamber, but he appointed that of forty cubits to be the sanctuary; and when he had cut a door-place out of the wall, he put therein doors of cedar, and over-laid them with a great deal of gold, and had sculptures upon it. He also had veils of blue, and purple, and scarlet, and the brightest and softest of linen, with the most curious flowers wrought upon them, which were to be drawn before those doors. He also dedicated for the most secret place, whose breadth

---

* These small rooms seem to have been no less than 20 cubits high a piece, otherwise there must have been a large interval between one and the other that was over it; and this with double floors, the one of six cubits distance from the floor beneath it.

BUILDING OF SOLOMON'S TEMPLE

was twenty cubits, and the length the same, two cherubims of solid gold; the height of each of them was five cubits:* they had each of them two wings stretched out as far as five cubits; wherefore Solomon set them up not far from each other, that with one wing they might touch the southern wall of the secret place, and with another the northern; their other wings, which joined to each other, were a covering to the ark, which was set between them: but nobody can tell, or even conjecture, what was the shape of these cherubims. He also laid the floor of the temple with plates of gold; and he added doors to the gate of the temple, agreeable to the measure of the height of the wall, but in breadth twenty cubits, and on them he glued gold plates; and, to say all in one word, he left no part of the temple, neither internal nor external, but what was covered with gold. He also had curtains drawn over these doors, in like manner as they were drawn over the inner doors of the most holy place; but the porch of the temple had nothing of that sort.

4. Now Solomon sent for an artificer out of Tyre, whose name was Hiram: he was by birth of the tribe of Naphtali, on the mother's side, (for she was of that tribe;) but his father was Ur, of the stock of the Israelites. This man was skilful in all sorts of work; but his chief skill lay in working in gold, in silver, and brass; by which were made all the mechanical works about the temple, according to the will of Solomon. Moreover, this Hiram made two [hollow] pillars, whose outsides were of brass; and the thickness of the brass was four fingers' breadth, and the height of the pillars was eighteen cubits, and their circumference twelve cubits; but there was cast with each of their chapiters lily-work, that stood upon the pillar, and it was elevated five cubits, round about which there was net-work interwoven with small palms, made of brass, and covered the lily-work. To this also were hung two hundred pomegranates, in two rows. The one of these pillars he set at the entrance of the porch on the right hand, and called it *Jachin;* and the other on the left hand, and called it *Booz.*

5. Solomon also cast a brazen sea, the figure of which was of a hemisphere. This brazen vessel was called *a sea* for its largeness, for the laver was ten feet in diameter, and cast of the thickness of a palm: its middle part rested on a short pillar, that had ten spirals round it, and that pillar was ten cubits in diameter. There stood round about it twelve oxen, that looked to the four winds of heaven, three to each wind, having their hinder parts depressed, that so the hemispherical vessel might rest upon them, which itself was also depressed round about inwardly. Now this sea contained three thousand baths.

6. He also made ten brazen bases for so many quadrangular lavers: the length of every one of these bases was five cubits, and the breadth four cubits, and the height six cubits. This vessel was partly turned, and was thus contrived: There were four small quadrangular pillars, that stood one at each corner; these had the sides of the base fitted to them on each quarter; they were parted into three parts; every interval had a border fitted to support [the laver;] upon which was engraven, in one place a lion, and in another place a bull, and an eagle. The small pillars had

the same animals engraven that were engraven on the sides. The whole work was elevated, and stood upon four wheels, which were also cast, which had also naves and felloes, and were a foot and a half in diameter. Any one who saw the spokes of the wheels, how exactly they were turned, and united to the sides of the bases, and with what harmony they agreed to the felloes, would wonder at them. However, their structure was this: certain shoulders of hands stretched out, held the corners above, upon which rested a short spiral pillar, that lay under the hollow part of the laver, resting upon the fore part of the eagle and the lion, which were adapted to them, insomuch, that those who viewed them would think they were of one piece: between these were engravings of palm trees. This was the construction of the ten bases: he also made ten large round brass vessels, which were the lavers themselves, each of which contained forty baths;† for it had its height four cubits, and its edges were as much distant from each other: he also placed these lavers upon the ten bases that were called Mechonoth: and he set five of the lavers on the left side of the temple,‡ which was on that side towards the north wind, and as many on the right side, towards the south, but looking towards the east; the same [eastern] way he also set the sea. Now, he appointed the sea to be for washing the hands and the feet of the priests when they entered into the temple and were to ascend the altar; but the lavers to cleanse the entrails of the beasts that were to be burnt-offerings, with their feet also.

7. He also made a brazen altar, whose length was twenty cubits, and its breadth the same, and its height ten, for the burnt-offerings; he also made all its vessels of brass; the pots, and the shovels, and the basons, and besides these, the snuffers and the tongs, and all its other vessels he made of brass, and such brass as was in splendour and beauty like gold. The king also dedicated a great number of tables, but one that was large and made of gold, upon which they set the loaves of God; and he made ten thousand more that resembled them, but were done after another manner, upon which lay the vials and the cups; those of gold were twenty thousand, those of silver were forty thousand. He also made ten thousand candlesticks, according to the command of Moses, one of which he dedicated for the temple, that it might burn in the daytime, according to the law; and one table with loaves upon it, on the north side of the temple, over against the candlestick; for this he set on the south side, but the golden altar stood between them. All these vessels were contained in that part of the holy house which was forty cubits long, and were before the veil of that most secret place wherein the ark was to be set.

8. The king also made pouring vessels, in number eighty thousand, and a hundred thousand golden vials, and twice as many silver

---

* Josephus says here that the cherubims were only five cubits high; while our Hebrew copies and the LXX both agree they were ten cubits high. I suppose the number here is falsely transcribed, and that Josephus wrote ten cubits also.

† The round or cylindrical lavers of four cubits in diameter, and four in height, must have contained a great deal more than these forty baths. Where the error lies is hard to say. In the meantime, the forty baths are probably the true quantity contained in each laver, since they went upon wheels, and were to be drawn by the Levites about the courts of the priests; had they held much more, they would have been too heavy to have been so drawn.

‡ Josephus by the right hand means what is against our left, when we suppose ourselves going up from the east gates of the courts towards the tabernacle and so *vice versa;* whence it follows, that the pillar Jachin, on the right hand of the temple, was on the south, against our left hand; and Booz on the north, against our right hand.

vials : of golden dishes, in order therein to offer kneaded fine flour at the altar, there were eighty thousand, and twice as many of silver. Of large basins also, wherein they mixed fine flour with oil, sixty thousand of gold, and twice as many of silver. Of the measures like those which Moses called the *Hin*, and the *Assaron*, (a tenth deal,) there were twenty thousand of gold, and twice as many of silver. The golden censers, in which they carried the incense to the altar, were twenty thousand : the other censers, in which they carried fire from the great altar to the little altar, within the temple, were fifty thousand. The sacerdotal garments which belong to the high priest, with the long robes, and the oracle, and the precious stones, were a thousand ; but the crown upon which Moses wrote [the name of God,] was only one, and hath remained to this very day. He also made ten thousand sacerdotal garments of fine linen, with purple girdles, for every priest ; and two hundred thousand trumpets, according to the command of Moses ; also two hundred thousand garments of fine linen, for the singers that were Levites ; and he made musical instruments, and such as were invented for singing of hymns, called *Nablæ* and *Cinyræ*, [psalteries and harps,] which were made of electrum, [the finest brass,] forty thousand.

9. Solomon made all these things for the honour of God, with great variety and magnificence, sparing no cost, but using all possible liberality in adorning the temple ; and these things he dedicated to the treasures of God. He also placed a partition round about the temple, which, in our tongue, we call *Gison*, but it is called *Thrigcos* by the Greeks, and he raised it up to the height of three cubits ; and it was for the exclusion of the multitude from coming into the temple, and shewing that it was a place that was free and open only for the priests. He also built beyond this court a temple, the figure of which was that of a quadrangle, and erected for it great and broad cloisters ; this was entered into by very high gates, each of which had its front exposed to one of the [four] winds, and were shut by golden doors. Into this temple all the people entered that were distinguished from the rest by being pure, and observant of the laws ; but he made that temple which was beyond this a wonderful one indeed, and such as exceeds all description in words ; nay, if I may so say, is hardly believed upon sight ; for when he had filled up great valleys with earth, which, on account of their immense depth, could not be looked on when you bended down to see them, without pain, and had elevated the ground four hundred cubits, he made it to be on a level with the top of the mountain on which the temple was built, and by this means the outmost temple which was exposed to the air, was even with the temple itself.* He encompassed this also with a building of a double row of cloisters, which stood on high upon pillars of native stone, while the roofs were of cedar, and were polished in a manner proper for such high roofs ; but he made all the doors of this temple of silver.

---

* When Josephus says that the floor of the outmost temple was with vast labour raised to be even, or of equal height with the floor of the inner temple, he must mean this in a gross estimation only ; for he and all others agree that the inner temple was a few cubits more elevated than the middle court, and that much more was the court of the priests elevated several cubits above the outmost court, since the middle was lower than the one and higher than the other.

CHAPTER IV

HOW SOLOMON REMOVED THE ARK INTO THE TEMPLE ; HOW HE MADE SUPPLICATION TO GOD, AND OFFERED PUBLIC SACRIFICES TO HIM

1. WHEN king Solomon had finished these works, these large and beautiful buildings, and had laid up his donations in the temple, and all this in the interval of seven years, and had given a demonstration of his riches and alacrity therein ; insomuch, that any one who saw it would have thought it must have been an immense time ere it could have been finished, and [would be surprised] that so much should be finished in so short a time ;—short, I mean, if compared with the greatness of the work : he also wrote to the rulers and elders of the Hebrews, and ordered all the people to gather themselves together to Jerusalem, both to see the temple which he had built, and to remove the ark of God into it ; and when this invitation of the whole body of the people to come to Jerusalem was everywhere carried abroad, it was the seventh month before they came together ; which month is, by our countrymen, called *Thisri* ; but by the Macedonians *Hyperberetæus*. The Feast of Tabernacles happened to fall at the same time, which was kept by the Hebrews as a most holy and most eminent feast. So they carried the ark and the tabernacle which Moses had pitched, and all the vessels that were for ministration to the sacrifices of God, and removed them to the temple.† The king himself, and all the people and the Levites, went before, rendering the ground moist with sacrifices and drink-offerings, and the blood of a great number of oblations, and burning an immense quantity of incense ; and this till the very air itself everywhere around was so full of these odours, that it met, in a most agreeable manner, persons at a great distance, and was an indication of God's presence, and, as men's opinion was, of his habitation with them in this newly-built and consecrated place, for they did not grow weary, either of singing hymns, or of dancing, until they came to the temple, and in this manner did they carry the ark : but when they should transfer it into the most secret places, the rest of the multitude went away, and only those priests that carried it set it between the two cherubims, which embracing it with their wings, (for so they were framed by the artificer,) they covered it, as under a tent or a cupola. Now the ark contained nothing else but those two tables of stone that preserved the ten commandments, which God spake to Moses in mount Sinai, and which were engraved upon them ; but they set the candlestick, and the table, and the golden altar, in the temple, before the most secret place, in the very same places wherein they stood till that time in the tabernacle. So they offered up the daily sacrifices ; but for the brazen altar, Solomon set it before the temple, over against the door, that when the door was opened, it might be exposed to sight, and the sacred solemnities, and the richness of the sacrifices, might be thence seen ; and all the rest of the vessels they gathered together, and put them within the temple.

2. Now, as soon as the priests had put all things in order about the ark, and were gone out, there came down a thick cloud, and stood

---

† This solemn removal of the ark from mount Sion to mount Moriah, confutes that notion of the modern Jews, as if those two were one and the same mountain.

there, and spread itself, after a gentle manner, into the temple : such a cloud it was as was diffused and temperate,—not such a rough one as we see full of rain in the winter season. This cloud so darkened the place, that one priest could not discern another; but it afforded to the minds of all a visible image and glorious appearance of God's having descended into this temple, and of his having gladly pitched his tabernacle therein. So these men were intent upon this thought; but Solomon rose up, (for he was sitting before,) and used such words to God as he thought agreeable to the Divine nature to receive, and fit for him to give;—for he said, "Thou hast an eternal house, O Lord, and such as thou hast created for thyself out of thine own works;—we know it to be the heaven, and the air, and the earth, and the sea, which thou pervadest, nor art thou contained within their limits. I have indeed built this temple to thee, and thy name, that from thence, when we sacrifice, and perform sacred operations, we may send our prayers up into the air, and may constantly believe that thou art present, and art not remote from what is thine own; for neither when thou seest all things, and hearest all things, nor now, when it pleases thee to dwell here, dost thou leave off the care of all men, but rather thou art very near to them all, but especially thou art present to those that address themselves to thee, whether by night or by day." When he had thus solemnly addressed himself to God, he converted his discourse to the multitude, and strongly represented the power and providence of God to them;—how he had shewn all things that were to come to pass to David his father, as many of those things had already come to pass, and the rest would certainly come to pass hereafter; and how he had given him his name, and told to David what he should be called before he was born; and foretold, that when he should be king after his father's death, he should build him a temple, which since they saw accomplished, according to his prediction, he required them to bless God, and by believing him, from the sight of what they had seen accomplished, never to despair of anything that he had promised for the future, in order to their happiness, or suspect that it would not come to pass.

3. When the king had thus discoursed to the multitude, he looked again towards the temple, and lifting up his right hand to the multitude, he said, " It is not possible by what men can do to return sufficient thanks to God for his benefits bestowed upon them, for the Deity stands in need of nothing, and is above any such requital; but so far as we have been made superior, O Lord, to other animals by thee, it becomes us to bless thy Majesty, and it is necessary for us to return thee thanks for what thou hast bestowed upon our house, and on the Hebrew people; for with what other instrument can we better appease thee, when thou art angry at us, or more properly preserve thy favour, than with our voice; which, as we have it from the air, so do we know that by that air it ascends upwards [towards thee.] I therefore ought myself to return thee thanks thereby, in the first place, concerning my father, whom thou hast raised from obscurity unto so great joy; and, in the next place, concerning myself, since thou hast performed all that thou hast promised unto this very day; and I beseech thee, for the time to come, to afford us whatsoever thou, O God, hast power to bestow on such as thou dost esteem; and to augment our house for all ages, as thou hast promised to David my father to do both in

his lifetime and at his death, that our kingdom shall continue, and that his posterity should successively receive it to ten thousand generations. Do not thou therefore fail to give us these blessings, and to bestow on my children that virtue in which thou delightest! and besides all this, I humbly beseech thee, that thou wilt let some portion of thy Spirit come down and inhabit in this temple, that thou mayest appear to be with us upon earth. As to thyself, the entire heavens, and the immensity of the things that are therein, are but a small habitation for thee; much more is this poor temple so; but I entreat thee to keep it as thine own house, from being destroyed by our enemies for ever, and to take care of it as thine own possession; but if this people be found to have sinned, and be thereupon afflicted by thee with any plague, because of their sin, as with dearth, or pestilence, or any other affliction which thou usest to inflict on those that transgress any of thy holy laws, and if they fly all of them to this temple, beseeching thee, and begging of thee to deliver them, then do thou hear their prayers, as being within thine own house, and have mercy upon them, and deliver them from their afflictions! nay, moreover, this help is what I implore of thee, not for the Hebrews only, when they are in distress, but when any shall come hither from any ends of the world whatsoever, and shall return from their sins and implore thy pardon, do thou then pardon them, and hear their prayer! for hereby all shall learn that thou thyself wast pleased with the building of this house for thee; and that we are not ourselves of an unsociable nature, nor behave ourselves like enemies to such as are not of our own people, but are willing that thy assistance should be communicated by thee to all men in common, and that they may have the enjoyment of thy benefits bestowed upon them."

4. When Solomon had said this, and had cast himself upon the ground, and worshipped a long time, he rose up and brought sacrifices to the altar; and when he had filled it with unblemished victims, he most evidently discovered that God had with pleasure accepted of all that he had sacrificed to him, for there came a fire running out of the air, and rushed with violence upon the altar, in the sight of all, and caught hold of and consumed the sacrifices. Now, when this divine appearance was seen, the people supposed it to be a demonstration of God's abode in the temple, and were pleased with it, and fell down upon the ground, and worshipped. Upon which the king began to bless God, and exhorted the multitude to do the same, as now having sufficient indications of God's favourable disposition to them; and to pray that they might always have the like indications from him, and that he would preserve in them a mind pure from all wickedness, in righteousness and religious worship, and that they might continue in the observation of those precepts which God had given them by Moses, because by that means the Hebrew nation would be happy, and indeed the most blessed of all nations among all mankind. He exhorted them also to be mindful, that by what methods they had attained their present good things, by the same they must preserve them sure to themselves, and make them greater, and more than they were at present; for that it was not sufficient for them to suppose they had received them on account of their piety and righteousness, but that they had no other way of preserving them for the time to come; for that it is not so great a thing for men to acquire somewhat which they want, as to preserve what they

have acquired, and to be guilty of no sin, whereby it may be hurt.

5. So when the king had spoken thus to the multitude, he dissolved the congregation, but not till he had completed his oblations, both for himself and for the Hebrews, insomuch that he sacrificed twenty and two thousand oxen, and a hundred and twenty thousand sheep; for then it was that the temple did first of all taste of the victims; and all the Hebrews, with their wives and children, feasted therein : nay, besides this, the king then observed splendidly and magnificently the feast which is called the *Feast of Tabernacles*, before the temple, for twice seven days, and he then feasted together with all the people.

6. When all these solemnities were abundantly satisfied, and nothing was omitted that concerned the divine worship, the king dismissed them; and every one went to their own homes, giving thanks to the king for the care he had taken of them, and the works he had done for them; and praying to God to preserve Solomon to be their king for a long time. They also took their journey home with rejoicing and making merry, and singing hymns to God : and indeed the pleasure they enjoyed took away the sense of the pains they all underwent in their journey home. So when they had brought the ark into the temple, and had seen its greatness, and how fine it was, and had been partakers of the many sacrifices that had been offered, and of the festivals that had been solemnised, they every one returned to their own cities. But a dream that appeared to the king in his sleep, informed him, that God had heard his prayers; and that he would not only preserve the temple, but would always abide in it; that is, in case his posterity and the whole multitude would be righteous. And for himself, it said, that if he continued according to the admonitions of his father, he would advance him to an immense degree of dignity and happiness, and that then his posterity should be kings of that country, of the tribe of Judah, for ever; but that still, if he should be found a betrayer of the ordinances of the law, and forget them, and turn away to the worship of strange gods, he would cut him off by the roots, and would neither suffer any remainder of his family to continue, nor would overlook the people of Israel, or preserve them any longer from afflictions, but would utterly destroy them with ten thousand wars and misfortunes; would cast them out of the land which he had given their fathers, and make them sojourners in strange lands; and deliver that temple which was now built, to be burnt and spoiled by their enemies; and that city to be utterly overthrown by the hands of their enemies; and make their miseries deserve to be a proverb, and such as should very hardly be credited for their stupendous magnitude, till their neighbours, when they should hear of them, should wonder at their calamities, and very earnestly inquire for the occasion, why the Hebrews, who had been so far advanced by God to such glory and wealth, should be then so hated by him? And that the answer that should be made by the remainder of the people should be, by confessing their sins, and the transgression of the laws of their country. Accordingly, we have it transmitted to us in writing, that thus did God speak to Solomon in his sleep.

CHAPTER V

HOW SOLOMON BUILT HIMSELF A ROYAL PALACE, VERY COSTLY AND SPLENDID; AND HOW HE SOLVED THE RIDDLES WHICH WERE SENT HIM BY HIRAM

1. AFTER the building of the temple, which, as we have before said, was finished in seven years, the king laid the foundation of his palace, which he did not finish under thirteen years; for he was not equally zealous in the building of this palace as he had been about the temple; for as to that, though it was a great work, and required wonderful and surprising application, yet God, for whom it was made, so far co-operated therewith, that it was finished in the forementioned number of years; but the palace, which was a building much inferior in dignity to the temple, both on account that its materials had not been so long beforehand gotten ready, nor had been so zealously prepared, and on account that this was only a habitation for kings, and not for God, it was longer in finishing. However, this building was raised so magnificently, as suited the happy state of the Hebrews, and of the king thereof; but it is necessary that I describe the entire structure and disposition of the parts, that so those that light upon this book may thereby make a conjecture, and, as it were, have a prospect of its magnitude.

2. This house was a large and curious building, and was supported by many pillars, which Solomon built to contain a multitude for hearing causes, and taking cognizance of suits. It was sufficiently capacious to contain a great body of men, who would come together to have their causes determined. It was a hundred cubits long, and fifty broad, and thirty high, supported by quadrangular pillars, which were all of cedar; but its roof was according to the Corinthian order, with folding doors, and their adjoining pillars of equal magnitude, each fluted with three cavities : which building was at once firm and very ornamental. There was also another house so ordered, that its entire breadth was placed in the middle : it was quadrangular, and its breadth was thirty cubits, having a temple over against it, raised upon massy pillars; in which temple there was a large and very glorious room, wherein the king sat in judgment. To this was joined another house, that was built for his queen. There were other smaller edifices for diet, and for sleep, after public matters were over; and these were all floored with boards of cedar. Some of these Solomon built with stones of ten cubits, and wainscotted the walls with other stones that were sawed, and were of great value, such as are dug out of the earth for the ornaments of temples, and to make fine prospects in royal palaces, and which make the mines whence they are dug famous. Now the contexture of the curious workmanship of these stones was in three rows, but the fourth row would make one admire its sculptures, whereby were represented trees, and all sorts of plants, with the shades that arose from their branches, and leaves that hung down from them. Those trees and plants covered the stone that was beneath them, and their leaves were wrought so prodigious thin and subtle that you would think they were in motion; but the other part, up to the roof, was plastered over, and, as it were, embroidered with colours and pictures. He, moreover, built other edifices for pleasure; as also very long cloisters, and those situate in an agreeable place of the palace; and among

them a most glorious dining-room, for feastings and compotations, and full of gold, and such other furniture as so fine a room ought to have for the conveniency of the guests, and where all the vessels were made of gold. Now it is very hard to reckon up the magnitude and the variety of the royal apartments; how many rooms there were of the largest sort, how many of a bigness inferior to those, and how many that were subterraneous and invisible; the curiosity of those that enjoyed the fresh air; and the groves for the most delightful prospect, for the avoiding the heat, and covering of their bodies. And to say all in brief, Solomon made the whole building entirely of white stone, and cedar-wood, and gold, and silver. He also adorned the roofs and walls with stones set in gold, and beautified them thereby in the same manner as he had beautified the temple of God with the like stones. He also made himself a throne of prodigious bigness, of ivory, constructed as a seat of justice, and having six steps to it; on every one of which stood, on each end of the step, two lions, two other lions standing above also; but at the sitting place of the throne, hands came out, and received the king; and when he sat backward, he rested on half a bullock, that looked towards his back; but still all was fastened together with gold.

3. When Solomon had completed all this in twenty years' time, because Hiram king of Tyre had contributed a great deal of gold, and more silver to these buildings, as also cedar-wood and pine-wood, he also rewarded Hiram with rich presents: corn he sent him also year by year, and wine and oil, which were the principal things that he stood in need of, because he inhabited an island, as we have already said. And besides these, he granted him certain cities of Galilee, twenty in number, that lay not far from Tyre; which when Hiram went to, and viewed, and did not like the gift, he sent word to Solomon that he did not want such cities as they were; and after that time those cities were called the land of Cabul; which name, if it be interpreted according to the language of the Phœnicians, denotes *what does not please*. Moreover, the king of Tyre sent sophisms and enigmatical sayings to Solomon, and desired he would solve them, and free them from the ambiguity that was in them. Now so sagacious and understanding was Solomon, that none of these problems were too hard for him; but he conquered them all by his reasonings, and discovered their hidden meaning, and brought it to light. Menander also, one who translated the Tyrian archives out of the dialect of the Phœnicians into the Greek language, makes mention of these two kings, where he says thus :—" When Abibalus was dead, his son Hiram received the kingdom from him, who, when he had lived fifty-three years, reigned thirty-four. He raised a bank in the large place, and dedicated the golden pillar which is in Jupiter's temple. He also went and cut down materials of timber out of the mountain called Libanus, for the roof of temples; and when he had pulled down the ancient temples, he both built the temple of Hercules and that of Astarte; and he first set up the temple of Hercules in the month Peritius; he also made an expedition against the Euchii [or Titii,] who did not pay their tribute; and when he had subdued them to himself, he returned. Under this king there was Abdemon, a very youth in age, who always conquered the difficult problems which Solomon, king of Jerusalem, commanded him to explain." Dius also makes mention of him, where he says thus :—" When Abibalus was

dead, his son Hiram reigned. He raised the eastern parts of the city higher, and made the city itself larger. He also joined the temple of Jupiter, which before stood by itself, to the city, by raising a bank in the middle between them; and he ordained it with donations of gold. Moreover, he went up to mount Libanus, and cut down materials of wood for the building of the temples." He says also, that "Solomon, who was then king of Jerusalem, sent riddles to Hiram, and desired to receive the like from him; but that he who could not solve them should pay money to them that did solve them; and that Hiram accepted the conditions; and when he was not able to solve the riddles [proposed by Solomon,] he paid a great deal of money for his fine; but that he afterward did solve the proposed riddles by means of Abdemon, a man of Tyre; and that Hiram proposed other riddles, which, when Solomon could not solve, he paid back a great deal of money to Hiram." This it is which Dius wrote.

CHAPTER VI

HOW SOLOMON FORTIFIED THE CITY OF JERUSALEM, AND BUILT GREAT CITIES; AND HOW HE BROUGHT SOME OF THE CANAANITES INTO SUBJECTION, AND ENTERTAINED THE QUEEN OF EGYPT, AND OF ETHIOPIA

1. Now when the king saw that the walls of Jerusalem stood in need of being better secured, and made stronger, (for he thought the walls that encompassed Jerusalem ought to correspond to the dignity of the city,) he both repaired them and made them higher, with great towers upon them; he also built cities which might be counted among the strongest, Hazor and Megiddo, and the third Gezer, which had indeed belonged to the Philistines; but Pharaoh, the king of Egypt, had made an expedition against it, and besieged it, and taken it by force; and when he had slain all its inhabitants, he utterly overthrew it, and gave it as a present to his daughter, who had been married to Solomon; for which reason the king rebuilt it, as a city that was naturally strong, and might be useful in wars, and the mutations of affairs that sometimes happen. Moreover, he built two other cities not far from it; Beth-horon was the name of one of them, and Balaath of the other. He also built other cities that lay conveniently for these, in order to the enjoyment of pleasures and delicacies in them, such as were naturally of a good temperature of the air, and agreeable for fruits ripe in their proper seasons, and well watered with springs. Nay, Solomon went as far as the desert above Syria, and possessed himself of it, and built there a very great city, which was distant two days' journey from the Upper Syria, and one day's journey from Euphrates, and six long days' journey from Babylon the Great. Now the reason why this city lay so remote from the parts of Syria that are inhabited, is this : That below there is no water to be had, and that it is in that place only that there are springs and pits of water. When he had therefore built this city, and encompassed it with very strong walls, he gave it the name of Tadmor, and that is the name it is still called by at this day among the Syrians; but the Greeks name it Palmyra.

2. Now Solomon the king was at this time engaged in building these cities. But if any inquire why all the kings of Egypt from Menes, who built Memphis, and was many years earlier

than our forefather Abraham, until Solomon, where the interval was more than one thousand three hundred years, were called Pharaohs, and took it from one Pharaoh that lived after the kings of that interval, I think it necessary to inform them of it, and this in order to cure their ignorance, and to make the occasion of that name manifest. Pharaoh, in the Egyptian tongue, signifies a *king*,* but I suppose they made use of other names from their childhood; but when they were made kings, they changed them into the name which, in their own tongue, denoted their authority; for thus it was also that the kings of Alexander, who were called formerly by other names, when they took the kingdom, were named Ptolemies, from their first king. The Roman emperors also were, from their nativity, called by other names, but are styled Cæsars, their empire and their dignity imposing that name upon them, and not suffering them to continue in those names which their fathers gave them. I suppose also that Herodotus of Halicarnassus, when he said there were three hundred and thirty kings of Egypt after Menes, who built Memphis, did therefore not tell us their names, because they were in common called Pharaohs; for when after their death there was a queen reigned, he calls her by her name Nicaule, as thereby declaring, that while the kings were of the male line, and so admitted of the same name, while a woman did not admit the same, he did therefore set down that her name, which she could not naturally have. As for myself, I have discovered from my own books, that after Pharaoh, the father-in-law of Solomon, no other king of Egypt did any longer use that name; and that it was after that time when the fore-named queen of Egypt and Ethiopia came to Solomon, concerning whom we shall inform the reader presently; but I have now made mention of these things, that I may prove that our books and those of the Egyptians agree together in many things.

3. But king Solomon subdued to himself the remnant of the Canaanites that had not before submitted to him;—those I mean that dwelt in mount Lebanon, and as far as the city Hamath; and ordered them to pay tribute. He also chose out of them every year such as were to serve him in the meanest offices, and to do his domestic works, and to follow husbandry; for none of the Hebrews were servants, [in such low employments;] nor was it reasonable that, when God had brought so many nations under their power, they should depress their own people to such mean offices of life, rather than those nations; but all the Israelites were concerned in warlike affairs, and were in armour, and were set over the chariots and the horses, rather than leading the life of slaves. He appointed also five hundred and fifty rulers over those Canaanites who were reduced to such domestic slavery, who received the entire care of them from the king, and instructed them in those labours and operations wherein he wanted their assistance.

4. Moreover, the king built many ships in the Egyptian Bay of the Red Sea, in a certain place called Ezion-geber; it is now called Berenice, and is not far from the city Eloth. This country belonged formerly to the Jews, and became useful for shipping, from the donations of Hiram, king of Tyre; for he sent a sufficient number of men thither for pilots, and such as were skilful in navigation; to whom Solomon gave this command: That they should go along with his own stewards to the land that was of old called Ophir, but now the Aurea Chersonesus, which belongs to India, to fetch him gold. And when they had gathered four hundred talents together, they returned to the king again.

5. There was then a woman, queen of Egypt and Ethiopia;† she was inquisitive into philosophy, and one that on other accounts also was to be admired. When this queen heard of the virtue and prudence of Solomon, she had a great mind to see him, and the reports that went every day abroad induced her to come to him, she being desirous to be satisfied by her own experience, and not by a bare hearing, (for reports thus heard, are likely enough to comply with a false opinion, while they wholly depend on the credit of the relators;) so she resolved to come to him, and that especially, in order to have a trial of his wisdom, while she proposed questions of very great difficulty, and entreated that he would solve their hidden meaning. Accordingly, she came to Jerusalem with great splendour and rich furniture; for she brought with her camels laden with gold, with several sorts of sweet spices, and with precious stones. Now, upon the king's kind reception of her, he both shewed a great desire to please her; and easily comprehending in his mind the meaning of the curious questions she propounded to him, he resolved them sooner than anybody could have expected. So she was amazed at the wisdom of Solomon, and discovered that it was more excellent upon trial than what she had heard by report beforehand; and especially she was surprised at the fineness and largeness of his royal palace, and not less so at the good order of the apartments, for she observed that the king had therein shewn great wisdom; but she was beyond measure astonished at the house which was called the *Forest of Lebanon*, as also at the magnificence of his daily table, and the circumstances of its preparation and ministration, with the apparel of his servants that waited, and the skilful and decent management of their attendance: nor was she less affected with those daily sacrifices which were offered to God, and the careful management which the priests and Levites used about them. When she saw this done every day, she was in the greatest admiration imaginable, insomuch that she was not able to contain the surprise she was in, but openly confessed how wonderfully she was affected; for she proceeded to discourse with the king, and thereby owned that she was overcome with admiration at the things before related; and said, "All things, indeed, O king, that came to our knowledge by report, came with uncertainty as to our belief of them; but as to those good things that to thee appertain, both such as thou thyself possessest, I mean wisdom and prudence, and the happiness thou hast from thy kingdom, certainly the same that came to us was no falsity; it was not only a true report, but it related thy happiness after a much lower manner than I now see it to be before my eyes. For as for the report, it only attempted to persuade our hearing, but did not so make known the dignity of the things themselves as does the sight of them, and being present among them. I, indeed, who did not believe

---

* This signification of the name Pharaoh appears to be true; but what Josephus adds presently, that no king of Egypt was called Pharaoh after Solomon's father-in-law, does hardly agree to our copies, which have long afterwards the names of Pharaoh Nechoh and Pharaoh Hophrah, (2 Kings xxiii 29; Jer. xliv. 30,) besides the frequent mention of that name in the prophets.

† That this queen of Sheba was a queen of Sabæa in South Arabia, and not of Egypt and Ethiopia, as Josephus here asserts, is now generally agreed.

what was reported, by reason of the multitude and grandeur of the things I inquired about, do see them to be much more numerous than they were reported to be. Accordingly, I esteem the Hebrew people, as well as thy servants and friends, to be happy, who enjoy thy presence and hear thy wisdom every day continually. One would therefore bless God, who hath so loved this country, and those that inherit therein, as to make thee king over them."

6. Now when the queen had thus demonstrated in words how deeply the king had affected her, her disposition was known by certain presents, for she gave him twenty talents of gold, and an immense quantity of spices and precious stones. (They say also that we possess the root of that balsam which our country still bears by this woman's gift.) Solomon also repaid her with many good things, and principally by bestowing upon her what she chose of her own inclination, for there was nothing that she desired which he denied her; and as he was very generous and liberal in his own temper, so did he shew the greatness of his soul in bestowing on her what she herself desired of him. So when this queen of Ethiopia had obtained what we have already given an account of, and had again communicated to the king what she had brought with her, she returned to her own kingdom.

CHAPTER VII

HOW SOLOMOM GREW RICH, AND FELL DESPERATELY IN LOVE WITH WOMEN, AND HOW GOD, BEING INCENSED AT IT, RAISED UP ADER AND JEROBOAM AGAINST HIM. CONCERNING THE DEATH OF SOLOMON

1. ABOUT the same time there were brought to the king from the Aurea Chersonesus, a country so called, precious stones and pine-trees, and these trees he made use of for supporting the temple and the palace, as also for the materials of musical instruments, the harps and the psalteries, that the Levites might make use of them in their hymns to God. The wood which was brought to him at this time was larger and finer than any that had ever been brought before; but let no one imagine that these pine-trees were like those which are now so named, and which take that their determination from the merchants, who so call them, that they may procure them to be admired by those that purchase them; for those we speak of were to the sight like the wood of the fig-tree, but were whiter and more shining. Now we have said thus much, that nobody may be ignorant of the difference between these sorts of wood, nor unacquainted with the nature of the genuine pine-tree; and we thought it both a seasonable and humane thing when we mentioned it, and the uses the king made of it, to explain this difference so far as we have done.

2. Now the weight of gold that was brought him was six hundred and sixty-six talents, not including in that sum what was brought by the merchants, nor what the toparchs and kings of Arabia gave him in presents. He also cast two hundred targets of gold, each of them weighing six hundred shekels: he also made three hundred shields, every one weighing three pounds of gold, and he had them carried and put into that house which was called the *Forest of Lebanon*. He also made cups of gold, and of [precious] stones, for the entertainment of his guests, and had them adorned in the most artificial manner; and he contrived that all his other furniture of vessels

should be of gold, for there was nothing then to be sold or bought for silver; for the king had many ships which lay upon the Sea of Tarsus; these he commanded to carry out all sorts of merchandise into the remotest nations; by the sale of which, silver and gold were brought to the king, and a great quantity of ivory, and Ethiopians, and apes; and they finished their voyage, going and returning, in three years' time.

3. Accordingly there went a great fame all around the neighbouring countries, which proclaimed the virtue and wisdom of Solomon, insomuch that all the kings everywhere were desirous to see him, as not giving credit to what was reported, on account of its being almost incredible: they also demonstrated the regard they had for him by the presents they made to him; for they sent him vessels of gold and silver, and purple garments, and many sorts of spices, and horses, and chariots, and as many mules for his carriages as they could find proper to please the king's eyes, by their strength and beauty. This addition that he made to those chariots and horses which he had before from those that were sent him, augmented the number of his chariots by above four hundred, for he had a thousand before, and augmented the number of his horses by two thousand, for he had twenty thousand before. These horses also were so much exercised, in order to their making a fine appearance, and running swiftly, that no others could, upon the comparison, appear either finer or swifter; but they were at once the most beautiful of all others, and their swiftness was incomparable also. Their riders also were a further ornament to them, being, in the first place, young men in the most delightful flower of their age, and being eminent for their largeness, and far taller than other men. They had also very long heads of hair hanging down, and were clothed in garments of Tyrian purple. They had also dust of gold every day sprinkled on their hair, so that their heads sparkled with the reflection of the sunbeams from the gold. The king himself rode upon a chariot in the midst of these men, who were still in armour, and had their bows fitted to them. He had on a white garment, and used to take his progress out of the city in the morning. There was a certain place, about fifty furlongs distant from Jerusalem, which is called Etham, very pleasant; it is in fine gardens, and abounding in rivulets of water;* thither did he use to go out in the morning, sitting on high [in his chariot.]

4. Now Solomon had a divine sagacity in all things, and was very diligent and studious to have things done after an elegant manner; so he did not neglect the care of the ways, but he laid a causeway of black stone along the roads that led to Jerusalem, which was the royal city, both to render them easy for travellers, and to manifest the grandeur of his riches and government. He also parted his chariots, and set them in a regular order, that a certain number of them should be in every city, still keeping a few about him; and those cities he called the *cities of his chariots;* and the king made silver as plentiful in Jerusalem as the stones in the street; and so multiplied cedar-trees in the plains of Judea, which

---

* Whether these fine gardens and rivulets of Etham, whither Solomon rode so often in state, be not those alluded to, (Eccles. ii. 5, 6,) and to the finest part whereof he seems to allude, when, in the Canticles, he compares his spouse to a "garden enclosed," to a "spring shut up," to a "fountain sealed," (chap. iv. 12,) cannot now be certainly determined, but may very probably be conjectured.

did not grow there before, that they were like to the multitude of the common sycamore-trees. He also ordained the Egyptian merchants that brought him their merchandise, to sell him a chariot, with a pair of horses, for six hundred drachmæ of silver, and he sent them to the kings of Syria, and to those kings that were beyond Euphrates.

5. But although Solomon was become the most glorious of kings, and the best beloved by God, and exceeded in wisdom and riches those that had been rulers of the Hebrews before him, yet did not he persevere in this happy state till he died. Nay, he forsook the observation of the laws of his father, and came to an end no way suitable to our foregoing history of him. He grew mad in his love of women, and laid no restraint on himself in his lusts; nor was he satisfied with the women of his country alone, but he married many wives out of foreign nations: Sidonians, and Tyrians, and Ammonites, and Edomites; and he transgressed the laws of Moses, which forbade Jews to marry any but those that were of their own people. He also began to worship their gods, which he did in order to the gratification of his wives, and out of his affection for them. This very thing our legislator suspected, and so admonished us beforehand, that we should not marry women of other countries, lest we should be entangled with foreign customs, and apostatise from our own; lest we should leave off to honour our own God, and should worship their gods. But Solomon was fallen headlong into unreasonable pleasures, and regarded not those admonitions; for when he had married seven hundred wives,* the daughters of princes, and of eminent persons, and three hundred concubines, and these besides the king of Egypt's daughter, he soon was governed by them, till he came to imitate their practices. He was forced to give them this demonstration of his kindness and affection to them, to live according to the laws of their countries. And as he grew into years, and his reason became weaker by length of time, it was not sufficient to recall to his mind the institutions of his own country; so he still more and more contemned his own God, and continued to regard the gods that his marriages had introduced: nay, before this happened, he sinned, and fell into an error about the observation of the laws, when he made the images of brazen oxen that supported the brazen sea,† and the images of lions about his own throne: for these he made, although it was not agreeable to piety so to do; and this he did, notwithstanding that he had his father as a most excellent and domestic pattern of virtue, and knew what a glorious character he had left behind him, because of his piety towards God; nor did he imitate David, although God had twice appeared to him in his sleep, and exhorted him to imitate his father: so he died ingloriously.

There came therefore a prophet to him, who was sent by God, and told him that his wicked actions were not concealed from God: and threatened him that he should not long rejoice in what he had done: that indeed the kingdom should not be taken from him while he was alive, because God had promised to his father David that he would make him his successor, but that he would take care that this should befall his son when he was dead; not that he would withdraw all the people from him, but that he would give ten tribes to a servant of his, and leave only two tribes to David's grandson for his sake, because he loved God, and for the sake of the city of Jerusalem, wherein he should have a temple.

6. When Solomon heard this, he was grieved, and greatly confounded, upon this change of almost all that happiness which had made him to be admired, into so bad a state; nor had there much time passed after the prophet had foretold what was coming, before God raised up an enemy against him, whose name was Ader, who took the following occasion of his enmity to him: —He was a child of the stock of the Edomites, and of the blood royal; and when Joab, the captain of David's host, laid waste the land of Edom, and destroyed all that were men grown, and able to bear arms, for six months' time, this Hadad fled away, and came to Pharaoh, the king of Egypt, who received him kindly, and assigned him a house to dwell in, and a country to supply him with food; and when he was grown up he loved him exceedingly, insomuch that he gave him his wife's sister, whose name was Taphenes, to wife, by whom he had a son, who was brought up with the king's children. When Hadad heard in Egypt that both David and Joab were dead, he came to Pharaoh, and desired that he would permit him to go to his own country: upon which the king asked what it was that he wanted, and what hardship he had met with, that he was so desirous to leave him; and when he was often troublesome to him, and entreated him to dismiss him, he did not then do it. But at the time when Solomon's affairs began to grow worse, on account of his forementioned transgressions,‡ and God's anger against him for the same, Hadad, by Pharaoh's permission, came to Edom; and when he was not able to make the people forsake Solomon, for it was kept under by many garrisons, and an innovation was not to be made with safety, he removed thence, and came into Syria; there he lighted upon one Rezon, who had run away from Hadadezer, king of Zobah, his master, and was become a robber in that country, and joined friendship with him, who had already a band of robbers about him. So he went up, and seized upon that part of Syria, and was made king thereof. He also made incursions into the land of Israel, and did it no small mischief, and spoiled it, and that in the lifetime of Solomon. And this was the calamity which the Hebrews suffered by Hadad.

7. There was also one of Solomon's own nation that made an attempt against him, Jeroboam, the son of Nebat, who had an expectation of rising, from a prophecy that had been made to him long before. He was left a child by his father, and brought up by his mother; and when Solomon saw that he was of an active and bold disposition, he made him the curator of the walls which he built round about Jerusalem;

* These 700 wives, and the 300 concubines, make 1000 in all; and are, I suppose, those very 1000 women intimated elsewhere by Solomon himself, when he speaks of his not having found one [good] woman among that very number, (Eccles. vii. 28.)

† Josephus is here certainly too severe upon Solomon, who, in making the cherubims and these twelve brazen oxen, seems to have done no more than imitate the patterns left him by David; which were all given David by divine inspiration; and although God gave no direction for the lions that adorned his throne, yet does not Solomon seem therein to have broken any law of Moses; for although the Pharisees extended the second commandment to forbid the very *making* of any image, though without any intention to have it worshipped, yet do not I suppose that Solomon so understood it, nor that it ought to be so understood.

‡ Since the beginning of Solomon's evil life and adversity was the time when Hadad or Ader began to give him disturbance, this implies that Solomon's evil life began early.

and he took such care of those works, and the king approved of his behaviour; and gave him, as a reward for the same, the charge of the tribe of Joseph. And when about that time, Jeroboam was once going out of Jerusalem, a prophet of the city Shilo, whose name was Ahijah, met him and saluted him; and when he had taken him a little aside, to a place out of the way, where there was not one other person present, he rent the garment he had on into twelve pieces, and bid Jeroboam take ten of them; and told him beforehand, that "this is the will of God; he will part the dominion of Solomon, and give one tribe, with that which is next it, to his son, because of the promise made to David for his succession, and will give ten tribes to thee, because Solomon hath sinned against him, and delivered up himself to women, and to their gods. Seeing, therefore, thou knowest the cause for which God hath changed his mind, and is alienated from Solomon, be thou righteous and keep the laws, because he hath proposed to thee the greatest of all rewards for thy piety, and the honour thou shalt pay to God, namely, to be as greatly exalted as thou knowest David to have been."

8. So Jeroboam was elevated by these words of the prophet; and being a young man,* of a warm temper, and ambitious of greatness, he could not be quiet; and when he had so great a charge in the government, and called to mind what had been revealed to him by Ahijah, he endeavoured to persuade the people to forsake Solomon, to make a disturbance, and to bring the government over to himself; but when Solomon understood his intention and treachery, he sought to catch him and kill him; but Jeroboam was informed of it beforehand, and fled to Shishak, the king of Egypt, and there abode till the death of Solomon; by which means he gained these two advantages,—to suffer no harm from Solomon, and to be preserved for the kingdom. So Solomon died when he was already an old man, having reigned eighty years, and lived ninety-four. He was buried in Jerusalem, having been superior to all other kings in happiness, and riches, and wisdom, excepting that when he was growing into years he was deluded by women, and transgressed the law; concerning which transgressions, and the miseries which befell the Hebrews thereby, I think proper to discourse at another opportunity.

CHAPTER VIII

HOW, UPON THE DEATH OF SOLOMON, THE PEOPLE FORSOOK HIS SON REHOBOAM, AND ORDAINED JEROBOAM KING OVER THE TEN TRIBES

1. Now when Solomon was dead, and his son Rehoboam (who was born of an Ammonite wife, whose name was Naamah) had succeeded him in the kingdom, the rulers of the multitude sent immediately into Egypt, and called back Jeroboam; and when he was come to them to the city Shechem, Rehoboam came to it also, for he had resolved to declare himself king to the Israelites, while they were there gathered together. So the rulers of the people, as well as Jeroboam,

came to him, and besought him, and said that he ought to relax, and to be gentler than his father, in the servitude he had imposed on them, because they had borne a heavy yoke, and that then they should be better affected to him, and be well contented to serve him under his moderate government, and should do it more out of love than fear; but Rehoboam told them they should come to him again in three days' time, when he would give an answer to their request. This delay gave occasion to a present suspicion, since he had not given them a favourable answer to their mind immediately, for they thought that he should have given them a humane answer off-hand, especially since he was but young. However, they thought that this consultation about it, and that he did not presently give them a denial afforded them some good hope of success.

2. Rehoboam now called his father's friends, and advised with them what sort of answer he ought to give to the multitude: upon which they gave him the advice which became friends, and those that knew the temper of such a multitude. They advised him to speak in a way more popular than suited the grandeur of a king, because he would thereby oblige them to submit to him with good-will, it being most agreeable to subjects that their kings should be almost upon the level with them;—but Rehoboam rejected this so good, and in general so profitable advice, (it was such at least, at that time when he was to be made king,) God himself, I suppose, causing what was most advantageous to be condemned by him. So he called for the young men who were brought up with him, and told them what advice the elders had given him, and bade them speak what they thought he ought to do. They advised him to give the following answer to the people, (for neither their youth nor God himself suffered them to discern what was best:)—That his little finger should be thicker than his father's loins; and if they had met with hard usage from his father, they should experience much rougher treatment from him; and if his father had chastised them with whips, they must expect that he would do it with scorpions.† The king was pleased with this advice, and thought it agreeable to the dignity of his government to give them such an answer. Accordingly, when the multitude was come together to hear his answer on the third day, all the people were in great expectation, and very intent to hear what the king would say to them, and supposed they should hear somewhat of a kind nature; but he passed by his friends, and answered as the young men had given him counsel. Now this was done according to the will of God, that what Ahijah had foretold might come to pass.

3. By these words the people were struck, as it were, by an iron hammer, and were so grieved at the words, as if they had already felt the effects of them; and they had great indignation at the king; and all cried out aloud, and said, "We will have no longer any relation to David or his posterity after this day;" and they said further, "We only leave to Rehoboam the temple which his father built;" and they threatened to forsake him. Nay, they were so bitter, and retained their wrath so long, that when he sent Adoram, who was over the tribute, that he might pacify them, and render them milder, and

---

* This youth of Jeroboam, when Solomon built the walls of Jerusalem, not very long after he had finished his twenty years' building of the temple and his own palace, or not very long after the twenty-fourth of his reign, and his youth here still mentioned, when Solomon's wickedness was become intolerable, fully confirm my former observation, that such his wickedness began early, and continued very long.

† By *scorpions* is not here meant that small animal so called, which was never used in corrections; but either a shrub with sharp prickles, like the stings of scorpions, such as our furze-brush, or else some terrible sort of whip of the like nature.

persuade them to forgive him, if he had said anything that was rash or grievous to them, in his youth, they would not hear it, but threw stones at him and killed him. When Rehoboam saw this, he thought himself aimed at by those stones with which they had killed his servant, and feared lest he should undergo the last of punishments in earnest; so he got immediately into his chariot, and fled to Jerusalem, where the tribe of Judah and that of Benjamin ordained him king; but the rest of the multitude forsook the sons of David from that day, and appointed Jeroboam to be the ruler of their public affairs. Upon this Rehoboam, Solomon's son, assembled a great congregation of those two tribes that submitted to him, and was ready to take a hundred and eighty thousand chosen men out of the army, to make an expedition against Jeroboam and his people, that he might force them by war to be his servants; but he was forbidden of God by the prophet [Shemaiah] to go to war; for that it was not just that brethren of the same country should fight one against another. He also said, that this defection of the multitude was according to the purpose of God. So he did not proceed in this expedition :—and now I will relate first the actions of Jeroboam, the king of Israel, after which we will relate what are therewith connected, the actions of Rehoboam, the king of the two tribes; by this means we shall preserve the good order of the history entire.

4. When therefore Jeroboam had built a palace in the city Shechem, he dwelt there. He also built him another at Penuel, a city so called; and now the Feast of Tabernacles was approaching in a little time, Jeroboam considered, if he should permit the multitude to go to worship God at Jerusalem, and there to celebrate the festival, they would probably repent of what they had done, and be enticed by the temple, and by the worship of God there performed, and would leave him, and return to their first king; and if so, he should run the risk of losing his own life. So he invented this contrivance : he made two golden heifers, and built two little temples for them, the one in the city Bethel, and the other in Dan, which last was at the fountains of the Lesser Jordan,* and he put the heifers into both the little temples, in the forementioned cities. And when he had called those ten tribes together, over whom he ruled, he made a speech to the people in these words. "I suppose my countrymen, that you know this, that every place hath God in it; nor is there any one determinate place in which he is, but he everywhere hears and sees those that worship him; on which account I do not think it right for you to go so long a journey to Jerusalem, which is an enemy's city, to worship him. It was a man that built the temple : I have also made two golden heifers, dedicated to the same God; and one of them I have consecrated in the city Bethel, and the other in Dan, to the end that those of you that dwell nearest those cities, may go to them, and worship God there : and I will ordain for you certain priests and Levites from among yourselves, that you may have no want of the tribe

of Levi, or of the sons of Aaron; but let him that is desirous among you of being a priest, bring to God a bullock and a ram, which they say Aaron the first priest brought also." When Jeroboam had said this, he deluded the people, and made them to revolt from the worship of their forefathers, and to transgress their laws. This was the beginning of miseries to the Hebrews, and the cause why they were overcome in war by foreigners, and so fell into captivity. But we shall relate those things in their proper places hereafter.

5. When the Feast [of Tabernacles] was just approaching, Jeroboam was desirous to celebrate it himself in Bethel, as did the two tribes celebrate it in Jerusalem. Accordingly he built an altar before the heifer, and undertook to be high priest himself. So he went up to the altar, with his own priests about him; but when he was going to offer the sacrifices and the burntofferings in the sight of all the people, a prophet, whose name was Jadon, was sent by God, and came to him from Jerusalem, who stood in the midst of the multitude, and in the hearing of the king, and directing his discourse to the altar, said thus :—" God foretells that there shall be a certain man of the family of David, Josiah by name, who shall slay upon thee those false priests that shall live at that time, and upon thee shall burn the bones of those deceivers of the people, those impostors and wicked wretches. However, that this people may believe that these things shall so come to pass, I foretell a sign to them that shall also come to pass ! This altar shall be broken to pieces immediately, and all the fat of the sacrifices that is upon it shall be poured upon the ground." When the prophet had said this, Jeroboam fell into a passion, and stretched out his hand, and bid them lay hold of him : but the hand which he stretched out was enfeebled, and he was not able to pull it in again to him, for it was become withered, and hung down as if it were a dead hand. The altar also was broken to pieces, and all that was upon it was poured out, as the prophet had foretold should come to pass. So the king understood that he was a man of veracity, and had a divine foreknowledge; and entreated him to pray to God that he would restore his right hand. Accordingly the prophet did pray to God to grant him that request. So the king having his hand recovered to its natural state, rejoiced at it, and invited the prophet to sup with him; but Jadon said, that he could not endure to come into his house, nor to taste of bread or water in this city, for that was a thing God had forbidden him to do : as also to go back by the same way which he came; but he said he was to return by another way. So the king wondered at the abstinence of the man; but was himself in fear, as suspecting a change of his affairs, for the worse, from what had been said to him.

* Whether these "fountains of the Lesser Jordan" were near a place called Dan, and the fountains of the Greater near a place called Jor, before their conjunction; or whether there was only one fountain, arising at the lake Phiala, and running to the Sea of Galilee, and so far called the Lesser Jordan, is hardly certain, even in Josephus himself, though the latter account be the most probable. However, the northern idolatrous calf, set up by Jeroboam, was where Little Jordan fell into Great Jordan, near a place called Daphnæ, as Josephus elsewhere informs us.

CHAPTER IX

HOW JADON THE PROPHET WAS PERSUADED BY ANOTHER LYING PROPHET, AND RETURNED [TO BETHEL,] AND WAS AFTERWARDS SLAIN BY A LION ; AS ALSO, WHAT WORDS THE WICKED PROPHET MADE USE OF TO PERSUADE THE KING, AND THEREBY ALIENATED HIS MIND FROM GOD

1. Now there was a certain wicked man in that city, who was a false prophet, whom Jeroboam had in great esteem, but was deceived by him and his flattering words. This man was

bedrid by reason of the infirmities of old age: however, he was informed by his sons concerning the prophet that was come from Jerusalem, and concerning the signs done by him; and how, when Jeroboam's right hand had been enfeebled, at the prophet's prayer he had revived it again. Whereupon he was afraid that this stranger and prophet should be in better esteem with the king than himself, and obtain greater honour from him; and he gave order to his sons to saddle his ass presently, and make all ready that he might go out. Accordingly they made haste to do what they were commanded, and he got upon the ass, and followed after the prophet; and when he had overtaken him, as he was resting himself under a very large oak-tree that was thick and shady, he at first saluted him, but presently he complained of him, because he had not come into his house, and partaken of his hospitality. And when the other said, that God had forbidden him to taste of any one's provision in that city,—he replied, that "for certain God had not forbidden that I should set food before thee, for I am a prophet as thou art, and worship God in the same manner that thou dost; and I am now come as sent by him, in order to bring thee into my house, and make thee my guest." Now Jadon gave credit to this lying prophet, and returned back with him. But when they were at dinner, and merry together, God appeared to Jadon, and said, that he should suffer punishment for transgressing his commands,— and he told him what that punishment should be; for he said that he should meet with a lion as he was going on his way, by which lion he should be torn in pieces, and be deprived of burial in the sepulchres of his fathers:—which things came to pass, as I suppose, according to the will of God, that so Jeroboam might not give heed to the words of Jadon, as of one that had been convicted of lying. However, as Jadon was again going to Jerusalem, a lion assaulted him, and pulled him off the beast he rode on, and slew him; yet did he not at all hurt the ass, but sat by him, and kept him, as also the prophet's body. This continued till some travellers that saw it, came and told it in the city to the false prophet, who sent his sons and brought the body into the city, and made a funeral for him at great expense. He also charged his sons to bury himself with him; and said, that all which he had foretold against that city, and the altar, and priests, and false prophets, would prove true; and that if he were buried with him, he should receive no injurious treatment after his death, the bones not being then to be distinguished asunder. But now, when he had performed those funeral rites to the prophet, and had given that charge to his sons, as he was a wicked and impious man, he goes to Jeroboam, and says to him, "And wherefore is it now that thou art disturbed at the words of this silly fellow?" And when the king had related to him what had happened about the altar, and about his own hand, and gave him the names of *divine man*, and *an excellent prophet*, he endeavoured, by a wicked trick, to weaken that his opinion; and by using plausible words concerning what had happened, he aimed to injure the truth that was in them; for he attempted to persuade him, that his hand was enfeebled by the labour it had undergone in supporting the sacrifices, and that upon its resting awhile it returned to its former nature again: and that as to the altar, it was but new, and had borne abundance of sacrifices, and those large ones too, and was accordingly broken to pieces, and fallen down by the weight of what had been laid upon it. He also in-

formed him of the death of him that had foretold those things, and how he perished; [whence he concluded that] he had not anything in him of a prophet, nor spake anything like one. When he had thus spoken, he persuaded the king, and entirely alienated his mind from God, and from doing works that were righteous and holy, and encouraged him to go on in his impious practices;* and accordingly, he was to that degree injurious to God, and so great a transgressor, that he sought for nothing every day but how he might be guilty of some new instances of wickedness, and such as would be more detestable than what he had been so insolent as to do before. And so much shall at present suffice to have said concerning Jeroboam.

CHAPTER X

CONCERNING REHOBOAM, AND HOW GOD INFLICTED PUNISHMENT UPON HIM FOR HIS IMPIETY, BY SHISHAK, [KING OF EGYPT.]

1. Now Rehoboam, the son of Solomon, who, as we said before, was king of the two tribes, built strong and large cities, Bethlehem, and Etam, and Tekoa, and Bethzur, and Shoco, and Adullam, and Ipan, and Maresha, and Ziph, and Adoriam, and Lachish, and Azekah, and Zorah, and Aijalon, and Hebron; these he built first of all in the tribe of Judah. He also built other large cities in the tribe of Benjamin, and walled them about, and put garrisons in them all, and captains, and a great deal of corn, and wine, and oil; and he furnished every one of them plentifully with other provisions that were necessary for sustenance: moreover, he put therein shields and spears for many ten thousand men. The priests also that were in all Israel, and the Levites, and if there were any of the multitude that were good and righteous men, they gathered themselves together to him, having left their own cities, that they might worship God in Jerusalem; for they were not willing to be forced to worship the heifers which Jeroboam had made; and they augmented the kingdom of Rehoboam for three years. And after he had married a woman of his own kindred, and had by her three children born to him, he married also another of his own kindred, who was daughter of Absalom by Tamar, whose name was Maachah; and by her he had a son, whom he named Abijah. He had moreover many other children by other wives, but he loved Maachah above them all. Now he had eighteen legitimate wives, and thirty concubines, and he had born to him twenty-eight sons and threescore daughters; but he appointed Abijah, whom he had by Maachah, to be his successor in the kingdom, and intrusted him already with the treasures and the strongest cities.

2. Now I cannot but think that the greatness of a kingdom, and its change into prosperity, often become the occasion of mischief and of transgression to men; for when Rehoboam saw that his kingdom was so much increased, he went out of the right way, unto unrighteous and irreligious practices, and he despised the worship

---

* How much a better copy Josephus had in this remarkable history of the true prophet of Judea, and his concern with Jeroboam, and with the false prophet of Bethel, than our other copies have, is evident at first sight. The prophet's very name, Jadon, is wanting in our other copies; and it is there said that God revealed Jadon the true prophet's death, not to himself, as here, but to the false prophet.

of God, till the people themselves imitated his wicked actions; for so it usually happens, that the manners of subjects are corrupted at the same time with those of their governors; which subjects then lay aside their own sober way of living, as a reproof of their governors' intemperate courses, and follow their wickedness as if it were virtue; for it is not possible to shew that men approve of the actions of their kings, unless they do the same actions with them. Agreeable whereto it now happened to the subjects of Rehoboam; for when he was grown impious, and a transgressor himself, they endeavoured not to offend him by resolving still to be righteous; but God sent Shishak, king of Egypt, to punish them for their unjust behaviour towards him; concerning whom Herodotus was mistaken, and applied his actions to Sesostris; for this Shishak,* in the fifth year of the reign of Rehoboam, made an expedition [into Judea] with many ten thousand men; for he had one thousand two hundred chariots in number that followed him, and threescore thousand horsemen, and four hundred thousand footmen. These he brought with him, and they were the greatest part of them Libyans and Ethiopians. Now, therefore, when he fell upon the country of the Hebrews, he took the strongest cities of Rehoboam's kingdom without fighting; and when he had put garrisons in them, he came last of all to Jerusalem.

3. Now when Rehoboam, and the multitude with him, were shut up in Jerusalem by the means of the army of Shishak, and when they besought God to give them the victory and deliverance, they could not persuade God to be on their side; but Shemaiah the prophet told them, that God threatened to forsake them, as they had forsaken his worship. When they heard this, they were immediately in a consternation of mind, and seeing no way of deliverance, they all earnestly set themselves to confess that God might justly overlook them, since they had been guilty of impiety towards him, and had let his laws lie in confusion. So when God saw them in that disposition, and that they acknowledged their sins, he told the prophet that he would not destroy them, but that he would, however, make them servants to the Egyptians, that they may learn whether they will suffer less by serving men or God. So when Shishak had taken the city without fighting, because Rehoboam was afraid, and received him into it, yet did not Shishak stand to the covenants he had made, but spoiled the temple, and emptied the treasures of God and those of the king, and carried off innumerable ten thousands of gold and silver, and left nothing at all behind him. He also took away the bucklers of gold, and the shields, which Solomon the king had made; nay, he did not leave the golden quivers which David had taken from the king of Zobah, and had dedicated to God; and when he had thus done, he returned to his own kingdom. Now Herodotus of Halicarnassus mentions this expedition, having only mistaken the king's name; and [in saying that] he made war upon many other nations also, and brought Syria and Palestine into subjection, and took the men that were therein prisoners without fighting. Now it is manifest that he intended to declare that our nation was subdued by him; for he saith, that he left behind him pillars in the land of these that delivered themselves up to him without fighting,

and engraved upon them the secret parts of women. Now our king Rehoboam delivered up our city without fighting. He says withal,† that the Ethiopians learned to circumcise their privy parts from the Egyptians; with this addition, that the Phœnicians and Syrians that live in Palestine confess that they learned it of the Egyptians; yet it is evident that no other of the Syrians that live in Palestine, besides us alone, are circumcised. But as to such matters, let every one speak what is agreeable to his own opinion.

4. When Shishak was gone away, king Rehoboam made bucklers and shields of brass, instead of those of gold, and delivered the same number of them to the keepers of the king's palace: so, instead of warlike expeditions, and that glory which results from those public actions, he reigned in great quietness, though not without fear, as being always an enemy to Jeroboam; and he died when he had lived fifty-seven years, and reigned seventeen. He was in his disposition a proud and a foolish man, and lost [part of his] dominions by not hearkening to his father's friends. He was buried in Jerusalem, in the sepulchres of the kings; and his son Abijah succeeded him in the kingdom, and this in the eighteenth year of Jeroboam's reign over the ten tribes; and this was the conclusion of these affairs. It must be now our business to relate the affairs of Jeroboam, and how he ended his life; for he ceased not, nor rested to be injurious to God, but every day raised up altars upon high mountains, and went on making priests out of the multitude.

CHAPTER XI

CONCERNING THE DEATH OF A SON OF JEROBOAM. HOW JEROBOAM WAS BEATEN BY ABIJAH, WHO DIED A LITTLE AFTERWARDS, AND WAS SUCCEEDED IN HIS KINGDOM BY ASA; AND ALSO HOW, AFTER THE DEATH OF JEROBOAM, BAASHA DESTROYED HIS SON NADAB, AND ALL THE HOUSE OF JEROBOAM

1. HOWEVER, God was in no long time ready to return Jeroboam's wicked actions, and the punishment they deserved, upon his own head, and upon the heads of all his house: and whereas a son of his lay sick at that time, who was called Abijah, he enjoined his wife to lay aside her robes, and to take the garments belonging to a private person, and to go to Ahijah the prophet, for that he was a wonderful man in foretelling futurities, it having been he who told Jeroboam that he should be king. He also enjoined her, when she came to him, to inquire concerning the child, as if she were a stranger, whether he should escape this distemper. So she did as her husband bade her, and changed her habit, and came to the city Shiloh, for there did Ahijah live: and as she was going into his house, his eyes being then dim with age, God appeared to him, and informed him of two things; that the wife of Jeroboam was come to him, and what answer he should make to her inquiry. Accordingly, as the woman was coming into the house

---

* This Shishak was not the same person with the famous Sesostris, as some have, in contradiction to all antiquity, supposed.

† Herodotus, as here quoted by Josephus, affirms, that "the Phœnicians and Syrians in Palestine [which last are generally supposed to denote the Jews] owned their receiving circumcision from the Egyptians;" whereas it is abundantly evident that the Jews received their circumcision from their patriarch Abraham. (Gen. xvii. 9-14; John vii. 22, 23,) as I conclude the Egyptian priests did also.

like a private person and a stranger, he cried out, "Come in, O thou wife of Jeroboam! Why concealest thou thyself? Thou art not concealed from God, who hath appeared to me, and informed me that thou wast coming, and hath given me in command what I shall say to thee." So he said that she should go away to her husband, and speak to him thus:—"Since I made thee a great man when thou wast little, or rather wast nothing, and rent the kingdom from the house of David, and gave it to thee, and thou hast been unmindful of these benefits, hast left off my worship, hast made thee molten gods, and honoured them, I will in like manner cast thee down again, and destroy all thy house, and make them food for the dogs and the fowls; for a certain king is rising up, by appointment, over all this people, who shall leave none of the family of Jeroboam remaining. The multitude also shall themselves partake of the same punishment, and shall be cast out of this good land, and shall be scattered into the places beyond Euphrates, because they have followed the wicked practices of their king, and have worshipped the gods that he made, and forsaken my sacrifices. But do thou, O woman, make haste back to thy husband, and tell him this message; but thou shalt then find thy son dead, for as thou enterest the city he shall depart this life; yet shall he be buried with the lamentation of all the multitude, and honoured with a general mourning, for he is the only person of goodness of Jeroboam's family." When the prophet had foretold these events, the woman went hastily away, with a disordered mind, and greatly grieved at the death of the forenamed child: so she was in lamentation as she went along the road, and mourned for the death of her son, that was just at hand. She was indeed in a miserable condition, at the unavoidable misery of his death, and went apace, but in circumstances very unfortunate, because of her son; for the greater haste she made, she would the sooner see her son dead, yet was she forced to make such haste, on account of her husband. Accordingly, when she was come back, she found that the child had given up the ghost, as the prophet had said; and she related all the circumstances to the king.

2. Yet did not Jeroboam lay any of these things to heart, but he brought together a very numerous army, and made a warlike expedition against Abijah, the son of Rehoboam, who had succeeded his father in the kingdom of the two tribes; for he despised him because of his age. But when he heard of the expedition of Jeroboam, he was not affrighted at it, but proved of a courageous temper of mind, superior both to his youth and to the hopes of his enemy; so he chose him an army out of the two tribes, and met Jeroboam at a place called Mount Zemaraim, and pitched his camp near the other, and prepared everything necessary for the fight. His army consisted of four hundred thousand, but the army of Jeroboam was double to it. Now, as the armies stood in array, ready for action and dangers, and were just going to fight, Abijah stood upon an elevated place, and, beckoning with his hand, he desired the multitude and Jeroboam himself to hear first with silence what he had to say. And when silence was made, he began to speak, and told them,—"God had consented that David and his posterity should be their rulers for all time to come, and this you yourselves are not unacquainted with; but I cannot but wonder how you should forsake my father, and join yourselves to his servant Jeroboam, and are now here with him to fight against those who, by God's own determination, are to

reign, and to deprive them of that dominion which they have still retained; for as to the greater part of it, Jeroboam is unjustly in possession of it. However, I do not suppose he will enjoy it any longer; but when he hath suffered that punishment which God thinks due to him for what is past, he will leave off the transgressions he hath been guilty of, and the injuries he hath offered to him, and which he hath still continued to offer, and hath persuaded you to do the same; yet when you were not any further unjustly treated by my father, than that he did not speak to you so as to please you, and this only in compliance with the advice of wicked men, you in anger forsook him, as you pretended, but, in reality, you withdrew yourselves from God, and from his laws, although it had been right for you to have forgiven a man that was young in age, and not used to govern people, not only some disagreeable words, but if his youth and unskilfulness in affairs had led him into some unfortunate actions, and that for the sake of his father Solomon, and the benefits you received from him; for men ought to excuse the sins of posterity on account of the benefaction of parents; but you considered nothing of all this then, neither do you consider it now, but come with so great an army against us. And what is it you depend upon for victory? Is it upon these golden heifers and the altars that you have on high places, which are demonstrations of your impiety, and not of religious worship? Or is it the exceeding multitude of your army which gives you such good hopes? Yet certainly there is no strength at all in an army of many ten thousands, when the war is unjust; for we ought to place our surest hope of success against our enemies in righteousness alone, and in piety towards God; which hope we justly have, since we have kept the laws from the beginning, and have worshipped our own God, who was not made by hands out of corruptible matter; nor was he formed by a wicked king, in order to deceive the multitude; but who is his own workmanship,* and the beginning and end of all things. I therefore give you counsel even now to repent, and to take better advice, and to leave off the prosecution of the war; to call to mind the laws of your country, and to reflect what it hath been that hath advanced you to so happy a state as you are now in."

3. This was the speech which Abijah made to the multitude. But while he was still speaking, Jeroboam sent some of his soldiers privately to encompass Abijah round about, on certain parts of the camp that were not taken notice of; and when he was thus within the compass of the enemy, his army was affrighted, and their courage failed them. But Abijah encouraged them, and exhorted them to place their hopes on God, for that he was not encompassed by the enemy. So they all at once implored the Divine assistance, while the priests sounded with the trumpet, and they made a shout, and fell upon their enemies, and God brake the courage, and cast down the force of their enemies, and made Abijah's army superior to them, for God vouchsafed to grant them a wonderful and very famous victory; and such a slaughter was now made of Jeroboam's army † as is never recorded to have

---

* This is a strange expression in Josephus. that God is his own workmanship, or that he made himself; perhaps he only means that he was not made by one, but was unoriginated.

† By this terrible slaughter God's indignation against that idolatry and rebellion fully appeared; the remainder were thereby seriously cautioned not to persist in them, and a kind of balance or equilibrium was

happened in any other war, whether it were of the Greeks or of the Barbarians, for they overthrew [and slew] five hundred thousand of their enemies, and they took their strongest cities by force, and spoiled them ; and besides those, they did the same to Bethel and her towns, and Jeshanah and her towns. And after this defeat, Jeroboam never recovered himself during the life of Abijah, who yet did not long survive, for he reigned but three years, and was buried in Jerusalem in the sepulchres of his forefathers. He left behind him twenty-two sons and sixteen daughters, and he had also those children by fourteen wives ; and Asa his son succeeded in the kingdom ; and the young man's mother was Michaiah. Under his reign the country of the Israelites enjoyed peace for ten years.

4. And so far concerning Abijah, the son of Rehoboam, the son of Solomon, as his history hath come down to us ; but Jeroboam, the king of the ten tribes, died when he had governed them two-and-twenty years ; whose son Nadab succeeded him, in the second year of the reign of Asa. Now Jeroboam's son governed two years, and resembled his father in impiety and wickedness. In these two years he made an expedition against Gibbethon, a city of the Philistines, and continued the siege in order to take it ; but he was conspired against while he was there, by a friend of his, whose name was Baasha, the son of Ahijah, and was slain ; which Baasha took the kingdom after the other's death, and destroyed the whole house of Jeroboam. It also came to pass, according as God had foretold, that some of Jeroboam's kindred that died in the city were torn to pieces and devoured by dogs ; and that others of them that died in the fields were torn and devoured by the fowls. So the house of Jeroboam suffered the just punishment of his impiety and of his wicked actions.

CHAPTER XII

HOW ZERAH, KING OF THE ETHIOPIANS, WAS BEATEN BY ASA ; AND HOW ASA, UPON BAASHA'S MAKING WAR AGAINST HIM, INVITED THE KING OF THE DAMASCENS TO ASSIST HIM ; AND HOW, ON THE DESTRUCTION OF THE HOUSE OF BAASHA, ZIMRI GOT THE KINGDOM, AS DID HIS SON AHAB AFTER HIM

1. Now Asa, the king of Jerusalem, was of an excellent character, and had a regard to God, and neither did nor designed anything but what had relation to the observation of the laws. He made a reformation of his kingdom, and cut off whatsoever was wicked therein, and purified it from every impurity. Now he had an army of chosen men, that were armed with targets and spears ; out of the tribe of Judah three hundred thousand ; and out of the tribe of Benjamin, that bore shields and drew bows, two hundred and fifty thousand ; but when he had already reigned ten years, Zerah, king of Ethiopia,* made an expedition against him, with a great army of nine hundred thousand footmen, and one hundred thousand horsemen, and three hundred chariots, and came as far as Mareshah, a city that belonged to the tribe of Judah. Now when

Zerah had passed so far with his own army, Asa met him and put his army in array over against him, in a valley called Zephathah, not far from the city ; and when he saw the multitude of the Ethiopians, he cried out, and besought God to give him the victory, and that he might kill many ten thousands of the enemy : "For," said he, "I depend on nothing else but that assistance which I expect from thee, which is able to make the fewer superior to the more numerous, and the weaker to the stronger ; and thence it is alone that I venture to meet Zerah and fight him."

2. While Asa was saying this, God gave him a signal of victory, and joining battle cheerfully on account of what God had foretold about it, he slew a great many of the Ethiopians ; and when he had put them to flight, he pursued them to the country of Gerar ; and when they left off killing their enemies, they betook themselves to spoiling them, (for the city Gerar was already taken,) and to spoiling their camp, so that they carried off much gold, and much silver, and a great deal of [other] prey, and camels, and great cattle, and flocks of sheep. Accordingly, when Asa and his army had obtained such a victory, and such wealth from God, they returned to Jerusalem. Now, as they were coming, a prophet, whose name was Azariah, met them on the road, and bade them stop their journey a little, and began to say to them thus : —That the reason why they had obtained this victory from God was this, that they had shewed themselves righteous and religious men, and had done everything according to the will of God ; that therefore, he said, if they persevered therein, God would grant that they should always overcome their enemies, and live happily ; but that if they left off his worship, all things shall fall out on the contrary ; and a time should come, wherein no true prophet shall be left in your whole multitude, nor a priest who shall deliver you a true answer from the oracle ; but your cities shall be overthrown, and your nation scattered over the whole earth, and live the life of strangers and wanderers. So he advised them, while they had time, to be good, and not to deprive themselves of the favour of God. When the king and the people heard this, they rejoiced ; and all in common, and every one in particular, took great care to behave themselves righteously. The king also sent some to take care that those in the country should observe the laws also.

3. And this was the state of Asa, king of the two tribes. I now return to Baasha, the king of the multitude of the Israelites who slew Nadab, the son of Jeroboam, and retained the government. He dwelt in the city Tirzah, having made that his habitation, and reigned twenty-four years. He became more wicked and impious than Jeroboam or his son. He did a great deal of mischief to the multitude, and was injurious to God, who sent the prophet Jehu, and told him beforehand, that his whole family should be destroyed, and that he would bring the same miseries on his house which had brought that of Jeroboam to ruin ; because when he had been made king by him, he had not requited his kindness, by governing the multitude righteously and religiously ; which things, in the first place, tended to their own happiness ; and, in the next place, were pleasing to God : that he had imitated this very wicked king Jeroboam ; and although that man's soul had perished, yet did he express to the life his wickedness ; and he said that he should therefore justly experience the like calamity with him, since he had been

---

made between the ten and the two tribes for the time to come ; while otherwise the perpetually idolatrous and rebellious ten tribes would naturally have been too powerful for the two tribes, which were pretty frequently free both from such idolatry and rebellion.

* The reader is to remember, that *Cush* is not Ethiopia, but Arabia.

guilty of the like wickedness. But Baasha, though he heard beforehand what miseries would befall him and his whole family for their insolent behaviour, yet did not he leave off his wicked practices for the time to come, nor did he care to appear to be other than worse and worse till he died; nor did he then repent of his past actions, nor endeavour to obtain pardon of God for them, but did as those do who have rewards proposed to them, when they have once in earnest set about their work, they do not leave off their labours; for thus did Baasha, when the prophet foretold to him what would come to pass, grow worse, as if what were threatened, the perdition of his family and the destruction of his house, (which are really among the greatest of evils,) were good things; and, as if he were a combatant for wickedness, he every day took more and more pains for it; and at last he took his army, and assaulted a certain considerable city called Ramah, which was forty furlongs distant from Jerusalem; and when he had taken it, he fortified it, having determined beforehand to leave a garrison in it, that they might thence make excursions, and do mischief to the kingdom of Asa.

4. Whereupon Asa was afraid of the attempts the enemy might make upon him; and considering with himself what mischiefs this army that was left in Ramah might do to the country over which he reigned, he sent ambassadors to the king of the Damascens, with gold and silver, desiring his assistance, and putting him in mind that we have had a friendship together from the times of our forefathers. So he gladly received that sum of money, and made a league with him, and broke the friendship he had with Baasha, and sent the commanders of his own forces unto the cities that were under Baasha's dominion, and ordered them to do them mischief. So they went and burnt some of them, and spoiled others: Ijon, and Dan, and Abelmain,* and many others. Now when the king of Israel heard this, he left off building and fortifying Ramah, and returned presently to assist his own people under the distresses they were in; but Asa made use of the materials that were prepared for building that city, for building in the same place two strong cities, the one of which was called Geba, and the other Mizpah; so that after this, Baasha had no leisure to make expeditions against Asa, for he was prevented by death, and was buried in the city Tirzah; and Elah, his son, took the kingdom, who, when he had reigned two years, died, being treacherously slain by Zimri, the captain of half his army; for when he was at Arza, his steward's house, he persuaded some of the horsemen that were under him to assault Elah, and by that means he slew him when he was without his armed men, and his captains, for they were all busied in the siege of Gibbethon, a city of the Philistines.

5. When Zimri, the captain of the army, had killed Elah, he took the kingdom himself, and according to Jehu's prophecy, slew all the house of Baasha; for it came to pass that Baasha's house utterly perished, on account of his impiety, in the same manner as we have already described the destruction of the house of Jero-

boam; but the army that was besieging Gibbethon, when they heard what had befallen the king, and that when Zimri had killed him he had gained the kingdom, they made Omri their general king, who drew off his army from Gibbethon, and came to Tirzah, where the royal palace was, and assaulted the city, and took it by force. But when Zimri saw that the city had none to defend it, he fled into the inmost part of the palace, and set it on fire, and burnt himself with it, when he had reigned only seven days. Upon which the people of Israel were presently divided, and part of them would have Tibni to be king, and part Omri; but when those that were for Omri's ruling had beaten Tibni, Omri reigned over all the multitude. Now it was in the thirtieth year of the reign of Asa that Omri reigned for twelve years; six of these years he reigned in the city of Tirzah, and the rest in the city called Semareon, but named by the Greeks Samaria; but he himself called it Semareon, from Semer, who sold him the mountain whereon he built it. Now Omri was no way different from those kings that reigned before him, but that he grew worse than they, for they all sought how they might turn the people away from God, by their daily wicked practices; and on that account it was that God made one of them to be slain by another, and that no one person of their families should remain. This Omri also died at Samaria, and Ahab his son succeeded him.

6. Now by these events we may learn what concern God hath for the affairs of mankind, and how he loves good men, and hates the wicked, and destroys them root and branch: for many of these kings of Israel, they and their families, were miserably destroyed, and taken away one by another, in a short time, for their transgression and wickedness; but Asa, who was king of Jerusalem, and of the two tribes, attained, by God's blessing, a long and a blessed old age, for his piety and righteousness and died happily, when he had reigned forty and one years; and when he was dead, his son Jehoshaphat succeeded him in the government. He was born of Asa's wife Azubah. And all men allowed that he followed the works of David his forefather, and this both in courage and piety; but we are not obliged now to speak any more of the affairs of this king.

CHAPTER XIII

HOW AHAB, WHEN HE HAD TAKEN JEZEBEL TO WIFE, BECAME MORE WICKED THAN ALL THE KINGS THAT HAD BEEN BEFORE HIM; OF THE ACTIONS OF THE PROPHET ELIJAH, AND WHAT BEFEL NABOTH

1. Now Ahab, the king of Israel, dwelt in Samaria, and held the government for twenty-two years; and made no alteration in the conduct of the kings that were his predecessors, but only in such things as were of his own invention for the worse, and in his most gross wickedness. He imitated them in their wicked courses, and in their injurious behaviour towards God; and more especially he imitated the transgression of Jeroboam; for he worshipped the heifers that he had made; and he contrived other absurd objects of worship beside those heifers; he also took to wife the daughter of Ethbaal, king of the Tyrians and Sidonians, whose name was Jezebel, of whom he learned to worship her own gods. This woman was active and bold, and fell

---

* This Abelmain, or Abellane, is supposed to be the same with Abel, or Abila, whence came Abilene. This may be that city so denominated from Abel the righteous, there buried; concerning the shedding of whose blood within the compass of the land of Israel, I understand our Saviour's words, about the fatal war and overthrow of Judea by Titus and his Roman army, (Matt. xxiii. 35, 36; Luke xi. 51.)

into so great a degree of impurity and wicked-ness, that she built a temple to the god of the Tyrians, which they called Belus, and planted a grove of all sorts of trees; she also appointed priests and false prophets to this god. The king also himself had many such about him; and so exceeded in madness and wickedness all [the kings] that went before him.

2. There was now a prophet of God Almighty, of Thesbon, a country in Gilead, that came to Ahab, and said to him, that God foretold he would not send rain nor dew in those years upon the country but when he should appear. And when he had confirmed this by an oath, he de-parted into the southern parts, and made his abode by a brook, out of which he had water to drink; for as for his food, ravens brought it to him every day; but when that river was dried up for want of rain, he came to Zarephath, a city not far from Sidon and Tyre, for it lay between them, and this at the command of God, for [God told him] that he should there find a woman, who was a widow, that should give him sus-tenance: so when he was not far off the city, he saw a woman that laboured with her own hands, gathering of sticks: so God informed him that this was the woman who was to give him sus-tenance: so he came and saluted her, and desired her to bring him some water to drink; but as she was going so to do, he called to her, and would have her to bring him a loaf of bread also; whereupon she affirmed upon oath, that she had at home nothing more than one handful of meal and a little oil, and that she was going to gather some sticks, that she might knead it, and make bread for herself and her son; after which, she said, they must perish, and be con-sumed by the famine, for they had nothing for themselves any longer. Hereupon he said, "Go on with good courage, and hope for better things; and first of all make me a little cake, and bring it to me, for I foretell to thee that this vessel of meal and this cruse of oil shall not fail until God send rain." When the prophet had said this, she came to him, and made him the before-named cake: of which she had part for herself, and gave the rest to her son, and to the prophet also; nor did anything of this fail until the drought ceased. Now Menander mentions this drought in his account of the acts of Eth-baal, king of the Tyrians; where he says thus: "Under him, there was a want of rain from the month Hyperberetæus till the month Hyper-beretæus of the year following; but when he made supplications, there came great thunders. This Ethbaal built the city Botrys, in Phœnicia, and the city Auza, in Libya." By these words he designed the want of rain that was in the days of Ahab; for at that time it was that Eth-baal also reigned over the Tyrians, as Menander informs us.

3. Now this woman, of whom we spake before, that sustained the prophet, when her son was fallen into a distemper till he gave up the ghost, and appeared to be dead, came to the prophet weeping, and beating her breasts with her hands, and sending out such expressions as her passions dictated to her, and complained to him that he had come to her to reproach her for her sins, and that on this account it was that her son was dead. But he bid her be of good cheer, and de-liver her son to him, for that he would deliver him again to her alive. So when she had de-livered her son up to him, he carried him into an upper room, where he himself lodged, and laid him down on the bed, and cried unto God, and said, that God had not done well in reward-ing the woman who had entertained him and

sustained him, by taking away her son; and he prayed that he would send again the soul of the child into him, and bring him to life again. Accordingly God took pity on the mother, and was willing to gratify the prophet, that he might not seem to have come to do her a mischief; and the child, beyond all expectation, came to life again. So the mother returned the prophet thanks, and said she was then clearly satisfied that God did converse with him.

4. After a little while Elijah came to king Ahab, according to God's will, to inform him that rain was coming. Now the famine had seized upon the whole country, and there was a great want of what was necessary for sustenance, insomuch that it was not only men that wanted it, but the earth itself also, which did not pro-duce enough for the horses and the other beasts, of what was useful for them to feed on, by reason of the drought. So the king called for Obadiah, who was steward over his cattle, and said to him, that he would have him go to the fountains of water and to the brooks, that if any herbs could be found for them, they might mow it down, and reserve it for the beasts. And when he had sent persons over all the habitable earth,* to discover the prophet Elijah, and they could not find him, he bade Obadiah accompany him: so it was resolved they should make a pro-gress, and divide the ways between them; and Obadiah took one road, and the king another. Now it happened, that the same time when queen Jezebel slew the prophets, this Obadiah had hidden a hundred prophets, and had fed them with nothing but bread and water. But when Obadiah was alone, and absent from the king, the prophet Elijah met him; and Obadiah asked him who he was; and when he had learned it from him, he worshipped him. Elijah then bid him go to the king, and tell him that I am here ready to wait on him. But Obadiah replied, "What evil have I done to thee, that thou sendest me to one who seeketh to kill thee, and hath sought over all the earth for thee? Or was he so ignorant as not to know that the king had left no place untouched unto which he had not sent persons to bring him back, in order, if they could take him, to have him put to death?" For he told him he was afraid lest God should appear to him again, and he should go away into another place; and that when the king should send him for Elijah, and he should miss of him, and not be able to find him anywhere upon earth, he should be put to death. He desired him therefore to take care of his preservation; and told him how diligently he had provided for those of his own profession, and had saved a hundred prophets, when Jezebel slew the rest of them, and had kept them concealed, and that they had been sustained by him. But Elijah bade him fear nothing, but go to the king; and he assured him upon oath, that he would certainly shew himself to Ahab that very day.

5. So when Obadiah had informed the king that Elijah was there, Ahab met him, and asked him in anger, if he were the man that afflicted the people of the Hebrews, and was the occasion of the drought they lay under? But Elijah, without any flattery, said that he was himself the man; he and his house, which brought such afflictions upon them; and that by introducing strange gods into their country, and worshipping

---

* Josephus here seems to mean, that this drought affected all the habitable earth, and presently all the earth, as our Saviour says it was upon all the earth, (Luke iv. 25.)

them, and by leaving their own, who was the only true God, and having no manner of regard to him. However, he bade him go his way, and gather together all the people to him, to mount Carmel, with his own prophets, and those of his wife, telling him how many there were of them, as also the prophets of the groves, about four hundred in number. And as all the men whom Ahab sent for, ran away to the forenamed mountain, the prophet Elijah stood in the midst of them, and said, "How long will you live thus in uncertainty of mind and opinion?" He also exhorted them, that in case they esteemed their own country God to be the true and only God, they would follow him and his commandments; but in case they esteemed him to be nothing, but had an opinion of the strange gods, and that they ought to worship them, his counsel was, that they should follow them. And when the multitude made no answer to what he said, Elijah desired, that, for a trial of the power of the strange gods and of their own God, he, who was his only prophet, while they had four hundred, might take a heifer and kill it as a sacrifice, and lay it upon pieces of wood, and not kindle any fire, and that they should do the same things, and call upon their own gods to set the wood on fire, for if that were done, they would thence learn the nature of the true God. This proposal pleased the people. So Elijah bade the prophets to choose out a heifer first, and kill it, and to call on their gods; but when there appeared no effect of the prayer or invocation, of the prophets upon their sacrifice, Elijah derided them, and bade them call upon their gods with a loud voice, for they might either be on a journey or asleep; and when these prophets had done so from morning till noon, and cut themselves with swords and lances,* according to the customs of their country, and he was about to offer his sacrifice, he bid [the prophets] go away; but bade [the people] come near and observe what he did, lest he should privately hide fire among the pieces of wood. So, upon the approach of the multitude, he took twelve stones, one of each tribe of the people of the Hebrews, and built an altar with them, and dug a very deep trench; and when he had laid the pieces of wood upon the altar, and upon them had laid the pieces of the sacrifices, he ordered them to fill four barrels, with water of the fountain, and to pour it upon the altar, till it ran over it, and till the trench was filled with the water poured into it. When he had done this, he began to pray to God, and to invocate him to make manifest his power to a people that had already been in an error a long time; upon which words a fire came on a sudden from heaven, in the sight of the multitude, and fell upon the altar, and consumed the sacrifice, till the very water was set on fire, and the place was become dry.

6. Now when the Israelites saw this, they fell down upon the ground, and worshipped one God, and called him *The great and the only true God;* but they called the others mere names, framed by the evil and wild opinions of men. So they caught their prophets, and, at the command of Elijah, slew them. Elijah also said to the king, that he should go to dinner without any further concern, for that in a little time he would see God send them rain. Accordingly, Ahab went his way; but Elijah went up to the highest top of mount Carmel, and sat down upon

the ground, and leaned his head upon his knees, and bade his servant go up to a certain elevated place, and look towards the sea, and when he should see a cloud rising anywhere, he should give notice of it, for till that time the air had been clear. When the servant had gone up, and had said many times that he saw nothing, at the seventh time of his going up, he said he saw a small black thing in the sky, not larger than a man's foot. When Elijah heard that, he sent to Ahab, and desired him to go away to the city before the rain came down. So he came to the city Jezreel; and in a little time the air was all obscured, and covered with clouds, and a vehement storm of wind came upon the earth, and with it a great deal of rain; and the prophet was under a divine fury, and ran along with the king's chariot unto Jezreel, a city of Izar† [Issachar.]

7. When Jezebel, the wife of Ahab, understood what signs Elijah had wrought, and how he had slain her prophets, she was angry, and sent messengers to him, and by them threatened to kill him, as he had destroyed her prophets. At this Elijah was affrighted, and fled to the city called Beersheba, which is situate at the utmost limits of the country belonging to the tribe of Judah, towards the land of Edom; and there he left his servant, and went away into the desert. He prayed also that he might die, for that he was not better than his fathers, nor need he be very desirous to live, when they were dead; and he lay and slept under a certain tree; and when somebody awakened him, and he was risen up, he found food set by him and water; so when he had eaten, and recovered his strength by that his food, he came to that mountain which is called Sinai, where it is related that Moses received his laws from God; and finding there a certain hollow cave, he entered into it, and continued to make his abode in it. But when a certain voice came to him, but from whence he knew not, and asked him, why he was come thither, and had left the city? he said, that because he had slain the prophets of the foreign gods, and had persuaded the people that he alone whom they had worshipped from the beginning was God, he was sought for by the king's wife to be punished for so doing. And when he had heard another voice, telling him that he should come out the next day into the open air, and should thereby know what he was to do, he came out of the cave the next day accordingly, when he both heard an earthquake, and saw the bright splendour of a fire; and after a silence made, a divine voice exhorted him not to be disturbed with the circumstances he was in, for that none of his enemies should have power over him. The voice also commanded him to return home, and to ordain Jehu, the son of Nimshi, to be king over their own multitude; and Hazael, of Damascus, to be over the Syrians; and Elisha, of the city Abel, to be a prophet in his stead: and that of the impious multitude, some should be slain by Hazael, and others by Jehu. So Elijah, upon hearing this charge, returned into the land of the Hebrews. And when he found Elisha, the son of Shaphat, ploughing, and certain others with him, driving twelve yoke of oxen, he came to him, and cast his own garment upon him; upon which Elisha began to prophesy presently, and leaving his oxen, he followed Elijah. And when he desired leave to salute his parents, Elijah gave him leave so to do: and when he had taken his leave of

---

* Spanheim takes notice here, that in the worship of Mithra (the god of the Persians) the priests cut themselves in the same manner as did these priests in the invocation of Baal, (the god of the Phœnicians.)

† For *Izar* we may here read *Issachar, i.e.* of the tribe of Issachar, for to that tribe did Jezreel belong.

them, he followed him, and became the disciple and the servant of Elijah all the days of his life. And thus have I despatched the affairs in which this prophet was concerned.

8. Now there was one Naboth, of the city Izar [Jezreel,] who had a field adjoining to that of the king : the king would have persuaded him to sell him that his field, which lay so near his own lands, at what price he pleased, that he might join them together, and make them one farm ; and if he would not accept of money for it, he gave him leave to choose any of his other fields in its stead. But Naboth said he would not do so, but would keep the possession of that land of his own, which he had by inheritance from his father. Upon this the king was grieved, as if he had received an injury, when he could not get another man's possession, and he would neither wash himself, nor take any food : and when Jezebel asked him what it was that troubled him, and why he would neither wash himself, nor eat either dinner nor supper, he related to her the perverseness of Naboth ; and how when he had made use of gentle words to him, and such as were beneath the royal authority, he had been affronted, and had not obtained what he desired. However, she persuaded him not to be cast down at this accident, but to leave off his grief, and return to the usual care of his body, for that she would take care to have Naboth punished : and she immediately sent letters to the rulers of the Israelites [Jezreelites] in Ahab's name, and commanded them to fast, and to assemble a congregation, and to set Naboth at the head of them, because he was of an illustrious family, and to have three bold men ready to bear witness that he had blasphemed God and the king, and then to stone him, and slay him in that manner. Accordingly, when Naboth had been thus testified against, as the queen had written to them, that he had blasphemed against God and Ahab the king, she desired him to take possession of Naboth's vineyard on free cost. So Ahab was glad at what had been done, and rose up immediately from the bed wherein he lay, to go to see Naboth's vineyard ; but God had great indignation at it, and sent Elijah the prophet to the field of Naboth, to speak to Ahab, and to say to him, that he had slain the true owner of that field unjustly. And as soon as he came to him, and the king had said that he might do with him what he pleased, (for he thought it a reproach to him to be thus caught in his sin,) Elijah said, that in that very place in which the dead body of Naboth was eaten by dogs, both his own blood and that of his wife's should be shed ; and that all his family should perish, because he had been so insolently wicked, and had slain a citizen unjustly and contrary to the laws of his country. Hereupon Ahab began to be sorry for the things he had done, and to repent of them ; and he put on sackcloth and went barefoot,* and would not touch any food : he also confessed his sins, and endeavoured thus to appease God. But God said to the prophet, that while Ahab was living, he would put off the punishment of his family, because he repented of those insolent crimes he had been guilty of, but that still he would fulfil his threatening under Ahab's son. Which message the prophet delivered to the king.

---

* " The Jews weep to this day," says Jerome, "and roll themselves upon sackcloth, in ashes, barefoot, upon such occasions." Spanheim adds, "that after the same manner Bernice, when his life was in danger, stood at the tribunal of Florus barefoot."

CHAPTER XIV.

HOW HADAD, KING OF DAMASCUS AND OF SYRIA, MADE TWO EXPEDITIONS AGAINST AHAB, AND WAS BEATEN

1. WHEN the affairs of Ahab were thus, at that very time the son of Hadad, [Benhadad,] who was king of the Syrians and of Damascus, got together an army out of all his country, and procured thirty-two kings beyond Euphrates, to be his auxiliaries : so he made an expedition against Ahab ; but because Ahab's army was not like that of Benhadad, he did not set it in array to fight him, but having shut up everything that was in the country, in the strongest cities he had, he abode in Samaria himself, for the walls about it were very strong, and it appeared to be not easily to be taken in other respects also. So the king of Syria took his army with him, and came to Samaria, and placed his army round about the city, and besieged it. He also sent a herald to Ahab, and desired he would admit the ambassadors he would send him, by whom he would let him know his pleasure. So upon the king of Israel's permission for him to send, those ambassadors came, and by their king's command spake thus :—That Ahab's riches, and his children, and his wives, were Benhadad's, and if he would make an agreement, and give him leave to take as much of what he had as he pleased, he would withdraw his army, and leave off the siege. Upon this Ahab bade the ambassadors to go back, and tell their king that both he himself, and all that he hath, were his possessions. And when these ambassadors had told this to Benhadad, he sent to him again, and desired, since he confessed that all he had was his, that he would admit those servants of his which he should send the next day ; and he commanded him to deliver to those whom he should send, whatsoever, upon their searching his palace and the houses of his friends and kindred, they should find to be excellent in its kind ; but that what did not please them they should leave to him. At this second embassage of the king of Syria, Ahab was surprised, and gathered together the multitude to a congregation, and told them, that for himself he was ready, for their safety and peace, to give up his own wives and children to the enemy, and to yield to him all his possessions, for that was what the Syrian king required at his first embassage ; but that now he desires to send his servants to search all their houses, and in them to leave nothing that is excellent in its kind, seeking an occasion of fighting against him, " as knowing that I would not spare what is mine own for your sakes, but taking a handle from the disagreeable terms he offers concerning you to bring a war upon us ; however, I will do what you shall resolve is fit to be done." But the multitude advised him to hearken to none of his proposals, but to despise him, and be in readiness to fight him. Accordingly, when he had given the ambassadors this answer to be reported, that he still continued in the mind to comply with what terms he at first desired, for the safety of the citizens ; but as for his second desires, he cannot submit to them,—he dismissed them.

2. Now when Benhadad heard this, he had indignation, and sent ambassadors to Ahab the third time, and threatened that his army would raise a bank higher than those walls, in confidence of whose strength he despised him, and that by only each man of his army taking a handful of earth ; hereby making a show of the great number of his army, and aiming to affright

him. Ahab answered, that he ought not to vaunt himself when he had only put on his armour, but when he should have conquered his enemies in the battle. So the ambassadors came back, and found the king at supper with his thirty-two kings, and informed him of Ahab's answer; who then immediately gave orders for proceeding thus:—To make lines round the city, and raise a bulwark, and to prosecute the siege all manner of ways. Now, as this was doing, Ahab was in a great agony, and all his people with him; but he took courage, and was freed from his fears, upon a certain prophet coming to him, and saying to him, that God had promised to subdue so many ten thousands of his enemies under him; and when he inquired by whose means the victory was to be obtained, he said, "By the sons of the princes; but under thy conduct as their leader, by reason of their unskilfulness [in war."] Upon which he called for the sons of the princes, and found them to be two hundred and thirty-two persons. So when he was informed that the king of Syria had betaken himself to feasting and repose, he opened the gates, and sent out the princes' sons. Now when the sentinels told Benhadad of it, he sent some to meet them, and commanded them, that if these men were come out for fighting, they should bind them, and bring them to him; and that if they came out peaceably they should do the same. Now Ahab had another army ready within the walls, but the sons of the princes fell upon the out-guard, and slew many of them, and pursued the rest of them to the camp; and when the king of Israel saw that these had the upper hand, he sent out all the rest of his army, which, falling suddenly upon the Syrians, beat them, for they did not think they would have come out; on which account it was that they assaulted them when they were naked* and drunk, insomuch that they left all their armour behind them when they fled out of the camp, and the king himself escaped with difficulty, by flying away on horseback. But Ahab went a great way in pursuit of the Syrians; and when he had spoiled their camp, which contained a great deal of wealth, and moreover a large quantity of gold and silver, he took Benhadad's chariots and horses, and returned to the city: but as the prophet told him he ought to have his army ready, because the Syrian king would make another expedition against him the next year, Ahab was busy in making provision for it accordingly.

3. Now Benhadad when he had saved himself, and as much of his army as he could, out of the battle, he consulted with his friends how he might make another expedition against the Israelites. Now those friends advised him not to fight with them on the hills, because their God was potent in such places, and thence it had come to pass that they had very lately been beaten; but they said, that if they joined battle with them in the plain they should beat them. They also gave him this further advice, to send home those kings whom he had brought as his auxiliaries, but to retain their army, and to set captains over it instead of kings, and to raise an army out of their country, and let them be in the place of the former who perished in the battle, together with horses and chariots. So he judged their counsel to be good, and acted according to it in the management of the army.

4. At the beginning of the spring, Benhadad took his army with him, and led it against the Hebrews; and when he was come to a certain city which was called Aphek, he pitched his camp in the Great Plain. Ahab also went to meet him with his army, and pitched his camp over against him, although his army was a very small one, if it were compared with the enemy's; but the prophet came again to him, and told him, that God would give him the victory, that he might demonstrate his own power to be not only on the mountains, but on the plains also; which it seems was quite contrary to the opinion of the Syrians. So they lay quiet in their camp seven days; but on the last of those days, when the enemies came out of their camp, and put themselves in array in order to fight, Ahab also brought out his own army; and when the battle was joined, and they fought valiantly, he put the enemy to flight, and pursued them, and pressed upon them, and slew them; nay, they were destroyed by their own chariots, and by one another; nor could any more than a few of them escape to their own city Aphek, who were also killed by the walls falling upon them, being in number twenty-seven thousand. Now there were slain in this battle a hundred thousand more; but Benhadad, the king of the Syrians, fled away, with certain others of his most faithful servants, and hid himself in a cellar under ground; and when these told him that the kings of Israel were humane and merciful men, and that they might make use of the usual manner of supplication, and obtain deliverance from Ahab, in case he would give them leave to go to him: he gave them leave accordingly. So they came to Ahab, clothed in sackcloth, with ropes about their heads, (for this was the ancient manner of supplication among the Syrians,) † and said that Benhadad desired he would save him; and that he would ever be a servant to him for that favour. Ahab replied he was glad that he was alive, and not hurt in the battle; and he further promised him the same honour and kindness that a man would shew to his brother. So they received assurances upon oath from him, that when he came to him he should receive no harm from him, and then went and brought him out of the cellar wherein he was hid, and brought him to Ahab as he sat in his chariot. So Benhadad worshipped him; and Ahab gave him his hand, and made him come up to him into his chariot, and kissed him, and bade him be of good cheer, and not to expect that any mischief should be done to him. So Benhadad returned him thanks, and professed that he would remember his kindness to him all the days of his life; and promised he would restore those cities of the Israelites which the former kings had taken from them, and grant that he should have leave to come to Damascus, as his forefathers had to come to Samaria. So they confirmed their covenant by oaths; and Ahab made him many presents, and sent him back to his own kingdom. And this was the conclusion of the war that Benhadad made against Ahab and the Israelites.

5. But a certain prophet, whose name was Micaiah,‡ came to one of the Israelites, and bade

---

* Reland notes here that the word *naked* does not always signify *entirely naked;* but sometimes without men's usual armour, without their usual robes or upper garments.

† This manner of supplication for men's lives among the Syrians, with ropes or halters about their heads or necks, is, I suppose, no strange thing in later ages, even in our own country.

‡ It is here remarkable that in Josephus's copy, this prophet, whose severe denunciation of a disobedient person's slaughter by a lion had lately come to pass, was no other than Micaiah, the son of Imlah, who, as he now denounced God's judgment on disobedient Ahab, seems directly to have been that very prophet whom

him smite him on the head, for by so doing he would please God; but when he would not do so, he foretold to him, that since he disobeyed the commands of God, he should meet with a lion and be destroyed by him. When this sad accident had befallen the man, the prophet came again to another, and gave him the same injunction; so he smote him, and wounded his skull: upon which he bound up his head, and came to the king, and told him that he had been a soldier of his, and had the custody of one of the prisoners committed to him by an officer, and that the prisoner being run away, he was in danger of losing his own life by the means of that officer, who had threatened him, that if the prisoner escaped he would kill him; and when Ahab had said that he would justly die, he took off the binding that was about his head, and was known by the king to be Micaiah the prophet, who made use of this artifice as a prelude to the following words; for he said that God would punish him who had suffered Benhadad, a blasphemer against him, to escape punishment; and that he would so bring it about, that he should die by the other's means,* and his people by the other's army. Upon which Ahab was very angry at the prophet, and gave commandment that he should be put in prison, and there kept; but for himself, he was in confusion at the words of Micaiah, and returned to his own house.

CHAPTER XV

CONCERNING JEHOSHAPHAT, THE KING OF JERUSALEM; AND HOW AHAB MADE AN EXPEDITION AGAINST THE SYRIANS, AND WAS ASSISTED THEREIN BY JEHOSHAPHAT, BUT WAS HIMSELF OVERCOME IN BATTLE, AND PERISHED THEREIN

1. AND these were the circumstances in which Ahab was. But I now return to Jehoshaphat, the king of Jerusalem, who, when he had augmented his kingdom, and had set garrisons in the cities of the countries belonging to his subjects, and had put such garrisons no less into these cities which were taken out of the tribe of Ephraim, by his grandfather Abijah, when Jeroboam reigned over the ten tribes [than he did into the other.] But then he had God favourable and assisting to him, as being both righteous and religious, and seeking to do somewhat every day that should be agreeable and acceptable to God. The kings also that were round about him honoured him with the presents they made him, till the riches he had acquired were immensely great, and the glory he had gained was of a most exalted nature.

2. Now, in the third year of his reign, he called together the rulers of the country, and the priests, and commanded them to go round the land, and teach all the people that were under him, city by city, the laws of Moses, and to keep them, and to be diligent in the worship of God. With this the whole multitude was so

the same Ahab, in 1 Kings, xxii. 8, 18, complains of "as one whom he hated, because he did not prophesy good concerning him, but evil;" and who, in that chapter, openly repeats his denunciations against him; all which came to pass accordingly.

* What is most remarkable in this history is this, that, during the Jewish theocracy, God acted entirely as the Supreme King of Israel, and the Supreme General of their armies; and always expected that the Israelites should be in such absolute subjection to him, as subjects and soldiers are to their earthly kings and generals, and that usually without knowing the particular reasons of their injunctions.

pleased, that they were not so eagerly set upon or affected with anything so much as the observation of the laws. The neighbouring nations also continued to love Jehoshaphat, and to be at peace with him. The Philistines paid their appointed tribute, and the Arabians supplied him every year with three hundred and sixty lambs, and as many kids of the goats. He also fortified the great cities, which were many in number, and of great consequence. He prepared also a mighty army of soldiers and weapons against their enemies. Now the army of men that wore their armour was three hundred thousand of the tribe of Judah, of whom Adnah was the chief; but John was chief of two hundred thousand. The same man was chief of the tribe of Benjamin, and had two hundred thousand archers under him. There was another chief, whose name was Jehozabad, who had a hundred and fourscore thousand armed men. This multitude was distributed to be ready for the king's service, besides those whom he sent to the best fortified cities.

3. Jehoshaphat took for his son Jehoram to wife, the daughter of Ahab, the king of the ten tribes, whose name was Athaliah. And when, after some time, he went to Samaria, Ahab received him courteously, and treated the army that followed him in a splendid manner, with great plenty of corn and wine, and of slain beasts; and desired that he would join with him in his war against the king of Syria, that he might recover from him the city Ramoth, in Gilead; for though it had belonged to his father, yet had the king of Syria's father taken it away from him; and upon Jehoshaphat's promise to afford him his assistance, (for indeed his army was not inferior to the other,) and his sending for his army from Jerusalem to Samaria, the two kings went out of the city, and each of them sat on his own throne, and each gave their orders to their several armies. Now Jehoshaphat bade them call some of the prophets, if there were any there, and inquire of them concerning this expedition against the king of Syria, whether they would give them counsel to make that expedition at this time, for there was peace at that time between Ahab and the king of Syria, which had lasted three years, from the time he had taken him captive till that day.

4. So Ahab called his own prophets, being in number about four hundred, and bade them inquire of God whether he would grant him the victory, if he made an expedition against Benhadad, and enable him to overthrow that city, for whose sake it was that he was going to war. Now these prophets gave their counsel for making this expedition; and said, that he would beat the king of Syria, and, as formerly, would reduce him under his power. But Jehoshaphat, understanding by their words that they were false prophets, asked Ahab whether there were not some other prophet, and he belonging to the true God, that we may have surer information concerning futurities. Hereupon Ahab said, there was indeed such a one, but that he hated him, as having prophesied evil to him, and having foretold that he should be overcome and slain by the king of Syria, and that for this cause he had him now in prison, and that his name was Micaiah, the son of Imlah. But upon Jehoshaphat's desire that he might be produced, Ahab sent a eunuch, who brought Micaiah to him. Now the eunuch had informed him by the way, that all the other prophets had foretold that the king should gain the victory; but he said, that it was not lawful for him to lie against God; but that he must speak what he should say to him

about the king, whatsoever it were. When he came to Ahab, and he had adjured him upon oath to speak the truth to him, he said that God had shewn to him the Israelites running away, and pursued by the Syrians, and dispersed upon the mountains by them, as flocks of sheep are dispersed when their shepherd is slain. He said further, that God signified to him that those Israelites should return in peace to their own home, and that he only should fall in the battle. When Micaiah had thus spoken, Ahab said to Jehoshaphat—"I told thee a little while ago the disposition of the man with regard to me, and that he uses to prophesy evil to me." Upon which Micaiah replied, that he ought to hear all, whatsoever it be, that God foretells; and that in particular, they were false prophets that encouraged him to make this war in hope of victory, whereas he must fight and be killed. Whereupon the king was in suspense with himself: but Zedekiah, one of those false prophets, came near, and exhorted him not to hearken to Micaiah, for he did not at all speak truth; as a demonstration of which he instanced in what Elijah had said, who was a better prophet in foretelling futurities than Micaiah;* for he foretold that the dogs should lick his blood in the city of Jezreel, in the field of Naboth, as they licked the blood of Naboth, who, by his means, was there stoned to death by the multitude; that therefore it was plain that this Micaiah was a liar, as contradicting a greater prophet than himself, and saying that he should be slain at three days' journey distance: "and [said he] you shall soon know whether he be a true prophet, and hath the power of the Divine Spirit; for I will smite him, and let him then hurt my hand, as Jadon caused the hand of Jeroboam the king to wither when he would have caught him; for I suppose thou hast certainly heard of that accident." So when, upon his smiting Micaiah, no harm happened to him, Ahab took courage, and readily led his army against the king of Syria; for, as I suppose, fate was too hard for him, and made him believe that the false prophets spake truer than the true one, that it might take an occasion of bringing him to his end. However, Zedekiah made horns of iron, and said to Ahab, that God made those horns signals, that by them he should overthrow all Syria. But Micaiah replied, that Zedekiah, in a few days, should go from one secret chamber to another, to hide himself, that he might escape the punishment of his lying. Then did the king give orders that they should take Micaiah away, and guard him to Amon, the governor of the city, and to give him nothing but bread and water.

5. Then did Ahab and Jehoshaphat the king of Jerusalem, take their forces, and marched to Ramoth, a city of Gilead; and when the king of Syria heard of this expedition, he brought out his army to oppose them, and pitched his camp not far from Ramoth. Now Ahab and Jehoshaphat had agreed that Ahab should lay aside his royal robes, but that the king of Jerusalem should put on his [Ahab's] proper habit, and stand before the army, in order to disprove, by this artifice, what Micaiah had foretold.† But

Ahab's fate found him out without his robes; for Benhadad the king of Assyria had charged his army, by means of their commanders, to kill nobody else but only the king of Israel. So when the Syrians, upon their joining battle with the Israelites, saw Jehoshaphat stand before the army, and conjectured that he was Ahab, they fell violently upon him, and encompassed him round; but when they were near, and knew that it was not he, they all returned back; and while the fight lasted from the morning light till late in the evening, and the Syrians were conquerors, they killed nobody, as their king had commanded them; and when they sought to kill Ahab alone, but could not find him, there was a young nobleman belonging to king Benhadad, whose name was Naaman; he drew his bow against the enemy, and wounded the king through his breastplate, in his lungs. Upon this Ahab resolved not to make his mischance known to his army, lest they should run away; but he bid the driver of his chariot to turn it back, and carry him out of the battle, because he was sorely and mortally wounded. However, he sat in his chariot and endured the pain till sunset, and then he fainted away and died.

6. And now the Syrian army, upon the coming on of the night, retired to their camp; and when the herald belonging to the camp gave notice that Ahab was dead, they returned home; and they took the dead body of Ahab to Samaria, and buried it there; but when they had washed his chariot in the fountain of Jezreel, which was bloody with the dead body of the king, they acknowledged that the prophecy of Elijah was true, for the dogs licked his blood, and the harlots continued afterwards to wash themselves in that fountain; but still he died at Ramoth, as Micaiah had foretold. And as what things were foretold should happen to Ahab by the two prophets came to pass, we ought thence to have high notions of God, and everywhere to honour and worship him, and never to suppose that what is pleasant and agreeable is worthy of belief before what is true; and to esteem nothing more advantageous than the gift of prophecy,‡ and that foreknowledge of future events which is derived from it, since God shews men thereby what we ought to avoid. We may also guess, from what happened to this king, and have reason to consider the power of fate, that there is no way of avoiding it, even when we know it. It creeps upon human souls, and flatters them with pleasing hopes, till it leads them about to the place where it will be too hard for them. Accordingly, Ahab appears to have been deceived thereby, till he disbelieved those that foretold his defeat; but by giving credit to such as foretold what was grateful to him, was slain; and his son Ahaziah succeeded him.

---

* These reasonings of Zedekiah the false prophet, in order to persuade Ahab not to believe Micaiah the true prophet, are plausible; and that some such objection was now raised against Micaiah is very likely, otherwise Jehoshaphat could never have been induced to accompany Ahab in those desperate circumstances.

† This reading of Josephus, that Jehoshaphat put on not his own but Ahab's robes, while Ahab was without

any robes at all, is exceeding probable. It gives great light also to this whole history, and shews, that although Ahab hoped Jehoshaphat would be mistaken for him, and run the only risk of being slain in the battle, yet was he entirely disappointed, while still the escape of Jehoshaphat, and the slaughter of Ahab, demonstrated the great distinction that Divine Providence made betwixt them.

‡ We have here a very wise reflection of Josephus about Divine Providence, and what is derived from it, *prophecy*; and that when wicked men think they take proper methods to elude what is denounced against them, and to escape the divine judgments thereby threatened them, without repentance, they are ever by Providence infatuated to bring about their own destruction, and thereby withal to demonstrate the perfect veracity of that God whose predictions they in vain endeavour to elude.

CHAPTER I

CONCERNING JEHOSHAPHAT AGAIN; HOW HE CONSTITUTED JUDGES, AND, BY GOD'S ASSISTANCE, OVERCAME HIS ENEMIES

1. WHEN Jehoshaphat the king was come to Jerusalem, from the assistance he had afforded Ahab, the king of Israel, when he fought with Benhadad, king of Syria, the prophet Jehu met him, and accused him for assisting Ahab, a man both impious and wicked; and said to him, that God was displeased with him for so doing, but that he delivered him from the enemy, notwithstanding he had sinned, because of his own proper disposition, which was good. Whereupon the king betook himself to thanksgivings and sacrifices to God; after which he presently went over all that country which he ruled round about, and taught the people, as well the laws which God gave them by Moses, as that religious worship was due to him. He also constituted judges in every one of the cities of his kingdom; and charged them to have regard to nothing so much in judging the multitude as to do justice, and not to be moved by bribes, nor by the dignity of men eminent for either their riches or their high birth, but to distribute justice equally to all, as knowing that God is conscious of every secret action of theirs. When he had himself instructed them thus, and gone over every city of the two tribes, he returned to Jerusalem. He there also constituted judges out of the priests and Levites, and principal persons of the multitude, and admonished them to pass all their sentences with care and justice.* And that if any of the people of his country had differences of great consequence, they should send them out of the other cities to these judges, who would be obliged to give righteous sentences concerning such causes; and this with the greater care, because it is proper that the sentences which are given in that city wherein the temple of God is, and wherein the king dwells, be given with great care and the utmost justice. Now he set over them Amariah the priest, and Zebediah, [both] of the tribe of Judah: and after this manner it was that the king ordered these affairs.

2. About the same time the Moabites and Ammonites made an expedition against Jehoshaphat, and took with them a great body of Arabians, and pitched their camp at Engedi, a city that is situate at the lake Asphaltitis, and distant three hundred furlongs from Jerusalem. In that place grows the best kind of palm-trees, and the opobalsamum. Now Jehoshaphat heard that the enemies had passed over the lake, and had made an irruption into that country which belonged to his kingdom; at which news he was affrighted, and called the people of Jerusalem to a congregation in the temple, and standing over

against the temple itself, he called upon God to afford him power and strength, so as to inflict punishment on those that made this expedition against them, (for that those who built this his temple had prayed that he would protect that city, and take vengeance on those that were so bold as to come against it;) for they are come to take from us that land which thou hast given us for a possession. When he had prayed thus, he fell into tears; and the whole multitude, together with their wives and children, made their supplications also: upon which a certain prophet, Jahaziel by name, came into the midst of the assembly, and cried out, and spake both to the multitude and to the king, that God heard their prayers, and promised to fight against their enemies. He also gave order that the king should draw his forces out the next day, for that he should find them between Jerusalem and the ascent of Engedi, at a place called *The Eminence*, and that he should not fight against them, but only stand still and see how God would fight against them. When the prophet had said this, both the king and the multitude fell on their faces, and gave thanks to God, and worshipped him: and the Levites continued singing hymns to God with their instruments of music.

3. As soon as it was day, and the king was come into that wilderness which is under the city of Tekoa, he said to the multitude, "that they ought to give credit to what the prophet had said, and not to set themselves in array for fighting; but to set the priests with their trumpets, and the Levites with the singers of hymns, to give thanks to God, as having already delivered our country from our enemies." This opinion of the king pleased [the people,] and they did what he advised them to do. So God caused a terror and a commotion to arise among the Ammonites, who thought one another to be enemies, and slew one another, insomuch that not one man out of so great an army escaped; and when Jehoshaphat looked upon that valley wherein their enemies had been encamped, and saw it full of dead men, he rejoiced at so surprising an event as was this assistance of God, while he himself by his own power, and without their labour, had given them the victory. He also gave his army leave to take the prey of the enemy's camp, and to spoil their dead bodies; and indeed so they did for three days together, till they were weary, so great was the number of the slain; and on the fourth day, all the people were gathered together, unto a certain hollow place or valley, and blessed God for his power and assistance; from which place had this name given it, the *Valley of* [Berachah, or] *Blessing*.

4. And when the king had brought his army back to Jerusalem, he betook himself to celebrate festivals, and offer sacrifices, and this for many days; and indeed, after this destruction of their enemies, and when it came to the ears of the foreign nations, they were all greatly affrighted, as supposing that God would openly fight for him hereafter. So Jehoshaphat from that time lived

---

* These judges were a kind of Jerusalem Sanhedrim, out of the priests, the Levites, and the principal of the people.

in great glory and splendour, on account of his righteousness and his piety towards God. He was also in friendship with Ahab's son, who was king of Israel; and he joined with him in the building of ships that were to sail to Pontus and the traffic cities of Thrace; * but he failed of his gains, for the ships were destroyed by being so great [and unwieldy,] on which account he was no longer concerned about shipping.—And this is the history of Jehoshaphat, the king of Jerusalem.

CHAPTER II

CONCERNING AHAZIAH, THE KING OF ISRAEL; AND AGAIN CONCERNING THE PROPHET ELIJAH

1. AND now Ahaziah, the son of Ahab, reigned over Israel, and made his abode in Samaria. He was a wicked man, and in all respects like to both his parents, and to Jeroboam, who first of all transgressed, and began to deceive the people. In the second year of his reign, the king of Moab fell off from his obedience, and left off paying those tributes which he before paid to his father Ahab. Now it happened that Ahaziah, as he was coming down from the top of his house, fell down from it, and in his sickness sent to the Fly, which was the god of Ekron, for that was this god's name, to inquire about his recovery :† but the God of the Hebrews appeared to Elijah the prophet, and commanded him to go and meet the messengers that were sent, and to ask them, whether the people of Israel had not a god of their own, that the king sent to a foreign god to inquire about his recovery? and to bid them return and tell the king that he would not escape this disease. And when Elijah had performed what God had commanded him, and the messengers had heard what he said, they returned to the king immediately; and when the king wondered how they could return so soon, and asked them the reason of it, they said, that a certain man met them, and forbade them to go on any further; but to return and tell thee, from the command of the God of Israel, that this disease will have a bad end. And when the king bade them describe the man that said this to them, they replied that he was a hairy man, and was girt about with a girdle of leather. So the king understood by this that the man who was described by the messengers was Elijah; whereupon he sent a captain to him, with fifty soldiers, and commanded them to bring Elijah to him; and when the captain that was sent found Elijah sitting upon the top of a hill, he commanded him to come down, and to come to the king, for so had he enjoined; but that in case he refused, he would carry him by force. Elijah said to him, "That you may have a trial whether I be a true prophet, I will pray that fire may fall from heaven, and destroy both the soldiers and yourself."‡ So he prayed, and a whirlwind of fire fell [from heaven,] and destroyed the captain and those that were with him. And when the king was informed of the destruction of these men, he was very angry, and sent another captain with the like number of armed men that were sent before. And when this captain also threatened the prophet, that unless he came down of his own accord he would take him and carry him away; upon his prayer against him, the fire [from heaven] slew this captain as well as the other. And when upon inquiry, the king was informed of what had happened to him, he sent out a third captain. But when this captain, who was a wise man, and of a mild disposition, came to the place where Elijah happened to be, and spake civilly to him, and said, that he knew that it was without his own consent, and only in submission to the king's command that he came to him; and that those that came before did not come willingly, but on the same account, —he therefore desired him to have pity on those armed men that were with him; and that he would come down and follow him to the king. So Elijah accepted of his discreet words and courteous behaviour, and came down and followed him. And when he came to the king he prophesied to him, and told him, that God said, —"Since thou hast despised him as not being God, and so unable to foretell the truth about thy distemper, but hast sent to the god of Ekron to inquire of him what will be the end of this thy distemper, know this, that thou shalt die."

2. Accordingly the king in a very little time died, as Elijah had foretold; but Jehoram his brother succeeded him in the kingdom, for he died without children: but for this Jehoram, he was like his father Ahab in wickedness, and reigned twelve years, indulging himself in all sorts of wickedness and impiety towards God, for, leaving off his worship, he worshipped foreign gods; but in other respects he was an active man. Now at this time it was that Elijah disappeared from among men, and no one knows of his death to this very day; but he left behind him his disciple Elisha, as we have formerly declared. And indeed, as to Elijah, and as to Enoch, who was before the Deluge, it is written in the sacred books that they disappeared; but so that nobody knew that they died.

CHAPTER III

HOW JORAM AND JEHOSHAPHAT MADE AN EXPEDITION AGAINST THE MOABITES; AS ALSO CONCERNING THE WONDERS OF ELISHA; AND THE DEATH OF JEHOSHAPHAT

1. WHEN Joram had taken upon him the kingdom, he determined to make an expedition against the king of Moab, whose name was Mesha; for, as we told you before, he was departed from his obedience to his brother [Ahaziah,] while he paid to his father Ahab two hundred thousand sheep, with their fleeces of wool. When therefore he had gathered his own army together, he sent also to Jehoshaphat, and en-

---

* What are here Pontus and Thrace are in our other copies Ophir and Tarshish, and the place whence the fleet sailed is in them Eziongeber, which lay on the Red Sea, whence it was impossible for any ships to sail to Pontus or Thrace. But we may conclude, that Josephus thought one Ophir to be somewhere in the Mediterranean, and not in the South Sea, though perhaps there might be another Ophir in that South Sea also, and that fleets might then sail both from Phœnicia and from the Red Sea, to fetch the gold of Ophir.

† This *God of Flies* seems to have been so called, as was the like god among the Greeks, from his supposed power over flies, in driving them away from the flesh of their sacrifices.

‡ This is esteemed a cruel action of Elijah, and it is owned by our Saviour, that it was an instance of greater severity than the spirit of the New Testament allows, (Luke ix. 54.) But then we must consider, that it is not unlikely that these captains and soldiers believed that they were sent to fetch the prophet, that he might be put to death for foretelling the death of the king, and this while they knew him to be the prophet of the true God, the Supreme King of Israel.

treated him, that since he had from the beginning been a friend to his father, he would assist him in the war that he was entering into against the Moabites, who had departed from their obedience, who not only himself promised to assist him, but would also oblige the king of Edom, who was under his authority, to make the same expedition also. When Joram had received these assurances of assistance from Jehoshaphat, he took his army with him, and came to Jerusalem; and when he had been sumptuously entertained by the king of Jerusalem, it was resolved upon by them to take their march against their enemies through the wilderness of Edom: and when they had taken a compass of seven days' journey, they were in distress for want of water for the cattle and for the army, from the mistake of their roads by the guides that conducted them, insomuch that they were all in an agony, especially Joram; and cried to God, by reason of their sorrow, and [desired to know] what wickedness had been committed by them that induced him to deliver three kings together, without fighting, unto the king of Moab. But Jehoshaphat, who was a righteous man, encouraged him, and bade him send to the camp and know whether any prophet of God was come along with them, that we might by him learn from God what we should do. And when one of the servants of Joram said that he had seen there Elisha, the son of Shaphat, the disciple of Elijah, the three kings went to him at the entreaty of Jehoshaphat: and when they were come at the prophet's tent, which tent was pitched out of the camp, they asked him what would become of the army? and Joram was particularly very pressing with him about it. And when he replied to him, that he should not trouble him, but go to his father's and his mother's prophets, for they [to be sure] were true prophets,—he still desired him to prophesy, and to save them. So he swore by God that he would not answer him, unless it were on account of Jehoshaphat, who was a holy and righteous man: and when, at his desire, they brought him a man that could play on the psaltery, the Divine Spirit came upon him as the music played, and he commanded them to dig many trenches in the valley; for, said he, "though there appear neither cloud, nor wind, nor storm of rain, ye shall see this river full of water, till the army and the cattle be saved for you by drinking of it; nor will this be all the favour that you shall receive from God, but you shall also overcome your enemies, and take the best and strongest cities of the Moabites, and you shall cut down their fruit-trees,* and lay waste their country, and stop up their fountains and rivers."

2. When the prophet had said this, the next day, before the sun-rising, a great torrent ran strongly; for God had caused it to rain very plentifully at the distance of three days' journey into Edom, so that the army and the cattle found water to drink in abundance. But when the Moabites heard that the three kings were coming upon them, and made their approach through the wilderness, the king of Moab gathered his army together presently, and commanded them to pitch their camp upon the mountains, that when the enemy should attempt to enter their country, they might not be concealed from them. But when, at the rising of the sun, they saw the

water in the torrent, for it was not far from the land of Moab, and that it was of the colour of blood, for at such a time the water especially looks red, by the shining of the sun upon it, they formed a false notion of the state of their enemies, as if they had slain one another for thirst; and that the river ran with their blood. However, supposing that this was the case, they desired their king would send them out to spoil their enemies; whereupon they all went in haste, as to an advantage already gained, and came to the enemy's camp, as supposing them destroyed already; but their hope deceived them, for as their enemies stood round about them, some of them were cut to pieces, and others of them were dispersed, and fled to their own country; and when the kings fell into the land of Moab, they overthrew the cities that were in it, and spoiled their fields, and marred them, filling them with stones out of the brooks, and cut down the best of their trees, and stopped up their fountains of water, and overthrew their walls to their foundations; but the king of Moab, when he was pursued, endured a siege, and seeing his city in danger of being overthrown by a force, made a sally, and went out with seven hundred men, in order to break through the enemy's camp with his horsemen, on that side where the watch seemed to be kept most negligently; and when, upon trial, he could not get away, for he lighted upon a place that was carefully watched, he returned into the city, and did a thing that shewed despair, and the utmost distress; for he took his eldest son, who was to reign after him, and lifting him up upon the wall, that he might be visible to all the enemies, he offered him as a whole burnt-offering to God, whom, when the kings saw, they commiserated the distress that was the occasion of it, and were so affected, in the way of humanity and pity, that they raised the siege, and every one returned to his own house. So Jehoshaphat came to Jerusalem, and continued in peace there, and outlived this expedition but a little time, and then died, having lived in all sixty years, and of them reigned twenty-five. He was buried in a magnificent manner in Jerusalem, for he had imitated the actions of David.

CHAPTER IV

JEHORAM SUCCEEDS JEHOSHAPHAT: HOW JORAM, HIS NAMESAKE, KING OF ISRAEL, FOUGHT WITH THE SYRIANS; AND WHAT WONDERS WERE DONE BY THE PROPHET ELISHA.

1. JEHOSHAPHAT had a good number of children; but he appointed his eldest son, Jehoram, to be his successor, who had the same name with his mother's brother, that was king of Israel, and the son of Ahab. Now when the king of Israel was come out of the land of Moab to Samaria, he had with him Elisha the prophet, whose acts I have a mind to go over particularly, for they were illustrious, and worthy to be related, as we have them set down in the sacred books.

2. For they say that the widow of Obadiah,†

---

* This practice of cutting down the fruit-trees was forbidden, even in ordinary wars, by the law of Moses, (Deut. xx. 19, 20;) and only allowed by God in this particular case, when the Moabites were to be punished and cut off in an extraordinary manner for their wickedness.

† That this woman was no other than the widow of Obadiah, is confirmed by the Chaldee paraphrast, and by the Rabbins and others. Nor is it unlikely that these debts were contracted by her husband for the support of those "hundred of the Lord's prophets, whom he maintained by fifty in a cave," in the days of Ahab and Jezebel, (1 Kings xviii. 4;) which circumstance rendered it highly fit that the prophet Elisha should provide her a remedy, and enable her to redeem herself and her

Ahab's steward, came to him, and said, that he was not ignorant how her husband had preserved the prophets that were to be slain by Jezebel, the wife of Ahab; for she said that he hid a hundred of them, and had borrowed money for their maintenance, and that, after her husband's death, she and her children were carried away to be made slaves by the creditors; and she desired of him to have mercy upon her on account of what her husband did, and afford her some assistance. And when he asked her what she had in the house, she said, "Nothing but a very small quantity of oil in a cruse." So the prophet bid her go away, and borrow a great many empty vessels of her neighbours, and when she had shut her chamber-door, to pour the oil into them all; for that God would fill them full. And when the woman had done what she was commanded to do, and bade her children bring every one of the vessels, and all were filled, and not one left empty, she came to the prophet, and told him that they were all full; upon which he advised her to go away, and sell the oil, and pay the creditors what was owing to them, for that there would be some surplus of the price of the oil, which she might make use of for the maintenance of her children:—and thus did Elisha discharge the woman's debts, and free her from the vexation of her creditors.

3. Elisha also sent a hasty message to Joram, and exhorted him to take care of that place, for that therein were some Syrians lying in ambush to kill him. So the king did as the prophet exhorted him, and avoided his going a-hunting; and when Benhadad missed of the success of his lying in ambush, he was wroth with his own servants, as if they had betrayed his ambushment to Joram; and he sent for them, and said they were the betrayers of his secret counsels; and he threatened that he would put them to death, since such their practice was evident, because he had intrusted this secret to none but them, and yet it was made known to his enemy: and when one that was present said, that he should not mistake himself, nor suspect that they had discovered to his enemy his sending men to kill him, but that he ought to know that it was Elisha the prophet who discovered all to him, and laid open all his counsels. So he gave order that they should send some to learn in what city Elisha dwelt. Accordingly, those that were sent brought word that he was in Dothan; wherefore Benhadad sent to that city a great army, with horses and chariots, to take Elisha; so they encompassed the city round about by night, and kept him therein confined; but when the prophet's servant in the morning perceived this, and that his enemies sought to take Elisha, he came running, and crying out after a disordered manner to him, and told him of it; but he encouraged him, and bade him not be afraid, and to despise the enemy, and trust in the assistance of God, and was himself without fear; and he besought God to make manifest to his servant his power and presence, so far as was possible, in order to the inspiring him with hope and courage. Accordingly, God heard the prayer of the prophet, and made the servant see a multitude of chariots and horses encompassing Elisha, till he laid aside his fear, and his courage revived at the sight of what he supposed was come to their assistance. After this Elisha did further entreat God, that he would dim the eyes of their enemies, and cast a mist before them, whereby they might not discern him. When this was done, he went into

the midst of his enemies, and asked them who it was that they came to seek; and when they replied, "The prophet Elisha," he promised he would deliver him to them, if they would follow him to the city where he was. So these men were so darkened by God in their sight and in their mind, that they followed him very diligently; and when Elisha had brought them to Samaria, he ordered Joram the king to shut the gates, and to place his own army round about them; and prayed to God to clear the eyes of these their enemies, and take the mist from before them. Accordingly, when they were freed from the obscurity they had been in, they saw themselves in the midst of their enemies; and as the Syrians were strangely amazed and distressed, as was but reasonable, at an action so divine and surprising; and as king Joram asked the prophet if he would give him leave to shoot at them, Elisha forbade him so to do; and said, that "it is just to kill those that are taken in battle; but that these men had done the country no harm, but, without knowing it, were come thither by the Divine Power;"—so that his counsel was to treat them in an hospitable manner at his table, and then send them away without hurting them.* Wherefore Joram obeyed the prophet; and when he had feasted the Syrians in a splendid and magnificent manner, he let them go to Benhadad their king.

4. Now when these men were come back, and had shewed Benhadad how strange an accident had befallen them, and what an appearance and power they had experienced of the God of Israel, he wondered at it, as also at that prophet with whom God was so evidently present; so he determined to make no more secret attempts upon the king of Israel, out of fear of Elisha, but resolved to make open war with them, as supposing he could be too hard for his enemies by the multitude of his army and power. So he made an expedition with a great army against Joram, who, not thinking himself a match for him, shut himself up in Samaria, and depended on the strength of its walls; but Benhadad supposed he should take the city, if not by his engines of war, yet that he should overcome the Samaritans by famine, and the want of necessaries, and brought his army upon them, and besieged the city; and the plenty of necessaries was brought so low with Joram, that from the extremity of want, an ass's head was sold in Samaria for fourscore pieces of silver; and the Hebrews bought a sextary of dove's dung, instead of salt, for five pieces of silver. Now Joram was in fear lest somebody should betray the city to the enemy, by reason of the famine, and went every day round the walls and the guards, to see whether any such were concealed among them; and by being thus seen, and taking such care, he deprived them of the opportunity of contriving any such thing; and if they had a mind to do it, he by this means prevented them; but upon a certain woman's crying out, "Have pity on me, my lord," while he thought that she was about to ask for somewhat to eat, he imprecated God's curse upon her, and said, he had neither thrashing-floor nor wine-press, whence he might give her anything at her petition. Upon which she said, she did not desire his aid in any such thing, nor trouble him about food, but desired that he would do her justice as to another woman; and

---

sons from the fear of that slavery which insolvent debtors were liable to by the law of Moses.

* Upon occasion of this stratagem of Elisha, in Josephus, we may take notice, that although Josephus was one of the greatest lovers of truth in the world; yet, in a just war, he seems to have had no manner of scruple upon him, by all such stratagems possible, to deceive public enemies.

when he bade her say on, and let him know what she desired, she said, she had made an agreement with the other woman, who was her neighbour and her friend, that because the famine and the want was intolerable, they should kill their children, each of them having a son of their own, "and we will live upon them ourselves for two days—the one day upon one son, and the other day upon the other; and," said she, "I have killed my son the first day, and we lived upon my son yesterday; but this other woman will not do the same thing, but hath broken her agreement, and hath hid her son." This story mightily grieved Joram when he heard it: so he rent his garment, and cried out with a loud voice, and conceived great wrath against Elisha the prophet, and set himself eagerly to have him slain, because he did not pray to God to provide them some exit and way of escape out of the miseries with which they were surrounded; and sent one away immediately to cut off his head, who made haste to kill the prophet; but Elisha was not unacquainted with the wrath of the king against him; for as he sat in his house by himself, with none but his disciples about him, he told them that Joram, who was the son of a murderer, had sent one to take away his head; "but," said he, "when he that is commanded to do this comes, take care that you do not let him come in, but press the door against him, and hold him fast there, for the king himself will follow him, and come to me, having altered his mind." Accordingly, they did as they were bidden, when he that was sent by the king to kill Elisha came; but Joram repented of his wrath against the prophet; and for fear he that was commanded to kill him should have done it before he came, he made haste to hinder his slaughter, and to save the prophet: and when he came to him, he accused him that he did not pray to God for their deliverance from the miseries they lay under, but saw them so sadly destroyed by them. Hereupon Elisha promised, that the very next day, at the very same hour in which the king came to him, they should have great plenty of food, and that two seahs of barley should be sold in the market for a shekel, and a seah of fine flour should be sold for a shekel. This prediction made Joram, and those that were present, very joyful, for they did not scruple believing what the prophet said, on account of the experience they had of the truth of his former predictions; and the expectation of plenty made the want they were in that day, with the uneasiness that accompanied it, appear a light thing to them; but the captain of the third band, who was a friend of the king, and on whose hand the king leaned, said, "Thou talkest of incredible things, O prophet! for as it is impossible for God to pour down torrents of barley, or fine flour, out of heaven, so is it impossible that what thou sayest should come to pass." To which the prophet made this reply—"Thou shalt see these things come to pass, but thou shalt not be in the least a partaker of them."

5. Now what Elisha had thus foretold came to pass in the manner following:—There was a law at Samaria,* that those that had the leprosy, and whose bodies were not cleansed from it, should abide without the city. And there were four men that on this account abode before the gates, while nobody gave them any food, by reason of the extremity of the famine; and as they were prohibited from entering into the city by the law, and they considered that if they were permitted to enter, they would miserably perish by the famine; as also, that if they stayed where they were, they should suffer in the same manner,—they resolved to deliver themselves up to the enemy, that in case they should spare them, they should live; but if they should be killed, that would be an easy death. So when they had confirmed this their resolution, they came by night to the enemy's camp. Now God had begun to affright and disturb the Syrians, and to bring the noise of chariots and armour to their ears, as though an army were coming upon them, and had made them suspect that it was coming nearer and nearer to them. In short, they were in such a dread of this army, that they left their tents, and ran together to Benhadad, and said that Joram, the king of Israel, had hired for auxiliaries both the king of Egypt and the king of the Islands, and led them against them; for they heard the noise of them as they were coming; and Benhadad believed what they said, (for there came the same noise to his ears as well as it did to theirs;) so they fell into a mighty disorder and tumult, and left their horses and beasts in their camp, with immense riches also, and betook themselves to flight. And those lepers who had departed from Samaria, and were gone to the camp of the Syrians, of whom we made mention a little before, when they were in the camp, saw nothing but great quietness and silence; accordingly they entered into it, and went hastily into one of their tents; and when they saw nobody there, they ate and drank, and carried garments, and a great quantity of gold, and hid it out of the camp; after which they went into another tent, and carried off what was in it, as they did at the former, and this did they for several times, without the least interruption from anybody; so they gathered thereby that the enemies were departed; whereupon they reproached themselves that they did not inform Joram and the citizens of it. So they came to the walls of Samaria, and called aloud to the watchmen, and told them in what state the enemies were, as did these tell the king's guards, by whose means Joram came to know of it; who then sent for his friends, and the captains of his host, and said to them, that he suspected that this departure of the king of Syria was by way of ambush and treachery; "and that out of despair of ruining you by famine, when you imagine them to be fled away, you may come out of the city to spoil their camp, and he may then fall upon you on a sudden, and may both kill you, and take the city without fighting;—whence it is that I exhort you to guard the city carefully, and by no means to go out of it, or proudly to despise your enemies, as though they were really gone away." And when a certain person said that he did very well and wisely to admit such a suspicion, but that he still advised him to send a couple of horsemen to search all the country as far as Jordan, that "if they were seized by an ambush of the enemy, they might be a security to your army, that they may not go out as if they suspected nothing, nor undergo the like misfortune; and," said he, "those horsemen may be numbered among those that have died by the famine, supposing they be caught and destroyed by the enemy." So the king was pleased with this opinion, and sent such as might search out the truth, who performed their journey over a road that was without any enemies; but found it full of provisions, and of weapons, that they had therefore thrown away, and left behind them, in order to their being light and expeditious in their flight. When the king

---

* This law of the Jews for the exclusion of lepers out of the camp in the wilderness, and out of the cities in Judea, is a known one, (Lev. xiii. 46; Numb. v. 1-4.)

heard this, he sent out the multitude to take the spoils of the camp; which gains of theirs were not of things of small value; but they took a great quantity of gold, and a great quantity of silver, and flocks of all kinds of cattle. They also possessed themselves of [so many] ten thousand measures of wheat and barley, as they never in the least dreamed of; and were not only freed from their former miseries, but had such plenty, that two seahs of barley were bought for a shekel, and a seah of fine flour for a shekel, according to the prophecy of Elisha. Now a seah is equal to an Italian modius and a half. The captain of the third band was the only man that received no benefit by this plenty; for as he was appointed by the king to oversee the gate, that he might prevent the too great crowd of the multitude, and they might not endanger one another to perish, by treading on one another in the press, he suffered himself in that very way, and died in that very manner, as Elisha had foretold this his death, when he alone of them all disbelieved what he said concerning that plenty of provisions which they should soon have.

6. Hereupon, when Benhadad, the king of Syria, had escaped to Damascus, and understood that it was God himself that cast all his army into this fear and disorder, and that it did not arise from the invasion of enemies, he was mightily cast down at his having God so greatly for his enemy, and fell into a distemper. Now it happened that Elisha the prophet, at that time, was gone out of his own country to Damascus, of which Benhadad was informed; he sent Hazael, the most faithful of all his servants, to meet him, and to carry him presents; and bade him inquire of him about his distemper, and whether he should escape the danger that it threatened. So Hazael came to Elisha with forty camels, that carried the best and most precious fruits that the country of Damascus afforded, as well as those which the king's palace supplied. He saluted him kindly, and said that he was sent to him by king Benhadad, and brought presents with him, in order to inquire concerning his distemper, whether he should recover from it or not. Whereupon the prophet bade him tell the king no melancholy news; but still he said he would die. So the king's servant was troubled to hear it; and Elisha wept also, and his tears ran down plenteously at his foresight at what miseries his people would undergo after the death of Benhadad; and when Hazael asked him what was the occasion of this confusion he was in, he said, that he wept out of commiseration for the multitude of the Israelites, and what terrible miseries they will suffer by thee; "for thou wilt slay the strongest of them, and wilt burn their strongest cities, and wilt destroy their children, and dash them against the stones, and wilt rip up their women with child." And when Hazael said, "How can it be that I should have power enough to do such things?" the prophet replied, that God had informed him that he should be king of Syria. So when Hazael was come to Benhadad, he told him good news concerning his distemper;* but on the next day he spread a wet cloth, in the nature of a net, over him, and

strangled him, and took his dominion. He was an active man, and had the good-will of the Syrians, and of the people of Damascus, to a great degree; by whom both Benhadad himself, and Hazael, who ruled after him, are honoured to this day as gods, by reason of their benefactions, and their building them temples, by which they adorned the city of the Damascens. They also every day do with great pomp pay their worship to these kings, and value themselves upon their antiquity; nor do they know that these kings are much later than they imagine, and that they are not yet eleven hundred years old. Now when Joram, the king of Israel, heard that Benhadad was dead, he recovered out of the terror and dread he had been in on his account, and was very glad to live in peace.

CHAPTER V

CONCERNING THE WICKEDNESS OF JEHORAM, KING OF JERUSALEM; HIS DEFEAT, AND DEATH

1. Now Jehoram, the king of Jerusalem, (for we have said before that he had the same name with the king of Israel,) as soon as he had taken the government upon him, betook himself to the slaughter of his brethren and his father's friends, who were governors under him, and thence made a beginning and a demonstration of his wickedness; nor was he at all better than those kings of Israel who at first transgressed against the laws of their country, and of the Hebrews, and against God's worship: and it was Athaliah, the daughter of Ahab, whom he had married, who taught him to be a bad man in other respects, and also to worship foreign gods. Now God would not quite root out this family, because of the promise he had made to David. However, Jehoram did not leave off the introduction of new sorts of customs to the propagation of impiety, and to the ruin of the customs of his own country. And when the Edomites about that time had revolted from him, and slain their former king, who was in subjection to his father, and had set up one of their own choosing, Jehoram fell upon the land of Edom, with the horsemen that were about him, and the chariots, by night, and destroyed those that lay near to his own kingdom; but did not proceed further. However, this expedition did him no service, for they all revolted from him, with those that dwelt in the country of Libnah. He was indeed so mad as to compel the people to go up to the high places of the mountains, and worship foreign gods.

2. As he was doing this, and had entirely cast his own country laws out of his mind, there was brought him an epistle from Elijah the prophet,† which declared, that God would execute judgments upon him, because he had not imitated his own fathers, but had followed the wicked courses of the kings of Israel; and had compelled the tribe of Judah and the citizens of Jerusalem to leave the holy worship of their own God, and to worship idols, as Ahab had compelled the Israelites to do, and because he

---

* Since Elijah did not live to anoint Hazael king of Syria himself, as he was empowered to do, (1 Kings xix. 15,) it was most probably now done, in his name, by his servant and successor Elisha; nor does it seem to me otherwise but that Benhadad immediately recovered of his disease, as the prophet foretold; and that Hazael, upon his being anointed to succeed him, though he ought to have stayed till he died by the

course of nature, was too impatient, and the very next day smothered or strangled him, in order to come directly to the succession.

† This epistle, in some copies of Josephus, is said to come to Joram from Elijah, with this addition, "for he was yet upon earth;" which could not be true of Elijah, who, as all agree, was gone from the earth above four years before. It is probable that the name of Elijah has crept into the text instead of Elisha.

had slain his brethren, and the men that were good and righteous. And the prophet gave him notice in this epistle what punishment he should undergo for these crimes, namely, the destruction of his people, with the corruption of the king's own wives and children; and that he should himself die of a distemper in his bowels, with long torments, those his bowels falling out by the violence of the inward rottenness of the parts, insomuch that, though he see his own misery, he shall not be able at all to help himself, but shall die in that manner. This it was which Elijah denounced to him in that epistle.

3. It was not long after this that an army of those Arabians that lived near to Ethiopia, and of the Philistines, fell upon the kingdom of Jehoram, and spoiled the country and the king's house; moreover, they slew his sons and his wives; one only of his sons was left him, who escaped the enemy; his name was Ahaziah; after which calamity, he himself fell into that disease which was foretold by the prophet, and lasted a great while, (for God inflicted this punishment upon him in his belly, out of his wrath against him,) and so he died miserably, and saw his own bowels fall out. The people also abused his dead body; I suppose it was because they thought that such his death came upon him by the wrath of God, and that therefore he was not worthy to partake of such a funeral as became kings. Accordingly, they neither buried him in the sepulchres of his fathers, nor vouchsafed him any honours, but buried him like a private man, and this when he had lived forty years, and reigned eight; and the people of Jerusalem delivered the government to his son Ahaziah.

CHAPTER VI

HOW JEHU WAS ANOINTED KING, AND SLEW BOTH JORAM AND AHAZIAH; AS ALSO WHAT HE DID FOR THE PUNISHMENT OF THE WICKED

1. Now Joram, the king of Israel, after the death of Benhadad, hoped that he might now take Ramoth, a city of Gilead, from the Syrians. Accordingly, he made an expedition against it, with a great army; but as he was besieging it, an arrow was shot at him by one of the Syrians, but the wound was not mortal: so he returned to have his wound healed in Jezreel, but left his whole army in Ramoth, and Jehu, the son of Nimshi, for their general,—for he had already taken the city by force; and he proposed, after he was healed, to make war with the Syrians; but Elisha the prophet sent one of his disciples to Ramoth, and gave him holy oil to anoint Jehu, and to tell him that God had chosen him to be their king. He also sent him to say other things to him, and bade him to take his journey as if he fled, that when he came away he might escape the knowledge of all men. So when he was come to the city, he found Jehu sitting in the midst of the captains of the army, as Elisha had foretold he should find him. So he came up to him, and said that he desired to speak with him about certain matters; and when he was arisen, and had followed him into an inward chamber, the young man took the oil, and poured it on his head, and said that God ordained him to be king, in order to his destroying the house of Ahab, and that he might revenge the blood of the prophets that were unjustly slain by Jezebel, that so their house might utterly perish, as those of Jeroboam the son of Nebat and of Baasha had perished for their

wickedness, and no seed might remain of Ahab's family. So when he had said this, he went away hastily out of the chamber, and endeavoured not to be seen by any of the army.

2. But Jehu came out, and went to the place where he before sat with the captains; and when they asked him, and desired him to tell them wherefore it was that this young man came to him, and added withal that he was mad,—he replied, "You guess right; for the words he spake were the words of a madman:"—and when they were eager about the matter, and desired he would tell them, he answered, that God had said he had chosen him to be king over the multitude. When he had said this, every one of them put off his garment,* and strewed it under him, and blew with trumpets, and gave notice that Jehu was king. So when he had gotten the army together, he was preparing to set out immediately against Joram, at the city of Jezreel, in which city, as we said before, he was healing of the wound which he had received in the siege of Ramoth. It happened also that Ahaziah, king of Jerusalem, was now come to Joram, for he was his sister's son, as we have said already, to see how he did after his wound, and this upon account of their kindred: but as Jehu was desirous to fall upon Joram and those with him on the sudden, he desired that none of the soldiers might run away and tell to Joram what had happened, for that this would be an evident demonstration of their kindness to him, and would shew that their real inclinations were to make him king.

3. So they were pleased with what he did, and guarded the roads, lest somebody should privately tell the thing to those that were at Jezreel. Now Jehu took his choice horsemen, and sat upon his chariot, and went on for Jezreel; and when he was come near, the watchman whom Joram had set there to spy out such as came to the city, saw Jehu marching on, and told Joram that he saw a troop of horsemen marching on. Upon which he immediately gave orders, that one of his horsemen should be sent out to meet them, and to know who it was that was coming. So when the horseman came up to Jehu, he asked him in what condition the army was, for that the king wanted to know it; but Jehu bade him not at all to meddle with such matters, but to follow him. When the watchman saw this, he told Joram that the horseman had mingled himself among the company, and came along with them. And when the king had sent a second messenger, Jehu commanded him to do as the former did: and as soon as the watchman told this also to Joram, he at last got upon his chariot himself, together with Ahaziah, the king of Jerusalem; for, as we said before, he was there to see how Joram did, after he had been wounded, as being his relation. So he went out to meet Jehu, who marched slowly,† and in good order; and when Joram met him in the field of Naboth, he asked him if all things were well in the camp; but Jehu reproached him bitterly, and ventured to call his mother a witch and a harlot. Upon this the king fearing what he intended, and suspecting he had no good meaning, turned his chariot about as soon as he could, and said to Ahaziah, "We are fought against by deceit and treachery." But Jehu drew his bow, and smote him, the arrow going through his heart: so Joram fell down immediately on his knee, and gave up

---

* Spanheim notes, that this was an Eastern custom.
† Our copies say that this "driving of the chariots was like the driving of Jehu, the son of Nimshi; for he driveth furiously," (2 Kings ix. 20.)

the ghost. Jehu also gave orders to Bidkar, the captain of the third part of his army, to cast the dead body of Joram into the field of Naboth, putting him in mind of the prophecy which Elijah prophesied to Ahab his father, when he had slain Naboth, that both he and his family should perish in that place; for that as they sat behind Ahab's chariot, they heard the prophet say so, and that it was now come to pass according to his prophecy. Upon the fall of Joram, Ahaziah was afraid of his own life, and turned his chariot into another road, supposing he should not be seen by Jehu; but he followed after him, and overtook him at a certain acclivity, and drew his bow, and wounded him; so he left his chariot, and got upon his horse, and fled from Jehu to Megiddo; and though he was under care, in a little time he died of that wound, and was carried to Jerusalem, and buried there, after he had reigned one year, and had proved a wicked man, and worse than his father.

4. Now when Jehu was come to Jezreel, Jezebel adorned herself and stood upon a tower, and said he was a fine servant that had killed his master! And when he looked up to her, he asked who she was, and commanded her to come down to him. At last he ordered the eunuchs to throw her down from the tower; and being thrown down, she besprinkled the wall with her blood, and was trodden upon by the horses, and so died. When this was done, Jehu came to the palace with his friends, and took some refreshment after his journey, both with other things, and by eating a meal. He also bade his servants to take up Jezebel and bury her, because of the nobility of her blood, for she was descended from kings; but those that were appointed to bury her found nothing else remaining but the extreme parts of her body, for all the rest were eaten by dogs. When Jehu heard this, he admired the prophecy of Elijah, for he foretold that she should perish in this manner at Jezreel.

5. Now Ahab had seventy sons brought up in Samaria. So Jehu sent two epistles, the one to them that brought up the children, the other to the rulers of Samaria, which said, that they should set up the most valiant of Ahab's sons for king, for that they had abundance of chariots, and horses, and armour, and a great army, and fenced cities, and that by so doing they might avenge the murder of Ahab. This he wrote to try the intentions of those of Samaria. Now when the rulers, and those that had brought up the children, had read the letters, they were afraid; and considering that they were not at all able to oppose him, who had already subdued two very great kings, they returned him this answer:—That they owned him for their lord, and would do whatsoever he bade them. So he wrote back to them such a reply as enjoined them to obey what he gave order for, and to cut off the heads of Ahab's sons, and send them to him. Accordingly the rulers sent for those that brought up the sons of Ahab, and commanded them to slay them, to cut off their heads, and send them to Jehu. So they did whatsoever they were commanded, without omitting any thing at all, and put them up in wicker baskets, and sent them to Jezreel. And when Jehu, as he was at supper with his friends, was informed that the heads of Ahab's sons were brought, he ordered them to make two heaps of them, one before each of the gates; and in the morning he went out to take a view of them, and when he saw them, he began to say to the people that were present, that he did himself make an expedition against his master [Joram,] and slew him; but

that it was not he that slew all these: and he desired them to take notice, that as to Ahab's family, all things had come to pass according to God's prophecy, and his house was perished, according as Elijah had foretold. And when he had further destroyed all the kindred of Ahab that were found in Jezreel, he went to Samaria; and as he was upon the road, he met the relations of Ahaziah, king of Jerusalem, and asked them, whither they were going? they replied, that they came to salute Joram, and their own king Ahaziah, for they knew not that he had slain them both. So Jehu gave orders that they should catch these, and kill them, being in number forty-two persons.

6. After these, there met him a good and a righteous man, whose name was Jehonadab, and who had been his friend of old. He saluted Jehu, and began to commend him, because he had done everything according to the will of God, in extirpating the house of Ahab. So Jehu desired him to come up into his chariot, and make his entry with him into Samaria; and told him that he would not spare one wicked man, but would punish the false prophets and false priests, and those that deceived the multitude, and persuaded them to leave the worship of God Almighty, and to worship foreign gods; and that it was a most excellent and a most pleasing sight to a good and a righteous man to see the wicked punished. So Jehonadab was persuaded by these arguments, and came up into Jehu's chariot, and came to Samaria. And Jehu sought out for all Ahab's kindred, and slew them. And being desirous that none of the false prophets, nor the priests of Ahab's god, might escape punishment, he caught them deceitfully by this wile: for he gathered all the people together, and said, that he would worship twice as many gods as Ahab worshipped, and desired that his priests, and prophets, and servants, might be present, because he would offer costly and great sacrifices to Ahab's god; and that if any of his priests were wanting, they should be punished with death. Now Ahab's god was called Baal: and when he had appointed a day on which he would offer these sacrifices, he sent messengers through all the country of the Israelites, that they might bring the priests of Baal to him. So Jehu commanded to give all the priests vestments; and when they had received them, he went into the house [of Baal,] with his friend Jehonadab, and gave orders to make search whether there were not any foreigner or stranger among them, for he would have no one of a different religion to mix among their sacred offices. And when they said that there was no stranger there, and they were beginning their sacrifices, he set fourscore men without, they being such of his soldiers as he knew to be most faithful to him, and bade them slay the prophets, and now vindicate the laws of their country, which had been a long time in disesteem. He also threatened, that if any one of them escaped, their own lives should go for them. So they slew them all with the sword; and burnt the house of Baal, and by that means purged Samaria of foreign customs, [idolatrous worship.] Now this Baal was the god of the Tyrians; and Ahab, in order to gratify his father-in-law, Ethbaal, who was the king of Tyre and Sidon, built a temple for him in Samaria, and appointed him prophets, and worshipped him with all sorts of worship, although, when this god was demolished, Jehu permitted the Israelites to worship the golden heifers. However, because he had done thus, and taken care to punish the wicked, God foretold by his prophet, that his sons should reign

over Israel for four generations: and in this condition was Jehu at this time.

CHAPTER VII

HOW ATHALIAH REIGNED OVER JERUSALEM FOR FIVE [SIX] YEARS, WHEN JEHOIADA THE HIGH PRIEST SLEW HER, AND MADE JEHOASH, THE SON OF AHAZIAH, KING

1. Now when Athaliah, the daughter of Ahab, heard of the death of her brother Joram, and of her son Ahaziah, and of the royal family, she endeavoured that none of the house of David might be left alive, but that the whole family might be exterminated, that no king might arise out of it afterward; and, as she thought, she had actually done it; but one of Ahaziah's sons was preserved, who escaped death after the manner following:—Ahaziah had a sister by the same father, whose name was Jehosheba, and she was married to the high priest Jehoiada. She went into the king's palace, and found Jehoash, for that was the little child's name, who was not above a year old, among those that were slain, but concealed with his nurse; so she took him with her into a secret bed-chamber, and shut him up there; and she and her husband Jehoiada brought him up privately in the temple six years, during which time Athaliah reigned over Jerusalem and the two tribes.

2. Now on the seventh year, Jehoiada communicated the matter to certain of the captains of hundreds, five in number, and persuaded them to be assisting to what attempts he was making against Athaliah, and to join with him in asserting the kingdom to the child. He also received such oaths from them as are proper to secure those that assist one another from the fear of discovery; and he was then of good hope that they should depose Athaliah. Now those men whom Jehoiada the priest had taken to be his partners, went into all the country, and gathered together the priests and the Levites, and the heads of the tribes out of it, and came and brought them to Jerusalem, to the high priest. So he demanded the security of an oath of them, to keep private whatsoever he should discover to them, which required both their silence and their assistance. So when they had taken the oath, and had thereby made it safe for him to speak, he produced the child that he had brought up, of the family of David, and said to them, "This is your king, of that house of which you know God hath foretold should reign over you for all time to come: I exhort you, therefore, that one-third part of you guard him in the temple, and that a fourth part keep watch at all the gates of the temple, and that the next part of you keep guard at the gate which opens and leads to the king's palace, and let the rest of the multitude be unarmed in the temple, and let no armed person go into the temple, but the priest only." He also gave them this order besides, "That a part of the priests and the Levites should be about the king himself, and be a guard to him, with their drawn swords, and to kill that man immediately, whoever he be, that should be so bold as to enter armed into the temple; and bade them be afraid of nobody, but persevere in guarding the king." So these men obeyed what the high priest advised them to, and declared the reality of their resolution by their actions. Jehoiada also opened that armoury which David had made in the temple, and distributed to the captains of hundreds, as also to the priests and Levites, all the spears and quivers, and what kind of weapons soever it contained, and set them armed round about the temple, so as to touch one another's hands, and by that means excluding those from entering that ought not to enter. So they brought the child into the midst of them, and put on him the royal crown, and Jehoiada anointed him with the oil, and made him king; and the multitude rejoiced, and made a noise, and cried, "God save the king!"

3. When Athaliah unexpectedly heard the tumult and the acclamations, she was greatly disturbed in her mind, and suddenly issued out of the royal palace with her own army: and when she was come to the temple, the priests received her; but as for those that stood round about the temple, as they were ordered by the high priest to do, they hindered the armed men that followed her from going in. But when Athaliah saw the child standing upon a pillar with the royal crown upon his head, she rent her clothes, and cried out vehemently, and commanded [her guards] to kill him that had laid snares for her, and endeavoured to deprive her of the government; but Jehoiada called for the captains of hundreds, and commanded them to bring Athaliah to the valley of Cedron, and slay her there, for he would not have the temple defiled with the punishments of this pernicious woman; and he gave order, that if any one came near to help her, he should be slain also; wherefore those that had the charge of her slaughter took hold of her, and led her to the gate of the king's mules, and slew her there.

4. Now as soon as what concerned Athaliah was, by this stratagem, after this manner, despatched, Jehoiada called together the people and armed men into the temple, and made them take an oath that they would be obedient to the king, and take care of his safety, and of the safety of his government; after which he obliged the king to give security [upon oath] that he would worship God, and not transgress the laws of Moses. They then ran to the house of Baal, which Athaliah and her husband Jehoram had built, to the dishonour of the God of their fathers, and to the honour of Ahab, and demolished it, and slew Mattan, that had his priesthood. But Jehoiada intrusted the care and custody of the temple to the priests and Levites, according to the appointment of king David, and enjoined them to bring their regular burnt-offerings twice a day, and to offer incense according to the law. He also ordained some of the Levites, with the porters, to be a guard to the temple, that no one that was defiled might come there.

5. And when Jehoiada had set these things in order, he, with the captains of hundreds, and the rulers, and all the people, took Jehoash out of the temple into the king's palace, and when he had set him upon the king's throne, the people shouted for joy, and betook themselves to feasting, and kept a festival for many days: but the city was quiet upon the death of Athaliah. Now Jehoash was seven years old when he took the kingdom: his mother's name was Zibiah, of the city Beersheba. And all the time that Jehoiada lived, Jehoash was careful that the laws should be kept, and very zealous in the worship of God; and when he was of age, he married two wives, who were given to him by the high priest, by whom were born to him both sons and daughters. And thus much shall suffice to have related concerning king Jehoash, how he escaped the treachery of Athaliah, and how he received the kingdom.

CHAPTER VIII

HAZAEL MAKES AN EXPEDITION AGAINST THE
PEOPLE OF ISRAEL AND THE INHABITANTS OF
JERUSALEM·; JEHU DIES, AND JEHOAHAZ SUC-
CEEDS IN THE GOVERNMENT; JEHOASH, THE
KING OF JERUSALEM, AT FIRST IS CAREFUL
ABOUT THE WORSHIP OF GOD, BUT AFTERWARDS
BECOMES IMPIOUS, AND COMMANDS ZECHARIAH
TO BE STONED ; WHEN JEHOASH [KING OF
JUDAH] WAS DEAD, AMAZIAH SUCCEEDS HIM IN
THE KINGDOM

1. Now Hazael, king of Syria, fought against
the Israelites and their king Jehu, and spoiled
the eastern parts of the country beyond Jordan,
which belonged to the Reubenites and Gadites,
and to [the half tribe of] Manassites; as also
Gilead and Bashan, burning and spoiling, and
offering violence to all that he laid his hands on,
and this without impeachment from Jehu, who
made no haste to defend the country when it
was under this distress: nay, he was become a
contemner of religion, and a despiser of holiness,
and of the laws, and died when he had reigned
over the Israelites twenty-seven years. He was
buried in Samaria, and left Jehoahaz his son his
successor in the government.

2. Now Jehoash, king of Jerusalem, had an
inclination to repair the temple of God; so he
called Jehoiada, and bade him send the Levites
and priests through all the country, to require
half a shekel of silver for every head, towards
the rebuilding and repairing of the temple, which
was brought to decay by Jehoram, and Athaliah
and her sons. But the high priest did not do
this, as concluding that no one would willingly
pay that money; but in the twenty-third year of
Jehoash's reign, when the king sent for him and
the Levites, and complained that they had not
obeyed what he enjoined them, and still commanded them to take care of the rebuilding the
temple, he used this stratagem for collecting
the money, with which the multitude was
pleased. He made a wooden chest, and closed
it up fast on all sides, but opened one hole in it;
he then set it in the temple beside the altar, and
desired every one to cast into it, through the
hole, what he pleased, for the repair of the temple. This contrivance was acceptable to the
people; and they strove one with another, and
brought in jointly large quantities of silver and
gold; and when the scribe and the priest that
were over the treasuries had emptied the chest,
and counted the money in the king's presence,
they then set it in its former place, and thus
did they every day. But when the multitude
appeared to have cast in as much as was wanted,
the high priest Jehoiada, and king Joash, sent
to hire masons and carpenters, and to buy large
pieces of timber, and of the most curious sort;
and when they had repaired the temple, they
made use of the remaining gold and silver,
which was not a little, for bowls, and basons,
and cups, and other vessels, and they went on
to make the altar every day fat with sacrifices of
great value. And these things were taken
suitable care of as long as Jehoiada lived.

3. But as soon as he was dead, (which was
when he had lived one hundred and thirty
years, having been a righteous, and in every
respect a very good man, and was buried in the
king's sepulchres at Jerusalem, because he had
recovered the kingdom to the family of David,)
king Joash betrayed his [want of] care about
God. The principal men of the people were
corrupted also together with him, and offended

against their duty, and what their constitution
determined to be most for their good. Hereupon
God was displeased with the change that was
made on the king, and on the rest of the people,
and sent prophets to testify to them what their
actions were, and to bring them to leave off their
wickedness: but they had gotten such a strong
affection, and so violent an inclination to it, that
neither could the examples of those that had
offered affronts to the laws, and had been so
severely punished, they and their entire families;
nor could the fear of what the prophets now
foretold bring them to repentance, and turn
them back from their course of transgression to
their former duty. But the king commanded
that Zechariah, the son of the high priest Jehoiada, should be stoned to death in the temple,
and forgot the kindnesses he had received from
his father; for when God had appointed him to
prophesy, he stood in the midst of the multitude, and gave this counsel to them and to the
king: That they should act righteously; and
foretold to them, that if they would not hearken
to his admonitions, they should suffer a heavy
punishment: but as Zechariah was ready to die,
he appealed to God as a witness of what he suffered for the good counsel he had given them,
and how he perished, after a most severe and
violent manner, for the good deeds his father had
done to Joash.

4. However, it was not long before the king
suffered punishment for his transgressions; for
when Hazael, king of Syria, made an irruption
into his country, and when he had overthrown
Gath, and spoiled it, he made an expedition
against Jerusalem; upon which Jehoash was
afraid, and emptied all the treasures of God, and
of the king [before him,] and took down the gifts
that had been dedicated [in the temple,] and sent
them to the king of Syria, and procured so much
by them, that he was not besieged, nor his kingdom quite endangered; but Hazael was induced,
by the greatness of the sum of money, not to
bring his army against Jerusalem; yet Jehoash
fell into a severe distemper, and was set upon by
his friends, in order to revenge the death of
Zechariah, the son of Jehoiada. These laid
snares for the king, and slew him. He was indeed buried in Jerusalem, but not in the royal
sepulchres of his forefathers, because of his impiety. He lived forty-seven years; and Amaziah his son succeeded him in the kingdom.

5. In the one-and-twentieth year of the reign
of Jehoash, Jehoahaz, the son of Jehu, took the
government of the Israelites in Samaria, and held
it seventeen years. He did not [properly] imitate his father, but was guilty of as wicked
practices as those that first had God in contempt.
But the king of Syria brought him low, and, by
expeditions against him, did so greatly reduce his
forces, that there remained no more of so great
an army than ten thousand armed men, and fifty
horsemen. He also took away from him his
great cities, and many of them also, and destroyed his army. And these were the things
that the people of Israel suffered, according to
the prophecy of Elisha, when he foretold that
Hazael should kill his master, and reign over the
Syrians and Damascens. But when Jehoahaz
was under such unavoidable miseries, he had recourse to prayer and supplication to God, and
besought him to deliver him out of the hands of
Hazael, and not overlook him, and give him up
into his hands. Accordingly, God accepted of
his repentance instead of virtue: and, being desirous rather to admonish those that might repent, and not to determine that they should be
utterly destroyed, he granted him deliverance

from war and dangers. So the country having obtained peace, returned again to its former condition, and flourished as before.

6. Now after the death of Jehoahaz, his son Joash took the kingdom, in the thirty-seventh year of Jehoash, the king of the tribe of Judah. This Joash then took the kingdom of Israel in Samaria, for he had the same name with the king of Jerusalem, and he retained the kingdom sixteen years. He was a good man,* and in his disposition was not at all like his father. Now at this time it was that when Elisha the prophet, who was already very old, and was now fallen into a disease, the king of Israel came to visit him; and when he found him very near death, he began to weep in his sight, and lament, to call him his father, and his weapons, because it was by his means that he never made use of his weapons against his enemies, but that he overcame his own adversaries by his prophecies, without fighting; and that he was now departing this life, and leaving him to the Syrians that were already armed, and to other enemies of his that were under their power; so he said it was not safe for him to live any longer, but that it would be well for him to hasten to his end, and depart out of this life with him. As the king was thus bemoaning himself, Elisha comforted him, and bade the king bend a bow that was brought him; and when the king had fitted the bow for shooting, Elisha took hold of his hands and bade him shoot; and when he had shot three arrows, and then left off, Elisha said, "If thou hadst shot more arrows, thou hadst cut the kingdom of Syria up by the roots; but since thou hast been satisfied with shooting three times only, thou shalt fight and beat the Syrians no more times than three, that thou mayest recover that country which they cut off from thy kingdom in the reign of thy father." So when the king had heard that, he departed; and a little while after the prophet died. He was a man celebrated for righteousness, and in eminent favour with God. He also performed wonderful and surprising works by prophecy, and such as were gloriously preserved in memory by the Hebrews. He also obtained a magnificent funeral, such a one indeed as it was fit a person so beloved of God should have. It also happened, that at that time certain robbers cast a man, whom they had slain, into Elisha's grave, and upon his dead body coming close to Elisha's body, it revived again. And thus far have we enlarged about the actions of Elisha the prophet, both such as he did while he was alive, and how he had a divine power after his death also.

7. Now upon the death of Hazael, the king of Syria, that kingdom came to Adad, his son, with whom Joash, king of Israel, made war; and when he had beaten him in three battles, he took from him all that country, and all those cities and villages, which his father Hazael had taken from the kingdom of Israel, which came to pass, however, according to the prophecy of Elisha. But when Joash happened to die, he was buried in Samaria; and the government devolved upon his son Jeroboam.

---

* This character of Joash given here seems a direct contradiction to our copies, which say (2 Kings xiii. 11) that "he did evil in the sight of the Lord; and that he departed not from all the sins of Jeroboam, the son of Nebat, who made Israel to sin: he walked therein." It is most likely that these different characters of Joash suited the different parts of his reign, and that, according to our copies, he was at first a wicked king, and afterwards was reclaimed, and became a good one, according to Josephus.

CHAPTER IX

HOW AMAZIAH MADE AN EXPEDITION AGAINST THE EDOMITES AND AMALEKITES, AND CONQUERED THEM; BUT WHEN HE AFTERWARDS MADE WAR AGAINST JOASH, HE WAS BEATEN, AND NOT LONG AFTER, WAS SLAIN; AND UZZIAH SUCCEEDED IN THE GOVERNMENT

1. Now, in the second year of the reign of Joash over Israel, Amaziah reigned over the tribe of Judah in Jerusalem. His mother's name was Jehoaddan, who was born at Jerusalem. He was exceeding careful of doing what was right, and this when he was very young; but when he came to the management of affairs, and to the government, he resolved that he ought first of all to avenge his father Jehoash, and to punish those friends that had laid violent hands upon him; so he seized upon them all, and put them to death; yet did he execute no severity on their children, but acted therein according to the laws of Moses, who did not think it just to punish children for the sins of their fathers. After this he chose him an army out of the tribe of Judah and Benjamin, of such as were in the flower of their age, and about twenty years old; and when he had collected about three hundred thousand of them together, he set captains of hundreds over them. He also sent to the king of Israel, and hired a hundred thousand of his soldiers for a hundred talents of silver, for he had resolved to make an expedition against the nations of the Amalekites, and Edomites, and Gebalites: but as he was preparing for his expedition, and ready to go out to the war, a prophet gave him counsel to dismiss the army of the Israelites, because they were bad men, and because God foretold that he should be beaten, if he made use of them as auxiliaries; but that he should overcome his enemies, though he had but a few soldiers, when it so pleased God. And when the king grudged at his having already paid the hire of the Israelites, the prophet exhorted him to do what God would have him, because he should thereby obtain much wealth from God. So he dismissed them, and said, that he still freely gave them their pay, and went himself with his own army, and made war with the nations before mentioned; and when he had beaten them in battle, he slew of them ten thousand, and took as many prisoners alive, whom he brought to the great rock which is in Arabia, and threw them down from it headlong. He also brought away a great deal of prey and vast riches from those nations; but while Amaziah was engaged in this expedition, those Israelites whom he had hired and then dismissed, were very uneasy at it, and taking their dismission for an affront, (as supposing that this would not have been done to them but out of contempt,) they fell upon his kingdom, and proceeded to spoil the country as far as Beth-horon, and took much cattle, and slew three thousand men.

2. Now upon the victory which Amaziah had gotten, and the great acts he had done, he was puffed up, and began to overlook God, who had given him the victory, and proceeded to worship the gods he had brought out of the country of the Amalekites. So a prophet came to him, and said, that he wondered how he could esteem these to be gods, who had been of no advantage to their own people who paid them honours, nor had delivered them from his hands, but had overlooked the destruction of many of them, and had suffered themselves to be carried captive, for that they had been carried to Jerusalem in the same

JONAH PREACHING AT NINEVEH

manner as any one might have taken some of the enemy alive, and led them thither. This reproof provoked the king to anger, and he commanded the prophet to hold his peace, and threatened to punish him if he meddled with his conduct. So he replied, that he should indeed hold his peace; but foretold withal, that God would not overlook his attempts for innovation; but Amaziah was not able to contain himself under that prosperity which God had given him, although he had affronted God thereupon; but in a vein of insolence he wrote to Joash, the king of Israel, and commanded that he and all his people should be obedient to him, as they had formerly been obedient to his progenitors, David and Solomon; and he let him know, that if he would not be so wise as to do what he commanded him, he must fight for his dominion. To which message Joash returned this answer in writing:—"King Joash to king Amaziah, There was a vastly tall cypress-tree in mount Lebanon, as also a thistle; this thistle sent to the cypress-tree to give the cypress-tree's daughter in marriage to the thistle's son; but as the thistle was saying this, there came a wild beast, and trode down the thistle: and this may be a lesson to thee, not to be so ambitious, and to have a care, lest upon thy good success in the fight against the Amalekites, thou growest so proud, as to bring dangers upon thyself, and upon thy kingdom."

3. When Amaziah had read this letter, he was more eager upon this expedition: which, I suppose, was by the impulse of God, that he might be punished for his offence against him. But as soon as he led out his army against Joash, and they were going to join battle with him, there came such a fear and consternation upon the army of Amaziah, as God, when he is displeased, sends upon men, and discomfited them, even before they came to a close fight. Now it happened, that as they were scattered about by the terror that was upon them, Amaziah was left alone, and was taken prisoner by the enemy: whereupon Joash threatened to kill him, unless he would persuade the children of Jerusalem to open their gates to him, and receive him and his army into the city. Accordingly Amaziah was so distressed, and in such fear of his life, that he made his enemy to be received into the city. So Joash overthrew a part of the wall, of the length of four hundred cubits, and drove his chariot through the breach into Jerusalem, and led Amaziah captive along with him; by which means he became master of Jerusalem, and took away the treasures of God, and carried off all the gold and silver that was in the king's palace, and then freed the king from captivity, and returned to Samaria. Now these things happened to the people of Jerusalem in the fourteenth year of the reign of Amaziah, who after this had a conspiracy made against him by his friends, and fled to the city Lachish, and was there slain by the conspirators, who sent men thither to kill him. So they took up his dead body, and carried it to Jerusalem, and made a royal funeral for him. This was the end of the life of Amaziah, because of his innovations in religion, and his contempt of God, when he had lived fifty-four years, and had reigned twenty-nine. He was succeeded by his son, whose name was Uzziah.

CHAPTER X

CONCERNING JEROBOAM, KING OF ISRAEL, AND JONAH, THE PROPHET; AND HOW, AFTER THE DEATH OF JEROBOAM, HIS SON ZECHARIAH

TOOK THE GOVERNMENT; HOW UZZIAH, KING OF JERUSALEM, SUBDUED THE NATIONS THAT WERE ROUND ABOUT HIM; AND WHAT BEFELL HIM WHEN HE ATTEMPTED TO OFFER INCENSE TO GOD

1. In the fifteenth year of the reign of Amaziah, Jeroboam the son of Joash reigned over Israel in Samaria forty years. This king was guilty of contumely against God,* and became very wicked in worshipping of idols, and in many undertakings that were absurd and foreign. He was also the cause of ten thousand misfortunes to the people of Israel. Now one Jonah, a prophet, foretold to him that he should make war with the Syrians, and conquer their army, and enlarge the bounds of his kingdom on the northern parts, to the city Hamath, and on the southern, to the lake Asphaltitis; for the bounds of the Canaanites originally were these, as Joshua their general had determined them. So Jeroboam made an expedition against the Syrians, and overran all their country, as Jonah had foretold.

2. Now I cannot but think it necessary for me, who have promised to give an accurate account of our affairs, to describe the actions of this prophet, so far as I have found them written down in the Hebrew books. Jonah had been commanded by God to go to the kingdom of Nineveh; and, when he was there, to publish it in that city, how it should lose the dominion it had over the nations. But he went not, out of fear: nay, he ran away from God to the city of Joppa, and finding a ship there, he went into it, and sailed to Tarsus, to Cilicia;† and upon the rise of a most terrible storm, which was so great that the ship was in danger of sinking, the mariners, the master, and the pilot himself, made prayers and vows, in case they escaped the sea. But Jonah lay still and covered [in the ship,] without imitating anything that the others did; but as the waves grew greater, and the sea became more violent by the winds, they suspected, as is usual in such cases, that some one of the persons that sailed with them was the occasion of this storm, and agreed to discover by lot which of them it was. When they had cast lots,‡ the lot fell upon the prophet; and when they asked him whence he came, and what he had done? he replied, that he was a Hebrew by nation, and a prophet of Almighty God; and he persuaded them to cast him into the sea, if they would escape the danger they were in, for that he was the occasion of the storm which was upon them. Now at the first they durst not do so, as esteeming it a wicked thing to cast a man, who was a stranger, and who had committed his life to them, into such manifest perdition; but at last, when their misfortunes overbore them, and the ship was just going to be drowned, and when they were animated to do it by the prophet

---

* What I have above noted concerning Jehoash, seems to me to have been true also concerning his son Jeroboam II.—viz., that although he began wickedly, and "was the cause of a vast number of misfortunes to the Israelites" in those his first years, so does it seem to me that he was afterwards reclaimed, and became a good king, and so was encouraged by the prophet Jonah, and had great successes afterwards.

† When Jonah is said in our Bibles to have gone to Tarshish, (Jonah i. 3,) Josephus understood it, that he went to Tarsus in Cilicia, or to the Mediterranean Sea, upon which Tarsus lay.

‡ This ancient piece of religion, of casting lots to discover great sinners, seems a remarkable remnant of the ancient tradition which prevailed of old over all mankind, that Providence used to interpose visibly in all human affairs, and never to bring notorious judgments but for notorious sins.

himself, and by the fear concerning their own safety, they cast him into the sea; upon which the sea became calm. It is also related that Jonah was swallowed down by a whale, and that when he had been there three days, and as many nights, he was vomited out upon the Euxine Sea, and this alive, and without any hurt upon his body; and there, on his prayer to God, he obtained pardon for his sins, and went to the city Nineveh, where he stood so as to be heard; and preached, that in a very little time they should lose the dominion of Asia; and when he had published this, he returned. Now, I have given this account about him, as I found it written [in our books.]

3. When Jeroboam the king had passed his life in great happiness, and had ruled forty years, he died, and was buried in Samaria, and his son Zechariah took the kingdom. After the same manner did Uzziah, the son of Amaziah, begin to reign over the two tribes in Jerusalem, in the fourteenth year of the reign of Jeroboam. He was born of Jecoliah, his mother, who was a citizen of Jerusalem. He was a good man, and by nature righteous and magnanimous, and very laborious in taking care of the affairs of his kingdom. He made an expedition also against the Philistines, and overcame them in battle, and took the cities of Gath and Jabneh, and brake down their walls; after which expedition, he assaulted those Arabs that adjoined to Egypt. He also built a city upon the Red Sea, and put a garrison into it. He after this overthrew the Ammonites, and appointed that they should pay tribute. He also overcame all countries as far as the bounds of Egypt, and then began to take care of Jerusalem itself for the rest of his life; for he rebuilt and repaired all those parts of the wall which had either fallen down by length of time, or by the carelessness of the kings his predecessors, as well as all that part which had been thrown down by the king of Israel, when he took his father Amaziah prisoner, and entered with him into the city. Moreover, he built a great many towers, of one hundred and fifty cubits high, and built walled towns in desert places, and put garrisons into them, and dug many channels for conveyance of water. He had also many beasts for labour, and an immense number of cattle; for his country was fit for pasturage. He was also given to husbandry, and took care to cultivate the ground, and planted it with all sorts of plants, and sowed it with all sorts of seeds. He had also about him an army composed of chosen men, in number three hundred and seventy thousand, who were governed by general officers and captains of thousands, who were men of valour and of unconquerable strength, in number two thousand. He also divided his whole army into bands and armed them, giving every one a sword, with brazen bucklers and breastplates, with bows and slings; and besides these, he made for them many engines of war for besieging of cities, such as cast stones and darts, with grapplers, and other instruments of that sort.

4. While Uzziah was in this state, and making preparations [for futurity,] he was corrupted in his mind by pride, and became insolent, and this on account of that abundance which he had of things that will soon perish, and despised that power which is of eternal duration, (which consisted in piety towards God, and in the observation of his laws;) so he fell by the occasion of the good success of his affairs, and was carried headlong into those sins of his father, which the splendour of that prosperity he enjoyed, and the glorious actions he had done, led him into,

while he was not able to govern himself well about them. Accordingly, when a remarkable day was come, and a general festival was to be celebrated, he put on the holy garment, and went into the temple to offer incense to God upon the golden altar, which he was prohibited to do by Azariah the high priest, who had fourscore priests with him, and who told him that it was not lawful for him to offer sacrifice, and that "none besides the posterity of Aaron were permitted so to do." And when they cried out, that he must go out of the temple, and not transgress against God, he was wroth at them, and threatened to kill them, unless they would hold their peace. In the meantime, a great earthquake shook the ground,* and a rent was made in the temple, and the bright rays of the sun shone through it, and fell upon the king's face, insomuch that the leprosy seized upon him immediately; and before the city, at a place called Eroge, half the mountain broke off from the rest on the west, and rolled itself four furlongs, and stood still at the east mountain, till the roads, as well as the king's gardens, were spoiled by the obstruction. Now, as soon as the priests saw that the king's face was infected with the leprosy, they told him of the calamity he was under, and commanded that he should go out of the city as a polluted person. Hereupon he was so confounded at the sad distemper, and sensible that he was not at liberty to contradict, that he did as he was commanded, and underwent this miserable and terrible punishment for an intention beyond what befitted a man to have, and for that impiety against God which was implied therein. So he abode out of the city for some time, and lived a private life, while his son Jotham took the government; after which he died with grief and anxiety at what had happened to him, when he had lived sixty-eight years, and reigned of them fifty-two; and was buried by himself in his own gardens.

CHAPTER XI

HOW ZECHARIAH, SHALLUM, MENAHEM, PEKA-HIAH, AND PEKAH, TOOK THE GOVERNMENT OVER THE ISRAELITES; AND HOW PUL AND TIGLATH - PILESER MADE AN EXPEDITION AGAINST THE ISRAELITES; HOW JOTHAM, THE SON OF UZZIAH, REIGNED OVER THE TRIBE OF JUDAH; AND WHAT THINGS NAHUM PROPHESIED AGAINST THE ASSYRIANS

1. Now when Zechariah, the son of Jeroboam, had reigned six months over Israel, he was slain by the treachery of a certain friend of his, whose name was Shallum, the son of Jabesh, who took the kingdom afterward, but kept it no longer than thirty days; for Menahem, the general of his army, who was at that time in the city of Tirzah, and heard of what had befallen Zechariah, removed thereupon with all his forces to Samaria, and joining battle with Shallum, slew him: and when he had made himself king, he went thence, and came to the city Tiphsah; but the citizens that were in it shut their gates, and barred them against the king, and would not admit him; but in order to be avenged on them, he burnt the country round about it, and took the city by force, upon a

* This account of an earthquake at Jerusalem, and of the consequences of the earthquake, is exceeding like to a prophecy in Zech. xiv. 4, 5; in which mention is made of "fleeing from that earthquake, as they fled from this earthquake in the days of Uzziah, king of Judah."

siege; and being very much displeased at what the inhabitants of Tiphsah had done, he slew them all, and spared not so much as the infants, without omitting the utmost instances of cruelty and barbarity; for he used such severity upon his own countrymen, as would not be pardonable with regard to strangers who had been conquered by him. And after this manner it was that this Menahem continued to reign with cruelty and barbarity for ten years; but when Pul, king of Assyria, had made an expedition against him, he did not think meet to fight or engage in battle with the Assyrians, but he persuaded him to accept of a thousand talents of silver, and to go away, and so put an end to the war. This sum the multitude collected for Menahem, by exacting fifty drachmæ as poll-money for every head;* after which he died, and was buried in Samaria, and left his son Pekahiah his successor in the kingdom, who followed the barbarity of his father, and so ruled but two years only, after which he was slain with his friends at a feast, by the treachery of one Pekah, the general of his horse, and the son of Remaliah, who had laid snares for him. Now this Pekah held the government twenty years, and proved a wicked man and a transgressor. But the king of Assyria, whose name was Tiglath-Pileser, when he had made an expedition against the Israelites, and had overrun all the land of Gilead, and the region beyond Jordan, and the adjoining country, which is called Galilee, and Kadesh, and Hazor, he made the inhabitants prisoners, and transplanted them into his own kingdom. And so much shall suffice to have related here concerning the king of Assyria.

2. Now Jotham, the son of Uzziah, reigned over the tribe of Judah in Jerusalem, being a citizen thereof by his mother, whose name was Jerusha. This king was not defective in any virtue, but was religious towards God, and righteous towards men, and careful of the good of the city, (for what part soever wanted to be repaired or adorned, he magnificently repaired and adorned them.) He also took care of the foundations of the cloisters in the temple, and repaired the walls that were fallen down, and built very great towers, and such as were almost impregnable; and if anything else in his kingdom had been neglected, he took great care of it. He also made an expedition against the Ammonites, and overcame them in battle, and ordered them to pay tribute, a hundred talents, and ten thousand cori of wheat, and as many of barley, every year, and so augmented his kingdom that his enemies could not despise it; and his own people lived happily.

3. Now there was at that time a prophet, whose name was Nahum, who spake after this manner concerning the overthrow of the Assyrians and of Nineveh:—"Nineveh shall be a pool of water in motion;† so shall all her people

be troubled, and tossed, and go away by flight, while they say one to another, Stand, stand still, seize their gold and silver, for there shall be no one to wish them well, for they will rather save their lives than their money; for a terrible contention shall possess them one with another, and lamentation, and loosing of the members, and their countenances shall be perfectly black with fear. And there will be the den of the lions, and the mother of the young lions! God says to thee, Nineveh, that they shall deface thee, and the lion shall no longer go out from thee to give laws to the world." And, indeed, this prophet prophesied many other things besides these concerning Nineveh, which I do not think necessary to repeat, and I here omit them, that I may not appear troublesome to my readers; all which things happened about Nineveh a hundred and fifteen years afterward:—so this may suffice to have spoken of these matters.

CHAPTER XII

HOW, UPON THE DEATH OF JOTHAM, AHAZ REIGNED IN HIS STEAD; AGAINST WHOM REZIN, KING OF SYRIA, AND PEKAH, KING OF ISRAEL, MADE WAR; AND HOW TIGLATH-PILESER, KING OF ASSYRIA, CAME TO THE ASSISTANCE OF AHAZ, AND LAID SYRIA WASTE, AND REMOVING THE DAMASCENS INTO MEDIA, PLACED OTHER NATIONS IN THEIR ROOM

1. Now Jotham died when he had lived forty-one years, and of them reigned sixteen, and was buried in the sepulchres of the kings; and the kingdom came to his son Ahaz, who proved most impious towards God, and a transgressor of the laws of his country. He imitated the kings of Israel, and reared altars in Jerusalem, and offered sacrifices upon them to idols; to which also he offered his own son as a burnt-offering, according to the practices of the Caananites. His other actions were also of the same sort. Now as he was going on in this mad course, Rezin, the king of Syria and Damascus, and Pekah, the king of Israel, who were now at amity one with another, made war with him; and when they had driven him into Jerusalem, they besieged that city a long while, making but a small progress, on account of the strength of its walls; and when the king of Syria had taken the city Elath, upon the Red Sea, and had slain the inhabitants, he peopled it with Syrians: and when he had slain those in the [other] garrisons, and the Jews in their neighbourhood, and had driven away much prey, he returned with his army back to Damascus. Now when the king of Jerusalem knew that the Syrians were returned home, he, supposing himself a match for the king of Israel, drew out his army against him, and joining battle with him was beaten; and this happened because God was angry with him on account of his many and great enormities. Accordingly, there were slain by the Israelites one hundred and twenty thousand of his men that day, whose general, Amaziah by name, slew Zechariah the king's son in his conflict with Ahaz, as well as the governor of the kingdom, whose name was Azricam. He also carried Elkanah, the general of the troops of the tribe of Judah, into captivity. They also carried the women and children of the tribe of Benjamin captives; and when they had gotten a great deal of prey, they returned to Samaria.

2. Now there was one Obed, who was a prophet at that time in Samaria; he met the army

---

* Dr Wall observes, "that when this Menahem is said to have exacted of each man fifty shekels of silver, to give Pul, the king of Assyria, a thousand talents, this is the first public money raised by any [Israelite] king by a tax on the people; that they used before to raise it out of the treasures of the house of the Lord, or of their own house; that it was a poll-money on the rich men, at the rate of £6 or £7 per head; and that God commanded, by Ezekiel, (ch. xlv. 8, and xlvi. 18,) that no such thing should be done, but the king should have land of his own.

† This passage is taken out of the prophet Nahum, (ch. ii. 8-13,) and is the only one that is given us almost *verbatim*, but a little abridged, in all Josephus's known writings: by which quotation we learn that he made use of the Hebrew original, as also we learn, that his Hebrew copy considerably differed from ours.

before the city walls, and with a loud voice told them that they had gotten the victory not by their own strength, but by reason of the anger God had against king Ahaz. And he complained that they were not satisfied with the good success they had had against him, but were so bold as to make captives out of their kinsmen the tribes of Judah and Benjamin. He also gave them counsel to let them go home without doing them any harm, for that if they did not obey God herein, they should be punished. So the people of Israel came together to their assembly, and considered of these matters, when a man whose name was Berechiah, and who was one of chief reputation in the government, stood up, and three others with him, and said,—"We will not suffer the citizens to bring these prisoners into the city, lest we be all destroyed by God: we have sins enough of our own that we have committed against him, as the prophets assure us; nor ought we therefore to introduce the practice of new crimes. When the soldiers heard that, they permitted them to do what they thought best. So the forenamed men took the captives and let them go, and took care of them, and gave them provisions, and sent them to their own country, without doing them any harm. However, these four went along with them, and conducted them as far as Jericho, which is not far from Jerusalem, and returned to Samaria.

3. Hereupon king Ahaz, having been so thoroughly beaten by the Israelites, sent to Tiglath-Pileser, king of the Assyrians, and sued for assistance from him in this war against the Israelites, and Syrians, and Damascens, with a promise to send him much money; he sent him also great presents at the same time. Now this king, upon the reception of those ambassadors, came to assist Ahaz, and made war upon the Syrians, and laid their country waste, and took Damascus by force, and slew Rezin their king, and transplanted the people of Damascus into the Upper Media, and brought a colony of Assyrians, and planted them in Damascus. He also afflicted the land of Israel, and took many captives out of it. While he was doing thus with the Syrians, king Ahaz took all the gold that was in the king's treasures, and the silver, and what was in the temple of God, and what precious gifts were there, and he carried them with him, and came to Damascus, and gave it to the king of Assyria, according to his agreement. So he confessed that he owed him thanks for all that he had done for him, and returned to Jerusalem. Now this king was so sottish and thoughtless of what was for his own good, that he would not leave off worshipping the Syrian gods when he was beaten by them, but he went on in worshipping them, as though they would procure him the victory; and when he was beaten again he began to honour the gods of the Assyrians; and he seemed more desirous to honour any other gods than his own paternal and true God, whose anger was the cause of his defeat: nay, he proceeded to such a degree of despite and contempt [of God's worship,] that he shut up the temple entirely, and forbade them to bring in the appointed sacrifices, and took away the gifts that had been given to it. And when he had offered these indignities to God, he died, having lived thirty-six years, and out of them reigned sixteen; and he left his son Hezekiah for his successor.

CHAPTER XIII

HOW PEKAH DIED BY THE TREACHERY OF HOSHEA, WHO WAS A LITTLE AFTER SUBDUED BY SHALMANESER; AND HOW HEZEKIAH REIGNED INSTEAD OF AHAZ; AND WHAT ACTIONS OF PIETY AND JUSTICE HE DID

1. ABOUT the same time Pekah the king of Israel died, by the treachery of a friend of his, whose name was Hoshea, who retained the kingdom nine years' time; but was a wicked man, and a despiser of the divine worship: and Shalmaneser, the king of Assyria, made an expedition against him, and overcame him, (which must have been because he had not God favourable nor assistant to him,) and brought him to submission, and ordered him to pay an appointed tribute. Now in the fourth year of the reign of Hoshea, Hezekiah, the son of Ahaz, began to reign in Jerusalem; and his mother's name was Abijah, a citizen of Jerusalem. His nature was good, and righteous, and religious; for when he came to the kingdom, he thought that nothing was prior, or more necessary, or more advantageous, to himself and to his subjects, than to worship God. Accordingly, he called the people together, and the priests, and the Levites, and made a speech to them, and said,—"You are not ignorant how, by the sins of my father, who transgressed that sacred honour which was due to God, you have had experience of many and great miseries, while you were corrupted in your mind by him, and were induced to worship those which he supposed to be gods: I exhort you, therefore, who have learned by sad experience how dangerous a thing impiety is, to put that immediately out of your memory, and to purify yourselves from your former pollutions, and to open the temple to these priests and Levites who are here convened, and to cleanse it with the accustomed sacrifices, and to recover all to the ancient honour which our fathers paid to it: for by this means we may render God favourable, and he will remit the anger he hath had to us."

2. When the king had said this, the priests opened the temple; and when they had set in order the vessels of God, and cast out what was impure, they laid the accustomed sacrifices upon the altar. The king also sent to the country that was under him, and called the people to Jerusalem to celebrate the feast of unleavened bread, for it had been intermitted a long time, on account of the wickedness of the forementioned kings. He also sent to the Israelites, and exhorted them to leave off their present way of living, and to return to their ancient practices, and to worship God, for that he gave them leave to come to Jerusalem, and to celebrate, all in one body, the feast of unleavened bread; and this he said was by way of invitation only, and to be done of their own good-will, and for their own advantage, and not out of obedience to him, because it would make them happy. But the Israelites, upon the coming of the ambassadors, and upon their laying before them what they had in charge from their own king, were so far from complying therewith, that they laughed the ambassadors to scorn, and mocked them as fools: as also they affronted the prophets who gave them the same exhortations, and foretold what they would suffer if they did not return to the worship of God, insomuch that at length they caught them, and slew them; nor did this degree of transgressing suffice them, but they had more wicked contrivances than what have

been described : nor did they leave off, before God, as a punishment for their impiety, brought them under their enemies :—but of that more hereafter. However, many there were of the tribe of Manasseh, and of Zebulon, and of Issachar, who were obedient to what the prophets exhorted them to do, and returned to the worship of God. Now all these came running to Jerusalem, to Hezekiah, that they might worship God [there.]

3. When these men were come, king Hezekiah went up into the temple, with the rulers and all the people, and offered for himself seven bulls, and as many rams, with seven lambs, and as many kids of the goats. The king also himself, and the rulers, laid their hands on the heads of the sacrifices, and permitted the priests to complete the sacred offices about them. So they both slew the sacrifices and burnt the burnt-offerings, while the Levites stood round about them, with their musical instruments, and sang hymns to God, and played on their psalteries, as they were instructed by David to do, and this while the rest of the priests returned the music, and sounded the trumpets which they had in their hands : and when this was done, the king and the multitude threw themselves down upon their faces, and worshipped God. He also sacrificed seventy bulls, one hundred rams, and two hundred lambs. He also granted the multitude sacrifices to feast upon six hundred oxen, and three thousand other cattle ; and the priests performed all things according to the law. Now the king was so pleased therewith, that he feasted with the people, and returned thanks to God : but as the feast of unleavened bread was now come, when they had offered that sacrifice which is called the Passover, they after that offered other sacrifices for seven days. When the king had bestowed on the multitude, besides what they sanctified of themselves, two thousand bulls, and seven thousand other cattle, the same was done by the rulers ; for they gave them a thousand bulls, and a thousand and forty other cattle. Nor had this festival been so well observed from the days of king Solomon, as it was now first observed with great splendour and magnificence ; and when the festival was ended, they went out into the country, and purged it; and cleansed the city of all the pollution of the idols. The king also gave order that the daily sacrifices should be offered, at his own charges, and according to the law ; and appointed that the tithes and first-fruits should be given by the multitude to the priests and Levites, that they might constantly attend upon divine service, and never be taken off from the worship of God. Accordingly, the multitude brought together all sorts of their fruits to the priests and the Levites. The king also made garners and receptacles for these fruits, and distributed them to every one of the priests and Levites, and to their children and wives ; and thus did they return to their old form of divine worship. Now when the king had settled these matters after the manner already described, he made war upon the Philistines, and beat them, and possessed himself of all the enemy's cities, from Gaza to Gath : but the king of Assyria sent to him, and threatened to overturn all his dominions, unless he would pay him the tribute which his father paid him formerly ; but king Hezekiah was not concerned at his threatenings, but depended on his piety towards God, and upon Isaiah the prophet, by whom he inquired, and accurately knew all future events :—and this much shall suffice for the present concerning this king Hezekiah.

CHAPTER XIV

HOW SHALMANESER TOOK SAMARIA BY FORCE, AND HOW HE TRANSPLANTED THE TEN TRIBES INTO MEDIA, AND BROUGHT THE NATION OF THE CUTHEANS INTO THEIR COUNTRY [IN THEIR ROOM.]

1. WHEN Shalmaneser, the king of Assyria, had it told him, that [Hoshea] the king of Israel had sent privately to So, the king of Egypt, desiring his assistance against him, he was very angry, and made an expedition against Samaria, in the seventh year of the reign of Hoshea ; but when he was not admitted [into the city] by the king,[*] he besieged Samaria three years, and took it by force in the ninth year of the reign of Hoshea, and in the seventh year of Hezekiah, king of Jerusalem, and quite demolished the government of the Israelites, and transplanted all the people into Media and Persia, among whom he took king Hoshea alive ; and when he had removed these people out of this their land, he transplanted other nations out of Cuthah, a place so called, (for there is [still] a river of that name in Persia,) into Samaria, and into the country of the Israelites. So the ten tribes of the Israelites were removed out of Judea, nine hundred and forty-seven years after their forefathers were come out of the land of Egypt, and possessed themselves of this country, but eight hundred years after Joshua had been their leader, and, as I have already observed, two hundred and forty years, seven months, and seven days, after they had revolted from Rehoboam, the grandson of David, and had given the kingdom to Jeroboam. And such a conclusion overtook the Israelites, when they had transgressed the laws, and would not hearken to the prophets, who foretold that this calamity would come upon them, if they would not leave off their evil doings. What gave birth to these evil doings, was that sedition which they raised against Rehoboam, the grandson of David, when they set up Jeroboam, his servant, to be their king, who, by sinning against God, and bringing them to imitate his bad example, made God to be their enemy, while Jeroboam underwent that punishment which he justly deserved.

2. And now the king of Assyria invaded all Syria and Phœnicia in a hostile manner. The name of this king is also set down in the archives of Tyre, for he made an expedition against Tyre in the reign of Eluleus ; and Menander attests to it, who, when he wrote his Chronology, and translated the Archives of Tyre into the Greek language, gives us the following history : —" One whose name was Eluleus, reigned thirty-six years : this king, upon the revolt of the Citteans, sailed to them, and reduced them again to a submission. Against these did the king of Assyria send an army, and in a hostile manner overrun all Phœnicia, but soon made peace with them all, and returned back; but Sidon, and Ace, and Palætyrus, revolted ; and many other cities there were which delivered themselves up to the king of Assyria. Accordingly, when the Tyrians would not submit to him, the king returned, and fell upon them again, while the Phœnicians had furnished him with threescore ships, and eight hundred men to row them ; and

* This siege of Samaria was so very long, no less than three years, that it was no way improbable but that parents, and particularly mothers, might therein be reduced to eat their own children, as the law of Moses had threatened upon their disobedience, (Lev. xxvi. 29 ; Deut. xxviii. 53-57.)

when the Tyrians had come upon them in twelve ships, and the enemy's ships were dispersed, they took five hundred men prisoners; and the reputation of all the citizens of Tyre was thereby increased; but the king of Assyria returned, and placed guards at their rivers and aqueducts, who should hinder the Tyrians from drawing water. This continued for five years; and still the Tyrians bore the siege, and drank of the water they had out of the wells they dug." And this is what is written in the Tyrian archives concerning Shalmaneser, the king of Assyria.

3. But now the Cutheans, who removed into Samaria, (for that is the name they have been called by to this time, because they were brought out of the country called Cuthah, which is a country of Persia, and there is a river of the same name in it,) each of them, according to their nations, which were in number five, brought their own gods into Samaria, and by worshipping them, as was the custom of their own countries, they provoked Almighty God to be angry and displeased at them, for a plague seized upon them, by which they were destroyed; and when they found no cure for their miseries, they learned by the oracle that they ought to worship Almighty God, as the method for their deliverance. So they sent ambassadors to the king of Assyria, and desired him to send them some of those priests of the Israelites whom he had taken captive. And when he thereupon sent them, and the people were by them taught the laws, and the holy worship of God, they worshipped him in a respectful manner, and the plague ceased immediately; and indeed they continue to make use of the very same customs to this very time, and are called in the Hebrew tongue *Cutheans*; but in the Greek *Samaritans*. And when they see the Jews in prosperity, they pretend that they are changed, and allied to them, and call them kinsmen, as though they were derived from Joseph, and had by that means an original alliance with them: but when they see them falling into a low condition, they say they are no way related to them, and that the Jews have no right to expect any kindness or marks of kindred from them, but they declare that they are sojourners that come from other countries. But of these we shall have a more seasonable opportunity to discourse hereafter.

BOOK X

CONTAINING THE INTERVAL OF ONE HUNDRED AND EIGHTY-TWO YEARS AND A HALF

FROM THE CAPTIVITY OF THE TEN TRIBES TO THE FIRST OF CYRUS

CHAPTER I

HOW SENNACHERIB MADE AN EXPEDITION AGAINST HEZEKIAH; WHAT THREATENINGS RABSHAKEH MADE TO HEZEKIAH WHEN SENNACHERIB WAS GONE AGAINST THE EGYPTIANS; HOW ISAIAH THE PROPHET ENCOURAGED HIM; HOW SENNACHERIB, HAVING FAILED OF SUCCESS IN EGYPT, RETURNED THENCE TO JERUSALEM; AND HOW, UPON HIS FINDING HIS ARMY DESTROYED, HE RETURNED HOME; AND WHAT BEFELL HIM A LITTLE AFTERWARD

1. It was now the fourteenth year of the government of Hezekiah, king of the two tribes, when the king of Assyria, whose name was Sennacherib, made an expedition against him with a great army, and took all the cities of the tribes of Judah and Benjamin by force; and when he was ready to bring his army against Jerusalem, Hezekiah sent ambassadors to him beforehand, and promised to submit, and pay what tribute he should appoint. Hereupon Sennacherib, when he heard of what offers the ambassadors made, resolved not to proceed in the war, but to accept of the proposals that were made him: and if he might receive three hundred talents of silver and thirty talents of gold, he promised that he would depart in a friendly manner; and he gave security upon oath to the ambassadors that he would then do him no harm, but go away as he came. So Hezekiah submitted, and emptied his treasures, and sent the money, as supposing he should be freed from his enemy, and from any further distress about his kingdom. Accordingly, the Assyrian king took it, and yet had no regard to what he had promised; but while he himself went to the war against the Egyptians and Ethiopians, he left his general Rabshakeh, and two other of his principal commanders, with great forces, to destroy Jerusalem. The names of the two other commanders were Tartan and Rabsaris.

2. Now as soon as they were come before the walls, they pitched their camp, and sent messengers to Hezekiah, and desired that they might speak with him; but he did not himself come out to them for fear, but he sent three of his most intimate friends: the name of the one was Eliakim, who was over the kingdom, and Shebna, and Joah the recorder. So these men came out, and stood over against the commanders of the Assyrian army; and when Rabshakeh saw them, he bade them go and speak to Hezekiah in the manner following:—That Sennacherib, the great king,* desires to know of him, on whom it is that he relies and depends, in flying from his lord, and will not hear him, nor admit his army into the city? Is it on account of the Egyptians, and in hopes that his army would be beaten by them? Whereupon he lets him know, that if this be what he expects, he is a foolish man, and like one who leans on a broken reed; while such a one will not only fall down, but will have his hand pierced and hurt by it. That he ought to know he makes this expedition against him by the will of God, who hath granted this favour to him, that he shall overthrow the kingdom of Israel, and that in the very same manner he shall destroy those that are his sub-

---

* This title of Great King, both in our Bibles, (2 Kings xviii. 19; Isa. xxxvi. 4,) and here in Josephus, is the very same that Herodotus gives this Sennacherib.

jects also.   When Rabshakeh had made this speech in the Hebrew tongue, for he was skilful in that language, Eliakim was afraid lest the multitude that heard him should be disturbed; so he desired him to speak in the Syrian tongue. But the general understanding what he meant, and perceiving the fear that he was in, he made his answer with a greater and a louder voice, but in the Hebrew tongue; and said, that "since they all heard what were the king's commands, they would consult their own advantage in delivering up themselves to us; for it is plain that both you and your king dissuade the people from submitting by vain hopes, and so induce them to resist; but if you be courageous, and think to drive our forces away, I am ready to deliver to you two thousand of these horses that are with me for your use, if you can set as many horsemen on their backs, and shew your strength; but what you have not, you cannot produce. Why, therefore, do you delay to deliver up yourselves to a superior force, who can take you without your consent? although it will be safer for you to deliver yourselves up voluntarily, while a forcible capture, when you are beaten, must appear more dangerous, and will bring further calamities upon you."

3. When the people, as well as the ambassadors, heard what the Assyrian commander said, they related it to Hezekiah, who thereupon put off his royal apparel, and clothed himself with sackcloth, and took the habit of a mourner, and, after the manner of his country, he fell upon his face, and besought God, and entreated him to assist them, now they had no other hope of relief. He also sent some of his friends, and some of the priests, to the prophet Isaiah, and desired that he would pray to God, and offer sacrifices for their common deliverance, and so put up supplications to him, that he would have indignation at the expectations of their enemies, and have mercy upon his people. And when the prophet had done accordingly, an oracle came from God to him, and encouraged the king and his friends that were about him; and foretold, that their enemies should be beaten without fighting, and should go away in an ignominious manner, and not with that insolence which they now shew, for that God would take care that they should be destroyed. He also foretold that Sennacherib, the king of Assyria, should fail of his purpose against Egypt, and that when he came home, he should perish by the sword.

4. About the same time also the king of Assyria wrote an epistle to Hezekiah, in which he said he was a foolish man in supposing that he should escape from being his servant, since he had already brought under many and great nations; and he threatened, that, when he took him, he would utterly destroy him, unless he now opened the gates, and willingly received his army into Jerusalem. When he had read this epistle, he despised it, on account of the trust that he had in God; but he rolled up the epistle, and laid it up within the temple; as he made his further prayers to God for the city, and for the preservation of all the people, the prophet Isaiah said, that God had heard his prayer, and that he should not at this time be besieged by the king of Assyria;* that, for the future, he

might be secure of not being at all disturbed by him; and that the people might go on peaceably, and without fear, with their husbandry and other affairs; but after a little while, the king of Assyria, when he had failed of his treacherous designs against the Egyptians, returned home without success on the following occasion:—He spent a long time in the siege of Pelusium; and when the banks that he had raised over against the walls were of a great height, and when he was ready to make an immediate assault upon them, but heard that Tirhaka, king of the Ethiopians, was coming, and bringing great forces to aid the Egyptians, and was resolved to march through the desert, and so to fall directly upon the Assyrians, this king Sennacherib was disturbed of the news; and, as I said before, left Pelusium, and returned back without success. Now, concerning this Sennacherib, Herodotus also says, in the second book of his histories, how "this king came against the Egyptian king, who was the priest of Vulcan; and that as he was besieging Pelusium, he broke up the siege on the following occasion:—This Egyptian priest prayed to God, and God heard his prayer, and sent a judgment upon the Arabian king." But in this Herodotus was mistaken when he called this king not king of the Assyrians, but of the Arabians; for he saith, that "a multitude of mice gnawed to pieces in one night both the bows and the rest of the armour of the Assyrians; and that it was on that account that the king, when he had no bows left, drew off his army from Pelusium." And Herodotus does indeed give us this history; nay, and Berosus, who wrote of the affairs of Chaldea, makes mention of this king Sennacherib, and that he ruled over the Assyrians, and that he made an expedition against all Asia and Egypt; and says thus:—

5. "Now when Sennacherib was returning from his Egyptian war to Jerusalem, he found his army under Rabshakeh his general in danger [by a plague,] for God had sent a pestilential distemper upon his army; and on the very first night of the siege, a hundred fourscore and five thousand, with their captains and generals, were destroyed. So the king was in a great dread, and in a terrible agony at this calamity; and being in great fear for his whole army, he fled with the rest of his forces to his own kingdom, and to his city Nineveh; and when he had abode there a little while, he was treacherously assaulted, and died by the hands of his elder sons,† Adrammelech and Seraser, and was slain in his own temple, which was called Araske. Now these sons of his were driven away, on account of the murder of their father, by the citizens, and went into Armenia, while Assarachoddas took the kingdom of Sennacherib." And this proved to be the conclusion of this Assyrian expedition against the people of Jerusalem.

CHAPTER II

HOW HEZEKIAH WAS SICK, AND READY TO DIE, AND HOW GOD BESTOWED UPON HIM FIFTEEN

---

* What Josephus says here is more distinct in our other copies, both of the Kings and of Isaiah, and deserves very great consideration.   The words are these :—"This shall be a sign unto thee : Ye shall eat this year such as groweth of itself ; and the second year that which springeth of the same ; and in the third year sow ye, and reap, and plant vineyards, and eat

the fruit thereof," (2 Kings xix. 20 ; Isa. xxxvii. 30 ;) which seem to me plainly to design a Sabbatic year, a year of jubilee next after it, and the succeeding usual labours and fruits of them on the third and following years.

† We are here to take notice, that these two sons of Sennacherib that ran away into Armenia, became the heads of two famous families there, the Arzerunii and Genunii.

YEARS LONGER LIFE, [AND SECURED THAT PRO-
MISE,] BY THE GOING BACK OF THE SHADOW
TEN DEGREES

1. Now Hezekiah being thus delivered, after
a surprising manner, from the dread he was in,
offered thank-offerings to God, with all his
people; because nothing else had destroyed
some of their enemies, and made the rest so
fearful of undergoing the same fate, that they
departed from Jerusalem, but that divine assistance: yet, while he was very zealous and diligent about the worship of God, did he soon
afterwards fall into a severe distemper, insomuch that the physicians despaired of him, and
expected no good issue of his sickness, as neither
did his friends: and besides the distemper itself,
there was a very melancholy circumstance that
disordered the king, which was the consideration
that he was childless, and was going to die, and
leave his house and his government without a
successor of his own body: so he was troubled
at the thoughts of this his condition, and lamented himself, and entreated of God that he
would prolong his life for a little while till he
had some children, and not suffer him to depart
this life before he was become a father. Hereupon God had mercy upon him, and accepted of
his supplication; because the trouble he was
under at his supposed death was not because he
was soon to leave the advantages he enjoyed in
the kingdom; nor did he on that account pray
that he might have a longer life afforded him,
but in order to have sons, that might receive
the government after him. And God sent
Isaiah the prophet, and commanded him to inform Hezekiah, that within three days' time he
should get clear of his distemper, and should
survive it fifteen years, and that he should have
children also. Now upon the prophet's saying
this, as God had commanded him, he could
hardly believe it, both on account of the distemper he was under, which was very sore, and
by reason of the surprising nature of what was
told him; so he desired that Isaiah would give
him some sign or wonder, that he might believe
him in what he had said, and be sensible that he
came from God: for things that are beyond expectation, and greater than our hopes, are made
credible by actions of the like nature. And
when Isaiah had asked him what sign he desired
to be exhibited, he desired that he would make
the shadow of the sun, which he had already
made to go down ten steps [or degrees] in his
house, to return again to the same place,* and
to make it as it was before. And when the prophet prayed to God to exhibit this sign to the
king, he saw what he desired to see, and was
freed from his distemper, and went up to the
temple, where he worshipped God and made
vows to him.

2. At this time it was that the dominion of the
Assyrians was overthrown by the Medes; † but

of these things I shall treat elsewhere. But the
king of Babylon, whose name was Baladan, sent
ambassadors to Hezekiah with presents, and desired he would be his ally and his friend So he
received the ambassadors gladly, and made them
a feast, and shewed them his treasures, and his
armoury, and the other wealth he was possessed
of, in precious stones, and in gold, and gave
them presents to be carried to Baladan, and sent
them back to him. Upon which the prophet
Isaiah came to him, and inquired of him whence
those ambassadors came: to which he replied,
that they came from Babylon, from the king;
and that he had shewed them all he had, that
by the sight of his riches and forces he might
thereby guess at [the plenty he was in,] and be
able to inform the king of it. But the prophet
rejoined, and said,—" Know thou, that, after a
little while, these riches of thine shall be carried
away to Babylon, and thy posterity shall be
made eunuchs there, and lose their manhood,
and be servants to the king of Babylon; for that
God foretold such things would come to pass."
Upon which words Hezekiah was troubled, and
said, that he was himself unwilling that his nation should fall into such calamities; yet, since
it is not possible to alter what God had determined, he prayed that there might be peace
while he lived. Berosus also makes mention of
this Baladan, king of Babylon. Now as to this
prophet [Isaiah,] he was, by the confession of
all, a divine and wonderful man in speaking
truth; and out of the assurance that he had
never written what was false, he wrote down
all his prophecies, and left them behind him in
books, that their accomplishment might be
judged of from the events by posterity. Nor
did this prophet do so alone; but the others,
which were twelve in number, did the same.
And whatsoever is done among us, whether it be
good, or whether it be bad, comes to pass according to their prophecies; but of every one of
these we shall speak hereafter.

CHAPTER III

HOW MANASSEH REIGNED AFTER HEZEKIAH; AND
HOW, WHEN HE WAS IN CAPTIVITY, HE RE-
TURNED TO GOD, AND WAS RESTORED TO HIS
KINGDOM, AND LEFT IT TO [HIS SON] AMON

1. WHEN king Hezekiah had survived the interval of time already mentioned, and had dwelt
all that time in peace, he died, having completed
fifty-four years of his life, and reigned twenty-
nine. But when his son Manasseh, whose
mother's name was Hephzibah, of Jerusalem,
had taken the kingdom, he departed from the
conduct of his father, and fell into a course of
life quite contrary thereto, and shewed himself
in his manners most wicked in all respects, and
omitted no sort of impiety, but imitated those
transgressions of the Israelites, by the commission of which against God, they had been destroyed; for he was so hardy as to defile the
temple of God, and the city, and the whole
country; for by setting out from a contempt of
God, he barbarously slew all the righteous men
that were among the Hebrews; nor would he
spare the prophets, for he every day slew some
of them, till Jerusalem was overflown with
blood. So God was angry at these proceedings,
and sent prophets to the king, and to the multitude, by whom he threatened the very same
calamities to them which their brethren the
Israelites upon the like affronts offered to God,

---

* As to this regress of the shadow, whether it were
physically done by the real miraculous revolution of
the earth in its diurnal motion backwards from east to
west for a while, and its return again to its old natural
revolution from west to east; or whether it were not
apparent only, and performed by an aerial phosphorus,
which imitated the sun's motion backwards, while a
cloud hid the real sun, cannot now be determined.
Philosophers and astronomers will naturally incline to
the latter hypothesis.

† This expression of Josephus seems to be too
strong; for although the Medes immediately cast off
the Assyrian yoke, and set up a king of their own, yet
it was some time before they overthrew Nineveh; and
some generations before they overthrew the Assyrian
or Babylonian empire and took Babylon.

were now under. But these men would not believe their words, by which belief they might
have reaped the advantage of escaping all those
miseries; yet did they in earnest learn that what
the prophets had told them was true.

2. And when they persevered in the same
course of life, God raised up war against them
from the king of Babylon and Chaldea, who
sent an army against Judea, and laid waste the
country; and caught king Manasseh by treachery,
and ordered him to be brought to him, and had
him under his power to inflict what punishment
he pleased upon him. But then it was that
Manasseh perceived what a miserable condition
he was in, and esteeming himself the cause of
all, he besought God to render his enemy humane and merciful to him. Accordingly, God
heard his prayer, and granted him what he
prayed for. So Manasseh was released by the
king of Babylon, and escaped the danger he was
in; and when he was come to Jerusalem, he
endeavoured, if it were possible, to cast out of
his memory those his former sins against God,
of which he now repented, and to apply himself
to a very religious life. He sanctified the temple, and purged the city, and for the remainder
of his days he was intent on nothing but to return his thanks to God for his deliverance, and
to preserve him propitious to him all his life
long. He also instructed the multitude to do
the same, as having very nearly experienced
what a calamity he was fallen into by a contrary
conduct. He also rebuilt the altar, and offered
the legal sacrifices, as Moses commanded; and
when he had re-established what concerned the
divine worship, as it ought to be, he took care of
the security of Jerusalem: he did not only repair the old walls with great diligence, but
added another wall to the former. He also
built very lofty towers, and the garrisoned
places before the city he strengthened, not only
in other respects, but with provisions of all sorts
that they wanted; and indeed, when he had
changed his former course, he so led his life for
the time to come, that from the time of his return to piety towards God, he was deemed a
happy man, and a pattern for imitation. When
therefore he had lived sixty-seven years, he
departed this life, having reigned fifty-five
years, and was buried in his own garden; and
the kingdom came to his son Amon, whose
mother's name was Meshulemeth, of the city of
Jotbath.

CHAPTER IV

HOW AMON REIGNED INSTEAD OF MANASSEH; AND
AFTER AMON, REIGNED JOSIAH; HE WAS BOTH
RIGHTEOUS AND RELIGIOUS. AS ALSO CON-
CERNING HULDAH THE PROPHETESS

1. THIS Amon imitated those works of his
father which he so insolently did when he was
young: so he had a conspiracy made against him
by his own servants, and was slain in his own
house, when he had lived twenty-four years, and
of them had reigned two; but the multitude
punished those that slew Amon, and buried him
with his father, and gave the kingdom to his son
Josiah, who was eight years old. His mother
was of the city of Boscath, and her name was
Jedidah. He was of a most excellent disposition, and naturally virtuous, and followed the
actions of king David, as a pattern and a rule to
him in the whole conduct of his life; and when
he was twelve years old, he gave demonstrations
of his religious and righteous behaviour; for he

brought the people to a sober way of living, and
exhorted them to leave off the opinion they had
of their idols, because they were not gods, but
to worship their own God; and by reflecting on
the actions of his progenitors, he prudently corrected what they did wrong, like a very elderly
man, and like one abundantly able to understand
what was fit to be done; and what he found
they had well done, he observed all the country
over, and imitated the same; and thus he acted
in following the wisdom and sagacity of his own
nature, and in compliance with the advice and
instruction of the elders; for by following the
laws it was that he succeeded so well in the
order of his government, and in piety with regard to the divine worship; and this happened
because the transgressions of the former kings
were seen no more, but quite vanished away;
for the king went about the city, and the whole
country, and cut down the groves, which were
devoted to strange gods, and overthrew their
altars; and if there were any gifts dedicated to
them by his forefathers, he made them ignominious, and plucked them down; and by this
means he brought the people back from their
opinion about them to the worship of God. He
also offered his accustomed sacrifices and burnt-
offerings upon the altar. Moreover, he ordained
certain judges and overseers, that they might
order the matters to them severally belonging,
and have regard to justice above all things, and
distribute it with the same concern they would
have about their own soul. He also sent over
all the country, and desired such as pleased to
bring gold and silver for the repairs of the temple, according to every one's inclinations and abilities; and when the money was brought in, he
made one Maaseiah the governor of the city, and
Shaphan the scribe, and Joah the recorder, and
Eliakim the high priest, curators of the temple,
and of the charges contributed thereto; who
made no delay, nor put the work off at all, but
prepared architects, and whatsoever was proper
for those repairs, and set closely about the work.
So the temple was repaired by this means, and
became a public demonstration of the king's
piety.

2. But when he was now in the eighteenth
year of his reign, he sent to Eliakim the high
priest, and gave order, that out of what money
was overplus, he should cast cups, and dishes,
and vials, for ministration [in the temple;] and
besides, that they should bring all the gold or
silver which was among the treasures, and expend that also in making cups and the like vessels: but as the high priest was bringing out the
gold, he lighted upon the holy books of Moses
that were laid up in the temple; and when he
had brought them out, he gave them to Shaphan
the scribe, who, when he had read them, came
to the king, and informed him that all was
finished which he had ordered to be done. He
also read over the books to him, who, when he
had heard them read, rent his garment, and
called for Eliakim, the high priest, and for
[Shaphan] the scribe, and for certain [other] of
his most particular friends, and sent them to
Huldah the prophetess, the wife of Shallum,
(which Shallum was a man of dignity, and of an
eminent family,) and bade them go to her and
say that [he desired] she would appease God,
and endeavour to render him propitious to them,
for that there was cause to fear lest, upon the
transgression of the laws of Moses by their
forefathers, they should be in peril of going into
captivity, and of being cast out of their own
country; lest they should be in want of all
things, and so end their days miserably. When

the prophetess had heard this from the messengers that were sent to her by the king, she bade them go back to the king, and say, that God had already given sentence against them, to destroy the people, and cast them out of their country, and deprive them of all the happiness they enjoyed; which sentence none could set aside by any prayers of theirs, since it was passed on account of their transgressions of the laws, and of their not having repented in so long a time, while the prophets had exhorted them to amend, and had foretold the punishments that would ensue on their impious practices; which threatening God would certainly execute upon them, that they might be persuaded that he is God, and had not deceived them in any respect as to what he had denounced by his prophets; that yet, because Josiah was a righteous man, he would at present delay those calamities, but that, after his death, he would send on the multitude what miseries he had determined for them.

3. So these messengers, upon this prophecy of the woman, came and told it to the king; whereupon he sent to the people everywhere, and ordered that the priests and the Levites should come together to Jerusalem; and commanded that those of every age should be present also; and when they were gathered together, he first read to them the holy books; after which he stood upon a pulpit, in the midst of the multitude, and obliged them to make a covenant, with an oath, that they would worship God and keep the laws of Moses. Accordingly, they gave their assent willingly, and undertook to do what the king had recommended to them. So they immediately offered sacrifices, and that after an acceptable manner, and besought God to be gracious and merciful to them. He also enjoined the high priest, that if there remained in the temple any vessel that was dedicated to idols, or to foreign gods, they should cast it out; so when a great number of such vessels were got together, he burnt them, and scattered their ashes abroad, and slew the priests of the idols that were not of the family of Aaron.

4. And when he had done thus in Jerusalem, he came into the country, and utterly destroyed what buildings had been made therein by king Jeroboam, in honour of strange gods; and he burnt the bones of the false prophets upon that altar which Jeroboam first built; and, as the prophet [Jadon,] who came to Jeroboam when he was offering sacrifice, and when all the people heard him, foretold what would come to pass—viz., that a certain man of the house of David, Josiah by name, should do what is here mentioned. And it happened that those predictions took effect after three hundred and sixty-one years.

5. After these things, Josiah went also to such other Israelites as had escaped captivity and slavery under the Assyrians, and persuaded them to desist from their impious practices, and to leave off the honours they paid to strange gods, but to worship rightly their own Almighty God, and adhere to him. He also searched the houses, and the villages, and the cities, out of a suspicion that somebody might have one idol or other in private; nay, indeed, he took away the chariots [of the Sun] that were set up in his royal palace,* which his predecessors had framed, and what thing soever there was besides which they wor-

shipped as a god. And when he had thus purged all the country, he called the people to Jerusalem, and there celebrated the feast of unleavened bread, and that called the Passover. He also gave the people for paschal sacrifices, young kids of the goats, and lambs, thirty thousand, and three thousand oxen for burnt-offerings. The principal of the priests also gave to the priests against the passover two thousand and six hundred lambs; the principal of the Levites also gave to the Levites five thousand lambs, and five hundred oxen, by which means there was great plenty of sacrifices; and they offered these sacrifices according to the laws of Moses, while every priest explained the matter, and ministered to the multitude. And indeed there had been no other festival thus celebrated by the Hebrews from the times of Samuel the prophet; and the plenty of sacrifices now was the occasion that all things were performed according to the laws, and according to the custom of their forefathers. So when Josiah had after this lived in peace, nay, in riches and reputation also, among all men, he ended his life in the manner following.

CHAPTER V

HOW JOSIAH FOUGHT WITH NECO [KING OF EGYPT,] AND WAS WOUNDED, AND DIED IN A LITTLE TIME AFTERWARDS; AS ALSO HOW NECO CARRIED JEHOAHAZ, WHO HAD BEEN MADE KING, INTO EGYPT, AND DELIVERED THE KINGDOM TO JEHOIAKIM; AND [LASTLY,] CONCERNING JEREMIAH AND EZEKIEL

1. Now Neco, king of Egypt, raised an army, and marched to the river Euphrates, in order to fight with the Medes and Babylonians, who had overthrown the dominions of the Assyrians,† for he had a desire to reign over Asia. Now when he was come to the city Mendes, which belonged to the kingdom of Josiah, he brought an army to hinder him from passing through his own country, in his expedition against the Medes. Now Neco sent a herald to Josiah, and told him, that he had not made his expedition against him, but was making haste to Euphrates; and desired that he would not provoke him to fight against him, because he obstructed his march to the place whither he had resolved to go. But Josiah did not admit of this advice of Neco, but put himself into a posture to hinder him from his intended march. I suppose it was fate that pushed him on to this conduct, that it might take an occasion against him; for as he was setting his army in array,‡ and rode about in his chariot, from one wing of his army to another, one of the Egyptians shot an arrow at him, and put an end to his eagerness for fighting; for, being sorely wounded, he commanded a retreat to be sounded for his army, and returned to Jerusalem, and died of that wound; and was magnificently buried in the sepulchre of his fathers, when he had lived thirty-nine years, and of them had reigned thirty-one. But all the people mourned greatly for him, lamenting and grieving on his account many days; and Jeremiah the prophet composed an elegy to lament him,§ which is extant till this

---

* It is hard to reconcile the account in the second book of Kings (ch. xxiii. 11) with this account in Josephus, whose copies are supposed to be here imperfect.

† This is a remarkable passage of chronology in Josephus, that about the latter end of the reign of Josiah, the Medes and Babylonians overthrew the empire of the Assyrians.

‡ This battle is esteemed the very same that Herodotus (b. ii. sect. 156) mentions, when he says, that "Necao joined battle with the Syrians [or Jews] at Magdolum [Megiddo,] and beat them."

§ Whether Josephus here means the book of the

time also. Moreover, this prophet denounced beforehand the sad calamities that were coming upon the city. He also left behind him in writing a description of that destruction of our nation which has lately happened in our days, and the taking of Babylon; nor was he the only prophet who delivered such predictions beforehand to the multitude; but so did Ezekiel also, who was the first person that wrote, and left behind him in writing two books, concerning these events. Now these two prophets were priests by birth, but of them Jeremiah dwelt in Jerusalem, from the thirteenth year of the reign of Josiah, until the city and temple were utterly destroyed. However, as to what befell this prophet, we will relate it in its proper place.

2. Upon the death of Josiah, which we have already mentioned, his son, Jehoahaz, by name, took the kingdom, being about twenty-three years old. He reigned in Jerusalem; and his mother was Hamutal, of the city Libnah. He was an impious man, and impure in his course of life; but as the king of Egypt returned from the battle, he sent for Jehoahaz to come to him to the city called Hamath,* which belongs to Syria; and when he was come, he put him in bands, and delivered the kingdom to a brother of his by the father's side, whose name was Eliakim, and changed his name to Jehoiakim, and laid a tribute upon the land of a hundred talents of silver, and a talent of gold; and this sum of money Jehoiakim paid by way of tribute; but Neco carried away Jehoahaz into Egypt, where he died, when he had reigned three months and ten days. Now Jehoiakim's mother was called Zebudah, of the city Rumah. He was of a wicked disposition, and ready to do mischief; nor was he either religious towards God, or good-natured towards men.

CHAPTER VI

HOW NEBUCHADNEZZAR, WHEN HE HAD CONQUERED THE KING OF EGYPT, MADE AN EXPEDITION AGAINST THE JEWS, AND SLEW JEHOIAKIM, AND MADE JEHOIACHIN, HIS SON, KING

1. Now in the fourth year of the reign of Jehoiakim, one whose name was Nebuchadnezzar took the government over the Babylonians, who at the same time went up with a great army to the city Carchemish, which was at Euphrates, upon a resolution he had taken to fight with Neco, king of Egypt, under whom all Syria then was. And when Neco understood the intention of the king of Babylon, and that this expedition was made against him, he did not despise his attempt, but made haste with a great band of men to Euphrates to defend himself from Nebuchadnezzar; and when they had joined battle, he was beaten, and lost many ten thousands [of his soldiers] in the battle. So the king of Babylon passed over Euphrates, and took all Syria, as far as Pelusium, excepting Judea. But when Nebuchadnezzar had already reigned four years, which was the eighth of Jehoiakim's government over the Hebrews, the king of Babylon made an

expedition with mighty forces against the Jews, and required tribute of Jehoiakim, and threatened, on his refusal, to make war against him. He was affrighted at his threatening, and bought his peace with money, and brought the tribute he was ordered to bring for three years.

2. But on the third year, upon hearing that the king of the Babylonians made an expedition against the Egyptians, he did not pay his tribute; yet was he disappointed of his hope, for the Egyptians durst not fight at this time. And indeed the prophet Jeremiah foretold every day how vainly they relied on their hopes from Egypt, and how the city would be overthrown by the king of Babylon, and Jehoiakim the king would be subdued by him. But what he thus spake proved to be of no advantage to them, because there were none that should escape; for both the multitude, and the rulers, when they heard him, had no concern about what they heard; but being displeased at what was said, as if the prophet were a diviner against the king, they accused Jeremiah; and bringing him before the court, they required that a sentence and a punishment might be given against him. Now all the rest gave their votes for his condemnation, but the elders refused, who prudently sent away the prophet from the court [of the prison,] and persuaded the rest to do Jeremiah no harm; for they said that he was not the only person who foretold what would come to the city, but that Micah signified the same before him, as well as many others, none of whom suffered anything of the kings that then reigned, but were honoured as the prophets of God. So they mollified the multitude with these words, and delivered Jeremiah from the punishment to which he was condemned. Now when this prophet had written all his prophecies, and the people were fasting, and assembled at the temple, on the ninth month of the fifth year of Jehoiakim, he read the book he had composed of his predictions of what was to befall the city, and the temple, and the multitude; and when the rulers heard of it, they took the book from him, and bade him and Baruch the scribe to go their ways, lest they should be discovered by one or other; but they carried the book, and gave it to the king; so he gave order in the presence of his friends, that his scribe should take it and read it. When the king heard what it contained, he was angry and tore it, and cast it into the fire, where it was consumed. He also commanded that they should seek for Jeremiah and Baruch the scribe, and bring them to him, that they might be punished. However, they escaped his anger.

3. Now a little time afterwards, the king of Babylon made an expedition against Jehoiakim, whom he received [into the city,] and this out of fear of the foregoing predictions of this prophet, as supposing that he should suffer nothing that was terrible, because he neither shut the gates, nor fought against him; yet when he was come into the city, he did not observe the covenants he had made; but he slew such as were in the flower of their age, and such as were of the greatest dignity, together with their king Jehoiakim, whom he commanded to be thrown before the walls, without any burial; and made his son Jehoiachin king of the country and of the city: he also took the principal persons in dignity for captives, three thousand in number, and led them away to Babylon; among whom was the prophet Ezekiel, who was then but young. And this was the end of king Jehoiakim, when he had lived thirty-six years, and of them reigned eleven. But Jehoiachin succeeded

---

Lamentations of Jeremiah, still extant, or to any other like melancholy poem now lost, but extant in the days of Josephus, cannot now be determined.

* This ancient city Hamath, which is joined with Arpad, or Aradus, and with Damascus, (2 Kings xviii. 34; Isa. xxxvi. 19; Jer. xlix. 23,) cities of Syria and Phœnicia, near the borders of Judea, was also itself evidently near the same borders.

him in the kingdom, whose mother's name was Nehushta; she was a citizen of Jerusalem. He reigned three months and ten days.

CHAPTER VII

THAT THE KING OF BABYLON REPENTED OF MAKING JEHOIACHIN KING, AND TOOK HIM AWAY TO BABYLON, AND DELIVERED THE KINGDOM TO ZEDEKIAH. THIS KING WOULD NOT BELIEVE WHAT WAS PREDICTED BY JEREMIAH AND EZEKIEL, BUT JOINED HIMSELF TO THE EGYPTIANS; WHO, WHEN THEY CAME INTO JUDEA, WERE VANQUISHED BY THE KING OF BABYLON; AS ALSO WHAT BEFELL JEREMIAH

1. BUT a terror seized on the king of Babylon, who had given the kingdom to Jehoiachin, and that immediately; he was afraid that he should bear him a grudge, because of his killing his father, and thereupon should make the country revolt from him: wherefore he sent an army, and besieged Jehoiachin in Jerusalem; but because he was of a gentle and just disposition, he did not desire to see the city endangered on his account, but he took his mother and kindred, and delivered them to the commanders sent by the king of Babylon, and accepted of their oaths, that neither should they suffer any harm, nor the city; which agreement they did not observe for a single year, for the king of Babylon did not keep it, but gave orders to his generals to take all that were in the city captives, both the youth and the handicraftsmen, and bring them bound to him; their number was ten thousand eight hundred and thirty-two; as also Jehoiachin, and his mother and friends; and when these were brought to him, he kept them in custody, and appointed Jehoiachin's uncle, Zedekiah, to be king; and made him take an oath, that he would certainly keep the kingdom for him, and make no innovation, nor have any league of friendship with the Egyptians.

2. Now Zedekiah was twenty and one years old when he took the government; and had the same mother with his brother Jehoiakim, but was a despiser of justice and of his duty, for truly those of the same age with him were wicked about him, and the whole multitude did what unjust and insolent things they pleased; for which reason the prophet Jeremiah came often to him, and protested to him, and insisted that he must leave off his impieties and transgressions, and take care of what was right, and neither give ear to the rulers, (among whom were wicked men,) nor give credit to their false prophets who deluded them, as if the king of Babylon would make no more war against him, and as if the Egyptians would make war against him, and conquer him, since what they said was not true; and the events would not prove such [as they expected.] Now as to Zedekiah himself, while he heard the prophet speak, he believed him, and agreed to everything as true, and supposed it was for his advantage; but then his friends perverted him, and dissuaded him from what the prophet advised, and obliged him to do what they pleased. Ezekiel also foretold in Babylon what calamities were coming upon the people, which, when he heard, he sent accounts of them unto Jerusalem; but Zedekiah did not believe their prophecies, for the reason following:—It happened that the two prophets agreed with one another in what they said as in all other things, that the city should be taken, and Zedekiah himself should be taken captive; but Ezekiel disagreed with him, and said, that Ze-

dekiah should not see Babylon; while Jeremiah said to him, that the king of Babylon should carry him away thither in bonds; and because they did not both say the same thing as to this circumstance, he disbelieved what they both appeared to agree in, and condemned them as not speaking truth therein, although all the things foretold did come to pass according to their prophecies, as we shall shew upon a fitter opportunity.

3. Now when Zedekiah had preserved the league of mutual assistance he had made with the Babylonians for eight years, he brake it, and revolted to the Egyptians, in hopes, by their assistance, of overcoming the Babylonians. When the king of Babylon knew this, he made war against him · he laid his country waste, and took his fortified towns, and came to the city Jerusalem itself to besiege it: but when the king of Egypt heard what circumstances Zedekiah his ally was in, he took a great army with him, and came into Judea, as if he would raise the siege; upon which the king of Babylon departed from Jerusalem, and met the Egyptians, and joined battle with them, and beat them; and when he had put them to flight, he pursued them, and drove them out of all Syria. Now as soon as the king of Babylon was departed from Jerusalem, the false prophets deceived Zedekiah, and said, that the king of Babylon would not any more make war against him or his people, nor remove them out of their own country into Babylon; and that those then in captivity would return, with all those vessels of the temple, of which the king of Babylon had despoiled that temple. But Jeremiah came among them, and prophesied what contradicted those predictions, and what proved to be true, that they did ill, and deluded the king; that the Egyptians would be of no advantage to them, but that the king of Babylon would renew the war against Jerusalem, and besiege it again, and would destroy the people by famine, and carry away those that remained into captivity, and would take away what they had as spoils, and would carry off those riches that were in the temple; nay, that, besides this, he would burn it, and utterly overthrow the city, and that they should serve him and his posterity seventy years; and then the Persians and the Medes should put an end to their servitude, and overthrow the Babylonians; "and that we shall be dismissed, and return to this land, and rebuild the temple, and restore Jerusalem."*— When Jeremiah said this, the greater part believed him; but the rulers, and those that were wicked, despised him, as one disordered in his senses. Now he had resolved to go elsewhere, to his own country, which was called Anathoth, and was twenty furlongs distant from Jerusalem; and as he was going, one of the rulers met him, and seized upon him, and accused him falsely, as though he were going as a deserter to the Babylonians; but Jeremiah said that he accused him falsely, and added, that he was only going to his own country; but the other would not believe him, but seized upon him, and led him away to the rulers, and laid an accusation against him, under whom he endured all sorts of torments and tortures, and was reserved to be punished; and this was the condition he was in for some time, while he suffered what I have already described unjustly.

4. Now, in the ninth year of the reign of Zede-

* Josephus says here, that Jeremiah prophesied not only of the return of the Jews from the Babylonian captivity, and this under the Persians and Medes, but of their rebuilding the temple, and even the city Jerusalem.

kiah, on the tenth day of the tenth month, the king of Babylon made a second expedition against Jerusalem, and lay before it eighteen months, and besieged it with the utmost application. There came upon them also two of the greatest calamities, at the same time that Jerusalem was besieged, a famine and a pestilential distemper, and made great havoc of them: and though the prophet Jeremiah was in prison, he did not rest, but cried out, and proclaimed aloud, and exhorted the multitude to open their gates, and admit the king of Babylon, for that, if they did so, they should be preserved, and their whole families; but if they did not so, they should be destroyed; and he foretold, that if any one stayed in the city, he should certainly perish by one of these ways,—either be consumed by the famine, or slain by the enemy's sword; but that if he would fly to the enemy he should escape death: yet did not these rulers who heard believe him, even when they were in the midst of their sore calamities; but they came to the king, and, in their anger, informed him what Jeremiah said, and accused him, and complained of the prophet as of a madman, and one that disheartened their minds, and, by the denunciation of miseries, weakened the alacrity of the multitude, who were otherwise ready to expose themselves to dangers for him and for their country, while he, in a way of threatening, warned them to fly to the enemy, and told them that the city should certainly be taken, and be utterly destroyed.

5. But for the king himself, he was not at all irritated against Jeremiah, such was his gentle and righteous disposition; yet, that he might not be engaged in a quarrel with those rulers at such a time, by opposing what they intended, he let them do with the prophet whatsoever they would: whereupon, when the king had granted them such a permission, they presently came into the prison and took him, and let him down with a cord into a pit full of mire, that he might be suffocated, and die of himself. So he stood up to the neck in the mire, which was all about him, and so continued: but there was one of the king's servants, who was in esteem with him, an Ethiopian by descent, who told the king what a state the prophet was in, and said that his friends and his rulers had done evil in putting the prophet into the mire, and by that means contriving against him that he should suffer a death more bitter than that by his bonds only. When the king heard this, he repented of his having delivered up the prophet to the rulers, and bade the Ethiopian take thirty men of the king's guards, and cords with them, and whatsoever else they understood to be necessary for the prophet's preservation, and to draw him up immediately. So the Ethiopian took the men that he was ordered to take, and drew up the prophet out of the mire, and left him at liberty in the prison.

6. But when the king had sent to call him privately, and inquired what he could say to him from God, which might be suitable to his present circumstances, and desired him to inform him of it, Jeremiah replied, that he had somewhat to say; but he said withal, he should not be believed, nor, if he admonished them, should he be hearkened to; "for," said he, "Thy friends have determined to destroy me, as though I had been guilty of some wickedness: and where are now those men who deceived us, and said that the king of Babylon would not come and fight against us any more? but I am afraid now to speak the truth, lest thou shouldest condemn me to die." And when the king had

assured him upon oath that he would neither himself put him to death, nor deliver him up to the rulers, he became bold upon that assurance that was given him, and gave him this advice: —That he should deliver the city up to the Babylonians; and he said, that it was God who prophesied this by him, that [he must do so] if he would be preserved, and escape out of the danger he was in, and that then neither should the city fall to the ground, nor should the temple be burned; but that [if he disobeyed,] he would be the cause of these miseries coming upon the citizens, and of the calamity that would befall his whole house. When the king heard this, he said that he would willingly do what he persuaded him to, and what he declared would be to his advantage, but that he was afraid of those of his own country that had fallen away to the Babylonians, lest he should be accused by them to the king of Babylon, and be punished. But the prophet encouraged him, and said he had no cause to fear such punishment, for that he should not have the experience of any misfortune, if he would deliver all up to the Babylonians; neither himself, nor his children, nor his wives, and that the temple should then continue unhurt. So when Jeremiah had said this, the king let him go, and charged him to betray what they had resolved on to none of the citizens, nor to tell any of these matters to any of the rulers, if they should have learned that he had been sent for, and should inquire of him what it was that he was sent for, and what he had said to him; but to pretend to them that he besought him that he might not be kept in bonds and in prison. And indeed he said so to them, for they came to the prophet, and asked him what advice it was that he came to give the king relating to them: and thus I have finished what concerns this matter.

CHAPTER VIII

HOW THE KING OF BABYLON TOOK JERUSALEM AND BURNT THE TEMPLE, AND REMOVED THE PEOPLE OF JERUSALEM AND ZEDEKIAH TO BABYLON. AS ALSO, WHO THEY WERE THAT HAD SUCCEEDED IN THE HIGH PRIESTHOOD UNDER THE KINGS

1. Now the king of Babylon was very intent and earnest upon the siege of Jerusalem; and he erected towers upon great banks of earth, and from them repelled those that stood upon the walls: he also made a great number of such banks round about the whole city, the height of which was equal to those walls. However, those that were within bore the siege with courage and alacrity, for they were not discouraged, either by famine or by the pestilential distemper, but were of cheerful minds in the prosecution of the war, although those miseries within oppressed them also; and they did not suffer themselves to be terrified, either by the contrivances of the enemy, or by their engines of war, but contrived still different engines to oppose all the other withal, till indeed there seemed to be an entire struggle between the Babylonians and the people of Jerusalem, who had the greater sagacity and skill; the former party supposing they should be thereby too hard for the other, for the destruction of the city; the latter placing their hopes of deliverance in nothing else but in persevering in such inventions, in opposition to the other, as might demonstrate the enemy's engines were useless to them; and this siege

they endured for eighteen months, until they were destroyed by the famine, and by the darts which the enemy threw at them from the towers.

2. Now the city was taken on the ninth day of the fourth month, in the eleventh year of the reign of Zedekiah. They were indeed only generals of the king of Babylon, to whom Nebuchadnezzar committed the care of the siege, for he abode himself in the city of Riblah. The names of these generals who ravaged and subdued Jerusalem, if any one desire to know them, were these: Nergal Sharezer, Samgar Nebo, Rabsaris, Sarsechim, and Rabmag; and when the city was taken about midnight, and the enemy's generals were entered into the temple, and when Zedekiah was sensible of it, he took his wives and his children, and his captains and friends, and with them fled out of the city, through the fortified ditch, and through the desert; and when certain of the deserters had informed the Babylonians of this, at break of day, they made haste to pursue after Zedekiah, and overtook him not far from Jericho, and encompassed him about. But for those friends and captains of Zedekiah who had fled out of the city with him, when they saw their enemies near them, they left him and dispersed themselves, some one way and some another, and every one resolved to save himself; so the enemy took Zedekiah alive, when he was deserted by all but a few, with his children and his wives, and brought him to the king. When he was come, Nebuchadnezzar began to call him a wicked wretch, and a covenant-breaker, and one that had forgotten his former words, when he promised to keep the country for him. He also reproached him for his ingratitude, that when he had received the kingdom from him, who had taken it from Jehoiachin, and given it him, he had made use of the power he gave him against him that gave it: "but," said he, "God is great, who hateth that conduct of thine, and hath brought thee under us." And when he had used these words to Zedekiah, he commanded his sons and his friends to be slain, while Zedekiah and the rest of the captains looked on; after which he put out the eyes of Zedekiah, and bound him, and carried him to Babylon. And these things happened to him,* as Jeremiah and Ezekiel had foretold to him, that he should be caught, and brought before the king of Babylon, and should speak to him face to face, and should see his eyes with his own eyes; and thus far did Jeremiah prophesy. But he was also made blind, and brought to Babylon, but did not see it, according to the prediction of Ezekiel.

3. We have said thus much, because it was sufficient to shew the nature of God to such as are ignorant of it, that it is various, and acts many different ways, and that all events happen after a regular manner, in their proper season, and that it foretells what must come to pass. It is also sufficient to shew the ignorance and incredulity of men, whereby they are not permitted to foresee anything that is future, and are, without any guard, exposed to calamities, so that it is impossible for them to avoid the experience of those calamities.

4. And after this manner have the kings of David's race ended their lives, being in number twenty-one, until the last king, who altogether reigned five hundred and fourteen years, and six months, and ten days: of whom Saul, who was their

first king, retained the government twenty years, though he was not of the same tribe with the rest.

5. And now it was that the king of Babylon sent Nebuzaradan, the general of his army, to Jerusalem, to pillage the temple; who had it also in command to burn it and the royal palace, and to lay the city even with the ground, and to transplant the people into Babylon. Accordingly, he came to Jerusalem, in the eleventh year of king Zedekiah, pillaged the temple, and carried out the vessels of God, both gold and silver, and particularly that large laver which Solomon dedicated, as also the pillars of brass, and their chapiters, with the golden tables and the candlesticks: and when he had carried these off, he set fire to the temple in the fifth month, the first day of the month, in the eleventh year of the reign of Zedekiah, and in the eighteenth year of Nebuchadnezzar; he also burnt the palace, and overthrew the city. Now the temple was burnt four hundred and seventy years, six months, and ten days, after it was built. It was then one thousand and sixty-two years, six months, and ten days, from the departure out of Egypt; and from the Deluge to the destruction of the temple, the whole interval was one thousand nine hundred and fifty-seven years, six months, and ten days; but from the generation of Adam, until this befell the temple, there were three thousand five hundred and thirteen years, six months, and ten days; so great was the number of years hereto belonging; and what actions were done during these years, we have particularly related. But the general of the Babylonian king now overthrew the city to the very foundations, and removed all the people, and took for prisoners the high priest Seraiah, and Zephaniah the priest that was next to him, and the rulers that guarded the temple, who were three in number, and the eunuch who was over the armed men, and seven friends of Zedekiah, and his scribe, and sixty other rulers; all whom, together with the vessels they had pillaged, he carried to the king of Babylon to Riblah, a city of Syria. So the king commanded the heads of the high priest and of the rulers to be cut off there; but he himself led all the captives and Zedekiah to Babylon. He also led Josedek the high priest away bound. He was the son of Seraiah the high priest, whom the king of Babylon had slain in Riblah, a city of Syria, as we just now related.

6. And now, because we have enumerated the succession of the kings, and who they were, and how long they reigned, I think it necessary to set down the names of the high priests, and who they were that succeeded one another in the high priesthood under the kings. The first high priest then at the temple which Solomon built was Zadok; after him his son Achimas received that dignity; after Achimas was Azarias; his son was Joram, and Joram's son was Isus; after him was Axioramus; his son was Phideas, and Phideas' son was Sudeas, and Sudeas' son was Juelus, and Juelus' son was Jotham, and Jotham's son was Nerias, and Nerias' son was Odeas, and his son was Sallumus, and Sallumus' son was Elcias, and his son [was Azarias, and his son] was Sareas,† and his son was Josedek, who was carried captive to Babylon. All these received the high priesthood by succession, the sons from their father.

7. When the king was come to Babylon, he kept Zedekiah in prison until he died, and buried

---

* This observation of Josephus about the seeming disagreement of Jeremiah, (ch. xxxii. 4; and xxxiv. 3; and Ezek. xii. 13,) but real agreement at last, concerning the fate of Zedekiah, is very true and very remarkable.

† I have here inserted in brackets this high priest Azarias, though he be omitted in all Josephus's copies, out of the Jewish chronicle, Seder Olam.

him magnificently, and dedicated the vessels he had pillaged out of the temple of Jerusalem to his own gods, and planted the people in the country of Babylon, but freed the high priest from his bonds.

CHAPTER IX

HOW NEBUZARADAN SET GEDALIAH OVER THE JEWS THAT WERE LEFT IN JUDEA, WHICH GEDALIAH WAS A LITTLE AFTERWARDS SLAIN BY ISHMAEL; AND HOW JOHANAN, AFTER ISHMAEL WAS DRIVEN AWAY, WENT DOWN INTO EGYPT WITH THE PEOPLE; WHICH PEOPLE NEBUCHADNEZZAR, WHEN HE MADE AN EXPEDITION AGAINST THE EGYPTIANS, TOOK CAPTIVE AND BROUGHT THEM AWAY TO BABYLON

1. Now the general of the army, Nebuzaradan, when he had carried the people of the Jews into captivity, left the poor, and those that had deserted, in the country; and made one, whose name was Gedaliah, the son of Ahikam, a person of a noble family, their governor; which Gedaliah was of a gentle and righteous disposition. He also commanded them that they should cultivate the ground, and pay an appointed tribute to the king. He also took Jeremiah the prophet out of prison, and would have persuaded him to go along with him to Babylon, for that he had been enjoined by the king to supply him with whatsoever he wanted; and if he did not like to do so, he desired him to inform him where he resolved to dwell, that he might signify the same to the king. But the prophet had no mind to follow him, nor to dwell anywhere else, but would gladly live in the ruins of his country, and in the miserable remains of it. When the general understood what his purpose was, he enjoined Gedaliah, whom he left behind, to take all possible care of him, and to supply him with whatsoever he wanted; so when he had given him rich presents, he dismissed him. Accordingly, Jeremiah abode in a city of that country, which was called Mispah; and desired of Nebuzaradan that he would set at liberty his disciple Baruch, the son of Neriah, one of a very eminent family, and exceeding skilful in the language of his country.

2. When Nebuzaradan had done thus, he made haste to Babylon; but as to those that fled away during the siege of Jerusalem, and had been scattered over the country, when they heard that the Babylonians were gone away, and had left a remnant in the land of Jerusalem, and those such as were to cultivate the same, they came together from all parts to Gedaliah to Mispah. Now the rulers that were over them were Johanan, the son of Kareah, and Jezaniah, and Seraiah, and others beside them. Now there was of the royal family one Ishmael, a wicked man, and very crafty, who, during the siege of Jerusalem, fled to Baalis, king of the Ammonites, and abode with him during that time; and Gedaliah persuaded them, now they were there, to stay with him, and to have no fear of the Babylonians, for that if they would cultivate the country, they should suffer no harm. This he assured them of by oath; and said that they should have him for their patron, and that if any disturbance should arise, they should find him ready to defend them. He also advised them to dwell in any city, as every one of them pleased; and that they would send men along with his own servants, and rebuild their houses upon the old foundations, and dwell there; and he admonished them beforehand, that they should make preparation, while the season lasted, of corn, and wine, and oil, that they might have whereon to feed during the winter. When he had thus discoursed to them, he dismissed them, that every one might dwell in what part of the country he pleased.

3. Now when this report was spread abroad as far as the nations that bordered on Judea, that Gedaliah kindly entertained those that came to him, after they had fled away, upon this [only] condition, that they should pay tribute to the king of Babylon, they also came readily to Gedaliah, and inhabited the country. And when Johanan, and the rulers that were with him, observed the country, and the humanity of Gedaliah, they were exceedingly in love with him, and told him that Baalis, the king of the Ammonites, had sent Ishmael to kill him by treachery, and secretly that he might have the dominion over the Israelites, as being of the royal family; and they said that he might deliver himself from this treacherous design, if he would give them leave to slay Ishmael, and nobody should know it, for they told him they were afraid that when he was killed by the other, the entire ruin of the remaining strength of the Israelites would ensue. But he professed that he did not believe what they said, when they told him of such a treacherous design, in a man that had been well treated by him; because it was not probable that one who, under such a want of all things, had failed of nothing that was necessary for him, should be found so wicked and ungrateful towards his benefactor, that when it would be an instance of wickedness in him not to save him had he been treacherously assaulted by others, to endeavour, and that earnestly, to kill him with his own hand: that, however, if he ought to suppose this information to be true, it was better for himself to be slain by the other, than destroy a man who fled to him for refuge, and intrusted his own safety to him, and committed himself to his disposal.

4. So Johanan, and the rulers that were with him, not being able to persuade Gedaliah, went away: but after the interval of thirty days was over, Ishmael came again to Gedaliah, to the city of Mispah, and ten men came with him: and when he had feasted Ishmael, and those that were with him, in a splendid manner at his table, and had given them presents, he became disordered in drink, while he endeavoured to be very merry with them: and when Ishmael saw him in that case, and that he was drowned in his cups to the degree of insensibility, and fallen asleep, he rose up on a sudden, with his ten friends, and slew Gedaliah and those that were with him at the feast; and when he had slain them, he went out by night, and slew all the Jews that were in the city, and those soldiers also which were left therein by the Babylonians; but the next day fourscore men came out of the country with presents to Gedaliah, none of them knowing what had befallen him; when Ishmael saw them, he invited them in to Gedaliah, and when they were come in, he shut up the court and slew them, and cast their dead bodies down into a certain deep pit, that they might not be seen; but of these fourscore men Ishmael spared those that entreated him not to kill them, till they had delivered up to him what riches they had concealed in the fields, consisting of their furniture, and garments, and corn: but he took captive the people that were in Mispah, with their wives and children; among whom were the daughters of king Zedekiah, whom Nebuzaradan, the general of the army of Babylon, had left with Gedaliah; and when he had done this, he came to the king of the Ammonites.

5. But when Johanan and the rulers with him heard of what was done at Mispah by Ishmael, and of the death of Gedaliah, they had indignation at it, and every one of them took his own armed men, and came suddenly to fight with Ishmael, and overtook him at the fountain in Hebron : and when those that were carried away captives by Ishmael saw Johanan and the rulers, they were very glad, and looked upon them as coming to their assistance, so they left him that had carried them captives, and came over to Johanan : then Ishmael, with eight men, fled to the king of the Ammonites ; but Johanan took those whom he had rescued out of the hands of Ishmael, and the eunuchs, and their wives and children, and came to a certain place called Mandara, and there they abode that day, for they had determined to remove from thence and go into Egypt, out of fear, lest the Babylonians should slay them, in case they continued in the country, and that out of anger at the slaughter of Gedaliah, who had been by them set over it for governor.

6. Now while they were under this deliberation, Johanan, the son of Kareah, and the rulers that were with him, came to Jeremiah the prophet, and desired that he would pray to God, that because they were at an utter loss what they are to do, he would discover it to them, and they sware that they would do whatsoever Jeremiah should say to them : and when the prophet said that he would be their intercessor with God, it came to pass, that after ten days God appeared to him, and said, that he should inform Johanan and the other rulers and all the people, that he would be with them while they continued in that country, and take care of them, and keep them from being hurt by the Babylonians, of whom they were afraid ; but that he would desert them if they went into Egypt ; and, out of his wrath against them, would inflict the same punishments upon them which they knew their brethren had already endured. So when the prophet had informed Johanan and the people that God had foretold these things, he was not believed, when he said that God commanded them to continue in that country ; but they imagined that he said so to gratify Baruch, his own disciple, and belied God, and that he persuaded them to stay there, that they might be destroyed by the Babylonians. Accordingly, both the people and Johanan disobeyed the counsel of God, which he gave them by the prophet, and removed into Egypt, and carried Jeremiah and Baruch along with them.

7. And when they were there, God signified to the prophet that the king of Babylon was about making an expedition against the Egyptians, and commanded him to foretell to the people that Egypt should be taken, and the king of Babylon should slay some of them, and should take others captive, and bring them to Babylon ; which things came to pass accordingly ; for on the fifth year after the destruction of Jerusalem, which was the twenty-third of the reign of Nebuchadnezzar, he made an expedition against Cœlesyria ; and when he had possessed himself of it, he made war against the Ammonites and Moabites ; and when he had brought all those nations under subjection, he fell upon Egypt, in order to overthrow it ; and he slew the king that then reigned,* and set up another : and he took those Jews that were there captives, and led

them away to Babylon ; and such was the end of the nation of the Hebrews, as it hath been delivered down to us, it having twice gone beyond Euphrates ; for the people of the ten tribes were carried out of Samaria by the Assyrians in the days of king Hoshea ; after which the people of the two tribes that remained after Jerusalem was taken [were carried away] by Nebuchadnezzar, the king of Babylon and Chaldea. Now as to Shalmanezer, he removed the Israelites out of their country, and placed therein the nation of the Cutheans, who had formerly belonged to the inner parts of Persia and Media, but were then called *Samaritans*, by taking the name of the country to which they were removed ; but the king of Babylon, who brought out the two tribes,† placed no other nation in their country, by which means all Judea and Jerusalem, and the temple, continued to be a desert for seventy years ; but the entire interval of time which passed from the captivity of the Israelites to the carrying away of the two tribes, proved to be a hundred and thirty years, six months, and ten days.

CHAPTER X

CONCERNING DANIEL, AND WHAT BEFELL HIM AT BABYLON

1. But now Nebuchadnezzar, king of Babylon, took some of the most noble of the Jews that were children, and the kinsmen of Zedekiah their king, such as were remarkable for the beauty of their bodies and the comeliness of their countenances, and delivered them into the hands of tutors, and to the improvement to be made by them. He also made some of them to be eunuchs ; which course he took also with those of other nations whom he had taken in the flower of their age, and afforded them their diet from his own table, and had them instructed in the institutes of the country, and taught the learning of the Chaldeans ; and they had now exercised themselves sufficiently in that wisdom which he had ordered they should apply themselves to. Now among these there were four of the family of Zedekiah, of most excellent dispositions ; the one of whom was called Daniel, another Ananias, another Misael, and the fourth Azarias : and the king of Babylon changed their names, and commanded that they should make use of other names. Daniel he called Baltasar ; Ananias, Shadrach ; Misael, Meshach ; and Azarias, Abednego. These the king had in esteem, and continued to love, because of the very excellent temper they were of, and because of their application to learning, and the progress they had made in wisdom.

2. Now Daniel and his kinsmen had resolved to use a severe diet, and to abstain from those kinds of food which came from the king's table, and entirely to forbear to eat of all living creatures : so he came to Ashpenaz, who was that eunuch to whom the care of them was committed,‡ and desired him to take and spend what was brought for them from the king ; but to give them pulse and dates for their food, and

---

* Herodotus says, this king of Egypt (Pharaoh, Hophra, or Apries) was slain by the Egyptians, as Jeremiah foretold his slaughter by his enemies, (Jer. xliv. 29, 30 ;) and that as a sign of the destruction of Egypt by Nebuchadnezzar.

† We see here that Judea was left in a manner desolate after the captivity of the two tribes, and was not re-peopled with foreign colonies, perhaps as an indication of Providence that the Jews were to re-people it without opposition themselves.

‡ That Daniel was made one of these eunuchs of whom Isaiah prophesied, (Isa. xxxix. 7,) and the three children his companions also, seems to me plain, both here in Josephus, and in our copies of Daniel (Dan. i. 3, 6, 7, 11, 18.)

anything else, besides the flesh of living creatures, that he pleased, for that their inclinations were to that sort of food, and that they despised the other. He replied, that he was ready to serve them in what they desired, but he suspected that they would be discovered by the king, from their meagre bodies, and the alteration of their countenances; because it could not be avoided but their bodies and colours must be changed with their diet, especially while they would be clearly discovered by the finer appearance of the other children, who would fare better, and thus they should bring him into danger, and occasion him to be punished: yet did they persuade Arioch, who was thus fearful to give them what food they desired for ten days, by way of trial; and in case the habit of their bodies were not altered, to go on in the same way, as expecting that they should not be hurt thereby afterwards; but if he saw them look meagre, and worse than the rest, he should reduce them to their former diet. Now when it appeared that they were so far from becoming worse by the use of this food, that they grew plumper and fuller in body than the rest, insomuch, that he thought those who fed on what came from the king's table seemed less plump and full, while those that were with Daniel looked as if they had lived in plenty, and in all sorts of luxury, Arioch, from that time, securely took himself what the king sent every day from his supper, according to custom, to the children, but gave them the forementioned diet, while they had their souls in some measure more pure, and less burdened, and so fitter for learning, and had their bodies in better tune for hard labour; for they neither had the former oppressed and heavy with variety of meats, nor were the other effeminate on the same account; so they readily understood all the learning that was among the Hebrews, and among the Chaldeans, as especially did Daniel, who, being already skilled in wisdom, was very busy about the interpretation of dreams: and God manifested himself to him.

3. Now two years after the destruction of Egypt, king Nebuchadnezzar saw a wonderful dream, the accomplishment of which God shewed him in his sleep; but when he arose out of his bed, he forgot the accomplishment: so he sent for the Chaldeans and magicians, and the prophets, and told them that he had seen a dream, and informed them that he had forgotten the accomplishment of what he had seen, and he enjoined them to tell him both what the dream was, and what was its signification; and they said that this was a thing impossible to be discovered by men; but they promised him, that if he would explain to them what dream he had seen, they would tell him its signification. Hereupon he threatened to put them to death, unless they told him his dream: and he gave command to have them all put to death, since they confessed they could not do what they were commanded to do. Now when Daniel heard that the king had given a command that all the wise men should be put to death, and that among them himself and his three kinsmen were in danger, he went to Arioch, who was captain of the king's guards, and desired to know of him what was the reason why the king had given command that all the wise men, and Chaldeans, and magicians, should be slain. So when he had learned that the king had had a dream, and he had forgotten it, and that when they were enjoined to inform the king of it, they had said they could not do it, and had thereby provoked him to anger, he desired of Arioch that he would go in to the king, and desire respite for the magicians for one night, and to put off their

slaughter so long, for that he hoped within that time to obtain, by prayer to God, the knowledge of the dream. Accordingly Arioch informed the king of what Daniel desired: so the king bid them delay the slaughter of the magicians till he knew what Daniel's promise would come to; but the young man retired to his own house, with his kinsmen, and besought God that whole night to discover the dream, and thereby deliver the magicians and Chaldeans, with whom they were themselves to perish, from the king's anger, by enabling him to declare his vision, and to make manifest what the king had seen the night before in his sleep, but had forgotten it. Accordingly, God, out of pity to those that were in danger, and out of regard to the wisdom of Daniel, made known to him the dream and its interpretation, that so the king might understand by him its signification also. When Daniel had obtained this knowledge from God, he arose very joyful, and told it his brethren, and made them glad, and to hope well that they should now preserve their lives, of which they despaired before, and had their minds full of nothing but the thoughts of dying. So when he had with them returned thanks to God, who had commiserated their youth, when it was day he came to Arioch, and desired him to bring him to the king, because he would discover to him that dream which he had seen the night before.

4. When Daniel was come in to the king, he excused himself first, that he did not pretend to be wiser than the other Chaldeans and magicians, when, upon their entire inability to discover his dream, he was undertaking to inform him of it; for this was not by his own skill, or on account of his having better cultivated his understanding than the rest; but he said, "God hath had pity upon us, when we were in danger of death, and when I prayed for the life of myself, and of those of my own nation, hath made manifest to me both the dream and the interpretation thereof; for I was not less concerned for thy glory than for the sorrow that we were by thee condemned to die, while thou didst so unjustly command men, both good and excellent in themselves, to be put to death, when thou enjoinedst them to do what was entirely above the reach of human wisdom, and requiredst of them what was only the work of God. Wherefore, as thou in thy sleep wast solicitous concerning those that should succeed thee in the government of the whole world, God was desirous to shew thee all those that should reign after thee, and to that end exhibited to thee the following dream:— Thou seemedst to see a great image standing before thee, the head of which proved to be of gold, the shoulders and arms of silver, and the belly and the thighs of brass, but the legs and the feet of iron; after which thou sawest a stone broken off from a mountain, which fell upon the image, and threw it down, and brake it to pieces, and did not permit any part of it to remain whole; but the gold, the silver, the brass, and the iron, became smaller than meal, which, upon the blast of a violent wind, was by force carried away, and scattered abroad; but the stone did increase to such a degree, that the whole earth beneath it seemed to be filled therewith. This is the dream which thou sawest, and its interpretation is as follows:—The head of gold denotes thee, and the kings of Babylon that have been before thee; but the two hands and arms signify this, that your government shall be dissolved by two kings; but another king that shall come from the west, armed with brass, shall destroy that government; and another government, that shall be like unto iron, shall put an end to the

power of the former, and shall have dominion over all the earth, on account of the nature of iron, which is stronger than that of gold, of silver, and of brass." Daniel did also declare the meaning of the stone to the king;* but I do not think proper to relate it, since I have only undertaken to describe things past or present, but not things that are future; yet if any one be so very desirous of knowing truth, as not to wave such points of curiosity, and cannot curb his inclination for understanding the uncertainties of futurity, and whether they will happen or not, let him be diligent in reading the book of Daniel, which he will find among the sacred writings.

5. When Nebuchadnezzar heard this, and recollected his dream, he was astonished at the nature of Daniel, and fell upon his face, and saluted Daniel in the manner that men worship God, and gave command that he should be sacrificed to as a god. And this was not all, for he also imposed the name of his own god upon him [Baltasar,] and made him and his kinsmen rulers of his whole kingdom; which kinsmen of his happened to fall into great danger by the envy and malice [of their enemies;] for they offended the king upon the occasion following:—He made an image of gold, the height of which was sixty cubits, and its breadth six cubits, and set it in the great plain of Babylon; and when he was going to dedicate the image, he invited the principal men out of all the earth that were under his dominions, and commanded them, in the first place, that when they should hear the sound of the trumpet, they should then fall down and worship the image; and he threatened, that those who did not do so, should be cast into a fiery fiurnace. When, therefore, all the rest, upon the hearing of the sound of the trumpet, worshipped the image, they relate that Daniel's kinsmen did not do it, because they would not transgress the laws of their country: so these men were convicted, and cast immediately into the fire, but were saved by Divine Providence, and after a surprising manner escaped death; for the fire did not touch them: and I suppose that it touched them not, as if it reasoned with itself that they were cast into it without any fault of theirs, and that, therefore, it was too weak to burn the young men when they were in it. This was done by the power of God, who made their bodies so far superior to the fire that it could not consume them. This it was which recommended them to the king as righteous men, and men beloved of God; on which account they continued in great esteem with him.

6. A little after this the king saw in his sleep again another vision; how he should fall from his dominion, and feed among the wild beasts; and that, when he had lived in this manner in the desert for seven years,† he should recover

his dominion again. When he had seen this dream, he called the magicians together again, and inquired of them about it, and desired them to tell him what it signified; but when none of them could find out the meaning of the dream, nor discover it to the king, Daniel was the only person that explained it; and as he foretold, so it came to pass; for after he had continued in the wilderness the forementioned interval of time, while no one durst attempt to seize his kingdom during those seven years, he prayed to God that he might recover his kingdom, and he returned to it. But let no one blame me for writing down every thing of this nature, as I find it in our ancient books; for as to that matter, I have plainly assured those that think me defective in any such point, or complain of my management, and have told them, in the beginning of this history, that I intended to do no more than translate the Hebrew books into the Greek language, and promised them to explain those facts, without adding anything to them of my own, or taking anything away from them.

CHAPTER XI

CONCERNING NEBUCHADNEZZAR AND HIS SUCCESSORS, AND HOW THEIR GOVERNMENT WAS DISSOLVED BY THE PERSIANS; AND WHAT THINGS BEFELL DANIEL IN MEDIA; AND WHAT PROPHECIES HE DELIVERED THERE

1. Now when king Nebuchadnezzar had reigned forty-three years,‡ he ended his life. He was an active man, and more fortunate than the kings that were before him. Now Berosus makes mention of his actions in the third book of his Chaldaic History, where he says thus:— "When his father Nebuchodonosor [Nabopollassar] heard that the governor whom he had set over Egypt, and the places about Cœlesyria and Phœnicia, had revolted from him, while he was not himself able any longer to undergo the hardships [of war,] he committed to his son Nebuchadnezzar, who was still but a youth, some parts of his army, and sent them against him. So when Nebuchadnezzar had given battle, and fought with the rebel, he beat him, and reduced the country from under his subjection, and made it a branch of his own kingdom; but about that time it happened that his father Nebuchodonosor [Nabopollassar] fell ill, and ended his life in the city of Babylon, when he had reigned twenty-one years;§ and when he was made sensible, as he was in a little time, that his father, Nebuchodonosor [Nabopollassar,] was dead, and having settled the affairs of Egypt, and the other countries, as also those that con-

---

* Of this most remarkable passage in Josephus, which he would not explain, but intimated to be a prophecy of futurity, and probably not safe for him to explain, as belonging to the destruction of the Roman empire by Jesus Christ, the true Messiah of the Jews, take the words of Havercamp: "Nor is this to be wondered at, that he would not now meddle with things future, for he had no mind to provoke the Romans, by speaking of the destruction of that city which they called the Eternal City."

† Since Josephus here explains the seven prophetic times which were to pass over Nebuchadnezzar to be seven years, we thence learn how he most probably must have understood those other parallel phrases, of "a time, times, and a half," of so many prophetic years also, though he withal lets us know, by his hint at the interpretation of the seventy weeks, as belonging to the fourth monarchy, and the destruction of Jerusalem by the Romans in the days of Josephus, that he did not think those years to be bare years, but rather days for

years; by which reckoning, and by which alone, could seventy weeks, or four hundred and ninety days, reach to the age of Josephus. But as to the truth of those seven years' banishment of Nebuchadnezzar from men, and his living so long among the beasts, the very small remains we have anywhere else of this Nebuchadnezzar, prevent our expectation of any other full account of it.

‡ These forty-three years for the duration of the reign of Nebuchadnezzar are the very same number in Ptolemy's canon.

§ These twenty-one years here ascribed to one Naboulassar, in the first book against Apion, or to Nabopollassar, the father of the great Nebuchadnezzar, are also the very same with those given in Ptolemy's canon. And note here, that what some modern chronologers say, that Nebuchadnezzar must have been a common name of other kings of Babylon, besides the great Nebuchadnezzar himself, is a groundless mistake, and destitute of all proper original authority.

cerned the captive Jews, and Phœnicians, and Syrians, and those of the Egyptian nations, and having committed the conveyance of them to Babylon to certain of his friends, together with the gross of his army, and the rest of their ammunition and provisions, he went himself hastily, accompanied with a few others, over the desert, and came to Babylon. So he took upon him the management of public affairs, and of the kingdom which had been kept for him by one that was the principal of the Chaldeans, and he received the entire dominions of his father, and appointed, that when the captives came, they should be placed as colonies, in the most proper places of Babylonia; but then he adorned the temple of Belus, and the rest of the temples, in a magnificent manner, with the spoils he had taken in the war. He also added another city to that which was there of old, and rebuilt it, that such as would besiege it hereafter might no more turn the course of the river, and thereby attack the city itself; he therefore built three walls round about the inner city, and three others about that which was the outer, and this he did with burnt brick. And after he had, after a becoming manner, walled the city, and adorned its gates gloriously, he built another palace before his father's palace, but so that they joined to it; to describe the vast height and immense riches of which, it would perhaps be too much for me to attempt; yet, as large and lofty as they were, they were completed in fifteen days.* He also erected elevated places for walking, of stone, and made it resemble mountains, and built it so that it might be planted with all sorts of trees. He also erected what was called a pensile paradise, because his wife was desirous to have things like her own country, she having been bred up in the palaces of Media." Megasthenes also, in his fourth book of his accounts of India, makes mention of these things, and thereby endeavours to shew that this king [Nebuchadnezzar] exceeded Hercules in fortitude, and in the greatness of his actions; for he saith, that he conquered a great part of Libya. Diocles also, in the second book of his Accounts of Persia, mentions this king; as does Philostratus, in his Accounts both of India and Phœnicia, say, that this king besieged Tyre thirteen years, while at the same time Ethbaal reigned at Tyre. These are all the histories that I have met with concerning this king.

2. But now, after the death of Nebuchadnezzar, Evil-Merodach his son succeeded in the kingdom, who immediately set Jeconiah at liberty, and esteemed him amongst his most intimate friends. He also gave him many presents, and made him honourable above the rest of the kings that were in Babylon; for his father had not kept his faith with Jeconiah, when he voluntarily delivered up himself to him, with his wives and children, and his whole kindred, for the sake of his country, that it might not be taken by siege, and utterly destroyed, as we said before. When Evil-Merodach was dead, after a reign of eighteen years, Neglissar his son took the government, and retained it forty years, and then ended his life; and after him the succession in the kingdom came to his son Labosordacus, who continued in

it in all but nine months; and when he was dead, it came to Baltasar,† who by the Babylonians was called Naboandelus; against him did Cyrus, the king of Persia, and Darius, the king of Media, make war; and when he was besieged in Babylon, there happened a wonderful and prodigious vision. He was sat down at supper in a large room, and there were a great many vessels of silver, such as were made for royal entertainments, and he had with him his concubines and his friends; whereupon he came to a resolution, and commanded that those vessels of God which Nebuchadnezzar had plundered out of Jerusalem, and had not made use of, but had put them into his own temple, should be brought out of that temple. He also grew so haughty as to proceed to use them in the midst of his cups, drinking out of them, and blaspheming against God. In the meantime, he saw a hand proceed out of the wall, and writing upon the wall certain syllables; at which sight, being disturbed, he called the magicians and Chaldeans together, and all that sort of men that are among these barbarians, and were able to interpret signs and dreams, that they might explain the writing to him. But when the magicians said they could discover nothing, nor did understand it, the king was in great disorder of mind, and under great trouble, at this surprising accident; so he caused it to be proclaimed through all the country, and promised, that to him who could explain the writing, and give the signification couched therein, he would give him a golden chain for his neck, and leave to wear a purple garment, as did the kings of Chaldea, and would bestow on him the third part of his own dominions. When this proclamation was made, the magicians ran together more earnestly, and were very ambitious to find out the importance of the writing; but still hesitated about it as much as before. Now when the king's grandmother saw him cast down at this accident,‡ she began to encourage him, and to say, that there was a certain captive who came from Judea, a Jew by birth, but brought away thence by Nebuchadnezzar when he had destroyed Jerusalem, whose name was Daniel, a wise man, and one of great sagacity in finding out what was impossible for others to discover, and what was known to God alone; who brought to light and answered such questions to Nebuchadnezzar as no one else was able to answer when they were consulted. She therefore desired that he would send for him, and inquire of him concerning the writing, and to condemn the unskilfulness of those that could not find their meaning, and this, although what God signified thereby should be of a melancholy nature.

3. When Baltasar heard this, he called for Daniel: and when he had discoursed to him what he had learned concerning him and his wisdom,

---

* These fifteen days for finishing such vast buildings at Babylon seem too absurd to be supposed to be the true number. Josephus assures us, that the walls of so much a smaller city as Jerusalem were two years and four months in building by Nehemiah, who yet hastened the work all that he could. I should think one hundred and fifteen days, or a year and fifteen days, much more proportionable to so great a work.

† It is here remarkable that Josephus, without the knowledge of Ptolemy's canon, should call the same king, whom he himself here styles Baltasar, or Belshazzar, from the Babylonian god Bel, Neboandelus also; and in the first book against Apion, from the same citation out of Berosus, Nabonnedon, from the Babylonian god Nabo, or Nebo. This last is not remote from the original pronunciation itself in Ptolemy's canon, Nabonadius; for both the place of this king in that canon, as the last of the Assyrian or Babylonian kings, and the number of years of his reign, seventeen, the same in both, demonstrate that it is one and the same king that is meant by them all.

‡ This grandmother, or mother of Baltasar, the queen-dowager of Babylon, for she is distinguished from his queen, seems to have been the famous Nitocris, who fortified Babylon against the Medes and Persians.

and how a divine spirit was with him, and that he alone was fully capable of finding out what others would never have thought of, he desired him to declare to him what this writing meant: that if he did so, he would give him leave to wear purple, and to put a chain of gold about his neck, and would bestow on him the third part of his dominion, as an honorary reward for his wisdom, that thereby he might become illustrious to those who saw him, and who inquired upon what occasion he obtained such honours. But Daniel desired that he would keep his gifts to himself; for what is the effect of wisdom and of divine revelation admits of no gifts, and bestows its advantages on petitioners freely; but that still he would explain the writing to him; which denoted that he should soon die, and this because he had not learnt to honour God, and not to admit things above human nature, by what punishments his progenitor had undergone for the injuries he had offered to God; and because he had quite forgotten how Nebuchadnezzar was removed to feed among wild beasts for his impieties, and did not recover his former life among men and his kingdom, but upon God's mercy to him, after many supplications and prayers; who did thereupon praise God all the days of his life, as one of almighty power, and who takes care of mankind. [He also put him in mind] how he had greatly blasphemed against God, and made use of his vessels amongst his concubines: that therefore God saw this, and was angry with him, and declared by his writing beforehand what a sad conclusion of his life he should come to. And he explained the writing thus:—"MANEH. This, if it be expounded in the Greek language, may signify a *Number*, because God hath numbered so long a time for thy life, and for thy government, and that there remains but a small portion. THEKEL. This signifies a *Weight*, and means that God hath weighed thy kingdom in a balance, and finds it going down already. PHARES. This also, in the Greek tongue, denotes a *Fragment;* God will therefore break thy kingdom in pieces, and divide it among the Medes and Persians."

4. When Daniel had told the king that the writing upon the wall signified these events, Baltasar was in great sorrow and affliction, as was to be expected, when the interpretation was so heavy upon him. However, he did not refuse what he had promised Daniel, although he were become a foreteller of misfortunes to him, but bestowed it all upon him: as reasoning thus, that what he was to reward was peculiar to himself, and to fate, and did not belong to the prophet, but that it was the part of a good and a just man to give what he had promised, although the events were of a melancholy nature. Accordingly, the king determined so to do. Now, after a little while, both himself and the city were taken by Cyrus, the king of Persia, who fought against him; for it was Baltasar, under whom Babylon was taken, when he had reigned seventeen years. And this is the end of the posterity of king Nebuchadnezzar, as history informs us; but when Babylon was taken by Darius, and when he, with his kinsman Cyrus, had put an end to the dominion of the Babylonians, he was sixty-two years old. He was the son of Astyages, and had another name among the Greeks. Moreover, he took Daniel the prophet, and carried him with him into Media, and honoured him very greatly, and kept him with him; for he was one of the three presidents whom he set over his three hundred and sixty provinces; for into so many did Darius part them.

5. However, while Daniel was in so great dignity, and in so great favour with Darius, and was alone intrusted with everything by him, as having somewhat divine in him, he was envied by the rest: for those that see others in greater honour than themselves with kings, envy them: and when those that were grieved at the great favour Daniel was in with Darius, sought for an occasion against him, he afforded them no occasion at all, for he was above all the temptations of money, and despised bribery, and esteemed it a very base thing to take anything by way of reward, even when it might be justly given him, he afforded those that envied him not the least handle for an accusation. So when they could find nothing for which they might calumniate him to the king, nothing that was shameful or reproachful, and thereby deprive him of the honour he was in with him, they sought for some other method whereby they might destroy him. When therefore they saw that Daniel prayed to God three times a day, they thought they had gotten an occasion, by which they might ruin him; so they came to Darius, and told him, that "the princes and governors had thought proper to allow the multitude a relaxation for thirty days, that no one might offer a petition or prayer either to himself, or to the gods, but that he who shall transgress this decree shall be cast into a den of lions, and there perish."

6. Whereupon the king, not being acquainted with their wicked design, nor suspecting that it was a contrivance of theirs against Daniel, said he was pleased with this decree of theirs, and he promised to confirm what they desired; he also published an edict to promulgate to the people that decree which the princes had made. Accordingly, all the rest took care not to transgress those injunctions, and rested in quiet; but Daniel had no regard to them, but, as he was wont, he stood and prayed to God in the sight of them all: but the princes having met with the occasion they so earnestly sought to find against Daniel, came presently to the king, and accused him, that Daniel was the only person that transgressed the decree, whilst not one of the rest durst pray to their gods. This discovery they made, not because of his impiety, but because they had watched him, and observed him out of envy; for supposing that Darius did thus out of a greater kindness to him than they expected, and that he was ready to grant him a pardon for this contempt of his injunctions, and envying this very pardon to Daniel, they did not become more favourable to him, but desired he might be cast into the den of lions, according to the law. So Darius, hoping that God would deliver him, and that he would undergo nothing that was terrible by the wild beasts, bade him bear this accident cheerfully; and when he was cast into the den, he put his seal to the stone that lay upon the mouth of the den, and went his way, but he passed all the night without food and without sleep, being in great distress for Daniel; but when it was day, he got up, and came to the den, and found the seal entire, which he had left the stone sealed withal; he also opened the seal, and cried out, and called to Daniel, and asked him if he were alive; and as soon as he heard the king's voice, and said that he had suffered no harm, the king gave order that he should be drawn up out of the den. Now when his enemies saw that Daniel had suffered nothing which was terrible, they would not own that he was preserved by God, and by his providence; but they said, that the lions had been filled full with food, and on that account it was, as they supposed, that the lions would not touch Daniel.

MENE MENE TEKEL
UPHARSIN

BALTASAR'S FEAST

nor come to him; and this they alleged to the king; but the king, out of an abhorrence of their wickedness, gave order that they should throw in a great deal of flesh to the lions; and when they had filled themselves, he gave further order that Daniel's enemies should be cast into the den, that he might learn whether the lions, now they were full, would touch them or not; and it appeared plain to Darius, after the princes had been cast to the wild beasts, that it was God who preserved Daniel,* for the lions spared none of them, but tore them all to pieces, as if they had been very hungry, and wanted food. I suppose, therefore, it was not their hunger, which had been a little before satisfied with abundance of flesh, but the wickedness of these men that provoked them [to destroy the princes :] for if it so please God, that wickedness might, by even those irrational creatures, be esteemed a plain foundation for their punishment.

7. When, therefore, those that had intended thus to destroy Daniel by treachery were themselves destroyed, king Darius sent [letters] over all the country, and praised that God whom Daniel worshipped, and said that he was the only true God, and had all power. He had also Daniel in very great esteem, and made him the principal of his friends. Now when Daniel was become so illustrious and famous, on account of the opinion men had that he was beloved of God, he built a tower at Ecbatana, in Media : it was a most elegant building, and wonderfully made, and it is still remaining, and preserved to this day; and to such as see it, it appears to have been lately built, and to have been no older than that very day when any one looks upon it, it is so fresh,† flourishing, and beautiful, and no way grown old in so long a time; for buildings suffer the same as men do, they grow old as well as they, and by numbers of years their strength is dissolved, and their beauty withered. Now they bury the kings of Media, of Persia, and Parthia, in this tower, to this day; and he who was intrusted with the care of it, was a Jewish priest; which thing is also observed to this day. But it is fit to give an account of what this man did, which is most admirable to hear; for he was so happy as to have strange revelations made to him, and those as to one of the greatest of the prophets, insomuch that while he was alive he had the esteem and applause both of the kings and of the multitude : and now he is dead, he retains a remembrance that will never fail, for the several books that he wrote and left behind him are still read by us till this time; and from them we believe that Daniel conversed with God; for he did not only prophecy of future events, as did the other prophets, but he also determined the time of their accomplishment; and while the prophets used to foretell misfortunes, and on that account were disagreeable both to the kings and to the multitude, Daniel was to them a prophet of good things, and this to such a degree, that, by the agreeable nature of his predictions, he

procured the good-will of all men; and by the accomplishment of them, he procured the belief of their truth, and the opinion of [a sort of] divinity for himself, among the multitude. He also wrote and left behind him what made manifest the accuracy and undeniable veracity of his predictions; for he saith, that when he was in Susa, the metropolis of Persia, and went out into the field with his companions, there was, on the sudden, a motion and concussion of the earth, and that he was left alone by himself, his friends flying away from him, and that he was disturbed, and fell on his face, and on his two hands, and that a certain person touched him, and at the same time bade him rise, and see what would befall his countrymen after many generations. He also related, that when he stood up, he was shewn a great ram, with many horns growing out of his head, and that the last was higher than the rest : that after this he looked to the west, and saw a he-goat carried through the air from that quarter; that he rushed upon the ram with violence, and smote him twice with his horns, and overthrew him to the ground, and trampled upon him : that afterwards he saw a very great horn growing out of the head of the he-goat; and that when it was broken off, four horns grew up that were exposed to each of the four winds, and he wrote that out of them arose another lesser horn, which, as he said, waxed great; and that God shewed to him, that it should fight against his nation, and take their city by force, and bring the temple-worship to confusion, and forbid the sacrifices to be offered for one thousand two hundred and ninety-six days. Daniel wrote that he saw these visions in the plain of Susa; and he hath informed us that God interpreted the appearance of this vision after the following manner :—He said that the ram signified the kingdoms of the Medes and Persians, and the horns those kings that were to reign in them; and that the last horn signified the last king, and that he should exceed all the kings in riches and glory; that the he-goat signified that one should come and reign from the Greeks, who should twice fight with the Persian, and overcome him in battle, and should receive his entire dominion; that by the great horn which sprang out of the forehead of the he-goat was meant the first king; and that the springing up of four horns upon its falling off, and the conversion of every one of them to the four quarters of the earth, signified the successors that should arise after the death of the first king, and the partition of the kingdom among them, and that they should be neither his children nor of his kindred that should reign over the habitable earth for many years; and that from among them there should arise a certain king that should overcome our nation and their laws, and should take away our political government, and should spoil the temple, and forbid the sacrifices to be offered for three years' time." And indeed it so came to pass, that our nation suffered these things under Antiochus Epiphanes, according to Daniel's vision, and what he wrote many years before they came to pass. In the very same manner Daniel also wrote concerning the Roman government, and that our country should be made desolate by them. All these things did this man leave in writing, as God had shewed them to him, insomuch that such as read his prophecies, and see how they have been fulfilled, would wonder at the honour wherewith God honoured Daniel; and may thence discover how the Epicureans are in an error, who cast providence out of human life, and do not believe that God takes care of the affairs of the world, nor

---

* It is no way improbable that Daniel's enemies might suggest this reason to the king, why the lions did not meddle with him, and that they might suspect the king's kindness to Daniel had procured these lions to be so filled beforehand, and that thence it was that he encouraged Daniel to submit to this experiment, in hopes of coming off safe; and that this was the true reason of making so terrible an experiment upon those his enemies, and all their families, (Dan. vi. 24.)

† What Josephus here says, that the stones of the sepulchres of the kings of Persia at this tower, or those perhaps of the same sort that are now commonly called the *Ruins of Persepolis*, continued so entire and unaltered in his days, as if they were lately put there, is confirmed by Reland.

that the universe is governed and continued in being by that blessed and immortal nature, but say that the world is carried along of its own accord, without a ruler and a curator; which, were it destitute of a guide to conduct, as they imagine, it would be like ships without pilots, which we see drowned by the winds, or like chariots without drivers, which are overturned; so would the world be dashed to pieces by its being carried without a Providence, and so perish and come to nought. So that, by the forementioned predictions of Daniel, those men seem to me very much to err from the truth, who determine that God exercises no providence over human affairs; for if that were the case, that the world went on by mechanical necessity, we should not see that all things would come to pass according to his prophecy. Now, as to myself, I have so described these matters as I have found them and read them; but if any one is inclined to another opinion about them, let him enjoy his different sentiments without any blame from me.

BOOK XI

CONTAINING THE INTERVAL OF TWO HUNDRED AND FIFTY-THREE YEARS FIVE MONTHS

FROM THE FIRST OF CYRUS TO THE DEATH OF ALEXANDER THE GREAT

CHAPTER I

HOW CYRUS, KING OF THE PERSIANS, DELIVERED THE JEWS OUT OF BABYLON, AND SUFFERED THEM TO RETURN TO THEIR OWN COUNTRY, AND TO BUILD THEIR TEMPLE; FOR WHICH WORK HE GAVE THEM MONEY

1. IN the first year of the reign of Cyrus,[*] which was the seventieth from the day that our people were removed out of their own land into Babylon, God commiserated the captivity and calamity of these poor people, according as he had foretold to them by Jeremiah the prophet, before the destruction of the city, that after they had served Nebuchadnezzar and his posterity, and after they had undergone that servitude seventy years, he would restore them again to the land of their fathers, and they should build their temple, and enjoy their ancient prosperity; and these things God did afford them; for he stirred up the mind of Cyrus, and made him write this throughout all Asia:—"Thus saith Cyrus the King:—Since God Almighty hath appointed me to be king of the habitable earth, I believe that he is that God which the nation of the Israelites worship; for indeed he foretold my name by the prophets, and that I should build him a house at Jerusalem, in the country of Judea."

2. This was known to Cyrus by his reading the book which Isaiah left behind him of his prophecies; for this prophet said that God had spoken thus to him in a secret vision:—"My will is, that Cyrus, whom I have appointed to be king over many and great nations, send back my people to their own land, and build my temple." This was foretold by Isaiah one hundred and forty years before the temple was demolished. Accordingly, when Cyrus read this, and admired the divine power, an earnest desire and ambition seized upon him to fulfil what was so written; so he called for the most eminent Jews that were in Babylon, and said to them, that he gave them leave to go back to their own country, and to rebuild their city Jerusalem,[†] and the temple of God, for that he would be their assistant, and that he would write to the rulers and governors that were in the neighbourhood of their country of Judea, that they should contribute to them gold and silver for the building of the temple, and, besides that, beasts for their sacrifices.

3. When Cyrus had said this to the Israelites, the rulers of the two tribes of Judah and Benjamin, with the Levites and priests, went in haste to Jerusalem, yet did many of them stay at Babylon, as not willing to leave their possessions; and when they were come thither, all the king's friends assisted them, and brought in, for the building of the temple, some gold, and some silver, and some a great many cattle and horses. So they performed their vows to God, and offered the sacrifices that had been accustomed of old time; I mean this upon the rebuilding of their city, and the revival of the ancient practices relating to their worship. Cyrus also sent back to them the vessels of God which king Nebuchadnezzar had pillaged out of the temple, and carried to Babylon. So he committed these things to Mithridates, the treasurer, to be sent away, with an order to give them to Sanabasar, that he might keep them till the temple was built; and when it was finished, he might deliver them to the priests and rulers of the multitude, in order to their being restored to the temple. Cyrus also sent an epistle to the governors that were in Syria, the contents whereof here follow:—

" KING CYRUS TO SISINNES AND SATHRABUZANES, SENDETH GREETING

"I have given leave to as many of the Jews that dwell in my country as please to return to their own country, and to rebuild their city, and to build the temple of God at Jerusalem, on the

---

* This Cyrus is called God's Shepherd by Xenophon, as well as by Isaiah, (Isa. xliv. 28.)

† This leave to build Jerusalem, and this epistle of Cyrus to the same purpose, are most unfortunately omitted in all our copies, but this best and completest copy of Josephus; and by such omission the famous prophecy of Isaiah, (Isa. xliv. 28,) could not hitherto be demonstrated from the sacred history to have been completely fulfilled, I mean as to that part of it which concerned his giving leave or commission for rebuilding the city of Jerusalem as distinct from the temple, the rebuilding of which is alone permitted or directed in the decree of Cyrus, in all our copies.

same place where it was before. I have also sent my treasurer, Mithridates, and Zorobabel, the governor of the Jews, that they may lay the foundations of the temple, and may build it sixty cubits high, and of the same latitude, making three edifices of polished stones, and one of the wood of the country, and the same order extends to the altar whereon they offer sacrifices to God. I require also, that the expenses for these things may be given out of my revenues. Moreover, I have also sent the vessels which king Nebuchadnezzar pillaged out of the temple, and have given them to Mithridates the treasurer, and to Zorobabel the governor of the Jews, that they may have them carried to Jerusalem, and may restore them to the temple of God. Now their number is as follows:—Fifty chargers of gold and five hundred of silver; forty Thericlean cups of gold, and five hundred of silver; fifty basons of gold, and five hundred of silver; thirty vessels for pouring [the drink-offerings,] and three hundred of silver, thirty vials of gold, and two thousand four hundred of silver; with a thousand other large vessels. I permit them to have the same honour which they were used to have from their forefathers, as also for their small cattle, and for wine and oil, two hundred and five thousand and five hundred drachmæ; and for wheat-flour twenty thousand and five hundred artabæ: and I give order that these expenses shall be given them out of the tributes due from Samaria. The priests shall also offer these sacrifices according to the laws of Moses in Jerusalem; and when they offer them, they shall pray to God for the preservation of the king and of his family, that the kingdom of Persia may continue. But my will is, that those who disobey these injunctions, and make them void, shall be hung upon a cross, and their substance brought into the king's treasury." And such was the import of this epistle. Now the number of those that came out of captivity to Jerusalem, were forty-two thousand four hundred and sixty-two.

CHAPTER II

HOW, UPON THE DEATH OF CYRUS, THE JEWS WERE HINDERED IN BUILDING OF THE TEMPLE BY THE CUTHEANS AND THE NEIGHBOURING GOVERNORS; AND HOW CAMBYSES ENTIRELY FORBADE THE JEWS TO DO ANY SUCH THING

1. WHEN the foundations of the temple were laying, and when the Jews were very zealous about building it, the neighbouring nations, and especially the Cutheans, whom Shalmanezer, king of Assyria, had brought out of Persia and Media, and had planted in Samaria, when he carried the people of Israel captive, besought the governors, and those that had the care of such affairs, that they would interrupt the Jews, both in the rebuilding of their city, and in the building of their temple. Now as these men were corrupted by them with money, they sold the Cutheans their interest for rendering this building a slow and a careless work, for Cyrus who was busy about other wars, knew nothing of all this; and it so happened, that when he had led his army against the Massagetæ, he ended his life.* But when Cambyses, the son

of Cyrus, had taken the kingdom, the governors in Syria, and Phœnicia, and in the countries of Ammon, and Moab, and Samaria, wrote an epistle to Cambyses; whose contents were as follow:—"To our Lord Cambyses. We thy servants, Rathumus the historiographer, and Semellius the scribe, and the rest that are thy judges in Syria and Phœnicia, send greeting: It is fit, O king, that thou shouldest know that those Jews who were carried to Babylon, are come into our country, and are building that rebellious and wicked city, and its market-places, and setting up its walls, and raising up the temple: know, therefore, that when these things are finished, they will not be willing to pay tribute, nor will they submit to thy commands, but will resist kings, and will choose rather to rule over others, than be ruled over themselves. We therefore thought it proper to write to thee, O king, while the works about the temple are going on so fast, and not to overlook this matter, that thou mayest search into the books of thy fathers, for thou wilt find in them that the Jews have been rebels, and enemies to kings, as hath their city been also, which, for that reason, hath been till now laid waste. We thought proper also to inform thee of this matter, because thou mayest otherwise perhaps be ignorant of it, that if this city be once inhabited, and be entirely encompassed with walls, thou wilt be excluded from the passage to Cœlesyria and Phœnicia."

2. When Cambyses had read the epistle, being naturally wicked, he was irritated at what they told him; and wrote back to them as follows: "Cambyses, the king, to Rathumus, the historiographer, to Beeltethemus, to Semellius the scribe, and the rest that are in commission, and dwelling in Samaria and Phœnicia, after this manner: I have read the epistle that was sent from you; and I gave order that the books of my forefathers should be searched into; and it is there found, that this city hath always been an enemy to kings, and its inhabitants have raised seditions and wars. We also are sensible that their kings have been powerful and tyrannical, and have exacted tribute of Cœlesyria and Phœnicia: wherefore I give order, that the Jews shall not be permitted to build that city, lest such mischief as they used to bring upon kings be greatly augmented." When this epistle was read, Rathumus, and Semellius the scribe, and their associates, got suddenly on horseback, and made haste to Jerusalem; they also brought a great company with them, and forbade the Jews to build the city and the temple. Accordingly, these works were hindered from going on till the second year of the reign of Darius, for nine years more; for Cambyses reigned six years, and within that time overthrew Egypt, and when he was come back, he died at Damascus.

CHAPTER III

HOW, AFTER THE DEATH OF CAMBYSES, AND THE SLAUGHTER OF THE MAGI, BUT UNDER THE REIGN OF DARIUS, ZOROBABEL WAS SUPERIOR TO THE REST IN THE SOLUTION OF PROBLEMS, AND THEREBY OBTAINED THIS FAVOUR OF THE KING, THAT THE TEMPLE SHOULD BE BUILT

1. AFTER the slaughter of the magi, who,

---

* Josephus here follows Herodotus, and those that related how Cyrus made war with the Scythians and Massagetes, near the Caspian Sea, and perished in it; while Xenophon's account, which appears never to have been seen by Josephus, that Cyrus died in peace

in his own country in Persia, is attested to by the writers of the affairs of Alexander the Great, when they agree that he found Cyrus's sepulchre at Pasargadæ, near Persepolis.

upon the death of Cambyses, attained the government of the Persians for a year, those families who were called the seven families of the Persians, appointed Darius, the son of Hystaspes, to be their king. Now he, while he was a private man, had made a vow to God, that if he came to be king, he would send all the vessels of God that were in Babylon to the temple at Jerusalem. Now it so fell out, that about this time Zorobabel, who had been made governor of the Jews that had been in captivity, came to Darius, from Jerusalem: for there had been an old friendship between him and the king. He was also, with two others, thought worthy to be guard of the king's body; and obtained that honour which he hoped for.

2. Now, in the first year of the king's reign, Darius feasted those that were about him, and those born in his house, with the rulers of the Medes, and princes of the Persians, and the toparchs of India and Ethiopia, and the generals of the armies of his hundred and twenty-seven provinces; but when they had eaten and drunken to satiety and abundantly, they every one departed to go to bed at their own houses, and Darius the king went to bed; but after he had rested a little part of the night, he awaked, and not being able to sleep any more, he fell into conversation with the three guards of his body, and promised, that to him who should make an oration about points that he should inquire of, such as should be most agreeable to truth, and to the dictates of wisdom, he would grant it as a reward for his victory, to put on a purple garment, and to drink in cups of gold, and to sleep upon gold, and to have a chariot with bridles of gold, and a head-tire of fine linen, and a chain of gold about his neck, and to sit next to himself, on account of his wisdom:—"And," says he, "he shall be called my cousin." Now when he had promised to give them these gifts, he asked the first of them, "Whether wine was not the strongest?"—the second, "Whether kings were not such?"—and the third, "Whether women were not such? or whether truth was not the strongest of all?" When he had proposed that they should make their inquiries about these problems, he went to rest; but in the morning he sent for his great men, his princes, and toparchs of Persia and Media, and set himself down in the place where he used to give audience, and bid each of the guards of his body to declare what they thought proper concerning the proposed questions, in the hearing of them all.

3. Accordingly, the first of them began to speak of the strength of wine; and demonstrated it thus: "When," said he, "I am to give my opinion of wine, O you men, I find that it exceeds everything, by the following indications: it deceives the mind of those that drink it, and reduces that of the king to the same state with that of the orphan, and he who stands in need of a tutor; and erects that of the slave to the boldness of him that is free; and that of the needy becomes like that of the rich man, for it changes and renews the souls of men when it gets into them; and it quenches the sorrow of those that are under calamities, and makes men forget the debts they owe to others, and makes them think themselves to be of all men the richest; it makes them talk of no small things, but of talents, and such other things as become wealthy men only; nay more, it makes them insensible of their commanders and of their kings, and takes away the remembrance of their friends and companions, for it arms men even against those that are dearest to them, and

makes them appear the greatest strangers to them; and when they are become sober, and they have slept out their wine in the night, they arise without knowing anything they have done in their cups. I take these for signs of power, and by them discover that wine is the strongest and most insuperable of all things.

4. As soon as the first had given the forementioned demonstrations of the strength of wine, he left off; and the next to him began to speak about the strength of a king, and demonstrated that it was the strongest of all, and more powerful than anything else that appears to have any force or wisdom. He began his demonstration after the following manner; and said, "They are men who govern all things: they force the earth and the sea to become profitable to them in what they desire, and over these men do kings rule, and over them they have authority. Now those who rule over that animal which is of all the strongest and most powerful, must needs deserve to be esteemed insuperable in power and force. For example, when these kings command their subjects to make wars, and undergo dangers, they are hearkened to; and when they send them against their enemies, their power is so great that they are obeyed. They command men to level mountains, and to pull down walls and towers; nay, when they are commanded to be killed and to kill, they submit to it, that they may not appear to transgress the king's commands; and when they have conquered, they bring what they have gained in war to the king. Those also who are not soldiers, but cultivate the ground, and plough it, after they have endured the labour, and all the inconveniences of such works of husbandry, when they have reaped and gathered in their fruits, they bring tributes to the king; and whatsoever it is which the king says or commands, it is done of necessity, and that without any delay, while he in the meantime is satiated with all sorts of food and pleasures, and sleeps in quiet. He is guarded by such as watch, and such as are, as it were, fixed down to the place through fear; for no one dares leave him, even when he is asleep, nor does any one go away and take care of his own affairs, but he esteems this one thing the only work of necessity, to guard the king; and accordingly to this he wholly addicts himself. How then can it be otherwise, but that it must appear that the king exceeds all in strength, while so great a multitude obeys his injunctions?"

5. Now when this man had held his peace, the third of them, who was Zorobabel, began to instruct them about women, and about truth, who said thus: "Wine is strong, as is the king also, whom all men obey, but women are superior to them in power; for it was a woman that brought the king into the world; and for those that plant the vines and make the wine, they are women who bear them, and bring them up; nor indeed is there anything which we do not receive from them; for these women weave garments for us, and our household affairs are by their means taken care of, and preserved in safety; nor can we live separate from women; and when we have gotten a great deal of gold and silver, and any other thing that is of great value, and deserving regard, and see a beautiful woman, we leave all these things, and with open mouth fix our eyes upon her countenance, and are willing to forsake what we have, that we may enjoy her beauty, and procure it to ourselves. We also leave father and mother, and the earth that nourishes us, and frequently forget our dearest friends, for the sake of women;

nay, we are so hardy as to lay down our lives for them; but what will chiefly make you take notice of the strength of women is this that follows: Do not we take pains, and endure a great deal of trouble, and that both by land and sea, and when we have procured somewhat as the fruit of our labours, do not we bring them to the women, as to our mistresses, and bestow them upon them? Nay, I once saw the king, who is lord of so many people, smitten on the face by Apame, the daughter of Rabases Themasius his concubine, and his diadem taken from him, and put upon her own head, while he bore it patiently; and when she smiled he smiled, and when she was angry he was sad; and according to the change of her passions, he flattered his wife, and drew her to reconciliation by the great humiliation of himself to her, if at any time he saw her displeased at him."

6. And when the princes and rulers looked one upon another, he began to speak about truth; and he said, "I have already demonstrated how powerful women are; but both these women themselves, and the king himself, are weaker than truth: for although the earth be large, and the heaven high, and the course of the sun swift, yet are all these moved according to the will of God, who is true and righteous, for which cause we also ought to esteem truth to be the strongest of all things, and that what is unrighteous is of no force against it. Moreover, all things else that have any strength are mortal, and short-lived, but truth is a thing that is immortal and eternal. It affords us not indeed such a beauty as will wither away by time, nor such riches as may be taken away by fortune, but righteous rules and laws. It distinguishes them from injustice, and puts what is unrighteous to rebuke."*

7. So when Zorobabel had left off his discourse about truth, and the multitude had cried out aloud that he had spoken the most wisely, and that it was truth alone that had immutable strength, and such as never would wax old, the king commanded that he should ask for somewhat over and above what he had promised, for that he would give it him because of his wisdom, and that prudence wherein he exceeded the rest; "and thou shalt sit with me," said the king, "and shalt be called my cousin." When he had said this, Zorobabel put him in mind of the vow he had made in case he should ever have the kingdom. Now this vow was, "to rebuild Jerusalem, and to build therein the temple of God, as also to restore the vessels which Nebuchadnezzar had pillaged, and carried to Babylon. And this," said he, "is that request which thou now permittest me to make, on account that I have been judged to be wise and understanding."

8. So the king was pleased with what he had said, and arose and kissed him; and wrote to the toparchs, and governors, and enjoined them to conduct Zorobabel and those that were going with him to build the temple. He also sent

letters to those rulers that were in Syria and Phœnicia to cut down and carry cedar-trees from Lebanon to Jerusalem, and to assist him in building the city. He also wrote to them, that all the captives who should go to Judea should be free; and he prohibited his deputies and governors to lay any king's taxes upon the Jews: he also permitted that they should have all the land which they could possess themselves of without tributes. He also enjoined the Idumeans and Samaritans, and the inhabitants of Cœlesyria, to restore those villages which they had taken from the Jews; and that, besides all this, fifty talents should be given them for the building of the temple. He also permitted them to offer their appointed sacrifices, and that whatsoever the high priest and the priests wanted, and those sacred garments wherein they used to worship God, should be made at his own charges; and that the musical instruments which the Levites used in singing hymns to God should be given them. Moreover, he charged them, that portions of land should be given to those that guarded the city and the temple, as also a determinate sum of money every year for their maintenance: and withal he sent the vessels. And all that Cyrus intended to do before him, relating to the restoration of Jerusalem, Darius also ordained should be done accordingly.

9. Now when Zorobabel had obtained these grants from the king, he went out of the palace, and looking up to heaven, he began to return thanks to God for the wisdom he had given him, and the victory he had gained thereby, even in the presence of Darius himself: for, said he, "I had not been thought worthy of these advantages, O Lord, unless thou had been favourable to me." When, therefore, he had returned these thanks to God for the present circumstances he was in, and had prayed to him to afford him the like favour for the time to come, he came to Babylon, and brought the good news to his countrymen of what grants he had procured for them from the king; who, when they heard the same, gave thanks also to God that he restored the land of their forefathers to them again. So they betook themselves to drinking and eating, and for seven days they continued feasting, and kept a festival, for the rebuilding and restoration of their country: after this they chose themselves rulers, who should go up to Jerusalem, out of the tribes of their forefathers, with their wives, and children, and cattle, who travelled to Jerusalem with joy and pleasure, under the conduct of those whom Darius sent along with them, and making a noise with songs, and pipes, and cymbals. The rest of the Jewish multitude also besides accompanied them with rejoicing.

10. And thus did these men go, a certain and determinate number out of every family, though I do not think it proper to recite particularly the names of those families, that I may not take off the minds of my readers from the connexion of the historical facts, and make it hard for them to follow the coherence of my narration: but the sum of those that went up, above the age of twelve years, of the tribes of Judah and Benjamin, was four hundred and sixty-two myriads and eight thousand;† the Levites were seventy-four; the number of the women and children mixed together was forty thousand seven hundred and forty-two; and besides these, there were

* The reader is to note, that although the speeches or papers of these three of the king's guard are much the same in the third book of Esdras, chap. iii. and iv., as they are here in Josephus, yet that the introduction of them is entirely different, while in Esdras the whole is related as the contrivance of the three of the king's guards themselves; and even the mighty rewards are spoken of as proposed by themselves, and the speeches are related to have been delivered by themselves to the king in writing, while all is contrary in Josephus. I need not say whose account is the most probable, the matters speak for themselves; and there can be no doubt but Josephus's history is here to be very much preferred before the other.

† This strange reading in Josephus of four millions instead of forty thousand, is a gross error, and ought to be corrected from Ezra ii. 64. 1 Esd. v. 40, and Neh. vii. 66, who all agree that the general sum was but about forty-two thousand three hundred and sixty.

singers of the Levites one hundred and twenty-eight, and porters one hundred and ten, and of the sacred ministers three hundred and ninety-two; there were also others besides these, who said they were Israelites, but were not able to shew their genealogies, six hundred and sixty-two : some there were also who were expelled out of the number and honour of the priests, as having married wives whose genealogies they could not produce, nor where they found in the genealogies of the Levites and priests; they were about five hundred and twenty-five; the multitude also of servants who followed those that went up to Jerusalem seven thousand three hundred and thirty-seven; singing men and singing women were two hundred and forty-five; the camels were four hundred and thirty-five; the beasts used to the yoke were five thousand five hundred and twenty-five; and the governors of all this multitude who numbered were Zorobabel, the son of Salathiel, of the posterity of David, and of the tribe of Judah; and Jeshua, the son of Josedek the high priest; and besides these there were Mordecai and Serebeus, who were distinguished from the multitude, and were rulers, who also contributed a hundred pounds of gold and five thousand of silver. By this means, therefore, the priests and the Levites, and a certain part of the entire people of the Jews that were in Babylon, came and dwelt in Jerusalem; but the rest of the multitude returned every one to their own countries.

CHAPTER IV

HOW THE TEMPLE WAS BUILT, WHILE THE CUTHEANS ENDEAVOURED IN VAIN TO OBSTRUCT THE WORK

1. Now in the seventh month after they were departed out of Babylon, both Jeshua the high priest, and Zorobabel the governor, sent messengers every way round about, and gathered those that were in the country together to Jerusalem universally, who came very gladly thither. He then built the altar on the same place it had formerly been built, that they might offer the appointed sacrifices upon it to God, according to the laws of Moses. But while they did this, they did not please the neighbouring nations, who all of them bare an ill will to them. They also celebrated the Feast of Tabernacles at that time, as the legislator had ordained concerning it; and after that they offered sacrifices, and what were called the daily sacrifices, and the oblations proper for the Sabbaths, and for all the holy festivals. Those also that had made vows performed them, and offered their sacrifices from the first day of the seventh month. They also began to build the temple, and gave a great deal of money to the masons and to the carpenters, and what was necessary for the maintenance of the workmen. The Sidonians also were very willing and ready to bring the cedar-trees from Libanus, to bind them together, and to make a united float of them, and to bring them to the port of Joppa, for that was what Cyrus had commanded at first, and what was now done at the command of Darius.

2. In the second year of their coming to Jerusalem, as the Jews were there, in the second month, the building of the temple went on apace; and when they had laid its foundations on the first day of the second month of that second year, they set, as overseers of the work, such Levites as were full twenty years old; and

Jeshua and his sons and brethren, and Codmiel, the brother of Judas, the son of Aminadab, with his sons; and the temple, by the great diligence of those that had the care of it, was finished sooner than any one would have expected. And when the temple was finished, the priests, adorned with their accustomed garments, stood with their trumpets, while the Levites, and the sons of Asaph, stood and sung hymns to God, according as David first of all appointed them to bless God. Now the priests and Levites, and the elder part of the families, recollecting with themselves how much greater and more sumptuous the old temple had been, seeing that now made how much inferior it was, on account of their poverty, to that which had been built of old, considered with themselves how much their happy state was sunk below what it had been of old, as well as their temple. Hereupon they were disconsolate, and not able to contain their grief, and proceeded so far as to lament and shed tears on those accounts; but the people in general were contented with their present condition; and because they were allowed to build them a temple, they desired no more, and neither regarded nor remembered, nor indeed at all tormented themselves with the comparison of that and the former temple, as if this were below their expectations. But the wailing of the old men, and of the priests, on account of the deficiency of this temple, in their opinion, if compared with that which had been domolished, overcame the sounds of the trumpets and the rejoicing of the people.

3. But when the Samaritans, who were still enemies to the tribes of Judah and Benjamin, heard the sound of the trumpets, they came running together, and desired to know what was the occasion of this tumult; and when they perceived that it was from the Jews who had been carried captive to Babylon, and were rebuilding their temple, they came to Zorobabel and to Jeshua, and to the heads of the families, and desired that they would give them leave to build the temple with them, and to be partners with them in building it; for they said, "We worship their God, and especially pray to him, and are desirous of their religious settlement, and this ever since Shalmanezer, the king of Assyria, transplanted us out of Cuthah and Media to this place." When they said thus, Zorobabel, and Jeshua the high priest, and the heads of the families of the Israelites, replied to them, that it was impossible for them to permit them to be their partners, whilst they [only] had been appointed to build that temple at first by Cyrus, and now by Darius, although it was indeed lawful for them to come and worship there if they pleased, and that they could allow them nothing, but in common with them, which was common to them with all other men, to come to their temple, and worship God there.

4. When the Cutheans heard this, for the Samaritans have that appellation, they had indignation at it, and persuaded the nations of Syria to desire of the governors, in the same manner as they had done formerly in the days of Cyrus, and again in the days of Cambysses afterwards, to put a stop to the temple, and to endeavour to delay and protract the Jews in their zeal about it. Now at this time Sisinnes, the governor of Syria and Phœnicia, and Sathrabuzanes, with certain others, came up to Jerusalem, and asked the rulers of the Jews, by whose grant it was that they built the temple in this manner, since it was more like a citadel than a temple? and for what reason it was that they built cloisters and walls, and those strong ones too,

about the city? To which Zorobabel and Jeshua the high priest replied, that they were the servants of God Almighty: that this temple was built for him by a king of theirs that lived in great prosperity, and one that exceeded all men in virtue; and that it continued a long time, but that because of their fathers' impiety towards God, Nebuchadnezzar, king of the Babylonians and of the Chaldeans, took their city by force, and destroyed it, and pillaged the temple, and burnt it down, and transplanted the people whom he had made captives, and removed them to Babylon; that Cyrus, who, after him, was king of Babylonia and Persia, wrote to them to build the temple, and committed the gifts and vessels, and whatsoever Nebuchadnezzar had carried out of it, to Zorobabel, and Mithridates the treasurer; and gave order to have them carried to Jerusalem, and to have them restored to their own temple when it was built; for he had sent to them to have it done speedily, and commanded Sanabassar to go up to Jerusalem, and to take care of the building of the temple; who, upon receiving that epistle from Cyrus, came and immediately laid its foundations:—"and although it hath been in building from that time to this, it hath not yet been finished, by reason of the malignity of our enemies. If therefore you have a mind, and think it proper, write this account to Darius, that when he hath consulted the records of the kings, he may find that we have told you nothing that is false about this matter."

5. When Zorobabel and the high priest had made this answer, Sisinnes, and those that were with him, did not resolve to hinder the building, until they had informed king Darius of all this. So they immediately wrote to him about these affairs; but as the Jews were now under terror, and afraid lest the king should change his resolution as to the building of Jerusalem, and of the temple, there were two prophets at that time amongst them, Haggai and Zechariah, who encouraged them, and bade them be of good cheer, and to suspect no discouragement from the Persians, for that God foretold this to them. So, in dependence on those prophets, they applied themselves earnestly to building, and did not intermit one day.

6. Now Darius, when the Samaritans had written to him, and in their epistle had accused the Jews how they fortified the city, and built the temple more like to a citadel than a temple; and said, that their doings were not expedient for the king's affairs; and besides, they shewed the epistle of Cambyses, wherein he forbade them to build the temple: and when Darius thereby understood that the restoration of Jerusalem was not expedient for his affairs, and when he had read the epistle that was brought him from Sisinnes and those that were with him, he gave order that what concerned these matters should be sought for among the royal records. Whereupon a book was found at Ecbatana, in the tower that was in Media, wherein was written as follows:—"Cyrus the king, in the first year of his reign, commanded that the temple should be built in Jerusalem; and the altar in height threescore cubits, and its breadth of the same, with three edifices of polished stone, and one edifice of stone of their own country; and he ordained that the expenses of it should be paid out of the king's revenue. He also commanded that the vessels which Nebuchadnezzar had pillaged, [out of the temple,] and had carried to Babylon, should be restored to the people of Jerusalem; and that the care of these things should belong to Sanabassar, the governor and

president of Syria and Phœnicia, and to his associates, that they may not meddle with that place, but may permit the servants of God, the Jews and their rulers, to build the temple. He also ordained that they should assist them in the work; and that they should pay to the Jews, out of the tribute of the country where they were governors, on account of the sacrifices, bulls, and rams, and lambs, and kids of the goats, and fine flour, and oil, and wine, and all other things that the priests should suggest to them; and that they should pray for the preservation of the king, and of the Persians: and that for such as transgressed any of these orders thus sent to them, he commanded that they should be caught, and hung upon a cross, and their substance confiscated to the king's use. He also prayed to God against them, that if any one attempted to hinder the building of the temple, God would strike him dead, and thereby restrain his wickedness."

7. When Darius had found this book among the records of Cyrus, he wrote an answer to Sisinnes and his associates, whose contents were these:—"King Darius to Sisinnes the governor, and to Sathrabuzanes, sendeth greeting. Having found a copy of this epistle among the records of Cyrus, I have sent it to you; and I will that all things be done as therein written.—Farewell." So when Sisinnes, and those that were with him, understood the intention of the king, they resolved to follow his directions entirely for the time to come. So they forwarded the sacred works, and assisted the elders of the Jews, and the princes of the Sanhedrim; and the structure of the temple was with great diligence brought to a conclusion, by the prophecies of Haggai and Zechariah, according to God's commands, and by the injunctions of Cyrus and Darius the kings. Now the temple was built in seven years' time: and in the ninth year of the reign of Darius, on the twenty-third day of the twelfth month, which is by us called *Adar*, but by the Macedonians *Dystrus*, the priests and the Levites, and the other multitude of the Israelites, offered sacrifices, as the renovation of their former prosperity after their captivity, and because they had now the temple rebuilt, a hundred bulls, two hundred rams, four hundred lambs, and twelve kids of the goats, according to the number of their tribes, (for so many are the tribes of the Israelites;) and this last for the sins of every tribe. The priests also, and the Levites, set the porters at every gate according to the laws of Moses. The Jews also built the cloisters of the inner temple that were round about the temple itself.

8. And as the feast of unleavened bread was at hand, in the first month, which according to the Macedonians, is called *Xanthicus*, but according to us *Nisan*, all the people ran together out of the villages to the city, and celebrated the festival, having purified themselves, with their wives and children, according to the law of their country; and they offered the sacrifice which was called the *Passover*, on the fourteenth day of the same month, and feasted seven days, and spared for no cost, but offered whole burnt-offerings to God, and performed sacrifices of thanksgiving, because God had led them again to the land of their fathers, and to the laws thereto belonging, and had rendered the mind of the king of Persia favourable to them. So these men offered the largest sacrifices on these accounts, and used great magnificence in the worship of God, and dwelt in Jerusalem, and made use of a form of government that was aristocratical, but mixed with an oligarchy, for the high

priests were at the head of their affairs, until the posterity of the Asamoneans set up kingly government; for before their captivity, and the dissolution of their polity, they at first had kingly government from Saul and David for five hundred and thirty-two years, six months, and ten days: but before those kings, such rulers governed them as were called Judges and Monarchs. Under this form of government, they continued for more than five hundred years, after the death of Moses, and of Joshua their commander.—And this is the account I had to give of the Jews who had been carried into captivity, but were delivered from it in the times of Cyrus and Darius.

9.* But the Samaritans, being evil and enviously disposed to the Jews, wrought them many mischiefs, by reliance on their riches, and by their pretence that they were allied to the Persians, on account that thence they came; and whatsoever it was that they were enjoined to pay the Jews by the king's order out of their tributes for the sacrifices, they would not pay it. They had also the governors favourable to them, and assisting them for that purpose; nor did they spare to hurt them, either by themselves or by others, as far as they were able. So the Jews determined to send an embassage to king Darius, in favour of the people of Jerusalem, and in order to accuse the Samaritans. The ambassadors were Zorobabel, and four others of the rulers; and as soon as the king knew from the ambassadors the accusations and complaints they brought against the Samaritans, he gave them an epistle to be carried to the governors and council of Samaria; the contents of which epistle were these:—"King Darius to Tanganas and Sambabas, the governors of the Samaritans; to Sadraces and Bobelo, and the rest of their fellow-servants that are in Samaria: Zorobabel, Ananias, and Mordecai, the ambassadors of the Jews, complain of you, that you obstruct them in the building of the temple, and do not supply them with the expenses which I commanded you to do for the offering of their sacrifices. My will therefore is this: That upon the reading of this epistle, you supply them with whatsoever they want for their sacrifices, and that out of the royal treasury, of the tributes of Samaria, as the priests shall desire, that they may not leave off their offering daily sacrifices, nor praying to God for me and the Persians;"—and these were the contents of that epistle.

CHAPTER V

HOW XERXES, THE SON OF DARIUS, WAS WELL-DISPOSED TO THE JEWS; AS ALSO CONCERNING ESDRAS AND NEHEMIAH

1. UPON the death of Darius, Xerxes his son took the kingdom; who, as he inherited his father's kingdom, so did he inherit his piety towards God, and honour of him; for he did all things suitably to his father relating to divine worship, and he was exceeding friendly to the Jews. Now about this time a son of Jeshua, whose name was Joacim, was the high priest. Moreover, there was now in Babylon a righteous man, and one that enjoyed a great reputation among the multitude; he was the principal priest of the people, and his name was Esdras. He was very skilful in the laws of Moses, and was well acquainted with king Xerxes. He had determined to go up to Jerusalem, and to

take with him some of those Jews that were in Babylon; and he desired that the king would give him an epistle to the governors of Syria, by which they might know who he was. Accordingly, the king wrote the following epistle to those governors:—"Xerxes, king of kings, to Esdras the priest, and reader of the divine law, greeting. I think it agreeable to that love which I bear to mankind, to permit those of the Jewish nation who are so disposed, as well as those of the priests and Levites that are in our kingdom, to go together to Jerusalem. Accordingly, I have given command for that purpose; and let every one that hath a mind go, according as it hath seemed good to me, and to my seven counsellors, and this in order to their review of the affairs of Judea, to see whether they be agreeable to the law of God. Let them also take with them those presents which I and my friends have vowed, with all that silver and gold which is found in the country of the Babylonians, as dedicated to God, and let all this be carried to Jerusalem, to God for sacrifices. Let it also be lawful for thee and thy brethren to make as many vessels of silver and gold as thou pleasest. Thou shalt also dedicate those holy vessels which have been given thee, and as many more as thou hast a mind to make, and shalt take the expenses out of the king's treasury. I have moreover written to the treasurers of Syria and Phœnicia, that they take care of those affairs that Esdras the priest, and reader of the laws of God, is sent about; and that God may not be at all angry with me, or with my children, I grant all that is necessary for sacrifices to God, according to the law, as far as a hundred cori of wheat; and I enjoin you not to lay any treacherous imposition, or any tributes, upon their priests or Levites, or sacred singers, or porters, or sacred servants, or scribes of the temple; and do thou, O Esdras, appoint judges according to the wisdom [given thee] of God, and those such as understand the law, that they may judge in all Syria and Phœnicia; and do thou instruct those also which are ignorant of it, that if any one of thy countrymen transgress the law of God, or that of the king, he may be punished, as not transgressing it out of ignorance, but as one that knows it indeed, but boldly despises and contemns it; and such may be punished by death, or by paying fines. Farewell."

2. When Esdras had received this epistle, he was very joyful, and began to worship God, and confessed that he had been the cause of the king's great favour to him, and that for the same reason he gave all the thanks to God. So he read the epistle at Babylon to those Jews that were there; but he kept the epistle itself, and sent a copy of it to all those of his own nation that were in Media; and when these Jews had understood what piety the king had towards God, and what kindness he had for Esdras, they were all greatly pleased; nay, many of them took their effects with them, and came to Babylon, as very desirous of going down to Jerusalem; but then the entire body of the people of Israel remained in that country; wherefore there are but two tribes in Asia and Europe subject to the Romans, while the ten tribes are beyond Euphrates till now, and are an immense multitude, and not to be estimated by numbers. Now there came a great number of priests, and Levites, and porters, and sacred singers, and sacred servants, to Esdras. So he gathered those that were in the captivity together beyond Euphrates, and stayed there three days, and ordained a fast for them, that they might make their prayers to God for their preservation, that they might suffer no misfor-

---

* The history contained in this section is entirely wanting in all our copies, both of Ezra and Esdras.

tunes by the way, either from their enemies, or from any other ill accident; for Esdras had said beforehand, that he had told the king how God would preserve them, and so he had not thought fit to request that he would send horsemen to conduct them. So when they had finished their prayers, they removed from Euphrates, on the twelfth day of the first month of the seventh year of the reign of Xerxes, and they came to Jerusalem on the fifth month of the same year. Now Esdras presented the sacred money to the treasurers, who were of the family of the priests, of silver six hundred and fifty talents, vessels of gold twenty talents, vessels of brass, that was more precious gold,* twelve talents by weight; for these presents had been made by the king and his counsellors, and by all the Israelites that stayed at Babylon. So when Esdras had delivered these things to the priests, he gave to God, as the appointed sacrifices of whole burnt-offerings, twelve bulls on account of the common preservation of the people, ninety rams, seventy-two lambs, and twelve kids of the goats, for the remission of sins. He also delivered the king's epistle to the king's officers, and to the governors of Cœlesyria and Phœnicia; and as they were under the necessity of doing what was enjoined by him, they honoured our nation, and were assistant to them in all their necessities.

3. Now these things were truly done under the conduct of Esdras; and he succeeded in them, because God esteemed him worthy of the success of his conduct, on account of his goodness and righteousness. But some time afterward there came some persons to him, and brought an accusation against certain of the multitude, and of the priests and Levites, who had transgressed their settlement, and dissolved the laws of their country, by marrying strange wives, and had brought the family of the priests into confusion. These persons desired him to support the laws, lest God should take up a general anger against them all, and reduce them to a calamitous condition again. Hereupon he rent his garment immediately, out of grief, and pulled off the hair of his head and beard, and cast himself upon the ground, because this crime had reached the principal men among the people; and considering that if he should enjoin them to cast out their wives, and the children they had by them, he should not be hearkened to, he continued lying upon the ground. However, all the better sort came running to him, who also themselves wept, and partook of the grief he was under for what had been done. So Esdras rose up from the ground, and stretched out his hands towards heaven, and said that he was ashamed to look towards it, because of the sins which the people had committed, while they had cast out of their memories what their fathers had undergone on account of their wickedness; and he besought God, who had saved a seed and a remnant out of the calamity and captivity they had been in, and had restored them again to Jerusalem, and to their own land, and had obliged the king of Persia to have compassion on them, that he would also forgive them their sins they had now committed, which, though they deserved death, yet was it agreeable to the mercy of God to remit even to these the punishment due to them.

4. After Esdras had said this, he left off praying; and when all those that came to him with their wives and children were under lamentation, one, whose name was Jechonias, a principal man in Jerusalem, came to him, and said, that they had sinned in marrying strange wives; and he persuaded him to adjure them all to cast those wives out, and the children born of them; and that those should be punished who would not obey the law. So Esdras hearkened to this advice, and made the heads of the priests, and of the Levites, and of the Israelites, swear that they would put away those wives and children, according to the advice of Jechonias; and when he had received their oaths, he went in haste out of the temple into the chamber of Johanan, the son of Eliasib, and as he had hitherto tasted nothing at all for grief, so he abode there that day; and when proclamation was made, that all those of the captivity should gather themselves together to Jerusalem, and those that did not meet there in two or three days should be banished from the multitude, and that their substance should be appropriated to the uses of the temple, according to the sentence of the elders, those that were of the tribes of Judah and Benjamin came together in three days—viz., on the twentieth day of the ninth month, which, according to the Hebrews, is called *Tebeth*, and according to the Macedonians, *Apelleius*. Now, as they were sitting in the upper room of the temple, where the elders also were present, but were uneasy because of the cold, Esdras stood up and accused them, and told them that they had sinned in marrying wives that were not of their own nation; but that now they would do a thing both pleasing to God and advantageous to themselves, if they would put those wives away. Accordingly, they all cried out that they would do so. That, however, the multitude was great, and that the season of the year was winter, and that this work would require more than one or two days. "Let their rulers, therefore, [said they,] and those that have married strange wives, come hither at a proper time, while the elders of every place, that are in common, to estimate the number of those that have thus married, are to be there also." Accordingly, this was resolved on by them; and they began the inquiry after those that had married strange wives on the first day of the tenth month, and continued the inquiry to the first day of the next month, and found a great many of the posterity of Jeshua the high priest, and of the priests and Levites, and Israelites, who had a greater regard to the observation of the law than to their natural affection,† and immediately cast out their wives, and the children which were born of them; and in order to appease God, they offered sacrifices, and slew rams, as oblations to him; but it does not seem to me to be necessary to set down the names of these men. So when Esdras had reformed this sin about the marriages of the forementioned persons, he reduced that practice to purity, so that it continued in that state for the time to come.

5. Now when they kept the feast of tabernacles in the seventh month,‡ and almost all

---

* This kind of brass or copper, or rather mixture of gold and brass or copper, was called *aurichalcum*, and was of old esteemed the most precious of all metals.

† This procedure of Esdras, after the Babylonish captivity, of reducing the Jewish marriages to the strictness of the law of Moses, without any regard to the greatness of those who had broken it, and without regard to natural affection for their heathen wives, and their children by them, deserves to be imitated in all attempts for reformation among Christians, the contrary conduct having ever been the bane of true religion, while political motives are suffered to take the place of the divine laws, and so the blessing of God is forfeited, and the Church still suffered to continue corrupt from one generation to another.

‡ This Jewish feast of tabernacles was imitated in several heathen solemnities.

the people were come together to it, they went up to the open part of the temple, to the gate which looked eastward, and desired Esdras that the laws of Moses might be read to them. Accordingly, he stood in the midst of the multitude and read them; and this he did from morning to noon. Now, by hearing the laws read to them, they were instructed to be righteous men for the present and for the future; but as for their past offences, they were displeased at themselves, and proceeded to shed tears on their account, as considering with themselves, that if they had kept the law, they had endured none of these miseries which they had experienced; but when Esdras saw them in that disposition, he bade them go home and not weep, for that it was a festival, and they ought not to weep thereon, for that it was not lawful so to do. He exhorted them rather to proceed immediately to feasting, and to do what was suitable to a feast, and what was agreeable to a day of joy; but to let their repentance and sorrow for their former sins be a security and a guard to them, that they fell no more into the like offences. So upon Esdras' exhortation they began to feast: and when they had so done for eight days, in their tabernacles, they departed to their own homes, singing hymns to God, and returning thanks to Esdras for his reformation of what corruptions had been introduced into their settlement. So it came to pass, that after he had obtained this reputation among the people, he died an old man, and was buried in a magnificent manner at Jerusalem. About the same time it happened also that Joacim, high priest, died; and his son Eliasib succeeded in the high priesthood.

6. Now there was one of those Jews who had been carried captive, who was cupbearer to king Xerxes; his name was Nehemiah. As this man was walking before Susa, the metropolis of the Persians, he heard some strangers that were entering the city, after a long journey, speaking to one another in the Hebrew tongue; so he went to them and asked from whence they came; and when their answer was, that they came from Judea, he began to inquire of them again in what state the multitude was, and in what condition Jerusalem was: and when they replied that they were in a bad state,* for that their walls were thrown down to the ground, and that the neighbouring nations did a great deal of mischief to the Jews, while in the daytime they overran the country and pillaged it, and in the night did them mischief, insomuch that not a few were led away captive out of the country, and out of Jerusalem itself, and that the roads were in the daytime found full of dead men. Hereupon Nehemiah shed tears, out of commiseration of the calamities of his countrymen; and, looking up to heaven, he said, "How long, O Lord, wilt thou overlook our nation, while it suffers so great miseries, and while we are made the prey and the spoil of all men?" And while he stayed at the gate, and lamented thus, one told him that the king was going to sit down to supper; so he made haste, and went as he was, without washing himself, to minister to the king in his office of cupbearer: but as the king was very pleasant after supper, and more cheerful than usual, he cast his eyes on Nehemiah, and seeing him look sad, he asked him why he was sad. Whereupon he prayed to God to give him favour, and afford the power of persuading by his words; and said, "How can I, O king,

appear otherwise than thus, and not be in trouble, while I hear that the walls of Jerusalem, the city where are the sepulchres of my fathers, are thrown down to the ground, and that its gates are consumed by fire? But do thou grant me the favour to go and build its wall, and to finish the building of the temple." Accordingly the king gave him a signal, that he freely granted him what he asked; and told him, that he should carry an epistle to the governors, that they might pay him due honour, and afford him whatsoever assistance he wanted, and as he pleased. "Leave off thy sorrow, then," said the king, "and be cheerful in the performance of thy office hereafter." So Nehemiah worshipped God, and gave the king thanks for his promise, and cleared up his sad and cloudy countenance, by the pleasure he had from the king's promises. Accordingly, the king called for him the next day, and gave him an epistle to be carried to Adeus, the governor of Syria, and Phœnicia, and Samaria; wherein he sent to him to pay due honour to Nehemiah, and to supply him with what he wanted for his building.

7. Now when he was come to Babylon, and had taken with him many of his countrymen, who voluntarily followed him, he came to Jerusalem in the twenty and fifth year of the reign of Xerxes; and when he had shewn the epistle to God,† he gave them to Adeus, and to the other governors. He also called together all the people to Jerusalem, and stood in the midst of the temple, and made the following speech to them: —"You know, O Jews, that God hath kept our fathers, Abraham, Isaac, and Jacob, in mind continually; and for the sake of their righteousness hath not left off the care of you. Indeed, he hath assisted me in gaining this authority of the king to raise up our wall, and finish what is wanting of the temple. I desire you, therefore, who well know the ill-will our neighbouring nations bear to us, and that when once they are made sensible that we are in earnest about building, they will come upon us, and contrive many ways of obstructing our works, that you will, in the first place, put your trust in God, as in him that will assist us against their hatred, and to intermit building neither night nor day, but to use all diligence, and to hasten on the work, now we have this especial opportunity for it." When he had said this, he gave order that the rulers should measure the wall, and part the work of it among the people, according to their villages and cities, as every one's ability should require. And when he had added this promise, that he himself, with his servants, would assist them, he dissolved the assembly. So the Jews prepared for the work: that is the name they are called by from the day that they came up from Babylon, which is taken from the tribe of Judah, which came first to these places, and thence both they and the country gained that appellation.

8. But now when the Ammonites, and Moabites, and Samaritans, and all that inhabited Cœlesyria, heard that the building went on apace, they took it heinously, and proceeded to lay snares for them, and to hinder their intentions. They also slew many of the Jews, and sought how they might destroy Nehemiah himself, by hiring some of the foreigners to kill him. They also put the Jews in fear, and disturbed

---

* This miserable condition of the Jews must have been after the death of Esdras, and before Nehemiah came commissioned to build the walls of Jerusalem.

† This shewing Xerxes' epistles to God, is very like the laying open the epistles of Sennacherib before him also by Hezekiah, (2 Kings xix. 14; Isa. xxxvii. 14;) although this last was for a memorial, to put him in mind of the enemies, in order to move the divine compassion, and the present as a token of gratitude for mercies already received.

them, and spread abroad rumours, as if many nations were ready to make an expedition against them, by which means they were harassed, and had almost left off the building. But none of these things could deter Nehemiah from being diligent about the work; he only set a number of men about him as a guard to his body, and so unweariedly persevered therein, and was insensible of any trouble, out of his desire to perfect this work. And thus did he attentively, and with great forecast, take care of his own safety; not that he feared death, but of this persuasion, that if he were dead, the walls for his citizens would never be raised. He also gave orders that the builders should keep their ranks, and have their armour on while they were building. Accordingly, the mason had his sword on, as well as he that brought the materials for building. He also appointed that their shields should lie very near them; and he placed trumpeters at every five hundred feet, and charged them, that if their enemies appeared, they should give notice of it to the people, that they might fight in their armour, and their enemies might not fall upon them naked. He also went about the compass of the city by night, being never discouraged, neither about the work itself, nor about his own diet and sleep, for he made no use of those things for his pleasure, but of necessity. And this trouble he underwent for two years and four months; * for in so long a time was the wall built, in the twenty-eighth year of the reign of Xerxes, in the ninth month. Now when the walls were finished, Nehemiah and the multitude offered sacrifices to God for the building of them; and they continued in feasting eight days. However, when the nations which dwelt in Syria heard that the building of the wall was finished, they had indignation at it; but when Nehemiah saw that the city was thin of people, he exhorted the priests and the Levites, that they would leave the country, and remove themselves to the city, and there continue; and he built them houses at his own expense; and he commanded that part of the people who were employed in cultivating the land, to bring the tithes of their fruits to Jerusalem, that the priests and Levites having whereof they might live perpetually, might not leave the divine worship; who willingly hearkened to the constitutions of Nehemiah, by which means the city Jerusalem came to be fuller of people than it was before. So when Nehemiah had done many other excellent things, and things worthy of commendation, in a glorious manner, he came to a great age, and then died. He was a man of a good and a righteous disposition, and very ambitious to make his own nation happy; and he hath left the walls of Jerusalem as an eternal monument for himself. Now this was done in the days of Xerxes.

CHAPTER VI

CONCERNING ESTHER, AND MORDECAI, AND HAMAN; AND HOW, IN THE REIGN OF ARTAXERXES, THE WHOLE NATION OF THE JEWS WAS IN DANGER OF PERISHING

1. AFTER the death of Xerxes, the kingdom came to be transferred to his son Cyrus, whom the Greeks called Artaxerxes. When this man had obtained the government over the Persians, the whole nation of the Jews,† with their wives and children, were in danger of perishing; the occasion whereof we shall declare in a little time; for it is proper, in the first place, to explain somewhat relating to this king, and how he came to marry a Jewish wife, who was herself of the royal family also, and who is related to have saved our nation; for when Artaxerxes had taken the kingdom, and had set governors over the hundred twenty and seven provinces, from India even unto Ethiopia, in the third year of his reign he made a costly feast for his friends, and for the nations of Persia, and for their governors, such a one as was proper for a king to make, when he had a mind to make a public demonstration of his riches, and this for a hundred and fourscore days; after which he made a feast for other nations, and for their ambassadors, at Shushan, for seven days. Now this feast was ordered after the manner following :—He caused a tent to be pitched, which was supported by pillars of gold and silver, with curtains of linen and purple spread over them, that it might afford room for many ten thousands to sit down. The cups with which the waiters ministered were of gold, and adorned with precious stones, for pleasure and for sight. He also gave order to the servants, that they should not force them to drink, by bringing them wine continually, as is the practice of the Persians, but to permit every one of the guests to enjoy himself according to his own inclination. Moreover, he sent messengers through the country, and gave order that they should have a remission of their labours, and should keep a festival many days, on account of his kingdom. In like manner did Vashti the queen gather her guests together, and made them a feast in the palace. Now the king was desirous to shew her, who exceeded all other women in beauty, to those that feasted with him, and he sent some to command her to come to his feast. But she, out of regard to the laws of the Persians, which forbid the wives to be seen by strangers, did not go to the king;‡ and though he oftentimes sent the eunuchs to her, she did nevertheless stay away, and refused to come, till the king was so much irritated, that he brake up the entertainment, and rose up, and called for those seven who had the interpretation of the laws committed to them, and accused his wife, and said, that he had been affronted by her, because that when she was frequently called by him to his feast, she did not obey him once. He therefore gave order that they should inform him what could be done by the law against her. So one of them, whose name was Memucan, said that this affront was offered not to him alone, but to all the Persians, who were in danger of leading their lives very ill with their wives, if they must be thus despised by them; for that none of their wives would have any reverence for their husbands, if they had " such an example of arrogance in the queen to-

---

* It may not be improper to remark here, with what an unusual accuracy Josephus determines these years of Xerxes, in which the wall of Jerusalem were built—viz., that Nehemiah came with this commission in the 25th of Xerxes; that the walls were two years and four months in building; and that they were finished on the 28th of Xerxes. It may also be remarked further, that Josephus hardly ever mentions more than one infallible astronomical character, I mean an eclipse of the moon, and this a little before the death of Herod the Great.

† Since some sceptical persons are willing to discard this book of Esther as no true history, I shall venture to say, that almost all the objections against this book of Esther are gone at once, if we place this history under Artaxerxes Longimanus, as do both the Septuagint interpreters and Josephus.

‡ If the Chaldee paraphrast be in the right, that Artaxerxes intended to shew Vashti to his guests naked, it is no wonder at all that she would not submit to such an indignity; but still if it were not so gross as that, yet it might, in the king's cups, be done in a way so indecent, as the Persian laws would not then bear, no more than the common laws of modesty.

wards thee, who rulest over all." Accordingly, he exhorted him to punish her, who had been guilty of so great an affront to him, after a severe manner; and when he had so done, to publish to the nations what had been decreed about the queen. So the resolution was to put Vashti away, and to give her dignity to another woman.

2. But the king having been fond of her, he did not well bear a separation, and yet by the law he could not admit of a reconciliation, so he was under trouble, as not having it in his power to do what he desired to do: but when his friends saw him so uneasy, they advised him to cast the memory of his wife, and his love for her, out of his mind, but to send abroad over all the habitable earth, and to search out for comely virgins, and to take her whom he should best like for his wife, because his passion for his former wife would be quenched by the introduction of another, and the kindness he had for Vashti would be withdrawn from her, and be placed on her that was with him. Accordingly, he was persuaded to follow this advice, and gave order to certain persons to chose out of the virgins that were in his kingdom those that were esteemed the most comely. So when a great number of these virgins were gathered together, there was found a damsel in Babylon, whose parents were both dead, and she was brought up with her uncle Mordecai, for that was her uncle's name. This uncle was of the tribe of Benjamin, and was one of the principal persons among the Jews. Now it proved that this damsel, whose name was Esther, was the most beautiful of all the rest, and that the grace of her countenance drew the eyes of the spectators principally upon her: so she was committed to one of the eunuchs to take the care of her; and she was very exactly provided with sweet odours, in great plenty, and with costly ointments, such as her body required to be anointed withal; and this was used for six months by the virgins, who were in number four hundred; and when the eunuch thought they had been sufficiently purified, in the forementioned time, and were now fit to go to the king's bed, he sent one to be with the king every day. So when he had accompanied with her, he sent her back to the eunuch; and when Esther had come to him, he was pleased with her, and fell in love with the damsel, and married her, and made her his lawful wife, and kept a wedding-feast for her on the twelfth month of the seventh year of his reign, which was called Adar. He also sent *angari*, as they are called, or messengers, unto every nation, and gave orders that they should keep a feast for his marriage, while he himself treated the Persians and the Medes, and the principal men of the nations, for a whole month, on account of this his marriage. Accordingly, Esther came to his royal palace, and he set a diadem on her head; and thus was Esther married, without making mention to the king what nation she was derived from. Her uncle also removed from Babylon to Shushan, and dwelt there, being every day about the palace, and inquiring how the damsel did, for he loved her as though she had been his own daughter.

3. Now the king had made a law,[*] that none of his own people should approach him unless they were called, when he sat upon his throne; and men, with axes in their hands, stood round about his throne, in order to punish such as approached to him without being called. How-

ever, the king sat with a golden sceptre in his hand, which he held out when he had a mind to save any one of those that approached to him without being called; and he who touched it was free from danger. But of this matter we have discoursed sufficiently.

4. Some time after this [two eunuchs] Bigthan and Teresh, plotted against the king; and Barnabazus, the servant of one of the eunuchs, being by birth a Jew, was acquainted with their conspiracy, and discovered it to the queen's uncle; and Mordecai, by means of Esther, made the conspirators known to the king. This troubled the king; but he discovered the truth, and hanged the eunuchs upon a cross, while at that time he gave no reward to Mordecai, who had been the occasion of his preservation. He only bade the scribe to set down his name in the records, and bade him stay in the palace, as an intimate friend of the king.

5. Now there was one Haman, the son of Amedatha, by birth an Amalekite, that used to go in to the king; and the foreigners and Persians worshipped him, as Artaxerxes had commanded that such honour should be paid to him; but Mordecai was so wise, and so observant of his own country's laws, that he would not worship the man.[†] When Haman observed this, he inquired whence he came; and when he understood that he was a Jew, he had indignation at him, and said within himself, that whereas the Persians, who were free men, worshipped him, this man, who was no better than a slave, does not vouchsafe to do so. And when he desired to punish Mordecai, he thought it too small a thing to request of the king that he alone might be punished; he rather determined to abolish the whole nation, for he was naturally an enemy to the Jews, because the nation of the Amalekites, of which he was, had been destroyed by them. Accordingly, he came to the king, and accused them, saying, "There is a certain wicked nation, and it is dispersed over all the habitable earth that was under his dominion; a nation separate from others, unsociable, neither admitting the same sort of divine worship that others do, nor using laws like to the laws of others, at enmity with thy people, and with all men, both in their manners and practices. Now, if thou wilt be a benefactor to thy subjects, thou wilt give order to destroy them utterly, and not leave the least remains of them, nor preserve any of them, either for slaves or for captives." But that the king might not be damnified by the loss of the tributes which the Jews paid him, Haman promised to give him out of his own estate forty thousand talents whensoever he pleased; and he said he would pay this money very willingly, that the kingdom might be freed from such a misfortune.

6. When Haman had made this petition, the king both forgave him the money, and granted him the men, to do what he would with them. So Haman, having gained what he desired, sent out immediately a decree, as from the king, to all nations, the contents whereof were these:— "Artaxerxes, the great king, to the rulers of the hundred and twenty-seven provinces, from India to Ethiopia, sends this writing. Whereas I have governed many nations, and obtained the

---

[*] Herodotus says that this law was first enacted by Deioces. Thus also stood guards, with their axes, about the throne of Tenus, or Tenudus, that the offender might by them be punished immediately.

[†] Whether this adoration required of Mordecai to Haman were by him deemed too like the adoration due only to God, or whether he thought he ought to pay no sort of adoration to an Amalekite, which nation had been such great sinners as to have been universally devoted to destruction by God himself, or whether both causes concurred, cannot now, I doubt, be certainly determined.

dominions of all the habitable earth, according to my desire, and have not been obliged to do anything that is insolent or cruel to my subjects by such my power, but have shewed myself mild and gentle, by taking care of their peace and good order, and have sought how they might enjoy those blessings for all time to come; and whereas I have been kindly informed by Haman, who, on account of his prudence and justice, is the first in my esteem, and in dignity, and only second to myself, for his fidelity and constant good-will to me, that there is an ill-natured nation intermixed with all mankind, that is averse to our laws, and not subject to kings, and of a different conduct of life from others, that hateth monarchy, and of a disposition that is pernicious to our affairs; I give order that these men, of whom Haman, our second father, hath informed us, be destroyed, with their wives and children, and that none of them be spared, and that none prefer pity to them before obedience to this decree; and this I will to be executed on the fourteenth day of the twelfth month of this present year, that so when all who have enmity to us are destroyed, and this in one day, we may be allowed to lead the rest of our lives in peace hereafter." Now when this decree was brought to the cities, and to the country, all were ready for the destruction and entire abolishment of the Jews, against the day before mentioned; and they were very hasty about it at Shushan, in particular. Accordingly, the king and Haman spent their time in feasting together with good cheer and wine; but the city was in disorder.

7. Now when Mordecai was informed of what was done, he rent his clothes, and put on sackcloth, and sprinkled ashes upon his head, and went about the city, crying out, that "a nation that had been injurious to no man was to be destroyed." And he went on saying thus as far as to the king's palace, and there he stood, for it was not lawful for him to go into it in that habit. The same thing was done by all the Jews that were in the several cities wherein this decree was published, with lamentation and mourning, on account of the calamities denounced against them. But as soon as certain persons had told the queen that Mordecai stood before the court in a mourning habit, she was disturbed at this report, and sent out such as should change his garments; but when he could not be induced to put off his sackcloth, because the sad occasion that forced him to put it on was not yet ceased, she called the eunuch Acratheus, for he was then present, and sent him to Mordecai, in order to know of him what sad accident had befallen him, for which he was in mourning, and would not put off the habit he had put on, at her desire. Then did Mordecai inform the eunuch of the occasion of his mourning, and of the decree which was sent by the king into all the country, and of the promise of money whereby Haman bought the destruction of their nation. He also gave him a copy of what was proclaimed at Shushan, to be carried to Esther; and he charged her to petition the king about this matter, and not to think it a dishonourable thing in her to put on a humble habit, for the safety of her nation, wherein she might deprecate the ruin of the Jews, who were in danger of it; for that Haman, whose dignity was only inferior to that of the king, had accused the Jews, and had irritated the king against them. When she was informed of this, she sent to Mordecai again, and told him that she was not called by the king, and that he who goes in to him without being called is to be slain, unless

when he is willing to save any one, he holds out his golden sceptre to him; but that to whomsoever he does so, although he go in without being called, that person is so far from being slain, that he obtains pardon, and is entirely preserved. Now when the eunuch carried this message from Esther to Mordecai, he bade him also tell her that she must not only provide for her own preservation, but for the common preservation of her nation, for that if she now neglected this opportunity, there would certainly arise help to them from God some other way; but she and her father's house would be destroyed by those whom she now despised. But Esther sent the very same eunuch back to Mordecai, [to desire him] to go to Shushan, and to gather the Jews that were there together to a congregation, and to fast, and abstain from all sorts of food, on her account, and [to let him know that] she with her maidens would do the same; and then she promised that she would go to the king, though it were against the law, and that if she must die for it, she would not refuse it.

8. Accordingly, Mordecai did as Esther had enjoined him, and made the people fast; and he besought God, together with them, not to overlook his nation, particularly at this time, when it was going to be destroyed; but that, as he had often before provided for them, and forgiven when they had sinned, so he would now deliver them from that destruction which was denounced against them; for although it was not all the nation that had offended, yet must they so ingloriously be slain, and that he was himself the occasion of the wrath of Haman, "Because," said he, "I did not worship him, nor could I endure to pay honour to him which I used to pay to thee, O Lord; for upon that his anger hath he contrived this present mischief against those that have not transgressed thy laws." The same supplications did the multitude put up; and entreated that God would provide for their deliverance, and free the Israelites that were in all the earth from this calamity which was now coming upon them, for they had it before their eyes, and expected its coming. Accordingly, Esther made supplication to God after the manner of her country, by casting herself down upon the earth, and putting on her mourning garments, and bidding farewell to meat and drink, and all delicacies, for three days' time; and she entreated God to have mercy upon her, and make her words appear persuasive to the king, and render her countenance more beautiful than it was before, that both by her words and beauty she might succeed, for the averting of the king's anger, in case he were at all irritated against her, and for the consolation of those of her own country, now they were in the utmost danger of perishing: as also that he would excite a hatred in the king against the enemies of the Jews, and those that had contrived their future destruction, if they proved to be contemned by him.

9. When Esther had used this supplication for three days, she put off those garments, and changed her habit, and adorned herself as became a queen, and took two of her handmaids with her, the one of which supported her, as she gently leaned upon her, and the other followed after, and lifted up her large train (which swept along the ground) with the extremities of her fingers: and thus she came to the king, having a blushing redness in her countenance, with a pleasant agreeableness in her behaviour, yet did she go in to him with fear; and as soon as she was come over against him, as he was sitting

on his throne, in his royal apparel, which was a garment interwoven with gold and precious stones, which made him seem to her more terrible, especially when he looked at her somewhat severely, and with a countenance on fire with anger, her joints failed her immediately, out of the dread she was in, and she fell down sideways in a swoon: but the king changed his mind, which happened, as I suppose, by the will of God, and was concerned for his wife, lest her fear should bring some very evil thing upon her, and he leaped from his throne, and took her in his arms, and recovered her, by embracing her, and speaking comfortably to her, and exhorting her to be of good cheer, and not to suspect anything that was sad on account of her coming to him without being called, because that law was made for subjects, but that she, who was a queen, as well as he a king, might be entirely secure: and as he said this, he put the sceptre into her hand, and laid his rod upon her neck, on account of the law; and so freed her from fear. And after she had recovered herself by these encouragements, she said, "My lord, it is not easy for me, on the sudden, to say what hath happened, for so soon as I saw thee to be great, and comely, and terrible, my spirit departed from me, and I had no soul left in me." And while it was with difficulty, and in a low voice, that she could say thus much, the king was in great agony and disorder, and encouraged Esther to be of good cheer, and to expect better fortune, since he was ready, if occasion should require it, to grant to her the half of his kingdom. Accordingly, Esther desired that he and his friend Haman would come to her to a banquet, for she said she had prepared a supper for him. He consented to it; and when they were there, as they were drinking, he bade Esther to let him know what she had desired; for that she should not be disappointed, though she should desire the half of his kingdom. But she put off the discovery of her petition till the next day, if he would come again, together with Haman, to her banquet.

10. Now when the king had promised so to do, Haman went away very glad, because he alone had the honour of supping with the king at Esther's banquet, and because no one else partook of the same honour with kings but himself; yet when he saw Mordecai in the court he was very much displeased, for he paid him no manner of respect when he saw him. So he went home and called for his wife Zeresh, and his friends, and when they were come, he shewed them what honour he enjoyed, not only from the king, but from the queen also, for as he alone had that day supped with her, together with the king, so was he also invited again for the next day; "Yet," said he, "am I not pleased to see Mordecai the Jew in the court." Hereupon his wife Zeresh advised him to give order that a gallows should be made fifty cubits high, and that in the morning he should ask it of the king that Mordecai might be hanged thereon. So he commended her advice, and gave order to his servants to prepare the gallows, and to place it in the court, for the punishment of Mordecai thereon, which was accordingly prepared. But God laughed to scorn the wicked expectations of Haman; and as he knew what the event would be, he was delighted at it, for that night he took away the king's sleep: and as the king was not willing to lose the time of his lying awake, but to spend it in something that might be of advantage to his kingdom, he commanded the scribe to bring him the chronicles of the former kings, and the records of his own

actions; and when he had brought them, and was reading them, one was found to have received a country on account of his excellent management on a certain occasion, and the name of the country was set down; another was found to have had a present made him on account of his fidelity: then the scribe came to Bigthan and Teresh, the eunuchs that had made a conspiracy against the king, which Mordecai had discovered; and when the scribe said no more but that, and was going on to another history, the king stopped him, and inquired, "Whether it was not added that Mordecai had a reward given him?" and when he said there was no such addition, he bade him leave off; and he inquired of those that were appointed for that purpose, what hour of the night it was; and when he was informed that it was already day, he gave order that, if they found any one of his friends already come, and standing before the court, they should tell him. Now it happened that Haman was found there, for he was come sooner than ordinary, to petition the king to have Mordecai put to death: and when the servants said, that Haman was before the court, he bade them call him in; and when he was come in, he said, "Because I know that thou art my only fast friend, I desire thee to give me advice how I may honour one that I greatly love, and that after a manner suitable to my magnificence." Now Haman reasoned with himself, that what opinion he should give it would be for himself, since it was he alone who was beloved by the king; so he gave that advice which he thought of all others the best; for he said, "If thou wouldst truly honour a man whom thou sayest thou dost love, give order that he may ride on horseback, with the same garment which thou wearest, and with a gold chain about his neck, and let one of thy intimate friends go before him, and proclaim through the whole city, that whosoever the king honoureth obtaineth this mark of his honour." This was the advice which Haman gave, out of a supposal that such reward would come to himself. Hereupon the king was pleased with the advice, and said, "Go thou, therefore, for thou hast the horse, the garment, and the chain, ask for Mordecai the Jew, and give him those things, and go before his horse and proclaim accordingly; for thou art," said he, "my intimate friend, and hast given me good advice; be thou then the minister of what thou hast advised me to. This shall be his reward from us, for preserving my life." When he heard this order, which was entirely unexpected, he was confounded in his mind, and knew not what to do. However, he went out and led the horse, and took the purple garment, and the golden chain for the neck, and finding Mordecai before the court, clothed in sackcloth, he bade him put that garment off, and put the purple garment on: but Mordecai not knowing the truth of the matter, but thinking that it was done in mockery, said, "O thou wretch, the vilest of all mankind, dost thou thus laugh at our calamities?" But when he was satisfied that the king bestowed this honour upon him, for the deliverance he had procured him when he convicted the eunuchs who had conspired against him, he put on that purple garment which the king always wore, and put the chain about his neck, and got on horseback, and went round the city, while Haman went before, and proclaimed, "This shall be the reward which the king will bestow on every one whom he loves, and esteems worthy of honour." And when they had gone round the city, Mordecai went in to the king; but Haman went home, out of shame, and informed his wife and friends of what had happened, and this with tears : who said that he would never be able to be revenged of Mordecai, for that God was with him.

11. Now while these men were thus talking one to another, Esther's eunuchs hastened Haman away to come to supper : but one of the eunuchs named Sabuchadas, saw the gallows that was fixed in Haman's house, and inquired of one of his servants for what purpose they had prepared it. So he knew that it was for the queen's uncle, because Haman was about to petition the king that he might be punished ; but at present he held his peace. Now when the king, with Haman, were at the banquet, he desired the king to tell him what gifts she desired to obtain, and assured her that she should have whatsoever she had a mind to. She then lamented the danger her people were in ; and that "she and her nation were given up to be destroyed, and that she on that account made this her petition : that she would not have troubled him if he had only given order that they should be sold into bitter servitude, for such a misfortune would not have been intolerable ; but she desired that they might be delivered from such destruction." And when the king inquired of her who was the author of this misery to them, she then openly accused Haman, and convicted him, that he had been the wicked instrument of this, and had formed this plot against them. When the king was hereupon in disorder, and was gone hastily out of the banquet into the gardens, Haman began to intercede with Esther, and to beseech her to forgive him, as to what he had offended, for he perceived that he was in a very bad case. And as he had fallen upon the queen's bed, and was making supplication to her, the king came in, and being still more provoked at what he saw, "O thou wretch," said he, "thou vilest of mankind, dost thou aim to force my wife?" And when Haman was astonished at this, and not able to speak one word more, Sabuchadas the eunuch came in, and accused Haman, and said, "He found a gallows at his house, prepared for Mordecai ; for that the servant told him so much, upon his inquiry, when he was sent to him to call him to supper:" he said further, that the gallows was fifty cubits high : which, when the king heard, he determined that Haman should be punished after no other manner than that which had been devised by him against Mordecai ; so he gave order immediately that he should be hung upon those gallows, and be put to death after the same manner. And from hence I cannot forbear to admire God, and to learn hence his wisdom and justice, not only in punishing the wickedness of Haman, but in so disposing it, that he should undergo the very same punishment which he had contrived for another ; as also, because thereby he teaches others this lesson, that what mischiefs any one prepares against another, he without knowing of it, first contrives it against himself.

12. Wherefore Haman, who had immoderately abused the honour he had from the king, was destroyed after this manner ; and the king granted his estate to the queen. He also called for Mordecai, (for Esther had informed him that she was akin to him,) and gave that ring to Mordecai ; which he had before given to Haman. The queen also gave Haman's estate to Mordecai ; and prayed the king to deliver the nation of the Jews from the fear of death, and shewed him what had been written over all the country by Haman the son of Ammedatha ; for that if her country were destroyed, and her countrymen were to perish, she could not bear to live herself

any longer. So the king promised her that he would not do anything that was disagreeable to her, nor contradict what she desired ; but he bade her write what she pleased about the Jews, in the king's name, and seal it with his seal, and send it to all his kingdom, for that those who read epistles whose authority is secured by having the king's seal to them, would no way contradict what was written therein. So he commanded the king's scribes to be sent for, and to write to the nations, on the Jew's behalf, and to his lieutenants and governors, that were over his hundred and twenty-seven provinces, from India to Ethiopia. Now the contents of this epistle were these :—"The great king Artaxerxes to our rulers, and those that are our faithful subjects, sendeth greeting.* Many men there are who, on account of the greatness of the benefits bestowed on them, and because of the honour which they have obtained from the wonderful kind treatment of those that bestowed it, are not only injurious to their inferiors, but do not scruple to do evil to those that have been their benefactors, as if they would take away gratitude from among men, and by their insolent abuse of such benefits as they never expected, they turn the abundance they have against those that are the authors of it, and suppose that they shall lie concealed from God in that case, and avoid that vengeance which comes from him. Some of these men, when they have had the management of affairs committed to them by their friends, and bearing private malice of their own against some others, by deceiving those that have the power, persuade them to be angry at such as have done them no harm, till they are in danger of perishing, and this by laying accusations and calumnies : nor is this state of things to be discovered by ancient examples, or such as we have learned by report only, but by some examples of such impudent attempts under our own eyes, so that it is not fit to attend any longer to calumnies and accusations, nor to the persuasion of others, but to determine what any one knows of himself to have been really done, and to punish what justly deserves it, and to grant favours to such as are innocent. This hath been the case of Haman, the son of Ammedatha, by birth an Amalekite, and alien from the blood of the Persians, who, when he was hospitably entertained by us, and partook of that kindness which we bear to all men to so great a degree, as to be called my father, and to be all along worshipped, and to have honour paid him by all in the second rank after the royal honour due to ourselves, he could not bear his good fortune, nor govern the magnitude of his prosperity with sound reason ; nay, he made a conspiracy against me and my life, who gave him his authority, by endeavouring to take away Mordecai, my benefactor, and my saviour, and basely and treacherously requiring to have Esther, the partner of my life, and of my dominion, brought to destruction ; for he contrived by this means to deprive me of my faithful friends, and transfer the government to others :†—but since

* The reason why Artaxerxes did not here revoke his former barbarous decree for the universal slaughter of the Jews, but only empowered the Jews to fight for their lives, and to kill their enemies, if they attempted their destruction, seems to have been that law of the Medes and Persians, that whatever decree was signed both by the king and his lords, could not be changed, but remained unalterable.

† These words give an intimation as if Artaxerxes suspected a deeper design in Haman than openly appeared—viz., that knowing the Jews would be faithful to him, and that he could never transfer the crown to his own family, who was an Agagite, (Esth. iii. 1, 10,) or of the posterity of Agag, the old king of the Amale-

I perceive that these Jews, that were by this pernicious fellow devoted to destruction, were not wicked men, but conducted their lives after the best manner, and were men dedicated to the worship of that God who hath preserved the kingdom to me and to my ancestors, I do not only free them from the punishment which the former epistle, which was sent by Haman, ordered to be inflicted on them,—to which if you refuse obedience you shall do well; but I will that they have all honour paid them. Accordingly, I have hanged up the man that contrived such things against them, with his family, before the gates of Shushan; that punishment being sent upon him by God, who seeth all things. And I give you in charge, that you publicly propose a copy of this epistle through all my kingdom, that the Jews may be permitted peaceably to use their own laws, and that you assist them, that at the same season whereto their miserable estate did belong, they may defend themselves the very same day from unjust violence, the thirteenth day of the twelfth month, which is Adar,—for God hath made that day a day of salvation, instead of a day of destruction to them; and may it be a good day to those that wish us well, and a memorial of the punishment of the conspirators against us : and I will that you take notice, that every city, and every nation, that shall disobey anything that is contained in this epistle, shall be destroyed by fire and sword. However, let this epistle be published through all the country that is under our obedience, and let all the Jews, by all means be ready against the day beforementioned, that they may avenge themselves upon their enemies."

13. Accordingly, the horsemen who carried the epistles, proceeded on the ways which they were to go with speed; but as for Mordecai, as soon as he had assumed the royal garment, and the crown of gold, and had put the chain about his neck, he went forth in a public procession; and when the Jews who were at Shushan saw him in so great honour with the king, they thought his good fortune was common to themselves also; and joy and a beam of salvation encompassed the Jews, both those that were in the cities and those that were in the countries, upon the publication of the king's letters, insomuch that many of other nations circumcised their foreskin for fear of the Jews, that they might procure safety to themselves thereby; for on the thirteenth day of the twelfth month, which according to the Hebrew, is called *Adar*, but according to the Macedonians, *Dystrus*, those that carried the king's epistle gave them notice, that the same day wherein their danger was to have been, on that very day should they destroy their enemies. But now the rulers of the provinces, and the tyrants, and the kings, and the scribes, had the Jews in esteem; for the fear they were in of Mordecai forced them to act with discretion. Now when the royal decree was come to all the country that was subject to the king, it fell out that the Jews at Shushan slew five hundred of their enemies: and when the king had told Esther the number of those that were slain in that city, but did not well know what had been done in the provinces, he asked her whether she would have anything further done against them, for that it should be done accordingly: upon which she desired that the Jews might be permitted to treat their remaining enemies in the same manner the next

day; as also, that they might hang the ten sons of Haman upon the gallows. So the king permitted the Jews so to do, as desirous not to contradict Esther. So they gathered themselves together again on the fourteenth day of the month Dystrus, and slew about three hundred of their enemies, but touched nothing of what riches they had. Now there were slain by the Jews that were in the country, and in the other cities, seventy-five thousand of their enemies, and these were slain on the thirteenth day of the month, and the next day they kept as a festival. In like manner the Jews that were in Shushan gathered themselves together, and feasted on the fourteenth day, and that which followed it; whence it is, that even now all the Jews that are in the habitable earth keep these days festivals, and send portions to one another. Mordecai also wrote to the Jews that lived in the kingdom of Artaxerxes to observe these days, and to celebrate them as festivals, and to deliver them down to posterity, that this festival might continue for all time to come, and that it might never be buried in oblivion; for since they were about to be destroyed on these days by Haman, they would do a right thing, upon escaping the danger in them, and on them inflicting punishment on their enemies, to observe those days, and give thanks to God on them; for which cause the Jews still keep the forementioned days, and call them days of Phurim, [or Purim.] And Mordecai became a great and illustrious person with the king, and assisted him in the government of the people. He also lived with the queen; so that the affairs of the Jews were, by their means, better than they could ever have hoped for. And this was the state of the Jews under the reign of Artaxerxes.

CHAPTER VII

HOW JOHN SLEW HIS BROTHER JESUS IN THE TEMPLE; AND HOW BAGOSES OFFERED MANY INJURIES TO THE JEWS; AND WHAT SANBALLAT DID

1. WHEN Eliasib the high priest was dead, his son Judas succeeded in the high priesthood: and when he was dead, his son John took that dignity; on whose account it was also that Bagoses, the general of another Artaxerxes' army, polluted the temple, and imposed tributes on the Jews, that out of the public stock, before they offered the daily sacrifices, they should pay for every lamb fifty shekels. Now Jesus was the brother of John, and was a friend of Bagoses, who had promised to procure him the high priesthood. In confidence of whose support, Jesus quarrelled with John in the temple, and so provoked his brother, that in his anger his brother slew him. Now it was a horrible thing for John, when he was high priest, to perpetrate so great a crime, and so much the more horrible, that there never was so cruel and impious a thing done, neither by the Greeks nor Barbarians. However, God did not neglect its punishment; but the people were on that very account enslaved, and the temple was polluted by the Persians. Now when Bagoses, the general of Artaxerxes' army, knew that John, the high priest of the Jews, had slain his own brother Jesus in the temple, he came upon the Jews immediately, and began in anger to say to them, "Have you had the impudence to perpetrate a murder in your temple?" And as he was aiming to go into the temple, they forbade him so to do;

kites, (1 Sam. xv. 8, 32, 33,) while they were alive, and spread over all his dominions, he therefore endeavoured to destroy them.

but he said to them, "Am not I purer than he that was slain in the temple?" And when he had said these words, he went into the temple. Accordingly, Bagoses made use of this pretence, and punished the Jews seven years for the murder of Jesus.

2. Now when John had departed this life, his son Jaddua succeeded in the high priesthood. He had a brother, whose name was Manasseh. Now there was one Sanballat, who was sent by Darius, the last king, [of Persia,] into Samaria. He was a Cuthean by birth; of which stock were the Samaritans also. This man knew that the city Jerusalem was a famous city, and that their kings had given a great deal of trouble to the Assyrians, and the people of Cœlesyria; so that he willingly gave his daughter, whose name was Nicaso, in marriage to Manasseh, as thinking this alliance by marriage would be a pledge and security that the nation of the Jews should continue their good-will to him.

CHAPTER VIII

CONCERNING SANBALLAT AND MANASSEH, AND THE TEMPLE WHICH THEY BUILT ON MOUNT GERIZZIM; AS ALSO HOW ALEXANDER MADE HIS ENTRY INTO THE CITY JERUSALEM; AND WHAT BENEFITS HE BESTOWED ON THE JEWS

1. ABOUT this time it was that Philip, king of Macedon, was treacherously assaulted and slain at Egæ by Pausanias, the son of Cerastes, who was derived from the family of Orestæ, and his son Alexander succeeded him in the kingdom; who, passing over the Hellespont, overcame the generals of Darius's army in a battle fought at Granicum. So he marched over Lydia, and subdued Ionia, and overran Caria, and fell upon the places of Pamphylia, as has been related elsewhere.

2. But the elders of Jerusalem being very uneasy that the brother of Jaddua the high priest, though married to a foreigner, should be a partner with him in the high priesthood, quarrelled with him; for they esteemed this man's marriage a step to such as would be desirous of transgressing about the marriage of [strange] wives, and that this would be the beginning of a mutual society with foreigners, although the offence of some about marriages, and their having married wives that were not of their own country, has been an occasion of their former captivity and of the miseries they then underwent; so they commanded Manasseh to divorce his wife, or not to approach the altar, the high priest himself joining with the people in their indignation against his brother, and driving him away from the altar. Whereupon Manasseh came to his father-in-law, Sanballat, and told him, that although he loved his daughter Nicaso, yet was he not willing to be deprived of his sacerdotal dignity on her account, which was the principal dignity in their nation, and always continued in the same family. And then Sanballat promised him not only to preserve to him the honour of his priesthood, but to procure for him the power and dignity of a high priest, and would make him governor of all the places he himself now ruled, if he would keep his daughter for his wife. He also told him further, that he would build him a temple like that at Jerusalem, upon Mount Gerizzim, which is the highest of all the mountains that are in Samaria; and he promised that he would do this with the approbation of Darius the king.

Manasseh was elevated with these promises, and stayed with Sanballat, upon a supposal that he should gain a high priesthood, as bestowed on him by Darius, for it happened Sanballat was then in years. But there was now a great disturbance among the people of Jerusalem, because many of those priests and Levites were entangled in such matches; for they all revolted to Manasseh, and Sanballat afforded them money, and divided among them land for tillage, and habitations also; and all this in order every way to gratify his son-in-law.

3. About this time it was that Darius heard how Alexander had passed over the Hellespont, and had beaten his lieutenants in the battle of Granicum, and was proceeding further; whereupon he gathered together an army of horse and foot, and determined that he would meet the Macedonians before they should assault and conquer all Asia. So he passed over the river Euphrates and came over Taurus, the Cilician mountain; and at Issus of Cilicia he waited for the enemy; as ready there to give him battle. Upon which Sanballat was glad that Darius was come down; and told Manasseh that he would suddenly perform his promises to him, and this as soon as ever Darius should come back, after he had beaten his enemies; for not he only, but all those that were in Asia also, were persuaded that the Macedonians would not so much as come to a battle with the Persians, on account of their multitude; but the event proved otherwise than they expected, for the king joined battle with the Macedonians, and was beaten, and lost a great part of his army. His mother also, and his wife and children, were taken captives, and he fled into Persia. So Alexander came into Syria, and took Damascus; and when he had obtained Sidon, he besieged Tyre, when he sent an epistle to the Jewish high priest, to send him some auxiliaries, and to supply his army with provisions; and that what presents he formerly sent to Darius, he would now send to him, and choose the friendship of the Macedonians, and that he should never repent of so doing; but the high priest answered the messengers, that he had given his oath to Darius not to bear arms against him; and he said that he would not transgress this while Darius was in the land of the living. Upon hearing this answer, Alexander was very angry; and though he determined not to leave Tyre, which was just ready to be taken, yet, as soon as he had taken it, he threatened that he would make an expedition against the Jewish high priest, and through him teach all men to whom they must keep their oaths. So when he had, with a good deal of pains during the siege, taken Tyre, and had settled its affairs, he came to the city of Gaza, and besieged both the city and him that was governor of the garrison, whose name was Babemeses.

4. But Sanballat thought he had now gotten a proper opportunity to make his attempt, so he renounced Darius, and taking with him seven thousand of his own subjects, he came to Alexander; and finding him beginning the siege of Tyre, he said to him, that he delivered up to him these men, who came out of places under his dominion, and did gladly accept of him for their lord instead of Darius. So when Alexander had received him kindly, Sanballat thereupon took courage, and spake to him about his present affair. He told him that he had a son-in-law, Manasseh, who was brother to the high priest Jaddua; and that there were many others of his own nation now with him, that were desirous to have a temple in the places subject to him; that it would be for the king's advantage to have

the strength of the Jews divided into two parts, lest when the nation is of one mind and united, upon any attempt for innovation, it prove troublesome to kings, as it had formerly proved to the kings of Assyria. Whereupon Alexander gave Sanballat leave so to do; who used the utmost diligence, and built the temple, and made Manasseh the priest, and deemed it a great reward that his daughter's children should have that dignity; but when the seven months of the siege of Tyre were over, and the two months of the siege of Gaza, Sanballat died. Now Alexander, when he had taken Gaza, made haste to go up to Jerusalem; and Jaddua the high priest, when he heard that, was in an agony, and under terror, as not knowing how he should meet the Macedonians, since the king was displeased at his foregoing disobedience. He therefore ordained that the people should make supplications, and should join with him in offering sacrifices to God, whom he sought to protect that nation, and to deliver them from the perils that were coming upon them; whereupon God warned him in a dream, which came upon him after he had offered sacrifice that he should take courage, and adorn the city, and open the gates; that the rest should appear in white garments, but that he and the priests should meet the king in the habits proper to their order, without the dread of any ill consequences, which the providence of God would prevent. Upon which, when he rose from his sleep, he greatly rejoiced; and declared to all the warning he had received from God. According to which dream he acted entirely, and so waited for the coming of the king.

5. And when he understood that he was not far from the city, he went out in procession, with the priests, and the multitude of citizens. The procession was venerable, and the manner of it different from that of other nations. It reached to a place called Sapha; which name, translated into Greek, signifies a *prospect*, for you have thence a prospect both of Jerusalem and of the temple; and when the Phoenicians and the Chaldeans that followed him, thought they should have liberty to plunder the city, and torment the high priest to death, which the king's displeasure fairly promised them, the very reverse of it happened; for Alexander, when he saw the multitude at a distance, in white garments, while the priests stood clothed with fine linen, and the high priest in purple and scarlet clothing, with his mitre on his head, having the golden plate whereon the name of God was engraved, he approached by himself, and adored that name, and first saluted the high priest. The Jews also did all together, with one voice, salute Alexander, and encompass him about; whereupon the kings of Syria and the rest were surprised at what Alexander had done, and supposed him disordered in his mind. However, Parmenio alone went up to him, and asked him how it came to pass that, when all others adored him, he should adore the high priest of the Jews? To whom he replied, "I did not adore him, but that God who hath honoured him with his high priesthood; for I saw this very person in a dream, in this very habit, when I was at Dios in Macedonia, who, when I was considering with myself how I might obtain the dominion of Asia, exhorted me to make no delay, but boldly to pass over the sea thither, for that he would conduct my army, and would give me the dominion over the Persians; whence it is, that having seen no other in that habit, and now seeing this person in it, and remembering that vision, and the exhortation which I had in my dream, I believe that I bring this army under the divine conduct, and shall therewith conquer Darius, and destroy the power of the Persians, and that all things will succeed according to what is in my own mind. And when he had said this to Parmenio, and had given the high priest his right hand, the priests ran along by him, and he came into the city; and when he went up into the temple, he offered sacrifice to God, according to the high priest's direction, and magnificently treated both the high priest and the priests. And when the book of Daniel was shewed him,[*] wherein Daniel declared that one of the Greeks should destroy the empire of the Persians, he supposed that himself was the person intended; and as he was then glad, he dismissed the multitude for the present, but the next day he called them to him, and bade them ask what favours they pleased of him; whereupon the high priest desired that they might enjoy the laws of their forefathers, and might pay no tribute on the seventh year. He granted all they desired; and when they entreated him that he would permit the Jews in Babylon and Media to enjoy their own laws also, he willingly promised to do hereafter what they desired: and when he said to the multitude, that if any of them would enlist themselves in his army on this condition, that they should continue under the laws of their forefathers, and live according to them, he was willing to take them with him, many were ready to accompany him in his wars.

6. So when Alexander had thus settled matters at Jerusalem, he led his army into the neighbouring cities; and when all the inhabitants, to whom he came, received him with great kindness, the Samaritans, who had then Shechem for their metropolis, (a city situate at Mount Gerizzim, and inhabited by apostates of the Jewish nation,) seeing that Alexander had so greatly honoured the Jews, determined to profess themselves Jews; for such is the disposition of the Samaritans, as we have already elsewhere declared, that when the Jews are in adversity they deny that they are of kin to them, and then they confess the truth; but when they perceive that some good fortune hath befallen them, they immediately pretend to have communion with them, saying, that they belong to them, and derive their genealogy from the posterity of Joseph, Ephraim, and Manasseh. Accordingly, they made their address to the king with splendour, and shewed great alacrity in meeting him at a little distance from Jerusalem; and when Alexander had commended them, the Shechemites approached to him, taking with them the troops that Sanballat had sent him, and they desired that he would come to their city, and do honour to their temple also; to whom he promised, that when he returned he would come to them; and when they petitioned that he would remit the tribute of the seventh year to them, because they did not now sow thereon, he asked who they were that made such a petition; and when they said that they were Hebrews, but had the name of Sidonians, living at Shechem, he asked them again whether they were Jews; and when they said they were not Jews, "It was to the Jews," said he, "that I granted that privilege; however, when I return, and am thoroughly informed by you of this matter, I will do what I shall think proper." And in this manner he took leave of the Shec-

---

[*] The place shewed Alexander might be Dan. vii. 6; viii. 3-8, 20, 21, 22; xi. 3; some or all of them very plain predictions of Alexander's conquests and successors

hemites; but ordered that the troops of Sanballat should follow him into Egypt, because
there he designed to give them lands, which he
did a little after in Thebais, when he ordered
them to guard that country.

7. Now when Alexander was dead, the government was parted among his successors; but the
temple upon Mount Gerizzim remained; and if
any one were accused by those of Jerusalem of
having eaten things common,* or of having

broken the Sabbath, or of any other crime of
the like nature, he fled away to the Shechemites, and said that he was accused unjustly
About this time it was that Jaddua the high
priest died, and Onias his son took the high
priesthood. This was the state of the affairs of
the people of Jerusalem at this time.

_____

* Here Josephus uses the word *Koinophagia*, "eat-

ing common things," for "eating things unclean;" as
does the New Testament, in Acts x. 14, 15, 28, and
xi. 8, 9; Rom. xiv. 14.

BOOK XII

CONTAINING THE INTERVAL OF A HUNDRED AND SEVENTY YEARS

FROM THE DEATH OF ALEXANDER THE GREAT TO THE DEATH OF JUDAS MACCABEUS

CHAPTER I

HOW PTOLEMY, THE SON OF LAGUS, TOOK JERUSA-
LEM AND JUDEA BY DECEIT AND TREACHERY,
AND CARRIED MANY OF THE JEWS THENCE, AND
PLANTED THEM IN EGYPT

1. Now when Alexander, king of Macedon, had
put an end to the dominion of the Persians, and
had settled the affairs of Judea after the forementioned manner, he ended his life; and as his
government fell among many, Antigonus obtained Asia; Seleucus, Babylon; and of the
other nations which were there, Lysimachus
governed the Hellespont, and Cassander possessed Macedonia; as did Ptolemy, the son of
Lagus, seize upon Egypt: and while these princes
ambitiously strove one against another, every
one for his own principality, it came to pass that
there were continual wars, and those lasting wars
too; and the cities were sufferers, and lost a
great many of their inhabitants in these times of
distress, insomuch that all Syria, by the means
of Ptolemy, the son of Lagus, underwent the reverse of that denomination of Saviour, which he
then had. He also seized upon Jerusalem, and
for that end made use of deceit and treachery;
for as he came into the city on a Sabbath-day, as
if he would offer sacrifice, he, without any trouble,
gained the city, while the Jews did not oppose
him, for they did not suspect him to be their
enemy; and he gained it thus, because they
were free from suspicion of him, and because on
that day they were at rest and quietness; and
when he had gained it, he reigned over it in a
cruel manner. Nay, Agatharchides of Cnidus,
who wrote the acts of Alexander's successors,
reproaches us with superstition, as if we, by it,
had lost our liberty; where he says thus: "There
is a nation called the nation of the Jews, who
inhabit a city strong and great, named Jerusalem.
These men took no care, but let it come into the
hands of Ptolemy, as not willing to take arms,
and thereby they submitted to be under a hard
master, by reason of their unseasonable superstition." This is what Agatharchides relates of
our nation. But when Ptolemy had taken a
great many captives, both from the mountainous
parts of Judea and from the places about Jerusalem and Samaria, and the places near mount

Gerizzim, he led them all into Egypt,* and settled them there. And as he knew that the people of Jerusalem were most faithful in the observation of oaths and covenants,—and this from the
answer they made to Alexander, when he sent an
embassage to them, after he had beaten Darius
in battle,—so he distributed many of them into
garrisons, and at Alexandria gave them equal
privileges of citizens with the Macedonians themselves; and required of them to take their oaths
that they would keep their fidelity to the posterity of those who committed these places to
their care. Nay, there were not a few other
Jews who, of their own accord, went into Egypt,
as invited by the goodness of the soil, and by the
liberality of Ptolemy. However, there were disorders among their posterity, with relation to
the Samaritans, on account of their resolution to
preserve that conduct of life which was delivered
to them by their forefathers, and they thereupon
contended one with another, while those of Jerusalem said that their temple was holy, and resolved to send their sacrifices thither; but the
Samaritans were resolved that they should be
sent to mount Gerizzim.

CHAPTER II

HOW PTOLEMY PHILADELPHUS PROCURED THE LAWS
OF THE JEWS TO BE TRANSLATED INTO THE GREEK
TONGUE; AND SET MANY CAPTIVES FREE; AND
DEDICATED MANY GIFTS TO GOD

1. WHEN Alexander had reigned twelve years,
and after him Ptolemy Soter forty years, Phila-

_____

* The great number of these Jews and Samaritans that
were formerly carried into Egypt by Alexander, and
now by Ptolemy, the son of Lagus, appear afterwards,
in the vast multitude who were soon ransomed by Philadelphus, and by him made free, before he sent for the
seventy-two interpreters; in the many garrisons, and
other soldiers of that nation in Egypt; in the famous
settlement of Jews, and the number of their synagogues
at Alexandria long afterward; and in the vehement
contention between the Jews and Samaritans under
Philometer, about the place appointed for public worship in the law of Moses, whether at the Jewish temple
of Jerusalem, or at the Samaritan temple of Gerizzim:
of all which our author treats hereafter.

delphus then took the kingdom of Egypt, and held it forty years within one. He procured the law to be interpreted, and set free those that were come from Jerusalem into Egypt, and were in slavery there, who were a hundred and twenty thousand. The occasion was this :—Demetrius Phalerius, who was library-keeper to the king, was now endeavouring, if it were possible, to gather together all the books that were in the habitable earth, and buying whatsoever was anywhere valuable, or agreeable to the king's inclination, (who was very earnestly set upon collecting of books ;) to which inclination of his, Demetrius was zealously subservient. And when once Ptolemy asked him how many ten thousands of books he had collected, he replied, that he had already about twenty times ten thousand ; but that, in a little time, he should have fifty times ten thousand. But he said he had been informed that there were many books of laws among the Jews worthy of inquiring after, and worthy of the king's library, but which, being written in characters and in a dialect of their own, will cause no small pains in getting them translated into the Greek tongue : that the character in which they are written seems to be like to that which is the proper character of the Syrians, and that its sound, when pronounced, is like to theirs also ; and that this sound appears to be peculiar to themselves. Wherefore, he said, that nothing hindered why they might not get those books to be translated also ; for while nothing is wanting that is necessary for that purpose, we may have their books also in this library. So the king thought that Demetrius was very zealous to procure him abundance of books, and that he suggested what was exceeding proper for him to do ; and therefore he wrote to the Jewish high priest that he should act accordingly.

2. Now there was one Aristeus, who was among the king's most intimate friends, and, on account of his modesty, very acceptable to him. This Aristeus resolved frequently, and that before now, to petition the king that he would set all the captive Jews in his kingdom free ; and he thought this to be a convenient opportunity for the making that petition. So he discoursed, in the first place, with the captains of the king's guards, Sosibius of Tarentum, and Andreas, and persuaded them to assist him in what he was going to intercede with the king for. Accordingly, Aristeus embraced the same opinion with those that have been before mentioned, and went to the king and made the following speech to him : "It is not fit for us, O king, to overlook things hastily, or to deceive ourselves, but to lay the truth open : for since we have determined not only to get the laws of the Jews transcribed, but interpreted also, for thy satisfaction, by what means can we do this, while so many of the Jews are now slaves in thy kingdom? Do thou then what will be agreeable to thy magnanimity, and to thy good-nature : free them from the miserable condition they are in, because that God, who supporteth thy kingdom, was the author of their laws, as I have learned by particular inquiry ; for both these people and we also worship the same God, the framer of all things. We call him, and that truly, by the name of Zηνα, [or life, or Jupiter,] because he breathes life into all men. Wherefore, do thou restore these men to their own country ; and this to do the honour of God, because these men pay a peculiarly excellent worship to him. And know this further, that though I be not of kin to them by birth, nor one of the same country with them, yet do I desire these favours to be done them. since all men are

the workmanship of God ; and I am sensible that he is well pleased with those that do good. I do therefore put up this petition to thee, to do good to them."

3. When Aristeus was saying thus, the king looked upon him with a cheerful and joyful countenance, and said, "How many ten thousands dost thou suppose there are of such as want to be made free?" To which Andreas replied, as he stood by, and said, "A few more than ten times ten thousand." The king made answer, "And is this a small gift that thou askest, Aristeus?" But Sosibius, and the rest that stood by, said that he ought to offer such a thank-offering as was worthy of his greatness of soul, to that God who had given him his kingdom. With this answer he was much pleased ; and gave order, that when they paid the soldiers their wages, they should lay down twenty drachmæ for every one of the slaves. And he promised to publish a magnificent decree about what they requested, which should confirm what Aristeus had proposed, and especially what God willed should be done ; whereby, he said, he would not only set those free who had been led away captive by his father and his army, but those who were in his kingdom before, and those also, if any such there were, who had been brought away since. And when they said that their redemption-money would amount to above four hundred talents, he granted it. A copy of which decree I have determined to preserve, that the magnanimity of this king may be made known. Its contents were as follows :—" Let all those who were soldiers under our father, and who, when they overran Syria and Phœnicia, and laid waste Judea, took the Jews captives, and made them slaves, and brought them into our cities, and into this country, and then sold them ; as also all those that were in my kingdom before them, and if there be any that have lately been brought thither, be made free by those that possess them ; and let them accept of [a hundred and] twenty drachmæ for every slave. And let the soldiers receive this redemption-money with their pay, but the rest out of the king's treasury : for I suppose that they were made captives without our father's consent, and against equity ; and that their country was harassed by the insolence of the soldiers, and that, by removing them into Egypt, the soldiers have made a great profit by them. Out of regard, therefore, to justice, and out of pity to those that have been tyrannised over contrary to equity, I enjoin those that have such Jews in their service to set them at liberty, upon the receipt of the before-mentioned sum ; and that no one use any deceit about them, but obey what is here commanded. And I will that they give in their names within three days after the publication of this edict, to such as are appointed to execute the same, and to produce the slaves before them also, for I think it will be for the advantage of my affairs : and let every one that will, inform against those that do not obey this decree ; and I will that their estates be confiscated into the king's treasury." When this decree was read to the king, it at first contained the rest that is here inserted, and only omitted those Jews that had formerly been brought, and those brought afterwards, which had not been distinctly mentioned ; so he added these clauses out of his humanity, and with great generosity. He also gave order that the payment, which was likely to be done in a hurry, should be divided among the king's ministers, and among the officers of his treasury. When this was over, what the king had decreed was quickly brought to a conclusion ; and this in

no more than seven days' time, the number of the talents paid for the captives being above four hundred and sixty, and this, because their masters required the [hundred and] twenty drachmæ for the children also, the king having, in effect, commanded that these should be paid for, when he said, in his decree, that they should receive the forementioned sum for every slave.

4. Now when this had been done after so magnificent a manner, according to the king's inclinations, he gave order to Demetrius to give him in writing his sentiments concerning the transcribing of the Jewish books; for no part of the administration is done rashly by these kings, but all things are managed with great circumspection. On which account I have subjoined a copy of these epistles, and set down the multitude of the vessels sent as gifts [to Jerusalem,] and the construction of every one, that the exactness of the artificers' workmanship, as it appeared to those that saw them, and which workmen made every vessel, may be made manifest, and this on account of the excellency of the vessels themselves. Now the copy of the epistle was to this purpose:—"Demetrius to the great king. When thou, O king, gavest me a charge concerning the collection of books that were wanting to fill your library, and concerning the care that ought to be taken about such as are imperfect, I have used the utmost diligence about those matters. And I let you know, that we want the books of the Jewish legislation, with some others; for they are written in the Hebrew characters, and being in the language of that nation, are to us unknown. It hath also happened to them, that they have been transcribed more carelessly than they should have been, because they have not had hitherto royal care taken about them. Now it is necessary that thou shouldst have accurate copies of them. And indeed this legislation is full of hidden wisdom, and entirely blameless, as being the legislation of God: for which cause it is, as Hecateus of Abdera says, that the poets and historians make no mention of it, nor of those men who lead their lives according to it, since it is a holy law, and ought not to be published by profane mouths. If then it please thee, O king, thou mayest write to the high priest of the Jews, to send six of the elders out of every tribe, and those such as are most skilful of the laws, that by their means we may learn the clear and agreeing sense of those books, and may obtain an accurate interpretation of their contents, and so may have such a collection of these as may be suitable to thy desire."

5. When this epistle was sent to the king, he commanded that an epistle should be drawn up for Eleazar, the Jewish high priest, concerning these matters; and that they should inform him of the release of the Jews that had been in slavery among them. He also sent fifty talents of gold for the making of large basons, and vials, and cups, and an immense quantity of precious stones. He also gave order to those who had the custody of the chests that contained those stones, to give the artificers leave to choose out what sorts of them they pleased. He withal appointed, that a hundred talents in money should be sent to the temple for sacrifices, and for other uses. Now I will give a description of these vessels, and the manner of their construction, but not till after I have set down a copy of the epistle which was written to Eleazar the high priest, who had obtained that dignity on the occasion following:—When Onias the high priest was dead, his son Simon became his suc-

cessor. He was called Simon the Just,[*] because of both his piety towards God, and his kind disposition to those of his own nation. When he was dead, and had left a young son, who was called Onias, Simon's brother Eleazar of whom we are speaking, took the high priesthood; and he it was to whom Ptolemy wrote, and that in the manner following:—"King Ptolemy to Eleazar the high priest, sendeth greeting. There are many Jews who now dwell in my kingdom, whom the Persians, when they were in power, carried captives. These were honoured by my father; some of whom he placed in the army, and gave them greater pay than ordinary; to others of them, when they came with him into Egypt, he committed his garrisons, and the guarding of them, that they might be a terror to the Egyptians; and when I had taken the government, I treated all men with humanity, and especially those that are thy fellow-citizens, of whom I have set free above a hundred thousand that were slaves, and paid the price of their redemption to their masters out of my own revenues; and those that are of a fit age, I have admitted into the number of my soldiers; and for such as are capable of being faithful to me, and proper for my court, I have put them in such a post, as thinking this [kindness done to them] to be a very great and an acceptable gift, which I devote to God for his providence over me; and as I am desirous to do what will be grateful to these, and to all the other Jews in the habitable earth, I have determined to procure an interpretation of your law, and to have it translated out of Hebrew into Greek, and to be deposited in my library. Thou wilt therefore do well to choose out and send to me men of a good character, who are now elders in age, and six in number out of every tribe. These, by their age, must be skilful in the laws, and of abilities to make an accurate interpretation of them; and when this shall be finished, I shall think that I have done a work glorious to myself; and I have sent to thee Andreas, the captain of my guard, and Aristeus, men whom I have in very great esteem; by whom I have sent those first-fruits which I have dedicated to the temple, and to the sacrifices, and to other uses, to the value of a hundred talents; and if thou wilt send to us, to let us know what thou wouldst have further, thou wilt do a thing acceptable to me."

6. When this epistle of the king was brought to Eleazar, he wrote an answer to it with all the respect possible:—"Eleazar the high priest to king Ptolemy, sendeth greeting. If thou and thy queen Arsinoe,[†] and thy children, be well, we are entirely satisfied. When we received thy epistle, we greatly rejoiced at thy intentions; and when the multitude were gathered together, we read it to them, and thereby made them sensible of the piety thou hast towards God. We also shewed them the twenty vials of gold, and thirty of silver, and the five large basons, and the table for the shew-bread; as also the hundred talents for the sacrifices, and for the making what shall be needful at the temple: which things Andreas and Aristeus, those most honoured friends of thine, have brought us; and truly they are persons of an excellent character, and of great learning, and worthy of thy virtue. Know then that we will gratify thee in what is

* We have a very great encomium of this Simon the Just, in the fiftieth chapter of the Ecclesiasticus, through the whole chapter.

† We are to remember here that Arsinoe was both his sister and his wife, according to the old custom of Persia, and of Egypt at this very time; nay, of the Assyrians long afterwards.

for thy advantage, though we do what we used not to do before; for we ought to make a return for the numerous acts of kindness which thou hast done to our countrymen. We immediately, therefore, offered sacrifices for thee and thy sister, with thy children and friends; and the multitude made prayers, that thy affairs may be to thy mind; and that thy kingdom may be preserved in peace, and that the translation of our law may come to the conclusion thou desirest, and be for thy advantage. We have also chosen six elders out of every tribe, whom we have sent, and the law with them. It will be thy part, out of thy piety and justice, to send back the law when it hath been translated; and to return those to us that bring it in safety.— Farewell."

7. This was the reply which the high priest made; but it does not seem to me to be necessary to set down the names of the seventy [two] elders who were sent by Eleazar, and carried the law, which yet were subjoined at the end of the epistle. However, I thought it not improper to give an account of those very valuable and artificially contrived vessels which the king sent to God, that all may see how great a regard the king had for God, for the king allowed a vast deal of expenses for these vessels, and came often to the workmen, and viewed their work, and suffered nothing of carelessness or negligence to be any damage to their operations; and I will relate how rich they were as well as I am able, although, perhaps, the nature of this history may not require such a description; but I imagine I shall thereby recommend the elegant taste and magnanimity of this king to those that read this history.

8. And, first, I will describe what belongs to the table. It was indeed in the king's mind to make this table vastly large in its dimensions; but then he gave orders that they should learn what was the magnitude of the table which was already at Jerusalem, and how large it was, and whether there were a possibility of making one larger than it; and when he was informed how large that was which was already there, and that nothing hindered but a larger might be made, he said that he was willing to have one made that should be five times as large as the present table; but his fear was, that it might be then useless in their sacred ministrations by its too great largeness; for he desired that the gifts he presented them should not only be there for show, but should be useful also in their sacred ministrations. According to which reasoning, that the former table was made of so moderate a size for use, and not for want of gold, he resolved that he would not exceed the former table in largeness, but would make it exceed it in the variety and elegancy of its materials; and as he was sagacious in observing the nature of all things, and in having a just notion of what was new and surprising, and where there were no sculptures, he would invent such as were proper by his own skill, and would shew them to the workmen, he commanded that such sculptures should now be made; and that those which were delineated should be most accurately formed, by a constant regard to their delineation.

9. When therefore the workmen had undertaken to make the table, they framed it in length two cubits [and a half,] in breadth one cubit, and in height one cubit and a half; and the entire structure of the work was of gold. They withal made a crown of a handbreadth round it, with wave-work wreathed about it, and with an engraving which imitated a cord, and was admirably turned on its three parts; for

as they were of a triangular figure, every angle had the same disposition of its sculptures, that when you turned them about, the very same form of them was turned about without any variation. Now that part of the crown-work that was enclosed under the table had its sculptures very beautiful; but that part which went round on the outside was more elaborately adorned with most beautiful ornaments, because it was exposed to sight, and to the view of the spectators; for which reason it was that both those sides which were extant above the rest were acute, and none of the angles, which we before told you were three, appeared less than another when the table was turned about. Now into the cord-work thus turned were precious stones inserted, in rows parallel one to the other, enclosed in golden buttons, which had ouches in them; but the parts which were on the side of the crown, and were exposed to the sight, were adorned with a row of oval figures obliquely placed, of the most excellent sort of precious stones, which imitated rods laid close, and encompassed the table round about; but under these oval figures thus engraven, the workmen had put a crown all round it, where the nature of all sorts of fruit was represented, insomuch that the bunches of grapes hung up; and when they had made the stones to represent all the kinds of fruit before mentioned, and that each in its proper colour, they made them fast with gold round the whole table. The like disposition of the oval figures, and of the engraved rods, was framed under the crown, that the table might on each side shew the same appearance of variety and elegancy of its ornaments, so that neither the position of the wave-work nor of the crown might be different, although the table were turned on the other side, but that the prospect of the same artificial contrivances might be extended as far as the feet; for there was made a plate of gold four fingers broad, through the entire breadth of the table, into which they inserted the feet, and then fastened them to the table by buttons and button-holes, at the place where the crown was situate, that so on what side soever of the table one should stand, it might exhibit the very same view of the exquisite workmanship, and of the vast expenses bestowed upon it; but upon the table itself they engraved a meander, inserting into it very valuable stones in the middle like stars, of various colours; the carbuncle and the emerald, each of which sent out agreeable rays of light to the spectators; with such stones of other sorts also as were most curious and best esteemed, as being most precious in their kind. Hard by this meander a texture of network ran round it, the middle of which appeared like a rhombus, into which were inserted rock-crystal and amber, which, by the great resemblance of the appearance they made, gave wonderful delight to those that saw them. The chapiters of the feet imitated the first budding of lilies, while their leaves were bent and laid under the table, but so that the chives were seen standing upright within them. Their bases were made of a carbuncle; and the place at the bottom, which rested on that carbuncle, was one palm deep, and eight fingers in breadth. Now they had engraven upon it, with a very fine tool, and with a great deal of pains, a branch of ivy, and tendrils of the vine, sending forth clusters of grapes, that you would guess they were nowise different from real tendrils; for they were so very thin, and so very far extended at their extremities, that they were moved with the wind, and made one believe that they were the product of nature, and not the representation of art. They also made the entire workmanship of the table appear to be threefold, while the joints of the several parts were so united together as to be invisible, and the places where they joined could not be distinguished. Now the thickness of the table was not less than half a cubit. So that this gift by the king's great generosity, by the great value of the materials, and the variety of its exquisite structure, and the artificer's skill in imitating nature with graving tools, was at length brought to perfection, while the king was very desirous, that though in largeness it were not to be different from that which was already dedicated to God, yet that in exquisite workmanship, and the novelty of the contrivances, and in the splendour of its construction, it should far exceed it, and be more illustrious than that was.

10. Now of the cisterns of gold there were two, whose sculpture was of scale-work, from its basis to its belt-like circle, with various sorts of stones enchased in the spiral circles. Next to which there was upon it a meander of a cubit in height: it was composed of stones of all sorts of colours; and next to this was the rod-work engraven; and next to that was a rhombus in a texture of network, drawn out to the brim of the basin, while small shields, made of stones, beautiful in their kind, and of four fingers' depth, filled up the middle parts. About the top of the basin were wreathed the leaves of lilies, and of the convolvulus, and the tendrils of vines in a circular manner; and this was the construction of the two cisterns of gold, each containing two firkins;—but those which were of silver were much more bright and splendid than looking-glasses; and you might in them see images that fell upon them more plainly than in the other. The king also ordered thirty vials; those of which the parts that were of gold, and filled up with precious stones, were shadowed over with the leaves of ivy and vines, artificially engraven; and these were the vessels that were, after an extraordinary manner, brought to this perfection, partly by the skill of the workmen, who were admirable in such fine work, but much more by the diligence and generosity of the king, who not only supplied the artificers abundantly, and with great generosity, with what they wanted, but he forbade public audiences for the time, and came and stood by the workmen, and saw the whole operation; and this was the cause why the workmen were so accurate in their performance, because they had regard to the king, and to his great concern about the vessels, and so the more indefatigably kept close to the work.

11. And these were what gifts were sent by Ptolemy to Jerusalem, and dedicated to God there. But when Eleazar the high priest had devoted them to God, and had paid due respect to those that brought them, and had given them presents to be carried to the king, he dismissed them. And when they were come to Alexandria, and Ptolemy heard that they were come, and that the seventy elders were come also, he presently sent for Andreas and Aristeus, his ambassadors, who came to him, and delivered him the epistle which they brought him from the high priest, and made answer to all the questions he put to them by word of mouth. He then made haste to meet the elders that came from Jerusalem for the interpretation of the laws; and he gave command, that everybody who came on other occasions should be sent away, which was a thing surprising, and what he did not use to do; for those that were drawn thither upon such occasions used to come to him

on the fifth day, but ambassadors at the month's end. But when he had sent those away, he waited for these that were sent by Eleazar; but as the old men came in with the presents, which the high priest had given them to bring to the king, and with the membranes, upon which they had their laws written in golden letters,* he put questions to them concerning those books; and when they had taken off the covers wherein they were wrapt up, they shewed him the membranes. So the king stood admiring the thinness of those membranes, and the exactness of the junctures, which could not be perceived, (so exactly were they connected one with another;) and this he did for a considerable time. He then said that he returned them thanks for coming to him, and still greater thanks to him that sent them; and, above all, to that God whose laws they appeared to be. Then did the elders, and those that were present with them, cry out with one voice, and wished all happiness to the king. Upon which he fell into tears by the violence of the pleasure he had, it being natural to men to afford the same indications in great joy that they do under sorrow. And when he had bidden them deliver the books to those that were appointed to receive them, he saluted the men, and said that it was but just to discourse, in the first place, of the errand they were sent about, and then to address himself to themselves. He promised, however, that he would make this day on which they came to him remarkable and eminent every year through the whole course of his life; for their coming to him, and the victory which he gained over Antigonus by sea, proved to be on the very same day. He also gave orders that they should sup with him; and gave it in charge that they should have excellent lodgings provided for them in the upper part of the city.

12. Now he that was appointed to take care of the reception of strangers, Nicanor by name, called for Dorotheus, whose duty it was to make provision for them, and bade him prepare for every one of them what should be requisite for their diet and way of living; which thing was ordered by the king after this manner: he took care that those that belonged to every city, which did not use the same way of living, that all things should be prepared for them according to the custom of those that came to him, that being feasted according to the usual method of their own way of living, they might be the better pleased, and might not be uneasy at anything done to them from which they were naturally averse. And this was now done in the case of these men by Dorotheus, who was put into this office because of his great skill in such matters belonging to common life: for he took care of all such matters as concerned the reception of strangers, and appointed them double seats for them to sit on, according as the king had commanded him to do; for he had commanded that half of their seats should be set at his right hand, and the other half behind his table, and took care that no respect should be omitted that could be shewn them. And when they were thus set down, he bid Dorotheus to minister to all those that were come to him from Judea, after the manner they used to be ministered to; for which cause he sent away their sacred heralds, and those that slew the sacrifices, and the rest that used to say grace: but called to one of those that were come to him, whose name was Eleazar, who was a priest, and

---

* The Talmudists say, that it is not lawful to write the law in letters of gold, contrary to this certain and very ancient example.

desired him to say grace : * who then stood in
the midst of them, and prayed that all prosperity might attend the king and those that
were his subjects. Upon which an acclamation
was made by the whole company, with joy and
a great noise ; and when that was over, they fell
to eating their supper, and to the enjoyment of
what was set before them. And at a little interval afterward, when the king thought a sufficient time had been interposed, he began to talk
philosophically to them, and he asked every one
of them a philosophical question,† and such a
one as might give light in those inquiries ; and
when they had explained all the problems that
had been proposed by the king about every
point, he was well pleased with their answers.
This took up the twelve days in which they were
treated ; and he that pleases may learn the particular questions in that book of Aristeus, which
he wrote on this very occasion.

13. And while not the king only, but the
philosopher Menedus also, admired them, and
said, that all things were governed by Providence, and that it was probable that thence it
was that such force or beauty was discovered in
these men's words,—they then left off asking
any more questions. But the king said that he
had gained very great advantages by their coming, for that he had received this profit from
them, that he had learned how he ought to rule
his subjects. And he gave order that they
should have every one three talents given them ;
and that those that were to conduct them to
their lodging should do it. Accordingly, when
three days were over, Demetrius took them, and
went over the causeway seven furlongs long : it
was a bank in the sea to an island. And when
they had gone over the bridge, he proceeded to
the northern parts, and shewed them where they
should meet, which was in a house which was
built near the shore, and was a quiet place, and
fit for their discoursing together about their
work. When he had brought them thither, he
entreated them, (now they had all things about
them which they wanted for the interpretation
of their law,) that they would suffer nothing to
interrupt them in their work. Accordingly,
they made an accurate interpretation, with great
zeal and great pains ; and this they continued to
do till the ninth hour of the day ; after which
time they relaxed and took care of their body,
while their food was provided for them in great
plenty : besides, Dorotheus, at the king's command, brought them a great deal of what was
provided for the king himself. But in the
morning they came to the court, and saluted
Ptolemy, and then went away to their former
place, where, when they had washed their
hands,‡ and purified themselves, they betook
themselves to the interpretation of the laws.
Now when the law was transcribed, and the

labour of interpretation was over, which came
to its conclusion in seventy-two days, Demetrius
gathered all the Jews together to the place
where the laws were translated, and where the
interpreters were, and read them over. The
multitude did also approve of those elders that
were the interpreters of the law. They withal
commended Demetrius for his proposal, as the
inventor of what was greatly for their happiness ; and they desired that he would give leave
to their rulers also to read the law. Moreover
they all, both the priests and the ancientest of
the elders, and the principal men of their commonwealth, made it their request, that since the
interpretation was happily finished, it might
continue in the state it now was, and might not
be altered. And when they all commended that
determination of theirs, they enjoined, that if
any one observed either anything superfluous, or
anything omitted, that he would take a view of
it again, and have it laid before them, and corrected ; which was a wise action of theirs, that
when the thing was judged to have been well
done, it might continue for ever.

14. So the king rejoiced when he saw that his design of this nature was brought to perfection, to so
great advantage : and he was chiefly delighted with
hearing the laws read to him ; and was astonished
at the deep meaning and wisdom of the legislator.
And he began to discourse with Demetrius,
" How it came to pass that, when this legislation
was so wonderful, no one, either of the poets or of
the historians, had made mention of it." Demetrius made answer, " that no one durst be so bold
as to touch upon the description of these laws,
because they were divine and venerable, and because some that had attempted it were afflicted
by God." He also told him, that " Theopompus
was desirous of writing somewhat about them,
but was thereupon disturbed in his mind for
above thirty days' time ; and upon some intermission of his distemper, he appeased God [by
prayer,] as suspecting that his madness proceeded
from that cause." Nay, indeed, he further saw
in a dream, that his distemper befell him while
he indulged too great a curiosity about divine
matters, and was desirous of publishing them
among common men ; but when he left off that
attempt, he recovered his understanding again.
Moreover, he informed him of Theodectes, the
tragic poet, concerning whom it was reported,
that when in a certain dramatic representation,
he was desirous to make mention of things that
were contained in the sacred books, he was
afflicted with a darkness in his eyes ; and that
upon his being conscious of the occasion of his
distemper, and appeasing God [by prayer,] he
was freed from that affliction.

15. And when the king had received these
books from Demetrius, as we have said already,
he adored them ; and gave order, that great care
should be taken of them, that they might remain
uncorrupted. He also desired that the interpreters would come often to him out of Judea, and
that both on account of the respect which he
would pay them, and on account of the presents
he would make them ; for he said, it was now
but just to send them away, although if, of their
own accord, they would come to him hereafter,
they should obtain all that their own wisdom
might justly require, and what his generosity
was able to give them. So he sent them away,
and gave to every one of them three garments
of the best sort, and two talents of gold, and a
cup of the value of one talent, and the furniture
of the room wherein they were feasted. And
these were the things he presented to them.
But by them he sent to Eleazar the high priest

---

* This is the most ancient example I have met with
of a grace, or thanksgiving, before meat. The next
example I have met with is that of the Essenes, both
before and after it ; those of our Saviour before it,
(Mark viii. 6 ; John vi. 11, 23 ; and St Paul, Acts
xxvii. 35,) and a form of such a grace or prayer for
Christians, at the end of the fifth book of the Apostolical Constitutions, which seems to have been intended
for both times, both before and after meat.

† They were rather political questions and answers,
tending to the good and religious government of mankind.

‡ This purification of the interpreters, by washing
in the sea, before they prayed to God every morning,
and before they set about translating, may be compared with the places of the Proseuchæ, or of prayer,
which were sometimes built near the sea or rivers
also.

ten beds, with feet of silver, and the furniture to them belonging, and a cup of the value of thirty talents ; and besides these, ten garments, and purple, and a very beautiful crown, and a hundred pieces of the finest woven linen; as also vials and dishes, and vessels for pouring, and two golden cisterns, to be dedicated to God. He also desired him, by an epistle, that he would give these interpreters leave, if any of them were desirous of coming to him ; because he highly valued a conversation with men of such learning, and should be very willing to lay out his wealth upon such men.   And this was what came to the Jews, and was much to their glory and honour, from Ptolemy and Philadelphus.

CHAPTER III

HOW THE KINGS OF ASIA HONOURED THE NATION OF THE JEWS, AND MADE THEM CITIZENS OF THOSE CITIES WHICH THEY BUILT

1. THE Jews also obtained honours from the kings of Asia, when they became their auxiliaries; for Seleucus Nicator made them citizens of those cities which he built in Asia, and in the Lower Syria, and in the metropolis itself, Antioch ; and gave them privileges equal to those of the Macedonians and Greeks, who were the inhabitants, insomuch that those privileges continue to this very day: an argument for which you have in this, that whereas the Jews do make use of oil prepared by foreigners,* they receive a certain sum of money from the proper officers belonging to their exercises as the value of that oil; which money, when the people of Antioch would have deprived them of, in the last war, Mucianus, who was then president of Syria, preserved it to them. And when the people of Alexandria and of Antioch did after that, at the time that Vespasian and Titus his son, governed the habitable earth, pray that these privileges of citizens might be taken away, they did not obtain their request.   In which behaviour any one may discern the equity and generosity of the Romans,† especially of Vespasian and Titus, who, although they had been at a great deal of pains in the war against the Jews, and were exasperated against them, because they did not deliver up their weapons to them, but continued the war to the very last, yet did not they take away any of their forementioned privileges belonging to them as citizens, but restrained their anger, and overcame the prayers of the Alexandrians and Antiochians, who were a very powerful people, insomuch that they did not yield to them, neither out of their favour to these people, nor out of their old grudge at those whose wicked opposition they had subdued in the war ; nor would they alter any of the ancient favours granted to the Jews, but said, that those who had borne arms against them, and fought them, had suffered punishment already, and that it was not just to deprive those

---

* The use of oil was much greater in Judea, and the neighbouring countries, than it is amongst us.   It was also, in the days of Josephus, thought unlawful for Jews to make use of any oil that was prepared by heathens, perhaps on account of some superstitions intermixed with its preparation by those heathens.   When, therefore, the heathens were to make them a present of oil, they paid them money instead of it.

† The justice, and equity, and generosity of the old Romans, both to the Jews and other conquered nations, affords us a very good reason why Almighty God, upon the rejection of the Jews for their wickedness, chose them for his people, and first established Christianity in that empire.

that had not offended of the privileges they enjoyed.

2. We also know that Marcus Agrippa was of the like disposition towards the Jews: for when the people of Ionia were very angry at them, and besought Agrippa, that they, and they only, might have those privileges of citizens which Antiochus, the grandson of Seleucus, (who by the Greeks was called *The God*,) had bestowed on them ; and desired that, if the Jews were to be joint-partakers with them, they might be obliged to worship the gods they themselves worshipped : but when these matters were brought to trial, the Jews prevailed, and obtained leave to make use of their own customs, and this under the patronage of Nicolaus of Damascus ; for Agrippa gave sentence, that he could not innovate.   And if any one hath a mind to know this matter accurately, let him peruse the hundred and twenty-third and hundred and twenty-fourth books of the history of this Nicolaus.   Now, as to this determination of Agrippa, it is not so much to be admired ; for at that time our nation had not made war against the Romans.   But one may well be astonished at the generosity of Vespasian and Titus, that after so great wars and contests which they had from us, they should use such moderation.   But I will now return to that part of my history whence I made the present digression.

3. Now it happened that in the reign of Antiochus the Great, who ruled over all Asia, that the Jews, as well as the inhabitants of Cœlesyria, suffered greatly, and their land was sorely harassed ; for while he was at war with Ptolemy Philopater, and with his son, who was called Epiphanes, it fell out that these nations were equally sufferers, both when he was beaten and when he beat the others: so that they were very like to a ship in a storm, which is tossed by the waves on both sides: and just thus were they in their situation in the middle between Antiochus's prosperity and its change to adversity. But at length, when Antiochus had beaten Ptolemy, he seized upon Judea: and when Philopater was dead, his son sent out a great army under Scopas, the general of his forces, against the inhabitants of Cœlesyria, who took many of their cities, and in particular our nation ; which, when he fell upon them, went over to him.   Yet was it not long afterward when Antiochus overcame Scopas, in a battle fought at the fountains of Jordan, and destroyed a great part of his army.   But afterward, when Antiochus subdued those cities of Cœlesyria which Scopas had gotten into his possession, and Samaria with them, the Jews, of their own accord, went over to him, and received him into the city [Jerusalem,] and gave plentiful provision to all his army, and to his elephants, and readily assisted him when he besieged the garrison which was in the citadel of Jerusalem.   Wherefore Antiochus thought it but just to requite the Jews' diligence and zeal in his service : so he wrote to the generals of his armies, and to his friends, and gave testimony to the good behaviour of the Jews towards him, and informed them what rewards he had resolved to bestow on them for that their behaviour.   I will set down presently the epistles themselves which he wrote to the generals concerning them, but will first produce the testimony of Polybius of Megalopolis ; for thus does he speak, in the sixteenth book of his history!—"Now Scopas, the general of Ptolemy's army, went in haste to the superior parts of the country, and in the winter-time overthrew the nation of the Jews." He also saith, in the same book, that "when Scopas was

conquered by Antiochus, Antiochus received Batanea and Samaria, and Abila and Gadara; and that, a while afterwards, there came in to him those Jews that inhabited near the temple which was called Jerusalem; concerning which, although I have more to say, and particularly concerning the presence of God about that temple, yet do I put off that history till another opportunity." This it is which Polybius relates; but we will return to the series of the history, when we have first produced the epistles of king Antiochus.

"KING ANTIOCHUS TO PTOLEMY, SENDETH GREETING

"Since the Jews, upon our first entrance on their country, demonstrated their friendship towards us; and when we came to their city, [Jerusalem,] received us in a splendid manner, and came to meet us with their senate, and gave abundance of provisions to our soldiers, and to the elephants, and joined with us in ejecting the garrison of the Egyptians that were in the citadel, we have thought fit to reward them, and to retrieve the condition of their city, which hath been greatly depopulated by such accidents as have befallen its inhabitants, and to bring those that have been scattered abroad back to the city; and, in the first place, we have determined, on account of their piety towards God, to bestow on them, as a pension, for their sacrifices of animals that are fit for sacrifice, for wine and oil, and frankincense, the value of twenty thousand pieces of silver, and [six] sacred artabræ of fine flour, with one thousand four hundred and sixty medimni of wheat, and three hundred and seventy-five medimni of salt; and these payments I would have fully paid them, as I have sent orders to you. I would also have the work about the temple finished, and the cloisters, and if there be anything else that ought to be rebuilt; and for the materials of wood, let it be brought them out of Judea itself, and out of the other countries, and out of Libanus, tax-free; and the same I would have observed as to those other materials which will be necessary, in order to render the temple more glorious; and let all of that nation live according to the laws of their own country; and let the senate and the priests, and the scribes of the temple, and the sacred singers, be discharged from poll-money and the crown-tax, and other taxes also; and that the city may the sooner recover its inhabitants, I grant a discharge from taxes for three years to its present inhabitants, and to such as shall come to it, until the month Hyperberetus. We also discharge them for the future from a third part of their taxes, that the losses they have sustained may be repaired; and all those citizens that have been carried away, and are become slaves, we grant them and their children their freedom; and give order that their substance be restored to them."

4. And these were the contents of this epistle. He also published a decree, through all his kingdom, in honour of the temple, which contained what follows:—"It shall be lawful for no foreigner to come within the limits of the temple round about; which thing is forbidden also to the Jews, unless to those who, according to their own custom, have purified themselves. Nor let any flesh of horses, or of mules, or of asses, be brought into the city, whether they be wild or tame; nor that of leopards, or foxes, or hares; and, in general, that of any animal which is forbidden for the Jews to eat. Nor let their skins be brought into it; nor let any such animal be bred up in the city. Let them only be permitted to use the sacrifices derived from their forefathers, with which they have been obliged to make acceptable atonements to God. And he that transgresseth any of these orders, let him pay to the priests three thousand drachmæ of silver." Moreover, this Antiochus bare testimony to our piety and fidelity, in an epistle of his, written when he was informed of a sedition in Phrygia and Lydia, at which time he was in the superior provinces, wherein he commanded Zeuxis, the general of his forces, and his most intimate friend, to send some of our nation out of Babylon into Phrygia. The epistle was this:—

"KING ANTIOCHUS TO ZEUXIS, HIS FATHER, SENDETH GREETING

"If you are in health, it is well. I also am in health. Having been informed that a sedition is arisen in Lydia and Phrygia, I thought the matter required great care; and upon advising with my friends what was fit to be done, it hath been thought proper to remove two thousand families of Jews, with their effects, out of Mesopotamia and Babylon, unto the castles and places that lie most convenient; for I am persuaded that they will be well-disposed guardians of our possessions, because of their piety towards God, and because I know that my predecessors have borne witness to them that they are faithful, and with alacrity do what they are desired to do. I will, therefore, though it be a laborious work, that thou remove these Jews; under a promise, that they shall be permitted to use their own laws: and when thou shalt have brought them to the places forementioned, thou shalt give every one of their families a place for building their houses, and a portion of land for their husbandry, and for the plantation of their vines; and thou shalt discharge them from paying taxes of the fruits of the earth for ten years; and let them have a proper quantity of wheat for the maintenance of their servants, until they receive bread-corn out of the earth; also let a sufficient share be given to such as minister to them in the necessaries of life, that by enjoying the effects of our humanity, they may shew themselves the more willing and ready about our affairs. Take care likewise of that nation, as far as thou art able, that they may not have any disturbance given them by any one."

Now these testimonials, which I have produced, are sufficient to declare the friendship that Antiochus the Great bare to the Jews.

CHAPTER IV

HOW ANTIOCHUS MADE A LEAGUE WITH PTOLEMY; AND HOW ONIAS PROVOKED PTOLEMY EUERGETES TO ANGER; AND HOW JOSEPH BROUGHT ALL THINGS RIGHT AGAIN, AND ENTERED INTO FRIENDSHIP WITH HIM; AND WHAT OTHER THINGS WERE DONE BY JOSEPH, AND HIS SON HYRCANUS

1. AFTER this Antiochus made a friendship and a league with Ptolemy, and gave him his daughter Cleopatra to wife, and yielded up to him Cœlesyria, and Samaria, and Judea, and Phœnicia, by way of dowry; and upon the division of the taxes between the two kings, all the principal men framed the taxes of their several countries, and collecting the sum that was settled for them, paid the same to the [two] kings. Now at this time the Samaritans were in a flourishing condition, and much distressed the Jews, cutting off parts of their land, and carry-

ing off slaves. This happened when Onias was high priest; for after Eleazar's death, his uncle Manasseh took the priesthood, and after he had ended his life, Onias received that dignity. He was son of Simon, who was called *The Just;* which Simon was the brother of Eleazar, as I said before. This Onias was one of a little soul, and a great lover of money; and for that reason, because he did not pay that tax of twenty talents of silver, which his forefathers paid to these kings, out of their own estates, he provoked king Ptolemy Euergetes to anger, who was the father of Philopater. Euergetes sent an ambassador to Jerusalem, and complained that Onias did not pay his taxes, and threatened, that if he did not receive them, he would seize upon their land, and send soldiers to live upon it. When the Jews heard this message of the king, they were confounded; but so sordidly covetous was Onias, that nothing of this nature made him ashamed.

2. There was now one Joseph, young in age, but of great reputation among the people of Jerusalem, for gravity, prudence, and justice. His father's name was Tobias; and his mother was the sister of Onias the high priest, who informed him of the coming of the ambassador; for he was then sojourning at a village named Phicol,* where he was born. Hereupon he came to the city [Jerusalem,] and reproved Onias for not taking care of the preservation of his countrymen, but bringing the nation into dangers, by not paying this money. For which preservation of them, he told him he had received the authority over them, and had been made high priest; but that, in case he was so great a lover of money, as to endure to see his country in danger on that account, and his countrymen suffer the greatest damages, he advised him to go to the king, and petition him to remit either the whole or a part of the sum demanded. Onias's answer was this:--That he did not care for his authority, and that he was ready, if the thing were practicable, to lay down his high priesthood; and that he would not go to the king, because he troubled not himself at all about such matters. Joseph then asked him if he would not give him leave to go ambassador on behalf of the nation; he replied, that he would give him leave. Upon which Joseph went up into the temple, and called the multitude together to a congregation, and exhorted them not to be disturbed nor affrighted, because of his uncle Onias's carelessness, but desired them to be at rest, and not terrify themselves with fear about it; for he promised them that he would be their ambassador to the king, and persuade him that they had done him no wrong; and when the multitude heard this, they returned thanks to Joseph. So he went down from the temple, and treated Ptolemy's ambassador in an hospitable manner. He also presented him with rich gifts, and feasted him magnificently for many days, and then sent him to the king before him, and told him that he would soon follow him; for he was now more willing to go to the king, by the encouragement of the ambassador, who earnestly persuaded him to come into Egypt, and promised him that he would take care that he should obtain every thing that he desired of Ptolemy; for he was highly pleased with his frank and liberal temper, and with the gravity of his deportment.

3. When Ptolemy's ambassador was come into

Egypt, he told the king of the thoughtless temper of Onias; and informed him of the goodness of the disposition of Joseph; and that he was coming to him, to excuse the multitude as not having done him any harm, for that he was their patron. In short, he was so very large in his encomiums upon the young man, that he disposed both the king and his wife Cleopatra to have a kindness for him before he came. So Joseph sent to his friends at Samaria, and borrowed money of them; and got ready what was necessary for his journey, garments and cups, and beasts for burden, which amounted to about twenty thousand drachmæ, and went to Alexandria. Now it happened that at this time all the principal men and rulers went up out of the cities of Syria and Phœnicia, to bid for their taxes; for every year the king sold them to the men of the greatest power in every city. So these men saw Joseph journeying on the way, and laughed at him for his poverty and meanness; but when he came to Alexandria, and heard that king Ptolemy was at Memphis, he went up thither to meet with him; which happened as the king was sitting in his chariot, with his wife, and with his friend Athenion, who was the very person who had been ambassador at Jerusalem, and had been entertained by Joseph. As soon therefore as Athenion saw him, he presently made him known to the king, how good and generous a young man he was. So Ptolemy saluted him first, and desired him to come up into his chariot; and as Joseph sat there he began to complain of the management of Onias: to which he answered, "Forgive him, on account of his age; for thou canst not certainly be unacquainted with this, that old men and infants have their minds exactly alike; but thou shalt have from us, who are young men, everything thou desirest, and shalt have no cause to complain." With this good humour and pleasantry of the young man, the king was so delighted, that he began already, as though he had had long experience of him, to have a still greater affection for him, insomuch that he bade him take his diet in the king's palace, and be a guest at his own table every day; but when the king was come to Alexandria, the principal men of Syria saw him sitting with the king, and were much offended at it.

4. And when the day came on which the king was to let the taxes of the cities to farm, and those that were the principal men of dignity in their several countries were to bid for them, the sum of the taxes together, of Cœlesyria and Phœnicia, and Judea, with Samaria, [as they were bidden for,] came to eight thousand talents. Hereupon Joseph accused the bidders, as having agreed together to estimate the value of the taxes at too low a rate; and he promised that he would himself give twice as much for them; but for those who did not pay, he would send the king home their whole substance; for this privilege was sold together with the taxes themselves. The king was pleased to hear that offer; and, because it augmented his revenues, he said he would confirm the sale of the taxes to him; but when he asked him this question, whether he had any sureties that would be bound for the payment of the money, he answered very pleasantly, "I will give such security, and those of persons good and responsible, and which you shall have no reason to distrust:" and when he bade him name them, who they were, he replied, "I give thee no other persons, O king, for my sureties, than thyself, and this thy wife; and you shall be security for both parties." So Ptolemy laughed at the proposal, and granted

* The name of this place is the very same with that of the chief captain of Abimelech's host, in the days of Abraham, (Gen. xxi. 22,) and might possibly be the place of his nativity or abode; for it seems to have been in the south part of Palestine, as that was.

him the farming of the taxes without any sureties. This procedure was a sore grief to those that came from the cities into Egypt, who were utterly disappointed; and they returned every one to their own country with shame.

5. But Joseph took with him two thousand foot soldiers from the king, for he desired he might have some assistance, in order to force such as were refractory in the cities to pay. And borrowing of the king's friends at Alexandria five hundred talents, he made haste back into Syria. And when he was at Askelon, and demanded the taxes of the people of Askelon, they refused to pay anything, and affronted him also: upon which he seized upon about twenty of the principal men, and slew them, and gathered what they had together, and sent it all to the king; and informed him what he had done. Ptolemy admired the prudent conduct of the man, and commended him for what he had done; and gave him leave to do as he pleased. When the Syrians heard of this they were astonished; and having before them a sad example in the men of Askelon that were slain, they opened their gates, and willingly admitted Joseph, and paid their taxes. And when the inhabitants of Scythopolis attempted to affront him, and would not pay him those taxes which they formerly used to pay, without disputing about them, he slew also the principal men of that city, and sent their effects to the king. By this means he gathered great wealth together, and made vast gains by this farming of the taxes; and he made use of what estate he had thus gotten, in order to support his authority, as thinking it a piece of prudence to keep what had been the occasion and foundation of his present good fortune; and this he did by the assistance of what he was already possessed of, for he privately sent many presents to the king, and to Cleopatra, and to their friends, and to all that were powerful about the court, and thereby purchased their good-will to himself.

6. This good fortune he enjoyed for twenty-two years; and was become the father of seven sons by one wife; he had also another son, whose name was Hyrcanus, by his brother Solymius's daughter, whom he married on the following occasion. He once came to Alexandria with his brother, who had along with him a daughter already marriageable, in order to give her in wedlock to some of the Jews of chief dignity there. He then supped with the king, and falling in love with an actress that was of great beauty, and came into the room where they feasted, he told his brother of it, and entreated him, because a Jew is forbidden by their law to come near to a foreigner, to conceal his offence, and to be kind and subservient to him, and to give him an opportunity of fulfilling his desires. Upon which his brother willingly entertained the proposal of serving him, and adorned his own daughter, and brought her to him by night, and put her into his bed. And Joseph being disordered with drink, knew not who she was, and so lay with his brother's daughter; and this did he many times, and loved her exceedingly; and said to his brother, that he loved this actress so well, that he should run the hazard of his life [if he must part with her,] and yet probably the king would not give him leave [to take her with him.] But his brother bade him be in no concern about that matter, and told him he might enjoy her whom he loved without any danger, and might have her for his wife; and opened the truth of the matter to him, and assured him that he chose rather to have his own daughter abused, than to overlook him, and see

him come to [public] disgrace. So Joseph commended him for this his brotherly love, and married his daughter; and by her begat a son whose name was Hyrcanus, as we said before. And when this his youngest son shewed, at thirteen years old, a mind that was both courageous and wise, and was greatly envied by his brethren, as being of a genius much above them, and such a one as they might well envy, Joseph had once a mind to know which of his sons had the best disposition to virtue; and when he sent them severally to those that had then the best reputation for instructing youth, the rest of his children, by reason of their sloth, and unwillingness to take pains, returned to him foolish and unlearned. After them he sent out the youngest, Hyrcanus, and gave him three hundred yoke of oxen, and bid him go two days' journey into the wilderness, and sow the land there, and yet kept back privately the yokes of the oxen that coupled them together. When Hyrcanus came to the place, and found he had no yokes with him, he contemned the drivers of the oxen, who advised him to send some to his father, to bring them some yokes; but he thinking that he ought not to lose his time while they should be sent to bring him the yokes, he invented a kind of stratagem, and what suited an age elder than his own; for he slew ten yoke of the oxen, and distributed their flesh among the labourers, and cut their hides into several pieces, and made him yokes, and yoked the oxen together with them; by which means he sowed as much land as his father had appointed him to sow, and returned to him. And when he was come back, his father was mightily pleased with his sagacity, and commended the sharpness of his understanding, and his boldness in what he did. And he still loved him the more, as if he were his only genuine son, while his brethren were much troubled at it.

7. But when one told him that Ptolemy had a son just born, and that all the principal men of Syria, and the other countries subject to him, were to keep a festival on account of the child's birthday, and went away in haste with great retinues to Alexandria, he was himself indeed hindered from going by old age; but he made trial of his sons, whether any of them would be willing to go to the king. And when the elder sons excused themselves from going, and said they were not courtiers good enough for such conversation, and advised him to send their brother Hyrcanus, he gladly hearkened to that advice, and called Hyrcanus, and asked him whether he would go to the king; and whether it was agreeable to him to go or not. And upon his promise that he would go, and his saying that he should not want much money for his journey, because he would live moderately, and that ten thousand drachmæ would be sufficient, he was pleased with his son's prudence. After a little while, the son advised his father not to send his presents to the king from thence, but to give him a letter to his steward at Alexandria, that he might furnish him with money, for purchasing what should be most excellent and most precious. So he thinking that the expense of ten talents would be enough for presents to be made to the king, and commending his son, as giving him good advice, wrote to Arion his steward, that managed all his money matters at Alexandria; which money was not less than three thousand talents on his account, for Joseph sent the money he received in Syria to Alexandria. And when the day appointed for the payment of the taxes to the king came, he wrote to Arion to pay them. So when the son had asked his father for a letter to this steward, and had

received it, he made haste to Alexandria. And when he was gone, his brethren wrote to all the king's friends, that they should destroy him.

8. But when he was come to Alexandria, he delivered his letter to Arion, who asked him how many talents he would have, (hoping he would ask for no more than ten, or a little more;) he said, he wanted a thousand talents. At which the steward was angry, and rebuked him, as one that intended to live extravagantly; and he let him know how his father had gathered together his estate by painstaking and resisting his inclinations, and wished him to imitate the example of his father: he assured him withal, that he would give him but ten talents, and that for a present to the king also. The son was irritated at this, and threw Arion into prison. But when Arion's wife had informed Cleopatra of this, with her entreaty, that she would rebuke the child for what he had done, (for Arion was in great esteem with her,) Cleopatra informed the king of it. And Ptolemy sent for Hyrcanus, and told him that he wondered, when he was sent to him by his father, that he had not yet come into his presence, but had laid the steward in prison. And he gave order, therefore, that he should come to him, and give an account of the reason of what he had done. And they report, that the answer he made to the king's messenger was this: That "there was a law of his that forbade a child that was born to taste of the sacrifice, before he had been at the temple, and sacrificed to God. According to which way of reasoning, he did not himself come to him in expectation of the present he was to make to him, as to one who had been his father's benefactor; and that he had punished the slave for disobeying his commands, for that it mattered not whether a master was little or great: so that unless we punish such as these, thou thyself mayest also expect to be despised by thy subjects." Upon hearing this his answer, he fell a-laughing, and wondered at the great soul of the child.

9. When Arion was apprised that this was the king's disposition, and that he had no way to help himself, he gave the child a thousand talents, and was let out of prison. So after three days were over, Hyrcanus came and saluted the king and queen. They saw him with pleasure, and feasted him in an obliging manner, out of the respect they bare to his father. So he came to the merchants privately, and bought a hundred boys, that had learning, and were in the flower of their ages, each at a talent a-piece; as also he bought a hundred maidens, each at the same price as the other. And when he was invited to feast with the king among the principal men of the country, he sat down the lowest of them all, because he was little regarded, as a child in age still; and this by those who placed every one according to their dignity. Now when all those that sat with him had laid the bones of the several parts in a heap before Hyrcanus, (for they had themselves taken away the flesh belonging to them,) till the table where he sat was filled full with them, Trypho, who was the king's jester, and was appointed for jokes and laughter at festivals, was now asked by the guests that sat at the table [to expose him to laughter.] So he stood by the king, and said, "Dost thou not see, my lord, the bones that lie by Hyrcanus? by this similitude thou mayest conjecture that his father made all Syria as bare as he hath made these bones." And the king laughing at what Trypho said, and asking of Hyrcanus, How he came to have so many bones before him? he replied, "Very rightfully, my

lord; for they are dogs that eat the flesh and bones together, as these thy guests have done, (looking in the meantime at those guests,) for there is nothing before them; but they are men that eat the flesh, and cast away the bones, as I, who am also a man, have now done." Upon which the king admired at his answer, which was so wisely made; and bade them all make an acclamation, as a mark of their approbation of his jest, which was truly a facetious one. On the next day Hyrcanus went to every one of the king's friends, and of the men powerful at court, and saluted them; but still inquired of the servants what present they would make the king on his son's birthday; and when some said that they would give twelve talents, and that others of greater dignity would every one give according to the quantity of their riches, he pretended to every one of them to be grieved that he was not able to bring so large a present; for that he had no more than five talents. And when the servants heard what he said, they told their masters; and they rejoiced in the prospect that Joseph would be disapproved, and would make the king angry, by the smallness of his present. When the day came, the others, even those that brought the most, offered the king not above twenty talents; but Hyrcanus gave to every one of the hundred boys and hundred maidens that he had bought a talent a-piece for them to carry, and introduced them, the boys to the king, and the maidens to Cleopatra: every body wondering at the unexpected richness of the presents, even the king and queen themselves. He also presented those that attended about the king with gifts to the value of a great number of talents, that he might escape the danger he was in from them; for to those it was that Hyrcanus's brethren had written to destroy him. Now Ptolemy admired at the young man's magnanimity, and commanded him to ask what gift he pleased. But he desired nothing else to be done for him by the king than to write to his father and brethren about him. So when the king had paid him very great respects, and had given him very large gifts, and had written to his father and his brethren, and all his commanders and officers, about him, he sent him away. But when his brethren heard that Hyrcanus had received such favours from the king, and was returning home with great honour, they went out to meet him, and to destroy him, and that with the privity of their father: for he was angry at him for the [large] sum of money that he bestowed for presents, and so had no concern for his preservation. However, Joseph concealed the anger he had at his son, out of fear of the king. And when Hyrcanus's brethren came to fight him, he slew many others of those that were with them, as also two of his brethren themselves; but the rest of them escaped to Jerusalem to their father. But when Hyrcanus came to the city, where nobody would receive him, he was afraid for himself, and retired beyond the river Jordan, and there abode; but obliging the Barbarians to pay their taxes.

10. At this time, Seleucus, who was called Soter, reigned over Asia, being the son of Antiochus the Great. And [now] Hyrcanus's father, Joseph, died. He was a good man, and of great magnanimity; and brought the Jews out of a state of poverty and meanness, to one that was more splendid. He retained the farm of the taxes of Syria, and Phœnicia, and Samaria, twenty-two years. His uncle also, Onias, died [about this time,] and left the high priesthood to his son Simon. And when he was dead, Onias

his son succeeded him in that dignity. To him it was that Areus, king of the Lacedemonians, sent an embassage, with an epistle; the copy whereof here follows:—

"AREUS, KING OF THE LACEDEMONIANS, TO ONIAS, SENDETH GREETING

"We have met with a certain writing, whereby we have discovered that both the Jews and the Lacedemonians are of one stock, and are derived from the kindred of Abraham.* It is but just, therefore, that you, who are our brethren, should send to us about any of your concerns as you please. We will also do the same thing. and esteem your concerns as our own, and will look upon our concerns as in common with yours. Demotoles, who brings you this letter, will bring your answer back to us. This letter is four-square; and the seal is an eagle, with a dragon in his claws."

11. And these were the contents of the epistle which was sent from the king of the Lacedemonians. But upon the death of Joseph, the people grew seditious, on account of his sons; for whereas the elders made war against Hyrcanus, who was the youngest of Joseph's sons, the multitude was divided, but the greater part joined with the elders in this war: as did Simon the high priest, by reason he was of kin to them. However, Hyrcanus determined not to return to Jerusalem any more, but seated himself beyond Jordan, and was at perpetual war with the Arabians, and slew many of them, and took many of them captives. He also erected a strong castle, and built it entirely of white stone to the very roof, and had animals of a prodigious magnitude engraven upon it. He also drew around it a great and deep canal of water. He also made caves of many furlongs in length, by hollowing a rock that was over-against him; and then he made large rooms in it, some for feasting, and some for sleeping, and living in. He introduced also a vast quantity of waters which ran along it, and which were very delightful and ornamental in the court. But still he made the entrances at the mouth of the caves so narrow, that no more than one person could enter by them at once. And the reason why he built them after that manner was a good one; it was for his own preservation, lest he should be besieged by his brethren, and run the hazard of being caught by them. Moreover, he built courts of greater magnitude than ordinary, which he adorned with vastly large gardens. And when he had brought the place to this state, he named it Tyre. This place is between Arabia and Judea, beyond Jordan, not far from the country of Heshbon. And he ruled over those parts for seven years, even all the time that Seleucus was king of Syria. But when he was dead, his brother Antiochus, who was called Epiphanes, took the kingdom. Ptolemy also, the king of Egypt, died, who was besides called Epiphanes. He left two sons, and both young in age; the elder of whom was called Philometer, and the younger Physcon. As for Hyrcanus, when he saw that Antiochus had a great army, and feared lest he should be caught by him, and

brought to punishment for what he had done to the Arabians, he ended his life, and slew himself with his own hand; while Antiochus seized upon all his substance.

CHAPTER V

HOW, UPON THE QUARRELS OF THE JEWS ONE AGAINST ANOTHER ABOUT THE HIGH PRIESTHOOD, ANTIOCHUS MADE AN EXPEDITION AGAINST JERUSALEM, TOOK THE CITY, AND PILLAGED THE TEMPLE, AND DISTRESSED THE JEWS: AS ALSO, HOW MANY OF THE JEWS FORSOOK THE LAWS OF THEIR COUNTRY; AND HOW THE SAMARITANS FOLLOWED THE CUSTOMS OF THE GREEKS, AND NAMED THEIR TEMPLE AT MOUNT GERIZZIM, THE TEMPLE OF JUPITER HELLENIUS

1. ABOUT this time, upon the death of Onias the high priest, they gave the high priesthood to Jesus his brother; for that son which Onias left [or Onias IV.] was yet but an infant; and, in its proper place, we will inform the reader of all the circumstances that befell this child. But this Jesus, who was the brother of Onias, was deprived of the high priesthood by the king, who was angry with him, and gave it to his younger brother, whose name also was Onias; for Simon had these three sons, to each of whom the priesthood came, as we have already informed the reader. This Jesus changed his name to Jason; but Onias was called Menelaus. Now as the former high priest, Jesus, raised a sedition against Menelaus, who was ordained after him, the multitude were divided between them both. And the sons of Tobias took the part of Menelaus, but the greater part of the people assisted Jason: and by that means Menelaus and the sons of Tobias were distressed, and retired to Antiochus, and informed him, that they were desirous to leave the laws of their country, and the Jewish way of living according to them, and to follow the king's laws, and the Grecian way of living: wherefore they desired his permission to build them a gymnasium at Jerusalem.† And when he had given them leave, they also hid the circumcision of their genitals, that even when they were naked they might appear to be Greeks. Accordingly, they left off all the customs that belonged to their own country, and imitated the practices of other nations.

2. Now Antiochus, upon the agreeable situation of the affairs of his kingdom, resolved to make an exp dition against Egypt, both because he had a desire to gain it, and because he contemned the son of Ptolemy, as now weak, and not yet of abilities to manage affairs of such consequence; so he came with great forces to Pelusium, and circumvented Ptolemy Philometer by treachery, and seized upon Egypt. He then came to the places about Memphis, and when he had taken them, he made haste to Alexandria, in hopes of taking it by siege, and of subduing Ptolemy, who reigned there. But he was driven not only from Alexandria, but out of all Egypt, by the declaration of the Romans, who charged him to let that country alone. Accordingly, as I have elsewhere formerly declared, I will now give a particular account of what concerns this king,—how he subdued Judea and the temple;

---

* These Lacedemonians, Grotius supposes, were derived from the Dores, that came of the Pelasgi. These are, by Herodotus, called Barbarians; and perhaps were derived from the Syrians and Arabians, the posterity of Abraham by Keturah. It may be further observed, that Eliezer, of Damascus, the servant of Abraham, (Gen. xv. 2, xxiv.,) was of old by some taken for his son. So that if the Lacedemonians were sprung from him, they might themselves to be of the posterity of Abraham, as well as the Jews, who were sprung from Isaac.

† This word, "gymnasium," properly denotes a place where the exercises were performed naked; which, because it would naturally distinguish circumcised Jews from uncircumcised Gentiles, these Jewish apostates endeavoured to appear uncircumcised, by means of a surgical operation, hinted at by St Paul, (1 Cor. vii. 18.)

for in my former work I mentioned those things very briefly, and have therefore now thought it necessary to go over that history again, and that with great accuracy.

3. King Antiochus returning out of Egypt,* for fear of the Romans, made an expedition against the city Jerusalem; and when he was there, in the hundred and forty-third year of the kingdom of the Seleucidæ, he took the city without fighting, those of his own party opening the gates to him. And when he had gotten possession of Jerusalem, and slew many of the opposite party; and when he had plundered it of a great deal of money, he returned to Antioch.

4. Now it came to pass, after two years, in the hundred and forty-fifth year, on the twenty-fifth day of that month which is by us called Chasleu, and by the Macedonians Appelus, in the hundred and fifty-third olympiad, that the king came up to Jerusalem, and, pretending peace, he got possession of the city by treachery: at which time he spared not so much as those that admitted him into it, on account of the riches that lay in the temple; but, led by his covetous inclination, (for he saw there was in it a great deal of gold, and many ornaments that had been dedicated to it of very great value,) and in order to plunder its wealth, he ventured to break the league he had made. So he left the temple bare, and took away the golden candlesticks, and the golden altar [of incense,] and table [of shew-bread,] and the altar [of burnt-offering;] and did not abstain from even the veils, which were made of fine linen and scarlet. He also emptied it of its secret treasures, and left nothing at all remaining; and by this means cast the Jews into great lamentation, for he forbade them to offer those daily sacrifices which they used to offer to God, according to the law. And when he had pillaged the whole city, some of the inhabitants he slew, and some he carried captive, together with their wives and children, so that the multitude of those captives that were taken alive amounted to about ten thousand. He also burnt down the finest buildings; and when he had overthrown the city walls, he built a citadel in the lower part of the city,† for the place was high, and overlooked the temple. on which account he fortified it with high walls and towers, and put into it a garrison of Macedonians. However, in that citadel dwelt the impious and wicked part of the [Jewish] multitude, from whom it proved that the citizens suffered many and sore calamities. And when the king had built an idol altar upon God's altar, he slew swine upon it, and so offered a sacrifice neither according to the law, nor the Jewish religious worship in that country. He also compelled them to forsake the worship which they paid their own God, and to adore those whom he took to be gods; and made them build temples, and raise idol altars, in every city and village, and offer swine upon them every day. He also commanded them not to circumcise their sons, and threatened to punish any that should be found to have transgressed his injunction.

He also appointed overseers, who should compel them to do what he commanded. And indeed many Jews there were who complied with the king's commands, either voluntarily, or out of fear of the penalty that was denounced: but the best men, and those of the noblest souls, did not regard him, but did pay a greater respect to the customs of their country than concern as to the punishment which he threatened to the disobedient; on which account they every day underwent great miseries and bitter torments; for they were whipped with rods, and their bodies were torn to pieces, and were crucified while they were still alive and breathed: they also strangled those women and their sons whom they had circumcised, as the king had appointed, hanging their sons about their necks as they were upon the crosses. And if there were any sacred book of the law found, it was destroyed; and those with whom they were found, miserably perished also.

5. When the Samaritans saw the Jews under these sufferings, they no longer confessed they were of their kindred, nor that the temple on Mount Gerizzim belonged to Almighty God. This was according to their nature, as we have already shewn. And they now said that they were a colony of Medes and Persians: and indeed they were a colony of theirs. So they sent ambassadors to Antiochus, and an epistle, whose contents are these:—"To king Antiochus the god Epiphanes, a memorial from the Sidonians, who live at Shechem. Our forefathers, upon certain frequent plagues, and as following a certain ancient superstition, had a custom of observing that day which by the Jews is called the Sabbath.‡ And when they had erected a temple at the mountain called Gerizzim, though without a name, they offered upon it the proper sacrifices. Now, upon the just treatment of these wicked Jews, those that manage their affairs, supposing that we were of kin to them, and practised as they do, make us liable to the same accusations, although we are originally Sidonians, as is evident from the public records. We therefore beseech thee, our benefactor and saviour, to give order to Apollonius, the governor of this part of the country, and to Nicanor, the procurator of thy affairs, to give us no disturbance, nor to lay to our charge what the Jews are accused for, since we are aliens from their nation and from their customs; but let our temple, which at present hath no name at all, be named the Temple of Jupiter Hellenius. If this were once done, we should be no longer disturbed, but should be more intent on our own occupation with quietness, and so bring in a greater revenue to thee." When the Samaritans had petitioned for this, the king sent them back the following answer in an epistle:—"King Antiochus to Nicanor. The Sidonians, who live at Shechem, have sent me the memorial inclosed. When therefore, we were advising with our friends about it, the messengers sent by them represented to us that they are no way concerned with accusations which belong to the Jews, but choose to live after the customs of the Greeks. Accordingly we declare them free from such accusations, and order that, agreeable to their petition, their temple be named the temple of Jupiter Hellenius." He also sent the like epistle to Appolonius, the governor of that part of the country, in the forty-sixth year, and the eighteenth day of the month Hecatombeon.

---

* Hereabout Josephus begins to follow the first book of the Maccabees.

† This citadel seems to have been a castle built on a hill, lower than mount Zion, though upon its skirts, and higher than mount Moriah, but between them both; which hill the enemies of the Jews now got possession of, and built on this citadel, and fortified it, till a good while afterwards the Jews regained it, demolished it, and levelled the hill itself with the common ground, that their enemies might no more recover it, and might thence overlook the temple itself, and do them such mischief as they had long undergone from it.

‡ This allegation of the Samaritans is remarkable, that though they were not Jews, yet did they, from ancient times, observe the Sabbath-day, and, as they elsewhere pretend, the Sabbatic year also.

CHAPTER VI

HOW, UPON ANTIOCHUS'S PROHIBITION TO THE
JEWS TO MAKE USE OF THE LAWS OF THEIR
COUNTRY, MATTATHIAS, THE SON OF ASAMONEUS,
ALONE DESPISED THE KING, AND OVERCAME THE
GENERALS OF ANTIOCHUS'S ARMY : AS ALSO CON-
CERNING THE DEATH OF MATTATHIAS, AND THE
SUCCESSION OF JUDAS

1. Now at this time there was one whose name
was Mattathias, who dwelt at Modin, the son of
John, the son of Simeon, the son of Asamoneus,
a priest of the order of Joarib, and a citizen of
Jerusalem. He had five sons ; John, who was
called Gaddis, and Simeon, who was called
Matthes, and Judas, who was called Maccabeus,*
and Eleazar, who was called Auran, and Jonathan, who was called Apphus. Now this Mattathias lamented to his children the sad state of
their affairs, and the ravage made in the city,
and the plundering of the temple, and the calamities the multitude were under; and he told
them that it was better for them to die for the
laws of their country, than live so ingloriously as
they then did.

2. But when those that were appointed by the
king were come to Modin, that they might compel the Jews to do what they were commanded,
and to enjoin those that were there to offer sacrifice, as the king had commanded, they desired
that Mattathias, a person of the greatest character among them, both on other accounts, and
particularly on account of such a numerous and
so deserving a family of children, would begin
the sacrifice, because his fellow-citizens would
follow his example, and because such a procedure would make him honoured by the king. But
Mattathias said that he would not do it ; and
that if all the other nations would obey the commands of Antiochus, either out of fear, or to
please him, yet would not he nor his sons leave
the religious worship of their country ; but as
soon as he had ended his speech, there came one
of the Jews into the midst of them, and sacrificed as Antiochus had commanded. At which
Mattathias had great indignation, and ran upon
him violently with his sons, who had swords
with them, and slew both the man himself that
sacrificed, and Apelles the king's general, who
compelled them to sacrifice, with a few of his
soldiers. He also overthrew the idol altar, and
cried out, " If," said he, "any one be zealous for
the laws of his country, and for the worship of
God, let him follow me ; " and when he had said
this, he made haste into the desert with his sons,
and left all his substance in the village. Many
others did the same also, and fled with their
children and wives into the desert and dwelt in
caves ; but when the king's generals heard this,
they took all the forces they then had in the
citadel at Jerusalem, and pursued the Jews into
the desert ; and when they had overtaken them,
they in the first place endeavoured to persuade
them to repent, and to chose what was most for
their advantage, and not put them to the necessity of using them according to the law of war ;
but when they would not comply with their persuasions, but continued to be of a different mind,
they fought against them on the Sabbath-day,
and they burnt them as they were in the caves,
without resistance, and without so much as stop-

* This appellation of Maccabee was not first of all
given to Judas Maccabeus, nor was derived from any
initial letters of the Hebrew words on his banner, "Mi
Kamoka Be Elim, Jehovah ?" ("Who is like unto thee
among the gods, O Jehovah ?" Exod. xv. 11,) as the
modern Rabbins vainly pretend.

ping up the entrances of the caves. And they
avoided to defend themselves on that day, because they were not willing to break in upon the
honour they owed the Sabbath, even in such distresses ; for our law requires that we rest upon
that day. There were about a thousand, with
their wives and children, who were smothered
and died in these caves : but many of those that
escaped joined themselves to Mattathias, and appointed him to be their ruler, who taught them
to fight even on the Sabbath-day ; and told them
that unless they would do so, they would become
their own enemies, by observing the law [so rigor-
ously,] while their adversaries would still assault
them on this day, and they would not then defend
themselves ; and that nothing could then hinder
but they must all perish without fighting. This
speech persuaded them ; and this rule continues
among us to this day, that if there be a necessity,
we may fight on Sabbath-days. So Mattathias
got a great army about him, and overthrew their
idol altars, and slew those that broke the laws,
even all that he could get under his power ; for
many of them were dispersed among the nations
round about them for fear of him. He also commanded that those boys who were not yet circumcised should be circumcised now ; and he
drove those away that were appointed to hinder
such their circumcision.

3. But when he had ruled one year, and was
fallen into a distemper, he called for his sons,
and set them round about him, and said, "O my
sons, I am going the way of all the earth ; and I
recommend to you my resolution, and beseech
you not to be negligent in keeping it, but to be
mindful of the desires of him who begat you, and
brought you up, and to preserve the customs of
your country, and to recover your ancient form
of government, which is in danger of being overturned, and not to be carried away with those
that, either by their own inclination, or out of
necessity, betray it, but to become such sons as
are worthy of me ; to be above all force and necessity, and so to dispose your souls, as to be
ready, when it shall be necessary, to die for your
laws ; as sensible of this, by just reasoning, that
if God see that you are so disposed he will not
overlook you, but will have a great value for your
virtue, and will restore to you again what you
have lost, and will return to you that freedom
in which you shall live quietly, and enjoy your
own customs. Your bodies are mortal, and subject to fate ; but they receive a sort of immortality, by the remembrance of what actions they
have done ; and I would have you so in love with
this immortality, that you may pursue after glory,
and that, when you have undergone the greatest
difficulties, you may not scruple, for such things,
to lose your lives. I exhort you especially to
agree one with another ; and in what excellency
any one of you exceeds another, to yield to him
so far, and by that means to reap the advantage
of every one's own virtues. Do you then esteem
Simon as your father, because he is a man of extraordinary prudence, and be governed by him
in what counsels he gives you. Take Maccabeus
for the general of your army, because of his
courage and strength, for he will avenge your
nation, and will bring vengeance on your enemies. Admit among you the righteous and religious, and augment their power."

4. When Mattathias had thus discoursed to
his sons, and had prayed to God to be their assistant, and to recover to the people their former
constitution, he died a little afterward, and was
buried at Modin ; all the people making great
lamentation for him. Whereupon his son Judas
took upon him the administration of public

affairs, in the hundred and forty-sixth year; and thus, by the ready assistance of his brethren and of others, Judas cast their enemies out of the country, and put those of their own country to death who had transgressed its laws, and purified the land of all the pollutions that were in it.

CHAPTER VII

HOW JUDAS OVERTHREW THE FORCES OF APOLLONIUS AND SERON, AND KILLED THE GENERALS OF THEIR ARMIES THEMSELVES; AND HOW WHEN, A LITTLE WHILE AFTERWARD, LYSIAS AND GORGIAS WERE BEATEN, HE WENT UP TO JERUSALEM, AND PURIFIED THE TEMPLE

1. WHEN Apollonius, the general of the Samaritan forces, heard this, he took his army, and made haste to go against Judas, who met him, and joined battle with him, and beat him, and slew many of his men, and among them Apollonius himself, their general, whose sword, being that which he happened then to wear, he seized upon and kept for himself; but he wounded more than he slew, and took a great deal of prey from the enemy's camp, and went his way; but when Seron, who was general of the army of Cœlesyria, heard that many had joined themselves to Judas, and that he had about him an army sufficient for fighting and for making war, he determined to make an expedition against him, as thinking it became him to endeavour to punish those that transgressed the king's injunctions. He then got together an army, as large as he was able, and joined to it the runagate and wicked Jews, and came against Judas. He then came as far as Bethoron, a village of Judea, and there pitched his camp; upon which Judas met him, and when he intended to give him battle, he saw that his soldiers were backward to fight, because their number were small, and because they wanted food, for they were fasting, he encouraged them, and said to them, that victory and conquest of enemies are not derived from the multitude in armies, but in the exercise of piety towards God; and that they had the plainest instances in their forefathers, who, by their righteousness, and exerting themselves on behalf of their own laws, and their own children, had frequently conquered many ten thousands,—for innocence is the strongest army. By this speech he induced his men to contemn the multitude of the enemy, and to fall upon Seron; and upon joining battle with him, he beat the Syrians; and when their general fell among the rest, they all ran away with speed, as thinking that to be their best way of escaping. So he pursued them unto the plain, and slew about eight hundred of the enemy; but the rest escaped to the region which lay near to the sea.

2. When king Antiochus heard of these things, he was very angry at what had happened; so he got together all his own army, with many mercenaries, whom he had hired from the islands, and took them with him, and prepared to break into Judea about the beginning of the spring; but when, upon his mustering his soldiers, he perceived that his treasures were deficient, and there was a want of money in them, for all the taxes were not paid, by reason of the seditions there had been among the nations, he having been so magnanimous and so liberal that what he had was not sufficient for him, he therefore resolved first to go into Persia, and collect the taxes of that country. Hereupon he left one whose name was Lysias, who was in great repute with him, governor of the kingdom, as far as the bounds of Egypt, and of the Lower Asia, and reaching from the river Euphrates, and committed to him a certain part of his forces, and of his elephants, and charged him to bring up his son Antiochus with all possible care, until he came back; and that he should conquer Judea, and take its inhabitants for slaves, and utterly destroy Jerusalem, and abolish the whole nation; and when king Antiochus had given these things in charge to Lysias, he went into Persia; and in the hundred and forty-seventh year, he passed over Euphrates, and went to the superior provinces.

3. Upon this Lysias chose Ptolemy, the son of Dorimenes, and Nicanor, and Gorgias, very potent men among the king's friends, and delivered to them forty thousand foot-soldiers and seven thousand horsemen, and sent them against Judea, who came as far as the city Emmaus, and pitched their camp in the plain country. There came also to them auxiliaries out of Syria, and the country round about; as also many of the runagate Jews; and besides these came some merchants to buy those that should be carried captives, (having bonds with them to bind those that should be made prisoners,) with that silver and gold which they were to pay for their price; and when Judas saw their camp, and how numerous their enemies were, he persuaded his own soldiers to be of good courage; and exhorted them to place their hopes of victory in God, and to make supplication to him, according to the custom of their country, clothed in sackcloth; and to shew what was their usual habit of supplication in the greatest dangers, and thereby to prevail with God to grant them the victory over their enemies. So he set them in their ancient order of battle used by their forefathers, under their captians of thousands, and other officers, and dismissed such as were newly married, as well as those that had newly gained possessions, that they might not fight in a cowardly manner, out of an inordinate love of life, in order to enjoy those blessings. When he had thus disposed his soldiers, he encouraged them to fight by the following speech, which he made to them:—"O my fellow-soldiers, no other time remains more opportune than the present for courage and contempt of dangers; for if you now fight manfully you may recover your liberty, which, as it is a thing of itself agreeable t̄ all men, so it proves to be to us much more desirable, by its affording us the liberty of worshipping God. Since, therefore, you are in such circumstances at present, you must either recover that liberty, and so regain a happy and blessed way of living, which is that according to our laws, and the customs of our country, or to submit to the most opprobrious sufferings; nor will any seed of your nation remain if you be beat in this battle. Fight therefore manfully; and suppose that you must die, though you do not fight; but believe, that besides such glorious rewards as those of the liberty of your country, of your laws, of your religion, you shall then obtain everlasting glory. Prepare yourselves, therefore, and put yourselves into such an agreeable posture, that you may be ready to fight with the enemy as soon as it is day to-morrow morning."

4. And this was the speech which Judas made to encourage them. But when the enemy sent Gorgias, with five thousand foot and one thousand horse, that he might fall upon Judas by night, and had for that purpose certain of the runagate Jews as guides, the son of Mattathias perceived it, and resolved to fall upon those enemies that were in their camp, now their forces

were divided. When they had therefore supped in good time, and had left many fires in their camp, he marched all night to those enemies that were at Emmaus; so that when Gorgias found no enemy in their camp, but suspected that they were retired and hidden themselves among the mountains, he resolved to go and seek them wheresoever they were. But, about break of day, Judas appeared to those enemies that were at Emmaus, with only three thousand men, and those ill-armed, by reason of their poverty; and when he saw the enemy very well and skilfully fortified in their camp, he encouraged the Jews, and told them, that they ought to fight, though it were with their naked bodies, for that God had sometimes of old given such men strength, and that against such as were more in number, and were armed also, out of regard to their great courage. So he commanded the trumpeters to sound for the battle: and by thus falling upon the enemy when they did not expect it, and thereby astonishing and disturbing their minds, he slew many of those that resisted him, and went on pursuing the rest as far as Gadara, and the plains of Idumea, and Ashdod, and Jamnia; and of these there fell about three thousand. Yet did Judas exhort his soldiers not to be too desirous of the spoils, for that still they must have a contest and battle with Gorgias, and the forces that were with him: but that, when they had once overcome them, then they might securely plunder the camp because they were the only enemies remaining, and they expected no others. And just as he was speaking to his soldiers, Gorgias's men looked down into that army which they left in their camp, and saw that it was overthrown, and the camp burnt; for the smoke that arose from it shewed them, even when they were a great way off, what had happened. When, therefore, those that were with Gorgias understood that things were in this posture, and perceived that those that were with Judas were ready to fight them, they also were affrighted, and put to flight; but then Judas, as though he had already beaten Gorgias's soldiers without fighting, returned and seized on the spoils. He took a great quantity of gold and silver, and purple, and blue, and then returned home with joy, and singing hymns to God for their good success: for this victory greatly contributed to the recovery of their liberty.

5. Hereupon Lysias was confounded at the defeat of the army which he had sent, and the next year he got together sixty thousand chosen men. He also took five thousand horsemen, and fell upon Judea; and he went up to the hill country of Bethsur, a village of Judea, and pitched his camp there, where Judas met him with ten thousand men; and when he saw the great number of his enemies, he prayed to God that he would assist him, and joined battle with the first of the enemy that appeared, and beat them, and slew about five thousand of them, and thereby became terrible to the rest of them. Nay, indeed, Lysias observing the great spirit of the Jews, how they were prepared to die rather than lose their liberty, and being afraid of their desperate way of fighting, as if it were real strength, he took the rest of the army back with him, and returned to Antioch, where he enlisted foreigners into the service, and prepared to fall upon Judea with a greater army.

6. When, therefore, the generals of Antiochus's armies had been beaten so often, Judas assembled the people together, and told them, that after these many victories which God had given them, they ought to go up to Jerusalem,

and purify the temple, and offer the appointed sacrifices. But as soon as he, with the whole multitude, was come to Jerusalem, and found the temple deserted, and its gates burnt down, and plants growing in the temple of their own accord, on account of its desertion, he and those that were with him began to lament, and were quite confounded at the sight of the temple; so he chose out some of his soldiers, and gave them order to fight against those guards that were in the citadel, until he should have purified the temple. When, therefore, he had carefully purged it, and had brought in new vessels, the candlestick, the table [of shew-bread,] and the altar [of incense,] which were made of gold, he hung up the veils at the gates, and added doors to them. He also took down the altar [of burnt offering,] and built a new one of stones that he gathered together, and not of such as were hewn with iron tools. So on the five and twentieth day of the month Casleu, which the Macedonians call Appelleus, they lighted the lamps that were on the candlestick, and offered incense upon the altar [of incense,] and laid the loaves upon the table [of shewbread,] and offered burnt offerings upon the new altar [of burnt-offering.] Now it so fell out, that these things were done on the very same day on which their divine worship had fallen off, and was reduced to a profane and common use, after three years' time; for so it was, that the temple was made desolate by Antiochus, and so continued for three years. This desolation happened to the temple in the hundred forty and fifth year, on the twenty-fifth day of the month Appelleus, and on the hundred and fifty-third olympiad; but it was dedicated anew, on the same day, the twenty-fifth of the month Appelleus, in the hundred and forty-eighth year, and on the hundred and fifty-fourth olympiad. And this desolation came to pass according to the prophecy of Daniel, which was given four hundred and eight years before; for he declared that the Macedonians would dissolve that worship [for some] time.

7. Now Judas celebrated the festival of the restoration of the sacrifices of the temple for eight days; and omitted no sort of pleasures thereon: but he feasted them upon very rich and splendid sacrifices; and he honoured God, and delighted them, by hymns and psalms. Nay, they were so very glad at the revival of their customs, when after a long time of intermission, they unexpectedly had regained the freedom of their worship, that they made it law for their posterity, that they should keep a festival, on account of the restoration of their temple worship, for eight days. And from that time to this we celebrate this festival, and call it Lights. I suppose the reason was, because this liberty beyond our hopes appeared to us; and that thence was the name given to that festival. Judas also rebuilt the walls round about the city, and reared towers of great height against the incursions of enemies, and set guards therein. He also fortified the city Bethsura, that it might serve as a citadel against any distresses that might come from our enemies.

CHAPTER VIII

HOW JUDAS SUBDUED THE NATIONS ROUND ABOUT; AND HOW SIMON BEAT THE PEOPLE OF TYRE AND PTOLEMAIS; AND HOW JUDAS OVERTHREW TIMOTHEUS, AND FORCED HIM TO FLY AWAY, AND DID MANY OTHER THINGS AFTER JOSEPH AND AZARIAS HAD BEEN BEATEN

1. WHEN these things were over, the nations

round about the Jews were very uneasy at the revival of their power, and rose up together, and destroyed many of them, as gaining advantage over them by laying snares for them, and making secret conspiracies against them. Judas made perpetual expeditions against these men, and endeavoured to restrain them from those incursions, and to prevent the mischiefs they did to the Jews. So he fell upon the Idumeans, the posterity of Esau, at Acrabattene, and slew a great many of them, and took their spoils. He also shut up the sons of Bean, that laid wait for the Jews; and he sat down about them, and besieged them, and burnt their towers, and destroyed the men [that were in them.] After this he went thence in haste against the Ammonites, who had a great and a numerous army, of which Timotheus was the commander. And when he had subdued them, he seized on the city Jazer, and took their wives and their children captives, and burnt the city, and then returned into Judea. But when the neighbouring nations understood that he was returned, they got together in great numbers in the land of Gilead, and came against those Jews that were at their borders, who then fled to the garrison of Dathema; and sent to Judas, to inform him that Timotheus was endeavouring to take the place whither they were fled. And as these epistles were reading, there came other messengers out of Galilee, who informed him that the inhabitants of Ptolemais, and of Tyre and Sidon, and strangers of Galilee, were gotten together.

2. Accordingly Judas, upon considering what was fit to be done with relation to the necessity both these cases required, gave order that Simon his brother should take three thousand chosen men, and go to the assistance of the Jews in Galilee, while he and another of his brothers, Jonathan, made haste into the land of Gilead with eight thousand soldiers. And he left Joseph, the son of Zacharias, and Azarias, to be over the rest of the forces; and charged them to keep Judea very carefully, and to fight no battles with any persons whomsoever until his return. Accordingly, Simon went into Galilee, and fought the enemy, and put them to flight, and pursued them to the very gates of Ptolemais, and slew about three thousand of them, and took the spoils of those that were slain, and those Jews whom they had made captives, with their baggage, and then returned home.

3. Now as for Judas Maccabeus, and his brother Jonathan, they passed over the river Jordan; and when they had gone three days' journey, they lighted upon the Nabateans, who came to meet them peaceably, and who told them how the affairs of those in the land of Galilee stood, and how many of them were in distress, and driven into garrisons, and into the cities of Galilee; and exhorted him to make haste to go against the foreigners, and to endeavour to save his countrymen out of their hands. To this exhortation Judas hearkened, and returned into the wilderness; and in the first place fell upon the inhabitants of Bosor, and took the city, and beat the inhabitants, and destroyed all the males, and all that were able to fight, and burnt the city. Nor did he stop even when night came on, but he journeyed in it to the garrison where the Jews happened to be then shut up, and where Timotheus lay round the place with his army: and Judas came upon the city in the morning; and when he found that the enemy were making an assault upon the walls, and that some of them brought ladders, on which they might get upon those

walls, and that others brought engines [to batter them,] he bid the trumpeter to sound his trumpet, and he encouraged his soldiers cheerfully to undergo dangers for the sake of their brethren and kindred; he also parted his army into three bodies, and fell upon the backs of their enemies. But when Timotheus's men perceived that it was Maccabeus that was upon them, of both whose courage and good success in war they had formerly had sufficient experience, they were put to flight; but Judas followed them with his army, and slew about eight thousand of them. He then turned aside to a city of the foreigners called Malle, and took it, and slew all the males, and burnt the city itself. He then removed from thence, and overthrew Casphom and Bosor, and many other cities of the land of Gilead.

4. But not long after this, Timotheus prepared a great army, and took many others as auxiliaries; and induced some of the Arabians, by the promise of rewards, to go with him in this expedition, and came with his army beyond the brook, over against the city Raphon: and he encouraged his soldiers, if it came to a battle with the Jews, to fight courageously, and to hinder their passing over the brook; for he said to them beforehand, that, "if they come over it, we shall be beaten." And when Judas heard that Timotheus prepared himself to fight, he took all his own army, and went in haste against Timotheus his enemy; and when he had passed over the brook, he fell upon his enemies, and some of them met him, whom he slew, and others of them he so terrified, that he compelled them to throw down their arms and fly; and some of them escaped, but some of them fled to what was called the Temple of Carnaim, and hoped thereby to preserve themselves; but Judas took the city, and slew them, and burnt the temple, and so used several ways of destroying his enemies.

5. When he had done this, he gathered the Jews together, with their children, and wives, and the substance that belonged to them, and was going to bring them back into Judea. But as soon as he was come to a certain city, the name of which was Ephron, that lay upon the road, (and as it was not possible for him to go any other way, so he was not willing to go back again,) he then sent to the inhabitants, and desired that they would open their gates, and permit them to go on their way through the city; for they had stopped up the gates with stones, and cut off their passage through it. And when the inhabitants of Ephron would not agree to this proposal, he encouraged those that were with him, and encompassed the city round, and besieged it, and lying round it, by day and night, took the city, and slew every male in it, and burnt it all down, and so obtained a way through it; and the multitude of those that were slain were so great, that they went over the dead bodies. So they came over Jordan, and arrived at the great plain, over against which is situate the city Bethshan, which is called by the Greeks Scythopolis.* And going away hastily from thence, they came into Judea, singing psalms and hymns as they went, and indulging such tokens of mirth as are usual in triumphs upon victory. They also offered thank-offerings, both for their good success, and for the preservation of

* The reason why Bethshan was called Scythopolis is well known from Herodotus—viz., that the Scythians, when they overran Asia, in the days of Josiah, seized on this city, and kept it as long as they continued in Asia; from which time it retained the name of Scythopolis, or the City of the Scythians.

their army, for not one of the Jews was slain in these battles.*

6. But as to Joseph, the son of Zacharias, and Azarias, whom Judas left generals [of the rest of his forces] at the same time when Simon was in Galilee, fighting against the people of Ptolemais, and Judas himself, and his brother Jonathan, were in the land of Gilead, did these men also affect the glory of being courageous generals in war, in order whereto they took the army that was under their command, and came to Jamnia. There Gorgias, the general of the forces of Jamnia, met them; and upon joining battle with him, they lost two thousand of their army,† and fled away, and were pursued to the very borders of Judea. And this misfortune befell them by their disobedience to what injunctions Judas had given them, not to fight with any one before his return. For besides the rest of Judas's sagacious counsels, one may well wonder at this concerning the misfortune that befell the forces commanded by Joseph and Azarias, which he understood would happen if they broke any of the injunctions he had given them. But Judas and his brethren did not leave off fighting with the Idumeans, but pressed upon them on all sides, and took from them the city of Hebron, and demolished all its fortifications, and set all its towers on fire, and burnt the country of the foreigners, and the city Marissa. They came also to Ashdod, and took it, and laid it waste, and took away a great deal of the spoils and prey that were in it, and returned to Judea.

CHAPTER IX

CONCERNING THE DEATH OF ANTIOCHUS EPI-PHANES; HOW ANTIOCHUS EUPATOR FOUGHT AGAINST JUDAS, AND BESIEGED HIM IN THE TEMPLE, AND AFTERWARDS MADE PEACE WITH HIM, AND DEPARTED; OF ALCIMUS AND ONIAS

1. ABOUT this time it was that king Antiochus, as he was going over the upper countries, heard that there was a very rich city in Persia, called Elymais; and therein a very rich temple of Diana, and that it was full of all sorts of donations dedicated to it; as also weapons and breastplates, which, upon inquiry, he found had been left there by Alexander, the son of Philip, king of Macedonia; and being incited by these motives, he went in haste to Elymais, and assaulted it, and besieged it. But as those that were in it were not terrified at his assault, nor at his siege, but opposed him very courageously, he was beaten off his hopes; for they drove him away from the city, and went out and pursued after him, insomuch that he fled away as far as Babylon, and lost a great many of his army; and when he was grieving for this disappointment, some persons told him of the defeat of his commanders whom he had left behind him to fight against Judea, and what strength the Jews had already gotten. When this concern about these affairs was added to the former, he was confounded, and, by the anxiety he was in, fell into a distemper, which, as it lasted a great while, and as his pains increased upon him, so he at length perceived he should die in a little time; so he called his friends to him, and told them that his distemper was severe upon him, and confessed withal, that this calamity was sent upon him for the miseries he had brought upon the Jewish nation, while he plundered their temple and contemned their God; and when he had said this, he gave up the ghost. Whence one may wonder at Polybius of Megalopolis, who, though otherwise a good man, yet saith that "Antiochus died, because he had a purpose to plunder the temple of Diana in Persia;" for the purposing to do a thing,‡ but not actually doing it, is not worthy of punishment. But if Polybius could think that Antiochus thus lost his life on that account, it is much more probable that this king died on account of his sacrilegious plundering of the temple at Jerusalem. But we will not contend about this matter with those who may think that the cause assigned by this Polybius of Megalopolis is nearer the truth than that assigned by us.

2. However, Antiochus, before he died, called for Philip, who was one of his companions, and made him the guardian of his kingdom, and gave him his diadem, and his garment, and his ring, and charged him to carry them, and deliver them to his son Antiochus; and desired him to take care of his education, and to preserve the kingdom for him.§ This Antiochus died in the hundred forty and ninth year: but it was Lysias that declared his death to the multitude, and appointed his son Antiochus to be king, (of whom at present he had the care,) and called him Eupator.

3. At this time it was that the garrison in the citadel at Jerusalem, with the Jewish runagates, did a great deal of harm to the Jews: for the soldiers that were in that garrison rushed out upon the sudden, and destroyed such as were going up to the temple in order to offer their sacrifices, for this citadel adjoined to and overlooked the temple. When these misfortunes had often happened to them, Judas resolved to destroy that garrison; whereupon he got all the people together, and vigorously besieged those that were in the citadel. This was in the hundred and fiftieth year of the dominion of the Seleucidæ. So he made engines of war, and erected bulwarks, and very zealously pressed on to take the citadel. But there were not a few of the runagates who were in the place, that went out by night into the country, and got together some other wicked men like themselves, and went to Antiochus the king, and desired of him that he would not suffer them to be neglected, under the great hardships that lay upon them from those of their own nation; and this because their sufferings were occasioned on his father's account, while they left the religious worship of their fathers, and preferred that which he had commanded them to follow: that there was danger lest the citadel, and those appointed to garrison it by the king, should be taken by Judas and those that were with him, unless he would

---

* This most providential preservation of all the religious Jews in this expedition, which was according to the will of God, is observable often among God's people, the Jews.

† Here is another great instance of providence, that when, even at the very time that Simon, and Judas, and Jonathan, were so miraculously preserved and blessed, in the just defence of their laws and religion, these other generals of the Jews, who went to fight for honour in a vainglorious way, and without any commission from God, or the family he had raised up to deliver them, were miserably disappointed and defeated.

‡ Since St Paul, a Pharisee, confesses that he had not known concupiscence to be sinful, had not the tenth commandment said, "Thou shalt not covet," (Rom. vii. 7;) the case seems to have been much the same with Josephus, who was of the same sect, that he had not a deep sense of the greatness of any sins that proceeded no further than the intention.

§ Antiochus Eupator, when he came to the crown, Appian informs us, was but nine years old.

send them succours. When Antiochus, who was but a child, heard this, he was angry, and sent for his captains and his friends, and gave order that they should get an army of mercenaries together, with such men also of his own kingdom as were of an age fit for war. Accordingly an army was collected of about a hundred thousand footmen, and twenty thousand horsemen, and thirty-two elephants.

4. So the king took this army, and marched hastily out of Antioch, with Lysias, who had the command of the whole, and came to Idumea, and thence went up to the city Bethsura, a city that was strong, and not to be taken without great difficulty. He set about this city, and besieged it ; and while the inhabitants of Bethsura courageously opposed him, and sallied out upon him, and burned his engines of war, a great deal of time was spent in the siege ; but when Judas heard of the king's coming, he raised the siege of the citadel, and met the king, and pitched his camp in certain straits, at a place called Bethzachariah, at the distance of seventy furlongs from the enemy ; but the king soon drew his forces from Bethsura, and brought them to those straits ; and as soon as it was day, he put his men in battle array, and made his elephants follow one another through the narrow passes, because they could not be set sideways by one another. Now round about every elephant there were a thousand footmen and five hundred horsemen. The elephants also had high towers [upon their backs,] and archers [in them ;] and he also made the rest of his army to go up the mountains, and put his friends before the rest ; and gave orders for the army to shout aloud, and so he attacked the enemy. He also exposed to sight their golden and brazen shields, so that a glorious splendour was sent from them ; and when they shouted, the mountains echoed again. When Judas saw this, he was not terrified, but received the enemy with great courage, and slew about six hundred of the first ranks. But when his brother Eleazar, whom they called Auran, saw the tallest of all the elephants armed with royal breastplates, and supposed that the king was upon him, he attacked him with great quickness and bravery. He also slew many of those that were about the elephant, and scattered the rest, and then went under the belly of the elephant, and smote him and slew him ; so the elephant fell upon Eleazar, and by his weight crushed him to death. And thus did this man come to his end, when he had first courageously destroyed many of his enemies.

5. But Judas, seeing the strength of the enemy, retired to Jerusalem, and prepared to endure a siege. As for Antiochus, he sent part of his army to Bethsura, to besiege it, and with the rest of his army he came against Jerusalem ; but the inhabitants of Bethsura were terrified at his strength ; and seeing that their provisions grew scarce, they delivered themselves up on the security of oaths that they should suffer no hard treatment from the king. And when Antiochus had thus taken the city, he did them no other harm than sending them out naked. He also placed a garrison of his own in the city : but as for the temple of Jerusalem, he lay at its siege a long time, while they within bravely defended it ; for what engines soever the kings set against them, they set other engines to oppose them. But then their provisions failed them ; what fruits of the ground they had laid up were spent, and the land being not ploughed that year, continued unsowed, because it was the seventh year, on which, by our laws, we are obliged to let it lie uncultivated. And withal, so many of the besieged ran away for want of necessaries, that but a few only were left in the temple.

6. And these happened to be the circumstances of such as were besieged in the temple. But then, because Lysias, the general of the army, and Antiochus the king, were informed that Philip was coming upon them out of Persia, and was endeavouring to get the management of public affairs to himself, they came into these sentiments, to leave the siege, and to make haste to go against Philip ; yet did they resolve not to let this be known to the soldiers or the officers ; but the king commanded Lysias to speak openly to the soldiers and the officers, without saying a word about the business of Philip ; and to intimate to them that the siege would be very long ; that the place was very strong ; that they were already in want of provisions ; that many affairs of the kingdom wanted regulation ; and that it was much better to make a league with the besieged, and to become friends to their whole nation, by permitting them to observe the laws of their fathers, while they broke out into this war only because they were deprived of them, and so to depart home. When Lysias had discoursed thus with them, both the army and the officers were pleased with this resolution.

7. Accordingly the king sent to Judas, and to those that were besieged with him, and promised to give them peace, and permit them to make use of and live according to the laws of their fathers ; and they gladly received his proposals ; and when they had gained security upon oath for their performance, they went out of the temple : but when Antiochus came into it, and saw how strong the place was, he broke his oaths, and ordered his army that was there to pluck down the walls to the ground ; and when he had so done, he returned to Antioch. He also carried with him Onias the high priest, who was also called Menelaus ; for Lysias advised the king to slay Menelaus, if he would have the Jews be quiet, and cause him no further disturbance, for that this man was the origin of all the mischief the Jews had done them, by persuading his father to compel the Jews to leave the religion of their fathers ; so the king sent Menelaus to Berea, a city of Syria, and had him put to death, when he had been high priest ten years. He had been a wicked and an impious man ; and, in order to get the government to himself, had compelled his nation to transgress their own laws. After the death of Menelaus, Alcimus, who was also called Jacimus, was made high priest. But when king Antiochus found that Philip had already possessed himself of the government, he made war against him, and subdued him, and took him, and slew him. Now, as to Onias, the son of the high priest, who, as we before informed you, was left a child when his father died, when he saw that the king had slain his uncle Menelaus, and given the high-priesthood to Alcimus, who was not of the high priest stock, but was induced by Lysias to translate that dignity from his family to another house, he fled to Ptolemy, king of Egypt ; and when he found he was in great esteem with him, and with his wife Cleopatra, he desired and obtained a place in the Nomus of Heliopolis, wherein he built a temple like to that at Jerusalem ; of which, therefore, we shall hereafter give an account, in a place more proper for it.

CHAPTER X

HOW BACCHIDES, THE GENERAL OF DEMETRIUS'S ARMY, MADE AN EXPEDITION AGAINST JUDEA,

AND RETURNED WITHOUT SUCCESS; AND HOW NICANOR WAS SENT A LITTLE AFTERWARD AGAINST JUDAS, AND PERISHED, TOGETHER WITH HIS ARMY; AS ALSO CONCERNING THE DEATH OF ALCIMUS, AND THE SUCCESSION OF JUDAS

1. ABOUT the same time Demetrius, the son of Seleucus, fled away from Rome, and took Tripoli, a city of Syria, and set the diadem on his own head. He also gathered certain mercenary soldiers together, and entered into his kingdom, and was joyfully received by all, who delivered themselves up to him; and when they had taken Antiochus the king, and Lysias, they brought them to him alive; both of whom were immediately put to death by the command of Demetrius, when Antiochus had reigned two years, as we have already elsewhere related; but there were now many of the wicked Jewish runagates that came together to him, and with them Alcimus the high priest, who accused the whole nation, and particularly Judas and his brethren; and said that they had slain all his friends; and that those in his kingdom that were of his party, and waited for his return, were by them put to death; that these men had ejected them out of their own country, and caused them to be sojourners in a foreign land; and they desired that he would send some one of his own friends, and know from him what mischief Judas's party had done.

2. At this Demetrius was very angry, and sent Bacchides, a friend of Antiochus Epiphanes,* a good man, and one that had been intrusted with all Mesopotamia, and gave him an army, and committed Alcimus the high priest to his care; and gave him charge to slay Judas, and those that were with him. So Bacchides made haste, and went out of Antioch with his army; and when he was come into Judea, he sent to Judas and his brethren, to discourse with him about a league of friendship and peace, for he had a mind to take him by treachery; but Judas did not give credit to him, for he saw that he came with so great an army as men do not bring when they come to make peace, but to make war. However, some of the people acquiesced in what Bacchides caused to be proclaimed; and supposing they should undergo no considerable harm from Alcimus, who was their countrymen, they went over to them; and when they had received oaths from both of them, that neither they themselves nor those of the same sentiments should come to any harm, they intrusted themselves with them; but Bacchides troubled not himself about the oaths he had taken, but slew threescore of them, although, by not keeping his faith with those that first went over, he deterred all the rest, who had intentions to go over to him, from doing it; but as he was gone out of Jerusalem, and was at the village called Bethzetho, he sent out, and caught many of the deserters, and some of the people also, and slew them all: and enjoined all that lived in the country to submit to Alcimus. So he left them there, with some part of the army, that he might have wherewith to keep the country in obedience, and returned to Antioch to king Demetrius.

3. But Alcimus was desirous to have the dominion more firmly assured to him; and understanding that, if he could bring it about that the multitude should be his friends, he should govern with greater security, he spake kind words to them all, and discoursed to each of them after an agreeable and pleasant manner; by which means he quickly had a great body of men and an army about him, although the greater part of them were of the wicked, and the deserters. With these, whom he used as his servants and soldiers, he went all over the country, and slew all that he could find of Judas's party; but when Judas saw that Alcimus was already become great, and had destroyed many of the good and holy men of the country, he also went all over the country and destroyed those that were of the other party; but when Alcimus saw that he was not able to oppose Judas, nor was equal to him in strength, he resolved to apply himself to king Demetrius for his assistance; so he came to Antioch, and irritated him against Judas, and accused him, alleging that he had undergone a great many miseries by this means, and that he would do more mischief unless he were prevented, and brought to punishment, which must be done by sending a powerful force against him.

4. So Demetrius, being already of opinion that it would be a thing pernicious to his own affairs to overlook Judas, now he was becoming so great, sent against him Nicanor, the most kind and most faithful of all his friends; for he it was who fled away with him from the city of Rome. He also gave him as many forces as he thought sufficient for him to conquer Judas withal, and bade him not to spare the nation at all. When Nicanor was come to Jerusalem, he did not resolve to fight Judas immediately, but judged it better to get him into his power by treachery; so he sent him a message of peace, and said there was no manner of necessity for them to fight and hazard themselves; and that he would give him his oath that he would do him no harm, for that he only came with some friends, in order to let him know what king Demetrius's intentions were, and what opinion he had of their nation. When Nicanor had delivered this message, Judas and his brethren complied with him, and suspecting no deceit, they gave him assurances of friendship, and received Nicanor and his army; but while he was saluting Judas, and they were talking together, he gave a certain signal to his own soldiers, upon which they were to seize upon Judas; but he perceived the treachery, and ran back to his own soldiers, and fled away with them. So upon this discovery of his purpose, and of the snares laid for Judas, Nicanor determined to make open war with him, and gathered his army together, and prepared for fighting him; and upon joining battle with him at a certain village called Capharsalama, he beat Judas,† and forced him to fly to that citadel which was at Jerusalem.

5. And when Nicanor came down from the citadel into the temple, some of the priests and elders met him, and saluted him; and shewed him the sacrifices which they said they offered to God for the king: upon which he blasphemed, and threatened them, that unless the people would deliver up Judas to him, upon his return he would pull down the temple. And when he had thus threatened them, he departed from Jerusalem: but the priests fell into tears out of grief at what he had said, and besought God to deliver them from their enemies. But now Nicanor, when he was gone out of Jerusalem,

---

* It is no way probable that Josephus would call Bacchides, that bitter and bloody enemy of the Jews, as our present copies have it, a good man. What Josephus probably means is, that he was a great man in the kingdom, and faithful to his king.

† Josephus's copies must have been corrupted when they here give victory to Nicanor, contrary to the words following, which imply, that he who was beaten fled into the citadel, which for certain belonged to the city of David or to mount Zion, and was in the possession of Nicanor's garrison, and not of Judas's.

and was at a certain village called Bethoron, he there pitched his camp,—another army out of Syria having joined him. And Judas pitched his camp at Adasa, another village, which was thirty furlongs distant from Bethoron, having no more than one thousand soldiers. And when he had encouraged them not to be dismayed at the multitude of their enemies, nor to regard how many there were against whom they were going to fight, but to consider who they themselves were, and for what great rewards they hazarded themselves, and to attack the enemy courageously, he led them out to fight, and joining battle with Nicanor, which proved to be a severe one, he overcame the enemy, and slew many of them; and at last Nicanor himself, as he was fighting gloriously, fell:—upon whose fall the army did not stay; but when they had lost their general, they were put to flight, and threw down their arms. Judas also pursued them and slew them; and gave notice by the sound of his trumpets to the neighbouring villages that he had conquered the enemy; which when the inhabitants heard, they put on their armour hastily, and met their enemies in the face as they were running away, and slew them, insomuch that not one of them escaped out of this battle; who were in number nine thousand. This victory happened to fall on the thirteenth day of that month which by the Jews is called Adar, and by the Macedonians Dystrus: and the Jews therein celebrate this victory every year, and esteem it as a festival day. After which the Jewish nation were, for a while, free from wars, and enjoyed peace; but afterward they returned into their former state of wars and hazards.

6. But now as the high priest Alcimus was resolving to pull down the wall of the sanctuary, which had been there of old time, and had been built by the holy prophets,* he was smitten suddenly by God, and fell down. This stroke made him fall down speechless upon the ground; and undergoing torments for many days, he at length died, when he had been high priest four years. And when he was dead, the people bestowed the high priesthood on Judas; who hearing of the power of the Romans, and that they had conquered in war Galatia, and Iberia, and Carthage, and Lybia; and that, besides these, they had subdued Greece, and their kings, Perseus, and Philip, and Antiochus the Great also, he resolved to enter into a league of friendship with them. He therefore sent to Rome some of his friends, Eupolemus the son of John, and Jason the son of Eleazar, and by them desired the Romans that they would assist them, and be their friends, and would write to Demetrius that he would not fight against the Jews. So the senate received the ambassadors that came from Judas to Rome, and discoursed with them about the errand on which they came, and then granted them a league of assistance. They also made a decree concerning it, and sent a copy of it into Judea. It was also laid up in the capital, and engraven in brass. The decree itself was this:—"The decree of the senate concerning a league of assistance and friendship with the nation of the Jews. It shall not be lawful for any that are subject to the Romans to make war with the nation of the Jews, nor to assist those that do so, either by sending them corn, or ships, or money.

And if any attack be made upon the Jews, the Romans shall assist them, as far as they are able; and again if any attack be made upon the Romans, the Jews shall assist them. And if the Jews have a mind to add to, or to take away anything from, this league of assistance, that shall be done with the common consent of the Romans. And whatsoever addition shall thus be made, it shall be of force." This decree was written by Eupolemus the son of John, and by Jason the son of Eleazar,† when Judas was high priest of the nation, and Simon his brother was general of the army. And this was the first league that the Romans made with the Jews, and was managed after this manner.

CHAPTER XI

THAT BACCHIDES WAS AGAIN SENT OUT AGAINST JUDAS; AND HOW JUDAS FELL AS HE WAS COURAGEOUSLY FIGHTING

1. BUT when Demetrius was informed of the death of Nicanor, and of the destruction of the army that was with him, he sent Bacchides again with an army in Judea, who marched out of Antioch, and came into Judea, and pitched his camp at Arbela, a city of Galilee; and having besieged and taken those that were in caves, (for many of the people fled into such places,) he removed, and made all the haste he could to Jerusalem. And when he had learned that Judas had pitched his camp at a certain village whose name was Bethzetho, he led his army against him: they were twenty thousand footmen, and two thousand horsemen. Now Judas had no more soldiers than three thousand. When these saw the multitude of Bacchides's men they were afraid, and left their camp, and fled all away, excepting eight hundred. Now when Judas was deserted by his own soldiers, and the enemy pressed upon him, and gave him no time to gather, he was disposed to fight with Bacchides's army, though he had but eight hundred men with him; so he exhorted these men to undergo the danger courageously, and encouraged them to attack the enemy. And when they said they were not a body sufficient to fight so great an army, and advised that they should retire now and save themselves, and that when he had gathered his own men together, then he should fall upon the enemy afterwards, his answer was this:—"Let not the sun ever see such a thing, that I should shew my back to the enemy; and although this be the time that will bring me to my end, and I must die in this battle, I will rather stand to it courageously, and bear whatsoever comes upon me, than by now running away, bring reproach upon my former great actions, or tarnish their glory." This was the speech he made to those that remained with him, and whereby he encouraged them to attack the enemy.

2. But Bacchides drew his army out of their camp, and put them in array for the battle. He set the horsemen on both the wings, and light soldiers and the archers he placed before the whole army, but was himself on the right wing. And when he had thus put his army in order of battle, and was going to join battle with the enemy, he commanded the trumpeter to give a

---

* This account of the miserable death of Alcimus or Jacimus, before the death of Judas, and of Judas's succession to him as high priest, directly contradicts 1 Mac. ix. 54-57, which places his death after the death of Judas, and says not a syllable of the high priesthood of Judas.

† This subscription is wanting, (1 Mac. viii. 17, 29,) and must be the words of Josephus, who, by mistake, thought that Judas was at this time high priest, and accordingly then reckoned his brother Jonathan to be the general of the army, which yet he seems not to have been till after the death of Judas.

signal of battle, and the army to make a shout, and to fall on the enemy. And when Judas had done the same, he joined battle with them; and as both sides fought valiantly, and the battle continued till sunset, Judas saw that Bacchides and the strongest part of the army was in the right wing, and thereupon took the most courageous men with him, and ran upon that part of the army, and fell upon those that were there, and broke their ranks, and drove them into the middle, and forced them to run away, and pursued them as far as to a mountain called Aza: but when those of the left wing saw that the right wing was put to flight, they encompassed Judas, and pursued him, and came behind him, and took him into the middle of their army; so not being able to fly, but encompassed round about with enemies, he stood still, and he and those that were with him fought; and when he had slain a great many of those that came against him, he at last was himself wounded, and fell, and gave up the ghost, and died in a way like to his former famous actions. When

Judas was dead, those that were with him had no one whom they could regard [as their commander;] but when they saw themselves deprived of such a general, they fled. But Simon and Jonathan, Judas's brethren, received his dead body by a treaty from the enemy, and carried it to the village Modin, where their father had been buried, and there buried him; while the multitude lamented him many days, and performed the usual solemn rites of a funeral to him. And this was the end that Judas came to. He had been a man of valour and a great warrior, and mindful of all the commands of their father Mattathias; and had undergone all difficulties, both in doing and suffering, for the liberty of his countrymen. And when his character was so excellent, [while he was alive,] he left behind him a glorious reputation and memorial, by gaining freedom for his nation, and delivering them from slavery under the Macedonians. And when he had retained the high priesthood three years, he died.

BOOK XIII

CONTAINING THE INTERVAL OF EIGHTY-TWO YEARS

FROM THE DEATH OF JUDAS MACCABEUS TO QUEEN ALEXANDRA'S DEATH

CHAPTER I

HOW JONATHAN TOOK THE GOVERNMENT AFTER HIS BROTHER JUDAS; AND HOW HE, TOGETHER WITH HIS BROTHER SIMON, WAGED WAR AGAINST BACCHIDES

1. BY what means the nation of the Jews recovered their freedom when they had been brought into slavery by the Macedonians, and what struggles, and how many great battles, Judas, the general of their army, ran through till he was slain as he was fighting for them, hath been related in the foregoing book: but after he was dead, all the wicked, and those that transgressed the laws of their forefathers, sprang up again in Judea, and grew upon them, and distressed them on every side. A famine also assisted their wickedness, and afflicted the country, till not a few, who by reason of their want of necessaries, and because they were not able to bear up against the miseries that both the famine and their enemies brought upon them, deserted their country, and went to the Macedonians. And now Bacchides gathered those Jews together who had apostatised from the accustomed way of living of their forefathers, and chose to live like their neighbours, and committed the care of the country to them; who also caught the friends of Judas, and those of his party, and delivered them up to Bacchides, who, when he had, in the first place, tortured and tormented them at his pleasure, he by that means at length killed them. And when this calamity of the Jews was become so great, as they had never had experience of the like since their return out of Babylon, those that remained of the companions of Judas, see-

ing that the nation was about to be destroyed after a miserable manner, came to his brother Jonathan, and desired him that he would imitate his brother, and that care which he took of his countrymen, for whose liberty in general he died also; and that he would not permit the nation to be without a governor, especially in those destructive circumstances wherein it now was. And when Jonathan said he was ready to die for them, and was indeed esteemed no way inferior to his brother, he was appointed to be the general of the Jewish army.

2. When Bacchides heard this, and was afraid that Jonathan might be very troublesome to the king and the Macedonians, as Judas had been before him, he sought how he might slay him by treachery: but this intention of his was not unknown to Jonathan, nor his brother Simon; but when these two were apprised of it, they took all their companions, and presently fled into that wilderness which was nearest to the city; and when they were come to a lake called Asphar, they abode there. But when Bacchides was sensible that they were in a low state, and were in that place, he hasted to fall upon them with all his forces, and pitching his camp beyond Jordan, he recruited his army: but when Jonathan knew that Bacchides was coming upon him, he sent his brother John, who was also called Gaddis, to the Nabatean Arabs, that he might lodge his baggage with them until the battle with Bacchides should be over, for they were the Jews' friends. And the sons of Ambri laid an ambush for John, from the city Medaba, and seized upon him, and upon those that were with him, and plundered all that they had with them: they also slew John, and all his companions. However, they were sufficiently punished for

what they now did by John's brethren, as we shall relate presently.

3. But when Bacchides knew that Jonathan had pitched his camp among the lakes of Jordan, he observed when their Sabbath-day came, and then assaulted him, [as supposing that he would not fight because of the law for resting on that day:] but he exhorted his companions [to fight;] and told them, that their lives were at stake, since they were encompassed by the river, and by their enemies, and had no way to escape, for that their enemies pressed upon them before, and the river was behind them. So, after he had prayed to God to give them the victory, he joined battle with the enemy, of whom he overthrew many: and as he saw Bacchides coming up boldly to him, he stretched out his right hand to smite him; but the other foreseeing and avoiding the stroke, Jonathan with his companions leaped into the river, and swam over it, and by that means escaped beyond Jordan, while the enemy did not pass over that river; but Bacchides returned presently to the citadel at Jerusalem, having lost about two thousand of his army. He also fortified many cities of Judea, whose walls had been demolished; Jericho, and Emmaus, and Bethoron, and Bethel, and Timna, and Pharatho, and Tecoa, and Gazara, and built towers in every one of these cities, and encompassed them with strong walls, that were very large also, and put garrisons into them, that they might issue out of them, and do mischief to the Jews. He also fortified the citadel at Jerusalem more than all the rest. Moreover, he took the sons of the principal Jews as pledges, and shut them up in the citadel, and in that manner guarded it.

4. About the same time, one came to Jonathan, and to his brother Simon, and told them that the sons of Ambri were celebrating a marriage, and bringing the bride from the city Gabatha, who was the daughter of one of the illustrious men among the Arabians, and that the damsel was to be conducted with pomp and splendour, and much riches: so Jonathan and Simon thinking this appeared to be the fittest time for them to avenge the death of their brother, and that they had forces sufficient for receiving satisfaction from them for his death, they made haste to Medaba, and lay in wait among the mountains for the coming of their enemies; and as soon as they saw them conducting the virgin and the bridegroom, and such a great company of their friends with them, as was to be expected at this wedding, they sallied out of their ambush and slew them all,— and took their ornaments, and all the prey that then followed them, and so returned, and received this satisfaction for their brother John from the sons of Ambri; for as well these sons themselves as their friends, and wives, and children, that followed them, perished, being in number about four hundred.

5. However, Simon and Jonathan returned to the lakes of the river, and abode there; but Bacchides, when he had secured all Judea with his garrisons, returned to the king; and then it was that the affairs of Judea were quiet for two years; but when the deserters and the wicked saw that Jonathan and those that were with him lived in the country very quietly, by reason of the peace, they sent to king Demetrius, and excited him to send Bacchides to seize upon Jonathan, which they said was to be done without any trouble, and in one night's time; and that if they fell upon them before they were aware, they might slay them all. So the king sent Bacchides, who, when he was come into Judea,

wrote to all his friends, both Jews and auxiliaries, that they should seize upon Jonathan, and bring him to him; and when, upon their endeavours, they were not able to seize upon Jonathan, for he was sensible of the snares they laid for him, and very carefully guarded against them, Bacchides was angry at these deserters, as having imposed upon him, and upon the king, and slew fifty of their leaders; whereupon Jonathan, with his brother, and those that were with him, retired to Bethagla, a village that lay in the wilderness, out of his fear of Bacchides. He also built towers in it, and encompassed it with walls, and took care that it should be safely guarded. Upon the hearing of which Bacchides led his own army along with him, and besides took his Jewish auxiliaries, and came against Jonathan, and made an assault upon his fortifications, and besieged him many days, but Jonathan did not abate of his courage at the zeal Bacchides used in the siege, but courageously opposed him; and while he left his brother Simon in the city to fight with Bacchides, he went privately out himself into the country, and got a great body of men together of his own party, and fell upon Bacchides's camp in the night-time, and destroyed a great many of them. His brother Simon knew also of this his falling upon them, because he perceived that the enemies were slain by him, so he sallied out upon them, and burnt the engines which the Macedonians used, and made a great slaughter of them; and when Bacchides saw himself encompassed with enemies, and some of them before, and some behind him, he fell into despair and trouble of mind, as confounded at the unexpected ill success of this siege. However, he vented his displeasure at these misfortunes upon those deserters who sent for him from the king, as having deluded him. So he had a mind to put an end to this siege after a decent manner, if it were possible for him so to do, and then to return home.

6. When Jonathan understood these his intentions, he sent ambassadors to him about a league of friendship and mutual assistance, and that they might restore those they had taken captive on both sides. So Bacchides thought this a pretty decent way of retiring home, and made a league of friendship with Jonathan, when they sware that they would not any more make war against one another. Accordingly, he restored the captives, and took his own men with him, and returned to the king at Antioch; and after this his departure, he never came into Judea again. Then did Jonathan take the opportunity of this quiet state of things, and went and lived in the city Michmash; and there governed the multitude, and punished the wicked and ungodly, and by that means purged the nation of them.

CHAPTER II

HOW ALEXANDER [BALA,] IN HIS WAR WITH DEMETRIUS, GRANTED JONATHAN MANY ADVANTAGES, AND APPOINTED HIM TO BE HIGH PRIEST, AND PERSUADED HIM TO ASSIST HIM, ALTHOUGH DEMETRIUS PROMISED HIM GREATER ADVANTAGES ON THE OTHER SIDE. CONCERNING THE DEATH OF DEMETRIUS

1. Now in the hundred and sixtieth year, it fell out that Alexander, the son of Antiochus Epiphanes,* came up into Syria, and took Ptole-

* This Alexander Bala, who pretended to be the son of Antiochus Epiphanes, and was owned for such by the Jews and Romans, and yet is by several historians

mais, the soldiers having betrayed it to him, for they were at enmity with Demetrius, on account of his insolence and difficulty of access: for he shut himself up in a palace of his that had four towers, which he had built himself, not far from Antioch, and admitted nobody. He was withal slothful and negligent about the public affairs, whereby the hatred of his subjects was the more kindled against him, as we have elsewhere already related. When, therefore, Demetrius heard that Alexander was in Ptolemais, he took his whole army, and led it against him; he also sent ambassadors to Jonathan, about a league of mutual assistance and friendship, for he resolved to be beforehand with Alexander, lest the other should treat with him first, and gain assistance from him; and this he did out of the fear he had lest Jonathan should remember how ill Demetrius had formerly treated him, and should join with him in this war against him. He therefore gave orders that Jonathan should be allowed to raise an army, and should get armour made, and should receive back those hostages of the Jewish nation whom Bacchides had shut up in the citadel of Jerusalem. When this good fortune had befallen Jonathan, by the concession of Demetrius, he came to Jerusalem, and read the king's letter in the audience of the people, and of those that kept the citadel. When these were read, these wicked men and deserters, who were in the citadel, were greatly afraid, upon the king's permission to Jonathan to raise an army, and to receive back the hostages: so he delivered every one of them to his own parents; and thus did Jonathan make his abode at Jerusalem, renewing the city to a better state, and reforming the buildings as he pleased; for he gave orders that the walls of the city should be rebuilt with square stones, that it might be more secure from their enemies; and when those that kept the garrisons that were in Judea saw this, they all left them, and fled to Antioch, excepting those that were in the city Bethsura, and those that were in the citadel of Jerusalem, for the greater part of these was of the wicked Jews and deserters, and on that account these did not deliver up their garrisons.

2. When Alexander knew what promises Demetrius had made Jonathan, and withal knew his courage, and what great things he had done when he fought the Macedonians, and besides what hardships he had undergone by the means of Demetrius, and of Bacchides, the general of Demetrius's army, he told his friends that he could not at present find any one else that might afford him better assistance than Jonathan, who was both courageous against his enemies, and had a particular hatred against Demetrius, as having both suffered many hard things from him, and acted many hard things against him. If, therefore, they were of opinion that they should make him their friend against Demetrius, it was more for their advantage to invite him to assist them now than at another time. It being therefore determined by him and his friends to send to Jonathan, he wrote to him this epistle: —"King Alexander to his brother Jonathan,

sendeth greeting. We have long ago heard of thy courage and thy fidelity, and for that reason have sent to thee, to make with thee a league of friendship and mutual assistance. We therefore do ordain thee this day the high priest of the Jews, and that thou beest called my friend. I have also sent thee, as presents, a purple robe and a golden crown, and desire that, now thou art by us honoured, thou wilt in like manner respect as also.

3. When Jonathan had received this letter, he put on the pontifical robe at the time of the feast of tabernacles, eight years after the death of his brother Judas, for at that time no high priest had been made. So he raised great forces, and had abundance of armour got ready. This greatly grieved Demetrius when he heard of it, and made him blame himself for his slowness, that he had not prevented Alexander, and got the good-will of Jonathan, but had given him time so to do. However, he also himself wrote a letter to Jonathan, and to the people, the contents whereof are these:—"King Demetrius to Jonathan, and to the nation of the Jews, sendeth greeting. Since you have preserved your friendship for us, and when you have been tempted by our enemies, you have not joined yourselves to them; I both commend you for this your fidelity, and exhort you to continue in the same disposition; for which you shall be repaid, and receive rewards from us: for I will free you from the greatest part of the tributes and taxes which you formerly paid to the kings my predecessors, and to myself; and I do now set you free from those tributes which you have ever paid; and besides, I forgive you the tax upon salt, and the value of the crowns which you used to offer to me:† and instead of the third part of the fruits [of the field,] and the half of the fruits of the trees, I relinquish my part of them from this day: and as to the poll-money, which ought to be given me for every head of the inhabitants of Judea, Samaria, and Galilee, and Perea, that I relinquish to you for this time, and for all time to come. I will also, that the city of Jerusalem be holy and inviolable, and free from the tithe, and from the taxes, unto its utmost bounds: and I so far recede from my title to the citadel, as to permit Jonathan your high priest to possess it, that he may place such a garrison in it as he approves of for fidelity and good-will to himself, that they may keep it for us. I also make free all those Jews who have been made captives and slaves in my kingdom. I also give order that the beasts of the Jews be not pressed for our service: and let their Sabbaths, and all their festivals, and three days before each of them, be free from any imposition. In the same manner, I set free the Jews that are inhabitants in my kingdom, and order that no injury be done them. I also give leave to such of them as are willing to enlist themselves in my army, that they may do it, and those as far as thirty thousand; which Jewish soldiers, wheresoever they go, shall have the same pay that my own army hath; and some of them I will place in my garrisons, and some as guards about mine own body, and as rulers over those that are in my court. I give them leave also to use the laws of their forefathers, and to observe them; and I will that they have power over the three toparchies that are added to Judea; and it shall be in the power of the high priest to take care that no one Jew shall

---

deemed to be a counterfeit, is, by Josephus, believed to have been the real son of that Antiochus, and by him always spoken of accordingly; and since the author of the first book of Maccabees, (chap. x. 2,) calls him by his father's name, Epiphanes, and says he was the son of Antiochus, I suppose the other writers are not to be followed against such evidence, though perhaps Epiphanes might have him by a woman of no family. The king of Egypt also, Philometor, gave him his daughter in marriage, which he would hardly have done had he believed him to be a counterfeit.

† "The Jews," says Grotius, "were wont to present crowns to the kings [of Syria;] afterwards that gold which was paid instead of those crowns, or which was expended in making them, was called the Crown-Gold and Crown-Tax."

have any other temple for worship but only that at Jerusalem. I bequeath also, out of my own revenues, yearly, for the expenses about the sacrifices, one hundred and fifty thousand [drachmæ;] and what money is to spare, I will that it shall be your own. I also release to you those ten thousand drachmæ which the kings received from the temple, because they appertain to the priests that minister in that temple. And whosoever shall fly to the temple at Jerusalem, or to the places thereto belonging, or who owe the king money, or are there on any other account, let them be set free, and let their goods be in safety. I also give you leave to repair and rebuild your temple, and that all be done at my expenses. I also allow you to build the walls of your city, and to erect high towers, and that they be erected at my charge. And if there be any fortified town that would be convenient for the Jewish country to have very strong, let it be so built at my expenses."

4. This was what Demetrius promised and granted to the Jews, by this letter. But king Alexander raised a great army of mercenary soldiers, and of those that deserted to him out of Syria, and made an expedition against Demetrius. And when it was come to a battle, the left wing of Demetrius put those who opposed them to flight, and pursued them a great way, and slew many of them, and spoiled their camp; but the right wing, where Demetrius happened to be, was beaten; and as for all the rest, they ran away. But Demetrius fought courageously, and slew a great many of the enemy; but as he was in pursuit of the rest, his horse carried him into a deep bog, where it was hard to get out, and there it happened, that upon his horse's falling down, he could not escape being killed; for when his enemies saw what had befallen him, they returned back, and encompassed Demetrius round, and they all threw their darts at him; but he, being now on foot, fought bravely. But at length he received so many wounds, that he was not able to bear up any longer, but fell. And this is the end that Demetrius came to, when he had reigned eleven years, as we have elsewhere related.

CHAPTER III

THE FRIENDSHIP THAT WAS BETWEEN ONIAS AND PTOLEMY PHILOMETOR; AND HOW ONIAS BUILT A TEMPLE IN EGYPT LIKE TO THAT AT JERUSALEM

1. BUT then the son of Onias the high priest, who was of the same name with his father, and who fled to king Ptolemy, who was called Philometor, lived now at Alexandria, as we have said already. When this Onias saw that Judea was oppressed by the Macedonians and their kings, out of a desire to purchase to himself a memorial and eternal fame, he resolved to send to king Ptolemy and queen Cleopatra, to ask leave of them that he might build a temple in Egypt like to that at Jerusalem, and might ordain Levites and priests out of their own stock. The chief reason why he was desirous so to do, was, that he relied upon the prophet Isaiah, who lived above six hundred years before, and foretold that there certainly was to be a temple built to Almighty God in Egypt by a man that was a Jew. Onias was elevated with this prediction, and wrote the following Epistle to Ptolemy and Cleopatra :—" Having done many and great things for you in the affairs of the war, by the assistance of God, and that in Cœlesyria and

Phœnicia, I came at length with the Jews to Leontopolis, and to other places of your nation, where I found that the greatest part of your people had temples in an improper manner, and that on this account they bare ill will one against another, which happens to the Egyptians by reason of the multitude of their temples, and the difference of opinion about divine worship. Now I found a very fit place in a castle that hath its name from the country Diana; this place is full of materials of several sorts, and replenished with sacred animals: I desire, therefore, that you will grant me leave to purge this holy place, which belongs to no master, and is fallen down, and to build there a temple to Almighty God, after the pattern of that in Jerusalem, and of the same dimensions, that may be for the benefit of thyself, and thy wife and children, that those Jews who dwell in Egypt may have a place whither they may come and meet together in mutual harmony one with another, and be subservient to thy advantages; for the prophet Isaiah foretold, that ' there should be an altar in Egypt to the Lord God :' and many other such things did he prophesy relating to that place."

2. And this was what Onias wrote to king Ptolemy. Now any one may observe his piety, and that of his sister and wife Cleopatra, by that epistle which they wrote in answer to it; for they laid the blame and the transgression of the law upon the head of Onias. And this was their reply :—" King Ptolemy and Queen Cleopatra to Onias, send greeting. We have read thy petition, wherein thou desirest leave to be given to thee to purge that temple which is fallen down at Leontopolis, in the Nomus of Heliopolis, and which is named from the country Bubastis; on which account we cannot but wonder that it should be pleasing to God to have a temple erected in a place so unclean, and so full of sacred animals. But since thou sayest that Isaiah the prophet foretold this long ago, we give thee leave to do it, if it may be done according to your law, and so that we may not appear to have at all offended God herein."

3. So Onias took the place, and built a temple, and an altar to God, like indeed to that at Jerusalem, but smaller and poorer. I do not think it proper for me now to describe its dimensions, or its vessels, which have been already described in my seventh book of the Wars of the Jews. However, Onias found other Jews like himself, together with priests and Levites, that there performed divine service. But we have said enough about this temple.

4. Now it came to pass that the Alexandrian Jews, and those Samaritans who paid their worship to the temple that was built in the days of Alexander at mount Gerizzim, did now make a sedition one against another, and disputed about their temples before Ptolemy himself, the Jews saying that, according to the law of Moses, the temple was to be built at Jerusalem; and the Samaritans saying that it was to be built at Gerizzim. They desired therefore the king to sit with his friends and hear the debates about these matters, and punish those with death who were baffled. Now Sabbeus and Theodosius managed the argument for the Samaritans, and Andronicus, the son of Messalamus, for the people of Jerusalem; and they took an oath by God and the king, to make their demonstrations according to the law; and they desired of Ptolemy, that whomsoever he should find that transgressed what they had sworn to, he would put him to death. Accordingly, the king took several of his friends into the council, and sat down, in order to hear what the pleaders said.

Now the Jews that were at Alexandria were in great concern for those men, whose lot it was to contend for the temple at Jerusalem; for they took it very ill that any should take away the reputation of that temple, which was so ancient and so celebrated all over the habitable earth. Now when Sabbeus and Theodosius had given leave to Andronicus to speak first, he began to demonstrate out of the law, and out of the successions of the high priests, how they every one in succession from his father had received that dignity, and ruled over the temple; and how all the kings of Asia had honoured that temple with their donations, and with the most splendid gifts dedicated thereto: but as for that at Gerizzim, he made no account of it, and regarded it, as if it had never had a being. By this speech, and other arguments, Andronicus persuaded the king to determine that the temple at Jerusalem was built according to the laws of Moses, and to put Sabbeus and Theodosius to death. And these were the events that befell the Jews at Alexandria in the days of Ptolemy Philometor.

CHAPTER IV

HOW ALEXANDER HONOURED JONATHAN AFTER AN EXTRAORDINARY MANNER; AND HOW DEMETRIUS, THE SON OF DEMETRIUS, OVERCAME ALEXANDER, AND MADE A LEAGUE OF FRIENDSHIP WITH JONATHAN

1. DEMETRIUS being thus slain in battle, as we have above related, Alexander took the kingdom of Syria; and wrote to Ptolemy Philometor, and desired his daughter in marriage; and said it was but just that he should be joined in affinity to one that had now received the principality of his forefathers, and had been promoted to it by God's providence, and had conquered Demetrius; and that was on other accounts not unworthy of being related to him. Ptolemy received this proposal of marriage gladly; and wrote him an answer, saluting him on account of his having received the principality of his forefathers; and promising him that he would give him his daughter in marriage; and assured him that he was coming to meet him at Ptolemais, and desired that he would there meet him, for that he would accompany her from Egypt so far, and would there marry his child to him. When Ptolemy had written thus, he came suddenly to Ptolemais, and brought his daughter Cleopatra along with him; and as he found Alexander there before him, as he desired him to come, he gave him his child in marriage, and for her portion gave her as much silver and gold as became such a king to give.

2. When the wedding was over, Alexander wrote to Jonathan, the high priest, and desired him to come to Ptolemais. So when he came to these kings, and had made them magnificent presents, he was honoured by them both. Alexander compelled him also to put off his own garment, and to take a purple garment, and made him sit with him on his throne; and commanded his captains that they should go with him into the middle of the city, and proclaim that it was not permitted to any one to speak against him, or to give him any disturbance. And when the captains had thus done, those that were prepared to accuse Jonathan, and who bore him ill-will, when they saw the honour that was done him by proclamation, and that by the king's order, ran away, and were afraid lest some mischief should befall them. Nay, king Alexander was so very kind to Jonathan, that he set him down as the principal of his friends.

3. But then, upon the hundred and sixty-fifth year, Demetrius, the son of Demetrius, came from Crete, with a great number of mercenary soldiers, which Lasthenes, the Cretan, brought him, and sailed to Cilicia. This thing cast Alexander into great concern and disorder when he heard it; so he made haste immediately out of Phœnicia, and came to Antioch, that he might put matters in a safe posture there before Demetrius should come. He also left Apollonius Daus* governor of Cœlesyria, who, coming to Jamnia with a great army, sent to Jonathan, the high priest, and told him that it was not right that he alone should live at rest, and with authority, and not be subject to the king; that this thing had made him a reproach among all men, that he had not yet made him subject to the king. "Do not thou therefore deceive thyself, and sit still among the mountains, and pretend to have forces with thee; but if thou hast any dependence on thy strength, come down into the plain, and let our armies be compared together, and the event of the battle will demonstrate which of us is the most courageous. However, take notice, that the most valiant men of every city are in my army, and that these are the very men who have always beaten thy progenitors; but let us have the battle in such a place of the country where we may fight with weapons, and not with stones, and where there may be no place whither those that are beaten may fly."

4. With this Jonathan was irritated; and choosing himself out ten thousand of his soldiers, he went out of Jerusalem in haste, with his brother Simon, and came to Joppa, and pitched his camp on the outside of the city, because the people of Joppa had shut their gates against him, for they had a garrison in the city put there by Apollonius. But when Jonathan was preparing to besiege them, they were afraid he would take them by force, and so they opened the gates to him. But Apollonius when he heard that Joppa was taken by Jonathan, took three thousand horsemen, and eight thousand footmen, and came to Ashdod; and removing thence, he made his journey silently and slowly, and going up to Joppa, he made as if he was retiring from the place, and so drew Jonathan into the plain, as valuing himself highly upon his horsemen, and having his hopes of victory principally in them. However, Jonathan sallied out, and pursued Apollonius to Ashdod; but as soon as Apollonius perceived that his enemy was in the plain, he came back and gave him battle. But Apollonius had laid a thousand horsemen in ambush in a valley, that they might be seen by their enemies as behind them; which when Jonathan perceived, he was under no consternation, but ordering his army to stand in a square battle array, he gave them a charge to fall on the enemy on both sides, and set them to face those that attacked them both before and behind; and while the fight lasted till the evening, he gave part of his forces to his brother Simon, and ordered him to attack the enemies; but for himself he charged those that were with him to cover themselves with their armour, and receive the darts of the horsemen, who did as they were commanded; so that the enemy's horsemen, while they threw their darts till they had no more left, did them no harm, for the darts that were thrown did not enter into their

---

* According to Dean Prideaux, this Apollonius Daus was the son of that Apollonius who had been made governor of Cœlesyria and Phœnicia by Seleucus Philopater.

bodies, being thrown upon the shields that were united and conjoined together, the closeness of which easily overcame the force of the darts, and they flew about without any effect. But when the enemy grew remiss in throwing their darts from morning till late at night, Simon perceived their weariness, and fell upon the body of men before him ; and because his soldiers shewed great alacrity, he put the enemy to flight : and when the horsemen saw the footmen ran away, neither did they stay themselves ; but they being very weary, by the duration of the fight till the evening, and their hope from the footmen being quite gone, they basely ran away, and in great confusion also, till they were separated one from another, and scattered over all the plain. Upon which Jonathan pursued them as far as Ashdod, and slew a great many of them, and compelled the rest, in despair of escaping, to fly to the temple of Dagon, which was at Ashdod : but Jonathan took the city on the first onset, and burnt it, and the villages about it ; nor did he abstain from the temple of Dagon itself, but burnt it also, and destroyed those that had fled to it. Now the entire multitude of the enemies that fell in the battle, and were consumed in the temple, were eight´thousand. When Jonathan therefore had overcome so great an army, he removed from Ashdod, and came to Askelon : and when he had pitched his camp without the city, the people of Askelon came out and met him, bringing him hospitable presents, and honouring him ; so he accepted of their kind intentions, and returned thence to Jerusalem with a great deal of prey, which he brought thence when he conquered his enemies. But when Alexander heard that Apollonius, the general of his army, was beaten, he pretended to be glad of it, because he had fought with Jonathan his friend and ally against his directions. Accordingly, he sent to Jonathan, and gave testimony to his worth ; and gave him honorary rewards, as a golden button,* which it is the custom to give the king's kinsmen, and allowed him Ekron and its toparchy for his own inheritance.

5. About this time it was that king Ptolemy, who was called Philometor, led an army, part by sea and part by land, and came to Syria, to the assistance of Alexander, who was his son-in-law ; and accordingly all the cities received him willingly, as Alexander had commanded them to do, and conducted him as far as Ashdod ; where they all made loud complaints about the temple of Dagon, which was burnt, and accused Jonathan of having laid it waste, and destroyed the country adjoining with fire, and slain a great number of them. Ptolemy heard these accusations, but said nothing. Jonathan also went to meet Ptolemy as far as Joppa, and obtained from him hospitable presents, and those glorious in their kinds, with all the marks of honour ; and when he had conducted him as far as the river called Eleutherus, he returned again to Jerusalem.

6. But as Ptolemy was at Ptolemais, he was very near to a most unexpected destruction ; for a treacherous design was laid for his life by Alexander, by the means of Ammonius, who was his friend : and as the treachery was very plain, Ptolemy wrote to Alexander, and required of him that he should bring Ammonius to condign punishment, informing him what snares had been laid for him by Ammonius, and desired that he might be accordingly punished for it ; but when

Alexander did not comply with his demands, he perceived that it was he himself who laid the design, and was very angry at him. Alexander had also formerly been on very ill terms with the people of Antioch, for they had suffered very much by this means ; yet did Ammonius at length undergo the punishment his insolent crimes had deserved, for he was killed in an opprobrious manner, like a woman, while he endeavoured to conceal himself in a feminine habit, as we have elsewhere related.

7. Hereupon Ptolemy blamed himself for having given his daughter in marriage to Alexander, and for the league he had made with him to assist him against Demetrius ; so he dissolved his relation to him, and took his daughter away from him, and immediately sent to Demetrius, and offered to make a league of mutual assistance and friendship with him, and agreed with him to give him his daughter in marriage, and to restore him to the principality of his fathers. Demetrius was well pleased with this embassage, and accepted of his assistance, and of the marriage of his daughter ; but Ptolemy had still one more hard task to do, and that was to persuade the people of Antioch to receive Demetrius, because they were greatly displeased at him, on account of the injuries his father Demetrius had done them ; yet did he bring this about ; for as the people of Antioch hated Alexander on Ammonius's account, as we have shewn already, they were easily prevailed with to cast him out of Antioch ; who, thus expelled out of Antioch, came into Cilicia. Ptolemy came then to Antioch, and was made king by its inhabitants, and by the army ; so that he was forced to put on his own two diadems, the one of Asia, the other of Egypt ; but being naturally a good and righteous man, and not desirous of what belonged to others, and besides these dispositions, being also a wise man in reasoning about futurities, he determined to avoid the envy of the Romans, so he called the people of Antioch together to an assembly, and persuaded them to receive Demetrius ; and assured them that he would not be mindful of what they did to his father in case he should be now obliged by them ; and he undertook that he would himself be a good monitor and governor to him ; and promised that he would not permit him to attempt any bad actions ; but that, for his own part, he was contented with the kingdom of Egypt. By which discourse he persuaded the people of Antioch to receive Demetrius.

8. But now Alexander made haste, with a numerous and great army, and came out of Cilicia into Syria, and burnt the country belonging to Antioch, and pillaged it ; whereupon Ptolemy, and his son-in-law Demetrius, brought their army against him, (for he had already given him his daughter in marriage,) and beat Alexander, and put him to flight ; and accordingly he fled into Arabia. Now, it happened in the time of the battle, that Ptolemy's horse, upon hearing the noise of an elephant, cast him off his back, and threw him on the ground ; upon the sight of which accident his enemies fell upon him, and gave him many wounds upon his head, and brought him into danger of death, for when his guards caught him up he was so very ill, that for four days' time he was not able either to understand or to speak. However, Zabdiel, a prince among the Arabians, cut off Alexander's head and sent it to Ptolemy, who recovering of his wounds, and returning to his understanding, on the fifth day, heard at once a most agreeable hearing, and saw a most agreeable sight, which were the death and the head of Alexander ; yet a

---

* The Phœnicians and Romans used to reward such as had deserved well of them, by presenting to them a golden button.

little after this his joy for the death of Alexander, with which he was so greatly satisfied, he also departed this life. Now Alexander, who was called Balas, reigned over Asia five years, as we have elsewhere related.

9. But when Demetrius, who was styled Nicator,* had taken the kingdom, he was so wicked as to treat Ptolemy's soldiers very hardly, neither remembering the league of mutual assistance that was between them, nor that he was his son-in-law and kinsman, by Cleopatra's marriage to him; so the soldiers fled from his wicked treatment to Alexandria; but Demetrius kept his elephants. But Jonathan the high priest levied an army out of all Judea, and attacked the citadel at Jerusalem, and besieged it. It was held by a garrison of Macedonians, and by some of those men who had deserted the customs of their forefathers. These men at first despised the attempts of Jonathan for taking the place, as depending on its strength; but some of those wicked men went out by night, and came to Demetrius, and informed him that the citadel was besieged; who was irritated with what he heard, and took his army, and came from Antioch, against Jonathan. And when he was at Antioch, he wrote to him, and commanded him to come to him quickly to Ptolemais: upon which Jonathan did not intermit the siege of the citadel, but took with him the elders of the people, and the priests, and carried with him gold and silver, and garments, and a great number of presents of friendship, and came to Demetrius, and presented him with them, and thereby pacified the king's anger. So he was honoured by him, and received from him the confirmation of his high priesthood, as he had possessed it by the grants of the kings his predecessors. And when the Jewish deserters accused him, Demetrius was so far from giving credit to them, that when he petitioned him that he would demand no more than three hundred talents for the tribute of all Judea, and the three toparchies of Samaria, and Perea, and Galilee, he complied with the proposal, and gave him a letter confirming those grants; the contents of which were as follows:—"King Demetrius to Jonathan his brother, and to the nation of the Jews, sendeth greeting. We have sent you a copy of that epistle which we have written to Lasthenes our kinsman, that you may know its contents.— 'King Demetrius to Lasthenes our father, sendeth greeting. I have determined to return thanks, and to shew favour to the nation of the Jews, who hath observed the rules of justice in our concerns. Accordingly, I remit to them the three prefectures, Apherima, and Lydda, and Ramatha, which have been added to Judea out of Samaria, with their appurtenances: as also what the kings my predecessors received from those that offered sacrifices in Jerusalem, and what are due from the fruits of the earth, and of the trees, and what else belongs to us; with the salt-pits, and the crowns that used to be presented to us. Nor shall they be compelled to pay any of those taxes from this time to all futurity. Take care, therefore, that a copy of this epistle be taken, and given to Jonathan, and be set up in an eminent place of their holy temple.'" And these were the contents of this writing. And now when Demetrius saw that there was peace everywhere, and that there was no danger, nor fear of war, he disbanded the greatest part of his army, and diminished their pay, and even retained in pay no others than such foreigners as came up with him from Crete, and from the other islands. However, this procured him ill-will and hatred from the soldiers, on whom he bestowed nothing from this time, while the kings before him used to pay them in time of peace, as they did before, that they might have their good-will, and that they might be very ready to undergo the difficulties of war, if any occasion should require it.

CHAPTER V

HOW TRYPHO, AFTER HE HAD BEATEN DEMETRIUS, DELIVERED THE KINGDOM TO ANTIOCHUS, THE SON OF ALEXANDER, AND GAINED JONATHAN FOR HIS ASSISTANT; AND CONCERNING THE ACTIONS AND EMBASSIES OF JONATHAN

1. Now there was a certain commander of Alexander's forces, an Apanemian by birth, whose name was Diodotus, and was also called Trypho, took notice of the ill-will the soldiers bare to Demetrius, and went to Malchus the Arabian, who brought up Antiochus, the son of Alexander, and told him what ill-will the army bare Demetrius, and persuaded him to give him Antiochus, because he would make him king, and recover to him the kingdom of his father. Malchus at first opposed him in this attempt, because he could not believe him; but when Trypho lay hard at him for a long time, he overpersuaded him to comply with Trypho's intentions and entreaties. And this was the state Trypho was now in.

2. But Jonathan the high priest, being desirous to get clear of those that were in the citadel of Jerusalem, and of the Jewish deserters and wicked men, as well as those in all the garrisons in the country, sent presents and ambassadors to Demetrius, and entreated him to take away his soldiers out of the strongholds of Judea. Demetrius made answer, that after the war, which he was now deeply engaged in, was over, he would not only grant him that, but greater things than that also: and he desired he would send him some assistance, and informed him that his army had deserted him. So Jonathan chose out three thousand of his soldiers, and sent them to Demetrius.

3. Now the people of Antioch hated Demetrius, both on account of what mischief he had himself done them, and because they were his enemies also on account of his father Demetrius, who had greatly abused them; so they watched some opportunity which they might lay hold on, to fall upon him. And when they were informed of the assistance that was coming to Demetrius from Jonathan, and considered at the same time that he would raise a numerous army, unless they prevented him and seized upon him, they took their weapons immediately, and encompassed his palace in the way of a siege, and seizing upon all the ways of getting out, they sought to subdue their king. And when he saw that the people of Antioch were become his bitter enemies, and that they were thus in arms, he took the mercenary soldiers which he had with him, and those Jews who were sent by Jonathan, and assaulted the Antiochians; but he was overpowered by them, for they were many ten thousands, and was beaten. But when the Jews saw that the Antiochians were superior, they went up to the top of the palace, and shot at them from thence; and because they were so remote from them by their height, that they suffered nothing on their side, but did great execution on the

---

* This name, Demetrius Nicator, or Demetrius the conqueror, is so written on his coins still extant.

others as fighting from such an elevation, they drove them out of the adjoining houses, and immediately set them on fire, whereupon the flame spread itself over the whole city, and burnt it all down. This happened by reason of the closeness of the houses, and because they were generally built of wood: so the Antiochians, when they were not able to help themselves, nor to stop the fire, were put to flight. And as the Jews leaped from the top of one house to another, and pursued them after that manner, it thence happened that the pursuit was very surprising. But when the king saw that the Antiochians were very busy in saving their children and their wives, and so did not fight any longer, he fell upon them in the narrow passages, and fought them, and slew a great number of them, till at last they were forced to throw down their arms, and to deliver themselves up to Demetrius. So he forgave them this their insolent behaviour, and put an end to the sedition: and when he had given rewards to the Jews out of the rich spoils he had gotten, and had returned them thanks, as the cause of his victory, he sent them away to Jerusalem to Jonathan, with an ample testimony of the assistance they had afforded him. Yet did he prove an ill man to Jonathan afterward, and broke the promises he had made: and he threatened that he would make war upon him, unless he would pay all that tribute which the Jewish nation owed to the first kings [of Syria.] And this he had done, if Trypho had not hindered him, and diverted his preparations against Jonathan to a concern for his own preservation; for he now returned out of Arabia into Syria, with the child Antiochus, for he was yet in age but a youth, and put the diadem on his head; and as the whole forces that had left Demetrius, because they had no pay, came to his assistance, he made war upon Demetrius, and joining battle with him, overcame him in the fight, and took from him both his elephants and the city of Antioch.

4. Demetrius, upon this defeat, retired into Cilicia: but the child Antiochus sent ambassadors and an epistle to Jonathan, and made him his friend and confederate, and confirmed to him the high priesthood, and yielded up to him the four prefectures which had been added to Judea. Moreover, he sent him vessels and cups of gold, and a purple garment, and gave him leave to use them. He also presented him with a golden button, and styled him one of his principal friends; and appointed his brother Simon to be the general over the forces, from the Ladder of Tyre unto Egypt. So Jonathan was so pleased with these grants made him by Antiochus, that he sent ambassadors to him and to Trypho, and professed himself to be their friend and confederate, and said he would join with him in a war against Demetrius, informing him that he had made no proper returns for the kindness he had done him; for that when he had received many marks of kindness from him, when he stood in great need of them, he, for such good turns, had requited him with further injuries.

5. So Antiochus gave Jonathan leave to raise himself a numerous army out of Syria and Phœnicia, and to make war against Demetrius's generals; whereupon he went in haste to the several cities, which received him splendidly indeed, but put no forces into his hands. And when he was come from thence to Askelon, the inhabitants of Askelon came and brought him presents, and met him in a splendid manner. He exhorted them, and every one of the cities of Cœlesyria, to forsake Demetrius, and to join with Antiochus, and in assisting him, to endeavour to punish Demetrius for what offences he had been guilty of against themselves; and told them there were many reasons for that their procedure, if they had a mind so to do. And when he had persuaded those cities to promise their assistance to Antiochus, he came to Gaza, in order to induce them also to be friends to Antiochus; but he found the inhabitants of Gaza much more alienated from him than he expected, for they had shut their gates against him; and although they had deserted Demetrius, they had not resolved to join themselves to Antiochus. This provoked Jonathan to besiege them, and to harass their country; for as he set a part of his army round about Gaza itself, so with the rest he overran their land, and spoiled it, and burdened what was in it. When the inhabitants of Gaza saw themselves in this state of affliction, and that no assistance came to them from Demetrius, that what distressed them was at hand, but what should profit them was still at a great distance, and it was uncertain whether it would come at all or not, they thought it would be prudent conduct to leave off any longer continuance with him, and to cultivate friendship with the other; so they sent to Jonathan, and professed they would be his friends, and afford him assistance; for such is the temper of men, that before they have had the trial of great afflictions, they do not understand what is for their advantage; but when they find themselves under such afflictions, they then change their minds, and what had been better for them to have done before they had been at all damaged, they choose to do, but not till after they have suffered such damages. However, he made a league of friendship with them, and took from them hostages for their performance of it, and sent these hostages to Jerusalem, while he went himself over all the country, as far as Damascus.

6. But when he heard that the generals of Demetrius's forces were come to the city Cadesh with a numerous army, (the place lies between the land of the Tyrians and Galilee,) for they supposed they should hereby draw him out of Syria, in order to preserve Galilee, and that he would not overlook the Galileans, who were his own people, when war was made upon them, he went to meet them, having left Simon in Judea, who raised as great an army as he was able out of the country, and then sat down before Bethsura, and besieged it, that being the strongest place in all Judea; and a garrison of Demetrius's kept it, as we have already related. But as Simon was raising banks, and bringing his engines of war against Bethsura, and was very earnest about the siege of it, the garrison was afraid lest the place should be taken of Simon by force, and they put to the sword; so they sent to Simon, and desired the security of his oath, that they should come to no harm from him, and that they would leave the place, and go away to Demetrius. Accordingly, he gave them his oath, and ejected them out of the city, and he put therein a garrison of his own.

7. But Jonathan removed out of Galilee, and from the waters which are called Gennesar, for there he was before encamped, and came into the plain that is called Asor, without knowing that the enemy was there. When therefore Demetrius's men knew a day beforehand that Jonathan was coming against them, they lay in ambush in the mountain, who were to assault him on the sudden, while they themselves met him with an army in the plain; which army when Jonathan saw ready to engage him, he also got ready his own soldiers for the battle as well as he was able. But those that were laid

in ambush by Demetrius's generals being behind them, the Jews were afraid lest they should be caught in the midst between two bodies, and perish; so they ran away in haste, and indeed all the rest left Jonathan, but a few that were in number about fifty, who stayed with him, and with them Mattathias, the son of Absalom; and Judas, the son of Chapseus, who were commanders of the whole army. These marched boldly, and like men desperate, against the enemy, and so pushed them, that by their courage they daunted them, and with their weapons in their hands, they put them to flight. And when those soldiers of Jonathan that had retired saw the enemy giving way, they got together after their flight, and pursued them with great violence; and this did they as far as Cadesh, where the camp of the enemy lay.

8. Jonathan having thus gotten a glorious victory, and slain two thousand of the enemy, returned to Jerusalem. So when he saw that all his affairs prospered according to his mind, by the providence of God, he sent ambassadors to the Romans, being desirous of renewing that friendship which their nation had with them formerly. He enjoined the same ambassadors, that, as they came back, they should go to the Spartans, and put them in mind of their friendship and kindred. So when the ambassadors came to Rome, they went in to their senate, and said what they were commanded by Jonathan their high priest to say, how he had sent them to confirm their friendship. The senate then confirmed what had been formerly decreed concerning their friendship with the Jews, and gave them letters to carry to all the kings of Asia and Europe, and to the governors of the cities, that they might safely conduct them to their own country. Accordingly, as they returned, they came to Sparta, and delivered the epistle which they had received of Jonathan to them; a copy of which here follows:—"Jonathan the high priest of the Jewish nation, and the senate, and body of the people of the Jews, to the ephori and senate, and body of the people of the Lacedemonians, send greeting. If you be well, and both your public and private affairs be agreeable to your mind, it is according to our wishes. We are well also. When in former times an epistle was brought to Onias, who was then our high-priest, from Areus, who at that time was your king, by Demoteles, concerning the kindred that was between us and you, a copy of which is here subjoined, we both joyfully received the epistle, and were well pleased with Demoteles and Areus, although we did not need such a demonstration, because we were well satisfied about it from the sacred writings,* yet did not we think fit first to begin the claim of this relation to you, lest we should seem too early in taking to ourselves the glory which is now given us by you. It is a long time since this relation of ours to you hath been renewed; and when we, upon holy and festival days, offer sacrifices to God, we pray to him for your preservation and victory. As to ourselves, although we have had many wars that have compassed us around, by reason of the covetousness of our neighbours, yet did not we determine to be troublesome either to you or to others that were related to us; but since we have now overcome our enemies, and have occasion to send Numenius, the

son of Antiochus, and Antipater, the son of Jason, who are both honourable men belonging to our senate, to the Romans, we gave them this epistle to you also, that they might renew that friendship which is between us. You will therefore do well yourselves to write to us, and send us an account of what you stand in need of from us, since we are in all things disposed to act according to your desires." So the Lacedemonians received the ambassadors kindly, and made a decree for friendship and mutual assistance, and sent it to them.

9. At this time there were three sects among the Jews, who had different opinions concerning human actions; the one was called the sect of the Pharisees, another the sect of the Sadducees, and the other the sect of the Essens. Now for the Pharisees,† they say that some actions, but not all, are the work of fate, and some of them are in our own power, and that they are liable to fate, but are not caused by fate. But the sect of the Essens affirm, that fate governs all things, and that nothing befalls men but what is according to its determination. And for the Sadducees, they take away fate, and say there is no such thing, and that the events of human affairs are not at its disposal; but they suppose that all our actions are in our power, so that we are ourselves the causes of what is good, and receive what is evil from our own folly. However, I have given a more exact account of these opinions in the second book of the Jewish War.

10. But now the generals of Demetrius being willing to recover the defeat they had had, gathered a greater army together than they had before, and came against Jonathan; but as soon as he was informed of their coming, he went suddenly to meet them, to the country of Hamath, for he resolved to give them no opportunity of coming into Judea; so he pitched his camp at fifty furlongs' distance from the enemy, and sent out spies to take a view of their camp, and after what manner they were encamped. When his spies had given him full information, and had seized upon some of them by night, who told him the enemy would soon attack him, he, thus apprised beforehand, provided for his security, and placed watchmen beyond his camp, and kept all his forces armed all night; and he gave them a charge to be of good courage, and to have their minds prepared to fight in the night-time, if they should be obliged so to do, lest their enemy's designs should seem concealed from them. But when Demetrius's commanders were informed that Jonathan knew what they intended, their counsels were disordered, and it alarmed them to find, that the enemy had discovered those their intentions; nor did they expect to overcome them any other way, now they had failed in the snares they had laid for them; for should they hazard an open battle, they did not think they should be a match for Jonathan's army, so they resolved to fly: and having lighted many fires, that when the enemy saw them they might suppose they were there still, they retired. But when Jonathan came to give them battle in the morning in their camp, and found it deserted, and understood they were fled, he pursued them; yet he could not overtake them, for they had already passed over the river Eleutherus, and were out of danger. So when Jonathan was re-

---

* This clause is rendered in the first book of Maccabees xii. 9: "For that we have the holy books of Scriptures in our hands to comfort us." The Hebrew original being lost, we cannot certainly judge which was the truest version, only the coherence favours Josephus.

† Josephus, who in his heart was a great admirer of the piety of the Essens, was yet in practice a Pharisee. And his account of this doctrine of the Pharisees is agreeable to his own opinion, who both fully allowed the freedom of human actions, and yet strongly believed the powerful interposition of Divine Providence.

turned thence, he went into Arabia, and fought against the Nabateans, and drove away a great deal of their prey, and took [many] captives, and came to Damascus, and there sold off what he had taken. About the same time it was that Simon his brother went over all Judea and Palestine, as far as Askelon, and fortified the strongholds; and when he had made them very strong, both in the edifices erected, and in the garrisons placed in them, he came to Joppa; and when he had taken it, he brought a great garrison into it, for he heard that the people of Joppa were disposed to deliver up the city to Demetrius's generals.

11. When Simon and Jonathan had finished these affairs, they returned to Jerusalem, where Jonathan gathered all the people together, and took counsel to restore the walls of Jerusalem, and to rebuild the wall that encompassed the temple, which had been thrown down, and to make the places adjoining stronger by very high towers; and besides that, to build another wall in the midst of the city, in order to exclude the market-place from the garrison, which was in the citadel, and by that means to hinder them from any plenty of provisions; and moreover, to make the fortresses that were in the country much stronger, and more defensible than they were before. And when these things were approved of by the multitude, as rightly proposed, Jonathan himself took care of the building that belonged to the city, and sent Simon away to make the fortresses in the country more secure than formerly. But Demetrius passed over [Euphrates,] and came into Mesopotamia, as desirous to retain that country still, as well as Babylon; and when he should have obtained the dominion of the upper provinces, to lay the foundation for recovering his entire kingdom; for these Greeks and Macedonians that dwelt there, frequently sent ambassadors to him, and promised that if he would come to them, they would deliver themselves up to him, and assist him in fighting against Arsaces,* the king of the Parthians. So he was elevated with these hopes, and came hastily to them, as having resolved that, if he had once overthrown the Parthians, and gotten an army of his own, he would make war against Trypho, and eject him out of Syria; and the people of that country received him with great alacrity. So he raised forces, with which he fought against Arsaces, and lost all his army; and was himself taken alive, as we have elsewhere related.

CHAPTER VI

HOW JONATHAN WAS SLAIN BY TREACHERY; AND HOW THEREUPON THE JEWS MADE SIMON THEIR GENERAL AND HIGH PRIEST: WHAT COURAGEOUS ACTIONS HE ALSO PERFORMED, ESPECIALLY AGAINST TRYPHO

1. Now when Trypho knew what had befallen Demetrius, he was no longer firm to Antiochus, but contrived by subtlety to kill him, and then take possession of his kingdom; but the fear that he was in of Jonathan was an obstacle to this his design, for Jonathan was a friend to Antiochus, for which cause he resolved first to take

* The king is both here and 1 Mac. xiv. 2, called by the family name Arsaces; but Appian says his proper name was Phraates. He is here called by Josephus the king of the Parthians, as the Greeks used to call them; but by the elder author of the First Maccabees, the king of the Persians and Medes, according to the language of the eastern nations.

Jonathan out of the way, and then to set about his design relating to Antiochus; but he judging it best to take him off by deceit and treachery, came from Antioch to Bethshan, which by the Greeks is called Scympolis, at which place Jonathan met him with forty thousand chosen men, for he thought that he came to fight him; but when he perceived that Jonathan was ready to fight, he attempted to gain him by presents and kind treatment, and gave order to his captains to obey him, and by these means was desirous to give assurance of his good-will, and to take away all suspicions out of his mind, that so he might make him careless and inconsiderate, and might take him when he was unguarded. He also advised him to dismiss his army, because there was no occasion for bringing it with him, when there was no war, but all was in peace. However, he desired him to retain a few about him, and go with him to Ptolemais, for that he would deliver the city up to him, and would bring all the fortresses that were in the country under his dominion; and he told him that he came with those very designs.

2. Yet did not Jonathan suspect anything at all by this his management, but believed that Trypho gave this advice out of kindness, and with a sincere design. Accordingly, he dismissed his army, and retained no more than three thousand of them with him, and left two thousand in Galilee; and he himself, with one thousand, came with Trypho to Ptolemais; but when the people of Ptolemais had shut their gates, as it had been commanded by Trypho to do, he took Jonathan alive, and slew all that were with him. He also sent soldiers against those two thousand that were left in Galilee, in order to destroy them: but those men having heard the report of what had happened to Jonathan, they prevented the execution, and before those that were sent by Trypho came, they covered themselves with their armour, and went away out of the country. Now when those that were sent against them saw that they were ready to fight for their lives, they gave them no disturbance, but returned back to Trypho.

3. But when the people of Jerusalem heard that Jonathan was taken, and that the soldiers who were with him were destroyed, they deplored his sad fate; and there was earnest inquiry made about him by everybody, and a great and just fear fell upon them, and made them sad, lest, now they were deprived of the courage and conduct of Jonathan, the nations about them should bear them ill-will; and as they were before quiet on account of Jonathan, they should now rise up against them, and by making war with them, should force them into the utmost dangers. And, indeed, what they suspected really befell them; for when those nations heard of the death of Jonathan, they began to make war with the Jews as now destitute of a governor; Trypho himself got an army together, and had an intention to go up to Judea, and make war against its inhabitants. But when Simon saw that the people of Jerusalem were terrified at the circumstances they were in, he desired to make a speech to them, and thereby to render them more resolute in opposing Trypho when he should come against them. He then called the people together into the temple, and thence began thus to encourage them:—" O my countrymen, you are not ignorant that our father, myself, and my brethren, have ventured to hazard our lives, and that willingly, for the recovery of your liberty; since I have therefore such plenty of examples before me, and we of our family have determined with ourselves to

die for our laws and our divine worship, there shall no terror be so great as to banish this resolution from our souls, nor to introduce in its place a love of life and a contempt of glory. Do you therefore follow me with alacrity whithersoever I shall lead you, as not destitute of such a captain as is willing to suffer, and to do the greatest things for you; for neither am I better than my brethren that I should be sparing of my own life, nor so far worse than they as to avoid and refuse what they thought the most honourable of all things,—I mean to undergo death for your laws, and for that worship of God which is peculiar to you; I will therefore give such proper demonstrations as will shew that I am their own brother; and I am so bold as to expect that I shall avenge their blood upon our enemies, and deliver you all, with your wives and children, from the injuries they intend against you, and, with God's assistance, to preserve your temple from destruction by them; for I see that these nations have you in contempt, as being without a governor, and that they thence are encouraged to make war against you."

4. By this speech of Simon he inspired the multitude with courage; and as they had before been dispirited through fear, they were now raised to a good hope of better things, insomuch that the whole multitude of the people cried out all at once, that Simon should be leader; and that instead of Judas and Jonathan his brethren, he should have government over them: and they promised that they would readily obey him in whatsoever he should command them. So he got together immediately all his own soldiers that were fit for war, and made haste in rebuilding the walls of the city, and strengthening them by very high and strong towers, and sent a friend of his, one Jonathan, the son of Absalom, to Joppa, and gave him order to eject the inhabitants out of the city, for he was afraid lest they should deliver up the city to Trypho; but he himself stayed to secure Jerusalem.

5. But Trypho removed from Ptolemais with a great army, and came into Judea, and brought Jonathan with him in bonds. Simon also met him with his army at the city Adida, which is upon a hill, and beneath it lie the plains of Judea. And when Trypho knew that Simon was by the Jews made their governor, he sent to him, and would have imposed upon him by deceit and treachery, and desired, if he would have his brother Jonathan released, that he would send him a hundred talents of silver, and two of Jonathan's sons as hostages, that when he shall be released, he may not make Judea revolt from the king; for that at present he was kept in bonds on account of the money he had borrowed of the king, and now owed it to him. But Simon was aware of the craft of Trypho; and although he knew that if he gave him the money he should lose it, and that Trypho would not set his brother free, and withal should deliver the sons of Jonathan to the enemy, yet because he was afraid that he should have a calumny raised against him among the multitude as the cause of his brother's death, if he neither gave the money, nor sent Jonathan's sons, he gathered his army together, and told them what offers Trypho had made; and added this, that the offers were ensnaring and treacherous, and yet that it was more eligible to send the money and Jonathan's sons, than to be liable to the imputation of not complying with Trypho's offers, and thereby refusing to save his brother. Accordingly, Simon sent the sons of Jonathan and the money; but when Trypho had received them, he did not keep his promise, nor set Jona-

than free, but took his army, and went about all the country, resolved to go afterwards to Jerusalem, by the way of Idumea, while Simon went over against him with his army, and all along pitched his camp over against his.

6. But when those that were in the citadel had sent to Trypho, and besought him to make haste and come to them, and to send them provisions, he prepared his cavalry as though he would be at Jerusalem that very night; but so great a quantity of snow fell in the night, that it covered the roads, and made them so deep, that there was no passing, especially for the cavalry. This hindered him from coming to Jerusalem; whereupon Trypho removed thence, and came into Cœlesyria, and falling vehemently upon the land of Gilead, he slew Jonathan there; and when he had given order for his burial, he returned himself to Antioch. However, Simon sent some to the city Basca to bring away his brother's bones, and buried them in their own city Modin; and all the people made a great lamentation over him. Simon also erected a very large monument for his father and his brethren, of white and polished stone, and raised it a great height, and so as to be seen a long way off, and made cloisters about it, and set up pillars, which were of one stone apiece; a work it was wonderful to see. Moreover, he built seven pyramids also for his parents and brethren, one for each of them, which were made very surprising, both for their largeness and beauty, and which have been preserved to this day; and we know that it was Simon who bestowed so much zeal about the burial of Jonathan, and the building of these monuments for his relations. Now Jonathan died when he had been high priest fourteen years, and had been also the governor of his nation. And these were the circumstances that concerned his death.

7. But Simon, who was made high priest by the multitude, on the very first year of his high priesthood, set his people free from their slavery under the Macedonians, and permitted them to pay tribute to them no longer; which liberty and freedom from tribute they obtained, after a hundred and seventy years * of the kingdom of the Assyrians, which was after Seleucus, who was called Nicator, got the dominion over Syria. Now the affection of the multitude towards Simon was so great, that in their contracts one with another, and in their public records, they wrote, "in the first year of Simon the benefactor, and ethnarch of the Jews;" for under him they were very happy, and overcame the enemies that were round about them; for Simon overthrew the city Gazara, and Joppa, and Jamnia. He also took the citadel of Jerusalem by siege, and cast it down to the ground, that it might not be any more a place of refuge to their enemies when they took it, to do them a mischief, as it had been till now. And when he had done this, he thought it their best way, and most for their advantage, to level the very mountain itself upon which the citadel happened to stand, that so the temple might be higher than it. And indeed, when he had called the multitude to an assembly, he persuaded them to have it so demolished, and this by putting them in mind what miseries they had suffered by its garrison and the Jewish deserters; and what miseries they might hereafter suffer in case any foreigner should obtain the kingdom, and put a garrison into

* These 170 years of the Assyrians mean no more than from the era of Seleucus. Dr Hudson truly observes, that the Syrians and Assyrians are sometimes confounded in ancient authors.

that citadel. This speech induced the multitude to a compliance, because he exhorted them to do nothing but what was for their own good: so they all set themselves to the work, and levelled the mountain, and in that work spent both day and night without intermission, which cost them three whole years before it was removed, and brought to an entire level with the plain of the rest of the city. After which the temple was the highest of all the buildings, now the citadel, as well as the mountain whereon it stood, were demolished. And these actions were thus performed under Simon.

CHAPTER VII

HOW SIMON CONFEDERATED HIMSELF WITH ANTIO-CHUS PIUS, AND MADE WAR AGAINST TRYPHO, AND, A LITTLE AFTERWARDS, AGAINST CENDE-BEUS, THE GENERAL OF ANTIOCHUS'S ARMY; AS ALSO HOW SIMON WAS MURDERED BY HIS SON-IN-LAW, PTOLEMY, AND THAT BY TREA-CHERY

1. * Now a little while after Demetrius had been carried into captivity, Trypho his governor destroyed Antiochus,† the son of Alexander, who was also called *The God*,‡ and this when he had reigned four years, though he gave it out that he died under the hands of the surgeons. He then sent his friends, and those that were most inti-mate with him, to the soldiers, and promised that he would give them a great deal of money if they would make him king. He intimated to them that Demetrius was made a captive by the Parthians; and that Demetrius's brother Antio-chus, if he came to be king, would do them a great deal of mischief, in way of revenge for re-volting from his brother. So the soldiers, in expectation of the wealth they should get by bestowing the kingdom upon Trypho, made him their ruler. However, when Trypho had gained the management of affairs, he demonstrated his disposition to be wicked; for while he was a private person, he cultivated a familiarity with the multitude, and pretended to great modera-tion, and so drew them on artfully to whatso-ever he pleased; but when he had once taken the kingdom, he laid aside any further dissimu-lation, and was the true Trypho; which beha-viour made his enemies superior to him; for the

soldiers hated him, and revolted from him to Cleopatra, the wife of Demetrius, who was then shut up in Seleucia with her children; but as Antiochus, the brother of Demetrius, who was called Soter, was not admitted by any of the cities, on account of Trypho, Cleopatra sent to him, and invited him to marry her, and to take the kingdom. The reasons why she made this invitation were these: That her friends per-suaded her to it, and that she was afraid for herself, in case some of the people of Seleucia should deliver up the city to Trypho.

2. As Antiochus was now come to Seleucia, and his forces increased every day, he marched to fight Trypho; and having beaten him in the battle, he ejected him out of the Upper Syria into Phœnicia, and pursued him thither, and besieged him in Dora, which was a fortress hard to be taken, whither he had fled. He also sent ambassadors to Simon the Jewish high priest, about a league of friendship and mutual assist-ance; who readily accepted of the invitation, and sent to Antiochus great sums of money and provisions for those that besieged Dora, and thereby supplied them very plentifully, so that for a little while he was looked upon as one of his most intimate friends; but still Trypho fled from Dora to Apamia, where he was taken during the siege, and put to death, when he had reigned three years.

3. However, Antiochus forgot the kind assist-ance that Simon had afforded him in his neces-sity, by reason of his covetous and wicked dis-position, and committed an army of soldiers to his friend Cendebeus, and sent him at once to ravage Judea, and to seize Simon. When Simon heard of Antiochus's breaking his league with him, although he were now in years, yet, pro-voked with the unjust treatment he had met with from Antiochus, and taking a resolution brisker than his age could well bear, he went like a young man to act as general of his army. He also sent his sons before among the most hardy of his soldiers, and he himself marched on with his army another way, and laid many of his men in ambushes in the narrow valleys between the mountains; nor did he fail of success in any one of his attempts, but was too hard for his enemies in every one of them. So he led the rest of his life in peace, and did also himself make a league with the Romans.

4. Now he was ruler of the Jews in all eight years; but at a feast came to his end. It was caused by the treachery of his son-in-law Ptolemy, who caught also his wife, and two of his sons, and kept them in bonds. He also sent some to kill John the third son, whose name was Hyrcanus: but the young man perceiving them coming, he avoided the danger he was in from them,§ and made haste into the city [Jerusalem,] as relying on the good-will of the multitude, because of the benefits they had received from his father, and because of the hatred the same multitude bare to Ptolemy; so that when Ptolemy was endeavouring to enter the city by another gate, they drove him away, as having already admitted Hyrcanus.

---

* It must here be noted that Josephus's copy of the first book of Maccabees, which he had so carefully fol-lowed, and faithfully abridged, as far as chap. xiii. 50, seems there to have ended. What few things there are afterwards common to both, might probably be learned by him from some other more imperfect records. How-ever, we must observe here, what the remaining part of that book of the Maccabees informs us of, and what Josephus would never have omitted had his copy con-tained so much,—that this Simon the Great, the Mac-cabee, made a league with Antiochus Soter, the son of Demetrius Soter, and brother of the other Demetrius, who was now a captive in Parthia; that upon his com-ing to the crown, about the 140th year before the Chris-tian era, he granted great privileges to the Jewish nation and to Simon their high priest and ethnarch: which privileges Simon seems to have taken of his own accord about three years before.

† How Trypho killed this Antiochus, the epitome of Livy informs us, chap. liii.—viz., that he corrupted his physicians or surgeons, who falsely pretended to the people that he was perishing with the stone, as they cut him for it, and killed him; which exactly agrees with Josephus.

‡ That this Antiochus, the son of Alexander Balas, was called "the God," is evident from his coins, which bear this inscription: "King Antiochus the God; Epiphanes the Victorious."

§ Here Josephus begins to follow and to abridge the next sacred Hebrew book, styled in the end of the first book of Maccabees, "The Chronicle of John's [Hyr-canus] High Priesthood;" but in some of the Greek copies, "the fourth book of Maccabees."

CHAPTER VIII

HYRCANUS RECEIVES THE HIGH PRIESTHOOD, AND
EJECTS PTOLEMY OUT OF THE COUNTRY; AN-
TIOCHUS MAKES WAR AGAINST HYRCANUS, AND
AFTERWARDS MAKES A LEAGUE WITH HIM

1. So Ptolemy retired to one of the fortresses
that was above Jericho, which was called Dagon.
But Hyrcanus having taken the high priesthood
that had been his father's before, and in the first
place propitiated God by sacrifices, he then made
an expedition against Ptolemy; and when he
made his attacks upon the place, in other points
he was too hard for him, but was rendered
weaker than he, by the commiseration he had for
his mother and his brethren, and by that only;
for Ptolemy brought them upon the wall, and
tormented them in sight of all, and threatened
that he would throw them down headlong, unless
Hyrcanus would leave off the siege; and as he
thought that, so far as he relaxed to the siege
and taking of the place, so much favour did he
shew to those that were dearest to him by preventing their misery, his zeal about it was cooled.
However, his mother spread out her hands, and
begged of him that he would not grow remiss on
her account, but indulge his indignation so much
the more, and that he would do his utmost to
take the place quickly, in order to get their
enemy under his power, and then to avenge upon
him what he had done to those that were dearest
to himself; for that death would be to her sweet,
though with torment, if that enemy of theirs
might but be brought to punishment for his
wicked dealings to them. Now when his mother
said so, he resolved to take the fortress immediately; but when he saw her beaten and
torn to pieces, his courage failed him, and he
could not but sympathise with what his mother
suffered, and was thereby overcome; and as the
siege was drawn out into length by this means,
that year on which the Jews use to rest came
on; for the Jews observe this rest every seventh
year, as they do every seventh day; so that
Ptolemy being for this cause released from the
war,* he slew the brethren of Hyrcanus and his
mother: and when he had so done, he fled to
Zeno, who was called Cotylas, who was then the
tyrant of the city Philadelphia.

2. But Antiochus being very uneasy at the
miseries that Simon had brought upon him, he
invaded Judea in the fourth year of his reign,
and the first year of the principality of Hyrcanus, in the hundred and sixty-second Olympiad.† And when he had burnt the country, he
shut up Hyrcanus in the city, which he encompassed round with seven encampments; but did
nothing at the first, because of the strength of
the walls, and because of the valour of the be-

siged, although they were once in want of
water, which yet they were delivered from by a
large shower of rain, which fell at the setting of
the Pleiades.‡ However, about the north part
of the wall, where it happened the city was upon
a level with the outward ground, the king raised
a hundred towers of three stories high, and
placed bodies of soldiers upon them; and as he
made his attacks every day, he cut a double
ditch, deep and broad, and confined the inhabitants within it as within a wall; but the besieged contrived to make frequent sallies out;
and if the enemy were not anywhere upon their
guard, they fell upon them, and did them a
great deal of mischief; and if they perceived
them, they then retired into the city with ease.
But because Hyrcanus discerned the inconvenience of so great a number of men in the city,
while the provisions were the sooner spent by
them, and yet, as is natural to suppose, those
great numbers did nothing, he separated the
useless part, and excluded them out of the city,
and retained that part only who were in the
flower of their age, and fit for war. However,
Antiochus would not let those that were excluded go away; who, therefore, wandering
about between the walls, and consuming away
by famine, died miserably; but when the feast
of tabernacles was at hand, those that were
within commiserated their condition, and received them in again. And when Hyrcanus
sent to Antiochus, and desired there might be a
truce for seven days, because of the festival, he
gave way to this piety towards God, and made
that truce accordingly; and besides that, he
sent in a magnificent sacrifice, bulls with their
horns gilded,§ with all sorts of sweet spices, and
with cups of gold and silver. So those that were
at the gates received the sacrifices from those
that brought them, and led them to the temple,
Antiochus the meanwhile feasting his army,
which was a quite different conduct from
Antiochus Epiphanes, who, when he had taken
the city, offered swine upon the altar, and
sprinkled the temple with the broth of their
flesh, in order to violate the laws of the Jews,
and the religion they derived from their forefathers; for which reason our nation made war
with him, and would never be reconciled to
him; but for this Antiochus, all men called him
Antiochus the Pious, for the great zeal he had
about religion.

3. Accordingly, Hyrcanus took this moderation of his kindly; and when he understood how
religious he was towards the Deity, he sent an
embassage to him, and desired that he would
restore the settlements they received from their
forefathers. So he rejected the counsel of those
that would have him utterly destroy the nation‖
by reason of their way of living, which was to
others unsociable, and did not regard what they
said. But being persuaded that all they did
was out of a religious mind, he answered the
ambassadors, that if the besieged would deliver
up their arms, and pay tribute for Joppa, and
the other cities which bordered upon Judea, and

---

* Hence we learn, that in the days of this excellent
high priest, John Hyrcanus, the observation of the
Sabbatic Year required a rest from war, as did that of
the weekly Sabbath from work; unless in the case of
necessity, when the Jews were attacked by their enemies, in which case, indeed, they then allowed defensive
fighting to be lawful even on the Sabbath-day. But
then it must be noted, that this rest from war no way
appears in the first book of Maccabees, (ch. xvi.,) but
the direct contrary; though indeed the Jews, in the
days of Antiochus Epiphanes, did not venture upon
fighting on the Sabbath-day, even in the defence of
their own lives, till the Asamoneans or Maccabees
decreed so to do.

† Josephus's copies say that this first year of John
Hyrcanus, which we have just now seen to be a Sabbatic Year, was in the 162d Olympiad, whereas it was
for certain the second year of the 161st.

‡ This helical setting of the Pleiades was, in the
days of Hyrcanus and Josephus, early in the spring,
about February, the time of the latter rain in Judea:
and this is the only astronomical character of time,
besides one eclipse of the moon in the reign of Herod,
that we meet with in all Josephus.

§ Dr Hudson tells us that this custom of gilding the
horns of those oxen that were to be sacrificed, is a
known thing both in the poets and orators.

‖ This account in Josephus, that the present Antiochus was persuaded, though in vain, not to make peace
with the Jews, but cut them off utterly, is fully confirmed by Diodorus Siculus.

HYRCANUS' SIEGE OF PTOLEMY AT DAGON

admit a garrison of his on these terms, he would make war against them no longer. But the Jews, although they were content with the other conditions, did not agree to admit the garrison, because they could not associate with other people, nor converse with them; yet were they willing, instead of the admission of the garrison, to give him hostages, and five hundred talents of silver; of which they paid down three hundred, and sent the hostages immediately, which king Antiochus accepted. One of those hostages was Hyrcanus's brother. But still he broke down the fortifications that encompassed the city. And upon these conditions Antiochus broke up the siege, and departed.

4. But Hyrcanus opened the sepulchre of David, who excelled all other kings in riches, and took out of it three thousand talents. He was also the first of the Jews that, relying on this wealth, maintained foreign troops. There was also a league of friendship and mutual assistance made between them, upon which Hyrcanus admitted him into the city, and furnished him with whatsoever his army wanted in great plenty, and with great generosity, and marched along with him when he made an expedition against the Parthians, of which Nicolaus of Damascus is a witness for us; who, in his history, writes thus:—"When Antiochus had erected a trophy at the river Lycus, upon his conquest of Indates, the general of the Parthians, he stayed there two days. It was the desire of Hyrcanus the Jew, because it was such a festival derived to them from their forefathers, whereon the law of the Jews did not allow them to travel." And truly he did not speak falsely in saying so; for that festival, which we call *Pentecost*, did then fall out to be the next day to the Sabbath: nor is it lawful for us to journey, either on the Sabbath-day, or on a festival day.* But when Antiochus joined battle with Arsaces, the king of Parthia, he lost a great part of his army, and was himself slain; and his brother Demetrius succeeded in the kingdom of Syria, by the permission of Arsaces, who freed him from his captivity at the same time that Antiochus attacked Parthia, as we have formerly related elsewhere.

CHAPTER IX

HOW, AFTER THE DEATH OF ANTIOCHUS, HYRCANUS MADE AN EXPEDITION AGAINST SYRIA, AND MADE A LEAGUE WITH THE ROMANS; CONCERNING THE DEATH OF KING DEMETRIUS AND ALEXANDER

1. BUT when Hyrcanus heard of the death of Antiochus, he presently made an expedition against the cities of Syria, hoping to find them destitute of fighting men, and of such as were able to defend them. However, it was not till the sixth month that he took Medaba, and that not without the greatest distress of his army. After this he took Samega, and the neighbouring places, and, besides these, Shechem and Gerizzim, and the nation of the Cutheans, who dwelt at the temple which resembled that temple which was at Jerusalem, and which Alexander permitted Sanballat, the general of his army, to build for the sake of Manasseh,

who was son-in-law to Jadua the high priest, as we have formerly related; which temple was now deserted two hundred years after it was built. Hyrcanus took also Dora and Marissa, cities of Idumea, and subdued all the Idumeans; and permitted them to stay in that country, if they would circumcise their genitals, and make use of the laws of the Jews; and they were so desirous of living in the country of their forefathers, that they submitted to the use of circumcision,† and the rest of the Jewish ways of living; at which time therefore this befell them, that they were hereafter no other than Jews.

2. But Hyrcanus the high priest was desirous to renew the league of friendship they had with the Romans: accordingly he sent an embassage to them; and when the senate had received their epistle, they made a league of friendship with them, after the manner following:—"Fanius, the son of Marcus, the prætor, gathered the senate together on the eighth day before the Ides of February, in the senate-house, when Lucius Manlius, the son of Lucius, of the Mentine tribe, and Caius Sempronius, the son of Caius, of the Falernian tribe, were present. The occasion was, that the ambassadors sent by the people of the Jews,‡ Simon the son of Dositheus, and Apollonius the son of Alexander, and Diodorus the son of Jason, who were good and virtuous men, had somewhat to propose about that league of friendship and mutual assistance which subsisted between them and the Romans, and about other public affairs, who desired that Joppa, and the havens, and Gazara, and the springs [of Jordan,] and the several other cities and countries of theirs, which Antiochus had taken from them in the war, contrary to the decree of the senate, might be restored to them; and that it might not be lawful for the king's troops to pass through their country, and the countries of those that are subject to them: and that what attempts Antiochus had made during that war, without the decree of the senate, might be made void: and that they would send ambassadors, who should take care that restitution be made them of what Antiochus had taken from them, and that they should make an estimate of the country that had been laid waste in the war: and that they would grant them letters of protection to the kings and free people, in order to their quiet return home. It was therefore decreed as to these points, to renew their league of friendship and mutual assistance with these good men, and who were sent by a good and friendly people."—But as to the letters desired, their answer was, that the senate would consult about that matter when their own affairs would give them leave; and that they would en-

---

* The Jews were not to march or journey on the Sabbath, or on such a great festival as was equivalent to the Sabbath, any further than a Sabbath-day's journey, or two thousand cubits.

† This account of the Idumeans admitting circumcision, and the entire Jewish law, from this time, or from the days of Hyrcanus afterwards, is confirmed by their entire history afterwards. This, in the opinion of Josephus, made them proselytes of justice, or entire Jews. However, Antigonus, the enemy of Herod, though Herod were derived from such a proselyte of justice for several generations, will allow him to be no more than a half Jew. Ammonius, a grammarian, says:—"The Jews are such by nature, and from the beginning, whilst the Idumeans were not Jews from the beginning, but Phœnicians and Syrians; but being afterwards subdued by the Jews and compelled to be circumcised, and to unite into one nation, and be subject to the same laws, they were called Jews." Dio also says:—"That country is also called Judea, and the people Jews; and this name is given also to as many as embrace their religion, though of other nations."

‡ In this decree of the Roman senate, it seems that these ambassadors were sent from the "people of the Jews," as well as from their prince or high priest John.

deavour, for the time to come, that no like injury should be done them ; and that their prætor Fanius should give them money out of the public treasury to bear their expenses home. And thus did Fanius dismiss the Jewish ambassadors, and gave them money out of the public treasury ; and gave the decree of the senate to those that were to conduct them, and to take care that they should return home in safety.

3. And thus stood the affairs of Hyrcanus the high priest. But as for king Demetrius, who had a mind to make war against Hyrcanus, there was no opportunity nor room for it, while both the Syrians and the soldiers bare ill-will to him, because he was an ill man. But when they had sent ambassadors to Ptolemy, who was called Physcon, that he would send them one of the family of Seleucus, in order to take the kingdom, and he sent them Alexander, who was called Zebina, with an army, and there had been a battle between them, Demetrius was beaten in the fight, and fled to Cleopatra his wife, to Ptolemais ; but his wife would not receive him. He went thence to Tyre, and was there caught ; and when he had suffered much from his enemies before his death, he was slain by them. So Alexander took the kingdom, and made a league with Hyrcanus. Yet, when he afterward fought with Antiochus the son of Demetrius, who was called Grypus, he was also beaten in the fight, and slain.

CHAPTER X

HOW, UPON THE QUARREL BETWEEN ANTIOCHUS GRYPUS AND ANTIOCHUS CYZICENUS, ABOUT THE KINGDOM, HYRCANUS TOOK SAMARIA, AND UTTERLY DEMOLISHED IT ; AND HOW HYRCANUS JOINED HIMSELF TO THE SECT OF THE SADDUCEES, AND LEFT THAT OF THE PHARISEES

1. WHEN Antiochus had taken the kingdom, he was afraid to make war against Judea, because he heard that his brother by the same mother, who was called Antiochus, was raising an army against him out of Cyzicum ; so he stayed in his own land, and resolved to prepare himself for the attack he expected from his brother, who was called Cyzicenus, because he had been brought up in that city. He was the son of Antiochus that was called Soter, who died in Parthia. He was the brother of Demetrius, the father of Grypus ; for it had so happened, that one and the same Cleopatra was married to two who were brethren, as we have related elsewhere. But Antiochus Cyzicenus coming into Syria, continued many years at war with his brother. Now Hyrcanus lived all this while in peace ; for after the death of Antiochus he revolted from the Macedonians,* nor did he any longer pay them the least regard, either as their subject or their friend, but his affairs were in a very improving and flourishing condition in the times of Alexander Zebina, and especially under these brethren, for the war which they had with one another gave Hyrcanus the opportunity of enjoying himself in Judea quietly, insomuch that he got an immense quantity of money. However, when Antiochus Cyzicenus distressed his land, he then openly shewed what he meant. And when he saw that Antiochus was destitute of Egyptian auxiliaries, and that both he and his

brother were in an ill condition in the struggles they had one with another, he despised them both.

2. So he made an expedition against Samaria, which was a very strong city ; of whose present name Sebaste, and its rebuilding by Herod, we shall speak at a proper time ; but he made his attack against it, and besieged it with a great deal of pains ; for he was greatly displeased with the Samaritans for the injuries they had done to the people of Marissa, a colony of the Jews, and confederate with them, and this in compliance to the kings of Syria. When he had therefore drawn a ditch, and built a double wall round the city, which was fourscore furlongs long, he set his sons Antigonus and Aristobulus over the siege ; which brought the Samaritans to that great distress by famine, that they were forced to eat what used not be eaten, and to call for Antiochus Cyzicenus to help them, who came readily to their assistance, but was beaten by Aristobulus ; and when he was pursued as far as Scythopolis by the two brethren, he got away : so they returned to Samaria, and shut them again within the wall, till they were forced to send for the same Antiochus a second time to help them, who procured about six thousand men from Ptolemy Lathyrus, which were sent them without his mother's consent, who had then in a manner turned him out of his government. With these Egyptians Antiochus did at first overrun and ravage the country of Hyrcanus after the manner of a robber, for he durst not meet him in the face to fight with him, as not having an army sufficient for that purpose, but only from this supposal, that by thus harassing his land he should force Hyrcanus to raise the siege of Samaria ; but because he fell into snares, and lost many of his soldiers therein, he went away to Tripoli, and committed the prosecution of the war against the Jews to Callimander and Epicrates.

3. But as to Callimander, he attacked the enemy too rashly, and was put to flight, and destroyed immediately ; and as to Epicrates, he was such a lover of money, that he openly betrayed Scythopolis, and other places near it, to the Jews ; but was not able to make them raise the siege of Samaria. And when Hyrcanus had taken the city, which was not done till after a year's siege, he was not contented with doing that only, but he demolished it entirely, and brought rivulets to it to drown it, for he dug such hollows as might let the waters run under it ; nay, he took away the very marks that there had ever been such a city there. Now a very surprising thing is related of this high priest Hyrcanus, how God came to discourse with him : for they say that on the very same day on which his sons fought with Antiochus Cyzicenus, he was alone in the temple, as high priest, offering incense, and heard a voice, that his sons had just then overcome Antiochus. And this he openly declared before all the multitude on his coming out of the temple ; and it accordingly proved true ; and in this posture were the affairs of Hyrcanus.

4. Now it happened at this time, that not only those Jews who were at Jerusalem and in Judea were in prosperity, but also those of them that were at Alexandria, and in Egypt, and Cyprus, for Cleopatra the queen was at variance with her son Ptolemy, who was called Lathyrus, and appointed for her generals, Chelcias and Ananias, the sons of that Onias who built the temple in the prefecture of Heliopolis, like that at Jerusalem, as we have elsewhere related. Cleopatra intrusted these men with her army ; and did

---

* Justin says, "The power of the Jews was now grown so great, that after this Antiochus, they would not bear any Macedonian king over them ; and that they set up a government of their own, and infested Syria with great wars."

nothing without their advice, as Strabo of Cappadocia attests, when he saith thus:—"Now the greater part, both those that came to Cyprus with us, and those that were sent afterward thither, revolted to Ptolemy immediately; only those that were called Onias's party, being Jews, continued faithful, because their countrymen Chelcias and Ananias were in chief fav with the queen." These are the words of Strabo.

5. However, this prosperous state of affairs moved the Jews to envy Hyrcanus; but they that were the worst disposed to him were the Pharisees,* who are one of the sects of the Jews, as we have informed you already. These have so great a power over the multitude, that when they say anything against the king or against the high priest, they are presently believed. Now Hyrcanus was a disciple of theirs, and greatly beloved by them. And when he once invited them to a feast, and entertained them very kindly, when he saw them in a good humour, he began to say to them, that they knew he was desirous to be a righteous man, and to do all things whereby he might please God, which was the profession of the Pharisees also. However, he desired, that if they observed him offending in any point, and going out of the right way, they would call him back and correct him. On which occasion they attested to his being entirely virtuous; with which commendation he was well pleased; but still there was one of his guests there, whose name was Eleazar, a man of an ill temper, and delighting in seditious practices. This man said, "Since thou desirest to know the truth, if thou wilt be righteous in earnest, lay down the high priesthood, and content thyself with the civil government of the people." And when he desired to know for what cause he ought to lay down the high priesthood, the other replied, "We have heard it from old men, that thy mother had been a captive under the reign of Antiochus Epiphanes."† This story was false, and Hyrcanus was provoked against him; and all the Pharisees had a very great indignation against him.

6. Now there was one Jonathan, a very great friend of Hyrcanus, but of the sect of the Sadducees, whose notions are quite contrary to those of the Pharisees. He told Hyrcanus that Eleazar had cast such a reproach upon him, according to the common sentiments of all the Pharisees, and that this would be made manifest if he would but ask him the question, What punishment they thought this deserved? for that he might depend upon it, that the reproach was not laid on him with their approbation, if they were for punishing him as his crime deserved. So the

Pharisees made answer, that he deserved stripes and bonds; but that it did not seem right to punish reproaches with death; and indeed the Pharisees, even upon other occasions, are not apt to be severe in punishments. At this gentle sentence, Hyrcanus was very angry, and thought that this man reproached him by their approbation. It was this Jonathan who chiefly irritated him, and influenced him so far, that he made him leave the party of the Pharisees, and abolish the decrees they had imposed on the people, and punish those that observed them. From this source arose that hatred which he and his sons met with from the multitude: but of these matters we shall speak hereafter. What I would now explain is this, that the Pharisees have delivered to the people a great many observances by succession from their fathers, which are not written in the law of Moses; and for that reason it is that the Sadducees reject them, and say that we are to esteem those observances to be obligatory which are in the written word, but are not to observe what are derived from the tradition of our forefathers; and concerning these things it is that great disputes and differences have arisen among them, while the Sadducees are able to persuade none but the rich, and have not the populace obsequious to them, but the Pharisees have the multitude of their side: but about these two sects, and that of the Essens, I have treated accurately in the second book of Jewish affairs.

7. But when Hyrcanus had put an end to this sedition, he after that lived happily, and administered the government in the best manner for thirty-one years. and then died,‡ leaving behind him five sons. He was esteemed by God worthy of the three privileges,—the government of his nation, the dignity of the high priesthood, and prophecy; for God was with him, and enabled him to know futurities; and to foretell this in particular, that, as to his two eldest sons, he foretold that they would not long continue in the government of public affairs; whose unhappy catastrophe will be worth our description, that we may thence learn how very much they were inferior to their father's happiness.

CHAPTER XI

HOW ARISTOBULUS, WHEN HE HAD TAKEN THE GOVERNMENT, FIRST OF ALL PUT A DIADEM ON HIS HEAD, AND WAS MOST BARBAROUSLY CRUEL TO HIS MOTHER AND HIS BRETHREN; AND HOW, AFTER HE HAD SLAIN ANTIGONUS, HE HIMSELF DIED

1. Now when their father Hyrcanus was dead, the eldest son Aristobulus, intending to change the government into a kingdom, for so he resolved to do, first of all put a diadem on his head, four hundred and eighty-one years and three months after the people had been delivered from the Babylonish slavery, and were returned to their own country again. This Aristobulus loved his next brother Antigonus, and treated him as his equal; but the others he held in bonds. He also cast his mother into prison, because she disputed the government with him;

---

* Dean Prideaux upon this the first public appearance of the Sadducees, says:—"Hyrcanus went over to the party of the Sadducees, that is, by embracing their doctrine against the traditions of the elders, added to the written law, and made of equal authority with it, but not their doctrine against the resurrection and a future state; for this cannot be supposed against so good and righteous a man as John Hyrcanus is said to be. It is most probable, that at this time the Sadducees had gone no further in the doctrines of that sect than to deny all their unwritten traditions, which the Pharisees were so fond of; for Josephus mentions no other difference at this time between them; neither does he say that Hyrcanus went over to the Sadducees in any other particular than in the abolishing of all the traditionary constitutions of the Pharisees, which our Saviour condemned as well as they."

† This slander, that arose from a Pharisee, has been preserved by their successors the Rabbins to these later ages; for David Gantz, in his Chronology, relates that Hyrcanus's mother was taken captive in mount Modinth.

‡ Here ends the life of this excellent person, and together with him the holy theocracy, or divine government of the Jewish nation, and its concomitant oracle by Urim. Now follows the profane and tyrannical Jewish monarchy, first, of the Asamoneans or Maccabees, and then of Herod the Great, the Idumean, till the coming of the Messiah.

for Hyrcanus had left her to be mistress of all. He also proceeded to that degree of barbarity, as to kill her in prison with hunger; nay, he was alienated from his brother Antigonus by calumnies, and added him to the rest whom he slew; yet he seemed to have an affection for him, and made him above the rest a partner with him in the kingdom. Those calumnies he at first did not give credit to, partly because he loved him, and so did not give heed to what was said against him, and partly because he thought the reproaches were derived from the envy of the relaters. But when Antigonus was once returned from the army, and that feast was then at hand when they make tabernacles to [the honour of] God, it happened that Aristobulus was fallen sick, and that Antigonus went up most splendidly adorned, and with his soldiers about him in their armour to the temple to celebrate the feast, and to put up many prayers for the recovery of his brother, when some wicked persons, who had a great mind to raise a difference between the brethren, made use of this opportunity of the pompous appearance of Antigonus, and of the great actions which he had done, and went to the king, and spitefully aggravated the pompous show of his at the feast, and pretended that all these circumstances were not like those of a private person; that these actions were indications of an affectation of royal authority; and that his coming with a strong body of men must be with an intention to kill him; and that his way of reasoning was this: That it was a silly thing in him, while it was in his power to reign himself, to look upon it as a great favour that he was honoured with a lower dignity by his brother.

2. Aristobulus yielded to these imputations, but took care both that his brother should not suspect him, and that he himself might not run the hazard of his own safety; so he ordered his guards to lie in a certain place that was underground, and dark, (he himself then lying sick in the tower which was called Antonia;) and he commanded them, that in case Antigonus came in to him unarmed, they should not touch any body, but if armed, they should kill him; yet did he send to Antigonus, and desired that he would come unarmed: but the queen, and those that joined with her in the plot against Antigonus, persuaded the messenger to tell him the direct contrary: how his brother had heard that he had made himself a fine suit of armour for war, and desired him to come to him in that armour, that he might see how fine it was. So Antigonus, suspecting no treachery, but depending on the good-will of his brother, came to Aristobulus armed as he used to be, with his entire armour, in order to shew it to him; but when he was come to a place which was called Strato's Tower, where the passages happened to be exceeding dark, the guards slew him; which death demonstrates that nothing is stronger than envy and calumny, and that nothing does more certainly divide the good-will and natural affections of men than those passions. But here one may take occasion to wonder at one Judas, who was of the sect of the Essens, and who never missed the truth in his predictions; for this man, when he saw Antigonus passing by the temple, cried to his companions and friends who abode with him as his scholars, in order to learn the art of foretelling things to come, "That it was good for him to die now, since he had spoken falsely about Antigonus, who is still alive, and I see him passing by, although he had foretold that he should die at the place called Strato's Tower that very day, while yet the place is six

hundred furlongs off where he had foretold he should be slain; and still this day is a great part of it already past, so that he was in danger of proving a false prophet." As he was saying this, and that in a melancholy mood, the news came that Antigonus was slain in a place underground, which itself was called also Strato's Tower, or of the same name with that Cesarea which is seated at the sea. This event put the prophet into a great disorder.

3. But Aristobulus repented immediately of his slaughter of his brother; on which account his disease increased upon him, and he was disturbed in his mind, upon the guilt of such wickedness, insomuch that his entrails were corrupted by his intolerable pain, and he vomited blood: at which time one of the servants that attended upon him, and was carrying his blood away, did, by divine providence, as I cannot but suppose, slip down and shed part of his blood at the very place where there were spots of Antigonus's blood then slain, still remaining; and when there was a cry made by the spectators, as if the servant had on purpose shed the blood on that place, Aristobulus heard it, and inquired what the matter was; and as they did not answer him, he was the more earnest to know what it was, it being natural to men to suspect that what is thus concealed is very bad: so upon his threatening, and forcing them by terrors to speak, they at length told him the truth; whereupon he shed many tears, in that disorder of mind which arose from his consciousness of what he had done, and gave a deep groan, and said, "I am not, therefore, I perceive to be concealed from God, in the impious and horrid crimes I have been guilty of; but a sudden punishment is coming upon me for the shedding the blood of my relations. And now, O thou most impudent body of mine, how long wilt thou retain a soul that ought to die, in order to appease the ghost of my brother and my mother? Why dost thou not give it all up at once? And why do I deliver up my blood, drop by drop, to those whom I have so wickedly murdered?" In saying which last words he died, having reigned a year. He was called a lover of the Grecians; and had conferred many benefits on his own country, and made war against Iturea, and added a great part of it to Judea, and compelled the inhabitants, if they would continue in that country, to be circumcised, and to live according to the Jewish laws. He was naturally a man of candour, and of great modesty, as Strabo bears witness in the name of Timagenes: who says thus:—"This man was a person of candour, and very serviceable to the Jews, for he added a country to them, and obtained a part of the nation of the Itureans for them, and bound them to them by the bond of the circumcision of their genitals."

CHAPTER XII

HOW ALEXANDER, WHEN HE HAD TAKEN THE GOVERNMENT, MADE AN EXPEDITION AGAINST PTOLEMAIS, AND THEN RAISED THE SIEGE, OUT OF FEAR OF PTOLEMY LATHYRUS; AND HOW PTOLEMY MADE WAR AGAINST HIM, BECAUSE HE HAD SENT TO CLEOPATRA TO PERSUADE HER TO MAKE WAR AGAINST PTOLEMY, AND YET PRETENDED TO BE IN FRIENDSHIP WITH HIM, WHEN HE WENT TO BEAT THE JEWS IN BATTLE

1. WHEN Aristobulus was dead, his wife Salome, who, by the Greeks, was called Alexandra, let his brethren out of prison, (for Aristobulus

had kept them in bonds, as we have said already,) and made Alexander Janneus king, who was the superior in age and in moderation. This child happened to be hated by his father as soon as he was born, and could never be permitted to come into his father's sight till he died. The occasion of which hatred is thus reported : when Hyrcanus chiefly loved the two eldest of his sons, Antigonus and Aristobulus, God appeared to him in his sleep, of whom he inquired which of his sons should be his successor. Upon God's representing to him the countenance of Alexander, he was grieved that he was to be the heir of all his goods, and suffered him to be brought up in Galilee. However, God did not deceive Hyrcanus, for after the death of Aristobulus, he certainly took the kingdom ; and one of his brethren who affected the kingdom he slew ; and the other who chose to live a private and quiet life, he had in esteem.

2. When Alexander Janneus had settled the government in the manner that he judged best, he made an expedition against Ptolemais ; and having overcome the men in battle, he shut them up in the city, and sat round about it, and besieged it ; for of the maritime cities there remained only Ptolemais and Gaza to be conquered, besides Strato's Tower and Dora, which were held by the tyrant Zoilus. Now while Antiochus Philometor, and Antiochus who was called Cyzicenus, were making war against one another, and destroying one another's armies, the people of Ptolemais could have no assistance from them ; but when they were distressed with this siege, Zoilus, who possessed Strato's Tower and Dora, and maintained a legion of soldiers, and, on occasion of the contest between the kings, affected tyranny himself, came and brought some small assistance to the people of Ptolemais ; nor indeed had the king such a friendship for them as that they should hope for any advantage from them. But both those kings were in the case of wrestling, who finding themselves deficient in strength, and yet being ashamed to yield, put off the fight by laziness, and by lying still as long as they can. The only hope they had remaining was from the kings of Egypt, and from Ptolemy Lathyrus, who now held Cyprus, and who came to Cyprus when he was driven from the government of Egypt by Cleopatra his mother : so the people of Ptolemais sent to this Ptolemy Lathyrus and desired him to come as a confederate, to deliver them, now they were in such danger, out of the hands of Alexander. And as the ambassadors gave him hopes, that if he would pass over into Syria, he would have the people of Gaza on the side of those of Ptolemais ; as they also said that Zoilus, and besides these the Sidonians and many others would assist them, so he was elevated at this, and got his fleet ready as soon as possible.

3. But in this interval Demetrius, one that was of abilities to persuade men to do as he would have them, and a leader of the populace, made those of Ptolemais change their opinions ; and said to them, that it was better to run the hazard of being subject to the Jews than to admit of evident slavery by delivering themselves up to a master ; and besides that, to have not only a war at present, but to expect a much greater war from Egypt ; for that Cleopatra would not overlook an army raised by Ptolemy for himself out of the neighbourhood, but would come against them with a great army of her own, and this because she was labouring to eject her son out of Cyprus also : that as for Ptolemy, if he fail of his hopes, he can still retire to Cyprus ; but that they will be left in the greatest danger

possible. Now Ptolemy, although he had heard of the change that was made in the people of Ptolemais, yet did he still go on with his voyage, and came to the country called Sycamine, and there set his army on shore. This army of his, in the whole horse and foot together, were about thirty thousand, with which he marched near to Ptolemais, and there pitched his camp : but when the people of Ptolemais neither received his ambassadors nor would hear what they had to say, he was under a very great concern.

4. But when Zoilus and the people of Gaza came to him, and desired his assistance, because their country was laid waste by the Jews, and by Alexander—Alexander raised the siege, for fear of Ptolemy : and when he had drawn off his army into his own country, he used a stratagem afterwards, by privately inviting Cleopatra to come against Ptolemy, but publicly pretending to desire a league of friendship and mutual assistance with him ; and promising to give him four hundred talents of silver, he desired that, by way of requital, he would take off Zoilus the tyrant, and give his country to the Jews. And then indeed Ptolemy with pleasure made such a league of friendship with Alexander, and subdued Zoilus : but when he afterwards heard that he had privily sent to Cleopatra his mother, he broke the league with him, which yet he had confirmed with an oath, and fell upon him, and besieged Ptolemais, because it would not receive him. However, leaving his generals, with some part of his forces, to go on with the siege, he went himself immediately with the rest to lay Judea waste : and when Alexander understood this to be Ptolemy's intention, he also got together about fifty thousand soldiers out of his own country ; nay, as some writers have said, eighty thousand. He then took his army and went to meet Ptolemy ; but Ptolemy fell upon Asochis, a city of Galilee, and took it by force on the Sabbath-day, and there he took about ten thousand slaves, and a great deal of other prey.

5. He then tried to take Sepphoris, which was a city not far from that which was destroyed, but lost many of his men ; yet did he then go to fight with Alexander. Alexander met him at the river Jordan, near a certain place called Saphoth, [not far from the river Jordan,] and pitched his camp near to the enemy. He had, however, eight thousand in the first rank, which he styled Hecatontomachi, having shields of brass.—Those in the first rank of Ptolemy's soldiers also had shields covered with brass : but Ptolemy's soldiers in other respects were inferior to those of Alexander, and therefore were more fearful of running hazards ; but Philostephanus, the camp-master, put great courage into them, and ordered them to pass the river, which was between their camps : nor did Alexander think fit to hinder their passage over it : for he thought that if the enemy had once gotten the river on their back, that he should the easier take them prisoners, when they could not flee out of the battle : in the beginning of which, the acts on both sides with their hands, and with their alacrity, were alike, and a great slaughter was made by both the armies ; but Alexander was superior, till Philostephanus opportunely brought up the auxiliaries, to help those that were giving way ; but as there were no auxiliaries to afford help to that part of the Jews that gave way, it fell out that they fled, and those near them did not assist them, but fled along with them. However, Ptolemy's soldiers acted quite otherwise ; for

they followed the Jews, and killed them, till at length those that slew them pursued after them when they had made them all run away, and slew them so long, that their weapons of iron were blunted, and their hands quite tired with the slaughter; for the report was, that thirty thousand men were then slain. Timagenes says, they were fifty thousand. As for the rest, they were part of them taken captives; and the other part ran away to their own country.

6. After this victory, Ptolemy overran all the country; and when night came on, he abode in certain villages of Judea, which when he found full of women and children, he commanded his soldiers to strangle them, and to cut them in pieces, and then to cast them into boiling caldrons, and then to devour their limbs as sacrifices. This commandment was given, that such as fled from the battle, and came to them, might suppose their enemies were cannibals, and eat men's flesh, and might on that account be still more terrified at them upon such a sight. And both Strabo and Nicholaus [of Damascus] affirm, that they used these people after this manner, as I have already related. Ptolemy also took Ptolemais by force, as we have declared elsewhere.

CHAPTER XIII

HOW ALEXANDER, UPON THE LEAGUE OF MUTUAL DEFENCE WHICH CLEOPATRA HAD AGREED WITH HIM, MADE AN EXPEDITION AGAINST CŒLESYRIA, AND UTTERLY OVERTHREW THE CITY OF GAZA; AND HOW HE SLEW MANY TEN THOUSANDS OF JEWS THAT HAD REBELLED AGAINST HIM; ALSO CONCERNING ANTIOCHUS GRYPUS, SELEUCUS, ANTIOCHUS CYZICENUS, AND ANTIOCHUS PIUS, AND OTHERS

1. WHEN Cleopatra saw that her son was grown great, and laid Judea waste without disturbance, and had gotten the city of Gaza under his power, she resolved no longer to overlook what he did, when he was almost at her gates; and she concluded that, now he was so much stronger than before, he would be very desirous of the dominion over the Egyptians; but she immediately marched against him, with a fleet at sea and an army of foot on land, and made Chelcias and Ananias, the Jews, generals of her whole army, while she sent the greatest part of her riches, her grandchildren, and her testament, to the people of Cos.* Cleopatra also ordered her son Alexander to sail with a great fleet to Phœnicia: and when that country had revolted, she came to Ptolemais; and because the people of Ptolemais did not receive her, she besieged the city; but Ptolemy went out of Syria, and made haste unto Egypt, supposing that he should find it destitute of an army, and soon take it, though he failed of his hopes. At this time Chelcias, one of Cleopatra's generals, happened to die in Cœlesyria, as he was in pursuit of Ptolemy.

2. When Cleopatra heard of her son's attempt, and that his Egyptian expedition did not succeed according to his expectations, she sent thither part of her army, and drove him out of that country; so when he was returned out of Egypt

again, he abode during the winter at Gaza, in which time Cleopatra took the garrison that was in Ptolemais by siege, as well as the city; and when Alexander came to her, he gave her presents, and such marks of respect as were but proper, since, under the miseries he endured by Ptolemy, he had no other refuge but her. Now there were some of her friends who persuaded her to seize Alexander, and to overrun and take possession of the country, not to sit still and see such a multitude of brave Jews subject to one man; but Ananias's counsel was contrary to theirs, who said that she would do an unjust action if she deprived a man that was her ally of that authority which belonged to him, and this a man who is related to us; "for (said he) I would not have thee ignorant of this, that what injustice thou dost to him will make all us that are Jews to be thine enemies." This desire of Ananias, Cleopatra complied with; and did no injury to Alexander, but made a league of mutual assistance with him at Scythopolis, a city of Cœlesyria.

3. So when Alexander was delivered from the fear he was in of Ptolemy, he presently made an expedition against Cœlesyria. He also took Gadara, after a siege of ten months. He took also Amathus, a very strong fortress belonging to the inhabitants above Jordan, where Theodorus, the son of Zeno, had his chief treasure, and what he esteemed most precious. This Zeno fell unexpectedly upon the Jews, and slew ten thousand of them, and seized upon Alexander's baggage: yet did not this misfortune terrify Alexander; but he made an expedition upon the maritime parts of the country, Raphia and Anthedon, (the name of which king Herod afterwards changed to Agrippias,) and took even that by force. But when Alexander saw that Ptolemy was retired from Gaza to Cyprus, and his mother Cleopatra was returned to Egypt, he grew angry at the people of Gaza, because they had invited Ptolemy to assist them, and besieged their city, and ravaged their country. But as Apollodotus, the general of the army of Gaza, fell upon the camp of the Jews by night, with two thousand foreign, and ten thousand of his own forces, while the night lasted, those of Gaza prevailed, because the enemy was made to believe that it was Ptolemy who attacked them; but when day was come on, and that mistake was corrected, and the Jews knew the truth of the matter, they came back again, and fell upon those of Gaza, and slew of them about a thousand. But as those of Gaza stoutly resisted them, and would not yield for either their want of anything, nor for the great multitude that were slain, (for they would rather suffer any hardship whatever, than come under the power of their enemies,) Aretas, king of the Arabians, a person then very illustrious, encouraged them to go on with alacrity, and promised them that he would come to their assistance; but it happened that, before he came, Apollodotus was slain; for his brother Lysimachus, envying him for the great reputation he had gained among the citizens, slew him, and got the army together, and delivered up the city to Alexander; who, when he came in at first, lay quiet, but afterwards set his army upon the inhabitants of Gaza, and gave them leave to punish them; so some went one way, and some went another, and slew the inhabitants of Gaza; yet were not they of cowardly hearts, but opposed them that came to slay them, and slew as many of the Jews; and some of them, when they saw themselves deserted, burnt their own houses, that the enemy might get none of their spoils: nay, some of them, with their own hands,

---

* This Cos is not that remote island in the Ægean Sea, famous for the birth of the great Hippocrates, but a city or island of the same name adjoining to Egypt, mentioned both by Stephanus and Ptolemy.

slew their children and their wives, having no other way but this of avoiding slavery for them; but the senators, who were in all five hundred, fled to Apollo's temple, (for this attack happened to be made as they were sitting,) whom Alexander slew; and when he had utterly overthrown their city he returned to Jerusalem, having spent a year in that siege.

4. About this very time Antiochus, who was called Grypus, died.[*] His death was caused by Heracleon's treachery, when he had lived forty-five years, and had reigned twenty-nine.[†] His son Seleucus succeeded him in the kingdom, and made war with Antiochus, his father's brother, who was called Antiochus Cyzicenus, and beat him, and took him prisoner, and slew him; but after a while Antiochus, the son of Cyzicenus, who was called Pius, came to Aradus, and put the diadem on his own head, and made war with Seleucus, and beat him, and drove him out of all Syria. But when he fled out of Syria, he came to Mopsuestia again, and levied money upon them: but the people of Mopsuestia had indignation at what he did, and burnt down his palace, and slew him, together with his friends. But when Antiochus, the son of Cyzicenus, was king of Syria, Antiochus,[‡] the brother of Seleucus, made war upon him, and was overcome, and destroyed, he and his army. After him, his brother Philip put on the diadem, and reigned over some part of Syria; but Ptolemy Lathyrus sent for his fourth brother Demetrius, who was called Eucerous, from Cnidus, and made him king of Damascus. Both these brothers did Antiochus vehemently oppose, but presently died; for when he was come as an auxiliary to Laodice, queen of the Gileadites,[§] when she was making war against the Parthians, and he was fighting courageously, he fell, while Demetrius and Philip governed Syria, as hath been elsewhere related.

5. As to Alexander, his own people were seditious against him; for at a festival which was then celebrated, when he stood upon the altar, and was going to sacrifice, the nation rose upon him and pelted him with citrons, [which they then had in their hands, because] the law of the Jews required, that at the feast of tabernacles every one should have branches of palm-tree and citron-tree: which thing we have elsewhere related. They also reviled him, as derived from a captive, and so unworthy of his dignity and of sacrificing. At this he was in a rage, and slew of them about six thousand. He also built a partition-wall of wood round the altar and the temple, as far as that partition within which it was only lawful for the priests to enter; and by this means he obstructed the multitude from coming at him. He also maintained foreigners of Pisidiæ and Cilicia; for as to the Syrians, he was at war with them, and so made no use of them. He also overcame the Arabians; such as the Moabites and Gileadites, and made them bring tribute. Moreover, he demolished Amathus, while Theodorus|| durst not fight with him; but as he had joined battle with Obedas,

king of the Arabians, and fell into an ambush in the places that were rugged and difficult to be travelled over, he was thrown down into a deep valley, by the multitude of the camels at Gadara, a village of Gilead, and hardly escaped with his life. From thence he fled to Jerusalem, where. besides his other ill success, the nation insulted him, and he fought against them for six years, and slew no fewer than fifty thousand of them; and when he desired that they would desist from their ill-will to him, they hated him so much the more, on account of what had already happened; and when he had asked them what he ought to do, they all cried out, that he ought to kill himself. They also sent to Demetrius Eucerus, and desired him to make a league of mutual defence with them.

CHAPTER XIV

HOW DEMETRIUS EUCERUS OVERCAME ALEXANDER, AND YET, IN A LITTLE TIME, RETIRED OUT OF THE COUNTRY FOR FEAR OF THE JEWS; AS ALSO HOW ALEXANDER SLEW MANY OF THE JEWS, AND THEREBY GOT CLEAR OF ALL HIS TROUBLES. CONCERNING THE DEATH OF DEMETRIUS

1. So Demetrius came with an army, and took those that invited him, and pitched his camp near the city Shechem; upon which Alexander with his six thousand two hundred mercenaries, and about twenty thousand Jews, who were of his party, went against Demetrius, who had three thousand horsemen, and forty thousand footmen. Now there were great endeavours used on both sides,—Demetrius trying to bring off the mercenaries that were with Alexander, because they were Greeks; and Alexander tried to bring off the Jews that were with Demetrius. However, when neither of them could persuade them so to do, they came to a battle, and Demetrius was the conqueror; in which all Alexander's mercenaries were killed, when they had given demonstration of their fidelity and courage. A great number of Demetrius's soldiers were also slain.

2. Now as Alexander fled to the mountains, six thousand of the Jews hereupon came together [from Demetrius] to him out of pity at the change of his fortune; upon which Demetrius was afraid, and retired out of the country; after which the Jews fought against Alexander, and being beaten, were slain in great numbers in the several battles which they had; and when he had shut up the most powerful of them in the city Bethome, he besieged them therein; and when he had taken the city, and gotten the men into his power, he brought them to Jerusalem, and did one of the most barbarous actions in the world to them; for as he was feasting with his concubines, in the sight of all the city, he ordered about eight hundred of them to be crucified; and while they were living, he ordered the throats of their children and wives to be cut before their eyes. This was indeed by way of revenge for the injuries they had done him; which punishment yet was of an inhuman nature, though we suppose that he had been ever so much distressed, as indeed he had been, by his wars with them, for he had by their means come to the last degree of hazard, both of his life and of his kingdom, while they were not satisfied by themselves only to fight against him, but introduced foreigners also for the same purpose; nay, at length they reduced him to that degree of necessity, that he was forced to deliver

---

* This account of the death of Antiochus Grypus is confirmed by Appian.

† Porphyry says that he reigned but twenty-six years.

‡ These two brothers, Antiochus and Philippus, are called *twins* by Porphyry; the fourth brother was king of Damascus.

§ This Laodicea was a city of Gilead, beyond Jordan. However, Porphyry says, that this Antiochus Pius did not die in this battle; but, running away, was drowned in the river Orontes. Appian says, that he was deprived of the kingdom of Syria by Tigranes; but Porphyry makes this Laodice queen of the Calamans.

|| This Theodorus was the son of Zeno, and was in possession of Amathus.

back to the king of Arabia the land of Moab and Gilead, which he had subdued, and the places that were in them, that they might not join with them in the war against him, as they had done ten thousand other things that tended to affront and reproach him. However, this barbarity seems to have been without any necessity, on which account he bare the name of a Thracian among the Jews;* whereupon the soldiers that had fought against him, being about eight thousand in number, ran away by night, and continued fugitives all the time that Alexander lived; who being now freed from any further disturbance from them, reigned the rest of his time in the utmost tranquillity.

3. But when Demetrius was departed out of Judea, he went to Berea, and besieged his brother Philip, having with him ten thousand footmen, and a thousand horsemen. However, Strato, the tyrant of Berea, the confederate of Philip, called in Zizon the ruler of the Arabian tribes, and Mithridates Sinax, the ruler of the Parthians, who coming with a great number of forces, and besieging Demetrius in his encampment, into which they had driven him with their arrows, they compelled those that were with him, by thirst, to deliver up themselves. So they took a great many spoils out of that country, and Demetrius himself, whom they sent to Mithridates, who was then king of Parthia; but as to those whom they took captives of the people of Antioch, they restored him to the Antiochians without any reward. Now Mithridates, the king of Parthia, had Demetrius in great honour, till Demetrius ended his life by sickness. So Philip, presently after the fight was over, came to Antioch, and took it, and reigned over Syria.

CHAPTER XV

HOW ANTIOCHUS, WHO WAS CALLED DIONYSIUS, AND AFTER HIM ARETAS, MADE EXPEDITIONS INTO JUDEA; AS ALSO HOW ALEXANDER TOOK MANY CITIES, AND THEN RETURNED TO JERUSALEM, AND AFTER A SICKNESS OF THREE YEARS DIED; AND WHAT COUNSEL HE GAVE TO ALEXANDRA

1. AFTER this, Antiochus, who was called Dionysius,† and was Philip's brother, aspired to the dominion, and came to Damascus, and got the power into his hands, and there he reigned; but as he was making war against the Arabians, his brother Philip heard of it, and came to Damascus, where Milesius, who had been left governor of the citadel, and the Damascenes themselves, delivered up the city so him; yet because Philip was become ungrateful to him, and had bestowed upon him nothing of that in hopes whereof he had received him into the city, but had a mind to have it believed that it was rather delivered up out of fear than by the kindness of Milesius, and because he had not rewarded him as he ought to have done, he became suspected by him, and so he was obliged to leave Damascus again; for Milesius caught him marching out of the Hippodrome, and shut him up in it, and kept Damascus for Antiochus [Eucerus,] who, hearing how Philip's affairs stood, came back

out of Arabia. He also came immediately, and made an expedition against Judea, with eight thousand armed footmen, and eight hundred horsemen. So Alexander, out of fear of his coming, dug a deep ditch, beginning at Chabarzaba, which is now called Antipatris, to the Sea of Joppa, on which part only his army could be brought against him. He also raised a wall, and erected wooden towers, and intermediate redoubts, for one hundred and fifty furlongs in length, and there expected the coming of Antiochus; but he soon burnt them all, and made his army pass by that way into Arabia. The Arabian king [Aretas] at first retreated, but afterward appeared on the sudden with ten thousand horsemen. Antiochus gave them the meeting, and fought desperately; and indeed when he had gotten the victory, and was bringing some auxiliaries to that part of his army that was in distress, he was slain. When Antiochus was fallen, his army fled to the village Cana, where the greatest part of them perished by famine.

2. After him‡ Aretas reigned over Cœlesyria, being called to the government by those that held Damascus, by reason of the hatred they bare to Ptolemy Menneus. He also made thence an expedition against Judea, and beat Alexander in battle, near a place called Adida; yet did he, upon certain conditions agreed on between them, retire out of Judea.

3. But Alexander marched again to the city Dios, and took it, and then made an expedition against Essa, where was the best part of Zeno's treasures, and there he encompassed the place with three walls; and when he had taken the city by fighting, he marched to Golan and Selucia; and when he had taken these cities, he, besides them, took that valley which is called *The Valley of Antiochus*, as also the fortress of Gamala. He also accused Demetrius, who was governor of those places, of many crimes, and turned him out; and after he had spent three years in this war, he returned to his own country; when the Jews joyfully received him upon this his good success.

4. Now at this time the Jews were in possession of the following cities that had belonged to the Syrians, and Idumeans, and Phœnicians: At the sea-side, Strato's Tower, Apollonia, Joppa, Jamnia, Ashdod, Gaza, Anthedon, Raphia, and Rhinocolura; in the middle of the country, near to Idumea, Adora, and Marissa; near the country of Samaria, mount Carmel, and mount Tabor, Scythopolis, and Gadara; of the country of the Gaulonites, Seleucia, and Gabala; in the country of Moab, Heshbon, and Medaba, Lemba, and Oronas, Gelithon, Zara, the valley of the Cilices, and Pella; which last they utterly destroyed, because its inhabitants would not bear to change their religious rites for those peculiar to the Jews.§ The Jews also possessed others of the principal cities of Syria, which had been destroyed.

---

* This name Thracida, which the Jews gave Alexander, must, by the coherence, denote *as barbarous as a Thracian*, or somewhat like it.

† This Antiochus Dionysius was the fifth son of Antiochus Grypus; and he is styled on the coins "Antiochus, Epiphanes, Dionysius."

‡ This Aretas was the first king of the Arabians who took Damascus, and reigned there; which name became afterwards common to such Arabian kings, both at Petra and at Damascus, as we learn from St Paul, 2 Cor. xi. 32.

§ Whatever countries the Asamoneans conquered from any of the neighbouring nations, they, after the days of Hyrcanus, compelled the inhabitants to leave their idolatry, and entirely to receive the law of Moses, as proselytes of justice, or else banished them into other lands. John Hyrcanus did it to the Idumeans, who lived then in the promised land, and this I suppose justly; but by what right the rest did it, even to the countries or cities that were no part of that land, I do not at all know. This looks like unjust persecution for religion.

5. After this, king Alexander, aitnough he fell into a distemper by hard drinking, and had a quartan ague which held him three years, yet would not leave off going out with his army, till he was quite spent with the labours he had undergone, and died in the bounds of Ragaba, a fortress beyond Jordan. But when his queen saw that he was ready to die, and had no longer any hopes of surviving, she came to him weeping and lamenting, and bewailed herself and her sons on the desolate condition they should be left in; and said to him, "To whom dost thou thus leave me and my children, who are destitute of all other supports, and this when thou knowest how much ill-will thy nation bears thee?" But he gave her the following advice: —That she need but follow what he would suggest to her in order to retain the kingdom securely, with her children: that she should conceal his death from the soldiers till she should have taken that place; after this, she should go in triumph, as upon a victory, to Jerusalem, and put some of her authority into the hands of the Pharisees; for that they would commend her for the honour she had done them, and would reconcile the nation to her; for he told her they had great authority among the Jews, both to do hurt to such as they hated, and to bring advantages to those to whom they were friendly disposed; for that they are then believed best of all by the multitude when they speak any severe thing against others, though it be only out of envy at them. And he said, that it was by their means that he had incurred the displeasure of the nation, whom indeed he had injured. "Do thou therefore," said he, "when thou art come to Jerusalem, send for the leading men among them, and shew them my body, and with great appearance of sincerity, give them leave to use it as they themselves please, whether they will dishonour the dead body by refusing it burial, as having severely suffered by my means, or whether in their anger they will offer any other injury to that body. Promise them also, that thou wilt do nothing without them in the affairs of the kingdom. If thou dost but say this to them, I shall have the honour of a more glorious funeral from them than thou couldst have made for me: and when it is in their power to abuse my dead body, they will do it no injury at all, and thou wilt rule in safety." * So when he had given his wife this advice, he died,—after he had reigned twenty-seven years, and lived fifty years, within one.

---

* It seems, by this dying advice of Alexander Janneus to his wife, that he had himself pursued the measures of his father Hyrcanus, and taken part with the Sadducees, who kept close to the written law, against the Pharisees, who had introduced their own traditions; and that he now saw a political necessity of submitting to the Pharisees, and their traditions hereafter, if his widow and family minded to retain their monarchical government over the Jewish nation; which sect were at last in a great measure the ruin of the Jews, and brought them into so wicked a state, that the vengeance of God came upon them to their utter excision. Just thus did Caiaphas politically advise the Jewish sanhedrim, (John xi. 50,) "that it was expedient for them that one man should die for the people, and that the whole nation perish not;" and this in consequence of their own political supposal, ver. 48, that, "if they let Jesus alone," with his miracles, "all men would believe on him; and the Romans would come and take away both their place and nation." Which political crucifixion of Jesus of Nazareth brought down the vengeance of God upon them, and occasioned those very Romans, of whom they seemed so much afraid, that to prevent it they put him to death, actually to "come and take away both their place and nation," within thirty-eight years afterwards.

CHAPTER XVI

HOW ALEXANDRA, BY GAINING THE GOOD-WILL OF THE PHARISEES, RETAINED THE KINGDOM NINE YEARS, AND THEN, HAVING DONE MANY GLORIOUS ACTIONS, DIED

1. So Alexandra, when she had taken the fortress, acted as her husband had suggested to her, and spoke to the Pharisees, and put all things into their power, both as to the dead body and as to the affairs of the kingdom, and thereby pacified their anger against Alexander, and made them bear good-will and friendship to him; who then came among the multitude, and made speeches to them, and laid before them the actions of Alexander, and told them that they had lost a righteous king; and by the commendation they gave him, they brought them to grieve, and to be in heaviness for him, so that he had a funeral more splendid than had any of the kings before him. Alexander left behind him two sons, Hyrcanus and Aristobulus, but committed the kingdom to Alexandra. Now, as to these two sons, Hyrcanus was indeed unable to manage public affairs, and delighted rather in a quiet life; but the younger, Aristobulus, was an active and a bold man; and for this woman herself, Alexandra, she was loved by the multitude, because she seemed displeased at the offences her husband had been guilty of.

2. So she made Hyrcanus high-priest because he was the elder, but much more because he cared not to meddle with politics, and permitted the Pharisees to do everything; to whom also she ordered the multitude to be obedient. She also restored again those practices which the Pharisees had introduced, according to the traditions of their forefathers, and which her father-in-law, Hyrcanus, had abrogated. So she had indeed the name of Regent; but the Pharisees had the authority; for it was they who restored such as had been banished, and set such as were prisoners at liberty, and, to say all at once, they differed in nothing from lords. However, the queen also took care of the affairs of the kingdom, and got together a great body of mercenary soldiers, and increased her own army to such a degree, that she became terrible to the neighbouring tyrants, and took hostages of them: and the country was entirely at peace, excepting the Pharisees; for they disturbed the queen, and desired that she would kill those that persuaded Alexander to slay the eight hundred men; after which they cut the throat of one of them, Diogenes: and after him they did the same to several, one after another, till the men that were the most potent came into the palace, and Aristobulus with them, for he seemed to be displeased at what was done; and it appeared openly that, if he had an opportunity, he would not permit his mother to go on so. These put the queen in mind what great dangers they had gone through, and great things they had done, whereby they had demonstrated the firmness of their fidelity to their master, insomuch that they had received the greatest marks of favour from him; and they begged of her, that she would not utterly blast their hopes, as it now happened, that when they had escaped the hazards that arose from their [open] enemies, they were to be cut off at home, by their [private] enemies, like brute beasts, without any help whatsoever. They said also, that if their adversaries would be satisfied with those that had been slain already, they would take what had been done patiently, on account of their natural love to their governors;

but if they must expect the same for the future also, they implored of her a dismission from her service; for they could not think of attempting any method for their deliverance without her, but would rather die willingly before the palace-gate, in case she would not forgive them. And that it was a great shame, both for themselves and for the queen, that when they were neglected by her, they should come under the lash of her husband's enemies; for that Aretas, the Arabian king, and the monarchs, would give any reward, if they could get such men as foreign auxiliaries, to whom their very names, before their voices be heard, may perhaps be terrible; but if they could not obtain this their second request, and if she had determined to prefer the Pharisees before them, they still insisted that she would place them every one in her fortresses; for if some fatal demon hath a constant spite against Alexander's house, they would be willing to bear their part, and to live in a private station there.

3. As these men said thus, and called upon Alexander's ghost for commiseration of those already slain, and those in danger of it, all the bystanders brake out into tears: but Aristobulus chiefly made manifest what were his sentiments, and used many reproachful expressions to his mother, [saying,] "Nay, indeed, the case is this, that they have been themselves the authors of their own calamities, who have permitted a woman who, against reason, was mad with ambition, to reign over them, when there were sons in the flower of their age fitter for it." So Alexandra, not knowing what to do with any decency, committed the fortresses to them, all but Hyrcania, and Alexandrium, and Macherus, where her principal treasures were. After a little while also, she sent her son Aristobulus with an army to Damascus against Ptolemy, who was called Meneus, who was such a bad neighbour to the city; but he did nothing considerable there, and so returned home.

4. About this time news was brought that Tigranes, the king of Armenia, had made an irruption into Syria with five hundred thousand soldiers,* and was coming against Judea. This news, as may well be supposed, terrified the queen and the nation. Accordingly they sent him many and very valuable presents, as also ambassadors, and that as he was besieging Ptolemais; for Selene the queen, the same that was also called Cleopatra, ruled then over Syria, who had persuaded the inhabitants to exclude Tigranes. So the Jewish ambassadors interceded with him, and entreated him that he would determine nothing that was severe about their queen or nation. He commended them for the respects they paid him at so great a distance: and gave them good hopes of his favour. But as soon as Ptolemais was taken, news came to Tigranes, that Lucullus, in his pursuit of Mithridates, could not light upon him, who was fled into Iberia, but was laying waste Armenia and besieging its cities. Now, when Tigranes knew this, he returned home.

5. After this, when the queen was fallen into a dangerous distemper, Aristobulus resolved to attempt the seizing of the government; so he stole away secretly by night, with only one of his servants, and went to the fortresses wherein his friends, that were such from the days of his father, were settled; for as he had been a great while displeased at his mother's conduct, so he was now much more afraid, lest, upon her death, their whole family should be under the power of the Pharisees; for he saw the inability of his brother, who was to succeed in the government: nor was any one conscious of what he was doing but only his wife, whom he left at Jerusalem with their children. He first of all came to Agaba, where was Galestes, one of the potent men before mentioned, and was received by him. When it was day the queen perceived that Aristobulus was fled; and for some time she supposed that his departure was not in order to make any innovation; but when messengers came one after another with the news that he had secured the first place, the second place, and all the places, (for as soon as one had begun, they all submitted to his disposal,) then it was that the queen and the nation were in the greatest disorder, for they were aware that it would not be long ere Aristobulus would be able to settle himself firmly in the government. What they were principally afraid of was this, that he would inflict punishment upon them for the mad treatment his house had had from them: so they resolved to take his wife and children into custody, and keep them in the fortress that was over the temple.† Now there was a mighty conflux of people that came to Aristobulus from all parts, insomuch that he had a kind of royal attendants about him; for in little more than fifteen days, he got twenty-two strong places, which gave him the opportunity of raising an army from Libanus and Trachonitis, and the monarchs; for men are easily led by the greater number, and easily submit to them. And besides this, that by affording him their assistance, when he could not expect it, they, as well as he, should have the advantages that would come by his being king, because they had been the occasion of his gaining the kingdom. Now the elders of the Jews, and Hyrcanus with them, went in unto the queen, and desired that she would give them her sentiments about the present posture of affairs, for that Aristobulus was in effect lord of almost all the kingdom by possessing of so many strongholds, and that it was absurd for them to take any counsel by themselves, how ill soever she were, whilst she was alive, and that the danger would be upon them in no long time. But she bade them do what they thought proper to be done: that they had many circumstances in their favour still remaining; a nation in good heart, an army, and money in their several treasuries; for that she had small concern about public affairs now, when the strength of her body already failed her.

6. Now a little while after she had said this to them, she died, when she had reigned nine years, and had in all lived seventy-three. A woman she was who shewed no signs of the weakness of her sex; for she was sagacious to the greatest degree in her ambition of governing, and demonstrated by her doings at once, that her mind was fit for action, and that sometimes men themselves shew the little understanding they have by the frequent mistakes they make in point of government; for she always preferred the present to futurity, and preferred the power of an imperious dominion above all things, and in comparison of that, had no regard to what was good or what was right. However, she brought the affairs of her house to such an unfortunate

---

* The number of 500,000, or even 300,000, for Tigranes's army, that came out of Armenia into Syria and Judea, seems much too large. Dr Hudson supposes them but 40,000.

† This fortress, whither the wife and children of Aristobulus were now sent, and which overlooked the temple, could be no other than what Hyrcanus I. built, and Herod the Great rebuilt, called the "Tower of Antonia."

condition, that she was the occasion of the taking away that authority from it, and that in no long time afterward, which she had obtained by a vast number of hazards and misfortunes, and this out of a desire of what does not belong to a woman, and all by a compliance in her sentiments with those that bare ill-will to their family, and by leaving the administration desti-tute of a proper support of great men ; and, indeed, her management during her administration, while she was alive, was such as filled the palace after her death with calamities and disturbance. However, although this had been her way of governing, she preserved the nation in peace ;—and this is the conclusion of the affairs of Alexandra.

BOOK XIV

CONTAINING THE INTERVAL OF THIRTY-TWO YEARS

FROM THE DEATH OF QUEEN ALEXANDRA TO THE DEATH OF ANTIGONUS

CHAPTER I

THE WAR BETWEEN ARISTOBULUS AND HYRCANUS ABOUT THE KINGDOM ; AND HOW THEY MADE AN AGREEMENT THAT ARISTOBULUS SHOULD BE KING, AND HYRCANUS LIVE A PRIVATE LIFE : AS ALSO, HOW HYRCANUS, A LITTLE AFTERWARDS, WAS PERSUADED BY ANTIPATER TO FLY TO ARETAS

1. WE have related the affairs of queen Alexandra, and her death, in the foregoing book, and will now speak of what followed, and was connected with those histories ; declaring, before we proceed, that we have nothing so much at heart as this, that we may omit no facts either through ignorance or laziness ; for we are upon the history and explication of such things as the greatest part are unacquainted withal, because of their distance from our times ; and we aim to do it with a proper beauty of style, so far as that is derived from proper words harmonically disposed, and from such ornaments of speech also as may contribute to the pleasure of our readers, that they may entertain the knowledge of what we write with some agreeable satisfaction and pleasure. But the principal scope that authors ought to aim at, above all the rest, is to speak accurately, and to speak truly, for the satisfaction of those that are otherwise unacquainted with such transactions, and obliged to believe what these writers inform them of.

2. Hyrcanus then began his high priesthood on the third year of the hundred and seventh Olympiad, when Quintus Hortensius and Quintus Metellus, who was called Metellus of Crete, were consuls at Rome ; when presently Aristobulus began to make war against him, and as it came to a battle with Hyrcanus at Jericho, many of his soldiers deserted him, and went over to his brother : upon which Hyrcanus fled into the citadel, where Aristobulus's wife and children were imprisoned by his mother, as we have said already, and attacked and overcame those his adversaries that had fled thither, and lay within the walls of the temple. So when he had sent a message to his brother about agreeing the matters between them, he laid aside his enmity to him on these conditions, that Aristobulus should be king, that he should live without intermeddling with public affairs, and quietly enjoy the estate he had acquired. When they had agreed upon these terms in the temple, and had confirmed the agreement with oaths, and the giving one another their right hands, and embracing one another in the sight of the whole multitude, they departed ; the one, Aristobulus, to the palace, and Hyrcanus, as a private man, to the former house of Aristobulus.

3. But there was a certain friend of Hyrcanus, an Idumean, called Antipater, who was very rich, and in his nature an active and a seditious man ; who was at enmity with Aristobulus, and had differences with him on account of his goodwill to Hyrcanus. It is true, that Nicolaus of Damascus says, that Antipater was of the stock of the principal Jews who came out of Babylon into Judea ; but that assertion of his was to gratify Herod, who was his son, and who, by certain revolutions of fortune came afterwards to be king of the Jews, whose history we shall give you in its proper place hereafter. However, this Antipater was at first called Antipas,[*] and that was his father's name also ; of whom they relate this : That king Alexander and his wife made him general of all Idumea, and that he made a league of friendship with those Arabians, and Gazites, and Ascalonites, that were of his own party, and had, by many and large presents, made them his fast friends ; but now this younger Antipater was suspicious of the power of Aristobulus, and was afraid of some mischief he might do him, because of his hatred to him ; so he stirred up the most powerful of the Jews, and talked against him to them privately ; and said, that it was unjust to overlook the conduct of Aristobulus, who had gotten the government unrighteously, and ejected his brother out of it who was the elder, and ought to retain what belonged to him by prerogative of his birth ; and the same speeches he perpetually made to Hyrcanus ; and told him that his own life would be in danger unless he guarded himself, and got quit of Aristobulus ; for he said that the friends of Aristobulus omitted no opportunity of advising him to kill him, as being then, and not before, sure to retain his principality. Hyrcanus gave no credit to these words of his, as being of a gentle disposition, and one that did not easily admit of calumnies against other men. This

---

[*] That the famous Antipater's or Antipas's father was also Antipater or Antipas, Josephus here assures us, though Eusebius indeed says it was Herod.

temper of his not disposing him to meddle with public affairs, and want of spirit, occasioned him to appear to spectators to be degenerated and unmanly ; while Aristobulus was of a contrary temper, an active man, and one of a great and generous soul.

4. Since therefore Antipater saw that Hyrcanus did not attend to what he said, he never ceased, day by day, to charge feigned crimes upon Aristobulus, and to calumniate him before him, as if he had a mind to kill him ; and so, by urging him perpetually, he advised him, and persuaded him to fly to Aretas, the king of Arabia ; and promised, that if he would comply with his advice, he would also himself assist him, [and go with him.] When Hyrcanus heard this, he said that it was for his advantage to fly away to Aretas. Now Arabia is a country that borders upon Judea. However, Hyrcanus sent Antipater first to the king of Arabia, in order to receive assurances from him, that when he should come in the manner of a supplicant to him, he would not deliver him up to his enemies. So Antipater having received such assurances, returned to Hyrcanus to Jerusalem. A while afterward he took Hyrcanus, and stole out of the city by night, and went a great journey, and came and brought him to the city called Petra, where the palace of Aretas was ; and as he was a very familiar friend of that king, he persuaded him to bring back Hyrcanus into Judea ; and this persuasion he continued every day without any intermission. He also proposed to make him presents on that account. At length he prevailed with Aretas in his suit. Moreover, Hyrcanus promised him, that when he had been brought thither, and had received his kingdom, he would restore that country, and those twelve cities which his father Alexander had taken from the Arabians ; which were these, Medaba, Naballo, Libyas, Tharabasa, Agala, Athone, Zoar, Orone, Marissa, Rudda, Lussa, and Oruba.

CHAPTER II

HOW ARETAS AND HYRCANUS MADE AN EXPEDITION AGAINST ARISTOBULUS, AND BESIEGED JERUSALEM ; AND HOW SCAURUS, THE ROMAN GENERAL, RAISED THE SIEGE. CONCERNING THE DEATH OF ONIAS

1. AFTER these promises had been given to Aretas, he made an expedition against Aristobulus, with an army of fifty thousand horse and foot, and beat him in the battle. And when after that victory many went over to Hyrcanus as deserters, Aristobulus was left desolate, and fled to Jerusalem ; upon which the king of Arabia took all his army and made an assault upon the temple, and besieged Aristobulus therein, the people still supporting Hyrcanus, and assisting him in the siege, while none but the priests continued with Aristobulus. So Aretas united the forces of the Arabians and of the Jews together, and pressed on the siege vigorously. As this happened at the time when the feast of unleavened bread was celebrated, which we call the Passover, the principal men among the Jews left the country, and fled into Egypt. Now there was one, whose name was Onias, a righteous man he was, and beloved of God, who, in a certain drought, had prayed to God to put an end to the intense heat, and whose prayers God had heard, and had sent them rain. This man had hid himself, because he saw that this sedition would last a great while. However, they brought him to the Jewish camp, and desired, that as by his prayers he had once put an end to the drought, so he would in like manner make imprecations on Aristobulus and those of his faction. And when, upon his refusal, and the excuses that he made, he was still by the multitude compelled to speak, he stood up in the midst of them, and said, "O God, the King of the whole world ! since those that stand now with me are thy people, and those that are besieged are also thy priests, I beseech thee, that thou wilt neither hearken to the prayers of those against these, nor bring to effect what these pray against those. Whereupon such wicked Jews as stood about him, as soon as he had made this prayer, stoned him to death.

2. But God punished them immediately for this their barbarity, and took vengeance of them for the murder of Onias, in the manner following :—While the priests and Aristobulus were besieged, it happened that the feast called the Passover was come, at which it is our custom to offer a great number of sacrifices to God ; but those that were with Aristobulus wanted sacrifices, and desired that their countrymen without would furnish them with such sacrifices, and assured them they should have as much money for them as they should desire ; and when they required them to pay a thousand drachmæ for each head of cattle, Aristobulus and the priests willingly undertook to pay for them accordingly ; and those within let down the money over the walls, and gave it them. But when the others had received it, they did not deliver the sacrifices, but arrived at that height of wickedness as to break the assurances they had given, and to be guilty of impiety towards God, by not furnishing those that wanted them with sacrifices. And when the priests found they had been cheated, and that the agreements they had made were violated, they prayed to God that he would avenge them on their countrymen. Nor did he delay that their punishment, but sent a strong and vehement storm of wind, that destroyed the fruits of the whole country, till a modius of wheat was then bought for eleven drachmæ.

3. In the meantime Pompey sent Scaurus into Syria, while he was himself in Armenia, and making war with Tigranes ; but when Scaurus was come to Damascus, and found that Lollius and Metellus had newly taken the city, he came himself hastily into Judea. And when he was come thither, ambassadors came to him, both from Aristobulus and Hyrcanus, and both desired he would assist them ; and when both of them promised to give him money, Aristobulus four hundred talents, and Hyrcanus no less, he accepted of Aristobulus's promise, for he was rich, and had a great soul, and desired to obtain nothing but what was moderate ; whereas the other was poor and tenacious, and made incredible promises in hope of greater advantages ; for it was not the same thing to take a city that was exceeding strong and powerful, as it was to eject out of the country some fugitives, with a great number of Nabateans, who were no very warlike people. He therefore made an agreement with Aristobulus, for the reason before mentioned, and took his money, and raised the siege, and ordered Aretas to depart, or else he should be declared an enemy to the Romans. So Scaurus returned to Damascus again ; and Aristobulus, with a great army, made war with Aretas and Hyrcanus, and fought them at a place called Papyron, and beat them in the battle, and slew about six thousand of the enemy, with whom fell Phalion also, the brother of Antipater.

CHAPTER III

HOW ARISTOBULUS AND HYRCANUS CAME TO POM-
PEY, IN ORDER TO ARGUE WHO OUGHT TO HAVE
THE KINGDOM ; AND HOW, UPON THE FLIGHT OF
ARISTOBULUS TO THE FORTRESS ALEXANDRIUM,
POMPEY LED HIS ARMY AGAINST HIM, AND OR-
DERED HIM TO DELIVER UP THE FORTRESS
WHEREOF HE WAS POSSESSED

1. A LITTLE afterward Pompey came to Damascus, and marched over Cœlesyria ; at which
time there came ambassadors to him from all
Syria, and Egypt, and out of Judea also, for
Aristobulus had sent him a great present, which
was a golden vine, of the value of five hundred
talents. Now Strabo of Cappadocia mentions
this present in these words:—"There came also
an embassage out of Egypt, and a crown of the
value of four thousand pieces of gold ; and out of
Judea there came another, whether you call it
a *vine* or a *garden ;* they called the thing Terpole,
the Delight. However, we ourselves saw the
present reposited at Rome, in the temple of
Jupiter Capitolinus, with this inscription : ' The
Gift of Alexander, the King of the Jews.' It
was valued at five hundred talents ; and the report is, that Aristobulus, the governor of the
Jews, sent it."

2. In a little time afterward came ambassadors
again to him, Antipater from Hyrcanus, and
Nicodemus from Aristobulus ; which last also
accused such as had taken bribes ; first Gabinius,
and then Scaurus,—the one three hundred
talents, and the other four hundred ; by which
procedure he made these two his enemies, besides those he had before ; and when Pompey had
ordered those that had controversies one with
another to come to him in the beginning of the
spring, he brought his army out of their winter
quarter , and marched into the country of Damascus ; nd as he went along he demolished the
citadel that was at Apamea, which Antiochus
Cyzicenus had built, and took cognizance of the
country of Ptolemy Menneus, a wicked man, and
not less so than Dionysius of Tripoli, who had
been beheaded, who was also his relation by marriage ; yet did he buy off the punishment of his
crimes for a thousand talents, with which money
Pompey paid the soldiers their wages. He also
conquered the place called Lysias, of which Silas
a Jew was tyrant ; and when he had passed over
the cities of Heliopolis and Chalcis, and got over
the mountain which is on the limit of Cœlesyria,
he came from Pella to Damascus ; and there it
was that he heard the causes of the Jews, and of
their governors Hyrcanus and Aristobulus, who
were at difference one with another, as also of
the nation against them both, which did not
desire to be under kingly government, because
the form of government they received from their
forefathers was that of subjection to the priests
of that God whom they worshipped ; and [they
complained,] that though these two were the
posterity of priests, yet did they seek to change
the government of their nation to another form,
in order to enslave them. Hyrcanus complained,
that although he were the elder brother, he was
deprived of the prerogative of his birth by Aristobulus, and that he had but a small part of the
country under him, Aristobulus having taken
away the rest from him by force. He also accused him, that the incursions which had been
made in their neighbours' countries, and the
piracies that had been at sea, were owing to him ;
and that the nation would not have revolted
unless Aristobulus had been a man given to

violence and disorder ; and there were no fewer
than a thousand Jews, of the best esteem among
them, who confirmed this accusation ; which
confirmation was procured by Antipater ; but
Aristobulus alleged against him, that it was
Hyrcanus's own temper, which was inactive, and
on that account contemptible, which caused him
to be deprived of the government ; and that for
himself he was necessitated to take it upon him,
for fear lest it should be transferred to others ;
and that as to his title [of king,] it was no other
than what his father had taken [before him.]
He also called for witnesses of what he said,
some persons who were both young and insolent ;
whose purple garments, fine heads of hair, and
other ornaments, were detested [by the court,]
and which they appeared in, not as though they
were to plead their cause in a court of justice,
but as if they were marching in a pompous procession.

3. When Pompey had heard the causes of
these two, and had condemned Aristobulus for
his violent procedure, he then spake civilly to
them, and sent them away ; and told them, that
when he came again into their country he would
settle all their affairs, after he had first taken a
view of the affairs of the Nabateans. In the
meantime, he ordered them to be quiet ; and
treated Aristobulus civilly, lest he should make
the nation revolt, and hinder his return ; which
yet Aristobulus did ; for without expecting any
further determination, which Pompey had promised them, he went to the city Delius, and thence
marched into Judea.

4. At this behaviour Pompey was angry ; and
taking with him that army which he was leading
against the Nabateans, and the auxiliaries that
came from Damascus, and the other parts of
Syria, with the other Roman legions which he
had with him, he made an expedition against
Aristobulus ; but as he passed by Pella and Scythopolis, he came to Coreæ, which is the first
entrance into Judea when one passes over the
midland countries, where he came to a most beautiful fortress that was built on the top of a mountain called Alexandrium, whither Aristobulus
had fled ; and thence Pompey sent his commands
to him, that he should come to him. Accordingly,
at the persuasion of many that he would not
make war with the Romans, he came down ; and
when he had disputed with his brother about the
right to the government, he went up again to
the citadel, as Pompey gave him leave to do ; and
this he did two or three times, as flattering
himself with the hopes of having the kingdom
granted him ; so that he still pretended he would
obey Pompey in whatsoever he commanded,
although at the same time he retired to the fortress, that he might not depress himself too low,
and that he might be prepared for a war, in
case it should prove, as he feared, that Pompey
would transfer the government to Hyrcanus : but
when Pompey enjoined Aristobulus to deliver up
the fortresses he held, and to send an injunction
to their governors under his own hand for that
purpose, for they had been forbidden to deliver
them up upon any other commands, he submitted indeed to do so ; but still he retired in displeasure to Jerusalem, and made preparations
for war. A little after this, certain persons came
out of Pontus, and informed Pompey, as he was
on the way, and conducting his army against
Aristobulus, that Mithridates was dead, and was
slain by his son Pharmaces.

CHAPTER IV

HOW POMPEY, WHEN THE CITIZENS OF JERUSALEM
SHUT THEIR GATES AGAINST HIM, BESIEGED THE
CITY, AND TOOK IT BY FORCE ; AND ALSO WHAT
OTHER THINGS HE DID IN JUDEA

1. Now when Pompey had pitched his camp
at Jericho, (where the palm-tree grows, and that
balsam which is an ointment of all the most precious, which, upon any incision made in the
wood with a sharp stone, distils out thence like a
juice,) he marched in the morning to Jerusalem.
Hereupon Aristobulus repented of what he was
doing, and came to Pompey, and [promised to]
give him money, and received him into Jerusalem, and desired that he would leave off the
war, and do what he pleased peaceably.   So
Pompey, upon his entreaty, forgave him, and
sent Gabinius; and soldiers with him, to receive
the money and the city : yet was no part of this
performed; but Gabinius came back, being both
excluded out of the city, and receiving none of
the money promised, because Aristobulus's soldiers would not permit the agreements to be
executed.   At this Pompey was very angry, and
put Aristobulus into prison, and came himself
to the city, which was strong on every side,
excepting the north, which was not so well fortified, for there was a broad and deep ditch, that
encompassed the city,* and included within it
the temple, which was itself encompassed about
with a very strong stone wall
2. Now there was a sedition of the men that
were within the city, who did not agree on what
was to be done in their present circumstances,
while some thought it best to deliver up the city
to Pompey; but Aristobulus's party exhorted
them to shut the gates, because he was kept in
prison.   Now these prevented the others, and
seized upon the temple, and cut off the bridge
which reached from it to the city, and prepared
themselves to abide a siege ; but the others
admitted Pompey's army in, and delivered up
both the city and the king's palace to him.   So
Pompey sent his lieutenant Piso with an army,
and placed garrisons both in the city and in the
palace, to secure them, and fortified the houses
that joined to the temple, and all those which
were more distant and without it.   And, in the
first place, he offered terms of accommodation to
those that were within; but when they would
not comply with what was desired, he encompassed all the places thereabout with a wall,
wherein Hyrcanus did gladly assist him on all
occasions ; but Pompey pitched his camp within
[the wall,] on the north part of the temple,
where it was most practicable ; but even on that
side there were great towers, and a ditch had
been dug, and a deep valley begirt it round
about, for on the parts towards the city were
precipices, and the bridge on which Pompey had
gotten in was broken down.   However, a bank
was raised, day by day, with a great deal of
labour, while the Romans cut down materials for
it from the places round about ; and when this
bank was sufficiently raised, and the ditch filled
up, though but poorly, by reason of its immense
depth, he brought his mechanical engines and
battering-rams from Tyre, and placing them on
the bank, he battered the temple with the stones
that were thrown against it; and had it not been
our practice, from the days of our forefathers, to
rest on the seventh day, this bank could never

have been perfected, by reason of the opposition
the Jews would have made ; for though our law
gives us leave then to defend ourselves against
those that begin to fight with us and assault us,
yet does it not permit us to meddle with our
enemies while they do anything else.
3. Which thing when the Romans understood
on those days which we call Sabbaths, they
threw nothing at the Jews, nor came to any
pitched battle with them, but raised up their
earthen banks, and brought their engines into
such forwardness, that they might do execution
the next days ; and any one may hence learn
how very great piety we exercise towards God,
and the observance of his laws, since the priests
were not at all hindered from their sacred ministrations, by their fear during this siege, but did
still twice each day, in the morning and about
the ninth hour, offer their sacrifices on the altar ;
nor did they omit those sacrifices, if any melancholy accident happened, by the stones that were
thrown among them ; for although the city was
taken on the third month, on the day of the
fast,† upon the hundred and seventy-ninth
Olympiad, when Caius Antonius and Marcus
Tullius Cicero were consuls, and the enemy then
fell upon them, and cut the throats of those that
were in the temple, yet could not those that
offered the sacrifices be compelled to run away,
neither by the fear they were in of their own
lives, nor by the number that were already slain,
as thinking it better to suffer whatever came
upon them at their very altars, than to omit anything that their laws required of them ; and that
this is not a mere brag, or an encomium to manifest a degree of our piety that was false, but is
the real truth, I appeal to those that have written of the acts of Pompey ; and among them,
to Strabo and Nicolaus [of Damascus ;] and besides these, to Titus Livius, the writer of the Roman History, who will bear witness of this thing.‡
4. But when the battering engine was brought
near, the greatest of the towers was shaken by
it, and fell down, and broke down a part of the
fortifications, so the enemy poured in apace ;
and Cornelius Faustus, the son of Sylla, with
his soldiers, first of all ascended the wall, and
next to him Furius the centurion, with those
that followed, on the other part ; while Fabius,
who was also a centurion, ascended it in the
middle, with a great body of men after him ; but
now all was full of slaughter ; some of the Jews
being slain by the Romans, and some by one
another ; nay, some there were who threw themselves down the precipices, or put fire to their
houses, and burnt them, as not able to bear the
miseries they were under.   Of the Jews there
fell twelve thousand ; but of the Romans very
few.   Absalom, who was at once both uncle and
father-in-law to Aristobulus, was taken captive ;
and no small enormities were committed about
the temple itself, which, in former ages, had
been inaccessible, and seen by none ; for Pompey
went into it, and not a few of those that were
with him also, and saw all that which was unlawful for any other men to see, but only for the

---

* From Strabo we learn that this ditch was 60 feet
deep, and 250 feet broad.

---

† That is, on the twenty-third of Sivan, the annual
fast for the defection and idolatry of Jeroboam, "who
made Israel to sin."
‡ Of this Pharisaical superstitious notion, that offensive fighting was unlawful to Jews, even under the utmost necessity, on the Sabbath-day, we hear nothing
before the times of the Maccabees. It was the occasion of
Jerusalem's being taken by Pompey, by Sossius, and by
Titus.   Our Saviour always opposed it, when the Pharisaical Jews insisted on it, as is evident in many places
in the New Testament, though he still intimated how
pernicious that superstition might prove to them in
their flight from the Romans, (Matt. xxiv. 20.)

high priests. There were in that temple the golden table, the holy candlestick, and the pouring vessels, and a great quantity of spices; and besides these there were among the treasures two thousand talents of sacred money; yet did Pompey touch nothing of all this,* on account of his regard to religion; and in this point also he acted in a manner that was worthy of his virtue. the next day he gave order to those that had the charge of the temple to cleanse it, and to bring what offerings the law required to God; and restored the high priesthood to Hyrcanus, both because he had been useful to him in other respects, and because he had hindered the Jews in the country from giving Aristobulus any assistance in his war with him. He also cut off those that had been the authors of that war; and bestowed proper rewards on Faustus, and those others that mounted the wall with such alacrity; and he made Jerusalem tributary to the Romans; and took away those cities of Cœlesyria which the inhabitants of Judea had subdued, and put them under the government of the Roman president, and confined the whole nation, which had elevated itself so high before, within its own bounds. Moreover, he rebuilt Gadara, which had been demolished a little before, to gratify Demetrius of Gadara, who was his freedman, and restored the rest of the cities, Hippos and Scythopolis, and Pella, and Dios, and Samaria, as also Marissa and Ashdod, and Jamnia, and Arethusa, to their own inhabitants: these were in the inland parts. Besides those that had been demolished, and also of the maritime cities, Gaza, and Joppa, and Dora, and Strato's Tower: which last Herod rebuilt after a glorious manner, and adorned with havens and temples; and changed its name to Cæsarea. All these Pompey left in a state of freedom, and joined them to the province of Syria.

5. Now the occasions of this misery which came upon Jerusalem were Hyrcanus and Aristobulus, by raising a sedition one against the other; for now we lost our liberty, and became subject to the Romans, and were deprived of that country which we had gained by our arms from the Syrians, and were compelled to restore it to the Syrians. Moreover, the Romans exacted of us, in a little time, above ten thousand talents; and the royal authority, which was a dignity formerly bestowed on those that were high priests, by the right of their family, became the property of private men; but of these matters we shall treat in their proper places. Now Pompey committed Cœlesyria, as far as the river Euphrates and Egypt, to Scaurus, with two Roman legions, and then went away to Cilicia, and made haste to Rome. He also carried bound along with him Aristobulus and his children; for he had two daughters, and as many sons; the one of whom ran away; but the younger, Antigonius, was carried to Rome, together with his sisters.

CHAPTER V

HOW SCAURUS MADE A LEAGUE OF MUTUAL ASSISTANCE WITH ARETAS; AND WHAT GABINIUS DID IN JUDEA, AFTER HE HAD CONQUERED ALEXANDER, THE SON OF ARISTOBULUS

1. SCAURUS made now an expedition against Petrea, in Arabia, and set on fire all the places round about it, because of the great difficulty of access to it; and as his army was pinched by fa-

mine, Antipater furnished him with corn out of Judea, and with whatever else he wanted, and this at the command of Hyrcanus; and when he was sent to Aretas as an ambassador, by Scaurus, because he had lived with him formerly, he persuaded Aretas to give Scaurus a sum of money, to prevent the burning of his country; and undertook to be his surety for three hundred talents. So Scaurus, upon these terms, ceased to make war any longer: which was done as much at Scaurus's desire, as at the desire of Aretas.

2. Some time after this, when Alexander, the son of Aristobulus, made an incursion into Judea, Gabinius came from Rome to Syria, as commander of the Roman forces. He did many considerable actions; and particularly made war with Alexander, since Hyrcanus was not yet able to oppose his power, but was already attempting to rebuild the wall of Jerusalem, which Pompey had overthrown, although the Romans who were there restrained him from his design. However, Alexander went over all the country round about, and armed many of the Jews, and suddenly got together ten thousand armed footmen, and fifteen hundred horsemen, and fortified Alexandrium, a fortress near to Coreæ, and Macherus, near the mountains of Arabia. Gabinius therefore came upon him, having sent Marcus Antonius, with other commanders, before. These armed such Romans as followed them; and, together with them, such Jews as were subject to them, whose leaders were Pitholaus and Malichus; and they took with them also their friends that were with Antipater, and met Alexander, while Gabinius himself followed with his legions. Hereupon Alexander retired to the neighbourhood of Jerusalem, where they fell upon one another, and it came to a pitched battle; in which the Romans slew of their enemies about three thousand, and took a like number alive.

3. At which time Gabinius came to Alexandrium, and invited those that were in it to deliver it up on certain conditions, and promised that then their former offences should be forgiven: but as a great number of the enemy had pitched their camp before the fortress, whom the Romans attacked, Marcus Antonius fought bravely, and slew a great number, and seemed to come off with the greatest honour. So Gabinius left part of his army there, in order to take the place, and he himself went into other parts of Judea, and gave order to rebuild all the cities that he met with that had been demolished; at which time were rebuilt Samaria, Ashdod, Scythopolis, Anthedon, Raphia, and Dora; Marissa also, and Gaza, and not a few others besides; and as the men acted according to Gabinius's command, it came to pass, that at this time these cities were securely inhabited, which had been desolate for a long time.

4. When Gabinius had done thus in the country he returned to Alexandrium; and when he urged on the siege of the place, Alexander sent an embassage to him, desiring that he would pardon his former offences; he also delivered up the fortresses Hyrcania and Macherus, and at last Alexandrium itself, which fortresses Gabinius demolished; but when Alexander's mother, who was of the side of the Romans, as having her husband and other children at Rome, came to him, he granted her whatsoever she asked; and when he had settled matters with her, he brought Hyrcanus to Jerusalem, and committed the care of the temple to him; and when he had ordained five councils, he distributed the nation into the same number of parts: so these councils governed the people; the first

---

* This is fully confirmed by the testimony of Cicero.

was at Jerusalem, the second at Gadara, the third at Amathus, the fourth at Jericho, and the fifth at Sepphoris, in Galilee. So the Jews were now freed from monarchic authority, and were governed by an aristocracy.

CHAPTER VI

HOW GABINIUS CAUGHT ARISTOBULUS AFTER HE HAD FLED FROM ROME, AND SENT HIM BACK TO ROME AGAIN; AND HOW THE SAME GABINIUS, AS HE RETURNED OUT OF EGYPT, OVERCAME ALEXANDER AND THE NABATEANS IN BATTLE

1. Now Aristobulus ran away from Rome to Judea, and set about the rebuilding of Alexandrium, which had been newly demolished: hereupon Gabinius sent soldiers against him, and for their commanders Sisenna, and Antonius, and Servilius, in order to hinder him from getting possession of the country, and to take him again; and indeed many of the Jews ran to Aristobulus on account of his former glory, as also because they should be glad of an innovation. Now there was one Pitholaus, a lieutenant at Jerusalem, who deserted to him with a thousand men, although a great number of those that came to him were unarmed; and when Aristobulus had resolved to go to Macherus, he dismissed those people, because they were unarmed; for they could not be useful to him in what actions he was going about; but he took with him eight thousand that were armed, and marched on; and as the Romans fell upon them severely, the Jews fought valiantly, but were beaten in the battle; and when they had fought with alacrity, but were overborne by the enemy, they were put to flight; of whom were slain about five thousand, and the rest being dispersed, tried, as well as they were able, to save themselves. However, Aristobulus had with him still above a thousand, and with them he fled to Macherus, and fortified the place; and though he had an ill success, he still had good hope of his affairs; but when he had struggled against the siege for two days' time, and had received many wounds, he was brought as a captive to Gabinius, with his son Antigonius, who also fled with him from Rome; and this was the fortune of Aristobulus, who was sent back again to Rome, and was there retained in bonds, having been both king and high priest for three years and six months; and was indeed an eminent person, and one of a great soul. However, the senate let his children go, upon Gabinius's writing to them that he had promised their mother so much when she delivered up the fortresses to him; and accordingly they then returned to Jerusalem.

2. Now when Gabinius was making an expedition against the Parthians, and had already passed over Euphrates, he changed his mind, and resolved to return into Egypt, in order to restore Ptolemy to his kingdom.* This hath also been related elsewhere. However, Antipater supplied his army, which he sent against Archelaus, with corn, and weapons, and money. He also made those Jews who were above Pelusium his friends and confederates, and had been the guardians of the passes that led into Egypt. But when he came back out of Egypt, he found

Syria in disorder with seditions and troubles; for Alexander, the son of Aristobulus, having seized on the government a second time by force, made many of the Jews revolt to him; and so he marched over the country with a great army, and slew all the Romans he could light upon, and proceeded to besiege the mountain called Gerizzim, whither they had retreated.

3. But when Gabinius found Syria in such a state, he sent Antipater, who was a prudent man, to those that were seditious, to try whether he could cure them of their madness, and persuade them to return to a better mind; and when he came to them, he brought many of them to a sound mind, and induced them to do what they ought to do. But he could not restrain Alexander, for he had an army of thirty thousand Jews, and met Gabinius, and, joining battle with him, was beaten, and lost ten thousand of his men about mount Tabor.

4. So Gabinius settled the affairs which belonged to the city Jerusalem, as was agreeable to Antipater's inclination, and went against the Nabateans, and overcame them in battle. He also sent away in a friendly manner, Mithridates and Orsanes, who were Parthian deserters, and came to him, though the report went abroad that they had run away from him. And when Gabinius had performed great and glorious actions, in his management of the affairs of the war, he returned to Rome, and delivered the government to Crassus. Now, Nicolaus of Damascus, and Strabo, of Cappadocia, both describe the expeditions of Pompey and Gabinius against the Jews, while neither of them say anything new which is not in the other.

CHAPTER VII

HOW CRASSUS CAME INTO JUDEA, AND PILLAGED THE TEMPLE; AND THEN MARCHED AGAINST THE PARTHIANS, AND PERISHED, WITH HIS ARMY. ALSO HOW CASSIUS OBTAINED SYRIA, AND PUT A STOP TO THE PARTHIANS, AND THEN WENT UP TO JUDEA

1. Now Crassus, as he was going upon his expedition against the Parthians, came into Judea, and carried off the money that was in the temple, which Pompey had left, being two thousand talents, and was disposed to spoil it of all the gold belonging to it, which was eight thousand talents. He also took a beam, which was made of solid beaten gold, of the weight of three hundred minæ, each of which weighed two pounds and a half. It was the priest who was guardian of the sacred treasures, and whose name was Eleazar, that gave him this beam, not out of a wicked design, for he was a good and a righteous man; but being intrusted with the custody of the veils belonging to the temple, which were of admirable beauty, and of very costly workmanship, and hung down from this beam, when he saw that Crassus was busy in gathering money, and was in fear of the entire ornaments of the temple, he gave him this beam of gold as a ransom for the whole, but this not till he had given his oath that he would remove nothing else out of the temple, but be satisfied with this only, which he should give him, being worth ten thousand [shekels.] Now, this beam was contained in a wooden beam that was hollow, but was known to no others; but Eleazar alone knew it; yet did Crassus take away this beam, upon the condition of touching nothing else that belonged to the temple,—and then brake his oath,

* Dr Hudson out of Livy, says, "A. Gabinius, the proconsul, restored Ptolemy to his kingdom of Egypt, and ejected Archelaus, whom they had set up for a king," &c.

and carried away all the gold that was in the temple.

2. And let no one wonder that there was so much wealth in our temple, since all the Jews throughout the habitable earth, and those that worshipped God, nay, even those of Asia and Europe, sent their contributions to it, and this from very ancient times. Nor is the largeness of these sums without its attestation; nor is that greatness owing to our vanity, as raising it without ground to so great a height: but there are many witnesses to it, and particularly Strabo of Cappadocia, who says thus:—"Mithridates sent to Cos, and took the money which queen Cleopatra had deposited there: as also eight hundred talents belonging to the Jews." Now we have no public money but only what appertains to God; and it is evident that the Asian Jews removed this money, out of fear of Mithridates; for it is not probable that those of Judea, who had a strong city and temple, should send their money to Cos; nor is it likely that the Jews who are inhabitants of Alexandria, should do so neither, since they were in no fear of Mithridates. And Strabo himself bears witness to the same thing in another place; that at the same time that Sylla passed over into Greece, in order to fight against Mithridates, he sent Lucullus to put an end to a sedition that our nation, of whom the habitable earth is full, had raised in Cyrene; where he speaks thus:—"There were four classes of men among those of Cyrene; that of citizens, that of husbandmen, the third of strangers, and the fourth of Jews. Now these Jews are already gotten into all cities; and it is hard to find a place in the habitable earth that hath not admitted this tribe of men, and is not possessed by them; and it hath come to pass that Egypt and Cyrene, as having the same governors, and a great number of other nations, imitate their way of living, and maintain great bodies of these Jews in a peculiar manner, and grow up to greater prosperity with them, and make use of the same laws with that nation also. Accordingly, the Jews have places assigned them in Egypt, wherein they inhabit, besides what is peculiarly allotted to this nation at Alexandria, which is a large part of that city. There is also an ethnarch allowed them, who governs the nation, and distributes justice to them, and takes care of their contracts, and of the laws to them belonging, as if he were the ruler of a free republic. In Egypt, therefore, this nation is powerful, because the Jews were originally Egyptians, and because the land wherein they inhabit, since they went thence, is near to Egypt. They also removed into Cyrene, because that this land adjoined to the government of Egypt, as well as does Judea, or rather was formerly under the same government." And this is what Strabo says.

3. So when Crassus had settled all things as he himself pleased, he marched into Parthia, where both he himself and all his army perished, as hath been related elsewhere. But Cassius, as he fled from Rome to Syria, took possession of it, and was an impediment to the Parthians, who, by reason of their victory over Crassus, made incursions upon it: and as he came back to Tyre, he went up into Judea also, and fell upon Taricheæ, and presently took it, and carried about thirty thousand Jews captives; and slew Pitholaus, who succeeded Aristobulus in his seditious practices, and that by the persuasion of Antipater, who proved to have great interest in him, and was at that time in great repute with the Idumeans also: out of which nation he married a wife, who was the daughter of one

of their eminent men, and her name was Cypros, * by whom he had four sons, Phasael and Herod, who was afterwards made king, and Joseph, and Pheroras; and a daughter named Salome. This Antipater cultivated also a friendship and mutual kindness with other potentates, but especially with the king of Arabia, to whom he committed his children, while he fought against Aristobulus. So Cassius removed his camp, and marched to Euphrates, to meet those that were coming to attack him, as hath been related by others.

4. But some time afterwards, Cæsar, when he had taken Rome, and after Pompey and the senate were fled beyond the Ionian Sea, freed Aristobulus from his bonds, and resolved to send him into Syria, and delivered two legions to him, that he might set matters right, as being a potent man in that country: but Aristobulus had no enjoyment of what he hoped for from the power that was given him by Cæsar; for those of Pompey's party prevented it, and destroyed him by poison; and those of Cæsar's party buried him. His dead body also lay, for a good while, embalmed in honey, till Antony afterwards sent it to Judea, and caused him to be buried in the royal sepulchre. But Scipio, upon Pompey's sending to him to slay Alexander, the son of Aristobulus, because the young man was accused of what offences he had been guilty of at first against the Romans, cut off his head; and thus did he die at Antioch. But Ptolemy, the son of Menneus, who was the ruler of Chalcis, under Mount Libanus, took his brethren to him, and sent his son Philippion to Askelon to Aristobulus's wife, and desired her to send back with him her son Antigonus and her daughters: the one of whom, whose name was Alexandra, Philippion fell in love with, and married her; though afterwards his father Ptolemy slew him, and married Alexandra, and continued to take care of her brethren.

CHAPTER VIII

THE JEWS BECOME CONFEDERATES WITH CÆSAR WHEN HE FOUGHT AGAINST EGYPT; THE GLORIOUS ACTIONS OF ANTIPATER, AND HIS FRIENDSHIP WITH CÆSAR; THE HONOURS WHICH THE JEWS RECEIVED FROM THE ROMANS AND ATHENIANS

1. Now after Pompey was dead, and after that victory Cæsar had gained over him, Antipater, who managed the Jewish affairs, became very useful to Cæsar when he made war against Egypt, and that by the order of Hyrcanus; for when Mithridates of Pergamus was bringing his auxiliaries, and was not able to continue his march through Pelusium, but obliged to stay at Askelon, Antipater came to him, conducting three thousand of the Jews, armed men: he had also taken care the principal men of the Arabians should come to his assistance; and on his account it was that all the Syrians assisted him also, as not willing to appear behindhand in their alacrity for Cæsar—viz., Jamblicus the ruler, and Ptolemy his son, and Tholomy the son of Sohemus, who dwelt at mount Libanus, and almost all the cities. So Mithridates marched out of Syria, and came to Pelusium;

---

* Dr Hudson observes, that this name was Cypros, as a Hebrew termination; but not Cypris, the Greek name for Venus, as some critics were ready to correct it.

and when its inhabitants would not admit him, he besieged the city. Now Antipater signalised himself here, and was the first who plucked down a part of the wall, and so opened a way to the rest, whereby they might enter the city, and by this means Pelusium was taken. But it happened that the Egyptian Jews, who dwelt in the country called Onion, would not let Antipater and Mithridates, with their soldiers, pass to Cæsar; but Antipater persuaded them to come over to their party, because he was of the same people with them, and that chiefly by shewing them the epistles of Hyrcanus the high priest, wherein he exhorted them to cultivate friendship with Cæsar; and to supply his army with money, and all sorts of provisions which they wanted; and accordingly, when they saw Antipater and the high priest of the same sentiments, they did as they were desired. And when the Jews about Memphis heard that these Jews were come over to Cæsar, they also invited Mithridates to come to them; so he came and received them also into his army.

2. And when Mithridates had gone over all Delta, as the place is called, he came to a pitched battle with the enemy, near the place called the Jewish Camp. Now Mithridates had the right wing, and Antipater the left; and when it came to fight, that wing where Mithridates was gave way, and was likely to suffer extremely, unless Antipater had come running to him with his own soldiers along the shore, when he had already beaten the enemy that opposed him; so he delivered Mithridates, and put those Egyptians who had been too hard for him to flight. He also took their camp, and continued in the pursuit of them. He also recalled Mithridates, who had been worsted, and was retired a great way off, of whose soldiers eight hundred fell; but of Antipater's fifty. So Mithridates sent an account of this battle to Cæsar, and openly declared that Antipater was the author of this victory, and of his own preservation; insomuch that Cæsar commended Antipater then, and made use of him all the rest of that war in the most hazardous undertakings: he also happened to be wounded in one of those engagements.

3. However, when Cæsar, after some time, had finished that war, and was sailed away for Syria, he honoured Antipater greatly, and confirmed Hyrcanus in the high priesthood; and bestowed on Antipater the privilege of a citizen of Rome, and a freedom from taxes everywhere; and it is reported by many, that Hyrcanus went along with Antipater in this expedition, and came himself into Egypt. And Strabo of Cappadocia bears witness to this, when he says thus, in the name of Asinius:—"After Mithridates had invaded Egypt, and with him Hyrcanus the high priest of the Jews." Nay, the same Strabo says thus again, in another place, in the name of Hypsicrates, that "Mithridates at first went out alone; but that Antipater, who had the care of the Jewish affairs, was called by him to Askelon, and that he had gotten ready three thousand soldiers to go along with him, and encouraged other governors of the country to go along with him also; and that Hyrcanus the high priest was also present in this expedition." This is what Strabo says.

4. But Antigonus, the son of Aristobulus, came at this time to Cæsar, and lamented his father's fate: and complained, that it was by Antipater's means that Aristobulus was taken off by poison, and his brother was beheaded by Scipio, and desired that he would take pity of him who had been ejected out of that principality which was due to him. He also accused Hyrcanus and Antipater as governing the nation by violence, and offering injuries to himself. Antipater was present, and made his defence as to the accusations that were laid against him. He demonstrated, that Antigonus and his party were given to innovation, and were seditious persons. He also put Cæsar in mind what difficult services he had undergone when he assisted him in his wars, and discoursed about what he was a witness of himself. He added, that Aristobulus was justly carried away to Rome, as one that was an enemy to the Romans, and could never be brought to be a friend to them, and that his brother had no more than he deserved from Scipio, as being seized in committing robberies; and that this punishment was not inflicted on him in a way of violence or injustice by him that did it.

5. When Antipater had made this speech, Cæsar appointed Hyrcanus to be high priest, and gave Antipater what principality he himself should choose, leaving the determination to himself; so he made him procurator of Judea. He also gave Hyrcanus leave to raise up the walls of his own city, upon his asking that favour of him, for they had been demolished by Pompey. And this grant he sent to the consuls of Rome, to be engraven in the capitol. The decree of the senate was this that follows:* "Lucius Valerius, the son of Lucius the prætor, referred this to the senate, upon the Ides of December, in the temple of Concord. There were present at the writing of this decree Lucius Coponius, the son of Lucius of the Colline tribe, and Papirius of the Quirine tribe, concerning the affairs which Alexander the son of Jason, and Numenius the son of Antiochus, and Alexander the son of Dositheus, ambassadors of the Jews, good and worthy men, proposed, who came to renew that league of good-will and friendship with the Romans which was in being before. They also brought a shield of gold, as a mark of confederacy, valued at fifty thousand pieces of gold; and desired that letters might be given them, directed both to the free cities and to the kings, that their country and their havens might be at peace, and that no one among them might receive any injury. It therefore pleased [the senate] to make a league of friendship and good-will with them, and to bestow on them whatsoever they stood in need of, and to accept of the shield which was brought by them. This was done in the ninth year of Hyrcanus the high priest and ethnarch, in the month Panemus." Hyrcanus also received honours from the people of Athens, as having been useful to them on many occasions; and when they wrote to him, they sent him this decree, as it here follows:— "Under the prutaneia and priesthood of Dionysius, the son of Esculapius, on the fifth day of the latter part of the month Panemus, this decree of the Athenians was given to their commanders, when Agathocles was archon, and Eucles, the

---

* Dr Hudson's note upon this place:—"Here is some mistake in Josephus; for when he had promised us a decree for the restoration of Jerusalem, he brings in a decree of far greater antiquity, and that a league of friendship and union only. One may easily believe that Josephus gave order for one thing, and his amanuensis performed another, by transposing decrees that concerned the Hyrcani, and as deluded by the sameness of their names; for that belongs to the first high priest of this name, [John Hyrcanus,] which Josephus here ascribes to one that lived later, [Hyrcanus, the son of Alexander Janneus.] However, the decree which he proposes to set down follows a little lower, in the collection of Roman decrees that concerned the Jews, and is that dated when Cæsar was consul the fifth time."

son of Menander of Alimusia, was the scribe. In the month Munychion, on the eleventh day of the Prutaneia, a council of the presidents was held in the theatre. Dorotheus the high priest, and the fellow-presidents with him, put it to the vote of the people. Dionysius, the son of Dionysius, gave the sentence. Since Hyrcanus, the son of Alexander, the high priest and ethnarch of the Jews, continues to bear good-will to our people in general, and to every one of our citizens in particular, and treats them with all sorts of kindness; and when any of the Athenians come to him, either as ambassadors, or on any occasion of their own, he receives them in an obliging manner, and sees that they are conducted back in safety, of which we have had several former testimonies: it is now also decreed, at the report of Theodosius, the son of Theodorus, and upon his putting the people in mind of the virtue of this man, and that his purpose is to do us all the good that is in his power, to honour him with a crown of gold, the usual reward according to the law, and to erect his statue in brass in the temple of Demus and of the Graces; and that this present of a crown shall be proclaimed publicly in the theatre, in the Dionysian shows, while the new tragedies are acting; and in the Panathenean, and Eleusinian, and Gymnical shows also; and that the commanders shall take care, while he continues in his friendship, and preserves his good-will to us, to return all possible honour and favour to the man for his affection and generosity; that by this treatment it may appear how our people receive the good kindly, and repay them a suitable reward; and he may be induced to proceed in his affection towards us, by the honours we have already paid him. That ambassadors be also chosen out of all the Athenians, who shall carry this decree to him, and desire him to accept the honours we do him, and to endeavour always to be doing some good to our city." And this shall suffice us to have spoken as to the honours that were paid by the Romans and by the people of Athens to Hyrcanus.

CHAPTER IX

HOW ANTIPATER COMMITTED THE CARE OF GALILEE TO HEROD, AND THAT OF JERUSALEM TO PHASAELUS; AS ALSO, HOW HEROD, UPON THE JEWS' ENVY AT ANTIPATER, WAS ACCUSED BEFORE HYRCANUS

1. Now when Cæsar had settled the affairs of Syria, he sailed away; and as soon as Antipater had conducted Cæsar out of Syria, he returned to Judea. He then immediately raised up the wall which had been thrown down by Pompey; and, by coming thither, he pacified that tumult which had been in the country, and this by both threatening and advising them to be quiet; for that, if they would be of Hyrcanus's side, they would live happily, and lead their lives without disturbance, in the enjoyment of their own possessions; but if they were addicted to the hopes of what might come by innovation, and aimed to get wealth thereby, they should have him a severe master, instead of a gentle governor, and Hyrcanus a tyrant instead of a king, and the Romans, together with Cæsar, their bitter enemies, instead of rulers, for that they would never bear him to be set aside whom they had appointed to govern. And when Antipater had said this to them, he himself settled the affairs of this country.

2. And seeing that Hyrcanus was of a slow and slothful temper, he made Phasaelus, his eldest son, governor of Jerusalem, and of the places that were about it, but committed Galilee to Herod, his next son, who was then a very young man, for he was but twenty-five years of age; but that youth of his was no impediment to him; but as he was a youth of great mind, he presently met with an opportunity of signalising his courage; for, finding there was one Hezekias, a captain of a band of robbers, who overran the neighbouring ports of Syria with a great troop of them, he seized him and slew him, as well as a great number of the other robbers that were with him; for which action he was greatly beloved by the Syrians; for when they were very desirous to have their country freed from this nest of robbers, he purged it of them: so they sung songs in his commendation in their villages and cities, as having procured them peace and the secure enjoyment of their possessions: and on this account it was that he became known to Sextus Cæsar, who was a relation of the great Cæsar, and was now president of Syria. Now Phasaelus, Herod's brother, was moved with emulation at his actions, and envied the fame he had thereby gotten, and became ambitious not to be behindhand with him in deserving it: so he made the inhabitants of Jerusalem bear him the greatest good-will while he held the city himself, but did neither manage its affairs improperly, nor abuse his authority therein. This conduct procured from the nation to Antipater such respect as is due to kings, and such honours as he might partake of if he were an absolute lord of the country. Yet did not this splendour of his, as frequently happens, in the least diminish in him that kindness and fidelity which he owed to Hyrcanus.

3. But now the principal men among the Jews, when they saw Antipater and his sons to grow so much in the good-will the nation bare to them, and in the revenues which they received out of Judea, and out of Hyrcanus's own wealth, they became ill-disposed to him; for indeed Antipater had contracted a friendship with the Roman emperors; and when he had prevailed with Hyrcanus to send them money, he took it to himself, and purloined the present intended, and sent it as if it were his own, and not Hyrcanus's gift to them. Hyrcanus heard of this management, but took no care about it; nay, he rather was glad of it: but the chief men of the Jews were therefore in fear, because they saw that Herod was a violent and bold man, and very desirous of acting tyrannically; so they came to Hyrcanus, and now accused Antipater openly, and said to him, "How long wilt thou be quiet under such actions as are now done? Or dost thou not see that Antipater and his sons have already seized upon the government, and that it is only the name of a king which is given thee? But do not thou suffer these things to be hidden from thee; nor do thou think to escape danger by being so careless of thyself and of thy kingdom; for Antipater and his sons are not now stewards of thine affairs; do not thou deceive thyself with such a notion; they are evidently absolute lords; for Herod, Antipater's son, hath slain Hezekiah and those that were with him, and hath thereby transgressed our law, which hath forbidden to slay any man, even though he were a wicked man, unless he had been first condemned to suffer death by the Sanhedrim,* yet hath he been

---

* None could be put to death in Judea but by the approbation of the Jewish Sanhedrim, there being an excellent provision in the law of Moses, that even in

so insolent as to do this, and that without any authority from thee."

4. Upon Hyrcanus hearing this, he complied with them. The mothers also of those who had been slain by Herod raised his indignation; for those women continued every day in the temple, persuading the king and the people that Herod might undergo a trial before the Sanhedrim for what he had done. Hyrcanus was so moved by these complaints, that he summoned Herod to come to his trial for what was charged upon him. Accordingly he came; but his father had persuaded him to come not like a private man, but with a guard, for the security of his person; and that when he had settled the affairs of Galilee in the best manner he could for his own advantage, he should come to his trial, but still with a body of men sufficient for his security on his journey, yet so that he should not come with so great a force as might look like terrifying Hyrcanus, but still such a one as might not expose him naked and unguarded [to his enemies.] However, Sextus Cæsar, president of Syria, wrote to Hyrcanus, and desired him to clear Herod, and dismiss him at his trial, and threatened him beforehand if he did not do it. Which epistle of his was the occasion of Hyrcanus delivering Herod from suffering any harm from the Sanhedrim, for he loved him as his own son; but when Herod stood before the Sanhedrim, with his body of men about him, he affrighted them all, and no one of his former accusers durst after that bring any charge against him, but there was a deep silence, and nobody knew what was to be done. When affairs stood thus, one whose name was Sameas,* a righteous man he was, and for that reason above all fear, rose up, and said, "O you that are assessors with me, and O thou that art our king, I neither have ever myself known such a case, nor do I suppose that any one of you can name its parallel, that one who is called to take his trial by us ever stood in such a manner before us; but every one, whosoever he be, that comes to be tried by this Sanhedrim, presents himself in a submissive manner, and like one that is in fear of himself, and that endeavours to move our compassion, with his hair dishevelled, and in a black and mourning garment; but this admirable man Herod, who is accused of murder, and called to answer so heavy an accusation, stands here clothed in purple, and with the hair of his head finely trimmed, and with his armed men about him, that if we shall condemn him by our law, he may slay us, and by overbearing justice may himself escape death; yet do not I make this complaint against Herod himself: he is to be sure more concerned for himself than for the laws; but my complaint is against yourselves and your king, who give him a licence so to do. However, take you notice, that God is great, and that this very man, whom you are going to absolve and dismiss, for the sake of Hyrcanus, will one day punish both you and your king himself also." Nor did Sameas mistake in any part of this prediction; for when Herod had received the kingdom, he slew all the members of this Sanhedrim, and Hyrcanus himself also, excepting Sameas, for he had a great honour for him on account of his righteousness, and because, when the city was afterwards besieged by Herod and Sosius, he persuaded the people to admit Herod into it; and told them, that for their sins they would not be able to escape his hands:—which things will be related by us in their proper places.

5. But when Hyrcanus saw that the members of the Sanhedrim were ready to pronounce the sentence of death upon Herod, he put off the trial to another day, and sent privately to Herod, and advised him to fly out of the city; for that by this means he might escape. So he retired to Damascus, as though he fled from the king; and when he had been with Sextus Cæsar, and had put his own affairs in a sure posture, he resolved to do thus:—That in case he were again summoned before the Sanhedrim to take his trial, he would not obey that summons. Hereupon the members of the Sanhedrim had great indignation at this posture of affairs, and endeavoured to persuade Hyrcanus that all these things were against him; which state of matters he was not ignorant of; but his temper was so unmanly and so foolish, that he was able to do nothing at all; but when Sextus had made Herod general of the army of Cœlesyria, for he sold him that post for money, Hyrcanus was in fear lest Herod should make war upon him; nor was the effect of what he feared long in coming upon him,— for Herod came, and brought an army along with him to fight with Hyrcanus, as being angry at the trial he had been summoned to undergo before the Sanhedrim; but his father Antipater, and his brother [Phasaelus] met him, and hindered him from assaulting Jerusalem; they also pacified his vehement temper, and persuaded him to do no overt action, but only to affright them with threatenings, and to proceed no further against one who had given him the dignity he had: they also desired him not only to be angry that he was summoned, and obliged to come to his trial, but to remember withal how he was dismissed without condemnation, and how he ought to give Hyrcanus thanks for the same; and that he was not to regard only what was disagreeable to him, and be unthankful for his deliverance. So they desired him to consider, that since it is God that turns the scales of war, there is great uncertainty in the issue of battles, and that therefore he ought not to expect the victory when he should fight with his king, and him that had supported him, and bestowed many benefits upon him, and had done nothing of itself very severe to him; for that his accusation, which was derived from evil counsellors, and not from himself, had rather the suspicion of some severity, than anything really severe in it. Herod was persuaded by these arguments, and believed that it was sufficient for his future hopes to have made a show of his strength before the nation, and done no more to it;—and in this state were the affairs of Judea at this time.

CHAPTER X

THE HONOURS THAT WERE PAID THE JEWS; AND THE LEAGUES THAT WERE MADE BY THE ROMANS, AND OTHER NATIONS, WITH THEM

1. Now when Cæsar was come to Rome, he was ready to sail into Africa to fight against Scipio and Cato, when Hyrcanus sent ambassadors to him, and by them desired that he would ratify that league of friendship and mutual alliance which was between them; and it seems to

---

criminal causes, and particularly where life was concerned, an appeal should lie from the lesser councils of seven in the other cities, to the supreme council of seventy-one at Jerusalem; and this is exactly according to our Saviour's words, when he says, "It could not be that a prophet should perish out of Jerusalem," (Luke xiii. 33.)

* This account, Reland observes, is confirmed by the Talmudists, who call this Sameas "Simeon the son of Shetach."

me to be necessary here to give an account of all the honours that the Romans and their emperors paid to our nation, and of the leagues of mutual assistance they have made with it, that all the rest of mankind may know what regard the kings of Asia and Europe have had to us, and that they have been abundantly satisfied of our courage and fidelity; for whereas many will not believe what hath been written about us by the Persians and Macedonians, because those writings are not everywhere to be met with, nor do lie in public places, but among us ourselves, and certain other barbarous nations, while there is no contradiction to be made against the decrees of the Romans, for they are laid up in the public places of the cities, and are extant still in the capitol, and engraven upon pillars of brass; nay, besides this, Julius Cæsar made a pillar of brass for the Jews at Alexandria, and declared publicly that they were citizens of Alexandria. Out of these evidences will I demonstrate what I say; and will now set down the decrees made both by the senate and by Julius Cæsar, which relate to Hyrcanus and to our nation.

2. "Caius Julius Cæsar, imperator and high priest, and dictator the second time, to the magistrates, senate, and people of Sidon, sendeth greeting. If you be in health, it is well. I also and the army are well. I have sent you a copy of that decree, registered on the tables, which concerns Hyrcanus, the son of Alexander, the high priest and ethnarch of the Jews, that it may be laid up among the public records; and I will that it be openly proposed in a table of brass, both in Greek and in Latin. It is as follows:—I Julius Cæsar, imperator the second time, and high priest, have made this decree, with the approbation of the senate: Whereas Hyrcanus, the son of Alexander the Jew, hath demonstrated his fidelity and diligence about our affairs, and this both now and in former times, both in peace and in war, as many of our generals have borne witness, and came to our assistance in the Alexandrian war, with fifteen hundred soldiers; and when he was sent up by me to Mithridates, shewed himself superior in valour to all the rest of that army;—for these reasons I will that Hyrcanus, the son of Alexander, and his children be ethnarchs of the Jews, and have the high priesthood of the Jews forever, according to the customs of their forefathers, and that he and his son be our confederates; and that besides this, every one of them be reckoned among our particular friends. I also ordain, that he and his children retain whatsoever privileges belong to the office of high priest, or whatsoever favours have been hitherto granted them; and if at any time hereafter there arise any questions about the Jewish customs, I will that he determine the same; and I think it not proper that they should be obliged to find us winter quarters, or that any money should be required of them."

3. "The decrees of Caius Cæsar, consul, containing what hath been granted and determined, are as follow:—That Hyrcanus and his children bear rule over the nation of the Jews, and have the profits of the places to them bequeathed; and that he, as himself the high priest and ethnarch of the Jews, defend those that are injured; and that ambassadors be sent to Hyrcanus, the son of Alexander the high priest of the Jews, that may discourse with him about a league of friendship and mutual assistance; and that a table of brass, containing the premises, be openly proposed in the capitol, and at Sidon, and Tyre, and Askelon, and in the temple, engraven in Roman and Greek letters: that this decree may

also be communicated to the quæstors and prætors of the several cities, and to the friends of the Jews: and that the ambassadors may have presents made them, and that these decrees be sent everywhere."

4. "Caius Cæsar, imperator, dictator, consul, hath granted, That out of regard to the honour, and virtue, and kindness of the man, and for the advantage of the senate, and of the people of Rome, Hyrcanus, the son of Alexander, both he and his children, be high priests and priests of Jerusalem, and of the Jewish nation, by the same right, and according to the same laws, by which their progenitors have held the priesthood."

5. "Caius Cæsar, consul the fifth time, hath decreed, that the Jews shall possess Jerusalem, and may encompass that city with walls; and that Hyrcanus, the son of Alexander, the high priest and ethnarch of the Jews, retain it, in the manner he himself pleases; and the Jews be allowed to deduct out of their tribute, every second year the land is let, [in the Sabbatic period,] a corus of that tribute; and that the tribute they pay be not let to farm, nor that they pay always the same tribute."

6. "Caius Cæsar, imperator the second time, hath ordained, That all the country of the Jews, excepting Joppa, do pay a tribute yearly for the city of Jerusalem, excepting the seventh, which they call the Sabbatical Year, because thereon they neither receive the fruits of their trees, nor do they sow their land; and that they pay their tribute to Sidon on the second year [of that Sabbatic period,] the fourth part of what was sown: and besides this, they are to pay the same tithes to Hyrcanus and his sons which they paid to their forefathers. And that no one, neither president nor lieutenant, nor ambassador, raise auxiliaries within the bounds of Judea, nor may soldiers exact money of them for winter quarters, or under any other pretence, but that they be free from all sorts of injuries: and that whatsoever they shall hereafter have, and are in possession of, or have bought, they shall retain them all. It is also our pleasure that the city Joppa, which the Jews had originally, when they made a league of friendship with the Romans, shall belong to them, as it formerly did; and that Hyrcanus, the son of Alexander, and his sons, have as tribute of that city, from those that occupy the land, for the country, and for what they export every year to Sidon, twenty thousand six hundred and seventy-five modii every year, the seventh year, which they call they Sabbatic Year, excepted; whereon they neither plough, nor receive the product of their trees. It is also the pleasure of the senate, that as to the villages which are in the great plain, which Hyrcanus and his forefathers formerly possessed, Hyrcanus and the Jews have them, with the same privileges with which they formerly had them also; and that the same original ordinances remain still in force which concern the Jews with regard to their high priests; and that they enjoy the same benefits which they have had formerly by the concession of the people, and of the senate; and let them enjoy the like privileges in Lydda. It is the pleasure also of the senate, that Hyrcanus the ethnarch, and the Jews, retain those places, countries, and villages, which belonged to the kings of Syria and Phœnicia, the confederates of the Romans, and which they had bestowed on them as their free gifts. It is also granted to Hyrcanus, and to his sons, and to the ambassadors by them sent to us, that in the fights between single gladiators, and in those with beasts,

they shall sit among the senators to see those shows; and that when they desire an audience, they shall be introduced into the senate by the dictator, or by the general of the horse; and when they have introduced them, their answers shall be returned them in ten days at the furthest, after the decree of the senate is made about their affairs."

7. "Caius Cæsar, imperator, dictator the fourth time, and consul the fifth time, declared to be perpetual dictator, made this speech concerning the rights and privileges of Hyrcanus, the son of Alexander, the high priest and ethnarch of the Jews. Since those imperators * that have been in the provinces before me have borne witness to Hyrcanus the high priest of the Jews, and to the Jews themselves, and this before the senate and people of Rome, when the people and senate returned their thanks to them, it is good that we now also remember the same, and provide that a requital be made to Hyrcanus, to the nation of the Jews, and to the sons of Hyrcanus, by the senate and people of Rome, and that suitably to what good will they have shewn us, and to the benefits they have bestowed upon us."

8. "Julius Caius, prætor [consul] of Rome, to the magistrates, senate, and people of the Parians, sendeth greeting. The Jews of Delos, and some other Jews that sojourn there, in the presence of your ambassadors, signified to us, that, by a decree of yours, you forbid them to make use of the customs of their forefathers, and their way of sacred worship. Now it does not please me that such decrees should be made against our friends and confederates, whereby they are forbidden to live according to their own customs, or to bring in contributions for common suppers and holy festivals, while they are not forbidden so to do even at Rome itself; for even Caius Cæsar, our imperator and consul, in that decree wherein he forbade the Bacchanal rioters to meet in the city, did yet permit these Jews, and these only, both to bring in their contributions, and to make their common suppers. Accordingly, when I forbid other Bacchanal rioters, I permit these Jews to gather themselves together, according to the customs and laws of their forefathers, and to persist therein. It will be therefore good for you, that if you have made any decree against these our friends and confederates, to abrogate the same, by reason of their virtue, and kind disposition towards us."

9. Now after Caius was slain, when Marcus Antonius and Publius Dolabella were consuls, they both assembled the senate, and introduced Hyrcanus's ambassadors into it, and discoursed of what they desired, and made a league of friendship with them. The senate also decreed to grant them all they desired. I add the decree itself, that those who read the present work may have ready by them a demonstration of the truth of what we say. The decree was this:—

10. The decree of the senate, copied out of the treasury, from the public tables belonging to the quæstors, when Quintus Rutilius and Caius Cornelius were quæstors, and taken out of the second table of the first class, on the third day before the ides of April, in the temple of Concord. There were present at the writing of this decree, Lucius Calpurnius Piso, of the Menenian tribe; Servius Papinias Potitus, of the Lemonian

tribe; Caius Caninius Rebilius, of the Terentine tribe; Publius Tidetius, Lucius Apulinus, the son of Lucius, of the Sergian tribe; Flavius, the son of Lucius, of the Lemonian tribe; Publius Platius, the son of Publius, of the Papyrian tribe; Marcus Acilius, the son of Marcus, of the Mecian tribe; Lucius Erucius, the son of Lucius, of the Stellatine tribe; Marcus Quintus Plancillus, the son of Marcus, of the Pollian tribe; and Publius Serius. Publius Dolabella and Marcus Antonius, the consuls, made this reference to the senate, that as to those things which, by the decree of the senate, Caius Cæsar had adjudged about the Jews, and yet had not hitherto that decree been brought into the treasury, it is our will, as it is also the desire of Publius Dolabella and Marcus Antonius, our consuls, to have these decrees put into the public tables, and brought to the city quæstors, that they may take care to have them put upon the double tables. This was done before the fifth of the ides of February, in the temple of Concord. Now the ambassadors from Hyrcanus the high priest were these:—Lysimachus, the son of Pausanias; Alexander, the son of Theodorus; Patroclus, the son of Chereas; and Jonathan, the son of Onias.

11. Hyrcanus sent also one of these ambassadors to Dolabella, who was then the prefect of Asia, and desired him to dismiss the Jews from military services, and to preserve to them the customs of their forefathers, and to permit them to live according to them. And when Dolabella had received Hyrcanus's letter, without any further deliberation, he sent an epistle to all the Asiatics, and particularly to the city of the Ephesians, the metropolis of Asia, about the Jews; a copy of which epistle here follows:—

12. "When Artemon was prytanis, on the first day of the month Leneon, Dolabella, imperator, to the senate and magistrates, and people of the Ephesians, sendeth greeting. Alexander, the son of Theodorus, the ambassador of Hyrcanus, the son of Alexander, the high priest and ethnarch of the Jews, appeared before me, to shew that his countrymen could not go into their armies, because they are not allowed to bear arms, or to travel on the Sabbath-days, nor there to procure themselves those sorts of food which they have been used to eat from the times of their forefathers,—I do therefore grant them a freedom from going into the army, as the former prefects have done, and permit them to use the customs of their forefathers, in assembling together for sacred and religious purposes, as their law requires, and for collecting oblations necessary for sacrifices; and my will is, that you write this to the several cities under your jurisdiction."

13. And these were the concessions that Dolabella made to our nation when Hyrcanus sent an embassage to him; but Lucius the consul's decree ran thus:—"I have at my tribunal set these Jews, who are citizens of Rome, and follow the Jewish religious rites, and yet live at Ephesus, free from going into the army, on account of the superstition they are under. This was done before the twelfth of the calends of October, when Lucius Lentulus and Caius Marcellus were consuls, in the presence of Titus Appius Balgus, the son of Titus and lieutenant of the Horatian tribe; of Titus Tongius, the son of Titus, of the Crustumine tribe; of Quintus Resius, the son of Quintus; of Titus Pompeius Longinus, the son of Titus; of Caius Servilius, the son of Caius, of the Terentine tribe; of Bracchus the military tribune; of Publius Lucius Gallus, the son of Publius, of the Veturian tribe; of Caius Sentius, the son of Caius, of the Sabbatine tribe; of

---

* Dr Hudson supposes that the Roman imperators, or generals of armies, here, were principally Pompey, Scaurus, and Gabinius.

Titus Atilius Bulbus, the son of Titus, lieutenant and vice-prætor to the magistrates, senate, and people of the Ephesians, sendeth greeting. Lucius Lentulus the consul freed the Jews that are in Asia from going into the armies, at my intercession for them; and when I had made the same petition some time afterward to Phanius the imperator, and to Lucius Antonius the vice-quæstor, I obtained the privilege of them also; and my will is, that you take care that no one give them any disturbance."

14. The decree of the Delians. "The answer of the prætors, when Beotus was archon, on the twentieth day of the month Thargeleon. While Marcus Piso the lieutenant lived in our city, who was also appointed over the choice of the soldiers, he called us, and many other of the citizens, and gave order, that if there be here any Jews who are Roman citizens, no one is to give them any disturbance about going into the army, because Cornelius Lentulus, the consul, freed the Jews from going into the army, on account of the superstition they are under,—you are therefore obliged to submit to the prætor:"—and the like decree was made by the Sardians about us also.

15. "Caius Phanius, the son of Caius, imperator and consul, to the magistrates of Cos, sendeth greeting. I would have you know that the ambassadors of the Jews have been with me, and desired they might have those decrees which the senate had made about them: which decrees are here subjoined. My will is, that you have a regard to and take care of these men, according to the senate's decree, that they may be safely conveyed home through your country."

16. The declaration of Lucius Lentulus the consul :—"I have dismissed those Jews who are Roman citizens, and who appear to me to have their religious rites, and to observe the laws of the Jews at Ephesus, on account of the superstition they are under. This act was done before the thirteenth of the calends of October."

17. "Lucius Antonius, the son of Marcus, vice-quæstor, and vice-prætor, to the magistrates, senate, and people of the Sardians, sendeth greeting. Those Jews that are our fellow-citizens of Rome, came to me, and demonstrated that they had an assembly of their own, according to the laws of their forefathers, and this from the beginning, as also a place of their own, wherein they determined their suits and controversies with one another. Upon their petition therefore to me, that these might be lawful for them, I give order that these their privileges be preserved, and they be permitted to do accordingly."

18. The declaration of Marcus Publius, the son of Spurius, and of Marcus, the son of Marcus, and of Lucius, the son of Publius :—"We went to the proconsul, and informed him of what Dositheus, the son of Cleopatrida of Alexandria, desired, that, if he thought good, he would dismiss those Jews who were Roman citizens, and were wont to observe the rites of the Jewish religion, on account of the superstition they were under. Accordingly he did dismiss them. This was done before the thirteenth of the calends of October."

19. "In the month Quintilis, when Lucius Lentulus and Caius Marcellus were consuls; and there were present Titus Appius Balbus, the son of Titus, lieutenant of the Horatian tribe; Titus Tongius of the Crustumine tribe; Quintus Resius, the son of Quintus, Titus Pompeius, the son of Titus, Cornelius Longinus, Caius Servilius Bracchus, the son of Caius, a military tribune, of the Terentine tribe; Publius Clusius Gallus,

the son of Publius, of the Veturian tribe; Caius Tentius, the son of Caius, a military tribune, of the Emilian tribe; Sextus Atilius Serranus, the son of Sextus, of the Esquiline tribe; Caius Pompeius, the son of Caius, of the Sabbatine tribe, Titus Appius Menander, the son of Titus, Publius Servilius Strabo, the son of Publius, Lucius Paccius Capito, the son of Lucius of the Colline tribe; Aulus Furius Tertius, the son of Aulus, and Appius Menas. In the presence of these it was that Lentulus pronounced this decree : I have before the tribunal dismissed those Jews that are Roman citizens, and are accustomed to observe the sacred rites of the Jews at Ephesus, on account of the superstition they are under."

20. "The magistrates of the Laodiceans to Caius Rubilius, the son of Caius, the consul, sendeth greeting. Sopater, the ambassador of Hyrcanus the high priest, hath delivered us an epistle from thee, whereby he lets us know that certain ambassadors were come from Hyrcanus, the high priest of the Jews, and brought an epistle written concerning their nation, wherein they desire that the Jews may be allowed to observe their Sabbaths and other sacred rites, according to the laws of their forefathers, and that they may be under no command, because they are our friends and confederates; and that nobody may injure them in our province. Now although the Trallians there present contradicted them, and were not pleased with these decrees, yet didst thou give order that they should be observed, and informed us that thou hadst been desired to write this to us about them. We therefore, in obedience to the injunctions we have received from thee, have received the epistle which thou sentest us, and have laid it up by itself among our public records; and as to the other things about which thou didst send to us, we will take care that no complaint be made against us."

21. "Publius Servilius, the son of Publius, of the Galban tribe, the proconsul, to the magistrates, senate, and people of the Milesians, sendeth greeting. Prytanes, the son of Hermes, a citizen of yours, came to me when I was at Tralles, and held a court there, and informed me that you used the Jews in a way different from my opinion, and forbade them to celebrate their Sabbaths, and to perform the sacred rites received from their forefathers, and to manage the fruits of the earth according to their ancient custom; and that he had himself been the promulger of your decree, according as your laws require; I would therefore have you know, that upon hearing the pleadings on both sides, I gave sentence that the Jews should not be prohibited to make use of their own customs."

22. The decree of those of Pergamus :—"When Cratippus was prytanis, on the first day of the month Desius, the decree of the prætors was this : Since the Romans, following the conduct of their ancestors, undertake dangers for the common safety of all mankind, and are ambitious to settle their confederates and their friends in happiness, and in firm peace, and since the nation of the Jews, and their high priest Hyrcanus, sent as ambassadors to them, Strato, the son of Theodatus, and Apollonius, the son of Alexander, and Eneas, the son of Antipater, and Aristobulus, the son of Amyntas, and Sosipater, the son of Philip, worthy and good men, who gave a particular account of their affairs, the senate thereupon made a decree about what they had desired of them, that Antiochus the king, the son of Antiochus, should do no injury to the Jews, the confederates of the Romans; and that the fortresses and the havens, and the country,

and whatever else he had taken from them, should be restored to them; and that it may be lawful for them to export their goods out of their own havens; and that no king nor people may have leave to export any goods, either out of the country of Júdea, or out of their havens, without paying customs, but only Ptolemy, the king of Alexandria, because he is our confederate and friend: and that, according to their desire, the garrison that is in Joppa may be ejected. Now Lucius Pettius, one of our senators, a worthy and good man, gave order that we should take care that these things should be done according to the senate's decree; and that we should take care also that their ambassadors might return home in safety. Accordingly we admitted Theodorus into our senate and assembly, and took the epistle out of his hands, as well as the decree of the senate: and as he discoursed with great zeal about the Jews, and described Hyrcanus's virtue and generosity, and how he was a benefactor to all men in common, and particularly to everybody that comes to him, we laid up the epistle in our public records; and made a decree ourselves, that since we also are in confederacy with the Romans, we would do everything we could for the Jews, according to the senate's decree. Theodorus also, who brought the epistle, desired of our prætors, that they would send Hyrcanus a copy of that decree, as also ambassadors to signify to him the affection of our people to him, and to exhort them to preserve and augment their friendship for us, and be ready to bestow other benefits upon us, as justly expecting to receive proper requitals from us; and desiring them to remember that our ancestors * were friendly to the Jews, even in the days of Abraham, who was the father of all the Hebrews, as we have [also] found it set down in our public records."

23. The decree of those of Halicarnassus:—"When Memnon, the son of Orestidas by descent, but by adoption of Euonymus, was priest, on the *** day of the month Aristerion, the decree of the people, upon the representation of Marcus Alexander, was this: Since we have ever a great regard to piety towards God, and to holiness; and since we aim to follow the people of the Romans, who are the benefactors of all men, and what they have written to us about a league of friendship and mutual assistance between the Jews and our city, and that their sacred offices and accustomed festivals and assemblies may be observed by them; we have decreed, that as many men and women of the Jews as are willing so to do, may celebrate their Sabbaths, and perform their holy offices, according to the Jewish laws; and may make their proseuchæ at the seaside, according to the customs of their forefathers; and if any one, whether he be a magistrate or a private person, hindereth them from so doing, he shall be liable to a fine, to be applied to the uses of the city."

24. The decree of the Sardians:—"This decree was made by the senate and people, upon the representation of the prætors:—Whereas those Jews who are our fellow-citizens, and live with us in this city, have ever had great benefits heaped upon them by the people, and have come now into the senate, and desired of the people, that upon the restitution of their law and their liberty, by the senate and people of Rome, they may assemble together, according to their ancient legal custom, and that we will not bring any suit against them about it; and that a place may be given them where they may have their congregations, with their wives and children, and may offer, as did their forefathers, their prayers and sacrifices to God. Now the senate and people have decreed to permit them to assemble together on the days formerly appointed, and to act according to their own laws; and that such a place be set apart for them by the prætors, for the building and inhabiting the same, as they shall esteem fit for that purpose: and that those that take care of the provisions for the city, shall take care that such sorts of food as they esteem fit for their eating, may be imported into the city."

25. The decree of the Ephesians:—"When Menophilus was prytanis, on the first day of the month Artemisius, this decree was made by the people:—Nicanor, the son of Euphemus, pronounced it, upon the representation of the prætors. Since the Jews that dwell in this city have petitioned Marcus Julius Pompeius, the son of Brutus, the proconsul, that they might be allowed to observe their Sabbaths, and to act in all things according to the customs of their forefathers, without impediment from anybody, the prætor hath granted their petition. Accordingly, it was decreed by the senate and people, that in this affair that concerned the Romans, no one of them should be hindered from keeping the Sabbath-day, nor be fined for so doing; but that they may be allowed to do all things according to their own laws."

26. Now there are many such decrees of the senate and imperators of the Romans,† and those different from these before us, which have been made in favour of Hyrcanus, and of our nation; as also, there have been more decrees of the cities, and rescripts of the prætors to such epistles as concerned our rights and privileges: and certainly such as are not ill-disposed to what we write, may believe that they are all to this purpose, and that by the specimens which we have inserted: for since we have produced evident marks that may still be seen, of the friendship we have had with the Romans, and demonstrated that those marks are engraven upon columns and tables of brass in the capitol, that are still in being, and preserved to this day, we have omitted to set them all down, as needless and disagreeable; for I cannot suppose any one so perverse as not to believe the friendship we have had with the Romans, while they have demonstrated the same by such a great number of their decrees relating to us; nor will they doubt of our fidelity as to the rest of these decrees, since we have shewn the same in those we have produced. And thus have we sufficiently explained that friendship and confederacy we at those times had with the Romans.

---

* We have here a most remarkable and authentic attestation of the citizens of Pergamus, that Abraham was the father of all the Hebrews; that their own ancestors were, in the oldest times, the friends of those Hebrews; and that the public acts of their city, then extant, confirmed the same; which evidence is too strong to be evaded by our present ignorance of the particular occasion of such ancient friendship and alliance between those people.

† If we compare Josephus's promise in sect. 4, to produce all the public decrees of the Romans in favour of the Jews, with his excuse here for omitting many of them, we may observe, that when he came to transcribe all those decrees he had collected, he found them so numerous that he thought he should too much tire his readers if he had attempted it, which he thought a sufficient apology for his omitting the rest of them.

CHAPTER XI

HOW MURCUS SUCCEEDED SEXTUS WHEN HE HAD
BEEN SLAIN BY BASUS'S TREACHERY; AND HOW,
AFTER THE DEATH OF CÆSAR, CASSIUS CAME
INTO SYRIA, AND DISTRESSED JUDEA; AS ALSO,
HOW MALICHUS SLEW ANTIPATER, AND WAS
HIMSELF SLAIN BY HEROD

1. Now it so fell out, that about this very
time the affairs of Syria were in great disorder,
and this on the occasion following: Cecilius
Bassus, one of Pompey's party, laid a treacherous design against Sextus Cæsar, and slew him,
and then took his army, and got the management of public affairs into his own hand; so
there arose a great war about Apamia, while
Cæsar's generals came against him with an army
of horsemen and footmen; to these Antipater
sent also succours, and his sons with them, as
calling to mind the kindnesses they had received
from Cæsar, and on that account he thought it
but just to require punishment for him, and to
take vengeance on the man that had murdered
him. And as the war was drawn out into a
great length, Murcus came from Rome to take
Sextus's government upon him: but Cæsar was
slain by Cassius and Brutus in the senate-house,
after he had retained the government three
years and six months. This fact, however, is
related elsewhere.

2. As the war that arose upon the death of
Cæsar was now begun, and the principal men
were all gone, some one way, and some another,
to raise armies, Cassius came from Rome into
Syria, in order to receive the [army that lay in
the] camp at Apamia; and having raised the
siege, he brought over both Bassus and Murcus
to his party. He then went over the cities, and
got together weapons and soldiers, and laid
great taxes upon those cities; and he chiefly
oppressed Judea, and exacted of it seven hundred talents: but Antipater, when he saw the
state to be in so great consternation and disorder, he divided the collection of that sum, and
appointed his sons to gather it; and so that part
of it was to be exacted by Malichus, who was
ill-disposed to him, and part by others. And
because Herod did exact what is required of
him from Galilee before others, he was in the
greatest favour with Cassius; for he thought it
a part of prudence to cultivate a friendship with
the Romans, and to gain their good-will at the
expense of others; whereas the curators of
other cities, with their citizens, were sold for
slaves; and Cassius reduced four cities into a
state of slavery, the two most potent of which
were Gophna and Emmaus; and, besides these,
Lydda and Thamna. Nay, Cassius was so very
angry at Malichus, that he had killed him, (for
he assaulted him,) had not Hyrcanus, by the
means of Antipater, sent him a hundred talents
of his own, and thereby pacified his anger against
him.

3. But after Cassius was gone out of Judea,
Malichus laid snares for Antipater, as thinking
that his death would be the preservation of
Hyrcanus's government; but his design was not
unknown to Antipater, which, when he perceived, he retired beyond Jordan, and got together an army, partly of Arabs, and partly of
his own countrymen. However, Malichus being
one of great cunning, denied that he had laid
any snares for him, and made his defence with
an oath, both to himself and his sons; and said
that while Phasaelus had a garrison in Jerusalem, and Herod had the weapons of war in his

custody, he could never have thought of any
such thing. So Antipater, perceiving the distress that Malichus was in, was reconciled to
him, and made an agreement with him: this
was when Murcus was president of Syria; who
yet perceiving that this Malichus was making a
disturbance in Judea, proceeded so far that he
had almost killed him; but still, at the intercession of Antipater, he saved him.

4. However, Antipater little thought that by
saving Malichus, he had saved his own murderer: for now Cassius and Murcus had got
together an army, and intrusted the entire care
of it with Herod, and made him general of the
forces of Cœlesyria, and gave him a fleet of ships,
and an army of horsemen and footmen; and
promised him, that after the war was over, they
would make him king of Judea; for a war was
already begun between Antony and the younger
Cæsar; but as Malichus was most afraid of
Antipater, he took him out of the way; and by
the offer of money, persuaded the butler of
Hyrcanus, with whom they were both to feast,
to kill him by poison. This being done, and
he having armed men with him, settled the
affairs of the city. But when Antipater's sons,
Herod and Phasaelus, were acquainted with
this conspiracy against their father, and had indignation at it, Malichus denied all, and utterly
renounced any knowledge of the murder. And
thus died Antipater, a man that had distinguished himself for piety and justice, and love
to his country. And whereas one of his sons,
Herod, resolved immediately to revenge their
father's death, and was coming upon Malichus
with an army for that purpose, the elder of his
sons, Phasaelus, thought it best rather to get
this man into their hands by policy, lest they
should appear to begin a civil war in the country; so he accepted of Malichus's defence for
himself, and pretended to believe him, that he
had had no hand in the violent death of Antipater his father, but erected a fine monument
for him. Herod also went to Samaria: and
when he found them in great distress, he revived their spirits, and composed their differences.

5. However, a little after this, Herod, upon
the approach of a festival, came with his soldiers into the city; whereupon Malichus was
affrighted, and persuaded Hyrcanus not to permit him to come into the city. Hyrcanus complied; and, for a pretence of excluding him,
alleged, that a rout of strangers ought not to be
admitted while the multitude were purifying
themselves. But Herod had little regard to the
messengers that were sent to him, and entered
the city in the night-time, and affrighted Malichus, yet did he remit nothing of his former
dissimulation, but wept for Antipater, and bewailed him as a friend of his, with a loud voice;
but Herod and his friends thought it proper not
openly to contradict Malichus's hypocrisy, but
to give him tokens of mutual friendship, in order
to prevent his suspicion of them.

6. However, Herod sent to Cassius, and informed him of the murder of his father; who
knowing what sort of man Malichus was as to
his morals, sent him back word, that he should
revenge his father's death; and also sent privately to the commanders of his army at Tyre,
with orders to assist Herod in the execution of a
very just design of his. Now when Cassius had
taken Laodicea, they all went together to him,
and carried him garlands and money: and
Herod thought that Malichus might be punished
while he was there; but he was somewhat ap-
prehensive of the thing, and designed to make

some great attempt, and because his son was then a hostage at Tyre, he went to that city, and resolved to steal him away privately, and to march thence into Judea; and as Cassius was in haste to march against Antony, he thought to bring the country to revolt, and to procure the government for himself. But Providence opposed his counsels; and Herod being a shrewd man, and perceiving what his intention was, he sent thither beforehand a servant, in appearance indeed to get a supper ready, for he had said before, that he would feast them all there, but in reality to the commanders of the army, whom he persuaded to go out against Malichus with their daggers. So they went out and met the man near the city, upon the sea-shore, and there stabbed him. Whereupon Hyrcanus was so astonished at what had happened, that his speech failed him; and when, after some difficulty, he had recovered himself, he asked Herod what the matter could be, and who it was that slew Malichus: and when he said that it was done by the command of Cassius, he commended the action; for that Malichus was a very wicked man, and one that conspired against his own country. And this was the punishment that was inflicted upon Malichus for what he wickedly did to Antipater.

7. But when Cassius was marched out of Syria, disturbances arose in Judea: for Felix, who was left at Jerusalem with an army, made a sudden attempt against Phasaelus, and the people themselves rose in arms; but Herod went to Fabius, the prefect of Damascus, and was desirous to run to his brother's assistance, but was hindered by a distemper that seized upon him, till Phasaelus himself had been too hard for Felix, and had shut him up in the tower, and there, on certain conditions, dismissed him. Phasaelus also complained of Hyrcanus, that although he had received a great many benefits from them, yet did he support their enemies; for Malichus's brother had made many places to revolt, and kept garrisons in them, and particularly Masada, the strongest fortress of them all. In the meantime, Herod was recovered of his disease, and came and took from Felix all the places he had gotten; and, upon certain conditions, dismissed him also.

CHAPTER XII

HEROD EJECTS ANTIGONUS, THE SON OF ARISTOBULUS, OUT OF JUDEA, AND GAINS THE FRIENDSHIP OF ANTONY, WHO WAS NOW COME INTO SYRIA, BY SENDING HIM MUCH MONEY; ON WHICH ACCOUNT HE WOULD NOT ADMIT OF THOSE THAT WOULD HAVE ACCUSED HEROD: AND WHAT IT WAS THAT ANTONY WROTE TO THE TYRIANS IN BEHALF OF THE JEWS

1. Now* Ptolemy, the son of Menneus, brought back into Judea Antigonus, the son of Aristobulus, who had already raised an army, and had, by money, made Fabius to be his friend, and this because he was of kin to him. Marion also gave him assistance. He had been left by Cassius to tyrannise over Tyre; for this Cassius was a man that seized on Syria, and then kept it under, in the way of a tyrant. Marion

* Gronovius truly observes, in his notes on the Roman decrees in favour of the Jews, that their rights and privileges were commonly purchased of the Romans with money. Accordingly, the chief captain confesses to St Paul that, "with a great sum had he obtained his freedom," (Acts xxii. 28.)

also marched into Galilee, which lay in his neighbourhood, and took three of its fortresses, and put garrisons into them to keep them. But when Herod came, he took all from him; but the Tyrian garrison he dismissed in a very civil manner; nay, to some of the soldiers he made presents out of the good-will he bare to that city. When he had despatched these affairs, and was gone to meet Antigonus, he joined battle with him, and beat him, and drove him out of Judea presently, when he was just come into its borders; but when he was come to Jerusalem, Hyrcanus and the people put garlands about his head; for he had already contracted an affinity with the family of Hyrcanus by having espoused a descendant of his, and for that reason Herod took the greater care of him, as being to marry the daughter of Alexander, the son of Aristobulus, and the grand-daughter of Hyrcanus; by which wife he became the father of three male and two female children. He had also married before this another wife, out of a lower family of his own nation, whose name was Doris, by whom he had his eldest son Antipater.

2. Now Antonius and Cæsar had beaten Cassius near Philippi, as others have related; but after the victory, Cæsar went into Gaul [Italy,] and Antony marched into Asia, who when he was arrived at Bithynia, he had ambassadors that met him from all parts. The principal men also of the Jews came thither, to accuse Phasaelus and Herod, and they said that Hyrcanus had indeed the appearance of reigning, but that these men had all the power; but Antony paid great respect to Herod, who was come to him to make his defence against his accusers, on which account his adversaries could not so much as obtain a hearing; which favour Herod had gained of Antony by money; but still, when Antony was come to Ephesus, Hyrcanus, the high priest, and our nation, sent an embassage to him, which carried a crown of gold with them, and desired that he would write to the governors of provinces, to set those Jews free who had been carried captive by Cassius, and this without their having fought against him, and to restore them that country which, in the days of Cassius, had been taken from them. Antony thought the Jews' desires were just, and wrote immediately to Hyrcanus, and to the Jews. He also sent, at the same time, a decree to the Tyrians; the contents of which were to the same purpose.

3. "Murcus Antonius, imperator, to Hyrcanus the high priest and ethnarch of the Jews, sendeth greeting. If you be in health, it is well; I am also in health, with the army. Lysimachus the son of Pausanias, and Josephus the son of Menneus, and Alexander the son of Theodorus, your ambassadors, met me at Ephesus, and have renewed the embassage which they had formerly been upon at Rome, and have diligently acquitted themselves of the present embassage, which thou and thy nation have intrusted to them, and have fully declared the good will thou hast for us. I am therefore satisfied, both by your actions and your words, that you are well-disposed to us; and I understand that your conduct of life is constant and religious; so I reckon you as our own; but when those that were adversaries to you, and to the Roman people, abstained neither from cities nor temples, and did not observe the agreement they had confirmed by oath, it was not only on account of our contest with them, but on account of all mankind in common, that we have taken vengeance on those who have been the authors of great injustice towards men, and of great wickedness towards the gods; for the sake of which we sup-

MALICHUS IS KILLED NEAR TYRE

pose that it was that the sun turned away his light from us,* as unwilling to view the horrid crime they were guilty of in the case of Cæsar. We have also overcome their conspiracies, which threatened the gods themselves, which Macedonia received, as it is a climate peculiarly proper for impious and insolent attempts; and we have overcome that confused rout of men, half mad with spite against us, which they got together at Philippi, in Macedonia, when they seized on the places that were proper for that purpose, and, as it were, walled them round with mountains to the very sea, and where the passage was open only through a single gate. This victory we gained, because the gods had condemned those wicked enterprises. Now Brutus, when he had fled as far as Philippi, was shut up by us, and became a partaker of the same perdition with Cassius; and now these have received their punishment, we suppose that we may enjoy peace for the time to come, and that Asia may be at rest from war. We therefore make that peace which God hath given us common to our confederates also, insomuch that the body of Asia is now recovered out of that distemper it was under by means of our victory. I, therefore, bearing in mind both thee and your nation, shall take care of what may be for your advantage. I have also sent epistles in writing to the several cities, that if any persons, whether freemen or bondmen, have been sold under the spear by Caius Cassius or his subordinate officers, they may be set free; and I will that you kindly make use of the favours which I and Dolabella have granted you. I also forbid the Tyrians to use any violence with you; and for what places of the Jews they now possess, I order them to restore them. I have withal accepted of the crown which thou sentest me."

4. "Murcus Antonius, imperator, to the magistrates, senate, and people of Tyre, sendeth greeting. The ambassadors of Hyrcanus, the high priest and ethnarch [of the Jews,] appeared before me at Ephesus, and told me that you are in possession of part of their country, which you entered upon under the government of our adversaries. Since, therefore, we have undertaken a war for the obtaining the government, and have taken care to do what was agreeable to piety and justice, and have brought to punishment those that had neither any remembrance of the kindness they had received, nor have kept their oaths, I will that you be at peace with those that are our confederates; as also, that what you have taken by the means of our adversaries shall not be reckoned your own, but be returned to those from whom you took them; for none of them took their provinces or their armies by the gift of the senate, but they seized them by force, and bestowed them by violence upon such as became useful to them in their unjust proceedings. Since, therefore, those men have received the punishment due to them, we desire that our confederates may retain whatsoever it was that they formerly possessed without disturbance, and that you restore all the places which belong to Hyrcanus, the ethnarch of the Jews, which you have had, though it were but one day before Caius Cassius began an unjustifiable war against us, and entered into our province; nor do you use any force against him, in order to weaken him, that he may not be able to dispose of that which is his own; but if you have any contest with him

about your respective rights, it shall be lawful for you to plead your cause when we come upon the places concerned, for we shall alike preserve the rights, and hear all the causes, of our confederates."

5. "Murcus Antonius, imperator, to the magistrates, senate, and people of Tyre, sendeth greeting. I have sent you my decree, of which I will that ye take care that it be engraven on the public tables, in Roman and Greek letters, and that it stand engraven in the most illustrious places, that it may be read by all. Murcus Antonius, imperator, one of the triumvirate over the public affairs, made this declaration:—Since Caius Cassius, in this revolt he hath made, hath pillaged that province which belonged not to him, and was held by garrisons there encamped, while they were our confederates, and hath spoiled that nation of the Jews which was in friendship with the Roman people, as in war; and since we have overcome his madness by arms, we now correct, by our decrees and judicial determinations, what he hath laid waste, that those things may be restored to our confederates; and as for what hath been sold of the Jewish possessions, whether they be bodies or possessions, let them be released: the bodies into that state of freedom they were originally in, and the possessions to their former owners. I also will, that he who shall not comply with this decree of mine, shall be punished for his disobedience; and if such a one be caught, I will take care that the offenders suffer condign punishment."

6. The same thing did Antony write to the Sidonians, and the Antiochians, and the Arabians. We have produced these decrees, therefore, as marks for futurity of the truth of what we have said, that the Romans had a great concern about our nation.

CHAPTER XIII

HOW ANTONY MADE HEROD AND PHASAELUS TETRARCHS, AFTER THEY HAD BEEN ACCUSED TO NO PURPOSE; AND HOW THE PARTHIANS, WHEN THEY BROUGHT ANTIGONUS INTO JUDEA, TOOK HYRCANUS AND PHASAELUS CAPTIVES. HEROD'S FLIGHT; AND WHAT AFFLICTIONS HYRCANUS AND PHASAELUS ENDURED

1. WHEN after this, Antony came into Syria, Cleopatra met him in Cilicia, and brought him to fall in love with her. And there came now also a hundred of the most potent of the Jews to accuse Herod and those about him, and set the men of the greatest eloquence among them to speak. But Messala contradicted them, on behalf of the young men, and all this in the presence of Hyrcanus, who was Herod's father-in-law† already. When Antony had heard both sides at Daphne, he asked Hyrcanus who they were that governed the nation best? He replied, Herod and his friends. Hereupon Antony, by reason of the old hospitable friendship he had made with his father [Antipater,] at that time when he was with Gabinius, he made both Herod and Phasaelus tetrarchs, and committed the public affairs of the Jews to them, and wrote letters to that purpose. He also bound fifteen

---

* This clause plainly alludes to that well-known but unusual and very long darkness of the sun, which happened upon the murder of Julius Cæsar by Brutus and Cassius; which is greatly taken notice of by Virgil, Pliny, and other Roman authors.

† We may here take notice that espousals alone were of old esteemed a sufficient foundation for affinity, Hyrcanus being here called *father-in-law* to Herod, because his grand-daughter Mariamne was betrothed to him, although the marriage was not completed till four years afterwards. See Matt. i. 16.

of their adversaries, and was going to kill them, but that Herod obtained their pardon.

2. Yet did not these men continue quiet when they were come back, but a thousand of the Jews came to Tyre to meet him there, whither the report was that he would come. But Antony was corrupted by the money which Herod and his brother had given him; and so he gave order to the governor of the place to punish the Jewish ambassadors, who were for making innovations, and to settle the government upon Herod: but Herod went out hastily to them, and Hyrcanus was with him, (for they stood upon the shore before the city;) and he charged them to go their ways, because great mischiefs would befall them if they went on with their accusation. But they did not acquiesce: whereupon the Romans ran upon them with their daggers, and slew some, and wounded more of them, and the rest fled away, and went home, and lay still in great consternation: and when the people made a clamour against Herod, Antony was so provoked at it that he slew the prisoners.

3. Now, in the second year, Pacorus, the king of Parthia's son, and Barzapharnes, a commander of the Parthians, possessed themselves of Syria. Ptolemy, the son of Menneus, also was now dead, and Lysanias his son took his government, and made a league of friendship with Antigonus, the son of Aristobulus: and in order to obtain it, made use of that commander, who had a great interest in him. Now Antigonus had promised to give the Parthians a thousand talents, and five hundred women, upon condition they would take the government away from Hyrcanus, and bestow it upon him, and withal kill Herod. And although he did not give them what he had promised, yet did the Parthians make an expedition into Judea on that account, and carried Antigonus with them. Pacorus went along the maritime parts; but the commander Barzapharnes through the midland. Now the Tyrians excluded Pacorus; but the Sidonians, and those of Ptolemais, received him. However, Pacorus sent a troop of horsemen into Judea, to take a view of the state of the country, and to assist Antigonus; and sent also the king's butler, of the same name with himself. So when the Jews that dwelt about mount Carmel came to Antigonus, and were ready to march with him into Judea, Antigonus hoped to get some part of the country by their assistance. The place is called Drymi; and when some others came and met them, the men privately fell upon Jerusalem; and when some more were come to them, they got together in great numbers, and came against the king's palace, and besieged it. But as Phasaelus's and Herod's party came to the other's assistance, and a battle happened between them in the market-place, the young men beat their enemies, and pursued them into the temple, and sent some armed men into the adjoining houses, to keep them in, who yet being destitute of such as should support them, were burnt, and the houses with them, by the people who rose up against them. But Herod was revenged on these seditious adversaries of his a little afterward for this injury they had offered him, when he fought with them, and slew a great number of them.

4. But while there were daily skirmishes, the enemy waited for the coming of the multitude out of the country to Pentecost, a feast of ours so called; and when that day was come, many ten thousands of the people were gathered together about the temple, some in armour, and some without. Now those that came guarded both the temple and the city, excepting what belonged to the palace, which Herod guarded with a few of his soldiers; and Phasaelus had the charge of the wall, while Herod, with a body of his men, sallied out upon the enemy, who lay in the suburbs, and fought courageously, and put many ten thousands to flight, some flying into the city, and some into the temple, and some into the outer fortifications, for some such fortifications there were in that place. Phasaelus came also to his assistance; yet was Pacorus the general of the Parthians, at the desire of Antigonus, admitted into the city, with a few of his horsemen, under pretence indeed as if he would still the sedition, but in reality to assist Antigonus in obtaining the government. And when Phasaelus met him, and received him kindly, Pacorus persuaded him to go himself as ambassador to Barzapharnes, which was done fraudulently. Accordingly, Phasaelus, suspecting no harm, complied with his proposal, while Herod did not give his consent to what was done, because of the perfidiousness of those barbarians, but desired Phasaelus rather to fight those that were come into the city.

5. So both Hyrcanus and Phasaelus went on the embassage; but Pacorus left with Herod two hundred horsemen, and ten men, who were called the *freemen;* and conducted the others on their journey; and when they were in Galilee, the governors of the cities there met them in their arms. Barzapharnes also received them at the first with cheerfulness, and made them presents, though he afterward conspired against them; and Phasaelus, with his horsemen, were conducted to the sea-side; but when they heard that Antigonus had promised to give the Parthians a thousand talents, and five hundred women, to assist him against them, they soon had a suspicion of the barbarians. Moreover, there was one who informed them that snares were laid for them by night, while a guard came about them secretly; and they had then been seized upon, had they not waited for the seizure of Herod by the Parthians that were about Jerusalem, lest, upon the slaughter of Hyrcanus and Phasaelus, he should have an intimation of it, and escape out of their hands. And these were the circumstances they were now in; and they saw who they were that guarded them. Some persons indeed would have persuaded Phasaelus to fly away on horseback, and not to stay any longer; and there was one Ophellius, who, above all the rest, was earnest with him to do so, for he had heard of this treachery from Saramalla, the richest of all the Syrians at that time, who also promised to provide him ships to carry him off; for the sea was just by them: but he had no mind to desert Hyrcanus, nor bring his brother into danger; but he went to Barzapharnes, and told him he did not act justly when he made such a contrivance against them, for that if he wanted money, he would give him more than Antigonus; and besides, that it was a horrible thing to slay those that came to him upon the security of their oaths, and that when they had done them no injury. But the barbarian swore to him that there was no truth in any of his suspicions, but that he was troubled with nothing but false proposals, and then went away to Pacorus.

6. But as soon as he was gone away, some men came and bound Hyrcanus and Phasaelus; while Phasaelus greatly reproached the Parthians for their perjury. However, that butler who was sent against Herod had it in command to get him without the walls of the city, and seize upon him; but messengers had been sent by

Phasaelus to inform Herod of the perfidiousness of the Parthians; and when he knew that the enemy had seized upon them, he went to Pacorus, and to the most potent of the Parthians, as to the lords of the rest, who, although they knew the whole matter, dissembled with him in a deceitful way; and said that he ought to go out with them before the walls, and meet those who were bringing him his letters, for that they were not taken by his adversaries, but were coming to give him an account of the good success Phasaelus had had. Herod did not give credit to what they said; for he had heard that his brother was seized upon by others also; and the daughter of Hyrcanus, whose daughter he had espoused, was his monitor also [not to credit them,] which made him still more suspicious of the Parthians; for although other people did not give heed to her, yet did he believe her as a woman of very great wisdom.

7. Now while the Parthians were in consultation what was fit to be done; for they did not think it proper to make an open attempt upon a person of his character; and while they put off the determination to the next day, Herod was under great disturbance of mind; and rather inclining to believe the reports he heard about his brother and the Parthians, than to give heed to what was said on the other side, he determined, that when the evening came on, he would make use of it for his flight, and not make any longer delay, as if the dangers from the enemy were not yet certain. He therefore removed with the armed men whom he had with him; and set his wives upon the beasts, as also his mother, and sister, and her whom he was about to marry [Mariamne,] the daughter of Alexander, the son of Aristobulus, with her mother, the daughter of Hyrcanus, and his youngest brother, and all their servants, and the rest of the multitude that was with him, and without the enemy's privity pursued his way to Idumea: nor could any enemy of his who then saw him in this case, be so hard-hearted, but would have commiserated his fortune, while the women drew along their infant children, and left their own country, and their friends in prison, with tears in their eyes, and sad lamentations, and in expectation of nothing but what was of a melancholy nature.

8. But for Herod himself, he raised his mind above the miserable state he was in, and was of good courage in the midst of his misfortunes; and, as he passed along, he bade them every one be of good cheer, and not to give themselves up to sorrow, because that would hinder them in their flight, which was now the only hope of safety that they had. Accordingly they tried to bear with patience the calamity they were under, as he exhorted them to do; yet was he once almost going to kill himself, upon the overthrow of a waggon, and the danger his mother was then in of being killed; and this on two accounts, because of his great concern for her, and because he was afraid lest, by this delay, the enemy should overtake him in the pursuit; but as he was drawing his sword, and going to kill himself therewith, those that were present restrained him, and being so many in number, were too hard for him; and told him that he ought not to desert them, and leave them a prey to their enemies, for that it was not the part of a brave man to free himself from the distresses he was in, and to overlook his friends that were in the same distress also. So he was compelled to let that horrid attempt alone, partly out of shame at what they said to him, and partly out of regard to the great number of those that would not permit him to do what he intended. So he en-

couraged his mother, and took all the care of her the time would allow, and proceeded on the way he proposed to go with the utmost haste, and that was to the fortress of Masada. And as he had many skirmishes with such of the Parthians as attacked him and pursued him, he was conqueror in them all.

9. Nor indeed was he free from the Jews all along as he was in his flight: for by the time he was gotten sixty furlongs out of the city, and was upon the road, they fell upon him, and fought hand to hand with him, whom he also put to flight, and overcame, not like one that was in distress and in necessity, but like one that was excellently prepared for war, and had what he wanted in great plenty. And in this very place where he overcame the Jews, it was that he some time afterwards built a most excellent palace, and a city round about it, and called it Herodium. And when he was come to Idumea, at a place called Thressa, his brother Joseph met him, and he then held a council to take advice about his affairs, and what was fit to be done in his circumstances, since he had a great multitude that followed him, besides his mercenary soldiers, and the place Masada, whither he proposed to fly, was too small to contain so great a multitude: so he sent away the greater part of his company, being above nine thousand, and bade them go, some one way, and some another, and so save themselves in Idumea, and gave them what would buy them provisions in their journey. But he took with him those that were the least encumbered, and were most intimate with him, and came to the fortress, and placed there his wives and his followers, being eight hundred in number, there being in the place a sufficient quantity of corn and water, and other necessaries, and went directly for Petra, in Arabia. But when it was day, the Parthians plundered all Jerusalem, and the palace, and abstained from nothing but Hyrcanus's money, which was three hundred talents. A great deal of Herod's money escaped, and principally all that the man had been so provident as to send into Idumea beforehand; nor indeed did what was in the city suffice the Parthians; but they went out into the country, and plundered it, and demolished the city Marissa.

10. And thus was Antigonus brought back into Judea by the king of the Parthians, and received Hyrcanus and Phasaelus for his prisoners; but he was greatly cast down because the women had escaped, whom he intended to have given the enemy, as having promised they should have them, with the money, for their reward: but being afraid that Hyrcanus, who was under the guard of the Parthians, might have his kingdom restored to him by the multitude, he cut off his ears, and thereby took care that the high priesthood should never come to him any more, because he was maimed, while the law required that this dignity should belong to none but such as had all their members entire.* But now one cannot but here admire the fortitude of Phasaelus, who, perceiving that he was to be put to death, did not think death any terrible thing at all; but to die thus by the means of his enemy, this he thought a most pitiable and dishonourable thing, and therefore since he had not his hands at liberty, for the bonds he was in prevented him from killing himself thereby, he dashed his head against a great stone, and thereby took away his own life, which he thought to be the best thing he could do in such a distress as he was in, and thereby put it out of the power

---

* This law of Moses is in Lev. xxi. 17-24.

of the enemy to bring him to any death he pleased. It is also reported, that when he had made a great wound in his head, Antigonus sent physicians to cure it, and, by ordering them to infuse poison into the wound, killed him. However, Phasaelus hearing, before he was quite dead, by a certain woman, that his brother Herod had escaped the enemy, underwent his death cheerfully, since he now left behind him one who would revenge his death, and who was able to inflict punishment on his enemies.

CHAPTER XIV

HOW HEROD GOT AWAY FROM THE KING OF ARABIA, AND MADE HASTE TO GO INTO EGYPT, AND THENCE WENT IN HASTE ALSO TO ROME; AND HOW, BY PROMISING A GREAT DEAL OF MONEY TO ANTONY, HE OBTAINED OF THE SENATE AND OF CÆSAR TO BE MADE KING OF THE JEWS

1. As for Herod, the great miseries he was in did not discourage him, but made him sharp in discovering surprising undertakings; for he went to Malchus, king of Arabia, whom he had formerly been very kind to, in order to receive somewhat by way of requital, now he was in more than ordinary want of it, and desired he would let him have some money, either by way of loan, or as his free gift, on account of the many benefits he had received from him; for not knowing what was become of his brother, he was in haste to redeem him out of the hand of his enemies, as willing to give three hundred talents for the price of his redemption. He also took with him the son of Phasaelus, who was a child of but seven years of age; for this very reason, that he might be a hostage for the repayment of the money. But there came messengers from Malchus to meet him, by whom he was desired to be gone, for that the Parthians had laid a charge upon him not to entertain Herod. This was only a pretence which he made use of, that he might not be obliged to repay him what he owed him; and this he was further induced to do, by the principal men among the Arabians, that they might cheat him of what sums they had received from [his father] Antipater, and which he had committed to their fidelity. He made answer, that he did not intend to be troublesome to them by his coming thither, but that he desired only to discourse with them about certain affairs that were to him of the greatest importance.

2. Hereupon he resolved to go away, and did go very prudently the road to Egypt; and then it was that he lodged in a certain temple; for he had left a great many of his followers there. On the next day he came to Rhinocolura, and there it was that he heard what had befallen his brother. Though Malchus soon repented of what he had done, and came running after Herod; yet with no manner of success, for he was gotten a very great way off, and made haste into the road to Pelusium; and when the stationary ships that lay there hindered him from sailing to Alexandria, he went to their captains, by whose assistance, and that out of much reverence of, and great regard to him, he was conducted into the city [Alexandria,] and was retained there by Cleopatra, yet was she not able to prevail with him to stay there, because he was making haste to Rome, even though the weather was stormy, and he was informed that the affairs of Italy were very tumultuous, and in great disorder.

3. So he set sail from thence to Pamphylia, and falling into a violent storm, he had much ado to escape to Rhodes, with the loss of the ship's burden; and there it was that two of his friends, Sappinas and Ptolemeus, met with him: and as he found that city very much damaged in the war against Cassius, though he were in necessity himself, he neglected not to do it a kindness, but did what he could to recover it to its former state. He also built there a three-decked ship, and set sail thence with his friends for Italy, and came to the port of Brundusium: and when he was come from thence to Rome, he first related to Antony what had befallen him in Judea, and how Phasaelus his brother was seized on by the Parthians, and put to death by them; and how Hyrcanus was detained captive by them, and how they had made Antigonus king, who had promised them a sum of money, no less than a thousand talents, with five hundred women, who were to be of the principal families, and of the Jewish stock; and that he had carried off the women by night; and that, by undergoing a great many hardships, he had escaped the hands of his enemies; as also that his own relations were in danger of being besieged and taken, and that he had sailed through a storm, and contemned all these terrible dangers, in order to come, as soon as possible, to him who was his hope and only succour at this time.

4. This account made Antony commiserate the change that had happened in Herod's condition;[*] and reasoning with himself that this was a common case among those that are placed in such great dignities, and that they are liable to the mutations that come from fortune, he was very ready to give him the assistance that he desired; and this because he called to mind the friendship he had had with Antipater, because Herod offered him money to make him king, as he had formerly given it to him to make him tetrarch, and chiefly because of his hatred to Antigonus, for he took him to be a seditious person, and an enemy to the Romans. Cæsar was also the forwarder to raise Herod's dignity, and to give him his assistance in what he desired, on account of the toils of war which he had himself undergone with Antipater his father in Egypt, and of the hospitality he had treated him withal, and the kindness he had always shewn him; as also to gratify Antony, who was very zealous for Herod. So a senate was convocated; and Messala first, and then Atratinus, introduced Herod into it, and enlarged upon the benefits they had received from his father, and put them in mind of the good-will he had borne to the Romans. At the same time, they accused Antigonus, and declared him an enemy, not only because of his former opposition to them, but that he had now overlooked the Romans, and taken the government from the Parthians. Upon this the senate was irritated; and Antony informed them further that it was for their advantage in the Parthian war that Herod should be king. This seemed good to all the senators; and so they made a decree accordingly.

5. And this was the principal instance of Antony's affection for Herod, that he not only procured him a kingdom which he did not expect, (for he did not come with an intention to ask the kingdom for himself, which he did not suppose the Romans would grant him, who used to bestow it on some of the royal family, but intended to desire it for his wife's brother, who was grandson by his father to Aristobulus, and

---

* Concerning the chronology of Herod, both principally derived from this and the two next chapters in Josephus, see the note on sect. 6, and chap. xv. sect. 10.

to Hyrcanus by his mother,) but that he procured it for him so suddenly, that he obtained what he did not expect, and departed out of Italy in so few days as seven in all. This young man [the grandson] Herod afterward took care to have slain, as we shall shew in its proper place. But when the senate was dissolved, Antony and Cæsar went out of the senate-house, with Herod between them, and with the consuls and other magistrates before them, in order to offer sacrifices, and to lay up their decrees in the capitol. Antony also feasted Herod the first day of his reign. And thus did this man receive the kingdom, having obtained it on the hundred and eighty-fourth Olympiad, when Caius Domitius Calvinus was consul the second time, and Caius Asinius Pollio [the first time.]

6. All this while Antigonus besieged those that were in Masada, who had plenty of all other necessaries, but were only in want of water,* insomuch that on this occasion Joseph, Herod's brother, was contriving to run away from it, with two hundred of his dependants, to the Arabians; for he had heard that Malchus repented of the offences he had been guilty of with regard to Herod; but God, by sending rain in the nighttime, prevented his going away, for their cisterns were thereby filled, and so he was under no necessity of running away on that account: but they were now of good courage, and the more so, because the sending that plenty of water which they had been in want of, seemed a mark of Divine Providence; so they made a sally, and fought hand to hand with Antigonus's soldiers, (with some openly, with some privately,) and destroyed a great number of them. At the same time, Ventidius, the general of the Romans, was sent out of Syria, to drive the Parthians out of it, and marched after them into Judea, on pretence indeed to succour Joseph; but in reality, the whole affair was no more than a stratagem, in order to get money of Antigonus; so they pitched their camp very near to Jerusalem, and stripped Antigonus of a great deal of money, and then he retired himself with the greater part of the army; but that the wickedness he had been guilty of might not be found out, he left Silo there, with a certain part of his soldiers, with whom also Antigonus cultivated an acquaintance, that he might cause him no disturbance, and was still in hopes that the Parthians would come again and defend him.

CHAPTER XV

HOW HEROD SAILED OUT OF ITALY TO JUDEA, AND FOUGHT WITH ANTIGONUS; AND WHAT OTHER THINGS HAPPENED IN JUDEA ABOUT THAT TIME

§ 1. BY this time Herod had sailed out of Italy to Ptolemais, and had gotten together no small army, both of strangers and of his own countrymen, and marched through Galilee against Antigonus. Silo also, and Ventidius, came and assisted him, being persuaded by Dellius, who was sent by Antony to assist in bringing back Herod. Now, for Ventidius, he was employed in composing the disturbances that had been made in the cities by the means of the Parthians; and for Silo, he was indeed in Judea, but corrupted by Antigonus. However, as Herod went along, his army increased every day, and all Galilee, with some small exception, joined him; but as he was

marching to those that were in Masada, (for he was obliged to endeavour to save those that were in that fortress, now they were besieged, because they were his relations,) Joppa was a hindrance to him; for it was necessary for him to take that place first, it being a city at variance with him, that no stronghold might be left in his enemies' hands behind him when he should go to Jerusalem. And when Silo made this a pretence for rising up from Jerusalem, and was thereupon pursued by the Jews, Herod fell upon them with a small body of men, and both put the Jews to flight and saved Silo, when he was very poorly able to defend himself; but when Herod had taken Joppa, he made haste to set free those of his family that were in Masada. Now of the people of the country, some joined him because of the friendship they had had with his father, and some because of the splendid appearance he made, and others by way of requital for the benefits they had received from both of them; but the greatest number came to him in hopes of getting somewhat from him afterward, if he were once firmly settled in the kingdom.

2. Herod had now a strong army; and as he marched on, Antigonus laid snares and ambushes in the passes and places most proper for them; but in truth he thereby did little or no damage to the enemy: so Herod received those of his family out of Masada, and the fortress Ressa, and then went on for Jerusalem. The soldiery also that was with Silo accompanied him all along, as did many of the citizens, being afraid of his power; and as soon as he had pitched his camp on the west side of the city, the soldiers that were set to guard that part shot their arrows, and threw their darts at him; and when some sallied out in a crowd, and came to fight hand to hand with the first ranks of Herod's army, he gave orders that they should, in the first place, make proclamation about the wall, that he came for the good of the people, and for the preservation of the city, and not to bear any old grudge at even his most open enemies, but ready to forget the offences which his greatest adversary had done him; but Antigonus, by way of reply to what Herod had caused to be proclaimed, and this before the Romans, and before Silo also, said, that they would not do justly if they gave the kingdom to Herod, who was no more than a private man, and an Idumean, i.e. a half Jew,† whereas they ought to bestow it on one of the royal family, as their custom was; for, that in case they at present bear an ill-will to him, and had resolved to deprive him of the kingdom, as having received it from the Parthians, yet were there many others of his family that might by their law take it, and these such as had no way offended the Romans; and being of the sacerdotal family, it would be an unworthy thing to put them by. Now while they said thus one to another, and fell to reproaching one another on both sides, Antigonus permitted his own men that were upon the wall to defend themselves; who, using their bows, and shewing great alacrity against their enemies, easily drove them away from the towers.

3. And now it was that Silo discovered that he

---

* This grievous want of water at Masada, till the place had like to have been taken by the Parthians, is an indication that it was now summer-time.

† This affirmation of Antigonus, spoken in the days of Herod, and in a manner to his face, seems to me of much greater authority than that pretence of his favourite and flatterer Nicolaus of Damascus, that he derived his pedigree from Jews as far backward as the Babylonish captivity. Accordingly Josephus always esteems him an Idumean, though he says his father Antipater was of the same people with the Jews, and a Jew by birth, as indeed all such proselytes of justice as the Idumeans, were in time esteemed the very same people with the Jews.

had taken bribes: for he set a great number of his soldiers to complain aloud of the want of provisions they were in, and to require money to buy them food; and that it was fit to let them go into places proper for winter quarters, since the places near the city were a desert, by reason that Antigonus's soldiers had carried all away; so he set his army upon removing, and endeavoured to march away; but Herod pressed Silo not to depart, and exhorted Silo's captains and soldiers not to desert him, when Cæsar and Antony, and the senate, had sent him thither, for that he would provide them plenty of all the things they wanted, and easily procure them a great abundance of what they required; after which entreaty, he immediately went into the country, and left not the least pretence to Silo for his departure, for he brought an unexpected quantity of provisions, and sent to those friends of his who inhabited about Samaria, to bring down corn, and wine, and oil, and cattle, and all other provisions, to Jericho, that there might be no want of a supply for the soldiers for the time to come. Antigonus was sensible of this, and sent presently over the country such as might restrain and lie in ambush for those that went out for provisions. So these men obeyed the orders of Antigonus, and got together a great number of armed men about Jericho, and sat upon the mountains, and watched those that brought the provisions. However, Herod was not idle in the meantime, for he took ten bands of soldiers, of whom five were of the Romans, and five of the Jews, with some mercenaries among them, and with some few horsemen, and came to Jericho; and as they found the city deserted, but that five hundred of them had settled themselves on the tops of the hills, with their wives and children, those he took and sent away; but the Romans fell upon the city and plundered it, and found the houses full of all sorts of good things. So the king left a garrison at Jericho, and came back again, and sent the Roman army to take their winter quarters in the countries that were come over to him, Judea, and Galilee, and Samaria. And so much did Antigonus gain of Silo for the bribes he gave him, that part of the army should be quartered at Lydda, in order to please Antony. So the Romans laid their weapons aside, and lived in plenty of all things.

4. But Herod was not pleased with lying still, but sent out his brother Joseph against Idumea with two thousand armed footmen, and four hundred horsemen, while he himself came to Samaria, and left his mother and his other relations there, for they were already gone out of Masada, and went into Galilee, and took certain places which were held by the garrisons of Antigonus; and he passed on to Sepphoris, as God sent a snow, while Antigonus's garrisons withdrew themselves, and had great plenty of provisions. He also went thence and resolved to destroy those robbers that dwelt in the caves, and did much mischief in the country; so he sent a troop of horsemen, and three companies of armed footmen against them. They were very near to a village called Arbela; and on the fortieth day after, he came himself with his whole army: and as the enemy sallied out boldly upon him, the left wing of his army gave way; but he appearing with a body of men, put those to flight who were already conquerors, and recalled his men that ran away. He also pressed upon his enemies, and pursued them as far as the river Jordan, though they ran away by different roads. So he brought over to him all Galilee, excepting those that dwelt in the caves, and distributed money to every one of his sol-

diers, giving them a hundred and fifty drachmæ apiece, and much more to their captains, and sent them into winter quarters; at which time Silo came to him, and his commanders with him, because Antigonus would not give them provisions any longer; for he supplied them for no more than one month; nay, he had sent to all the country round about, and ordered them to carry off the provisions that were there, and retire to the mountains, that the Romans might have no provisions to live upon, and so might perish by famine; but Herod committed the care of that matter to Pheroras, his youngest brother, and ordered him to repair Alexandrium also. Accordingly, he quickly made the soldiers abound with great plenty of provisions, and rebuilt Alexandrium, which had been before desolate.

5. About this time it was that Antony continued some time at Athens, and that Ventidius, who was now in Syria, sent for Silo, and commanded him to assist Herod, in the first place, to finish the present war, and then to send for their confederates for the war they were themselves engaged in; but as for Herod, he went in haste against the robbers that were in the caves, and sent Silo away to Ventidius, while he marched against them. These caves were in mountains that were exceedingly abrupt, and in their middle were no other than precipices, with certain entrances into the caves, and those caves were encompassed with sharp rocks, and in these did the robbers lie concealed, with all their families about them; but the king caused certain chests to be made, in order to destroy them, and to be hung down, bound about with iron chains, by an engine, from the top of the mountain, it being not possible to get up to them, by reason of the sharp ascent of the mountains, nor to creep down to them from above. Now these chests were filled with armed men, who had long hooks in their hands, by which they might pull out such as resisted them, and then tumble them down, and kill them by so doing; but the letting the chests down proved to be a matter of great danger, because of the vast depth they were to be let down, although they had their provisions in the chests themselves; but when the chests were let down, and not one of those in the mouths of the caves durst come near them, but lay still out of fear, some of the armed men girt on their armour, and by both their hands took hold of the chain by which the chests were let down, and went into the mouths of the caves, because they fretted that such delay was made by the robbers not daring to come out of the caves; and when they were at any of those mouths, they first killed many of those that were in the mouths with their darts, and afterwards pulled those to them that resisted them with their hooks, and tumbled them down the precipices, and afterwards went into the caves, and killed many more, and then went into the chests again, and lay still there; but, upon this, terror seized the rest, when they heard the lamentations that were made, and they despaired of escaping; however, when the night came on, that put an end to the whole work; and as the king proclaimed pardon by a herald to such as delivered themselves up to him, many accepted of the offer. The same method of assault was made use of the next day; and they went further, and got out in baskets to fight them, and fought them at their doors, and sent fire among them, and set their caves on fire, for there was a great deal of combustible matter within them. Now there was one old man who was caught within one of these caves, with seven

children and a wife; these prayed him to give them leave to go out, and yield themselves up to the enemy; but he stood at the cave's mouth, and always slew that child of his who went out, till he had destroyed them every one, and after that he slew his wife, and cast their dead bodies down the precipice, and himself after them, and so underwent death rather than slavery: but before he did this, he greatly reproached Herod with the meanness of his family, although he was then king. Herod also saw what he was doing, and stretched out his hand, and offered him all manner of security for his life; by which means all these caves were at length subdued entirely.

6. And when the king had set Ptolemy over these parts of the country as his general, he went to Samaria with six hundred horsemen and three thousand armed footmen, as intending to fight Antigonus; but still this command of the army did not succeed well with Ptolemy, but those that had been troublesome to Galilee before attacked him; and when they had done this, they fled among the lakes and places almost inaccessible, laying waste and plundering whatsoever they could come at in those places; but Herod soon returned, and punished them for what they had done; for some of those rebels he slew, and others of them, who had fled to the strongholds, he besieged, and both slew them and demolished their strongholds; and when he had thus put an end to their rebellion, he laid a fine upon the cities of a hundred talents.

7. In the meantime, Pacorus was fallen in a battle, and the Parthians were defeated, when Ventidius sent Macheras to the assistance of Herod, with two legions and a thousand horsemen, while Antony encouraged him to make haste; but Macheras, at the instigation of Antigonus, without the approbation of Herod, as being corrupted by money, went about to take a view of his affairs; but Antigonus, suspecting this intention of his coming, did not admit him into the city, but kept him at a distance, with throwing stones at him, and plainly shewed what he himself meant; but when Macheras was sensible that Herod had given him good advice, and that he had made a mistake himself in not hearkening to that advice, he retired to the city Emmaus; and what Jews he met with he slew them, whether they were enemies or friends, out of the rage he was in at what hardships he had undergone. The king was provoked at this conduct of his, and went to Samaria, and resolved to go to Antony about these affairs, and to inform him that he stood in no need of such helpers, who did him more mischief than he did his enemies; and that he was able of himself to beat Antigonus. But Macheras followed him, and desired that he would not go to Antony; or, if he was resolved to go, that he would join his brother Joseph with them, and let them fight against Antigonus. So he was reconciled to Macheras, upon his earnest entreaties. Accordingly, he left Joseph there with his army, but charged him to run no hazards, nor to quarrel with Macheras.

8. But for his own part, he made haste to Antony (who was then at the siege of Samosata, a place upon Euphrates) with his troops, both horsemen and footmen, to be auxiliaries to him; and when he came to Antioch, and met there a great number of men gotten together that were very desirous to go to Antony, but durst not venture to go, out of fear, because the barbarians fell upon men on the road, and slew many, so he encouraged them, and became their conductor upon the road. Now when they were within two days' march of Samosata, the barbarians had laid an ambush there to disturb those that came to Antony, and where the woods made the passes narrow, as they led to the plains, there they laid not a few of their horsemen, who were to lie still until those passengers were gone by into the wide place. Now as soon as the first ranks were gone by, (for Herod brought on the rear,) those that lay in ambush, who were about five hundred, fell upon them on the sudden, and when they had put the foremost to flight, the king came riding hard, with the forces that were about him, and immediately drove back the enemy; by which means he made the minds of his own men courageous, and emboldened them to go on, insomuch that those who ran away before, now returned back, and the barbarians were slain on all sides. The king also went on killing them, and recovered all the baggage, among which were a great number of beasts for burden, and of slaves, and proceeded on in his march; and whereas there were a great number of those in the woods that attacked them, and were near the passage that led into the plain, he made a sally upon these also with a strong body of men, and put them to flight, and slew many of them, and thereby rendered the way safe for those that came after; and these called Herod their saviour and protector.

9. And when he was near to Samosata, Antony sent out his army in all their proper habiliments to meet him, in order to pay Herod this respect, and because of the assistance he had given him; for he had heard what attacks the barbarians had made upon him [in Judea.] He also was very glad to see him there, as having been made acquainted with the great actions he had performed upon the road; so he entertained him very kindly, and could not but admire his courage. Antony also embraced him as soon as he saw him, and saluted him after a most affectionate manner, and gave him the upper hand, as having himself lately made him a king; and in a little time Antiochus delivered up the fortress, and on that account this war was at an end; then Antony committed the rest to Sossius, and gave him orders to assist Herod, and went himself to Egypt. Accordingly, Sossius sent two legions before into Judea to the assistance of Herod, and he followed himself with the body of the army.

10. Now Joseph was already slain in Judea, in the manner following:—He forgot what charge his brother Herod had given him when he went to Antony; and when he had pitched his camp among the mountains, for Macheras had lent him five regiments, with these he went hastily to Jericho, in order to reap the corn thereto belonging; and as the Roman regiments were but newly raised, and were unskilful in war, for they were in great part collected out of Syria, he was attacked by the enemy, and caught in those places of difficulty, and was himself slain, as he was fighting bravely, and the whole army was lost, for there were six regiments slain. So when Antigonus had got possession of the dead bodies, he cut off Joseph's head, although Pheroras his brother would have redeemed it at the price of fifty talents. After which defeat, the Galileans revolted from their commanders, and took those of Herod's party, and drowned them in the lake; and a great part of Judea was become seditious: but Macheras fortified the place Gitta [in Samaria.]

11. At this time messengers came to Herod, and informed him of what had been done; and when he was come to Daphne by Antioch, they told him of the ill fortune that had befallen his

brother, which yet he expected, from certain visions that appeared to him in his dreams, which clearly foreshewed his brother's death. So he hastened his march; and when he came to mount Libanus, he received about eight hundred men of that place, having already with him one Roman legion, and with these he came to Ptolemais. He also marched thence by night with his army, and proceeded along Galilee. Here it was that the enemy met him, and fought him, and were beaten, and shut up in the same place of strength whence they had sallied out the day before. So he attacked the place in the morning; but, by reason of a great storm that was then very violent, he was able to do nothing, but drew off his army into the neighbouring villages; yet as soon as the other legion that Antony sent him was come to his assistance, those that were in garrison in the place were afraid, and deserted it in the night time. Then did the king march hastily to Jericho, intending to avenge himself on the enemy for the slaughter of his brother; and when he had pitched his tents, he made a feast for the principal commanders, and after this collation was over, and he had dismissed his guests, he retired to his own chamber: and here may one see what kindness God had for the king, for the upper part of the house fell down when nobody was in it, and so killed none, insomuch that all the people believed that Herod was beloved of God, since he had escaped such a great and surprising danger.

12. But the next day six thousand of the enemy came down from the tops of the mountains to fight the Romans, which greatly terrified them; and the soldiers that were in light armour came near, and pelted the king's guards that were come out with darts and stones, and one of them hit him on the side with a dart. Antigonus also sent a commander against Samaria, whose name was Pappus, with some forces, being desirous to shew the enemy how potent he was, and that he had men to spare in his war with them. He sat down to oppose Macheras; but Herod, when he had taken five cities, took such as were left in them, being about two thousand, and slew them, and burnt the cities themselves, and then returned to go against Pappus, who was encamped at a village called Isanas; and there ran in to him many out of Jericho and Judea, near to which places he was, and the enemy fell upon his men, so stout were they at this time, and joined battle with them, but he beat them in the fight; and in order to be revenged on them for the slaughter of his brother, he pursued them sharply, and killed them as they ran away; and as the houses were full of armed men,* and many of them ran as far as the tops of the houses, he got them under his power, and pulled down the roofs of the houses, and saw the lower rooms full of soldiers that were caught, and lay all on a heap; so they threw stones down upon them as they lay piled one upon another, and thereby killed them: nor was there a more frightful spectacle in all the war than this, where, beyond the walls, an immense multitude of dead men lay heaped one upon another. This action it was which chiefly brake the spirits of the enemy,

who expected now what would come; for there appeared a mighty number of people that came from places far distant, that were now about the village, but then ran away; and had it not been for the depth of winter, which then restrained them, the king's army had presently gone to Jerusalem, as being very courageous at this good success, and the whole work had been done immediately; for Antigonus was already looking about how he might fly away and leave the city.

13. At this time the king gave orders that the soldiers should go to supper, for it was late at night, while he went into a chamber to use the bath, for he was very weary: and here it was that he was in the greatest danger, which yet, by God's providence, he escaped; for as he was naked, and had but one servant that followed him, to be with him while he was bathing in an inner room, certain of the enemy who were, in their armour, and had fled thither out of fear, were then in the place; and as he was bathing, the first of them came out with his naked sword drawn, and went out at the doors, and after him a second, and a third, armed in like manner, and were under such a consternation, that they did no hurt to the king, and thought themselves to have come off very well in suffering no harm themselves in their getting out of the house. However, on the next day, he cut off the head of Pappus, for he was already slain, and sent it to Pheroras, as a punishment of what their brother had suffered by his means, for he was the man that slew him with his own hand.

14. When the rigour of winter was over, Herod removed his army, and came near to Jerusalem, and pitched his camp hard by the city. Now this was the third year since he had been made king at Rome; and as he removed his camp, and came near that part of the wall where it could be most easily assaulted, he pitched that camp before the temple, intending to make his attacks in the same manner as did Pompey. So he encompassed the place with three bulwarks, and erected towers, and employed a great many hands about the work, and cut down the trees that were round about the city; and when he had appointed proper persons to oversee the works, even while the army lay before the city, he himself went to Samaria, to complete his marriage, and to take to wife the daughter of Alexander, the son of Aristobulus; for he had betrothed her already, as I have before related.

CHAPTER XVI

HOW HEROD, WHEN HE HAD MARRIED MARIAMNE, TOOK JERUSALEM, WITH THE ASSISTANCE OF SOSIUS, BY FORCE; AND HOW THE GOVERNMENT OF THE ASAMONEANS WAS PUT AN END TO

1. AFTER the wedding was over, came Sosius through Phœnicia, having sent out his army before him over the midland parts. He also, who was their commander, came himself, with a great number of horsemen and footmen. The king also came himself from Samaria, and brought with him no small army, besides that which was there before, for they were about thirty thousand; and they all met together at the walls of Jerusalem, and encamped at the north wall of the city, being now an army of eleven legions, armed men on foot, and six thousand horsemen, with other auxiliaries out of Syria. The generals were two: Sosius, sent by

---

* It may be worth our observation here, that these soldiers of Herod could not have gotten upon the tops of these houses which were full of enemies, in order to pull up the upper floors and destroy them beneath, but by ladders from the outside; which illustrates some texts in the New Testament, by which it appears that men used to ascend thither by ladders on the outside. See Matt. xxiv. 17; Mark xiii. 15; Luke v. 19; xvii. 31.

Antony to assist Herod, and Herod on his own account, in order to take the government from Antigonus, who was declared an enemy to Rome, and that he might himself be king, according to the decree of the senate.

2. Now the Jews that were inclosed within the walls of the city fought against Herod with great alacrity and zeal, (for the whole nation was gathered together;) they also gave out many prophecies about the temple, and many things agreeable to the people, as if God would deliver them out of the danger they were in; they had also carried off what was out of the city, that they might not leave anything to afford sustenance either for men or for beasts; and, by private robberies, they made the want of necessaries greater. When Herod understood this, he opposed ambushes in the fittest places against their private robberies, and he sent legions of armed men to bring in provisions, and that from remote places, so that in a little time they had great plenty of provisions. Now the three bulwarks were easily erected, because so many hands were continually at work upon it; for it was summer-time, and there was nothing to hinder them in raising their works, neither from the air nor from the workmen: so they brought their engines to bear, and shook the walls of the city, and tried all manner of ways to get in: yet did not those within discover any fear, but they also contrived not a few engines to oppose their engines withal. They also sallied out, and burnt not only those engines that were not yet perfected, but those that were; and when they came hand to hand, their attempts were not less bold than those of the Romans, though they were behind them in skill. They also erected new works when the former were ruined, and making mines under ground, they met each other, and fought there; and making use of brutish courage rather than of prudent valour, they persisted in this war to the very last; and this they did while a mighty army lay round about them, and while they were distressed by famine and the want of necessaries, for this happened to be a Sabbatic Year. The first that scaled the walls were twenty chosen men; the next were Sosius's centurions; for the first wall was taken in forty days, and the second in fifteen more, when some of the cloisters that were about the temple were burnt, which Herod gave out to have been burnt by Antigonus, in order to expose him to the hatred of the Jews. And when the outer court of the temple, and the lower city, were taken, the Jews fled into the inner court of the temple, and into the upper city; but now, fearing lest the Romans should hinder them from offering their daily sacrifices to God, they sent an embassage, and desired that they would only permit them to bring in beasts for sacrifices, which Herod granted, hoping they were going to yield; but when he saw that they did nothing of what he supposed, but bitterly opposed him, in order to preserve the kingdom to Antigonus, he made an assault upon the city, and took it by storm; and now all parts were full of those that were slain, by the rage of the Romans at the long duration of the siege, and by the zeal of the Jews that were on Herod's side, who were not willing to leave one of their adversaries alive; so they were murdered continually in the narrow streets and in the houses by crowds, and as they were flying to the temple for shelter, and there was no pity taken of either infants or the aged, nor did they spare so much as the weaker sex; nay, although the king sent about, and besought them to spare the people, yet nobody

restrained their hands from slaughter, but, as if they were a company of madmen, they fell upon persons of all ages, without distinction; and then Antigonus, without regard to either his past or present circumstances, came down from the citadel, and fell down at the feet of Sosius, who took no pity of him, in the change of his fortune, but insulted him beyond measure, and called him Antigone, [i.e., a woman, and not a man;] yet did he not treat him as if he were a woman, by letting him go at liberty, but put him into bonds, and kept him in close custody.

3. And now Herod having overcome his enemies, his care was to govern those foreigners who had been his assistants, for the crowd of strangers rushed to see the temple, and the sacred things in the temple; but the king thinking a victory to be a more severe affliction than a defeat, if any of those things which it was not lawful to see should be seen by them, used entreaties and threatenings, and even sometimes force itself, to restrain them. He also prohibited the ravage that was made in the city, and many times asked Sosius, whether the Romans would empty the city both of money and men, and leave him king of a desert; and told him, that he esteemed dominion over the whole habitable earth as by no means an equivalent satisfaction for such a murder of his citizens: and when he said that this plunder was justly to be permitted the soldiers for the siege they had undergone, he replied, that he would give every one his reward out of his own money; and by this means he redeemed what remained of the city from destruction; and he performed what he had promised him, for he gave a noble present to every soldier, and a proportionable present to their commanders; but a most royal present to Sosius himself, till they all went away full of money.

4. This destruction befell the city of Jerusalem when Marcus Agrippa and Caninius Gallus were consuls at Rome,* on the hundred and eighty-fifth Olympiad, on the third month, on the solemnity of the fast, as if a periodical revolution of calamities had returned since that which befell the Jews under Pompey; for the Jews were taken by him on the same day, and this was after twenty-seven years' time. So when Sosius had

* Note here, that Josephus frequently assures us, that there passed above three years between Herod's first obtaining the kingdom at Rome and his second obtaining it upon the taking of Jerusalem and death of Antigonus. The present history of this interval twice mentions the army going into winter quarters, which perhaps belonged to two several winters (chap. xv. sect. 3, 4;) and though Josephus says nothing how long they lay in those quarters, yet does he give such an account of the long and studied delays of Ventidius, Silo, and Macheras, who were to see Herod settled in his new kingdom, and gives us such particular accounts of the many great actions of Herod during the same interval, as fairly imply that interval, before Herod went to Samosata, to have been very considerable. However, what is wanting in Josephus, is fully supplied by Moses Chorenensis, the Armenian historian, in his history of that interval, who directly assures us that Tigranes, then king of Armenia, and the principal manager of this Parthian war, reigned two years after Herod was made king at Rome, and yet Antony did not hear of his death, in that very neighbourhood, at Samosata, till he was come thither to besiege it; after which Herod brought him an army, which was three hundred and forty miles' march, and through a difficult country, full of enemies also, and joined with him in the siege of Samosata till that city was taken; then Herod and Sosius marched back with their large armies the same number of three hundred and forty miles; and when, in a little time, they sat down to besiege Jerusalem, they were not able to take it but by a siege of five months. All which put together, fully supplies what is wanting in Josephus, and secures the entire chronology of these times beyond contradiction.

dedicated a crown of gold to God, he marched away from Jerusalem, and carried Antigonus with him in bonds to Antony; but Herod was afraid lest Antigonus should be kept in prison [only] by Antony, and that when he was carried to Rome by him, he might get his cause to be heard by the senate, and might demonstrate, as as he was himself of the royal blood, and Herod but a private man, that therefore it belonged to his sons, however, to have the kingdom, on account of the family they were of, in case he had himself offended the Romans by what he had done. Out of Herod's fear of this it was that he, by giving Antony a great deal of money, endeavoured to persuade him to have Antigonus slain, which, if it were once done, he should be free from that fear. And thus did the government of the Asamoneans cease, a hundred and twenty-six years after it was first set up. This family was a splendid and an illustrious one, both on account of the nobility of their stock, and of the dignity of the high priesthood, as also for the glorious actions their ancestors had performed for our nation: but these men lost the government by their dissensions one with another, and it came to Herod, the son of Antipater, who was of no more than a vulgar family, and of no eminent extraction, but one that was subject to other kings. And this is what history tells us was the end of the Asamonean family.

BOOK XV

CONTAINING THE INTERVAL OF EIGHTEEN YEARS

FROM THE DEATH OF ANTIGONUS TO THE FINISHING OF THE TEMPLE BY HEROD

CHAPTER I

CONCERNING POLLIO AND SAMEAS. HEROD SLAYS THE PRINCIPAL OF ANTIGONUS'S FRIENDS, AND SPOILS THE CITY OF ITS WEALTH. ANTONY BEHEADS ANTIGONUS

1. How Sosius and Herod took Jerusalem by force; and besides that, how they took Antigonus captive, has been related by us in the foregoing book. We will now proceed in the narration. And since Herod had now the government of all Judea put into his hands, he promoted such of the private men of the city as had been of his party, but never left off avenging and punishing every day those that had chosen to be of the party of his enemies; but Pollio the Pharisee, and Sameas, a disciple of his, were honoured by him above all the rest; for when Jerusalem was besieged, they advised the citizens to receive Herod; for which advice they were well requited. But this Pollio, at the time when Herod was once upon his trial of life and death, foretold, in a way of reproach, to Hyrcanus and the other judges, how this Herod, whom they suffered now to escape, would afterward inflict punishment on them all; which had its completion in time, while God fulfilled the words he had spoken.

2. At this time Herod, now he had got Jerusalem under his power, carried off all the royal ornaments, and spoiled the wealthy men of what they had gotten; and when, by these means, he had heaped together a great quantity of silver and gold, he gave it all to Antony, and his friends that were about him. He also slew forty-five of the principal men of Antigonus's party, and set guards at the gates of the city, that nothing might be carried out together with their dead bodies. They also searched the dead, and whatsoever was found, either of silver or gold, or other treasure, it was carried to the king; nor was there any end of the miseries he brought upon them; and this distress was in part occasioned by the covetousness of the prince regent, who was still in want of more, and in part by the Sabbatic Year, which was still going on, and forced the country to lie still uncultivated, since we are forbidden to sow the land in that year. Now when Antony had received Antigonus as his captive, he determined to keep him against his triumph; but when he heard that the nation grew seditious, and that, out of their hatred to Herod, they continued to bear good-will to Antigonus, he resolved to behead him at Antioch, for otherwise the Jews could no way be brought to quiet. And Strabo of Cappadocia attests to what I have said, when he thus speaks:—"Antony ordered Antigonus the Jew to be brought to Antioch, and there to be beheaded; and this Antony seems to me to have been the very first man who beheaded a king, as supposing he could no other way bend the minds of the Jews so as to receive Herod, whom he had made king in his stead; for by no torments could they be forced to call him king, so great a fondness they had for their former king; so he thought that this dishonourable death would diminish the value they had for Antigonus's memory, and at the same time would diminish the hatred they bear to Herod." Thus far Strabo.

CHAPTER II

HOW HYRCANUS WAS SET AT LIBERTY BY THE PARTHIANS, AND RETURNED TO HEROD; AND WHAT ALEXANDRA DID WHEN SHE HEARD THAT ANANELUS WAS MADE HIGH PRIEST

1. Now after Herod was in possession of the kingdom, Hyrcanus the high priest, who was then a captive among the Parthians, came to him again, and was set free from his captivity in the manner following:—Barzapharnes and Pacorus, the generals of the Parthians, took Hyrcanus, who was first made high priest and afterwards king, and Herod's brother, Phasaelus, captives, and were carrying them away into Parthia. Phasaelus indeed could not bear the reproach of being in bonds; and thinking that death with

glory was better than any life whatsoever, he became his own executioner, as I have formerly related.

2. But when Hyrcanus was brought into Parthia, the king of Phraates treated him after a very gentle manner, as having already learned of what an illustrious family he was; on which account he set him free from his bonds, and gave him a habitation at Babylon,* where there were Jews in great numbers. These Jews honoured Hyrcanus as their high priest and king, as did all the Jewish nation that dwelt as far as Euphrates, which respect was very much to his satisfaction. But when he was informed that Herod had received the kingdom, new hopes came upon him, as having been himself still of a kind disposition towards him; and expecting that Herod would bear in mind what favour he had received from him, and when he was upon his trial, and when he was in danger that a capital sentence would be pronounced against him, he delivered him from that danger, and from all punishment. Accordingly, he talked of that matter with the Jews that came often to him with great affection; but they endeavoured to retain him among them, and desired that he would stay with them, putting him in mind of the kind offices and honours they did him, and that those honours they paid him were not at all inferior to what they could pay to either their high priests or their kings: and what was a greater motive to determine him, they said, was this, that he could not have those dignities [in Judea] because of that maim in his body, which had been inflicted on him by Antigonus; and that kings do not use to requite men for those kindnesses which they received when they were private persons, the height of their fortune making usually no small changes in them.

3. Now, although they suggested these arguments to him for his own advantage, yet did Hyrcanus still desire to depart. Herod also wrote to him, and persuaded him to desire of Phraates, and the Jews that were there, that they should not grudge him the royal authority, which he should have jointly with himself, for that now was the proper time for himself to make him amends for the favours he had received from him, as having been brought up by him, and saved by him also, as well as for Hyrcanus to receive it. And as he wrote thus to Hyrcanus, so did he send also Saramallas his ambassador to Phraates, and many presents with him, and desired him in the most obliging way, that he would be no hindrance to his gratitude towards his benefactor. But this zeal of Herod's did not flow from that principle, but because he had been made governor of that country without having any just claim to it, he was afraid, and that upon reasons good enough, of a change in his condition, and so made what haste he could to get Hyrcanus into his power, or indeed to put him quite out of the way; which last thing he effected afterwards.

4. Accordingly, when Hyrcanus came, full of assurance, by the permission of the king of Parthia, and at the expense of the Jews, who supplied him with money, Herod received him with all possible respect, and gave him the upper place at public meetings, and set him above all the rest at feasts, and thereby deceived him. He called him his father, and endeavoured, by all the ways possible, that he might have no suspicion of any treacherous design against him. He also did other things, in order to secure his government, which yet occasioned a sedition in his own family; for being cautious how he made any illustrious person the high priest of God,† he sent for an obscure priest out of Babylon, whose name was Ananelus, and bestowed the high priesthood upon him.

5. However, Alexandra, the daughter of Hyrcanus, and wife of Alexander, the son of Aristobulus the king, who had also brought Alexander [two] children, could not bear this indignity. Now this son was one of the greatest comeliness, and was called Aristobulus; and the daughter, Mariamne, was married to Herod, and eminent for her beauty also. This Alexandra was much disturbed, and took this indignity offered to her son exceeding ill, that while he was alive, any one else should be sent to have the dignity of the high priesthood conferred upon him. Accordingly, she wrote to Cleopatra (a musician assisting her in taking care to have her letters carried) to desire her intercession with Antony, in order to gain the high priesthood for her son.

6. But as Antony was slow in granting this request, his friend Dellius came into Judea upon some affairs, and when he saw Aristobulus, he stood in admiration at the tallness and handsomeness of the child, and no less at Mariamne, the king's wife, and was open in his commendations of Alexandra, as the mother of most beautiful children: and when she came to discourse with him, he persuaded her to get pictures drawn of them both, and to send them to Antony, for that when he saw them, he would deny her nothing that she would ask. Accordingly, Alexandra was elevated with these words of his, and sent the pictures to Antony. Dellius also talked extravagantly, and said that these children seemed not derived from men, but from some god or other. His design in doing so was to entice Antony into lewd pleasures with them, who was ashamed to send for the damsel, as being the wife of Herod, and avoided it because of the reproaches he should have from Cleopatra on that account; but he sent in the most decent manner he could for the young man; but added this withal, unless he thought it hard upon him so to do. When this letter was brought to Herod, he did not think it safe for him to send one so handsome as was Aristobulus, in the prime of his life, for he was sixteen years of age, and of so noble a family, and particularly not to Antony, the principal man among the Romans, and one that would abuse him in his amours, and besides, one that openly indulged himself in such pleasures as his power allowed him, without control. He therefore wrote back to him, that if this boy should only go out of the country, all would be in a state of war and uproar; because the Jews were in hopes of a change in the government, and to have another king over them.

7. When Herod had thus excused himself to Antony, he resolved that he would not entirely permit the child of Alexandra to be treated dishonourably: but his wife Mariamne lay vehemently at him to restore the high priesthood to her brother; and he judged it was for his advantage so to do, because if he once had that dignity, he could not go out of the country. So he called all his friends together, and told

---

* The city here called "Babylon" by Josephus, seems to be one which was built by some of the Seleucidæ, upon the Tigris; which, long after the utter desolation of Old Babylon, was commonly so called, just as the later adjoining city Bagdat is often called by the same old name of Babylon.

† Here we have an example of Herod's worldly and profane politics, when, by the abuse of his unlawful and usurped power, to make whom he pleased high priest, in the person of Ananelus, he occasioned such disturbances in his kingdom, and in his own family, as suffered him to enjoy no lasting peace or tranquillity ever afterwards.

them that Alexandra privately conspired against his royal authority, and endeavoured, by the means of Cleopatra, so to bring it about, that he might be deprived of the government, and that by Antony's means this youth might have the management of public affairs in his stead; and that this procedure of hers was unjust, since she would at the same time deprive her daughter of the dignity she now had, and would bring disturbances upon the kingdom, for which he had taken a great deal of pains, and had gotten it with extraordinary hazards: that yet, while he well remembered her wicked practices, he would not leave off doing what was right himself, but would even now give the youth the high priesthood; and that he formerly set up Ananelus, because Aristobulus was then so very young a child. Now when he had said this, not at random, but as he thought with the best discretion he had, in order to deceive the women, and those friends whom he had taken to consult withal, Alexandra, out of the great joy she had at this unexpected promise, and out of fear from the suspicions she lay under, fell a weeping; and made the following apology for herself, and said, that as to the [high] priesthood, she was very much concerned for the disgrace her son was under, and so did her utmost endeavours to procure it for him, but that as to the kingdom, she had made no attempts, and that if it were offered her [for her son,] she would not accept it; and that now she would be satisfied with her son's dignity, while he himself held the civil government, and she had thereby the security that arose from his peculiar ability in governing, to all the remainder of her family: that she was now overcome by his benefits, and thankfully accepted of this honour shewn by him to her son, and that she would hereafter be entirely obedient; and she desired him to excuse her, if the nobility of her family, and that freedom of acting which she thought that allowed her, had made her act too precipitately and imprudently in this matter. So when they had spoken thus to one another, they came to an agreement; and all suspicions, so far as appeared, were vanished away.

CHAPTER III

HOW HEROD, UPON HIS MAKING ARISTOBULUS HIGH PRIEST, TOOK CARE THAT HE SHOULD BE MURDERED IN A LITTLE TIME; AND WHAT APOLOGY HE MADE TO ANTONY ABOUT ARISTOBULUS: AS ALSO CONCERNING JOSEPH AND MARIAMNE

1. So king Herod immediately took the high priesthood away from Ananelus, who, as we said before, was not of this country, but one of those Jews that had been carried captive beyond Euphrates; for there were not a few ten thousands of this people that had been carried captives, and dwelt about Babylonia, whence Ananelus came. He was one of the stock of the high priests,* and had been of old a particular friend of Herod; and when he was first made king, he conferred that dignity upon him, and now put him out of it again, in order to quiet the troubles in his family, though what he did was plainly unlawful, for at no other time [of old] was any

one that had once been in that dignity deprived of it. It was Antiochus Epiphanes who first broke that law, and deprived Jesus, and made his brother Onias high priest in his stead. Aristobulus was the second that did so, and took that dignity from his brother [Hyrcanus;] and this Herod was the third who took that high office away [from Ananelus,] and gave it to this young man, Aristobulus, in his stead.

2. And now Herod seemed to have healed the divisions in his family; yet was he not without suspicion, as is frequently the case of people seeming to be reconciled to one another, but thought that, as Alexandra had already made attempts tending to innovations, so did he fear that she would go on therein, if she found a fit opportunity for so doing; so he gave a command that she should dwell in the palace, and meddle with no public affairs: her guards also were so careful, that nothing she did in private life every day was concealed. All these hardships put her out of patience, by little and little, and she began to hate Herod; for as she had the pride of a woman to the utmost degree, she had great indignation at this suspicious guard that was about her, as desirous rather to undergo anything that could befall her than to be deprived of her liberty of speech, and, under the notion of an honorary guard, to live in a state of slavery and terror. She therefore sent to Cleopatra, and made a long complaint of the circumstances she was in, and entreated her to do her utmost for her assistance. Cleopatra hereupon advised her to take her son with her, and come away immediately to her into Egypt. This advice pleased her; and she had this contrivance for getting away: She got two coffins made, as if they were to carry away two dead bodies, and put herself into one, and her son into the other, and gave orders to such of her servants as knew of her intentions, to carry them away in the night-time. Now their road was to be thence to the sea-side; and there was a ship ready to carry them into Egypt. Now Æsop, one of her servants, happened to fall upon Sabion, one of her friends, and spake of this matter to him, as thinking he had known of it before. When Sabion knew this (who had formerly been an enemy of Herod, and had been esteemed one of those that laid snares for and gave poison to [his father] Antipater,) he expected that this discovery would change Herod's hatred into kindness; so he told the king of this private stratagem of Alexandra: whereupon he suffered her to proceed to the execution of her project, and caught her in the very fact; but still he passed by her offence: and though he had a great mind to do it, he durst not inflict anything that was severe upon her, for he knew that Cleopatra would not bear that he should have her accused, on account of her hatred to him; but made a show as if it were rather the generosity of his soul, and his great moderation, that made him forgive them. However, he fully proposed to himself to put this young man out of the way, by one means or other; but he thought he might in all probability be better concealed in doing it, if he did it not presently nor immediately after what had lately happened.

3. And now, upon the approach of the feast of tabernacles, which is a festival very much observed among us, he let those days pass over, and both he and the rest of the people were therein very merry; yet did the envy which at this time arose in him, cause him to make haste to do what he was about, and provoke him to it; for when this youth, Aristobulus, who was now in the seventeenth year of his age, went up

---

* When Josephus says here that this Ananelus was "of the stock of the high priests," it contradicts what he had been just telling us that he was a priest of an obscure family or character (chap. ii. sect. 4.)

to the altar, according to the law, to offer the
sacrifices, and this with the ornaments of his
high priesthood, and when he performed the
sacred offices,* he seemed to be exceedingly
comely, and taller than men usually were at
that age, and to exhibit in his countenance a
great deal of that high family he was sprung
from,—a warm zeal and affection towards him
appeared among the people, and the memory of
the actions of his grandfather Aristobulus was
fresh in their minds; and their affections got
so far the mastery of them, that they could not
forbear to shew their inclinations to him. They
at once rejoiced and were confounded, and
mingled with good wishes their joyful acclamations which they made to him, till the good-
will of the multitude was made too evident;
and they more rashly proclaimed the happiness
they had received from his family than was fit
under a monarchy to have done. Upon all this,
Herod resolved to complete what he had intended against this young man. When therefore the festival was over, and he was feasting
at Jericho with Alexandra, who entertained him
there, he was then very pleasant with the young
man, and drew him into a lonely place, and at
the same time played with him in a juvenile
and ludicrous manner. Now the nature of that
place was hotter than ordinary; so they went
out in a body, and of a sudden, and in a vein of
madness; and as they stood by the fish ponds,
of which there were large ones about the house,
they went to cool themselves [by bathing,]
because it was in the midst of a hot day. At
first they were only spectators of Herod's servants and acquaintance as they were swimming;
but after a while, the young man, at the instigation of Herod, went into the water among
them, while such of Herod's acquaintance as he
had appointed to do it, dipped him as he was
swimming, and plunged him under water, in
the dark of the evening, as if it had been done
in sport only; nor did they desist till he was
entirely suffocated. And thus was Aristobulus
murdered, being not eighteen years old, and
having kept the high priesthood one year only;
which high priesthood Ananelus now recovered
again.

4. When this sad accident was told the women,
their joy was soon changed into lamentation, at
the sight of the dead body that lay before them,
and their sorrow was immoderate. The city
also [of Jerusalem,] upon the spreading of this
news, was in very great grief, every family looking on this calamity as if it had not belonged to
another, but that one of themselves was slain:
but Alexandra was more deeply affected, upon
her knowledge that he had been destroyed [on
purpose.] Her sorrow was greater than that of
others, by her knowing how the murder was
committed; but she was under the necessity of
bearing up under it, out of her prospect of a
greater mischief that might otherwise follow;
and she sometimes came to an inclination to
destroy herself with her own hand, but still she
restrained herself, in hopes she might live long
enough to revenge the unjust murder thus privately committed; nay, she further resolved to
endeavour to live longer, and to give no occasion
to think she suspected that her son was slain on
purpose, and supposed that she might thereby
be in a capacity of revenging it at a proper opportunity. Thus did she restrain herself, that
she might not be noted for entertaining any such

suspicion. However, Herod endeavoured that
none abroad should believe that the child's
death was caused by any design of his; and for
this purpose he did not only use the ordinary
signs of sorrow, but fell into tears also, and exhibited a real confusion of soul; and perhaps
his affections were overcome on this occasion,
when he saw the child's countenance so young
and so beautiful, although his death was supposed to tend to his own security. So far at
least this grief served as to make some apology
for him; and as for his funeral, that he took
care should be very magnificent, by making
great preparation for a sepulchre to lay his body
in, and providing a great quantity of spices, and
burying many ornaments together with him, till
the very women, who were in such deep sorrow,
were astonished at it, and received in this way
some consolation.

5. However, no such things could overcome
Alexandra's grief; but the remembrance of this
miserable case made her sorrow both deep and
obstinate. Accordingly, she wrote an account
of this treacherous scene to Cleopatra, and how
her son was murdered; but Cleopatra, as she
had formerly been desirous to give her what
satisfaction she could, and commiserating Alexandra's misfortunes, made the case her own,
and would not let Antony be quiet, but excited
him to punish the child's murder: for that it
was an unworthy thing that Herod, who had
by him been made a king of a kingdom that no
way belonged to him, should be guilty of such
horrid crimes against those that were of the
royal blood in reality. Antony was persuaded
by these arguments; and when he came to Laodicea, he sent and commanded Herod to come
and make his defence as to what he had done to
Aristobulus, for that such a treacherous design
was not well done, if he had any hand in it.
Herod was now in fear, both of the accusation
and of Cleopatra's ill-will to him, which was
such that she was ever endeavouring to make
Antony hate him. He therefore determined to
obey his summons, for he had no possible way
to avoid it: so he left his uncle Joseph procurator for his government and for the public affairs,
and gave him a private charge, that if Antony
should kill him, he also should kill Mariamne
immediately; for that he had a tender affection
for this his wife, and was afraid of the injury
that should be offered him, if, after his death,
she, for her beauty, should be engaged to some
other man: but his intimation was nothing but
this at the bottom, that Antony had fallen in
love with her, when he formerly heard somewhat of her beauty. So when Herod had given
Joseph this charge, and had indeed no sure
hopes of escaping with his life, he went away
to Antony.

6. But as Joseph was administering the public
affairs of the kingdom, and for that reason was
very frequently with Mariamne, both because
his business required it, and because of the
respects he ought to pay to the queen, he frequently let himself into discourses about Herod's
kindness, and great affection towards her; and
when the women, especially Alexandra, used to
turn his discourses into feminine raillery, Joseph
was so over-desirous to demonstrate the king's
inclinations, that he proceeded so far as to mention the charge he had received, and thence drew
his demonstration, that Herod was not able to
live without her; and that if he should come to
any ill end, he could not endure a separation
from her, even after he was dead. Thus spake
Joseph. But the women, as was natural, did
not take this to be an instance of Herod's strong

* This entirely confutes the Talmudists, who pretend that no one under twenty years of age could officiate as high priest among the Jews.

affection for them, but of his severe usage of them, that they could not escape destruction, nor a tyrannical death, even when he was dead himself: and this saying [of Joseph] was a foundation for the women's severe suspicions about him afterwards.

7. At this time a report went about the city of Jerusalem, among Herod's enemies, that Antony had tortured Herod, and put him to death. This report, as is natural, disturbed those that were about the palace, but chiefly the women: upon which Alexandra endeavoured to persuade Joseph to go out of the palace, and fly away with them to the ensigns of the Roman legions which then lay encamped about the city, as a guard to the kingdom, under the command of Julius; for that by this means, if any disturbance should happen about the palace, they should be in greater security, as having the Romans favourable to them; and that besides, they hoped to obtain the highest authority, if Antony did but once see Mariamne, by whose means they should recover the kingdom, and want nothing which was reasonable for them to hope for, because of their royal extraction.

8. But as they were in the midst of these deliberations, letters were brought from Herod about all his affairs, and proved contrary to the report, and of what they before expected; for when he was come to Antony, he soon recovered his interest with him, by the presents he made him, which he had brought with him from Jerusalem; and he soon induced him, upon discoursing with him, to leave off his indignation at him, so that Cleopatra's persuasions had less force than the arguments and presents he brought to regain his friendship: for Antony said, that it was not good to require an account of a king, as to the affairs of his government, for at this rate he could be no king at all, but that those who had given him that authority ought to permit him to make use of it. He also said the same things to Cleopatra, that it would be best for her not busily to meddle with the acts of the king's government. Herod wrote an account of these things; and enlarged upon the other honours which he had received from Antony: how he sat by him at his hearing causes, and took his diet with him every day, and that he enjoyed those favours from him, notwithstanding the reproaches that Cleopatra so severely laid against him, who having a great desire of his country, and earnestly entreating Antony that the kingdom might be given to her, laboured with her utmost diligence to have him out of the way; but that he still found Antony just to him, and had no longer any apprehensions of hard treatment from him; and that he was soon upon his return, with a firmer additional assurance of his favour to him, in his reigning and managing public affairs; and that there was no longer any hope for Cleopatra's covetous temper, since Antony had given her Cœlesyria instead of what she desired; by which means he had at once pacified her, and got clear of the entreaties which she made him to have Judea bestowed upon her.

9. When these letters were brought, the women left off their attempt for flying to the Romans, which they thought of while Herod was supposed to be dead; yet was not that purpose of theirs a secret; but when the king had conducted Antony on his way against the Parthians, he returned to Judea, when both his sister Salome, and his mother, informed him of Alexandra's intentions. Salome also added somewhat further against Joseph, though it was no more than a calumny, that he had often had criminal conversation with Mariamne. The rea-

son of her saying so was this, that she for a long time bare her ill-will; for when they had differences with one another, Mariamne took great freedoms, and reproached the rest for the meanness of their birth. But Herod, whose affection to Mariamne was always very warm, was presently disturbed at this, and could not bear the torments of jealousy, but was still restrained from doing any rash thing to her by the love he had for her; yet did his vehement affection and jealousy together make him ask Mariamne by herself about this matter of Joseph; but she denied it upon her oath, and said all that an innocent woman could possibly say in her own defence; so that by little and little the king was prevailed upon to drop the suspicion, and left off his anger at her; and being overcome with his passion for his wife, he made an apology to her for having seemed to believe what he had heard about her, and returned her a great many acknowledgments of her modest behaviour, and professed the extraordinary affection and kindness he had for her, till at last, as is usual between lovers, they both fell into tears, and embraced one another with a most tender affection. But as the king gave more and more assurances of his belief of her fidelity, and endeavoured to draw her to a like confidence in him, Mariamne said, "Yet was not that command thou gavest, that if any harm came to thee from Antony, I, who had been no occasion of it, should perish with thee, a sign of thy love to me?" When these words were fallen from her, the king was shocked at them, and presently let her go out of his arms, and cried out, and tore his hair with his own hands, and said, that now he had an evident demonstration that Joseph had had criminal conversation with his wife; for that he would never have uttered what he had told him alone by himself, unless there had been such a great familiarity and firm confidence between them. And while he was in this passion he had liked to have killed his wife; but being still overborne by his love to her, he restrained this his passion, though not without a lasting grief and disquietness of mind. However, he gave order to slay Joseph without permitting him to come into his sight; and as for Alexandra, he bound her, and kept her in custody, as the cause of all this mischief.

CHAPTER IV

HOW CLEOPATRA, WHEN SHE HAD GOTTEN FROM ANTONY SOME PARTS OF JUDEA AND ARABIA, CAME INTO JUDEA; AND HOW HEROD GAVE HER MANY PRESENTS, AND CONDUCTED HER ON HER WAY BACK TO EGYPT

1. Now at this time the affairs of Syria were in confusion by Cleopatra's constant persuasions to Antony to make an attempt upon every body's dominions; for she persuaded him to take those dominions away from their several princes, and bestow them upon her; and she had a mighty influence upon him, by reason of his being enslaved to her by his affections. She was also by nature very covetous, and stuck at no wickedness. She had already poisoned her brother, because she knew that he was to be king of Egypt, and this when he was but fifteen years old; and she got her sister Arsinoe to be slain, by the means of Antony, when she was a supplicant at Diana's temple at Ephesus; for if there were but any hopes of getting money, she would violate both temples and sepulchres. Nor was there any holy place that was esteemed the most

inviolable, from which she would not fetch the ornaments it had in it; nor any place so profane, but was to suffer the most flagitious treatment possible from her, if it could but contribute somewhat to the covetous humour of this wicked creature; yet did not all this suffice so extravagant a woman, who was a slave to her lusts, but she still imagined that she wanted everything she could think of, and did her utmost to gain it; for which reason she hurried Antony on perpetually to deprive others of their dominions, and give them to her; and as she went over Syria with him, she contrived to get it into her possession; so he slew Lysanias the son of Ptolemy, accusing him of his bringing the Parthians upon those countries. She also petitioned Antony to give her Judea and Arabia; and, in order thereto, desired him to take these countries away from their present governors. As for Antony, he was so entirely overcome by this woman, that one would not think her conversation only could do it, but that he was some way or other bewitched to do whatsoever she would have him; yet did the grossest parts of her injustice make him so ashamed, that he would not always hearken to her to do those flagrant enormities she would have persuaded him to. That therefore he might not totally deny her, nor by doing everything which she enjoined him, appear openly to be an ill man, he took some parts of each of those countries away from their former governors, and gave them to her. Thus he gave her the cities that were within the river Eleutherus, as far as Egypt, excepting Tyre and Sidon, which he knew to have been free cities from their ancestors, although she pressed him very often to bestow those on her also.

2. When Cleopatra had obtained thus much, and had accompanied Antony in his expedition to Armenia, as far as Euphrates, she returned back, and came to Apamia and Damascus, and passed on to Judea; where Herod met her, and farmed of her her parts of Arabia, and those revenues that came to her from those regions about Jericho. This country bears that balsam, which is the most precious drug that is there, and grows there alone. The place bears also palm-trees, both many in number, and those excellent in their kind. When she was there, and was very often with Herod, she endeavoured to have criminal conversation with the king: nor did she affect secresy in the indulgence of such sort of pleasures; and perhaps she had in some measure a passion of love to him, or rather, what is most probable, she laid a treacherous snare for him, by aiming to obtain such adulterous conversation from him; however, upon the whole, she seemed overcome with love to him. Now Herod had a great while borne no good-will to Cleopatra, as knowing that she was a woman irksome to all; and at that time he thought her particularly worthy of his hatred, if this attempt proceeded out of lust: he had also thought of preventing her intrigues, by putting her to death, if such were her endeavours. However, he refused to comply with her proposals, and called a counsel of his friends to consult with them whether he should not kill her, now he had her in his power; for that he should thereby deliver all those from a multitude of evils to whom she was already become irksome, and was expected to be still so for the time to come; and that this very thing would be much for the advantage of Antony himself, since she would certainly not be faithful to him, in case any such season or necessity should come upon him as that he should stand in need of her fidelity. But when he thought to follow this advice, his friends would

not let him; and told him, that, in the first place, it was not right to attempt so great a thing, and run himself thereby into the utmost danger; and they laid hard at him, and begged him to undertake nothing rashly, for that Antony would never bear it, no, not though any one should evidently lay before his eyes that it was for his own advantage; and that the appearance of depriving him of her conversation, by this violent and treacherous method, would probably set his affections more on a flame than before. Nor did it appear that he could offer anything of tolerable weight in his defence, this attempt being against such a woman as was of the highest dignity of any of her sex at that time in the world; and as to any advantage to be expected from such an undertaking, if any such could be supposed in this case, it would appear to deserve condemnation on account of the insolence he must take upon him in doing it: which considerations made it very plain, that in so doing he would find his government filled with mischiefs, both great and lasting, both to himself and his posterity, whereas it was still in his power to reject that wickedness she would persuade him to, and to come off honourably at the same time. So by thus affrighting Herod, and representing to him the hazards he must, in all probability, run by this undertaking, they restrained him from it. So he treated Cleopatra kindly, and made her presents, and conducted her on her way to Egypt.

3. But Antony subdued Armenia, and sent Artabazes, the son of Tigranes, in bonds, with his children and procurators, to Egypt, and made a present of them, and of all the royal ornaments which he had taken out of that kingdom, to Cleopatra; and Artaxias, the eldest of his sons, who had escaped at that time, took the kingdom of Armenia; who yet was ejected by Archelaus and Nero Cæsar, when they restored Tigranes, his younger brother, to that kingdom: but this happened a good while afterward.

4. But then, as to the tributes which Herod was to pay Cleopatra for that country which Antony had given her, he acted fairly with her, as deeming it not safe for him to afford any cause for Cleopatra to hate him. As for the king of Arabia, whose tribute Herod had undertaken to pay her, for some time indeed he paid him as much as came to two hundred talents; but he afterward became very niggardly and slow in his payments, and could hardly be brought to pay some parts of it, and was not willing to pay even them without some deductions.

CHAPTER V

HOW HEROD MADE WAR WITH THE KING OF ARABIA, AND AFTER THEY HAD FOUGHT MANY BATTLES, AT LENGTH CONQUERED HIM, AND WAS CHOSEN BY THE ARABS TO BE GOVERNOR OF THAT NATION; AS ALSO CONCERNING A GREAT EARTHQUAKE

1. HEREUPON Herod held himself ready to go against the king of Arabia, because of his ingratitude to him, and because, after all, he would do nothing that was just to him, although Herod made the Roman war an occasion of delaying his own; for the battle of Actium was now expected, which fell into the hundred and eighty-seventh Olympiad, where Cæsar and Antony were to fight for the supreme power of the world; but Herod having enjoyed a country that was very fruitful, and that now for a long time, and having received

great taxes, and raised great armies therewith, got together a body of men, and carefully furnished them with all necessaries, and designed them as auxiliaries for Antony; but Antony said he had no want of his assistance; but he commanded him to punish the king of Arabia, for he had heard, both from him and from Cleopatra, how perfidious he was; for this was what Cleopatra desired, who thought it for her own advantage that these two kings should do one another as great mischief as possible. Upon this message from Antony, Herod returned back, but kept his army with him, in order to invade Arabia immediately. So when his army of horsemen and footmen was ready, he marched to Diospolis, whither the Arabians came also to meet them, for they were not unapprised of this war that was coming upon them; and after a great battle had been fought, the Jews had the victory; but afterward there were gotten together another numerous army of the Arabians, at Cana, which is a place of Cœlesyria. Herod was informed of this beforehand: so he marched against them with the greatest part of the forces he had; and when he was come near Cana, he resolved to encamp himself; and he cast up a bulwark, that he might take a proper season for attacking the enemy; but as he was giving those orders, the multitude of the Jews cried out that he should make no delay, but lead them against the Arabians. They went with great spirit, as believing they were in very good order; and those especially were so that had been in the former battle and had been conquerors, and had not permitted their enemies so much as to come to a close fight with them; and when they were so tumultuous, and shewed such great alacrity, the king resolved to make use of that zeal the multitude then exhibited; and when he had assured them he would not be behindhand with them in courage, he led them on, and stood before them in all his armour, all the regiments following him in their several ranks; whereupon a consternation fell upon the Arabians; for when they perceived that the Jews were not to be conquered, and were full of spirit, the greater part of them ran away, and avoided fighting; and they had been quite destroyed, had not Athenio fallen upon the Jews, and distressed them; for this man was Cleopatra's general over the soldiers she had there, and was at enmity with Herod, and very wistfully looked on to see what the event of the battle would be. He had also resolved, that in case the Arabians did anything that was brave and successful, he would lie still; but in case they were beaten, as it really happened, he would attack the Jews with those forces he had of his own, and with those that the country had gotten together for him: so he fell upon the Jews unexpectedly, when they were fatigued, and thought they had already vanquished the enemy, and made a great slaughter of them; for as the Jews had spent their courage upon their known enemies, and were about to enjoy themselves in quietness after their victory, they were easily beaten by these that attacked them afresh; and in particular received a great loss in places where the horses could not be of any service, and which were very stony, and where those that attacked them were better acquainted with the places than themselves; and when the Jews had suffered this loss, the Arabians raised their spirits after their defeat, and returning back again, slew those that were already put to flight; and indeed all sorts of slaughter were now frequent, and of those that escaped, a few only returned into the camp. So king Herod, when he despaired of the battle, rode up to them to bring them assistance, yet

did he not come time enough to do them any service, though he laboured hard to do it; but the Jewish camp was taken, so that the Arabians had unexpectedly a most glorious success, having gained that victory which of themselves they were no way likely to have gained, and slaying a great part of the enemy's army; whence afterward Herod could only act like a private robber, and make excursions upon many parts of Arabia, and distress them by sudden incursions, while he encamped among the mountains, and avoided by any means to come to a pitched battle; yet did he greatly harass the enemy by his assiduity, and the hard labour he took in this matter. He also took great care of his own forces, and used all the means he could to restore his affairs to their old state.

2. At this time it was that the fight happened at Actium, between Octavius Cæsar and Antony, in the seventh year of the reign of Herod;* and then it was also that there was an earthquake in Judea, such a one as had not happened at any other time, and which earthquake brought a great destruction upon the cattle in that country. About ten thousand men also perished by the fall of houses; but the army, which lodged in the field, received no damage by this sad accident. When the Arabians were informed of this, and when those that hated the Jews, and pleased themselves with aggravating the reports, told them of it, they raised their spirits, as if their enemy's country was quite overthrown, and the men were utterly destroyed, and thought there now remained nothing that could oppose them. Accordingly, they took the Jewish ambassadors, who came to them after all this had happened, to make peace with them, and slew them, and came with great alacrity against their army; but the Jews durst not withstand them, and were so cast down by the calamities they were under, that they took no care of their affairs, but gave up themselves to despair, for they had no hope that they should be so upon a level again with them in battles, nor obtain any assistance elsewhere, while their affairs at home were in such great distress also. When matters were in this condition, the king persuaded the commanders by his words, and tried to raise their spirits, which were quite sunk: and first he endeavoured to encourage and embolden some of the better sort beforehand, and then ventured to make a speech to the multitude, which he had before avoided to do, lest he should find them uneasy thereat, because of the misfortunes which had happened: so he made a consolatory speech to the multitude, in the manner following:—

3. "You are not unacquainted, my fellow-soldiers, that we have had, not long since, many accidents that have put a stop to what we are about; and it is probable, that even those that are most distinguished above others for their courage, can hardly keep up their spirits in such circumstances; but since we cannot avoid fighting, and nothing that hath happened is of such a nature but it may by ourselves be recovered into a good state, and this by one brave action only well performed, I have proposed to myself both to give you some encouragement, and, at the same time, some information; both which parts of my design will tend to this point, that you may still continue in your own proper fortitude. I will, then, in the first place, demon-

* It is here to be noticed, that this seventh year of the reign of Herod, and all the other years of his reign, in Josephus, are dated from the death of Antigonus, and never from his first obtaining the kingdom at Rome, above three years before.

strate to you, that this war is a just one on our side, and that on this account it is a war of necessity, and occasioned by the injustice of our adversaries ; for, if you be once satisfied of this, it will be a real cause of alacrity to you ; after which I will further demonstrate, that the misfortunes we are under are of no great consequence, and that we have the greatest reason to hope for victory. I shall begin with the first, and appeal to yourselves as witnesses to what I shall say. You are not ignorant certainly of the wickedness of the Arabians, which is to that degree as to appear incredible to all other men, and to include somewhat that shews the grossest barbarity and ignorance of God. The chief things wherein they have affronted us have arisen from covetousness and envy ; and they have attacked us in an insidious manner, and on the sudden. And what occasion is there for me to mention many instances of such their procedure ? When they were in danger of losing their own government of themselves, and of being slaves to Cleopatra, what others were they that freed them from that fear? for it was the friendship I had with Antony, and the kind disposition he was in towards us, that hath been the occasion that even these Arabians have not been utterly undone ; Antony being unwilling to undertake anything which might be suspected by us of unkindness : but when he had a mind to bestow some parts of each of our dominions on Cleopatra, I also managed that matter so, that by giving him presents of my own, I might obtain a security to both nations, while I undertook myself to answer for the money, and gave him two hundred talents, and became surety for those two hundred more which were imposed upon the land which was subject to this tribute : and this they have defrauded us of, although it was not reasonable that Jews should pay tribute to any man living, or allow part of their land to be taxable ; but although that was to be, yet ought we not to pay tribute for these Arabians, whom we have ourselves preserved ; nor is it fit that they who have professed (and that with great integrity and sense of our kindness) that it is by our means that they keep their principality, should injure us, and deprive us of what is our due, and this while we have been still not their enemies but their friends. And whereas observation of covenants takes place among the bitterest enemies, but among friends is absolutely necessary,—this is not observed among these men, who think gain to be the best of all things, let it be by any means whatsoever, and that injustice is no harm, if they may but get money by it : is it therefore a question with you, whether the unjust are to be punished or not? when God himself hath declared his mind that so it ought to be,—and hath commanded that we ever should hate injuries and injustice, which is not only just but necessary in wars between several nations ; for these Arabians have done what both the Greeks and Barbarians own to be an instance of the grossest wickedness, with regard to our ambassadors, whom they have beheaded, while the Greeks declare that such ambassadors are sacred and inviolable.* And for ourselves, we have learned from God the most excellent of our doctrines, and the most holy part of our law, by angels or ambas-

sadors ; for this name brings God to the knowledge of mankind, and is sufficient to reconcile enemies one to another. What wickedness, then, can be greater than the slaughter of ambassadors, who come to treat about doing what is right ? And when such have been their actions, how is it possible they can either live securely in common life. or be successful in war? In my opinion, this is impossible. But perhaps some will say, that what is holy, and what is righteous, is indeed on our side, but that the Arabians are either more courageous or more numerous than we are. Now, as to this, in the first place, it is not fit for us to say so, for with whom is what is righteous, with them is God himself ; now, where God is, there is both multitude and courage. But to examine our own circumstances a little, we were conquerors in the first battle ; and when we fought again, they were not able to oppose us, but ran away, and could not endure our attacks or our courage ; but when we had conquered them, then came Athenio, and made war against us without declaring it ; and pray, is this an instance of their manhood, or is it not a second instance of their wickedness and treachery? Why are we therefore of less courage, on account of that which ought to inspire us with stronger hopes ? and why are we terrified at these, who, when they fight upon a level, are continually beaten, and when they seem to be conquerors, they gain it by wickedness? and if we suppose that any one should deem them to be men of real courage, will he not be excited by that very consideration to do his utmost against them? for true valour is not shewn by fighting against weak persons, but in being able to overcome the most hardy. But then, if the distresses we ourselves are under, and the miseries that have come by the earthquake, have affrighted any one, let him consider, in the first place, that this very thing will deceive the Arabians, by their supposal that what hath befallen us is greater than it really is. Moreover, it is not right that the same thing that emboldens them should discourage us ; for these men, you see, do not derive their alacrity from any advantageous virtue of their own, but from their hope, as to us, that we are quite cast down by our misfortunes ; but when we boldly march against them, we shall soon pull down their insolent conceit of themselves, and shall gain this by attacking them, that they will not be so insolent when we come to the battle ; for our distresses are not so great, nor is what hath happened an indication of the anger of God against us, as some imagine ; for such things are accidental, and adversities that come in the usual course of things ; and if we allow that this was done by the will of God, we must allow that it is now over by his will also, and that he is satisfied with what hath already happened ; for had he been willing to afflict us still more thereby, he had not changed his mind so soon. And as for the war we are engaged in, he hath himself demonstrated that he is willing it should go on, and that he knows it to be a just war ; for while some of the people in the country have perished, all you who were in arms have suffered nothing, but are all preserved alive ; whereby God makes it plain to us, that if you had universally, with your children and wives, been in the army, it had come to pass that you had not undergone anything that would have much hurt you. Consider these things, and, what is more than all the rest, that you have God at all times for your protector ; and prosecute these men with a just bravery, who in point of friendship, are unjust, in their battles perfidious, towards am-

---

* Herod says here, that as ambassadors were sacred when they carried messages to others, so did the laws of the Jews derive a sacred authority by being delivered from God by angels [or divine ambassadors ;] which is St Paul's expression about the same laws, (Gal. iii. 16 ; Heb. ii. 2.)

bassadors impious, and always inferior to you in valour."

4. When the Jews heard this speech, they were much raised in their minds, and more disposed to fight than before. So Herod when he had offered the sacrifices appointed by the law,* made haste, and took them, and led them against the Arabians; and in order to that, passed over Jordan, and pitched his camp near to that of the enemy. He also thought fit to seize upon a certain castle that lay in the midst of them, as hoping it would be for his advantage, and would the sooner produce a battle; and that if there were occasion for delay, he should by it have his camp fortified; and as the Arabians had the same intentions upon that place, a contest arose about it; at first they were but skirmishes, after which there came more soldiers, and it proved a sort of fight, and some fell on both sides, till those of the Arabian side were beaten, and retreated. This was no small encouragement to the Jews immediately; and when Herod observed that the enemy's army were disposed to anything rather than to come to an engagement, he ventured boldly to attempt the bulwark itself, and to pull it to pieces, and so to get nearer to their camp, in order to fight them; for when they were forced out of their trenches, they went out in disorder, and had not the least alacrity, or hope of victory; yet did they fight hand to hand, because they were no more in number than the Jews, and because they were in such a disposition of war that they were under a necessity of coming on boldly; so they came on to a terrible battle, while not a few fell on each side. However, at length the Arabians fled; and so great a slaughter was made upon their being routed, that they were not only killed by their enemies, but became the authors of their own deaths also, and were trodden down by the multitude, and the great current of people in disorder, and were destroyed by their own armour; so five thousand men lay dead upon the spot, while the rest of the multitude soon ran within the bulwark [for safety,] but had no firm hope of safety, by reason of their want of necessaries, and especially of water. The Jews pursued them, but could not get in with them, but sat round about the bulwark, and watched any assistance that would get into them, and prevented any there that had a mind to it from running away.

5. When the Arabians were in these circumstances, they sent ambassadors to Herod, in the first place, to propose terms of accommodation, and after that to offer him, so pressing was their thirst upon them, to undergo whatsoever he pleased, if he would free them from their present distress; but he would admit of no ambassadors, of no price of redemption, nor of any other moderate terms whatever, being very desirous to revenge those unjust actions which they had been guilty of towards his nation. So they were necessitated by other motives, and particularly by their thirst, to come out, and deliver themselves up to him, to be carried away captives; and in five days' time, the number of four thousand were taken prisoners, while all the rest resolved to make a sally upon their enemies, and to

fight it out with them, choosing rather, if so it must be, to die therein, than to perish gradually and ingloriously. When they had taken this resolution, they came out of their trenches, but could no way sustain the fight, being too much disabled, both in mind and body, and having not room to exert themselves, and thought it an advantage to be killed, and a misery to survive; so at the first onset there fell about seven thousand of them, after which stroke, they let all the courage they had put on before fall, and stood amazed at Herod's warlike spirit under his own calamities; so for the future they yielded, and made him ruler of their nation; whereupon he was greatly elevated at so seasonable a success, and returned home, taking great authority upon him, on account of so bold and glorious an expedition as he had made.

CHAPTER VI

HOW HEROD SLEW HYRCANUS, AND THEN HASTED AWAY TO CÆSAR, AND OBTAINED THE KINGDOM FROM HIM ALSO; AND HOW, A LITTLE TIME AFTERWARD, HE ENTERTAINED CÆSAR IN A MOST HONOURABLE MANNER

1. HEROD'S other affairs were now very prosperous, and he was not to be easily assaulted on any side. Yet did there come upon him a danger that would hazard his entire dominions, after Antony had been beaten at the battle of Actium by Cæsar [Octavian;] for at that time both Herod's enemies and friends despaired of his affairs, for it was not probable that he would remain without punishment, who had shewn so much friendship for Antony. So it happened that his friends despaired, and had no hopes of his escape; but for his enemies, they all outwardly appeared troubled at his case, but were privately very glad of it, as hoping to obtain a change for the better. As for Herod himself, he saw that there was no one of royal dignity left but Hyrcanus, and therefore he thought it would be for his advantage not to suffer him to be an obstacle in his way any longer; for that in case he himself survived, and escaped the danger he was in, he thought it was the safest way to put it out of the power of such a man to make any attempt against him at such junctures of affairs, as was more worthy of the kingdom than himself; and in case he should be slain by Cæsar, his envy prompted him to desire to slay him that would otherwise be king after him.

2. While Herod had these things in his mind, there was a certain occasion afforded him; for Hyrcanus was of so mild a temper, both then and at other times, that he desired not to meddle with public affairs, nor to concern himself with innovations, but left all to fortune, and contented himself with what that afforded him: but Alexandra [his daughter] was a lover of strife, and was exceeding desirous of a change of the government; and spoke to her father not to bear for ever Herod's injurious treatment of their family, but to anticipate their future hopes, as he safely might; and desired him to write about these matters to Malchus, who was then governor of Arabia, to receive them, and to secure them [from Herod,] for that if they went away, and Herod's affairs proved to be, as it was likely they would be by reason of Cæsar's enmity to him, they should then be the only persons that could take the government; and this, both on account of the royal family they were of, and on account of the good disposition of the multi-

---

* This piece of religion is worth remarking, because it is the only example of this nature that Josephus ever mentions of this Herod; and it was when he had been in mighty distress—such times of affliction making men most religious; nor was he disappointed of his hopes here, but immediately gained a most signal victory over the Arabians, while they who just before had been so great victors were now under a strange consternation, and hardly able to fight at all.

tude to them. While she used these persuasions, Hyrcanus put off her suit; but as she shewed that she was a woman, and a contentious woman too, and would not desist either night or day, but would always be speaking to him about these matters, and about Herod's treacherous designs, she at last prevailed with him to entrust Dositheus, one of his friends, with a letter, wherein his resolution was declared; and he desired the Arabian governor to send him some horsemen, who should receive him, and conduct him to the lake Asphaltites, which is from the bounds of Jerusalem three hundred furlongs: and he did therefore trust Dositheus with his letter, because he was a careful attendant on him and on Alexandra, and had no small occasion to bear ill-will to Herod; for he was a kinsman of one Joseph, whom he had slain, and a brother of those that were formerly slain at Tyre by Antony: yet could not these motives induce Dositheus to serve Hyrcanus in this affair; for preferring the hopes he had from the present king to those he had from him, he gave Herod the letter. So he took his kindness in good part, and bade him besides do what he had already done, that is, go on in serving him, by rolling up the epistle and sealing it again, and delivering it to Malchus, and then to bring back the letter in answer to it; for it would be much better if he could know Malchus's intentions also. And when Dositheus was ready to serve him in this point also, the Arabian governor returned back for answer, that he would receive Hyrcanus, and all that should come with him, and even all the Jews that were of his party: that he would, moreover, send forces sufficient to secure them in their journey; and that he should be in no want of anything he should desire. Now as soon as Herod had received this letter, he immediately sent for Hyrcanus, and questioned him about the league he had made with Malchus; and when he denied it, he shewed the letter to the Sanhedrim, and put the man to death immediately.

3. And this account we give the reader, as it is contained in the commentaries of king Herod: but other historians do not agree with them, for they suppose that Herod did not find, but rather made this an occasion for thus putting him to death, and that by treacherously laying a snare for him; for thus do they write:—That Herod and he were once at a treat, and that Herod had given no occasion to suspect [that he was displeased at him,] but put this question to Hyrcanus, Whether he had received any letters from Malchus? and when he answered that he had received letters, but those of salutation only; and when he asked further, whether he had not received any presents from him? and when he had replied, that he had received no more than four horses to ride on, which Malchus had sent him, they pretended that Herod charged these upon him as the crimes of bribery and treason, and gave orders that he should be led away and slain. And in order to demonstrate that he had been guilty of no offence, when he was thus brought to his end, they allege how mild his temper had been; and that even in his youth he had never given any demonstration of boldness or rashness, and that the case was the same when he came to be king, but that he even then committed the management of the greatest part of public affairs to Antipater: and that he was now above fourscore years old, and knew that Herod's government was in a secure state. He also came over Euphrates, and left those who greatly honoured him beyond that river, though he were to be entirely under Herod's government; and that it was a most incredible thing that he should

enterprise anything by way of innovation, and not at all agreeable to his temper, but that this was a plot of Herod's own contrivance.

4. And this was the fate of Hyrcanus; and thus did he end his life, after he had endured various and manifold turns of fortune in his lifetime; for he was made high priest of the Jewish nation in the beginning of his mother Alexandra's reign, who held the government nine years; and when, after his mother's death, he took the kingdom himself, and held it three months, he lost it, by the means of his brother Aristobulus. He was then restored by Pompey, and received all sorts of honour from him, and enjoyed them forty years; but when he was again deprived by Antigonus, and was maimed in his body, he was made a captive by the Parthians, and thence returned home again after some time, on account of the hopes that Herod had given him; none of which came to pass according to his expectation; but he still conflicted with many misfortunes through the whole course of his life: and, what was the heaviest calamity of all, as we have related already, he came to an end which was undeserved by him. His character appeared to be that of a man of a mild and moderate disposition, who suffered the administration of affairs to be generally done by others under him. He was averse to much meddling with the public, nor had shrewdness enough to govern a kingdom: and both Antipater and Herod came to their greatness by reason of his mildness; and at last he met with such an end from them as was not agreeable either to justice or piety.

5. Now Herod, as soon as he had put Hyrcanus out of the way, made haste to Cæsar; and because he could not have any hopes of kindness from him, on account of the friendship he had for Antony, he had a suspicion of Alexandra, lest she should take this opportunity to bring the multitude to a revolt, and introduce a sedition into the affairs of the kingdom; so he committed the care of everything to his brother Pheroras, and placed his mother Cyprus, and his sister [Salome,] and the whole family, at Masada, and gave him a charge, that if he should hear any sad news about him, he should take care of the government: but as to Mariamne his wife, because of the misunderstanding between her and his sister, and his sister's mother, which made it impossible for them to live together, he placed her at Alexandrium, with Alexandra her mother, and left his treasurer Joseph and Sohemus of Iturea, to take care of that fortress. These two had been very faithful to him from the beginning, and were now left as a guard to the women. They also had it in charge, that if they should hear any mischief had befallen him, they should kill them both; and, as far as they were able, to preserve the kingdom for his sons, and for his brother Pheroras.

6. When he had given them this charge, he made haste to Rhodes, to meet Cæsar; and when he had sailed to that city, he took off his diadem, but remitted nothing else of his usual dignity: and when, upon his meeting him, he desired that he would let him speak to him, he therein exhibited a much more noble specimen of a great soul, for he did not betake himself to supplications, as men usually do upon such occasions, nor offered him any petition, as if he were an offender; but, after an undaunted manner, gave an account of what he had done; for he spake thus to Cæsar:—That he had the greatest friendship for Antony, and did everything that he could that he might attain the government: that he was not indeed in the army

with him, because the Arabians had diverted him, but that he had sent him both money and corn, which was but too little in comparison of what he ought to have done for him; "for if a man owns himself to be another's friend and knows him to be a benefactor, he is obliged to hazard everything, to use every faculty of his soul, every member of his body, and all the wealth he hath, for him; in which I confess I have been too deficient. However, I am conscious to myself, that so far I have done right, that I have not deserted him on his defeat at Actium : nor upon the evident change of his fortune have I transferred my hopes from him to another, but have preserved myself, though not as a valuable fellow-soldier, yet certainly as a faithful counsellor to Antony, when I demonstrated to him that the only way he had to save himself, and not lose all his authority, was to slay Cleopatra; for when she was once dead, there would be room for him to retain his authority, and rather to bring thee to make a composition with him, than to continue at enmity any longer. None of which advices would he attend to, but preferred his own rash resolutions before them. which have happened unprofitably for him, but profitably for thee. Now, therefore, in case thou determinest about me, and my alacrity in serving Antony, according to thy anger at him, I own there is no room for me to deny what I have done, nor will I be ashamed to own, and that publicly too, that I had a great kindness for him; but if thou wilt put him out of the case, and only examine how I behave myself to my benefactors in general, and what sort of friend I am, thou wilt find by experience that we shall do and be the same to thyself, for it is but changing the names, and the firmness of friendship that we shall bear thee will not be disapproved by thee."

7. By this speech, and by his behaviour, which shewed Cæsar the frankness of his mind, he greatly gained upon him, who was himself of a generous and magnificent temper, insomuch that those very actions, which were the foundation of the accusation against him, procured him Cæsar's good-will. Accordingly, he restored him his diadem again; and encouraged him to exhibit himself as great a friend to himself as he had been to Antony, and then had him in great esteem. Moreover, he added this, that Quintus Didius had written to him that Herod had very readily assisted him in the affair of the gladiators. So when he had obtained such a kind reception, and had, beyond all his hopes, procured his crown to be more entirely and firmly settled upon him than ever, by Cæsar's donation, as well as by that decree of the Romans, which Cæsar took care to procure for his greater security, he conducted Cæsar on his way to Egypt, and made him presents, even beyond his ability, to both him and his friends; and in general behaved himself with great magnanimity. He also desired that Cæsar would not put to death one Alexander, who had been a companion of Antony; but Cæsar had sworn to put him to death, and so he could not obtain that his petition : and now he returned to Judea again with greater honour and assurance than ever, and affrighted those that had expectations to the contrary, as still acquiring from his very dangers greater splendour than before, by the favour of God to him. So he prepared for the reception of Cæsar as he was going out of Syria to invade Egypt; and when he came he entertained him at Ptolemais with all royal magnificence. He also bestowed presents on the army, and brought them provisions in abundance. He

also proved to be one of Cæsar's most cordial friends, and put the army in array, and rode along with Cæsar, and had a hundred and fifty men, well appointed in all respects, after a rich and sumptuous manner, for the better reception of him and his friends. He also provided them with what they should want, as they passed over the dry desert, insomuch that they lacked neither wine nor water, which last the soldiers stood in the greatest need of; and besides, he presented Cæsar with eight hundred talents, and procured to himself the good-will of them all, because he was assisting to them in a much greater and more splendid degree than the kingdom he had obtained could afford; by which he more and more demonstrated to Cæsar the firmness of his friendship, and his readiness to assist him : and what was of the greatest advantage to him was this, that his liberality came at a seasonable time also; and when they returned again out of Egypt, his assistances were no way inferior to the good offices he had formerly done them.

CHAPTER VII

HOW HEROD SLEW SOHEMUS AND MARIAMNE, AND AFTERWARDS ALEXANDRA AND COSTOBARUS, AND HIS MOST INTIMATE FRIENDS, AND, AT LAST, THE SONS OF BABBAS ALSO

1. HOWEVER, when he came into his kingdom again, he found his house in disorder, and his wife Mariamne and her mother Alexandra very uneasy; for, as they supposed, (what was easy to be supposed,) that they were not put into that fortress [Alexandrium] for the security of their persons, but as into a garrison for their imprisonment, and that they had no power over anything, either of others or of their own affairs, they were very uneasy; and Mariamne, supposing that the king's love to her was but hypocritical, and rather pretended (as advantageous to himself) than real, she looked upon it as fallacious. She also was grieved that he would not allow her any hopes of surviving him, if he should come to any harm himself. She also recollected what commands he had formerly given to Joseph, insomuch that she endeavoured to please, her keepers, and especially Sohemus, as well apprised how all was in his power; and at the first Sohemus was faithful to Herod, and neglected none of the things he had given him in charge. But when the women, by kind words and liberal presents, had gained his affections over to them, he was by degrees overcome, and at length discovered to them all the king's injunctions, and this on that account principally, that he did not so much as hope he would come back with the same authority he had before, so that he thought he should both escape any danger from him, and supposed that he did hereby much gratify the women, who were likely not to be overlooked in the settling of the government, nay, that they would be able to make him abundant recompense, since they must either reign themselves, or be very near to him that should reign. He had a further ground of hope also, that though Herod should have all the success he could wish for, and should return again, he could not contradict his wife in what she desired, for he knew that the king's fondness for his wife was inexpressible. These were the motives that drew Sohemus to discover what injunctions had been given him. So Mariamne was greatly displeased to hear that there was no end of the dangers she

was under from Herod, and was greatly uneasy at it, and wished that he might obtain no favours [from Cæsar,] and esteemed it almost an insupportable task to live with him any longer; and this she afterwards openly declared, without concealing her resentment.

2. And now Herod sailed home with joy, at the unexpected good success he had had; and went, first of all, as was proper, to this his wife, and told her, and her only, the good news, as preferring her before the rest, on account of his fondness for her, and the intimacy there had been between them, and saluted her; but it so happened, that as he told her of the good success he had had, she was so far from rejoicing at it, that she rather was sorry for it; nor was she able to conceal her resentments, but depending on her dignity, and the nobility of her birth, in return for his salutations, she gave a groan, and declared evidently that she rather grieved than rejoiced at his success,—and this till Herod was disturbed at her, as affording him, not only marks of her suspicion, but evident signs of her dissatisfaction. This much troubled him, to see that this surprising hatred of his wife to him was not concealed, but open; and he took this so ill, and yet was so unable to bear it, on account of the fondness he had for her, that he could not continue long in any one mind, but sometimes was angry at her, and sometimes reconciled himself to her; but by always changing one passion for another, he was still in great uncertainty, and thus was entangled between hatred and love, and was frequently disposed to inflict punishment on her for her insolence towards him; but being deeply in love with her in his soul, he was not able to get quit of this woman. In short, as he would gladly have her punished, so was he afraid lest, ere he were aware, he should, by putting her to death, bring a heavier punishment upon himself at the same time.

3. When Herod's sister and mother perceived that he was in this temper with regard to Mariamne, they thought they had now got an excellent opportunity to exercise their hatred against her, and provoked Herod to wrath by telling him such long stories and calumnies about her as might at once excite his hatred and his jealousy. Now, though he willingly enough heard their words, yet had not he courage enough to do anything to her as if he believed them, but still he became worse and worse disposed to her, and these ill passions were more and more inflamed on both sides, while she did not hide her disposition towards him; and he turned his love to her into wrath against her; but when he was just going to put this matter past all remedy, he heard the news that Cæsar was the victor in the war, and that Antony and Cleopatra were both dead, and that he had conquered Egypt; whereupon he made haste to go to meet Cæsar, and left the affairs of his family in their present state. However, Mariamne recommended Sohemus to him, as he was setting out on his journey, and professed that she owed him thanks for the care he had taken of her, and asked of the king for him a place in the government; upon which an honourable employment was bestowed upon him accordingly. Now, when Herod was come into Egypt, he was introduced to Cæsar with great freedom, as already a friend of his, and received very great favours from him; for he made him a present of those four hundred Galatians who had been Cleopatra's guards, and restored that country to him again, which, by her means, had been taken away from him. He also added to his kingdom Gadara, Hippos, and

Samaria; and, besides those, the maritime cities, Gaza, Anthedon, Joppa, and Strato's Tower.

4. Upon these new acquisitions, he grew more magnificent, and conducted Cæsar as far as Antioch; but upon his return, as much as his prosperity was augmented by the foreign additions that had been made him, so much the greater were the distresses that came upon him in his own family, and chiefly in the affair of his wife, wherein he formerly appeared to have been most of all fortunate; for the affection he had for Mariamne was no way inferior to the affections of such as are on that account celebrated in history, and this very justly. As for her, she was in other respects a chaste woman, and faithful to him; yet had she somewhat of a woman rough by nature, and treated her husband imperiously enough, because she saw he was so fond of her as to be enslaved to her. She did not also consider seasonably with herself that she lived under a monarchy, and that she was at another's disposal, and accordingly would behave herself after a saucy manner to him, which yet he usually put off in a jesting way, and bore with moderation and good temper. She would also expose his mother and his sister openly, on account of the meanness of their birth, and would speak unkindly of them, insomuch that there was before this a disagreement and unpardonable hatred among the women, and it was now come to greater reproaches of one another than formerly, which suspicions increased, and lasted a whole year after Herod returned from Cæsar. However, these misfortunes, which had been kept under some decency for a great while, burst out all at once upon such an occasion as was now offered; for as the king was one day about noon lain down on his bed to rest him, he called for Mariamne, out of the great affection he had always for her. She came in accordingly, but would not lie down by him; and when he was very desirous of her company, she shewed her contempt of him; and added, by way of reproach, that he had caused her grandfather and her brother to be slain; and when he took this injury very unkindly, and was ready to use violence to her, in a precipitate manner, the king's sister, Salome, observing that he was more than ordinarily disturbed, sent into the king his cupbearer, who had been prepared long beforehand for such a design, and bade him tell the king how Mariamne had persuaded him to give his assistance in preparing a love-potion for him; and if it appeared to be greatly concerned, and to ask what that love-potion was, to tell him that she had the potion, and that he was desired only to give it him; but in case he did not appear to be much concerned at this potion, to let the thing drop; and that if he did so, no harm should thereby come to him. When she had given him these instructions, she sent him at this time to make such a speech. So he went in after a composed manner, to gain credit to what he should say, and yet somewhat hastily; and said, that Mariamne had given him presents, and persuaded him to give him a love-potion; and when this moved the king, he said that this love-potion was a composition that she had given him, whose effects he did not know, which was the reason of his resolving to give him this information, as the safest course he could take, both for himself and for the king. When Herod heard what he said, and was in an ill disposition before, his indignation grew more violent; and he ordered that eunuch of Mariamne, who was most faithful to her, to be brought to torture about this potion, as well knowing it was not

possible that anything small or great could be done without him; and when the man was under the utmost agonies, he could say nothing concerning the thing he was tortured about, but so far he knew, that Mariamne's hatred against him was occasioned by somewhat that Sohemus had said to her. Now, as he was saying this, Herod cried out aloud, and said, that Sohemus, who had been at all other times the most faithful to him, and to his government, would not have betrayed what injunctions he had given him, unless he had had a nearer conversation than ordinary with Mariamne. So he gave orders that Sohemus should be seized on and slain immediately; but he allowed his wife to take her trial; and got together those that were most faithful to him, and laid an elaborate accusation against her for this love-potion and composition, which had been charged upon her by way of calumny only. However, he kept no temper in what he said, and was in too great a passion for judging well about this matter. Accordingly, when the court was at length satisfied that he was so resolved, they passed the sentence of death upon her; but when the sentence was passed upon her, this temper was suggested by himself, and by some others of the court, that she should not be thus hastily put to death, but be laid in prison in one of the fortresses belonging to the kingdom; but Salome and her party laboured hard to have the woman put to death; and they prevailed with the king to do so, and advised this out of caution, lest the multitude should be tumultuous if she were suffered to live; and thus was Mariamne led to execution.

5. When Alexandra observed how things went, and that there were small hopes that she herself should escape the like treatment from Herod, she changed her behaviour to quite the reverse of what might have been expected from her former boldness, and this after a very indecent manner; for out of her desire to shew how entirely ignorant she was of the crimes laid against Mariamne, she leaped out of her place, and reproached her daughter, in the hearing of all the people; and cried out, that she had been an ill woman, and ungrateful to her husband, and that her punishment came justly upon her for such her insolent behaviour, for that she had not made proper returns to him who had been their common benefactor. And when she had for some time acted in this hypocritical manner, and had been so outrageous as to tear her hair, this indecent dissembling behaviour, as was to be expected, was greatly condemned by the rest of the spectators, as it was principally by the poor woman who was to suffer; for at the first she gave her not a word, nor was discomposed at her peevishness, and only looked at her, yet did she, out of a greatness of soul, discover her concern for her mother's offence, and especially for exposing herself in a manner so unbecoming her: but as for herself, she went to her death with an unshaken firmness of mind, and without changing the colour of her face, and thereby evidently discovered the nobility of her descent to the spectators, even in the last moments of her life.

6. And thus died Mariamne, a woman of an excellent character, both for chastity and greatness of soul; but she wanted moderation, and had too much of contention in her nature, yet had she all that can be said in the beauty of her body, and her majestic appearance in conversation; and thence arose the greatest part of the occasions why she did not prove so agreeable to the king, nor live so pleasantly with him as she

might otherwise have done; for while she was most indulgently used by the king, out of his fondness for her, and did not expect that he could do anything hard to her, she took too unbounded a liberty. Moreover, that which most afflicted her, was what he had done to her relations; and she ventured to speak of all they had suffered by him, and at last greatly provoked both the king's mother and sister, till they became enemies to her; and even he himself also did the same, on whom alone she depended for her expectations of escaping the last of punishments.

7. But when she was once dead, the king's affections for her were kindled in a more outrageous manner than before, whose old passion for her we have already described; for his love to her was not of a calm nature, nor such as we usually meet with among other husbands; for at its commencement it was of an enthusiastic kind; nor was it, by their long cohabitation and free conversation together, brought under his power to manage; but at this time his love to Mariamne seemed to seize him in such a peculiar manner, as looked like divine vengeance upon him for taking away her life; for he would frequently call for her, and frequently lament for her, in a most indecent manner. Moreover, he bethought him of everything he could make use of to divert his mind from thinking of her, and contrived feasts and assemblies for that purpose, but nothing would suffice; he therefore laid aside the administration of public affairs, and was so far conquered by his passion, that he would order his servants to call for Mariamne, as if she were still alive, and could still hear them; and when he was in this way, there arose a pestilential disease, and carried off the greatest part of the multitude, and of his best and most esteemed friends, and made all men suspect that this was brought upon them by the anger of God, for the injustice that had been done to Mariamne. This circumstance affected the king still more, till at length he forced himself to go into desert places, and there, under pretence of going a hunting, bitterly afflicted himself; yet had he not borne his grief there many days before he fell into a most dangerous distemper himself; he had an inflammation upon him, and a pain in the hinder part of his head, joined with madness; and for the remedies that were used, they did him no good at all, but proved contrary to his case, and so at length brought him to despair. All the physicians also that were about him, partly because the medicines they brought for his recovery could not at all conquer the disease, and partly because his diet could be no other than what his disease inclined him to, desired him to eat whatever he had a mind to, and so left the small hopes they had of his recovery in the power of that diet, and committed him to fortune. And thus did his distemper go on, while he was at Samaria, now called Sebaste.

8. Now Alexandra abode at this time at Jerusalem; and being informed what condition Herod was in, she endeavoured to get possession of the fortified places that were about the city, which were two, the one belonging to the city itself, the other belonging to the temple; and those that could get them into their hands had the whole nation under their power, for without the command of them it was not possible to offer their sacrifices; and to think of leaving off those sacrifices, is to every Jew plainly impossible, who are still more ready to lose their lives than to leave off that divine worship which they have been wont to pay to God. Alexandra, therefore, discoursed with those that had the keeping of those strongholds, that it was proper

for them to deliver the same to her, and to Herod's sons, lest, upon his death, any other person should seize upon the government; and that upon his recovery none could keep them more safely for him than those of his own family. These words were not by them at all taken in good part; and, as they had been in former times faithful [to Herod,] they resolved to continue so more than ever, both because they hated Alexandra, and because they thought it a sort of impiety to despair of Herod's recovery while he was yet alive, for they had been his old friends; and one of them, whose name was Achiabus, was his cousin-german. They sent messengers, therefore, to acquaint him with Alexandra's design; so he made no longer delay, but gave orders to have her slain; yet was it with difficulty, and after he had endured great pain, that he got clear of his distemper. He was still sorely afflicted, both in mind and body, and made very uneasy, and readier than ever upon all occasions to inflict punishment upon those that fell under his hand. He also slew the most intimate of his friends, Costobarus, and Lysimachus, and Gadias, who was also called Antipater; as also Dositheus, and that upon the following occasion.

9. Costobarus was an Idumean by birth, and one of principal dignity among them, and one whose ancestors had been priests to the Koze, whom the Idumeans had [formerly] esteemed as a god; but after Hyrcanus had made a change in their political government, and made them receive the Jewish customs and law, Herod made Costobarus governor of Idumea and Gaza, and gave him his sister Salome to wife; and this was upon his slaughter of [his uncle] Joseph, who had that government before, as we have related already. When Costobarus had gotten to be so highly advanced, it pleased him, and was more than he hoped for, and he was more and more puffed up by his good success, and in a little while he exceeded all bounds, and did not think fit to obey what Herod, as their ruler, commanded him, or that the Idumeans should make use of the Jewish customs, or be subject to them. He therefore sent to Cleopatra, and informed her that the Idumeans had been always under his progenitors, and that for the same reason it was but just that she should desire that country for him of Antony, for that he was ready to transfer his friendship to her: and this he did, not because he was better pleased to be under Cleopatra's government, but because he thought that, upon the diminution of Herod's power, it would not be difficult for him to obtain himself the entire government over the Idumeans, and somewhat more also; for he raised his hopes still higher, as having no small pretences, both by his birth and by these riches which he had gotten by his constant attention to filthy lucre; and accordingly it was not a small matter that he aimed at. So Cleopatra desired this country of Antony, but failed of her purpose. An account of this was brought to Herod, who was thereupon ready to kill Costobarus; yet, upon the entreaties of his sister and mother, he forgave him, and vouchsafed to pardon him entirely, though he still had a suspicion of him afterwards for this his attempt.

10. But some time afterward, when Salome happened to quarrel with Costobarus, she sent him a bill of divorce,* and dissolved her marriage with him, though this was not according to the Jewish laws; for with us it is lawful for a husband to do so; but a wife if she departs from her husband, cannot of herself be married to another, unless her former husband put her away. However, Salome chose not to follow the law of her country, but the law of her authority, and so renounced her wedlock; and told her brother Herod, that she left her husband out of her good-will to him, because she perceived that he, with Antipater, and Lysimachus, and Dositheus, were raising a sedition against him: as an evidence whereof, she alleged the case of the sons of Babas, that they had been by him preserved alive already for the interval of twelve years, which proved to be true. But when Herod thus unexpectedly heard of it, he was greatly surprised at it, and was the more surprised, because the relation appeared incredible to him. As for the fact relating to these sons of Babas, Herod had formerly taken great pains to bring them to punishment, as being enemies to his government; but they were now forgotten by him, on account of the length of time [since he had ordered them to be slain.] Now the cause of his ill-will and hatred to them arose hence: that while Antigonus was king, Herod, with his army, besieged the city of Jerusalem, where the distress and miseries which the besieged endured were so pressing, that the greater number of them invited Herod into the city, and already placed their hopes on him. Now, the sons of Babas were of great dignity, and had power among the multitude, and were faithful to Antigonus, and were always raising calumnies against Herod, and encouraged the people to preserve the government to that royal family which held it by inheritance. So these men acted thus politically, and, as they thought, for their own advantage; but when the city was taken, and Herod had gotten the government into his own hands, and Costobarus was appointed to hinder men from passing out at the gates, and to guard the city, that those citizens that were guilty, and of the party opposite to the king, might not get out of it,—Costobarus being sensible that the sons of Babas were had in respect and honour by the whole multitude, and supposing that their preservation might be of great advantage to him in the changes of government afterward, he set them by themselves, and concealed them in his own farms; and when this thing was suspected, he assured Herod upon oath that he really knew nothing of that matter, and so overcame the suspicions that lay upon him; nay, after that, when the king had publicly proposed a reward for the discovery, and had put in practice all sorts of methods for searching out this matter, he would not confess it; but being persuaded that when he had first denied it, if the men were found, he should not escape unpunished, he was forced to keep them secret, not only out of his good-will to them, but out of a necessary regard to his own preservation also. But when the king knew this thing, by his sister's information, he sent men to the places where he had the intimation they were concealed, and ordered both them and those that were accused as guilty with them, to be slain, insomuch that there were now none at all left of the kindred of Hyrcanus; and the kingdom was entirely in Herod's power, and there was nobody remaining of such dignity as could put a stop to what he did against the Jewish laws.

---

* Here is a plain example of a Jewish lady giving a divorce to her husband, though in the days of Josephus it was not esteemed lawful for a woman so to do. However, the Christian law, when it allowed divorce for adultery, (Matt. v. 32,) allowed the innocent wife to divorce her guilty husband, as well as the innocent husband to divorce his guilty wife, as we learn from the Shepherd of Hermas, and from the Second Apology of Justin Martyr, where a persecution was brought upon the Christians upon such a divorce.

CHAPTER VIII

HOW TEN MEN OF THE CITIZENS [OF JERUSALEM] MADE A CONSPIRACY AGAINST HEROD, FOR THE FOREIGN PRACTICES HE HAD INTRODUCED, WHICH WAS A TRANSGRESSION OF THE LAWS OF THEIR COUNTRY. CONCERNING THE BUILDING OF SEBASTE AND CESAREA, AND OTHER EDIFICES OF HEROD

1. On this account it was that Herod revolted from the laws of his country, and corrupted their ancient constitution, by the introduction of foreign practices, which constitution yet ought to have been preserved inviolable; by which means we became guilty of great wickedness afterwards, while those religious observances which used to lead the multitude to piety, were now neglected: for, in the first place, he appointed solemn games to be celebrated every fifth year, in honour of Cæsar, and built a theatre at Jerusalem, as also a very great amphitheatre in the plain. Both of them were indeed costly works, but opposite to the Jewish customs; for we have had no such shows delivered down to us as fit to be used or exhibited by us, yet did he celebrate these games every five years, in the most solemn and splendid manner. He also made proclamation to the neighbouring countries, and called men together out of every nation. The wrestlers, and the rest of those that strove for the prizes in such games, were invited out of every land, both by the hopes of the rewards there to be bestowed, and by the glory of victory to be there gained. So the principal persons that were the most eminent in these sorts of exercises, were gotten together, for there were very great rewards for victory proposed, not only to those that performed their exercises naked, but to those that played the musicians also, and were called *Thymelici;* and he spared no pains to induce all persons, the most famous for such exercises, to come to this contest for victory. He also proposed no small rewards to those who ran for the prizes in chariot races, when they were drawn by two, or three, or four pair of horses. He also imitated everything, though ever so costly and magnificent, in other nations, out of an ambition that he might give most public demonstration of his grandeur. Inscriptions also of the great actions of Cæsar, and trophies of those nations which he had conquered in his wars, and all made of the purest gold and silver, encompassed the theatre itself: nor was there anything that could be subservient to his design, whether it were precious garments, or precious stones set in order, which was not also exposed to sight in these games. He had also made a great preparation of wild beasts, and of lions themselves in great abundance, and of such other beasts as were either of uncommon strength, or of such a sort as were rarely seen. These were prepared either to fight one with another, or that men who were condemned to death were to fight with them. And truly foreigners were greatly surprised and delighted at the vastness of the expenses here exhibited, and at the great dangers that were here seen; but to natural Jews this was no better than a dissolution of these customs for which they had so great a veneration.* It

appeared also no better than an instance of barefaced impiety to throw men to the wild beasts, for the affording delight to the spectators, and it appeared an instance of no less impiety, to change their own laws for such foreign exercises, but, above all the rest, the trophies gave most distaste to the Jews; for, as they imagined them to be images, included within the armour that hung round about them, they were sorely displeased at them, because it was not the custom of their country to pay honours to such images.

2. Nor was Herod unacquainted with the disturbance they were under; and, as he thought it unseasonable to use violence with them, so he spake to some of them by way of consolation; and in order to free them from that superstitious fear they were under, yet could not he satisfy them, but they cried out with one accord, out of their great uneasiness at the offences they thought he had been guilty of, that although they should think of bearing all the rest, yet would they never bear images of men in their city, meaning the trophies, because this was disagreeable to the laws of their country. Now when Herod saw them in such a disorder, and that they would not easily change their resolution unless they received satisfaction in this point, he called to him the most eminent men among them, and brought them upon the theatre, and shewed them the trophies, and asked them, what sort of things they took these trophies to be; and when they cried out that they were the images of men, he gave order that they should be stripped of these outward ornaments which were about them, and shewed them the naked pieces of wood; which pieces of wood, now without any ornaments, became matter of great sport and laughter to them, because they had before always had the ornaments of images themselves in derision.

3. When therefore Herod had thus got clear of the multitude, and had dissipated the vehemency of passion under which they had been, the greatest part of the people were disposed to change their conduct, and not to be displeased at him any longer; but still some of them continued in their displeasure against him, for his introduction of new customs, and esteemed the violation of the laws of their country as likely to be the origin of very great mischiefs to them, so that they deemed it an instance of piety rather to hazard themselves [to be put to death,] than to seem as if they took no notice of Herod, who, upon the change he had made in their government, introduced such customs, and that in a violent manner, which they had never been used to before, as indeed in pretence a king, but in reality one that shewed himself an enemy to their whole nation; on which account ten men that were citizens [of Jerusalem,] conspired together against him, and sware to one another to undergo any dangers in the attempt, and took daggers with them under their garments [for the purpose of killing Herod.] Now there was a certain blind man among those conspirators who had thus sworn to one another, on account of the indignation he had against what he heard to have been done; he was not indeed able to afford the rest any assistance in the undertaking, but was ready to undergo any suffering with them, if so be they should come to any harm, insomuch that he became a very great encourager of the rest of the undertakers.

4. When they had taken this resolution, and

---

* These grand plays and shows, and Thymelici, or music-meetings, and chariot-races, &c., were still, as we see here, looked on by the sober Jews as heathenish sports, and tending not only to corrupt the manners of the Jewish nation, and to bring them in love with paganish idolatry and paganish conduct of life, but to the dissolution of the law of Moses. Nor is the case of our modern masquerades, plays, operas, and the like "pomps and vanities of this wicked world," of any better tendency under Christianity.

GREAT AMPHITHEATRE OF HEROD

that by common consent, they went into the theatre, hoping that, in the first place, Herod should not escape them, as they should fall on him so unexpectedly; and supposing, however, that if they missed him, they should kill a great many of those that were about him; and this resolution they took, though they should die for it, in order to suggest to the king what injuries he had done to the multitude. These conspirators therefore, standing thus prepared beforehand, went about their design with great alacrity; but there was one of those spies of Herod that were appointed for such purposes, to fish out and inform him of any conspiracies that should be made against him, who found out the whole affair, and told the king of it, as he was about to go into the theatre. So when he reflected on the hatred which he knew the greatest part of the people bore him, and on the disturbances that arose upon every occasion, he thought this plot against him not to be improbable. Accordingly, he retired into his palace, and called those that were accused of this conspiracy before him by their several names; and as, upon the guards falling upon them, they were caught in the very fact, and knew they could not escape, they prepared themselves for their ends with all the decency they could, and so as not at all to recede from their resolute behaviour, for they shewed no shame for what they were about, nor denied it; but when they were seized, they shewed their daggers, and professed, that the conspiracy they had sworn to was a holy and a pious action; that what they intended to do was not for gain, or out of any indulgence to their passions, but principally for those common customs of their country, which all the Jews were obliged to observe, or to die for them. This was what these men said, out of their undaunted courage in this conspiracy. So they were led away to execution by the king's guards that stood about them, and patiently underwent all the torments inflicted on them till they died. Nor was it long before that spy who had discovered them, was seized on by some of the people, out of the hatred they bore to him; and was not only slain by them, but pulled to pieces, limb from limb, and given to the dogs. This execution was seen by many of the citizens, yet would not one of them discover the doers of it, till upon Herod's making a strict scrutiny after them, by bitter and severe tortures, certain women that were tortured confessed what they had seen done; the authors of which fact were so terribly punished by the king, that their entire families were destroyed for this their rash attempt; yet did not the obstinacy of the people, and the undaunted constancy they shewed in the defence of their laws, make Herod any easier to them, but he still strengthened himself after a more secure manner, and resolved to encompass the multitude every way, lest such innovations should end in an open rebellion.

5. Since, therefore, he had now the city fortified by the palace in which he lived, and by the temple, which had a strong fortress by it, called Antonia, and was rebuilt by himself, he contrived to make Samaria a fortress for himself also against all the people, and called it Sebaste, supposing that this place would be a stronghold against the country, not inferior to the former. So he fortified that place, which was a day's journey distant from Jerusalem, and which would be useful to him in common, to keep both the country and the city in awe. He also built another fortress for the whole nation: it was of old called Strato's Tower: but was by him named Cesarea. Moreover, he chose out some select horsemen, and placed them in the great plain; and built [for them] a place in Galilee, called Gaba, with Hesebonitis, in Perea; and these were the places which he particularly built, while he always was inventing somewhat further for his own security, and encompassing the whole nation with guards, that they might by no means get from under his power, nor fall into tumults, which they did continually upon any small commotion; and that if they did make any commotions, he might know of it, while some of his spies might be upon them from the neighbourhood, and might both be able to know what they were attempting, and to prevent it; and when he went about building the wall of Samaria, he contrived to bring thither many of those that had been assisting him in his wars, and many of the people in that neighbourhood also, whom he made fellow-citizens with the rest. This he did, out of an ambitious desire of building a temple, and out of a desire to make the city more eminent than it had been before, but principally because he contrived that it might at once be for his own security, and a monument of his magnificence. He also changed its name, and called it Sebaste. Moreover, he parted the adjoining country, which was excellent in its kind, among the inhabitants of Samaria, that they might be in a happy condition, upon their first coming to inhabit. Besides all which, he encompassed the city with a wall of great strength, and made use of the acclivity of the place for making its fortifications stronger; nor was the compass of the place made now so small as it had been before, but was such as rendered it not inferior to the most famous cities, for it was twenty furlongs in circumference. Now within, and about the middle of it, he built a sacred place, of a furlong and a half [in circuit,] and adorned it with all sorts of decorations, and therein erected a temple, which was illustrious, on account of both its largeness and beauty; and as to the several parts of the city, he adorned them with decorations of all sorts also; and as to what was necessary to provide for his own security, he made the walls very strong for that purpose, and made it for the greatest part a citadel; and as to the elegance of the building, it was taken care of also, that he might leave monuments of the fineness of his taste, and of his beneficence, to future ages.

CHAPTER IX

CONCERNING THE FAMINE THAT HAD HAPPENED IN JUDEA AND SYRIA; AND HOW HEROD, AFTER HE HAD MARRIED ANOTHER WIFE, REBUILT CESAREA, AND OTHER GRECIAN CITIES

1. Now on this very year, which was the thirteenth year of the reign of Herod, very great calamities came upon the country; whether they were derived from the anger of God, or whether this misery returns again naturally in certain periods of time;* for, in the first place, there were perpetual droughts, and for that reason the ground was barren, and did not bring forth the same quantity of fruits that it used to produce; and after this barrenness of the soil, that change

---

* Here we have an eminent example of the language of Josephus in his writing to Gentiles, different from that when he wrote to Jews; in his writing to whom he derives all such judgments from the anger of God; but because he knew many of the Gentiles thought they might naturally come in certain periods, he complies with them in the following sentence.

of food which the want of corn occasioned, produced distempers in the bodies of men, and a pestilential disease prevailed, one misery following upon the back of another; and these circumstances, that they were destitute both of methods of cure and of food, made the pestilential distemper, which began after a violent manner, the more lasting. The destruction of men also, after such a manner, deprived those that survived of all their courage, because they had no way to provide remedies sufficient for the distresses they were in. When therefore the fruits of that year were spoiled, and whatsoever they had laid up beforehand was spent, there was no foundation of hope for relief remaining, but the misery, contrary to what they expected, still increased upon them; and this, not only on that year, while they had nothing for themselves left [at the end of it,] but what seed they had sown perished also, by reason of the ground not yielding its fruits on the second year.* This distress they were in made them also, out of necessity, to eat many things that did not use to be eaten: nor was the king himself free from this distress any more than other men, as being deprived of that tribute he used to have from the fruits of the ground; and having already expended what money he had, in his liberality to those whose cities he had built; nor had he any people that were worthy of his assistance, since this miserable state of things had procured him the hatred of his subjects; for it is a constant rule, that misfortunes are still laid to the account of those that govern.

2. In these circumstances he considered with himself how to procure some seasonable help; but this was a hard thing to be done, while their neighbours had no food to sell them; and their money also was gone, had it been possible to purchase a little food at a great price. However, he thought it his best way, by all means, not to leave off his endeavours to assist his people; so he cut off the rich furniture that was in his palace, both of silver and gold, insomuch that he did not spare the finest vessels he had, or those that were made with the most elaborate skill of the artificers, but sent the money to Petronius, who had been made prefect of Egypt by Cæsar; and as not a few had already fled to him under their necessities, and as he was particularly a friend to Herod, and desirous to have his subjects preserved, he gave leave to them, in the first place, to export corn, and assisted them every way, both in purchasing and exporting the same; so that he was the principal, if not the only person, who afforded them what help they had. And Herod, taking care the people should understand that this help came from himself, did thereby not only remove the ill opinion of those that formerly hated him, but gave them the greatest demonstration possible of his good-will to them, and care of them: for, in the first place, as for those who were able to provide their own food, he distributed to them their portion

* This famine for two years that affected Judea and Syria seems to have been more terrible during this time than was that in the days of Jacob, (Gen. xli. xlii.) And what makes the comparison the more remarkable is this:—That now, as well as then, the relief they had was from Egypt also; then from Joseph the governor of Egypt, under Pharaoh king of Egypt, and now from Petronius the prefect of Egypt, under Augustus, the Roman Emperor. It is also well worth our observation here, that these two years were a Sabbatic Year and a year of jubilee, for which Providence, during the theocracy, used to provide a triple crop beforehand; but which became now, when the Jews had forfeited that blessing, the greatest years of famine to them ever since the days of Ahab.

of corn in the exactest manner; but for those many that were not able, either by reason of their old age, or any other infirmity, to provide food for themselves, he made this provision for them that the bakers should make their bread ready for them. He also took care that they might not be hurt by the danger of winter, since they were in great want of clothing also, by reason of the utter destruction and consumption of their sheep and goats, till they had no wool to make use of, nor anything else to cover themselves withal. And when he had procured these things for his own subjects, he went further, in order to provide necessaries for their neighbours; and gave seed to the Syrians; which things turned greatly to his own advantage also, this charitable assistance being afforded most seasonably to their fruitful soil, so that every one had now a plentiful provision of food. Upon the whole, when the harvest of the land was approaching, he sent no fewer than fifty thousand men, whom he had sustained, into the country; by which means he both repaired the afflicted condition of his own kingdom with great generosity and diligence, and lightened the afflictions of his neighbours, who were under the same calamities; for there was nobody who had been in want, that was left destitute of a suitable assistance by him; nay, further, there were neither any people, nor any cities, nor any private men, who were to make provision for the multitudes; and on that account were in want of support, and had recourse to him, but received what they stood in need of, insomuch that it appeared, upon a computation, that the number of cori of wheat, of ten Attic medimni apiece, that were given to foreigners, amounted to ten thousand; and the number that was given in his own kingdom was fourscore thousand. Now it happened that this care of his and this seasonable benefaction, had such influence on the Jews, and was so cried up among other nations, as to wipe off that old hatred which his violation of some of their customs, during his reign, had procured him among all the nation, and that this liberality of his assistance in this their greatest necessity was full satisfaction for all that he had done of that nature, as also it procured him great fame among foreigners; and it looked as if these calamities that afflicted his land to a degree plainly incredible, came in order to raise his glory, and to be to his great advantage: for the greatness of his liberality in these distresses, which he now demonstrated beyond all expectation, did so change the disposition of the multitude towards him, that they were ready to suppose he had been from the beginning not such a one as they had found him to be by experience, but such a one as the care he had taken of them in supplying their necessities proved him now to be.

3. About this time it was that he sent five hundred chosen men out of the guards of his body as auxiliaries to Cæsar, whom Ælius Gallus † led to the Red Sea, and who were of great service to him there. When, therefore, his affairs were thus improved, and were again in a flourishing condition, he built himself a palace in the upper city, raising the rooms to a very great height, and adorning them with the most costly furniture of gold, and marble seats, and beds; and these were so large that they could contain very many companies of men. These apartments were also of distinct magnitudes,

† This Ælius Gallus seems to be no other than that Ælius Largus whom Dio speaks of as conducting an expedition that was about this time made into Arabia Felix.

and had particular names given them; for one apartment was called Cæsar's, another Agrippa's. He also fell in love again, and married another wife, not suffering his reason to hinder him from living as he pleased. The occasion of this his marriage was as follows :—There was one Simon, a citizen of Jerusalem, the son of one Boethus, a citizen of Alexandria, and a priest of great note there : this man had a daughter, who was esteemed the most beautiful woman of that time ; and when the people of Jerusalem began to speak much in her commendation, it happened that Herod was much affected with what was said of her : and when he saw the damsel, he was smitten with her beauty, yet did he entirely reject the thoughts of using his authority to abuse her; as believing, what was the truth, that by so doing he should be stigmatised for violence and tyranny : so he thought it best to take the damsel to wife. And while Simon was of a dignity too inferior to be allied to him, but still too considerable to be despised, he governed his inclinations after the most prudent manner, by augmenting the dignity of the family, and making them more honourable ; so he immediately deprived Jesus the son of Phabet of the high priesthood, and conferred that dignity on Simon, and so joined an affinity with him [by marrying his daughter.]

4. When this wedding was over, he built another citadel in that place where he had conquered the Jews, when he was driven out of his government, and Antigonus enjoyed it. This citadel is distant from Jerusalem about threescore furlongs. It was strong by nature, and fit for such a building. It is a sort of moderate hill, raised to a further height by the hand of man. till it was of the shape of a woman's breast. It is encompassed with circular towers, and hath a straight ascent up to it, which ascent is composed of steps of polished stones, in number two hundred. Within it are royal and very rich apartments, of a structure that provided both for security and for beauty. About the bottom there are habitations of such a structure as are well worth seeing, both on other accounts, and also on account of the water which is brought thither from a great way off, and at vast expenses ; for the place itself is destitute of water. The plain that is about this citadel is full of edifices, not inferior to any city in largeness, and having the hill above it in the nature of a castle.

5. And now, when all Herod's designs had succeeded according to his hopes, he had not the least suspicion that any troubles could arise in his kingdom, because he kept his people obedient, as well by the fear they stood in of him, for he was implacable in the infliction of his punishments, as by the provident care he had shewn towards them, after the most magnanimous manner, when they were under their distresses ; but still he took care to have external security for his government, as a fortress against his subjects ; for the orations he made to the cities were very fine, and full of kindness ; and he cultivated a seasonable good understanding with their governors, and bestowed presents on every one of them, inducing them thereby to be more friendly to him, and using his magnificent disposition so as his kingdom might be better secured to him, and this till all his affairs were every way more and more augmented. But then, this magnificent temper of his, and that submissive behaviour and liberality which he exercised towards Cæsar, and the most powerful men of Rome, obliged him to transgress the customs of his nation, and to set aside many of their laws, by building cities after an extravagant manner, and erecting temples,—not in Judea indeed, for that would not have been borne, it being forbidden for us to pay any honour to images, or representations of animals, after the manner of the Greeks ; but still he did this in the country [properly] out of our bounds, and in the cities thereof.* The apology which he made to the Jews for these things was this :—That all was done, not out of his own inclinations, but by the commands and injunctions of others, in order to please Cæsar and the Romans ; as though he had not the Jewish customs so much in his eye as he had the honour of those Romans, while yet he had himself entirely in view all the while, and indeed was very ambitious to leave great monuments of his government to posterity ; whence it was that he was so zealous in building such fine cities, and spent such vast sums of money upon them.

6. Now upon his observation of a place near the sea, which was very proper for containing a city, and was before called Strato's Tower, he set about getting a plan for a magnificent city there, and erected many edifices all over it, and this of white stone. He also adorned it with most sumptuous palaces, and large edifices for containing the people ; and what was the greatest and most laborious work of all, he adorned it with a haven, that was always free from the waves of the sea. Its largeness was not less than the Pyræum [at Athens ;] and had towards the city a double station for ships. It was of excellent workmanship ; and this was the more remarkable for its being built in a place that of itself was not suitable to such noble structures, but was to be brought to perfection by materials from other places, and at very great expense. This city is situate in Phœnicia, in the passage by sea to Egypt, between Joppa and Dora, which are lesser maritime cities, and not fit for havens, on account of the impetuous south winds that beat upon them, which, rolling the sands that come from the sea against the shores, do not admit of ships lying in their station ; but the merchants are generally there forced to ride at their anchors in the sea itself. So Herod endeavoured to rectify this inconvenience, and laid out such a compass towards the land as might be sufficient for a haven, wherein the great ships might lie in safety ; and this he effected by letting down vast stones of above fifty feet in length, not less than eighteen in breadth, and nine in depth, into twenty fathoms deep ; and as some were lesser, so were others bigger, than those dimensions. This mole which he built by the seaside was two hundred feet wide, the half of which was opposed to the current of the waves, so as to keep off those waves which were to break upon them, and so was called Procymatia, or the first breaker of the waves ; but the other half had upon it a wall, with several towers, the largest of which was named Drusus, and was a work of very great excellence, and had its name from Drusus, the son-in-law of Cæsar, who died young. There were also a great number of arches, where the mariners dwelt : there was also before them a quay [or landing-place,] which ran round the entire haven, and was a most agreeable walk to such as had a mind to that exercise ; but the entrance or

---

* It may here be noticed how tyrannical and extravagant soever Herod were in himself, and in his Grecian cities, as to those plays, and shows, and temples for idolatry, yet durst even he introduce very few of them into the cities of the Jews, who, as Josephus here notes, would not even then have borne them, so zealous were they still for many of the laws of Moses.

mouth of the port was made on the north quarter, on which side was the stillest of the winds of all in this place : and the basis of the whole circuit on the left hand, as you enter the port, supported a round turret, which was made very strong, in order to resist the greatest waves ; while, on the right hand, as you enter, stood two vast stones, and those each of them larger than the turret, which was over against them : these stood upright, and were joined together. Now there were edifices all along the circular haven, made of the most polished stone, with a certain elevation, whereon was erected a temple, that was seen a great way off by those that were sailing for that haven, and had in it two statues, the one of Rome, the other of Cæsar. The city itself was called Cesarea, which was also itself built of fine materials, and was of a fine structure ; nay, the very subterranean vaults and cellars had no less of architecture bestowed on them than had the buildings above ground. Some of these vaults carried things at even distances to the haven and to the sea ; but one of them ran obliquely, and bound all the rest together, that both the rain and the filth of the citizens were together carried off with ease, and the sea itself, upon the flux of the tide from without, came into the city, and washed it all clean. Herod also built therein a theatre of stone ; and on the south quarter, behind the port, an amphitheatre also, capable of holding a vast number of men, and conveniently situated for a prospect to the sea. So this city was thus finished in twelve years ; during which time the king did not fail to go on both with the work, and to pay the charges that were necessary.

CHAPTER X

HOW HEROD SENT HIS SONS TO ROME ; HOW ALSO HE WAS ACCUSED BY ZENODORUS AND THE GADARENS, BUT WAS CLEARED OF WHAT THEY ACCUSED HIM OF, AND WITHAL GAINED TO HIMSELF THE GOOD-WILL OF CÆSAR. CONCERNING THE PHARISEES, THE ESSENS, AND MANAHEM

1. WHEN Herod was engaged in such matters, and when he had already re-edified Sebaste [Samaria,] he resolved to send his sons Alexander and Aristobulus to Rome, to enjoy the company of Cæsar ; who, when they came thither, lodged at the house of Pollio,* who was very fond of Herod's friendship : and they had leave to lodge in Cæsar's own palace, for he received these sons of Herod with all humanity, and gave Herod leave to give his kingdom to which of his sons he pleased ; and, besides all this, he bestowed on him Trachon, and Batanea, and Auranitis, which he gave him on the occasion following :—One Zenodorus† had hired what was called the house of Lysanias, who, as he was not satisfied with his revenues, became a partner with the robbers that inhabited the Trachonites, and so procured him a larger income ; for the inhabitants of those places lived in a mad way, and pillaged the country of the Damascenes, while Zenodorus did not restrain them, but partook of the prey they acquired. Now, as the neighbouring people

were hereby great sufferers, they complained to Varro, who was the president [of Syria,] and entreated him to write to Cæsar about this injustice of Zenodorus. When these matters were laid before Cæsar, he wrote back to Varro to destroy those nests of robbers, and give the land to Herod, that by his care the neighbouring countries might be no longer disturbed with these doings of the Trachonites, for it was not an easy thing to restrain them, since this way of robbery had been their usual practice, and they had no other way to get their living, because they had neither any city of their own, nor lands in their possession, but only some receptacles and dens in the earth, and there they and their cattle lived in common together : however, they had made contrivances to get pools of water, and laid up corn in granaries for themselves, and were able to make great resistance, by issuing out on the sudden against any that attacked them ; for the entrances of their caves were narrow, in which but one could come in at a time, and the places within incredibly large, and made very wide ; but the ground over their habitations was not very high, but rather on a plain, while the rocks are altogether hard and difficult to be entered upon, unless any one gets into the plain road by the guidance of another, for these roads are not straight, but have several revolutions. But when these men are hindered from their wicked preying upon their neighbours, their custom is to prey one upon another, insomuch that no sort of injustice comes amiss to them. But when Herod had received this grant from Cæsar, and was come into this country, he procured skilful guides, and put a stop to their wicked robberies, and procured peace and quietness to the neighbouring people.

2. Hereupon Zenodorus was grieved, in the first place, because his principality was taken away from him, and still more so, because he envied Herod, who had gotten it ; so he went up to Rome to accuse him, but returned back again without success. Now Agrippa was [about this time] sent to succeed Cæsar in the government of the countries beyond the Ionian Sea, upon whom Herod lighted when he was wintering about Mitylene, for he had been his particular friend and companion, and then returned into Judea again. However, some of the Gadarens came to Agrippa, and accused Herod, whom he sent back bound to the king, without giving them the hearing : but still the Arabians, who of old bare ill-will to Herod's government, were nettled, and at that time attempted to raise a sedition in his dominions, and, as they thought, upon a more justifiable occasion ; for Zenodorus, despairing already of success as to his own affairs, prevented [his enemies,] by selling to those Arabians a part of his principality, called Auranitis, for the value of fifty talents ; but as this was included in the donations of Cæsar, they contested the point with Herod, as unjustly deprived of what they had bought. Sometimes they did this by making incursions upon him, and sometimes by attempting force against him, and sometimes by going to law with him. Moreover they persuaded the poorer soldiers to help them, and were troublesome to him, out of a constant hope that they should reduce the people to raise a sedition ; in which designs those that are in the most miserable circumstances of life are still the most earnest ; and although Herod had been a great while apprized of these attempts, yet did not he indulge any severity to them, but by rational methods aimed to mitigate things, as not willing to give any handle for tumult.

3. Now when Herod had already reigned seven-

---

* This Pollio, with whom Herod's sons lived at Rome, was not Pollio the Pharisee, already mentioned by Josephus, but Asinius Pollio, the Roman.

† The character of this Zenodorus is so like that of a famous robber of the same name in Strabo, and that about this very country, and about this very time also, that there is little doubt they were the same.

teen years, Cæsar came into Syria; at which time the greatest part of the inhabitants of Gadara clamoured against Herod, as one that was heavy in his injunctions, and tyrannical. These reproaches they mainly ventured upon by the encouragemant of Zenodorus, who took his oath that he would never leave Herod till he had procured that they should be severed from Herod's kingdom, and joined to Cæsar's province. The Gadarens were induced hereby, and made no small cry against him; and that the more boldly, because those that had been delivered up by Agrippa were not punished by Herod, who let them go, and did them no harm; for indeed he was the principal man in the world who appeared almost inexorable in punishing crimes in his own family; but very generous in remitting the offences that were committed elsewhere. And while they accused Herod of injuries and plunderings, and subversion of temples, he stood unconcerned, and was ready to make his defence. However, Cæsar gave him his right hand, and remitted nothing of his kindness to him, upon this disturbance of the multitude; and indeed these things were alleged the first day, but the hearing proceeded no further; for as the Gadarens saw the inclination of Cæsar and of his assessors, and expected, as they had reason to do, that they should be delivered up to the king, some of them, out of a dread of the torments they might undergo, cut their own throats in the night-time, and some of them threw themselves down precipices, and others of them cast themselves into the river, and destroyed themselves of their own accord; which accidents seemed a sufficient condemnation of the rashness and crimes they had been guilty of; whereupon Cæsar made no longer delay, but cleared Herod from the crimes he was accused of. Another happy accident there was, which was a further great advantage to Herod at this time; for Zenodorus's belly burst, and a great quantity of blood issued from him in his sickness, and he thereby departed this life at Antioch in Syria; so Cæsar bestowed his country, which was no small one, upon Herod; it lay between Trichon and Galilee, and contained Ulatha, and Paneas, and the country round about. He also made him one of the procurators of Syria, and commanded that they should do everything with his approbation; and, in short, he arrived at that pitch of felicity, that whereas there were but two men that governed the vast Roman empire, first Cæsar and then Agrippa, who was his principal favourite, Cæsar preferred no one to Herod besides Agrippa; and Agrippa made no one his greater friend than Herod beside Cæsar; and when he had acquired such freedom, he begged of Cæsar a tetrarchy * for his brother Pheroras, while he did himself bestow upon him a revenue of a hundred talents out of his own kingdom, that in case he came to any harm himself, his brother might be in safety, and that his sons might not have dominion over him. So when he had conducted Cæsar to the sea, and was returned home, he built him a most beautiful temple, of the whitest stone in Zenodorus's country, near the place called Panium. This is a very fine cave in a mountain, under which there is a great cavity in the earth, and the cavern is abrupt, and prodigiously deep, and full of a still water; over it hangs a vast mountain; and under the caverns arise the springs of the river Jordan. Herod adorned this place, which was already a very remarkable

one, still further by the erection of this temple, which he dedicated to Cæsar.

4. At which time Herod released to his subjects the third part of their taxes, under pretence indeed of relieving them after the dearth they had had; but the main reason was, to recover their good-will, which he now wanted; for they were uneasy at him, because of the innovations he had introduced in their practices of the dissolution of their religion, and of the disuse of their own customs, and the people everywhere talked against him, like those that were still more provoked and disturbed at his procedure; against which discontents he greatly guarded himself, and took away the opportunities they might have to disturb him, and enjoined them to be always at work; nor did he permit the citizens either to meet together, or to walk, or eat together, but watched everything they did, and when any were caught, they were severely punished; and many there were who were brought to the citadel Hyrcania, both openly and secretly, and were there put to death; and there were spies set everywhere, both in the city and in the roads, who watched those that met together; nay, it is reported that he did not himself neglect this part of caution, but that he would oftentimes himself take the habit of a private man, and mix among the multitude in the night-time, and make trial what opinion they had of his government; and as for those that could be no way reduced to acquiesce under his scheme of government, he persecuted them all manner of ways; but for the rest of the multitude, he required that they should be obliged to take an oath of fidelity to him, and at the same time compelled them to swear that they would bear him good-will, and continue certainly so to do, in his management of the government; and indeed a great part of them, either to please him, or out of fear of him, yielded to what he required of them; but for such as were of a more open and generous disposition, and had indignation at the force he used to them, he by one means or other made away with them. He endeavoured also to persuade Pollio the Pharisee, and Sameas, and the greatest part of their scholars, to take the oath; but these would neither submit so to do, nor were they punished together with the rest, out of the reverence he bore to Pollio. The Essens also, as we call a sect of ours, were excused from this imposition. These men live the same kind of life as do those whom the Greeks call Pythagoreans; concerning whom I shall discourse more fully elsewhere. However, it is but fit to set down here the reasons wherefore Herod had these Essens in such honour, and thought higher of them than their mortal nature required; nor will this account be unsuitable to the nature of this history, as it will shew the opinion men had of these Essens.

5. Now there was one of these Essens, whose name was Manahem, who had this testimony, that he not only conducted his life after an excellent manner, but had the foreknowledge of future events given him by God also. This man once saw Herod when he was a child, and going to school, and saluted him as king of the Jews; but he, thinking that either he did not know him, or that he was in jest, put him in mind that he was but a private man; but Manahem smiled to himself, and clapped him on his backside with his hand, and said, "However that be, thou wilt be king, and wilt begin thy reign happily, for God finds thee worthy of it; and do thou remember the blows that Manahem hath given thee, as being a signal of the change of

---

* A *tetrarchy* properly and originally denoted the fourth part of an entire kingdom or country, and a *tetrarch* one that was ruler of such a fourth part.

thy fortune; and truly this will be the best reasoning for thee, that thou love justice [towards men,] and piety towards God, and clemency towards thy citizens; yet do I know how thy whole conduct will be, that thou wilt not be such a one, for thou wilt excel all men in happiness, and obtain an everlasting reputation, but wilt forget piety and righteousness; and these crimes will not be concealed from God at the conclusion of thy life, when thou wilt find that he will be mindful of them and punish thee for them." Now at that time Herod did not at all attend to what Manahem said, as having no hopes of such advancement; but a little afterward, when he was so fortunate as to be advanced to the dignity of king, and was in the height of his dominion, he sent for Manahem, and asked him how long he should reign. Manahem did not tell him the full length of his reign; wherefore, upon that silence of his he asked him further, whether he should reign ten years or not? He replied, "Yes, twenty, nay, thirty years;" but did not assign the just determinate limit of his reign. Herod was satisfied with these replies, and gave Manahem his hand, and dismissed him, and from that time he continued to honour all the Essens. We have thought it proper to relate these facts to our readers, how strange soever they be, and to declare what hath happened among us, because many of these Essens have, by their excellent virtue, been thought worthy of this knowledge of divine revelations.

CHAPTER XI

HOW HEROD REBUILT THE TEMPLE, AND RAISED IT HIGHER, AND MADE IT MORE MAGNIFICENT THAN IT WAS BEFORE; AND ALSO CONCERNING THAT TOWER WHICH HE CALLED ANTONIA

1. AND now Herod, in the eighteenth year of his reign, and after the acts already mentioned, undertook a very great work, that is, to build of himself the temple of God,* and make it larger in compass, and to raise it to a most magnificent altitude, as esteeming it to be the most glorious of all his actions, as it really was, to bring it to perfection, and this would be sufficient for an everlasting memorial of him; but as he knew the multitude were not ready nor willing to assist him in so vast a design, he thought to prepare them first by making a speech to them, and then set about the work itself: so he called them together, and spake thus to them;—"I think I need not speak to you, my countrymen, about such other works as I have done since I came to the kingdom, although I may say they have been performed in such a manner as to bring more security to you than glory to myself; for I have neither been negligent in the most difficult times about what tended to ease your necessities, nor have the buildings I have made been so proper to preserve me as yourselves from injuries; and I imagine that, with God's assistance, I have advanced the nation of the Jews to a degree of happiness which they never had before; and for the particular edifices belonging to your own country, and to your own cities, as also to those cities that we have lately acquired, which we have erected and greatly adorned, and

* The fancy of the modern Jews, in calling this temple, which was really the third of their temples, the second temple, followed so long by later Christians, seems to be without any solid foundation.

thereby augmented the dignity of your nation, it seems to me a needless task to enumerate them to you, since you well know them yourselves; but as to that undertaking which I have a mind to set about at present, and which will be a work of the greatest piety and excellence that can possibly be undertaken by us, I will now declare it to you. Our fathers, indeed, when they were returned from Babylon, built this temple to God Almighty, yet does it want sixty cubits of its largeness and altitude; for so much did that first temple which Solomon built exceed this temple: nor let any one condemn our fathers for their negligence or want of piety herein, for it was not their fault that the temple was no higher; for they were Cyrus, and Darius the son of Hystaspes, who determined the measures for its rebuilding; and it hath been by reason of the subjection of those fathers of ours to them and to their posterity, and after them to the Macedonians, that they had not the opportunity to follow the original model of this pious edifice, nor could raise it to its ancient altitude; but since I am now, by God's will, your governor, and I have had peace a long time, and have gained great riches and large revenues, and, what is the principal thing of all, I am at amity with and well regarded by the Romans, who, if I may so say, are the rulers of the whole world, I will do my endeavour to correct that imperfection which hath arisen from the necessity of our affairs and the slavery we have been under formerly, and to make a thankful return, after the most pious manner to God, for what blessings I have received from him, by giving me this kingdom, and that by rendering his temple as complete as I am able."

2. And this was the speech which Herod made to them: but still this speech affrighted many of the people, as being unexpected by them, and because it seemed incredible, it did not encourage them, for they were afraid that he would pull down the whole edifice, and not be able to bring his intentions to perfection for its rebuilding; and this danger appeared to them to be very great, and the vastness of the undertaking to be such as could hardly be accomplished. But while they were in this disposition, the king encouraged them, and told them he would not pull down their temple till all things were gotten ready for building it up entirely again. And as he promised them this beforehand, so he did not break his word with them, but got ready a thousand waggons, that were to bring stones for the building, and chose out ten thousand of the most skilful workmen, and bought a thousand sacerdotal garments for the priests, and had some of them taught the arts of stonecutters, and others of carpenters, and then began to build; but this not till everything was well prepared for the work.

3. So Herod took away the old foundations, and laid others, and erected the temple upon them, being in length a hundred cubits, and in height twenty additional cubits, which [twenty,] upon the sinking of their foundations, fell down: and this part it was that we resolved to raise again in the days of Nero. Now the temple was built of stones that were white and strong, and each of their length was twenty-five cubits, their height was eight, and their breadth about twelve; and the whole structure, as also the structure of the royal cloister, was on each side much lower, but the middle was much higher, till they were visible to those that dwelt in the country for a great many furlongs, but chiefly to such as lived over against them, and those that approached to them. The temple had doors

also at the entrance, and lintels over them, of the same height with the temple itself. They were adorned with embroidered veils, with their flowers of purple, and pillars interwoven: and over these, but under the crown-work, was spread out a golden vine, with its branches hanging down from a great height, the largeness and fine workmanship of which was a surprising sight to the spectators, to see what vast materials there were, and with what great skill the workmanship was done. He also encompassed the entire temple with very large cloisters, contriving them to be in a due proportion thereto; and he laid out larger sums of money upon them than had been done before him, till it seemed that no one else had so greatly adorned the temple as he had done. There was a large wall to both the cloisters; which wall was itself the most prodigious work that was ever heard of by man. The hill was a rocky ascent, that declined by degrees towards the east parts of the city, till it came to an elevated level. This hill it was which Solomon, who was the first of our kings, by divine revelation, encompassed with a wall; it was of excellent workmanship upwards, and round the top of it. He also built a wall below, beginning at the bottom, which was encompassed by a deep valley; and at the south side he laid rocks together, and bound them one to another with lead, and included some of the inner parts, till it proceeded to a great height, and till both the largeness of the square edifice and its altitude were immense, and till the vastness of the stones in the front were plainly visible on the outside, yet so that the inward parts were fastened with iron, and preserved the joints immovable for all future times. When this work [for the foundation] was done in this manner, and joined together as a part of the hill itself to the very top of it, he wrought it all into one outward surface, and filled up the hollow places which were about the wall, and made it a level on the external upper surface, and a smooth level also. This hill was walled all round, and in compass four furlongs, [the distance of] each angle containing in length a furlong: but within this wall, and on the very top of all, there ran another wall of stone also, having, on the east quarter, a double cloister, of the same length with the wall; in the midst of which was the temple itself. This cloister looked to the gates of the temple; and it had been adorned by many kings in former times; and round about the entire temple were fixed the spoils taken from barbarous nations; all these had been dedicated to the temple by Herod, with the addition of those he had taken from the Arabians.

4. Now on the north side [of the temple] was built a citadel, whose walls were square and strong, and of extraordinary firmness. This citadel was built by the kings of the Asamonean race, who were also high priests before Herod, and they called it the Tower, in which were reposited the vestments of the high priest, which the high priest only put on at the time when he was to offer sacrifice. These vestments king Herod kept in that place; and after his death they were under the power of the Romans, until the time of Tiberius Cæsar; under whose reign Vitellius, the president of Syria, when he once came to Jerusalem, and had been most magnificently received by the multitude, he had a mind to make them some requital for the kindness they had shewn him; so, upon their petition to have those holy vestments in their own power, he wrote about them to Tiberius Cæsar, who granted his request: and this their power over

the sacerdotal vestments continued with the Jews till the death of king Agrippa; but after that, Cassius Longinus, who was president of Syria, and Cuspius Fadus, who was procurator of Judea, enjoined the Jews to reposit those vestments in the tower of Antonia, for that they ought to have them in their power, as they formerly had. However, the Jews sent ambassadors to Claudius Cæsar, to intercede with him for them; upon whose coming, king Agrippa, junior, being then at Rome, asked for and obtained the power over them from the emperor; who gave command to Vitellius, who was then commander in Syria, to give them it accordingly. Before that time they were kept under the seal of the high priest, and of the treasurers of the temple; which treasurers, the day before a festival, went up to the Roman captain of the temple-guards, and viewed their own seal, and received the vestments; and again when the festival was over, they brought it to the same place, and shewed the captain of the temple-guards their seal, which corresponded with his seal, and reposited them there. And that these things were so, the afflictions that happened to us afterward [about them] are sufficient evidence: but for the tower itself, when Herod the king of the Jews had fortified it more firmly than before, in order to secure and guard the temple, he gratified Antonius, who was his friend, and the Roman ruler, and then gave it the name of the Tower of Antonia.

5. Now, in the western quarter of the enclosures of the temple there were four gates; the first led to the king's palace, and went to a passage over the intermediate valley; two more led to the suburbs of the city; and the last led to the other city, where the road descended down into the valley by a great number of steps, and thence up again by the ascent; for the city lay over against the temple in the manner of a theatre, and was encompassed with a deep valley along the entire south quarter; but the fourth front of the temple, which was southward, had indeed itself gates in its middle, as also it had the royal cloisters, with three walks, which reached in length from the east valley unto that on the west, for it was impossible it should reach any further: and this cloister deserves to be mentioned better than any other under the sun; for while the valley was very deep, and its bottom could not be seen, if you looked from above into the depth, this further vastly high elevation of the cloister stood upon that height, insomuch that if any one looked down from the top of the battlements, or down both these altitudes, he would be giddy, while his sight could not reach to such an immense depth. This cloister had pillars that stood in four rows one over against the other all along, for the fourth row was interwoven into the wall, which [also was built of stone;] and the thickness of each pillar was such, that three men might, with their arms extended, fathom it round, and join their hands again, while its length was twenty-seven feet, with a double spiral at its basis; and the number of all the pillars [in that court] was an hundred and sixty-two. Their chapiters were made with sculptures after the Corinthian order, and caused an amazement [to the spectators,] by reason of the grandeur of the whole. These four rows of pillars included three intervals for walking in the middle of this cloister; two of which walks were made parallel to each other, and were contrived after the same manner; the breadth of each of them was thirty feet, the length was a furlong, and the height fifty feet:

but the breadth of the middle part of the cloister was one and a half of the other, and the height was double, for it was much higher than those on each side; but the roofs were adorned with deep sculptures in wood, representing many sorts of figures: the middle was much higher than the rest, and the wall of the front was adorned with beams, resting upon pillars, that were interwoven into it, and that front was all of polished stone, insomuch that its fineness, to such as had not seen it, was incredible, and to such as had seen it, was greatly amazing. Thus was the first enclosure. In the midst of which, and not far from it, was the second, to be gone up to by a few steps: this was encompassed by a stone wall for a partition, with an inscription, which forbade any foreigner to go in under pain of death. Now this inner inclosure had on its southern and northern quarters three gates [equally] distant from one another; but on the east quarter, towards the sun-rising, there was one large gate through which such as were pure came in, together with their wives; but the temple further inward in that gate was not allowed to the women; but still more inward was there a third [court of the] temple, whereinto it was not lawful for any but the priests alone to enter. The temple itself was within this; and before that temple was the altar, upon which we offer our sacrifices and burnt-offerings to God. Into none of these three did king Herod enter,* for he was forbidden, because he was not a priest. However, he took care of the cloisters and the outer enclosures; and these he built in eight years.

---

* "Into none of these three did king Herod enter," —i. e., 1. Not into the court of the priests; 2. Nor into the holy house itself; 3. Nor into the separate place belonging to the altar, as the words following imply; for none but priests, or their attendants the Levites, might come into any of them.

6. But the temple itself was built by the priests in a year and six months,—upon which all the people were full of joy; and presently they returned thanks, in the first place, to God; and in the next place, for the alacrity the king had shewn. They feasted and celebrated this rebuilding of the temple: and for the king, he sacrificed three hundred oxen to God; as did the rest, every one according to his ability: the number of which sacrifices it is not possible to set down; for it cannot be that we should truly relate it; for at the same time with this celebration for the work about the temple, fell also the day of the king's inauguration, which he kept of an old custom as a festival, and it now coincided with the other; which coincidence of them both made the festival most illustrious.

7. There was also an occult passage built for the king: it led from Antonia to the inner temple, at its eastern gate; over which also he erected for himself a tower, that he might have the opportunity of a subterraneous ascent to the temple, in order to guard against any sedition which might be made by the people against their kings. It is also reported,† that during the time that the temple was building, it did not rain in the day time, but that the showers fell in the nights, so that the work was not hindered. And this our fathers have delivered to us; nor is it incredible, if any have regard to the manifestations of God. And thus was performed the work of the rebuilding of the temple.

---

† This tradition which Josephus here mentions, of this remarkable circumstance relating to the building of Herod's temple, is a demonstration that its building was a known thing in Judea at this time. He was born but forty-six years after it is related to have been finished, and might himself have seen and spoken with some of the builders themselves, and with a great number of those who had seen its building.

BOOK XVI

CONTAINING THE INTERVAL OF TWELVE YEARS

FROM THE FINISHING OF THE TEMPLE BY HEROD TO THE DEATH OF ALEXANDER AND ARISTOBULUS

CHAPTER I

A LAW OF HEROD'S ABOUT THIEVES. SALOME AND PHERORAS CALUMNIATE ALEXANDER AND ARISTOBULUS, UPON THEIR RETURN FROM ROME, FOR WHOM HEROD YET PROVIDES WIVES

1. As king Herod was very zealous in the administration of his entire government, and desirous to put a stop to particular acts of injustice which were done by criminals about the city and country, he made a law, no way like our original laws, and which he enacted himself, to expose housebreakers to be ejected out of his kingdom; which punishment was not only grievous to be borne by the offenders, but contained in it a dissolution of the customs of our forefathers; for this slavery to foreigners, and

such as did not live after the manner of Jews, and this necessity that they were under to do whatsoever such men should command, was an offence against our religious settlement, rather than a punishment to such as were found to have offended, such a punishment being avoided in our original laws; for those laws ordain, that the thief shall restore fourfold; and that if he have not so much, he shall be sold indeed, but not to foreigners, nor so that he be under perpetual slavery, for he must have been released after six years. But this law, thus enacted in order to introduce a severe and illegal punishment, seemed to be a piece of insolence of Herod, when he did not act as a king but as a tyrant, and thus contemptuously, and without any regard to his subjects, did he venture to introduce such a punishment. Now this penalty thus brought into practice, was like Herod's other actions, and became a part of his accusation, and an occasion of the hatred he lay under.

2. Now at this time it was that he sailed to Italy, as very desirous to meet with Cæsar, and to see his sons who lived at Rome : and Cæsar was not only very obliging to him in other respects, but delivered him his sons again, that he might take them home with him, as having already completed themselves in the sciences ; but as soon as the young men were come from Italy, the multitude were very desirous to see them, and they became conspicuous among them all, as adorned with great blessings of fortune, and having the countenances of persons of royal dignity. So they soon appeared to be the objects of envy to Salome, the king's sister, and to such as had raised calumnies against Mariamne ; for they were suspicious, that when these came to the government, they should be punished for the wickedness they had been guilty of against their mother ; so they made this very fear of theirs a motive to raise calumnies against them also. They gave it out that they were not pleased with their father's company, because he had put their mother to death, as if it were not agreeable to piety to appear to converse with their mother's murderer. Now, by carrying these stories, that had indeed a true foundation, [in the fact,] but were only built on probabilities as to the present accusation, they were able to do them mischief, and to make Herod take away that kindness from his sons which he had before borne to them, for they did not say these things to him openly, but scattered abroad such words among the rest of the multitude ; from which words, when carried to Herod, he was induced [at last] to hate them, and which natural affection itself, even in length of time, was not able to overcome ; yet was the king at that time in a condition to prefer the natural affection of a father before all the suspicions and calumnies his sons lay under : so he respected them as he ought to do, and married them to wives, now they were of an age suitable thereto. To Aristobulus he gave for a wife Bernice, Salome's daughter ; and to Alexander, Glaphyra, the daughter of Archelaus, king of Cappadocia.

CHAPTER II

HOW HEROD TWICE SAILED TO AGRIPPA ; AND HOW UPON THE COMPLAINT OF THE JEWS IN IONIA AGAINST THE GREEKS, AGRIPPA CONFIRMED THE LAWS OF THE JEWS TO THEM

1. WHEN Herod had despatched these affairs, and he understood that Marcus Agrippa had sailed again out of Italy into Asia, he made haste to him, and besought him to come to him into his kingdom, and to partake of what he might justly expect from one that had been his guest, and was his friend. This request he greatly pressed, and to it Agrippa agreed, and came into Judea : whereupon Herod omitted nothing that might please him. He entertained him in his new-built cities, and shewed him the edifices he had built, and provided all sorts of the best and most costly dainties for him and his friends, and that at Sebaste and Cesarea, about that port that he had built, and at the fortresses which he had erected at great expenses, Alexandrium, and Herodium, and Hyrcania. He also conducted him to the city Jerusalem, where all the people met him in their festival garments, and received him with accla-

mations. Agrippa also offered a hecatomb of sacrifices to God ; and feasted the people, without omitting any of the greatest dainties that could be gotten. He also took so much pleasure there, that he abode many days with them, and would willingly have stayed longer, but that the season of the year made him haste away ; for as winter was coming on, he thought it not safe to go to sea later, and yet he was of necessity to return again to Ionia.

2. So Agrippa went away, when Herod had bestowed on him, and on the principal of those that were with him, many presents ; but king Herod, when he had passed the winter in his own dominions, made haste to get to him again in the spring, when he knew he designed to go to a campaign at the Bosphorus. So when he had sailed by Rhodes and by Cos, he touched at Lesbos, as thinking he should have overtaken Agrippa there ; but he was taken short here by a north wind, which hindered his ship from going to the shore ; so he continued many days at Chius, and there he kindly treated a great many that came to him, and obliged them by giving them royal gifts. And when he saw that the portico of the city was fallen down, which as it was overthrown in the Mithridatic war, and was a very large and fine building, so was it not so easy to rebuild that as it was the rest, yet did he furnish a sum not only large enough for that purpose, but what was more than sufficient to finish the building ; and ordered them not to overlook that portico, but to rebuild it quickly, that so the city might recover its proper ornaments. And when the high winds were laid, he sailed to Mitylene, and thence to Byzantium ; and when he heard that Agrippa was sailed beyond the Cyanean rocks, he made all the haste possible to overtake him, and came up with him about Synope, in Pontus. He was seen sailing by the shipmen most unexpectedly, but appeared to their great joy ; and many friendly salutations there were between them, insomuch that Agrippa thought he had received the greatest marks of the king's kindness and humanity towards him possible, since the king had come so long a voyage, and at a very proper season, for his assistance, and had left the government of his own dominions, and thought it more worth his while to come to him. Accordingly, Herod was all in all to Agrippa, in the management of the war, and a great assistant in civil affairs, and in giving him counsel as to particular matters. He was also a pleasant companion for him when he relaxed himself, and a joint partaker with him in all things ; in troubles because of his kindness ; and in prosperity, because of the respect Agrippa had for him. Now as soon as those affairs of Pontus were finished, for whose sake Agrippa was sent thither, they did not think fit to return by sea, but passed through Paphlagonia and Cappadocia, they then travelled thence over great Phrygia, and came to Ephesus, and then they sailed from Ephesus to Samos. And indeed the king bestowed a great many benefits on every city that he came to, according as they stood in need of them ; for as for those that wanted either money or kind treatment, he was not wanting to them ; but he supplied the former himself out of his own expenses : he also became an intercessor with Agrippa for all such as sought after his favour, and he brought things so about, that the petitioners failed in none of their suits to him, Agrippa being himself of a good disposition, and of great generosity, and ready to grant all such requests as might be advantageous to the petitioners, provided they were not to the

detriment of others. The inclination of the king was of great weight also, and still excited Agrippa, who was himself ready to do good; for he made a reconciliation between the people of Ilium, at whom he was angry, and paid what money the people of Chius owed to Cæsar's procurators, and discharged them of their tributes; and helped all others, according as their several necessities required.

3. But now, when Agrippa and Herod were in Ionia, a great multitude of Jews, who dwelt in their cities, came to them, and laying hold of the opportunity and the liberty now given them, laid before them the injuries which they suffered, while they were not permitted to use their own laws, but were compelled to prosecute their law suits, by the ill usage of the judges, upon their holy days, and were deprived of the money they used to lay up at Jerusalem, and were forced into the army, and upon such other offices as obliged them to spend their sacred money; from which burdens they always used to be freed by the Romans, who had still permitted them to live according to their own laws. When this clamour was made, the king desired of Agrippa that he would hear their cause, and assigned Nicolaus, one of his friends, to plead for those their privileges. Accordingly, when Agrippa had called the principal of the Romans, and such of the kings and rulers as were there, to be his assessors, Nicolaus stood up, and pleaded for the Jews as follows :—"It is of necessity incumbent on such as are in distress to have recourse to those that have it in their power to free them from those injuries they lie under; and for those that now are complainants, they approach you with great assurance; for as they have formerly often obtained your favour, so far as they have even wished to have it, they now only entreat that you, who have been the donors, will take care that those favours you have already granted them may not be taken away from them. We have received these favours from you, who alone have power to grant them, but have them taken from us by such as are no greater than ourselves, and by such as we know are as much subjects as we are; and certainly, if we have been vouchsafed great favours, it is to our commendation who have obtained them, and having been found deserving of such great favours; and if those favours be but small ones, it would be barbarous for the donors not to confirm them to us : and for those that are the hindrance of the Jews, and use them reproachfully, it is evident that they affront both the receivers, while they will not allow those to be worthy men to whom their excellent rulers themselves have borne their testimony, and the donors, while they desire those favours already granted may be abrogated. Now if any one should ask these Gentiles themselves, which of the two things they should choose to part with, their lives, or the customs of their forefathers, their solemnities, their sacrifices, their festivals, which they celebrate in honour of those they suppose to be gods; I know very well that they would choose to suffer anything whatsoever rather than a dissolution of any of the customs of their forefathers; for a great many of them have rather chosen to go to war on that account, as very solicitous not to transgress in those matters; and indeed we take an estimate of that happiness which all mankind do now enjoy by your means from this very thing, that we are allowed every one to worship as our own institutions require, and yet live [in peace;] and although they would not be thus treated themselves, yet do they endeavour to compel others to comply with them, as if it were

not as great an instance of impiety, profanely to dissolve the religious solemnities of any others, as to be negligent in the observation of their own towards their gods. And let us now consider the one of these practices :—Is there any people, or city, or community of men, to whom your government and the Roman power does not appear to be the greatest blessing? Is there any one that can desire to make void the favours they have granted? No one is certainly so mad; for there are no men but such as have been partakers of their favours, both in public and private ; and indeed those that take away what you have granted, can have no assurance, but every one of their own grants made them by you may be taken from them also; which grants of yours can yet never be sufficiently valued; for if they consider the old governments under kings, together with your present government, besides the great number of benefits which this government hath bestowed on them in order to their happiness, that is instead of all the rest, that they appear to be no longer in a state of slavery, but of freedom. Now the privileges we desire, even when we are in the best circumstances, are not such as deserve to be envied, for we are indeed in a prosperous state by your means, but this is only in common with others, and it is no more than this which we desire, to preserve our religion without any prohibition, which, as it appears not in itself a privilege to be envied us, so it is for the advantage of those that grant it to us, for if the Divinity delights in being honoured, he must delight in those that permit him to be honoured. And there are none of our customs which are inhuman, but all tending to piety, and devoted to the preservation of justice; nor do we conceal those injunctions of ours by which we govern our lives, they being memorials of piety, and of a friendly conversation among men. And the seventh day we set apart from labour; it is dedicated to the learning of our customs and laws,* we thinking it proper to reflect on them, as well as on any [good] thing else, in order to our avoiding of sin. If any one therefore examine into our observances, he will find they are good in themselves, and that they are ancient also, though some think otherwise, insomuch that those who have received them cannot easily be brought to depart from them, out of that honour they pay to the length of time they have religiously enjoyed them and observed them. Now our adversaries take these our privileges away in the way of injustice; they violently seize upon that money of ours which is offered to God, and called sacred money, and this openly, after a sacrilegious manner; and they impose tributes upon us, and bring us before tribunals on holy days, and then require other like debts of us, not because the contracts require it, and for their own advantage, but because they would put an affront on our religion, of which they are conscious as well as we, and have indulged themselves in an unjust, and to them involuntary hatred; for your government over all is one, tending to the establishing of benevolence, and abolishing of ill-will among such as are disposed to it. This is therefore what we implore from thee, most excellent Agrippa, that we may not be ill-treated; that we may not be abused; that we may not be hindered from making use of our own customs, nor be despoiled of our goods; nor be forced by these

---

* Observe here the ancient practice of the Jews, of dedicating the Sabbath-day, not to idleness, but to the learning their sacred rites and religious customs, and to the meditation on the law of Moses.

men to do what we ourselves force nobody to do: for these privileges of ours are not only according to justice, but have formerly been granted us by you: and we are able to read to you many decrees of the senate, and the tables that contain them, which are still extant in the capitol concerning these things, which it is evident were granted after you had experience of our fidelity towards you, which ought to be valued, though no such fidelity had been, for you have hitherto preserved what people were in possession of, not to us only, but almost to all men, and have added greater advantages than they could have hoped for, and thereby your government is become a great advantage to them. And if any one were able to enumerate the prosperity you have conferred on every nation, which they possess by your means, he could never put an end to his discourse; but that we may demonstrate that we are not unworthy of all those advantages we have obtained, it will be sufficient for us to say nothing of other things, but to speak freely of this king who now governs us, and is now one of thy assessors: and indeed in what instance of good-will, as to your house, hath he been deficient? What mark of fidelity to it hath he omitted? What token of honour hath he not devised? What occasion for his assistance of you hath he not regarded at the very first? What hindereth, therefore, but that your kindness may be as numerous as his so great benefits to you have been? It may also perhaps be fit not here to pass over in silence the valour of his father Antipater, who, when Cæsar made an expedition into Egypt, assisted him with two thousand armed men, and proved inferior to none, neither in the battles on land, nor in the management of the navy; and what need I say anything of how great weight those soldiers were at that juncture? or how many, and how great presents they were vouchsafed by Cæsar? And truly I ought before now to have mentioned the epistle which Cæsar wrote to the senate; and how Antipater had honours, and the freedom of the city of Rome, bestowed upon him; for these are demonstrations both that we have received these favours by our own deserts, and do on that account petition thee for thy confirmation of them, from whom we had reason to hope for them, though they had not been given us before, both out of regard to our king's disposition towards you, and your disposition towards him; and further, we have been informed by those Jews that were there, with what kindness thou camest into our country, and how thou offeredst the most perfect sacrifices to God, and honouredst him with remarkable vows, and how thou gavest the people a feast, and acceptedst of their own hospitable presents to thee. We ought to esteem all these kind entertainments made by both our nation and our city, to a man who is the ruler and manager of so much of the public affairs, as indications of that friendship which thou hast returned to the Jewish nation, and which had been procured them by the family of Herod. So we put them in mind of these things before the king, now sitting by thee, and make our request for no more but this, that what you have given us yourselves, you will not see taken away by others from us."

4. When Nicolaus had made this speech, there was no opposition made to it by the Greeks, for this was not an inquiry made, as in a court of justice, but an intercession to prevent violence to be offered to the Jews any longer; nor did the Greeks make any defence of themselves, or deny what it was supposed they had done. Their pretence was no more than this, that while the Jews inhabited in their country, they were entirely unjust to them [in not joining in their worship] but they demonstrated their generosity in this, that though they worshipped according to their own institutions, they did nothing that ought to grieve them. So when Agrippa perceived that they had been oppressed by violence, he made this answer:—That, on account of Herod's good-will and friendship, he was ready to grant the Jews whatsoever they should ask him, and that their requests seemed to him in themselves just; and that if they requested anything further, he should not scruple to grant it them, provided they were no way to the detriment of the Roman government; but that, while their request was no more than this, that what privileges they had already given them might not be abrogated, he confirmed this to them, that they might continue in the observation of their own customs, without any one offering them the least injury; and when he had said thus, he dissolved the assembly: upon which Herod stood up and saluted him, and gave him thanks for the kind disposition he shewed to them. Agrippa also took this in a very obliging manner, and saluted him again, and embraced him in his arms; after which he went away from Lesbos; but the king determined to sail from Samos to his own country; and when he had taken his leave of Agrippa, he pursued his voyage, and landed at Cesarea in a few days' time, as having favourable winds; from whence he went to Jerusalem, and there gathered all the people together to an assembly, not a few being there out of the country also. So when he came to them, he gave them a particular account of all his journey, and of the affairs of all the Jews in Asia, how by his means they would live without injurious treatment for the time to come. He also told them of the entire good fortune he had met with, and how he had administered the government, and had not neglected anything which was for their advantage; and as he was very joyful, he now remitted to them the fourth part of their taxes for the last year. Accordingly, they were so pleased with his favour and speech to them, that they went their ways with great gladness, and wished the king all manner of happiness.

CHAPTER III

HOW GREAT DISTURBANCES AROSE IN HEROD'S FAMILY ON HIS PREFERRING ANTIPATER, HIS ELDEST SON, BEFORE THE REST, TILL ALEXANDER TOOK THAT INJURY VERY HEINOUSLY

1. BUT now the affairs in Herod's family were in more and more disorder, and became more severe upon him, by the hatred of Salome to the young men [Alexander and Aristobulus,] which descended as it were by inheritance [from their mother Mariamne:] and as she had fully succeeded against their mother, so she proceeded to that degree of madness and insolence, as to endeavour that none of her posterity might be left alive, who might have it in their power to revenge her death. The young men had also somewhat of a bold and uneasy disposition towards their father, occasioned by the remembrance of what their mother had unjustly suffered, and by their own affectation of dominion. The old grudge was also renewed; and they cast reproaches on Salome and Pheroras, who requited the young men with malicious designs, and actually laid treacherous snares for them. Now, as for this hatred, it was equal on both sides, but

the manner of exerting that hatred was different; for as for the young men, they were rash, reproaching and affronting the others openly, and were inexperienced enough to think it the most generous to declare their minds in that undaunted manner; but the others did not take that method, but made use of calumnies after a subtle and spiteful manner, still provoking the young men, and imagining that their boldness might in time turn to the offering violence to their father, for inasmuch as they were not ashamed of the pretended crime of their mother, nor thought she suffered justly, these supposed that might at length exceed all bounds, and induce them to think they ought to be avenged on their father, though it were by despatching him with their own hands. At length it came to this, that the whole city was full of their discourses, as is usual in such contests, the unskilfulness of the young men was pitied; but the contrivance of Salome was too hard for them, and what imputations she laid upon them came to be believed, by means of their own conduct; for they were so deeply affected with the death of their mother, that while they said both she and themselves were in a miserable case, they vehemently complained of her pitiable end, which indeed was truly such, and said that they were themselves in a pitiable case also, because they were forced to live with those that had been her murderers, and to be partakers with them.

2. These disorders increased greatly, and the king's absence abroad had afforded a fit opportunity for that increase; but as soon as Herod was returned, and had made the forementioned speech to the multitude, Pheroras and Salome let fall words immediately as if he were in great danger, and as if the young men openly threatened that they would not spare him any longer, but revenge their mother's death upon him. They also added another circumstance, that their hopes were fixed on Archelaus, the king of Cappadocia, that they should be able by his means to come to Cæsar, and accuse their father. Upon hearing such things, Herod was immediately disturbed; and indeed was the more astonished because the same things were related to him by some others also. He then called to mind his former calamity, and considered that the disorders in his family had hindered him from enjoying any comfort from those that were dearest to him, or from his wife whom he loved so well; and suspecting that his future troubles would soon be heavier and greater than those that were past, he was in great confusion of mind, for Divine Providence had in reality conferred upon him a great many outward advantages for his happiness, even beyond his hopes,— but the troubles he had at home were such as he never expected to have met with, and rendered him unfortunate; nay, both sorts came upon him to such a degree as no one could imagine, and made it a doubtful question, whether, upon the comparison of both, he ought to have exchanged so great a success of outward good things for so great misfortunes at home, or whether he ought not to have chosen to avoid the calamities relating to his family, though he had, for a compensation, never been possessed of the admired grandeur of a kingdom.

3. As he was thus disturbed and afflicted, in order to depress these young men, he brought to court another of his sons, that was born to him when he was a private man; his name was Antipater: yet did he not then indulge him as he did afterwards, when he was quite overcome by him, and let him do everything as he pleased, but rather with a design of depressing the insolence of the sons of Mariamne, and managing this elevation of his son, that it might be for a warning to them; for this bold behaviour of theirs [he thought] would not be so great, if they were once persuaded that the succession to the kingdom did not appertain to them alone, or must of necessity come to them. So he introduced Antipater as their antagonist, and imagined that he made a good provision for discouraging their pride, and that after this was done to the young men, there might be a proper season for expecting these to be of a better disposition: but the event proved otherwise than he intended, for the young men thought he did them a very great injury; and as Antipater was a shrewd man, when he had once obtained this degree of freedom, and began to expect greater things than he had before hoped for, he had but one single design in his head, and that was to distress his brethren, and not at all to yield to them the pre-eminence, but to keep close to his father, who was already alienated from them by the calumnies he heard about them, and ready to be brought upon in any way his zeal against them should advise him to pursue, that he might be continually more and more severe against him. Accordingly, all the reports that were spread abroad came from him, while he avoided himself the suspicion, as if those discoveries proceeded from him; but he rather chose to make use of those persons for his assistants that were unsuspected, and such as might be believed to speak truth by reason of the good-will they bore to the king; and indeed there were already not a few who cultivated their friendship with Antipater, in hopes of gaining somewhat by him, and these were the men who most of all persuaded Herod, because they appeared to speak thus out of their good-will to him: and while these joint accusations, which, from various foundations, supported one another's veracity, the young men themselves afforded further occasions to Antipater also; for they were observed to shed tears often, on account of the injury that was offered them, and had their mother in their mouths; and among their friends they ventured to reproach their father, as not acting justly by them; all which things were with an evil intention reserved in memory by Antipater against a proper opportunity; and when they were told to Herod, with aggravations, increased the disorder so much, that it brought a great tumult into the family; for while the king was very angry at imputations that were laid upon the sons of Mariamne, and was desirous to humble them, he still increased the honour that he had bestowed on Antipater, and was at last so overcome by his persuasions, that he brought his mother to court also. He also wrote frequently to Cæsar in favour of him, and more earnestly recommending him to his care particularly. And when Agrippa was returned to Rome, after he had finished his ten years' government in Asia, Herod sailed from Judea; and when he met with him, he had none with him but Antipater, whom he delivered to Agrippa, that he might take him along with him, together with many presents, that so he might become Cæsar's friend, insomuch that things already looked as if he had all his father's favour, and that the young men were already entirely rejected from any hopes of the kingdom.

CHAPTER IV

HOW, DURING ANTIPATER'S ABODE AT ROME, HEROD BROUGHT ALEXANDER AND ARISTOBULUS BEFORE CÆSAR, AND ACCUSED THEM. ALEXANDER'S DEFENCE OF HIMSELF BEFORE CÆSAR, AND RECONCILIATION TO HIS FATHER

1. AND now what happened during Antipater's absence augmented the honour to which he had been promoted, and his apparent eminence above his brethren, for he made a great figure at Rome, because Herod had sent recommendations of him to all his friends there; only he was grieved that he was not at home, nor had proper opportunities of perpetually calumniating his brethren; and his chief fear was, lest his father should alter his mind, and entertain a more favourable opinion of the sons of Mariamne; and as he had this in his mind, he did not desist from his purpose, but continually sent from Rome any such stories as he hoped might grieve and irritate his father against his brethren, under pretence indeed of a deep concern for his preservation, but in truth, such as his malicious mind dictated, in order to purchase a greater hope of the succession, which yet was already great in itself : and thus he did till he had excited such a degree of anger in Herod, that he was already become very ill disposed towards the young men; but still while he delayed to exercise so violent a disgust against them, and that he might not either be too remiss or too rash, and so offend, he thought it best to sail to Rome, and there accuse his sons before Cæsar, and not indulge himself in any such crime as might be heinous enough to be suspected of impiety. But as he was going up to Rome, it happened that he made such haste as to meet with Cæsar at the city Aquilei:* so when he came to the speech of Cæsar, he asked for a time for hearing this great cause, wherein he thought himself very miserable, and presented his sons there, and accused them of their mad actions, and of their attempts against him:—That they were enemies to him; and by all the means they were able, did their endeavours to shew their hatred to their own father, and would take away his life, and so obtain his kingdom, after the most barbarous manner: that he had power from Cæsar to dispose of it, not by necessity, but by choice, to him who shall exercise the greatest piety towards him; while these my sons are not so desirous of ruling, as they are upon a disappointment thereof, to expose their own life, if so be they may but deprive their father of his life; so wild and polluted is their mind by time become, out of their hatred to him: that whereas he had a long time borne this his misfortune, he was now compelled to lay it before Cæsar, and to pollute his ears with such language, while he himself wants to know what severity they have ever suffered from him, or what hardships he had ever laid upon them to make them complain of him; and how they can think it just that he should not be lord of that kingdom which he in a long time, and with great danger, had gained, and not allow him to keep it, and dispose of it to him who should deserve best; and this, with other advantages, he proposes as a reward for the piety of such a one as will hereafter imitate the care he hath taken of it, and that such a one may gain so great a requital as that is: and that it is an impious thing for them to pretend to meddle with it beforehand, for he who hath ever the kingdom in his view, at the same time reckons upon procuring the death of his father, because otherwise he cannot come at the government; that as for himself, he had hitherto given them all that he was able, and what was agreeable to such as are subject to the royal authority, and the sons of a king: what ornaments they wanted, with servants and delicate fare, and had married them into the most illustrious families, the one [Aristobulus] to his sister's daughter, but Alexander to the daughter of king Archelaus; and, what was the greatest favour of all, when their crimes were so very bad, and he had authority to punish them, yet had he not made use of it against them, but had brought them before Cæsar, their common benefactor, and had not used the severity which either as a father who had been impiously abused, or as a king who had been assaulted treacherously, he might have done, but made them stand upon the level with him in judgment: that, however, it was necessary that all this should not be passed over without punishment, nor himself live in the greatest fears; nay, that it was not for their own advantage to see the light of the sun after what they had done, although they should escape at this time, since they had done the vilest things, and would certainly suffer the greatest punishments that ever were known among mankind.

2. These were the accusations which Herod laid with great vehemency against his sons before Cæsar. Now the young men, both while he was speaking, and chiefly at his concluding, wept, and were in confusion. Now as to themselves, they knew in their own conscience they were innocent, but because they were accused by their father, they were sensible, as the truth was, that it was hard for them to make their apology, since though they were at liberty to speak their minds freely as the occasion required, and might with force and earnestness refute the accusation, yet was it not now decent so to do. There was therefore a difficulty how they should be able to speak; and tears, and at length a deep groan followed, while they were afraid, that if they said nothing, they should seem to be in this difficulty from a consciousness of guilt,—nor had they any defence ready, by reason of their youth, and the disorder they were under; yet was not Cæsar unapprised, when he looked upon them in the confusion they were in, that their delay to make their defence did not arise from any consciousness of great enormities, but from their unskilfulness and modesty. They were also commiserated by those that were there in particular; and they moved their father's affections in earnest, till he had much ado to conceal them.

3. But when they saw there was a kind disposition arisen both in him and in Cæsar, and that every one of the rest did either shed tears, or at least did all grieve with them, the one of them, whose name was Alexander, called to his father, and attempting to answer his accusation, said, "O father, the benevolence thou hast shewed to us is evident, even in this very judicial procedure, for hadst thou any pernicious intentions about us, thou hadst not produced us here before the common saviour of all, for it was in thy power, both as a king and as a father, to punish the guilty; but by thus bringing us to Rome, and making Cæsar himself a witness to what is done, thou intimatest that thou intendest to save us; for no one that hath a design to slay a man will bring him to the temples, and to the altars; yet are our circumstances still worse,

---

* Although Herod met Augustus at Aquilei, yet was this accusation of his sons deferred till they came to Rome.

for we cannot endure to live ourselves any longer, if it be believed that we have injured such a father; nay, perhaps it would be worse for us to live with this suspicion upon us, that we have injured him, than to die without such guilt: and if our open defence may be taken to be true, we shall be happy, both in pacifying thee, and in escaping the danger we are in; but if this calumny so prevails, it is more than enough for us that we have seen the sun this day; which why should we see, if this suspicion be fixed upon us? Now it is easy to say of young men, that they desired to reign: and to say further, that this evil proceeds from the case of our unhappy mother. This is abundantly sufficient to produce our present misfortune out of the former; but consider well, whether such an accusation does not suit all such young men, and may not be said of them all promiscuously; for nothing can hinder him that reigns, if he have children, and their mother be dead, but the father may have a suspicion upon all his sons, as intending some treachery to him: but a suspicion is not sufficient to prove such an impious practice. Now let any man say, whether we have actually and insolently attempted any such thing, whereby actions otherwise incredible used to be made credible? Can anybody prove that poison hath been prepared? or prove a conspiracy of our equals, or the corruption of servants, or letters written against thee? though indeed there are none of those things but have sometimes been pretended by way of calumny, when they were never done; for a royal family that is at variance with itself is a terrible thing; and that which thou callest a reward of piety, often becomes, among very wicked men, such a foundation of hope, as makes them leave no sort of mischief untried. Nor does any one lay any wicked practices to our charge; but as to calumnies by hearsay, how can we put an end to them, who will not hear what we have to say? Have we talked with too great freedom? yes; but not against thee, for that would be unjust, but against those that never conceal anything that is spoken to them. Hath either of us lamented our mother? yes; but not because she is dead, but because she was evil spoken of by those that had no reason so to do. Are we desirous of that dominion which we know our father is possessed of? For what reason can we do so? If we already have royal honours, as we have, should not we labour in vain? And if we have them not, yet are not we in hopes of them? Or supposing that we had killed thee, could we expect to obtain thy kingdom? while neither the earth would let us tread upon it, nor the sea let us sail upon it, after such an action as that: nay, the religion of all your subjects, and the piety of the whole nation, would have prohibited parricides from assuming the government, and from entering into that most holy temple which was built by thee.* But suppose we had made light of other dangers, can any murderer go off unpunished while Cæsar is alive? We are thy

*Since some men have indulged a suspicion that Josephus's history of Herod's rebuilding the temple is no better than a fable, it may not be amiss to take notice of this clause in the speech of Alexander before his father Herod, in his and his brother's vindication, which mentions the temple as known by every body to have been built by Herod. See John ii. 20. See also another speech of Herod's own to the young men that pulled down his golden eagle from the front of the temple, where he takes notice how the building of the temple cost him a vast sum; and that the Asamoneans, in those one hundred and twenty-five years they held the government, were not able to perform so great a work to the honour of God as this was.

sons, and not so impious, or so thoughtless as that comes to, though perhaps more unfortunate than is convenient for thee. But in case thou neither findest any causes of complaint, nor any treacherous designs, what sufficient evidence hast thou to make such a wickedness of ours credible? Our mother is dead indeed, but then what befell her might be an instruction to us to caution, and not an incitement to wickedness. We are willing to make a larger apology for ourselves; but actions never done do not admit of discourse: nay, we will make this agreement with thee, and that before Cæsar, the lord of all, who is now a mediator between us, if thou, O father, canst bring thyself by the evidence of truth, to have a mind free from suspicion concerning us, let us live, though even then we shall live in an unhappy way, for to be accused of great acts of wickedness, though falsely, is a terrible thing; but if thou hast any fear remaining, continue thou on in thy pious life, we will give this reason for our own conduct; our life is not so desirable to us as to desire to have it, if it tend to the harm of our father who gave it us."

4. When Alexander had thus spoken, Cæsar, who did not before believe so gross a calumny, was still more moved by it, and looked intently upon Herod, and perceived he was a little confounded: the persons there present were under an anxiety about the young men, and the fame that was abroad made the king hated, for the very incredibility of the calumny, and the commiseration of the flower of youth, the beauty of body, which were in the young men, pleaded strongly for assistance, and the more so on this account, that Alexander had made their defence with great dexterity and prudence; nay, they did not themselves any longer continue in their former countenances, which had been bedewed with tears, and cast downwards to the ground, but now there arose in them hopes of the best: and the king himself appeared not to have had foundation enough to build such an accusation upon, he having no real evidence wherewith to convict them. Indeed he wanted some apology for making the accusation; but Cæsar, after some delay, said, that although the young men were thoroughly innocent of that for which they were calumniated, yet had they been so far to blame, that they had not demeaned themselves towards their father so as to prevent that suspicion which was spread abroad concerning them. He also exhorted Herod to lay all such suspicions aside, and to be reconciled to his sons; for that it was not just to give credit to any such reports concerning his own children; and that this repentance on both sides might heal those breaches that had happened between them, and might improve that their good-will to one another, whereby those on both sides, excusing the rashness of their suspicions, might resolve to bear a greater degree of affection towards each other than they had before. After Cæsar had given them this admonition, he beckoned to the young men. When, therefore, they were disposed to fall down to make intercession to their father, he took them up, and embraced them, as they were in tears, and took each of them distinctly in his arms, till not one of those that were present, whether freeman or slave, but was deeply affected with what they saw.

5. Then did they return thanks to Cæsar, and went away together; and with them went Antipater, with a hypocritical pretence that he rejoiced at this reconciliation. And in the last days they were with Cæsar, Herod made him a present of three hundred talents, as he was then exhibiting shows and largesses to the people of

Rome; and Cæsar made him a present of half the revenue of the copper mines in Cyprus, and committed the care of the other half to him, and honoured him with other gifts and incomes: and as to his own kingdom, he left it in his power to appoint which of his sons he pleased for his successor, or to distribute it in parts to every one, that the dignity might thereby come to them all; and when Herod was disposed to make such a settlement immediately, Cæsar said he would not give him leave to deprive himself, while he was alive, of the power over his kingdom, or over his sons.

6. After this, Herod returned to Judea again; but during his absence, no small part of his dominions about Trachon had revolted, whom yet the commanders he left there had vanquished, and compelled to a submission again. Now, as Herod was sailing with his sons, and was come over against Cilicia, to [the island] Eleusa, which hath now changed its name for Sebaste, he met with Archelaus, king of Cappadocia, who received him kindly, as rejoicing that he was reconciled to his sons, and that the accusation against Alexander who had married his daughter, was at an end. They also made one another such presents as it became kings to make. From thence Herod came to Judea and to the temple, where he made a speech to the people concerning what had been done in this his journey:—he also discoursed to them about Cæsar's kindness to him, and about as many of the particulars he had done as he thought it for his advantage other people should be acquainted with. At last he turned his speech to the admonition of his sons; and exhorted those that lived at court, and the multitude, to concord; and informed them that his sons were to reign after him; Antipater first, and then Alexander and Aristobulus, the sons of Mariamne; but he desired that at present they should all have regard to himself, and esteem him king and lord of all, since he was not yet hindered by old age, but was in that period of life when he must be the most skilful in governing; and that he was not deficient in other arts of management that might enable him to govern the kingdom well, and to rule over his children also. He further told the rulers under him, and the soldiery, that in case they would look upon him alone, their life would be led in a peaceable manner, and they would make one another happy; and when he had said this, he dismissed the assembly. Which speech was acceptable to the greatest part of the audience, but not so to them all; for the contention among his sons, and the hopes he had given them, occasioned thoughts and desires of innovations among them.

CHAPTER V

HOW HEROD CELEBRATED THE GAMES THAT WERE TO RETURN EVERY FIFTH YEAR, UPON THE BUILDING OF CESAREA; AND HOW HE BUILT AND ADORNED MANY OTHER PLACES AFTER A MAGNIFICENT MANNER; AND DID MANY OTHER ACTIONS GLORIOUSLY

1. ABOUT this time it was that Cesarea Sebaste, which he had built, was finished. The entire building being accomplished in the tenth year, the solemnity of it fell into the twenty-eighth year of Herod's reign, and into the hundred and ninety-second olympiad; there was accordingly a great festival, and most sumptuous preparations made presently, in order to its dedication; for he had appointed a contention in music, and games to be performed naked; he had also gotten ready a great number of those that fight single combats, and of beasts for the like purpose; horse races also, and the most chargeable of such sports and shows as used to be exhibited at Rome, and in other places. He consecrated this combat to Cæsar, and ordered it to be celebrated every fifth year. He also sent all sorts of ornaments for it out of his own furniture, that it might want nothing to make it decent; nay, Julia, Cæsar's wife, sent a great part of her most valuable furniture [from Rome,] insomuch that he had no want of anything; the sum of them all was estimated at five hundred talents. Now when a great multitude was come to that city to see the shows, as well as the ambassadors whom other people sent, on account of the benefits they had received [from Herod,] he entertained them all in the public inns, and at public tables, and with perpetual feasts; this solemnity having in the daytime the diversions of fights, and in the night-time such merry meetings as cost vast sums of money, and publicly demonstrated the generosity of his soul; for in all his undertakings he was ambitious to exhibit what exceeded whatsoever had been done before of the same kind; and it is related that Cæsar and Agrippa often said, that the dominions of Herod were too little for the greatness of his soul; for that he deserved to have both all the kingdom of Syria, and that of Egypt also.

2. After this solemnity and these festivals were over, Herod erected another city in the plain called Capharsaba, where he chose out a fit place, both for plenty of water and goodness of soil, and proper for the production of what was there planted, where a river encompassed the city itself, and a grove of the best trees for magnitude was round about it: this he named Antipatris, from his father Antipater. He also built upon another spot of ground above Jericho, of the same name with his mother, a place of great security, and very pleasant for habitation, and called it Cyprus. He also dedicated the finest monuments to his brother Phasaelus, on account of the great natural affection there had been between them, by erecting a tower in the city itself, not less than the tower of Pharos, which he named Phasaelus, which was at once a part of the strong defences of the city, and a memorial for him that was deceased, because it bare his name. He also built a city of the same name in the valley of Jericho, as you go from it northward, whereby he rendered the neighbouring country more fruitful, by the cultivation its inhabitants introduced, and this also he called Phasaelus.

3. But as for his other benefits, it is impossible to reckon them up, those which he bestowed on cities, both in Syria and in Greece, and in all the places he came to in his voyages; for he seems to have conferred, and that after a most plentiful manner, what would minister to many necessities, and the building of public works, and gave them the money that was necessary to such works as wanted it, to support them upon the failure of their other revenues; but what was the greatest and most illustrious of all his works, he erected Apollo's temple at Rhodes, at his own expense, and gave them a great number of talents of silver for the repair of their fleet. He also built the greatest part of the public edifices for the inhabitants of Nicopolis, at Actium;[*] and for the Antiochians, the in-

---

[*] Suetonius says concerning this Nicopolis, when Augustus rebuilt it:—"And that the memory of the victory at Actium might be celebrated the more after

habitants of the principal city of Syria, where a broad street cuts through the place lengthways, he built cloisters along it on both sides, and laid the open road with polished stone, which was of very great advantage to the inhabitants; and as to the olympic games, which were in a very low condition, by reason of the failure of their revenues, he recovered their reputation, and appointed revenues for their maintenance, and made that solemn meeting more venerable, as to the sacrifices and other ornaments; and by reason of this vast liberality, he was generally declared in their inscriptions to be one of the perpetual managers of those games.

4. Now some there are who stand amazed at the diversity of Herod's nature and purposes; for when we have respect to his magnificence, and the benefits which he bestowed on all mankind, there is no possibility for even those that had the least respect for him to deny, or not openly to confess, that he had a nature vastly beneficent; but when any one looks upon the punishments he inflicted, and the injuries he did, not only to his subjects, but to his nearest relations, and takes notice of his severe and unrelenting disposition there, he will be forced to allow that he was brutish, and a stranger to all humanity; insomuch that these men suppose his nature to be different, and sometimes at contradiction with itself; but I am myself of another opinion, and imagine that the occasion of both these sorts of actions was one and the same; for being a man ambitious of honour, and quite overcome by that passion, he was induced to be magnificent wherever there appeared any hopes of future memorial, or of reputation at present; and as his expenses were beyond his abilities, he was necessitated to be harsh with his subjects; for the persons on whom he expended his money were so many, that they made him a very bad procurer of it; and because he was conscious that he was hated by those under him, for the injuries he did them, he thought it not an easy thing to amend his offences, for that was inconvenient for his revenue; he therefore strove on the other side to make their ill-will an occasion of his gains. As to his own court, therefore, if any one was not very obsequious to him in his language, and would not confess himself to be his slave, or but seeming to think of any innovation in his government, he was not able to contain himself, but prosecuted his very kindred and friends, and punished them as if they were enemies; and this wickedness he undertook out of a desire that he might be himself alone honoured. Now for this my assertion about that passion of his, we have the greatest evidence, by what he did to honour Cæsar and Agrippa, and his other friends; for with what honours he paid his respects to them who were his superiors, the same did he desire to be paid to himself; and what he thought the most excellent present he could make another, he discovered an inclination to have the like presented to himself; but now the Jewish nation is by their law a stranger to all such things, and accustomed to prefer righteousness to glory; for which reason that nation was not agreeable to him, because it was out of their power to flatter the king's ambition with statues or temples, or any other such performances; and this seems to me to have been at once the occasion of Herod's crimes as to his own courtiers and counsellors, and of his benefactions as to foreigners and those that had no relation to him.

---

ward, he built Nicopolis at Actium, and appointed public shows to be there exhibited every fifth year."

CHAPTER VI

AN EMBASSAGE OF THE JEWS IN CYRENE AND ASIA TO CÆSAR, CONCERNING THE COMPLAINTS THEY HAD TO MAKE AGAINST THE GREEKS; WITH COPIES OF THE EPISTLES WHICH CÆSAR AND AGRIPPA WROTE TO THE CITIES FOR THEM

1. Now the cities ill-treated the Jews in Asia, and all those also of the same nation which lived at Libya, which joins to Cyrene, while the former kings had given them equal privileges with the other citizens; but the Greeks affronted them at this time, and that so far as to make away their sacred money, and to do them mischief on other particular occasions. When, therefore, they were thus afflicted, and found no end of the barbarous treatment they met with among the Greeks, they sent ambassadors to Cæsar on those accounts; who gave them the same privileges as they had before, and sent letters to the same purpose to the governors of the provinces, copies of which I subjoin here, as testimonials of the ancient favourable disposition the Roman emperors had towards us.

2. "Cæsar Augustus, high priest and tribune of the people, ordains thus:—Since the nation of the Jews have been found grateful to the Roman people, not only at this time, but in times past also, and chiefly Hyrcanus the high priest, under my father,* Cæsar the emperor, it seemed good to me and my counsellors, according to the sentence and oath of the people of Rome, that the Jews have liberty to make use of their own customs, according to the law of their forefathers, as they made use of them under Hyrcanus, the high priest of Almighty God; and that their sacred money be not touched, but be sent to Jerusalem, and that it be committed to the care of the receivers at Jerusalem; and that they be not obliged to go before any judge on the Sabbath-day, nor on the day of the preparation to it, after the ninth hour;† but if any one be caught stealing their holy books, or their sacred money, whether it be out of the synagogue or public school, he shall be deemed a sacrilegious person, and his goods shall be brought into the public treasury of the Romans. And I give order, that the testimonial which they have given me, on account of my regard to that piety which I exercise toward all mankind, and out of regard to Caius Marcus Censorinus, together with the present decree, he proposed in that most eminent place which hath been consecrated to me by the community of Asia at Ancyra. And if any one transgress any part of what is above decreed, he shall be severely punished." This was inscribed upon a pillar in the temple of Cæsar.

3. "Cæsar to Norbanus Flaccus, sendeth greeting. Let those Jews, how many soever they be, who have been used, according to their ancient customs, to send their sacred money to Jerusalem, do the same freely." These were the decrees of Cæsar.

4. Agrippa also did himself write, after the manner following, on behalf of the Jews:— "Agrippa, to the magistrates, senate, and people of the Ephesians, sendeth greeting. I will that the care and custody of the sacred money that is carried to the temple at Jerusalem be left

---

* Augustus here calls Julius Cæsar his *father*, though by birth he was only his *uncle*, on account of his adoption by him.

† This is authentic evidence that the Jews, in the days of Augustus, began to prepare for the celebration of the Sabbath at the ninth hour on Friday.

to the Jews of Asia, to do with it according to their ancient customs; and that such as steal that sacred money of the Jews, and fly to a sanctuary, shall be taken thence and delivered to the Jews, by the same law that sacrilegious persons are taken thence. I have also written to Sylvanus the prætor, that no one compel the Jews to come before a judge on the Sabbath-day."

5. "Marcus Agrippa to the magistrates, senate, and people of Cyrene, sendeth greeting. The Jews of Cyrene have interceded with me for the performance of what Augustus sent orders about to Flavius, the then prætor of Libya, and to the other procurators of that province, that the sacred money may be sent to Jerusalem freely, as hath been their custom from their forefathers, they complaining that they are abused by certain informers, and under pretence of taxes which were not due, are hindered from sending them; which I command to be restored without any diminution or disturbance given to them: and if any of that sacred money in the cities be taken from their proper receivers, I further enjoin that the same be exactly returned to the Jews in that place."

6. "Caius Norbanus Flaccus, proconsul, to the magistrates of the Sardians, sendeth greeting. Cæsar hath written to me, and commanded me not to forbid the Jews, how many soever they be, from assembling together according to the customs of their forefathers, nor from sending their money to Jerusalem: I have therefore written to you, that you may know that both Cæsar and I would have you act accordingly."

7. Nor did Julius Antonius, the proconsul, write otherwise. "To the magistrates, senate, and people of the Ephesians, sendeth greeting. As I was dispensing justice at Ephesus, on the ides of February, the Jews that dwell in Asia demonstrated to me that Augustus and Agrippa had permitted them to use their own laws and customs, and to offer those their first fruits, which every one of them freely offers to the Deity on account of piety, and to carry them in a company together to Jerusalem without disturbance. They also petitioned me, that I would confirm what had been granted by Augustus and Agrippa by my own sanction. I would therefore have you take notice, that according to the will of Augustus and Agrippa, I permit them to use and do according to the customs of their forefathers without disturbance."

8. I have been obliged to set down these decrees, because the present history of our own acts will go generally among the Greeks; and I have hereby demonstrated to them, that we have formerly been in great esteem, and have not been prohibited by those governors we were under from keeping any of the laws of our forefathers; nay, that we have been supported by them, while we followed our own religion, and the worship we paid to God: and I frequently make mention of these decrees, in order to reconcile other people to us, and to take away the causes of that hatred which unreasonable men bear to us. As for our customs,* there is no nation which always makes use of the same, and

in every city almost we meet with them different from one another; but natural justice is most agreeable to the advantage of all men equally, both Greeks and barbarians, to which our laws have the greatest regard, and thereby render us, if we abide in them after a pure manner, benevolent and friendly to all men, on which account we have reason to expect the like return from others, and to inform them that they ought not to esteem difference of positive institutions a sufficient cause of alienation, but [join with us in] the pursuit of virtue and probity, for this belongs to all men in common, and of itself alone is sufficient for the preservation of human life. I now return to the thread of my history.

CHAPTER VII

HOW, UPON HEROD'S GOING DOWN INTO DAVID'S SEPULCHRE, THE SEDITION IN HIS FAMILY GREATLY INCREASED

1. As for Herod, he had spent vast sums about the cities, both without and within his own kingdom: and as he had before heard that Hyrcanus, who had been king before him, had opened David's sepulchre, and taken out of it three thousand talents of silver, and that there was a much greater number left behind, and indeed enough to suffice all his wants, he had a great while an intention to make the attempt; and at this time he opened that sepulchre by night, and went into it, and endeavoured that it should not be at all known in the city, but took only his faithful friends with him. As for any money, he found none, as Hyrcanus had done, but that furniture of gold, and those precious goods that were laid up there; all which he took away. However, he had a great desire to make a more diligent search, and to go further in, even as far as the very bodies of David and Solomon; where two of his guards were slain, by a flame that burst out upon those that went in, as the report was. So he was terribly affrighted, and went out, and built a propitiatory monument of that fright he had been in; and this of white stone, at the mouth of the sepulchre, and that at a great expense also. And even Nicolaus his historiographer makes mention of this monument built by Herod, though he does not mention his going down into the sepulchre, as knowing that action to be of ill repute; and many other things he treats of in the same manner in his book; for he wrote in Herod's lifetime, and under his reign, and so as to please him, and as a servant to him, touching upon nothing but what tended to his glory, and openly excusing many of his notorious crimes, and very diligently concealing them. And as he was desirous to put handsome colours on the death of Mariamne and her sons, which were barbarous actions in the king, he tells falsehoods about the incontinence of Mariamne, and the treacherous designs of his sons upon him; and thus he proceeded in his whole work, making a pompous encomium upon what just actions he had done, but earnestly apologising for his unjust ones. Indeed, a man, as I said, may have a great deal to say by way of excuse for Nicolaus, for he did not so properly write this as a history for others, as somewhat that might be subservient to the king himself. As for ourselves, who come of a family nearly allied to the Asamonean kings, and on that account have an honourable place, which is the priesthood, we

---

* The remaining part of this chapter is remarkable, as justly distinguishing natural justice, religion, and morality, from positive institutions, and evidently preferring the former before the latter, as did the true prophets of God always under the Old Testament, and Christ and his apostles always under the New; whence Josephus seems to have been at this time nearer Christianity than were the Scribes and Pharisees of his age; who, as we know from the New Testament, were entirely of a different opinion and practice.

think it indecent to say anything that is false about them, and accordingly we have described their actions after an unblemished and upright manner. And although we reverence many of Herod's posterity, who still reign, yet do we pay a greater regard to truth than to them, and this though it sometimes happens that we incur their displeasure by so doing.

2. And indeed Herod's troubles in his family seemed to be augmented by reason of this attempt he made upon David's sepulchre; whether divine vengeance increased the calamities he lay under, in order to render them incurable, or whether fortune made an assault upon him, in those cases wherein the seasonableness of the cause made it strongly believed that the calamities came upon him for his impiety; for the tumult was like a civil war in his palace; and their hatred to one another was like that where each one strove to exceed another in calumnies. However, Antipater used stratagems perpetually against his brethren, and that very cunningly: while abroad he loaded them with accusations, but still took upon him frequently to apologise for them, that this apparent benevolence to them might make him be believed, and forward his attempts against them; by which means he, after various manners, circumvented his father, who believed that all he did was for his preservation. Herod also recommended Ptolemy, who was a great director of the affairs of his kingdom, to Antipater; and consulted with his mother about the public affairs also. And indeed these were all in all, and did what they pleased, and made the king angry against any other persons, as they thought it might be to their own advantage; but still the sons of Mariamne were in a worse and worse condition perpetually; and while they were thrust out, and set in a more dishonourable rank, who yet by birth were the most noble, they could not bear the dishonour. And for the women, Glaphyra, Alexander's wife, the daughter of Archelaus, hated Salome, both because of her love to her husband, and because Glaphyra seemed to behave herself somewhat insolently towards Salome's daughter, who was the wife of Aristobulus, which equality of hers to herself Glaphyra took very impatiently.

3. Now, besides this second contention that had fallen among them, neither did the king's brother Pheroras keep himself out of trouble, but had a particular foundation for suspicion and hatred; for he was overcome with the charms of his wife to such a degree of madness, that he despised the king's daughter, to whom he had been betrothed, and wholly bent his mind to the other, who had been but a servant. Herod also was grieved by the dishonour that was done him, because he had bestowed many favours upon him, and had advanced him to that height of power that he was almost a partner with him in the kingdom; and saw that he had not made him a due return for his favours, and esteemed himself unhappy on that account. So upon Pheroras's unworthy refusal, he gave the damsel to Phasaelus's son; but after some time, when he thought the heat of his brother's affections was over, he blamed him for his former conduct, and desired him to take his second daughter, whose name was Cypros. Ptolemy also advised him to leave off affronting his brother, and to forsake her whom he had loved, for that it was a base thing to be so enamoured of a servant, as to deprive himself of the king's good-will to him, and become an occasion of his trouble, and make himself hated by him. Pheroras knew that this advice would be for his own advantage, particularly because he had been

accused before, and forgiven; so he put his wife away, although he had already had a son by her, and engaged to the king that he would take his second daughter, and agreed that the thirtieth day after should be the day of his marriage; and sware he would have no further conversation with her whom he had put away; but when the thirty days were over, he was such a slave to his affections, that he no longer performed anything he had promised, but continued still with his former wife. This occasioned Herod to grieve openly, and made him angry, while the king dropped one word or other against Pheroras perpetually; and many made the king's anger an opportunity for raising calumnies against him. Nor had the king any longer a single quiet day or hour, but occasions of one fresh quarrel or another arose among his relations, and those that were dearest to him; for Salome was of a harsh temper, and ill-natured to Mariamne's sons; nor would she suffer her own daughter, who was the wife of Aristobulus, one of these young men, to bear a good-will to her husband, but persuaded her to tell her if he said anything to her in private, and when any misunderstandings happened, as is common, she raised a great many suspicions out of it: by which means she learned all their concerns, and made the damsel ill-natured to the young man. And in order to gratify her mother, she often said that the young men used to mention Mariamne when they were by themselves; and that they hated their father, and were continually threatening, that if they had once got the kingdom, they would make Herod's sons by his other wives country schoolmasters, for that the present education which was given them, and their diligence in learning, fitted them for such an employment. And as for the women, whenever they saw them adorned with their mother's clothes, they threatened, that instead of their present gaudy apparel, they should be clothed in sackcloth, and confined so closely that they should not see the light of the sun. These stories were presently carried by Salome to the king, who was troubled to hear them, and endeavoured to make up matters: but these suspicions afflicted him, and becoming more and more uneasy, he believed everybody against everybody. However, upon his rebuking his sons, and hearing the defence they made for themselves, he was easier for a while, though a little afterwards much worse accidents came upon him.

4. For Pheroras came to Alexander, the husband of Glaphyra, who was the daughter of Archelaus, as we have already told you, and said that he had heard from Salome, that Herod was enamoured of Glaphyra, and that his passion for her was incurable. When Alexander heard that, he was all on fire, from his youth and jealousy; and he interpreted the instances of Herod's obliging behaviour to her, which were very frequent, for the worse, which came from those suspicions he had on account of that word which fell from Pheroras; nor could he conceal his grief at the thing, but informed him what words Pheroras had said. Upon which Herod was in a greater disorder than ever; and not bearing such a false calumny, which was to his shame, was much disturbed at it: and often did he lament the wickedness of his domestics, and how good he had been to them, and how ill requitals they had made him. So he sent for Pheroras, and reproached him, and said, "Thou vilest of all men! art thou come to that unmeasurable and extravagant degree of ingratitude, as not only to suppose such things of me, but to speak of them? I now indeed perceive

what thy intentions are: it is not thy only aim to reproach me, when thou usest such words to my son, but thereby to persuade him to plot against me, and get me destroyed by poison; and who is there, if he had not a good genius at his elbow, as hath my son, that would bear such a suspicion of his father, but would revenge himself upon him? Dost thou suppose that thou hast only dropped a word for him to think of, and not rather hast put a sword into his hand to slay his father? And what dost thou mean, when thou really hatest both him and his brother, to pretend kindness to them, only in order to raise a reproach against me, and talk of such things as no one but such an impious wretch as thou art could either devise in their mind, or declare in their words? Begone, thou that art such a plague to thy benefactor and thy brother; and may that evil conscience of thine go along with thee; while I still overcome my relations by kindness, and am so far from avenging myself of them, as they deserve, that I bestow greater benefits upon them than they are worthy of."

5. Thus did the king speak. Whereupon Pheroras, who was caught in the very act of his villany, said, that "it was Salome who was the framer of this plot, and that the words came from her;" but as soon as she heard that, for she was at hand, she cried out, like one that would be believed, that no such thing ever came out of her mouth; that they all earnestly endeavoured to make the king hate her, and to make her away, because of the good-will she bore to Herod, and because she was always foreseeing the dangers that were coming upon him, and that at present there were more plots against him than usual: for while she was the only person who persuaded her brother to put away the wife he now had, and to take the king's daughter, it was no wonder if she were hated by him. As she said this, and often tore her hair, and often beat her breast, her countenance made her denial to be believed, but the perverseness of her manners declared at the same time her dissimulation in these proceedings; but Pheroras was caught between them, and had nothing plausible to offer in his own defence, while he confessed that he had said what was charged upon him, but was not believed when he said he had heard it from Salome; so the confusion among them was increased, and their quarrelsome words one to another. At last the king, out of his hatred to his brother and sister, sent them both away; and when he had commended the moderation of his son, and that he had himself told him of the report, he went in the evening to refresh himself. After such a contest as this had fallen out among them, Salome's reputation suffered greatly, since she was supposed to have first raised the calumny; and the king's wives were grieved at her, as knowing that she was a very ill-natured woman, and would sometimes be a friend, and sometimes an enemy, at different seasons; so they perpetually said one thing or another against her; and somewhat that now fell out, made them the bolder in speaking against her.

5. There was one Obodas, king of Arabia, an inactive and slothful man in his nature; but Sylleus managed most of his affairs for him. He was a shrewd man, although he was but young, and was handsome withal. This Sylleus, upon some occasion coming to Herod, and supping with him, saw Salome, and set his heart upon her: and understanding that she was a widow, he discoursed with her. Now because Salome was at this time less in favour with her brother, she looked upon Sylleus with some

passion, and was very earnest to be married to him; and on the days following there appeared many, and those very great, indications of their agreement together. Now the women carried this news to the king, and laughed at the indecency of it; whereupon Herod inquired about it further of Pheroras, and desired him to observe them at supper, how their behaviour was one towards another; who told him, that by the signals which came from their heads and their eyes, they both were evidently in love. After this, Sylleus the Arabian being suspected, went away, but came again in two or three months afterwards, as it were on that very design, and spake to Herod about it, and desired that Salome might be given him to wife; for that his affinity might not be disadvantageous to his affairs, by a union with Arabia, the government of which country was already in effect under his power, and more evidently would be his hereafter. Accordingly, when Herod discoursed with his sister about it, and asked her whether she were disposed to this match, she immediately agreed to it; but when Sylleus was desired to come over to the Jewish religion, and then he should marry her, and that it was impossible to do it on any other terms, he could not bear that proposal, and went away; for he said, that if he should do so, he should be stoned by the Arabs. Then did Pheroras reproach Salome for her incontinency, as did the women much more; and said that Sylleus had debauched her. As for that damsel which the king had betrothed to his brother Pheroras, but he had not taken her, as I have before related, because he was enamoured of his former wife, Salome desired Herod she might be given to her son by Costobarus: which match he was very willing to, but was dissuaded from it by Pheroras, who pleaded, that this young man would not be kind to her since her father had been slain by him, and that it was more just that his son, who was to be his successor in the tetrarchy, should have her; so he begged his pardon, and persuaded him to do so. Accordingly the damsel, upon this change of her espousals, was disposed of to this young man, the son of Pheroras, the king giving for her portion a hundred talents.

CHAPTER VIII

HOW HEROD TOOK UP ALEXANDER, AND BOUND HIM; WHOM YET ARCHELAUS, KING OF CAPPADOCIA, RECONCILED TO HIS FATHER HEROD AGAIN

1. BUT still the affairs of Herod's family were no better, but perpetually more troublesome. Now this accident happened, which arose from no decent occasion, but proceeded so far as to bring great difficulties upon him. There were certain eunuchs which the king had, and on account of their beauty was very fond of them; and the care of bringing him drink was intrusted to one of them; of bringing him his supper, to another; and of putting him to bed to a third, who also managed the principal affairs of the government; and there was one told the king that these eunuchs were corrupted by Alexander the king's son, by great sums of money: and when they were asked whether Alexander had had criminal conversation with them, they confessed it, but said they knew of no further mischief of his against his father; but when they were more severely tortured, and were in the utmost extremity, and the tormentors, out of

compliance with Antipater, stretched the rack to the very utmost, they said that Alexander bare ill-will and innate hatred to his father; and that he told them that Herod despaired to live much longer; and that, in order to cover his great age, he coloured his hair black, and endeavoured to conceal what would discover how old he was; but that if he would apply himself to him, when he should attain the kingdom, which in spite of his father, could come to no one else, he should quickly have the first place in that kingdom under him, for that he was now ready to take the kingdom, not only as his birthright, but by the preparations he had made for obtaining it, because a great many of the rulers, and a great many of his friends, were of his side, and those no ill men n ither, ready both to do and to suffer whatsoever should come on that account.

2. When Herod heard this confession, he was all over anger and fear, some parts seeming to him reproachful, and some made him suspicious of dangers that attended him, insomuch, that on both accounts he was provoked, and bitterly afraid lest some more heavy plot was laid against him than he should be then able to escape from; whereupon he did not now make an open search, but sent about spies to watch such as he suspected, for he was now overrun with suspicion and hatred against all about him; and indulging abundance of those suspicions, in order to his preservation, he continued to suspect those that were guiltless: nor did he set any bounds to himself; but supposing that those who stayed with him had the most power to hurt him, they were to him very frightful; and for those that did not use to come to him, it seemed enough to name them [to make them suspected,] and he thought himself safer when they were destroyed: and at last his domestics were come to that pass, that being no way secure of escaping themselves, they fell to accusing one another, and imagining that he who first accused another, was most likely to save himself; yet, when any had overthrown others, they were hated; and they were thought to suffer justly, who unjustly accused others; and they only thereby prevented their own accusation: nay, they now executed their own private enmities by this means, and when they were caught, they were punished in the same way. Thus these men contrived to make use of this opportunity as an instrument and a snare against their enemies; yet, when they tried it, were themselves caught also in the same snare which they laid for others: and the king soon repented of what he had done, because he had no clear evidence of the guilt of those whom he had slain; and yet what was still more severe in him, he did not make use of his repentance, in order to leave off doing the like again, but in order to inflict the same punishment upon their accusers.

3. And in this state of disorder were the affairs of the palace; and he had already told many of his friends directly, that they ought not to appear before him, nor come into the palace; and the reason of this injunction was, that [when they were there] he had less freedom of acting, or a greater restraint on himself on their account; for at this time it was that he expelled Andromachus and Gemellus, men who had of old been his friends, and been very useful to him in the affairs of his kingdom, and been of advantage to his family by their embassages and counsels; and had been tutors to his sons, and had in a manner the first degree of freedom with him. He expelled Andromachus, because his son Demetrius was a companion to Alexander; and Gemellus, because he knew that he wished him well, which arose from his having been with him in his youth, when he was at school, and absent at Rome. These he expelled out of his palace, and was willing enough to have done worse by them; but that he might not seem to take such liberty against men of so great reputation, he contented himself with depriving them of their dignity, and of their power to hinder his wicked proceedings.

4. Now it was Antipater who was the cause of all this; who when he knew what a mad and licentious way of acting his father was in, and had been a great while one of his counsellors, he hurried him on, and then thought he should bring him to do somewhat to purpose, when every one that could oppose him was taken away. When therefore Andromachus and his friends were driven away, and had no discourse nor freedom with the king any longer, the king in the first place examined by torture all whom he thought to be faithful to Alexander, whether they knew of any of his attempts against him: but these died without having anything to say to that matter, which made the king more zealous [after discoveries,] when he could not find out what evil proceedings he suspected them of. As for Antipater, he was very sagacious to raise a calumny against those that were really innocent, as if their denial was only their constancy and fidelity [to Alexander,] and thereupon provoked Herod to discover by the torture of great numbers what attempts were still concealed. Now there was a certain person among the many that was tortured, who said he knew that the young man had often said, that when he was commended as a tall man in his body, and a skilful marksman, and that in his other commendable exercises, he exceeded all men, these qualifications given him by nature, though good in themselves, were not advantageous to him, because his father was grieved at them, and envied him for them; and that when he walked along with his father, he endeavoured to depress and shorten himself, that he might not appear too tall; and that when he shot at anything he was hunting, when his father was by, he missed his mark on purpose; for he knew how ambitious his father was of being superior in such exercises. So when the man was tormented about this saying, and had ease given his body after it, he added, that he had his brother Aristobulus for his assistance, and contrived to lie in wait for their father, as they were hunting, and kill him; and when they had done so, to fly to Rome, and desire to have the kingdom given them. There were also letters of the young man found, written to his brother; wherein he complained that his father did not act justly in giving Antipater a country, whose [yearly] revenues amounted to ten hundred talents. Upon these confessions Herod presently thought he had somewhat to depend on, in his own opinion, as to his suspicion about his sons: so he took up Alexander and bound him; yet did he still continue to be uneasy, and was not quite satisfied of the truth of what he had heard; and when he came to recollect himself, he found that they had only made juvenile complaints and contentions, and that it was an incredible thing, that when his son should have slain him, he should openly go to Rome [to beg the kingdom;] so he was desirous to have some surer mark of his son's wickedness, and was very solicitous about it, that he might not appear to have condemned him to be put in prison too rashly; so he tortured the principal of Alexander's friends, and put not a few of them to death, without getting any of the things out of

them which he suspected. And while Herod was very busy about this matter, and the palace was full of terror and trouble, one of the younger sort, when he was in the utmost agony, confessed that Alexander had sent to his friends at Rome, and desired that he might be quickly invited thither by Cæsar, and that he could discover a plot against him; that Mithridates, the king of Parthia, was joined in friendship with his father against the Romans, and that he had a poisonous potion ready prepared at Askelon.

5. To these accusations Herod gave credit, and enjoyed hereby, in his miserable case, some sort of consolation, in excuse of his rashness, as flattering himself with finding things in so bad a condition; but as for the poisonous potion which he laboured to find, he could find none. As for Alexander, he was very desirous to aggravate the vast misfortunes he was under, so he pretended not to deny the accusations, but punished the rashness of his father with a greater crime of his own; and perhaps he was willing to make his father ashamed of his easy belief of such calumnies: he aimed especially, if he could gain belief to his story, to plague him and his whole kingdom; for he wrote four letters and sent them to him, that "he did not need to torture any more persons, for he had plotted against him; and that he had for his partners, Pheroras and the most faithful of his friends; and that Salome came in to him by night, and that she lay with him whether he would or not; and that all men were come to be of one mind to make away with him as soon as they could, and so get clear of the continual fear they were in from him." Among these were accused Ptolemy and Sapinnius, who were the most faithful friends to the king. And what more can be said, but that those who before were the most intimate friends, were become wild beasts to one another, as if a certain madness had fallen upon them, while there was no room for defence or refutation, in order to the discovery of the truth, but all were at random doomed to destruction; so that some lamented those that were in prison, some those that were put to death, and others lamented that they were in expectation of the same miseries; and a melancholy solitude rendered the kingdom deformed, and quite the reverse to that happy state it was formerly in. Herod's own life also was entirely disturbed; and, because he could trust nobody, ne was sorely punished by the expectation of further misery; for he often fancied in his imagination, that his son had fallen upon him, or stood by him with a sword in his hand; and thus was his mind night and day intent upon this thing, and revolved it over and over, and no otherwise than if he were under a distraction. And this was the sad condition Herod was now in.

6. But when Archelaus. king of Cappadocia, heard of the state that Herod was in, and being in great distress about his daughter, and the young man [her husband,] and grieving with Herod as with a man that was his friend, on account of so great a disturbance as he was under, he came [to Jerusalem] on purpose to compose their differences; and, when he found Herod in such a temper, he thought it wholly unseasonable to reprove him, or to pretend that he had done anything rashly, for that he should thereby naturally bring him to dispute the point with him, and by still more and more apologising for himself to be the more irritated: he went, therefore, another way to work, in order to correct the former misfortunes, and appeared angry at the young man, and said that Herod had been so very mild a man that he had not acted a rash

part at all. He also said he would dissolve his daughter's marriage with Alexander, nor could in justice spare his own daughter, if she were conscious of anything, and did not inform Herod of it. When Archelaus appeared to be of this temper, and otherwise than Herod expected or imagined, and for the main took Herod's part, and was angry on his account, the king abated of his harshness, and took occasion from his appearing to have acted justly hitherto, to come by degrees to put on the affection of a father, and was on both sides to be pitied; for when some persons refuted the calumnies that were laid on the young man, he was thrown into a passion; but when Archelaus joined in the accusation, he was dissolved into tears and sorrow after an affectionate manner. Accordingly, he desired that he would not dissolve his son's marriage, and became not so angry as before for his offences. So when Archelaus had brought him to a more moderate temper, he transferred the calumnies upon his friends; and said it must be owing to them that so young a man, and one unacquainted with malice, was corrupted; and he supposed that there was more reason to suspect the brother than the son. Upon which Herod was very much displeased at Pheroras, who indeed now had no one that could make a reconciliation between him and his brother. So when he saw that Archelaus had the greatest power with Herod, he betook himself to him in the habit of a mourner, and like one that had all the signs upon him of an undone man. Upon this Archelaus did not overlook the intercession he made to him, nor yet did he undertake to change the king's disposition towards him immediately; and he said that it was better for him to come himself to the king, and confess himself the occasion of all; that this would make the king's anger not to be extravagant towards him, and that then he would be present to assist him. When he had persuaded him to this, he gained his point with both of them; and the calumnies raised against the young man were, beyond all expectation, wiped off. And Archelaus, as soon as he had made the reconciliation, went then away to Cappadocia, having proved at this juncture of time the most acceptable person to Herod in the world; on which account he gave him the richest presents, as tokens of his respects to him, and being on other occasions magnanimous, he esteemed him one of his dearest friends. He also made an agreement with him that he would go to Rome, because he had written to Cæsar about these affairs; so they went together as far as Antioch, and there Herod made a reconciliation between Archelaus and Titus, the president of Syria, who had been greatly at variance, and so returned back to Judea.

CHAPTER IX

CONCERNING THE REVOLT OF THE TRACHONITES; HOW SYLLEUS ACCUSED HEROD BEFORE CÆSAR; AND HOW HEROD, WHEN CÆSAR WAS ANGRY AT HIM, RESOLVED TO SEND NICOLAUS TO ROME

1. WHEN Herod had been at Rome, and was come back again, a war arose between him and the Arabians, on the occasion following:—The inhabitants of Trachonitis, after Cæsar had taken the country away from Zenodorus, and added it to Herod, had not now power to rob, but were forced to plough the land, and to live quietly, which was a thing they did not like; and when they did take that pains, the ground did not pro-

duce much fruit for them. However, at the first the king would not permit them to rob; and so they abstained from that unjust way of living upon their neighbours, which procured Herod a great reputation for his care. But when he was sailing to Rome, it was at that time when he went to accuse his son Alexander, and to commit Antipater to Cæsar's protection, the Trachonites spread a report as if he were dead, and revolted from his dominion, and betook themselves again to their accustomed way of robbing their neighbours; at which time the king's commanders subdued them during his absence; but about forty of the principal robbers, being terrified by those that had been taken, left the country, and retired into Arabia, Sylleus entertaining them, after he had missed of marrying Salome, and gave them a place of strength, in which they dwelt. So they overran not only Judea, but all Cœlesyria also, and carried off the prey, while Sylleus afforded them places of protection and quietness during their wicked practices. But when Herod came back from Rome, he perceived that his dominions had greatly suffered by them, and since he could not reach the robbers themselves, because of the secure retreat they had in that country, and which the Arabian government afforded them, and yet being very uneasy at the injuries they had done him, he went all over Trachonitis, and slew their relations; whereupon these robbers were more angry than before, it being a law among them to be avenged on the murderers of their relations by all possible means; so they continued to tear and rend everything under Herod's dominion with impunity; then did he discourse about the robberies to Saturninus and Volumnius, and required that they should be punished; upon which occasion they still the more confirmed themselves in their robberies, and became more numerous, and made very great disturbances, laying waste the countries and villages that belonged to Herod's kingdom, and killing those men whom they caught, till these unjust proceedings came to be like a real war, for the robbers were now become about a thousand;—at which Herod was sore displeased, and required the robbers, as well as the money which he had lent Obodas, by Sylleus, which was sixty talents, and since the time of payment was now past, he desired to have it paid him: but Sylleus, who had laid Obodas aside, and managed all by himself, denied that the robbers were in Arabia, and put off the payment of the money; about which there was a hearing before Saturninus and Volumnius, who were then the presidents of Syria.* At last, he, by their means, agreed, that within thirty days' time Herod should be paid his money, and that each of them should deliver up the other subjects reciprocally. Now, as to Herod, there was not one of the other's subjects found in his kingdom, either as doing any injustice, or on any other account; but it was proved that the Arabians had the robbers amongst them.

2. When the day appointed for payment of the money was past, without Sylleus's performing any part of his agreement, and he was gone to Rome, Herod demanded the payment of the money, and that the robbers that were in Arabia should be delivered up; and, by the permission of Saturninus and Volumnius, executed the judgment himself upon those that were refractory. He took an army that he had, and led it into Arabia, and in three days' time marched

seven *mansiones;* and when he came to the garrison wherein the robbers were, he made an assault upon them, and took them all, and demolished the place, which was called Raepta, but did no harm to any others. But as the Arabians came to their assistance, under Naceb their captain, there ensued a battle, wherein a few of Herod's soldiers, and Naceb, the captain of the Arabians, and about twenty of his soldiers fell, while the rest betook themse es to flight. So when he had brought these to punishment, he placed three thousand Idumeans in Trachonitis, and thereby restrained the robbers that were there. He also sent an account to the captains that were about Phœnicia, and demonstrated that he had done nothing but what he ought to do in punishing the refractory Arabians, which, upon an exact inquiry, they found to be no more than what was true.

3. However, messengers were hasted away to Sylleus to Rome, and informed him what had been done, and, as is usual, aggravated everything. Now Sylleus had already insinuated himself into the knowledge of Cæsar, and was then about the palace; and as soon as he heard of those things, he changed his habit into black, and went in, and told Cæsar that Arabia was afflicted with war, and that all his kingdom was in great confusion, upon Herod's laying it waste with his army; and he said, with tears in his eyes, that two thousand five hundred of the principal men among the Arabians had been destroyed, and that their captain Nacebus, his familiar friend and kinsman, was slain; and that the riches that were at Raepta were carried off; and that Obodas was despised, whose infirm state of body rendered him unfit for war; on which account neither he nor the Arabian army were present. When Sylleus said so, and added invidiously, that he would not himself have come out of the country, unless he had believed that Cæsar would have provided that they should all have peace one with another, and that, had he been there, he would have taken care that the war should not have been to Herod's advantage. Cæsar was provoked when this was said; and asked no more than this one question, both of Herod's friends that were there, and of his own friends who were come from Syria, Whether Herod had led an army thither? And when they were forced to confess so much, Cæsar, without staying to hear for what reason he did it, and how it was done, grew very angry, and wrote to Herod sharply. The sum of his epistle was this, that whereas of old he had used him as his friend, he should now use him as his subject. Sylleus also wrote an account of this to the Arabians; who were so elevated with it, that they neither delivered up the robbers that had fled to them, nor paid the money that was due: they retained those pastures also which they had hired, and kept them without paying their rent, and all this because the king of the Jews was now in a low condition, by reason of Cæsar's anger at him. Those of Trachonitis also made use of this opportunity, and rose up against the Idumean garrison, and followed the same way of robbing with the Arabians, who had pillaged their country, and were more rigid in their unjust proceedings, not only in order to get by it, but by way of revenge also.

4. Now Herod was forced to bear all this, that confidence of his being quite gone with which Cæsar's favour used to inspire him; for Cæsar would not admit so much as an embassage from him, to make an apology for him; and when they came again, he sent them away without success: so he was cast into sadness and fear;

---

* These joint presidents of Syria, Saturninus and Volumnius, were not perhaps of equal authority, but the latter like a procurator under the former.

and Sylleus's circumstances grieved him exceedingly, who was now believed by Cæsar, and was present at Rome, nay sometimes aspiring higher. Now it came to pass that Obodas was dead : and Æneas, whose name was Aretas,* took the government, for Sylleus endeavoured by calumnies to get him turned out of his principality, that he might himself take it ; with which design he gave much money to the courtiers, and promised much money to Cæsar, who indeed was angry that Aretas had not sent to him first before he took the kingdom, yet did Æneas send an epistle to Cæsar, and a crown of gold of the weight of many talents. Now that epistle accused Sylleus as having been a wicked servant, and having killed Obodas by poison ; and that while he was alive he had governed him as he pleased ; and had also debauched the wives of the Arabians ; and had borrowed money, in order to obtain the dominion for himself : yet did not Cæsar give heed to these accusations, but sent his ambassadors back without receiving any of his presents. But in the meantime the affairs of Judea and Arabia became worse and worse, partly because of the anarchy they were under, and partly because, bad as they were, nobody had power to govern them ; for of the two kings, the one was not yet confirmed in his kingdom, and so had not authority sufficient to restrain the evil-doers ; and as for Herod, Cæsar was immediately angry at him for having avenged himself, and so he was compelled to bear all the injuries that were offered him. At length, when he saw no end of the mischief which surrounded him, he resolved to send ambassadors to Rome again, and see whether his friends had prevailed to mitigate Cæsar, and to address themselves to Cæsar himself ; and the ambassador he sent thither was Nicolaus of Damascus.

CHAPTER X

HOW EURYCLES FALSELY ACCUSED HEROD'S SONS ; AND HOW THEIR FATHER BOUND THEM, AND WROTE TO CÆSAR ABOUT THEM. OF SYLLEUS ; AND HOW HE WAS ACCUSED BY NICOLAUS

1. THE disorders about Herod's family and children about this time grew much worse; for it now appeared certain, nor was it unforeseen beforehand, that fortune threatened the greatest and most insupportable misfortunes possible to his kingdom. Its progress and augmentation at this time arose on the occasion following :—One Eurycles, a Lacedemonian (a person of note there, but a man of a perverse mind, and so cunning in his ways of voluptuousness and flattery, as to indulge both, and yet seem to indulge neither of them) came in his travels to Herod, and made him presents, but so that he received more presents from him. He also took such proper seasons for insinuating himself into his friendship, and he became one of the most intimate of the king's friends. He had his lodging in Antipater's house ; but he had not only access, but free conversation, with Alexander, as pretending to him that he was in great favour with Archelaus, the king of Cappadocia ; whence he pretended much respect to Glaphyra, and, in an occult manner, cultivated a friendship with them all, but always attending to what was said and

done, that he might be furnished with calumnies to please them all. In short, he behaved himself so to everybody in his conversation, as to appear to be his particular friend, and he made others believe that his being anywhere was for that person's advantage. So he won upon Alexander, who was but young ; and persuaded him, that he might open his grievances to him with assurance, and with nobody else. So he declared his grief to him, how his father was alienated from him. He related to him also the affairs of his mother, and of Antipater ; that he had driven them from their proper dignity, and had the power over everything himself ; that no part of this was tolerable, since his father was already come to hate them ; and he added, that he would neither admit them to his table nor his conversation. Such were the complaints, as was but natural, of Alexander about the things that troubled him : and these discourses Eurycles carried to Antipater, and told him, he did not inform him of this on his own account, but that being overcome by his kindness, the great importance of the thing obliged him to do it : and he warned him to have a care of Alexander, for that what he said was spoken with vehemency, and that, in consequence of what he said, he would certainly kill him with his own hand. Whereupon Antipater, thinking him to be his friend by this advice, gave him presents upon all occasions, and at length persuaded him to inform Herod of what he had heard. So when he related to the king Alexander's ill temper, as discovered by the words he had heard him speak, he was easily believed by him ; and he thereby brought the king to that pass, turning him about by his words, and irritating him till he increased his hatred to him, and made him implacable, which he shewed at that very time, for he immediately gave Eurycles a present of fifty talents ; who, when he had gotten them, went to Archelaus, king of Cappadocia, and commended Alexander before him, and told him that he had been many ways of advantage to him, in making a reconciliation between him and his father. So he got money from him also, and went away, before his pernicious practices were found out ; but when Eurycles was returned to Lacedemon, he did not leave off doing mischief ; and so, for his many acts of injustice, he was banished from his own country.

2. But as for the king of the Jews, he was not now in the temper he was in formerly towards Alexander and Aristobulus, when he had been content with the hearing their calumnies when others told him of them, but he was now come to that pass as to hate them himself, and to urge men to speak against them, though they did not do it of themselves. He also observed all that was said, and put questions, and gave ear to every one that would but speak, if they could but say anything against them, till at length he heard that Euratus of Cos was a conspirator with Alexander ; which thing to Herod was the most agreeable and sweetest news imaginable.

3. But still a greater misfortune came upon the young men ; while the calumnies against them were continually increased, and, as a man may say, one would think it was every one's endeavour to lay some grievous thing to their charge, which might appear to be for the king's preservation. There were two guards of Herod's body, who were in great esteem for their great strength and tallness, Jucundus and Tyrannus ; these men had been cast off by Herod, who was displeased at them ; these now used to ride along with Alexander, and for their skill in their exercises were in great esteem with him, and had some gold and other gifts bestowed on them.

---

* This Aretas was now become so established a name for the kings of Arabia [at Petra and Damascus,] that when the crown came to this Æneas, he changed his name to Aretas.

Now the king, having an immediate suspicion of these men, had them tortured; who endured the torture courageously for a long time; but at last confessed that Alexander would have persuaded them to kill Herod when he was in pursuit of the wild beasts, that it might be said he fell from his horse, and was run through with a spear, for that he had once such a misfortune formerly. They also shewed where there was money hidden in the stable, under ground; and these convicted the king's chief hunter, that he had given the young men the royal huntingspears and weapons to Alexander's dependants, and at Alexander's command.

4. After these, the commander of the garrison of Alexandrium was caught and tortured; for he was accused to have promised to receive the young men into his fortress, and to supply them with that money of the king's which was laid up in that fortress, yet did not he acknowledge anything of it himself; but his son came in, and said it was so, and delivered up the writing, which, so far as could be guessed, was in Alexander's hand. Its contents were these :—"When we have finished, by God's help, all that we have proposed to do, we will come to you; but do your endeavours, as you have promised, to receive us into your fortress." After this writing was produced, Herod had no doubt about the treacherous designs of his sons against him; but Alexander said that Diophantus, the scribe, had imitated his hand, and that the paper was maliciously drawn up by Antipater; for Diophantus appeared to be very cunning in such practices; and as he was afterwards convicted of forging other papers, he was put to death for it.

5. So the king produced those that had been tortured before the multitude at Jericho, in order to have them accuse the young men, which accusers many of the people stoned to death; and when they were going to kill Alexander and Aristobulus likewise, the king would not permit them to do so, but restrained the multitude, by means of Ptolemy and Pheroras. However, the young men were put under a guard, and kept in custody, that nobody might come at them; and all that they did or said was watched, and the reproach and fear they were in was little or nothing different from those of condemned criminals; and one of them, who was Aristobulus, was so deeply affected, that he brought Salome, who was his aunt, and his mother-in-law, to lament with him for his calamities, and to hate him who had suffered things to come to that pass; when he said to her, "Art thou not in danger of destruction also, while the report goes that thou hadst disclosed beforehand all our affairs to Sylleus, when thou wast in hopes of being married to him?" But she immediately carried those words to her brother: upon which he was out of patience, and gave command to bind him; and enjoined them both, now they were kept separate one from the other, to write down all the ill things they had done against their father, and bring the writing to him. So when this was enjoined them, they wrote this : that they had laid no treacherous designs, nor made any preparations against their father, but that they had intended to fly away; and that by the distress they were in, their lives being now uncertain and tedious to them.

6. About this time there came an ambassador out of Cappadocia from Archelaus, whose name was Melas; he was one of the principal rulers under him. So Herod being desirous to shew Archelaus's ill-will to him, called for Alexander, as he was in his bonds, and asked him again concerning his flight, whither and how they had resolved to retire; Alexander replied,—To Archelaus, who had promised to send them away to Rome; but that they had no wicked or mischievous designs against their father, and that nothing of that nature which their adversaries had charged upon them was true; and that their desire was, that he might have examined Tyrannus and Jucundus more strictly, but that they had been suddenly slain by the means of Antipater, who put his own friends among the multitude [for that purpose.]

7. When this was said, Herod commanded that both Alexander and Melas should be carried to Glaphyra, Archelaus's daughter, and that she should be asked, whether she did not know somewhat of Alexander's treacherous designs against Herod? Now as soon as they were come to her, and she saw Alexander in bonds, she beat her head, and in great consternation, gave a deep and a moving groan. The young man also fell into tears. This was so miserable a spectacle to those present, that, for a great while, they were not able to say or to do any thing; but at length Ptolemy, who was ordered to bring Alexander, bade him say whether his wife was conscious of his actions. He replied,— "How is it possible that she, whom I love better than my own soul, and by whom I have had children, should not know what I do?" Upon which she cried out, that she knew of no wicked designs of his; but that yet, if her accusing herself falsely would tend to his preservation, she would confess it all. Alexander replied,— "There is no such wickedness as those (who ought the least of all so to do) suspect, which either I have imagined, or thou knowest of, but this only, that we had resolved to retire to Archelaus, and from thence to Rome." Which she also confessed. Upon which Herod, supposing that Archelaus's ill-will to him was fully proved, sent a letter by Olympus and Volumnius; and bade them, as they sailed by, to touch at Eleusa of Cilicia, and give Archelaus the letter. And that when they had expostulated with him, that he had a hand in his son's treacherous designs against him, they should from thence sail to Rome; and that, in case they found Nicolaus had gained any ground, and that Cæsar was no longer displeased at him, he should give him his letters, and the proof which he had ready to shew against the young men. As to Archelaus, he made his defence for himself, that he had promised to receive the young men, because it was both for their own and their father's advantage so to do, lest some too severe procedure should be gone upon in that anger and disorder they were in on occasion of the present suspicions; but that still he had not promised to send them to Cæsar; and that he had not promised anything else to the young men that could shew any ill-will to him.

8. When these ambassadors were come to Rome, they had a fit opportunity to deliver their letters to Cæsar, because they found him reconciled to Herod; for the circumstances of Nicolaus's embassage had been as follows :—As soon as he was come to Rome, and was about the court, he did not first of all set about what he was come for only, but he thought fit also to accuse Sylleus. Now, the Arabians, even before he came to talk with them, were quarrelling one with another; and some of them left Sylleus's party, and joining themselves to Nicolaus, informed him of all the wicked things that had been done; and produced to him evident demonstrations of the slaughter of a great number of Obodas's friends by Sylleus; for when these men left Sylleus, they had carried off with them

those letters whereby they could convict him. When Nicolaus saw such an opportunity afforded him, he made use of it, in order to gain his own point afterward, and endeavoured immediately to make a reconciliation between Cæsar and Herod; for he was fully satisfied, that if he should desire to make a defence for Herod directly, he should not be allowed that liberty; but that if he desired to accuse Sylleus, there would an occasion present itself of speaking on Herod's behalf. So when the cause was ready for hearing, and the day was appointed, Nicolaus, while Aretas's ambassadors were present, accused Sylleus, and said that he imputed to him the destruction of the king [Obodas,] and of many others of the Arabians: that he had borrowed money for no good design; and he proved that he had been guilty of adultery, not only with the Arabian, but Roman women also. And he added, that above all the rest he had alienated Cæsar from Herod; and that all that he had said about the actions of Herod were falsities. When Nicolaus was come to this topic, Cæsar stopped him from going on, and desired him only to speak to this affair of Herod, and to shew that he had not led an army into Arabia, nor slain two thousand five hundred men there, nor taken prisoners, nor pillaged the country. To which Nicolaus made this answer:—"I shall principally demonstrate, that either nothing at all, or but a very little, of those imputations are true, of which thou hast been informed; for had they been true, thou mightest justly have been still more angry at Herod." At this strange assertion, Cæsar was very attentive; and Nicolaus said, that there was a debt due to Herod of five hundred talents, and a bond, wherein it was written, that if the time appointed be elapsed, it should be lawful to make a seizure out of any part of his country. "As for the pretended army," he said, "it was no army, but a party sent out to require the just payment of the money: that this was not sent immediately, nor so as the bond allowed, but that Sylleus had frequently come before Saturninus and Volumnius, the presidents of Syria: and that at last he had sworn at Berytus, by thy fortune,* that he would certainly pay the money within thirty days, and deliver up the fugitives that were under his dominion. And that when Sylleus had performed nothing of this, Herod came again before the presidents; and upon their permission to make a seizure for the money, he, with difficulty, went out of his country with a party of soldiers for that purpose. And this is all the war which these men so tragically describe; and this is the affair of the expedition into Arabia. And how can this be called a war, when thy presidents permitted it, the covenants allowed it, and it was not executed till thy name, O Cæsar, as well as that of the other gods, had been profaned? And now I must speak in order about the captives. There were robbers that dwelt in Trachonitis:—at first their number was no more than forty, but they became more afterwards, and they escaped the punishment Herod would have inflicted on them, by making Arabia their refuge. Sylleus received them, and supported them with food, that they might be mischievous to all mankind; and gave them a country to inhabit, and himself received the gains they made by robbery; yet did he promise that he would deliver up these men, and that by the

same oaths and same time that he sware and fixed for payment of his debt: nor can he by any means shew that any other persons have at this time been taken out of Arabia besides these, and indeed not all these neither, but only so many as could not conceal themselves. And thus does the calumny of the captives, which hath been so odiously represented, appear to be no better than a fiction and a lie, made on purpose to provoke thy indignation; for I venture to affirm, that when the forces of the Arabians came upon us, and one or two of Herod's party fell, he then only defended himself, and there fell Nacebus their general, and in all about twenty-five others, and no more; whence Sylleus, by multiplying every single soldier to a hundred, he reckons the slain to have been two thousand five hundred."

9. This provoked Cæsar more than ever: so he turned to Sylleus full of rage, and asked him how many of the Arabians were slain. Hereupon he hesitated, and said he had been imposed upon. The covenants were also read about the money he had borrowed, and the letters of the presidents of Syria, and the complaints of the several cities, so many as had been injured by the robbers. The conclusion was this, that Sylleus was condemned to die, and that Cæsar was reconciled to Herod, and owned his repentance for what severe things he had written to him, occasioned by calumny, insomuch that he told Sylleus, that he had compelled him, by his lying account of things, to be guilty of ingratitude against a man that was his friend. At the last all came to this, Sylleus was sent away to answer Herod's suit, and to repay the debt that he owed, and after that to be punished [with death;] but still Cæsar was offended with Aretas, that he had taken upon himself the government, without his consent first obtained, for he had determined to bestow Arabia upon Herod; but that the letters he had sent hindered him from so doing; for Olympus and Volumnius, perceiving that Cæsar was now become favourable to Herod, thought fit immediately to deliver him the letters they were commanded by Herod to give him concerning his sons. When Cæsar had read them, he thought it would not be proper to add another government to him, now he was old, and in an ill state with relation to his sons, so he admitted Aretas's ambassadors; and after he had just reproved him for his rashness, in not tarrying till he received the kingdom from him, he accepted of his presents, and confirmed him in his government.

CHAPTER XI

HOW HEROD, BY PERMISSION FROM CÆSAR, ACCUSED HIS SONS BEFORE AN ASSEMBLY OF JUDGES AT BERYTUS; AND WHAT TERO SUFFERED, FOR USING A BOUNDLESS AND MILITARY LIBERTY OF SPEECH. CONCERNING ALSO THE DEATH OF THE YOUNG MEN, AND THEIR BURIAL AT ALEXANDRIUM

1. So Cæsar was now reconciled to Herod, and wrote thus to him:—That he was grieved for him on account of his sons; and that in case they had been guilty of any profane and insolent crimes against him, it would behove him to punish them as parricides, for which he gave him power accordingly; but if they had only contrived to fly away, he would have him give them an admonition, and not proceed to extremity with them. He also advised him to

---

* This oath, *by the fortune of Cæsar*, was put to Polycarp, a bishop of Smyrna, by the Roman governor, to try whether he were a Christian, as they were then esteemed who refused to swear that oath.

get an assembly together, and to appoint some place near Berytus,* which is a city belonging to the Romans, and to take the presidents of Syria, and Archelaus, king of Cappadocia, and as many more as he thought to be illustrious for their friendship to him, and the dignities they were in, and determine what should be done by their approbation. These were the directions that Cæsar gave him. Accordingly Herod, when the letter was brought to him, was immediately very glad of Cæsar's reconciliation to him, and very glad also that he had a complete authority given him over his sons. And it strangely came about, that whereas before, in his adversity, though he had indeed shewn himself severe, yet had he not been very rash, nor hasty, in procuring the destruction of his sons; he now, in his prosperity, took advantage of this change for the better, and the freedom he now had, to exercise his hatred against them, after an unheard-of manner; he therefore sent and called as many as he thought fit to this assembly, excepting Archelaus; for as for him, he either hated him, so that he would not invite him, or thought he would be an obstacle to his designs.

2. When the presidents, and the rest that belonged to the cities, were come to Berytus, he kept his sons in a certain village belonging to Sidon, called Platana, but near to this city, that if they were called he might produce them. for he did not think fit to bring them before the assembly: and when there were one hundred and fifty assessors present, Herod came by himself alone, and accused his sons, and in such a way as if it were not a melancholy accusation, and not made but out of necessity, and upon the misfortunes he was under; indeed, in such a way as was very indecent for a father to accuse his sons, for he was very vehement and disordered when he came to the demonstration of the crime they were accused of, and gave the greatest signs of passion and barbarity: nor would he suffer the assessors to consider of the weight of the evidence, but asserted them to be true by his own authority, after a manner most indecent in a father against his sons, and read himself what they themselves had written, wherein there was no confession of any plots or contrivances against him, but only how they had contrived to fly away, and containing withal certain reproaches against him, on account of the ill-will he bare them; and when he came to those reproaches, he cried out most of all, and exaggerated what they said, as if they had confessed the design against him,—and took his oath that he had rather lose his life than hear such reproachful words. At last he said that he had sufficient authority, both by nature and by Cæsar's grant to him, [to do what he thought fit.] He also added an allegation of a law of their country, which enjoined this:—That if parents laid their hands on the head of him that was accused, the standers-by were obliged to cast stones at him, and thereby slay him: which though he were ready to do in his own country and kingdom, yet did he wait for their determination; and yet they came thither not so much as judges, to condemn them for such manifest designs against him, whereby he had almost perished by his sons' means, but as per-

sons that had an opportunity of shewing their detestation of such practices, and declaring how unworthy a thing it must be in any, even the most remote, to pass over such treacherous designs [without punishment.]

3. When the king had said this, and the young men had not been produced to make any defence for themselves, the assessors perceived there was no room for equity and reconciliation; so they confirmed his authority. And in the first place, Saturninus, a person that had been consul, and one of great dignity, pronounced his sentence, but with great moderation and trouble; and said, that he condemned Herod's sons; but did not think they should be put to death. He had sons of his own; and to put one's son to death, is a greater misfortune than any other that could befall him by their means. After him Saturninus's sons, for he had three sons that followed him, and were his legates, pronounced the same sentence with their father. On the contrary, Volumnius's sentence was to inflict death on such as had been so impiously undutiful to their father; and the greatest part of the rest said the same, insomuch that the conclusion seemed to be, that the young men were condemned to die. Immediately after this Herod came away from thence, and took his sons to Tyre, where Nicolaus met him in his voyage from Rome; of whom he inquired, after he had related to him what had passed at Berytus, what his sentiments were about his sons, and what his friends at Rome thought of the matter. His answer was, "That what they had determined to do to thee was impious, and that thou oughtest to keep them in prison: and if thou thinkest anything further necessary, thou mayest indeed so punish them, that thou mayest not appear to indulge thy anger more than to govern thyself by judgment; but if thou inclinest to the milder side, thou mayest absolve them, lest perhaps thy misfortunes be rendered incurable: and this is the opinion of the greater part of thy friends at Rome also." Whereupon Herod was silent, and in great thoughtfulness, and bade Nicolaus sail along with him.

4. Now as they came to Cesarea, everybody was there talking of Herod's sons; and the kingdom was in suspense, and the people in great expectation of what would become of them, for a terrible fear seized upon all men, lest the ancient disorders of the family should come to a sad conclusion, and they were in great trouble about their sufferings; nor was it without danger to say any rash thing about this matter, nor even to hear another saying it, but men's pity was forced to be shut up in themselves, which rendered the excess of their sorrow very irksome, but very silent; yet was there an old soldier of Herod's, whose name was Tero, who had a son of the same age as Alexander, and his friend, who was so very free as openly to speak out what others thought about the matter; and was forced to cry out often among the multitude, and said, in the most unguarded manner, that truth was perished, and justice taken away from men, while lies and ill-will prevailed, and brought such a mist before public affairs, that the offenders were not able to see the greatest mischiefs that can befall men. And as he was so bold, he seemed not to have kept himself out of danger, by speaking so freely; but the reasonableness of what he said moved men to regard him as having behaved himself with great manhood, and this at a proper time also, for which reason every one heard what he said with pleasure: and although they first took care of their own safety by keeping silent themselves,

---

* What Josephus relates Augustus to have here said, that Berytus was a city belonging to the Romans, is confirmed by Spanheim:—"It was," says he, "a colony placed there by Augustus. The colony of Berytus was rendered famous by the benefits of Cæsar; and thence it is, that among the coins of Augustus, we meet with some having this inscription: 'The happy colony of Augustus at Berytus.'"

yet did they kindly receive the great freedom he took; for the expectation they were in of so great an affliction, put a force upon them to speak of Tero whatsoever they pleased.

5. This man had thrust himself into the king's presence with the greatest freedom, and desired to speak with him by himself alone, which the king permitted him to do; where he said this:—"Since I am not able, O king, to bear up under so great a concern as I am under, I have preferred the use of this bold liberty that I now take, which may be for thy advantage, if thou mind to get any profit by it, before my own safety. Whither is thy understanding gone, and left thy soul empty? Whither is that extraordinary sagacity of thine gone, whereby thou hast performed so many and such glorious actions? Whence comes this solitude, and desertion of thy friends and relations? Of which I cannot but determine that they are neither thy friends nor relations, while they overlook such horrid wickedness in thy once happy kingdom. Dost not thou perceive what is doing? Wilt thou slay these two young men, born of thy queen, who are accomplished with every virtue in the highest degree, and leave thyself destitute in thy old age, but exposed to one son, who hath very ill managed the hopes thou hast given him, and to relations whose death thou hast so often resolved on thyself? Dost not thou take notice, that the very silence of the multitude at once sees the crime, and abhors the fact? The whole army and the officers have commiseration on the poor unhappy youths, and hatred to those that are the actors in this matter."—These words the king heard, and for some time with good temper. But what can one say? When Tero plainly touched upon the bad behaviour and perfidiousness of his domestics, he was moved at it; but Tero went on further, and by degrees used an unbounded military freedom of speech, nor was he so well disciplined as to accommodate himself to the time: so Herod was greatly disturbed, and seemed to be rather reproached by this speech, than to be hearing what was for his advantage; while he learned thereby that both the soldiers abhorred the thing he was about, and the officers had indignation at it, he gave order that all whom Tero had named, and Tero himself, should be bound and kept in prison.

6. When this was over, one Trypho, who was the king's barber, took the opportunity, and came and told the king that Tero would often have persuaded him, when he trimmed him with a razor, to cut his throat, for that by this means he should be among the chief of Alexander's friends, and receive great rewards from him. When he had said this, the king gave order that Tero, and his son, and the barber, should be tortured, which was done accordingly; but while Tero bore up himself, his son, seeing his father already in a sad case, and with no hope of deliverance, and perceiving what would be the consequence of his terrible sufferings, said, that if the king would free him and his father from these torments for what he should say, he would tell the truth. And when the king had given his word to do so, he said that there was an agreement made, that Tero should lay violent hands on the king, because it was easy for him to come when he was alone; and that if, when he had done the thing, he should suffer death for it, as was not unlikely, it would be an act of generosity done in favour of Alexander. This was what Tero's son said, and thereby freed his father from the distress he was in; but uncertain it is whether he had been thus forced to

speak what was true, or whether it were a contrivance of his in order to procure his own and his father's deliverance from their miseries.

7. As for Herod, if he had before any doubt about the slaughter of his sons, there was now no longer any room left in his soul for it; but he had banished away whatsoever might afford him the least suggestion of reasoning better about this matter, so he already made haste to bring his purpose to a conclusion. He also brought out three hundred of the officers that were under an accusation, as also Tero and his son, and the barber that accused them, before an assembly, and brought an accusation against them all; whom the multitude stoned with whatsoever came to hand, and thereby slew them. Alexander also and Aristobulus were brought to Sebaste, by their father's command, and there strangled; but their dead bodies were in the night time carried to Alexandrium, where their uncle, by the mother's side, and the greatest part of their ancestors, had been deposited.

8.* And now perhaps it may not seem unreasonable to some, that such an inveterate hatred might increase so much [on both sides,] as to proceed further, and overcome nature; but it may justly deserve consideration, whether it be to be laid to the charge of the young men, that they gave such an occasion to their father's anger, and led him to do what he did, and by going on long in the same way, put things past remedy, and brought him to use them so unmercifully; or whether it be to be laid to the father's charge, that he was so hard-hearted, and so very tender in the desire of government, and of other things that would tend to his glory, that he would take no one into a partnership with him, that so whatsoever he would have done himself might continue immovable; or, indeed, whether fortune has not greater power than all prudent reasonings: whence we are persuaded that human actions are thereby determined beforehand by an inevitable necessity, and we call her Fate, because there is nothing which is not done by her; wherefore I suppose it will be sufficient to compare this notion with that other, which attributes somewhat to ourselves, and renders men not unaccountable for the different conducts of their lives; which notion is no other than the philosophical determination of our ancient law. Accordingly, of the two other causes of this sad event, anybody may lay the blame on the young men, who acted by youthful vanity, and pride of their royal birth, that they should bear to hear the calumnies that were raised against their father, while certainly they were not equitable judges of the actions of his life, but ill-natured in suspecting, and intemperate in speaking of it, and on both accounts easily caught by those that observed them, and revealed them to gain favour: yet cannot their father be thought worthy of excuse, as to that horrid impiety which he was guilty of about them, while he ventured, without any certain evidence of their treacherous designs against him, and without any proofs that they had made preparations for such an attempt, to kill his own sons, who were of very comely bodies, and the great darlings of other men, and no way deficient in their conduct, whether it were in hunting, or in warlike exercises, or in speaking upon occasional topics of discourse; for in all these they were skilful, and especially Alexander, who was the eldest; for

---

* This eighth section is entirely wanting in the old Latin version, arising probably from the great difficulty of an exact translation

certainly it had been sufficient, even though he had condemned them, to have kept them alive in bonds, or to let them live at a distance from his dominions in banishment, while he was surrounded by the Roman forces, which were a strong security to him, whose help would prevent his suffering anything by a sudden onset, or by open force; but for him to kill them on the sudden, in order to gratify a passion that governed him, was a demonstration of insufferable impiety. He also was guilty of so great a crime in his old age; nor will the delays that he made, and the length of time in which the thing was done, plead at all for his excuse; for when a man is on a sudden amazed, and in commotion of mind, and then commits a wicked ac-

tion, although this be a heavy crime, yet it is a thing that frequently happens; but to do it upon deliberation, and after frequent attempts, and as frequent puttings off, to undertake it at last, and accomplish it, was the action of a murderous mind, and such as was not easily moved from that which was evil: and this temper he shewed in what he did afterward, when he did not spare those that seemed to be the best beloved of his friends that were left, wherein, though the justice of the punishment caused those that perished to be the less pitied, yet was the barbarity of the man here equal, in that he did not abstain from their slaughter also. But of those persons we shall have occasion to discourse more hereafter.

BOOK XVII

CONTAINING THE INTERVAL OF FOURTEEN YEARS

FROM ALEXANDER AND ARISTOBULUS'S DEATH TO THE BANISHMENT OF ARCHELAUS

CHAPTER I

HOW ANTIPATER WAS HATED BY ALL THE NATION [OF THE JEWS] FOR THE SLAUGHTER OF HIS BRETHREN; AND HOW, FOR THAT REASON, HE GOT INTO PECULIAR FAVOUR WITH HIS FRIENDS AT ROME, BY GIVING THEM MANY PRESENTS; AS HE DID ALSO WITH SATURNINUS, THE PRESIDENT OF SYRIA, AND THE GOVERNORS WHO WERE UNDER HIM; AND CONCERNING HEROD'S WIVES AND CHILDREN

1. WHEN Antipater had thus taken off his brethren, and had brought his father into the highest degree of impiety, till he was haunted with furies for what he had done, his hopes did not succeed to his mind, as to the rest of his life; for although he was delivered from the fear of his brethren being his rivals as to the government, yet did he find it a very hard thing, and almost impracticable, to come at the kingdom, because the hatred of the nation against him on that account was become very great: and, besides this very disagreeable circumstance, the affairs of the soldiery grieved him still more, who were alienated from him, from which yet these kings derived all the safety which they had, whenever they found the nation desirous of innovation: and all this danger was drawn upon him by his destruction of his brethren. However, he governed the nation jointly with his father, being indeed no other than a king already; and he was for that very reason trusted, and more firmly depended on, for which he ought himself to have been put to death, as appearing to have betrayed his brethren out of his concern for the preservation of Herod, and not rather out of his ill-will to them, and before them, to his father himself; and this was the accursed state he was in. Now, all Antipater's contrivances tended to make his way to take off Herod, that he might have nobody to accuse him in the vile practices he was devising; and that Herod might have no refuge, nor any to afford him their assistance, since they must

thereby have Antipater for their open enemy; insomuch that the very plots he had laid against his brethren, were occasioned by the hatred he bore his father. But at this time he was more than ever set upon the execution of his attempts against Herod, because, if he were once dead, the government would now be firmly secured to him; but if he were suffered to live any longer, he should be in danger upon a discovery of that wickedness of which he had been the contriver, and his father would then of necessity become his enemy. And on this account it was that he became very bountiful to his father's friends, and bestowed great sums on several of them, in order to surprise men with his good deeds, and take off their hatred against them. And he sent great presents to his friends at Rome, particularly to gain their good-will; and, above all, to Saturninus, the president of Syria. He also hoped to gain the favour of Saturninus's brother with the large presents he bestowed on him; as also he used the same art to [Salome] the king's sister, who had married one of Herod's chief friends. And when he counterfeited friendship to those with whom he conversed, he was very subtle in gaining their belief, and very cunning to hide his hatred against any that he really did hate. But he could not impose upon his aunt, who understood him of a long time, and was a woman not easily to be deluded, especially while she had already used all possible caution in preventing his pernicious designs. Although Antipater's uncle by the mother's side was married to her daughter, and this by his own connivance and management, while she had before been married to Aristobulus, and while Salome's other daughter by that husband was married to the son of Calleas; yet that marriage was no obstacle to her, who knew how wicked he was, in her discovering his designs, as her former kindred to him could not prevent her hatred of him. Now Herod had compelled Salome, while she was in love with Sylleus the Arabian, and had taken a fondness to him, to marry Alexas; which match was by her submitted to at the instance of Julia, who persuaded Salome not to refuse it, lest she should herself be their open enemy, since Herod had sworn that he would never be friends with Salome if she would not accept of Alexas for her husband; so she submitted to Julia, as being Cæsar's wife; and besides that, she advised her to nothing but what was very much for her own advantage. At this time also it was that Herod sent back king Archelaus's daughter, who had been Alexander's wife, to her father, returning the portion he had with her out of his own estate, that there might be no dispute between them about it.

2. Now Herod brought up his sons' children with great care; for Alexander had two sons by Glaphyra; and Aristobulus had three sons by Bernice, Salome's daughter, and two daughters; and as his friends were once with him, he presented the children before them; and deploring the hard fortune of his own sons, he prayed that no such ill-fortune would befall these who were their children, but that they might improve in virtue, and obtain what they justly deserved, and might make him amends for his care of their education. He also caused them to be betrothed against they should come to the proper age of marriage; the elder of Alexander's sons to Pheroras's daughter, and Antipater's daughter to Aristobulus's eldest son. He also allotted one of Aristobulus's daughters to Antipater's son, and Aristobulus's other daughter to Herod, a son of his own, who was born to him by the high priest's daughter: for it is the ancient practice among us to have many wives at the same time. Now the king made these espousals for the children, out of commiseration of them now they were fatherless, as endeavouring to render Antipater kind to them by these intermarriages. But Antipater did not fail to bear the same temper of mind to his brothers' children which he had borne to his brothers themselves; and his father's concern about them provoked his indignation against them upon his supposal, that they would become greater than ever his brothers had been; while Archelaus, a king, would support his daughter's sons, and Pheroras, a tetrarch, would accept of one of the daughters as a wife to his son. What provoked him also was this, that all the multitude would so commiserate these fatherless children, and so hate him, [for making them fatherless,] that all would come out, since they were no strangers to his vile disposition towards his brethren. He contrived, therefore, to overturn his father's settlements, as thinking it a terrible thing that they should be so related to him, and be so powerful withal. So Herod yielded to him, and changed his resolution at his entreaty; and the determination now was, that Antipater himself should marry Aristobulus's daughter, and Antipater's son should marry Pheroras's daughter. So the espousals for the marriages were changed after this manner, even without the king's real approbation.

3. Now Herod the king had at this time nine wives; one of them Antipater's mother, and another the high priest's daughter, by whom he had a son of his own name. He had also one who was his brother's daughter, and another his sister's daughter; which two had no children. One of his wives also was of the Samaritan nation, whose sons were Antipas and Archelaus, and whose daughter was Olympias; which daughter was afterwards married to Joseph, the king's brother's son; but Archelaus and Antipas were brought up with a certain private man at Rome. Herod had also to wife Cleopatra of Jerusalem,

and by her he had his sons Herod and Philip, which last was also brought up at Rome: Pallas was also one of his wives, who bare him his son Phasaelus; and besides these, he had for his wives Phedra and Elpis, by whom he had his daughters Roxana and Salome. As for his elder daughters by the same mother with Alexander and Aristobulus, and whom Pheroras neglected to marry, he gave the one in marriage to Antipater, the king's sister's son, and the other to Phasaelus, his brother's son;—and this was the posterity of Herod.

CHAPTER II

CONCERNING ZAMARIS, THE BABYLONIAN JEW; CONCERNING THE PLOTS LAID BY ANTIPATER AGAINST HIS FATHER; AND SOMEWHAT ABOUT THE PHARISEES

1. AND now it was that Herod, being desirous to secure himself on the side of the Trachonitis, resolved to build a village as large as a city for the Jews, in the middle of that country, which might make his own country difficult to be assaulted, and whence he might be at hand to make sallies upon them, and do them a mischief. Accordingly, when he understood that there was a man who was a Jew come out of Babylon, with five hundred horsemen, all of whom could shoot their arrows as they rode on horseback, and, with a hundred of his relations, had passed over Euphrates, and now abode at Antioch by Daphne of Syria, where Saturninus, who was then president, had given them a place for habitation called Valatha, he sent for this man, with the multitude that followed him, and promised to give him land in the toparchy called Batanea, which country is bounded with Trachonitis, as desirous to make that his habitation a guard to himself. He also engaged to let him hold the country free from tribute, and that they should dwell entirely without paying such customs as used to be paid, and gave it him tax free.

2. The Babylonian was induced by these offers to come hither; so he took possession of the land, and built in it fortresses and a village, and named it Bathyra. Whereby this man became a safeguard to the inhabitants against the Trachonites, and preserved those Jews who came out of Babylon, to offer their sacrifices at Jerusalem, from being hurt by the Trachonite robbers; so that a great number came to him from all those parts where the ancient Jewish laws were observed, and the country became full of people, by reason of their universal freedom from taxes. This continued during the life of Herod; but when Philip, who was [tetrarch] after him, took the government, he made them pay some small taxes, and that for a little while only; and Agrippa the Great, and his son of the same name, although they harassed them greatly, yet would they not take their liberty away. From whom, when the Romans have now taken the government into their own hands, they still gave them the privilege of their freedom, but oppress them entirely with the imposition of taxes. Of which matter I shall treat more accurately in the progress of this history.*

3. At length Zamaris the Babylonian, to whom Herod had given that country for a possession, died; having lived virtuously, and left children of a good character behind him; one of whom was Jacim, who was famous for his valour, and

---

* This is now wanting.

taught his Babylonians how to ride their horses; and a troop of them were guards to the fore-mentioned kings; and when Jacim was dead in his old age, he left a son whose name was Philip, one of great strength in his hands, and in other respects also more eminent for his valour than any of his contemporaries; on which account there was a confidence and firm friendship between him and king Agrippa. He had also an army which he maintained, as great as that of a king; which he exercised and led wheresoever he had occasion to march.

4. When the affairs of Herod were in the condition I have described, all the public affairs depended upon Antipater; and his power was such, that he could do good turns to as many as he pleased, and this by his father's concession; in hopes of his good-will and fidelity to him; and this till he ventured to use his power still further, because his wicked designs were concealed from his father, and he made him believe everything he said. He was also formidable to all, not so much on account of the power and authority he had, as for the shrewdness of his vile attempts beforehand; but he who principally cultivated a friendship with him was Pheroras, who received the like marks of his friendship; while Antipater had cunningly encompassed him about by a company of women, whom he placed as guards about him; for Pheroras was greatly enslaved to his wife, and to her mother, and to her sister; and this notwithstanding the hatred he bare them, for the indignities they had offered to his virgin daughters. Yet did he bear them; and nothing was to be done without the women, who had got this man into their circle, and continued still to assist each other in all things, insomuch that Antipater was entirely addicted to them both by himself and by his mother; for these four women* said all one and the same thing; but the opinions of Pheroras and Antipater were different in some points of no consequence. But the king's sister [Salome] was their antagonist, who for a good while had looked about all their affairs, and was apprised that this their friendship was made, in order to do Herod some mischief, and was disposed to inform the king of it; and since these people knew that their friendship was very disagreeable to Herod, as tending to do him a mischief, they contrived that their meetings should not be discovered; so they pretended to hate one another, and abuse one another when time served, and especially when Herod was present, or when any one was there that would tell him; but still their intimacy was firmer than ever, when they were private; and this was the course they took. But they could not conceal from Salome neither their first contrivance, when they set about these their intentions, nor when they had made some progress in them; but she searched out everything, and, aggravating the relations to her brother, declared to him, as well their secret assemblies and compotations, as their counsels taken in a clandestine manner, which, if they were not in order to destroy him, they might well enough have been open and public; but to appearance they are at variance, and speak about one another as if they intended one another a mischief, but agree so well together when they are out of the sight of the multitude; for when they are alone by themselves they act in concert, and profess that they will never leave off their friendship, but will fight against those from whom they conceal their designs: and thus did she search out these things, and get a perfect

* Pheroras's wife, and her mother and sister, and Doris, Antipater's mother.

knowledge of them, and then told her brother of them, who understood also of himself a great deal of what she said, but still durst not depend upon it, because of the suspicions he had of his sister's calumnies; for there was a certain sect of men that were Jews, who valued themselves highly upon the exact skill they had in the law of their fathers, and made men believe they were highly favoured by God, by whom this set of women were inveigled. These are those that are called the sect of the Pharisees, who were in a capacity of greatly opposing kings. A cunning sect they were, and soon elevated to a pitch of open fighting and doing mischief. Accordingly, when all the people of the Jews gave assurance of their good-will to Cæsar, and to the king's government, these very men did not swear, being above six thousand; and when the king imposed a fine upon them, Pheroras's wife paid their fine for them. In order to requite which kindness of hers, since they were believed to have the fore-knowledge of things to come by divine inspiration, they foretold how God had decreed that Herod's government should cease, and his posterity should be deprived of it; but that the kingdom should come to her and Pheroras. These predictions were not concealed from Salome, but were told the king; as also how they had perverted some persons about the palace itself. So the king slew such of the Pharisees as were principally accused, and Bagoas the eunuch, and one Carus, who exceeded all men of that time in comeliness, and one that was his catamite. He slew also all those of his own family who had consented to what the Pharisees foretold; and for Bagoas, he had been puffed up by them, as though he should be named the father and the benefactor of him who, by the prediction, was foretold to be their appointed king; for that this king would have all things in his power, and would enable Bagoas to marry, and to have children of his own body begotten.

CHAPTER III

CONCERNING THE ENMITY BETWEEN HEROD AND PHERORAS; HOW HEROD SENT ANTIPATER TO CÆSAR; AND OF THE DEATH OF PHERORAS

1. WHEN Herod had punished those Pharisees who had been convicted of the foregoing crimes, he gathered an assembly together of his friends and accused Pheroras's wife; and ascribing the abuses of the virgins to the impudence of that woman, brought an accusation against her for the dishonour she had brought upon them: that she had studiously introduced a quarrel between him and his brother; and, by her ill temper, had brought them into a state of war, both by her words and actions: that the fines which he had laid had not been paid, and the offenders had escaped punishment by her means; and that nothing which had of late been done, had been done without her: "for which reason Pheroras would do well, if he would of his own accord, and by his own command, and not at my entreaty, or as following my opinion, put this his wife away, as one that will still be the occasion of war between thee and me. And now, Pheroras, if thou valuest thy relation to me, put this wife of thine away; for by this means thou wilt continue to be a brother to me, and wilt abide in thy love to me." Then said Pheroras, (although he was pressed hard by the former words,) that as he would not do so unjust a thing as to renounce his brotherly relation to

him, so would he not leave off his affection for his wife; that he would rather choose to die, than to live and be deprived of a wife that was so dear unto him. Hereupon Herod put off his anger against Pheroras on these accounts, although he himself thereby underwent a very uneasy punishment. However, he forbade Antipater and his mother to have any conversation with Pheroras, and bade them to take care to avoid the assemblies of the women: which they promised to do, but still got together when occasion served; and both Pheroras and Antipater had their own merry meetings. The report went also, that Antipater had criminal conversation with Pheroras's wife, and that they were brought together by Antipater's mother.

2. But Antipater had now a suspicion of his father, and was afraid that the effects of his hatred to him might increase; so he wrote to his friends at Rome, and bade them send to Herod, that he would immediately send Antipater to Cæsar; which when it was done, Herod sent Antipater thither, and sent most noble presents along with him; as also his testament, wherein Antipater was appointed to be his successor: and that if Antipater should die first, his son [Herod Philip,] by the high priest's daughter, should succeed. And, together with Antipater, there went to Rome, Sylleus the Arabian, although he had done nothing of all that Cæsar had enjoined him. Antipater also accused him of the same crimes of which he had been formerly accused by Herod. Sylleus was also accused by Aretas, that without his consent he had slain many of the chief Arabians at Petra; and particularly Soemus, a man that deserved to be honoured by all men, and that he had slain Fabatus, a servant of Cæsar. These were the things of which Sylleus was accused, and that on the occasion following:—There was one Corinthus, belonging to Herod, of the guards of the king's body, and one who was greatly trusted by him. Sylleus had persuaded this man with the offer of a great sum of money to kill Herod; and he had promised to do it. When Fabatus had been made acquainted with this, for Sylleus had himself told him of it, he informed the king of it; who caught Corinthus, and put him to the torture, and thereby got out of him the whole conspiracy. He also caught two other Arabians, who were discovered by Corinthus; the one the head of a tribe, and the other a friend to Sylleus, who both were by the king brought to torture, and confessed that they were to come to encourage Corinthus not to fail of doing what he had undertaken to do; and to assist him with their own hands in the murder, if need should require their assistance. So Saturninus, upon Herod's discovering the whole to him, sent them to Rome.

3. At this time Herod commanded Pheroras, that since he was so obstinate in his affection for his wife, he should retire into his own tetrarchy; which he did very willingly, and sware many oaths that he would not come again till he heard that Herod was dead. And indeed when upon a sickness of the king, he was desired to come to him before he died, that he might intrust him with some of his injunctions, he had such a regard to his oath, that he would not come to him; yet did not Herod so retain his hatred to Pheroras, but remitted of his purpose [not to see him] which he before had, and that for such great causes as have been already mentioned: but as soon as he began to be ill he came to him, and this without being sent for; and when he was dead he took care of his funeral, and had his body brought to Jerusalem, and buried there,

and appointed a solemn mourning for him. This [death of Pheroras] became the origin of Antipater's misfortunes, although he had already sailed for Rome, God now being about to punish him for the murder of his brethren. I will explain the history of this matter very distinctly, that it may be for a warning to mankind, that they take care of conducting their whole lives by the rules of virtue.

CHAPTER IV

PHERORAS'S WIFE IS ACCUSED BY HIS FREEDMEN AS GUILTY OF POISONING HIM; AND HOW HEROD, UPON EXAMINING OF THE MATTER BY TORTURE, FOUND THE POISON; BUT SO THAT IT HAD BEEN PREPARED FOR HIMSELF BY HIS SON ANTIPATER; AND UPON AN INQUIRY BY TORTURE, HE DISCOVERED THE DANGEROUS DESIGNS OF ANTIPATER

1. As soon as Pheroras was dead, and his funeral was over, two of Pheroras's freedmen, who were much esteemed by him, came to Herod, and entreated him not to leave the murder of his brother without avenging it, but to examine into such an unreasonable and unhappy death. When he was moved with these words, for they seemed to him to be true, they said that Pheroras supped with his wife the day before he fell sick, and that a certain potion was brought to him in a sort of food as he was not used to eat; but that when he had eaten it he died of it: that this potion was brought out of Arabia by a woman, under pretence indeed as a love potion, for that was its name, but in reality to kill Pheroras; for that the Arabian women are skilful in making such poisons: and the woman to whom they ascribe this, was confessedly a most intimate friend of one of Sylleus's mistresses; and that both the mother and the sister of Pheroras's wife had been at the place where she lived, and had persuaded her to sell them this potion, and had come back and brought it with them the day before that of his supper. Hereupon the king was provoked, and put the women slaves to the torture, and some that were free with them; and as the fact did not yet appear, because none of them would confess it, at length one of them, under the utmost agonies, said no more but this, that she prayed that God would send the like agonies upon Antipater's mother who had been the occasion of these miseries to all of them. This prayer induced Herod to increase the women's tortures, till thereby all was discovered: their merry meetings, their secret assemblies, and the disclosing of what he had said to his son alone unto Pheroras's* women. (Now what Herod had charged Antipater to conceal, was the gift of a hundred talents to him, not to have any conversation with Pheroras.) And what hatred he bore to his father; and that he complained to his mother how very long his father lived; and that he was himself almost an old man, insomuch that if the kingdom should come to him, it would not afford him any great pleasure; and that there were a great many of his brothers, or brothers' children, bringing up, that might have hopes of the kingdom as well as himself; all which made his own hopes of it uncertain; for that even now, if he should himself not live, Herod had ordained that the government should be conferred, not on his son, but rather on a brother. He also had accused the

---

* His wife, her mother, and sister.

king of great barbarity, and of the slaughter of his sons; and that it was out of the fear he was under, lest he should do the like to him, that made him contrive this his journey to Rome, and Pheroras contrive to go to his own tetrarchy.*

2. These confessions agreed with what his sister had told him, and tending greatly to corroborate her testimony, and to free her from the suspicion of her unfaithfulness to him. So the king having satisfied himself of the spite which Doris, Antipater's mother, as well as himself, bore to him, took away from her all her fine ornaments, which were worth many talents, and sent her away, and entered into friendship with Pheroras's women. But he who most of all irritated the king against his son, was one Antipater, the procurator of Antipater the king's son, who, when he was tortured, among other things, said that Antipater had prepared a deadly potion, and given it to Pheroras, with his desire that he would give it to his father during his absence, and when he was too remote to have the least suspicion cast upon him thereto relating; that Antiphilus, one of Antipater's friends, brought that potion out of Egypt; and that it was sent to Pheroras by Theudion, the brother of the mother of Antipater, the king's son, and by that means came to Pheroras's wife, her husband having given it her to keep. And when the king asked her about it, she confessed it; and as she was running to fetch it, she threw herself down from the house top, yet did she not kill herself, because she fell upon her feet: by which means, when the king had comforted her, and promised her and her domestics pardon, upon condition of their concealing nothing of the truth from him, but had threatened her with the utmost miseries if she proved ungrateful [and concealed anything;] so she promised him, and swore that she would speak out everything, and tell after what manner everything was done; and said what many took to be entirely true, that the potion was brought out of Egypt by Antiphilus, and that his brother, who was a physician, had procured it; and that, "when Theudion brought it us, she kept it upon Pheroras's committing it to her; and that it was prepared by Antipater for thee. When, therefore, Pheroras was fallen sick, and thou camest to him and tookest care of him, and when he saw the kindness thou hadst for him, his mind was overborne thereby. So he called me to him, and said to me, 'O woman: Antipater hath circumvented me in this affair of his father and my brother, by persuading me to have a murderous intention to him, and procuring a potion to be subservient thereto: do thou, therefore, go and fetch my potion, (since my brother appears to have still the same virtuous disposition towards me which he had formerly, and I do not expect to live long myself, and that I may not defile my forefathers by the murder of a brother,) and burn it before my face;' that accordingly she immediately brought it, and did as her husband bade her; and that she burnt the greatest part of the potion; but a little of it was left, that if the king, after Pheroras's death, should treat her ill, she might poison herself, and thereby get

clear of her miseries." Upon her saying thus, she brought out the potion, and the box in which it was, before them all. Nay, there was another brother of Antiphilus, and his mother also, who, by the extremity of pain and torture, confessed the same things, and owned the box [to be that which was brought out of Egypt.] The high priest's daughter also, who was the king's wife, was accused to have been conscious of all this, and had resolved to conceal it; for which reason Herod divorced her, and blotted her son out of his testament, wherein he had been mentioned as one that was to reign after him; and he took the high priesthood away from his father-in-law, Simeon the son of Boethus, and appointed Matthias the son of Theophilus, who was born at Jerusalem, to be high priest in his room.

3. While this was doing, Bathyllus also, Antipater's freedman, came from Rome, and upon torture was found to have brought another potion, to give it into the hands of Antipater's mother, and of Pheroras, that if the former potion did not operate upon the king, this at least might carry him off. There came also letters from his friends at Rome, by the approbation and at the suggestion of Antipater, to accuse Archelaus and Philip, as if they calumniated their father on account of the slaughter of Alexander and Aristobulus, and as if, because they commiserated their deaths, and as if, because they were sent for home, (for their father had already recalled them,) they concluded they were themselves also to be destroyed. These letters had been procured by great rewards, by Antipater's friends; but Antipater himself wrote to his father about them, and laid the heaviest things to their charge; yet did he entirely excuse them of any guilt, and said they were but young men, and so imputed their words to their youth. But he said, that he had himself been very busy in the affair relating to Sylleus, and in getting interest among the great men; and on that account had bought splendid ornaments to present them withal, which cost him two hundred talents. Now, one may wonder how it came about, that while so many accusations were laid against him in Judea during seven months before this time, he was not made acquainted with any of them. The causes of which were, that the roads were exactly guarded, and that men hated Antipater; for there was nobody who would run any hazards himself to gain him any advantages.

CHAPTER V

ANTIPATER'S NAVIGATION FROM ROME TO HIS FATHER; AND HOW HE WAS ACCUSED BY NICOLAUS OF DAMASCUS, AND CONDEMNED TO DIE BY HIS FATHER, AND BY QUINTILIUS VARUS, WHO WAS THEN PRESIDENT OF SYRIA; AND HOW HE WAS THEN BOUND TILL CÆSAR SHOULD BE INFORMED OF HIS CAUSE.

1. Now Herod, upon Antipater's writing to him, that having done all that he was to do, and this in the manner he was to do it, he would suddenly come to him, concealed his anger against him, and wrote back to him, and bade him not delay his journey, lest any harm should befall himself in his absence. At the same time also he made some little complaint about his mother, but promised that he would lay those complaints aside when he should return. He withal expressed his entire affection for him, as fearing lest he should have some suspicion of him, and defer his journey to him; and lest,

---

* It seems to me, by this whole story put together, that Pheroras was not himself poisoned, as is commonly supposed; for Antipater had persuaded him to poison Herod, (ch. v. sect. 1,) which would fall to the ground if he were himself poisoned: nor could the poisoning of Pheroras serve any design that appears now going forward; it was only the supposal of two of his freedmen, that this love-potion, or poison, which they knew was brought to Pheroras's wife, was made use of for poisoning him; whereas it appears to have been brought for her husband to poison Herod withal, as the future examinations demonstrate.

while he lived at Rome, he should lay plots for the kingdom, and moreover do somewhat against himself. This letter Antipater met with in Cilicia; but had received an account of Pheroras's death before at Tarentum. The last news affected him deeply; not out of any affection for Pheroras, but because he was dead without having murdered his father, which he had promised him to do. And when he was at Celendris in Cilicia, he began to deliberate with himself about his sailing home, as being much grieved with the ejection of his mother. Now, some of his friends advised him that he should tarry awhile somewhere, in expectation of further information. But others advised him to sail home without delay; for that if he were once come thither, he would soon put an end to all accusations, and that nothing afforded any weight to his accusers at present but his absence. He was persuaded by these last, and sailed on, and landed at the haven called Sebastus, which Herod had built at vast expenses in honour of Cæsar, and called Sebastus. And now was Antipater evidently in a miserable condition, while nobody came to him nor saluted him, as they did at his going away, with good wishes or joyful acclamations; nor was there now anything to hinder them from entertaining him, on the contrary, with bitter curses, while they supposed he was come to receive his punishment for the murder of his brethren.

2. Now Quintilius Varus was at this time at Jerusalem, being sent to succeed Saturninus as president of Syria, and was come as an assessor to Herod, who had desired his advice in his present affairs; and as they were sitting together, Antipater came upon them, without knowing anything of the matter; so he came into the palace clothed in purple. The porters indeed received him in, but excluded his friends. And now he was in great disorder, and presently understood the condition he was in, while, upon his going to salute his father, he was repulsed by him, who called him a murderer of his brethren, and a plotter of destruction against himself, and told him that Varus should be his auditor and his judge the very next day; so he found, that what misfortunes he now heard of was already upon him, with the greatness of which he went away in confusion; upon which his mother and his wife met him, (which wife was the daughter of Antigonus, who was king of the Jews before Herod,) from whom he learned all circumstances which concerned him, and then prepared himself for his trial.

3. On the next day Varus and the king sat together in judgment, and both their friends were also called in, as also the king's relations, with his sister Salome, and as many as could discover anything, and such as had been tortured; and besides these, some slaves of Antipater's mother, who were taken up a little before Antipater's coming, and brought with them a written letter, the sum of which was this: That he should not come back, because all was come to his father's knowledge; and that Cæsar was the only refuge he had left to prevent both his and her delivery into his father's hands. Then did Antipater fall down at his father's feet, and besought him not to prejudge his case, but that he might be first heard by his father, and that his father would keep himself still unprejudiced. So Herod ordered him to be brought into the midst, and then lamented himself about his children, from whom he had suffered such great misfortunes; and because Antipater fell upon him in his old age. He also reckoned up what maintenance, and what education he had

given them; and what seasonable supplies of wealth he had afforded them, according to their own desires; none of which favours had hindered them from contriving against him, and from bringing his very life into danger in order to gain his kingdom, after an impious manner, by taking away his life before the course of nature, their father's wishes, or justice, required that that kingdom should come to them: and that he wondered what hopes could elevate Antipater to such a pass as to be hardy enough to attempt such things; that he had by his testament in writing declared him his successor in the government; and while he was alive, he was in no respect inferior to him; either in his illustrious dignity, or in power and authority, he having no less than fifty talents for his yearly income, and had received for his journey to Rome no fewer than thirty talents. He also objected to him the case of his brethren whom he had accused; and if they were guilty, he had imitated their example; and if not, he had brought him groundless accusations against his near relations; for that he had been acquainted with all those things by him, and by nobody else, and had done what was done by his approbation, and whom he now absolved from all that was criminal, by becoming the inheritor of the guilt of such their parricide.

4. When Herod had thus spoken, he fell aweeping, and was not able to say any more; but at his desire Nicolaus of Damascus, being the king's friend, and always conversant with him, and acquainted with whatsoever he did, and with the circumstances of his affairs, proceeded with what remained, and explained all that concerned the demonstrations and evidences of the facts. Upon which Antipater, in order to make his legal defence, turned himself to his father, and enlarged upon the many indications he had given of his good-will to him; and instanced in the honours that had been done him, which yet had not been done, had he not deserved them by his virtuous concern about him; for that he had made provision for everything that was fit to be foreseen beforehand, as to giving him his wisest advice; and whenever there was occasion for the labour of his own hands, he had not grudged any such pains for him. And that it was almost impossible that he, who had delivered his father from so many treacherous contrivances laid against him, should be in a plot against him, and so lose all the reputation he had gained for his virtue, by his wickedness which succeeded it; and this while he had nothing to prohibit him, who was already appointed his successor, to enjoy the royal honour with his father also at present; and that there was no likelihood that a person who had the one half of that authority, without any danger, and with a good character, should hunt after the whole with infamy and danger, and this when it was doubtful whether he could obtain it or not; and when he saw the sad example of his brethren before him, and was both the informer and accuser against them, at a time when they might not otherwise have been discovered; nay, was the author of the punishment inflicted upon them, when it appeared evidently that they were guilty of a wicked attempt against their father; and that even the contentions that were in the king's family, were indications that he had ever managed affairs out of the sincerest affection to his father. And as to what he had done at Rome, Cæsar was a witness thereto, who was yet no more to be imposed upon than God himself; of whose opinions his letters sent hither are sufficient evidence: and that it was

not reasonable to prefer the calumnies of such as proposed to raise disturbances, before those letters; the greatest part of which calumnies had been raised during his absence, which gave scope to his enemies to forge them, which they had not been able to do if he had been there. Moreover, he shewed the weakness of the evidence obtained by torture, which was commonly false; because the distress men are in under such tortures naturally obliges them to say many things in order to please those that govern them. He also offered himself to the torture.

5. Hereupon there was a change observed in the assembly, while they greatly pitied Antipater, who, by weeping and putting on a countenance suitable to his sad case, made them commiserate the same; insomuch that his very enemies were moved to compassion; and it appeared plainly that Herod himself was affected in his own mind, although he was not willing it should be taken notice of. Then did Nicolaus begin to prosecute what the king had begun, and that with great bitterness; and summed up all the evidence which arose from the tortures, or from the testimonies. He principally and largely cried up the king's virtues, which he had exhibited in the maintenance and education of his sons; while he never could gain any advantage thereby, but still fell from one misfortune to another. Although he owned that he was not so much surprised with that thoughtless behaviour of his former sons, who were but young, and were besides corrupted by wicked counsellors, who were the occasion of their wiping out of their minds all the righteous dictates of nature, and this out of a desire of coming to the government sooner than they ought to do; yet that he could not but justly stand amazed at the horrid wickedness of Antipater, who, although he had not only had great benefits bestowed on him by his father, enough to tame his reason, yet could not be more tamed than the most envenomed serpents; whereas even those creatures admit of some mitigation, and will not bite their benefactors, while Antipater hath not let the misfortunes of his brethren be any hindrance to him, but he hath gone on to imitate their barbarity notwithstanding. "Yet wast thou, O Antipater! (as thou hast thyself confessed) the informer as to what wicked actions they had done, and the searcher out of the evidence against them, and the author of the punishment they underwent upon their detection. Nor do we say this as accusing thee for being so zealous in thy anger against them, but are astonished at thy endeavours to imitate their profligate behaviour; and we discover thereby, that thou didst not act thus for the safety of thy father, but for the destruction of thy brethren, that by such outside hatred of their impiety thou mightest be believed a lover of thy father, and mightest thereby get thee power enough to do mischief with the greatest impunity; which design thy actions indeed demonstrate. It is true, thou tookest thy brethren off, because thou didst convict them of their wicked designs; but thou didst not yield up to justice those who were their partners; and thereby didst make it evident to all men that thou madest a covenant with them against thy father, when thou chosest to be the accuser of thy brethren, as desirous to gain to thyself alone this advantage of laying plots to kill thy father, and so to enjoy double pleasure, which is truly worthy of thy evil disposition,—which thou hast openly shewn against thy brethren; on which account thou didst rejoice, as having done a most famous exploit: nor was that behaviour unworthy of thee; but if

thy intention were otherwise, thou art worse than they: while thou didst contrive to hide thy treachery against thy father, thou didst hate them; not as plotters against thy father, for in that case thou hadst not fallen upon the like crime, but as successors of his dominions, and more worthy of that succession than thyself. Thou wouldest kill thy father after thy brethren, lest thy lies raised against them might be detected; and lest thou shouldst suffer what punishment thou hadst deserved, thou hadst a mind to exact that punishment of thy unhappy father, and didst devise such a sort of uncommon parricide as the world never yet saw;—for thou who art his son didst not only lay a treacherous design against thy father, and didst it while he loved thee, and had been thy benefactor,—had made thee in reality his partner in the kingdom, and had openly declared thee his successor, while thou wast not forbidden to taste the sweetness of authority already, and hadst the firm hope of what was future by thy father's determination, and the security of a written testament; but for certain thou didst not measure these things according to thy father's various disposition, but according to thy own thoughts and inclinations; and wast desirous to take the part that remained away from thy too indulgent father, and soughtest to destroy him with thy deeds, whom thou in words pretendest to preserve. Nor wast thou content to be wicked thyself, but thou filledst thy mother's head with thy devices, and raisedst disturbance among thy brethren, and hadst the boldness to call thy father a wild beast; while thou hadst thyself a mind more cruel than any serpent, whence thou sentest out that poison among thy nearest kindred and greatest benefactors, and invitedst them to assist thee and guard thee, and didst hedge thyself in on all sides by the artifices of both men and women against an old man,—as though that mind of thine was not sufficient of itself to support so great a hatred as thou barest to him; and here thou appearest, after the tortures of freemen, of domestics, of men and women, which have been examined on thy account, and after the informations of thy fellow-conspirators, as making haste to contradict the truth; and has thought on ways not only how to take thy father out of the world, but to disannul that written law which is against thee, and the virtue of Varus, and the nature of justice; nay, such is that impudence of thine on which thou confidest, that thou desirest to be put to the torture thyself, while thou allegest that the tortures of those already examined thereby have made them tell lies; that those that have been the deliverers of thy father may not be allowed to have spoken the truth; but that thy tortures may be esteemed the discoverers of truth. Wilt not thou, O Varus! deliver the king from the injuries of his kindred? Wilt not thou destroy this wicked wild beast, which hath pretended kindness to his father, in order to destroy his brethren; while yet he is himself alone ready to carry off the kingdom immediately, and appears to be the most bloody butcher to him of them all? for thou art sensible that parricide is a general injury both to nature and to common life; and that the intention of parricide is not inferior to its preparation; and he who does not punish it, is injurious to nature itself."

6. Nicolaus added further what belonged to Antipater's mother, and whatsoever she had prattled like a woman; as also about the predictions and the sacrifices relating to the king; and whatsoever Antipater had done lasciviously in

his cups and his amours among Pheroras's women; the examination upon torture; and whatsoever concerned the testimonies of the witnesses, which were many, and of various kinds: some prepared beforehand, and others were sudden answers, which further declared and confirmed the foregoing evidence. For those men who were not acquainted with Antipater's practices, but had concealed them out of fear, when they saw that he was exposed to the accusations of the former witnesses, and that his great good fortune, which had supported him hitherto, had now evidently betrayed him into the hands of his enemies, who were now insatiable in their hatred to him, told all they knew of him; and his ruin was now hastened, not so much by the enmity of those who were his accusers, by his gross, impudent, and wicked contrivances, and by his ill-will to his father and his brethren; while he had filled their house with disturbance, and caused them to murder one another; and was neither fair in his hatred nor kind in his friendship, but just so far as served his own turn. Now, there were a great number who for a long time beforehand had seen all this, and especially such as were naturally disposed to judge of matters by the rules of virtue, because they were used to determine about affairs without passion, but had been restrained from making any open complaints before; these, upon the leave now given them, produced all that they knew before the public. The demonstrations also of these wicked facts could no way be disproved: because the many witnesses there were did neither speak out of favour to Herod, nor were they obliged to keep what they had to say silent, out of suspicion of any danger they were in; but they spake what they knew, because they thought such actions very wicked, and that Antipater deserved the greatest punishment; and indeed not so much for Herod's safety, as on account of the man's own wickedness. Many things were also said, and those by a great number of persons, who were no way obliged to say them: insomuch that Antipater, who used generally to be very shrewd in his lies and impudence, was not able to say one word to the contrary. When Nicolaus had left off speaking, and had produced the evidence, Varus bade Antipater to betake himself to making his defence, if he had prepared anything whereby it might appear that he was not guilty of the crimes he was accused of; for that, as he was himself desirous, so did he know that his father was in like manner desirous also to have him found entirely innocent; but Antipater fell down on his face, and appealed to God and to all men, for testimonials of his innocency, desiring that God would declare, by some evident signals, that he had not laid any plots against his father. This being the usual method of all men destitute of virtue, that, when they set about any wicked undertakings, they fall to work according to their own inclinations, as if they believed that God was unconcerned in human affairs; but when once they are found out, and are in danger of undergoing the punishment due to their crimes, they endeavour to overthrow all the evidence against them, by appealing to God; which was the very thing which Antipater now did; for whereas he had done everything as if there were no God in the world, when he was on all sides distressed by justice, and when he had no other advantage to expect from any legal proofs, by which he might disprove the accusations laid against him, he impudently abused the majesty of God, and ascribed it to his power, that he hath been preserved hitherto; and produced before them all

what difficulties he had ever undergone in his bold acting for his father's preservation.

7. So when Varus, upon asking Antipater what he had to say for himself, found that he had nothing to say besides his appeal to God, and saw that there was no end of that, he bade them bring the potion before the court, that he might see what virtue still remained in it; and when it was brought, and one that was condemned to die had drank it by Varus's command, he died presently. Then Varus got up and departed out of the court, and went away the day following to Antioch, where his usual residence was, because that was the palace of the Syrians; upon which Herod laid his son in bonds: but what were Varus's discourses to Herod, was not known to the generality, and upon what words it was that he went away; though it was also generally supposed, that whatever Herod did afterward about his son, was done with his approbation; but when Herod had bound his son, he sent letters to Rome to Cæsar about him, and such messengers withal as should by word of mouth, inform Cæsar of Antipater's wickedness. Now, at this very time there was seized a letter of Antiphilus, written to Antipater out of Egypt, (for he lived there:) and, when it was opened by the king, it was found to contain as follows:—"I have sent thee Acme's letter, and hazarded my own life; for thou knowest that I am in danger from two families, if I be discovered. I wish thee good success in thy affair." These were the contents of this letter; but the king made inquiry about the other letter also, for it did not appear; but Antiphilus's slave, who brought the letter which had been read, denied that he had received the other: but while the king was in doubt about it, one of Herod's friends seeing a seam upon the inner coat of the slave, and a doubling of the cloth, (for he had two coats on,) he guessed that the letter might be within that doubling; which accordingly proved to be true. So they took out the letter; and its contents were these:—"Acme to Antipater. I have written such a letter to thy father as thou desiredest me. I have also taken a copy and sent it, as if it came from Salome to my Lady [Livia;] which, when thou readest, I know that Herod will punish Salome, as plotting against him." Now, this pretended letter of Salome to her lady was composed by Antipater, and in the name of Salome, as to its meaning, but in the words of Acme. The letter was this:—"Acme to king Herod. I have done my endeavour that nothing that is done against thee should be concealed from thee. So, upon my finding a letter of Salome written to my lady against thee, I have written out a copy and sent it to thee; with hazard to myself, but for thy advantage. The reason why she wrote it was this,—that she had a mind to be married to Sylleus. Do thou therefore tear this letter in pieces, that I may not come into danger of my life." Now Acme had written to Antipater himself, and informed him, that in compliance with his command, she had both herself written to Herod, as if Salome had laid a sudden plot entirely against him, and had herself sent a copy of an epistle, as coming from Salome to her lady. Now Acme was a Jew by birth, and a servant to Julia, Cæsar's wife: and did this out of her friendship for Antipater, as having been corrupted by him with a large present of money, to assist in his pernicious designs against his father and his aunt.

8. Hereupon Herod was so amazed at the prodigious wickedness of Antipater, that he was ready to have ordered him to be slain imme-

diately, as a turbulent person in the most important concerns, and as one that had laid a plot not only against himself, but against his sister also; and even corrupted Cæsar's own domestics. Salome also provoked him to it, beating her breast, and bidding him kill her, if he could produce any credible testimony that she had acted in that manner. Herod also sent for his son, and asked him about this matter, and bade him contradict it if he could, and not suppress anything he had to say for himself; and when he had not one word to say, he asked him, since he was every way caught in his villany, that he would make no further delay but discover his associates in these his wicked designs. So he laid all upon Antiphilus; but discovered nobody else. Hereupon Herod was in such great grief, that he was ready to send his son to Rome to Cæsar, there to give an account of these his wicked contrivances. But he soon became afraid, lest he might there, by the assistance of his friends, escape the danger he was in: so he kept him bound as before, and sent more ambassadors and letters [to Rome] to accuse his son, and an account of what assistance Acme had given him in his wicked designs, with copies of the epistles before mentioned.

CHAPTER VI

CONCERNING THE DISEASE THAT HEROD FELL INTO, AND THE SEDITION WHICH THE JEWS RAISED THEREUPON; WITH THE PUNISHMENT OF THE SEDITIOUS

1. Now Herod's ambassadors made haste to Rome; but sent, as instructed beforehand, what answers they were to make to the questions put to them. They also carried the epistles with them. But Herod now fell into a distemper, and made his will, and bequeathed his kingdom to [Antipas] his youngest son; and this out of that hatred to Archelaus and Philip, which the calumnies of Antipater had raised against them. He also bequeathed a thousand talents to Cæsar, and five hundred to Julia, Cæsar's wife, to Cæsar's children, and friends and freedmen. He also distributed among his sons and their sons his money, his revenue, and his lands. He also made Salome, his sister, very rich, because she had continued faithful to him in all his circumstances, and was never so rash as to do him any harm. And as he despaired of recovering, for he was now about the seventieth year of his age, he grew fierce, and indulged the bitterest anger upon all occasions; the cause whereof was this, that he thought himself despised, and that the nation was pleased with his misfortunes; besides which, he resented a sedition which some of the lower sort of men excited against him, the occasion of which was as follows:—

2. There was one Judas, the son of Saripheus, and Matthias, the son of Margalothus, two of the most eloquent men among the Jews, and most celebrated intrepreters of the Jewish laws, and men well beloved by the people, because of their education of their youth; for all those that were studious of virtue frequented their lectures every day. These men, when they found that the king's distemper was incurable, excited the young men that they would pull down all those works which the king had erected contrary to the law of their fathers, and thereby obtain the reward which the law will confer on them for such actions of piety; for that it was truly on account of Herod's rashness in making such things as the law had forbidden, that his other misfortunes, and this distemper also, which was so unusual among mankind, and with which he was now afflicted, came upon him: for Herod had caused such things to be made, which were contrary to the law, of which he was accused by Judas and Matthias; for the king had erected over the great gate of the temple a large golden eagle, of great value, and had dedicated it to the temple. Now, the law forbids those that propose to live according to it, to erect images,* or representations of any living creature. So these wise men persuaded [their scholars] to pull down the golden eagle: alleging, that although they should incur any danger which might bring them to their deaths, the virtue of the action now proposed to them would appear much more advantageous to them than the pleasures of life; since they would die for the preservation and observation of the law of their fathers; since they would also acquire an everlasting fame and commendation; since they would be both commended by the present generation, and leave an example of life that would never be forgotten to posterity; since that common calamity of dying cannot be avoided by our living so as to escape any such dangers: that therefore it is a right thing for those who are in love with a virtuous conduct, to wait for that fatal hour by such a behaviour as may carry them out of the world with praise and honour; and that this will alleviate death to such a degree, thus to come at it by the performance of brave actions, which bring us into danger of it; and at the same time to leave that reputation behind them to their children, and to all their relations, whether they be men or women, which will be of great advantage to them afterward.

3. And with such discourses as this did these men excite the young men to this action; and a report being come to them that the king was dead, this was an addition to the wise men's persuasions, so, in the very middle of the day they got upon the place, they pulled down the eagle, and cut it into pieces with axes, while a great number of the people were in the temple. And now the king's captain, upon hearing what the undertaking was, and supposing it a thing of higher nature than it proved to be, came up thither, having a great band of soldiers with him, such as was sufficient to put a stop to the multitude of those who pulled down what was dedicated to God: so he fell upon them unexpectedly, and as they were upon this bold attempt, in a foolish presumption rather than a cautious circumspection, as is usual with the multitude, and while they were in disorder, and incautious of what was for their advantage,—so he caught no fewer than forty of the young men, who had the courage to stay behind when the rest ran away, together with the authors of this bold attempt, Judas and Matthias, who thought it an ignominious thing to retire upon his approach, and led them to the king. And when they were come to the king, and he had asked them if they had been so bold as to pull down what he had dedicated to God, "Yes," said they, "what was contrived we contrived, and what hath been performed we performed it; and that with such a virtous courage as become men; for we have given our assistance to those things which were dedicated to the majesty of God, and we have provided for what we have learned by hearing the law: and it ought not to be wondered at, if

---

* That the making of images, without an intention to worship them, was not unlawful to the Jews, see the note on Antiq. b. viii. chap. vii. sect. 5.

we esteem those laws which Moses had suggested to him, and were taught him by God, and which he wrote and left behind him, more worthy of observation than thy commands. Accordingly we will undergo death, and all sorts of punishments which thou canst inflict upon us, with pleasure, since we are conscious to ourselves that we shall die, not for any unrighteous actions, but for our love to religion." And thus they all said, and their courage was still equal to their profession, and equal to that with which they readily set about this undertaking. And when the king had ordered them to be bound, he sent them to Jericho, and called together the principal men among the Jews; and when they were come, he made them assemble in the theatre, and because he could not himself stand, he lay upon a couch, and enumerated the many labours he had long endured on their account, and his building of the temple, and what a vast charge that was to him; while the Asamoneans, during the hundred and twenty-five years of their government, had not been able to perform any so great a work for the honour of God as that was: that he had also adorned it with very valuable donations; on which account he hoped that he had left himself a memorial, and procured himself a reputation after his death. He then cried out, that these men had not abstained from affronting him, even in his lifetime, but that, in the very daytime, and in sight of the multitude, they had abused him to that degree, as to fall upon what he had dedicated, and in that way of abuse, had pulled it down to the ground. They pretended indeed, that they did it to affront him; but if any one consider the thing truly, they will find that they were guilty of sacrilege against God therein.

4. But the people, on account of Herod's barbarous temper, and for fear he should be so cruel as to inflict punishment on them, said what was done, was done without approbation, and that it seemed to them that the actors might well be punished for what they had done. But as for Herod, he dealt more mildly with others [of the assembly;] but he deprived Matthias of the high priesthood, as in part on occasion of this action, and made Joazar, who was Matthias's wife's brother, high priest in his stead. Now it happened, that during the time of the high priesthood of this Matthias, there was another person made high priest for a single day, that very day which the Jews observe as a fast. The occasion was this:—This Matthias the high priest, on the night before that day when the fast was to be celebrated, seemed, in a dream,* to have conversation with his wife; and because he could not officiate himself on that account, Joseph, the son of Ellemus, his kinsman, assisted him in that sacred office. But Herod deprived this Matthias of the high priesthood, and burnt the other Matthias, who had raised the sedition, with his companions, alive. And that very night there was an eclipse of the moon.†

5. But now Herod's distemper greatly increased upon him after a severe manner, and this by God's judgment upon him for his sins: for a fire glowed in him slowly, which did not

so much appear to the touch outwardly, as it augmented his pains inwardly; for it brought upon him a vehement appetite to eating, which he could not avoid to supply with one sort of food or other. His entrails were also exulcerated, and the chief violence of his pain lay on his colon; an aqueous and transparent liquor also had settled itself about his feet, and a like matter afflicted him at the bottom of his belly. Nay, further, his privy-member was putrified, and produced worms; and when he sat upright he had a difficulty of breathing, which was very loathsome, on account of the stench of his breath and the quickness of its returns; he had also convulsions in all parts of his body, which increased his strength to an insufferable degree. It was said by those who pretended to divine, and who were endued with wisdom to foretell such things, that God inflicted this punishment on the king on account of his great impiety; yet was he still in hopes of recovering, though his afflictions seemed greater than any one could bear. He also sent for physicians, and did not refuse to follow what they prescribed for his assistance; and went beyond the river Jordan, and bathed himself in warm baths that were at Callirrhoe, which, besides their other general virtues, were also fit to drink; which water runs into the lake called Asphaltitis. And when the physicians once thought fit to have him bathed in a vessel full of oil, it was supposed that he was just dying; but, upon the lamentable cries of his domestics, he revived; and having no longer the least hopes of his recovering, he gave order that every soldier should be paid fifty drachmæ; and he also gave a great deal to their commanders, and to his friends, and came again to Jericho, where he grew so choleric, that it brought him to do all things like a madman; and though he were near his death, he contrived the following wicked designs. He commanded that all the principal men of the entire Jewish nation, wheresoever they lived, should be called to him. Accordingly, there were a great number that came, because the whole nation was called, and all men heard of this call, and death was the penalty of such as should despise the epistles that were sent to call them. And now the king was in a wild rage against them all, the innocent as well as those that had afforded him ground for accusations; and when they were come, he ordered them all to be shut up in the hippodrome, and sent for his sister Salome, and her husband Alexas, and spake thus to them:—" I shall die in a little time, so great are my pains; which death ought to be cheerfully borne, and to be welcomed by all men; but what principally troubles me is this, that I shall die without being lamented, and without such mourning as men usually expect at a king's death." For that he was not unacquainted with the temper of the Jews, that his death would be a thing very desirable, and exceedingly acceptable to them; because during his lifetime they were ready to revolt from him, and to abuse the donations he had dedicated to God: that it therefore was their business to resolve to afford him some alleviation of his great sorrows on this occasion; for that if they do not refuse him their consent in what he desires, he shall have a great mourning at his funeral, and such as never any king had before him; for then the whole nation would mourn from their very soul, which otherwise would be done in sport and mockery only. He desired therefore that as soon as they see he hath given up the ghost, they shall place soldiers round the hippodrome, while they do not know that he is dead; and that they shall not

---

* This fact is attested both in the Mishna and Talmud.

† This eclipse of the moon (which is the only eclipse mentioned by Josephus) is of the greatest consequence for the determination of the time for the death of Herod and Antipater, and for the birth and entire chronology of Jesus Christ. It happened March 13th, in the year of the Julian period 4710, and the 4th year before the Christian æra.

declare his death to the multitude till this is done, but that they shall give orders to have those that are in custody shot with their darts; and that this slaughter of them all will cause that he shall not miss to rejoice on a double account; that as he is dying, they will make him secure that his will shall be executed in what he charges them to do; that he shall have the honour of a memorable mourning at his funeral. So he deplored his condition, with tears in his eyes, and obtested them by the kindness due from them, as of his kindred, and by the faith they owed to God, and begged of them that they would not hinder him of this honourable mourning at his funeral. So they promised him not to transgress his commands.

6. Now any one may easily discover the temper of this man's mind, which not only took pleasure in doing what he had done formerly against his relations, out of the love of life, but by those commands of his which savoured of no humanity; since he took care, when he was departing out of this life, that the whole nation should be put into mourning, and indeed made desolate of their dearest kindred, when he gave order that one out of every family should be slain, although they had done nothing that was unjust, or against him, nor were they accused of any other crimes; while it is usual for those who have any regard to virtue, to lay aside their hatred at such a time, even with respect to those they justly esteemed their enemies.

CHAPTER VII

HEROD HAS THOUGHTS OF KILLING HIMSELF WITH HIS OWN HAND; AND A LITTLE AFTERWARDS HE ORDERS ANTIPATER TO BE SLAIN

As he was giving these commands to his relations, there came letters from his ambassadors, who had been sent to Rome unto Cæsar, which when they were read, their purport was this:—That Acme was slain by Cæsar, out of his indignation at what hand she had in Antipater's wicked practices; and that as to Antipater himself, Cæsar left it to Herod to act as became a father and a king, and either to banish him or to take away his life, which he pleased. When Herod heard this, he was somewhat better, out of the pleasure he had from the contents of the letters, and was elevated at the death of Acme, and at the power that was given him over his son; but, as his pains were become very great, he was now ready to faint for want of something to eat; so he called for an apple and a knife; for it was his custom formerly to pare the apple himself, and soon afterwards to cut it, and eat it. When he had got the knife, he looked about, and had a mind to stab himself with it; and he had done it, had not his first cousin, Achiabus, prevented him, and cried out loudly. Whereupon a woful lamentation echoed through the palace, and great tumult was made, as if the king were dead. Upon which Antipater, who verily believed his father was deceased, grew bold in his discourse, as hoping to be immediately and entirely released from his bonds, and to take the kingdom into his hands, without any more ado; so he discoursed with the jailer about letting him go, and in that case promised him great things, both now and hereafter, as if that were the only thing now in question; but the jailer did not only refuse to do what Antipater would have him, but informed the king of his intentions, and how many solicitations he had

from him [of that nature.] Hereupon Herod, who had formerly no affection nor good-will towards his son to restrain him, when he heard what the jailer said, he cried out, and beat his head, although he was at death's door, and raised himself upon his elbow, and sent for some of his guards, and commanded them to kill Antipater without any further delay, and to do it presently, and to bury him in an ignoble manner at Hyrcania.

CHAPTER VIII

CONCERNING HEROD'S DEATH, AND TESTAMENT, AND BURIAL

1. AND now Herod altered his testament upon the alteration of his mind; for he appointed Antipas, to whom he had before left the kingdom, to be tetrarch of Galilee and Berea, and granted the kingdom to Archelaus. He also gave Gaulonitis, and Trachonitis, and Paneas, to Philip, who was his son, but own brother to Archelaus,* by the name of a tetrarchy; and bequeathed Jamnia, and Ashdod, and Phasaelis, to Salome his sister, with five hundred thousand [drachmæ] of silver that was coined. He also made provision for all the rest of his kindred, by giving them sums of money and annual revenues, and so left them all in a wealthy condition. He bequeathed also to Cæsar ten millions [of drachmæ] of coined money; besides both vessels of gold and silver, and garments exceeding costly, to Julia, Cæsar's wife; and to certain others, five millions. When he had done those things, he died, the fifth day after he had caused Antipater to be slain; having reigned, since he had procured Antigonus to be slain, thirty-four years; but since he had been declared king by the Romans, thirty-seven.—A man he was of great barbarity towards all men equally, and a slave to his passions; but above the consideration of what was right; yet was he favoured by fortune as much as any man ever was, for from a private man he became a king; and though he were encompassed with ten thousand dangers, he got clear of them all, and continued his life till a very old age; but then, as to the affairs of his family and children, in which, indeed, according to his own opinion, he was also very fortunate, because he was able to conquer his enemies; yet, in my opinion, he was herein very unfortunate.

2. But then Salome and Alexas, before the king's death was made known, dismissed those that were shut up in the hippodrome, and told them that the king ordered them to go away to their own lands, and take care of their own affairs, which was esteemed by the nation a great benefit; and now the king's death was made public, when Salome and Alexas gathered the soldiery together in the amphitheatre at Jericho; and the first thing they did was, they read Herod's letter, written to the soldiery, thanking them for their fidelity and good-will to him, and exhorting them to afford his son Archelaus, whom he had appointed for their king, like fidelity and good-will. After which Ptolemy, who had the king's seal intrusted to

* When it is said that Philip and Archelaus were *own brothers*, or born of the same father and mother, there must be some mistake; because they had indeed the same father, Herod, but different mothers: the former Cleopatra, and Archelaus, Malthace. They were indeed brought up together at Rome like own brothers, which intimacy is perhaps all that Josephus intended by the words before us.

him, read the king's testament, which was to be
of force no otherwise than as it should stand
when Cæsar had inspected it; so there was
presently an acclamation made to Archelaus, as
king; and the soldiers came by bands, and their
commanders with them, and promised the same
good-will to him, and readiness to serve him,
which they had exhibited to Herod; and they
prayed God to be assistant to him.

3. After this was over, they prepared for his
funeral, it being Archelaus's care that the procession to his father's sepulchre should be very
sumptuous. Accordingly, he brought out all
his ornaments to adorn the pomp of the funeral.
The body was carried upon a golden bier, embroidered with very precious stones of great
variety, and it was covered over with purple, as
well as the body itself; he had a diadem upon
his head, and above it a crown of gold; he had
also a sceptre in his right hand. About the bier
were his sons and his numerous relations; next
to these was the soldiery distinguished according to their several countries and denominations; and they were put into the following
order:—First of all went his guards; then the
band of Thracians; and after them the Germans; and next the band of Galatians, every
one in their habiliments of war; and behind
these marched the whole army in the same
manner as they used to go out to war, and as
they used to be put in array by their muster-
masters and centurions: these were followed by
five hundred of his domestics, carrying spices.
So they went eight furlongs,* to Herodium; for
there, by his own command, he was to be
buried;—and thus did Herod end his life.

4. Now Archelaus paid him so much respect,
as to continue his mourning till the seventh day;
for so many days are appointed for it by the law
of our fathers; and when he had given a treat
to the multitude, and left off his mourning, he
went up into the temple; he had also acclamations and praises given him, which way soever
he went, every one striving with the rest who
should appear to use the loudest acclamations.
So he ascended a high elevation made for him,
and took his seat, in a throne made of gold, and
spake kindly to the multitude, and declared
with what joy he received their acclamations,
and the marks of the good-will they shewed to
him; and returned them thanks that they did
not remember the injuries his father had done
them, to his disadvantage; and promised them
he would endeavour not to be behindhand with
them in rewarding their alacrity in his service,
after a suitable manner; but that he should abstain at present from the name of King; and
that he should have the honour of that dignity,
if Cæsar should confirm and settle that testament which his father had made; and that it
was on this account, that when the army would
have put the diadem on him at Jericho, he
would not accept of that honour, which is
usually so much desired, because it was not yet
evident that he who was to be principally concerned in bestowing it, would give it him; although, by his acceptance of the government, he
should not want the ability of rewarding their
kindness to him; and that it should be his endeavour, as to all things wherein they were concerned, to prove in every respect better than his
father. Whereupon the multitude, as it is
usual with them, supposed that the first days of

those that enter upon such governments, declare
the intentions of those that accept them; and
so by how much Archelaus spake the more
gently and civilly to them, by so much did they
more highly commend him, and made application to him for the grant of what they desired.
Some made a clamour that he would ease them
of some of their annual payments; but others
desired him to release those that were put into
prison by Herod, who were many, and had been
put there at several times; others of them required that he would take away those taxes
which had been severely laid upon what was
publicly sold and bought. So Archelaus contradicted them in nothing, since he pretended to
do all things so as to get the good-will of the
multitude to him, as looking upon that good-will
to be a great step towards his preservation of the
government. Hereupon he went and offered
sacrifice to God, and then betook himself to feast
with his friends.

CHAPTER IX

HOW THE PEOPLE RAISED A SEDITION AGAINST ARCHELAUS, AND HOW HE SAILED TO ROME

1. At this time also it was that some of the
Jews got together out of a desire of innovation.
They lamented Matthias, and those that were
slain with him by Herod, who had not any respect
paid them by a funeral mourning, out of the fear
men were in of that man; they were those who
had been condemned for pulling down the golden
eagle. The people made a great clamour and
lamentation hereupon, and cast out some reproaches against the king also, as if that tended
to alleviate the miseries of the deceased. The
people assembled together, and desired of Archelaus, that, in way of revenge on their account,
he would inflict punishment on those who had
been honoured by Herod; and that, in the first
and principal place, he would deprive that high
priest whom Herod had made, and would choose
one more agreeable to the law, and of greater
purity, to officiate as high priest. This was
granted by Archelaus, although he was mightily
offended at their importunity, because he proposed to himself to go to Rome immediately,
to look after Cæsar's determination about him.
However, he sent the general of his forces to
use persuasions, and to tell them that the death
which was inflicted on their friends, was according to the law; and to represent to them, that
their petitions about these things were carried
to a great height of injury to him; that the
time was not now proper for such petitions, but
required their unanimity until such time as he
should be established in the government by the
consent of Cæsar, and should then be come back
to them; for that he would then consult with
them in common concerning the purport of their
petitions; but that they ought at present to be
quiet, lest they should seem seditious persons.

2. So when the king had suggested these
things, and instructed his general in what he
was to say, he sent him away to the people; but
they made a clamour, and would not give him
leave to speak, and put him in danger of his life,
and as many more as were desirous to venture
upon saying openly anything which might reduce
them to a sober mind, and prevent their going
on in their present courses,—because they had
more concern to have all their own wills performed than to yield obedience to their governors; thinking it to be a thing insufferable that,
while Herod was alive, they should lose those

---

* At eight *stadia* or furlongs a day, Herod's funeral,
conducted to Herodium, which lay at the distance from
Jericho, where he died. of 200 *stadia* or furlongs, must
have taken up no less than twenty-five days.

that were the most dear to them, and that when he was dead, they could not get the actors to be punished. So they went on with their designs after a violent manner, and thought all to be lawful and right which tended to please them, and being unskilful in foreseeing what dangers they incurred; and when they had suspicion of such a thing, yet did the present pleasure they took in the punishment of those they deemed their enemies overweigh all such considerations; and although Archelaus sent many to speak to them, yet they treated them not as messengers sent by him, but as persons that came of their own accord to mitigate their anger, and would not let one of them speak. The sedition, also, was made by such as were in a great passion; and it was evident that they were proceeding further in seditious practices, by the multitude running so fast upon them.

3. Now, upon the approach of that feast of un-leavened bread, which the law of their fathers had appointed for the Jews at this time, which feast is called the Passover,* and is a memorial of their deliverance out of Egypt, (when they offer sacrifices with great alacrity; and when they are required to slay more sacrifices in num-ber than at any other festival; and when an innumerable multitude came thither out of the country, nay, from beyond its limits also, in order to worship God,) the seditious lamented Judas and Matthias, those teachers of the laws, and kept together in the temple, and had plenty of food, because these seditious persons were not ashamed to beg it. And as Archelaus was afraid lest some terrible thing should spring up by means of these men's madness, he sent a regiment of armed men, and with them a captain of a thousand, to suppress the violent efforts of the seditious, before the whole multitude should be infected with the like madness; and gave them this charge, that if they found any much more openly seditious than others, and more busy in tumultuous practices, they should bring them to him. But those that were seditious on account of those teachers of the law, irritated the people by the noise and clamours they used to encourage the people in their designs; so they made an assault upon the soldiers, and came up to them, and stoned the greatest part of them, although some of them ran away wounded, and their cap-tain among them; and when they had thus done, they returned to the sacrifices which were al-ready in their hands. Now Archelaus thought there was no way to preserve the entire govern-ment, but by cutting off those who made this attempt upon it; so he sent out the whole army upon them, and sent the horsemen to prevent those that had their tents without the temple, and to kill such as ran away from the footmen when they thought themselves out of danger; which horsemen slew three thousand men, while the rest went to the neighbouring mountains. Then did Archelaus order proclamation to be made to them all, that they should retire to their own homes; so they went away, and left the festival, out of fear of somewhat worse which would follow, although they had been so bold by reason of their want of instruction. So Arche-laus went down to the sea with his mother, and took with him Nicolaus and Ptolemy, and many others of his friends, and left Philip his brother as governor of all things belonging both to his own family and to the public. There went out

also with him Salome, Herod's sister, who took with her her children, and many of her kindred were with her; which kindred of hers went, as they pretended, to assist Archelaus in gaining the kingdom, but in reality to oppose him, and chiefly to make loud complaints of what he had done in the temple. But Sabinus, Cæsar's steward for Syrian affairs, as he was making haste into Judea, to preserve Herod's effects, met with Archelaus at Cæsarea; but Varus, (president of Syria,) came at that time, and re-strained him from meddling with them, for he was there as sent for by Archelaus by means of Ptolemy. And Sabinus, out of regard to Varus, did neither seize upon any of the castles that were among the Jews, nor did he seal up the treasures in them, but permitted Archelaus to have them, until Cæsar should declare his re-solution about them; so that, upon this his promise, he tarried still at Cæsarea. But after Archelaus was sailed for Rome, and Varus was removed to Antioch, Sabinus went to Jerusalem, and seized on the king's palace. He also sent for the keepers of the garrisons, and for all those that had the charge of Herod's effects, and declared publicly that he should require them to give an account of what they had; and he disposed of the castles in the manner he pleased: but those who kept them did not neglect what Archelaus had given them in command, but con-tinued to keep all things in the manner they had been enjoined them; and their pretence was, that they kept them all for Cæsar.

4. At the same time also did Antipas, another of Herod's sons, sail to Rome, in order to gain the government; being buoyed up by Salome with promises that he should take that govern-ment; and that he was a much honester and fitter man than Archelaus for that authority, since Herod had, in his former testament, deemed him the worthiest to be made king; which ought to be esteemed more valid than his latter testament. Antipas also brought with him his mother, and Ptolemy the brother of Nicolaus, one that had been Herod's most ho-oured friend, and was now zealous for Antipas: but it was Irenæus the orator, and one who, on account of his reputation for sagacity, was in-trusted with the affairs of the kingdom, who most of all encouraged him to attempt to gain the kingdom; by whose means it was that, when some advised him to yield to Archelaus, as to his elder brother, and who had been declared king by their father's last will, he would not submit so to do. And when he was come to Rome, all his relations revolted to him: not out of their good-will to him, but out of their hatred to Archelaus; though indeed they were most of all desirous of gaining their liberty, and to be put under a Roman governor; but, if there were too great an opposition made to that, they thought Antipas preferable to Archelaus, and so joined with him, in order to procure the king-dom for him. Sabinus also, by letters, accused Archelaus to Cæsar.

5. Now when Archelaus had sent in his papers to Cæsar, wherein he pleaded his right to the kingdom and his father's testament, with the accounts of Herod's money, and with Ptolemy, who brought Herod's seal, he so expected the event; but when Cæsar had read these papers, and Varus's and Sabinus's letters, with the ac-counts of the money, and what were the annual incomes of the kingdom, and understood that Antipas had also sent letters to lay claim to the kingdom, he summoned his friends together, to know their opinions, and with them Caius, the son of Agrippa, and of Julia his daughter, whom

---

* This passover, when the sedition here mentioned was moved against Archelaus, was not one, but thir-teen months after the eclipse of the moon, already men-tioned.

he had adopted, and took him, and made him sit first of all, and desired such as pleased to speak their minds about the affairs now before them. Now, Antipater, Salome's son, a very subtle orator, and a bitter enemy to Archelaus, spake first to this purpose :—"That it was ridiculous in Archelaus to plead now to have the kingdom given him, since he had, in reality, taken already the power over it to himself, before Cæsar had granted it to him; and appealed to those bold actions of his, in destroying so many at the Jewish festival; and, if the men had acted unjustly, it was but fit the punishing of them should have been reserved to those that were out of the country, but had the power to punish them, and not been executed by a man that, if he pretended to be a king, he did an injury to Cæsar, by usurping that authority before it was determined for him by Cæsar; but, if he owned himself to be a private person, his case was much worse, since he who was putting in for the kingdom, could by no means expect to have that power granted him, of which he had already deprived Cæsar [by taking it to himself.] He also touched sharply upon him, and appealed to his changing the commanders in the army, and his sitting in the royal throne beforehand, and his determination of law-suits; all done as if he were no other than a king. He appealed also to his concessions to those that petitioned him on a public account, and indeed doing such things, than which he could devise no greater if he had been already settled in the kingdom by Cæsar. He also ascribed to him the releasing of the prisoners that were in the Hippodrome, and many other things, that either had been done certainly by him, or were believed to be done, and easily might be believed to have been done, because they were of such a nature as to be usually done by young men, and by such as, out of a desire of ruling, seize upon the government too soon. He also charged him with his neglect of the funeral mourning for his father, and with having merry meetings the very night in which he died; and that it was thence the multitude took the handle of raising a tumult; and if Archelaus could thus requite his dead father, who had bestowed such benefits upon him, and bequeathed such great things to him, by pretending to shed tears for him in the daytime, like an actor on the stage, but every night making mirth for having got the government, he would appear to be the same Archelaus with regard to Cæsar, if he granted him the kingdom, which he hath been to his father; since he had then dancing and singing, as though an enemy of his were fallen, and not as though a man were carried to his funeral that was so nearly related, and had been so great a benefactor to him. But he said that the greatest crime of all was this, that he came now before Cæsar to obtain the government by his grant, while he had before acted in all things as he could have acted, if Cæsar himself, who ruled all, had fixed him firmly in the government. And what he most aggravated in his pleading, was the slaughter of those about the temple, and the impiety of it, as done at the festival; and they were slain like sacrifices themselves, some of whom were foreigners, and others of their own country, till the temple was full of dead bodies : and all this was done, not by an alien, but by one who pretended to the lawful title of a king, that he might complete the wicked tyranny which his nature prompted him to, and which is hated by all men. On which account his father never so much as dreamed of making him his successor in the kingdom, when he was of a sound mind,

because he knew his disposition; and, in his former and more authentic testament, he appointed his antagonist Antipas to succeed; but that Archelaus was called by his father to that dignity, when he was in a dying condition, both of body and mind; while Antipas was called when ripest in his judgment, and of such strength of body as made him capable of managing his own affairs : and if his father had the like notion of him formerly that he hath now shewn, yet he hath given a sufficient specimen what a king he is likely to be when he hath [in effect] deprived Cæsar of that power of disposing of the kingdom, which he justly hath, and hath not abstained from making a terrible slaughter of his fellow-citizens in the temple, while he was but a private person."

6. So when Antipater had made this speech, and had confirmed what he had said by producing many witnesses from among Archelaus's own relations, he made an end of his pleading. Upon which Nicolaus arose up to plead for Archelaus, and said, "That what had been done at the temple was rather to be attributed to the mind of those that had been killed, than to the authority of Archelaus; for that those who were the authors of such things, are not only wicked in the injuries they do of themselves, but in forcing sober persons to avenge themselves upon them. Now, it is evident that what these did in way of opposition was done under pretence, indeed against Archelaus, but in reality against Cæsar himself, for they, after an injurious manner, attacked and slew those who were sent by Archelaus, and who came only to put a stop to their doings. They had no regard, either to God or to the festival, whom Antipater yet is not ashamed to patronise, whether it be out of his indulgence of an enmity to Archelaus, or out of his hatred of virtue and justice. For as to those who begin such tumults, and first set about such unrighteous actions, they are the men who force those that punish them to betake themselves to arms even against their will. So that Antipater in effect ascribes the rest of what was done, to all those who were of counsel to the accusers; for nothing which is here accused of injustice has been done, but what was derived from them as its authors; nor are those things evil in themselves, but so represented only in order to do harm to Archelaus. Such is these men's inclination to do an injury to a man that is of their kindred, their father's benefactor, and familiarly acquainted with them, and that hath ever lived in friendship with them; for that, as to this testament, it was made by the king when he was of a sound mind, and so ought to be of more authority than his former testament; and that for this reason, because Cæsar is therein left to be the judge and disposer of all therein contained; and for Cæsar, he will not, to be sure, at all imitate the unjust proceedings of those men, who, during Herod's whole life, had on all occasions been joint-partakers of power with him, and yet do zealously endeavour to injure his determination, while they have not themselves had the same regard to their kinsman [which Archelaus had.] Cæsar will not therefore disannul the testament of a man whom he had entirely supported, of his friend and confederate, and that which is committed to him in trust to ratify; nor will Cæsar's virtuous and upright disposition, which is known and uncontested through all the habitable world, imitate the wickedness of these men in condemning a king as a madman, and as having lost his reason, while he hath bequeathed the succession to a good son of his, and to one who flies to

Cæsar's upright determination for refuge. Nor can Herod at any time have been mistaken in his judgment about a successor, while he shewed so much prudence as to submit all to Cæsar's determination."

7. Now when Nicolaus had laid these things before Cæsar, he ended his plea: whereupon Cæsar was so obliging to Archelaus, that he raised him up when he had cast himself down at his feet, and said, that he well deserved the kingdom: and he soon let them know that he was so far moved in his favour, that he would not act otherwise than his father's testament directed, and that was for the advantage of Archelaus. However, while he gave this encouragement to Archelaus to depend on him securely, he made no full determination about him; and, when the assembly was broken up, he considered by himself whether he should confirm the kingdom to Archelaus, or whether he should part it among all Herod's posterity; and this, because they all stood in need of much assistance to support them.

CHAPTER X

A SEDITION OF THE JEWS AGAINST SABINUS; AND HOW VARUS BROUGHT THE AUTHORS OF IT TO PUNISHMENT

1. BUT before these things could be brought to a settlement, Malthace, Archelaus's mother, fell into a distemper, and died of it; and letters came from Varus, the president of Syria, which informed Cæsar of the revolt of the Jews; for, after Archelaus was sailed, the whole nation was in a tumult. So Varus, since he was there himself, brought the authors of the disturbance to punishment; and when he had restrained them for the most part from this sedition, which was a great one, he took his journey to Antioch, leaving one legion of his army at Jerusalem to keep the Jews quiet, who were now very fond of innovation. Yet did not this at all avail to put an end to their sedition, for, after Varus was gone away, Sabinus, Cæsar's procurator, stayed behind, and greatly distressed the Jews, relying on the forces that were left there, that they would by their multitude protect him; for he made use of them, and armed them as his guards, thereby so oppressing the Jews, and giving them so great disturbance, that at length they rebelled; for he used force in seizing the citadels, and zealously pressed on the search after the king's money, in order to seize upon it by force, on account of his love of gain, and his extraordinary covetousness.

2. But on the approach of Pentecost, which is a festival of ours, so called from the days of our forefathers, a great many ten thousands of men got together; nor did they come only to celebrate the festival, but out of their indignation at the madness of Sabinus, and at the injuries he offered them. A great number there was of Galileans, and Idumeans, and many men from Jericho, and others who had passed over the river Jordan, and inhabited those parts. This whole multitude joined themselves to all the rest, and were more zealous than the others in making an assault on Sabinus, in order to be avenged on him; so they parted themselves into three bands, and encamped themselves in the places following:—some of them seized on the Hippodrome; and of the other two bands, one pitched themselves from the northern part of the temple to the southern, on the east quarter;

but the third band held the western part of the city, where the king's palace was. Their work tended entirely to besiege the Romans, and to enclose them on all sides. Now Sabinus was afraid of these men's number, and of their resolution, who had little regard to their lives, but were very desirous not to be overcome, while they thought it a point of puissance to overcome their enemies; so he sent immediately a letter to Varus, and, as he used to do, was very pressing with him, and entreated him to come quickly to his assistance; because the forces he had left were in imminent danger, and would probably, in no long time, be seized upon, and cut to pieces; while he did himself get up to the highest tower of the fortress Phasaelus, which had been built in honour of Phasaelus, king Herod's brother, and called so when the Parthians had brought him to his death. So Sabinus gave thence a signal to the Romans to fall upon the Jews, although he did not himself venture so much as to come down to his friends, and thought he might expect that the others should expose themselves first to die on account of his avarice. However, the Romans ventured to make a sally out of their place, and a terrible battle ensued; wherein, though it is true the Romans beat their adversaries, yet were not the Jews daunted in their resolutions, even when they had the sight of that terrible slaughter that was made of them; but they went round about, and got upon those cloisters which encompassed the outer court of the temple, where a great fight was still continued, and they cast stones at the Romans, partly with their hands, and partly with slings, as being much used to those exercises. All the archers also in array did the Romans a great deal of mischief, because they used their hands dexterously from a place superior to the others, and because the others were at an utter loss what to do; for when they tried to shoot their arrows against the Jews upwards, these arrows could not reach them, insomuch that the Jews were easily too hard for their enemies. And this sort of fight lasted a great while, till at last the Romans, who were greatly distressed by what was done, set fire to the cloisters so privately, that those who were gotten upon them did not perceive it. This fire,* being fed by a great deal of combustible matter, caught hold immediately on the roof of the cloisters; so the wood, which was full of pitch and wax, and whose gold was laid on it with wax, yielded to the flame presently, and those vast works, which were of the highest value and esteem, were destroyed utterly, while those that were on the roof, unexpectedly perished at the same time; for as the roof tumbled down, some of these men tumbled down with it, and others of them were killed by their enemies who encompassed them. There was a great number more, who out of despair of saving their lives, and out of astonishment at the misery that surrounded them, did either cast themselves into the fire, or threw themselves upon their own swords, and so got out of their misery. But as to those that retired behind the same way by which they ascended, and thereby escaped, they were all killed by the Romans, as being unarmed men, and their courage failing them; their wild fury being now not able to help them, because they were destitute of armour, insomuch that of those that went up to the top of the roof, not one escaped.

---

* These great devastations made about the temple seem not to have been fully re-edified in the days of Nero; till whose time there were eighteen thousand workmen continually employed in rebuilding and repairing that temple.

The Romans also rushed through the fire, where it gave them room so to do, and seized on that treasure where the sacred money was reposited: a great part of which was stolen by the soldiers; and Sabinus got openly four hundred talents.

3. But this calamity of the Jews' friends, who fell in this battle, grieved them, as did also this plundering of the money dedicated to God in the temple. Accordingly, that body of them which continued best together, and was the most warlike, encompassed the palace, and threatened to set fire to it, and kill all that were in it. Yet still they commanded them to go out presently, and promised that if they would do so, they would not hurt them, nor Sabinus neither; at which time the greatest part of the king's troops deserted to them, while Rufus and Gratus, who had three thousand of the most warlike of Herod's army with them, who were men of active bodies, went over to the Romans. There was also a band of horsemen under the command of Rufus, which itself went over to the Romans also. However, the Jews went on with the siege, and dug mines under the palace-walls, and besought those that were gone over to the other side not to be their hindrance, now they had such a proper opportunity for the recovery of their country's ancient liberty; and for Sabinus, truly he was desirous of going away with his soldiers, but was not able to trust himself with the enemy, on account of what mischief he had already done them; and he took this great [pretended] lenity of theirs for an argument why he should not comply with them; and so, because he expected that Varus was coming, he still bore on the siege.

4. Now, at this time there were ten thousand other disorders in Judea, which were like tumults, because a great number put themselves into a warlike posture, either out of hopes of gain to themselves, or out of enmity to the Jews. In particular, two thousand of Herod's old soldiers, who had been already disbanded, got together in Judea itself, and fought against the king's troops, although Achiabus, Herod's first cousin, opposed them: but as he was driven out of the plains into the mountainous parts by the military skill of those men, he kept himself in the fastnesses that were there, and saved what he could.

5. There was also Judas,* the son of that Ezekias who had been head of the robbers; which Ezekias was a very strong man, and had with great difficulty been caught by Herod. This Judas having gotten together a multitude of men of a profligate character about Sepphoris in Galilee, and made an assault upon the palace [there,] and seized upon all the weapons that were laid up in it, and with them armed every one of those that were with him, and carried away what money was left there; and he became terrible to all men, by tearing and rending those that came near him; and all this in order to raise himself, and out of an ambitious desire of the royal dignity; and he hoped to obtain that as the reward, not of his virtuous skill in war, but of his extravagance in doing injuries.

6. There was also Simon, who had been a slave of Herod the king, but in other respects a comely person, of a tall and robust body; he was one that was much superior to others of his

order, and had had great things committed to his care. This man was elevated at the disorderly state of things, and was so bold as to put a diadem on his head, while a certain number of the people stood by him. and by them he was declared to be a king, and thought himself more worthy of that dignity than any one else. He burnt down the royal palace at Jericho, and plundered what was left in it. He also set fire to many others of the king's houses in several places of the country, and utterly destroyed them, and permitted those that were with him to take what was left in them for a prey; and he would have done greater things, unless care had been taken to repress him immediately; for Gratus, when he had joined himself to some Roman soldiers, took the forces he had with him, and met Simon, and after a great and a long fight, no small part of those that came from Perea, who were a disordered body of men, and fought rather in a bold than in a skilful manner, were destroyed; and although Simon had saved himself by flying away through a certain valley, yet Gratus overtook him, and cut off his head. The royal palace, also, at Amathus, by the river Jordan, was burnt down, by a party of men that were got together, as were those belonging to Simon. And thus did a great and wild fury spread itself over the nation, because they had no king to keep the multitude in good order; and because those foreigners, who came to reduce the seditious to sobriety, did, on the contrary, set them more in a flame, because of the injuries they offered them, and the avaricious management of their affairs.

7. But because Athronges, a person neither eminent by the dignity of progenitors, nor for any great wealth he was possessed of, but one that had in all respects been a shepherd only, and was not known by anybody; yet because he was a tall man, and excelled others in the strength of his hands, he was so bold as to set up for king. This man thought it so sweet a thing to do more than ordinary injuries to others, that although he should be killed, he did not so much care, if he lost his life in so great a design. He had also four brethren, who were tall men themselves, and were believed to be superior to others in the strength of their hands, and thereby were encouraged to aim at great things, and thought that strength of theirs would support them in retaining the kingdom. Each of these ruled over a band of men of their own; for those they got together to them were very numerous. They were every one of them also commanders; but, when they came to fight, they were subordinate to him, and fought for him, while he put a diadem upon his head, and assembled a council to debate about what things should be done; and all things were done according to his pleasure. And this man retained his power a great while; he was also called king, and had nothing to hinder him from doing what he pleased. He also, as well as his brethren, slew a great many both of the Romans and of the king's forces, and managed matters with the like hatred to each of them. The king's forces they fell upon, because of the licentious conduct they had been allowed under Herod's government; and they fell upon the Romans, because of the injuries they had so lately received from them. But in process of time they grew more cruel to all sorts of men; nor could any one escape from one or other of these seditions, since they slew some out of the hopes of gain, and others from a mere custom of slaying men. They once attacked a company of Romans at Emmaus, who were bringing corn and weapons

---

* Unless this Judas be the same with that Theudas mentioned in Acts v. 36, Josephus must have omitted him; for that other Theudas, whom he afterwards mentions under Fadus, the Roman governor, (b. xx. ch. v. sect. 1,) is much too late to correspond to him that is mentioned in the Acts. The names Theudas, Thaddeus, and Judas, differ but little.

to the army, and fell upon Arius, the centurion, who commanded the company, and shot forty of the best of his foot-soldiers; but the rest of them were affrighted at their slaughter, and left their dead behind them, but saved themselves by the means of Gratus, who came with the king's troops that were about him to their assistance. Now, these four brethren continued the war a long while by such sort of expeditions, and much grieved the Romans, (but did their own nation also a great deal of mischief;) yet were they afterwards subdued; one of them in a fight with Gratus, another with Ptolemy; Archelaus also took the eldest of them prisoner; while the last of them was so dejected at the others' misfortune, and saw so plainly that he had no way now left to save himself, his army being worn away with sickness and continual labours, that he also delivered himself up to Archelaus, upon his promise and oath to God to [preserve his life.] But these things came to pass a good while afterward.

8. And now Judea was full of robberies; and, as the several companies of the seditious lighted upon any one to head them, he was created a king immediately, in order to do mischief to the public. They were in some small measure, indeed, and in small matters, hurtful to the Romans, but the murders they committed upon their own people lasted a long while.

9. As soon as Varus was once informed of the state of Judea, by Sabinus's writing to him, he was afraid for the legion he had left there; so he took the two other legions, (for there were three legions in all belonging to Syria,) and four troops of horsemen, with the several auxiliary forces which either the kings or certain of the tetrarchs afforded him, and made what haste he could to assist those that were then besieged in Judea. He also gave order, that all that were sent out for this expedition should make haste to Ptolemais. The citizens of Berytus also gave him fifteen hundred auxiliaries, as he passed through their city. Aretas also, the king of Arabia Petrea, out of his hatred to Herod, and in order to purchase the favour of the Romans, sent him no small assistance, besides their footmen and horsemen: and, when he had now collected all their forces together, he committed part of them to his son, and to a friend of his, and sent them upon an expedition into Galilee, which lies in the neighbourhood of Ptolemais; who made an attack upon the enemy, and put them to flight, and took Sepphoris, and made its inhabitants slaves, and burnt the city. But Varus himself pursued his march to Samaria with his whole army: yet did not he meddle with the city of that name, because it had not at all joined with the seditious, but pitched his camp at a certain village that belonged to Ptolemy, whose name was Arus, which the Arabians burnt, out of their hatred to Herod, and out of the enmity they bore to his friends; whence they marched to another village, whose name was Sampho, which the Arabians plundered and burnt, although it was a fortified and strong place; and all along this march nothing escaped them, but all places were full of fire and of slaughter. Emmaus was also burnt by Varus's order, after its inhabitants had deserted it, that he might avenge those that had there been destroyed. From thence he now marched to Jerusalem; whereupon the Jews, whose camp lay there, and who had besieged the Roman legion, not bearing the coming of this army, left the siege imperfect: but as to the Jerusalem Jews, when Varus reproached them bitterly for what had been done, they cleared themselves of the accusation; and alleged that the conflux of the people was occasioned by the feast; that the war was not made with their approbation, but by the rashness of the strangers; while they were on the side of the Romans, and besieged together with them, rather than having any inclination to besiege them. There also came beforehand to meet Varus, Joseph, the cousin-german of king Herod, as also Gratus and Rufus, who brought their soldiers along with them, together with those Romans who had been besieged: but Sabinus did not come into Varus's presence, but stole out of the city privately, and went to the seaside.

10. Upon this, Varus sent a part of his army into the country, to seek out those that had been the authors of the revolt; and when they were discovered, he punished some of them that were most guilty, and some he dismissed: now the number of those that were crucified on this account were two thousand: after which he disbanded his army, which he found nowise useful to him in the affairs he came about; for they behaved themselves very disorderly, and disobeyed his orders, and what Varus desired them to do; and this out of regard to that gain which they made by the mischief they did. As for himself, when he was informed that ten thousand Jews had gotten together, he made haste to catch them; but they did not proceed so far as to fight him, but, by the advice of Achiabus, they came together, and delivered themselves up to him: hereupon Varus forgave the crime of revolting to the multitude, but sent their several commanders to Cæsar, many of whom Cæsar dismissed; but for the several relations of Herod who had been among these men in this war, they were the only persons whom he punished, who, without the least regard to justice, fought against their own kindred.

CHAPTER XI

AN EMBASSAGE OF THE JEWS TO CÆSAR; AND HOW CÆSAR CONFIRMED HEROD'S TESTAMENT

1. So when Varus had settled these affairs, and had placed the former legion at Jerusalem, he returned back to Antioch; but as for Archelaus, he had new sources of trouble come upon him at Rome, on the occasions following: for an embassage of the Jews was come to Rome, Varus having permitted the nation to send it, that they might petition for the liberty of living by their own laws. Now, the number of the ambassadors that were sent by the authority of the nation, were fifty, to which they joined above eight thousand of the Jews that were at Rome already. Hereupon Cæsar assembled his friends, and the chief men among the Romans, in the temple of Apollo, which he had built at a vast charge; whither the ambassadors came, and a multitude of the Jews that were there already, came with them, as did also Archelaus and his friends; but as for the several kinsmen which Archelaus had, they would not join themselves with him, out of their hatred to him: and yet they thought it too gross a thing for them to assist the ambassadors [against him,] as supposing it would be a disgrace to them in Cæsar's opinion to think of thus acting in opposition to a man of their own kindred: Philip* also was come hither out of Syria, by the persuasion of Varus, with this principal intention to assist his brother

---

* He was tetrarch afterwards.

[Archelaus;] for Varus was his great friend: but still so, that if there should any change happen in the form of government, (which Varus suspected there would,) and if any distribution should be made on account of the number that desired the liberty of living by their own laws, that he might not be disappointed, but might have his share in it.

2. Now, upon the liberty that was given to the Jewish ambassadors to speak, they who hoped to obtain a dissolution of kingly government, betook themselves to accuse Herod of his iniquities ; and they declared that he was indeed in name a king, but that he had taken to himself an uncontrollable authority, which tyrants exercise over their subjects, and had made use of that authority for the destruction of the Jews, and did not abstain from making many innovations among them besides, according to his own inclinations; and that whereas there were a great many who perished by that destruction he brought upon them, so many indeed as no other history relates, they that survived were far more miserable than those that suffered under him, not only by the anxiety they were under from his looks and disposition towards them, but from the danger their estates were in of being taken away by him. That he did never leave off adorning these cities that lay in their neighbourhood, but were inhabited by foreigners ; but so that the cities belonging to his own government were ruined, and utterly destroyed; that whereas, when he took the kingdom, it was in an extraordinary flourishing condition, he had filled the nation with the utmost degree of poverty : and when, upon unjust pretences, he had slain any of the nobility, he took away their estates : and when he permitted any of them to live, he condemned them to the forfeiture of what they possessed. And, besides the annual impositions which he laid upon every one of them, they were to make liberal presents to himself, to his domestics and friends, and to such of his slaves as were vouchsafed the favour of being his tax-gatherers; because there was no way of obtaining a freedom from unjust violence, without giving either gold or silver for it. That they would say nothing of the corruption of the chastity of their virgins, and the reproach laid on their wives for incontinency, and those things acted after an insolent and inhuman manner ; because it was not a smaller pleasure to the sufferers to have such things concealed, than it would have been not to have suffered them. That Herod had put such abuses upon them as a wild beast would not have put on them, if he had power given him to rule over us : and that, although their nation had passed through many subversions and alterations of government, their history gave no account of any calamity they had ever been under, that could be compared with this which Herod had brought upon their nation ; that it was for this reason that they thought they might justly and gladly salute Archelaus as king, upon this supposition, that whosoever should be set over their kingdom, he would appear more mild to them than Herod had been ; and that they had joined with him in the mourning for his father, in order to gratify him, and were ready to oblige him in other points also, if they could meet with any degree of moderation from him ; but that he seemed to be afraid lest he should not be deemed Herod's own son ; and so, without any delay, he immediately let the nation understand his meaning, and this before his dominion was well established, since the power of disposing of it belonged to Cæsar, who could either give it to him or not, as he pleased.

That he had given a specimen of his future virtue to his subjects, and with what kind of moderation and good administration he would govern them, by that his first action which concerned them, his own citizens, and God himself also, when he made the slaughter of three thousand of his own countrymen at the temple. How, then, could they avoid the just hatred of him, who, to the rest of his barbarity, hath added this as one of our crimes, that we have opposed and contradicted him in the exercise of his authority? Now, the main thing they desired, was this : That they might be delivered from kingly and the like forms of government,* and might be added to Syria, and be put under the authority of such presidents of theirs as should be sent to them ; for that it would thereby be made evident, whether they be really a seditious people, and generally fond of innovations, or whether they would live in an orderly manner, if they might have governors of any sort of moderation set over them.

3. Now when the Jews had said this, Nicolaus vindicated the kings from these accusations, and said, that as for Herod, since he had never been thus accused all the time of his life, it was not fit for those that might have accused him of lesser crimes than those now mentioned, and might have procured him to be punished during his lifetime, to bring an accusation against him now he is dead. He also attributed the actions of Archelaus to the Jews' injuries to him, who, affecting to govern contrary to the laws, and going about to kill those that would have hindered them from acting unjustly, when they were by him punished for what they had done, made their complaints against him ; so he accused them of their attempts for innovation, and of the pleasure they took in sedition, by reason of their not having learned to submit to justice and to the laws, but still desiring to be superior in all things. This was the substance of what Nicolaus said.

4. When Cæsar had heard these pleadings, he dissolved the assembly ; but a few days afterwards he appointed Archelaus, not indeed to be king of the whole country, but ethnarch of one half of that which had been subject to Herod, and promised to give him the royal dignity hereafter, if he governed that part virtuously. But as for the other half, he divided it into two parts, and gave it to two other of Herod's sons, to Philip and to Antipas, that Antipas who disputed with Archelaus for the whole kingdom. Now, to him it was that Perea and Galilee paid their tribute, which amounted annually to 200 talents,† while Batanea with Trachonitis, as well as Auranitis, with a certain part of what was called the *House of Zenodorus*, paid the tribute of one hundred talents to Philip ; but Idumea, and Judea, and the country of Samaria, paid tribute to Archelaus, but had now a fourth part of that tribute taken off by order of Cæsar, who

---

* If any one compare the divine prediction concerning the tyrannical power which the Jewish kings would exercise, if the Israelites would be so foolish as to prefer it before their ancient theocracy or aristocracy, (1 Sam. viii. 1-22,) he will soon find that it was fulfilled in the days of Herod, and that to such a degree, that the nation seemed to repent of their ancient choice, in opposition to God's better choice for them, and had much rather be subject to even a pagan Roman government, and their deputies, than to be any longer under the oppression of the family of Herod.

† Since Archelaus had one half of the kingdom of Herod, and his annual income was 600 talents; we may therefore gather what was Herod the Great's yearly income, I mean about 1600 talents, which, at the value of 3000 shekels to a talent, and about 2s. 10d. to a shekel, in the days of Josephus, amounts to £680,000 sterling per annum.

decreed them that mitigation, because they did not join in this revolt with the rest of the multitude. There were also certain of the cities which paid tribute to Archelaus :—Strato's Tower and Sebaste, with Joppa and Jerusalem; for as to Gaza, Gadara, and Hippos, they were Grecian cities, which Cæsar separated from his government, and added them to the province of Syria. Now the tribute money that came to Archelaus every year from his own dominions amounted to six hundred talents.

5. And so much came to Herod's sons from their father's inheritance; but Salome, besides what her brother left her by his testament, which were Jamnia, Ashdod, and Phasaelis, and five hundred thousand [drachmæ] of coined silver, Cæsar made her a present of a royal habitation at Askelon; in all, her revenues amounted to sixty talents by the year, and her dwelling-house was within Archelaus's government. The rest also of the king's relations received what his testament allotted them. Moreover, Cæsar made a present to each of Herod's two virgin daughters, besides what their father left them, of two hundred and fifty thousand [drachmæ] of silver, and married them to Pheroras's sons: he also granted all that was bequeathed unto himself to the king's sons, which was one thousand five hundred talents, excepting a few of the vessels, which he reserved for himself; and they were acceptable to him, not so much for the great value they were of, as because they were memorials of the king to him.

CHAPTER XII

CONCERNING A SPURIOUS ALEXANDER

1. WHEN these affairs had been thus settled by Cæsar, a certain young man, by birth a Jew, but brought up by a Roman freedman in the city of Sidon, ingrafted himself into the kindred of Herod, by the resemblance of his countenance, which those saw him attested to be that of Alexander, the son of Herod, whom he had slain; and this was an incitement to him to endeavour to obtain the government; so he took to him as an assistant, a man of his own country, (one that was well acquainted with the affairs of the palace, but, on other accounts, an ill man, and one whose nature made him capable of causing great disturbances to the public, and one that became a teacher of such a mischievous contrivance to the other,) and declared himself to be Alexander, and the son of Herod, but stolen away by one of those that were sent to slay him, who, in reality, slew other men, in order to deceive the spectators, but saved both him and his brother Aristobulus. Thus was this man elated, and able to impose on those that came to him; and when he was come to Crete, he made all the Jews that came to discourse with him believe him to be [Alexander.] And when he had gotten much money which had been presented to him there, he passed over to Melos, where he got much more money than he had before, out of the belief they had that he was of the royal family, and their hopes that he would recover his father's principality, and reward his benefactors; so he made haste to Rome, and was conducted thither by those strangers who entertained him. He was also so fortunate as, upon his landing at Dicearchia, to bring the Jews that were there unto the same delusion; and not only other people, but also all those who had been great with Herod, or had a kind-

ness for him, joined themselves to this man as to their king. The cause of it was this, that men were glad of his pretences, which were seconded by the likeness of his countenance, which made those that had been acquainted with Alexander strongly to believe that he was no other but the very same person, which they also confirmed to others by oath; insomuch that when the report went about him that he was coming to Rome, the whole multitude of Jews that were there went out to meet him, ascribing it to Divine Providence that he had so unexpectedly escaped, and being very joyful on account of his mother's family. And when he was come, he was carried in a royal litter through the streets; and all the ornaments about him were such as kings are adorned withal; and this was at the expense of those that entertained him. The multitude also flocked about him greatly, and made mighty acclamations to him, and nothing was omitted which could be thought suitable to such as had been so unexpectedly preserved.

2. When this thing was told Cæsar, he did not believe it, because Herod was not easily to be imposed upon in such affairs as were of great concern to him; yet, having some suspicion it might be so, he sent one Celadus, a freedman of his, and one that had conversed with the young men themselves, and bade him bring Alexander into his presence: so he brought him, being no more accurate in judging about him than the rest of the multitude. Yet did he not deceive Cæsar; for although there was a resemblance between him and Alexander, yet it was not so exact as to impose on such as were prudent in discerning; for this spurious Alexander had his hands rough, by the labours he had been put to; and instead of that softness of body which the other had, and this as derived from his delicate and generous education, this man, for the contrary reason, had a rugged body. When, therefore, Cæsar saw how the master and the scholar agreed in this lying story, and in a bold way of talking, he inquired about Aristobulus, and asked what became of him, who (it seems) was stolen away together with him, and for what reason it was that he did not come along with him, and endeavour to recover that dominion which was due to his high birth also. And when he said that he had been left in the isle of Crete, for fear of the dangers of the sea, that, in case any accident should come to himself, the posterity of Mariamne might not utterly perish, but that Aristobulus might survive, and punish those that laid such treacherous designs against them; and when he persevered in his affirmations, and the author of the imposture agreed in supporting it, Cæsar took the young man by himself, and said to him, "If thou wilt not impose upon me, thou shalt have this for thy reward, that thou shalt escape with thy life; tell me, then, who thou art, and who it was that had boldness enough to contrive such a cheat as this. For this contrivance is too considerable a piece of villany to be undertaken by one of thy age." Accordingly, because he had no other way to take, he told Cæsar the contrivance, and after what manner, and by whom, it was laid together. So Cæsar, upon observing the spurious Alexander to be a strong active man, and fit to work with his hands, that he might not break his promise to him, put him among those that were to row among the mariners, but slew him that induced him to do what he had done; for as for the people of Melos, he thought them sufficiently punished, in having thrown away so much of their money upon this

spurious Alexander. And such was the ignominious conclusion of this bold contrivance about the spurious Alexander.

CHAPTER XIII

HOW ARCHELAUS, UPON A SECOND ACCUSATION, WAS BANISHED TO VIENNA

1. WHEN Archelaus was entered on his ethnarchy, and was come into Judea, he accused Joazar the son of Boethus, of assisting the seditious, and took away the high priesthood from him, and put Eleazar his brother in his place. He also magnificently rebuilt the royal palace that had been at Jericho, and he diverted half the water with which the village of Neara used to be watered, and drew off that water into the plain, to water those palm-trees which he had there planted: he also built a village, and put his own name upon it, and called it Archelais. Moreover, he transgressed the law of our fathers,* and married Glaphyra, the daughter of Archelaus, who had been the wife of his brother Alexander, which Alexander had three children by her, while it was a thing detestable among the Jews to marry the brother's wife. Nor did this Eleazar abide long in the high priesthood, —Jesus, the son of Sie, being put in his room while he was still living.

2. But in the tenth year of Archelaus's government, both his brethren and the principal men of Judea and Samaria, not being able to bear his barbarous and tyrannical usage of them, accused him before Cæsar, and that especially because they knew he had broken the commands of Cæsar, which obliged him to behave himself with moderation among them. Whereupon Cæsar, when he heard it, was very angry, and called for Archelaus's steward, who took care of his affairs at Rome, and whose name was Archelaus also; and thinking it beneath him to write to Archelaus, he bade him sail away as soon as possible, and bring him to Rome; so the man made haste in his voyage, and when he came into Judea he found Archelaus feasting with his friends; so he told him what Cæsar had sent him about, and hastened him away. And when he was come [to Rome] to Cæsar, upon hearing what certain accusers of his had to say, and what reply he could make, both banished him, and appointed Vienna, a city of Gaul, to be the place of his habitation, and took his money away from him.

3. Now, before Archelaus was gone up to Rome upon this message, he related this dream to his friends: That he saw ears of corn, in number ten, full of wheat, perfectly ripe; which ears, as it seemed to him, were devoured by oxen. And when he was awake and gotten up, because the vision appeared to be of great importance to him, he sent for the diviners, whose study was employed about dreams. And while

some were of one opinion and some of another, (for all their interpretations did not agree,) Simon, a man of the sect of the Essens, desired to speak his mind freely, and said, that the vision denoted a change in the affairs of Archelaus, and that not for the better; that oxen, because that animal takes uneasy pains in his labours, denoted afflictions, and indeed denoted further, a change of affairs; because that land which is ploughed by oxen cannot remain in its former state; and that the ears of corn being ten, determined the like number of years, because an ear of corn grows in one year; and that the time of Archelaus's government was over. And thus did this man expound the dream. Now, on the fifth day after this dream came first to Archelaus, the other Archelaus, that was sent to Judea by Cæsar to call him away, came hither also.

4. The like accident befell Glaphyra his wife, who was the daughter of king Archelaus, who, as I said before, was married, while she was a virgin, to Alexander, the son of Herod, and brother of Archelaus; but since it fell out so that Alexander was slain by his father, she was married to Juba, the king of Libya; and when he was dead, and she lived in widowhood in Cappadocia with her father, Archelaus divorced his former wife Mariamne, and married her, so great was his affection for her; who, during her marriage to him, saw the following dream:—She thought she saw Alexander standing by her; at which she rejoiced, and embraced him with great affection; but that he complained of her, and said,—"O Glaphyra; thou provest that saying to be true, which assures us that women are not to be trusted. Didst thou not pledge thy faith to me? and wast thou not married to me when thou wast a virgin? and had we not children between us? Yet hast thou forgotten the affection I bare to thee, out of a desire of a second husband. Nor hast thou been satisfied with that injury thou didst me, but thou hast been so bold as to procure thee a third husband to lie by thee, and in an indecent and imprudent manner hast entered into my house, and hast been married to Archelaus, thy husband and my brother. However, I will not forget thy former kind affection for me; but will set thee free from every such reproachful action, and cause thee to be mine again, as thou once wast." When she had related this to her female companions, in a few days' time she departed this life.

5. Now, I did not think these histories improper for the present discourse, both because my discourse now is concerning kings, and otherwise also on account of the advantage hence to be drawn, as well for the confirmation of the immortality of the soul, as of the providence of God over human affairs, I thought them fit to be set down; but if any one does not believe such relations, let him indeed enjoy his own opinion, but let him not hinder another that would thereby encourage himself in virtue. So Archelaus's country was laid to the province of Syria; and Cyrenius, one that had been consul, was sent by Cæsar to take account of people's effects in Syria, and to sell the house of Archelaus.

---

* Spanheim observes here, that it was forbidden the Jews to marry their brother's wife when she had children by her first husband; and Zenoras interprets the clause before us accordingly.

BOOK XVIII

FROM THE BANISHMENT OF ARCHELAUS TO THE DEPARTURE OF THE JEWS FROM BABYLON

CHAPTER I

HOW CYRENIUS WAS SENT BY CÆSAR TO MAKE A TAXATION OF SYRIA AND JUDEA; AND HOW COPONIUS WAS SENT TO BE PROCURATOR OF JUDEA; CONCERNING JUDAS OF GALILEE, AND CONCERNING THE SECTS THAT WERE AMONG THE JEWS

1. Now Cyrenius, a Roman senator, and one who had gone through other magistracies, and had passed through them till he had been consul, and one who, on other accounts, was of great dignity, came at this time into Syria, with a few others, being sent by Cæsar to be a judge of that nation, and to take an account of their substance: Coponius also, a man of the equestrian order, was sent together with him, to have the supreme power over the Jews. Moreover, Cyrenius came himself into Judea, which was now added to the province of Syria, to take an account of their substance, and to dispose of Archelaus's money; but the Jews, although at the beginning they took the report of a taxation heinously, yet did they leave off any further opposition to it, by the persuasion of Joazar, who was the son of Boethus, and high priest. So they, being over-persuaded by Joazar's words, gave an account of their estates, without any dispute about it; yet there was one Judas, a Gaulonite,* of a city whose name was Gamala, who taking with him Sadduc,† a Pharisee, became zealous to draw them to a revolt, who said that this taxation was no better than an introduction to slavery, and exhorted the nation to assert their liberty; as if they could procure them happiness and security for what they possessed, and an assured enjoyment of a still greater good, which was that of the honour and glory they would thereby acquire for magnanimity. They also said that God would not otherwise be assisting to them, than upon their joining with one another in such counsels as might be successful, and for their own advantage; and this especially, if they would set about great exploits, and not grow weary in executing the same; so men received what they said with pleasure, and this bold attempt proceeded to a great height. All sorts of misfortunes also sprang from these men, and the nation was infected with this doctrine to an incredible degree; one violent war came upon us after another, and

we lost our friends, who used to alleviate our pain; there were also very great robberies and murders of our principal men. This was done in pretence indeed for the public welfare, but in reality for the hopes of gain to themselves; whence arose seditions, and from them murders of men, which sometimes fell on those of their own people, (by the madness of these men towards one another, while their desire was that none of the adverse party might be left,) and sometimes on their enemies; a famine also coming upon us, reduced us to the last degree of despair, as did also the taking and demolishing of cities; nay, the sedition at last increased so high, that the very temple of God was burnt down by their enemy's fire. Such were the consequences of this, that the customs of our fathers were altered, and such a change was made, as added a mighty weight toward bringing all to destruction, which these men occasioned by thus conspiring together; for Judas and Sadduc, who excited a fourth philosophic sect among us, and had a great many followers therein, filled our civil government with tumults at present, and laid the foundation of our future miseries, by this system of philosophy, which we were before unacquainted withal; concerning which I shall discourse a little, and this the rather, because the infection which spread thence among the younger sort, who were zealous for it, brought the public to destruction.

2. The Jews had for a great while three sects of philosophy peculiar to themselves; the sect of the Essens, and the sect of the Sadducees, and the third sort of opinions was that of those called Pharisees; of which sects, although I have already spoken in the second book of the Jewish War, yet will I a little touch upon them now.

3. Now, for the Pharisees, they live meanly, and despise delicacies in diet; and they follow the conduct of reason; and what that prescribes to them as good for them, they do; and they think they ought earnestly to strive to observe reason's dictates for practice. They also pay a respect to such as are in years; nor are they so bold as to contradict them in anything which they have introduced; and, when they determine that all things are done by fate, they do not take away the freedom from men of acting as they think fit; since their notion is, that it hath pleased God to make a temperament, whereby what he wills is done, but so that the will of men can act virtuously or viciously. They also believe that souls have an immortal vigour in them, and that under the earth there will be rewards or punishments, according as they have lived virtuously or viciously in this life; and the latter are to be detained in an everlasting prison, but that the former shall have power to revive and live again; on account of which doctrines, they are able greatly to persuade the body of the people; and whatsoever they do about divine worship, prayers, and sac-

---

* Since St Luke once, (Acts v. 37,) and Josephus four several times previously, calls this Judas a Galilean, but here a Gaulonite, of the city of Gamala; it is a great question where this Judas was born, whether in Galilee on the west side, or in Gaulonitis on the east side of the river Jordan.

† It seems not very improbable to me that this Sadduc, the Pharisee, was the very same man of whom the Rabbins speak, as the unhappy but undesigning occasion of the impiety or infidelity of the Sadducees; nor perhaps had the men this name of Sadducees till this very time, though they were a distinct sect long before.

rifices, they perform them according to their direction; insomuch that the cities gave great attestations to them on account of their entire virtuous conduct, both in the actions of their lives and their discourses also.

4. But the doctrine of the Sadducees is this: That souls die with the bodies; nor do they regard the observation of anything besides what the law enjoins them; for they think it an instance of virtue to dispute with those teachers of philosophy whom they frequent; but this doctrine is received but by a few, yet by those still of the greatest dignity; but they are able to do almost nothing of themselves; for when they become magistrates, as they are unwillingly and by force sometimes obliged to be, they addict themselves to the notions of the Pharisees, because the multitude would not otherwise bear them.

5. The doctrine of the Essens is this: That all things are best ascribed to God. They teach the immortality of souls, and esteem that the rewards of righteousness are to be earnestly striven for: and when they send what they have dedicated to God into the temple, they do not offer sacrifices,* because they have more pure lustrations of their own; on which account they are excluded from the common court of the temple, but offer their sacrifices themselves; yet is their course of life better than that of other men; and they entirely addict themselves to husbandry. It also deserves our admiration, how much they exceed all other men that addict themselves to virtue, and this in righteousness: and indeed to such a degree, that as it hath never appeared among any other men, neither Greeks nor barbarians, no, not for a little time, so hath it endured a long while among them. This is demonstrated by that institution of theirs, which will not suffer anything to hinder them from having all things in common; so that a rich man enjoys no more of his own wealth than he who hath nothing at all. There are about four thousand men that live in this way, and neither marry wives, nor are desirous to keep servants; as thinking the latter tempts men to be unjust, and the former gives the handle to domestic quarrels; but as they live by themselves, they minister one to another. They also appoint certain stewards to receive the incomes of their revenues, and of the fruits of the ground; such as are good men and priests, who are to get their corn and their food ready for them. They none of them differ from others of the Essens in their way of living, but do the most resemble those Dacæ who are called *Polistæ* † [dwellers in cities.]

6. But of the fourth sect of Jewish philosophy, Judas the Galilean was the author. These men agree in all other things with the Pharisaic notions; but they have an inviolable attachment to liberty; and they say that God is to be their only Ruler and Lord. They also do not value dying any kinds of death, nor indeed do they heed the deaths of their relations and friends, nor can any such fear make them call any man Lord; and since this immovable resolution of

theirs is well known to a great many, I shall speak no further about that matter; nor am I afraid that anything I have said of them should be disbelieved, but rather fear, that what I have said is beneath the resolution they shew when they undergo pain; and it was in Gessius Florus's time that the nation began to grow mad with this distemper, who was our procurator, and who occasioned the Jews to go wild with it by the abuse of his authority, and to make them revolt from the Romans; and these are the sects of Jewish philosophy.

CHAPTER II

HOW HEROD AND PHILIP BUILT SEVERAL CITIES IN HONOUR OF CÆSAR. CONCERNING THE SUCCESSION OF PRIESTS AND PROCURATORS; AS ALSO WHAT BEFELL PHRAATES AND THE PARTHIANS

1. WHEN Cyrenius had now disposed of Archelaus's money, and when the taxings were come to a conclusion, which were made in the thirty-seventh year of Cæsar's victory over Antony at Actium, he deprived Joazar of the high priesthood, which dignity had been conferred on him by the multitude, and he appointed Ananus, the son of Seth, to be high priest; while Herod and Philip had each of them received their own tetrarchy, and settled the affairs thereof. Herod also built a wall about Sepphoris, (which is the security of all Galilee,) and made it the metropolis of the country. He also built a wall round Betharamphtha, which was itself a city also, and called it Julias, from the name of the emperor's wife. When Philip, also, had built Paneas, a city, at the fountains of Jordan, he named it Cesarea. He also advanced the village Bethsaida, situate at the lake of Gennesareth, unto the dignity of a city, both by the number of inhabitants it contained, and its other grandeur, and called it by the name of Julias, the same name with Cæsar's daughter.

2. As Coponius, who we told you was sent along with Cyrenius, was exercising his office of procurator, and governing Judea, the following accidents happened. As the Jews were celebrating the feast of unleavened bread, which we call the Passover, it was customary for the priests to open the temple-gates just after midnight. When, therefore, those gates were first opened, some of the Samaritans came privately into Jerusalem, and threw about dead men's bodies in the cloisters; on which account the Jews afterwards excluded them out of the temple, which they had not used to do at such festivals; and on other accounts also they watched the temple more carefully than they had formerly done. A little after which accident, Coponius returned to Rome, and Marcus Ambivius came to be his successor in that government; under whom Salome, the sister of king Herod, died, and left to Julia, [Cæsar's wife,] Jamnia, all its toparchy, and Phasaelis in the plain, and Archelaus, where is a great plantation of palm-trees, and their fruit is excellent in its kind.— After him came Annius Rufus, under whom died Cæsar, the second emperor of the Romans, the duration of whose reign was fifty-seven years, besides six months and two days, (of which time Antonius ruled together with him fourteen years; but the duration of his life was seventy-seven years;) upon whose death Tiberius Nero, his wife Julia's son, succeeded. He was now the third emperor; and he sent Valerius

---

* It seems by what Josephus says here, that these Essens did not use to go to the Jewish festivals at Jerusalem, or to offer sacrifices there, which may be one great occasion why they are never mentioned in the ordinary books of the New Testament.

† Who these *Polistæ* in Josephus, among the Pythagoric Dacæ, were, it is not easy to determine. Scaliger conjectures that some of those Dacæ lived alone, like monks, in tents or caves; but that others of them lived together in built cities, and thence were called by such names as implied the same.

Gratus to be procurator of Judea, and to succeed Annius Rufus. This man deprived Ananus of the high priesthood, and appointed Ismael, the son of Phabi, to be high priest. He also deprived him in a little time, and ordained Eleazar, the son of Ananus, who had been high priest before, to be high priest : which office, when he had held for a year, Gratus deprived him of it, and gave the high priesthood to Simon, the son of Camithus ; and, when he had possessed that dignity no longer than a year, Joseph Caiaphas was made his successor. When Gratus had done those things, he went back to Rome, after he had tarried in Judea eleven years, when Pontius Pilate came as his successor.

3. And now Herod the tetrarch, who was in great favour with Tiberius, built a city of the same name with him, and called it Tiberias. He built it in the best part of Galilee, at the lake of Gennesareth. There are warm baths at a little distance from it, in a village named Emmaus. Strangers came and inhabited this city ; a great number of the inhabitants were Galileans also ; and many were necessitated by Herod to come thither out of the country belonging to him, and were by force compelled to be its inhabitants ; some of them were persons of condition. He also admitted poor people, such as those that were collected from all parts, to dwell in it. Nay, some of them were not quite freemen ; and these he was a benefactor to, and made them free in great numbers ; but obliged them not to forsake the city, by building them very good houses at his own expenses, and by giving them land also ; for he was sensible, that to make this place a habitation was to transgress the Jewish ancient laws, because many sepulchres were to be here taken away, in order to make room for the city Tiberias :* whereas our law pronounces, that such inhabitants are unclean for seven days, (Num. xix. 11.)

4. About this time died Phraates, king of the Parthians, by the treachery of Phraataces his son, upon the occasion following : — When Phraates had had legitimate sons of his own, he had also an Italian maid-servant, whose name was Thermusa, who had been formerly sent to him by Julius Cæsar, among other presents. He first made her his concubine ; but he being a great admirer of her beauty, in process of time having a son by her, whose name was Phraataces, he made her his legitimate wife, and had a great respect for her. Now, she was able to persuade him to do anything that she said, and was earnest in procuring the government of Parthia for her son ; but still she saw that her endeavours would not succeed, unless she could contrive how to remove Phraates's legitimate sons [out of the kingdom ;] so she persuaded him to send those his sons as pledges of his fidelity to Rome ; and they were sent to Rome accordingly, because it was not easy for him to contradict her commands. Now, while Phraataces was alone brought up in order to succeed in the government, he thought it very tedious to expect that government by his father's donation, [as his successor ;] he therefore formed a treacherous design against his father, by his mother's assistance, with whom, as the report went, he had criminal conversation also. So he was hated for both these vices, while his subjects esteemed this [wicked] love of his mother to be no way inferior to his parricide ; and he was by them, in a sedi-

tion, expelled out of the country before he grew too great, and died. But, as the best sort of Parthians agreed together, that it was impossible they should be governed without a king, while also it was their constant practice to choose one of the family of Arsaces [nor did their law allow of any others ; and they thought this kingdom had been sufficiently injured already by the marriage with an Italian concubine, and by her issue,] they sent ambassadors, and called Orodes [to take the crown ;] for the multitude would not otherwise have borne them ; and though he was accused of very great cruelty, and was of an untractable temper, and prone to wrath, yet still he was one of the family of Arsaces. However, they made a conspiracy against him, and slew him, and that, as some say, at a festival, and among their sacrifices (for it is the universal custom there to carry their swords with them ;) but, as the more general report is, they slew him when they had drawn him out a hunting. So they sent ambassadors to Rome, and desired they would send one of those that were there as pledges, to be their king. Accordingly, Vonones was preferred before the rest, and sent to them, (for he seemed capable of such great fortune, which two of the greatest kingdoms under the sun now offered him, his own and a foreign one.) However, the barbarians soon changed their minds, they being naturally of a mutable disposition, upon the supposal that this man was not worthy to be their governor ; for they could not think of obeying the commands of one that had been a slave, (for so they called those that had been hostages,) nor could they bear the ignominy of that name ; and this was the more intolerable, because then the Parthians must have such a king set over them, not by right of war, but in time of peace. So they presently invited Artabanus, king of Media, to be their king, he being also of the race of Arsaces. Artabanus complied with the offer that was made him, and came to them with an army. So Vonones met him ; and at first the multitude of the Parthians stood on his side, and he put his army in array ; but Artabanus was beaten, and fled to the mountains of Media. Yet did he a little after, gather a great army together, and fought with Vonones, and beat him ; whereupon Vonones fled away on horseback, with a few of his attendants about him, to Selucia, [upon Tigris.] So when Artabanus had slain a great number, and this after he had gotten the victory by reason of the very great dismay the barbarians were in, he retired to Ctesiphon with a great number of his people ; and so he now reigned over the Parthians. But Vonones fled away to Armenia ; and as soon as he came thither, he had an inclination to have the government of the country given him, and sent ambassadors to Rome [for that purpose.] But because Tiberius refused it him, and because he wanted courage, and because the Parthian king threatened him, and sent ambassadors to him to denounce war against him if he proceeded, and because he had no way to take to regain any other kingdom, (for the people of authority among the Armenians about Niphates joined themselves to Artabanus,) he delivered up himself to Silanus, the president of Syria, who, out of regard to his education at Rome, kept him in Syria, while Artabanus gave Armenia to Orodes, one of his own sons.

5. At this time died Antiochus, the king of Commagene ; whereupon the multitude contended with the nobility, and both sent ambassadors [to Rome ;] for the men of power were desirous that their form of government might be

---

* We may here take notice, that after the death of Herod the Great, and the succession of Archelaus, Josephus is very brief in his accounts of Judea, till near his own time. I suppose the reason is, that he had but few good histories of those times before him.

changed into that of a Roman province; as were the multitude desirous to be under kings, as their fathers had been. So the senate made a decree, that Germanicus should be sent to settle the affairs of the east, fortune hereby taking a proper opportunity for depriving him of his life; for when he had been in the east, and settled all affairs there, his life was taken away by the poison which Piso gave him.

CHAPTER III

SEDITION OF THE JEWS AGAINST PONTIUS PILATE; CONCERNING CHRIST, AND WHAT BEFELL PAULINA AND THE JEWS AT ROME

1. BUT now Pilate, the procurator of Judea, removed the army from Cesarea to Jerusalem, to take their winter-quarters there, in order to abolish the Jewish laws. So he introduced Cæsar's effigies, which were upon the ensigns, and brought them into the city; whereas our law forbids us the very making of images; on which account the former procurators were wont to make their entry into the city with such ensigns as had not those ornaments. Pilate was the first who brought these images to Jerusalem, and set them up there; which was done without the knowledge of the people, because it was done in the night-time; but as soon as they knew it, they came in multitudes to Cesarea, and interceded with Pilate many days, that he would remove the images; and when he would not grant their requests, because it would tend to the injury of Cæsar, while yet they persevered in their request, on the sixth day he ordered his soldiers to have their weapons privately, while he came and sat upon his judgment-seat, which seat was so prepared in the open place of the city, that it concealed the army that lay ready to oppress them; and when the Jews petitioned him again, he gave a signal to the soldiers to encompass them round, and threatened that their punishment should be no less than immediate death, unless they would leave off disturbing him, and go their ways home. But they threw themselves upon the ground, and laid their necks bare, and said they would take their deaths very willingly, rather than the wisdom of their laws should be transgressed; upon which Pilate was deeply affected with their firm resolution to keep their laws inviolable, and presently commanded the images to be carried back from Jerusalem to Cesarea.

2. But Pilate undertook to bring a current of water to Jerusalem, and did it with the sacred money, and derived the origin of the stream from the distance of two hundred furlongs. However, the Jews * were not pleased with what had been done about this water; and many ten thousands of the people got together, and made a clamour against him, and insisted that he should leave off that design. Some of them also used reproaches, and abused the man, as crowds of such people usually do. So he habited a great number of his soldiers in their habit, who carried daggers under their garments, and sent them to a place where they might surround them. So he bade the Jews himself go away; but they boldly casting reproaches upon him, he gave the soldiers that signal which had been beforehand agreed on; who laid upon them much greater blows than Pilate had commanded them, and equally punished those that were tumultuous, and those that were not, nor did they spare them in the least; and since the people were unarmed, and were caught by men prepared for what they were about, there were a great number of them slain by this means, and others of them ran away wounded; and thus an end was put to this sedition.

3. Now, there was about this time, Jesus, a wise man, if it be lawful to call him a man, for he was a doer of wonderful works,—a teacher of such men as receive the truth with pleasure. He drew over to him both many of the Jews, and many of the Gentiles. He was [the] Christ; and when Pilate, at the suggestion of the principal men amongst us, had condemned him to the cross,† those that loved him at the first did not forsake him, for he appeared to them alive again the third day,‡ as the divine prophets had foretold these and ten thousand other wonderful things concerning him; and the tribe of Christians, so named from him, are not extinct at this day.

4. About the same time also another sad calamity put the Jews into disorder; and certain shameful practices happened about the temple of Isis that was at Rome. I will now first take notice of the wicked attempt about the temple of Isis, and will then give an account of the Jewish affairs. There was at Rome a woman whose name was Paulina; one who, on account of the dignity of her ancestors, and by the regular conduct of a virtuous life, had a great reputation: she was also very rich; and although she was of a beautiful countenance, and in that flower of her age wherein women are the most gay, yet did she lead a life of great modesty. She was married to Saturninus, one that was every way answerable to her in an excellent character. Decius Mundus fell in love with this woman, who was a man very high in the equestrian order; and as she was of too great dignity to be caught by presents, and had already rejected them, though they had been sent in great abundance, he was still more inflamed with love to her, insomuch that he promised to give her two hundred thousand Attic drachmæ for one night's lodging; and when this would not prevail upon her, and he was not able to bear his misfortune in his amours, he thought it the best way to famish himself to death for want of food, on account of Paulina's sad refusal; and he determined with himself to die after such a manner, and he went on with his purpose accordingly. Now, Mundus had a freed-woman, who had been made free by his father, whose name was Ide, one skilful in all sorts of mischief. This woman was very much grieved at the young man's resolution to kill himself (for he did not conceal his intentions to destroy himself from others) and came to him, and encouraged him by her discourse, and made him to hope, by some promises she gave him, that he might obtain a night's lodging with Paulina; and when he joyfully hearkened to her entreaty, she said she wanted no more than fifty thousand drachmæ for the entrapping of the woman. So when she had encouraged the young man, and gotten as much money as she required, she did not take the same methods as had been taken before, because she perceived that the woman was by

---

* These Jews, as they are here called, whose blood Pilate shed on this occasion, may very well be those very Galilean Jews, "whose blood Pilate had mingled with their sacrifices," (Luke xiii. 1, 2:) these tumults being usually excited at some of the Jews' great festivals, when they slew abundance of sacrifices, and the Galileans being commonly much more busy in such tumults than those of Judea and Jerusalem.

† A.D. 33, April 3.   ‡ April 5.

no means to be tempted by money; but as she knew that she was very much given to the worship of the goddess Isis, she devised the following stratagem:—She went to some of Isis's priests, and upon the strongest assurances [of concealment,] she persuaded them by words, but chiefly by the offer of money, of twenty-five thousand drachmæ in hand, and as much more when the thing had taken effect; and told them the passion of the young man, and persuaded them to use all means possible, to beguile the woman. So they were drawn in to promise so to do, by that large sum of gold they were to have. Accordingly the oldest of them went immediately to Paulina; and upon his admittance, he desired to speak with her by herself. When that was granted him, he told her that he was sent by the god Anubis, who was fallen in love with her, and enjoined her to come to him. Upon this she took the message very kindly, and valued herself greatly upon this condescension of Anubis; and told her husband that she had a message sent her, and was to sup and lie with Anubis; so he agreed to her acceptance of the offer, as fully satisfied with the chastity of his wife. Accordingly, she went to the temple; and after she had supped there, and it was the hour to go to sleep, the priest shut the doors of the temple; when, in the holy part of it, the lights were also put out. Then did Mundus leap out (for he was hidden therein) and did not fail of enjoying her, who was at his service all the night long, as supposing he was the god; and when he was gone away, which was before those priests who knew nothing of this stratagem were stirring, Paulina came early to her husband, and told him how the god Anubis had appeared to her. Among her friends also she declared how great a value she put upon this favour, who partly disbelieved the thing, when they reflected on its nature, and partly were amazed at it, as having no pretence for not believing it, when they considered the modesty and the dignity of the person; but now, on the third day after what had been done, Mundus met Paulina, and said,—"Nay, Paulina, thou hast saved me two hundred thousand drachmæ, which sum thou mightest have added to thy family; yet hast thou not failed to be at my service in the manner I invited thee. As for the reproaches thou hast laid upon Mundus, I value not the business of names; but I rejoice in the pleasure I reaped by what I did, while I took to myself the name of Anubis." When he had said this, he went his way: but now she began to come to the sense of the grossness of what she had done, and rent her garments, and told her husband of the horrid nature of this wicked contrivance, and prayed him not to neglect to assist her in this case. So he discovered the fact to the emperor; whereupon Tiberius inquired into the matter thoroughly, by examining the priests about it, and ordered them to be crucified, as well as Ide, who was the occasion of their perdition, and who had contrived the whole matter, which was so injurious to the woman. He also demolished the temple of Isis, and gave order that her statue should be thrown into the river Tiber; while he only banished Mundus, but did no more to him, because he supposed that what crime he had committed, was done out of the passion of love; and these were the circumstances which concerned the temple of Isis, and the injuries occasioned by her priests.—I now return to the relation of what happened about this time to the Jews at Rome, as I formerly told you I would.

5. There was a man who was a Jew, but had been driven away from his own country by an accusation laid against him for transgressing their laws, and by the fear he was under of punishment for the same; but in all respects a wicked man:—he then living at Rome, professed to instruct men in the wisdom of the laws of Moses. He procured also three other men, entirely of the same character with himself, to be his partners. These men persuaded Fulvia, a woman of great dignity, and one that had embraced the Jewish religion, to send purple and gold to the temple at Jerusalem; and, when they had gotten them, they employed them for their own uses, and spent the money themselves; on which account it was that they at first required it of her. Whereupon Tiberius, who had been informed of the thing by Saturninus, the husband of Fulvia, who desired inquiry might be made about it, ordered all the Jews to be banished out of Rome; at which time the consuls enlisted four thousand men out of them, and sent them to the island Sardinia; but punished a greater number of them, who were unwilling to become soldiers on account of keeping the laws of their forefathers. Thus were these Jews banished out of the city by the wickedness of four men.

CHAPTER IV

HOW THE SAMARITANS MADE A TUMULT, AND PILATE DESTROYED MANY OF THEM; AND HOW PILATE WAS ACCUSED, AND WHAT THINGS WERE DONE BY VITELLIUS RELATING TO THE JEWS AND THE PARTHIANS

1. BUT the nation of the Samaritans did not escape without tumults. The man who excited them to it, was one who thought lying a thing of little consequence, and who contrived everything so, that the multitude might be pleased; so he bade them get together upon mount Gerizzim, which is by them looked upon as the most holy of all mountains, and assured them that, when they were come thither, he would shew them those sacred vessels which were laid under that place, because Moses put them there.* So they came thither armed, and thought the discourse of the man probable; and as they abode at a certain village, which was called Tirathaba, they got the rest together to them, and desired to go up the mountain in a great multitude together. But Pilate prevented their going up, by seizing upon the roads with a great band of horsemen and footmen, who fell upon those that were gotten together in the village; and when they came to an action, some of them they slew, and others of them they put to flight, and took a great many alive, the principal of whom, and also the most potent of those that fled away, Pilate ordered to be slain.

2. But when this tumult was appeased, the Samaritan senate sent an embassy to Vitellius, a man that had been consul, and who was now president of Syria, and accused Pilate of the murder of those that were killed; for that they did not go to Tirathaba in order to revolt from the Romans, but to escape the violence of Pilate.

---

* Since Moses never came himself beyond Jordan, nor particularly to mount Gerizzim, and since these Samaritans have a tradition among them, that in the days of Uzzi or Ozis the high priest, (1 Chron. vi. 6,) the ark and other sacred vessels were, by God's command, laid up or hidden in mount Gerizzim, it is highly probable that this was the foolish foundation the present Samaritans went upon, in the sedition here described.

CHRIST CONDEMNED TO THE CROSS

So Vitellius sent Marcellus, a friend of his, to take care of the affairs of Judea, and ordered Pilate to go to Rome, to answer before the emperor to the accusation of the Jews. So Pilate, when he had tarried ten years in Judea, made haste to Rome, and this in obedience to the orders of Vitellius, which he durst not contradict; but before he could get to Rome, Tiberius was dead.

3. But Vitellius came into Judea, and went up to Jerusalem; it was at the time of that festival which is called the Passover. Vitellius was there magnificently received, and released the inhabitants of Jerusalem from all the taxes upon the fruits that were bought and sold, and gave them leave to have the care of the high priest's vestments, with all their ornaments, and to have them under the custody of the priests in the temple; which power they used to have formerly, although at this time they were laid up in the tower of Antonia, the citadel so called, and that on the occasion following: —There was one of the [high] priests named Hyrcanus, and as there were many of that name, he was the first of them; this man built a tower near the temple, and when he had so done, he generally dwelt in it, and had these vestments with him; because it was lawful for him alone to put them on, and he had them there reposited when he went down into the city, and took his ordinary garments; the same things were continued to be done by his sons, and by their sons after them; but when Herod came to be king, he rebuilt this tower, which was very conveniently situated, in a magnificent manner; and because he was a friend to Antonius, he called it by the name of Antonia; and as he found these vestments lying there, he retained them in the same place, as believing that, while he had them in his custody, the people would make no innovations against him. The like to what Herod did was done by his son Archelaus, who was made king after him; after whom the Romans, when they entered on the government, took possession of these vestments of the high priest, and had them reposited in a stone chamber, under the seal of the priests, and of the keepers of the temple, the captain of the guard lighting a lamp there every day; and seven days before a festival * they were delivered to them by the captain of the guard. when the high priest having purified them, and made use of them, laid them up again in the same chamber where they had been laid up before, and this the very next day after the feast was over. This was the practice at the three yearly festivals, and on the fast-day; but Vitellius put those garments into our own power, as in the days of our forefathers, and ordered the captain of the guard not to trouble himself to inquire where they were laid, or when they were to be used; and this he did as an act of kindness, to oblige the nation to him. Besides which he also deprived Joseph, who was called Caiphas, of the high priesthood, and appointed Jonathan, the son of Ananus, the former high priest, to succeed him. After which he took his journey back to Antioch.

4. Moreover, Tiberius sent a letter to Vitellius, and commanded him to make a league of friendship with Artabanus, the king of Parthia; for while he was his enemy, he terrified him, because he had taken Armenia away from him, lest he should proceed further, and told him he should no otherwise trust him than upon his giving him hostages, and especially his son Artabanus. Upon Tiberius's writing thus to Vitellius, by the offer of great presents of money, he persuaded both the king of Iberia and the king of Albania to make no delay, but to fight against Artabanus; and although they would not do it themselves, yet did they give the Scythians a passage through their country, and opened the Caspian gates to them, and brought them upon Artabanus. So Armenia was again taken from the Parthians, and the country of Parthia was filled with war, and the principal of their men were slain, and all things were in disorder among them: the king's son also himself fell in these wars, together with many ten thousands of his army. Vitellius had also sent such great sums of money to Artabanus's father's kinsmen and friends, that he had almost procured him to be slain by the means of those bribes which they had taken. And when Artabanus perceived that the plot laid against him was not to be avoided, because it was laid by the principal men, and those a great many in number, and that it would certainly take effect,—when he had estimated the number of those that were truly faithful to him, as also of those who were already corrupted, but were deceitful in the kindness they professed to him, and were likely upon trial, to go over to his enemies, he made his escape to the upper provinces, where he afterwards raised a great army out of the Dahæ and Sacæ, and fought with his enemies, and retained his principality.

5. When Tiberius had heard of these things, he desired to have a league of friendship made between him and Artabanus; and when, upon this invitation, he received the proposal kindly, Artabanus and Vitellius went to Euphrates, and as a bridge was laid over the river, they each of them came with their guards about them, and met one another on the midst of the bridge. And when they had agreed upon the terms of peace, Herod the tetrarch erected a rich tent on the midst of the passage, and made them a feast there. Artabanus also, not long afterwards, sent his son Darius as a hostage, with many presents, among which there was a man seven cubits tall, a Jew he was by birth, and his name was Eleazar, who, for his tallness, was called a giant. After which Vitellius went to Antioch, and Artabanus to Babylon; but Herod [the tetrarch,] being desirous to give Cæsar the first information that they had obtained hostages, sent posts with letters, wherein he had accurately described all the particulars, and had left nothing for the consular Vitellius to inform him of. But when Vitellius's letters were sent, and Cæsar had let him know that he was acquainted with the affairs already, because Herod had given him an account of them before, Vitellius was very much troubled at it; and supposing that he had been thereby a greater sufferer than he really was, he kept up a secret anger upon this occasion, till he could be revenged upon him; which he was after Caius had taken the government.

6. About this time it was that Philip, Herod's brother, departed this life, in the twentieth year of the reign of Tiberius,† after he had been tetrarch of Trachonitis, and Gaulonitis, and of the

---

* This mention of the high priest's sacred garments received seven days before a festival, and purified in those days against a festival, as having been polluted by being in the custody of heathens, in Josephus, agrees with the traditions of the Talmudists.

† This calculation is exactly right; for since Herod died about September, in the fourth year before the Christian era, and Tiberius began, as is well known, Aug. 19, A.D. 14, it is evident that the 37th year of Philip, reckoned from his father's death, was the 20th of Tiberius, or near the end of A.D. 33, (the very year of our Saviour's death also,) or, however, in the beginning of the next year, A.D. 34.

nation of the Bataneans also, thirty-seven years. He had shewn himself a person of moderation and quietness in the conduct of his life and government; he constantly lived in that country which was subject to him; he used to make his progress with a few chosen friends; his tribunal also, on which he sat in judgment, followed him in his progress; and when any one met him who wanted his assistance, he made no delay, but had his tribunal set down immediately, wheresoever he happened to be, and sat down upon it, and heard his complaint: he there ordered the guilty that were convicted to be punished, and absolved those that had been accused unjustly. He died at Julias; and when he was carried to that monument which he had already erected for himself beforehand, he was buried with great pomp. His principality Tiberius took, (for he left no sons behind him,) and added it to the province of Syria, but gave order that the tributes which arose from it should be collected, and laid up in his tetrarchy.

CHAPTER V

HEROD THE TETRARCH MAKES WAR WITH ARETAS, THE KING OF ARABIA, AND IS BEATEN BY HIM; AS ALSO CONCERNING THE DEATH OF JOHN THE BAPTIST. HOW VITELLIUS WENT UP TO JERUSALEM; TOGETHER WITH SOME ACCOUNT OF AGRIPPA, AND OF THE POSTERITY OF HEROD THE GREAT

1. ABOUT this time Aretas (the king of Arabia Petrea) and Herod had a quarrel, on the account following: Herod the tetrarch had married the daughter of Aretas, and had lived with her a great while; but when he was once at Rome, he lodged with Herod,* who was his brother indeed, but not by the same mother; for this Herod was the son of the high priest Simon's daughter. However, he fell in love with Herodias, this last Herod's wife, who was the daughter of Aristobulus their brother, and the sister of Agrippa the Great. This man ventured to talk to her about a marriage between them; which address when she admitted, an agreement was made for her to change her habitation, and come to him as soon as he should return from Rome: one article of this marriage also was this, that he should divorce Aretas's daughter. So Antipas, when he had made this agreement, sailed to Rome; but when he had done there the business he went about, and was returned again, his wife having discovered the agreement he had made with Herodias, and having learned it before he had notice of her knowledge of the whole design, she desired him to send her to Macherus, which is a place on the borders of the dominions of Aretas and Herod, without informing him of any of her intentions. Accordingly Herod sent her thither, as thinking his wife had not perceived anything; now she had sent a good while before to Macherus, which was subject to her father, and so all things necessary for her journey were made ready for her by the general of Aretas's army, and by that means she soon came to Arabia, under the conduct of the several generals, who carried her from one to another successively; and she soon came to her father, and told him of Herod's intentions. So Aretas made

* This Herod seems to have had the additional name of Philip, as Antipas was named Herod-Antipas: and as Antipas and Antipater seem to be in a manner the very same name, yet were the names of two sons of Herod the Great, so might Philip the tetrarch and this Herod-Philip be two different sons of the same father.

this the first occasion of his enmity between him and Herod, who had also some quarrel with him about their limits at the country of Gamalitis. So they raised armies on both sides, and prepared for war, and sent their generals to fight instead of themselves; and, when they had joined battle, all Herod's army was destroyed by the treachery of some fugitives, though they were of the tetrarchy of Philip, joined with Aretas's army. So Herod wrote about these affairs to Tiberius; who, being very angry at the attempt made by Aretas, wrote to Vitellius, to make war upon him, and either to take him alive, and bring him to him in bonds, or to kill him, and send him his head. This was the charge that Tiberius gave to the president of Syria.

2. Now, some of the Jews thought that the destruction of Herod's army came from God, and that very justly, as a punishment of what he did against John, that was called the *Baptist*; for Herod slew him, who was a good man, and commanded the Jews to exercise virtue, both as to righteousness towards one another, and piety towards God, and so to come to baptism; for that the washing [with water] would be acceptable to him, if they made use of it, not in order to the putting away, [or the remission] of some sins [only,] but for the purification of the body: supposing still that the soul was thoroughly purified beforehand by righteousness. Now, when [many] others came to crowd about him, for they were greatly moved [or pleased] by hearing his words, Herod, who feared lest the great influence John had over the people might put it into his power and inclination to raise a rebellion, (for they seemed ready to do anything he should advise,) thought it best, by putting him to death, to prevent any mischief he might cause, and not bring himself into difficulties, by sparing a man who might make him repent of it when it should be too late. Accordingly he was sent a prisoner, out of Herod's suspicious temper, to Macherus, the castle I before mentioned, and was there put to death. Now the Jews had an opinion that the destruction of this army was sent as a punishment upon Herod, and a mark of God's displeasure against him.

3. So Vitellius prepared to make war with Aretas, having with him two legions of armed men; he also took with him all those of light armature, and of the horsemen which belonged to them, and were drawn out of the kingdoms which were under the Romans, and made haste for Petra, and came to Ptolemais. But as he was marching very busily, and leading his army through Judea, the principal men met him, and desired that he would not thus march through their land; for that the laws of their country would not permit them to overlook those images which were brought into it, of which there were a great many in their ensigns; so he was persuaded by what they said, and changed that resolution of his, which he had before taken in this matter. Whereupon he ordered the army to march along the great plain, while he himself, with Herod the tetrarch, and his friends, went up to Jerusalem to offer sacrifice to God, an ancient festival of the Jews being then just approaching; and when he had been there, and been honourably entertained by the multitude of Jews, he made a stay there for three days, within which time he deprived Jonathan of the high priesthood, and gave it to his brother Theophilus; but when on the fourth day letters came to him, which informed him of the death of Tiberius, he obliged the multitude to take an oath of fidelity to Caius; he also recalled his army, and made them every one go home, and

take their winter-quarters there, since, upon the devolution of the empire upon Caius, he had not the like authority of making this war which he had before. It was also reported, that when Aretas heard of the coming of Vitellius to fight him, he said, upon his consulting with the diviners, that it was impossible that this army of Vitellius's could enter Petra; for that one of the rulers would die, either he that gave orders for the war, or he that was marching at the other's desire, in order to be subservient to his will, or else he against whom this army is prepared. So Vitellius truly retired to Antioch; but Agrippa, the son of Aristobulus, went up to Rome, a year before the death of Tiberius, in order to treat of some affairs with the emperor, if he might be permitted so to do. I have now a mind to describe Herod and his family, how it fared with them, partly because it is suitable to this history to speak of that matter, and partly because this thing is a demonstration of the interposition of Providence; how a multitude of children is of no advantage, no more than any other strength, that mankind set their hearts upon, besides those acts of piety which are done towards God; for it happened, that within the revolution of a hundred years, that the posterity of Herod, who were a great many in number, were, excepting a few, utterly destroyed.* One may well apply this for the instruction of mankind, and learn thence how unhappy they were: it will also shew us the history of Agrippa, who, as he was a person most worthy of admiration, so was he from a private man, beyond all the expectation of those that knew him, advanced to great power and authority. I have said something of them formerly; but I shall now also speak accurately about them.

4. Herod the Great had two daughters by Mariamne, the [grand] daughter of Hyrcanus; the one was Salampsio, who was married to Phasaelus, her first cousin, who was himself the son of Phasaelus, Herod's brother, her father making the match: the other was Cypros, who was herself married also to her first cousin Antipater, the son of Salome, Herod's sister. Phasaelus had five children by Salampsio; Antipater, Herod, and Alexander, and two daughters, Alexandra and Cypros: which last, Agrippa, the son of Aristobulus, married; and Timius of Cyprus married Alexandra; he was a man of note, but had by her no children. Agrippa had by Cypros two sons and three daughters, which daughters were named Bernice, Mariamne, and Drusilla; but the names of the sons were Agrippa and Drusus, of which Drusus died before he came to the years of puberty; but their father, Agrippa, was brought up with his other brethren, Herod and Aristobulus, for these were also the sons of the son of Herod the Great by Bernice; but Bernice was the daughter of Costobarus and of Salome, who was Herod's sister. Aristobulus left these infants when he was slain by his father, together with his brother Alexander, as we have already related; but when they were arrived at the years of puberty, this Herod, the brother of Agrippa, married Mariamne, the daughter of Olympias, who was the daughter of Herod the king, and of Joseph, the son of Joseph, who was brother to Herod the king, and had by her a son, Aristobulus; but Aristobulus, the third

brother of Agrippa, married Jotape, the daughter of Sampsigeramus, king of Emesa; they had a daughter who was deaf, whose name also was Jotape; and these hitherto were the children of the male line; but Herodias, their sister, was married to Herod, [Philip,] the son of Herod the Great, who was born of Mariamne, the daughter of Simon the high priest, who had a daughter Salome; after whose birth, Herodias took upon her to confound the laws of our country, and divorce herself from her husband, while he was alive, and was married to Herod, [Antipas,] her husband's brother by the father's side; he was tetrarch of Galilee; but her daughter Salome was married to Philip, the son of Herod, the tetrarch of Trachonitis: and, as he died childless, Aristobulus, the son of Herod, the brother of Agrippa, married her: they had three sons, Herod, Agrippa, and Aristobulus; and this was the posterity of Phasaelus and Salampsio; but the daughter of Antipater by Cypros, was Cypros, whom Alexas Selcias, the son of Alexas, married; they had a daughter, Cypros; but Herod and Alexander, who, as we told you, were the brothers of Antipater, died childless. As to Alexander, the son of Herod the king, who was slain by his father, he had two sons, Alexander and Tigranes, by the daughter of Archelaus, king of Cappadocia. Tigranes, who was king of Armenia, was accused at Rome, and died childless; Alexander had a son of the same name with his brother Tigranes, and was sent to take possession of the kingdom of Armenia by Nero; he had a son, Alexander, who married Jotape, the daughter of Antiochus, the king of Commagena; Vespasian made him king of an island in Cilicia. But these descendants of Alexander, soon after their birth, deserted the Jewish religion, and went over to that of the Greeks; but for the rest of the daughters of Herod the king, it happened that they died childless; and as these descendants of Herod whom we have enumerated were in being at the same time that Agrippa the Great took the kingdom, and I have now given an account of them, it now remains that I relate the several hard fortunes which befell Agrippa, and how he got clear of them, and was advanced to the greatest height of dignity and honour.

CHAPTER VI

OF THE NAVIGATION OF KING AGRIPPA TO ROME, TO TIBERIUS CÆSAR; AND HOW, UPON HIS BEING ACCUSED BY HIS OWN FREEDMAN, HE WAS BOUND; HOW ALSO HE WAS SET AT LIBERTY BY CAIUS, AFTER TIBERIUS'S DEATH, AND WAS MADE KING OF THE TETRARCHY OF PHILIP

1. A LITTLE before the death of Herod the king, Agrippa lived at Rome, and was generally brought up and conversed with Drusus, the emperor Tiberius's son, and contracted a friendship with Antonia, the wife of Drusus the Great, who had his mother Bernice in great esteem, and was very desirous of advancing her son. Now, as Agrippa was by nature magnanimous and generous in the presents he made while his mother was alive, this inclination of his mind did not appear, that he might be able to avoid her anger for such his extravagance; but when Bernice was dead, and he was left to his own conduct, he spent a great deal extravagantly in his daily way of living, and a great deal in the immoderate presents he made, and those chiefly among Cæsar's freedmen, in

* Whether this sudden extinction of almost the entire lineage of Herod the Great, was not in part as a punishment for the gross incests they were frequently guilty of, in marrying their own nephews and nieces, well deserves to be considered. See Lev. xviii. 6, 7, xxi. 10.

order to gain their assistance, insomuch that he was in a little time reduced to poverty, and could not live at Rome any longer. Tiberius also forbade the friends of his deceased son to come into his sight, because on seeing them he should be put in mind of his son, and his grief would thereby be revived.

2. For these reasons he went away from Rome, and sailed to Judea, but in evil circumstances, being dejected with the loss of that money which he once had, and because he had not wherewithal to pay his creditors, who were many in number, and such as gave no room for escaping them. Whereupon he knew not what to do; so for shame of his present condition, he retired to a certain tower at Malatha, in Idumea, and had thoughts of killing himself; but his wife Cyprus perceived his intentions, and tried all sorts of methods to divert him from his taking such a course: so she sent a letter to his sister Herodias, who was now the wife of Herod the tetrarch, and let her know Agrippa's present design, and what necessity it was which drove him thereto, and desired her, as a kinswoman of his, to give him her help, and to engage her husband to do the same, since she saw how she alleviated these her husband's troubles all she could, although she had not the like wealth to do it withal. So they sent for him and allotted him Tiberias for his habitation, and appointed him some income of money for his maintenance, and made him a magistrate of that city, by way of honour to him. Yet did not Herod long continue in that resolution of supporting him, though even that support was not sufficient for him; for, as once they were at a feast at Tyre, and in their cups, and reproaches were cast upon one another, Agrippa thought that was not to be borne, while Herod hit him in the teeth with his poverty, and with his owing his necessary food to him. So he went to Flaccus, one that had been consul, and had been a very great friend to him at Rome formerly, and was now president of Syria.

3. Hereupon Flaccus received him kindly, and he lived with him. Flaccus had also with him there, Aristobulus, who was indeed Agrippa's brother, but was at variance with him; yet did not their enmity to one another hinder the friendship of Flaccus to them both; but still they were honourably treated by him. However, Aristobulus did not abate of his ill-will to Agrippa, till at length he brought him into ill terms with Flaccus; the occasion of bringing on which estrangement was this:—The Damascenes were at difference with the Sidonians about their limits, and when Flaccus was about to hear the cause between them, they understood that Agrippa had a mighty influence upon him; so they desired that he would be of their side, and for that favour promised him a great deal of money; so he was zealous in assisting the Damascenes as far as he was able. Now Aristobulus had gotten intelligence of this promise of money to him, and accused him to Flaccus of the same; and when, upon a thorough examination of the matter, it appeared plainly so to be, he rejected Agrippa out of the number of his friends. So he was reduced to the utmost necessity, and came to Ptolemais; because he knew not where else to get a livelihood, he thought to sail to Italy; but as he was restrained from so doing by want of money, he desired Marsyas, who was his freed-man, to find some method for procuring him so much as he wanted for that purpose, by borrowing such a sum of some person or other. So Marsyas desired of Peter, who was the freed-man of Bernice, Agrippa's mother,

and by the right of her testament was bequeathed to Antonia, to lend so much upon Agrippa's own bond and security: but he accused Agrippa of having defrauded him of certain sums of money, and so obliged Marsyas, when he made the bond of twenty thousand Attic drachmæ, to accept of twenty-five hundred drachmæ less than what he desired; which the other allowed of, because he could not help it. Upon the receipt of this money, Agrippa came to Anthedon, and took shipping, and was going to set sail; but Herennius Capito, who was the procurator of Jamnia, sent a band of soldiers to demand of him three hundred thousand drachmæ of silver, which were by him owing to Cæsar's treasury while he was at Rome, and so forced him to stay. He then pretended that he would do as he bade him; but when night came on, he cut his cables, and went off, and sailed to Alexandria, where he desired Alexander the alabarch to lend him two hundred thousand drachmæ; but he said he would not refuse it to Cypros, as greatly astonished at her affection to her husband, and at the other instances of her virtue; so she undertook to repay it. Accordingly, Alexander paid them five talents at Alexandria, and promised to pay them the rest of that sum at Dicearchia, [Puteoli;] and this he did out of the fear he was in that Agrippa would soon spend it. So this Cypros set her husband free, and dismissed him to go on with his navigation to Italy, while she and her children departed for Judea.

4. And now Agrippa was come to Puteoli, whence he wrote a letter to Tiberius Cæsar, who then lived at Capreæ, and told him that he was come so far in order to wait on him, and to pay him a visit; and desired that he would give him leave to come over to Capreæ: So Tiberius made no difficulty, but wrote to him in an obliging way in other respects; and withal told him he was glad of his safe return, and desired him to come to Capreæ; and, when he was come, he did not fail to treat him as kindly as he had promised him in his letter to do. But the next day came a letter to Cæsar from Herennius Capito, to inform him that Agrippa had borrowed three hundred thousand drachmæ, and not paid it at the time appointed; but, when it was demanded of him, he ran away like a fugitive, out of the places under his government, and put it out of his power to get the money of him. When Cæsar had read this letter, he was much troubled at it, and gave orders that Agrippa should be excluded from his presence until he had paid that debt: upon which he was no way daunted at Cæsar's anger, but entreated Antonia, the mother of Germanicus, and Claudius, who was afterwards Cæsar himself, to lend him those three hundred thousand drachmæ, that he might not be deprived of Tiberius's friendship; so, out of regard to the memory of Bernice his mother, (for those two women were very familiar with one another,) and out of regard of his and Claudius's education together, she lent him the money; and, upon the payment of this debt, there was nothing to hinder Tiberius's friendship to him. After this, Tiberius Cæsar recommended to him his grandson, and ordered that he should always accompany him when he went abroad. But, upon Agrippa's kind reception by Antonia, he betook him to pay his respects to Caius, who was her grandson, and in very high reputation by reason of the good-will they bare his father. Now there was one Thallus, a freedman of Cæsar's of whom he borrowed a million of drachmæ, and thence repaid Antonia the debt he owed her; and by spending the overplus

in paying his court to Caius, became a person of great authority with him.

5. Now, as the friendship which Agrippa had for Caius was come to a great height, there happened some words to pass between them, as they were once in a chariot together, concerning Tiberius; Agrippa praying [to God] (for they two sat by themselves) that Tiberius might soon go off the stage, and leave the government to Caius, who was in every respect more worthy of it. Now, Eutychus, who was Agrippa's freed-man, and drove his chariot, heard these words, and at that time said nothing of them; but when Agrippa accused him of stealing some garments of his, (which was certainly true,) he ran away from him; but when he was caught, and brought before Piso, who was governor of the city, and the man was asked why he ran away, he replied, that he had somewhat to say to Cæsar that tended to his security and preservation: so Piso bound him, and sent him to Capreæ. But Tiberius, according to his usual custom, kept him still in bonds, being a delayer of affairs, if ever there was any other king or tyrant that was so; for he did not admit ambassadors quickly, and no successors were despatched away as governors or procurators of the provinces that had been formerly sent, unless they were dead; whence it was that he was so negligent in hearing the causes of prisoners; insomuch that when he was asked by his friends what was the reason of his delay in such cases, he said that he delayed to hear ambassadors lest, upon their quick dismission, other ambassadors should be appointed, and return upon him; and so he should bring trouble upon himself in their public reception and dismission: that he permitted those governors who had been sent once to their governments [to stay there a great while] out of regard to the subjects that were under them; for that all governors are naturally disposed to get as much as they can; and that those who are not to fix there, but to stay a short time, and that at an uncertainty when they shall be turned out, do the more severely hurry themselves on to fleece the people; but that, if their government be long continued to them, they are at last satiated with the spoils, as having gotten a vast deal, and so become at length less sharp in their pillaging; but that, if successors are sent quickly, the poor subjects, who are exposed to them as a prey, will not be able to bear the new ones, while they shall not have the same time allowed them wherein their predecessors had filled themselves, and so grow more unconcerned about getting more; and this because they are removed before they have had time [for their oppressions.] He gave them an example to shew his meaning:—A great number of flies came about the sore places of a man that had been wounded, upon which, one of the standers-by pitied the man's misfortune, and thinking he was not able to drive away those flies himself, was going to drive them away for him; but he prayed him to let them alone; the other, by way of reply, asked him the reason of such a preposterous proceeding, in preventing relief from his present misery; to which he answered, "If thou drivest these flies away, thou wilt hurt me worse; for as these are already full of my blood, they do not crowd about me, nor pain me so much as before, but are sometimes more remiss, while the fresh ones that come, almost famished, and find me quite tired down already, will be my destruction. For this cause, therefore, it is that I am myself careful not to send such new governors perpetually to those my subjects, who are already sufficiently harassed by many oppressions, as may, like these flies, further distress them; and so, besides their natural desire of gain, may have this additional incitement to it, that they expect to be suddenly deprived of that pleasure which they take in it." And as a further attestation to what I say of the dilatory nature of Tiberius, I appeal to this his practice itself; for although he was emperor twenty-two years, he sent in all but two procurators to govern the nation of the Jews,—Gratus, and his successor in the government, Pilate. Nor was he in one way of acting with respect to the Jews, and in another with respect to the rest of his subjects. He further informed them, that even in the hearing of the causes of prisoners, he made such delays, because immediate death to those that must be condemned to die, would be an alleviation of their present miseries, while those wicked wretches have not deserved any favour; "but I do it that, by being harassed with the present calamity, they may undergo greater misery."

6. On this account it was that Eutychus could not obtain a hearing, but was kept still in prison. However, some time afterward, Tiberius came from Capreæ to Tusculanum, which is about a hundred furlongs from Rome. Agrippa then desired of Antonia that she would then procure a hearing for Eutychus, let the matter whereof he accused him prove what it would. Now, Antonia was greatly esteemed by Tiberius on all accounts, from the dignity of her relation to him, who had been his brother Drusus's wife, and from her eminent chastity;* for though she was still a young woman, she continued in her widowhood, and refused all other matches, although Augustus had enjoined her to be married to somebody else; yet did she all along preserve her reputation free from reproach. She had also been the greatest benefactress to Tiberius, when there was a very dangerous plot laid against him by Sejanus, a man who had been her husband's friend, and who had the greatest authority, because he was general of the army, and when many members of the senate, and many of the freed-men, joined with him, and the soldiery was corrupted, and the plot was come to a great height. Now Sejanus had certainly gained his point, had not Antonia's boldness been more wisely conducted than Sejanus's malice; for, when she had discovered his designs against Tiberius, she wrote him an exact account of the whole, and gave the letter to Pallas, the most faithful of her servants, and sent him to Capreæ to Tiberius, who, when he understood it, slew Sejanus and his confederates; so that Tiberius, who had her in great esteem before, now looked upon her with still greater respect, and depended upon her in all things. So, when Tiberius was desired by this Antonia to examine Eutychus, he answered, "If indeed Eutychus hath falsely accused Agrippa in what he hath said of him, he hath had sufficient punishment by what I have done to him already; but if, upon examination, the accusation appears to be true, let Agrippa have a care, lest, out of desire of punishing his freed-man, he do not rather bring a punishment

* This high commendation of Antonia for marrying but once, and this notwithstanding the strongest temptations, shews how honourable single marriages were both among the Jews and Romans, in the days of Josephus and of the apostles, and takes away much of that surprise which the modern Protestants have at those laws of the apostles, where no widows, but those who had been the wives of one husband only, are taken into the church list; and no bishops, priests, or deacons, are allowed to marry more than once, without leaving off to officiate as clergymen any longer. See Luke ii. 36; 1 Tim. v. 11, 12, iii. 2, 12; Tit. i. 10.

upon himself." Now, when Antonia told Agrippa of this, he was still much more pressing that the matter might be examined into; so Antonia, upon Agrippa's lying hard at her continually to beg this favour, took the following opportunity:—As Tiberius lay once at his ease upon his sedan, and was carried about, and Caius, her grandson, and Agrippa, were before him after dinner, she walked by the sedan, and desired him to call Eutychus, and have him examined; to which he replied, "O Antonia! the gods are my witnesses that I am induced to do what I am going to do, not by my own inclination, but because I am forced to it by thy prayers." When he had said this, he ordered Macro, who succeeded Sejanus, to bring Eutychus to him; accordingly, without any delay, he was brought. Then Tiberius asked him what he had to say against a man who had given him his liberty. Upon which he said, "O my lord! this Caius, and Agrippa with him, were once riding in a chariot, when I sat at their feet, and, among other discourses that passed, Agrippa said to Caius, Oh that the day would once come when this old fellow will die, and name thee for the governor of the habitable earth! for then this Tiberius, his grandson, would be no hindrance, but would be taken off by thee, and that earth would be happy, and I happy also." Now, Tiberius took these to be truly Agrippa's words, and bearing a grudge withal at Agrippa, because, when he had commanded him to pay his respects to Tiberius, his grandson, and the son of Drusus, Agrippa had not paid him that respect, but had disobeyed his commands, and transferred all his regards to Caius; he said to Macro, "Bind this man." But Macro, not distinctly knowing which of them it was whom he bade him bind, and not expecting that he would have any such thing done to Agrippa, he forbore, and came to ask more distinctly what it was that he said. But when Cæsar had gone round the hippodrome, he found Agrippa standing:—"For certain," said he, "Macro, this is the man I meant to have bound;" and when he still asked, which of these is to be bound? he said, Agrippa. Upon which Agrippa betook himself to make supplication for himself, putting him in mind of his son, with whom he was brought up, and of Tiberius [his grandson] whom he had educated, but all to no purpose, for they led him about bound even in his purple garments. It was also very hot weather, and they had but little wine to their meal, so that he was very thirsty; he was also in a sort of agony, and took this treatment of him heinously: as he therefore saw one of Caius's slaves, whose name was Thaumastus, carrying some water in a vessel, he desired that he would let him drink: so the servant gave him some water to drink; and he drank heartily, and said, "O thou boy! this service of thine to me will be for thy advantage; for, if I once get clear of these my bonds, I will soon procure thee thy freedom from Caius, who has not been wanting to minister to me now I am in bonds, in the same manner as when I was in my former state and dignity." Nor did he deceive him in what he promised him, but made him amends for what he had now done: for, when afterwards Agrippa was come to the kingdom, he took particular care of Thaumastus, and got him his liberty from Caius, and made him the steward over his own estate; and when he died, he left him to Agrippa his son, and to Bernice his daughter, to minister to them in the same capacity. The man also grew old in that honourable post, and therein died. But all this happened a good while later.

7. Now Agrippa stood in his bonds before the royal palace, and leaned on a certain tree for grief, with many others, who were in bonds also; and as a certain bird sat upon the tree on which Agrippa leaned (the Romans called this bird bubo,) [an owl,] one of those that were bound, a German by nation, saw him, and asked a soldier who that man in purple was; and when he was informed that his name was Agrippa, and that he was by nation a Jew, and one of the principal men in that nation, he asked leave of the soldier to whom he was bound, to let him come near to him, to speak with him; for that he had a mind to inquire of him about some things relating to his country; which liberty, when he had obtained, as he stood near him, he said thus to him by an interpreter,—"This sudden change of thy condition, O young man! is grievous to thee, as bringing on thee a manifold and very great adversity; nor wilt thou believe me, when I foretell how thou wilt get clear of this misery which thou art now under, and how Divine Providence will provide for thee. Know therefore (and I appeal to my own country gods, as well as to the gods of this place, who have awarded these bonds to us) that all I am going to say about thy concerns, shall neither be said for favour nor bribery, nor out of an endeavour to make thee cheerful without cause: for such predictions, when they come to fail, make the grief at last, and in earnest, more bitter than if the party had never heard of any such thing. However, though I run the hazard of my own self, I think it fit to declare to thee the prediction of the gods. It cannot be that thou shouldst long continue in these bonds; but thou wilt soon be delivered from them, and wilt be promoted to the highest dignity and power, and thou wilt be envied by all those who now pity thy hard fortune; and thou wilt be happy till thy death, and leave thy happiness to the children whom thou shalt have. But, do thou remember, when thou seest this bird again, that thou wilt then live but five days longer. This event will be brought to pass by that God who hath sent this bird hither to be a sign unto thee. And I cannot but think it unjust to conceal from thee what I foreknow concerning thee, that, by thy knowing beforehand what happiness is coming upon thee, thou mayest not regard thy present misfortunes. But, when this happiness shall actually befall thee, do not forget what misery I am in myself, but endeavour to deliver me." So when the German had said this, he made Agrippa laugh at him as much as he afterwards appeared worthy of admiration. But now Antonia took Agrippa's misfortune to heart: however, to speak to Tiberius on his behalf, she took to be a very difficult thing, and indeed quite impracticable as to any hope of success; yet did she procure of Macro, that the soldiers that kept him should be of a gentle nature, and that the centurion who was over them, and was to diet with him, should be of the same disposition, and that he might have leave to bathe himself every day, and that his freed-men and friends might come to him, and that other things that tended to ease him might be indulged him. So his friend Silas came in to him, and two of his freed-men, Marsyas and Stechus, who brought him such sorts of food as he was fond of, and indeed took great care of him; they also brought him garments under pretence of selling them, and, when night came on, they laid them under him; and the soldiers assisted them, as Macro had given them order to do beforehand. And this was Agrippa's condition for six months' time; and in this case were his affairs.

8. But as for Tiberius, upon his return to Capreæ, he fell sick. At first his distemper was
but gentle; but, as that distemper increased
upon him, he had small or no hopes of recovery.
Hereupon he bade Euodus, who was the freed-
man whom he most of all respected, to bring the
children to him, for that he wanted to talk to
them before he died. Now he had at present no
sons of his own alive; for Drusus's son Tiberius
was still living, whose additional name was Gemellus: there was also living Caius, the son of
Germanicus, who was the son of his brother
[Drusus.] He was now grown up, and had had
a liberal education, and was well improved by
it, and was in esteem and favour with the people,
on account of the excellent character of his father Germanicus, who had attained the highest
honour among the multitude, by the firmness of
his virtuous behaviour, by the easiness and
agreeableness of his conversing with the multitude, and because the dignity he was in did not
hinder his familiarity with them all, as if they
were his equals; by which behaviour he was not
only greatly esteemed by the people and the senate, but by every one of those nations that
were subject to the Romans; some of whom
were affected when they came to him, with the
gracefulness of their reception by him; and
others were affected in the same manner by the
report of the others that had been with him:
and, upon his death, there was a lamentation
made by all men; not such a one as was to be
made in way of flattery to their rulers, while
they did but counterfeit sorrow, but such as was
real; while everybody grieved at his death, as if
they had lost one that was near to them. And
truly such had been his easy conversation with
men, that it turned greatly to the advantage of
his son among all; and, among others, the soldiery were so peculiarly affected to him, that
they reckoned it an eligible thing, if need were,
to die themselves, if he might but attain to the
government.

9. But when Tiberius had given order to Euodus to bring the children to him the next day in
the morning, he prayed to his country gods to
shew him a manifest signal, which of those children should come to the government; being
very desirous to leave it to his son's son, but
still depending upon what God would foreshew
concerning them, more than upon his own opinion and inclination; so he made this to be the
omen, that the government should be left to
him who should come to him first the next day.
When he had thus resolved within himself, he
sent to his grandson's tutor, and ordered him to
bring the child to him early in the morning, as
supposing that God would permit him to be
made emperor. But God proved opposite to his
designation; for, while Tiberius was thus contriving matters, and as soon as it was all day, he
bid Euodus to call in that child which should be
there ready. So he went out, and found Caius
before the door, for Tiberius was not yet come,
but staid waiting for his breakfast; for Euodus
knew nothing of what his lord intended; so he
said to Caius, "Thy father calls thee," and then
brought him in. As soon as Tiberius saw Caius,
and not before, he reflected on the power of God,
and how the ability of bestowing the government on whom he would was entirely taken from
him; and thence he was not able to establish
what he had intended. So he greatly lamented
that his power of establishing what he had before
contrived was taken from him, and that his
grandson Tiberius was not only to lose the Roman empire by his fatality, but his own safety
also; because his preservation would now depend upon such as would be more potent than
himself, who would think it a thing not to be
borne, that a kinsman should live with them,
and so his relation would not be able to protect
him: but he would be feared and hated by him
who had the supreme authority, partly on account of his being next to the empire, and
partly on account of his perpetually contriving
to get the government, both in order to preserve
himself, and to be at the head of affairs also.
Now Tiberius had been very much given to as-
trology, and the calculation of nativities; and
had spent his life in the esteem of what predictions had proved true more than those whose
profession it was. Accordingly, when he once
saw Galba coming in to him, he said to his most
intimate friends, that there came in a man that
would one day have the dignity of the Roman
empire. So that this Tiberius was more addicted to all such sorts of diviners than any other of
the Roman emperors, because he had found
them to have told the truth in his own affairs;
and indeed he was now in great distress upon
this accident that had befallen him, and was
very much grieved at the destruction of his son's
son, which he foresaw, and complained of himself, that he should have made use of such a
method of divination beforehand, while it was
in his power to have died without grief by his
knowledge of futurity; whereas he was now
tormented by his foreknowledge of the misfortune of such as were dearest to him, and must
die under that torment. Now, although he was
disordered at this unexpected revolution of the
government to those for whom he did not intend
it, he spake thus to Caius, though unwillingly,
and against his own inclination:—"O child, although Tiberius be nearer related to me than
thou art, I, by my own determination, and the
conspiring suffrage of the gods, do give, and put
into thy hand, the Roman empire; and I desire
thee never to be unmindful when thou comest
to it, either of my kindness to thee, who set
thee in so high a dignity, or of thy relation to
Tiberius: but as thou knowest that I am, together with and after the gods, the procurer of
so great a happiness to thee, so I desire that thou
wilt make me a return for my readiness to assist thee, and wilt take care of Tiberius because
of his near relation to thee. Besides which,
thou art to know, that, while Tiberius is alive,
he will be a security to thee, both as to empire
and as to thy own preservation; but, if he die,
that will be but a prelude to thy own misfortunes; for to be alone under the weight of such
vast affairs, is very dangerous; nor will the gods
suffer those actions which are unjustly done,
contrary to that law which directs men to do
otherwise, to go off unpunished." This was the
speech which Tiberius made; which did not persuade Caius to act accordingly, although he promised so to do; but, when he was settled in the
government, he took off this Tiberius, as was
predicted by the other Tiberius; as he was also
himself, in no long time afterwards, slain by a
secret plot laid against him.

10. So when Tiberius had at this time appointed Caius to be his successor, he outlived
but a few days, and then died, after he had held
the government twenty-two years, five months
and three days. Now Caius was the fourth emperor: but when the Romans understood that
Tiberius was dead, they rejoiced at the good
news, but had not courage to believe it; not
because they were unwilling it should be true,
for they would have given large sums of money
that it might be so, but because they were afraid
that, if they had shewn their joy, when the

news proved false, their joy should be openly known, and they should be accused for it, and be thereby undone; for this Tiberius had brought a vast number of miseries on the best families of the Romans, since he was easily inflamed with passion in all cases, and was of such a temper as rendered his anger irrevocable, till he had executed the same, although he had taken a hatred against men without reason; for he was by nature fierce in all the sentences he gave, and made death the penalty for the slightest offence; insomuch that when the Romans heard the rumour about his death gladly, they were restrained from the enjoyment of that pleasure by the dread of such miseries as they foresaw would follow, if their hopes proved ill-grounded. Now Marsyas, Agrippa's freed-man, as soon as he heard of Tiberius's death, came running to tell Agrippa the news; and finding him going out to the bath, he gave him a nod, and said, in the Hebrew tongue, "The lion* is dead;" who, understanding his meaning, and being overjoyed at the news, "Nay," said he, "but all sorts of thanks and happiness attend thee for this news of thine; only I wish that what thou sayest may prove true." Now the centurion who was set to keep Agrippa, when he saw with what haste Marsyas came, and what joy Agrippa had from what he said, he had a suspicion that his words implied some great innovation of affairs, and he asked them about what was said. They at first diverted the discourse; but upon his further pressing, Agrippa, without more ado, told him, for he had already become his friend; so he joined with him in that pleasure which this news occasioned, because it would be fortunate for Agrippa, and made him a supper: but, as they were feasting, and the cups went about, there came one who said, that Tiberius was still alive, and would return to the city in a few days. At which news the centurion was exceedingly troubled, because he had done what might cost him his life, to have treated so joyfully a prisoner, and this upon the news of the death of Cæsar; so he thrust Agrippa from the couch whereon he lay, and said, "Dost thou think to cheat me by a lie about the emperor without punishment? and shalt thou not pay for this thy malicious report at the price of thine head?" When he had so said, he ordered Agrippa to be bound again, (for he had loosed him before,) and kept a severer guard over him than formerly, and in that evil condition was Agrippa that night; but the next day the rumour increased in the city, and confirmed the news that Tiberius was certainly dead; insomuch that men durst now openly and freely talk about it; nay, some offered sacrifices on that account. Several letters also came from Caius; one of them to the senate, which informed them of the death of Tiberius, and of his own entrance on the government; another to Piso, the governor of the city, which told him the same thing. He also gave order that Agrippa should be removed out of the camp, and go to that house where he lived before he was put in prison; so that he was now out of fear as to his own affairs; for, although he was still in custody, yet it was now with ease to his own affairs. Now, as soon as Caius was come to Rome, and had brought Tiberius's dead body with him, and had made a sumptuous funeral for him, according to the laws of his country, he was much disposed to set Agrippa at liberty that very day; but Antonia

hindered him, not out of any ill-will to the prisoner, but out of regard to decency in Caius, lest that should make men believe that he received the death of Tiberius with pleasure, when he loosed one whom he had bound, immediately. However, there did not many days pass, ere he sent for him to his house, and had him shaved, and made him change his raiment; after which he put a diadem upon his head, and appointed him to be king of the tetrarchy of Philip. He also gave him the tetrarchy of Lysanias,† and changed his iron chain for a golden one of equal weight. He also sent Marullus to be procurator of Judea.

11. Now, in the second year of the reign of Caius Cæsar, Agrippa desired leave to be given him to sail home, and settle the affairs of his government; and he promised to return again when he had put the rest in order, as it ought to be put. So, upon the emperor's permission, he came into his own country, and appeared to them all unexpectedly as a king, and thereby demonstrated to the men that saw him, the power of fortune, when they compared his former poverty with his present happy affluence; so some called him a happy man; and others could not well believe that things were so much changed with him for the better.

CHAPTER VII

HOW HEROD THE TETRARCH WAS BANISHED

1. BUT Herodias, Agrippa's sister, who now lived as wife to that Herod who was tetrarch of Galilee and Perea, took this authority of her brother in an envious manner, particularly when she saw that he had a greater dignity bestowed on him than her husband had; since, when he ran away, he was not able to pay his debts; and now he was come back, it was because he was in a way of dignity and of great fortune. She was therefore grieved and much displeased at so great a mutation of his affairs; and chiefly when she saw him marching among the multitude with the usual ensigns of royal authority, she was not able to conceal how miserable she was, by reason of the envy she had towards him; but she excited her husband, and desired him that he would sail to Rome, to court honours equal to his; for she said, that she could not bear to live any longer, while Agrippa, the son of that Aristobulus, who was condemned to die by his father, one that came to her husband in such extreme poverty, that the necessaries of life were forced to be entirely supplied him day by day; and when he fled away from his creditors by sea, he now returned a king: while he was himself the son of a king, and while the near relation he bare to royal authority, called upon him to gain the like dignity, he sat still, and was contented with a private life. "But then, Herod, although thou wast formerly not concerned to be in a lower condition than thy father, from whom thou wast derived, had been, yet do thou now seek after the dignity which thy kinsman hath attained to; and do not thou bear this contempt, that a man who admired thy riches should be in greater honour than thyself, nor suffer his poverty to shew itself able to purchase greater things than our abundance: nor do thou esteem it other than a shameful thing to be inferior to one who, the other day, lived upon thy charity.

---

* The name of a lion is often given to tyrants, especially by the Jews, such as Agrippa, and probably his freed-man Marsyas, in effect, were, Ezek. xix. 1, 9; Esth. iv. 13; 2 Tim. iv. 17

† Although Caius now promised to give Agrippa the tetrarchy of Lysanias, yet was it not actually conferred upon him till the reign of Claudius.

But let us go to Rome, and let us spare no pains nor expenses, either of silver or gold, since they cannot be kept for any better use than for the obtaining of a kingdom.

2. But for Herod, he opposed her request at this time, out of the love of ease, and having a suspicion of the trouble he should have at Rome; so he tried to instruct her better. But the more she saw him draw back, the more she pressed him to it, and desired him to leave no stone unturned in order to be king: and at last she left not off till she engaged him, whether he would or not, to be of her sentiments, because he could no otherwise avoid her importunity. So he got all things ready, after as sumptuous a manner as he was able, and spared for nothing, and went up to Rome, and took Herodias along with him. But Agrippa, when he was made sensible of their intentions and preparations, he also prepared to go thither; and as soon as he heard they set sail, he sent Fortunatus, one of his freed-men, to Rome, to carry presents to the emperor, and letters against Herod, and to give Caius a particular account of those matters, if he should have any opportunity. This man followed Herod so quick, and had so prosperous a voyage, and came so little after Herod, that while Herod was with Caius, he came himself, and delivered his letters; for they both sailed to Dicearchia, and found Caius at Baiæ, which is itself a little city of Campania, at the distance of about five furlongs from Dicearchia. There are in that place royal palaces, with sumptuous apartments, every emperor still endeavouring to outdo his predecessor's magnificence: the place also affords warm baths, that spring out of the ground of their own accord, which are of advantage for the recovery of the health of those that make use of them; and, besides, they minister to men's luxury also. Now Caius saluted Herod, for he first met with him, and then looked upon the letters which Agrippa had sent him, and which were written in order to accuse Herod; wherein he accused him, that he had been in confederacy with Sejanus, against Tiberius's government, and that he was now confederate with Artabanus, the king of Parthia, in opposition to the government of Caius; as a demonstration of which, he alleged, that he had armour sufficient for seventy thousand men ready in his armoury. Caius was moved at this information, and asked Herod, whether what was said about the armour was true; and when he confessed there was such armour there, for he could not deny the same, the truth of it being too notorious, Caius took that to be a sufficient proof of the accusation, that he intended to revolt. So he took away from him his tetrarchy, and gave it by way of addition to Agrippa's kingdom; he also gave Herod's money to Agrippa, and, by way of punishment, awarded him a perpetual banishment, and appointed Lyons, a city of Gaul, to be his place of habitation. But when he was informed that Herodias was Agrippa's sister, he made her a present of what money was her own, and told her that it was her brother who prevented her being put under the same calamity with her husband. But she made this reply:—"Thou, indeed, O emperor! actest after a magnificent manner, and as becomest thyself, in what thou offerest me; but the kindness which I have for my husband, hinders me from partaking of the favour of thy gift; for it is not just that I, who have been made a partner in his prosperity, should forsake him in his misfortunes." Hereupon Caius was angry at her, and sent her with Herod into banishment, and gave her estate to Agrippa. And thus did

God punish Herodias for her envy at her brother, and Herod also for giving ear to the vain discourses of a woman. Now, Caius managed public affairs with great magnanimity during the first and second year of his reign, and behaved himself with such moderation, that he gained the good-will of the Romans themselves, and of his other subjects. But, in process of time, he went beyond the bounds of human nature in his conceit of himself, and, by reason of the vastness of his dominions, made himself a god, and took upon himself to act in all things to the reproach of the Deity itself.

CHAPTER VIII

CONCERNING THE EMBASSAGE OF THE JEWS TO CAIUS;[*] AND HOW CAIUS SENT PETRONIUS INTO SYRIA, TO MAKE WAR AGAINST THE JEWS, UNLESS THEY WOULD RECEIVE HIS STATUE

1. THERE was now a tumult arisen at Alexandria, between the Jewish inhabitants and the Greeks; and three ambassadors were chosen out of each party that were at variance, who came to Caius. Now, one of these ambassadors from the people of Alexandria was Apion, who uttered many blasphemies against the Jews; and, among other things that he said, he charged them with neglecting the honours that belonged to Cæsar; for that while all who were subject to the Roman empire built altars and temples to Caius, and in other regards universally received him as they received the gods, these Jews alone thought it a dishonourable thing for them to erect statues in honour of him, as well as to swear by his name. Many of these severe things were said by Apion, by which he hoped to provoke Caius to anger at the Jews, as he was likely to be. But Philo, the principal of the Jewish embassage, a man eminent on all accounts, brother to Alexander the alabarch,[†] and one not unskilful in philosophy, was ready to betake himself to make his defence against those accusations; but Caius prohibited him, and bade him begone: he was also in such a rage, that it openly appeared he was about to do them some very great mischief. So Philo, being thus affronted, went out, and said to those Jews that were about him, that they should be of good courage, since Caius's words indeed shewed anger at them, but in reality had already set God against himself.

2. Hereupon Caius, taking it very heinously that he he should be thus despised by the Jews alone, sent Petronius to be president of Syria, and successor in the government to Vitellius, and gave him order to make an invasion into Judea, with a great body of troops, and, if they would admit of his statue willingly, to erect it in the temple of God; but, if they were obstinate, to conquer them by war, and then to do it. Accordingly Petronius took the government of Syria, and made haste to obey Cæsar's epistle. He got together as great a number of auxiliaries as he possibly could, and took with him two legions of the Roman army, and came to Ptole-

* This is a most remarkable chapter, as containing such instances of the interposition of Providence as have been always very rare among the other idolatrous nations, but of old very many among the posterity of Abraham, the worshippers of the true God.
† This Alexander, the alabarch, or governor of the Jews, at Alexandria, and brother to Philo, is supposed to be the same with that Alexander who is mentioned by St Luke, as of the kindred of the high priests, (Acts iv. 6.)

mais, and there wintered, as intending to set about the war in the spring. He also wrote word to Caius what he had resolved to do; who commended him for his alacrity, and ordered him to go on, and to make war with them, in case they would not obey his commands. But there came many ten thousands of the Jews to Petronius, to Ptolemais, to offer their petitions to him, that he would not compel them to transgress and violate the law of their forefathers; "but if," said they, "thou art entirely resolved to bring this statue, and erect it, do thou first kill us, and then do what thou hast resolved on, for while we are alive we cannot permit such things as are forbidden us to be done by the authority of our legislator, and by our forefathers' determination that such prohibitions are instances of virtue." But Petronius was angry at them, and said, "If indeed I were myself emperor, and were at liberty to follow my own inclination, and then had designed to act thus, these your words would be justly spoken to me; but now Cæsar hath sent to me, I am under the necessity of being subservient to his decrees, because a disobedience to them will bring upon me inevitable destruction." Then the Jews replied, "Since, therefore, thou art so disposed, O Petronius! that thou wilt not disobey Caius's epistles, neither will we transgress the commands of our law; and as we depend upon the excellency of our laws, and, by the labours of our ancestors, have continued hitherto, without suffering them to be transgressed, we dare not by any means suffer ourselves to be so timorous as to transgress those laws out of the fear of death, which God hath determined are for our advantage; and, if we fall into misfortunes we will bear them, in order to preserve our laws, as knowing that those who expose themselves to dangers, have good hope of escaping them: because God will stand on our side when, out of regard to him, we undergo afflictions, and sustain the uncertain turns of fortune. But, if we should submit to thee, we should be greatly reproached for our cowardice, as thereby shewing ourselves ready to transgress our law; and we should incur the great anger of God also, who, even thyself being judge, is superior to Caius."

3. When Petronius saw by their words, that their determination was hard to be removed, and that, without a war, he should not be able to be subservient to Caius in the dedication of his statue, and that there must be a great deal of blood shed, he took his friends, and the servants that were about him, and hasted to Tiberias, as wanting to know in what posture the affairs of the Jews were; and many ten thousands of the Jews met Petronius again, when he came to Tiberias. These thought they must run a mighty hazard if they should have a war with the Romans, but judged that the transgression of the law was of much greater consequence, and made supplication to him, that he would by no means reduce them to such distresses, nor defile their city with the dedication of the statue. Then Petronius said to them, "Will you then make war with Cæsar, without considering his great preparations for war, and your own weakness?" They replied, "We will not by any means make war with him; but still we will die before we will see our laws transgressed." So they threw themselves down upon their faces, and stretched out their throats, and said they were ready to be slain; and this they did for forty days together, and in the meantime left off the tilling of their ground, and that while the season of the year required them to sow it. Thus they continued firm in their resolution, and

proposed to themselves to die willingly, rather than to see the dedication of the statue.

4. When matters were in this state, Aristobulus, king Agrippa's brother, and Helcias the Great, and the other principal men of that family with them, went in unto Petronius, and besought him, that, since he saw the resolution of the multitude, he would not make any alteration, and thereby drive them to despair; but would write to Caius, that the Jews had an insuperable aversion to the reception of the statue, and how they continued with him, and left off the tillage of their ground; that they were not willing to go to war with him, because they were not able to do it, but were ready to die with pleasure, rather than suffer their laws to be transgressed: and how, upon the land's continuing unsown, robberies would grow up, on the inability they would be under of paying their tributes; and that perhaps Caius might be thereby moved to pity, and not order any barbarous action to be done to them, nor think of destroying the nation: that if he continues inflexible in his former opinion to bring a war upon them, he may then set about it himself. And thus did Aristobulus, and the rest with him, supplicate Petronius. So Petronius,* partly on account of the pressing instances which Aristobulus and the rest with him made, and because of the great consequence of what they desired, and the earnestness wherewith they made their supplication, —partly on account of the firmness of the opposition made by the Jews, which he saw, while he thought it a horrible thing for him to be such a slave to the madness of Caius, as to slay so many ten thousand men, only because of their religious disposition towards God, and after that to pass his life in expectation of punishment; Petronius, I say, thought it much better to send to Caius, and to let him know how intolerable it was for him to bear the anger he might have against him for not serving him sooner, in obedience to his epistle, for that perhaps he might persuade him; and that, if this mad resolution continued, he might then begin the war against them; nay, that in case he should turn his hatred against himself, it was fit for virtuous persons even to die for the sake of such vast multitudes of men. Accordingly he determined to hearken to the petitions in this matter.

5. He then called the Jews together to Tiberias, who came many ten thousands in number; he also placed that army he now had with him opposite to them: but did not discover his own meaning, but the commands of the emperor, and told them that his wrath would, without delay, be executed on such as had the courage to disobey what he had commanded, and this immediately; and that it was fit for him who had received so great a dignity by his grant, not to contradict him in anything:—"Yet," said he, "I do not think it just to have such a regard to my own safety and honour, as to refuse to sacrifice them for your preservation, who are so many in number, and endeavour to preserve the regard that is due to your law; which, as it hath come down to you from your forefathers, so do you esteem it worthy of your utmost contention to preserve it: nor, with the supreme assistance and power of God, will I be so hardy as to suffer your temple

---

* This Publius Petronius was after this still president of Syria, under Claudius, and, at the desire of Agrippa, published a severe decree against the inhabitants of Dora, who, in a sort of imitation of Caius, had set up a statue of Claudius in a Jewish synagogue there. This decree is extant, and greatly confirms the present account of Josephus, as do the other decrees of Claudius, relating to the other Jewish affairs.

to fall into contempt by the means of the imperial authority. I will, therefore, send to Caius, and let him know what your resolutions are, and will assist your suit as far as I am able, that you may not be exposed to suffer on account of the honest designs you have proposed to yourselves ; and may God be your assistant for his authority is beyond all the contrivances and power of men ; and may he procure you the preservation of your ancient laws, and may not he be deprived, though without your consent, of his accustomed honours. But if Caius be irritated, and turn the violence of his rage upon me, I will rather undergo all that danger and that affliction that may come either on my body or my soul, than see so many of you perish, while you are acting in so excellent a manner. Do you, therefore, every one of you, go your way about your own occupations, and fall to the cultivation of your ground ; I will myself send to Rome, and will not refuse to serve you in all things, both by myself and by my friends."

6. When Petronius had said this, and had dismissed the assembly of the Jews, he desired the principal of them to take care of their husbandry, and to speak kindly to the people, and encourage them to have good hope of their affairs. Thus did he readily bring the multitude to be cheerful again. And now did God shew his presence to Petronius, and signify to him, that he would afford him his assistance in his whole design ; for he had no sooner finished the speech that he made to the Jews, but God sent down great showers of rain, contrary to human expectation ; for that day was a clear day, and gave no sign, by the appearance of the sky, of any rain ; nay, the whole year had been subject to a great drought, and made men despair of any water from above, even when at any time they saw the heavens overcast with clouds ; insomuch, that when such a great quantity of rain came, and that in an unusual manner and without any other expectation of it, the Jews hoped that Petronius would by no means fail in his petition for them. But as to Petronius, he was mightily surprised when he perceived that God evidently took care of the Jews, and gave very plain signs of his appearance, and this to such a degree, that those that were in earnest much inclined to the contrary, had no power left to contradict it. This was also among those other particulars which he wrote to Caius, which all tended to dissuade him, and by all means to entreat him not to make so many ten thousands of these men go distracted ; whom if he should slay (for without war they would by no means suffer the laws of their worship to be set aside) he would lose the revenue they paid him, and would be publicly cursed by them for all future ages. Moreover, that God, who was their governor, had shewn his power most evidently on their account, and that such a power of his as left no room for doubt about it ;—and this was the business that Petronius was now engaged in.

7. But king Agrippa, who now lived at Rome, was more and more in the favour of Caius ; and when he had once made him a supper, and was careful to exceed all others, both in expenses and in such preparations as might contribute most to his pleasure ; nay, it was so far from the ability of others, that Caius himself could never equal, much less exceed it, (such care had he taken beforehand to exceed all men, and particularly to make all agreeable to Cæsar ;) hereupon Caius admired his understanding and magnificence, that he should force himself to do all to please him, even beyond such expenses as he could bear, and was desirous not to be behind

Agrippa in that generosity which he exerted, in order to please him. So Caius, when he had drunk wine plentifully, and was merrier than ordinary, and said thus during the feast, when Agrippa had drunk to him :—" I knew before now how great a respect thou hast had for me, and how great kindness thou hast shewn me, though with those hazards to thyself, which thou underwentest under Tiberius on that account ; nor hast thou omitted anything to shew thy good-will towards us, even beyond thy ability ; whence it would be a base thing for me to be conquered by thy affection. I am therefore desirous to make thee amends for everything in which I have been formerly deficient ; for all that I have bestowed on thee, that may be called *my gifts*, is but little. Everything that may contribute to thy happiness shall be at thy service, and that cheerfully, and so far as my ability will reach ;" *—and this was what Caius said to Agrippa, thinking he would ask for some large country, or the revenues of certain cities ; but, although he had prepared beforehand what he would ask, yet had he not discovered his intentions, but made this answer to Caius immediately, that it was not out of any expectation of gain that he formerly paid his respects to him, contrary to the commands of Tiberius, nor did he now do anything relating to him out of regard to his own advantage, and in order to receive anything from him : that the gifts he had already bestowed upon him were great, and beyond the hopes of even a craving man ; for although they may be beneath thy power, [who art the donor,] yet are they greater than my inclination and dignity, who am the receiver ;— and, as Caius was astonished at Agrippa's inclinations, and still the more pressed him to make his request for somewhat which he might gratify him with, Agrippa replied, " Since thou, O my Lord, declarest such is thy readiness to grant, that I am worthy of thy gifts, I will ask nothing relating to my own felicity ; for what thou hast already bestowed upon me has made me excel therein ; but I desire somewhat which may make thee glorious for piety, and render the Divinity assistant to thy designs, and may be for an honour to me among those that inquire about it, as shewing that I never once fail of obtaining what I desire of thee ; for my petition is this, that thou wilt no longer think of the dedication of that statue which thou hast ordered to be set up in the Jewish temple by Petronius."

8. And thus did Agrippa venture to cast the die upon this occasion, so great was the affair in his opinion, and in reality, though he knew how dangerous a thing it was so to speak ; for, had not Caius approved it, it had tended to no less than the loss of his life. So Caius, who was mightily taken with Agrippa's obliging behaviour, and on other accounts thinking it a dishonourable thing to be guilty of falsehood before so many witnesses, in points wherein he had with such alacrity forced Agrippa to become a petitioner, so that it would look as if he had already repented of what he had said, and because he greatly admired Agrippa's virtue, in not desiring him at all to augment his own dominions, either with larger revenues, or other authority, but took care of the public tranquillity, of the laws, and of the Divinity itself, he granted him what he requested. He also wrote thus to Petronius, commending him for his assembling his army, and then consulting him about these affairs.

---

* This behaviour of Caius to Agrippa is very like that of Herod Antipas, his uncle, to Herodias, Agrippa's sister, about John the Baptist, (Matt. xiv. 6-11.)

"If, therefore," said he, "thou hast already erected my statue, let it stand; but if thou hast not yet dedicated it, do not trouble thyself further about it, but dismiss thy army, go back, and take care of those affairs which I sent thee about at first, for I have now no occasion for the erection of that statue. This I have granted as a favour to Agrippa, a man whom I honour so very greatly, that I am not able to contradict what he would have, or what he desired me to do for him." And this was what Caius wrote to Petronius, which was before he received his letter, informing him that the Jews were very ready to revolt about this statue, and that they seemed resolved to threaten war against the Romans, and nothing else. When, therefore, Caius was much displeased that any attempt should be made against his government, as he was a slave to base and vicious actions on all occasions, and had no regard to what was virtuous and honourable, and against whomsoever he resolved to shew his anger, and that for any cause whatsoever, he suffered not himself to be restrained by any admonition, but thought the indulging his anger to be a real pleasure, he wrote thus to Petronius:—"Seeing thou esteemest the presents made thee by the Jews to be of greater value than my commands, and art grown insolent enough to be subservient to their pleasure, I charge thee to become thy own judge, and to consider what thou art to do, now thou art under my displeasure; for I will make thee an example to the present and to all future ages, that they may not dare to contradict the commands of their emperor."

9. This was the epistle which Caius wrote to Petronius; but Petronius did not receive it while Caius was alive, that ship which carried it sailed so slow, the other letters came to Petronius before this, by which he understood that Caius was dead; for God would not forget the dangers Petronius had undertaken on account of the Jews, and of his own honour. But when he had taken Caius away, out of his indignation of what he had so insolently attempted, in assuming to himself divine worship, both Rome and all that dominion conspired with Petronius, especially those that were of the senatorian order, to give Caius his due reward, because he had been unmercifully severe to them; for he died not long after he had written to Petronius that epistle which threatened him with death. But as for the occasion of his death, and the nature of the plot against him, I shall relate them in the progress of this narration. Now, that epistle which informed Petronius of Caius's death came first; and a little afterward came that which commanded him to kill himself with his own hands. Whereupon he rejoiced at this coincidence as to the death of Caius, and admired God's providence, who, without the least delay, and immediately, gave him a reward for the regard he had to the temple, and the assistance he afforded the Jews for avoiding the dangers they were in. And by this means Petronius escaped that danger of death which he could not foresee.

CHAPTER IX

WHAT BEFELL THE JEWS THAT WERE IN BABYLON ON OCCASION OF ASINEUS AND ANILEUS, TWO BRETHREN

1. A VERY sad calamity now befell the Jews that were in Mesopotamia, and especially those that dwelt in Babylonia. Inferior it was to none of the calamities which had gone before, and came together with a great slaughter of them, and that greater than any upon record before; concerning all which I shall speak more accurately, and shall explain the occasions whence these miseries came upon them. There was a city of Babylonia called Neerda; not only a very populous one, but one that had a good and large territory about it; and, besides its other advantages, full of men also. It was, besides, not easily to be assaulted by enemies, from the river Euphrates encompassing it all round, and from the walls that were built about it. There was also the city Nisibis, situate on the same current of the river. For which reason the Jews, depending on the natural strength of these places, deposited in them that half shekel which every one, by the custom of our country, offers unto God, as well as they did other things devoted to him; for they made use of these cities as a treasury, whence at a proper time they were transmitted to Jerusalem; and many ten thousand men undertook the carriage of those donations, out of fear of the ravages of the Parthians, to whom the Babylonians were then subject. Now, there were two men, Asineus and Anileus, of the city Neerda by birth, and brethren to one another. They were destitute of a father; and their mother put them to learn the art of weaving curtains, it not being esteemed a disgrace among them for men to be weavers of cloth. Now, he that taught them that art, and was set over them, complained that they came too late to their work, and punished them with stripes; but they took this just punishment as an affront, and carried off all the weapons which were kept at that house, which were not a few, and went into a certain place where was a partition of the rivers, and was a place naturally very fit for the feeding of cattle, and for preserving such fruits as were usually laid up against winter. The poorest sort of the young men also resorted to them, whom they armed with the weapons they had gotten, and became their captains; and nothing hindered them from being their leaders into mischief; for, as soon as they were become invincible, and had built them a citadel, they sent to such as fed cattle, and ordered them to pay them so much tribute out of them as might be sufficient for their maintenance, proposing also that they would be their friends, if they would submit to them, and that they would defend them from all their other enemies on every side; but that they would kill the cattle of those that refused to obey them. So they hearkened to their proposals, (for they could do nothing else,) and sent them as many sheep as were required of them; whereby their forces grew greater, and they became lords over all they pleased, because they marched suddenly and did them mischief, insomuch that everybody who had to do with them chose to pay them respect; and they became formidable to such as came to assault them, till the report about them came to the ears of the king of Parthia himself.

2. But when the governor of Babylonia understood this, and had a mind to put a stop to them before they grew greater, and before greater mischiefs should arise from them he got together as great an army as he could, both of Parthians and Babylonians, and marched against them, thinking to attack them and destroy them before any one should carry them the news that he had got an army together. He then encamped at a lake, and lay still; but on the next day (it was the Sabbath, which is among the Jews a day of rest from all sorts of

work) he supposed that the enemy would not dare to fight him thereon, but that he would take them and carry them away prisoners, without fighting. He therefore proceeded gradually, and thought to fall upon them on the sudden. Now Asineus was sitting with the rest, and their weapons lay by them; upon which he said, "Sirs, I hear a neighing of horses; not of such as are feeding, but such as have men on their backs; I also hear such a noise of their bridles, that I am afraid that some enemies are coming upon us to encompass us round. However, let somebody go to look about, and make report of what reality there is in the present state of things: and may what I have said prove a false alarm!" And when he had said this, some of them went out to spy out what was the matter; and they came again immediately, and said to him, that "neither hast thou been mistaken in telling us what our enemies were doing, nor will those enemies permit us to be injurious to people any longer. We are caught by their intrigues like brute beasts, and there is a large body of cavalry marching upon us, while we are destitute of hands to defend ourselves withal, because we are restrained from doing it by the prohibition of our law, which obliges us to rest [on this day."] But Asineus did not by any means agree with the opinion of his spy as to what was to be done, but thought it more agreeable to the law to pluck up their spirits in this necessity they were fallen into, and break their law by avenging themselves, although they should die in the action, than by doing nothing to please their enemies in submitting to be slain by them. Accordingly he took up his weapons, and infused courage into those that were with him, to act as courageously as himself. So they fell upon their enemies, and slew a great many of them, because they despised them, and came as to a certain victory, and put the rest to flight.

3. But when the news of this fight came to the king of Parthia, he was surprised at the boldness of these brethren, and was desirous to see them, and speak with them. He therefore sent the most trusty of all his guards to say thus to them:—"That king Artabanus, although he has been unjustly treated by you, who have made an attempt against his government, yet hath he more regard to your courageous behaviour than to the anger he bears to you, and hath sent me to give you his right hand* and security; and he permits you to come to him safely, and without any violence upon the road, and he wants to have you address yourselves to him as friends, without meaning any guile or deceit to you. He also promises to make you presents, and to pay you those respects which will make an addition of his power to your courage, and thereby be of advantage to you." Yet did Asineus himself put off his journey thither, but sent his brother Anileus with all such presents as he could procure. So he went, and was admitted to the king's presence; and when Artabanus saw Anileus coming alone, he inquired into the reason why Asineus avoided to come along with him; and when he understood that he was afraid, and stayed by the lake, he took an oath, by the gods of his country, that he would do them no harm, if they came to him upon the assurances he gave them, and gave them his right hand. This is of the greatest force there with all these barbarians, and affords a firm security to those who converse with them;

for none of them will deceive you when once they have given you their right hands, nor will any one doubt their fidelity, when that is once given, even though they were before suspected of injustice. When Artabanus had done this, he sent away Anileus to persuade his brother to come to him. Now this the king did, because he wanted to curb his own governors of provinces by the courage of these Jewish brethren, lest they should make a league with them; for they were ready for a revolt, and were disposed to rebel, had they been sent on an expedition against them. He was also afraid, lest when he was engaged in a war, in order to subdue those governors of provinces that had revolted, the party of Asineus and those in Babylonia should be augmented, and either make war upon him when they should hear of that revolt, or, if they should be disappointed in that case, they would not fail of doing further mischief to him.

4. When the king had these intentions, he sent away Anileus; and Anileus prevailed on his brother [to come to the king,] when he had related to him the king's good-will, and the oath that he had taken. Accordingly they made haste to go to Artabanus, who received them, when they were come with pleasure, and admired Asineus's courage in the actions he had done, and this because he was a little man to see to, and at first appeared contemptible also, and such as one might deem a person of no value at all. He also said to his friends, how, upon the comparison, he shewed his soul to be, in all respects, superior to his body; and when, as they were drinking together, he once shewed Asineus to Abdagases, one of the generals of his army, and told him his name, and described the great courage he was of in war, and Abdagases had desired leave to kill him, and thereby to inflict upon him a punishment for those injuries he had done to the Parthian government, the king replied, "I will never give thee leave to kill a man who hath depended on my faith, especially not after I have sent him my right hand, and endeavoured to gain his belief by oaths made by the gods. But, if thou beest a truly warlike man, thou standest not in need of my perjury. Go thou then, and avenge the Parthian government; attack this man, when he is returned back, and conquer him by the forces that are under thy command, without my privity." Hereupon the king called for Asineus, and said to him, "It is time for thee, O thou young man! to return home, and not provoke the indignation of my generals in this place any further, lest they attempt to murder thee, and that without my approbation. I commit to thee the country of Babylonia in trust, that it may, by thy care, be preserved free from robbers, and from other mischiefs. I have kept my faith inviolable to thee, and that not in trifling affairs, but in those that concerned thy safety, and do therefore deserve thou shouldst be kind to me." When he had said this, and given Asineus some presents, he sent him away immediately; who, when he was come home, built fortresses, and became great in a little time, and managed things with such courage and success, as no other person, that had no higher a beginning, ever did before him. Those Parthian governors also, who were sent that way, paid him great respect; and the honour that was paid him by the Babylonians seemed to them too small, and beneath his deserts, although he were in no small dignity and power there: nay, indeed, all the affairs of Mesopotamia depended upon him; and he more and more flourished in this happy condition of his for fifteen years.

---

* The joining of the right hands was esteemed among the Persians and Parthians, in particular, a most inviolable obligation to fidelity.

5. But as their affairs were in so flourishing a state, there sprang up a calamity among them on the following occasion. When once they had deviated from that course of virtue whereby they had gained so great power, they affronted and transgressed the laws of their forefathers, and fell under the dominion of their lusts and pleasures. A certain Parthian, who came as general of an army into these parts, had a wife following him, who had a vast reputation for other accomplishments, and particularly was admired above all other women for her beauty. Anileus, the brother of Asineus, either heard of that her beauty from others, or perhaps saw her himself also, and so became at once her lover and her enemy ; partly because he could not hope to enjoy this woman but by obtaining power over her as a captive, and partly because he thought he could not conquer his inclinations for her. As soon, therefore, as her husband had been declared an enemy to them, and was fallen in the battle, the widow of the deceased was married to this her lover. However, this woman did not come into their house, without producing great misfortunes, both to Anileus himself, and to Asineus also ; but brought great mischiefs on them on the occasion following. Since she was led away captive, on the death of her husband, she concealed the images of those gods which were their country gods, common to her husband and to herself : now it is the custom* of that country for all to have the idols they worship in their own houses, and to carry them along with them when they go into a foreign land ; agreeably to which custom of theirs she carried her idols with her. Now, at first, she performed her worship to them privately, but when she was become Anileus's married wife, she worshipped them in her accustomed manner, and with the same appointed ceremonies which she used in her former husband's days ; upon which their most esteemed friends blamed him at first, that he did not act after the manner of the Hebrews, nor perform what was agreeable to their laws, in marrying a foreign wife, and one that transgressed the accurate appointments of their sacrifices and religious ceremonies ; that he ought to consider, lest by allowing himself in many pleasures of the body, he might lose his principality, on account of the beauty of a wife, and that high authority which, by God's blessing, he had arrived at. But when they prevailed not at all upon him, he slew one of them for whom he had the greatest respect, because of the liberty he took with him ; who, when he was dying, out of regard to the laws, imprecated a punishment upon his murderer Anileus, and upon Asineus also, and that all their companions might come to a like end from their enemies ; upon the two first as the principal actors of this wickedness, and upon the rest as those that would not assist him when he suffered in the defence of their laws. Now these latter were sorely grieved, yet did they tolerate these doings, because they remembered that they had arrived at their present happy state by no other means than their fortitude. But when they also heard of the worship of those gods whom the Parthians adore, they thought the injury that Anileus offered to their laws was to be borne no longer ; and a greater number of them came to Asineus, and loudly complained of Anileus, and told him, that it had been well that he had of himself seen what was advantageous to them ; but that how-

ever, it was now high time to correct what had been done amiss, before the crime that had been committed proved the ruin of himself and all the rest of them. They added, that the marriage of this woman was made without their consent, and without a regard to their old laws ; and that the worship which this woman paid [to her gods] was a reproach to the God whom they worshipped. Now Asineus was sensible of his brother's offence, that it had been already the cause of great mischiefs, and would be so for the time to come ; yet did he tolerate the same from the good-will he had to so near a relation, and forgiving it to him, on account that his brother was quite overborne by his wicked inclinations. But as more and more still came about him every day, and the clamours about it became greater, he at length spake to Anileus about these clamours, reproving him for his former actions, and desiring him for the future to leave them off, and send the woman back to her relations. But nothing was gained by these reproofs ; for, as the woman perceived what a tumult was made among the people on her account, and was afraid for Anileus, lest he should come to any harm for his love to her, she infused poison into Asineus's food, and thereby took him off, and was now secure of prevailing, when her lover was to be judge of what should be done about her.

6. So Anileus took the government upon himself alone, and led his army against the villages of Mithridates, who was a man of principal authority in Parthia, and had married king Artabanus's daughter ; he also plundered them, and among that prey was found much money, and many slaves, as also a great number of sheep, and many other things, which, when gained, make men's condition happy. Now, when Mithridates, who was there at this time, heard that his villages were taken, he was very much displeased to find that Anileus had first begun to injure him, and to affront him in his present dignity, when he had not offered any injury to him beforehand : and he got together the greatest body of horsemen he was able, and those out of that number which were of an age fit for war, and came to fight Anileus : and when he was arrived at a certain village of his own, he lay still there, as intending to fight him on the day following, because it was the Sabbath, the day on which the Jews rest. And when Anileus was informed of this, by a Syrian stranger of another village, who not only gave him an exact account of other circumstances, but told him where Mithridates would have a feast, he took his supper at a proper time, and marched by night, with an intent of falling upon the Parthians while they were unapprised what they should do ; so he fell upon them about the fourth watch of the night ; and some of them he slew while they were asleep, and others he put to flight, and took Mithridates alive, and set him naked upon an ass,† which, among the Parthians, is esteemed the greatest reproach possible. And when he had brought him into a wood with such a resolution, and his friends desired him to kill Mithridates, he soon told them his own mind to the contrary, and said, that it was not right to kill a man who was of one of the principal families among the Parthians, and greatly honoured with matching into the royal family ; that so far as they had hitherto gone was tolerable, for although they had injured Mithridates, yet, if they preserved his life, this benefit would

---

* This custom of the Mesopotamians to carry their household gods along with them wherever they travelled, is as old as the days of Jacob, when Rachel his wife did the same, (Gen. xxxi. 19, 30-35.)

† This custom is still kept up at Damascus in Syria ; where, in order to shew their despite against the Christians, the Turks will not suffer them to hire horses, but asses only, when they go abroad to see the country.

be remembered by him to the advantage of those that gave it him; but that if he were once put to death, the king would not be at rest till he had made a great slaughter of the Jews that dwelt at Babylon; "to whose safety we ought to have a regard, both on account of our relation to them, and because, if any misfortune befall us, we have no place to retire to, since he hath gotten the flower of their youth under him." By this thought, and this speech of his made in council, he persuaded them to act accordingly; so Mithridates was let go. But, when he was got away, his wife reproached him, that although he was son-in-law to the king, he neglected to avenge himself on those that had injured him, while he took no care about it, but was contented to have been made a captive by the Jews, and to have escaped them; and she bade him either to go back like a man of courage, or else she sware by the gods of their royal family, that she would certainly dissolve her marriage with him. Upon which, partly because he could not bear the daily trouble of her taunts, and partly because he was afraid of her insolence, lest she should in earnest dissolve their marriage, he unwillingly, and against his inclinations, got together again as great an army as he could, and marched along with them, as himself thinking it a thing not to be borne any longer, that he, a Parthian, should owe his preservation to the Jews, when they had been too hard for him in the war.

7. But as soon as Anileus understood that Mithridates was marching with a great army against him, he though it too ignominious a thing to tarry about the lakes, and not to take the first opportunity of meeting his enemies, and he hoped to have the same success, and to beat their enemies as they did before; as also he ventured boldly upon the like attempts. Accordingly he led out his army; and a great many more joined themselves to that army, in order to betake themselves to plunder the people, and in order to terrify the enemy again, by their numbers. But when they had marched ninety furlongs, while the road had been through dry [and sandy] places, and about the midst of the day, they were become very thirsty: and Mithridates appeared, and fell upon them as they were in distress for want of water, on which account, and on account of the time of the day, they were not able to bear their weapons. So Anileus and his men were put to an ignominious rout, while men in despair were to attack those that were fresh, and in good plight; so a great slaughter was made, and many ten thousand men fell. Now Anileus, and all that stood firm about him, ran away, as fast as they were able, into a wood, and afforded Mithridates the pleasure of having gained a great victory over them. But there now came in to Anileus, a conflux of bad men, who regarded their lives very little, if they might but gain some present ease, insomuch that they, by thus coming to him, compensated the multitude of those that perished in the fight. Yet were not these men like those that fell, because they were rash, and unexercised in war: however, with these he came upon the villages of the Babylonians, and a mighty devastation of all things was made there by the injuries that Anileus did them. So the Babylonians, and those that had already been in the war, sent to Neerda to the Jews there, and demanded Anileus. But, although they did not agree to their demands, (for if they had been willing to deliver him up, it was not in their power so to do;) yet did they desire to make peace with them. To which the other replied, that they also wanted to settle conditions

of peace with them, and sent men, together with the Babylonians, who discoursed with Anileus about them. But the Babylonians, upon taking a view of his situation, and having learned where Anileus and his men lay, fell secretly upon them as they were drunk and fallen asleep, and slew all that they caught of them, without any fear, and killed Anileus himself also.

8. The Babylonians were now freed from Anileus's heavy incursions, which had been a great restraint to the effects of that hatred they bore to the Jews: for they were almost always at variance, by reason of the contrariety of their laws; and which party soever grew boldest before the other, they assaulted the other: and at this time in particular it was, that upon the ruin of Anileus's party, the Babylonians attacked the Jews, which made those Jews so vehemently to resent the injuries they received from the Babylonians, that, being neither able to fight them, nor bearing to live with them, they went to Seleucia, the principal city of those parts, which was built by Seleucus Nicator. It was inhabited by many of the Macedonians, but by more of the Grecians; not a few of the Syrians also dwelt there; and thither did the Jews fly, and lived there five years, without any misfortunes. But, on the sixth year, a pestilence came upon these at Babylon, which occasioned new removals of men's habitations out of that city; and because they came to Seleucia, it happened that a still heavier calamity came upon them on that account,—which I am going to relate immediately.

9. Now the way of living of the people of Seleucia, who were Greeks and Syrians, was commonly quarrelsome, and full of discords, though the Greeks were too hard for the Syrians. When, therefore, the Jews were come thither, and dwelt among them, there arose a sedition; and the Syrians were too hard for the other, by the assistance of the Jews, who are men that despise dangers, and very ready to fight upon any occasion. Now, when the Greeks had the worst in this sedition, and saw that they had but one way of recovering their former authority, and that was, if they could prevent the agreement between the Jews and Syrians, they every one discoursed with such of the Syrians as were formerly their acquaintance, and promised they would be at peace and friendship with them. Accordingly, they gladly agreed so to do; and when this was done by the principal men of both nations, they soon agreed to a reconciliation; and when they were so agreed, they both knew that the great design of such their union, would be their common hatred to the Jews. Accordingly they fell upon them, and slew about fifty thousand of them; nay, the Jews were all destroyed, excepting a few who escaped, either by the compassion which their friends or neighbours afforded them in order to let them fly away. These retired to Ctesiphon, a Grecian city, and situated near to Seleucia, where the king [of Parthia] lives in winter every year, and where the greatest part of his riches are deposited; but the Jews had here no certain settlement, those of Seleucia having little concern for the king's honour. Now the whole nation of the Jews were in fear both of the Babylonians and of the Seleucians, because all the Syrians that live in those places agreed with the Seleucians in the war against the Jews; so the most of them gathered themselves together, and went to Neerda and Nisibis, and obtained security there by the strength of those cities; besides which, their inhabitants, who were a great many, were all warlike men. And this was the state of the Jews at this time in Babylonia.

CHAPTER I

HOW CAIUS * WAS SLAIN BY CHEREA

1. Now this Caius † did not demonstrate his madness in offering injuries only to the Jews at Jerusalem, or to those that dwelt in the neighbourhood, but suffered it to extend itself through all the earth and sea, so far as was in subjection to the Romans, and filled it with ten thousand mischiefs; so many indeed in number as no former history relates. But Rome itself felt the most dismal effects of what he did, while he deemed that not to be any way more honourable than the rest of the cities; but he pulled and hauled its other citizens, but especially the senate, and particularly the nobility, and such as had been dignified by illustrious ancestors; he also had ten thousand devices against such of the equestrian order, as it was styled, who were esteemed by the citizens equal in dignity and wealth with the senators, because out of them the senators were themselves chosen; these he treated after an ignominious manner, and removed them out of his way while they were at once slain, and their wealth plundered; because he slew men generally in order to seize on their riches. He also asserted his own divinity, and insisted on greater honours to be paid him by his subjects than are due to mankind. He also frequented that temple of Jupiter which they style the Capitol, which is with them the most holy of all temples, and had boldness enough to call himself the brother of Jupiter. And other pranks he did like a madman; as when he laid a bridge from the city Dicearchia, which belongs to Campania, to Misenum, another city upon the sea-side, from one promontory to another, of the length of thirty furlongs, as measured over the sea. And this was done, because he esteemed it to be a most tedious thing to row over in a small ship, and thought withal that it became him to make that bridge, as he was lord of the sea, and might oblige it to give marks of obedience as well as the earth; so he enclosed the whole bay within his bridge, and drove his chariot over it; and thought, that as he was a god, it was fit for him to travel over such roads as this was. Nor did he abstain from the plunder of any of the Grecian temples, and gave order that all the engravings and sculptures, and the rest of the ornaments of the statues and do-

nations therein dedicated, should be brought to him, saying that the best things ought to be set nowhere but in the best place, and that the city of Rome was the best place. He also adorned his own house and his gardens with the curiosities brought from those temples, together with the houses he lay at when he travelled all over Italy; whence he did not scruple to give a command that the statue of Jupiter Olympius, so called because he was honoured at the Olympian games by the Greeks, which was the work of Phidias the Athenian, should be brought to Rome. Yet did not he compass his end, because the architect told Memmius Regulus, who was commanded to remove the statue of Jupiter, that the workmanship was such as would be spoiled, and would not bear the removal. It was also reported that Memmius, both on that account, and on account of some such mighty prodigies as are of an incredible nature, put off the taking it down, and wrote to Caius those accounts, as his apology for not having done what his epistle required of him; and that when he was thence in danger of perishing, he was saved by Caius being dead himself, before he had put him to death.

2. Nay, Caius's madness came to this height, that when he had a daughter born, he carried her into the capitol, and put her upon the knees of the statue, and said that the child was common to him and to Jupiter, and determined that she had two fathers,—but which of these fathers were the greatest, he left undetermined; and yet mankind bore him in such his pranks. He also gave leave to slaves to accuse their masters of any crimes whatsoever they pleased; for all such accusations were terrible, because they were in great part made to please him, and at his suggestion, insomuch that Pollux, Claudius's slave, had the boldness to lay an accusation against Claudius himself; and Caius was not ashamed to be present at his trial of life and death, to hear the trial of his own uncle, in hopes of being able to take him off, although he did not succeed to his mind: but when he had filled the whole habitable world which he governed, with false accusations and miseries, and had occasioned the greatest insults of slaves against their masters, who indeed, in a great measure, ruled them, there were many secret plots now laid against him; some in anger, and in order for men to revenge themselves, on account of the miseries they had already undergone from him; and others made attempts upon him, in order to take him off before they should fall into such great miseries, while his death came very fortunately for the preservation of the lives of all men, and had a great influence upon the public welfare; and this happened most happily for our nation in particular, which had almost utterly perished if he had not been suddenly slain; and I confess I have a mind to give a full

---

* In this and the next three chapters, we have, I think, a more distinct account of the slaughter of Caius, and the succession of Claudius, than we have of any such ancient facts whatsoever elsewhere, caused probably by Josephus's bitter hatred against tyranny; and the pleasure he took in giving the history of the slaughter of such a barbarous tyrant as was this Caius Caligula, as also the deliverance his own nation had by that slaughter.

† Called *Caligula* by the Romans.

account of this matter particularly, because it will afford great assurance of the power of God, and great comfort to those that are under affliction, and wise caution to those who think their happiness will never end, nor bring them at length to the most lasting miseries, if they do not conduct their lives by the principles of virtue.

3. Now there were three several conspiracies made, in order to take off Caius, and each of these three was conducted by excellent persons. Emilius Regulus, born at Corduba in Spain, got some men together, and was desirous to take Caius off, either by them or by himself. Another conspiracy there was laid by them, under the conduct of Cherea Cassius, the tribune [of the pretorian band;] Minucianus Annius was also one of great consequence among those that were prepared to oppose his tyranny. Now the several occasions of these men's several hatred and conspiracy against Caius were these: —Regulus had indignation and hatred against all injustice, for he had a mind naturally angry, and bold, and free, which made him not conceal his counsels; so he communicated them to many of his friends, and to others who seemed to him persons of activity and vigour; Minucianus entered into this conspiracy, because of the injustice done to Lepidus his particular friend, and one of the best character of all the citizens, whom Caius had slain, as also because he was afraid of himself, since Caius's wrath tended to the slaughter of all alike: and for Cherea, he came in, because he thought it a deed worthy of a free ingenuous man to kill Caius, and was ashamed of the reproach he lay under from Caius, as though he were a coward; as also because he was himself in danger every day from his friendship with him, and the observance he paid him. These men proposed this attempt to all the rest that were concerned, who saw the injuries that were offered them, and were desirous that Caius's slaughter might succeed by their mutual assistance of one another, that they might themselves escape being killed by the taking off Caius; that perhaps they should gain their point, and that it would be a happy thing if they should gain it, to approve themselves to so many excellent persons as earnestly wished to be partakers with them in their design, for the delivery of the city and of the government, even at the hazard of their own lives; but still Cherea was the most zealous of them all, both out of a desire of getting himself the greatest name, and also by reason of his access to Caius's presence with less danger, because he was tribune, and could therefore the more easily kill him.

4. Now, at this time came on the horse-races [Circensian games;] the view of which games was eagerly desired by the people of Rome, for they come with great alacrity into the hippodrome [circus] at such times, and petition their emperors, in great multitudes, for what they stand in need of; who usually did not think fit to deny them their requests, but readily and gratefully granted them. Accordingly they most importunately desired that Caius would now ease them in their tributes, and abate somewhat of the rigour of the taxes imposed upon them; but he would not hear their petition; and, when their clamours increased, he sent soldiers, some one way and some another, and gave order that they should lay hold on those that made the clamours, and without any more ado, bring them out and put them to death. These were Caius's commands, and those who were commanded executed the same; and the number of those who were slain on this occasion was very great. Now the people saw this, and bore it so far, that they left off clamouring, because they saw with their own eyes that this petition to be relieved as to the payment of their money brought immediate death upon them. These things made Cherea more resolute to go on with his plot in order to put an end to this barbarity of Caius against men. He then, at several times, thought to fall upon Caius as he was feasting, yet did he restrain himself by some considerations; not that he had any doubt on him about killing him, but as watching for a proper season, that the attempt might not be frustrated, but that he might give the blow so that he might certainly gain his purpose.

5. Cherea had been in the army a long time, yet was he not pleased with conversing so much with Caius; but Caius had set him to require the tributes, and other dues, which, when not paid in due time, were forfeited to Cæsar's treasury; and he had made some delays in requiring them, because those burdens had been doubled; and had rather indulged his own mild disposition than performed Caius's command; nay, indeed, he provoked Caius to anger by his sparing men, and pitying the hard fortunes of those from whom he demanded the taxes; and Caius upbraided him with his sloth and effeminacy in being so long about collecting the taxes; and indeed he did not only affront him in other respects, but when he gave him the watch-word of the day, to whom it was to be given by his place, he gave him feminine words, and those of a nature very reproachful; and these watchwords he gave out, as having been initiated in the secrets of certain mysteries which he had been himself the author of. Now, although he had sometimes put on woman's clothes, and had been wrapt in some embroidered garments to them belonging, and done a great many other things in order to make the company mistake him for a woman; yet did he, by way of reproach, object the like womanish behaviour to Cherea. But when Cherea received the watch-word from him, he had indignation at it, but had greater indignation at the delivery of it to others, as being laughed at by those that received it; insomuch that his fellow-tribunes made him the subject of their drollery; for they would foretell that he would bring them some of his usual watch-words when he was about to take the watch-word from Cæsar, and would thereby make him ridiculous; on which account he took the courage of assuming certain partners to him, as having just reasons for his indignation against Caius. Now there was one Pompedius, a senator, and one who had gone through almost all posts in the government, but otherwise an Epicurean, and for that reason loved to lead an inactive life. Now Timidius, an enemy of his, had informed Caius that he had used indecent reproaches against him, and he made use of Quintilia for a witness to them; a woman she was much beloved by many that frequented the theatre, and particularly by Pompedius, on account of her great beauty. Now this woman thought it a horrible thing to attest to an accusation that touched the life of her lover, which was also a lie. Timidius, however, wanted to have her brought to the torture. Caius was irritated at this reproach upon him, and commanded Cherea, without any delay, to torture Quintilia, as he used to employ Cherea in such bloody matters, and those that required the torture, because he thought he would do it the more barbarously, in order to avoid that imputation of effeminacy which he had laid upon him.

But Quintilia, when she was brought to the rack trod upon the foot of one of her associates, and let him know that he might be of good courage, and not be afraid of the consequence of her tortures, for that she would bear them with magnanimity. Cherea tortured this woman after a cruel manner; unwillingly indeed, but because he could not help it. He then brought her, without being the least moved at what she had suffered, into the presence of Caius, and that in such a state as was sad to behold; and Caius, being somewhat affected with the sight of Quintilia, who had her body miserably disordered by the pains she had undergone, freed both her and Pompedius of the crime laid to their charge. He also gave her money to make her an honourable amends, and comfort her for that maiming of her body which she had suffered, and for her glorious patience under such unsufferable torments.

6. This matter sorely grieved Cherea, as having been the cause, as far as he could, or the instrument, of those miseries to men, which seemed worthy of consolation to Caius himself; on which account he said to Clement and to Papinius, (of whom Clement was general of the army, and Papinius was a tribune:) "To be sure, O Clement, we have no way failed in our guarding the emperor; for as to those that have made conspiracies against his government, some have been slain by our care and pains, and some have been by us tortured, and this to such a degree, that he hath himself pitied them. How great then is our virtue in submitting to conduct his armies!" Clement held his peace, but shewed the shame he was under in obeying Caius's orders, both by his eyes and his blushing countenance, while he thought it by no means right to accuse the emperor in express words, lest their own safety should be endangered thereby. Upon which Cherea took courage, and spake to him without fear of the dangers that were before him, and discoursed largely of the sore calamities under which the city and the government then laboured, and said, "We may indeed pretend in words, that Caius is the person unto whom the cause of such miseries ought to be imputed; but, in the opinion of such as are able to judge uprightly, it is I, O Clement! and this Papinius, and before us thou thyself, who bring these tortures upon the Romans, and upon all mankind. It is not done by our being subservient to the commands of Caius, but it is done by our own consent; for whereas it is in our power to put an end to the life of this man, who hath so terribly injured the citizens and his subjects, we are his guard in mischief and his executioners, instead of his soldiers, and are the instruments of his cruelty. We bear these weapons, not for our liberty, not for the Roman government, but only for his preservation, who hath enslaved both their bodies and their minds; and we are every day polluted with the blood that we shed, and the torments we inflict upon others; and this we do, till somebody becomes Caius's instrument in bringing the like miseries upon ourselves. Nor does he thus employ us, because he hath a kindness for us, but rather because he hath a suspicion of us, as also because, when abundance more have been killed, (for Caius will set no bounds to his wrath, since he aims to do all not out of regard to justice, but to his own pleasure,) we shall also ourselves be exposed to his cruelty; whereas we ought to be the means of confirming the security and liberty of all, and at the same time to resolve to free ourselves from dangers."

7. Hereupon Clement openly commended Cherea's intentions, but bade him hold his tongue; for that in case his words should get out among many, and such things should be spread abroad as were fit to be concealed, the plot would come to be discovered before it was executed, and they should be brought to punishment; but that they should leave all to futurity, and the hope which thence arose, that some fortunate event would come to their assistance: that, as for himself, his age would not permit him to make any attempt in that case. "However, although perhaps I could not suggest what may be safer than what thou, Cherea, hast contrived and said, yet how is it possible for any one to suggest what is more for thy reputation?" So Clement went his way home, with deep reflections on what he had heard, and what he had himself said. Cherea also was under a concern, and went quickly to Cornelius Sabinus, who was himself one of the tribunes, and whom he otherwise knew to be a worthy man, and a lover of liberty, and on that account very uneasy at the present managemant of public affairs, he being desirous to come immediately to the execution of what had been determined, and thinking it right for him to propose it to the other, and afraid lest Clement should discover them, and besides looking upon delays and puttings-off to be the next to desisting from the enterprise.

8. But as all was agreeable to Sabinus, who had himself, equally with Cherea, the same design, but had been silent for want of a person to whom he could safely communicate that design; so having now met with one, who not only promised to conceal what he heard, but who had already opened his mind to him, he was much more encouraged, and desired of Cherea that no delay might be made therein. Accordingly they went to Minucianus, who was as virtuous a man, and as zealous to do glorious actions as themselves, and suspected by Caius on occasion of the slaughter of Lepidus; for Minucianus and Lepidus were intimate friends, and both in fear of the dangers that they were under; for Caius was terrible to all the great men, as appearing ready to act a mad part towards each of them in particular, and towards all of them in general; and these men were afraid of one another, while they were yet uneasy at the posture of affairs, but avoided to declare their mind and their hatred against Caius to one another, out of fear of the dangers they might be in thereby, although they perceived by other means their mutual hatred against Caius, and on that account were not averse to a mutual kindness one towards another.

9. When Minucianus and Cherea had met together, and saluted one another, (as they had been used in former conversations to give the upper hand to Minucianus, both on account of his eminent dignity, for he was the noblest of all the citizens, and highly commended by all men, especially when he made speeches to them,) Minucianus, began first, and asked Cherea what was the watch-word he had received that day from Caius; for the affront which was offered Cherea in giving the watch-word was famous over the city. But Cherea made no delay so long as to reply to that question, out of the joy he had that Minucianus would have such confidence in him as to discourse with him. "But do thou," said he, "give me the watch-word of liberty. And I return thee my thanks, that thou hast so greatly encouraged me to exert myself after an extraordinary manner; nor do I stand in need of many words to encourage me, since both thou and I are of the same mind, and partakers of the same resolutions, and this be-

fore we have conferred together. I have indeed but one sword girt on, but this one will serve us both. Come on, therefore, let us set about the work. Do thou go first, if thou hast a mind, and bid me follow thee; or else I will go first, and thou shalt assist me, and we will assist one another and trust one another. Nor is there a necessity for even one sword to such as have a mind disposed to such works, by which mind the sword uses to be successful. I am zealous about this action, nor am I solicitous what I may myself undergo; for I am not at leisure to consider the danger that may come upon myself, so deeply am I troubled at the slavery our once free country is now under, and at the contempt cast upon our excellent laws, and at the destruction which hangs over all men, by the means of Caius. I wish that I may be judged by thee, and that thou mayest esteem me worthy of credit in these matters, seeing we are both of the same opinion, and there is herein no difference between us."

10. When Minucianus saw the vehemency with which Cherea delivered himself, he gladly embraced him, and encouraged him in his bold attempt, commending him, and embracing him; so he let him go with his good wishes; and some affirm, that he thereby confirmed Minucianus in the prosecution of what had been agreed among them; for, as Cherea entered into the court, the report runs, that a voice came from among the multitude to encourage him, which bid him finish what he was about, and take the opportunity that Providence offered; and that Cherea at first suspected that some one of the conspirators had betrayed him, and he was caught; but at length perceived that it was by way of exhortation. Whether somebody,* that was conscious of what he was about, gave a signal for his encouragement, or whether it was God himself, who looks upon the actions of men, that encouraged him to go on boldly in his design, is uncertain. The plot was now communicated to a great many, and they were all in their armour; some of the conspirators being senators, and some of the equestrian order, and as many of the soldiery as were made acquainted with it; for there was not one of them who would not reckon it a part of his happiness to kill Caius; and on that account they were all very zealous in the affair, by what means soever any one could come at it, that he might not be behindhand in these virtuous designs, but might be ready with all his alacrity or power, both by words and actions, to complete this slaughter of a tyrant. And besides these, Callistus also, who was a freed-man of Caius's, and was the only man that had arrived at the greatest degree of power under him,— such a power, indeed, as was in a manner equal to the power of the tyrant himself; by the dread that all men had of him, and by the great riches he had acquired; for he took bribes most plenteously, and committed injuries without bounds; and was more extravagant in the use of his power in unjust proceedings than any other. He also knew the disposition of Caius to be implacable, and never to be turned from what he had resolved on. He had withal many other reasons why he thought himself in danger, and the vastness of his wealth was not one of the least of them: on which account he privately ingratiated himself with Cladius, and transferred his courtship to him, out of this hope, that in case, upon the removal of Caius, the government

should come to him, his interest in such changes should lay a foundation for his preserving his dignity under him, since he laid in beforehand a stock of merit, and did Claudius good offices in his promotion. He also had the boldness to pretend that he had been persuaded to make away with Claudius, by poisoning him; but had still invented ten thousand excuses for delaying to do it. But it seems probable to me that Callistus only counterfeited this in order to ingratiate himself with Claudius; for if Caius had been in earnest resolved to take off Claudius, he would not have admitted of Callistus's excuses, nor would Callistus, if he had been enjoined to do such an act as was desired by Caius, have put it off, nor, if he had disobeyed those injunctions of his master, had he escaped immediate punishment; while Claudius was preserved from the madness of Caius by a certain divine providence, and Callistus pretended to such a piece of merit as he no way deserved.

11. However, the execution of Cherea's designs was put off from day to day, by the sloth of many therein concerned; for, as to Cherea himself, he would not willingly make any delay in that execution, thinking every time a fit time for it, for frequent opportunities offered themselves; as when Caius went up to the capitol to sacrifice for his daughter, or when he stood upon his royal palace, and threw gold and silver pieces of money among the people, he might be pushed down headlong, because the top of the palace that looks towards the market-place, was very high; and also when he celebrated the mysteries, which he had appointed at that time; for he was then no way secluded from the people, but solicitous to do everything carefully and decently; and was free from all suspicion that he should be then assaulted by anybody; and although the gods should afford him no divine assistance to enable him to take away his life, yet had he strength himself sufficient to despatch Caius even without a sword. Thus was Cherea angry at his fellow-conspirators, for fear they should suffer a proper opportunity to pass by; and they were themselves sensible that he had just cause to be angry at them, and that his eagerness was for their advantage; yet did they desire he would have a little longer patience, lest, upon any disappointment they might meet with, they should put the city in disorder, and an inquisition should be made after the conspiracy, and should render the courage of those that were to attack Caius without success, while he would then secure himself more carefully than ever against them; that it would therefore be the best to set about the work when the shows were exhibited in the palace. These shows were acted in honour of that Cæsar who first of all changed the popular government, and transferred it to himself; galleries being fixed before the palace, where the Romans that were patricians, became spectators, together with their children and their wives, and Cæsar himself was to be also a spectator; and they reckoned among those many ten thousands who would there be crowded into a narrow compass, they should have a favourable opportunity to make their attempt upon him as he came in; because his guards that should protect him, if any of them should have a mind to do it, would not here be able to give him any assistance.

12. Cherea consented to this delay; and when the shows were exhibited, it was resolved to do the work the first day. But fortune, which allowed a further delay to his slaughter, was too hard for their foregoing resolution: and, as three days of the regular time for these shows

---

* Just such a voice as this is related to be, came, and from an unknown original also, to the famous Polycarp, as he was going to martyrdom, bidding him "play the man."

were now over, they had much ado to get the business done on the last day. Then Cherea called the conspirators together, and spake thus to them :—"So much time passed away without effect is a reproach to us, as delaying to go through such a virtuous design as we are engaged in ; but more fatal will this delay prove if we be discovered, and the design be frustrated ;—for Caius will then become more cruel in his unjust proceedings. Do not we see how long we deprive all our friends of their liberty, and give Caius leave still to tyrannise over them ? while we ought to have procured them security for the future, and, by laying a foundation for the happiness of others, gain to ourselves great admiration and honour for all time to come." Now, while the conspirators had nothing tolerable to say by way of contradiction, and yet did not quite relish what they were doing, but stood silent and astonished, he said further, "O my brave comrades ! why do we make such delays ? Do not you see that this is the last day of these shows, and that Caius is about to go to sea ! for he is preparing to sail to Alexandria, in order to see Egypt. Is it therefore for your honour to let a man go out of your hands who is a reproach to mankind, and to permit him to go after a pompous manner, triumphing both at land and sea ? shall not we be justly ashamed of ourselves if we give leave to some Egyptian or other, who shall think his injuries insufferable to freemen, to kill him : as for myself, I will no longer bear your slow proceedings, but will expose myself to the dangers of the enterprise this very day, and bear cheerfully whatsoever shall be the consequence of the attempt ; nor, let them be ever so great, will I put them off any longer : for, to a wise and courageous man, what can be more miserable than that, while I am alive, any one else should kill Caius, and deprive me of the honour of so virtuous an action ?"

13. When Cherea had spoken thus, he zealously set about the work, and inspired courage into the rest to go on with it ; and they were all eager to fall to it without further delay. So he was at the palace in the morning, with his equestrian sword girt on him ; for it was the custom that the tribunes should ask for the watch-word with their swords on, and this was the day on which Cherea was by custom to receive the watch-word ; and the multitude were already come to the palace, to be soon enough for seeing the shows, and that in great crowds, and one tumultuously crushing another, while Caius was delighted with this eagerness of the multitude ; for which reason their was no order observed in the seating men, nor was any peculiar place appointed for the senators, or for the equestrian order ; but they sat at random, men and women together, and freemen were mixed with the slaves. So Caius came out in a solemn manner, and offered sacrifice to Augustus Cæsar, in whose honour indeed these shows were celebrated. Now it happened, upon the fall of a certain priest, that the garment of Asprenas, a senator, was filled with blood, which made Caius laugh, although this was an evident omen to Asprenas, for he was slain at the same time with Caius. It is also related, that Caius was that day, contrary to his usual custom, so very affable and good-natured in his conversation, that every one of those that were present were astonished at it. After the sacrifice was over, Caius betook himself to see the shows, and sat down for that purpose, as did also the principal of his friends sit near him. Now the parts of the theatre were so fastened together, as it used

to be every year, in the manner following :—It had two doors ; the one door led to the open air, the other was for going into, or going out of, the cloisters, that those within the theatre might not be thereby disturbed ; but out of one gallery there went an inward passage, parted into partitions also, which led into another gallery, to give room to the combatants, and to the musicians, to go out as occasion served. When the multitude were set down, and Cherea, with the other tribunes were set down also, and the right corner of the theatre was allotted to Cæsar, one Vatinius, a senator, commander of the Pretorian band, asked of Cluvius, one that sat by him, and was of consular dignity also,—Whether he had heard anything of the news or not ?—but took care that nobody should hear what he said ; and when Cluvius replied, that he had heard no news,—"Know then," said Vatinius, "that the game of the slaughter of tyrants is to be played this day." But Cluvius replied, "O brave comrade ! hold thy peace, lest some one of the Achaians hear thy tale." And as there was abundance of autumnal fruit thrown among the spectators, and a great number of birds, that were of great value to such as possessed them, on account of their rareness, Caius was pleased with the birds fighting for the fruits, and with the violence wherewith the spectators seized upon them ; and here he perceived two prodigies that happened there ; for an actor was introduced, by whom a leader of robbers was crucified, and the pantomime brought in a play called Cinyras, wherein he himself was to be slain, as well as his daughter Myrrha, and wherein a great deal of fictitious blood was shed, both about him that was crucified and also about Cinyras. It is also confessed that this was the same day wherein Pausanias, a friend of Philip, the son of Amyntas, who was king of Macedonia, slew him as he was entering into the theatre. And now Caius was in doubt whether he should tarry to the end of the shows, because it was the last day, or whether he should not go first to the bath, and to dinner, and then return and sit down as before. Hereupon Minucianus, who sat over Caius, and was afraid that the opportunity should fail them, got up, because he saw Cherea was already gone out, and made haste out, to confirm him in his resolution ; but Caius took hold of his garment in an obliging way, and said to him,—"O brave man ! whither art thou going ?" Whereupon, out of reverence to Cæsar, as it seemed, he sat down again ; but his fear prevailed over him, and in a little time he got up again, and then Caius did no way oppose his going out, as thinking that he went out to perform some necessities of nature. And Asprenas, who was one of the confederates, persuaded Caius to go out to the bath, and to dinner, and then to come in again ; as desirous that what had been resolved on might be brought to a conclusion immediately.

14. So Cherea's associates placed themselves in order, as the time would permit them, and they were obliged to labour hard, that the place which was appointed them should not be left by them ; they had an indignation at the tediousness of the delays, and that what they were about should be put off any longer, for it was already about the ninth* hour of the day ; and Cherea, upon Caius's tarrying so long, had a great mind to go in, and fall upon him in his seat, although he foresaw that this could not be

---

* Suetonius says Caius was slain about the seventh hour of the day, Josephus about the ninth. The series of the narration favours Josephus.

done without much bloodshed, both of the senators and of those of the equestrian order that were present; and although he knew this must happen, yet had he a great mind to do so, as thinking it a right thing to procure security and freedom to all at the expense of such as might perish at the same time. And as they were just going back into the entrance to the theatre, word was brought them that Caius was arisen, whereby a tumult was made; hereupon the conspirators thrust away the crowd, under pretence as if Caius was angry at them, but in reality as desirous to have a quiet place, that should have none in it to defend him, while they set about Caius's slaughter. Now Claudius, his uncle, was gone out before, and Marcus Vinicius, his sister's husband, as also Valerius of Asia; whom, though they had had such a mind to put out of their places, the reverence to their dignity hindered them so to do; then followed Caius, with Paulus Arruntius: and because Caius was now gotten within the palace, he left the direct road, along which those his servants stood that were in waiting, and by which road Claudius had gone out before, Caius turned aside into a private narrow passage, in order to go to the place for bathing, as also in order to take a view of the boys that came out of Asia, who were sent thence partly to sing hymns in these mysteries which were now celebrated, and partly to dance in the Pyrrhic way of dancing upon the theatres. So Cherea met him, and asked him for the watchword; upon Caius's giving him one of his ridiculous words he immediately reproached him, and drew his sword and gave him a terrible stroke with it, yet was not this stroke mortal. And although there be those that say it was so contrived on purpose by Cherea that Caius should not be killed at one blow, but should be punished more severely by a multitude of wounds, yet does this story appear to be incredible; because the fear men are under in such actions does not allow them to use their reason. And if Cherea was of that mind, I esteem him the greatest of all fools, in pleasing himself in his spite against Caius, rather than immediately procuring safety to himself and to his confederates from the dangers they were in; because there might many things still happen for helping Caius's escape, if he had not already given up the ghost; for certainly Cherea would have regard, not so much to the punishment of Caius, as to the affliction himself and his friends were in, while it was in his power, after such success, to keep silent, and to escape the wrath of Caius's defenders, and not leave it to uncertainty whether he should gain the end he aimed at or not; and after an unreasonable manner to act as if he had a mind to ruin himself, and lose the opportunity that lay before him. But everybody may guess as he pleases about this matter. However, Caius was staggered with the pain that the blow gave him; for the stroke of the sword falling in the middle, between the shoulder and neck, was hindered by the first bone of the breast from proceeding any further. Nor did he either cry out, (in such astonishment was he,) nor did he call out for any of his friends; whether it were that he had no confidence in them, or that his mind was otherwise disordered, but he groaned under the pain he endured, and presently went forward and fled,—when Cornelius Sabinus, who was already prepared in mind so to do, thrust him down upon his knee, where many of them stood round about him, and struck him with their swords, and they cried out, and encouraged one another all at once to strike him again; but all agree that Aquila gave him the finishing stroke, which directly killed him. But one may justly ascribe this act to Cherea; for although many concurred in the act itself, yet was he the first contriver of it, and began long before all the rest to prepare for it; and was the first man that boldly spake of it to the rest; and upon their admission of what he said about it, he got the dispersed conspirators together: he prepared everything after a prudent manner, and by suggesting good advice, shewed himself far superior to the rest, and made obliging speeches to them, insomuch that he even compelled them to go on, who otherwise had not courage enough for that purpose; and when opportunity served to use his sword in hand, he appeared first of all ready so to do, and gave the first blow in this virtuous slaughter; he also brought Caius easily into the power of the rest, and almost killed him himself, insomuch that it is but just to ascribe all that the rest did to the advice, and bravery, and labours of the hands of Cherea.

15. Thus did Caius come to his end, and lay dead by the many wounds which had been given him. Now Cherea and his associates, upon Caius's slaughter, saw that it was impossible for them to save themselves, if they should all go the same way, partly on account of the astonishment they were under; for it was no small danger they had incurred by killing an emperor, who was honoured and loved by the madness of the people, especially when the soldiers were likely to make a bloody inquiry after his murderers. The passages also were narrow wherein the work was done, which were also crowded with a great multitude of Caius's attendants, and of such of the soldiers as were of the emperor's guard that day; whence it was that they went by other ways, and came to the house of Germanicus, the father of Caius, whom they had now killed, (which house adjoined to the palace; for while the edifice was one, it was built in its several parts by those particular persons who had been emperors, and those parts bare the names of those that built them, or the name of him who had begun to build any of its parts.) So they got away from the insults of the multitude, and then were for the present out of danger, that is so long as the misfortune which had overtaken the emperor was not known. The Germans were the first who perceived that Caius was slain. These Germans were Caius's guard, and carried the name of the country whence they were chosen, and composed the Celtic legion. The men of that country are naturally passionate, which is commonly the temper of some other of the barbarous nations also, as being not used to consider much about what they do; they are of robust bodies, and fall upon their enemies as soon as ever they are attacked by them; and which way soever they go, they perform great exploits. When therefore, these German guards understood that Caius was slain, they were very sorry for it, because they did not use their reason in judging about public affairs, but measured all by the advantages themselves received, Caius being beloved by them, because of the money he gave them, by which he had purchased their kindness to him: so they drew their swords, and Sabinus led them on. He was one of the tribunes, not by the means of the virtuous actions of his progenitors, for he had been a gladiator, but he had obtained that post in the army by his having a robust body. So these Germans marched along the houses in quest of Cæsar's murderers, and cut Asprenas to pieces, because he was the first man they fell upon, and whose garment it was that the blood of the sacrifices stained, as I have said already, and which fore-

told that this his meeting the soldiers would not be for his good. Then did Norbanus meet them, who was one of the principal nobility of the city, and could shew many generals of armies among his ancestors; but they paid no regard to his dignity: yet was he of such great strength that he wrested the sword of the first of those that assaulted him out of his hands, and appeared plainly not to be willing to die without a struggle for his life, until he was surrounded by a great number of assailants, and died by the multitude of the wounds which they gave him. The third man was Anteius, a senator, and a few others with him. He did not meet with these Germans by chance, as the rest did before, but came to shew his hatred to Caius, and because he loved to see Caius lie dead with his own eyes, and took a pleasure in that sight; for Caius had banished Anteius's father, who was of the same name with himself, and, being not satisfied with that, he sent out his soldiers, and slew him; so he was come to rejoice at the sight of him, now he was dead. But as the house was now all in a tumult, when he was aiming to hide himself, he could not escape that accurate search which the Germans made, while they barbarously slew those that were guilty and those that were not guilty, and this equally also. And thus were these [three] persons slain.

16. But when the rumour that Caius was slain reached the theatre, they were astonished at it, and could not believe it: even some that entertained his destruction with great pleasure, and were more desirous of its happening than almost any other satisfaction that could come to them, were under such a fear that they could not believe it. There were also those who greatly distrusted it, because they were unwilling that any such thing should come to Caius, nor could believe it, though it were ever so true, because they thought that no man could possibly have so much power as to kill Caius. These were the women, and the children, and the slaves, and some of the soldiery. This last sort had taken his pay, and in a manner tyrannised with him, and had abused the best of the citizens, in being subservient to his unjust commands, in order to gain honours and advantages to themselves; but for the women and the youth, they had been inveigled with shows, and the fighting of the gladiators, and certain distributions of flesh-meat among them, which things in pretence were designed for the pleasing of the multitude, but in reality to satiate the barbarous cruelty and madness of Caius. The slaves also were sorry, because they were by Caius allowed to accuse and to despise their masters, and they could have recourse to his assistance when they had unjustly affronted them; for he was easy in believing them against their masters, even when they accused them falsely; and, if they would discover what money their masters had, they might soon obtain both riches and liberty, as the rewards of their accusation, because the reward of these informers was the eighth * part of the criminal's substance. As to the nobles, although the report appeared credible to some of them, either because they knew of the plot beforehand, or because they wished it might be true; however, they concealed not only the joy they had at the relation of it, but that they had heard anything at all about it. These last acted so, out of the fear they had that if the report proved false, they should be punished for having so

* This reward proposed by the Roman laws to informers was sometimes an eighth part of the criminal's goods, as here; and sometimes a fourth part.

soon let men know their minds. But those that knew Caius was dead, because they were partners with the conspirators, they concealed all still more cautiously, as not knowing one another's minds; and fearing lest they should speak of it to some of those to whom the continuance of tyranny was advantageous; and, if Caius should prove to be alive, they might be informed against and punished. And another report went about, that although Caius had been wounded indeed, yet was not he dead, but alive still, and under the physician's hands. Nor was any one looked upon by another as faithful enough to be trusted, and to whom any one would open his mind; for he was either a friend to Caius, and therefore suspected to favour his tyranny, or he was one that hated him, who therefore might be suspected to desire the less credit because of his ill-will to him. Nay, it was said by some (and this indeed it was that deprived the nobility of their hopes, and made them sad) that Caius was in a condition to despise the dangers he had been in, and took no care of healing his wounds, but was gotten away into the market-place, and, bloody as he was, was making a harangue to the people. And these were the conjectural reports of those that were so unreasonable as to endeavour to raise tumults, which they turned different ways, according to the opinions of the hearers. Yet did they not leave their seats, for fear of being accused, if they should go out before the rest; for they should not be sentenced according to the real intention with which they went out, but according to the supposals of the accuser and of the judges.

17. But now a multitude of Germans had surrounded the theatre with their swords drawn: all the spectators looked for nothing but death; and at every one's coming in, a fear seized upon them, as if they were to be cut in pieces immediately; and in great distress they were, as neither having courage enough to go out of the theatre, nor believing themselves safe from dangers if they tarried there. And when the Germans came upon them, the cry was so great, that the theatre rang again with the entreaties of the spectators to the soldiers, pleading that they were entirely ignorant of everything that related to such seditious contrivances, and if there were any sedition raised, they knew nothing of it; they therefore begged that they would spare them, and not punish those that had not the least hand in such bold crimes as belonged to other persons, while they neglected to search after such as had really done whatsoever it be that hath been done. Thus did these people appeal to God, and deplore their infelicity with shedding of tears and beating their faces, and said everything that the most imminent danger, and the utmost concern for their lives, could dictate to them. This brake the fury of the soldiers, and made them repent of what they minded to do to the spectators, which would have been the greatest instance of cruelty. And so it appeared to even these savages, when they had once fixed the heads of those that were slain with Asprenas upon the altar; at which sight the spectators were sorely afflicted, both upon the consideration of the dignity of the persons, and out of a commiseration of their sufferings; nay, indeed, they were almost in as great disorder at the prospect of the danger themselves were in, seeing it was still uncertain whether they should entirely escape the like calamity. Whence it was that such as thoroughly and justly hated Caius, could yet no way enjoy the pleasure of his death, because they were them-

selves in jeopardy of perishing together with him; nor had they hitherto any firm assurance of surviving.

18. There was at this time one Euaristus Arruntius, a public crier in the market, and therefore of a strong and audible voice, who vied in wealth with the richest of the Romans, and was able to do what he pleased in the city, both then and afterward. This man put himself into the most mournful habit he could, although he had a greater hatred against Caius than any one else; his fear and his wise contrivance to gain his safety, taught him so to do, and prevailed over his present pleasure; so he put on such a mournful dress as he would have done had he lost his dearest friends in the world; this man came into the theatre, and informed them of the death of Caius, and by this means put an end to that state of ignorance that men had been in. Arruntius also went round about the pillars, and called out to the Germans, as did the tribunes with him, bidding them put up their swords, and telling them that Caius was dead; and this proclamation it was plainly which saved those that were collected together in the theatre, and all the rest who any way met the Germans; for while they had hopes that Caius had still any breath in him, they abstained from no sort of mischief; and such an abundant kindness they still had for Caius, that they would willingly have prevented the plot against him, and procured his escape from so sad a misfortune, at the expense of their own lives; but they now left off the warm zeal they had to punish his enemies, now they were fully satisfied that Caius was dead, because it was now in vain for them to shew their zeal and kindness to him, when he who should reward them was perished. They were also afraid that they should be punished by the senate, if they should go on in doing such injuries, that is, in case the authority of the supreme governor should revert to them; and thus at length a stop was put, though not without difficulty, to that rage which possessed the Germans on account of Caius's death.

19. But Cherea was so much afraid for Minucianus, lest he should light upon the Germans, now they were in their fury, that he went and spake to every one of the soldiers, and prayed them to take care of his preservation, and made himself great inquiry about him, lest he should have been slain; and for Clement, he let Minucianus go, when he was brought to him, and, with many other of the senators, affirmed the action was right, and commended the virtue of those that contrived it, and had courage enough to execute it; and said, that "tyrants do indeed please themselves and look big for a while, upon having the power to act unjustly; but do not, however, go happily out of the world, because they are hated by the virtuous; and that Caius, together with all his unhappiness was become a conspirator against himself, before these other men who attacked him, did so; and, by becoming intolerable, in setting aside the wise provision the laws had made, taught his dearest friends to treat him as an enemy; insomuch, that although in common discourse these conspirators were those that slew Caius, yet that, in reality, he lies now dead as perishing by his own self."

20. Now by this time the people in the theatre were arisen from their seats, and those that were within made a very great disturbance: the cause of which was this, that the spectators were too hasty in getting away. There was also one Alcyon, a physician, who hurried away, as if to cure those that were wounded, and, under that pretence, he sent those that were with him to fetch what things were necessary for the healing of those wounded persons, but in reality to get them clear of the present dangers they were in. Now the senate, during this interval, had met, and the people also assembled together in the accustomed form, and were both employed in searching after the murderers of Caius. The people did it very zealously, but the senate in appearance only; for there was present Valerius of Asia, one that had been consul; this man went to the people, as they were in disorder, and very uneasy that they could not yet discover who they were that had murdered the emperor; he was then earnestly asked by them all who it was that had done it. He replied,—"I wish I had been the man." The consuls also published an edict, wherein they accused Caius, and gave order to the people then got together, and to the soldiers, to go home, and gave the people hopes of the abatement of the oppressions they lay under; and promised the soldiers, if they lay quiet as they used to do, and would not go abroad to do mischief unjustly, that they would bestow rewards upon them; for there was reason to fear lest the city might suffer harm by their wild and ungovernable behaviour, if they should once betake themselves to spoil the citizens, or plunder the temples. And now the whole multitude of the senators were assembled together, and especially those that had conspired to take away the life of Caius, who put on at this time an air of great assurance, and appeared with great magnanimity, as if the administration of public affairs were already devolved upon them.

CHAPTER II

HOW THE SENATORS DETERMINED TO RESTORE THE DEMOCRACY; BUT THE SOLDIERS WERE FOR PRESERVING THE MONARCHY. CONCERNING THE SLAUGHTER OF CAIUS'S WIFE AND DAUGHTER. A CHARACTER OF CAIUS'S MORALS

1. WHEN the public affairs were in this posture, Claudius was on the sudden hurried away out of his house; for the soldiers had a meeting together: and when they had debated about what was to be done, they saw that a democracy was incapable of managing such a vast weight of public affairs: and that if it should be set up, it would not be for their advantage; and in case any one of those already in the government should obtain the supreme power, it would in all respects be to their grief, if they were not assisting to him in this advancement: that it would therefore be right for them, while the public affairs were unsettled, to choose Claudius emperor, who was uncle to the deceased Caius, and of a superior dignity and worth to every one of those who were assembled together in the senate, both on account of the virtues of his ancestors, and of the learning he had acquired in his education; and who, if once settled in the empire, would reward them according to their deserts, and bestow largesses upon them. These were their consultations, and they executed the same immediately. Claudius was therefore seized upon suddenly by the soldiery. But Cneus Sentius Saturninus, although he understood that Claudius was seized, and that he intended to claim the government, unwillingly indeed in appearance, but in reality by his own free consent, stood up in the senate, and, without being dismayed, made an exhortatory oration to them.

and such a one indeed as was fit for men of freedom and generosity, and spake thus :—

2. " Although it be a thing incredible, O Romans! because of the great length of time, that so unexpected an event hath happened, yet are we now in possession of liberty. How long indeed this will last is uncertain, and lies at the disposal of the gods, whose grant it is: yet such it is as is sufficient to make us rejoice, and be happy for the present, although we may soon be deprived of it; for one hour is sufficient to those that are exercised in virtue, wherein we may live with a mind accountable only to ourselves, in our own country, now free, and governed by such laws as this country once flourished under. As for myself, I cannot remember our former time of liberty, as being born after it was gone; but I am beyond measure filled with joy at the thoughts of our present freedom. I also esteem those that were born and brought up in that our former liberty happy men, and that those men are worthy of no less esteem than the gods themselves, who have given us a taste of it in this age; and I heartily wish that this quiet enjoyment of it, which we have at present, might continue to all ages. However, this single day may suffice for our youth, as well as for us that are in years. It will seem an age to our old men, if they might die during its happy duration : it may also be for the instruction of the younger sort, what kind of virtue those men, from whose loins we are derived, were exercised in. As for ourselves, our business is, during the space of time, to live virtuously,—than which nothing can be more to our advantage; which course of virtue it is alone that can preserve our liberty; for as to our ancient state, I have heard of it by the relations of others; but as to our late state, during my life-time, I have known it by experience, and learned thereby what mischief tyrannies have brought upon this commonwealth, discouraging all virtue, and depriving persons of magnanimity of their liberty, and proving the teachers of flattery and slavish fear, because it leaves the public administration not to be governed by wise laws, but by the humour of those that govern. For, since Julius Cæsar took it into his head to dissolve our democracy, and, by overbearing the regular system of our laws, to bring disorders into our administration, and to get above right and justice, and to be a slave to his own inclinations, there is no kind of misery but what hath tended to the subversion of this city; while all those that have succeeded him, have striven one with another to overthrow the ancient laws of their country, and have left it destitute of such citizens as were of generous principles; because they thought it tended to their safety to have vicious men to converse withal, and not only to break the spirits of those that were best esteemed for their virtue, but to resolve upon their utter destruction. Of all which emperors, who have been many in number, and who laid upon us insufferable hardships during the times of their government, this Caius, who hath been slain to-day, hath brought more terrible calamities upon us than did all the rest, not only by exercising his ungoverned rage upon his fellow-citizens, but also upon his kindred and friends, and alike upon all others, and by inflicting still greater miseries upon them, as punishments, which they never deserved, he being equally furious against men and against the gods; for tyrants are not content to gain their sweet pleasure, and this by acting injuriously, and in the vexation they bring both upon men's estates and their wives,—but they look upon them to be their principal advantage,

when they can utterly overthrow the entire families of their enemies; while all lovers of liberty are the enemies of tyranny. Nor can those who patiently endure what miseries they bring on them gain their friendship; for as they are conscious of the abundant mischiefs they have brought on these men, and how magnanimously they have borne their hard fortunes, they cannot but be sensible what evils they have done, and thence only depend on security from what they are suspicious of, if it may be in their power to take them quite out of the world. Since, then, we are now gotten clear of such great misfortunes, and are only accountable to one another, (which form of government affords us the best assurance of our present concord, and promises us the best security from all evil designs, and will be most for our own glory in settling the city in good order,) you ought, every one of you in particular, to make provision for his own, and in general, for the public utility: or, on the contrary, they may declare their dissent to such things as have been proposed, and this without any hazard of danger to come upon them,—because they have now no lord set over them, who, without fear of punishment, could do mischief to the city, and had an uncontrollable power to take off those freely that declared their opinions. Nor has anything so much contributed to this increase of tyranny of late, as sloth, and a timorous forbearance of contradicting the emperor's will; while men had an over great inclination to the sweetness of peace, and had learned to live like slaves, and as many of us as either heard of intolerable calamities that happened at a distance from us, or saw the miseries that were near us, out of the dread of dying virtuously, endured a death joined with the utmost infamy. We ought then, in the first place, to decree the greatest honours we are able to those that have taken off the tyrant, especially to Cherea Cassius; for, this one man, with the assistance of the gods, hath, by his counsel and by his actions, been the procurer of our liberty. Nor ought we to forget him now we have recovered our liberty, who, under the foregoing tyranny, took counsel beforehand, and beforehand hazarded himself for our liberties; but ought to decree him proper honours, and thereby freely declare, that he from the beginning acted with our approbation. And certainly it is a very excellent thing, and what becomes freemen, to requite their benefactors, as this man hath been a benefactor to us all, though not at all like Cassius and Brutus, who slew Caius Julius [Cæsar ;] for these men laid the foundations of sedition and civil wars in our city;—but this man, together with his slaughter of the tyrant, hath set our city free from all those sad miseries which arose from the tyranny."

3. And this was the purport of Sentius's oration, which was received with pleasure by the senators, and by as many of the equestrian order as were present. And now one Trebellius Maximus rose up hastily, and took from Sentius's finger a ring, which had a stone, with the image of Caius engraven upon it, and which, in his zeal in speaking, and his earnestness in doing what he was about, as it was supposed, he had forgotten to take off himself. This sculpture was broken immediately. But as it was now far in the night, Cherea demanded of the consuls the watchword, who gave him this word, Liberty. These facts were the subjects of admiration to themselves, and almost incredible; for it was a hundred years since the democracy had been laid aside, when this giving the watch-word returned to the consuls; for, before the city was subject

to tyrants, they were the commanders of the soldiers. But when Cherea had received the watch-word, he delivered it to those who were on the senate's side, which were four regiments, who esteemed the government without emperors, to be preferable to tyranny. So these went away with their tribunes. The people also now departed very joyful, and full of hope and courage, as having recovered their former democracy, and no longer under an emperor: and Cherea was in very great esteem with them.

4. And now Cherea was very uneasy that Caius's daughter and wife were still alive, and that all his family did not perish with him, since whosoever was left of them must be left for the ruin of the city and of the laws. Moreover, in order to finish this matter with the utmost zeal, and in order to satisfy his hatred of Caius, he sent Julius Lupus, one of the tribunes, to kill Caius's wife and daughter. They proposed this office to Lupus, as to a kinsman of Clement, that he might be so far a partaker of this murder of the tyrant, and might rejoice in the virtue of having assisted his fellow-citizens, and that he might appear to have been a partaker with those that were first in their designs against him; yet did this action appear to some of the conspirators to be too cruel, as to this using such severity to a woman, because Caius did more indulge his own ill-nature than use her advice in all that he did; from which ill-nature it was that the city was in so desperate a condition with the miseries that were brought on it, and the flower of the city was destroyed; but others accused her of giving her consent to these things; nay, they ascribed all that Caius had done to her as the cause of it, and said she had given a potion to Caius, which had made him obnoxious to her, and had tied him down to love her by such evil methods; insomuch that she, having rendered him distracted, was become the author of all the mischiefs that had befallen the Romans, and that habitable world which was subject to them. So that at length it was determined that she must die; nor could those of the contrary opinion at all prevail to have her saved; and Lupus was sent accordingly. Nor was there any delay made in executing what he went about, but he was subservient to those that sent him on the first opportunity, as desirous to be no way blameable in what might be done for the advantage of the people. So, when he was come into the palace, he found Cesonia, who was Caius's wife, lying by her husband's dead body, which also lay down on the ground, and destitute of all such things as the law allows to the dead, and all over herself besmeared with the blood of her husband's wounds, and bewailing the great affliction she was under, her daughter lying by her also; and nothing else was heard in these her circumstances, but her complaint of Caius, as if he had not regarded what she had often told him of beforehand; which words of hers were taken in a different sense even at that time, and are now esteemed equally ambiguous, by those that hear of them, and are still interpreted according to the different inclinations of people. Now some said that the words denoted, that she had advised him to leave off his mad behaviour, and his barbarous cruelty to the citizens, and to govern the public with moderation and virtue, lest he should perish by the same way, upon their using him as he had used them. But some said, that as certain words had passed concerning the conspirators, she desired Caius to make no delay, but immediately to put them all to death; and this whether they were guilty or not, and that thereby he would be out of the fear of any

danger; and that this was what she reproached him for when she advised him so to do, but he was too slow and tender in the matter. And this was what Cesonia said; and what the opinions of men were about it. But when she saw Lupus approach, she shewed him Caius's dead body, and persuaded him to come nearer, with lamentation and tears; and as she perceived that Lupus was in disorder, and approached her in order to execute some design disagreeable to himself, she was well aware for what purpose he came, and stretched out her naked throat, and that very cheerfully to him, bewailing her case, like one utterly despairing of her life, and bidding him not to boggle at finishing the tragedy they had resolved upon relating to her. So she boldly received her death's wound at the hand of Lupus, as did the daughter after her. So Lupus made haste to inform Cherea of what he had done.

5. This was the end of Caius, after he had reigned four years, within four months. He was, even before he came to be emperor, ill-natured, and one that had arrived at the utmost pitch of wickedness; a slave to his pleasures, and a lover of calumny; greatly affected by every terrible accident, and on that account of a very murderous disposition where he durst shew it. He enjoyed his exorbitant power to this only purpose, to injure those who least deserved it, with unreasonable insolence, and got his wealth by murder and injustice. He laboured to appear above regarding either what was divine or agreeable to the laws, but was a slave to the commendations of the populace; and whatsoever the laws determined to be shameful, and punished, that he esteemed more honourable than what was virtuous. He was unmindful of his friends, how intimate soever, and though they were persons of the highest character; and, if he was once angry at any of them, he would inflict punishment upon them on the smallest occasions; and esteemed every man that endeavoured to lead a virtuous life his enemy! And whatsoever he commanded, he would not admit of any contradiction to his inclinations; whence it was that he had criminal conversation with his own sister;* from which occasion chiefly it was also that a bitter hatred first sprang up against him among the citizens, that sort of incest not having been known of a long time; and so this provoked men to distrust him, and to hate him that was guilty of it. And for any great or royal work that he ever did, which might be for the present and future ages, nobody can name any such, but only the haven that he made about Rhegium and Sicily, for the reception of the ships that brought corn from Egypt; which was indeed a work without dispute very great in itself, and of very great advantage to the navigation. Yet was not this work brought to perfection by him, but was the one half of it left imperfect by reason of his want of application to it; the cause of which was this, that he employed his studies about useless matters, and that by spending his money upon such pleasures as concerned no one's benefit but his own, he could not exert his liberality in things that were undeniably of great consequence. Otherwise he was an excellent orator, and thoroughly acquainted with the Greek tongue, as well as with his own country or Roman language. He was also able, off-hand and readily, to give answers to compositions

---

* Spanheim here notes, that the name of Caius's sister, with whom he was guilty of incest, was Drusilla; and that Suetonius adds, he was guilty of the same crime with all his sisters also.

made by others, of considerable length and accuracy. He was also more skilful in persuading others to very great things than any one else, and this from a natural affability of temper, which had been improved by much exercise and painstaking; for as he was the grandson * of the brother of Tiberius, whose successor he was, this was a strong inducement to his acquiring of learning, because Tiberius aspired after the highest pitch of that sort of reputation: and Caius aspired after the like glory for eloquence, being induced thereto by the letters of his kinsman and his emperor. He was also among the first rank of his own citizens. But the advantages he received from his learning did not countervail the mischief he brought upon himself in the exercise of his authority; so difficult it is for those to obtain the virtue that is necessary for a wise man, who have the absolute power to do what they please without control. At the first he got himself such friends as were in all respects the most worthy, and was greatly beloved by them, while he imitated their zealous application to the learning and to the glorious actions of the best men; but when he became insolent towards them, they laid aside the kindness they had for him, and began to hate him; from which hatred came that plot which they raised against him, and wherein he perished.

CHAPTER III

HOW CLAUDIUS WAS SEIZED UPON, AND BROUGHT OUT OF HIS HOUSE, AND BROUGHT TO THE CAMP; AND HOW THE SENATE SENT AN EMBASSAGE TO HIM

1. Now Claudius, as I said before, went out of that way along which Caius was gone; and as the family was in a mighty disorder upon the sad accident of the murder of Caius, he was in great distress how to save himself, and was found to have hidden himself in a certain narrow place,† though he had no other occasion for suspicion of any danger, besides the dignity of his birth; for while he was a private man, he behaved himself with moderation, and was contented with his present fortune, applying himself to learning, and especially to that of the Greeks, and keeping himself entirely clear from everything that might bring on any disturbance. But at this time the multitude were under a consternation, and the whole palace was full of the soldiers' madness, and the very emperor's guards seemed under the like fear and disorder with private persons, the band called *pretorian*, which was the purest part of the army, was in consultation what was to be done at this juncture. Now all those that were at this consultation had little regard to the punishment Caius had suffered, because he justly deserved such his fortune; but they were rather considering their own circumstances, how they might take the best care of themselves, especially while the Germans were busy in punishing the murderers of Caius; which yet was rather done to gratify their own savage temper, than for the good of the public; all which things disturbed Claudius, who was afraid of his own safety, and this particularly because he saw the heads of Asprenas

and his partners carried about. His station had been on a certain elevated place, whither a few steps led him, and whither he had retired in the dark by himself. But when Gratus, who was one of the soldiers that belonged to the palace, saw him, but did not well know by his countenance who he was, because it was dark, though he could well judge that it was a man who was private there on some design, he came nearer to him; and when Claudius desired that he would retire, he discovered who he was, and owned him to be Claudius. So he said to his followers, "This is a Germanicus; ‡ come on, let us choose him for our emperor." But when Claudius saw they were making preparations for taking him away by force, and was afraid they would kill him as they had killed Caius, he besought them to spare him, putting them in mind how quietly he had demeaned himself, and that he was unacquainted with what had been done. Hereupon Gratus smiled upon him, and took him by the right hand, and said, "Leave off, sir, these low thoughts of saving yourself, while you ought to have greater thoughts, even of obtaining the empire, which the gods, out of their concern for the habitable world, by taking Caius out of the way, commits to thy virtuous conduct. Go to, therefore, and accept of the throne of thy ancestors." So they took him up and carried him, because he was not then able to go on foot, such was his dread and his joy at what was told him.

2. Now there was already gathered together about Gratus, a great number of the guards; and when they saw Claudius carried off, they looked with a sad countenance, as supposing that he was carried to execution for the mischiefs that had been lately done; while yet they thought him a man who never meddled with public affairs all his life long, and one that had met with no contemptible dangers under the reign of Caius; and some of them thought it reasonable that the consuls should take cognisance of these matters; and, as still more and more of the soldiery got together, the crowd about him ran away, and Claudius could hardly go on, his body was then so weak; and those who carried his sedan, upon an inquiry that was made about his being carried off, ran away and saved themselves, as despairing of their lord's preservation. But, when they were come into the large court of the palace, (which, as the report goes about it, was inhabited first of all the parts of the city of Rome,) and had just reached the public treasury, many more soldiers came about him, as glad to see Claudius's face, and thought it exceeding right to make him emperor on account of their kindness for Germanicus, who was his brother, and had left behind him a vast reputation among all that were acquainted with him. They reflected also on the covetous temper of the leading men of the senate, and what great errors they had been guilty of when the senate had the government formerly; they also considered the impossibility of such an undertaking, as also what dangers they should be in, if the government should come to a single person, and that such a one should possess it as they had no hand in advancing, and not to Claudius, who would take it as their grant, and as gained by their good-will to him, and would remember the favours they had

---

* This Caius was the son of Germanicus, who was the son of Drusus the brother of Tiberius the emperor.

† The first place Claudius came to was inhabited, and called Hermeum.

‡ How Claudius, another son of Drusus, which Drusus was the father of Germanicus, could be here himself called Germanicus, Suetonius informs us, when he assures us that, by a decree of the senate, the surname of Germanicus was bestowed upon Drusus and his posterity also.

done him, and would make them a sufficient recompense for the same.

3. These were the discourses the soldiers had one with another by themselves, and they communicated them to all such as came in to them. Now those that inquired about this matter willingly embraced the invitation that was made them to join with the rest : so they carried Claudius into the camp, crowding about him as his guard, and encompassing him about, one chairman still succeeding another, that their vehement endeavours might not be hindered. But as to the populace and senators, they disagreed in their opinions. The latter were very desirous to recover their former dignity, and were zealous to get clear of the slavery that had been brought on them by the injurious treatment of the tyrants, which the present opportunity afforded them ; but for the people, who were envious against them, and knew that the emperors were capable of curbing their covetous temper, and were a refuge from them, they were very glad that Claudius had been seized upon, and brought to them, and thought, that if Claudius were made emperor, he would prevent a civil war, such as there was in the days of Pompey. But when the senate knew that Claudius was brought into the camp by the soldiers, they sent to him those of their body which had the best character for their virtues, that they might inform him that he ought to do nothing by violence, in order to gain the government ; that he who was a single person, one either already, or hereafter to be a member of their body, ought to yield to the senate, which consisted of so great a number ; that he ought to let the law take place in the disposal of all that related to the public order, and to remember how greatly the former tyrants had afflicted their city, and what dangers both he and they had escaped under Caius ; and that he ought not to hate the heavy burden of tyranny, when the injury is done by others, while he did himself wilfully treat his country after a mad and insolent manner ; that if he would comply with them, and demonstrate that his firm resolution was to live quietly and virtuously, he would have the greatest honours decreed on him that a free people could bestow ; and by subjecting himself to the law, would obtain this branch of commendation, that he acted like a man of virtue, both as a ruler and a subject ; but that if he would act foolishly, and learn no wisdom by Caius's death, they would not permit him to go on ; that a great part of the army was got together for them, with plenty of weapons, and a great number of slaves, which they could make use of : that good hope was a great matter in such cases, as was also good fortune, and that the gods would never assist any others, but those that undertook to act with virtue and goodness, who can be no other than such as fight for the liberty of their country.

4. Now the ambassadors, Veranius and Brocchus, who were both of them tribunes of the people, made this speech to Claudius ; and, falling down upon their knees, they begged of him that he would not throw the city into wars and misfortunes ; but when they saw what a multitude of soldiers encompassed and guarded Claudius, and that the forces that were with the consuls were, in comparison of them, perfectly inconsiderable, they added, that if he did desire the government, he should accept of it as given by the senate ; that he would prosper better, and be happier if he came to it, not by injustice, but by the good-will of those that would bestow it upon him.

CHAPTER IV

WHAT THINGS KING AGRIPPA DID FOR CLAUDIUS ; AND HOW CLAUDIUS, WHEN HE HAD TAKEN THE GOVERNMENT, COMMANDED THE MURDERERS OF CAIUS TO BE SLAIN

1. Now Claudius, though he was sensible after what an insolent manner the senate had sent to him, yet did he, according to their advice, behave himself for the present with moderation ; but not so far that he could not recover himself out of his fright : so he was encouraged [to claim the government] partly by the boldness of the soldiers, and partly by the persuasion of king Agrippa, who exhorted him not to let such a dominion slip out of his hands, when it came thus to him of its own accord. Now this Agrippa, with relation to Caius, did what became one that had been so much honoured by him ; for he embraced Caius's body after he was dead, and laid it upon a bed, and covered it as well as he could, and went out to the guards, and told them Caius was still alive ; but he said that they should call for physicians, since he was very ill of his wounds. But when he had learned that Claudius was carried away violently by the soldiers, he rushed through the crowd to him, and when he found that he was in disorder, and ready to resign up the government to the senate, he encouraged him, and desired him to keep the government ; but when he had said this to Claudius, he retired home. And, upon the senate's sending for him, he anointed his head with ointment, as if he had lately accompanied with his wife, and had dismissed her, and then came to them : he also asked of the senators what Claudius did ; who told him the present state of affairs, and then asked his opinion about the settlement of the public. He told them in words, that he was ready to lose his life for the honour of the senate, but desired them to consider what was for their advantage, without any regard to what was most agreeable to them ; for that those who grasp at government, will stand in need of weapons and soldiers to guard them, unless they will set up without any preparation for it, and so fall into danger. And when the senate replied, that they would bring in weapons in abundance, and money, and that as to an army, a part of it was already collected together for them, and they would raise a larger one by giving the slaves their liberty,—Agrippa made answer, " O senators ! may you be able to compass what you have a mind to ; yet will I immediately tell you my thoughts, because they tend to your preservation. Take notice, then, that the army which will fight for Claudius hath been long exercised in warlike affairs ; but our army will be no better than a rude multitude of raw men, and those such as have been unexpectedly made free from slavery, and ungovernable ; we must then fight against those that are skilful in war, with men who know not so much as how to draw their swords. So that my opinion is, that we should send some persons to Claudius, to persuade him to lay down the government ; and I am ready to be one of your ambassadors."

2. Upon this speech of Agrippa, the senate complied with him, and he was sent among others, and privately informed Claudius of the disorder the senate was in, and gave him instructions to answer them in a somewhat commanding strain, and as one invested with dignity and authority. Accordingly, Claudius said to the ambassadors, that he did not wonder the senate had no mind to have an emperor over them, be-

cause they had been harassed by the barbarity of those that had formerly been at the head of their affairs; but that they should taste of an equitable government under him, and moderate times, while he should only be their ruler in name, but the authority should be equally common to them all; and since he had passed through many and various scenes of life before their eyes, it would be good for them not to distrust him. So the ambassadors, upon their hearing this his answer, were dismissed. But Claudius discoursed with the army which was there gathered together, who took oaths that they would persist in their fidelity to him; upon which he gave the guards every man five thousand* drachmæ a-piece, and a proportionable quantity to their captains, and promised to give the same to the rest of the armies, wheresoever they were.

3. And now the consuls called the senate together, into the temple of Jupiter the Conqueror, while it was still night; but some of those senators concealed themselves in the city, being uncertain what to do, upon the hearing of this summons; and some of them went out of the city to their own farms, as foreseeing whether the public affairs were going, and despairing of liberty; nay, these supposed it much better for them to be slaves without danger to themselves, and to live a lazy and inactive life, than by claiming the dignity of their forefathers, to run the hazard of their own safety. However, a hundred, and no more, were gotten together; and as they were in consultation about the present posture of affairs, a sudden clamour was made by the soldiers that were on their side, desiring that the senate would choose them an emperor, and not bring the government into ruin by setting up a multitude of rulers. So they fully declared to be for the giving the government not to all, but to one; but they gave the senate leave to look out for a person worthy to be set over them, insomuch, that now the affairs of the senate were much worse than before; because they had not only failed in the recovery of their liberty, which they boasted themselves of, but were in dread of Claudius also. Yet there were those that hankered after the government, both on account of the dignity of their families, and that accruing to them by their marriages; for Marcus Minucianus was illustrious, both by his own nobility and by his having married Julia, the sister of Caius, who accordingly was very ready to claim the government, although the consuls discouraged him, and made one delay after another in proposing it: that Minucianus also, who was one of Caius's murderers, restrained Valerius of Asia from thinking of such things; and a prodigious slaughter there had been, if leave had been given to these men to set up for themselves, and oppose Claudius. There was also a considerable number of gladiators besides, and of those soldiers who kept watch by night in the city, and rowers of ships, who all ran into the camp; insomuch, that of those who put in for the government, some left off their pretensions, in order to spare the city, and others out of fear of their own persons.

4. But as soon as ever it was day, Cherea, and those that were with him, came into the senate, and attempted to make speeches to the soldiers. However, the multitude of those soldiers, when they saw they were making signals for silence with their hands, and were ready to begin to speak to them, grew tumultuous, and would not let them speak at all, because they were zealous to be under a monarchy; and they demanded of the senate one for their ruler, as not enduring any longer delays. But the senate hesitated about either their own governing, or how they should be governed, while the soldiers would not admit them to govern; and the murderers of Caius would not permit the soldiers to dictate to them. When they were in these circumstances, Cherea was not able to contain the anger he had, and promised, that if they desired an emperor, he would give them one, if one would bring him the watch-word from Eutychus. Now, this Eutychus was charioteer of the green-band faction, styled Prasine, and a great friend of Caius, who used to harass the soldiery with building stables for horses, and spent his time in ignominious labours, which occasioned Cherea to reproach them with him, and to abuse them with much other scurrilous language; and told them he would bring them the head of Claudius; and that it was an amazing thing that, after their former madness, they should commit their government to a fool. Yet were they not moved with his words, but drew their swords, and took up their ensigns, and went to Claudius, to join in taking the oath of fidelity to him. So the senate were left without anybody to defend them; and the very consuls differed nothing from private persons. They were also under consternation and sorrow, men not knowing what would become of them, because Claudius was very angry at them; so they fell a reproaching one another, and repented of what they had done. At which juncture Sabinus, one of Caius's murderers, threatened that he would sooner come into the midst of them and kill himself, than consent to make Claudius emperor, and see slavery returning upon them; he also abused Cherea for loving his life too well, while he who was the first in his contempt of Caius, could think it a good thing to live, when, even by all that they had done for the recovery of their liberty, they had found it impossible to do it. But Cherea said he had no manner of doubt upon him about killing himself; yet he would first sound the intentions of Claudius before he did it.

5. These were the debates [about the senate;] but in the camp everybody was crowding on all sides to pay their court to Claudius; and the other consul, Quintus Pomponius, was reproached by the soldiery as having rather exhorted the senate to recover their liberty; whereupon they drew their swords, and were going to assault him, and they had done it, if Claudius had not hindered them, who snatched the consul out of the danger he was in, and set him by him. But he did not receive that part of the senate which was with Quintus in the like honourable manner; nay, some of them received blows, and were thrust away as they came to salute Claudius; nay, Aponius went away wounded, and they were all in danger. However, king Agrippa went up to Claudius, and desired he would treat the senators more gently; for if any mischief should come to the senate, he would have no others over whom to rule. Claudius complied with him, and called the senate together into the palace, and was carried thither himself through the city, while the soldiery conducted him, though this was to the great vexation of the multitude; for Cherea and Sabinus, two of Caius's murderers, went in the fore-front of them, in an open manner, while Pollio, whom Claudius, a little before, had made captain of his guards, had sent them an epistolary edict, to forbid them to appear in public. Then did

---

* This number of drachmæ to be distributed to each private soldier, equal to £161 sterling, seems much too large, and is perhaps a mistake of the transcriber's.

Claudius, upon his coming to the palace, get his friends together, and desired their suffrages about Cherea. They said that the work he had done was a glorious one; but they accused him that he did it of perfidiousness, and thought it just to inflict the punishment [of death] upon him, to discountenance such actions for the time to come. So Cherea was led to his execution, and Lupus and many other Romans with him. Now it is reported that Cherea bore his calamity courageously; and this not only by the firmness of his own behaviour under it, but by the reproaches he laid upon Lupus, who fell into tears; for when Lupus had laid his garment aside and complained of the cold,* he said, that cold was never hurtful to Lupus [i.e., a wolf.] And as a great many men went along with them to see the sight, when Cherea came to the place, he asked the soldier who was to be their executioner, whether this office was what he was used to, or whether this was the first time of his using his sword in that manner; and desired him to bring him that very sword with which he himself slew Caius. So he was happily killed at one stroke. But Lupus did not meet with such good fortune in going out of the world, since he was timorous, and had many blows levelled at his neck, because he did not stretch it out boldly [as he ought to have done.]

6. Now a few days after this, as the Parental Solemnities were just at hand, the Roman multitude made their usual oblations to their several ghosts, and put portions into the fire in honour of Cherea, and besought him to be merciful to them, and not continue his anger against them for their ingratitude. And this was the end of the life that Cherea came to. But for Sabinus, although Claudius not only set him at liberty, but gave him leave to retain his former command in the army, yet did he think it would be unjust in him to fail of performing his obligations to his fellow-confederates; so he fell upon his sword, and killed himself, the wound reaching up to the very hilt of the sword.

CHAPTER V

HOW CLAUDIUS RESTORED TO AGRIPPA HIS GRANDFATHER'S KINGDOMS, AUGMENTED HIS DOMINIONS; AND HOW HE PUBLISHED AN EDICT IN BEHALF OF THE JEWS

1. Now, when Claudius had taken out of the way all those soldiers whom he suspected, which he did immediately, he published an edict, and therein confirmed that kingdom to Agrippa which Caius had given him, and therein commended the king highly. He also made an addition to it of all that country over which Herod, who was his grandfather, had reigned, that is, Judea and Samaria; and this he restored to him as due to his family. But for Abila † of Lysanias, and all that lay at mount Libanus, he

bestowed them upon him, as out of his own territories. He also made a league with this Agrippa, confirmed by oaths, in the middle of the forum, in the city of Rome: he also took away from Antiochus that kingdom which he was possessed of, but gave him a certain part of Cilicia and Commagena: he also set Alexander Lysimachus, the alabarch, at liberty, who had been his old friend, and steward to his mother Antonia, but had been imprisoned by Caius, whose son [Marcus] married Bernice, the daughter of Agrippa. But when Marcus, Alexander's son, was dead, who had married her when she was a virgin, Agrippa gave her in marriage to his brother Herod, and begged for him of Claudius the kingdom of Chalcis.

2. Now, about this time there was a sedition between the Jews and the Greeks, at the city of Alexandria; for, when Caius was dead, the nation of the Jews, which had been very much mortified under the reign of Caius, and reduced to very great distress by the people of Alexandria, recovered itself, and immediately took up their arms to fight for themselves. So Claudius sent an order to the president of Egypt, to quiet that tumult; he also sent an edict, at the request of king Agrippa and king Herod, both to Alexandria and to Syria, whose contents were as follows:—" Tiberius Claudius Cæsar Augustus Germanicus, high priest, and tribune of the people, ordains thus:—Since I am assured that the Jews of Alexandria, called Alexandrians, have been joint inhabitants in the earliest times with the Alexandrians, and have obtained from their kings equal privileges with them, as is evident by the public records that are in their possession, and the edicts themselves; and that after Alexandria had been subjected to our empire by Augustus, their rights and privileges have been preserved by those presidents who have at divers times been sent thither; and that no dispute had been raised about those rights and privileges, even when Aquila was governor of Alexandria; and that when the Jewish ethnarch was dead, Augustus did not prohibit the making such ethnarchs, as willing that all men should be so subject [to the Romans] as to continue in the observation of their own customs, and not be forced to transgress the ancient rules of their own country religion; but that, in the time of Caius, the Alexandrians became insolent to the Jews that were among them, which Caius, out of his great madness, and want of understanding, reduced the nation of the Jews very low, because they would not transgress the religious worship of their country, and call him a god: I will, therefore, that the nation of the Jews be not deprived of their rights and privileges on account of the madness of Caius; but that those rights and privileges, which they formerly enjoyed, be preserved to them, and that they may continue in their own customs. And I charge both parties to take very great care that no troubles may arise after the promulgation of this edict."

3. And such were the contents of this edict on behalf of the Jews, that was sent to Alexandria. But the edict that was sent into the other parts of the habitable earth was this which follows:—" Tiberius Claudius Cæsar Augustus Germanicus, high priest, tribune of the people, chosen consul the second time, ordains thus:—Upon the petition of king Agrippa and king Herod, who are persons very dear to me, that I would grant the same rights and privileges should be preserved to the Jews which are in all the Roman empire, which I have granted to those of Alexandria, I very willingly comply therewith; and this grant I make not only for the

---

* This piercing cold here complained of by Lupus, agrees well with the time of the year when Claudius began his reign; it being for certain about the months of November, December, or January, and most probably a few days after January 24, and a few days before the Roman Parentalia.

† Here St Luke is in some measure confirmed, when he informs us, (chap. iii. 1,) that Lysanias was some time before tetrarch of Abilene, whose capital was Abila; as he is further confirmed by Ptolemy, when he calls that city Abila of Lysanias. This principality seems to have belonged to the land of Canaan originally, to have been the burying-place of Abel, and referred to as such, (Matt. xxiii. 36; Luke xi. 51.)

sake of the petitioners, but as judging those Jews for whom I have been petitioned, worthy of such a favour, on account of their fidelity and friendship to the Romans. I think it also very just that no Grecian city should be deprived of such rights and privileges, since they were preserved to them under the great Augustus. It will therefore be fit to permit the Jews, who are in all the world under us, to keep their ancient customs without being hindered so to do. And I do charge them also to use this my kindness to them with moderation, and not to shew a contempt of the superstitious observances of other nations, but to keep their own laws only. And I will that this decree of mine be engraven on tables by the magistrates of the cities and colonies, and municipal places, both those within Italy and those without it, both kings and governors, by the means of the ambassadors, and to have them exposed to the public for full thirty days, in such a place, whence it may plainly be read from the ground."*

CHAPTER VI

WHAT THINGS WERE DONE BY AGRIPPA AT JERUSALEM WHEN HE WAS RETURNED BACK INTO JUDEA; AND WHAT IT WAS THAT PETRONIUS WROTE TO THE INHABITANTS OF DORIS, IN BEHALF OF THE JEWS

1. Now Claudius Cæsar, by these decrees of his which were sent to Alexandria and to all the habitable earth, made known what opinion he had of the Jews. So he soon sent Agrippa away to take his kingdom, now he was advanced to a more illustrious dignity than before, and sent letters to the presidents and procurators of the provinces, that they should treat him very kindly. Accordingly, he returned in haste, as was likely he would, now he returned in much greater prosperity than he had before. He also came to Jerusalem and offered all the sacrifices that belonged to him, and omitted nothing which the law required; on which account he ordered that many of the Nazarites should have their heads shorn. And for the golden chain which had been given him by Caius, of equal weight with that iron chain wherewith his royal hands had been bound, he hung it up within the limits of the temple, over the treasury,† that it might be a memorial of the severe fate he had lain under, and a testimony of his change for the better; that it might be a demonstration how the greatest prosperity may have a fall, and that God sometimes raises what is fallen down: for this chain thus dedicated, afforded a document to all men, that king Agrippa had been once bound in a chain for a small cause, but recovered his former dignity again; and a little while afterwards got out of his bonds, and was advanced to be a more illustrious king than he was before. Whence men may understand, that all that partake of human nature, how great soever they are, may fall; and that those that fall may gain their former illustrious dignity again.

2. And when Agrippa had entirely finished all the duties of the divine worship, he removed Theophilus, the son of Ananus, from the high priesthood, and bestowed that honour of his on Simon, the son of Boethus, whose name was also Cantheras, whose daughter king Herod had married, as I have related above. Simon, therefore, had the [high] priesthood with his brethren, and with his father, in like manner as the sons of Simon, the son of Onias, who were three, had it formerly under the government of the Macedonians, as we have related in a former book.

3. When the king had settled the high priesthood after this manner, he returned the kindness which the inhabitants of Jerusalem had shewn him; for he released them from the tax upon houses, every one of whom paid it before, thinking it a good thing to requite the tender affection of those that loved him. He also made Silas the general of his forces, as a man who had partaken with him in many of his troubles. But after a very little while, the young men of Doris, preferring a rash attempt before piety, and being naturally bold and insolent, carried a statue of Cæsar into a synagogue of the Jews, and erected it there. This procedure of theirs greatly provoked Agrippa; for it plainly tended to the dissolution of the laws of his country. So he came without delay to Publius Petronius, who was then president of Syria, and accused the people of Doris. Nor did he less resent what was done than did Agrippa; for he judged it a piece of impiety to transgress the laws that regulate the actions of men. So he wrote the following letter to the people of Doris, in an angry strain:— "Publius Petronius, the president under Tiberius Claudius Cæsar Augustus Germanicus, to the magistrates of Doris, ordains as follows:—Since some of you have had the boldness, or madness rather, after the edict of Claudius Cæsar Augustus Germanicus was published, for permitting the Jews to observe the laws of their country, not to obey the same, but have acted in entire opposition thereto, as forbidding the Jews to assemble together in the synagogue, by removing Cæsar's statue, and setting it up therein, and thereby have offended not only the Jews, but the emperor himself, whose statue is more commodiously placed in his own temple than in a foreign one, where is the place of assembling together; while it is but a part of natural justice, that every one should have the power over the place belonging peculiarly to themselves, according to the determination of Cæsar,—to say nothing of my own determination, which it would be ridiculous to mention after the emperor's edict, which gives the Jews leave to make use of their own customs, as also gives order that they enjoy equally the rights of citizens with the Greeks themselves,—I therefore ordain, that Proculus Vitellius, the centurion, bring those men to me, who, contrary to Augustus's edict, have been so insolent as to do this thing, at which those very men who appear to be of principal reputation among them, have an indignation also, and allege for themselves that it was not done with their consent, but by the violence of the multitude, that they might give an account of what hath been done. I also exhort the principal magistrates among them, unless they have a mind to have this action esteemed to be done with their consent, to inform the centurion of those that were guilty of it, and take care that no handle be hence taken for raising a sedition or quarrel among them, which those seem to me to hunt after, who encourage such doings; while both I myself, and king Agrippa, for whom I have the highest honour, have nothing more

---

* This form was so known and frequent among the Romans, that it used to be thus represented at the bottom of their edicts by the initial letters only, U. D. P. R. L. P., Unde De Plano Recte Lege Possit: "Whence it may be plainly read from the ground."

† This treasury-chamber seems to have been the very same in which our Saviour taught, and where the people offered their charity money, for the repairs or other uses of the temple, (Mark xii. 41, &c.; Luke xxii. 1; John viii. 20.)

under our care than that the nation of the Jews may have an occasion given them of getting together, under the pretence of avenging themselves, and become tumultuous. And that it may be more publicly known what Augustus hath resolved upon this whole matter, I have subjoined those edicts which he hath lately caused to be published at Alexandria, and which, although they may be well known to all, yet did king Agrippa, for whom I have the highest honour, read them at that time before my tribunal, and pleaded that the Jews ought not to be deprived of those rights which Augustus hath granted them. I therefore charge you, that you do not, for the time to come, seek for any occasion of sedition or disturbance, but that every one be allowed to follow their own religious customs."

4. Thus did Petronius take care of this matter, that such a breach of the law might be corrected, and that no such thing might be attempted afterwards against the Jews. And now king Agrippa took the [high] priesthood away from Simon Cantheras, and put Jonathan, the son of Ananus, into it again, and owned that he was more worthy of that dignity than the other. But this was not a thing acceptable to him, to recover that his former dignity. So he refused it, and said, "O king! I rejoice in the honour that thou hast for me, and take it kindly that thou wouldst give me such a dignity of thy own inclinations, although God hath judged that I am not at all worthy of the high priesthood. I am satisfied with having once put on the sacred garments; for I then put them on after a more holy manner than I should now receive them again. But, if thou desirest that a person more worthy than myself should have this honourable employment, give me leave to name thee such a one. I have a brother that is pure from all sin against God, and of all offences against thyself; I recommend him to thee, as one that is fit for this dignity." So the king was pleased with these words of his, and passed by Jonathan, and according to his brother's desire, bestowed the high priesthood upon Matthias. Nor was it long before Marcus succeeded Petronius, as president of Syria.

CHAPTER VII

CONCERNING SILAS,—AND ON WHAT ACCOUNT IT WAS THAT KING AGRIPPA WAS ANGRY AT HIM. HOW AGRIPPA BEGAN TO ENCOMPASS JERUSALEM WITH A WALL; AND WHAT BENEFITS HE BESTOWED ON THE INHABITANTS OF BERYTUS

1. Now Silas, the general of the king's horse, because he had been faithful to him under all his misfortunes, and had never refused to be a partaker with him in any of his dangers, but had oftentimes undergone the most hazardous dangers for him, was full of assurance, and thought he might expect a sort of equality with the king, on account of the firmness of the friendship he had shewn to him. Accordingly, he would nowhere let the king sit as his superior, and took the like liberty in speaking to him upon all occasions, till he became troublesome to the king, when they were merry together, extolling himself beyond measure, and oft putting the king in mind of the severity of fortune he had undergone, that he might by way of ostentation demonstrate what zeal he had shewn in his service; and was continually harping upon this string, what pains he had taken for him, and much enlarged still

upon that subject. The repetition of this so frequently seemed to reproach the king, insomuch that he took this ungovernable liberty of talking very ill at his hands. For the commemoration of times when men have been under ignominy is by no means agreeable to them; and he is a very silly man who is perpetually relating to a person what kindness he had done him. At last therefore, Silas had so thoroughly provoked the king's indignation, that he acted rather out of passion than good consideration, and did not only turn Silas out of his place, as general of his horse, but sent him in bonds into his own country. But the edge of his anger wore off by length of time, and made room for more just reasonings as to his judgment about this man; and he considered how many labours he had undergone for his sake. So when Agrippa was solemnising his birthday, and he gave festival entertainments to all his subjects, he sent for Silas on the sudden to be his guest. But, as he was a very frank man, he thought he had now a just handle given him to be angry; which he could not conceal from those that came for him, but said to them, "What honour is this the king invites me to, which I conclude will soon be over? For the king hath not let me keep those original marks of the good-will I bore him, which I once had from him; but he hath plundered me, and that unjustly also. Does he think that I can leave off that liberty of speech, which, upon the consciousness of my deserts, I shall use more loudly than before, and shall relate how many misfortunes I have delivered him from? how many labours I have undergone for him, whereby I procured him deliverance and respect? as a reward for which I have borne the hardships of bonds and a dark prison! I shall never forget this usage. Nay, perhaps, my very soul, when it is departed out of the body, will not forget the glorious actions I did on his account." This was the clamour he made; and he ordered the messengers to tell it to the king. So he perceived that Silas was incurable in his folly, and still suffered him to lie in prison.

2. As for the walls of Jerusalem, that were adjoining to the new city [Bezetha,] he repaired them at the expense of the public, and built them wider in breadth and higher in altitude; and he had made them too strong for all human power to demolish, unless Marcus, the then president of Syria, had by letter informed Claudius Cæsar of what he was doing. And when Claudius had some suspicion of attempts for innovation, he sent to Agrippa to leave off the building of those walls presently. So he obeyed, as not thinking it proper to contradict Claudius.

3. Now, this king was by nature very beneficent and liberal in his gifts, and very ambitious to oblige people with such large donations; and he made himself very illustrious by the many chargeable presents he made them. He took delight in giving, and rejoiced in living with good reputation. He was not at all like that Herod who reigned before him; for that Herod was ill-natured, and severe in his punishments, and had no mercy on them that he hated; and every one perceived that he was more friendly to the Greeks than to the Jews; for he adorned foreign cities with large presents in money; with building them baths and theatres besides; nay, in some of those places, he erected temples, and porticoes in others; but he did not vouchsafe to raise one of the least edifices in any Jewish city, or make them any donation that was worth mentioning. But Agrippa's temper was mild, and equally liberal to all men. He was humane to foreigners, and made them sensible of his liber-

ality. He was in like manner rather of a gentle and compassionate temper. Accordingly, he loved to live continually at Jerusalem, and was exactly careful in the observance of the laws of his country. He therefore kept himself entirely pure : nor did any day pass over his head without its appointed sacrifice.

4. However, there was a certain man of the Jewish nation at Jerusalem, who appeared to be very accurate in the knowledge of the law. His name was Simon. This man got together an assembly, while the king was absent at Cesarea, and had the insolence to accuse him as not living holily, and that he might justly be excluded out of the temple, since it belonged only to native Jews. But the general of Agrippa's army informed him that Simon had made such a speech to the people. So the king sent for him; and, as he was then sitting in the theatre, he bade him sit down by him, and said to him with a low and gentle voice,—"What is there done in this place that is contrary to the law?" But he had nothing to say for himself, but begged his pardon. So the king was more easily reconciled to him than one could have imagined, as esteeming mildness a better quality in a king than anger; and knowing that moderation is more becoming in great men than passion. So he made Simon a small present and dismissed him.

5. Now, as Agrippa was a great builder in many places, he paid a peculiar regard to the people of Berytus : for he erected a theatre for them, superior to many others of that sort, both in sumptuousness and elegance, as also an amphitheatre, built at vast expenses; and besides these he built them baths and porticoes, and spared for no costs in any of his edifices, to render them both handsome and large. He also spent a great deal upon their dedication, and exhibited shows upon them, and brought thither musicians of all sorts, and such as made the most delightful music of the greatest variety. He also shewed his magnificence upon the theatre, in his great number of gladiators; and there it was that he exhibited the several antagonists, in order to please the spectators; no fewer indeed than seven hundred men to fight with seven hundred other men; and allotted all the malefactors he had for this exercise, that both the malefactors might receive their punishment, and that this operation of war might be a recreation in peace. And thus were these criminals all destroyed at once.

CHAPTER VIII

WHAT OTHER ACTS WERE DONE BY AGRIPPA UNTIL HIS DEATH; AND AFTER WHAT MANNER HE DIED

1. WHEN Agrippa had finished what I have above related at Berytus, he removed to Tiberias, a city of Galilee. Now he was in great esteem among other kings. Accordingly there came to him Antiochus, king of Commagena, Sampsigeramus, king of Emesa, and Cotys, who was king of the lesser Armenia, and Polemo, who was king of Pontus, as also Herod his brother, who was king of Chalcis. All these he treated with agreeable entertainments, and after an obliging manner, and so as to exhibit the greatness of his mind,—and so as to appear worthy of those respects which the kings paid to him, by coming thus to see him. However, while these kings stayed with him, Marcus, the

president of Syria, came thither. So the king, in order to preserve the respect that was due to the Romans, went out of the city to meet him, as far as seven furlongs. But this proved to be the beginning of a difference between him and Marcus; for he took with him in his chariot those other kings as his assessors. But Marcus had a suspicion what the meaning could be of so great a friendship of these kings one with another, and did not think so close an agreement of so many potentates to be for the interest of the Romans. He therefore sent some of his domestics to every one of them, and enjoined them to go their ways home without further delay. This was very ill taken by Agrippa, who after that became his enemy. And now he took the high-priesthood away from Matthias, and made Elioneus, the son of Cantheras, high priest in his stead.

2. Now, when Agrippa had reigned three years over all Judea, he came to the city Cesarea, which was formerly called Strato's Tower; and there he exhibited shows in honour of Cæsar, upon his being informed that there was a certain festival celebrated to make vows for his safety. At which festival, a great multitude was gotten together of the principal persons, and such as were of dignity through his province. On the second day of which shows he put on a garment made wholly of silver, and of a contexture truly wonderful, and came into the theatre early in the morning; at which time the silver of his garment being illuminated by the fresh reflection of the sun's rays upon it, shone out after a surprising manner, and was so resplendent as to spread a horror over those that looked intently upon him : and presently his flatterers cried out, one from one place, and another from another, (though not for his good,) that he was a god : and they added,—"Be thou merciful to us; for although we have hitherto reverenced thee only as a man, yet shall we henceforth own thee as superior to mortal nature." Upon this the king did neither rebuke them, nor reject their impious flattery. But, as he presently afterwards looked up, he saw an owl sitting on a certain rope over his head, and immediately understood that this bird was the messenger of ill tidings, as it had once been the messenger of good tidings to him; and fell into the deepest sorrow. A severe pain also arose in his belly, and began in a most violent manner. He therefore looked upon his friends, and said,—"I, whom you call a god, am commanded presently to depart this life; while Providence thus reproves the lying words you just now said to me; and I, who was by you called immortal, am immediately to be hurried away by death. But I am bound to accept of what Providence allots, as it pleases God; for we have by no means lived ill, but in a splendid and happy manner." When he had said this, his pain was become violent. Accordingly he was carried into the palace; and the rumour went abroad everywhere, that he would certainly die in a little time. But the multitude presently sat in sackcloth, with their wives and children, after the law of their country, and besought God for the king's recovery. All places were also full of mourning and lamentation. Now the king rested in a high chamber, and as he saw them below lying prostrate on the ground, he could not himself forbear weeping. And when he had been quite worn out by the pain in his belly for five days, he departed this life, being in the fifty-fourth year of his age, and the seventh year of his reign; for he reigned four years under Caius Cæsar, three of them were over Philip's tetrar-

chy only, and on the fourth he had that of Herod added to it; and he reigned besides those, three years under the reign of Claudius Cæsar: in which time he reigned over the fore-mentioned countries, and also had Judea added to them, as also Samaria and Cesarea. The revenues that he received out of them were very great, no less than twelve millions of drachmæ.* Yet did he borrow great sums from others; for he was so very liberal, that his expenses exceeded his income; and his generosity was boundless.

3. But before the multitude were made acquainted with Agrippa's being expired, Herod the king of Chalcis, and Helcias the master of his horse, and the king's friend, sent Aristo, one of the king's most faithful servants, and slew Silas, who had been their enemy, as if it had been done by the king's own command.

CHAPTER IX

WHAT THINGS WERE DONE AFTER THE DEATH OF AGRIPPA; AND HOW CLAUDIUS, ON ACCOUNT OF THE YOUTH AND UNSKILFULNESS OF AGRIPPA, JUNIOR, SENT CUSPIUS FADUS TO BE PROCURATOR OF JUDEA, AND OF THE ENTIRE KINGDOM

§ 1. AND thus did king Agrippa depart this life. But he left behind him a son, Agrippa by name, a youth in the seventeenth year of his age, and three daughters, one of whom, Bernice was married to Herod, his father's brother, and was sixteen years old; the other two, Mariamne and Drusilla, were still virgins; the former was ten years old, and Drusilla six. Now these his daughters were thus espoused by their father; Mariamne to Julius Archelaus Epiphanes, the son of Antiochus, the son of Chelcias; and Drusilla to the son of Commagena. But when it was known that Agrippa was departed this life, the inhabitants of Cesarea and of Sebaste forgot the kindnesses he had bestowed on them, and acted the part of the bitterest enemies; for they cast such reproaches upon the deceased as are not fit to be spoken of: and so many of them as were then soldiers, which were a great number, went to his house, and hastily carried off the statues† of this king's daughters, and

---

* This sum, which is equal to £425,000 sterling, was Agrippa the Great's yearly income, or about three quarters of his grandfather Herod's income, he having abated the tax upon houses at Jerusalem, and was not so tyrannical as Herod had been to the Jews.

† Photius says, they were not the statues or images, but the ladies themselves, who were thus basely abused by the soldiers.

all at once carried them into the brothel-houses, and when they had set them on the tops of those houses, they abused them to the utmost of their power, and did such things to them as are too indecent to be related. They also laid themselves down in the public places, and celebrated general feastings, with garlands on their heads, and with ointments and libations to Charon, and drinking to one another for joy that the king was expired. Nay, they were not only unmindful of Agrippa, who had extended his liberality to them in abundance, but of his grandfather Herod also, who had himself rebuilt their cities, and had raised them havens and temples at vast expenses.

2. Now Agrippa, the son of the deceased, was at Rome, and brought up with Claudius Cæsar. And when Cæsar was informed that Agrippa was dead, and that the inhabitants of Sebaste and Cesarea had abused him, he was sorry for the first news, and was displeased with the ingratitude of those cities. He was therefore disposed to send Agrippa, junior, away presently to succeed his father in the kingdom, and was willing to confirm him in it by his oath. But those freemen and friends of his who had the greatest authority with him, dissuaded him from it, and said that it was a dangerous experiment to permit so large a kingdom to come under the government of so very young a man, and one hardly yet arrived at the years of discretion, who would not be able to take sufficient care of its administration; while the weight of a kingdom is heavy enough to a grown man. So Cæsar thought what they said to be reasonable.—Accordingly he sent Cuspius Fadus to be procurator of Judea, and of the entire kingdom, and paid that respect to the deceased as not to introduce Marcus, who had been at variance with him, into his kingdom. But he determined, in the first place, to send orders to Fadus, that he should chastise the inhabitants of Cesarea and Sebaste for those abuses they had offered to him that was deceased, and their madness towards his daughters that were still alive; and that he should remove that body of soldiers that were at Cesarea and Sebaste, with the five regiments, into Pontus, that they might do their military duty there, and that he should choose an equal number of soldiers out of the Roman legions that were in Syria, to supply their place. Yet were not those that had such orders actually removed; for by sending ambassadors to Claudius, they mollified him, and got leave to abide in Judea still; and these were the very men that became the source of very great calamities to the Jews in after-times, and sowed the seeds of that war which began under Florus; whence it was that, when Vespasian had subdued the country, he removed them out of his province.

BOOK XX

CONTAINING THE INTERVAL OF TWENTY-TWO YEARS

FROM FADUS THE PROCURATOR TO FLORUS

CHAPTER I

A SEDITION OF THE PHILADELPHIANS AGAINST THE JEWS; AND ALSO CONCERNING THE VESTMENTS OF THE HIGH PRIEST

1. UPON the death of king Agrippa, which we have related in the foregoing book, Claudius Cæsar sent Cassius Longinus as successor to Marcus, out of regard to the memory of king Agrippa, who had often desired of him by letters, while he was alive, that he would not suffer Marcus to be any longer president of Syria. But Fadus, as soon as he was come procurator into Judea, found quarrelsome doings between the Jews that dwelt in Perea and the people of Philadelphia, about their borders, at a village called Mia, that was filled with men of a warlike temper; for the Jews of Perea had taken up arms without the consent of their principal men, and had destroyed many of the Philadelphians. When Fadus was informed of this procedure, it provoked him very much that they had not left the determination of the matter to him, if they thought that the Philadelphians had done them any wrong, but had rashly taken up arms against them. So he seized upon three of their principal men, who were also the causes of this sedition, and ordered them to be bound, and afterward had one of them slain, whose name was Hannibal; and he banished the other two, Amram and Eleazar; Tholomy also, the arch robber, was, after some time, brought to him bound, and slain, but not till he had done a world of mischief to Idumea and the Arabians. And indeed, from that time, Judea was cleared of robberies by the care and providence of Fadus. He also at this time sent for the high priests and the principal citizens of Jerusalem, and this at the command of the emperor, and admonished them that they should lay up the long garment and the sacred vestment, which it is customary for nobody but the high priest to wear, in the tower of Antonia, that it might be under the power of the Romans, as it had been formerly. Now the Jews durst not contradict what he had said, but desired Fadus, however, and Longinus, (which last was come to Jerusalem, and had brought a great army with him, out of a fear that the [rigid] injunctions of Fadus should force the Jews to rebel,) that they might, in the first place, have leave to send ambassadors to Cæsar, to petition him that they might have the holy vestments under their own power; and that, in the next place, they would tarry till they knew what answer Claudius would give to that their request. So they replied, that they would give them leave to send their ambassadors, provided they would give their sons as pledges [for their peaceable behaviour.] And when they had agreed so to do, and had given them the pledges they desired, the ambassadors were sent accordingly. But when, upon their coming to Rome, Agrippa, junior, the son of the deceased, understood the reason why they came, (for he dwelt with Claudius Cæsar, as we said before,) he besought Cæsar to grant the Jews their request about the holy vestments, and to send a message to Fadus accordingly.

2. Hereupon Claudius called for the ambassadors, and told them that he granted their request; and bade them to return their thanks to Agrippa for this favour which had been bestowed on them upon his entreaty. And, besides these answers of his, he sent the following letter by them:—" Claudius Cæsar Germanicus, tribune of the people the fifth time, and designed consul the fourth time, and imperator the tenth time, the father of his country, to the magistrates, senate, and people, and the whole nation of the Jews, sendeth greeting. Upon the representation of your ambassadors to me by Agrippa my friend, whom I have brought up, and have now with me, and who is a person of very great piety, who are come to give me thanks for the care I have taken of your nation, and to entreat me, in an earnest and obliging manner, that they may have the holy vestments, with the crown belonging to them, under their power,—I grant their request, as that excellent person Vitellius, who is very dear to me, had done before me. And I have complied with your desire, in the first place, out of regard to that piety which I profess, and because I would have every one worship God according to the laws of their own country; and this I do also, because I shall hereby highly gratify king Herod and Agrippa, junior, whose sacred regards to me, and earnest good-will to you, I am well acquainted with, and with whom I have the greatest friendship, and whom I highly esteem, and look on as persons of the best character. Now I have written about these affairs to Cuspius Fadus, my procurator. The names of those that brought me your letter are Cornelius, the son of Cero, Trypho, the son of Theudio, Dorotheus, the son of Nathaniel, and John, the son of John. This is dated before the fourth of the calends of July, when Rufus and Pompeius Sylvanus are consuls."

3. Herod also, the brother of the deceased Agrippa, who was then possessed of the royal authority over Chalcis, petitioned Claudius Cæsar for the authority over the temple, and the money of the sacred treasure, and the choice of the high priests, and obtained all that he petitioned for. So that after that time this authority continued among all his descendants till the end of the war.* Accordingly Herod removed the last high priest, called Cantheras, and bestowed that dignity on his successor Joseph, the son of Camus.

---

* Here is some mistake of Josephus; for the power of appointing high priests, after Herod king of Chalcis was dead, and Agrippa junior was made king of Chalcis in his room, belonged to him; and he exercised the same all along till Jerusalem was destroyed.

CHAPTER II

HOW HELENA, THE QUEEN OF ADIABENE, AND
HER SON IZATES, EMBRACED THE JEWISH RELI-
GION; AND HOW HELENA SUPPLIED THE POOR
WITH CORN WHEN THERE WAS A GREAT FAMINE
AT JERUSALEM

1. ABOUT this time it was that Helena, queen of Adiabene, and her son Izates, changed their course of life, and embraced the Jewish customs, and this on the occasion following:—Monobazus, the king of Adiabene, who had also the name of Bazeus, fell in love with his sister Helena, and took her to be his wife, and begat her with child. But as he was in bed with her one night, he laid his hand upon his wife's belly, and fell asleep, and seemed to hear a voice, which bade him take his hand off his wife's belly, and not to hurt the infant that was therein, which, by God's providence, would be safely born, and have a happy end. This voice put him into disorder; so he awaked immediately, and told the story to his wife; and when his son was born, he called him Izates. He had indeed Monobazus, his elder brother, by Helena also, as he had other sons by other wives besides. Yet did he openly place all his affections on this his only-begotten* son Izates, which was the origin of that envy which his other brethren, by the same father, bore to him; while on this account they hated him more and more, and were all under great affliction that their father should prefer Izates before them all. Now, although their father was very sensible of these their passions, yet did he forgive them, as not indulging those passions out of an ill disposition, but out of a desire each of them had to be beloved by their father. However, he sent Izates, with many presents, to Abennerig, the king of Charax-Spasini, and that out of the great dread he was in about him, lest he should come to some misfortunes by the hatred his brethren bore him; and he committed his son's preservation to him. Upon which Abennerig gladly received the young man, and had a great affection for him, and married him to his own daughter, whose name was Samacha: he also bestowed a country upon him, from which he received large revenues.

2. But when Monobazus was grown old, and saw that he had but a little time to live, he had a mind to come to the sight of his son before he died. So he sent for him, and embraced him after the most affectionate manner, and bestowed on him the country called Carræ; it was a soil that bare amomum in great plenty: there was also in it the remains of that ark, wherein it is related that Noah escaped the deluge, and where they are still shewn to such as are desirous to see them.† Accordingly Izates abode in that country until his father's death. But the very day that Monobazus died, queen Helena sent for all the grandees and governors of the kingdom, and for those that had the armies committed to their command; and when they were come, she made the following speech to them:—"I believe you are not unacquainted that my husband was desirous that Izates should

succeed him in the government, and thought him worthy so to do. However, I wait your determination; for, happy is he who receives a kingdom, not from a single person only, but from the willing suffrages of a great many." This she said, in order to try those that were invited, and to discover their sentiments. Upon the hearing of which, they first of all paid their homage to the queen, as their custom was, and then they said that they confirmed the king's determination, and would submit to it; and they rejoiced that Izates's father had preferred him before the rest of his brethren, as being agreeable to all their wishes: but that they were desirous first of all to slay his brethren and kinsmen, that so the government might come securely to Izates; because if they were once destroyed, all that fear would be over which might arise from their envy and hatred to him. Helena replied to this, that she returned them her thanks for their kindness to herself and to Izates; but desired that they would however defer the execution of this slaughter of Izates's brethren till he should be there himself, and give his approbation to it. So since these men had not prevailed with her when they advised her to slay them, they exhorted her at least to keep them in bonds till he should come, and that for their own security; they also gave her counsel to set up some one whom she could put the greatest trust in, as governor of the kingdom in the meantime. So queen Helena complied with this counsel of theirs, and set up Monobazus, the eldest son, to be king, and put the diadem upon his head, and gave him his father's ring, with its signet; as also the ornament which they called Sampser, and exhorted him to administer the affairs of the kingdom till his brother should come; who came suddenly upon hearing that his father was dead, and succeeded his brother Monobazus, who resigned up the government to him.

3. Now, during the time Izates abode at Charax-Spasini, a certain Jewish merchant, whose name was Ananias, got among the women that belonged to the king, and taught them to worship God according to the Jewish religion. He, moreover, by their means became known to Izates; and persuaded him, in like manner, to embrace that religion; he also, at the earnest entreaty of Izates, accompanied him when he was sent for by his father to come to Adiabene; it also happened that Helena, about the same time, was instructed by a certain other Jew, and went over to them. But, when Izates had taken the kingdom, and was come to Adiabene, and there saw his brethren and other kinsmen in bonds, he was displeased at it; and as he thought it was an instance of impiety either to slay or imprison them, but still thought it a hazardous thing for to let them have their liberty, with the remembrance of the injuries that had been offered them, he sent some of them and their children for hostages to Rome, to Claudius Cæsar, and sent the others to Artabanus, the king of Parthia, with the like intentions.

4. And when he perceived that his mother was highly pleased with the Jewish customs, he made haste to change, and to embrace them entirely; and as he supposed that he could not be thoroughly a Jew unless he were circumcised, he was ready to have it done. But when his mother understood what he was about, she endeavoured to hinder him from doing it, and said to him that this thing would bring him into danger: and that as he was a king, he would thereby bring himself into great odium among his sub-

---

* Josephus here uses the word *monogene*, an only-begotten son, for no other than one best-beloved, as does both the Old and the New Testament; I mean where there were one or more sons besides, (Gen. xxii. 2; Heb. xi. 7.)

† It is here very remarkable, that the remains of Noah's ark were believed to be still in being in the days of Josephus.

jects, when they should understand that he was so fond of rites that were to them strange and foreign ; and that they would never bear to be ruled over by a Jew. This it was that she said to him, and for the present persuaded him to forbear. And when he had related what she said to Ananias, he confirmed what his mother had said ; and when he had also threatened to leave him, unless he complied with him, he went away from him ; and said he was afraid lest such an action being once become public to all, he should himself be in danger of punishment for having been the king's instructor in actions that were of ill reputation ; and he said, that he might worship God without being circumcised, even though he did resolve to follow the Jewish law entirely ; which worship of God was of a superior nature to circumcision. He added, that God would forgive him, though he did not perform the operation, while it was omitted out of necessity, and for fear of his subjects. So the king at that time complied with these persuasions of Ananias. But afterwards, as he had not quite left off his desire of doing this thing, a certain other Jew that came out of Galilee, whose name was Eleazar, and who was esteemed very skilful in the learning of his country, persuaded him to do the thing ; for as he entered into his palace to salute him, and found him reading the law of Moses, he said to him, " Thou dost not consider, O king! that thou unjustly breakest the principal of those laws, and art injurious to God himself, [by omitting to be circumcised ;] for thou oughtest not only to read them, but chiefly to practice what they enjoin thee. How long wilt thou continue uncircumcised? but, if thou hast not yet read the law about circumcision, and dost not know how great impiety thou art guilty of by neglecting it, read it now." When the king had heard what he said, he delayed no longer, but retired to another room, and sent for a surgeon, and did what he was commanded to do. He then sent for his mother, and Ananias his tutor, and informed them that he had done the thing ; upon which they were presently struck with astonishment and fear, and that to a great degree, lest the thing should be openly discovered and censured, and the king should hazard the loss of his kingdom, while his subjects would not bear to be governed by a man who was so zealous in another religion ; and lest they should themselves run some hazard, because they would be supposed the occasion of his so doing. But it was God himself who hindered what they feared from taking effect ; for he preserved both Izates himself and his sons when they fell into many dangers, and procured their deliverance when it seemed to be impossible, and demonstrated thereby, that the fruit of piety does not perish as to those that have regard to him, and fix their faith upon him only : *—but these events we shall relate hereafter.

5. But as to Helena, the king's mother, when she saw that the affairs of Izates's kingdom were in peace, and that her son was a happy man, and admired among all men, and even among foreigners, by the means of God's providence over him, she had a mind to go to the city of Jerusalem, in order to worship at that temple of God which was so very famous among all men, and to offer her thank-offerings there. So she de-

sired her son to give her leave to go thither : upon which he gave his consent to what she desired very willingly, and made great preparations for her dismission, and gave her a great deal of money, and she went down to the city Jerusalem, her son conducting her on her journey a great way. Now her coming was of very great advantage to the people of Jerusalem ; for whereas a famine did oppress them at that time, and many people died for want of what was necessary to procure food withal, queen Helena sent some of her servants to Alexandria with money to buy a great quantity of corn, and others of them to Cyprus, to bring a cargo of dried figs ; and as soon as they were come back, and had brought those provisions, which was done very quickly, she distributed food to those that were in want of it, and left a most excellent memorial behind her of this benefaction, which she bestowed on our whole nation ; and when her son Izates was informed of this famine,† he sent a great sum of money to the principal men in Jerusalem.

CHAPTER III

HOW ARTABANUS, THE KING OF PARTHIA, OUT OF FEAR OF THE SECRET CONTRIVANCES OF HIS SUBJECTS AGAINST HIM, WENT TO IZATES, AND WAS BY HIM REINSTATED IN HIS GOVERNMENT ; AS ALSO HOW BARDANES, HIS SON, DENOUNCED WAR AGAINST IZATES

1. BUT now Artabanus, king of the Parthians, perceiving that the governors of the provinces had framed a plot against him, did not think it safe for him to continue among them ; but resolved to go to Izates, in hopes of finding some way for his preservation by his means, and, if possible, for his return to his own dominions. So he came to Izates, and brought a thousand of his kindred and servants with him, and met him upon the road, while he well knew Izates, but Izates did not know him. When Artabanus stood near him, and in the first place, he then said to him, " O king! do not thou overlook me thy servant, nor do thou proudly reject the suit I make thee ; for as I am reduced to a low estate, by the change of fortune, and of a king am become a private man, I stand in need of thy assistance. Have regard, therefore, unto the uncertainty of my fortune, and esteem the care thou shalt take of me to be taken of thyself also ; for if I be neglected, and my subjects go off unpunished, many other subjects will become more insolent towards other kings also." And this speech Artabanus made with tears in his eyes, and with a dejected countenance. Now, as soon as Izates heard Artabanus's name, and saw him stand as a supplicant before him, he leaped down from his horse immediately, and said to him, " Take courage, O king! nor be disturbed at thy present calamity, as if it were incurable ; for the change of thy sad condition shall be sudden ; for thou shalt find me to be more thy friend and thy assistant than thy hopes can promise thee ; for I will either re-establish thee in the kingdom of Parthia, or lose my own."

---

* Josephus is very full and express in these three chapters (iii. iv. and v.) in observing how carefully Divine Providence preserved this Izates, king of Adiabene, and his sons, while he did what he thought was his bounden duty, notwithstanding the strongest political motives to the contrary.

† Of this terrible famine itself in Judea, Dr Hudson says :—" This is that famine foretold by Agabus, Acts xi. 28 ; which happened when Claudius was consul the fourth time ; and not that other which happened when Claudius was consul the second time, and Cæsina was his colleague.

2. When he had said this, he set Artabanus upon his horse, and followed him on foot, in honour of a king whom he owned as greater than himself;—which when Artabanus saw, he was very uneasy at it, and sware by his present fortune and honour, that he would get down from his horse, unless Izates would get upon his horse again and go before him. So he complied with his desire, and leaped upon his horse; and, when he had brought him to his royal palace, he shewed him all sorts of respect when they sat together,—and he gave him the upper place at festivals also, as regarding not his present fortune, but his former dignity; and that upon this consideration also, that the changes of fortune are common to all men. He also wrote to the Parthians, to persuade them to receive Artabanus again; and gave them his right hand and his faith, that he should forget what was past and done, and that he would undertake for this as a mediator between them. Now the Parthians did not themselves refuse to receive him again, but pleaded that it was not now in their power so to do, because they had committed the government to another person, who had accepted of it, and whose name was Cinnamus; and that they were afraid lest a civil war should arise on this account. When Cinnamus understood their intentions, he wrote to Artabanus himself, for he had been brought up by him, and was of a nature good and gentle also, and desired him to put confidence in him, and to come and take his own dominions again. Accordingly Artabanus trusted him, and returned home; when Cinnamus met him, worshipped him, and saluted him as a king, and took the diadem off his own head, and put it on the head of Artabanus.

3. And thus was Artabanus restored to his kingdom again by the means of Izates, when he had lost it by the means of the grandees of the kingdom. Nor was he unmindful of the benefits he had conferred upon him, but rewarded him with such honours as were of the greatest esteem among them; for he gave him leave to wear his tiara upright,* and to sleep upon a golden bed, which are privileges and marks of honour peculiar to the kings of Parthia. He also cut off a large and fruitful country from the king of Armenia, and bestowed it upon him. The name of the country is Nisibis, wherein the Macedonians had formerly built that city which they called Antioch of Mygodonia. And these were the honours that were paid Izates by the king of the Parthians.

4. But in no long time Artabanus died, and left his kingdom to his son Bardanes. Now this Bardanes came to Izates, and would have persuaded him to join him with his army, and to assist him in the war he was preparing to make with the Romans; but he could not prevail with him. For Izates so well knew the strength and good fortune of the Romans, that he took Bardanes to attempt what was impossible to be done; and having, besides, sent his sons, five in number, and they but young also, to learn accurately the language of our nation, together with our learning, as well as he had set his mother to worship at our temple, as I have said already, was the more backward to a compliance; and restrained Bardanes, telling him perpetually of the great armies and famous actions of the Romans, and thought thereby to terrify him, and desired thereby to hinder him from that expedition. But the Parthian king was provoked at

* This privilege of wearing the tiara upright, or with the tip of the cone erect, is known to have been of old peculiar to great kings, from Xenophon and others.

this his behaviour, and denounced war immediately against Izates. Yet did he gain no advantage by this war, because God cut off all his hopes therein; for the Parthians, perceiving Bardanes's intention, and how he had determined to make war with the Romans, slew him, and gave his kingdom to his brother Gotarzes. He also, in no long time, perished by a plot made against him, and Vologases, his brother, succeeded him, who committed two of his provinces to two of his brothers by the same father;—that of the Medes to the elder, Parcorus; and Armenia to the younger, Tiridates.

CHAPTER IV

HOW IZATES WAS BETRAYED BY HIS OWN SUBJECTS, AND FOUGHT AGAINST BY THE ARABIANS; AND HOW IZATES, BY THE PROVIDENCE OF GOD, WAS DELIVERED OUT OF THEIR HANDS

1. Now when the king's brother, Monobazus, and his other kindred, saw how Izates, by his piety to God, was become greatly esteemed by all men, they also had a desire to leave the religion of their country, and to embrace the customs of the Jews; but that act of theirs was discovered by Izates's subjects. Whereupon the grandees were much displeased, and could not contain their anger at them, but had an intention, when they should find a proper opportunity, to inflict a punishment upon them. Accordingly, they wrote to Abia, king of the Arabians, and promised him great sums of money, if he would make an expedition against their king: and they further promised him, that, on the first onset, they would desert their king, because they were desirous to punish him, by reason of the hatred he had to their religious worship; then they obliged themselves by oaths to be faithful to each other, and desired that he would make haste in this design. The king of Arabia complied with their desires, and brought a great army into the field, and marched against Izates; and, in the beginning of the first onset, and before they came to a close fight, those grandees, as if they had a panic terror upon them, all deserted Izates, as they had agreed to do, and, turning their backs upon their enemies, ran away. Yet was not Izates dismayed at this; but when he understood that the grandees had betrayed him, he also retired into his camp, and made inquiry into the matter; and as soon as he knew who they were that had made this conspiracy with the king of Arabia, he cut off those that were found guilty; and renewing the fight on the next day, he slew the greatest part of his enemies, and forced all the rest to betake themselves to flight. He also pursued their king, and drove him into a fortress called Arsamus, and, following on the siege vigorously, he took that fortress. And, when he had plundered it of all the prey that was in it, which was not small, he returned to Adiabene; yet did he not take Abia alive; because, when he found himself encompassed upon every side, he slew himself.

2. But although the grandees of Adiabene had failed in their first attempt, as being delivered up by God into their king's hands, yet would they not even then be quiet, but wrote again to Vologases, who was then king of Parthia, and desired that he would kill Izates, and set over them some other potentate, who should be of a Parthian family; for they said that they hated their own king for abrogating the laws of their

forefathers, and embracing foreign customs. When the king of Parthia heard this, he boldly made war upon Izates; and, as he had no just pretence for this war, he sent to him and demanded back those honourable privileges which had been bestowed on him by his father, and threatened, on his refusal, to make war upon him. Upon hearing of this, Izates was under no small trouble of mind, as thinking it would be a reproach upon him to appear to resign those privileges that had been bestowed upon him out of cowardice; yet, because he knew, that though the king of Parthia should receive back those honours, yet would he not be quiet, he resolved to commit himself to God, his protector, in the present danger he was in of his life; and as he esteemed him to be his principal assistant, he intrusted his children and his wives to a very strong fortress, and laid up his corn in his citadels, and set the hay and the grass on fire. And when he had thus put things in order, as well as he could, he awaited the coming of the enemy. And when the king of Parthia was come, with a great army of footmen and horsemen, which he did sooner than was expected, (for he marched in great haste,) and had cast up a bank at the river that parted Adiabene from Media,—Izates also pitched his camp not far off, having with him six thousand horsemen. But there came a messenger to Izates, sent by the king of Parthia, who told him how large his dominions were, as reaching from the river Euphrates to Bactria, and enumerated that king's subjects: he also threatened him that he should be punished, as a person ungrateful to his lords; and said that the God whom he worshipped could not deliver him out of the king's hands. When the messenger had delivered this his message, Izates replied, that he knew the king of Parthia's power was much greater than his own; but that he knew also that God was much more powerful than all men. And when he had returned him this answer, he betook himself to make supplication to God, and threw himself on the ground, and put ashes upon his head, in testimony of his confusion, and fasted, together with his wives and children.* Then he called upon God, and said, "O Lord and Governor, if I have not in vain committed myself to thy goodness, but have justly determined that thou only art the Lord and principal of all beings, come now to my assistance, and defend me from my enemies, not only on my own account, but on account of their insolent behaviour with regard to thy power, while they have not feared to lift up their proud and arrogant tongue against thee." Thus did he lament and bemoan himself, with tears in his eyes; whereupon God heard his prayer. And immediately that very night Vologases received letters, the contents of which were these, that a great band of Dahæ and Sacæ, despising him, now he was gone so long a journey from home, had made an expedition, and laid Parthia waste; so that he [was forced to] retire back, without doing anything. And thus it was that Izates escaped the threatenings of the Parthians by the providence of God.

3. It was not long ere Izates died, when he had completed fifty-five years of his life, and had ruled his kingdom twenty-four years. He left behind him twenty-four sons and twenty-four daughters. However, he gave order that his brother Monobazus should succeed in the

government, thereby requiting him, because, while he was himself absent, after their father's death, he had faithfully preserved the government for him. But when Helena, his mother, heard of her son's death, she was in great heaviness, as was but natural, upon her loss of such a most dutiful son; yet was it a comfort to her that she heard the succession came to her eldest son. Accordingly she went to him in haste; and when she was come into Adiabene, she did not long outlive her son Izates. But Monobazus sent her bones, as well as those of Izates, his brother, to Jerusalem, and gave orders that they should be buried at the pyramids* which their mother had erected; they were three in number, and distant no more than three furlongs from the city of Jerusalem.

CHAPTER V

CONCERNING THEUDAS, AND THE SONS OF JUDAS THE GALILEAN; AS ALSO WHAT CALAMITY FELL UPON THE JEWS ON THE DAY OF THE PASSOVER

1. Now it came to pass, that while Fadus was procurator of Judea, that a certain magician, whose name was Theudas,† persuaded a great part of the people to take their effects with them, and follow him to the river Jordan; for he told them he was a prophet, and that he would, by his own command, divide the river, and afford them an easy passage over it; and many were deluded by his words. However, Fadus did not permit them to make any advantage of his wild attempt, but sent a troop of horsemen out against them; who falling upon them unexpectedly, slew many of them, and took many of them alive. They also took Theudas alive, and cut off his head, and carried it to Jerusalem. This was what befell the Jews in the time of Cuspius Fadus's government.

2. Then came Tiberius Alexander as successor to Fadus; he was the son of Alexander the alabarch of Alexandria; which Alexander was a principal person among all his contemporaries, both for his family and wealth: he was also more eminent for his piety than this his son Alexander, for he did not continue in the religion of his country. Under these procurators that great famine happened in Judea, in which queen Helena bought corn in Egypt at a great expense, and distributed it to those that were in want, as I have related already; and besides this, the sons of Judas of Galilee were now slain; I mean of that Judas who caused the people to revolt, when Cyrenius came to take an account of the estates of the Jews, as we have shewn in a foregoing book. The names of those sons were James and Simon, whom Alexander commanded to be crucified; but now Herod, king of Chalcis, removed Joseph, the son of Camydus, from the high priesthood, and made Ananias, the son of Nebedeus, his successor; and now it was that Cumanus came as successor to Tiberius Alexander; as also that Herod, brother of Agrippa the great king, departed this life, in the eighth year of the reign of Claudius Cæsar. He left behind him three sons, Aristo-

* This conduct of Izates is a plain sign that he was become either a Jew or an Ebonite Christian, who indeed differed not much from proper Jews. However, his supplications were heard, and he was providentially delivered from that imminent danger he was in.

* These pyramids or pillars, erected by Helena, queen of Adiabene, near Jerusalem, three in number, are mentioned by Eusebius. They are also mentioned by Pausanias. Reland also guesses that that now called Absalom's Pillar may be one of them.

† This Theudas, who arose under Fadus the procurator, about A.D. 45 or 46, could not be that Theudas who arose in the days of the taxing under Cyrenius; or about A.D. 7, Acts v. 36, 37.

bulus, whom he had by his first wife, with Bernicianus and Hyrcanus, both whom he had by Bernice, his brother's daughter; but Claudius Cæsar bestowed his dominions on Agrippa, junior.

3. Now, while the Jewish affairs were under the administration of Cumanus, there happened a great tumult at the city of Jerusalem, and many of the Jews perished therein; but I shall first explain the occasion whence it was derived. When that feast which is called the Passover was at hand, at which time our custom is to use unleavened bread, and a great multitude was gathered together from all parts to that feast, Cumanus was afraid lest some attempt of innovation should then be made by them; so he ordered that one regiment of the army should take their arms, and stand in the temple cloisters, to repress any attempts of innovation, if perchance any such should begin; and this was no more than what the former procurators of Judea did at such festivals; but on the fourth day of the feast, a certain soldier let down his breeches, and exposed his privy members to the multitude, which put those that saw him into a furious rage, and made them cry out that this impious action was not done to reproach them, but God himself; nay, some of them reproached Cumanus, and pretended that the soldier was set on by him; which, when Cumanus heard, he was also himself not a little provoked at such reproaches laid upon him; yet did he exhort them to leave off such seditious attempts, and not to raise a tumult at the festival; but when he could not induce them to be quiet, for they still went on in their reproaches to him, he gave order that the whole army should take their entire armour, and come to Antonia, which was a fortress, as we have said already, which overlooked the temple; but when the multitude saw the soldiers there, they were affrighted at them, and ran away hastily; but as the passages out were but narrow, and as they thought their enemies followed them, they were crowded together in their flight, and a great number were pressed to death in those narrow passages; nor indeed was the number fewer than twenty thousand that perished in this tumult. So, instead of a festival they had at last a mournful day of it; and they all of them forgot their prayers and sacrifices, and betook themselves to lamentation and weeping; so great an affliction did the impudent obsceneness of a single soldier bring upon them.*

4. Now, before this their first mourning was over, another mischief befell them also; for some of those that had raised the foregoing tumult, when they were travelling along the public road, about a hundred furlongs from the city, robbed Stephanus, a servant of Cæsar, as he was journeying, and plundered him of all that he had with him; which things when Cumanus heard of, he sent soldiers immediately, and ordered them to plunder the neighbouring villages, and to bring the most eminent persons among them in bonds to him. Now, as this devastation was making, one of the soldiers seized the Laws of Moses, that lay in one of those villages, and brought them out before the eyes of all present, and tore them to pieces; and this was done with reproachful language, and much scurrility; which things when the Jews heard of, they ran together, and that

in great numbers, and came down to Cesarea, where Cumanus then was, and besought him that he would avenge, not themselves, but God himself, whose laws had been affronted; for that they could not bear to live any longer, if the laws of their forefathers must be affronted after this manner. Accordingly Cumanus, out of fear lest the multitude should go into a sedition, and by the advice of his friends also, took care that the soldier who had offered the affront to the laws should be beheaded; and thereby put a stop to the sedition which was ready to be kindled a second time.

CHAPTER VI

HOW THERE HAPPENED A QUARREL BETWEEN THE JEWS AND THE SAMARITANS; AND HOW CLAUDIUS PUT AN END TO THEIR DIFFERENCES

1. Now there arose a quarrel between the Samaritans and the Jews on the occasion following:—It was the custom of the Galileans, when they came to the holy city at the festivals, to take their journeys through the country of the Samaritans;* and at this time there lay, in the road they took, a village that was called Ginea, which was situated in the limits of Samaria and the great plain, where certain persons thereto belonging, fought with the Galileans, and killed a great many of them; but, when the principal of the Galileans were informed of what had been done, they came to Cumanus, and desired him to avenge the murder of those that were killed; but he was induced by the Samaritans, with money, to do nothing in the matter; upon which the Galileans were much displeased, and persuaded the multitude of the Jews to betake themselves to arms, and to regain their liberty, saying, that slavery was in itself a bitter thing, but that, when it was joined with direct injuries, it was perfectly intolerable. And when their principal men endeavoured to pacify them, and promised to endeavour to persuade Cumanus to avenge those that were killed, they would not hearken to them, but took their weapons, and entreated the assistance of Eleazar, the son of Dineus, a robber, who had many years made his abode in the mountains, with which assistance they plundered many villages of the Samaritans. When Cumanus heard of this action of theirs, he took the band of Sebaste, with four regiments of footmen, and armed the Samaritans, and marched out against the Jews, and caught them, and slew many of them, and took a great number of them alive; whereupon those that were the most eminent persons at Jerusalem, and that both in regard to the respect that was paid them, and the families they were of, as soon as they saw to what a height things were gone, put on sackcloth, and heaped ashes upon their heads, and by all possible means besought the seditious, and persuaded them that they would set before their eyes the utter subversion of their country, the conflagration of their temple, and the slavery of themselves, their wives, and children,† which

---

* This and many more tumults and seditions, which arose at the Jewish festivals, in Josephus, illustrate the cautious procedure of the Jewish governors, when they said, Matt. xxvi. 5, "Let us not take Jesus on the feast-day, lest there be an uproar among the people."

* This constant passage of the Galileans through the country of Samaria, as they went to Judea and Jerusalem, illustrates several passages in the Gospels. (See Luke xvii.; 1 John iv. 4.)

† Our Saviour had foretold that the Jews' rejection of his gospel would bring upon them, among other miseries, these three, which they themselves here shew they expected would be the consequences of their present tumults and seditions—the utter subversion of their country, the conflagration of their temple, and the slavery of themselves, their wives, and children. (See Luke xxi. 6-23.)

would be the consequence of what they were doing, and would alter their minds, would cast away their weapons, and for the future be quiet, and return to their own homes. These persuasions of theirs prevailed upon them. So the people dispersed themselves, and the robbers went away again to their places of strength; and after this time all Judea was overrun with robberies.

2. But the principal of the Samaritans went to Ummidius Quadratus, the president of Syria, who at that time was at Tyre, and accused the Jews of setting their villages on fire, and plundering them; and said withal, that they were not so much displeased at what they had suffered, as they were at the contempt thereby shewn to the Romans; while, if they had received any injury, they ought to have made them the judges of what had been done, and not presently to make such devastations as if they had not the Romans for their governors; on which account they came to him in order to obtain that vengeance they wanted. This was the accusation which the Samaritans brought against the Jews. But the Jews affirmed that the Samaritans were the authors of this tumult and fighting, and that, in the first place, Cumanus had been corrupted by their gifts, and passed over the murder of those that were slain in silence;—which allegations when Quadratus heard, he put off the hearing of the cause, and promised that he would give sentence when he should come into Judea, and should have a more exact knowledge of the truth of that matter. So these men went away without success. Yet was it not long ere Quadratus came to Samaria; where, upon hearing the cause, he supposed that the Samaritans were the authors of that disturbance. But when he was informed that certain of the Jews were making innovations, he ordered those to be crucified whom Cumanus had taken captive. From whence he came to a certain village called Lydda, which was not less than a city in largeness, and there heard the Samaritan cause a second time before his tribunal, and there learned from a certain Samaritan, that one of the chief of the Jews, whose name was Dortus, and some other innovators with him, four in number, persuaded the multitude to a revolt from the Romans; whom Quadratus ordered to be put to death: but still he sent away Ananias the high priest, and Ananus the commander of [the temple,] in bonds to Rome, to give an account of what they had done to Claudius Cæsar. He also ordered the principal men, both of the Samaritans and Jews, as also Cumanus the procurator, and Celer the tribune, to go to Italy to the emperor, that he might hear their cause, and determine their differences one with another. But he came again to the city of Jerusalem, out of his fear that the multitude of Jews should attempt some innovation; but he found the city in a peaceable state, and celebrating one of the usual festivals of their country to God. So he believed that they would not attempt any innovations, and left them at the celebration of the festival, and returned to Antioch.

3. Now Cumanus and the principal of the Samaritans, who were sent to Rome, had a day appointed them by the emperor, whereupon they were to have pleaded their cause about the quarrels they had one with another. But now Cæsar's freed-men and his friends were very zealous on the behalf of Cumanus and the Samaritans; and they had prevailed over the Jews, unless Agrippa, junior, who was then at Rome, had seen the principal of the Jews hard set, and had earnestly entreated Agrippina, the emperor's wife, to persuade her husband to hear the cause, so as was agreeable to his justice, and to condemn those to be punished who were really the authors of this revolt from the Roman government:—whereupon Claudius was so well disposed beforehand, that when he had heard the cause, and found that the Samaritans had been the ringleaders in those mischievous doings, he gave order that those who came up to him should be slain, and that Cumanus should be banished. He also gave order that Celer the tribune should be carried back to Jerusalem, and should be drawn through the city in the sight of all the people, and then should be slain.

CHAPTER VII

FELIX IS MADE PROCURATOR OF JUDEA; AS ALSO CONCERNING AGRIPPA, JUNIOR, AND HIS SISTERS

1. So Claudius sent Felix, the brother of Pallas, to take care of the affairs of Judea; and, when he had already completed the twelfth year of his reign, he bestowed upon Agrippa the tetrarchy of Philip, and Batanea, and added thereto Trachonites, with Abila; which last had been the tetrarchy of Lysanius; but he took from him Chalcis, when he had been governor thereof four years. And when Agrippa had received these countries as the gift of Cæsar, he gave his sister Drusilla in marriage to Azizus, king of Emesa, upon his consent to be circumcised; for Epiphanes, the son of king Antiochus, had refused to marry her, because, after he had promised her father formerly to come over to the Jewish religion, he would not now perform that promise. He also gave Mariamme in marriage to Archelaus, the son of Helcias, to whom she had formerly been betrothed by Agrippa her father; from which marriage was derived a daughter, whose name was Bernice.

2. But for the marriage of Drusilla with Azizus, it was in no long time afterward dissolved, upon the following occasion:—While Felix was procurator of Judea, he saw this Drusilla, and fell in love with her; for she did indeed exceed all other women in beauty; and he sent to her a person whose name was Simon,* one of his friends; a Jew he was, and by birth a Cypriot, and one who pretended to be a magician; and endeavoured to persuade her to forsake her present husband, and marry him; and promised, that if she would not refuse him, he would make her a happy woman. Accordingly she acted ill, and because she was desirous to avoid her sister Bernice's envy, for she was very ill-treated by her on account of her beauty, was prevailed upon to transgress the laws of her forefathers, and to marry Felix; and when he had had a son by her, he named him Agrippa. But after what manner that young man, with his wife, perished at the conflagration of the mountain Vesuvius, in the days of Titus Cæsar, shall be related hereafter. †

3. But as for Bernice, she lived a widow a long while after the death of Herod [king of

---

* This Simon, a friend of Felix, a Jew, born in Cyprus, though he pretended to be a magician, and seems to have been wicked enough, could hardly be that famous Simon the magician, in the Acts of the Apostles (viii. 9, &c.,) as some are ready to suppose. The Simon mentioned in the Acts was not properly a Jew, but a Samaritan, of the town of Gittæ, in the country of Samaria.

† This is now wanting.

Chalcis,] who was both her husband and her uncle. But, when the report went that she had criminal conversation with her brother [Agrippa, junior] she persuaded Polemo, who was king of Cilicia, to be circumcised, and to marry her, as supposing, that by this means she should prove those calumnies upon her to be false; and Polemo was prevailed upon, and that chiefly on account of her riches. Yet did not this matrimony endure long; but Bernice left Polemo, and, as was said, with impure intentions. So she forsook at once this matrimony, and the Jewish religion: and at the same time, Mariamme put away Archelaus, and was married to Demetrius, the principal man among the Alexandrian Jews, both for his family and his wealth; and indeed he was then their alabarch. So she named her son whom she had by him Agrippinus.

CHAPTER VIII

AFTER WHAT MANNER, UPON THE DEATH OF CLAUDIUS, NERO SUCCEEDED IN THE GOVERNMENT; AS ALSO WHAT BARBAROUS THINGS HE DID. CONCERNING THE ROBBERS, MURDERERS, AND IMPOSTORS, THAT AROSE WHILE FELIX AND FESTUS WERE PROCURATORS OF JUDEA

1. Now Claudius Cæsar died when he had reigned thirteen years, eight months, and twenty days;* and a report went about that he was poisoned by his wife Agrippina. Her father was Germanicus, the brother of Cæsar. Her husband was Domitius Ænobarbus, one of the most illustrious persons that was in the city of Rome; after whose death, and her long continuance in widowhood, Claudius took her to wife. She brought along with her a son, Domitius, of the same name with his father. He had before this slain his wife Messalina, out of jealousy, by whom he had his children Britannicus and Octavia; their eldest sister was Antonia, whom he had by Pelina his first wife. He also married Octavia to Nero; for that was the name that Cæsar gave him afterward, upon his adopting him for his son.

2. But now Agrippina was afraid, lest when Britannicus should come to man's estate, he should succeed his father in the government, and desired to seize upon the principality beforehand for her own son [Nero:] upon which the report went, that she thence compassed the death of Claudius. Accordingly she sent Burrhus, the general of the army, immediately, and with him the tribunes and such also of the freed-men as were of the greatest authority, to bring Nero away into the camp, and to salute him emperor. And when Nero had thus obtained the government, he got Britannicus to be so poisoned, that the multitude should not perceive it; although he publicly put his own mother to death not long afterward, making her this requital, not only for being born of her, but for bringing it so about by her contrivances, that he obtained the Roman empire. He also slew Octavia his own wife, and many other illustrious persons, under this pretence, that they plotted against him.

3. But I omit any further discourse about these affairs; for there have been a great many

who have composed the history of Nero; some of whom have departed from the truth of facts, out of favour, as having received benefits from him; while others, out of hatred to him, have so impudently raved against him with their lies, that they justly deserved to be condemned. Nor do I wonder at such as have told lies of Nero, since they have not in their writings preserved the truth of history as to those facts that were earlier than his time, even when the actors could have no way incurred their hatred, since those writers lived a long time after them; but as to those that have no regard to truth, they may write as they please,—for in that they take delight; but as to ourselves, who have made truth our direct aim, we shall briefly touch upon what only belongs remotely to this undertaking, but shall relate what hath happened to us Jews with great accuracy, and shall not grudge our pains in giving an account both of the calamities we have suffered and of the crimes we have been guilty of.—I will now therefore return to the relation of our own affairs.

4. For in the first year of the reign of Nero, upon the death of Azizus, king of Emesa, Soemus, his brother, succeeded in his kingdom, and Aristobulus, the son of Herod, king of Chalcis, was intrusted by Nero with the government of the Lesser Armenia. Cæsar also bestowed on Agrippa a certain part of Galilee, Tiberias and Taricheæ,* and ordered them to submit to his jurisdiction. He gave him also Julias, a city of Perea, with fourteen villages that lay about it.

5. Now, as for the affairs of the Jews, they grew worse and worse continually; for the country was again filled with robbers and impostors, who deluded the multitude. Yet did Felix catch and put to death many of those impostors every day, together with the robbers. He also caught Eleazar, the son of Dineus, who had gotten together a company of robbers; and this he did by treachery; for he gave him assurance that he should suffer no harm, and thereby persuaded him to come to him; but when he came, he bound him and sent him to Rome. Felix also bore an ill-will to Jonathan, the high priest, because he frequently gave him admonitions about governing the Jewish affairs better than he did, lest he should himself have complaints made of him by the multitude, since he it was who had desired Cæsar to send him as procurator of Judea. So Felix contrived a method whereby he might get rid of him, now he was become so continually troublesome to him; for such continual admonitions are grievous to those who are disposed to act unjustly. Wherefore Felix persuaded one of Jonathan's most faithful friends, a citizen of Jerusalem, whose name was Doras, to bring the robbers upon Jonathan, in order to kill him; and this he did by promising to give him a great deal of money for so doing. Doras complied with the proposal, and contrived matters so, that the robbers might murder him after the following manner:—Certain of those robbers went up to the city, as if they were going to worship God, while they had daggers under their garments; and, by thus mingling themselves among the multitude, they slew Jonathan;† and as this

---

* This duration of the reign of Claudius agrees with Dio, as he also remarks that Nero's name, which was at first L. Domitius Ænobarbus, after Claudius had adopted him was Nero Claudius Cæsar Drusus Germanicus.

* This agrees with Josephus's frequent accounts elsewhere in his own Life, that Tiberius, and Taricheæ, and Gamala, were under this Agrippa, junior, till Justus, the son of Pistus, seized upon them for the Jews, upon the breaking out of the war.

† This treacherous and barbarous murder, by the contrivance of Felix, was the immediate occasion of the ensuing murders by the *sicarii* or ruffians, and

murder was never avenged, the robbers went up with the greatest security at the festivals after this time; and having weapons concealed in 'like manner as before, and mingling themselves among the multitude, they slew certain of their own enemies, and were subservient to other men for money; and slew others not only in remote parts of the city, but in the temple itself also; for they had the boldness to murder men there, without thinking of the impiety of which they were guilty. And this seems to me to have been the reason why God, out of his hatred to these men's wickedness, rejected our city; and as for the temple, he no longer esteemed it sufficiently pure for him to inhabit therein, but brought the Romans upon us, and threw a fire upon the city to purge it; and brought upon us, our wives, and children, slavery,—as desirous to make us wiser by our calamities.

6. These works that were done by the robbers, filled the city with all sorts of impiety. And now these impostors and deceivers persuaded the multitude to follow them into the wilderness, and pretended that they would exhibit manifest wonders and signs, that should be performed by the providence of God. And many that were prevailed on by them suffered the punishment of their folly; for Felix brought them back, and then punished them. Moreover, there came out of Egypt* about this time to Jerusalem, one that said he was a prophet, and advised the multitude of the common people to go along with him to the mount of Olives, as it was called, which lay over against the city, and at the distance of five furlongs. He said further, that he would shew them from hence, how, at his command, the walls of Jerusalem would fall down; and he promised them that he would procure them an entrance into the city through those walls, when they were fallen down. Now when Felix was informed of these things, he ordered his soldiers to take their weapons, and came against them with a great number of horsemen and footmen, from Jerusalem, and attacked the Egyptian and the people that were with him. He also slew four hundred of them, and took two hundred alive. But the Egyptian himself escaped out of the

fight, but did not appear any more. And again the robbers stirred up the people to make war with the Romans, and said they ought not to obey them at all; and when any persons would not comply with them, they set fire to their villages, and plundered them.

7. And now it was that a great sedition arose between the Jews that inhabited Cesarea, and the Syrians who dwelt there also, concerning their equal right to the privileges belonging to citizens; for the Jews claimed the pre-eminence, because Herod their king was the builder of Cesarea, and because he was by birth a Jew. Now the Syrians did not deny what was alleged about Herod; but they said that Cesarea was formerly called Strato's Tower, and that then there was not one Jewish inhabitant. When the presidents of that country heard of these disorders, they caught the authors of them on both sides, and tormented them with stripes, and by that means put a stop to the disturbance for a time. But the Jewish citizens depending on their wealth, and on that account despising the Syrians, reproached them again, and hoped to provoke them by such reproaches. However, the Syrians, though they were inferior in wealth, yet valuing themselves highly on this account, that the greatest part of the Roman soldiers that were there, were either of Cesarea or Sebaste, they also for some time used reproachful language to the Jews also; and thus it was, till at length they came to throwing stones at one another; and several were wounded, and fell on both sides, though still the Jews were the conquerors. But when Felix saw that this quarrel was become a kind of war, he came upon them on the sudden, and desired the Jews to desist; and when they refused so to do, he armed his soldiers, and sent them out upon them, and slew many of them, and took more of them alive, and permitted his soldiers to plunder some of the houses of the citizens, which were full of riches. Now those Jews that were more moderate, and of principal dignity among them, were afraid of themselves, and desired of Felix that he would sound a retreat to his soldiers, and spare them for the future, and afford them room for repentance for what they had done; and Felix was prevailed upon to do so.

8. About this time king Agrippa gave the high priesthood to Ismael, who was the son of Fabi. And now arose a sedition between the high priests and the principal men of the multitude of Jerusalem; each of whom got them a company of the boldest sort of men, and of those that loved innovations, about them, and became leaders to them; and when they struggled together, they did it by casting reproachful words against one another, and by throwing stones also. And there was nobody to reprove them; but these disorders were after a licentious manner in the city, as if it had no government over it. And such was the impudence* and boldness that had seized on the high priests, that they had the hardness to send their servants into the thrashing-floors, to take away those tithes that were due to the priests, insomuch that it so fell out that the poorer sort of the priests died for want. To this degree did the violence of the seditious prevail over all right and justice.

9. Now, when Porcius Festus was sent as successor to Felix by Nero, the principal of the Jewish inhabitants at Cesarea went up to Rome to accuse Felix; and he had certainly been

---

one great cause of the following horrid cruelties and miseries of the Jewish nation, as Josephus here supposes. And since we are soon coming to the catalogue of Jewish high priests, it may not be amiss to insert this Jonathan among them; and to transcribe his particular catalogue of the last twenty-eight high-priests, and begin with Ananelus, who was made by Herod the Great. 1. Ananelus. 2. Aristobulus. 3. Jesus, the son of Fabus. 4. Simon, the son of Boethus. 5. Marthias, the son of Theophilus. 6. Joazar, the son of Boethus. 7. Eleazar, the son of Boethus. 8. Jesus, the son of Sic. 9. [Annas, or] Ananus, the son of Seth. 10. Ismael, the son of Fabus. 11. Eleazar, the son of Ananus. 12. Simon, the son of Camithus. 13. Josephus Caiaphas, the son-in-law to Ananus. 14. Jonathan, the son of Ananus. 15. Theophilus, his brother, and son of Ananus. 16. Simon the son of Boethus. 17. Matthias, the brother of Jonathan, and son of Ananus. 18. Aljoneus. 19. Josephus, the son of Camydus. 20. Ananias, the son of Nebedeus. 21. Jonathas. 22. Ismael, the son of Fabi. 23. Joseph Cabi, the son of Simon. 24. Ananus, the son of Ananus. 25. Jesus, the son of Damneus. 26. Jesus, the son of Gamaliel. 27. Matthias, the son of Theophilus. 28. Phanias, the son of Samuel.—Ananus and Joseph Caiaphas, mentioned about the middle of this catalogue, are no other than those Anas and Caiaphas so often mentioned in the Four Gospels; and Ananias, the son of Nebedeus, was that high priest before whom St Paul pleaded his own cause, (Acts xxiv.)

* Of this Egyptian impostor, and the number of his followers in Josephus, see Acts xxi. 38.

* The wickedness here was very peculiar and extraordinary, that the high priests should so oppress their brethren the priests, as to starve the poorest of them to death.

brought to punishment, unless Nero had yielded to the importunate solicitations of his brother Pallas, who was at that time had in the greatest honour by him. Two of the principal Syrians in Cesarea persuaded Burrhus, who was Nero's tutor, and secretary for his Greek epistles, by giving him a great sum of money, to disannul that equality of the Jewish privileges of citizens which they hitherto enjoyed. So Burrhus, by his solicitations, obtained leave of the emperor, that an epistle should be written to that purpose. This epistle became the occasion of the following miseries that befell our nation; for, when the Jews of Cesarea were informed of the contents of this epistle to the Syrians, they were more disorderly than before, till a war was kindled.

10. Upon Festus's coming into Judea, it happened that Judea was afflicted by the robbers, while all the villages were set on fire, and plundered by them. And then it was that the *sicarii*, as they were called, who were robbers, grew numerous. They made use of small swords, not much different in length from the Persian *acinacæ*, but somewhat crooked, and like the Roman *sicæ*, [or sickles,] as they were called; and from these weapons these robbers got their denomination; and with these weapons they slew a great many; for they mingled themselves among the multitude at their festivals, when they were come up in crowds from all parts to the city to worship God, as we said before, and easily slew those that they had a mind to slay. They also came frequently upon the villages belonging to their enemies, with their weapons, and plundered them, and set them on fire. So Festus sent forces, both horsemen and footmen, to fall upon those that had been seduced by a certain impostor, who promised them deliverance and freedom from the miseries they were under, if they would but follow him as far as the wilderness. Accordingly those forces that were sent destroyed both him that had deluded them and those that were his followers also.

11. About the same time king Agrippa built himself a very large dining-room in the royal palace at Jerusalem, near to the portico. Now this palace had been erected of old by the children of Asamoneus, and was situate upon an elevation, and afforded a most delightful prospect to those that had a mind to take a view of the city, which prospect was desired by the king; and there he could lie down, and eat, and thence observe what was done in the temple; which thing, when the chief men at Jerusalem saw, they were very much displeased at it; for it was not agreeable to the institutions of our country or law that what was done in the temple should be viewed by others, especially what belonged to the sacrifices. They therefore erected a wall upon the uppermost building which belonged to the inner court of the temple towards the west; which wall, when it was built, did not only intercept the prospect of the dining-room in the palace, but also of the western cloisters that belonged to the outer court of the temple also, where it was that the Romans kept guards for the temple at the festivals. At these doings both king Agrippa and principally Festus the procurator, were much displeased; and Festus ordered them to pull the wall down again: but the Jews petitioned him to give them leave to send an embassage about this matter to Nero; for they said they could not endure to live if any part of the temple should be demolished; and when Festus had given them leave so to do, they sent ten of their principal men to Nero, as also Ismael the high priest, and Helcias, the keeper of the sacred treasure. And when Nero had heard what they had to say, he not only forgave* them what they had already done, but also gave them leave to let the wall they had built stand. This was granted in order to gratify Poppea, Nero's wife, who was a religious woman, and had requested these favours of Nero, and who gave orders to the ten ambassadors to go their way home; but retained Helcias and Ismael as hostages with herself. As soon as the king heard this news, he gave the high priesthood to Joseph, who was called Cabi, the son of Simon, formerly high priest.

CHAPTER IX

CONCERNING ALBINUS, UNDER WHOSE PROCURATORSHIP JAMES WAS SLAIN; AS ALSO WHAT EDIFICES WERE BUILT BY AGRIPPA

1. AND now Cæsar, upon hearing of the death of Festus, sent Albinus into Judea as procurator; but the king deprived Joseph of the high priesthood, and bestowed the succession to that dignity on the son of Ananus, who was also himself called Ananus. Now the report goes, that this elder Ananus proved a most fortunate man; for he had five sons, who had all performed the office of a high priest to God, and he had himself enjoyed that dignity a long time formerly, which had never happened to any other of our high priests; but this younger Ananus, who, as we have told you already, took the high priesthood, was a bold man in his temper, and very insolent; he was also of the sect of the Sadducees,† who were very rigid in judging offenders, above all the rest of the Jews, as we have already observed; when, therefore, Ananus was of this disposition, he thought he had now a proper opportunity [to exercise his authority.] Festus was now dead, and Albinus was but upon the road; so he assembled the sanhedrim of the judges, and brought before them the brother of Jesus, who was called Christ, whose name was James, and some others, [or some of his companions;] and when he had formed an accusation against them as breakers of the law, he delivered them to be stoned: but as for those who seemed the most equitable of the citizens, and such as were the most uneasy at the breach of the laws, they disliked what was done; they also sent to the king [Agrippa,] desiring him to send to Ananus that he should act so no more, for that what he had already done was not to be justified: nay, some of them went also to meet Albinus, as he was upon his journey from Alexandria, and informed him that it was not lawful for Ananus to assemble a sanhedrim without his consent:‡—whereupon Albinus complied with

* We have here an eminent example of Nero's mildness and goodness in his government towards the Jews, during the first five years of his reign. However, this generous act of kindness was obtained of Nero by his queen Poppea, who was a religious lady, and perhaps privately a Jewish proselyte, and so were not owing entirely to Nero's own goodness.

† It hence evidently appears that Sadducees might be high priests in the days of Josephus, and that these Sadducees were usually very severe and inexorable judges, while the Pharisees were much milder, and more merciful.

‡ The sanhedrim condemned our Saviour, but could not put him to death without the approbation of the Roman procurator; nor could therefore Ananias and his sanhedrim do more here, since they never had Albinus's approbation for the putting of James to death.

what they had said, and wrote in anger to Ananus, and threatened that he would bring him to punishment for what he had done; on which king Agrippa took the high priesthood from him, when he had ruled but three months, and made Jesus, the son of Damneus, high priest.

2. Now, as soon as Albinus was come to the city of Jerusalem, he used all his endeavours and care that the country might be kept in peace, and this by destroying many of the *sicarii;* but as for the high priest Ananias,* he increased in glory every day, and this to a great degree, and had obtained the favour and esteem of the citizens in a signal manner; for he was a great hoarder up of money: he therefore cultivated the friendship of Albinus, and of the high priest [Jesus,] by making them presents; he also had servants who were very wicked, who joined themselves to the boldest sort of the people, and went to the thrashing-floors, and took away the tithes that belonged to the priests by violence, and did not refrain from beating such as would not give these tithes to them. So the other high priests acted in the like manner, as did those his servants, without any one being able to prohibit them; so that [some of the] priests, that of old were wont to be supported with those tithes, died for want of food.

3. But now the *sicarii* went into the city by night, just before the festival, which was now at hand, and took the scribe belonging to the governor of the temple, whose name was Eleazar, who was the son of Ananus (Ananias) the high priest, and bound him, and carried him away with them; after which they sent to Ananias, and said that they would send the scribe to him, if he would persuade Albinus to release ten of those prisoners which he had caught of their party; so Ananias was plainly forced to persuade Albinus, and gained his request of him. This was the beginning of greater calamities; for the robbers perpetually contrived to catch some of Ananias's servants; and when they had taken them alive, they would not let them go till they thereby recovered some of their own *sicarii;* and as they were again become no small number, they grew bold, and were a great affliction to the whole country.

4. About this time it was that Agrippa built Cesarea Philippi larger than it was before, and, in honour of Nero, named it Neronias; and when he had built a theatre at Berytus, with vast expenses, he bestowed on them shows, to be exhibited every year, and spent therein many ten thousand [drachmæ;] he also gave the people a largess of corn, and distributed oil among them, and adorned the entire city with statues of his own donation, and with original images made by ancient hands; nay, he almost transferred all that was most ornamental in his own kingdom thither. This made him more than ordinarily hated by his subjects; because he took those things away that belonged to them, to adorn a foreign city; and now Jesus the son of Gamaliel became the successor of Jesus, the son of Damneus, in the high priesthood, which the king had taken from the other; on which account a sedition arose between the high priests, with regard to one another; for they got together bodies of the people, and frequently came, from reproaches, to throwing of stones at each other; but Ananias was too hard for the rest, by his riches,—which enabled him to gain those that were the most ready to receive. Costobarus, also, and Saulus,

did themselves get together a multitude of wicked wretches, and this because they were of the royal family; and so they obtained favour among them, because of their kindred to Agrippa: but still they used violence with the people, and were very ready to plunder those that were weaker than themselves. And from that time it principally came to pass, that our city was greatly disordered, and that all things grew worse and worse among us.

5. But when Albinus heard that Gessius Florus was coming to succeed him, he was desirous to appear to do somewhat that might be grateful to the people of Jerusalem: so he brought out all those prisoners who seemed to him to be the most plainly worthy of death, and ordered them to be put to death accordingly. But as to those who had been put into prison on some trifling occasion, he took money of them, and dismissed them; by which means the prisons were indeed emptied, but the country was filled with robbers.

6. Now, as many of the Levites,† which is a tribe of ours, as were singers of hymns, persuaded the king to assemble a sanhedrim, and to give them leave to wear linen garments as well as the priests: for they said this would be a work worthy the times of his government, that he might have a memorial of such a novelty, as being his doing. Nor did they fail of obtaining their desire; for the king, with the suffrages of those that came into the sanhedrim, granted the singers of hymns this privilege, that they might lay aside their former garments, and wear such a linen one as they desired; and as a part of this tribe ministered in the temple, he also permitted them to learn those hymns as they had besought him for. Now all this was contrary to the laws of our country, which whenever they have been transgressed, we have never been able to avoid the punishment of such transgressions.

7. And now it was that the temple was finished. So, when the people saw that the workmen were unemployed, who were above eighteen thousand, and that they, receiving no wages, were in want, because they had earned their bread by their labours about the temple; and while they were unwilling to keep them by their treasuries that were there deposited, out of fear of [their being carried away by] the Romans; and while they had a regard to the making provision for the workmen, they had a mind to expend those treasures upon them; for if any one of them did but labour for a single hour, he received his pay immediately; so they persuaded him to rebuild the eastern cloisters. These cloisters belonged to the outer court, and were situated in a deep valley, and had walls that reached four hundred cubits [in length,] and were built of square and very white stones, the length of each of which stones was twenty cubits, and their height six cubits. This was the work of king Solomon, who first of all built the entire temple. But king Agrippa, who had the care of the temple committed to him by Claudius Cæsar, considered that it is easy to demolish any building, but hard to build it up again, and that it was particularly hard to do it to those cloisters, which would require a considerable time, and great sums of money, he denied the petitioners their request about that matter; but he did not obstruct them when they desired the city might

---

* This Ananias was not the son of Nebedeus, as I take it, but he who was called Annas, or Ananus the Elder, the ninth in the catalogue, and who had been esteemed high priest for a long time.

† This insolent petition of some of the Levites, to wear the sacerdotal garments when they sung hymns to God in the temple, was very probably owing to the great depression and contempt the haughty high priests had brought their brethren the priests into.

be paved with white stone. He also deprived Jesus, the son of Gamaliel, of the high priesthood, and gave it to Matthias, the son of Theophilus, under whom the Jews' war with the Romans took its beginning.

CHAPTER X

AN ENUMERATION OF THE HIGH PRIESTS

1. AND now I think it proper and agreeable to history to give an account of our high priests; how they began, who those are which are capable of that dignity, and how many of them there had been at the end of the war. In the first place, therefore, history informs us that Aaron, the brother of Moses, officiated to God as a high priest; and that, after his death, his sons succeeded him immediately; and that this dignity hath been continued down from them all to their posterity. Whence it is a custom of our country, that no one should take the high priesthood of God but he who is of the blood of Aaron, while every one that is of another stock, though he were a king, can never obtain that high priesthood. Accordingly, the number of all the high priests from Aaron, of whom we have already spoken as the first of them, until Phanas, who was made high priest during the war by the seditious, was eighty-three; of whom thirteen officiated as high priests in the wilderness, from the days of Moses, while the tabernacle was standing, until the people came into Judea, when king Solomon erected the temple to God; for at first they held the high priesthood till the end of their life, although afterward they had successors while they were alive. Now these thirteen, who were the descendants of two of the sons of Aaron, received this dignity by succession, one after another; for their form of government was an aristocracy, and after that a monarchy, and in the third place the government was regal. Now, the number of years during the rule of these thirteen, from the days when our fathers departed out of Egypt, under Moses their leader, until the building of that temple which king Solomon erected at Jerusalem, was six hundred and twelve. After those thirteen high priests, eighteen took the high priesthood at Jerusalem, one in succession to another, from the days of king Solomon until Nebuchadnezzar, king of Babylon, made an expedition against that city, and burnt the temple, and removed our nation into Babylon, and then took Josadek, the high priest, captive; the time of these high priests were four hundred and sixty-six years, six months, and ten days, while the Jews were still under the regal government. But after the term of seventy years' captivity under the Babylonians, Cyrus king of Persia, sent the Jews from Babylon to their own land again, and gave them leave to rebuild their temple; at which time Jesus, the son of Josadek, took the high priesthood over the captives when they were returned home. Now he and his posterity, who were in all fifteen, unto king Antiochus Eupator, were under a democratical government for four hundred and fourteen years; and then the forementioned Antiochus and Lysias the general of his army, deprived Onias, who was called Menelaus, of the high priesthood, and slew him at Berea; and driving away the son [of Onias the third,] put Jacimus into the high priest's place, one that was indeed of the stock of Aaron, but not of the family of Onias. On which account Onias, who was the nephew of Onias that was dead, and bore the same name with his father, came into Egypt, and got into the friendship of Ptolemy Philometor, and Cleopatra his wife, and persuaded them to make him the high priest of that temple which he built to God in the prefecture of Heliopolis, and this in imitation of that at Jerusalem; but as for the temple which was built in Egypt, we have spoken of it frequently already. Now when Jacimus had retained the priesthood three years, he died, and there was no one that succeeded him, but the city continued seven years without a high priest. But then the posterity of the sons of Asamoneus, who had the government of the nation conferred upon them when they had beaten the Macedonians in war, appointed Jonathan to be their high priest, who ruled over them seven years. And when he had been slain by the treacherous contrivance of Trypho, as we have related somewhere, Simon his brother took the high priesthood; and when he was destroyed at a feast by the treachery of his son-in-law, his own son, whose name was Hyrcanus, succeeded him, after he had held the high priesthood one year longer than his brother. This Hyrcanus enjoyed that dignity thirty years, and died an old man, leaving the succession to Judas, who was also called Aristobulus, whose brother Alexander was his heir; which Judas died of a sore distemper, after he had kept the priesthood, together with the royal authority; for this Judas was the first that put on his head a diadem for one year. And when Alexander had been both king and high priest twenty-seven years, he departed this life, and permitted his wife Alexandra to appoint him that should be high priest; so she gave the high priesthood to Hyrcanus, but retained the kingdom herself nine years, and then departed this life. The like duration [and no longer] did her son Hyrcanus enjoy the high priesthood; for after her death his brother Aristobulus fought against him, and beat and deprived him of his principality; and he did himself both reign and perform the office of high priest to God. But when he had reigned three years, and as many months, Pompey came upon him, and not only took the city of Jerusalem by force, but put him and his children in bonds, and sent them to Rome. He also restored the high priesthood to Hyrcanus, and made him governor of the nation, but forbade him to wear a diadem. This Hyrcanus ruled, besides his first nine years, twenty-four years more, when Barzapharnes and Pacorus, the generals of the Parthians, passed over Euphrates, and fought with Hyrcanus, and took him alive, and made Antigonus, the son of Aristobulus, king; and when he had reigned three years and three months, Sosius and Herod besieged him, and took him, when Antony had him brought to Antioch, and slain there. Herod was then made king by the Romans, but did no longer appoint high priests out of the family of Asamoneus; but made certain men to be so that were of no eminent families, but barely of those that were priests, excepting that he gave that dignity to Aristobulus; for when he had made this Aristobulus, the grandson of that Hyrcanus who was then taken by the Parthians, and had taken his sister Mariamme to wife, he thereby aimed to win the good-will of the people, who had a kind remembrance of Hyrcanus, [his grandfather.] Yet did he afterward, out of his fear lest they should all bend their inclinations to Aristobulus, put him to death, and that by contriving how to have him suffocated, as he was swimming at Jericho, as we have already related that matter; but after this

man, he never intrusted the high priesthood to the posterity of the sons of Asamoneus. Archelaus also, Herod's son, did like his father in the appointment of the high priests, as did the Romans also, who took the government over the Jews into their hands afterward. Accordingly, the number of the high priests, from the days of Herod until the day when Titus took the temple and the city, and burnt them, were in all twenty-eight; the time also that belonged to them was a hundred and seven years. Some of these were the political governors of the people under the reign of Herod, and under the reign of Archelaus his son, although, after their death, the government became an aristocracy, and the high priests were intrusted with a dominion over the nation. And thus much may suffice to be said concerning our high priests.

CHAPTER XI

CONCERNING FLORUS THE PROCURATOR, WHO NECESSITATED THE JEWS TO TAKE UP ARMS AGAINST THE ROMANS. THE CONCLUSION

1. Now Gessius Florus, who was sent as successor to Albinus by Nero, filled Judea with abundance of miseries. He was by birth of the city of Clazomenæ, and brought along with him his wife Cleopatra, (by whose friendship with Poppea, Nero's wife, he obtained this government,) who was no way different from him in wickedness. This Florus was so wicked, and so violent in the use of his authority, that the Jews took Albinus to have been [comparatively] their benefactor; so excessive were the mischiefs that he brought upon them. For Albinus concealed his wickedness, and was careful that it might not be discovered to all men; but Gessius Florus, as though he had been sent on purpose to shew his crimes to everybody, made a pompous ostentation of them to our nation, as never omitting any sort of violence, nor any unjust sort of punishment; for he was not to be moved by pity, and never was satisfied with any degree of gain that came in his way; nor had he any more regard to great than to small acquisitions, but became a partner with the robbers themselves; for a great many fell then into that practice without fear, as having him for their security, and depending on him, that he would save them harmless in their particular robberies; so that there were no bounds set to the nation's miseries; but the unhappy Jews, when they were not able to bear the devastations which the robbers made among them, were all under a necessity of leaving their own habitations, and of flying away, as hoping to dwell more easily anywhere else in the world among foreigners [than in their own country.] And what need I say any more upon this head? since it was this Florus who necessitated us to take up arms against the Romans, while we thought it better to be destroyed at once, than by little and little. Now this war began in the second year of the government of Florus, and the twelfth year of the reign of Nero. But then what actions we were forced to do, or what miseries we were enabled to suffer, may be accurately known by such as will peruse those books which I have written about the Jewish war.

2. I shall now, therefore, make an end here of my Antiquities; after the conclusion of which events, I began to write that account of the war; and these Antiquities contain what hath been delivered down to us from the original creation of man, until the twelfth year of the reign of Nero, as to what hath befallen the Jews, as well in Egypt as in Syria, and in Palestine, and what we have suffered from the Assyrians and Babylonians, and what afflictions the Persians and Macedonians, and after them the Romans, have brought upon us; for I think I may say that I have composed this history with sufficient accuracy in all things. I have attempted to enumerate those high priests that we have had during the interval of two thousand years; I have also carried down the succession of our kings, and related their actions, and political administration, without [considerable] errors, as also the power of our monarchs; and all according to what is written in our sacred books; for this it was that I promised to do in the beginning of this history. And I am so bold as to say, now I have so completely perfected the work I proposed to myself to do, that no other person, whether he were a Jew or a foreigner, had he ever so great an inclination to it, could so accurately deliver these accounts to the Greeks as is done in these books. For those of my own nation freely acknowledge that I far exceed them in the learning belonging to the Jews; I have also taken a great deal of pains to obtain the learning of the Greeks, and understand the elements of the Greek language, although I have so long accustomed myself to speak our own tongue, that I cannot pronounce Greek with sufficient exactness: for our nation does not encourage those that learn the languages of many nations, and so adorn their discourses with the smoothness of their periods; because they look upon this sort of accomplishment as common, not only to all sorts of freemen, but to as many of the servants as please to learn them. But they give him the testimony of being a wise man who is fully acquainted with our laws, and is able to interpret their meaning; on which account, as there have been many who have done their endeavours with great patience to obtain this learning, there have yet hardly been so many as two or three that have succeeded therein, who were immediately well rewarded for their pains.

3. And now it will not be perhaps an invidious thing if I treat briefly of my own family, and of the actions of my own life,* while there are still living such as can either prove what I say to be false, or can attest that it is true; with which accounts I shall put an end to these Antiquities, which are contained in twenty books, and sixty thousand verses. And if God permit me, I will briefly run over this war again, with what befell us therein to this very day, which is the thirteenth year of the reign of Cæsar Domitian, and the fifty-sixth of my own life. I have also an intention to write three books concerning our Jewish opinions about God and his essence, and about our laws; why, according to them, some things are permitted us to do, and others are prohibited.

---

* The Life here referred to, will be found at the beginning of the volume.

THE WARS OF THE JEWS;

OR

THE HISTORY OF THE DESTRUCTION OF JERUSALEM

PREFACE

1. *WHEREAS the war which the Jews made with the Romans hath been the greatest of all those, not only that have been in our times, but, in a manner, of those that ever were heard of; both of those wherein cities have fought against cities, or nations against nations; while some men who were not concerned in the affair themselves, have gotten together vain and contradictory stories by hearsay, and have written them down after a sophistical manner; and while those that were there present have given false accounts of things, and this either out of a humour of flattery to the Romans, or of hatred to the Jews; and while their writings contain sometimes accusations, and sometimes encomiums, but nowhere the accurate truth of the facts, I have proposed to myself, for the sake of such as live under the government of the Romans, to translate those books into the Greek tongue, which I formerly composed in the language of our own country, and sent to the Upper Barbarians;† I Joseph, the son of Matthias, by birth a Hebrew, a priest also, and one who at first fought against the Romans myself, and was forced to be present at what was done afterwards, [am the author of this work.]

2. Now at the time when this great concussion of affairs happened, the affairs of the Romans themselves were in great disorder. Those Jews also, who were for innovations, then arose when the times were disturbed; they were also in a flourishing condition for strength and riches, insomuch that the affairs of the east were exceeding tumultuous, while some hoped for gain, and others were afraid of loss in such troubles; for the Jews hoped that all of their nation which were beyond Euphrates would have raised an insurrection together with them. The Gauls also, in the neighbourhood of the Romans, were in motion, and the Celtæ were not quiet; but all was in disorder after the death of Nero. And the opportunity now offered induced many to aim at the royal power: and the soldiery affected change, out of the hopes of getting money. I thought it therefore an absurd thing to see the truth falsified in affairs of such great consequence, and to take no notice of it; but to suffer those Greeks and Romans that were not in the wars to be ignorant of these things, and to read either flatteries or fictions, while the Parthians, and the Babylonians, and the remotest Arabians, and of those our nation beyond Euphrates, with the Adiabeni, by my means, knew accurately both when the war begun, what miseries it brought upon us, and after what manner it ended.

3. It is true, these writers have the confidence to call their accounts histories; wherein yet they seem to me to fail of their own purpose, as well as to relate nothing that is sound; for they have a mind to demonstrate the greatness of the Romans, while they still diminish and lessen the actions of the Jews, as not discerning how it cannot be that those must appear to be great who have only conquered those that were little; nor are they ashamed to overlook the length of the war, the multitude of the Roman forces which so greatly suffered in it, or the might of the commanders,—whose great labours about Jerusalem will be deemed inglorious if what they achieved be reckoned but a small matter.

4. However, I will not go to the other extreme, out of opposition to those men who extol the Romans, nor will I determine to raise the actions of my countrymen too high; but I will prosecute the actions of both parties with accuracy. Yet shall I suit my language to the passions I am under, as to the affairs I describe, and must be allowed to indulge some lamentations upon the miseries undergone by my own country; for that it was a seditious temper of our own that destroyed it; and that they were the tyrants among the Jews who brought the Roman power upon us, who unwillingly attacked us, and occasioned the burning of our holy temple; Titus Cæsar, who destroyed it, is himself a witness, who, during the entire war, pitied the people who were kept under by the seditious, and did often voluntarily delay the taking of

---

* I have already observed that this history of the Jewish War was Josephus's first work, and published about A.D. 75, when he was but thirty-eight years of age; and that when he wrote it, he was not thoroughly acquainted with several circumstances of history from the days of Antiochus Epiphanes, with which it begins, till near his own times, contained in the first and former part of the second book, and so committed many involuntary errors therein: that he published his Antiquities eighteen years afterward, in the 13th year of Domitian, A.D. 93, when he was much more completely acquainted with those ancient times, and after he had perused those most ancient histories, the first book of Maccabees, and the Chronicles of the Priesthood of John Hyrcanus, &c.: that accordingly he then reviewed those parts of this work, and gave the public a more faithful, complete, and accurate account of the facts therein related; and honestly corrected the errors he had before run into.

† These Upper Barbarians were the Parthians and Babylonians, and remotest Arabians, [or the Jews among them;] besides the Jews beyond Euphrates, and the Adiabeni, or Assyrians.

the city, and allowed time to the siege, in order to let the authors have opportunity for repentance. But if any one makes an unjust accusation against us, when we speak so passionately about the tyrants, or the robbers, or sorely bewail the misfortunes of our country, let him indulge our affections herein, though it be contrary to the rules for writing history; because it had so come to pass, that our city Jerusalem had arrived at a higher degree of felicity than any other city under the Roman government, and yet at last fell into the sorest calamities again. Accordingly it appears to me, that the misfortunes of all men, from the beginning of the world, if they be compared to these of the Jews,* are not so considerable as they were; while the authors of them were not foreigners neither. This makes it impossible for me to contain my lamentations. But, if any one be inflexible in his censures of me, let him attribute the facts themselves to the historical part, and the lamentations to the writer himself only.

5. However, I may justly blame the learned men among the Greeks, who, when such great actions have been done in their own times, which, upon the comparison, quite eclipse the old wars, do yet sit as judges of those affairs, and pass bitter censures upon the labours of the best writers of antiquity; which moderns, although they may be superior to the old writers in eloquence, yet are they inferior to them in the execution of what they intended to do. While these also write new histories about the Assyrians and Medes, as if the ancient writers had not described their affairs as they ought to have done; although these be as far inferior to them in abilities as they are different in their notions from them; for of old, every one took upon them to write what happened in his own time; where their immediate concern in the actions made their promises of value; and where it must be reproachful to write lies, when they must be known by the reader to be such. But then, an undertaking to preserve the memory of what hath not been before recorded, and to represent the affairs of one's own time to those that come afterwards, is really worthy of praise and commendation. Now, he is to be esteemed to have taken good pains in earnest, not who does no more than change the disposition and order of other men's works, but he who not only relates what had not been related before, but composes an entire body of history of his own: accordingly, I have been at great charges, and have taken very great pains, [about this history,] though I be a foreigner; and do dedicate this work, as a memorial of great actions, both to the Greeks and to the Barbarians. But, for some of our own principal men, their mouths are wide open, and their tongues loosed presently, for gain and law-suits, but quite muzzled up when they are to write history, where they must speak truth and gather facts together with a great deal of pains; and so they leave the writing of such histories to weaker people, and to such as are not acquainted with the actions of princes. Yet shall the real truth of historical facts be preferred by us, how much soever it be neglected among the Greek historians.

6. To write concerning the Antiquities of the Jews, who they were [originally,] and how they revolted from the Egyptians, and what country they travelled over, and what countries they seized upon afterward, and how they were removed out of them, I think this not to be a fit opportunity, and, on other accounts, also superfluous; and this because many Jews before me have composed the histories of our ancestors very exactly; as have some of the Greeks done it also, and have translated our histories into their own tongue, and have not much mistaken the truth in their histories. But then, where the writers of these affairs and our prophets leave off, thence shall I take my rise, and begin my history. Now, as to what concerns that war which happened in my own time, I will go over it very largely, and with all the diligence I am able; but for what preceded mine own age, that I shall run over briefly.

7. [For example, I shall relate] how Antiochus, who was named Epiphanes, took Jerusalem by force, and held it three years and three months, and was then ejected out of the country by the sons of Asamoneus: after that, how their posterity quarrelled about the government, and brought upon their settlement the Romans and Pompey; how Herod also, the son of Antipater, dissolved their government, and brought Socius upon them; as also how our people made a sedition upon Herod's death, while Augustus was the Roman emperor, and Quintilius Varus was in that country; and how the war broke out in the twelfth year of Nero, with what happened to Cestius; and what places the Jews assaulted in a hostile manner in the first sallies of the war.

8. As also [I shall relate] how they built walls about the neighbouring cities; and how Nero, upon Cestius's defeat, was in fear of the entire event of the war, and thereupon made Vespasian general in this war; and how this Vespasian, with the elder of his sons, † made an expedition into the country of Judea; what was the number of the Roman army that he made use of; and how many of his auxiliaries were cut off in all Galilee; and how he took some of its cities entirely, and by force, and others of them by treaty, and on terms. Now, when I am come so far, I shall describe the good order of the Romans in war, and the discipline of their legions: the amplitude of both the Galilees, with their nature, and the limits of Judea. And, besides this, I shall particularly go over what is peculiar to the country, the lakes and fountains that are in them, and what miseries happened to every city as they were taken; and all this with accuracy, as I saw the things done, or suffered in them; for I shall not conceal any of the calamities I myself endured, since I shall relate them to such as know the truth of them.

9. After this [I shall relate] how, when the Jews' affairs were become very bad, Nero died; and Vespasian, when he was going to attack Jerusalem, was called back to take the government upon him; what signs happened to him relating to his gaining that government, and what mutations of government then happened at Rome, and how he was unwillingly made emperor by his soldiers; and how, upon his departure to Egypt, to take upon him the government of the empire, the affairs of the Jews became very tumultuous; as also how the tyrants rose up against them, and fell into dissensions amongst themselves.

10. Moreover [I shall relate] how Titus marched out of Egypt into Judea the second time; as also how and where, and how many forces he got together; and in what state the city was,

* That these calamities of the Jews, who were our Saviour's murderers, were to be the greatest that had ever been since the beginning of the world, our Saviour had directly foretold, (Matt. xxiv. 21; Mark xiii. 19; Luke xxi. 23, 24:) and that they proved to be such accordingly, Josephus is here a most authentic witness.

† Titus.

by means of the seditious, at his coming; what attacks he made, and how many ramparts he cast up; of the three walls that encompassed the city, and of their measures; of the strength of the city, and the structure of the temple and holy house; and besides, the measures of those edifices, and of the altar, and all accurately determined. A description also of certain of their festivals, and seven purifications or days of purity, and the sacred ministrations of the priests, with the garments of the priests, and of the high priests; and of the nature of the most holy place of the temple; without concealing anything, or adding anything to the known truth of things.

11. After this, I shall relate the barbarity of the tyrants towards the people of their own nation, as well as the indulgence of the Romans in sparing foreigners; and how often Titus, out of his desire to preserve the city and the temple, invited the seditious to come to terms of accommodation. I shall also distinguish the sufferings of the people, and their calamities; how far they were afflicted by the sedition, and how far by the famine, and at length were taken.

Nor shall I omit to mention the misfortunes of the deserters, nor the punishments inflicted on the captives; as also how the temple was burnt against the consent of Cæsar; and how many sacred things that had been laid up in the temple, were snatched out of the fire; the destruction also of the entire city, with the signs and wonders that went before it; and the taking the tyrants captive, and the multitude of those that were made slaves, and into what different misfortunes they were every one distributed. Moreover, what the Romans did to the remains of the wall; and how they demolished the strong-holds that were in the country; and how Titus went over the whole country, and settled its affairs; together with his return into Italy, and his triumph.

12. I have comprehended all these things in seven books; and have left no occasion for complaint or accusation to such as have been acquainted with this war; and I have written it down for the sake of those that love truth, but not for those that please themselves [with fictitious relations.] And I will begin my account of these things with what I call my First Chapter.

BOOK I

CONTAINING THE INTERVAL OF ONE HUNDRED AND SIXTY-SEVEN YEARS

FROM ANTIOCHUS EPIPHANES TAKING JERUSALEM TO THE DEATH OF HEROD THE GREAT

CHAPTER I

HOW THE CITY OF JERUSALEM WAS TAKEN, AND THE TEMPLE PILLAGED [BY ANTIOCHUS EPIPHANES.] AS ALSO CONCERNING THE ACTIONS OF THE MACCABEES, MATTHIAS AND JUDAS; AND CONCERNING THE DEATH OF JUDAS

1. AT the same time that Antiochus, who was called Epiphanes, had a quarrel with the sixth Ptolemy about his right to the whole country of Syria, a great sedition fell among the men of power in Judea, and they had a contention about obtaining the government; while each of those that were of dignity could not endure to be subject to their equals. However, Onias, one of the high priests, got the better, and cast the sons of Tobias out of the city; who fled to Antiochus, and besought him to make use of them for his leaders, and to make an expedition into Judea. The king being thereto disposed beforehand, complied with them, and came upon the Jews with a great army, and took their city by force, and slew a great multitude of those that favoured Ptolemy, and sent out his soldiers to plunder them without mercy. He also spoiled the temple, and put a stop to the constant practice of offering a daily sacrifice of expiation for three years and six months. But Onias, the high priest, fled to Ptolemy, and received a place from him in the Nomus of Heliopolis, where he built a city resembling Jerusalem, and a temple that was like its temple; concerning which we shall speak more in its proper place hereafter.

2. Now Antiochus was not satisfied either with his unexpected taking of the city, or with its pillage, or with the great slaughter he had made there; but being overcome with his violent passions, and remembering what he had suffered during the siege, he compelled the Jews to dissolve the laws of their country, and to keep their infants uncircumcised, and to sacrifice swine's flesh upon the altar; against which they all opposed themselves, and the most approved among them were put to death. Bacchides also, who was sent to keep the fortresses, having these wicked commands, joined to his own natural barbarity, indulged all sorts of the extremest wickedness, and tormented the worthiest of the inhabitants, man by man, and threatened their city every day with open destruction; till at length he provoked the poor sufferers, by the extremity of his wicked doings, to avenge themselves.

3. Accordingly Matthias, the son of Asamoneus, one of the priests who lived in a village called Modin, armed himself, together with his own family, which had five sons of his in it, and slew Bacchides with daggers; and thereupon, out of the fear of the many garrisons [of the enemy] he fled to the mountains; and so many of the people followed him, that he was encouraged to come down from the mountains, and to give battle to Antiochus's generals, when he beat them, and drove them out of Judea. So he came to the government by this his success, and became the prince of his own people by their own free consent, and then died, leaving the government to Judas, his eldest son.

4. Now Judas, supposing that Antiochus would not lie still, gathered an army out of his own countrymen, and was the first that made a league of friendship with the Romans, and drove Epiphanes out of the country when he had made a second expedition into it, and this by giving him a great defeat there; and when he was warmed by this great success, he made an assault upon the garrison that was in the city, for it had not been cut off hitherto; so he ejected them out of the upper city, and drove the soldiers into the lower, which part of the city was called the Citadel. He then got the temple under his power, and cleansed the whole place, and walled it round about, and made new vessels for sacred ministrations, and brought them into the temple, because the former vessels had been profaned. He also built another altar, and began to offer the sacrifices; and when the city had already received its sacred constitution again, Antiochus died; whose son Antiochus succeeded him in the kingdom, and in his hatred to the Jews also.

5. So this Antiochus got together fifty thousand footmen, and five thousand horsemen, and four score elephants, and marched through Judea into the mountainous parts. He then took Bethsura, which was a small city; but at a place called Bethzacharias, where the passage was narrow, Judas met him with his army. However, before the forces joined battle, Judas's brother, Eleazar, seeing the very highest of the elephants adorned with a large tower, and with military trappings of gold to guard him, and supposing that Antiochus himself was upon him, he ran a great way before his own army, and cutting his way through the enemy's troops, he got up to the elephant: yet could not reach him who seemed to be the king, by reason of his being so high; but still he ran his weapon into the belly of the beast, and brought him down upon himself, and was crushed to death, having done no more than attempted great things, and shewed that he preferred glory before life. Now he that governed the elephant was but a private man; but had he proved to be Antiochus, Eleazar had performed nothing more by this bold stroke than that it might appear he chose to die, when he had the bare hope of thereby doing a glorious action; nay, this disappointment proved an omen to his brother [Judas] how the entire battle would end. It is true that the Jews fought it out bravely for a long time; but the king's forces, being superior in number, and having fortune on their side, obtained the victory; and when a great many of his men were slain, Judas took the rest with him, and fled to the toparchy of Gophnas. So Antiochus went to Jerusalem, and stayed there but a few days, for he wanted provisions, and so he went his way. He left indeed a garrison behind him, such as he thought sufficient to keep the place; but drew the rest of his army off, to take their winter-quarters in Syria.

6. Now, after the king was departed, Judas was not idle; for as many of his own nation came to him, so did he gather those that had escaped out of the battle together, and gave battle again to Antiochus's generals at a village called Adasa; and being too hard for his enemies in the battle, and killing a great number of them, he was at last himself slain also. Nor was it many days afterward that his brother John had a plot laid against him by Antiochus's party, and was slain by them.

CHAPTER II

CONCERNING THE SUCCESSORS OF JUDAS, WHO WERE JONATHAN, SIMEON, AND JOHN HYRCANUS

1. WHEN Jonathan who was Judas's brother, succeeded him, he behaved with great circumspection in other respects, with relation to his own people; and he corroborated his authority by preserving his friendship with the Romans. He also made a league with Antiochus the son. Yet was not all this sufficient for his security; for the tyrant Trypho, who was guardian to Antiochus's son, laid a plot against him; and, besides that, endeavoured to take off his friends, and caught Jonathan by a wile, as he was going to Ptolemais to Antiochus, with a few persons in his company, and put them in bonds, and then made an expedition against the Jews; but when he was afterward driven away by Simeon, who was Jonathan's brother, and was enraged at his defeat, he put Jonathan to death.

2. However, Simeon managed the public affairs after a courageous manner, and took Gazaro, and Joppa, and Jamnia, which were cities in the neighbourhood. He also got the garrison under, and demolished the citadel. He was afterwards an auxiliary to Antiochus, against Trypho, whom he besieged in Dora, before he went on his expedition against the Medes; yet could not he make the king ashamed of his ambition, though he had assisted him in killing Trypho; for it was not long ere Antiochus sent Cendebeus his general with an army to lay waste Judea, and to subdue Simeon; yet he, though he was now in years, conducted the war as if he were a much younger man. He also sent his sons with a band of strong men against Antiochus, while he took part of the army himself with him, and fell upon him from another quarter: he also laid a great many men in ambush in many places of the mountains, and was superior in all his attacks upon them. And when he had been conqueror after so glorious a manner, he was made high priest, and also freed the Jews from the dominion of the Macedonians, after a hundred and seventy years of the empire [of Seleucas.]

3. This Simeon had also a plot laid against him, and was slain at a feast by his son-in-law Ptolemy, who put his wife and two sons into prison, and sent some persons to kill John, who was also called Hyrcanus. But when the young man was informed of their coming beforehand, he made much haste to get to the city, as having a very great confidence in the people there, both on account of the memory of the glorious actions of his father, and of the hatred they could not but bear to the injustice of Ptolemy. Ptolemy also made an attempt to get into the city by another gate, but was repelled by the people, who had just then admitted Hyrcanus; so he retired presently to one of the fortresses that were above Jericho, which was called Dagon. Now, when Hyrcanus had received the high priesthood, which his father had held before, and had offered sacrifice to God, he made great haste to attack Ptolemy, that he might afford relief to his mother and brethren.

4. So he laid siege to the fortress, and was superior to Ptolemy in other respects, but was overcome by him as to the just affection [he had for his relations;] for when Ptolemy was distressed, he brought forth his mother and his brethren, and set them upon the wall, and beat them with rods in everybody's sight, and threatened, that, unless he would go away immedi-

ELEAZAR'S ATTEMPT TO KILL ANTIOCHUS

ately, he would throw them down headlong; at which sight Hyrcanus's commiseration and concern were too hard for his anger. But his mother was not dismayed, neither at the stripes she received, nor at the death with which she was threatened, but stretched out her hands, and prayed her son not to be moved with the injuries that she suffered, to spare the wretch; since it was to her better to die by the means of Ptolemy than to live ever so long, provided he might be punished for the injuries he had done to their family. Now John's case was this:—When he considered the courage of his mother, and heard her entreaty, he set about his attacks; but when he saw her beaten, and torn to pieces with the stripes, he grew feeble, and was entirely overcome by his affections. And as the siege was delayed by this means, the year of rest came on, upon which the Jews rest every seventh year as they do on every seventh day. On this year, therefore, Ptolemy was freed from being besieged, and slew the brethren of John, with their mother, and fled to Zeno, who was also called Cotylas, who was the tyrant of Philadelphia.

5. And now Antiochus was so angry at what he had suffered from Simeon, that he made an expedition into Judea, and sat down before Jerusalem, and besieged Hyrcanus: but Hyrcanus opened the sepulchre of David, who was the richest of all kings, and took thence about three thousand talents in money, and induced Antiochus, by the promise of three thousand talents, to raise the siege. Moreover, he was the first of the Jews that had money enough, and began to hire foreign auxiliaries also.

6. However, at another time, when Antiochus was gone upon an expedition against the Medes, and so gave Hyrcanus an opportunity of being avenged upon him, he immediately made an attack upon the cities of Syria, as thinking, what proved to be the case with them, that he should find them empty of good troops. So he took Medaba and Samea, with the towns in their neighbourhood, as also Shechem and Gerizzim; and besides these [he subdued] the nation of the Cutheans, who dwelt round about that temple which was built in imitation of the temple at Jerusalem: he also took a great many other cities of Idumea, with Adoreon and Marissa.

7. He also proceeded as far as Samaria, where is now the city Sebaste, which was built by Herod the king, and encompassed it all round with a wall, and set his sons, Aristobulus and Antigonus, over the siege; who pushed it on so hard, that a famine so far prevailed with the city, that they were forced to eat what never was esteemed food. They also invited Antiochus, who was called Cyzicenus, to come to their assistance; whereupon he got ready, and complied with their invitation, but was beaten by Aristobulus and Antigonus; and indeed he was pursued as far as Scythopolis by these brethren, and fled away from them. So they returned back to Samaria, and shut the multitude again within the wall; and when they had taken the city they demolished it, and made slaves of its inhabitants. And, as they had still great success in their undertakings, they did not suffer their zeal to cool, but marched with an army as far as Scythopolis, and made an incursion upon it, and laid waste all the country that lay within mount Carmel.

8. But then these successes of John and of his sons made them be envied, and occasioned a sedition in the country; and many there were who got together, and would not be at rest till they brake out into open war, in which war they were beaten. So John lived the rest of his life very happily, and administered the government after a most extraordinary manner, and this for thirty-three entire years together. He died, leaving five sons behind him. He was certainly a very happy man, and afforded no occasion to have any complaint made of fortune on his account. He it was who alone had three of the most desirable things in the world,—the government of his nation, and the high priesthood, and the gift of prophecy; for the Deity conversed with him,—and he was not ignorant of anything that was to come afterwards; insomuch that he foresaw and foretold that his two eldest sons would not continue masters of the government: and it will highly deserve our narration to describe their catastrophe, and how far inferior these men were to their father in felicity.

CHAPTER III

HOW ARISTOBULUS WAS THE FIRST THAT PUT A DIADEM ABOUT HIS HEAD; AND, AFTER HE HAD PUT HIS MOTHER AND BROTHER TO DEATH, DIED HIMSELF, WHEN HE HAD REIGNED NO MORE THAN A YEAR

1. FOR after the death of their father, the elder of them, Aristobulus, changed the government into a kingdom, and was the first that put a diadem upon his head, four hundred and seventy-one years and three months after our people came down into this country, when they were set free from the Babylonian slavery. Now, of his brethren, he appeared to have an affection for Antigonus, who was next to him, and made him his equal; but, for the rest, he bound them, and put them in prison. He also put his mother in bonds, for her contesting the government with him; for John had left her to be the governess of public affairs. He also proceeded to that degree of barbarity as to cause her to be pined to death in prison.

2. But vengeance circumvented him in the affair of his brother Antigonus, whom he loved, and whom he made his partner in the kingdom; for he slew him by the means of the calumnies which ill men about the palace contrived against him. At first, indeed, Aristobulus would not believe their reports, partly out of the affection he had for his brother, and partly because he thought that a great part of these tales were owing to the envy of their relaters: however, as Antigonus came once in a splendid manner from the army to that festival, wherein our ancient custom is to make tabernacles for God, it happened in those days that Aristobulus was sick, and that, at the conclusion of the feast, Antigonus came up to it, with his armed men about him, and this when he was adorned in the finest manner possible; and that, in a great measure, to pray to God on the behalf of his brother. Now, at this very time it was that these ill men came to the king, and told him in what a pompous manner the armed men came, and with what insolence Antigonus marched, and that such his insolence was too great for a private person, and that accordingly he was come with a great band of men to kill him; for that he could not endure this bare enjoyment of royal honour, when it was in his power to take the kingdom himself.

3. Now Aristobulus, by degrees, and unwillingly, gave credit to these accusations; and accordingly he took care not to discover his suspicion openly, though he provided to be secure against any accidents; so he placed the guards

of his body in a certain dark subterraneous passage; for he lay sick in a certain place called formerly the Citadel, though afterwards its name was changed to Antonia; and he gave orders, that if Antigonus came unarmed, they should let him alone; but if he came to him in his armour, they should kill him. He also sent some to let him know beforehand, that he should come unarmed. But, upon this occasion, the queen very cunningly contrived the matter with those that plotted his ruin, for she persuaded those that were sent, to conceal the king's message; but to tell Antigonus how his brother had heard he had got a very fine suit of armour, made with fine martial ornaments, in Galilee; and because his present sickness hindered him from coming and seeing all that finery, he very much desired to see him now in his armour, because, said he, in a little time thou art going away from me.

4. As soon as Antigonus heard this, the good temper of his brother not allowing him to suspect any harm from him, he came along with his armour on, to shew it to his brother; but when he was going along that dark passage, which was called Strato's Tower, he was slain by the body guards, and became an eminent instance how calumny destroys all good-will and natural affection, and how none of our good affections are strong enough to resist envy perpetually.

5. And truly any one would be surprised at Judas upon this occasion. He was of the sect of the Essenes, and had never failed or deceived men in his predictions before. Now, this man saw Antigonus as he was passing along by the temple, and cried out to his acquaintance, (they were not a few who attended upon him as his scholars,) "Oh, strange!" said he, "it is good for me to die now, since truth is dead before me, and somewhat that I have foretold hath proved false; for this Antigonus is this day alive, who ought to have died this day; and the place where he ought to be slain, according to that fatal decree, was Strato's Tower, which is at the distance of six hundred furlongs from this place, and yet four hours of this day are over already; which point of time renders the prediction impossible to be fulfilled." And when the old man had said this he was dejected in his mind, and so continued. But in a little time news came that Antigonus was slain in a subterraneous place, which was itself also called Strato's Tower, by the same name with that Cesarea which lay by the sea-side; and this ambiguity it was which caused the prophet's disorder.

6. Hereupon Aristobulus repented of the great crime he had been guilty of, and this gave occasion to the increase of the distemper. He also grew worse and worse, and his soul was constantly disturbed at the thought of what he had done, till his very bowels being torn to pieces by the intolerable grief he was under, he threw up a great quantity of blood. And, as one of those servants that attended him carried out that blood, he, by some supernatural providence, slipped and fell down in the very place where Antigonus had been slain; and so he spilt some of the murderer's blood upon the spots of the blood of him that had been murdered, which still appeared. Hereupon a lamentable cry arose among the spectators, as if the servant had spilled the blood on purpose in that place; and, as the king heard that cry, he inquired what was the cause of it; and while nobody durst tell him, he pressed them so much the more to let him know what was the matter; so, at length, when he had threatened them, and forced them to speak out, they told; whereupon he burst into tears, and groaned, and said, "So I perceive I

am not like to escape the all-seeing eye of God, as to the great crimes I have committed; but the vengeance of the blood of my kinsman pursues me hastily. O thou most impudent body! how long wilt thou retain a soul that ought to die, on account of that punishment it ought to suffer for a mother and a brother slain! how long shall I myself spend my blood drop by drop! let them take it all at once; and let their ghosts no longer be disappointed by a few parcels of my bowels offered to them." As soon as he had said these words, he presently died, when he had reigned no longer than a year.

CHAPTER IV.

WHAT ACTIONS WERE DONE BY ALEXANDER JANNEUS, WHO REIGNED TWENTY-SEVEN YEARS.

1. AND now the king's wife loosed the king's brethren, and made Alexander king, who appeared both elder in age and more moderate in his temper than the rest; who, when he came to the government, slew one of his brethren, as affecting to govern himself; but had the other of them in great esteem, as loving a quiet life, without meddling with public affairs.

2. Now it happened that there was a battle between him and Ptolemy, who was called Lathyrus, who had taken the city Asochis. He indeed slew a great many of his enemies; but the victory rather inclined to Ptolemy. But, when this Ptolemy was pursued by his mother Cleopatra, and retired into Egypt, Alexander besieged Gadara, and took it; as also he did Amathus, which was the strongest of all the fortresses that were about Jordan, and therein were the most precious of all the possessions of Theodorus the son of Zeno. Whereupon Theodorus marched against him, and took what belonged to himself, as well as the king's baggage, and slew ten thousand of the Jews. However, Alexander recovered this blow, and turned his face towards the maritime parts, and took Raphia, and Gaza, with Anthedon also, which was afterwards called Agrippias by king Herod.

3. But when he had made slaves of the citizens of all these cities, the nation of the Jews made an insurrection against him at a festival; for at those feasts seditions are generally begun: and it looked as if he should not be able to escape the plot they had laid for him, had not his foreign auxiliaries, the Pisidians and Cilicians, assisted him; for, as to the Syrians, he never admitted them among his mercenary troops, on account of their innate enmity against the Jewish nation. And when he had slain more than six thousand of the rebels, he made an incursion into Arabia, and when he had taken that country, together with the Gileadites and Moabites, he enjoined them to pay him tribute, and returned to Amathus; and as Theodorus was surprised at his great success, he took the fortress, and demolished it.

4. However, when he fought with Obodas, king of the Arabians, who had laid an ambush for him near Golan, and a plot against him, he lost his entire army, which was crowded together in a deep valley, and broken to pieces by the multitude of camels; and when he had made his escape to Jerusalem, he provoked the multitude, who hated him before, to make an insurrection against him, and this on account of the greatness of the calamity that he was under. However, he was then too hard for them: and,

in the several battles that were fought on both sides, he slew not fewer than fifty thousand of the Jews, in the interval of six years. Yet had he no reason to rejoice in these victories, since he did but consume his own kingdom; till at length he left off fighting, and endeavoured to come to a composition with them, by talking with his subjects; but this mutability and irregularity of his conduct made them hate him still more; and when he asked them why they so hated him, and what he should do, in order to appease them, they said, by killing himself; for that it would be then all they could do, to be reconciled to him who had done such tragical things to them, even when he was dead. At the same time they invited Demetrius, who was called Eucerus, to assist them; and as he readily complied with their request, in hopes of great advantages, and came with his army, the Jews joined with those their auxiliaries about Shechem.

5. Yet did Alexander meet both these forces with one thousand horsemen, and eight thousand mercenaries that were on foot. He had also with him that part of the Jews which favoured him, to the number of ten thousand; while the adverse party had three thousand horsemen, and fourteen thousand footmen. Now, before they joined battle, the kings made proclamation, and endeavoured to draw off each other's soldiers, and make them revolt; while Demetrius hoped to induce Alexander's mercenaries to leave him,—and Alexander hoped to induce the Jews that were with Demetrius to leave him; but, since neither the Jews would leave off their rage, nor the Greeks prove unfaithful, they came to an engagement, and to a close fight with their weapons. In which battle Demetrius was the conqueror, although Alexander's mercenaries shewed the greatest exploits, both in soul and body. Yet did the upshot of this battle prove different from what was expected, as to both of them; for neither did those that invited Demetrius to come to them continue firm to him, though he was conqueror; and six thousand Jews, out of pity to the change of Alexander's condition, when he was fled to the mountains, came over to him. Yet could not Demetrius bear this turn of affairs; but, supposing that Alexander was already become a match for him again, and that all the nation would [at length] run to him, he left the country, and went his way.

6. However, the rest of the [Jewish] multitude did not lay aside their quarrels with him, when the [foreign] auxiliaries were gone; but they had a perpetual war with Alexander, until he had slain the greatest part of them, and driven the rest into the city Bemeselis; and when he had demolished that city, he carried the captives to Jerusalem. Nay, his rage was grown so extravagant, that his barbarity proceeded to a degree of impiety: for when he had ordered eight hundred to be hung upon crosses in the midst of the city, he had the throats of their wives and children cut before their eyes; and these executions he saw as he was drinking and lying down with his concubines. Upon which, so deep a surprise seized on the people, that eight thousand of his opposers fled away the very next night, out of all Judea, whose flight was only terminated by Alexander's death; so at last, though not till late, and with great difficulty, he, by such actions, procured quiet to his kingdom, and left off fighting any more.

7. Yet did that Antiochus, who was also called Dionysius, become an origin of troubles again. This man was the brother of Demetrius, and the last of the race of the Seleucidæ.* Alexander was afraid of him, when he was marching against the Arabians; so he cut a deep trench between Antipatris, which was near the mountains, and the shores of Joppa; he also erected a high wall before the trench, and built wooden towers in order to hinder any sudden approaches; but still he was not able to exclude Antiochus, for he burnt the towers, and filled up the trenches, and marched on with his army; and as he looked upon taking his revenge on Alexander for endeavouring to stop him, as a thing of less consequence, he marched directly against the Arabians, whose king retired into such parts of the country as were fittest for engaging the enemy, and then on the sudden made his horse turn back, which were in number ten thousand, and fell upon Antiochus's army while they were in disorder, and a terrible battle ensued. Antiochus's troops, so long as he was alive, fought it out, although a mighty slaughter was made among them by the Arabians; but when he fell, for he was in the fore-front, in the utmost danger, in rallying his troops, they all gave ground, and the greatest part of his army were destroyed, either in the action or the flight; and for the rest, who fled to the village of Cana, it happened that they were all consumed by want of necessaries, a few only excepted.

8. About this time it was that the people of Damascus, out of their hatred to Ptolemy, the son of Menneus, invited Aretas [to take the government,] and made him king of Cœlesyria. This man also made an expedition against Judea, and beat Alexander in battle; but afterwards retired by mutual agreement. But Alexander, when he had taken Pella, marched to Gerasa again, out of the covetous desire he had of Theodorus's possessions; and when he had built a triple wall about the garrison, he took the place by force. He also demolished Golan, and Seleucia, and what was called the Valley of Antiochus; besides which, he took the strong fortress of Gamala, and stripped Demetrius, who was governor therein, of what he had, on account of the many crimes he laid to his charge, and then returned into Judea, after he had been three whole years in this expedition; and now he was kindly received of the nation, because of the good success he had. So, when he was at rest from war, he fell into a distemper; for he was afflicted with a quartan ague, and supposed that, by exercising himself again in martial affairs, he should get rid of this distemper; but, by making such expeditions at unseasonable times, and forcing his body to undergo greater hardships than he was able to bear, he brought himself to his end. He died, therefore, in the midst of his troubles, after he had reigned seven-and-twenty years.

CHAPTER V

ALEXANDRA REIGNS NINE YEARS; DURING WHICH TIME THE PHARISEES WERE THE REAL RULERS OF THE NATION

1. Now Alexander left the kingdom to Alexandra his wife, and depended upon it that the Jews would now very readily submit to her; because she had been very averse to such cruelty

---

* Josephus here calls this Antiochus the last of the Seleucidæ, although there remained still a shadow of another king of that family, Antiochus Asiaticus, or Commagenus, who reigned, or rather lay hid, till Pompey quite turned him out.

as he had treated them with, and had opposed his violation of their laws, and had thereby got the good-will of the people. Nor was he mistaken as to his expectations; for this woman kept the dominion, by the opinion that the people had of her piety; for she chiefly studied the ancient customs of her country, and cast those men out of the government that offended against their holy laws. And as she had two sons by Alexander, she made Hyrcanus, the elder, high priest, on account of his age; as also, besides that, on account of his inactive temper no way disposing him to disturb the public. But she retained the younger, Aristobulus, with her as a private person, by reason of the warmth of his temper.

2. And now the Pharisees joined themselves to her to assist her in the government. These are a certain sect of the Jews that appear more religious than others, and seem to interpret the laws more accurately. Now, Alexandra hearkened to them to an extraordinary degree, as being herself a woman of great piety towards God. But these Pharisees artfully insinuated themselves into her favour by little and little, and became themselves the real administrators of the public affairs: they banished and reduced whom they pleased; they bound and loosed [men] at their pleasure;* and, to say all at once, they had the enjoyment of the royal authority, whilst the expenses and the difficulties of it belonged to Alexandra. She was a sagacious woman in the management of great affairs, and intent always upon gathering soldiers together; so that she increased the army the one half, and procured a great body of foreign troops, till her own nation became not only very powerful at home, but terrible also to foreign potentates, while she governed other people, and the Pharisees governed her.

3. Accordingly they themselves slew Diogenes, a person of figure, and one that had been a friend to Alexander; and accused him as having assisted the king with his advice, for crucifying the eight hundred men [before mentioned.] They also prevailed with Alexandra to put to death the rest of those who had irritated him against them. Now, she was so superstitious as to comply with their desires, and accordingly they slew whom they pleased themselves. But the principal of those that were in danger fled to Aristobulus, who persuaded his mother to spare the men on account of their dignity, but to expel them out of the city, unless she took them to be innocent; so they were suffered to go unpunished, and were dispersed all over the country. But when Alexandra sent out her army to Damascus, under pretence that Ptolemy was always oppressing that city, she got possession of it; nor did it make any considerable resistance. She also prevailed with Tigranes, king of Armenia, who lay with his troops about Ptolemais and besieged Cleopatra,† by agreements and presents, to go away. Accordingly, Tigranes soon arose from the siege by reason of those domestic tumults which happened upon Lucullus's expedition into Armenia.

4. In the meantime, Alexandra fell sick, and Aristobulus, her younger son, took hold of this opportunity, with his domestics, of which he had a great many, who were all of them his friends, on account of the warmth of their youth, and got possession of all the fortresses. He also used the sums of money he found in them to get together a number of mercenary soldiers, and made himself king; and besides this, upon Hyrcanus's complaint to his mother, she compassionated his case, and put Aristobulus's wife and his sons under restraint in Antonia, which was a fortress that joined to the north part of the temple. It was, as I have already said, of old called the Citadel, but afterwards got the name of Antonia, when Antony was lord [of the east,] just as the other cities, Sebaste and Agrippias, had their names changed, and these given them from Sebastus, and Agrippa. But Alexandra died before she could punish Aristobulus, for his disinheriting his brother, after she had reigned nine years.

CHAPTER VI

WHEN HYRCANUS, WHO WAS ALEXANDER'S HEIR, RECEDED FROM HIS CLAIM TO THE CROWN, ARISTOBULUS IS MADE KING; AND AFTERWARDS THE SAME HYRCANUS, BY THE MEANS OF ANTIPATER, IS BROUGHT BACK BY ARETAS. AT LAST POMPEY IS MADE THE ARBITRATOR OF THE DISPUTE BETWEEN THE BROTHERS

1. Now Hyrcanus was heir to the kingdom' and to him did his mother commit it before she died: but Aristobulus was superior to him in power and magnanimity; and when there was a battle between them, to decide the dispute about the kingdom, near Jericho, the greatest part deserted Hyrcanus, and went over to Aristobulus; but Hyrcanus, with those of his party who stayed with him, fled to Antonia, and got into his power the hostages which might be for his preservation, (which were Aristobulus's wife, with her children;) but they came to an agreement before things should come to extremities, that Aristobulus should be king, and Hyrcanus should resign that up, but retain all the rest of his dignities, as being the king's brother. Hereupon they were reconciled to each other in the temple, and embraced one another in a very kind manner, while the people stood round about them: they also changed their houses; while Aristobulus went to the royal palace, and Hyrcanus retired to the house of Aristobulus.

2. Now, those other people who were at variance with Aristobulus were afraid, upon his unexpectedly obtaining the government; and especially this concerned Antipater, whom Aristobulus hated of old. He was by birth an Idumean, and one of the principal of that nation, on account of his ancestors and riches, and other authority to him belonging; he also persuaded Hyrcanus to fly to Aretas, the king of Arabia, and to lay claim to the kingdom: as also he persuaded Aretas to receive Hyrcanus, and to bring him back to his kingdom: he also cast reproaches upon Aristobulus, as to his morals, and gave great commendation to Hyrcanus, and exhorted Aretas to receive him, and told him how becoming a thing it would be for him, who ruled so great a kingdom, to afford assistance to such as are injured; alleging that Hyrcanus was treated unjustly, by being deprived of that dominion which belonged to him by the prerogative of his birth. And when he had predisposed them both to do what he would have them, he took Hyrcanus by night, and ran away from the city;

---

* Matt. xvi. 19, xvii. 18. Here we have the oldest and most authentic Jewish exposition of binding and loosing, for punishing or absolving men; not for declaring actions lawful or unlawful.

† Strabo relates, that this Selene Cleopatra was besieged by Tigranes, not in Ptolemais, as here, but after she had left Syria, in Seleucia, a citadel in Mesopotamia, and adds, that when he had kept her a while in prison, he put her to death.

and, continuing his flight with great swiftness, he escaped to the place called Petra, which is the royal seat of the king of Arabia, where he put Hyrcanus into Aretas's hands; and by discoursing much with him, and gaining upon him with many presents, he prevailed with him to give him an army that might restore him to his kingdom. This army consisted of fifty thousand footmen and horsemen, against which Aristobulus was not able to make resistance, but was deserted in the first onset, and was driven to Jerusalem: he also had been taken at first by force, if Scaurus, the Roman general, had not come and seasonably interposed himself, and raised the siege. This Scaurus was sent into Syria from Armenia by Pompey the Great, when he fought against Tigranes; so Scaurus came to Damascus, which had been lately taken by Metellus and Lollius, and caused them to leave the place; and, upon his hearing how the affairs of Judea stood, he made haste thither as to a certain booty.

3. As soon, therefore, as he was come into the country, there came ambassadors from both the brothers, each of them desiring his assistance; but Aristobulus's three hundred talents had more weight with him than the justice of the cause; which sum, when Scarus had received, he sent a herald to Hyrcanus and the Arabians, and threatened them with the resentment of the Romans and of Pompey, unless they would raise the siege. So Aretas was terrified, and retired out of Judea to Philadelphia, as did Scaurus return to Damascus again: nor was Aristobulus satisfied with escaping [out of his brother's hands,] but gathered all his forces together and pursued his enemies, and fought them at a place called Papyron, and slew above six thousand of them, and, together with them, Antipater's brother Phalion.

4. When Hyrcanus and Antipater were thus deprived of their hopes from the Arabians, they transferred the same to their adversaries; and because Pompey had passed through Syria, and was come to Damascus, they fled to him for assistance; and, without any bribes, they made the same equitable pleas that they had used to Aretas, and besought him to hate the violent behaviour of Aristobulus, and to bestow the kingdom upon him to whom it justly belonged, both on account of his good character, and on account of his superiority in age. However, neither was Aristobulus wanting to himself in this case, as relying on the bribes that Scaurus had received: he was also there himself, and adorned himself after a manner the most agreeable to royalty that he was able. But he soon thought it beneath him to come in such a servile manner, and could not endure to serve his own ends in a way so much more abject than he was used to; so he departed from Diospolis.

5. At this his behaviour Pompey had great indignation; Hyrcanus also and his friends made great intercession to Pompey; so he took not only his Roman forces, but many of his Syrian auxiliaries, and marched against Aristobulus. But when he had passed by Pella and Scythopolis, and was come to Corea, where you enter into the country of Judea, when you go up to it through the Mediterranean parts, he heard that Aristobulus was fled to Alexandrium, which is a stronghold, fortified with the utmost magnificence, and situated upon a high mountain, and he sent to him, and commanded him to come down. Now his inclination was to try his fortune in a battle, since he was called in such an imperious manner, rather than to comply with that call. However, he saw the multi-

tude were in great fear, and h[...] him to consider what the pow[...] was, and how it was irresistib[...] with their advice, and came [...] and when he had made a lo[...] self, and for the justness of h[...] the government, he returned [...] And when his brother invited h[...] plead his cause,] he came down and sp[...] the justice of it, and then went away without any hindrance from Pompey; so he was between hope and fear. And when he came down, it was to prevail with Pompey to allow him the government entirely; and when he went up to the citadel, it was that he might not appear to debase himself too low. However, Pompey commanded him to give up his fortified places, and forced him to write to every one of their governors to yield them up; they having had this charge given them, to obey no letters but what were of his own handwriting. Accordingly he did what he was ordered to do; but had still an indignation at what was done, and retired to Jerusalem, and prepared to fight with Pompey.

6. But Pompey did not give him time to make any preparations [for a siege,] but followed him at his heels; he was also obliged to make haste in his attempt, by the death of Mithridates, of which he was informed about Jericho. Now here is the most fruitful country about Judea, which bears a vast number of palm-trees, besides the balsam-tree, whose sprouts they cut with sharp stones, and at the incisions they gather the juice, which drops down like tears. So Pompey pitched his camp in that place one night, and then hasted away next morning to Jerusalem; but Aristobulus was so affrighted at his approach, that he came and met him by way of supplication. He also promised him money, and that he would deliver up both himself and the city into his disposal;—and thereby he mitigated the anger of Pompey. Yet did not he perform any of the conditions he had agreed to; for Aristobulus's party would not so much as admit Gabinius into the city, who was sent to receive the money that he had promised.

CHAPTER VII

HOW POMPEY HAD THE CITY OF JERUSALEM DELIVERED UP TO HIM, BUT TOOK THE TEMPLE [BY FORCE.] HOW HE WENT INTO THE HOLY OF HOLIES; AS ALSO WHAT WERE HIS OTHER EXPLOITS IN JUDEA

1. AT this treatment Pompey was very angry, and took Aristobulus into custody; and when he was come to the city he looked about where he might make his attack; for he saw the walls were so firm that it would be hard to overcome them, and that the valley before the walls was terrible; and that the temple, which was within that valley, was itself encompassed with a very strong wall, insomuch that if the city were taken, the temple would be a second place of refuge for the enemy to retire to.

2. Now, as he was long in deliberating about this matter, a sedition arose among the people within the city; Aristobulus's party being willing to fight, and to set their king at liberty, while the party of Hyrcanus were for opening the gates to Pompey; and the dread people were in, occasioned these last to be a very numerous party, when they looked upon the excellent order the Roman soldiers were in. So Aristobulus's

was worsted, and retired into the temple, and cut off the communication between the temple and the city, by breaking down the bridge that joined them together, and prepared to make an opposition to the utmost; but as the others had received the Romans into the city, and had delivered up the palace to him, Pompey sent Piso, one of his great officers, into that palace with an army, who distributed a garrison about the city, because he could not persuade any one of those that had fled to the temple to come to terms of accommodation; he then disposed all things that were round about them so as might favour their attacks, as having Hyrcanus's party very ready to afford them both counsel and assistance.

3. But Pompey himself filled up the ditch that was on the north side of the temple, and the entire valley also, the army itself being obliged to carry the materials for that purpose. And indeed it was a hard thing to fill up that valley, by reason of its immense depth, especially as the Jews used all the means possible to repel them from their superior station; nor had the Romans succeeded in their endeavours, had not Pompey taken notice of the seventh days, on which the Jews abstain from all sorts of work on a religious account, and raised his bank, but restrained his soldiers from fighting on those days; for the Jews only acted defensively on Sabbath-days. But as soon as Pompey had filled up the valley, he erected high towers upon the bank, and brought those engines which they had fetched from Tyre near to the wall, and tried to batter it down; and the slingers of stones beat off those that stood above them, and drove them away: but the towers on this side of the city made very great resistance, and were indeed extraordinary both for largeness and magnificence.

4. Now, here it was that, upon the many hardships which the Romans underwent, Pompey could not but admire not only at the other instances of the Jews' fortitude, but especially that they did not at all intermit their religious services, even when they were encompassed with darts on all sides; for, as if the city were in full peace, their daily sacrifices and purifications, and every branch of their religious worship, were still performed to God with the utmost exactness. Nor, indeed, when the temple was actually taken, and they were every day slain about the altar, did they leave off the instances, of their divine worship that were appointed by their law; for it was in the third month of the siege before the Romans could even with great difficulty overthrow one of the towers, and get into the temple. Now he that first of all ventured to get over the wall was Faustus Cornelius, the son of Sylla; and next after him were two centurions, Furius and Fabius; and every one of these was followed by a cohort of his own, who encompassed the Jews on all sides, and slew them; some of them as they were running for shelter to the temple, and others as they, for a while, fought in their own defence.

5. And now did many of the priests, even when they saw their enemies assailing them with swords in their hands, without any disturbance, go on with their divine worship, and were slain while they were offering their drink-offerings and burning their incense, as preferring the duties about their worship to God before their own preservation. The greatest part of them were slain by their own countrymen of the adverse faction, and an innumerable multitude threw themselves down precipices; nay, some there were who were so distracted among the insuperable difficulties they were under, that they

set fire to the buildings that were near to the wall, and were burnt together with them. Now of the Jews were slain twelve thousand; but of the Romans very few were slain, but a greater number was wounded.

6. But there was nothing that affected the nation so much, in the calamities they were then under, as that their holy place, which had been hitherto seen by none, should be laid open to strangers; for Pompey, and those that were about him, went into the temple itself, whither it was not lawful for any to enter but the high priest, and saw what was reposited therein, the candlestick with its lamps, and the table, and the pouring vessels, and the censers, all made entirely of gold, as also a great quantity of spices heaped together, with two thousand talents of sacred money. Yet did not he touch the money, nor anything else that was there reposited; but he commanded the ministers about the temple, the very next day after he had taken it, to cleanse it, and to perform their accustomed sacrifices. Moreover, he made Hyrcanus high priest, as one that not only in other respects had shewn great alacrity, on his side, during the siege, but as he had been the means of hindering the multitude that was in the country from fighting for Aristobulus, which they were otherwise very ready to have done: by which means he acted the part of a good general, and reconciled the people to him more by benevolence than by terror. Now among the captives, Aristobulus's father-in-law was taken, who was also his uncle: so those that were the most guilty he punished with decollation; but rewarded Faustus, and those with him that had fought so bravely, with glorious presents; and laid a tribute upon the country, and upon Jerusalem itself.

7. He also took away from the nation all those cities they had formerly taken, and that belonged to Cœlesyria, and made them subject to him that was at that time appointed to be the Roman president there, and reduced Judea within its proper bounds. He also rebuilt * Gadara, that had been demolished by the Jews, in order to gratify one Demetrius, who was of Gadara, and was one of his own freed-men. He also made other cities free from their dominion, that lay in the midst of the country,—such, I mean, as they had not demolished before that time; Hippos, and Scythopolis, as also Pella, and Samaria, and Marissa: and besides these, Ashdod, and Jamnia, and Arethusa; and in like manner dealt he with the maritime cities, Gaza, and Joppa, and Dora, and that which was anciently called Strato's Tower, but was afterwards rebuilt with the most magnificent edifices, and had its name changed to Cesarea, by king Herod. All which he restored to their own citizens, and put them under the province of Syria; which province, together with Judea, and the countries as far as Egypt, and Euphrates, he committed to Scaurus as their governor, and gave him two legions to support him; while he made all the haste he could himself to go through Cilicia, in his way to Rome, having Aristobulus and his children along with him, as his captives. They were two daughters and two sons; the one of which sons, Alexander, ran away as he was going; but the younger, Antigonus, with his sisters, were carried to Rome.

* The coin of this Gadara, still extant, with its date from this era, is a certain evidence of its rebuilding by Pompey.

POMPEY STORMS THE TEMPLE

CHAPTER VIII

ALEXANDER, THE SON OF ARISTOBULUS, WHO RAN
AWAY FROM POMPEY, MAKES AN EXPEDI-
TION AGAINST HYRCANUS ; BUT BEING OVERCOME BY
GABINIUS, HE DELIVERS UP THE FORTRESSES TO
HIM. AFTER THIS, ARISTOBULUS ESCAPES FROM
ROME, AND GATHERS AN ARMY TOGETHER ; BUT
BEING BEATEN BY THE ROMANS, HE IS BROUGHT
BACK TO ROME ; WITH OTHER THINGS RELATING
TO GABINIUS, CRASSUS, AND CASSIUS

1. IN the meantime Scaurus made an expedition into Arabia, but was stopped by the difficulty
of the places about Petra. However, he laid
waste the country about Pella, though even
there he was under great hardship, for his army
was afflicted with famine. In order to supply
which want, Hyrcanus afforded him some assistance, and sent him provisions by the means of
Antipater ; whom also Scaurus sent to Aretas, as
one well acquainted with him, to induce him to
pay him money to buy his peace. The king of
Arabia complied with the proposal, and gave him
three hundred talents ; upon which Scaurus drew
his army out of Arabia.*

2. But as for Alexander, that son of Aristobulus who ran away from Pompey, in some time
he got a considerable band of men together, and
lay heavy upon Hyrcanus, and over-ran Judea,
and was likely to overturn him quickly ; and indeed he had come to Jerusalem, and had ventured to rebuild its wall that was thrown down
by Pompey, had not Gabinius, who was sent as
successor to Scaurus into Syria, shewn his
bravery, as in many other points, so in making
an expedition against Alexander, who, as he was
afraid he would attack him, so he got together
a large army, composed of ten thousand armed
footmen, and fifteen hundred horsemen. He
also built walls about proper places ; Alexandrium, and Hyrcanium, and Macherus, that lay
upon the mountains of Arabia.

3. However, Gabinius sent before him Marcus
Antonius, and followed himself with his whole
army ; but for the select body of soldiers that
were about Antipater, and another body of Jews
under the command of Malichus and Pitholaus,
these joined themselves to those captains that
were about Marcus Antonius, and met Alexander ; to which body came Gabinius with his
main army soon afterward ; and as Alexander
was not able to sustain the charge of the enemies' forces, now they were joined, he retired.
But when he was come near to Jerusalem, he
was forced to fight, and lost six thousand men
in the battle ; three thousand of whom fell down
dead, and three thousand were taken alive ; so
he fled with the remainder to Alexandrium.

4. Now, when Gabinius was come to Alexandrium, because he found a great many there encamped, he tried, by promising them pardon for
their former offences, to induce them to come
over to him before it came to a fight ; but when
they would hearken to no terms of accommodation, he slew a great number of them, and shut
a great number of them in the citadel. Now
Marcus Antonius, their leader, signalised himself

in this battle, who, as he always shewed great
courage, so did he never shew it so much as
now ; but Gabinius, leaving forces to take the
citadel, went away himself, and settled the cities
that had not been demolished, and rebuilt those
that had been destroyed. Accordingly, upon
his injunction, the following cities were restored—Scythopolis, Samaria, Anthedon, Apollonia, Jamnia, Raphia, Marissa, Adoreus, Gamala, Ashdod, and many others ; while a great
number of men readily ran to each of them, and
became their inhabitants.

5. When Gabinius had taken care of these
cities, he returned to Alexandrium, and pressed
on the siege. So when Alexander despaired of
ever obtaining the government, he sent ambassadors to him, and prayed him to forgive what he
had offended him in, and gave up to him the remaining fortresses, Hyrcanium and Macherus, as
he put Alexandrium into his hands afterwards :
all which Gabinius demolished, at the persuasion
of Alexander's mother, that they might not be
receptacles of men in a second war. She was
now there, in order to mollify Gabinius, out of
her concern for her relations that were captives
at Rome, which were her husband and her other
children. After this, Gabinius brought Hyrcanus to Jerusalem, and committed the care of the
temple to him ; but ordained the political government to be by an aristocracy. He also
parted the whole nation into five conventions,
assigning one portion to Jerusalem, another to
Gadara, that another should belong to Amathus, a fourth to Jericho, and to the fifth division was allotted Sepphoris, a city of Galilee.
So the people were glad to be thus freed from
monarchical government, and were governed for
the future by an aristocracy.

6. Yet did Aristobulus afford a new foundation for other disturbances. He fled away from
Rome, and got together again many of the Jews
that were desirous of a change, such as had
borne an affection to him of old ; and when he
had taken Alexandrium in the first place, he attempted to build a wall about it : but as soon as
Gabinius had sent an army against him under
Sisenna, Antonius, and Servilius, he was aware
of it, and retreated to Macherus. And as for
the unprofitable multitude, he dismissed them,
and only marched on with those that were
armed, being to the number of eight thousand,
among whom was Pitholaus, who had been the
lieutenant at Jerusalem, but deserted to Aristobulus with a thousand of his men : so the Romans followed him, and when it came to a battle,
Aristobulus's party for a long time fought courageously ; but at length they were overborne by
the Romans, and of them five thousand fell
dead, and about two thousand fled to a certain
little hill, but the thousand that remained with
Aristobulus brake through the Roman army,
and marched together to Macherus ; and, when
the king had lodged the first night on its ruins,
he was in hopes of raising another army, if the
war would but cease a while ; accordingly, he
fortified that stronghold, though it was done
after a poor manner. But the Romans falling
upon him, he resisted, even beyond his abilities,
for two days, and then was taken, and brought a
prisoner to Gabinius, with Antigonus his son,
who had fled away together with him from
Rome ; and from Gabinius he was carried to
Rome again. Wherefore the senate put him
under confinement, but returned his children
back to Judea, because Gabinius informed them
by letters that he had promised Aristobulus's
mother to do so, for her delivering the fortresses
up to him.

---

* Aldrich says, regarding this submission of Aretas
to Scaurus :—"Hence is derived that old and famous
denarius belonging to the Emilian family, wherein
Aretas appears in a posture of supplication, and taking
hold of a camel's bridle with his left hand, and with his
right hand presenting a branch of the frankincense-
tree, with this inscription : M. SCAURUS UX. S. C. ;
and beneath, REX ARETAS."

7. But now as Gabinius was marching to the war against the Parthians, he was hindered by Ptolemy, whom, upon his return from Euphrates, he brought back into Egypt, making use of Hyrcanus and Antipater to provide everything that was necessary for this expedition ; for Antipater furnished him with money, and weapons, and corn, and auxiliaries ; he also prevailed with the Jews that were there, and guarded the avenues at Pelusium, to let them pass. But now, upon Gabinius's absence, the other part of Syria was in motion, and Alexander, the son of Aristobulus, brought the Jews to revolt again. Accordingly, he got together a very great army, and set about killing all the Romans that were in the country : hereupon Gabinius was afraid (for he was come back already out of Egypt, and obliged to come back quickly by these tumults,) and sent Antipater, who prevailed with some of the revolters to be quiet. However, thirty thousand still continued with Alexander, who was himself eager to fight also ; accordingly, Gabinius went out to fight, when the Jews met him ; and, as the battle was fought near Mount Tabor, ten thousand of them were slain, and the rest of the multitude dispersed themselves, and fled away. So Gabinius came to Jerusalem, and settled the government as Antipater would have it ; thence he marched, and fought and beat the Nabateans : as for Mithridates and Orsanes, who fled out of Parthia, he sent them away privately, but gave it out among the soldiers that they had run away.

8. In the meantime, Crassus came as successor to Gabinius in Syria. He took away all the rest of the gold belonging to the temple of Jerusalem, in order to furnish himself for his expedition against the Parthians. He also took away the two thousand talents which Pompey had not touched ; but when he had passed over Euphrates, he perished himself, and his army with him ; concerning which affairs this is not a proper time to speak [more largely.]

9. But now Cassius, after Crassus, put a stop to the Parthians, who were marching in order to enter Syria. Cassius had fled into that province, and when he had taken possession of the same, he made a hasty march into Judea ; and upon his taking Taricheæ, he carried thirty thousand Jews into slavery. He also slew Pitholaus, who had supported the seditious followers of Aristobulus : and it was Antipater who advised him so to do. Now this Antipater married a wife of an eminent family among the Arabians, whose name was Cypros, and had four sons born to him by her, Phasaelus and Herod, who was afterwards king, and besides, Joseph and Pheroras ; and he had a daughter, whose name was Salome. Now, as he made himself friends among the men of power everywhere, by the kind offices he did them, and the hospitable manner that he treated them, so did he contract the greatest friendship with the king of Arabia, by marrying his relation ; insomuch that when he made war with Aristobulus, he sent and intrusted his children with him. So when Cassius had forced Alexander to come to terms and to be quiet, he returned to Euphrates, in order to prevent the Parthians from repassing it.

CHAPTER IX

ARISTOBULUS IS TAKEN OFF BY POMPEY'S FRIENDS, AS IS HIS SON ALEXANDER BY SCIPIO. ANTIPATER CULTIVATES A FRIENDSHIP WITH CÆSAR,

AFTER POMPEY'S DEATH ; HE ALSO PERFORMS GREAT ACTIONS IN THAT WAR, WHEREIN HE ASSISTED MITHRIDATES

1. Now, upon the flight of Pompey and of the senate beyond the Ionian Sea, Cæsar got Rome and the empire under his power, and released Aristobulus from his bonds. He also committed two legions to him, and sent him in haste into Syria, as hoping that by his means he should easily conquer that country, and the parts adjoining to Judea. But envy prevented any effect of Aristobulus's alacrity and the hopes of Cæsar ; for he was taken off by poison given him by those of Pompey's party ; and, for a long while, he had not so much as a burial vouchsafed him in his own country ; but his dead body lay [above ground,] preserved in honey, until it was sent to the Jews by Antony, in order to be buried in the royal sepulchres.

2. His son Alexander also was beheaded by Scipio at Antioch, and that by the command of Pompey, and upon an accusation laid against him before his tribunal, for the mischiefs he had done to the Romans. But Ptolemy, the son of Menneus, who was then ruler of Chalcis, under Libanus, took his brethren to him, by sending his son Philipio for them to Ascalon ; who took Antigonus, as well as his sisters, away from Aristobulus's wife, and brought them to his father ; and falling in love with the younger daughter, he married her, and was afterward slain by his father on her account ; for Ptolemy himself, after he had slain his son, married her, whose name was Alexandra ; on account of which marriage he took the greater care of her brother and sister.

3. Now, after Pompey was dead, Antipater changed sides, and cultivated a friendship with Cæsar. And, since Mithridates of Pergamus, with the forces he led against Egypt, was excluded from the avenues about Pelusium, and was forced to stay at Ascalon, he persuaded the Arabians among whom he had lived to assist him, and came himself to him, at the head of three thousand men. He also encouraged the men of power in Syria to come to his assistance ; as also of the inhabitants of Libanus, Ptolemy, and Jamblicus, and another Ptolemy ; by which means the cities of that country came readily into this war ; insomuch that Mithridates ventured now, in dependence upon the additional strength that he had gotten by Antipater, to march forward to Pelusium ; and when they refused him a passage through it, he besieged the city ; in the attack of which place Antipater principally signalised himself, for he brought down that part of the wall which was over against him, and leaped first of all into the city, with the men that were about him.

4. Thus was Pelusium taken. But still, as they were marching on, those Egyptian Jews that inhabited the country, called the country of Onias, stopped them. Then did Antipater not only persuade them not to stop them, but to afford provisions for their army ; on which account even the people about Memphis would not fight against them, but, of their own accord, joined Mithridates. Whereupon he went round about Delta, and fought the rest of the Egyptians at a place called the Jews' Camp : nay, when he was in danger in the battle with all his right wing Antipater wheeled about, and came along the bank of that river to him ; for he had beaten those that opposed him as he led the left wing. After which success he fell upon those that pursued Mithridates, and slew a great many of them, and pursued the remainder so far, that he took their camp, while he lost no more than fourscore of his own men ; as Mithridates lost, during the pursuit that was made after him, about eight hundred. He was also himself saved unexpectedly, and became an unreproachable witness to Cæsar of the great actions of Antipater.

5. Whereupon Cæsar encouraged Antipater to undertake other hazardous enterprises for him, and that by giving him great commendations and hopes of reward. In all which enterprises he readily exposed himself to many dangers, and became a most courageous warrior ; and had many wounds all over his body, as demonstrations of his valour. And when Cæsar had settled the affairs of Egypt, and was returning into Syria again, he gave him the privilege of a Roman citizen, and freedom from taxes, and rendered him an object of admiration by the honours and marks of friendship he bestowed upon him. On this account it was that he also confirmed Hyrcanus in the high priesthood.

CHAPTER X

CÆSAR MAKES ANTIPATER PROCURATOR OF JUDEA ; AS DOES ANTIPATER APPOINT PHASAELUS TO BE GOVERNOR OF JERUSALEM, AND HEROD GOVERNOR OF GALILEE ; WHO, IN SOME TIME, WAS CALLED TO ANSWER FOR HIMSELF [BEFORE THE SANHEDRIM,] WHERE HE IS ACQUITTED, SEXTUS CÆSAR IS TREACHEROUSLY KILLED BY BASSUS, AND IS SUCCEEDED BY MARCUS

1. ABOUT this time it was that Antigonus, the son of Aristobulus, came to Cæsar, and became, in a surprising manner, the occasion of Antipater's further advancement ; for, whereas he ought to have lamented that his father appeared to have been poisoned on account of his quarrels with Pompey, and to have complained of Scipio's barbarity towards his brother, and not to mix any invidious passion when suing for mercy ; instead of those things, he came before Cæsar, and accused Hyrcanus and Antipater, how they had driven him and his brethren entirely out of their native country, and had acted in a great many instances unjustly and extravagantly with regard to their nation ; and that as to the assistance they had sent him into Egypt, it was not done out of good-will to him, but out of the fear they were in from former quarrels, and in order to gain pardon for their friendship to [his enemy] Pompey.

2. Hereupon Antipater threw away his garments, and shewed the multitude of the wounds he had, and said, that as to his good-will to Cæsar, he had no occasion to say a word, because his body cried aloud, though he said nothing himself : that he wondered at Antigonus s boldness, while he was himself no other than the son of an enemy to the Romans, and of a fugitive, and had it by inheritance from his father to be fond of innovations and seditions, that he should undertake to accuse other men before the Roman governor, and endeavour to gain some advantages to himself, when he ought to be contented that he was suffered to live ; for that the reason of his desire of governing public affairs was not so much because he was in want of it, but because, if he could once obtain the same, he might stir up a sedition among the Jews, and use what he should gain for the Romans, to the disservice of those that gave it him.

3. When Cæsar heard this, he declared Hyrcanus to be the most worthy of the high priesthood, and gave leave to Antipater to choose what authority he pleased : but he left the determination of such dignity to him that bestowed the dignity upon him ; so he was constituted procurator of all Judea, and obtained leave, moreover, to rebuild those walls of his country that had been thrown down. These honorary grants Cæsar sent orders to have engraved in the Capitol, that they might stand there as indications of his own justice, and of the virtue of Antipater.

4. But as soon as Antipater had conducted Cæsar out of Syria he returned to Judea, and the first thing he did was to rebuild that wall of his own country [Jerusalem,] which Pompey had overthrown, and then to go over the country, and to quiet the tumults that were therein ; where he partly threatened, and partly advised, every one, and told him that, in case they would submit to Hyrcanus, they would live happily and peaceably, and enjoy what they possessed, and that with universal peace and quietness ; but that in case they hearkened to such as had some frigid hopes, by raising new troubles, to get themselves some gain, they should then find him to be their lord, instead of their procurator, and find Hyrcanus to be a tyrant, instead of a king,— and both the Romans and Cæsar to be their enemies, instead of rulers ; for that they would not suffer him to be removed from the government, whom they had made their governor ; and, at the same time that he said this, he settled the affairs of the country by himself, because he saw that Hyrcanus was inactive, and not fit to manage the affairs of the kingdom. So he constituted his eldest son, Phasaelus, governor of Jerusalem, and of the parts about it ; he also sent his next son, Herod, who was very young, [twenty-five years of age,] with equal authority into Galilee.

5. Now Herod was an active man, and soon found proper materials for his active spirit to work upon. As therefore he found that Hezekias, the head of the robbers, ran over the neighbouring parts of Syria with a great band of men, he caught him and slew him, and many more of the robbers with him ; which exploit was chiefly grateful to the Syrians, insomuch that hymns were sung in Herod's commendation, both in the villages and in the cities, as having procured their quietness, and having preserved what they possessed to them ; on which occasion he became acquainted with Sextus Cæsar, a kinsman of the great Cæsar, and president of Syria. A just emulation of his glorious actions excited Phasaelus also to imitate him. Accordingly he procured the good-will of the inhabitants of Jerusalem, by his own management of the city affairs, and did not abuse his power in any disagreeable manner ; whence it came to pass that the nation paid Antipater the respects that were due only to a king, and the honours due to an absolute lord ; yet did he not abate any part of that good-will or fidelity which he owed to Hyrcanus.

6. However, he found it impossible to escape envy in such his prosperity : for the glory of these young men affected even Hyrcanus himself already privately, though he said nothing of it to anybody ; but what he principally was grieved at was the great actions of Herod, and that so many messengers came one before another, and informed him of the great reputation he got in all his undertakings. There were also many people in the royal palace itself who inflamed his envy at him ; those, I mean, who were obstructed in their designs by the prudence either of the young men or of Antipater. These men said that, by committing the public affairs

to the management of Antipater and of his sons, he sat with nothing but the bare name of a king, without any of its authority; and they asked him how long he would so far mistake himself as to breed up kings against his own interest; for that they did not now conceal their government of affairs any longer, but were plainly lords of the nation, and had thrust him out of his authority; that this was the case when Herod slew so many men without his giving him any command to do it, either by word of mouth or by his letter, and this in contradiction to the law of the Jews; who therefore, in case he be not a king, but a private man, still ought to come to his trial, and answer it to him, and to the laws of his country, which do not permit any one to be killed till he had been condemned in judgment.

7. Now Hyrcanus was by degrees inflamed with these discourses, and at length could bear no longer, but summoned Herod to take his trial. Accordingly, by his father's advice, and as soon as the affairs of Galilee would give him leave, he came up [to Jerusalem,] when he had first placed garrisons in Galilee: however, he came with a sufficient body of soldiers, so many indeed that he might not appear to have with him an army able to overthrow Hyrcanus's government, nor yet so few as to expose him to the insults of those that envied him. However, Sextus Cæsar was in fear for the young man, lest he should be taken by his enemies, and brought to punishment; so he sent some to denounce expressly to Hyrcanus, that he should acquit Herod of the capital charge against him; who acquitted him accordingly, as being otherwise inclined also so to do, for he loved Herod.

8. But Herod, supposing that he had escaped punishment without the consent of the king, retired to Sextus, to Damascus, and got everything ready, in order not to obey him if he should summon him again; whereupon those that were evil-disposed irritated Hyrcanus, and told him that Herod was gone away in anger, and was prepared to make war upon him; and as the king believed what they said, he knew not what to do, since he saw his antagonist was stronger than he was himself; and now, since Herod was made general of Cœlesyria and Samaria by Sextus Cæsar, he was formidable, not only from the good-will which the nation bore him, but by the power he himself had; insomuch that Hyrcanus fell into the utmost degree of terror, and expected he would presently march against him with his army.

9. Nor was he mistaken in the conjecture he made; for Herod got his army together, out of the anger he bare him for his threatening him with the accusation in a public court, and led it to Jerusalem, in order to throw Hyrcanus down from his kingdom; and this he had soon done, unless his father and brother had gone out together and broken the force of his fury, and this by exhorting him to carry his revenge no farther than to threatening and affrighting, but to spare the king, under whom he had been advanced to such a degree of power; and that he ought not to be so much provoked at his being tried, as to forget to be thankful that he was acquitted; nor so long to think upon what was of a melancholy nature, as to be ungrateful for his deliverance; and if we ought to reckon that God is the arbitrator of success in war, an unjust cause is of more disadvantage than an army can be of advantage; and that therefore he ought not to be entirely confident of success in a case where he is to fight against his king, his supporter, and one that had often been his benefactor, and that

had never been severe to him any otherwise than as he had hearkened to evil counsellors, and this no farther than by bringing a shadow of injustice upon him. So Herod was prevailed upon by these arguments, and supposed that what he had already done was sufficient for his future hopes, and that he had enough shewn his power to the nation.

10. In the meantime, there was a disturbance among the Romans about Apamia, and a civil war occasioned by the treacherous slaughter of Sextus Cæsar, by Cecilius Bassus, which he perpetrated out of his good-will to Pompey; he also took the authority over his forces; but, as the rest of Cæsar's commanders attacked Bassus with their whole army, in order to punish him for the murder of Cæsar, Antipater also sent them assistance by his sons, both on account of him that was murdered, and on account of that Cæsar who was still alive, both of whom were their friends; and as this war grew to be of a considerable length, Marcus came out of Italy as successor to Sextus.

CHAPTER XI.

HEROD IS MADE PROCURATOR OF ALL SYRIA; MALICHUS IS AFRAID OF HIM, AND TAKES ANTIPATER OFF BY POISON: WHEREUPON THE TRIBUNES OF THE SOLDIERS ARE PREVAILED WITH TO KILL HIM.

1. THERE was at this time a mighty war raised among the Romans, upon the sudden and treacherous slaughter of Cæsar by Cassius and Brutus, after he had held the government for three years and seven months.[*] Upon this murder there were very great agitations, and the great men were mightily at difference one with another, and every one betook himself to that party where they had the greatest hopes of advancing themselves. Accordingly, Cassius came into Syria, in order to receive the forces that were at Apamia, where he procured a reconciliation between Bassus and Marcus, and the legions which were at difference with him: so he raised the siege of Apamia, and took upon him the command of the army, and went about exacting tribute of the cities, and demanding their money to such a degree as they were not able to bear.

2. So he gave command that the Jews should bring in seven hundred talents: whereupon Antipater, out of his dread of Cassius's threats, parted the raising of this sum among his sons, and among others of his acquaintance, and to be done immediately; and among them he required one Malichus, who was at enmity with him, to do his part also, which necessity forced him to do. Now Herod, in the first place, mitigated the passion of Cassius, by bringing his share out of Galilee, which was a hundred talents, on which account he was in the highest favour with him; and when he reproached the rest for being tardy, he was angry at the cities themselves; so he made slaves of Gophna and Emmaus, and two others of less note: nay, he proceeded as if he would kill Malichus, because he had not made greater haste in exacting his tribute; but Antipater prevented the ruin of this man, and of

* In the Antiquities, the duration of the reign of Julius Cæsar is three years six months; but here three years seven months. It is probable the real duration might be three years and between six and seven months.

the other cities, and got into Cassius's favour by bringing in a hundred talents immediately.*

3. However, when Cassius was gone, Malichus forgot the kindness that Antipater had done him, and laid frequent plots against him that had saved him, as making haste to get him out of the way, who was an obstacle to his wicked practices; but Antipater was so much afraid of the power and cunning of the man, that he went beyond Jordan, in order to get an army to guard himself against his treacherous designs; but when Malichus was caught in this plot, he put upon Antipater's sons by his impudence, for he thoroughly deluded Phasaelus, who was the guardian of Jerusalem, and Herod who was intrusted with the weapons of war, and this by a great many excuses and oaths, and persuaded them to procure his reconciliation to their father. Thus was he preserved again by Antipater, who dissuaded Marcus, the then president of Syria, from his resolution of killing Malichus, on account of his attempts for innovation.

4. Upon the war between Cassius and Brutus on one side, against the younger Cæsar [Augustus] and Antony on the other, Cassius and Marcus got an army out of Syria; and because Herod was likely to have a great share in providing necessaries, they then made him procurator of all Syria, and gave him an army of foot and horse. Cassius promised him also, that after the war was over, he would make him king of Judea; but it so happened that the power and hopes of his son became the cause of his perdition; for, as Malichus was afraid of this, he corrupted one of the king's cup-bearers with money, to give a poisonous potion to Antipater; so he became a sacrifice to Malichus's wickedness, and died at a feast. He was a man, in other respects, active in the management of affairs, and one that recovered the government to Hyrcanus, and preserved it in his hands.

5. However, Malichus, when he was suspected of poisoning Antipater, and when the multitude was angry with him for it, denied it, and made the people believe he was not guilty. He also prepared to make a greater figure, and raised soldiers; for he did not suppose that Herod would be quiet, who indeed came upon him with an army presently, in order to revenge his father's death; but upon hearing the advice of his brother Phasaelus, not to punish him in an open manner, lest the multitude should fall into a sedition, he admitted of Malichus's apology, and professed that he cleared him of his suspicion; he also made a pompous funeral for his father.

6. So Herod went to Samaria, which was then in a tumult, and settled the city in peace; after which at the [Pentecost] festival, he returned to Jerusalem, having his armed men with him; hereupon Hyrcanus, at the request of Malichus, who feared his approach, forbade them to introduce foreigners to mix themselves with the people of the country, while they were purifying themselves; but Herod despised the pretence, and him that gave that command, and came in by night. Upon which Malichus came to him, and bewailed Antipater; Herod also made him believe, [he admitted of his lamentation as real,] although he had much ado to restrain his passion at him; however, he did himself bewail the murder of his father in his letters to Cassius, who on other accounts also

hated Malichus. Cassius sent him word back that he should avenge his father's death upon him, and privately gave order to the tribunes that were under him that they should assist Herod in a righteous action he was about.

7. And because, upon the taking of Laodicea by Cassius, the men of power were gotten together from all quarters, with presents and crowns in their hands, Herod allotted this time for the punishment of Malichus. When Malichus suspected that, and was at Tyre, he resolved to withdraw his son privately from among the Tyrians, who was a hostage there, while he got ready to fly away into Judea; the despair he was in of escaping excited him to think of greater things; for he hoped that he should raise the nation to a revolt from the Romans, while Cassius was busy about the war against Antony, and that he should easily depose Hyrcanus, and get the crown for himself.

8. But fate laughed at the hopes he had, for Herod foresaw what he was so zealous about, and invited both Hyrcanus and him to supper; but calling one of the principal servants that stood by him to him, he sent him out, as though it were to get things ready for supper, but in reality to give notice beforehand about the plot that was laid against him; accordingly they called to mind what orders Cassius had given them, and went out of the city with their swords in their hands upon the sea-shore, where they encompassed Malichus round about, and killed him with many wounds. Upon which Hyrcanus was immediately affrighted, till he swooned away, and fell down at the surprise he was in; and it was with difficulty that he was recovered, when he asked who it was that had killed Malichus. And when one of the tribunes replied that it was done by the command of Cassius, "Then," said he, "Cassius hath saved both me and my country, by cutting off one that was laying plots against them both." Whether he spake according to his own sentiments, or whether his fear was such that he was obliged to commend the action by saying so, is uncertain; however, by this method Herod inflicted punishment upon Malichus.

CHAPTER XII.

PHASAELUS IS TOO HARD FOR FELIX; HEROD ALSO OVERCOMES ANTIGONUS IN BATTLE: AND THE JEWS ACCUSE BOTH HEROD AND PHASAELUS; BUT ANTONIUS ACQUITS THEM, AND MAKES THEM TETRARCHS.

1. WHEN Cassius was gone out of Syria, another sedition arose at Jerusalem, wherein Felix assaulted Phasaelus with an army, that he might revenge the death of Malichus upon Herod, by falling upon his brother. Now Herod happened then to be with Fabius, the governor of Damascus, and as he was going to his brother's assistance, he was detained by sickness; in the meantime, Phasaelus was by himself too hard for Felix, and reproached Hyrcanus on account of his ingratitude, both for what assistance he had afforded Malichus, and for overlooking Malichus's brother, when he possessed himself of the fortresses; for he had gotten a great many of them already, and among them the strongest of them all, Masada.

2. However, nothing could be sufficient for him against the force of Herod, who, as soon as he was recovered, took the other fortresses again, and drove him out of Masada in the posture of

---

* It appears evidently that this Cassius was a bitter oppressor and exacter of tribute in Judea. These 700 talents amount to about £300,000 sterling, and are about half the yearly revenue of king Herod afterwards.

a supplicant; he also drove away Marion, the tyrant of the Tyrians, out of Galilee, when he had already possessed himself of three fortified places; but as to those Tyrians whom he had caught he preserved them all alive; nay, some of them he gave presents to, and so sent them away, and thereby procured good-will to himself from the city, and hatred to the tyrant. Marion had indeed obtained this tyrannical power of Cassius, who set tyrants over all Syria; * and out of hatred to Herod it was that he assisted Antigonus, the son of Aristobulus, and principally on Fabius's account, whom Antigonus had made his assistant by money, and had him accordingly on his side when he made his descent; but it was Ptolemy, the kinsman of Antigonus, that supplied all that he wanted.

3. When Herod had fought against these in the avenues of Judea, he was conqueror in the battle, and drove away Antigonus, and returned to Jerusalem, beloved by everybody for the glorious action he had done; for those who did not before favour him did join themselves to him now, because of his marriage into the family of Hyrcanus; for as he had formerly married a wife out of his own country of no ignoble blood, who was called Doris, of whom he begat Antipater, so did he now marry Mariamne, the daughter of Alexander, the son of Aristobulus, and the grand-daughter of Hyrcanus, and was become thereby a relation of the king.

4. But when Cæsar and Antony had slain Cassius near Philippi, and Cæsar was gone to Italy, and Antony to Asia, amongst the rest of the cities which sent ambassadors to Antony unto Bithynia, the great men of the Jews came also, and accused Phasaelus and Herod, that they kept the government by force, and that Hyrcanus had no more than an honourable name. Herod appeared ready to answer this accusation; and, having made Antony his friend by the large sums of money he gave him, he brought him to such a temper as not to hear the others speak against him; and thus did they part at this time.

5. However, after this there came a hundred of the principal men among the Jews to Daphne by Antioch, to Antony, who was already in love with Cleopatra to the degree of slavery; these Jews put those men that were the most potent, both in dignity and eloquence, foremost, and accused the brethren.† But Messala opposed them, and defended the brethren, and that while Hyrcanus stood by him, on account of his relation to them. When Antony had heard both sides, he asked Hyrcanus which party was the fittest to govern; who replied, that Herod and his party was fittest. Antony was glad of that answer, for he had been formerly treated in an hospitable and obliging manner by his father Antipater, when he marched into Judea with Gabinius; so he constituted the brethren tetrarchs, and committed to them the government of Judea.

6. But when the ambassadors had indignation at this procedure, Antony took fifteen of them and put them into custody, whom he was also going to kill presently, and the rest he drove away with disgrace; on which occasion a still greater tumult arose at Jerusalem; so they sent again a thousand ambassadors to Tyre, where Antony now abode, as he was marching to Jerusalem; upon these men who made a clamour,

he sent out the governor of Tyre, and ordered him to punish all that he could catch of them. and to settle those in the administration whom he had made tetrarchs.

7. But before this, Herod and Hyrcanus went out upon the sea-shore, and earnestly desired of these ambassadors that they would neither bring ruin upon themselves, nor war upon their native country, by their rash contentions; and when they grew still more outrageous, Antony sent out armed men, and slew a great many, and wounded more of them: of whom those that were slain were buried by Hyrcanus, as were the wounded put under the care of physicians by him; yet would not those that had escaped be quiet still, but put the affairs of the city into such disorder, and so provoked Antony, that he slew those whom he had put into bonds also.

CHAPTER XIII

THE PARTHIANS BRING ANTIGONUS BACK INTO JUDEA, AND CAST HYRCANUS AND PHASAELUS INTO PRISON. THE FLIGHT OF HEROD, AND THE TAKING OF JERUSALEM, AND WHAT HYRCANUS AND PHASAELUS SUFFERED

1. Now two years afterward, when Barzapharnes, a governor among the Parthians, and Pacorus, the king's son, had possessed themselves of Syria, and when Lysanias had already succeeded upon the death of his father Ptolemy, the son of Menneus, in the government, [of Chalcis,] he prevailed with the governor, by a promise of a thousand talents, and five hundred women, to bring back Antigonus to his kingdom, and to turn Hyrcanus out of it. Pacorus was by these means induced so to do, and marched along the sea-coast, while he ordered Barzapharnes to fall upon the Jews as he went along the Mediterranean part of the country; but of the maritime people, the Tyrians would not receive Pacorus, although those of Ptolemais and Sidon had received him; so he committed a troop of his horse to a certain cup-bearer belonging to the royal family, of his own name, [Pacorus,] and gave him orders to march into Judea, in order to learn the state of affairs among their enemies, and to help Antigonus when he should want his assistance.

2. Now, as these men were ravaging Carmel, many of the Jews ran together to Antigonus, and shewed themselves ready to make an incursion into the country; so he sent them before into that place called Drymus, [the woodland, ‡] to seize upon the place; whereupon a battle was fought between them; and they drove the enemy away, and pursued them, and ran after them as far as Jerusalem, and as their numbers increased, they proceeded as far as the king's palace; but as Hyrcanus and Phasaelus received them with a strong body of men, there happened a battle in the market-place, in which Herod's party beat the enemy, and shut them up in the temple, and set sixty men in the houses adjoining as a guard on them. But the people that were tumultuous against the brethren came in and burnt those men; while Herod, in his rage for killing them, attacked and slew many of the people, till one party made incursions on the other by turns, day by day, in the way of am-

---

* Here we see that Cassius set tyrants over all Syria; so that his assisting to destroy Cæsar does not seem to have proceeded from his true zeal for public liberty, but from a desire to be a tyrant himself.

† Phasaelus and Herod.

‡ This large and noted wood, or woodland, belonging to Carmel, is mentioned in the Old Testament, (2 Kings xix. 25; and Isa. xxxvi. 24.)

bushes : and slaughters were made continually among them.

3. Now when that festival which we call Pentecost was at hand, all the places about the temple, and the whole city, was full of a multitude of people that were come out of the country, and who were the greatest part of them armed also, at which time Phasaelus guarded the wall, and Herod, with a few, guarded the royal palace; and when he made an assault upon his enemies, as they were out of their ranks, on the north quarter of the city, he slew a great number of them, and put them all to flight; and some of them he shut up within the city, and others within the outward rampart. In the meantime Antigonus desired that Pacorus might be admitted to be a reconciler between them; and Phasaelus was prevailed upon to admit the Parthian into the city with five hundred horse, and to treat him in an hospitable manner, who pretended that he came to quell the tumult, but in reality he came to assist Antigonus ; however, he laid a plot for Phasaelus, and persuaded him to go as an ambassador to Barzapharnes, in order to put an end to the war, although Herod was very earnest with him to the contrary, and exhorted him to kill the plotter, but not expose himself to the snares he had laid for him, because the barbarians are naturally perfidious. However, Pacorus went out and took Hyrcanus with him, that he might be the less suspected ; he also * left some of the horsemen, called the Freemen, with Herod, and conducted Phasaelus with the rest.

4. But now, when they were come to Galilee, they found that the people of that country had revolted, and were in arms, who came very cunningly to their leader, and besought him to· conceal his treacherous intentions by an obliging behaviour to them; accordingly, he at first made them presents, and afterward, as they went way, laid ambushes for them ; and, when they were come to one of the maritime cities called Ecdippon, they perceived that a plot was laid for them : for they were there informed of a promise of a thousand talents, and how Antigonus had devoted the greatest number of the women that were there with them, among the five hundred, to the Parthians ; they also perceived that an ambush was always laid for them by the barbarians in the night-time; they had also been seized on before this, unless they had waited for the seizure of Herod first at Jerusalem, because, if he were once informed of this treachery of theirs, he would take care of himself : nor was this a mere report, for they saw the guards already not far off them.

5. Nor would Phasaelus think of forsaking Hyrcanus and flying away, although Ophellius earnestly persuaded him to it; for this man had learned the whole scheme of the plot from Samaralla, the richest of all the Syrians. But Phasaelus went up to the Parthian governor, and reproached him to his face for laying this treacherous plot against them, and chiefly because he had done it for money; and he promised him that he would give him more money for their preservation than Antigonus had promised to give for the kingdom. But the sly Parthian endeavoured to remove all his suspicion by apologies and by oaths, and then went to [the other] Pacorus ; immediately after which those Parthians who were left, and had it in charge, seized upon Phasaelus and Hyrcanus, who could do no more than curse their perfidiousness and their perjury.

6. In the meantime the cup-bearer was sent, [back,] and laid a plot how to seize upon Herod, by deluding him, and getting him out of the city, as he was commanded to do. But Herod suspected the barbarians from the beginning; and having then received intelligence that a messenger, who was to bring him the letters that informed him of the treachery intended, had fallen among the enemy, he would not go out of the city ; though Pacorus said, very positively, that he ought to go out, and meet the messengers that brought the letters, for that the enemy had not taken them, and that the contents of them were not accounts of any plots upon them, but of what Phasaelus had done ; yet Herod had heard from others that his brother was seized; and Alexandra,† the shrewdest woman in the world, Hyrcanus's daughter, begged of him that he would not go out, nor trust himself to those barbarians, who now were come to make an attempt upon him openly.

7. Now, as Pacorus and his friends were considering how they might bring their plot to bear privately, because it was not possible to circumvent a man of so great prudence by openly attacking him, Herod prevented them, and went off with the persons that were the most nearly related to him by night, and this without their enemies being apprised of it. But, as soon as the Parthians perceived it, they pursued after them; and, as he gave orders for his mother, and sister, and the young woman who was betrothed to him, with her mother, and his youngest brother, to make the best of their way, he himself, with his servants, took all the care they could to keep off the barbarians; and when, at every assault, he had slain a great many of them, he came to the stronghold of Masada.

8. Nay, he found by experience that the Jews fell more heavily upon him than did the Parthians, and created him troubles perpetually, and this ever since he was gotten sixty furlongs from the city ; these sometimes brought it to a sort of regular battle. Now, in the place where Herod beat them, and killed a great number of them, there he afterward built a citadel, in memory of the great actions he did there, and adorned it with the most costly palaces, and erected very strong fortifications, and called it, from his own name, Herodium. Now, as they were in their flight, many joined themselves to him every day ; and at a place called Thressa of Idumea, his brother Joseph met him, and advised him to ease himself of a great number of his followers, because Masada would not contain so great a multitude, which were above nine thousand. Herod complied with this advice, and sent away the most cumbersome part of his retinue, that they might go into Idumea, and gave them provisions for their journey ; but he got safe to the fortress with his nearest relations, and retained with him only the stoutest of his followers; and there it was that he left eight hundred of his men as a guard for the women, and provisions sufficient for a siege; but he made haste himself to Petra of Arabia.

9. As for the Parthians in Jerusalem, they betook themselves to plundering, and fell upon the houses of those that were fled, and upon the king's palace, and spared nothing but Hyrcanus's money, which was not above three hundred talents. They lighted on other men's money also, but not so much as they hoped for; for Herod, having a long while had a suspicion of the per-

---

* These accounts, that the Parthians fought chiefly on horseback, and that only some few of their soldiers were freemen, perfectly agree with Trogus Pompeius.

† Mariamne here, in the copies.

fidiousness of the barbarians, had taken care to have what was most splendid among his treasures conveyed into Idumea, as every one belonging to him had in like manner done also. But the Parthians proceeded to that degree of injustice, as to fill all the country with war without denouncing it, and to demolish the city Marissa, and not only set up Antigonus for king, but to deliver Phasaelus and Hyrcanus bound into his hands, in order to their being tormented by him. Antigonus himself also bit off Hyrcanus's ears with his own teeth, as he fell down upon his knees to him, that so he might never be able, upon any mutation of affairs, to take the high priesthood again; for the high priests that officiated were to be complete, and without blemish.

10. However, he failed in his purpose of abusing Phasaelus, by reason of his courage, for though he neither had the command of his sword nor of his hands, he prevented all abuses by dashing his head against a stone; so he demonstrated himself to be Herod's own brother, and Hyrcanus a most degenerate relation, and died with great bravery and made the end of his life agreeable to the actions of it. There is also another report about his end—viz., that he recovered of that stroke, and that a surgeon, who was sent by Antigonus to heal him, filled the wound with poisonous ingredients, and so killed him. Whichsoever of these deaths he came to, the beginning of it was glorious. It is also reported, that before he expired, he was informed by a certain poor woman how Herod had escaped out of their hands, and that he said thereupon, "I now die with comfort, since I leave behind me one alive that will avenge me of mine enemies."

11. This was the death of Phasaelus; but the Parthians, although they had failed of the women they chiefly desired, yet did they put the government of Jerusalem into the hands of Antigonus, and took away Hyrcanus, and bound him, and carried him to Parthia.

CHAPTER XIV

WHEN HEROD IS REJECTED IN ARABIA, HE MAKES HASTE TO ROME, WHERE ANTONY AND CÆSAR JOIN THEIR INTEREST TO MAKE HIM KING OF THE JEWS

1. Now Herod did the more zealously pursue his journey into Arabia, as making haste to get money of the king, while his brother was yet alive; by which money alone it was that he hoped to prevail upon the covetous temper of the barbarians to spare Phasaelus; for he reasoned thus with himself:—That if the Arabian king was too forgetful of his father's friendship with him, and was too covetous to make him a free gift, he would, however, borrow as much of him as might redeem his brother, and put into his hands, as a pledge, the son of him that was to be redeemed. Accordingly, he led his brother's son along with him, who was of the age of seven years. Now he was ready to give three hundred talents for his brother, and intended to desire the intercession of the Tyrians, to get them accepted; however, fate had been too quick for his diligence; and since Phasaelus was dead, Herod's brotherly love was now in vain. Moreover, he was not able to find any lasting friendship among the Arabians; for the king, Malichus, sent to him immediately, and commanded him to return back out of his coun-

try, and used the name of the Parthians as a pretence for so doing, as though these had denounced to him by their ambassadors to cast Herod out of Arabia; while in reality they had a mind to keep back what they owed to Antipater, and not be obliged to make requital to his sons for the free gifts the father had made them. He also took the imprudent advice of those who, equally with himself, were willing to deprive Herod of what Antipater had deposited among them; and these men were the most potent of all whom he had in his kingdom.

2. So when Herod had found that the Arabians were his enemies, and this for those very reasons whence he hoped they would have been the most friendly, and had given them such an answer as his passion suggested, he returned back and went for Egypt. Now he lodged the first evening at one of the temples of that country, in order to meet with those whom he left behind; but on the next day word was brought him, as he was going to Rhinocurura, that his brother was dead, and how he came by his death; and when he had lamented him as much as his present circumstances could bear, he soon laid aside such cares, and proceeded on his journey. But now, after some time, the king of Arabia repented of what he had done, and sent presently away messengers to call him back: Herod had prevented them, and was come to Pelusium, where he could not obtain a passage from those that lay with the fleet, so he besought their captains to let him go by them; accordingly, out of the reverence they bore to the fame and dignity of the man, they conducted him to Alexandria; and when he came into the city, he was received by Cleopatra with great splendour,—who hoped he might be persuaded to be commander of her forces in the expedition she was now about. But he rejected the queen's solicitations, and being neither affrighted at the height of that storm which then happened, nor at the tumults that were now in Italy, he sailed for Rome.

3. But as he was in peril about Pamphylia, and obliged to cast out the greatest part of the ship's lading, he, with difficulty got safe to Rhodes, a place which had been grievously harassed in the war with Cassius. He was there received by his friends, Ptolemy and Sappinius; and although he was then in want of money, he fitted up a three-decked ship of very great magnitude, wherein he and his friends sailed to Brundusium,* and went to Rome with all speed; where he first of all went to Antony, on account of the friendship his father had with him, and laid before him the calamities of himself and his family; and that he had left his nearest relations besieged in a fortress, and had sailed to him through a storm, to make supplication to him for assistance.

4. Hereupon Antony was moved to compassion at the change that had been made in Herod's affairs, and this both upon his calling to mind how hospitably he had been treated by Antipater, but more especially on account of Herod's own virtue; so he then resolved to get him made king of the Jews, whom he had himself formerly made tetrarch. The contest also that he had with Antigonus was another inducement, and that of no less weight than the great regard he had for Herod; for he looked upon Antigonus as a seditious person, and an enemy of the Romans: and as for Cæsar, Herod found him better prepared than Antony, as remember-

_____

* This Brentesium or Brundusium has coins still preserved.

ing very fresh the wars he had gone through together with his father, the hospitable treatment he had met with from him, and the entire good-will he had shewn to him ; besides the activity which he saw in Herod himself. So he called the senate together, wherein Messalas, and after him Atratinus, produced Herod before them, and gave a full account of the merits of his father, and his own good-will to the Romans. At the same time they demonstrated that Antigonus was their enemy, not only because he soon quarrelled with them, but because he now overlooked the Romans, and took the government by the means of the Parthians. These reasons greatly moved the senate, at which juncture Antony came in, and told them that it was for their advantage in the Parthian war that Herod should be king ; so they all gave their votes for it. And when the senate was separated, Antony and Cæsar went out, with Herod between them ; while the consul and the rest of the magistrates went before them, in order to offer sacrifices, and to lay the decree in the capitol. Antony also made a feast for Herod on the first day of his reign.

CHAPTER XV

ANTIGONUS BESIEGES THOSE THAT WERE IN MASADA, WHOM HEROD FREES FROM CONFINEMENT WHEN HE CAME BACK FROM ROME, AND PRESENTLY MARCHES TO JERUSALEM, WHERE HE FINDS SILO CORRUPTED BY BRIBES

1. Now during this time, Antigonus besieged those that were in Masada, who had all other necessaries in sufficient quantity, but were in want of water ; on which account Joseph, Herod's brother, was disposed to run away to the Arabians, with two hundred of his own friends, because he had heard that Malichus repented of his offences with regard to Herod ; and he had been so quick as to have been gone out of the fortress already, unless, on that very night when he was going away, there had fallen a great deal of rain, insomuch that his reservoirs were full of water, and so he was under no necessity of running away. After which, therefore, they made an irruption upon Antigonus's party, and slew a great many of them, some in open battles, and some in private ambush ; nor had they always success in their attempts, for sometimes they were beaten, and ran away.

2. In the meantime Ventidius, the Roman general, was sent out of Syria, to restrain the incursions of the Parthians ; and after he had done that, he came into Judea, in pretence indeed to assist Joseph and his party, but in reality to get money of Antigonus ; and when he had pitched his camp very near to Jerusalem, as soon as he had got money enough, he went away with the greatest part of his forces ; yet still did he leave Silo with some part of them, lest if he had taken them all away, his taking of bribes might have been too openly discovered. Now Antigonus hoped that the Parthians would come to his assistance, and therefore cultivated a good understanding with Silo in the meantime, lest any interruption should be given to his hopes.

3. Now by this time Herod had sailed out of Italy, and had come to Ptolemais : and as soon as he had gotten together no small army of foreigners, and of his own countrymen, he marched through Galilee against Antigonus, wherein he was assisted by Ventidius and Silo, both of whom

Dellius,* a person sent by Antony, persuaded to bring Herod [into his kingdom.] Now Ventidius was at this time among the cities, and composing the disturbances which had happened by means of the Parthians, as was Silo in Judea corrupted by the bribes that Antigonus had given him ; yet was not Herod himself destitute of power, but the number of his forces increased every day as he went along, and all Galilee, with few exceptions, joined themselves to him. So he proposed to himself to set about his most necessary enterprise, and that was Masada, in order to deliver his relations from the siege they endured But still Joppa stood in his way, and hindered his going thither : for it was necessary to take that city first, which was in the enemies' hands, that when he should go to Jerusalem, no fortress might be left in the enemies' power behind him. Silo also willingly joined him, as having now a plausible occasion of drawing off his forces [from Jerusalem ;] and when the Jews pursued him, and pressed upon him [in his retreat,] Herod made an excursion upon them with a small body of his men, and soon put them to flight, and saved Silo when he was in distress.

4. After this, Herod took Joppa, and then made haste to Masada to free his relations. Now, as he was marching, many came in to him ; some induced by their friendship to his father, some by the reputation he had already gained himself, and some in order to repay the benefits they had received from both ; but still what engaged the greatest number on his side, was the hopes from him, when he should be established in his kingdom ; so that he had gotten together an army hard to be conquered. But Antigonus laid an ambush for him as he marched out, in which he did little or no harm to his enemies. However, he easily recovered his relations again that were in Masada, as well as the fortress Ressa, and then marched to Jerusalem, where the soldiers that were with Silo joined themselves to his own, as did many out of the city, from a dread of his power.

5. Now, when he had pitched his camp on the west side of the city, the guards who were there shot their arrows and threw their darts at them, while others ran out in companies, and attacked those in the fore-front ; but Herod commanded proclamation to be made at the wall, that he was come for the good of the people and the preservation of the city, without any design to be revenged on his open enemies, but to grant oblivion to them, though they had been the most obstinate against him. Now the soldiers that were for Antigonus made a contrary clamour, and did neither permit anybody to hear that proclamation, nor to change their party ; so Antigonus gave order to his forces to beat the enemy from the walls : accordingly, they soon threw their darts at them from the towers, and put them to flight.

6. And here it was that Silo discovered he had taken bribes ; for he set many of the soldiers to clamour about their want of necessaries, and to require their pay, in order to buy themselves food, and to demand that he would lead them into places convenient for their winter quarters ; because all the parts about the city were laid waste by the means of Antigonus's army, which had taken all things away. By this he moved the army, and attempted to get them off the siege ; but Herod went to the captains that were under Silo, and to a great many of the soldiers,

---

* This Dellius is famous, or rather infamous, in the history of Mark Antony.

and begged of them not to leave him, who was sent thither by Cæsar and Antony, and the senate; for that he would take care to have their wants supplied that very day. After the making of which entreaty he went hastily into the country, and brought hither so great an abundance of necessaries, that he cut off all Silo's pretences; and, in order to provide that for the following days they should not want supplies, he sent to the people that were about Samaria (which city had joined itself to him) to bring corn, wine, and oil, and cattle to Jericho. When Antigonus heard of this, he sent some of his party with orders to hinder, and lay ambushes for these collectors of corn. This command was obeyed, and a great number of armed men were gathered together about Jericho, and lay upon the mountains to watch those that brought the provisions. Yet was Herod not idle, but took with him ten cohorts, five of them were Romans, and five Jewish cohorts, together with some mercenary troops intermixed among them, and besides those a few horsemen, and came to Jericho; and when he came he found the city deserted, but that there were five hundred men, with their wives and children, who had taken possession of the tops of the mountains; these he took and dismissed them, while the Romans fell upon the rest of the city, and plundered it, having found the houses full of all sorts of good things. So the king left a garrison at Jericho, and came back, and sent the Roman army into those cities which were come over to him, to take their winter quarters there, —viz., into Judea [or Idumea,] and Galilee, and Samaria. Antigonus also, by bribes, obtained of Silo to let a part of his army be received at Lydda, as a compliment to Antonius.

CHAPTER XVI

HEROD TAKES SEPPHORIS, AND SUBDUES THE ROBBERS THAT WERE IN THE CAVES: HE AFTER THAT AVENGES HIMSELF UPON MACHERAS, AS UPON AN ENEMY OF HIS, AND GOES TO ANTONY, AS HE WAS BESIEGING SAMOSATA

1. So the Romans lived in plenty of all things, and rested from war. However, Herod did not lie at rest, but seized upon Idumea, and kept it, with two thousand footmen, and four hundred horsemen; and this he did by sending his brother Joseph thither, that no innovation might be made by Antigonus. He also removed his mother, and all his relations, who had been in Masada, to Samaria; and when he had settled them securely, he marched to take the remaining parts of Galilee, and to drive away the garrisons placed there by Antigonus.

2. But when Herod had reached Sepphoris,* in a very great snow, he took the city without any difficulty, the guards that should have kept it flying away before it was assaulted; where he gave an opportunity to his followers that had been in distress to refresh themselves, there being in that city a great abundance of necessaries. After which he hasted away to the robbers that were in the caves, who overran a great part of the country, and did as great mischief to its inhabitants as a war itself could have done. Accordingly he sent beforehand three cohorts of footmen, and one troop of horsemen, to the village of Arbela, and came himself forty

days afterwards† with the rest of his forces. Yet were not the enemy affrighted at his assault, but met him in arms; for their skill was that of warriors, but their boldness was that of robbers; when, therefore, it came to a pitched battle, they put to flight Herod's left wing with their right one: but Herod, wheeling about on the sudden from his own right wing, came to their assistance, and both made his own left wing return back from its flight, and fell upon the pursuers, and cooled their courage, till they could not bear the attempts that were made directly upon them, and so turned back and ran away.

3. But Herod followed them, and slew them as he followed them, and destroyed a great part of them, till those that remained were scattered beyond the river [Jordan;] and Galilee was freed from the terrors they had been under, excepting from those that remained, and lay concealed in caves, which required longer time ere they could be conquered. In order to which, Herod, in the first place, distributed the fruits of their former labours to the soldiers, and gave every one of them a hundred and fifty drachmæ of silver, and a great deal more to their commanders, and sent them into their winter quarters. He also sent to his youngest brother Pheroras, to take care of a good market for them, where they might buy themselves provisions, and to build a wall about Alexandrium; who took care of both those injunctions accordingly.

4. In the meantime Antony abode at Athens, while Ventidius called for Silo and Herod to come to the war against the Parthians, but ordered them first to settle the affairs of Judea: so Herod willingly dismissed Silo to go to Ventidius; but he made an expedition himself against those that lay in the caves. Now these caves were in the precipices of craggy mountains, and could not be come at from any side, since they had only some winding pathways,. very narrow, by which they got up to them; but the rock that lay on their front had beneath it valleys of a vast depth, and of an almost perpendicular declivity; insomuch that the king was doubtful for a long time what to do, by reason of a kind of impossibility there was of attacking the place. Yet did he at length make use of a contrivance that was subject to the utmost hazard; for he let down the most hardy of his men in chests, and set them at the mouths of the dens. Now these men slew the robbers and their families, and when they made resistance, they sent in fire upon them, [and burnt them;] and as Herod was desirous of saving some of them, he had proclamation made, that they should come and deliver themselves up to him; but not one of them came willingly to him; and of those that were compelled to come, many preferred death to captivity. And here a certain old man, the father of seven children, whose children, together with their mother, desired him to give them leave to go out, upon the assurance and right hand that was offered them, slew them after the following manner:—He ordered every one of them to go out, while he stood himself at the cave's mouth, and slew that son of his perpetually who went out. Herod was near enough to see this sight, and his bowels of compassion were moved at it, and he stretched out his right hand to the old man, and besought

---

* This Sepphoris, the metropolis of Galilee, so often mentioned by Josephus, has coins still remaining.

† This way of speaking, "after forty days," is interpreted by Josephus himself, "on the fortieth day." In like manner, when Josephus says that Herod lived "after" he had ordered Antipater to be slain "five days;" this is by himself interpreted, that he died "on the fifth day afterward."

him to spare his children; yet did he not relent at all upon what he said, but over and above reproached Herod on the lowness of his descent, and slew his wife as well as his children, and when he had thrown their dead bodies down the precipice, he at last threw himself down after them.

5. By this means Herod subdued these caves, and the robbers that were in them. He then left there a part of his army, as many as he thought sufficient to prevent any sedition, and made Ptolemy their general, and returned to Samaria: he led also with him three thousand armed footmen, and six hundred horsemen, against Antigonus. Now here those that used to raise tumults in Galilee, having liberty so to do upon his departure, fell unexpectedly upon Ptolemy, the general of his forces, and slew him: they also laid the country waste, and then retired to the bogs, and to places not easily to be found; but when Herod was informed of this insurrection, he came to the assistance of the country immediately, and destroyed a great number of the seditious, and raised the sieges of all those fortresses they had besieged; he also exacted the tribute of a hundred talents of his enemies, as a penalty for the mutations they had made in the country.

6. By this time (the Parthians being already driven out of the country, and Parcorus slain) Ventidius, by Antony's command, sent a thousand horsemen, and two legions, as auxiliaries to Herod, against Antigonus. Now Antigonus besought Macheras, who was their general, by letter, to come to his assistance, and made a great many mournful complaints about Herod's violence, and about the injuries he did to the kingdom; and promised to give him money for such his assistance: but he complied not with his invitation to betray his trust, for he did not contemn him that sent him, especially while Herod gave him more money [than the other offered.] So he pretended friendship to Antigonus, but came as a spy to discover his affairs, although he did not herein comply with Herod, who dissuaded him from so doing; but Antigonus perceived what his intentions were beforehand, and excluded him out of the city, and defended himself against him as against an enemy, from the walls; till Macheras was ashamed of what he had done, and retired to Emmaus to Herod; and, as he was in a rage at his disappointment, he slew all the Jews whom he met with, without sparing those that were for Herod, but using them all as if they were for Antigonus.

7. Hereupon Herod was very angry at him, and was going to fight against Macheras as his enemy; but he restrained his indignation, and marched to Antony to accuse Macheras of maladministration; but Macheras was made sensible of his offences, and followed after the king immediately, and earnestly begged and obtained that he would be reconciled to him. However, Herod did not desist from his resolution of going to Antony; but when he heard that he was besieging Samosata* with a great army, which is a strong city near to the Euphrates, he made the greater haste; as observing that this was a proper opportunity for shewing at once his courage, and for doing what would greatly oblige Antony. Indeed, when he came, he soon made an end of that siege, and slew a great number of the barbarians, and took from them a large prey; insomuch that Antony, who admired his courage

* This Samosata, the metropolis of Commagena, is well known from its coins.

formerly, did now admire it still more. Accordingly, he heaped many more honours upon him, and gave him more assured hopes that he should gain his kingdom: and now king Antiochus was forced to deliver up Samosata.

CHAPTER XVII

THE DEATH OF JOSEPH, [HEROD'S BROTHER,] WHICH HAD BEEN SIGNIFIED TO HEROD IN DREAMS. HOW HEROD WAS PRESERVED TWICE, AFTER A WONDERFUL MANNER. HE CUTS OFF THE HEAD OF PAPPUS, WHO WAS THE MURDERER OF HIS BROTHER, AND SENDS THAT HEAD TO [HIS OTHER BROTHER] PHERORAS. AND IN NO LONG TIME HE BESIEGES JERUSALEM, AND MARRIES MARIAMNE

1. IN the meantime Herod's affairs in Judea were in an ill state. He had left his brother Joseph with full power, but had charged him to make no attempts against Antigonus till his return; for that Macheras would not be such an assistant as he could depend on, as it appeared by what he had done already; but as soon as Joseph heard that his brother was at a very great distance, he neglected the charge he had received, and marched towards Jericho with five cohorts, which Macheras sent with him. This movement was intended for seizing on the corn, as it was now in the midst of summer; but when his enemies attacked him in the mountains, and its places which were difficult to pass, he was both killed himself, as he was very bravely fighting in the battle, and the entire Roman cohorts were destroyed; for these cohorts were new raised men, gathered out of Syria, and there was no mixture of those called veteran soldiers among them, who might have supported those that were unskilful in war.

2. This victory was not sufficient for Antigonus; but he proceeded to that degree of rage, as to treat the dead body of Joseph barbarously; for when he had gotten possession of the bodies of those that were slain, he cut off his head, although his brother Pheroras would have given fifty talents as a price of redemption for it. And now the affairs of Galilee were put into such disorder after this victory of Antigonus, that those of Antigonus's party brought the principal men that were on Herod's side to the lake, and there drowned them. There was a great change made also in Idumea, where Macheras was building a wall about one of the fortresses, that was called Gittha. But Herod had not yet been informed of these things; for after the taking of Samosata, and when Antony had set Sosius over the affairs of Syria, and given him orders to assist Herod against Antigonus, he departed into Egypt. But Sosius sent two legions before him into Judea, to assist Herod, and followed himself soon after with the rest of his army.

3. Now when Herod was at Daphne, by Antioch, he had some dreams which clearly foreboded his brother's death; and as he leaped out of his bed in a disturbed manner, there came messengers that acquainted him with that calamity. So when he had lamented this misfortune for a while, he put off the main part of his mourning, and made haste to march against his enemies; and when he had performed a march that was above his strength, and was gone as far as Libanus, he got eight hundred men of those that lived near to that mountain, as his assistants, and joined with them one Roman legion,

with which, before it was day, he made an irruption into Galilee, and met his enemies, and drove them back to the place which they had left. He also made an immediate and continued attack upon the fortress. Yet was he forced, by a most terrible storm, to pitch his camp in a neighbouring village before he could take it. But when, after a few days' time, the second legion, that came from Antony, joined themselves to him, the enemy were affrighted at his power, and left their fortifications in the night-time.

4. After this he marched through Jericho, as making what haste he could to be avenged on his brother's murderers: where happened to him a providential sign, out of which when he had unexpectedly escaped, he had the reputation of being very dear to God; for that evening there feasted with him many of the principal men; and after that feast was over, and all the guests were gone out, the house fell down immediately. And as he judged this to be a common signal of what dangers he should undergo, and how he should escape them in the war that he was going about, he in the morning set forward with his army, when about six thousand of his enemies came running down from the mountains, and began to fight with those in his fore-front; yet durst they not be so very bold as to engage the Romans hand to hand, but threw stones and darts at them at a distance, by which means they wounded a considerable number; in which action Herod's own side was wounded with a dart.

5. Now as Antigonus had a mind to appear to exceed Herod not only in the courage, but in the number of his men, he sent Pappus, one of his companions, with an army against Samaria, whose fortune it was to oppose Macheras. But Herod overran the enemy's country, and demolished five little cities, and destroyed two thousand men that were in them, and burned their houses, and then returned to his camp; but his head-quarters were at the village called Cana.

6. Now a great multitude of Jews resorted to him every day, both out of Jericho and the other parts of the country. Some were moved so to do out of their hatred to Antigonus, and some out of regard to the glorious actions Herod had done; but others were led on by unreasonable desire of change; so he fell upon them immediately. As for Pappus and his party, they were not terrified either at their number or at their zeal, but marched out with great alacrity to fight them; and it came to a close fight. Now other parts of their army made resistance for a while: but Herod, running the utmost hazard, out of the rage he was in at the murder of his brother, that he might be avenged on those that had been the authors of it, soon beat those that opposed him; and, after he had beaten them, he always turned his force against those that stood to it still, and pursued them all; so that a great slaughter was made, while some were forced back into that village whence they came out; he also pressed hard upon the hindermost, and slew a vast number of them; he also fell into the village with the enemy, where every house was filled with armed men, and the upper rooms were crowded above with soldiers for their defence; and when he had beaten those that were on the outside, he pulled the houses to pieces, and plucked out those that were within; upon many he had the roofs shaken down, whereby they perished by heaps; and as for those that fled out of the ruins, the soldiers received them with their swords in their hands; and the multitude of those slain and lying in heaps was so great, that the conquerors could not pass along the roads. Now the enemy could not bear this blow, so that when the multitude of them which was gathered together, saw that those in the villages were slain, they dispersed themselves and fled away; upon the confidence of which victory, Herod had marched immediately to Jerusalem, unless he had been hindered by the depth of winter's [coming on.] This was the impediment that lay in the way of this his entire glorious progress, and was what hindered Antigonus from being now conquered, who was already disposed to forsake the city.

7. Now when at the evening Herod had already dismissed his friends to refresh themselves after their fatigue, and when he was gone himself, while he was still hot in his armour, like a common soldier, to bathe himself, and had but one servant that attended him, and before he was gotten into the bath, one of the enemies met him in the face with a sword in his hand, and then a second, and a third, and after that more of them; these were men who had run away out of the battle into the bath in their armour, and they had lain there for some time in great terror, and in privacy; and when they saw the king, they trembled for fear, and ran by him in a fright, although he was naked, and endeavoured to get off into the public road. Now there was by chance nobody else at hand that might seize upon these men; and for Herod, he was contented to have come to no harm himself, so that they all got away in safety.

8. But on the next day Herod had Pappus's head cut off, who was the general of Antigonus, and was slain in the battle, and sent it to his brother Pheroras, by way of punishment for their slain brother; for he was the man that slew Joseph. Now as winter was going off, Herod marched to Jerusalem, and brought his army to the wall of it; this was the third year since he had been made king at Rome; so he pitched his camp before the temple, for on that side it might be besieged; and there it was that Pompey took the city. So he parted the work among the army, and demolished the suburbs, and raised three banks, and gave orders to have towers built upon those banks, and left the most laborious of his acquaintance at the works. But he went himself to Samaria, to take the daughter of Alexander, the son of Aristobulus, to wife, who had been betrothed to him before, as we have already said; and thus he accomplished this by the by, during the siege of the city, for he had his enemies in great contempt already.

9. When he had thus married Mariamne, he came back to Jerusalem with a greater army. Sosius also joined him with a large army, both of horsemen and footmen, which he sent before him through the midland parts, while he marched himself along Phœnicia; and when the whole army was gotten together, which were eleven regiments of footmen, and six thousand horsemen, besides the Syrian auxiliaries, which were no small part of the army, they pitched their camp near the north wall. Herod's dependence was upon the decree of the senate, by which he was made king; and Sosius relied upon Antony, who sent the army that was under him to Herod's assistance.

CHAPTER XVIII

HOW HEROD AND SOSIUS TOOK JERUSALEM BY FORCE; AND WHAT DEATH ANTIGONUS CAME TO. ALSO, CONCERNING CLEOPATRA'S AVARICIOUS TEMPER

§ 1. Now the multitude of the Jews that were

in the city were divided into several factions, for the people that crowded about the temple, being the weaker part of them, gave it out that, as the times were, he was the happiest and most religious man who should die first. But as to the more bold and hardy men, they got together in bodies, and fell a robbing others after various manners, and these particularly plundered the places that were about the city, and this because there was no food left either for the horses or the men; yet some of the warlike men, who were used to fight regularly, were appointed to defend the city during the siege, and these drove those that raised the banks away from the wall; and these were always inventing some engine or another to be a hindrance to the engines of the enemy; nor had they so much success any way as in the mines under ground.

2. Now, as for the robberies which were committed, the king contrived that ambushes should be so laid, that they might restrain their excursions; and as for the want of provisions, he provided that they should be brought to them from great distances. He was also too hard for the Jews, by the Romans' skill in the art of war: although they were bold to the utmost degree, now they durst not come to a plain battle with the Romans, which was certain death; but through their mines under ground they would appear in the midst of them on the sudden, and before they could batter down one wall, they built them another in its stead; and to sum up all at once, they did not shew any want of either painstaking or of contrivances, as having resolved to hold out to the very last. Indeed, though they had so great an army lying round about them, they bore a siege of five months, till some of Herod's chosen men ventured to get upon the wall, and fell into the city, as did Sosius's centurions after them; and now the first of all seized upon what was about the temple; and upon the pouring in of the army, there was slaughter of vast multitudes everywhere, by reason of the rage the Romans were in at the length of the siege, and by reason that the Jews that were about Herod earnestly endeavoured that none of their adversaries might remain; so they were cut to pieces by great multitudes, and as they were crowded together in narrow streets, and in houses, or were running away to the temple; nor was there any mercy shewn either to infants or to the aged, or to the weaker sex; insomuch, that although the king sent about and desired them to spare the people, nobody could be persuaded to withhold their right hand from slaughter, but they slew people of all ages like madmen. Then it was that Antigonus, without any regard to his former and present fortune, came down from the citadel and fell down at Sosius's feet, who, without pitying him at all, upon the change of his condition, laughed at him beyond measure, and called him Antigona.* Yet did he not treat him like a woman, or let him go free, but put him into bonds, and kept him in custody.

3. But Herod's concern at present, now he had gotten his enemies under his power, was to restrain the zeal of his foreign auxiliaries; for the multitude of the strange people were very eager to see the temple, and what was sacred in the holy house itself; but the king endeavoured to restrain them, partly by his exhortations, partly by his threatenings, nay, partly by force, as thinking the victory worse than a defeat to him, if anything that ought not to be seen were seen by them. He also forbade, at the same

time, the spoiling of the city, asking Sosius in the most earnest manner, whether the Romans, by thus emptying the city of money and men, had a mind to leave him king of a desert,—and told him, that he judged the dominion of the habitable earth too small a compensation for the slaughter of so many citizens. And when Sosius said, that it was but just to allow the soldiers this plunder, as a reward for what they had suffered during the siege, Herod made answer, that he would give every one of the soldiers a reward out of his own money. So he purchased the deliverance of his country, and performed his promises to them, and made presents after a magnificent manner to each soldier, and proportionably to their commanders, and with a most royal bounty to Sosius himself, whereby nobody went away but in a wealthy condition. Hereupon Sosius dedicated a crown of gold to God, and then went away from Jerusalem, leading Antigonus away in bonds to Antony; then did the axe bring him to his end, who still had a fond desire of life, and some frigid hopes of it to the last; but by his cowardly behaviour well deserved to die by it.

4. Hereupon king Herod distinguished the multitude that was in the city; and for those that were of his side, he made them still more his friends by the honours he conferred on them; but for those of Antigonus's party, he slew them: and as his money ran low, he turned all the ornaments he had into money, and sent it to Antony, and to those about him. Yet could he not hereby purchase an exemption from all sufferings; for Antony was now bewitched by his love to Cleopatra, and was entirely conquered by her charms. Now Cleopatra had put to death all her kindred, till no one near her in blood remained alive, and after that she fell a slaying those no way related to her. So she calumniated the principal men among the Syrians to Antony, and persuaded him to have them slain, that so she might easily gain to be mistress of what they had; nay, she extended her avaricious humour to the Jews and Arabians, and secretly laboured to have Herod and Malichus, the kings of both those nations, slain by his order.

5. Now as to these her injunctions to Antony, he complied in part; for though he esteemed it too abominable a thing to kill such good and great kings, yet was he thereby alienated from the friendship he had for them. He also took away a great deal of their country; nay even the plantation of palm-trees at Jericho, where also grows the balsam-tree, and bestowed them upon her; as also all the cities on this side the river Eleutherus, Tyre and Sidon expected. And when she was become mistress of these, and had conducted Antony in his expedition against the Parthians, as far as Euphrates, she came by Apamia and Damascus into Judea; and there did Herod pacify her indignation at him by large presents. He also hired of her those places which had been torn away from his kingdom, at the yearly rent of two hundred talents. He conducted her also as far as Pelusium, and paid her all the respect possible. Now it was not long after this that Antony was come back from Parthia, and led with him Artabazes, Tigrane's son, captive, as a present to Cleopatra; for this Parthian was presently given her, with his money, and all the prey that was taken with him.

---

* This is a woman, not a man.

CHAPTER XIX

HOW ANTONY, AT THE PERSUASION OF CLEOPATRA, SENT HEROD TO FIGHT AGAINST THE ARABIANS;

AND HOW, AFTER SEVERAL BATTLES,. HE AT LENGTH GOT THE VICTORY. AS ALSO CONCERNING A GREAT EARTHQUAKE

1. Now when the war about Actium was begun, Herod prepared to come to the assistance of Antony, as being already freed from his troubles in Judea, and having gained Hyrcania, which was a place that was held by Antigonus's sister. However, he was cunningly hindered from partaking of the hazards that Antony went through by Cleopatra; for since, as we have already noted, she had laid a plot against the kings [of Judea and Arabia,] she prevailed with Antony to commit the war against the Arabians to Herod; that so, if he got the better, she might become mistress of Arabia, or, if he were worsted, of Judea; and that she might destroy one of those kings by the other.

2. However, this contrivance tended to the advantage of Herod; for at the very first he took hostages from the enemy, and got together a great body of horse, and ordered them to march against them about Diospolis; and he conquered that army, although it fought resolutely against him. After which defeat, the Arabians were in great motion, and assembled themselves together at Kanatha, a city of Cœlesyria, in a vast multitude, and waited for the Jews. And when Herod was come thither, he tried to manage this war with particular prudence, and gave orders that they should build a wall about their camp; yet did not the multitude comply with those orders, but were so emboldened by their foregoing victory, that they presently attacked the Arabians, and beat them at the first onset, and then pursued them; yet were there snares laid for Herod in that pursuit; while Athenio, who was one of Cleopatra's generals, and always an antagonist to Herod, sent out of Kanatha the men of that country against him; for upon this fresh onset, the Arabians took courage, and returned back, and both joined their numerous forces about stony places, that were hard to be gone over, and there put Herod's men to the rout, and made a great slaughter of them; but those that escaped out of the battle fled to Ormiza, where the Arabians surrounded their camp and took it, with all the men in it.

3. In a little time after this calamity, Herod came to bring them succours; but he came too late. Now the occasion of that blow was this, that the officers would not obey his orders; for had not the fight begun so suddenly, Athenio had not found a proper season for the snares he laid for Herod; however, he was even with the Arabians afterward, and overran their country, and did them more harm than their single victory could compensate. But as he was avenging himself on his enemies there fell upon him another providential calamity; for in the seventh* year of his reign, when the war about Actium was at the height, at the beginning of the spring, the earth was shaken, and destroyed an immense number of cattle, and thirty thousand men; but the army received no harm, because it lay in the open air. In the meantime, the fame of this earthquake elevated the Arabians to greater courage, and this by augmenting it to a fabulous height, as is constantly the case in melancholy

accidents, and pretending that all Judea was overthrown. Upon this supposal, therefore, that they could easily get a land that was destitute of inhabitants into their power, they first sacrificed those ambassadors who were come to them from the Jews, and then marched into Judea immediately. Now the Jewish nation were affrighted at this invasion, and quite dispirited at the greatness of their calamities one after another; whom yet Herod got together, and endeavoured to encourage to defend themselves by the following speech which he made to them:—

4. "The present dread you are under, seems to me to have seized upon you very unseasonably. It is true, you might be justly dismayed at the providential chastisement which hath befallen you; but to suffer yourselves to be equally terrified at the invasion of men, is unmanly. As for myself, I am so far from being affrighted at our enemies after this earthquake, that I imagine that God hath thereby laid a bait for the Arabians, that we may be avenged on them; for their present invasion proceeds more from our accidental misfortunes, than that they have any great dependence on their weapons, or their own fitness for action. Now that hope which depends not on men's own power, but on other's ill success, is a very ticklish thing; for there is no certainty among men, either in their bad or good fortunes; but we may easily observe, that fortune is mutable, and goes from one side to another; and this you may readily learn from examples among yourselves; for when you were once victors in the former fight, your enemies overcame you at last; and very likely it will now happen so, that these who think themselves sure of beating you, will themselves be beaten; for when men are very confident, they are not upon their guard, while fear teaches men to act with caution; insomuch, that I venture to prove from your very timorousness, that you ought to take courage; for when you were more bold than you ought to have been, and than I would have had you, and marched on, Athenio's treachery took place; but your present slowness and seeming dejection of mind, is to me a pledge and assurance of victory; and indeed it is proper beforehand to be thus provident: but when we come to action, we ought to erect our minds, and to make our enemies, be they ever so wicked, believe, that neither any human, no, nor any providential misfortune can ever depress the courage of the Jews while they are alive; nor will any of them ever overlook an Arabian, or suffer such a one to become lord of his good things, whom he has in a manner taken captive, and that many times also:—and do not disturb yourselves at the quaking of inanimate creatures, nor do not imagine that this earthquake is a sign of another calamity; for such affections of the elements are according to the course of nature; nor does it import anything further to men, than what mischief it does immediately of itself. Perhaps, there may come some short sign beforehand in the case of pestilences, and famines, and earthquakes; but these calamities themselves have their force limited by themselves, [without foreboding any other calamity;] and indeed what greater mischief can the war, though it should be a violent one, do to us, than the earthquake hath done? Nay, there is a signal of your enemies' destruction visible, and that a very great one also; and this is not a natural one, nor deprived from the hands of foreigners neither, but it is this, that they have barbarously murdered our ambassadors, contrary to the common law of mankind; and they have destroyed so many, as if they esteemed them sacrifices for

* This seventh year of the reign of Herod, with the great earthquake in the beginning of the same spring, which are here fully implied to be not much before the fight at Actium, and which is known to have been in the beginning of September, in the 31st year before the Christian era, determines the chronology of Josephus as to the reign of Herod—viz., that he began in the year 37.

God, in relation to this war; but they will not avoid his great eye, nor his invincible right hand; and we shall be revenged on them presently in case we still retain any of the courage of our forefathers, and rise up boldly to punish these covenant-breakers. Let every one therefore go on and fight, not so much for his wife or his children, or for the danger his country is in, as for these ambassadors of ours; those dead ambassadors will conduct this war of ours better than we ourselves who are alive; and if you will be ruled by me, I will myself go before you into danger; for you know this well enough, that your courage is irresistible, unless you hurt yourselves by acting rashly."*

5. When Herod had encouraged them by this speech, and he saw with what alacrity they went, he offered sacrifice to God; and after that sacrifice, he passed over the river Jordan with his army, and pitched his camp about Philadelphia, near the enemy, and about a fortification that lay between them. He then shot at them at a distance, and was desirous to come to an engagement presently; for some of them had been sent beforehand to seize upon that fortification: but the king sent some who immediately beat them out of the fortification, while he himself went in the fore-front of the army, which he put in battle array every day, and invited the Arabians to fight; but as none of them came out of their camp, for they were in a terrible fright, and their general, Elthemus, was not able to say a word for fear,—so Herod came upon them, and pulled their fortification to pieces, by which means they were compelled to come out to fight, which they did in disorder, and so that the horsemen and footmen were mixed together. They were indeed superior to the Jews in number, but inferior in their alacrity, although they were obliged to expose themselves to danger by their very despair of victory.

6. Now while they made opposition, they had not a great number slain; but as soon as they turned their backs, a great many were trodden to pieces by the Jews, and a great many by themselves, and so perished, till five thousand were fallen down dead in their flight, while the rest of the multitude prevented their immediate death by crowding into the fortification. Herod encompassed these around, and besieged them; and while they were ready to be taken by their enemies in arms, they had another additional distress upon them, which was thirst and want of water; for the king was above hearkening to their ambassadors; and when they offered five hundred talents, as the price of their redemption, he pressed still harder upon them; and as they were burnt up by their thirst, they came out and voluntarily delivered themselves up by multitudes to the Jews, till in five days' time four thousand of them were put into bonds; and on the sixth day the multitude that were left despaired of saving themselves, and came out to fight: with these Herod fought, and slew again about seven thousand, insomuch that he punished Arabia so severely, and so far extinguished the spirits of the men, that he was chosen by the nation for their ruler.

---

* This speech of Herod is set down twice by Josephus, to the very same purpose, but by no means in the same words; whence it appears that the sense was Herod's, but the composition Josephus's.

CHAPTER XX

HEROD IS CONFIRMED IN HIS KINGDOM BY CÆSAR, AND CULTIVATES A FRIENDSHIP WITH THE EMPEROR BY MAGNIFICENT PRESENTS; WHILE CÆSAR RETURNS HIS KINDNESS BY BESTOWING ON HIM THAT PART OF HIS KINGDOM WHICH HAD BEEN TAKEN AWAY FROM IT BY CLEOPATRA, WITH THE ADDITION OF ZENODORUS'S COUNTRY ALSO

1. BUT now Herod was under immediate concern about a most important affair, on account of his friendship with Antony, who was already overcome at Actium by Cæsar, yet he was more afraid than hurt; for Cæsar did not think he had quite undone Antony, while Herod continued his assistance to him. However, the king resolved to expose himself to dangers: accordingly he sailed to Rhodes, where Cæsar then abode, and came to him without his diadem, and in the habit and appearance of a private person, but in his behaviour as a king. So he concealed nothing of the truth, but spake thus before his face:—"O Cæsar, as I was made king of the Jews by Antony, so do I profess I have used my royal authority in the best manner, and entirely for his advantage; nor will I conceal this further, that thou hadst certainly found me in arms, and an inseparable companion of his, had not the Arabians hindered me. However, I sent him as many auxiliaries as I was able, and many ten thousand [cori] of corn. Nay, indeed, I did not desert my benefactor after the blow that was given him at Actium; but I gave him the best advice I was able, when I was no longer able to assist him in the war; and I told him there was but one way of recovering his affairs, and that was to kill Cleopatra; and I promised him, that if she were once dead, I would afford him money and walls for his security, with an army and myself to assist him in his war against thee: but his affection for Cleopatra stopped his ears, as did God himself also, who hath bestowed the government on thee. I own myself also to be overcome together with him; and with his last fortune I have laid aside my diadem, and am come hither to thee, having my hopes of safety in thy virtue; and I desire that thou wilt first consider how faithful a friend, and not whose friend, I have been."

2. Cæsar replied to him thus:—"Nay, thou shalt not only be in safety, but shalt be a king, and that more firmly than thou wast before; for thou art worthy to reign over a great many subjects, by reason of the fastness of thy friendship; and do thou endeavour to be equally constant in thy friendship to me upon my good success, which is what I depend upon from the generosity of thy disposition. However, Antony hath done well in preferring Cleopatra to thee; for by this means we have gained thee by her madness, and thus thou hast begun to be my friend before I began to be thine; on which account Quintus Didius hath written to me that thou sentest him assistance against the gladiators. I do therefore assure thee that I will confirm the kingdom to thee by a decree; I shall also endeavour to do thee some further kindness hereafter, that thou mayest find no loss in the want of Antony."

3. When Cæsar had spoken such obliging things to the king, and had put the diadem again about his head, he proclaimed what he had bestowed on him by a decree, in which he enlarged in the commendation of the man after a magnificent manner. Whereupon Herod obliged him

to be kind to him by the presents he gave him, and he desired him to forgive Alexander, one of Antony's friends, who was become a supplicant to him. But Cæsar's anger against him prevailed, and he complained of the many and very great offences the man whom he petitioned for had been guilty of; and by that means he rejected his petition. After this, Cæsar went for Egypt through Syria, when Herod received him with royal and rich entertainments; and then did he first of all ride along with Cæsar, as he was reviewing his army about Ptolemais, and feasted him with all his friends, and then distributed among the rest of the army what was necessary to feast them withal. He also made a plentiful provision of water for them, when they were to march as far as Pelusium, through a dry country, which he did also in like manner on their return thence; nor were there any necessaries wanting to that army. It was therefore the opinion, both of Cæsar and of his soldiers, that Herod's kingdom was too small for those generous presents he made them; for which reason, when Cæsar was come into Egypt, and Cleopatra and Antony were dead, he did not only bestow other marks of honour upon him, but made an addition to his kingdom, by giving him not only the country which had been taken from him by Cleopatra, but, besides that, Gadara, and Hippos, and Samaria; and, moreover, of the maritime cities, Gaza, and Anthedon, and Joppa, and Strato's Tower. He, also made a present of four hundred Galls [Galatians] as a guard for his body, which they had been to Cleopatra before. Nor did anything so strongly induce Cæsar to make these presents as the generosity of him that received them.

4. Moreover, after the first games at Actium, he added to his kingdom both the region called Trachonitis, and what lay in its neighbourhood, Batanea, and the country of Auranitis; and that on the following occasion:—Zenodorus, who had hired the house of Lysanias, had all along sent robbers out of Trachonitis among the Damascens; who thereupon had recourse to Varro, the president of Syria, and desired of him that he would represent the calamity they were in to Cæsar. When Cæsar was acquainted with it, he sent back orders that this nest of robbers should be destroyed. Varro therefore made an expedition against them, and cleared the land of those men, and took it away from Zenodorus. Cæsar did also afterward bestow it on Herod, that it might not again become a receptacle for those robbers that had come against Damascus. He also made him a procurator of all Syria, and this on the tenth year afterward, when he came again into that province; and this was so established, that the other procurators could not do anything in the administration without his advice: but when Zenodorus was dead, Cæsar bestowed on him all that land which lay between Trachonitis and Galilee. Yet, what was still of more consequence to Herod, he was beloved by Cæsar next after Agrippa, and by Agrippa next after Cæsar; whence he arrived at a very great degree of felicity; yet did the greatness of his soul exceed it; and the main part of his magnanimity was extended to the promotion of piety.

CHAPTER XXI

OF THE [TEMPLE AND] CITIES THAT WERE BUILT BY HEROD, AND ERECTED FROM THE VERY FOUNDATIONS; AS ALSO OF THOSE OTHER EDIFICES

THAT WERE ERECTED BY HIM: AND WHAT MAGNIFICENCE HE SHEWED TO FOREIGNERS; AND HOW FORTUNE WAS IN ALL THINGS FAVOURABLE TO HIM

1. ACCORDINGLY, in the fifteenth year of his reign, Herod rebuilt the temple, and encompassed a piece of land about it with a wall; which land was twice as large as that before enclosed. The expenses he laid out upon it were vastly large also, and the riches about it were unspeakable. A sign of which you have in the great cloisters that were erected about the temple and the citadel* which were on its north side. The cloisters he built from the foundation, but the citadel he repaired at a vast expense; nor was it other than a royal palace, which he called Antonia, in honour of Antony. He also built himself a palace in the upper city, containing two very large and most beautiful apartments; to which the holy house itself could not be compared [in largeness.] The one apartment he named Cæsareum, and the other Agrippium, from his [two great] friends.

2. Yet did he not preserve their memory by particular buildings only, with their names given them, but his generosity went as far as entire cities; for when he had built a most beautiful wall round a country in Samaria, twenty furlongs long, and had brought six thousand inhabitants into it, and had allotted it a most fruitful piece of land, and in the midst of this city, thus built, had erected a very large temple to Cæsar, and had laid round about it a portion of sacred land of three furlongs and a half, he called the city Sebaste, from Sebastus, or Augustus, and settled the affairs of the city after a most regular manner.

3. And when Cæsar had further bestowed upon him another additional country, he built there also a temple of white marble, hard by the fountains of Jordan: the place is called Panium, where is a top of a mountain that is raised to an immense height, and at its side, beneath, or at its bottom, a dark cave opens itself; within which there is a horrible precipice, that descends abruptly to a vast depth: it contains a mighty quantity of water, which is immovable; and when anybody lets down anything to measure the depth of the earth beneath the water, no length of cord is sufficient to reach it. Now the fountains of Jordan rise at the roots of this cavity outwardly; and, as some think, this is the utmost origin of Jordan: but we shall speak of that matter more accurately in our following history.

4. But the king erected other places at Jericho also, between the citadel Cypros and the former palace, such as were better and more useful than the former for travellers, and named them from the same friends of his. To say all at once, there was not any place of his kingdom fit for the purpose, that was permitted to be without somewhat that was for Cæsar's honour; and when he had filled his own country with temples, he poured out the like plentiful marks of his esteem into his province, and built many cities which he called Cesareas.

5. And when he observed that there was a city by the sea-side that was much decayed (its name

---

* This fort was built, as is supposed, by John Hyrcanus, and called "Baris," the Tower or Citadel. It was afterwards rebuilt, with great improvements, by Herod, under the government of Antonius, and was named from him "the Tower of Antonia;" and about the time when Herod rebuilt the temple, he seems to have put his last hand to it. It lay on the north-west side of the temple, and was a quarter as large.

was Strato's Tower) but that the place, by the happiness of its situation, was capable of great improvements from his liberality, he rebuilt it all with white stone, and adorned it with several most splendid palaces, wherein he especially demonstrated his magnanimity; for the case was this, that all the sea-shore between Dora and Joppa, in the middle, between which this city is situated, had no good haven, insomuch that every one that sailed from Phœnicia for Egypt was obliged to lie in the stormy sea, by reason of the south winds that threatened them; which wind, if it blew but a little fresh, such vast waves are raised, and dash upon the rocks, that upon their retreat, the sea is in a great ferment for a long way. But the king, by the expenses he was at, and the liberal disposal of them, overcame nature, and built a haven larger than was the Pyrecum [at Athens;] and in the inner retirements of the water he built another deep station [for the ships also.]

6. Now, although the place where he built was greatly opposite to his purposes, yet did he so fully struggle with that difficulty, that the firmness of his building could not easily be conquered by the sea; and the beauty and the ornament of the works were such, as though he had not had any difficulty in the operation; for when he had measured out as large a space as we have before mentioned, he let down stones into twenty-fathom water, the greatest part of which were fifty feet in length, and nine in depth, and ten in breadth, and some still larger. But when the haven was filled up to that depth, he enlarged that wall which was thus already extant above the sea, till it was two hundred feet wide; one hundred of which had buildings before it, in order to break the force of the waves, whence it was called Procumatia, or the first breaker of the waves; but the rest of the space was under a stone wall that ran round it. On this wall were large towers, the principal and most beautiful of which was called Drusium, from Drusus, who was son-in-law to Cæsar.

7. There were also a great number of arches, where the mariners dwelt; and all the places before them round about was a large valley, or walk, for a quay [or landing-place] to those that came on shore; but the entrance was on the north, because the north wind was the most gentle of all the winds. At the mouth of the haven were on each side three great Colossi, supported by pillars, where those Colossi that are on your left hand as you sail into the port, are supported by a solid tower; but those on the right hand are supported by two upright stones joined together, which stones were larger than that tower which was on the other side of the entrance. Now there were continual edifices joined to the haven, which were also themselves of white stone; and to this haven did the narrow streets of the city lead, and were built at equal distances one from another. And over against the mouth of the haven, upon an elevation, there was a temple for Cæsar, which was excellent both for beauty and largeness; and therein was a Colossus of Cæsar, not less than that of Jupiter Olympius, which it was made to resemble. The other Colossus of Rome was equal to that of Juno at Argos. So he dedicated the city to the province, and the haven to the sailors there; but the honour of the building he ascribed to Cæsar,* and named it Cesarea accordingly.

8. He also built the other edifices, the amphitheatre, and theatre, and market-place, in a manner agreeable to that denomination; and appointed games every fifth year, and called them in like manner, Cæsar's Games; and he first himself proposed the largest prizes upon the hundred and ninety-second Olympiad; in which not only the victors themselves, but these that came next to them, and even those that came in the third place, were partakers of his royal bounty. He also rebuilt Anthedon, a city that lay on the coast, and had been demolished in the wars, and named it Agrippeum. Moreover, he had so very great a kindness for his friend Agrippa, that he had his name engraved upon that gate which he had himself erected in the temple.

9. Herod was also a lover of his father, if any other person ever was so; for he made a monument for his father, even that city which he built in the finest plain that was in his kingdom, and which had rivers and trees in abundance, and named it Antipatris. He also built a wall about a citadel that lay above Jericho, and was a very strong and very fine building, and dedicated it to his mother, and called it Cypros. Moreover, he dedicated a tower that was at Jerusalem, and called it by the name of his brother Phasaelus, whose structure, largeness, and magnificence, we shall describe hereafter. He also built another city in the valley that leads northward from Jericho, and named it Phasaelus.

10. And as he transmitted to eternity his family and friends, so did he not neglect a memorial for himself, but built a fortress upon a mountain towards Arabia, and named it from himself Herodium;† and he called that hill that was of the shape of a women's breast, and was sixty furlongs distant from Jerusalem, by the same name. He also bestowed much curious art upon it with great ambition, and built round towers all about the top of it, and filled up the remaining space with the most costly palaces round about, insomuch that not only the sight of the inner apartments was splendid, but great wealth was laid out on the outward walls, and partitions, and roofs also. Besides this, he brought a mighty quantity of water from a great distance, and at vast charges, and raised an ascent to it of two hundred steps of the whitest marble, for the hill was itself moderately high, and entirely factitious. He also built other palaces about the roots of the hill, sufficient to receive the furniture that was put into them, with his friends also, insomuch that on account of its containing all necessaries, the fortress might seem to be a city, but, by the bounds it had, a palace only.

11. And when he had built so much, he shewed the greatness of his soul to no small number of foreign cities. He built palaces for exercise at Tripoli, and Damascus, and Ptolemais; he built a wall about Byblus, as also large rooms, and cloisters, and temples, and marketplaces, at Berytus and Tyre, with theatres at Sidon and Damascus. He also built aqueducts for those Laodiceans who lived by the sea-side; and for those of Ascalon he built baths and costly fountains, as also cloisters round a court, that were admirable both for their workmanship and largeness. Moreover, he dedicated groves

---

* These buildings of cities by the name of Cæsar, and institution of solemn games in honour of Augustus Cæsar, related of Herod by Josephus, the Roman his-

torians attest to as things then frequent in the province of that empire.

† There were two cities, or citadels, called Herodium, in Judea; one of them was 200, and the other 60 furlongs distant from Jerusalem.

and meadows to some people; nay, not a few cities there were who had lands of his donation, as if they were parts of his own kingdom. He also bestowed annual revenues, and those for ever also, on the settlements for exercises, and appointed for them, as well as for the people of Cos, that such rewards should never be wanting. He also gave corn to all such as wanted it, and conferred upon Rhodes large sums of money for building ships; and this he did in many places, and frequently also. And when Apollo's temple had been burnt down, he rebuilt it at his own charges, after a better manner than it was before. What need I speak of the presents he made to the Lycians and Samnians! or of his great liberality through all Ionia! and that according to every body's wants of them. And are not the Athenians, and Lacedemonians, and Nicopolitans, and that Pergamus which is in Mysia, full of donations that Herod presented them withal! And as for that large open place belonging to Antioch in Syria, did not he pave it with polished marble, though it were twenty furlongs long! and this when it was shunned by all men before, because it was full of dirt and filthiness; when he besides adorned the same place with a cloister of the same length.

12. It is true a man may say, these were favours peculiar to those particular places on which he bestowed his benefits; but then what favours he bestowed on the Eleans was a donation not only in common to all Greece, but to all the habitable earth, as far as the glory of the Olympic games reached; for when he perceived that they were come to nothing, for want of money, and that the only remains of ancient Greece were in a manner gone, he not only became one of the combatants in that return of the fifth year games, which in his sailing to Rome he happened to be present at, but he settled upon them revenues of money for perpetuity, insomuch that his memorial as a combatant there can never fail. It would be an infinite task if I should go over his payments of people's debts, or tributes, for them, as he eased the people of Phasaelus, of Batanea, and of the small cities about Cilicia, of those annual pensions they before paid. However, the fear he was in much disturbed the greatness of his soul, lest he should be exposed to envy, or seem to hunt after greater things than he ought, while he bestowed more liberal gifts upon these cities than did their owners themselves.

13. Now Herod had a body suited to his soul, and was ever a most excellent hunter, where he generally had good success, by means of his great skill in riding horses; for in one day he caught forty wild beasts :* that country breeds also bears; and the greatest part of it is replenished with stags and wild asses. He was also such a warrior as could not be withstood : many men therefore there are who have stood amazed at his readiness in his exercises, when they saw him throw the javelin directly forward, and shoot the arrow upon the mark; and then, besides those performances of his depending on his own strength of mind and body, fortune was also very favourable to him, for he seldom failed of success in his wars; and when he failed, he was not himself the occasion of such failings, but he either was betrayed by some, or the rashness of his own soldiers procured his defeat.

---

* Here seems to be a small defect in the copies, which describe the wild beasts which were hunted in a certain country by Herod, without naming any such country at all.

CHAPTER XXII

THE MURDER OF ARISTOBULUS AND HYRCANUS, THE HIGH PRIESTS; AS ALSO OF MARIAMNE THE QUEEN

1. HOWEVER, fortune was avenged on Herod in his external great successes, by raising him up domestic troubles; and he began to have wild disorders in his family, on account of his wife, of whom he was so very fond; for when he came to the government, he sent away her whom he had before married when he was a private person, and who was born at Jerusalem, whose name was Doris, and married Mariamne, the daughter of Alexander, the son of Aristobulus; on whose account disturbances arose in his family, and that in part very soon, but chiefly after his return from Rome; for, first of all, he expelled Antipater the son of Doris, for the sake of his sons by Mariamne, out of the city, and permitted him to come thither at no other times than at the festivals. After this he slew his wife's grandfather, Hyrcanus, when he was returned out of Parthia to him, under this pretence, that he suspected him of plotting against him. Now this Hyrcanus had been carried captive to Barzapharnes, when he overran Syria; but those of his own country beyond Euphrates were desirous he would stay with them, and this out of the commiseration they had for his condition; and had he complied with their desires, when they exhorted him not to go over the river to Herod, he had not perished : but the marriage of his granddaughter [to Herod] was his temptation; for as he relied upon him, and was over-fond of his own country, he came back to it. Herod's provocation was this :—not that Hyrcanus made an attempt to gain the kingdom, but that it was fitter for him to be their king than for Herod.

2. Now of the five children which Herod had by Mariamne, two of them were daughters, and three were sons; and the youngest of these sons was educated at Rome, and there died; but the two eldest he treated as those of royal blood, on account of the nobility of their mother, and because they were not born till he was king; but then what was stronger than all this, was the love that he bare to Mariamne, and which inflamed him every day to a great degree, and so far conspired with the other motives that he felt no other troubles, on account of her he loved so entirely; but Mariamne's hatred to him was not inferior to his love to her. She had indeed but too just a cause of indignation, from what he had done, while her boldness proceeded from his affection to her; so she openly reproached him with what he had done to her grandfather Hyrcanus, and to her brother Aristobulus, for he had not spared this Aristobulus, though he were but a child; for when he had given him the high priesthood at the age of seventeen, he slew him quickly after he had conferred that dignity upon him; but when Aristobulus had put on the holy vestments, and had approached to the altar at a festival, the multitude, in great crowds, fell into tears; whereupon the child was sent by night to Jericho, and was there dipped by the Galls, at Herod's command, in a pool till he was drowned.

3. For these reasons Mariamne reproached Herod, and his sister and mother, after a most contumelious manner, while he was dumb on account of his affection for her; yet had the women great indignation at her, and raised a

calumny against her, that she was false to his bed : which thing they thought most likely to move Herod to anger. They also contrived to have many other circumstances believed, in order to make the thing more credible, and accused her of having sent her picture into Egypt to Antony, and that her lust was so extravagant, as to have thus shewn herself, though she was absent, to a man that ran mad after women, and to a man that had it in his power to use violence to her. This charge fell like a thunderbolt upon Herod, and put him into disorder ; and that especially, because his love to her occasioned him to be jealous, and because he considered with himself that Cleopatra was a shrewd woman, and that on her account Lysanias the king was taken off as well as Malichus the Arabian, for his fear did not only extend to the dissolving of his marriage, but to the danger of his life.

4. When therefore he was about to take a journey abroad, he committed his wife to Joseph, his sister Salome's husband, as to one who would be faithful to him, and bare him good-will on account of their kindred : he also gave him a secret injunction, that if Antony slew him, he should slay her ; but Joseph, without any ill design, and only in order to demonstrate the king's love to his wife, how he could not bear to think of being separated from her, even by death itself, discovered of this grand secret to her ; upon which, when Herod was come back, and as they talked together, and he confirmed his love to her by many oaths, and assured her that he had never such an affection for any other woman as he had for her,—" Yes," says she, " thou didst, to be sure, demonstrate thy love to me by the injunctions thou gavest Joseph, when thou commandedst him to kill me." *

5. When he heard that this grand secret was discovered, he was like a distracted man, and said, that Joseph would never have disclosed that injunction of his unless he had debauched her. His passion also made him stark mad, and leaping out of his bed, he ran about the palace after a wild manner ; at which time his sister Salome took the opportunity also to blast her reputation, and confirmed his suspicion about Joseph ; whereupon, out of his ungovernable jealousy and rage, he commanded both of them to be slain immediately ; but as soon as ever his passion was over, he repented of what he had done, and as soon as his anger was worn off, his affections were kindled again ; and indeed the flame of his desires for her was so ardent, that he could not think she was dead, but would appear, under his disorders, to speak to her as if she was still alive, till he were better instructed by time, when his grief and trouble, now she was dead, appeared as great as his affection had been for her while she was living.

CHAPTER XXIII

CALUMNIES AGAINST THE SONS OF MARIAMNE; ANTIPATER IS PREFERRED BEFORE THEM ; THEY ARE ACCUSED BEFORE CÆSAR, AND HEROD IS RECONCILED TO THEM

1. Now Mariamne's sons were heirs to that

---

* Here is either a defect or a great mistake ; for Mariamne did not now reproach Herod with this his first injunction to Joseph to kill her, if he himself were slain by Antony, but that he had given the like command a second time to Soemus also, when he was afraid of being slain by Augustus.

hatred which had been borne their mother ; and when they considered the greatness of Herod's crime towards her, they were suspicious of him as of an enemy of theirs ; and this first while they were educated at Rome, but still more when they were returned to Judea. This temper of theirs increased upon them as they grew up to be men ; and when they were come to an age fit for marriage, the one of them married their aunt Salome's daughter, which Salome had been the accuser of their mother ; the other married the daughter of Archelaus, king of Cappadocia. And now they used boldness in speaking, as well as bore hatred in their minds. Now those that calumniated them took a handle from such their boldness, and certain of them spake now more plainly to the king, that there were treacherous designs laid against him by both his sons ; and he that was son-in-law to Archelaus, relying upon his father-in-law, was preparing to fly away, in order to accuse Herod before Cæsar ; and when Herod's head had been long enough filled with these calumnies, he brought Antipater, whom he had by Doris, into favour again, as a defence to him against his other sons, and began all the ways he possibly could to prefer him before them.

2. But these sons were not able to bear this change in their affairs ; for when they saw him that was born of a mother of no family, the nobility of their birth made them unable to contain their indignation ; but whensoever they were uneasy, they shewed the anger they had at it ; and as these sons did day after day improve in that their anger, Antipater already exercised all his own abilities, which were very great, in flattering his father, and in contriving many sorts of calumnies against his brethren, while he told some stories of them himself, and put it upon other proper persons to raise other stories against them ; till at length he entirely cut his brethren off from all hopes of succeeding to the kingdom ; for he was already publicly put into his father's will as his successor. Accordingly he was sent with royal ornaments, and other marks of royalty, to Cæsar, excepting the diadem. He was also able in time to introduce his mother again into Mariamne's bed. The two sorts of weapons he made use of against his brethren, were flattery and calumny, whereby he brought matters privately to such a pass, that the king had thoughts of putting his sons to death.

3. So the father drew Alexander as far as Rome, and charged him with an attempt of poisoning him, before Cæsar. Alexander could hardly speak for lamentation ; but having a judge that was more skilful than Antipater, and more wise than Herod, he modestly avoided laying any imputation upon his father, but with great strength of reason confuted the calumnies laid against him ; and when he had demonstrated the innocency of his brother, who was in the like danger with himself, he at last bewailed the craft of Antipater, and the disgrace they were under. He was enabled also to justify himself, not only by a clear conscience, which he carried with him, but by his eloquence ; for he was a shrewd man in making speeches. And upon his saying at last, that if his father objected this crime to them, it was in his power to put them to death, he made all the audience weep ; and he brought Cæsar to that pass, as to reject the accusations, and to reconcile their father to them immediately. But the conditions of this reconciliation were these, that they should in all things be obedient to their father, and that he should have power to leave the kingdom to which of them he pleased.

4. After this the king came back from Rome, and seemed to have forgiven his sons upon these accusations; but still so, that he was not without his suspicions of them. They were followed by Antipater, who was the fountain-head of those accusations; yet did not he openly discover his hatred to them, as revering him that had reconciled them. But as Herod sailed by Cilicia, he touched at Eleusa,* where Archelaus treated them in the most obliging manner, and gave him thanks for the deliverance of his son-in-law, and was much pleased at their reconciliation; and this the more, because he had formerly written to his friends at Rome that they should be assisting to Alexander at his trial. So he conducted Herod as far as Zaphyrium, and made him presents to the value of thirty talents.

5. Now when Herod was come to Jerusalem, he gathered the people together, and presented to them his three sons, and gave them an apologetic account of his absence, and thanked God greatly, and thanked Cæsar greatly also, for settling his house when it was under disturbances, and had procured concord among his sons, which was of greater consequence than the kingdom itself,—"and which I will render still more firm; for Cæsar hath put into my power to dispose of the government, and to appoint my successor. Accordingly, in way of requital for his kindness, and in order to provide for mine own advantage, I do declare that these three sons of mine shall be kings. And, in the first place, I pray for the approbation of God to what I am about; and, in the next place, I desire your approbation also. The age of one of them, and the nobility of the other two, shall procure them the succession. Nay, indeed, my kingdom is so large, that it may be sufficient for more kings. Now do you keep those in their places whom Cæsar hath joined and their father hath appointed; and do not you pay undue or unequal respects to them, but to every one according to the prerogative of their births; for he that pays such respects unduly, will thereby not make him that is honoured beyond what his age requires, so joyful as he will make him that is dishonoured sorrowful. As for the kindred and friends that are to converse with them, I will appoint them to each of them, and will so constitute them, that they may be securities for their concord; as well knowing that the ill tempers of those with whom they converse, will produce quarrels and contentions among them; but that, if these with whom they converse be of good tempers, they will preserve their natural affections for one another. But still I desire, that not these only, but all the captains of my army have for the present their hopes placed on me alone; for I do not give away my kingdom to these my sons, but give them royal honours only; whereby it will come to pass that they will enjoy the sweet parts of the government as rulers themselves, but that the burden of administration will rest upon myself whether I will or not. And let every one consider what age I am of; how I have conducted my life, and what piety I have exercised; for my age is not so great, that men may soon expect the end of my life; nor have I indulged such a luxurious way of living as cuts men off when they are young; and we have been so religious towards God, that we [have reason to hope we] may arrive at a very

great age. But for such as cultivate a friendship with my sons, so as to aim at my destruction, they shall be punished by me on their account. I am not one who envy my own children, and therefore forbid men to pay them great respect; but I know that such [extravagant] respects are the way to make them insolent. And if every one that comes near them does but revolve this in his mind, that if he proves a good man he shall receive a reward from me, but that if he prove seditious, his ill-intended complaisance shall get him nothing from him to whom it is shewn, I suppose they will all be of my side, that is, of my sons' side; for it will be for their advantage that I reign, and that I be at concord with them. But do you, O my good children, reflect upon the holiness of nature itself, by whose means natural affection is preserved, even among wild beasts; in the next place, reflect upon Cæsar, who hath made this reconciliation among us; and, in the third place, reflect upon me, who entreat you to do what I have power to command you,—continue brethren, I give you royal garments, and royal honours; and I pray to God to preserve what I have determined, in case you be at concord one with another." When the king had thus spoken, and had saluted every one of his sons after an obliging manner, he dismissed the multitude; some of whom gave their assent to what he said, and wished it might take effect accordingly; but for those who wished for a change of affairs, they pretended they did not so much as hear what he said.

CHAPTER XXIV

THE MALICE OF ANTIPATER AND DORIS. ALEXANDER IS VERY UNEASY ON GLAPHYRA'S ACCOUNT. HEROD PARDONS PHERORAS, WHOM HE SUSPECTED, AND SALOME, WHOM HE KNEW TO MAKE MISCHIEF AMONG THEM. HEROD'S EUNUCHS ARE TORTURED, AND ALEXANDER IS BOUND

1. BUT now the quarrel that was between them still accompanied these brethren when they parted, and the suspicions they had one of the other grew worse. Alexander and Aristobulus were much grieved that the privilege of the first-born was confirmed to Antipater; as was Antipater very angry at his brethren, that they were to succeed him. But then the last being of a disposition that was mutable and politic, he knew how to hold his tongue, and used a great deal of cunning, and thereby concealed the hatred he bore to them; while the former, depending on the nobility of their births, had everything upon their tongues which was in their minds. Many also there were who provoked them further, and many of their [seeming] friends insinuated themselves into their acquaintance, to spy out what they did. Now everything that was said by Alexander was presently brought to Antipater, and from Antipater it was brought to Herod with additions. Nor could the young man say anything in the simplicity of his heart, without giving offence, but what he said was still turned to calumny against him. And if he had been at any time a little free in his conversation, great imputations were forged from the smallest occasions. Antipater also was perpetually setting some to provoke him to speak, that the lies he raised of him might seem to have some foundation of truth; and if, among the many stories that were given out, but one

* That this island Eleusa, afterward called Sebaste, near Cilicia, had in it the royal palace of this Archelaus, king of Cappadocia, Strabo testifies. Stephanus of Byzantium also calls it "an island in Cilicia, which is now Sebaste."

of them could be proved true, that was supposed to imply the rest to be true also. And as to Antipater's friends, they were all either naturally so cautious in speaking, or had been so far bribed to conceal their thoughts, that nothing of these grand secrets got abroad by their means. Nor should one be mistaken if he called the life of Antipater a mystery of wickedness; for he either corrupted Alexander's acquaintance with money, or got into their favour by flatteries; by which two means he gained all his designs, and brought them to betray their master, and to steal away, and reveal what he either did or said. Thus did he act a part very cunningly in all points, and wrought himself a passage by his calumnies with the greatest shrewdness; while he put on a face as if he were a kind brother to Alexander and Aristobulus, but suborned other men to inform of what they did to Herod. And when anything was told against Alexander, he would come in and pretend, [to be of his side,] and would begin to contradict what was said; but would afterward contrive matters so privately, that the king should have an indignation at him. His general aim was this:—To lay a plot, and to make it be believed that Alexander lay in wait to kill his father; for nothing afforded so great a confirmation of those calumnies as did Antipater's apologies for him.

2. By these methods Herod was inflamed, and, as much as his natural affection to the young men did every day diminish, so much did it increase towards Antipater. The courtiers also inclined to the same conduct; some of their own accord, and others by the king's injunction, as particularly Ptolemy, the king's dearest friend, as also the king's brethren, and all his children; for Antipater was all in all: and what was the bitterest part of all to Alexander, Antipater's mother was also all in all: she was one that gave counsel against them, and was more harsh than a step-mother, and one that hated the queen's sons more than is usual to hate sons-in-law. All men did therefore already pay their respects to Antipater, in hopes of advantage; and it was the king's command which alienated everybody [from the brethren,] he having given this charge to his most intimate friends, that they should not come near, nor pay any regard, to Alexander, or to his friends. Herod was also become terrible, not only to his domestics about the court, but to his friends abroad; for Cæsar had given such a privilege to no other king as he had given to him, which was this:—that he might fetch back any one that fled from him, even out of a city that was not under his own jurisdiction. Now the young men were not acquainted with the calumnies raised against them; for which reason they could not guard themselves against them, but fell under them; for their father did not make any public complaints against either of them; though in a little time they perceived how things were, by his coldness to them, and by the great uneasiness he shewed upon anything that troubled him. Antipater had also made their uncle Pheroras to be their enemy, as well as their aunt Salome, while he was always talking with her as with a wife, and irritating her against them. Moreover, Alexander's wife, Glaphyra, augmented this hatred against them, by deriving her nobility and genealogy [from great persons,] and pretending that she was a lady superior to all others in that kingdom, as being derived by her father's side from Temenus, and by her mother's side from Darius, the son of Hystaspes. She also frequently reproached Herod's sister and

wives with the ignobility of their descent; and that they were every one chosen by him for their beauty, but not for their family. Now those wives of his were not a few; it being of old permitted to the Jews to marry many wives,* —and this king delighted in many; all whom hated Alexander, on account of Glaphyra's boasting and reproaches.

3. Nay, Aristobulus had raised a quarrel between himself and Salome, who was his mother-in-law, besides the anger she had conceived at Glaphyra's reproaches; for he perpetually upbraided his wife with the meanness of her family, and complained, that as he had married a woman of a low family, so had his brother Alexander married one of royal blood. At this Salome's daughter wept, and told it her with this addition, that Alexander threatened the mothers of his other brethren, that when he should come to the crown, he would make them weave with their maidens, and would make those brothers of his country schoolmasters; and break this jest upon them, that they had been very carefully instructed, to fit them for such an employment. Hereupon Salome could not contain her anger, but told all to Herod; nor could her testimony be suspected, since it was against her own son-in-law. There was also another calumny that ran abroad, and inflamed the king's mind; for he heard that these sons of his were perpetually speaking of their mother, and, among the lamentations for her, did not abstain from cursing him; and that when he made presents of any of Mariamne's garments to his later wives, these threatened, that in a little time, instead of royal garments, they would clothe them in no better than haircloth.

4. Now upon these accounts, though Herod was somewhat afraid of the young men's high spirit, yet did he not despair of reducing them to a better mind; but before he went to Rome, whither he was now going by sea, he called them to him, and partly threatened them a little, as a king; but for the main, he admonished them as a father, and exhorted them to love their brethren; and told them that he would pardon their former offences, if they would amend for the time to come. But they refuted the calumnies that had been raised of them, and said they were false, and alleged that their actions were sufficient for their vindication; and said withal, that he himself ought to shut his ears against such tales, and not to be too easy in believing them, for that there would never be wanting those that would tell lies to their disadvantage, as long as any would give ear to them.

5. When they had thus soon pacified him, as being their father, they got clear of the present fear they were in. Yet did they see occasion for sorrow some time afterwards; for they knew that Salome, as well as their uncle Pheroras, were their enemies; who were both of them heavy and severe persons, and especially Pheroras, who was a partner with Herod in all the

---

* That it was an immemorial custom among the Jews and their forefathers, the patriarchs, to have sometimes more wives, or wives and concubines, than one at the same time, and that this polygamy was not directly forbidden in the law of Moses, is evident; but that polygamy was ever properly and distinctly permitted in that law of Moses, (Deut. xvii. 16, 17, or xxi. 15,) or indeed any where else, does not appear to me. And what our Saviour says about the common Jewish divorces, which may lay much greater claim to such a permission than polygamy, seems to me true in this case also; that Moses, "for the hardness of their hearts," suffered them to have several wives at the same time; but that "from the beginning it was not so," (Matt. xix. 8; Mark x. 5.)

affairs of the kingdom, excepting his diadem. He had also a hundred talents of his own revenues, and enjoyed the advantage of all the land beyond Jordan, which he had received as a gift from his brother, who had asked of Cæsar to make him a tetrarch, as he was made accordingly. Herod had also given him a wife out of the royal family, who was no other than his own wife's sister; and after her death, had solemnly espoused to him his own eldest daughter, with a dowry of three hundred talents; but Pheroras refused to consummate this royal marriage, out of his affection to a maid-servant of his. Upon which account Herod was very angry, and gave that daughter in marriage to a brother's son of his, [Joseph,] who was slain afterwards by the Parthians; but in some time he laid aside his anger against Pheroras, and pardoned him, as one not able to overcome his foolish passion for the maid-servant.

6. Nay, Pheroras had been accused long before, while the queen [Mariamne] was alive, as if he were in a plot to poison Herod; and there came so great a number of informers. that Herod himself, though he was an exceeding lover of his brethren, was brought to believe what was said, and to be afraid of it also; and when he had brought many of those that were under suspicion to the torture, he came at last to Pheroras's own friends; none of whom did openly confess the crime, but they owned that he had made preparation to take her whom he loved, and run away to the Parthians. Costobarus also, the husband of Salome, to whom the king had given her in marriage, after her former husband had been put to death for adultery, was instrumental in bringing about this contrivance and flight of his. Nor did Salome escape all calumny upon herself; for her brother Pheroras accused her, that she had made an agreement to marry Sylleus, the procurator of Obodas, king of Arabia, who was at bitter enmity with Herod; but when she was convicted of this, and of all that Pheroras had accused her of, she obtained her pardon. The king also pardoned Pheroras himself the crimes he had been accused of.

7. But the storm of the whole family was removed to Alexander; and all of it rested upon his head. There were three eunuchs who were in the highest esteem with the king, as was plain by the offices they were in about him; for one of them was appointed to be his butler, another of them got his supper ready for him, and the third put him to bed, and lay down by him. Now Alexander had prevailed with these men, by large gifts, to let him use them after an obscene manner; which when it was told the king, they were tortured, and found guilty, and presently confessed the criminal conversation he had with them. They also discovered the promises by which they were induced so to do, and how they were deluded by Alexander, who had told them that they ought not to fix their hopes upon Herod, an old man, and one so shameless as to colour his hair, unless they thought that would make him young again; but that they ought to fix their attention to him who was to be his successor in the kingdom, whether he would or not; and who in no long time would avenge himself on his enemies, and make his friends happy and blessed, and themselves in the first place; and the men of power did already pay respects to Alexander privately, and that the captains of the soldiery, and the officers, did secretly come to him.

8. These confessions did so terrify Herod that he durst not immediately publish them; but he sent spies abroad privately, by night and by day, who should make a close inquiry after all that was done and said; and when any were but suspected [of treason] he put them to death, insomuch that the palace was full of horribly unjust proceedings; for everybody forged calumnies, as they were themselves in a state of enmity or hatred against others; and many there were who abused the king's bloody passion to the disadvantage of those with whom they had quarrels, and lies were easily believed, and punishments were inflicted sooner than the calumnies were forged. He who had just then been accusing another, was accused himself, and was led away to execution together with him whom he had convicted; for the danger the king was in of his life made examinations be very short. He also proceeded to such a degree of bitterness, that he could not look on any one of those that were not accused with a pleasant countenance, but was in the most barbarous disposition towards his friends. Accordingly, he forbade a great many of them to come to the court, and to those whom he had not power to punish actually, he spake harshly; but for Antipater, he insulted Alexander, now he was under his misfortunes, and got a stout company of his kindred together, and raised all sorts of calumny against him; and for the king, he was brought to such a degree of terror by those prodigious slanders and contrivances, that he fancied he saw Alexander coming to him with a drawn sword in his hand. So he caused him to be seized upon immediately and bound, and fell to examining his friends by torture, many of whom died [under the torture,] but would discover nothing, nor say anything against their consciences; but some of them, being forced to speak falsely by the pain they endured, said that Alexander, and his brother Aristobulus, plotted against him, and waited for an opportunity to kill him as he was hunting, and then fly away to Rome. These accusations, though they were of an incredible nature, and only framed upon the great distress they were in, were readily believed by the king, who thought it some comfort to him, after he had bound his son, that it might appear he had not done it unjustly.

CHAPTER XXV

ARCHELAUS PROCURES A RECONCILIATION BETWEEN ALEXANDER, PHERORAS, AND HEROD

1. Now as to Alexander, since he perceived it impossible to persuade his father [that he was innocent,] he resolved to meet his calamities, how severe soever they were; so he composed four books against his enemies, and confessed that he had been in a plot; but declared withal that the greatest part [of the courtiers] were in a plot with him, and chiefly Pheroras and Salome: nay, that Salome once came and forced him to lie with her in the night-time, whether he would or no. These books were put into Herod's hands, and made a great clamour against the men of power. And now it was that Archelaus came hastily into Judea, as being affrighted for his son-in-law and his daughter; and he came as a proper assistant, and in a very prudent manner, and by a stratagem he obliged the king not to execute what he had threatened; for when he was come to him, he cried out, "Where in the world is this wretched son-in-law of mine? Where shall I see the head of him who had contrived to murder his father, which I will tear to pieces with my own hands? I will do the same also to my daughter, who hath such a fine hus-

band ; for although she be not a partner in the plot, yet, by being the wife of such a creature, she is polluted. And I cannot but admire at thy patience, against whom this plot is laid, if Alexander be still alive; for as I came with what haste I could from Cappadocia, I expected to find him put to death for his crimes long ago ; but still in order to make an examination with thee about my daughter, whom, out of regard to thee, and thy dignity, I had espoused to him in marriage, but now we must take counsel about them both, and if thy paternal affection be so great, that thou canst not punish thy son, who hath plotted against thee, let us change our right hands, and let us succeed one to the other in expressing our rage upon this occasion."

2. When he had made this pompous declaration, he got Herod to remit of his anger, though he was in disorder, who thereupon gave him the books which Alexander had composed to be read by him ; and as he came to every head, he considered of it, together with Herod. So Archelaus took hence the occasion for that stratagem which he had made use of, and by degrees he laid the blame on these men whose names were in these books, and especially upon Pheroras; and when he saw that the king believed him [to be earnest,] he said, " We must consider whether the young man be not himself plotted against by such a number of wicked wretches, and not thou plotted against by the young man ; for I cannot see any occasion for his falling into so horrid a crime, since he enjoys the advantages of royalty already, and has the expectation of being one of thy successors ; I mean this, unless there were some persons that persuade him to it, and such persons as make an ill use of the facility they know there is to persuade young men : for by such persons, not only young men are sometimes imposed upon, but old men also ; and by them sometimes are the most illustrious families and kingdoms overturned."

3. Herod assented to what he had said, and, by degrees, abated of his anger against Alexander; but was more angry at Pheroras, who perceived that the king's inclination changed on a sudden, and that Archelaus's friendship could do everything with him, and that he had no honourable method of preserving himself, he procured his safety by his impudence. So he left Alexander, and had recourse to Archelaus; who told him that he did not see how he could get him excused, now he was directly caught in so many crimes, whereby it was evidently demonstrated that he had plotted against the king, and had been the cause of those misfortunes which the young man was now under, unless he would moreover leave off his cunning knavery and his denials of what he was charged withal, and confess the charge, and implore pardon of his brother, who still had a kindness for him ; but that if he would do so, he would afford him all the assistance he was able.

4. With this advice Pheroras complied, and, putting himself into such a habit as might most move compassion, he came with black cloth upon his body, and tears in his eyes, and threw himself down at Herod's feet, and begged his pardon for what he had done, and confessed that he had acted very wickedly, and was guilty of everything that he had been accused of, and lamented that disorder of his mind and distraction which his love to a woman, he said, had brought him to. So when Archelaus had brought Pheroras to accuse and bear witness against himself, he then made an excuse for him, and mitigated Herod's anger towards him. and this by using certain domestic examples ; for that when

he had suffered much greater mischiefs from a brother of his own, he preferred the obligations of nature before the passion of revenge ; because it is in kingdoms as it is in gross bodies, where some member or other is ever swelled by the body's weight ; in which case it is not proper to cut off such member, but to heal it by a gentle method of cure.

5. Upon Archelaus's saying this, and much more to the same purpose, Herod's displeasure against Pheroras was mollified ; yet did he persevere in his own indignation against Alexander, and said he would have his daughter divorced and taken away from him, and this till he had brought Herod to that pass, that contrary to his former behaviour to him, he petitioned Archelaus for the young man, and that he would let his daughter continue espoused to him : but Archelaus made him strongly believe that he would permit her to be married to any one else, but not to Alexander; because he looked upon it as a very valuable advantage, that the relation they had contracted by that affinity, and the privileges that went along with it, might be preserved : and when the king said that his son would take it for a great favour done to him if he would not dissolve the marriage, especially since they had already children between the young man and her, and since that wife of his was so well beloved by him, and that as while she remains his wife she would be a great preservative to him, and keep him from offending, as he had formerly done ; so if she should be torn away from him, she would be the cause of his falling into despair ; because such men's attempts are best mollified when they are diverted from them by settling their affections at home. So Archelaus complied with what Herod desired, but not without difficulty, and was both himself reconciled to the young man and reconciled his father to him also. However, he said he must, by all means, be sent to Rome to discourse with Cæsar, because he had already written a full account to him of this whole matter.

6. Thus a period was put to Archelaus's stratagem, whereby he delivered his son-in-law out of the dangers he was in : but when these reconciliations were over, they spent their time in feastings and agreeable entertainments ; and when Archelaus was going away, Herod made him a present of seventy talents, with a golden throne set with precious stones, and some eunuchs, and a concubine who was called Pannychis. He also paid due honours to every one of his friends according to their dignity. In like manner did all the king's kindred, by his command, make glorious presents to Archelaus ; and so he was conducted on his way by Herod and his nobility as far as Antioch.

CHAPTER XXVI

HOW EURYCLES* CALUMNIATED THE SONS OF MARIAMNE ; AND HOW EUARATUS'S APOLOGY HAD NO EFFECT

1. Now a little afterward there came into

---

* This vile fellow seems to have been the same who is mentioned by Plutarch, as a companion to Mark Antony, and as living with Herod, whence he might easly insinuate himself into the acquaintance of Herod's sons, Antipater and Alexander. The reason why his being a Spartan rendered him acceptable to the Jews, as we here see he was, is visible from the public records of the Jews and Spartans, owing those Spartans to be of kin to the Jews, and derived from their common ancestor Abraham, the first patriarch of the Jewish nation.

Judea a man that was much superior to Archelaus's stratagems, who did not only overturn that reconciliation that had been so wisely made with Alexander, but proved the occasion of his ruin. He was a Lacedemonian, and his name was Eurycles. He was so corrupt a man, that out of the desire of getting money, he chose to live under a king, for Greece could not suffice his luxury. He presented Herod with splendid gifts as a bait which he laid, in order to compass his ends, and quickly received them back again manifold; yet did he esteem bare gifts as nothing, unless he imbrued the kingdom in blood by his purchases. Accordingly, he imposed upon the king by flattering him, and by talking subtlely to him, as also by the lying encomiums which he made upon him: for as he soon perceived Herod's blind side, so he said and did everything that might please him, and thereby became one of his most intimate friends; for both the king and all that were about him, had a great regard for this Spartan, on account of his country.

2. Now as soon as this fellow perceived the rotten parts of the family, and what quarrels the brothers had one with another, and in what disposition the father was towards each of them, he chose to take his lodging at the first in the house of Antipater, but deluded Alexander with a pretence of friendship to him, and falsely claimed to be an old acquaintance of Archelaus; for which reason he was presently admitted into Alexander's familiarity as a faithful friend. He also soon recommended himself to his brother Aristobulus; and when he had thus made trial of these several persons, he imposed upon one of them by one method, and upon another by another; but he was principally hired by Antipater, and so betrayed Alexander, and this by reproaching Antipater, because, while he was the eldest son, he overlooked the intrigues of those who stood in the way of his expectations; and by reproaching Alexander, because he who was born of a queen and was married to a king's daughter, permitted one that was born of a mean woman to lay claim to the succession, and this when he had Archelaus to support him in the most complete manner. Nor was his advice thought to be other than faithful by the young man, because of his pretended friendship with Archelaus: on which account it was that Alexander lamented to him Antipater's behaviour with regard to himself, and this without concealing anything from him; and how it was no wonder if Herod, after he had killed their mother, should deprive them of her kingdom. Upon this Eurycles pretended to commiserate his condition, and to grieve with him. He also, by a bait that he laid for him, procured Aristobulus to say the same things. Thus did he inveigle both the brothers to make complaints of their father, and then went to Antipater, and carried these grand secrets to him. He also added a fiction of his own, as if his brothers had laid a plot against him, and were almost ready to come upon him with their drawn swords. For this intelligence he received a great sum of money, and on that account he commended Antipater before his father, and at length undertook the work of bringing Alexander and Aristobulus to their graves, and accused them before their father. So he came to Herod and told him that he would save his life, as a requital for the favours he had received from him, and would preserve his light [of life] by way of retribution for his kind entertainment; for that a sword had been long whetted, and Alexander's right hand had long been stretched out against him; but that he had laid impediments in his

way, prevented his speed, and that by pretending to assist him in his design: how Alexander said, that Herod was not contented to reign in a kingdom that belonged to others, and to make dilapidations in their mother's government after he had killed her; but besides all this, that he introduced a spurious successor, and proposed to give the kingdom of their ancestors to that pestilent fellow Antipater:—that he would now appease the ghosts of Hyrcanus and Mariamne, by taking vengeance on him; for that it was not fit for him to take the succession to the government from such a father without bloodshed; that many things happen every day to provoke him so to do, insomuch that he can say nothing at all, but it affords occasion for calumny against him; for that, if any mention be made of nobility or birth, even in other cases, he is abused unjustly, while his father would say that nobody, to be sure, is of noble birth but Alexander, and that his father was inglorious for want of such nobility. If they be at any time hunting, and he says nothing, he gives offence; and if he commends anybody, they take it in way of jest: that they always find their father unmercifully severe, and have no natural affection for any of them but for Antipater; on which accounts, if this plot does not take he is very willing to die; but that in case he kill his father he hath sufficient opportunity for saving himself. In the first place, he hath Archelaus his father-in-law, to whom he can easily fly; and, in the next place, he hath Cæsar, who had never known Herod's character to this day; for that he shall not appear then before him with that dread he used to do when his father was there to terrify him; and that he will not then produce the accusations that concerned himself alone, but would, in the first place, openly insist on the calamities of their nation, and how they are taxed to death, and in what ways of luxury and wicked practices that wealth is spent which was gotten by bloodshed; what sort of persons they are that get our riches, and to whom those cities belong, upon whom he bestows his favours; that he would have inquiry made what became of his grandfather [Hyrcanus,] and his mother [Mariamne,] and would openly proclaim the gross wickedness that was in the kingdom; on which accounts he should not be deemed a parricide.

3. When Eurycles had made this portentous speech, he greatly commended Antipater, as the only child that had an affection for his father, and on that account was an impediment to the other's plot against him. Hereupon the king, who had hardly repressed his anger upon the former accusations, was exasperated to an incurable degree. At which Antipater took another occasion to send in other persons to his father to accuse his brethren, and to tell him that they had privately discoursed with Jucundus and Tyrannus, who had once been masters of the horse to the king, but for some offences had been put out of that honourable employment. Herod was in a very great rage at these informations, and presently ordered those men to be tortured: yet did not they confess anything of what the king had been informed; but a certain letter was produced, as written by Alexander to the governor of a castle, to desire him to receive him and Aristobulus into the castle when he had killed his father, and to give them weapons, and what other assistance he could, upon that occasion. Alexander said that this letter was a forgery of Diophantus. This Diophantus was the king's secretary, a bold man, cunning in counterfeiting any one's hand; and after he had counterfeited

a great number, he was at last put to death for it. Herod did also order the governor of the castle to be tortured; but got nothing out of him of what the accusations suggested.

4. However, although Herod found the proofs too weak, he gave order to have his sons kept in custody; for till now they had been at liberty. He also called that pest of his family, and forger of all this vile accusation, Eurycles, his saviour and benefactor, and gave him a reward of fifty talents. Upon which he prevented any accurate accounts that could come of what he had done, by going immediately into Cappadocia, and there he got money of Archelaus, having the impudence to pretend that he had reconciled Herod to Alexander. He thence passed over into Greece, and used what he had thus wickedly gotten to the like wicked purposes. Accordingly, he was twice accused before Cæsar, that he had filled Achaia with sedition, and had plundered its cities; so he was sent into banishment. And thus was he punished for what wicked actions he had been guilty of about Aristobulus and Alexander.

5. But it will be now worth while to put Euaratus of Cos in opposition to this Spartan; for as he was one of Alexander's most intimate friends, and came to him in his travels at the same time that Eurycles came; so the king put the question to him, whether those things of which Alexander was accused were true? He assured him upon oath that he had never heard any such things from the young men; yet did this testimony avail nothing for the clearing these miserable creatures; for Herod was only disposed the most readily to hearken to what was made against them, and every one was most agreeable to him that would believe they were guilty, and shewed their indignation at them.

CHAPTER XXVII

HEROD, BY CÆSAR'S DIRECTION, ACCUSES HIS SONS AT BERYTUS. THEY ARE NOT PRODUCED BEFORE THE COURT, BUT YET ARE CONDEMNED; AND IN A LITTLE TIME ARE SENT TO SEBASTE, AND STRANGLED THERE

1. MOREOVER, Salome exasperated Herod's cruelty against his sons; for Aristobulus was desirous to bring her, who was his mother-in-law and his aunt, into the like dangers with themselves: so he sent to her to take care of her own safety, and told her that the king was preparing to put her to death, on account of the accusation that was laid against her, as if when she formerly endeavoured to marry herself to Sylleus the Arabian, she had discovered the king's grand secrets to him, who was the king's enemy; and this it was that came as the last storm, and entirely sunk the young men who were in great danger before; for Salome came running to the king, and informed him of what admonition had been given her; whereupon he could bear no longer, but commanded both the young men to be bound, and kept the one asunder from the other. He also sent Volumnius, the general of his army, to Cæsar immediately, as also his friend Olympus with him, who carried the informations in writing along with them. Now, as soon as they had sailed to Rome and delivered the king's letters to Cæsar, Cæsar was mightily troubled at the case of the young men; yet did not he think he ought to take the power from the father of condemning his sons; so he wrote back to him, and appointed him to have the power over his sons; but said withal, that he would do well to make an examination into this matter of the plot against him in a public court, and to take for his assessors his own kindred, and the governors of the province;—and if those sons be found guilty, to put them to death; but if they appear to have thought of no more than only flying away from him, that he should, in that case, moderate their punishment.

2. With these directions Herod complied, and came to Berytus, where Cæsar had ordered the court to be assembled, and got the judicature together. The presidents sat first, as Cæsar's letters had appointed, who were Saturninus and Pedanius, and their lieutenants that were with them, with whom was the procurator Volumnius also; next to them sat the king's kinsmen and friends, with Salome also, and Pheroras; after whom sat the principal men of all Syria, excepting Archelaus; for Herod had a suspicion of him, because he was Alexander's father-in-law. Yet did not he produce his sons in open court; and this was done very cunningly, for he knew well enough that, had they but appeared openly, they would certainly have been pitied; and if withal they had been suffered to speak, Alexander would easily have answered what they were accused of; but they were in custody at Platane, a village of the Sidonians.

3. So the king got up, and inveighed against his sons as if they were present; and as for that part of the accusation that they had plotted against him, he urged it but faintly, because he was destitute of proofs; but he insisted before the assessors on the reproaches, and jests, and injurious carriage, and ten thousand the like offences against them, which were heavier than death itself; and when nobody contradicted him, he moved them to pity his case, as though he had been condemned himself, now he had gained a bitter victory over his sons. So he asked every one's sentence; which sentence was first of all given by Saturninus, and was this:—That he condemned the young men, but not to death; for that it was not fit for him, who had three sons of his own now present, to give his vote for the destruction of the sons of another. The two lieutenants also gave the like vote; some others there were also who followed their example; but Volumnius began to vote on the more melancholy side, and all those that came after him condemned the young men to die; some out of flattery, and some out of hatred to Herod; but none out of indignation at their crimes. And now all Syria and Judea was in great expectation, and waited for the last act of this tragedy; yet did nobody suppose that Herod would be so barbarous as to murder his children: however, he carried them away to Tyre, and thence sailed to Cesarea, and then he deliberated with himself what sort of death the young men should suffer.

4. Now there was a certain old soldier of the king's, whose name was Tero, who had a son that was very familiar with, and a friend to Alexander, and who himself particularly loved the young men. This soldier was in a measure distracted, out of the excess of the indignation he had at what was doing; and at first he cried out aloud, as he went about, that justice was trampled under foot; that truth was perished, and nature confounded; and that the life of man was full of iniquity, and everything else that passion could suggest to a man who spared not his own life; and at last he ventured to go to the king, and said, "Truly, I think, thou art a most miserable man, when thou hearkenest to most wicked wretches, against those that ought

to be dearest to thee; since thou hast frequently resolved that Pheroras and Salome should be put to death, and yet believest them against thy sons; while these, by cutting off the succession of thine own sons, leave all wholly to Antipater, and thereby choose to have thee such a king as may be thoroughly in their own power. However, consider whether this death of Antipater's brethren will not make him hated by the soldiers; for there is nobody but commiserates the young men; and of the captains, a great many shew their indignation at it openly." Upon his saying this, he named those that had such indignation; but the king ordered those men, with Tero himself, and his son, to be seized upon immediately.

5. At which time there was a certain barber, whose name was Trypho. This man leaped out from among the people in a kind of madness, and accused himself, and said, "this Tero endeavoured to persuade me also to cut thy throat with my razor when I trimmed thee; and promised that Alexander should give me large presents for so doing." When Herod heard this, he examined Tero, with his son and the barber, by the torture; but as the others denied the accusation, and he said nothing further, Herod gave order that Tero should be racked more severely: but his son, out of pity to his father, promised to discover the whole to the king, if he would grant [that his father should be no longer tortured.] When he had agreed to this, he said, that his father, at the persuasion of Alexander, had an intention to kill him. Now some said this was forged, in order to free his father from his torments; and some said it was true.

6. And now Herod accused the captains and Tero in an assembly of the people, and brought the people together in a body against them; and accordingly there were they put to death, together with [Trypho] the barber; they were killed by the pieces of wood and the stones that were thrown at them. He also sent his sons to Sebaste, a city not far from Cesarea, and ordered them to be there strangled; and as what he had ordered was executed immediately, so he commanded that their dead bodies should be brought to the fortress Alexandrium, to be buried with Alexander, their grandfather by the mother's side. And this was the end of Alexander and Aristobulus.

CHAPTER XXVIII

HOW ANTIPATER IS HATED OF ALL MEN; AND HOW THE KING ESPOUSES THE SONS OF THOSE THAT HAD BEEN SLAIN TO HIS KINDRED; BUT THAT ANTIPATER MADE HIM CHANGE THEM FOR OTHER WOMEN. OF HEROD'S MARRIAGES AND CHILDREN

1. BUT an intolerable hatred fell upon Antipater from the nation, though he had now an indisputable title to the succession; because they all knew that he was the person who contrived all the calumnies against his brethren. However, he began to be in a terrible fear, as he saw the posterity of those that had been slain growing up; for Alexander had two sons by Glaphyra, Tigranes and Alexander; and Aristobulus had Herod, and Agrippa, and Aristobulus, his sons, with Herodias and Mariamne, his daughters; and all by Bernice, Salome's daughter. As for Glaphyra, Herod, as soon as he had killed Alexander, sent her back, together with her portion, to Cappadocia. He married Ber-

nice, Aristobulus's daughter, to Antipater's uncle by his mother, and it was Antipater who, in order to reconcile her to him, when she had been at variance with him, contrived this match; he also got into Pheroras's favour, and into the favour of Cæsar's friends, by presents, and other ways of obsequiousness, and sent no small sums of money to Rome; Saturninus also, and his friends in Syria, were all well replenished with the presents he made them; yet, the more he gave the more he was hated, as not making these presents out of generosity, but spending his money out of fear. Accordingly it so fell out that the receivers bore him no more goodwill than before, but that those to whom he gave nothing were his most bitter enemies. However, he bestowed his money every day more and more profusely, on observing that, contrary to his expectations, the king was taking care about the orphans, and discovering at the same time his repentance for killing their fathers, by his commiseration of those that sprang from them.

2. Accordingly, Herod got together his kindred and friends, and set before them the children, and with his eyes full of tears, said thus to them: "It was an unlucky fate that took away from me these children's fathers, which children are recommended to me by that natural commiseration which their orphan condition requires; however, I will endeavour, though I have been a most unfortunate father, to appear a better grandfather, and to leave these children such curators after myself as are dearest to me. I therefore betroth thy daughter, Pheroras, to the elder of these brethren, the children of Alexander, that thou mayest be obliged to take care of them. I also betroth to thy son, Antipater, the daughter of Aristobulus; be thou therefore a father to that orphan; and my son Herod [Philip] shall have her sister, whose grandfather, by the mother's side, was high priest. And let every one that loves me be of my sentiments in these dispositions, whom none that hath an affection for me will abrogate. And I pray God that he will join these children together in marriage to the advantage of my kingdom, and of my posterity; and may he look down with eyes more serene upon them than he looked upon their fathers!"

3. While he spake these words, he wept, and joined the children's right hands together: after which he embraced them every one after an affectionate manner, and dismissed the assembly. Upon this Antipater was in great disorder immediately, and lamented publicly at what was done; for he supposed that this dignity, which was conferred on these orphans, was for his own destruction, even in his father's lifetime, and that he should run another risk of losing the government if Alexander's sons should have both Archelaus [a king,] and Pheroras a tetrarch, to support them. He also considered how he was himself hated by the nation, and how they pitied these orphans: how great affection the Jews bare to those brethren of his when they were alive, and how gladly they remembered them, now they had perished by his means. So he resolved by all the ways possible to get these espousals dissolved.

4. Now he was afraid of going subtlely about this matter with his father, who was hard to be pleased, and was presently moved upon the least suspicion: so he ventured to go to him directly, and to beg of him before his face, not to deprive him of that dignity which he had been pleased to bestow upon him; and that he might not have the bare name of a king, while the power was in

other persons; for that he should never be able to keep the government, if Alexander's son was to have both his grandfather Archelaus and Pheroras for his curators; and he besought him earnestly, since there were so many of the royal family alive, that he would change those [intended] marriages. Now the king had nine wives,* and children by seven of them; Antipater was himself born of Doris, and Herod [Philip] of Marianne, the high priest's daughter; Antipas also and Archelaus were by Malthace, the Samaritan, as was his daughter Olympias, which his brother Joseph's† son had married. By Cleopatra of Jerusalem he had Herod and Philip; and by Pallas, Phasaelus; he had also two daughters, Roxana and Salome, the one by Phedra, and the other by Elpis: he had also two wives who had no children, the one his first cousin, and the other his niece; and besides these he had two daughters, the sisters of Alexander and Aristobulus, by Marianne. Since, therefore, the royal family was so numerous, Antipater prayed him to change these intended marriages.

5. When the king perceived what disposition he was in towards the orphans, he was angry at it, and a suspicion came into his mind as to those sons whom he had put to death, whether that had not been brought about by the false tales of Antipater; so at that time he made Antipater a long and peevish answer, and bade him begone. Yet was he afterwards prevailed upon cunningly by his flatteries, and changed the marriages; he married Aristobulus's daughter to him, and his son to Pheroras's daughter.

6. Now one may learn, in this instance, how very much this flattering Antipater could do,—even what Salome in the like circumstances could not do; for when she, who was his sister, had by the means of Julia, Cæsar's wife, earnestly desired leave to be married to Sylleus the Arabian, Herod swore he would esteem her his bitter enemy, unless she would leave off that project: he also caused her, against her own consent, to be married to Alexas, a friend of his, and that one of her daughters should be married to Alexas's son, and the other to Antipater's uncle by the mother's side. And for the daughters that the king had by Mariamne, the one was married to Antipater, his sister's son, and the other to his brother's son, Phasaelus.

CHAPTER XXIX

ANTIPATER BECOMES INTOLERABLE; HE IS SENT TO ROME, AND CARRIES HEROD'S TESTAMENT WITH HIM; PHERORAS LEAVES HIS BROTHER, THAT HE MAY KEEP HIS WIFE; HE DIES AT HOME

1. Now when Antipater had cut off the hopes of the orphans, and had contracted such affini-

ties as would be most for his own advantage, he proceeded briskly, as having a certain expectation of the kingdom; and as he had now assurances added to his wickedness, he became intolerable; for not being able to avoid the hatred of all people, he built his security upon the terror he struck into them. Pheroras also assisted him in his designs, looking upon him as already fixed in the kingdom. There was also a company of women in the court, who excited new disturbances; for Pheroras's wife, together with her mother and sister, as also Antipater's mother, grew very impudent in the palace. She also was so insolent as to affront the king's two daughters,* on which account the king hated her to a great degree; yet although these women were hated by him, they domineered over others: there was only Salome who opposed their good agreement, and informed the king of their meetings, as not being for the advantage of his affairs; and when those women knew what calumnies she had raised against them, and how much Herod was displeased, they left off their public meetings and friendly entertainments of one another; nay, on the contrary, they pretended to quarrel one with another when the king was within hearing. The like dissimulation did Antipater make use of; and when matters were public, he opposed Pheroras: but still they had private cabals, and merry-meetings in the night-time; nor did the observation of others do any more than confirm their mutual agreement. However, Salome knew everything they did, and told everything to Herod.

2. But he was inflamed with anger at them, and chiefly at Pheroras's wife; for Salome had principally accused her. So he got an assembly of his friends and kindred together, and there accused this woman of many things, and particularly of the affronts she had offered his daughters; and that she had supplied the Pharisees with money, by way of rewards for what they had done against him, and had procured his brother to become his enemy, by giving him love-potions. At length he turned his speech to Pheroras, and told him that he would give him his choice of these two things:—Whether he would keep in with his brother, or with his wife? And when Pheroras said that he certainly would die rather than forsake his wife, —Herod, not knowing what to do further in that matter, turned his speech to Antipater, and charged him to have no intercourse either with Pheroras's wife, or with Pheroras himself, or with any one belonging to her. Now, though Antipater did not transgress that his injunction publicly, yet did he in secret come to their night-meetings: and because he was afraid that Salome observed what he did, he procured, by the means of his Italian friends, that he might go and live at Rome; for when they wrote that it was proper for Antipater to be sent to Cæsar for some time, Herod made no delay, but sent him, and that with a splendid attendance, and a great deal of money, and gave him his testament to carry with him,—wherein Antipater had the kingdom bequeathed to him, and wherein Herod was named for Antipater's successor; that Herod, I mean, who was the son of Mariamne, the high priest's daughter.

3. Sylleus also, the Arabian, sailed to Rome, without any regard to Cæsar's injunctions, and this in order to oppose Antipater with all his

---

* Dean Aldrich takes notice here, that these nine wives of Herod were alive at the same time, and that if the celebrated Mariamne, who was now dead, be reckoned, those wives were in all ten. Yet it is remarkable that he had no more than fifteen children by them all.

† To prevent confusion, it may not be amiss to distinguish between four Josephs in the history of Herod. 1. Joseph, Herod's uncle, and the [second] husband of his sister Salome, slain by Herod on account of Mariamne. 2. Joseph, Herod's quæstor, or treasurer, slain on the same account. 3. Joseph, Herod's brother, slain in battle against Antigonus. 4. Joseph, Herod's nephew, the husband of Olympias, mentioned in this place.

* These daughters of Herod, whom Pheroras's wife affronted, were Salome and Roxana, two virgins, who were born to him of his two wives, Elpis and Phedra.

might, as to that law-suit which Nicolaus had with him before. This Sylleus had also a great contest with Aretas his own king; for he had slain many others of Aretas's friends, and particularly Sohemus, the most potent man in the city Petra. Moreover, he had prevailed with Phabatus, who was Herod's steward, by giving him a great sum of money, to assist him against Herod; but when Herod gave him more, he induced him to leave Sylleus, and by his means he demanded of him all that Cæsar had required of him to pay; but when Sylleus paid nothing of what he was to pay, and did also accuse Phabatus to Cæsar, and said that he was not a steward for Cæsar's advantage, but for Herod's, Phabatus was angry at him on that account, but was still in very great esteem with Herod, and discovered Sylleus's grand secrets, and told the king that Sylleus had corrupted Corinthus, one of the guards of his body, by bribing him, and of whom he must therefore have a care. Accordingly the king complied; for this Corinthus, though he was brought up in Herod's kingdom, yet was by birth an Arabian; so the king ordered him to be taken up immediately, and not only him, but two other Arabians, who were caught with him; the one of them was Sylleus's friend, the other the head of a tribe. These last, being put to the torture, confessed that they had prevailed with Corinthus, for a large sum of money, to kill Herod; and when they had been further examined before Saturninus, the president of Syria, they were sent to Rome.

4. However, Herod did not leave off importuning Pheroras, but proceeded to force him to put away his wife; yet could he not devise any way by which he could bring the woman herself to punishment, although he had many causes of hatred to her; till at length he was in such great uneasiness at her, that he cast both her and his brother out of his kingdom. Pheroras took this injury very patiently, and went away into his own tetrarchy, [Perea, beyond Jordan,] and sware that there should be but one end put to his flight, and that should be Herod's death; and that he would never return while he was alive. Nor indeed would he return when his brother was sick, although he earnestly sent for him to come to him, because he had a mind to leave some injunctions with him before he died: but Herod unexpectedly recovered. A little afterward Pheroras himself fell sick, when Herod shewed great moderation; for he came to him and pitied his case, and took care of him; but his affection for him did him no good, for Pheroras died a little afterward. Now, though Herod had so great an affection for him to the last day of his life, yet was a report spread abroad that he had killed him by poison. However, he took care to have his dead body carried to Jerusalem, and appointed a very great mourning to the whole nation for him, and bestowed a a most pompous funeral upon him; and this was the end that one of Alexander's and Aristobulus's murderers came to.

CHAPTER XXX

WHEN HEROD MADE INQUIRY ABOUT PHERORAS'S DEATH, A DISCOVERY WAS MADE THAT ANTIPATER HAD PREPARED A POISONOUS DRAUGHT FOR HIM. HEROD CASTS DORIS AND HER ACCOMPLICES, AS ALSO MARIAMNE, OUT OF THE PALACE, AND BLOTS HER SON HEROD OUT OF HIS TESTAMENT

1. BUT now the punishment was transferred unto the original author, Antipater, and took its rise from the death of Pheroras; for certain of his freedmen came with a sad countenance to the king, and told him that his brother had been destroyed by poison, and that his wife had brought him somewhat that was prepared after an unusual manner, and that upon his eating it, he presently fell into his distemper; that Antipater's mother and sister, two days before, brought a woman out of Arabia that was skilful in mixing such drugs, that she might prepare a love potion for Pheroras; and that instead of a love potion, she had given him deadly poison; and that this was done by the management of Sylleus, who was acquainted with that woman.

2. The king was deeply affected with so many suspicions, and had the maid-servants and some of the free women also tortured; one of whom cried out in her agonies, "May that God that governs the earth and the heaven, punish the author of all these our miseries, Antipater's mother!" The king took a handle from this confession, and proceeded to inquire further into the truth of this matter. So this woman discovered the friendship of Antipater's mother to Pheroras and Antipater's women, as also their secret meetings, and that Pheroras and Antipater had drunk with them for a whole night together as they returned from the king, and would not suffer anybody, either man-servant or maid-servant, to be there; while one of the free women discovered the whole of the matter.

3. Upon this, Herod tortured the maid-servants, every one by themselves separately; who all unanimously agreed in the foregoing discoveries, and that accordingly by agreement they went away, Antipater to Rome, and Pheroras to Perea; for that they oftentimes talked to one another thus:—That after Herod had slain Alexander and Aristobulus, he would fall upon them, and upon their wives, because, after he had not spared Mariamne and her children, he would spare nobody; and that for this reason it was best to get as far off the wild beast as they were able:—and that Antipater oftentimes lamented his own case before his mother; and said to her, that he had already gray hairs upon his head, and that his father grew younger again every day, and that perhaps death would overtake him before he should begin to be a king in earnest; and that in case Herod should die, which yet nobody knew when it would be, the enjoyment of the succession could certainly be but for a little time; for that these heads of Hydra, the sons of Alexander and Aristobulus, were growing up: that he was deprived by his father of the hopes of being succeeded by his children, for that his successor after his death was not to be any one of his own sons, but Herod the son of Mariamne:—that in this point Herod was plainly distracted, to think that his testament should therein take place; for he would take care that none of his posterity should remain, because he was, of all fathers, the greatest hater of his children. Yet does he hate his brother still worse; whence it was that he awhile ago gave himself a hundred talents, that he should not have any intercourse with Pheroras. And when Pheroras said, wherein have we done him any harm? Antipater replied,—"I wish he would but deprive us of all we have, and leave us naked and alive only; but it is indeed impossible to escape this wild beast, who is thus given to murder; who will not permit us to love any person openly, although we be together privately; yet may we be so openly too, if we are but endowed with the courage and the hands of men."

4. These things were said by the women upon the torture: as also that Pheroras resolved to fly with them to Perea. Now Herod gave credit to all they said, on account of the affair of the hundred talents; for he had had no discourse with any body about them, but only with Antipater. So he vented his anger first of all against Antipater's mother, and took away from her all the ornaments which he had given her, which cost a great many talents, and cast her out of the palace a second time. He also took care of Pheroras's women after their tortures, as being now reconciled to them; but he was in great consternation himself, and inflamed upon every suspicion, and had many innocent persons led to the torture, out of his fear, lest he should perhaps leave any guilty person untortured.

5. And now it was that he betook himself to examine Antipater of Samaria, who was the steward of [his son] Antipater; and upon torturing him, he learnt that Antipater had sent for a potion of deadly poison for him out of Egypt, by Antiphilus, a companion of his; that Theudio, the uncle of Antipater, had it from him, and delivered it to Pheroras; for that Antipater had charged him to take his father off while he was at Rome, and so free him from the suspicion of doing it himself: that Pheroras also committed this potion to his wife. Then did the king send for her, and bade her bring to him what she had received immediately. So she came out of her house as if she would bring it with her, but threw herself down from the top of the house, in order to prevent any examination and torture from the king. However, it came to pass, as it seems by the providence of God when he intended to bring Antipater to punishment, that she fell not upon her head but upon other parts of her body, and escaped. The king, when she was brought to him, took care of her (for she was at first quite senseless upon her fall,) and asked her why she had thrown herself down; and gave her his oath, that if she would speak the real truth, he would excuse her from punishment; but that if she concealed anything, he would have her body torn to pieces by torments, and leave no part of it to be buried.

6. Upon this the woman paused a little, and then said, "Why do I spare to speak of these grand secrets, now Pheroras is dead! that would only tend to save Antipater, who is all our destruction. Hear, then, O king, and be thou, and God himself, who cannot be deceived, witnesses to the truth of what I am going to say. When thou didst sit weeping by Pheroras as he was dying, then it was that he called me to him, and said,—'My dear wife, I have been greatly mistaken as to the disposition of my brother towards me, and have hated him that is so affectionate to me, and have contrived to kill him who is in such disorder for me before I am dead. As for myself, I receive the recompense of my impiety; but·do thou bring what poison was left with us by Antipater, and which thou keepest, in order to destroy him, and consume it immediately in the fire in my sight, that I may not be liable to the avenger in the invisible world.' This I brought as he bade me, and emptied the greatest part of it into the fire, but reserved a little of it for my own use against uncertain futurity, and out of my fear of thee."

7. When she had said this, she brought the box, which had a small quantity of this potion in it: but the king let her alone, and transferred the tortures to Antiphilus's mother and brother; who both confessed that Antiphilus brought the box out of Egypt, and that they had received the potion from a brother of his, who was a physician at Alexandria. Then did the ghosts of Alexander and Aristobulus go round all the palace, and became the inquisitors and discoverers of what could not otherwise have been found out, and brought such as were the freest from suspicion to be examined; whereby it was discovered that Mariamne, the high priest's daughter, was conscious of this plot; and her very brothers, when they were tortured, declared it so to be. Whereupon the king avenged this insolent attempt of the mother upon the son, and blotted Herod, whom he had by her, out of his testament, who had been before named therein as successor to Antipater.

CHAPTER XXXI

ANTIPATER IS CONVICTED BY BATHYLLUS; BUT HE STILL RETURNS FROM ROME, WITHOUT KNOWING IT. HEROD BRINGS HIM TO HIS TRIAL

1. AFTER these things were over, Bathyllus came under examination, in order to convict Antipater, who proved the concluding attestation to Antipater's designs; for indeed he was no other than his freedman. This man came, and brought another deadly potion, the poison of asps and the juices of other serpents, that if the first potion did not do the business, Pheroras and his wife might be armed with this also to destroy the king. He brought also an addition to Antipater's insolent attempts against his father, which was the letters which he wrote against his brethren, Archelaus and Philip, who were the king's sons, and educated at Rome, being yet youths, but of generous dispositions. Antipater set himself to get rid of these as soon as he could, that they might not be prejudicial to his hopes; and to that end he forged letters against them, in the name of his friends at Rome. Some of these he corrupted by bribes, to write how they grossly reproached their father, and did openly bewail Alexander and Aristobulus, and were uneasy at their being recalled; for their father had already sent for them, which was the very thing that troubled Antipater.

2. Nay indeed, while Antipater was in Judea, and before he was upon his journey to Rome, he gave money to have the like letters against them sent from Rome, and then came to his father, who as yet had no suspicion of him, apologised for his brethren, and alleged on their behalf, that some of the things contained in those letters were false, and others of them were only youthful errors. Yet at the same time that he expended a great deal of his money, by making presents to such as wrote against his brethren, did he aim to bring his accounts into confusion, by buying costly garments, and carpets of various contextures, with silver and gold cups, and a great many more curious things, that so, among the very great expenses laid out upon such furniture, he might conceal the money he had used in hiring men [to write the letters;] for he brought in an account of his expenses, amounting to two hundred talents, his main pretence for which, was the law-suit that he had been in with Sylleus. So while all his rogueries, even those of a lesser sort, were covered by his great villany, while all the examinations by torture proclaimed his attempt to murder his father, and the letters proclaimed his second attempt to murder his brethren,—yet did no one of those that came to Rome inform him of his misfortunes in Judea, although seven months

had intervened between his conviction and his return,—so great was the hatred which they all bore to him. And perhaps they were the ghosts of those brethren of his that had been murdered, that stopped the mouths of those that intended to have told him. He then wrote from Rome, and informed his [friends] that he would soon come to them, and how he was dismissed with honour by Cæsar.

3. Now the king being desirous to get this plotter against him into his hands, and being also afraid lest he should some way come to the knowledge how his affairs stood, and be upon his guard, he dissembled his anger in his epistle to him, as in other points he wrote kindly to him, and desired him to make haste, because, if he came quickly, he would then lay aside the complaints he had against his mother; for Antipater was not ignorant that his mother had been expelled out of the palace. However he had before received a letter, which contained an account of the death of Pheroras, at Tarentum,*—and made great lamentations at it; for which some commended him, as being for his own uncle; though probably this confusion arose on account of his having thereby failed in his plot [on his father's life;] and his tears were more for the loss of him that was to have been subservient therein, than for [an uncle] Pheroras; moreover, a sort of fear came upon him as to his designs, lest the poison should have been discovered. However, when he was in Cilicia he received the forementioned epistle from his father, and made great haste accordingly. But when he had sailed to Celenderis, a suspicion came into his mind relating to his mother's misfortunes; as if his soul foreboded some mischief to itself. Those therefore of his friends who were the most considerate, advised him not rashly to go to his father, till he had learned what were the occasions why his mother had been ejected, because they were afraid that he might be involved in the calumnies that had been cast upon his mother; but those that were less considerate, and had more regard to their own desires of seeing their native country than to Antipater's safety, persuaded him to make haste home, and not, by delaying his journey, afford his father ground for an ill suspicion, and give a handle to those that raised stories against him; for that in case anything had been moved to his disadvantage, it was owing to his absence, which durst not have been done had he been present;— and they said it was absurd to deprive himself of certain happiness, for the sake of an uncertain suspicion, and not rather to return to his father, and take the royal authority upon him, which was in a state of fluctuation on his account only. Antipater complied with this last advice; for Providence hurried him on [to his destruction.] So he passed over the sea, and landed at Sebastus, the haven of Cesarea.

4. And here he found a perfect and unexpected solitude, while everybody avoided him, and nobody durst come at him; for he was equally hated by all men; and now that hatred had liberty to shew itself, and the dread men were in of the king's anger made men keep from him; for the whole city [of Jerusalem] was filled with the rumours about Antipater, and Antipater himself was the only person who was ignorant of them; for as no man was dismissed more magnificently when he began his voyage to Rome, so was no man now received back with greater ignominy. And indeed he began already to suspect what misfortunes there were in Herod's

family; yet did he cunningly conceal his suspicion; and while he was inwardly ready to die for fear, he put on a forced boldness of countenance. Nor could he now fly any whither, nor had he any way of emerging out of the difficulties which encompassed him; nor indeed had he there any certain intelligence of the affairs of the royal family, by reason of the threats the king had given out; yet had he some small hopes of better tidings, for perhaps nothing had been discovered; or, if any discovery had been made, perhaps he should be able to clear himself by impudence and artful tricks, which were the only things he relied upon for his deliverance.

5. And with these hopes did he screen himself, till he came to the palace, without any friends with him; for these were affronted, and shut out at the first gate. Now Varus, the president of Syria, happened to be in the palace [at this juncture;] so Antipater went in to his father, and, putting on a bold face, he came near to salute him. But Herod stretched out his hands, and turned his head away from him, and cried out, "Even this is an indication of a parricide, to be desirous to get me into his arms, when he is under such heinous accusations. God confound thee, thou vile wretch; do not thou touch me till thou hast cleared thyself of these crimes that are charged upon thee. I appoint thee a court where thou art to be judged: and this Varus, who is very seasonably here, to be thy judge; and get thou thy defence ready against to-morrow, for I give thee so much time to prepare suitable excuses for thyself." And as Antipater was so confounded that he was able to make no answer to this charge, he went away; but his mother and wife came to him, and told him of all the evidence they had gotten against him. Hereupon he recollected himself, and considered what defence he should make against the accusations.

CHAPTER XXXII

ANTIPATER IS ACCUSED BEFORE VARUS, AND IS CONVICTED OF LAYING A PLOT [AGAINST HIS FATHER] BY THE STRONGEST EVIDENCE. HEROD PUTS OFF HIS PUNISHMENT TILL HE SHOULD BE RECOVERED, AND IN THE MEANTIME ALTERS HIS TESTAMENT

1. Now the day following, the king assembled a court of his kinsmen and friends, and called in Antipater's friends also. Herod himself, with Varus, were the presidents; and Herod called for all the witnesses, and ordered them to be brought in; among whom some of the domestic servants of Antipater's mother were brought in also, who had but a little while before been caught, as they were carrying the following letter from her to her son:—"Since all those things have been already discovered to thy father, do not thou come to him, unless thou canst procure some assistance from Cæsar." When this and the other witnesses were introduced, Antipater came in, and falling on his face before his father's feet, he said, "Father, I beseech thee, do not thou condemn me beforehand, but let thy ears be unbiassed, and attend to my defence; for if thou wilt give me leave, I will demonstrate that I am innocent."

2. Hereupon Herod cried out to him to hold his peace, and spake thus to Varus:—"I cannot but think that thou, Varus, and every other upright judge, will determine that Antipater is

---

* This Tarentum has coins still extant.

a vile wretch. I am also afraid that thou wilt abhor my ill fortune, and judge me also myself worthy of all sorts of calamity for begetting such children; while yet I ought rather to be pitied, who have been so affectionate a father to such wretched sons; for when I had settled the kingdom on my former sons, even when they were young, and when, besides the charges of their education at Rome, I had made them the friends of Cæsar, and made them envied by other kings, I found them plotting against me. These have been put to death, and that, in a great measure, for the sake of Antipater; for as he was then young, and appointed to be my successor, I took care chiefly to secure him from danger: but this profligate wild beast, when he had been over and above satiated with that patience which I shewed him, he made use of that abundance I had given him against myself; for I seemed to him to live too long, and he was very uneasy at the old age I had arrived at; nor could he stay any longer, but would be a king by parricide. And justly I am served by him for bringing him back out of the country to court, when he was of no esteem before, and for thrusting out those sons of mine that were born of the queen, and for making him a successor to my dominions. I confess to thee, O Varus, the great folly I was guilty of; for I provoked those sons of mine to act against me, and cut off their just expectations for the sake of Antipater; and indeed what kindness did I do to them, that could equal what I have done to Antipater! to whom I have, in a manner, yielded up my royal authority while I am alive, and whom I have openly named for the successor to my dominions in my testament, and given him a yearly revenue of his own of fifty talents, and supplied him with money to an extravagant degree out of my own revenue; and when he was about to sail to Rome, I gave him three hundred talents, and recommended him, and him alone of all my children, to Cæsar, as his father's deliverer. Now what crimes were these other sons of mine guilty of like those of Antipater! and what evidence was there brought against them so strong as there is to demonstrate this son to have plotted against me! Yet does this parricide presume to speak for himself, and hopes to obscure the truth by his cunning tricks. Thou, O Varus, must guard thyself against him; for I know the wild beast, and I foresee how plausibly he will talk, and his counterfeit lamentation. This was he who exhorted me to have a care of Alexander, when he was alive, and not to intrust my body with all men! This was he who came to my very bed, and looked about, lest any one should lay snares for me! This was he who took care of my sleep, and secured me from any fear of danger, who comforted me under the trouble I was in upon the slaughter of my sons, and looked to see what affection my surviving brethren bore me! This was my protector, and the guardian of my body! And when I call to mind, O Varus, his craftiness upon every occasion, and his art of dissembling, I can hardly believe that I am still alive, and I wonder how I have escaped such a deep plotter of mischief! However, since some fate or other makes my house desolate, and perpetually raises up those that are dearest to me against me, I will, with tears, lament my hard fortune, and privately groan under my lonesome condition; yet am I resolved that no one who thirsts after my blood shall escape punishment, although the evidence should extend itself to all my sons."

3. Upon Herod's saying this, he was interrupted by the confusion he was in; but ordered Nicolaus, one of his friends, to produce the evidence against Antipater. But in the meantime Antipater lifted up his head (for he lay on the ground before his father's feet) and cried out aloud, "Thou, O father, hast made my apology for me; for how can I be a parricide, whom thou thyself confessest to have always had for thy guardian? Thou callest my filial affection prodigious lies and hypocrisy! how then could it be that I, who was so subtle in other matters, should here be so mad as not to understand that it was not easy that he who committed so horrid a crime should be concealed from men, but impossible that he should be concealed from the Judge of Heaven, who sees all things, and is present everywhere? or did not I know what end my brethren came to, on whom God inflicted so great a punishment for their evil designs against thee? And indeed what was there that could possibly provoke me against thee? Could the hope of being a king do it? I was a king already. Could I suspect hatred from thee? No: was I not beloved by thee? and what other fear could I have? Nay, by preserving thee safe, I was a terror to others. Did I want money? No: for who was able to expend so much as myself? Indeed, father, had I been the most execrable of mankind, and had I had the soul of the most execrable wild beast, must I not have been overcome with the benefits thou hadst bestowed on me? whom, as thou thyself sayest, thou broughtest [into the palace;] whom thou didst prefer before so many of thy sons; whom thou madest a king in thine own lifetime, and, by the vast magnitude of the other advantages thou bestowedst on me, thou madest me an object of envy. O miserable man! that thou shouldest undergo that bitter absence, and thereby afford a great opportunity for envy to rise against thee, and a long space for such as were laying designs against thee! Yet was I absent, father, on thy affairs, that Sylleus might not treat thee with contempt in thine old age. Rome is a witness to my filial affection, and so is Cæsar, the ruler of the habitable earth, who oftentimes called me Philopater.* Take here the letters he hath sent thee, they are more to be believed than the calumnies raised here; these letters are my only apology; these I use as the demonstration of that natural affection I have to thee. Remember, that it was against my own choice that I sailed [to Rome,] as knowing that latent hatred that was in the kingdom against me. It was thou, O father, however unwillingly, who hast been my ruin, by forcing me to allow time for the calumnies against me, and envy at me. However, I am come hither, and am ready to hear the evidence there is against me. If I be a parricide, I have passed by land and by sea, without suffering any misfortunes on either of them: but this method of trial is no advantage to me; for it seems, O father, that I am already condemned, both before God and before thee; and as I am already condemned, I beg that thou wilt not believe the others that have been tortured, but let fire be brought to torment me; let the racks march through my bowels; have no regard to any lamentations that this polluted body can make; for if I be a parricide, I ought not to die without torture." Thus did Antipater cry out with lamentation and weeping, and moved all the rest, and Varus in particular, to commiserate his case. Herod was the only person whose passion was too strong to permit him to weep, as knowing that the testimonies against him were true.

4. And now it was that, at the king's com-

---

* A lover of his father.

mand, Nicolaus, when he had premised a great deal about the craftiness of Antipater, and had prevented the effects of their commiseration to him, afterwards brought in a bitter and large accusation against him, ascribing all the wickedness that had been in the kingdom to him, and especially the murder of his brethren, and demonstrated that they had perished by the calumnies he had raised against them. He also said that he had laid designs against them that were still alive, as if they were laying plots for the succession; and (said he) how can it be supposed that he who prepared poison for his father, should abstain from mischief as to his brethren? He then proceeded to convict him of the attempt to poison Herod, and gave an account, in order, of the several discoveries that had been made; and had great indignation as to the affair of Pheroras, because Antipater had been for making him murder his brother, and had corrupted those that were dearest to the king, and filled the whole palace with wickedness; and when he had insisted on many other accusations, and the proofs of them, he left off.

5. Then Varus bade Antipater make his defence; but he lay long in silence, and said no more but this:—"God is my witness that I am entirely innocent." So Varus asked for the potion, and gave it to be drunk by a condemned malefactor, who was then in prison, who died upon the spot. So Varus, when he had had a very private discourse with Herod, and had written an account of this assembly to Cæsar, went away, after a day's stay. The king also bound Antipater, and sent away to inform Cæsar of his misfortunes.

6. Now after this, it was discovered that Antipater had laid a plot against Salome also; for one of Antiphilus's domestic servants came, and brought letters from Rome, from the maidservant of Julia, [Cæsar's wife,] whose name was Acme. By her a message was sent to the king, that she had found a letter written by Salome, among Julia's papers, and had sent it to him privately, out of her good will to him. This letter of Salome contained the most bitter reproaches of the king, and the highest accusation against him. Antipater had forged this letter, and had corrupted Acme, and persuaded her to send it to Herod. This was proved by her letter to Antipater, for thus did this woman write to him:—"As thou desirest, I have written a letter to thy father, and have sent that letter; and am persuaded that the king will not spare his sister when he reads it. Thou wilt do well to remember what thou hast promised, when all is accomplished."

7. When this epistle was discovered, and what the epistle forged against Salome contained, a suspicion came into the king's mind, that perhaps the letters against Alexander were also forged: he was moreover greatly disturbed, and in a passion because he had almost slain his sister on Antipater's account. He did no longer delay therefore to bring him to punishment for all his crimes; yet when he was eagerly pursuing Antipater, he was restrained by a severe distemper he fell into. However, he sent an account to Cæsar about Acme, and the contrivances against Salome: he sent also for his testament, and altered it, and therein made Antipas king, as taking no care of Archelaus and Philip, because Antipater had blasted their reputation with him; but he bequeathed to Cæsar, besides other presents that he gave him, a thousand talents; as also to his wife, and children, and friends, and freedmen about five hundred: he also bequeathed to all others a great quantity of land, and of money, and shewed his respects to Salome his sister, by giving her most splendid gifts. And this was what was contained in his testament, as it was now altered.

CHAPTER XXXII

THE GOLDEN EAGLE IS CUT TO PIECES. HEROD'S BARBARITY WHEN HE WAS READY TO DIE. HE ATTEMPTS TO KILL HIMSELF. HE COMMANDS ANTIPATER TO BE SLAIN. HE SURVIVES HIM FIVE DAYS, AND THEN DIES

1. Now Herod's distemper became more and more severe to him, and this because these his disorders fell upon him in his old age, and when he was in a melancholy condition; for he was already almost seventy years of age, and had been brought low by the calamities that happened to him about his children, whereby he had no pleasure in life, even when he was in health; the grief also that Antipater was still alive aggravated his disease, whom he resolved to put to death now, not at random, but as soon as he should be well again, and resolved to have him slain [in a public manner.]

2. There also now happened to him among his other calamities, a certain popular sedition. There were two men of learning in the city, [Jerusalem,] who were thought the most skilful in the laws of their country, and were on that account had in very great esteem all over the nation; they were the one Judas, the son of Sepphoris, and the other Matthias, the son of Margalus. There was a great concourse of the young men came to these men when they expounded the laws, and there got together every day a kind of an army of such as were growing up to be men. Now when these men were informed that the king was wearing away with melancholy, and with a distemper, they dropped words to their acquaintance, how it was now a very proper time to defend the cause of God, and to pull down what had been erected contrary to the laws of their country; for it was unlawful there should be any such thing in the temple as images, or faces, or the like representation of any animal whatsoever. Now the king had put up a golden eagle over the great gate of the temple, which these learned men exhorted them to cut down: and told them that if there should any danger arise, it was a glorious thing to die for the laws of their country; because that the soul was immortal, and that an eternal enjoyment of happiness did await such as died on that account; while the mean-spirited, and those that were not wise enough to shew a right love of their souls, preferred death by a disease, before that which is the result of a virtuous behaviour.

3. At the same time that these men made this speech to their disciples, a rumour was spread abroad that the king was dying, which made the young men set about the work with greater boldness; they therefore let themselves down from the top of the temple with thick cords, and this at mid-day, and while a great number of people were in the temple, and cut down that golden eagle with axes. This was presently told to the king's captain of the temple, who came running with a great body of soldiers, and caught about forty of the young men, and brought them to the king. And when he asked them, first of all, whether they had been so hardy as to cut down the golden eagle, they confessed they had done so; and when he asked them by whose

GOLDEN EAGLE TORN DOWN

command they had done it, they replied at the command of the law of their country; and when he further asked them how they could be so joyful when they were to be put to death, they replied, because they should enjoy greater happiness after they were dead.

4. At this the king was in such an extravagant passion, that he overcame his disease, [for the time,] and went out, and spake to the people; wherein he made a terrible accusation against those men, as being guilty of sacrilege, and as making greater attempts under pretence of their law; and he thought they deserved to be punished as impious persons. Whereupon the people were afraid lest a great number should be found guilty, and desired that when he had first punished those that put them upon this work, and then those that were caught in it, he would leave off his anger as to the rest. With this the king complied, though not without difficulty; and ordered those that had let themselves down, together with their rabbins, to be burnt alive; but delivered the rest that were caught to the proper officers, to be put to death by them.

5. After this the distemper seized his whole body, and greatly disordered all its parts with various symptoms; for there was a gentle fever upon him, and an intolerable itching over all the surface of his body, and continual pains in his colon, and dropsical tumours about his feet, and an inflammation of the abdomen,—and a putrefaction of his privy member, that produced worms. Besides which he had a difficulty of breathing upon him, and could not breathe but when he sat upright, and had a convulsion of all his members; insomuch that the diviners said those diseases were a punishment upon him for what he had done to the rabbins. Yet did he struggle with his numerous disorders, and still had a desire to live, and hoped for recovery, and considered several methods of cure. Accordingly, he went over Jordan, and made use of those hot baths at Callirrhoe, which run into the lake Asphaltitis, but are themselves sweet enough to be drunk. And here the physicians thought proper to bathe his whole body in warm oil, by letting it down into a large vessel full of oil; whereupon his eyes failed him, and he came and went as if he were dying; and as a tumult was then made by his servants, at their voice he revived again. Yet did he after this despair of recovery, and gave orders that each soldier should have fifty drachmæ a-piece, and that his commanders and friends should have great sums of money given them.

6. He then returned back and came to Jericho, in such a melancholy state of body as almost threatened him with present death, when he proceeded to attempt a horrid wickedness; for he got together the most illustrious men of the whole Jewish nation, out of every village, into a place called the Hippodrome, and there shut them in. He then called for his sister Salome, and her husband Alexas, and made his speech to them:—"I know well enough that the Jews will keep a festival upon my death; however, it is in my power to be mourned for on other accounts, and to have a splendid funeral, if you will but be subservient to my commands. Do you but take care to send soldiers to encompass these men that are now in custody, and slay them immediately upon my death, and then all Judea, and every family of them, will weep at it whether they will or no."

7. These were the commands he gave them: when there came letters from his ambassadors at Rome, whereby information was given that Acme was put to death at Cæsar's command,

and that Antipater was condemned to die; however, they write withal, that if Herod had a mind rather to banish him, Cæsar permitted him so to do. So he for a little while revived, and had a desire to live; but presently after he was overborne by his pains, and was disordered by want of food, and by a convulsive cough, and endeavoured to prevent a natural death; so he took an apple, and asked for a knife, for he used to pare apples and eat them; he then looked round about to see that there was nobody to hinder him, and lifted up his right hand as if he would stab himself; but Achiabus, his first cousin, came running to him, and held his hand, and hindered him from so doing; on which occasion a very great lamentation was made in the palace as if the king were expiring. As soon as ever Antipater heard that, he took courage, and with joy in his looks, besought his keepers, for a sum of money, to loose him and let him go; but the principal keeper of the prison did not only obstruct him in that his intention, but ran and told the king what his design was; hereupon the king cried out louder than his distemper would well bear, and immediately sent some of his guards and slew Antipater; he also gave order to have him buried at Hyrcanium, and altered his testament again,—and therein made Archelaus, his eldest son, and the brother of Antipas, his successor; and made Antipas tetrarch.

8. So Herod, having survived the slaughter of his son five days, died, having reigned thirty-four years, since he had caused Antigonus to be slain, and obtained his kingdom; but thirty-seven years since he had been made king by the Romans. Now, as for his fortune, it was prosperous in all other respects, if ever any other man could be so; since, from a private man, he obtained the kingdom, and kept it so long, and left it to his own sons; but still in his domestic affairs, he was a most unfortunate man. Now before the soldiers knew of his death, Salome and her husband came out and dismissed those that were in bonds, whom the king had commanded to be slain, and told them he had altered his mind, and would have every one of them sent to their own homes. When these men were gone, Salome told the soldiers [the king was dead,] and got them and the rest of the multitude together to an assembly, in the amphitheatre at Jericho, where Ptolemy, who was intrusted by the king with his signet-ring, came before them, and spake of the happiness the king had attained, and comforted the multitude, and read the epistle which had been left for the soldiers, wherein he earnestly exhorted them to bear good-will to his successor; and after he had read the epistle, he opened and read his testament, wherein Philip was to inherit Trachonitis, and the neighbouring countries, and Antipas was to be tetrarch, as we said before, and Archelaus was made king. He had also been commanded to carry Herod's ring to Cæsar, and the settlements he had made, sealed up, because Cæsar was to be lord of all the settlements he had made, and was to confirm his testament; and he ordered that the dispositions he had made were to be kept as they were in his former testament.

9. So there was an acclamation made to Archelaus to congratulate him upon his advancement; and the soldiers, with the multitude, went round about in troops, and promised him their good-will, and besides, prayed God to bless his government. After this, they betook themselves to prepare for the king's funeral; and Archelaus omitted nothing of magnificence therein, but

brought out all the royal ornaments to augment the pomp of the deceased. There was a bier all of gold, embroidered with precious stones, and a purple bed of various contexture with the dead body upon it, covered with purple; and a diadem was put upon his head, and a crown of gold above it, and a sceptre in his right hand; and near to the bier were Herod's sons, and a multitude of his kindred; next to whom came his guards, and the regiment of Thracians, the Germans also and Gauls, all accoutred as if they were going to war; but the rest of the army went foremost, armed, and following their captains and officers in a regular manner: after whom, five hundred of his domestic servants and freedmen followed, with sweet spices in their hands; and the body was carried two hundred furlongs, to Herodium, where he had given order to be buried. And this shall suffice for the conclusion of the life of Herod.

BOOK II

CONTAINING THE INTERVAL OF SIXTY-NINE YEARS

FROM THE DEATH OF HEROD TILL VESPASIAN WAS SENT TO SUBDUE THE JEWS BY NERO

CHAPTER I

ARCHELAUS MAKES A FUNERAL FEAST FOR THE PEOPLE, ON ACCOUNT OF HEROD. AFTER WHICH A GREAT TUMULT IS RAISED BY THE MULTITUDE, AND HE SENDS THE SOLDIERS OUT UPON THEM, WHO DESTROY ABOUT THREE THOUSAND OF THEM

1. Now the necessity which Archelaus was under of taking a journey to Rome was the occasion of new disturbances; for when he had mourned for his father seven days, and had given a very expensive funeral feast to the multitude (which custom is the occasion of poverty to many of the Jews, because they are forced to feast the multitude; for if any one omits it, he is not esteemed a holy person,) he put on a white garment, and went up to the temple, where the people accosted him with various acclamations. He also spake kindly to the multitude, from an elevated seat and a throne of gold, and returned them thanks for the zeal they had shewn about his father's funeral, and the submission they had made to him, as if he were already settled in the kingdom; but he told them withal, that he would not at present take upon him either the authority of a king, or the names thereto belonging, until Cæsar, who is made lord of this whole affair by the testament, confirms the succession; for that when the soldiers would have set the diadem on his head at Jericho, he would not accept of it; but that he would make abundant requitals, not to the soldiers only, but to the people, for their alacrity and good-will to him, when the superior lords [the Romans] should have given him a complete title to the kingdom; for that it should be his study to appear in all things better than his father.
2. Upon this the multitude was pleased, and presently made a trial of what he intended, by asking great things of him; for some made a clamour that he would ease them in their taxes; others, that he would take off the duties upon commodities; and some, that he would loose those that were in prison; in all which cases he answered readily to their satisfaction, in order to get the good-will of the multitude; after which he offered [the proper] sacrifices, and feasted with his friends. And here it was that

a great many of those that desired innovations came in crowds towards evening, and began then to mourn on their own account, when the public mourning for the king was over. These lamented those that were put to death by Herod, because they had cut down the golden eagle that had been over the gate of the temple. Nor was this mourning of a private nature, but the lamentations were very great, the mourning solemn, and the weeping such as was loudly heard all over the city, as being for those men who had perished for the laws of their country, and for the temple. They cried out, that a punishment ought to be inflicted for these men upon those that were honoured by Herod; and that, in the first place, the man whom he had made high-priest should be deprived; and that it was fit to choose a person of greater piety and purity than he was.
3. At these clamours Archelaus was provoked; but restrained himself from taking vengeance on the authors, on account of the haste he was in of going to Rome, as fearing lest, upon his making war on the multitude, such an action might detain him at home. Accordingly, he made trial to quiet the innovators by persuasion rather than by force, and sent his general in a private way to them, and by him exhorted them to be quiet. But the seditious threw stones at him, and drove him away, as he came into the temple, and before he could say anything to them. The like treatment they shewed to others, who came to them after him, many of whom were sent by Archelaus, in order to reduce them to sobriety, and these answered still on all occasions after a passionate manner; and it openly appeared that they would not be quiet, if their numbers were but considerable. And indeed, at the feast of unleavened bread, which was now at hand, and is by the Jews called the passover, and used to be celebrated with a great number of sacrifices, and an innumerable multitude of people came out of the country to worship: some of these stood in the temple bewailing the rabbins [that had been put to death], and procured their sustenance by begging, in order to support their sedition. At this Archelaus was affrighted, and privately sent a tribune, with a cohort of soldiers, upon them, before the disease should spread over the whole multitude, and gave orders that they should constrain those that

began the tumult, by force, to be quiet. At these the whole multitude was irritated, and threw stones at many of the soldiers, and killed them ; but the tribune fled away wounded, and had much ado to escape so. After which they betook themselves to their sacrifices, as if they had done no mischief ; nor did it appear to Archelaus that the multitude could be restrained without bloodshed ; so he sent his whole army upon them, the footmen in great multitudes, by the way of the city, and the horsemen by the way of the plain, who, falling upon them on the sudden, as they were offering their sacrifices, destroyed about three thousand of them ; but the rest of the multitude were dispersed upon the adjoining mountains : these were followed by Archelaus's heralds, who commanded every one to retire to their own homes ; whither they all went, and left the festival.

CHAPTER II

ARCHELAUS GOES TO ROME WITH A GREAT NUM-
BER OF HIS KINDRED : HE IS THERE ACCUSED
BEFORE CÆSAR BY ANTIPATER ; BUT IS SUPERIOR
TO HIS ACCUSERS IN JUDGMENT, BY THE MEANS
OF THAT DEFENCE WHICH NICOLAUS MADE FOR
HIM

1. ARCHELAUS went down now to the sea-side, with his mother and his friends, Poplas, and Ptolemy, and Nicolaus, and left behind him Philip, to be his steward in the palace, and to take care of his domestic affairs. Salome went also along with him with her sons, as did also the king's brethren and sons-in-law. These, in appearance, went to give him all the assistance they were able, in order to secure his succession, but in reality to accuse him for his breach of the laws by what he had done at the temple.

2. But as they were come to Cesarea, Sabinus, the procurator of Syria, met them ; he was going up to Judea, to secure Herod's effects ; but Varus, [president of Syria,] who was come thither, restrained him from going any further. This Varus, Archelaus had sent for, by the earnest entreaty of Ptolemy. At this time, indeed, Sabinus, to gratify Varus, neither went to the citadels, nor did he shut up the treasuries where his father's money was laid up, but promised that he would lie still until Cæsar should have taken cognisance of the affair. So he abode at Cesarea ; but as soon as those that were his hindrance were gone, when Varus was gone to Antioch, and Archelaus was sailed to Rome, he immediately went on to Jerusalem, and seized upon the palace ; and when he had called for the governors of the citadels, and the stewards [of the king's private affairs,] he tried to sift out the accounts of the money, and to take possession of the citadels. But the governors of those citadels were not unmindful of the commands laid upon them by Archelaus, and continued to guard them, and said, the custody of them rather belonged to Cæsar than to Archelaus.

3. In the meantime Antipas went also to Rome, to strive for the kingdom, and to insist that the former testament, wherein he was named to be king, was valid before the latter testament. Salome had also promised to assist him, as had many of Archelaus's kindred, who sailed along with Archelaus himself also. He also carried along with him his mother, and Ptolemy, the brother of Nicolaus, who seemed one of great weight, on account of the great trust Herod put in him, he having been one of his most honoured friends. However, Antipas depended chiefly upon Ireneus, the orator ; upon whose authority he had rejected such as advised him to yield to Archelaus, because he was his elder brother, and because the second testament gave the kingdom to him. The inclinations also of all Archelaus's kindred, who hated him, were removed to Antipas, when they came to Rome ; although, in the first place, every one rather desired to live under their own laws [without a king,] and to be under a Roman governor ; but if they should fail in that point, these desired that Antipas might be their king.

4. Sabinus did also afford these his assistance to the same purpose by the letters he sent, wherein he accused Archelaus before Cæsar, and highly commended Antipas. Salome also, and those with her, put the crimes which they accused Archelaus of in order, and put them into Cæsar's hands ; and after they had done that, Archelaus wrote down the reasons of his claim, and, by Ptolemy, sent in his father's ring, and his father's accounts ; and when Cæsar had maturely weighed by himself what both had to allege for themselves, as also had considered of the great burden of the kingdom, the largeness of the revenues, and withal the number of children Herod had left behind him, and had moreover read the letters he had received from Varus and Sabinus on this occasion, he assembled the principal persons among the Romans together (in which assembly Caius, the son of Agrippa, and his daughter Julias, but by himself adopted for his own son, sat in the first seat) and gave the pleaders leave to speak.

5. Then stood up Salome's son, Antipater (who of all Archelaus's antagonists was the shrewdest pleader,) and accused him in the following speech :—That Archelaus did in words contend for the kingdom, but that in deeds he had long exercised royal authority, and so did insult Cæsar in desiring to be now heard on that account, since he had not stayed for his determination about the succession, and since he had suborned certain persons, after Herod's death, to move for putting the diadem upon his head ; since he had set himself down in the throne, and given answers as a king, and altered the disposition of the army, and granted to some higher dignities : that he had also complied in all things with the people in the requests they had made to him as to their king, and had also dismissed those that had been put into bonds by his father, for most important reasons. Now, after all this, he desires the shadow of that royal authority, whose substance he had already seized to himself, and so hath made Cæsar lord, not of things, but of words. He also reproached him further, that his mourning for his father was only pretended, while he put on a sad countenance in the daytime, but drank to great excess in the night ; from which behaviour, he said, the late disturbances among the multitude came, while they had an indignation thereat ; and indeed the purport of his whole discourse was to aggravate Archelaus's crime in slaying such a multitude about the temple, which multitude came to the festival, but were barbarously slain in the midst of their own sacrifices ; and he said there was such a vast number of dead bodies heaped together in the temple, as even a foreign war, should that come upon them [suddenly,] before it was denounced, could not have heaped together ; and he added, that it was the foresight his father had of that his barbarity, which made him never give him any hopes of the kingdom ; but when his mind was more infirm than his body, and he was not able to

reason soundly, and did not well know what was the character of that son, whom in his second testament he made his successor; and this was done by him at a time when he had no complaints to make of him whom he had named before, when he was sound in body, and when his mind was free from all passion. That, however, if any one should suppose Herod's judgment, when he was sick, was superior to that at another time, yet had Archelaus forfeited his kingdom by his own behaviour, and those his actions, which were contrary to the law and to its disadvantage. Or what sort of a king will this man be, when he hath obtained the government from Cæsar, who hath slain so many before he hath obtained it!

6. When Antipater had spoken largely to this purpose, and had produced a great number of Archelaus's kindred as witnesses, to prove every part of the accusation, he ended his discourse. Then stood up Nicolaus to plead for Archelaus. He alleged that the slaughter in the temple could not be avoided; that those that were slain were become enemies not to Archelaus's kingdom only, but to Cæsar, who was to determine about him. He also demonstrated, that Archelaus's accusers had advised him to perpetrate other things of which he might have been accused; but he insisted that the latter testament should, for this reason, above all others, be esteemed valid, because Herod had therein appointed Cæsar to be the person who should confirm the succession; for he who shewed such prudence as to recede from his own power, and yield it up to the lord of the world, cannot be supposed mistaken in his judgment about him that was to be his heir; and he that so well knew whom to choose for arbitrator of the succession could not be unacquainted with him whom he chose for his successor.

7. When Nicolaus had gone through all he had to say, Archelaus came, and fell down before Cæsar's knees, without any noise;—upon which he raised him up, after a very obliging manner, and declared, that truly he was worthy to succeed his father. However, he still made no firm determination in his case; but when he had dismissed those assessors that had been with him that day, he deliberated by himself about the allegations which he had heard, whether it were fit to constitute any of those named in the testaments for Herod's successor, or whether the government should be parted among all his posterity; and this because of the number of those that seemed to stand in need of support therefrom.

CHAPTER III

THE JEWS FIGHT A GREAT BATTLE WITH SABINUS'S SOLDIERS, AND A GREAT DESTRUCTION IS MADE AT JERUSALEM

1. Now before Cæsar had determined anything about these affairs, Malthace, Archelaus's mother, fell sick and died. Letters also were brought out of Syria from Varus, about a revolt of the Jews. This was foreseen by Varus, who accordingly, after Archelaus was sailed, went up to Jerusalem to restrain the promoters of the sedition, since it was manifest that the nation would not be at rest; so he left one of those legions which he brought with him out of Syria in the city, and went himself to Antioch. But Sabinus came, after he was gone, and gave them an occasion of making innovations; for he compelled the keeper of the citadels to deliver them up to him, and made a bitter search after the king's money, as depending not only on the soldiers who were left by Varus, but on the multitude of his own servants, all whom he armed and used as the instruments of his covetousness. Now when that feast, which was observed after seven weeks, and which the Jews called Pentecost (i.e., the 50th day) was at hand, its name being taken from the number of the days [after the Passover,] the people got together, but not on account of the accustomed divine worship, but of the indignation they had [at the present state of affairs.] Wherefore an immense multitude ran together, out of Galilee, and Idumea, and Jericho, and Perea that was beyond Jordan; but the people that naturally belonged to Judea itself were above the rest both in number and in the alacrity of the men. So they distributed themselves into three parts, and pitched their camps in three places; one at the north side of the temple, another at the south side, by the Hippodrome, and the third part were at the palace on the west. So they lay round about the Romans on every side, and besieged them.

2. Now Sabinus was affrighted, both at their multitude and at their courage, and sent messengers to Varus continually, and besought him to come to his succour quickly, for that, if he delayed, his legion would be cut to pieces. As for Sabinus himself, he got up to the highest tower of the fortress, which was called Phasaelus; it is of the same name with Herod's brother, who was destroyed by the Parthians; and then he made signs to the soldiers of that legion to attack the enemy; for his astonishment was so great, that he durst not go down to his own men. Hereupon the soldiers were prevailed upon, and leaped out into the temple, and fought a terrible battle with the Jews; in which, while there were none over their heads to distress them, they were too hard for them, by their skill, and the others' want of skill in war; but when once many of the Jews had gotten up to the top of the cloisters and threw their darts downward upon the heads of the Romans, there were a great many of them destroyed. Nor was it easy to avenge themselves upon those that threw their weapons from on high, nor was it more easy for them to sustain those who came to fight them hand to hand.

3. Since therefore the Romans were sorely afflicted by both these circumstances, they set fire to the cloisters, which were works to be admired, both on account of their magnitude and costliness. Whereupon those that were above them were presently encompassed with the flame, and many of them perished therein; as many of them also were destroyed by the enemy, who came suddenly upon them; some of them also threw themselves down from the walls backward, and some there were, who, from the desperate condition they were in, prevented the fire, by killing themselves with their own swords; but so many of them as crept out from the walls, and came upon the Romans, were easily mastered by them, by reason of the astonishment they were under; until at last some of the Jews being destroyed, and others dispersed by the terror they were in, the soldiers fell upon the treasure of God, which was now deserted, and plundered about four hundred talents, of which sum Sabinus got together all that was not carried away by the soldiers.

4. However, this destruction of the works [about the temple,] and of the men, occasioned a much greater number, and those of a more

warlike sort, to get together, to oppose the Romans. These encompassed the palace round, and threatened to destroy all that were in it, unless they went their ways quickly; for they promised that Sabinus should come to no harm if he should go out with his legion. There were also a great many of the king's party who deserted the Romans, and assisted the Jews; yet did the most warlike body of them all, who were three thousand of the men of Sebaste, go over to the Romans. Rufus also, and Gratus, their captains, did the same, (Gratus having the foot of the king's party under him, and Rufus the horse;) each of whom, even without the forces under them, were of great weight, on account of their strength and wisdom, which turns the scales in war. Now the Jews persevered in the siege, and tried to break down the walls of the fortress, and cried out to Sabinus and his party, that they should go their ways, and not prove a hindrance to them, now they hoped after a long time to recover that ancient liberty which their forefathers had enjoyed. Sabinus indeed was well contented to go out of the danger he was in; but he distrusted the assurances the Jews gave him, and suspected such gentle treatment was but a bait laid as a snare for them: this consideration, together with the hopes he had of succour from Varus, made him bear the siege still longer.

CHAPTER IV

HEROD'S VETERAN SOLDIERS BECOME TUMULTUOUS. THE ROBBERIES OF JUDAS. SIMON AND ATHRONGEUS TAKE THE NAME OF KING UPON THEM

1. AT this time there were great disturbances in the country, and that in many places; and the opportunity that now offered itself induced a great many to set up for kings; and indeed in Idumea two thousand of Herod's veteran soldiers got together, and armed themselves, and fought against those of the king's party; against whom Achaibus, the king's first cousin, fought, and that out of some of the places that were the most strongly fortified; but so as to avoid a direct conflict with them in the plains. In Sepphoris also, a city of Galilee, there was one Judas, (the son of the arch-robber Hezekias, who formerly over-ran the country, and had been subdued by king Herod;) this man got no small multitude together, and broke open the place where the royal armour was laid up, and armed those about him, and attacked those that were so earnest to gain the dominion.

2. In Perea also, Simon, one of the servants to the king, relying upon the handsome appearance, and tallness of his body, put a diadem upon his own head also; he also went about with a company of robbers that he had gotten together, and burnt down the royal palace that was at Jericho, and many other costly edifices besides, and procured himself very easily spoils by rapine, as snatching them out of the fire; and he had soon burnt down all the fine edifices, if Gratus, the captain of the foot of the king's party, had not taken the Trachonite archers, and the most warlike of Sebaste, and met the man. His footmen were slain in the battle in abundance; Gratus also cut to pieces Simon himself, as he was flying along a strait valley, when he gave him an oblique stroke upon his neck, as he ran away, and brake it. The royal palaces that were near Jordan at Betharamptha,

were also burnt down by some other of the seditious that came out of Perea.

3. At this time it was that a certain shepherd ventured to set himself up for a king: he was called Athrongeus. It was his strength of body that made him expect such a dignity, as well as his soul, which despised death; and besides these qualifications, he had four brethren like himself. He put a troop of armed men under each of these his brethren, and made use of them as his generals and commanders, when he made his incursions, while he did himself act like a king, and meddled only with the more important affairs; and at this time he put a diadem about his head, and continued after that to over-run the country for no little time with his brethren, and became their leader in killing both the Romans and those of the king's party; nor did any Jew escape him, if any gain could accrue to him thereby. He once ventured to encompass a whole body of Romans at Emmaus, who were carrying corn and weapons to their legion: his men shot their arrows and darts, and thereby slew their centurion Arius, and forty of the stoutest of his men, while the rest of them, who were in danger of the same fate, upon the coming of Gratus, with those of Sebaste, to their assistance, escaped; and when these men had thus served both their own countrymen and foreigners, and that through this whole war, three of them were after some time subdued; the eldest by Archelaus, the two next by falling into the hands of Gratus and Ptolemeus; but the fourth delivered himself up to Archelaus, upon his giving him his right hand for his security. However, this their end was not till afterward, while at present they filled all Judea with a piratic war.

CHAPTER V

VARUS COMPOSES THE TUMULTS IN JUDEA, AND CRUCIFIES ABOUT TWO THOUSAND OF THE SEDITIOUS

1. UPON Varus's reception of the letters that were written by Sabinus and the captains, he could not avoid being afraid for the whole legion [he had left there.] So he made haste to their relief, and took with him the other two legions, with the four troops of horsemen to them belonging, and marched to Ptolemais—having given orders for the auxiliaries that were sent by the kings and governors of cities to meet him there. Moreover, he received from the people of Berytus, as he passed through their city, fifteen hundred armed men. Now as soon as the other body of auxiliaries were come to Ptolemais, as well as Aretas the Arabian, (who out of the hatred he bore to Herod, brought a great army of horse and foot,) Varus sent a part of his army presently to Galilee, which lay near to Ptolemais, and Caius, one of his friends, for their captain. This Caius put those that met him to flight, and took the city Sepphoris and burnt it, and made slaves of its inhabitants. But as for Varus himself, he marched to Samaria with his whole army, where he did not meddle with the city itself, because he found that it had made no commotion during those troubles, but pitched his camp about a certain village which was called Arius. It belonged to Ptolemy, and on that account was plundered by the Arabians, who were very angry even at Herod's friends also. He thence marched on to the village Sampho, another fortified place,

which they plundered, as they had done the other. As they carried off all the money they lighted upon belonging to the public revenues, all was now full of fire and bloodshed, and nothing could resist the plunders of the Arabians. Emmaus was also burnt, upon the flight of its inhabitants, and this at the command of Varus, out of his rage at the slaughter of those that were about Arius.

2. Thence he marched on to Jerusalem, and as soon as he was but seen by the Jews, he made their camps disperse themselves: they also went away, and fled up and down the country. But the citizens received him, and cleared themselves of having any hand in this revolt, and said that they had raised no commotions, but had only been forced to admit the multitude, because of the festival, and that they were rather besieged together with the Romans, than assisted those that had revolted. There had before this met him Joseph, the first cousin of Archelaus, and Gratus, together with Rufus, who led those of Sebaste, as well as the king's army: there also met him those of the Roman legion, armed after their accustomed manner; for as to Sabinus, he durst not come into Varus's sight, but was gone out of the city before this, to the sea-side. But Varus sent a part of his army into the country, against those that had been the authors of this commotion, and as they caught great numbers of them, those that appeared to have been the least concerned in these tumults he put into custody, but such as were the most guilty he crucified; these were in number about two thousand.

3. He was also informed that there continued in Idumea ten thousand men still in arms; but when he found that the Arabians did not act like auxiliaries, but managed the war according to their own passions, and did mischief to the country otherwise than he intended, and this out of their hatred to Herod, he sent them away, but made haste, with his own legions, to march against those that had revolted; but these, by the advice of Achiabus, delivered themselves up to him before it came to a battle. Then did Varus forgive the multitude their offences, but sent their captains to Cæsar to be examined by him. Now Cæsar forgave the rest, but gave orders that certain of the king's relations (for some of those that were among them were Herod's kinsmen) should be put to death, because they had engaged in a war against a king of their own family. When, therefore, Varus had settled matters at Jerusalem after this manner, and had left the former legion there as a garrison, he returned to Antioch.

CHAPTER VI

THE JEWS GREATLY COMPLAIN OF ARCHELAUS, AND DESIRE THAT THEY MAY BE MADE SUBJECT TO ROMAN GOVERNORS. BUT WHEN CÆSAR HAD HEARD WHAT THEY HAD TO SAY, HE DISTRIBUTED HEROD'S DOMINIONS AMONG HIS SONS, ACCORDING TO HIS OWN PLEASURE

1. BUT now came another accusation from the Jews against Archelaus at Rome, which he was to answer to. It was made by those ambassadors who, before the revolt, had come, by Varus's permission, to plead for the liberty of their country; those that came were fifty in number, but there were more than eight thousand of the Jews at Rome who supported them; and when Cæsar had assembled a council of the principal Romans in Apollo's * temple, that was in the palace, (this was what he had himself built and adorned, at a vast expense,) the multitude of the Jews stood with the ambassadors, and on the other side stood Archelaus, with his friends: but as for the kindred of Archelaus, they stood on neither side; for to stand on Archelaus's side, their hatred to him, and envy at him, would not give them leave; while yet they were afraid to be seen by Cæsar with his accusers. Besides these, there were present Archelaus's brother, Philip, being sent thither beforehand, out of kindness, by Varus, for two reasons: the one was this, that he might be assisting to Archelaus; and the other was this, that in case Cæsar should make a distribution of what Herod possessed among his posterity, he might obtain some share of it.

2. And now, upon the permission that was given the accusers to speak, they, in the first place, went over Herod's breaches of their law, and said that he was not a king, but the most barbarous of all tyrants, and that they had found him to be such by the sufferings they underwent from him: that when a very great number had been slain by him, those that were left had endured such miseries, that they called those that were dead happy men; that he had not only tortured the bodies of his subjects, but entire cities, and had done much harm to the cities of his own country, while he adorned those that belonged to foreigners; and he shed the blood of Jews in order to do kindness to those people who were out of their bounds: that he had filled the nation full of poverty, and of the greatest iniquity, instead of that happiness and those laws which they had anciently enjoyed; that, in short, the Jews had borne more calamities from Herod, in a few years, than had their forefathers during all that interval of time that had passed since they had come out of Babylon, and returned home in the reign of Xerxes:† that, however, the nation was come to so low a condition, by being inured to hardships, that they submitted to his successor of their own accord, though he brought them into bitter slavery; that accordingly they readily called Archelaus, though he was the son of so great a tyrant, *king,* after the decease of his father, and joined with him in mourning for the death of Herod, and in wishing him good success in that his succession; while yet this Archelaus, lest he should be in danger of not being thought the genuine son of Herod, began his reign with the murder of three thousand citizens; as if he had a mind to offer so many bloody sacrifices to God for his government, and to fill the temple with the like number of dead bodies at that festival: that, however, those that were left after so many miseries, had just reason to consider now at last the calamities they had undergone, and to oppose themselves, like soldiers in war, to receive those stripes upon their faces. [but not upon their backs as hitherto.] Whereupon they prayed that the Romans would have compassion upon the [poor] remains of Judea, and not expose what was left of them to such as barbarously tore them to pieces, and that they would join their country to Syria, and administer the go-

* This holding of a council in the temple of Apollo, in the emperor's palace at Rome, by Augustus, and even the building of this temple magnificently by himself in that palace, are exactly agreeable to Augustus in his elder years.

† Here we have a strong confirmation that it was Xerxes, and not Artaxerxes, under whom the main part of the Jews returned out of the Babylonian captivity; i.e., in the days of Ezra and Nehemiah.

vernment by their own commanders, whereby it would [soon] be demonstrated that those who are now under the calumny of seditious persons, and lovers of war, know how to bear governors that are set over them, if they be but tolerable ones. So the Jews concluded their accusations with this request. Then rose up Nicolaus, and confuted the accusations that were brought against the kings, and himself accused the Jewish nation, as hard to be ruled, and as naturally disobedient to kings. He also reproached all those kinsmen of Archelaus who had left him, and were gone over to his accusers.

3. So Cæsar, after he had heard both sides, dissolved the assembly for that time; but a few days afterward, he gave the one half of Herod's kingdom to Archelaus, by the name of Ethnarch, and promised to make him king also afterward, if he rendered himself worthy of that dignity; but as to the other half, he divided it into two tetrarchies, and gave them to two other sons of Herod, the one of them to Philip, and the other to that Antipas who contested the kingdom with Archelaus. Under this last was Perea and Galilee, with a revenue of two hundred talents: but Batanea, and Trachonitis, and Auranitis, and certain parts of Zeno's house about Jamnia, with a revenue of a hundred talents, were made subject to Philip; while Idumea, and all Judea, and Samaria, were parts of the ethnarchy of Archelaus, although Samaria was eased of one quarter of its taxes, out of regard to their not having revolted with the rest of the nation. He also made subject to him the following cities, viz. Strato's Tower, and Sebaste, and Joppa, and Jerusalem; but as to the Grecian cities Gaza and Gadara, and Hippos, he cut them off from the kingdom, and added them to Syria. Now the revenue of the country that was given to Archelaus, was four hundred talents. Salome also, besides what the king had left her in his testaments, was now made mistress of Jamnia, and Ashdod, and Phasaelis. Cæsar did moreever bestow upon her the royal palace of Ascalon; by all which she got together a revenue of sixty talents; but he put her house under the ethnarchy of Archelaus; and for the rest of Herod's offspring, they received what was bequeathed to them in his testaments; but, besides that, Cæsar granted to Herod's two virgin daughters five hundred thousand [drachmæ] of silver, and gave them in marriage to the sons of Pheroras: but after this family distribution, he gave between them what had been bequeathed to him by Herod, which was a thousand talents, reserving to himself only some inconsiderable presents in honour of the deceased.

CHAPTER VII

THE HISTORY OF THE SPURIOUS ALEXANDER. ARCHELAUS IS BANISHED, AND GLAPHYRA DIES, AFTER WHAT WAS TO HAPPEN TO BOTH OF THEM HAD BEEN SHEWN THEM IN DREAMS

1. IN the meantime there was a man, who was by birth a Jew, but brought up at Sidon with one of the Roman freedmen, who falsely pretended, on account of the resemblance of their countenances, that he was that Alexander who was slain by Herod. This man came to Rome, in hopes of not being detected. He had one who was his assistant, of his own nation, and who knew all the affairs of the kingdom, and instructed him to say how those that were sent

to kill him and Aristobulus had pity upon them, and stole them away, by putting bodies that were like theirs in their places. This man deceived the Jews that were at Crete, and got a great deal of money of them, for travelling in splendour; and thence sailed to Melos, where he was thought so certainly genuine, that he got a great deal more money, and prevailed with those who had treated him to sail along with him to Rome. So he landed at Dicearchia [Puteoli,] and got very large presents from the Jews who dwelt there, and was conducted by his father's friends as if he were a king; nay, the resemblance in his countenance procured him so much credit, that those who had seen Alexander, and had known him very well, would take their oaths that he was the very same person. Accordingly, the whole body of the Jews that were at Rome ran out in crowds to see him, and an innumerable multitude there was who stood in the narrow places through which he was carried; for those of Melos were so far distracted, that they carried him in a sedan, and maintained a royal attendance for him at their own proper charges.

2. But Cæsar, who knew perfectly well the lineaments of Alexander's face, because he had been accused by Herod before him, discerned the fallacy in his countenance, even before he saw the man. However, he suffered the agreeable fame that went of him to have some weight with him, and sent Celadus, one who well knew Alexander, and ordered him to bring the young man to him. But when Cæsar saw him, he immediately discerned a difference in his countenance; and when he had discovered that his whole body was of a more robust texture and like that of a slave, he understood the whole was a contrivance. But the impudence of what he said greatly provoked him to be angry at him; for when he was asked about Aristobulus, he said that he was also preserved alive, and was left on purpose in Cyprus, for fear of treachery, because it would be harder for plotters to get them both into their power while they were separate. Then did Cæsar take him by himself privately, and said to him,—" I will give thee thy life, if thou wilt discover who it was that persuaded thee to forge such stories." So he said that he would discover him, and followed Cæsar, and pointed to that Jew who abused the resemblance of his face to get money; for that he had received more presents in every city than ever Alexander did when he was alive. Cæsar laughed at the contrivance, and put this spurious Alexander among his rowers, on account of the strength of his body; but ordered him that persuaded him to be put to death. But for the people of Melos, they had been sufficiently punished for their folly, by the expenses they had been at on his account.

3. And now Archelaus took possession of his ethnarchy, and used not the Jews only, but the Samaritans also, barbarously; and this out of his resentment of their old quarrels with him. Whereupon they both of them sent ambassadors against him to Cæsar; and in the ninth year of his government he was banished to Vienna, a city of Gaul, and his effects were put into Cæsar's treasury. But the report goes, that before he was sent for by Cæsar, he seemed to see nine ears of corn, full and large, but devoured by oxen. When, therefore he had sent for the diviners, and some of the Chaldeans, and inquired of them what they thought it portended; and when one of them had one interpretation, and another had another, Simon, one of the sect of the Essens, said that he thought that the ears

of corn denoted years; and the oxen denoted a mutation of things, because by their ploughing they made an alteration of the country. That therefore he should reign as many years as there were ears of corn; and after he passed through various alternations of fortune, should die. Now five days after Archelaus had heard this interpretation, he was called to his trial.

4. I cannot but think it worthy to be recorded what dream Glaphyra, the daughter of Archelaus, king of Cappadocia, had, who had at first been wife to Alexander, who was the brother of Archelaus, concerning whom we have been discoursing. This Alexander was the son of Herod the king, by whom he was put to death, as we have already related. This Glaphyra was married, after his death, to Juba, king of Libya; and, after his death, was returned home, and lived a widow with her father. Then it was that Archelaus, the ethnarch, saw her, and fell so deeply in love with her, that he divorced Mariamne, who was then his wife, and married her. When, therefore, she was come into Judea, and had been there for a little while, she thought she saw Alexander stand by her, and that he said to her,—"Thy marriage with the king of Libya might have been sufficient for thee; but thou wast not contented with him, but art returned again to my family, to a third husband; and him, thou impudent woman, hast thou chosen for thine husband, who is my brother. However, I shall not overlook the injury thou hast offered me; I shall [soon] have thee again, whether thou wilt or no." Now Glaphyra hardly survived the narration of this dream of hers two days.

CHAPTER VIII

ARCHELAUS'S ETHNARCHY IS REDUCED INTO A [ROMAN] PROVINCE. THE SEDITION OF JUDAS OF GALILEE. THE THREE SECTS OF THE JEWS

1. AND now Archelaus's part of Judea was reduced into a province, and Coponius, one of the equestrian order among the Romans, was sent as a procurator, having the power of [life and] death put into his hands by Cæsar. Under his administration it was that a certain Galilean, whose name was Judas, prevailed with his countrymen to revolt; and said they were cowards if they would endure to pay a tax to the Romans, and would, after God, submit to mortal men as their lords. This man was a teacher of a peculiar sect of his own, and was not at all like the rest of those their leaders.

2. For there are three philosophical sects among the Jews. The followers of the first of whom are the Pharisees; of the second the Sadducees; and the third sect, who pretends to a severer discipline, are called Essens. These last are Jews by birth, and seem to have a greater affection for one another than the other sects have. These Essens reject pleasures as an evil, but esteem continence, and the conquest over our passions, to be virtue. They neglect wedlock, but choose out other persons' children, while they are pliable, and fit for learning; and esteem them to be of their kindred, and form them according to their own manners. They do not absolutely deny the fitness of marriage, and the succession of mankind thereby continued; but they guard against the lascivious behaviour of women, and are persuaded that none of them preserve their fidelity to one man.

3. These men are despisers of riches, and so

very communicative as raises our admiration. Nor is there any one to be found among them who hath more than another; for it is a law among them, that those who come to them must let what they have be common to the whole order,—insomuch, that among them all there is no appearance of poverty or excess of riches, but every one's possessions are intermingled with every other's possessions; and so there is, as it were, one patrimony among all the brethren. They think that oil is a defilement; and if one of them be anointed without his own approbation, it is wiped off his body; for they think to be sweaty is a good thing, as they do also to be clothed in white garments. They also have stewards appointed to take care of their common affairs, who every one of them have no separate business for any, but what is for the use of them all.

4. They have no certain city, but many of them dwell in every city; and if any of their sect come from other places, what they have lies open for them, just as if it were their own; and they go into such as they never knew before, as if they had been ever so long acquainted with them. For which reason they carry nothing with them when they travel into remote parts, though still they take their weapons with them, for fear of thieves. Accordingly there is, in every city where they live, one appointed particularly to take care of strangers, and provide garments and other necessaries for them. But the habit and management of their bodies are such as children use who are in fear of their masters. Nor do they allow of the change of garments, or of shoes, till they be first entirely torn to pieces, or worn out by time. Nor do they either buy or sell anything to one another; but every one of them gives what he hath to him that wanteth it, and receives from him again in lieu of it what may be convenient for himself; and although there be no requital made, they are fully allowed to take what they want of whomsoever they please.

5. And as for their piety towards God, it is very extraordinary; for before sunrising they speak not a word about profane matters, but put up certain prayers which they have received from their forefathers, as if they made a supplication for its rising. After this every one of them are sent away by their curators, to exercise some of those arts wherein they are skilled, in which they labour with great diligence till the fifth hour. After which they assemble themselves together again into one place; and when they have clothed themselves in white veils, they then bathe their bodies in cold water. And after this purification is over, they every one meet together in an apartment of their own, into which it is not permitted to any of another sect to enter; while they go, after a pure manner, into the dining-room, as into a certain holy temple, and quietly set themselves down; upon which the baker lays them loaves in order; the cook also brings a single plate of one sort of food, and sets it before every one of them; but a priest says grace before meat; and it is unlawful for any one to taste of the food before grace be said. The same priest when he hath dined, says grace again after meat; and when they begin, and when they end, they praise God, as he that bestows their food upon them; after which they lay aside their [white] garments, and betake themselves to their labours again till the evening; then they return home to supper, after the same manner; and if there be any strangers there, they sit down with them. Nor is there ever any clamour or disturbance to pollute their

house, but they give every one leave to speak in their turn; which silence thus kept in their house appears to foreigners like some tremendous mystery; the cause of which is that perpetual sobriety they exercise, and some settled measure of meat and drink that is allotted to them, and that such as is abundantly sufficient for them.

6. And truly, as for other things, they do nothing but according to the injunctions of their curators; only these two things are done among them at every one's own free will, which are, to assist those that want it, and to shew mercy; for they are permitted of their own accord to afford succour to such as deserve it, when they stand in need of it, and to bestow food on those that are in distress; but they cannot give anything to their kindred without the curators. They dispense their anger after a just manner, and restrain their passion. They are eminent for fidelity, and are the ministers of peace; whatsoever they say also is firmer than an oath; but swearing is avoided by them, and they esteem it worse than perjury;* for they say, that he who cannot be believed without [swearing by] God, is already condemned. They also take great pains in studying the writings of the ancients, and choose out of them what is most for the advantage of their soul and body; and they inquire after such roots and medicinal stones as may cure their distempers.

7. But now, if any one hath a mind to come over to their sect, he is not immediately admitted, but he is prescribed the same method of living which they use, for a year, while he continues excluded; and they give him a small hatchet, and the forementioned girdle, and the white garment. And when he hath given evidence, during that time, that he can observe their continence, he approaches nearer to their way of living, and is made a partaker of the waters of purification; yet is he not even now admitted to live with them; for after this demonstration of his fortitude, his temper is tried two more years, and if he appear to be worthy, they then admit him into their society. And before he is allowed to touch their common food, he is obliged to take tremendous oaths; that, in the first place, he will exercise piety towards God; and then, that he will observe justice towards all men; and that he will do no harm to any one, either of his own accord, or by the command of others; that he will always hate the wicked, and be assistant to the righteous; that he will ever shew fidelity to all men, and especially to those in authority, he will at no time whatever abuse his authority, nor endeavour to outshine his subjects, either in his garments, or any other finery; that he will be perpetually a lover of truth, and propose to himself to reprove those that tell lies; that he will keep his hands clear from theft, and his soul from unlawful gains; and that he will neither conceal anything from those of his own sect, nor discover any of their doctrines to others, no, not though any one should compel him so to do at the hazard of his life. Moreover, he swears to communicate their doctrines to no one any otherwise than as he received them himself; that he will abstain from robbery, and will equally preserve the books belonging to their sect, and the names of the angels† [or messen-

gers.] These are the oaths by which they secure their proselytes to themselves.

8. But for those that are caught in any heinous sins, they cast them out of their society; and he who is thus separated from them, does often die after a miserable manner; for as he is bound by the oath he hath taken, and by the customs he hath been engaged in, he is not at liberty to partake of that food that he meets with elsewhere, but is forced to eat grass, and to famish his body with hunger till he perish; for which reason they receive many of them again when they are at their last gasp, out of compassion to them, as thinking the miseries they have endured till they come to the very brink of death to be a sufficient punishment for the sins they had been guilty of.

9. But in the judgments they exercise they are most accurate and just; nor do they pass sentence by the votes of a court that is fewer than a hundred. And as to what is once determined by that number, it is unalterable. What they most of all honour, after God himself, is the name of their legislator [Moses;] whom, if any one blaspheme, he is punished capitally. They also think it a good thing to obey their elders, and the major part. Accordingly, if ten of them be sitting together, no one of them will speak while the other nine are against it. They also avoid spitting in the midst of them, or on the right side. Moreover, they are stricter than any other of the Jews in resting from their labours on the seventh day; for they not only get their food ready the day before, that they may not be obliged to kindle a fire on that day, but they will not remove any vessel out of its place, nor go to stool thereon. Nay, on the other days they dig a small pit, a foot deep, with a paddle (which kind of hatchet is given them when they are first admitted among them;) and covering themselves round with their garment, that they may not affront the divine rays of light, they ease themselves into that pit, after which they put the earth that was dug out again into the pit; and even this they do only in the more lonely places, which they choose out for this purpose; and although this easement of the body be natural, yet it is a rule with them to wash themselves after it, as if it were a defilement to them.

10. Now after the time of their preparatory trial is over, they are parted into four classes; and so far are the juniors inferior to the seniors, that if the seniors should be touched by the juniors, they must wash themselves, as if they had intermixed themselves with the company of a foreigner. They are long-lived also; insomuch that many of them live above a hundred years, by means of the simplicity of their diet; nay, as I think, by means of the regular course of life they observe also. They contemn the miseries of life, and are above pain, by the generosity of their mind. And as for death, if it will be for their glory, they esteem it better than living always; and indeed our war with the Romans gave abundant evidences what great souls they had in their trials, wherein, although they were tortured and distorted, burnt and torn to pieces, and went through all kinds of instruments of torment, that they might be forced either to blaspheme their legislator or to eat what was forbidden them, yet could they not be made to do either of them, no, nor once to flatter their tormentors, nor to shed a tear; but

---

* This practice of the Essens is delivered here in general words, as are the parallel injunctions of our Saviour, Matt. vi. 34, xxiii. 16; and of St James v. 12; but all admit of particular exceptions for solemn causes, and on great and necessary occasions.

† This mention of the "names of angels," so particularly preserved by the Essens, looks like a prelude to that "worshipping of angels," blamed by St Paul, as superstitious and unlawful, in some such sort of people as these Essens were, (Coloss. ii. 8.)

they smiled in their very pains, and laughed those to scorn who inflicted the torments upon them, and resigned up their souls with great alacrity, as expecting to receive them again.

11. For their doctrine is this:—"That bodies are corruptible, and that the matter they are made of is not permanent; but that the souls are immortal, and continue for ever; and that they come out of the most subtile air, and are united to their bodies as in prisons, into which they are drawn by a certain natural enticement; but that when they are set free from the bonds of the flesh, they then, as released from a long bondage, rejoice and mount upward. And this is like the opinion of the Greeks, that good souls have their habitations beyond the ocean, in a region that is neither oppressed with storms of rain or snow, nor with intense heat, but that this place is such as is refreshed by the gentle breathing of a west wind, that is perpetually blowing from the ocean; while they allot to bad souls a dark and tempestuous den, full of never-ceasing punishments. And indeed the Greeks seem to me to have followed the same notion, when they allot the islands of the blessed to their brave men, whom they call heroes and demigods; and to the souls of the wicked, the region of the ungodly, in Hades, where their fables relate that certain persons, such as Sisyphus, and Tantalus, and Ixion, and Tityus, are punished; which is built first on this supposition, that souls are immortal; and thence are those exhortations to virtue, and dehortations from wickedness collected; whereby good men are bettered in the conduct of their life, by the hope they have of reward after their death, and whereby the vehement inclinations of bad men to vice are restrained, by the fear and expectation they are in, that although they should lie concealed in this life, they should suffer immortal punishment after death. These are the divine doctrines of the Essens about the soul, which lay an unavoidable bait for such as have once had a taste for their philosophy.

12. There are also among them who undertake to foretell things to come, by reading the holy books, and using several sorts of purifications, and being perpetually conversant in the discourses of the prophets; and it is but seldom that they miss in their predictions.

13. Moreover, there is another order of Essens, who agree with the rest as to their way of living, and customs, and laws, but differ from them in the point of marriage, as thinking that by not marrying they cut off the principal part of human life, which is the prospect of succession; nay rather, that if all men should be of the same opinion, the whole race of mankind would fail. However, they try their spouses for three years; and if they find that they have their natural purgations thrice, as trials that they are likely to be fruitful, they then actually marry them. But they do not use to accompany with their wives when they are with child, as a demonstration that they do not marry out of regard to pleasure, but for the sake of posterity. Now the women go into the baths with some of their garments on, as the men do with somewhat girded about them. And these are the customs of this order of Essens.

14. But then as to the two other orders at first mentioned; the Pharisees are those who are esteemed most skilful in the exact explication of their laws, and introduce the first sect. These ascribe all to fate [or providence,] and to God, and yet allow, that to act what is right, or the contrary, is principally in the power of men, although fate does co-operate in every action.

They say that all souls are incorruptible; but that the souls of good men are only removed into other bodies,—but that the souls of bad men are subject to eternal punishment. But the Sadducees are those that compose the second order, and take away fate entirely, and suppose that God is not concerned in our doing or not doing what is evil; and they say, that to act what is good, or what is evil, is at men's own choice, and that the one or the other belongs so to every one, that they may act as they please. They also take away the belief of the immortal duration of the soul, and the punishments and rewards in Hades. Moreover, the Pharisees are friendly to one another, and are for the exercise of concord and regard for the public. But the behaviour of the Sadducees one towards another is in some degrees wild; and their conversation with those that are of their own party is as barbarous as if they were strangers to them. And this is what I had to say concerning the philosophic sects among the Jews.

CHAPTER IX

THE DEATH OF SALOME. THE CITIES WHICH HEROD AND PHILIP BUILT. PILATE OCCASIONS DISTURBANCES. TIBERIUS PUTS AGRIPPA INTO BONDS, BUT CAIUS FREES HIM FROM THEM AND MAKES HIM KING. HEROD ANTIPAS IS BANISHED

1. AND now, as the ethnarchy of Archelaus was fallen into a Roman province, the other sons of Herod, Philip, and that Herod who was called Antipas, each of them took upon them the administration of their own tetrarchies; for when Salome died, she bequeathed to Julia, the wife of Augustus, both her toparchy, and Jamnia, as also her plantation of palm-trees that were in Phasaelis. But when the Roman empire was translated to Tiberius, the son of Julia, upon the death of Augustus, who had reigned fifty-seven years, six months, and two days, both Herod and Philip continued in their tetrarchies; and the latter of them built the city Cesarea, at the fountains of Jordan, and in the region of Paneas; as also the city Julias, in the lower Gaulonitis. Herod also built the city Tiberias in Galilee, and in Perea [beyond Jordan] another that was also called Julias.

2. Now Pilate, who was sent as procurator into Judea by Tiberius, sent by night those images of Cæsar that are called ensigns, into Jerusalem. This excited a very great tumult among the Jews when it was day; for those that were near them were astonished at the sight of them, as indications that their laws were trodden under foot: for those laws do not permit any sort of images to be brought into the city. Nay, besides the indignation which the citizens themselves had at this procedure, a vast number of people came running out of the country. These come zealously to Pilate to Cesarea, and besought him to carry those ensigns out of Jerusalem, and to preserve them their ancient laws inviolable; but upon Pilate's denial of their request, they fell down prostrate upon the ground, and continued immovable in that posture for five days and as many nights.

3. On the next day Pilate sat upon his tribunal, in the open market-place, and called to him the multitude, as desirous to give them an answer; and then gave a signal to the soldiers that they should all by agreement at once encompass the Jews with their weapons; so the band of

soldiers stood round about the Jews in three ranks. Pilate also said to them, that they should be cut in pieces, unless they would admit of Cæsar's images; and gave intimation to the soldiers to draw their naked swords. Hereupon the Jews, as it were at one signal, fell down in vast numbers together, and exposed their necks bare, and cried out that they were sooner ready to be slain, than that their law should be transgressed. Hereupon Pilate was greatly surprised at their prodigious superstition, and gave orders that the ensigns should be presently carried out of Jerusalem.

4. After this he raised another disturbance, by expending that sacred treasure which is called Corban* upon aqueducts, whereby he brought water from the distance of four hundred furlongs. At this the multitude had great indignation; and when Pilate was come to Jerusalem, they came about his tribunal, and made a clamour at it. Now when he was apprised beforehand of this disturbance, he mixed his own soldiers in their armour with the multitude, and ordered them to conceal themselves under the habits of private men, and not indeed to use their swords, but with staves to beat those that made the clamour. He then gave the signal from his tribunal [to do as he had bidden them.] Now the Jews were so sadly beaten, that many of them perished by the stripes they received, and many of them perished as trodden to death, by which means the multitude was astonished at the calamity of those that were slain, and held their peace.

5. In the meantime Agrippa, the son of that Aristobulus who had been slain by his father Herod, came to Tiberius to accuse Herod the tetrarch; who not admitting of his accusation, he staid at Rome, and cultivated a friendship with others of the men of note, but principally with Caius the son of Germanicus, who was then but a private person. Now this Agrippa, at a certain time, feasted Caius; and as he was very complaisant to him on several other accounts, he at length stretched out his hands, and openly wished that Tiberius might die, and that he might quickly see him emperor of the world. This was told to Tiberius by one of Agrippa's domestics; who thereupon was very angry, and ordered Agrippa to be bound, and had him very ill treated in the prison for six months, until Tiberius died, after he had reigned twenty-two years, and six months, and three days.

6. But when Caius was made Cæsar, he released Agrippa from his bonds, and made him king of Philip's tetrarchy, who was now dead; but when Agrippa had arrived at that degree of dignity, he inflamed the ambitious desires of Herod the tetrarch, who was chiefly induced to hope for the royal authority by his wife Herodias, who reproached him for his sloth, and told him that it was only because he would not sail to Cæsar that he was destitute of that great dignity; for since Cæsar had made Agrippa a king, from a private person, much more would he advance him from a tetrarch to that dignity. These arguments prevailed with Herod, so that he came to Caius, by whom he was punished for his ambition, by being banished into Spain; for Agrippa followed him, in order to accuse him; to whom also Caius gave his tetrarchy, by way of addition. So Herod died in Spain, whither his wife had followed him.

CHAPTER X

CAIUS COMMANDS THAT HIS STATUE SHOULD BE SET UP IN THE TEMPLE ITSELF; AND WHAT PETRONIUS DID THEREUPON

1. Now Caius Cæsar did so grossly abuse the fortune he had arrived at, as to take himself to be a god, and to desire to be so called also, and to cut off those of the greatest nobility out of his country. He also extended his impiety as far as the Jews. Accordingly, he sent Petronius with an army to Jerusalem, to place his statues in the temple,† and commanded him that, in case the Jews would not admit of them, he should slay those that opposed it, and carry all the rest of the nation into captivity: but God concerned himself with these his commands. However, Petronius marched out of Antioch into Judea, with three legions, and many Syrian auxiliaries. Now as to the Jews, some of them could not believe the stories that spake of a war; but those that did believe them were in the utmost distress how to defend themselves, and the terror diffused itself presently through them all: for the army was already come to Ptolemais.

2. This Ptolemais is a maritime city of Galilee, built in the great plain. It is encompassed with mountains: that on the east side, sixty furlongs off, belongs to Galilee; but that on the south belongs to Carmel, which is distant from it a hundred and twenty furlongs; and that on the north is the highest of them all, and is called by the people of the country, The Ladder of the Tyrians, which is at the distance of a hundred furlongs. The very small river Belus ‡ runs by it, at the distance of two furlongs; near which there is Memnon's monument, § and hath near it a place no larger than a hundred cubits, which deserves admiration; for the place is round and hollow, and affords such sand as glass is made of; which place when it hath been emptied by the many ships there loaded, it is filled again by the winds, which bring into it, as it were on purpose, that sand which lay remote, and was no more than bare common sand, while this mine presently turns it into glassy sand; and what is to me still more wonderful, that glassy sand which is superfluous, and is once removed out of the place, becomes bare common sand again; and this is the nature of the place we are speaking of.

3. But now the Jews got together in great numbers, with their wives and children, into that plain that was by Ptolemais, and made supplication to Petronius, first for their laws, and, in the next place, for themselves. So he was prevailed upon by the multitude of the supplicants, and by their supplications, and left his army and statues at Ptolemais, and then went forward into Galilee, and called together the multitude and all the men of note to Tiberias, and shewed them the power of the Romans, and the threatenings of Cæsar; and, besides this, proved that their petition was unreasonable, because while all the nations in subjection

---

* This use of corban or oblation, as here applied to the sacred money dedicated to God in the treasury of the temple, illustrates our Saviour's words, **Mark vii. 11. 12.**

† Tacitus owns that Caius commanded the Jews to place his effigies in their temple, though he be mistaken when he adds that the Jews thereupon took arms.

‡ This account of a place near the mouth of the river Belus in Phœnicia, whence came that sand out of which the ancients made their glass, is a known thing in history; particularly in Tacitus and Strabo, and more largely in Pliny.

§ This Memnon had several monuments; and one of them appears to have been in Syria, and not improbably in this very place.

to them had placed the images of Cæsar in their several cities, among the rest of their gods,—for them alone to oppose it, was almost like the behaviour of revolters, and was injurious to Cæsar.

4. And when they insisted on their law, and the custom of their country, and how it was not only not permitted them to make either an image of God, or indeed of a man, and to put it in any despicable part of their country, much less in the temple itself, Petronius replied, "And am not I also," said he, "bound to keep the laws of my own lord? For if I transgress it, and spare you, it is but just that I perish; while he that sent me, and not I, will commence a war against you; for I am under command as well as you." Hereupon the multitude cried out, that they were ready to suffer for their law. Petronius then quieted them, and said to them, "Will you then make war against Cæsar?" The Jews said, "We offer sacrifices twice every day for Cæsar, and for the Roman people;" but that if he would place the images among them, he must first sacrifice the whole Jewish nation; and that they were ready to expose themselves, together with their children and wives, to be slain. At this Petronius was astonished, and pitied them on account of the inexpressible sense of religion the men were under, and that courage of theirs which made them ready to die for it; so they were dismissed without success.

5. But on the following days, he got together the men of power privately, and the multitude publicly, and sometimes he used persuasions to them, and sometimes he gave them his advice; but he chiefly made use of threatenings to them, and insisted upon the power of the Romans, and the anger of Caius; and besides, upon the necessity he was himself under [to do as he was enjoined.] But as they could no way be prevailed upon, and he saw that the country was in danger of lying without tillage (for it was about seed-time that the multitude continued for fifty days together idle,) so he at last got them together, and told them that it was best for him to run some hazard himself; "for either, by the divine assistance, I shall prevail with Cæsar; and shall myself escape the danger as well as you, which will be matter of joy to us both; or, in case Cæsar continue in his rage, I will be ready to expose my own life for such a great number as you are." Whereupon he dismissed the multitude, who prayed greatly for his prosperity; and he took the army out of Ptolemais, and returned to Antioch; from whence he presently sent an epistle to Cæsar, and informed him of the irruption he had made into Judea, and of the supplications of the nation; and that unless he had a mind to lose both the country and the men in it, he must permit them to keep their law, and must countermand his former injunction. Caius answered that epistle in a violent way, and threatened to have Petronius put to death for his being so tardy in the execution of what he had commanded. But it happened that those who brought Caius's epistle were tossed by a storm, and were detained on the sea three months, while others that brought the news of Caius's death had a good voyage. Accordingly, Petronius received the epistle concerning Caius, seven-and-twenty days before he received that which was against himself.

CHAPTER XI

CONCERNING THE GOVERNMENT OF CLAUDIUS, AND THE REIGN OF AGRIPPA. CONCERNING THE DEATH OF AGRIPPA AND OF HEROD, AND WHAT CHILDREN THEY BOTH LEFT BEHIND THEM

1. Now when Caius had reigned three years and eight months, and had been slain by treachery, Claudius was hurried away by the armies that were at Rome to take the government upon him; but the senate, upon the reference of the consuls, Sentius Saturninus, and Pomponius Secundus, gave orders to the three regiments of soldiers that stayed with them, to keep the city quiet, and went up into the Capitol in great numbers, and resolved to oppose Claudius by force, on account of the barbarous treatment they had met with from Caius; and they determined either to settle the nation under an aristocracy, as they had of old been governed, or at least to choose by vote such a one for emperor as might be worthy of it.

2. Now it happened, that at this time Agrippa sojourned at Rome, and that both the senate called him to consult with them, and at the same time Claudius sent for him out of the camp, that he might be serviceable to him, as he should have occasion for his service. So he, perceiving that Claudius was in effect made Cæsar already, went to him, who sent him, as an ambassador to the senate, to let them know what his intentions were: that, in the first place, it was without his seeking, that he was hurried away by the soldiers; moreover, that he thought it was not just to desert those soldiers in such their zeal for him, and that if he should do so, his own fortune would be in uncertainty; for that it was a dangerous case to have been once called to the empire. He added further, that he would administer the government as a good prince, and not like a tyrant; for that he would be satisfied with the honour of being called Emperor, but would, in every one of his actions, permit them all to give him their advice; for that although he had not been by nature for moderation, yet would the death of Caius afford him a sufficient demonstration how soberly he ought to act in that station.

3. This message was delivered by Agrippa; to which the senate replied, that since they had an army, and the wisest counsels on their side, they would not endure a voluntary slavery. When Claudius heard what answer the senate had made, he sent Agrippa to them again, with the following message:—That he could not bear the thoughts of betraying them that had given their oaths to be true to him; and that he saw he must fight, though unwillingly, against such as he had no mind to fight; that, however, [if it must come to that,] it was proper to choose a place without the city for the war: because it was not agreeable to piety to pollute the temples of their own city with the blood of their own countrymen, and this only on occasion of their imprudent conduct. And when Agrippa had heard this message, he delivered it to the senators.

4. In the meantime, one of the soldiers belonging to the senate drew his sword, and cried out, "O my fellow-soldiers, what is the meaning of this choice of ours, to kill our brethren, and to use violence to our kindred that are with Claudius! while we may have him for our emperor whom no one can blame, and who hath so many just reasons [to lay claim to the government!] and this with regard to those against whom we are going to fight!" When he had said this, he marched through the whole senate, and carried all the soldiers along with him. Upon which all the patricians were immediately in a great fright at their being thus deserted.

But still, because there appeared no other way whither they could turn themselves for deliverance, they made haste the same way with the soldiers, and went to Claudius. But those that had the greatest luck in flattering the good fortune of Claudius betimes, met them before the walls with their naked swords, and there was reason to fear that those that came first might have been in danger, before Claudius could know what violence the soldiers were going to offer them, had not Agrippa run before, and told him what a dangerous thing they were going about, and that unless he restrained the violence of these men, who were in a fit of madness against the patricians, he would lose those on whose account it was most desirable to rule, and would be emperor over a desert.

5. When Claudius heard this he restrained the violence of the soldiery, and received the senate into the camp, and treated them after an obliging manner, and went out with them presently, to offer their thank-offerings to God, which were proper upon his first coming to the empire. Moreover, he bestowed upon Agrippa his whole paternal kingdom immediately, and added to it, besides those countries that had been given by Augustus to Herod, Trachonitis, and Auranitis, and still besides these, that kingdom which was called the kingdom of Lysanias. This gift he declared to the people by a decree, but ordered the magistrates to have the donation engraved on the tables of brass, and to be set up in the Capitol. He bestowed on his brother Herod, who was also his son-in law, by marrying [his daughter] Bernice, the kingdom of Chalcis.

6. So now riches flowed in to Agrippa by his enjoyment of so large a dominion; nor did he abuse the money he had on small matters, but he began to encompass Jerusalem with such a wall, which, had it been brought to perfection, had made it impracticable for the Romans to take it by siege; but his death, which happened at Cesarea, before he had raised the walls to their due height, prevented him. He had then reigned three years, as he had governed his tetrarchies three other years. He left behind him three daughters, born to him by Cypros,— Bernice, Mariamne, and Drusilla; and a son born of the same mother, whose name was Agrippa: he was left a very young child, so that Claudius made the country a Roman province, and sent Cuspius Fadus to be its procurator, and after him Tiberius Alexander, who, making no alterations of the ancient laws, kept the nation in tranquillity. Now after this, Herod the king of Chalcis died, and left behind him two sons, born to him of his brother's daughter Bernice; their names were Bernicianus, and Hyrcanus. [He also left behind him] Aristobulus, whom he had by his former wife Mariamne. There was besides, another brother of his that died a private person, his name was also Aristobulus, who left behind him a daughter, whose name was Jotape: and these, as I have formerly said, were the children of Aristobulus, the son of Herod; which Aristobulus and Alexander were born to Herod by Mariamne, and were slain by him. But as for Alexander's posterity, they reigned in Armenia.

CHAPTER XII

MANY TUMULTS UNDER CUMANUS, WHICH WERE COMPOSED BY QUADRATUS. FELIX IS PROCURATOR OF JUDEA. AGRIPPA IS ADVANCED FROM CHALCIS TO A GREATER KINGDOM

1. Now after the death of Herod, king of Chal-

cis, Claudius set Agrippa, the son of Agrippa, over his uncle's kingdom, while Cumanus took upon him the office of procurator of the rest, which was a Roman province, and therein he succeeded Alexander; under which Cumanus began the troubles, and the Jews' ruin came on; for when the multitude were come together to Jerusalem, to the feast of unleavened bread, and a Roman cohort stood over the cloisters of the temple, (for they always were armed and kept guard at the festivals, to prevent any innovation which the multitude thus gathered together might make,) one of the soldiers pulled back his garment, and cowering down after an indecent manner, turned his breech to the Jews, and spake such words as you might expect upon such a posture. At this the whole multitude had indignation, and made a clamour to Cumanus, that he would punish the soldier; while the rasher part of the youth, and such as were naturally the most tumultuous, fell to fighting, and caught up stones, and threw them at the soldiers. Upon which Cumanus was afraid lest all the people should make an assault upon him, and sent to call for more armed men, who, when they came in great numbers into the cloisters, the Jews were in a very great consternation; and being beaten out of the temple, they ran into the city; and the violence with which they crowded to get out was so great, that they trod upon each other, and squeezed one another, till ten thousand of them were killed, insomuch that this feast became the cause of mourning to the whole nation, and every family lamented [their own relations.]

2. Now there followed after this another calamity, which arose from a tumult made by robbers; for at the public road of Beth-horen, one Stephen, a servant of Cæsar, carried some furniture, which the robbers fell upon and seized. Upon this Cumanus sent men to go round about to the neighbouring villages, and to bring their inhabitants to him bound, as laying it to their charge that they had not pursued after the thieves, and caught them. Now here it was that a certain soldier finding the sacred book of the law, tore it to pieces, and threw it into the fire.* Hereupon the Jews were in great disorder, as if their whole country were in a flame, and assembled themselves so many of them by their zeal for their religion, as by an engine; and ran together with united clamour to Cesarea, to Cumanus, and made supplication to him that he would not overlook this man, who had offered such an affront to God, and to his law; but punish him for what he had done. Accordingly, he, perceiving that the multitude would not be quiet unless they had a comfortable answer from him, gave order that the soldier should be brought, and drawn through those that required to have him punished, to execution; which being done, the Jews went their ways.

3. After this there happened a fight between the Galileans and the Samaritans; it happened at a village called Geman, which is situate in the great plain of Samaria; where, as a great number of Jews were going up to Jerusalem to the feast [of tabernacles], a certain Galilean was slain; and besides, a vast number of people ran together out of Galilee, in order to fight with the Samaritans. But the principal men among them came to Cumanus, and besought that, before the evil became incurable, he would come into Galilee and bring the authors of this murder to punishment; for that there was no other way

---

* The Talmud, in recounting ten sad accidents for which the Jews ought to rend their garments, reckons this for one:—"When they hear that the law of God is burnt."

to make the multitude separate, without coming to blows. However, Cumanus postponed their supplications to the other affairs he was then about, and sent the petitioners away without success.

4. But when the affair of this murder came to be told at Jerusalem, it put the multitude into disorder, and they left the feast; and without any generals to conduct them, they marched with great violence to Samaria; nor would they be ruled by any of the magistrates that were set over them; but they were managed by one Eleazar, the son of Dineus, and by Alexander, in these their thievish and seditious attempts. These men fell upon those that were in the neighbourhood of the Acrabatene toparchy, and slew them, without sparing any age, and set the villages on fire.

5. But Cumanus took one troop of horsemen, called the troop of Sebaste, out of Cesarea, and came to the assistance of those that were spoiled; he also seized upon a great number of those that followed Eleazar, and slew more of them. And as for the rest of the multitude of those that went so zealously to fight with the Samaritans, the rulers of Jerusalem ran out, clothed with sackcloth, and having ashes on their heads, and begged of them to go their ways, lest by their attempt to revenge themselves upon the Samaritans, they should provoke the Romans to come against Jerusalem; to have compassion upon their country and temple, their children and their wives, and not bring the utmost dangers of destruction upon them, in order to avenge themselves upon one Galilean only. The Jews complied with these persuasions of theirs, and dispersed themselves; but still there were a great number who betook themselves to robbing, in hopes of impunity; and rapines and insurrections of the bolder sort happened over the whole country. And the men of power among the Samaritans came to Tyre, to Ummidius Quadratus,* the president of Syria, and desired that they that had laid waste the country might be punished: the great men also of the Jews, and Jonathan the son of Ananus, the high-priest, came thither, and said that the Samaritans were the beginners of the disturbance, on account of that murder they had committed; and that Cumanus had given occasion to what had happened by his unwillingness to punish the original authors of that murder.

6. But Quadratus put both parties off for that time, and told them, that when he should come to those places he would make a diligent inquiry after every circumstance. After which he went to Cesarea, and crucified all those whom Cumanus had taken alive; and when from thence he was come to the city Lydda, he heard the affair of the Samaritans, and sent for eighteen of the Jews, whom he had learned to have been concerned in that fight, and beheaded them; but he sent two others of those that were of the greatest power among them, and both Jonathan and Ananias, the high priests, as also Ananus the son of this Ananias, and certain others that were eminent among the Jews, to Cæsar; as he did in like manner by the most illustrious of the Samaritans. He also ordered that Cumanus [the procurator] and Celer the tribune should sail to Rome, in order to give an account of what had been done to Cæsar. When he had finished these matters, he went up from Lydda to Jerusalem, and finding the multitude celebrating the

feast of unleavened bread without any tumult, he returned to Antioch.

7. Now when Cæsar at Rome had heard what Cumanus and the Samaritans had to say, (where it was done in the hearing of Agrippa, who zealously espoused the cause of the Jews, as in like manner many of the great men stood by Cumanus,) he condemned the Samaritans, and commanded that three of the most powerful men among them should be put to death: he banished Cumanus, and sent Celer bound to Jerusalem, to be delivered over to the Jews to be tormented; that he should be drawn round the city, and then beheaded.

8. After this, Cæsar sent Felix,† the brother of Pallas, to be procurator of Galilee, and Samaria, and Perea, and removed Agrippa from Chalcis into a greater kingdom; for he gave him the tetrarchy which had belonged to Philip, which contained Batanea, Trachonitis, and Gaulonitis: he also added to it the kingdom of Lysanias, and that province [Abilene] which Varus had governed. But Claudius himself, when he had administered the government thirteen years eight months and twenty days, died, and left Nero to be his successor in the empire, whom he had adopted by his wife Agrippina's delusions, in order to be his successor, although he had a son of his own whose name was Britanicus, by Messalina his former wife, and a daughter whose name was Octavia, whom he had married to Nero; he had also another daughter by Petina, whose name was Antonia.

CHAPTER XIII

NERO ADDS FOUR CITIES TO AGRIPPA'S KINGDOM: BUT THE OTHER PART OF JUDEA WERE UNDER FELIX. THE DISTURBANCES WHICH WERE RAISED BY THE SICARII, THE MAGICIANS, AND AN EGYPTIAN FALSE PROPHET. THE JEWS AND SYRIANS HAVE A CONTEST AT CESAREA

1. Now as to the many things in which Nero acted like a madman, out of the extravagant degree of the felicity and riches which he enjoyed, and by that means used his good fortune to the injury of others; and after what manner he slew his brother, and wife, and mother; from whom his barbarity spread itself to others that were most nearly related to him; and how, at last, he was so distracted that he became an actor in the scenes, and upon the theatre,—I omit to say any more about them, because there are writers enough upon those subjects everywhere; but I shall turn myself to those actions of his time in which the Jews were concerned.

2. Nero therefore bestowed the kingdom of the lesser Armenia upon Aristobulus, Herod's son,‡ and he added to Agrippa's kingdom four cities, with the toparchies to them belonging: I mean Abila, and that Julias which is in Perea, Tarichea also, and Tiberias of Galilee; but over the rest of Judea he made Felix procurator. This Felix took Eleazar the arch-robber, and many that were with him, alive, when they had

---

* This Ummidius, or Numidius, or, as Tacitus calls him, Vinidius Quadratus, is mentioned in an ancient inscription, still preserved, which calls him *Ummidius Quadratus*.

† Take the character of this Felix (who is well known from the Acts of the Apostles, particularly from his trembling when St Paul discoursed of "righteousness, chastity, and judgment to come,"—(Acts xxiv. 25;) in the words of Tacitus, produced here by Dean Aldrich:— "Felix exercised the authority of a king, with the disposition of a slave, and relying upon the great power of his brother Pallas at court, thought he might safely be guilty of all kinds of wicked practices."

‡ *i. e.* Herod, king of Chalcis.

ravaged the country for twenty years together, and sent them to Rome; but as to the number of the robbers whom he caused to be crucified, and of whom were caught among them, and those he brought to punishment, they were a multitude not to be enumerated.

3. When the country was purged of these, there sprang up another sort of robbers in Jerusalem, which were called Sicarii, who slew men in the daytime, and in the midst of the city; this they did chiefly at the festivals, when they mingled themselves among the multitude, and concealed daggers under their garments, with which they stabbed those that were their enemies; and when any fell down dead, the murderers became a part of those that had indignation against them; by which means they appeared persons of such reputation, that they could by no means be discovered. The first man who was slain by them was Jonathan the high priest, after whose death many were slain every day, while the fear men were in of being so served was more afflicting than the calamity itself; and while everybody expected death every hour, as men do in war, so men were obliged to look before them, and to take notice of their enemies at a great distance; nor, if their friends were coming to them, durst they trust them any longer; but, in the midst of their suspicions and guarding of themselves, they were slain. Such was the celerity of the plotters against them, and so cunning was their contrivance.

4. There was also another body of wicked men gotten together, not so impure in their actions, but more wicked in their intentions, who laid waste the happy state of the city no less than did these murderers. These were such men as deceived and deluded the people under pretence of divine inspiration, but were for procuring innovations and changes of the government; and these prevailed with the multitude to act like madmen, and went before them into the wilderness, as pretending that God would there shew them the signal of liberty; but Felix thought this procedure was to be the beginning of a revolt; so he sent some horsemen and footmen, both armed, who destroyed a great number of them.

5. But there was an Egyptian false prophet that did the Jews more mischief than the former; for he was a cheat, and pretended to be a prophet also, and got together thirty thousand men that were deluded by him; these he led round about from the wilderness to the mount which is called the Mount of Olives, and was ready to break into Jerusalem by force from that place; and if he could but once conquer the Roman garrison and the people, he intended to domineer over them by the assistance of those guards of his who were to break into the city with him; but Felix prevented his attempt, and met him with his Roman soldiers, while all the people assisted him in his attack upon him, insomuch that when it came to a battle, the Egyptian ran away with a few others, while the greatest part of those that were with him were either destroyed or taken alive; but the rest of the multitude were dispersed every one to their own homes, and there concealed themselves.

6. Now when these were quieted, it happened, as it does in a diseased body, that another part was subject to an inflammation; for a company of deceivers and robbers got together, and persuaded the Jews to revolt, and exhorted them to assert their liberty, inflicting death on those that continued in obedience to the Roman government, and saying, that such as willingly chose slavery ought to be forced from such their desired inclinations; for they parted themselves into different bodies, and lay in wait up and down the country, and plundered the houses of the great men, and slew the men themselves, and set the villages on fire; and this till all Judea was filled with the effects of their madness. And thus the flame was every day more and more blown up, till it came to a direct war.

7. There was also another disturbance at Cesarea: those Jews who were mixed with the Syrians that lived there, raising a tumult against them. The Jews pretended that the city was theirs, and said that he who built it was a Jew; meaning king Herod. The Syrians confessed also that its builder was a Jew; but they still said, however, that the city was a Grecian city; for that he who set up statues and temples in it could not design it for Jews. On which account both parties had a contest with one another; and this contest increased so much, that it came at last to arms, and the bolder sort of them marched out to fight; for the elders of the Jews were not able to put a stop to their own people that were disposed to be tumultuous, and the Greeks thought it a shame for them to be overcome by the Jews. Now these Jews exceeded the others in riches and strength of body; but the Grecian part had the advantage of assistance from the soldiery; for the greatest part of the Roman garrison was raised out of Syria; and being thus related to the Syrian part, they were ready to assist it. However, the governors of the city were concerned to keep all quiet, and whenever they caught those that were most for fighting on either side, they punished them with stripes and bonds. Yet did not the sufferings of those that were caught affright the remainder, or make them desist; but they were still more and more exasperated, and deeper engaged in the sedition. And as Felix came once into the market-place, and commanded the Jews, when they had beaten the Syrians, to go their ways, and threatened them if they would not, and they would not obey him, he sent his soldiers out upon them, and slew a great many of them, upon which it fell out that what they had was plundered. And as the sedition still continued, he chose out the most eminent men on both sides as ambassadors to Nero, to argue about their several privileges.

CHAPTER XIV

FESTUS SUCCEEDS FELIX, WHO IS SUCCEEDED BY ALBINUS, AS HE IS BY FLORUS; WHO, BY THE BARBARITY OF HIS GOVERNMENT, FORCES THE JEWS INTO THE WAR

1. Now it was that Festus succeeded Felix as procurator, and made it his business to correct those that made disturbances in the country. So he caught the greatest part of the robbers, and destroyed a great many of them. But then Albinus, who succeeded Festus, did not execute his office as the other had done; nor was there any sort of wickedness that could be named but he had a hand in it. Accordingly, he did not only, in his political capacity, steal and plunder every one's substance, nor did he only burden the whole nation with taxes, but he permitted the relations of such as were in prison for robbery, and had been laid there, either by the senate of every city, or by the former procurators, to redeem them for money; and nobody remained in the prisons as a malefactor but he who

gave him nothing. At this time it was that the enterprises of the seditious at Jerusalem were very formidable; the principal men among them purchasing leave of Albinus to go on with their seditious practices; while that part of the people who delighted in disturbances joined themselves to such as had fellowship with Albinus: and every one of these wicked wretches were encompassed with his band of robbers, while he himself, like an arch-robber, or a tyrant, made a figure among his company, and abused his authority over those about him, in order to plunder those that lived quietly. The effect of which was this, that those who lost their goods were forced to hold their peace, when they had reason to shew great indignation at what they had suffered; but those who had escaped were forced to flatter him that deserved to be punished, out of the fear they were in of suffering equally with the others. Upon the whole, nobody durst speak their minds, for tyranny was generally tolerated; and at this time were those seeds sown which brought the city to destruction.

2. And although such was the character of Albinus, yet did Gessius Florus, who succeeded him, demonstrate him to have been a most excellent person, upon the comparison: for the former did the greatest part of his rogueries in private, and with a sort of dissimulation; but Gessius did his unjust actions to the harm of the nation after a pompous manner; and as though he had been sent as an executioner to punish condemned malefactors, he omitted no sort of rapine, or of vexation: where the case was really pitiable, he was most barbarous; and in things of the greatest turpitude, he was most impudent; nor could any one outdo him in disguising the truth; nor could any one contrive more subtle ways of deceit than he did. He indeed thought it but a petty offence to get money out of single persons; so he spoiled whole cities, and ruined entire bodies of men at once, and did almost publicly proclaim it all the country over, that they had liberty given them to turn robbers, upon this condition, that he might go shares with them in the spoils. Accordingly, this his greediness of gain was the occasion that entire toparchies were brought to desolation; and a great many of the people left their own country, and fled into foreign provinces.

3. And truly, while Cestius Gallus was president of the province of Syria, nobody durst do so much as send an embassage to him against Florus; but when he was come to Jerusalem, upon the approach of the feast of unleavened bread, the people came about him not fewer in number than three millions:* these besought him to commiserate the calamities of their nation, and cried out upon Florus as the bane of their country. But as he was present, and stood by Cestius, he laughed at their words. However, Cestius, when he had quieted the multitude, and had assured them that he would take care that Florus should hereafter treat them in a more gentle manner, returned to Antioch; Florus also conducted him as far as Cesarea, and deluded him, though he had at that very time the purpose of shewing his anger at the nation, and procuring a war upon them, by which means alone it was that he supposed he might conceal his enormities; for he expected

that, if the peace continued, he should have the Jews for his accusers before Cæsar; but that if he could procure them to make a revolt, he should divert their laying lesser crimes to his charge, by a misery that was so much greater; he therefore did every day augment their calamities, in order to induce them to a rebellion.

4. Now at this time it happened that the Grecians at Cesarea had been too hard for the Jews, and had obtained of Nero the government of the city, and had brought the judicial determination: at the same time began the war, in the twelfth year of the reign of Nero, and the seventeenth of the reign of Agrippa, in the month of Artemissus [Jyar.] Now the occasion of this war was by no means proportionable to those heavy calamities which it brought upon us; for the Jews that dwelt at Cesarea had a synagogue near the place, whose owner was a certain Cesarean Greek: the Jews had endeavoured frequently to have purchased the possession of the place, and had offered many times its value for its price; but as the owner overlooked their offers, so did he raise other buildings upon the place, in way of affront to them, and made working-shops of them, and left them but a narrow passage, and such as was very troublesome for them to go along to their synagogue; whereupon the warmer part of the Jewish youth went hastily to the workmen, and forbade them to build there; but as Florus would not permit them to use force, the great men of the Jews, with John the publican, being in the utmost distress what to do, persuaded Florus, with the offer of eight talents, to hinder the work. He then, being intent upon nothing but getting money, promised he would do for them all they desired of him, and then went away from Cesarea to Sebaste, and left the sedition to take its full course, as if he had sold a licence to the Jews to fight it out.

5. Now on the next day, which was the seventh day of the week, when the Jews were crowding apace to their synagogue, a certain man of Cesarea, of a seditious temper, got an earthen vessel, and set it, with the bottom upward, at the entrance of that synagogue, and sacrificed birds. This thing provoked the Jews to an incurable degree, because their laws were affronted, and the place was polluted; whereupon the sober and moderate part of the Jews thought it proper to have recourse to their governors again, while the seditious part, and such as were in the fervour of their youth, were vehemently inflamed to fight. The seditious also among [the Gentiles of] Cesarea stood ready for the same purpose; for they had, by agreement, sent the man to sacrifice beforehand [as ready to support him;] so that it soon came to blows. Hereupon Jucundus, the master of the horse, who was ordered to prevent the fight, came thither, and took away the earthen vessel, and endeavoured to put a stop to the sedition, but when he was overcome by the violence of the people of Cesarea, the Jews caught up their book of the law, and retired to Narbata, which is a place to them belonging, distant from Cesarea sixty furlongs. But John, and twelve of the principal men with him, went to Florus, to Sebaste, and made a lamentable complaint of their case, and besought him to help them; and with all possible decency, put him in mind of the eight talents they had given him; but he had the men seized upon, and put in prison, and accused them for carrying the books of the law out of Cesarea.

6. Moreover, as to the citizens of Jerusalem, although they took this matter very ill, yet did they restrain their passion; but Florus acted

---

* Here we may note, that 3,000,000 of the Jews were present at the passover, A.D. 65; which confirms what Josephus elsewhere informs us of, that at a passover a little later, they counted 256,500 paschal lambs; which, at twelve to each lamb, which is no immoderate calculation, come to 3,078,000. See b. vi. chap. ix. sect. 3.

DESECRATION OF THE SYNAGOGUE AT CESAREA

herein as if he had been hired, and blew up the war into a flame, and sent some to take seventeen talents out of the sacred treasure, and pretended that Cæsar wanted them. At this the people were in confusion immediately, and ran together to the temple, with prodigious clamours, and called upon Cæsar by name, and besought him to free them from the tyranny of Florus. Some also of the seditious cried out upon Florus, and cast the greatest reproaches upon him, and carried a basket about, and begged some spells of money for him, as for one that was destitute of possessions, and in a miserable condition. Yet was not he made ashamed hereby of his love of money, but was more enraged and provoked to get still more; and instead of coming to Cesarea, as he ought to have done, and quenched the flame of war, which was beginning thence, and so take away the occasion of any disturbances, on which account it was that he had received a reward [of eight talents,] he marched hastily with an army of horsemen and footmen against Jerusalem, that he might gain his will by the arms of the Romans, and might, by his terror, and by his threatenings, bring the city into subjection.

7. But the people were desirous of making Florus ashamed of his attempt, and met his soldiers with acclamations, and put themselves in order to receive him very submissively; but he sent Capito, a centurion, beforehand, with fifty soldiers, to bid them go back, and not now make a show of receiving him in an obliging manner, whom they had so foully reproached before; and said that it was incumbent on them, in case they had generous souls, and free speakers, to jest upon him to his face, and appear to be lovers of liberty, not only in words but with their weapons also. With this message was the multitude amazed; and upon the coming of Capito's horsemen into the midst of them, they were dispersed before they could salute Florus, or manifest their submissive behaviour to him. Accordingly they retired to their own houses, and spent that night in fear and confusion of face.

8. Now at this time Florus took up his quarters at the palace; and on the next day he had his tribunal set before it, and sat upon it, when the high priests, and the men of power, and those of the greatest eminence in the city, came all before that tribunal; upon which Florus commanded them to deliver up to him those that had reproached him, and told them that they should themselves partake of the vengeance to them belonging, if they did not produce the criminals; but these demonstrated that the people were peaceably disposed, and they begged forgiveness for those that had spoken amiss; for that it was no wonder at all that in so great a multitude there should be some more daring than they ought to be, and by reason of their younger age, foolish also; and that it was impossible to distinguish those that offended from the rest, while every one was sorry for what he had done, and denied it out of fear of what would follow: that he ought, however, to provide for the peace of the nation, and to take such counsels as might preserve the city for the Romans, and rather, for the sake of a great number of innocent people, to forgive a few that were guilty, than for the sake of a few of the wicked, to put so large and good a body of men into disorder.

9. Florus was more provoked at this, and called out aloud to the soldiers to plunder that which was called the Upper Market Place, and to slay such as they met with. So the soldiers, taking this exhortation of their commander in a

sense agreeable to their desire of gain, did not only plunder the place they were sent to, but forcing themselves into every house, they slew its inhabitants; so the citizens fled along the narrow lanes, and the soldiers slew those that they caught, and no method of plunder was omitted; they also caught many of the quiet people, and brought them before Florus, whom he first chastised with stripes, and then crucified. Accordingly, the whole number of those that were destroyed that day, with their wives and children (for they did not spare the infants themselves,) was about three thousand six hundred; and what made this calamity the heavier, was this new method of Roman barbarity; for Florus ventured then to do what no one had done before, that is, to have men of the equestrian order whipped,* and nailed to the cross before his tribunal; who, although they were by birth Jews, yet were they of Roman dignity notwithstanding.

CHAPTER XV

CONCERNING BERNICE'S PETITION TO FLORUS, TO SPARE THE JEWS, BUT IN VAIN; AS ALSO HOW, AFTER THE SEDITIOUS FLAME WAS QUENCHED, IT WAS KINDLED AGAIN BY FLORUS

1. ABOUT this very time king Agrippa was going to Alexandria, to congratulate Alexander upon his having obtained the government of Egypt from Nero; but as his sister Bernice was come to Jerusalem, and saw the wicked practices of the soldiers, she was sorely affected at it, and frequently sent the masters of her horse and her guards to Florus, and begged of him to leave off these slaughters; but he would not comply with her request nor have any regard either to the multitude of those already slain, or to the nobility of her that interceded, but only to the advantage he should make by his plundering; nay, this violence of the soldiers broke out to such a degree of madness, that it spent itself on the queen herself; for they did not only torment and destroy those whom they had caught under her very eyes, but indeed had killed herself also, unless she had prevented them by flying to the palace, and had stayed there all night with her guards, which she had about her for fear of an insult from the soldiers. Now she dwelt then at Jerusalem, in order to perform a vow† which she had made to God; for it is usual with those that had been either afflicted with a distemper, or with any other distresses, to make vows; and for thirty days before they are to offer their sacrifices, to abstain from wine, and to shave the hair of their head. Which things Bernice was now performing, and stood barefoot before Florus's tribunal, and besought him [to spare the Jews.] Yet could she neither have reverence

---

* Here we have examples of native Jews who were of the equestrian order among the Romans, and so ought never to have been whipped or crucified, according to the Roman laws. See almost the like case in St Paul himself, Acts xxii. 25-29.

† This vow which Bernice came now to accomplish at Jerusalem, was not that of a Nazarite, but such a one as religious Jews used to make, in hopes of any deliverance from a disease, or other danger. However, these thirty days' abode at Jerusalem seems to be too long, unless it were wholly voluntary in this great lady. It is not required in the law of Moses relating to Nazarites, Num. vi.; and is very different from St Paul's time for such preparation, which was but one day, Acts xxi. 26.

paid to her, nor could she escape without some danger of being slain herself.

2. This happened upon the sixteenth day of the month Artemissus, [Jyar.] Now on the next day, the multitude, who were in a great agony, ran together to the upper market-place, and made the loudest lamentations for those that had perished; and the greatest part of the cries were such as reflected on Florus; at which the men of power were affrighted, together with the high priests, and rent their garments, and fell down before each of them, and besought them to leave off, and not to provoke Florus to some incurable procedure, besides what they had already suffered. Accordingly, the multitude complied immediately, out of reverence to those that had desired it of them, and out of the hope they had that Florus would do them no more injuries.

3. So Florus was troubled that the disturbances were over, and endeavoured to kindle the flame again, and sent for the high priests, with the other eminent persons, and said the only demonstration that the people would not make any other innovations should be this,—that they must go out and meet the soldiers that were ascending from Cesarea, whence two cohorts were coming; and while these men were exhorting the multitude so to do, he sent beforehand, and gave directions to the centurions of the cohorts, that they should give notice to those that were under them, not to return the Jews' salutations; and that if they made any reply to his disadvantage, they should make use of their weapons. Now the high priests assembled the multitude in the temple, and desired them to go and meet the Romans, and to salute the cohorts very civilly, before their miserable case should become incurable. Now the seditious part would not comply with these persuasions; but the consideration of those that had been destroyed made them incline to those that were boldest for action.

4. At this time it was that every priest, and every servant of God, brought out the holy vessels, and the ornamental garments wherein they used to minister in sacred things.—The harpers also, and the singers of hymns, came out with their instruments of music, and fell down before the multitude, and begged of them they would preserve those holy ornaments to them, and not to provoke the Romans to carry off those sacred treasures. You might also see then the high priests themselves, with dust sprinkled in great plenty upon their heads, with bosoms deprived of any covering but what was rent; these besought every one of the eminent men by name, and the multitude in common, that they would not for a small offence betray their country to those that were desirous to have it laid waste; saying, "What benefit will it bring to the soldiers to have a salutation from the Jews? or what amendment of affairs will it bring you, if you do not now go out to meet them? and that if they saluted them civilly, all handle would be cut off from Florus to begin a war; that they should thereby gain their country, and freedom from all further sufferings; and that, besides, it would be a sign of great want of command of themselves, if they should yield to a few seditious persons, while it was fitter for them who were so great a people to force the others to act soberly."

5. By these persuasions, which they used to the multitude and to the seditious, they restrained some by threatenings, and others by the reverence that was paid them. After this they led them out, and they met the soldiers

quietly, and after a composed manner, and when they were come up with them, they saluted them; but when they made no answer, the seditious exclaimed against Florus, which was the signal given for falling upon them. The soldiers therefore encompassed them presently, and struck them with their clubs, and as they fled away, the horsemen trampled them down; so that a great many fell down dead by the strokes of the Romans, and more by their own violence in crushing one another. Now there was a terrible crowding about the gates, and while every body was making haste to get before another, the flight of them all was retarded, and a terrible destruction there was among those that fell down, for they were suffocated, and broken to pieces by the multitude of those that were uppermost; nor could any of them be distinguished by his relations, in order to the care of his funeral: the soldiers also who beat them, fell upon those whom they overtook, without shewing them any mercy, and thrust the multitude through the place called Bezetha, as they forced their way, in order to get in and seize upon the temple, and the tower Antonia. Florus also, being desirous to get those places into his possession, brought such as were with him out of the king's palace, and would have compelled them to get as far as the citadel [Antonia;] but his attempt failed, for the people immediately turned back upon him, and stopped the violence of his attempt; and as they stood upon the tops of their houses, they threw their darts at the Romans, who, as they were sorely galled thereby, because those weapons came from above, and they were not able to make a passage through the multitude, which stopped up the narrow passages, they retired to the camp which was at the palace.

6. But for the seditious, they were afraid lest Florus should come again, and get possession of the temple, through Antonia; so they got immediately upon those cloisters of the temple that joined to Antonia, and cut them down. This cooled the avarice of Florus; for whereas he was eager to obtain the treasures of God [in the temple,] and on that account was desirous of getting into Antonia, as soon as the cloisters were broken down he left off his attempt; he then sent for the high priests and the sanhedrim, and told them that he was indeed himself going out of the city, but that he would leave them as large a garrison as they should desire. Hereupon they promised that they would make no innovations, in case he would leave them one band; but not that which had fought with the Jews, because the multitude bore ill-will against that band on account of what they had suffered from it; so he changed the band as they desired, and with the rest of his forces returned to Cesarea.

CHAPTER XVI

CESTIUS SENDS NEOPOLITANUS THE TRIBUNE TO SEE IN WHAT CONDITION THE AFFAIRS OF THE JEWS WERE. AGRIPPA MAKES A SPEECH TO THE PEOPLE OF THE JEWS, THAT HE MAY DIVERT THEM FROM THEIR INTENTIONS OF MAKING WAR WITH THE ROMANS

1. HOWEVER, Florus contrived another way to oblige the Jews to begin the war, and sent to Cestius and accused the Jews falsely of revolting [from the Roman government,] and imputed the beginning of the former fight to them, and pre-

tended they had been the authors of that disturbance, wherein they were only the sufferers. Yet were not the governors of Jerusalem silent upon this occasion, but did themselves write to Cestius, as did Bernice also, about the illegal practices of which Florus had been guilty against the city; who upon reading both accounts, consulted with his captains [what he should do.] Now some of them thought it best for Cestius to go up with his army, either to punish the revolt, if it was real, or to settle the Roman affairs on a surer foundation, if the Jews continued quiet under them; but he thought it best himself to send one of his intimate friends beforehand, to see the state of affairs, and to give him a faithful account of the intentions of the Jews. Accordingly, he sent one of his tribunes, whose name was Neopolitanus, who met with king Agrippa as he was returning from Alexandria, at Jamnia, and told him who it was that sent him, and on what errands he was sent.

2. And here it was that the high priests and men of power among the Jews, as well as the sanhedrim, came to congratulate the king [upon his safe return;] and after they had paid their respects, they lamented their own calamities, and related to him what barbarous treatment they had met with from Florus. At which barbarity Agrippa had great indignation, but transferred, after a subtle manner, his anger towards those Jews whom he really pitied, that he might beat down their high thoughts of themselves, and would have them believe that they had not been so unjustly treated, in order to dissuade them from avenging themselves. So these great men, as of better understanding than the rest, and desirous of peace, because of the possessions they had, understood that this rebuke which the king gave them was intended for their good; but as to the people, they came sixty furlongs out of Jerusalem, and congratulated both Agrippa and Neopolitanus; but the wives of those that had been slain came running first of all and lamenting. The people also when they heard their mourning, fell into lamentations also, and besought Agrippa to assist them: they also cried out to Neopolitanus, and complained of the many miseries they had endured under Florus; and they shewed them, when they were come into the city, how the market-place was made desolate, and the houses plundered. They then persuaded Neopolitanus, by the means of Agrippa, that he would walk round the city, with only one servant, as far as Siloam, that he might inform himself that the Jews submitted to all the rest of the Romans, and were only displeased at Florus, by reason of his exceeding barbarity to them. So he walked round, and had sufficient experience of the good temper the people were in, and then went up to the temple, where he called the multitude together, and highly commended them for their fidelity to the Romans, and earnestly exhorted them to keep the peace; and having performed such parts of divine worship at the temple as he was allowed to do, he returned to Cestius.

3. But as for the multitude of the Jews, they addressed themselves to the king, and to the high priests, and desired they might have leave to send ambassadors to Nero against Florus, and not by their silence afford a suspicion that they had been the occasion of such great slaughters as had been made, and were disposed to revolt, alleging that they should seem to have been the first beginners of the war, if they did not prevent the report by shewing who it was that began it; and it appeared openly that they would not be quiet, if anybody should hinder them from sending such an embassage. But Agrippa, although he thought it too dangerous a thing for them to appoint men to go as the accusers of Florus, yet did he not think it fit for him to overlook them, as they were in a disposition for war. He therefore called the multitude together into a large gallery, and placed his sister Bernice in the house of the Asamoneans, that she might be seen by them, (which house was over the gallery, at the passage to the upper city, where the bridge joined the temple to the gallery,) and spake to them as follows:—

4. * "Had I perceived that you were all zealously disposed to go to war with the Romans, and that the purer and more sincere part of the people did not propose to live in peace, I had not come out to you, nor been so bold as to give you counsel; for all discourses that tend to persuade men to do what they ought to do is superfluous, when the hearers are agreed to do the contrary. But because some are earnest to go to war because they are young, and without experience of the miseries it brings; and because some are for it, out of an unreasonable expectation of regaining their liberty, and because others hope to get by it, and are therefore earnestly bent upon it; that in the confusion of your affairs they may gain what belongs to those that are too weak to resist them, I have thought proper to get you all together, and to say to you what I think to be for your advantage; that so the former may grow wiser, and change their minds, and that the best men may come to no harm by the ill conduct of some others. And let not any one be tumultuous against me, in case what they hear me say do not please them; for as to those that admit of no cure, but are resolved upon a revolt, it will still be in their power to retain the same sentiments after my exhortation is over; but still my discourse will fall to the ground, even with relation to those that have a mind to hear me, unless you will all keep silence. I am well aware that many make a tragical exclamation concerning the injuries that have been offered you by your procurators, and concerning the glorious advantages of liberty; but before I begin the inquiry, who you are that must go to war, and who they are against whom you must fight, —I shall first separate those pretences that are by some connected together; for if you aim at avenging yourselves on those that have done you injury, why do you pretend this to be a war for recovering your liberty? but if you think all servitude intolerable, to what purpose serve your complaints to particular governors? for if they treated you with moderation, it would still be equally an unworthy thing to be in servitude. Consider now the several cases that may be supposed, how little occasion there is for your going to war. Your first occasion is, the accusations you have to make against your procurators: now here you ought to be submissive to those in authority, and not give them any provocation: but when you reproach men greatly for small offences, you excite those whom you reproach to be your adversaries; for this will only make them leave off hurting you privately, and with some degree of modesty, and to lay what you have waste openly. Now nothing so much damps the force of strokes as bearing them with patience; and the quietness of those who are in-

---

* In this speech of king Agrippa we have an authentic account of the extent and strength of the Roman empire when the Jewish war began. He is the same Agrippa who said to Paul, "Almost thou persuadest me to be a Christian," Acts xxvi. 28; and of whom St Paul said, "He was expert in all the customs and questions of the Jews," v. 3.

jured, diverts the injurious persons from afflicting. But let us take it for granted that the Roman ministers are injurious to you, and are incurably severe; yet are they not all the Romans who thus injure you; nor hath Cæsar, against whom you are going to make war, injured you: it is not by their command that any wicked governor is sent to you; for they who are in the west cannot see those that are in the east; nor indeed is it easy for them there even to hear what is done in these parts. Now it is absurd to make war with a great many for the sake of one; to do so with such mighty people, for a small cause; and this when these people are not able to know of what you complain: nay, such crimes as we complain of may soon be corrected, for the same procurator will not continue for ever; and probable it is that the successors will come with more moderate inclinations. But as for war, if it be once begun, it is not easily laid down again, nor borne without calamities coming therewith. However, as to the desire of recovering your liberty, it is unseasonable to indulge it so late; whereas you ought to have laboured earnestly in old time that you might never have lost it: for the first experience of slavery was hard to be endured, and the struggle that you might never have been subject to it would have been just; but that slave who hath once been brought into subjection, and then runs away, is rather a refractory slave than a lover of liberty; for it was then the proper time for doing all things that was possible, that you might have never admitted the Romans [into your city] when Pompey first came into the country. But so it was, that our ancestors and their kings, who were in much better circumstances than we are, both as to money and [strong] bodies, and [valiant] souls, did not bear the onset of a small body of the Roman army. And yet you who have not accustomed yourselves to obedience from one generation to another, and who are so much inferior to those who first submitted in your circumstances, will venture to oppose the entire empire of the Romans; while those Athenians, who, in order to preserve the liberty of Greece, did once set fire to their own city; who pursued Xerxes, that proud prince, when he sailed upon the sea; and could not be contained by the seas, but conducted such an army as was too broad for Europe; and made him run away like a fugitive in a single ship, and brake so great a part of Asia at the lesser Salamis, are yet at this time servants to the Romans; and those injunctions which are sent from Italy, become laws to the principal governing city of Greece.—Those Lacedemonians also, who got the great victories at Thermopylæ and Platea, and had Agesilaus, [for their king,] and searched every corner of Asia, are content to admit the same lords. These Macedonians also, who still fancy what great men their Philip and Alexander were, and see that the latter had promised them the empire over the world, these bear so great a change, and pay their obedience to those whom fortune hath advanced in their stead.—Moreover, ten thousand other nations there are, who had greater reason than we to claim their entire liberty, and yet do submit. You are the only people who think it a disgrace to be servants to those to whom all the world hath submitted. What sort of an army do you rely on? What are the arms you depend on? Where is your fleet that may sieze upon the Roman seas? and where are those treasures that may be sufficient for your undertakings? Do you suppose, I pray you, that you are to make war with the Egyptians, and with the Arabians?

Will you not carefully reflect upon the Roman empire? Will you not estimate your own weakness? Hath not your army been often beaten even by your neighbouring nations, while the power of the Romans is invincible in all parts of the habitable earth? nay, rather they seek for somewhat still beyond that, for all Euphrates is not a sufficient boundary for them on the east side, nor the Danube on the north, and for their southern limit, Lybia has been searched over by them, as far as countries uninhabited, as is Cadiz their limit on the west, nay, indeed, they have sought for another habitable earth beyond the ocean, and have carried their arms as far as such British islands as were never known before. What therefore do you pretend to do? Are you richer than the Gauls, stronger than the Germans, wiser than the Greeks, more numerous than all the men upon the habitable earth?— What confidence is it that elevates you to oppose the Romans? Perhaps it will be said, it is hard to endure slavery. Yes; how much harder is it to the Greeks, who were esteemed the noblest of all people under the sun? These, although they inhabit a large country, are in subjection to six bundles of Roman rods. It is the same case with the Macedonians, who have juster reason to claim their liberty than you have. What is the case of five hundred cities of Asia? do they not submit to a single governor, and to the consular bundle of rods? What need I speak of the Heniochi, and Colchi, and the nation of Tauri, those that inhabit the Bosphorus, and the nations about Pontus, and Meotis, who formerly knew not so much as a lord of their own, but are now subject to three thousand armed men, and where forty long ships keep the sea in peace, which before was not navigable, and very tempestuous? How strong a plea may Bithynia, and Cappadocia, and the people of Pamphylia, the Lycians, and Cilicians, put in for liberty! but they are made tributary without an army. What are the circumstances of the Thracians, whose country extends in breadth five days' journey, and in length seven, and is of a much more harsh constitution, and much more defensible than yours, and, by the rigour of its cold, sufficient to keep off armies from attacking them? do not they submit to two thousand men of the Roman garrisons? Are not the Illyrians, who inhabit the country adjoining, as far as Dalmatia and the Danube, governed by barely two legions? by which also they put a stop to the incursions of the Dacians; and for the Dalmatians, who have made such frequent insurrections, in order to regain their liberty, and who could never before be so thoroughly subdued, but that they always gathered their forces together again, and revolted, yet are they now very quiet under one Roman legion. Moreover, if great advantages might provoke any people to revolt, the Gauls might do it best of all, as being so thoroughly walled round by nature; on the east side of the Alps, on the north by the river Rhine, on the south by the Pyrenean mountains, and on the west by the ocean.—Now, although these Gauls have such obstacles before them to prevent any attack upon them, and have no fewer than three hundred and five nations among them, nay, have, as one may say, the fountains of domestic happiness within themselves, and send out plentiful streams of happiness over almost the whole world, these bear to be tributary to the Romans, and derive their prosperous condition from them; and they undergo this, not because they are of effeminate minds, or because they are of an ignoble stock, as having borne a war of eighty years, in order to preserve their liberty; but by reason of the great regard they have to the power of the Romans, and their good fortune, which is of greater efficacy than their arms. These Gauls, therefore, are kept in servitude by twelve hundred soldiers, who are hardly so many as are their cities; nor hath the gold dug out of the mines of Spain been sufficient for the support of a war to preserve their liberty, nor could their vast distance from the Romans by land and by sea do it; nor could the martial tribes of the Lusitanians and Spaniards escape; no more could the ocean, with its tide, which yet was terrible to the ancient inhabitants. Nay, the Romans have extended their arms beyond the pillars of Hercules, and have walked among the clouds, upon the Pyrenean mountains, and have subdued these nations; and one legion is a sufficient guard for these people, although they were so hard to be conquered, and at a distance so remote from Rome. Who is there among you that hath not heard of the great number of the Germans? You have, to be sure, yourselves seen them to be strong and tall, and that frequently, since the Romans have them among their captives everywhere; yet these Germans, who dwell in an immense country, who have minds greater than their bodies, and a soul that despises death, and who are in rage more fierce than wild beasts, have the Rhine for the boundary of their enterprises, and are tamed by eight Roman legions. Such of them as were taken captives became their servants; and the rest of the entire nation were obliged to save themselves by flight. Do you also, who depend on the walls of Jerusalem, consider what a wall the Britons had: for the Romans sailed away to them, and subdued them while they were encompassed by the ocean, and inhabited an island that is not less than [the continent of] this habitable earth, and four legions are a sufficient guard to so large an island: and why should I speak much more about this matter, while the Parthians, that most warlike body of men, and lords of so many nations, and encompassed with such mighty forces, send hostages to the Romans; whereby you may see, if you please, even in Italy, the noblest nation of the east under the notion of peace, submitting to serve them. Now, when almost all people under the sun submit to the Roman arms, will you be the only people that make war against them? and this without regarding the fate of the Carthaginians, who, in the midst of their brags of the great Hannibal, and the nobility of their Phenician original, fell by the hand of Scipio. Nor indeed have the Cyrenians, derived from the Lacedemonians, nor the Marmaridæ, a nation extended as far as the regions uninhabitable for want of water, nor have the Syrtes, a place terrible to such as barely hear it described, the Nasamons and Moors, and the immense multitude of the Numidians, been able to put a stop to the Roman valour; and as for the third part of the habitable earth [Africa,] whose nations are so many, that it is not easy to number them, and which is bounded by the Atlantic Sea, and the Pillars of Hercules, and feeds an innumerable multitude of Ethiopians, as far as the Red Sea, these have the Romans subdued entirely. And besides the annual fruits of the earth, which maintain the multitude of the Romans for eight months in the year, this, over and above, pays all sorts of tribute, and affords revenues suitable to the necessities of the government. Nor do they, like you, esteem such injunctions a disgrace to them, although they have but one Roman legion that abides among them; and indeed what occasion

is there for shewing you the power of the Romans over remote countries, when it is so easy to learn it from Egypt, in your neighbourhood? This country is extended as far as the Ethiopians, and Arabia the Happy, and borders upon India; it hath seven millions five hundred thousand men, besides the inhabitants of Alexandria, as may be learned from the revenue of the poll-tax; yet it is not ashamed to submit to the Roman government, although it hath Alexandria as a grand temptation to a revolt, by reason it is so full of people and of riches, and is besides exceeding large, its length being thirty furlongs, and its breadth no less than ten; and it pays more tribute to the Romans in one month than you do in a year: nay, besides what it pays in money, it sends corn to Rome that supports it for four months [in the year:] it is also walled round on all sides, either by almost impassable deserts, or seas that have no havens, or by rivers, or by lakes; yet have none of these things been found too strong for the Roman good fortune; however, two legions that lie in that city are a bridle both for the remoter parts of Egypt, and for the parts inhabited by the more noble Macedonians. Where, then, are those people whom you are to have for your auxiliaries? Must they come from parts of the world that are uninhabited? for all that are in the habitable earth are [under the] Romans.—Unless any of you extend his hopes as far as beyond the Euphrates, and suppose that those of your own nation that dwell in Adiabene will come to your assistance, (but certainly these will not embarrass themselves with an unjustifiable war, nor if they should follow such ill advice, will the Parthians permit them so to do;) for it is their concern to maintain the truce that is between them and the Romans, and they will be supposed to break the covenants between them, if any under their government march against the Romans. What remains therefore, is this, that you have recourse to divine assistance; but this is already on the side of the Romans; for it is impossible that so vast an empire should be settled without God's providence. Reflect upon it, how impossible it is your zealous observation of your religious customs to be here preserved, which are hard to be observed, even when you fight with those whom you are able to conquer; and how can you then hope for God's assistance, when, by being forced to transgress his law, you will make him turn his face from you? and if you do observe the custom of the Sabbath-days, and will not be prevailed on to do anything thereon, you will easily be taken, as was your forefathers by Pompey, who was the busiest in his siege on those days on which the besieged rested; but if in time of war you transgress the law of your country, I cannot tell on whose account you will afterward go to war; for your concern is but one, that you do nothing against any of your forefathers; and how will you call upon God to assist you, when you are voluntarily transgressing against his religion? Now, all men that go to war, do it either as depending on divine or on human assistance; but since your going to war will cut off both those assistances, those that are for going to war choose evident destruction. What hinders you from slaying your children and wives with your own hands, and burning this most excellent native city of yours? for by this mad prank you will, however, escape the reproach of being beaten; but it were best, O my friends, it were best, while the vessel is still in the haven, to foresee the impending storm, and not to set sail out of the port into the middle of the hurricanes; for we justly pity those who fall into great misfortunes without foreseeing them; but for him who rushes into manifest ruin, he gains reproaches [instead of commiseration.] But certainly no one can imagine that you can enter into a war as by an agreement, or that when the Romans have got you under their power, they will use you with moderation, or will not rather, for an example to other nations, burn your holy city, and utterly destroy your whole nation; for those of you who shall survive the war will not be able to find a place whither to flee, since all men have the Romans for their lords already, or are afraid they shall have hereafter. Nay, indeed, the danger concerns not those Jews that dwell here only, but those of them who dwell in other cities also; for there is no people upon the habitable earth which have not some portion of you among them, whom your enemies will slay, in case you go to war, and on that account also; and so every city that hath Jews in it will be filled with slaughter for the sake only of a few men, and they who slay them will be pardoned; but if that slaughter be not made by them, consider how wicked a thing it is to take arms against those that are so kind to you. Have pity, therefore, if not on your children and wives, yet upon this your metropolis, and its sacred walls; spare the temple and preserve the holy house, with its holy furniture, for yourselves; for if the Romans get you under their power, they will no longer abstain from them, when their former abstinence shall have been so ungratefully requited. I call to witness your sanctuary, and the holy angels of God, and this country common to us all, that I have not kept back anything that is for your preservation; and if you will follow that advice which you ought to do, you will have that peace which will be common to you and to me; but if you indulge your passions, you will run those hazards which I shall be free from."

5. When Agrippa had spoken thus, both he and his sister wept, and by their tears repressed a great deal of the violence of the people; but still they cried out, that they would not fight against the Romans but against Florus, on account of what they had suffered by his means. To which Agrippa replied, that what they had already done was like such as make war against the Romans; "for you have not paid the tribute which is due to Cæsar;* and you have cut off the cloisters [of the temple] from joining to the tower Antonia. You will therefore prevent any occasion of revolt, if you will but join these together again, and if you will but pay your tribute; for the citadel does not now belong to Florus, nor are you to pay the tribute-money to Florus."

CHAPTER XVII

HOW THE WAR OF THE JEWS WITH THE ROMANS BEGAN; AND CONCERNING MANAHEM

1. THIS advice the people hearkened to, and went up into the temple with the king and Bernice, and began to rebuild the cloisters: the rulers also and senators divided themselves into the villages, and collected the tributes, and soon got together forty talents, which was the sum that was deficient. And thus did Agrippa then put a stop to that war which was threatened.

Moreover, he attempted to persuade the multitude to obey Florus, until Cæsar should send one to succeed him; but they were hereby more provoked, and cast reproaches upon the king, and got him excluded out of the city; nay, some of the seditious had the impudence to throw stones at him. So when the king saw that the violence of those that were for innovations was not to be restrained, and being very angry at the contumelies he had received, he sent their rulers, together with their men of power, to Florus, to Cesarea, that he might appoint whom he thought fit to collect the tribute in the country, while he retired into his own kingdom.

2. And at this time it was that some of those that principally excited the people to go to war, made an assault upon a certain fortress called Masada. They took it by treachery, and slew the Romans that were there, and put others of their own party to keep it. At the same time Eleazar, the son of Ananias the high priest, a very bold youth, who was at that time governor of the temple, persuaded those that officiated in the divine service to receive no gift or sacrifice for any foreigner. And this was the true beginning of our war with the Romans: for they rejected the sacrifice of Cæsar on this account: and when many of the high priests and principal men besought them not to omit the sacrifice, which it was customary for them to offer for their princes, they would not be prevailed upon. These relied much upon their multitude, for the most flourishing part of the innovators assisted them; but they had the chief regard to Eleazar, the governor of the temple.

3. Hereupon the men of power got together, and conferred with the high priests, as did also the principal of the Pharisees; and thinking all was at stake, and that their calamities were becoming incurable, took counsel what was to be done. Accordingly, they determined to try what they could do with the seditious by words, and assembled the people before the brazen gate, which was that gate of the inner temple [court of the priests] which looked towards the sunrising. And, in the first place, they shewed the great indignation they had at this attempt for a revolt, and for their bringing so great a war upon their country: after which they confuted their pretence as unjustifiable, and told them, that their forefathers had adorned their temple in great part with donations bestowed on them by foreigners, and had always received what had been presented to them from foreign nations; and that they had been so far from rejecting any person's sacrifice, (which would be the highest instance of impiety,) that they had themselves placed those donations about the temple which were still visible, and had remained there so long a time: that they did now irritate the Romans to take arms against them, and invited them to make war upon them, and brought up novel rules of strange divine worship, and determined to run the hazard of having their city condemned for impiety, while they would not allow any foreigners but Jews only, either to sacrifice or to worship therein. And if such a law should ever be introduced in the case of a single person only, he would have indignation at it, as an instance of inhumanity determined against him; while they have no regard to the Romans or to Cæsar, and forbade even their oblations to be received also; that however they cannot but fear, lest, by thus rejecting their sacrifices, they shall not be allowed to offer their own; and that this city will lose its principality, unless they grow wiser quickly, and restore the sacrifices as formerly; and indeed amend the in-

---

* Julius Cæsar had decreed, that the Jews of Jerusalem should pay an annual tribute to the Romans, excepting the city of Joppa, and for the Sabbatical year.

jury [they have offered to foreigners,] before the report of it comes to the ears of those that have been injured.

4. And as they said these things, they produced those priests that were skilful in the customs of their country, who made the report, that all their forefathers had received the sacrifices from foreign nations.—But still not one of the innovators would hearken to what was said; nay, those that ministered about the temple would not attend their divine service, but were preparing matters for beginning the war. So the men of power, perceiving that the sedition was too hard for them to subdue, and that the danger which would arise from the Romans would come upon them first of all, endeavoured to save themselves, and sent ambassadors; some to Florus, the chief of whom was Simon the son of Ananias; and others to Agrippa, among whom the most eminent was Saul, and Antipas, and Costobarus, who were of the king's kindred; and they desired of them both that they would come with an army to the city, and cut off the sedition before it should be too hard to be subdued. Now this terrible message was good news to Florus; and because his design was to have a war kindled, he gave the ambassadors no answer at all. But Agrippa was equally solicitous for those that were revolting, and for those against whom the war was to be made, and was desirous to preserve the Jews for the Romans, and the temple and metropolis for the Jews; he was also sensible that it was not for his own advantage that the disturbances should proceed; so he sent three thousand horsemen to the assistance of the people out of Auranitis, and Batanea, and Trachonitis, and these under Darius, the master of his horse; and Philip the son of Jacimus, the general of his army.

5. Upon this the men of power, with the high priest, as also all the part of the multitude that were desirous of peace, took courage, and seized upon the upper city [Mount Zion;] for the seditious part had the lower city and the temple in their power: so they made use of stones and slings perpetually against one another, and threw darts continually on both sides! and sometimes it happened that they made excursions by troops, and fought it out hand to hand, while the seditious were superior in boldness, but the king's soldiers in skill. These last strove chiefly to gain the temple, and to drive those out of it who profaned it; as did the seditious, with Eleazar (besides what they had already) labour to gain the upper city. Thus were their perpetual slaughters on both sides for seven days' time; but neither side would yield up the parts they had seized upon.

6. Now the next day was the festival of Xylophory; upon which the custom was for every one to bring wood for the altar, (that their might never be a want of fuel for that fire which was unquenchable and always burning.) Upon that day they excluded the opposite party from the observation of this part of religion. And when they had joined to themselves many of the Sicarii, who crowded in among the weaker people, (that was the name of such robbers as had under their bosoms swords called Sicæ,) they grew bolder, and carried their undertakings further, insomuch that the king's soldiers were overpowered by their multitude and boldness; and so they gave way, and were driven out of the upper city by force. The others then set fire to the house of Ananias the high priest, and to the palaces of Agrippa and Bernice; after which they carried the fire to the place where the archives were reposited, and made haste to burn the contracts belonging to their creditors, and thereby dissolve their obligations for paying their debts; and this was done, in order to gain the multitude of those who had been debtors, and that they might persuade the poorer sort to join in their insurrection with safety against the more wealthy; so the keepers of the records fled away, and the rest set fire to them. And when they had thus burnt down the nerves of the city, they fell upon their enemies; at which time some of the men of power, and of the high priests, went into the vaults under ground, and concealed themselves, while others fled with the king's soldiers to the upper palace, and shut the gates immediately: among whom were Ananias the high priest, and the ambassadors that had been sent to Agrippa. And now the seditious were contented with the victory they had gotten, and the buildings they had burnt down, and proceeded no further.

7. But on the next day, which was the fifteenth of the month Lous [Ab,] they made an assault upon Antonia, and besieged the garrison which was in it two days, and then took the garrison, and slew them, and set the citadel on fire; after which they marched to the palace, whither the king's soldiers were fled, and parted themselves into four bodies, and made an attack upon the walls. As for those that were within it, no one had the courage to sally out, because those that assaulted them were so numerous; but they distributed themselves into breastworks and turrets, and shot at the besiegers, whereby many of the robbers fell under the walls; nor did they cease to fight one with another either by night or by day; while the seditious supposed that those within would grow weary for want of food; and those within supposed the others would do the like by the tediousness of the siege.

8. In the meantime one Manahem, the son of Judas, that was called the Galilean (who was a very cunning sophister, and had formerly reproached the Jews under Cyrenius, that after God they were subject to the Romans) took some of the men of note with him, and retired to Masada, where he broke open king Herod's armoury, and gave arms not only to his own people, but to other robbers also. These he made use of for a guard, and returned in the state of a king to Jerusalem; and became the leader of the sedition, and gave orders for continuing the siege; but they wanted proper instruments, and it was not practicable to undermine the wall, because the darts came down upon them from above. But still they dug a mine, from a great distance, under one of the towers, and made it totter; and having done that, they set on fire what was combustible, and left it; and when the foundations were burnt below, the tower fell down suddenly. Yet did they meet with another wall that had been built within, for the besieged were sensible beforehand of what they were doing, and probably the tower shook as it was undermining; so they provided themselves with another fortification; which when the besiegers unexpectedly saw, while they thought they had already gained the place, they were under some consternation. However, those that were within sent to Manahem, and to the other leaders of the sedition, and desired that they might go out upon a capitulation; this was granted to the king's soldiers and their own countrymen only, who went out accordingly; but the Romans that were left alone were greatly dejected, for they were not able to force their way through such a multitude; and to desire them to give them their right hand for their

security, they thought would be a reproach to them; and besides if they should give it them, they durst not depend upon it; so they deserted their camp, as easily taken, and ran away to the royal towers,—that called Hippicus, that called Phasaelus, and that called Mariamne. But Manahem and his party fell upon the place whence the soldiers were fled, and slew as many of them as they could catch before they got up to the towers, and plundered what they left behind them, and set fire to the camp. This was executed on the sixth day of the month Gorpieus [Elul.]

9. But on the next day the high priest was caught where he had concealed himself in an aqueduct; he was slain, together with Hezekiah his brother, by the robbers: hereupon the seditious besieged the towers, and kept them guarded, lest any one of the soldiers should escape. Now the overthrow of the places of strength, and the death of the high priest Ananias, so puffed up Manahem, that he became barbarously cruel; and as he thought he had no antagonist to dispute the management of affairs with him, he was no better than an insupportable tyrant: but Eleazar and his party, when words had passed between them, how it was not proper when they revolted from the Romans, out of the desire of liberty, to betray that liberty to any of their own people, and to bear a lord, who, though he should be guilty of no violence, was yet meaner than themselves; as also, that, in case they were obliged to set some one over their public affairs, it was fitter they should give that privilege to any one rather than to him, they made an assault upon him in the temple; for he went up thither to worship in a pompous manner, and adorned with royal garments, and had his followers with him in their armour. But Eleazar and his party fell violently upon him, as did also the rest of the people, and taking up stones to attack him withal, they threw them at the sophister, and thought that if he were once ruined, the entire sedition would fall to the ground. Now Manahem and his party made resistance for a while; but when they perceived that the whole multitude were falling upon them, they fled which way every one was able; those that were caught were slain, and those that hid themselves were searched for. A few there were of them who privately escaped to Masada, among whom was Eleazar, the son of Jarius, who was of kin to Manahem, and acted the part of a tyrant at Masada afterward. As for Manahem himself, he ran away to the place called Ophla, and there lay skulking in private; but they took him alive, and drew him out before them all; they then tortured him with many sorts of torments, and after all slew him, as they did by those that were captains under him also, and particularly by the principal instrument of his tyranny whose name was Apsalom.

10 And, as I said, so far truly the people assisted them, while they hoped this might afford some amendment to the seditious practices; but the others were not in haste to put an end to the war, but hoped to prosecute it with less danger, now they had slain Manahem. It is true, that when the people earnestly desired that they would leave off besieging the soldiers, they were the most earnest in pressing it forward, and this till Metilius, who was the Roman general, sent to Eleazar, and desired that they would give them security to spare their lives only; but agreed to deliver up their arms, and what else they had with them. The others readily complied with their petition, sent to them Gorion, the son of Nicodemus, and Ananias, the son of Sadduk, and Judas, the son of Jonathan, that they might give them the security of their right hands, and of their oaths: after which Metilius brought down his soldiers; which soldiers, while they were in arms, were not meddled with by any of the seditious, nor was there any appearance of treachery: but as soon as, according to the articles of capitulation, they had all laid down their shields and their swords, and were under no further suspicion of any harm, but were going away, Eleazar's men attacked them after a violent manner, and encompassed them round, and slew them, while they neither defended themselves nor entreated for mercy, but only cried out upon the breach of their articles of capitulation and their oaths. And thus were all these men barbarously murdered, excepting Metilius; for when he entreated for mercy, and promised he would turn Jew, and be circumcised, they saved him alive, but none else. This loss to the Romans was but light, there being no more than a few slain out of an immense army; but still it appeared to be a prelude to the Jews' own destruction, while men made public lamentation when they saw that such occasions were afforded for a war as were incurable; that the city was all over polluted with such abominations, from which it was but reasonable to expect some vengeance, even though they should escape revenge from the Romans; so that the city was filled with sadness, and every one of the moderate men in it were under great disturbance, as likely themselves to undergo punishment for the wickedness of the seditious; for indeed it so happened that this murder was perpetrated on the Sabbath day, on which day the Jews have a respite from their works on account of divine worship.

CHAPTER XVIII

THE CALAMITIES AND SLAUGHTERS THAT CAME UPON THE JEWS

1. Now the people of Cesarea had slain the Jews that were among them on the very same day and hour [when the soldiers were slain,] which one would think must have come to pass by the direction of Providence; insomuch that in one hour's time above twenty thousand Jews were killed, and all Cesarea was emptied of its Jewish inhabitants; for Florus caught such as ran away, and sent them in bonds to the galleys. Upon which stroke that the Jews received at Cesarea, the whole nation was greatly enraged; so they divided themselves into several parties, and laid waste the villages of the Syrians, and their neighbouring cities, Philadelphia, and Sebonitis, and Gerasa, and Pella, and Scythopolis, and after them Gadara, and Hippos; and falling upon Gaulonitis, some cities they destroyed there and some they set on fire, and then they went to Kedasa, belonging to the Tyrians, and to Ptolemais, and to Gaba, and to Cesarea; nor was either Sebaste (Samaria) or Askelon able to oppose the violence with which they were attacked; and when they had burned these to the ground, they entirely demolished Anthedon and Gaza; many also of the villages that were about every one of those cities were plundered, and an immense slaughter was made of the men who were caught in them.

2. However, the Syrians were even with the Jews in the multitude of the men whom they slew; for they killed those whom they caught in their cities, and that not only out of the

hatred they bare them, as formerly, but to prevent the danger under which they were from them; so that the disorders in all Syria were terrible, and every city was divided into two armies encamped one against another, and the preservation of the one party was in the destruction of the other; so the daytime was spent in shedding blood, and the night in fear,—which was of the two the more terrible; for when the Syrians thought they had ruined the Jews, they had the Judaisers in suspicion also; and as each side did not care to slay those whom they only suspected on the other, so did they greatly fear them when they were mingled with the other, as if they were certainly foreigners. Moreover, greediness of gain was a provocation to kill the opposite party, even to such as had of old appeared very mild and gentle towards them; for they without fear plundered the effects of the slain, and carried off the spoil of those whom they slew to their own houses, as if they had been gained in a set battle; and he was esteemed a man of honour who got the greatest share, as having prevailed over the greatest number of his enemies. It was then common to see cities filled with dead bodies, still lying unburied, and those of old men, mixed with infants all dead and scattered about together; women also lay amongst them, without any covering for their nakedness: you might then see the whole province full of inexpressible calamities, while the dread of still more barbarous practices which were threatened, was everywhere greater than what had been already perpetrated.

3. And thus far the conflict had been between Jews and foreigners; but when they made excursions to Scythopolis, they found Jews that acted as enemies; for they stood in battle array with those of Scythopolis, and preferred their own safety before their relation to us, they fought against their own countrymen; nay, their alacrity was so very great, that those of Scythopolis suspected them. These were afraid, therefore, lest they should make an assault upon the city in the night-time, and to their great misfortune, should thereby make an apology for themselves to their own people for their revolt from them. So they commanded them, that in case they would confirm their agreement and demonstrate their fidelity to them, who were of a different nation, they should go out of the city, with their families, to a neighbouring grove: and when they had done as they were commanded, without suspecting anything, the people of Scythopolis lay still for the interval of two days, to tempt them to be secure; but on the third night they watched their opportunity, and cut all their throats, some of them as they lay unguarded, and some as they lay asleep. The number that was slain was above thirteen thousand, and then they plundered them of all that they had.

4. It will deserve our relation what befell Simon: he was the son of one Saul, a man of reputation among the Jews. This man was distinguished from the rest by the strength of his body, and the boldness of his conduct, although he abused them both to the mischieving of his countrymen; for he came every day and slew a great many of the Jews of Scythopolis, and he frequently put them to flight, and became himself alone the cause of his army's conquering. But a just punishment overtook him for the murders he had committed upon those of the same nation with him; for when the people of Scythopolis threw their darts at them in the grove, he drew his sword, but did not attack any of the enemy; for he saw that he could do nothing against such a multitude; but he cried out, after a very moving manner, and said,— "O you people of Scythopolis, I deservedly suffer for what I have done with relation to you, when I gave you such security of my fidelity to you, by slaying so many of those that were related to me. Wherefore we very justly experience the perfidiousness of foreigners, while we acted after a most wicked manner against our own nation. I will therefore die, polluted wretch as I am, by mine own hands; for it is not fit I should die by the hand of our enemies; and let the same action be to me both a punishment for my great crimes, and a testimony of my courage to my commendation, that so no one of our enemies may have it to brag of, that he it was that slew me; and no one may insult upon me as I fall." Now when he had said this, he looked round about him upon his family with eyes of commiseration and of rage, (that family consisted of a wife and children, and his aged parents;) so, in the first place, he caught his father by his gray hairs and ran his sword through him,—and after him he did the same to his mother, who willingly received it; and after them he did the same to his wife and children, every one almost offering themselves to his sword, as desirous to prevent being slain by their enemies; so when he had gone over all his family, he stood upon their bodies to be seen by all, and stretching out his right hand, that this action might be observed by all, he sheathed his entire sword into his own bowels. This young man was to be pitied, on account of the strength of his body and the courage of his soul; but since he had assured foreigners of his fidelity [against his own countrymen] he suffered deservedly.

5. Besides this murder at Scythopolis, the other cities rose up against the Jews that were among them: those of Askelon slew two thousand five hundred, and those of Ptolemais two thousand, and put not a few into bonds; those of Tyre also put a great number to death, but kept a greater number in prison; moreover, those of Hippos and those of Gadara did the like, while they put to death the boldest of the Jews, but kept those of whom they were most afraid in custody; as did the rest of the cities of Syria, according as they every one either hated them or were afraid of them; only the Antiochians, the Sidonians, and Apamians, spared those that dwelt with them, and they would not endure either to kill any of the Jews, or to put them in bonds. And perhaps they spared them because their own number was so great that they despised their attempts. But I think that the greatest part of this favour was owing to their commiseration of those whom they saw to make no innovations. As for the Gerasens, they did no harm to those that abode with them; and for those who had a mind to go away, they conducted them as far as their borders reached.

6. There was also a plot laid against the Jews in Agrippa's kingdom; for he was himself gone to Cestius Gallus, to Antioch, but had left one of his companions, whose name was Noarus, to take care of the public affairs; which Noarus was of kin to king Sohemus.* Now there came certain men, seventy in number, out of Batanea, who were the most considerable for their families and prudence of the rest of the people; these desired to have an army put into their hands, that if any tumult should happen, they might have about them a guard sufficient to restrain

* Of this Sohemus we have mention made by Tacitus. We also learn from Dio, that his father was king of the Arabians of Iturea, which Iturea is mentioned by St Luke, iii. 1.

such as might rise up against them. This Noarus sent out some of the king's armed men by night, and slew all those [seventy] men; which bold action he ventured upon without the consent of Agrippa, and was such a lover of money, that he chose to be so wicked to his own countrymen, although he brought ruin on the kingdom thereby; and thus cruelly did he treat that nation, and this contrary to the laws also, until Agrippa was informed of it, who did not indeed dare to put him to death, out of regard to Sohemus; but still he put an end to his procuratorship immediately. But as to the seditious, they took the citadel which was called Cypros, and was above Jericho, and cut the throats of the garrison, and utterly demolished the fortifications. This was about the same time that the multitude of the Jews that were at Macherus persuaded the Romans who were in garrison to leave the place, and deliver it up to them. These Romans being in great fear, lest the place should be taken by force, made an agreement with them to depart upon certain conditions; and when they had obtained the security they desired, they delivered up the citadel, into which the people of Macherus put a garrison for their own security, and held it in their own power.

7. But for Alexandria, the sedition of the people of the place against the Jews was perpetual, and this from that very time when Alexander [the Great], upon finding the readiness of the Jews in assisting him against the Egyptians, and as a reward for such their assistance, gave them equal privileges in this city with the Grecians themselves;—which honorary reward continued among them under his successors, who also set apart for them a particular place, that they might live without being polluted [by the Gentiles,] and were thereby not so much intermixed with foreigners as before: they also gave them this further privilege, that they should be called Macedonians. Nay, when the Romans got possession of Egypt, neither the first Cæsar, nor any one that came after him, thought of diminishing the honours which Alexander had bestowed on the Jews. But still conflicts perpetually arose with the Grecians; and although the governors did every day punish many of them, yet did the sedition grow worse; but at this time especially, when there were tumults in other places also, the disorders among them were put into a greater flame; for when the Alexandrians had once a public assembly, to deliberate about an embassage they were sending to Nero, a great number of Jews came flocking to the theatre; but when their adversaries saw them, they immediately cried out, and called them their enemies, and said they came as spies upon them; upon which they rushed out and laid violent hands upon them; and as for the rest, they were slain as they ran away; but there were three men whom they caught, and hauled them along, in order to have them burnt alive; but all the Jews came in a body to defend them, who at first threw stones at the Grecians; but after that they took lamps, and rushed with violence into the theatre, and threatened that they would burn the people to a man; and this they had soon done, unless Tiberius Alexander, the governor of the city, had restrained their passions. However this man did not begin to teach them wisdom by arms, but sent among them privately some of the principal men, and thereby entreated them to be quiet, and not provoke the Roman army against them; but the seditious made a jest of the entreaties of Tiberius, and reproached him for so doing.

8. Now when he perceived that those that were for innovations would not be pacified till some great calamity should overtake them, he sent out upon them those two Roman legions that were in the city, and together with them five thousand other soldiers, who, by chance, were come together out of Lybia, to the ruin of the Jews. They were also permitted not only to kill them, but to plunder them of what they had, and set fire to their houses. These soldiers rushed violently into that part of the city which was called Delta, where the Jewish people lived together, and did as they were bidden though not without bloodshed on their own side also; for the Jews got together, and set those that were the best armed among them in the forefront, and made resistance for a great while; but when once they gave back, they were destroyed unmercifully; and this their destruction was complete, some being caught in the open field, and others forced into their houses, which houses were first plundered of what was in them, and then set on fire by the Romans; wherein no mercy was shewn to the infants, and no regard had to the aged; but they went on in the slaughter of persons of every age, till all the place was overflowed with blood, and fifty thousand of them lay dead upon heaps; nor had the remainder been preserved, had they not betaken themselves to supplication. So Alexander commiserated their condition, and gave orders to the Romans to retire: accordingly, these, being accustomed to obey orders, left off killing at the first intimation; but the populace of Alexandria bare so very great hatred to the Jews, that it was difficult to recall them; and it was a hard thing to make them leave their dead bodies.

9. And this was the miserable calamity which at this time befell the Jews at Alexandria. Hereupon Cestius thought fit no longer to lie still, while the Jews were everywhere up in arms; so he took out of Antioch the twelfth legion entire, and out of each of the rest he selected two thousand, with six cohorts of footmen, and four troops of horsemen, besides those auxiliaries which were sent by the kings; of which Antiochus sent two thousand horsemen, and three thousand footmen, with so many archers; and Agrippa sent the same number of footmen, and one thousand horsemen; Sohemus also followed with four thousand, a third part whereof were horsemen, but most part were archers, and thus did he march to Ptolemais. There were also great numbers of auxiliaries gathered together from the [free] cities, who indeed had not the same skill in martial affairs, but made up in their alacrity and in their hatred to the Jews what they wanted in skill. There came also along with Cestius, Agrippa himself, both as a guide in his march over the country, and a director of what was fit to be done; so Cestius took part of his forces, and marched hastily to Zebulon, a strong city of Galilee, which was called the *City of Men*, and divides the country of Ptolemais from our nation; this he found deserted by its men, the multitude having fled to the mountains, but full of all sorts of good things; those he gave leave to the soldiers to plunder, and set fire to the city, although it was of admirable beauty, and had its houses built like those in Tyre, and Sidon, and Berytus. After this he overran all the country, and seized upon whatsoever came in his way, and set fire to the villages that were round about them, and then returned to Ptolemais. But when the Syrians, and especially those of Berytus, were busy in plundering, the Jews plucked up their courage again, for they knew that Cestius was

retired, and fell upon those that were left behind unexpectedly, and destroyed about two thousand of them.

10. And now Cestius himself marched from Ptolemais, and came to Cesarea; but he sent part of his army before him to Joppa, and gave orders, that if they could take that city [by surprise] they should keep it; but that in case the citizens should perceive they were coming to attack them, they then should stay for him, and for the rest of the army. So some of them made a brisk march by the sea-side, and some by land, and so coming upon them on both sides, they took the city with ease; and as the inhabitants had made no provision aforehand for a flight, nor had gotten anything ready for fighting, the soldiers fell upon them, and slew them all, with their families, and then plundered and burnt the city. The number of the slain was eight thousand four hundred. In like manner Cestius sent also a considerable body of horsemen to the toparchy of Narbatene, that adjoined to Cesarea, who destroyed the country, and slew a great multitude of its people; they also plundered what they had, and burnt their villages.

11. But Cestius sent Gallus, the commander of the twelfth legion, into Galilee, and delivered to him as many of his forces as he supposed sufficient to subdue that nation. He was received by the strongest city of Galilee, which was Sepphoris, with acclamations of joy: which wise conduct of that city occasioned the rest of the cities to be in quiet; while the seditious part and the robbers ran away to that mountain which lies in the very middle of Galilee, and is situated over against Sepphoris; it is called Asamon. So Gallus brought his forces against them; but while those men were in the superior parts, above the Romans, they easily threw their darts upon the Romans, as they made their approaches, and slew about two hundred of them; but when the Romans had gone round the mountains, and were gotten into the parts above their enemies, the others were soon beaten; nor could they who had only light armour on, sustain the force of them that fought them armed all over; nor when they were beaten could they escape the enemy's horsemen; insomuch that only some few concealed themselves in certain places hard to be come at, among the mountains, while the rest, above two thousand in number, were slain.

CHAPTER XIX

WHAT CESTIUS DID AGAINST THE JEWS; AND HOW, UPON HIS BESIEGING JERUSALEM, HE RETREATED FROM THE CITY, WITHOUT ANY JUST OCCASION IN THE WORLD. AS ALSO WHAT SEVERE CALAMITIES HE UNDERWENT FROM THE JEWS IN HIS RETREAT

1. AND now Gallus seeing nothing more that looked towards an innovation in Galilee, returned with his army to Cesarea: but Cestius removed with his whole army, and marched to Antipatris; and when he was informed that there was a great body of Jewish forces gotten together in a certain tower called Aphek, he sent a party before to fight them; but this party dispersed the Jews by affrighting them before it came to a battle: so they came, and finding their camp deserted, they burnt it, as well as the villages that lay about it. But when Cestius had marched from Antipatris to Lydda, he found the city empty of its men, for the whole multitude were gone up to Jerusalem to the feast of the tabernacles; yet did he destroy fifty of those that shewed themselves, and burnt the city, and so marched forwards; and ascending by Bethoron, he pitched his camp at a certain place called Gabao, fifty furlongs distant from Jerusalem.

2. But as for the Jews, when they saw the war approaching to their metropolis, they left the feast, and betook themselves to their arms; and taking courage greatly from their multitude, went in a sudden and disorderly manner to the fight, with a great noise, and without any consideration had of the rest of the seventh day, although the Sabbath was the day to which they had the greatest regard; but that rage which made them forget the religious observation [of the Sabbath,] made them too hard for their enemies in the fight: with such violence, therefore, did they fall upon the Romans, as to break into their ranks, and to march through the midst of them, making a great slaughter as they went, insomuch that unless the horsemen, and such part of the footmen as were not yet tired in the action, had wheeled round, and succoured that part of the army which was not yet broken, Cestius, with his whole army, had been in danger: however, five hundred and fifteen of the Romans were slain, of which number four hundred were footmen, and the rest horsemen, while the Jews lost only twenty-two, of whom the most valiant were the kinsmen to Monobazus, king of Adiabene, and their names were Monobazus and Kenedeus; and next to them were Niger of Perea, and Silas of Babylon, who had deserted from King Agrippa to the Jews; for he had formerly served in his army. When the front of the Jewish army had been cut of, the Jews retired into the city; but still Simon, the son of Giora, fell upon the backs of the Romans as they were ascending Bethoron, and put the hindmost of the army into disorder, and carried off many of the beasts that carried the weapons of war, and led them into the city; but as Cestius tarried there three days, the Jews seized upon the elevated parts of the city, and set watches at the entrances into the city, and appeared openly resolved not to rest when once the Romans should begin to march.

3. And now when Agrippa observed that even the affairs of the Romans were likely to be in danger, while such an immense multitude of their enemies had seized upon the mountains round about, he determined to try what the Jews would agree to by words, as thinking that he should either persuade them all to desist from fighting, or, however, that he should cause the sober part of them to separate themselves from the opposite party. So he sent Borceus and Phebus, the persons of his party that were the best known among them, and promised them that Cestius should give them his right hand, to secure them of the Romans' entire forgiveness for what they had done amiss, if they would throw away their arms, and come over to them: but the seditious, fearing lest the whole multitude, in hopes of security to themselves, should go over to Agrippa, resolved immediately to fall upon and kill the ambassadors: accordingly they slew Phebus before he said a word, but Borceus was only wounded, and prevented his fate by flying away. And when the people were very angry at this, they had the seditious beaten with stones and clubs, and drove them before them into the city.

4. But now Cestius, observing that the disturbances that were begun among the Jews afforded him a proper opportunity to attack them, took his whole army along with him, and put

the Jews to flight, and pursued them to Jerusalem. He then pitched his camp upon the elevation called Scopus [or watch-tower,] which was distant seven furlongs from the city ; yet did he not assault them in three days' time, out of expectation that those within might perhaps yield a little ; and in the meantime he sent out a great many of his soldiers into the neighbouring villages, to seize upon their corn; and on the fourth day, which was the thirtieth of the month Hyperberetus [Tisri,] when he put his army in array, he brought it into the city. Now as for the people, they were kept under by the seditious; but the seditious themselves were greatly affrighted at the good order of the Romans, and retired from the suburbs, and retreated into the inner part of the city, and into the temple. But when Cestius was come into the city, he set the part called Bezetha, which is also called Cenopolis, [or the new city,] on fire ; as he did also to the timber-market : after which he came into the upper city, and pitched his camp over against the royal palace ; and had he but at this very time attempted to get within the walls by force, he had won the city presently, and the war had been put an end to at once ; but Tyrannius Priscus, the muster-master of the army, and a great number of the officers of the horse, had been corrupted by Florus, and diverted him from that his attempt ; and that was the occasion that this war lasted so very long, and thereby the Jews were involved in such incurable calamities.

5. In the meantime, many of the principal men of the city were persuaded by Ananus, the son of Jonathan, and invited Cestius into the city, and were about to open the gates for him ; but he overlooked this offer, partly out of his anger at the Jews, and partly because he did not thoroughly believe they were in earnest ; whence it was that he delayed the matter so long, that the seditious perceived the treachery, and threw Ananus and those of his party down from the wall, and pelting them with stones, drove them into their houses ; but they stood themselves at proper distances in the towers, and threw their darts at those that were getting over the wall. Thus did the Romans make their attack against the wall for five days, but to no purpose. But on the next day, Cestius took a great many of his choicest men, and with them the archers, and attempted to break into the temple at the northern quarter of it : but the Jews beat them off from the cloisters, and repulsed them several times when they were gotten near to the wall, till at length the multitude of the darts cut them off, and made them retire ; but the first rank of the Romans rested their shields upon the wall, and so did those that were behind them, and the like did those that were still more backward, and guarded themselves with what they call Testudo, [the back of] a tortoise, upon which the darts that were thrown fell, and slided off without doing them any harm ; so the soldiers undermined the wall, without being themselves hurt, and got all things ready for setting fire to the gate of the temple.

6. And now it was that a horrid fear seized upon the seditious, insomuch that many of them ran out of the city, as though it were to be taken immediately ; but the people upon this took courage, and where the wicked part of the city gave ground, thither did they come, in order to set open the gates, and to admit Cestius as their benefactor, who, had he but continued the siege a little longer, had certainly taken the city ; but it was, I suppose, owing to the aversion God had already at the city and the sanctuary, that he was hindered from putting an end to the war that very day.

7. It then happened that Cestius was not conscious either how the besieged despaired of success, nor how courageous the people were for him ; and so he recalled his soldiers from the place, and by despairing of any expectation of taking it, without having received any disgrace, he retired from the city, without any reason in the world. When the robbers perceived this unexpected retreat of his, they resumed their courage, and ran after the hinder parts of his army, and destroyed a considerable number of both their horsemen and footmen; and now Cestius lay all night at the camp, which was at Scopus ; and as he went off further next day, he thereby invited the enemy to follow him, who still fell upon the hindmost, and destroyed them ; they also fell upon the flank on each side of the army, and threw darts upon them obliquely, nor durst those that were hindmost turn back upon those who wounded them behind, as imagining that the multitude of those that pursued them was immense ; nor did they venture to drive away those that pressed upon them on each side, because they were heavy with their arms, and were afraid of breaking their ranks to pieces, and because they saw the Jews were light and ready for making incursions upon them. And this was the reason why the Romans suffered greatly, without being able to revenge themselves upon their enemies ; so they were galled all the way, and their ranks were put into disorder, and those that were thus put out of their ranks were slain ; among whom were Priscus the commander of the sixth legion, and Longinus the tribune, and Emilius Secundus, the commander of a troop of horsemen. So it was not without difficulty that they got to Gabao, their former camp, and that not without the loss of a great part of their baggage. There it was that Cestius stayed two days ; and was in great distress to know what he should do in these circumstances ; but when, on the third day, he saw a still greater number of enemies, and all the parts round about him full of Jews, he understood that his delay was to his own detriment, and that if he stayed the longer there, he should have still more enemies upon him.

8. That therefore he might fly the faster, he gave orders to cast away what might hinder his army's march ; so they killed the mules and other creatures, excepting those that carried their darts and machines, which they retained for their own use, and this principally because they were afraid lest the Jews should seize upon them. He then made his army march on as far as Bethoron. Now the Jews did not so much press upon them when they were in large open places ; but when they were penned up in their descent through narrow passages, then did some of them get before, and hindered them from getting out of them ; and others of them thrust the hindermost down into the lower places ; and the whole multitude extended themselves over-against the neck of the passage, and covered the Roman army with their darts. In which circumstances, as the footmen knew not how to defend themselves, so the danger pressed the horsemen still more, for they were so pelted, that they could not march along the road in their ranks, and the ascents were so high, that the cavalry were not able to march against the enemy ; the precipices also, and valleys into which they frequently fell, and tumbled down, were such on each side of them, that there was neither place for their flight, nor any contrivance could be thought of for their defence ; till the distress

they were at last in was so great, that they betook themselves to lamentations, and to such mournful cries as men use in the utmost despair: the joyful acclamations of the Jews also, as they encouraged one another, echoed the sounds back again, these last composing a noise of those that a; once rejoiced and were in a rage. Indeed these things were come to such a pass, that the Jews had almost taken Cestius's entire army prisoners, had not the night come on, when the Romans fled to Bethoron, and the Jews seized upon all the places round about them, and watched for their coming out [in the morning.]

9. And then it was that Cestius, despairing of obtaining room for a public march, contrived how he might best run away; and when he had selected four hundred of the most courageous of his soldiers, he placed them at the strongest of their fortifications; and gave order, that when they went up to the morning guard, they should erect their ensigns, that the Jews might be made to believe that the entire army was there still, while he himself took the rest of his forces with him, and marched, without any noise, thirty furlongs. But when the Jews perceived, in the morning, that the camp was empty, they ran upon those four hundred who had deluded them, and immediately threw their darts at them, and slew them; and then pursued after Cestius. But he had already made use of a great part of the night in his flight, and still marched quicker when it was day; insomuch, that the soldiers, through the astonishment and fear they were in, left behind them their engines for sieges, and for throwing of stones, and a great part of the instruments of war. So the Jews went on pursuing the Romans as far as Antipatris; after which, seeing they could not overtake them, they came back and took the engines, and spoiled the dead bodies; and gathered the prey together which the Romans had left behind them, and came back running and singing to their metropolis; while they had themselves lost a few only, but had slain of the Romans five thousand and three hundred footmen, and three hundred and eighty horsemen. This defeat happened on the eighth day of the month Dius [Marhesvan,] in the twelfth year of the reign of Nero.

CHAPTER XX

CESTIUS SENDS AMBASSADORS TO NERO. THE PEOPLE OF DAMASCUS SLAY THOSE JEWS THAT LIVED WITH THEM. THE PEOPLE OF JERUSALEM, AFTER [THEY HAD LEFT OFF] PURSUING CESTIUS, RETURN TO THE CITY, AND GET THINGS READY FOR ITS DEFENCE, AND MAKE A GREAT MANY GENERALS FOR THEIR ARMIES, AND PARTICULARLY JOSEPHUS, THE WRITER OF THESE BOOKS. SOME ACCOUNT OF HIS ADMINISTRATION

1. AFTER this calamity had befallen Cestius, many of the most eminent of the Jews swam away from the city, as from a ship when it was going to sink; Costobarus, therefore, and Saul, who were brethren, together with Philip, the son of Jacimus, who was the commander of King Agrippa's forces, ran away from the city, and went to Cestius. But then how Antipas, who had been besieged with them in the king's palace, but would not fly away with them, was afterward slain by the seditious, we shall relate hereafter. However, Cestius sent Saul and his friends, at their own desire, to Achia, to Nero, to inform him of the great distress they were in;

and lay the blame of their kindling the war upon Florus, as hoping to alleviate his own danger, by provoking his indignation against Florus.

2. In the meantime, the people of Damascus, when they were informed of the destruction of the Romans, set about the slaughter of those Jews that were among them; and as they had them already cooped up together in the place of public exercises, which they had done out of the suspicion they had of them, they thought they should meet with no difficulty in the attempt; yet did they distrust their own wives, which were almost all of them addicted to the Jewish religion; on which account it was that their greatest concern was how they might conceal these things from them; so they came upon the Jews, and cut their throats, as being in a narrow place, in number ten thousand, and all of them unarmed, and this in one hour's time, without anybody to disturb them.

3. But as to those who had pursued after Cestius, when they were returned back to Jerusalem, they overbore some of those that favoured the Romans by violence, and some they persuaded [by entreaties] to join with them, and got together in great numbers in the temple, and appointed a great many generals for the war. Joseph also, the son of Gorion, and Ananus the high priest, were chosen as governors of all affairs within the city, and with a particular charge to repair the walls of the city; for they did not ordain Eleazar the son of Simon to that office, although he had gotten into his possession the prey they had taken from the Romans, and the money they had taken from Cestius, together with a great part of the public treasures, because they saw he was of a tyrannical temper; and that his followers were, in their behaviour, like guards about him. However, the want they were in of Eleazar's money, and the subtle tricks used by him, brought all so about, that the people were circumvented, and submitted themselves to his authority in all public affairs.

4. They also chose other generals for Idumea; Jesus the son of Sapphias, one of the high priests; and Eleazar, the son of Ananias, the high priest; they also enjoined Niger, the then governor of Idumea,* who was of a family that belonged to Perea, beyond Jordan, and was thence called the Peraite, that he should be obedient to those forenamed commanders. Nor did they neglect the care of other parts of the country; but Joseph the son of Simon was sent as general to Jericho, as was Manasseh to Perea, and John, the Essene, to the toparchy of Thamma; Lydda was also added to his portion, and Joppa and Emmaus. But John, the son of Matthias, was made the governor of the toparchies of Gophnitica and Acrabastene; as was Josephus, the son of Matthias, of both the Galilees. Gamala also, which was the strongest city in those parts, was put under his command.

5. So every one of the other commanders administered the affairs of his portion with that alacrity and prudence they were masters of; but as to Josephus, when he came into Galilee, his first care was to gain the good-will of the people of that country, as sensible that he should thereby have in general good success, although he should fail in other points. And being conscious to himself that if he communicated part of his power to the great men, he should make them his fast friends; and that he should gain the same favour from the multitude, if he exe-

---

* The Idumeans, as having been proselytes of justice since the days of John Hyrcanus, were now esteemed as part of the Jewish nation, and are here provided with a Jewish commander accordingly.

cuted his commands by persons of their own country, and with whom they were well acquainted; he chose out seventy* of the most prudent men, and those elders in age, and appointed them to be rulers of all Galilee, as he chose seven judges in every city to hear the lesser quarrels; for as to the greater causes, and those wherein life and death were concerned, he enjoined they should be brought to him and the seventy elders.

6. Josephus also, when he had settled these rules for determining causes by the law, with regard to the people's dealings one with another, betook himself to make provisions for their safety against external violence; and as he knew the Romans would fall upon Galilee, he built walls in proper places about Jotapata, and Bersabee, and Salamis; and besides these about Caphareccho, and Japha, and Sigo, and what they call mount Tabor, and Taricheæ, and Tiberias. Moreover, he built walls about the caves near the lake of Gennessar, which places lay in the Lower Galilee; the same as he did to the places of Upper Galilee, as well as to the rock called the rock of Achabari, and to Seph, and Jamnith, and Meroth; and in Gaulanitis he fortified Seleucia, and Sogane, and Gamala; but as to those of Sepphoris, they were the only people to whom he gave leave to build their own walls, and this because he perceived they were rich and wealthy, and ready to go to war, without standing in need of any injunctions for that purpose. The case was the same with the Gischala, which had a wall built about it by John the son of Levi himself, but with the consent of Josephus; but for the building of the rest of the fortresses, he laboured together with all the other builders, and was present to give all the necessary orders for that purpose. He also got together an army out of Galilee, of more than a hundred thousand young men, all of whom he armed with the old weapons which he had collected together and prepared for them.

7. And when he had considered that Roman power became invincible, chiefly by their readiness in obeying orders, and the constant exercise of their arms, he despaired of teaching these his men the use of their arms, which was to be obtained by experience; but observing that their readiness in obeying orders was owing to the multitude of their officers, he made his partitions in his army more after the Roman manner, and appointed a great many subalterns. He also distributed the soldiers into various classes, whom he put under captains of tens, and captains of hundreds, and then under captains of thousands; and besides these he had commanders of larger bodies of men. He also taught them to give the signals one to another, and to call and recall the soldiers by the trumpets, how to expand the wings of an army, and make them wheel about; and when one wing hath had success, to turn again and assist those that were hard set, and to join in the defence of what had most suffered. He also continually instructed them in what concerned the courage of the soul and the hardiness of the body; and, above all, he exercised them for war, by declaring to them distinctly the good order of the Romans, and that they were to fight with men who, both by the strength of their bodies and courage of their souls, had conquered in a manner the whole habitable earth. He told them that he should make trial of the good order they would observe

in war, even before it came to any battle, in case they would abstain from the crimes they used to indulge themselves in, such as theft, and robbery, and rapine, and from defrauding their own countrymen, and never to esteem the harm done to those that were so near of kin to them to be any advantage to themselves; for that wars are then managed the best when the warriors preserve a good conscience; but that such as are ill men in private life will not only have those for enemies which attack them, but God himself also for their antagonist.

8. And thus did he continue to admonish them. Now he chose for the war such an army as was sufficient, i.e., sixty thousand footmen, and two hundred and fifty horsemen; and besides these, on which he put the greatest trust, there were about four thousand five hundred mercenaries: he had also six hundred men as guards of his body. Now the cities easily maintained the rest of his army, excepting the mercenaries; for one of the cities enumerated before sent out half their men to their army, and retained the other half at home, in order to get provisions for them; insomuch that the one part went to the war, and the other part to their work: and so those that sent out their corn were paid for it by those that were in arms, by that security which they enjoyed from them.

CHAPTER XXI

CONCERNING JOHN OF GISCHALA. JOSEPHUS USES STRATAGEMS AGAINST THE PLOTS JOHN LAID AGAINST HIM, AND RECOVERS CERTAIN CITIES WHICH HAD REVOLTED FROM HIM

1. Now, as Josephus was thus engaged in the administration of the affairs of Galilee, there arose a treacherous person, a man of Gischala, the son of Levi, whose name was John. His character was that of a very cunning, and very knavish person, beyond the ordinary rate of the other men of eminence there; and for wicked practices he had not his fellow anywhere. Poor he was at first, and for a long time his wants were a hindrance to him in his wicked designs. He was a ready liar, and yet very sharp in gaining credit to his fictions: he thought it a point of virtue to delude people, and would delude even such as were the dearest to him. He was a hypocritical pretender to humanity, but when he had hopes of gain he spared not the shedding of blood: his desires were ever carried to great things, and he encouraged his hopes from those mean wicked tricks which he was the author of. He had a peculiar knack at thieving; but in some time he got certain companions in his impudent practices: at first they were but few, but as he proceeded on in his evil course, they became still more and more numerous. He took care that none of his partners should be easily caught in their rogueries, but chose such out of the rest as had the strongest constitutions of body, and the greatest courage of soul, together with great skill in martial affairs; so he got together a band of four hundred men, who came principally out of the country of Tyre, and were vagabonds who had run away from its villages; and by the means of these he laid waste all Galilee, and irritated a considerable number, who were in great expectation of a war then suddenly to arise among them.

2. However, John's want of money had hitherto restrained him in his ambition after command, and in his attempts to advance himself; but

---

* We see here how Josephus exactly imitated his legislator Moses, in appointing seven lesser judges for smaller causes in particular cities.

when he saw that Josephus was highly pleased with the activity of his temper, he persuaded him, in the first place, to intrust him with the repairing of the walls of his native city [Gischala;] in which work he got a great deal of money from the rich citizens. He after that contrived a very shrewd trick, and pretending that the Jews who dwelt in Syria were obliged to make use of oil that was made by others than those of their own nation, he desired leave of Josephus to send oil to their borders; so he bought four amphoræ with such Tyrian money as was of the value of four Attic drachmæ, and sold every half amphoræ at the same price; and as Galilee was very fruitful in oil, and was peculiarly so at that time, by sending away great quantities, and having the sole privilege so to do, he gathered an immense sum of money together, which money he immediately used to the disadvantage of him who gave him that privilege; and as he supposed that if he could once overthrow Josephus, he should himself obtain the government of Galilee; so he gave order to the robbers that were under his command to be more zealous in their thieving expeditions, that by the rise of many that desired innovations in the country, he might either catch their general in his snares, as he came to the country's assistance, and then kill him; or if he should overlook the robbers, he might accuse him for his negligence to the people of the country. He also spread abroad a report far and near that Josephus was delivering up the administration of affairs to the Romans;—and many such plots did he lay in order to ruin him.

3. Now at the same time that certain young men of the village of Dabaritta, who kept guard in the great Plain, laid snares for Ptolemy, who was Agrippa's and Bernice's steward, and took from him all that he had with him: among which things there were a great many costly garments, and no small number of silver cups, and six hundred pieces of gold; yet they were not able to conceal what they had stolen, but brought it all to Josephus, to Taricheæ. Hereupon he blamed them for the violence they had offered to the king and queen, and deposited what they brought to him with Eneas, the most potent man of Taricheæ, with an intention of sending the things back to the owners at a proper time; which act of Josephus brought him into the greatest danger; for those that had stolen the things had an indignation at him, both because they gained no share of it for themselves, and because they perceived beforehand what was Josephus's intention, and that he would freely deliver up what had cost so much pains to the king and queen. These ran away by night to their several villages, and declared to all men that Josephus was going to betray them; they also raised great disorders in all the neighbouring cities, insomuch that in the morning a hundred thousand armed men came running together; which multitude was crowded together in the hippodrome at Taricheæ, and made a very peevish clamour against him; while some cried out that they should depose the traitor, and others that they should burn him. Now John irritated a great many, as did also one Jesus, the son of Sapphias, who was then governor of Tiberias. Then it was that Josephus's friends, and the guards of his body, were so affrighted at this violent assault of the multitude, that they all fled away but four; and as he was asleep, they waked him, as the people were going to set fire to the house; and although those four that remained with him persuaded him to run away, he was neither surprised at his being himself deserted, nor at the great multitude that came against him, but leaped out to them with his clothes rent, and ashes sprinkled on his head, with his hands behind him, and his sword hanging at his neck. At this sight his friends, especially those of Taricheæ, commiserated his condition; but those that came out of the country, and those in their neighbourhood, to whom his government seemed burdensome, reproached him, and bade him produce the money which belonged to them all immediately, and to confess the agreement he had made to betray them; for they imagined, from the habit in which he appeared, that he could deny nothing of what they suspected concerning him, and that it was in order to obtain pardon, that he had put himself entirely into so pitiable a posture; but this humble appearance was only designed as preparatory to a stratagem of his, who thereby contrived to set those that were so angry at him at variance one with another about the things they were angry at. However, he promised he would confess all: hereupon he was permitted to speak, when he said, "I did neither intend to send this money back to Agrippa, nor to gain it myself; for I did never esteem one that was your enemy to be my friend, nor did I look upon what would tend to your disadvantage to be my advantage. But, O you people of Taricheæ, I saw that your city stood in more need than others of fortification for your security, and that it wanted money in order for the building it a wall. I was also afraid lest the people of Tiberias and other cities should lay a plot to seize upon these spoils, and therefore it was that I intended to retain this money privately, that I might encompass you with a wall. But if this does not please you, I will produce what was brought me, and leave it to you to plunder it: but if I have conducted myself so well as to please you, you may, if you please, punish your benefactor."

4. Hereupon the people of Taricheæ loudly commended him; but those of Tiberias, with the rest of the company, gave him hard names, and threatened what they would do to him; so both sides left off quarrelling with Josephus, and fell to quarrelling with one another. So he grew bold upon the dependence he had on his friends, which were the people of Taricheæ, and about forty thousand in number, and spake more freely to the whole multitude, and reproached them greatly for their rashness; and told them, that with this money he would build walls about Taricheæ, and would put the other cities in a state of security also; for that they should not want money, if they would but agree for whose benefit it was to be procured, and would not suffer themselves to be irritated against him who had procured it for them.

5. Hereupon the rest of the multitude that had been deluded retired; but yet so that they went away angry, and two thousand of them made an assault upon him in their armour; and as he was already gone to his own house, they stood without and threatened him. On which occasion Josephus again used a second stratagem to escape them; for he got upon the top of the house, and with his right hand desired them to be silent, and said to them, "I cannot tell what you would have, nor can hear what you say, for the confused noise you make:" but he said he would comply with all their demands, in case they would but send some of their number in to him that might talk with him about it. And when the principal of them, with their leaders, heard this, they came into the house. He then drew them to the most retired part of the house,

and shut the door of that hall where he put them, and then had them whipped till every one of their inward parts appeared naked. In the meantime the multitude stood round the house, and supposed that he had a long discourse with those that were gone in, about what they claimed of him. He had then the doors set open immediately, and sent the men out all bloody, which so terribly affrighted those that had before threatened him, that they threw away their arms and ran away.

6. But as for John, his envy grew greater [upon this escape of Josephus,] and he framed a new plot against him; he pretended to be sick, and by a letter desired that Josephus would give him leave to use the hot baths that were at Tiberias, for the recovery of his health. Hereupon Josephus, who hitherto suspected nothing of John's plots against him, wrote to the governors of the city, that they would provide a lodging and necessaries for John; which favours, when he had made use of, in two days' time he did what he came about; some he corrupted with delusive frauds, and others with money, and so persuaded them to revolt from Josephus. This Silas, who was appointed guardian of the city by Josephus, wrote to him immediately, and informed him of the plot against him; which epistle, when Josephus had received, he marched with great diligence all night, and came early in the morning to Tiberias; at which time the rest of the multitude met him. But John, who suspected that his coming was not for his advantage, sent, however, one of his friends, and pretended that he was sick, and that being confined to his bed he could not come to pay him his respects. But as soon as Josephus had got the people of Tiberias together in the stadium, and tried to discourse with them about the letters that he had received, John privately sent some armed men, and gave them orders to slay him. But when the people saw that the armed men were about to draw their swords, they cried out;—at which cry Josephus turned himself about, and when he saw that the swords were just at his throat, he marched away in great haste to the sea-shore, and left off that speech which he was going to make to the people, upon an elevation of six cubits high. He then seized on a ship which lay in the haven, and leaped into it, with two of his guards, and fled away into the midst of the lake.

7. But now the soldiers he had with him took up their arms immediately, and marched against the plotters, but Josephus was afraid lest a civil war should be raised by the envy of a few men, and bring the city to ruin; so he sent some of his party to tell them that they should do no more than provide for their own safety; that they should not kill anybody, nor accuse any for the occasion they had afforded [of a disorder.] Accordingly these men obeyed his orders, and were quiet; but the people of the neighbouring country, when they were informed of this plot, and of the plotter, got together in great multitudes to oppose John. But he prevented their attempt, and fled away to Gischala, his native city, while the Galileans came running out of their several cities to Josephus; and as they were now become many ten thousands of armed men, they cried out, that they were come against John, the common plotter against their interest, and would at the same time burn him, and that city which had received him. Hereupon Josephus told them that he took their good-will to him kindly, but still he restrained their fury, and intended to subdue his enemies by prudent conduct, rather than by slaying them; so he ex-

cepted those of every city which had joined in this revolt with John, by name, who had readily been shewn him by those that came from every city, and caused public proclamation to be made, that he would seize upon the effects of those that did not forsake John within five days' time, and would burn both their houses and their families with fire. Whereupon three thousand of John's party left him immediately, who came to Josephus, and threw their arms down at his feet. John then betook himself, together with his two thousand Syrian runagates, from open attempts, to more secret ways of treachery. Accordingly, he privately sent messengers to Jerusalem, to accuse Josephus, as having too great power, and to let them know that he would soon come as a tyrant to their metropolis, unless they prevented him. This accusation the people were aware of beforehand, but had no regard to it. However, some of the grandees, out of envy, and some of the rulers also, sent money to John privately, that he might be able to get together mercenary soldiers, in order to fight Josephus; they also made a decree of themselves, and this for recalling him from his government, yet did they not think that decree sufficient; so they sent withal two thousand five hundred armed men, and four persons of the highest rank amongst them; Joazar the son of Nomicus, and Ananias the son of Sadduk; as also Simon and Judas, the sons of Jonathan, (all very able men in speaking,) that these persons might withdraw the good-will of the people from Josephus. These had it in charge, that if he would voluntarily come away, they should permit him to [come and] give an account of his conduct; but if he obstinately insisted upon continuing in his government, they should treat him as an enemy. Now, Josephus's friends had sent him word that an army was coming against him, but they gave him no notice beforehand what the reason of their coming was, that being only known among some secret councils of his enemies; and by this means it was that four cities revolted from him immediately, Sepphoris, and Gamala, and Gischala and Tiberias. Yet did he recover these cities without war; and when he had routed those four commanders by stratagems, and had taken the most potent of their warriors, he sent them to Jerusalem; and the people [of Galilee] had great indignation at them, and were in a zealous disposition to slay, not only these forces, but those that sent them also, had not these forces prevented it by running away.

8. Now John was detained afterward within the walls of Gischala, by the fear he was in of Josephus; but within a few days Tiberias revolted again, and the people within it invited king Agrippa [to return to the exercise of his authority there;] and when he did not come at the time appointed, and when a few Roman horsemen appeared that day, they expelled Josephus out of the city. Now, this revolt of theirs was presently known at Taricheæ; and as Josephus had sent out all the soldiers that were with him to gather corn, he knew not how either to march out alone against the revolters, or to stay where he was, because he was afraid the king's soldiers might prevent him if he tarried, and might get into the city; for he did not intend to do anything on the next day, because it was the Sabbath-day, and would hinder his proceeding. So he contrived to circumvent the revolters by a stratagem; and in the first place, he ordered the gates of Taricheæ to be shut, that nobody might go out and inform [those of Tiberias,] for whom it was intended, what stratagem he was about; he then got together all the

ships that were upon the lake, which were found to be two hundred and thirty, and in each of them he put no more than four mariners. So he sailed to Tiberias with haste, and kept at such a distance from the city, that it was not easy for the people to see the vessels, and ordered that the empty vessels should float up and down there, while himself, who had but seven of his guards with him, and those unarmed also, went so near as to be seen; but when his adversaries, who were still reproaching him, saw him from the walls, they were so astonished that they supposed all the ships were full of armed men, and threw down their arms, and by signals of intercession they besought him to spare the city.

9. Upon this, Josephus threatened them terribly, and reproached them, that when they were the first that took up arms against the Romans, they should spend their forces beforehand in civil dissensions, and do what their enemies desired above all things; and that besides, they should endeavour so hastily to seize upon him, who took care of their safety, and had not been ashamed to shut the gates of the city against him that built their walls; that, however, he would admit of any intercessors from them that might make some excuse for them, and with whom he would make such agreements as might be for the city's security. Hereupon ten of the most potent men of Tiberias came down to him presently, and when he had taken them into one of his vessels, he ordered them to be carried a great way off from the city. He then commanded that fifty others of their senate, such as were men of the greatest eminence, should come to him, that they also might give him some security on their behalf. After which, under one new pretence or another, he called forth others, one after another, to make the league between them. He then gave order to the masters of those vessels which he had thus filled, to sail away immediately for Tarichææ, and to confine those men in the prison there; till at length he took all their senate, consisting of six hundred persons, and about two thousand of the populace, and carried them away to Tarichææ.

10. And when the rest of the people cried out, that it was one Clitus that was the chief author of this revolt, they desired him to spend his anger upon him [only;] but Josephus, whose intention it was to slay nobody, commanded one Levius, belonging to his guards, to go out of the vessel, in order to cut off both Clitus's hands; yet was Levius afraid to go out by himself alone, to such a large body of enemies, and refused to go. Now Clitus saw that Josephus was in a great passion in the ship, and ready to leap out of it, in order to execute the punishment himself; he begged therefore from the shore that he would leave him one of his hands, which Josephus agreed to upon condition that he would himself cut off the other hand; accordingly he drew his sword, and with his right hand cut off his left, so great was the fear he was in of Josephus himself. And thus he took the people of Tiberias prisoners, and recovered the city again with empty ships and seven of his guard. Moreover, a few days afterward he retook Gischala, which

had revolted with the people of Sepphoris, and gave his soldiers leave to plunder it; yet did he get all the plunder together, and restored it to the inhabitants; and the like he did to the inhabitants of Sepphoris and Tiberias: for when he had subdued those cities, he had a mind, by letting them be plundered, to give them some good instruction, while at the same time he regained their good-will by restoring them their money again.

CHAPTER XXII

THE JEWS MAKE ALL READY FOR THE WAR; AND SIMON, THE SON OF GIORAS, FALLS TO PLUNDERING

1. AND thus were the disturbances of Galilee quieted, when, upon their ceasing to prosecute their civil dissensions, they betook themselves to make preparations for the war with the Romans. Now in Jerusalem the high priest Ananus, and as many of the men of power as were not in the interest of the Romans, both repaired the walls, and made a great many warlike instruments, insomuch that, in all parts of the city, darts and all sorts of armour were upon the anvil. Although the multitude of the young men were engaged in exercises, without any regularity, and all places were full of tumultuous doing: yet the moderate sort were exceedingly sad; and a great many there were who, out of the prospect they had of the calamities that were coming upon them made great lamentations. There were also such omens observed as were understood to be forerunners of evils, by such as loved peace, but were by those that kindled the war interpreted so as to suit their own inclinations; and the very state of the city, even before the Romans came against it, was that of a place doomed to destruction. However, Ananus's concern was this, to lay aside for a while the preparations for the war, and to persuade the seditious to consult their own interest, and to restrain the madness of those that had the name of zealots: but their violence was too hard for him; and what end he came to we shall relate hereafter.

2. But as for the Acrabbene toparchy, Simon, the son of Gioras, got a great number of those that were fond of innovations together, and betook himself to ravage the country; nor did he only harass the rich men's houses, but tormented their bodies, and appeared openly and beforehand to affect tyranny in his government. And when an army was sent against him by Ananus, and the other rulers, he and his band retired to the robbers that were at Masada, and stayed there, and plundered the country of Idumea with them, till both Ananus and his other adversaries were slain; and until the rulers of that country were so afflicted with the multitude of those that were slain, and with the continual ravage of what they had, that they raised an army, and put garrisons into the villages, to secure them from these insults. And in this state were the affairs of Judea at that time.

BOOK III

FROM VESPASIAN'S COMING TO SUBDUE THE JEWS TO THE TAKING OF GAMALA

CHAPTER I

VESPASIAN IS SENT INTO SYRIA BY NERO TO MAKE WAR WITH THE JEWS

1. WHEN Nero was informed of the Romans' ill success in Judea, a concealed consternation and terror, as is usual in such cases, fell upon him; although he openly looked very big, and was very angry, and said, that what had happened was rather owing to the negligence of the commander than to any valour of the enemy: and as he thought it fit for him who bare the burden of the whole empire to despise such misfortunes, he now pretended so to do, and to have a soul superior to all such sad accidents whatsoever. Yet did the disturbance that was in his soul plainly appear by the solicitude he was in [how to recover his affairs again.]

2. And as he was deliberating to whom he should commit the care of the East, now it was in so great a commotion, and who might be best able to punish the Jews for their rebellion, and might prevent the same distemper from seizing upon the neighbouring nations also,—he found no one but Vespasian equal to the task, and able to undergo the great burden of so mighty a war, seeing he was growing an old man already in the camp, and from his youth had been exercised in warlike exploits: he was also a man that had long ago pacified the west, and made it subject to the Romans, when it had been put into disorder by the Germans: he had also recovered to them Britain by his arms, which had been little known before; * whereby he procured to his father Claudius to have a triumph bestowed on him without any sweat or labour of his own.

3. So Nero esteemed these circumstances as favourable omens, and saw that Vespasian's age gave him sure experience, and great skill, and that he had his sons as hostages for his fidelity to himself, and that the flourishing age they were in would make them fit instruments under their father's prudence. Perhaps also there was some interposition of Providence, which was paving the way for Vespasian's being himself emperor afterwards. Upon the whole, he sent this man to take upon him the command of the armies that were in Syria; but this not without great encomiums and flattering compellations, such as necessity required, and such as might mollify him into complaisance. So Vespasian sent his son Titus from Achaia, where he had been with Nero, to Alexandria, to bring back with him from thence the fifth and tenth legions, while he himself, when he had passed over the Hellespont, came by land into Syria, where he gathered together the Roman forces, with a consi-

derable number of auxiliaries from the kings in that neighbourhood.

CHAPTER II

A GREAT SLAUGHTER OF THE JEWS AT ASCALON. VESPASIAN COMES TO PTOLEMAIS

1. Now the Jews, after they had beaten Cestius, were so much elevated with their unexpected success, that they could not govern their zeal, but, like people blown up into a flame by their good fortune, carried the war to remoter places. Accordingly they presently got together a great multitude of all their most hardy soldiers, and marched away for Ascalon. This is an ancient city that is distant from Jerusalem five hundred and twenty furlongs, and was always an enemy to the Jews; on which account they determined to make their first effort against it, and to make their approaches to it as near as possible. This excursion was led on by three men, who were the chief of them all, both for strength and sagacity: Niger, called the Peraite, Silas of Babylon, and besides them, John the Essene. Now Ascalon was strongly walled about, but had almost no assistance to be relied on [near them,] for the garrison consisted of one cohort of footmen, and one troop of horsemen, whose captain was Antonius.

2. These Jews, therefore, out of their anger, marched faster than ordinary, and, as if they had come but a little way, approached very near the city, and were come even to it; but Antonius, who was not unapprised of the attack they were going to make upon the city, drew out his horsemen beforehand, and being neither daunted at the multitude nor at the courage of the enemy, received their first attacks with great bravery; and when they crowded to the very walls, he beat them off. Now the Jews were unskilful in war, but were to fight with those who were skilful therein; they were footmen to fight with horsemen; they were in disorder, to fight with those that were united together; they were poorly armed, to fight those that were completely so; they were to fight more by their rage than by sober counsel, and were exposed to soldiers that were exactly obedient, and did everything they were bidden upon the least intimation. So they were easily beaten; for as soon as ever their first ranks were once in disorder, they were put to flight by the enemy's cavalry, and those of them that came behind such as crowded to the wall, fell upon their own party's weapons, and became one another's enemies; and this so long till they were all forced to give way to the attacks of the horsemen, and were dispersed all the plain over, which plain was wide, and all fit for the horsemen; which circumstance was very commodious for the Ro-

---

* Suetonius confirms this: "In the reign of Claudius, Vespasian, for the sake of Narcissus, was sent as a lieutenant of a legion into Germany. Thence he removed into Britain, and fought thirty battles with the enemy." In Vesp. sect. 4.

mans, and occasioned the slaughter of the greatest number of the Jews; for such as ran away, they could overrun them, and make them turn back; and when they had brought them back after their flight, and driven them together, they ran them through, and slew a vast number of them, insomuch that others encompassed others of them, and drove them before them whithersoever they turned themselves, and slew them easily with their arrows; and the great number there were of the Jews seemed a solitude to themselves, by reason of the distress they were in, while the Romans had such good success with their small number, that they seemed to themselves to be the greater multitude; and as the former strove zealously under their misfortunes, out of the shame of a sudden flight, and hopes of a change in their success, so did the latter fear no weariness by reason of their good fortune; insomuch that the fight lasted till the evening, till ten thousand men of the Jews' side lay dead, with two of their generals, John and Silas; and the greater part of the remainder were wounded, with Niger, their remaining general, who fled away together to a small city of Idumea, called Sallis. Some few also of the Romans were wounded in this battle.

3. Yet were not the spirits of the Jews broken by so great a calamity, but the losses they had sustained rather quickened their resolution for other attempts; for, overlooking the dead bodies which lay under their feet, they were enticed by their former glorious actions to venture on a second destruction; so when they had lain still so little a while that their wounds were not yet thoroughly cured, they got together all their forces, and came with greater fury, and in much greater numbers, to Ascalon; but their former ill fortune followed them, as the consequence of their unskilfulness, and other deficiencies in war; for Antonius laid ambushes for them in the passages they were to go through, where they fell into snares unexpectedly, and where they were encompassed about with horsemen before they could form themselves into a regular body for fighting, and were above eight thousand of them slain: so all the rest of them ran away, and with them Niger, who still did a great many bold exploits in his flight. However, they were driven along together by the enemy, who pressed hard upon them, into a certain strong tower belonging to a village called Bezedel. However, Antonius and his party, that they might neither spend any considerable time about this tower, which was hard to be taken, nor suffer their commander, and the most courageous man of them all, to escape from them, they set the wall on fire; and as the tower was burning, the Romans went away rejoicing, as taking it for granted that Niger was destroyed; but he leaped out of the tower into a subterraneous cave, in the innermost part of it, and was preserved; and on the third day afterward he spake out of the ground to those that with great lamentations were searching for him, in order to give him a decent funeral; and when he was come out he filled all the Jews with an unexpected joy, as though he were preserved by God's providence to be their commander for the time to come.

4. And now Vespasian took along with him his army from Antioch (which is the metropolis of Syria, and, without dispute, deserves the place of the third city in the habitable earth that was under the Roman empire,* both in mag-

nitude and other marks of prosperity) where he found King Agrippa with all his forces, waiting for his coming, and marched to Ptolemais. At this city also the inhabitants of Sepphoris of Galilee met him, who were for peace with the Romans. These citizens had beforehand taken care of their own safety, and being sensible of the power of the Romans, they had been with Cestius Gallus, before Vespasian came, and had given their faith to him, and received the security of his right hand; and had received a Roman garrison; and at this time withal they received Vespasian, the Roman general, very kindly, and readily promised that they would assist him against their own countrymen. Now the general delivered them, at their desire, as many horsemen and footmen as he thought sufficient to oppose the incursions of the Jews, if they should happen to come against them;—and indeed the danger of losing Sepphoris would be no small one, in this war that was now beginning, seeing it was the largest city in Galilee, and built in a place by nature very strong, and might be a security of the whole nation's [fidelity to the Romans.]

CHAPTER III

A DESCRIPTION OF GALILEE, SAMARIA, AND JUDEA

1. Now Phœnicia and Syria encompass about the Galilees, which are two, and called the Upper Galilee and the Lower. They are bounded towards the sun-setting, with the borders of the territory belonging to Ptolemais, and by Carmel; which mountain had formerly belonged to the Galileans, but now belonged to the Tyrians; to which mountain adjoins Gaba, which is called the *City of Horsemen*, because those horsemen that were dismissed by Herod the king, dwelt therein; they are bounded on the south with Samaria and Scythopolis, as far as the river Jordan; on the east with Hippene and Gadaris, and also with Gaulanitis, and the borders of the kingdom of Agrippa; its northern parts are bounded by Tyre, and the country of the Tyrians. As for that Galilee which is called the Lower, it extends in length from Tiberias to Zebulon, and of the maritime places, Ptolemais is its neighbour; its breadth is from the village called Xaloth, which lies in the great plain, as far as Bersabe, from which beginning also is taken the breadth of the Upper Galilee, as far as the village Baca, which divides the land of the Tyrians from it; its length is also from Meloth to Thella, a village near to Jordan.

2. These two Galilees, of so great largeness, and encompassed with so many nations of foreigners, have always been able to make a strong resistance on all occasions of war; for the Galileans are inured to war from their infancy, and have been always very numerous; nor hath the country been ever destitute of men of courage, or wanted a numerous set of them; for their soil is universally rich and fruitful, and full of the plantations of trees of all sorts, insomuch that it invites the most slothful to take pains in its cultivation, by its fruitfulness: accordingly, it is all cultivated by its inhabitants, and no part of it lies idle. Moreover, the cities lie here very thick; and the very many villages there are here, are everywhere so full of people, by the richness of their soil, that the very least of them contain above fifteen thousand inhabitants.

3. In short, if any one will suppose that Gali-

---

* Spanheim and Reland both agree, that the two cities here esteemed greater than Antioch, the metropolis of Syria, were Rome and Alexandria.

lee is inferior to Perea in magnitude, he will be obliged to prefer it before it in its strength : for this is all capable of cultivation, and is everywhere fruitful; but for Perea, which is indeed much larger in extent, the greater part of it is a desert, and rough, and much less disposed for the production of the milder kinds of fruits ; yet hath it a moist soil [in other parts,] and produces all kinds of fruits, and its plains are planted with trees of all sorts, while yet the olive-tree, the vine, and the palm-tree, are chiefly cultivated there. It is also sufficiently watered with torrents, which issue out of the mountains, and with springs that never fail to run, even when the torrents fail them, as they do in the dog-days. Now the length of Perea is from Macherus to Pella, and its breadth from Philadelphia to Jordan ; its northern parts are bounded by Pella, as we have already said, as well as its western with Jordan ; the land of Moab, is its southern border, and its eastern limits reach to Arabia, and Sibonitis, and besides to Philadelphene and Gerasa.

4. Now, as to the country of Samaria, it lies between Judea and Galilee ; it begins at a village that is in the great plain called Ginea, and ends at the Acrabbene toparchy, and is entirely of the same nature with Judea ; for both countries are made up of hills and valleys, and are moist for agriculture, and are very fruitful. They have abundance of trees, and are full of autumnal fruit, both that which grows wild, and that which is the effect of cultivation. They are not naturally watered with many rivers, but derive their chief moisture from rainwater, of which they have no want; and for those rivers which they have, all their waters are exceeding sweet : by reason also of the excellent grass they have, their cattle yield more milk than do those in other places ; and, what is the greatest sign of excellency and abundance, they each of them are very full of people

5. In the limits of Samaria and Judea lies the village Anuath, which is also named Borceos. This is the northern boundary of Judea. The southern parts of Judea, if they be measured lengthways, are bounded by a village adjoining to the confines of Arabia ; the Jews that dwell there call it Jordan. However, its breadth is extended from the river Jordan to Joppa. The city Jerusalem is situated in the very middle ; on which account some have, with sagacity enough, called that city the navel of the country. Nor indeed is Judea destitute of such delights as come from the sea, since its maritime places extend as far as Ptolemais ; it was parted into eleven portions, of which the royal city Jerusalem was the supreme, and presided over all the neighbouring country, as the head does over the body. As to the other cities that were inferior to it, they presided over their several toparchies ; Gophna was the second of those cities, and next to that Acrabatta, after them Thamna, and Lydda, and Emmaus, and Pella, and Idumea, and Engaddi, and Herodium, and Jericho ; and after them came Jamnia and Joppa, as presiding over the neighbouring people ; and besides these there was the region of Gamala, and Gaulanitis, and Batanea, and Trachonitis, which are also parts of the kingdom of Agrippa. This [last] country begins at mount Libanus, and the fountains of Jordan, and reaches breadthways to the lake of Tiberias ; and in length is extended from a village called Arpha, as far as Julias. Its inhabitants are a mixture of Jews and Syrians.—And thus have I, with all possible brevity, described the country of Judea, and those that lie round about it.

CHAPTER IV

JOSEPHUS MAKES AN ATTEMPT UPON SEPPHORIS, BUT IS REPELLED TITUS COMES WITH A GREAT ARMY TO PTOLEMAIS

1. Now the auxiliaries who were sent to assist the people of Sepphoris, being a thousand horsemen, and six thousand footmen, under Placidus the tribune, pitched their camp in two bodies in the great plain. The foot were put into the city to be a guard to it ; but the horse lodged abroad in the camp. These last, by marching continually one way or other, and overrunning the parts of the adjoining country, were very troublesome to Josephus and his men ; they also plundered all the places that were out of the city's liberty, and intercepted such as durst go abroad. On this account it was that Josephus marched against the city, as hoping to take what he had lately encompassed with so strong a wall, before they revolted from the rest of the Galileans, that the Romans would have much ado to take it : by which means he proved too weak, and failed of his hopes, both as to forcing the place, and to his prevailing with the people of Sepphoris to deliver it up to him. By this means he provoked the Romans to treat the country according to the law of war ; nor did the Romans, out of the anger they bore at this attempt, leave off either by night or by day, burning the places in the plain, or stealing away the cattle that was in the country, and killing whatsoever appeared capable of fighting perpetually, and leading the weaker people as slaves into captivity ; so that Galilee was all over filled with fire and blood, nor was it exempted from any kind of misery or calamity ; for the only refuge they had was this, that when they were pursued, they could retire to the cities which had walls built them by Josephus.

2. But as to Titus, he sailed over from Achaia to Alexandria, and that sooner than the winter season did usually permit ; so he took with him those forces he was sent for, and marching with great expedition, he came suddenly to Ptolemais and there finding his father, together with the two legions, the fifth and tenth, which were the most eminent legions of all, he joined them to that fifteenth legion which was with his father : eighteen cohorts followed these legions ; there came also five cohorts from Cesarea, with one troop of horsemen, and five other troops of horsemen from Syria. Now these ten cohorts had severally a thousand footmen, but the other thirteen cohorts had no more than six hundred footmen apiece, with a hundred and twenty horsemen. There were also a considerable number of auxiliaries got together, that came from the kings Antiochus and Agrippa, and Sohemus, each of them contributing one thousand footmen that were archers, and a thousand horsemen. Malchus also, the king of Arabia, sent a thousand horsemen, besides five thousand footmen, the greatest part of whom were archers ; so that the whole army, including the auxiliaries sent by the kings, as well horsemen as footmen, when all were united together, amounted to sixty thousand, besides the servants, who, as they followed in vast numbers, so because they had been trained up in war with the rest, ought not to be distinguished from the fighting men ; for as they were in their masters' service in times of peace, so did they undergo the like dangers with them in times of war, insomuch that they were inferior to none, either in skill or in strength, only they were subject to their masters.

CHAPTER V

A DESCRIPTION OF THE ROMAN ARMIES AND ROMAN CAMPS; AND WHAT THE ROMANS ARE COMMENDED FOR

1. Now here one cannot but admire at the precaution of the Romans, in providing themselves of such household servants, as might not only serve at other times for the common offices of life, but might also be of advantage to them in their wars; and, indeed, if any one does but attend to the other parts of their military discipline, he will be forced to confess that their obtaining so large a dominion, hath been the acquisition of their valour, and not the bare gift of fortune; for they do not begin to use their weapons first in time of war, nor do they then put their hands first into motion, while they avoided so to do in times of peace; but as if their weapons did always cling to them, they have never any truce from warlike exercises; nor do they stay till times of war admonish them to use them; for their military exercises differ not at all from the real use of their arms, but every soldier is every day exercised, and that with great diligence, as if it were in time of war, which is the reason why they bear the fatigue of battle so easily; for neither can any disorder remove them from their usual regularity, nor can fear affright them out of it, nor can labour tire them; which firmness of conduct makes them to overcome those that have the same firmness; nor would he be mistaken that should call those their exercises unbloody battles, and their battles bloody exercises.   Nor can their enemies easily surprise them with the suddenness of their incursions; for as soon as they have marched into an enemy's land, they do not begin to fight till they have walled their camp about; nor is the fence they raise rashly made, or uneven; nor do they all abide in it, nor do those that are in it take their places at random; but if it happens that the ground is uneven, it is first levelled: their camp is also four-square by measure, and carpenters are ready, in great numbers, with their tools, to erect their buildings for them.*

2. As for what is within the camp, it is set apart for tents, but the outward circumference hath the resemblance of a wall, and is adorned with towers at equal distances, where between the towers stand the engines for throwing arrows and darts, and for slinging stones, and where they lay all other engines that can annoy the enemy, all ready for their several operations. They also erect four gates, one at every side of the circumference, and those large enough for the entrance of the beasts, and wide enough for making excursions, if occasion should require. They divide the camp within into two streets, very conveniently, and place the tents of the commanders in the middle; but in the very midst of all is the general's own tent in the nature of a temple, insomuch that it appears to be a city built on the sudden, with its market-

place, and place for handicraft trades, and with seats for the officers, superior and inferior; where, if any differences arise, their causes are heard and determined. The camp, and all that is in it, is encompassed with a wall all round about, and that sooner than one would imagine, and this by the multitude and the skill of the labourers; and, if occasion require, a trench is drawn round the whole, whose depth is four cubits, and its breadth equal.

3. When they have thus secured themselves, they live together by companies with quietness and decency, as are all their other affairs managed with good order and security.   Each company hath also their wood, and their corn, and their water brought them, when they stand in need of them; for they neither sup nor dine as they please themselves singly, but all together. Their times also for sleeping, and watching, and rising, are notified beforehand by the sound of trumpets, nor is anything done without such a signal; and in the morning the soldiery go every one to their centurions, and these centurions to their tribunes, to salute them; with whom all the superior officers go to the general of the whole army, who then gives them of course the watch-word and other orders, to be by them carried to all that are under their command; which is also observed when they go to fight, and thereby they turn themselves about on the sudden, when there is occasion for making sallies, as they come back when they are recalled, in crowds also.

4. When they are to go out of their camp, the trumpet gives a sound, at which time nobody lies still, but at the first intimation they take down their tents, and all is made ready for their going out; then do the trumpets sound again, to order them to get ready for the march; then do they lay their baggage suddenly upon their mules and other beasts of burden, and stand, at the place for starting, ready to march; when also they set fire to their camp, and this they do because it will be easy for them to erect another camp, and that it may not ever be of use to their enemies.   Then do the trumpets give a sound the third time, that they are to go out in order to excite those that on any account are a little tardy, that so no one may be out of his rank when the army marches.   Then does the crier stand at the general's right hand, and asks them thrice, in their own tongue, whether they be ready to go out to war or not.   To which they reply as often, with a loud and cheerful voice, saying, "We are ready." And this they do almost before the question is asked them; they do this as filled with a kind of martial fury, and at the time that they so cry out, they lift up their right hands also.

5 When, after this, they are gone out of their camp, they all march without noise, and in a decent manner, and every one keeps his own rank, as if they were going to war. The footmen are armed with breastplates and headpieces, and have swords on each side; but the sword which is upon their left side is much longer than the other; for that on the right side is not longer than a span.   Those footmen also that are chosen out from amongst the rest to be about the general himself, have a lance and a buckler; but the rest of the foot-soldiers have a spear and a long buckler, besides a saw and a basket, a pick-axe and an axe, a thong of leather, and a hook, with provisions for three days; so that a footman hath no great need of a mule to carry his burdens. The horsemen have a long sword on their right sides, and a long pole in their hand: a shield also lies by them obliquely

---

* This description of the exact symmetry and regularity of the Roman army, and of the Roman encampments, with the sounding their trumpets, &c., and order of war, described in this and the next chapter, is so very like to the symmetry and regularity of the people of Israel in the wilderness that one cannot well avoid the supposal, that the one was the ultimate pattern of the other, and that the tactics of the ancients were taken from the rules given by God to Moses.   And it is thought by some skilful in these matters, that these accounts of Josephus, as to the Roman camp and armour, and conduct in war, are preferable to those in the Roman authors themselves.

on one side of their horses, with three or more
darts that are borne in their quiver, having broad
points, and no smaller than spears. They have
also head-pieces and breastplates, in like manner as have all the footmen. And for those
that are chosen to be about the general, their armour no way differs from that of the horsemen
belonging to other troops; and he always leads
the legions forth, to whom the lot assigns that
employment.

6. This is the manner of the marching and
resting of the Romans, as also these are the several sorts of weapons they use. But when they
are to fight, they leave nothing without forecast,
nor to be done off-hand, but counsel is ever first
taken before any work is begun, and what hath
been there resolved upon is put in execution
presently; for which reason they seldom commit
any errors; and if they have been mistaken at
any time, they easily correct those mistakes.
They also esteem any errors they commit upon
taking counsel beforehand, to be better than
such rash success as is owing to fortune only;
because such a fortuitous advantage tempts them
to be inconsiderate, while consultation, though
it may sometimes fail of success, hath this good
in it, that it makes men more careful hereafter;
but for the advantages that arise from chance,
they are not owing to him that gains them;
and as to what melancholy accidents happen unexpectedly, there is this comfort in them, that
they had however taken the best consultations
they could to prevent them.

7. Now they so manage their preparatory exercises of their weapons, that not the bodies of
the soldiers only, but their souls, may also become
stronger: they are moreover hardened for war
by fear; for their laws inflict capital punishments, not only for soldiers running away from
their ranks, but for slothfulness and inactivity,
though it be but in a lesser degree; as are their
generals more severe than their laws, for they
prevent any imputation of cruelty towards those
under condemnation, by the great rewards they
bestow on the valiant soldiers; and the readiness of obeying their commanders is so great,
that it is very ornamental in peace; but when
they come to a battle, the whole army is but one
body, so well coupled together are their ranks,
so sudden are their turnings about, so sharp their
hearing as to what orders are given them, so
quick their sight of the ensigns, and so nimble
are their hands when they set to work; whereby it comes to pass, that what they do is done
quickly, and what they suffer they bear with
the greatest patience. Nor can we find any examples whereby they have been conquered in
battle, when they came to a close fight, either
by the multitude of the enemies, or by their
stratagems, or by the difficulties in the places
they were in; no, nor by fortune neither, for
their victories have been surer to them than fortune could have granted them. In a case, therefore, where counsel still goes before action, and
where, after taking the best advice, that advice
is followed by so active an army, what wonder is
it that Euphrates on the east, the ocean on the
west, the most fertile regions of Lybia on the
south, and the Danube and the Rhine on the
north, are the limits of this empire? One might
well say, that the Roman possessions are not inferior to the Romans themselves.

8. This account I have given the reader, not
so much with the intention of commending the
Romans, as of comforting those that have been
conquered by them, and for deterring others
from attempting innovations under their government. This discourse of the Roman military

conduct may also perhaps be of use to such
of the curious as are ignorant of it, and yet have
a mind to know it. I return now from this
digression.

CHAPTER VI

PLACIDUS ATTEMPTS TO TAKE JOTAPATA, AND IS
BEATEN OFF. VESPASIAN MARCHES INTO GALI-
LEE

1. AND now Vespasian, with his son Titus,
had tarried some time at Ptolemais, and had put
his army in order. But when Placidus, who had
overrun Galilee, and had besides slain a number
of those whom he had caught, (which were only
the weaker part of the Galileans, and such as
were of timorous souls,) saw that the warriors
ran always to those cities whose walls had been
built by Josephus, he marched furiously against
Jotapata, which was of them all the strongest,
as supposing he should easily take it by a sudden
surprise, and that he should thereby obtain great
honour to himself among the commanders, and
bring a great advantage to them in their future
campaign; because if this strongest place of them
all were once taken, the rest would be so affrighted as to surrender themselves. But he was
mightily mistaken in his undertaking; for the
men of Jotapata were apprised of his coming to attack them, and came out of the city, and expected
him there. So they fought the Romans briskly
when they least expected it, being both many in
number, and prepared for fighting, and of great
alacrity, as esteeming their country, their wives,
and their children, to be in danger, and easily
put the Romans to flight, and wounded many of
them, and slew seven of them; because their retreat was not made in a disorderly manner, because the strokes only touched the surface of
their bodies, which were covered with their
armour in all parts, and because the Jews did rather throw their weapons upon them from a great
distance, than venture to come hand to hand
with them, and had only light armour on, while
the others were completely armed. However,
three men of the Jews' side were slain and a few
wounded; so Placidus, finding himself unable to
assault the city, ran away.

2. But as Vespasian had a great mind to fall
upon Galilee, he marched out from Ptolemais,
having put his army into that order wherein the
Romans used to march. He ordered those auxiliaries which were lightly armed, and the archers, to march first, that they might prevent any
sudden assaults from the enemy, and might search
out the woods that looked suspiciously, and were
capable of ambuscades. Next to these followed
that part of the Romans who were most completely armed, both footmen and horsemen.
Next to these followed ten out of every hundred,
carrying along with them their arms, and what
was necessary to measure out a camp withal;
and after them, such as were to make the road
even and straight, and if it were anywhere rough
and hard to be passed over, to plane it, and to
cut down the woods that hindered their march,
that the army might not be in distress, or tired
with their march. Behind these he set such
carriages of the army as belonged both to himself and to the other commanders, with a considerable number of their horsemen for their security. After these he marched himself, having
with him a select body of footmen, and horsemen, and pikemen. After these came the peculiar cavalry of his own legion, for there were an
hundred and twenty horsemen that peculiarly

belonged to every legion. Next to these came the mules that carried the engines for sieges, and the other warlike machines of that nature. After these came the commanders of the cohorts, and tribunes, having about them soldiers chosen out of the rest. Then came the ensigns encompassing the eagle, which is at the head of every Roman legion, the king, and the strongest of all birds, which seems to them a signal of dominion, and an omen that they shall conquer all against whom they march; these sacred ensigns are followed by the trumpeters. Then came the main army in their squadrons and battalions, with six men in depth, which were followed at last by a centurion, who, according to custom, observed the rest. As for the servants of every legion, they all followed the footmen, and led the baggage of the soldiers, which was borne by the mules and other beasts of burden. But behind all the legions came the whole multitude of the mercenaries; and those that brought up the rear came last of all for the security of the whole army, being both footmen, and those in their armour also, with a great number of horsemen.

3. And thus did Vespasian march with his army, and came to the bounds of Galilee, where he pitched his camp and restrained his soldiers, who were eager for war; he also shewed his army to the enemy in order to affright them, and to afford them a season for repentance, to see whether they would change their minds before it came to a battle, and at the same time he got things ready for besieging their strongholds. And indeed this sight of the general brought many to repent of their revolt, and put them all into a consternation: for those that were in Josephus's camp, which was at the city called Garis, not far from Sepphoris, when they heard that the war was come near them, and that the Romans would suddenly fight them hand to hand, dispersed themselves and fled, not only before they came to a battle, but before the enemy ever came in sight, while Josephus and a few others were left behind; and as he saw that he had not an army sufficient to engage the enemy, that the spirits of the Jews were sunk, and that the greater part would willingly come to terms, if they might be credited, he already despaired of the success of the whole war, and determined to get as far as he possibly could, out of danger; so he took those that stayed along with him, and fled to Tiberias.

CHAPTER VII

VESPASIAN, WHEN HE HAS TAKEN THE CITY GADARA, MARCHES TO JOTAPATA. AFTER A LONG SIEGE, THE CITY IS BETRAYED BY A DESERTER, AND TAKEN BY VESPASIAN

1. So Vespasian marched to the city Gadara, and took it upon the first onset, because he found it destitute of a considerable number of men grown up and fit for war. He came then into it, and slew all the youth, the Romans having no mercy on any age whatsoever; and this was done out of the hatred they bore the nation, and because of the iniquity they had been guilty of in the affair of Cestius. He also set fire, not only to the city itself, but to all the villas and small cities that were round about it; some of them were quite destitute of inhabitants; and out of some of them he carried the inhabitants as slaves into captivity.

2. As to Josephus, his retiring into that city which he chose as the most fit for his security, put it into great fear; for the people of Tiberias did not imagine that he would have run away, unless he had entirely despaired of the success of the war; and indeed, as to that point, they were not mistaken about his opinion; for he saw whither the affairs of the Jews would tend at last, and was sensible that they had but one way of escaping, and that was by repentance. However, although he expected that the Romans would forgive him, yet did he choose to die many times over rather than to betray his country, and to dishonour that supreme command of the army which had been intrusted to him, or to live happily under those against whom he was sent to fight. He determined, therefore, to give an exact account of affairs to the principal men at Jerusalem by a letter, that he might not, by too much aggrandising the power of the enemy, make them too timorous; nor by relating that their power beneath the truth, might encourage them to stand out when they were perhaps disposed to repentance. He also sent them word, that if they thought of coming to terms, they must suddenly write him an answer; or if they resolve upon war, they must send him an army sufficient to fight the Romans. Accordingly he wrote these things, and sent messengers immediately to carry his letter to Jerusalem.

3. Now Vespasian was very desirous of demolishing Jotapata, for he had got intelligence that the greatest part of the enemy had retired thither; and that it was, on other accounts, a place of great security to them. Accordingly, he sent both footmen and horsemen to level the road, which was mountainous and rocky, not without difficulty to be travelled over by footmen, but absolutely impracticable for horsemen. Now these workmen accomplished what they were about in four days' time, and opened a broad way for the army. On the fifth day, which was the twenty-first of the month Artimisius (Jyar) Josephus prevented him, and came from Tiberias, and went into Jotapata, and raised the drooping spirits of the Jews. And a certain deserter told this good news to Vespasian, that Josephus had removed himself thither, which made him make haste to the city, as supposing, that with taking that he should take all Judea, in case he could but withal get Josephus under his power. So he took this news to be of the vastest advantage to him, and believed it to be brought about by the providence of God, that he who appeared to be the most prudent man of all their enemies had, of his own accord, shut himself up in a place of sure custody. Accordingly, he sent Placidus with a thousand horsemen, and Ebutius, a decurion, a person that was of eminency both in council and in action, to encompass the city round, that Josephus might not escape away privately.

4. Vespasian also, the very next day, took his whole army and followed them, and by marching till late in the evening, arrived then at Jotapata; and bringing his army to the northern side of the city, he pitched his camp on a certain hill which was seven furlongs from the city, and still greatly endeavoured to be well seen by the enemy, to put them into consternation, which was indeed so terrible to the Jews immediately, that no one of them durst go out beyond the wall. Yet did the Romans put off the attack at that time, because they had marched all the day, although they placed a double row of battalions round the city, with a third row beyond them round the whole, which consisted of cavalry, in order to stop up every way for an exit; which thing making the Jews despair of escaping, excited them to act more boldly; for nothing

makes men fight so desperately in war as necessity.

5. Now when an assault was made the next day by the Romans, the Jews at first stayed out of the walls, and opposed them; and met them, as having formed themselves a camp before the city walls. But when Vespasian had set against them the archers and slingers, and the whole multitude that could throw to a great distance, he permitted them to go to work, while he himself, with the footmen, got upon an acclivity, whence the city might easily be taken. Josephus was then in fear for the city, and leaped out, and all the Jewish multitude with him; these fell together upon the Romans in great numbers, and drove them away from the wall, and performed a great many glorious and bold actions. Yet did they suffer as much as they made the enemy suffer; for as despair of deliverance encouraged the Jews, so did a sense of shame equally encourage the Romans. These last had skill as well as strength; the other had only courage, which armed them, and made them fight furiously. And when the fight had lasted all day, it was put an end to by the coming on of night. They had wounded a great many of the Romans, and killed of them thirteen men; of the Jews' side seventeen were slain, and six hundred wounded.

6. On the next day the Jews made another attack upon the Romans, and went out of the walls, and fought a much more desperate battle with them than before; for they were now become more courageous than formerly, and that on account of the unexpected good opposition they had made the day before, as they found the Romans also to fight more desperately; for a sense of shame inflamed these into a passion, as esteeming their failure of a sudden victory to be a kind of defeat. Thus did the Romans try to make an impression upon the Jews till the fifth day continually, while the people of Jotapata made sallies out, and fought at the walls most desperately; nor were the Jews affrighted at the strength of the enemy, nor were the Romans discouraged at the difficulties they met with in taking the city.

7. Now Jotapata is almost all of it built upon a precipice, having on all the other sides of it every way valleys immensely deep and steep, insomuch that those who would look down would have their sight fail them before it reached to the bottom. It is only to be come at on the north side, where the utmost part of the city is built on the mountain, as it ends obliquely at a plain. This mountain Josephus had encompassed with a wall when he fortified the city, that its top might not be capable of being seized upon by the enemies. The city is covered all round with other mountains, that can no way be seen till a man comes just upon it. And this was the strong situation of Jotapata.

8. Vespasian, therefore, in order to try how he might overcome the natural strength of the place, as well as the bold defence of the Jews, made a resolution to prosecute the siege with vigour.—To that end he called the commanders that were under him to a council of war, and consulted with them which way the assault might be managed to the best advantage; and when the resolution was there taken to raise a bank against that part of the wall which was practicable, he sent his whole army abroad to get the materials together. So when they had cut down all the trees on the mountains that adjoined to the city, and had gotten together a vast heap of stones, besides the wood they had cut down, some of them brought hurdles, in order to avoid the effects of the darts that were shot from above them. These hurdles they spread over their banks, under cover whereof they formed their bank, and so were little or nothing hurt by the darts that were thrown upon them from the wall, while others pulled the neighbouring hillocks to pieces, and perpetually brought earth to them; so that while they were busy three sorts of ways, nobody was idle. However, the Jews cast great stones from the walls upon the hurdles which protected the men, with all sorts of darts also; and the noise of what could not reach them was yet so terrible, that it was some impediment to the workmen.

9. Vespasian then set the engines for throwing stones and darts round about the city; the number of the engines was in all a hundred and sixty; and bade them fall to work, and dislodge those that were upon the wall. At the same time such engines as were intended for that purpose, threw at once lances upon them with great noise, and stones of the weight of a talent were thrown by the engines that were prepared for that purpose, together with fire, and a vast multitude of arrows, which made the wall so dangerous, that the Jews durst not only not come upon it, but durst not come to those parts within the walls which were reached by the engines, for the multitude of the Arabian archers, as well also as all those that threw darts and slung stones, fell to work at the same time with the engines. Yet did not the others lie still when they could not throw at the Romans from a higher place; for they then made sallies out of the city like private robbers, by parties, and pulled away the hurdles that covered the workmen, and killed them when they were thus naked; and when those workmen gave way, these cast away the earth that composed the bank, and burnt the wooden parts of it, together with the hurdles, till at length Vespasian perceived that the intervals there were between the works were of disadvantage to him; for those spaces of ground afforded the Jews a place for assaulting the Romans. So he united the hurdles, and at the same time joined one part of the army to the other, which prevented the private excursions of the Jews.

10. And when the bank was now raised, and brought nearer than ever to the battlements that belonged to the walls, Josephus thought it would be entirely wrong in him if he could make no contrivances in opposition to theirs, and that might be for the city's preservation; so he got together his workmen, and ordered them to build the wall higher; and when they said that this was impossible to be done while so many darts were thrown at them, he invented this sort of cover for them:—He bade them fix piles, and expand before them raw hides of oxen newly killed, and these hides by yielding and hollowing themselves when the stones were thrown at them might receive them, for that the other darts would slide off them, and the fire that was thrown would be quenched by the moisture that was in them; and these he set before the workmen; and under them these workmen went on with their works in safety, and raised the wall higher, and that both by day and by night, till it was twenty cubits high. He then built a good number of towers upon the wall, and fitted it to strong battlements. This greatly discouraged the Romans, who in their own opinions were already gotten within the walls, while they were now at once astonished at Josephus's contrivance, and at the fortitude of the citizens that were in the city.

11. And now Vespasian was plainly irritated

at the great subtlety of this stratagem, and at the boldness of the citizens of Jotapata ; for taking heart again upon the building of this wall, they made fresh sallies upon the Romans, and had every day conflicts with them by parties, together with all such contrivances as robbers make use of, and with the plundering of all that came to hand, as also with the setting fire to all the other works ; and this till Vespasian made his army leave off fighting them, and resolved to lie round the city, and to starve them into a surrender, as supposing that either they would be forced to petition him for mercy by the want of provisions, or if they should have the courage to hold out till the last they should perish by famine : and he concluded he should conquer them the more easily in fighting, if he gave them an interval, and then to fall upon them when they were weakened by famine ; but still he gave orders that they should guard against their coming out of the city.

12. Now the besieged had plenty of corn within the city, and indeed of all other necessaries, but they wanted water, because there was no fountain in the city, and the people being there usually satisfied with rain-water ; yet it is a rare thing in that country to have rain in summer, and at this season during the siege, they were in great distress for some contrivance to satisfy their thirst ; and they were very sad at this time particularly, as if they were already in want of water entirely, for Josephus seeing that the city abounded with other necessaries, and that the men were of good courage, and being desirous to protract the siege to the Romans longer than they expected, ordered their drink to be given them by measure : but this scanty distribution of water by measure was deemed by them as a thing more hard upon them than the want of it ; and their not being able to drink as much as they would, made them more desirous of drinking than they otherwise had been ; nay, they were so much disheartened thereby as if they were come to the last degree of thirst. Nor were the Romans unacquainted with the state they were in, for when they stood over against them beyond the wall, they could see them running together, and taking their water by measure, which made them throw their javelins thither, the place being within their reach, and kill a great many of them.

13. Hereupon Vespasian hoped that their receptacles of water would in no long time be emptied, and that they would be forced to deliver up the city to him ; but Josephus being minded to break such his hope, gave command that they should wet a great many of their clothes and hang them out about the battlements, till the entire walls was of a sudden all wet with the running down of water. At this sight the Romans were discouraged, and under consternation, when they saw them able to throw away in sport so much water, when they supposed them not to have enough to drink themselves. This made the Roman general despair of taking the city by their want of necessaries, and to betake himself again to arms, and to try to force them to surrender, which was what the Jews greatly desired ; for as they despaired of either themselves or their city being able to escape, they preferred a death in battle before one by hunger and thirst.

14. However, Josephus contrived another stratagem besides the foregoing, to get plenty of what they wanted.—There was a certain rough and uneven place that could hardly be ascended, and on that account was not guarded by the soldiers ; so Josephus sent out certain persons along the western parts of the valley, and by them sent letters to whom he pleased of the Jews that were out of the city, and procured from them what necessaries soever they wanted in the city in abundance ; he enjoined them also to creep generally along by the watch as they came into the city, and to cover their backs with such sheep skins as had their wool upon them, that if any one should spy them in the nighttime, they might be believed to be dogs. This was done till the watch perceived their contrivance, and encompassed that rough place about themselves.

15. And now it was that Josephus perceived that the city could not hold out long, and that his own life would be in doubt if he continued in it ; so he consulted how he and the most potent men of the city might fly out of it. When the multitude understood this, they came all round about him, and begged of him not to overlook them while they entirely depended on him, and him alone ; for that there was still hope of the city's deliverance if he would stay with them, because everybody would undertake any pains with great cheerfulness on his account, and in that case there would be some comfort for them also, though they should be taken : that it became him neither to fly from his enemies, nor to desert his friends, nor to leap out of that city, as out of a ship that was sinking in a storm, into which he came when it was quiet and in a calm ; for that by going away he would be the cause of drowning the city, because nobody would then venture to oppose the enemy when he was once gone, upon whom they wholly confided.

16. Hereupon Josephus avoided letting them know that he was to go away to provide for his own safety, but told them that he would go out of the city for their sakes ; for that if he stayed with them, he should be able to do them little good while they were in a safe condition ; and that if they were once taken, he should only perish with them to no purpose ; but that if he were once gotten free from this siege, he should be able to bring them very great relief ; for that he would then immediately get the Galileans together, out of the country, in great multitudes, and draw the Romans off their city by another war. That he did not see what advantage he could bring to them now, by staying among them, but only provoke the Romans to besiege them more closely, as esteeming it a most valuable thing to take him ; but that if they were once informed that he was fled out of the city, they would greatly remit of their eagerness against it. Yet did not this plea move the people, but inflamed them the more to hang about him. Accordingly, both the children and the old men, and the women with their infants, came mourning to him and fell down before him, and all of them caught hold of his feet, and held him fast, and besought him, with great lamentations, that he would take his share with them in their fortune ;—and I think they did this, not that they envied his deliverance, but that they hoped for their own ; for they could not think they should suffer any great misfortune, provided Josephus would but stay with them.

17. Now, Josephus thought, that if he resolved to stay, it would be ascribed to their entreaties ; and if he resolved to go away by force, he should be put into custody. His commiseration also of the people under their lamentations, had much broken that of his eagerness to leave them : so he resolved to stay, and arming himself with the common despair of the citizens, he said to them, " Now is the time to begin to fight in earnest, when there is no hope of deliverance left. It is

a brave thing to prefer glory before life, and to set about some such noble undertaking as may be remembered by late posterity." Having said this he fell to work immediately, and made a sally, and dispersed the enemies' out-guards, and ran as far as the Roman camp itself, and pulled the coverings of their tents to pieces, that were upon their banks, and set fire to their works. And this was the manner in which he never left off fighting, neither the next day nor the day after it, but went on with it for a considerable number of both days and nights.

18. Upon this, Vespasian, when he saw the Romans distressed by these sallies (although they were ashamed to be made to run away by the Jews; and when at any time they made the Jews run away, their heavy armour would not let them pursue them far; while the Jews, when they had performed any action, and before they could be hurt themselves, still retired into the city,) ordered his armed men to avoid their onset, and not to fight it out with men under desperation, while nothing is more courageous than despair; but that their violence would be quenched when they saw they failed of their purposes, as fire is quenched when it wants fuel; and that it was most proper for the Romans to gain their victories as cheap as they could, since they are not forced to fight, but only to enlarge their own dominions. So he repelled the Jews in great measure by the Arabian archers, and the Syrian slingers, and by those that threw stones at them, nor was there any intermission of the great number of their offensive engines. Now, the Jews suffered greatly by these engines, without being able to escape from them; and when these engines threw their stones or javelins a great way, and the Jews were within their reach, they pressed hard upon the Romans, and fought desperately, without sparing either soul or body, one part succouring another by turns, when it was tired down.

19. When, therefore, Vespasian looked upon himself as in a manner besieged by these sallies of the Jews, and when his banks were now not far from the walls, he determined to make use of his battering ram. This battering ram is a vast beam of wood like the mast of a ship; its fore-part is armed with a thick piece of iron at the head of it, which is so carved as to be like the head of a ram, whence its name is taken. This ram is slung in the air by ropes passing over its middle, and is hung like the balance in a pair of scales from another beam, and braced by strong beams that pass on both sides of it in the nature of a cross. When this ram is pulled backward by a great number of men with united force, and then thrust forward by the same men, with a mighty noise, it batters the walls with that iron part which is prominent; nor is there any tower so strong, or walls so broad, that can resist any more than its first batteries, but all are forced to yield to it at last. This was the experiment which the Roman general betook himself to when he was eagerly bent upon taking the city, and found lying in the field so long to be to his disadvantage, because the Jews would never let him be quiet. So these Romans brought the several engines for galling an enemy nearer to the walls, that they might reach such as were upon the wall, and endeavoured to frustrate their attempts; these threw stones and javelins at them; in the like manner did the archers and slingers come both together closer to the wall. This brought matters to such a pass that none of the Jews durst mount the walls, and then it was that the Romans brought the battering ram that was cased with hurdles all over, and in the

upper part was secured with skins that covered it, and this both for the security of themselves and of the engine. Now, at the very first stroke of this engine, the wall was shaken, and a terrible clamour was raised by the people within the city, as if they were already taken.

20. And now, when Josephus saw this ram still battering the same place, and that the wall would quickly be thrown down by it, he resolved to elude for a while the force of the engine. With this design he gave orders to fill sacks with chaff, and to hang them down before that place where they saw the ram always battering, that the stroke might be turned aside, or that the place might feel less of the strokes by the yielding nature of the chaff. This contrivance very much delayed the attempts of the Romans, because let them remove their engine to what part they pleased, those that were above it removed their sacks, and placed them over-against the strokes it made, insomuch that the wall was no way hurt, and this by diversion of the strokes, till the Romans made an opposite contrivance of long poles, and by tying hooks at their ends, cut off the sacks. Now, when the battering ram, thus recovered its force, and the wall having been but newly built, was giving way, Josephus and those about him, had afterward immediate recourse to fire, to defend themselves withal; whereupon they took what materials soever they had that were but dry, and made a sally three ways, and set fire to the machines and to the hurdles, and the banks of the Romans themselves; nor did the Romans well know how to come to their assistance, being at once under a consternation at the Jews' boldness, and being prevented by the flames from coming to their assistance; for the materials being dry with the bitumen and pitch that were among them, as was brimstone also, the fire caught hold of every thing immediately; and what cost the Romans a great deal of pains was in one hour consumed.

21. And here a certain Jew appeared worthy of our relation and commendation; he was the son of Sameas, and was called Eleazar, and was born at Saab in Galilee. This man took up a stone of vast bigness, and threw it down from the wall upon the ram, and this with so great a force that it broke off the head of the engine. He also leaped down and took up the head of the ram from the midst of them, without any concern, carried it to the top of the wall, and this while he stood as a fit mark to be pelted by all his enemies. Accordingly, he received the strokes upon his naked body, and was wounded with five darts; nor did he mind any of them while he went up to the top of the wall, where he stood in sight of them all, as an instance of the greatest boldness: after which he threw himself on a heap with his wounds upon him, and fell down, together with the head of the ram. Next to him, two brothers shewed their courage; their names were Netir and Philip, both of them of the village Ruma, and both of them Galileans also; these men leaped upon the soldiers of the tenth legion, and fell upon the Romans with such a noise and force as to disorder their ranks, and put to flight all upon whomsoever they made their assaults.

22. After these men's performances, Josephus, and the rest of the multitude with him, took a great deal of fire, and burnt both the machines, and their coverings, with the works belonging to the fifth, and to the tenth legion, which they put to flight; when others followed them immediately, and buried those instruments and all their materials under ground. However, about the evening the Romans erected the battering

ASSAULT OF JOTAPATA

ram again, against that part of the wall which had suffered before; where a certain Jew that defended the city from the Romans, hit Vespasian with a dart in his foot, and wounded him a little, the distance being so great, that no mighty impression could be made by the dart thrown so far off. However, this caused the greatest disorder among the Romans; for when those who stood near him saw his blood, they were disturbed at it, and a report went abroad, through the whole army, that the general was wounded, while the greatest part left the siege, and came running together with surprise and fear to the general; and before them all came Titus, out of the concern he had for his father, insomuch that the multitude were in great confusion, and this out of the regard they had for their general, and by reason of the agony that the son was in. Yet did the father soon put an end to the son's fear, and to the disorder the army was under, for being superior to his pains, and endeavouring soon to be seen by all that had been in the fright about him, he excited them to fight the Jews more briskly; for now everybody was willing to expose himself to danger immediately in order to avenge their general; and then they encouraged one another with loud voices, and ran hastily to the walls.

23. But still Josephus and those with him, although they fell down dead one upon another, by the darts and stones which the engines threw upon them, yet did not they desert the wall, but fell upon those who managed the ram, under the protection of the hurdles, with fire, and iron weapons, and stones; and these could do little or nothing, but fell themselves perpetually, while they were seen by those whom they could not see, for the light of their own flame shone about them, and made them a most visible mark to the enemy, as they were in the day-time, while the engines could not be seen at a great distance, and so what was thrown at them was hard to be avoided; for the force with which these engines threw stones and darts made them hurt several at a time, and the violent noise of the stones that were cast by the engines was so great, that they carried away the pinnacles of the wall, and broke off the corners of the towers; for no body of men could be so strong as not to be overthrown to the last rank by the largeness of the stones; and any one may learn the force of the engines by what happened this very night; for as one of those that stood round about Josephus was near the wall, his head was carried away by such a stone, and his skull was flung as far as three furlongs. In the day-time also, a woman with child had her belly so violently struck, as she was just come out of her house, that the infant was carried to the distance of half a furlong; so great was the force of that engine. The noise of the instruments themselves was very terrible, the sound of the darts and stones that were thrown by them was so also; of the same sort was that noise the dead bodies made, when they were dashed against the wall; and indeed dreadful was the clamour which these things raised in the women within the city, which was echoed back at the same time by the cries of such as were slain; while the whole space of ground whereon they fought ran with blood, and the wall might have been ascended over by the bodies of the dead carcasses; the mountains also contributed to increase the noise by their echoes; nor was there on that night anything of terror wanting that could either affect the hearing or the sight: yet did a great part of those that fought so hard for Jotapata fall manfully, as were a great part of

them wounded. However the morning watch was come ere the wall yielded to the machines employed against it, though it had been battered without intermission. However, those within covered their bodies with their armour, and raised works over against that part which was thrown down, before those machines were laid by which the Romans were to ascend into the city.

24. In the morning Vespasian got his army together, in order to take the city [by storm,] after a little recreation upon the hard pains they had been at the night before; and as he was desirous to draw off those that opposed him from the places where the wall had been thrown down, he made the most courageous of the horsemen get off their horses, and placed them in three ranks over against those ruins of the walls, but covered with their armour on every side, and with poles in their hands, that so these might begin their ascent as soon as the instruments for such ascent were laid; behind them he placed the flower of the footmen; but for the rest of the horse, he ordered them to extend themselves over against the wall, upon the whole hilly country, in order to prevent any from escaping out of the city when it should be taken; and behind these he placed the archers round about, and commanded them to have all their darts ready to shoot. The same command he gave to the slingers, and to those that managed the engines, and bade them to take up other ladders and have them ready to lay upon those parts of the wall which were yet untouched, that the besieged might be engaged in trying to hinder their ascent by them, and leave the guard of the parts that were thrown down, while the rest of them should be overborne by the darts cast at them, and might afford his men an entrance into the city.

25. But Josephus, understanding the meaning of Vespasian's contrivance, set the old men, together with those that were tired out, at the sound parts of the wall, as expecting no harm from those quarters, but set the strongest of his men at the place where the wall was broken down, and before them all, six men by themselves, among whom he took his share of the first and greatest danger. He also gave orders, that when the legions made a shout they should stop their ears, that they might not be affrighted at it, and that, to avoid the multitude of the enemies' darts, they should bend down on their knees, and cover themselves with their shields, and that they should retreat a little backward for a while, till the archers should have emptied their quivers; but that, when the Romans should lay their instruments for ascending the walls, they should leap out on the sudden, and with their own instruments should meet the enemy, and that every one should strive to do his best, in order not to defend his own city, as if it were possible to be preserved, but in order to revenge it, when it was already destroyed; and that they should set before their eyes how their old men were to be slain, and their children and their wives to be killed immediately by the enemy; and that they would beforehand spend all their fury, on account of the calamities just coming upon them, and pour it out on the actors.

26. And thus did Josephus dispose of both his bodies of men; but then for the useless part of the citizens, the women and children, when they saw their city encompassed by a threefold army, (for none of the usual guards that had been fighting before were removed,) when they also saw not only the walls thrown down, but their enemies with swords in their hands, as also the

hilly country above them shining with their weapons, and the darts in the hands of the Arabian archers, they made a final and lamentable outcry of the destruction, as if the misery were not only threatened, but actually come upon them already. But Josephus ordered the women to be shut up in their houses, lest they should render the warlike actions of the men too effeminate, by making them commiserate their condition, and commanded them to hold their peace, and threatened them if they did not, while he came himself before the breach, where his allotment was; for all those who brought ladders to the other place, he took no notice of them, but earnestly waited for the shower of arrows that was coming.

27. And now the trumpeters of the several Roman legions sounded together, and the army made a terrible shout; and the darts, as by order, flew so fast that they intercepted the light. However, Josephus's men remembered the charges he had given them, they stopped their ears at the sounds, and covered their bodies against the darts; and as to the engines that were set ready to go to work, the Jews ran out upon them, before those that should have used them were gotten upon them. And now, on the ascending of the soldiers, there was a great conflict, and many actions of the hands and of the soul were exhibited, while the Jews did earnestly endeavour, in the extreme danger they were in, not to shew less courage than those who, without being in danger, fought so stoutly against them; nor did they leave struggling with the Romans till they either fell down dead themselves, or killed their antagonists. But the Jews grew weary with defending themselves continually, and had not enow to come in their places to succour them,—while, on the side of the Romans, fresh men still succeeded those that were tired; and still new men soon got upon the machines for ascent, in the room of those that were thrust down; those encouraging one another, and joining side to side with their shields, which were a protection to them, they became a body of men not to be broken; and as this band thrust away the Jews, as though they were themselves but one body, they began already to get upon the wall.

28. Then did Josephus take necessity for his counsellor in this utmost distress, (which necessity is very sagacious in invention, when it is irritated by despair,) and gave orders to pour scalding oil upon those whose shields protected them. Whereupon they soon got it ready, being many that brought it, and what they brought being a great quantity also, and poured it on all sides upon the Romans, and threw down upon them their vessels as they were still hissing from the heat of the fire: this so burnt the Romans, that it dispersed that united band, who now tumbled down from the wall with horrid pains, for the oil did easily run down the whole body from head to foot, under their entire armour, and fed upon their flesh like flame itself, its fat and unctuous nature rendering it soon heated and slowly cooled; and as the men were cooped up in their head-pieces and breast-plates they could no way get free from this burning oil; they could only leap and roll about in their pains, as they fell down from the bridges they had laid. And as they were thus beaten back, and retired to their own party, who still pressed them forward, they were easily wounded by those that were behind them.

29. However, in this ill success of the Romans, their courage did not fail them, nor did the Jews want prudence to oppose them; for

the Romans, although they saw their own men thrown down, and in a miserable condition, yet were they vehemently bent against those that poured the oil upon them, while every one reproached the man before him as a coward, and one that hindered him from exerting himself; while the Jews made use of another stratagem to prevent their ascent, and poured boiling fenugreek upon the boards, in order to make them slip and fall down; by which means neither could those that were coming up, nor those that were going down, stand upon their feet; but some of them fell backward upon the machines on which they ascended, and were trodden upon; many of them fell down upon the bank they had raised, and when they were fallen upon it were slain by the Jews; for when the Romans could not keep their feet, the Jews being freed from fighting hand to hand, had leisure to throw their darts at them. So the general called off his soldiers in the evening that had suffered so sorely, of whom the number of the slain was not a few, while that of the wounded was still greater; but of the people of Jotapata no more than six men were killed, although more than three hundred were carried off wounded. This fight happened on the twentieth day of the month Desius, [Sivan.]

30. Hereupon Vespasian comforted his army on occasion of what had happened, and as he found them angry indeed, but rather wanting somewhat to do than any further exhortations, he gave orders to raise the banks still higher, and to erect three towers, each fifty feet high, and that they should cover them with plates of iron on every side, that they might be both firm by their weight, and not easily liable to be set on fire. These towers he set upon the banks, and placed upon them such as could shoot darts and arrows, with the lighter engines for throwing stones and darts also; and besides these, he set upon them the stoutest men among the slingers, who not being to be seen by reason of the height they stood upon, and the battlements that protected them, might throw their weapons at those that were upon the wall, and were easily seen by them. Hereupon the Jews, not being easily able to escape those darts that were thrown down upon their heads, nor to avenge themselves on those whom they could not see, and perceiving that the height of the towers was so great, that a dart which they threw with their hand could hardly reach it, and that the iron plates about them made it very hard to come at them by fire, they ran away from the walls, and fled hastily out of the city, and fell upon those that shot at them. And thus did the people of Jotapata resist the Romans, while a great number of them were every day killed, without their being able to retort the evil upon their enemies; nor could they keep them out of the city without danger to themselves.

31. About this time it was that Vespasian sent out Trajan against a city called Japha, that lay near to Jotapata, and that desired innovations; and was puffed up with the unexpected length of the opposition of Jotapata. This Trajan was the commander of the tenth legion, and to him Vespasian committed one thousand horsemen and two thousand footmen. When Trajan came to the city, he found it hard to be taken, for besides the natural strength of its situation, it was also secured by a double wall; but when he saw the people of this city coming out of it, and ready to fight him, he joined battle with them, and after a short resistance which they made, he pursued after them: and as they fled to their first wall, the Romans followed them so closely, that they

fell in together with them : but when the Jews were endeavouring to get again within their second wall, their fellow-citizens shut them out, as being afraid that the Romans would force themselves in with them. It was certainly God, therefore, who brought the Romans to punish the Galileans, and did then expose the people of the city every one of them manifestly to be destroyed by their bloody enemies ; for they fell upon the gates in great crowds, and earnestly calling to those that kept them, and that by their names also, yet had they their throats cut in the very midst of their supplications; for the enemy shut the gates of the first wall, and their own citizens shut the gates of the second, so they were enclosed between two walls, and were slain in great numbers together ; many of them were run through by the swords of their own men, and many by their own swords, besides an immense number that were slain by the Romans ; —nor had they any courage to revenge themselves ; for there was added to the consternation they were in from the enemy, their being betrayed by their own friends, which quite broke their spirits : and at last they died, cursing not the Romans, but their own citizens, till they were all destroyed, being in number twelve thousand. So Trajan gathered that the city was empty of people that could fight, and although there should a few of them be therein, he supposed that they would be too timorous to venture upon any opposition ; so he reserved the taking of the city to the general. Accordingly he sent messengers to Vespasian, and desired him to send his son Titus to finish the victory he had gained. Vespasian hereupon imagining there might be some pains still necessary, sent his son with an army of five hundred horsemen, and one thousand footmen. So he came quickly to the city, and put his army in order, and set Trajan over the left wing, while he had the right himself, and led them to the siege : and when the soldiers brought ladders to be laid against the wall on every side, the Galileans opposed them from above for a while ; but soon afterwards they left the walls. Then did Titus's men leap into the the city, and seized upon it presently ; but when those that were in it were gotten together, there was a fierce battle between them ; for the men of power fell upon the Romans in the narrow streets, and the women threw whatsoever came next to hand at them, and sustained a fight with them of six hours' time; but when the fighting men were spent, the rest of the multitude had their throats cut, partly in the open air and partly in their own houses, both young and old together. So there were no males now remaining, besides infants, who with the women were carried as slaves into captivity ; so that the number of the slain, both now in the city and at the former fight, was fifteen thousand, and the captives were two thousand one hundred and thirty. This calamity befell the Galileans on the twenty-fifth day of the month Desius [Sivan.]

32. Nor did the Samaritans escape their share of misfortune at this time ; for they assembled themselves together upon the mountain called Gerizim, which is with them a holy mountain, and there they remained ; which collection of theirs, as well as the courageous minds they shewed, could not but threaten somewhat of war ; nor were they rendered wiser by the miseries that had come upon their neighbouring cities. They also, notwithstanding the great success the Romans had, marched on in an unreasonable manner, depending on their own weakness, and were disposed for any tumult upon its first appearance. Vespasian therefore thought it best to prevent their motions, and to cut off the foundation of their attempts; for although all Samaria had ever garrisons settled among them, yet did the number of those that were come to mount Gerizim, and their conspiracy together, give ground to fear what they would be at ; he therefore sent thither Cerealis, the commander of the fifth legion, with six hundred horsemen and three thousand footmen, who did not think it safe to go up to the mountain and give them battle, because many of the enemy were on the higher part of the ground ; so he encompassed all the lower part of the mountain with his army, and watched them all that day. Now it happened that the Samaritans, who were now destitute of water, were inflamed with a violent heat (for it was summer-time, and the multitude had not provided themselves with necessaries) insomuch that some of them died that very day with heat, while others of them preferred slavery before such a death as that was, and fled to the Romans ; by whom Cerealis understood that those who still stayed there were very much broken by their misfortunes. So he went up to the mountain, and having placed his forces round about the enemy, he, in the first place, exhorted them to take the security of his right hand, and come to terms with him, and thereby save themselves; and assured them, that if they would lay down their arms, he would secure them from any harm ; but when he could not prevail with them, he fell upon them and slew them all, being in number eleven thousand and six hundred. This was done on the twenty-seventh day of the month Desius [Sivan.] And these were the calamities that befell the Samaritans at this time.

33. But as the people of Jotapata still held out manfully, and bore up under their miseries beyond all that could be hoped for, on the forty-seventh day [of the siege] the banks cast up by the Romans were become higher than the wall ; on which day a certain deserter went to Vespasian, and told him, how few were left in the city, and how weak they were, and that they had been so worn out with perpetual watching, and also perpetual fighting, that they could not now oppose any force that came against them, and that they might be taken by stratagem, if any one would attack them ; for that about the last watch of the night, when they thought they might have some rest from the hardships they were under, and when a morning sleep used to come upon them, as they were thoroughly weary, he said the watch used to fall asleep : accordingly his advice was, that they should make their attack at that hour. But Vespasian had a suspicion about this deserter, as knowing how faithful the Jews were to one another, and how much they despised any punishments that could be inflicted on them ; this last because one of the people of Jotapata had undergone all sorts of torments, and though they made him pass through a fiery trial of his enemies in his examination, yet would he inform them nothing of the affairs within the city, and as he was crucified, smiled at them! However, the probability there was in the relation itself did partly confirm the truth of what the deserter told him, and they thought he might probably speak the truth. However, Vespasian thought they should be no great sufferers if the report was a sham ; so he commanded them to keep the man in custody, and prepared the army for taking the city.

34. According to which resolution they marched without noise, at the hour that had been told them, to the wall ; and it was Titus himself that first got upon it, with one of his tribunes, Domitius Sabinus, and a few of the fifteenth legion

along with him. So they cut the throats of the watch, and entered the city very quietly. After these came Cerealis the tribune, and Placidus, and led on those that were under them. Now when the citadel was taken, and the enemy were in the very midst of the city, and when it was already day, yet was not the taking of the city known by those that held it; for a great many of them were fast asleep, and a great mist, which then by chance fell upon the city, hindered those that got up from distinctly seeing the case they were in, till the whole Roman army was gotten in, and they were raised up only to find the miseries they were under; and as they were slaying, they perceived the city was taken. And for the Romans, they so well remembered what they had suffered during the siege, that they spared none, nor pitied any, but drove the people down the precipice from the citadel, and slew them as they drove them down; at which time the difficulties of the place hindered those that were still able to fight from defending themselves; for as they were distressed in the narrow streets, and could not keep their feet sure along the precipice, they were overpowered with the crowd of those that came fighting them down from the citadel. This provoked a great many, even of those chosen men that were about Josephus, to kill themselves with their own hands; for when they saw they could kill none of the Romans, they resolved to prevent being killed by the Romans, and got together in great numbers, in the utmost parts of the city, and killed themselves.

35. However, such of the watch as at the first perceived they were taken, and ran away as fast as they could, went up into one of the towers on the north side of the city, and for a while defended themselves there; but as they were encompassed with a multitude of enemies, they tried to use their right hands, when it was too late, and at length they cheerfully offered their necks to be cut off by those that stood over them. And the Romans might have boasted that the conclusion of that siege was without blood [on their side,] if there had not been a centurion, Antonius, who was slain at the taking of the city. His death was occasioned by the following treachery: for there was one of those that fled into the caverns, which were a great number, who desired that this Antonius would reach him his right hand for his security, and would assure him that he would preserve him, and give him his assistance in getting up out of the cavern; accordingly, he incautiously reached him his right hand, when the other man prevented him, and stabbed him under his loins with a spear, and killed him immediately.

36. And on this day, the Romans slew all the multitude that appeared openly; but on the following days they searched the hiding-places, and fell upon those that were under ground, and in the caverns, and went thus through every age, excepting the infants and the women, and of these there were gathered together as captives twelve hundred; and as for those that were slain at the taking of the city, and in the former fights, they were numbered to be forty thousand. So Vespasian gave order that the city should be entirely demolished, and all the fortifications burnt down. And thus was Jotapata taken, in the thirteenth year of the reign of Nero, on the first day of the month Panemus [Tamuz.]

CHAPTER VIII

HOW JOSEPHUS WAS DISCOVERED BY A WOMAN, AND WAS WILLING TO DELIVER HIMSELF UP TO THE ROMANS; AND WHAT DISCOURSE HE HAD WITH HIS OWN MEN WHEN THEY ENDEAVOURED TO HINDER HIM; AND WHAT HE SAID TO VESPASIAN, WHEN HE WAS BROUGHT TO HIM; AND AFTER WHAT MANNER VESPASIAN USED HIM AFTERWARDS

1. AND now the Romans searched for Josephus, both out of the hatred they bore him, and because their general was very desirous to have him taken; for he reckoned that if he were once taken, the greatest part of the war would be over. They then searched among the dead, and looked into the most concealed recesses of the city; but as the city was first taken, he was assisted by a certain supernatural providence; for he withdrew himself from the enemy when he was in the midst of them, and leaped into a certain deep pit, whereto there adjoined a large den at one side of it, which den could not be seen by those that were above ground; and here he met with forty persons of eminence that had concealed themselves, and with provisions enough to satisfy them for not a few days. So in the day-time he hid himself from the enemy, who had seized upon all places; and in the night-time he got up out of the den, and looked about for some way of escaping, and took exact notice of the watch: but as all places were guarded everywhere on his account, that there was no way of getting off unseen, he went down again into the den. Thus he concealed himself two days: but on the third day, when they had taken a woman who had been with them, he was discovered. Whereupon Vespasian sent immediately and zealously two tribunes, Paulinus and Gallicanus, and ordered them to give Josephus their right hands as a security for his life, and to exhort him to come up.

2. So they came and invited the man to come up, and gave him assurances that his life should be preserved; but they did not prevail with him; for he gathered suspicions from the probability there was that one who had done so many things against the Romans must suffer for it, though not from the mild temper of those that invited him. However, he was afraid that he was invited to come up in order to be punished, until Vespasian sent besides these a third tribune, Nicanor, to him; he was one that was well known to Josephus, and had been his familiar acquaintance in old time. When he was come, he enlarged upon the natural mildness of the Romans towards those they have once conquered; and told him, that he had behaved himself so valiantly, that the commanders rather admired than hated him; that the general was very desirous to have him brought to him, not in order to punish him, for that he could do though he should not come voluntarily, but that he was determined to preserve a man of his courage. He moreover added this, that Vespasian, had he been resolved to impose upon him, would not have sent to him a friend of his own, nor put the fairest colour upon the vilest action, by pretending friendship and meaning perfidiousness; nor would he have himself acquiesced, or come to him, had it been to deceive him.

3. Now, as Josephus began to hesitate with himself about Nicanor's proposal, the soldiery were so angry, that they ran hastily to set fire to the den; but the tribune would not permit them so to do, as being very desirous to take the man alive. And now, as Nicanor lay hard at Josephus to comply, and he understood how the multitude of the enemy threatened him, he called to mind the dreams which he had dreamed

in the night-time, whereby God had signified to him beforehand both the future calamities of the Jews, and the event that concerned the Roman emperors. Now Josephus was able to give shrewd conjectures about the interpretation of such dreams as have been ambiguously delivered by God. Moreover, he was not unacquainted with the prophecies contained in the sacred books, as being a priest himself, and of the posterity of priests : and just then was he in an ecstasy ; and setting before him the tremendous images of the dreams he had lately had, he put up a secret prayer to God, and said, —"Since it pleaseth thee, who hast created the Jewish nation, to depress the same, and since all their good fortune is gone over to the Romans, and since thou hast made choice of this soul of mine to foretell what is to come to pass hereafter, I willingly give them my hands, and am content to live. And I protest openly, that I do not go over to the Romans as a deserter of the Jews, but as a minister from thee."

4. When he had said this, he complied with Nicanor's invitation. But when those Jews who had fled with him understood that he yielded to those that invited him to come up, they came about him in a body, and cried out, "Nay, indeed, now may the laws of our forefathers, which God ordained himself, well groan to purpose ; that God we mean who hath created the souls of the Jews of such a temper that they despise death. O Josephus : art thou still fond of life ; and canst thou bear to see the light in a state of slavery ? How soon hast thou forgotten thyself ! How many hast thou persuaded to lose their lives for liberty ! Thou hast therefore had a false reputation for manhood, and a like false reputation for wisdom, if thou canst hope for preservation from those against whom thou hast fought so zealously, and art however willing to be preserved by them, if they be in earnest. But although the good fortune of the Romans hath made thee forget thyself, we ought to take care that the glory of our forefathers may not be tarnished. We will lend thee our right hand and a sword ; and if thou wilt die willingly, thou wilt die as general of the Jews ; but if unwillingly, thou wilt die as a traitor to them." As soon as they said this, they began to thrust their swords at him, and threatened they would kill him, if he thought of yielding himself to the Romans.

5. Upon this, Josephus was afraid of their attacking him, and yet thought he should be a betrayer of the commands of God if he died before they were delivered. So he began to talk like a philosopher to them in the distress he was then in, when he said thus to them :—"O my friends, why are we so earnest to kill ourselves ? and why do we set our soul and body, which are such dear companions, at such variance ? Can any one pretend that I am not the man I was formerly ? Nay, the Romans are sensible how that matter stands well enough. It is a brave thing to die in war ; but so that it be according to the law of war, by the hand of conquerors. If, therefore, I avoid death from the sword of the Romans, I am truly worthy to be killed by my own sword, and my own hand ; but if they admit of mercy, and would spare their enemy, how much more ought we to have mercy upon ourselves, and to spare ourselves ! for it is certainly a foolish thing to do that to ourselves which we quarrel with them for doing unto us. I confess freely that it is a brave thing to die for liberty ; but still so that it be in war, and done by those who take that liberty from us ; but at present our enemies do neither meet us in battle, nor do they kill us. Now, he is equally a coward who will not die when he is obliged to die, and he who will die when he is not obliged so to do. What are we afraid of, when we will not go up to the Romans ? Is it death ? If so, what are we afraid of, when we but suspect our enemies will inflict it on us, shall we inflict it on ourselves for certain ? But it may be said, we must be slaves. And are we, then, in a clear state of liberty at present ? It may also be said, that it is a manly act for one to kill himself. No, certainly, but a most unmanly one ; as I should esteem that pilot to be an arrant coward who, out of fear of a storm, should sink his ship of his own accord. Now, self-murder is a crime most remote from the common nature of all animals, and an instance of impiety against God our Creator : nor indeed is there an animal that dies by its own contrivance, or by its own means ; for the desire of life is a law engraven in them all ; on which account we deem those that openly take it away from us to be our enemies, and those that do it by treachery, are punished for so doing. And do you not think that God is very angry when a man does injury to what he hath bestowed on him ? for from him it is that we have received our being ; and we ought to leave it to his disposal to take that being away from us. The bodies of all men are indeed mortal, and are created out of corruptible matter ; but the soul is ever immortal, and is a portion of the Divinity that inhabits our bodies. Besides, if any one destroys or abuses a *depositum* he hath received from a mere man, he is esteemed a wicked and perfidious person ; but then if any one cast out of his body this divine *depositum*, can we imagine that he who is there affronted doth not know of it ? Moreover, our law justly ordains, that slaves who run away from their masters shall be punished, though the masters they ran away from may have been wicked masters to them. And shall we endeavour to run away from God, who is the best of all masters, and not think ourselves highly guilty of impiety ? Do not you know that those who depart out of this life, according to the law of nature, and pay that debt which was received from God, when he that lent it us is pleased to require it back, enjoy eternal fame ? that their houses and their posterity are sure, that their souls are pure and obedient, and obtain a most holy place in heaven, from whence, in the revolution of ages, they are again sent into pure bodies ; while the souls of those whose hands have acted madly against themselves, are received by the darkest place in Hades, and while God, who is their father, punishes those that offend against either of them in their posterity ? for which reason God hates such doings, and the crime is punished by our most wise legislator. Accordingly our laws determine, that the bodies of such as kill themselves should be exposed till the sun be set, without burial, although at the same time it be allowed them to be lawful to bury our enemies [sooner.] The laws of other nations also enjoin such men's hands to be cut off when they are dead, which had been made use of in destroying themselves when alive, while they reckoned that as the body is alien from the soul, so is the hand alien from the body. It is therefore, my friends, a right thing to reason justly, and not add to the calamities which men bring upon us, impiety towards our Creator. If we have a mind to preserve ourselves, let us do it ; for to be preserved by those our enemies, to whom we have given so many demonstrations of our courage, is no way inglorious ; but if we have a mind

to die, it is good to die by the hand of those that have conquered us. For my part, I will not run over to our enemies' quarters, in order to be a traitor to myself; for certainly I should then be much more foolish than those that deserted to the enemy, since they did it in order to save themselves, and I should do it for my own destruction. However, I heartily wish the Romans may prove treacherous in this matter; for if, after their offer of their right hand for security, I be slain by them, I shall die cheerfully, and carry away with me the sense of their perfidiousness as a consolation greater than victory itself."

6. Now these and many the like motives did Josephus use to these men, to prevent their murdering themselves; but desperation had shut their ears, as having long ago devoted themselves to die, and they were irritated at Josephus. They then ran upon him with their swords in their hands, one from one quarter, and another from another, and called him a coward, and every one of them appeared openly as if he were ready to smite him; but he, calling to one of them by name, and looking like a general to another, and taking a third by the hand, and making a fourth ashamed of himself, by praying him to forbear, and being in this condition distracted with various passions (as he well might in the great distress he was then in,) he kept off every one of their swords from killing him, and was forced to do like such wild beasts as are encompassed about on every side, who always turn themselves against those that last touched them. Nay, some of their right hands were debilitated by the reverence they bare to their general in these fatal calamities, and their swords dropped out of their hands; and not a few of them were there, who, when they aimed to smite him with their swords, were not thoroughly either willing or able to do it.

7. However, in this extreme distress, he was not destitute of his usual sagacity; but trusting himself to the providence of God, he put his life into hazard [in the manner following]:—"And now," said he, "since it is resolved among you that you will die, come on, let us commit our mutual deaths to determination by lot. He whom the lot falls to first, let him be killed by him that hath the second lot, and thus fortune shall make its progress through us all; nor shall any of us perish by his own right hand, for it would be unfair if, when the rest are gone, somebody should repent and save himself." This proposal appeared to them to be very just; and when he had prevailed with them to determine this matter by lots, he drew one of the lots for himself also. He who had the first lot laid his neck bare to him who had the next, as supposing that the general would die among them immediately; for they thought death, if Josephus might die with them, was sweeter than life; yet was he with another left to the last, whether we must say it happened so by chance, or whether by the providence of God: and as he was very desirous neither to be condemned by the lot, nor, if he had been left to the last, to imbrue his right hand in the blood of his countryman, he persuaded him to trust his fidelity to him, and to live as well as himself.

8. Thus Josephus escaped in the war with the Romans, and in this his own war with his friends, and was led by Nicanor to Vespasian; but now all the Romans ran together to see him, and as the multitude pressed one upon another about their general, there was a tumult of a various kind; while some rejoiced that Josephus was taken, and some threatened him, and some crowded to see him very near; but those that were more remote cried out to have this their enemy put to death, while those that were near called to mind the actions he had done, and a deep concern appeared at the change of his fortune. Nor were there any of the Roman commanders, how much soever they had been enraged at him before, but relented when they came to the sight of him. Above all the rest, Titus's own valour, and Josephus's own patience under his afflictions, made him pity him, as did also the commiseration of his age, when he recalled to mind that but a little while ago he was fighting, but lay now in the hands of his enemies, which made him consider the power of fortune, and how quick is the turn of affairs in war, and how no state of men is sure; for which reason he then made a great many more to be of the same pitiful temper with himself, and induced them to commiserate Josephus. He was also of great weight in persuading his father to preserve him. However, Vespasian gave strict orders that he should be kept with great caution, as though he would, in a very little time, send him to Nero.

9. When Josephus heard him give those orders, he said that he had somewhat in his mind that he would willingly say to himself alone. When therefore they were all ordered to withdraw, excepting Titus, and two of their friends, he said, "Thou, O Vespasian, thinkest no more than that thou hast taken Josephus himself captive; but I come to thee as a messenger of greater tidings; for had not I been sent by God to thee, I knew what was the law of the Jews in this case, and how it becomes generals to die. Dost thou send me to Nero? For why? Are Nero's successors till they come to thee still alive? Thou O Vespasian, art Cæsar and emperor, thou, and thy son. Bind me now still faster, and keep me for thyself, for thou, O Cæsar, art not only lord over me, but over the land and sea, and all mankind; and certainly I deserve to be kept in closer custody than I am now in, in order to be punished, if I rashly affirm anything of God." When he had said this, Vespasian at present did not believe him, but supposed that Josephus said this as a cunning trick, in order to his own preservation; but in a little time he was convinced, and believed what he said to be true, God himself erecting his expectations, so as to think of obtaining the empire, and by other signs foreshewing his advancement. He also found Josephus to have spoken the truth on other occasions; for one of those friends that were present at that secret conference, said to Josephus, "I cannot but wonder how thou couldst not foretell to the people of Jotapata that they should be taken, nor couldst fortell this captivity which hath happened to thyself, unless what thou now sayest to be a vain thing, in order to avoid the rage that is risen against thyself." To which Josephus replied, "I did foretell to the people of Jotapata that they would be taken on the forty-seventh day, and that I should be caught alive by the Romans." Now when Vespasian had inquired of the captives privately about these predictions, he found them to be true, and then he began to believe those that concerned himself. Yet did he not set Josephus at liberty from his bonds, but bestowed on him suits of clothes, and other precious gifts; he treated him also in a very obliging manner, and continued so to do, Titus still joining his interest in the honours that were done him.

CHAPTER IX

HOW JOPPA WAS TAKEN, AND TIBERIAS DELIVERED UP

1. Now Vespasian returned to Ptolemais on the fourth day of the month Panemus [Tamus,] and from thence he came to Cesarea, which lay by the seaside. This was a very great city of Judea, and for the greatest part inhabited by Greeks: the citizens here received both the Roman army and its general with all sorts of acclamations and rejoicings, and this partly out of the goodwill they bore to the Romans, but principally out of the hatred they bore to those that were conquered by them; on which account they came clamouring against Josephus in crowds, and desired he might be put to death; but Vespasian passed over this petition concerning him, as offered by the injudicious multitude, with a bare silence. Two of the legions also he placed at Cesarea, that they might there take their winter-quarters, as perceiving the city very fit for such a purpose; but he placed the fifth and tenth at Scythopolis, that he might not distress Cesarea with the entire army. This place was warm, even in winter, as it was suffocating hot in the summer-time, by reason of its situation in a plain, and near to the sea [of Galilee.]

2. In the meantime there were gathered together, as well such as had seditiously got out from among their enemies, as those that had escaped out of the demolished cities, which were in all a great number, and repaired Joppa, which had been left desolate by Cestius, that it might serve them for a place of refuge; and because the adjoining region had been laid waste in the war, and was not capable of supporting them, they determined to go off to sea. They also built themselves a great many piratical ships, and turned pirates upon the seas near to Syria, and Phœnicia, and Egypt, and made those seas unnavigable to all men. Now, as soon as Vespasian knew of their conspiracy, he sent both footmen and horsemen to Joppa, which was unguarded in the nighttime; however, those that were in it perceived that they should be attacked, and were afraid of it; yet did they not endeavour to keep the Romans out, but fled to their ships, and lay at sea all night, out of the reach of their darts.

3. Now Joppa is not naturally a haven, for it ends in a rough shore, where all the rest of it is straight; but the two ends bend towards each other, where there are deep precipices, and great stones that jut out into the sea, and where the chains wherewith Andromeda was bound have left their footsteps, which attest to the antiquity of that fable; but the north wind opposes and beats upon the shore, and dashes mighty waves against the rocks which receive them, and renders the haven more dangerous than the country they had deserted. Now as those people of Joppa were floating about in this sea, in the morning there fell a violent wind upon them; it is called by those that sail there "the black north wind," and there dashed their ships one against another, and dashed some against the rocks, and carried many of them by force, while they strove against the opposite waves, into the main sea; for the shore was so rocky, and had so many of the enemy upon it, that they were afraid to come to land; nay, the waves rose so very high, that they drowned them; nor was there any place whither they could fly, nor any way to save themselves; while they were thrust out of the sea, by the violence of the wind, if they stayed where they were, and out of the city by the violence of the Romans; and much lamentation there was when the ships were dashed one against another, and a terrible noise when they were broken to pieces; and some of the multitude that were in them were covered with the waves, and so perished, and a great many were embarrassed with shipwrecks; but some of them thought that to die by their own swords was lighter than by the sea, and so they killed themselves before they were drowned! although the greatest part of them were carried by the waves and dashed to pieces against the abrupt parts of the rocks, insomuch that the sea was bloody a long way, and the maritime parts were full of dead bodies; for the Romans came upon those that were carried to the shore, and destroyed them; and the number of the bodies that were thus thrown out of the sea was four thousand and two hundred. The Romans also took the city without opposition, and utterly destroyed it.

4. And thus was Joppa taken twice by the Romans in a little time; but Vespasian, in order to prevent these pirates from coming thither any more, erected a camp there, where the citadel of Joppa had been, and left a body of horse in it, with a few footmen; that these last might stay there and guard the camp, and the horsemen might spoil the country that lay round it, and might destroy the neighbouring villages and smaller cities. So these troops overran the country, as they were ordered to do, and every day cut to pieces and laid desolate the whole region.

5. But now, when the fate of Jotapata was related at Jerusalem, a great many at the first disbelieved it, on account of the vastness of the calamity, and because they had no eye-witness to attest the truth of what was related about it; for not one person was saved to be a messenger of that news, but a fame was spread abroad at random that the city was taken, as such fame usually spreads bad news about. However, the truth was known by degrees, from the places near Jotapata, and appeared to all to be too true. Yet were there fictitious stories added to what was really done; for it was reported that Josephus was slain at the taking of the city; which piece of news filled Jerusalem full of sorrow. In every house also, and among all to whom any of the slain were allied, there was a lamentation for them; but the mourning for the commander was a public one; and some mourned for those that had lived with them, others for their kindred, others for their friends, and others for their brethren, but all mourned for Josephus; insomuch that the lamentation did not cease in the city before the thirtieth day; and a great many hired mourners,* with their pipes, who should begin the melancholy ditties for them.

6. But as the truth came out in time, it appeared how the affairs of Jotapata really stood; yet it was found that the death of Josephus was a fiction; and when they understood that he was alive, and was among the Romans, and that the commanders treated him at another rate than they treated captives, they were as vehemently angry at him now as they had shewn their goodwill before, when he appeared to have been dead. He was also abused by some as having been a coward, and by others as a deserter; and the city was full of indignation at him, and of reproaches cast upon him; their rage was also aggravated by their afflictions, and more inflamed by their ill-success; and what usually becomes an occasion of caution to wise men, I mean

---

* These public mourners, hired upon the supposed death of Josephus, and the real death of many more, illustrate some passages in the Bible, which suppose the same custom, as Matt. xii. 17.

affliction, became a spur to them to venture on further calamities, and the end of one misery became still the beginning of another; they therefore resolved to fall on the Romans the more vehemently, as resolving to be revenged on him in revenging themselves on the Romans. And this was the state of Jerusalem as to the troubles which now came upon it.

7. But Vespasian, in order to see the kingdom of Agrippa, while the king persuaded himself so to do, (partly, in order to his treating the general and his army in the best and most splendid manner his private affairs would enable him to do, and partly that he might, by their means, correct such things as were amiss in his government,) he removed from that Cesarea which was by the seaside, and went to that which is called Cesarea Philippi;* and there he refreshed his army for twenty days, and was himself feasted by king Agrippa, where he also returned public thanks to God for the good success he had had in his undertakings. But as soon as he was informed that Tiberias was fond of innovations, and that Taricheæ had revolted, both which cities were parts of the kingdom of Agrippa, and was satisfied within himself that the Jews were everywhere perverted [from their obedience to their governors,] he thought it seasonable to make an expedition against those cities, and that for the sake of Agrippa, and in order to bring his cities to reason. So he sent away his son Titus to [the other] Cesarea, that he might bring the army that lay there to Scythopolis, which is the largest city of Decapolis, and in the neighbourhood of Tiberias, whither he came, and where he waited for his son. He then came with three legions, and pitched his camp thirty furlongs off Tiberias, at a certain station easily seen by the innovators; it is named Sennabris. He also sent Valerian, a decurion, with fifty horsemen, to speak peaceably to those that were in the city, and to exhort them to give him assurances of their fidelity; for he had heard that the people were desirous of peace, but were obliged by some of the seditious part to join with them, and so were forced to fight for them. When Valerian had marched up to the place, and was near the wall, he alighted off his horse, and made those that were with him do the same, that they might not be thought to come to skirmish with them; but before they could come to a discourse one with another, the most potent men among the seditious made a sally upon them armed; their leader was one whose name was Jesus, the Son of Shaphat, the principal head of a band of robbers. Now Valerian, neither thinking it safe to fight contrary to the commands of the general, though he were secure of a victory, and knowing that it was a very hazardous undertaking for a few to fight with many, for those that were unprovided to fight those that were ready, and being on other accounts surprised at this unexpected onset of the Jews, he ran away on foot, as did five of the rest in like manner, and left their horses behind them; which horses Jesus led away into the city, and rejoiced as if they had taken them in battle, and not by treachery.

8. Now the seniors of the people, and such as were of principal authority among them, fearing what would be the issue of this matter, fled to the camp of the Romans; they then took their king along with them, and fell down before Vespasian, to supplicate his favour, and besought him not to overlook them, nor to impute the madness of a few to the whole city, to spare a people that had been ever civil and obliging to the Romans; but to bring the authors of this revolt to due punishment, who had hitherto so watched them, that though they were zealous to give them the security of their right hands of a long time, yet could they not accomplish the same. With those supplications the general complied, although he was very angry at the whole city about the carrying off his horses, and this because he saw that Agrippa was under a great concern for them. So when Vespasian and Agrippa had accepted of their right hands by way of security, Jesus and his party thought it not safe for them to continue at Tiberias, so they ran away to Taricheæ. The next day Vespasian sent Trajan before, with some horsemen to the citadel, to make trial of the multitude, whether they were all disposed for peace; and as soon as he knew that the people were of the same mind with the petitioners, he took his army, and went to the city; upon which the citizens opened to him their gates, and met him with acclamations of joy, and called him their saviour and benefactor. But as the army was a great while in getting in at the gates, they were so narrow, Vespasian commanded the south wall to be broken down, and so made a broad passage for their entrance. However, he charged them to abstain from rapine and injustice, in order to gratify the king; and on his account spared the rest of the wall, while the king undertook for them that they should continue [faithful to the Romans] for the time to come. And thus did he restore this city to a quiet state, after it had been grievously afflicted by the sedition.

CHAPTER X

HOW TARICHEÆ WAS TAKEN; A DESCRIPTION OF THE RIVER JORDAN, AND OF THE COUNTRY OF GENNESARETH

1. AND now Vespasian pitched his camp between this city and Taricheæ, but fortified his camp more strongly, as suspecting that he should be forced to stay there, and have a long war; for all the innovators had gotten together at Taricheæ, as relying upon the strength of the city, and on the lake that lay by it. This lake is called by the people of the country the *Lake of Gennesareth*. The city itself is situated like Tiberias, at the bottom of a mountain; and on those sides which are not washed by the sea, had been strongly fortified by Josephus, though not so strongly as Tiberias; for the wall of Tiberias had been built at the beginning of the Jews' revolt, when he had great plenty of money, and great power, but Taricheæ partook only the remains of that liberality. Yet had they a great number of ships gotten ready upon the lake, that in case they were beaten at land, they might retire to them; and they were so fitted up, that they might undertake a sea fight also. But as the Romans were building a wall about their camp, Jesus and his party were neither affrighted at their number nor at the good order they were in, but made a sally upon them; and at the very first onset the builders of the wall were dispersed; and these pulled what little they had before built to pieces; but as soon as they saw the armed men getting together, and before they had suffered anything

* Of this Cesarea Philippi, twice mentioned in our New Testament, (Matt. xvi. 13; Mark viii. 27,) there are coins still extant.

themselves, they retired to their own men. But then the Romans pursued them, and drove them into their ships, where they launched out as far as might give them an opportunity of reaching the Romans with what they threw at them, and then cast anchor, and brought their ships close, as in a line of battle, and thence fought the enemy from the sea, who were themselves at land. But Vespasian, hearing that a great multitude of them were gotten together in the plain that was before the city, he thereupon sent his son, with six hundred chosen horsemen, to disperse them.

2. But when Titus perceived that the enemy was very numerous, he sent to his father, and informed him that he should want more forces. But as he saw a great many of the horsemen eager to fight, and that before any succours could come to them, and that yet some of them were privately under a sort of consternation at the Jews, he stood in a place whence he might be heard, and said to them, "My brave Romans! for it is right for me to put you in mind what nation you are, in the beginning of my speech, that so you may not be ignorant who you are, and who they are against whom we are going to fight. For as to us, Romans, no part of the habitable earth hath been able to escape our hands hitherto; but as for the Jews, that I may speak of them too, though they have been already beaten, yet do they not give up the cause; and a sad thing it would be for us to grow weary under good success, when they bear up under their misfortunes. As to the alacrity which you shew publicly, I see it, and rejoice at it; yet am I afraid lest the multitude of the enemy should bring a concealed fright upon some of you; let such a one consider again, who we are that are to fight; and who those are against whom we are to fight. Now these Jews, though they be very bold and great despisers of death, are but a disorderly body, and unskilful in war, and may rather be called a rout than an army; while I need say nothing of our skill and our good order; for this is the reason why we Romans alone are exercised for war in time of peace, that we may not think of number for number when we come to fight with our enemies; for what advantage should we reap by our continual sort of warfare, if we must still be equal in number to such as have not been used to war! Consider further, that you are to have a conflict with men in effect unarmed, while you are well armed; with footmen, while you are horsemen; with those that have no good general, while you have one, and as these advantages make you in effect manifold more than you are, so do their disadvantages mightily diminish their number. Now it is not the multitude of men, though they be soldiers, that manage wars with success, but it is their bravery that does it, though they be but a few; for a few are easily set in battle array, and can easily assist one another, while over-numerous armies are more hurt by themselves than by their enemies. It is boldness and rashness, the effects of madness, that conduct of the Jews. Those passions indeed make a great figure when they succeed, but are quite extinguished upon the least ill success; but we are led on by courage, and obedience, and fortitude, which shews itself indeed in our good fortune, but still does not for ever desert us in our ill fortune. Nay, indeed, your fighting is to be on greater motives than those of the Jews; for although they run the hazard of war for liberty, and for their country, yet what can be a greater motive to us than glory? and that it may never be said, that after we have got dominion of the habitable earth, the Jews are able to confront us. We must also reflect upon this, that there is no fear of our suffering any incurable disaster in the present case; for those that are ready to assist us are many and at hand also; yet it is in our power to seize upon this victory ourselves, and I think we ought to prevent the coming of those my father is sending to us for our assistance, that our success may be peculiar to ourselves, and of greater reputation to us; and I cannot but think this an opportunity wherein my father, and I, and you, shall be all put to the trial, whether he be worthy of his former glorious performances, whether I be his son in reality, and whether you be really my soldiers; for it is usual for my father to conquer; and for myself, I should not bear the thoughts of returning to him if I were once taken by the enemy; and how will you be able to avoid being ashamed, if you do not shew equal courage with your commander, when he goes before you into danger? For you know very well that I shall go into danger first, and make the first attack upon the enemy. Do not you therefore desert me, but persuade yourselves that God will be assisting to my onset. Know this also before we begin, that we shall now have better success than we should have, if we were to fight at a distance."

3. As Titus was saying this, an extraordinary fury fell upon the men; and as Trajan was already come before the fight began, with four hundred horsemen, they were uneasy at it, because the reputation of the victory would be diminished by being common to so many. Vespasian had also sent both Antonius and Silo, with two thousand archers, and had given them in charge to seize upon the mountain that was over-against the city, and repel those that were upon the wall; which archers did as they were commanded, and prevented those that attempted to assist them that way; and now Titus made his own horse march first against the enemy, as did the others with a great noise after him, and extended themselves upon the plain as wide as the enemy who confronted them; by which means they appeared much more numerous than they really were. Now the Jews, although they were surprised at their onset, and at their good order, made resistance against their attacks for a little while; but when they were pricked with their long poles, and overborne by the violent noise of the horsemen, they came to be trampled under their feet; many also of them were slain on every side, which made them disperse themselves and run to the city, as fast as every one was able. So Titus pressed upon the hindmost, and slew them; and of the rest, some he fell upon as they stood on heaps, and some he prevented, and met them in the mouth, and run them through; many also he leaped upon as they fell one upon another, and trod them down, and cut off all the retreat they had to the wall, and turned them back into the plain, till at last they forced a passage by their multitude, and got away, and ran into the city.

4. But now there fell out a terrible sedition among them within the city; for the inhabitants themselves, who had possessions there, and to whom the city belonged, were not disposed to fight from the very beginning; and now the less so, because they had been beaten: but the foreigners who were very numerous, would force them to fight so much the more, insomuch that there was a clamour and a tumult among them, as all mutually angry at one another; and when Titus heard this tumult, for he was not far from the wall, he cried out, "Fellow-soldiers, now is the time; and why do we make any delay, when

God is giving up the Jews to us? Take the victory which is given you: do not you hear what a noise they make? Those that have escaped our hands are in an uproar against one another. We have the city if we make haste; but besides haste, we must undergo some labour, and use some courage; for no great thing used to be accomplished without danger; accordingly we must not only prevent their uniting again, which necessity will soon compel them to do, but we must also prevent the coming of our own men to our assistance, that as few as we are we may conquer so great a multitude, and may ourselves alone take the city.

5. As soon as ever Titus had said this, he leaped upon his horse, and rode apace down to the lake; by which lake he marched, and entered into the city the first of them all, as did the others soon after him. Hereupon those that were upon the walls were seized with a terror at the boldness of the attempt, nor durst any one venture to fight with him, or to hinder him; so they left guarding the city, and some of these that were about Jesus fled over the country, while others of them ran down to the lake, and met the enemy in the teeth, and some were slain as they were getting up into ships, but others of them, as they attempted to overtake those that were already gone aboard. There was also a great slaughter made in the city, while those foreigners that had not fled away already, made opposition; but the natural inhabitants were killed without fighting; for in hopes of Titus's giving them his right hand for their security, and out of the consciousness that they had not given any consent to the war, they avoided fighting, till Titus had slain the authors of this revolt, and then put a stop to any further slaughters, out of commiseration of these inhabitants of the place; but for those that had fled to the lake, upon seeing the city taken, they sailed as far as they possibly could from the enemy.

6. Hereupon Titus sent one of his horsemen to his father, and let him know the good news of what he had done; at which, as was natural, he was very joyful, both on account of the courage and glorious actions of his son; for he thought that now the greatest part of the war was over. He then came thither himself, and set men to guard the city, and gave them command to take care that nobody got privately out of it, but to kill such as attempted so to do; and on the next day he went down to the lake, and commanded that vessels should be fitted up, in order to pursue those that had escaped in the ships. These vessels were quickly gotten ready accordingly, because there was great plenty of materials, and a great number of artificers also.

7. Now this lake of Gennesareth is so called from the country adjoining to it. Its breadth is forty furlongs, and its length one hundred and forty; its waters are sweet, and very agreeable for drinking, for they are finer than the thick waters of other fens; the lake is also pure, and on every side ends directly at the shores and at the sand; it is also of a temperate nature when you draw it up, and of a more gentle nature than river or fountain water, and yet always cooler than one could expect in so diffuse a place as this is. Now, when this water is kept in the open air, it is as cold as that snow which the country people are accustomed to make by night in summer. There are several kinds of fish in it, different both to the taste and the sight from those elsewhere: it is divided into two parts by the river Jordan. Now Panium is thought to be the fountain of Jordan, but in reality it is carried thither after an occult manner from the

place called Phiala: this place lies as you go up to Trachonitis, and is a hundred and twenty furlongs from Cesarea, and is not far out of the road on the right hand; and indeed it hath its name of Phiala [vial or bow] very justly, from the roundness of its circumference, as being round like a wheel; its water continues always up to its edges, without either sinking or running over; and as this origin of Jordan was formerly not known, it was discovered so to be when Philip was tetrarch of Trachonitis; for he had chaff thrown into Phiala, and it was found at Panium, where the ancients thought the fountain-head of the river was, whither it had been therefore carried [by the waters.] As for Panium itself, its natural beauty hath been improved by the royal liberality of Agrippa, and adorned at his expenses. Now Jordan's visible stream arises from this cavern, and divides the marshes and fens of the lake Semechonitis: when it hath run another hundred and twenty furlongs, it first passes by the city Julias, and then passes through the middle of the lake Gennesareth; after which it runs a long way over a desert, and then makes its exit into the lake Asphaltitis.

8. The country also that lies over against this lake hath the same name of Gennesareth; its nature is wonderful as well as its beauty; its soil is so fruitful that all sorts of trees can grow upon it, and the inhabitants accordingly plant all sorts of trees there; for the temper of the air is so well mixed, that it agrees very well with those several sorts, particularly walnuts, which require the coldest air, flourish there in vast plenty; there are palm-trees also, which grow best in hot air; fig-trees also and olives grow near them, which yet require an air that is more temperate. One may call this place the ambition of nature, where it forces those plants that are naturally enemies to one another to agree together: it is a happy contention of the seasons, as if every one of them laid claim to this country; for it not only nourishes different sorts of autumnal fruit beyond men's expectation, but preserves them a great while; it supplies men with the principal fruits, with grapes and figs continually, during ten months in the year,* and the rest of the fruits as they become ripe together, through the whole year; for besides the good temperature of the air, it is also watered from a most fertile fountain. The people of the country call it Capharnaum. Some have thought it to be a vein of the Nile, because it produces the Coracin fish as well as that lake does which is near to Alexandria. The length of this country extends itself along the banks of this lake that bears the same name, for thirty furlongs, and is in breadth twenty; and this is the nature of that place.

9. But now, when the vessels were gotten ready, Vespasian put upon ship-board as many of his forces as he thought sufficient to be too hard for those that were upon the lake, and set sail after them. Now these which were driven into the lake could neither fly to the land, where all was in their enemies' hand, and in war against them, nor could they fight upon the level of the sea, for their ships were small and fitted only for piracy; they were too weak to fight with Vespasian's vessels, and the mariners that were in them were so few, that they were afraid to come near the Romans, who attacked them in great numbers. However, as they sailed round about the

---

* It may be worth our while to observe here, that near this lake of Gennesareth grapes and figs hang on the trees ten months of the year.

vessels, and sometimes as they came near them, they threw stones at the Romans when they were a good way off, or came closer and fought them ; yet did they receive the greatest harm themselves in both cases. As for the stones they threw at the Romans, they only made a sound one after another, for they threw them against such as were in their armour, while the Roman darts could reach the Jews themselves ; and when they ventured to come near the Romans, they became sufferers themselves before they could do any harm to the other, and were drowned, they and their ships together. As for those that endeavoured to come to an actual fight, the Romans ran many of them through with their long poles. Sometimes the Romans leaped into their ships, with swords in their hands, and slew them ; but when some of them met the vessels, the Romans caught them by the middle, and destroyed at once their ships and themselves who were taken in them. And for such as were drowning in the sea, if they lifted their heads up above the water they were either killed by the darts, or caught by the vessels ; but if, in the desperate case they were in, they attempted to swim to their enemies, the Romans cut off either their heads or their hands : and indeed they were destroyed after various manners everywhere, till the rest, being put to flight, were forced to get upon the land, while the vessels encompassed them about [on the sea ;] but as many of these were repulsed when they were getting ashore as were killed by the darts upon the lake ; and the Romans leaped out of their vessels, and destroyed a great many more upon the land : one might then see the lake all bloody, and full of dead bodies, for not one of them escaped. And a terrible stink, and a very sad sight there was on the following days over that country ; for as for the shores, they were full of shipwrecks, and of dead bodies all swelled ; and as the dead bodies were inflamed by the sun, and putrified, they corrupted the air, insomuch that the misery was not only the object of commiseration to the Jews, but to those that hated them, and had been the authors of that misery. This was the upshot of the sea-fight. The number of the slain, including those that were killed in the city before, was six thousand and five hundred.

10. After this fight was over, Vespasian sat upon his tribunal at Tarichea, in order to distinguish the foreigners from the old inhabitants ; for those foreigners appeared to have begun the war. So he deliberated with the other commanders, whether he ought to save those old inhabitants or not. And when the commanders alleged that the dismission of them would be to his own disadvantage, because when they were once set at liberty, they would not be at rest, since they would be people destitute of proper habitations, and would be able to compel such as they fled to, to fight against us. Vespasian acknowledged that they did not deserve to be saved, and that if they had leave given them to fly away, they would make use of it against those that gave them that leave. But still he considered with himself after what manner they should be slain ; * for if he had then slain them, he suspected the people of the country would thereby become his enemies ; for that to be sure they never would bear it, that so many that had been supplicants to him should be killed ; and to offer violence to them, after he had given them assurance of their lives, he could not himself bear to do it. However, his friends were too hard for him, and pretended that nothing against the Jews could be any impiety, and that he ought to prefer what was profitable before what was fit to be done, where both could not be made consistent. So he gave them an ambiguous liberty to do as they advised, and permitted the prisoners to go along no other road than that which led to Tiberias only, So they readily believed what they desired to be true, and went along securely, with their effects, the way which was allowed them, while the Romans seized upon all the road that led to Tiberias, that none of them might go out of it, and shut them up in the city. Then came Vespasian, and ordered them all to stand in the stadium, and commanded them to kill the old men, together with the others that were useless, who were in number a thousand and two hundred. Out of the young men he chose six thousand of the strongest, and sent them to Nero, to dig through the Isthmus, and sold the remainder for slaves, being thirty thousand and four hundred, besides such as he made a present of to Agrippa ; for as to those that belonged to his kingdom, he gave him leave to do what he pleased with them ; however, the king sold these also for slaves ; but for the rest of the multitude, who were Trachonites, and Gaulanites, and of Hippos, and some of Gadara, the greatest part of them were seditious persons and fugitives, who were of such shameful characters that they preferred war before peace. These prisoners were taken on the eighth day of the month Gorpiæus [Elul.]

---

* This is the most cruel and barbarous action that Vespasian ever did in this whole war, as he did it with great reluctance also. It was done both after public assurance given of sparing the prisoners' lives, and when all knew and confessed that these prisoners were no way guilty of any sedition against the Romans.

BOOK IV

FROM THE SIEGE OF GAMALA TO THE COMING OF TITUS TO BESIEGE JERUSALEM

CHAPTER I

THE SIEGE AND TAKING OF GAMALA

1. Now all those Galileans who, after the taking of Jotapata, had revolted from the Romans, did, upon the conquest of Tariche, deliver themselves up to them again. And the Romans received all the fortresses and the cities, excepting Gischala and those that had seized upon Mount Tabor; Gamala also, which is a city over against Tariche, but on the other side of the lake, conspired with them. This city lay upon the borders of Agrippa's kingdom, as also did Sogana and Seleucia. And these were both parts of Gaulanitis; for Sogana was a part of that called the Upper Gaulanitis, as was Gamala of the Lower; while Seleucia was situated at the lake Semechonitis, which lake is thirty furlongs in breadth, and sixty in length; its marshes reach as far as the place Daphne, which, in other respects, is a delicious place, and hath such fountains as supply water to what is called Little Jordan, under the temple of the golden calf, where it is sent into Great Jordan. Now Agrippa had united Sogana and Seleucia by leagues to himself, at the very beginning of the revolt from the Romans; yet did not Gamala accede to them, but relied upon the difficulty of the place, which was greater than that of Jotapata, for it was situated upon a rough ridge of a high mountain, with a kind of neck in the middle: where it begins to ascend, it lengthens itself, and declines as much downward before as behind, insomuch that it is like a camel in figure, from whence it is so named, although the people of the country do not pronounce it accurately. Both on the side and the face there are abrupt parts divided from the rest, and ending in vast deep valleys; yet are the parts behind, where they are joined to the mountain, somewhat easier of ascent than the other; but then the people belonging to the place have cut an oblique ditch there, and made that hard to be ascended also. On its acclivity, which is straight, houses are built, and those very thick and close to one another. The city also hangs so strangely, that it looks as if it would fall down upon itself, so sharp is it at the top. It is exposed to the south; and its southern mount, which reaches to an immense height, was in the nature of a citadel to the city; and above that was a precipice, not walled about, but extending itself to an immense depth. There was also a spring of water within the wall, at the utmost limits of the city.

2. As this city was naturally hard to be taken, so had Josephus, by building a wall about it, made it still stronger, as also by ditches and mines under ground. The people that were in it were made more bold by the nature of the place than the people of Jotapata had been, but it had much fewer fighting men in it; and they had such a confidence in the situation of the place, that they thought the enemy could not be too many for them; for the city had been filled with those that had fled to it for safety, on account of its strength; on which account they had been able to resist those whom Agrippa sent to besiege it for seven months together.

3. But Vespasian removed from Emmaus, where he had last pitched his camp before the city Tiberias, (now Emmaus, if it be interpreted, may be rendered "a warm bath," for therein is a spring of warm water, useful for healing,) and came to Gamala; yet was its situation such that he was not able to encompass it all round with soldiers to watch it; but where the places were practical, he set men to watch it, and seized on the mountain which was over it. And as the legions, according to their usual custom, were fortifying their camp upon that mountain, he began to cast up banks at the bottom, at the part towards the east, where the highest tower of the whole city was, and where the fifteenth legion pitched their camp; while the fifth legion did duty over against the midst of the city, and whilst the tenth legion filled up the ditches and valleys. Now at this time it was that as king Agrippa was come nigh the walls, and was endeavouring to speak to those that were on the walls about a surrender, he was hit with a stone on his right elbow by one of the slingers; he was then immediately surrounded with his own men. But the Romans were excited to set about the siege, by their indignation on the king's account, and by their fear on their own account, as concluding that these men would omit no kinds of barbarity against foreigners and enemies, who were so enraged against one of their own nation, and one that advised them to nothing but what was for their own advantage.

4. Now when the banks were finished, which was done on a sudden, both by the multitude of hands and by their being accustomed to such work, they brought the machines; but Chares and Joseph, who were the most potent men of the city, set their armed men in order, though already in a fright, because they did not suppose that the city could hold out long, since they had not a sufficient quantity either of water, or of other necessaries. However, these their leaders encouraged them, and brought them out upon the wall, and for a while indeed they drove away those that were bringing the machines; but when those machines threw darts and stones at them, they retired into the city; then did the Romans bring battering rams to three several places, and made the wall shake [and fall.] They then poured in over the parts of the wall that were thrown down, with a mighty sound of trumpets and noise of armour, and with a shout

of the soldiers, and brake in by force upon those that were in the city; but these men fell upon the Romans for some time, at their first entrance, and prevented their going any farther, and with great courage beat them back; and the Romans were so overpowered by the greater multitude of the people, who beat them on every side that they were obliged to run into the upper parts of the city. Whereupon the people turned about, and fell upon their enemies, who had attacked them, and thrust them down to the lower parts, and as they were distressed by the narrowness and difficulty of the place, slew them; and as these Romans could neither beat those back that were above them, nor escape the force of their own men that were forcing their way forward, they were compelled to fly into their enemies' houses, which were low; but these houses being thus full of soldiers, whose weight they could not bear, fell down suddenly; and when one house fell, it shook down a great many of those that were under it, as did those do to such as were under them. By this means a vast number of the Romans perished; for they were so terribly distressed, that although they saw the houses subsiding, they were compelled to leap upon the tops of them; so that a great many were ground to powder by these ruins, and a great many of those that got from under them lost some of their limbs, but still a greater number were suffocated by the dust that arose from those ruins. The people of Gamala supposed this to be an assistance afforded them by God, and without regarding what damage they suffered themselves, they pressed forward, and thrust the enemy upon the tops of their houses; and when they stumbled in the sharp and narrow streets, and were perpetually tumbling down, they threw their stones or darts at them, and slew them. Now the very ruins afforded them stones enow; and for iron weapons, the dead men of the enemy's side afforded them what they wanted; for drawing the swords of those that were dead, they made use of them to despatch such as were only half dead; nay, there were a great number who, upon their falling down from the tops of the houses, stabbed themselves, and died after that manner; nor indeed was it easy for those that were beaten back to fly away; for they were so unacquainted with the ways, and the dust was so thick, that they wandered about without knowing one another, and fell down dead among the crowd.

5. Those therefore that were able to find the ways out of the city retired. But now Vespasian always stayed among those that were hard set; for he was deeply affected with seeing the ruins of the city falling upon his army, and forgot to take care of his own preservation. He went up gradually towards the highest parts of the city before he was aware, and was left in the midst of dangers, having only a very few with him; for even his son Titus was not with him at that time, having been sent into Syria to Mucianus. However, he thought it not safe to fly, nor did he esteem it a fit thing for him to do; but calling to mind the actions he had done from his youth, and recollecting his courage, as if he had been excited by a divine fury, he covered himself and those that were with him with their shields, and formed a testudo over both their bodies and their armour, aad bore up the enemy's attacks, who came running down from the top of the city; and without shewing any dread at the multitude of the men or of their darts, he endured all, until the enemy took notice of that divine courage that was within him, and remitted of their attacks;

and when they pressed less zealously upon him, he retired, though without shewing his back to them, till he was gotten out of the walls of the city. Now a great number of the Romans fell in this battle, among whom was Ebutius, the decurion, a man who appeared not only in this engagement, wherein he fell, but everywhere, and in former engagements, to be of the truest courage, and one that had done very great mischief to the Jews. But there was a centurion, whose name was Gallus, who, during this disorder, being encompassed about, and ten other soldiers, privately crept into the house of a certain person, where he heard them talking at supper what the people intended to do against the Romans, or about themselves (for both the man himself and those with him were Syrians.) So he got up in the night-time, and cut all their throats, and escaped, together with his soldiers, to the Romans.

6. And now Vespasian comforted his army, which was much dejected, by reflecting on their ill success, and because they had never before fallen into such a calamity, and besides this, because they were greatly ashamed that they had left their general alone in great dangers. As to what concerned himself, he avoided to say any thing, that he might by no means seem to complain of it; but he said that "we ought to bear manfully what usually falls out in war, and this by considering what the nature of war is, and how it can never be that we must conquer without bloodshed on our own side; for there stands about us that fortune which is of its own nature mutable; that while they had killed so many ten thousands of the Jews, they had now paid their small share of the reckoning to fate; and as it is the part of weak people to be too much puffed up with good success, so is it the part of cowards to be too much affrighted at that which is ill; for the change from the one to the other is sudden on both sides; and he is the best warrior who is of a sober mind under misfortunes, that he may continue in that temper, and cheerfully recover what hath been lost formerly; and as for what had now happened, it was neither owing to their effeminacy nor to the valour of the Jews, but the difficulty of the place was the occasion of their advantage, and of our disappointment. Upon reflecting on which matter one might blame your zeal as perfectly ungovernable; for when the enemy had retired to their highest fastnesses, you ought to have restrained yourselves, and not, by presenting yourselves at the top of the city to be exposed to dangers; but upon your having obtained the lower parts of the city, you ought to have provoked those that had retired thither to a safe and settled battle; whereas, in rushing so hastily upon victory, you took no care of your own safety. But this incautiousness in war, and this madness of zeal, is not a Roman maxim. While we perform all that we attempt by skill and good order, that procedure is on the part of barbarians, and is what the Jews chiefly support themselves by. We ought therefore to return to our own virtue, and to be rather angry than any longer dejected at this unlucky misfortune; and let every one seek for his own consolation from his own hand; for by this means he will avenge those that have been destroyed, and punish those that have killed them. For myself, I will endeavour, as I have now done, to go first before you against your enemies in every engagement, and to be the last that retires from it."

7. So Vespasian encouraged his army by this speech; but for the people of Gamala, it happened that they took courage for a little while,

upon such great and unaccountable success as they had. But when they considered with themselves that they had now no hopes of any terms of accommodation, and reflecting upon it that they could not get away, and that their provisions began already to be short, they were exceedingly cast down, and their courage failed them; yet they did not neglect what might be for their preservation, so far as they were able, but the most courageous among them guarded those parts of the wall which were beaten down, while the more infirm did the same to the rest of the wall that still remained round the city. And as the Romans raised their banks, and attempted to get into the city a second time, a great many of them fled out of the city through impracticable valleys, where no guards were placed, as also through subterranean caverns; while those that were afraid of being caught, and for that reason stayed in the city, perished for want of food; for what food they had was brought together from all quarters, and reserved for the fighting men.

8. And these were the hard circumstances the people of Gamala were in. But now Vespasian went about other work by the by, during this siege, and that was to subdue those that had seized upon Mount Tabor, a place that lies in the middle between the great plain and Scythopolis, whose top is elevated as high as three furlongs, and is hardly to be ascended on its north side; its top is a plain of six furlongs, and all encompassed with a wall. Now, Josephus erected this so long a wall in forty days' time, and furnished it with other materials, and with water from below, for the inhabitants only made use of rain water; as therefore there was a great number of people gotten together upon this mountain, Vespasian sent Placidus, with six hundred horsemen thither. Now, as it was impossible for him to ascend the mountain, he invited many of them to peace by the offer of his right hand for their security, and of his intercession for them. Accordingly they came down, but with a treacherous design, as well as he had the like treacherous design upon them on the other side; for Placidus spoke mildly to them, as aiming to take them when he got them into the plain; they also came down, as complying with his proposals, but it was in order to fall upon him when he was not aware of it; however, Placidus's stratagem was too hard for theirs; for when the Jews began to fight, he pretended to run away, and when they were in pursuit of the Romans, he enticed them a great way along the plain, and then made his horsemen turn back; whereupon he beat them, and slew a great number of them, and cut off the retreat of the rest of the multitude, and hindered their return. So they left Tabor, and fled to Jerusalem, while the people of the country came to terms with him, for their water failed them, and so they delivered up the mountain and themselves to Placidus.

9. But of the people of Gamala, those that were of the bolder sort fled away and hid themselves, while the more infirm perished by famine; but the men of war sustained the siege till the two-and-twentieth day of the month Hyperberetæus [Tisri,] when three soldiers of the fifteenth legion, about the morning-watch, got under a high tower that was near, and undermined it without making any noise; nor when they either came to it, which was in the nighttime, nor when they were under it, did those that guarded it perceive them. These soldiers then, upon their coming, avoided making a noise, and when they had rolled away five of its strongest stones, they went away hastily; where-

upon the tower fell down on a sudden, with a great noise, and its guard fell headlong with it; so that those that kept guard at other places were under such disturbance that they ran away; the Romans also slew many of those that ventured to oppose them, among whom was Joseph, who was slain by a dart, as he was running away over that part of the wall that was broken down: but as those that were in the city were greatly affrighted at the noise, they ran hither and thither, and a great consternation fell upon them, as though all the enemy had fallen in at once upon them. Then it was that Chares, who was ill, and under the physicians' hands, gave up the ghost, the fear he was in greatly contributing to make his distemper fatal to him. But the Romans so well remembered their former ill success, that they did not enter the city till the three-and-twentieth day of the forementioned month.

10. At which time Titus, who was now returned, out of the indignation he had at the destruction the Romans had undergone while he was absent, took two hundred chosen horsemen, and ome footmen with him, and entered without noise into the city. Now, as the watch perceived that he was coming, they made a noise, and betook themselves to their arms; and as this his entrance was presently known to those that were in the city, some of them caught hold of their children and their wives, and drew them after them, and fled away to the citadel, with lamentations and cries, while others of them went to meet Titus, and were killed presently; but so many of them as were hindered from running up to the citadel, not knowing what in the world to do, fell among the Roman guards; while the groans of those that were killed were prodigiously great everywhere, and blood ran down over all the lower parts of the city, from the upper. But then Vespasian himself came to his assistance against those that had fled to the citadel, and brought his whole army with him: now this upper part of the city was every way rocky, and difficult of ascent, and elevated to a vast altitude, and very full of people on all sides, and encompassed with precipices, whereby the Jews cut off those that came up to them, and did much mischief to others by their darts and the large stones which they rolled down upon them, while they were themselves so high that the enemy's darts could hardly reach them. However, there arose such a divine storm against them as was instrumental to their destruction; this carried the Roman darts upon them, and made those which they threw return back, and drove them obliquely away from them: nor could the Jews indeed stand upon their precipices, by reason of the violence of the wind, having nothing that was stable to stand upon, nor could they see those that were ascending up to them; so the Romans got up and surrounded them, and some they slew before they could defend themselves, and others as they were delivering up themselves; and the remembrance of those that were slain at their former entrance into the city increased their rage against them now; a great number also of those that were surrounded on every side, and despaired of escaping, threw their children and their wives, and themselves, also down the precipices, into the valley beneath, which, near the citadel, had been dug hollow to a vast depth; but so it happened, that the anger of the Romans appeared not to be so extravagant as was the madness of those that were now taken, while the Romans slew but four thousand, whereas the number of those that had thrown themselves down was

COLLAPSE OF THE TOWER AT GAMALA

found to be five thousand : nor did any one escape except two women, who were the daughters of Philip, and Philip himself, who was the son of a certain eminent man called Jacimus, who had been general of king Agrippa's army ; and these did therefore escape, because they lay concealed from the sight of the Romans when the city was taken ; for otherwise they spared not so much as the infants, of whom many were flung down by them from the citadel. And thus was Gamala taken on the three-and-twentieth day of the month Hyperberetæus [Tisri,] whereas the city had first revolted on the four-and-twentieth day of the month Gorpiæus [Elul.]

CHAPTER II

THE SURRENDER OF THE SMALL CITY OF GISCHALA; JOHN FLIES FROM IT TO JERUSALEM

§ 1. Now, no place of Galilee remained to be taken but the small city of Gischala, whose inhabitants were yet desirous of peace ; for they were generally husbandmen, and always applied themselves to cultivate the fruits of the earth. However, there were a great number that belonged to a band of robbers, that were already corrupted, and had crept in among them, and some of the governing part of the citizens were sick of the same distemper. It was John, the son of a certain man whose name was Levi, that drew them into this rebellion, and encouraged them in it. He was a cunning knave, and of a temper that could put on various shapes ; very rash in expecting great things, and very sagacious in bringing about what he hoped for. It was known to everybody that he was fond of war, in order to thrust himself into authority ; and the seditious part of the people of Gischala were under his management, by whose means the populace, who seemed ready to send ambassadors in order to a surrender, waited for the coming of the Romans in battle array. Vespasian sent against them Titus, with a thousand horsemen, but withdrew the tenth legion to Scythopolis, while he returned to Cesarea, with the other two legions, that he might allow them to refresh themselves after their long and hard campaign, thinking withal that the plenty which was in those cities would improve their bodies and their spirits, against the difficulties they were to go through afterwards ; for he saw there would be occasion for great pains about Jerusalem, which was not yet taken, because it was the royal city, and the principal city of the whole nation ; and because those that had run away from the war in other places got all together thither. It was also naturally strong, and the walls that were built round it made him not a little concerned about it. Moreover, he esteemed the men that were in it to be so courageous and bold, that even without the consideration of the walls, it would be too hard to subdue them ; for which reason he took care of and exercised his soldiers beforehand for the work, as they do wrestlers before they begin their undertakings.

2. Now Titus, as he rode up to Gischala, found it would be easy for him to take the city upon the first onset : but knew withal, that if he took it by force, the multitude would be destroyed by the soldiers without mercy. (Now he was already satiated with the shedding of blood, and pitied the major part, who would then perish, without distinction, together with the guilty.) So he was rather desirous the city might be surrendered up to him on terms. Accordingly, when

he saw the wall full of those men that were of the corrupted party, he said to them,—That he could not but wonder what it was they depended on, when they alone stayed to fight the Romans, after every other city was taken by them ; especially when they have seen cities much better fortified than theirs is, overthrown by a single attack upon them ; while as many as have intrusted themselves to the security of the Romans' right hand which he now offers to them, without regarding their former insolence, do enjoy their own possessions in safety ; for that while they had hopes of recovering their liberty, they might be pardoned ; but their continuance still in their opposition, when they saw that to be impossible, was inexcusable ; for that, if they will not comply with such humane offers, and right hands for security, they have experience of such a war as would spare nobody, and should soon be made sensible that their wall would be but a trifle, when battered by the Roman machines ; in depending on which, they demonstrate themselves to be the only Galileans that were no better than arrogant slaves and captives.

3. Now none of the populace durst not only make a reply, but durst not so much as get upon the wall, for it was all taken up by the robbers, who were also the guard at the gates, in order to prevent any of the rest from going out, in order to propose terms of submission, and from receiving any of the horsemen into the city. But John returned Titus this answer,—that for himself he was content to hearken to his proposals, and that he would either persuade or force those that pursued them. Yet he said, that Titus ought to have such regard to the Jewish law, as to grant them leave to celebrate that day, which was the seventh day of the week, on which it was unlawful not only to remove their arms, but even to treat of peace also ; and that even the Romans were not ignorant how the period of the seventh day was among them a cessation from all labours ; and that he who should compel them to transgress the law about that day, would be equally guilty with those that were compelled to transgress it : and that this delay could be of no advantage to him ; for why should anybody think of doing anything in the night, unless it was to fly away ? which he might prevent by placing his camp round about them : and that they should think it a great point gained, if they might not be obliged to transgress the laws of their country ; and that it would be a right thing for him, who designed to grant them peace, without their expectation of such a favour, to preserve the laws of those they saved inviolable. Thus did this man put a trick upon Titus, not so much out of regard to the seventh day, as to his own preservation, for he was afraid lest he should be quite deserted if the city should be taken, and had his hopes of life in that night, and in his flight therein. Now this was the work of God, who therefore preserved this John, that he might bring on the destruction of Jerusalem ; as also it was his work that Titus was prevailed with by this pretence for a delay, and that he pitched his camp further off the city at Cydessa. This Cydessa was a strong Mediterranean village of the Tyrians, which always hated and made war against the Jews ; it had also a great number of inhabitants, and was well fortified ; which made it a proper place for such as were enemies to the Jewish nation.

4. Now, in the night-time, when John saw that there was no Roman guard about the city, he seized the opportunity directly, and, taking with him not only the armed men that were

about him, but a considerable number of those that had little to do, together with their families, he fled to Jerusalem. And indeed, though the man was making haste to get away, and was tormented with fears of being a captive, or of losing his life, yet did he prevail with himself to take out of the city along with him a multitude of women and children, as far as twenty furlongs; but there he left them as he proceeded further on his journey, where those that were left behind made sad lamentations; for the farther every one was come from his own people, the nearer they thought themselves to be to their enemies. They also affrighted themselves with this thought, that those who would carry them into captivity were just at hand, and still turned themselves back at the mere noise they made themselves in this their hasty flight, as if those from whom they fled were just upon them. Many also of them missed their ways; and the earnestness of such as aimed to outgo the rest, threw down many of them. And indeed there was a miserable destruction made of the women and children; while some of them took courage to call their husbands and kinsmen back, and to beseech them, with the bitterest lamentions, to stay for them; but John's exhortation, who cried out to save themselves, and fly away, prevailed. He said also, that if the Romans should seize upon those whom they left behind, they would be revenged on them for it. So this multitude that ran thus away was dispersed abroad, according as each of them was able to run, one faster or slower than another.

5. Now on the next day Titus came to the wall, to make the agreement; whereupon the people opened their gates to him, and came out to him, with their children and wives, and made acclamations of joy to him, as to one that had been their benefactor, and had delivered the city out of custody; they also informed him of John's flight, and besought him to spare them, and to come in and bring the rest of those that were for innovations to punishment; but Titus, not so much regarding the supplications of the people, sent part of his horsemen to pursue after John, but they could not overtake him, for he was gotten to Jerusalem before; they also slew six thousand of the women and children who went out with him, but returned back and brought with them almost three thousand. However, Titus was greatly displeased that he had not been able to bring this John, who had deluded him, to punishment: yet he had captives enough, as well as the corrupted part of the city, to satisfy his anger, when it missed of John. So he entered the city in the midst of acclamations of joy; and when he had given orders to the soldiers to pull down a small part of the wall, as of a city taken in war, he repressed those that had disturbed the city rather by threatenings than by executions; for he thought that many would accuse innocent persons, out of their own animosities and quarrels, if he should attempt to distinguish those that were worthy of punishment from the rest; and that it was better to let a guilty person alone in his fears than to destroy with him any one that did not deserve it; for that probably such a one might be taught prudence, by the fear of the punishment he had deserved, and have a shame upon him for his former offences, when he had been forgiven; but that the punishment of such as have been once put to death could never be retrieved. However, he placed a garrison in the city for its security, by which means he should restrain those that were for innovations, and should leave those that were peaceably disposed

in greater security. And thus was all Galilee taken; but this not till after it had cost the Romans much pains before it could be taken by them.

CHAPTER III

CONCERNING JOHN OF GISCHALA; CONCERNING THE ZEALOTS, AND THE HIGH PRIEST ANANUS; AS ALSO HOW THE JEWS RAISED SEDITIONS ONE AGAINST ANOTHER [IN JERUSALEM.]

1. Now, upon John's entry into Jerusalem, the whole body of the people were in an uproar, and ten thousand of them crowded about every one of the fugitives that were come to them, and inquired of them what miseries had happened abroad, when their breath was so short, and hot, and quick, that of itself it declared the great distress they were in; yet did they talk big under their misfortunes, and pretended to say that they had not fled away from the Romans, but came thither in order to fight them with less hazard; for that it would be an unreasonable and a fruitless thing for them to expose themselves to desperate hazards about Gischala, and such weak cities, whereas they ought to lay up their weapons and their zeal, and reserve it for their metropolis. But when they related to them the taking of Gischala, and their decent departure, as they pretended, from that place, many of the people understood it to be no better than a flight; and especially when the people were told of those that were made captives, they were in great confusion, and guessed those things to be plain indications that they should be taken also; but for John, he was very little concerned for those whom he had left behind him, but went about among all the people, and persuaded them to go to war, by the hopes he gave them. He affirmed that the affairs of the Romans were in a weak condition, and extolled his own power. He also jested upon the ignorance of the unskilful, as if those Romans, although they should take to themselves wings, could never fly over the walls of Jerusalem, who found such great difficulties in taking the villages of Galilee, and had broken their engines of war against their walls.

2. These harangues of John's corrupted a great part of the young men, and puffed them up for the war; but as to the most prudent part, and those in years, there was not a man of them but foresaw what was coming, and made lamentation on that account, as if the city was already undone, and in this confusion were the people; but then it must be observed, that the multitude that came out of the country were at discord before the Jerusalem sedition began; for Titus went from Gischala to Cesarea; and Vespasian from Cesarea to Jamnia and Azotus, and took them both; and when he had put garrisons into them, he came back with a great number of the people, who were come over to him, upon his giving them his right hand for their preservation. There were, besides, disorders and civil wars in every city; and all those that were at quiet from the Romans turned their hands one against another. There was also a bitter contest between those that were fond of war, and those that were desirous of peace. At the first this quarrelsome temper caught hold of private families, who could not agree among themselves; after which those people that were the dearest to one another brake through all restraints with regard to each other, and every one associated with those of his own opinion,

and began already to stand in opposition one to another; so that seditions arose everywhere, while those that were for innovations, and were desirous of war, by their youth and boldness, were too hard for the aged and the prudent men; and, in the first place, all the people of every place betook themselves to rapine; after which they got together in bodies, in order to rob the people of the country, insomuch that for barbarity and iniquity those of the same nation did no way differ from the Romans; nay, it seemed to be a much lighter thing to be ruined by the Romans than by themselves.

3. Now the Roman garrisons, which guarded the cities, partly out of their uneasiness to take such trouble upon them, and partly out of the hatred they bare to the Jewish nation, did little or nothing towards relieving the miserable, till the captains of these troops of robbers, being satiated with rapines in the country, got all together from all parts, and became a band of wickedness, and all together crept into Jerusalem, which was now become a city without a governor, and, as the ancient custom was, received without distinction all that belonged to their nation; and these they then received, because all men supposed that those who came so fast into the city, came out of kindness, and for their assistance, although these very men, besides the seditions they raised, were otherwise the direct cause of the city's destruction also; for as they were an unprofitable and a useless multitude, they spent those provisions beforehand, which might otherwise have been sufficient for the fighting men. Moreover, besides the bringing on of the war, they were the occasion of sedition and famine therein.

4. There were, besides these, other robbers that came out of the country, and came into the city, and joining to them those that were worse than themselves, omitted no kind of barbarity; for they did not measure their courage by their rapines and plundering only, but proceeded as far as murdering men; and this not in the night-time or privately, or with regard to ordinary men, but did it openly in the day-time, and began with the most eminent persons in the city; for the first man they meddled with was Antipas, one of the royal lineage, and the most potent man in the whole city, insomuch that the public treasures were committed to his care; him they took and confined, as they did in the next place to Levias, a person of great note, with Sophas, the son of Raguel: both of whom were of royal lineage also. And besides these, they did the same to the principal men of the country. This caused a terrible consternation among the people; and every one contented himself with taking care of his own safety, as they would do if the city had been taken in war.

5. But these were not satisfied with the bonds into which they had put the men forementioned; nor did they think it safe for them to keep them thus in custody long, since they were men very powerful, and had numerous families of their own that were able to avenge them. Nay, they thought the very people would perhaps be so moved at these unjust proceedings, as to rise in a body against them: it was therefore resolved to have them slain. Accordingly, they sent one John, who was the most bloody-minded of them all, to do that execution: this man was also called "the son of Dorcas," in the language of the country. Ten more men went along with him into the prison, with their swords drawn, and so they cut the throats of those that were in custody there. The grand lying pretence these

men made for so flagrant an enormity was this, that these men had had conferences with the Romans for a surrender of Jerusalem to them; and so they said they had slain only such as were traitors to their common liberty. Upon the whole, they grew the more insolent upon this bold prank of theirs, as though they had been the benefactors and saviours of the city.

6. Now the people were come to that degree of meanness and fear, and these robbers to that degree of madness, that these last took upon upon them to appoint high priests.* So when they had disannulled the succession, according to those families out of whom the high priests used to be made, they ordained certain unknown and ignoble persons for that office, that they might have their assistance in their wicked undertakings; for such as obtained this highest of all honours, without any desert, were forced to comply with those that bestowed it on them. They also set the principal men at variance one with another, by several sorts of contrivances and tricks, and gained the opportunity of doing what they pleased, by the mutual quarrels of those who might have obstructed their measures; till at length, when they were satiated with the unjust actions they had done towards men, they transferred their contumelious behaviour to God himself, and came into the sanctuary with polluted feet.

7. And now the multitude were going to rise against them already; for Ananus, the ancientest of the high priests, persuaded them to it. He was a very prudent man, and had perhaps saved the city if he could but have escaped the hands of those that plotted against him. Those men made the temple of God a stronghold for them, and a place whither they might resort, in order to avoid the troubles they feared from the people; the sanctuary was now become a refuge, and a shop of tyranny. They also mixed jesting among the miseries they introduced, which was more intolerable than what they did; for, in order to try what surprise the people would be under, and how far their own power extended, they undertook to dispose of the high priesthood by casting lots for it, whereas, as we have said already, it was to descend by succession in a family. The pretence they made for this strange attempt was an ancient practice, while they said that of old it was determined by lot; but in truth, it was no better than a dissolution of an undeniable law, and a cunning contrivance to seize upon the government, derived from those that presumed to appoint governors as they themselves pleased.

8. Hereupon they sent for one of the pontifical tribes, which is called Eniachim,† and cast lots which of it should be the high priest. By fortune, the lot so fell as to demonstrate their iniquity after the plainest manner, for it fell upon one whose name was Phannias, the son of Samuel, of the village Aphtha. He was a man not only unworthy of the high priesthood, but that

---

* Here we may discover the utter disgrace and ruin of the high priesthood among the Jews, when undeserving, ignoble, and vile persons were advanced to that office by the seditious; which sort of high priests were thereupon obliged to comply with and assist those that advanced them in their impious practices. The names of these high priests were Jesus the son of Damneus, Jesus the son of Gamaliel, Matthias the son of Theophilus, and Phannias, the son of Samuel; all whom we shall meet with in Josephus's future history of this war.

† This tribe or course of the high priests, here called Eniachim, seems to Mr Lowth, to be that in 1 Chron. xxiv. 12, "the course of Jakin," where some copies have "the course of Eliakim," and I think this to be by no means an improbable conjecture.

did not well know what the high priesthood was; such a mere rustic was he! yet did they hail this man, without his own consent out of the country, as if they were acting a play upon the stage, and adorned him with a counterfeit face; they also put upon him the sacred garments, and upon every occasion instructed him what he was to do. This horrid piece of wickedness was sport and pastime with them, but occasioned the other priests, who at a distance saw their law made a jest of, to shed tears, and sorely lament the dissolution of such a sacred dignity.

9. And now the people could no longer bear the insolence of this procedure, but did altogether run zealously in order to overthrow that tyranny; and indeed they were Gorian the son of Josephus, and Symeon the son of Gamaliel, who encouraged them, by going up and down when they were assembled together in crowds, and as they saw them alone, to bear no longer, but to inflict punishment upon these pests and plagues of their freedom, and to purge the temple of these bloody polluters of it. The best esteemed also of the high priests, Jesus the son of Gamala, and Ananus the son of Ananus, when they were at their assemblies, bitterly reproached the people for their sloth, and excited them against the zealots; for that was the name they went by, as if they were zealous in good undertakings, and were not rather zealous in the worst actions, and extravagant in them beyond the example of others.

10. And now, when the multitude were gotten together to an assembly, and every one was in indignation at these men's siezing upon the sanctuary, at their rapine and murders, but had not yet begun their attacks upon them (the reason of which was this, that they imagined it to be a difficult thing to suppress these zealots, as indeed the case was,) Ananus stood in the midst of them, and casting his eyes frequently at the temple, and having a flood of tears in his eyes, he said,—" Certainly it had been good for me to die before I had seen the house of God full of so many abominations, or these sacred places that ought not to be trodden on at random, filled with the feet of these blood-shedding villains; yet do I, who am clothed with the vestments of the high priesthood, and am called by that most venerable name [of high priest,] still live, and am but too fond of living, and cannot endure to undergo a death which would be the glory of my old age; and if I were the only person concerned and, as it were, in a desert, I would give up my life, and that alone for God's sake; for to what purpose is it to live among a people insensible of their calamities, and where there is no notion remaining of any remedy for the miseries that are upon them? for when you are seized upon you bear it! and when you are beaten, you are silent! and when the people are murdered, nobody dare so much as send out a groan openly! O bitter tyranny that we are under! But why do I complain of the tyrants? Was it not you, and your sufferance of them, that have nourished them? Was it not you that overlooked those that first of all got together, for they were then but a few, and by your silence made them grow to be many; and by conniving at them when they took arms, in effect armed them against yourselves? You ought to have then prevented their first attempts, when they fell a reproaching your relations; but by neglecting that care in time, you have encouraged these wretches to plunder men. When houses were pillaged, nobody said a word, which was the occasion why they carried off the owners of those houses; and when they were drawn through the midst of the

city, nobody came to their assistance. They then proceeded to put those whom you had betrayed into their hands, into bonds. I do not say how many, and of what characters those men were whom they thus served, but certainly they were such as were accused by none, and condemned by none; and since nobody succoured them when they were in bonds, the consequence was, that you saw the same persons slain. We have seen this also; so that still the best of the herd of brute animals, as it were, have been still led to be sacrificed, when yet nobody said one word, or moved his right hand for their preservation. Will you bear, therefore,—will you bear to see your sanctuary trampled on? and will you lay steps for these profane wretches, upon which they may mount to higher degrees of insolence? Will not you pluck them down from their exaltation? for even by this time, they had proceeded to higher enormities, if they had been able to overthrow anything greater than the sanctuary. They have seized upon the strongest place of the whole city; you may call it the temple, if you please, though it be like a citadel or fortress. Now, while you have tyranny in so great a degree walled in, and see your enemies over your heads, to what purpose is it to take counsel? and what have you to support your minds withal? Perhaps you wait for the Romans, that they may protect our holy places: are our matters then brought to that pass? and are we come to that degree of misery, that our enemies themselves are expected to pity us? O wretched creatures! will not you rise up, and turn upon those that strike you? which you may observe in wild beasts themselves, that they will avenge themselves on those that strike them. Will not you call to mind, every one of you, the calamities you yourselves have suffered? nor lay before your eyes what afflictions you yourselves have undergone? and will not such things sharpen your souls to revenge? Is therefore that most honourable and most natural of our passions utterly lost, I mean the desire of liberty? Truly, we are in love with slavery, and in love with those that lord it over us, as if we had received that principle of subjection from our ancestors! yet did they undergo many and great wars for the sake of liberty, nor were they so far overcome by the power of the Egyptians, or the Medes, but that they still did what they thought fit, notwithstanding their commands to the contrary. And what occasion is their now for a war with the Romans? (I meddle not with determining whether it be an advantageous and profitable war or not.) What pretence is there for it? Is it not that we may enjoy our liberty? Besides, shall we not bear the lords of the habitable earth to be lords over us, and yet bear tyrants of our own country? Although I must say that submission to foreigners may be borne, because fortune hath already doomed us to it, while submission to wicked people of our own nation is too unmanly, and brought upon us by our own consent. However, since I have had occasion to mention the Romans, I will not conceal a thing that, as I am speaking, comes into my mind, and affects me considerably;—it is this, that though we should be taken by them (God forbid the event should be so!) yet can we undergo nothing that will be harder to be borne than what these men have already brought upon us. How, then, can we avoid shedding of tears, when we see the Roman donations in our temples, while we withal see those of our own nation taking our spoils, and plundering our glorious metropolis, and slaughtering our men, from which enormities those Romans themselves would have abstained? to see those Romans never going beyond the bounds allotted to profane persons, nor venturing to break in upon any of our sacred customs; nay, having horror upon their minds when they view at a distance those sacred walls, while some have been born in this very country, and brought up in our customs, and called Jews, do walk about in the midst of the holy places, at the very time when their hands are still warm with the slaughter of their own countrymen. Besides, can any one be afraid of a war abroad, and that with such as will have comparatively much greater moderation than our own people have? For truly, if we may suit our words to the things they represent, it is probable one may hereafter find the Romans to be supporters of our laws, and those within ourselves the subverters of them. And now I am persuaded that every one of you here comes satisfied before I speak, that these overthrowers of our liberties deserve to be destroyed, and that nobody can so much as devise a punishment that they have not deserved by what they have done, and that you are all provoked against them by those their wicked actions, whence you have suffered so greatly. But perhaps many of you are affrighted at the multitude of those zealots, and at their audaciousness, as well as at the advantage they have over us in their being higher in place than we are; for these circumstances, as they have been occasioned by your negligence, so will they become still greater by being still longer neglected; for their multitude is every day augmented, by every ill man's running away to those that are like to themselves, and their audaciousness is therefore inflamed because they meet with no obstruction to their designs. And for their higher place, they will make use of it for engines also, if we give them time to do so; but be assured of this, that if we go up to fight them, they will be made tamer by their own consciences, and what advantages they have in the height of their situation they will lose by the opposition of their reason; perhaps also God himself, who hath been affronted by them, will make what they throw at us return against themselves, and these impious wretches will be killed by their own darts: let us but make our appearance before them, and they will come to nothing. However, it is a right thing, if there should be any danger in the attempt, to die before these holy gates, and to spend our very lives, if not for the sake of our children and wives, yet for God's sake, and for the sake of his sanctuary. I will assist you, both with my counsel and with my hand; nor shall any sagacity of ours be wanting for your support; nor shall you see that I will be sparing of my body neither."

11. By these motives Ananus encouraged the multitude to go against the zealots, although he knew how difficult it would be to disperse them, because of their multitude, and their youth, and the courage of their souls; but chiefly because of the consciousness of what they had done, since they would not yield, as not so much as hoping for pardon at the last for those their enormities. However, Ananus resolved to undergo whatever sufferings might come upon him, rather than overlook things, now they were in such great confusion. So the multitude cried out to him to lead them on against those whom he has described in his exhortations to them; and every one of them was most readily disposed to run any hazard whatsoever on that account.

12. Now, while Ananus was choosing out his men, and putting those that were proper for his purpose in array for fighting, the zealots got in-

formation of his undertaking (for there were some who went to them, and told them all that the people were doing) and were irritated at it; and leaping out of the temple in crowds, and by parties, spared none whom they met with. Upon this, Ananus got the populace together on the sudden, who were more numerous indeed than the zealots, but inferior to them in arms, because they had not been regularly put into array for fighting; but the alacrity that everybody shewed, supplied all their defects on both sides, the citizens taking up so great a passion as was stronger than arms, and deriving a degree of courage from the temple, more forcible than any multitude whatsoever; and indeed these citizens thought it was not possible for them to dwell in the city, unless they cut off the robbers that were in it. The zealots also thought that unless they prevailed, there would be no punishment so bad, but it would be inflicted on them. So their conflicts were conducted by their passions; and at the first they only cast stones at each other in the city, and threw their javelins at a distance; but when either of them were too hard for the other, they made use of their swords; and great slaughter was made on both sides, and a great number were wounded. As for the dead bodies of the people, their relations carried them out to their own houses; but when any of the zealots were wounded, he went up into the temple and defiled that sacred floor with his blood, insomuch that one may say it was their blood alone that polluted our sanctuary. Now in these conflicts the robbers always sallied out of the temple, and were too hard for their enemies; but the populace grew very angry, and became more and more numerous, and reproached those that gave back, and those behind would not afford room to those that were going off, but forced them on again, till at length they made their whole body to turn against their adversaries, and the robbers could no longer oppose them, but were forced gradually to retire into the temple; when Ananus and his party fell into it at the same time together with them.* This horribly affrighted the robbers, because it deprived them of the first court; so they fled into the inner court immediately, and shut the gates. Now, Ananus did not think fit to make any attack against the holy gates, although the other threw their stones and darts at them from above. He also deemed it unlawful to introduce the multitude into that court before they were purified; he therefore choose out of them all by lot, six thousand armed men, and placed them as guards in the cloisters; so there was a sucession of such guards one after another, and every one was forced to attend in his course; although many of the chief of the city were dismissed by those that then took on them the government, upon their hiring some of the poorer sort, and sending them to keep the guard in their stead.

13. Now it was John who, as we told you, ran away from Gischala, and was the occasion of all these being destroyed. He was a man of great craft, and bore about him in his soul a great passion after tyranny, and at a distance was the

---

* It was worth noting here, that this Ananus, the best of the Jews at this time, and the high priest who was so very uneasy at the profanation of the Jewish courts of the temple by the zealots, did not, however, scruple the profanation of the "court of the Gentiles;" as in our Saviour's days it was very much profaned by the Jews, and made a market-place, nay, "a den of thieves," without scruple, Matt. xxi. 12, 13; Mark xi. 15, 16, 17. Accordingly Josephus himself, when he speaks of the two inner courts, calls them both *hagia*, or *holy places;* but, so far as I remember, never gives that character to the court of the Gentiles.

adviser in these actions; and indeed at this time he pretended to be of the people's opinion, and went all about with Ananus when he consulted the great every day, and in the night-time also when he went round the watch; but he divulged their secrets to the zealots; and everything that the people deliberated about was by his means known to their enemies, even before it had been well agreed upon by themselves; and by way of contrivance how he might not be brought into suspicion, he cultivated the greatest friendship possible with Ananus, and with the chief of the people; yet did this overdoing of his turn against him, for he flattered them so extravagantly, that he was but the more suspected; and his constant attendance everywhere, even when he was not invited to be present, made him strongly suspected of betraying their secrets to the enemy; for they plainly perceived that they understood all the resolutions taken against them at their consultations. Nor was there any one whom they had so much reason to suspect of that discovery as this John; yet was it not easy to get quit of him, so potent was he grown by his wicked practices. He was also supported by many of those eminent men, who were to be consulted upon all considerable affairs; it was therefore thought reasonable to oblige him to give them assurance of his good-will upon oath; accordingly John took such an oath readily, that he would be on the people's side, and would not betray any of their counsels or practices to their enemies, and would assist them in overthrowing those that attacked them, and that both by his hand and his advice. So Ananus and his party believed his oath, and did now receive him to their consultations without further suspicion; nay, so far did they believe him, that they sent him as their ambassador into the temple to the zealots, with proposals of accommodation; for they were very desirous to avoid the pollution of the temple as much as they possibly could, and that no one of their nation should be slain therein.

14. But now this John, as if his oath had been made to the zealots, and for confirmation of his good-will to them, and not against them, went into the temple, and stood in the midst of them, and spake as follows: that he had run many hazards on their account, and in order to let them know of everything that was secretly contrived against them by Ananus and his party; but that both he and they should be cast into the most inevitable danger, unless some providential assistance were afforded them; for that Ananus made no longer delay, but had prevailed with the people to send ambassadors to Vespasian to invite him to come presently and take the city; and that he had appointed a fast for the next day against them, that they might obtain admission into the temple on a religious account, or gain it by force, and fight with them there; that he did not see how long they could either endure a siege, or how they could fight against so many enemies. He added farther, that it was by the providence of God he was himself sent as an ambassador to them for an accommodation; for that Ananus did therefore offer them such proposals, that he might come upon them when they were unarmed; that they ought to choose one of those two methods; either to intercede with those that guarded them, to save their lives, or to provide some foreign assistance for themselves; that if they fostered themselves with the hopes of pardon, in case they were subdued, they had forgotten what desperate things they had done, or could suppose, that as soon as the actors repented, those that

had suffered by them must be presently reconciled to them; while those that have done injuries, though they pretend to repent of them, are frequently hated by the others for that sort of repentance; and that the sufferers, when they get the power into their hands, are usually still more severe upon the actors; that the friends and kindred of those that had been destroyed would always be laying plots against them, and that a large body of people were very angry on account of their gross breaches of their laws and [illegal] judicatures, insomuch that although some part might commiserate them, those would be quite overborne by the majority.

CHAPTER IV

THE IDUMEANS BEING SENT FOR BY THE ZEALOTS, CAME IMMEDIATELY TO JERUSALEM: AND WHEN THEY WERE EXCLUDED OUT OF THE CITY, THEY LAY ALL NIGHT THERE. JESUS, ONE OF THE HIGH PRIESTS, MAKES A SPEECH TO THEM; AND SIMON THE IDUMEAN MAKES A REPLY TO IT

1. Now, by this crafty speech, John made the zealots afraid; yet durst he not directly name what foreign assistance he meant, but in a covert way only intimated at the Idumeans; but now that he might particularly irritate the leaders of the zealots, he calumniated Ananus, that he was about a piece of barbarity, and did in a special manner threaten them. These leaders were Eleazar, the son of Simon, who seemed the most plausible man of them all, both in considering what was fit to be done, and in the execution of what he had determined upon, and Zecharias, the son of Phalek; both of whom derived their families from the priests. Now, when these two men had heard, not only the common threatenings which belonged to them all, but those peculiarly levelled against themselves; and besides, how Ananus and his party, in order to secure their own dominion, had invited the Romans to come to them, for that also was part of John's lie, they hesitated a great while what they should do, considering the shortness of the time by which they were straitened; because the people were prepared to attack them very soon, and because the suddenness of the plot laid against them had almost cut off their hopes of getting any foreign assistance; for they might be under the height of their afflictions before any of their confederates could be informed of it. However, it was resolved to call in the Idumeans; so they wrote a short letter to this effect: —That Ananus had imposed on the people, and was betraying their metropolis to the Romans; that they themselves had revolted from the rest, and were in custody in the temple, on account of the preservation of their liberty; that there was but a small time left, wherein they might hope for their deliverance; and that unless they would come immediately to their assistance, they should themselves be soon in the power of Ananus, and the city would be in the power of the Romans. They also charged the messengers to tell many more circumstances to the rulers of the Idumeans. Now, there were two active men proposed for the carrying of this message, and such as were well able to speak, and to persuade them that things were in this posture, and, what was a qualification still more necessary than the former, they were very swift of foot; for they knew well enough that these would immediately comply with their desires, as being ever a tumultuous and disorderly nation, always on the

watch upon every motion, delighting in mutations; and upon your flattering them ever so little, and petitioning them, they soon take their arms, and put themselves into motion, and make haste to a battle, as if it were to a feast. There was indeed occasion for quick despatch in the carrying of this message; in which point the messengers were no way defective. Both their names were Ananias; and they soon came to the rulers of the Idumeans.

2. Now, these rulers were greatly surprised at the contents of the letter, and at what those that came with it further told them; whereupon they ran about the nation like madmen, and made proclamation that the people should come to war; so a multitude was suddenly got together, sooner indeed than the time appointed in the proclamation, and everybody caught up their arms, in order to maintain the liberty of their metropolis; and twenty thousand of them were put into battle array, and came to Jerusalem, under four commanders, John, and Jacob the son of Sosas; and besides these were Simon, the son of Cathlas, and Phineas, the son of Clusothus.

3. Now this exit of the messengers was not known either to Ananus, or to the guards; but the approach of the Idumeans was known to him; for as he knew of it before they came, he ordered the gates to be shut against them, and that the walls should be guarded. Yet did not he by any means think of fighting against them, but, before they came to blows, to try what persuasions would do. Accordingly, Jesus, the eldest of the high priests next to Ananus, stood upon the tower that was over against them, and said thus:—"Many troubles indeed, and those of various kinds, have fallen upon this city, yet in none of them have I so much wondered at her fortune as now, when you are come to assist wicked men, and this after a manner very extraordinary; for I see that you are come to support the vilest of men against us, and this with so great alacrity, as you could hardly put on the like, in case our metropolis had called you to her assistance against barbarians; and if I had perceived that your army was composed of men like unto those who invited them, I had not deemed your attempt so absurd; for nothing does so much cement the minds of men together as the alliance there is between their manners; but now for these men who have invited you, if you were to examine them one by one, every one of them would be found to have deserved ten thousand deaths; for the very rascality and offscouring of the whole country, who have spent in debauchery their own substance and, by way of trial beforehand, have madly plundered the neighbouring villages and cities, in the upshot of all, have privately run together into this holy city. They are robbers, who by their prodigious wickedness have profaned this most sacred floor, and who are to be now seen drinking themselves drunk in the sanctuary, and expending the spoils of those whom they have slaughtered upon their unsatiable bellies. As for the multitude that is with you, one may see them so decently adorned in their armour, as it would become them to be, had their metropolis called them to her assistance against foreigners. What can a man call this procedure of yours but the sport of fortune, when he sees a whole nation coming to protect a sink of wicked wretches? I have for a good while been in doubt what it could possibly be that should move you to do this so suddenly; because certainly you would not take on your armour on the behalf of robbers, and against a people of kin to you, without some

very great cause for your so doing; but we have an item that the Romans are pretended, and that we are supposed to be going to betray this city to them; for some of your men have lately made a clamour about those matters, and have said they are come to set their metropolis free. Now, we cannot but admire at these wretches in their devising such a lie as this against us; for they knew there was no other way to irritate against us men that were naturally desirous of liberty, and on that account the best disposed to fight against foreign enemies, but by framing a tale as if we were going to betray that most desirable thing, liberty. But you ought to consider what sort of people they are that raise this calumny, and against what sort of people that calumny is raised, and to gather the truth of things, not by fictitious speeches, but out of the actions of both parties; —for what occasion is there for us to sell ourselves to the Romans, while it was in our power not to have revolted from them at the first, or, when we had once revolted, to have returned under their dominion again, and this while the neighbouring countries were not yet laid waste? whereas it is not an easy thing to be reconciled to the Romans, if we were desirous of it, now they have subdued Galilee, and are thereby become proud and insolent; and to endeavour to please them at the time when they are so near us, would bring such a reproach upon us as were worse than death. As for myself, indeed I should have preferred peace with them before death; but now we have once made war upon them, and fought with them, I prefer death with reputation, before living in captivity under them. But farther, whether do they pretend that we, who are the rulers of the people, have sent thus privately to the Romans, or hath it been done by the common suffrages of the people? If it be ourselves only that have done it, let them name those friends of ours that have been sent as our servants to manage this treachery. Hath any one been caught as he went out in this errand, or seized upon as he came back? Are they in possession of our letters? How could we be concealed from such a vast number of our fellow-citizens, among whom we are conversant every hour, while what is done privately in the country is, it seems, known by the zealots, who are but few in number, and under confinement also, and are not able to come out of the temple into the city! Is this the first time that they are become sensible how they ought to be punished for their insolent actions! For while these men were free from the fear they are now under, there was no suspicion raised that any of us were traitors. But if they lay this charge against the people, this must have been done at public consultation, and not one of the people must have dissented from the rest of the assembly: in which case the public fame of this matter would have come to you sooner than any particular indication. But how could that be? Must there not, then, have been ambassadors sent to confirm the agreements? And let them tell us who this ambassador was, that was ordained for that purpose. But this is no other than a pretence of such men as are loath to die, and are labouring to escape those punishments that hang over them; for if fate had determined that this city was to be betrayed into its enemies' hands, no other than these men that accuse us falsely could have the impudence to do it, there being no wickedness wanting to complete their impudent practices, but this only that they become traitors. And now, you Idumeans are come hither already with your arms, it is your duty, in the first place, to be assisting to your metropolis, and to join with us in cutting off those tyrants that have infringed the rules of our regular tribunals, that have trampled upon our laws, and made their swords the arbitrators of right and wrong; for they have seized upon men of great eminence, and under no accusation, as they stood in the midst of the market-place, and tortured them with putting them into bonds, and, without bearing to hear what they had to say, or what supplications they made, they destroyed them. You may, if you please, come into this city, though not in the way of war, and take a view of the marks still remaining of what I now say, and may see the houses that have been depopulated by their rapacious hands, with those wives and families that are in black, mourning for their slaughtered relations; as also you may hear their groans and lamentations all the city over; for there is nobody but hath tasted of the incursions of these profane wretches, who have proceeded to that degree of madness, as not only to have transferred their impudent robberies out of the country, and the remote cities, into this city, the very face and head of the whole nation, but out of the city into the temple also; for that is now made their receptacle and refuge, and the fountain-head whence their preparations are made against us. And this place, which is adored by the habitable world, and honoured by such as only know it by report, as far as the ends of the earth, is trampled upon by these wild beasts born among ourselves. They now triumph in the desperate condition they are already in, when they hear that one people is going to fight against another people, and one city against another city, and that your nation hath gotten an army together against its own bowels. Instead of which procedure, it were highly fit and reasonable, as I said before, for you to join with us in cutting off these wretches, and in particular to be revenged on them for putting this very cheat upon you; I mean, for having the impudence to invite you to assist them, of whom they ought to have stood in fear, as ready to punish them. But if you have some regard to these men's invitation of you, yet may you lay aside your arms, and come into the city under the notion of our kindred, and take upon you a middle name between that of auxiliaries and of enemies, and so become judges in this case. However, consider what those men will gain by being called into judgment before you, for such undeniable and such flagrant crimes, who would not vouchsafe to hear such as had no accusations laid against them to speak a word for themselves. However, let them gain this advantage by your coming. But still, if you will neither take our part in that indignation we have at these men, nor judge between us, the third thing I have to propose is this, that you let us both alone, and neither insult upon our calamities, nor abide with these plotters against their metropolis; for though you should have ever so great a suspicion that some of us have discoursed with the Romans, it is in your power to watch the passages into the city; and in case anything that we have been accused of is brought to light, then to come and defend your metropolis, and to inflict punishment on those that are found guilty; for the enemy cannot prevent you who are so near to the city. But if, after all, none of these proposals seem acceptable and moderate, do not you wonder that the gates are shut against you, while you bear your arms about you."

4. Thus spake Jesus; yet did not the multitude of the Idumeans give any attention to what he said, but were in a rage, because they did not meet with a ready entrance into the city. The generals also had indignation at the offer of laying down their arms, and looked upon it as equal to a captivity to throw them away at any man's injunctions whomsoever. But Simon, the son of Cathlas, one of their commanders, with much ado quieted the tumult of his own men, and stood so that the high priests might hear him, and said as follows:—" I can no longer wonder that the patrons of liberty are under custody in the temple, since there are those that shut the gates of our common city * to their own nation, and at the same time are preparing to admit the Romans into it; nay, perhaps are disposed to crown the gates with garlands at their coming, while they speak to the Idumeans from their own towers, and enjoin them to throw down their arms which they have taken up for the preservation of its liberty; and while they will not intrust the guard of our metropolis to their kindred, profess to make them judges of the differences that are among them; nay, while they accuse some men of having slain others without a legal trial, they do themselves condemn a whole nation, after an ignominious manner, and have now walled up that city from their own nation, which used to be open even to foreigners that came to worship there. We have indeed come in great haste to you, and to a war against our own countrymen; and the reason why we have made such haste is this, that we may preserve that freedom which you are so unhappy as to betray. You have probably been guilty of the like crimes against those whom you keep in custody, and have, I suppose, collected together the like plausible pretences against them also that you make use of against us; after which you have gotten the mastery of those within the temple, and keep them in custody, while they are only taking care of the public affairs. You have also shut the gates of the city in general against nations that are the most nearly related to you; and while you give such injurious commands to others, you complain that you have been tyrannised over by them, and fix the name of unjust governors upon such as are tyrannised over by yourselves. Who can bear this, your abuse of words, while they have a regard to the contrariety of your actions, unless you mean this—that those Idumeans do now exclude you out of your metropolis, whom you exclude from the sacred offices of your own country! One may indeed justly complain of those that are besieged in the temple, that when they had courage enough to punish those tyrants, whom you call eminent men, and free from any accusations, because of their being your companions in wickedness, they did not begin with you, and thereby cut off beforehand the most dangerous parts of this treason. But if these men have been more merciful than the public necessity required, we that are Idumeans will preserve this house of God, and will fight for our common country, and will oppose by war as well those that attack them from abroad, as those that betray them from within. Here will we abide before the walls in our armour, until either the Romans grow weary in waiting for

---

* This appellation of Jerusalem, "the common city" of the Idumeans, who were proselytes of justice, as well as of the original native Jews, greatly confirms that maxim of the rabbins, that "Jerusalem was not assigned, or appropriated, to the tribe of Benjamin or Judah, but every tribe had equal right to it [at their coming to worship there at the secret festivals.")

you, or you become friends to liberty, and repent of what you have done against it."

5. And now did the Idumeans make an acclamation to what Simon had said; but Jesus went away sorrowful, as seeing that the Idumeans were against all moderate counsels, and that the city was besieged on both sides; nor indeed were the minds of the Idumeans at rest; for they were in a rage at the injury that had been offered them by their exclusion out of the city; and when they thought the zealots had been strong, but saw nothing of theirs to support them, they were in doubt about the matter, and many of them repented that they had come thither. But the shame that would attend them in case they returned without doing anything at all, so far overcame their repentance, that they lay all night before the wall, though in a very bad encampment; for there broke out a prodigious storm in the night, with the utmost violence, and very strong winds, with the largest showers of rain, and continual lightnings, terrible thunderings, and amazing concussions and bellowings of the earth, that was in an earthquake. These things were a manifest indication that some destruction was coming upon men, when the system of the world was put into this disorder; and any one would guess that these wonders foreshewed some grand calamities that were coming.

6. Now the opinion of the Idumeans and of the citizens was one and the same. The Idumeans thought that God was angry at their taking arms, and that they would not escape punishment for their making war upon their metropolis. Ananus and his party thought that they had conquered without fighting, and that God acted as a general for them; but truly they proved both ill conjectures at what was to come, and made those events to be ominous to their enemies, while they were themselves to undergo the ill effects of them; for the Idumeans fenced one another by uniting their bodies into one band, and thereby kept themselves warm, and connecting their shields over their heads, were not so much hurt by the rain. But the zealots were more deeply concerned for the danger these men were in than they were for themselves, and got together, and looked about them, to see whether they could devise any means of assisting them, the hotter sort of them thought it best to force their guards with their arms, and after that to fall into the midst of the city, and publicly open the gates to those that came to their assistance; as supposing the guards would be in disorder, and give way at such an unexpected attempt of theirs, especially as the greater part of them were unarmed and unskilful in the affair of war; and that besides, the multitude of the citizens would not to be easily gathered together, but confined to their houses by the storm; and that if there were any hazard in their undertaking, it became them to suffer anything whatsoever themselves, rather than to overlook so great a multitude as were miserably perishing on their account. But the more prudent part of them disapproved of this forcible method, because they saw not only the guards about them very numerous, but the walls of the city itself carefully watched, by reason of the Idumeans. They also supposed that Ananus would be everywhere, and visit the guards every hour; which indeed was done upon other nights, but was omitted that night, not by reason of any slothfulness of Ananus, but by the overbearing appointment of fate, that so both he himself might perish, and the multitude of the guards might perish with him; for truly, as the night was far gone, and the storm very terrible, Ananus gave the guards in the cloisters leave to go to sleep; while it came into the heads of the zealots to make use of the saws belonging to the temple, and to cut the bars of the gates to pieces. The noise of the wind, and the not inferior sound of the thunder, did here also conspire with their designs, that the noise of the saws was not heard by the others.

7. So they secretly went out of the temple to the wall of the city, and made use of their saws, and opened that gate which was over-against the Idumeans. Now at first there came a fear upon the Idumeans themselves, which disturbed them, as imagining that Ananus and his party were coming to attack them, so that every one of them had his right hand upon his sword, in order to defend himself; but they soon came to know who they were that came to them, and were entered the city. And had the Idumeans then fallen upon the city, nothing could have hindered them from destroying the people, every man of them, such was the rage that were in them at that time; but they first of all made haste to get the zealots out of custody, which those that brought them in earnestly desired them to do, and not overlook those for whose sake they were come, in the midst of their distresses, nor to bring them into a still greater danger; for that when they had once seized upon the guards, it would be easy for them to fall upon the city; but that if the city were once alarmed, they would not then be able to overcome those guards, because as soon as they should perceive they were there, they would put themselves in order to fight them, and would hinder their coming into the temple.

CHAPTER V

THE CRUELTY OF THE IDUMEANS, WHEN THEY WERE GOTTEN INTO THE TEMPLE, DURING THE STORM; AND OF THE ZEALOTS. CONCERNING THE SLAUGHTER OF ANANUS, AND JESUS, AND ZACHARIAS; AND HOW THE IDUMEANS RETIRED HOME

1. THIS advice pleased the Idumeans, and they ascended through the city to the temple. The zealots were also in great expectation of their coming, and earnestly waited for them. When therefore these were entering, they also came boldly out of the inner temple, and mixing themselves with the Idumeans, they attacked the guards; and those that were upon the watch, but were fallen asleep, they killed as they were asleep; but as those that were now awakened made a cry, the whole multitude arose, and in the amazement they were in caught hold of their arms immediately, and betook themselves to their own defence; and so long as they thought they were only the zealots that attacked them, they went on boldly, as hoping to overpower them by their number; but when they saw others pressing in upon them also, they perceived the Idumeans were got in; and the greater part of them laid aside their arms, together with their courage, and betook themselves to lamentations. But some few of the younger sort covered themselves with their armour, and valiantly received the Idumeans, and for a while protected the old men. Others, indeed, gave a signal to those that were in the city of the calamities they were in; but when these were also made sensible that the Idumeans were come in, none of them durst come to their assistance; only they returned the terrible echo of wailing, and lamenting their mis-

fortunes. A great howling of the women was excited also, and every one of the guards were in danger of being killed. The zealots also joined in the shouts raised by the Idumeans; and the storm itself rendered the cry more terrible; nor did the Idumeans spare anybody; for as they are naturally a barbarous and bloody nation, and had been distressed by the tempest, they made use of their weapons against those that had shut the gates against them, and acted in the same manner as to those that supplicated for their lives, and to those that fought them, insomuch that they ran those through with their swords who desired them to remember the relation there was between them, and begged of them to have regard to their common temple. Now there was at present neither any place for flight nor any hope for preservation; but as they were driven one upon another in heaps, so were they slain. Thus the greater part were driven together by force, as there was now no place of retirement, and the murderers were upon them; and, having no other way, threw themselves down headlong into the city; whereby, in my opinion, they underwent a more miserable destruction than that which they avoided, because that was a voluntary one. And now the outer temple was all of it overflowed with blood; and that day, as it came on, saw eight thousand five hundred dead bodies there.

2. But the rage of the Idumeans was not satiated by these slaughters; but they now betook themselves to the city, and plundered every house, and slew every one they met; and for the multitude, they esteemed it needless to go on with killing them, but they sought for the high priests, and the generality went with the greatest zeal against them; and as soon as they caught them they slew them, and then standing upon their dead bodies, in way of jest upbraided Ananus with his kindness to the people, and Jesus with his speech made to them from the wall. Nay, they proceeded to that degree of impiety, as to cast away their bodies without burial, although the Jews used to take so much care of the burial of men, that they took down those that were condemned and crucified, and buried them before the going down of the sun. I should not mistake if I said that the death of Ananus was the beginning of the destruction of the city, and that from this very day may be dated the overthrow of her wall, and the ruin of her affairs, whereon they saw their high priest, and the procurer of their preservation slain in the midst of the city. He was on other accounts a venerable, and very just man; and besides the grandeur of that nobility, and dignity, and honour, of which he was possessed, he had been a lover of a kind of parity, even with regard to the meanest of the people; he was a prodigious lover of liberty, and an admirer of democracy in government; and did ever prefer the public welfare before his own advantage, and preferred peace above all things; for he was thoroughly sensible that the Romans were not to be conquered. He also foresaw that of necessity a war should follow; and that unless the Jews made up matters very dexterously, they would be destroyed: to say all in a word, if Ananus had survived they had certainly compounded matters; for he was a shrewd man in speaking and persuading the people, and had already gotten the mastery of those that opposed his designs, or were for the war. And the Jews had then put abundance of delays in the way of the Romans, if they had had such a general as he was. Jesus was also joined with him; and although he was inferior to him upon the comparison, he was

superior to the rest; and I cannot but think that it was because God had doomed this city to destruction, as a polluted city, and was resolved to purge his sanctuary by fire, that he cut off these its great defenders and well-wishers, while those that a little before had worn the sacred garments, and had presided over the public worship, and had been esteemed venerable by those that dwelt on the whole habitable earth when they came into our city, were cast out naked, and seen to be the food of dogs and wild beasts. And I cannot but imagine that virtue itself groaned at these men's case, and lamented that she was here so terribly conquered by wickedness. And this at last was the end of Ananus and Jesus.

3. Now after these were slain, the zealots and the multitude of the Idumeans fell upon the people as upon a flock of profane animals, and cut their throats; and, for the ordinary sort, they were destroyed in what place soever they caught them. But for the noblemen and the youth, they first caught them and bound them, and shut them up in prison, and put off their slaughters, in hopes that some of them would turn over to their party; but none of them would comply with their desires, but all of them preferred death before being enrolled among such wicked wretches as acted against their own country. But this refusal of theirs brought upon them terrible torments; for they were so scourged and tormented, that their bodies were not able to sustain their torments, till at length, and with difficulty, they had the favour to be slain. These whom they caught in the daytime, were slain in the night, and then their bodies were carried out and thrown away, that there might be room for other prisoners; and the terror that was upon all the people was so great, that no one had courage enough either to weep openly for the dead man that was related to him, or bury him: but those that were shut up in their own houses, could only shed tears in secret, and durst not even groan without great caution, lest any of their enemies should hear them; for if they did, those that mourned for others soon underwent the same death with those whom they mourned for. Only in the night-time they would take up a little dust and throw it upon their bodies; and even some that were the most ready to expose themselves to danger, would do it in the day-time: and there were twelve thousand of the better sort who perished in this manner.

4. And now these zealots and Idumeans were quite weary of barely killing men, so they had the impudence of setting up fictitious tribunals and judicatures for that purpose; and as they intended to have Zacharias,* the son of Baruch, one of the most eminent of the citizens, slain,— so what provoked them against him was that hatred of wickedness and love of liberty which were so eminent in him: he was also a rich man, so that by taking him off, they did not only hope

---

* Some commentators are ready to suppose that this "Zacharias, the son of Baruch," was the very same person with "Zacharias, the son of Barachias," Matt. xxiii. 35. This is a somewhat strange exposition; since Zechariah the prophet was really "the son of Barachiah," and "grandson of Iddo," (Zech. i. 1;) and how he died, we have no other account, than that before us in St Matthew; while this "Zacharias" was "the son of Baruch:" since the slaughter was past when our Saviour spake those words, the Jews then had already slain him; whereas the slaughter of "Zacharias, the son of Baruch," was then about thirty-four years future: and since that slaughter was "between the temple and the altar," in the court of the priests, one of the most sacred and remote parts of the whole temple; while this was in the middle of the temple.

to seize his effects, but also to get rid of a man that had great power to destroy them. So they called together, by a public proclamation, seventy of the principal men of the populace, for a show, as if they were real judges, while they had no proper authority. Before these was Zacharias accused of a design to betray their polity to the Romans, and having traitorously sent to Vespasian for that purpose. Now there appeared no proof or sign of what he was accused; but they affirmed themselves that they were well persuaded that so it was, and desired that such their affirmation might be taken for sufficient evidence. Now when Zacharias clearly saw that there was no way remaining for his escape from them, as having been treacherously called before them, and then put in prison, but not with any intention of a legal trial, he took great liberty of speech, in that despair of life he was under. Accordingly he stood up, and laughed at their pretended accusation, and in a few words confuted the crimes laid to his charge; after which he turned his speech to his accusers, and went over distinctly all their transgressions of the law, and made heavy lamentations upon the confusion they had brought public affairs into: in the meantime the zealots grew tumultuous, and had much ado to abstain from drawing their swords, although they designed to preserve the appearance and show of judicature to the end. They were also desirous, on other accounts to try the judges, whether they would be mindful of what was just at their own peril. Now the seventy judges brought in their verdict, that the person accused was not guilty, — as choosing rather to die themselves with him, than to have his death laid at their doors; hereupon there arose a great clamour of the zealots upon his acquittal, and they all had indignation at the judges, for not understanding that the authority that was given them was but in jest. So two of the boldest of them fell upon Zacharias in the middle of the temple, and slew him; and as he fell down dead they bantered him, and said, "Thou hast also our verdict, and this will prove a more sure acquittal to thee than the other." They also threw him down out of the temple immediately in the valley beneath it. Moreover they struck the judges with the backs of their swords, by way of abuse, and thrust them out of the court of the temple, and spared their lives with no other design than that, when they were dispersed among the people in the city, they might become their messengers to let them know they were no better than slaves.

5. But by this time the Idumeans repented of their coming, and were displeased at what had been done; and when they were assembled together by one of the zealots, who had come privately to them, he declared to them what a number of wicked pranks they had themselves done in conjunction with those that invited them, and gave a particular account of what mischiefs had been done against their metropolis.— He said, that they had taken arms, as though the high priests were betraying their metropolis to the Romans, but had found no indication of any such treachery: but that they had succoured those that had pretended to believe such a thing, while they did themselves the works of war and tyranny after an insolent manner. It had been indeed their business to have hindered them from such their proceedings at the first, but seeing they had once been partners with them in shedding the blood of their own countrymen, it was high time to put a stop to such crimes, and not continue to afford any more assistance to such as are subverting the laws of their forefathers; for that if any had taken it ill that the gates had been shut against them, and they had not been permitted to come into the city, yet that those who had excluded them have been punished, and Ananus is dead, and that almost all those people have been destroyed in one night's time. That one may perceive many of themselves now repenting for what they had done, and might see the horrid barbarity of those that had invited them, and that they had no regard to such as had saved them; that they were so impudent as to perpetrate the vilest things, under the eyes of those who had supported them, and that their wicked actions would be laid to the charge of the Idumeans, and would be so laid to their charge, till somebody obstructs their proceedings, or separates himself from the same wicked action; that they therefore ought to retire home, since the imputation of treason appears to be a calumny, and that there was no expectation of the coming of the Romans at this time, and that the government of the city was secured by such walls as cannot easily be thrown down; and, by avoiding any other fellowship with these bad men, to make some excuse for themselves, as to what they had been so far deluded, as to have been partners with them hitherto.

CHAPTER VI

HOW THE ZEALOTS, WHEN THEY WERE FREED FROM THE IDUMEANS, SLEW A GREAT MANY MORE OF THE CITIZENS; AND HOW VESPASIAN DISSUADED THE ROMANS, WHEN THEY WERE VERY EARNEST TO MARCH AGAINST THE JEWS, FROM PROCEEDING IN THE WAR AT THAT TIME

1. THE Idumeans complied with these persuasions; and in the first place, they set those that were in the prisons at liberty, being about two thousand of the populace, who thereupon fled away immediately to Simon, one whom we shall speak of presently. After which these Idumeans retired from Jerusalem, and went home; which departure of theirs was a great surprise to both parties; for the people, not knowing of their repentance, pulled up their courage for a while, as eased of so many of their enemies, while the zealots grew more insolent, not as deserted by their confederates, but as freed from such men as might hinder their designs, and put some stop to their wickedness. Accordingly they made no longer any delay, nor took any deliberation in their enormous practises, but made use of the shortest methods for all their executions; and what they had once resolved upon, they put in practice sooner than any one could imagine; but their thirst was chiefly after the blood of valiant men, and men of good families; the one sort of whom they destroyed out of envy, the other out of fear; for they thought their whole security lay in leaving no potent men alive; on which account they slew Gorion, a person eminent in dignity, and on account of his family also; he was also for democracy, and of as great boldness and freedom of spirit as were any of the Jews whosoever; the principal thing that ruined him, added to his other advantages, was his free-speaking. Nor did Niger of Perea escape their hands; he had been a man of great valour in their war with the Romans, but was now drawn through the middle of the city, and, as he went, he frequently cried out, and shewed the scars of his wounds; and when he was drawn out of the gates, and despaired of his preservation, he besought them

to grant him a burial; but as they had threatened him beforehand not to grant him any spot of earth for a grave, which he chiefly desired of them, so did they slay him [without permitting him to be buried.] Now when they were slaying him, he made this imprecation upon them, that they might undergo both famine and pestilence in this war, and besides all that, they might come to the mutual slaughter of one another; all which imprecations God confirmed against these impious men, and was what came most justly upon them, when not long afterward they tasted of their own madness in their mutual seditions one against another. So when this Niger was killed, their fears of being overturned were diminished, and indeed there was no part of the people but they found out some pretence to destroy them; for some were therefore slain because they had had differences with some of them; and as to those that had not opposed them in times of peace, they watched seasonable opportunities to gain some accusation against them; and if any one did not come near them at all, he was under their suspicion as a proud man; if any one came with boldness, he was esteemed a contemner of them; and if any one came as aiming to oblige them, he was supposed to have some treacherous plot against them; while the only punishment of crimes, whether they were of the greatest or smallest sort, was death. Nor could any one escape, unless he were very inconsiderable, either on account of the meanness of his birth, or on account of his fortune.

2. And now all the rest of the commanders of the Romans deemed this sedition among their enemies to be of great advantage to them, and were very earnest to march to the city; and they urged Vespasian as their lord and general in all cases, to make haste, and said to him, that "+he providence of God is on our side, by setting our enemies at variance against one another; that still the change in such cases may be sudden, and the Jews may quickly be at one again, either because they may be tired out with their civil miseries, or repent them of such doings." But Vespasian replied, that they were greatly mistaken in what they thought fit to be done, as those that, upon the theatre love to make a show of their hands, and of their weapons, but do it at their own hazard, without considering what was for their advantage and for their security; for that if they now go and attack the city immediately, they shall but occasion their enemies to unite together, and shall convert their force, now it is in its height, against themselves; but if they stay a while they shall have fewer enemies, because they will be consumed in this sedition: that God acts as general of the Romans better than he can do, and is giving the Jews up to them without any pains of their own, and granting their army a victory without any danger; that therefore it is their best way, while their enemies are destroying each other with their own hands, and falling into the greatest misfortunes, which is that of sedition, to sit still as spectators of the dangers they run into, rather than to fight hand to hand with men that love murdering, and are mad one against another. "But if any one imagines that the glory of victory, when it is gotten without fighting, will be more insipid, let him know thus much, that a glorious success, quietly obtained, is more profitable than the dangers of a battle; for we ought to esteem those that do what is agreeable to temperance and prudence, no less glorious than those that have gained great reputation by their actions in war: that he shall lead on his army with greater force

when their enemies are diminished, and his own army refreshed after the continual labours they had undergone. However, that this is not a proper time to propose to ourselves the glory of victory; for that the Jews are not now employed in making of armour or building of walls, nor indeed of getting together auxiliaries, while the advantage will be on their side who gave them such opportunity of delay; but that the Jews are vexed to pieces every day by their civil wars and dissensions, and are under greater misfortunes than, if they were once taken, could be inflicted on them by us. Whether therefore, any one has regard to what is for our safety, he ought to suffer those Jews to destroy one another; or whether he hath regard to the greater glory of the action, we ought by no means to meddle with these men, now they are afflicted with a distemper at home; for should we conquer them, it would be said the conquest was not owing to our bravery, but to their sedition."

3. And now the commanders joined in their approbation of what Vespasian had said, and it was soon discovered how wise an opinion he had given; and indeed many there were of the Jews that deserted every day, and fled away from the zealots, although their flight was very difficult, since they had guarded every passage out of the city, and slew every one that was caught at them, as taking it for granted they were going over to the Romans; yet did he that gave them money get clear off, while he that gave them none was voted a traitor. So the upshot was this, that the rich purchased their flight by money, while none but the poor were slain. Along all the roads also vast numbers of dead bodies lay in heaps, and even many of those that were so zealous in deserting, at length chose rather to perish within the city; for the hopes of burial made death in their own city appear of the two less terrible to them. But these zealots came at last to that degree of barbarity, as not to bestow a burial either on those slain in the city, or on those that lay along the roads; but as if they had made an agreement to cancel both the laws of their country and the laws of nature, and, at the same time that they defiled men with their wicked actions, they would pollute the Divinity itself also, they left the dead bodies to putrify under the sun: and the same punishment was allotted to such as buried any, as to those that deserted, which was no other than death; while he that granted the favour of a grave to another, would presently stand in need of a grave himself. To say all in a word, no other gentle passion was so entirely lost among them as mercy; for what were the greatest objects of pity did most of all irritate these wretches, and they transferred their rage from the living to those that had been slain, and from the dead to the living. Nay, the terror was so very great, that he who survived called them that were first dead happy, as being at rest already; as did those that were under torture in the prisons, declare, that, upon this comparison, those that lay unburied were the happiest. These men, therefore, trampled upon all the laws of man, and laughed at the laws of God; and for the oracles of the prophets, they ridiculed them as the tricks of jugglers; yet did these prophets foretell many things concerning [the rewards of] virtue, and [punishments of] vice, which when these zealots violated, they occasioned the fulfilling of those very prophecies belonging to their own country: for there was a certain ancient oracle of those men, that the city should then be taken and the sanctuary burnt, by right of war, when a sedition should invade

the Jews, and their own hands should pollute the temple of God. Now, while these zealots did not [quite] disbelieve these predictions, they made themselves the instruments of their accomplishment.

CHAPTER VII

HOW JOHN TYRANNISED OVER THE REST; AND WHAT MISCHIEFS THE ZEALOTS DID AT MASADA. HOW ALSO VESPASIAN TOOK GADARA; AND WHAT ACTIONS WERE PERFORMED BY PLACIDIUS

1. BY this time John was beginning to tyrannise, and thought it beneath him to accept of barely the same honours that others had; and joining to himself by degrees a party of the most wicked of them all, he broke off from the rest of the faction. This was brought about by his still disagreeing with the opinions of others, and in giving out injunctions of his own, in a very imperious manner; so that it was evident he was setting up a monarchical power. Now, some submitted to him out of their fear of him, and others out of their good-will to him; for he was a shrewd man to entice men to him, both by deluding them and putting cheats upon them. Nay, many there were that thought they should be safer themselves, if the causes of their past insolent actions should now be reduced to one head, and not to a great many. His activity was so great, and that both in action and counsel, that he had not a few guards about him; yet was there a great party of his antagonists that left him; among whom envy at him weighed a great deal, while they thought it a very heavy thing to be in subjection to one that was formerly their equal. But the main reason that moved men against him was the dread of monarchy, for they could not hope easily to put an end to his power, if he had once obtained it; and yet they knew that he would have this pretence always against them, that they had opposed him when he was first advanced; while every one chose rather to suffer anything whatsoever in war, than that, when they had been in a voluntary slavery for some time, they should afterwards perish. So the sedition was divided into two parts, and John reigned in opposition to his adversaries over one of them: but for their leaders, they watched one another, nor did they at all, or at least very little, meddle with arms in their quarrels; but they fought earnestly against the people, and contended one with another which of them should bring home the greatest prey. But because the city had to struggle with three of the greatest misfortunes, war, and tyranny, and sedition, it appeared, upon the comparison, that the war was the least troublesome to the populace of them all. Accordingly they ran away from their own houses to foreigners, and obtained that preservation from the Romans which they despaired to obtain among their own people.

2. And now a fourth misfortune arose, in order to bring our nation to destruction. There was a fortress of very great strength not far from Jerusalem, which had been built by our ancient kings, both as a repository for their effects in the hazards of war, and for the preservation of their bodies at the same time. It is called Masada. Those that were called *Sicarii* had taken possession of it formerly; but at this time they overran the neighbouring countries, aiming only to procure to themselves necessaries; for the fear they were then in prevented

their future ravages; but when once they were informed that the Roman army lay still, and that the Jews were divided between sedition and tyranny, they boldly undertook greater matters; and at the feast of unleavened bread, which the Jews celebrate in memory of their deliverance from their Egyptian bondage, when they were sent back into the country of their forefathers, they came down by night, without being discovered by those that could have prevented them, and overran a certain small city called Engaddi:—in which expedition they prevented those citizens that could have stopped them, before they could arm themselves and fight them. They also dispersed them, and cast them out of the city. As for such as could not run away, being women and children, they slew of them above seven hundred. Afterward, when they had carried everything out of their houses, and had seized upon all the fruits that were in a flourishing condition, they brought them into Masada. And indeed these men laid all the villages that were about the fortress waste, and made the whole country desolate; while there came to them every day from all parts not a few men as corrupt as themselves. At this time all the other regions of Judea that had hitherto been at rest were in motion, by means of the robbers. Now as it is in a human body, if the principal part be inflamed, all the members are subject to the same distemper, so by means of the sedition and disorder that was in the metropolis had the wicked men that were in the country opportunity to ravage the same. Accordingly, when every one of them had plundered their own villages, they then retired into the desert; yet were these men that now got together and joined in the conspiracy by parties, too small for an army, and too many for a gang of thieves: and thus did they fall upon the holy places* and the cities; yet did it now so happen that they were sometimes very ill treated by those upon whom they fell with such violence, and were taken by them as men are taken in war: but still they prevented any farther punishment as do robbers, who as soon as their ravages [are discovered,] run their way. Nor was there now any part of Judea that was not in a miserable condition, as well as its most eminent city also.

3. These things were told Vespasian by deserters; for although the seditious watched all the passages out of the city, and destroyed all, whosoever they were, that came thither, yet were there some who had concealed themselves, and, when they had fled to the Romans, persuaded their general to come to their city's assistance, and save the remainder of the people; informing him withal, that it was upon account of the people's good-will to the Romans that many of them were already slain, and the survivors in danger of the same treatment. Vespasian did indeed already pity the calamities these men were in, and arose, in appearance, as though he were going to besiege Jerusalem,—but in reality to deliver them from a [worse] siege they were already under. However, he was obliged first to overthrow what remained elsewhere, and to leave nothing out of Jerusalem behind him that might interrupt him in that siege. Accordingly, he marched against Gadara, the metropolis of Perea, which is a place of strength, and entered that city on the fourth day of the month Dystrus

---

* By these *hiera*, or "holy places," as distinct from cities, must be meant *proseuchæ*, or "houses of prayer" out of cities; of which we find mention made in the New Testament and other authors. See Luke vi. 12; Acts xvi. 13, 16.

[Adar;] for the men of power had sent an embassage to him, without the knowledge of the seditious, to treat about a surrender; which they did out of the desire they had of peace, and for saving their effects, because many of the citizens of Gadara were rich men. This embassy the opposite party knew nothing of, but discovered it as Vespasian was approaching near the city. However, they despaired of keeping possession of the city, as being inferior in number to their enemies who were within the city, and seeing the Romans very near to the city; so they resolved to fly, but thought it dishonourable to do it without shedding some blood, and revenging themselves on the authors of this surrender; so they seized upon Dolesus (a person not only the first in rank and family in the city, but one that seemed the occasion of sending such an embassy) and slew him, and treated his dead body after a barbarous manner, so very violent was their anger at him, and then ran out of the city. And now as the army was just upon them, the people of Gadara admitted Vespasian with joyful acclamations, and received from him the security of his right hand, as also a garrison of horsemen and footmen, to guard them against the excursions of the runagates; for as to their wall, they had pulled it down before the Romans desired them so to do, that they might thereby give them assurance that they were lovers of peace, and that, if they had a mind, they could not now make war against them.

4. And now Vespasian sent Placidus against those that had fled from Gadara, with five hundred horsemen, and three thousand footmen, while he returned himself to Cesarea, with the rest of the army. But as soon as these fugitives saw the horsemen that pursued them just at their backs, and before they came to a close fight, they ran together to a certain village, which was called Bethennabris, where, finding a great multitude of young men, and arming them, partly by their own consent and partly by force, they rashly and suddenly assaulted Placidus and the troops that were with him. These horsemen at the first onset gave way a little, as contriving to entice them farther off the wall; and when they had drawn them into a place fit for their purpose, they made their horse encompass them around, and threw their darts at them. So the horsemen cut off the flight of the fugitives, while the foot terribly destroyed those that fought against them; for those Jews did no more than shew their courage, and then were destroyed; for as they fell upon the Romans when they were joined close together, and, as it were, walled about with their entire armour, they were not able to find any place where the darts could enter, nor were they any way able to break their ranks, while they were themselves run through by the Roman darts, and, like the wildest of wild beasts, rushed upon the points of the others' swords; so some of them were destroyed as cut with their enemies' swords upon their faces, and others were dispersed by the horsemen.

5. Now Placidus's concern was to exclude them in their flight from getting into the village; and causing his horsemen to march continually on that side of them, he then turned short upon them, and at the same time his men made use of their darts, and easily took their aim at those that were the nearest to them, as they made those that were farther off turn back by the terror they were in, till at last the most courageous of them brake through those horsemen, and fled to the wall of the village. And now those that guarded the wall were in great doubt what to do; for though they could not bear the thoughts of excluding these that came from Gadara, because of their own people that were among them; and yet if they should admit them, they expected to perish with them, which came to pass accordingly; for as they were crowding together at the wall, the Roman horsemen were just ready to fall in with them. However, the guards prevented them, and shut the gates, when Placidus made an assault upon them, and, fighting courageously till it was dark, he got possession of the wall, and of the people that were in the city, when the useless multitude were destroyed; but those that were more potent ran away; and the soldiers plundered the houses, and set the village on fire. As for those that ran out of the village, they stirred up such as were in the country, and exaggerating their own calamities, and telling them that the whole army of the Romans were upon them, they put them into great fear on every side; so they got together in great numbers, and fled to Jericho, for they knew no other place that could afford them any hope of escaping, it being a city that had a strong wall, and a great multitude of inhabitants. But Placidus, relying much upon his horsemen and his former good success, followed them, and slew all that he overtook, as far as Jordan; and when he had driven the whole multitude to the river side, where they were stopped by the current, (for it had been augmented lately by rains, and was not fordable,) he put his soldiers in array over against them; so the necessity the others were in provoked them to hazard a battle, because there was no place whither they could flee. They then extended themselves a very great way along the banks of the river, and sustained the darts that were thrown at them as well as the attacks of the horsemen, who beat many of them, and pushed them into the current. At which fight, hand to hand, fifteen thousand of them were slain, while the number of those that were unwillingly forced to leap into Jordan was prodigious. There were besides, two thousand and two hundred taken prisoners. A mighty prey was taken also, consisting of asses, and sheep, and camels, and oxen.

6. Now this destruction that fell upon the Jews, as it was not inferior to any of the rest in itself, so did it still appear greater than it really was; and this, because not only the whole of the country through which they had fled was filled with slaughter, and Jordan could not be passed over, by reason of the dead bodies that were in it, but because the lake Asphaltitis was also full of dead bodies, that were carried down into it by the river. And now Placidus, after this good success that he had, fell violently upon the neighbouring smaller cities and villages; when he took Abila, and Julias, and Bezemoth, and all those that lay as far as the lake Asphaltitis, and put such of the deserters into each of them as he thought proper. He then put his soldiers on board the ships, and slew such as had fled to the lake, insomuch that all Perea had either surrendered themselves, or were taken by the Romans, as far as Macherus.

CHAPTER VIII

HOW VESPASIAN, UPON HEARING OF SOME COMMOTIONS IN GALL,* MADE HASTE TO FINISH THE

---

* Gr. Galatia, and so everywhere.

JEWISH WAR; A DESCRIPTION OF JERICHO, AND OF THE GREAT PLAIN; WITH AN ACCOUNT, BESIDES, OF THE LAKE ASPHALTITIS

1. IN the meantime, an account came that there were commotions in Gall, and that Vindex, together with the men of power in that country, had revolted from Nero; which affair is more accurately described elsewhere. This report thus related to Vespasian, excited him to go on briskly with the war; for he foresaw already the civil wars which were coming upon them, nay, that the very government was in danger; and he thought, if he could first reduce the eastern parts of the empire to peace, he should make the fears for Italy the lighter; while therefore the winter was his hindrance [from going into the field,] he put garrisons into the villages and smaller cities for their security; he put decurions also into the villages, and centurions into the cities; he besides this rebuilt many of the cities that had been laid waste; but at the beginning of the spring he took the greatest part of his army, and led it from Cesarea to Antipatris, where he spent two days in settling the affairs of that city, and then, on the third day, he marched on, laying waste and burning all the neighbouring villages. And when he had laid waste all the places about the toparchy of Thamnas, he passed on to Lydda and Jamnia; and when both those cities had come over to him, he placed a great many of those that had come over to him [from other places] as inhabitants therein, and then came to Emmaus, where he seized upon the passages which led thence to their metropolis, and fortified his camp, and leaving the fifth legion therein, he came to the toparchy of Bethletephon. He then destroyed that place, and the neighbouring places, by fire, and fortified, at proper places, the strongholds all about Idumea; and when he had seized upon two villages, which were in the very midst of Idumea, Betaris, and Caphartobas, he slew above ten thousand of the people, and carried into captivity above a thousand, and drove away the rest of the multitude, and placed no small part of his own forces in them, who overran and laid waste the whole mountainous country; while he, with the rest of his forces, returned to Emmaus, whence he came down through the country of Samaria, and hard by the city, by others called Neapolis (or Sichem) but by the people of that country Mabortha, to Corea, where he pitched his camp, on the second day of the month Dæsius [Sivan;] and on the day following he came to Jericho; on which day Trajan, one of his commanders, joined him with the forces he brought out of Perea, all the places beyond Jordan being subdued already.

2. Hereupon a great multitude prevented their approach, and came out of Jericho, and fled to those mountainous parts that lay over against Jerusalem, while that part which was left behind was in a great measure destroyed; they also found the city desolate. It is situated in a plain; but a naked and barren mountain, of a great length, hangs over it, which extends itself to the land about Scythopolis northward, but as far as the country of Sodom, and the utmost limits of the lake Asphaltitis southward. This mountain is all of it very uneven and uninhabited, by reason of its barrenness: there is an opposite mountain that is situated over-against it, on the other side of Jordan; this last begins at Julias and the northern quarters, and extends itself southward as far as Somorrhon, which is the bounds of Petra, in Arabia. In this ridge of mountains there is one called the Iron Mountain, that runs in length as far as Moab. Now the region that lies in the middle between these ridges of mountains, is called the Great Plain; it reaches from the village Ginnabris, as far as the lake Asphaltitis; its length is two hundred and thirty furlongs, and its breadth a hundred and twenty, and it is divided in the midst by Jordan. It hath two lakes in it; that of Asphaltitis, and that of Tiberias, whose natures are opposite to each other; for the former is salt and unfruitful; but that of Tiberias is sweet and fruitful. This plain is much burnt up in summer-time, and, by reason of the extraordinary heat, contains a very unwholesome air; it is all destitute of water excepting the river Jordan, which water of Jordan is the occasion why those plantations of palm-trees that are near its banks, are more flourishing, and much more fruitful, as those that are remote from it not so flourishing and fruitful.

3. Notwithstanding which, there is a fountain by Jericho, that runs plentifully, and is very fit for watering the ground: it arises near the old city, which Joshua, the son of Nun, the general of the Hebrews, took the first of all the cities of the land of Canaan, by right of war. The report is, that this fountain, at the beginning, caused not only the blasting of the earth and the trees, but of the children born of women; and that it was entirely of a sickly and corruptive nature to all things whatsoever, but that it was made gentle, and very wholesome and fruitful, by the prophet Elisha. This prophet was familiar with Elijah, and was his successor, who when he once was the guest of the people of Jericho, and the men of the place had treated him very kindly, he both made them amends as well as the country, by a lasting favour; for he went out of the city to this fountain, and threw into the current an earthen vessel full of salt; after which he stretched out his righteous hand unto heaven, and, pouring out a mild drink-offering, he made this supplication,—That the current might be mollified, and that the veins of fresh water might be opened: that God also would bring into the place a more temperate and fertile air for the current, and would bestow upon the people of that country plenty of the fruits of the earth, and a succession of children; and that this prolific water might never fail them, while they continued to be righteous. To these prayers Elisha joined proper operations of his hands, after a skilful manner, and changed the fountain; and that water, which had been the occasion of barrenness and famine before from that time did supply a numerous posterity and afforded great abundance to the country. Accordingly, the power of it is so great in watering the ground, that if it do but once touch a country it affords a sweeter nourishment than other waters do, when they lie so long upon them, till they are satiated with them. For which reason, the advantage gained from other waters, when they flow in great plenty, is but small, while that of this water is great when it even flows in little quantities. Accordingly it waters a larger space of ground than any other waters do, and passes along a plain of seventy furlongs long, and twenty broad; wherein it affords nourishment to those most excellent gardens that are thick set with trees. There are in it many sorts of palm-trees that are watered by it, different from each other in taste and name; the better sort of them, when they are pressed, yield an excellent kind of honey, not much inferior in sweetness to other honey. This country withal produces honey from bees: it also bears that balsam which is the most precious of all the fruits in

that place, cypress-trees also, and those that bear myrobalanum; so that he who should pronounce this place to be divine would not be mistaken, wherein is such plenty of trees produced as are very rare, and of the most excellent sort. And indeed, if we speak of those other fruits, it will not be easy to light on any climate in the habitable earth that can well be compared to it, —what is here sown comes up in such clusters: the cause of which seems to me to be the warmth of the air and the fertility of the waters; the warmth calling forth the sprouts, and making them spread, and the moisture making every one of them take root firmly, and supplying that virtue which it stands in need of in summer time. Now, this country is then so sadly burnt up, that nobody cares to come at it; and if the water be drawn up before sun-rising, and after that exposed to the air, it becomes exceeding cold, and becomes of a nature quite contrary to the ambient air: as in winter again it becomes warm; and if you go into it, it appears very gentle. The ambient air is here also of so good a temperature, that the people of the country are clothed in linen only, even when snow covers the rest of Judea. This place is one hundred and fifty furlongs from Jerusalem, and sixty from Jordan. The country, as far as Jerusalem, is desert and stony; but that as far as Jordan and the lake Asphaltitis lies lower indeed, though it be equally desert and barren. But so much shall suffice to have been said about Jericho, and of the great happiness of its situation.

4. The nature of the lake Asphaltitis is also worth describing. It is, as I have said already, bitter and unfruitful. It is so light [or thick] that it bears up the heaviest things that are thrown into it; nor is it easy for any one to make things sink therein to the bottom, if he had a mind so to do. Accordingly when Vespasian went to see it, he commanded that some who could not swim, should have their hands tied behind them, and be thrown into the deep, when it so happened that they all swam as if a wind had forced them upwards. Moreover, the change of the colour of this lake is wonderful, for it changes its appearance thrice every day; and as the rays of the sun fall differently upon it, the light is variously reflected. However, it casts up black clods of bitumen in many parts of it; these swim at the top of the water, and resemble both in shape and bigness headless bulls: and when the labourers that belong to the lake come to it, and catch hold of it as it hangs together, they draw it into their ships; but when the ship is full, it is not easy to cut off the rest, for it is so tenacious as to make the ship hang upon its clods till they set it loose with the menstrual blood of women, and with urine, to which alone it yields. This bitumen is not only useful for the caulking of ships, but for the cure of men's bodies: accordingly it is mixed in a great many medicines. The length of this lake is five hundred and eighty furlongs, where it is extended as far as Zoar, in Arabia; and its breadth is a hundred and fifty. The country of Sodom borders upon it. It was of old a most happy land, both for the fruits it bore and the riches of its cities, although it be now all burnt up. It is related how for the impiety of its inhabitants, it was burnt by lightning; in consequence of which there are still the remainders of that divine fire; and the traces [or shadows] of the five cities are still to be seen, as well as the ashes growing in their fruits, which fruits have a colour as if they were fit to be eaten; but if you pluck them with your hands, they dissolve into smoke and ashes. And thus what is related of this land of Sodom hath these marks of credibility which our very sight affords us.

CHAPTER IX

THAT VESPASIAN, AFTER HE HAD TAKEN GADARA, MADE PREPARATION FOR THE SIEGE OF JERUSALEM; BUT THAT, UPON HIS HEARING OF THE DEATH OF NERO, HE CHANGED HIS INTENTIONS: AS ALSO, CONCERNING SIMON OF GERASA

1. AND now Vespasian had fortified all the places round about Jerusalem, and erected citadels at Jericho and Adida, and placed garrisons in them both, partly out of his own Romans, and partly out of the body of his auxiliaries. He also sent Lucius Annius to Gerasa, and delivered to him a body of horsemen, and a considerable number of footmen. So when he had taken the city, which he did at the first onset, he slew a thousand of those young men who had not prevented him by flying away; but he took their families captive, and permitted his soldiers to plunder them of their effects; after which he set fire to their houses, and went away to the adjoining villages, while the men of power fled away, and the weaker part were destroyed, and what was remaining was all burnt down. And now the war having gone through all the mountainous country, and all the plain country also, those that were at Jerusalem were deprived of the liberty of going out of the city; for as to such as had a mind to desert, they were watched by the zealots; and as to such as were not yet on the side of the Romans, their army kept them in, by encompassing the city round about on all sides.

2. Now as Vespasian was returned to Cesarea, and was getting ready with all his army to march directly to Jerusalem, he was informed that Nero was dead, after he had reigned thirteen years and eight days. But as to any narration after what manner he abused his power in the government, and committed the management of affairs to those vile wretches, Nymphidius and Tigellinus, his unworthy freed-men; and how he had a plot laid against him by them, and was deserted by all his guards, and ran away with four of his most trusty freed-men, and slew himself in the suburbs of Rome; and how those that occasioned his death were, in no long time, brought themselves to punishment; how also the war in Gall ended; and how Galba was made emperor,* and returned out of Spain to Rome; and how he was accused by the soldiers as a pusillanimous person, and slain by treachery in the middle of the market-place at Rome, and Otho was made emperor; with his expedition against the commanders of Vitellius, and his destruction thereupon; and besides what troubles there were under Vitellius, and the fight that was about the Capitol; as also how Antonius Primus and Mucianus slew Vitellius, and his German legions, and thereby put an end to that civil war,—I have omitted to give an exact account of them, because they are well known by all, and they are described by a great number of Greek and Roman authors; yet for the sake of the connection of matters, and that

---

* Of these Roman affairs and tumults under Galba, Otho, and Vitellius, see Tacitus, Suetonius, and Dio. However, we may observe that Josephus writes the name of the second of them not Otto, but Otho.

my history may not be incoherent, I have just touched upon everything briefly. Wherefore Vespasian put off at first his expedition against Jerusalem, and stood waiting whither the empire would be transferred after the death of Nero. Moreover, when he heard that Galba was made emperor, he attempted nothing till he also should send him some directions about the war : however, he sent his son Titus to him, to salute him, and to receive his commands about the Jews. Upon the very same errand did king Agrippa sail along with Titus to Galba ; but as they were sailing in their long ships by the coasts of Achaia, for it was winter time, they heard that Galba was slain, before they could get to him, after he had reigned seven months and as many days. After whom Otho took the government, and undertook the management of public affairs. So Agrippa resolved to go on to Rome without any terror on account of the change in the government ; but Titus, by a divine impulse, sailed back from Greece to Syria, and came in great haste to Cesarea, to his father. And now they were both in suspense about the public affairs, the Roman empire being then in a fluctuating condition, and did not go on with their expedition against the Jews, but thought that to make any attack upon foreigners was now unseasonable, on account of the solicitude they were in for their own country.

3. And now there arose another war at Jerusalem. There was a son of Giora, one Simon, by birth of Gerasa, a young man, not so cunning indeed as John [of Gischala,] who had already seized upon the city, but superior in strength of body and courage ; on which account, when he had been driven away from that Acrabattene toparchy, which he once had, by Ananus the high priest, he came to those robbers who had seized upon Masada. At first they suspected him, and only permitted him to come with the women he brought with him into the lower part of the fortress, while they dwelt in the upper part of it themselves. However, his manner so well agreed with theirs, and he seemed so trusty a man, that he went out with them, and ravaged and destroyed the country with them about Masada ; yet when he persuaded them to undertake greater things, he could not prevail with them so to do ; for as they were accustomed to dwell in that citadel, they were afraid of going far from that which was their hiding-place ; but he affecting to tyrannise, and being fond of greatness, when he had heard of the death of Ananus, left them, and went into the mountainous part of the country. So he proclaimed liberty to those in slavery, and a reward to those already free, and got together a set of wicked men from all quarters.

4. And as he had now a strong body of men about him, he over-ran the villages that lay in the mountainous country, and when there were still more and more that came to him, he ventured to go down to the lower parts of the country, and since he was now become formidable to the cities, many of the men of power were corrupted by him ; so that his army was no longer composed of slaves and robbers, but a great many of the populace were obedient to him as to their king. He then over-ran the Acrabattene toparchy, and the places that reached as far as the Great Idumea ; for he built a wall at a certain village called Nain, and made use of that as a fortress for his own party's security ; and at the valley called Paran, he enlarged many of the caves, and many others he found ready for his purpose ; these he made use of as repositories for his treasures, and receptacles for his prey,

and therein he laid up the fruits that he had got by rapine ; and many of his partizans had their dwelling in them ; and he made no secret of it that he was exercising his men beforehand, and making preparation for the assault of Jerusalem.

5. Whereupon the zealots, out of the dread they were in of his attacking them, and being willing to prevent one that was growing up to oppose them, went out against him with their weapons. Simon met them, and joining battle with them, slew a considerable number of them, and drove the rest before him into the city : but durst not trust so much upon his forces as to make an assault upon the walls ; but he resolved first to subdue Idumea, and as he had now twenty thousand armed men, he marched to the borders of their country. Hereupon the rulers of the Idumeans got together on the sudden the most warlike part of their people, about twenty-five thousand in number, and permitted the rest to be guard to their own country, by reason of the incursions that were made by the *Sicarii* that were at Masada. Thus they received Simon at their borders, where they fought him, and continued the battle all that day ; and the dispute lay whether they had conquered him or been conquered by him. So he went back to Nain, as did the Idumeans return home. Nor was it long ere Simon came violently again upon their country ; when he pitched his camp at a certain village called Thecoe, and sent Eleazar, one of his companions, to those that kept garrison at Herodium, and in order to persuade them to surrender that fortress to him. The garrison received this man readily, while they knew nothing of what he came about ; but as soon as he talked of the surrender of the place, they fell upon him with their drawn swords, till he found he had no place for flight, when he threw himself down from the wall into the valley beneath ; so he died immediately : but the Idumeans, who were already much afraid of Simon's power, thought fit to take a view of the enemy's army before they hazarded a battle with him.

6. Now, there was one of their commanders, named Jacob, who offered to serve them readily upon that occasion, but had it in his mind to betray them. He went therefore from the village Alurus, wherein the army of the Idumeans were gotten together, and came to Simon, and at the very first he agreed to betray his country to him, and took assurances upon oath from him that he should always have him in esteem, and then promised him that he would assist him in subduing all Idumea under him ; upon which account he was feasted after an obliging manner by Simon, and elevated by his mighty promises ; and when he was returned to his own men, he at first belied the army of Simon, and said it was manifold more in number than it was ; after which, he dexterously persuaded the commanders, and by degrees the whole multitude, to receive Simon, and to surrender the whole government up to him without fighting ; and as he was doing this, he invited Simon by his messengers, and promised him to disperse the Idumeans, which he performed also ; for as soon as their army was nigh them, he first of all got upon his horse, and fled, together with those whom he had corrupted : hereupon a terror fell upon the whole multitude ; and before it came to a close fight, they broke their ranks, and every one retired to his own home.

7. Thus did Simon unexpectedly march into Idumea, without bloodshed, and made a sudden attack upon the city Hebron, and took it ;

wherein he got possession of a great deal of prey, and plundered it of a vast quantity of fruit. Now, the people of the country say, that it is an ancienter city, not only than any in that country, but than Memphis in Egypt, and accordingly its age is reckoned at two thousand and three hundred years. They also relate that it had been the habitation of Abraham, the progenitor of the Jews, after he had removed out of Mesopotamia; and they say that his posterity descended from thence into Egypt, whose monuments are to this very time shewn in that small city; the fabric of which monuments are of the most excellent marble, and wrought after the most elegant manner. There is also there shewn, at the distance of six furlongs from the city, a very large turpentine-tree; and the report goes, that this tree has continued ever since the creation of the world. Thence did Simon make his progress over all Idumea, and did not only ravage the cities and villages, but laid waste the whole country; for, besides those that were completely armed, he had forty thousand men that followed him, insomuch that he had not provisions enough to suffice such a multitude. Now, besides this want of provisions that he was in, he was of a barbarous disposition, and bore great anger at this nation, by which means it came to pass that Idumea was greatly depopulated; and as one may see all the woods behind despoiled of their leaves by locusts, after they have been there, so was there nothing left behind Simon's army but a desert. Some places they burnt down, some they utterly demolished, and whatever grew in the country, they either trod it down or fed upon it, and by their marches they made the ground that was cultivated, harder and more untractable than that which was barren. In short, there was no sign remaining of those places that had been laid waste, that ever they had had a being.

8. This success of Simon excited the zealots afresh; and though they were afraid to fight him openly in a fair battle, yet did they lay ambushes in the passes, and seized upon his wife, with a considerable number of her attendants; whereupon they came back to the city rejoicing, as if they had taken Simon himself captive, and were in present expectation that he would lay down his arms, and make supplication to them for his wife; but instead of indulging any merciful affection, he grew very angry at them for seizing his beloved wife; so he came to the wall of Jerusalem, and, like wild beasts when they are wounded, and cannot overtake those that wounded them, he vented his spleen upon all persons that he met with. Accordingly, he caught all those that were come out of the city-gates, either to gather herbs or sticks, who were unarmed and in years; he then tormented them and destroyed them, out of the immense rage he was in, and was almost ready to taste the very flesh of their dead bodies. He also cut off the hands of a great many, and sent them into the city to astonish his enemies, and in order to make the people fall into a sedition, and desert those that had been the authors of his wife's seizure. He also enjoined them to tell the people that Simon swore by the God of the universe, who sees all things, that unless they will restore him his wife, he will break down their wall, and inflict the like punishment upon all the citizens, without sparing any age, and without making any distinction between the guilty and the innocent. Those threatenings so greatly affrighted, not the people only, but the zealots themselves also, that they sent his wife back to

him,—when he became a little milder, and left off his perpetual blood-shedding.

9. But now sedition and civil war prevailed, not only over Judea, but in Italy also; for now Galba was slain in the midst of the Roman market-place; then was Otho made emperor, and fought against Vitellius, who set up for emperor also; for the legions in Germany had chosen him; but when he gave battle to Valens and Cecinna, who were Vitellius's generals, at Betriacum, in Gall, Otho gained the advantage on the first day; but on the second day Vitellius's soldiers had the victory; and after much slaughter, Otho slew himself, when he had heard of this defeat at Brixia, and after he had managed the public affairs three months and two days. Otho's army also came over to Vitellius's generals, and he came himself down to Rome with his army; but in the meantime Vespasian removed from Cesarea, on the fifth day of the month Dæsius [Sivan,] and marched against those places of Judea which were not yet overthrown. So he went up to the mountainous country, and took those two toparchies that were called the Gophnitick and Acrabattene toparchies. After which he took Bethel and Ephraim, two small cities; and when he had put garrisons into them, he rode as far as Jerusalem, in which march he took many prisoners, and many captives. But Cerealis, one of his commanders, took a body of horsemen and footmen, and laid waste that part of Idumea which was called the Upper Idumea, and attacked Caphethra, which pretended to be a small city, and took it at the first onset, and burnt it down. He also attacked Capharabim, and laid siege to it, for it had a very strong wall; and when he expected to spend a very long time in that siege, those that were within opened their gates on the sudden, and came to beg pardon, and surrendered themselves up to him. When Cerealis had conquered them he went to Hebron, another very ancient city. I have told you already, that this city is situated in a mountainous country not far off Jerusalem; and when he had broken into the city by force, what multitude and young men were left therein he slew, and burnt down the city; so that now all the places were taken, excepting Herodium, and Masada, and Macherus, which were in the possession of the robbers, so Jerusalem was what the Romans at present aimed at.

10. And now as soon as Simon had set his wife free, and recovered her from the zealots, he returned back to the remainder of Idumea, and driving the nation all before him from all quarters, he compelled a great number of them to retire to Jerusalem; he followed them himself also to the city, and encompassed the wall all round again; and when he lighted upon any labourers that were coming thither out of the country, he slew them. Now this Simon, who was without the wall, was a greater terror to the people than the Romans themselves, as were the zealots who were within it more heavy upon them than both of the other; and during this time did the mischievous contrivances and courage [of John] corrupt the body of the Galileans; for these Galileans had advanced this John, and made him very potent, who made them a suitable requital from the authority he had obtained by their means; for he permitted them to do all things that any of them desired to do, while their inclination to plunder was insatiable, as was their zeal in searching the houses of the rich; and for the murdering of the men, and abusing of the women, it was sport to them. They also devoured what spoils they had taken,

together with their blood, and indulged themselves in feminine wantonness, without any disturbance, till they were satiated therewith: while they decked their hair, and put on women's garments, and were besmeared over with ointments; and that they might appear very comely, they had paints under their eyes, and imitated, not only the ornaments, but also the lusts of women, and were guilty of such intolerable uncleanness, that they invented unlawful pleasures of that sort. And thus did they roll themselves up and down the city, as in a brothel-house, and defiled it entirely with their impure actions: nay, while their faces looked like the faces of women, they killed with their right hands; and when their gait was effeminate, they presently attacked men, and became warriors, and drew their swords from under their finely-dyed cloaks, and ran everybody through whom they alighted upon. However, Simon waited for such as ran away from John, and was the more bloody of the two: and he who had escaped the tyrant within the wall, was destroyed by the other that lay before the gates. So that all attempts of flying and deserting to the Romans were cut off, if any had a mind so to do.

11. Yet did the army that was under John raise a sedition against him; and all the Idumeans separated themselves from the tyrant, and attempted to destroy him, and this out of their envy at his power, and hatred of his cruelty; so they got together, and slew many of the zealots, and drove the rest before them into that royal palace that was built by Grapte, who was a relation of Izates, the king of Adiabene; the Idumeans fell in with them, and drove the zealots out thence into the temple, and betook themselves to plunder John's effects; for both he himself was in that palace, and therein had he laid up the spoils he had acquired by his tyranny. In the meantime the multitude of those zealots that were dispersed over the city ran together to the temple unto those that had fled thither, and John prepared to bring them down against the people and the Idumeans, who were not so much afraid of being attacked by them, (because they were themselves better soldiers than they,) as at their madness, lest they should privately sally out of the temple and get among them, and not only destroy them, but set the city on fire also. So they assembled themselves together, and the high priests with them, and took counsel after what manner they should avoid their assault. Now it was God who turned their opinions to the worst advice, and thence they devised such a remedy to get themselves free, as was worse than the disease itself. Accordingly, in order to overthrow John, they determined to admit Simon, and earnestly to desire the introduction of a second tyrant into the city; which resolution they brought to perfection, and sent Matthias, the high priest, to beseech this Simon to come in to them, of whom they had so often been afraid. Those also that had fled from the zealots in Jerusalem joined in this request to him, out of the desire they had of preserving their houses and their effects. Accordingly he, in an arrogant manner, granted them his lordly protection, and came into the city, in order to deliver it from the zealots. The people also made joyful acclamations to him, as their saviour and preserver; but when he was come in, with his army, he took care to secure his own authority, and looked upon those that had invited him to be no less his enemies than those against whom the invitation was intended.

12. And thus did Simon get possession of Jerusalem, in the third year of the war, in the month Xanthicus [Nisan;] whereupon John, with his multitude of zealots, as being both prohibited from coming out of the temple, and having lost their power in the city (for Simon and his party had plundered them of what they had) were in despair of deliverance. Simon also made an assault upon the temple, with the assistance of the people, while the others stood upon the cloisters and the battlements, and defended themselves from their assaults. However, a considerable number of Simon's party fell, and many were carried off wounded; for the zealots threw their darts easily from a superior place, and seldom failed of hitting their enemies; but having the advantage of situation, and having withal erected four very large towers aforehand, that their darts might come from higher places, one at the north-east corner of the court, one above the Xystus, the third at another corner over against the lower city, and the last was erected above the top of the Pastophoria, where one of the priests stood of course, and gave a signal beforehand, with a trumpet,* at the beginning of every seventh day, in the evening twilight, as also at the evening when the day was finished, as giving notice to the people when they were to leave off work, and when they were to go to work again. These men also set their engines to cast darts and stones withal, upon those towers, with their archers and slingers. And now Simon made his assault upon the temple more faintly, by reason that the greatest part of his men grew weary of that work; yet did he not leave off his opposition, because his army was superior to the others, although the darts which were thrown by the engines were carried a great way, and slew many of those that fought for him.

CHAPTER X

HOW THE SOLDIERS, BOTH IN JUDEA AND EGYPT, PROCLAIMED VESPASIAN EMPEROR; AND HOW VESPASIAN RELEASED JOSEPHUS FROM HIS BONDS

1. Now, about this time it was that heavy calamities came about Rome on all sides; for Vitellius was come from Germany with his soldiery, and drew along with him a great multitude of other men besides. And when the spaces allotted for soldiers could not contain them, he made all Rome itself his camp, and filled all the houses with armed men; which men, when they saw the riches of Rome with those eyes which had never seen such riches before, and found themselves shone round about on all sides with silver and gold, they had much ado to contain their covetous desires, and were ready to betake themselves to plunder, and to the slaughter of such as should stand in their way. And this was the state of affairs in Italy at that time.

2. But when Vespasian had overthrown all the places that were near to Jerusalem, he returned to Cesarea, and heard of the troubles that were at Rome, and that Vitellius was emperor. This produced indignation in him, although he well knew how to be governed, as well as to govern, and could not with any satisfaction own him for his lord who acted so madly, and seized upon the government as if it were absolutely destitute of a governor. And as this sorrow of his was vio-

* This beginning and ending the observation of the Jewish Seventh Day, or Sabbath, with a priest's blowing of a trumpet, is remarkable, and nowhere else mentioned, that I know of.

lent, he was not able to support the torments he was under, nor to apply himself further in other wars when his native country was laid waste; but then, as much as his passion excited him to avenge his country, so much was he restrained by the consideration of his distance therefrom; because fortune might prevent him, and do a world of mischief before he could himself sail over the sea of Italy, especially as it was still the winter season; so he restrained his anger, how vehement soever it was at this time.

3. But now his commanders and soldiers met in several companies, and consulted openly about changing the public affairs;—and, out of their indignation, cried out, how "at Rome there are soldiers that live delicately, and when they have not ventured so much as to hear the fame of war, they ordain whom they please for our governors, and in hopes of gain make them emperors; while you, who have gone through so many labours, and are grown into years under your helmets, give leave to others to use such a power, when yet you have among yourselves one more worthy to rule than any whom they have set up. Now, what juster opportunity shall they ever have of requiting their generals, if they do not make use of this that is now before them? while there is so much juster reason for Vespasian's being emperor than for Vitellius; as they are themselves more deserving than those that made the other emperors; for that they have undergone as great wars as have the troops that come from Germany; nor are they inferior in war to those that have brought that tyrant to Rome, nor have they undergone smaller labours than they; for that neither will the Roman senate, nor people, bear such a lascivious emperor as Vitellius, if he be compared with their chaste Vespasian; nor will they endure a most barbarous tyrant, instead of a good governor, nor choose one that hath no child, to preside over them, instead of him that is a father; because the advancement of men's own children to dignities is certainly the greatest security kings can have for themselves. Whether, therefore we estimate the capacity of governing from the skill of a person in years, we ought to have Vespasian,—or whether from the strength of a young man, we ought to have Titus; for by this means we shall have the advantage of both their ages, for that they will afford strength to those that shall be made emperors, they having already three legions, besides other auxiliaries from the neighbouring kings and will have further all the armies in the east to support them, as also those in Europe, so far as they are out of the distance and dread of Vitellius, besides such auxiliaries as they may have in Italy itself; that is Vespasian's brother, and his other son [Domitian;] the one of whom will bring in a great many of those young men that are of dignity, while the other is intrusted with the government of the city, which office of his will be no small means of Vespasian's obtaining the government. Upon the whole the case may be such, that if we ourselves make further delays, the senate may choose an emperor, whom the soldiers, who are the saviours of the empire, will have in contempt.

4. These were the discourses the soldiers had in their several companies; after which they got together in a great body, and, encouraging one another, they declared Vespasian emperor,* and exhorted him to save the government which was now in danger. Now Vespasian's concern had been for a considerable time about the public,

yet did not he intend to set up governor for himself, though his actions shewed him to deserve it, while he preferred that safety which is in a private life before the dangers in a state of such dignity; but when he refused the empire, the commanders insisted the more earnestly upon his acceptance; and the soldiers came about him with their drawn swords in their hands, and threatened to kill him, unless he would now live according to his dignity. And when he had shewn his reluctance a great while, and had endeavoured to thrust away this dominion from him, he at length, being not able to persuade them, yielded to their solicitations that would salute him emperor.

5. So upon the exhortations of Mucianus and the other commanders, that he would accept of the empire, and upon that of the rest of the army, who cried out that they were willing to be led against all his opposers, he was in the first place intent upon gaining the dominion over Alexandria, as knowing that Egypt was of the greatest consequence, in order to obtain the entire government, because of its supplying corn [to Rome;] which corn, if he could be master of, he hoped to dethrone Vitellius, supposing he should aim to keep the empire by force (for he would not be able to support himself, if the multitude at Rome should once be in want of food;) and because he was desirous to join the two legions that were at Alexandria to the other legions that were with him. He also considered with himself, that he should then have that country for a defence to himself against the uncertainty of fortune; for Egypt† is hard to be entered by land, and hath no good havens by sea. It hath on the west the dry deserts of Libya; and on the south Syene, that divides it from Ethiopia, as well as the cataracts of the Nile, that cannot be sailed over; and on the east the Red Sea, extending as far as Coptus; and it is fortified on the north by the land that reaches to Syria, together with that called the Egyptian Sea, having no haven in it for ships. And thus is Egypt walled about on every side. Its length between Pelusium and Syene is two thousand furlongs, and the passage by sea from Plinthine to Pelusium, is three thousand six hundred furlongs. Its river Nile is navigable as far as the city called Elephantine, the forenamed cataracts hindering ships from going any farther. The haven also of Alexandria is not entered by the mariners without difficulty, even in times of peace; for the passage inward is narrow, and full of rocks, that lie under the water, which oblige mariners to turn from a straight direction: its left side is blocked up by works made by men's hands on both sides; on which right side lies the island called Pharus, which is situated just before the entrance, and supports a very great tower, that affords the sight of a fire to such as sail within three hundred furlongs of it, that ships may cast anchor a great way off in the night-time, by reason of the difficulty of sailing nearer. About this island are built very great piers, the handiwork of men, against which when the sea dashes itself, and its waves are broken against those boundaries, the navigation becomes very troublesome, and the entrance through so narrow a passage is rendered very dangerous: yet is the haven itself, when you are got into it, a very safe one, and of thirty furlongs in largeness; into which is brought what the country wants, in order to its happiness; as also

---

* It is plain by the nature of the thing, as well as by Josephus and Eutropius, that Vespasian was first of all saluted emperor in Judea, and not till some time afterward in Egypt.

† Here we have an authentic description of the bounds and circumstances of Egypt in the days of Vespasian and Titus.

what abundance the country affords more than it wants itself, is hence distributed into all the habitable earth.

6. Justly therefore did Vespasian desire to obtain that government, in order to corroborate his attempts upon the whole of the empire: so he immediately sent to Tiberius Alexander, who was then governor of Egypt and of Alexandria, and informed him what the army had put him upon, and now he, being forced to accept of the burden of the government, was desirous to have him for his confederate and supporter. Now as soon as ever Alexander had read this letter, he readily obliged the legions and the multitude to take the oath of fidelity to Vespasian, both of whom willingly complied with him, as already acquainted with the courage of the man, from that his conduct in their neighbourhood. Accordingly Vespasian, looking upon himself as already intrusted with the government, got all things ready for his journey [to Rome.] Now fame carried this news abroad more suddenly than any one could have thought, that he was emperor over the east, upon which every city kept festivals, and celebrated sacrifices and oblations for such good news; the legions also that were in Mysia and Pannonia, who had been in commotion a little before, on account of this insolent attempt of Vitellius, were very glad to take the oath of fidelity to Vespasian, upon his coming to the empire. Vespasian then removed from Cesarea to Berytus, where many embasaages came to him from Syria, and many from other provinces, bringing with them from every city crowns, and the congratulations of the people. Mucianus came also, who was the president of the province, and told him with what alacrity the people [received the news of his advancement,] and how the people of every city had taken the oath of fidelity to him.

7. So Vespasian's good fortune succeeded to his wishes everywhere, and the public affairs were, for the greatest part, already in his hands; upon which he considered that he had not arrived at the government without Divine Providence, but that a righteous kind of fate had brought the empire under his power; for as he called to mind the other signals, which had been a great many everywhere, that foretold he should obtain the government, so did he remember what Josephus had said to him when he ventured to foretell his coming to the empire while Nero was alive; so he was much concerned that this man was still in bonds with him. He then called for Mucianus, together with his other commanders and friends, and in the first place, he informed them what a valiant man Josephus had been, and what great hardships he had made him undergo in the siege of Jotapata. After that he related those predictions of his* which he had then suspected as fictions, suggested out of the fear he was in, but which had by time been demonstrated to be divine. "It is a shameful thing (said he) that this man who hath fore-

told my coming to the empire beforehand, and been the minister of a divine message to me, should still be retained in the condition of a captive or prisoner." So he called for Josephus, and commanded that he should be set at liberty; whereupon the commanders promised themselves glorious things, from this requital Vespasian made to a perfect stranger. Titus was then present with his father, and said, "O father, it is but just that the scandal [of a prisoner] should be taken off Josephus, together with his iron chain; for if we do not barely loose his bonds, but cut them to pieces, he will be like a man that hath never been bound at all." For that is the usual method as to such as have been bound without cause. This advice was agreed to by Vespasian also; so there came a man in, and cut the chain to pieces; while Josephus received this testimony of his integrity for a reward, and was moreover esteemed a person of credit as to futurities also.

CHAPTER XI

THAT UPON THE CONQUEST AND SLAUGHTER OF VITELLIUS, VESPASIAN HASTENED HIS JOURNEY TO ROME; BUT TITUS HIS SON RETURNED TO JERUSALEM

1. AND now, when Vespasian had given answers to the embassages, and had disposed of the places of power justly,† and according to every one's deserts, he came to Antioch, and consulting which way he had best take, he preferred to go to Rome rather than to march to Alexandria, because he saw that Alexandria was sure to him already, but that the affairs at Rome were put into disorder by Vitellius; so he sent Mucianus to Italy, and committed a considerable army both of horsemen and footmen to him; yet was Mucianus afraid of going by sea, because it was the middle of winter; so he led his army on foot through Cappadocia and Phrygia.

2. In the meantime Antonius Primus took the third of the legions that were in Mysia, for he was president of that province, and made haste, in order to fight Vitellius; whereupon Vitellius sent away Cecinna, with a great army, having a mighty confidence in him, because of his having beaten Otho. This Cecinna marched out of Rome in great haste, and found Antonius about Cremona in Gall, which city is in the borders of Italy; but when he saw there that the enemy were numerous and in good order, he durst not fight them; and as he thought a retreat dangerous, so he began to think of betraying his army to Antonius. Accordingly, he assembled the centurions and tribunes that were under his command, and persuaded them to go over to Antonius, and this by diminishing the reputation of Vitellius, and by exaggerating the power of Vespasian. He also told them, that with the one there was no more than the bare name of dominion; but with the other was the power of it; and that it was better for them to prevent necessity, and gain favour, and, while they were likely to be overcome in battle, to avoid the danger beforehand, and go over to Antonius willingly; that Vespasian was able of himself to subdue what had not yet submitted, without their assistance, while Vitellius could not preserve what he had already with it.

---

* As Daniel was preferred by Darius and Cyrus, on account of his having foretold the destruction of the Babylonian monarchy by their means, and the consequent exaltation of the Medes and Persians, Dan. v. vi.; or rather, as Jeremiah was set at liberty and honourably treated by Nebuzaradan, at the command of Nebuchadnezzar, on account of his having foretold the destruction of Jerusalem by the Babylonians, Jer. xl. 1-7; so was our Josephus set at liberty and honourably treated, on account of his having foretold the advancement of Vespasian and Titus to the Roman empire. All these are most eminent instances of the interposition of Divine Providence, and of the certainty of divine predictions in the great revolutions of the four monarchies.

† This is well observed by Josephus, that Vespasian, in order to secure his success, and establish his government at first, distributed his offices and places upon the foot of justice, and bestowed them on such as best deserved them, and were best fit for them.

3. Cecinna said this, and much more to the same purpose, and persuaded them to comply with him; and both he and his army deserted; but still the very same night the soldiers repented of what they had done, and a fear seized on them, lest perhaps Vitellius who sent them should get the better; and drawing their swords. they assaulted Cecinna, in order to kill him; and the thing had been done by them, if the tribunes had not fallen upon their knees, and besought them not to do it: so the soldiers did not kill him, but put him in bonds, as a traitor, and were about to send him to Vitellius. When [Antonius] Primus heard of this, he raised up his men immediately, and made them put on their armour, and led them against those that had revolted; hereupon they put themselves in order of battle, and made resistance for a while, but were soon beaten, and fled to Cremona; then did Primus take his horsemen, and cut off their entrance into the city, and encompassed and destroyed a great multitude of them before the city, and fell into the city together with the rest, and gave leave to his soldiers to plunder it. And here it was that many strangers, who were merchants, as well as many of the people of that country, perished, and among them Vitellius's whole army, being thirty thousand and two hundred, while Antonius lost no more of those that came with him from Mysia than four thousand and five hundred; he then loosed Cecinna, and sent him to Vespasian, to tell him the good news. So he came, and was received by him; and covered the scandal of his treachery by the unexpected honours he received from Vespasian.

4. And now, upon the news that Antonius was approaching, Sabinus took courage at Rome, and assembled those cohorts of soldiers that kept watch by night, and in the night-time seized upon the capitol; and, as the day came on, many men of character came over to him, with Domitian, his brother's son, whose encouragement was of very great weight for encompassing the government. Now, Vitellius was not much concerned at this Primus, but was very angry with those that had revolted with Sabinus; and thirsting, out of his natural barbarity, after noble blood, he sent out part of the army which came along with him to fight against the capitol; and many bold actions were done on this side and on the side of those that held the temple. But at last, the soldiers that came from Germany, being too numerous for the others, got the hill in their possession, where Domitian, any many other of the principal Romans, providentially escaped, while the rest of the multitude were entirely cut to pieces, and Sabinus himself was brought to Vitellius and then slain: the soldiers also plundered the temple of its ornaments, and set it on fire. But now within a day's time came Antonius, with his army, and was met by Vitellius and his army; and having had a battle in three several places, the last were all destroyed. Then did Vitellius come out of his palace, in his cups, and satiated with an extravagant and luxurious meal, as in the last extremity and being drawn along through the multitude, and abused with all sorts of torments, had his head cut off in the midst of Rome, having retained the government eight months and five days; and had he lived much longer, I cannot but think the empire would not have been sufficient for his lust. Of the others that were slain, were numbered above fifty thousand. This battle was fought on the third day of the month Appelleus [Casleu;] on the next day Mucianus came into the city with his army, and ordered Antonius and his men to leave off killing; for they were still searching the houses, and killing many of Vitellius's soldiers and many of the populace, as supposing them to be of his party, prevented by their rage any accurate distinction between them and others. He then produced Domitian, and recommended him to the multitude, until his father should come himself: so the people being now freed from their fears, made acclamations of joy for Vespasian, as for their emperor, and kept festival-days for his confirmation, and for the destruction of Vitellius.

5. And now, as Vespasian was come to Alexandria, this good news came from Rome, and at the same time came embassies from all his own habitable earth, to congratulate him upon his advancement; and though this Alexandria was the greatest of all cities next to Rome, it proved too narrow to contain the multitude that then came to it. So upon this confirmation of Vespasian's entire government, which was now settled, and upon the unexpected deliverance of the public affairs of the Romans from ruin, Vespasian turned his thoughts to what remained unsubdued in Judea. However, he himself made haste to go to Rome as the winter was now almost over, and soon set the affairs of Alexandria in order, but sent his son Titus, with a select part of his army, to destroy Jerusalem. So Titus marched on foot as far as Nicopolis, which is distant twenty furlongs from Alexandria; there he put his army on board some long ships, and sailed upon the river along the Mendesian Nomus, as far as the city Thmuis; there he got out of the ships, and walked on foot, and lodged all night at a small city called Tanis. His second station was Heracleopolis, and his third Pelusium; he then refreshed his army at that place for two days; and on the third passed over the mouths of the Nile at Pelusium; he then proceeded one station over the desert, and pitched his camp at the temple of Casian Jupiter,* and on the next day at Ostracine. This station had no water; but the people of the country make use of water brought from other places. After this he rested at Rhinocolura, and from thence he went to Raphia, which was his fourth station. This city is the beginning of Syria. For his fifth station he pitched his camp at Gaza; after which he came to Ascalon, and from thence to Jamnia, and after that to Joppa, and from Joppa to Cesarea, having taken a resolution to gather all his other forces together at that place.

---

* There are coins of this Casian Jupiter still extant.

BOOK V

FROM THE COMING OF TITUS TO BESIEGE JERUSALEM TO THE GREAT EXTREMITY TO WHICH THE JEWS WERE REDUCED

CHAPTER I

CONCERNING THE SEDITIONS AT JERUSALEM, AND WHAT TERRIBLE MISERIES AFFLICTED THE CITY BY THEIR MEANS

1. WHEN therefore Titus had marched over that desert which lies between Egypt and Syria, in the manner forementioned, he came to Cesarea, having resolved to set his forces in order at that place, before he began the war. Nay, indeed, while he was assisting his father at Alexandria, in settling that government which had been newly conferred upon them by God, it so happened that the sedition at Jerusalem was revived, and parted into three factions, and that one faction fought against the other; which partition in such evil cases may be said to be a good thing, and the effect of divine justice. Now, as to the attack the zealots made upon the people, and which I esteem the beginning of the city's destruction, it hath been already explained after an accurate manner; as also whence it arose, and to how great a mischief it was increased; but for the present sedition, one should not mistake if he called it a sedition begotten by another sedition, and to be like a wild beast grown mad, which for the want of food from abroad, fell now upon eating its own flesh.

2. For Eleazar, the son of Simon, who made the first separation of the zealots from the people, and made them retire into the temple, appeared very angry at John's insolent attempts, which he made every day upon the people; for this man never left off murdering: but the truth was, that he could not bear to submit to a tyrant who set up after him. So he being desirous of gaining the entire power and dominion to himself, revolted from John, and took to his assistance Judas the son of Chelcias, and Simon the son of Ezron, who were among the men of greatest power. There was also with him Hezekiah the son of Chobar, a person of eminence. Each of these were followed by a great many of the zealots; these seized upon the inner court of the temple,* and laid their arms upon the holy gates, and over the holy fronts of that court; and because they had plenty of provisions, they were of good courage, for there was a great abundance of what was consecrated to sacred uses, and they scrupled not the making use of them; yet were they afraid, on account of their small number; and when they had laid up their arms there, they did not stir from the place they were in. Now as to John, what advantage he

had above Eleazar in the multitude of his followers, the like disadvantage he had in the situation he was in, since he had his enemies over his head; and as he could not make any assault upon them without terror, so was his anger too great to let them be at rest; nay, although he suffered more mischief from Eleazar and his party than he could inflict upon them, yet would not he leave off assaulting them, insomuch that there were continual sallies made one against another, as well as darts thrown at one another, and the temple was defiled everywhere with murders.

3. But now the tyrant Simon, the son of Gioras, whom the people had invited in, out of the hopes they had of his assistance in the great distresses they were in, having in his power the upper city, and a great part of the lower, did now make more vehement assaults upon John and his party, because they were fought against from above also; yet was he beneath their situation, when he attacked them, as they were beneath the attacks of the others above them. Whereby it came to pass, that John did both receive and inflict great damage, and that easily, as he was fought against on both sides; and the same advantage that Eleazar and his party had over him, since he was beneath them, the same advantage had he, by his higher situation, over Simon. On which account he easily repelled the attacks that were made from beneath, by the weapons thrown from their hands only; but was obliged to repel those that threw darts from the temple above him, by his engines of war; for he had such engines as threw darts, and javelins, and stones, and that in no small number, by which he did not only defend himself from such as fought against him, but slew moreover many of the priests, as they were about their sacred ministrations; for notwithstanding these men were mad with all sorts of impiety, yet did they still admit those that desired to offer their sacrifices, although they took care to search the people of their own country beforehand, and both suspected and watched them; while they were not so much afraid of strangers, who, although they had gotten leave of them, to come into that court, were yet often destroyed by this sedition: for those darts that were thrown by the engines came with that force, that they went over all the buildings, and the temple itself, and fell upon the priests, and those† that were about the sacred offices; insomuch that many persons who came thither with great zeal from the ends of the earth, to offer sacrifices at this celebrated place, which was esteemed holy by all mankind, fell down before their own sacrifices themselves, and sprinkled that altar, which was venerable among all men, both Greeks and barbarians, with their own blood; till the dead bodies of strangers were mingled together with those of

---

* This appears to be the first time that the zealots ventured to polute this most sacred court of the temple, which was the court of the priests, wherein the temple itself and the altar stood. So that the conjecture of those that would interpret that Zacharias, who was slain "between the temple and the altar" several months before, as if he were slain there by the zealots, is groundless.

† The Levites.

their own country, and those of profane persons with those of the priests, and the blood of all sorts of dead carcases stood in lakes in the holy courts themselves. And now, "O most wretched city, what misery so great as this didst thou suffer from the Romans, when they came to purify thee from thy intestine hatred! For thou couldst be no longer a place fit for God, nor couldst thou longer continue in being, after thou hadst been a sepulchre for the bodies of thine own people, and hadst made the holy house itself a burying-place in this civil war of thine! Yet mayst thou again grow better, if perchance thou wilt hereafter appease the anger of that God who is the author of thy destruction." But I must restrain myself from these passions by the rules of history, since this is not a proper time for domestic lamentation, but for historical narrations; I therefore return to the operations that follow in this sedition.

4. And now there were three treacherous factions in the city, the one parted from the other. Eleazar and his party, that kept the sacred first-fruits, came against John in their cups. Those that were with John plundered the populace, and went out with zeal against Simon. This Simon had his supply of provisions from the city, in opposition to the seditious. When, therefore, John was assaulted on both sides, he made his men turn about, throwing his darts upon those citizens that came up against him, from the cloisters he had in his possession, while he opposed those that attacked him from the temple by his engines of war; and if at any time he was freed from those that were above him, which happened frequently, from their being drunk and tired, he sallied out with a great number upon Simon and his party; and this he did always in such parts of the city as he could come at, till he set on fire those houses that were full of corn, and of all other provisions.* The same thing was done by Simon, when, upon the others' retreat, he attacked the city also; as if they had, on purpose done it to serve the Romans, by destroying what the city had laid up against the siege, and by thus cutting off the nerves of their own power. Accordingly, it so came to pass, that all the places that were about the temple were burnt down, and were become an intermediate desert space, ready for fighting on both sides; and that almost all the corn was burnt, which would have been sufficient for a siege of many years. So they were taken by the means of famine, which it was impossible they should have been, unless they had thus prepared the way for it by this procedure.

5. And now, as the city was engaged in a war on all sides, from these treacherous crowds of wicked men, the people of the city, between them, were like a great body torn in pieces. The aged men and women were in such distress by their internal calamities, that they wished for the Romans, and earnestly hoped for an external war, in order to their delivery from their domestic miseries. The citizens themselves were under a terrible consternation and fear; nor had they any opportunity of taking counsel, and of changing their conduct; nor were their any hope of coming to an agreement with their enemies; nor could such as had a mind flee away; for guards were set at all places, and the heads of the robbers, although they were seditious one against another in other respects, yet did they agree in

killing those that were for peace with the Romans, or were suspected of an inclination to desert them, as their common enemies. They agreed in nothing but this, to kill those that were innocent. The noise also of those that were fighting was incessant, both by day and by night; but the lamentations of those that mourned exceeded the other; nor was there ever any occasion for them to leave off their lamentations, because their calamities came perpetually one upon another, although the deep consternation they were in prevented their outward wailing; but being constrained by their fear to conceal their inward passions, they were inwardly tormented, without daring to open their lips in groans. Nor was any regard paid to those that were still alive, by their relations; nor was there any care taken of burial for those that were dead; the occasion of both which was this, that every one despaired of himself; for those that were not among the seditious, had no great desire of anything, as expecting for certain that they should very soon be destroyed; but for the seditious themselves, they fought against each other, while they trod upon the dead bodies as they lay heaped one upon another, and taking up a mad rage from those dead bodies that were under their feet, became the fiercer thereupon. They, moreover, were still inventing somewhat or other that was pernicious against themselves; and when they had resolved upon anything, they executed it without mercy, and omitted no method of torment or of barbarity. Nay, John abused the sacred materials, and employed them in the construction of his engines of war; for the people and the priests had formerly determined to support the temple, and raise the holy house twenty cubits higher; for king Agrippa had at a very great expense, and with very great pains, brought thither such materials as were proper for that purpose, being pieces of timber very well worth seeing, both for their straightness and their largeness: but the war coming on, and interrupting the work, John had them cut, and prepared for the building him towers, he finding them long enough to oppose from them those his adversaries that fought him from the temple that was above him. He also had them brought and erected behind the inner court over against the west end of the cloisters, where alone he could erect them; whereas, the other sides of that court had so many steps as would not let them come nigh enough the cloisters.

6. Thus did John hope to be too hard for his enemies by these engines constructed by his impiety; but God himself demonstrated that his pains would prove of no use to him, by bringing the Romans upon him before he had reared any of his towers; for Titus, when he had gotten together part of his forces about him, and had ordered the rest to meet him at Jerusalem, marched out of Cesarea. He had with him those three legions that had accompanied his father, when he laid Judea waste, together with that twelfth legion which had been formerly beaten with Cestius; which legion, as it was otherwise remarkable for its valour, so did it march on now with greater alacrity to avenge themselves on the Jews, as remembering what they had formerly suffered from them. Of these legions, he ordered the fifth to meet him, by going through Emmaus, and the tenth to go up by Jericho; he also moved himself, together with the rest; besides whom marched those auxiliaries that came from the kings, being now more in number than before, together with a considerable number that came to his assistance from Syria. Those also that had been selected out of

---

* This destruction of such a vast quantity of corn and other provisions, as was sufficient for many years, was the direct occasion of that terrible famine, which consumed incredible numbers of Jews in Jerusalem during its siege

these four legions, and sent with Mucianus to Italy, had their places filled up out of these soldiers that came out of Egypt with Titus, who were two thousand men, chosen out of the armies at Alexandria. There followed him also three thousand, drawn from those that guarded the river Euphrates; as also, there came Tiberius Alexander, who was a friend of his, most valuable, both for his good-will to him, and for his prudence. He had formerly been governor of Alexandria, but was now thought worthy to be general of the army [under Titus.] The reason of this was, that he had been the first who encouraged Vespasian very lately to accept this his new dominion, and joined himself to him with great fidelity, when things were uncertain, and fortune had not yet declared for him. He also followed Titus as a counsellor, very useful to him in this war, both by his age and skill in such affairs.

CHAPTER II

HOW TITUS MARCHED TO JERUSALEM, AND HOW HE WAS IN DANGER, AS HE WAS TAKING A VIEW OF THE CITY. OF THE PLACE ALSO WHERE HE PITCHED HIS CAMP

1. Now, as Titus was upon his march into the enemy's country, the auxiliaries that were sent by the kings marched first, having all the other auxiliaries with them; after whom followed those that were to prepare the roads, and measure out the camp; then came the commander's baggage, and after that the other soldiers, who were completely armed to support them; then came Titus himself, having with him another select body; and then came the pikemen; after whom came the horse belonging to that legion. All these came before the engines; and after these engines followed the tribunes and the leaders of the cohorts, with their select bodies; after these came the ensigns, with the eagle; and before those ensigns, came the trumpeters belonging to them; next these came the main body of the army in their ranks, every rank being six deep; the servants belonging to every legion came after these; and before these last their baggage; the mercenaries came last, and those that guarded them brought up the rear. Now Titus, according to the Roman usage, went in the front of the army after a decent manner, and marched through Samaria to Gophna, a city that had been formerly taken by his father, and was then garrisoned by Roman soldiers; and when he had lodged there one night, he marched on in the morning; and when he had gone as far as a day's march, he pitched his camp at that valley which the Jews, in their own tongue, call "the Valley of Thorns," near a certain village called Gabaothsaul, which signifies "the Hill of Saul," being distant from Jerusalem about thirty furlongs. There it was that he chose out six hundred select horsemen, and went to take a view of the city, to observe what strength it was of, and how courageous the Jews were; whether, when they saw him, and before they came to a direct battle, they would be affrighted and submit; for he had been informed, what was really true, that the people who were fallen under the power of the seditious, and the robbers, were greatly desirous of peace; but being too weak to rise up against the rest, they lay still.

2. Now, so long as he rode along the straight road which led to the wall of the city, nobody appeared out of the gates; but when he went out of that road, and declined towards the tower Psephinus, and led the band of horsemen obliquely, an immense number of the Jews leaped out suddenly at the towers called the "Women's Towers," through that gate which was over against the monuments of queen Helena, and intercepted his horse; and standing directly opposite to those that still ran along the road, hindered them from joining those that had declined out of it. They intercepted Titus also, with a few others. Now it was here impossible for him to go forward, because all the places had trenches dug in them from the wall, to preserve the gardens round about, and were full of gardens obliquely situated, and of many hedges; and to return back to his own men, he saw it was also impossible, by reason of the multitude of the enemies that lay between them; many of whom did not so much as know that the king was in any danger, but supposed him still among them. So he perceived, that his preservation must be wholly owing to his own courage, and turned his horse about, and cried out aloud to those that were about him to follow him, and ran with violence into the midst of his enemies, in order to force his way through them to his own men. And hence we may principally learn, that both the success of war, and the dangers that kings are in, are under the providence of God; for while such a number of darts were thrown at Titus, when he had neither his head-piece on, nor his breast-plate, (for, as I told you, he went out not to fight, but to view the city,) none of them touched his body, but went aside without hurting him; as if all of them missed him on purpose, and only made a noise as they passed by him. So he diverted those perpetually with his sword that came on his side, and overturned many of those that directly met him, and made his horse ride over those that were overthrown. The enemy indeed made a great shout at the boldness of Cæsar, and exhorted one another to rush upon him. Yet did these against whom he marched, fly away, and go off from him in great numbers; while those that were in the same danger with him, kept up close to him, though they were wounded both on their backs, and on their sides; for they had each of them but this one hope of escaping, if they could assist Titus in opening himself a way, that he might not be encompassed round by his enemies before he got away from them. Now, there were two of those that were with him, but at some distance; the one of whom the enemy encompassed round, and slew him with their darts, and his horse also; but the other they slew, as he leaped down from his horse, and carried off his horse with them. But Titus escaped with the rest, and came safe to the camp. So this success of the Jews' first attack, raised their minds, and gave them an ill-grounded hope; and this short inclination of fortune on their side, made them very courageous for the future.

3. But now, as soon as that legion that had been at Emmaus was joined to Cæsar at night, he removed thence, when it was day, and came to a place called Scopus; from whence the city began already to be seen, and a plain view might be taken of the great temple. Accordingly, this place, on the north quarter of the city and adjoining thereto, was a plain, and very properly named Scopus [the prospect;] and was no more than seven furlongs from it. And here it was that Titus ordered a camp to be fortified for two legions that were to be together; but ordered another camp to be fortified, at three furlongs farther distance behind them, for the fifth le-

gion; for he thought that, by marching in the night, they might be tired, and might deserve to be covered from the enemy, and with less fear might fortify themselves: and, as these were now beginning to build, the tenth legion, which came through Jericho, was already come to the place, where a certain part of armed men had formerly lain, to guard that pass into the city, and had been taken before by Vespasian. These legions had orders to encamp at the distance of six furlongs from Jerusalem, at the mount called the Mount of Olives, which lies over against the city on the east side, and is parted from it by a deep valley, interposed between them, which is named Cedron.

4. Now, when hitherto the several parties in the city had been dashing one against another perpetually, this foreign war, now suddenly come upon them after a violent manner, put the first stop to their contentions one against another; and, as the seditious now saw with astonishment the Romans pitching three several camps, they began to think of an awkward sort of concord, and said one to another,—"What do we here, and what do we mean, when we suffer three fortified walls to be built to coop us in, that we shall not be able to breathe freely? while the enemy is securely building a kind of city in opposition to us, and while we sit still within our own walls, and become spectators only of what they are doing, with our hands idle, and our armour laid by, as if they were about somewhat that was for our good and advantage. We are, it seems," so did they cry out, "only courageous against ourselves, while the Romans are likely to gain the city without bloodshed by our sedition." Thus did they encourage one another when they were gotten together, and took their armour immediately, and ran out upon the tenth legion, and fell upon the Romans with great eagerness, and with a prodigious shout, as they were fortifying their camp. These Romans were caught in different parties, and this in order to perform their several works, and on that account had in great measure laid aside their arms; for they thought the Jews would not have ventured to make a sally upon them; and had they been disposed so to do they supposed their sedition would have distracted them. So they were put into disorder unexpectedly; when some of them left their works they were about, and immediately marched off, while many ran to their arms, but were smitten and slain before they could turn back upon the enemy. The Jews became still more and more in number, as encouraged by the good success of those that first made the attack; and, while they had such good fortune, they seemed, both to themselves and to the enemy, to be many more than they really were. The disorderly way of their fighting at first put the Romans also to a stand, who had been constantly used to fighting skilfully in good order, and with keeping their ranks, and obeying the orders that were given them; for which reason the Romans were caught unexpectedly, and were obliged to give way to the assaults that were made upon them. Now when these Romans were overtaken, and turned back upon the Jews, they put a stop to their career; yet, when they did not take care enough of themselves through the vehemency of their pursuit, they were wounded by them; but, as still more and more Jews sallied out of the city, the Romans were at length brought into confusion, and put to flight, and ran away from their camp. Nay, things looked as though the entire legion would have been in danger, unless Titus had been informed of the case they were

in, and had sent them succours immediately. So he reproached them for their cowardice, and brought those back that were running away, and fell himself upon the Jews on their flank, with those select troops that were with him, and slew a considerable number, and wounded more of them, and put them all to flight, and made them run away hastily down the valley. Now as these Jews suffered greatly in the declivity of the valley, so, when they were gotten over it, they turned about, and stood over against the Romans, having the valley between them, and there fought with them. Thus did they continue the fight till noon; but, when it was already a little after noon, Titus set those that came to the assistance of the Romans with him, and those that belonged to the cohorts, to prevent the Jews from making any more sallies, and then sent the rest of the legion to the upper part of the mountain, to fortify their camp.

5. This march of the Romans seemed to the Jews to be a flight; and as the watchman, who was placed upon the wall, gave a signal by shaking his garment, there came out a fresh multitude of Jews, and that with such mighty violence, that one might compare it to the running of the most terrible wild beasts. To say the truth, none of these that opposed them could sustain the fury with which they made their attacks; but, as if they had been cast out of an engine, they brake the enemies' ranks to pieces, who were put to flight, and ran away to the mountain; none but Titus himself, and a few others with him, being left in the midst of the acclivity. Now these others, who were his friends, despised the danger they were in, and were ashamed to leave their general, earnestly exhorting him to give way to these Jews that are fond of dying, and not to run into such dangers before those that ought to stay before him; to consider what his fortune was, and not, by supplying the place of a common soldier, to venture to turn back upon the enemy so suddenly; and this because he was general in the war, and lord of the habitable earth, on whose preservation the public affairs do all depend. These persuasions Titus seemed not so much as to hear, but opposed those that ran upon him, and smote them on the face; and, when he had forced them to go back, he slew them: he also fell upon great numbers as they marched down the hill, and thrust them forward; while those men were so amazed at his courage and his strength, that they could not fly directly to the city, but declined from him on both sides, and pressed after those that fled up the hill; yet did he still fall upon their flank, and put a stop to their fury. In the meantime, a disorder and a terror fell again upon those that were fortifying their camp at the top of the hill, upon their seeing those beneath them running away, insomuch that the whole legion was dispersed, while they thought that the sallies of the Jews upon them were plainly insupportable, and that Titus was himself put to flight; because they took it for granted that, if he had stayed, the rest would never have fled for it. Thus were they encompassed on every side by a kind of panic fear, and some dispersed themselves one way, and some another, till certain of them saw their general in the very midst of an action, and, being under great concern for him, they loudly proclaimed the danger he was in to the entire legion; and now shame made them turn back, and they reproached one another, that they did worse than run away, by deserting Cæsar. So they used their utmost force against the Jews, and declining from the straight declivity, they drove them in heaps into the

bottom of the valley. Then did the Jews turn about and fight them; but as they were themselves retiring, and now, because the Romans had the advantage of the ground, and were above the Jews, they drove them into the valley. Titus also pressed upon those that were near him, and sent the legion again to fortify their camp; while he, and those that were with him before, opposed the enemy, and kept them from doing further mischief; insomuch that, if I may be allowed neither to add anything out of flattery, nor to diminish anything out of envy, but to speak the plain truth, Cæsar did twice deliver that entire legion when it was in jeopardy, and gave them a quiet opportunity of fortifying their camp.

CHAPTER III

HOW THE SEDITION WAS AGAIN REVIVED WITHIN JERUSALEM, AND YET THE JEWS CONTRIVED SNARES FOR THE ROMANS. HOW TITUS ALSO THREATENED HIS SOLDIERS FOR THEIR UNGOVERNABLE RASHNESS

1. As now the war abroad ceased for a while, the sedition within was revived; and on the feast of unleavened bread, which was now come, it being the fourteenth day of the month Xanthicus [Nisan] when it is believed the Jews were first freed from the Egyptians, Eleazar and his party opened the gates of this [inmost court of the] temple, and admitted such of the people as were desirous to worship God into it.* But John made use of this festival as a cloak for his treacherous designs and armed the most inconsiderable of his own party, the greater part of whom were not purified, with weapons concealed under their garments, and sent them with great zeal into the temple, in order to seize upon it; which armed men, when they were gotten in, threw their garments away, and presently appeared in their armour. Upon which their was a very great disorder and disturbance about the holy house: while the people who had no concern in the sedition, supposed that this assault was made against all without distinction, as the zealots thought it was made against themselves only. So these left off guarding the gates any longer, and leaped down from their battlements before they came to an engagement, and fled away into the subterranean caverns of the temple; while the people that stood trembling at the altar, and about the holy house, were rolled on heaps together, and trampled upon, and were beaten both with wooden and with iron weapons without mercy. Such, also, as had differences with others, slew many persons that were quiet, out of their own private enmity and hatred, as if they were opposite to the seditious; and all those that had formerly offended any of these plotters, were now known, and were now led away to the slaughter; and, when they had done abundance of horrid mischief to the guiltless, they granted a truce to the guilty, and let these go off that came out of the caverns. These followers of John also did now seize upon this inner temple, and upon all

the warlike engines therein, and then ventured to oppose Simon. And thus that sedition, which had been divided into three factions, was now reduced to two.

2. But Titus, intending to pitch his camp nearer to the city than Scopus, placed as many of his choice horsemen and footmen as he thought sufficient, opposite to the Jews, to prevent their sallying out upon them, while he gave orders for the whole army to level the distance, as far as the wall of the city. So they threw down all the hedges and walls which the inhabitants had made about their gardens and groves of trees, and cut down all the fruit-trees that lay between them and the wall of the city, and filled up all the hollow places and the chasms, and demolished the rocky precipices with iron instruments; and thereby made all the places level from Scopus to Herod's monuments, which adjoined to the pool called the serpent's pool.

3. Now at this very time, the Jews contrived the following stratagem against the Romans. The bolder sort of the seditious went out at the towers, called the Women's Towers, as if they had been ejected out of the city by those who were for peace, and rambled about as if they were afraid of being assaulted by the Romans, and were in fear of one another; while those that stood upon the wall, and seemed to be of the people's side, cried out aloud for peace, and entreated they might have security for their lives given them, and called for the Romans, promising to open the gates to them; and as they cried out after that manner, they threw stones at their own people, as though they would drive them away from the gates. These also pretended that they were excluded by force, and that they petitioned those that were within to let them in; and rushing upon the Romans perpetually, with violence, they then came back, and seemed to be in great disorder. Now the Roman soldiers thought this cunning stratagem of theirs was to be believed real, and thinking they had the one party under their power, and could punish them as they pleased, and hoping that the other party would open their gates to them set to the execution of their designs accordingly. But for Titus himself, he had this surprising conduct of the Jews in suspicion; for whereas he had invited them to come to terms of accommodation, by Josephus, but one day before, he could then receive no civil answer from them; so he ordered the soldiers to stay where they were. However, some of them that were set in the front of the works prevented him, and catching up their arms ran to the gates; whereupon those that seemed to have been ejected, at the first retired; but as soon as the soldiers were gotten between the towers on each side of the gate, the Jews ran out, and encompassed them round, and fell upon them behind, while that multitude which stood upon the wall, threw a heap of stones and darts of all kinds at them, insomuch that they slew a considerable number, and wounded many more; for it was not easy for the Romans to escape, by reason those behind them pressed them forward; besides which the shame they were under for being mistaken, and the fear they were in of their commanders, engaged them to persevere in their mistake, wherefore they fought with their spears a great while, and received many blows from the Jews, though indeed they gave them as many blows again, and at last repelled those that had encompassed them about, while the Jews pursued them as they retired, and followed them, and threw darts at them as far as the monuments of queen Helena.

4. After this, these Jews, without keeping any

---

* Here we see the true occasion of those vast numbers of Jews that were in Jerusalem during this siege by Titus, and perished therein; that the siege began at the feast of the passover, when such prodigious multitudes of Jews and proselytes of the gate were come from all parts of Judea, and from other countries, in order to celebrate that great festival.

decorum, grew insolent upon their good fortune, and jested upon the Romans, for being deluded by the trick they had put upon them, and making a noise with beating their shields, leaped for gladness, and made joyful exclamations: while these soldiers were received with threatenings by their officers, and with indignation by Cæsar himself, [who spake to them thus:] These Jews, who are only conducted by their madness, do everything with care and circumspection; they contrive stratagems, and lay ambushes, and fortune gives success to their stratagems, because they are obedient, and preserve their good-will and fidelity to one another, while the Romans, to whom fortune uses to be ever subservient, by reason of their good order, and ready submission to their commanders, have now had ill success by their contrary behaviour, and by not being able to restrain their hands from action, they have been caught; and that which is the most to their reproach, they have gone on without their commanders, in the very presence of Cæsar. "Truly," says Titus, "the laws of war cannot but groan heavily, as will my father also himself, when he shall be informed of this wound that hath been given us, since he, who is grown old in wars, did never make so great a mistake. Our laws of war do also ever inflict capital punishment on those that in the least break into good order, while at this time they have seen an entire army run into disorder. However, those that have been so insolent, shall be made immediately sensible, that even they who conquer, among the Romans, without orders for fighting, are to be under disgrace." When Titus had enlarged upon this matter before the commanders, it appeared evident that he would execute the law against all those that were concerned; so these soldiers' minds sunk down in despair, as expecting to be put to death, and that justly and quickly. However, the other legions came round about Titus, and entreated his favour to these their fellow-soldiers, and made supplication to him, that he would pardon the rashness of a few, on account of the better obedience of all the rest; and promised for them that they should make amends for their present fault, by their more virtuous behaviour for the time to come.

5. So Cæsar complied with their desires, and with what prudence dictated to him also; for he esteemed it fit to punish single persons by real executions, but that the punishment of great multitudes should proceed no farther than reproofs; so he was reconciled to the soldiers, but gave them a special charge to act more wisely for the future; and he considered with himself how he might be even with the Jews for their stratagem. And now when the space between the Romans and the wall had been levelled, which was done in four days; and as he was desirous to bring the baggage of the army, with the rest of the multitude that followed him, safely to the camp, he set the strongest part of his army over against that wall which lay on the north quarter of the city, and over against the western part of it, and made his army seven deep, with the footmen placed before them, and the horsemen behind them, each of the last in their ranks, whilst the archers stood in the midst in seven ranks. And now as the Jews were prohibited, by so great a body of men, from making sallies upon the Romans, both the beasts that bare the burdens, and belonged to the three legions, and the rest of the multitude, marched on without any fear. But as for Titus himself, he was but about two furlongs distant from the wall, at that part of it where was the corner,* and over against that tower which was called Psephinus, at which tower, the compass of the wall belonging to the north bended, and extended itself over against the west; but the other part of the army fortified themselves at the tower called Hippicus, and was distant, in like manner, but two furlongs from the city. However, the tenth legion continued in its own place, upon the Mount of Olives.

CHAPTER IV

THE DESCRIPTION OF JERUSALEM

1. THE city of Jerusalem was fortified with three walls, on such parts as were not encompassed with unpassable valleys; for in such places it had but one wall. The city was built upon two hills which are opposite to one another, and have a valley to divide them asunder; at which valley the corresponding rows of houses on both hills end. Of these hills, that which contains the upper city is much higher, and in length more direct. Accordingly, it was called the "Citadel," by king David; he was the father of that Solomon who built this temple at the first; but it is by us called the "Upper Marketplace." But the other hill, which was called "Acra," and sustains the lower city, is of the shape of a moon when she is horned; over-against this was a third hill, but naturally lower than Acra, and parted formerly from the other by a broad valley. However, in those times when the Asamoneans reigned, they filled up that valley with earth, and had a mind to join the city to the temple. They then took off part of the height of Acra, and reduced it to be of less elevation than it was before, that the temple might be superior to it. Now the Valley of the Cheesemongers, as it was called, and was that which we told you before, distinguished the hill of the upper city from that of the lower, extended as far as Siloam; for that is the name of a fountain which hath sweet waters in it, and this in great plenty also. But on the outsides, these hills are surrounded by deep valleys, and by reason of the precipices to them belonging on both sides, they are everywhere unpassable.

2. Now, of these three walls, the old one was hard to be taken, both by reason of the valleys, and of that hill on which it was built, and which was above them. But besides that great advantage, as to the place where they were situated, it was also built very strong; because David and Solomon, and the following kings, were very zealous about this work. Now that wall began on the north, at the tower called "Hippicus," and extended as far as the "Xistus," a place so called, and then joining at the council-house, ended at the west cloister of the temple. But if we go the other way westward, it began at the same place, and extended through a place called "Bethso," to the gate of the Essens; and after that it went southward, having its bending above the fountain Siloam, where it also bends again towards the east at Solomon's pool, and reaches as far as a certain place which they called "Ophlas," where it was joined to the eastern cloister of the temple. The second wall took its beginning from that gate which they called "Gennath," which belonged to the first wall; it only encompassed the northern quarter of the city, and

---

* Perhaps, says Dr Hudson, here was that gate, called the "Gate of the Corner," in 2 Chr. xxvi. 9. See ch. iv. sect. 2.

reached as far as the tower Antonia. The beginning of the third wall was at the tower Hippicus, whence it reached as far as the north quarter of the city, and the tower Psephinus, and then was so far extended till it came over against the monuments of Helena, which Helena was queen of Adiabene, the daughter of Izates; it then extended further to a great length, and passed by the sepulchral caverns of the kings, and bent again at the tower of the corner, at the monument which is called the "Monument of the Fuller," and joined to the old wall at the valley called the "Valley of Cedron." It was Agrippa who encompassed the parts added to the old city with this wall, which had been all naked before; for as the city grew more populous, it gradually crept beyond its old limits, and those parts of it that stood northward of the temple, and joined that hill to the city, made it considerably larger, and occasioned that hill, which is in number the fourth, and is called "Bezetha," to be inhabited also. It lies over against the tower Antonia, but is divided from it by a deep valley, which was dug on purpose, and that in order to hinder the foundations of the tower of Antonia from joining to this hill, and thereby affording an opportunity for getting to it with ease, and hindering the security that arose from its superior elevation; for which reason also that depth of the ditch made the elevation of the towers more remarkable. This new-built part of the city was called "Bezetha," in our language, which, if interpreted in the Grecian language, may be called the "New City." Since, therefore, its inhabitants stood in need of a covering, the father of the present king, and of the same name with him, Agrippa, began that wall we spoke of; but he left off building it when he had only laid the foundation, out of the fear he was in of Claudius Cæsar, lest he should suspect that so strong a wall was built in order to make some innovation in public affairs; for the city could no way have been taken if that wall had been finished in the manner it was begun; as its parts were connected together by stones twenty cubits long, and ten cubits broad, which could never have been easily undermined by any iron tools, or shaken by any engines. The wall was, however, ten cubits wide, and it would probably have had a height greater than that, had not his zeal who began it been hindered from exerting itself. After this it was erected with great diligence by the Jews, as high as twenty cubits, above which it had battlements of two cubits, and turrets of three cubits altitude, insomuch that the entire altitude extended as far as twenty-five cubits.

3. Now the towers that were upon it were twenty cubits in breadth and twenty cubits in height; they were square and solid, as was the wall itself, wherein the niceness of the joints and the beauty of the stones were no way inferior to those of the holy house itself. Above this solid altitude of the towers, which was twenty cubits, there were rooms of great magnificence, and over them upper rooms, and cisterns to receive rain-water. They were many in number, and the steps by which you ascended up to them were every one broad; of these towers then the third wall had ninety, and the spaces between them were each two hundred cubits; but in the middle wall were forty towers, and the old wall was parted into sixty, while the whole compass of the city was thirty-three furlongs. Now the third wall was all of it wonderful; yet was the tower Psephinus elevated above it at the northwest corner, and there Titus pitched his own tent; for being seventy cubits high, it both afforded a prospect of Arabia at sun-rising, as well

as it did of the utmost limits of the Hebrew possessions at the sea westward. Moreover, it was an octagon, and over against it was the tower Hippicus; and hard by two others were erected by king Herod, in the old wall. These were for largeness, beauty, and strength, beyond all that were in the habitable earth: for besides the magnanimity of his nature, and his munificence towards the city on other occasions, he built these after such an extraordinary manner, to gratify his own private affections, and dedicated these towers to the memory of those three persons who had been the dearest to him, and from whom he named them. They were his brother, his friend, and his wife. This wife he had slain out of his love [and jealousy,] as we have already related; the other two he lost in war, as they were courageously fighting. Hippicus, so named from his friend, was square; its length and breadth each twenty-five cubits, and its height thirty, and it had no vacuity in it. Over this solid building, which was composed of great stones united together, there was a reservoir twenty cubits deep, over which there was a house of two stories, whose height was twenty-five cubits, and divided into several parts; over which were battlements of two cubits, and turrets all round of three cubits high, insomuch that the entire height added together amounted to fourscore cubits. The second tower which he named from his brother Phasaelus, had its breadth and its height equal, each of them forty cubits; over which a cloister went round about, whose height was ten cubits, and it was covered from enemies by breast-works and bulwarks. There was also built over that cloister another tower, parted into magnificent rooms and a place for bathing; so that this tower wanted nothing that might make it appear to be a royal palace. It was also adorned with battlements and turrets, more than was the foregoing, and the entire altitude was about ninety cubits; the appearance of it resembled the tower of Pharus, which exhibited a fire to such as sailed to Alexandria, but was much larger than it in compass. This was now converted to a house, wherein Simon exercised his tyrannical authority. The third tower was Mariamne, for that was his queen's name; it was solid as high as twenty cubits; its breadth and its length were twenty cubits, and were equal to each other; its upper buildings were more magnificent, and had greater variety than the other towers had; for the king thought it most proper for him to adorn that which was denominated from his wife, better than those denominated from men, as those were built stronger than this that bore his wife's name. The entire height of this tower was fifty cubits.

4. Now as these towers were so very tall, they appeared much taller by the place on which they stood; for that very old wall wherein they were was built on a high hill, and was itself a kind of elevation that was still thirty cubits taller; over which were the towers situated, and thereby were made much higher to appearance. The largeness also of the stones was wonderful, for they were not made of common small stones, nor of such large ones only as men could carry, but they were of white marble, cut out of the rock; each stone was twenty cubits in length, and ten in breadth, and five in depth. They were so exactly united to one another, that each tower looked like one entire rock of stone, so growing naturally, and afterwards cut by the hands of the artificers into present shape and corners; so little or not at all, did their joints or connexion appear. Now as these towers were themselves on the north side of the wall, the

king had a palace inwardly thereto adjoined, which exceeds all my ability to describe it; for it was so very curious as to want no cost or skill in its construction, but was entirely walled about to the height of thirty cubits, and was adorned with towers at equal distances, and with large bed-chambers, that would contain beds for a hundred guests a-piece, in which the variety of the stones is not to be expressed; for a large quantity of those that were rare of that kind was collected together. Their roofs were also wonderful, both for the length of the beams and the splendour of their ornaments. The number of the rooms was also very great, and the variety of the figures that were about them was prodigious; their furniture was complete, and the greatest part of the vessels that were put in them was of silver and gold. There were besides many porticoes, one beyond another, round about, and in each of those porticoes curious pillars; yet were all the courts that were exposed to the air everywhere green. There were moreover several groves of trees, and long walks through them, with deep canals, and cisterns, that in several parts were filled with brazen statues, through which the water ran out. There were withal many dove-courts of tame pigeons about the canals; but, indeed, it is not possible to give a complete description of these palaces; and the very remembrance of them is a torment to one, as putting one in mind what vastly rich buildings that fire which was kindled by the robbers hath consumed; for these were not burnt by the Romans, but by these internal plotters, as we have already related, in the beginning of their rebellion. That fire began at the tower of Antonia, and went on to the palaces, and consumed the upper parts of the three towers themselves.

CHAPTER V

A DESCRIPTION OF THE TEMPLE

1. Now this temple, as I have already said, was built upon a strong hill. At first the plain at the top was hardly sufficient for the holy house and the altar, for the ground about it was very uneven, and like a precipice; but when king Solomon, who was the person that built the temple, had built a wall to it on its east side, there was then added one cloister founded on a bank cast up for it, and on the other parts the holy house stood naked; but in future ages the people added new banks, and the hill became a larger plain. They then broke down the wall on the north side, and took in as much as sufficed afterward for the compass of the entire temple; and when they had built walls on three sides of the temple round about, from the bottom of the hill, and had performed a work that was greater than could be hoped for (in which work long ages were spent by them, as well as all their sacred treasures were exhausted, which were still replenished by those tributes which were sent to God from the whole habitable earth,) they then encompassed their upper courts with cloisters, as well as they [afterward] did the lowest [court of the] temple. The lowest part of this was erected to the height of three hundred cubits, and in some places more; yet did not the entire depth of the foundations appear, for they brought earth, and filled up the valleys, as being desirous to make them on a level with the narrow streets of the city; wherein they made use of stones of forty cubits

in magnitude; for the great plenty of money they then had, and the liberality of the people, made this attempt of theirs to succeed to an incredible degree; and what could not be so much as hoped for as ever to be accomplished was, by perseverance and length of time, brought to perfection.

2. Now, for the works that were above these foundations, these were not unworthy of such foundations; for all the cloisters were double, and the pillars to them belonging were twenty-five cubits in height, and supported the cloisters. These pillars were of one entire stone each of them, and that stone was white marble; and the roofs were adorned with cedar, curiously graven. The natural magnificence, and excellent polish, and the harmony of the joints in these cloisters, afforded a prospect that was very remarkable; nor was it on the outside adorned with any work of the painter or engraver. The cloisters [of the outmost court] were in breadth thirty cubits, while the entire compass of it was, by measure, six furlongs, including the tower of Antonia; those entire courts that were exposed to the air were laid with stones of all sorts. When you go through these [first] cloisters, unto the second [court of the] temple, there was a partition made of stone all round, whose height was three cubits: its construction was very elegant; upon it stood pillars, at equal distances from one another, declaring the law of purity, some in Greek, and some in Roman letters, that "no foreigner should go within that sanctuary;" for that second [court of the] temple was called "the Sanctuary," and was ascended to by fourteen steps from the first court. This court was four-square, and had a wall about it peculiar to itself; the height of its buildings, although it was on the outside forty cubits, was hidden by the steps, and on the inside that height was but twenty-five cubits; for it being built over against a higher part of the hill with steps, it was no farther to be entirely discerned within, being covered by the hill itself. Beyond these fourteen steps there was the distance of ten cubits: this was all plain, whence there were other steps, each of five cubits a-piece that leads to the gates, which gates on the north and south sides were eight, on each of those sides four, and of necessity two on the east; for since there was a partition built for the women on that side, as the proper place wherein they were to worship, there was a necessity of a second gate for them; this gate was cut out of its wall, over against the first gate. There was also on the other sides one southern and one northern gate, through which was a passage into the court of the women; for as to the other gates, the women were not allowed to pass through them; nor when they went through their own gate could they go beyond their own wall. This place was allotted to the women of our own country, and of other countries, provided they were of the same nation, and that equally; the western part of this court had no gate at all, but the wall was built entire on that side; but then the cloisters which were betwixt the gates, extended from the wall inward, before the chambers; for they were supported by very fine and large pillars. These cloisters were single, and, excepting their magnitude, were no way inferior to those of the lower court.

3. Now nine of these gates were on every side covered over with gold and silver, as were the jambs of their doors and their lintels; but there was one gate that was without [the inward court of] the holy house, which was of Corin-

thian brass, and greatly excelled those that were only covered over with silver and gold. Each gate had two doors, whose height was severally thirty cubits, and their breadth fifteen. However, they had large spaces, within of thirty cubits, and had on each side rooms, and those, both in breadth and in length, built like towers, and their height was above forty cubits. Two pillars did also support these rooms, and were in circumference twelve cubits. Now the magnitudes of the other gates were equal one to another; but that over the Corinthian gate, which opened on the east over against the gate of the holy house itself, was much larger: for its height was fifty cubits; and its doors were forty cubits; and it was adorned after a most costly manner, as having much richer and thicker plates of silver and gold upon them than the other. These nine gates had that silver and gold poured upon them by Alexander, the father of Tiberius. Now there were fifteen steps, which led away from the wall of the court of the women to this greater gate; whereas those that led thither from the other gates were five steps shorter.

4. As to the holy house itself, which was placed in the midst [of the inmost court] that most sacred part of the temple, it was ascended to by twelve steps; and in front its height and its breadth were equal, and each a hundred cubits, though it was behind thirty cubits narrower; for on its front it had what may be styled shoulders on each side, that passed twenty cubits farther. Its first gate was seventy cubits high, and twenty-five cubits broad; but this gate had no doors; for it represented the universal visibility of heaven, and that it cannot be excluded from any place. Its front was covered with gold all over, and through it the first part of the house, that was more inward did all of it appear; which, as it was very large, so did all the parts about the more inward gate appear to shine to those that saw them; but then, as the entire house was divided into two parts within, it was only the first part of it that was open to our view. Its height extended all along to ninety cubits in height, and its length was fifty cubits, and its breadth twenty; but that gate which was at this end of the first part of the house, as we have already observed, all over covered with gold, as was its whole wall about it: it had also golden vines above it, from which clusters of grapes hung as tall as a man's height; but then this house, as it was divided into two parts, the inner part was lower than the appearance of the outer, and had golden doors of twenty-five cubits altitude, and sixteen in breadth; but before these doors there was a veil of equal largeness with the doors. It was a Babylonian curtain, embroidered with blue and fine linen, and scarlet, and purple, and of a contexture that was truly wonderful. Nor was this mixture of colours without its mystical interpretation, but was a kind of image of the universe; for by the scarlet, there seemed to be enigmatically signified fire, by the fine flax the earth, by the blue the air, and by the purple the sea; two of them having their colours this foundation of this resemblance; but the fine flax and the purple have their own origin for that foundation, the earth producing the one, and the sea the other. This curtain had also embroidered upon it all that was mystical in the heavens, excepting that of the [twelve] signs, representing living creatures.

5. When any person entered into the temple, its floor received them. This part of the temple therefore was in height sixty cubits, and its length the same; whereas its breadth was but twenty cubits: but still that sixty cubits in length was divided again, and the first part of it cut off at forty cubits, and had in it three things that were very wonderful and famous among all mankind; the candlestick, the table [of shewbread,] and the altar of incense. Now the seven lamps signified the seven planets; for so many there were springing out of the candlestick. Now, the twelve loaves that were upon the table signified the circle of the zodiac and the year; but the altar of incense, by its thirteen kinds of sweet-smelling spices with which the sea replenished it, signified that God is possessor of all things that are both in the uninhabitable and habitable parts of the earth, and that they are all to be dedicated to his use. But the inmost part of the temple of all was twenty cubits. This was also separated from the outer part by a veil. In this there was nothing at all. It was inaccessible and inviolable, and not to be seen by any; and was called the Holy of Holies. Now, about the sides of the lower part of the temple there were little houses, with passages out of one into another; there were a great many of them, and they were three stories high; there were also entrances on each side into them from the gate of the temple. But the superior part of the temple had no such little houses any farther, because the temple was there narrower, and forty cubits higher, and of a smaller body than the lower parts of it. Thus we collect that the whole height, including the sixty cubits from the floor, amounted to a hundred cubits.

6. Now the outward face of the temple in its front wanted nothing that was likely to surprise either men's minds or their eyes: for it was covered all over with plates of gold of great weight, and, at the first rising of the sun, reflected back a very fiery splendour, and made those who forced themselves to look upon it to turn their eyes away, just as they would have done at the sun's own rays. But this temple appeared to strangers, when they were at a distance, like a mountain covered with snow; for, as to those parts of it that were not gilt, they were exceeding white. On its top it had spikes with sharp points, to prevent any pollution of it by birds sitting upon it. Of its stones, some of them were forty-five cubits in length, five in height, and six in breadth. Before this temple stood the altar, fifteen cubits high, and equal both in length and breadth; each of which dimensions was fifty cubits. The figure it was built in was a square, and it had corners like horns; and the passage up to it was by an insensible acclivity. It was formed without any iron tool, nor did any such iron tool so much as touch it at any time. There was a wall of partition, about a cubit in height, made of fine stones, and so as to be grateful to the sight; this encompassed the holy house and the altar, and kept the people that were on the outside off from the priests. Moreover those that had the gonorrhœa and the leprosy were excluded out of the city entirely; women also, when their courses were upon them, were shut out of the temple; nor when they were free from that impurity, were they allowed to go beyond the limit beforementioned; men also, that were not thoroughly pure were prohibited to come into the inner [court of the] temple; nay, the priests themselves that were not pure, were prohibited to come into it also.

7. Now all those of the stock of the priests that could not minister by reason of some defect in their bodies, came within the partition to-

gether with those that had no such imperfection, and had their share with them by reason of their stock, but still made use of none except their own private garments; for nobody but he that officiated had on his sacred garments; but then these priests that were without any blemish upon them, went up to the altar clothed in fine linen. They abstained chiefly from wine, out of this fear, lest otherwise they should transgress some rules of their ministration. The high priest did also go up with them; not always indeed, but on the seventh days and new moons, and if any festival belonging to our nation, which we celebrate every year, happened. When he officiated, he had on a pair of breeches that reached beneath his privy parts to his thighs, and had on an inner garment of linen, together with a blue garment, round, without seam, with fringe-work and reaching to the feet. There were also golden bells that hung upon the fringes, and pomegranates intermixed among them. The bells signified thunder, and the pomegranates lightning. But that girdle that tied the garment to the breast was embroidered with five rows of various colours of gold, and purple, and scarlet, as also of fine linen and blue; with which colours, we told you before, the veils of the temple were embroidered also. The like embroidery was upon the ephod; but the quantity of gold therein was greater. Its figure was that of a stomacher for the breast. There were upon it two golden buttons like small shields, which buttoned the ephod to the garment: in these buttons were enclosed two very large and very excellent sardonyxes, having the names of that nation engraved upon them: on the other part were hung twelve stones, three in a row one way, and four in the other; a sardius, a topaz, and an emerald: a carbuncle, a jasper, and a sapphire; an agate, an amethyst, and a ligure; an onyx, a beryl, and a chrysolite; upon every one of which was again engraved one of the forementioned names of the tribes. A mitre also of fine linen encompassed his head, which was tied by a blue riband, about which there was another golden crown, in which was engraven the sacred name [of God:] it consists of four vowels. However, the high-priest did not wear these garments at other times, but a more plain habit; he only did it when he went into the most sacred part of the temple, which he did but once a year, on that day when our custom is for all of us to keep a fast to God. And thus much concerning the city and the temple; but for the customs and laws hereto relating, we shall speak more accurately another time; for there remain a great many things thereto relating which have not been here touched upon.

8. Now, as to the tower of Antonia, it was situated at the corner of two cloisters of the court of the temple; of that on the west and that on the north; it was erected upon a rock of fifty cubits in height, and was on a great precipice; it was the work of king Herod, wherein he demonstrated his natural magnanimity. In the first place, the rock itself was covered over with smooth pieces of stone, from its foundation, both for ornament, and that any one who would either try to get up, or to go down it, might not be able to hold his feet upon it. Next to this, and before you come to the edifice of the tower itself, there was a wall three cubits high; but within that wall all the space of the tower of Antonia itself was built upon, to the height of forty cubits. The inward parts had the largeness and form of a palace, it being parted into all kinds of rooms and other conveniences, such as courts, and places for bathing, and broad spaces for camps; insomuch that, by having all conveniences that cities wanted, it might seem to be composed of several cities, but by its magnificence, it seemed a palace; and as the entire structure resembled that of a tower, it contained also four other distinct towers at its four corners; whereof the others were but fifty cubits high; whereas that which lay upon the south-east corner was seventy cubits high, that from thence the whole temple might be viewed; but on the corner where it joined to the two cloisters of the temple, it had passages down to them both, through which the guard (for there always lay in this tower a Roman legion) went several ways among the cloisters, with their arms, on the Jewish festivals, in order to watch the people, that they might not there attempt to make any innovations; for the temple was a fortress that guarded the city, as was the tower of Antonia a guard to the temple; and in that tower were the guards of those three. There was also a peculiar fortress belonging to the upper city, which was Herod's palace; but for the hill Bezetha, it was divided from the tower of Antonia, as we have already told you; and as that hill on which the tower of Antonia stood, was the highest of these three, so did it adjoin to the new city, and was the only place that hindered the sight of the temple on the north. And this shall suffice at present to have spoken about the city and the walls about it, because I have proposed to myself to make a more accurate description of it elsewhere.

CHAPTER VI

CONCERNING THE TYRANTS SIMON AND JOHN. HOW ALSO, AS TITUS WAS GOING ROUND THE WALL OF THE CITY, NICANOR WAS WOUNDED BY A DART; WHICH ACCIDENT PROVOKED TITUS TO PRESS ON THE SIEGE

1. Now the warlike men that were in the city, and the multitude of the seditious that were with Simon, were ten thousand, besides the Idumeans. Those ten thousand had fifty commanders, over whom this Simon was supreme. The Idumeans that paid him homage were five thousand, and had eight commanders, among whom those of the greatest fame were Jacob, the son of Sosas, and Simon, the son of Cathlas. John, who had seized upon the temple, had six thousand armed men, under twenty commanders; the zealots also that had come over to him, and left off their opposition, were two thousand four hundred, and had the same commander they had formerly, Eleazar, together with Simon, the son of Arinus. Now, while these factions fought one against another, the people were their prey on both sides, as we have said already; and that part of the people who would not join with them in their wicked practices, were plundered by both factions. Simon held the upper city, and the great wall as far as Cedron, and as much of the old wall as bent from Siloam to the east, and which went down to the palace of Monobazus, who was king of the Adiabeni, beyond Euphrates; he also held the fountain, and the Acra, which was no other than the lower city; he also held all that reached to the palace of queen Helena, the mother of Monobazus; but John held the temple, and the parts thereto adjoining, for a great way, as also Ophla, and the valley called the "Valley of Cedron;" and when the parts that were interposed between their possessions were burnt by them, they left a space wherein they might fight with each

other ; for this internal sedition did not cease, even when the Romans were encamped near their very walls. But although they had grown wiser at the first onset the Romans made upon them, this lasted but a while ; for they returned to their former madness, and separated one from another, and fought it out, and did everything that the besiegers could desire them to do ; for they never suffered anything that was worse from the Romans than they made each other suffer ; nor was there any misery endured by the city after these men's actions that could be esteemed new. But it was most of all unhappy before it was overthrown, while those that took it did it a greater kindness ; for I venture to affirm, that the sedition destroyed the city, and the Romans destroyed the sedition, which it was a much harder thing to do than to destroy the walls ; so that we may justly ascribe our misfortunes to our own people, and the just vengeance taken on them by the Romans ; as to which matter let every one determine by the actions on both sides.

2. Now, when affairs within the city were in this posture, Titus went round the city on the outside with some chosen horsemen, and looked about for a proper place where he might make an impression upon the walls ; but as he was in doubt where he could possibly make an attack on any side, (for the place was no way accessible where the valleys were, and on the other side the first wall appeared too strong to be shaken by the engines,) he therefore thought it best to make his assault upon the monument of John the high priest ; for there it was that the first fortification was lower, and the second was not joined to it, the builders neglecting to build the wall strong where the new city was not much inhabited ; here also was an easy passage to the third wall, through which he thought to take the upper city, and, through the tower of Antonia, the temple itself. But at this time, as he was going round about the city, one of his friends, whose name was Nicanor, was wounded with a dart on his left shoulder, as he approached, together with Josephus, too near the wall, and attempted to discourse to those that were upon the wall, about terms of peace ; for he was a person known by them. On this account it was that Cæsar, as soon as he knew their vehemence that they would not bear even such as approached them to what tended to their own preservation, was provoked to press on the siege. He also at the same time gave his soldiers leave to set the suburbs on fire, and ordered that they should bring timber together, and raise banks against the city ; and when he had parted his army into three parts, in order to set about those works, he placed those that shot darts and the archers in the midst of the banks that were then raising ; before whom he placed those engines that threw javelins, and darts, and stones, that he might prevent the enemy from sallying out upon their works, and might hinder those that were upon the wall from being able to obstruct them. So the trees were now cut down immediately, and the suburbs left naked. But now while the timber was carrying to raise the banks, and the whole army was earnestly engaged in their works, the Jews were not, however, quiet ; and it happened that the people of Jerusalem, who had been hitherto plundered and murdered, were now of good courage, and supposed they should have a breathing-time, while the others were very busy in opposing their enemies without the city, and that they should now be avenged on those that had been the authors of their miseries, in case the Romans did but get the victory.

3. However, John stayed behind, out of his fear of Simon, even while his own men were earnest in making a sally upon their enemies without. Yet did not Simon lie still, for he lay near the place of the siege : he brought his engines of war, and disposed of them at due distances upon the wall, both those which they took from Cestius formerly, and those which they got when they seized the garrison that lay in the tower of Antonia. But though they had these engines in their possession, they had so little skill in using them, that they were in a great measure useless to them ; but a few there were who had been taught by deserters how to use them, which they did use, though after an awkward manner. So they cast stones and arrows at those that were making the banks ; they also ran out upon them by companies, and fought with them. Now those that were at work covered themselves with hurdles spread over their banks, and their engines were opposed to them when they made their excursions. The engines, that all the legions had ready prepared for them, were admirably contrived ; but still more extraordinary ones belonged to the tenth legion : those that threw darts and those that threw stones, were more forcible and larger than the rest, by which they not only repelled the excursions of the Jews, but drove those away that were upon the walls also. Now, the stones that were cast, were of the weight of a talent, and were carried two furlongs and further. The blow they gave was no way to be sustained, not only by those that stood first in the way, but by those that were beyond them for a great space. As for the Jews, they at first watched the coming of the stone, for it was of a white colour, and could therefore not only be perceived by the great noise it made, but could be seen also before it came, by its brightness ; accordingly, the watchmen that sat upon the towers gave them notice when the engine was let go, and the stone came from it, and cried out aloud, in their own country language, "THE STONE COMETH ;" so those that were in its way stood off, and threw themselves down upon the ground ; by which means, and by their thus guarding themselves, the stone fell down and did them no harm. But the Romans contrived how to prevent that, by blacking the stone, who then could aim at them with success, when the stone was not discerned beforehand, as it had been till then ; and so they destroyed many of them at one blow. Yet did not the Jews, under all this distress, permit the Romans to raise their banks in quiet ; but they shrewdly and boldly exerted themselves, and repelled them both by night and by day.

4. And now, upon the finishing the Roman works, the workmen measured the distance there was from the wall, and this by lead and line, which they threw to it from their banks ; for they could not measure it any otherwise, because the Jews would shoot at them, if they came to measure it themselves ; and when they found that the engines could reach the wall, they brought them thither. Then did Titus set his engines at proper distances, so much nearer to the wall, that the Jews might not be able to repel them, and gave orders that they should go to work ; and then thereupon a prodigious noise echoed round about from three places, and on the sudden there was a great noise made by the citizens that were within the city, and no less a terror fell upon the seditious themselves ; whereupon both sorts, seeing the common danger they were in, contrived to make a like defence. So those of different factions cried out one to another, that they acted entirely as in concert

with their enemies; whereas, they ought, however, notwithstanding God did not grant them a lasting concord, in their present circumstances, to lay aside their enmities one against another, and to unite together against the Romans. Accordingly, Simon gave those that came from the temple leave, by proclamation, to go upon the wall; John also himself, though he could not believe Simon was in earnest, gave them the same leave. So on both sides they laid aside their hatred and their peculiar quarrels, and formed themselves into one body; they then ran round the walls, and having a vast number of torches with them, they threw them at the machines, and shot darts perpetually upon those that impelled those engines which battered the wall; nay, the bolder sort leaped out by troops upon the hurdles that covered the machines, and pulled them to pieces, and fell upon those that belonged to them, and beat them, not so much by any skill they had, as principally by the boldness of their attacks. However, Titus himself sent assistance to those that were the hardest set, and placed both horsemen and archers on the several sides of the engines, and thereby beat off those that brought the fire to them; he also thereby repelled those that shot stones or darts from the towers, and then set the engines to work in good earnest; yet did not the wall yield to these blows, excepting where the battering-ram of the fifteenth legion moved the corner of a tower, while the wall itself continued unhurt; for the wall was not presently in the same danger with the tower, which was extant far above it; nor could the fall of that part of the tower, easily break down any part of the wall itself together with it.

5. And now the Jews intermitted their sallies for a while; but when they observed the Romans dispersed all abroad at their works, and in their several camps (for they thought the Jews had retired out of weariness and fear) they all at once made a sally at the tower Hippicus, through an obscure gate, and at the same time brought fire to burn the works, and went boldly up to the Romans, and to their very fortifications themselves, where, at the cry they made, those that were near them came presently to their assistance, and those farther off came running after them; and here the boldness of the Jews was too hard for the good order of the Romans; and as they beat those whom they first fell upon, so they pressed upon those that were now gotten together. So this fight about the machines was very hot, while the one side tried hard to set them on fire, and the other side to prevent it; on both sides there was a confused cry made, and many of those in the fore-front of the battle were slain. However, the Jews were now too hard for the Romans, by the furious assaults they made like madmen; and the fire caught hold of the works, and both all these works and the engines themselves, had been in danger of being burnt, had not many of those select soldiers that came from Alexandria opposed themselves to prevent it, and had they not behaved themselves with greater courage than they themselves supposed they could have done; for they outdid those in this fight that had greater reputation than themselves before. This was the state of things till Cæsar took the stoutest of his horsemen and attacked the enemy, while he himself slew twelve of those that were in the fore-front of the Jews; which death of these men, when the rest of the multitude saw, they gave way, and he pursued them, and drove them all into the city, and saved the works from the fire. Now it happened at this fight, that a cer-

tain Jew was taken alive, who, by Titus's orders, was crucified before the wall, to see whether the rest of them would be affrighted, and abate of their obstinacy. But after the Jews were retired, John, who was commander of the Idumeans, and was talking to a certain soldier of his acquaintance before the wall, was wounded by a dart shot at him by an Arabian, and died immediately, leaving the greatest lamentation to the Jews, and sorrow to the seditious; for he was a man of great eminence, both for his actions and his conduct also.

CHAPTER VII

HOW ONE OF THE TOWERS ERECTED BY THE ROMANS FELL DOWN OF ITS OWN ACCORD; AND HOW THE ROMANS, AFTER GREAT SLAUGHTER HAD BEEN MADE, GOT POSSESSION OF THE FIRST WALL. HOW ALSO TITUS MADE HIS ASSAULTS UPON THE SECOND WALL; AS ALSO CONCERNING LONGINUS THE ROMAN, AND CASTOR THE JEW

1. Now, on the next night, a most surprising disturbance fell upon the Romans; for whereas Titus had given orders for the erection of three towers of fifty cubits high, that by setting men upon them at every bank, he might from thence drive those away who were upon the wall, it so happened that one of these towers fell down about midnight; and as its fall made a very great noise, fear fell upon the army, and they, supposing that the enemy was coming to attack them, ran all to their arms. Whereupon a disturbance and a tumult arose among the legions, and as nobody could tell what had happened, they went on after a disconsolate manner; and seeing no enemy appear, they were afraid one of another, and every one demanded of his neighbour the watch-word with great earnestness, as though the Jews had invaded their camp. And now they were like people under a panic fear, till Titus was informed of what had happened, and gave orders that all should be acquainted with it; and then, though with some difficulty, they got clear of the disturbance they had been under.

2. Now, these towers were very troublesome to the Jews, who otherwise opposed the Romans very courageously; for they shot at them out of their lighter engines than those towers, as they did also by those that threw darts, and the archers, and those that slung stones. For neither could the Jews reach those that were over them, by reason of their height; and it was not practicable to take them, nor to overturn them, they were so heavy, nor to set them on fire, because they were covered with plates of iron. So they retired out of the reach of the darts, and did no longer endeavour to hinder the impression of their rams, which, by continually beating upon the wall, did gradually prevail against it; so that the wall already gave way to the Nico, for by that name did the Jews themselves call the greatest of their engines, because it conquered all things. And now, they were for a long while grown weary of fighting, and of keeping guards, and were retired to lodge in the night-time at a distance from the wall. It was on other accounts also thought by them to be superfluous to guard the wall, there being, besides that, two other fortifications still remaining, and they being slothful, and their counsels having been ill-concerted on all occasions; so a great many grew lazy, and retired. Then the Romans mounted

the breach, where Nico had made one, and all the Jews left the guarding the wall, and retreated to the second wall; so those that had gotten over the wall, opened the gates, and received all the army within it. And thus did the Romans get possession of this first wall, on the fifteenth day of the siege, which was the seventh day of the month Artemisius [Jyar,] when they demolished a great part of it, as well as they did of the northern parts of the city, which had been demolished also by Cestius formerly.

3. And now Titus pitched his camp within the city, at that place which was called "the camp of the Assyrians," having seized upon all that lay as far as Cedron, but took care to be out of the reach of the Jews' darts. He then presently began his attacks, upon which the Jews divided themselves into several bodies, and courageously defended that wall; while John and his faction did it from the tower of Antonia, and from the northern cloister of the temple, and fought the the Romans before the monument of king Alexander; and Simon's army also took for their share the spot of ground that was near John's monument, and fortified it as far as to that gate where water was brought in to the tower Hippicus. However, the Jews made violent sallies, and that frequently also, and in bodies together out of the gates, and there fought the Romans; and when they were pursued all together to the wall, they were beaten in those fights, as wanting the skill of the Romans. But when they fought them from the walls, they were too hard for them, the Romans being encouraged by their power, joined to their skill, as were the Jews by their boldness, which was nourished by the fear they were in, and that hardiness which is natural to our nation under calamities; they were also encouraged still by the hope of deliverance, as were the Romans by the hopes of subduing them in a little time. Nor did either side grow weary, but attacks and fightings upon the walls and perpetual sallies out in bodies were practised all the day long; nor were there any sort of warlike engagements that were not then put in use. And the night itself had much ado to part them, when they began to fight in the morning; nay, the night itself was passed without sleep on both sides, and was more uneasy than the day to them, while the one was afraid lest the wall should be taken, and the others lest the Jews should make sallies upon their camps; both sides also lay in their armour during the night-time, and thereby were ready at the appearance of light to go to the battle. Now, among the Jews the ambition was who should undergo the first dangers, and thereby gratify their commanders. Above all, they had a great veneration and dread of Simon; and to that degree was he regarded by every one of those that were under him, that at his command they were ready to kill themselves with their own hands. What made the Romans so courageous, was their usual custom of conquering and disuse of being defeated, their constant wars, and perpetual warlike exercises, and the grandeur of their dominion; and what was now the chief encouragement,—Titus, who was present everywhere with them all; for it appeared a terrible thing to grow weary while Cæsar was there, and fought bravely as well as they did, and was himself at once an eye-witness of such as behaved themselves valiantly, and he who was to reward them also. It was besides esteemed an advantage at present to have any one's valour known by Cæsar; on which account many of them appeared to have more alacrity than strength to answer it. And now, as the Jews were about this time standing in array before the wall, and that in a strong body, and while both parties were throwing their darts at each other, Longinus, one of the equestrian order, leaped out of the army of the Romans, and leaped into the very midst of the army of the Jews, and as they dispersed themselves upon this attack, he slew two of their men of the greatest courage; one of them he struck in his mouth, as he was coming to meet him; the other was slain by that very dart that he drew out of the body of the other, with which he ran this man through his side as he was running away from him; and when he had done this, he first of all ran out of the midst of his enemies to his own side. So this man signalized himself for his valour, and many there were who were ambitious of gaining the like reputation. And now the Jews were unconcerned at what they suffered themselves from the Romans, and were only solicitous about what mischief they could do them; and death itself seemed a small matter to them, if at the same time they could but kill any one of their enemies. But Titus took care to secure his own soldiers from harm, as well as to have them overcome their enemies. He also said that inconsiderate violence was madness; and that this alone was the true courage that was joined with good conduct. He therefore commanded his men to take care, when they fought their enemies, that they received no harm from them at the same time; and thereby shew themselves to be truly valiant men.

4. And now Titus brought one of his engines to the middle tower of the north part of the wall, in which a certain crafty Jew, whose name was Castor, lay in ambush, with ten others like himself, the rest being fled away by reason of the archers. These men lay still for a while, as in great fear, under their breast-plates; but when the tower was shaken, they arose; and Castor did then stretch out his hand, as a petitioner, and called for Cæsar, and by his voice moved his compassion, and begged of him to have mercy upon them: and Titus in the innocency of his heart, believing him to be in earnest, and hoping that the Jews did now repent, stopped the working of the battering-ram, and forbade them to shoot at the petitioners, and bade Castor say what he had a mind to say to him. He said that he would come down, if he would give him his right hand for his security. To which Titus replied, that he was well pleased with such his agreeable conduct, and would be well pleased if all the Jews would be of his mind; and that he was ready to give the like security to the city. Now five of the ten dissembled with him, and pretended to beg for mercy; while the rest cried out aloud, that they would never be slaves to the Romans, while it was in their power to die in a state of freedom. Now while these men were quarrelling for a long while, the attack was delayed; Castor also sent to Simon, and told him that they might take some time for consultation about what was to be done, because he would elude the power of the Romans for a considerable time. And at the same time that he sent thus to him, he appeared openly to exhort those that were obstinate to accept of Titus's hand for their security; but they seemed very angry at it, and brandished their naked swords upon the breast-works, and struck themselves upon their breast, and fell down as if they had been slain. Hereupon Titus, and those with him were amazed at the courage of the men; and as they were not able to see exactly what was done, they admired at their great fortitude, and pitied their calamity. During this interval, a certain person shot a dart

at Castor, and wounded him in his nose; whereupon he presently pulled out the dart, and shewed it to Titus, and complained that this was unfair treatment: so Cæsar reproved him that shot the dart, and sent Josephus, who then stood by him, to give his right hand to Castor. But Josephus said that he would not go to him, because these pretended petitioners meant nothing that was good; he also restrained those friends of his who were zealous to go to him. But still there was one Æneas, a deserter, who said he would go to him. Castor also called to them, that somebody should come and receive the money which he had with him; this made Æneas the more earnestly to run to him with his bosom open. Then did Castor take up a great stone, and threw it at him, which missed him, because he guarded himself against it; but still it wounded another soldier that was coming to him. When Cæsar understood that this was a delusion, he perceived that mercy in war is a pernicious thing, because such cunning tricks have less place under the exercise of greater severity. So he caused the engine to work more strongly than before, on account of his anger at the deceit put upon him. But Castor and his companions set the tower on fire when it began to give way, and leaped through the flame into a hidden vault that was under it; which made the Romans further suppose that they were men of great courage, as having cast themselves into the fire.

CHAPTER VIII

HOW THE ROMANS TOOK THE SECOND WALL TWICE, AND GOT ALL READY FOR TAKING THE THIRD WALL

1. Now Cæsar took this wall there on the fifth day after he had taken the first; and when the Jews had fled from him, he entered into it with a thousand armed men, and those of his choice troops, and this at a place where were the merchants of wool, the braziers, and the market for cloth, and where the narrow streets led obliquely to the wall. Wherefore, if Titus had either demolished a larger part of the wall immediately, or had come in, and according to the law of war, had laid waste what was left, his victory would not, I suppose, have been mixed with any loss to himself; but now, out of the hope he had that he should make the Jews ashamed of their obstinacy, by not being willing, when he was able to afflict them more than he needed to do, he did not widen the breach of the wall in order to make a safer retreat upon occasion; for he did not think they would lay snares for him that did them such a kindness. When therefore he came in, he did not permit of his soldiers to kill any of those they caught, nor to set fire to their houses neither; nay, he gave leave to the seditious, if they had a mind, to fight without any harm to the people, and promised to restore the people's effects to them; for he was very desirous to preserve the city for his own sake, and the temple for the sake of the city. As to the people, he had them of a long time ready to comply with his proposals; but as to the fighting men, this humanity of his seemed a mark of his weakness; and they imagined that he made these proposals because he was not able to take the rest of the city. They also threatened death to the people, if they should any one of them say a word about a surrender. They moreover cut the throats of such as talked of a peace, and then attacked those Romans that were come within the wall. Some of them they met in the narrow streets, and some they fought against from their houses, while they made a sudden sally out at the upper gates, and assaulted such Romans as were beyond the wall till those that guarded the wall were so affrighted, that they leaped down from their towers, and retired to their several camps; upon which a great noise was made by the Romans that were within, because they were encompassed round on every side by their enemies; as also by them that were without, because they were in fear for those that were left in the city. Thus did the Jews grow more numerous perpetually, and had great advantage over the Romans, by their full knowledge of those narrow lanes; and they wounded a great many of them, and fell upon them, and drove them out of the city. Now these Romans were at present forced to make the best resistance they could; for they were not able, in great numbers, to get out at the breach in the wall, it was so narrow. It is also probable that all those that were gotten within had been cut to pieces, if Titus had not sent them succours; for he ordered the archers to stand at the upper ends of these narrow lanes; and he stood himself where was the greatest multitude of his enemies, and with his darts he put a stop to them; as with him did Domitius Sabinus also, a valiant man, and one that in this battle appeared so to be. Thus did Cæsar continue to shoot darts at the Jews continually, and to hinder them from coming upon his men, and this until all his soldiers had retreated out of the city.

2. And thus were the Romans driven out, after they had possessed themselves of the second wall. Whereupon the fighting men that were in the city were lifted up in their minds, and were elevated upon this their good success, and began to think that the Romans would never venture to come into the city any more; and that, if they kept within it themselves, they should not be any more conquered; for God had blinded their minds for the transgressions they had been guilty of, nor could they see how much greater forces the Romans had than those that were now expelled, no more than they could discern how a famine was creeping upon them; for hitherto they had fed themselves out of the public miseries, and drank the blood of the city. But now poverty had for a long time seized upon the better part, and a great many had died already for want of necessaries; although the seditious indeed supposed the destruction of the people to be an easement to themselves, for they desired that none others might be preserved but such as were against a peace with the Romans, and were resolved to live in opposition to them, and they were pleased when the multitude of those of a contrary opinion were consumed, as being then freed from a heavy burden: and this was their disposition of mind with regard to those that were within the city, while they covered themselves with their armour, and prevented the Romans, when they were trying to get into the city again, and made a wall of their own bodies over against that part of the wall that was cast down. Thus did they valiantly defend themselves for three days; but on the fourth day they could not support themselves against the vehement assaults of Titus, but were compelled by force to fly whither they had fled before; so he quietly possessed himself again of that wall, and demolished it entirely; and when he had put a garrison into the towers that were on the south parts of the city, he contrived how he might assault the third wall.

CHAPTER IX

TITUS, WHEN THE JEWS WERE NOT AT ALL MOLLI-
FIED BY HIS LEAVING OFF THE SIEGE FOR A
WHILE, SET HIMSELF AGAIN TO PROSECUTE THE
SAME; BUT SOON SENT JOSEPHUS TO DISCOURSE
WITH HIS OWN COUNTRYMEN ABOUT PEACE

1. A RESOLUTION was now taken by Titus, to
relax the siege for a little while, and to afford
the seditious an interval for consideration, and
to see whether the demolishing of their second
wall would not make them a little more compli-
ant, or whether they were not somewhat afraid
of a famine, because the spoils they had gotten
by rapine would not be sufficient for them long;
so he made use of this relaxation, in order to
compass his own designs. Accordingly, as the
usual appointed time when he must distribute
subsistence-money to the soldiers, was now come,
he gave orders that the commanders should put
the army into battle array, in the face of the
enemy, and then give every one of the soldiers
their pay. So the soldiers, according to custom, opened the cases wherein their arms before
lay covered, and marched with their breastplates
on; as did the horsemen lead their horses in
their fine trappings. Then did the places that
were before the city, shine very splendidly for a
great way; nor was there anything so grateful
to Titus's own men, or so terrible to the enemy
as that sight; for the whole old wall and the
north side of the temple were full of spectators,
and one might see the houses full of such as
looked at them; nor was there any part of the
city which was not covered over with their multitudes; nay, a very great consternation seized
upon the hardiest of the Jews themselves, when
they saw all the army in the same place, together
with the fineness of their arms, and the good
order of their men; and I cannot but think that
the seditious would have changed their minds at
that sight, unless the crimes they had committed against the people had been so horrid,
that they despaired of forgiveness from the Romans; but as they believed death with torments must be their punishment, if they did
not go on in the defence of the city, they thought
it much better to die in war. Fate also prevailed
so far over them, that the innocent were to perish
with the guilty, and the city was to be destroyed
with the seditious that were in it.

2. Thus did the Romans spend four days in
bringing this subsistence-money to the several
legions; but, on the fifth day, when no signs of
peace appeared to come from the Jews, Titus divided his legions, and began to raise banks, both
at the tower of Antonia, and at John's monument. Now, his designs were to take the upper
city at that monument, and the temple at the
tower of Antonia; for if the temple were not
taken, it would be dangerous to keep the city
itself; so at each of these parts he raised him
banks, each legion raising one. As for those
that wrought at John's monument, the Idumeans, and those that were in arms with Simon,
made sallies upon them, and put some stop to
them; while John's party and the multitude of
zealots with them, did the like to those that
were before the tower of Antonia. These Jews
were now too hard for the Romans, not only in
direct fighting, because they stood upon the
higher ground, but because they had now
learned to use their own engines; for their continual use of them, one day after another, did
by degrees improve their skill about them; for
of one sort of engines for darts they had three

hundred, and forty for stones; by the means of
which they made it more tedious for the Romans to raise their banks; but then Titus,
knowing that the city would be either saved or
destroyed for himself, did not only proceed earnestly in the siege, but did not omit to have the
Jews exhorted to repentance; so he mixed good
counsel with his works for the siege; and being
sensible that exhortations are frequently more
effectual than arms, he persuaded them to surrender the city, now in a manner already taken,
and thereby to save themselves, and sent Josephus to speak to them in their own language;
for he imagined they might yield to the persuasion of a countryman of their own.

3. So Josephus went round about the wall,
and tried to find a place that was out of the
reach of their darts, and yet within their hearing, and besought them, in many words, to spare
themselves, to spare their country and their
temple, and not to be more obdurate in these
cases than foreigners themselves; for that the
Romans, who had no relation to those things,
had a reverence for their sacred rites and places,
although they belonged to their enemies, and
had till now kept their hands off from meddling
with them; while such as were brought up
under them, and, if they be preserved, will be
the only people that will reap the benefit of
them, hurry on to have them destroyed. That
certainly they have seen their strongest walls
demolished, and that the wall that was still remaining,
was weaker than those that were already taken.
That they must know the Roman power was invincible, and that they had been used to serve
them; for, that in case it be allowed a right
thing to fight for liberty, that ought to have
been done at first; but for them that have once
fallen under the power of the Romans, and have
now submitted to them for so many long years,
to pretend to shake off that yoke afterward,
was the work of such as had a mind to die miserably, not of such as were lovers of liberty. Besides, men may well enough grudge at the dishonour of owning ignoble masters over them,
but ought not to do so to those who have all
things under their command; for what part of
the world is there that hath escaped the Romans, unless it be such as are of no use, for violent heat or violent cold? And evident it is,
that fortune is on all hands gone over to them;
and that God, when he had gone round the nations with this dominion, is now settled in Italy.
That, moreover, it is a strong and fixed law,
even among brute beasts, as well as among men,
to yield to those that are too strong for them;
and to suffer those to have dominion who are
too hard for the rest in war; for which reason it
was that their forefathers, who were far superior to them both in their souls and bodies, and
other advantages, did yet submit to the Romans;
which they would not have suffered, had they
not known that God was with them. As for
themselves, what can they depend on in this
their opposition, when the greatest part of the
city is already taken? and when those that are
within it are under greater miseries than if they
were taken, although their walls be still standing? For that the Romans are not unacquainted
with that famine which is in the city, whereby
the people are already consumed, and the fighting men will in a little time be so too; for
although the Romans should leave off the siege,
and not fall upon the city with their swords in
their hands, yet was there an insuperable war
that beset them within, and was augmented
every hour, unless they were able to wage war
with famine, and fight against it, or could alone

conquer their natural appetites. He added this farther, How right a thing it was to change their conduct, before their calamities were become incurable, and to have recourse to such advice as might preserve them, while opportunity was offered them for so doing; for that the Romans would not be mindful of their past actions to their disadvantage, unless they persevered in their insolent behaviour to the end; because they were naturally mild in their conquests, and preferred what was profitable, before what their passions dictated to them; which profit of theirs lay not in leaving the city empty of inhabitants, nor the country a desert; on which account Cæsar did now offer them his right hand for their security. Whereas, if he took the city by force, he would not save any one of them, and this especially, if they rejected his offers in these their utmost distresses; for the walls that were already taken, could not but assure them that the third wall would quickly be taken also; and though their fortifications should prove too strong for the Romans to break through them, yet would the famine fight for the Romans against them.

4. While Josephus was making this exhortation to the Jews, many of them jested upon him from the wall, many reproached him; nay, some threw their darts at him; but when he could not himself persuade them by such open good advice, he betook himself to the histories belonging to their own nations; and cried out aloud, "O miserable creatures! Are you so unmindful of those that used to assist you, that you will fight by your weapons and by your hands against the Romans? When did we ever conquer any other nation by such means? and when was it that God, who is the Creator of the Jewish people, did not avenge them when they had been injured? Will not you turn again, and look back, and consider whence it is that you fight with such violence, and how great a Supporter you have profanely abused? Will you recall to mind the prodigious things done for your forefathers and this holy place, and how great enemies of yours were by him subdued under you? I even tremble myself in declaring the works of God before your ears, that are unworthy to hear them: however, hearken to me that you may be informed how you fight, not only against the Romans but against God himself. In old times there was one Necao, king of Egypt, who was also called Pharaoh: he came with a prodigious army of soldiers, and seized queen Sarah, the mother of our nation. What did Abraham our progenitor then do? Did he defend himself from this injurious person by war, although he had three hundred and eighteen captains under him, and an immense army under each of them? Indeed, he deemed them to be no number at all without God's assistance, and only spread out his hands towards this holy place,* which you have now polluted, and reckoned upon him as upon his invincible supporter, instead of his own army. Was not our queen sent back, without any defilement, to her husband, the very next evening?—while the king of Egypt fled away, adoring this place

---

* Josephus supposes, in this speech to the Jews, that not Abraham only, but Pharaoh king of Egypt, prayed towards a temple at Jerusalem, or towards Jerusalem itself, in which were Mount Sion and Mount Moriah, on which the tabernacle and temple did afterwards stand; and this long before either the Jewish tabernacle or temple was built; nor is the famous command given by God to Abraham, to go two or three days' journey, on purpose to offer up his son Isaac there, unfavourable to such a notion.

---

which you have defiled by shedding thereon the blood of your countrymen; and he also trembled at those visions which he saw in the night-season, and bestowed both silver and gold on the Hebrews, as on a people beloved of God. Shall I say nothing, or shall I mention the removal of our fathers into Egypt, who, when they were used tyrannically, and were fallen under the power of foreign kings for four hundred years together, and might have defended themselves by war and by fighting, did yet do nothing but commit themselves to God? Who is there that does not know that Egypt was over-run with all sorts of wild beasts, and consumed by all sorts of distempers? how their land did not bring forth his fruit? how the Nile failed of water; how the ten plagues of Egypt followed one upon another? and how, by those means, our fathers were sent away, under a guard, without any bloodshed, and without running any dangers, because God conducted them as his peculiar servants? Moreover, did not Palestine groan under the ravage the Assyrians made, when they carried away our sacred ark? as did their idol Dagon, and as also did that entire nation of those that carried it away, how they were smitten with a loathsome distemper in the secret parts of their bodies, when their very bowels came down together with what they had eaten, till those hands that stole it away were obliged to bring it back again, and that with the sound of cymbals and timbrels, and other oblations, in order to appease the anger of God for their violation of his holy ark. It was God who then became our general, and accomplished these great things for our fathers, and this because they did not meddle with war and fighting, but committed it to him to judge about their affairs. When Sennacherib, king of Assyria, brought along with him all Asia, and encompassed this city round with his army, did he fall by the hands of men? were not those hands lifted up to God in prayers, without meddling with their arms, when an angel of God destroyed that prodigious army in one night? when the Assyrian king, as he rose next day, found a hundred fourscore and five thousand dead bodies, and when he, with the remainder of his army, fled away from the Hebrews, though they were unarmed, and did not pursue them! You are also acquainted with the slavery we were under at Babylon, where the people were captives for seventy years; yet were they not delivered into freedom again before God made Cyrus his gracious instrument in bringing it about; accordingly they were set free by him, and did again restore the worship of their Deliverer at his temple. And, to speak in general, we can produce no example wherein our fathers got any success by war, or failed of success, when without war they committed themselves to God. When they stayed at home they conquered, as pleased their Judge; but when they went out to fight they were always disappointed: for example, when the king of Babylon besieged this very city, and our king Zedekiah fought against him, contrary to what predictions were made to him by Jeremiah the prophet, he was at once taken prisoner, and saw the city and the temple demolished. Yet how much greater was the moderation of that king, than is that of your present governors, and that of the people then under him, than is that of you at this time! for when Jeremiah cried out aloud, how very angry God was at them, because of their transgressions, and told them that they should be taken prisoners, unless they would surrender up their city, neither did the king nor the people put him to death; but for you (to pass over what you have done within the city, which I am not able to describe, as your wickedness deserves) you abuse me, and throw darts at me, who only exhort you to save yourselves, as being provoked when you are put in mind of your sins, and cannot bear the very mention of those crimes which you every day perpetrate. For another example, when Antiochus, who was called Epiphanes, lay before this city, and had been guilty of many indignities against God, and our forefathers met him in arms, they then were slain in the battle, this city was plundered by our enemies, and our sanctuary made desolate for three years and six months. And what need I bring any more examples! Indeed, what can it be that hath stirred up an army of the Romans against our nation? Is it not the impiety of the inhabitants? Whence did our servitude commence? Was it not derived from the seditions that were among our forefathers, when the madness of Aristobulus and Hyrcanus, and our mutual quarrels, brought Pompey upon this city, and when God reduced those under subjection to the Romans, who were unworthy of the liberty they had enjoyed? After a siege, therefore, of three months, they were forced to surrender themselves, although they had been guilty of such offences with regard to our sanctuary and our laws, as you have; and this while they had much greater advantages to go to war than you have. Do not we know what end Antigonus, the son of Aristobulus, came to, under whose reign God provided that this city should be taken again upon account of the people's offences? When Herod, the son of Antipater, brought upon us Sosius, and Sosius brought upon us the Roman army, they were then encompassed and besieged for six months, till, as a punishment for their sins they were taken, and the city was plundered by the enemy. Thus it appears, that arms were never given to our nation; but that we are always given up to be fought against, and to be taken; or I suppose, that such as inhabit this holy place ought to commit the disposal of all things to God, and then only to disregard the assistance of men when they resign themselves up to their arbitrator, who is above. As for you, what have you done of those things that are recommended by our legislator! and what have you not done of those things that he hath condemned! How much more impious are you than those who were so quickly taken! You have not avoided so much as those sins which are usually done in secret; I mean thefts, and treacherous plots against men, and adulteries. You are quarrelling about rapines and murders, and invent strange ways of wickedness. Nay, the temple itself is become the receptacle of all, and this divine place is polluted by the hands of those of our country; which place hath yet been reverenced by the Romans when it was at a distance from them, when they have suffered many of their own customs to give place to our law. And, after all this, do you expect Him whom you have so impiously abused to be your supporter? To be sure then you have a right to be petitioners, and to call on Him to assist you, so pure are your hands! Did your king [Hezekiah] lift up such hands in prayer to God against the king of Assyria, when he destroyed that great army in one night? And do the Romans commit such wickedness as did the king of Assyria, that you may have reason to hope for the like vengeance upon them? Did not that king accept of money from our king upon this condition, that he should not destroy the city, and yet, contrary to the oath he had taken, he came down to burn the temple? while the Romans do demand no more than that accustomed tribute which our fathers paid to their fathers; and if they may but once obtain that, they neither aim to destroy this city, nor to touch this sanctuary; nay, they will grant you besides, that your posterity shall be free, and your possessions secured to you, and will preserve your holy laws inviolate to you. And it is plain madness to expect that God should appear as well disposed towards the wicked as towards the righteous, since he knows when it is proper to punish men for their sins immediately; accordingly he brake the power of the Assyrians the very first night that they pitched their camp. Wherefore, had he judged that our nation was worthy of freedom, or the Romans of punishment, he had immediately inflicted punishment upon those Romans, as he did upon the Assyrians, when Pompey began to meddle with our nation, or when after him Sosius came up against us, or when Vespasian laid waste Galilee, or lastly, when Titus came first of all near to this city: although Magnus and Sosius did not only suffer nothing, but took the city by force: as did Vespasian go from the war he made against you to receive the empire; and as for Titus, those springs that were formerly almost dried up when they were under your power, since he is come, run more plentifully than they did before; accordingly, you know that Siloam, as well as all the other springs that were without the city, did so far fail, that water was sold by distinct measures; whereas they now have such a great quantity of water for your enemies, as is sufficient not only for drink both for themselves and their cattle, but for watering their gardens also. The same wonderful sign you had also experience of formerly, when the fore-mentioned king of Babylon made war against us, and when he took the city and burnt the temple; while yet I believe the Jews of that age were not so impious as you are. Wherefore I cannot but suppose that God is fled out of his sanctuary, and stands on the side of those against whom you fight. Now, even a man, if he be but a good man, will fly from an impure house, and will hate those that are in it; and do you persuade yourselves that God will abide with you in your iniquities, who sees all secret things, and hears what is kept most private! Now, what crime is there, I pray you, that is so much as kept secret among you, or is concealed by you! nay, what is there that is not open to your very enemies! for you shew your transgressions after a pompous manner, and contend one with another which of you shall be more wicked than another; and you make a public demonstration of your injustice, as if it were virtue! However, there is a place left for preservation, if you be willing to accept of it; and God is easily reconciled to those that confess their faults, and repent of them. O hard-hearted wretches as you are! cast away all your arms, and take pity of your country already going to ruin; return from your wicked ways, and have regard to the excellency of that city which you are going to betray, to that excellent temple with the donations of so many countries in it. Who could bear to be the first to set that temple on fire? who could be willing that these things should be no more? and what is there that can better deserve to be preserved? O insensible creatures, and more stupid than are the stones themselves! And if you cannot look at these things with discerning eyes, yet, however, have pity upon your families, and set before every one of your eyes your children, and wives, and parents, who will be gradually consumed either by famine or by war. I am sensible that this danger will extend to my mother, and wife, and to that family of mine who have been by no means ignoble, and indeed to one that hath been very eminent in old time; and perhaps you may imagine that it is on their account only that I give you this advice: if that be all, kill them: nay, take my own blood as a reward, if it may but procure your preservation; for I am ready to die in case you will but return to a sound mind after my death."

CHAPTER X

HOW A GREAT MANY OF THE PEOPLE EARNESTLY ENDEAVOURED TO DESERT TO THE ROMANS; AS ALSO WHAT INTOLERABLE THINGS THOSE THAT STAYED BEHIND SUFFERED BY FAMINE, AND THE SAD CONSEQUENCES THEREOF

1. As Josephus was speaking thus with a loud voice, the seditious would neither yield to what he said, nor did they deem it safe for them to alter their conduct; but as for the people, they had a great inclination to desert to the Romans; accordingly, some of them sold what they had, and even the most precious things that had been laid up as treasures by them, for a very small matter, and swallowed down pieces of gold, that they might not be found out by the robbers; and when they had escaped to the Romans, went to stool, and had wherewithal to provide plentifully for themselves; for Titus let a great number of them go away into the country, whither they pleased: and the main reasons why they were so ready to desert were these: That now they should be freed from those miseries which they had endured in that city, and yet should not be in slavery to the Romans: however, John and Simon, with their factions, did more carefully watch these men's going out than they did the coming in of the Romans; and, if any one did but afford the least shadow of suspicion of such an intention, his throat was cut immediately.

2. But as for the richer sort, it proved all one to them whether they stayed in the city or attempted to get out of it, for they were equally destroyed in both cases; for every such person was put to death under this pretence, that they were going to desert,—but in reality that the robbers might get what they had. The madness of the seditious did also increase together with their famine, and both those miseries were every day inflamed more and more; for their was no corn which anywhere appeared publicly, but the robbers came running into, and searched men's private houses; and if they found none, they tormented them worse, because they supposed they had more carefully concealed it. The indication they made use of whether they had any or not, was taken from the bodies of these miserable wretches; which, if they were in good case, they supposed they were in no want at all of food; but if they were wasted away, they walked off without searching any further; nor did they think it proper to kill such as these, because they saw they would very soon die of themselves for want of food. Many there were indeed who sold what they had for one measure; it was of wheat, if they were of the richer sort; but of barley, if they were poorer. When these had so done, they shut themselves up in the inmost rooms of their houses, and ate the corn they had gotten; some did it without grinding it, by reason of the extremity of the want they were in, and others baked bread of it, according as ne-

cessity and fear dictated to them: a table was nowhere laid for a distinct meal, but they snatched the bread out of the fire, half baked, and ate it very hastily.

3. It was now a miserable case, and a sight that would justly bring tears into our eyes, how men stood as to their food, while the more powerful had more than enough, and the weaker were lamenting [for want of it.] But the famine was too hard for all other passions, and it is destructive to nothing so much as to modesty; for what was otherwise worthy of reverence, was in this case despised; insomuch that children pulled the very morsels that their fathers were eating, out of their very mouths, and what was still more to be pitied, so did the mothers do as to their infants: and when those that were most dear were perishing under their hands, they were not ashamed to take from them the very last drops that might preserve their lives; and while they ate after this manner, yet were they not concealed in so doing; but the seditious everywhere came upon them immediately, and snatched away from them what they had gotten from others; for when they saw any house shut up, this was to them a signal that the people within had gotten some food; whereupon they broke open the doors, and ran in, and took pieces of what they were eating, almost up out of their very throats and this by force; the old men, who held their food fast, were beaten; and if the women hid what they had within their hands, their hair was torn for so doing; nor was there any commiseration shewn either to the aged or to infants, but they lifted up children from the ground as they hung upon the morsels they had gotten, and shook them down upon the floor; but still were they more barbarously cruel to those that had prevented their coming in, and had actually swallowed down what they were going to seize upon, as if they had been unjustly defrauded of their right. They also invented terrible methods of torment to discover where any food was, and they were these: to stop up the passages of the privy parts of the miserable wretches, and to drive sharp stakes up their fundaments! and a man was forced to bear what it is terrible even to hear, in order to make him confess that he had but one loaf of bread, or that he might discover a handful of barley-meal that was concealed; and this was done when these tormentors were not themselves hungry; for the thing had been less barbarous had necessity forced them to it; but this was done to keep their madness in exercise, and as making preparations of provisions for themselves on the following days. These men went also to meet those that had crept out of the city by night, as far as the Roman guards, to gather some plants and herbs that grew wild; and when those people thought they had got clear of the enemy, these snatched from them what they had brought with them, even while they had frequently entreated them, and that by calling upon the tremendous name of God, to give them back some part of what they had brought; though these would not give them the least crumb; and they were to be well contented that they were only spoiled, and not slain at the same time.

4. These were the afflictions which the lower sort of people suffered from these tyrants' guards; but for the men that were in dignity, and withal were rich, they were carried before the tyrants themselves; some of whom were falsely accused of laying treacherous plots, and so were destroyed; others of them were charged with designs of betraying the city to the Romans: but the readiest way of all was this, to suborn some-

body to affirm that they were resolved to desert to the enemy; and he who was utterly despoiled of what he had by Simon, was sent back again to John, as of those who had been already plundered by John, Simon got what remained; insomuch that they drank the blood of the populace to one another, and divided the dead bodies of the poor creatures between them; so that although, on account of their ambition after dominion, they contended with each other, yet did they very well agree in their wicked practices; for he that did not communicate what he had got by the miseries of others to the other tyrant, seemed to be too little guilty, and in one respect only; and he that did not partake of what was so communicated to him, grieved at this, as at the loss of what was a valuable thing, that he had no share in such barbarity.

5. It is therefore impossible to go distinctly over every instance of these men's iniquity. I shall therefore speak my mind here at once briefly:— That neither did any other city ever suffer such miseries, nor did any age ever breed a generation more fruitful in wickedness than this was, from the beginning of the world. Finally, they brought the Hebrew nation into contempt, that they might themselves appear comparatively less impious with regard to strangers. They confessed what was true, that they were the slaves, the scum, and the spurious abortive and offspring of our nation, while they overthrew the city themselves, and forced the Romans whether they would or no, to gain a melancholy reputation, by acting gloriously against them and did almost draw that fire upon the temple, which they seemed to think came too slowly; and, indeed, when they saw the temple burning, from the upper city, they were neither troubled at it, nor did they shed any tears on that account, while yet these passions were discovered among the Romans themselves: which circumstances we shall speak of hereafter in their proper place, when we come to treat of such matters.

CHAPTER XI

HOW THE JEWS WERE CRUCIFIED BEFORE THE WALLS OF THE CITY. CONCERNING ANTIOCHUS EPIPHANES; AND HOW THE JEWS OVERTHREW THE BANKS THAT HAD BEEN RAISED BY THE ROMANS

1. So now Titus's banks were advanced a great way, notwithstanding his soldiers had been very much distressed from the wall. He then sent a party of horsemen, and ordered they should lay ambushes for those that went out into the valleys to gather food. Some of these were indeed, fighting men, who were not contented with what they got by rapine; but the greater part of them were poor people, who were deterred from deserting, by the concern they were under for their own relations: for they could not hope to escape away, together with their wives and children, without the knowledge of the seditious; nor could they think of leaving these relations to be slain by the robbers on their account; nay, the severity of the famine made them bold in thus going out: so nothing remained but that, when they were concealed from the robbers, they should be taken by the enemy; and when they were going to be taken, they were forced to defend themselves, for fear of being punished: as, after they had fought, they thought it too late to make any supplications for mercy: so they were first whipped, and then tormented with all sorts of tortures before they died, and were then crucified before the wall of the city. This miserable procedure made Titus greatly to pity them, while they caught every day five hundred Jews; nay, some days they caught more; yet did it not appear to be safe for him to let loose those that were taken by force to go their way; and to set a guard over so many, he saw would be to make such as guarded them useless to him. The main reason why he did not forbid that cruelty, was this, that he hoped the Jews might perhaps yield at that sight, out of fear lest they might themselves afterwards be liable to the same cruel treatment. So the soldiers, out of the wrath and hatred they bore the Jews, nailed those they caught, one after one way, and another after another, to the crosses, by way of jest; when their multitude was so great, that room was wanting for the crosses, and crosses wanting for the bodies.*

2. But so far were the seditious from repenting at this sad sight, that, on the contrary, they made the rest of the multitude believe otherwise; for they brought the relations of those that had deserted, upon the wall, with such of the populace as were very eager to go over upon the security offered them, and shewed them what miseries those underwent, who fled to the Romans; and told them that those who were caught, were supplicants to them, and not such as were taken prisoners. This sight kept many of those within the city who were so eager to desert, till the truth was known; yet did some of them run away immediately, as unto certain punishment, esteeming death from their enemies to be a quiet departure, if compared with that by famine. So Titus commanded that the hands of many of those that were caught should be cut off, that they might not be thought deserters, and might be credited on account of the calamity they were under, and sent them in to John and Simon, with this exhortation, that they would now at length leave off [their madness,] and not force him to destroy the city, whereby they would have those advantages of repentance, even in their utmost distress, that they would preserve their own lives, and so fine a city of their own, and that temple which was their peculiar. He then went round about the banks that were cast up, and hastened them, in order to shew that his words should in no long time be followed by his deeds. In answer to which, the seditious cast reproaches upon Cæsar himself, and upon his father also, and cried out with a loud voice, that they contemned death, and did well to prefer it before slavery; that they would do all the mischief to the Romans they could while they had breath in them; and that for their own city, since they were, as he said, to be destroyed, they had no concern about it, and that the world itself was a better temple to God than this. That yet this temple would be preserved by him that inhabited therein, whom they still had for their assistant in this war, and did therefore laugh at all his threatenings, which would come to nothing; because the conclusion of the whole depended upon God only. These words were mixed with reproaches, and with them they made a mighty clamour.

3. In the meantime Antiochus Epiphanes came to the city, having with him a considerable number of other armed men, and a band called the Macedonian Band about him, all of the same age, tall, and just past their childhood, armed,

---

* Reland notices here how justly this judgment came upon the Jews, since they had brought it on themselves by the crucifixion of their Messiah.

and instructed after the Macedonian manner, whence it was that they took that name. Yet were many of them unworthy of so famous a nation; for it had so happened, that the king of Commagene had flourished more than other kings that were under the power of the Romans, till a change happened in his condition; and when he was become an old man, he declared plainly that we ought not to call any man happy before he is dead. But this son of his, who was then come hither before his father was decaying, said that he could not but wonder what made the Romans so tardy in making their attacks upon the wall. Now he was a warlike man, and naturally bold in exposing himself to dangers; he was also so strong a man, that his boldness seldom failed of having success. Upon this, Titus smiled, and said he would share the pains of an attack with him. However, Antiochus went as he then was, and with his Macedonians made a sudden assault upon the wall; and, indeed, for his own part, his strength and skill were so great, that he guarded himself from the Jewish darts, and yet shot his darts at them, while yet the young men with him, were almost all sorely galled; for they had so great a regard to the promises that had been made of their courage, that they would needs persevere in their fighting, and at length many of them retired, but not till they were wounded; and then they perceived that true Macedonians, if they were to be conquerors, must have Alexander's good fortune also.

4. Now, as the Romans began to raise their banks on the twelfth day of the month Artemisius [Jyar,] so had they much ado to finish them by the twenty-ninth day of the same month, after they had laboured hard for seventeen days continually; for there were now four great banks raised, one of which was at the tower of Antonia; this was raised by the fifth legion, over against the middle of that pool which is called Struthius. Another was cast up by the twelfth legion, at the distance of about twenty cubits from the other. But the labours of the tenth legion, which lay a great way off these, were at the north quarter, and at the pool called Amygdalon; as was that of the fifteenth legion about thirty cubits from it, and at the high priest's monument. And now, when the engines were brought, John had from within undermined the space that was over against the tower of Antonia, as far as the banks themselves, and had supported the ground over the mine with beams laid across one another, whereby the Roman works stood upon an uncertain foundation. Then did he order such materials to be brought in, as were daubed over with pitch and bitumen, and set them on fire; and as the cross beams that supported the banks were burning, the ditch yielded on the sudden, and the banks were shaken down, and fell into the ditch with a prodigious noise. Now at the first there arose a very thick smoke and dust, as the fire was choked with the fall of the bank; but as the suffocated materials were now gradually consumed, a plain flame brake out; on which sudden appearance of the flame a consternation fell upon the Romans, and the shrewdness of the contrivance discouraged them: and indeed, this accident coming upon them at a time when they thought they had already gained their point, cooled their hopes for the time to come. They also thought it would be to no purpose to take the pains to extinguish the fire, since, if it were extinguished, the banks were swallowed up already [and become useless] to them.

5. Two days after this, Simon and his party made an attempt to destroy the other banks; for the Romans had brought their engines to bear there, and began already to make the wall shake. And here one Tephtheus, of Garsis, a city of Galilee, and Megassarus, one who was derived from some of queen Mariamne's servants, and with them one from Adiabene, he was the son of Nabateus, and called by the name of Chagiras, from the ill fortune he had, the word signifying "a lame man," snatched some torches, and ran suddenly upon the engines. Nor were there, during this war, any men who ever sallied out of the city who were their superiors, either in their own boldness, or in the terror they struck into their enemies; for they ran out upon the Romans, not as if they were enemies, but friends, without fear or delay; nor did they leave their enemies till they had rushed violently through the midst of them, and set their machines on fire; and though they had darts thrown at them on every side, and were on every side assaulted with their enemies' swords, yet did they not withdraw themselves out of the dangers they were in, till the fire had caught hold of the instruments; but when the flame went up, the Romans came running from their camp to save their engines. Then did the Jews hinder their succours from the wall, and fought with those that endeavoured to quench the fire, without any regard to the danger their bodies were in. So the Romans pulled the engines out of the fire, while the hurdles that covered them were on fire; but the Jews caught hold of the battering-rams through the flame itself, and held them fast, although the iron upon them was become red-hot; and now the fire spread itself from the engines to the banks, and prevented those that came to defend them: and all this while the Romans were encompassed round about with the flame; and, despairing of saving their works from it, they retired to their camp. Then did the Jews become still more and more in number by the coming of those that were within the city to their assistance; and as they were very bold upon the good success they had had, their violent assaults were almost irresistible; nay, they proceeded as far as the fortifications of the enemy's camp, and fought with their guards. Now there stood a body of soldiers in array before that camp, which succeeded one another by turns in their armour; and as to those, the law of the Romans was terrible, that he who left his post there, let the occasion be whatsoever it might, he was to die for it; so that body of soldiers, preferring rather to die in fighting courageously, than as a punishment for their own cowardice, stood firm; and at the necessity these men were in of standing to it, many of the others that had run away, out of shame, turned back again; and when they had set their engines against the wall, they kept the multitude from coming more of them out of the city; [which they could the more easily do] because they had made no provision for preserving or guarding their bodies at this time; for the Jews fought now hand to hand with all that came in their way, and, without any caution, fell against the points of their enemies' spears, and attacked them bodies against bodies; for they were now too hard for the Romans, not so much by their other warlike actions, as by these courageous assaults they made upon them; and the Romans gave way more to their boldness than they did to the sense of the harm they had received from them.

6. And now Titus was come from the tower of

CONFLAGRATION OF ROMAN FIELD WEAPONS

Antonia, whither he was gone to look out for a place for raising other banks, and reproached the soldiers greatly for permitting their own walls to be in danger, when they had taken the walls of their enemies and sustained the fortune of men besieged, while the Jews were allowed to sally out against them, though they were already in a sort of prison. He then went round about the enemy with some chosen troops, and fell upon their flank himself; so the Jews, who had been before assaulted in their faces, wheeled about to Titus, and continued the fight. The armies also were now mixed one among another, and the dust that was raised so far hindered them from seeing one another, and the noise that was made so far hindered them from hearing one another, that neither side could discern an enemy from a friend. However, the Jews did not flinch, though not so much from their real strength, as from their despair of deliverance. The Romans also would not yield, by reason of the regard they had to glory, and to their reputation in war, and because Cæsar himself went into the danger before them; insomuch that I cannot but think the Romans would in the conclusion have now taken the whole multitude of the Jews, so very angry were they at them, had these not prevented the upshot of the battle, and retired into the city. However, seeing the banks of the Romans demolished, these Romans were very much cast down upon the loss of what had cost them so long pains, and this in one hour's time; and many indeed despaired of taking the city with their usual engines of war only.

CHAPTER XII

TITUS THOUGHT FIT TO ENCOMPASS THE CITY ROUND WITH A WALL; AFTER WHICH THE FAMINE CONSUMED THE PEOPLE BY WHOLE HOUSES AND FAMILIES TOGETHER

1. AND now did Titus consult with his commanders what was to be done. Those that were of the warmest tempers thought he should bring the whole army against the city and storm the wall; for that hitherto no more than a part of their army had fought with the Jews; but that in case the entire army was to come at once, they would not be able to sustain their attacks, but would be overwhelmed by their darts: but of those that were for a more cautious management, some were for raising their banks again; and others advised to let the banks alone, but to lie still before the city, to guard against the coming out of the Jews, and against their carrying provisions into the city, and so to leave the enemy to the famine, and this without direct fighting with them; for that despair was not to be conquered, especially as to those who are desirous to die by the sword, while a more terrible misery is reserved for them. However, Titus did not think it fit for so great an army to lie entirely idle, and that yet it was in vain to fight with those that would be destroyed one by another; he also shewed them how impracticable it was to cast up any more banks, for want of materials, and to guard against the Jews coming out, still more impracticable; as also, to encompass the whole city round with his army, was not very easy, by reason of its magnitude and the difficulty of the situation; and on other accounts dangerous, upon the sallies the Jews might make out of the city; for although they might guard the known passages out of the place, yet would they, when they found them-

selves under the greatest distress, contrive secret passages out, as being well acquainted with all such places; and if any provisions were carried in by stealth, the siege would thereby be longer delayed. He also owned, that he was afraid that the length of time thus to be spent, would diminish the glory of his success; for though it be true, that length of time will perfect everything, yet, that to do what we do in a little time, is still necessary to the gaining reputation: that therefore his opinion was, that if they aimed at quickness joined with security, they must build a wall round about the whole city; which was, he thought, the only way to prevent the Jews from coming out any way, and that then they would either entirely despair of saving the city, and so would surrender it up to him, or be still the more easily conquered when the famine had farther weakened them; for that besides this wall, he would not lie entirely at rest afterward, but would take care then to have banks raised again, when those that would oppose them were become weaker: but that if any one should think such a work to be too great and to be finished without much difficulty, he ought to consider that it is not fit for Romans to undertake any small work, and that none but God himself could with ease accomplish any great think whatsoever.

2. These arguments prevailed with the commanders. So Titus gave orders that the army should be distributed to their several shares of this work; and indeed there now came upon the soldiers a certain divine fury, so that they did not only part the whole wall that was to be built among them, nor did only one legion strive with another, but the lesser divisions of the army did the same; insomuch that each soldier was ambitious to please his decurion, each decurion his centurion, each centurion his tribune, and the ambition of the tribunes was to please their superior commanders, while Cæsar himself took notice of and rewarded the like contention in those commanders; for he went round about the works many times every day, and took a view of what was done. Titus began the wall from the Camp of the Assyrians, where his own camp was pitched, and drew it down to the lower parts of Cenepolis; thence it went along the valley of Cedron to the Mount of Olives; it then bent towards the south, and encompassed the mountain as far as the rock called Peristereon, and that other hill which lies next it, and is over the valley which reaches to Siloam; whence it bended again to the west, and went down to the valley of the Fountain, beyond which it went up again at the monument of Ananus the high priest, and encompassing that mountain where Pompey had formerly pitched his camp, it returned back to the north side of the city, and was carried on as far as a certain village called "The House of the Erebinthi;" after which it encompassed Herod's monument, and there on the east, was joined to Titus's own camp, where it began. Now the length of this wall was forty furlongs, one only abated. Now at this wall without were erected thirteen places to keep garrisons in, the circumference of which, put together, amounted to ten furlongs; the whole was completed in three days: so that what would naturally have required some months, was done in so short an interval as is incredible. When Titus had therefore encompassed the city with this wall, and put garrisons into proper places, he went round the wall at the first watch of the night, and observed how the guard was kept; the second watch he allotted to Alexander; the commanders of legions

took the third watch. They also cast lots among themselves who should be upon the watch in the night-time, and who should go all night long round the spaces that were interposed between the garrisons.

3. So all hope of escaping was now cut off from the Jews, together with their liberty of going out of the city. Then did the famine widen its progress, and devoured the people by whole houses and families; the upper rooms were full of women and children that were dying by famine; and the lanes of the city were full of the dead bodies of the aged; the children also and the young men wandered about the market-places like shadows, all swelled with famine, and fell down dead wheresoever their misery seized them. As for burying them, those that were sick themselves were not able to do it; and those that were hearty and well were deterred from doing it by the great multitude of those dead bodies, and by the uncertainty there was how soon they should die themselves; for many died as they were burying others, and many went to their coffins before that fatal hour was come! Nor was there any lamentation made under these calamities, nor were heard any mournful complaints; but the famine confounded all natural passions; for those who were just going to die, looked upon those that were gone to their rest before them with dry eyes and open mouths. A deep silence also, and a kind of deadly night, had seized upon the city; while yet the robbers were still more terrible than these miseries were themselves; for they brake open those houses which were no other than graves of dead bodies, and plundered them of what they had; and carrying off the coverings of their bodies, went out laughing, and tried the points of their swords on their dead bodies; and, in order to prove what mettle they were made of, they thrust some of those through that still lay alive upon the ground; but for those that entreated them to lend them their right hand, and their sword to despatch them, they were too proud to grant their requests, and left them to be consumed by the famine. Now every one of these died with their eyes fixed upon the temple, and left the seditious alive behind them. Now the seditious at first gave orders that the dead should be buried out of the public treasury, as not enduring the stench of their dead bodies. But afterwards, when they could not do that, they had them cast down from the walls into the valleys beneath.

4. However, when Titus, in going his rounds along those valleys, saw them full of dead bodies, and the thick putrefaction running about them, he gave a groan; and spreading out his hands to heaven, called God to witness that this was not his doing: and such was the sad case of the city itself. But the Romans were very joyful, since none of the seditious could now make sallies out of the city, because they were themselves disconsolate; and the famine already touched them also. These Romans besides had great plenty of corn and other necessaries out of Syria, and out of the neighbouring provinces; many of whom would stand near to the wall of the city, and shew the people what great quantities of provisions they had, and so make the enemy more sensible of their famine, by the great plenty, even to satiety, which they had themselves. However, when the seditious still shewed no inclination of yielding, Titus, out of his commiseration of the people that remained, and out of his earnest desire of rescuing what was still left out of these miseries, began to raise his banks again, although materials for them were hard to be come at; for all the trees that were about the city had been already cut down for the making of the former banks. Yet did the soldiers bring with them other materials from the distance of ninety furlongs, and thereby raised banks in four parts, much greater than the former, though this was done only at the tower of Antonia. So Cæsar went his rounds through the legions, and hastened on the works, and shewed the robbers that they were now in his hands. But these men, and these only, were incapable of repenting of the wickedness they had been guilty of; and separating their souls from their bodies, they used them both, as if they belonged to other folks, and not to themselves. For no gentle affection could touch their souls, nor could any pain affect their bodies, since they could still tear the dead bodies of the people as dogs do, and fill the prisons with those that were sick.

CHAPTER XIII

THE GREAT SLAUGHTERS AND SACRILEGE THAT WERE IN JERUSALEM

1. ACCORDINGLY Simon would not suffer Matthias, by whose means he got possession of the city, to go off without torment. This Matthias was the son of Bœthus, and was one of the high priests, one that had been very faithful to the people, and in great esteem with them: he, when the multitude were distressed by the zealots, among whom John was numbered, persuaded the people to admit this Simon to come in to assist them, while he had made no terms with him, nor expected anything that was evil from him. But when Simon was come in, and had gotten the city under his power, he esteemed him that had advised them to admit him, as his enemy equally with the rest, as looking upon that advice as a piece of his simplicity only: so he had him then brought before him, and condemned to die for being on the side of the Romans, without giving him leave to make his defence. He condemned also his three sons to die with him; for as to the fourth, he prevented him by running away to Titus before. And when he begged for this, that he might be slain before his sons, and that as a favour, on account that he had procured the gates of the city to be opened to him, he gave orders that he should be slain the last of them all; so he was not slain till he had seen his sons slain before his eyes, and that by being produced over against the Romans; for such a charge had Simon given to Ananus, the son of Bamadus, who was the most barbarous of all his guards. He also jested upon him, and told him that he might now see whether those to whom he intended to go over, would send him any succours or not; but still he forbade their dead bodies should be buried. After the slaughter of these, a certain priest, Ananias, the son of Masambulus, a person of eminency, as also Aristeus the scribe of the Sanhedrim, and born at Emmaus, and with them fifteen men of figure among the people were slain. They also kept Josephus's father in prison, and made public proclamation, that no citizen whosoever should either speak to him himself, or go into his company among others, for fear he should betray them. They also slew such as joined in lamenting these men, without any further examination.

2. Now when Judas, the son of Judas, who was one of Simon's under officers, and a person intrusted by him to keep one of the towers, saw

this procedure of Simon, he called together ten of those under him that were most faithful to him (perhaps this was done, partly out of pity to those that had so barbarously been put to death; but, principally, in order to provide for his own safety) and spoke thus to them :—"How long shall we bear these miseries; or, what hopes have we of deliverance by thus continuing faithful to such wicked wretches? Is not the famine already come against us? Are not the Romans in a manner gotten within the city? Is not Simon become unfaithful to his benefactors? and is there not reason to fear he will very soon bring us to the like punishment, while the security the Romans offer us is sure? Come on, let us surrender up this wall, and save ourselves and the city. Nor will Simon be very much hurt, if, now he despairs of deliverance, he be brought to justice a little sooner than he thinks on." Now these ten were prevailed upon by those arguments; so he sent the rest of those that were under him, some one way and some another, that no discovery might be made of what they had resolved upon. Accordingly he called to the Romans from the tower, about the third hour; but they, some of them out of pride, despised what he said, and others of them did not believe him to be in earnest, though the greatest number delayed the matter, as believing they should get possession of the city in a little time, without any hazard: but when Titus was just coming thither with his armed men, Simon was acquainted with the matter before he came, and presently took the tower into his own custody, before it was surrendered, and seized upon these men, and put them to death in the sight of the Romans themselves; and when he had mangled their dead bodies, he threw them down before the wall of the city.

3. In the meantime, Josephus, as he was going round the city, had his head wounded by a stone that was thrown at him; upon which he fell down as giddy. Upon which fall of his, the Jews made a sally, and he had been hurried away into the city, if Cæsar had not sent men to protect him immediately; and, as these men were fighting, Josephus was taken up, though he heard little of what was done. So the seditious supposed they had now slain the man whom they were the most desirous of killing, and made thereupon a great noise, by way of rejoicing. This accident was told in the city; and the multitude that remained became very disconsolate at the news, as being persuaded that he was really dead, on whose account alone they could venture to desert to the Romans; but when Josephus's mother heard in prison that her son was dead, she said to those that watched about her, That she had always been of opinion, since the siege of Jotapata, [that he would be slain,] and she would never enjoy him alive any more. She also made great lamentation privately to the maidservants that were about her, and said, That this was all the advantage she had of bringing so extraordinary a person as this son into the world; that she should not be able even to bury that son of hers, by whom she expected to have been buried herself. However, this false report did not put his mother to pain, nor afford merriment to the robbers long; for Josephus soon recovered of his wound, and came out, and cried out aloud, That it would not be long ere they should be punished for this wound they had given him. He also made a fresh exhortation to the people to come out, upon the security that would be given them. This sight of Josephus encouraged the people greatly, and brought a great consternation upon the seditious.

4. Hereupon some of the deserters, having no other way, leaped down from the wall immediately, while others of them went out of the city with stones, as if they would fight them; but thereupon they fled away to the Romans :—but here a worse fate accompanied these than what they had found within the city; and they met with a quicker despatch from the too great abundance they had among the Romans, than they could have done from the famine among the Jews; for when they came first to the Romans, they were puffed up by the famine, and swelled like men in a dropsy; after which they all on the sudden over-filled those bodies that were before empty, and so burst asunder, excepting such only as were skilful enough to restrain their appetites, and, by degrees, took in their food into bodies unaccustomed thereto. Yet did another plague seize upon those that were thus preserved; for there was found among the Syrian deserters a certain person who was caught gathering pieces of gold out of the excrements of the Jews' bellies; for the deserters used to swallow such pieces of gold, as we told you before, when they came out; and for these did the seditious search them all; for there was a great quantity of gold in the city, insomuch that as much was now sold [in the Roman camp] for twelve Attic [drams] as was sold before for twenty-five; but when this contrivance was discovered in one instance, the fame of it filled their several camps, that the deserters came to them full of gold. So the multitude of the Arabians, with the Syrians, cut up those that came as supplicants, and searched their bellies. Nor does it seem to me that any misery befell the Jews that was more terrible than this, since in one night about two thousand of these deserters were thus dissected.

5. When Titus came to the knowledge of this wicked practice, he had like to have surrounded those that had been guilty of it with his horse, and shot them dead; and he had done it, had not their number been so very great, and those that were liable to this punishment would have been manifold more than those whom they had slain. However, he called together the commanders of the auxiliary troops he had with him, as well as the commanders of the Roman legions, (for some of his own soldiers had also been guilty herein, as he had been informed,) and had great indignation against both sorts of them, and spoke to them as follows :—"What! have any of my own soldiers done such things as this, out of the uncertain hope of gain, without regarding their own weapons, which are made of silver and gold? Moreover, do the Arabians and Syrians now first of all begin to govern themselves as they please, and to indulge their appetites in a foreign war, and then, out of their barbarity in murdering men, and out of their hatred to the Jews, get it ascribed to the Romans?"— for this infamous practice was said to be spread among some of his own soldiers also. Titus then threatened that he would put such men to death, if any of them were discovered to be so insolent as to do so again; moreover, he gave it in charge to the legions that they should make a search after such as were suspected, and should bring them to him; but it appeared that the love of money was too hard for all their dread of punishment, and a vehement desire of gain is natural to men, and no passion is so venturesome as covetousness; otherwise such passions have certain bounds, and are subordinate to fear; but in reality it was God who condemned the whole nation, and turned every course that was taken for their preservation to their destruction. This,

therefore, which was forbidden by Cæsar under such a threatening, was ventured upon privately against the deserters, and these barbarians would go out still, and meet those that ran away, before any saw them, and looking about them to see that no Romans spied them, they dissected them, and pulled this polluted money out of their bowels; which money was still found in a few of them, while yet a great many were destroyed by the bare hope there was of thus getting by them, which miserable treatment made many that were deserting to return back again into the city.

6. But as for John, when he could no longer plunder the people, he betook himself to sacrilege, and melted down many of the sacred utensils, which had been given to the temple; as also many of those vessels which were necessary for such as ministered about holy things,—the caldrons, the dishes, and the table; nay, he did not abstain from those pouring-vessels that were sent them by Augustus and his wife; for the Roman emperors did ever both honour and adorn this temple: whereas this man, who was a Jew, seized upon what were the donations of foreigners; and said to those that were with him, that it was proper for them to use divine things while they were fighting for the Divinity, without fear, and that such whose warfare is for the temple should live of the temple; on which account he emptied the vessels of that sacred wine and oil which the priests kept to be poured on the burnt-offerings, and which lay in the inner court of the temple, and distributed it among the multitude, who, in their anointing themselves and drinking, used [each of them] above an hin of them; and here I cannot but speak my mind, and what the concern I am under dictates to me, and it is this:—I suppose that had the Romans made any longer delay in coming against these villains, the city would either have been swallowed up by the ground opening upon them, or been overflowed by water, or else been destroyed by such thunder as the country of Sodom perished by, for it had brought forth a generation of men much more

atheistical than were those that suffered such punishments; for by their madness it was that all the people came to be destroyed.

7. And indeed why do I relate these particular calamities?—while Manneus, the son of Lazarus, came running to Titus at this very time, and told him that there had been carried out through that one gate which was intrusted to his care no fewer than a hundred and fifteen thousand eight hundred and eighty dead bodies, in the interval between the fourteenth day of the month Xanthicus, [Nisan,] when the Romans pitched their camp by the city, and the first day of the month Panemus, [Tamuz.] This was itself a prodigious multitude; and though this man was not himself set as a governor at that gate, yet was he appointed to pay the public stipend for carrying these bodies out, and so was obliged of necessity to number them, while the rest were buried by their relations, though all their burial was but this, to bring them away, and cast them out of the city. After this man there ran away to Titus many of the eminent citizens, and told him the entire number of the poor that were dead; and that no fewer than six hundred thousand were thrown out at the gates, though still the number of the rest could not be discovered; and they told him farther, that when they were no longer able to carry out the dead bodies of the poor, they laid their corpses on heaps in very large houses, and shut them up therein; as also that a medimnus of wheat was sold for a talent; and that when, a while afterward, it was not possible to gather herbs, by reason all the city was walled about, some persons were driven to that terrible distress as to search the common sewers and old dung-hills of cattle, and to eat the dung which they got there; and what they of old could not so much as endure to see they now used for food. When the Romans barely heard all this, they commiserated their case; while the seditious, who saw it also, did not repent, but suffered the same distress to come upon themselves; for they were blinded by that fate, which was already coming upon the city, and upon themselves also.

BOOK VI

CONTAINING THE INTERVAL OF ABOUT ONE MONTH

FROM THE GREAT EXTREMITY TO WHICH THE JEWS WERE REDUCED TO THE TAKING OF JERUSALEM BY TITUS

CHAPTER I

THAT THE MISERIES OF THE JEWS STILL GREW WORSE; AND HOW THE ROMANS MADE AN ASSAULT UPON THE TOWER OF ANTONIA

1. THUS did the miseries of Jerusalem grow worse and worse every day, and the seditious were still more irritated by the calamities they were under, even while the famine preyed upon themselves, after it had preyed upon the people. And indeed the multitude of carcases that lay in heaps one upon another was a horrible sight, and produced a pestilential stench, which was a

hindrance to those that would make sallies out of the city, and fight the enemy: but as those were to go in battle array, who had been already used to ten thousand murders, and must tread upon those dead bodies as they marched along, so were not they terrified, nor did they pity men as they marched over them: nor did they deem this affront offered to the deceased to be any ill omen to themselves; but as they had their right hands already polluted with the murders of their own countrymen, and in that condition ran out to fight with foreigners, they seem to me to have cast a reproach upon God himself, as if he were too slow in punishing them; for the war was not now gone on with as if they had any hope of victory, for they gloried after a brutish manner in that despair of deliverance they were already in. And now the Romans, although they were greatly distressed in getting together their materials, raised their banks in one-and-twenty days, after they had cut down all the trees that were in the country that adjoined to the city, and that for ninety furlongs round about, as I have already related. And truly the very view itself of the country was a melancholy thing; for those places which were before adorned with trees and pleasant gardens were now become a desolate country every way, and its trees were all cut down: nor could any foreigner that had formerly seen Judea, and the most beautiful suburbs of the city, and now saw it as a desert, but lament and mourn sadly at so great a change: for the war had laid all signs of beauty quite waste: nor, if any one that had known the place before had come on a sudden to it now, would he have known it again; but though he were at the city itself, yet would he have inquired for it notwithstanding.

2. And now the banks were finished, they afforded a foundation for fear both to the Romans and to the Jews; for both the Jews expected that the city would be taken, unless they could burn those banks, as did the Romans expect that, if these were once burnt down, they should never be able to take it; for there was a mighty scarcity of materials, and the bodies of the soldiers began to fail with such hard labours, as did their souls faint with so many instances of ill success; nay, the very calamities themselves that were in the city proved a greater discouragement to the Romans than to those within the city; for they found the fighting men of the Jews to be not at all mollified among such their sore afflictions, while they had themselves perpetually less and less hopes of success, and their banks were forced to yield to the stratagems of the enemy, their engines to the firmness of their wall, and their closest fights to the boldness of their attack; and, what was their greatest discouragement of all, they found the Jews' courageous souls to be superior to the multitude of the miseries they were under by their sedition, their famine, and the war itself; insomuch that they were ready to imagine that the violence of their attacks was invincible, and the alacrity they shewed would not be discouraged by their calamities; for what would not those be able to bear if they should be fortunate, who turned their very misfortunes to the improvement of their valour! These considerations made the Romans keep a stronger guard about their banks than they formerly had done.

3. But now John and his party took care for securing themselves afterward, even in case this wall should be thrown down, and fell to their work before the battering-rams were brought against them. Yet did they not compass what they endeavoured to do, but as they were gone out with their torches, they came back under great discouragement, before they came near to the banks; and the reasons were these: that in the first place, their conduct did not seem unanimous, but they went out in distinct parties, and at distinct intervals, and after a slow manner, and timorously, and, to say all in a word, without a Jewish courage; for they were now defective in what is peculiar to our nation, that is, in boldness, in violence of assault, and in running upon the enemy altogether, and in persevering in what they go about, though they do not at first succeed in it; but they now went out in a more languid manner than usual and at the same time found the Romans set in array, and more courageous than ordinary, and that they guarded their banks both with their bodies and their entire armour, and this to such a degree on all sides, that they left no room for the fire to get among them, and that every one of their souls was in such good courage, that they would sooner die than desert their ranks; for besides their notion that all their hopes were cut off, in case their works were once burnt, the soldiers were greatly ashamed that subtilty should be quite too hard for courage, madness for armour, multitude for skill, and Jews for Romans. The Romans had now also another advantage, in that their engines for sieges co-operated with them in throwing darts and stones as far as the Jews, when they were coming out of the city; whereby the man that fell became an impediment to him that was next to him, as did the danger of going farther make them less zealous in their attempts; and for those that had run under the darts, some of them were terrified by the good order and closeness of the enemies' ranks before they came to a close fight, and others were pricked with their spears, and turned back again; at length they reproached one another for their cowardice, and retired without doing anything. This attack was upon the first day of the month Panemus, [Tamuz.] So, when the Jews were retreated, the Romans brought their engines, although they had all the while stones thrown at them from the tower of Antonia, and were assaulted by fire and sword, and by all sorts of darts, which necessity afforded the Jews to make use of; for although these had great dependence on their own wall, and a contempt of the Roman engines, yet did they endeavour to hinder the Romans from bringing them. Now these Romans struggled hard, on the contrary, to bring them, as deeming that this zeal of the Jews was in order to avoid any impression to be made on the tower of Antonia, because its wall was but weak, and its foundations rotten. However, that tower did not yield to the blows given it from the engines; yet did the Romans bear the impressions made by the enemies' darts which were perpetually cast at them, and did not give way to any of those dangers that came upon them from above, and so they brought their engines to bear; but then as they were beneath the other, and were sadly wounded by the stones thrown down upon them, some of them threw their shields over their bodies, and partly with their hands, and partly with their bodies, and partly with crows, they undermined its foundations, and with great pains they removed four of its stones. Then night came upon both sides, and put an end to this struggle for the present; however, that night the wall was so shaken by the battering-rams in that place where John had used his stratagem before, and had undermined their banks, that the ground then gave way, and the wall fell down suddenly.

4. When this accident had unexpectedly happened, the minds of both parties were variously affected: for though one would expect that the Jews would be discouraged, because this fall of their wall was unexpected by them, and they had made no provision in that case, yet did they pull up their courage, because the tower of Antonia itself was still standing; as was the unexpected joy of the Romans at this fall of the wall soon quenched by the sight they had of another wall, which John and his party had built within it. However, the attack of this second wall appeared to be easier than that of the former, because it seemed a thing of greater facility to

get up to it through the parts of the former wall that were now thrown down. This new wall appeared also to be much weaker than the tower of Antonia, and accordingly the Romans imagined that it had been erected so much on the sudden, that they should soon overthrow it : yet did not anybody venture now to go up to this wall : for that such as first ventured so to do must certainly be killed.

5. And now Titus, upon consideration that the alacrity of soldiers in war is chiefly excited by hopes and good words, and that exhortations and promises do frequently make men to forget the hazards they run, nay, and sometimes to despise death itself, got together the most courageous part of his army, and tried what he could do with his men by these methods :—"O fellow-soldiers," said he, "to make an exhortation to men to do what hath no peril in it, is on that very account inglorious to such to whom that exhortation is made ; and indeed so it is in him that makes the exhortation, an argument of his own cowardice also. I therefore think, that such exhortations ought then only to be made use of when affairs are in a dangerous condition, and yet are worthy of being attempted by every one themselves ; accordingly, I am fully of the same opinion with you, that it is a difficult task to go up this wall ; but that it is proper for those that desire reputation for their valour to struggle with difficulties in such cases, will then appear, when I have particularly shewn that it is a brave thing to die with glory, and that the courage here necessary shall not go unrewarded in those that first begin the attempt ; and let my first argument to move you to it be taken from what probably some would think reasonable to dissuade you—I mean the constancy and patience of these Jews, even under their ill successes ; for it is unbecoming you, who are Romans and my soldiers, who have in peace been taught how to make wars, and who have also been used to conquer in those wars, to be inferior to Jews, either in action of the hand or in courage of the soul, and this especially when you are at the conclusion of your victory, and are assisted by God himself ; for as to our misfortunes, they have been owing to the madness of the Jews, while their sufferings have been owing to your valour, and to the assistance God hath afforded you ; for as to the seditions they have been in, and the famine they are under and the siege they now endure, and the fall of their walls without our engines, what can they all be but demonstrations of God's anger against them, and of his assistance afforded us ? It will not therefore be proper for you, either to shew yourselves inferior to those to whom you are really superior, or to betray that divine assistance which is afforded you ; and indeed, how can it be esteemed otherwise than a base and unworthy thing, that while the Jews, who need not be much ashamed if they be deserted, because they have long learned to be slaves to others, do yet despise death, that they may be so no longer, —and do make sallies into the very midst of us frequently, not in hopes of conquering us, but merely for a demonstration of their courage ; we, who have gotten possession of almost all the world that belongs to either land or sea, to whom it will be a great shame if we do not conquer them, do not once undertake any attempt against our enemies wherein there is much danger, but sit still idle, with such brave arms as we have, and only wait till the famine and fortune do our business themselves, and this when we have it in our power, with some small hazard, to gain all that we desire ! For if we go up to this tower of Antonia, we gain the city ; for if there should

be any more occasion for fighting against those within the city, which I do not suppose there will, since we shall then be upon the top of the hill,[*] and be upon our enemies before they can have taken breath, these advantages promise us no less than a certain and sudden victory. As for myself, I shall at present wave any commendations of those who die in war,[†] and omit to speak of the immortality of those men who are slain in the midst of their martial bravery ; yet cannot I forbear to imprecate upon those who are of a contrary disposition, that they may die in time of peace, by some distemper or other, since their souls are already condemned to the grave, together with their bodies ; for what man of virtue is there who does not know that those souls which are severed from their fleshy bodies in battles by the sword are received by the ether, that purest of elements, and joined to that company which are placed among the stars ; that they become good demons, and propitious heroes, and shew themselves as such to their posterity afterwards ? while upon those souls that wear away in and with their distempered bodies comes a subterranean night to dissolve them to nothing, and a deep oblivion to take away all the remembrance of them, and this notwithstanding they be clean from all spots and defilements of this world ; so that, in this case, the soul at the same time comes to the utmost bounds of its life, and of its body, and of its memorial also ; but since fate has determined that death is to come of necessity upon all men, a sword is a better instrument for that purpose than any disease whatsoever. Why, is it not then a very mean thing for us not to yield up that to the public benefit which we must yield up to fate ? And this discourse have I made, upon the supposition that those who at first attempt to go upon this wall must needs be killed in the attempt, though still men of true courage have a chance to escape even in the most hazardous undertakings ; for, in the first place, that part of the former wall that is thrown down is easily to be ascended ; and for the new-built wall, it is easily destroyed. Do you, therefore, many of you, pull up your courage, and set about this work, and do you mutually encourage and assist one another ; and this your bravery will soon break the hearts of your enemies ; and perhaps such a glorious undertaking as yours is may be accomplished without bloodshed ; for although it be justly to be supposed that the Jews will try to hinder you at your first beginning to go up to them, yet when you have once concealed yourselves from them, and driven them away by force, they will not be able to sustain your efforts against them any longer, though but a few of you prevent them, and get over the wall. As for that person who first mounts the wall, I should blush for shame if I did not make him to be envied of others, by those rewards I would bestow upon him. If such a one escape with his life, he shall have the command of others that are now but his equals ; although it be true also, that the greatest rewards will accrue to such as die in the attempt."

6. Upon this speech of Titus, the rest of the multitude were affrighted at so great a danger.

---

[*] Roland notes here that the tower of Antonia stood higher than the floor of the temple or court adjoining to it ; and that accordingly they descended thence into the temple.

[†] In this speech of Titus we may see the notions which the Romans then had of death, and of the happy state of those who died bravely in war, and the contrary estate of those who died ignobly in their beds by sickness.

But there was one whose name was Sabinus, a soldier that served among the cohorts, and a Syrian by birth, who appeared to be of very great fortitude, both in the actions he had done, and the courage of his soul he had shewn ; although anybody would have thought, before he came to his work, that he was of such a weak constitution of body, that he was not fit to be a soldier ; for his colour was black, his flesh was lean and thin, and lay close together ; but there was a certain heroic soul that dwelt in this small body, which body was indeed much too narrow for that peculiar courage which was in him. Accordingly he was the first that rose up ; when he thus spake :—"I readily surrender myself to thee, O Cæsar : I first ascend the wall, and I heartily wish that my fortune may follow my courage and my resolution. And if some ill-fortune grudge me the success of my undertaking, take notice that my ill-success will not be unexpected, but that I choose death voluntarily for thy sake." When he had said this, and had spread out his shield over his head with his left hand, and had, with his right hand, drawn his sword, he marched up to the wall just about the sixth hour of the day. There followed him eleven others, and no more, that resolved to imitate his bravery ; but still this was the principal person of them all, and went first, as excited by a divine fury. Now, those that guarded the wall shot at them from thence, and cast innumerable darts upon them from every side ; they also rolled very large stones upon them, which overthrew some of those eleven that were with him. But as for Sabinus himself, he met the darts that were cast at him, and though he was overwhelmed with them, yet did he not leave off the violence of his attack before he had gotten up on the top of the wall, and had put the enemy to flight. For as the Jews were astonished at his great strength, and the bravery of his soul ; and as, withal, they imagined more of them had got upon the wall than really had, they were put to flight. And now one cannot but complain here of fortune, as still envious of virtue, and always hindering the performance of glorious achievements ; this was the case of the man before us, when he had just obtained his purpose ; for he then stumbled at a certain large stone, and fell down upon it headlong, with a very great noise. Upon which the Jews turned back, and when they saw him to be alone, and fallen down also, they threw darts at him from every side. However, he got upon his knee, and covered himself with his shield, and at the first defended himself against them, and wounded many of those that came near him ; but he was soon forced to relax his right hand, by the multitude of the wounds that had been given him, till at length he was quite covered over with darts before he gave up the ghost. He was one who deserved a better fate, by reason of his bravery ; but, as might be expected, he fell under so vast an attempt. As for the rest of his partners, the Jews dashed three of them to pieces with stones, and slew them as they were gotten up to the top of the wall ; the other eight being wounded, were pulled down and carried back to the camp. These things were done upon the third day of the month Panemus, [Tamuz.]

7. Now two days afterward, twelve of these men that were on the fore-front, and kept watch upon the banks, got together, and called to them the standard-bearer of the fifth legion, and two others of a troop of horsemen, and one trumpeter ; these went without noise about the ninth hour of the night, through the ruins to the tower of Antonia ; and when they had cut the throats of the first guards of the place, as they were asleep, they got possession of the wall, and ordered the trumpeter to sound his trumpet. Upon which the rest of the guard got up on the sudden, and ran away before any body could see how many they were that were gotten up ; for partly from the fear they were in, and partly from the sound of the trumpet which they heard, they imagined a great number of the enemy were gotten up. But as soon as Cæsar heard the signal, he ordered the army to put on their armour immediately, and came thither with his commanders, and first of all ascended, as did the chosen men that were with him. And as the Jews were flying away to the temple, they fell into that mine which John had dug under the Roman banks. Then did the seditious of both the bodies of the Jewish army, as well that belonging to John as that belonging to Simon, drive them away ; and indeed were no way wanting as to the highest degree of force and alacrity ; for they esteemed themselves entirely ruined if once the Romans got into the temple, as did the Romans look upon the same thing as the beginning of their entire conquest. So a terrible battle was fought at the entrance of the temple, while the Romans were forcing their way, in order to get possession of that temple, and the Jews were driving them back to the tower of Antonia ; in which battle the darts were on both sides useless, as well as the spears, and both sides drew their swords, and fought it out hand to hand. Now during this struggle, the positions of the men were undistinguished on both sides, and they fought at random, the men being intermixed one with another, and confounded, by reason of the narrowness of the place ; while the noise that was made fell on the ear after an indistinct manner, because it was so very loud. Great slaughter was now made on both sides, and the combatants trod upon the bodies and the armour of those that were dead, and dashed them to pieces. Accordingly, to which side soever the battle inclined, those that had the advantage exhorted one another to go on, as did those that were beaten make great lamentations. But still there was no room for flight, nor for pursuit, but disorderly revolutions and retreats, while the armies were intermixed one with another ; but those that were in the first ranks were under the necessity of killing or being killed, without any way for escaping ; for those on both sides that came behind forced those before them to go on, without leaving any space between the armies. At length the Jews' violent zeal was too hard for the Romans' skill, and the battle already inclined entirely that way ; for the fight had lasted from the ninth hour of the night till the seventh hour of the day, while the Jews came on in crowds, and had the danger the temple was in for their motive ; the Romans having no more here than a part of their army ; for those legions, on which the soldiers on that side depended, were not come up to them. So it was at present thought sufficient by the Romans to take possession of the tower of Antonia.

8. But there was one Julian, a centurion, that came from Bithynia ; a man he was of great reputation, whom I had formerly seen in that war, and one of the highest fame, both for his skill in war, his strength of body, and the courage of his soul. This man, seeing the Romans giving ground, and in a sad condition, (for he stood by Titus at the tower of Antonia,) leaped out, and of himself alone put the Jews to flight when they were already conquerors, and made them retire as far as the corner of the inner

court of the temple: from him the multitude fled away in crowds, as supposing that neither his strength nor his violent attacks could be those of a mere man. Accordingly he rushed through the midst of the Jews, as they were dispersed all abroad, and killed those that he caught. Nor, indeed, was there any sight that appeared more wonderful in the eyes of Cæsar, or more terrible to others than this. However, he was himself pursued by fate, which it was not possible that he who was but a mortal man should escape; for as he had shoes all full of sharp and thick nails, as had every one of the other soldiers, so when he ran on the pavement of the temple, he slipped, and fell down upon his back with a very great noise, which was made by his armour. This made those that were running away to turn back; whereupon those Romans that were in the tower of Antonia set up a great shout, as if they were in fear for the man. But the Jews got about him in crowds, and struck at him with their spears and with their swords on all sides. Now he received a great many of the strokes of these iron weapons upon his shield, and often attempted to get up again, but was thrown down by those that struck at him; yet did he, as he lay along, stab many of them with his sword. Nor was he soon killed, as being covered with his helmet and his breastplate in all those parts of his body where he might be mortally wounded; he also pulled his neck close to his body, till all his other limbs were shattered, and nobody durst come to defend him, and then he yielded to his fate. Now Cæsar was deeply affected on account of this man of so great fortitude, and especially as he was killed in the sight of so many people; he was desirous himself to come to his assistance, but the place would not give him leave, while such as could have done it were too much terrified to attempt it. Thus, when Julian had struggled with death a great while, and had let but few of those that had given him his mortal wound go off unhurt, he had at last his throat cut, though not without some difficulty; and left behind him a great fame, not only among the Romans and with Cæsar himself, but among his enemies also; then did the Jews catch up his dead body, and put the Romans to flight again, and shut them up in the tower of Antonia. Now those that most signalised themselves, and fought most zealously in this battle of the Jewish side, were one Alexas and Gyphtheus, of John's party; and of Simon's party were Malachias, and Judas the son of Merto, and James the son of Sosas, the commander of the Idumeans; and of the zealots, two brethren, Simon and Judas, the sons of Jairus.

CHAPTER II

HOW TITUS GAVE ORDERS TO DEMOLISH THE TOWER OF ANTONIA, AND THEN PERSUADED JOSEPHUS TO EXHORT THE JEWS AGAIN, [TO A SURRENDER.]

1. AND now Titus gave orders to his soldiers that were with him to dig up the foundations of the tower of Antonia, and make him a ready passage for his army to come up; while he himself had Josephus brought to him (for he had been informed that on that very day, which was the seventeenth day[*] of Panemus, [Tamuz,] the

sacrifice called "the Daily Sacrifice" had failed, and had not been offered to God for want of men to offer it, and that the people were grievously troubled at it) and commanded him to say the same things to John that he had said before, that if he had any malicious inclination for fighting, he might come out with as many of his men as he pleased, in order to fight, without the danger of destroying either his city or temple; but that he desired he would not defile the temple, nor thereby offend against God. That he might, if he pleased, offer the sacrifices which were now discontinued, by any of the Jews whom he should pitch upon. Upon this, Josephus stood in such a place where he might be heard, not by John only, but by many more, and then declared to them what Cæsar had given him in charge, and this in the Hebrew language. So he earnestly prayed them to spare their own city, and to prevent that fire which was just ready to seize upon the temple, and to offer their usual sacrifices to God therein. At these words of his a great sadness and silence were observed among the people. But the tyrant himself cast many reproaches upon Josephus, with imprecations besides; and at last added this withal, that he did never fear the taking of the city, because it was God's own city. In answer to which, Josephus said thus, with a loud voice: —"To be sure, thou hast kept this city wonderfully pure for God's sake! the temple also continues entirely unpolluted! Nor hast thou been guilty of any impiety against him, for whose assistance thou hopest! He still receives his accustomed sacrifices! Vile wretch that thou art! if any one should deprive thee of thy daily food, thou wouldst esteem him to be an enemy to thee; but thou hopest to have that God for thy supporter in this war whom thou hast deprived of his everlasting worship! and thou imputest those sins to the Romans, who to this very time take care to have our laws observed, and almost compel these sacrifices to be still offered to God, which have by thy means been intermitted! Who is there can avoid groans and lamentations at the amazing change that is made in this city? since very foreigners and enemies do now correct that impiety which thou hast occasioned: while thou, who art a Jew, and was educated in our laws, art become a greater enemy to them than the others! But still, John, it is never dishonourable to repent, and amend what hath been done amiss, even at the last extremity. Thou hast an instance before thee in Jechoniah, the king of the Jews, if thou hast a mind to save the city, who, when the king of Babylon made war against him, did, of his own accord, go out of this city before it was taken, and did undergo a voluntary captivity with his family, that the sanctuary might not be delivered up to the enemy, and that he might not see the house of God set on fire: on which account he is celebrated among all the Jews, in their sacred memorials, and his memory is become immortal, and will be conveyed fresh down to our posterity through all ages. This, John, is an excellent example in such a time of danger; and I dare venture to promise that the Romans shall still forgive thee. And take notice, that I, who make this exhortation to thee, am one of thine own nation; I, who am a Jew, do make this promise to thee. And it will become thee to consider who I am that give thee this

---

[*] This was a very remarkable day indeed, the seventeenth of Panemus, [Tamuz,] A.D. 70, when, according to Daniel's prediction, 606 years before, the Romans

"in half a week caused the sacrifice and oblation to cease," Dan. ix. 27; for from the month of February, A.D. 66, about which time Vespasian entered on this war, to this very time, was just three years and a half.

counsel, and whence I am derived; for while I am alive I shall never be in such slavery as to forego my own kindred, or forget the laws of our forefathers. Thou hast indignation at me again, and makest a clamour at me, and reproachest me; indeed, I cannot deny but I am worthy of worse treatment than all this amounts to, because, in opposition to fate, I make this kind invitation to thee, and endeavour to force deliverance upon those whom God hath condemned. And who is there that does not know what the writings of the ancient prophets contain in them,—and particularly that oracle which is just now going to be fulfilled upon this miserable city?—for they foretold that this city should be then taken when somebody shall begin the slaughter of his own countrymen! and are not both the city and the entire temple now full of the dead bodies of your countrymen? It is God therefore, it is God himself who is bringing on this fire, to purge that city and temple by means of the Romans,* and is going to pluck up this city, which is full of your pollutions."

2. As Josephus spoke these words with groans, and tears in his eyes, his voice was intercepted by sobs. However, the Romans could not but pity the affliction he was under, and wonder at his conduct. But for John, and those that were with him, they were but the more exasperated against the Romans on this account, and were desirous to get Josephus also into their power: yet did that discourse influence a great many of the better sort; and truly some of them were so afraid of the guards set by the seditious, that they tarried where they were, but still were satisfied that both they and the city were doomed to destruction. Some also there were who, watching for a proper opportunity when they might quietly get away, fled to the Romans, of whom were the high priests Joseph and Jesus, and of the sons of high priests three, whose father was Ishmael, who was beheaded in Cyrene, and four sons of Matthias, as also one son of the other Matthias, who ran away after his father's death, and whose father was slain by Simon, the son of Gioras, with three of his sons, as I have already related: many also of the other nobility went over to the Romans, together with the high priests. Now Cæsar not only received these men very kindly in other respects, but, knowing they would not willingly live after the customs of other nations, he sent them to Gophna, and desired them to remain there for the present, and told them, that when he was gotten clear of this war, he would restore each of them to their possessions again; so they cheerfully retired to that small city which was allotted them, without fear of any danger. But as they did not appear, the seditious gave out again that these deserters were slain by the Romans,—which was done in order to deter the rest from running away by fear of the like treatment. This trick of theirs succeeded now for a while, as did the like trick before; for the rest were hereby deterred from deserting, by fear of the like treatment.

3. However, when Titus had recalled those men from Gophna, he gave orders that they should go round the wall, together with Josephus, and shew themselves to the people; upon which a great many fled to the Romans. These

men also got in a great number together, and stood before the Romans, and besought the seditious, with groans, and tears in their eyes, in the first place to receive the Romans entirely into the city, and save that their own place of residence again; but that if they would not agree to such a proposal, they would at least depart out of the temple, and save the holy house for their own use; for that the Romans would not venture to set the sanctuary on fire, but under the most pressing necessity. Yet did the seditious still more and more contradict them; and while they cast loud and bitter reproaches upon these deserters, they also set their engines for throwing of darts, and javelins, and stones upon the sacred gates of the temple, at due distances from one another, insomuch that all the space round about within the temple might be compared to a burying-ground, so great was the number of the dead bodies therein; as might the house itself be compared to a citadel. Accordingly, these men rushed upon these holy places in their armour, that were otherwise unapproachable, and that while their hands were yet warm with the blood of their own people which they had shed; nay, they proceeded to such great transgressions, that the very same indignation which Jews would naturally have against Romans, had they been guilty of such abuses against them, the Romans now had against the Jews, for their impiety in regard to their own religious customs. Nay, indeed, there were none of the Roman soldiers who did not look with a sacred horror upon the holy house, and adored it, and wished that the robbers would repent before their miseries became incurable.

4. Now Titus was deeply affected with this state of things, and reproached John and his party, and said to them, "Have not you, vile wretches that you are, by our permission, put up this partition-wall † before your sanctuary? Have not you been allowed to put up the pillars thereto belonging, at due distances, and on it to engrave in Greek, and in your own letters, this prohibition, that no foreigner should go beyond that wall? Have we not given you leave to kill such as go beyond it, though he were a Roman? And what do you do now, you pernicious villains? Why do you trample upon dead bodies in this temple? and why do you pollute this holy house with the blood both of foreigners and Jews themselves? I appeal to the gods of my own country, and to every god that ever had any regard to this place, (for I do not suppose it to be now regarded by any of them;) I also appeal to my own army, and to those Jews that are now with me, and even to you yourselves, that I do not force you to defile this your sanctuary; and if you will but change the place whereon you will fight, no Roman shall either come near your sanctuary, or offer any affront to it; nay, I will endeavour to preserve you your holy house, whether you will or not."‡

5. As Josephus explained these things from the mouth of Cæsar, both the robbers and the tyrant thought that these exhortations proceeded from Titus's fear, and not from his good-will to them, and grew insolent upon it; but when Titus saw that these men were neither to be moved by commiseration towards themselves,

---

* Josephus speaks so, that it is most evident he was fully satisfied that God was on the Romans' side, and made use of them now for the destruction of the Jews, which was for certain the true state of this matter, as the prophet Daniel first, and our Saviour himself afterwards, had clearly foretold.

† Of this partition-wall separating Jews and Gentiles, with its pillars and inscription, see the description of the temples, chap. xv.

‡ That these seditious Jews were the direct occasions of their own destruction, and of the conflagration of their city and temple, and that Titus earnestly and constantly laboured to save both, is here and everywhere most evident in Josephus.

nor had any concern upon them to have the holy house spared, he proceeded, unwillingly, to go on again with the war against them. He could not indeed bring all his army against them, the place was so narrow; but choosing thirty soldiers of the most valiant out of every hundred, and committing a thousand to each tribune, and making Cerealis their commander-in-chief, he gave orders that they should attack the guards of the temple about the ninth hour of that night; but as he was now in his armour, and preparing to go down with them, his friends would not let him go, by reason of the greatness of the danger, and what the commanders suggested to them; for they said that he would do more by sitting above in the tower of Antonia, as a dispenser of rewards to those that signalised themselves in the fight, than by coming down and hazarding his own person in the fore-front of them; for that they would all fight stoutly while Cæsar looked upon them. With this advice Cæsar complied, and said, that the only reason he had for such compliance with the soldiers was this, that he might be able to judge of their courageous actions, and that no valiant soldier might lie concealed, and miss of his reward; and no cowardly soldier might go unpunished; but that he might himself be an eye-witness, and able to give evidence of all that was done, who was to be the disposer of punishments and rewards to them. So he sent the soldiers about their work, at the hour forementioned, while he went out himself to a higher place in the tower of Antonia, whence he might see what was done, and there waited with impatience to see the event.

6. However, the soldiers that were sent did not find the guards of the temple asleep, as they hoped to have done; but were obliged to fight with them immediately hand to hand, as they rushed with violence upon them with a great shout. Now, as soon as the rest within the temple heard that shout of those that were upon the watch, they ran out in troops upon them. Then did the Romans receive the onset of those that came first upon them; but those that followed them fell upon their own troops, and many of them treated their own soldiers as if they had been enemies: for the great confused noise that was made on both sides hindered them from distinguishing one another's voices, as did the darkness of the night hinder them from the like distinction by the sight, besides that blindness which arose otherwise also from the passion and the fear they were in at the same time; for which reason, it was all one to the soldiers who it was they struck at. However, this ignorance did less harm to the Romans than to the Jews, because they were joined together under their shields, and made their sallies more regularly than the others did, and each of them remembered their watchword; while the Jews were perpetually dispersed abroad, and made their attacks and retreats at random, and so did frequently seem to one another to be enemies; for every one of them received those of their own men that came back in the dark as Romans, and made an assault upon them; so that more of them were wounded by their own men than by the enemy, till, upon the coming on of the day, the nature of the fight was discerned by the eye afterward. Then did they stand in battle-array in distinct bodies, and cast their darts regularly, and regularly defended themselves; nor did either side yield or grow weary. The Romans contended with each other who should fight the most strenuously, both single men and entire regiments, as being under the eye of Titus; and every one concluded that this day would bring

his promotion if he fought bravely. The great encouragements which the Jews had in view to act vigorously were their fear for themselves and for the temple, and the presence of their tyrant, who exhorted some, and beat and threatened others to act courageously. Now, it so happened that this fight was for the most part a stationary one, wherein the soldiers went on, and came back in a short time, and suddenly; for there was no long space of ground for either of their flights or pursuits; but still there was a tumultuous noise among the Romans from the tower of Antonia, who loudly cried out upon all occasions for their own men to press on courageously, when they were too hard for the Jews, and to stay when they were retiring backward; so that here was a kind of theatre of war; for what was done in this fight could not be concealed either from Titus or from those that were about him. At length, it appeared that this fight, which began at the ninth hour of the night, was not over till past the fifth hour of the day; and that, in the same place where the battle began, neither party could say they had made the other to retire; but both the armies left the victory almost in uncertainty between them; wherein those that signalised themselves on the Roman side were a great many: but on the Jewish side, and of those that were with Simon, Judas the son of Merto, and Simon the son of Josias; of the Idumeans, James and Simon, the latter of whom was the son of Cathlas, and James was the son of Sosas; of those that were with John, Gyphtheus and Alexas; and, of the zealots, Simon the son of Jairus.

7. In the meantime, the rest of the Roman army had, in seven days' time, overthrown [some] foundations of the tower of Antonia, and had made a ready and broad way to the temple. Then did the legions come near the first court,* and began to raise their banks. The one bank was over against the north-west corner of the inner temple;† another was at that northern edifice which was between the two gates; and of the other two, one was at the western cloister of the outer court of the temple; the other against its northern cloister. However, these works were thus far advanced by the Romans, not without great pains and difficulty, and particularly by being obliged to bring their materials from the distance of a hundred furlongs. They had further difficulties also upon them; sometimes, by the over great security they were in that they should overcome the Jewish snares laid for them, and by that boldness of the Jews which their despair of escaping had inspired them withal; for some of their horsemen, when they went out to gather wood or hay, let their horses feed, without having their bridles on during the time of foraging; upon which horses the Jews sallied out in whole bodies, and seized them: and when this was continually done, and Cæsar believed, what the truth was, that the horses were stolen more by the negligence of his own men than by the valour of the Jews, he determined to use greater severity to oblige the rest to take care of their horses; so he commanded that one of those soldiers who had lost their horses should be capitally punished; whereby he so terrified the rest, that they preserved their horses for the time to come; for they did not any longer let them go from them to feed by themselves, but, as if they had grown to them, they went always along with them when they wanted necessaries. Thus did the Romans

---

* The Court of the Gentiles   † The Court of Israel.

still continue to make war against the temple, and to raise their banks against it.

8. Now, after one day had been interposed since the Romans ascended the breach, many of the seditious were so pressed by the famine, upon the present failure of their ravages, that they got together, and made an attack on those Roman guards that were upon the Mount of Olives, and this about the eleventh hour of the day, as supposing first, that they would not expect such an onset, and, in the next place, that they were then taking care of their bodies, and that therefore they should very easily beat them; but the Romans were apprised of their coming to attack them, beforehand, and running together from the neighbouring camps on the sudden, prevented them from getting over their fortification, or forcing the wall that was built about them. Upon this came on a sharp fight, and here many great actions were performed on both sides; while the Romans shewed both their courage and their skill in war, as did the Jews come on them with immoderate violence and intolerable passion. The one party were urged on by shame, and the other by necessity; for it seemed a very shameful thing to the Romans to let the Jews go, now they were taken in a kind of net; while the Jews had but one hope of saving themselves, and that was, in case they could by violence break through the Roman wall:— and one, whose name was Pedanius, belonging to a party of horsemen, when the Jews were already beaten and forced down into the valley together, spurred his horse on their flank with great vehemence, and caught up a certain young man belonging to the enemy by his ankle, as he was running away. The man was, however, of a robust body, and in his armour; so low did Pedanius bend himself downward from his horse, even as he was galloping away, and so great was the strength of his right hand, and of the rest of his body, as also such skill had he in horsemanship. So this man seized upon that his prey, as upon a precious treasure, and carried him as his captive to Cæsar: whereupon Titus admired the man that had seized the other, for his great strength, and ordered the man that was caught to be punished, [with death,] for his attempt against the Roman wall, but betook himself to the siege of the temple, and to pressing on the raising of the banks.

9. In the meantime the Jews were so distressed by the fights they had been in, as the war advanced higher and higher, and creeping up to the holy house itself, that they, as it were, cut off those limbs of their body which were infected, in order to prevent the distemper's spreading farther; for they set the north-west cloister, which was joined to the tower of Antonia, on fire, and after that brake off about twenty cubits of that cloister, and thereby made a beginning in burning the sanctuary: two days after which, or on the twenty-fourth day of the forenamed month, [Panemus, or Tamuz,] the Romans set fire to the cloister that joined to the other, when the fire went fifteen cubits farther. The Jews, in like manner, cut off its roof; nor did they entirely leave off what they were about, till the tower of Antonia was parted from the temple, even when it was in their power to have stopped the fire; nay, they lay still while the temple was first set on fire, and deemed this spreading of the fire to be for their own advantage. However, the armies were still fighting one against another about the temple; and the war was managed by continual sallies of particular parties against one another.

10. Now there was at this time a man among the Jews; low of stature he was, and of a despicable appearance; of no character either as to his family, or in other respects: his name was Jonathan. He went out at the high priest John's monument, and uttered many other insolent things to the Romans, and challenged the best of them all to a single combat; but many of those that stood there in the army huffed him, and many of them, (as they might well be,) were afraid of him. Some of them also reasoned thus, and that justly enough: that it was not fit to fight with a man that desired to die, because that those that utterly despaired of deliverance had, besides other passions, a violence in attacking men that could not be opposed, and had no regard to God himself; and that to hazard one's self with a person whom if you overcome you do no great matter, and by whom it is hazardous that you may be taken prisoner, would be an instance, not of manly courage, but of unmanly rashness. So there being nobody that came out to accept the man's challenge, and the Jew cutting them with a great number of reproaches, as cowards, (for he was a very haughty man in himself, and a great despiser of the Romans,) one whose name was Pudens, of the body of horsemen, out of his abomination of the other's words, and of his impudence withal, and perhaps out of an inconsiderate arrogance, on account of the other's lowness of stature, ran out to him, and was too hard for him in other respects, but was betrayed by his ill-fortune; for he fell down, and as he was down, Jonathan came running to him, and cut his throat, and then standing upon his dead body, he brandished his sword, bloody as it was, and shook his shield with his left hand, and made many acclamations to the Roman army, and exulted over the dead man, and jested upon the Romans; till at length one Priscus, a centurion, shot a dart at him as he was leaping and playing the fool with himself, and thereby pierced him through: upon which a shout was set up both by the Jews and the Romans, though on different accounts. So Jonathan grew giddy by the pain of his wounds, and fell down upon the body of his adversary—a plain instance how suddenly vengeance may come upon men that have success in war, without any just deserving of the same.

CHAPTER III

CONCERNING A STRATAGEM THAT WAS DEVISED BY THE JEWS, BY WHICH THEY BURNT MANY OF THE ROMANS; WITH ANOTHER DESCRIPTION OF THE TERRIBLE FAMINE THAT WAS IN THE CITY

1. But now the seditious that were in the temple did every day openly endeavour to beat off the soldiers that were upon the banks, and on the twenty-seventh day of the fore-named month, [Panemus, or Tamuz,] contrived such a stratagem as this:—They filled that part of the western cloister* which was between the beams, and the roof under them, with dry materials, as also with bitumen and pitch, and then retired from that place as though they were tired with the pains they had taken; at which procedure of theirs, many of the most inconsiderate among the Romans, who were carried away with violent passions, followed hard after them as they were retiring, and applied ladders to the cloister, and

---

* Of the Court of the Gentiles.

got up to it suddenly; but the prudent part of them, when they understood this unaccountable retreat of the Jews, stood still where they were before. However, the cloister was full of those that were gone up the ladders; at which time the Jews set it all on fire; and as the flames burst out everywhere on the sudden, the Romans that were out of the danger were seized with a very great consternation, as were those that were in the midst of the danger in the utmost distress. So when they perceived themselves surrounded with the flames, some of them threw themselves down backwards into the city, and some among their enemies, [in the temple;] as did many leap down to their own men, and broke their limbs to pieces: but a great number of those that were going to take these violent methods were prevented by the fire; though some prevented the fire by their own swords. However, the fire was on the sudden carried so far as to surround those who would have otherwise perished. As for Cæsar himself, he could not, however, but commiserate those that thus perished, although they got up thither without any order for so doing, since there was no way of giving them any relief. Yet was this some comfort to those that were destroyed that everybody might see that person grieve, for whose sake they came to their end; for he cried out openly to them, and leaped up, and exhorted those that were about him to do their utmost to relieve them. So every one of them died cheerfully, as carrying along with him these words and this intention of Cæsar as a sepulchral monument. Some there were, indeed, who retired into the wall of the cloister, which was broad, and were preserved out of the fire, but were then surrounded by the Jews; and although they made resistance against the Jews for a long time, yet were they wounded by them, and at length they all fell down dead.

2. At the last a young man among them, whose name was Longus, became a decoration to this sad affair, and while every one of them that perished were worthy of a memorial, this man appeared to deserve it beyond all the rest. Now the Jews admired this man for his courage, and were farther desirous of having him slain; so they persuaded him to come down to them, upon security given him for his life. But Cornelius, his brother, persuaded him, on the contrary, not to tarnish his own glory nor that of the Roman army. He complied with this last advice, and lifting up his sword before both armies, he slew himself. Yet was there one Artorius among those surrounded with the fire, who escaped by his subtlety; for when he had with a loud voice called to him Lucius, one of his fellow-soldiers that lay with him in the same tent, and said to him, "I do leave thee heir of all I have, if thou wilt come and receive me." Upon this he came running to receive him readily; Artorius then threw himself down upon him, and saved his own life, while he that received him was dashed so vehemently against the stone pavement by the other's weight, that he died immediately. This melancholy accident made the Romans sad for a while, but still it made them more upon their guard for the future, and was of advantage to them against the delusions of the Jews, by which they were greatly damaged, through their unacquaintedness with the places, and with the nature of the inhabitants. Now this cloister was burnt down as far as John's tower which he built in the war he made against Simon over the gates that led to the Xystus. The Jews also cut off the rest of that cloister from the temple, after they had destroyed those

that got up to it. But the next day the Romans burnt down the northern cloister entirely, as far as the east cloister, whose common angle joined to the valley that was called Cedron, and was built over it; on which account the depth was frightful. And this was the state of the temple at that time.

3. Now of those that perished by famine in the city, the number was prodigious, and the miseries they underwent were unspeakable; for if so much as the shadow of any kind of food did anywhere appear, a war was commenced presently; and the dearest friends fell a-fighting one with another about it, snatching from each other the most miserable supports of life. Nor would men believe that those who were dying had no food; but the robbers would search them when they were expiring, lest any one should have concealed food in their bosoms, and counterfeited dying: nay, these robbers gaped for want, and ran about stumbling and staggering along like mad dogs, and reeling against the doors of the houses like drunken men; they would also, in the great distress they were in, rush into the very same houses two or three times in one and the same day. Moreover, their hunger was so intolerable, that it obliged them to chew everything, while they gathered such things as the most sordid animals would not touch, and endured to eat them; nor did they at length abstain from girdles and shoes; and the very leather which belonged to their shields they pulled off and gnawed: the very wisps of old hay became food to some; and some gathered up fibres, and sold a very small weight of them for four Attic, [drachmæ.] But why should I describe the shameless impudence that the famine brought on men in their eating inanimate things, while I am going to relate a matter of fact, the like to which no history relates, either among the Greeks or Barbarians! It is horrible to speak of it, and incredible when heard. I had indeed willingly omitted this calamity of ours, that I might not seem to deliver what is so portentous to posterity, but that I have innumerable witnesses to it in my own age; and besides, my country would have had little reason to thank me for suppressing the miseries that she underwent at this time.

4. Now there was a certain woman that dwelt beyond Jordan, her name was Mary; her father was Eleazar, of the village Bethezub, which signifies *the House of Hyssop*. She was eminent for her family and her wealth, and had fled away to Jerusalem with the rest of the multitude, and was with them besieged therein at this time. The other effects of this woman had been already seized upon; such I mean as she had brought with her out of Perea, and removed to the city. What she had treasured up besides, as also what food she had contrived to save, had also been carried off by the rapacious guards, who came every day running into her house for that purpose. This put the poor woman into a very great passion, and by the frequent reproaches and imprecations she cast at these rapacious villains, she had provoked them to anger against her; but none of them, either out of the indignation she had raised against herself, or out of the commiseration of her case, would take away her life; and if she found any food, she perceived her labours were for others, and not for herself; and it was now become impossible for her any way to find any more food, while the famine pierced through her very bowels and marrow, when also her passion was fired to a degree beyond the famine itself: nor did she consult with anything but with her pas-

sion and the necessity she was in. She then attempted a most unnatural thing; and snatching up her son, who was a child sucking at her breast, she said, "O thou miserable infant! for whom shall I preserve thee in this war, this famine, and this sedition? As to the war with the Romans, if they preserve our lives, we must be slaves! This famine also will destroy us, even before that slavery comes upon us; yet are these seditious rogues more terrible than both the other. Come on; be thou my food, and be thou a fury to these seditious varlets and a byeword to the world, which is all that is now wanting to complete the calamities of us Jews." As soon as she had said this, she slew her son; and then roasted him, and ate the one half of him, and kept the other half by her concealed. Upon this the seditious came in presently, and smelling the horrid scent of this food, they threatened her that they would cut her throat immediately if she did not shew them what food she had gotten ready. She replied, that she had saved a very fine portion of it for them; and withal uncovered what was left of her son. Hereupon they were seized with a horror and amazement of mind, and stood astonished at the sight; when she said to them, "This is mine own son; and what hath been done was mine own doing! Come, eat of this food; for I have eaten of it myself! Do not you pretend to be either more tender than a woman, or more compassionate than a mother; but if you be so scrupulous, and do abominate this my sacrifice, as I have eaten the one half, let the rest be reserved for me also." After which, those men went out trembling, being never so much affrighted at anything as they were at this, and with some difficulty they left the rest of that meat to the mother. Upon which, the whole city was full of horrid action immediately; and while everybody laid this miserable case before their own eyes, they trembled, as if this unheard-of action had been done by themselves. So those that were thus distressed by the famine were very desirous to die; and those already dead were esteemed happy, because they had not lived long enough either to hear or see such miseries.

5. This sad instance was quickly told to the Romans, some of whom could not believe it, and others pitied the distress which the Jews were under; but there were many of them who were hereby induced to a more bitter hatred than ordinary against our nation;—but for Cæsar, he excused himself before God as to this matter, and said that he had proposed peace and liberty to the Jews, as well as an oblivion of all their former insolent practices; but that they, instead of concord, had chosen sedition; instead of peace, war; and before satiety and abundance, a famine. That they had begun with their own hands to burn down that temple, which we have preserved hitherto; and that therefore they deserved to eat such food as this was. That, however, this horrid action of eating one's own child, ought to be covered with the overthrow of their very country itself; and men ought not to leave such a city upon the habitable earth to be seen by the sun, wherein mothers are thus fed, although such food be fitter for the fathers than for the mothers to eat of, since it is they that continue still in a state of war against us, after they have undergone such miseries as these. And at the same time that he said this, he reflected on the desperate condition these men must be in; nor could he expect that such men could be recovered to sobriety of mind, after they had endured those very sufferings, for the avoiding

whereof it only was probable they might have repented.

CHAPTER IV

WHEN THE BANKS WERE COMPLETED, AND THE BATTERING-RAMS BROUGHT, AND COULD DO NOTHING, TITUS GAVE ORDERS TO SET FIRE TO THE GATES OF THE TEMPLE; IN NO LONG TIME AFTER WHICH THE HOLY HOUSE ITSELF WAS BURNT DOWN, EVEN AGAINST HIS CONSENT

1. AND now two of the legions had completed their banks on the eighth day of the month Lous, [Ab.] Whereupon Titus gave orders that the battering-rams should be brought and set over against the western edifice of the inner temple; for before these were brought, the firmest of all the other engines had battered the wall for six days together without ceasing, without making any impression upon it; but the vast largeness and strong connexion of the stones were superior to that engine, and to the other battering-rams also. Other Romans did indeed undermine the foundations of the northern gate, and, after a world of pains, removed the outermost stones, yet was the gate still upheld by the inner stones, and stood still unhurt; till the workmen, despairing of all such attempts by engines and crows, brought their ladders to the cloisters. Now the Jews did not interrupt them in so doing; but when they were gotten up, they fell upon them and fought with them; some of them they thrust down and threw them backwards headlong; others of them they met and slew; they also beat many of those that went down the ladders again and slew them with their swords before they could bring their shields to protect them; nay, some of the ladders they threw down from above when they were full of armed men; a great slaughter was made of the Jews also at the same time, while those that bare the ensigns fought hard for them, as deeming it a terrible thing, and what would tend to their great shame, if they permitted them to be stolen away. Yet did the Jews at length get possession of these engines, and destroyed those that had gone up the ladders, while the rest were so intimidated by what those suffered who were slain, that they retired: although none of the Romans died without having done good service before his death. Of the seditious, those that had fought bravely in the former battles did the like now; as besides them did Eleazar, the brother's son of Simon the tyrant. But when Titus perceived that his endeavours to spare a foreign temple turned to the damage of his soldiers and made them be killed, he gave orders to set the gates on fire.

2. In the meantime there deserted to him Ananus, who came from Emmaus, the most bloody of all Simon's guards, and Archelaus, the son of Magadatus, they hoping to be still forgiven, because they left the Jews at a time when they were the conquerors. Titus objected this to these men, as a cunning trick of theirs; and as he had been informed of their other barbarities toward the Jews, he was going in all haste to have them both slain. He told them that they were only driven to this desertion because of the utmost distress they were in, and did not come away of their own good disposition; and that those did not deserve to be preserved by whom their own city was set on fire, out of which fire they now hurried themselves away. However, the security he had promised deserters overcame his resentments, and he dismissed them accordingly.

though he did not give them the same privileges that he had afforded to others; and now the soldiers had already put fire to the gates, and the silver that was over them quickly carried the flames to the wood that was within it, whence it spread itself all on the sudden, and caught hold of the cloisters. Upon the Jews seeing this fire all about them, their spirits sunk, together with their bodies, and they were under such astonishment that not one of them made any haste either to defend himself or to quench the fire, but they stood as mute spectators of it only. However, they did not so grieve at the loss of what was now burning as to grow wiser thereby for the time to come; but as though the holy house itself had been on fire already, they whetted their passions against the Romans. This fire prevailed during that day and the next also; for the soldiers were not able to burn all the cloisters that were round about together at one time, but only by pieces.

3. But then on the next day, Titus commanded part of his army to quench the fire, and to make a road for the more easy marching up of the legions, while he himself gathered the commanders together. Of those there were asembled the six principal persons: Tiberius Alexander, the commander [under the general] of the whole army; with Sextus Cerealis, the commander of the fifth legion; and Larcius Lepidus, the commander of the tenth legion; and Titus Frigius, the commander of the fifteenth legion: there was also with them Eternius, the leader of the two legions that came from Alexandria; and Marcus Antonius Julianus, procurator of Judea: after these came together all the rest of the procurators and tribunes. Titus proposed to these that they should give him their advice what should be done about the holy house. Now, some of these thought it would be the best way to act according to the rules of war, [and demolish it;] because the Jews would never leave off rebelling while that house was standing; at which house it was that they used to get all together. Others of them were of opinion, that in case the Jews would leave it, and none of them would lay their arms up in it, he might save it; but that in case they got upon it, and fought any more, he might burn it; because it must then be looked upon not as a holy house, but as a citadel: and that the impiety of burning it would then belong to those that forced this to be done, and not to them. But Titus said, that "although the Jews should get upon that holy house, and fight us thence, yet ought we not to revenge ourselves on things that are inanimate, instead of the men themselves;" and that he was not in any case for burning down so vast a work as that was, because this would be a mischief to the Romans themselves, as it would be an ornament to their government while it continued. So Fronto, and Alexander, and Cerealis, grew bold upon that declaration, and agreed to the opinion of Titus. Then was this assembly dissolved, when Titus had given orders to the commanders that the rest of their forces should lie still; but that they should make use of such as were most courageous in this attack. So he commanded that the chosen men that were taken out of the cohorts should make their way through the ruins and quench the fire.

4. Now it is true, that on this day the Jews were so weary, and under such consternation, that they refrained from any attacks; but on the next day they gathered their whole force together, and ran upon those that guarded the outward court of the temple, very boldly, through the east gate, and this about the second

hour of the day. These guards received that their attack with great bravery, and by covering themselves with their shields before, as if it were with a wall, they drew their squadrons close together; yet was it evident that they could not abide there very long, but would be overborne by the multitude of those that sallied out upon them, and by the heat of their passion. However, Cæsar seeing, from the tower of Antonia, that this squadron was likely to give way, he sent some chosen horsemen to support them. Hereupon the Jews found themselves not able to sustain their onset, and upon the slaughter of those in the fore-front, many of the rest were put to flight; but as the Romans were going off, the Jews turned upon them and fought them; and as those Romans came back upon them, they retreated again, until about the fifth hour of the day they were overborne, and shut themselves up in the inner [court of the] temple.

5. So Titus retired into the tower of Antonia, and resolved to storm the temple the next day, early in the morning, with his whole army, and to encamp round about the holy house; but, as for that house, God had for certain long ago doomed it to the fire; and now that fatal day was come, according to the revolution of ages: it was the tenth day of the month Lous, [Ab,] upon which it was formerly burnt by the king of Babylon; although these flames took their rise from the Jews themselves, and were occasioned by them; for upon Titus's retiring, the seditious lay still for a little while, and then attacked the Romans again, when those that guarded the holy house fought with those that quenched the fire that was burning in the inner [court of the] temple; but these Romans put the Jews to flight, and proceeded as far as the holy house itself. At which time one of the soldiers, without staying for any orders, and without any concern or dread upon him at so great an undertaking, and being hurried on by a certain divine fury, snatched somewhat out of the materials that were on fire, and being lifted up by another soldier, he set fire to a golden window, through which there was a passage to the rooms that were round about the holy house, on the north side of it. As the flames went upward the Jews made a great clamour, such as so mighty an affliction required, and ran together to prevent it; and now they spared not their lives any longer, nor suffered anything to restrain their force, since that holy house was perishing, for whose sake it was that they kept such a guard about it.

6. And now a certain person came running to Titus, and told him of this fire, as he was resting himself in his tent after the last battle; whereupon he rose up in great haste, and as he was, ran to the holy house, in order to have a stop put to the fire; after him followed all his commanders, and after them followed the several legions, in great astonishment; so there was a great clamour and tumult raised, as was natural upon the disorderly motion of so great an army. Then did Cæsar, both by calling to the soldiers that were fighting, with a loud voice, and by giving a signal to them with his right hand, order them to quench the fire; but they did not hear what he said, though he spake so loud, having their ears already dinned by a greater noise another way; nor did they attend to the signal he made with his right hand neither, as still some of them were distracted with fighting, and others with passion; but as for the legions that came running thither, neither any persuasions nor any threatenings could restrain their violence, but each one's own passion was his commander

at this time; and as they were crowding into the temple together, many of them were trampled on by one another, while a great number fell among the ruins of the cloisters, which were still hot and smoking, and were destroyed in the same miserable way with those whom they had conquered : and when they were come near the holy house, they made as if they did not so much as hear Cæsar's orders to the contrary; but they encouraged those that were before them to set it on fire. As for the seditious they were in too great distress already to afford their assistance, [toward quenching the fire;] they were everywhere slain, and everywhere beaten; and as for a great part of the people, they were weak and without arms, and had their throats cut wherever they were caught. Now, round about the altar lay dead bodies heaped one upon another; as at the steps * going up to it ran a great quantity of their blood, whither also the dead bodies that were slain above [on the altar] fell down.

7. And now, since Cæsar was no way able to restrain the enthusiastic fury of the soldiers, and the fire proceeded on more and more, he went into the holy place of the temple, with his commanders, and saw it, with what was in it, which he found to be far superior to what the relations of foreigners contained, and not inferior to what we ourselves boasted of and believed about it; but as the flame had not as yet reached to its inward parts, but was still consuming the rooms that were about the holy house, and Titus supposing what the fact was, that the house itself might yet be saved, he came in haste and endeavoured to persuade the soldiers to quench the fire, and gave order to Liberalius the centurion, and one of those spearmen that were about him, to beat the soldiers that were refractory with their staves, and to restrain them! yet were their passions too hard for the regard they had for Cæsar, and the dread they had for him who forbade them, as was their hatred of the Jews, and a certain vehement inclination to fight them, too hard for them also. Moreover, the hope of plunder induced many to go on, as having this opinion, that all the places within were full of money, and as seeing that all round about it was made of gold; and besides, one of those that went into the place prevented Cæsar, when he ran so hastily out to restrain the soldiers, and threw the fire upon the hinges of the gate, in the dark; whereby the flame burst out from within the holy house itself immediately, when the commanders retired, and Cæsar with them, and when nobody any longer forbade those that were without to set fire to it; and thus was the holy house burnt down, without Cæsar's approbation.

8. Now, although any one would justly lament the destruction of such a work as this was, since it was the most admirable of all the works that we have seen or heard of, both for its curious structure and its magnitude, and also for the vast wealth bestowed upon it, as well as for the glorious reputation it had for its holiness; yet might such a one comfort himself with this thought, that it was fate that decreed it so to be, which is inevitable, both as to living creatures and as to works and places also. However, one cannot but wonder at the accuracy of this period thereto relating; for the same month and day were now observed, as I said before, wherein the holy house was burnt formerly by the Babylonians. Now the number of years that passed from its first foundation, which was laid by king Solomon, till this its destruction, which happened in the second year of the reign of Vespasian, are collected to be one thousand one hundred and thirty, besides seven months and fifteen days; and from the second building of it, which was done by Haggai, in the second year of Cyrus the king, till its destruction under Vespasian, there were six hundred and thirty-nine years and forty-five days.

CHAPTER V

THE GREAT DISTRESS THE JEWS WERE IN UPON THE CONFLAGRATION OF THE HOLY HOUSE CONCERNING A FALSE PROPHET, AND THE SIGNS THAT PRECEDED THIS DESTRUCTION

1. WHILE the holy house was on fire, everything was plundered that came to hand, and ten thousand of those that were caught were slain; nor was there a commiseration of any age, or any reverence of gravity; but children, and old men, and profane persons, and priests, were all slain in the same manner; so that this war went round all sorts of men, and brought them to destruction, and as well those that made supplication for their lives, as those that defended themselves by fighting. The flame was also carried a long way, and made an echo, together with the groans of those that were slain; and because this hill was high, and the works at the temple were very great, one would have thought that the whole city had been on fire. Nor can one imagine anything either greater or more terrible than this noise; for there was at once a shout of the Roman legions, who were marching all together, and a sad clamour of the seditious, who were now surrounded with fire and sword. The people also that were left above were beaten back upon the enemy, and under a great consternation, and made sad moans at the calamity they were under; the multitude also that was in the city joined in this outcry with those that were upon the hill; and besides many of those that were worn away by the famine, and their mouths almost closed when they saw the fire of the holy house, they exerted their utmost strength, and brake out into groans and outcries again: Perea did also return the echo, as well as the mountains round about, [the city,] and augmented the force of the entire noise. Yet was the misery itself more terrible than this disorder; for one would have thought that the hill itself, on which the temple stood, was seething-hot, as full of fire on every part of it, that the blood was larger in quantity than the fire, and those that were slain more in number than those that slew them; for the ground did nowhere appear visible, for the dead bodies that lay on it; but the soldiers went over heaps of these bodies, as they ran upon such as fled from them. And now it was that the multitude of the robbers were thrust out [of the inner court of the temple] by the Romans, and had much ado to get into the outer court, and from thence into the city, while the remainder of the populace fled into the cloister of that outer court. As for the priests, some of them plucked up from the holy house the spikes that were upon it, with their bases, which were made of lead, and shot them

---

* These steps to the altar of burnt-offering seem either an improper and inaccurate expression of Josephus, since it was unlawful to make ladder-steps, or else those steps or stairs we now use were invented before the days of Herod the Great, and had been here built by him; though the latter Jews always deny it, and say that even Herod's altar was ascended to by an acclivity only.

at the Romans instead of darts. But then as they gained nothing by so doing, and as the fire burst out upon them, they retired to the wall that was eight cubits broad, and there they tarried; yet did two of these of eminence among them, who might have saved themselves by going over to the Romans, or have borne up with courage, and taken their fortune with the others, throw themselves into the fire, and were burnt together with the holy house; their names were Meirus the son of Belgas, and Joseph the son of Daleus.

2. And now the Romans, judging that it was in vain to spare what was round about the holy house, burnt all those places, as also the remains of the cloisters and the gates, two excepted; the one on the east side, and the other on the south; both which, however, they burnt afterward. They also burnt down the treasury-chambers, in which was an immense quantity of money, and an immense number of garments, and other precious goods, there reposited; and, to speak all in a few words, there it was that the entire riches of the Jews were heaped up together, while the rich people had there built themselves chambers, [to contain such furniture.] The soldiers also came to the rest of the cloisters that were in the outer [court of the] temple, whither the women and children and a great mixed multitude of the people fled, in number about six thousand. But before Cæsar had determined anything about these people, or given the commanders any orders relating to them, the soldiers were in such a rage, that they set the cloister on fire; by which means it came to pass that some of these were destroyed by throwing themselves down headlong, and some were burnt in the cloisters themselves. Nor did any one of these escape with his life. A false prophet* was the occasion of these people's destruction, who had made a public proclamation in the city that very day, that God commanded them to get up upon the temple, and that there they should receive miraculous signs of their deliverance. Now, there was then a great number of false prophets suborned by the tyrants to impose upon the people, who denounced this to them, that they should wait for deliverance from God; and this was in order to keep them from deserting, and that they might be buoyed up above fear and care by such hopes. Now, a man that is in adversity does easily comply with such promises; for when such a seducer makes him believe that he shall be delivered from those miseries which oppress him, then it is that the patient is full of hopes of such deliverance.

3. Thus were the miserable people persuaded by these deceivers, and such as belied God himself; while they did not attend, nor give credit, to the signs that were so evident, and did so plainly foretell their future desolation; but, like men infatuated, without either eyes to see or minds to consider, did not regard the denunciations that God made to them. Thus there was a star resembling a sword, which stood over the city, and a comet, that continued a whole year. Thus also, before the Jews' rebellion, and before those commotions which preceded the war, when the people were come in great crowds to the feast of unleavened bread, on the eighth day of the month Xanthicus,† [Nisan,] and at

the ninth hour of the night, so great a light shone round the altar and the holy house, that it appeared to be bright day-time; which light lasted for half an hour. This light seemed to be a good sign to the unskilful, but was so interpreted by the sacred scribes as to portend those events that followed immediately upon it. At the same festival also, a heifer, as she was led by the high priest to be sacrificed, brought forth a lamb in the midst of the temple. Moreover, the eastern gate of the inner, [court of the temple,] which was of brass, and vastly heavy, and had been with difficulty shut by twenty men, and rested upon a basis armed with iron, and had bolts fastened very deep into the firm floor, which was there made of one entire stone, was seen to be opened of its own accord about the sixth hour of the night. Now, those that kept watch in the temple came thereupon running to the captain of the temple, and told him of it; who then came up thither, and not without great difficulty was able to shut the gate again. This also appeared to the vulgar to be a very happy prodigy, as if God did thereby open them the gate of happiness. But the men of learning understood it, that the security of their holy house was dissolved of its own accord, and that the gate was opened for the advantage of their enemies. So these publicly declared, that this signal foreshewed the desolation that was coming upon them. Besides these, a few days after that feast, on the one-and-twentieth day of the month Artemisius, [Jyar,] a certain prodigious and incredible phenomenon appeared; I suppose the account of it would seem to be a fable, were it not related by those that saw it, and were not the events that followed it of so considerable a nature as to deserve such signals; for, before sun-setting, chariots and troops of soldiers in their armour were seen running about among the clouds, and surrounding of cities. Moreover, at that feast which we call Pentecost, as the priests were going by night into the inner‡ [court of the] temple, as their custom was, to perform their sacred ministrations, they said that, in the first place, they felt a quaking, and heard a great noise, and after that they heard a sound as of a great multitude, saying, "Let us remove hence." But, what is still more terrible, there was one Jesus, the son of Ananus, a plebeian, and an husbandman, who, four years before the war began, and at a time when the city was in very great peace and prosperity, came to that feast whereon it is our custom for every one to make tabernacles to God in the temple, began on a sudden to cry aloud, "A voice from the east, a voice from the west, a voice from the four winds, a voice against Jerusalem and the holy house, a voice against the bridegrooms and the brides, and a voice against this whole people!" This was his cry, as he went about by day and by night, in all the lanes of the city. However, certain of the most eminent among the populace had great indignation at this dire cry of his, and took up the man, and gave him a great number of severe stripes; yet did not he either say anything for himself, or anything peculiar to those that chastised him, but still he went on with the same words which he cried before. Hereupon our rulers supposing, as the case proved to be, that this was a sort of divine fury in the man, brought him to the Roman procurator—

* Reland here justly takes notice that these Jews who had despised the true Prophet, were deservedly abused and deluded by these false ones.

† Since Josephus still uses the Syro-Macedonian month Xanthicus, for the Jewish month Nisan, this eighth, or, as Nicephorus reads it, this ninth of Xanthicus, or Nisan, was almost a week before the

Passover, on the fourteenth: about which time we learn from St John that many used to go "out of the country to Jerusalem, to purify themselves," (John xi. 55, with xii. 1.)

‡ This here seems to be the court of the priests.

where he was whipped till his bones were laid bare; yet did he not make any supplication for himself, nor shed any tears, but turning his voice to the most lamentable tone possible, at every stroke of the whip his answer was, "Woe, woe to Jerusalem!" And when Albinus (for he was then our procurator) asked him, Who he was? and whence he came? and why he uttered such words? he made no manner of reply to what he said, but still did not leave off his melancholy ditty, till Albinus took him to be a madman, and dismissed him. Now, during all the time that passed before the war began, this man did not go near any of the citizens, nor was seen by them while he said so; but he every day uttered these lamentable words, as if it were his premeditated vow, "Woe, woe to Jerusalem!" Nor did he give ill words to any of those that beat him every day, nor good words to those that gave him food; but this was his reply to all men, and indeed no other than a melancholy presage of what was to come. This cry of his was the loudest at the festivals; and he continued this ditty for seven years and five months, without growing hoarse, or being tired therewith, until the very time that he saw his presage in earnest fulfilled in our siege, when it ceased; for, as he was going round upon the wall, he cried out with his utmost force, "Woe, woe to the city again, and to the people, and to the holy house!" And just as he added at the last,—"Woe, woe to myself also!" there came a stone out of one of the engines, and smote him, and killed him immediately: and as he was uttering the very same presages, he gave up the ghost.

4. Now, if any one consider these things, he will find that God takes care of mankind, and by all ways possible foreshews to our race what is for their preservation; but that men perish by those miseries which they madly and voluntarily bring upon themselves; for the Jews, by demolishing the tower of Antonia, had made their temple four-square, while at the same time they had it written in their sacred oracles,—"That then should their city be taken, as well as their holy house, when once their temple should become four-square." But now, what did most elevate them in undertaking this war was an ambiguous oracle that was also found in their sacred writings, how, "about that time, one from their country should become governor of the habitable earth." The Jews took this prediction to belong to themselves in particular; and many of the wise men were thereby deceived in their determination. Now, this oracle certainly denoted the government of Vespasian, who was appointed emperor in Judea. However, it is not possible for men to avoid fate, although they see it beforehand. But these men interpreted some of these signals according to their own pleasure; and some of them they utterly despised, until their madness was demonstrated, both by the taking of their city and their own destruction.

CHAPTER VI

HOW THE ROMANS CARRIED THEIR ENSIGNS TO THE TEMPLE, AND MADE JOYFUL ACCLAMATIONS TO TITUS. THE SPEECH THAT TITUS MADE TO THE JEWS WHEN THEY MADE SUPPLICATION FOR MERCY. WHAT REPLY THEY MADE THERETO; AND HOW THAT REPLY MOVED TITUS'S INDIGNATION AGAINST THEM

1. AND now the Romans, upon the flight of the seditious into the city, and upon the burning of the holy house itself, and of all the buildings lying round about it, brought their ensigns to the temple,* and set them over against its eastern gate; and there did they offer sacrifices to them, and there did they make Titus imperator,† with the greatest acclamations of joy. And now all the soldiers had such vast quantities of the spoils which they had gotten by plunder, that in Syria a pound weight of gold was sold for half its former value. But as for those priests that kept themselves still upon the wall of the holy house,‡ there was a boy that, out of the thirst he was in, desired some of the Roman guards to give him their right hands as a security for his life, and confessed he was very thirsty. These guards commiserated his age, and the distress he was in, and gave him their right hands accordingly. So he came down himself, and drank some water, and filled the vessel he had with him when he came to them with water, and then went off, and fled away to his own friends; nor could any of those guards overtake him; but still they reproached him for his perfidiousness. To which he made this answer:—"I have not broken the agreement; for the security I had given me was not in order to my staying with you, but only in order to my coming down safely, and taking up some water; both which things I have performed, and thereupon think myself to have been faithful to my engagement." Hereupon those whom the child had imposed upon admired at his cunning, and that on account of his age. On the fifth day afterward, the priests that were pined with the famine came down, and when they were brought to Titus by the guards, they begged for their lives: but he replied, that the time of pardon was over as to them; and that this very holy house, on whose account alone they could justly hope to be preserved, was destroyed; and that it was agreeable to their office that priests should perish with the house itself to which they belonged. So he ordered them to be put to death.

2. But as for the tyrants themselves, and those that were with them, when they found that they were encompassed on every side, and, as it were, walled round, without any method of escaping, they desired to treat with Titus by word of mouth. Accordingly, such was the kindness of his nature, and his desire of preserving the city from destruction, joined to the advice of his friends, who now thought the robbers were come to a temper, that he placed himself on the other side of the outer [court of the] temple; for there were gates on that side above the Xystus, and a bridge that connected the upper city to the temple. This bridge it was that lay between the tyrants and Cæsar, and parted them; while the multitude stood on each side,—those of the Jewish nation about Simon and John, with great hope of pardon; and the Romans about Cæsar, in great expectation how Titus would receive their supplication. So Titus charged his soldiers to restrain their rage, and to let their darts

---

* Havercamp says here:—"This is a remarkable place; and Tertullian truly says that the entire religion of the Roman camp almost consisted in worshipping the ensigns, in swearing by the ensigns, and in preferring the ensigns before all the [other] gods."

† This declaring Titus imperator by the soldiers, upon such signal success, and the slaughter of such a vast number of enemies, was according to the usual practice of the Romans in like cases.

‡ The Jews of later times agree with Josephus, that there were hiding-places or secret chambers about the holy house.

alone, and appointed an interpreter between them, which was a sign that he was the conqueror, and first began the discourse, and said, "I hope you, sirs, are now satisfied with the miseries of your country, who have not had any just notions either of our great power or of your own great weakness; but have, like madmen, after a violent and inconsiderate manner, made such attempts as have brought your people, your city, and your holy house to destruction. You have been the men that have never left off rebelling since Pompey first conquered you; and have, since that time, made open war with the Romans. Have you depended on your multitude, while a very small part of the Roman soldiery have been strong enough for you? Have you relied on the fidelity of your confederates? and what nations are there, out of the limits of our dominion, that would choose to assist the Jews before the Romans? Are your bodies stronger than ours? nay, you know that the [strong] Germans themselves are our servants. Have you stronger walls than we have? Pray, what greater obstacle is there than the wall of the ocean, with which the Britons are encompassed, and yet do adore the arms of the Romans? Do you exceed us in courage of soul, and in the sagacity of your commanders? Nay, indeed, you cannot but know that the very Carthaginians have been conquered by us. It can therefore be nothing certainly but the kindness of us Romans which hath excited you against us; who, in the first place, have given you this land to possess; and, in the next place, have set over you kings of your own nation; and, in the third place, have preserved the laws of your forefathers to you, and have withal permitted you to live, either by yourselves or among others, as it should please you; and, what is our chief favour of all, we have given you leave to gather up that tribute which is paid to God,* with such other gifts that are dedicated to him; nor have we called those that carried these donations to account, nor prohibited them; till at length you became richer than we ourselves, even when you were our enemies; and you made preparations for war against us with our own money: nay, after all, when you were in the enjoyment of all these advantages, you turned your too great plenty against those that gave it you, and, like merciless serpents, have thrown out your poison against those that treated you kindly. I suppose, therefore, that you might despise the slothfulness of Nero, and, like limbs of the body that are broken or dislocated, you did then lie quiet, waiting for some other time, though still with a malicious intention, and have now shewn your distemper to be greater than ever, and have extended your desires as far as your impudent and immense hopes would enable you to do it. At this time my father came into this country, not with a design to punish you for what you had done under Cestius, but to admonish you; for, had he come to overthrow your nation, he had run directly to your fountainhead, and had immediately laid this city waste; whereas, he went and burnt Galilee, and the neighbouring parts, and thereby gave you time for repentance; which instance of humanity you took for an argument of his weakness, and nourished up your impudence by our mildness. When Nero was gone out of the world, you did as the wickedest wretches would have done, and encouraged yourselves to act against us by our

civil dissensions, and abused that time when both I and my father were gone away to Egypt, to make preparations for this war. Nor were you ashamed to raise disturbances against us when we were made emperors, and this while you had experienced how mild we had been, when we were no more than generals of the army; but when the government was devolved upon us, and all other people did thereupon lie quiet, and even foreign nations sent embassies and congratulated our access to the government, then did you Jews shew yourselves to be our enemies. You sent embassies to those of your nation that are beyond Euphrates, to assist you in your raising disturbances; new walls were built by you round your city, seditions arose, and one tyrant contended against another, and a civil war broke out among you; such, indeed, as became none but so wicked a people as you are. I then came to this city, as unwillingly sent by my father, and received melancholy injunctions from him. When I heard that the people were disposed to peace, I rejoiced at it: I exhorted you to leave off these proceedings before I began this war; I spared you even when you had fought against me a great while; I gave my right hand as security to the deserters; I observed what I had promised faithfully. When they fled to me, I had compassion of many of those that I had taken captive; I tortured those that were eager for war, in order to restrain them. It was unwillingly that I brought my engines of war against your walls; I always prohibited my soldiers, when they were set upon your slaughter, from their severity against you. After every victory I persuaded you to peace, as though I had been myself conquered. When I came near your temple I again departed from the laws of war, and exhorted you to spare your own sanctuary, and to preserve your holy house to yourselves. I allowed you a quiet exit out of it, and security for your preservation: nay, if you had a mind, I gave you leave to fight in another place. Yet have you still despised every one of my proposals, and have set fire to your holy house with your own hands. And now, vile wretches, do you desire to treat with me by word of mouth? To what purpose is it that you would save such a holy house as this was, which is now destroyed? What preservation can you now desire after the destruction of your temple? Yet do you stand still at this very time in your armour; nor can you bring yourselves so much as to pretend to be supplicants even in this your utmost extremity! O miserable creatures! what is it you depend on? Are not your people dead? is not your holy house gone? is not your city in my power? and are not your own very lives in my hands? And do you still deem it a part of valour to die? However, I will not imitate your madness. If you throw down your arms, and deliver up your bodies to me, I grant you your lives; and I will act like a mild master of a family; what cannot be healed shall be punished, and the rest I will preserve for my own use."

3. To that offer of Titus they made this reply:—That they could not accept of it, because they had sworn never to do so; but they desired they might have leave to go through the wall that had been made about them, with their wives and children; for that they would go into the desert, and leave the city to him. At this Titus had great indignation; that, when they were in the case of men already taken captives, they should pretend to make their own terms with him, as if they had been conquerors! So he ordered this proclamation to be made to them,

---

* Spanheim notes here, that the Romans used to permit the Jews to collect their sacred tribute, and send it to Jerusalem.

That they should no more come out to him as deserters, nor hope for any further security; for that he would henceforth spare nobody, but fight them with his whole army; and that they must save themselves as well as they could; for that he would from henceforth treat them according to the laws of war. So he gave orders to the soldiers both to burn and plunder the city; who did nothing indeed that day; but on the next day they set fire to the repository of the archives, to Acra, to the council-house, and to the place called Ophlas; at which time the fire proceeded as far as the palace of queen Helena, which was in the middle of Acra: the lanes also were burnt down, as were also those houses that were full of the dead bodies of such as were destroyed by famine.

4. On the same day it was that the sons and brethren of Izates the king, together with many others of the eminent men of the populace, got together there, and besought Cæsar to give them his right hand for their security. Upon which, though he was very angry at all that were now remaining, yet did he not lay aside his old moderation, but received these men. At that time, indeed, he kept them all in custody, but still bound the king's sons and kinsmen, and led them with him to Rome, in order to make them hostages for their country's fidelity to the Romans.

CHAPTER VII

WHAT AFTERWARDS BEFELL THE SEDITIOUS, WHEN THEY HAD DONE A GREAT DEAL OF MISCHIEF, AND SUFFERED MANY MISFORTUNES: AS ALSO HOW CÆSAR BECAME MASTER OF THE UPPER CITY

1. AND now the seditious rushed into the royal palace, into which many had put their effects, because it was so strong, and drove the Romans away from it. They also slew all the people that had crowded into it, who were in number about eight thousand four hundred, and plundered them of what they had. They also took two of the Romans alive; the one was a horseman, and the other a footman. They then cut the throat of the footman, and immediately had him drawn through the whole city, as revenging themselves upon the whole body of the Romans by this one instance. But the horseman said he had somewhat to suggest to them, in order to their preservation; whereupon he was brought before Simon; but he having nothing to say when he was there, he was delivered to Ardalas, one of his commanders, to be punished, who bound his hands behind him, and put a riband over his eyes, and then brought him out over against the Romans, as intending to cut off his head. But the man prevented that execution, and ran away to the Romans, and this while the Jewish executioner was drawing out his sword. Now when he was gotten away from the enemy, Titus could not think of putting him to death; but because he deemed him unworthy of being a Roman soldier any longer, on account that he had been taken alive by the enemy, he took away his arms, and ejected him out of the legion whereto he had belonged; which, to one that had a sense of shame, was a penalty severer than death itself.

2. On the next day the Romans drove the robbers out of the lower city, and set all on fire as far as Siloam. These soldiers were indeed glad to see the city destroyed. But they missed the plunder, because the seditious had carried off all their effects, and were retired into the upper city; for they did not yet at all repent of the mischiefs they had done, but were insolent, as if they had done well; for, as they saw the city on fire, they appeared cheerful, and put on joyful countenances, in expectation, as they said, of death to end their miseries. Accordingly, as the people were now slain, the holy house was burnt down, and the city was on fire, there was nothing further left for the enemy to do. Yet did not Josephus grow weary, even in this utmost extremity, to beg of them to spare what was left of the city; he spake largely to them about their barbarity and impiety, and gave them his advice in order to their escape, though he gained nothing thereby more than to be laughed at by them; and as they could not think of surrendering themselves up, because of the oath they had taken, nor were strong enough to fight with the Romans any longer upon the square, as being surrounded on all sides, and a kind of prisoners already, yet were they so accustomed to kill people, that they could not restrain their right hands from acting accordingly. So they dispersed themselves before the city, and laid themselves in ambush among its ruins, to catch those that attempted to desert to the Romans; accordingly, many such deserters were caught by them, and were all slain; for these were too weak, by reason of their want of food, to fly away from them; so their dead bodies were thrown to the dogs. Now every sort of death was thought more tolerable than the famine, insomuch that, though the Jews despaired now of mercy, yet would they fly to the Romans, and would themselves, even of their own accord, fall among the murderous rebels also. Nor was there any place in the city that had no dead bodies in it, but what was entirely covered with those that were either killed by the famine or the rebellion; and all was full of the dead bodies of such as had perished, either by that sedition or by that famine.

3. So now the last hope which supported the tyrants, and the crew of robbers who were with them, was in the caves and caverns under ground; whither, if they could once fly, they did not expect to be searched for; but endeavoured that, after the whole city should be destroyed, and the Romans gone away, they might come out again, and escape from them. This was no better than a dream of theirs; for they were not able to lie hid either from God or from the Romans. However, they depended on these under-ground subterfuges, and set more places on fire than did the Romans themselves; and those that fled out of their houses, thus set on fire, into ditches they killed without mercy, and pillaged them also; and if they discovered food belonging to any one, they seized upon it and swallowed it down, together with their blood also; nay, they were now come to fight one with another about their plunder; and I cannot but think that, had not their destruction prevented it, their barbarity would have made them taste of even the dead bodies themselves.

CHAPTER VIII

HOW CÆSAR RAISED BANKS ROUND ABOUT THE UPPER CITY, [MOUNT ZION,] AND WHEN THEY WERE COMPLETED, GAVE ORDERS FOR THE MACHINES TO BE BROUGHT. HE THEN POSSESSED HIMSELF OF THE WHOLE CITY

1. Now, when Cæsar perceived that the upper

city was so steep, that it could not possibly be taken without raising banks against it, he distributed the several parts of that work among his army, and this on the twentieth day of the month Lous, [Ab.] Now, the carriage of the materials was a difficult task, since all the trees, as I have already told you, that were about the city, within the distance of a hundred furlongs, had their branches cut off already, in order to make the former banks. The works that belonged to the four legions were erected on the west side of the city, over against the royal palace; but the whole body of the auxiliary troops, with the rest of the multitude that were with them, [erected their banks] at the Xystus, whence they reached to the bridge, and that tower of Simon, which he had built as a citadel for himself against John, when they were at war one with another.

2. It was at this time that the commanders of the Idumeans got privately together, and took counsel about surrendering themselves up to the Romans. Accordingly, they sent five men to Titus, and entreated him to give them his right hand for their security. So Titus, thinking that the tyrants would yield if the Idumeans, upon whom a great part of the war depended, were once withdrawn from them, after some reluctance and delay, complied with them, and gave them security for their lives, and sent the five men back; but as these Idumeans were preparing to march out, Simon perceived it, and immediately slew the five men that had gone to Titus, and took their commanders, and put them in prison, of whom the most eminent was Jacob, the son of Sosas; but as for the multitude of the Idumeans, who did not at all know what to do, now their commanders were taken from them, he had them watched, and secured the walls by a more numerous garrison. Yet could not that garrison resist those that were deserting; for although a great number of them were slain, yet were the deserters many more in number. These were all received by the Romans, because Titus himself grew negligent as to his former orders for killing them, and because the very soldiers grew weary of killing them, and because they hoped to get some money by sparing them; for they left only the populace, and sold the rest of the multitude,* with their wives and children, and every one of them at a very low price, and that because such as were sold were very many, and the buyers very few; and although Titus had made proclamation beforehand that no deserter should come alone by himself, that so they might bring out their families with them, yet did he receive such as these also. However, he set over them such as were to distinguish some from others, in order to see if any of them deserved to be punished; and indeed the number of those that were sold was immense; but of the populace above forty thousand were saved, whom Cæsar let go whither every one of them pleased.

3. But now at this time it was that one of the priests, the son of Thebuthus, whose name was Jesus, upon his having security given him by the oath of Cæsar that he should be preserved upon condition that he should deliver to him certain of the precious things that had been reposited in the temple, came out of it, and delivered him from the wall of the holy house two candlesticks like to those that lay in the holy house, with tables, and cisterns, and vials, all made of solid gold, and very heavy. He also delivered to him the veils and the garments, with the precious stones, and a great number of other precious vessels that belonged to their sacred worship. The treasurer of the temple also, whose name was Phineas, was seized on, and shewed Titus the coats and girdles of the priests, with a great quantity of purple and scarlet, which were there reposited for the use of the veil, as also a great deal of cinnamon and cassia, with a large quantity of other sweet spices,† which used to be mixed together, and offered as incense to God every day. A great many other treasures were also delivered to him, with sacred ornaments of the temple not a few; which things thus delivered to Titus, obtained of him for this man the same pardon that he had allowed to such as deserted of their own accord.

4. And now were the banks finished on the seventh day of the month Gorpieus, [Elul,] in eighteen days' time, when the Romans brought their machines against the wall; but for the seditious, some of them, as despairing of saving the city, retired from the wall to the citadel; others of them went down into the subterranean vaults, though still a great many of them defended themselves against those that brought the engines for the battery; yet did the Romans overcome them by their number and by their strength; and, what was the principal thing of all, by going cheerfully about their work, while the Jews were quite dejected and become weak. Now, as soon as a part of the wall was battered down, and certain of the towers yielded to the impression of the battering-rams, those that opposed themselves fled away, and such a terror fell upon the tyrants as was much greater than the occasion required; for before the enemy got over the breach they were quite stunned, and were immediately for flying away; and now one might see these men, who had hitherto been so insolent and arrogant in their wicked practices, to be cast down and to tremble, insomuch that it would pity one's heart to observe the change that was made in those vile persons. Accordingly, they ran with great violence upon the Roman wall that encompassed them, in order to force away those that guarded it, and to break through it, and get away; but when they saw that those who had formerly been faithful to them had gone away, (as indeed they were fled whithersoever the great distress they were in persuaded them to flee,) as also when those that came running before the rest told them that the western wall was entirely overthrown, while others said the Romans were gotten in, and others that they were near, and looking out for them, which were only the dictates of their fear, which imposed upon their sight, they fell upon their faces, and greatly lamented their own mad conduct; and their nerves were so terribly loosed, that they could not flee away; and here one may chiefly reflect on the power of God exercised upon these wicked wretches, and on the good fortune of the Romans; for these tyrants did now wholly deprive themselves of the security

---

* This was an eminent completion of God's ancient threatening by Moses, that if they apostatised from obedience to his laws, they should be "sold unto their enemies for bondmen and bondwomen," (Deut. xxviii. 68.) But one thing here is peculiarly remarkable, that Moses adds,—Though they should be "sold" for slaves, yet "no man should buy them;" i. e. either they should have none to redeem them from this sale into slavery; or rather that the slaves to be sold should be more than were the purchasers for them, and so they should be sold for little or nothing; which is what Josephus here affirms to have been the case at this time.

† These various sorts of spices, even more than those four which Moses prescribed, (Exod. xxxi. 34,) we see were used in their public worship under Herod's temple, particularly cinnamon and cassia.

they had in their own power, and came down from those very towers of their own accord, wherein they could have never been taken by force, nor indeed by any other way than by famine. And thus did the Romans, when they had taken such great pains about weaker walls, get by good fortune what they could never have gotten by their engines; for three of these towers were too strong for all mechanical engines whatsoever; concerning which we have treated of before.

5. So they now left these towers of themselves, or rather they were ejected out of them by God himself, and fled immediately to that valley which was under Siloam, where they again recovered themselves out of the dread they were in for a while, and ran violently against that part of the Roman wall which lay on that side; but as their courage was too much depressed to make their attacks with sufficient force, and their power was now broken with fear and affliction, they were repulsed by the guards, and dispersing themselves at distances from each other, went down into the subterranean caverns. So the Romans being now become masters of the walls, they both placed their ensigns upon the towers, and made joyful acclamations for the victory they had gained, as having found the end of this war much lighter than its beginning; for when they had gotten upon the last wall without any bloodshed, they could hardly believe what they found to be true; but seeing nobody to oppose them, they stood in doubt what such an unusual solitude could mean. But when they went in numbers into the lanes of the city with their swords drawn, they slew those whom they overtook without mercy, and set fire to the houses whither the Jews were fled, and burnt every soul in them, and laid waste a great many of the rest; and when they were come to the houses to plunder them, they found in them entire families of dead men, and the upper rooms full of dead corpses, that is of such as died by the famine; they then stood in a horror at this sight, and went out without touching any thing. But although they had this commiseration for such as were destroyed in that manner, yet had they not the same for those that were still alive, but they ran every one through whom they met with, and obstructed the very lanes with their dead bodies, and made the whole city run down with blood, to such a degree indeed that the fire of many of the houses was quenched with these men's blood. And truly so it happened, that though the slayers left off at the evening, yet did the fire greatly prevail in the night; and as all was burning, came that eighth day of the month Gorpieus [Elul] upon Jerusalem; a city that had been liable to so many miseries during this siege, that, had it always enjoyed as much happiness from its first foundation, it would certainly have been the envy of the world. Nor did it on any other account so much deserve these sore misfortunes, as by producing such a generation of men as were the occasions of this its overthrow.

CHAPTER IX

WHAT INJUNCTIONS CÆSAR GAVE WHEN HE WAS COME WITHIN THE CITY. THE NUMBER OF THE CAPTIVES, AND OF THOSE THAT PERISHED IN THE SIEGE; AS ALSO CONCERNING THOSE THAT ESCAPED INTO THE SUBTERRANEAN CAVERNS, AMONG WHOM WERE THE TYRANTS SIMON AND JOHN THEMSELVES

1. Now, when Titus was come into this [upper] city, he admired not only some other places of strength in it, but particularly those strong towers which the tyrants, in their mad conduct, had relinquished; for when he saw their solid altitude, and the largeness of their several stones, and the exactness of their joints, as also how great was their breadth, and how extensive their length, he expressed himself after the following manner:—" We have certainly had God for our assistant in this war, and it was no other than God that ejected the Jews out of these fortifications; for what could the hands of men, or any machines, do towards overthrowing these towers!" At which time he had many such discourses to his friends; he also let such go free as had been bound by the tyrants, and were left in the prisons. To conclude, when he entirely demolished the rest of the city, and overthrew its walls, he left these towers as a monument of his good fortune, which had proved his auxiliaries, and enabled him to take what could not otherwise have been taken by him.

2. And now, since his soldiers were already quite tired with killing men, and yet there appeared to be a vast multitude still remaining alive, Cæsar gave orders that they should kill none but those that were in arms, and opposed them, but should take the rest alive. But, together with those whom they had orders to slay, they slew the aged and the infirm; but for those that were in their flourishing age, and who might be useful to them, they drove them together into the temple, and shut them up within the walls of the court of the women; over which Cæsar set one of his freedmen, as also Fronto, one of his own friends; which last was to determine every one's fate, according to his merits. So this Fronto slew all those that had been seditious and robbers, who were impeached one by another; but of the young men, he chose out the tallest and most beautiful, and reserved them for the triumph; and as for the rest of the multitude that were above seventeen years old, he put them into bonds, and sent them to the Egyptian mines.[*] Titus also sent a great number into the provinces, as a present to them, that they might be destroyed upon their theatres, by the sword and by the wild beasts; but those that were under seventeen years of age were sold for slaves. Now, during the days wherein Fronto was distinguishing these men there perished, for want of food, eleven thousand; some of whom did not taste any food, through the hatred their guards bore to them; and others would not take in any when it was given them. The multitude also was so very great, that they were in want even of corn for their sustenance.

3. Now the number[†] of those that were carried captive during this whole war was collected to be ninety-seven thousand; as was the number of those that perished during the whole siege, eleven hundred thousand, the greater part of whom were indeed of the same nation, [with the citizens of Jerusalem,] but not belonging to the city itself; for they were come up from all the country to the feast of unleavened bread, and were on a sudden shut up by an army, which, at the very first, occasioned so great a straitness among them, that there came a pestilential de-

---

[*] See the several predictions that the Jews, if they became obstinate in their idolatry and wickedness, should be sent again, or sold into Egypt for their punishment, (Deut. xxviii. 68 ; Jer. xliv. 7 ; Hos. viii. 13, ix. 3, xi. 35.)

[†] The whole multitude of the Jews that were destroyed during the entire seven years before this time amounts to 1,337,490

struction upon them, and soon afterward such a famine as destroyed them more suddenly. And that this city could contain so many people in it is manifest by that number of them which was taken under Cestius, who being desirous of informing Nero of the power of the city, who otherwise was disposed to contemn that nation, entreated the high priests, if the thing were possible, to take the number of their whole multude. So these high priests, upon the coming of their feast which is called the Passover, when they slay their sacrifices, from the ninth hour to the eleventh, but so that a company not less than ten belong to every sacrifice, (for it is not lawful for them to feast singly by themselves,) and many of us are twenty in a company, found the number of sacrifices was two hundred and fifty-six thousand five hundred; which, upon the allowance of no more than ten that feast together, amounts to two millions seven hundred thousand and two hundred persons that were pure and holy; for as to those that have the leprosy, or the gonorrhœa, or women that have their monthly courses, or such as are otherwise polluted, it is not lawful for them to be partakers of this sacrifice; nor indeed for any foreigners neither, who come hither to worship.

4. Now this vast multitude is indeed collected out of the remote places, but the entire nation was now shut up by fate as in a prison, and the Roman army encompassed the city when it was crowded with inhabitants. Accordingly, the multitude of those that therein perished exceeded all the destructions that either men or God ever brought upon the world; for to speak only of what was publicly known, the Romans slew some of them, some they carried captives, and others they made search for under ground, and when they found where they were, they broke up the ground and slew all they met with. There were also found slain there above two thousand persons, partly by their own hands, and partly by one another, but chiefly destroyed by the famine; but then, the ill savour of the dead bodies was most offensive to those that lighted upon them, insomuch that some were obliged to get away immediately, while others were so greedy of gain, that they would go in among the dead bodies that lay in heaps, and tread upon them; for a great deal of treasure was found in these caverns, and the hope of gain made every way of getting it to be esteemed lawful. Many also of those that had been put in prison by the tyrants were now brought out; for they did not leave off their barbarous cruelty at the very last: yet did God avenge himself upon them both, in a manner agreeable to justice. As for John, he wanted food, together with his brethren, in these caverns, and begged that the Romans would now give him their right hand for his security, which he had often proudly rejected before; but for Simon, he struggled hard with the distress he was in, till he was forced to surrender himself, as we shall relate hereafter; so he was reserved for the triumph, and to be then slain: as was John condemned to perpetual imprisonment: and now the Romans set fire to the extreme parts of the city, and burnt them down, and entirely demolished its walls.

CHAPTER X

THAT WHEREAS THE CITY OF JERUSALEM HAD BEEN FIVE TIMES TAKEN FORMERLY, THIS WAS THE SECOND TIME OF ITS DESOLATION. A BRIEF ACCOUNT OF ITS HISTORY

1. AND thus was Jerusalem taken, in the second year of the reign of Vespasian, on the eighth day of the month Gorpieus, [Elul.] It had been taken five * times before, though this was the second time of its desolation; for Shishak, the king of Egypt, and after him Antiochus, and after him Pompey, and after him Sosius and Herod took the city, but still preserved it; but before all these, the king of Babylon conquered it, and made it desolate, one thousand four hundred and sixty-eight years and six months after it was built. But he who first built it was a potent man among the Canaanites, and is in our tongue called [Melchisedek] the Righteous King, for such he really was; on which account he was [there] the first priest of God, and first built a temple, [there,] and called the city Jerusalem, which was formerly called Salem. However, David, the king of the Jews, ejected the Canaanites, and settled his own people therein. It was demolished entirely by the Babylonians, four hundred and seventy-seven years and six months after him. And from king David, who was the first of the Jews who reigned therein, to this destruction under Titus, were one thousand one hundred and seventy-nine years; but from its first building, till this last destruction, were two thousand one hundred and seventy-seven years; yet hath not its great antiquity, nor its vast riches, nor the diffusion of its nation over all the habitable earth, nor the greatness of the veneration paid to it on a religious account, been sufficient to preserve it from being destroyed. And thus ended the siege of Jerusalem.

---

* Besides these five, who had taken Jerusalem of old, Josephus, upon further recollection, reckons a sixth, (Antiq. b. xii. ch. i. sect 1,) who should have been here inserted in the second place—Ptolemy, the son of Lagus.

BOOK VII

FROM THE TAKING OF JERUSALEM BY TITUS, TO THE SEDITION OF THE JEWS AT CYRENE

CHAPTER I

HOW THE ENTIRE CITY OF JERUSALEM WAS DEMO-
LISHED, EXCEPTING THREE TOWERS; AND HOW
TITUS COMMENDED HIS SOLDIERS, IN A SPEECH
MADE TO THEM, AND DISTRIBUTED REWARDS TO
THEM, AND THEN DISMISSED MANY OF THEM

1. Now, as soon as the army had no more
people to slay or to plunder, because there remained none to be the objects of their fury, (for
they would not have spared any, had there remained any other such work to be done,) Cæsar
gave orders that they should now demolish the
entire city and temple, but should leave as many
of the towers standing as were of the greatest
eminency; that is, Phasaelus, and Hippicus,
and Mariamne, and so much of the wall as enclosed the city on the west side. This wall was
spared, in order to afford a camp for such as
were to lie in garrison; as were the towers also
spared, in order to demonstrate to posterity
what kind of city it was, and how well fortified,
which the Roman valour had subdued; but for
all the rest of the wall, it was so thoroughly laid
even with the ground by those that dug it up
to the foundation, that there was left nothing to
make those that came thither believe it had ever
been inhabited. This was the end which Jerusalem came to by the madness of those that
were for innovations; a city otherwise of great
magnificence, and of mighty fame among all
mankind.

2. But Cæsar resolved to leave there as a
guard the tenth legion, with certain troops of
horsemen, and companies of footmen. So, having entirely completed this war, he was desirous
to commend his whole army, on account of the
great exploits they had performed, and to bestow
proper rewards on such as had signalised themselves therein. He had therefore a great tribunal
made for him in the midst of the place where he
had formerly encamped, and stood upon it with
his principal commanders about him, and spake
so as to be heard by the whole army in the
manner following:—That he returned them
abundance of thanks for their good-will which
they had shewn to him; he commended them
for that ready obedience they had exhibited in
this whole war;—which obedience had appeared
in the many and great dangers they had courageously undergone; as also for that courage
they had shewn, and had thereby augmented of
themselves their country's power, and had made
it evident to all men that neither the multitude

of their enemies, nor the strength of their places,
nor the largeness of their cities, nor the rash
boldness and brutish rage of their antagonists,
were sufficient at any time to get clear of the
Roman valour, although some of them may
have fortune in many respects on their side.
He said further, that it was but reasonable for
them to put an end to this war, now it had
lasted so long, for they had nothing better to
wish for when they entered into it; and that
this happened more favourably for them, and
more for their glory, that all the Romans had
willingly accepted of those for their governors,
and the curators of their dominions, whom they
had chosen for them, and had sent into their
own country for that purpose, which still
continued under the management of those
whom they had pitched on, and were thankful
to them for pitching upon them. That accordingly, although he did both admire and tenderly regard them all, because he knew that
every one of them had gone as cheerfully about
their work as their abilities and opportunities
would give them leave, yet, he said, that he
would immediately bestow rewards and dignities on those that had fought the most bravely,
and with greater force, and had signalised their
conduct in the most glorious manner, and had
made his army more famous by their noble exploits: and that no one who had been willing to
take more pains than another should miss of a
just retribution for the same; for that he had
been exceedingly careful about this matter, and
that the more, because he had much rather reward the virtues of his fellow-soldiers than
punish such as had offended.

3. Hereupon Titus ordered those whose business it was, to read the list of all that had performed great exploits in this war, whom he
called to him by their names, and commended
them before the company, and rejoiced in them
in the same manner as a man would have rejoiced
in his own exploits. He also put on their heads
crowns of gold, and golden ornaments about their
necks, and gave them long spears of gold, and
ensigns that were made of silver, and removed
every one of them to a higher rank: and besides
this, he plentifully distributed among them, out
of the spoils and the other prey they had taken,
silver, and gold, and garments. So when they
had all these honours bestowed on them, according to his own appointment made to every one,
and he had wished all sorts of happiness to the
whole army, he came down, among the great
acclamations which were made to him, and then
betook himself to offer thank-offerings, [to the
gods,] and at once sacrificed a vast number of
oxen, that stood ready at the altars, and distributed them among the army to feast on; and
when he had stayed three days among the principal commanders, and so long feasted with them,
he sent away the rest of his army to the several
places where they would be every one best situ-

***⁎** This is the proper place for such as have closely
attended to these latter books of the War to peruse,
and that with equal attention, those distinct and plain
predictions of Jesus of Nazareth, in the Gospels thereto
relating, as compared with their exact completions in
Josephus's history; upon which completions, Dr Whitby
well observes, no small part of the evidence for the
truth of the Christian religion does depend.

ated; but permitted the tenth legion to stay, as a guard at Jerusalem, and did not send them away beyond Euphrates, where they had been before; and as he remembered that the twelfth legion had given way to the Jews, under Cestius their general, he expelled them out of all Syria, for they had lain formerly at Raphanea, and sent them away to a place called Melesine, near Euphrates, which is in the limits of Armenia and Cappadocia; he also thought fit that two of the legions should stay with him till he should go to Egypt. He then went down with his army to that Cesarea which lay by the sea-side, and there laid up the rest of his spoils in great quantities, and gave order that the captives should be kept there; for the winter season hindered him then from sailing into Italy.

CHAPTER II

HOW TITUS EXHIBITED ALL SORTS OF SHOWS AT CESAREA PHILLIPPI. CONCERNING SIMON THE TYRANT, HOW HE WAS TAKEN, AND RESERVED FOR THE TRIUMPH

1. Now at the same time that Titus Cæsar lay at the siege of Jerusalem, did Vespasian go on board a merchant-ship, and sailed from Alexandria to Rhodes; whence he sailed away in ships with three rows of oars; and as he touched at several cities that lay in his road, he was joyfully received by them all, and so passed over from Ionia into Greece; whence he set sail from Corcyra to the promontory of Iapyx, whence he took his journey by land. But as for Titus, he marched from that Cesarea which lay by the sea side, and came to that which is named Cesarea Phillippi, and stayed there a considerable time, and exhibited all sorts of shows there; and here a great number of the captives were destroyed, some being thrown to wild beasts, and others in multitudes forced to kill one another, as if they were enemies. And here it was that Titus was informed of the seizure of Simon, the son of Gioras, which was made after the manner following:—This Simon, during the siege of Jerusalem, was in the upper city; but when the Roman army were gotten within the walls, and were laying the city waste, he then took the most faithful of his friends with him, and among them some that were stone-cutters, with those iron tools that belonged to their occupation, and as great a quantity of provisions as would suffice them for a long time, and let himself and them all down into a certain subterraneous cavern that was not visible above ground. Now, so far as had been digged of old, they went onward along it without disturbance; but where they met with solid earth, they dug a mine under ground, and this in hopes that they should be able to proceed so far as to rise from under ground, in a safe place, and by that means escape; but when they came to make the experiments, they were disappointed of their hope; for the miners could make but small progress, and that with difficulty also: insomuch that their provisions, though they distributed them by measure, began to fail them. And now Simon, thinking he might be able to astonish and delude the Romans, put on a white frock, and buttoned upon him a purple cloak, and appeared out of the ground in the place where the temple had formerly been. At the first, indeed, those that saw him were greatly astonished, and stood still where they were; but afterward they came nearer to him, and asked him who he was.

Now Simon would not tell them, but bade them call for their captain; and when they ran to call him, Terentius Rufus,* who was left to command the army there, came to Simon, and learned of him the whole truth, and kept him in bonds, and let Cæsar know that he was taken. Thus did God bring this man to be punished for what bitter and savage tyranny he had exercised against his countrymen, by those who were his worst enemies; and this while he was not subdued by violence, but voluntarily delivered himself up to them to be punished, and that on the very same account that he had laid false accusations against many Jews, as if they were falling away to the Romans, and had barbarously slain them; for wicked actions do not escape the divine anger, nor is justice too weak to punish offenders, but in time overtakes those that transgress its laws, and inflicts its punishments upon the wicked in a manner so much more severe, as they expected to escape it on account of their not being punished immediately.† Simon was made sensible of this by falling under the indignation of the Romans. This rise of his out of the ground did also occasion the discovery of a great number of others of the seditious at that time, who had hidden themselves under ground; but for Simon, he was brought to Cæsar in bonds, when he was come back to that Cesarea which was on the sea side; who gave orders that he should be kept against that triumph which he was to celebrate at Rome upon this occasion.

CHAPTER III

HOW TITUS, UPON THE CELEBRATION OF HIS BROTHER'S AND FATHER'S BIRTHDAYS, HAD MANY OF THE JEWS SLAIN. CONCERNING THE DANGER THE JEWS WERE IN AT ANTIOCH, BY MEANS OF THE TRANSGRESSION AND IMPIETY OF ONE ANTIOCHUS, A JEW

1. WHILE Titus was at Cesarea, he solemnised the birthday of his brother [Domitian] after a splendid manner, and inflicted a great deal of the punishment intended for the Jews in honour of him: for the number of those that were now slain in fighting with the beasts, and were burnt, and fought with one another, exceeded two thousand five hundred. Yet did all this seem to the Romans, when they were thus destroying ten thousand several ways, to be a punishment beneath their deserts. After this, Cæsar came to Berytus,‡ which is a city of Phœnicia, and a Roman colony, and stayed there a longer time, and exhibited a still more pompous solemnity about his father's birthday, both in the magnificence of the shows, and in the other vast expenses he was at in his devices thereto belonging; so that a great multitude of the captives were here destroyed after the same manner as before.

2. It happened also about this time that the Jews who remained at Antioch were under accusations, and in danger of perishing, from the disturbances that were raised against them by

---

* This Terentius Rufus is the same person whom the Talmudists call *Turnus Rufus*; of whom they relate, that "he ploughed up Sion as a field, and made Jerusalem become as heaps, and the mountain of the house as the high places of a forest;" which was long before foretold by the prophet Micah, (iii. 12,) and quoted from him in the prophecies of Jeremiah, (xxvi. 18.)

† See Eccles. viii. 11.

‡ This Berytus was certainly a Roman colony, and has coins extant that witness the same.

SIMON EMERGING FROM CAVERN

the Antiochians, and this both on account of the slanders spread abroad at this time against them, and on account of what pranks they had played not long before; which I am obliged to describe without fail, though briefly, that I may the better connect my narration of future actions with those that went before.

3. For as the Jewish nation is widely dispersed over all the habitable earth among its inhabitants, so it is very much intermingled with Syria by reason of its neighbourhood, and had the greatest multitudes in Antioch by reason of the largeness of the city, wherein the kings, after Antiochus, had afforded them a habitation with the most undisturbed tranquillity; for though Antiochus, who was called Epiphanes, laid Jerusalem waste, and spoiled the temple, yet did those that succeeded him in the kingdom restore all the donations that were made of brass to the Jews of Antioch, and dedicated them to their synagogue; and granted them the enjoyment of equal privileges of citizens with the Greeks themselves; and as the succeeding kings treated them after the same manner, they both multiplied to a great number, and adorned their temple, [their synagogue,] gloriously by fine ornaments, and with great magnificence, in the use of what had been given them. They also made proselytes of a great many of the Greeks perpetually, and thereby, after a sort, brought them to be a portion of their own body. But about this time when the present war began, and Vespasian was newly sailed to Syria, and all men had taken up a great hatred against the Jews, then it was that a certain person, whose name was Antiochus, being one of the Jewish nation, and greatly respected on account of his father, who was governor of the Jews at Antioch,* came upon the theatre at a time when the people of Antioch were assembled together, and became an informer against his father; and accused both him and others that they had resolved to burn the whole city in one night; he also delivered up to them some Jews that were foreigners, as partners in their resolutions. When the people heard this they could not refrain their passion, but commanded that those who were delivered up to them should have fire brought to burn them: who were accordingly all burnt upon the theatre immediately. They did also fall violently upon the multitude of the Jews, as supposing that by punishing them suddenly they should save their own city. As for Antiochus, he aggravated the rage they were in, and thought to give them a demonstration of his own conversion, and his hatred of the Jewish customs, by sacrificing after the manner of the Greeks: he persuaded the rest also to compel them to do the same, because they would by that means discover who they were that had plotted against them, since they would not do so; and when the people of Antioch tried the experiment, some few complied; but those that would not do so were slain. As for Antiochus himself, he obtained soldiers from the Roman commander, and became a severe master over his own citizens, not permitting them to rest on the seventh day, but forcing them to do all that they usually did on other days; and to that degree of distress did he reduce them in this matter, that the rest of the seventh day was

dissolved not only at Antioch, but the same thing, which took thence its rise, was done in other cities also, in like manner, for some small time.

4. Now, after these misfortunes had happened to the Jews at Antioch, a second calamity befell them, the description of which when we were going about, we premised the account foregoing: for upon this accident, whereby the four-square market-place was burnt down, as well as the archives, and the place where the public records were preserved, and the royal palaces, (and it was not without difficulty that the fire was then put a stop to, which was likely, by the fury wherewith it was carried along, to have gone over the whole city,) Antiochus accused the Jews as the occasion of all the mischief that was done. Now this induced the people of Antioch, who were now under the immediate persuasion, by reason of the disorder they were in, that this calumny was true; and would have been under the same persuasion, even though they had not borne an ill-will to the Jews before, to believe this man's accusation, especially when they considered what had been done before; and this to such a degree, that they all fell violently upon those that were accused; and this, like madmen, in a very furious rage also, even as if they had seen the Jews in a manner setting fire themselves to the city; nor was it without difficulty that one Cneius Collegas, the legate, could prevail with them to permit the affairs to be laid before Cæsar; for as to Cesennius Petus, the president of Syria, Vespasian had already sent him away; and so it happened, that he was not yet come back thither. But when Collegas had made a careful inquiry into the matter, he found out the truth, and that not one of those Jews that were accused by Antiochus had any hand in it; but that all was done by some vile persons greatly in debt, who supposed that if they could once set fire to the market-place, and burn the public records, they should have no further demands made upon them. So the Jews were under great disorder and terror, in the uncertain expectations of what would be the upshot of those accusations against them.

CHAPTER IV

HOW VESPASIAN WAS RECEIVED AT ROME; AS ALSO HOW THE GERMANS REVOLTED FROM THE ROMANS, BUT WERE SUBDUED. THAT THE SAMARITANS OVERRAN MYSIA, BUT WERE COMPELLED TO RETURN TO THEIR OWN COUNTRY AGAIN

1. AND now Titus Cæsar, upon the news that was brought him concerning his father, that his coming was much desired by all the Italian cities, and that Rome especially received him with great alacrity and splendour, betook himself to rejoicing and pleasures to a great degree, as now freed from the solicitude he had been under, after the most agreeable manner. For all men that were in Italy shewed their respects to him in their minds, before he came thither, as if he were already come, as esteeming the very expectation they had of him to be his real presence on account of the great desires they had to see him, and because the good-will they bore him was entirely free and unconstrained; for it was a desirable thing to the senate, who well remembered the calamities they had undergone in the late changes of their governors, to receive a governor who was adorned with the

---

* The Jews at Antioch and Alexandria had allowed them, both by the Macedonians, and afterwards by the Romans, a governor of their own. He was called sometimes barely "governor," sometimes "ethnarch," and [at Alexandria] "alabarch." They had the like governor or governors allowed them at Babylon under their captivity there.

gravity of old age, and with the highest skill in the actions of war, whose advancement would be, as they knew, for nothing else but for the preservation of those that were to be governed. Moreover, the people had been so harassed by their civil miseries, that they were still more earnest for his coming immediately, as supposing they should then be firmly delivered from their calamities, and believed they should then recover their secure tranquillity and prosperity; and for the soldiery, they had the principal regard to him, for they were chiefly apprised of his great exploits in war; and since they had experienced the want of skill and want of courage in other commanders, they were very desirous to be freed from that great shame they had undergone by their means, and heartily wished to receive such a prince as might be a security and an ornament to them; and as this good-will to Vespasian was universal, those that enjoyed any remarkable dignities could not have patience enough to stay at Rome, but made haste to meet him at a very great distance from it; nay, indeed, none of the rest could endure the delay of seeing him, but did all pour out of the city in such crowds, and were so universally possessed with the opinion that it was easier and better for them to go out than to stay there, that this was the very first time that the city joyfully perceived itself almost empty of its citizens; for those that stayed within were fewer than those that went out; but as soon as the news was come that he was hard by, and those that had met him at first related with what good humour he received every one that came to him, then it was that the whole multitude that had remained in the city, with their wives and children, came into the road, and waited for him there; and for those whom he passed by, they made all sorts of acclamations on account of the joy they had to see him, and the pleasantness of his countenance, and styled him their Benefactor and Saviour, and the only person who was worthy to be ruler of the city of Rome; and now the city was like a temple, full of garlands and sweet odours; nor was it easy for him to come to the royal palace for the multitude of people that stood about him, where yet at last he performed his sacrifices of thanksgiving to his household gods for his safe return to the city. The multitude did also betake themselves to feasting; which feasts and drink-offerings they celebrated by their tribes, and their families, and their neighbourhoods, and still prayed to God to grant that Vespasian, his sons, and all their posterity, might continue in the Roman government for a very long time, and that his dominion might be preserved from all opposition. And this was the manner in which Rome so joyfully received Vespasian, and thence grew immediately into a state of great prosperity.

2. But before this time, and while Vespasian was about Alexandria, and Titus was lying at the siege of Jerusalem, a great multitude of the Germans were in commotion, and tended to rebellion; and as the Gauls in their neighbourhood joined with them, they conspired together, and had thereby great hopes of success, and that they should free themselves from the dominion of the Romans. The motives that induced the Germans to this attempt for a revolt, and for beginning the war, were these:—In the first place, the nature, [of the people,] which was destitute of just reasonings, and ready to throw themselves rashly into danger upon small hopes; in the next place, the hatred they bore to those that were their governors, while their nation had never been conscious of subjection to any

but to the Romans, and that by compulsion only. Besides these motives, it was the opportunity that now offered itself which above all the rest prevailed with them so to do; for when they saw the Roman government in a great internal disorder, by the continual changes of its rulers, and understood that every part of the habitable earth under them was in an unsettled and tottering condition, they thought this was the best opportunity that could afford itself for themselves to make a sedition, when the state of the Romans was so ill. Classicus* also, and Civilis, two of their commanders, puffed them up with such hopes. These had for a long time been openly desirous of such an innovation, and were induced by the present opportunity to venture upon the declaration of their sentiments; the multitude was also ready; and when these men told them of what they intended to attempt, that news was gladly received by them. So when a great part of the Germans had agreed to rebel, and the rest were no better disposed, Vespasian, as guided by divine Providence, sent letters to Petilius Cerealis, who had formerly had the command of Germany, whereby he declared him to have the dignity of consul, and commanded him to take upon him the government of Britain; so he went whither he was ordered to go, and when he was informed of the revolt of the Germans, he fell upon them as soon as they were gotten together, and put his army in battle-array, and slew a great multitude of them in the fight, and forced them to leave off their madness, and to grow wiser; nay, had he not fallen thus suddenly upon them on the place, it had not been long ere they would however have been brought to punishment; for as soon as ever the news of their revolt was come to Rome, and Cæsar Domitian was made acquainted with it, he made no delay even at that his age, when he was exceeding young, but undertook this weighty affair. He had a courageous mind, from his father, and had made greater improvements than belonged to such an age: accordingly, he marched against the barbarians immediately; whereupon their hearts failed them at the rumour of his approach, and they submitted themselves to him with fear, and thought it a happy thing that they were brought under their old yoke again without suffering any further mischiefs. When, therefore, Domitian had settled all the affairs of Gaul in such good order that it would not be easily put into disorder any more, he returned to Rome with honour and glory, as having performed such exploits as were above his own age, and worthy of such a father.

3. At the very same time with the fore-mentioned revolt of the Germans did the bold attempt of the Scythians against the Romans occur; for those Scythians who are called Sarmatians, being a very numerous people, transported themselves over the Danube into Mysia, without being perceived; after which, by their violence, and entirely unexpected assault, they slew a great many of the Romans that guarded the frontiers; and as the consular legate Fonteius Agrippa came to meet them, and fought courageously against them, he was slain by them. They then overran all the region that had been subject to him, tearing and rending everything that fell in their way; but when Vespasian was in-

* This Classicus, and Civilis, and Cerealis, are names well known in Tacitus: the two former as moving sedition against the Romans, and the last as sent to repress them by Vespasian, just as they are here described by Josephus; which is the case also of Fonteius Agrippa and Rubrius Gallus, in sect 3.

formed of what had happened, and how Mysia was laid waste, he sent away Rubrius Gallus to punish these Sarmatians; by whose means many of them perished in the battles he fought against them, and that part which escaped fled with fear to their own country. So when this general had put an end to the war, he provided for the future security of the country also; for he placed more and more numerous garrisons in the place, till he made it altogether impossible for the barbarians to pass over the river any more; and thus had this war in Mysia a sudden conclusion.

CHAPTER V

CONCERNING THE SABBATIC RIVER WHICH TITUS SAW AS HE WAS JOURNEYING THROUGH SYRIA; AND HOW THE PEOPLE OF ANTIOCH CAME WITH A PETITION TO TITUS AGAINST THE JEWS, BUT WERE REJECTED BY HIM; AS ALSO CONCERNING TITUS'S AND VESPASIAN'S TRIUMPH

1. Now Titus Cæsar tarried some time at Berytus, as we told you before. He thence removed, and exhibited magnificent shows in all those cities of Syria through which he went, and made use of the captive Jews as public instances of the destruction of that nation. He then saw a river as he went along, of such a nature as deserves to be recorded in history; it runs in the middle between Arcea, belonging to Agrippa's kingdom, and Raphanea. It hath somewhat very peculiar in it; for when it runs, its current is strong, and has plenty of water; after which its springs fail for six days together, and leave its channel dry, as any one may see; after which days it runs on the seventh day as it did before, and as though it had undergone no change at all: it hath also been observed to keep this order perpetually and exactly; whence it is that they call it the Sabbatic River,—that name being taken from the sacred seventh day among the Jews.

2. But when the people of Antioch were informed that Titus was approaching, they were so glad at it, that they could not keep within their walls, but hasted away to give him the meeting; nay, they proceeded as far as thirty furlongs, and more, with that intention. These were not the men only, but a multitude of women also with their children did the same; and when they saw him coming up to them they stood on both sides of the way, and stretched out their right hands, saluting him, and making all sorts of acclamations to him, and turned back together with him. They also, among all the acclamations they made to him, besought him, all the way they went, to eject the Jews out of their city; yet did not Titus at all yield to this their petition, but gave them the bare hearing of it quietly. However, the Jews were in a great deal of terrible fear, under the uncertainty they were in what his opinion was, and what he would do to them: for Titus did not stay at Antioch, but continued his progress immediately to Zeugma, which lies upon the Euphrates, whither came to him messengers from Vologeses, king of Parthia, and brought him a crown of gold upon the victory he had gained over the Jews; which he accepted of, and feasted the king's messengers, and then came back to Antioch. And when the senate and people of Antioch earnestly entreated him to come upon their theatre, where their whole multitude was assembled, and expected him, he complied with great humanity; but when they pressed him with much earnestness, and continually begged of him that he would eject the Jews out of their city, he gave them this very pertinent answer:— "How can this be done, since that country of theirs, whither the Jews must be obliged then to retire, is destroyed, and no place will receive them besides?" Whereupon the people of Antioch, when they had failed of success in this their first request, made him a second; for they desired that he would order those tables of brass to be removed, on which the Jews' privileges were engraven. However, Titus would not grant that neither, but permitted the Jews of Antioch to continue to enjoy the very same privileges in that city which they had before, and then departed for Egypt; and as he came to Jerusalem in his progress, and compared the melancholy condition he saw it then in with the ancient glory of the city, and called to mind the greatness of its present ruins, as well as its ancient splendour, he could not but pity the destruction of the city,—so far was he from boasting that so great and goodly a city as that was had been by him taken by force; nay, he frequently cursed those that had been the authors of their revolt, and had brought such a punishment upon the city; insomuch that it only appeared that he did not desire that such a calamity as this punishment of theirs amounted to should be a demonstration of his courage. Yet was there no small quantity of the riches that had been in that city still found among its ruins, a great deal of which the Romans dug up; but the greatest part was discovered by those who were captives, and so they carried it away— I mean the gold and the silver, and the rest of that most precious furniture which the Jews had, and which the owners had treasured up under ground, against the uncertain fortunes of war.

3. So Titus took the journey he intended into Egypt, and passed over the desert very suddenly, and came to Alexandria, and took up a resolution to go to Rome by sea. And as he was accompanied by two legions, he sent each of them again to the places whence they had before come; the fifth he sent to Mysia; and the fifteenth to Pannonia: as for the leaders of the captives, Simon and John, with the other seven hundred men, whom he had selected out of the rest as being eminently tall and handsome of body, he gave order that they should be soon carried to Italy, as resolving to produce them in his triumph. So when he had had a prosperous voyage to his mind, the city of Rome behaved itself in his reception, and their meeting him at a distance, as it did in the case of his father. But what made the most splendid appearance in Titus's opinion was, when his father met him, and received him; but still the multitude of the citizens conceived the greatest joy when they saw them all three together,* as they did at this time: nor were many days overpast when they determined to have but one triumph, that should be common to both of them, on account of the glorious exploits they had performed, although the senate had decreed each of them a separate triumph by himself. So when notice had been given beforehand of the day appointed for this pompous solemnity to be made, on account of their victories, not one of the immense multitude was left in the city, but everybody went out so far as to gain only a station where they might stand, and left only such a passage as was necessary for those that were to be seen to go along it.

---

* Vespasian and his two sons, Titus and Domitian.

4. Now, all the soldiery marched out beforehand by companies, and in their several ranks, under their several commanders, and in the night-time, and were about the gates, not of the upper palaces, but those near the temple of Isis; for there it was that the emperors had rested the foregoing night. And as soon as ever it was day, Vespasian and Titus came out crowned with laurel, and clothed in those ancient purple habits which were proper to their family, and then went as far as Octavian's Walks; for there it was that the senate, and the principal rulers, and those that had been recorded as of the equestrian order, waited for them. Now a tribunal had been erected before the cloisters, and ivory chairs had been set upon it, when they came and sat down upon them. Whereupon the soldiery made an acclamation of joy to them immediately, and all gave them attestations of their valour; while they were themselves without their arms, and only in their silken garments, and crowned with laurel: then Vespasian accepted of these shouts of theirs; but while they were still disposed to go on in such acclamations, he gave them a signal of silence. And when everybody entirely held their peace, he stood up, and covering the greatest part of his head with his cloak, he put up the accustomed solemn prayers; the like prayers did Titus put up also; after which prayers Vespasian made a short speech to all the people, and then sent away the soldiers to a dinner prepared for them by the emperors. Then did he retire to that gate which was called the Gate of the Pomp, because pompous shows do always go through that gate, there it was that they tasted some food, and when they had put on their triumphal garments, and had offered sacrifices to the gods that were placed at the gate, they sent the triumph forward, and marched through the theatres, that they might be the more easily seen by the multitude.

5. Now, it is impossible to describe the multitude of the shows as they deserve, and the magnificence of them all; such indeed as man could not easily think of as performed either by the labour of workmen, or the variety of riches, or the rarities of nature; for almost all such curiosities as the most happy men ever get by piece-meal were here heaped one upon another, and those both admirable and costly in their nature; and all brought together on that day, demonstrated the vastness of the dominions of the Romans; for there was here to be seen a mighty quantity of silver, and gold, and ivory, contrived into all sorts of things, and did not appear as carried along in pompous show only, but, as a man may say, running along like a river. Some parts were composed of the rarest purple hangings, and so carried along; and others accurately represented to the life what was embroidered by the arts of the Babylonians. There were also precious stones that were transparent, some set in crowns of gold, and some in other ouches, as the workmen pleased; and of these such a vast number brought, that we could not but thence learn how vainly we imagined any of them to be rarities. The images of the gods were also carried, being as well wonderful for their largeness, as made very artificially, and with great skill of the workmen; nor were any of these images of any other than very costly materials; and many species of animals were brought, every one in their own natural ornaments. The men also who brought every one of these shows were great multitudes, and adorned with purple garments, all over interwoven with gold; those that were chosen for carrying these pompous shows, having also about them such magnificent ornaments as were both

extraordinary and surprising. Besides these, one might see that even the great number of the captives was not unadorned, while the variety that was in their garments, and their fine texture, concealed from the sight the deformity of their bodies. But what afforded the greatest surprise of all, was the structure of the pageants that were borne along; for indeed he that met them could not but be afraid that the bearers would not be able firmly enough to support them, such was their magnitude; for many of them were so made, that they were on three or even four stories, one above another. The magnificence also of their structure afforded one both pleasure and surprise; for upon many of them were laid carpets of gold. There was also wrought gold and ivory fastened about them all; and many resemblances of the war, and those in several ways, and variety of contrivances, affording a most lively portraiture of itself; for there was to be seen a happy country laid waste, and entire squadrons of enemies slain; while some of them ran away, and some were carried into captivity; with walls of great altitude and magnitude overthrown and ruined by machines; with the strongest fortifications taken, and the walls of most populous cities upon the tops of hills seized on, and an army pouring itself within the walls; as also every place full of slaughter, and supplications of the enemies, when they were no longer able to lift up their hands in way of opposition. Fire also sent upon temples was here represented, and houses overthrown and falling upon their owners: rivers also, after they came out of a large and melancholy desert, ran down, not into a land cultivated, nor as drink for men, or for cattle, but through a land still on fire upon every side; for the Jews related that such a thing they had undergone during this war. Now the workmanship of these representations was so magnificent and lively in the construction of the things, that it exhibited what had been done to such as did not see it, as if they had been there really present. On the top of every one of these pageants was placed the commander of the city that was taken, and the manner wherein he was taken. Moreover, there followed those pageants a great number of ships; and for the other spoils, they were carried in great plenty. But for those that were taken in the temple of Jerusalem, they made the greatest figure of them all; that is the golden table, of the weight of many talents; the candlestick also, that was made of gold, though its construction were now changed from that which we made use of; for its middle shaft was fixed upon a basis, and the small branches were produced out of it to a great length, having the likeness of a trident in their position, and had every one a socket made of brass for a lamp at the tops of them. These lamps were in number seven, and represented the dignity of the number seven among the Jews; and the last of all the spoils, was carried the Law of the Jews. After these spoils passed by a great many men, carrying the images of Victory, whose structure was entirely either of ivory or of gold. After which Vespasian marched in the first place, and Titus followed him; Domitian also rode along with them, and made a glorious appearance, and rode on a horse that was worthy of admiration.

6. Now, the last part of this pompous show was at the temple of Jupiter Capitolinus, whither when they were come, they stood still; for it was the Romans' ancient custom to stay till somebody brought the news that the general of the enemy was slain. This general was Simon,

the son of Gioras, who had then been led in this triumph among the captives; a rope had also been put upon his head, and he had been drawn into a proper place in the forum, and had withal been tormented by those that drew him along; and the law of the Romans required, that malefactors condemned to die should be slain there. Accordingly, when it was related that there was an end of him, and all the people had set up a shout for joy, they then began to offer those sacrifices which they had consecrated, in the prayers used in such solemnities; which when they had finished, they went away to the palace. And as for some of the spectators, the emperors entertained them at their own feast; and for all the rest there were noble preparations made for their feasting at home; for this was a festival-day to the city of Rome, as celebrated for the victory obtained by their army over their enemies, for the end that was now put to their civil miseries, and for the commencement of their hopes of future prosperity and happiness.

7. After these triumphs were over, and after the affairs of the Romans were settled on the surest foundations, Vespasian resolved to build a temple to Peace, which he finished in so short a time, and in so glorious a manner, as was beyond all human expectation and opinion: for he having now by Providence a vast quantity of wealth, besides what he had formerly gained in his other exploits, he had this temple adorned with pictures and statues; for in this temple were collected and deposited all such rarities as men aforetime used to wander all over the habitable world to see, when they had a desire to see them one after another: he also laid up therein, as ensigns of his glory, those golden vessels and instruments that were taken out of the Jewish temple. But still he gave order that they should lay up their law, and the purple veils of the holy place, in the royal palace itself, and keep them there.

CHAPTER VI

CONCERNING THE CITY CALLED MACHÆRUS; AND HOW LUCILIUS BASSUS TOOK THE CITADEL, AND OTHER PLACES

1. Now, Lucilius Bassus was sent as legate into Judea, and there he received the army from Cerealis Vitellius, and took that citadel which was in Herodium, together with the garrison that was in it; after which he got together all the soldiery that was there, (which was a large body, but dispersed into several parties,) with the tenth legion, and resolved to make war upon Machærus; for it was highly necessary that this citadel should be demolished, lest it might be a means of drawing away many into a rebellion, by reason of its strength; for the nature of the place was very capable of affording the surest hopes of safety to those who possessed it, as well as delay and fear to those that should attack it; for what was walled in was itself a very rocky hill, elevated to a very great height; which circumstance alone made it very hard to be subdued. It was also so contrived by nature, that it could not be easily ascended; for it is, as it were, ditched about with such valleys on all sides, and to such a depth, that the eye cannot reach their bottoms, and such as are not easily to be passed over, and even such as it is impossible to fill up with earth; for that valley which cuts it on the west, extends to threescore fur-

longs, and did not end till it came to the lake Asphaltitis; on the same side it was also that Machærus had the tallest top of its hill elevated above the rest. But then for the valleys that lay on the north and south sides, although they are not so large as that already described, yet is it in like manner an impracticable thing to think of getting over them; and for the valley that lies on the east side, its depth is found to be no less than a hundred cubits. It extends as far as a mountain that lies over against Machærus, with which it is bounded.

2. Now when Alexander [Janneus,] the king of the Jews, observed the nature of this place, he was the first to build a citadel here, which afterwards was demolished by Gabinius, when he made war against Aristobulus; but when Herod came to be king, he thought the place to be worthy of the utmost regard, and of being built upon in the firmest manner, and this especially because it lay so near to Arabia; for it is seated in a convenient place on that account, and hath a prospect toward that country; he therefore surrounded a large space of ground with walls and towers, and built a city there, out of which city there was a way that led up to the very citadel itself on the top of the mountain; nay, more than this, he built a wall round that top of the hill, and erected towers at the corners, of a hundred and sixty cubits high; in the middle of which place he built a palace, after a magnificent manner, wherein were large and beautiful edifices. He also made a great many reservoirs for the reception of water, that there might be plenty of it ready for all uses, and those in the properest places that were afforded him there. Thus did he, as it were, contend with the nature of the place, that he might exceed its natural strength and security (which yet itself rendered it hard to be taken) by those fortifications which were made by the hands of men. Moreover, he put a large quantity of darts and other machines of war into it, and contrived to get everything thither that might any way contribute to its inhabitants' security, under the longest siege possible.

3. Now, within this place there grew a sort of rue, that deserves our wonder on account of its largeness, for it was no way inferior to any figtree whatsoever, either in height or in thickness; and the report is, that it had lasted ever since the times of Herod, and would probably have lasted much longer, had it not been cut down by those Jews who took possession of the place afterward: but still in that valley which encompasses the city on the north side, there is a certain place called Baaras, which produces a root of the same name with itself; its colour is like to that of flame, and towards the evening it sends out a certain ray like lightning: it is not easily taken by such as would do it, but recedes from their hands, nor will yield itself to be taken quietly, until either the urine of a woman, or her menstrual blood, be poured upon it; nay, even then it is certain death to those that touch it, unless any one take and hang the root itself down from his hand, and so carry it away. It may also be taken another way, without danger, which is this: they dig a trench quite round about it, till the hidden part of the root be very small, they then tie a dog to it, and when the dog tries hard to follow him that tied him, this root is easily plucked up, but the dog dies immediately, as if it were instead of the man that would take the plant away; nor after this need any one be afraid of taking it into their hands. Yet, after all this pains in getting it, it is only valuable on account of one virtue it hath,

that if it only be brought to sick persons, it quickly drives away those called Demons, which are no other than the spirits of the wicked, which enter into men that are alive, and kill them, unless they can obtain some help against them. Here are also fountains of hot water, that flow out of this place, which have a very different taste one from the other; for some of them are bitter, and others of them are plainly sweet. Here are also many eruptions of cold waters, and this not only in the places that lie lower, and have their fountains near one another, but, what is still more wonderful, here is to be seen a certain cave hard by, whose cavity is not deep, but it is covered over by a rock that is prominent: above this rock there stand up two [hills or] breasts, as it were, but a little distant one from another, the one of which sends out a fountain that is very cold, and the other sends out one that is very hot; which waters, when they are mingled together, compose a most pleasant bath; they are medicinal indeed for other maladies, but especially good for strengthening the nerves. This place has in it also mines of sulphur and alum.

4. Now, when Bassus had taken a full view of this place, he resolved to besiege it by filling up the valley that lay on the east side; so he fell hard to work, and took great pains to raise his banks as soon as possible, and by that means to render the siege easy. As for the Jews that were caught in this place, they separated themselves from the strangers that were with them, and they forced those strangers, as an otherwise useless multitude, to stay in the lower part of the city, and undergo the principal dangers, while they themselves seized on the upper citadel, and held it, and this both on account of its strength, and to provide for their own safety. They also supposed they might obtain their pardon, in case they should at last surrender the citadel. However, they were willing to make trial, in the first place, whether the hopes they had of avoiding a siege would come to any-thing; with which intention they made sallies every day, and fought with those that met them; in which conflicts they were many of them slain, as they therein slew many of the Romans; but still it was the opportunities that presented themselves which chiefly gained both sides their victories; these were gained by the Jews, when they fell upon the Romans as they were off their guard; but by the Romans, when, upon the others' sallies against their banks, they foresaw their coming, and were upon their guard when they received them; but the conclusion of the siege did not depend upon these bickerings, but a certain surprising accident, relating to what was done in this siege, forced the Jews to surrender the citadel. There was a certain young man among the besieged, of great bold-ness, and very active of his hand, his name was Eleazar; he greatly signalized himself in those sallies, and encouraged the Jews to go out in great numbers, in order to hinder the raising of the banks, and did the Romans a vast deal of mischief when they came to fighting: he so managed matters, that those who sallied out, made their attacks easily, and returned back without danger, and this by still bringing up the rear himself. Now, it happened, that on a certain time when the fight was over, and both sides were parted, and retired home, he, in way of contempt of the enemy, and thinking that none of them would begin the fight again at that time, stayed without the gates, and talked with those that were upon the wall, and his mind was wholly intent upon what they said. Now, a cer-

tain person belonging to the Roman camp, whose name was Rufus, by birth an Egyptian, ran upon him suddenly, when nobody expected such a thing, and carried him off, with his armour itself; while, in the meantime, those that saw it from the wall, were under such an amazement, that Rufus prevented their assistance, and carried Eleazar to the Roman camp. So the general of the Romans ordered that he should be taken up naked, set before the city to be seen, and sorely whipped before their eyes. Upon this sad accident that befell the young man, the Jews were terribly confounded, and the city, with one voice, sorely lamented him, and the mourning proved greater than could well be sup-posed, upon the calamity of a single person. When Bassus perceived that, he began to think of using a stratagem against the enemy, and was desirous to aggravate their grief, in order to pre-vail with them to surrender the city for the pre-servation of that man. Nor did he fail of his hope; for he commanded them to set up a cross, as if he were just going to hang Eleazar upon it immediately: the sight of this occasioned a sore grief among those that were in the citadel, and they groaned vehemently, and cried out, that they could not bear to see him thus destroyed. Whereupon Eleazar besought them not to dis-regard him now he was going to suffer a most miserable death, and exhorted them to save themselves, by yielding to the Roman power and good fortune, since all other people were now conquered by them. These men were greatly moved with what he said, there being also many within the city that interceded for him, because he was of an eminent and very numerous family; so they now yielded to their passion of commise-ration, contrary to their usual custom. Accord-ingly they sent out immediately certain mes-sengers, and treated with the Romans, in order to a surrender of the citadel to them, and de-sired that they might be permitted to go away, and take Eleazar along with them. Then did the Romans and their general accept of these terms; while the multitude of strangers that were in the lower part of the city, hearing of the agreement that was made by the Jews for themselves alone, were resolved to fly away privately in the night-time; but as soon as they had opened their gates, those that had come to terms with Bassus told him of it; whether it were that they envied the others' deliverance, or whether it were done out of fear, lest an occasion should be taken against them upon their escape, is uncertain. The most courageous, therefore, of those men that went out, prevented the enemy, and got away, and fled for it; but for those men that were caught within, they were slain, to the number of one thousand seven hundred, as were the women and children made slaves; but as Bassus thought he must perform the covenant he had made with those that had surrendered the citadel, he let them go, and re-stored Eleazar to them.

5. When Bassus had settled these affairs, he marched hastily to the forest of Jarden, as it is called; for he had heard that a great many of those that had fled from Jerusalem and Macherus formerly, were there gotten together. When he was therefore come to the place, and understood that the former news was no mistake, he, in the first place, surrounded the whole place with his horsemen, that such of the Jews as had boldness enough to try to break through, might have no way possible for escaping, by reason of the situa-tion of these horsemen; and for the footmen, he ordered them to cut down the trees that were in the wood whither they were fled. So the Jews

were under a necessity of performing some glorious exploit, and of greatly exposing themselves in a battle, since they might perhaps thereby escape. So they made a general attack, and with a great shout fell upon those that surrounded them, who received them with great courage; and so while the one side fought desperately, and the others would not yield, the fight was prolonged on that account. But the event of the battle did not answer the expectation of the assailants; for so it happened, that no more than twelve fell on the Roman side, with a few that were wounded; but not one of the Jews escaped out of this battle for they were all killed, being in the whole not fewer in number than three thousand, together with Judas the son of Jairus, their general; concerning whom we have before spoken, that he had been captain of a certain band at the siege of Jerusalem, and by going down into a certain vault under ground, had privately made his escape.

6. About the same time it was that Cæsar sent a letter to Bassus, and to Liberius Maximus, who was the procurator [of Judea,] and gave order that all Judea should be exposed to sale;* for he did not found any city there, but reserved the country for himself. However he assigned a place for eight hundred men only, whom he had dismissed from his army, which he gave them for their habitation; it is called Emmaus,† and is distant from Jerusalem threescore furlongs. He also laid a tribute upon the Jews wheresoever they were, and enjoined every one of them to bring two drachmæ every year into the Capitol, as they used to pay the same to the temple at Jerusalem. And this was the state of the Jewish affairs at this time.

CHAPTER VII

CONCERNING THE CALAMITY THAT BEFELL ANTIOCHUS, KING OF COMMAGENE. AS ALSO CONCERNING THE ALANS, AND WHAT GREAT MISCHIEF THEY DID TO THE MEDES AND ARMENIANS

1. AND now, in the fourth year of the reign of Vespasian, it came to pass, that Antiochus, the king of Commagene, with all his family, fell into very great calamities. The occasion was this:— Cesennius Petus, who was president of Syria at this time, whether it were done out of regard to truth, or whether out of hatred to Antiochus (for which was the real motive was never thoroughly discovered,) sent an epistle to Cæsar, and therein told him that Antiochus, with his son Epiphanes, had resolved to rebel against the Romans, and had made a league with the king of Parthia to that purpose: that it was therefore fit to prevent them, lest they prevent us, and begin such a war as may cause a general disturbance in the Roman empire. Now Cæsar was disposed to take some care about the matter, since this discovery was made; for the neighbourhood of the kingdoms made the affair worthy of greater regard; for Samosata, the capital of Commagene, lies upon Euphrates, and,

upon any such design, could affor[d] [pas]sage over it to the Parthians a[nd] afford them a secure reception. [...] accordingly believed, and had auth[orized] him of doing what he should think p[roper in this] case; so he set about it without dela[y, and fell] upon Commagene before Antiochu[s and his] people had the least expectation of his coming: he had with him the tenth legion, as also some cohorts and troops of horsemen. These kings also came to his assistance:—Aristobulus, king of the country called Chalcidene, and Sohemus, who was called king of Emesa: nor was there any opposition made to his forces when they entered the kingdom; for no one of that country would so much as lift up his hand against them. When Antiochus heard this unexpected news, he could not think in the least of making war with the Romans, but determined to leave his whole kingdom in the state wherein it now was, and to retire privately, with his wife and children, as thinking thereby to demonstrate himself to the Romans to be innocent as to the accusation laid against him. So he went away from that city as far as a hundred and twenty furlongs, into a plain, and there pitched his tents.

2. Petus then sent some of his men to seize upon Samosata, and by their means took possession of that city, while he went himself to attack Antiochus with the rest of his army. However, the king was not prevailed upon by the distress he was in to do anything in the way of war against the Romans, but bemoaned his own hard fate, and endured with patience what he was not able to prevent. But his sons, who were young and unexperienced in war, but of strong bodies, were not easily induced to bear this calamity without fighting. Epiphanes, therefore, and Callineius betook themselves to military force; and as the battle was a sore one, and lasted all the day long, they shewed their own valour in a remarkable manner; and nothing but the approach of night put a period thereto, and that without any diminution of their forces; yet would not Antiochus, upon this conclusion of the fight, continue there by any means, but took his wife and his daughters, and fled away with them to Cilicia; and, by so doing, quite discouraged the minds of his own soldiers. Accordingly, they revolted, and went over to the Romans, out of the despair they were in of his keeping the kingdom, and his case was looked upon by all as quite desperate. It was therefore necessary that Epiphanes and his soldiers should get clear of their enemies before they became entirely destitute of any confederates; nor were there any more than ten horsemen with him, who passed with him over Euphrates, whence they went undisturbed to Vologoses, the king of Parthia, where they were not disregarded, as fugitives; but had the same respect paid them as if they had retained their ancient prosperity.

3. Now when Antiochus was come to Tarsus in Cilicia, Petus ordered a centurion to go to him, and send him in bonds to Rome. However, Vespasian could not endure to have a king brought to him in that manner, but thought it fit rather to have a regard to the ancient friendship that had been between them, than to preserve an inexorable anger upon pretence of this war. Accordingly, he gave orders that they should take off his bonds, while he was still upon the road, and that he should not come to Rome, but should now go and live at Lacedemon; he also gave him large revenues, that he might not only live in plenty, but like a king also. When Epiphanes, who was before in great fear for his

---

* It is very remarkable that Titus did not people this now desolate country of Judea, but ordered it to be all sold; nor indeed is it properly peopled at this day, but lies ready for its old inhabitants the Jews, at their future restoration.

† This city of Emmaus which was the place of the government of Julius Africanus in the beginning of the third century, and which he then procured to be rebuilt, and after which rebuilding it was called Nicopolis, is entirely different from that Emmaus which is mentioned by St. Luke.

...her, was informed of this, their minds were freed from that great and almost incurable concern they had been under. He also hoped that Cæsar would be reconciled to them, upon the intercession of Vologoses; for although he lived in plenty, he knew not how to bear living out of the Roman empire. So Cæsar gave him leave, after an obliging manner, and he came to Rome; and as his father came quickly to him from Lacedemon, he had all sorts of respect paid him there, and there he remained.

4. Now, there was a nation of the Alans inhabiting at the lake Meotis. This nation about this time laid a design of falling upon Media and the parts beyond it, in order to plunder them; with which intention they treated with the king of Hyrcania; for he was master of that passage which king Alexander [the Great] shut up with iron gates. This king gave them leave to come through them; so they came in great multitudes, and fell upon the Medes unexpectedly, and plundered their country, which they found full of people, and replenished with abundance of cattle, while nobody durst make any resistance against them; for Pacorus, the king of the country, had fled away for fear, into places where they could not easily come at him, and had yielded up everything he had to them, and had only saved his wife and his concubines from them, and that with difficulty also, after they had been made captives, by giving them a hundred talents for their ransom. These Alans therefore plundered the country without opposition, and with great ease, and then proceeded as far as Armenia, laying all waste before them. Now, Tiridates was king of that country, who met them, and fought them, but had like to have been taken alive in the battle; for a certain man threw a net over him from a great distance, and had soon drawn him to him, unless he had immediately cut the cord with his sword, and ran away and prevented it. So the Alans, being still more provoked by this sight, laid waste the country, and drove a great multitude of the men, and a great quantity of the other prey they had gotten out of both kingdoms, along with them, and then retreated back to their own country.

CHAPTER VIII

CONCERNING MASADA AND THOSE SICARII WHO KEPT IT; AND HOW SILVA BETOOK HIMSELF TO FORM THE SIEGE OF THAT CITADEL. ELEAZAR'S SPEECHES TO THE BESIEGED

1. WHEN Bassus was dead in Judea, Flavius Silva succeeded him as a procurator there; who when he saw that all the rest of the country was subdued in this war, and that there was but one only stronghold that was still in rebellion, he got all his army together that lay in different places, and made an expedition against it. This fortress was called Masada. It was one Eleazar, a potent man, and the commander of these Sicarii, that had seized upon it. He was a descendant from that Judas who had persuaded abundance of the Jews, as we have formerly related, not to submit to the taxation, when Cyrenius was sent into Judea to make one; for then it was that the Sicarii got together against those that were willing to submit to the Romans, and treated them in all respects as if they had been their enemies, both by plundering them of what they had, by driving away their cattle, and by setting fire to their houses: for they said, that they differed not at all from foreigners,

by betraying, in so cowardly a manner, that freedom which Jews thought worthy to be contended for to the utmost, and by owning that they preferred slavery under the Romans before such a contention. Now, this was in reality no better than a pretence, and a cloak for the barbarity which was made use of by them, and to colour over their own avarice, which they afterwards made evident by their own actions; for those that were partners with them in their rebellion, joined also with them in the war against the Romans, and went further lengths with them in their impudent undertakings against them; and when they were again convicted of dissembling in such their pretences, they still more abused those that justly reproached them for their wickedness; and indeed that was a time most fertile in all manner of wicked practices, insomuch that no kind of evil deeds were then left undone; nor could any one so much as devise any bad thing that was new, so deeply were they all infected, and strove with one another in their single capacity, and in their communities, who should run the greatest lengths in impiety towards God, and in unjust actions towards their neighbours; the men of power oppressing the multitude, and the multitude earnestly labouring to destroy the men of power. The one part were desirous of tyrannizing over others; and the rest of offering violence to others, and of plundering such as were richer than themselves. They were the Sicarii who first began these transgressions, and first became barbarous towards those allied to them, and left no words of reproach unsaid, and no works of perdition untried, in order to destroy those whom their contrivances affected. Yet did John demonstrate by his actions, that these Sicarii were more moderate than he was himself, for he not only slew such as gave him good counsel to what was right, but treated them worst of all, as the most bitter enemies that he had among all the citizens; nay, he filled his entire country with ten thousand instances of wickedness, such as a man who was already hardened sufficiently in his impiety towards God, would naturally do; for the food was unlawful that was set upon his table, and he rejected those purifications that the law of his country had ordained; so that it was no longer a wonder if he, who was so mad in his impiety towards God did, not observe any rules of gentleness and common affection towards men. Again, therefore, what mischief was there which Simon the son of Gioras did not do? or what kind of abuses did he abstain from as to those very free men who had set him up for a tyrant? What friendship or kindred were there that did not make him more bold in his daily murders? for they looked upon the doing of mischief to strangers as only a work beneath their courage, but thought their barbarity towards their nearest relations would be a glorious demonstration thereof. The Idumeans also strove with these men who should be guilty of the greatest madness; for they [all,] vile wretches as they were, cut the throats of the high priests, that so no part of a religious regard to God might be preserved; they thence proceeded to destroy utterly the least remains of a political government, and introduced the most complete scene of iniquity in all instances that were practicable; under which scene, that sort of people that were called Zealots grew up, and who indeed corresponded to the name; for they imitated every wicked work; nor, if their memory suggested any evil thing that had formerly been done, did they avoid zealously to pursue the same; and although they gave themselves that name from their zeal for what was good, yet did it agree to them only by way of irony, on account of those they had unjustly treated by their wild and brutish disposition, or as thinking the greatest mischiefs to be the greatest good. Accordingly, they all met with such ends as God deservedly brought upon them in way of punishment; for all such miseries have been sent upon them as man's nature is capable of undergoing, till the utmost period of their lives, and till death came upon them in various ways of torment : yet might one say justly that they suffered less than they had done, because it was impossible they could be punished according to their deserving: but to make a lamentation according to the deserts of those who fell under these men's barbarity, this is not a proper place for it:—I therefore now return again to the remaining part of the present narration.

2. For now it was that the Roman general came, and led his army against Eleazar and those Sicarii who held the fortress Masada together with him; and for the whole country adjoining, he presently gained it, and put garrisons into the most proper places of it; he also built a wall quite round the entire fortress, that none of the besieged might easily escape : he also set his men to guard the several parts of it : he also pitched his camp in such an agreeable place as he had chosen for the siege, and at which place the rock belonging to the fortress did make the nearest approach to the neighbouring mountain, which yet was a place of difficulty for getting plenty of provisions; for it was not only food that was to be brought from a great distance [to the army,] and this with a great deal of pain to those Jews who were appointed for that purpose, but water was also to be brought to the camp, because the place afforded no fountain that was near it. When therefore Silva had ordered these affairs beforehand, he fell to besieging the place; which siege was likely to stand in need of a great deal of skill and pains, by reason of the strength of the fortress, the nature of which I will now describe.

3. There was a rock not small in circumference, and very high. It was encompassed with valleys of such vast depth downward, that the eye could not reach their bottoms; they were abrupt, and such as no animal could walk upon, excepting at two places of the rock, where it subsides, in order to afford a passage for ascent, though not without difficulty, Now, of the ways that lead to it, one is that from the lake Asphaltitis, towards the sun-rising, and another on the west, where the ascent is easier : the one of these ways is called the *Serpent*, as resembling that animal in its narrowness, and its perpetual windings ; for it is broken off at the prominent precipices of the rock, and returns frequently into itself, and lengthening again by little and little, hath much ado to proceed forward ; and he that would walk along it must first go on one leg, and then on the other ; there is also nothing but destruction, in case your feet slip ; for on each side there was a vastly deep chasm and precipice, sufficient to quell the courage of everybody by the terror it infuses into the mind. When, therefore, a man hath gone along this way for thirty furlongs, the rest is the top of the hill,—not ending at a small point, but is no other than a plain upon the highest part of the mountain. Upon this top of the hill Jonathan the high priest first of all built a fortress and called it *Masada ;* after which the rebuilding of this place employed the care of king Herod to a great degree ; he also built a wall round about the entire top of the hill, seven furlongs long ; it was composed of white stone ; its height was

twelve, and its breadth eight cubits ; there was also erected upon that wall thirty-eight towers, each of them fifty cubits high ; out of which you might pass into lesser edifices, which were built on the inside, round the entire wall ; for the king reserved the top of the hill, which was of a fat soil and better mould than any valley for agriculture, that such as committed themselves to this fortress for their preservation, might not even there be quite destitute of food, in case they should ever be in want of it from abroad. Moreover, he built a palace therein at the western ascent : it was within and beneath the walls of the citadel, but inclined to its north side. Now, the wall of this palace was very high and strong, and had at its four corners towers sixty cubits high. The furniture also of the edifices, and of the cloisters, and of the baths, was of great variety, and very costly ; and these buildings were supported by pillars of single stones on every side : the wall also and the floors of the edifices were paved with stones of several colours. He also had cut many and great pits, as reservoirs for water out of the rocks, at every one of the places that were inhabited, both above and around about the palace, and before the wall ; and by this contrivance he endeavoured to have water for several uses, as if there had been fountains there. Here was also a road digged from the palace, and leading to the very top of the mountain, which yet could not be seen by such as were without [the walls;] nor indeed could enemies easily make use of the plain roads ; for the road on the east side, as we have already taken notice, could not be walked upon, by reason of its nature ; and for the western road, he built a large tower at its narrowest place, at no less a distance from the top of the hill than a thousand cubits ; which tower could not possibly be passed by, nor could it be easily taken ; nor indeed could those that walked along it without any fear (such was its contrivance) easily get to the end of it ; and after such a manner was this citadel fortified, both by nature and by the hands of men, in order to frustrate the attacks of enemies.

4. As for the furniture that was within this fortress, it was still more wonderful on account of its splendour and long continuance ; for here was laid up corn in large quantities, and such as would subsist men for a long time ; here was also wine and oil in abundance, with all kinds of pulse and dates heaped up together ; all which Eleazar found there, when he and his *Sicarii* got possession of the fortress by treachery. These fruits were also fresh and full ripe, and no way inferior to such fruits newly laid in, although they were little short of a hundred years from the laying in these provisions [by Herod,] till the place was taken by the Romans ; nay, indeed, when the Romans got possession of those fruits that were left, they found them not corrupted all that while : nor should we be mistaken, if we supposed that the air was here the cause of their enduring so long, this fortress being so high, and so free from the mixture of all terrene and muddy particles of matter. There was also found here a large quantity of all sorts of weapons of war, which had been treasured up by that king, and were sufficient for ten thousand men ; there was cast iron, and brass, and tin, which shew that he had taken much pains to have all things here ready for the greatest occasions ; for the report goes how Herod thus prepared this fortress on his own account, as a refuge against two kinds of danger ; the one for fear of the multitude of the Jews, lest they should depose him and re-

store their former kings to the government; the other danger was greater and more terrible, which arose from Cleopatra, queen of Egypt, who did not conceal her intentions, but spoke often to Antony, and desired him to cut off Herod, and entreated him to bestow the kingdom of Judea upon her. And certainly it is a great wonder that Antony did never comply with her commands in this point, as he was so miserably enslaved to his passion for her; nor should any one have been surprised if she had been gratified in such her request. So the fear of these dangers made Herod rebuild Masada, and thereby leave it for the finishing stroke of the Romans in this Jewish war.

5. Since therefore the Roman commander Silva had now built a wall on the outside, round about this whole place, as we have said already, and had thereby made a most accurate provision to prevent any one of the besieged running away, he undertook the siege itself, though he found but one single place that would admit of the banks he was to raise; for behind that tower which secured the road that led to the palace, and to the top of the hill from the west, there was a certain eminency of the rock, very broad and very prominent, but three hundred cubits beneath the highest part of Masada; it was called the White Promontory. Accordingly, he got upon that part of the rock, and ordered the army to bring earth; and when they fell to that work with alacrity, and abundance of them together, the bank was raised, and became solid for two hundred cubits in height. Yet was not this bank thought sufficiently high for the use of the engines that were to be set upon it; but still another elevated work of great stones compacted together was raised upon that bank: this was fifty cubits, both in breadth and height. The other machines that were now got ready were like to those that had been first devised by Vespasian, and afterwards by Titus, for sieges. There was also a tower made of the height of sixty cubits, and all over plated with iron, out of which the Romans threw darts and stones from the engines, and soon made those that fought from the walls of the place to retire, and would not let them lift up their heads above the works. At the same time, Silva ordered that great battering-ram which he had made, to be brought thither, and to be set against the wall, and to make frequent batteries against it, which with some difficulty, broke down a part of the wall, and quite overthrew it. However, the *Sicarii* made haste, and presently built another wall within that, which should not be liable to the same misfortune from the machines with the other: it was made soft and yielding, and so was capable of avoiding the terrible blows that affected the other. It was framed after the following manner: They laid together great beams of wood lengthways, one close to the end of another, and the same way in which they were cut: there were two of these rows parallel to one another, and laid at such a distance from each other as the breadth of the wall required, and earth was put into the space between those rows. Now, that the earth might not fall away upon the elevation of this bank to a greater height, they farther laid other beams over across them, and thereby bound those beams together that lay lengthways. This work of theirs was like a real edifice; and when the machines were applied, the blows were weakened by its yielding; and as the materials by such concussion were shaken closer together, the pile by that means became firmer than before. When Silva

saw this, he thought it best to endeavour the taking of this wall by setting fire to it; so he gave orders that the soldiers should throw a great number of burning torches upon it: accordingly, as it was chiefly made of wood, it soon took fire; and when it was once set on fire, its hollowness made that fire spread to a mighty flame. Now, at the very beginning of this fire, a north wind that then blew proved terrible to the Romans; for by bringing the flame downward, it drove it upon them, and they were almost in despair of success, as fearing their machines would be burnt: but after this, on a sudden the wind changed into the south, as if it were done by divine providence: and blew strongly the contrary way, and carried the flame, and drove it against the wall, which was now on fire through its entire thickness. So the Romans, having now assistance from God, returned to their camp with joy, and resolved to attack their enemies the very next day; on which occasion they set their watch more carefully that night, lest any of the Jews should run away from them without being discovered.

6. However, neither did Eleazar once think of flying away, nor would he permit any one else to do so; but when he saw their wall burnt down by the fire, and could devise no other way of escaping, or room for their farther courage, and setting before their eyes what the Romans would do to them, their children, and their wives, if they got them into their power, he consulted about having them all slain. Now, as he judged this to be the best thing they could do in their present circumstances, he gathered the most courageous of his companions together, and encouraged them to take that course by a speech, which he made to them in the manner following:—"Since we, long ago, my generous friends, resolved never to be servants to the Romans, nor to any other than to God himself, who alone is the true and just Lord of mankind, the time is now come that obliges us to make that resolution true in practice. And let us not at this time bring a reproach upon ourselves for self-contradiction, while we formerly would not undergo slavery, though it were then without danger, but must now, together with slavery, choose such punishments also as are intolerable; I mean this, upon the supposition that the Romans once reduce us under their power while we are alive. We were the very first that revolted from them, and we are the last that fight against them; and I cannot but esteem it as a favour that God hath granted us, that it is still in our power to die bravely, and in a state of freedom, which hath not been the case with others who were conquered unexpectedly. It is very plain that we shall be taken within a day's time; but it is still an eligible thing to die after a glorious manner, together with our dearest friends. This is what our enemies themselves cannot by any means hinder, although they be very desirous to take us alive. Nor can we propose to ourselves any more to fight them and beat them. It had been proper indeed for us to have conjectured at the purpose of God much sooner, and at the very first, when we were so desirous of defending our liberty, and when we received such sore treatment from one another, and worse treatment from our enemies, and to have been sensible that the same God, who had of old taken the Jewish nation into his favour, had now condemned them to destruction; for had he either continued favourable, or been but in a lesser degree displeased with us, he had not overlooked the destruction of so many men, or delivered his most holy city to be burnt and

demolished by our enemies. To be sure, we weakly hoped to have preserved ourselves, and ourselves alone, still in a state of freedom, as we had been guilty of no sins ourselves against God, nor been partners with those of others; we also taught other men to preserve their liberty. Wherefore, consider how God hath convinced us that our hopes were in vain, by bringing such distress upon us in the desperate state we are now in, and which is beyond all our expectations; for the nature of this fortress, which was in itself unconquerable, hath not proved a means of our deliverance; and even while we have still great abundance of food, and a great quantity of arms and other necessaries more than we want, we are openly deprived by God himself of all hope of deliverance; for that fire which was driven upon our enemies did not, of its own accord, turn back upon the wall which we had built: this was the effect of God's anger against us for our manifold sins, which we have been guilty of in a most insolent and extravagant manner with regard to our own countrymen; the punishments of which let us not receive from the Romans, but from God himself, as executed by our own hands, for these will be more moderate than the other. Let our wives die before they are abused, and our children before they have tasted of slavery; and after we have slain them, let us bestow that glorious benefit upon one another mutually, and preserve ourselves in freedom, as an excellent funeral monument for us. But first let us destroy our money and the fortress by fire; for I am well assured that this will be a great grief to the Romans, that they shall not be able to seize upon our bodies, and shall fail of our wealth also: and let us spare nothing but our provisions; for they will be a testimonial when we are dead that we were not subdued for want of necessaries; but that, according to our original resolution, we have preferred death before slavery."

7. This was Eleazar's speech to them. Yet did not the opinions of all the soldiers acquiesce therein; but although some of them were very zealous to put his advice in practice, and were in a manner filled with pleasure at it, and thought death to be a good thing, yet had those that were most effeminate a commiseration for their wives and families; and when these men were especially moved by the prospect of their own certain death, they looked wistfully at one another, and by the tears that were in their eyes, declared their dissent from his opinion. When Eleazar saw these people in such fear, and that their souls were dejected at so prodigious a proposal, he was afraid lest perhaps these effeminate persons should, by their lamentations and tears, enfeeble those that heard what he had said courageously; so he did not leave off exhorting them, but stirred up himself, and recollecting proper arguments for raising their courage, he undertook to speak more briskly and fully to them, and that concerning the immortality of the soul. So he made a lamentable groan, and fixing his eyes intently on those that wept, he spake thus:—"Truly, I was greatly mistaken when I thought to be assisting to brave men who struggled hard for their liberty, and to such as were resolved either to live with honour, or else to die; but I find that you are such people as are no better than others, either in virtue or in courage, and are afraid of dying, though you be delivered thereby from the greatest miseries, while you ought to make no delay in this matter, nor to await any one to give you good advice; for the laws of our country, and of God himself,

have, from ancient times, and as soon as ever we could use our reason, continually taught us, and our forefathers have corroborated the same doctrine, by their actions, and by their bravery of mind, that it is life that is a calamity to men, and not death; for this last affords our souls their liberty, and sends them by a removal into their own place of purity, where they are to be insensible to all sorts of misery; for while souls are tied down to a mortal body, they are partakers of its miseries; and, to speak the truth, they are themselves dead; for the union of what is divine to what is mortal is disagreeable. It is true, the power of the soul is great, even when it is imprisoned in a mortal body; for by moving it after a way that is invisible, it makes the body a sensible instrument, and causes it to advance further in its actions than mortal nature could otherwise do. However, when it is freed from that weight which draws it down to the earth, and is connected with it, it obtains its own proper place, and does then become a partaker of that blessed power, and those abilities, which are then every way incapable of being hindered in their operations. It continues invisible, indeed, to the eyes of men, as does God himself; for certainly it is not itself seen, while it is in the body; for it is thereafter an invisible matter, and when it is freed from it, it is still not seen. It is this soul which hath one nature, and that an incorruptible one also; but yet is it the cause of the change that is made in the body; for whatsoever it be which the soul touches, that lives and flourishes; and from whatsoever it is removed, that withers away and dies; such a degree is there in it of immortality. Let me produce the state of sleep as a most evident demonstration of the truth of what I say; wherein souls, when the body does not distract them, have the sweetest rest depending on themselves, and conversing with God, by their alliance to him; they then go everywhere, and foretell many futurities beforehand; and why are we afraid of death, while we are pleased with the rest that we have in sleep? and how absurd a thing is it to pursue after liberty while we are alive, and yet to envy it to ourselves where it will be eternal! We, therefore, who have been brought up in a discipline of our own, ought to become an example to others of our readiness to die; yet if we do not stand in need of foreigners to support us in this matter, let us regard those Indians who profess the exercise of philosophy; for these good men do but unwillingly undergo the time of life, and look upon it as a necessary servitude, and make haste to let their souls loose from their bodies; nay, when no misfortune presses them to it, nor drives them upon it, these have such a desire of a life of immortality, that they tell other men beforehand that they are about to depart; and nobody hinders them, but every one thinks them happy men, and gives them letters to be carried to their familiar friends [that are dead;] so firmly and certainly do they believe that souls converse with one another [in the other world.] So when these men have heard all such commands that were to be given them, they deliver their body to the fire; and, in order to their getting their soul a separation from the body, in the greatest purity, they die in the midst of hymns of commendations made to them; for their dearest friends conduct them to their death more readily than do any of the rest of mankind conduct their fellow-citizens when they are going a very long journey, who, at the same time, weep on their own account, but look upon the others as happy persons, as so soon to be made partakers of the immortal order of beings. Are not we, therefore, ashamed to have lower notions than the Indians? and by our own cowardice to lay a base reproach upon the laws of our country, which are so much desired and imitated by all mankind? But put the case that we had been brought up under another persuasion, and taught that life is the greatest good which men are capable of, and that death is a calamity: however, the circumstances we are now in, ought to be an inducement to us to bear such calamity courageously, since it is by the will of God, and by necessity, that we are to die: for it now appears that God hath made such a decree against the whole Jewish nation, that we are to be deprived of this life which [he knew] we would not make a due use of; for do not you ascribe the occasion of your present condition to yourselves, nor think the Romans are the true occasion that this war we have had with them is become so destructive to us all: these things have not come to pass by their power, but a more powerful cause hath intervened, and made us afford them an occasion of their appearing to be conquerors over us. What Roman weapons, I pray you, were those, by which the Jews of Cesarea were slain? On the contrary, when they were no way disposed to rebel, but were all the while keeping their seventh day festival, and did not so much as lift up their hands against the citizens of Cesarea, yet did those citizens run upon them in great crowds, and cut their throats, and the throats of their wives and children, and this without any regard to the Romans themselves, who never took us for their enemies, till we revolted from them. But some may be ready to say, that truly the people of Cesarea had always a quarrel against those that lived among them, and that when an opportunity offered itself, they only satisfied the old rancour they had against them. What then shall we say to those of Scythopolis, who ventured to wage war with us on account of the Greeks? Nor did they do it by way of revenge upon the Romans, when they acted in concert with our countrymen. Wherefore you see how little our good-will and fidelity to them that profited us, while they were slain, they and their whole families after the most inhuman manner; which was all the requital that was made them for the assistance they had afforded to the others; for that very same destruction which they had prevented from falling upon the others, did they suffer themselves from them, as if they had been ready to be the actors against them. It would be too long for me to speak at this time of every destruction brought upon us: for you cannot but know, that there was not any one Syrian city which did not slay their Jewish inhabitants, and were not more bitter enemies to us than were the Romans themselves: nay, even those of Damascus, when they were able to allege no tolerable pretence against us, filled their city with the most barbarous slaughter of our people, and cut the throats of eighteen thousand Jews, with their wives and children. And as to the multitude of those that were slain in Egypt, and that with torments also, we have been informed there were more than sixty thousand; those indeed being in a foreign country, and so naturally meeting with nothing to oppose against their enemies, were killed in the manner forementioned. As for all those of us who have waged war against the Romans in our country, had we not sufficient reason to have sure hopes of victory? For we had arms, and walls, and fortresses so prepared as not to be easily taken, and courage not to be moved by any dangers in the cause of liberty, which encouraged us all to revolt from

the Romans. But then, these advantages sufficed us but for a short time, and only raised our hopes, while they really appeared to be the origin of our miseries; for all we had, hath been taken from us, and all hath fallen under our enemies, as if these advantages were only to render their victory over us the more glorious, and were not disposed for the preservation of those by whom these preparations were made. And as for those that were already dead in the war, it is reasonable we should esteem them blessed, for they are dead in defending, and not in betraying their liberty; but as to the multitude of those that are now under the Romans, who would not pity their condition? and who would not make haste to die, before he would suffer the same miseries with them? Some of them have been put upon the rack, and tortured with fire and whippings, and so died. Some have been half-devoured by wild beasts, and yet have been reserved alive to be devoured by them a second time, in order to afford laughter and sport to our enemies; and such of those as are alive still, are to be looked on as the most miserable, who, being so desirous of death, could not come at it. And where is now that great city, the metropolis of the Jewish nation, which was fortified by so many walls round about, which had so many fortresses and large towers to defend it, which could hardly contain the instruments prepared for the war, and which had so many ten thousands of men to fight for it? Where is this city that was believed to have God himself inhabiting therein? It is now demolished to the very foundations; and hath nothing but that monument of it preserved, I mean the camp of those that have destroyed it, which still dwells upon its ruins; some unfortunate old men also lie upon the ashes of the temple, and a few women are there preserved alive by the enemy, for our bitter shame and reproach. Now, who is there that revolves these things in his mind, and yet is able to bear the sight of the sun, though he might live out of danger? Who is there so much his country's enemy, or so unmanly, and so desirous of living, as not to repent that he is still alive? And I cannot but wish that we had all died before we had seen that holy city demolished by the hands of our enemies, or the foundations of our holy temple dug up after so profane a manner. But since we had a generous hope that deluded us, as if we might perhaps have been able to avenge ourselves on our enemies on that account, though it be now become vanity, and hath left us alone in this distress, let us make haste to die bravely. Let us pity ourselves, our children, and our wives, while it is in our power to shew pity to them; for we are born to die, as well as those were whom we have begotten; nor is it in the power of the most happy of our race to avoid it. But for abuses and slavery, and the sight of our wives led away after an ignominious manner, with their children, these are not such evils as are natural and necessary among men; although such as do not prefer death before those miseries, when it is in their power so to do, must undergo even them, on account of their own cowardice. We revolted from the Romans with great pretensions to courage; and when at the very last they invited us to preserve ourselves, we would not comply with them. Who will not, therefore, believe that they will certainly be in a rage at us, in case they can take us alive? Miserable will then be the young men, who will be strong enough in their bodies to sustain many torrents! miserable also will be those of elder years, who will not be able to bear those calamities which young men might sustain! One man will be obliged to hear the voice of his son imploring help of his father, when his hands are bound : But certainly our hands are still at liberty, and have a sword in them : let them then be subservient to us in our glorious design ; let us die before we become slaves under our enemies, and let us go out of the world, together with our children and our wives, in a state of freedom. This it is that our laws command us to do ; this it is that our wives and children crave at our hands ; nay, God himself hath brought this necessity upon us ; while the Romans desire the contrary, and are afraid lest any man should die before we are taken. Let us therefore make haste, and instead of affording them so much pleasure, as they hope for in getting us under their power, let us leave them an example which shall at once cause their astonishment at our death, and their admiration of our hardiness therein."

CHAPTER IX

HOW THE PEOPLE THAT WERE IN THE FORTRESS WERE PREVAILED ON BY THE WORDS OF ELEAZAR, TWO WOMEN AND FIVE CHILDREN ONLY EXCEPTED, AND ALL SUBMITTED TO BE KILLED BY ONE ANOTHER

1. Now as Eleazar was proceeding on in this exhortation, they all cut him off short, and made haste to do the work, as full of an unconquerable ardour of mind, and moved with a demoniacal fury. So they went their ways, as one still endeavouring to be before another, and as thinking that this eagerness would be a demonstration of their courage and good conduct, if they could avoid appearing in the last class : so great was the zeal they were in to slay their wives and children, and themselves also ! Nor indeed, when they came to the work itself, did their courage fail them as one might imagine it would have done ; but they then held fast the same resolution, without wavering, which they had upon the hearing of Eleazar's speech, while yet every one of them still retained the natural passion of love to themselves and their families, because the reasoning they went upon, appeared to them to be very just, even with regard to those that were dearest to them ; for the husbands tenderly embraced their wives and took their children into their arms, and gave the longest parting kisses to them, with tears in their eyes. Yet at the same time did they complete what they had resolved on, as if they had been executed by the hands of strangers, and they had nothing else for their comfort but the necessity they were in of doing this execution, to avoid that prospect they had of the miseries they were to suffer from their enemies. Nor was there at length any one of these men found that scrupled to act their part in this terrible execution, but every one of them despatched his dearest relations. Miserable men indeed were they! whose distress forced them to slay their own wives and children with their own hands, as the lightest of those evils that were before them. So they not being able to bear the grief they were under for what they had done, any longer, and esteeming it an injury to those they had slain, to live even the shortest space of time after them—they presently laid all they had in a heap, and set fire to it. They then chose ten men by lot out of them, to slay all the rest ; every one of whom laid himself down by his wife and children on the ground, and threw his arms about them, and they offered their necks to the stroke of those who by lot executed that melancholy office ; and when these ten had, without fear, slain them all, they made the same rule for casting lots for themselves, that he whose lot it was should first kill the other nine, and after all, should kill himself. Accordingly, all those had courage sufficient to be no way behind one another, in doing or suffering ; so, for a conclusion, the nine offered their necks to the executioner, and he who was the last of all, took a view of all the other bodies, lest perchance some or other among so many that were slain should want his assistance to be quite despatched ; and when he perceived that they were all slain, he set fire to the palace, and with the great force of his hand ran his sword entirely through himself, and fell down dead near to his own relations. So these people died with this intention, that they would not have so much as one soul among them all alive to be subject to the Romans. Yet was there an ancient woman, and another who was of kin to Eleazar, and superior to most women in prudence and learning, with five children, who had concealed themselves in caverns under ground, and had carried water thither for their drink, and were hidden there when the rest were intent upon the slaughter of one another. These others were nine hundred and sixty in number, the women and children being withal included in that computation. This calamitous slaughter was made on the fifteenth day of the month [Xanthicus] Nisan.

2. Now for the Romans, they expected that they should be fought in the morning, when accordingly they put on their armour, and laid bridges of planks upon their ladders from their banks, to make an assault upon the fortress, which they did ; but saw nobody as an enemy, but a terrible solitude on every side, with a fire within the place, as well as a perfect silence. So they were at a loss to guess at what had happened. At length they made a shout, as if it had been at a blow given by a battering-ram, to try whether they could bring any one out that was within ; the women heard this noise and came out of their underground cavern, and informed the Romans what had been done, as it was done ; and the second of them clearly described all both what was said and what was done, and the manner of it ; yet did they not easily give their attention to such a desperate undertaking, and did not believe it could be as they said ; they also attempted to put the fire out, and quickly cutting themselves a way through it, they came within the palace, and so met with the multitude of the slain, but could take no pleasure in the fact, though it were done to their enemies. Nor could they do other than wonder at the courage of their resolution, and at the immovable contempt of death which so great a number of them had shown, when they went through with such an action as that was.

CHAPTER X

THAT MANY OF THE SICARII FLED TO ALEXANDRIA ALSO, AND WHAT DANGERS THEY WERE IN THERE ; ON WHICH ACCOUNT THAT TEMPLE, WHICH HAD FORMERLY BEEN BUILT BY ONIAS, THE HIGH PRIEST, WAS DESTROYED

1. WHEN Masada was thus taken, the general left a garrison in the fortress to keep it, and he himself went away to Cesarea ; for there were now no enemies left in the country, it being all overthrown by so long a war. Yet did this war afford disturbances and dangerous disorders even

in places very far remote from Judea; for still it came to pass that many Jews were slain at Alexandria in Egypt; for as many of the *Sicarii* as were able to fly thither, out of the seditious wars in Judea, were not content to have saved themselves, but must needs be undertaking to make new disturbances, and persuaded many of those that entertained them to assert their liberty, to esteem the Romans to be no better than themselves, and to look upon God as their only Lord and Master. But when part of the Jews of reputation opposed them, they slew some of them, and with the others they were very pressing in their exhortations to revolt from the Romans; but when the principal men of the senate saw what madness they were come to, they thought it no longer safe for themselves to overlook them. So they got all the Jews together to an assembly, and accused the madness of the *Sicarii*, and demonstrated that they had been the authors of all the evils that had come upon them. They said also, that "these men, now they were run away from Judea, having no sure hope of escaping, because as soon as ever they shall be known, they will be soon destroyed by the Romans, they come hither and fill us full of those calamities which belong to them, while we have not been partakers with them in any of their sins." Accordingly they exhorted the multitude to have a care, lest they should be brought to destruction by their means, and to make their apology to the Romans for what had been done, by delivering these men up to them; who being thus apprized of the greatness of the danger they were in, complied with what was proposed, and ran with great violence upon the *Sicarii*, and seized upon them; and, indeed, six hundred of them were caught immediately: but as to all those that fled into Egypt, and to the Egyptian Thebes, it was not long ere they were caught also, and brought back,— whose courage, or whether we ought to call it madness, or hardiness in their opinions, everybody was amazed at; for when all sorts of torments and vexations of their bodies that could be devised were made use of to them, they could not get any one of them to comply so far as to confess, or seem to confess, that Cæsar was their lord; but they preserved their own opinion, in spite of all the distress they were brought to, as if they received these torments and the fire itself with bodies insensible of pain, and with a soul that in a manner rejoiced under them. But what was most of all astonishing to the beholders, was the courage of the children; for not one of these children was so far overcome by these torments, as to name Cæsar for their lord. So far does the strength of the courage [of the soul] prevail over the weakness of the body.

2. Now, Lupus did then govern Alexandria, who presently sent Cæsar word of this commotion; who having in suspicion the restless temper of the Jews for innovation, and being afraid lest they should get together and persuade some others to join with them, gave orders to Lupus to demolish that Jewish temple which was in the region called Onion, and was in Egypt, which was built and had its denomination from the occasion following:—Onias, the son of Simon, one of the Jewish high priests, fled from Antiochus, the king of Syria, when he made war with the Jews, and came to Alexandria; and as Ptolemy received him very kindly on account of his hatred to Antiochus, he assured him, that if he would comply with his proposal, he would bring all the Jews to his assistance; and when the king agreed to do it so far as he was able, he desired him to give

him leave to build a temple somewhere in Egypt, and to worship God according to the customs of his own country; for that the Jews would then be so much readier to fight against Antiochus, who had laid waste the temple at Jerusalem, and that they would then come to him with greater good-will; and that, by granting them liberty of conscience, very many of them would come over to him.

3. So Ptolemy complied with his proposals, and gave him a place one hundred and eighty furlongs distant from Memphis. That Nomos was called the Nomos of Heliopolis, where Onias built a fortress and a temple, not like to that at Jerusalem, but such as resembled a tower. He built it of large stones to the height of sixty cubits; he made the structure of the altar an imitation of that in our own country, and in like manner adorned with gifts, excepting the make of the candlestick, for he did not make a candlestick, but had a [single] lamp hammered out of a piece of gold, which illuminated the place with its rays, and which he hung by a chain of gold; but the entire temple was encompassed with a wall of burnt brick, though it had gates of stone. The king also gave him a large country for a revenue in money, that both the priests might have a plentiful provision made for them, and that God might have great abundance of what things were necessary for his worship. Yet did not Onias do this out of a sober disposition, but he had a mind to contend with the Jews at Jerusalem, and could not forget the indignation he had for being banished thence. Accordingly, he thought by building this temple he should draw away a great number from them to himself. There had been also a certain ancient prediction made by a [prophet] whose name was Isaiah, about six hundred years before, that this temple should be built by a man that was a Jew in Egypt, (Isa. xix. 18-23.) And this is the history of the building of that temple.

4. And now Lupus, the governor of Alexandria, upon the receipt of Cæsar's letter, came to the temple and carried out of it some of the donations dedicated thereto, and shut up the temple itself; and as Lupus died a little afterward, Paulinus succeeded him. This man left none of these donations there, and threatened the priests severely if they did not bring them all out; nor did he permit any who were desirous of worshipping God there, so much as to come near the whole sacred place; but when he had shut up the gates, he made it entirely inaccessible, insomuch that there remained no longer the least footsteps of any divine worship that had been in that place. Now, the duration of the time from the building of this temple till it was shut up again, was three hundred and forty-three years.

CHAPTER XI.

CONCERNING JONATHAN, ONE OF THE SICARII, THAT STIRRED UP A SEDITION IN CYRENE, AND WAS A FALSE ACCUSER [OF THE INNOCENT.]

1. AND now did the madness of the *Sicarii*, like a disease, reach as far as the cities of Cyrene; for one Jonathan, a vile person, and by trade a weaver, came thither, and prevailed with no small number of the poorer sort to give ear to him; he also led them into the desert, upon promising them that he would shew them signs and apparitions; and as for the other Jews at Cyrene, he concealed his knavery from them,

and put tricks upon them; but those of the greatest dignity among them informed Catullus, the governor of the Libyan Pentapolis, of his march into the desert, and of the preparations he had made for it. So he sent out after him both horsemen and footmen, and easily overcame them, because they were unarmed men: of these, many were slain in the fight, but some were taken alive, and brought to Catullus. As for Jonathan, the head of this plot, he fled away at this time; but, upon a great and very diligent search which was made all the country over for him, he was at last taken; and when he was brought to Catullus, he devised a way whereby he both escaped punishment himself and afforded an occasion to Catullus of doing much mischief; for he falsely accused the richest men among the Jews, and said that they had put him upon what he did.

2. Now, Catullus easily admitted of these his calumnies; and aggravated matters greatly, and made tragical exclamations that he might also be supposed to have had a hand in the finishing of the Jewish war; but what was still harder, he did not only give a too easy belief to his stories, but he taught the *Sicarii* to accuse men falsely. He bade this Jonathan, therefore, name one Alexander, a Jew, (with whom he had formerly had a quarrel, and openly professed that he hated him;) he also got him to name his wife Bernice, as concerned with him. These two, Catullus ordered to be slain in the first place; nay, after them he caused all the rich and wealthy Jews to be slain, being no fewer in all than three thousand. This, he thought, he might do safely, because he confiscated their effects, and added them to Cæsar's revenues.

3. Nay, indeed, lest any Jews that lived elsewhere, should convict him of his villainy, he extended his false accusations farther, and persuaded Jonathan, and certain others that were caught with him, to bring an accusation of attempts for innovation against the Jews that were of the best character both at Alexandria and at Rome. One of these, against whom this treacherous accusation was laid, was Josephus, the writer of these books. However, this plot, thus contrived by Catullus, did not succeed according to his hopes: for though he came himself to Rome, and brought Jonathan and his companions along with him in bonds, and thought he should have no farther inquisition made as to those lies that were forged under his government, or by his means, yet did Vespasian suspect the matter, and make an inquiry how far it was true; and when he understood that the accusation laid against the Jews was an unjust one, he cleared them of the crimes charged upon them; and this, on account of Titus's concern about the matter, and brought a deserved punishment upon Jonathan; for he was first tormented, and then burnt alive.

4. But as to Catullus, the emperors were so gentle to him, that he underwent no severe condemnation at this time: yet was it not long before he fell into a complicated and almost incurable distemper, and died miserably. He was not only afflicted in body, but the distemper in his mind was more heavy upon him than the other; for he was terribly disturbed, and continually cried out, that he saw the ghosts of those whom he had slain, standing before him. Whereupon he was not able to contain himself, but leaped out of his bed, as if both torments and fire were brought to him. This his distemper grew still a great deal worse and worse continually, and his very entrails were so corroded, that they fell out of his body, and in that condition he died. Thus he became as great an instance of divine providence as ever was, and demonstrated that God punishes wicked men.

5. And here we shall put an end to this our history; wherein we formerly promised to deliver the same with all accuracy, to such as should be desirous of understanding after what manner this war of the Romans with the Jews was managed. Of which history, how good the style is, must be left to the determination of the readers; but for the agreement with the facts, I shall not scruple to say, and that boldly, that truth hath been what I have alone aimed at through its entire composition.

ANTIQUITY OF THE JEWS

FLAVIUS JOSEPHUS AGAINST APION*

BOOK I

1. I SUPPOSE that, by my books of the Antiquities of the Jews, most excellent Epaphroditus,† I have made it evident to those who peruse them, that our Jewish nation is of very great antiquity, and had a distinct subsistence of its own originally ; as also, I have therein declared how we came to inhabit this country wherein we now live. Those Antiquities contain the history of five thousand years, and are taken out of our sacred books ; but are translated by me into the Greek tongue. However, since I observe a considerable number of people giving ear to the reproaches that are laid against us by those who bear ill-will to us, and will not believe what I have written concerning the antiquity of our nation, while they take it for a plain sign that our nation is of a late date, because they are not so much as vouchsafed a bare mention by the most famous historiographers among the Grecians, I therefore have thought myself under an obligation to write somewhat briefly about these subjects, in order to convict those that reproach us, of spite and voluntary falsehood, and to correct the ignorance of others, and withal to instruct all those who are desirous of knowing the truth of what great antiquity we really are. As for the witnesses whom I shall produce for the proof of what I say, they shall be such as are esteemed to be of the greatest reputation for truth, and the most skilful in the knowledge of all antiquity, by the Greeks themselves. I will also shew that those who have written so reproachfully and falsely about us, are to be convicted by what they have written themselves to the contrary. I shall also endeavour to give an account of the reasons why it hath so happened, that there hath not been a great number of Greeks who have made mention of our nation in their histories. I will, however, bring those Grecians to light who have not omitted such

our history, for the sake of those that either do not know them, or pretend not to know them already.

2. And now, in the first place, I cannot but greatly wonder at those men who suppose that we must attend to none but Grecians when we are inquiring about the most ancient facts, and must inform ourselves of their truth from them only, while we must not believe ourselves nor other men ; for I am convinced that the very reverse is the truth of the case. I mean this,— if we will not be led by vain opinions, but will make inquiry after truth from facts themselves ; for they will find, that almost all which concerns the Greeks happened not long ago ; nay, one may say, is of yesterday only. I speak of the building of their cities, the invention of their arts, and the description of their laws ; and as for their care about the writing down of their histories, it is very near the last thing they set about. However, they acknowledge themselves so far, that they were the Egyptians, the Chaldeans and Phœnicians, (for I will not now reckon ourselves among them,) that have preserved the memorials of the most ancient and most lasting traditions of mankind ; for almost all these nations inhabit such countries as are least subject to destruction from the world about them ; and these also have taken especial care to have nothing omitted of what was [remarkably] done among them ; but their history was esteemed sacred, and put into public tables, as written by men of the greatest wisdom they had among them ; but as for the place where the Grecians inhabit, ten thousand destructions have overtaken it and blotted out the memory of former actions ; so that they were ever beginning a new way of living, and supposed that every one of them was the origin of their new state. It was also late, and with difficulty, that they came to know the letters they now use ; for those who would advance their use of these letters to the greatest antiquity, pretend that they learned them from the Phœnicians and from Cadmus ; yet is nobody able to demonstrate that they have any writing preserved from that time, neither in their temples, nor in any other public monuments. This appears, because the time when those lived who went to the Trojan war, so many years afterward, is in great doubt, and great inquiry is made whether the Greeks used their letters at that time ; and the most prevailing opinion, and that nearest the truth, is, that their present way of using those letters was unknown at that time. However, there is not any writing which the Greeks agree to be genuine among them ancienter than Homer's poems, who must

plainly be confessed later than the siege of Troy; nay, the report goes, that even he did not leave his poems in writing, but that their memory was preserved in songs, and they were put together afterward; and this is the reason of such a number of variations as are found in them. As for those who set themselves about writing their histories, I mean such as Cadmus of Miletus, and Acusilaus of Argos, and any others that may be mentioned as succeeding Acusilaus, they lived but a little while before the Persian expedition into Greece. But then for those that first introduced philosophy, and the consideration of things celestial and divine among them, such as Pherecydes the Syrian, and Pythagoras, and Thales, all with one consent agree, that they learned what they knew of the Egyptians and Chaldeans, and wrote but little. And these are the things which are supposed to be the oldest of all among the Greeks; and they have much ado to believe that the writings ascribed to those men are genuine.

3. How can it then be other than an absurd thing for the Greeks to be so proud, and to vaunt themselves to be the only people that are acquainted with antiquity, and that have delivered the true accounts of those early times after an accurate manner! Nay, who is there that cannot easily gather from the Greek writers themselves, that they knew but little on any good foundation when they set to write, but rather wrote their histories from their own conjectures? Accordingly, they confute one another in their own books to purpose, and are not ashamed to give us the most contradictory accounts of the same things; and I should spend my time to little purpose, if I should pretend to teach the Greeks that which they know better than I already, what a great disagreement there is between Hellanicus and Acusilaus about their genealogies; in how many cases Acusilaus corrects Hesiod: or after what manner Ephorus demonstrates Hellanicus to have told lies in the greatest part of his history: as does Timeus in like manner as to Ephorus, and the succeeding writers do to Timeus, and all the later writers do to Herodotus; nor could Timeus agree with Antiochus and Philistius, or with Callias, about the Sicilian History, no more than do the several writers of the Atthidæ follow one another about the Athenian affairs; nor do the historians the like, that wrote the Argolics, about the affairs of the Argives. And now what need I say any more about particular cities and smaller places, while in the most approved writers of the expedition of the Persians, and of the actions which were therein performed, there are so great differences! Nay, Thucydides himself is accused by some as writing what is false, although he seems to have given us the exactest history of the affairs of his own time.

4. As for the occasions of this so great disagreement of theirs, there may be assigned many that are very probable, if any have a mind to make an inquiry about them; but I ascribe these contradictions chiefly to two causes, which I will now mention, and still think what I shall mention in the first place, to be the principal of all; for if we remember, that in the beginning the Greeks had taken no care to have public records of their several transactions preserved, this must for certain have afforded those that would afterward write about those ancient transactions the opportunity of making mistakes, and the power of making lies also; for this original recording of such ancient transactions hath not only been neglected by the other states of Greece, but even among the Athenians themselves also, who pretend to be Aborigines, and to have applied themselves to learning, there are no such records extant; nay, they say themselves, that the laws of Draco concerning murders, which are now extant in writing, are the most ancient of their public records; which Draco yet lived but a little time before the tyrant Pisistratus.* For as to the Arcadians, who make such boasts of their antiquity, what need I speak of them in particular, since it was still later before they got their letters, and learned them, and that with difficulty also.

5. There must therefore naturally arise great differences among writers, when they had no original records to lay for their foundation, which might at once inform those who had an inclination to learn, and contradict those that would tell lies. However, we are to suppose a second occasion besides the former of these contradictions; it is this:—That those who were the most zealous to write history, were not solicitous for the discovery of truth, although it was very easy for them always to make such a profession; but their business was to demonstrate that they could write well, and make an impression upon mankind thereby; and in what manner of writing they thought they were able to exceed others, to that did they apply themselves. Some of them betook themselves to the writing of fabulous narrations; some of them endeavoured to please the cities or the kings, by writing in their commendation; others of them fell to finding faults with transactions, or with the writers of such transactions, and thought to make a great figure by so doing; and indeed these do what is of all things the most contrary to true history; for it is the great character of true history that all concerned therein both speak and write the same things; while these men, by writing differently about the same things, think they shall be believed to write with the greatest regard to truth. We therefore [who are Jews] must yield to the Grecian writers as to language and eloquence of composition; but then we shall give them no such preference as to the verity of ancient history; and least of all as to that part which concerns the affairs of our own several countries.

6. As to the care of writing down the records from the earliest antiquity among the Egyptians and Babylonians; that the priests were intrusted therewith, and employed a philosophical concern about it; that they were the Chaldean priests that did so among the Babylonians; and that the Phœnicians, who were mingled among the Greeks, did especially make use of their letters, both for the common affairs of life, and for the delivering down the history of common transactions, I think I may omit any proof, because all men allow it so to be: but now as to our forefathers, that they took no less care about writing such records (for I will not say they took greater care than the others I spoke of) and that they committed that matter to their high priests and to their prophets, and that these records have been written all along down to our own times with the utmost accuracy; nay, if it be not too bold for me to say it, our history will be so written hereafter;—I shall endeavour briefly to inform you.

7. For our forefathers did not only appoint the best of these priests, and those that attended upon the divine worship, for that design from the beginning, but made profession that the stock of the priests should continue unmixed and pure; for he who is partaker of the priest-

---

* About the day of Cyrus and Daniel.

hood, must propagate of a wife of the same nation, without having any regard to money, or any other dignities; but he is to make a scrutiny, and take his wife's genealogy from the ancient tables, and procure many witnesses to it;* and this is our practice, not only in Judea, but wheresoever any body of men of our nation do live; and even there, an exact catalogue of our priests' marriages is kept: I mean at Egypt and at Babylon, or in any other place of the rest of the habitable earth, whithersoever our priests are scattered; for they send to Jerusalem the ancient names of their parents in writing, as well as those of their remoter ancestors, and signify who are the witnesses also; but if any war falls out, such as have fallen out a great many of them already, when Antiochus Epiphanes made an invasion upon our country, as also when Pompey the Great and Quintilius Varus did so also, and principally in the wars that have happened in our own times, those priests that survive them, compose new tables of genealogy out of the old records, and examine the circumstances of the women that remain; for still they do not admit of those that have been captives, as suspecting that they had conversation with some foreigners; but what is the strongest argument of our exact management in this matter is what I am now going to say, that we have the names of our high priests, from father to son, set down in our records, for the interval of two thousand years; and if any one of these have been transgressors of these rules, they are prohibited to present themselves at the altar, or to be partakers of any other of our purifications; and this is justly, or rather necessarily done, because every one is not permitted of his own accord to be a writer, nor is there any disagreement in what is written; they being only prophets that have written the original and earliest accounts of things as they learned them of God himself by inspiration; and others have written what hath happened in their own times, and that in a very distinct manner also.

8. For we have not an innumerable multitude of books among us, disagreeing from and contradicting one another [as the Greeks have,] but only twenty-two books, which contain the records of all the past times; which are justly believed to be divine; and of them, five belong to Moses, which contain his laws, and the traditions of the origin of mankind till his death. This interval of time was little short of three thousand years; but as to the time from the death of Moses till the reign of Artaxerxes king of Persia, who reigned after Xerxes, the prophets, who were after Moses, wrote down what was done in their times in thirteen books. The remaining four books contain hymns to God, and precepts for the conduct of human life. It is true, our history hath been written since Artaxerxes, very particularly, but hath not been esteemed of the like authority with the former by our forefathers, because there hath not been an exact succession of prophets since that time; and how firmly we have given credit to those books of our own nation is evident by what we do; for during so many ages as have already passed, no one has been so bold as either to add anything to them or take anything from them, or to make any change in them; but it becomes natural to all Jews, immediately and from their very birth, to esteem those books to contain divine doctrines, and to persist in them, and, if

occasion be, willingly to die for them. For it is no new thing for our captives, many of them in number, and frequently in time, to be seen to endure racks and deaths of all kinds upon the theatres, that they may not be obliged to say one word against our laws, and the records that contain them; whereas, there are none at all among the Greeks who would undergo the least harm on that account, no, nor in case all the writings that are among them were to be destroyed; for they take them to be such discourses as are framed agreeably to the inclinations of those that write them; and they have justly the same opinion of the ancient writers, since they see some of the present generation bold enough to write about such affairs, wherein they were not present, nor had concern enough to inform themselves about them from those that knew them; examples of which may be had in this late war of ours, where some persons have written histories, and published them, without having been in the place concerned, or having been near them when the actions were done; but these men put a few things together by hearsay, and insolently abuse the world, and call these writings by the name of Histories.

9. As for myself, I have composed a true history of that whole war, and all the particulars that occurred therein, as having been concerned in all its transactions; for I acted as general of those among us that are named Galileans, as long as it was possible for us to make any opposition. I was then seized on by the Romans, and became a captive. Vespasian also and Titus had kept me under a guard, and forced me to attend them continually. At the first I was put into bonds; but was set at liberty afterward, and sent to accompany Titus when he came from Alexandria to the siege of Jerusalem; during which time there was nothing done which escaped my knowledge; for what happened in the Roman camp I saw, and wrote down carefully; and what informations the deserters brought [out of the city] I was the only man that understood them. Afterward I got leisure at Rome; and when all my materials were prepared for that work, I made use of some persons to assist me in learning the Greek tongue, and by these means I composed the history of those transactions; and I was so well assured of the truth of what I related, that I first of all appealed to those that had the supreme command in that war, Vespasian and Titus, as witnesses for me, for to them I presented those books first of all, and after them to many of the Romans who had been in that war. I also told them to many of our own men who understood the Greek philosophy; among whom were Julius Archelaus, Herod [king of Chalcis,] a person of great gravity, and king Agrippa himself, a person that deserved the greatest admiration. Now all these men bore their testimony to me, that I had the strictest regard to truth; who yet would not have dissembled the matter, nor been silent, if I, out of ignorance, or out of favour to any side, either had given false colours to actions, or omitted any of them.

10. There have been indeed some bad men, who have attempted to calumniate my history, and took it to be a kind of scholastic performance for the exercise of young men. A strange sort of accusation and calumny this! since every one that undertakes to deliver the history of actions truly, ought to know them accurately himself in the first place, as either having been concerned in them himself, or been informed of them by such as knew them. Now, both these methods of knowledge I may very properly pretend to in

---

* Of this accuracy of the Jews, before and in our Saviour's time, in carefully preserving the genealogies all along, particularly those of the priests, see Josephus's Life, sect. I.

the composition of both my works; for, as I said, I have translated the Antiquities out of our sacred books; which I easily could do, since I was a priest by my birth, and have studied that philosophy which is contained in those writings: and as for the History of the War, I wrote it as having been an actor myself in many of its transactions, an eye-witness in the greatest part of the rest, and was not unacquainted with anything whatsoever that was either said or done in it. How impudent, then, must those deserve to be esteemed who undertake to contradict me about the true state of those affairs! who, although they pretend to have made use of both the emperors' own memoirs, yet they could not be acquainted with our affairs who fought against them.

11. This digression I have been obliged to make out of necessity, as being desirous to expose the vanity of those that profess to write histories; and I suppose I have sufficiently declared that this custom of transmitting down the histories of ancient times, hath been better preserved by those nations which are called Barbarians, than by the Greeks themselves. I am now willing, in the next place, to say a few things to those who endeavour to prove that our constitution is but of late time, for this reason, as they pretend that the Greek writers have said nothing about us: after which I shall produce testimonies for our antiquity out of the writings of foreigners: I shall also demonstrate, that such as cast reproaches upon our nation do it very unjustly.

12. As for ourselves, therefore, we neither inhabit a maritime country, nor do we delight in merchandise, nor in such a mixture with other men as arises from it; but the cities we dwell in are remote from the sea, and having a fruitful country for our habitation, we take pains in cultivating that only. Our principle care of all is this, to educate our children well; and we think it to be the most necessary business of our whole life, to observe the laws that have been given us, and to keep those rules of piety that have been delivered down to us. Since, therefore, besides what we have already taken notice of, we have had a peculiar way of living of our own, there was no occasion offered us in ancient ages for intermixing among the Greeks, as they had for mixing among the Egyptians, by their intercourse of exporting and importing their several goods; as they also mixed with the Phœnicians, who lived by the sea-side, by means of their love of lucre in trade and merchandise. Nor did our forefathers betake themselves, as did some others, to robbery; nor did they, in order to gain more wealth, fall into foreign wars, although our country contained many ten thousands of men of courage sufficient for that purpose; for this reason it was that the Phœnicians themselves came soon by trading and navigation to be known to the Grecians, and by their means the Egyptians became known to the Grecians also, as did all those people whence the Phœnicians in long voyages over the seas carried wares to the Grecians. The Medes also and the Persians, when they were lords of Asia, became well known to them; and this was especially true of the Persians, who led their armies as far as the other continent, [Europe.] The Thracians were also known to them by the nearness of their countries, and Scythians by the means of those that sailed to Pontus; for it was so in general that all maritime nations, and those that inhabited near the eastern or western seas, became most known to those that were desirous to be writers; but such as had their habitations further

from the sea, were for the most part unknown to them; which things appear to have happened as to Europe also, where the city of Rome, that hath this long time been possessed of so much power, and hath performed such great actions in war, is never yet mentioned by Herodotus, nor by Thucydides, nor by any one of their contemporaries; and it was very late, and with great difficulty, that the Romans became known to the Greeks. Nay, those that were reckoned the most exact historians (and Ephorus for one) were so very ignorant of the Gauls and the Spaniards, that he supposed the Spaniards, who inhabited so great a part of the western regions of the earth, to be no more than one city. Those historians also have ventured to describe such customs as were made use of by them, which they never had either done or said; and the reason why these writers did not know the truth of their affairs, was this, that they had not any commerce together;—but the reason why they wrote such falsities was this, that they had a mind to appear to know things which others had not known. How can it then be any wonder, if our nation was no more known to many of the Greeks, nor had given them any occasion to mention them in their writings, while they were so remote from the sea, and had a conduct of life so peculiar to themselves?

13. Let us now put the case, therefore, that we made use of this argument concerning the Grecians, in order to prove that their nation was not ancient, because nothing is said of them in our records; would they not laugh at us all, and probably give the same reasons for our silence that I have now alleged, and would produce their neighbouring nations as witnesses to their own antiquity? Now, the very same thing will I endeavour to do; for I will bring the Egyptians and Phœnicians as my principal witnesses, because nobody can complain of their testimony as false, on account that they are known to have borne the greatest ill-will towards us; I mean this as to the Egyptians, in general all of them, while of the Phœnicians, it is known the Tyrians have been most of all in the same ill dispositions towards us: yet do I confess that I cannot say the same of the Chaldeans, since our first leaders and ancestors were derived from them; and they do make mention of us Jews in their records, on account of the kindred there is between us. Now, when I shall have made my assertions good, so far as concerns the others. I will demonstrate that some of the Greek writers have made mention of us Jews also, that those who envy us may not have even this pretence for contradicting what I have said about our nation.

14. I shall begin with the writings of the Egyptians; not indeed of those that have written in the Egyptian language, which it is impossible for me to do. But Manetho was a man who was by birth an Egyptian, yet had he made himself master of the Greek learning, as is very evident; for he wrote the history of his own country in the Greek tongue, by translating it, as he saith himself, out of their sacred records: he also finds great fault with Herodotus for his ignorance and false relations of Egyptian affairs. Now, this Manetho, in the second book of his Egyptian History, writes concerning us in the following manner. I will set down his very words, as if I were to bring the very man himself into a court for a witness:—"There was a king of ours, whose name was Timaus. Under him it came to pass, I know not how, that God was averse to us, and there came, after a surprising manner, men of ignoble birth out of the eastern parts, and had boldness enough to make

an expedition into our country, and with ease subdued it by force, yet without our hazarding a battle with them. So when they had gotten those that governed us under their power, they afterwards burnt down our cities, and demolished the temples of the gods, and used all the inhabitants after a most barbarous manner: nay, some they slew, and led their children and their wives into slavery. At length they made one of themselves king, whose name was Salatis; he also lived at Memphis, and made both the upper and lower regions pay tribute, and left garrisons in places that were the most proper for them. He chiefly aimed to secure the eastern parts, as foreseeing that the Assyrians, who had then the greatest power, would be desirous of that kingdom and invade them; and as he found in the Saite Nomos [Seth-roite] a city very proper for his purpose, and which lay upon the Bubastic channel, but with regard to a certain theologic notion was called *Avaris*, this he rebuilt, and made very strong by the walls he built about it, and by a most numerous garrison of two hundred and forty thousand armed men whom he put into it to keep it. Thither Salatis came in summer-time, partly to gather his corn, and pay his soldiers their wages, and partly to exercise his armed men, and thereby to terrify foreigners. When this man had reigned thirteen years, after him reigned another, whose name was Beon, for forty-four years; after him reigned another, called Apachnas, thirty-six years and seven months: after him Apophis reigned sixty-one years, and then Jonias fifty years and one month; after all these reigned Assis forty-nine years and two months. And these six were the first rulers among them, who were all along making war with the Egyptians, and were very desirous gradually to destroy them to the very roots. This whole nation was styled Hycsos, that is, *Shepherd-kings*; for the first syllable Hyc, according to the sacred dialect denotes *a king*, as is Sos, *a shepherd*—but this according to the ordinary dialect; and of these is compounded Hycsos: but some say that these people were Arabians." Now, in another copy it is said, that this word does not denote *Kings*, but, on the contrary, denotes *Captive Shepherds*, and this on account of the particle Hyc; for that Hyc, with the aspiration, in the Egyptian tongue again denotes *Shepherds*, and that expressly also; and this to me seems the more probable opinion, and more agreeable to ancient history. [But Manetho goes on]:—"These people, whom we have before named *kings*, and called *shepherds* also, and their descendants," as he says, "kept possession of Egypt five hundred and eleven years." After these, he says, "That the kings of Thebais and of the other parts of Egypt made an insurrection against the shepherds, and that there a terrible and long war was made between them." He says further, "That under a king, whose name was Alisphragmuthosis, the shepherds were subdued by him, and were indeed driven out of other parts of Egypt, but were shut up in a place that contained ten thousand acres: this place was named Avaris." Manetho says, "That the shepherds built a wall round all this place, which was a large and strong wall, and this in order to keep all their possessions and their prey within a place of strength, but that Thummosis the son of Alisphragmuthosis made an attempt to take them by force and by siege with four hundred and eighty thousand men to lie round about them; but that, upon his despair of taking the place by that siege, they came to a composition with them, that they should leave Egypt, and go

without any harm to be done them, whithersoever they would; and that, after this composition was made, they went away with their whole families and effects, not fewer in number than two hundred and forty thousand, and took their journey from Egypt, through the wilderness, for Syria: but that, as they were in fear of the Assyrians, who had then the dominion over Asia, they built a city in that country which is now called Judea, and that large enough to contain this great number of men, and called it Jerusalem."* Now Manetho, in another book of his, says, "That this nation, thus called Shepherds, was also called Captives, in their sacred books." And this account of his is the truth; for feeding of sheep was the employment of our forefathers in the most ancient ages; and as they led such a wandering life in feeding sheep, they were called Shepherds. Nor was it without reason that they were called Captives by the Egyptians, since one of our ancestors, Joseph, told the king of Egypt that he was a captive, and afterwards sent for his brethren into Egypt by the king's permission.

15. But now I shall produce the Egyptians as witnesses to the antiquity of our nation. I shall therefore here bring in Manetho again, and what he writes as to the order of the times in this case, and thus he speaks:—"When this people or shepherds were gone out of Egypt to Jerusalem, Tethmosis the king of Egypt, who drove them out, reigned afterward twenty-five years and four months, and then died; after him his son Chebron took the kingdom for thirteen years; after whom came Amenophis, for twenty years and seven months: then came his sister Amesses, for twenty-one years and nine months; after her came Mephres, for twelve years and nine months; after him was Mephramuthosis, for twenty-five years and ten months; after him was Tethmosis, for nine years and eight months; after him came Amenophis, for thirty years and ten months; after him came Orus, for thirty-six years and five months; then came his daughter Acenchres, for twelve years and one month; then was her brother Rathotis, for nine years; then was Acencheres, for twelve years and five months; then came another Acencheres, for twelve years and three months; after him Armais, for four years and one month; after him was Rameeses, for one year and four months: after him came Armesses Miammoun, for sixty years and two months; after him Amenophis, for nineteen years and six months; after him came Sethosis, and Ramesses, who had an army of horse, and naval force. This king appointed his brother Armais, to be his deputy over Egypt." [In another copy it stood thus:—After him came Sethosis, and Ramesses, two brethren, the former of whom had a naval force, and in a hostile manner destroyed those that met him upon the sea: but as he slew Ramesses in no long time afterward, so he appointed another of his brethren to be his deputy over Egypt.] "He also gave him all the other authority of a king, but with these only injunctions, that he should not wear the diadem, nor be injurious to the queen, the mother of his children, and that he should not meddle with the other concubines of the king; while he made an expedition against Cyprus and Phœnicia, and besides against the Assyrians and the Medes. He then subdued them all, some by his arms, some without fighting, and some by the terror

---

* Here we have an account of the first building of the city of Jerusalem, according to Manetho, when the Phœnician shepherds were expelled out of Egypt, about thirty-seven years before Abraham came out of Haran.

of his great army; and being puffed up by the great successes he had had, he went on still the more boldly, and overthrew the cities and countries that lay in the eastern parts; but after some considerable time, Armais, who was left in Egypt, did all those very things, by way of opposition, which his brother had forbidden him to do, without fear; for he used violence to the queen, and continued to make use of the rest of the concubines, without sparing any of them; nay, at the persuasion of his friends he put on the diadem, and set up to oppose his brother; but then, he who was set over the priests of Egypt, wrote letters to Sethosis, and informed him of all that had happened, and how his brother had set up to oppose him: he therefore returned back to Pelusium immediately, and recovered his kingdom again. The country also was called from his name *Egypt*: for Manetho says that Sethosis himself was called Egyptus, as was his brother Armais called Danaus."

16. This is Manetho's account; and evident it is from the number of years by him set down belonging to this interval, if they be summed up together, that these shepherds, as they are here called, who were no others than our forefathers, were delivered out of Egypt, and came thence, and inhabited this country three hundred and ninety-three years before Danaus came to Argos; although the Argives look upon him as their most ancient king. Manetho, therefore, bears this testimony to two points of the greatest consequence to our purpose, and those from the Egyptian records themselves. In the first place, that we came out of another country into Egypt; and that withal our deliverance out of it was so ancient in time, as to have preceded the siege of Troy almost a thousand years; but then, as to those things which Manetho adds, not from the Egyptian records, but, as he confesses himself, from some stories of an uncertain original, I will disprove them hereafter particularly, and shall demonstrate that they are no better than incredible fables.

17. I will now, therefore, pass from these records, and come to those that belong to the Phœnicians, and concern our nation, and shall produce attestations to what I have said out of them. There are then records among the Tyrians that take in the history of many years, and these are public writings, and are kept with great exactness, and include accounts of the facts done among them, and such as concern their transactions with other nations also, those I mean which were worthy of remembering. Therein it was recorded that the temple was built by king Solomon at Jerusalem, one hundred forty-three years and eight months before the Tyrians built Carthage; and in their annals the building of our temple is related: for Hirom, the king of Tyre, was the friend of Solomon our king, and had such friendship transmitted down to him from his forefathers. He thereupon was ambitious to contribute to the splendour of this edifice of Solomon; and made him a present of one hundred and twenty talents of gold. He also cut down the most excellent timber out of that mountain which is so called Libanus, and sent it to him for adorning its roof. Solomon also not only made him many other presents, by way of requital, but gave him a country in Galilee also, that was called Chabulon; * but there was another passion, a philosophic inclination of theirs, which cemented the friendship that was betwixt them;

for they sent mutual problems to one another, with a desire to have them unriddled by each other; wherein Solomon was superior to Hirom, as he was wiser than he in other respects; and many of the epistles that passed between them are still preserved among the Tyrians. Now, that this may not depend on my bare word, I will produce for a witness, Dius, one that is believed to have written the Phœnician History after an accurate manner. This Dius, therefore, writes thus, in his Histories of the Phœnicians:—" Upon the death of Abibalus, his son Hirom took the kingdom. This king raised banks at the eastern parts of the city, and enlarged it: he also joined the temple of Jupiter Olympius, which stood before in an island by itself, to the city, by raising a causey between them, and adorned that temple with donations of gold. He moreover went up to Libanus, and had timber cut down for the building of temples. They say farther, that Solomon, when he was king of Jerusalem, sent problems to Hirom to be solved, and desired he would send others back for him to solve, and that he who could not solve the problems proposed to him, should pay money to him that solved them; and when Hirom had agreed to the proposals, but was not able to solve the problems, he was obliged to pay a great deal of money, as a penalty for the same. As also they relate, that one Abdemon, a man of Tyre, did solve the problems, and proposed others which Solomon could not solve, upon which he was obliged to repay a great deal of money to Hirom." These things are attested to by Dius, and confirm what we have said upon the same subjects before.

18. And now I shall add Menander the Ephesian, as an additional witness. This Menander wrote the Acts that were done both by the Greeks and Barbarians, under every one of the Tyrian kings; and had taken much pains to learn their history out of their own records. Now, when he was writing about those kings that had reigned at Tyre, he came to Hirom, and says thus:—" Upon the death of Abibalus, his son Hirom took the kingdom; he lived fifty-three years, and reigned thirty-four. He raised a bank on that called the Broad place, and dedicated that golden pillar which is in Jupiter's temple; he also went and cut down timber from the mountain called Libanus, and got timber of cedar for the roofs of the temples. He also pulled down the old temples, and built new ones: besides this, he consecrated the temples of Hercules and Astarte. He first built Hercules's temple, in the month Peritus, and that of Astarte when he made his expedition against the Tityans, who would not pay him their tribute; and when he had subdued them to himself, he returned home. Under this king there was a younger son of Abdemon, who mastered the problems which Solomon, king of Jerusalem, had recommended to be solved." Now the time from this king to the building of Carthage, is thus calculated:—" Upon the death of Hirom, Beleazarus his son took the kingdom; he lived forty-three years, and reigned seven years: after him succeeded his son Abdastartus; he lived twenty-nine years, and reigned nine years. Now four sons of his nurse plotted against him and slew him, the eldest of whom reigned twelve years; after them came Astartus the son of Deleastartus: he lived fifty-four years, and reigned twelve years; after him came his brother Aserymus; he lived fifty-four years, and reigned nine years: he was slain by his brother Pheles, who took the kingdom and reigned but eight months, though he lived fifty years: he was slain by

* 1 Kings ix. 13.

Ithobalus, the priest of Astarte, who reigned thirty-two years, and lived sixty-eight years; he was succeeded by his son Badezorus, who lived forty-five years, and reigned six years; he was succeeded by Matgenus his son: he lived thirty-two years, and reigned nine years: Pygmalion succeeded him: he lived fifty-six years, and reigned forty-seven years. Now, in the seventh year of his reign, his sister fled away from him, and built the city of Carthage in Libya." So the whole time from the reign of Hirom till the building of Carthage, amounts to the sum of one hundred and fifty-five years and eight months. Since then the temple was built at Jerusalem in the twelfth year of the reign of Hirom, there were from the building of the temple until the building of Carthage, one hundred forty-three years and eight months. Wherefore, what occasion is there for alleging any more testimonies out of the Phœnician histories [on behalf of our nation,] since what I have said is so thoroughly confirmed already? and to be sure our ancestors came into this country long before the building of the temple; for it was not till we had gotten possession of the whole land by war that we built our temple. And this is the point that I have clearly proved out of our sacred writings in my Antiquities.

19. I will now relate what hath been written concerning us in the Chaldean histories; which records have a great agreement with our books in other things also. Berosus shall be witness to what I say; he was by birth a Chaldean, well known by the learned, on account of his publication of the Chaldean books of astronomy and philosophy among the Greeks. This Berosus, therefore, following the most ancient records of that nation, gives us a history of the deluge of waters that then happened, and of the destruction of mankind thereby, and agrees with Moses's narration thereof. He also gives us an account of that ark wherein Noah, the origin of our race, was preserved, when it was brought to the highest part of the Armenian mountains: after which he gives us a catalogue of the posterity of Noah, and adds the years of their chronology, and at length comes down to Nabolassar, who was king of Babylon, and of the Chaldeans. And when he was relating the acts of this king, he describes to us how he sent his son Nabuchodonosor against Egypt, and against our land, with a great army, upon his being informed that they had revolted from him; and how, by that means, he subdued them all, and set our temple that was at Jerusalem on fire; nay, and removed our people entirely out of their own country, and transferred them to Babylon; when it so happened that our city was desolate during the interval of seventy years, until the days of Cyrus king of Persia. He then says, "That this Babylonian king conquered Egypt, and Syria, and Phœnicia, and Arabia; and exceeded in his exploits all that had reigned before him in Babylon and Chaldea." A little after which Berosus subjoins what follows in his History of Ancient Times. I will set down Berosus's own accounts, which are these:—"When Nabolassar, father of Nabuchodonosor, heard that the governor whom he had set over Egypt and over the parts of Celesyria and Phœnicia, had revolted from him, he was not able to bear it any longer; but committing certain parts of his army to his son Nabuchodonosor, who was then but young, he sent him against the rebel: Nabuchodonosor joined battle with him, and conquered him, and reduced the country under his dominion again. Now it so fell out, that his father Nabolassar fell into a distemper at this time, and died in the

city of Babylon, after he had reigned twenty-nine years. But as he understood, in a little time, that this father Nabolassar was dead, he set the affairs of Egypt and the other countries in order, and committed the captives he had taken from the Jews, and Phœnicians, and Syrians, and of the nations belonging to Egypt, to some of his friends, that they might conduct that part of the forces that had on heavy armour, with the rest of the baggage, to Babylonia; while he went in haste, having but a few with him, over the desert to Babylon; whither when he was come, he found the public affairs had been managed by the Chaldeans, and that the principal persons among them had preserved the kingdom for him. Accordingly he now entirely obtained all his father's dominions. He then came, and ordered the captives to be placed as colonies in the most proper places of Babylonia: but for himself, he adorned the temple of Belus, and the other temples, after an elegant manner, out of the spoils he had taken in this war. He also rebuilt the old city, and added another to it on the outside, and so far restored Babylon, that none who should besiege it afterwards might have it in their power to divert the river, so as to facilitate an entrance into it; and this he did by building three walls about the inner city, and three about the outer. Some of these walls he built of burnt brick and bitumen, and some of brick only. So when he had thus fortified the city with walls, after an excellent manner, and had adorned the gates magnificently, he added a new palace to that which his father had dwelt in, and this close by it also, and that more eminent in its height, and in its great splendour. It would perhaps require too long a narration, if any one were to describe it. However, as prodigiously large and magnificent as it was, it was finished in fifteen days. Now in this palace he erected very high walks, supported by stone pillars, and by planting what was called a *pensile paradise*, and replenishing it with all sorts of trees, he rendered the prospect of an exact resemblance of a mountainous country. This he did to please his queen, because she had been brought up in Media, and was fond of a mountainous situation."

20. This is what Berosus relates concerning the forementioned king, as he relates many other things about him also in the third book of his Chaldean History; wherein he complains of the Grecian writers for supposing, without any foundation, that Babylon was built by Semiramis, queen of Assyria, and for her false pretence to those wonderful edifices thereto relating, as if they were her own workmanship; as indeed in these affairs the Chaldean History cannot but be the most creditable. Moreover, we meet with a confirmation of what Berosus says, in the archives of the Phœnicians, concerning this king Nabuchodonosor, that he conquered all Syria and Phœnicia; in which case Philostratus agrees with the others in that history which he composed, where he mentions the siege of Tyre; so does Megasthenes also, in the fourth book of his Indian History, wherein he pretends to prove that the forementioned king of the Babylonians was superior to Hercules in strength and the greatness of his exploits; for he says that he conquered a great part of Libya, and conquered Iberia also. Now, as to what I have said before, about the temple at Jerusalem, that it was fought against by the Babylonians, and burnt by them, but was opened again when Cyrus had taken the kingdom of Asia, shall now be demonstrated from what Berosus adds further upon that head; for thus he says in his third book:—

"Nabuchodonosor, after he had begun to build the forementioned wall, fell sick, and departed this life, when he had reigned forty-three years; whereupon his son Evilmerodach obtained the kingdom. He governed public affairs after an illegal and impure manner, and had a plot laid against him by Neriglissoor, his sister's husband, and was slain by him when he had reigned but two years. After he was slain, Neriglissoor, the person who plotted against him, succeeded him in the kingdom, and reigned four years; his son Laborosoarchod obtained the kingdom, though he was but a child, and kept it nine months; but by reason of the very ill-temper and ill practices he exhibited to the world, a plot was laid against him also by his friends, and he was tormented to death. After his death, the conspirators got together, and by common consent put the crown upon the head of Nabonnedus, a man of Babylon, and one who belonged to that insurrection. In his reign it was that the walls of the city of Babylon were curiously built with burnt brick and bitumen; but when he was come to the seventeenth year of his reign, Cyrus came out of Persia with a great army; and having already conquered all the rest of Asia, he came hastily to Babylonia. When Nabonnedus perceived he was coming to attack him, he met him with his forces, and joining battle with him, was beaten; and fled away with a few of his troops with him, and was shut up within the city Borsippus. Hereupon Cyrus took Babylon, and gave order that the outer walls of the city should be demolished, because the city had proved very troublesome to him, and cost him a great deal of pains to take it. He then marched away to Borsippus, to besiege Nabonnedus; but as Nabonnedus did not sustain the siege, but delivered himself into his hands, he was at first kindly used by Cyrus, who gave him Carmania, as a place for him to inhabit in, but sent him out of Babylonia. Accordingly Nabonnedus spent the rest of his time in that country, and there died."

21. These accounts agree with true history in our books; for in them it is written that Nebuchadnezzar, in the nineteenth year of his reign, laid our temple desolate, and so it lay in that state of obscurity for fifty years; but that in the second year of the reign of Cyrus, its foundations were laid and it was finished again in the second year of Darius. I will now add the records of the Phœnicians; for it will not be altogether superfluous to give the reader demonstrations more than enow on this occasion. In them we have this enumeration of the times of their several kings:—"Nabuchodonosor besieged Tyre for thirteen years in the days of Ithobal, their king; after him reigned Baal, ten years; after him were judges appointed, who judged the people: Ecnibalus, the son of Balsacus, two months; Chelbes, the son of Abdeus, ten months; Abbar, the high priest, three months; Mitgonus Gerastratus, the sons of Abdelemus, were judges six years; after whom Balatorus reigned one year; after his death, they sent and fetched Merbalus from Babylon, who reigned four years; after his death, they sent for his brother Hirom, who reigned twenty years. Under his reign Cyrus became king of Persia." So that the whole interval is fifty-four years besides three months; for in the seventh year of the reign of Nebuchadnezzar, he began to besiege Tyre; and Cyrus the Persian, took the kingdom in the fourteenth year of Hirom. So that the records of the Chaldeans and Tyrians, agree with our writings about this temple; and the testimonies here produced are an indisputable and undeniable attestation to the antiquity of our nation: and I suppose that what I have already said, may be sufficient to such as are not very contentious.

22. But now it is proper to satisfy the inquiry of those that disbelieve the records of barbarians, and think none but Greeks to be worthy of credit, and to produce many of these very Greeks who were acquainted with our nation, and to set before them such as upon occasion have made mention of us in their own writings. Pythagoras, therefore, of Samos, lived in very ancient times, and was esteemed a person superior to all philosophers, in wisdom and piety towards God. Now it is plain that he did not only know our doctrines, but was in very great measure a follower and admirer of them. There is not indeed extant any writing that is owned for his; * but many there are who have written his history, of whom Hermippus is the most celebrated, who was a person very inquisitive in all sorts of history. Now, this Hermippus, in his first book concerning Pythagoras, speaks thus:—"That Pythagoras, upon the death of one of his associates, whose name was Calliphon, a Crotoniate by birth, affirmed that this man's soul conversed with him both night and day, and enjoined him not to pass over a place where an ass had fallen down; as also not to drink of such waters as caused thirst again; and to abstain from all sorts of reproaches." After which he adds thus :—"This he said in imitation of the doctrines of the Jews and Thracians, which he transferred into his own philosophy." For it is very truly affirmed of this Pythagoras, that he took a great many of the laws of the Jews into his own philosophy. Nor was our nation unknown of old to several of the Grecian cities, and indeed was thought worthy of imitation by some of them. This is declared by Theophrastus, in his writings concerning laws; for he says that "the laws of the Tyrians forbid men to swear foreign oaths." Among which he enumerates some others, and particularly that called Corban; which oath can only be found among the Jews, and declares what a man may call "a thing devoted to God." Nor indeed was Herodotus of Halicarnassus unacquainted with our nation, but mentions it after a way of his own, when he saith thus, in the second book concerning the Colchians. His words are these:—"The only people who were circumcised in their privy members originally, were the Colchians, the Egyptians, and the Ethiopians; but the Phœnicians and those Syrians that are in Palestine, confess that they learned it from the Egyptians; and as for those Syrians who live about the rivers Thermodon and Parthenius, and their neighbours the Macrones, they say they have already learned it from the Colchians; for these are the only people that are circumcised among mankind, and appear to have done the very same thing with the Egyptians; but as for the Egyptians and Ethiopians themselves, I am not able to say which of them received it from the other." This therefore is what Herodotus says, that "the Syrians that are in Palestine are circumcised." But there are no inhabitants of Palestine that are circumcised, excepting the Jews; and therefore it must be his knowledge of them that enabled him to speak so much concerning them. Cherilus also, a still ancienter writer, and a poet, makes mention of our nation,

---

* It is well known by the learned, that we are not secure that we have any genuine writings of Pythagoras; those Golden Verses, which are his best remains, being generally supposed to have been written not by himself but by some of his scholars only.

and informs us that it came to the assistance of king Xerxes, in his expedition against Greece; for in his enumeration of all those nations, he last of all inserts ours among the rest, when he says :—" At the last there passed over a people, wonderful to be beheld ; for they spake the Phœnician tongue with their mouths ; they dwelt in the Solymean mountains, near a broad lake : their heads were sooty ; they had round rasures on them : their heads and faces were like nasty horse-heads also, that had been hardened in the smoke." I think, therefore, that it is evident to everybody that Cherilus means us, because the Solymean mountains are in our country, wherein we inhabit, as is also the lake Asphaltitis ; for this is a broader and larger lake than any other that is in Syria : and thus does Cherilus make mention of us. But now that not only the lowest sort of the Grecians, but those that are held in the greatest admiration for their philosophic improvements among them, did not only know the Jews, but, when they lighted upon any of them, admired them also, it is easy for any one to know ; for Clearchus, who was the scholar of Aristotle, and inferior to no one of the Peripatetics whomsoever, in his first book concerning sleep, says that "Aristotle, his master, related what follows of a Jew," and sets down Aristotle's own discourse with him. The account is this, as written down by him : "Now, for a great part of what this Jew said, it would be too long to recite it ; but what includes in it both wonder and philosophy, it may not be amiss to discourse of. Now, that I may be plain with thee, Hyperochides, I shall herein seem to thee to relate wonders, and what will resemble dreams themselves. Hereupon Hyperochides answered modestly, and said, For that very reason it is that all of us are very desirous of hearing what thou art going to say. Then replied Aristotle, For this cause it will be the best way to imitate that rule of the Rhetoricians, which requires us first to give an account of the man and of what nation he was, that so we may not contradict our master's directions. Then said Hyperochides, Go on, if it so pleases thee. This man then [answered Aristotle,] was by birth a Jew, and came from Celesyria ; these Jews are derived from the Indian philosophers ; they are named by the Indians *Calami*, and by the Syrians *Judæi*, and took their name from the country they inhabit, which is called Judea ; but for the name of their city it is a very awkward one, for they call it Jerusalem. Now, this man, when he was hospitably treated by a great many, came down from the upper country to the places near the sea, and became a Grecian, not only in his language, but in his soul also ; insomuch that when we ourselves happened to be in Asia about the same places whither he came, he conversed with us and with all other philosophical persons, and made a trial of our skill in philosophy ; and as he had lived with many learned men, he communicated to us more information than he received from us." This is Aristotle's account of the matter, as given us by Clearchus : which Aristotle discoursed also particularly of the great and wonderful fortitude of this Jew in his diet, and continent way of living, as those that please may learn more about him from Clearchus's book itself ; for I avoid setting down any more than is sufficient for my purpose. Now Clearchus said this by way of digression, for his main design was of another nature ; but for Hecateus of Abdera, who was both a philosopher, and one very useful in an active life, he was contemporary with king Alexander in his youth, and afterward was with Ptolemy,

the son of Lagus : he did not write about the Jewish affairs by the by only, but composed an entire book concerning the Jews themselves ; out of which book I am willing to run over a few things, of which I have been treating by way of epitome. And in the first place, I will demonstrate the time when this Hecateus lived ; for he mentions the fight that was between Ptolemy and Demetrius about Gaza, which was fought in the eleventh year after the death of Alexander, and in the hundred and seventeenth Olympiad, as Castor says in his history. For when he had set down this olympiad, he says further, that " on this olympiad Ptolemy the son of Lagus, beat in battle Demetrius the son of Antigonus, who was named Poliocretes, at Gaza." Now, it is agreed by all, that Alexander died in the hundred and fourteenth olympiad ; it is therefore evident that our nation flourished in his time, and in the time of Alexander. Again, Hecateus says to the same purpose as follows :—"Ptolemy got possession of the places in Syria after the battle at Gaza ; and many, when they heard of Ptolemy's moderation and humanity, went along with him to Egypt, and were willing to assist him in his affairs ; one of whom (Hecateus says) was Hezekiah,* the high priest of the Jews ; a man of about sixty-six years of age, and in great dignity among his own people. He was a very sensible man, and could speak very movingly, and was very skilful in the management of affairs, if any other man ever was so ; although, as he says, all the priests of the Jews took tithes of the products of the earth, and managed public affairs, and were in number not above fifteen hundred at the most." Hecateus mentions this Hezekiah a second time, and says, that "as he was possessed of so great a dignity, and was become familiar with us, so did he take certain of those that were with him, and explained to them all the circumstances of their people ; for he had all their habitations and polity down in writing." Moreover, Hecateus declares again, "what regard we have for our laws, and that we resolve to endure anything rather than transgress them, because we think it right for us to do so. Whereupon he adds that, although they are in a bad reputation among their neighbours, and among all those that come to them, and have been often treated injuriously by the kings and governors of Persia, yet can they not be dissuaded from acting what they think best ; but that when they are stripped on this account, and have torments inflicted upon them, and they are brought to the most terrible kinds of death, they meet them after a most extraordinary manner, beyond all other people, and will not renounce the religion of their forefathers." Hecateus also produces demonstrations not a few of this their resolute tenaciousness of their laws, when he speaks thus :—"Alexander was once at Babylon, and had an intention to rebuild the temple of Belus that was fallen to decay, and in order thereto, he commanded all his soldiers in general to bring earth thither. But the Jews, and they only, would not comply with that command ; nay, they underwent stripes and great losses of what they had on this account, till the king forgave them, and permitted them to live in quiet." He adds farther, that "when the Macedonians came to them into that country, and demolished the [old] temples and the altars, they assisted them in demolishing them all ; but [for not assisting them in

---

* This Hezekiah is not named in Josephus's catalogue ; the real high-priest at that time being rather Onias, as Archbishop Usher supposes. However, Josephus often uses the word *high priests* in the plural number, as if there were many living at the same time.

rebuilding them] they either underwent losses, or sometimes obtained forgiveness." He adds farther, that "these men deserve to be admired on that account." He also speaks of the mighty populousness of our nation, and says, that "the Persians formerly carried away many ten thousands of our people to Babylon, as also that not a few ten thousands were removed after Alexander's death into Egypt and Phœnicia, by reason of the sedition that was arisen in Syria." The same person takes notice in his history, how large the country is which we inhabit, as well as of its excellent character, and says, that "the land in which the Jews inhabit contains three millions of arouræ,* and is generally of a most excellent and most fruitful soil ; nor is Judea of lesser dimensions." The same man describes our city of Jerusalem also itself as of a most excellent structure, and very large, and inhabited from the most ancient times. He also discourses of the multitude of men in it, and of the construction of our temple, after the following manner : —"There are many strong places and villages (says he) in the country of Judea ; but one strong city there is, about fifty furlongs in circumference, which is inhabited by a hundred and twenty thousand men, or thereabouts : they call it Jerusalem. There is about the middle of the city, a wall of stone, the length of which is five hundred feet, and the breadth a hundred cubits, with double cloisters ; wherein there is a square altar, not made of hewn stone, but composed of white stones gathered together, having each side twenty cubits long, and its altitude ten cubits. Hard by it is a large edifice, wherein there is an altar and a candlestick, both of gold, and in weight two talents ; upon these there is a light that is never extinguished, neither by night nor by day. There is no image, nor anything, nor any donations therein ; nothing at all is there planted, neither grove nor any thing of that sort. The priests abide therein both nights and days, performing certain purifications, and drinking not the least drop of wine while they are in the temple." Moreover, he attests that we Jews went as auxiliaries along with king Alexander ; after him with his successors. I will add further what he says he learned when he was himself with the same army, concerning the actions of a man that was a Jew. His words are these :—"As I was myself going to the Red Sea, there followed us a man, whose name was Mosollam ; he was one of the Jewish horsemen who conducted us ; he was a person of great courage, and a strong body, and by all allowed to be the most skilful archer that was either among the Greeks or barbarians. Now, this man, as people were in great numbers passing along the road, and a certain augur was observing an augury by a bird, and requiring

them all to stand still, inquired what they stayed for. Hereupon the augur shewed him the bird from whence he took his augury, and told him that if the bird stayed where he was, they ought all to stand still ; but that if he got up, and flew onward, they must go forward ; but that if he flew backward, they must retire again. Mosollam made no reply, but drew his bow, and shot at the bird, and hit him, and killed him ; and as the augur and some others were very angry, and wished imprecations upon him, he answered them thus :—Why are you so mad as to take this most unhappy bird into your hands? for how can this bird give us any true information concerning our march, which could not foresee to save himself? for had he been able to foreknow what was future, he would not have come to this place, but would have been afraid lest Mosollam the Jew would shoot at him, and kill him." But of Hecateus's testimonies we have said enough ; for as to such as desire to know more of them, they may easily obtain them from his book itself. However, I shall not think it too much for me to name Agatharchides, as having made mention of us Jews, though in way of derision at our simplicity, as he supposes it to be ; for when he was discoursing of the affairs of Stratonice, "how she came out of Macedonia into Syria, and left her husband Demetrius, while yet Seleucus would not marry her as she expected, but during the time of his raising an army at Babylon, stirred up a sedition about Antioch ; and how after that the king came back, and upon his taking of Antioch, she fled to Seleucia, and had it in her power to sail away immediately, yet did she comply with a dream which forbade her so to do, and so was caught and put to death." When Agatharchides had premised this story, and had jested upon Stratonice for her superstition, he gives a like example of what was reported concerning us, and writes thus :—"There are a people called Jews, who dwell in a city the strongest of all other cities, which the inhabitants call Jerusalem, and are accustomed to rest on every seventh day ;† at which times they make no use of their arms, nor meddle with husbandry, nor take care of any affairs of life, but spread out their hands in their holy places, and pray till the evening. Now it came to pass, that when Ptolemy, the son of Lagus, came into this city with his army, these men, in observing this mad custom of theirs, instead of guarding the city, suffered their country to submit itself to a bitter lord ; and their law was openly proved to have commanded a foolish practice.‡ This accident taught all other men but the Jews to disregard such dreams as these were, and not to follow the like idle suggestions delivered as a law, when, in such uncertainty of human reasonings, they are at a loss what they should do." Now this our procedure seems a ridiculous thing to Agatharchides, but will appear to such as consider it without prejudice a great thing, and what deserved a great many encomiums ; I mean, when certain men constantly prefer the observation of their laws, and their religion towards God, before the preservation of themselves and their country.

23. Now, that some writers have omitted to mention our nation, not because they knew nothing of us, but because they envied us, or for some other unjustifiable reasons, I think

---

* This number of arouræ or Egyptian acres, as contained in the country of Judea, will be about one-third of the entire number of arouræ in the whole land of Judea ; supposing it one hundred and sixty miles long, and seventy miles broad ; which estimation, for the fruitful parts of it, as perhaps here in Hecateus, is not therefore very wide from the truth. The fifty furlongs in compass for the city of Jerusalem presently are not very wide from the truth also, as Josephus himself makes its wall thirty-three furlongs, besides the suburbs and gardens ; nay, he says that Titus's wall about it at some small distance, after the gardens and suburbs were destroyed, was not less than thirty-nine furlongs. Nor perhaps were its constant inhabitants, in the days of Hecateus, many more than these 120,000, because room was always to be left for vastly greater numbers which came up at the three great festivals ; to say nothing of the probable increase in their number between the days of Hecateus and Josephus, which was at least three hundred years.

† A glorious testimony this of the observation of the Sabbath by the Jews.

‡ Not their law, but the superstitious interpretation of their leaders, which neither the Maccabees nor our blessed Saviour did ever approve of.

I can demonstrate by particular instances; for Hieronymus, who wrote the History of [Alexander's] Successors, lived at the same time with Hecateus, and was a friend of king Antigonus, and president of Syria. Now, it is plain that Hecateus wrote an entire book concerning us, while Hieronymus never mentions us in his history, although he was bred up very near to the places where we live. Thus different from one another are the inclinations of men; while the one thought we deserved to be carefully remembered, so some ill-disposed passion blinded the other's mind so entirely, that he could not discern the truth. And now certainly the foregoing records of the Egyptians, and Chaldeans, and Phœnicians, together with so many of the Greek writers, will be sufficient for the demonstration of our antiquity. Moreover, besides those forementioned, Theophilus, and Theodotus, and Mnaseas, and Aristophanes, and Hermogenes, Euhemerus also, and Conon, and Zopyrion, and perhaps many others (for I have not lighted upon all the Greek books) have made distinct mention of us. It is true, many of the men beforementioned have made great mistakes about the true accounts of our nation in the earliest times, because they had not perused our sacred books; yet have they all of them afforded their testimony to our antiquity, concerning which I am now treating. However, Demetrius Phalereus, and the elder Philo, with Eupolemus, have not greatly missed the truth about our affairs; whose lesser mistakes ought therefore to be forgiven them; for it was not in their power to understand our writings with the utmost accuracy.

24. One particular there is still remaining behind of what I at first proposed to speak to, and that is to demonstrate that those calumnies and reproaches, which some have thrown upon our nation, are lies, and to make use of those writers' own testimonies against themselves: and that in general this self-contradiction hath happened to many other authors by reason of their ill-will to some people, I conclude, is not unknown to such as have read histories with sufficient care; for some of them have endeavoured to disgrace the nobility of certain nations, and of some of the most glorious cities, and have cast reproaches upon certain forms of government. Thus hath Theopompus abused the city of Athens, Polycrates that of Lacedemon, as hath he that wrote the Tripoliticus (for he is not Theopompus, as is supposed by some) done by the city of Thebes. Timeus also hath greatly abused the foregoing people and others also; and this ill-treatment they use chiefly when they have a contest with men of the greatest reputation: some, out of envy and malice,—and others as supposing that by this foolish talking of theirs they may be thought worthy of being remembered themselves; and indeed they do by no means fail of their hopes, with regard to the foolish part of mankind, but men of sober judgment still condemn them of great malignity.

25. Now the Egyptians were the first that cast reproaches upon us; in order to please which nation, some others undertook to pervert the truth, while they would neither own that our forefathers came into Egypt from another country, as the fact was, nor give a true account of our departure thence; and indeed the Egyptians took many occasions to hate us and envy us: in the first place, because our ancestors had had the dominion over their country, and when they were delivered from them, and gone to their own country again, they lived there in prosperity. In the next place, the difference of our

religion from theirs hath occasioned great enmity between us, while our way of divine worship did as much exceed that which their laws appointed, as does the nature of God exceed that of brute beasts; for so far they all agree through the whole country, to esteem such animals as gods, although they differ from one another in the peculiar worship they severally pay to them; and certainly men they are entirely of vain and foolish minds, who have thus accustomed themselves from the beginning to have such bad notions concerning their gods, and could not think of imitating that decent form of divine worship which we made use of, though, when they saw our institutions approved of by many others, they could not but envy us on that account; for some of them have proceeded to that degree of folly and meanness in their conduct, as not to scruple to contradict their own ancient records, nay, to contradict themselves also in their writings, and yet were so blinded by their passions as not to discern it.

26. And now I will turn my discourse to one of their principal writers, whom I have a little before made use of as a witness to our antiquity; I mean Manetho.* He promised to interpret the Egyptian history out of their sacred writings, and premised thus: that "our people had come into Egypt, many ten thousands in number, and subdued its inhabitants;" and when he had further confessed, that "we went out of that country afterward, and settled in that country which is now called Judea, and there built Jerusalem and its temple." Now, thus far he followed his ancient records; but after this he permits himself, in order to appear to have written what rumours and reports passed abroad about the Jews, and introduces incredible narrations, as if he would have the Egyptian multitude, that had the leprosy and other distempers to have been mixed with us, as he says they were, and that they were condemned to fly out of Egypt together; for he mentions Amenophis, a fictitious king's name, though on that account he durst not set down the number of years of his reign, which yet he had accurately done as to the other kings he mentions; he then ascribes certain fabulous stories to this king, as having in a manner forgotten how he had already related that the departure of the shepherds for Jerusalem had been five hundred and eighteen years before; for Tethmosis was king when they went away. Now, from his days, the reigns of the intermediate kings, according to Manetho, amounted to three hundred and ninety-three years, as he says himself, till the two brothers Sethos and Hermeus; the one of whom, Sethos, was called by that other name of Egyptus; and the other, Hermeus, by that of Danaus. He also says that Sethos cast the other out of Egypt, and reigned fifty-nine years, as did his eldest son Rhampses reign after him sixty-six years. When Manetho therefore acknowledged that our forefathers were gone out of Egypt so many years ago, he introduces his fictitious king Amenophis, and says thus:—"This king was desirous to become a spectator of the gods, as had Orus, one of his predecessors in that kingdom, desired the same before him; he also communicated that his desire to his namesake Amenophis, who was the

* In reading this and the remaining sections of this book, and some parts of the next, one may easily perceive that our usually cool and candid author, Josephus, was too highly offended with the imprudent calumnies of Manetho, and the other bitter enemies of the Jews, with whom he had now to deal, and was thereby betrayed into a greater heat and passion than ordinary, and that by consequence he does not hear reason with his usual fairness and impartiality.

son of Papis, and one that seemed to partake of a divine nature, both as to wisdom and the knowledge of futurities." Manetho adds "how this namesake of his told him that he might see the gods, if he would clear the whole country of the lepers and of the other impure people; that the king was pleased with this injunction, and got together all that had any defects in their bodies out of Egypt. And that their number was eighty thousand; whom he sent to those quarries which are on the east side of the Nile, that they might work in them, and might be separated from the rest of the Egyptians." He says farther, that "there were some of the learned priests that were polluted with the leprosy; but that still this Amenophis, the wise man and the prophet, was afraid that the gods would be angry at him and at the king, if there should appear to have been violence offered them; who also added this farther [out of his sagacity about futurities,] that certain people would come to the assistance of these polluted wretches, and would conquer Egypt, and keep it in their possession thirteen years: that, however, he durst not tell the king of these things, but that he left a writing behind him about all those matters, and then slew himself, which made the king disconsolate." After which he writes thus, *verbatim*:—" After those that were sent to work in the quarries had continued in that miserable state for a long while, the king was desired that he would set apart the city Avaris, which was then left desolate of the shepherds, for their habitation and protection; which desire he granted them. Now this city, according to the ancient theology, was Trypho's city. But when these men were gotten into it, and found the place fit for a revolt, they appointed themselves a ruler out of the priests of Heliopolis, whose name was Osarsiph, and they took their oaths that they would be obedient to him in all things. He then, in the first place, made this law for them, That they should neither worship the Egyptian gods, nor should abstain from any one of those sacred animals which they have in the highest esteem, but kill and destroy them all; that they should join themselves to nobody but to those that were of this confederacy.—When he had made such laws as these, and many more such as were mainly opposite to the customs of the Egyptians,* he gave order that they should use the multitude of the hands they had in building walls about their city, and make themselves ready for a war with king Amenophis, while he did himself take into his friendship the other priests and those that were polluted with them, and sent ambassadors to those shepherds who had been driven out of the land by Tethmosis to the city called Jerusalem; whereby he informed them of his own affairs, and of the state of those others that had been treated after such an ignominious manner, and desired that they would come with one consent to his assistance in this war against Egypt. He also promised that he would, in the first place, bring them back to their ancient city and country Avaris, and provide a plentiful maintenance for their multitude; that he would protect them and fight for them as occasion should require, and would easily reduce the country under their dominion. These shepherds were all very glad of this message, and came away with alacrity all together, being in number two hundred thousand men; and in a little time they came to

Avaris. And now Amenophis the king of Egypt, upon his being informed of their invasion, was in great confusion, as calling to mind what Amenophis, the son of Papis, had foretold him; and, in the first place, he assembled the multitude of the Egyptians, and took counsel with their leaders, and sent for their sacred animals to him, especially the priests distinctly, that they should hide for those that were principally worshipped in the temples, and gave a particular charge to the images of their gods with the utmost care. He also sent his son Sethos, who was also named Ramesses from his father Rhampses, being but five years old, to a friend of his. He then passed on with the rest of the Egyptians, being three hundred thousand of the most warlike of them, against the enemy, who met them. Yet did he not join battle with them; but thinking that would be to fight against the gods, he returned back and came to Memphis, where he took Apis and the other sacred animals which he had sent for to him, and presently marched into Ethiopia, together with his whole army and multitude of Egyptians; for the king of Ethiopia was under an obligation to him, on which account he received him, and took care of all the multitude that was with him, while the country supplied all that was necessary for the food of the men. He also allotted cities and villages for this exile, that was to be from its beginning during those fatally determined thirteen years. Moreover, he pitched a camp for his Ethiopian army, as a guard to king Amenophis, upon the borders of Egypt. And this was the state of things in Ethiopia. But for the people of Jerusalem, when they came down together with the polluted Egyptians, they treated the men in such a barbarous manner, that those who saw how they subdued the forementioned country, and the horrid wickedness they were guilty of, thought it a most dreadful thing; for they did not only set the cities and villages on fire, but were not satisfied till they had been guilty of sacrilege, and destroyed the images of the gods, and used them in roasting those sacred animals that used to be worshipped, and forced the priests and prophets to be the executioners and murderers of those animals, and then ejected them naked out of the country. It was also reported that the priest, who ordained their polity and their laws, was by birth of Heliopolis; and his name Osarsiph from Osiris, who was the god of Heliopolis; but that when he was gone over to these people, his name was changed, and he was called Moses."

27. This is what the Egyptians relate about the Jews, with much more, which I omit for the sake of brevity. But still Manetho goes on, that "After this, Amenophis returned from Ethiopia with a great army, as did his son Rhampses with another army also, and that both of them joined battle with the shepherds and the polluted people, and beat them and slew a great many of them, and pursued them to the bounds of Syria." These and the like accounts are written by Manetho. But I will demonstrate that he trifles, and tells arrant lies, after I have made a distinction which will relate to what I am going to say about him; for this Manetho had granted and confessed that this nation was not originally Egyptian, but that they had come from another country, and subdued Egypt, and went away again out of it. But that those Egyptians who were thus diseased in their bodies were not mingled with us afterward, and that Moses who brought the people out was not one of that company, but

---

* This is a very valuable testimony of Manetho, that the laws of Osarsiph, or Moses, were not made in compliance with, but in opposition to the customs of the Egyptians.

lived many generations earlier, I shall endeavour to demonstrate from Manetho's own accounts themselves.

28. Now, for the first occasion of this fiction, Manetho supposes what is no better than a ridiculous thing; for he says that "King Amenophis desired to see the gods." What gods, I pray, did he desire to see? If he meant the gods whom their laws ordained to be worshipped, the ox, the goat, the crocodile, and the baboon, he saw them already; but for the heavenly gods, how could he see them, and what should occasion this his desire? To be sure, it was because another king before him had already seen them. He had then been informed what sort of gods they were, and after what manner they had been seen, insomuch that he did not stand in need of any new artifice for obtaining this sight. However, the prophet by whose means the king thought to compass his design was a wise man. If so, how came he not to know that such his desire was impossible to be accomplished? for the event did not succeed. And what pretence could there be to suppose that the gods would not be seen by reason of the people's maims in their bodies, or leprosy? for the gods are not angry at the imperfection of bodies but at wicked practices; and as to eighty thousand lepers, and those in an ill state also, how is it possible to have them gathered together in one day? nay, how came the king not to comply with the prophet? for his injunction was, that those that were maimed should be expelled out of Egypt, while the king only sent them to work in the quarries, as if he were rather in want of labourers, than intended to purge his country. He says farther, that "this prophet slew himself, as foreseeing the anger of the gods, and those events which were to come upon Egypt afterward; and that he left this prediction for the king in writing." Besides, how came it to pass that this prophet did not foreknow his own death at the first? nay, how came he not to contradict the king in his desire to see the gods immediately? how came that unreasonable dread upon him of judgments that were not to happen in his life-time; or what worse thing could he suffer, out of the fear of which he made haste to kill himself? But now let us see the silliest thing of all:—the king, although he had been informed of these things, and terrified with the fear of what was to come, yet did not he even then eject these maimed people out of his country, when it had been foretold him that he was to clear Egypt of them; but, as Manetho says, "He then, upon their request, gave them that city to inhabit, which had formerly belonged to the shepherds, and was called Avaris; whither when they were gone in crowds (he says) they chose one that had formerly been priest of Heliopolis; and that this priest first ordained that they should neither worship the gods, nor abstain from those animals that were worshipped by the Egyptians, but should kill and eat them all, and should associate with nobody but those that had conspired with them; and that he bound the multitude by oaths to be sure to continue in these laws; and that when he had built a wall about Avaris, he made war against the king." Manetho adds also, that "this priest sent to Jerusalem to invite that people to come to his assistance, and promised to give them Avaris; for that it had belonged to the forefathers of those that were coming from Jerusalem, and that when they were come, they made a war immediately against the king, and got possession of all Egypt." He says also, that "the Egyptians came with an army of two hundred thousand men, and that Amenophis, the king of Egypt, not thinking that he ought to fight against the gods, ran away presently into Ethiopia, and committed Apis and certain others of their sacred animals to the priests, and commanded them to take care of preserving them." He says further, that "the people of Jerusalem came accordingly upon the Egyptians, and overthrew their cities, and burnt their temples, and slew their horsemen, and in short abstained from no sort of wickedness nor barbarity: and for that priest who settled their polity and their laws," he says, "he was by birth of Heliopolis, and his name was Osarsiph, from Osiris the god of Heliopolis; but that he changed his name, and called himself Moses." He then says, that "on the thirteenth year afterward, Amenophis, according to the fatal time of the duration of his misfortunes, came upon them out of Ethiopia with a great army, and joining battle with the shepherds and with the polluted people, overcame them in battle, and slew a great many of them, and pursued them as far as the bounds of Syria."

29. Now Manetho does not reflect upon the improbability of his lie; for the leprous people, and the multitude that was with them, although they might formerly have been angry at the king, and at those that had treated them so coarsely, and this according to the prediction of the prophet; yet certainly, when they were come out of the mines, and had received of the king a city, and a country, they would have grown milder towards him. However, had they ever so much hated him in particular, they might have laid a private plot against himself, but would hardly have made war against all the Egyptians; I mean this on the account of the great kindred they who were so numerous must have had among them. Nay, still, if they had resolved to fight with the men, they would not have had impudence enough to fight with their gods; nor would they have ordained laws quite contrary to those of their own country, and to those in which they had been bred up themselves. Yet are we beholden to Manetho, that he does not lay the principal charge of those horrid transgressions upon those that came from Jerusalem, but says that the Egyptians themselves were the most guilty, and that they were their priests that contrived these things, and made the multitude take their oaths for doing so; but still how absurd is it to suppose that none of these people's own relations or friends should be prevailed with to revolt, nor to undergo the hazards of war with them; while these polluted people were forced to send to Jerusalem, and bring their auxiliaries from thence! What friendship, I pray, or what relation was there formerly, between them that required this assistance? On the contrary, these people were enemies, and greatly differed from them in their customs. He says, indeed, that they complied immediately, upon their promising them that they should conquer Egypt; as if they did not themselves very well know that country out of which they had been driven by force. Now, had these men been in want, or lived miserably, perhaps they might have undertaken so hazardous an enterprise; but as they dwelt in a happy city, and had a large country, and one better than Egypt itself, how came it about, that for the sake of those that had of old been their enemies, of those that were maimed in their bodies, and of those whom none of their own relations would endure, they should run such hazards in assisting them? For they could not foresee that the king would run away from them; on the

contrary, he saith himself, that "Amenophis's son had three hundred thousand men with him, and met them at Pelusium." Now, to be sure, those that came could not be ignorant of this; but for the king's repentance and flight, how could they possibly guess at it? He then says, that "those who came from Jerusalem, and made this invasion, got the granaries of Egypt into their possession, and perpetrated many of the most horrid actions there." And thence he reproaches them, as though he had not himself introduced them as enemies, or as though he might accuse such as were invited from another place, for so doing, when the natural Egyptians themselves had done the same things before their coming, and had taken oaths so to do. However, "Amenophis, some time afterward, came upon them, and conquered them in a battle, and slew his enemies, and drove them before him as far as Syria." As if Egypt were so easily taken by people that came from any place whatsoever; and as if those that had conquered it by war, when they were informed that Amenophis was alive, did neither fortify the avenues of Ethiopia into it, although they had great advantages for doing it, nor did get their other forces ready for their defence! but that he followed them over the sandy desert, and slew them as far as Syria; while yet it is not an easy thing for an army to pass over that country, even without fighting.

30. Our nation, therefore, according to Manetho, was not derived from Egypt, nor were any of the Egyptians mingled with us; for it is to be supposed that many of the leprous and distempered people were dead in the mines, since they had been there a long time, and in so ill a condition; many others must be dead in the battles that happened afterward, and more still in the last battle and flight after it.

31. It now remains that I debate with Manetho about Moses. Now the Egyptians acknowledge him to have been a wonderful, and a divine person; nay, they would willingly lay claim to him themselves, though after a most abusive and incredible manner: and pretend that he was of Heliopolis, and one of the priests of that place, and was ejected out of it among the rest, on account of his leprosy; although it had been demonstrated out of their records, that he lived five hundred and eighteen years earlier, and then brought our forefathers out of Egypt into the country that is now inhabited by us. But now that he was not subject in his body to any such calamity, is evident from what he himself tells us: for he forbade those that had the leprosy either to continue in a city or to inhabit a village, but commanded that they should go about by themselves with their clothes rent; and declares that such as either touch them, or live under the same roof with them, should be esteemed unclean; nay more, if any one of their diseases be healed, and he recover his natural constitution again, he appointed them certain purifications and washings with spring-water, and the shaving of all their hair, and enjoins that they shall offer many sacrifices, and those of several kinds, and then at length admitted into the holy city; although it were to be expected that, on the contrary, if he had been under the same calamity, he should have taken care of such persons beforehand, and have had them treated after a kinder manner, as affected with a concern for those that were to be under the like misfortunes with himself. Nor was it only those leprous people for whose sake he made these laws, but also for such as should be maimed in the smallest part of their body, who yet are not permitted by him to officiate as priests; nay, although any priest already initiated, should have such a calamity fall upon him afterward, he ordered him to be deprived of his honour of officiating. How can it then be supposed that Moses should ordain such laws against himself, to his own reproach and damage who so ordained them? Nor indeed is that other notion of Manetho at all probable, wherein he relates the change of his name, and says, that "he was formerly called Osarsiph;" and this a name no way agreeable to the other, while his true name was Moüses, and signifies a person who is preserved out of the water, for the Egyptians call water Moü. I think, therefore, I have made it sufficiently evident that Manetho, while he followed his ancient records, did not much mistake the truth of the history; but that when he had recourse to fabulous stories, without any certain author, he either forged them himself without any probability, or else gave credit to some men who spake so, out of their ill-will to us.

32. And now I have done with Manetho, I will inquire into what Cheremon says; for he also, when he pretended to write the Egyptian history, sets down the same name for this king that Manetho did, Amenophis, as also of his son Ramesses, and then goes on thus:—"The goddess Isis appeared to Amenophis in his sleep, and blamed him that her temple had been demolished in the war; but that Phritiphantes, the sacred scribe, said to him, that in case he would purge Egypt of the men that had pollutions upon them, he should be no longer troubled with such frightful apparitions. That Amenophis accordingly chose out two hundred and fifty thousand of those that were thus diseased, and cast them out of the country: that Moses and Joseph were scribes, and Joseph was a sacred scribe; that their names were Egyptian originally; that of Moses had been Tisithene, and that of Joseph Peteseph: that these two came to Pelusium, and lighted upon three hundred and eighty thousand that had been left there by Amenophis, he not being willing to carry them into Egypt; that these scribes made a league of friendship, with them and made with them an expedition against Egypt: that Amenophis could not sustain their attacks, but immediately fled into Ethiopia, and left his wife with child behind him, who lay concealed in certain caverns, and there brought forth a son, whose name was Messene, and who, when he was grown up to man's estate, pursued the Jews into Syria, being about two hundred thousand men, and then received his father Amenophis out of Ethiopia."

33. This is the account Cheremon gives us. Now, I take it for granted, that what I have said already hath plainly proved the falsity of both these narrations; for had there been any real truth at the bottom, it was impossible that they should so greatly disagree about the particulars; but for those that invent lies, what they write will easily give us very different accounts, while they forge what they please out of their own heads. Now, Manetho says that the king's desire of seeing the gods was the origin of the ejection of the polluted people; but Cheremon feigns that it was a dream of his own, sent upon him by Isis, that was the occasion of it. Manetho says that the person who foreshewed this purgation of Egypt to the king, was Amenophis; but this man says it was Phritiphantes. As to the numbers of the multitude that were expelled, they agree exceedingly well,* the former reckoning them eighty thousand, and the

---

* By way of irony, I suppose.

latter about two hundred and fifty thousand! Now, for Manetho, he describes these polluted persons as sent first to work in the quarries, and says, that after that the city Avaris was given them for their habitation. As also, he relates that it was not till after they had made war with the rest of the Egyptians, that they invited the people of Jerusalem to come to their assistance; while Cheremon says only, that they were gone out of Egypt, and lighted upon three hundred and eighty thousand men about Pelusium, who had been left there by Amenophis, and so they invaded Egypt with them again; that thereupon Amenophis fled into Ethiopia; but then, this Cheremon commits a most ridiculous blunder in not informing us who this army of so many ten thousands were, or whence they came; whether they were native Egyptians, or whether they came from a foreign country. Nor indeed has this man, who forged a dream from Isis about the leprous people, assigned the reason why the king would not bring them into Egypt. Moreover, Cheremon sets down Joseph as driven away at the same time with Moses, who yet died four generations * before Moses; which four generations make almost one hundred and seventy years. Besides all this, Ramesses, the son of Amenophis, by Manetho's account, was a young man, and assisted his father in his war, and left the country at the same time with him, and fled into Ethiopia: but Cheremon makes him to have been born in a certain cave, after his father was dead, and that he had then overcame the Jews in battle, and drove them into Syria, being in number about two hundred thousand. O the levity of the man! for he neither told us who these three hundred and eighty thousand were, nor how the four hundred and thirty thousand perished; whether they fell in war, or went over to Ramesses; and, what is strangest of all, it is not possible to learn out of him, who they were whom he calls Jews, or to which of these two parties he applies that denomination, whether to the two hundred and fifty thousand leprous people, or to the three hundred and eighty thousand that were about Pelusium. But perhaps it will be looked upon as a silly thing in me to make any larger confutation of such writers as sufficiently confute themselves; for had they been only confuted by other men, it had been more tolerable.

34. I shall now add to these accounts about Manetho and Cheremon, somewhat about Lysimachus, who hath taken the same topic of falsehood, with those forementioned, but hath gone far beyond them in the incredible nature of his forgeries; which plainly demonstrates that he contrived them out of his virulent hatred of our nation. His words are these:—" The people of the Jews being leprous and scabby, and subject to certain other kinds of distemper, in the days of Bocchoris, king of Egypt, they fled to the temples, and got their food there by begging; and as the numbers were very great that were fallen under these diseases, there arose a scarcity in Egypt. Hereupon, Bocchoris, the king of Egypt, sent some to consult the oracle of [Jupiter] Hammon about this scarcity. The god's answer was this, that he must purge his temples of impure and impious men, by expelling them out of those temples into desert places; but as to the scabby and leprous people, he must drown them, and purge his temples, the sun having an indignation at these men being suffered to live;

and by this means the land will bring forth its fruits. Upon Bocchoris's having received these oracles, he called for their priests, and the attendants upon their altars, and ordered them to make a collection of the impure people, and to deliver them to the soldiers, to carry them away into the desert; but to take the leprous people, and wrap them in sheets of lead, and let them down into the sea. Hereupon the scabby and leprous people were drowned, and the rest were gotten together, and sent into desert places, in order to be exposed to destruction. In this case they assembled themselves together, and took counsel what they should do; and determined that, as the night was coming on, they should kindle fires and lamps, and keep watch; that they also should fast the next night, and propitiate the gods, in order to obtain deliverance from them. That on the next day there was one Moses, who advised them that they should venture upon a journey, and go along one road till they should come to places fit for habitation; that he charged them to have no kind regards for any man, nor give good counsel to any, but always to advise them for the worst; and to overturn all those temples and altars of the gods they should meet with: that the rest commended what he had said with one consent, and did what they had resolved on, and so travelled over the desert. But that the difficulties of the journey being over, they came to a country inhabited, and that there they abused the men, and plundered and burnt their temples, and then came into that land which is called Judea, and there they built a city and dwelt therein, and that their city was named *Hierosyla*, from this their robbing of the temples; but that still, upon the success they had afterwards, they through course of time, changed its denomination, that it might not be a reproach to them, and called the city *Hierosolyma*, and themselves *Hierosolymites*."

35. Now this man did not discover and mention the same king with the others, but feigned a newer name, and passing by the dream and the Egyptian prophet, he brings to him [Jupiter] Hammon, in order to gain oracles about the scabby and leprous people; for he says that the multitude of Jews were gathered together at the temples. Now, it is uncertain whether he ascribes this name to these lepers, or to those that were subject to such diseases among the Jews only; for he describes them as a people of the Jews. What people does he mean? foreigners, or those of that country? Why, then, dost thou call them Jews, if they were Egyptians? But if they were foreigners, why dost thou not tell us whence they came? And how could it be that, after the king had thrown many of them into the sea, and ejected the rest into desert places, there should be still so great a multitude remaining? Or after what manner did they pass over the desert, and get the land which we now dwell in, and build our city, and that temple which hath been so famous among all mankind? And besides, he ought to have spoken more about our legislator than by giving us his bare name; and to have informed us of what nation he was, and what parents he was derived from; and to have assigned the reasons why he undertook to make such laws concerning the gods, and concerning matters of injustice with regard to men during that journey. For, in case the people were by birth Egyptians, they would not on the sudden have so easily changed the customs of their country; and in case they had been foreigners, they had for certain some laws or other which had been kept by them from long custom. It is true, that with regard to those

* Here we see that Josephus esteemed a generation between Joseph and Moses to be about 42 or 43 years; which, if taken between the earlier children, well agrees with the duration of human life in those ages.

who had ejected them, they might have sworn never to bear good-will to them, and might have had a plausible reason for so doing. But if these men resolved to wage an implacable war against all men, in case they had acted as wickedly as he relates of them, and this while they wanted the assistance of all men, this demonstrates a kind of mad conduct indeed; but not of the men themselves, but very greatly so of him that tells such lies about them. He hath also impudence enough to say that a name, implying "Robbers of the temples,"* was given to their city, but that this name was afterwards changed. The

* That is the meaning of *Hierosyla* in Greek, not in Hebrew.

reason of which is plain, that the former name brought reproach and hatred upon them in the times of their prosperity, while it seems those that built the city thought they did honour to the city by giving it such a name. So we see that this fine fellow had such an unbounded inclination to reproach us, that he did not understand that robbery of temples is not expressed by the same word and name among the Jews as it is among the Greeks. But why should a man say any more to a person who tells such impudent lies! However, since this book is arisen to a competent length, I will make another beginning, and endeavour to add what still remains to perfect my design, in the following book.

BOOK II

1. IN the former book, most honoured Epaphroditus, I have demonstrated our antiquity, and confirmed the truth of what I have said, from the writings of the Phœnicians, and Chaldeans, and Egyptians. I have, moreover, produced many of the Grecian writers, as witnesses thereto. I have also made a refutation of Manetho and Cheremon, and of certain others of our enemies. I shall now* therefore begin a confutation of the remaining authors who have written anything against us; although I confess I have had a doubt upon me about Apion,† the grammarian, whether I ought to take the trouble of confuting him or not; for some of his writings contain much the same accusations which the others have laid against us, some things that he hath added are very frigid and contemptible, and for the greatest part of what he says, it is very scurrilous; and, to speak no more than the plain truth, it shews him to be a very unlearned person; and what he lays together looks like the work of a man of very bad morals, and of one no better in his whole life than a mountebank. Yet, because there are a great many men so very foolish that they are rather caught by such orations than by what is written with care, and take pleasure in reproaching other men, and cannot abide to hear them commended, I thought it to be necessary not to let this man go off without examination, who had written such an accusation against us, as if he would bring us to make an answer in open court. For I also have observed, that many men are very much delighted when they see a man who first began to reproach another, to be himself exposed to contempt on account of the vices he hath himself been guilty of. However, it is not a very easy thing to go over this man's discourse, nor to know plainly what he means; yet does he seem amidst great confusion and disorder in his falsehoods, to produce, in the first place, such things as resemble what we have examined already, and relate to the departure of our forefathers out of Egypt; and, in the second place, he accuses those Jews that are inhabitants of Alex-

* The former part of this book is written against the calumnies of Apion, and then more briefly against the like calumnies of Apollonius Molo. But after that, Josephus leaves off any more particular reply to those adversaries of the Jews, and gives us a large and excellent description and vindication of that theocracy which was settled for the Jewish nation by Moses, their great legislator.

† Called by Tiberius *Cymbalum Mundi*—the drum of the world.

andria; as, in the third place, he mixes with these things such accusations as concern the sacred purifications, with the other legal rites used in the temple.

2. Now, although I cannot but think that I have already demonstrated, and that abundantly, more than was necessary, that our fathers were not originally Egyptians, nor were thence expelled, either on account of bodily diseases, or any other calamities of that sort, yet will I briefly take notice of what Apion adds upon that subject; for in his third book, which relates to the affairs of Egypt, he speaks thus:— "I have heard of the ancient men of Egypt, that Moses was of Heliopolis, and that he thought himself obliged to follow the customs of his forefathers, and offered his prayers in the open air, towards the city walls; but that he reduced them all to be directed towards the sun-rising, which was agreeable to the situation of Heliopolis; that he also set up pillars instead of gnomons,‡ under which was represented a cavity like that of a boat, and the shadow that fell from their tops fell down upon that cavity, that it might go round about the like course as the sun itself goes round in the other." This is that wonderful relation which we have given us by this great grammarian. But that it is a false one is so plain, that it stands in need of few words to prove it, but is manifest from the works of Moses; for when he erected the first tabernacle to God, he did himself neither give order for any such kind of representation to be made at it, nor ordain that those who came after him should make such a one. Moreover, when in a future age Solomon built his temple in Jerusalem, he avoided all such needless decorations as Apion hath here devised. He says farther, "how he had heard of the ancient men that Moses was of Heliopolis." To be sure that was because, being a younger man himself, he believed those that by their elder age were acquainted and conversed with him. Now, this [man,] grammarian as he was, could not certainly tell which was the poet Homer's country, no more than he could which was the country of Pythagoras, who lived comparatively but a little while ago; yet does he thus easily determine

‡ This seems to have been the first dial that had been made in Egypt, and was a little before the time that Ahaz made his [first] dial in Judea, and about anno 755, in the first year of the seventh olympaid, as we shall see presently. See 2 Kings xx. 11; Isa. xxxviii. 8.

the age of Moses, who preceded them such a vast number of years, as depending on his ancient men's relation, which shews how notorious a liar he was. But then as to this chronological determination of the time when he says he brought the leprous people, the blind, and the lame, out of Egypt, see how well this most accurate grammarian of ours agrees with those that have written before him! Manetho says that the Jews departed out of Egypt in the reign of Tethmosis, three hundred and ninety-three years before Danaus fled to Argos; Lysimachus says it was under king Bocchoris, that is, one thousand seven hundred years ago; Molo and some others determined it as every one pleased: but this Apion of ours, as deserving to be believed before them, hath determined it exactly to have been in the seventh olympiad, and the first year of that olympiad; the very same year in which he says that Carthage was built by the Phœnicians. The reason why he added this building of Carthage was, to be sure, in order, as he thought, to strengthen his assertion by so evident a character of chronology. But he was not aware that this character confutes his assertion; for if we may give credit to the Phœnician records as to the time of the first coming of their colony to Carthage, they relate that Hirom their king was above one hundred and fifty years earlier than the building of Carthage; concerning whom I have formerly produced testimonials out of those Phœnician records, as also that this Hirom was a friend of Solomon when he was building the temple of Jerusalem, and gave him great assistance in his building that temple; while still Solomon himself built that temple six hundred and twelve years after the Jews came out of Egypt. As for the number of those that were expelled out of Egypt, he hath contrived to have the very same number with Lysimachus, and says they were a hundred and ten thousand. He then assigns a certain wonderful and plausible occasion for the name of Sabbath; for he says, that "when the Jews had travelled a six days' journey, they had buboes in their groins: and that on this account it was that they rested on the seventh day, as having got safely to that country which is called Judea; that then they preserved the language of the Egyptians, and called that day the Sabbath, for that malady of buboes in their groin, was named Sabbatosis by the Egyptians." And would not a man now laugh at this fellow's trifling, or rather hate his impudence in writing thus? We must, it seems, take it for granted, that all these hundred and ten thousand men must have had these buboes! But, for certain, if those men had been blind and lame, and had all sorts of distempers upon them, as Apion says they had, they could not have gone one single day's journey; but if they had been all able to travel over a large desert, and, besides that, to fight and conquer those that opposed them, they had not all of them had buboes in their groins after the sixth day was over; for no such distemper comes naturally and of necessity upon those that travel; but still, when there are many ten thousands in a camp together, they constantly march a settled space [in a day.] Nor is it at all probable that such a thing should happen by chance; this would be prodigiously absurd to be supposed. However, our admirable author Apion hath before told us, that "they came to Judea in six days' time;" and again, that "Moses went up to a mountain that lay between Egypt and Arabia, which was called Sinai, and was concealed there forty days, and that when he came down from thence, he gave

laws to the Jews." But then, how is it possible for them to tarry forty days in a desert place, where there was no water, and at the same time to pass all over the country between that and Judea in the six days? And as for this grammatical translation of the word Sabbath, it either contains an instance of his great impudence or gross ignorance; for the words *Sabbo* and *Sabbath* are widely different from one another; for the word Sabbath in the Jewish language denotes *rest* from all sorts of work; but the word Sabbo, as he affirms, denotes among the Egyptians, the malady of a *bubo* in the groin.

3. This is that novel account which the Egyptian Apion gives us concerning the Jews' departure out of Egypt, and is no better than a contrivance of his own. But why should we wonder at the lies he tells us about our forefathers, when he affirms them to be of Egyptian original, when he lies about himself? for although he was born at Oasis in Egypt, he pretends to be, as a man may say, the top man of all the Egyptians; yet does he forswear his real country and progenitors, and by falsely pretending to be born at Alexandria, cannot deny the pravity of his family; for you see how justly he calls those Egyptians whom he hates, and endeavours to reproach; for had he not deemed Egyptians to be a name of great reproach, he would not have avoided the name of an Egyptian himself; as we know that those who brag of their own countries, value themselves upon the denomination they acquire thereby, and reprove such as unjustly lay claim thereto. As for the Egyptians' claim to be of our kindred, they do it on one of the following accounts: I mean, either as they value themselves upon it, and pretend to bear that relation to us; or else as they would draw us in to be partakers of their own infamy. But this fine fellow, Apion, seems to broach this reproachful appellation against us [that we were originally Egyptians] in order to bestow it on the Alexandrians as a reward for the privilege they had given him of being a fellow-citizen with them; he also is apprised of the ill-will the Alexandrians bear to those Jews who are their fellow-citizens, and so proposes to himself to reproach them, although he must thereby include all the other Egyptians also; while in both cases he is no better than an impudent liar.

4. But let us now see what those heavy and wicked crimes are, which Apion charges upon the Alexandrian Jews. "They came" (says he) "out of Syria, and inhabited near the tempestuous sea, and were in the neighbourhood of the dashing of the waves." Now, if the place of habitation includes anything that is reproachful, this man reproaches not his own real country, [Egypt,] but what he pretends to be of his own country, Alexandria; for all are agreed in this, that the part of that city which is near to the sea, is the best part of all for habitation. Now, if the Jews gained that part of the city by force, and have kept it hitherto without impeachment, this is a mark of their valour; but in reality it was Alexander himself that gave them that place for their habitation, when they obtained equal privileges there with the Macedonians. Nor can I devise what Apion would have said, had their habitation been at Necropolis, and not been fixed hard by the royal palace [as it is;] nor had their nation had the denomination of Macedonians given till this very day [as they have.] Had this man now read the epistles of king Alexander, or those of Ptolemy the son of Lagus, or met with the writings of the succeeding kings, or that pillar

which is still standing at Alexandria, and contains the privileges which the great [Julius] Cæsar bestowed upon the Jews; had this man, I say, known these records, and yet hath the impudence to write in contradiction to them, he hath shewn himself to be a wicked man: but if he knew nothing of these records, he hath shewn himself to be a man very ignorant: nay, when he appears to wonder how Jews could be called Alexandrians, this is another like instance of his ignorance; for all such as are called out to be colonists, although they be ever so far remote from one another in their original, receive their names from those that bring them to their new habitations. And what occasion is there to speak of others, when those of us Jews that dwell at Antioch, are named Antiochians, because Seleucus, the founder of that city, gave them the privileges belonging thereto? After the like manner do those Jews that inhabit Ephesus and the other cities of Ionia enjoy the same name with those that were originally born there, by the grant of the succeeding princes; nay, the kindness and humanity of the Romans hath been so great, that it hath granted leave to almost all others to take the same name of Romans upon them; I mean not particularly men only, but entire and large nations themselves also; for those anciently named Iberi, and Tyrrheni, and Sobini, are now called Romani: and if Apion reject this way of obtaining the privilege of a citizen of Alexandria, let him abstain from calling himself an Alexandrian hereafter; for otherwise, how can he who was born in the very heart of Egypt be an Alexandrian, if this way of accepting such a privilege, of which he would have us deprived, be once abrogated? Although indeed these Romans, who are now the lords of the habitable earth, have forbidden the Egyptians to have the privileges of any city whatsoever, while this fine fellow, who is willing to partake of such a privilege himself as he is fobidden to make use of, endeavours by calumnies to deprive those of it that have justly received it: for Alexander did not therefore get some of our nation to Alexandria because he wanted inhabitants for this his city, on whose building he had bestowed so much pains; but this was given to our people as a reward; because he had, upon a careful trial, found them all to have been men of virtue and fidelity to him; for, as Hecateus says concerning us, "Alexander honoured our nation to such a degree, that, for the equity and the fidelity which the Jews exhibited to him, he permitted them to hold the country of Samaria free from tribute. Of the same mind was Ptolemy the son of Lagus, as to those Jews who dwelt at Alexandria." For he intrusted the fortresses of Egypt into their hands, as believing they would keep them faithfully and valiantly for them; and when he was desirous to secure the government of Cyrene, and the other cities of Libya to himself, he sent a party of Jews to inhabit them. And as for his successor Ptolemy, who was called Philadelphus, he did not only set all those of our nation free, who were captives under him, but did give a great deal of money [for their ransom]; and, what was his greatest work of all, he had a great desire of knowing our laws, and of obtaining the books of our sacred scriptures: accordingly he desired that such men might be sent him as might interpret our law to him; and in order to have them well compiled, he committed that care to no ordinary persons, but ordained that Demetrius Phalereus, and Andreas, and Aristeas; the first, Demetrius, the most

learned person of his age, and the others, such as were intrusted with the guard of his body, should take the care of this matter: nor would he certainly have been so desirous of learning our law and the philosophy of our nation, had he despised the men that made use of it, or had he not indeed had them in great admiration.

5. Now, this Apion was unacquainted with almost all the kings of those Macedonians whom he pretends to have been his progenitors,—who were yet very well affected towards us; for the third of those Ptolemies, who were called Euergetes, when he had gotten possession of all Syria by force, did not offer his thank-offerings to the Egyptian gods for his victory, but came to Jerusalem, and, according to our own laws, offered many sacrifices to God, and dedicated to Him such gifts as were suitable to such a victory; and as for Ptolemy Philometer and his wife Cleopatra, they committed their whole kingdom to Jews, when Onias and Dositheus, both Jews, whose names are laughed at by Apion, were the generals of their whole army; but certainly, instead of reproaching them, he ought to admire their actions, and return them thanks for saving Alexandria, whose citizen he pretends to be; for when these Alexandrians were making war with Cleopatra the queen, and were in danger of being utterly ruined, these Jews brought them to terms of agreement, and freed them from the miseries of a civil war. "But then (says Apion) Onias brought a small army afterward upon the city, at the time when Thermus the Roman ambassador, was there present." Yes, do I venture to say, and that he did rightly and very justly in so doing; for that Ptolemy who was called Physco, upon the death of his brother Philometer, came from Cyrene, and would have ejected Cleopatra as well as her sons out of her kingdom, that he might obtain it for himself unjustly. For this cause then it was that Onias undertook a war against him on Cleopatra's account; nor would he desert that trust the royal family had reposed in him in their distress. Accordingly, God gave a remarkable attestation to his righteous procedure; for when Ptolemy Physco had the presumption to fight against Onias's army, and had caught all the Jews that were in the city, [Alexandria,] with their children and wives, and exposed them naked and in bonds to his elephants, that they might be trodden upon and destroyed, and when he had made those elephants drunk for that purpose, the event proved contrary to his preparations; for these elephants left the Jews who were exposed to them, and fell violently upon Physco's friends, and slew a great number of them; nay, after this, Ptolemy saw a terrible ghost, which prohibited his hurting those men; his very concubine, whom he loved so well (some call her Ithaca, and others Irene), making supplication to him, that he would not perpetrate so great a wickedness. So he complied with her request, and repented of what he either had already done, or was about to do; whence it is well known that the Alexandrian Jews do with good reason celebrate this day, on the account that they had thereon been vouchsafed such an evident deliverance from God. However, Apion, the common calumniator of men, hath the presumption to accuse the Jews for making this war against Physco, when he ought to have commended them for the same. This man also makes mention of Cleopatra, the last Queen of Alexandria, and abuses us, because she was ungrateful to us; whereas he ought to have reproved her, who indulged herself in all kinds of injustice and wicked practices, both with regard

to her nearest relations, and husbands who had loved her, and indeed in general with regard to all the Romans, and those emperors that were her benefactors; who also had her sister Arsinoe slain in a temple, when she had done her no harm: moreover, she had her brother slain by private treachery, and she destroyed the gods of her country, and the sepulchres of her progenitors; and while she had received her kingdom from the first Cæsar, she had the impudence to rebel against his son* and successor; nay, she corrupted Antony with her love-tricks, and rendered him an enemy to his country, and made him treacherous to his friends, and [by his means] despoiled some of their royal authority, and forced others in her madness to act wickedly; but what need I enlarge upon this head any farther, when she left Antony in his fight at sea, though he were her husband, and the father of their common children, and compelled him to resign up his government, with the army, and to follow her [into Egypt;] nay, when last of all, Cæsar had taken Alexandria, she came to that pitch of cruelty, that she declared she had some hope of preserving her affairs still, in case she could kill the Jews, though it were with her own hand; to such a degree of barbarity and perfidiousness had she arrived; and doth any one think that we cannot boast ourselves of anything, if, as Apion says, this queen did not at a time of famine, distribute wheat among us? However, she at length met with the punishment she deserved. As for us Jews, we appeal to the great Cæsar what assistance we brought him, and what fidelity we shewed to him against the Egyptians; as also to the senate and its decrees, and the epistles of Augustus Cæsar, whereby our merits [to the Romans] are justified. Apion ought to have looked upon those epistles, and in particular to have examined the testimonies given on our behalf under Alexander and all the Ptolemies, and the decrees of the senate and of the greatest Roman emperors; and if Germanicus was not able to make a distribution of corn to all the inhabitants of Alexandria, that only shews what a barren time it was, and how great a want there was then of corn, but tends nothing to the accusation of the Jews; for what all the emperors have thought of the Alexandrian Jews is well known, for this distribution of wheat was no otherwise omitted with regard to the Jews, than it was with regard to the other inhabitants of Alexandria; but they still were desirous to preserve what the kings had formerly intrusted to their care, I mean the custody of the river: nor did those kings think them unworthy of having the entire custody thereof upon all occasions.

6. But besides this, Apion objects to us thus: —"If the Jews (says he) be citizens of Alexandria, why do not they worship the same gods with the Alexandrians?" To which I give this answer:—Since you are yourselves Egyptians, why do you fight one against another, and have implacable wars about your religion? At this rate we must not call you all Egyptians, nor indeed, in general, men, because you breed up with great care beasts of a nature quite contrary to that of men, although the nature of all men seems to be one and the same. Now, if their be such differences in opinion among you Egyptians, why are you surprised that those who came to Alexandria from another country, and had original laws of their own before, should persevere in the observance of those laws? But still he charges us with being the authors of sedition:

which accusation if it be a just one, why is it not laid against us all, since we are known to be all of one mind? Moreover, those that search into such matters will soon discover that the authors of sedition have been such citizens of Alexandria as Apion is; for while they were the Grecians and Macedonians who were in possession of this city, there was no sedition raised against us, and we were permitted to observe our ancient solemnities; but when the number of the Egyptians therein, came to be considerable, the times grew confused, and then these seditions brake out still more and more, while our people continued uncorrupted. These Egyptians, therefore, were the authors of these troubles, who not having the constancy of Macedonians, nor the prudence of Grecians, indulged all of them the evil manners of the Egyptians, and continued their ancient hatred against us; for what is here so presumptuously charged upon us, is owing to the differences that are amongst themselves; while many of them have not obtained the privileges of citizens in proper times, but style those who are well known to have had that privilege extended to them all, no other than foreigners; for it does not appear that any of the kings have ever formerly bestowed those privileges of citizens upon Egyptians, no more than have the emperors done it more lately; while it was Alexander who introduced us into this city at first, the kings augmented our privileges therein, and the Romans have been pleased to preserve them always inviolable. Moreover, Apion would lay a blot upon us, because we do not erect images to our emperors, as if those emperors did not know this before, or stood in need of Apion as their defender: whereas he ought rather to have admired the magnanimity and modesty of the Romans, whereby they do not compel those that are subject to them to transgress the laws of their countries, but are willing to receive the honours due to them after such a manner as those who are to pay them esteem consistent with piety and with their own laws; for they do not thank people for conferring honours upon them, when they are compelled by violence so to do. Accordingly, since the Grecians and some other nations think it a right thing to make images, nay, when they have painted the pictures of their parents, and wives, and children, they exult for joy; and some there are who take pictures for themselves of such persons as were no way related to them: nay, some take the pictures of such servants as they were fond of. What wonder is it then if such as these appear willing to pay the same respect to their princes and lords? But then our legislator had forbidden us to make images, not by way of denunciation beforehand, that the Roman authority was not to be honoured, but as despising a thing that was neither necessary nor useful for either God or man; and he forbade them, as we shall prove hereafter, to make these images for any part of the animal creation, and much less for God himself, who is no part of such animal creation. Yet hath our legislator nowhere forbidden us to pay honours to worthy men, provided they be of another kind, and inferior to those we pay to God; with which honours we willingly testify our respect to our emperors, and to the people of Rome; we also offer perpetual sacrifices for them; nor do we only offer them every day at the common expenses of all the Jews; but although we offer no other such sacrifices out of our common expenses, no not for our own children, yet do we this as a peculiar honour to the emperors, and to them alone, while we do the same to no other person whomsoever. And let this suffice for an answer in general, to Apion,

---

* Sister's son, and adopted son.

as to what he says with relation to the Alexandrian Jews.

7. However, I cannot but admire those other authors who furnished this man with such his materials; I mean Posidonious and Apollonius Molo, who, while they accuse us for not worshipping the same gods whom others worship, they think themselves not guilty of impiety when they tell lies of us, and frame absurd and reproachful stories about our temple; whereas it is a most shameful thing for freemen to forge lies on any occasion, and much more so to forge them about our temple, which was so famous over all the world, and was preserved so sacred by us; for Apion hath the impudence to pretend, that "the Jews placed an ass's head in their holy place;" and he affirms that this was discovered when Antiochus Epiphanes spoiled our temple, and found that ass's head there made of gold, and worth a great deal of money. To this my first answer shall be this, that had there been any such thing among us, an Egyptian ought by no means to have thrown it in our teeth, since an ass is not a more contemptible animal than ——,* and goats, and other such creatures which among them are gods. But besides this answer, I say further, how comes it about that Apion does not understand this to be no other than a palpable lie, and to be confuted by the thing itself as utterly incredible? For we Jews are always governed by the same laws, in which we constantly persevere; and although many misfortunes have befallen our city, as the like have befallen others, and although Theos [Epiphanes,] and Pompey the Great, and Licinius Crassus, and last of all Titus Cæsar, have conquered us in war, and gotten possession of our temple, yet has none of them found any such thing there, nor indeed anything but what was agreeable to the strictest piety; although what they found we are not at liberty to reveal to other nations. But for Antiochus [Epiphanes,] he had no just cause for that ravage in our temple that he made; he only came to it when he wanted money, without declaring himself our enemy, and attacked us while we were his associates and his friends; nor did he find anything there that was ridiculous. This is attested by many worthy writers; Polybius of Megalopolis, Strabo of Cappadocia, Nicolaus of Damascus, Timagenes, Castor the chronologer, and Apollodorus,† who all say that it was out of Antiochus's want of money that he broke his league with the Jews, and despoiled their temple when it was full of gold and silver. Apion ought to have had a regard to these facts, unless he had himself had either an ass's heart or a dog's impudence; of such a dog I mean as they worship; for he had no other external reasons for the lies he tells of us. As for us Jews, we ascribe no honour or power to asses, as do the Egyptians to crocodiles and asps, when they esteem such as are seized upon by the former, or bitten by the latter, to be happy persons, and persons worthy of God. Asses are the same with us which they are with other wise men, viz., creatures that bear the burdens which we lay upon them; but if they come to our threshing-floors and eat our corn, or do not perform what we impose upon them, we beat them with a great many stripes: because it is their business to minister to us in our husbandry affairs. But this Apion of ours was either perfectly unskilful in the composition of such fallacious discourses, or however, when he began [somewhat better,] he was not able to persevere in what he had undertaken, since he hath no manner of success in these reproaches he casts upon us.

8. He adds another Grecian fable, in order to reproach us. In reply to which, it would be enough to say that we who presume to speak about divine worship ought not to be ignorant of this plain truth, that it is a degree of less impurity to pass through temples, than to forge wicked calumnies of its priests. Now, such men as he are more zealous to justify a sacrilegious king than to write what is just and what is true about us, and about our temple; for when they are desirous of gratifying Antiochus, and of concealing that perfidiousness and sacrilege which he was guilty of, with regard to our nation, when he wanted money, they endeavour to disgrace us, and tell lies even relating to futurities. Apion becomes other men's prophet upon this occasion, and says, that "Antiochus found in our temple a bed and a man lying upon it, with a small table before him, full of dainties, from the [fishes of the] sea, and the fowls of the dry land; that this man was amazed at these dainties thus set before him; that he immediately adored the king, upon the coming in, as hoping that he would afford him all possible assistance; that he fell down upon his knees, and stretched out to him his right hand, and begged to be released; and that when the king bade him sit down, and tell him who he was, and why he dwelt there, and what was the meaning of those various sorts of food that were set before him, the man made a lamentable complaint, and with sighs, and tears in his eyes, gave him this account of the distress he was in; and said that he was a Greek, and that as he went over this province, in order to get his living, he was seized upon by foreigners, on a sudden, and brought to this temple, and shut up therein, and was seen by nobody, but was fattened by these curious provisions thus set before him: and that truly at the first such unexpected advantages seemed to him matter of great joy; that, after a while they brought a suspicion upon him, and at length astonishment, what their meaning should be; that at last he inquired of the servants that came to him, and was by them informed that it was in order to the fulfilling a law of the Jews, which they must not tell him, that he was thus fed; and that they did the same at a set time every year: that they used to catch a Greek foreigner, and fatten him thus up every year, and then lead him to a certain wood, and kill him, and sacrifice with their accustomed solemnities, and taste of his entrails, and take an oath upon this sacrificing a Greek, that they would ever be at enmity with the Greeks; and that then they threw the remaining parts of the miserable wretch into a certain pit." Apion adds further, that "the man said there were but a few days to come ere he was to be slain, and implored Antiochus that, out of the reverence he bore to the Grecian gods, he would disappoint the snares the Jews laid for his blood, and would deliver him from the miseries with which he was encompassed." Now, this is such a most tragical fable, as is full of nothing but cruelty and impudence; yet does it not excuse Antiochus of his sacrilegious attempts, as those who wrote it in his vindication are willing to suppose; for he could not presume beforehand that he should meet with any such thing in com-

---

* *Furiones* in the Latin, which, what animal it denotes, does not now appear.

† These six Pagan authors, here mentioned to have described the famous profanation of the Jewish temple by Antiochus Epiphanes are all lost; I mean so far of their writings as contained that description; though it is plain Josephus perused them all, as extant in his time.

ing to the temple, but must have found it unexpectedly. He was therefore still an impious person, that was given to unlawful pleasures, and had no regard to God in his actions. But [as for Apion] he hath done whatever his extravagant love of lying hath dictated to him, as it is most easy to discover by a consideration of his writings; for the difference of our laws is known not to regard the Grecians only, but they are principally opposite to the Egyptians, and to some other nations also: for while it so falls out, that men of all countries come sometimes and sojourn among us, how comes it about that we take an oath, and conspire only against the Grecians, and that by the effusion of their blood also? Or how is it possible that all the Jews should get together to these sacrifices, and the entrails of one man should be sufficient for so many thousands to taste of them, as Apion pretends? Or why did not the king carry this man, whosoever he was, and whatsoever was his name, (which is not set down in Apion's book,) with great pomp back into his own country? when he might thereby have been esteemed a religious person himself, and a mighty lover of the Greeks, and might thereby have procured himself great assistance from all men against that hatred the Jews bore to him. But I leave this matter; for the proper way of confuting fools is not to use bare words, but to appeal to the things themselves that make against them. Now, then, all such as ever saw the construction of our temple, of what nature it was, know well enough how the purity of it was never to be profaned; for it had four several courts, encompassed with cloisters round about, every one of which had by our law a peculiar degree of separation from the rest. Into the first court everybody was allowed to go, even foreigners; and none but women, during their courses, were prohibited to pass through it; all the Jews went into the second court, as well as their wives, when they were free from all uncleanness; into the third went the Jewish men when they were clean and purified; into the fourth went the priests, having on their sacerdotal garments; but for the most sacred place, none went in but the high priests, clothed in their peculiar garments. Now, there is so great caution used about these offices of religion, that the priests are appointed to go into the temple but at certain hours: for, on the morning, at the opening of the inner temple, those that are to officiate receive the sacrifices, as they do again at noon, till the doors are shut. Lastly, it is not so much as lawful to carry any vessel into the holy house; nor is there anything therein, but the altar [of incense,] the table of [shew bread,] the censer, and the candlestick, which are all written in the law: for there is nothing further there, nor are there any mysteries performed that may not be spoken of; nor is there any feasting within the place. For what I have now said is publicly known, and supported by the testimony of the whole people, and their operations are very manifest; for although there be four courses of the priests, and every one of them have above five thousand men in them, yet do they officiate on certain days only; and when those days are over, other priests succeed in the performance of their sacrifices, and assemble together at mid-day, and receive the keys of the temple, and the vessels by tale, without anything relating to food or drink being carried into the temple; nay, we are not allowed to offer such things at the altar, excepting what is prepared for the sacrifices.

9. What then can we say of Apion, but that he examined nothing that concerned these things, while still he uttered incredible things about them! But it is a great shame for a grammarian not to be able to write true history. Now, if he knew the purity of our temple, he hath entirely omitted to take notice of it; but he forges a story about the seizing of a Grecian, about ineffable food, and the most delicious preparation of dainties; and pretends that strangers could go into a place whereinto the noblest men among the Jews are not allowed to enter, unless they be priests. This, therefore, is the utmost degree of impiety, and a voluntary lie, in order to the delusion of those who will not examine into the truth of matters. Whereas, such unspeakable mischiefs as are above related have been occasioned by such calumnies that are raised upon us.

10. Nay, this miracle of piety derides us further, and adds the following pretended facts to his former fable; for he says that this man related how, "while the Jews were once in a long war with the Idumeans, there came a man out of one of the cities of the Idumeans, who there had worshipped Apollo. This man, whose name is said to have been Zabidus, came to the Jews, and promised that he would deliver Apollo, the god of Dora, into their hands, and that he would come to our temple, if they would all come up with him, and bring the whole multitude of the Jews with them; that Zabidus made him a certain wooden instrument, and put it round about him, and set three rows of lamps therein, and walked after such a manner, that he appeared to those that stood a great way off him to be a kind of star walking upon the earth: that the Jews were terribly frighted at so surprising an appearance, and stood very quiet at a distance; and that Zabidus, while they continued so very quiet, went into the holy house, and carried off that golden head of an ass, (for so facetiously does he write,) and then went his way back again to Dora in great haste." And say you so, sir! as I may reply; then does Apion load the ass, that is himself, and lays on him a burden of fooleries and lies; for he writes of places that have no being; and not knowing the cities he speaks of, he changes their situation; for Idumea borders upon our country, and is near to Gaza, in which there is no such city as Dora, although there be, it is true, a city named Dora in Phoenicia, near Mount Carmel, but it is four days' journey from Idumea. Now, then, why does this man accuse us, because we have not gods in common like other nations? If our forefathers were so easily persuaded upon to have Apollo come to them, and thought they saw him walking upon the earth, and the stars with him; for certainly those who have so many festivals, wherein they light lamps, must yet, at this rate, have never seen a candlestick! But still it seems that while Zabidus took his journey over the country, where were so many ten thousands of people, nobody met him. He also, it seems, even in a time of war, found the walls of Jerusalem destitute of guards. I omit the rest. Now the doors of the holy house were seventy cubits high, and twenty cubits broad; they were all plated over with gold, and almost of solid gold itself; and there were no fewer than twenty men required to shut them every day; nor was it lawful ever to leave them open, though it seems this lamp-bearer of ours opened them easily, or thought he opened them, as he thought he had the ass's head in his hand. Whether, therefore, he returned it to us again, or whether Apion took it and brought it into the temple again, that Antiochus might find it, and afford a handle for a second fable of Apion, is uncertain.

11. Apion also tells a false story, when he mentions an oath of ours, as if we "swore by God, the maker of the heaven, and earth, and sea, to bear no good-will to any foreigner, and particularly to none of the Greeks." Now this liar ought to have said directly that "we would bear no good-will to any foreigner, and particularly to none of the Egyptians." For then his story about the oath would have squared with the rest of his original forgeries, in case our forefathers had been driven away by their kinsmen the Egyptians, not on account of any wickedness they had been guilty of, but on account of the calamities they were under; for as to the Grecians, we are rather remote from them in place than different from them in our institutions, insomuch that we have no enmity with them, nor any jealousy of them. On the contrary, it hath so happened, that many of them have come over to our laws, and some of them have continued in their observation, although others of them had not courage enough to persevere, and so departed from them again; nor did ever anybody hear this oath sworn by us: Apion, it seems, was the only person that heard it, for he indeed was the first composer of it.

12. However, Apion deserves to be admired for his great prudence as to what I am going to say, which is this, "That there is a plain mark among us that we neither have just laws, nor worship God as we ought to do, because we are not governors, but are rather in subjection to Gentiles, sometimes to one nation, and sometimes to another; and that our city hath been liable to several calamities, while their city [Alexandria] hath been of old time an imperial city, and not used to be in subjection to the Romans." But now this man had better leave off his bragging; for everybody but himself would think that Apion said what he hath said against himself; for there are very few nations that have had the good fortune to continue many generations in the principality, but still the mutations in human affairs have put them into subjection under others; and most nations have been often subdued, and brought into subjection by others. Now, for the Egyptians, perhaps they are the only nation that have had this extraordinary privilege, to have never served any of those monarchs who subdued Asia and Europe, and this on account, as they pretend, that the gods fled into their country and saved themselves, by being changed into the shapes of wild beasts. Whereas these Egyptians* are the very people that appear to have never, in all the past ages, had one day of freedom, no not so much as from their own lords. For I will not reproach them with relating the manner how the Persians used them, and this not once only, but many times, when they laid their cities waste, demolished their temples, and cut the throats of those animals whom they esteemed to be gods; for it is not reasonable to imitate the clownish ignorance of Apion, who hath no regard to the misfortunes of the Athenians, or of the Lacedemonians, the latter of whom were styled by all men the most courageous, and the former the most religious, of the Grecians. I say nothing of such kings as have been famous

for piety, particularly of one of them whose name was Cresus, nor what calamities he met with in his life; I say nothing of the citadel of Athens, of the temple at Ephesus, of that at Delphi, nor of ten thousand others which have been burnt down, while nobody casts reproaches on those that were the sufferers, but on those that were the actors therein. But now we have met with Apion, an accuser of our nation, though one that still forgets the miseries of his own people, the Egyptians; but it is that Sesostris, who was once so celebrated a king of Egypt, that hath blinded him. Now, we will not boast of our kings, David and Solomon, though they conquered many nations; accordingly we will let them alone. However, Apion is ignorant of what everybody knows, that the Egyptians were servants to the Persians, and afterwards to the Macedonians, when they were lords of Asia, and were no better than slaves, while we have enjoyed liberty formerly; nay, more than that, have had the dominion of the cities that lie round about us, and this nearly for a hundred and twenty years together, until Pompeius Magnus. And when all the kings everywhere were conquered by the Romans, our ancestors were the only people who continued to be esteemed their confederates and friends, on account of their fidelity to them.

13. "But," says Apion, "we Jews have not had any wonderful men amongst us, not any inventors of arts, nor any eminent for wisdom." He then enumerates Socrates, and Zeno, and Cleanthes, and some others of the same sort; and after all, he adds himself to them, which is the most wonderful thing of all that he says, and pronounces Alexandria to be happy, because it hath such a citizen as he is in it; for he was the fittest man to be a witness to his own deserts, although he hath appeared to all others no better than a wicked mountebank, of a corrupt life, and ill discourses; on which account one may justly pity Alexandria, if it should value itself upon such a citizen as he is. But as to our own men, we have had those who have been as deserving of commendation as any other whatsoever; and such as have perused our Antiquities cannot be ignorant of them.

14. As to the other things which he sets down as blameworthy, it may perhaps be the best way to let them pass without apology, that he may be allowed to be his own accuser, and the accuser of the rest of the Egyptians. However, he accuses us for sacrificing animals, and for abstaining from swine's flesh, and laughs at us for the circumcision of our privy members. Now, as for our slaughter of tame animals for sacrifices, it is common to us and to all other men; but this Apion, by making it a crime to sacrifice them, demonstrates himself to be an Egyptian; for had he been either a Grecian or a Macedonian, [as he pretends to be,] he had not shewn an uneasiness at it; for those people glory in sacrificing whole hecatombs to the gods, and make use of those sacrifices for feasting; and yet is not the world thereby rendered destitute of cattle, as Apion was afraid would come to pass. Yet, if all men had followed the manners of the Egyptians, the world had certainly been made desolate as to mankind, but had been filled full of the wildest sort of brute beasts, which, because they suppose them to be gods, they carefully nourish. However, if any one should ask Apion which of the Egyptians he thinks to be the most wise, and most pious of them all, he would certainly acknowledge the priests to be so; for the histories say that two things were originally committed to their care by their kings'

---

* This notorious disgrace belonging peculiarly to the people of Egypt, ever since the times of the old prophets of the Jews, may be confirmed by the testimony of Isidorus, an Egyptian of Pelusium, (Epist. lib. i. Ep. 489.) And this is a remarkable completion of the ancient prediction of God, by Ezekiel, (xxix. 14, 15,) that the Egyptians should "be a base kingdom, the basest of kingdoms," and that "it should not exalt itself any more above the nations."

injunctions, the worship of the gods, and the support of wisdom and philosophy. Accordingly, these priests are all circumcised, and abstain from swine's flesh; nor does any one of the other Egyptians assist them in slaying those sacrifices they offer to the gods. Apion was therefore quite blinded in his mind when, for the sake of the Egyptians, he contrived to reproach us, and to accuse such others as not only make use of that conduct of life which he so much abuses, but have also taught other men to be circumcised, as says Herodotus; which makes me think that Apion is hereby justly punished for his casting such reproaches on the laws of his own country; for he was circumcised himself of necessity, on account of an ulcer in his privy member; and when he received no benefit by such circumcision, but his member became putrid, he died in great torment. Now, men of good tempers ought to observe their own laws concerning religion accurately, and to persevere therein, but not presently to abuse the laws of other nations, while this Apion deserted his own laws, and told lies about ours; and this was the end of Apion's life, and this shall be the conclusion of our discourse about him.

15. But now, since Apollonius Molo, and Lysimachus, and some others write treatises about our lawgiver Moses and about our laws which are neither just nor true, and this partly out of ignorance, but chiefly out of ill-will to us, while they calumniate Moses as an impostor and deceiver, and pretend that our laws teach us wickedness, but nothing that is virtuous, I have a mind to discourse briefly, according to my ability, about our whole constitution of government, and about the particular branches of it; for I suppose it will thence become evident that the laws we have given us are disposed after the best manner for the advancement of piety, for mutual communion with one another, for a general love of mankind, as also for justice, and for sustaining labours with fortitude, and for a contempt of death; and I beg of those that shall peruse this writing of mine to read it without partiality; for it is not my purpose to write an encomium upon ourselves, but I shall esteem this as a most just apology for us, and taken from those our laws, according to which we lead our lives, against the many and the lying objections that have been made against us. Moreover, since this Apollonius does not do like Apion, and lay a continued accusation against us, but does it only by starts, and up and down his discourse, while he sometimes reproaches us as atheists, and man-haters, and sometimes hits us in the teeth with our want of courage, and yet sometimes, on the contrary, accuses us of too great boldness, and madness in our conduct; nay, he says that we are the weakest of all the barbarians, and this is the reason why we are the only people who have made no improvements in human life; now I think I shall have then sufficiently disproved all these his allegations, when it shall appear that our laws enjoin the very reverse of what he says, and that we very carefully observe those laws ourselves; and if I be compelled to make mention of the laws of other nations, that are contrary to ours, those ought deservedly to thank themselves for it, who have pretended to depreciate our laws in comparison of their own; nor will there, I think, be any room after that for them to pretend either that we have no such laws ourselves, an epitome of which I will present to the reader, or that we do not, above all men, continue in the observation of them.

16. To begin then a good way backward, I would advance this, in the first place, that those who have been admirers of good order, and of living under common laws, and who began to introduce them, may well have this testimony, that they are better than other men, both for moderation and such virtue as is agreeable to nature Indeed, their endeavour was to have everything they ordained believed to be very ancient, that they might not be thought to imitate others, but might appear to have delivered a regular way of living to others after them. Since then this is the case, the excellency of a legislator is seen in providing for the people's living after the best manner, and in prevailing with those that are to use the laws he ordains for them, to have a good opinion of them, and in obliging the multitude to persevere in them, and to make no changes in them, neither in prosperity nor adversity. Now, I venture to say, that our legislator is the most ancient of all the legislators whom we have anywhere heard of; for as for the Lycurguses, and Solons, and Zaleucus Locrenses, and all those legislators who are so admired by the Greeks, they seem to be of yesterday, if compared with our leglslator, insomuch as the very name of a law was not so much as known in old times among the Grecians. Homer is a witness to the truth of this observation, who never uses that term in all his poems, for indeed there was then no such thing among them, but the multitude was governed by wise maxims, and by the injunctions of their king. It was also a long time that they continued in the use of these unwritten customs, although they were always changing them upon several occasions; but for our legislator, who was of so much greater antiquity than the rest, (as even those that speak against us upon all occasions do always confess,) he exhibited himself to the people as their best governor and counsellor, and included in his legislation the entire conduct of their lives, and prevailed with them to receive it, and brought it so to pass, that those that were made acquainted with his laws did most carefully observe them.

17. But let us consider his first and greatest work; for when it was resolved on by our forefathers to leave Egypt and return to their own country, this Moses took the many ten thousands that were of the people, and saved them out of many desperate distresses, and brought them home in safety. And certainly it was here necessary to travel over a country without water, and full of sand, to overcome their enemies, and, during these battles, to preserve their children and their wives, and their prey; on all which occasions he became an excellent general of an army, and a most prudent counsellor, and one that took the truest care of them all: he also so brought it about that the whole multitude depended upon him; and while he had them always obedient to what he enjoined, he made no manner of use of his authority for his own private advantage, which is the usual time when governors gain great powers to themselves, and pave the way for tyranny, and accustom the multitude to live very dissolutely; whereas, when our legislator was in so great authority, he, on the contrary, thought he ought to have regard to piety, and to shew his great good-will to the people; and by this means he thought he might shew the great degree of virtue that was in him, and might procure the most lasting security to those who had made him their governor. When he had therefore come to such a good resolution, and had performed such wonderful exploits, we had just reason to look upon ourselves as having him for a divine governor and counsel-

lor; and when he had at first persuaded him-self* that his actions and designs were agreeable to God's will, he thought it his duty to impress, above all things, that notion upon the multi-tude; for those who have once believed that God is the inspector of their lives will not per-mit themselves in any sin; and this is the char-acter of our legislator: he was no impostor, no deceiver, as his revilers say, though unjustly, but such a one as they brag Minos† to have been among the Greeks, and other legislators after him; for some of them suppose that they had their laws from Jupiter, while Minos said that the revelation of his laws was to be referred to Apollo, and his oracle at Delphi, whether they really thought they were so derived, or supposed, however, that they could persuade the people easily that so it was; but which of these it was who made the best laws, and which had the greatest reason to believe that God was their author, it will be easy, upon comparing those laws themselves together, to determine; for it is time that we came to that point. Now there are innumerable differences in the particular cus-toms and laws that are among all mankind, which a man may briefly reduce under the fol-lowing heads:—Some legislators have permitted their governments to be under monarchies, others put them under oligarchies, and others under a republican form; but our legislator had no re-gard to any of these forms, but he ordained our government to be what, by a strained expression, may be termed a Theocracy,‡ by ascribing the authority and the power to God, and by per-suading all the people to have a regard to him, as the author of all the good things enjoyed either in common by all mankind, or by each one in particular, and of all that they themselves obtained by praying to him in their greatest dif-ficulties. He informed them that it was impos-sible to escape God's observation, either in any of our outward actions, or in any of our in-ward thoughts. Moreover, he represented God as unbegotten,§ and immutable, through all eter-nity, superior to all mortal conceptions in pul-chritude; and though known to us by his power, yet unknown to us as to his essence. I do not now explain how these notions of God are the sentiments of the wisest among the Grecians, and how they were taught them upon the prin-

* This language, that Moses "persuaded himself" that what he did was according to God's will can mean no more than that he was "firmly persuaded," that he had "fully satisfied himself," that so it was— viz., by the many revelations he had received from God, and the numerous miracles God had enabled him to work.

† That is, Moses really was what the heathen legis-lators pretended to be, under a divine direction.

‡ This expression itself, that "Moses ordained the Jewish government to be a Theocracy," may be illus-trated by that parallel expression in the Antiq. b. iii. ch. viii. sect. 9, that "Moses left it to God to be pre-sent at his sacrifices when he pleased; and when he pleased, to be absent." Both ways of speaking sound harsh in the ears of Jews and Christians, but still they were not very improper in him, when he thought fit to accommodate himself to the notions and language of the Greeks and Romans, and this as far as ever truth would give him leave.

§ These excellent accounts of the divine attributes, and that God is not to be at all known in his essence, as also some other clear expressions about the resur-rection of the dead, and the state of departed souls, &c., look more like the exalted notions of the Essenes, or rather Ebionite Christians, than those of a mere Jew or Pharisee. The following large accounts also of the laws of Moses seem to shew a regard to the higher interpretations and improvements of Moses's laws, de-rived from Jesus Christ, than to the bare letter of them in the Old Testament.

ciples that he afforded them. However, they testify with great assurance that these notions are just, and agreeable to the nature of God, and to his majesty; for Pythagoras, and Anaxagoras, and Plato, and the Stoic philosophers that suc-ceeded them, and almost all the rest, are of the same sentiments, and had the same notions of the nature of God; yet durst not these men dis-close those true notions to more than a few, be-cause the body of the people were prejudiced with other opinions beforehand. But our legis-lator, who made his actions agree to his laws, did not only prevail with those that were his contemporaries to agree with these his notions, but so firmly imprinted this faith in God upon all their posterity, that it could never be re-moved. The reason why the constitution of this legislation was ever better directed to the utility of all than other legislations were is this, that Moses did not make religion a part of virtue, but he saw and he ordained other virtues to be a part of religion—I mean justice, and fortitude, and temperance, and a universal agreement of the members of the community with one an-other; for all our actions and studies, and all our words, [in Moses's settlement,] have a reference to piety towards God; for he hath left none of these in suspense, or undetermined; for there are two ways of coming at any sort of learning, and a moral conduct of life: the one is by in-struction in words, the other by practical exer-cises. Now, other lawgivers have separated these two ways in their opinions, and choosing one of those ways of instruction, or that which best pleased every one of them, neglected the other. Thus did the Lacedemonians and the Cretans teach by practical exercises, but not by words; while the Athenians, and almost all the other Grecians, made laws about what was to be done, or left undone, but had no regard to the exercising them thereto in practice.

18. But for our legislator, he very carefully joined these two methods of instruction toge-ther; for he neither left these practical exercises to go on without verbal instruction, nor did he permit the hearing of the law to proceed without the exercises for practice; but beginning im-mediately from the earliest infancy, and the ap-pointment of every one's diet, he left nothing of the very smallest consequence to be done at the pleasure and disposal of the person himself. Ac-cordingly, he made a fixed rule of law, what sorts of food they should abstain from, and what sorts they should use; as also, what communion they should have with others, what great dili-gence they should use in their occupations, and what times of rest should be interposed, that, by living under that law as under a father and a master, we might be guilty of no sin, neither voluntary nor out of ignorance; for he did not suffer the guilt of ignorance to go on without punishment, but demonstrated the law to be the best and the most necessary instruction of all others, permitting the people to leave off their other employments, and to assemble together for the hearing of the law, and learning it exactly, and this not once or twice, or oftener, but every week; which thing all the other legislators seem to have neglected.

19. And indeed the greatest part of mankind are so far from living according to their own laws that they hardly know them; but when they have sinned they learn from others that they have transgressed the law. Those also who are in the highest and principal posts of the government confess they are not acquainted with those laws, and are obliged to take such persons for their assessors in public administra-

tions as profess to have skill in those laws; but for our people, if anybody do but ask any one of them about our laws, he will more readily tell them all than he will tell his own name, and this in consequence of our having learned them immediately as soon as ever we became sensible of anything, and of our having them, as it were, engraven on our souls. Our transgressors of them are but few; and it is impossible, when any do offend, to escape punishment.

20. And this very thing it is that principally creates such a wonderful agreement of minds amongst us all; for this entire agreement of ours in all our notions concerning God, and our having no difference in our course of life and manners, procures among us the most excellent concord of these our manners that is anywhere among mankind; for no other people but we Jews have avoided all discourses about God that any way contradict one another, which yet are frequent among other nations; and this is true not only among ordinary persons, according as every one is affected, but some of the philosophers have been insolent enough to indulge such contradictions, while some of them have undertaken to use such words as entirely take away the nature of God, as others of them have taken away his providence over mankind. Nor can any one perceive amongst us any difference in the conduct of our lives; but all our works are common to us all. We have one sort of discourse concerning God, which is conformable to our law, and affirms that he sees all things; as also, we have but one way of speaking concerning the conduct of our lives, that all other things ought to have piety for their end; and this anybody may hear from our women and servants themselves.

21. Hence hath arisen that accusation which some make against us, that we have not produced men that have been the inventors of new operations, or of new ways of speaking; for others think it a fine thing to persevere in nothing that has been delivered down from their forefathers, and these testify it to be an instance of the sharpest wisdom when these men venture to transgress those traditions; whereas we, on the contrary, suppose it to be our only wisdom and virtue to admit no actions nor supposals that are contrary to our original laws; which procedure of ours is a just and sure sign that our law is admirably constituted; for such laws as are not thus well made are convicted upon trial to want amendment.

22. But while we are ourselves persuaded that our law was made agreeably to the will of God, it would be impious for us not to observe the same; for what is there in it that anybody would change? and what can be invented better? or what can we take out of other people's laws that will exceed it? Perhaps some would have the entire settlement of our government altered. And where shall we find a better or more righteous constitution than ours, while this makes us esteem God to be the governor of the universe, and permits the priests in general to be the administrators of the principal affairs, and withal intrusts the government over the other priests to the chief high priest himself! which priests our legislator, at their first appointment, did not advance to that dignity for their riches, or any abundance of other possessions, or any plenty they had as the gifts of fortune; but he intrusted the principal management of divine worship to those that exceeded others in an ability to persuade men, and in prudence of conduct. These men had the main care of the law and of the other parts of the people's conduct committed to them; for they were the priests who were ordained to be the inspectors of all, and the judges in doubtful cases, and the punishers of those that were condemned to suffer punishment.

23. What form of government then can be more holy than this? what more worthy kind of worship can be paid to God than we pay, where the entire body of the people are prepared for religion, where an extraordinary degree of care is required in the priests, and where the whole polity is so ordered as if it were a certain religious solemnity? For what things foreigners, when they solemnise such festivals, are not able to observe for a few days' time, and call them Mysteries and Sacred Ceremonies, we observe with great pleasure and an unshaken resolution during our whole lives. What are the things, then, that we are commanded or forbidden? They are simply and easily known. The first command is concerning God, and affirms that God contains all things, and is a being every way perfect and happy, self-sufficient, and supplying all other beings; the beginning, the middle, and the end of all things. He is manifest in his works and benefits, and more conspicuous than any other being whatsoever; but as to his form and magnitude, he is most obscure. All materials, let them be ever so costly, are unworthy to compose an image for him; and all arts are unartful to express the notion we ought to have of him. We can neither see nor think of anything like him, nor is it agreeable to piety to form a resemblance of him. We see his works, the light, the heaven, the earth, the sun and the moon, the waters, the generations of animals, the productions of fruits. These things hath God made, not with hands, not with labour, nor as wanting the assistance of any to co-operate with him; but as his will resolved they should be made, and be good also, they were made, and became good immediately. All men ought to follow this Being, and to worship him in the exercise of virtue; for this way of worship of God is the most holy of all others.

24. There ought also to be but one temple for one God; for likeness is the constant foundation of agreement. This temple ought to be common to all men, because he is the common God of all men. His priests are to be continually about his worship, over whom he that is the first by his birth is to be their ruler perpetually. His business must be to offer sacrifices to God, together with those priests that are joined with him, to see that the laws be observed, to determine controversies, and to punish those that are convicted of injustice; while he that does not submit to him shall be subject to the same punishment as if he had been guilty of impiety towards God himself. When we offer sacrifices to him, we do it not in order to surfeit ourselves, or to be drunken; for such excesses are against the will of God, and would be an occasion of injuries and of luxury; but by keeping ourselves sober, orderly, and ready for our other occupations, and being more temperate than others. And for our duty at the sacrifices themselves, we ought in the first place to pray for the common welfare of all, and after that our own; for we are made for fellowship one with another; and he who prefers the common good before what is peculiar to himself is above all acceptable to God. And let our prayers and supplications be made humbly to God, not [so much] that he would give us what is good, (for he hath already given that of his own accord, and hath proposed the same publicly to all,) as that we may duly receive it, and when we have received

it, may preserve it. Now, the law has appointed several purifications at our sacrifices, whereby we are cleansed after a funeral, after what sometimes happens to us in bed, and after accompanying with our wives, and upon many other occasions, too long now to set down. And this is our doctrine concerning God and his worship, and is the same that the law appoints for our practice.

25. But, then, what are our laws about marriage? That law owns no other mixture of sexes but that which nature hath appointed, of a man with his wife, and that this be used only for the procreation of children. But it abhors the mixture of a male with a male; and if any one do that, death is his punishment. It commands us also, when we marry, not to have regard to portion, nor to take a woman by violence, nor to persuade her deceitfully and knavishly; but demand her in marriage of him who hath power to dispose of her, and is fit to give her away by the nearness of his kindred; for, saith the Scripture, "A woman is inferior to her husband in all things." * Let her, therefore, be obedient to him; not so that he should abuse her, but that she may acknowledge her duty to her husband; for God hath given the authority to the husband. A husband, therefore, is to lie only with his wife whom he hath married; but to have to do with another man's wife is a wicked thing; which, if any one venture upon, death is inevitably his punishment: no more can he avoid the same who forces a virgin betrothed to another man, or entices another man's wife. The law, moreover, enjoins us to bring up all our offspring, and forbids women to cause abortion of what is begotten, or to destroy it afterward; and if any woman appears to have done so, she will be a murderer of her child, by destroying a living creature, and diminishing human kind; if any one, therefore, proceeds to such fornication, or murder, he cannot be clean. Moreover, the law enjoins that after the man and wife have lain together in a regular way they shall bathe themselves; for there is a defilement contracted thereby, both in soul and body, as if they had gone into another country; for indeed the soul, by being united to the body, is subject to miseries, and is not freed therefrom again but by death; on which account, the law requires this purification to be entirely performed.

26. Nay, indeed, the law does not permit us to make festivals at the births of our children, and thereby afford occasion of drinking to excess; but it ordains that the very beginning of our education should be immediately directed to sobriety. It also commands us to bring those children up in learning, and to exercise them in the laws, and make them acquainted with the acts of their predecessors, in order to their imitation of them, and that they may be nourished up in the laws from their infancy, and might neither transgress them nor yet have any pretence for their ignorance of them.

27. Our law has also taken care of the decent burial of the dead, but without any extravagant expenses for their funerals, and without the erection of any illustrious monuments for them; but hath ordered that their nearest relations should perform their obsequies; and hath shewn it to be regular, that all who pass by when any one is buried should accompany the funeral, and join in the lamentation. It also ordains, that the house and its inhabitants should be purified after the funeral is over, that every one

may thence learn to keep at a great distance from the thoughts of being pure, if he hath been once guilty of murder.

28. The law ordains also, that parents should be honoured immediately after God himself, and delivers that son who does not requite them for the benefits he hath received from them, but is deficient on any such occasion, to be stoned. It also says, that the young men should pay due respect to every elder, since God is the eldest of all beings. It does not give leave to conceal anything from our friends, because that is not true friendship which will not commit all things to their fidelity : it also forbids the revelation of secrets, even though an enmity arise between them. If any judge takes bribes, his punishment is death : he that overlooks one that offers him a petition, and this when he is able to relieve him, he is a guilty person. What is not by any one intrusted to another ought not to be required back again. No one is to touch another's goods. He that lends money must not demand usury for its loan. These, and many more of the like sort, are the rules that unite us in the bands of society one with another.

29. It will also be worth our while to see what equity our legislator would have us to exercise in our intercourse with strangers; for it will thence appear that he made the best provision he could possibly, both that we should not dissolve our own constitution, nor shew an envious mind towards those that would cultivate a friendship with us. Accordingly, our legislator admits all those that have a mind to observe our laws so to do; and this after a friendly manner, as esteeming that a true union which not only extends to our own stock, but to those that would live after the same manner with us; yet does he not allow those that come to us by accident only to be admitted into communion with us.

30. However, there are other things which our legislator ordained for us beforehand, which of necessity we ought to do in common to all men; as to afford fire, and water, and food to all such as want it; to shew them the roads; and not to let any one lie unburied. He also would have us treat those that are esteemed our enemies with moderation; for he doth not allow us to set their country on fire, nor permit us to cut down those trees that bear fruit : nay, farther, he forbids us to spoil those that have been slain in war. He hath also provided for such as are taken captive that they may not be injured, and especially that the women may not be abused. Indeed he hath taught us gentleness and humanity so effectually, that he hath not despised the care of brute beasts, by permitting no other than a regular use of them, and forbidding any other; and if any of them come to our houses, like suppliants, we are forbidden to slay them : nor may we kill the dams together with their young ones; but we are obliged, even in an enemy's country, to spare and not to kill those creatures that labour for mankind. Thus hath our lawgiver contrived to teach us an equitable conduct every way, by using us to such laws as instruct us therein; while at the same time he hath ordained that such as break these laws should be punished, without the allowance of any excuse whatsover.

31. Now, the greatest part of offences with us are capital—as if any one be guilty of adultery; if any one force a virgin; if any one be so impudent as to attempt sodomy with a male; or if, upon another's making an attempt upon him, he submits to be so used. There is also a law for slaves of the like nature, that can never be avoided. Moreover, if any one cheats another in measures or weights, or makes a knavish bargain

---

* This text is nowhere in our present copies of the Old Testament.

and sale, in order to cheat another; if any one steal what belongs to another, and takes what he never deposited; all these have punishments allotted them, not such as are met with among other nations, but more severe ones. And as for attempts of unjust behaviour towards parents, or impiety against God, though they be not actually accomplished, the offenders are destroyed immediately. However, the reward for such as live exactly according to the laws, is not silver or gold; it is not a garland of olive-branches or of smallage, nor any such public sign of commendation: but every good man hath his own conscience bearing witness to himself, and by virtue of our legislator's prophetic spirit, and of the firm security God himself affords such a one, he believes that God hath made this grant to those that observe these laws, even though they be obliged readily to die for them, that they shall come into being again, and at a certain revolution of things, receive a better life than they had enjoyed before. Nor would I venture to write thus at this time, were it not well known to all by our actions that many of our people have many a time bravely resolved to endure any sufferings, rather than speak one word against our law.

32. Nay, indeed, in case it had so fallen out, that our nation had not been so thoroughly known among all men as they are, and our voluntary submission to our laws had not been so open and manifest as it is, but that somebody had pretended to have written these laws himself, and had read them to the Greeks, or had pretended that he had met with them out of the limits of the known world, that had such reverend notions of God, and had continued for a long time in the firm observance of such laws as ours, I cannot but suppose that all men would admire them on a reflection upon the frequent changes they had therein been themselves subject to; and this while those that have attempted to write somewhat of the same kind for politic government, and for laws, are accused as composing monstrous things, and are said to have undertaken an impossible task upon them. And here I will say nothing of those other philosophers who have undertaken anything of this nature in their writings. But even Plato himself, who is so admired by the Greeks on account of that gravity in his manner and force in his words, and that ability he had to persuade men beyond all other philosophers, is little better than laughed at, and exposed to ridicule on that account, by those that pretend to sagacity in political affairs; although he that shall diligently peruse his writings, will find his precepts to be somewhat gentle, and pretty near to the customs of the generality of mankind. Nay, Plato himself confesseth that it is not safe to publish the true notion concerning God among the ignorant multitude. Yet do some men look upon Plato's discourses as no better than certain idle words set off with great artifice. However, they admire Lycurgus as the principal lawgiver; and all men celebrate Sparta for having continued in the firm observance of his laws for a very long time. So far then we have gained, that it is to be confessed a mark of virtue to submit to laws.* But then let such as admire this in the Lacedemonians compare that duration of theirs with

more than two thousand years, which our political government hath continued; and let them further consider, that though the Lacedemonians did seem to observe their laws exactly while they enjoyed their liberty, yet that when they underwent a change in their fortune, they forgot almost all those laws; while we, having been under ten thousand changes in our fortune by the changes that happened among the kings of Asia, have never betrayed our laws under the most pressing distresses we have been in; nor have we neglected them either out of sloth or for a livelihood.† Nay, if any one will consider it, the difficulties and labours laid upon us have been greater than what appears to have been borne by the Lacedemonian fortitude, while they neither ploughed their land, nor exercised any trades, but lived in their own city, free from all such pains-taking, in the enjoyment of plenty, and using such exercises as might improve their bodies, while they made use of other men as their servants for all the necessaries of life, and had their food prepared for them by the others: and these good and humane actions they do for no other purpose but this, that by their actions and their sufferings, they may be able to conquer all those against whom they make war. I need not add this, that they have not been fully able to observe their laws; for not only a few single persons, but multitudes of them, have in heaps neglected those laws, and have delivered themselves, together with their arms, into the hands of their enemies.

33. Now as for ourselves, I venture to say, that no one can tell of so many; nay, not of more than one or two that have betrayed our laws, no not out of fear of death itself; I do not mean such an easy death as happens in battles, but that which comes with bodily torments, and seems to be the severest kind of death of all others. Now I think, those that have conquered us have put us to such deaths, not out of their hatred to us when they had subdued us, but rather out of their desire of seeing a surprising sight, which is this, whether there be such men in the world who believe that no evil is to them so great as to be compelled to do or to speak anything contrary to their own laws. Nor ought men to wonder at us, if we are more courageous in dying for our laws than all other men are; for other men do not easily submit to the easier things in which we are instituted; I mean working with our hands, and eating but little, and being contented to eat and drink, not at random, or at every one's pleasure, or being under inviolable rules in lying with our wives, in magnificent furniture, and again in the observation of our times of rest; while those that can use their swords in war, and can put their enemies to flight when they attack them, cannot bear to submit to such laws about their way of living: whereas our being accustomed willingly to submit to laws in these instances, renders us fit to shew our fortitude upon other occasions also.

34. Yet do the Lysimachi and the Molones, and some other writers (unskilful sophists as they are, and the deceivers of young men) reproach us as the vilest of all mankind. Now I have no mind to make an inquiry into the laws of other nations; for the custom of our country is to keep our own laws, but not to accuse the laws of others. And indeed, our legislator hath expressly forbidden us to laugh at and revile those that are esteemed gods by other people,

---

* It may not be amiss to set down here a very remarkable testimony of the great philosopher, Cicero, as to the preference of "laws to philosophy:"—"I will boldly declare my opinion, though the whole world be offended at it. I prefer this little book of the Twelve Tables alone to all the volumes of the philosophers. I find it to be not only of more weight, but also much more useful."—De Oratore.

† Or, We have observed our times of rest, and sorts of food allowed us [during our distresses.]

on account of the very name of God ascribed to them. But since our antagonists think to run us down upon the comparison of their religion and ours, it is not possible to keep silence here, especially while what I shall say to confute these men will not be now first said, but hath been already said by many, and these of the highest reputation also; for who is there among those that have been admired among the Greeks for wisdom, who hath not greatly blamed both the most famous poets and most celebrated legislators, for spreading such notions originally among the body of the people concerning the gods? such as these, that they may be allowed to be as numerous as they have a mind to have them; that they are begotten one by another, and that after all the kinds of generation you can imagine. They also distinguish them in their places and ways of living, as they would distinguish several sorts of animals : as some to be under the earth; some to be in the sea; and the ancientest of them all to be bound in hell; and for those to whom they have allotted heaven, they have set over them one, who in title is their father, but in his actions a tyrant and a lord; whence it came to pass that his wife, and brother, and (daughter, which daughter he brought forth from his own head,) made a conspiracy against him to seize upon him and confine him, as he had himself seized upon and confined his own father before.

35. And justly have the wisest men thought these notions deserved severe rebukes; they also laugh at them for determining that we ought to believe some of the gods to be beardless and young, and others of them to be old, and to have beards accordingly; that some are set to trades; that one god is a smith, and another goddess is a weaver; that one god is a warrior, and fights with men; that some of them are harpers, or delight in archery; and besides, that mutual seditions arise among them, and that they quarrel about men, and this so far, that they not only lay hands upon one another, but that they are wounded by men, and lament, and take on for such their afflictions; but what is the grossest of all in point of lasciviousness, are those unbounded lusts ascribed to almost all of them, and their amours; which how can it be other than a most absurd supposal, especially when it reaches to the male Gods, and to the female goddesses also? Moreover, the chief of all their gods, and their first father himself, overlooks those goddesses whom he hath deluded and begotten with child, and suffers them to be kept in prison, or drowned in the sea. He is also so bound up by fate, that he cannot save his own offspring, nor can he bear their deaths without shedding of tears.—These are fine things indeed! as are the rest that follow. Adulteries truly are so impudently looked on in heaven by the gods, that some of them have confessed they envied those that were found in the very act; and why should they not do so, when the eldest of them, who is their king also, hath not been able to restrain himself, in the violence of his lust, from lying with is wife so long as they might get into their bed-chamber? Now, some of the gods are servants to men, and will sometimes be builders for a reward, and sometimes will be shepherds; while others of them, like malefactors, are bound in a prison of brass; and what sober person is there who would not be provoked at such stories, and rebuke those that forged them, and condemn the great silliness of those that admit them for true! Nay, others there are that have advanced a certain timorousness and fear, as also madness and fraud, and any other of the vilest passions, into the nature and form of gods, and have persuaded whole cities to offer sacrifices to the better sort of them; on which account they have been absolutely forced to esteem some gods as the givers of good things, and to call others of them averters of evil. They also endeavour to move them, as they would the vilest of men, by gifts and presents, as looking for nothing else than to receive some great mischief from them, unless they pay them such wages.

36. Wherefore it deserves our inquiry what should be the occasion of this unjust management, and of these scandals about the Deity. And truly I suppose it to be derived from the imperfect knowledge the heathen legislators had at first of the true nature of God. Nor did they explain to the people even so far as they did comprehend of it; nor did they compose the other parts of their political settlements according to it, but omitted it as a thing of very little consequence, and gave leave both to the poets to introduce what gods they pleased, and those subject to all sorts of passions, and to the orators to procure political decrees from the people for the admission of such foreign gods as they thought proper. The painters also, and statuaries of Greece, had herein great power, as each of them could contrive a shape [proper for a god;] the one to be formed out of clay, and the other by making a bare picture of such a one; but those workmen that were principally admired, had the use of ivory and of gold as the constant materials for their new statues; [whereby it comes to pass that some temples are quite deserted, while others are in great esteem, and adorned with all the rites of all kinds of purification.] Besides this, the first gods, who have long flourished in the honours done them, are now grown old, [while those that flourished after them are come in their room as a second rank, that I may speak the most honourably of them that I can :] nay, certain other gods there are who are newly introduced, and newly worshipped [as we, by way of digression, have said already, and yet have left their places of worship desolate;] and for their temples, some of them are already left desolate, and others are built anew, according to the pleasure of men; whereas they ought to have preserved their opinion about God and that worship which is due to him, always and immutably the same.

37. But now, this Apollonius Molo was one of these foolish and proud men. However, nothing that I have said was unknown to those that were real philosophers among the Greeks; nor were they unacquainted with those frigid pretences of allegories [which had been alleged for such things :] on which account they justly despised them, but have still agreed with us as to the true and becoming notions of God; whence it was that Plato would not have political settlements to admit of any one of the other poets, and dismisses even Homer himself, with a garland on his head, and with ointment poured upon him, and this because he should not destroy the right notions of God with his fables. Nay, Plato principally imitated our legislator in this point, that he enjoined his citizens to have the main regard to this precept, " That every one of them should learn their laws accurately." He also ordained, that they should not admit of foreigners intermixing with their own people at random, and provided that the commonwealth should keep itself pure, and consist of such only as persevered in their own laws. Apollonius Molo did no way consider this, when he made it one branch of his accusation against us, that we do not admit of such as have different notions

about God, nor will we have fellowship with those that choose to observe a way of living different from ourselves; yet is not this method peculiar to us, but common to all other men; not among the ordinary Grecians only; but among such of those Grecians as are of the greatest reputation among them. Moreover, the Lacedemonians continued in their way of expelling foreigners and would not, indeed, give leave to their own people, to travel abroad, as suspecting that those two things would introduce a dissolution of their own laws: and perhaps there may be some reason to blame the rigid severity of the Lacedemonians; for they bestowed the privilege of their city on no foreigners, nor would give leave to them to stay among them: whereas we, though we do not think fit to imitate other institutions, yet do we willingly admit of those that desire to partake of ours, which I think I may reckon to be a plain indication of our humanity, and at the same time of our magnanimity also.

38. But I shall say no more of the Lacedemonians. As for the Athenians, who glory in having made their city to be common to all men, what their behaviour was, Apollonius did not know, while they punished those that spoke contrary to their laws about the gods, without mercy; for on what other account was it that Socrates was put to death by them? Certainly, he neither betrayed their city to its enemies, nor was he guilty of sacrilege with regard to their temples; but on this account, that he swore certain new oaths, and that he affirmed, either in earnest, or, as some say, only in jest, that a certain demon used to make signs to him [what he should not do]. For these reasons he was condemned to drink poison, and kill himself. His accuser also complained that he corrupted the young men, by inducing them to despise the political settlement and laws of their city: and thus was Socrates, the citizen of Athens, punished. There was also Anaxagoras, who, although he was of Clazomenæ, was within a few suffrages of being condemned to die, because he said the sun, which the Athenians thought to be a god, was a ball of fire. They also made this public proclamation, "That they would give a talent to any one who would kill Diagoras of Melos," because it was reported that he laughed at their mysteries: Protagoras also, who was thought to have written somewhat that was not owned for truth by the Athenians about the gods, had been seized upon, and put to death, if he had not fled immediately. Nor need we wonder that they thus treated such considerable men, when they did not even spare women; for they very lately slew a certain priestess, because she was accused by somebody that she initiated people into the worship of strange gods, it having been forbidden so to do by one of their laws; and a capital punishment had been decreed to such as introduced a strange god; it being manifest, that they who make use of such a law, do not believe those of other nations to be really gods, otherwise they had not envied themselves the advantage of more gods than they already had; and this was the happy administration of the affairs of the Athenians! Now, as to the Scythians, they take a pleasure in killing men, and differ little from brute beasts; yet do they think it reasonable to have their institutions observed. They also slew Anacharsis, a person greatly admired for his wisdom among the Greeks, when he returned to them, because he appeared to come fraught with Grecian customs. We find many punished among the Persians, on the same account. Apollonius was greatly pleased with the laws of the Persians, and was an admirer of them, because the Greeks enjoyed the advantage of their courage, and had the very same opinion about the gods which they had. This last was exemplified in the temples they burnt, and their courage in coming and almost entirely enslaving the Grecians. However, Apollonius had imitated all the Persian institutions, and that by his offering violence to other men's wives, and castrating his own sons. Now, with us, it is a capital crime, if any one does thus abuse even a brute beast; and as for us, neither hath the fear of our governors, nor a desire of following what other nations have in so great esteem, been able to withdraw us from our laws; nor have we exerted our courage in raising up wars to increase our wealth, but only for the observation of our laws; and when we with patience bear other losses, yet when any persons would compel us to break our laws, then it is that we choose to go to war, though it be beyond our ability to pursue it, and bear the greatest calamities to the last with much fortitude; and indeed, what reason can there be why we should desire to imitate the laws of other nations, while we see they are not observed by their own legislators? And why do not the Lacedemonians think of abolishing that form of their government which suffers them not to associate with any others, as well as their contempt of matrimony? And why do not the Eleans and Thebans abolish that unnatural and impudent lust, which makes them lie with males? For they will not shew a sufficient sign of their repentance of what they of old thought to be very excellent, and very advantageous in their practices, unless they entirely avoid all such actions for the time to come: nay, such things are inserted into the body of their laws, and had once such a power among the Greeks, that they ascribed these sodomitical practices to the gods themselves, as part of their good character; and indeed it was according to the same manner that the gods married their own sisters. This the Greeks contrived as an apology for their own absurd and unnatural pleasures.

39. I omit to speak concerning punishments, and how many ways of escaping them the greatest part of legislators have afforded malefactors, by ordaining that, for adulteries, fines in money should be allowed, and for corrupting [virgins] they need only marry them; as also what excuses they may have in denying the facts, if any one should attempt to inquire into them; for amongst most other nations it is a studied art how men may transgress their laws! but no such thing is permitted amongst us; for though we be deprived of our wealth, of our cities, or of other advantages we have, our law continues immortal; nor can any Jew go so far from his own country, nor be so affrighted at the severest lord, as not to be more affrighted at the law than at him. If, therefore, this be the disposition we are under, with regard to the excellency of our laws, let our enemies make use of this concession, that our laws are most excellent; and if still they imagine that though we so firmly adhere to them, yet are they bad laws notwithstanding, what penalties then do they deserve to undergo who do not observe their own laws, which they esteem superior? Whereas, therefore, length of time is esteemed to be the truest touchstone in all cases, I would make that a testimonial of the excellency of our laws, and of that belief thereby delivered to us concerning God; for as there hath been a very long time for this comparison, if any one will but compare its duration with the duration of the

laws made by other legislators, he will find our legislator to have been the most ancient of them all.

40. We have already demonstrated that our laws have been such as have always inspired admiration and imitation into all other men: nay, the earliest Grecian philosophers, though in appearance they observed the laws of their own countries, yet did they, in their actions and their philosophic doctrines, follow our legislator, and instructed men to live sparingly, and to have friendly communication one with another. Nay, farther, the multitude of mankind itself have had a great inclination for a long time to follow our religious observances; for there is not any city of the Grecians, nor any of the barbarians, nor any nation whatsoever, whither our custom of resting on the seventh day hath not come, and by which our fasts and lighting up lamps, and many of our prohibitions as to our food, are not observed; they also endeavour to imitate our mutual concord with one another, and the charitable distribution of our goods, and our diligence in our trades, and our fortitude in undergoing the distresses we are in, on account of our laws; and, what is here matter of the greatest admiration, our law hath no bait of pleasure to allure men to it, but it prevails by its own force; and as God himself pervades all the world, so hath our law passed through all the world also. So that if any one will but reflect on his own country, and his own family, he will have reason to give credit to what I say. It is therefore but just, either to condemn all mankind of indulging a wicked disposition, when they have been so desirous of imitating laws that are to them foreign and evil in themselves, rather than following laws of their own that are of a better character, or else our accusers must leave off their spite against us; nor are we guilty of any envious behaviour towards them, when we honour our own legislator, and believe what he, by his prophetic authority, hath taught us concerning God; for though we should not be able ourselves to understand the excellency of our own laws, yet would the great multitude of those that desire to imitate them justify us in greatly valuing ourselves upon them.

41. But as for the [distinct] political laws by which we are governed, I have delivered them accurately in my books of Antiquities; and have only mentioned them now, so far as was necessary to my present purpose, without proposing to myself either to blame the laws of other nations, or to make an encomium upon our own, —but in order to convict those that have written about us unjustly, and in an impudent affectation of disguising the truth. And now I think I have sufficiently completed what I proposed in writing these books; for whereas our accusers have pretended that our nation are a people of very late original, I have demonstrated that they are exceeding ancient; for I have produced as witnesses thereto, many ancient writers, who have made mention of us in their books, while they had said no such writer had so done. Moreover, they had said that we were sprung from the Egyptians, while I have proved that we came from another country into Egypt; while they had told lies of us, as if we were expelled thence on account of diseases on our bodies, it has appeared on the contrary, that we returned to our country by our own choice, and with sound and strong bodies. Those accusers reproached our legislator as a vile fellow; whereas God in old time bare witness to his virtuous conduct; and since that testimony of God, time itself hath been discovered to have borne witness to the same thing.

42. As to the laws themselves, more words are unnecessary, for they are visible in their own nature, and appear to teach not impiety, but the truest piety in the world. They do not make men hate one another, but encourage people to communicate what they have to one another freely; they are enemies to injustice, they take care of righteousness, they banish idleness and expensive living, and instruct men to be content with what they have, and to be laborious in their callings; they forbid men to make war from a desire of getting more, but make men courageous in defending the laws; they are inexorable in punishing malefactors; they admit no sophistry of words, but are always established by actions themselves, which actions we ever propose as surer demonstrations than what is contained in writing only; on which account I am so bold as to say that we are become the teachers of other men, in the greatest number of things, and those of the most excellent nature only; for what is more excellent than inviolable piety? what is more just than submission to laws? and what is more advantageous than mutual love and concord? and this so far that we are to be neither divided by calamities, nor to become injurious and seditious in prosperity, but to contemn death when we are in war, and in peace to apply ourselves to our mechanical occupations, or to our tillage of the ground; while we in all things, and in all ways, are satisfied that God is the inspector and governor of our actions. If these precepts had either been written at first, or more exactly kept by any others before us, we should have owed them thanks as disciples owe to their masters; but if it be visible that we have made use of them more than any other men, and if we have demonstrated that the orignal invention of them is our own, let the Apions, and the Molones, with all the rest of those that delight in lies and reproaches, stand confuted; but let this and the foregoing book be dedicated to thee, Epaphroditus, who art so great a lover of truth, and by thy means to those that have been in like manner desirous to be acquainted with the affairs of our nation.

AN EXTRACT

OUT OF

JOSEPHUS' DISCOURSE TO THE GREEKS CONCERNING HADES

1. Now as to Hades, wherein the souls of the righteous and unrighteous are detained, it is necessary to speak of it. Hades is a place in the world not regularly finished; a *subterraneous* region, where the light of this world does not shine; from which circumstance, that in this place the light does not shine, it cannot be but there must be in it perpetual *darkness*. This region is allowed as a place of custody for souls, in which angels are appointed as guardians to them, who distribute to them *temporary punishments*, agreeable to every one's behaviour and manners.

2. In this region there is a certain place set apart, as *a lake of unquenchable fire*, wherein we suppose no one hath hitherto been cast; but it is prepared for a day afore-determined by God, in which one righteous sentence shall deservedly be passed upon all men; when the unjust and those that have been disobedient to God, and have given honour to such idols as have been the vain operations of the hands of men, as to God himself, shall be adjudged to this *everlasting punishment*, as having been the causes of defilement; while the just shall obtain *an incorruptible* and never-fading *kingdom*. These are now indeed confined in Hades, but not in the same place wherein the unjust are confined.

3. For there is one descent into this region, at whose *gate* we believe there stands an archangel with an host; which *gate* when those pass through that are conducted down by the angels appointed over souls, they do not go the same way; but the just are guided to the *right hand*, and are led with hymns sung by the *angels* appointed over that place, unto a region of *light*, in which the just have dwelt from the beginning of the world; not constrained by necessity, but ever enjoying the prospect of the good things they see, and rejoice in the expectation of those new enjoyments which will be peculiar to every one of them, and esteeming those things beyond what we have here; with whom their is no place of toil, no burning heat, no piercing cold, nor are any briers there; but the countenance of the *fathers* and of the just, which they see, always smiles upon them, while they wait for that rest and *eternal* new *life in heaven*, which is to succeed this region. This place we call *The Bosom of Abraham*.

4. But as to the unjust, they are dragged by force to the *left hand*, by the angels allotted for punishment, no longer going with a good-will, but as prisoners driven by violence; to whom are sent the angels appointed over them to reproach them and to threaten them with their terrible looks, and to thrust them still downwards. Now those angels that are set over these souls, drag them into the neighbourhood of hell itself; who, when they are hard by it, continually hear the noise of it, and do not stand clear of the hot vapour itself; but when they have a nearer view of this spectacle, as of a terrible and exceeding great prospect of fire, they are struck with a fearful expectation of a future judgment, and in effect punished thereby; and not only so, but where they see the place [or choir] of the *fathers* and of the just, even hereby are they punished; for a *chaos* deep and large is fixed between them; insomuch that a just man that hath compassion upon them, cannot be admitted, nor can one that is unjust, if he were bold enough to attempt it, pass over it.

5. This is the discourse concerning Hades, wherein the souls of all men are confined until a proper season, which God hath determined, when he will make a resurrection of all men from the dead, not procuring a transmigration of souls from one body to another, but raising again those very bodies, which you Greeks, seeing to be dissolved, do not believe [their resurrection :] but learn not to disbelieve it; for while you believe that the soul is created, and yet is made immortal by God, according to the doctrine of Plato, and this in time, be not incredulous, but believe that God is able, when he hath raised to life that body which was made as a compound of the same elements, to make it immortal; for it must never be said of God that he is able to do some things, and unable to do others. We have therefore believed that the body will be raised again; for although it be dissolved, it is not perished; for the earth receives its remains, and preserves them; and while they are like *seed*, and are mixed among the more fruitful soil, they flourish, and what is *sown* is indeed sown *bare grain;* but at the mighty sound of God the Creator, it will sprout up, and be raised in a *clothed* and *glorious* condition, though not before it has been dissolved, and mixed [with the earth.] So that we have not rashly believed the resurrection of the body; for although it be dissolved for a time on account of the original transgression, it exists still, and is cast into the earth as into a potter's furnace, in order to be formed again, not in order to rise again such as it was before, but in a state of purity, and so as never to be destroyed any more: and to every body shall its own soul be restored; and when it hath *clothed itself* with that body, it will not

be subject to misery, but, being itself pure, it will continue with its pure body, and rejoice with it, with which it having walked righteously now in this world, and never having had it as a snare, it will receive it again with great gladness; but as for the unjust, they will receive their bodies not changed, not freed from diseases or distempers, nor made glorious, but with the same diseases wherein they died; and such as they were in their unbelief, the same shall they be when they shall be faithfully judged.

6. For all men, the just as well as the unjust, shall be brought before *God the word*; for to him hath *the Father committed all judgment*; and he, in order to *fulfil the will of his Father*, shall come as judge, whom we call *Christ*. For Minos and Rhadamanthus are not judges, as you Greeks do suppose, but he whom *God even the Father hath glorified*; CONCERNING WHOM WE HAVE ELSEWHERE GIVEN A MORE PARTICULAR ACCOUNT, FOR THE SAKE OF THOSE WHO SEEK AFTER TRUTH. This person, exercising the righteous judgment of the Father towards all men, hath prepared a just sentence for every one, according to his works; at whose judgment-seat when all men, and angels, and demons shall stand, they will send forth one voice, and say, JUST IS THY JUDGMENT; the rejoinder to which will bring a just sentence upon both parties, by giving justly to those that have done well an *everlasting fruition*; but allotting to the lovers of wicked works *eternal punishment*. To these belong *the unquenchable fire*, and that without end, and a certain fiery *worm never dying*, and not destroying the body, but continuing its eruption out of the body with never-ceasing grief; neither will sleep give ease to these men, nor will the night afford them comfort; death will not free them from their punishment, nor will the interceding prayers of their kindred profit them; for the just are no longer seen by them, nor are they thought worthy of remembrance; but the just shall remember only their righteous actions, whereby they have attained *the heavenly kingdom*, in which there is no sleep, no sorrow, no corruption, no care, no night, no day measured by time, no sun driven in his course along the circle of heaven by necessity, and measuring out the bounds and conversions of the seasons, for the better illumination of the life of men; no moon decreasing and increasing, or introducing a variety of seasons, nor will she then moisten the earth; no burning sun, no Bear turning round [the pole,] no Orion to rise, no wandering of innumerable stars. The earth will not then be difficult to be passed over, nor will it be hard to find out the court of Paradise, nor will there be any fearful roaring of the sea, forbidding the passengers to walk on it: even that will be made easily passable to the just, though it will not be void of moisture. Heaven will not then be uninhabitable by men; and it will not be impossible to discover the way of ascending thither. The earth will not be uncultivated, nor require too much labour of men, but will bring forth its fruits of its own accord, and will be well adorned with them. There will be no more generations of wild beasts, nor will the substance of the rest of the animals shoot out any more; for it will not produce men, but the number of the righteous will continue, and never fail, together with righteous angels, and spirits [of God,] and with his word, as a choir of righteous men and women that never grow old, and continue in an incorruptible state, singing hymns to God, who hath advanced them to that happiness, by the means of a regular institution of life; with whom the whole creation also will lift up a perpetual hymn from *corruption to incorruption*, as glorified by a splendid and pure spirit. It will not then be restrained by a bond of necessity, but with a lively freedom shall offer up a voluntary hymn, and shall praise him that made them, together with the angels, and spirits, and men now *freed from all bondage*.

7. And now, if you Gentiles will be persuaded by these motives, and leave your vain imaginations about your pedigrees, and gaining of riches and philosophy, and will not spend your time about subtleties of words, and thereby lead your minds into error, and if you will apply your ears to the hearing of the inspired prophets, the interpreters, both of God and of his word, and will believe in God, you shall both be partakers of these things, and obtain the good things that are to come; you shall see the ascent into the immense heaven plainly, and that kingdom which is there; for what God hath now concealed in silence [will be then made manifest,] *what neither eye hath seen, nor ear hath heard, nor hath it entered into the heart of man, the things that God hath prepared for them that love him.*

8. *In whatsoever ways I shall find you, in them shall I judge you entirely*; so cries the END of all things. And he who hath at first lived a virtuous life, but towards the latter end falls into vice, these labours by him before endured, shall be altogether vain and unprofitable, even as in a play, brought to an ill catastrophe. Whosoever shall have lived wickedly and luxuriously may repent; however, there will be need of much time to conquer an evil habit, and even after repentance his whole life must be guarded with great care and diligence, after the manner of a body, which, after it hath been a long time afflicted with a distemper, requires a stricter diet and method of living; for though it may be possible, perhaps, to break off the chain of our irregular affections at once, yet our amendment cannot be secured without the grace of God, the prayers of good men, the help of the brethren, and our own sincere repentance and constant care. It is a good thing not to sin at all; it is also good, having sinned, to repent, as it is best to have health always; but it is a good thing to recover from a distemper. *To God be glory and dominion for ever and ever. Amen.*

APPENDIX.

DISSERTATION I

THE TESTIMONIES OF JOSEPHUS CONCERNING JESUS CHRIST, JOHN THE BAPTIST, AND JAMES THE JUST, VINDICATED

SINCE we meet with several important testimonies in Josephus, the Jewish historian, concerning John the Baptist, the forerunner of Jesus of Nazareth, concerning Jesus of Nazareth himself, and concerning James the Just, the brother of Jesus of Nazareth; and since the principal testimony, which is that concerning Jesus of Nazareth himself, has of late been greatly questioned by many, and rejected by some of the learned as spurious, it will be fit for me, who have ever declared my firm belief that these testimonies were genuine, to set down fairly some of the *original evidence and citations* I have met with in the first fifteen centuries concerning them; and then to make proper *observations* upon that evidence, for the reader's more complete satisfaction.

But before I produce the citations themselves, out of Josephus, give me leave to prepare the reader's attention, by setting down the sentiments of perhaps the most learned person, and the most competent judge that ever was, as to the authority of Josephus, I mean of Joseph Scaliger, in the Prolegomena to his book *De Emendatione Temporum*, p. 17. "Josephus is the most diligent and the greatest lover of truth of all writers: nor are we afraid to affirm of him, that it is more safe to believe him, not only as to the affairs of the Jews, but also as to those that are foreign to them, than all the Greek and Latin writers; and this, because his fidelity and his compass of learning are everywhere conspicuous."

THE ANCIENT CITATIONS OF THE TESTIMONIES OF JOSEPHUS, FROM HIS OWN TIME TILL THE END OF THE FIFTEENTH CENTURY

About A.D. 110. *Tacit. Annal.* lib. xv. cap. 44.—Nero, in order to stifle the rumour, [as if he himself had set Rome on fire,] ascribed it to those people who were hated for their wicked practices, and called by the vulgar, *Christians:* these he punished exquisitely. *The author of this name was Christ, who, in the reign of Tiberius, was brought to punishment by Pontius Pilate the procurator.*

About A.D. 147. *Just. Mart. Dialog. cum Tryph.* p. 230—You [Jews] knew that Jesus was risen from the dead, and ascended into heaven, as the prophecies did foretell was to happen.

About A.D. 230. *Origen. Comment. in Matth.* p. 234.—This James was of so shining a character among the people, on account of his righteous-

ness, that Flavius Josephus, when, in his twentieth book of the Jewish Antiquities, he had a mind to set down what was the cause why the people suffered such miseries, till the very holy house was demolished, he said, that these things befell them by the anger of God, on account of what they had dared to do to James, the brother of Jesus, who was called *Christ;* and wonderful it is, that while he did not receive Jesus for Christ, he did nevertheless bear witness that James was so righteous a man. He says farther, that the people thought they had suffered these things for the sake of James.

About. A.D. 250. *Id. Contr. Cels.* lib. i. p. 35, 36.—I would say to Celsus, who personates a Jew, that admitted of John the Baptist and how he baptized Jesus, that one who lived but a little while after John and Jesus, wrote, how that John was a baptizer unto the remission of sins; for Josephus testifies in the eighteenth book of his Jewish Antiquities, that John was the Baptist, and that he promised purification to those that were baptized. The same Josephus, also, although he did not believe in Jesus as Christ, when he was inquiring after the cause of the destruction of Jerusalem, and of the demolition of the temple, and ought to have said that their machinations against Jesus were the cause of those miseries coming on the people, because they had slain that Christ who was foretold by the prophets, he, though as it were unwillingly, and yet as one not remote from the truth, says, "these miseries befell the Jews by way of revenge for James the Just, who was the brother of Jesus that was called Christ; because they had slain him who was a most righteous person." Now this James was he whom that genuine disciple of Jesus, Paul, said he had seen *as the Lord's brother* [Gal. i. 19;] which relation implies not so much nearness of blood, or the sameness of education, as it does the agreement of manners and preaching. If, therefore, he says the desolation of Jerusalem befell the Jews for the sake of James, with how much greater reason might he have said that it happened for the sake of Jesus? &c.

About A.D. 324. *Euseb. Demonstr. Evan.* lib. iii. p. 124.—Certainly, the attestation of those I have already produced concerning our Saviour may be sufficient. However, it may not be amiss, if, over and above, we make use of Josephus the Jew for a farther witness; who, in the eighteenth book of his Antiquities, when he was writing the history of what happened under

Pilate, makes mention of our Saviour in these words:—" Now there was about this time, Jesus, a wise man, if it be lawful to call him a man ; for he was a doer of wonderful works, a teacher of such men as had a veneration for truth. He drew over to him both many of the Jews and many of the Gentiles : he was the Christ. And when Pilate, at the suggestion of the principal men among us, had condemned him to the cross, those that loved him at first did not forsake him ; for he appeared unto them alive again the third day, as the divine prophets had spoken of these and ten thousand other wonderful things concerning him : whence the tribe of Christians, so named from him, are not extinct at this day." If, therefore, we have this historian's testimony, that he not only brought over to himself the twelve apostles, with the seventy disciples, but many of the Jews, and many of the Gentiles also, he must manifestly have had somewhat in him extraordinary, above the rest of mankind ; for how otherwise could he draw over so many of the Jews and of the Gentiles, unless he performed admirable and amazing works, and used a method of teaching that was not common ? Moreover, the scripture of the Acts of the Apostles (xxi. 20.) bears witness, that there were many ten thousands of Jews, who were persuaded that he was the Christ of God, who was foretold by the prophets.

About A.D. 330. Id. Hist. Eccles. lib. i. cap. 11.—Now the divine scripture of the Gospels makes mention of John the Baptist as having his head cut off by the younger Herod. Josephus also concurs in this history, and makes mention of Herodias by name, as the wife of his brother, whom Herod had married, upon divorcing his former lawful wife. She was the daughter of Aretas, king of the Petrean Arabians ; and which Herodias he had parted from her husband while he was alive ; on which account also, when he had slain John, he made war with Aretas [Aretas made war with him,] because his daughter had been used dishonourably : in which war, when it came to a battle, he says, that all Herod's army was destroyed, and that he suffered this because of his wicked contrivance against John. Moreover, the same Josephus, by acknowledging John to have been a most righteous man, and the Baptist, conspires in his testimony with what is written in the Gospels. He also relates, that Herod lost his kingdom for the sake of the same Herodias, together with whom he was himself condemned to be banished to Vienna, a city of Gaul ; and this is his account in the eighteenth book of the Antiquities, where he writes this of John *verbatim :* —" Some of the Jews thought that the destruction of Herod's army came from God, and that very justly, as a punishment for what he did against John that was called the *Baptist ;* for Herod slew him, who was a good man, and one that commanded the Jews to exercise virtue, both as to righteousness towards one another, and piety towards God, and so to come to baptism, for that by this means, the washing [with water] would appear acceptable to him, when they made use of it, not in order to the putting away [or the remission] of some sins [only,]—but for the purification of the body, supposing still that the soul was thoroughly purified beforehand by righteousness. Now, when [many] others came in crowds about him, for they were greatly delighted in hearing his words, Herod was afraid that this so great power of persuading men might tend to some sedition or other ; for they seemed to be disposed to do every thing he should advise them to ; so he supposed it better to prevent

any attempt for a mutation from him, by cutting him off, than after any such mutation should be brought about, and the public should suffer, to repent [of such negligence.] Accordingly, he was sent a prisoner, out of Herod's suspicious temper, to Macherus, the castle I before mentioned, and was there put to death."—When Josephus had said this of John, he makes mention also of our Saviour, in the same history, after this manner :—" Now there was about this time, one Jesus, a wise man, if it be lawful to call him a man ; for he was a doer of wonderful works, a teacher of such men as receive the truth with pleasure. He drew over to him both many of the Jews and many of the Gentiles also :—he was the Christ. And when Pilate, at the suggestion of the principal men among us, had condemned him to the cross, those that loved him at the first did not forsake him ; for he appeared to them alive again the third day, as the divine prophets had foretold these and ten thousand other wonderful things concerning him : and still the tribe of Christians, so named from him, are not extinct at this day." And since this writer, sprung from the Hebrews themselves, hath delivered these things above, in his own work, concerning John the Baptist and our Saviour, what room is there for any further evasion ? &c.

Now James was so wonderful a person, and was so celebrated by all others for righteousness, that the judicious Jews thought this to have been the occasion of that siege of Jerusalem, which came on presently after his martyrdom ; and that it befell them for no other reason than that impious fact they were guilty of against him. Josephus, therefore, did not refuse to attest thereto in writing, by the words following :— " These miseries befell the Jews by way of revenge for James the Just, who was the brother of Jesus that was called Christ, on account that they had slain him who was a most righteous person."

The same Josephus declares the manner of his death in the twentieth book of the Antiquities, in these words :—" Cæsar sent Albinus into Judea to be procurator, when he had heard that Festus was dead. Now Ananus, junior, who, as we said, had been admitted to the high priesthood, was in his temper bold and daring in an extraordinary manner. He was also of the sect of the Sadducees, who are more savage in judgment than any of the other Jews, as we have already signified. Since therefore this was the character of Ananus, he thought he had now a proper opportunity [to exercise his authority,] because Festus was dead, and Albinus was but upon the road ; so he assembles the sanhedrim of judges, and brings before them James, the brother of Jesus who was called Christ, and some others [of his companions ;] and when he had formed an accusation against them, as breakers of the law, he delivered them to be stoned : but as for those who seemed the most equitable of the citizens, and those who were the most uneasy at the breach of the laws, they disliked what was done. They also sent to the king [Agrippa,] desiring him to send to Ananus that he should act so no more, for that what he had already done could not be justified," &c.

About A.D. 360. Ambrose, or Hegesippus de Excid. Urb. Hierosolym. lib. ii. cap. 12.—We have discovered that it was the opinion and belief of the Jews, as Josephus affirms (who is an author not to be rejected, when he writes against himself,) that Herod lost his army, not by the deceit of men, but by the anger of God and that justly, as an effect of revenge for what he did to John the Baptist, a just man, who had said to him, *It is not lawful for thee to have thy brother's wife.*

The Jews themselves also bear witness to Christ. as appears by Josephus, the writer of their history, who says thus:—"That there was at that time a wise man, if (says he) it be lawful to have him called a man, a doer of wonderful works, who appeared to his disciples after the third day from his death, alive again, according to the writings of the prophets, who foretold these and innumerable other miraculous events concerning him: from whom began the congregation of Christians, and hath penetrated among all sorts of men: nor does there remain any nation in the Roman world which continues strangers to his religion." If the Jews do not believe us, let them at least believe their own writers. Josephus, whom they esteem a very great man, hath said this, and yet hath he spoken truth after such a manner; and so far was his mind wandered from the right way, that even he was not a believer as to what he himself said; but thus he spake, in order to deliver historical truth, because he thought it was not lawful for him to deceive, while yet he was no believer, because of the hardness of his heart and his perfidious intention. However, it was no prejudice to the truth that he was not a believer; but this adds more weight to his testimony, that while he was an unbeliever, and unwilling this should be true, he has not denied it to be so.

About A.D. 400. *Hieronym. de Vir. Illustr. in Josepho.*—Josephus, in the eighteenth book of Antiquities, most expressly acknowledges that Christ was slain by the Pharisees, on account of the greatness of his miracles; and that John the Baptist was truly a prophet; and that Jerusalem was demolished on account of the slaughter of James the apostle. Now, he wrote concerning our Lord after this manner:—"At the same time there was Jesus, a wise man, if yet it be lawful to call him a man; for he was a doer of wonderful works, a teacher of those who willingly receive the truth. He had many followers, both of the Jews and of the Gentiles:—he was believed to be Christ. And when by the envy of our principal men, Pilate had condemned him to the cross, yet notwithstanding those who had loved him at first persevered, for he appeared to them alive on the third day, as the oracles of the prophets had foretold many of these and other wonderful things concerning him: and the sect of Christians, so named from him, are not extinct at this day."

About A.D. 410. *Isidorus Pelusiota, the Scholar of Chrysostom*, lib. iv. epist. 225.—There was one Josephus, a Jew of the greatest reputation, and one that was zealous of the law; one also that paraphrased the Old Testament with truth, and acted valiantly for the Jews, and had showed that their settlement was nobler than can be described by words. Now since he made their interest give place to truth, for he would not support the opinion of impious men, I think it necessary to set down his words. What then does he say? "Now there was about that time Jesus, a wise man, if it be lawful to call him a man; for he was a doer of wonderful works, a teacher of such men as receive the truth with pleasure. He drew over to him both many of the Jews and many of the Gentiles:—he was the Christ. And when Pilate, at the suggestion of the principal men among us, had condemned him to the cross, those that loved him at first did not forsake him; for he appeared to them the third day alive again, as the divine prophets had said these and a vast number of other wonderful things concerning him: and the tribe of

Christians, so named from him, are not extinct at this day." Now I cannot but wonder greatly at this great man's love of truth in many respects, but chiefly where he says, "Jesus was a teacher of men who received the truth with pleasure"

About A.D. 440. *Sozomen. Hist. Eccles.* lib. i. cap. 1.—Now Josephus, the son of Matthias, a priest, a man of very great note, both among the Jews and the Romans, may well be a witness of credit as to the truth of Christ's history; for he scruples to call him a man, as being a doer of wonderful works, and a teacher of the words of truth. He names him Christ openly, and is not ignorant that he was condemned to the cross, and appeared on the third day alive, and that ten thousand other wonderful things were foretold of him by the divine prophets. He testifies also, that those whom he drew over to him, being many of the Gentiles, as well as of the Jews, continued to love him, and that the tribe named from him was not then extinct. Now he seems to me by this relation almost to proclaim that Christ is God. However, he appears to have been so affected with the strangeness of the thing, as to run, as it were, in a sort of middle way, so as not to put any indignity upon believers in him, but rather to afford his suffrage to them.

About A.D. 510. *Cassiodorus Hist. Tripartit. e Sozomeno.*—Now Josephus, the son of Matthias, and a priest, a man of great nobility among the Jews, and of great dignity among the Romans, shall be a truth of Christ's history: for he dares not call him a man, as a doer of famous works, and a teacher of true doctrines: he names him Christ openly, and is not ignorant that he was condemned to the cross, and appeared on the third day alive, and that an infinite number of other wonderful things were foretold of him by the holy prophets. Moreover, he testifies also, that there were then alive many whom he had chosen, both Greeks and Jews, and that they continued to love him, and that the sect which was named from him was by no means extinct at that time.

About A.D. 640. *Chron. Alex.* p. 514.—Now Josephus also relates in his eighteenth book of the Antiquities, how John the Baptist, that holy man, was beheaded, on account of Herodias, the wife of Philip, the brother of Herod himself; for Herod had divorced his former wife, who was still alive, and had been his lawful wife: she was the daughter of Aretas, king of the Petreans. When therefore Herod had taken Herodias away from her husband, while he was yet alive (on whose account he slew John also,) Aretas made war against Herod, because his daughter had been dishonourably treated. In which war, he says, that all Herod's army was destroyed, and that he suffered that calamity because of the wickedness he had been guilty of against John. The same Josephus relates, that Herod lost his kingdon on account of Herodias, and that with her he was banished to Lyons, &c.

P. 526, 527.] Now that our Saviour taught his preaching three years, is demonstrated both by other necessary reasonings, as also out of the holy Gospels, and out of Josephus's writings, who was a wise man among the Hebrews, &c.

P. 584, 586.] Josephus relates, in the fifth book of the [Jewish] war, that Jerusalem was taken in the third [second] year of Vespasian, as after forty years since they had dared to put Jesus to death: in which time he says, that James the brother of our Lord, and bishop of Jerusalem, was thrown down [from the temple,] and slain of them, by stoning.

About A.D. 740. *Anastasius Abbas contr. Jud.*—Now Josephus, an author and writer of your own, says of Christ, that he was a just and good man, shewed and declared so to be by divine grace, who gave aid to many by signs and miracles.

About A.D. 790. *Georgius Syncellus Chron.* p. 339.—These miseries befell the Jews by way of revenge for James the Just, who was the brother of Jesus that was called Christ, on the account that they had slain him who was a most righteous person. Now as Ananus, a person of that character, thought he had a proper opportunity, because Festus was dead, and Albinus was but upon the road, so he assembles the sanhedrim of judges, and brings before them James, the brother of Jesus, who was called Christ, and some of his companions; and when he had formed an accusation against them, as breakers of the law, he delivered them to be stoned; but as for those that seemed the most equitable of the citizens, and those that were the most uneasy at the breach of the laws, they disliked what was done. They also sent to the king [Agrippa,] desiring him to send to Ananus that he should act so no more, for that what he had already done could not be justified, &c.

About A.D. 850. *Johan. Malela Chron.* lib. x. —From that time began the destruction of the Jews, as Josephus, the philosopher of the Jews, hath written; who also said this, that from the time the Jews crucified Christ, who was a good and a righteous man (that is, if it be fit to call such a one a man, and not God,) the land of Judea was never free from trouble. These things the same Josephus the Jew has related in his writings.

About A.D. 860. *Photius Cod.* lib. xlviii.—I have read the treatise of Josephus *About the Universe,* whose title I have elsewhere read to be, *Of the Substance of the Universe.* It is contained in two very small treatises. He treats of the origin of the world in a brief manner. However, he speaks of the divinity of Christ, who is our true God, in a way very like to what we use, declaring that the same name of Christ belongs to him, and writes of his ineffable generation of the Father after such a manner as cannot be blamed; which thing may perhaps raise a doubt in some, whether Josephus was the author of the work, though the phraseology does not at all differ from this man's other works. However, I have found in some papers that this discourse was not written by Josephus, but by one Caius, a presbyter.

Cod. ccxxxviii.] Herod, the tetrarch of Galilee and of Perea, the son of Herod the Great, fell in love, as Josephus says, with the wife of his brother Philip, whose name was Herodias, who was the grand-daughter of Herod the Great, by his son Aristobulus, whom he had slain. Agrippa was also her brother. Now Herod took her away from her husband, and married her. This is he that slew John the Baptist, that great man, the forerunner [of Christ,] being afraid (as Josephus says) lest he should raise a sedition among his people; for they all followed the directions of John, on account of the excellency of his virtue. In his time was the passion of our Saviour.

Cod. xxxiii.] I have read the Chronicle of Justus of Tiberias. He omits the greatest part of what was necessary to be related; but, as infected with Jewish prejudices, being also himself a Jew by birth, he makes no mention at all of the advent, or of the acts done, or of the miracles wrought, by Christ.

The time uncertain, Macarius in Actis Sancto-

rum, tom. v. p. 149. *ap. Fabric. Joseph.* p. 61.— Josephus, a priest of Jerusalem, and one that wrote with truth the history of the Jewish affairs, bears witness that Christ, the true God, was incarnate, and crucified, and the third day rose again; whose writings are reposited in the public library. Thus he says:—Now there was about this time Jesus, a wise man, if it be lawful to call him a man; for he was a doer of wonderful works, a teacher of such men as receive the truth with pleasure. He drew over to him both many of the Jews and many of the Gentiles also: this was the Christ. And when Pilate, at the suggestion of the principal men among us, had condemned him to the cross, those that loved him at the first did not forsake him; for he appeared to them alive again on the third day, as the divine prophets had foretold these and ten thousand other wonderful things concerning him: and still the tribe of Christians, so named from him, are not extinct at this day." Since, therefore, the writer of the Hebrews has engraven this testimony concerning our Lord and Saviour in his own books, what defence can there remain for the unbelievers?

About A.D. 980. *Suidas in voce* Ἰησους.— We have found Josephus, who hath written about the taking of Jerusalem (of whom Eusebius Pamphilii makes frequent mention in his Ecclesiastical History,) saying openly in his Memoirs of the Captivity, that Jesus officiated in the temple with the priests. Thus have we found Josephus saying—a man of ancient times, and not very long after the apostles, &c.

About A.D. 1060. *Cedrenus. Compend. Histor.* p. 196.—Josephus does indeed write concerning John the Baptist as follows:—Some of the Jews thought that the destruction of Herod's army came from God, and that he was punished very justly for what punishment he had inflicted on John, that was called the *Baptist;* for Herod slew him, who was a good man, and commanded the Jews to exercise virtue, both by righteousness towards one another and piety towards God, and so to come to baptism. But as concerning Christ, the same Josephus says, that about that time there was Jesus, a wise man, if it be lawful to call him a man; for he was a doer of wonderful works, and a teacher of such men as receive the truth with pleasure: for that Christ drew over many even from the Gentiles; whom when Pilate had crucified, those who at first had loved him did not leave off to preach concerning him, for he appeared to them the third day alive again, as the divine prophets had testified, and spoke these and other wonderful things concerning him.

About A.D. 1080. *Theophylact. in Joan.* lib. xiii.—The city of the Jews was taken, and the wrath of God was kindled against them: as also Josephus witnesses, that this came upon them on account of the death of Jesus.

About A.D. 1120. *Zonaras Annal.* tom. i. p. 267.—Josephus in the eighteenth book of Antiquities, writes thus concerning our Lord and God Jesus Christ:—Now, there was about this time Jesus, a wise man, if it be lawful to call him a man; for he was a doer of wonderful works, a teacher of such men as receive the truth with pleasure. He drew over to him many of the Jews, and many of the Gentiles: —he was the Christ. And when Pilate, at the suggestion of the principal men among us, had condemned him to the cross, those that loved him at first did not forsake him; for he appeared to them the third day alive again, as the divine prophets had said these and ten thousand other wonderful things concerning him : and the tribe of Christians, so named from him, are not extinct at this day.

About A.D. 1120. *Glycus Annal.* p. 234.— Then did Philo, that wise man, and Josephus, flourish. This last was styled *The Lover of Truth,* because he commended John, who baptized our Lord ; and because he bore witness that Christ, in like manner, was a wise man, and the doer of great miracles ; and that, when he was crucified, he appeared the third day.

About A.D. 1170. *Gotfridus Viterbiensis Chron.* p. 366. *e Vers. Rufini.*—Josephus relates that a very great war arose between Aretas, king of the Arabians, and Herod, on account of the sin which Herod had committed against John. Moreover, the same Josephus writes thus concerning Christ : There was at this time Jesus, a wise man, if at least it be lawful to call him a man ; for he was a doer of wonderful works, a teacher of such men as willingly hear truth. He also drew over to him many of the Jews and many of the Gentiles :—he was Christ. And when Pilate, at the accusation of the principal men of our nation, had decreed that he should be crucified, those that had loved him from the beginning did not forsake him ; for he appeared to them the third day alive again, according to what the divinely inspired prophets had foretold, that these and innumerable other miracles should come to pass about him. Moreover, both the name and sect of Christians, who were named from him, continue in being unto this day.

About A.D. 1360. *Nicephorus Callistus Hist. Eccles.* lib. i. p. 90, 91.—Now this [concerning Herod the tetrarch] is attested to, not only by the book of the Holy Gospels, but by Josephus, that lover of truth : who also makes mention of Herodias his brother's wife, whom Herod had taken away from him while he was alive, and married her ; having divorced his former lawful wife, who was the daughter of Aretas, king of the Petrean Arabians. This Herodias he had married, and lived with her : on which account also, when he had slain John, he made war with Aretas, because his daughter had been dishonourably used ; in which war he relates that all Herod's army was destroyed, and that he suffered this on account of the most unjust slaughter of John. He also adds, that John was a most righteous man. Moreover he makes mention of his baptism, agreeing in all points thereto relating with the gospel. He also informs us, that Herod lost his kingdom on account of Herodias, with whom also he was condemned to be banished to Vienna, which was their place of exile, and a city bordering upon Gaul, and lying near the utmost bounds of the west.

About A.D. 1450. *Hardmannus Schedelius Chron.* p. 110.—Josephus the Jew, who was called Flavius, a priest, and the son of Matthias, a priest of that nation, a most celebrated historian, and very skilful in many things ; he was certainly a good man, and of an excellent character, who had the highest opinion of Christ.

About A.D. 1480. *Platina de Vitis Pontificum, in Christo.*—I shall avoid mentioning what Christ did until the 30th year of his age, when he was baptized by John, the son of Zacharias, because not only the Gospels and Epistles are full of those acts of his, which he did in the most excellent and most holy manner, but the books of such as were quite remote from his way of living, and acting, and ordaining, are also full of the same. Flavius Josephus himself, who wrote twenty books of Jewish Antiquities in the Greek tongue,

when he had proceeded as far as the government of the emperor Tiberius, says, There was in those days Jesus, a certain wise man, if at least it be lawful to call him a man ; for he was a doer of wonderful works, and a teacher of men, of such especially as willingly hear the truth. On this account he drew over to him many, both of the Jews and Gentiles :—he was Christ. But when Pilate, instigated by the principal men of our nation, had decreed that he should be crucified, yet did not those that had loved him from the beginning forsake him ; and besides, he appeared to them the third day after his death alive, as the divinely inspired prophets had foretold, that these and innumerable other miracles should come to pass about him : and the famous name of *Christians,* taken from him, as well as their sect, do still continue in being.

The same Josephus also affirms, That John the Baptist, a true prophet, and on that account one that was had in esteem by all men, was slain by Herod, the son of Herod the Great, a little before the death of Christ, in the castle of Macherus,—not because he was afraid for himself and his kingdom, as the same author says, —but because he had incestuously married Herodias, the sister of Agrippa, and the wife of that excellent person his brother Philip.

About A.D. 1480. *Trithemius Abbas de Scriptor. Eccles.*—Josephus the Jew, although he continued to be a Jew, did frequently commend the Christians ; and in the eighteenth book of his Antiquities, wrote down an eminent testimony concerning our Lord Jesus Christ.

OBSERVATIONS FROM THE FOREGOING EVIDENCE AND CITATIONS

I. THE *style* of all these original testimonies belonging to Josephus, is exactly the style of the same Josephus, and especially the style about those parts of his Antiquities wherein we find these testimonies. This is denied by nobody, as to the other concerning John the Baptist and James the Just, and is now become equally undeniable as to that concerning Christ.

II. These testimonies therefore being confessedly and undeniably written by Josephus himself, it is next to impossible that he should wholly omit some testimony concerning Jesus Christ ; nay, while his testimonies of John the Baptist and of James the Just are so honourable, and gave them so great characters, it is also impossible that this testimony concerning Christ should be other than very honourable, or such as afforded him a still greater character also. Could the very same author who gave such a full and advantageous character of John the Baptist, the forerunner of Jesus of Nazareth, all whose disciples were by him directed to Jesus of Nazareth as to the true Messias, and all whose disciples became afterwards the disciples of Jesus of Nazareth, say nothing honourable of that Jesus of Nazareth himself ?—and this in a history of those very times in which he was born and lived and died, and that while the writer lived but a little after him in the same country in which he was born, and lived, and died. This is almost incredible. And further, could the very same author, who gave such an advantageous character of James the Just, and this under the very appellation of *James, the brother of Jesus, who was called Christ,* which James was one of the principal disciples or apostles of this Jesus Christ, and had been many years the only Christian bishop of the believing Jews of Judea and Jerusalem, in the very days and in the very country of this writer ;—could he, I say, wholly omit any, nay, a very honourable account of Jesus Christ himself, whose disciple and bishop this James most certainly was? This is almost incredible. Hear what Ittigius, one of the wisest and learnedest of all those who have lately inclined to give up the testimony concerning Christ, as it stands in our copies, for spurious, says upon this occasion: —" If any one object to me, that Josephus hath not omitted John the Baptist, the forerunner of Christ, nor James the disciple of Christ, and that therefore he could not have done the part of a good historian, if he had been entirely silent concerning Christ, I shall freely grant that Josephus was not entirely silent concerning Christ; nay, I shall further grant, that when Josephus was speaking of Christ, he did not abstain from his commendation; for we are not to determine from that inveterate hatred which the modern Jews bear to Christ, what was the behaviour of those Jews, upon whom the miracles that were daily wrought by the apostles in the name of Christ imprinted a sacred horror."

III. The famous clause in this testimony of Josephus concerning Christ, *This was Christ*, or *the Christ*, does not mean that this Jesus was the *Christ of God*, or the *true Messiah* of the Jews; but that this Jesus was distinguished from all others of that name, of which there were not a few, as mentioned by Josephus himself, by the addition of the other name of Christ; or that this person was no other than he whom all the world knew by the name of *Jesus Christ*, and his followers by the name of *Christians*. This I esteem to be a clear case, and that from the arguments following:—

(1.) The Greeks and Romans, for whose use Josephus wrote his Antiquities, could no otherwise understand these words. The Jews indeed, and afterwards the Christians, who knew that a great Messias, a person that was to be Christ, the *annointed* of God, and that was to perform the office of a *King*, a *Priest*, and a *Prophet*, to God's people, might readily so understand this expression; but Josephus, as I have already noted, wrote here not to Jews or Christians, but to Greeks and Romans, who knew nothing of this: but knew very well that an eminent person, living in Judea, whose name was *Jesus Chrest*, or *Jesus Christ*, had founded a new and numerous sect, which took the latter of those names, and were everywhere, from him, called *Chrestians*, or *Christians;* in which sense alone they could understand these words of Josephus, and in which sense I believe he desired they should understand them; nor does Josephus ever use the Hebrew term *Messiah* in any of his writings, nor the Greek term *Christ*, in any such acceptation elsewhere.

(2.) Josephus himself as good as exlpains his own meaning, and that by the last clause of this very passage, where he says the Christians were named from this Christ, without a syllable as though he really meant he was the true Messiah, or *Christ of God*. He farther seems to me to explain this his meaning in that other place where alone he elsewhere mentions this name of Christ; that is, when upon occasion of the mention of James, when he was condemned by Ananus, he calls him *the Brother of Jesus*, not that was the *true Messiah*, or *the true Christ*, but only *that was called Christ*.

(3.) It was quite beside the purpose of Josephus to declare himself here to be a Christian, or a believer in Jesus as the true Messiah. Had he intended so to do, he would surely have explained the meaning of the word *Christ* to his Greek and Roman readers; he would surely have been a great deal fuller and larger in his accounts

of Christ, and of the Christian religion; nor would such a declaration at that time have recommended him, or his nation, or his writings, to either the Greeks or the Romans; of his reputation with both which people he is known to have been, in the writing of these Antiquities, very greatly solicitous.

(4.) Josephus's usual way of writing is historical and declarative of facts, and of the opinions of others, and but rarely such as directly informs us of his own opinion, unless we prudently gather it from what he says historically, or as the opinions of others. This is very observable in the writings of Josephus, and in particular as to what he says of John the Baptist, and of James the Just; so that this interpretation is most probable, as most agreeable to Josephus's way of writing in parallel cases.

(5.) This seems to be the universal sense of all the ancients, without exception, who cite this testimony from him; and though they almost everywhere own this to be the true reading, yet do they everywhere suppose Josephus to be still an unbelieving Jew, and not a believing Christian; nay, Jerome appears so well assured of this interpretation, and that Josephus did not mean to declare any more by these words, than a common opinion that, according to his usual way of interpreting authors, not to the words but to the sense (of which we have, I think, two more instances in his accounts out of Josephus now before us,) he renders this clause, *Credebatur esse Christus*, i.e. *He was believed to be Christ*. Nor is the parallel expression of Pilate to be otherwise understood, when he made that inscription upon the cross, *This is Jesus, the King of the Jews* (Matt. xxvii. 31;) which is well explained by himself elsewhere, and corresponds to the import of the present clause, *What shall I do with Jesus, who is called Christ?* (Matt. xxvii, 17, 22.) And we may full as well prove from Pilate's inscription upon the cross, that he hereby declared himself *a believer in Christ*, for the *real king of the Jews*, as we can from these words of Josephus, that he thereby declared himself to be a real believer in him, as the true Messiah.

IV. Though Josephus did not design here to declare himself openly to be a Christian, yet could he not possibly believe all that he here asserts concerning Jesus Christ, unless he were so far a Christian as the Jewish Nazarenes or Ebionites then were, who believed Jesus of Nazareth to be the true Messiah, without believing he was more than a man: who also believed the necessity of the observation of the ceremonial law of Moses in order to salvation for all mankind, which were the two main articles of those Jewish Christians' faith, though in opposition to all the thirteen apostles of Jesus Christ in the first century, and in opposition to the whole Catholic Church of Christ in the following centuries also. Accordingly, I have elsewhere proved, that Josephus was no other in his own mind and conscience than a Nazarene or Ebionite Jewish Christian; and have observed, that this entire testimony, and all that Josephus says of John the Baptist and of James, as well as his absolute silence about all the rest of the apostles and their companions, exactly agree to him under that character and no other; and indeed to me it is most astonishing, that all our learned men, who have of late considered these testimonies of Josephus, except the converted Jew Galatinus, should miss such an obvious and natural observation. We all know this from St James's own words, (Acts xxi. 20,) that *so many ten thousands of Jews as believed in Christ*, in the first century, *were all zealous of the ceremonial law*, or were no other than Nazarene or Ebionite Christians; and, by consequence, if there were any reason to think our Josephus to be in any sense a believer or a Christian, as from all these testimonies there were very great ones, all those and many other reasons could not but conspire to assure us, he was no other than a Nazarene or Ebionite Christian; and this I take to be the plain and evident key of this whole matter.

V. Since therefore Josephus appears to have been, in his own heart and conscience, no other than a Nazarene or Ebionite Christian, and, by consequence, with them rejected all our Greek Gospels and Greek books of the New Testament, and received only the Hebrew Gospels of the Nazarenes or Ebionites, styled by them, the *Gospel according to the Hebrews*, or *according to the Twelve Apostles*, or even *according to Matthew*, we ought always to have that Nazarene or Ebionite Gospel, with the other Nazarene or Ebionite fragments, in view, when we consider any passages of Josephus relating to Christ or to Christianity. Thus, since that Gospel omitted all that is in the beginning of our St Matthew's and St Luke's Gospels, and began with the ministry of John the Baptist, in which first parts of the Gospel History are the accounts of the slaughter of the infants, and of the enrolment or taxation under Augustus Cæsar and Herod, it is no great wonder that Josephus has not taken care particularly and clearly to preserve those histories to us. Thus, when we find that Josephus calls James the brother of Christ, by the name of *James the Just*, and describes him as a *most just or righteous man*, in an especial manner, we are to remember that such is his name and character in the Gospel according to the Hebrews, and the other Ebionite remains of Hegesippus, but nowhere else, that I remember, in the earliest antiquity; nor are we to suppose they herein referred to any other than that *righteousness which was by the Jewish law*, wherein St Paul (Philip. iii. 4, 5, 6,) before he embraced Christianity, professed himself to have been *blameless*. Thus when Josephus, with other Jews, ascribed the miseries of that nation under Vespasian and Titus, with the destruction of Jerusalem, to the barbarous murder of James the Just, we must remember what we learn from the Ebionite fragments of Hegesippus, that these Ebionites interpreted a prophecy of Isaiah as foretelling this very murder, and those consequent miseries :—*Let us take away the just one, for he is unprofitable to us : therefore shall they eat the fruit of their own ways* (Isaiah iii. 10.) Thus when Josephus says, as we have seen, that the most equitable citizens of Jerusalem, and those that were most zealous of the law, were very uneasy at the condemnation of this James, and some of his friends and fellow-Christians, by the high priest and sanhedrim, about A.D. 62, and declares that he himself was one of those Jews who thought the terrible miseries of that nation effects of the vengeance of God for their murder of this James, about A.D. 68, we may easily see those opinions could only be the opinions of converted Jews or Ebionites. The high priest and sanhedrim, who always persecuted the Christians, and now condemned these Christians, and the body of these unbelieving Jews, who are supposed to suffer for murdering this James, the head of the Nazarene or Ebionite Christians in Judea, could not, to be sure, be of that opinion; nor could Josephus himself be of the same opinion, as he declares he was, without the strongest inclinations to the Christian religion, or without being secretly a Christian Jew, *i. e.* a Nazarene or Ebionite;

which thing is, by the way, a very great additional argument that such he was, and no other. Thus, lastly, when Josephus is cited in Suidas, as affirming that Jesus officiated with the priests in the temple, this account is by no means disagreeable to the pretensions of the Ebionites. Hegesippus affirms the very same of James the Just also.

VI. In the first citation of the famous testimony concerning our Saviour, from Tacitus, almost all that was true of the Jews is directly taken by him out of Josephus, as will be demonstrated under the Third Dissertation hereafter.

VII. The second author I have alleged for it is Justin Martyr, one so nearly coeval with Josephus, that he might be born about the time when he wrote his Antiquities : he appeals to the same Antiquities by that very name; and though he does not here directly quote them, yet does he seem to me to allude to this very testimony in them concerning our Saviour, when he affirms, in this place, to Trypho the Jew, that *his nation originally knew that Jesus was risen from the dead, and ascended into heaven, as the prophecies did foretell was to happen*. Since there neither now is, nor probably in the days of Justin was, any other Jewish testimony extant which is so agreeable to what Justin here affirms of those Jews, as is this of Josephus the Jew before us; nor indeed does he seem to me to have had anything else particularly in his view here, but this very testimony, where Josephus says, "That Jesus appeared to his followers alive the third day after his crucifixion, as the divine prophets had foretold these and ten thousand other wonderful things concerning him."

VIII. The third author I have quoted for Josephus's testimonies of John the Baptist, of Jesus of Nazareth, and of James the Just, is Origen, who is indeed allowed on all hands to have quoted him for the excellent character of John the Baptist, and of James the Just; but whose supposed entire silence about this testimony concerning Christ is usually alleged as the principal argument against its being genuine, and particularly as to the clause, *This was the Christ :* and that, as we have seen, because he twice assures us that, in his opinion, *Josephus himself did not acknowledge Jesus for Christ*. Now, as to this latter clause, I have already shewn that Josephus did not here, in writing to Greeks and Romans, mean any such thing by those words, as Jews and Christians naturally understand by them : I have also observed, that all the ancients allow still, with Origen, that Josephus did not, in the Jewish and Christian sense, acknowledge Jesus for the true Messiah, or the true Christ of God, notwithstanding their express quotation of that clause in Josephus as genuine; so that unless we suppose Origen to have had a different notion of these words from all the other ancients, we cannot conclude from this assertion of Origen, that he had not those words in his copy, not to say that it is, after all, much more likely that his copy a little differed from the other copies in this clause, or indeed omitted it entirely, than that he, on its account, must be supposed not to have had the rest of this testimony therein, though indeed I see no necessity of making any such supposal at all. However, it seems to me that Origen affords us four several indications that the main parts at least of this testimony itself were in his copy :—

(1.) When Origen introduces Josephus's testimony concerning James the Just, that he thought the miseries of the Jews were an instance of the divine vengeance on that nation for putting James to death instead of Jesus, he uses an expression no way necessary to his purpose, nor occasioned by any words of Josephus there, that they had slain *that Christ which was foretold in the prophecies.* Whence could this expression come here into Origen's mind, when he was quoting a testimony of Josephus concerning the brother of Christ, but from his remembrance of a clause in the testimony of the same Josephus concerning Christ himself, that *the prophets had foretold his death and resurrection, and ten thousand other wonderful things concerning him*

(2) How came Origen to be so surprised at Josephus's ascribing the destruction of Jerusalem to the Jews' murdering of James the Just, and not to their murdering of Jesus, as we have seen he was, if he had not known that Josephus had spoken of Jesus and his death before, and that he had a very good opinion of Jesus, which yet he could learn no way so authentically as from this testimony? Nor do the words he here uses, that Josephus was not *remote from the truth,* perhaps allude to anything else but to this very testimony before us.

(3.) How can the same Origen, upon another slight occasion, when he had just set down that testimony of Josephus concerning James the Just, the brother of Jesus, who was called Christ, say that, "it may be questioned whether the Jews thought Jesus to be a man, or whether they did not suppose him to be a being of a diviner kind?" This looks so very like the fifth and sixth clauses of this testimony in Josephus, that *Jesus was a wise man, if it be lawful to call him a man,* that it is highly probable Origen thereby alluded to them; and this is the more to be depended on, because all the unbelieving Jews, and all the rest of the Nazarene Jews, esteemed Jesus, with one consent, as a *mere man,* the son of Joseph and Mary; and it is not, I think, possible to produce any one Jew but Josephus, who in a sort of compliance with the Romans and the Catholic Christians, who thought him a God, would say anything like his *being a God.*

(4.) How came Origen to affirm twice, so expressly, that *Josephus did not himself own,* in the Jewish and Christian sense, *that Jesus was Christ,* notwithstanding his quotations of such eminent testimonies out of him for John the Baptist his forerunner, and for James the Just, his brother, and one of his principal disciples? There is no passage in all Josephus so likely to persuade Origen of this, as is the famous testimony before us, wherein, as he and all the ancients understood it, he was generally called Christ indeed, but not any otherwise than as the common name whence the sect of Christians was derived, and where he all along speaks of those Christians as a sect then in being, whose author was a wonderful person, and his followers great lovers of him and of the truth, yet as *such a sect as he had not joined himself to;* which exposition, as it is a very natural one, so was it, I doubt, but too true of our Josephus at that time; nor can I devise any other reason but this, and the parallel language of Josephus elsewhere, when he speaks of James as the *brother,* not *of Jesus who was Christ,* but *of Jesus who was called Christ,* that could so naturally induce Origen and others to be of that opinion.

IX. There are two remarkable passages in Suidas and Theophylact, already set down as citing Josephus; the former, *that Jesus officiated with the priests in the temple;* and the latter, that the destruction of Jerusalem, and miseries of the Jews, were owing to their *putting Jesus to death,* which are in none of our present copies, nor cited thence by any ancienter authors, nor indeed do they seem altogether consistent with the other most authentic testimonies. However, since Suidas cites his passage from a treatise of Josephus, called "*Memoirs of the Jews' Captivity,*" a book never heard of elsewhere, and since both citations are not at all disagreeable to Josephus's character as a Nazarene or Ebionite, I dare not positively conclude they are spurious, but must leave them in suspense, for the further consideration of the learned.

X. As to that great critic Photius, in the ninth century, who is supposed not to have had this testimony in his copy of Josephus, or else to have esteemed it spurious; because in his extracts out of Josephus's Antiquities, it is not expressly mentioned,—this is a strange thing indeed!—that a section, which had been cited out of Josephus's copies all along before the days of Photius, as well as it has been all along cited out of them since his days, should be supposed not to be in his copy, because he does not directly mention it in certain short and imperfect extracts, no way particularly relating to such matters. Those who lay a stress on this silence of Photius, seem little to have attended to the nature and brevity of those extracts. They contain little or nothing, as he in effect professes at their entrance, but what concerns Antipater, Herod the Great, and his brethren and family, with their exploits, till the days of Agrippa junior, and Cumanus, the governor of Judea, fifteen years after the death of our Saviour, without one word of Pilate, or what happened under his government, which yet was the only proper place in which this testimony could come to be mentioned. However, since Photius seems therefore, as we have seen, to suspect the treatise ascribed by some to Josephus, *Of the Universe,* because it speaks very high things of the eternal generation and divinity of Christ, this looks very like his knowledge and belief of somewhat really in the same Josephus, which spake in a lower manner of him, which could be hardly any other passage than this testimony before us; and since, as we have also seen, when he speaks of the Jewish History of Justus of Tiberias, as infected with the prejudices of the Jews in taking no manner of notice of the advent, of the acts, and of the miracles of Jesus Christ, while yet he never speaks so of Josephus himself, this most naturally implies also, that there was not the like occasion here as there; but that Josephus had not wholly omitted that advent, those acts, or miracles which yet he has done everywhere else, in the books seen by Photius, as well as Justus of Tiberias, but in this famous testimony before us, so that it is most probable Photius not only had this testimony in his copy, but believed it to be genuine also.

XI. As to the silence of Clement of Alexandria, who cites the Antiquities of Josephus, but never cites any of the testimonies now before us, it is no strange thing at all, since he never cites Josephus but once, and that for a point of chronology only, to determine how many years had passed from the days of Moses to the days of Josephus,—so that his silence may almost as well be alleged against a hundred other remarkable passages in Josephus's works as against these before us.

XII. Nor does the like silence of Tertullian imply that these testimonies, or any of them, were not in the copies of his age. Tertullian never once hints at any treatises of Josephus but those against Apion, and that in general only, for a point of chronology; nor does it any way appear that Tertullian ever saw any of Josephus's writings besides, and far from being certain that he saw even those. He had particular occasion in his dispute against the Jews to quote Josephus, above any other writer, to prove the completion of the prophecies of the Old Testament in the destruction of Jerusalem and miseries of the Jews at that time, of which he there discourses, yet does he never once quote him upon that solemn occasion; so that it seems to me that Tertullian never read either the Greek Antiquities of Josephus, or his Greek books of the Jewish wars : nor is this at all strange in Tertullian, a Latin writer, that lived in Africa, by none of which African writers is there any one clause, that I know of, cited out of any of Josephus's writings ; nor is it worth my while in such numbers of positive citations of these clauses, to mention the silence of other later writers as being here of very small consequence.

DISSERTATION II

CONCERNING GOD'S COMMAND TO ABRAHAM TO OFFER UP ISAAC, HIS SON, FOR A SACRIFICE.

SINCE this command of God to Abraham (Gen. xxii.) has of late been greatly mistaken by some who venture to reason about very ancient facts from very modern notions, and this without a due regard to either the customs, or opinions, or circumstances of the times whereto those facts belong, or indeed to the true reasons of the facts themselves ; since the mistakes about those customs, opinions, circumstances and reasons, have of late so far prevailed, that the very same action of Abraham, which was so celebrated by St Paul (Rom. iv. 16–25,) St James (chap. ii. 21, 22,) the author to the Hebrews (chap. xi. 17–19,) Philo and Josephus, in the first century, and by innumerable others since, as an uncommon instance of signal virtue, of heroic faith in God, and piety towards him ; nay, is in the sacred history (Gen. xxii. 15–18) highly commended by the divine *Angel of the Covenant*, in the name of God himself, and promised to be plentifully rewarded ; since this command, I say, is now at last, in the eighteenth century, become a *stone of stumbling and a rock of offence* among us, and that sometimes to persons of otherwise good sense, and of a religious disposition of mind also, I shall endeavour to set this matter in its true, *i. e.* in its ancient and original light, for the satisfaction of the inquisitive. In order whereto we are to consider,

1. That till this very profane age, it has been, I think, universally allowed by all sober persons, who owned themselves the creatures of God, that the Creator has a just right over all his rational creatures, to protract their lives to what length he pleases,—to cut them off when and by what instruments he pleases,—to afflict them with what sicknesses he pleases,—and to remove them from one state or place in this his great palace of the universe to another, as he pleases ; and that all those rational creatures are bound in duty and interest to acquiesce under the divine disposal, and to resign themselves up to the good providence of God in all such his dispensations towards them. I do not mean to intimate that God may, or ever does, act in these cases after a mere arbitrary manner, or without sufficient reason, believing, according to the whole tenor of natural and revealed religion, that *he hateth nothing that he hath made* (Wisdom xi. 14); that whatsoever he does, how melancholy soever it may appear at first sight to us, is really intended for the good of his creatures, and at the upshot of things, will fully appear so to be : but that still he is not obliged, nor does in general give his creatures an account of the particular reasons of such his dispensations towards them immediately, but usually tries and exercises their faith and patience, their resignation and obedience, in their present state of probation, and reserves those reasons to the last day, *the day of the revelation of the righteous judgment of God.* (Rom. ii. 5.)

2. That the entire histories of the past ages, from the days of Adam till now, shew that Almighty God has ever exercised his power over mankind, and that without giving them an immediate account of the reasons of such his conduct ; and that withal, the best and wisest men of all ages, Heathens as well as Jews and Christians,—Marcus Antoninus as well as the patriarch Abraham and St Paul, have ever humbly submitted themselves to this conduct of the Divine Providence, and always confessed that they were obliged to the undeserved goodness and mercy of God for every enjoyment, but could not demand any of them of his justice ;— no, not so much as the continuance of that life whereto those enjoyments do appertain. When God was pleased to sweep the wicked race of men away by a flood, the young innocent infants, as well as the guilty old sinners ; when he was pleased to shorten the lives of men after the Flood, and still downward till the days of David and Solomon ; when he was pleased to destroy impure Sodom and Gomorrah by fire and brimstone from heaven, and to extirpate the main body of the Amorites out of the land of Canaan, as soon as *their iniquities were full*, (Gen. xv. 16,) and in these instances included the young innocent infants, together with the old hardened sinners ; when God was pleased to send an angel, and by him to destroy 185,000 Assyrians (the number attested to by Berosus the Chaldean, as well as by our own Bibles) in the days of Hezekiah, most of whom seem to have had no other peculiar guilt upon them than that common to soldiers in war, of obeying without reserve their king Sennacherib, his generals and captains ; and, when, at the plague of Athens, London, Marseilles, &c., so many thousand righteous men and women, with innocent babes, were swept away on a sudden, by a fatal contagion,—I do not remember that sober men have complained that God dealt unjustly with such his creatures, in those to us seemingly severe dispensations. Nor are we certain when any such seemingly severe dispensations are really such, nor do we know but shortening the lives of men may sometimes be the greatest blessing to them, and prevent or put a stop to those courses of gross

wickedness which might bring them to a greater misery in the world to come; nor is it fit for such poor, weak, and ignorant creatures as we are, in the present state, to call our almighty, and all-wise, and all-good Creator and Benefactor to an account upon any such occasions,—since we cannot but acknowledge that it is *He that hath made us, and not we ourselves* (Psalm c. 3,) that we are nothing, and have nothing of ourselves independent of him, but that all we are, all we have, and all we hope for, is derived from him, from his free and undeserved bounty, which therefore he may justly take from us in what way soever and whensoever he pleases; all wise and good men still saying in such cases with the pious Psalmist (Ps. xxxix. 9,) *I was dumb, I opened not my mouth, because thou didst it;* and with patient Job (ch. i. 21; ii. 10,) *Shall we receive good at the hand of God, and shall not we receive evil? The Lord gave, and the Lord hath taken away, blessed be the name of the Lord.* If therefore this shortening or taking away the lives of men be an objection against any divine command for that purpose, it is full as strong against the present system of the world, against the conduct of Divine Providence in general, and against natural religion, which is founded on the justice of that Providence, and is no way peculiar to revealed religion, or to the fact of Abraham now before us; nor in this case much different from what was soon after the days of Abraham thoroughly settled, after Job's and his friends' debates, by the inspiration of Elihu, and the determination of God himself, where the Divine Providence was at length thoroughly cleared and justified before all the world, as it will be, no question, more generally cleared and justified at the final judgment.

3. That till this profane age, it has also, I think, been universally allowed by all sober men, that a command of God, when sufficiently made known to be so, is abundant authority for the taking away the life of any person whomsoever. I doubt both ancient and modern princes, generals of armies, and judges, even those of the best reputation also, have ventured to take many men's lives away upon much less authority; nor indeed do the most sceptical of the moderns care to deny this authority directly; they rather take a method of objecting somewhat more plausible, though it amounts to much the same: they say that the apparent disagreement of any command to the moral attributes of God, such as this of the slaughter of an only child seems plainly to be, will be a greater evidence that such a command does not come from God, than any pretended revelation can be that it does; but as to this matter, although divine revelations have now so long ceased, that we are not well acquainted with the manner of conveying such revelations with certainty to men, and by consequence the apparent disagreement of a command with the moral attributes of God, ought at present, generally, if not constantly, to deter men from acting upon such a pretended revelation, yet was there no such uncertainty in the days of the old prophets of God, or of Abraham, the friend of God (Isa. xli. 8,) who are ever found to have had an entire certainty of those their revelations; and what evidently shews they were not deceived, is this, that the events and consequences of things afterwards always corresponded, and secured them of the truth of such divine revelations. Thus the first miraculous voice from heaven (Gen xxii. 11, 12,) calling to Abraham not to execute this command, and the performance of those eminent promises made by the second voice (Gen. xxii 17, 18,) on account

of his obedience to that command, are demonstrations that Abraham's commission for what he did was truly divine, and are an entire justificacation of his conduct in this matter. The words of the first voice from heaven will come hereafter to be set down in a fitter place; but the glorious promises made to Abraham's obedience by the second voice, must here be produced from verse 15—18. "And the angel of the Lord called unto Abraham out of heaven the second time, and said, By myself have I sworn, saith the Lord; for because thou hast done this thing, and hast not withheld thy son, thine only son, from me, that in blessing I will bless thee, and in multiplying I will multiply thy seed as the stars of heaven, and as the sand which is upon the sea-shore; and thy seed shall possess the gate of his enemies; and in thy seed shall all the nations of the earth be blessed, because thou hast obeyed my voice." Every one of which promises have been eminently fulfilled; and, what is chiefly remarkable, the last and principal of them, that *in Abraham's* SEED *all the nations of the earth should be blessed*, was never promised till this time. It had been twice promised him (chap. xii. 3; and xviii. 18,) that *in himself should all the families of the earth be blessed*; but that this blessing was to belong to future times, and to be bestowed by the means of one of his late posterity, the Messias, that great *son* and *seed* of Abraham only, was never revealed before, but on such an amazing instance of his faith and obedience as was this his readiness to offer up his only-begotten son Isaac, was now first promised, and has been long ago performed in the birth of Jesus of Nazareth, *the son of David, the son of Abraham*, (Matt. i. 1,) which highly deserves our observation in this place; nor can we suppose that anything else than clear conviction that this command came from God could induce so good a man and so tender a father as Abraham was, to sacrifice his own beloved son, and to lose thereby all the comfort he received from him at present, and all the expectation he had of a numerous and happy posterity from him hereafter.

4. That long before the days of Abraham, the demons or heathen gods had required and received human sacrifices, and particularly that of the offerer's own children, and this both before and after the Deluge. This practice had been indeed so long left off in Egypt, and the custom of sacrificing animals there, was confined to so few kinds in the days of Herodotus, that he would not believe they had ever offered human sacrifices at all: for he says, that "the fable, as if Hercules was sacrificed to Jupiter in Egypt, was feigned by the Greeks, who were entirely unacquainted with the nature of the Egyptians and their laws; for how should they sacrifice men, with whom it is unlawful to sacrifice any brute beast, boars and bulls, and pure calves and ganders only excepted?" However, it is evident from Sanchoniatho, Manetho, Pausanias, Diodorus Siculus, Philo, Plutarch, and Porphyry, that such sacrifices were frequent both in Phœnicia and Egypt, and that long before the days of Abraham, as Sir John Marsham and Bishop Cumberland have fully proved; nay, that in other places (though not in Egypt) this cruel practice continued long after Abraham, and this till the very third, if not also to the fifth century of Christianity, before it was quite abolished. Take the words of the original authors in English, as most of them occur in their originals, in Sir John Marsham's Chronicon, p. 76 – 78, 300 –304.

"Chronus offered up his only-begotten son as

a burnt-offering, to his father Uranus, when there was a famine and a pestilence."

"Chronus, whom the Phœnicians name *Israel* [it should be *Il*,] and who was, after his death, consecrated into the star Saturn, when he was king of the country, and had by a nymph of that country, named Anobret, an only begotten son, whom, on that account, they called *Jeul*, (the Phœnicians to this day calling an only begotten son by that name,) he in his dread of very great dangers that lay upon the country from war, adorned his son with royal apparel, and built an altar, and offered him in sacrifice."

"The Phœnicians, when they were in great dangers by war, by famine, or by pestilence, sacrificed to Saturn one of the dearest of their people, whom they chose by public suffrage for that purpose; and Sanchoniatho's Phœnician history is full of such sacrifices." [These hitherto I take to have been before the Flood.]

"In Arabia, the Dumatii sacrificed a child every year."

"They relate, that of old the [Egyptian] kings sacrificed such men as were of the same colour with Typho, at the sepulchre of Osiris."

"Manetho relates, that they burnt Typhonean men alive in the city Idithyia [or Ilithyia,] and scattered their ashes like chaff that is winnowed; and this was done publicly, and at an appointed season in the dog-days."

"The barbarous nations did a long time admit of the slaughter of children, as of a holy practice, and acceptable to the gods; and this thing, both private persons, and kings, and entire nations, practise at proper seasons."

"The human sacrifices that were enjoined by the Dodonean oracle, mentioned in Pausanias's Achaics, in the tragical story of Coresus and Calirrhoe, sufficiently intimate that the Phœnician and the Egyptian priests had set up this Dodonean oracle before the time of Amosis, who destroyed that barbarous practice in Egypt."

——*Isque adytis hæc tristia dicta reportat :*
Sanguine placastis ventos, et virgine cæsa,
Cum primum Iliacas Danai venistis ad oras ;
Sanguine quærendi reditus, animaque litandum
Argolica——
VIRG. Æn. ii. 115.
He from the gods this dreadful answer brought ;
O Grecians, when the Trojan shores you sought;
Your passage with a virgin's blood was bought !
So must your safe return be bought again,
And Grecian blood once more atone the main.
DRYDEN.

These bloody sacrifices were, for certain, instances of the greatest degree of impiety, tyranny, and cruelty in the world : that either wicked demons or wicked men, who neither made nor preserved mankind, who had therefore no right over them, nor were they able to make them amends in the next world for what they thus lost or suffered in this, should, after so inhuman a manner, command the taking away the lives of men, and particularly of the offerer's own children, without the commission of any crime; this was, I think, an abomination derived from him who was *a murderer from the beginning*, (John viii. 44;) a crime truly and properly diabolical.

5. That accordingly Almighty God himself, under the Jewish dispensation, vehemently condemned the Pagans, and sometimes the Jews themselves, for this crime; and for this, among other heinous sins, cast the idolatrous nations (nay, sometimes the Jews too) out of Palestine. Take the principal texts hereto relating, as they lie in order in the Old testament :—

"Thou shalt not let any of thy seed pass through the fire to Molech. Defile not yourselves in any of these things, for in all these the nations are defiled, which I cast out before you," &c. (Lev. xviii. 21.)

"Whosoever he be of the children of Israel, or of the strangers that sojourn in Israel, that giveth any of his seed unto Molech, he shall surely be put to death; the people of the land shall stone him with stones." (Lev. xx. 2.)

"Take heed to thyself, that thou be not snared by following the nations, after that they be destroyed from before thee; and that thou inquire not after their gods, saying, How did these nations serve their gods, even so will I do likewise. Thou shalt not do so unto the Lord thy God; for every abomination of the Lord, which he hateth, have they done unto their gods; for even their sons and their daughters have they burnt in the fire to their gods." Deut. xii. 30, 31. See chap. xviii. 10, and 2 Kings xvii. 17.

"And Ahaz made his son to pass through the fire, according to the abominations of the heathen, whom the Lord cast out before the children of Israel." (2 Kings xvi 3.)

"Moreover, Ahaz burnt incense in the valley of the son of Hinnom, and burnt his children (his son, in Josephus) in the fire, after the abominations of the heathen, whom the Lord had cast out before the children of Israel." (2 Chron. xxviii. 3.)

"And the Sepharvites burnt their children in the fire to Adrammelech and Anamelech, the gods of Sepharvaim," &c. (2 Kings xvii. 31.)

"And Josiah defiled Tophet, which is in the valley of the children of Hinnom, that no man might make his son or his daughter to pass through the fire unto Molech." (2 Kings xxiii. 10.)

"Yea they sacrificed their sons and their daughters unto demons; and shed innocent blood, the blood of their sons and of their daughters, whom they sacrificed unto the idols of Canaan; and the land was polluted with blood." (Ps. cvi. 37, 38. See Isa. lvii. 5.)

"The children of Judah have done evil in my sight, saith the Lord; they have set their abominations in the house which is called by my name to pollute it; and they have built the high places of Tophet, which is in the valley of the son of Hinnom, to burn their sons and their daughters in the fire, which I commanded them not, nor came it into my heart." (Jer. vii. 30–32.)

"Thus saith the Lord of Hosts the God of Israel, Behold I will bring evil upon this place, the which whosoever heareth, his ears shall tingle, because they have forsaken me, and have estranged this place, and have burnt incense unto other gods, whom neither they nor their fathers have known, nor the kings of Judah, and have filled this place with the blood of innocents. They have built also the high places of Baal, to burn their sons with fire for burnt offerings unto Baal, which I commanded not, nor spake it, neither came it into my mind," &c. (Jer. xix. 3–5.)

"They built the high places of Baal, which are in the valley of the son of Hinnom, to cause their sons and their daughters to pass through the fire unto Molech, which I commanded them not, neither came it into my mind that they should do this abomination, to cause Judah to sin." (Jer. xxxii. 35.)

"Moreover, thou hast taken thy sons and thy daughters, whom thou hast born unto me, and these hast thou sacrificed unto them to be devoured. Is this of thy whoredoms a small matter, that thou hast slain my children, and delivered them to cause them to pass through the fire for them?" (Ezek. xvi. 20, 21. See chap. xx. 26; 1 Cor x. 20.)

"Thou hatest the old inhabitants of thy holy land, for doing most odious works of witchcraft and wicked sacrifices; and also those merciless murderers of children, and devourers of man's flesh, and feasts of blood, with their priests, out of the midst of their idolatrous crew, and the parents that killed with their own hands souls destitute of help."—(Wisd. xii. 4-6.)

6. That Almighty God never permitted, in any one instance, that such a human sacrifice should actually be offered to himself (though he had a right to have required it, if he had so pleased) under the whole Jewish dispensation, which yet was full of many other kinds of sacrifices, and this at a time when mankind generally thought such sacrifices of the greatest virtue for the procuring pardon of sin and the divine favour. This the ancient records of the heathen world attest. Take their notion, in the words of Philo Biblius, the translator of Sanchoniatho:—"It was the custom of the ancients, in the greatest calamities and dangers, for the governors of the city or nation, in order to avert the destruction of all, to devote their beloved son to be slain, as a price of redemption to the punishing [or avenging] demons; and those so devoted were killed after a mystical manner." This the history of the king of Moab (2 Kings iii. 27,) when he was in great distress in his war against Israel and Judah, informs us of; who then "took his eldest son, that should have reigned in his stead, and offered him for a burnt-offering upon the city-wall." This also the Jewish prophet Micah (chap. vi. 6-8) implies, when he inquires, "Wherewith shall I come before the Lord, and bow myself before the High God? Shall I come before him with burnt-offerings, with calves of a year old? Will the Lord be pleased with thousands of rams, and ten thousands of fat kids of the goats? Shall I give my first born for my transgression, the fruit of my body for the sin of my soul?" No, certainly; "For he hath shewed thee, O man, what is good; and what doth the Lord require of thee, but to do justly, and to love mercy, and to humble thyself to walk with thy God?"

It is true, God did here try the faith and obedience of Abraham to himself, whether they were as strong as the Pagans exhibited to their demons or idols, yet did he withal take effectual care, and that by a miraculous interposition also, to prevent the execution, and provided himself a ram, as a vicarious substitute, to supply the place of Isaac immediately:—"And the angel of the Lord called unto Abraham, and said, Abraham, Abraham!—and he said, Here am I: —and he said, Lay not thine hand upon the lad, neither do thou any thing unto him; for now I know that thou fearest God, seeing thou hast not withheld thy son, thine only son from me. And Abraham lifted up his eyes, and looked, and behold a ram caught in a thicket by his horns; and Abraham went and took the ram, and offered him up for a burnt-offering in the stead of his son." (Gen. xxii. 11-13.) Thus though Jephtha (Judg. xi. 36-39,) has, by many, been thought to have vowed to offer up his daughter and only child for a sacrifice, and that as bound on him, upon supposition of his vow, by a divine law (Lev. xxvii. 28, 29,) of which I was once myself; yet upon more mature consideration, I have, for some time, thought this to be a mistake, and that his vow extended only to her being devoted to serve God at the tabernacle,

or elsewhere, in a state of perpetual virginity; and that neither that law did enjoin any human sacrifices, nor do we meet with any example of its execution in this sense afterwards. Philo never mentions any such law, no more than Josephus; and when Josephus thought that Jephtha had made such a vow, and executed it, he is so far from hinting at its being done in compliance with any law of God, that he expressly condemns him for it, as having acted contrary thereto; or, in his own words, "as having offered an oblation neither conformable to the law, nor acceptable to God, nor weighing with himself what opinion the hearers would have of such a practice."

7. That Isaac being at this time, according to Josephus, who is herein justly followed by Archbishop Usher, no less than twenty-five years of age, and Abraham being, by consequence, one hundred and twenty-five, it is not to be supposed that Abraham could bind Isaac, in order to offer him in sacrifice, but by his own free consent; which free consent of the party who is to suffer, seems absolutely necessary in all such cases; and which free consent St Clement, as well as Josephus, distinctly takes notice of on this occasion. St Clement describes it thus:—"Isaac being fully persuaded of what he knew was to come, cheerfully yielded himself up for a sacrifice." And for Josephus, after introducing Abraham in a pathetic speech laying before Isaac the divine command, and exhorting him patiently and joyfully to submit to it, he tells us that "Isaac very cheerfully consented;" and then introduces him in a short, but very pious answer, acquiescing in the proposal; and adds, that "he then immediately, and readily, went to the altar to be sacrificed." Nor did Jephtha (Judges xi. 36, 37) perform his rash vow, whatever it were, till his daughter had given her consent to it.

8. It appears to me that Abraham never despaired entirely of the interposition of Providence for the preservation of Isaac, although in obedience to the command he prepared to sacrifice him to God. This seems to me intimated in Abraham's words to his servants on the third day, when he was in sight of the mountain on which he was to offer his son Isaac: "We will go and worship, and we will come again to you." As also in his answer to his son, when he inquired, "Behold, the fire and the wood; but where is the lamb for a burnt-offering?—and Abraham said, My son, God will provide himself a lamb for a burnt-offering." (Gen. xxii. 5-7.) Both these passages look to me somewhat like such an expectation. However,

9. It appears most evident that Abraham, and I suppose Isaac also, firmly believed, that if God should permit Isaac to be actually slain as a sacrifice, he would certainly and speedily raise him again from the dead. This, to be sure, is supposed in the words already quoted, that both "he and his son would go and worship, and come again to the servants;" and is clearly and justly collected from this history by the author to the Hebrews (chap. xi. 17, 18, 19:) "By faith, Abraham, when he was tried, offered up Isaac; and he that had received the promises offered up his only begotten, of whom it was said, That in Isaac shall thy seed be called, accounting [or reasoning] that God was able to raise him from the dead." And this reasoning was at once very obvious and wholly undeniable, that since God was truth itself, and had over and over promised that he would "multiply Abraham exceedingly; that he should be a father of many nations; that his name should be no longer Abram but Abra-

ham, because a father of many nations God had made him," &c. ; that "Sarai his wife should be called Sarah ; that he would bless her, and give Abraham a son also of her ;" and that "he would bless him ; and she should become nations ; and kings of people should be of her," &c. (Gen xvii. 2, 4, 5, 6, 16;) and that "in Isaac should his seed be called," (Gen. xxi. 12 :) —and since withal it is here supposed that Isaac was to be slain as a sacrifice before he was married, or had any seed, God was, for certain, obliged by his promises, in these circumstances, to raise Isaac again from the dead ; and this was an eminent instance of that *faith* whereby "Abraham believed God, and it was imputed to him for righteousness," (Gen. xv. 6,) viz. that if God should permit Isaac to be sacrificed, he would certainly and quickly raise him up again from the dead, "from whence also he received him in a figure," as the author to the Hebrews (chap. xi. 19) here justly observes.

10 That the firm and just foundation of Abraham's faith and assurance in God for such a resurrection was this, besides the general consideration of the divine veracity, that during the whole time of his sojourning in strange countries, in Canaan and Egypt, ever since he had been called out of Chaldea or Mesopotamia at seventy-five years of age (Gen. xii. 4,) he had had constant experience of a special, of an over-ruling, of a kind and gracious Providence over him, till his 125th year, which, against all human views, had continually blessed him and enriched him, and, in his elder age, had given him first Ishmael by Hagar, and afterward promised him Isaac to "spring from his own body now dead, and from the deadness of Sarah's womb (Rom. iv. 19,) when she was past age (Heb. xi. 11,) and when it ceased to be with Sarah after the manner of women (Gen. xviii. 11,) and had actually performed that and every other promise, how improbable soever that performance had appeared, he had ever made to him, and this during fifty entire years together ; so that although, at his first exit out of Chaldea or Mesopotamia, he might have been tempted *to stagger at such a promise of God, through unbelief,* yet might he now, after fifty years' constant experience, be justly *strong in faith, giving glory to God, as being fully persuaded that what God had promised,* (the resurrection of Isaac) *he was both able and willing to perform,* (Rom. iv. 20, 21.)

11. That this assurance therefore, that God, if he permitted Isaac to be slain, would infallibly raise him again from the dead, entirely alters the state of the case of Abraham's sacrificing Isaac to the true God, from that of all other human sacrifices whatsoever offered to false ones, all those others being done without the least promise or prospect of such a resurrection ; and this indeed takes away all pretence of injustice in the divine command, as well as of all inhumanity or cruelty in Abraham's obedience to it.

12. That upon the whole, this command to Abraham and what followed upon it, looks so very like an intention of God to typify or represent beforehand, in Isaac, *a beloved* or *only begotten son,* what was to happen long afterwards to the great *Son* and *seed of Abraham, the Messiah,* the beloved and *the only begotten of the Father, whose day Abraham saw by faith beforehand, and rejoiced to see it,* (John viii. 56,) viz., that he, *by the determinate counsel and foreknowledge of God, should be crucified and slain,* as a sacrifice, and should *be raised again the third day,* (Acts ii. 22-32,) and this *at Jerusalem also;* and that in the meantime, God would accept of the sacrifices of rams and the like animals, at the same city, Jerusalem, that one cannot easily avoid the application. This seems the reason why Abraham was obliged to go to the land of Moriah, or Jerusalem, and why it is noted that it was *the third day,* (Gen. xxii. 2, 4,) that he came to the place, which implies that the return back, after the slaying of the sacrifice, would naturally be *the third day* also ; and why this sacrifice was not Ishmael the *son after the flesh* only, but Isaac the *son by promise,* the *beloved son* of Abraham ; and why Isaac was styled the *only son,* or *only begotten son* of Abraham, (Heb. xi. 17,) though he had Ishmael besides ; and why Isaac himself was to *bear the wood* on which he was to be sacrificed, (Gen. xxii. 6 ; John xix. 17 ;) and why the place was no other than *the land of Moriah,* or *vision, i. e.* most probably a place where the Shechinah or Messiah had been *seen,* and God by him worshipped, even before the days of Abraham, and where lately lived, and perhaps now lived, Melchisedeck, the grand type of the Messiah, (who might then possibly be present at the sacrifice ;) and why this sacrifice was to be offered either on the mountain called afterwards distinctly *Moriah,* where the temple stood, and where all the Mosaic sacrifices were afterwards to be offered, as Josephus and the generality suppose, or perhaps, as others suppose, that where the Messiah himself was to be offered,—its neighbour Mount Calvary. This seems also the reason why the ram was substituted as a vicarious sacrifice instead of Isaac. These circumstances seem to me very peculiar and extraordinary, and to render the present hypothesis extremely probable. Nor perhaps did St Clement mean anything else, when, in his fore-cited passage, he says, that "Isaac was fully persuaded of what he knew was to come," and therefore "cheerfully yielded himself up for a sacrifice." Nor indeed does that name of this place, *Jehovah-Jireh,* which continued till the days of Moses, and signified *God will see,* or rather *God will provide,* seem to be given it by Abraham, on any other account, than that God would then, in the fulness of time, *provide himself a lamb,* (that *Lamb of God,* (John i. 29,) *which was to take away the sin of the world,) for a burnt-offering.*

But now, if after all it be objected, that how peculiar and how typical soever the circumstances of Abraham and Isaac might be in themselves, of which the heathens about them could have little notion, yet such a divine command to Abraham for slaying his beloved son Isaac, must however be of very ill example to the Gentile world, and that it probably did either first occasion, or at least greatly encourage, their wicked practices, in offering their children for sacrifices to their idols, I answer by the next consideration :—

13. That this objection is so far from truth, that God's public and miraculous prohibition of the execution and this command to Abraham (which command itself the Gentiles would not then at all be surprised at, because it was so like to their own usual practices,) as well as God's substitution of a vicarious oblation, seems to have been the very occasion of the immediate *abolition* of those impious sacrifices by Tethmosis or Amosis, among the neighbouring Egyptians, and of the *substitution* of more inoffensive ones there instead of them. Take the account of this abolition, which we shall presently prove was about the time of Abraham's offering up his son Isaac, as it is preserved by Porphyry, from Manetho, the famous Egyptian historian and chronologer, which is also cited from Porphyry

by Eusebius and Theodoret :—" Amosis," says Porphyry, "abolished the laws for slaying of men at Heliopolis in Egypt, as Manetho bears witness in his book of Antiquity and Piety. They were sacrificed to Juno, and were examined, as were the pure calves, that were also sealed with them : they were sacrificed three in a day. In whose stead Amosis commanded that men of wax of the same number, should be substituted."

Now, I have lately shewn that these Egyptians had Abraham in great veneration, and that *all the wisdom of those Egyptians, in which Moses was afterwards learned*, was derived from no other than Abraham. Now, it appears evidently by the forecited passage, that the first abolition of these human sacrifices, and the substitution of waxen images in their stead, and particularly at Heliopolis, in the north-east of Egypt, in the neighbourhood of Beersheba, in the south of Palestine, where Abraham now lived, at the distance of about a hundred and twenty miles only, was in the days, and by the order of Tethmosis or Amosis, who was the first of the Egyp-

tian kings, after the expulsion of the Phœnician shepherds. Now, therefore, we are to inquire when this Tethmosis or Amosis lived, and compare his time with the time of the sacrifice of Isaac. Now, if we look into my Chronological Table, published A.D. 1721, we shall find that the hundred and twenty-fifth year of Abraham, or, which is all one, the twenty-fifth year of Isaac, falls into A.M. 2573, or into the thirteenth year of Tethmosis or Amosis, which is the very middle of his twenty-five years' reign ; so that this abolition of human sacrifices in Egypt, and substitution of others in their room, seems to have been occasioned by the solemn prohibition of such a sacrifice in the case of Abraham, and by the following substitution of a ram in its stead : which account of this matter not only takes away the groundless suspicions of the moderns, but shews the great seasonablenes of the divine prohibition of the execution of this command to Abraham, as probably the direct occasion of putting a stop to the barbarity of the Egyptians in offering human sacrifices, and that for many, if not for all, generations afterwards.

DISSERTATION III

TACITUS'S ACCOUNT OF THE ORIGIN OF THE JEWISH NATION, AND OF THE PARTICULARS OF THE LAST JEWISH WAR; THAT THE FORMER WAS PROBABLY WRITTEN IN OPPOSITION TO JOSEPHUS'S ANTIQUITIES, AND THAT THE LATTER WAS CERTAIN ALMOST ALL DIRECTLY TAKEN FROM JOSEPHUS'S HISTORY OF THE JEWISH WAR

SINCE Tacitus, the famous Roman historian, who has written more largely and professedly about the origin of the Jewish nation, about the chorography of Judea, and the last Jewish war under Cestius, Vespasian, and Titus, than any other old Roman historian ; and since both Josephus and Tacitus were in favour with the same Roman emperors,—Vespasian, Titus, and Domitian ; and since Tacitus was an eminent pleader and writer of history at Rome during the time, or not long after, our Josephus had been there studying the Greek language, reading the Greek books, and writing his own works in the same Greek language, which language was almost universally known at Rome in that age ; and since therefore it is next to impossible to suppose that Tacitus could be unacquainted with the writings of Josephus, it cannot but be highly proper to compare their accounts of Judea, of the Jews, and Jewish affairs, together. Nor is it other than a very surprising paradox to me, how it has been possible for learned men, particularly for the several learned editors of Josephus and Tacitus, to be so very silent about this matter as they have hitherto been, especially when not only the correspondence of the authors as to time and place, but the likeness of the subject matter and circumstances, is so often so very remarkable ; nay, indeed, since so many of the particular facts belonged peculiarly to the region of Judea, and to the Jewish nation, and are such as could hardly be taken by a foreigner from any other author than from our Josephus,—this strange silence is almost unaccountable, if not inexcusable. The two only other writers whom we know of, whence such Jewish affairs might be

supposed to be taken by Tacitus, who never appears to have been in Judea himself, are Justus of Tiberias, a Jewish historian, contemporary with Josephus, and one Antonius Julianus, once mentioned by Minutius Felix, in his Octavius (sect. 33,) as having written on the same subject with Josephus, and both already mentioned by me on another occasion (Dissert. I.) As to Justus of Tiberias, he could not be the historian whence Tacitus took his Jewish affairs ; because, as we have seen in the place just cited, the principal passage in Tacitus of that nature, concerning Christ and his sufferings under the emperor Tiberius, and by his procurator Pontius Pilate, was not there, as we know from the testimony of Photius (Cod. xxx.;)—and as to Antonius Julianus, his very name shews him to have been not a Jew, but a Roman. He is never mentioned by Josephus ; and so probably knew no more of the country or affairs of Judea than Tacitus himself. He was, I suppose, rather an epitomizer of Josephus, and not so early as Tacitus, than an original historian himself before him. Nor could so exact a writer as Tacitus ever take up with such poor and almost unknown historians as these were, while Josephus's seven books of the Jewish War were then so common ; were in such great reputation at Rome ; were attested to, and recommended by Vespasian and Titus, the emperors, by king Agrippa, and king Archelaus, and Herod, king of Chalcis ; and he was there honoured with a statue ; and these his books were reposited in the public library at Rome, as we know from Josephus himself, from Eusebius, and Jerome, while we never hear of any other history of the Jews, that had then and there any such attestations or recommendations. Some things indeed Tacitus might take from the Roman records of this war. I mean from the Commentaries of Vespasian, which are mentioned by Josephus himself, in his own Life (sect. 65,) and some others from the relations of Roman people, where the affairs of Rome were concerned: as also other affairs might be remembered by old officers and soldiers that had been in the Jewish war. Accordingly I still suppose that Tacitus had some part of his information these ways, and particularly where he a little differs from or makes additions to Josephus: but then, as this will all reach no farther than three or four years during this war, so will it by no means account for that abridgment of the geography of the country, and entire series of the principal facts of history thereto relating, which are in Tacitus, from the days of Antiochus Epiphanes, two hundred and forty years before that war, with which Antiochus both Josephus and Tacitus begin their distinct histories of the Jews, preparatory to the history of this last war. Nor could Tacitus take the greatest part of those earlier facts belonging to the Jewish nation from the days of Moses, or to Christ and the Christians in the days of Tiberius, from Roman authors; of which Jewish and Christian affairs those authors had usually very little knowledge, and which the heathens generally did grossly pervert and shamefully falsify; and this is so true as to Tacitus's own accounts of the origin of the Jewish nation, that the reader may almost take it for a constant rule, that when Tacitus contradicts Josephus's Jewish Antiquities, he either tells direct falsehoods, or truths so miserably disguised, as renders them little better than falsehoods, and hardly ever lights upon any thing relating to them that is true and solid, but when the same is in those Antiquities at this day:—of which matters more will be said in the notes on this history immediately following.

HISTORY OF THE JEWS.

BOOK V. CHAP. II

Since we are now going to relate the final period of this famous city [Jerusalem,] it seems proper to give an account of its original. The tradition is, that the Jews ran away from the island of Crete, and settled themselves on the coast of Libya, and this at the time when Saturn was driven out of his kingdom by the power of Jupiter: an argument for it is fetched from their name. The mountain Ida is famous in Crete; and the neighbouring inhabitants are named Idæi, which, with a barbarous argument, becomes the name of Judæi [Jews.] Some say they were a people that were very numerous in Egypt, under the reign of Isis; and that the Egyptians got free from that burden, by sending them into the adjacent countries, under their captains Hierosolymus and Judas. The greatest part say they were those Ethiopians whom fear and hatred obliged to change their habitations, in the reign of king Cepheus There are those who report that they were Assyrians, who, wanting lands, got together, and obtained part of Egypt, and soon afterward settled themselves in cities of their own, in the land of the Hebrews, and the parts of Syria that lay nearest to them. Others pretend their origin to be more eminent, and that the Solymi, a people celebrated in Homer's poems, were the founders of this nation, and gave this their own name Hierosolyma to the city which they built there.

Chap. III.] Many authors agree, that when once an infectious distemper was arisen in Egypt, and made men's bodies impure, Bocchoris, their king, went to the oracle of [Jupiter] Hammon, and begged he would grant him some relief against this evil, and that he was enjoined to purge his nation of them, and to banish this kind of men into other countries, as hateful to the gods. That when he had sought for, and gotten them all together, they were left in a vast desert: that hereupon the rest devoted themselves to weeping and inactivity; but one of those exiles, Moses by name, advised them to look for no assistance from any of the gods, or from any of mankind, since they had been abandoned by both, but made them believe in him, as in a celestial leader, by whose help they had already gotten clear of their present miseries. They agreed to it; and though they were unacquainted with every thing, they began their journey at random; but nothing tired them so much as the want of water; and now they laid themselves down on the ground to a great extent, as just ready to perish, when a herd of wild asses came from feeding, and went to a rock overshadowed by a grove of trees. Moses followed them, as conjecturing that there was [thereabouts] some grassy soil, and so he opened large sources of water for them. That was an ease to them; and when they had journeyed continually six entire days, on the seventh day they drove out the inhabitants, and obtained those lands wherein their city and temple were dedicated

Chap. IV.] As for Moses, in order to secure the nation firmly to himself, he ordained new rites, and such as were contrary to those of other men. All things are with them profane which with us are sacred: and again, those practices are allowed among them which are by us esteemed most abominable.

They place the image of that animal in their most holy place, by whose indication it was that they had escaped their wandering condition and their thirst.

They sacrifice rams by way of reproach to [Jupiter] Hammon. An ox is also sacrificed, which the Egyptians worship under the name of Apis.

They abstain from swine's flesh, as a memorial of that miserable destruction which the mange, to which that creature is liable, brought on them, and with which they had been defiled.

That they had endured a long famine, they attest still by their frequent fastings: and that they stole the fruits of the earth, we have an argument from the bread of the Jews, which is unleavened.

It is generally supposed that they rest on the seventh day; because that day gave them [the first] rest from their labours. Besides which, they are idle on every seventh year, as being pleased with a lazy life. Others say that they do honour thereby to Saturn; or perhaps the Idæi gave them this part of their religion, who [as we said above] were expelled, together with Saturn, and who, as we have been informed, were the founders of this nation; or else it was because the star Saturn moves in the highest orb, and of the seven planets exerts the principal part of that energy whereby mankind are governed; and indeed the most of the heavenly bodies exert their power and perform their courses according to the number Seven.

Chap. V.] These rites, by what manner soever they were first begun, are supported by their antiquity. The rest of their institutions are awkward, impure, and got ground by their pravity; for every vile fellow, despising the rites of his forefathers, brought thither their tribute and contributions, by which means the Jewish commonwealth was augmented; and because among themselves there is an unalterable fidelity and kindness always ready at hand, but bitter enmity towards all others; they are a people separated from all others in their food and in their beds; though they be the lewdest nation upon earth, yet will they not corrupt foreign women, though nothing be esteemed unlawful among themselves.

They have ordained circumcision of the part used in generation, that they may thereby be distinguished from other people. The proselytes to their religion have the same usage.

They are taught nothing sooner than to despise the gods, to renounce their country, and to have their parents, children, and brethren in the utmost contempt; but still they take care to increase and multiply, for it is esteemed utterly unlawful to kill any of their children.

They also look on the souls of those that die in battle, or are put to death for their crimes, as eternal. Hence comes their love of posterity and contempt of death.

They derive their custom of burying, instead of burning their dead, from the Egyptians; they have also the same care of the dead with them, and the same persuasion about the invisible world below; but of the gods above their opinion is contrary to theirs. The Egyptians worship abundance of animals, and images of various sorts.

The Jews have no notion of any more than one Divine Being; and that known only by the mind. They esteem such to be profane who frame images of gods out of perishable matter, and in the shape of men; that this Being is supreme and eternal, immutable and unperishable, is their doctrine. Accordingly, they have no images in their cities, much less in their temples; they never grant this piece of flattery to kings, or this kind of honour to emperors. But because their priests, when they play on the pipe and the timbrels, wear ivy round their head, and a golden vine has been found in their temple, some have thought that they worshipped our father Bacchus, the conqueror of the East; whereas the ceremonies of the Jews do not at all agree with those of Bacchus, for he appointed rites that were of a jovial nature, and fit for festivals, while the practices of the Jews are absurd and sordid.

CHAP. VI.] The limits of Judea easterly are bounded by Arabia; Egypt lies on the south; on the west are Phœnicia and the [Great] Sea. They have a prospect of Syria on their north quarter, as at some distance from them.

The bodies of the men are healthy, and such as will bear great labours.

They have not many showers of rain: their soil is very fruitful; the produce of their land is like ours, in great plenty.

They have also, besides ours, two trees peculiar to themselves, the balsam-tree, and the palm-tree. Their groves of palms are tall and beautiful. The balsam-tree is not very large. As soon as any branch is swelled, the veins quake as for fear, if you bring an iron knife to cut them. They are to be opened with the broken piece of a stone, or with the shell of a fish. The juice is useful in physic.

Libanus is their principal mountain, and is very high; and yet, what is very strange to be related, it is always shadowed with trees, and never free from snow. The same mountain supplies the river Jordan with water, and affords it its fountains also. Nor is this Jordan carried into the sea: it passes through one and a second lake undiminished; but it is stopped by the third.

This third lake is vastly great in circumference, as if it were a sea. It is of an ill taste; and is pernicious to the adjoining inhabitants by its strong smell. The wind raises no waves there, nor will it maintain either fishes or such birds as use the water. The reason is uncertain, but the fact is thus, that bodies cast into it are borne up as by somewhat solid. Those who can, and those who cannot swim, are equally borne up by it. At a certain time of the year it casts out bitumen; the manner of gathering it, like other arts, has been taught by experience. The liquor is of its own nature, of a black colour; and, if you pour vinegar upon it, it clings together, and swims on the top. Those whose business it is, take it in their hands, and pull it into the upper parts of the ship, after which it follows, without farther attraction, and fills the ship full, till you cut it off, nor can you cut it off either with a brass or an iron instrument; but it cannot bear the touch of blood, or of a cloth wet with the menstrual purgations of women, as the ancient authors say; but those that are acquainted with the place assure us, that these waves of bitumen are driven along, and by the hand drawn to the shore, and that when they are dried by the warm steams from the earth, and the force of the sun, they are cut in pieces with axes and wedges, as timber and stones are cut in pieces.

CHAP. VII.] Not far from this lake are those plains, which are related to have been of old fertile, and to have had many cities full of people, but to have been burnt up by a stroke of lightning: it is also said that the footsteps of that destruction still remain; and that the earth itself appears as burnt earth, and has lost its natural fertility; and that as an argument thereof, all the plants that grow of their own accord, or are planted by the hand, whether they arrive at the degree of an herb, or of a flower, or at complete maturity, become black and empty, and, as it were, vanish into ashes. As for myself, as I am willing to allow that these once famous cities were burnt by fire from heaven, so would I suppose that the earth is infected with the vapour of the lake, and the spirit [or air] that is over it thereby corrupted, and that by this means the fruits of the earth, both corn and grapes, rot away, both the soil and the air being equally unwholesome.

The river Belus does also run into the sea of Judea; and the sands that are collected about its mouth, when you mix nitre with them, are melted into glass; this sort of shore is but small, but its sand, for the use of those that carry it off, is inexhaustible.

CHAP. VIII.] A great part of Judea is composed of scattered villages; it also has larger towns; Jerusalem is the capital city of the whole nation. In that city there was a temple of immense wealth; in the first parts that are fortified is the city itself; next it the royal palace. The temple is inclosed in its most inward recesses. A Jew can come no farther than the gates; all but the priests are excluded by their threshold. While the East was under the dominion of the Assyrians, the Medes, and the Persians, the Jews were of all slaves the most despicable.

After the dominion of the Macedonians prevailed, King Antiochus tried to conquer their superstition, and to introduce the customs of the Greeks; but he was disappointed of his design, which was to give this most profligate nation a change for the better; and that was by his war with the Parthians, for at this time Arsaces had fallen off [from the Macedonians] Then it was that the Jews set kings over them, because the Macedonians were become weak, the Parthians were not yet very powerful, and the Romans were very remote; which kings, when they had been expelled by the mobility of the vulgar, and had recovered their dominion by war, attempted the same things that kings used to do, I mean they introduced the destruction of cities, the slaughter of brethren, of wives, and parents, but still went on in their superstition: for they took upon them withal the honourable dignity of the high priesthood, as a firm security to their power and authority.

CHAP. IX.] The first of the Romans that conquered the Jews was Cneius Pompeius, who entered the temple by right of victory. Thence the report was everywhere divulged, that therein was no image of a god, but an empty place, and mysteries, most secret places that have nothing in them. The walls of Jerusalem were then destroyed, but the temple continued still. Soon afterward arose a civil war among us; and when therein these provinces were reduced under Marcus Antonius, Pacorus, king of the Parthians, got possession of Judea, but was himself slain by Paulus Ventidius, and the Parthians were driven beyond Euphrates; and for the Jews, Caius Sosius subdued them. Antonius gave the kingdom to Herod; and when Augustus conquered Antonius he still augmented it.

After Herod's death, one Simon, without waiting for the disposition of Cæsar, took upon him the title of *King*, who was brought to punishment by [or under] Quinctilius Varus, when he was president of Syria. Afterward the nation was reduced, and the children of Herod governed it in three partitions.

Under Tiberius the Jews had rest. After some time, they were enjoined to place Caius Cæsar's statue in the temple; but rather than permit that they took up arms; which sedition was put an end to by the death of Cæsar.

Claudius, after the kings were either dead or reduced to smaller dominions, gave the province of Judea to Roman knights, or to freed men, to be governed by them; among whom was Antonius Felix, one that exercised all kinds of barbarity and extravagance, as if he had royal authority, but with the disposition of a slave. He had married Drusilla, the grand-daughter of Antonius: so that Felix was the grand-daughter's husband, and Claudius the grand-son of the same Antonius.

ANNALS, BOOK XII

BUT he that was the brother of Pallas, whose surname was Felix, did not act with the same moderation [as did Pallas himself.] He had been a good while ago set over Judea, and thought he might be guilty of all sorts of wickedness with impunity while he relied on so sure an authority.

The Jews had almost given a specimen of sedition: and even after the death of Caius was known, and they had not obeyed his command, there remained a degree of fear lest some future prince should renew that command [for the setting up the prince's statue in their temple;] and in the meantime, Felix, by the use of unseasonable remedies, blew up the coals of sedition into a flame, and was imitated by his partner in the government, Ventidius Cumanus, the country

being thus divided between them; that the nation of the Galileans were under Cumanus, and the Samaritans under Felix; which two nations were of old at variance, but now, out of contempt of their governors, did less restrain their hatred: they then began to plunder one another, to send in parties of robbers to lie in wait, and sometimes to fight battles, and withal to bring spoils and prey to the procurators [Cumanus and Felix.] Whereupon these procurators began to rejoice; yet when the mischief grew considerable, soldiers were sent to quiet them, but the soldiers were killed; and the province had been in a flame of war, had not Quadratus, the president of Syria, afforded his assistance. Nor was it long in dispute whether the Jews, who had killed the soldiers in the mutiny, should be put to death: it was agreed they should die,—only Cumanus and Felix occasioned a delay; for Claudius, upon hearing the causes as to this rebellion, had given [Quadratus] authority to determine the case, even as to the procurators themselves; but Quadratus shewed Felix among the judges, and took him into his seat of judgment, on purpose that he might discourage his accusers. So Cumanus was condemned for those flagitious actions, of which both he and Felix had been guilty, and peace was restored to the province.

HISTOR. BOOK V. CHAP. X

HOWEVER, the Jews had patience till Gessius Florus was made procurator. Under him it was that the war began. Then Cestius Gallus, the president of Syria, attempted to appease it, and tried several battles, but generally with ill success.

Upon his death, whether it came by fate, or that he was weary of his life, is uncertain, Vespasian had the good fortune, by his reputation, and excellent officers, and a victorious army, in the space of two summers, to make himself master of all the open country and of all the cities, Jerusalem excepted.

[Flavius Vespasianus, whom Nero had chosen for his general, managed the Jewish war with three legions. Histor. b. i. ch. x.]

The next year, which was employed in a civil war [at home,] so far as the Jews were concerned, passed over in peace. When Italy was pacified, the care of foreign parts was revived. The Jews were the only people that stood out; which increased the rage of [the Romans.] It was also thought most proper that Titus should stay with the army, to prevent any accident or misfortune which the new government might be liable to.

[Vespasian had put end to the Jewish war; the siege of Jerusalem was the only enterprise remaining, which was a work hard and difficult; but rather from the nature of the mountain and the obstinacy of the Jewish superstition, than because the besieged had strength enough to undergo the distresses [of a siege.] We have already informed [the reader] that Vespasian had with him three legions well exercised in war. Histor. b. ii. ch. v.]

When Vespasian was a very young man, it was promised him that he should arrive at the very highest pitch of fame: but what did first of all seem to confirm the omen, was his triumphs, and consulship, and the glory of his victories over the Jews. When he had once obtained these, he believed it was portended that he should come to the empire.

There is between Judea and Syria a mountain and a god, both called by the same name of *Car-*

mel, though our predecessors have informed us that this god had no image, and no temple, and indeed no more than an altar and solemn worship. Vespasian was once offering a sacrifice there, at a time when he had some secret thought in his mind ; the priest, whose name was *Basilides*, when he, over and over, looked at the entrails, said, "Vespasian, whatever thou art about, whether the building of thy house or enlargement of thy lands, or augmentation of thy slaves, thou art granted a mighty seat, very large bounds, and a huge number of men." These doubtful answers were soon spread abroad by fame, and at the time were explained ; nor was anything so much in public vogue, and very many discourses of that nature were made before him, and the more, because they foretold what he expected.

Mucianus and Vespasianus went away, having fully agreed on their designs ; the former to Antioch, the latter to Cesarea. Antioch is the capital of Syria, and Cesarea the capital of Judea. The commencement of Vespasian's advancement to the empire was at Alexandria, where Tiberius Alexander made such haste, that he obliged the legions to take the oath of fidelity to him on the kalends of July, which was ever after celebrated as the day of his inauguration, although the army in Judea had taken that oath on the fifth of the Nones of July, with that eagerness, that they would not stay for his son Titus, who was then on the road, returning out of Syria, ch. lxxix. . Vespasian delivered over the strongest part of his forces to Titus, to enable him to finish what remained of the Jewish war. Histor. b. iv. ch. li.

During these months in which Vespasian continued at Alexandria, waiting for the usual set time of the summer-gales of wind, and stayed for settled fair weather at sea, many miraculous events happened ; by which the good-will of Heaven, and a kind of inclination of the Deity in his favour, was declared.

A certain man of the vulgar sort at Alexandria, well known for the decay of his eyes, kneeled down by him and groaned, and begged of him the cure of his blindness, as by the admonition of Serapis, the god which this superstitious nation worships above others. He also desired that the emperor would be pleased to put some of his spittle upon the balls of his eyes. Another infirm man there, who was lame of his hand, prayed Cæsar, as by the same god's suggestion, to tread upon him with his foot. Vespasian at first began to laugh at them, and to reject them ; and when they were instant with him, he sometimes feared he should have the reputation of a vain person, and sometimes, upon the solicitation of the infirm, he flattered himself, and others flattered him, with the hopes of succeeding. At last he ordered the physicians to give their opinion, whether this sort of blindness and lameness were curable by the art of man or not ? The physicians answered uncertainly, that the one had not the visual faculty utterly destroyed, and that it might be restored, if the obstacles were removed : that the other's limbs were disordered, but if a healing virtue were made use of, they were capable of being made whole. Perhaps, said they, the gods are willing to assist, and that the emperor is chosen by divine interposition. However, they said at last, that if the cures succeeded, Cæsar would have the glory ; if not, the poor miserable objects would only be laughed at. Whereupon Vespasian imagined that his good fortune would be universal, and that nothing on that account could be incredible ; so he looked cheerfully, and in the sight of the multitude, who stood in great expectation, he did what they desired him ; upon which the lame hand was recovered, and the blind man saw immediately. Both these cures are related to this day by those that were present, and when speaking falsely will get no reward.

BOOK V. CHAP. I

At the beginning of the same year, Titus Cæsar, who was pitched upon by his father to finish the conquest of Judea, and, while both he and his father were private persons, was celebrated for his martial conduct, acted now with greater vigour and hopes of reputation, the kind inclinations both of the provinces and of the armies striving one with another who should most encourage him. He was also himself in a disposition to shew that he was more than equal to his fortune ; and when he appeared in arms, he did all things after such a ready and graceful way, treating all after such an affable manner, and with such kind words, as invited the good-will and good wishes of all. He appeared also in his actions and in his place in the troops ; he mixed with the common soldiers, yet without any stain to his honour as a general. He was received in Judea by three legions, the fifth, and the tenth, and the fifteenth, who were Vespasian's old soldiers. Syria also afforded him the twelfth, and Alexandria soldiers out of the twenty-second and twenty-third legions. Twenty cohorts of auxiliaries accompanied, as also eight troops of horse.

King Agrippa also was there, and king Sohemus, and the auxiliaries of king Antiochus, and a strong body of Arabians, who, as is usual in nations that are neighbours to one another, went with their accustomed hatred against the Jews, with many others out of the city of Rome, as every one's hopes led him, of getting early into the general's favour, before others should prevent them.

He entered into the borders of the enemy's country with these forces, in exact order of war ; and looking carefully about him, and being ready for battle, he pitched his camp not far from Jerusalem.

Chap. X.] When therefore he had pitched his camp, as we said just now, before the walls of Jerusalem, he pompously shewed his legions ready for an engagement.

Chap. XI.] The Jews formed their camp under the very wall [of the city ;] and if they succeeded, they resolved to venture farther ; but if they were beaten back, that was their place of refuge. When a body of cavalry were sent against them, and with them cohorts that were expedite and nimble, the fight was doubtful ; but soon afterwards the enemies gave ground, and on the following days there were frequent skirmishes before the gates, till after many losses they were driven into the city. The Romans then betook themselves to the siege, for it did not seem honourable to stay till the enemies were reduced by famine. The soldiers were very eager to expose themselves to dangers ; part of them out of true valour, and many out of a brutish fierceness, and out of a desire of reward.

Titus had Rome, and the riches and pleasures of it, before his eyes ; all which seemed to be too long delayed, unless Jerusalem could be soon destroyed.

The city stood on a high elevation, and it had great works and ramparts to secure it, such indeed as were sufficient for its fortification, had it been on plain ground ; for there were two hills of a vast height, which were enclosed by walls made crooked by art, or [naturally] bending inwards, that they might flank the besiegers, and cast darts on them sideways. The extreme parts of the rock were craggy, and the towers, when they had the advantage of the ground, were sixty feet high; when they were built on the plain ground they were not lower than one hundred and twenty feet: they were of uncommon beauty, and to those who looked at them at a great distance, they seemed equal. Other walls there were beneath the royal palace, besides the tower of Antonia, with its top particularly conspicuous. It was called so by Herod, in honour of Marcus Antonius.

Chap. XII.] The temple was like a citadel, having walls of its own, which had more labour and pains bestowed on them than the rest. The cloisters wherewith the temple was enclosed were an excellent fortification.

They had a fountain of water that ran perpetually, and the mountains were hollowed under ground; they had moreover pools and cisterns for the preservation of the rain-water.

They that built this city foresaw, that from the difference of their conduct of life from their neighbours, they should have frequent wars; thence it came to pass that they had provision for a long siege. After Pompey's conquest also, their fear and experience had taught them generally what they should want.

Moreover, the covetous temper that prevailed under Claudius, gave the Jews an opportunity of purchasing for money leave to fortify Jerusalem; so they built walls in time of peace, as if they were going to war, they being augmented in number by those rude multitudes of people that retired thither on the ruin of the other cities; for every obstinate fellow ran away thither, and there became more seditious than before.

There were three captains, and as many armies. Simon had the remotest and largest parts of the walls under him. John, who was also called *Bar Gioras* (the son of Gioras,) had the middle parts of the city under him; and Eleazar had fortified the temple itself. John and Simon were superior in multitude and strength of arms, Eleazar was superior by his situation, but battles, factions, and burnings, were common to them all; and a great quantity of corn was consumed by fire. After a while, John sent some, who, under the pretence of offering sacrifices, might slay Eleazar and his body of troops, which they did, and got the temple under their power. So the city was now parted into two factions, until, upon the coming of the Romans, this war abroad produced peace between these that were at home.

Chap. XIII.] Such prodigies had happened, as this nation, which is superstitious enough in its own way, would not agree to expiate by the ceremonies of the Roman religion, nor would they atone the gods by sacrifices and vows, as these used to do on the like occasions. Armies were seen to fight in the sky, and their armour looked of a bright light colour, and the temple shone with sudden flashes of fire out of the clouds. The doors of the temple were opened on a sudden, and a voice greater than human was heard, that the gods were retiring, and at the same time there was a great motion perceived, as if they were going out of it, which some esteemed to be causes of terror. The greater part had a firm belief that it was contained in the old sacerdotal books, that at this very time the East would prevail, and that some that came out of Judea, should obtain the empire of the world, which obscure oracle foretold

Vespasian and Titus; but the generality of the common people, as usual, indulged their own inclinations, and when they had once interpreted all to forbode grandeur to themselves, adversity itself could not persuade them to change their minds, though it were from falsehood to truth.

We have been informed, that the number of the besieged, of every age and of both sexes, male and female, was six hundred thousand. There were weapons for all that could carry them: and more than could be expected, for their number, were bold enough to do so. The men and the women were equally obstinate; and when they supposed they were to be carried away captive, they were more afraid of life than of death.

Against this city and nation Titus Cæsar resolved to fight, by ramparts and ditches, since the situation of the place did not admit of taking it by storm or surprise. He parted the duty among the legions; and there were no farther engagements, until whatever had been invented for the taking of cities by the ancients, or by the ingenuity of the moderns, was got ready.

ANNALS, BOOK XV

Nero, in order to stifle the rumour [as if he had himself set Rome on fire,] ascribed it to those people who were hated for their wicked practices, and called by the vulgar *Christians;* these he punished exquisitely. The author of this name was *Christ,* who in the reign of Tiberius was brought to punishment by Pontius Pilate, the procurator. For the present this pernicious superstition was in part suppressed; but it brake out again, not only over Judea, whence this mischief first sprang, but in the city of Rome also, whither do run from every quarter and make a noise, all the flagrant and shameful enormities. At first, therefore, those were seized who confessed; afterward a vast multitude were detected by them, and were convicted, not so much as really guilty of setting the city on fire, but as hating all mankind; nay, they made a mock of them as they perished, and destroyed them by putting them into the skins of wild beasts, and setting dogs upon them to tear them to pieces: some were nailed to crosses, and others flamed to death: they were also used in the night-time instead of torches for illumination. Nero had offered his own gardens for this spectacle. He also gave them Circensian games, and dressed himself like the driver of a chariot, sometimes appearing among the common people, sometimes in the circle itself; whence a commiseration arose, though the punishments were levelled at guilty persons, and such as deserved to be made the most flagrant examples, as if these people were destroyed,—not for the public advantage, but to satisfy the barbarous humour of one man.

*** Since I have set down all the vile calumnies of Tacitus upon the Christians as well as the Jews, it will be proper, before I come to my Observations, to set down two heathen records in their favour, and those hardly inferior in antiquity, and of much greater authority than Tacitus; I mean Pliny's Epistle to Trajan when he was proconsul of Bithynia; with Trajan's Answer or rescript to Pliny, cited by Tertullian, Eusebius, and Jerome. These are records of so great esteem with Havercamp, the last editor of Josephus, that he thinks they not only deserve to be *read,* but almost to be *learned by heart also.*

PLINY'S EPISTLE TO TRAJAN

ABOUT A.D. 112

Sir,

It is my constant method to apply myself to you for the resolution of all my doubts; for who can better govern my dilatory way of proceeding or instruct my ignorance? I have never been present at the examination of the Christians [by others,] on which account I am unacquainted with what uses to be inquired into, and what, and how far they used to be punished; nor are my doubts small, whether there be not a distinction to be made between the ages [of the accused?] and whether tender youth ought to have the same punishment with strong men? Whether there be not room for pardon upon repentance? or whether it may not be an advantage to one that had been a Christian, that he has forsaken Christianity? Whether the bare name, without any crimes besides, or the crimes adhering to that name, be to be punished? In the meantime I have taken this course about those who have been brought before me as Christians. I asked them whether they were Christians or not? If they confessed that they were Christians, I asked them again, and a third time, intermixing threatenings with the questions. If they persevered in their confessions, I ordered them to be executed; for I did not doubt but, let their confessions be of any sort whatsoever, this positiveness and inflexible obstinacy deserved to be punished. There have been some of this mad sect whom I took notice of in particular as Roman citizens, that they might be sent to that city. After some time, as is usual in such examinations, the crime spread itself, and many more cases came before me. A libel was sent to me, though without an author, containing many names [of persons accused.] These denied that they were Christians now, or ever had been. They called upon the gods, and supplicated to your image, which I caused to be brought to me for that purpose, with frankincense and wine; they also cursed Christ; none of which things, it is said, can any of those that are really Christians be compelled to do: so I thought fit to let them go. Others of them that were named in the libel, said they were Christians, but presently denied it again; that indeed they had been Christians, but had ceased to be so, some three years, some many more; and one there was that said he had not been so these twenty years. All these worshipped your image, and the images of our gods; these also cursed Christ. However, they assured me that the main of their fault, or of their mistake, was this:—That they were wont, on a stated day, to meet together before it was light, and to sing a hymn to Christ, as to a god, alternately; and to oblige themselves by a sacrament [or oath,] not to do anything that was ill; but that they would commit no theft, or pilfering, or adultery; that they would not break their promises, or deny what was deposited with them, when it was required back again; after which it was their custom to depart, and to meet again at a common but innocent meal, which they had left off upon that edict which I published at your command, and wherein I had forbidden any such conventicles. These examinations made me think it necessary to inquire by torments what the truth was; which I did of two servant-maids, who were called Deaconesses: but still I discovered no more than that they were addicted to a bad and to an extravagant superstition. Hereupon I have put off any further examinations, and have recourse to you, for the affair seems to be well worth consultation, especially on account of the number of those that are in danger; for there are many of every age, of every rank, and of both sexes, who are now and hereafter likely to be called to account, and to be in danger; for this superstition is spread like a contagion, not only into cities and towns, but into country villages also, which yet there is reason to hope may be stopped and corrected. To be sure, the temples, which were almost forsaken, begin already to be frequented; and the holy solemnities, which were long intermitted, begin to be revived. The sacrifices begin to sell well everywhere, of which very few purchasers had of late appeared; whereby it is easy to suppose how great a multitude of men may be amended, if place for repentance be admitted.

TRAJAN'S EPISTLE TO PLINY

My Pliny,—You have taken the method which you ought in examining the causes of those that had been accused as Christians, for indeed no certain and general form of judging can be ordained in this case. These people are not to be sought for; but if they be accused and convicted, they are to be punished; but with this caution, that he who denies himself to be a Christian, and makes it plain that he is not so by supplicating to our gods, although he had been so formerly, may be allowed pardon, upon his repentance. As for libels sent without an author, they ought to have no place in any accusation whatsoever, for that would be a thing of very ill example, and not agreeable to my reign.

OBSERVATIONS

UPON THE PASSAGES TAKEN OUT OF TACITUS

I. We see here what a great regard the best of the Roman historians of that age, Tacitus, had to the history of Josephus, while though he never names him, as he very rarely names any of those Roman authors whence he derives other parts of his history, yet does it appear that he refers to his seven books of the Jewish Wars several times in a very few pages, and almost always depends on his accounts of the affairs of the Romans and Parthians, as well as of the Jews, during no fewer than 240 years, to which those books extend.

II. Yet does it appear that when he now and then followed other historians, or reports concerning the Romans, the Parthians, or the Jews, during that long interval, he was commonly mistaken in them, and had better have kept close to Josephus than hearken to any of his other authors or informers.

III. It also appears highly probable that Tacitus had seen the Antiquities of Josephus, and knew that the most part of the accounts he produced of the origin of the Jewish nation entirely contradicted those Antiquities. He also could hardly avoid seeing that those accounts contradicted one another also, and were childish, absurd, and supported by no good evidence whatsoever: as also, he could hardly avoid seeing that Josephus's accounts in those Antiquities were authentic, substantial, and thoroughly attested to by the ancient records of that nation, and of the neighbouring nations also, which indeed no one can now avoid seeing, that carefully peruses and considers them.

IV. Tacitus therefore, in concealing the greatest part of the true ancient history of the Jewish nation, which lay before him in Josephus, and producing such fabulous, ill-grounded, and partial histories, which he had from the heathens, acted a most unfair part; and this procedure of his is here the more gross, in regard he professes such great impartiality (Hist. b. i. ch. i., and is allowed indeed to have observed that impartiality as to the Roman affairs.

V. Tacitus's hatred and contempt of God's peculiar people, the Jews, and his attachment to the grossest idolatry, superstition, and astral fatality of the Romans, were therefore so strong in him, as to overbear all restraints of sober reason and equity in the case of those Jews, though he be allowed so exactly to have followed them on other occasions relating to the Romans.

VI. Since therefore Tacitus was so bitter against the Jews, and since he knew that Christ was a Jew himself, and that his apostles and first followers were Jews, and also knew that the Christian religion was derived into the Roman provinces from Judea,—it is no wonder that his hatred and contempt of the Jews extended itself to the Christians also, whom the Romans usually confounded with the Jews; as therefore his hard words of the Jews appear to have been generally groundless, and hurt his own reputation instead of theirs, so ought we to esteem his alike hard words of the Christians to be blots upon his own character, and not upon theirs.

VII. Since therefore Tacitus, soon after the publication of Josephus's Antiquities, and in contradiction to them, was determined to produce such idle stories about the Jews, and since one of those idle stories is much the same with that published in Josephus, against Apion, from Manetho and Lysimachus, and nowhere else met with so fully in all antiquity, it is most probable that those Antiquities of Josephus were the very occasion of Tacitus giving us these stories; as we know from Josephus himself, against Apion, b. i. sect. 1, that the same Antiquities were the very occasion of Apion's publication of his equally scandalous stories about them, and which Josephus so thoroughly confuted in these two books, written against him; and if Tacitus, as I suppose, had also read these two books, his procedure in publishing such stories after he had seen so thorough a confutation of them, was still more highly criminal. Nor will Tacitus's fault be much less, though we suppose he neither saw the Antiquities, nor the books against Apion: because it was very easy for him, then at Rome, to have had more authentic accounts of the origin of the Jewish nation, and of the nature of the Jewish and Christian religions, from the Jews and Christians themselves, who he owns were very numerous in his days; so that his publication of such idle stories is still utterly inexcusable.

VIII. It is therefore very plain, after all, that notwithstanding the encomiums of several of our learned critics upon Tacitus, and hard suspicions upon Josephus, all the (involuntary) mistakes of Josephus, in all his large works put together, their *quality* as well as *quantity* considered, do not amount to near so great a sum as do these gross errors and misrepresentations of Tacitus about the Jews amount to in a few pages; so little reason have some of our later and lesser critics to prefer the Greek and Roman historians and writers to the Jewish, and

particularly to Josephus. Such later and lesser critics should have learned more judgment and modesty from their great father Joseph Scaliger, when, as we have seen, after all his deeper inquiries, he solemnly pronounces (*De Emend. Temp. Prolegom.* p. 17,) that "Josephus was the most diligent and the greatest lover of truth of all writers;" and is not afraid to affirm, that "it is more safe to believe him, not only as to the affairs of the Jews, but also as to those that are foreign to them, than all the Greek and Latin writers; and this because his fidelity and compass of learning are everywhere conspicuous."

N. B. Since there is another somewhat particular heathen account of the origin and ancient history of the Jews already mentioned, written by Trogus Pompeius, about the days of our Saviour, and abridged by Justin, about the days of Antoninus Pius, which is fit to be compared with the Bible and with Josephus, I shall here set it down entire, with a few brief notes, and refer to it hereafter, as occasion shall require.

JUSTIN, BOOK XXXVI. CHAP. I

ANTIOCHUS [Sidetes] conquered the Jews also, who had asserted their liberty during the empire of the Macedonians, under his father Demetrius.[1] They had now become so strong, that after this king they would not bear any other of the Macedonian race; nay, they set up a government of their own, and afflicted Syria with great wars.[2]

CHAP. *II.*] For the origin of the Jews was from Damascus,[3] that most eminent city of Syria; whence also sprung the Assyrian kings by queen Semiramis. Its name was taken from its king, Damascus; in honour of whom the Syrians worship at the sepulchre of Arathes his wife, as at a temple, and esteem of her as of a goddess that deserved the highest religious veneration. After Damascus, Azel was king, and afterwards Ador,[4] and Abraham, and Israhel. But Israhel was made more famous than his ancestors by the good fortune of having ten sons.[5] He therefore parted his kingdom into ten shares, and bequeathed it so parted among his sons; and named them all Jews, after the name of Judas, who died after the partition was made; and he ordered that they should all honour Judas's memory.[6] However, his share was added to all the other shares. The name of the youngest of these

---

[1] This is true. See Antiq. B. XIII, ch. v., vi., vii., x., xi.; ch. viii. sect. 2, & c. Only here is a mistake, when it is said that this Antiochus was the son of this Demetrius. He was his brother, and the son of the former Demetrius.

[2] This is very true. See Of the War, B. I. ch. ii., &c.; Antiq. B. XIII. ch. vi., &c.; I Macc. xiii., &c.

[3] I know no other foundation for this, but that Abraham, in his journey from Haran to Canaan, seems to have staid and reigned some time at Damascus; as Nicolaus of Damascus says, in Josephus, Antiq. B. I. ch. vii. sect. 2. Or else, that Eleazar of Damascus, the servant of Abraham, and by some thought to have been his son, was supposed to be one of the Jews' ancestors. See the note on Antiq. B. XII. ch. iv. sect. 10.

[4] These two names seem to mean Azael and Adod, or, as it is often written, Ador; the same kings, I suppose, which Josephus informs us the Syrians to his days worshipped as gods, Antiq. B. IX. ch. iv. sect. 6.

[5] Ten sons for twelve.

[6] There were twelve tribes, but never more than two kingdoms. Nor did Judas die sooner than the rest of his brethren. However, the name of *Judaei*, or Jews, is allowed by all to have been taken from this Judas.

brethren was Joseph,[6] of whose extraordinary abilities his other brethren were afraid; and on that account[7] they caught him in a close manner, and sold him to foreign merchants. And when they had carried him into Egypt, he learnt the magic arts there with great sagacity,[8] and in a little time became very dear to the king himself. For he was a most skilful expounder of prodigies, and first reduced the art of interpreting dreams to a rule. Nor did any thing of Divine or human laws seem unknown to him. Insomuch that he foresaw a dearth of provisions many years beforehand; and all Egypt had perished by famine, had not the king, at his suggestion, given a command that the fruits of the earth should be laid up. In short, such great evidences were given of his skill, that the answers he made seemed to be the answers of a god, and not of a man.[9] Moses was his son,[10] who was in great esteem, not only from the knowledge he inherited from his father, but from the beauty of his countenance also.[11] But as for the Egyptians, when they were afflicted with the scab and leprosy, they were admonished by an oracle to banish him, and those afflicted persons with him, lest that pestilential distemper should spread further. He therefore became the leader of these exiles, and stole away the Egyptian gods;[12] which when the Egyptians went armed to recover, they were forced by tempests to return home again.[13] Moses therefore, in order to return to their old country of Damascus, seized upon Mount Syna: in which journey, which was through the deserts of Arabia, when he and his people were tired with fasting seven days, they came at length to that place, and in the language of that nation called the seventh day the Sabbath; and consecrated it for ever to fasting,[14] because that day had put an end to their fasting, and to their wandering condition; and because they remembered that they were driven out of Egypt, for fear their distemper should spread; and that they might not, on the same account, be odious among their neighbours, they took care to have no communication with foreigners: which order, begun on this occasion only, by degrees became a real part of their religion. After Moses, his son Arvas succeeded to priest. After which time[15] it became a constant custom among the Jews to have the same persons for their kings and their priests. And incredible it is how greatly they flourished by this union of justice and religion together.

Chap. III.] The riches of the nation lay in the gains they made of their balsam, which grows only in these countries.[1] For here is a valley shut up between ridges of continued mountains, as if it were by a wall. The valley contains the space of two hundred acres; its name is Jericho. In that valley there is a grove of trees, eminent both for its fertility and pleasant situation; nor can it be otherwise, considering that it is divided between the palm trees and the balsam trees. The balsam trees in shape are like the turpentine trees, only they do not grow so tall, and they are cultivated after the manner of vines. The balsam itself perspires out of the trees at a certain time of the year. Nor is this place to be less admired on account of its coolness than of its fertility. I say this because the sun, which in this whole climate is exceeding hot, is yet here rendered naturally temperate, and that by a constant breeze of cool air. In this country is the lake Asphaltites, which is called the *Dead Sea*, because it is very large, and because the waters are immovable. For it is neither moved by the winds; (the bitumen, which here makes the whole lake a sort of stagnant pool, hindering the effect of those winds;) nor will it bear navigable vessels, for whatsoever is without life sinks downright to the bottom; nor does it bear up any material thing but what is covered over with alum. Xerxes, king of Persia, was the first who subdued the Jews.[2] They afterward came, together with the Persians, under the dominion of Alexander the Great; and they were a long while under the power of the Macedonian empire, and subject to the kingdom of Syria. When they fell off from Demetrius, they sought the friendship of the Romans, and were the first people of the East that obtained their liberty; the Romans, at that time, easily disposing of what did not belong to them.

N. B. We may here observe, that none of these heathen historians but Tacitus and Suetonius wrote with spite and bitterness against either the Jews or the Christians, but with a tolerable degree of candour. It seems to me that the Antiquities of Jo-

---

[6] Benjamin was the youngest, and not Joseph.

[7] The reason of this is to be taken out of the Bible and Josephus, and not from uncertain guesses of the pagans.

[8] All power of working wonders was then included under magic arts.

[9] Here is a great deal that is very true. One would wonder whence Trogus Pompeius had it. This is nearest the sacred history of almost any heathen accounts that concerned the Jews, excepting the beginning of Ovid's Metamorphoses, which whence it was taken I do not know also.

[10] Moses was some generations after Joseph, and not of his family nor tribe.

[11] This beauty of Moses is every where celebrated, but chiefly by Josephus, Antiq. B. II. ch. ix. sect. 6, 7.

[12] These Egyptian gods were not stolen by the Israelites, but were carried by the Egyptians themselves into the Red Sea, and were drowned with them. See Essay on the Old Test. Append. p. 239.

[13] Of these tempests, when the Egyptians were drowned, see the same Append. p. 154, 155.

[14] It should be rather to feasting; for the sabbath was always a festival among the Jews.

[15] Arvas, or Aaron, was not the son, but the brother of Moses; he did not succeed to the kingdom, but became the first high priest.

[16] Not till above one thousand four hundred years after the death of Moses and Aaron, by my chronology.

[1] See Josephus, Of the War, B. I. ch. vi. sect. 6; Antiq. B. XIV. ch. iv. sect. 1; B. XV. ch. iv. sect. 2.

[2] Xerxes never subdued the Jews, but was always their great friend. See Josephus, Antiq. B. XI. ch. v. The rest is true, and agreeable to Josephus, and to the history of the Maccabees.

sephus, which were published at Rome, A. D. 93, in the thirteenth of Domitian, when he with his Romans were become bitter persecutors of the Jews and Christians, was the occasion of this spite and bitterness in Tacitus and Suetonius, as well as in Apion and others, confuted by Josephus upon that occasion afterward. Nor can persecutors ever bear the affront, as to allow that those whom they persecute are other than wicked and vile men; as all such persecutors, how profligate and how barbarous soever they themselves are, and how virtuous and innocent soever those whom they persecute, do naturally describe them as thus wicked and vile, in vindication of their own honour among posterity.

DISSERTATION IV

PROVING

THAT THE COPY OF THE BOOKS OF THE OLD TESTAMENT LAID UP IN HEROD'S TEMPLE,
AND THENCE USED BY JOSEPHUS, THE JEWISH HISTORIAN, IN HIS ANTIQUITIES, WAS
NO OTHER THAN THAT MOST ANCIENT COLLECTION OR LIBRARY MADE BY NEHEMIAH, IN
THE DAYS OF ARTAXERXES, THE SON OF XERXES; AND WAS FREE FROM THE SEVERAL
ADDITIONS AND ALTERATIONS MADE AFTERWARDS IN THE OTHER COPIES WHICH ARE
NOW EXTANT

THIS APPEARS BY THE ARGUMENTS FOLLOWING

1. I. It is expressly told us, in the public epistle sent by the Jews of Jerusalem to their brethren in Egypt, in the hundred and forty-fourth year before the Christian era, and preserved in the Second Book of Maccabees, that as Judas Maccabeus had made a collection of the sacred books of the Jews after the persecution by Antiochus Epiphanes;[1] so had Nehemiah done the like long before it, and not very long after the captivity of Babylon, and the rebuilding the Jewish temple by Zorobabel. The words are these: *The same things also are related in the writings and commentaries of Nehemiah; how he founded a library, and gathered together the acts of the kings, and of the prophets, and of David, and the epistles of the kings concerning the holy gifts. In like manner also Judas gathered together all those things [books] that were lost, by reason of the war we had, and they remain with us. Wherefore if ye have need thereof, send some to fetch them unto you,* 2 Macc. ii. 13—15. Nor is there reason to doubt but such authentic collections, made by governors of the Jewish nation, would naturally be reposited in the Jewish temple; (whence Grotius justly concludes that Nehemiah's library itself was erected in that very temple;[2]) and would there be preserved, and thence removed into Herod's temple, when it was rebuilt: out of which temple, as I have elsewhere proved from Josephus's own words,[3] he received that copy which he made principal use of in his Antiquities. And because this is the great foundation of my present proposition, take the evidence at large, in the terms I formerly gave it. "It well deserves our further remark, that Josephus, when he wrote his Antiquities, seems not only to have had the use of one or more ordinary Hebrew copy, but probably of the most authentic copy in the whole nation; I mean that which had

been laid up in the temple itself: which very book seems to have been given him, or, however, the use freely allowed him, after the destruction of the temple, and when he wrote his Antiquities. For thus stand his own accounts: 'Titus Cæsar,' says Josephus, 'when the city of Jerusalem was taken by force, persuaded me frequently to take whatever I pleased out of the ruins of my country; for he told me that he gave me leave so to do. But there being nothing that I much valued, now my country was destroyed, I only asked of Titus liberty for myself and my family, as the only comfort now remaining in my calamities; *I also had the holy books by his concession.*' From all which facts laid together, it is plain that either Josephus had the authentic copy of the holy books, that was found in the temple, given him by Titus entirely; or at least that such authentic copy was at his command in the emperor's palace at Rome, in which city he wrote his Antiquities. And if we compare these things with his own assertion,—that two of the accounts he had given, [*viz.* that of the miracle of *water out of the rock,* and *of the sun's standing still,*[4]] and one of them, even of a miracle, not contained in the Pentateuch, but in Joshua, was extant *in the Scriptures laid up in the temple,* we shall see reason to believe, not only that he still made use of the Hebrew copies in general, but even of that very most authentic copy of all, which used to be laid up in the temple at Jerusalem."

Whether the Pentateuch made a part of Nehemiah's collection the text of the Maccabees does not directly inform us, though one cannot easily believe it was wanting in his library. Possibly Nehemiah supposed the vulgar copies of the Pentateuch perfect enough, and thought there was little occasion for that operose collection which he perceived necessary about the other books and papers.

N. B. Though it may be an objection to the authentic nature of this epistle of the Jews at Jeru-

---

[1] See Authent. Rec. p. 220—232.

[2] In locum.

[3] Essay on the Old Testament, p. 190—195.

[4] Antiq. B. III. ch. 1. sect 7; B. V. ch. 1. sect. 17.

salem, that the festival of dedication in the days of Nehemiah (the observation of which is therein recommended to the Jews in Egypt) is there said to have been *after he had builded the temple and the altar*, 2 Macc. i. 18; Neh. ii. 8, of which our copies of the book of Nehemiah say very little; yet is this objection taken away by the better copy of Josephus, who informs us that Nehemiah desired of the king to let him go, not only to *build the walls of Jerusalem*, but to *finish the building of the temple also;* and introduces Nehemiah in his speech to the whole body of the Jews in the midst of their temple, informing them of the king's grant to him of leave, not only to *build those walls*, but to *finish that temple also.* Which testimonies are strong attestations to the truth of this epistle.

2. II. That Josephus's copy was not a little different from even the Samaritan and Septuagint copies, as they stood in his age, and much more from the Masorete copy, as it has been since the days of Barchocab, is most evident. That his copy was, generally speaking, more perfect and authentic than those other copies, will certainly appear by a critical comparison of them all along; and has been frequently observed and proved in my Essay towards restoring the true text of the Old Testament, and in my Supplement to the Literal Accomplishment of Scripture Prophecies. And that this copy of Josephus's was not a common copy, but one laid up in the temple, we know from his own affirmations, just now set down. What Bible then could this be, but that which we know was collected by Nehemiah, about five hundred and twenty years before Josephus had his copy out of Herod's temple, and five hundred and forty before he wrote his Antiquities, and this in the same city Jerusalem, and in all probability reposited by him in its temple also?

3. III. That Josephus followed a better copy of the historical books, written after the Babylonish captivity, I mean of Esdras, of Nehemiah, and of Esther, than either the present Masorete copy or even the Septuagint version contains, appears by the particular character of those books, or of the materials out of which they were composed, in this very letter of the Jews; viz. that they principally contained the epistles of the kings of Persia, concerning their sacred donations to the people of the Jews; of which epistles we have the fewest accounts and copies in the Masorete Bible, more in the Septuagint version, and most of all in Josephus's Antiquities.

4. IV. It is evident that Josephus made use of an uncommon copy, or materials for a copy, of Nehemiah, as to the building the walls of Jerusalem, not under Artaxerxes, but Xerxes, contrary to all our Masorete and Septuagint copies; and this still in such a certain agreement with the chronology of Ptolemy's canon, and of Daniel's seventy weeks, (which seventy weeks could never be cleared till this copy was made use of,) as is very extraordinary. See Lit. Accomp. of Proph. Supplem. p.

56—93. This implies that Josephus had a most authentic copy of this book of Nehemiah, or of part at least of those materials out of which it was afterward composed; and such a one as neither the Masoretes nor the Septuagint interpreters appear to have had. All which exactly agrees to this collection or library of Nehemiah before us, and to no other. I am still obliged to speak cautiously concerning the histories after the captivity, without determining concerning them, whether they were already reduced into the books of Esdras, Nehemiah, and Esther; or whether they were then only a collection of materials, out of which those books were afterward to be composed. For these three histories being all, in a manner, contemporary with Nehemiah, and the two last entirely so, it is a great question whether their materials were digested into books as early as the collection of Nehemiah's library, or not. The words here are, that this last part of the library had, not these books, but only the *epistles of the kings concerning the holy gifts:* which way of speaking, somewhat different from what went before, seems to me rather to imply authentic papers out of which the books were to be afterward composed, than the books themselves when they were already composed.

5. V. There is a large branch of the book of Nehemiah which all our Masorete, Septuagint, and vulgar Latin copies give us as part of his book, though it be rather an appendix to the book of Esdras, and is undoubtedly later than the rest of the book of Nehemiah; [being neither in his name, in the first person,[1] as is the rest of his book, nor continued with it in the vulgar Latin; but exhibited as a distinct history when it is introduced; and containing accounts as late as Jaddua, who was high priest under Alexander the Great, long after the days of Ezra and Nehemiah;] the branch I mean is from chap. vii. 70, to chap. xii. 26. Now since it is plain that this entire branch could not be in Nehemiah's copy or library, and yet is in all the other copies, we may hence draw a strong κριτηριον or character to determine, whether Josephus followed the other copies, or that of Nehemiah himself only. If he own this branch, he must have used some later copy; if not, he must have used Nehemiah's. Now it is very plain, and taken notice of by me several years ago, that though Josephus abridges some of the foregoing and following parts of this book, yet does it not appear that he had a syllable out of that branch. See Essay on the Old Testament, p. 55, which plainly shows us that he made use of Nehemiah's own copy, and of no other.

6. VI. Josephus, in his first book against Apion, sect. 8, is so peculiarly express, as to the very different regard the Jews paid to the holy books *before* and *after* the reign of *Artaxerxes, the son of Xerxes;* or, which is much the same, before and after Nehemiah's government; to which time he reckons the

---

[1] See Suppl. to Lit. Accompl. of Proph. p. 57—59.

constant succession of the prophets extended, but not longer; [which so different regard does however no where else appear in any other original author; no, not in the Septuagint version itself;] that it is exceeding remarkable, and affords us no small foundation for conjecture, that the Bible he had out of the Jewish temple ended in the days of Nehemiah, and in all probability was no other than Nehemiah's own collection or library. Which argument will be the stronger, if we consider,

7. VII. That the prophecy of Malachi, a book ever owned as sacred by the whole Jewish nation, was written after the days of Artaxerxes and Nehemiah, as I have elsewhere proved.[1] This book will therefore afford us another κριτήριον or character of Josephus's copy. If he had Malachi in his Bible, he must have had a later copy, or such a one as the Masoretes or Septuagint give us; but if he had not Malachi, he must have had this earlier Bible of Nehemiah. Now it is clear that Josephus, though he mention by name Isaiah, Jeremiah, Baruch, Ezekiel, Daniel, Jonah, Nahum, Haggai, and Zechariah, never says one word of Malachi, or of his prophecy; which yet, had it concluded his most authentic Old Testament, as it hath done the most authentic Old Testament of the rest of his nation in all the later ages, he would hardly have omitted; especially since he omits no other Hebrew book, whether historical or prophetical, in or after the Babylonish captivity. Nor if Josephus had read Malachi in his copy, would he surely have ended his succession of the prophets, and his catalogue of the most sacred books of his nation, with Artaxerxes the son of Xerxes; but either with Darius Nothus, or Artaxerxes Mnemon; in one of whose reigns, in all probability, this prophet wrote his prophecy. Which character therefore determines, and that with great probability, that it was Nehemiah's Bible which was used by Josephus, and no other.

8. VIII. This further appears by Josephus's entire omission of the book of Canticles, and I think only of that book in the whole Old Testament, now extant, earlier than Nehemiah; which yet is in all our Masorete, Septuagint, and other copies; though it can make no just pretence to the title of a sacred book, as I have elsewhere proved.[2] Nor is this other than a considerable κριτήριον or character that Josephus used no later copy than that of Nehemiah; there being not the least sign that the Jews so early admitted that strange book into their canon, though it appear some of them, at least, did so when the Septuagint version was made, about two hundred years afterward. I mean this if their later copies be in that case like the original ones.

9. IX. Josephus, by his perpetual using the Hebrew original of the first book of Apocryphal Esdras, as we now call it, instead of the Hebrew canonical Ezra, which is indeed a kind of epitome, or rather

an imperfect copy of the other, though perhaps as old as the Septuagint version, affords us another κριτήριον or character which Bible he used; I mean one older than that Hebrew canonical Ezra, which he never once cites in his large and particular accounts of that entire history. I say only perhaps this canonical Ezra is as old as the Septuagint version. For though it stand now in all our copies of that version, yet we having no citations from it, that I know of, till long after the days of Barchocab,[3] I am doubtful about such its antiquity. Possibly it may be of equal date with our imperfect Hebrew Nehemiah and Esther; and that they were all distinct original compositions from some such authentic papers which Nehemiah's library contained, but those very imperfect and ill digested. It also contains some Chaldee chapters, as does our Hebrew Daniel. For which Chaldee chapters of these two books we have, I think, no evidence older than Barchocab. So that I a little suspect this Hebrew and Chaldee Ezra to be no earlier than his time. By all which it appears that Josephus's Bible was different from and older than the present Masorete and Septuagint Bibles; or, in other words, that it was Nehemiah's Bible, and no other.

10. X. But the principa κριτήριον or character that Josephus's Bible was that of Nehemiah, is the general state of the book of Nehemiah itself, in all our later copies, as compared with Josephus's accounts of his history. If Josephus had used a copy of Nehemiah that extended to all the acts of his life, and in particular during the most publicly remarkable part of it, his twelve years' government of Judea, from the twentieth to the thirty-second of king Artaxerxes, Neh. v. 14; xiii. 6, as our copies now do, we might suppose he had made use of a copy of this book like ours, and as late or later than those twelve years' government extended to. But if he used only Nehemiah's own papers, as they stood collected in his own library, he could proceed no further than that part of his life which preceded that collection. Now this is the certain state of Josephus's history of Nehemiah. For though he intimate his knowledge of Nehemiah's later glorious acts, and particularly, as we have seen, of his *finishing the temple*, yet do his distinct accounts reach no further than the days of Xerxes; and contain very little more than the building the walls of Jerusalem, or about three years of the latter end of that reign of Xerxes, without a syllable of his twelve years' government under Artaxerxes. Accordingly, while the third book of Esdras in the complete Greek and Latin editions has four hundred and thirty-four verses, and the book of Esther has about two hundred and seventy verses, and in all editions the book of Nehemiah has four hundred and six verses, Josephus's account of Esdras is no less, in the Cologne edition, without notes, than fourteen pages. And his account of Esther is almost

---

[1] Lit. Accompl. of Proph. Suppl. p. 79—81.

[2] Suppl. to the Essay on the Old Testament, p 25—29. See the entire Supplement.

[3] Essay on the Old Testament, p. 50—53.

ten pages, in a near proportion to their largeness. While his whole account of Nehemiah, which by a just proportion ought to be above thirteen, is no more than two pages. Nor indeed does Josephus contain any part of this history that is in our present copies any further than what is in part of the first, in part of the second, in part of the fourth, in part of the twelfth, and in part of the thirteenth chapters; while he omits part of the first, part of the second, all the third, part of the fourth, all the fifth, sixth, seventh, eighth, ninth, tenth, eleventh, part of the twelfth, and part of the thirteenth chapters. And what parts of our copies are not omitted, are yet told us by him in such a different and better manner, and with such a different and better chronology, as demonstrates he did not take even those small parts from our present copies, but from other original papers, not a little different from them, and more authentic than they were. Which things are highly worthy the consideration of the learned.

N. B. To confirm this argument from the great disproportion there is in Josephus's account of the book of Nehemiah, as compared with his accounts of the other historical books in the canon of the Old Testament, I observe, that while there are one with another three hundred and eighty-two pages of the same edition of Josephus, which correspond to four hundred and thirty-six chapters of our Bible, from Genesis to Esther, which is almost a page to a chapter, we have in Nehemiah only those two pages to those thirteen chapters; which is a proportion utterly unexampled, I think, through Josephus's whole eleven books of Antiquities, which include that entire history. Nor is there, I believe, room for any other solution than what I have here given the inquisitive reader.

N. B. Since therefore Josephus's materials for the historical books, after the captivity, reach as far as the entire history of Esther, chap. iii. 7, i. e. to the twelfth of Artaxerxes, the son of Xerxes, and yet did not extend to the government of Nehemiah, from his twentieth to the thirty-second year, we ought to state the time of the collection of Nehemiah's library after the twelfth, but little or nothing later than the twentieth, of Artaxerxes. Accordingly I should, all things considered, determine the time to that very twentieth of Artaxerxes, upon Nehemiah's return to his government, that he and his people might have authentic copies of those sacred books ready at hand, by which his authority and their obedience were to be directed ever afterwards.

11. XI. The *order* of the several parts of the Pentateuch, and of other histories of the Old Testament, is in Josephus so frequently different from and better than either that in the Masorete copy, or the Septuagint version, or even sometimes than that in the Samaritan Pentateuch itself, that he must have had an earlier and more uncorrupt copy than were any of the others.

12. XII. Not only the *order*, but many *portions of sacred history* themselves are so much fuller

and more exact, consistent and agreeable with *chronology*, with *natural religion*,[1] and with one another, in Josephus, than they are in any of our other copies, that he must have had an earlier and more uncorrupt copy than any we now have. These two last observations have forced themselves upon me in my late careful comparison of the Masorete copy, in our common Bibles, with the eleven first books of Josephus's Antiquities. And I dare boldly affirm, that when other learned Christians will take the pains to make the like careful comparison, they will hardly be able to avoid making the same observations. And what immense light such an entire comparison of the other copies with Josephus's Antiquities, and their improvements and corrections from those Antiquities, will cast upon many of those sacred books, and indeed upon the entire Old Testament history, and upon many of the prophecies also, I had much rather other learned men should discover by their own trials, than take my bare affirmations or observations for the truth of it.

13. XIII. There are none of those passages in Josephus's Antiquities which appear not to be so ancient as the times of Moses, or Joshua, or of the other original sacred historians, though they be in the Masorete Hebrew and Septuagint version, and even several times in the Samaritan Pentateuch itself; which passages have afforded a plausible handle to many, since the days of Aben Ezra, to suppose those books themselves in general later than the authors to whom they are ascribed. This is an observation, as I think, entirely new, and of very great consequence; and will therefore well deserve a thorough consideration. I shall trace all the several expressions or additions at large, in the order they lie in our Bibles, and compare the places all along with Josephus.

(1.) Gen. xii. 6, when Abraham was newly come out of Mesopotamia, it is taken notice of in the Hebrew and Samaritan texts, and in the Septuagint version, that *the Canaanite or Canaanites were then in the land.* And,

(2.) Again, Gen. xiii. 7, That *the Canaanite and Perizzite dwelt then in the land.* Which could hardly be remarked, as worth notice, that the land of Canaan had Canaanites in it, till after Joshua had driven those Canaanites out of it; which we all know was not done till after the death of Moses. Now we have both these histories in Josephus, but not a syllable of either of these passages. Nor are these passages either quoted or alluded to, that I know of, in any other book afterwards, before the making of the Septuagint version; which is to be supposed of the other examples, to be here given, without any special repetition.

(3.) Gen. xiv. 18, it is said, not only in all the other copies, but in Josephus also, that Abram pursued after those that had taken Lot prisoner *unto Dan:* which place is by some supposed to be

---

[1] See Suppl. to Lit. Accomp. of Proph. p. 75—77.

the old city Laish, called afterwards Dan, Judg. xviii. 29, from a colony of the tribe of Dan there settled, considerably later than the death of Moses. But then, as it is no way certain that by Dan is here meant the city of Laish, afterward called Dan, or indeed any city at all ; so Josephus directly assures us that the place whither Abram pursued his enemies was rather one of the fountains of Jordan, which was called Dan, than any city whatsoever. And as to the city Laish, when it was rebuilt by the Danites, and named Dan, Josephus mentions that its rebuilding, and this its new name ; but seems to have had no notion that this was the place whither Abram pursued his enemies. And if we observe that in Josephus's copy here it was the *fifth night* that Abram overtook them ; see also B. V. ch. i. sect. 18 ; and that, upon their defeat, it was the *second day* afterward when they were fled no further than Hobah, *on the left side of Damascus ;* and consider, that when an army flies for their lives they march much swifter than at other times ; we shall look for this place Dan nearer the sea of Galilee, than either to the fountains of Jordan or the city Laish, which was not far from them. Nor indeed do I take it to be any other than that Dan in the tribe of Naphtali, which was situate thereabout, Josh. xix. 38, with 1 Kings xv. 20 ; 2 Chron. xvi. 4. If indeed the Masorete Hebrew, and Roman copy of the Septuagint, could be depended on, God showed Moses from Mount Nebo *all the land of Gilead unto Dan,* Deut. xxxiv. 1, which must then have been a place about the fountains of Jordan, according to Josephus's opinion. But since both the Samaritan and the Alexandrian copy of the Septuagint, as well as Josephus, have no such text there, I still prefer this conjecture, that it was Dan near the sea of Tiberias whither Abram pursued his enemies, and no other ; which might well be its name in the days of Moses himself. As for that common phrase, *from Dan even to Beersheba,* as the entire length of the land of Canaan in after-ages, we meet not with it till after the city of Laish was called Dan, Judg. xx. 1, and for certain means no other place in all the Old Testament. But this is of no consequence in our present inquiry.

(4.) Gen. xix. 37, Moses informs us that Moab, the son of Lot, by his elder daughter, was the father of the Moabites *unto this day :* and, (5.) ver. 38, that Ammi, or Ammon, the other son of Lot, by his younger daughter, was the father of the Ammonites *unto this day.* These expressions are in all copies, and in Josephus also ; and very well do they suit to the days of Moses, under whose government these Moabites and Ammonites were considerable nations, with which he and the Israelites were greatly concerned, during the forty years' abode in their neighbourhood in the wilderness.

(6.) Gen. xxvi. 26, 32, 33, our present copies inform us that the city Beer-sheba, or the *well of the oath,* was so called, because Isaac there sware to Abimelech king of Gerar, to Ahuzza and Phicol his courtiers, at a well dug by him, without the least notice that this well was dug in the days of Abraham, and that there Abraham sware unto the same Abimelech king of Gerar, and to the same Ahuzza and Phicol his courtiers, about ninety years before, Gen. xxi. 22, 30—32. Certainly this is a later addition or repetition ; certainly this is a mistake of Isaac for Abraham. But then we have not a word of this here in Josephus.

(7.) It is said by some that the city Hebron, so called in the Pentateuch itself, had not that name till it was given to Hebron, the [grand] son of Caleb by Joshua, after the death of Moses, Gen. xxiii. 2 ; Numb. xiii. 22. But certainly this is a great mistake. Hebron was given to Caleb himself, and to none else, Josh. xiv. 14 ; xxi. 11, 12 ; upon which, probably, it was that Caleb's grandson was called Hebron. Nor does Josephus give us the least intimation that the name Hebron was of so late an original as the days of Joshua. I have elsewhere suggested that Kiriath Arba was built, or rather rebuilt, by Hebron, the second king of Tanis, or Zoan ; and thenceforward called after his own name.[1] Whereas its name, when Abraham came first thither, was no other than Kiriath Arba ; though long before Moses wrote the Pentateuch its name was changed to Hebron ; it being built or rebuilt seven years before Zoan in Egypt. See Gen. xxiii. 2 ; Josh. xiv. 15 ; Judg. i. 10, and my Chronological Table.

(8.) Gen. xxxii. 32, we learn, that the children of Israel eat not of a certain sinew of the thigh of animals *unto this day.* This is in all copies, even in Josephus also ; and was equally true when Moses and when Josephus wrote, and is equally true at this very day.

I pass over (9.) the clause in the Septuagint, Gen. xxxv. 4, that Jacob destroyed the teraphim or idols, which some of his family had brought out of Mesopotamia with them *to this very day,* as being in no other copy or version whatsoever.

(10.) Gen. xxxv. 20, the text informs us, that the pillar set up by Jacob upon Rachel's grave was there *unto this day,* of which Josephus is entirely silent ; as indeed he omits the setting up of the pillar itself also ; though we are sure her grave or monument was known in the days of Samuel, about six hundred years afterwards, 1 Sam. x. 2.

(11.) Gen. xxxvi. 31, &c., [and 1 Chron. i. 43, &c.,] we have a complete catalogue of the *kings that reigned in the land of Edom, before there reigned any king over the children of Israel.* Which language seems to imply, that at the time of writing this catalogue there had been one or more kings that reigned over the children of Israel ; of whom yet king Saul is supposed the first, long after the days of Moses. And the number of the kings of Edom here being eight, it is supposed they might possibly reach as low as Saul. But I take all this to be very uncertain. God had lately promised or

[1] See Authent. Rec. p. 971.

foretold that *kings should come out of Jacob's loins*, chap. xxxv. 11. Moses himself is said, both in the Hebrew and Samaritan, to have been *king in Jeshurun*, Deut. xxxiii. 5. The interval between Joshua and the Judges is described both in the Hebrew and Septuagint as a state of anarchy, *when there was no king in Israel*, Judg. xvii. 6; xviii. 1, as an unusual thing in those days, and among that people. And Abimelech, one of the judges, denotes *my father the king*, and the text assures us, Judg. ix. 6, that all the men of Shechem went and *made Abimelech king*. Nor does it at all appear that these kings of Edom reigned till the days of Saul. Eight kings might reign not much above a century, and the last reign might be over before the Exodus out of Egypt. Nay, we really know that Edom was governed by dukes, who succeeded these eight kings, when the Israelites came first into the wilderness, Exod. xv. 15. However, certain it is that all the latter part of Gen. xxxvi., from ver. 20 to the end, including these kings of Edom, is omitted in Josephus. So that we can have no evidence that he had here either our present language, or our present catalogue of the kings of Edom, in his temple copy.

(12.) Gen. xlviii. 26, we are assured that the law which Joseph made for the Egyptians, that the king should have the fifth part of all the lands of Egypt, excepting those belonging to the priests, continued *unto this day*, or, in Josephus's phrase, *unto the later kings*, or *to the kings afterwards*. This agrees well to the days of Moses, when there had been about nine kings of Egypt, in Manetho, since the coming of Jacob into that country. See my Chronological Table.

14. (13.) Exod. vi. 26, 27, after an enumeration of the ancestors of Moses and Aaron, in the twelve foregoing verses, we have this addition, *These are that Aaron and Moses to whom the Lord said, Bring out the children of Israel from the land of Egypt, according to their armies. These are they which spake to Pharaoh king of Egypt, to bring out the children of Israel from Egypt: these are that Moses and Aaron.* These words do not, for certain, look like the words of Moses himself, no more than does the whole genealogy seem to fit the place wherein it now stands in all our copies. Accordingly Josephus entirely omits, not only these two verses, but the whole genealogy in this place.

(14.) Exod. xvi. 32—34, Moses enjoins Aaron to lay up the pot of manna *before the Lord,—before the testimony, to be kept for their generations:* and Aaron, in obedience thereto, lays it up there accordingly, and this before the tabernacle, with its *tables of the testimony* and *ark of the testimony*, were in being. Sure this is a dislocation. And if we consult Josephus, we shall see that the last five verses of this chapter, wherein both this command and its execution are related, are themselves wholly omitted; and so very probably he had them not in

his temple copy in this place.

(15.) Exod. xvi. 35, it is said that *the Israelites did eat manna forty years, until they came to a land inhabited; they did eat manna, till they came unto the borders of the land of Canaan.* This text is in all copies, even in Josephus's copy also; and exactly agrees to the end of the life of Moses; and might easily be written by himself, as Josephus would naturally suppose; or might be added by Joshua, when he also added the history of the death of Moses, a little afterwards.

15. (16.) Numb. xii. 3, we have this verse, by way of parenthesis, inserted into the Masorete Hebrew, into the Samaritan Pentateuch, and into the Septuagint version, *Now the man Moses was very meek, above all the men who were upon the face of the earth.* This great commendation of Moses for his unexampled meekness does by no means, to be sure, look like Moses's own writing. *Let another man praise thee, and not thine own mouth; a stranger, and not thine own lips*, Prov. xxvii. 2, is an undoubted maxim of wisdom in Solomon, and not likely to be transgressed by Moses, the meekest of men. Josephus does not give us the history into which this parenthesis is inserted, so we cannot have any reason to suppose it was in his copy. And indeed, to add this further, I have not observed that in Josephus's frequent and great commendations of Moses, he ever particularly celebrates this his extraordinary meekness; as did those that used the later Hebrew, or the Septuagint copies, wherein this commendation of Moses is extant. I mean the father of Sirach; the apostles, or Clement, in the Constitutions; and Ignatius, in his Epistles both to the Ephesians and Magnesians.[1] So that it is most probable Josephus's copy had neither this history nor this clause inserted into it; and that both were additions later than the days of Nehemiah.

(17.) Numb. xxi. 1—3, we have this account, that *Arad the Canaanite, which dwelt in the south* of Palestine, westward of Jordan, *fought against Israel, and took some of them prisoners;* and that, on the Israelites devoting their cities to utter destruction, as God had commanded them, God heard their prayer, and the people with their cities were utterly destroyed; and that *utter destruction* gave the name *Hormah*, of which that is the signification, to the place afterwards. This history plainly belongs to the time after the death of Joshua, Judg. i. 16, 17, and there we find it also in its proper place. But how it came into our Hebrew, Samaritan, and Septuagint copies of the book of Numbers I cannot tell; for it is certain that the Israelites could have no war on that side Jordan during the life of Moses. It is true, we are further told, Numb. xxxiii. 4, that when Aaron died at Mount Hor, king *Arad heard of the coming*

---

[1] Ecclus. xlv. 4. Constitut. vi. 3; vii. 7. Ignat. ad Eph. sect. 10, ad Magnes. sect. 12.

of the children of Israel; which is all that could belong to the days of Moses. However, Josephus entirely omits this history, in this mistaken place; though it be touched upon by him in its proper place of the book of Judges. So that it still appears Josephus's copy was purer and more uncorrupt than any of those other copies now extant.

(18.) Numb. xxxii. 41, and Deut. iii. 14, we are told that the country or cities Bashan-Havoth-Jair were so named by Jair the son of Manasseh *unto this day.* Now all this rather belongs to the days of the judges, one of which was this Jair, of the tribe of Manasseh, as Josephus agrees; but not a syllable of this in Josephus, till the days of the judges; nor even there a syllable of the continuance of the names of these cities or villages *unto this day.*

16. (19.) Deut. i. 1, we have this text, *These are the words which Moses spake unto all Israel beyond Jordan;* and chap. iii. 8, Moses is introduced again speaking thus, *And we took at that time out of the hand of the two kings of the Amorites the land that was beyond Jordan.* This expression *beyond Jordan* is in these and other places in the Masorete Hebrew, and Samaritan texts, as well as in the Septuagint version. Yet because the place where Moses now was could not yet be styled the *land beyond Jordan* till the Israelites had been on the other side of Jordan, which did not happen till after the death of Moses, our English and other versions have ventured to render the original, directly against its natural signification, *on this side Jordan.* Josephus is so far from acknowledging so strange an expression, as we find in our copies, that he introduces Moses here telling the Israelites, very truly, that God did not permit him to go *beyond Jordan,* nor to enjoy the good things he would there bestow upon them, as it were in opposition to all our other and later copies.

(20, 21.) Deut. ii. 21, in the LXXII. we are informed that the Ammonites conquered and dwelt in the land of the Rephaim, instead of the Rephaim, *unto this day.* And, ver. 22, in the Hebrew and Samaritan, that the children of Esau conquered *and dwelt in Seir,* instead of the Horites, *even unto this day;* of whom, ver. 12, the same succession is described; with this addition, that these children of Esau conquered and *dwelt in the stead of the Horites, as Israel did unto the land of his possession, which the Lord gave unto them:* as if these accounts were written after the Israelites were settled in the land of Canaan, or after the death of Moses. But of all this we have not a word in Josephus.

(22.) Deut. xxxiv. 6, it is affirmed that no one knows of the place were Moses was buried *unto this day.* But no such affirmation appears in Josephus.

N. B. I do not here set down the three last verses of the book of Deuteronomy, chap. xxxiv. 10—12, concerning Moses, that *there arose no prophet like him* afterward, which though extant in all copies, and in the copy of Josephus also, are plainly no part of either Moses's or Joshua's writing; but a very proper appendix to the Pentateuch; and could not have any other author than one of the later Jewish prophets, or the governors of the Jewish church, about or after the Babylonish captivity. Nor is it at all improbable but Ezra and Nehemiah, with one or both their contemporary prophets, Haggai and Zechariah, might add this remarkable clause, to prepare the Jewish nation to look hereafter from Moses and the old prophets, to the great *Prophet like unto Moses,* or to King Messiah; to whom they were entirely *to hearken,* upon the penalty of *excision from among their people,* Deut. xviii. 15—19. However, I venture to say that common readers ought not to be deluded by seeing these verses stand as a part of the original book of Deuteronomy, which are so clearly no other than a later appendix to it.

17. (23.) Josh. iv. 9, we meet with this assertion, that the twelve stones, which were set up by Joshua in the midst of Jordan when they came over it, are there *unto this day.* But no such assertion is in Josephus.

(24.) Josh. v. 9, we are acquainted that the place of Joshua's encampment was called Gilgal *unto this day;* of which we find no sign in Josephus. To say nothing of the addition to the anathema on the builder of Jericho, in the LXXII., Josh. vi. 26, as evidently taken from its completion long afterward, 1 Kings xvi. 34, and not elsewhere, and wanting in the Hebrew. I observe that,

(25.) Josh. vi. 25, it is noted that Rahab, the inn-keeper, who saved the spies at Jericho, dwelt in Israel *unto this day.* But no such note is set down in Josephus.

(26, 27.) Josh. vii. 26, it is related, that the Israelites raised over Achar or Achor a great heap of stones *unto this day*—and that therefore the name of that place was called the valley of Achor *unto this day.* But no such language appears here in Josephus.

(28.) Josh. viii. 28, we find this passage, that Joshua made Ai an heap for ever, a desolation, *unto this day.* But we find no such thing in Josephus. And,

(29.) Josh. viii. 29, that the carcass of the king of Ai was cast in at the entering of the gate of the city Ai, and a great heap of stones raised thereon *unto this day,* without the least countenance from Josephus.

(30.) Josh. ix. 23, in the Hebrew, we find that the Gibeonites were doomed by Joshua and the elders to be *hewers of wood and drawers of water for the house of God,* or for the *temple,* which was not built till long after the days of Joshua. Now whether *the house of God* here denote the *temple,* or only the *tabernacle,* which was already erected in the days of Joshua, I shall not now inquire, because Josephus has no such expression, but only that they were doomed to be *public serv-ants*, as both the Hebrew and Septuagint copies have it, ver. 21, 27, or that they should be *hewers of wood and drawers of water to all the congre-gation unto this day ;* which was probably the old reading in ver. 23 also. Now the Septuagint have no mention of the *house* of God here ; and Jose-phus acknowledges not the addition, *unto this day*.

(31.) Josh. x. 10, it is said that the Canaanites were *chased along the way that goeth up to Beth-horon*. This name of Bethhoron is in the Hebrew and Septuagint, as well as in Josephus ; yet are we told, 1 Chron. vii. 24, that this city Bethhoron was *built by Sherah, the daughter* or *granddaughter of Ephraim*, after the Israelites were settled in Canaan, and not at the time when it is here mentioned. Now this is so common in old times, to say a city was built when it was rebuilt, or greatly improved, that it is not worth our while to make any further apolo-gy for such an expression. See Judg. xviii. 28, 29 ; xxi. 23 ; 1 Kings xii. 25 ; 2 Chron. xi. 5—10. Nor do I see any reason to believe that Bethhoron had not that name till this re-edification by Sherah ; but suppose it the old name when Joshua first came into the land of Canaan.

(32.) Josh. x. 14, we have these words, upon occasion of the sun's standing still, that there was *no day like that before it nor after it*. This ex-pression looks like a much later addition. But then we have not a syllable like it in Josephus, upon this occasion.

(33.) Josh. x. 27, we find this history, that the children of Israel laid great stones in the cave's mouth of five kings of the Amorites *until this very day*. But this is not mentioned by Josephus.

(34.) Josh. xiii. 13, we learn that the Geshur-ites and Maachathites dwelt among the Israelites *unto this day*. But nothing of this is in Josephus.

(35.) Josh. xv. 13—19, we have a particular account of Caleb's driving away the Anakims, and taking Debir, and Kirjath-sepher, and giving his daughter Achsah to wife to Othniel the son of Ke-naz, who took it ; with other occurrences, all be-longing to the interval after Joshua's death ; and they are accordingly repeated in their proper place of the book of Judges, chap. i. 10—15. This clause is in both our Masorete and Septuagint copies ; but not a syllable of it in Josephus under Joshua ; but only in its proper place, under the judges. But it would be too tedious to give here all the examples of books, clauses, and facts dislo-cated, both in the Masorete and even the Samaritan Hebrew copies, and in the Septuagint version, but set in their proper places by Josephus, from his better copy. See many of these taken notice of in my Essay on the Old Testament, and Literal Ac-complishment of Scripture Prophecies, with its Supplement.

(36.) Josh. xv. 63, we are informed that the Jebusites dwelt with the children of Judah at Jeru-salem *unto this day*. But we have no mention of this in Josephus.

(37.) Josh. xvi. 10, we read that the Canaanites dwelt among the Ephraimites *unto this day*. And in the Septuagint we have this much later addition : *Until Pharaoh king of Egypt came up, and took the city,* [Gazer,] *and burnt it with fire ; and he persecuted the Canaanites, and Perizzites, and the inhabitants of Gazer : and Pharaoh gave it in dowry to his daughter* [as 1 Kings ix. 15]. But of all this Josephus says nothing. And so far the additional passages to the Pentateuch and to Joshua are found to be peculiar to our other and later copies, and to have had no place in the temple or Nehemiah's copy made use of by Josephus. And so far is abundantly sufficient for the vindication of the original texts of Moses and Joshua from the objections arising from these later additions, of the continuance of certain names and memorials *until this day*, or until some time considerably later than the history itself. Now the Pentateuch and Joshua are the principal books liable to this sort of ex-ceptions. For as to other books, that contain the history of several hundred years, such expressions *might* properly enough be added about ancient facts when those books were composed and published, without any such suspicion upon them. Though it will appear, as we go along, that Josephus had not very many of those expressions in his copy, unless when they were equally true in his own time as they were at the time of the original books' publication. To proceed therefore to the remaining examples.

(38.) Josh. xix. 27, we have, in both our copies, mention made of a place or city in the borders of the tribe of Aser, called Cabul ; which is supposed to be in that country which was not called Cabul till the days of Solomon, as we find 1 Kings ix. 13, where it is added, that this country retained that name of Cabul *unto this day*. But then Josephus has neither that name in the history of Joshua, nor a syllable of its retaining that name *unto this day* in the history of Solomon.

(39.) At the end of the book of Joshua, in the Septuagint, we have this additional clause, that the Israelites put the flint knives, wherewith Joshua circumcised the children of Israel in Gilgal, into Joshua's monument at Timnath-serah ; and that they are there *unto this day*. But of this not a syllable in any other copy.

18. (40.) Judg. i. 21, we are assured that the Jebus-ites dwelt with the children of Benjamin *unto this day*. But this is not in Josephus.

(41.) And ver. 26, that Luz, so named between the death of Joshua and Othniel the first judge, was the name of a town *unto this day*. But this is not in Josephus.

(42.) And ver. 27, the Septuagint, and they only, say that the tribe of Manasseh did not possess Bethel, [Bethsan,] *which is Scythopolis*. This must be a very late addition, though perhaps earlier than the Septuagint version, as all the learned very well know. But we have nothing of this in Josephus.

(43.) Judg. vi. 24, we learn that Gideon's altar is *unto this day yet* in Ophrah of the Abiezrites. But of this Josephus says nothing.

(44.) Judg. xv. 19, we are told that the place where Samson slew the Philistines with the jawbone of an ass was called Lehi *unto this day*. This text was in Josephus's copy, and was true, not only when the book of Judges was published, and when Josephus wrote, but as late as the days of Glycas, or the twelfth century of Christianity, also. See Reland's Palæstina in Lechi and Eleutheropolis.

(45.) Judg. xviii. 12, it is said that the place where the six hundred Danites first pitched their camp in the tribe of Judah, when they went upon the expedition to Laish, was called Mahaneh-dan, or the *camp of Dan, unto this day*. But of this Josephus makes no mention.

(46.) Judg. xviii. 30, it is said that the idolatry of Micah lasted *until the day of the captivity of the land*, i. e. either to the captivity of the ark by the Philistines in the days of Eli, or to the captivity of the ten tribes in the days of Nebuchadnezzar.

(47.) And ver. 31, that it lasted *all the time that the house of God was in Shiloh*, which favours the first interpretation. However, both these clauses seem to me to be additions, later than the book of Judges itself. But, then, Josephus omits the entire history of this idolatry of Micah; and so we can have no reason to suppose that he had either of those clauses in his copy.

19. (48.) 1 Sam. v. 5, we learn that the priests of Dagon, and his worshippers, in memory of their god's falling upon the threshold of his temple before the ark of the true God, *did not tread on that threshold unto this day*. But nothing of this is in Josephus.

(49.) 1 Sam. vi. 18, that the stone on which the inhabitants of Beth-shemesh sacrificed, upon the ark's return from the country of the Philistines, *remained to this day in the field of Joshua the Beth-shemite*. But not a word of this in Josephus.

(50.) 1 Sam. vii. 15, it is said, that *Samuel judged Israel all the days of his life;* which could hardly be written by Samuel himself. Accordingly the clause is wanting in Josephus.

(51.) 1 Sam. ix. 9, we have a parenthesis added, both in the Hebrew and Greek copies : *Beforetime in Israel, when a man went to inquire of God, thus he spake, Come, and let us go to the seer: [for he that is now called a Prophet was beforetime called a Seer.]* How far these last words are true, or who inserted them, I know not. But so far I know, that we have no footsteps of their truth in any other text, but rather the contrary. The word *seer* is never once before used ; and the word *prophet* very often, in all the preceding books of the Old Testament. However, Josephus is so far from confirming this parenthesis, that, on the contrary, he uses no other than the word *prophet* through this whole history. As for myself, I suspect a disorder in the present text, from what hand soever it came, and that it originally ran thus : *Beforetime in Israel, when a man went to inquire of God, thus he spake, Come, and let us go to the prophet: for he that is now* [sometimes] *called a Seer was before* [always] *called a Prophet*. Which exactly agrees to the fact, even in all our present copies of the Old Testament ; wherein the word *prophet* is always used before this time, and after it both the words are used promiscuously.

(52.) 1 Sam. xxvii. 6, the history informs us, that *Ziklag*, given to David by Achish king of Gath, *pertaineth to the kings of Judah unto this day;* which could not well be written till after the days of David. Accordingly this addition is wanting in Josephus.

(53.) 1 Sam. xxx. 25, we learn that David's ordinance to divide the spoils equally among those that went out to the battle, and those who continued in and guarded the camp, was *a statute and an ordinance for Israel unto this day*, or when this history was published. And this ordinance is mentioned by Josephus also, and I suppose lasted not only to the times of the Maccabees, 2 Mac. viii. 28, but also to his own time. And no wonder, since it is rather a revival, an explication, and execution of an old law of Moses, Numb. xxi. 35, &c. ; Josh. xxi. 8, than the enacting of a new one. Nor do I know that David had, at this time, any power to enact new laws; though he were certainly obliged to obey the old ones.

20. (54.) 2 Sam. iv. 3, it is said that the Beerothites fled to Gittaim, after the death of Saul, and were sojourners there *unto this day*. But we meet with no such addition in Josephus.

(55.) 2 Sam. vi. 8, and 1 Chron. xiii. 11, it is observed that the place where Uzzah was slain for taking hold on the ark, being no priest, see Numb. iv. 15, was called Perez-uzzah, or the breach of Uzzah, *to this day*. This is in all the copies, even in Josephus ; and might well retain its name, not only when these books were published, but when Josephus himself wrote also.

(56.) 2 Sam. viii. 7, in the Septuagint version we have this addition to the series of the history, as to those bracelets or shields of gold which David took from the servants of Hadadezer, king of Zobah, and brought them to Jerusalem, that *Sousakim*, or *Shishac, king of Egypt, took them, when he came up to Jerusalem, in the days of Rehoboam the son of Solomon*. And the same clause was in Josephus's Hebrew copy ; and was a very proper addition when these books of the Kings were finished and published, some time after the reign of Rehoboam. Though how it has come to pass that our present Masorete Hebrew wants this clause, which was extant in Josephus's Hebrew, I cannot determine.

(57.) 2 Sam. xiv. 27, we have just such another addition, in the Septuagint, as to Tamar the daughter of Absalom, that *she became the wife of Roboam the son of Solomon, and bare him Abia.* And the same clause was in Josephus's Hebrew copy; and in both with the same propriety, though in the same manner wanting in our present Hebrew also.

(58.) 2 Sam. xviii. 18, we are informed that Absalom's pillar or place was so called *unto this day.* But this is omitted in Josephus.

(59.) 2 Sam. xxiv. 25, in the Septuagint version we have this addition to the series of the history, concerning the altar on which David offered sacrifices at the threshingfloor of Araunah the Jebusite, *and Solomon added to* [enlarged] *the altar at last, for it was too little at first.* But of this we have not a syllable either in our Masorete Hebrew copies, or in Josephus.

21. (60.) 1 Kings viii. 8, and 2 Chron. v. 9, we read that the ark, or its staves, were in the most holy place of Solomon's temple *unto this day*, or when the books of Kings and Chronicles were published; of which additional clause Josephus says not a word. But we must note here, that this clause could not be true in the days of the author of the book of Chronicles, unless that book were published before the carrying away the ark in the days of Zedekiah. Whence the two last verses of that book, which are verbatim the same with the two first of Ezra, concerning the decree of Cyrus for the return of the Jews, are plainly a later and a very inaccurate addition; as indeed the last eight verses of chap. xxxv. and the whole xxxvi. chapter seem to be such an addition, and in our present copies a very inaccurate addition also.

(61.) 1 Kings ix. 21, and 2 Chron. viii. 8, we read that Solomon laid a tribute upon the remains of the seven nations of Canaan *unto this day.* But this clause is not in Josephus.

(62.) 1 Kings xii. 19, and 2 Chron. v. 19, we find this passage, that Israel rebelled against the house of David, from the foolish answer of Rehoboam to the twelve tribes at Sichem, *unto this day;* though Josephus has no such passage.

22. (63.) 2 Kings ii. 22, it is said that the waters at Jericho were healed by Elisha *unto this day.* This addition seems here to have been in Josephus also. Nor was it less true when he wrote, than when these books of Kings were published; nor is it less true at this day, as the travellers inform us.[1]

(64.) 2 Chron. xx. 26, we learn that the *valley of Berachah,* or *Blessing,* was so *called* from the solemn *blessing* of God there, after Jehoshaphat had received a wonderful deliverance therein, *unto this day.* Josephus has all the rest of the history, but without those additional words *unto this day.*

(65.) 2 Kings viii. 22, and 2 Chron. xxi. 10, we

are informed that Edom revolted from under the hand of Judah *unto this day;* which is omitted in Josephus.

(66.) 2 Kings x. 27, we are informed that Jehu and his forces made the house of Baal a draughthouse *unto this day.* But Josephus says nothing of this addition.

(67.) 2 Kings xiv. 7, we are assured that Amaziah, king of Judah, took Selah, or a rock, by war, and called the name of it Joktheel *unto this day.* But we have nothing of this addition in Josephus.

(68.) 2 Kings xvi. 6, we are told that the Syrians, who had taken Elath from Ahaz, dwelt there *to this day.* But we have no such addition in Josephus.

(69.) 2 Kings xvii. 23, and 1 Chron. v. 26, we learn that Israel was carried captive to Assyria *unto this day;* without any confirmation of it from Josephus.

(70.) Ver. 34, 41, we learn further, that the Samaritans or Cuthites, that came into the deserted parts of the country of the ten tribes, *feared the Lord, and served their graven images, both their children, and their children's children; as did their fathers, so do they to this day.* And this they did when this book was published, and in the days of Josephus, as he here and elsewhere informs us; nay, so did they still lower, till the days of Nero; as I have shown elsewhere, Lit. Accomp. of Proph. p. 155, 156; Proposals, p. 13.

(71.) 2 Kings xviii., and 2 Chron. xxxv. 20, *ap.* LXXII., we read that after Hezekiah, as well as before him, there was *none like him among all the kings of Judah.* And,

(72.) The very same is said of Josiah, 2 Kings xxiii. 25, without the least confirmation to either of the clauses in Josephus's history of those kings.

23. (73, 74.) 1 Chron. iv. 41, 43, we read of certain Simeonites, that in the days of Hezekiah, king of Judah, smote a certain people, of Arabia, perhaps, and devoted them to destruction *unto this day;* and that others of them, five hundred in number, smote the rest of the Amalekites that were escaped, and dwelt there *unto this day.* But Josephus entirely omitting all the former nine genealogical chapters of this book, we can have no pretence for supposing these additions to have been in his copy.

(75.) 1 Chron. v. 18—22, we read that the tribes beyond Jordan made war with the neighbouring Arabians, and conquered them, and made a great slaughter of them, and *dwelt in their stead until the captivity* [under Pul, and Tiglath Pul Assar, ver. 26.] This addition was a very natural one when these books of Chronicles were published, long after those captivities; but cannot be discovered to have been in Josephus's copy, for the reason before mentioned.

24. (76.) 2 Chron. xxxv. 25, and 3 Esdras i. 32, we are informed, that the Israelites made lamentation for Josiah *unto this day;* and that this was given out for an ordinance, to be done continually in all the nation of Israel. And well might this

be added when this last branch of this book of Chronicles and when Esdras were written, after the captivity; though as to Josephus, who takes all out of this apocryphal Esdras, and not out of the canonical Ezra, we find no such clause in his history.

(77.) 2 Kings xxiii. 32, and 2 Chron. xxxvi. 2, in the LXXII. we are informed that Jehoahaz did evil in the sight of the Lord, *according to all that his fathers had done.* And 2 Kings xxiii. 37, and 2 Chron. xxxvi. 5, in the LXXII. we have the same expression of his brother Jehoiakim, while yet of their four immediate ancestors, Hezekiah, Manasses, Amon, and Josias, the first and last were among the best of the kings of Judah. So that one may doubt of the propriety of the expression in both these cases; and that not only because it is sometimes dropped in the Hebrew, but because it is entirely omitted by Josephus in both these histories.

Upon the whole, there does not appear so much as one of these sort of passages which ought to be supposed later than the original finishing and publishing of the historical books of the Old Testament, in all the Antiquities of Josephus; and by consequence we have not the least evidence that his temple copy had any one of them. However, the reader will excuse me if I conclude this catalogue with two observations of a somewhat different nature from most of the foregoing, though not foreign to my present design.

(78.) 2 Chron. xxxvi. 6, we have this account of Jehoiakim's end, *that Nebuchadnezzar bound him in fetters to carry him to Babylon;* or, as the Septuagint have it, *and brought him to Babylon;* and in the same Septuagint is added, ver. 18, in contradiction thereto, that *Jehoiakim slept with his fathers,* and *they buried him in Ganosan,* [i. e. with Manasseh in the garden of Uzza, 2 Kings xxi. 18.] How these accounts agree one with another, or with Jeremiah's predictions, that the Babylonians should be so far from giving leave to bury the bodies of the Jews their enemies, that they should *give them for meat to the fowls of the heaven,* and *for the beasts of the earth, and that none should fray them away,* Jer. vii. 33; that, in particular, they should *bring out the bones of the kings of Judah, and the bones of the princes, and the bones of the priests,* &c., *out of their graves, and should spread them before the sun, and the moon, and all the host of heaven,* with which they had committed idolatry; that they should *not be gathered, nor be buried,* but should be *for dung upon the face of the earth,* chap. viii. 1, 2; nay, that, in a most especial manner, this Jehoiakim should be *buried with the burial of an ass, drawn and cast forth beyond the gates of Jerusalem,* chap. xxii. 19: how these accounts and the predictions of Jeremiah agree, I am not able to say. But then, as I have already observed, p. 945 *prius,* and as he that will compare the Hebrew and Septuagint will

soon see, the eight last verses of the thirty-fifth and all the thirty-sixth chapter of the Second Book of Chronicles, are too late and too inaccurate additions to that book to be depended on against any sacred authority. Nor do I know that Josephus ever owns any facts peculiar to these chapters; which seem indeed no other than a part of the present book of Ezra, never owned by Josephus. However, so far is plain, that Josephus's temple copy of the sacred history agrees here with Jeremiah's predictions. And he thence assures us that the carcass of Jehoiakim was ordered to be *cast out unburied before the walls of Jerusalem,* exactly according to the predictions of Jeremiah; which account highly deserves the consideration of the inquisitive.

25. (79.) 1 Sam. xvii. 50—58, we have an account, both in the Hebrew and Septuagint, that king Saul, when he saw David go forth against Goliath, the Philistine, did not know him, or at least did not know who was his father; which seems a later addition. For it looks like an impossibility that Saul should be so ignorant at that time, considering how long David, the son of Jesse, had been his servant and armour-bearer; and that by Jesse his father's leave, as we read in the end of the foregoing chapter; and the following chapter is but the history of about forty or fifty days. But of this whole history, and of what follows it, in the next five verses, chap. xviii. 1—5, we have not a word in Josephus. And indeed this seems to me a portion of true history, but entirely dislocated or removed out of its proper place; and that it happened, not when David went out against Goliath, but when he had formerly gone out against some other of the same Philistines. For we read, that when David was first sent for to live with Saul, he was recommended to him as *a mighty valiant man,* and *a man of war,* chap. xvi. 18; to which character so early Josephus agrees also. Now it is very probable that this martial character of David was not acquired without some martial exploits, and those against the Philistines, the known enemies of his nation and religion; at one of which earlier exploits it is most likely Saul made this inquiry before us, and not at the time specified in our copies. Nor is the occasion of this dislocation unobvious, viz. that it might be at a time when David had slain another Philistine, and had that Philistine's head in his hand; which likeness of circumstances might easily induce a later compiler to place it to this time, when he had Goliath's head in his hand, long afterward. However, Josephus's perfect silence about this history, and about what follows it, and his connexion of the foregoing victory to the song of the women dancers, chap. xviii. 6, are plain indications that either some mistake or some transposition has here happened in our later copies; of which he saw no footsteps in his temple copy.

26. N. B. We have in many places of the historical books of the Old Testament quotations of, or references to, other old Jewish books, or to other records not now preserved, as confirming or enlarging the histories contained in our Bible. Whether these quotations or references were original, or were afterward added, I cannot certainly say. Only I must here take notice, that I have never observed the least traces of any of these quotations or references in all Josephus's Antiquities.

27. *Corollary* 1. It appears by what has been already proved, that the voluntary additions, omissions, or dislocations which we may observe in the present copies of the Old Testament are of a bare human original; and that we have no evidence of any such till after the days of Nehemiah and Xerxes, or indeed during the constant succession of prophets among the Jews. For this deserves to be particularly remarked, that these additions appear in almost every historical book of the Old Testament till the days of Nehemiah, but no further. Nor has either the book of Nehemiah or Esther in any copy one example; and, indeed, the books of Ezra and Esdras have but one such example in our other copies, and not one in Josephus's copy, as we have seen already; although there were otherwise not less occasions for inserting them into those, than into the other historical books of the Old Testament.

Corol. 2. Yet are most of these later additional passages, which speak of many of the old names of places and monuments of that nation as still in being *at this day*, or after the days of Nehemiah, *i. e.* many hundred years after most of the histories themselves were written, strong attestations to the truth of those histories, and great evidence that such histories were all along publicly owned to be true by the Jewish nation.

Corol. 3. It is therefore now incumbent upon the learned Christians, and especially upon the bishops and pastors of the church, to publish better and more authentic editions and versions of the Old Testament than has hitherto been done. I mean with the text of the Pentateuch according to the Samaritan, the text of the rest according to the Septuagint version; together with the various readings of Josephus and of the Masorete Hebrew; which are all the original remains of those books now extant among us.

Corol. 4. No learned and judicious commentators ought hereafter to pronounce about any books or clauses of consequence and difficulty in the Old Testament, without consulting the remains we now have of these four several editions of those holy books; especially not without consulting the Antiquities of Josephus, who used the best of them.

28. N. B. There is among many other things that Josephus's copy appears to want, but which are in the other copies, one omission of so important a nature as ought to be particularly taken notice of

in this place; I mean of the heinous sin of the golden calf, or the idolatrous worship paid to it in the wilderness, by the people of Israel. What makes it stranger is this, that Josephus's account is not only negative, by a bare omission; but positive, by affording an exact coherence without it, nay, such a coherence as is plainly inconsistent with it. And what still makes it the more surprising is, that Josephus frequently professes, in these Antiquities, neither to *add to* nor *take away from* the sacred books which lay before him. And when he thought proper to digest many of the laws of Moses into a regular system,[1] and this only in an order different from that in which they were delivered, and in which they stood in the Pentateuch, he does not venture upon that procedure but with great caution, and with giving a distinct intimation of it; that so he might not incur any blame among his brethren of the Jewish nation, as having made some unwarrantable alteration in their Bible. Accordingly he, in the most solemn manner, appeals to all original records, sacred or profane, and to those that please to compare his accounts with those originals, for his justification upon all occasions. Nor do we need to trust his bare affirmations and protestations, but have abundant evidence from his entire works, that he really did all along regard, not the honour or reputation of his nation, or of the great men of it, but the real truth of facts, whether they were to their honour or dishonour; of which the reader will meet with innumerable instances every where in his writings. One example I shall give, because it is so exactly to the present case, and it is that of the later idolatry of the ten tribes with the two golden calves at Dan and Bethel; which he is so far from omitting, that he does not so much as attempt to disguise it, but plainly sets it down in its proper place, and always owns that the captivity of those ten tribes was the punishment of that idolatry. All which notwithstanding, and notwithstanding the great reputation he has ever obtained among the best judges for his fidelity and integrity, this omission is universally ascribed to him, and laid against him, and that sometimes with the highest aggravations. *But all this without any real evidence at all.* It is plain that his copy was taken out of the temple, and was not a little different from our other copies. It is pretty plain also, as I have proved, that he used Nehemiah's own copy or library; and what parts were wanting in that copy we have no other way to know at present but by Josephus himself. So that this accusation is entirely a *supposition without proof.* Those indeed who have suffered themselves to be imposed upon by the later Jewish Rabbins, and have been by them made to believe that the original copies of the sacred books of the Old Testament were the very same with those we have had from them since the days of Barchocab, may charge

---

[1] Antiq. B. IV. ch. 8. sect. 4.

this and many other omissions, and additions, and corrections upon Josephus, as their author, and may blame him for corrupting the sacred text in these cases; but those who will have the patience that I have had, in comparing the ancient Samaritan, Septuagint, and Masorete copies, with that of Josephus all along, and will therein use the same impartial sagacity which they would think proper in comparing the copies of other ancient authors, will see a very different state of things before them. They will particularly admire and adore the good providence of God, in preserving not only the oldest and most authentic version of the Septuagint interpreters in a considerable degree of purity; but chiefly the Samaritan Pentateuch, and the eleven first books of Josephus's Antiquities, and this last as a faithful extract out of Nehemiah's library, collected about two hundred and seventy years earlier than the Septuagint version was made, and above six hundred years earlier then Barchocab, the Jews' spurious Messiah, was set up; from which time I date our present Masorete copy. Any sober inquirer, who compares all these copies, will soon discover such varieties in them, and gain such great light by the comparison of those varieties, as will greatly surprise, and, if I be not much mistaken, will greatly please him also. Thus he will soon find, on such a comparison, that the heinous sins of David, as to his adultery and murder, as well as his punishments for them; as also the heinous sins of his son Solomon, in his polygamy and idolatry; are entirely omitted in our books of Chronicles. He will also soon find that most of the glorious things done by Jehoshaphat, and God's miraculous delivery of him and his people in the sudden and dangerous invasion by the Moabites, Ammonites, and the inhabitants of Mount Seir, as also the famous repentance and restoration of Manasseh, are entirely omitted in our books of Kings, to give no more examples at present, though they be all preserved in other books of our Bible, and are all thence faithfully described in Josephus's Antiquities. But the examples of this kind are too many to be here set down; so many, indeed, that I am satisfied this omission in Josephus is no sufficient evidence of his want of integrity; but rather an evidence of a great degree of it, in following his temple copy even where it so greatly differed from all the other copies, and where it might expose him to the censure of his countrymen for an omission of a very famous history, always owned for true and genuine by that nation. It may well enough be supposed that Nehemiah's copy might deliver this account nearly as it is in Josephus. I mean that Moses came down the *first* time from Mount Sinai, or Horeb, with two large *tables of the laws of righteousness*, contained Exod. xxi.—xxiii., like those *two great stones* in the Samaritan text, chap. xx. 17, for the very same purpose afterwards; and with the *description of the tabernacle*, contained chap. xxv.—xxx.; and that the people had not then of-

fended, and did then receive Moses with great joy and a ready obedience to those laws; as Josephus assures us they did. Although when he went a *second* time to receive the *two* small *tables of the covenant*, containing the *ten words*, they made the *golden calf*, as we find in all our other copies. Those Jews seem to have had a notion of some such thing who supposed Moses to have been three distinct times in the mount for forty days. [See Bishop Patrick on Deut. ix. 25.] And if we consider the words of our ordinary copies, Exod. xxiv. 12, *I will give thee* [Moses] *tables of stones; the law and the commandments which I have written;* and compare the language of Scripture, still distinguishing the *covenant* and the *ten words* delivered solemnly by God himself at Mount Sinai, from these other *laws* and *commandments* delivered by Moses, as I have long ago observed; we shall not perhaps be averse to such an interpretation. See Prim. Christ. Revived, Vol. III. p. 56, 57. However, I must not here conceal a remarkable fragment produced from the Greek Catenæ by Vossius[1] out of Josephus, which seems to belong to this very matter, and to be an intimation that this idolatry by the golden calf was not of old omitted in all the copies of Josephus. The words are these: *He* [Moses] *concluded that it was absurd for the people, when they were drunk, and in their transgression, to receive the legislation of God;* which passage highly deserves the reflection of the learned upon this occasion. But the reader will judge better of such matters after he has considered better of my next observation.

29. N. B. It will be fit to observe here the several occasions, steps, and methods by which the sacred books of the Old Testament have come down to us in their present form, and in so imperfect and disordered a manner as we now find them. We all know there have been many distresses, idolatries, persecutions, and captivities which the Israelites fell into after the days of Moses, and before the days of Christ: under which not only some of their old books have been entirely lost; a catalogue of which Mr. Du Pin has given us;[2] but many of the rest have either lost some parts, or had those parts greatly disordered and dislocated by collectors and compilers, when they put them together afterward. The first of the moderns who seems to have been thoroughly sensible of these disorders and dislocations, I speak it on my own personal knowledge, was the most learned bishop Lloyd; though he very rarely let the public into that his discovery. Possibly his interlined Bible, that great treasure of sacred learning, if once deciphered, would afford us many excellent observations of this kind. In the mean time, take this small sketch of my own observations on this subject. To omit then the observation,

---

[1] De 70 Inter. Apud Ittig. Prolegom.
[2] Bibliotheca, Prelim. Dissert. p. 30. See also 3 Kings viii. 53. *ap.* LXXII.

that after nine chapters of the book of Proverbs are over, the tenth begins like a new collection of them, The proverbs of Solomon, we find in the first place a collection, or rather an improvement of an ancienter collection, of the sacred books in the days of Hezekiah king of Judah, about seven hundred and ten years before the Christian era, when the xxv., xxvi., xxvii., xxviii., and xxix. chapters were added to the book of Proverbs; which chapters begin thus: *These are also proverbs of Solomon, which the men of Hezekiah, king of Judah, copied out.* And perhaps the two last chapters, ascribed, the former to *Agur, the son of Jakeh,* and the latter to *king Lemuel,* [or to Solomon himself,] might be added not long afterwards. I interpret king Lemuel of king Solomon, because we meet with no king whose proper name was Lemuel, and because the last part of the chapter ascribed to him is quoted in the Apostolical Constitutions[1] as Solomon's. Though I confess the subject of these verses is so different from the rest of the foregoing chapter, and its manner of handling so different also, that it may pass for a distinct chapter, and may possibly belong to a distinct author. Thus after the long and, for the greatest part, most wicked and idolatrous reign of Manasseh, and the short, but alike wicked and idolatrous, reign of his son Amon, there was found by Hilkiah, the high priest, upon repairing the temple in the days of Josiah, 2 Kings xxii. 8, &c.; 2 Chron. xxxiv. 14, &c., the original copy of the book *of the law,* òr of the principal laws of Moses; and that, as Josephus informs us, not ἐν τῷ ἱερῷ, in the buildings about the courts of the temple only, in which he supposes the entire collection of sacred books to have been placed, but particularly ἐν τῷ ναῷ, in the holy house itself, the proper place for that small most sacred book of the *laws of righteousness;* and, as I suppose, written by Moses's own hand. Of the contents of which book see Horeb Covenant Revived, p. 107, 108. Upon this discovery it was, probably, that those principal laws of Moses came to be inserted into the Pentateuch, where we now find them. This I may call the *second* collection, or rather an improvement of such collection, which we meet with any intimation of in ancient records. Next to this we may reckon Nehemiah's, as a *third* collection, of which largely already. Only upon its particular nomination of the *acts* or works of David, as distinct from the *acts* or works *of the kings, and of the prophets,* it may not improbably be supposed that the present collection of David's Psalms into five books, or parts, was now made; though Josephus never mentioning this fivefold division as belonging to his copy, I cannot be at all positive about it. This collection of the holy books by Nehemiah is justly called a *library;*[2] and is, I think, one of the earliest examples of such a collection under that name of a *library* in all antiquity. This original collection of

the holy books of the Old Testament, this Biblia, or Bible, appears to have been met with by Josephus, upon the sacking and burning of Herod's temple by Titus Vespasian, when it was given him by Titus; but had perhaps lain concealed many years in that temple; as had the forementioned original *book of the law* lain probably long concealed till the days of Josiah in Solomon's temple. And had not this last temple been sacked and burnt by Titus when Josephus was there, and the former being repaired by Josiah when Hilkiah was there, it is possible to be supposed that neither of these inestimable treasures had been recovered by us.

Thus the prophet Esdras, 4 Esd. i. 39, 40, not long after the days of Nehemiah, added, in the *fourth* place, the *prophecy of Malachi* to the ancienter sacred catalogue; and thereby completed the Hebrew canon of Jerusalem; at least if we include the prophet Esdras's own book or books. Of which see the Appendix to the fourth volume of Primitive Christianity Revived, and the Authentic Records, p. 46—161.

Thus there was, in the *fifth* place, about a century later, an addition made to the book of Esdras the scribe, though now inserted into the book of Nehemiah, reaching as low as the days of Jaddua the high priest, in or near the days of Alexander the Great, already intimated. This was probably done by those who made that collection which the Septuagint interpreters followed, in the days of Ptolemy Lagi and Ptolemy Philadelphus; in which edition we find that insertion. About, or perhaps before, this time, it seems to me, in the *sixth* place, the Samaritan Pentateuch obtained its present form; as being much of kin to, and greatly supported by, the Septuagint Greek copy of that Pentateuch, though it be a more full and a much better copy than the other. Whether it came to the first Christians from the Samaritans themselves, or from the proper Jews, I cannot certainly say, for want of historical memoirs concerning it. Though it reaching no further than the Pentateuch looks more like a derivation from the Samaritans, who owned no more than that Pentateuch, than from the proper Jews, who owned all the other books. The reason of the difficulty is this, that, as I have elsewhere proved, not the Samaritan Bible only, but the Jewish also, was all written in no other than the Samaritan character, till the days of Barchocab. See Essay on the Old Testament, p. 149—171. But then, in the *seventh* place, the most entire collection of the sacred books of the Jews, preserved in any language, which may be called the Hellenistical, as the former the Hebrew canon, seems to have been reserved for Ptolemy Philadelphus, and for the enriching of his famous Alexandrian library. The remains of which Hellenistical canon we have chiefly in the Synopsis Sacræ Scripturæ, and in the Septuagint Bible, including now some books written a little after that version was made. Which Hellenistical canon is attested to by the known

1 Constitut. I. 8
2 See Esth. ii. 23. *ap.* LXXII.

books of the New Testament, by the Apostolical Constitutions, and by all other apostolical and most primitive Christian writers, who always quote the books of the Old Testament according to that version. Thus we know, in the *eighth* place, that Judas Maccabeus made a collection of the holy books at Jerusalem, after the persecution by Antiochus Epiphanes, 2 Macc. ii. 14, which seems to have been the last public Hebrew collection that was made, till, in the *ninth* and last place, the Jews fixed upon us their later collection or edition (called by me the Masorete copy) when they set up their spurious Messiah Barchocab, in the former part of the second century of Christianity; of whose imperfections I have largely treated in my Essay on the Old Testament.

30. N. B. The result of my long and laborious inquiries about the genuine copies, editions, and readings of the sacred books of the Old Testament is plainly this: That although the modern Jews, and almost all the modern Christians, who, by an unhappy fatality, have been deluded by them, are very positive for a kind of perfection in our Masorete Hebrew copy; and it has been a long while accordingly styled, The Hebrew Verity; yet is the truth of the case for certain far otherwise. That, on the contrary, those books have come down to us in a very imperfect and disordered condition, even in all our copies. That even Nehemiah's own copy, as given us by Josephus, though by far the oldest and best of them all, was by no means perfect; I mean this as to the oldest books; though, without doubt, the latest were much more perfect and uncorrupt; especially those that were written under or after the Babylonian captivity; I mean Daniel, Haggai, Zechariah, Esdras, Nehemiah, and Esther. That the copy which we call the Samaritan, being that which has alone preserved the original Hebrew character ever used by the Jews till the days of Barchocab,[1] has been preserved in the next degree of perfection, and, had it not been confined to the Pentateuch alone, would have been a treasure still more inestimable. That the copy used by the Septuagint interpreters was still more imperfect. That Judas Maccabeus's copy or collection, being not now extant, we cannot tell what perfection it had; only so far, that it contained some ancient histories or sacred books which none of the remaining copies have preserved to us, 2 Macc. i., ii. That, for certain, the present Masorete copy is the most imperfect and corrupt of them all. But that still, upon the view of the whole, any judicious and impartial inquirer will not only be satisfied of the general nature of the laws, the general truth of the histories, the general purport of the prophecies, and the general wisdom of the moral instructions all along; (the very worst copy no way appearing to have been altered so much as *one-tenth*, perhaps not *one-twentieth*, of the whole;) but will common-

ly be able, upon the comparison of them all together, and of the ancient citations made from them in different ages, to distinguish the true genuine readings and the true genuine order from the mistakes and disorders of our present copies: nay, that he will soon discover that almost all our present difficulties and seeming contradictions in those sacred books, as compared together, had no place in the original writings themselves; but have still arisen sometimes from the bare mistakes of modern Rabbins and commentators, but much oftener from the mistakes of our modern copies and versions. Nor does it appear to me that Josephus, in his use of the temple or Nehemiah's copy, was ever sensible of more than *one* text in that copy which so much as *seemingly contradicted* any other; I mean Gen. xv. 13,[2] as compared with Exod. xii. 40, 41; how numerous and difficult soever those *seeming contradictions* do now appear in our present copies, and are noted by every commentator at this day; which thing highly deserves the most serious consideration.

31. N. B. If we could suppose that Josephus meant all the twenty-two volumes of the Jews' Hebrew Bible, by that *law of the Jews* which he assures us was carried in triumph at Rome by Titus,[3] we might suppose that the box, or somewhat like it, now supporting the candlestick upon Titus's triumphal arch,[4] either was or included the very receptacle of those twenty-two volumes, and that this receptacle was the very book-case of Nehemiah's library, then taken out of the Jewish temple. However, since Josephus rather means the Pentateuch by the *law of the Jews* on other occasions; and since he assures us that he himself lived in Vespasian's own house,[5] which he had before he was emperor, and by consequence there used the temple copy of the sacred books given him by Titus; it is not impossible that library of Nehemiah may be still remaining among the ruins of Rome; though I doubt, if it should be dug up and known, the letters must long ago, by length of time, have become illegible; we having no manuscript, now remaining legible, so old as Josephus, much less so old as Nehemiah. Otherwise, if such book-case, with its library, were once discovered, and the letters were legible, I venture to say that it would deserve to be esteemed a much greater treasure than all the other treasures of antiquity in that famous city put together.

32. N. B. Since it appears to me very evident, that when Josephus wrote his Antiquities, and therein gave us the remarkable testimonies already recited concerning John the Baptist, Jesus Christ, and his brother James the Just, he was, in his own conscience, a Nazarene or Ebionite Christian, it may not be amiss to inquire at what time of his life and writings he became such. Now this time must,

---

[1] See Essay on the Old Testament, p. 149—164.

[2] Antiq. B. I. ch. x. sect. 3, and B. II. ch. ix. sect. 2, with ch. xv. sect. 2.   [3] Of the War, B. VII. ch. v. sect. 5.
[4] Vid. Reland. de Spoliis Templi, p. 6.
[5] De Vita suà, sect. 76.

I think, be determined to be after the finishing of his seven books of the Jewish Wars, about A. D. 75, but long before his finishing his twenty books of the Jewish Antiquities, A. D. 93. My reasons are these:

(1.) That though all the facts which concerned Monobazus, or Abgarus, and Helena, and their conversion to Josephus's Judaism, i. e. to Nazarene or Ebionite Christianity, produced in the Authentic Records, p. 954—961, and all that concerned John the Baptist, Jesus Christ, and James his brother, already produced in these papers, were within the compass of the seven books of the Wars of the Jews; yet have we not a word of any of them there, but only in the Antiquities; which looks very like such a concern for Christianity, when he wrote the Jewish Antiquities, as he had not when he wrote the Jewish Wars. Nor do I remember the least passage in those books of the Wars relating at all to Christianity; which silence Photius observes, as we have noted already, p. 913 *prius*, to have been usual when unbelieving Jews wrote any histories of that age.

(2.) The great progress the gospel had made after Josephus had written his books of the Jewish Wars, and long before he finished his books of Antiquities, and this particularly as to the Greeks and Romans, among whom he then lived, might very naturally excite in him a great curiosity to make an exact inquiry into it, and into the miracles that supported it; the effect of which would naturally be his conviction of their truth, and his conversion to Christianity.

(3.) The great disappointments Josephus had met with in the deaths of Vespasian and his son Titus, to both whom he had foretold their coming to the Roman empire, and from both whom he must naturally have had great expectations to the advantage of his people the Jews, together with the continued deplorable estate that people were under ever since the destruction of Jerusalem, must naturally make him cast his eyes elsewhere. And since any deliverance from the Romans could now be only hoped for from the Jews' Messiah, Josephus's circumstances and notions directly led him to consider whether that Messiah was not already come, and so directly prepared him for the examination and belief of Christianity; which therefore most probably commenced soon after the death of Vespasian, A. D. 79, or however of Titus, A. D. 81.

(4.) The nature of his books of Antiquities, which frequently brought before him the Scripture prophecies, and particularly those that gave characters of the Jews' Messiah, would naturally make him inquisitive into their completion. The effect of which would also naturally be his conviction that Jesus was to be acknowledged by those characters to be the true Messiah; which effect those prophecies frequently had in that age in other Jews' conversion to Christianity also. But especially,

(5.) The nature of those his books of Antiquities brought before him the prophecies of Daniel, concerning the four monarchies; and concerning the Messiah's fifth monarchy or kingdom to succeed them; concerning the death of the Messiah, after seventy weeks of years from the days of Nehemiah; concerning the destruction of Jerusalem by the fourth or Roman monarchy, which destruction he saw; and concerning the Messiah's future overthrow of that monarchy; all which predictions he seems to me to have rightly and Christianly applied. So that he could not well avoid seeing, that by Daniel's prophecies Jesus of Nazareth was that Messiah. And very remarkable it is, that the prophecies in this book of Daniel, which have the strongest and clearest proofs for the Jewish and Christian religion of all others, appear to have affected Josephus far more than any or all the other prophecies in the sacred writings; his accounts of these alone being in those his Antiquities far larger than the like accounts therein of all the other Scripture prophecies put together. Nor can I do other than suspect that it was his thorough consideration of these prophecies of Daniel, when in the course of his narration he came naturally to treat of them, and with which he appears so greatly affected, that principally contributed to his conversion to Christianity. Nor are we to forget that Josephus seems ever, in his Wars of the Jews, to apply Daniel's prediction of *time, times, and a half*, Dan. vii. 25; xii. 7, to the profanation by Antiochus, as if it had lasted *three years and a half*, Of the War, Prœeme, sect. 7; B. I. ch. i. sect. 1; B. V. ch. ix. sect. 4; while he does as often leave off that application in his Antiquities, B. X. ch. xi. sect. 7; B. XII. ch. vii. sect. 6, *bis*, and honestly own, with the original authors of the two books of the Maccabees, that such profanation continued but *three years only :* which last is also, I think, a remarkable application of one of Daniel's prophecies, I mean that of the one thousand one hundred evenings and one thousand one mornings, two thousand two hundred in all, Dan. viii. 14, which seems to have been the number in Josephus's copy, as Jerome says some would have it in his time; instead of those two thousand three hundred in our Masorete Hebrew, in Clem. Alex. in Africanus, in the MS. Alex., and those two thousand four hundred in our Vatican copy. So that, upon the whole, it is most probable, that when Josephus wrote his seven books of the Jewish Wars, about A. D. 75, he was an unbelieving Jew; but that when he was writing the tenth book of his Antiquities, about A. D. 84, he became a Christian. Nor is there, I think, any more indication in the former nine books of Antiquities that he was so at that time, than in the seven books of the Jewish Wars; though afterward we have frequent indications of it in the eleven following books of those Antiquities.

DISSERTATION V

UPON THE CHRONOLOGY OF JOSEPHUS

1. In order to state this difficult point, of the genuine chronology of Josephus, I shall make use of the labours of Dr. Wills, in his small, but very valuable, dissertation upon this subject, prefixed to Sir Roger Le Strange's edition of Josephus in English; and of the improvements I formerly made upon it, in my Essay towards restoring the true Text of the Old Testament, Prop. X., XI., p. 195—219, together with such additional light as I have since gained from further observations upon reading Havercamp's accurate edition of this author. Now since it is but too evident, that not a few of Josephus's numbers, both in his present Greek copies, and those of the old Latin versions, (I mean that of Rufinus of the seven books Of the Wars, and perhaps of the two books against Apion; and that of Cassiodorus's friend, supposed to be Epiphanius Scholasticus, of the twenty books of Antiquities,) have been grossly corrupted since the days of Josephus; we must, with Dr. Wills, of necessity have recourse to the citations made from his books in early ages, before those alterations were made, that so we may see what was his own genuine chronology. In order therefore to our discovery of that chronology, we must in the entrance, and by way of a preliminary, observe, that Josephus appears to have finished and published his Greek books of the Jewish War about A. D. 75, or when he was no more than thirty-eight years of age; and that it was about eighteen years afterwards, or in the thirteenth of Domitian, A. D. 93, i. e. when he was fifty-six years of age, that he published his Antiquities; as also that he published his two books against Apion still later, after those Antiquities had been read and censured by the Greeks or Gentiles. All which is plainly proved by Fabricius, edit. Havercamp, vol. II. p. 57, &c. As to his own Life, which he intended as an appendix to his Antiquities, it could not be finished till after the third of Trajan, A. D. 100, or after he was sixty-three years of age; as is clear, though contrary to the common opinion, from his mentioning therein Agrippa II. as then dead, sect. 65, who yet did not die till that third of Trajan; as the words of a contemporary writer, Justus of Tiberias, to be produced hereafter out of Photius, directly inform us. See the note upon Justus of Tiberias's Fragment, after the Life of Josephus, and Havercamp's edition, vol. II. p. 40, 58—63. And that his two books against Apion were written after the fore-going, will appear probable hereafter. I proceed therefore to my present design; I mean, to state the genuine chronology of Josephus from the ancient citations. And in order thereto I observe,

2. (1.) That Josephus certainly reckoned *almost three thousand years*, and no more, *from the creation of Adam to the death of Moses.* This is Josephus's own express computation in all his present MSS. and printed copies, Greek and Latin; and that in his latest work, against Apion, B. I. sect. 8. And this number is not only in all the present MSS. and printed copies, but was also in those very ancient copies made use of by Eusebius; who quotes the same number from him, Hist. Eccl. B. III. ch. x. sect. 85, and whose MSS. still appear, by Valesius's notes, to have the same number. That number is also quoted by Nicephorus, and was in the version used by Hermannus Contractus, both in the eleventh century; nay, was cited accordingly by Bede, about the end of the seventh century, without the least variation. See Niceph. Hist. Eccl. p. 162; Herm. Contr. at A. M. 2493; Bede De Natur. Rer. fol. 76; and De Rat. Temp. Epist. Apologet. So that here we may securely fix our foot, and affirm, that Josephus, for certain, originally reckoned *almost* three thousand years, and no more, *from the creation of Adam till the death of Moses.*

3. (2.) That Josephus did also, for certain, reckon about 1770, 1780, or 1790 years, from the days of Moses, or the Exodus out of Egypt, till the destruction of Jerusalem by Titus Vespasian, A. D. 70. This computation is most probably taken from Antiq. B. VIII. ch. iii. sect. 1, and Of the War, B. VI. ch. x., and is cited in Clement of Alexandria, by a still earlier anonymous author, who wrote but seventy-seven years after that destruction, and but fifty-four years after Josephus finished his Antiquities. The remarkable words of this citation are these, Strom. I. p. 341: " Flavius Josephus the Jew, who composed the history of that nation, when he collected the series of years, says, That from Moses to David [from the Exodus out of Egypt to the death of David] there were 585 years [change ὲ, or 5, into ἠ, or 8, and you will have the exact number 588, as frequently in Josephus elsewhere]. From David to the second year of Vespasian [A. D. 70] 1179. From whence to the tenth year of Antoninus

[A. D. 147] are 77. So that the whole sum from Moses to the tenth year of Antoninus is 1833 [it should be 1841 or 1844] years." Now 585+ 1179=1764, and 588+1179=1767. And what greatly confirms that ancient citation is this, that these numbers agree, within a few years, with those particular sums which even all the present copies of Josephus give us, and that as to both parts of this entire interval: the one, from the going out of Egypt, in the days of Moses, to the death of David, which is usually in Josephus, at this day, the sum of 588 years, as we shall show hereafter. The other, from the death of David to the destruction of Jerusalem, in the second year of Vespasian, A. D. 70, is not only in the place cited just 1179 years, Of the War, B. VI. ch. x., but is nearly the sum of the particular years at the conclusion of the twentieth book of Antiquities. Nor does the whole sum in this last place, from Moses to the second of Vespasian, differ above twenty-six years from the sum before us, taken out of Josephus very near to his own time, as the reader may easily satisfy himself by the following table, taken out of the end of the twentieth book of Antiquities, and on all accounts highly worthy to be transcribed in this place.

HIGH PRIESTS OF THE JEWS

[Eighty-three in number.]

	Years.
Thirteen from Moses to Solomon . .	612
Eighteen to the burning of the temple	466½
Duration of the captivity . . .	70
Sixteen high priests from Josedek to Eupator	414
Jacimus	3
Without a high priest . . .	7
Jonathan	7
Simon	8
Hyrcanus I.	31
Aristobulus I.	1
Alexander	27
Hyrcanus II.	9
Aristobulus II.	3¼
Hyrcanus II. again . . .	24
Antigonus	3¼
Twenty-eight from Herod . .	107
	Sum, 1793

So that we have great reason to believe that Josephus reckoned almost 3000 years, and no more, from the creation of Adam to the death of Moses, and about 1770, 1780, or 1790 years from the Exodus, to the destruction of Jerusalem by Titus Vespasian, A. D. 70.

4. (3.) That those numbers are also nearly according to Josephus's own mind, is further evident from certain numbers still preserved in other uncorrupt places of his present copies. Thus in the procme to his Antiquities, even as it now stands,

he affirms, "That the holy books of the Jews, whence he took his materials, contained the history of five thousand years." Thus he also more fully declares, in the beginning of his first book against Apion, "That his books of Antiquities, which brought the affairs of the Jews down to his own time, contained the history of five thousand years." Which chronology, for a round and large sum, is the nearest possible; nay, is almost the exact sum, upon the foot of that Egyptian chronology made use of by him in his books against Apion. Of which more hereafter, sect. 35. And as this chronology does not admit of his present number of years before the deluge, which in the copies is no less than two thousand six hundred and fifty-six, and which would make the whole much nearer to six thousand than to five thousand years; so the exact number four thousand seven hundred and sixty-eight years, which we shall soon see the particulars amount to in his own last corrections, agree tolerably to the present number of five thousand. Thus we are informed, Antiq. B. IX. ch. iv. sect. 6, that in Josephus's chronology, Hadad, or Benhadad, and Hazael, the two successive kings of Syria, in the days of Jehosaphat and Joram kings of Judah, and of Ahab and Joram kings of Israel, though they had been deified by the Syrians, and looked on by them as exceeding ancient, did not live eleven hundred years before Josephus published his Antiquities. Accordingly, by the present chronology, it will appear, that, in the opinion of Josephus, there were but one thousand and forty-one years from the death of Jehosaphat to the thirteenth of Domitian, when Josephus published his Antiquities. Thus Josephus says, Of the War, B. IV. ch. ix. sect 7, that Hebron was ancienter than Memphis in Egypt, and two thousand three hundred years older than his own time. But since he no where determines the exact time when Memphis was built in the history of the Old Testament; and since in his Antiquities, B. I. ch. viii. sect. 3, he rightly corrects Memphis, for Tanis or Zoan, as Numb. xiii. 22, and leaves out the number of years from the building of Hebron and Tanis to his own time; this number two thousand three hundred gives us but a very gross and uncertain determination of Josephus's chronology. Though I cannot say that it properly disagrees to his other characters of this period; at least not to his largest Egyptian chronology, of which hereafter, sect. 35.

5. (4.) That this calculation is still further confirmed, as to those branches from Abraham or Melchizedek, and from Moses to Josephus, by no fewer than eight other numbers in his present copies, Antiq. Procme, sect. 3, and B. XX. ch. xi. sect. 2, and Against Apion, B. I. sect. 7, and B. II. sect. 31, and Of the War, B. VI. ch. x. sect. 1. In the four first of which places the numbers do all agree; and recount, in a general way, two thousand years from Moses to Josephus. Nor is this other than

the nearest large number, and does not ill agree with those exacter ones of about one thousand eight hundred and seventy, one thousand eight hundred and eighty, and one thousand eight hundred and ninety years, which this chronology affords us, from the birth of Moses till the days of Josephus, as we have in part seen already, and shall more fully see presently. And if any wonder that the Jews should then reckon this period to be so long, they ought to know that Philo, who was one of the same nation with Josephus, and lived a little earlier than he, though in the same century, counted it in his days *more than two thousand years.* Although it must be confessed he at the same time makes this apology for himself, that he did not then enter into the nicety of such computations.[1] As for the four numbers in the last place just now cited, that from the building of Jerusalem by a righteous king Melchisedek, in the days of Abraham, to the destruction of the same city by Nebuchadnezzar, were one thousand four hundred and sixty-eight years; that from David to the same destruction, as will be again recited hereafter, were four hundred and seventy-seven years; that from David to the destruction by Titus, in the days of Josephus, were, as above recited, one thousand one hundred and seventy-nine years; and, after all, that from its building by Melchisedek, till its destruction by Titus, were two thousand one hundred and seventy-seven years: these are all so agreeable to one another, to the former determinations, and to what the several parts will amount to, as is, in general, a very strong confirmation of our present chronology of Josephus.

(5.) This general computation of about five thousand years from the creation of Adam to the days of Josephus, as compounded of almost three thousand years to the death of Moses, and of about two thousand years from Moses to Josephus, is considerably attested to by Origen; who, when he probably had an eye to Josephus, as well as to the Septuagint Bible, informs us, " That there were four thousand eight hundred and thirty years from the creation to the birth of Christ, and four thousand nine hundred to the seventieth year of his economy." [2] The same is also pretty nearly confirmed by the same Origen's other observation, that it was as long from Adam to Noah [or from the creation to the flood] as from Moses to Christ; our present chronology of Josephus allowing, in gross, about one thousand six hundred years to each of these intervals, as will more distinctly appear when we come to the particulars.

6. In order to which we must first of all set down the genealogical table of the patriarchs, from the creation of Adam to the birth of Abraham, according to our known copies of the Hebrew, the Samaritan, and the Septuagint; as also that of Josephus, both according to the present corrupted

numbers, and what I esteem the genuine numbers of Josephus. Which table follows.

7. The numbers here first set down for Josephus's numbers are those in his common copies; and those set down afterward are what will be proved to have been his true original numbers, written by himself. Those in the Samaritan column for Mathusela and Lamech are double; the former what the copies of Eusebius, and Syncellus, and the present copies afford us; the latter what Jerome gives us from his copy. The like variety there is under Nahor, both in Josephus and the Septuagint; as also for the age of Terah when he died, in Josephus, whether at two hundred and five, or one hundred and forty-five; of the former of which in its proper place hereafter, and of the latter immediately. For whereas the present Hebrew and Septuagint prolong the age of Terah to two hundred and five, and Josephus's present copies afford us the same large number, I have here set down that larger number from those copies; but I have set down also the smaller number one hundred and forty-five as corrected from the Samaritan. The reason of which correction must be given in this place. All ancient copies, versions, and testimonies agree that Terah *was* no more than *seventy years old when he begat Abraham, Nahor, and Haran.* All ancient copies, versions, and testimonies agree that Abraham, when he departed out of Haran, after the death of Terah his father there, was no more than *seventy-five years old.* Whence it follows most obviously, that Terah could be no more than one hundred and forty-five years old at his death. Yet do all the present copies of the Hebrew, Josephus, and the Septuagint directly affirm, that Terah was no fewer than *two hundred and five years old* at his death. Though if we have recourse to the Samaritan Pentateuch, we shall there find as directly that Terah was then no more than one hundred and forty-five years old. And this certainly is the *true reading*, as the reasoning already made use of from the two other texts, which are undisputed in all copies, does plainly assure us. And that this was the *ancient reading* also, the older copies of the LXXII., in the days of Philo, as well as the series of the reasoning in Josephus himself upon this occasion, does secure us; and both of them do thereby plainly discover that great corruption which the Masorete Hebrew has introduced into our Bible in this place. For as to the Septuagint copy, in the days of Philo, he assures us, De Somniis, p. 5721, " That Jacob's grandfather Abraham could not, in his opinion, for a certain reason, endure to live any long time in Haran. Accordingly, says he, we read that Abraham (born when his father Terah was seventy) *was* (only) *seventy-five years old when he departed out of Haran;* although his father Terah had lived there to his death." Which reasoning, if Philo *spake* exactly, implies that Terah could be no more than one hundred and forty-five years old at the utmost when

[1] Ap Euseb. Præp. Evang. VIII. 6. p. 357.
[2] Homil. XXIX. in Matth. p. 139.

A GENEALOGICAL TABLE OF THE PATRIARCHS BEFORE AND AFTER THE DELUGE

Joseph. Antiq. B. I. ch. ii., iii.; ch. iii. sect. 2—4, 9; ch. vi. sect. 5; B. VII. ch. i. sect. 1.

	Before the son's birth.					After the son's birth.			Length of lives.				Years bef. the Christ. era
	Heb.	Jos. vulg.	Jos. vers.	Sam.	LXXII.	Heb.	Sam.	LXXII.	Heb.	Jos.	Sam.	LXXII.	
Adam	130	230	130	130	230	800	800	700	930	930	930	930	4485
Seth	105	205	105	105	205	807	807	707	912	912	912	912	4355
Enos	90	190	90	90	190	815	815	715	905	905	905	905	4250
Cainan	70	170	70	70	170	840	840	740	910	910	910	910	4160
Maleleel	65	165	65	65	165	830	830	730	895	895	895	895	4090
Jared	162	162	62	62	162	800	785	800	962	962	847	962	4025
Enoch	65	65	65	65	165	300	300	200	365	365	365	365	3963
Mathusela	187	187	187	$\frac{67}{187}$	167	782	653	802	969	969	720	969	3898
Lamech	182	182	182	$\frac{53}{182}$	188	595	600	565	777	777	653	753	3711
Noah	600	600	600	600	600				950	950	950	950	3529
To the Deluge.	1656	2256	1556	$\frac{1307}{1356}$	2242								2929
Sem *after Del.*	2	12	2	2	2	500	500	500			600		
Arphaxad	35	135	135	135	135	403	303	330			438		2927
Cainan II.	0	0	0	0	130	0	0	330	0	0	0		2792
Sala	30	130	130	130	130	403	303	336			433		0000
Eber	34	134	134	134	134	430	270	270			404		2662
Phaleg	30	130	130	130	130	209	109	209			239		2528
Ragau	32	132	132	132	132	207	107	207			239		2398
Sarug	30	130	130	130	130	200	100	200			230		2266
Nahor	29	79	[28] or 29	79	$\frac{79}{179}$	119	69	125			148		2136
Terah *at the birth of Abram*	70	70	70	70	70				205	$\frac{204}{145}$	145	205	2107
Sum to the birth of Abram	292	952	892	942	$\frac{1072}{1172}$								2037

Thence to the death of Moses $75 + 430 + 40 = 545 = 2037 = 545 = 1492$.

he died, according to his copy of the Septuagint. And as to Josephus's Hebrew copy of the Pentateuch, it is plain by his own reasoning, Antiq. B. I. ch. vi. sect. 5, that it did not exhibit the larger number, two hundred and five, but the smaller, one hundred and forty-five. His words are these, even in all his present copies: " They buried Terah when he was dead at Haran, after he had lived two hundred and five years ; FOR the life of man was already cut short, and became shorter till the birth of Moses." Now this reason given by Josephus, upon occasion of the particular number of years of the life of Terah, " That they were not to be wondered at, though they were comparatively but few ; since God had already shortened the life of man, and was going on to shorten it still," is an excellent reason, if his number were so few as one hundred and forty-five, with the Samaritan ; but sufficiently absurd, if it were so many as two hundred and five, with his present copies, with the present Hebrew, and Septuagint. For that number is no fewer than fifty-seven years more than the years of his father Nahor in all copies. Nor is the other number in him and in Philo still remaining, where Abraham is said to be born at the seventieth year of Terah, at all reconcilable to the other hypothesis. Nor will Josephus's famous number, of *almost three thousand years*, and no more, *from the creation of Adam to the death of Moses*, permit us to believe that his copy could have here the number two hundred and five, which would imply that Terah was one hundred and thirty years old when Abraham was born, as those that allow that number are all forced to determine ; which indeed increases the chronology sixty years, and renders the number aforementioned fifty-three years above three thousand, contrary, as we have seen, to the most undeniable authority of all the copies of Josephus, both ancient and modern.

8. *Corollary.* Hence we may observe, in general, that Josephus's genuine chronology agreed nearer to the Samaritan Pentateuch, especially as it stood in Jerome's copy, than either to the present Hebrew or to the present Septuagint Greek copies ; I mean, from the creation of Adam to the death of Moses : Josephus affording us almost three thousand, or exactly, as we shall see presently, two thousand nine hundred and ninety-three ; the Samaritan two thousand seven hundred and ninety-four, in Jerome's copy three thousand and forty-three ; the present Hebrew two thousand four hundred and ninety-three ; and the present Septuagint three thousand eight hundred and fifty-nine years ; as the foregoing table of the genealogy of the patriarchs demonstrates. The common Samaritan copy being less than Josephus two hundred and six, that of Jerome's exceeding it fifty years only, while the Septuagint copy exceeds it no less than eight hundred and sixty-six years, and the Masorete Hebrew wants no fewer than five hundred years.

9. And now, since I have stated Josephus's chronology in general, it will be fit to enter into the particular periods of it ; which appear to me, upon a careful examination, to have originally stood thus.

		Years.
(1.)	From the creation of Adam till the deluge of Noah . . .	1556
(2.)	From the deluge till the birth of Abraham . . .	892
(3.)	From the birth of Abraham till his departure out of Haran . .	75
(4.)	From that departure out of Haran till the Exodus out of Egypt .	430
	From that Exodus to the death of Moses . . .	40
	[From the creation of Adam till the death of Moses . . .	2993]
(5.)	From the Exodus out of Egypt till the building of the temple, at first 592, but at last corrected by Josephus himself to . . .	612
(6.)	From the building of the temple till its conflagration, at the first 470, but at last corrected by Josephus himself to . . .	466
(7.)	From the conflagration to the first of Cyrus, when the Jews returned out of captivity	70
(8.)	From the first of Cyrus to the twelfth of Nero, where the history in the Antiquities ends	639
(9.)	Thence to the second of Vespasian, or the destruction of Jerusalem .	4
(10.)	Thence to the thirteenth of Domitian, A. D. 93, when Josephus finished his Antiquities	23
	From the birth of Moses till the thirteenth of Domitian, at first 1878, but to be corrected to	1894
	From the creation of Adam till the thirteenth of Domitian, at first 4751, but to be corrected to . . .	4767

10. As to the two first periods, 1556 years till the flood, and 892 years till the birth of Abraham, if the reader consult the genealogical table of the patriarchs, set down sect. 6 already, he will see how the sums are made up, viz. by adding together the several years of the patriarchs, both before and after the flood, when their sons were born, and noting the result. What I am here to do is to show the footsteps of these numbers in Josephus.

As to the *first* period, 1556 years from the creation of Adam till the deluge, the sum, in the present copies of Josephus, is uncertain; what the generality of the copies have, 2656, is utterly inconsistent with that fundamental character of *not quite* 3000 *years to the death of Moses*, and is little better than a set of corrections or corruptions from the Septuagint. One MS. however seems more genuine, and has 1-56, without the figure for the hundreds; so that we are still left in good measure in the dark between the numbers 1656 from the Hebrew, and 1556 from Jerome's Samaritan; but then, we having been assured that Josephus accounted not quite 3000 *years till the death of Moses*, this implies that he could have no more than 1556, the other number 1656, which is now in the Hebrew, being 93 years too many for that interval. So that it hence appears Josephus's copy gave Jared but 62 years when his son Enoch was born, according to the Samaritan; and that the present Hebrew, and probably even Origen's Septuagint, which gave him 162, have unjustly enlarged this period 100 years. And as to the lesser number 1556, it is so far confirmed elsewhere in Josephus's present copies, Antiq. B. X. ch. viii. sect. 5, that if you deduct the years there reckoned between the flood and the burning of the temple by Nebuchadnezzar, 1957, from the years reckoned in the same place between the creation of Adam and that burning of the temple, 3513, in almost all his Greek and Latin copies, and in Zonaras's and Freculphus's citations, though both 500 years too small, there will remain the just sum of 1556 years from the creation to the flood; which is no very inconsiderable confirmation of the truth of the same number.

N. B. If any reader wonder at the 2929th year before the Christian era here set down in the table, as my own correspondent year for the deluge, while I myself, in the latter editions of my New Theory, determine that deluge to have begun in Anno 2926, edit. 4, p. 39 and 218, he is to take notice, that the present chronology is made from the sacred books themselves, without mixing my own hypothesis of the cause of the deluge by the comet, referred to in that Theory; and supposes the years in the ten generations to Abraham to be all complete years, without the addition or subtraction of any odd months or days; which is by no means probable to have been so in fact, as is there observed. So that the absolute or chronological number might well be no more than 2926, though the addition of the several numbers in the Bible put together amount to 2929, which former number indeed is my real opinion of that matter.

11. As to the *second* period in this chronology of Josephus's, 892 *years from the flood to the birth of Abraham*, it is supported, for the main, by the Samaritan and Septuagint, and even the present copies of Josephus's also. For although these copies have now the bare *sum* of the present

Hebrew, 292, yet do the *particulars* of which that sum is to be composed amount in the same copies at least to 892, which small number 292 is therefore too gross a corruption to be derived from Josephus himself. Nor in that case would the sum to the death of Moses be any whit near to 3000 years, as we have already proved it certainly was. Yet is there, in reality, no other difference of this sum 892 from the particulars, which make up 942, than 50 years, which must be here accounted for. This difference wholly arises from the variety of the readings of the number for the age of Nahor when his son Terah was born, whether it should be 28, or 29, or 79 (to say nothing of some other numbers, too extravagant, and too little supported, to be here taken notice of, which may be seen in Dr. Wills, p. 18). In these numbers the MSS. greatly differ. Now though I confess here, that both the Samaritan and present Septuagint have 79, yet does it appear to me most probable, as the number is cited by Origen also, if Dr. Wills be in the right, that Josephus wrote either 28 or 29; this last being in the Hebrew and vulgar Latin, as well as 28 is in several MSS. of Josephus. However, these two numbers are so nearly the same, that which of them is the true number is not worth much dispute. But that the one of them was Josephus's real number, in opposition to the larger numbers elsewhere, is plain, both from those MSS. that have 28, and especially from that grand and sure standard of the chronology of Josephus, which does not allow quite 3000 *years to the death of Moses;* which, if his number were here 79, would be exceeded by no fewer than 43 years. Nor indeed ought Josephus to be supposed herein to agree *exactly* with the Samaritan and Septuagint, as he would had he 79 years; since Freculphus in the ninth century informs us, that he did then *nearly*, but not exactly, agree with them. I say nothing here of the 12 *years* which all the present copies of Josephus interpose between the flood and the birth of Arphaxad, instead of 2 years, which I think all the other copies and versions have in this place, not only because it is unsupported by any collateral evidence, but also because it is entirely inconsistent with that grand character of *not quite* 3000 *years* till the death of Moses. Nor does this number seem to be any more than the bare mistake of transcribers.

12. As to the *third* period, 75 *years till Abraham's departure out of Haran*, upon the death of his father Terah, it is without dispute on all sides and in all copies; I mean when that gross error about Terah's death not before he was 205 years old, and Abraham's consequent birth not before the 130th of Terah, is corrected. Of which already, sect. 7.

13. As to the *fourth* period, 430 *years from Abraham's departure out of Haran till the Exodus out of Egypt*, it is also fully agreed to by

Josephus; and is indeed the express assertion of two texts of Scripture, Exod. xii. 40, 41, and that to *a day* also; Antiq. B. II. ch. xv. sect. 2. I mean as they were read and understood by him, and as they still are read both in the Samaritan and Septuagint even at this day, and as they therefore ought to stand in our Hebrew copies also. But this hath been cleared elsewhere; Essay on the Old Testament, p. 62. I need also say nothing of that branch of the next period, which assigns 40 *years from the Exodus out of Egypt till the death of Moses*, because it is known to every one, and is the very same in Josephus, Antiq. B. III. ch. i. sect. 6; B. IV. ch. 4. sect. 6; ch. viii. sect. 49; B. V. ch. i. sect. 4, 29, and in all other sacred accounts whatsoever. Only it will be proper to observe here, how accurately the sum of our present accounts hitherto, *viz.* 2993 *years till the death of Moses*, agrees with Josephus's own affirmation, so often mentioned, of *almost* 3000 *years* to that time.

14. The entire *fifth* period in Josephus, from the Exodus out of Egypt to the building of the temple, 592 at first, and as corrected at last by Josephus himself, 612 years, is so often repeated in him, one way or other, and that usually with the former number 592, and is so fully confirmed by that ancient quotation from Josephus before mentioned, sect. 3, which gives 585 or rather 588 years from the Exodus to the death of David, near 4 years before that building began, that, within the latitude of somewhat above 20 years, there is no room at all to doubt of his opinion herein. Thus, Antiq. B. VII. ch. iii. sect. 2, Josephus reckons 515 years from the days of Joshua to David's taking Jerusalem. Add 33 of David's reign afterwards, and near 4 of Solomon's before he began to build the temple, and the 40 years in that wilderness, including the whole period before us, and they make in even years 592, from the Exodus to the building of Solomon's temple. Thus the interval of 592 years is express in Antiq. B. VIII. ch. iii. sect. 1, in the Greek copies.

	Josephus's computation. YEARS.	ANTIQ. B. / ch. / sect.	My own computation. YEARS.	Began ANNO
Moses in the wilderness	40	IV. viii. 49	40	1532
Joshua	25	V. i. 29	25	1492
Interregnum	18	VI. v. 4	18	1467
Slavery under Cushan	8	V. iii. 2	8	1449
Othniel judge	40	V. iii. 2	40	1441
Slavery under the Moabites	18	V. iv. 1	18	1401
Ehud judge	80	V. iv. 3	8	1383
Shamgar judge	1	V. iv. 3	1	1375
Slavery under Jabin	20	V. v. 2	20	1374
Deborah and Barak judges	40	V. v. 4	40	1354
Slavery under the Midianites	7	V. vi. 1	7	1314
Gideon judge	40	V. vi. 1	40	1307
Abimelech king or judge	3	V. vii. 2	3	1267
Thola judge	23]	— — —	23	1264
Jair judge	22	V. vii. 6	22	1241
Slavery under the Ammonites [and the incursion of the Philistines, B. V. ch. vii. 1; viii. 1.]	18	V. vii. 10	18	1219
			Sum 291	
Jephtha judge	6	V. vii. 12	6	1201
Ibsan judge	7	V. vii. 13	7	1195
Elon judge	10	V. vii. 14	10	1188
Abdon judge	[8]	V. vii. 15	8	1178
Slavery under the Philistines	40	V. viii. 1	42½	1170
Samson judge under the Philistines	20	V. viii. 12	—	
Eli judge under the Philistines	20	V. xi. 3	—	
Samuel judge 12+22½	32½	VI. xiii. 5	12½	1148
Saul king	20	VI. xiv. 9	20	1116
David king	40	VII. xv. 2	40	1096
Solomon king before he built the temple	3½	VIII. iii. 1	3½	1056
	Sum 610		temple built	1052
			149	149
			291	291
			40	40
			480	480

Again, Antiq. B. X. ch. viii. sect. 5, we are told that Nebuchadnezzar burnt the temple 470 years after its building by Solomon; and in the 1950th year, or rather, as other copies have it, 1957th from the Exodus out of Egypt. Take the former number out of the latter, and there will remain 580, or rather 587, years from the Exodus to the building of Solomon's temple, which is but 5 years different from the greatest part of the other numbers of the period before us. Again, the sum of the years of the fifth, sixth, and seventh books of the Antiquities, 476+32+40=548, together with the 40 years in the wilderness, and the first 4 years of Solomon's reign, including the whole period before us, amount to just 592 years. To say nothing of Josephus's general number of *above* 500 *years* after the death of Moses and Joshua, before kings were set up, B. XI. ch. iv. sect. 8. And so far go Josephus's computations before his later review, at the end of his Antiquities. But there the number is altered, as well in all our present Greek and Latin copies, as in the fourth century copy of Hegesippus or Ambrose, where he increases this interval 20 years, and makes it 612; as he does also in his final review in the second book against Apion, sect. 2. Nor do I at all suppose this number to be an error of the copies, but a correction made by Josephus himself. See sect. 3 before.

15. Let us now see how the particulars answer to his general sum in Josephus. See table.
This sum of the several particulars, 610, is but 2 years too small for Josephus's largest and most correct number already stated, 612.

16. Under this period, however, we have several difficulties as to these particulars in the present copies of Josephus, though the sum be so near the sum in other places; especially that largest number 612 in the conclusion of the Antiquities, and in the second book against Apion already quoted. Those difficulties here follow.

(1.) Thola the judge with his 23 years is wholly omitted. But this seems not at all owing to Josephus himself, but to his transcribers only, especially while all agree that his own sum includes those 23 years also.

(2.) Though Abdon the judge be set down in Josephus, yet are the eight years of his government omitted. But this seems also no way owing to Josephus, but to his transcribers only.

(3.) Josephus says, Antiq. B. VIII. ch. iii. sect. 1, that the temple was built but 1440 years after the deluge. Now take 1397, the sum already determined *from the deluge to the Exodus*, out of 1440, *from the deluge to the building of the temple*, and there remain 43 years only, instead of those 592 or 612 years which we have seen Josephus gives us *from that Exodus to the building of the temple*. But this number 1440 is too gross a mistake to be supposed Josephus's own. It must certainly be derived from the transcribers only.

(4.) Josephus, Antiq. B. VI. ch. i. sect. 4, with ch. ii. sect. 1, allows that there were full 20 years from the death of Eli to Samuel's victory over the Philistines at Eben-Ezer, as in 1 Sam. vii.; which is utterly inconsistent with no more than 12 years' government of Samuel, as here specified, unless we allow of an interregnum between Eli and Samuel, equal to those 20 years; which yet neither Josephus, nor any other chronologer, appears to have done. Nor is there, I think, any just foundation at all for so doing.

(5.) Josephus says, Antiq. B. V. ch. v. sect. 1, that the *rest* under Ehud, which has here and in our other copies no fewer than 80 years ascribed to it, was *hardly a breathing time;* which well agrees to 8, but by no means to 80 years' duration of this *rest*, till the death of Ehud.

Of these five particulars there remain therefore but two; the *fourth* and *fifth*, which seem to belong to Josephus himself, and deserve a distinct consideration. As to the former number, 20 years, from the death of Eli to the victory of Samuel, it seems not to have been attended to by Josephus, when he stated Samuel's government, before the anointing of Saul, at 12 years. They were only implied in the ark's being 20 years at Kirjathjearim after the death of Eli, before the Israelites brought it to Mispeh, just before Samuel's victory at Eben-Ezer. Which though it certainly implies that Samuel's government, or the interregnum before it, must then have been full 20 years, and this some considerable time before Saul was anointed king; yet were not those 20 years expressed either in the catalogue of the judges, or under the servitudes; and so might at first be easily overlooked by Josephus. Though perhaps it was the later observation of these 20 years, which he had formerly omitted, that obliged him at last to increase his number for this entire period from 592 to 612 years. As for the latter number, 8 instead of 80, for Ehud, it is not in any of our copies at present; but was in Theophilus's copy in the second century, Ad Autolyc. III. 24; and being a clear consequence of Josephus's own reasoning, it ought by no means to be rejected; especially while a number is much more easily mistaken by transcribers than a series of plain reasoning. Nor indeed can either Jephtha's 300 years' possession of the land of Sihon and Og, Judg. xi. 26, or so small a number as 480 till the building of the temple, be reconciled to these 80 years; but both strongly enforce the reading of 8 years only in its stead. I therefore look upon these two numbers, 80 and 8, to have been both truly in some of Josephus's copies: the former and larger 80 in those copies which he followed when he made this whole period 592 or 612 years, out of the books of Judges and Samuel: for without it they cannot be completed: the latter and smaller 8 in those copies which he followed when he made use of that famous text,

1 Kings vi. 1, for his standard, which expressly determines this entire interval to be no more than 480 years; and of the existence of which text in some of Josephus's copies this small number 8 is, I think, the only indication; and without which lesser number it is not possible fairly to reduce the particulars in the books of Judges and Samuel within so small a compass.

17. Now if inquiry be made, why Josephus should choose to desert the plain text in the book of Kings that had no ambiguity; and to prefer a more uncertain reasoning from the books of Judges and Samuel; I shall venture to propose this conjecture, that not being able to reduce the numbers in the books of Judges and Samuel within the compass of the 480 years in the book of Kings, (as neither have the modern chronologers been better able, while all their copies have had 80 instead of 8 years' rest under Ehud,) and being naturally desirous of advancing Moses to as great antiquity as he could, which appears plain every where, he at length left the text in the Kings, and gave us a much longer computation from the books of Judges and Samuel. However, I must here further suggest this to the reader, that Josephus seems to have been no way singular in this his procedure; but that both St. Paul, when, Acts xiii. 20, he stated the bare duration of the judges, besides the 40 years in the wilderness, and the reigns of Saul and David, at about 450 years, seems to have followed the like long computation; and Philo, when he estimated the interval between Moses's and his own age, which was somewhat earlier than the age of Josephus, at above 2000 years, as in sect. 5 before; seems to have been of the very same opinion also. Though I confess several strong reasons persuade me that 480 years is the only true number for this entire period. See Essay on the Old Testament, p. 210, 211.

18. Nor, indeed, in case we follow Josephus's reasoning, and Theophilus's number, and take 8 years instead of 80 for Ehud's government, shall we be very much puzzled in reconciling the numbers in the books of Judges and Samuel with the 300 years of Jephtha, or with the 480 years in the book of Kings. I mean this if we take notice, That (1.) Samuel was *born* when Eli was high priest, 1 Sam. i., and yet was an *old man* before he anointed Saul, chap. viii. 1, 5, which must imply that he was then at least near seventy years of age. That (2.) the slavery under the Ammonites, and the contemporary part of the incursions by the Philistines, began about the very same time, though in different parts of the land, as Sir John Marsham well observes from Judg. x. 7—9. See my Chronol. of the Old Test. p. 80. Though it seems the Philistines could do little against the Israelites till two or three years after the four following judges were all dead; at which time I suppose the 40 years of proper slavery under the Philistines did commence. That (3.) the chronological table, sect. 15 above, gives us directly 291 years from the conquest of Sihon and Og, to the end of the slavery under the Ammonites; which Jephtha might well call, in a round number, 300 years, Judg. xi. 26; Antiq. B. V. ch. vii. sect. 9. That (4.) Samson's 20 years were expressly *in the days of the Philistines*, Judg. xiv. 11, 20, and so are not to be reckoned apart; as Sir John Marsham, in the place just now cited, rightly observes also. That (5.) Eli has but 20 years in the Septuagint, 1 Sam. iv. 18; and that when the Hebrew and Josephus call them 40 years, they must of necessity include those other 20 years under the former judges, while he was high priest only, before the latter years of the slavery under the Philistines began. For it is undeniable that he died at 98, 20 years and 7 months before Samuel put an end to their 40 years' tyranny, by the great victory at Eben-Ezer, 1 Sam. vii. And the reader is to observe further, that although, for the carrying on the series of the chronology, I have set down in the foregoing table but 42½ years for the Philistines, as the nature of such chronology required; yet do I rather believe that those Philistines not only began their incursions upon the Israelites in the southwest at the same time with the incursions of the Ammonites in the north-east, as the text implies, Judg. x. 7—9, and continued those incursions during the 31 years of the Ammonites, of Jephtha and Ibsan, of Elon and Abdon; but that till a few years after the death of Abdon their success was not so great as to denominate the Israelites slaves to them. From which period I therefore date these 40 years of the Philistines, as continuing from that time to Samuel's victory at Eben-Ezer. Nor does it seem to me improbable that all these 71 years are called in general *the days of the Philistines;* under which the 20 years of Samson's judicature, and the 20 or 40 years of Eli's high priesthood and judicature, are also to be included; although in the north-east parts those other judges, Jephtha, Ibsan, Elon, and Abdon were their contemporaries also. However, we must further take notice, That (6.) the reign of Saul is evidently to be esteemed no more than 20 years, as Josephus rightly determines it. See sect. 31 hereafter. And when St. Paul ascribes to him 40 years, Acts xiii. 21, it must be from the popular opinion of that time only. Of which more in the place referred to hereafter. According to which *postulata* my own computation, sect. 15, naturally produces the just number of 480 years from the Exodus out of Egypt to the fourth year of Solomon, when he began to build the temple. Which table I therefore take for the true chronology of this period.

19. As to the *sixth* period in Josephus, at first of 470, and at last corrected to 466 *years, from the building to the conflagration of the temple,* it is several times in, and by several ways gathered from, Josephus. Thus he expressly assures us, Antiq. B. X. ch. viii. sect. 5, that 470 years is the

true number for this interval. He there also secures us that this number was what he really meant, by informing us further, that from the Exodus to the burning of the temple were 1062 years. Take out thence the 592 years from the Exodus till the building of the temple, already determined from him, and there remain 470 from the building to the burning of that temple. Which reading of this place is confirmed by Zonaras and Freculphus. Again, in the same place, the kings of the race of David reigned 514 years; from which number subtract 40 years for David, and 4 for Solomon, there will remain 470 years. Again, Antiq. B. XI. ch. iv. sect. 8, the kings (including Saul) reigned 532 years. Take away for Saul 20, for David 40, and for Solomon 4, there will remain, from the building of the temple to its conflagration, 468 years; only 2 years shorter, and somewhat more exact, than the former 470 years. Nor is the more inaccurate determination in the books of the War,

B. VI. ch. x., of this burning of the temple after the death of David, of 477 years, above 3 or 4 years different in excess from the former. But that number which is the most accurate of all is what we meet with at the end of the Antiquities, where this period is but 466 years.

20. However, some other difficulties occur in this period, which must be here considered; and they relating chiefly to the years of the kings of Israel, and their distinct sum, as compared with the years of the kings of Judah contemporary with them, till that kingdom was carried captive by Salmanassar, and their distinct sum, I shall, in imitation of the learned Peter Brinch, ap. Havercamp. p. 296, set down these successive kings of Judah and Israel from Josephus, with the several years of their reigns, and their sums, and then compare them together.

Anno	Kings of Judah.	Years.	ANTIQ. B.	ch.	sect.
	Solomon, after the temple began to be built, reigned	76	VIII.	vii.	8.
976	Rehoboam	17	VIII.	x.	4.
959	Abia	3	VIII.	xi.	3.
957	Asa	41	VIII.	xii.	6.
916	Jehosaphat	25	IX.	iii.	2.
894	Joram	8	IX.	v.	3.
887	Ahaziah	1	IX.	vi.	3.
885	Athaliah	6	IX.	vii.	1.
879	Joash	40	IX. vii. 1,2. / IX. viii. 4.		
840	Amasiah	29	IX.	ix.	3.
811	Uzziah	52	IX.	x.	4.
759	Jotham	16	IX.	xii.	1.
744	Ahaz	16	IX.	xii.	3.
728	Hezekiah	29	X.	iii.	1.
699	Manasseh	55	X.	iii.	2.
643	Amon	2	X.	iv.	1.
641	Josiah	31	X.	v.	1.
610	Joahaz	¼	X.	v.	2.
610	Jehoiakim	11	X.	vi.	3.
599	Jehoiachin	¼	X.	vi.	3.
599	Zedechiah	11	X.	viii. 2,5.	

Sum 469½ or 470

Anno	Kings of Israel.	Years.	ANTIQ. B.	ch.	sect.
975	Jeroboam I. reign.	22	VIII.	xi.	4.
955	Nadab	2	VIII.	xi.	4.
954	Baasha	24	VIII.	xii.	3.
931	Elah	2	VIII.	xii.	4.
931	Zimri 7 days		VIII.	xii.	5.
930	Omri	12	VIII.	xii.	5.
919	Ahab	22	VIII.	xiii.	1.
899	Ahaziah	2	IX.	ii.	1.
898	Joram	12	IX.	ii.	2.
885	Jehu	27	IX.	viii.	1.
857	Jehoahaz	17	IX.	xviii.	5.
842	Joash	16	IX.	ix. 1,3.	
826	Jeroboam II.	40	IX.	x.	13.
773	Zachariah	½	IX.	xi.	1.
77⅔	Shallum	$\frac{1}{12}$	IX.	xi.	1.
772	Menahem	10	IX.	xi.	1.
762	Pekahiah	2	IX.	xi.	1.
760	Pekah	20	IX.	xi.	1.
731	Hoshea	9	IX.	xiii.	1.

Sum 239½ or 240

N. B. These reigns of Judah and Israel are exactly even to months connected to the years of the Julian period in tables engraven on copper, in my Chronol. of the Old Test. p. 96, and thence the years before the Christian era in which they began are placed before each reign in this table.

21. When we cast up the numbers for Judah, they amount to the very same sum which Josephus has so often given us, from the building to the burning of the temple, 470. Which sum therefore he, in all probability, took from these very numbers,

without connecting them to the kings of Israel, or allowing for either deficient or redundant months; which yet is very necessary to be done, when we will be exact; and which I suppose was afterward done by Josephus himself, at the end of his Antiquities; where this entire period is reduced to 466 years, and is very little different from the most accurate number 424¼, at which I long ago stated it in my Chronol. of the Old Test. p. 69, 83—94. I mean this when we allow 80 years for the reign of Solomon, as it is rightly determined by Josephus;

instead of those 40 which alone our other copies ascribe to him. See sect. 58 hereafter, and Essay on the Old Test., p. 31, 32. To which arguments I shall here add another that is in a manner decretory. It is this, That Solomon must in all have reigned about 80 years, because both in Josephus's and in our own common copies Rehoboam, his son and successor, was born of Naamah an Ammonitess; who could not be married to the father till he had left his piety, and was fallen in love with his foreign and idolatrous women, Antiq. B. VIII. ch. vii. sect. 5; 1 Kings xi. 1. Yet was he, in all our Hebrew and Greek copies, no less than 41 years old, and in Josephus's copy no less than 40, when he began to reign after his father's death, 1 Kings xiv. 21; 2 Chron. xii. 13; and though, Antiq. B. VIII. ch. x. sect. 4, the book of Chronicles and Josephus call Rehoboam a *young man* when he came to the crown, which is not in these latter ages usual in one of 40 or 41 years of age, Antiq. B. VIII. ch. viii. sect. 1; 2 Chron. xiii. 7, yet did not Josephus, or others of old, avoid that way of speaking, at the like considerable ages. See the notes on Antiq. B. I. ch. xii. sect. 3, and B. XIV. ch. ix. sect. 2. Nor is this any thing else, I suppose, than a remains of the ancientest way of speaking, when the lives of men were much longer, and so youth lasted much later, than in these latter ages of the world; which indeed is most of all remarkable in Hesiod, who, speaking of those ancienter ages when the lives of men were vastly long, calls one of *an hundred* years old μέγα νήπιον, *a great infant*, Op. et Dier. ver. 130. See the note on Antiq. B. I. ch. iii. sect. 9. However, the sum of the years from the revolt under Jeroboam to the captivity of the ten tribes, which amounts to somewhat above 239 years, or, in the next round and decimal number, to 240 years, is plainly taken by Josephus, Antiq. B. IX. ch. xiv. sect. 1, for the true number, without the least attempt for connecting the particular numbers to those of the kingdom of Judah, or allowing for either deficient or redundant months, or indeed for two *interregna* which seem here very material, and are esteemed no shorter than 20 years, as may be seen in my Chronology of the Old Testament, p. 89; and either Jeroboam the Second's reign must be enlarged 11 or 12 years, (see the Six Dissertations, printed in 8vo, 1734, p. 233,) or both those *interregna* will be necessary for adjusting the two collateral branches of this period together. We may also note here, that Josephus never corrected this deficiency in the kingdom of Israel afterward. Nor ought the critics therefore to make any emendations here of 260 for 240 years; nor elsewhere, Antiq. B. X. ch. ix. sect. 7, of 133 for 130, in the interval between the captivity of the ten and of the two tribes, although both may be more exact numbers in chronology than the other; since I think it pretty plain that Josephus did not in either of these places enter into such niceties; but gave us the gross numbers, as they stood in his copies, without any further adjustment or correction whatsoever.

22. N. B. It is worth our regard here, before we leave this period, that the number of years, Antiq. B. X. ch. iv. sect. 4, from the prophet Jadon's denunciation to Jeroboam, that the bones of the idolatrous priests, now set up by Jeroboam at Bethel, should by a future king, Josiah by name, be burnt on his altar, to the actual burning them by Josiah, in the eighteenth year of his reign, is said by Josephus to have been 361, which is only 4 years too long, as in the table of the kings of Judah before us; and so, within that latitude, confirms those numbers from Rehoboam to Josiah, as really the numbers in Josephus's copies. However, since the Vatican copy of Josephus here names the prophet whom he meant, Achias, who foretold to Jeroboam that he should be king about 4 or 5 years before Jadon foretold the burning those bones by Josiah, in Bishop Lloyd's chronology, there might be reason to suspect that Josephus's memory a little failed him in this matter, and that, by mistake, he confounded the number of years belonging to Achias, which were really about 362 or 361, with those belonging to Jadon, which were but 357. Which emendation, if it be admitted, this number 361 will be the exact sum of the years concerned, according to this table, and strongly confirm the duration before us, which includes the greatest part of this period. But because this no way agrees to Josephus's account of Solomon, I cannot insist upon it. See the notes on B. VIII. ch. vii. sect. 6, 8.

23. As to the *seventh* period, 70 *years from the conflagration of the temple to the first of Cyrus*, when the captive Jews returned to their own land, it is certainly Josephus's own calculation; and very frequently either set down by him expressly, or plainly supposed in his reasoning. So that how ill soever he has placed the beginning of that seventy years' captivity of the two tribes, which I think appears, by the best evidence, to have been above 18 years before that conflagration of the temple, as I have showed elsewhere, Chronology of the Old Testament, p. 48—52, and table, p. 96; (and of which interval Josephus himself seems at last to have been sensible in his first book against Apion, sect. 21, of which presently;) yet will it not bear a dispute that thus did he generally estimate this branch of sacred chronology. Thus, Antiq. B. X. ch. ix. sect. 7, he affirms, that the temple, as well as the country of Judea and the city Jerusalem, lay desolate 70 years. Thus, B. XI. ch. 1. sect. 1, the first of Cyrus is the 70th of the Jewish captivity, and this twice repeated. In the same place Josephus says that from Isaiah, who foretold Cyrus by name, to the burning of the temple, were 140 years, and from the same Isaiah to the first of Cyrus were 210 years. Subtract the former number from the latter, and there remain just 70 years. Thus also, B. XX. ch. x. sect. 1, from the burning of the temple to

the return of the Jews, at the first of Cyrus, are exactly 70 years. It is true that Josephus's present copies, Antiq. B. X. ch. xi. sect. 1 ; ch. ii. sect. 4, give us a chronology of the kings of Babylon, from the eighteenth of Nebuchadnezzar, when, according to Josephus, the temple was burnt, to Cyrus, which contradicts this determination; they ascribing to Nebuchadnezzar full 25 years after the conflagration, [in all 43,] then to Evil-merodach 18, then 40 to Niglassar, [or Niricassolassar; perhaps the same with Nergal-sharezer, Jer. xxxix. 3,] then to Labosordachus 9 months, and then to Baltasar [or Nabonadius] 17 years; in all 100 years and 9 months. But certainly some of these numbers are too grossly mistaken, and too much contradict Ptolemy's Astronomical Canon, as well as Josephus's former determinations from the sacred history, to be ascribed to himself. Nebuchadnezzar reigned in the Canon, as well as here, 43 years; [Baltasar or] Nabonadius there, as well as here, 17 years; and Niglassar, or Niricassolassar, 4 the Canon, and the like number in Berosus, as set down in the first book against Apion by Josephus himself, sect. 19, and in Syncellus also. For which we have here, by a gross mistake of the transcribers, 40. So that when these numbers are rightly placed from that Canon, we shall find that Evil-merodach [or Ilvarodamus] only ought here to have 22 years instead of 2 in the Canon, and those instead of the 18 in our copies of Josephus. So these 70 years will be then easily adjusted after this manner, though in reality 20 years too long.

	Years.
Nebuchadnezzar, after the burning of the temple	25¼
Evil-merodach	22
Niglassar	4
Labosordachus	¾
Baltasar	17
The first of Cyrus	1
	Sum 70

But then it is true that in one of Josephus's last books of all, I mean his first book against Apion, sect. 21, he gives us, from the Tyrian Annals, a series of kings and judges down from Ithobaal and Nebuchadnezzar to Cyrus, amounting to 54 years and 3 months; wherein he says the temple lay waste, not 70 years, as he had formerly so often said, but only 50 years, which is very near the truth, by the Astronomical Canon itself, and may probably be his own correction in his old age. The copies indeed do not suit this number; but have, without all probability, 7 years only; as if it were the remains of the old number 70. Yet because two ancient citations of this place, both by Eusebius and Syncellus, as Dr. Hudson here observes, have the true number 50, as well as one copy another false number 13, those oldest citations may well be preferred, though I dare not venture with Dr. Hudson to put it into the text itself.

24. The *eighth* period, *from the first of Cyrus to the second of Vespasian*, A. D. 70, when Jerusalem was destroyed, contained 642½ years. This number is collected many ways from Josephus's present copies; as will best appear by the partition of it into several branches, and going over each branch distinctly.

	Years.
(1.) From the first of Cyrus, to the conquest of the last Darius, i. e. the entire duration of the Persian monarchy	246
(2.) Thence to the Greek era of Seleucus	18
(3.) Thence to Mattathias the Maccabee	145½
[Thence to the beginning of the government of Asamoneans or Maccabees, about	3½]
(4.) Thence to the death of Antigonus, and beginning of the reign of Herod the Great	126
(5.) Thence to the destruction of the temple, in the second year of Vespasian	107
	Sum 642½

25. As to the *first* part of the period, containing 246 years, it is thus proved from Josephus. In Antiq. B. XII. ch. vii. sect. 7, we are informed, that from the prophecy of Daniel, in the first year of that Darius who, with Cyrus, conquered the Babylonian monarchy, to the profanation of the temple by Antiochus Epiphanes, in the 145th year of the Greeks or of Seleucus, were 408 years. See Lit. Accompl. of Proph. p. 106—108. This number is also quoted by Cedrenus in the eleventh century. Now the era of Seleucus is known to have begun 18 years after the end of the Persian monarchy. Add there-

fore 144 and 18, which give 162, and subtract that number from 408, there remain 246 years for the duration of the Persian monarchy. Thus, Antiq. B. XX. ch. x. sect. 1, from the first year of the Jewish liberty, or the beginning of Cyrus, to Antiochus Eupator, the son and successor of Antiochus Epiphanes, there were 414 years, which number is cited from Josephus by Hegesippus in the fourth century. Now Josephus says, Antiq. B. XII. ch. ix. sect. 2, that Antiochus Epiphanes dying in the 149th year of Seleucus's Greek era, left the kingdom to his son Eupator. If Eupator's first year therefore be the 150th of Seleucus, and 18 years be added, from the conquest of Darius by Alexander the Great, they make 168 years; and this sum deducted from 414, there remain 246 years for the duration of the Persian monarchy. Thus the sum of the eleventh book of Antiquities is 253⅓ years, and contains the interval from the beginning of Cyrus to the death of Alexander the Great; which death, as is well known, happened 7 years after his conquest of Darius. Now deduct 7 from 253⅓, and there remain 246⅓ years, the duration of the Persian monarchy. It must indeed be confessed that Josephus was greatly mistaken in the length of this Persian monarchy, and esteemed it 38 or 39 years longer than it really was by Ptolemy's own Canon, which ascribes no more than 207 years to it. But the ancients were not able to distinguish that beginning of Cyrus, when he first came at the head of the Persian army, used by all the Greek chronologers, 30 years before his death, from that beginning of it in Ptolemy's Canon, upon the taking of Babylon, 9 years before his death; much less from that beginning of it, upon the death of Cyaxares or Darius the Mede, which we know from Xenophon's Cyropædia was hardly 7 years before his death; see Lit. Accompl. of Proph. Supplem. p. 74; which error, joined to that further error, as if the number of years ascribed by Josephus to Xerxes above 21 (see the same Supplem. p. 72) were distinct from the 41 years of Artaxerxes his son and successor, and perhaps some other errors in the length of some of the rest of the Persian reigns, have occasioned this great mistake in Josephus of 38 or 39 years' excess in the duration of the Persian monarchy.

26. The *second* part, or that of 18 *years to the era of Seleucus*, has been already taken as a known interval, and by the reverse of the former reasoning from Josephus, appears to have been known to him in particular. For if we deduct his 246 years' duration of the Persian monarchy from 253, his number from its beginning to the death of Alexander, there remain 7 years' interval from the end of the Persian monarchy to the death of Alexander. If we also deduct 150 of the era of Seleucus, or the first year of Eupator, and 253 from the first of Cyrus to the death of Alexander, which put together are 403, out of 414 from the first of Cyrus to the first of Eupator, both which have been already stated from Josephus, there remain 11 years between the death of Alexander and the beginning of the era of Seleucus. Nor are these two last determinations of 7 and 11, that is of 18 years, at all different, that I have observed, from Ptolemy's Canon, or any other valuable chronology of that time.

27. The *third* part, or 145 *years to Mattathias the Maccabee*, is thus proved from Josephus. We read expressly, Antiq. B. XII. ch. vi. sect. 3, 4, that Mattathias died, after having been the captian of the Jews a year, in the year of Seleucus 146. Nor

is there any other passage in him that contradicts this. Only he seems to me, either, by inadvertence, to have here confounded the two beginnings of Herod's reign, as Dr. Wills supposes; or rather not to have dated the government of the Asamoneans or Maccabees till 3 or 4 years afterwards, as we shall see presently.

28. The *fourth* part, for the *duration of the Asamoneans* or Maccabees, till Herod the Great began his reign, upon the death of Antigonus, of 126 years, is expressly in Josephus, Antiq. B. XIV. at the end; though it be elsewhere said by Herod to have been but 125 years, B. XVII. ch. vi. sect. 3. The larger number is for certain the truer. So this number reaches from the 145th year of Seleucus to the 271st year of Seleucus, and no further; which, to be sure, is not later than Herod's first obtaining the kingdom at Rome, if it reach so far. Yet does Josephus end this part of the present period with the death of Antigonus, between 3 and 4 years afterward. So that it is probable, as I just now hinted, that he did not here begin to reckon the government of the Asamoneans or Maccabees at the first attempt for liberty, made by Mattathias the father, but at the time when Judas Maccabeus his son vanquished Lysias, and restored the worship of God at the temple, 3 or 4 years afterward, from which date there were, for certain, about 126 years to the death of Antigonus. It is true that, Antiq. B. XV. ch. vi. sect. 4, we are told by Josephus that Hyrcanus II., during his mother Alexandra's reign, was high priest 9 years; that after her death he reigned 3 months, and then was set aside by his younger brother Aristobulus; and that he was afterward restored by Pompey, and officiated both as king and as high priest for 40 years. This is some way or other grossly erroneous. In Josephus's last determination, B. XX. ch. x., set down already, sect. 3, Hyrcanus II. has first 9 years allowed him, as high priest, then comes Aristobulus II. 3 years, [or, as in B. XIV. ch. vi. sect. 1, 3 years and 6 months,] and then Hyrcanus II. again 24 years. The whole sum is but 33 years for Hyrcanus II., or, including the 3 years of Aristobulus II., but 36 years in all. Perhaps for τεσσαράκοντα, or 40, Josephus wrote εἰκοσιτέσσαρα, or 24, which perfectly agrees with his last determination.

However, see this error otherwise corrected in Dean Prideaux's Connexion, at the year 70 before the Christian era. Before we proceed further, we must take notice, that Josephus, in his War of the Jews, B. I. ch. iii. sect. 1, tells us that Aristobulus first put a diadem on his head 471 years after the return from the captivity, which was in the first of Cyrus. In Freculphus's citation the number is 475, and in Antiq. B. XIII. ch. xi. sect. 1, 481 years. The number 471 seems nearest the truth, and by that the other are to be corrected. Now this number is thus to be made out from Josephus, very nearly.

Years.

From the first of Cyrus to the era of Seleucus, as before . . . 264
Thence to the government of the Maccabees, as before . . . 148
Thence to Simon the high priest, in the 170th year of Seleucus, Of the War, B. I. ch.
    ii. sect. 2; Antiq. B. XIII. ch. vi. sect. 5; 1 Macc. xiii. 41 . . . 22
The duration of Simon's high priesthood, Antiq. B. XX. ch. x. . . . 8
The duration of John Hyrcanus's high priesthood and reign 30, or 31, or 33 years, Of
    the War, B. I. ch. ii. sect. 8; Antiq. B. XX. ch. x., or rather, as will appear here-
    after, no more than 29

                                      Sum 471

But now, before we proceed to the next period, it may not be improper to confirm some part of this last, and of a former branch of Josephus's chronology, by a remarkable passage in the same Josephus, Antiq. B. XIII. ch. iii. sect. 1, where he informs us that Onias, the banished high priest of the Jews, about the 149th year before the Christian era, and the 32nd of Ptolemy Philometor, king of Egypt, desired leave of this Ptolemy to build a temple to the God of the Jews in Egypt; he alleging that such a temple had been foretold to be built in that country *above* 600 *years* before, by the prophet Isaiah, chap. xix. 18, 19; and this temple was now built accordingly. Add 600 years to the 149th year before the Christian era, the sum is the 749th year before the same era; *before* which time that prophecy must therefore have been delivered in Josephus's chronology. Now as that has been already stated, this year 749 falls about the latter end of the reign of Hezekiah; which is the last reign in which Isaiah prophesied, chap. i. 1. Though indeed by my own determination that prophecy was delivered in the 14th of Hezekiah, anno 714, or 35 years after that year 749, Authent. Rec. Part II. p. 755. So much does my chronology here differ from that of Josephus; which is no wonder, if the reader considers that I have corrected from Ptolemy's Canon those 38 or 39 years by which Josephus had unjustly enlarged the Persian monarchy, as I have very lately observed. Nor will it be improper to mention another small attestation to our chronology of Josephus, which is taken from Book II. against Apion, sect. 11, where Josephus asserts, that the Jews had not only their own liberty, but some authority and dominion over other nations for 120 years before Pompey came and subdued them. Now Hyrcanus, the son of Joseph, and grandson of Tobias, about anno 183 or 182, set up a small principality beyond Jordan, and kept it 7 years; soon after which the Asamoneans or Maccabees set up their government, which lasted free till the coming of Pompey, anno 63, for 120 years.

29. The *fifth* and *last* part of the foregoing period, 107 *years from the death of Antigonus to the destruction of the temple* in the second of Vespasian, A. D. 70, is the express reckoning of Josephus himself in the most accurate scheme of his chronology, Antiq. B. XX. ch. x. It is true that,

Antiq. B. XIV. ch. vi. sect. 4, Josephus, in all his copies, and as he is cited in Syncellus, as from Eusebius, says that 27 years were interposed after Jerusalem was taken by Pompey, till it was taken by Sosius and Herod; or that it was taken on the very same day of the year after 27 years. Whereas our present account of Josephus's chronology allows no more than 26 complete years for that interval. Whether this error of one year be a mistake of Josephus's own, or owing to his transcribers, I cannot tell. In the mean time, I own it to be a mistake, though a very small one, and of no great consequence, as to our present general determination of Josephus's chronology. It is true also that there is, Antiq. B. XIV. ch. ix. sect. 2, a seeming strange assertion, that Herod, when he was *very young*, or a youth of 15 *years of age*, was made governor of Galilee. But then the entire series of his reign in Josephus requiring it to be 25 years instead of 15; and it being usual in those days to say persons were *young, very young*, at 25 years of age and more; and there being many other chronological characters in the reign of Herod which demonstrate he was about 25 years old at that time, as will fully appear in the notes; I conclude that this is only an error of transcribers, and is no way to be imputed to Josephus.

30. It will be now proper to sum up the several numbers prefixed at the beginning of the several twenty books of the Antiquities, and to compare them with the numbers already determined.

The reader is here to take notice, that the particular numbers set down in this index are the same that Josephus's present copies afford us; excepting the first, 3833, which has been demonstrated not to be Josephus's own number, but rather the second, 2733; see sect. 1, 2; which is therefore summed up with the rest. Whether these numbers were placed at the beginning of every book by Josephus himself, or by some late author or transcriber, I cannot certainly tell. They differ so little from Josephus's own numbers, excepting the first already corrected, that I do not see but they might be his own doing; the small differences in that case arising, either from some difference of opinion at different times of Josephus's life, or from some errors of the scribes, or from both. There is also some small difference in the numbers in the old Latin version from these in our Greek copies. But since Dr. Wills informs us that the sum of the ten last books in that version differs from those in our Greek copies but 3 years and 5 months, that difference seems very inconsiderable also.

Book					
I.	3833	.	.	.	[2733]
II.	.	.	.	.	220
III.	.	.	.	.	2
IV.	.	.	.	.	38
V.	.	.	.	.	476
VI.	.	.	.	.	32
VII.	.	.	.	.	40
VIII.	.	.	.	.	163
IX.	.	.	.	.	157
X.	.	.	.	.	182½
XI.	.	.	.	.	253½
XII.	.	.	.	.	170
XIII.	.	.	.	.	82
XIV.	.	.	.	.	32
XV.	.	.	.	.	18
XVI.	.	.	.	.	12
XVII.	.	.	.	.	14
XVIII.	.	.	.	.	32
XIX.	.	.	.	.	3½
XX.	.	.	.	.	22

From the twelfth of Nero, A. D. 66, where the twentieth book ends, to the second of Vespasian, A. D. 70, when Jerusalem was destroyed . . } 4

Sum 4686½

Thence to the thirteenth of Domitian, A. D. 93, when Josephus finished his Antiquities . . . } 23

Sum 4709½

Take 4709½ from 4751, the difference is 41½. Take the same 4709½ from 4767, the difference is 56½. See sect. 9 before.

31. Some other numbers there are in Josephus's present copies, and that both in the series of the chronology, and in occasional computations, which are too gross mistakes to be supposed owing to himself.

Thus, Antiq. B. VI. ch. xiii. sect. 5, and ch. xiv. sect. 9, Josephus informs us that Saul reigned 18 years during the life of Samuel, and, as the Greek copies add, 22 years after his death; which together make 40 years, that is indeed the number St. Paul ascribes to him also, in all Dr. Wills's copies and versions, excepting the Arabic version, which omits the number entirely, Acts xiii. 21. Yet does the old Latin version of Josephus give us here only 2 years, instead of 20; and, in agreement thereto, Josephus gives him, in another place, but 20 years in all, and that expressly, Antiq. B. X. ch. viii. sect. 4; as, most probably from him, does Theophilus of Antioch, Ad Autol. III. p. 135. Which two years

only, after the death of Samuel, best agrees with 1 Sam. xiii. 1, where he is directly said to have reigned but 2 *years over Israel*. Perhaps the words *after the death of Samuel* are wanting; though the rest of the text being corrupted in the Hebrew, and omitted both in the Septuagint and Josephus, and Samuel being then alive himself, I cannot depend on that testimony. See my note on Antiq. B. VI. ch. vi. sect. 1. However, the same 2 years and no more after the death of Samuel entirely agree to the number at the beginning of the book, 32 years for Samuel and Saul, after the victory of Eben-Ezer, and best of all agrees to the series of the history and the few things related of Saul and Samuel's death in all the copies, and contained in the five last chapters of the First Book of Samuel. Clement of Alexandria, Strom. I. p. 325, confirms the same 2 years only; and that, probably, as taken from the ancient copies of Josephus. Nor can we any way confine this whole period within the known 480 years, if Saul be allowed 40 of them. The prediction also of God by Samuel, 1 Sam. xiii. 13, 14, and Jos. Antiq. B. VI. ch. vi. sect. 2, that Saul's kingdom upon his disobedience *should not continue*, seems to forbid us to ascribe to him so many as 22 years after the death of Samuel. So this error of the 40 years' reign of Saul is to be ascribed to later transcribers, correctors, or corrupters of Josephus, and to them only.

Thus we have already hinted, sect. 16, before, at another error in the present copies of Josephus, Antiq. B. VIII. ch. iii. sect. 1, of 1440 years only, from the deluge to the building of Solomon's temple, instead of 1989. We have also another error in the same place, that from Adam to the building of the temple were 3102 years only, instead of 3545.

Thus, Antiq. B. IX. ch. xiv. sect. 1, we have, from Joshua to the captivity of the ten tribes, 800 years, instead of 907.

Thus, Antiq. B. X. ch. viii. sect. 5, we have 1950, or rather, as in some copies, 1957 years, instead of 2450, or rather 2457, from the deluge to the conflagration of the temple by Nebuchadnezzar. As also we have, in the same place, 3513 years, instead of 4013, from the creation of Adam till the same conflagration, and both just 500 years too little, as has been already noted, sect. 10, before. Those therefore must not be Josephus's own numbers, but owing to correctors or transcribers; which is here peculiarly very evident, because the two other numbers in the same place, 470 years from the building of the temple, and 1062 years from the Exodus out of Egypt, and both to the same conflagration; are evidently right, or according to Josephus's mind, and yet entirely inconsistent with the two foregoing numbers.

Thus also, Antiq. B. VII. at the end, we have, in our present copies, 1300 years from David's burial to Hyrcanus's opening his sepulchre; and so Freculphus read this number in the ninth century.

And yet Josephus's own larger chronology will allow no more than 980, or at most, in a round number, 1000 years.

These, and perhaps some few other numbers which I may have overlooked, seem to me too grossly erroneous, and too contrary to the known chronology of Josephus, to be supposed derived from himself; and accordingly I ascribe them all to the transcribers, correctors, or corrupters since his time.

32. However, there are many numbers which are discovered not to be exactly right, where yet the mistakes are so small, or so agreeable to Josephus's ways of writing his chronology, in one part or other of his life, that it is no way impossible but several of them at least might be owing to Josephus himself, either for want of accuracy in some books or copies he made use of, or by failure of memory, or by inattention or haste in writing, such as the best authors are sometimes subject to in things of such great difficulty. I shall give a few chronological instances out of his latter writings, his Antiquities, and his first book against Apion; with not a few both chronological and historical errors out of his first writings, I mean his two former books of the Jewish War. The notes in Havercamp's edition generally mention them.

(1.) Thus, Antiq. B. IX. ch. xiv. sect. 1, we have 947 years from Joshua to the captivity of the ten tribes by Salmanassar. This is too much. But if instead of Joshua we take the Exodus out of Egypt, which was also in the days of Joshua, and is one of Josephus's most common epochas, till the captivity of the ten tribes, and this by Josephus's last corrected numbers, they will be 612+[750] 76+260=[947 or] 948, which is either the same, or so near the number 947, that it is very probable Josephus himself made the mistake, and that this date, as from Joshua, was owing to his inattention only.

(2.) Thus in the same place we have but 240 years from the defection under Jeroboam to the captivity of the ten tribes; which was rather by Josephus's own chronology, as appears above, and as I have just now taken for granted, 260 years. This smaller number 240, as I have already noted, sect. 20, 21, above, is the just sum of the reigns of the kings of Israel, beginning with Jeroboam, till that captivity of the ten tribes, without the consideration of any connexion with the kings of Judah; which shows the necessity of allowing two *interregna*, or somewhat equivalent thereto, of 20 years, which may supply the 20 years wanting in this period. So that I suspect this *inaccuracy* or *overmuch accuracy*, the reader may call it which he pleases, was not owing to transcribers or correctors, but to Josephus himself.

(3.) Thus in his first book against Apion, sect. 19, we have a famous quotation out of Berosus; which we have also in his Antiquities, B. X. ch. xi. sect. 1. In the place last mentioned Naboco-

lassar, or rather Nabopolassar, the father of the great Nabocolassar, or Nebuchadnezzar, is said to have reigned ἔτη εἴκοσι ἐν, or 21 years. In the other ἔτη εἴκοσι εννέα, or 29 years. The number 21 is that in Ptolemy's Canon; and therefore is to be supposed the true number, and the other 29 false. But whether Josephus himself, or the transcribers, only mistook the Greek words, which are very much alike, I do not know.

(4.) Thus in the first book of the Jewish War, Procœme, sect. 7, and B. I. ch. i. sect. 1, and B. V. ch. ix. sect. 4, Josephus thrice ascribes 3½ *years* to the profanation of the temple by Antiochus Epiphanes; while yet, in his Antiquities, B. X. ch. xi. sect. 7 once, and B. XII. ch. vii. sect. 6 *twice*, he honestly owns that it was but 3 *years;* which last we know to be true from the original historians, the authors of the two books of the Maccabees, 1 Macc. i. 54, 59, with iv. 52, and 2 Macc. x. 3, 5. See the Six Dissertations, p. 131, 132.

(5.) Thus, in the same B. I. ch. i. sect. 1, Josephus ascribes the beginning of the Jewish apostacy to Onias the high priest; whereas it appears by his Antiquities, B. XII. ch. v. sect. 1, and by 2 Macc. iv. 7, &c., that it was Jason, the brother of Onias, who was the cause of that apostacy.

(6.) Thus both in the Procœme, sect. 7, and in the B. I. ch. i. sect. 2, 5, Josephus says that Antiochus took Jerusalem κατὰ κράτος, *by force;* and so says the author of the Second Book of Maccabees, ch. v. 11. But the same Josephus, in his Antiquities, B. XII. ch. v. sect. 2, says that it was taken ἀμαχητὶ, *without fighting.*

(7.) Thus, B. I. ch. i. sect. 2, Josephus says Bacchides was sent to oppress and tyrannize over the Jews by Antiochus; whereas it appears to have been not Bacchides, but Apelles, Antiq. B. XII. ch. vi. sect. 1, 2.

(8.) Thus, B. I. ch. i. sect. 3, Mattathias is called the *son* of Asamoneus; whereas we are informed, Antiq. B. XII. ch. vi. sect. 1, that he was his *great grandson.*

(9.) Thus, B. I. ch. i. sect. 4, Josephus places the first league of Judas Maccabeus with the Romans in the lifetime of Antiochus Epiphanes; whereas we learn from Antiq. B. XII. ch. x. sect. 6, that it was after the death of Epiphanes, and of his son Eupator; and from 1 Macc. viii., that it was at least after the death of Epiphanes.

(10.) Thus, B. I. ch. i. sect. 5, we meet with the number of Eupator's army to be 50,000 footmen; but in the Antiquities, B. XII. ch. viii. sect. 3, 100,000, as 1 Macc. vi. 30; and in 2 Macc. xi. 2, they are no fewer than 80,000; to say nothing of the other variations.

(11.) Thus, B. I. ch. i. sect. 6, we have an account of a battle fought by Judas with the generals of Eupator at Akedosa or Adasa, in which Judas was slain. Whereas that battle was fought with the commanders of Demetrius Soter. Nor was Judas slain in this battle, but long afterward. All which we learn from the Antiquities, B. XII. ch. x. sect. 5, and from 1 Macc. vii. 40—50, and from 2 Macc. xv. 36.

(12.) Thus, B. I. ch. ii. sect. 7, the surname of an Antiochus there mentioned is Aspendius; while we learn from the Antiquities, B. XIII. ch. x. sect. 1, and otherwise, that it was not Aspendius, but Cyzicenus. The late editors have ventured to put this last into the text here, without any copy to support them; which procedure I dare not imitate in my translation.

(13.) Thus, B. I. ch. ii. sect. 8, Josephus gives to John Hyrcanus's high priesthood 33 *entire years;* whereas in his Antiquities, B. XIII. ch. i. sect. 1, and B. XX. ch. x., he never gives him more than 31. Nay, Eusebius, Demonst. VIII. 11, and Jerome on Dan. ix., assign him but 29; and both most probably had that number from their ancient copies of Josephus. Nor will the rest of Josephus's and the Maccabees' chronology about this time at all admit of these 33 years; nay, hardly of 31.

(14.) Thus, B. I. ch. iv. sect. 5, Josephus reckons up king Alexander's army at 1000 horse, with auxiliaries and foot 8000, and Jews particularly come to his assistance 10,000; whereas in his Antiquities, B. XIII. ch. xiv. sect. 1, he reckons the auxiliaries to be 6200, and the additional Jews about 20,000.

(15.) Thus, B. I. ch. viii. sect. 2, we have Gabinius sent, as the successor of Scaurus, into Syria: whereas there were two between them, Philip and Lentulus; though they both continued so little a while in their governments, but 2 years in all, that some others, as well as Josephus, seem to have known nothing of them. Accordingly, this mistake is not corrected in the parallel place of the Antiquities, B. XIV. ch. v. sect. 2.

(16.) Thus, B. I. ch. viii. sect. 9, Josephus promises that he would elsewhere speak of Cassius's expedition against the Parthians; but never does it. In the Antiquities he only says, B. XIV. ch. vii. sect. 3, " As others have related." Nor indeed are several more of Josephus's passages referred to by himself in his other writings found in his present copies; as will appear in the note on Antiq. B. XII. ch. v. sect. 2. See there my conjecture about them.

(17.) Thus, B. I. ch. ix. sect. 4, Josephus reckons that Antipater lost 80 men in an action, while in his Antiquities, B. XIV. ch. viii. sect. 2, he informs us they were no more than 50.

(18.) Thus, B. I. ch. x. sect. 8, Josephus says that Herod thought he escaped punishment against king Hyrcanus's consent; yet does the same Herod own, in the Antiquities, B. XIV. ch. ix. sect. 4, 5, that Hyrcanus was the cause of that his escape.

(19.) Thus, B. I. ch. xiii. sect. 6, Josephus calls the famous Mariamne the daughter of Hyrcanus; whereas it appears evidently in the Antiquities, in many places, that Alexandra her mother was the daughter, and she herself the grand-daughter, of Hyrcanus. But because in this very Book, ch. xxii. sect. 1, 2, and ch. xxvi. sect. 2, Hyrcanus is styled her grandfather, and she his grand-daughter, the former may be only a false reading.

(20.) Thus, B. I. ch. xvii. sect. 5, Josephus describes the station of a camp as at Cana [in Galilee]; whereas in his Antiquities, B. XIV. ch. xv. sect. 2, 12, it was at Isana [in Samaria]. Though this may be merely the mistake of transcribers, from the nearness of the sound and writing of the two places.

(21.) Thus, B. I. ch. xvii. sect. 7, the circumstances of Herod's escape at the bath are some small matter different from those in the Antiquities. Here Herod is not yet gotten into the house wherein was the bath; and several other soldiers are said to pass by him, besides the three distinctly mentioned. Whereas, in the Antiquities, B. XIV. ch. xv. sect. 13, Herod was actually in the house; and no more soldiers than those three are mentioned to have passed by him.

(22.) Thus, B. I. ch. xviii. sect. 5, Josephus informs us that Antony made war with the Parthians, and made a present of Artabazes, the son of Tigranes, the Parthian, to Cleopatra: whereas Tigranes and Artabazes were not Parthians, but Armenians; and in the Antiquities, B. XV. ch. iv. sect. 3, this war was made against the Armenians, and so also is this history in Moses Chorenensis, p. 121.

(23.) Thus, B. I. ch. xix. sect. 3, the number of people destroyed in Judea by an earthquake is 30,000; but in the Antiquities they are no more than 10,000, though it must be taken notice of that some copies have there also 30,000.

(24.) Thus, B. I. ch. xxi. sect. 1, Josephus informs us that Herod rebuilt the temple in the 15th year of his reign [from the conquest or death of Antigonus]; whereas it is most evident from the Antiquities, B. XV. ch. xi. sect. 1, that it was not *begun* till his 18th year, from the same date. Of which matter see more, Chronol. of the Old Testament, p. 144.

(26.) Thus, B. I. ch. xxii. sect. 3, Josephus speaks of the slaughter of Lysanias and of Malichus by Herod. This slaughter of Lysanias is confirmed in the Antiquities, B. XV. ch. iv. sect. 1, as also by Dio, XLIX. p. 411. That of Malichus, (which indeed he had related before, ch. xviii. 4, as sought for and put upon Herod,) by Cleopatra, is neither related in the Antiquities nor by Dio; nor by any other, that Dean Aldrich can remember.

(27.) Thus, B. I. ch. xxii. sect. 5, our Josephus writes as if Joseph and Mariamne were slain immediately after Herod's return from Antony; whereas it appears by the Antiquities, B. XV. ch. iii. sect. 9, that Josephus was indeed slain immediately, but Mariamne not till [about a year] afterward.

(28.) Thus, B. I. ch. xxvi. sect. 3, Josephus informs us that some persons who were tormented, in order to extort a confession about treasonable practices in Herod's sons, Alexander and Aristobulus, against him, confessed nothing of what they were accused; whereas in the same history in the Antiquities, B. XVI. ch. x. sect. 4, he relates their confession of several such practices.

(29.) Thus, B. I. ch. xxvii. sect. 2, 3, we have but *two* of Saturninus's legates mentioned; but, Antiq. B. XVI. ch. xi. sect. 3, we have mention of *three* of them.

33. (30.) Thus, B. II. ch. vi. sect. 3, Josephus states the yearly revenues of Judea at 400 talents, and of Galilee and Perea at 200, and of the tetrarchy of Philip at 100 talents; which yet is much under the sum implied in the Antiquities, B. XVII. ch. xi. sect. 4. See the note there.

(31.) Thus, in the same place, Josephus says that Herod, by his will, gave Archelaus a territory that brought him in 400 talents per annum; which in the Antiquities, B. XVII. ch. xiii. sect. 4, are 600 talents.

(32.) Thus, in the same place, he also reckons up certain cities as added to Herod's gift to Salome his sister by Cæsar; whereas in the Antiquities, B. XVII. ch. viii. sect. 1, and ch. xiii. sect. 4, they are part of Herod's own gift to her, and only confirmed by Cæsar.

(33.) He also adds presently, that Cæsar bequeathed to two of Herod's virgin daughters what Herod had left him, being 1000 talents; whereas in the Antiquities, B. XVII. ch. xiii. sect. 5, that sum is 1500 talents.

(34.) Thus, B. II. ch. vii. sect. 3, Josephus informs us of a dream that Archelaus had, a little before he was banished, relating to nine ears of corn, that foreboded nine years of his reign, and no more: whereas in his Antiquities, B. XVII. ch. xiii. sect. 3, he reckons ten ears of corn, that foreboded ten years of his reign, before he was to be banished. Which last number is fully confirmed from Josephus's own family records; whence he assures us that his own father was born on that tenth year of Archelaus, Of his own Life, sect. 1; though indeed it appears very plain that Archelaus reigned but a part of that tenth year.

(35.) Thus, B. II. ch. ix. sect. 4, Josephus says that Pilate brought water to Jerusalem from the distance of 400 furlongs; but in the Antiquities, B. XVIII. ch. iii. sect. 2, from only 200 furlongs, which is much the most probable.

(36.) Thus, B. II. ch. ix. sect. 5, Agrippa is said to have gone to Tiberius, and to have accused Herod Antipas, *about the time* when Pilate had murdered a great number of the Jews; whereas it appears by the Antiquities, B. XVIII. ch. iv. sect. 8, that this accusation was full eight years afterward.

(37.) Thus, in the same section, Josephus says that the dangerous words of Agrippa, for which he was imprisoned by Tiberius, were spoken at a feast; whereas he assures us in his Antiquities, B. XVIII. ch. vii. sect. 4, they were spoken in a chariot.

(38.) Thus, in the same section, Josephus says that Tiberius reigned 22 years, 6 months, 3 days; whereas in his Antiquities, B. XVIII. ch. vi. sect. 10, the number is 22 years, 5 months, 3 days; but as in Zonaras, supposed to be cited from Josephus, 22 years, 7 months, 7 days, which being the very same that is in Dio, is probably the true number, and Josephus's original number also.

(39.) Thus, B. II. ch. ix. sect. 6, Josephus says that Herod Antipas was banished into Spain; but in his Antiquities, B. XVIII. ch. vii. sect. 2, that it was to Lyons in Gaul: which best agrees with the testimony of Strabo, who says he was banished *to the Allobroges*, Lib. XV. p. 765; and of Dio, who says only he was banished *beyond the Alps*, Lib. LV. p. 649.

(40.) Thus, B. II. ch. xi. sect. 1, Josephus says the cohorts that staid with the senate were but *three;* but in the Antiquities, B. XIX. ch. ii. sect. 3, he tells us they were *four*.

(41.) Thus, B. II. ch. xii. sect. 5, Josephus says, that in a battle with Eleazar, Cumanus took *many* prisoners, but slew *more;* whereas in the Antiquities, B. XX. ch. v. sect. 1, he says the direct contrary, that he slew *many*, but took *more* prisoners.

(42.) Thus, B. II. ch. xii. sect. 6, he tells us that Quadratus came to execute justice on some rebellious Jews and Samaritans to Cesarea; whereas the Antiquities, B. XX. ch. v. sect. 2, say that he came to Samaria.

(43.) Thus, B. II. ch. xiii. sect. 5, Josephus makes those rebels who followed that Egyptian impostor, who is also mentioned Acts xxi. 38, to have been in number 30,000, while St. Luke, who then lived, mentions only 4000. Accordingly Josephus, Antiq. B. XX. ch. viii. sect. 6, agrees well with St. Luke; for as he there says nothing of so great a number as 30,000, so he says that the number slain by Felix, when he subdued them, was no more than 400, and 200 taken prisoners. These smaller numbers much better agree to 4000 than to the 30,000.

(44.) Thus, B. II. ch. xx. sect. 5, Josephus takes no notice of the two other priests, Joazar and Judas, which were for some time joined with him in the government of Galilee; whom yet he distinctly mentions in his Life, sect. 7, &c., long afterwards.

(45.) Thus, B. II. ch. xxi. sect. 3, Josephus says that, in a great distress he was in at Tarichea, all his friends and guards left him but *four;* whereas in his Life, sect. 28, he assures us they all left him but *one*, whose name was Simon.

(46.) Thus, B. II. ch. xxi. sect. 7, Josephus says, that when he once came to Tiberias, his great enemy John of Giscala pretended to be sick, and so staid at home, when the rest came to salute him; whereas long afterward, in his Life, sect. 17, he acknowledges that John did come with the rest, and salute him, though after an awkward manner.

(47.) Thus, B. IV. ch. ix. sect. 7, Josephus says that Chebron or Hebron in Palestine was older than Memphis in Egypt ; whereas in all our other copies, Numb. xiii. 22, and in the Antiquities, B. I. ch. viii. sect. 3, it was Zoan or Tanis, and not Memphis, that was built at that time. It is probable that Chebron, the second king of Tanis or Zoan, in my chronological catalogue of them, taken out of Manetho, was the founder of this Palestine city Chebron, or Hebron, in the south of that country nearest to Egypt, and gave it his own name also. See Dissert. IV. sect. 13.

(48.) Thus, B. V. ch. v. sect. 1, in a speech of Josephus's own to the Jews, he says, that when Abraham went to deliver Lot from captivity, with his 'three hundred and eighteen servants, those servants were captains, and had an *immense number* of soldiers under them. But when he afterward came to that history in his Antiquities, he more truly observes, that Abraham demonstrated how much the alacrity and courage of soldiers in war is beyond their number and multitude, by conquering so great an army as was that of the four Assyrian kings, with his three hundred and eighteen servants, and three of his friends ; which reasoning entirely supposes they were all single persons, and not captains of regiments, contrary to his former determination. See another error in this section corrected in the note upon it.

(49.) Thus, B. VI. ch. iv. sect. 8, we have the interval, from the building of Solomon's temple to its destruction by Titus, 1130 years instead of 1180, from the Antiquities. See sect. 15 and 20, as before. As also, from the building of the second temple, in the second year of Cyrus, by Haggai, till the same destruction, 639 instead of 643 years. Wherein there seem to be two more mistakes also : I mean the supposal that the temple was built in the second of Cyrus, which was indeed the second of Darius : and that other supposal, that Haggai built it in that second of Cyrus ; whereas Haggai was only a prophet, that encouraged Zorobabel and Jeshua in building it ; and this not at the second of Cyrus, but of Darius, as all our copies, and Josephus himself among the rest in his Antiquities, inform us. These are complicated errors, and such

as Josephus does not use to be guilty of in his Antiquities.

(50.) Thus, B. VII. ch. x. sect. 2, Onias III., the high priest who built the temple Onion in Egypt, is called the *son of Simon ;* whereas, Antiq. B. XIII. ch. iii. sect. 1, he more truly says he was the *son of Onias.* See the note on B. XII. ch. v. sect. 1.

(51.) Thus, lastly, in the same place, we have the duration of that temple determined to 343 years ; which ought, by Josephus's own accounts, to be rather 223, for it was built about the 32nd year of Philometor, or anno 149, and was destroyed not long after the destruction of Jerusalem, about A. D. 74. See Dr. Prideaux, Connect. at anno 149.

N. B. I do not here speak particularly of Josephus's chronology under Jehoiakim, Jehoiachin, and Zedekiah, with the 70 years' duration of the captivity of the two tribes till the first of Cyrus. Josephus seems here to have been not a little perplexed ; and to suppose that Daniel was carried captive in the days of Zedekiah, and not of Jehoiakim ; that Ezekiel was carried captive under Jehoiakim, and not Jehoiachin ; and that the temple was burnt in the 11th of Zedekiah, instead of the beginning of his 12th year ; and this in the 18th of Nebuchadnezzar, instead of the 19th, as our other copies inform us. In short, for want of the Astronomical Canon, and for want of observing that Nebuchadnezzar's reign began in Judea $2\frac{1}{2}$ years before his father died in Babylon, whence that Canon dates the son's reign ; and because he sometimes thought 70 years might be counted from the burning of the temple under Zedekiah, and yet reach no further than the first of Cyrus, and the like errors, some of them almost unavoidable at that time, and in that country ; I have therefore not altered any thing in my former chronology of the Old Testament with relation to these times : it appearing to me that our other copies of the sacred books, when compared with the Astronomical Canon, and with Xenophon's Cyropædia, two inestimable records for those times, but neither of them seen by Josephus, give us a much more accurate chronology here than can be discovered in Josephus's history.

N. B. There are certain odd months and days noted by Josephus which have not been hitherto mentioned, as follows :

	years.	mon.	days.	
Thus we have	240	7	7	From the beginning of Jeroboam to the captivity of the ten tribes, Antiq. B. IX. ch. xiv. sect. 1.
	514	6	10	From the beginning of Saul to the end of Zedekiah, Antiq. B. X. ch. viii. sect. 4.
	470	6	10	From the building to the burning of the temple, Antiq. B. X. ch. viii. sect. 5.
	1062	6	10	From the Exodus to the burning of that temple, ibid.
	3513	6	10	From the creation of Adam to the burning of the temple, ibid.
	466	6	10	The duration of the high priests before the Babylonish captivity, Antiq. B. XX. ch. 10.
	468	6	0	From the building of Solomon's temple till the burning of it by Titus, Of the War, B. VI. ch. x. sect. 6.
	467	6	0	From David's [Solomon's] building Jerusalem [the temple] till it was overthrown by the Babylonians, ibid.

Not one of which numbers, either of months or days, can, I think, be made out by what he has preserved to us of the dates hereto belonging: those dates also that he has preserved generally disagree to such a pretended accuracy. So that Josephus can hardly be supposed the author of such niceties, unless the transcribers or correctors have grossly disguised the numbers originally written by him. Only the three last numbers seem to mean the very same interval, though a little mistaken either by Josephus himself, or by his transcribers, as the reader will easily remark upon comparing them together.

34. N. B. The foregoing 51 are the principal examples of such mistakes in Josephus's present copies, as seem to me generally to be his own real mistakes, and not owing to his transcribers or correctors; and the reader will readily observe, that they are chiefly confined to the two first books of the Jewish War, belonging to older times, and written when he was comparatively but a young man, under thirty-eight years of age, when he had read comparatively but a few books, and those not always the most authentic; when in particular he appears never to have seen either the First Book of Maccabees, or the following Chronicle of John Hyrcanus, 1 Macc. xvi. 23, 24, both written in Hebrew, and both the authentic originals, whence he ought to have drawn the principal facts he was to relate; and which, accordingly, he closely followed, and carefully abridged, when, many years afterward, he wrote his Antiquities. As for the five books of Jason of Cyrene, or their abridgement, the Second Book of Maccabees, which were written in Greek, he seems never to have seen them at all. To be sure he has made little or no use of them. Nor is the comparative inaccuracy of Josephus's history in these first parts of his writings to be denied. Nor was he himself afterward insensible of it, when, in his Antiquities, B. XII. ch. v. sect. 2, he begins the history of Antiochus Epiphanes, with whose history his first book Of the War had also begun, after this manner: " I will now relate distinctly," says Josephus, " what concerns this king; and how he seized upon Judea and the temple. For when I formerly wrote that history, I mentioned the facts only by way of epitome. Wherefore I think it necessary now to go over that history again, and this after an accurate manner." And greatly does it tend to the honour of Josephus, that he was so willing in his *latter* works to correct the errors of his *former*, as he appears frequently to have done, though his commentators do hardly ever take notice of it; but instead thereof frequently puzzle and perplex themselves, though generally to little purpose, in *reconciling* such passages in his following works to the parallel ones in his first; while they ought rather to have acknowledged them to be not seldom plainly *irreconcilable*, and to have taken particular notice of the later passages as no other than honest *emendations* of the former. Nor is it any wonder at all that the Antiquities, published, as I said, about 18 years after the books of the Jewish War, and his account of his own Life, which was an appendix to them, together with two books against Apion, which I think were written still later, should be more authentic and more accurate than the earliest of all his writings, the first and second book of the Jewish War. For the reader is to take special notice, that no further does this great inaccuracy extend; the rest of the history of that war generally belonging to his own times, and being derived from the most undeniable evidence, what his own eyes saw, or his own ears heard; or from the original information of those whose eyes saw or ears heard what he relates to us. And thus far concerning Josephus's Jewish chronology, as it was faithfully taken by him from the known Hebrew records of that nation.

35. But then we must take notice further, what has not, that I remember, been distinctly taken notice of by any hitherto, that Josephus, in his former book against Apion, sect. 14—16, 26, 31, has another different system of ancient chronology, relating, as he thought, to the Jews also; and this taken from Manetho, the great Egyptian chronologer and historian, and his accounts of the Phœnician shepherds; those *Hic-Sos*, which Josephus assures us signified either *shepherd kings*, or *shepherd captives;* and which he understood to have been the children of Israel, who came from Phœnicia or Canaan, and were, for certain, by occupation shepherds, when they dwelt in Egypt, from the days of Jacob till the days of Moses; under which Moses Manetho himself confesses the Israelites departed out of Egypt. But by Manetho's chronology these Phœnician shepherds, which had for many years oppressed and tyrannized over the natural Egyptians, went away out of the country, no fewer than 393 years before Danaus came to Argos, and 518 years before Amenophis, the uncertain king of Egypt, in the same Manetho; and so, in Josephus's opinion, near 1000 years before the Trojan war. Which departure of the Phœnician shepherds happened, in the sacred chronology, even as stated by Josephus himself, considerably before Jacob and the patriarchs his sons came into Egypt. See my chronological table. This Egyptian chronology however Josephus follows in his books against Apion, where he debates matters with the Greeks, who despised the Jews and their sacred books, and would by no means allow them even that less considerable antiquity which Josephus laid claim to from the sacred writings. And if Josephus's notion, that these old Phœnician shepherds in Egypt were the Israelites, could have been supported, his argument for their so great antiquity had been, as to Manetho and his heathen followers, perfectly undeniable. However, Josephus seems to have

thought they were so, and was the proper occasion that the ancientest Christian chronologers thought so also, till the great Eusebius corrected that grossest of all Josephus's mistakes, and demonstrated that the abode of the Israelites in Egypt was long after the expulsion of those shepherds out of that country, as the very learned Bp. Cumberland has fully settled that antiquity of the Phœnician shepherds in his Sanchoniatho, Lib. II. sect. 3, 4, p. 350—415: see also Marsham's Chronicon, p. 6, 98—104, 134, 135. Nor is this large chronology peculiar to Josephus, in his debates with Manetho, in the former of these two books, styled the books against Apion, but in the debates with Apion himself, and Lysimachus, &c., in the latter book; where, in sect. 2, he affirms, that from Bocchoris, who was burnt alive by *Sabachon the cruel*, king of Egypt, to his own time, were no fewer than 1700 years, which very long interval can no way be made out but on the foot of this Egyptian chronology: see Authent. Rec. vol. II. p. 970. When therefore we remember with what writers Josephus had to do in these his latest books, and what seems to have been his own opinion concerning these Phœnician shepherds; as also that Josephus's proper business was to make the fathers of the Jews as ancient as he could, in opposition to such as would not admit them to be of any considerable antiquity at all; we are not much to wonder that he reasons there, not from the Jewish records, which they denied, but from those Egyptian records, which they could not deny; and this while he had before, from the Jewish chronology, stated the interval from Moses to his own age at almost 1900, and in a round number had called it several times 2000 years, as we have already seen; I say we are not much to wonder that he now advanced it, according to that Egyptian chronology, as he understood it, to *above* 2000 years, Contr. Apion, B. II. sect. 31, as it is also cited in Eusebius's Præp. Evang. VIII. 8. p. 369.

36. This observation affords us a very proper occasion to enter into the very secrets of Josephus's heart in writing the history of the Jewish War, his Antiquities, and other works, *viz.* That he did not so much undertake to *reconcile* ancient chronological and historical accounts of the world, and particularly of their nation; or to make *hypotheses* of his own for their adjustment, which the moderns perpetually do; as to produce fairly and candidly the ancient accounts themselves, whether those of his own or those of other nations, and honestly leave them to the judgment of unprejudiced readers. I mean this in particular cases, where such accounts seemed to contradict one another. For where those accounts agreed, as, for the main, they usually did, he most frequently observes such their agreement, and thereby strongly confirms the Jewish chronology and history upon all occasions. But that Josephus thought himself obliged to that uncommon

degree of fidelity in ancient authors, sacred as well as profane, he several times assures us, and protests that he neither *added to* nor *took from* them. See Essay on the Old Testament, p. 190—195, and Antiq. B. VIII. ch. ii. sect. 8. I mean in any other sense than an *epitome*, written for the use of foreigners, and designed for their approbation and instruction, must omit some, and embellish other histories after a more polite manner than the ancient brevity of the Hebrew language, and the simplicity of the ancient Hebrew composition, presented them to him in their originals. This appears to be true, not only by those his affirmations, but by the general process of his accounts also. And this exact fidelity I take to be the distinguishing character of Josephus, perhaps beyond that of almost any other but the sacred historians themselves. See Dissertat. IV. sect. 28. Thus we find him *twice* setting down the 400 *years* foretold for the affliction of Abraham's posterity in Egypt, from Gen. xv. 13, Antiq. B. I. ch. x. sect. 3, and B. II. ch. ix. sect. 1. Although he seems no more able to reconcile his copy there to other texts of Scripture, which plainly imply that the Israelites were in Egypt but 215 years, as Josephus also believed, Antiq. B. II. ch. xv. sect. 2, and were not in affliction there near one half of that time neither, than we are to reconcile ours at this day. [The word *until* 400 *years* would set all right; it being indeed but 405 years from the birth of Isaac to the Exodus out of Egypt.] Thus we may find Josephus honestly setting down the weight of the pollings of Absalom's hair at 200 shekels, or 5 pounds, 2 Sam. xxiv. 26, Antiq. B. VII. ch. viii. sect. 5, without giving us any account how that weight could be supposed true in one week's time; for so often he thought Absalom polled his head. Nor perhaps could he solve that difficulty any better than we can at this day. See my own conjecture, [that this weight included the *sum* of all those pollings at the time of his death, and not the single weight of his hair cut off at each polling,] Lit. Accompl. of Proph. Supplem. p. 77, 78. Thus Josephus directly mentions the assumption of Enoch and Elijah to heaven, the speaking of Balaam's ass, the abode of Jonas in the whale's belly, and his being cast out in the Euxine Sea, in their proper places, with other wonders, the least credible among the heathen, without any scruple. Thus also he records the epistle of Elijah the prophet to king Joram, Antiq. B. IX. ch. v. sect. 2, as he found it in his copies, and as it still stands in all our copies; although he had himself related his translation to heaven, or disappearing, about 4 years before. See the note on that place. Thus also he makes no difficulty to set down the age of Ahaz when he began to reign of barely 20 years, with almost all the other copies, Antiq. B. IX. ch. xii. sect. 3; as also, with all the other copies, that he reigned but 16 years, and that Hezekiah his son was 25 years old when he began to reign, B. X. ch. iii. sect. 1; although it thence follow, that Ahaz was but about

11 years old when Hezekiah was born, and used to afford one of the most insuperable difficulties in all the Bible history. Of which see the note on the former of those places. Thus he tells us, Antiq. B. IX. ch. x. sect. 1, with our other copies, that Jeroboam II., the son of Joash, was a very wicked man; nay, he adds, that *he was the cause of a vast number of misfortunes to the Israelites;* none of which either he or our other copies enumerate: but, on the contrary, he with them gives us a different account, and reckons up the great things he did for that nation, and the blessings of God upon him and them immediately, which I take to have been after his repentance and amendment; which yet is omitted in all our copies, as well as it was in those of Josephus. Of which in due place hereafter. Thus we have seen how Josephus at first estimated the interval between the first defection of Jeroboam, and the captivity of the ten tribes, at no more than 240 years, which is the just sum of the reigns of the several kings of Israel during that interval; as also how he at first estimated the interval from the building of the temple by Solomon, to its burning by Nebuchadnezzar, at 470 years, which is his just sum of the reigns of the several kings of Judah during that interval also, without adjusting the reigns in the two kingdoms together, which was but necessary, and which he seems afterward to have attempted, and that with no bad success, at the end of his Antiquities. Which scheme therefore I look on as the judicious result of his own later inquiries into sacred chronology. But as to that larger Egyptian chronology from Manetho; it is true that Josephus's Books against Apion are later than his Antiquities, and perhaps not a few years later also; and so it is possible that in the mean time he might have met with some other Jewish copies or records that might then dispose him to think Manetho's chronology of the Phœnician shepherds, even as understood of the Israelites when they were in Egypt, not to be utterly unjustifiable. But since we have no intimation of this, even in those books against Apion, we cannot be assured of any such thing. And Eusebius's later discovery, now generally and justly received, that the kingdom of these Phœnician shepherds was several centuries ancienter than the abode of the Israelites in Egypt, renders it highly unlikely that there ever were any such records extant, as carried Moses to the antiquity here supposed by Josephus. Nor need we, perhaps, ascribe this hypothesis of Josephus to any thing else than to his great inclination to make Moses, the Jewish legislator, *as much ancienter*, as possible, than all the famous heathen legislators; and his observation *ad hominem*, as we speak, that, in his opinion, the Egyptian chronology of Manetho's implied the same very great antiquity, without any further concern of his to compare it with or adjust it to the Jewish chronology.

37. And now I shall take leave to make some further reflections on Josephus's sacred chronology.

The impartial reader, upon perusal of the foregoing pages, will easily remark, how very near the several particulars of this chronology, even taken generally from Josephus's present copies, carefully and fairly considered and compared, come to those ancient surer general numbers for the three grand branches of it: (1.) From the creation of Adam till the death of Moses, [2993 or] *almost* 3000 *years.* (2.) From the days of Moses, or the Exodus out of Egypt, till the days of David, or till the death of David, 585 [or rather 588] years. And, (3.) From the days or from the death of David, till the second year of Vespasian, A. D. 70, just 1179 years. These sure ancient numbers put together are 4757, or rather 4760 years; and are very nearly the same which the ten several distinct periods in Josephus's Antiquities, sect. 9 before, do afford us. He will also readily discover, upon the like perusal of these papers, that the learned Peter Brinch, as well as other moderns, when they so greatly run down Josephus on account of his pretended very numerous and very great errors in chronology, ap. Havercamp, p. 291—304, have not entered candidly into this matter, nor gone to the bottom of it; nor indeed judged wisely about it: but have frequently ascribed the gross errors of more modern scribes and correctors to Josephus himself; have several times overlooked his own second thoughts and emendations; and have not seldom blamed him unjustly, because he had not by him Ptolemy's Canon, or Xenophon's Cyropædia, or other lately discovered helps in his chronology; or indeed sometimes because he does not agree with the numbers of other later and corrupter copies of the sacred books of the Old Testament, which his better temple copy corrected; or with certain modern hypotheses not well supported by such more authentic evidence as lay before him. The learned, especially those who are critically and peevishly disposed, are here not seldom very sharp-sighted in finding faults in Josephus; and while they, upon weak conjectures of their own, do on many occasions carp at and set aside histories of great consequence in Josephus, for which we have no reason to doubt but he had good authority, they are very fond of exposing his supposed mistakes about them. Josephus was but a man, and so sometimes liable to mistakes, as all men are. Yet had he very evidently at least one much better copy of the books of the Old Testament than the moderns, as I have proved at large in the fourth Dissertation prefixed. He had also, by the index of authors in his two last editions, and repeated in this, at least eighty old heathen authors to consult, when he wrote his Antiquities and his books against Apion; of which we have now scarce fourteen remaining. He was also a most diligent inquirer into history, and a great lover of truth. And after all this, do the moderns think they can now have sufficient evidence from their other much later and much more imperfect copies of the Old Testament, and much fewer remains of heathen antiquity, to reject and set aside his accounts upon so many occasions as they venture to do? The perpetual rule and standard of our assent ought ever to be this, that we reject nothing affirmed by Josephus, or other ancient writers that have ever been esteemed faithful and honest, and lovers of truth, till our evidence against it *preponderate* the attestation of those authors. And I confess I cannot but read sometimes with indignation many of our modern learned writers, even the excellent Dean Prideaux himself; who, while they frequently know little of very many transactions of ancient times but what they borrow from Josephus, do yet presume to set several of them aside, without any real contradictory evidence at all, and barely from certain ill-grounded supposals or suspicions of their own. But this is not a proper place to enlarge upon these matters, excepting such as are of a chronological nature; which yet have been, I think, sufficiently treated of in this Dissertation already.

38. N. B. Since I have now finished what I had to propose concerning the chronology of Josephus, it may not be amiss to do as I did formerly in the like case, Essay on the Old Testament, p. 214, 215, and to set down what I myself do now esteem the true sacred chronology all the way: and that will be done by little more than transcribing my former table of the Essay; I not seeing evidence enough to make any considerable alterations in any period of that chronology. I mean this, unless we prefer Eusebius's and our copies of the Samaritan Pentateuch, before Jerome's copy of that Pentateuch; which last agrees nearly with Josephus's copy, as to two readings before the flood; which correction would make the first period 246 years shorter, as has appeared, sect. 6 and 8 before. Of which see also Authentic Records, Part I. p. 463, 464, and Essay on the Old Testament, p. 21, 22.

		Years.
(1.) From the autumnal equinox next after the creation of Adam, to that at the end of the deluge		1556
(2.) Thence to the departure of Abraham out of Haran, at the Jewish passover, about the vernal equinox		$966\frac{1}{2}$
(3.) Thence to the Exodus out of Egypt, at the Jewish passover . .		430
(Thence to the death of Moses, six weeks before the Jewish passover . .		40)
(4.) From the Exodus out of Egypt to the building of Solomon's temple .		480
(5.) Thence to the temple's conflagration		$464\frac{1}{2}$
(6.) Thence to the passover, on the first year of the Christian era . .		$587\frac{2}{3}$
	Sum	$4484\frac{1}{2}$

Therefore from the death of Moses, to the passover in the first year of the Christian era, are . . . . $1492\frac{1}{3}$

N. B. Not knowing what deficient or redundant months there were in the 80 years' reign of Solomon, given us by Josephus; who, with our Bibles, calls David's 40 years and 6 months' reign but 40 years in the whole; I allow here the 480 years, in 1 Kings vi. 1, to be *complete*, instead of *current*, as are the particulars also that compose the same general sum, sect. 15 before, which allowance brings this number 1492 exactly to that in my chronological table, published A. D. 1721. According to which table I determine the chronology all along the margin of this version of Josephus.

39. Since that excellent person Mons. Toinard has, I think, in his celebrated Harmony of the Gospels, p. 9, truly determined, in agreement with the plain sense of the law of Moses, Lev. xxv. 8—11, as well as with the most learned Jews, and particularly with our Josephus, Antiq. III. ch. xii. sect. 3, and Maimonides, in Bp. Patrick on Lev. xxv. 12, that the *Jewish year of jubilee* was always the first of a sabbatic week of years; and thence the 50th year also, i. e. the first of the next week of years after the $7 \times 7 = 49$ years were over. So that every 49th and 50th year were, the former a *sabbatic year*, and the latter a *year of jubilee*, without any interruption of the sabbatic cycles by the jubilees. It will be fit here to try Josephus's and others' chronologies, and particularly my former chronology made from the Masorete Hebrew, and my present made chiefly from the Samaritan, Septuagint, and Josephus, jointly considered, both which were made without all regard thereto, by this admirable and decretory characteristic, and to see whether any of them can approve themselves to be true and genuine by their agreement to it.

40. It is true, learned men have hardly been able hitherto to observe, either in any of our copies of the books of Scripture, or in Josephus's Antiquities, one certain *year of jubilee*, either proclaimed or celebrated, as we do several *sabbatical years*. See Literal Accomplishment of Prophecies, p. 75. Yet have I very lately taken notice of a most remarkable one, as it seems to me, in the history of the Old Testament, as well as in Josephus; though he gives us no hint of his knowledge that such year was properly a *year of jubilee*: as I had long ago taken notice of another, perhaps not less remarkable, in a *prophecy of Isaiah*. By that in the

history of the Old Testament I mean the very *first year of jubilee* of all, the year when Moses died, and Joshua introduced the Israelites into the land of Canaan, and took its first-fruits, the city of Jericho. We know that, by the law of Moses, every *year of jubilee* was still to be proclaimed by a very *loud and joyful sound*, or by what is peculiarly styled the *trumpet of jubilee*, Lev. xxv. 8, &c. And certainly, as this was the very first year when a *jubilee* could possibly be proclaimed in Judea; so was no one other *year of jubilee* so remarkably proclaimed by these *trumpets of Jobel* or *Jobelim* as this was. These trumpets our translators have strangely rendered *trumpets of rams' horns*, without any foundation either in the Hebrew, the Samaritan, the Septuagint, or Josephus. *Jobel* never signifies a ram's horn; and though that miserable kind of trumpet might be sometimes used on some smaller occasions, or in a stratagem, as in the case of Gideon, Judg. vii. 16—18, where the Septuagint and Josephus call his trumpets *rams' horns;* yet is there not the least pretence that those poor *rams' horns* were used as trumpets of a *loud and joyful sound*, as *trumpets of jubilee*. Nor, indeed, excepting that amazing *sound* of an angelic and metaphoric *trumpet*, at the solemn delivery of the law on Mount Sinai, Exod. xix. 13, is this word ever used but for the *trumpet of jubilee*, both in the laws relating to the *year of jubilee*, and in the account of the siege of Jericho. In the laws no fewer than eighteen times, Lev. xxv. 10—12, twice, 15, 28, 30, 31, 33, 40, 52, 54; xxvii. 17, 18, 21, 23, 24; Numb. xxxvi. 4: and in the siege five times; four times in the plural, *Jobelim*, and once in the singular, *Jobel*, Josh. vi. 4—6, 8, 13. This year of jubilee seems to have begun in the lifetime of Moses, with the *feast of trumpets*, or *new-year's day*, the 1st of Tisri, Numb. xxix. 1. It seems to have proceeded with *blowing trumpets* against the Midianites, soon afterward; perhaps on the 10th of Tisri, the time appointed by the law for blowing the *trumpets of jubilee*, had the Jews then been in the Promised Land, Lev. xxv. 9; or, however, at the feast of tabernacles, presently after it, Numb. xxxi. 6. But still they were not entered into Canaan; and so could not yet make that *loud and joyful sound*, the *sound of liberty:* which Josephus, in agreement with the law, Lev. xxv. 10, says is the signification of *Jobel*.

However, as soon as they were entered into Canaan, Josephus thinks on the first day of the passover, they were enjoined to go round Jericho with the priests sounding the *trumpets of jubilee*, and so once on each of five more days, the five next days of the passover, in the opinion of Josephus; and seven times on the seventh day, the seventh and last day of the passover, in the opinion of Josephus; without any other noise than that of these *trumpets of jubilee:* till at the seventh time, on the seventh day, heaven and earth rang with the united sounds of the *shoutings of the people*, and of the *trumpets*

of jubilee: till the walls of Jericho fell down, and the city was taken and destroyed. How it has come to pass that we have all so long overlooked this most solemn *proclamation* of a *year of jubilee*, I can but guess. But certainly, as I have already noted, this was more solemnly proclaimed by these *trumpets of jubilee*, than ever any other *year of jubilee* was proclaimed, from the days of Moses till the destruction of Jerusalem by Titus Vespasian. Nor indeed can any year suit better, as the first of six years before the sabbatic year, than this; while the following history, both in our own Bibles and in Josephus's Antiquities, assures us that Joshua's want lasted no longer than the *sixth* year, counting this for one; and that accordingly the people *rested* in their new acquisitions on the next year, the first *seventh* or *sabbatic year*, Josh. xiv. 10; xxi. 43, 44; xxii. 4; Antiq. B. V. ch. i. sect. 19.

41. We have also, what is perhaps not less remarkable, both in the history of the Kings and in the book of Isaiah, an account of a *sabbatic year*, and a *year of jubilee* immediately following it, and this in a prophecy of Isaiah's. It belongs to part of the 18th and part of the 19th year of Hezekiah. This interpretation is almost intimated by Archbishop Usher at that year, the year of the world, according to him, 3295, and for certain the 710th before the Christian era. And I have long supposed this to be its true interpretation; though I know not how it has happened, that I never till now in earnest considered it, and examined any chronological tables by it. The words of God by Isaiah are these: *This shall be a sign unto thee, Ye shall eat this year such as* groweth of itself; (as the Jews were always to do on a *sabbatic year*, Lev. xxv. 1—7;) *and the second year that which springeth of the same :* (as the Jews were always to do on a *year of jubilee* also, ver. 11 :) *and in the third year sow ye, and reap, and plant vineyards, and eat the fruit thereof*, 2 Kings xix. 29; Isa. xxxvii. 30. *i. e.* "You shall be so far from being disturbed by Sennacherib, of whom you are now so terribly afraid, that you shall be able to keep your *two* years of rest, which are already begun, your ordinary *sabbatic year*, and your extraordinary *year of jubilee*, without any molestation from Sennacherib, till you fall to your ordinary occupations the *third* year, as ye were wont to do in times of the greatest peace and quietness."

42. And to confirm this interpretation, if we supply what seems most evidently to be lost out of a context of the book of Leviticus, relating to this very matter, we have an express promise that God would do to them in this case, as he did with the falling of the manna in the wilderness, as to the sabbath or day of rest, when on the *sixth* day of the week he sent them a *double* quantity of that heavenly food, Exod. xvi. 22—26; that is, he not only would give the Jews a *double* crop on the common *sixth* year, to supply food for *two* years;

for that *sixth* year itself, and for the following ordinary *seventh* or *sabbatic year :* but that he would moreover give them a *triple* crop on the extraordinary *sixth* year, to supply food for *three* years; for that *sixth* year itself, and for the two following years of rest, the *sabbatic year* and the *year of jubilee.*   The present text runs thus, after the foregoing laws for the observation of the *sabbatic years,* and the *years of jubilee,* Lev. xxv. 20—22 : *And if ye shall say, What shall we eat the seventh year ? behold, we shall not sow, nor gather in our increase: then I will command my blessing upon you in the sixth year, and it shall bring forth fruit for three years. And ye shall sow the eighth year, and eat of old fruits until the ninth year ; until her fruits come in ye shall eat of the old.*   This is not intelligible as it now stands in all our copies; how the rest of *one* year only should distress them for *three,* the rest of the *seventh* year only distress them till the *ninth ?* nor have the commentators any thing material to offer as a solution of these difficulties.   Accordingly, Ainsworth and Dr. Wall make no attempt towards any solution at all.   The context, and the nature of the things themselves, evidently require that it be supplied after the following manner : *And if ye shall say,* (in the ordinary case of a *sabbatic year,) What shall we eat the seventh year ? behold, we shall not sow, nor gather in our increase : then I will command my blessing on the sixth year, and the land shall bring forth fruit for two years.   And ye shall sow the eighth year.   But if ye shall say,* (in the extraordinary case of a *year of jubilee,) What shall we eat the eighth year ? behold, we shall not sow, nor gather in our increase* [neither on the *seventh* nor *eighth* year] : *then I will command my blessing on you in the sixth year, and it shall bring forth fruit for three years.   And ye shall eat of old fruit until the ninth year ; until her fruits come in ye shall eat of the old.*   And if we take notice, that the Jews did not sow in *one* year, and reap the product in *another ;* did not sow in the *eighth year,* and reap its product in the *ninth year ;* but that the *sabbatic years* and *years of jubilee,* as is well known, began in the autumn before seed time, and lasted till after harvest; we shall be forced to allow of this emendation.   Nor indeed can I avoid a strong suspicion, that the Jews themselves, after the days of Hezekiah, but before the Samaritan obtained its present form, and dropped the various readings of the Hebrew text, and before the Septuagint interpreters made their version, abridged and corrupted this context, when they had once left off the strict observation of the rest on the years of jubilee ; as loth to permit an express law, that notoriously contradicted their own practice, to stand in its full perfection against them in their Pentateuch.   The Rabbins pretend, as Bishop Patrick informs us, on Lev. xxv. 10, that " after

the tribes of Reuben, and Gad, and the half tribe of Manasseh were carried captive, jubilees ceased."   This cannot well be true, because we have very probably found a jubilee observed in the days of Hezekiah still later, even after the captivity of the ten tribes by Salmanassar.   I rather think their careful observation of the rest for the land, both on *sabbatic years* and *years of jubilee,* at least of the *years of jubilee,* was left off by the ten tribes from the days of wicked Jeroboam, *who made Israel to sin :* but that the observation of the *years of jubilee* at least, if not of the *sabbatic years* also, was left off from the days of wicked Manasseh, into whose 40th year fell a jubilee ; or, however, during the Babylonish captivity, about whose 44th year fell the death of Nebuchadnezzar, and a year of jubilee also.   I say, they seem to me to have been left off at least so soon, even by the two tribes ; suspecting, however, that neither the *sabbatic years* nor *years of jubilee* were duly observed, I mean only as to the rest of the land thereon, under the several apostacies of the Jews to idolatry, whether in the days of the judges or of the kings of Judah.   My reasons are *two :* the *one* taken from the perfect silence of the sacred historians and of Josephus about their observation all that time ; the *other* taken from the distinct mention of the neglect of 70 years of such *rest* for the land, and of its punishment by 70 years' entire and continued *rest* of the same land, during so many years' captivity of the two tribes, or as many years as they had not allowed it to rest, according to the law of Moses.   Compare Lev. xxvi. 33—35, with 2 Chron. xxxvi. 21.   Now 70 sabbatic years belong to 490 years, if they be taken by themselves ; but if we include the years of jubilee, they are 8 in every 49 years, and belong to 430 years.   Now these 430 years must end at the burning of the temple, and entire desolation of the land by Nebuchadnezzar, at the conclusion of the reign of Zedekiah.   And if we examine the duration of the several apostacies of all the tribes to idolatry under the judges, and of the two tribes under the kings, till that captivity, they may well be estimated at about 430 years also.   Nor was the Jewish settlement after the captivity so complete, during several periods of jubilees, as to oblige us to expect their restoration any more ; I mean as to the observation of the strict rest of the land on those years.   None living had then seen any such rest on a year of jubilee ; and so those years would naturally vanish out of the people's minds, unless the prophets of God or their religious governors had taken care of their restoration.   Now I do not find that any one year of jubilee fell out during the times when Haggai, or Zechariah, or even Malachi, prophesied among them ; or during the governments of either Zorobabel, Ezra, or Nehemiah.   Though I do not indeed suppose the abridgement or corruption of the text before us to have been made till after the days of Nehemiah, whose copy of the sacred books I have proved to have been used by Josephus.

43. But as for that common supposal of the moderns, that it would be very hard upon the Jews ever to have *two* years of rest for the land together, it is already answered by the genuine text, as I have restored it, in Leviticus; and seems to me altogether of a piece with that other false supposal of the modern Rabbins, that it would be too hard upon the Jews to pay *three* tithes every *third* year: which yet was certainly a part of the law of Moses, Deut. xiv. 28, 29; xxvi. 12, 13; was certainly practised by good Tobit, even under the Assyrian captivity, Tob. i. 6—8; and was so understood by Josephus himself, Antiq. B. IV. ch. viii. sect. 22, and, I suppose, so practised by religious Jews in his time also. It is moreover of a piece with a supposal that might be made, that it had not been safe for the males that were grown up to go up to Jerusalem at the three festivals every year, as they certainly were commanded to do, and as they certainly did, lest their enemies should come and ravage and plunder their country, and destroy their wives and children, at such festivals; which, humanly speaking, it was very easy for those enemies to do. He who required *three* tithes every *third* year, and had intimated that by such ways *their barns should be filled with plenty, and their presses should burst out with new wine*, Prov. iii. 10; [see the like under the Jewish Christian church in the Apostol. Constitut. VII. 29;] he who had promised and performed it, that *no man should desire their land, at their going up thrice in a year* to their festivals, Exod. xxxiv. 24; could and did always make the land sufficiently fruitful in the *third* and *sixth* years, to reward the conscientious observers of those laws. As was such extraordinary fruitfulness a certain demonstration of that especial Divine Providence which presided over that nation in all those ages; I mean this whilst they submitted to God, as to their supreme King and Governor; and continued in obedience to his laws, given them by the hand of Moses; but no longer. Nor do we find any Sadducees or sceptics in religion among the Jews till long after their rejection of those their Divine laws, and after their settlement under political governments, when they were abandoned by God, and had forfeited all the peculiar regards of Divine Providence; which is an observation worthy the deepest consideration of the sceptics of the present age.

44. It will therefore be here worth our while to make a careful inquiry into the state of the land of Judea all along, as to that rest that was to be afforded it on *sabbatic years*, and especially when those years were succeeded by *years of jubilee* also; and to see whether the *sixth* year had a more plentiful crop or not, according to this promise in the book of Leviticus; I mean, as before, only while

the Jews took care of the observance of the rest of the laws of Moses, and of these in particular also. Now here, since we have but ten or eleven instances of such years at all remarkable in the Jewish history, so far as I have observed, even from the days of Joshua to the destruction of Jerusalem by Titus Vespasian, let us examine every one of them distinctly.

45. The *first* and most remarkable instance is that already mentioned, in the days of good king Hezekiah, anno 709 before the Christian era; where the nature of that joyful promise made to the people, that Sennacherib should not interrupt them in the peaceable performance of the duties of those two years of rest, inclines one to believe that they had store enough laid up already from the foregoing *sixth* year to serve them the two next; otherwise it would have been small comfort for them that Sennacherib should not come to and disturb and plunder them, if for want of a harvest the foregoing year they were to be starved the two next by famine. And if the character of this land was now taken by Rabshakeh from his experience of it while he was in it, on that *sixth* and beginning of the *seventh* year, as it is not unreasonable to do, he recommended the land of Assyria by its resemblance to the land of Judea, and owned it was then *a land of corn and wine, a land of bread and vineyards, a land of oil-olive and of honey*, 2 Kings xviii. 32; Isa. xxxvi. 17; which is a proper description of it in such a plentiful year as this naturally was, according to the Divine promise in Leviticus.

46. The *second* instance is that in the ninth year of wicked Zedekiah, anno 590 before the Christian era; in whose reign we have no marks of any intention to observe the rest of this sabbatic year; nay, in whose reign we know it was not observed, and this where the non-observance of it was accounted one cause of the entire rest of the land during the 70 years' captivity, especially since on this very year the nation brake through a covenant they had made to observe one part of their duty on that year, and reduced those their bond servants, whom they had once released on this *year of release*, into bondage again, which was done on purpose, perhaps, that they might plough and sow for them on that sabbatic year, in defiance of the law of Moses to the contrary, Jer. xxxiv. 8—17. Accordingly, we may remark that the city of Jerusalem suffered greatly by *famine* soon afterward, Jer. xxxiv. 17; xxxvii. 21; xxxviii. 9; as if the Divine Providence had cursed and not blessed the land on the foregoing *sixth* year.

47. The *third* sabbatic year that I take notice of, is that when the temple began to be rebuilt, in the second year of Darius Hystaspes, the 520th before the Christian era, which was before the sabbatic years were revived after the captivity. And what the state of the foregoing *sixth* year was, be-

fore they set about the building of the temple, we may learn from Hag. ii. 15—19, *When one came to an heap of twenty measures, there were but ten : when one came to the press-fat, for to draw out fifty vessels out of the press, there were but twenty : when God smote them with blasting, and with mildew, and with hail, in all the labours of their hands.* As also what that state should be when they should have complied with Haggai and Zechariah, and the temple should be rebuilt, as it was seven years afterward, Joseph. Antiq. B. XI. ch. iv. sect. 7, which was also a *sabbatic year*, and the next a *year of jubilee :* Hag. ii. 19, *Is the seed yet in the barn ? yea, as yet the vine, and the fig tree, and the pomegranate, and the olive tree hath not brought forth : from this day will I bless you.* As if still the blessing or curse of God went along with the Jews' obedience and disobedience in the observation or profanation of the years of rest for the land, as well as in the like instance of obedience or disobedience to his other commandments.

48. As to the *fourth* and *fifth* sabbatic years known, the *former* by the solemn reading of the law by good Ezra the scribe, and the *latter* by the release of debts and mortgages under good Nehemiah, the governor, the 8th and 29th of Xerxes, see Lit. Accompl. of Proph. Supplem. p. 62, 63. In the former of them there is a very good sign of the people's honest intentions to observe this rest on the sabbatic year; I mean their desire that Ezra would now read the law solemnly to them at the beginning of this sabbatic year; as also their *weeping when they heard the words of the law*, Neh. viii.; 1 Esd. ix., as conscious of the grossness of their former transgressions of it, and probably of their former breaches of this law among others, and as ready to obey it for the time to come. Accordingly, they *made them booths and kept the feast of tabernacles according to the law* immediately, and *entered into a covenant to keep all God's laws by* Moses, and this of the *seventh year* in particular, Neh. x. 28—31. So that there is no doubt but this year was kept as a year of *rest*, or a *sabbatic year.* Nor do we find the least sign of want at this time, now the *sixth* year was just over. On the contrary, the Jews, at the exhortation of Ezra or Nehemiah, now *went their way to eat the fat, and drink the sweet ; and to send portions to them for whom nothing was prepared ; and to make great mirth*, Neh. viii. 9, 11 ; 1 Esd. ix. 50, 54, as was naturally to be done in a year of plenty and abundance. As for the latter sabbatic year, the 29th of Xerxes, Neh. v. 1—13, we find that the rich Jews had been before very oppressive and tyrannical over their poor brethren, instead of being desirous to observe the sabbatic year, which was also a *year of release*, and that in the days of Nehemiah it was very hard to make them rest even on the *sabbath day*, Neh. xiii. 15. So that

there is no suspicion of their keeping the *sabbatic year* at this time. Whence we find that according to these evil doings of the Jews there had been a great *dearth* among them, Neh. v. 5; as if in this case also there had been a curse on the land the foregoing *sixth year* instead of a blessing. Nor did Nehemiah insist on any thing then, but their *release* of those oppressive debts which the poor had been forced to contract; as supposing, perhaps, that any further attempt for the observation of the *rest* of that year was utterly impracticable.

49. The *sixth* sabbatic year that I find was that in the days of good Judas the Maccabee, when Antiochus Eupator besieged him in the temple, anno 163. This year was observed as a *rest* for the land, 1 Macc. vi. 49, 53 ; Antiq. B. XII. ch. ix. sect. 5. And here indeed we may take notice, that too many had crowded into Bethsura and the temple for the *residue of the store* laid up the former year to supply, during the sieges of those places, 1 Macc. vi. 53; and that a *famine* prevailed in the temple. But then we find no complaints among the besiegers, or in the country of Judea, or any want of provisions there ; nor indeed any sign of a barren *sixth year* at all. On the contrary, the mention of that *residue of the store which they of Judea that were delivered from the Gentiles had eaten up*, supposes the foregoing year to have been so plentiful, as to have afforded an overplus to be *stored up* against this sabbatic year, though that *store* had been imprudently consumed before the besieged required it. However, Providence now remarkably made the nation amends ; and saved the Jews, that were now obedient, but were besieged in the temple, when they were reduced to great distress ; and unexpectedly sent a pretender to the crown of Syria out of Persia, Philip by name, who obliged Eupator not only to draw off his army from the temple, but to make a league with the whole nation of the Jews, and to suffer them to live according to their own laws afterward, 1 Macc. vi. 55—60, which was a greater and more seasonable blessing to them than the greatest plenty.

50. The *seventh* sabbatic year was that at the end of Simon, and the beginning of John Hyrcanus, anno 135, which Josephus supposes was observed, at least by resting from war, Of the War, B. I. ch. ii. sect. 4 ; Antiq. B. XIII. ch. viii. sect. 1 ; but in contradiction to the First Book of Maccabees, chap. xvi. 11—22, which shows it to have been so far from a year of *rest* to the land, that it was a year of great fighting, war, and cruelty. So that we have no reason to believe that it was observed as a sabbatic year ; nor do we at all know what crop there was the foregoing year ; nor does the author of the Book of Maccabees take any notice of this as of a sabbatic year, as it did of that forementioned in the days of Judas. And thus far I esteem the Jewish nation under a theocracy, under the oracle of

Urim, and peculiarly regarded by Divine Providence; but the future sabbatic years I esteem as belonging to a political monarchy. See the note on Antiq. B. III. ch. viii. sect. 9. However, since the Jews still kept those years, by allowing the land to rest on them, let us go over such of them as are mentioned by Josephus distinctly.

51. The *eighth* instance of a *sixth* year before a *sabbatic year* may that be esteemed which we meet with in Josephus, at anno 66 or 65 before the Christian era, where, on a notorious breach of covenants and impiety of the Jews in Jerusalem, when they were besieged by Aretas and Hyrcanus, there was sent upon them such a pestilential wind as destroyed the fruits of the whole land, and occasioned a modius of wheat to be sold for eleven drachmæ, which was then esteemed an extravagant price, Antiq. B. XIV. ch. ii. sect. 2. Nor is it unlikely that it was the circumstance of the sabbatic year, when they had no new harvest, that occasioned the price of grain to be so extravagant and severe to them. This was many years after the Jews in Judea had deserted God's true religion, and God had thereupon deserted them, that so sad a scarcity and dearth came upon them on the *sixth* and on the *sabbatic year*, which otherwise God would certainly have preserved them from. Of which their desertion of God, and God's desertion of them, more presently.

52. The *ninth* instance we have of a sabbatic year observed by the Jews was that when Sosius and Herod fought against and took Jerusalem by force, anno 37. And then indeed Josephus takes notice that there was in Judea a *famine, or great scarcity of provisions, on account of the sabbatic year*, Antiq. B. XIV. ch. xvi. sect. 2. This is the first plain instance that I have met with of the failure of a plentiful crop on the *sixth* year, when the *seventh* was observed as a year of *rest*, or sabbatic year. And no wonder is it at all that it thus failed. For now the theocracy of the Jews in Judea had been long become a secular, a political, and a tyrannical monarchy; the Urim, that Divine oracle peculiar to this theocracy, had been long taken from them, as has been noted already, sect. 50 before, and the nation had been long very corrupt and very wicked; the Pharisees had long set up their rest in external obedience to rituals, one of which was this law of rigorous resting on the *sabbatic day* and *sabbatic year*, without any concern for inward holiness and real religion; the honest spirit of the old Jewish piety and charity was quite gone; and the present war was so far from a religious war, according to the law, or for the defence of the Mosaic settlement, that it was a mere carnal and secular war, between an ambitious and wicked high priest, Antigonus, with his heathen and idolatrous Parthians, on one side; and a no less ambitious and wicked king, Herod, with his heathen and idolatrous Romans, on the other. See Authent. Rec. Part I. p.

204. So that it is no wonder that God had now withdrawn his good providence from his ancient peculiar people the Jews, in this and the like instances, since they had long rejected his government, and were become as bad, if not worse, than many of the heathen nations round about them.

53. The *tenth* instance of a *sabbatic year*, and this such a one as immediately preceded a *year of jubilee*, was that in the 13th of Herod, anno 2⅕. This, though not expressly said by Josephus to be such, is yet strongly implied in the account he gives us of a terrible famine and pestilence beginning in the 13th year of Herod, or anno 24, Antiq. B. XV. ch. ix., extending to both Syria and Judea, and occasioned by a terrible drought and pestilential disposition of the air before the sabbatic year began, or in the summer anno 24. For he says there, chap. ix. sect. 2, that Herod gave vast quantities of the corn that came out of Egypt *to the Syrians* for seed, against the next year, without a word of any given then for seed *to the Jews;* who yet, had it not been a sabbatic year in which they could not sow, would have wanted it all themselves for the same purpose. Nor is there any question but the following year was a sabbatic year in Judea. And what is here very remarkable is this, that the sabbatic year, still observed, was such a one as, for certain, immediately preceded a year of jubilee, which was not observed anno 2¾, as the table, to be soon set down, will demonstrate; but which ought to have been observed also, as well as the other. It is moreover very remarkable, that this terrible drought and pestilential disposition of the air fell out at the very time when Providence, under the theocracy, as we have seen, used to furnish a *triple* crop against the *two years of rest*, I mean the *sabbatic year* and the *year of jubilee;* during both which years, as Josephus takes particular notice, sect. 1, these countries were sorely afflicted with this famine, till the Syrian crop came to their relief in the second year. Whether this famine and pestilential air may not be looked on as providential, and as punishments for the Jews' rejection of their theocracy, and their breaking those laws God had given them under that theocracy, and this, among others, for a rest of the land on the year of jubilee, and for setting up a political government in its stead, will very well deserve our serious consideration.

54. The *eleventh* and concluding instance of a sabbatic year, is that in the last year of Caius, the Roman emperor, A. D. 41, when Josephus informs us that the Jews had a great drought all the year, till on their amazing zeal against the pollution of their temple by idolatry, or against admitting the emperor's idol statue into it; the president of Syria Petronius's most religious resolution, at the hazard of his life, not to force them to it; God, in a very extraordinary manner, sent them rain, and that immediately. See Antiq. B. XVIII. ch. viii. sect. 5, 6, and the note there. And these are all the *sabbatic*

years and *years of jubilee* of which I have found any distinct accounts, either in the Bible or in Josephus, till the utter destruction of the Jewish worship and polity under Titus Vespasian.

55. Now, therefore, to return to my main design, which is the determination of the *years of jubilee*. If from the $\frac{19}{38}$ of Hezekiah, the fundamental year of jubilee determined by the prophet Isaiah, as I have already noted; which answers to the latter part of the 709th and to the former part of the 708th year before the Christian era, as may be seen in Archbishop Usher, in Dean Prideaux, and in my tables of the kings of Judah and Israel in the Chronology of the Old Testament; being parts of the 4004th and 4005th years of the Julian period, and without dispute the 50th year after the 49 years of the sabbatic period, according to the law of Moses, Lev. xxv. 8—11, and by consequence

a *year of jubilee*: if, I say, we proceed from this fundamental year, both upward, by addition, and downward, by subtraction of 49 years; from the days of Moses to the days of Tiberius Cæsar, when John the Baptist put an end to the legal and began the evangelical dispensation, we shall find just 31 intervals of 49 years apiece, = 1519 years. But if we both begin and end with a year of jubilee, as we are obliged to do here, our entire period will include in all 32 jubilees, and 1520 years: I mean this before Jerusalem was destroyed, when all the remains of *sabbatic years* and *years of jubilee*, with the entire civil and ecclesiastical constitution of the Jewish nation, was dissolved. Accordingly, upon these principles the 32 jubilees, without dispute, fall on the several years following; 31 of them falling into the years before the Christian era began, and the last after that era was begun.

THIRTY-ONE JUBILEES BEFORE THE CHRISTIAN ERA, WITH ONE AFTERWARD

	$178\frac{5}{6}$	
	$173\frac{6}{7}$	
	$168\frac{2}{8}$	
	$164\frac{0}{9}$	
	$159\frac{1}{6}$	
	$154\frac{4}{1}$	
I.	$149\frac{3}{4}$	my first jubilee.
II.	$144\frac{1}{4}$	
III.	$139\frac{4}{4}$	Abp. Usher's and M. Toinard's first jubilees.
IV.	$134\frac{6}{5}$	
V.	$129\frac{7}{6}$	
VI.	$124\frac{8}{7}$	
VII.	$119\frac{9}{8}$	
VIII.	$114\frac{0}{49}$	
IX.	$110\frac{1}{4}$	
X.	$105\frac{3}{4}$	
XI.	$100\frac{3}{4}$	
XII.	$95\frac{4}{3}$	
XIII.	$90\frac{1}{4}$	
XIV.	$85\frac{6}{5}$	
XV.	$80\frac{7}{6}$	
XVI.	$75\frac{8}{7}$	
XVII.	$70\frac{9}{8}$	
XVIII.	$66\frac{0}{9}$	
XIX.	$61\frac{1}{0}$	
XX.	$56\frac{3}{4}$	
XXI.	$51\frac{3}{4}$	
XXII.	$46\frac{4}{4}$	
XXIII.	$41\frac{4}{4}$	
XXIV.	$36\frac{6}{5}$	
XXV.	$31\frac{7}{0}$	
XXVI.	$26\frac{8}{7}$	
XXVII.	$21\frac{9}{8}$	
XXVIII.	$17\frac{0}{0}9$	
XXIX.	$12\frac{1}{0}$	
XXX.	$7\frac{4}{4}$	
XXXI.	$2\frac{3}{4}$	
XXXII.	$2\frac{7}{8}$ A. D.	

Only the reader is to note, that I here take in 6 earlier years of jubilee also, for the sake of such chronologies as extend further backward than mine does. The first number being all along that year before the Christian era in which the jubilee began, in autumn ; and the second that in which it ended, in autumn also; the former including about one quarter, and the latter about three quarters, of each year of jubilee : from the first, that began in the year 1493, and ended 1492, before the Christian era ; to the last, which began A. D. 27, and ended A. D. 28.

56. N. B. Since Archbishop Usher, by mistake, supposed that *years of jubilee* always fell upon *sabbatic years*, his years of jubilee, after they are once begun, cannot be nearer to mine than one year ; as accordingly they are one year before mine all the way : but Mons. Toinard rightly supposing that the *years of jubilee* were only the next to *sabbatic years* may agree with mine ; as they exactly do all the way, after they are begun. Only neither of these learned chronologers supposing that the jubilees began with Joshua's entry into Canaan, but some time afterwards ; nor knowing the true year when he entered ; their jubilees do not begin till near a century after mine. Thus my first jubilee begins in anno 1493, and ends anno 1492. Archbishop Usher's first jubilee begins anno 1396, and ends anno 1395. While Mons. Toinard's first jubilee begins anno 1395, and ends anno 1394. This note was to be thus nicely set down, to prevent any possible mistake in such as make use of the chronologies of those very learned persons, relating to *sabbatic years* and *years of jubilee.*

57. Now, in order to compare several chronologies, and see whether any of them will correspond to this κριτήριον, this *distinguishing character ;* I mean whether any of them place the death of Moses, and the entrance of Joshua into Canaan about a month after it, upon the first of a week of years in the sabbatic period, and also upon that particular first of a week of years which was a jubilee ; I shall here exhibit to the reader the year, as estimated before the Christian era, according to such chronologers as I have met with, both ancient and modern ; together with the distances, if they be distant, of their supposed year from the jubilee nearest to them ; many of which accounts I have drawn from Ricciolus's Chronology, p. 290—292, as follows :

	Years	Dist. from a jubilee
According to Africanus and Julius Hilarion	1756	19
Dr. Cary's larger chronology from the LXXII.	1725	12
Josephus's largest chronology, as above, sect. 9	1681	7
Josephus's shorter chronology, as above, sect. 14	1661	22
Nicephorus Callistus	1631	8
Mons. Vignol	1619	20
Isaac Vossius	1616	23
Clement of Alexandria	1617	20
Vignere	1583	7
Dr. Brett	1574	16
Megerlin	1564	23
Capellus	1555	14
Ricciolus	1552	11
Josephus's shortest chronology, as sect. 16	1549	8
Mr. Whiston's present chronology, sect. 38	1492	0
Petavius	1491	1
Sir Walter Raleigh	1479	13
Eusebius and his followers	1472	20
Funccius, Marianus Scotus, and Massæus	1470	22
Lanquetus, Salianus, and Torniellus	1469	23
Scaliger, Calvisius, Helvicus, Mr. Talents, Isaacson, and à Lapide	1457	14
Origanus, Ubbo Emmius, and Mr. Bedford	1456	13
Simson, and Dr. Howel	1455	12
Archbishop Usher, Bishop Lloyd, Mons. Toinard, and Mr. Whiston in his former chronology, all from the Hebrew	1451	8
Dr. Cary's shorter chronology, from the Hebrew	1450	7
Henry Philippi, and Sir John Marsham	1447	4
Herwartus	1409	15
Arias Montanus	1361	16
Gordon	1357	12
Tirinus	1317	21
The Jewish Rabbins	1272	24

58. If the reader wonder how so great a chronologer as Petavius, without allowing more than 40 years to the reign of Solomon, should here, in a manner, agree with my latest determination, when I follow Josephus, and allow him no fewer than 80 years; he is to know, that Petavius was so greatly distressed in his attempt to reduce the years in the wilderness, those of Joshua, the Judges, Samuel, Saul, and David, as they stand in the Hebrew copy, within the express number of 480, according to the same Hebrew copy, 1 Kings vi. 1, that he most absurdly expounded the Exodus out of Egypt, whence those 480 years were dated, as including the entire interval of the 40 years in the wilderness also, and thereby weakly augmented that number from 480 to 520 years. However, he thought the *year of jubilee* to be a *sabbatic year* also, and had no certain *year of jubilee* from whence to compute; so that his so near agreement with me is merely accidental, and only shows the necessity of allowing Solomon 80 years, with Josephus, in order to comply with this most excellent character of sacred chronology, that the entry into Canaan must therein fall into a *year of jubilee*. And till any chronologers can adjust the sacred numbers so, that this κριτήριον may be as true in their systems as it is in mine, which I believe to be utterly impossible, they ought to come into this determination, and confess that this appears to be the true chronology of the Bible from the death of Moses till this very day. Nor is this my determination the consequence of the observation of that first jubilee: the same chronology was published 14 years ago, in my chronological table; and therein the 1492nd year before the Christian era is the 2993rd year of the world, and is correspondent to the death of Moses; though till very lately I did not at all know that it was to be, or was that *first year of jubilee*. I knew indeed several years ago, that by comparing seven *sabbatic years* with Ptolemy's Canon, the First Book of Maccabees, Josephus, &c., the sacred chronology had been by me and others rightly determined ever since the captivity of the ten tribes, or during 3228 years backward. See Lit. Accomp.

of Proph. Supplem. p. 75. Yet it is but very lately that this chronological character from the *year of jubilee* has enabled me to extend it so far backward as 3227 complete years; it being plainly so long since the middle of that first year of jubilee till Easter in the present year, 1736. Nor may it be amiss to add, that since the 40 years in the wilderness, after the Exodus, and before Joshua entered Canaan, at the full moon of passover, and the 430 years, even to the *selfsame day*, from Abraham's coming out of Haran to that Exodus at the passover, as we read Exod. xii. 40, 41, make 470 years, and are undisputed in all copies, we may add those 470 years to the former sum; which is then 3697 years: so that I think we may now safely pronounce, that from the full moon when Abraham came out of Haran, April 13th, anno 1962, till the full moon last March 15th, are just 3693 lunisolar years; or, which is in a manner the same, 3697 tropical years. Which accuracy of computation, and this upon such authentic foundations, is to me highly satisfactory, greatly to the reputation of Josephus's temple copy, and well worthy the consideration of our most learned chronologers.

60. N. B. The chronological numbers in the margin and notes of this edition of Josephus take their date either *backward*, before the Christian era, with the bare notation of Anno; or *forward*, after that era, with the common notation of A. D. And these numbers before Abraham came out of Haran are peculiar to this chronology: from thence till the end of the reign of Solomon they usually differ 40 or 41 years from those in Bishop Lloyd's Bible, or Mr. Marshal's Tables of Chronology, or Archbishop Usher's Annals, and are commonly so many years larger than theirs. But after Solomon they are usually the same with theirs, and with the like in Dr. Prideaux's Connexion. The reasons of which have already appeared in this Dissertation. In which I hope that many greater mistakes will not be found than of years *current* for years *complete*, or the reverse; for which I must not say that I can always be answerable.

DISSERTATION VI

TO PROVE

THAT THE FRAGMENT OR EXTRACT OUT OF AN HOMILY CONCERNING HADES BELONGS TO JOSEPHUS, THE JEWISH HISTORIAN; AND WAS BY HIM PREACHED OR WRITTEN WHEN HE WAS BISHOP OF JERUSALEM, ABOUT THE END OF TRAJAN.

1. IN Photius's Bibliotheca, Cod. XLVIII., we have an account of a little Greek book, containing two very small treatises, Concerning the Universe, as in some copies; or, Concerning the Cause of the Universe, as in others; or, Concerning the Substance of the Universe, as in those of a third sort. The

like title there was to a treatise of Hippolytus's, as standing on his famous monument. The like title there was also to a treatise of Caius's, the presbyter; who was the author of a discourse called the Labyrinth; wherein he says he wrote such a treatise. To which title there was usually this addition, κατὰ Πλάτωνα, *according to Plato;* or rather, κατὰ Πλάτωνος, *against Plato.* Photius read this small work; and he informs us, that some ascribed it to Josephus, some to Justin Martyr, and some to Irenæus; but that he supposed it written by Caius. We have also a few MSS. copies of an extract, or fragment, or homily, being the latter of two discourses or homilies *concerning the place* or *state of demons,* and *concerning Hades.* The former, concerning demons, is not now extant; but the latter is preserved, and seems to me a most valuable remainder of most primitive antiquity. Hœschelius first published it in Greek, from a MS. copy given him by Max. Marguntius, in his notes on Photius, p. 9—12, but did not translate it into Latin. Le Moyne lighted upon another MS. copy, very little differing from the former; he published it in Greek and Latin, as belonging to Hippolytus; though I think that name is in no MS., but only that of Josephus. So that he ventured upon a supposal, an almost wholly groundless supposal, as if this were the same small treatise that is mentioned on his monument *concerning the universe.* Fabricius also mentions a MS. of it in Cardinal Coislin's library. Dr. Humphreys has also published it from a Baroccian MS. at the end of his English Athenagoras, by the leave of Dr. Hicks, and out of Dr. Grabe's papers. This copy is much the most valuable, because it is about a fourth part larger than the other; and yet appears equally genuine. The former copy has been of late also published in the works of Josephus, as a fragment ascribed to him; though very few of the learned have esteemed it to be genuine. See Havercamp's edition, Tom. II. Addend. p. 145—147. Its title is, Extracts out of Josephus's Exhortation to the Greeks, with this groundless addition, either before or after the other, *according to* or *against Plato,* concerning the Cause of the Universe. And this counterfeit part of the title has so far imposed on our modern critics, that they all agree our fragment to be one part of the same book that is mentioned by Photius. See Le Moyne's edition: Arlenius's Preface, ap. Havercamp, p. 74; J. Higius's Prolegom. ap. eund. p. 95; and Fabricius, Of Josephus, ap. eund. p. 64. A strange opinion this! while, excepting the spurious part of the title, in which there is indeed a great resemblance, their characters and contents are entirely different. Photius's small treatises were concerning the *cause,* or *substance,* *of the universe;* our fragment, concerning *Hades.* Photius's treatises confuted Plato; our fragment mentions him but once, and that with approbation. Photius's treatises showed that Plato contradicted

himself in his doctrines of the soul, and of matter, and of the resurrection; our fragment has nothing of those notions of Plato at all. Photius's treatises confuted the philosopher Alcinous; of whom our fragment says not one word. Nor does it yet appear that this Alcinous lived before the third, or even the fourth century, long after the days of Josephus; and perhaps not a little later than Justin Martyr, Irenæus, Hippolytus, and Caius, its other several supposed authors. See Fabric. Biblioth. Græc. Book IV. Part II. sect. 2. Photius's treatises showed, that the nation of the Jews was older than that of the Greeks; of which not a syllable in our fragment. Photius's treatises had such wild notions about the constituent parts of mankind at first out of the four elements, as, in the opinion of Photius, were unworthy of Jews, and particularly of Josephus; concerning which our fragment says nothing directly; but, by consequence of what it says of the resurrection of the body, rather contradicts such opinions. Photius's treatises contained Photian or Athanasian notions about Christ's ineffable generation and Divinity; our fragment has not a syllable tending that way, and only styles *Christ God the Word,* and one *to whom the Father had committed the power of judging the world,* &c., exactly like the genuine writings of the apostolic age. Photius's treatises were, as he thought, perfectly of the style of Josephus's other works; (though indeed in the small citation of the author's own words by him that does not appear;) while Josephus, as all the learned know, wrote in the Attic dialect, and the style of our fragment is almost entirely Hellenistical. So that it is amazing how the critics have come to be so grossly mistaken in this matter; those small treatises mentioned by Photius being evidently not now extant; nor do they appear to have been cited by any other author, ancient or modern, now known, but by Philoponus, about A. D. 600, L. III. C. 16. Nor is there the least direct evidence in the world that Photius ever saw our fragment. And so much for this last work, cited by Philoponus and Photius.

2. Let us now come to our fragment *concerning Hades,* still extant; and search for the *internal characters,* and *external testimonies,* as to its *age* and its *author;* whose *contents* are, for certain, very admirable, greatly affecting, and of the highest importance to mankind. And first for the *internal characters.*

(1.) The general doctrine of the *intermediate state* of souls in *Hades,* between death and the resurrection, is here the very same with that of the first ages of the gospel; though that doctrine gradually dropped in some later ages.

(2.) The *temporary punishments* inflicted in *Hades* on sinners not yet hopeless, by angels allotted to that office, in order to their entire reformation and complete recovery, sect. 1, is very like the doctrine of Hermas, a writer of the apostolic age;

not only as to punishments in this life, but as to those in *Hades* also, Vis. III. sect. 2, 7; Simil. VII. sect. 23; VIII. sect. 3, 8; IX. sect. 6, 9, 13, 16. Part of this doctrine has been long ago lost also.

(3.) That most primitive doctrine, which Dr. Grabe, in his Spicilegium, sect. 1, p. 353, declares to be not only the doctrine of Enoch, but of the apostles, and of the church apostolical, is clear in this fragment, sect. 2, that none of the wicked, whether demons or men, were then cast into *Gehenna*, or *hell-fire;* nor indeed should be cast into it till the day of judgment; as in Matt. viii. 29; Jude 9; Enoch, sect. 6; in the Authentic Records, Part I. p. 265; all before or in the first century; the torments they undergo beforehand arising rather from the sense they have of that misery, and what they must expect at the last day, than from the actual feeling the torments of hell before it, sect. 4, though this doctrine was soon, in good measure, dropped also among Christians.

(4.) The good are here described as going at their death to the *right hand*, into *light;* and the bad to the *left hand*, into *darkness;* and that through a gate also, sect. 1, 3, like the accounts 4 Esd. vii. 13, 14; viii. 12; Matt. xxiii. 13; xxv. 30; all before or in the first century.

(5.) The good, as soon as they are dead, are here conducted *by angels;* and this to a place called Abraham's bosom, sect. 3, as in Luke xvi. 22, 23, and Constitut. VIII. 41; in the first century.

(6.) Here is mention made of the *chaos* or *great gulf* interposed between the righteous and the wicked in *Hades*, sect. 4, as Luke xvi. 23, &c., in the first century; where the sight of the good in a happy state, while they are themselves excluded out of it, increases the misery of the bad, as Luke xiii. 28, in the same century.

(7.) Here the bodies in the grave are compared to *seed sown*, and to *bare grain*, that fructifies again, sect. 5; and the reasoning about the *resurrection* is much like that of St. Paul's, 1 Cor. xv. 37, 38, and that in the Apostolical Constitutions V. 7; both in the first century.

(8.) The expression here used of ἐπενδυσάμενος, sect. 5, being *clothed upon* with a glorified body at the resurrection, is St. Paul's also, 2 Cor. v. 2, in the first century.

(9.) The descriptions of the person and office of Christ in this fragment or homily are these: that he is Θεὸς Λόγος, *God the Word*, in distinction from *God the Father;* and that he is the *Judge of the world, by the appointment of the Father,* sect. 6, as John i. 1, and Acts xvi. 31; which are most primitive and apostolical descriptions, and free from all the philosophical notions and terms of the latter ages.

(10.) The descriptions of the punishments of *Gehenna*, or *hell*, as distinct from *Hades*, by an *unquenchable fire*, and a *never-dying worm*, sect. 2, 6, are exactly those of our Saviour himself, Mark ix. 44, 46, 48, in the first century.

(11.) St. Paul's words, citing a text out of the Old Testament, now lost, or corrupted, are here set down *verbatim;* that the happiness of heaven will be such as *eye hath not seen, nor ear heard, neither hath it entered into the heart of man, the things that God hath prepared for them that love him*, sect. 7, as 1 Cor. ii. 9, in the first century.

(12.) The citation here made of some words of our Saviour's, not contained in any of our Gospels, Ἐφ' οἷς ἂν εὕρω ὑμᾶς, ἐπὶ τέτοις κρινῶ παρ' ἕκαστα· βοᾷ τὸ τέλος τῶν ἁπάντων; *In whatsoever state I shall find you, in that I will judge you; as the end of all things proclaims to us*, sect. 8; contains a double mark of original antiquity. For the citation itself is in Justin Martyr, and that for our Saviour's own words, as in this place; and that very probably out of the Gospel according to the Hebrews or Nazarenes, as this its citation by Josephus most probably implies. See Grabe's Spicileg. Sect. I. p. 14 and 327. And this name by which our Lord is here called, the *end of all things*, is a direct imitation of the latter part of his name thrice in the Apocalypse, chap. i. 8; xxi. 6; xxii. 13, where he is styled the *beginning and the end*. This is a plain indication that the author of this fragment or homily had seen and owned the Apocalypse of St. John. Both which characters perfectly agree to the circumstances of our Josephus, who certainly lived till the reign of Trajan, and several years later than the writing the Apocalypse. The allusion to which is the very latest character of chronology that I have observed in this homily.

(13.) The doxology at the end of all, *To God be glory and dominion for ever and ever, Amen,* is the very doxology of Peter, the apostle of the circumcision, twice, 1 Pet. iv. 11, and v. 11; and once of St. John, the beloved disciple, Apoc. i. 6; both Jews of the first century.

(14.) The nature of this fragment or homily is like that of the apostolical Epistles of St. Paul, who at their conclusion, whatever his premises were, almost constantly adds moral and Christian exhortations for practice; and just thus does our author conclude this fragment or homily also, in a serious and practical exhortation to the Greeks or Gentiles his hearers, sect. 7, 8; which I esteem another character that it belonged to those earliest and most serious times of Christianity.

(15.) To conclude this head of the *internal characters;* the *style* of this fragment or homily is, for certain, almost entirely *Hellenistical;* which is the known Christian style of the apostolical age; and lasted properly in the church no later than the martyrdom of Polycarp, somewhat before the middle of the second century. Nor is there, I think, the least internal character later than the first or beginning of the second century. Nor do the entire contents for certain agree to any other time whatsoever.

3. And now, before I can proceed to my second head, the arguments and testimonies which fix this fragment or homily to the church of the circumcision at Jerusalem, and to Josephus himself, while he was bishop there, I must premise somewhat concerning the history of Josephus, and the circumstances he was in during the latter part of his life. It will be observed in the beginning of my notes upon Josephus, that he published his history of the Jewish War in the Greek language, about A. D. 75, in the days of Vespasian; that he published his Antiquities in the thirteenth of Domitian, A. D. 93; as also he wrote his own Life, for an Appendix to those Antiquities, after the third of Trajan, or A. D. 100. I have also observed in the fourth Dissertation prefixed, sect. 32, that Josephus never affords us the least indication of his being so much as a Nazarene or Ebionite Christian till he came to the book of Daniel, in the course of his Antiquities, some time before A. D. 93, and that yet he afterward affords us many such indications. But then, where he lived and what he did after A. D. 93, the world has not hitherto at all known. And Dr. Cave, when he speaks of him in his Historia Literaria, truly remarks, that " He was still alive in the year of Christ 93; [he might have said in the year 100;] but what became of him after that time does not appear." While yet, if we attend, we may find no obscure indications concerning him then in his own known works, and in Eusebius's Ecclesiastical History thereto relating; especially as compared with this fragment or homily ascribed to him. He informs us, at the end of his own Life, how very kind Vespasian, and his two sons, Titus and Domitian, had been to him, in making him a citizen of Rome, in giving him a pension, and assigning him lands near his native city Jerusalem, and others in a remoter part of the plain country of Judea, not named by him; and, in particular, that Domitian made his lands tax free; which, he says, was an especial favour: but he never says one word that either Nerva or Trajan took any notice of him. It also appears there that he continued at Rome almost all that time. But where he lived, and what he did after the death of Domitian, his last patron at Rome, as I have already noted, I could never find he directly informs us. However, in his first book against Apion, he lets us know thrice that he, as well as his people the Jews, were then in Judea, sect. 1, 31, 35, where he calls Judea the *country which we now possess*, χώραν ἦν νῦν ἔχομεν· and the *country which is now inhabited by us*, χώραν τὴν νῦν οἰκουμένην ὑφ᾽ ἡμῶν· and lastly, the *country which we now inhabit*, χώρας ἧς νῦν κατοικοῦμεν. He also intimates such an assurance of his nation preserving their history exactly in future ages, as well as they had done it in those that were past, sect. 6, as plainly implies they were then not barely scattered over the heathen world, but resettled in Judea again. And since Josephus,

at the end of his Antiquities, tells us that he had a mind to continue his history of the Jewish War and Jewish affairs till the thirteenth of Domitian; I take the present intimation to mean, that as he had before written their history with great care, till the destruction of Jerusalem, he intended himself to continue it during his own time, which he could no way promise to do in the like authentic manner as he had written his former works, had he not now lived in Judea, among his own people. Now that the Jews were resettled in Judea in the reign of Trajan is very well known, since they soon raised such a terrible sedition there, under their spurious Messias Barchocab, as was not appeased but by the slaughter of 580,000 of them. And that Josephus did not only in the foregoing three passages in general include himself among his nation, while he was at Rome, but meant that he was himself there also, appears by his constant use of the first plural, *we* and *us*, in all the three places, without any variation; and by the plain circumstances of Josephus himself after the death of his last patron Domitian. He had now no pretences to the favour of Nerva or Trajan; especially not towards the end of Trajan, when the Jews, his countrymen, were meditating a grand rebellion against the Romans. In these circumstances, whither could our Josephus go for security and maintenance, but to his own country of Judea, and to his native city Jerusalem? near which part of his lands given him by the former emperors lay. So that all the evidence agrees, that in this reign of Trajan Josephus must have lived in Judea; and, in all probability, at Jerusalem also. And since it has appeared already that he was a Nazarene or Ebionite Christian long before this time, see Dissertat. I. per tot., what can we suppose, but that he must join with the Nazarene or Ebionite Christians at Jerusalem, and might very probably accept of the bishopric of Jerusalem among them also? Now it appears from the very few records that Eusebius could meet with about this church of Jerusalem, after its destruction by Titus, and before its second destruction by Adrian, Hist. Eccles. IV. 4, and Præp. Evang. III. 5, that it was a very considerable church; that it observed the laws of Moses, together with those of Christ; and that it had no fewer than fifteen bishops of the circumcision, including James the brother of our Lord, though he could not learn when each of those bishops began or ended, nor how long any of them continued in that see; see Pearson, De Success. Rom. Episc. p. 7, 8; that terrible destruction under Adrian having, it seems, together with the people, almost utterly destroyed the records of that nation which belonged to this period. Nor would Eusebius have omitted an account of the death of those brethren of our Saviour, who were bishops of Jerusalem, as Hegesippus implies, ap. Euseb. Hist. Eccl. III. 20, or of the death of the famous Josephus, had he known them. However, he assures us he lighted upon a written catalogue of these fifteen bishops, and that the name of the fourteenth was Joseph; whom I suppose to have been no other than our Nazarene, or Ebionite, or perhaps now catholic Christian Josephus; though, with the rest of his church, he might still observe the laws of Moses. For the apostles themselves being Jews, as is well known, together with their Christianity observed the ceremonial laws of Moses, especially when they were in Judea; and permitted their Jewish converts to do the same, provided that there were no *necessity* laid on them for such its observation, that *justification* and *salvation* were not expected by that law, but by the Christian dispensation, and that the Gentile Christians were allowed to be entirely free from that bondage.

4. This being premised, let us now proceed to the remaining arguments, several of which are *external testimonies;* whereby it will appear that no other than such a Jewish Christian of the circumcision as Josephus could be the author of this fragment or homily now before us. And,

(1.) The general language of this address to these unbelievers, when it all along styles them Ἕλληνες, Greeks, or Gentiles, seems to me to imply that the author was himself a believing Jew, and not a Gentile; that being the original grand distinction between the several branches of mankind, with regard to religion, into Jews and Greeks, or Gentiles, as every one knows that hath but read over the New Testament. Since therefore this homily is entirely addressed to these Greeks or Gentiles, and this not improbably as distinguished from that people to which the author himself belonged, he must most probably have been himself a Jew, as was our Josephus.

(2.) The entire genius and composition of this whole homily seems to me to be just like those in our New Testament, or in St. Barnabas's Epistle; the writers of which were every one Jews; and not so like to the genius and composition of the Apostolical Constitutions, the Epistles of Clement, of Ignatius, or Polycarp, or the writings of any other apostolical man that was of Gentile extraction. For the truth of this observation I must appeal to every skilful critic, and leave it with them for their sober determination. And if that prove to be on my side, this will exactly agree with our Jew, Josephus.

(3.) The nature of this fragment, both in its addresses at the beginning and middle, and its doxology at the end, to say nothing of the general nature of its contents, bespeak it to be nothing else than what I have so often called it, a Christian homily. Now such treatises or homilies as were preserved to posterity were in the earliest times almost wholly confined to the bishops, who were then the wisest, the learnedest, and the most considerable persons in the Christian church. This any one may observe in Eusebius's catalogues of the treatises and homilies of the three first centuries; and this observation exactly agrees to my opinion, that Josephus a Christian bishop was its author.

(4.) The mention here made of the *smiles of the fathers*, and of the place or *choir of the fathers* seen out of *Hades*, sect. 3, 4, as distinct from those of the *righteous* in general, most naturally implies that the author of this homily esteemed those fathers, Abraham, and Isaac, and Jacob, &c., to have been *his fathers* also, as Luke xiii. 28; xvi. 24, 25, 27; and by consequence, that he was one of the Jewish nation, as was our Josephus. It is also not quite unworthy of our observation, that this author does not speak of *our fathers*, as one Jew speaking to other Jews might naturally say; but *the fathers*, as a Jew preaching to Gentiles would be obliged to speak.

(5.) The character here given of Christ, sect. 6, that he is Θεὸς Λόγος, *God the Word*, was hardly used in the first ages, but in the Apostolical Constitutions, V. 16, 19, 20; VI. 11; VII. 26; VIII. 1, 12, and also in the writers belonging to Judea, or to its neighbourhood Antioch and Alexandria. See Ignatius, bishop of Antioch, Ad Magnes. sect. 6; Ad Philadelph. sect. 4, 6; Ad Smyrn. sect. 1. Clement of Alexandria, Exhort. p. 74, 75. Origen of Alexandria, that lived also some time in Judea, Comment. in Joann. p. 49. Council of Antioch, ap. Prim. Christ. Revived, vol. III. p. 430. Eusebius, bishop of Cesarea in Palestine, twice, ib. p. 443; and the Creed of Arius and Euzoius presented to the Council of Jerusalem, ib. p. 487. This phrase is also no fewer than sixteen times made use of by Athanasius of Alexandria before the Council of Nice, to say nothing of those his works that are later. See the Collection of Ancient Monuments, p. 73. So that this character best of all agrees to our Josephus, a converted Jew in Judea, and probably now a Christian bishop of the circumcision at Jerusalem. Now this acknowledgment of the Divinity of Christ, in opposition to the first Ebionites, who said he was barely the son of Joseph and Mary, Constitut. VI. 6, exactly agrees to Eusebius's character of this church of Jerusalem, under these fifteen bishops of the circumcision; that *they received the knowledge of Christ after a sincere manner*, or after such a manner as Eusebius thought to be the truth. This seems to imply their belief of the *Divinity of Christ*, in the ancient sense of it; as Suspicius Severus well explains it, when he says that *this church did almost universally believe in Christ as God, under the observation of the law*, Lib. II. sect. 45, which character does, for certain, so far agree to Josephus; that as he was ever a zealous advocate for the *law of Moses*, so did he, in his famous passage concerning Christ, Antiq. B. XVIII. ch. iii. sect. 3, show himself even then not averse to the belief of his *Divinity* also. I mean when he styles him, *A wise man, if it be lawful to call him a man.* See the note on Antiq. B. I. ch. xii. sect. 2. Now as Josephus appears to have been a long while an Ebionite, so do we know from Origen that one sort of these Ebionites agreed to that his Divinity, Contr. Cels. V. p. 272, 274. Though I must confess the author of this fragment or homily refers here so often to our books of the New Testament, and peculiarly to St. Paul's Epistles, whom the Nazarenes or Ebionites hated above all the apostles, that he seems to have now embraced catholic Christianity, though probably together with the observation of the law of Moses. Which is also justly believed to have been the case not of our Josephus only, supposing him now bishop of Jerusalem, but of almost all the Christian church in Judea in his time; though indeed the unhappy loss of its records hinders us from any more distinct knowledge of this matter; the present fragment or homily being perhaps, with St. James's Epistle, the only genuine remains of that church now extant in the world.

(6.) The use of two uncommon Greek words, βρασμὸς and ἐκϐράσσων, elsewhere used by our Josephus, Of the War, B. III. ch. vii. sect. 28, and I think very rarely used by the Hellenists, is a further internal argument that Josephus was the author of this fragment.

(7.) There is one particular observation belonging to the contents of this fragment or homily that seems to me to be decretory, and to determine the question that some of this Jewish church that used the Hebrew copy of the Old Testament, nay, rather that Josephus himself in particular, was the author of it. The observation is this, that in the present address to the Greeks, or Gentiles, there are near forty references or allusions to texts of the New Testament in Greek; and not one to any of the Old Testament, either in Hebrew or Greek; and this in a discourse concerning Hades, which yet is almost five times as often mentioned in the Old Testament as in the New. What can be the reason of this, but that the Jewish *church* at Jerusalem used the Hebrew Bible alone, which those Greeks, or Gentiles, to whom the address is here made, could not understand; and that our Josephus in particular always and only used the same Hebrew Bible, and the books written in Hebrew; as I have elsewhere largely proved from his own words, Essay on the Old Test. p. 184—195, and Suppl. p. 45—48? So that the author of this fragment or homily was now forced to wave the consideration of the Old Testament, which was written in Hebrew; and confine himself to the New Testament, which was all written in Greek [even St. Matthew's Gospel as well as the rest; as the many references or allusions here made to it in Greek fully imply, and as I have elsewhere proved, Essay on the Old Test. p. 182, 183]. It is true, there are two passages here that may allude to the Fourth Book of the prophet Esdras, belonging to the Old Testament; the one concerning the original disobedience of our first parents, as the cause of man's mortality,

4 Esd. iii. 7, &c.; and the other concerning the insignificancy of the intercession of relations for the wicked at the day of judgment, chap. vii. 35—47. But then these references or allusions, if they be allowed to be such, are so far from *contradicting*, that they further *confirm* the present observation, because this was a book, so far as we now know, extant only in Greek in the days of Josephus; and so not unfit to be made use of in this address of his to the Greeks, as well as the New Testament.

5. I come now to the *external arguments*, or *ancient citations* and testimonies; and go on with the former numbers.

(8.) Porphyry, in his fourth book περὶ ἀποχῆς, gives a large account of the Essens, out of three books of our Josephus; the second book of the War, the eighteenth of the Antiquities, and the second of two books or discourses which he addressed Πρὸς τὲς Ἕλληνας, *To the Greeks ;* which can be no other, that I know of, but the second of the two discourses before us, addressed in like manner, Πρὸς τὲς Ἕλληνας, *To the Greeks*, and whose doctrine is very nearly allied to the notions of the Essens. Had we the entire discourse, it is probable the matter would be still plainer; though as it is there is no particular occasion for dispute about it. For as for what all the critics have said hitherto, that Porphyry means the second book against Apion, while that is never called by this name, and while it has nothing in it about the Essens at all, is entirely groundless.

(9.) This fragment or homily is quoted as, without dispute, Josephus's work, in the eighth century, by John Damascen, in his Parallels, p. 789, of Lequien's edition. And some clauses there quoted are esteemed by Fabricius as more correct than they stand in our present copies, ap. Havercamp. p. 64.

(10.) It is also quoted as, without dispute, belonging to Josephus, by Zonaras, Annal. I. p. 267 Now Zonaras was one very well versed in the writings of Josephus. This was in the eleventh century.

(11.) The four MSS. we have of it do all, I think, ascribe it to Josephus, and to no other, as to its true author.

(12.) It is inserted, just so much of it I mean as is cited by Zonaras, in one MS. of Josephus's history of the Jewish War, B. II. ch. ix. sect. 1, and this after the insertion of the famous testimony concerning Christ, as it is in Zonaras also, in the place above cited. So that there is great reason to suspect that the insertion of both these eminent passages into that single MS., and out of both their proper places, was only derived by the transcribers from Zonaras. Whence I lay but small stress on these citations in the MS. as distinct from those in Zonaras himself.

(13.) However, this fragment or homily must be

written by one who had *elsewhere given a more particular account of Christ, for the sake of those who sought after truth*, than was here done : Περὶ ὧ ἐν ἑτέροις λεπτομερέστερον διεληλύθαμεν, πρὸς τὸς ἐπιζητὸντας τὴν ἀλήθειαν, sect. 6. This so naturally belongs to Josephus, and his famous testimony concerning Christ, and is a part of the MS. of Josephus before mentioned also, as well as, in Zonaras, and all our other copies, that I think it a strong attestation, both to the genuine authority of that testimony, in which view it has been already quoted, in the first Dissertation prefixed, sect. 8, and to this fragment or homily, as belonging both to the same author, Josephus.

Corollary. This fragment therefore, taken in its general tenor, and as concluding with a Christian doxology, seems to be no other than an extract from, or perhaps in the largest copy an entire homily of, Josephus's, when he was bishop of Jerusalem, in his old age, about the end of Trajan ; and was certainly directed to an audience of Greeks or Gentiles. And as I esteem it a homily highly valuable ; so do I earnestly wish that the former part of this fragment, or extract, or homily, or perhaps a former homily itself, *concerning demons*, here intimated to. have gone before this, sect. 1, were extant also. But, alas ! *Non licet nobis adeo esse beatis !*

As for the objection, that Josephus having had three wives, as he tells us in his own Life, sect. 75, 76, was by the known apostolical rules incapable of being made a Christian bishop, see the note on Antiq. B. XVIII. ch. vi. sect. 6, the answer is obvious, that the words of the seventeenth Apostolical Canon are these, *He who hath been twice married after his baptism—cannot be made a bishop,* &c., plainly implying that what marriages any man had contracted before his baptism did no way exclude him from the episcopal function. And since there is not the least reason to suppose that our Josephus was twice or at all married, after he became a catholic Christian, and had been baptized, this objection vanishes to nothing. See Authent. Rec. Part II. p. 960.

As for the *style* of this homily, so much more Hellenistical than what appears in Josephus's earlier works, it would be the natural consequence of his leaving off his other Greek writers, which he read formerly at Rome, and his frequent perusal of the books of the New Testament, and the rest of the sacred and Christian writers then extant in Judea, who all wrote in that Hellenistic dialect. Nor could this be well otherwise. For as his frequent reading the Attic Greek writers, when he was comparatively young, made him then imitate their style ; so would his frequent reading the Hellenistic writers, in his old age, naturally make him imitate their style afterwards.

POSTSCRIPT

Since I finished the sixth Dissertation foregoing, upon Josephus's homily concerning *Hades*, I have received a very full and very accurate account of the citations made out of it in John Damascen's Parallels, of Le Quien's edition, which I had not myself met with before when I wrote that Dissertation ; as the reader may easily observe in my short mention of it out of Fabricius, sect. 5. The account I have of it is from my great and learned friend Mr. Richard Allin ; which, at my desire, he hath since favoured me withal. The entire account is too long for this place, but the result in brief is this : That John Damascen's Parallels, or passages taken out of ancient authors, as found in the different MSS., are collections made, partly by himself, in the eighth century, about A. D. 730 ; and partly by an earlier author, whose name is not preserved, in the seventh century, about A. D. 615, which earlier collection Damascen also transcribed into his own book. That in this earlier collection there are two large passages taken out of this homily.

The larger of the two stands under the name of Josephus ; the other under that of Meletius, bishop of Antioch, about the middle of the fourth century, or about A. D. 360, who had, it seems, himself transcribed it, either from some still earlier collector, or from this homily itself. For which citations, also, as made in Damascen, we have the authority of Zonaras, in the twelfth century, about A. D. 1120. But still the reader is to remark, (1.) That the words of Porphyry, the first author now extant that cites this work, are these : " And such are the institutions of the Essens, as Josephus writes in several parts of his works. For [he describes them] in the second book of his Jewish history, which he completely delivered in seven books ; and in the eighteenth book of his Antiquities, which work contains twenty books. As also in his second [book] πρυς τὸς "Ελληνας, *addressed to the Greeks ;* of which there are two books." (2.) That there immediately follows in Porphyry a very large extract out of Josephus's second book of the Jewish War, ch. viii. sect. 2—13; in which place of Josephus we have a particular account of the Essens' religious disposition towards God; and their doctrines about *Hades*, and the resurrection of the body, and the future state of the good in happiness, and of the wicked in misery; in perfect agreement with this homily before us. Part of which accounts are also transcribed thence by Porphyry, just after the words foregoing, sect. 11—13. (3.) That although this homily, as now extant, does not directly mention the Essens, as do the two other places cited from Josephus; yet is it probable that it might have done so, if we had it complete; whereas we have no more than a fragment, or extract out of it. And how much larger the whole might be, we may partly guess at by the largest copy, fragment, or extract, which contains no less than one quarter more than the other copies. (4.) Whereas Porphyry directly cites here the *second* book, or discourse of Josephus made to the Greeks, this extract is directly part of such a *second* book, or discourse, as the first words show; which assure us that the *former* of them was concerding *demons;* as is this *second* concerning *Hades*, the resurrection, and future state. (5.) That what is cited in Damascen, as out of Meletius bishop of Antioch, contains a remarkable expression, which is in no other copy or MS., that our Saviour Christ is Θεὸς ἐνανθρωπήσας, *A God in a man.* This language was, I think, never used till the fourth century, when Meletius lived; and seems an indication that he added it as his own paraphrase, to accommodate the other older language of Josephus to the language and taste of the age in which he lived. The Christians in the days of Josephus would rather have called him Θεὸς ἐνσαρκωθεὶς, *A God incarnate.* (6.) That the learned Ittigius himself, who yet does not own the fragment to be genuine, allows this to be one argument that it may be Josephus's own, that therein the accounts of the state and place of separate souls in *Hades* are agreeable to those that Josephus elsewhere gives us concerning those matters, Prolegom. apud Havercamp, p. 95. (7.) That the contents of this homily do certainly demonstrate its author to have been a catholic Christian when he preached or wrote it. This is not only evident through the whole contexture, and by its frequent allusions to our books of the New Testament; but particularly by his calling our Saviour *God the Word; to whom God hath committed all judgment; who, fulfilling the will of the Father, is to come as*

Judge; whom we call Christ; and whom God the Father hath glorified, &c. (8.) That if this discourse were written only, and not preached; or were written by Josephus when he was no more than a presbyter, instead of a bishop; the consequences will be very little different from those that follow from what I have already asserted on those two heads. Though I should think he who is once convinced that this discourse does really belong to our Josephus, will have no great reason to quarrel with me for believing it a homily of his, and that when he delivered it he was the fourteenth bishop of Jerusalem.

To conclude the whole. Since the many and plain *internal characters* persuade, nay, almost enforce, us to believe this extract, or fragment, to be the genuine work of our Josephus; and that, with the greatest probability, it was a homily of his, delivered publicly to the Greeks, who were always allowed to hear such homilies, when he was a catholic Christian bishop of Jerusalem; and since, withal, it is expressly quoted by name as his, by Porphyry, in the third century; since a large quotation is taken out of it by Meletius, bishop of Antioch, in the fourth century; since a still larger quotation is taken out of it, as his, in the seventh century; since both these large quotations are confirmed by John Damascen's insertion of them into his Parallels, in the eighth century; since another large citation out of it is inserted into one of Josephus's own MSS., and the same repeated as his, and Damascen's citations of it confirmed by Zonaras in the twelfth century; since we have no fewer than four MSS. copies of it, very well agreeing with one another, and all ascribing it to our Josephus, in the several centuries and places when and where those copies were written; and since, withal, we have no proper *internal characters*, or *external testimonies* in the world, to contradict the foregoing evidence on its side; I cannot but conclude, with the greatest justice, that it ought most certainly to be owned by all as the genuine work of our Josephus; and that, most probably, it was a homily of his when he was bishop of Jerusalem.

Here follows the homily itself, in the original Greek; with all the various readings out of the four MSS. copies, and out of the ancient citations. What I esteem to have been the true original reading is by me inserted in the text, and what I esteem otherwise is thrown into the margin.

Ἐσσαῖοι τοιῦτο ἐποιῦντο τὸ πολίτευμα· ὡς πολλαχῦ Ἰώσηπος τῶν πραγματειῶν ἀνέγραψεν. About
Καὶ γὰρ ἐν τῷ δευτέρῳ τῆς Ἰυδαϊκῆς Ἱςορίας, ἣν δι' ἑπτὰ βιβλίων συνεπλήρωσε. Καὶ ἐν   A. D. 270.
τῷ ὀκτωκαιδεκάτῳ τῆς ἀρχαιολογίας, ἣν δι' εἴκοσι βιβλίων ἐπραγματεύσατο. Καὶ ἐν τῷ
δευτέρῳ τῷ πρὸς τὲς Ἕλληνας· Εἰσὶ δὲ δύο τὰ βιβλία. Porphyr. Περὶ Ἀποχῆς, De
Abstinentiâ, L. IV. sect. 11. p. 158.

VARIÆ LECTIONES.

C. MS. Coislin.   H. Edit. Hœschel.
M. Le Moyne.   D. Damascen.
G. Grabe.   L. B. MS. Jose-
Z. Zonaras.   phi, Lug. Bat.

a Ἰώσηπος, G.
b ἐν τῷ πρὸς Ἕλληνας λόγῳ, Z.
Which words are omitted in Grabe's
MS., though the thing itself be thrice
in the body of the fragment there,
and twice in the other copies.

a "Ἰώσηπυ," b ἐκ τῦ πρὸς Ἕλληνας λόγυ·" Περὶ "Ἄδυ, ἐν ᾧ συνέχονται
ψυχαὶ δικαίων τε καὶ ἀδίκων.

[Of the spurious addition to this title, see sect. 1.]

c Ναὶ, C.
d τόπος, M. G., but see afterward,
sect. 5.   *ᴧ αἱ, D.

† ᴧ περ, καὶ ὑπόγειος, M.

‖ ᴧ ὃ, G.

e ἑκάτυ, D.

f τόπων, D.

g λίμνη, C. H. M. τῆς λύμνης, G.

h καταρρερίφθαι, C. H. M. G.
i ἐσκεύασθη.
k παρὰ, D.

l προσενέχθαι, G.

m deest, G.

n συνέχονται, G.
o ὡς οἱ δίκαιοι, D.

p deest, D.

q deest, G.

r θεωρίας, D.   ᴧ ὁρωμένων, G.
s βελτίονα, D. C·   t οὗ, D.
u deest, D.

x βιωτὴν, G.   y τῦτον δὲ ὀνό-
μᾳτι, G.

z deest, C. H. G. M.

ᴧ ἐπιτελῦντες, G. ἐπιγελῶντες, D.
a ἀπονειδίζοντες, G. D.
b deest, H. D. M.   c ἐς ἀγομένας,
M. H.
d ἐγγίονες, D. G.
e ὑπακύυσι, D. H. M.

f deest, M. H.

g καταπεπλήγασι, G.   h deest, D.

i ὃ, H. G. M. C.

k deest, M.

l μήτε, D.

ᴧ αἱ, D.   m μέχρι, D

n ποιησάμενος, D.

1. cΚΑΙ" ὗτος μὲν ὁ περὶ δαιμόνων dλόγος." Περὶ δὲ "Ἄδυ, ἐν ᾧ συνέχονται *ᴧ ψυχαὶ δικαίων τε καὶ ἀδίκων, ἀναγκαῖον εἰπεῖν. Ὁ "Ἄδης τόπος
ἐςὶν ἐν τῇ κτίσει ἀκατασκεύαςος· †ᴧ χωρίον ὑπόγειον· ἐν ᾧ φῶς κόσμυ οὐκ
ἐπιλάμπει. φωτὸς τοίνυν ἐν τέτῳ τῷ χωρίῳ μὴ καταλάμποντος, ἀνάγκη σκό-
τος διηνεκῶς τυγχάνειν. Τῦτο τὸ χωρίον ‖ᴧ ὡς φρύριον ἀπενεμήθη ψυχαῖς·
ἐφ' ᾧ κατεςάθησαν ἄγγελοι φρυροὶ, πρὸς τὰς fἑκάςων" πράξεις διανέμοντες
τὰς τῶν fτρόπων" προσκαίρυς κολάσεις.

2. Ἐν τέτῳ δὲ τῷ χωρίῳ τόπος ἀφώρισται τῆς gλίμνης" πυρὸς ἀσβέςυ· ἐν
ᾧ μὲν ὑδέπω τινὰ hκατερρίφθαι" ὑπειλήφαμεν. iἘσκεύαςαι" δὲ εἰς τὴν
προωρισμένην ἡμέραν kὑπὸ" Θεῦ, ἐν ᾗ δικαίας κρίσεως ἀπόφασις μία πᾶσιν
ἀξίως lπροσενεχθεῖν." καὶ οἱ μὲν ἄδικοι, καὶ Θεῷ ἀπειθήσαντες, τάτε μάταια
ἔργα χειρῶν ἀνθρώπων κατεσκευασμένα εἴδωλα, ὡς Θεὸν τιμήσαντες, ταύτης
τῆς ἀϊδίυ κολάσεως, mὡς" αἴτιοι μιασμάτων γενόμενοι, προσκριβῶσι. οἱ δὲ
δίκαιοι τῆς ἀφθάρτυ καὶ ἀνεκλείπτυ βασιλείας τύχωσιν· οἱ ἐν τῷ "Ἄδῃ
νῦν μὲν nσυνέχονται," ἀλλ' ὑ τῷ αὐτῷ τόπῳ oᾧ" καὶ οἱ ἄδικοι."

3. Μία γὰρ εἰς τῦτο τὸ χωρίον κάθοδος· ὑ τῇ πύλῃ ἐφεςῶτα ἀρχάγγελον,
ἅμα ςρατιᾷ, πεπιςεύκαμεν· ἣν πύλην διελθόντες οἱ καταγόμενοι ὑπὸ τῶν ἐπὶ
τὰς ψυχὰς τεταγμένων pἀγγέλων," ὑ μιᾷ ὁδῷ πορεύονται· ἀλλ' οἱ μὲν
δίκαιοι εἰς δεξιὰ φωταγωγύμενοι, καὶ ὑπὸ τῶν ἐφεςώτων κατὰ τόπον ἀγγέλων
ὑμνέμενοι, ἄγονται εἰς χωρίον φωτεινόν. Ἐν ᾧ οἱ ἀπ' ἀρχῆς δίκαιοι πολι-
τεύονται· ὑχ' ὑπ' ἀνάγκης κρατύμενοι, ἀλλὰ τῆς τῶν ὁρωμένων qἀγαθῶν"
rθέας" ἀεὶ ἀπολαύοντες, καὶ τῇ τῶν ἑκάςοτε καινῶν ᴧ προσδοκίᾳ ἡδόμενοι,
κἀκεῖνα τέτων sβελτίω" ἡγύμενοι. tοἷς" ὁ τόπος ὑ καματηφόρος γίνεται, ὑ
καύσων, ὑ κρύος, ὑ τρίβολος ἐν αὐτῷ· ἀλλ' ἡ τῶν πατέρων δικαίων uτε"
ὁρωμένη ὄψις πάντοτε μειδιᾷ, ἀναμενόντων τὴν μετὰ τῦτο τὸ χωρίον ἀνά-
παυσιν, καὶ αἰωνίαν xἀναβίωσιν" ἐν ὑρανῷ. yτέτῳ δὲ ὄνομα" κικλήσκομεν
κόλπον Ἀβραάμ.

4. Οἱ δὲ ἄδικοι zεἰς" ἀριςερὰ ἕλκονται ὑπὸ ἀγγέλων κολαςῶν, ὑκέτ-
εκυσίως πορευόμενοι, ἀλλὰ μετὰ βίας, ὡς δέσμιοι ἑλκόμενοι· οἷς οἱ ἐφεςῶτες
ἄγγελοι ᴧ διαπέμπονται ἀονειδίζοντες," καὶ φοβερῷ ὄμματι ἐπαπειλῦντες, εἰς
τὰ κατώτερα bμέρη" ὠθῦντες· ὑς ἀγομένυς" ἕλκυσιν οἱ ἐφεςῶτε· ἕως πλη-
σίον τῆς γεέννης. Οἱ dἔγγιον" ὄντες, τῦ μὲν βρασμῦ ἀδιαλείπτως
eἐπακύυσι," καὶ τῦ τῆς θερμῆς ἀτμῦ οὐκ ἀμοιρῦσιν· αὐτῆς δὲ τῆς ἐγγίονος
ὄψεως τὴν φοβερὰν καὶ ὑπερβαλλόντως fξάνθην" θέαν -ῦ πυρὸς ὁρῶντες,
gκαταπεπήγασι." τῇ προσδοκίᾳ τῆς μελλύσης κρίσεως ἤδη hδυνάμει" κολαζόμενοι. Ἀλλὰ καὶ ὗτοι τὸν τῶν πατέρων χορὸν, καὶ τὲς δικαίυς ὁρῶσι,
καὶ ἐπ' αὐτῷ kτύτῳ" κολαζόμενοι. Χάος γὰρ βαθὺ καὶ μέγα ἀναμέσον
ἐςήρικται· ὥςε lμὴ" δίκαιον συμπαθήσαντα προσδέξασθαι, μήτε ἄδικον τολ-
μήσαντα διελθεῖν.

5. Οὗτος ὁ περὶ "Ἄδυ λόγος· ἐν ᾧ ᴧ ψυχαὶ πάντων κατέχονται mἄχρι καιρῦ,
ὃν ὁ Θεὸς ὥρισεν, ἀνάςασιν τότε πάντων nποιησόμενος" ὑ ψυχὰς μετενσω-

ματῶν, ἀλλ' αὐτὰ τὰ σώματα ἀνιϛῶν· ἃ λελυμένα ὁρῶντες ἀπιϛεῖτε Ἕλληνες, μάθετε μὴ ἀπιϛεῖν. Τὴν γὰρ ψυχὴν γεητὴν καὶ ἀθάνατον ὑπὸ Θεῶ γεγονέναι πιϛεύσαντες, κατὰ τὸν Πλάτωνος λόγον, χρόνῳ, μὴ ἀπιϛήσητε, [a]ὡς" καὶ τὸ σῶμα ἐκ τῶν αὐτῶν ϛοιχείων [b]σύνθετον" γενόμενον δυνατὸς ὁ Θεὸς ἀναβιώσας ἀθάνατον ποιεῖν. Οὐ τὸ μὲν δυνατὸς, τὸ δὲ ἀδύνατον ῥηθήσεται ﹏περὶ Θεῶ. Ἡμεῖς ἒν καὶ σῶμα ἀνίϛασθαι πεπιϛεύκαμεν. Εἰ γὰρ φθείρεται, ἀλλ' οὐκ ἀπόλλυται. τότε γὰρ τὰ λείψανα [c]ὑποδεχομένη ἡ γῆ," τηρεῖ· καὶ δίκην σπόρῳ ﹏γενόμενα, καὶ τῷ γῆς λιπαρωτέρῳ [d]συμπλεκόμενα, ἀνθεῖ." Καὶ τὸ μὲν σπαρὲν κόκκος γυμνὸς σπείρεται, [e]κελεύσματι" δὲ τῶ δημιωργήσαντος Θεῶ θάλλων, ἠμφιεσμένος καὶ ἔνδοξος ἐγείρεται. ὃ πρότερον, εἰ μὴ ἀποθανὼν λυθῇ καὶ [f]συμμιγῇ." ὥϛε τὴν ἀνάϛασιν τῶ σώματος ὁ μάτην πεπιϛεύκαμεν. ἀλλ' εἰ καὶ λύεται πρὸς καιρὸν, διὰ τὴν ἀπ' ἀρχῆς γενομένην, παρακοὴν, ὡς εἰς χωνευτήριον εἰς γῆν καθίϛαται, πάλιν ἀναπλασθησόμενον· ὁ τοιῶτον [g]ἀνιϛάμενον," ἀλλὰ καθαρὸν, καὶ μηκέτι φθειρόμενον· [h]καὶ" ἑκάϛῳ σώματι ἡ ἰδία ψυχὴ ἀποδοθήσεται, [i]καὶ" τῶτο ἐπενδυσαμένη, οὐκ ἀνιαθήσεται, ἀλλὰ συγχαρήσεται καθαρὰ καθαρῷ παραμείνασα. ᾦ ἐν τῷ κόσμῳ νῦν δικαίως συνοδεύσασα, καὶ μὴ ἐπίβωλον ἐν πᾶσιν ἔχωσα, μετὰ πάσης ἀγαλλιάσεως ἀπολήψεται. Οἱ δὲ ἄδικοι οὐκ ἀλλοιωθέντα τὰ σώματα, ὁδὲ πάθως ἢ νόσω μεταϛάντα, ὁδὲ ἐνδοξασθέντα ἀπολήψονται· ἀλλ' ἐν οἷς νοσήμασιν ἐτελεύτων, καὶ ὁποῖοι ἐν ἀπιϛίᾳ γεγέννηνται, τοιῶτοι πιϛῶς κριθήσονται.

6. Πάντες [k]γὰρ" δίκαιοί τε καὶ ἄδικοι ἐνώπιον τοῦ Θεῶ Λόγω ἀχθήσονται· τότῳ γὰρ ὁ πατὴρ τὴν [l]κρίσιν πᾶσαν" δέδωκε, καὶ αὐτὸς βωλὴν πατρὸς ἐπιτελῶν κριτὴς παραγίνεται, ὃν Χριϛὸν προσαγορεύομεν. ﹏Οὐδὲ γὰρ Μίνως [m]καὶ Ῥαδάμανθος κριταὶ [n]οἳ" καθ' ὑμᾶς, Ἕλληνες, ἀλλ' ὃν ὁ Θεὸς [o]καὶ πατὴρ ἐδόξασε·" περὶ ὧ ἐν ἑτέροις λεπτομερέϛερον διεληλύθαμεν, πρὸς τὰς [p]ἐπιζητῶντας" τὴν ἀλήθειαν. ὅτος τὴν πατρὸς [q]εἰς πάντας" [r]δικαιοκρισίαν" ποιόμενος, [s]ἑκάϛῳ" κατὰ [t]τὰ ἔργα" παρεσκεύασε τὸ [u]δικαιον. ὃ ﹏κρίσει παραϛάντες [x]πάντες ἄνθρωποί τε, καὶ ἄγγελοι, καὶ δαίμονες," μίαν ἀποφθέγξονται ﹏φωνὴν, [y]ὅτως" λέγοντες, ΔΙΚΑΙΑ ﹏ΣΟΥ 'Η ΚΡΙΣΙΣ." [z]Ἧς φωνῆς τὸ ἀντυπόδομα ἐπ' ἀμφοτέρως [a]ἐπάγει τὸ δίκαιον" τοῖς μὲν εὖ πράξασι, [b]καὶ" δικαίως τὴν ἀΐδιον [c]τῶν ἀγαθῶν" ἀπόλαυσιν [d]παρασχόντος" τοῖς δὲ τῶν φαύλων [e]ἐργάταις" τὴν [f]αἰώνιον κόλασιν ἀπονείμαντος." Καὶ τέτοις μὲν τὸ πῦρ ἄσβεϛον διαμένει [g]καὶ ἀτελεύτητον," σκόληξ δέ τις ἔμπυρος μὴ τελευτῶν, μηδὲ σῶμα διαφθείρων, ἀπαύϛῳ [h]δὲ" ὀδύνῃ ἐκ [i]σώματος" ἐκβράσσων παραμένει. ‖ Τέτως οὐκ ὕπνος ἀναπαύσει, [k]ὁ νὺξ παρηγορήσει, ὁ θάνατος τῆς κολάσεως ἀπολύσει," ὁ παράκλησις συγγενῶν μεσιτευσάντων ὀνήσει· ὁ γὰρ ἔτι δίκαιοι ὑπ' αὐτῶν ὁρῶνται, ὁδὲ μνήμης γίνονται ἄξιοι· [l]μόνοι" δὲ οἱ δίκαιοι δικαίων [m]μεμνήσονται" ἔργων, δι' ὧν ἐπὶ τὴν ἐρανίαν βασιλείαν κατήντησαν· ἐν ᾗ οὐκ ὕπνος, ὁ λύπη, ὁ φθορὰ, ὁ φρον[n]τις," ὁδὲ νὺξ, ὁδὲ ἡμέρα, χρόνῳ μετρωμένη· ὁκ ἥλιος ἀνάγκῃ κύκλον ἐρανῶ δρόμῳ ἐλαυνόμενος· ὡρῶν μέτρα ἢ κέντρα πρὸς εὔγνωϛον ἀνθρώπων βίον διαμετρωμένα, ὡροθετῶντος. ὁ σελήνη φθίνωσα, ἢ αὔξωσα, ἢ τροπὰς καιρῶν [o]ἐπάγωσα" οὐκ ὑγραίνωσα γῆν, ὁδὲ ἥλιος ἐπικαίων, οὐκ ἄρκτος ϛρεφομένη οὐκ ὡρίων γενώμενος, οὐκ ἄϛρων πλάνη ἐνάριθμος, ὁ δύσβατος γῆ, ὁδὲ δυσεύρετος παραδεί﹏ αὐλὴ, ὁδὲ δεινὸν θαλάσσης φρύαγμα, κωλύον ἐπιβάντα πατεῖν. εὔβατος δὲ καὶ αὕτη τοῖς δικαίοις γενήσεται, ὅτε τῶ ὑγρῶ ϛερεωμένη, [p]ὁδὲ τοῦ ϛερῶ διὰ τὸ κωφὸν ἰχνῶ πατωμένη," οὐκ ἐρανὸς ἀοίκητος ἀνθρώποις, ὁδὲ τότε [q]τῆς" ἀναβάσεως [r]ἡ ὁδὸς" ἀνεύρετος, ὁ γῆ ἀνέργαϛος, ὁδὲ ἀνθρώποις ἐπίπονος· αὐτομάτη δὲ φύωσα κάρπης πρὸς ἐνκοσμίαν, [s]ᾗ προσάξει ὁ δεσπότων." ὁ θηρίων [t]γενέσεις" πάλιν, ὁδὲ τῶν λοιπῶν [u]ζώων" ἐκβρασσομένη ὁσία· ὁδὲ γὰρ [x]ἄνθρωπος" πάλιν γεννᾷ· ἀλλ' ὁ [y]τῶν" δικαίων ἀριθμὸς διαμένει ἀνέκλειπτος, ἅμα δικαίοις ἀγγέλοις, καὶ πνεύμασι. [z]Θεῷ," καὶ τῷ τότω Λόγῳ ὡς τῶν δικαίων χορὸς ἀνδρῶν τε καὶ γυναικῶν ἀγήρως καὶ ἀφθάρτως διαμένει· ὑμνῶν τὸν ἐπὶ ταῦτα προαγόμενον Θεὸν, διὰ τῆς τοῦ ἐν βίῳ εὐτάκτω νομοθεσίας. Σὺν οἷς καὶ πᾶσα κτίσις ἀδιάλειπτον ὕμνον ἀνοίσει, ἀπὸ τῆς φθορᾶς εἰς ἀφθαρσίαν, διαυγεῖ καὶ καθαρῷ πνεύματος δεδοξασμένη. Οὐκ ὑπ' ἀνάγκης δεσμῶ συσχεθήσεται, ἀλλὰ

[a] deest, G.   [b] deest, D.

[c] γῆ ὑποδεξαμένη, G.
﹏ πιανομένῳ, G. [d] συμπλεκομένῳ ἀνθήσει, G.
[e] κελεύσιμόν τι, M. H.

[f] γῆ συμπηγῇ, G.

[g] φθειρόμενον, G.

[h] ὡς, G. [i] deest, G.

[k] δὲ, D. Z. G.

[l] πᾶσαν κρίσιν, D. deest πᾶσαν, ap. Zon. et L. B.
﹏ Θεὸν ἐνανθρωπήσαντα, D.
[m] ἢ, D. [n] deest, Z. L. B.
[o] ἐδόξασε καὶ πατὴρ, D.
[p] ζητῶντας, Z. L. B.
[s] ἑκάϛω, Z. L. B. [r] δικαίαν κρίσιν, D.
﹏ πᾶσι, Z. L. B. ﹏ τῇ, D.
[t] τὸ ἴδιον, D. [u] deest, D.
[x] οἱ πάντες, G. ἄγγελοί τε, καὶ ἄνθρωποι, καὶ δαίμονες, D.
﹏ αὐτῷ, D. [y] deest, D.
[z] 'Η ΚΡΙΣΙΣ ΣΟΥ, D.
[a] τὸ δίκαιον ἐπάγει, D.
[b] deest, C. H. G. M. Z. L. B.
[c] desunt, C. H. G. Z. L. B. M.
[d] παρέχον, D.
[e] ἐραϛαῖς, C. Z. L. B. H. G. M.
[f] ἀΐδιον κόλασιν ἀπονέμοντος, D. ἀπονέμοντος, L. Β. [g] desunt, D.
[h] deest, D. [i] ϛώματος, D.
[k] [Καὶ ἄλλα ἐπὶ τέτοις φησὶν·] Z. desunt, D.

[l] μόνον, D. [m] μέμνηνται, Ε
[n] ὁ πόνος, ὁ λύπη, ὁ φρόντις, D.

[o] ἀπάγωσα, G.

[p] desunt, H. M.

[q] deest, G. [r] ὁδὸς, G.

[s] desunt, H. M.

[t] γένεσις, G. [u] deest, G.

[x] ἀνθρώπως, M. ἀνθρώποις, H.
[y] deest, G.
[z] Θεῶ, G. H. M. C. want the greatest part of the rest to the end.

ἐλευθερία ζῶσα ἑκύσιον τὸν ὕμνον, ἅμα τοῖς ἐλευθερωθεῖσιν πάσης δυλείας
ἀγγέλοις τε καὶ πνεύμασιν, καὶ ἀνθρώποις αἴνεσιν τὸν πεποιηκότα.

7. [a]Τέτοις" [b]ἐὰν" πεισθέντες Ἕλληνες, καταλείψητε τὴν ματαιότητα τῆς
περὶ γένυς, καὶ χρημάτων πόρυ, σοφίας, καὶ μὴ περὶ λέξαις ῥημάτων ἀσχο-
λύμενοι, τὸν νῦν εἰσπλανῆσαι νω—ητε· ἀλλὰ τοῖς θεοπνεύτοις προφήταις,
καὶ Θεῦ καὶ Λόγυ ἐξηγηταῖς ἐγχειρίσαντες τὰς ἀκοὰς, Θεῷ πιστεύσητε,
[c]ἔσεσθε καὶ τέτων κοινωνοὶ," καὶ τῶν μελλόντων [d]τεύξεσθε" ἀγαθῶν,
ἀμέτρυ τε ἐρανῦ ἀνάβασιν, καὶ τὴν ἐκεῖ βασιλείαν ὄψεσθε φανερῶς. εἰ γὰρ
ὁ Θεὸς, ἃ νῦν σεσιώπεται, ἃ ὕτε ὀφθαλμὸς εἶδεν, ὕτε ὖς ἤκυσεν, ὕτε ἐπὶ
[e]καρδίαν" ἀνθρώπυ ἀνέβη, ὅσα [f]ἑτοίμασεν ὁ Θεὸς" τοῖς ἀγαπῶσιν αὐτόν.

8. Ἐφ᾽ οἷς ἂν εὕρω ὑμᾶς, ἐπὶ τύτοις κρινῶ παρ᾽ ἕκαστα· βοᾷ τὸ Τέλος τῶν
ἁπάντων. ὥστε καὶ ταῦτα εὐπεποιηκότι τὸν βίον, λήξαντος καὶ τοῦ καὶ ὅλυ
τέλυς ἐξώκηλαν, τῇ πρὸς κακίαν ἀνόητοι οἱ πρόσθεα πόνοι, ἐπὶ τῇ καταστροφῇ
τοῦ δράματος ἐξάθλῳ γενομένῳ. Τῶτε χεῖρον καὶ ἐπισεσυρμένως βιώσαντι
πρότερον, ἐστιν ὕστερον μετανοήσαντι πολλῦ χρόνυ πολιτείαν πονηρὰν ἐκνι-
κῆσαι, τῷ μετὰ τὴν μετάνοιαν χρόνῳ. ἀκριβείας δὲ δεῖται πολλῆς, ὑπὲρ τῆς
μακρὰν ὅσῳ πεποιηκόσι σώμασι διαίτης χρεία, καὶ προσοχῆς πλείονος ἐστιν
μέν. δυνατὸν γὰρ ἴσως ἀθρόως ἀποκόψαι πάθη σύστροφα, ἀλλὰ μετὰ Θεῦ
δυνάμεος, καὶ ἀνθρώπων ἱκησίας, καὶ ἀδελφῶν βοηθείας, καὶ εἰλικρινῦς με-
τανοίας, καὶ συνεχῦς μελέτης καταρθῶται. Καλὸν μὲν τὸ μὴ ἁμαρτάνειν·
ἀγαθὸν δὲ καὶ τὸ ἁμαρτάνοντα μετανοεῖν. ὥσπερ ἄριστον τὸ ὑγιαίνειν ἀεὶ,
καλὸν δὲ καὶ τὸ ἀνασφῆλαι μετὰ τὴν νόσον. [g]Τῷ Θεῷ" δόξα, καὶ τὸ κράτος,
εἰς τὺς αἰῶνας τῶν αἰώνων· Ἀμήν.

[a] τέτυς, G.   [b] οἱ πεισθέντες
τοῖς λόγοις ἄνθρωποι, H. τέτοις
οἱ πεισθέντες, M.

[c] ἔσεσθε καὶ τῶν δικαίων κοινωνοὶ,
H. ἔσεσθαι, M.
[d] τεύξεσθαι, H.

[e] καρδίας, L. M.
[f] ὁ Θεὸς ἑτοίμασε, H

[g] Αὐτῷ ἡ, H. M. G.

DISSERTATION VII

OF THE

LEARNED CHRISTOPHER CELLARIUS:

WHEREIN

THE HISTORY OF THE FAMILY OF HEROD BY FLAVIUS JOSEPHUS IS VINDICATED, AS IT DE-
SERVES, FROM THE LEARNED JOHN HARDUIN'S SUSPICIONS OF FORGERY; AND THAT HIS-
TORY IS SHOWED TO BE AGREEABLE TO ANCIENT COINS.

1. SINCE we are about to discourse of the family of Herod, we must explain whose fidelity it is we rely upon in this history : it is that of Flavius Josephus, the most excellent author of the History of the Jews ; whose authority has been esteemed so great by the ancients, by the moderns, and by those of the middle ages, that they cannot ascribe greater authority to any other historian. For how great is the reputation he was in with Jerome, when in his twenty-second Epistle to Eustochium, ch. xv., he compares him with the very best historian we have, and styles him the Grecian Livy ! that is, he styles him one whose abilities, industry, and fidelity are not less admired by all men, than are the like qualities in Titus Livius of Padua ; of whom it is related by Pliny, Book II. Epistle III., as also by

Jerome, Epistle CIII. chap. i., that *a certain person of Cadiz came from the utmost part of the earth on purpose to see him, and as soon as he had seen him went away.* Eusebius, who is himself an author greatly esteemed, in his Ecclesiastical History, Book III. chap. ix., calls Josephus *an author worthy of credit.* And, that I may add the testimony of one only of the moderns, but he of the highest reputation, Josephus is called by the great Scaliger, in the Prolegomena to his Emendatio Temporum, the *greatest lover of truth* of all historians, and that not undeservedly.

2. The greater commendations therefore Josephus has received, and that from persons themselves greatly commended, and this by uninterrupted consent, the greater is the wonder we naturally

have that a person of great fame, and one who has procured himself extraordinary commendation for his learning, both by his Notes upon Pliny, and his illustrating of the geography of cities and nations from coins, we mean John Harduin, in the Prolusion to his Chronology restored from Coins, lately printed at Paris, speaks with so much derogation of the authority of Josephus, that he takes him for a foolish, a forged, and a supposititious author; and this, as he says, he is induced to do, upon the credit of coins, which commonly contradict Josephus's narrations in the history of Herod's family. For myself, as I have a great value for ancient coins, and believe that many things in history and chronology may be corrected from them; so have not I yet seen reason to alter my opinion on account of these coins which are produced by Harduin, or thence to slight the agreeing opinion of antiquity and of the past ages about Josephus; nor shall I permit his reputation to be entirely eluded, despised, or subverted by them. I shall therefore apply myself, with the greatest industry I am able, to lay before every one's eyes the coins alleged by this author, together with his reasonings upon them, and add their interpretation; and this in a manner so agreeable to the truth, that we may give our assent to such coins as are genuine, and yet, at the same time, Josephus's history may have its reputation preserved inviolable.

3. The tradition concerning the family of the Herods, derived from Josephus, is well known by all the learned, and hitherto agreed to by general consent; and is briefly repeated in my Antiqua Historia, with the places out of Josephus every where noted. It is this: that Herod, the son of Antipater, which Herod was born of an illustrious family of the proselytes of Idumea, received the supreme authority over Palestine from his father, (he having received it from Julius Cæsar,) and lost it again upon the invasion of Antigonus, the last of the race of the Hasmoneans, assisted by the Parthians; but that he in a little time recovered it again, by the aid of Antony, together with the title of king: and that by this means, under the patronage of Augustus Cæsar, who had confirmed him in his kingdom, he governed, in a severe manner, and for a great number of years, all Palestine, in its utmost extent, between Syria, Arabia, and Egypt. That Archelaus, the son of this Herod, was banished into Gaul, when he had reigned over Judea and Samaria nine years, by the name of ethnarch; and that then a Roman province was erected out of his possessions, which was governed by the procurators of Cæsar. That his other sons, Herod Antipas and Philip, did each of them govern their several tetrarchies; the former having under him Galilee and Perea, the latter Iturea and Trachonitis: and that when the latter was dead, and the former banished, Agrippa, the grandson of the first Herod, by his son Aristobulus, whom he had slain, received that entire kingdom which had belonged to his grandfather,

by the favour of Claudius Cæsar, its provincial government being dissolved. But that when he was dead, which happened in a few years, Judea became a Roman province again; yet so that his son, who was Agrippa junior, was made king of Chalcis, and afterward of Abylene, and of the tetrarchy of Philip.

4. Harduin dissents from this history in several points. First, he says that Herod began to have dominion by the help of Julius Cæsar; and that he was king, not over all Palestine, but over Judea and Samaria only. That Archelaus succeeded his father in the same kingdom, and had in like manner the title of king; but that Galilee, with other parts, was under the dominion of Zenodorus the tetrarch, who was succeeded, during their father's lifetime, by Herod the son of Herod, and Philip his brother, each of them a tetrarch, upon a partition of his possession; and that this Herod the tetrarch was the murderer of *John the Baptist*, and was not a Jew, nor a proselyte, but a Gentile, and afterward made king; and the same person who slew James, and cast Peter into prison; and that he is unjustly distinguished from [Herod] the tetrarch, under the name of Agrippa. That Judea, which once had received the form of a province, after the death of Archelaus, (whose banishment he denies,) did never recover the state of a kingdom again, as Josephus relates. These and others are the paradoxical opinions of this man. Let us examine them every one distinctly.

5. This very learned man's opinion of the commencement of the dominion of Herod, p. 24, is as follows: *Judea was bestowed on Herod, as at present appears to me,* [says Harduin,] *on this occasion. Julius Cæsar, when he was dictator, owed Herod a great sum of money, as we may conjecture from Tully's words to Atticus,* Book VI. Epist. 1. BUT YOU, SIR, HAVE YOU EXTORTED FIFTY ATTIC TALENTS OF CÆSAR, BY THE MEANS OF HEROD? A strange, that I may not say a ridiculous, thing this! The Epistle was written by Cicero in Asia, when he was proconsul, and Cæsar was still in Gaul. How therefore could Herod the Idumean's money come to him, who before the Alexandrian war was not so much as known to Cæsar? Besides this, the place has such puzzling various readings, that some do not read *Herodes*, but *Orodes:* and some for *jamne vos* have a monstrous reading, *Genuarios;* whence some there are who can discover Genuæos, the name of a city among the Allobroges. How much more clear and intelligible is the history of Josephus, that Antipater, the father of Herod, the friend of Hyrcanus the king, had given great assistance to Cæsar in Egypt, when he besieged and took Pelusium, and at other battles; from whom he received this reward of his labours, that he should be either made a coadjutor to Hyrcanus the king, in the exercise of the government; or that he should exercise it alone, and Hyrcanus, who was also the high priest, should govern in

sacred rather than in civil affairs! See Josephus, Of the War, B. I. ch. xviii.

6. We are now to determine the bounds of Herod's kingdom. While his father was alive, he was governor of Galilee. By which means he came into the friendship of Sextus Cæsar, the proconsul of Syria. But upon the death of his father, who was taken out of the way by Malichus's fraud, that is, he was poisoned, the war happened with Antigonus, who was supported by the Parthians : in which war king Hyrcanus was carried away into captivity; Phasaelus, Herod's brother, killed himself in prison; and Herod himself escaped with difficulty into Italy ; where when, by the assistance of Antony, he was declared king by the Roman senate, he disputed his title with Antigonus for some time, till Antigonus was overcome by the arms of the Romans, and by Sosius, their general, was taken and beheaded. By this means Herod came to the possession of the entire kingdom of the Hasmoneans, a part of which was Galilee and the neighbouring countries. On the contrary, the learned Harduin affirms, p. 24, that the ethnarchy and royalty of Herod appertained only to Judea and Samaria.

7. The arguments which induce him so to determine are such as these. In the first place, that, Luke i. 5, he is only called *king of Judea.* But certainly, if we take Judea in so narrow a sense, he must not have reigned over Samaria neither. But if it be taken in a larger acceptation, it comprehends Galilee and Perea as well as Samaria. After this, he objects the succession of Archelaus to these two parts only, [Judea and Samaria,] when yet he is said, Matt. ii. 22, to have *reigned in the stead of his father ;* as if this language must signify that the entire inheritance of his father was left to him his son. It is true, those words do signify what this learned man would have, unless a testament intervene, or a different disposition from a superior lord, such as was Augustus ; by both which two only of the four parts of the kingdom came to the elder son, and the other two to his brethren, the tetrarchs, Antipas and Philip. He further supposes that there is another consideration which restrains the kingdom of Herod [to Judea and Samaria], that he built no cities in Galilee, as monuments of his fidelity and regard to the Romans, as he built Cesarea and Sebaste elsewhere. But neither did he build any in Idumea ; and, if we speak strictly, nor in Judea itself, for Cesarea was out of the limits of Judea, as appears from Acts xii. 19. It is sufficient that he built such cities in some parts of his dominion ; it is not necessary that he should build such in every part of them.

8. At length he urges this, as his principal argument, that in the times of Herod Galilee belonged to Zenodorus the tetrarch ; and that Herod's sons must have received it from him, either by some intermarriage, or by some other title, and not by paternal inheritance. This he believes to be true

upon the credit of one or two coins, which have the face of Octavian, and on the reverse the face of Zenodorus, without any diadem, and with this inscription ; ΖΗΝΟΔΩΡΟΣ ΤΕΤΡΑΡΧΗ . . . . ΓΗ . . . . . and in another ΖΗΝΟΔΟΡΟΥ ΤΕΤΡΑΡΧΟΥ . . . . with the other letters so far erased that they are not legible. In the former, the era of the Greeks is visible, and thus expressed, L. ΒΡΣ, that is, CLXXXII. But how does this contribute to the diminution of the kingdom of Herod ? Josephus, in his Jewish Antiquities, B. XV. ch. ix., assigns to Zenodorus Trachonitis, with the neighbouring countries, and expressly distinguishes them from Galilee ; which countries Augustus bestowed on Herod not till after the death of Zenodorus ; which thing is confirmed by Dio Cassius, Book LIV. p. 526, at the year of the building of Rome DCCXXXIV., *Augustus bestowed on Herod the tetrarchy of Zenodorus.* This tetrarchy was nearly the same with that which Philip afterward received by paternal inheritance, including then Paneas, as says Josephus ; but still all of it out of the bounds of Galilee. But Harduin, p. 30, says, *I incline to believe that Zenodorus was at the same time tetrarch of Galilee.* But since he produces no evidence but his own *inclination,* that is, nothing but *conjecture,* we have greater reason to believe, and so do firmly assert, that from the extent of the kingdom of the Hasmoneans [into which Herod succeeded] it appears that Galilee was not among the possessions of Zenodorus. As to what he alleges of [Octavian's and Zenodorus's] faces, a thing unaccustomed in Jewish coins, we turn it upon its author, that because Galilee was always inhabited by Jews, as is abundantly known from the Gospels, coins with faces upon them, such as are these of Zenodorus, cannot belong to a governor of Galilee. Only I must not omit one thing concerning Herod, after his father's death, but before the Parthian war, ere I proceed to what remains ; that he, as well as his brother Phasaelus, were declared *tetrarchs,* as Josephus informs us, Antiq. B. XIV. ch. xiii. sect. 1 ; but that when Hyrcanus was taken prisoner, and his brother Phasaelus dead, he made use of the name of *ethnarch,* as we are taught by that most illustrious person Ezekiel Spanheim, the most learned of all men in this kind of literature, De Præst. et Usu Numism. p. 447, where he produces a coin with this inscription, ΗΡΩΔΟΥ ΕΘΝΑΡ . . . . which he, out of his great sagacity, thinks to be no other than this first Herod, before he obtained of the Romans the name of king. [But see the note on the War, B. II. ch. vii. sect. 3.]

9. Let us now make some inquiry about Archelaus, to whom Josephus ascribes the dignity of *ethnarch,* but not of *king,* as given him by Augustus, Antiq. B. XVII. ch. xiii. ; and he relates that Archelaus himself, before he had the possession confirmed by Augustus, *avoided the taking upon him the name of king,* ch. xi., because that entirely

depended on the authority and assent of Cæsar. But Harduin is persuaded that he was equally a king with his father, because, Matt. ii. 22, he is said to have *reigned*, and to have succeeded his father. But who is there so ignorant as not to know that the sacred writers often speak with the vulgar? which vulgar, especially those of the Jewish nation, call also lesser princes *kings*. As is the other Herod, in the same history, called by Matthew, chap. xiv. 1, and by Luke, chap. ix. 7, and this according to the genius and decree of the Romans, the *tetrarch;* yet is he called by Mark, in a popular way of speaking, a *king*, chap. vi. 14. Archelaus did indeed succeed in the room of his father, but only in part, which is there styled Judea, by way of restriction, not in the entire kingdom; nor indeed in the name of king, which was not hereditary, but to be granted by the liberality of the Romans.

10. There is no small dissent also about the years of Archelaus, and the time of his death. Josephus, at the end of his seventeenth book, says that Archelaus was accused by his brethren, and banished to Vienna in Gaul, by Augustus, in the tenth year of his principality; that is, after his ninth year was over. Dio Cassius, Book LV. p. 567, consents to the thing itself. *Herod of Palestine*, says he, *was accused by his brethren, and was banished beyond the Alps.* Which banishment happened, according to his enumeration of the consuls of every year, on the eighth year before the death of Augustus, which was nearly the eighth year of Christ's age [rather the tenth. See the Addenda to my fifth of the Six Dissertations, p. 335—355]. But by Josephus's computation could not happen before the eleventh year of Christ's age; which to Harduin, p. 38, appears repugnant to the Holy Scripture, where it is said that our Lord Christ, before he was twelve years of age, frequented the temple every year; which seems most probably to be meant from his eighth year, that we may believe that four years at least before that time he had gone up to the temple, which he would not have done while Archelaus was alive, from whom he had fled [into Egypt]. This can hardly be proved from the context in Luke, (chap. ii.,) where *according to custom* is not to be referred to the child Christ, but to his parents, or to the feast days, and their ceremonies; unless the words, *supposing him to have been in the company*, refer to it; as many interpreters do refer them to that matter, and thence collect the same age of Christ. Against which opinion I say nothing. Nor do I believe that, because he [once] fled from Archelaus, it can be firmly concluded that he came not to the temple while he was alive. When his parents returned from Egypt with the child, they did not so much fly from Archelaus, as he was Herod's son; (for then they would not have trusted themselves to another son of his, who ruled in Galilee;) but they were afraid that their place of abode at Bethlehem would be discovered to him.

11. But as to numbers of years, I am not much concerned, especially when they are written in figures, wherein some mistakes very easily happen. There are no genuine coins of Archelaus remaining [yet see the note cited on sect. 8 before]. That which can be clearly and certainly collected from the coin which Harduin shows us is no more but this, that Archelaus was removed before the thirty-ninth year of the victory at Actium. For that coin having an *ear of corn*, the symbol of fertility; and a *palm tree*, the glory of Judea; shows the name of CÆSAR only, and the number XXXIX. Whence we conjecture, that it was coined not in a kingdom, or ethnarchy, but in Judea, as now become a province. But on what year soever of Archelaus his government ceased, there is a greater controversy about the manner of its ceasing. In Josephus he is banished. In Harduin he died without an heir. Now because Dio Cassius agrees with Josephus, and that Dio calls him Herod, by the common name of the family, whom others call Archelaus, as has been usual in the instances of Antipas and Agrippa, we do the more firmly adhere to our opinion; and the rather so, because the Jews approach very near to the same. For Ben Gorion, at the end of his sixty-first chapter, says that *the fifth day after Archelaus's dream, the Roman army came up against Archelaus, whose commander bound him with chains, and sent him to Rome, where he died.* This author agrees [to Josephus] in his transportation; though he mistake in the determination both of the manner and the place.

12. But, as we said before, the greatest controversy is about Herod the tetrarch, and Agrippa the king; which two are distinguished by Josephus, as the one the son of Herod, the murderer of the Baptist, by his peculiar name Antipas, and the very same a tetrarch of Galilee, but not a king, and banished into Gaul by Caius Cæsar. The other Agrippa Herod, the grandson of Herod the Great, by Aristobulus, whom he had slain; dignified by Caius Cæsar with the tetrarchies of. Philip and Lysanias, and with the name of king; and had afterward, for an augmentation, the tetrarchy of Antipas given him by Claudius, as also the countries of Judea and Samaria; one who reigned not long, but perished after a most fatal manner, when the third year of Claudius was hardly expired. Both these are with Harduin one and the same Herod, for a long time a tetrarch, and at last a king; and so the same person who slew John the Baptist and James the brother of John. It is incumbent on me now to examine very diligently into this matter.

13. The first thing that Harduin undertakes is this, to persuade us that Herod the tetrarch was neither Jew nor proselyte, but a Gentile, p. 54, &c. Now certainly he who was born of a Jewish father, and derived from a nation which had universally, full ninety years before, joined itself to the Jews, as proselytes; and who governed the Jewish people, such as the Galileans were: and who went to Je-

rusalem, to Jewish festivals every year, and heard John the Baptist gladly; shall we deny that such a one was initiated into the Jewish religion? He was born of Herod the king, an observer of the Jewish law; as appears not only from Josephus, but even from that joke of Augustus's in Macrobius, Saturnal. II. 4, *It is better to be Herod's hog than his son.* It is not indeed set down in the Holy Scriptures that this tetrarch was Herod's son, which Josephus affirms. But if we will not believe Josephus, an ancient inscription will evince it to be true, which is brought to light by that most diligent author Jac. Spon. Miscell. Erud. Antiq. fol. 338; ʽΗΡΩ-ΔΗΝ ʽΗΡΩΔΟΥ ΒΑΣΙΛΕΩΣ ʽΥΙΟΝ ΤΕΤΡΑΡΧΗΝ, *Herod the tetrarch, the son of Herod the king.* Nor were the Idumeans, from whom Herod sprung, in this age proselytes, but Jews, having been admitted into the Jewish religion a long time; insomuch that Scaliger proves, in his Animadversions on Eusebius, p. 165, that the first Herod was the great great-grandchild of a *proselyte.* Which arguments sufficiently assure us that the case was not the same with the tetrarch as with the Greeks, John xii. 20, as Harduin believes, when he went up to Jerusalem to worship; but like a Jew, and one that made a full profession of the Jews' religion. And for the argument he deduces from that unlawful matrimony with his brother's wife, disapproved of by John, against the tetrarch's being of the Jewish religion, the contrary seems to me to be clear; nor does this argument appear to me to require many words in answer to it.

14. After this he brings an accusation against Josephus, as a falsifier, from a coin, and the number of years inscribed on it. It is thus engraven in Greek letters; ʽΗΡΩΔΗΣ ΤΕΤΡΑΡΧΗΣ ΜΓ., and on the reverse ΓΑΙΩ ΚΑΙΣΑ. ΤΕΡΜ. ΣΕΒ. Or, as that great man Hen. Noris, in his particular dissertation upon the coin of Herod Antipas, expresses it in his copper cut: On the laurel of the forepart, ΓΑΙΩ ΚΑΙΣΑΡ ΓΕΡ . . . . . ΝΙΚΩ. On the reverse, about a palm tree, ʽΗΡΩΔΗΣ ΤΕΤΡΑΡΚΗΣ; with the letters of the year ΜΓ. Whence it seems to be certain that Herod was in the forty-third year of his reign in the days of Caius Caligula. But then this is not repugnant to Josephus's history, who relates that the tetrarch was banished in no other reign than that of Caius the emperor, and indeed in his last year. See Antiq. B. XVIII. ch. ix. And Noris, just now quoted, so orders his calculation, in which he was very skilful, that the last year of Caius well agrees to the forty-third year of the tetrarchy. [See this more exactly computed in the note on the War, B. I. ch. xxxiii. sect. 8.] And if, in the vulgar way of computation, the number of the tetrarchy be too great, it will be no inconvenience to say that Antipas was made governor of Galilee while his father was alive, or some years before he died; as was his father Herod made by Antipater his father while he was alive, and had

the supreme power, as we said above. This hypothesis will be sufficient to support that calculation, even though we suppose there be no other epocha here to be understood besides that of the tetrarchate. [All this is needless; for this coin exactly agrees with the true chronology of Herod the Great, and strongly confirms it; as is shown in the note already referred to.]

15. Moreover, Harduin thinks that the tetrarch and the king were one and the same person, from the common name of Herod given to both; while the Scripture never names either Antipas, or Agrippa the Great. But he gains nothing by this; for although the Scripture does not mention those names of distinction, which Josephus does, yet has it other characters of distinction sufficiently clear; while, Acts xii., xiii., in both their beginnings, the one Herod is called *king*, and the other *tetrarch*, which are different dignities and offices. And how often is it that other writers name the Antiochuses and the Ptolemies, without the addition of other proper titles, by which they were distinguished! It is true, Justin Martyr, in his Dialogue against Trypho, p. 330, calls Herod the son of Herod, in whose reign Christ was born, *king;* but while he calls him *king* of the Jews, and his *father's successor*, he sufficiently exposes his unskilfulness in history.

16. This learned man [Harduin] therefore appeals to another coin, whereon it is written ΒΑΣΙ-ΛΕΥΣ ʽΗΡΩΔ . . . . . ΥΔΙΟΣ; and on the reverse ΚΛΑΥΔΙΩ ΚΑΙΣΑΡΙ ΣΕΒΑΣΤΩ ΕΤ Γ.: *King Herod, a lover of Claudius;* and, *To Claudius Cæsar Augustus, the third year.* What cogent argument is there why we must needs understand this of Herod, *the son of Herod?* Or what hinders but that, with the same great man, whom I again name to do myself honour, Ez. Spanheim, p. 443, we may understand it of Agrippa the Great? To be sure he lived three years in that kingdom, which was augmented for his sake by Claudius, as Josephus testifies, at the end of his nineteenth book; as a mark of his gratitude for which favour he desired to be called *A lover of Claudius*, and named some cities of his kingdom, as Gaba and Tiberias, *Claudian cities*, as the forequoted Henry Noris has informed us also from coins. To which class I think that coin ought also to be referred, which Lucas Holstenius, who was once the glory of the Germans in Italy, produced out of the treasury of the Barberini; ΒΑΣΙΛΕΥΣ ʽΗΡΩΔΗΣ; and on the reverse, ΚΛΑΥΔΙΑ ΚΑΙΣΑΡΕΑ: *King Herod; the Claudian Cesarea.*

17. This is that Herod whom Josephus calls Agrippa the Great, who is mentioned in the twelfth chapter of the Acts of the Apostles. But if this very learned man [Harduin] contemns, as he uses to do, the testimony of Josephus, there will however be no foundation for despising the opinion of the most ancient Syrian interpreter, who, to take

away all scruple, acts here not like an interpreter, but a paraphrast, in expounding a text of a doubtful sense, Acts xii. 1, with the utmost perspicuity; *Herod the king, who was named Agrippa.* What could be said more clearly, and that in a version of so great antiquity, that it is difficult for us to find a record more ancient? So it is in all the copies; nor has there ever been the least variety of reading, whence a conjecture might have arisen of its novelty, or of an interpolation.

18. Since therefore this learned person alleges nothing from the coins which might overthrow the common opinion concerning the family of Herod, derived from Josephus, I must persist in this opinion, that in Acts xii. we are to understand Herod Agrippa, the son of Aristobulus, on whom Claudius Cæsar had bestowed the kingdom of his grandfather. He had been cast into prison by Tiberius, to whom he had made an imprecation; and was released by Caius Cæsar, and made king over the tetrarchies of Philip and Lysanias. After the third year was over, he received the possession of the tetrarchy of Herod; and soon after received from Claudius Samaria also, as well as Judea. So that he, at length, was in the possession of all Palestine, or land of Israel, for three years, until his fatal death; which death is described by Josephus, as well as by St. Luke; though not so distinctly by Josephus as by St. Luke. See Antiq. B. XIX. at the end; and Dio Cassius, Book LIX. p. 645, and Book LX. p. 670.

19. We have another testimony to add, and that from an enemy, I mean Justus of Tiberias; between whom and Josephus, who was his contemporary, there was a bitter enmity. However, he agrees to the distinction he has made between the Herods. Photius, in his Bibliotheca, makes the following extract out of his Chronicon, Cod. XXXIII. " Justus begins his history from Moses, and ends it not till the death of Agrippa, the seventh [ruler] in the family of Herod, and the last king of the Jews; who took the government under Claudius, had it augmented under Nero, and still more augmented by Vespasian. He died in the third year of Trajan." That is, in the royal family of Herod, Agrippa jun., was the the seventh and last, who began to reign under Claudius, and died in the third year of Trajan. Which number agrees well with Josephus, in whom these are the rulers: I. Herod the Great. II. Archelaus. III. Philip. IV. Antipas. V. Agrippa the elder. VI. Herod of Chalcis. VII. Agrippa jun.

20. Harduin denies that the Herod mentioned in the Acts of the Apostles ruled over Judea, or that what was once a Roman province could ever be made a kingdom again. But how many examples are there in Asia, in Cilicia, in Pontus, and in Syria Commagena, where the form of a province has been abrogated, and kingdoms restored! All these examples do most evidently appear in the tables subjoined

to my Antiqua Historia. But perhaps Herod the tetrarch, to whom Pilate sent our Saviour bound, was only a stranger at Jerusalem; and Cæsar's procurator sent back the apostles, as Galileans, to the governor of Galilee, who happened to be there; especially in a cause that belonged not to the civil power, but to the Jewish religion. So does Harduin, whom we have so often cited, think, and so does he explain this matter. But this is by no means sufficient for the explication of the sense of St. Luke. If he were only a stranger, whence came his power of punishing the soldiers of the Roman president, when they had not carefully kept the prison? for, ver. 19 of that chapter, ἐκέλευσε ἀπαχθῆναι, he *commanded* them to be *led away* to be punished, and to be beheaded; which the Latins also express by being *led away* only. So says Pliny of the Christians, in his Epistle to Trajan; *Those that persevered in their religion, I commanded to be led away.* See what I have noted upon that place. The Syriac interpreter hath here a perspicuous paraphrase; *He condemned those keepers of the prison, and commanded them to be slain.* I add this, If he were only a stranger, why did he go from Jerusalem to Cesarea, and οιετριξεν, *inhabit* there, as in his royal palace? Now when Judea was a province, Cesarea was the seat of the Roman president, not of the governor of Galilee, as is most evident out of the history of Felix and Festus.

21. That very coin, upon which Harduin vaunts himself, with its inscription, ΒΑΣΙΛΕΥΣ ΜΕΓΑΣ ΑΓΡΙΠΠΑΣ ΦΙΛΟΚΛΑΥΔΙΟΣ, *The great king Agrippa, the lover of Claudius*, is the strongest argument on the side of Josephus. For if he were a *great king*, as he was by the testimony of this coin, it certainly follows that he had possessions greater than those of the two tetrarchies which are ascribed to him by Harduin, I mean that of Galilee and that of Philip; (see p. 65;) which were esteemed dominions hardly worthy the name of a *common*, or even of a *small king;* much less did they deserve the name of the possessions of a *great king*. Now Josephus celebrates this Agrippa as lord of a larger kingdom, or that which his grandfather had, which extended over all Palestine: this less disagrees with so pompous a title.

22. We have spoken already about the religion of this Herod the tetrarch. And since we have demonstrated that the Herod who is mentioned Acts xii. was different from him, it will be somewhat worth our while to consider what was his religion. Harduin, who supposes the tetrarch and the king to be one and the same person, denies, in the same place, that he who slew James was a Jew. St. Luke, says he, p. 55, plainly declares that he was neither a proselyte nor a Jew, when he relates, that it was not on a religious motive, but BECAUSE IT PLEASED THE JEWS, that he made war with the Christians. Are not then those Jews who study to please Jews? By this reasoning, neither must they have been Romans who were called *popular*

patriots, and spent their estates that they might please the people, obtain their favour, and the affection of the people to themselves. Nor must those emperors be Romans who, as Eutropius says, did, for the same reason, behave themselves with the utmost *civility* in the government.

23. The brother of this Agrippa was Herod, the king of Chalcis, as Josephus assures us, Of the War, B. II. ch. xi. sect. 5. A coin of which Herod Peter Seguin, one exceeding skilful in this kind of learning, has produced, with this inscription on the laurel; ΚΛΑΥΔΙΩ ΚΑΙΣΑΡΙ ΣΕΒΑΣΤΩ ΕΤ Ε;

that is, *To Claudius Cæsar Augustus in the fifth year.* And on the reverse this inscription is upon an old head, adorned with a royal diadem; ΒΑΣΙ-ΛΕΥΣ ῙΗΡΩΔ . . . . ΥΔΙΟΣ; *King Herod, the lover of Claudius.* On the contrary, Harduin, p. 58, says, What if there not only never was any Herod king of Chalcis, but no such kingdom at all as that of Chalcis? Thus does he most readily suppose, in his prejudice, that whatsoever depends on the single history of Josephus is false. Now Josephus says, Antiq. B. XIX. ch. v. sect. 1, that Herod, the brother of Agrippa, was governor of Chalcis; and, Of the War. B. II. ch. xi. sect. 5, he says of the same Herod that he reigned over Chalcis. Nay, he is styled a *king* by Claudius, in his epistle, set down by Josephus, Antiq. B. XX. ch. i. The force of which reasoning depends on this question, whether Herod Agrippa was alive on the fifth of Claudius? which is not probable, and is also contrary to Eusebius, who in his Chronicon says he perished in the fourth year of that emperor; which determination is commended and approved by Scaliger, in his Animadversions on that Chronicon, p. 189 [and by Pearson, Annal. Paulin. p. 51. Nay, moreover, Dio Cassius, an author of unsuspected credit, says of Claudius Cæsar, Book LX. p. 670, that *he gave the brother of Agrippa the great a certain principality;* which Josephus expressly assures us was no other than that of Chalcis, Antiq. B. XIX. ch. v. We have not therefore sufficient reason to reject Josephus and Eusebius, with whom, as we have just now seen, Dio also does very well agree.

24. There now remains Agrippa the son, mentioned Acts xxv. [23,] together with his sister Bernice. He was at Rome with Claudius, a youth of 17 years of age, when the news came of his father's death. And Claudius had made him successor to his father, unless his friends had suggested him this piece of advice, "that it was a dangerous thing to commit a kingdom, that lay at the bounds of the empire, such as was the kingdom of Judea, to so young a king." Accordingly, Judea was again reduced into the form of a province, together with the rest of Agrippa's possessions; and Cuspius Fadus was sent as the ordinary procurator to take care of it, and govern it. See Josephus, at the conclusion of his nineteenth book. Harduin denies that Judea was reduced into a province again; which he

thinks was ever so since it was made first a province under Augustus. We have already replied to this, sect. 20, by alleging the examples of countries in Asia, which, of Roman provinces, had been made kingdoms, and afterwards had been made provinces again. I shall now add the concurrent testimony of Tacitus, out of his History, V. 9: "Claudius, after the kings were dead, or reduced to smaller dominions, gave the province of Judea to Roman knights, or to freed-men, to be governed by them."

25. Nor was Agrippa, the son of Agrippa, without a kingdom, though he did not obtain it immediately after his father's death. So says Joseph Scaliger, upon Euseb. p. 189: "The kingdom was not delivered to him immediately after his father's death; but was governed so long in the name of Cæsar, until the king should be of age to govern it himself." The same Scaliger, a little after, when he comes to Tacitus's words, in his Annals, "The Itureans and Jews, when their kings Sohemus and Agrippa were dead, were joined to the province of Syria," says, "We must so understand this, that the Itureans were joined to Syria for perpetuity; but that the Jews were so only till Agrippa jun. should be of age to govern them himself. But that this should be five years after the death of Agrippa sen. who can believe? excepting one who forgets * that Cornelius Tacitus does several times, and greatly, mistake in his Chronology, and in his History of other Nations." I wish so great a man had written otherwise; for Tacitus and Josephus agree very well together. The death of Agrippa sen., as has been shown already out of Josephus and Eusebius, fell into the fourth year of Claudius. Agrippa jun., a youth of seventeen years of age, did not succeed his father; whose kingdom was turned into a Roman province, or added to the province of Syria. The emperor Claudius, in the beginning of the ninth year of his reign, that is, when C. Pompeius and Q. Verannius were consuls, put Agrippa, the son of Agrippa, in the place of his uncle Herod, in the kingdom of Chalcis, who was then to be sure dying. But four years afterward, that is, in the twelfth year of his reign, he took from him Chalcis, and bestowed on him the tetrarchies of Philip and Lysanias; that is, Trachonitis, Battanea, and Abilene: while, in the mean time, Judea, Samaria, and Galilee, and the other parts under the same jurisdiction, were governed by a Roman procurator, till the destruction of the city. See Josephus, Antiq. B. XX. ch. v. &c. Agrippa reigned a long while, or 50 years, from the ninth of Claudius to the third of Trajan. For Photius the patriarch, in his Bibliotheca, Cod. XXXIII., relates these words out of Justus of Tiberias, who was contemporary with Josephus; which words have been already set down: " Justus begins his history from Moses, and ends it not till the death of Agrippa, the seventh [ruler] in the

* remembers, Lat.

family of Herod, and the last king of the Jews; who took the government under Claudius, had it augmented under Nero, and still more augmented by Vespasian. He died in the third year of Trajan." There are a great many coins of this king remaining, with the images of Vespasian, Titus, and Domitian; which are exhibited by my great patron Ez. Spanheim, De Præst. et Usu Numismatum, p. 864. Of which that with the effigies of Vespasian has on the reverse this inscription, ΕΤΟΥ ΚΘ ΒΑ ΑΓΡΙΠΠΑ, *In the twenty-ninth year of king Agrippa;* which is a sufficient argument that he reigned a long time.

26. And so much for the family of Herod, and their order and succession. What remains of the objections made by Harduin against Josephus we now undertake to answer. In order to render the reputation of Josephus suspected, he objects, in the first place, that the name of Antipas, which we owe to Josephus, does not appear either in the inscription produced sect. 13 before, or on the coins. But certainly, if this argument be valid, the name Archelaus might be also suspected; because, as Harduin confesses, it is not met with on the coins; and, instead of that, we find the name Herod in Dio Cassius. But what sort of name Antipas is Ben Gorion shows, chap. lxiii. at the beginning; who calls him Antipater, by a Greek name; from whence Antipas is derived: as in Pliny's Epistles, X. 5, Harpocrates is derived from Harpocras. Harduin proceeds to object falsity to Josephus, when he sometimes says he was banished into Gaul, and sometimes into Spain. But the reconciliation of these places is easy: while he might first be banished into Gaul; and then, to aggravate his punishment, he might be carried as far as Spain, a country very remote from that wherein he was born. Ben Gorion, chap. lxiii., confirms that place, [Of the War,] while he says he was banished into a place called Sepharad, which is the Jews' word for Spain. [The truth is, Josephus frequently, in his Antiquities, corrects the errors of his two former books Of the War, as I have largely observed and proved in the fifth Dissertation prefixed, where this is one of the examples. See there sect. 33.] Moreover, he would render Josephus suspected, p. 51, because he writes that Claudius was assisted in obtaining the empire by Agrippa, who then happened to be at Rome; while it is not easy to believe

that a little king over a barbarous country should be partaker of the counsels and determinations of the Roman senate. But here Dio Cassius is not wanting to Josephus, but rises up in his defence, Book LX. p. 670, where he says of Claudius, " That he augmented the kingdom of Agrippa of Palestine, who had assisted him in procuring the dominion; for he happened to be then at Rome."

27. And now this learned man makes his attempt against Josephus another way, when he objects that the rebuilding of the temple at Je-

rusalem, which he attributes to Herod, is a fiction of his, for the increasing the magnificence of Herod, p. 32. Now that this rebuilding the temple is not a fiction, may be proved pretty plainly from the sacred writer, John ii. 20. For those forty-six years cannot be understood of the building the temple of Zorobabel, which was finished in four years, Ezra vi. 15. Nor when Judea was become a province of the Roman empire did the reparation of the temple cease. Nor were such repairs made under the conduct of the Roman procurator. For the Cæsars left this care of the temple and of sacred things to some prince of the Jewish nation, as was done when Agrippa sen. died. Claudius then granted it to his brother Herod, king of Chalcis, Joseph. Antiq. B. XX. ch. i., iii, which privilege continued afterward with Agrippa jun. to the destruction of the temple and city. See there chap. vii., and especially chap. viii. sect. 2. where it is said of Agrippa the king, that Claudius committed the care of the temple to him, although at the same times neither had Herod nor Agrippa any right in Judea or Jerusalem, which was all vested in the president or procurator.

28. Harduin charges Josephus with another crime, whence he thinks it certain that that author never saw Palestine, and this because he places Cesarea of Palestine in Phœnicia. A new crime, and never heard of before! Of which, if Josephus be to be accused, Strabo, the prince of geographers, must be first condemned. For in Book XVI. p. 520, he says, Having now gone over Celesyria, we pass to Phœnice. And when he had enumerated the cities, he concludes, p. 523, with these words, So far concerning Phœnice. In the middle of which description, and among the thickest of the Phœnician cities, he says, *After Ace* (i. e. Ptolemais) *is the tower of Strato, having an haven.* This very city is Cesarea. So says Pliny, V. 13, *Strato's tower, the same is Cesarea; it was built by Herod.* By what right is Josephus accused, who is of the same sentiments with Strabo? Some geographers and historians make Phœnicia to extend further into the south, though others make that limit shorter. Livy, xxxv. 13, says that *king Antiochus gave his daughter in marriage at Raphia, in Phœnice, to Ptolemy king of Egypt: and then, at the conclusion of the winter, came to Ephesus.* Now Raphia is at the sea-shore, near to the borders of Egypt.

29. At length Harduin accuses Josephus of falsehood, about the *kingdom of the Hasmoneans.* But then Strabo, long before Josephus, Book XVI. p. 524, when he is giving an account of Syria and Judea, says, *Alexander did first of all set up himself for a king, instead of a priest.* This Alexander was called Jannæus, the father of Hyrcanus and Aristobulus. Which is sufficient to wipe off this imputation, as if Josephus were a *fabulous* author, which Harduin lays to his charge. Although Strabo is here to be so far corrected, that Alexander was

not the *first* who made use of a crown, and of the title of king, but his brother Aristobulus assumed the same honour before him. [See the note on Antiq. B. XIII. ch. x. sect. 7.] I believe this learned man was induced to charge Josephus thus, because he had met with no coins of the Hasmonean *kings*. But by the same way of reasoning some of the principal branches of history may be denied: *v. gr.* The Trapezuntine empire, which was founded by Alexias Comnenus, when Constantinople came into the hands of the Latins, and lasted CCL years. This kingdom has not hitherto been illustrated by coins, nor could it be so illustrated; the most skilful not calling to mind that they ever saw any such coins. Yet is not that which Nicetas, Gregoras, Paulus Venetus, and Chalcocondyles have related concerning it to be esteemed fabulous.

30. Lastly, Harduin brings an indictment against Josephus before the grammarians. " I say nothing," says he, " of Josephus's solecism, when he uses Αγρίππȣ, as it is also read in the MSS., for Αγρίππα, in the genitive case; which last yet is in the coins of that Agrippa with whom he pretends to have been a contemporary." But softly, sir; that is not a solecism which the best authors in the Greek language have used. There are two forms of the genitive case in these names; and Αγρίππα is found Acts xxv. 23, and in Xiphiline in Vespasian, both in Stephens's edition, p. 222, and that of Sylburgius, p. 322. Nor is the other termination, ȣ, a solecism, which not Plutarch only, in Antonius, p. 946, but Dio Cassius, Book LII. in the beginning, and Appian of Alexandria, Of the Civil War, Book V., and that imitator of elegancy of expression, Zonaras, in Augustus, have made use of. Will Harduin then accuse these writers of solecism? Nor is this unusual in other proper names that end in ας, *v. gr.* Αἰνείȣ, Ἀρέτȣ, Μαικήνȣ. Theodorus Gaza, Isagog. Book I. p. 4, says the word Αἰνείας is declined Αἰνείȣ. And a coin lately produced by Andrew Morellius, a most sagacious searcher into antiquity, in his Specimina, Table XXIII.; ΒΑΣΙΛΕΩΣ ΑΡΕΘΟΥ ΦΙΛΕΛΛΗΝΟΣ. And Dio Cassius himself, in the place forecited, Μετά τε τȣ Ἀγρίππȣ, καὶ τȣ Μαικήνȣ. Nor was our Josephus unacquainted with that other form, which Harduin thinks to be alone agreeable to the Greek language; which it will be sufficient to prove by one example, Antiq. B. XIV. ch. ii. Πέτρα, τὰ Βασίλεια τȣ Ἀρέτα.

31. It remains now to suppose, with Harduin, that Josephus has on purpose omitted the murder of the infants, and therefore seems not to have read so much as the sacred books of the New Testament. Even Scaliger, in his Animadversions on Eusebius, p. 176, owns, *That it is strange, that an example of so brutish a cruelty should be overlooked by Josephus, when he so diligently lays open the rest of Herod's barbarous enormities.* I also wonder at it myself. Yet do not I think this omis-

sion sufficient to prove the fraud of the writer, as Harduin would have it. For this might be owing to some other cause; and if there be any thing here that is culpable, it is to be laid to the charge of Nicolaus of Damascus, rather than of Josephus. For there is little doubt but he passed it over, because he wrote while Herod was alive, whose friend he was, and for whose cause he pleaded before Augustus. Whom when Josephus followed closely, as he does not deny he did, perhaps that happened to him which we know hath happened to many others, that this detestable fact escaped his mind, his memory, and his hand, while he was writing; not on purpose, but partly by slipping out of his memory, and partly by his exactly adhering to the author that wrote before him. [Here are several mistakes. Josephus was an Ebionite Christian when he wrote this part of his Antiquities, as I have proved already, Authent. Rec. p. 954—960, and Dissert. I. prefixed p. 911, and did not then believe our Gospels, but only the Nazarene or Ebionite *Gospel according to the Hebrews:* which began with the preaching of John the Baptist, long after this slaughter of the infants. Josephus did not confine himself to Nicolaus of Damascus's flattering history of Herod, but consulted more impartial writers: see the note on Antiq. B. XVI. ch. vii. sect. 1. Nor does he quite omit this murder of the infants, nor the other important accidents that then happened; but gives us them as the Nazarenes or Ebionites had given them to him. Of which see the Addenda to the fifth of the Six Dissertations, p. 335—344.

N. B. Upon the whole, this attempt of Harduin's to lessen the reputation of Josephus, thus thoroughly confuted by Cellarius, does in reality strongly support it; and is become an undeniable attestation to his exact knowledge in the affairs of the family of Herod, and to his great fidelity and accuracy in the histories of those times.

N. B. It will deserve to be here considered, that whereas the New Testament, with Josephus, calls the successor of Herod the Great, Archelaus; one of the coins, with Dio, calls even him Herod, sect. 8 prius: and whereas the New Testament calls Josephus's Agrippa the Great, Herod, that his name is also upon another coin, sect. 16 prius: and whereas he whom the New Testament calls Philip, the brother of Herod the tetrarch, whose wife he stole away from her husband and married, is by Josephus called Herod: all these examples show that most of the posterity of Herod the Great were called of some by the general name of Herod, and of others by their peculiar names, Archelaus, Antipas, Agrippa, Philip, &c., and that these ancient authors are thus easily reconciled together in these their several names ascribed to them.

April 28, 1737 WILL. WHISTON

TABLE

OF THE

JEWISH WEIGHTS AND MEASURES;

PARTICULARLY OF THOSE MENTIONED

IN JOSEPHUS' WORKS

BEFORE I can authenticly state these Jewish weights and measures, I must first set down all the passages I have met with in Josephus' writings that can give any light to these matters.

Antiq. B. III. ch. i. sect. 6, Josephus makes Assaron the same measure which we render a tenth deal, i. e. the tenth part of a Bath, or Epha. It is otherwise styled an Omer.

Ch. vi. sect. 6, he says that this Assaron [or Omer] was equal to 7 Attic Cotulæ.

Sect. 7, he says, that the Talent was called Cinchares by the Hebrews, and was equal to 100 Manehs, Mnas [or pounds].

Ch. viii. sect. 2, he affirms that the Siclus or Shekel was equal to 4 Attic Drachmæ.

Sect. 10, he mentions the coins called Darics.

Ch. ix. sect. 4, he informs us that the Hin was equal to 2 Attic Chouses [or 2 Roman Congii].

Ch. xv. sect. 3, he reckons 70 Cori [or Chomers] equal to 31 Sicilian and to 41 Attic Medimni.

B. VIII. ch. ii. sect. 9, he says, that the Badus or Bath was equal to 72 Xestæ [or Sextaries].

B. IX. ch. iv. sect. 5, he says, [Seah or] Saton was equal to an Italian Modius and a half.

B. XIV. ch. vii. sect. 1, he affirms Maneh or Mna to be equal to 2½ Litræ [Libræ, or pounds, each of 12 Avoirdupois ounces].

B. XV. ch. ix. sect. 2, he affirms the Corus [or Chomer] to be equal to 10 Attic Medimni.

Of the War, B. II. ch. xxi. sect. 2, he mentions a Tyrian coin, and says it was equal to 4 Attic Drachmæ; which is the same weight that he gives to the Jewish Siclus, or Shekel.

N. B. Antonius Augustinus weighed two Carthaginian coins, which proved to be full 4 Drachmæ apiece, or equal to Josephus' shekel. Now it is well known that the Carthaginians were a colony of the Tyrians. See Cumberland's Weights and Measures, p. 106.

OF THE JEWISH MEASURES OF LENGTH

	Cubits.	Inches.	Feet.	Inches.
Cubit, the standard		21	1	9
Zereth, or large span	$\frac{1}{2}$	10.5	0	0
Small span	$\frac{1}{3}$	7	0	0
Palm, or hand's breadth	$\frac{1}{6}$	3.5	0	0
Inch, or thumb's breadth	$\frac{1}{18}$	1.16	0	0
Digit, or finger's breadth	$\frac{1}{24}$	.875	0	0
Ορуυία, or fathom	4	84	7	0
Ezekiel's Canna, or reed	6	126	10	6
Arabian Canna, or pole	8	168	14	0
Schœnus, line, or chain	80	1680	140	0
Sabbath-day's journey	2000	42000	3500	0
Jewish mile	4000	84000	7000	0
Stadium, or furlong, $\frac{1}{10}$	400	8400	700	0
Parasang	12000	252000	21000	0

See Cumberland's Weights and Measures, p. 57, 58, 135, 136.

Since I have always determined, both in my Description of the Temples, chap. viii., and in my Authentic Records, Part II. p. 875—877, that the Jewish cubit was nearly 21 inches, English measure, nor see any room to believe the Jews ever had any other or larger cubit among them, the Jewish measures of length derived from it will be easily determined. Nor is there any thing, that I know of, in Josephus's writings, that contradicts these determinations. But as to the origin of cubits, and other like measures of length, and their differences; and how they were taken from the members of human bodies, of different statures, in different ages; see Lamy, De Tabernac. et Templ. L. I. c. i. sect. 3, and c. viii., ix., with the forecited place of the Authentic Records.

OF THE JEWISH MEASURES OF CAPACITY

Before I can authenticly state these Jewish measures of capacity, I must set down such English, and Attic, and Roman measures as the Jewish are usually compared with, together with the best determinations of their quantity in cubical inches; as also in such pints or pounds as contain 29 cubical inches (which is very near our wine pint, the half of our wine quart, and the eighth part of our wine gallon). Whence they may be reduced into any other measures, at every one's pleasure.

	Cub. Inches.	Pints, or Pounds.
Wine gallon contains	231	7.96
Corn gallon contains	272	9.38
Culæus Romanus	33129.6	
Medimnus Atticus	2484.72	85.68
Amphora Romana	1656.48	
Modius Italicus,—16 Sextaries	552	18.8
Attic Chous, or Roman Congius, equal to 120 ounces of water, Avoirdupois	207.06	.714
Chœnix,—30 ounces of water	51.76	1.78
Cotyla Attica, 10 ounces of water	17.25	.59
Xestes or Roman Sextary,—2 Cotylæ,—20 ounces of water	34.5	1.18

N. B. Josephus, from his own knowledge, and his Old Testament, assures us, in all his copies, both Greek and Latin, seen by Dr. Hudson, that the brazen sea in the temple was a hemisphere, and contained 3000 Baths; that it was 10 cubits in diameter; and consequently about 30 cubits, by a gross estimation, in circumference. Our Hebrew and Greek copies, 1 Kings vii. 23—26, do also agree to the same diameter, and circumference, and depth; and that it was *round all about*, or a real hemisphere. Only they say that it contained but 2000 Baths. While the same Hebrew and Greek copies, in 2 Chron. iv. 2—5, agree in all things with the Book of Kings excepting the number of Baths this sea contained; which is there constantly 3000, as in Josephus's copies. It is true that the Geneva edition of Josephus has but 2000. But then Dr. Hudson thinks the editors took that number not from any MS., but from the Bible, in the place already mentioned of the Kings. However, because Josephus himself gives us the contents of Assaron or Omer, the known $\frac{1}{10}$ of Bath or Epha, Exod. xvi. 36, to be seven [Attic] Cotylæ, or 1207.5 cubical inches, this only agrees to the number 2000, as in the Book of Kings. Now I confess I see no other foundation for doubt in this whole matter, but only about the number of the Baths contained in this sea, whether they were 2000 or 3000. In which the direct evidences appear to me so equally balanced, that I am not able to determine between them. So I shall wave the more uncertain authority of the modern Rabbins, and modern writers depending on them, and state the Jewish Bath or Epha by geometrical calculation from these surer premises; and thence deduce the rest of the Jewish measures of capacity which bear a known proportion to it; and this upon both the hypotheses, that the brazen sea held only 2000, or that it held 3000, Baths. The cube of 10 cubits, or of 210 inches=9261000 solid or cubical inches. Now the geometricians know, that as 1 to .532 decimals, or as 1000 to 532 integers; so is that cube to a sphere of the same diameter=4843503 solid or cubical inches. Its half, or the hemisphere, is therefore 2421751 such inches. Divide that sum by 2000 and by 3000, the numbers of the Baths contained in that hemisphere, upon the two hypotheses before mentioned, the quotients will be equal to one Bath or Epha; i. e. either to 1210.911 or to 807.274 such inches; i. e. they will, in the former case, be equal to $\frac{3}{23}$, or above $\frac{1}{8}$, and in the second case to $\frac{2}{23}$, or exactly to the mean, between the $\frac{1}{11}$ and $\frac{1}{12}$ of the cube of the cubit, i. e. in English measure, either 41.74 or 27.83 English pints, or pounds. See Cumberland's Weights and Measures, p. 86 and 137. Accordingly, my table is double, and contains the Jewish measures of capacity, according to both those estimations, and that as well in cubical inches as in pints or pounds also.

N. B. Josephus's present copies, Antiq. B. VIII. ch. ii. sect. 9, affirm that the Badus, or Bath, the tenth part of Corus, or Chomer, was equal to 72 Xestæ, or Sextaries; i. e. to about 2484.72 cubical inches; which is the content of the Medimnus Atticus. As also, B. XV. ch. ix. sect. 2, they affirm that the Corus, or Chomer, which is 10 Baths, contained 10 Medimni; both which estimations agree, although they be wide from all our computations in

excess. Yet do the same copies say elsewhere, B. III. ch. xv. sect. 3, that 70 Cori, or Chomers, are equal to no more than 31 Sicilian, and to 41 Attic, Medimni, which is but 1454 solid or cubical inches for a single Corus or Chomer. As if the same measure were equal to 24847.2 and to no more than 1454 cubical inches, or were above 17 times as large as itself. This number is very wide from all our computations in defect. These quantities are therefore so entirely contradictory to one another, that I must be forced to drop them on both sides in my present determinations, and to proceed upon the principles foregoing only.

	At 3000 Baths		At 2000 Baths	
	Cub. inches.	Pints, or pounds.	Cub. inches.	Pints, or pounds.
Bath, or Epha	807.274	27.83	1210.911	41.74
Corus, or Chomer,—10 Baths, or Ephas	8072.74	278.3	12109.11	417.4
Seah, or Saton,—⅓ of Epha	269.091	9.266	403.64	13.994
Seah, or Saton, according to Josephus, —1½ Modius Italicus	828	28.3	828	28.3
Hin, according to the Rabbins,—⅙ of Epha	134.54	4.4633	201.81	6.694
Hin, according to Josephus, equal to 2 Attic Chouses	414.12	14.3	414.12	14.3
Omer, or Assaron,—1/10 of Epha	80.727	2.78	121.09	4.17
Cab,—1/18 of Epha	44.859	1.544	67.288	2.316
Log,—1/72 of Epha	11.21	.39	16.81	.585
Metretes, or Syrian firkin, John ii. 6	207	7.125	207	7.125

See Cumberland, p. 86, 90, 91, 92, 137

N. B. Josephus's Seah or Saton is so far from being only ⅓ of the Bath or Epha, as the Rabbins esteem it, that it is larger than that Bath or Epha itself upon the hypothesis of the brazen sea's containing 3000 Baths or Ephas. And even upon the hypothesis of its containing but 2000, it contains above ⅔ of it. So we are still greatly at a loss in this matter.

N. B. Since Josephus's larger quantity of the Hin best agrees with the 1500 shekels, or 750 ounces, or 47 pounds weight of dry spices, to be moistened for a *holy oil* or *ointment* by an Hin of oil olive, Exod. xxx. 22—33; and since the Rabbins' smaller quantity best agrees with the ¼ of a Hin of beaten oil, commanded to be mingled with a tenth deal or Omer of flour, for a cake at the daily meat-offering, Exod. xxix. 40; I cannot, by those calculations, determine between these different measures, either of the Hin, or of the 3000 and 2000 Baths in the

brazen sea. So I suffer those computations to balance one another, without preponderating one above another. Yet shall I venture to propose another argument, which has nothing, that I know of, to counterbalance it, and which is directly on the side of the 3000 Baths, and its first series of measures; which argument I have elsewhere insisted on for the same purpose. This is taken from the quantity of the manna which was allotted by God himself to be every man's daily portion in the wilderness, an Omer apiece: this is full as large, on that hypothesis, as every man required, and much too large on the other hypothesis. Of which see Authent. Records, Part II. p. 880, 881, and Cumberland, p. 87, 88. And thus, upon the whole, I am still obliged to prefer the number 3000, and its first series of measures, before the number 2000, and its second series, as I did formerly also.

OF THE JEWISH WEIGHTS AND COINS

Now before I can authenticly determine the weight and value of the Jewish shekel, and other weights and coins derived therefrom, I must set down such other weights and coins as the shekel hath been esteemed very nearly equal to; which are as follow:

		s.	d.
Four Attic Drachmæ, according to Breerwood		2	6
according to Bernard		2	8½
according to Greaves 67 grains,		2	9½

	s.	d
The mean quantity is	2	8
Two Alexandrian Drachmæ,—4 Attic Drachmæ	2	8
A Tyrian coin	2	8
Four Drachmæ, Troy weight,—240 grains	2	7
Four Drachmæ, Avoirdupois,—219 grains, or ½ an ounce	2	4¼
Four Roman Denarii, or pence	2	7
Shekel itself, as weighed by Bernard, about	3	0
by Cumberland	2	4½
by Villalpandus	2	9½
by Abp. Usher	2	5
Duke of Devonshire's shekel, weighed by Mr. Barker	2	4½
The mean weight of the shekel (excepting that of Dr. Bernard)	2	5¼

Mean quantity of 4 Attic and 2 Alexandrian Drachmæ; of 4 Drachmæ Troy, and as many Avoirdupois; of a Tyrian coin; of 4 Denarii; and of the several shekels themselves; very nearly   2   6

Hence I now state the Jewish coins and weights as follows :

	£	s.	d.
Stater, Siclus, or shekel of the sanctuary, the standard	0	2	6
Tyrian coin, equal to the shekel	0	2	6
Bekah, half of the shekel	0	1	3
Drachma Attica, one-fourth	0	0	7½
Drachma Alexandrina, or Darchmon, or Adarchmon, one-half	0	1	3
Gerah, or Obolus, one-twentieth	0	0	1½
Maneh, or Mna,—100 shekels in weight,—21900 grains Troy.			
Maneh, Mna, or Mina, as a coin—60 shekels	7	10	0
Talent of silver—3000 shekels	375	0	0
Drachma of gold, not more than	0	1	1
Shekel of gold, not more than	0	4	4
Daric of gold	1	0	4
Talent of gold, not more than	648	0	0

N. B. The Roman coins mentioned in the New Testament are to be thus valued. See Cumberland, p. 117, 118, 139.

	s.	d.	f.
The Denarius	0	7	3
Their As or Assis	0	0	3.1
Their Assarium	0	0	1.5
Their Quadrans	0	0	.75
Their Mite	0	0	.333

N. B. Since our ancient testimonies, and the weight of our present shekels, conspire to assure us that a Hebrew shekel was nearly equal to 4 Attic and 2 Alexandrian Drachmæ, to 4 Drachmæ Troy, and to as many Avoirdupois, to a Tyrian coin, and to 4 Denarii, I thence deduce its mean quantity to have been 2s. 6d.; allowing somewhat for the wearing of such shekels as are now extant while they passed as coins; and laying aside that unexampled quantity in Dr. Bernard, as some way mistaken (on which single example yet, so far as appears to me, the shekel is supposed, both by himself and by Dean Prideaux, to have been no less than 3s. in value). See Prid. Connexion, pref. p. 20, 21.

It is true, that some of the learned Jews pretend, that their later shekels were one-fifth larger than their ancient ones; which later shekels might be then at least 2s. 10d. But since no such larger shekels have been yet seen, (unless that weighed by Dr. Bernard were of that sort,) I cannot depend upon such a Rabbinical assertion without further evidence. And though there should have been any such coined in later times, the estimate of the shekel under the Old and New Testament, and the days of Josephus, will hardly be affected by it. See the note on Joseph. Antiq. B. III. ch. viii. sect. 2.

As for the Drachma, Shekel, and Talent of gold among the Jews, I state them no higher than as

19 to 11 (the specific gravity of gold to that of silver) larger than those of silver. Which yet have been hitherto most unhappily and extravagantly esteemed 14, or 15, or even 16 times as high in value as silver; and this without due consideration of the several instances wherein such pieces of gold have been mentioned in the Old Testament. See the Description of the Temples, chap. xiii., and Cumberland, p. 138, 139.

As to those golden Darics mentioned by Josephus, when he supplies them in Numb. vii., instead of shekels, which we supply, I follow Bishop Cumberland in their estimation. See his book, p. 115.

N. B. It being so evident, and known by all, that a Hebrew talent of silver was just 3000 shekels; when Josephus's present copies say that such talent was equal to 100 Manehs, Mnas, or Minæ, which we should render pounds, of 30 ounces, or 60 shekels apiece; this talent will still be as large again as it ought to be. Though I cannot easily suppose that Josephus could himself be guilty of so great a mistake. But whence it has arisen I cannot at all tell. Nor do I find that the correctors or corrupters of Josephus's numbers have been less busy, or less successful, in those belonging to his weights and measures, than they have been in those relating to his chronology. Of which largely in the fifth Dissertation prefixed.

A TABLE OF THE JEWISH MONTHS

IN JOSEPHUS AND OTHERS, WITH THE SYRO-MACEDONIAN NAMES JOSEPHUS GIVES THEM, AND THE NAMES OF THE JULIAN OR ROMAN MONTHS CORRESPONDING TO THEM, OUT OF THE VERY LEARNED EZEKIEL SPANHEIM, IN HAVERCAMP'S EDITION, P. 407, WITH SOME SMALL IMPROVEMENTS.

	Hebrew names	Syro-Macedonian Names	Roman Names
(1.)	Nisan	Xanthicus	March and April
(2.)	Jyar	Artemisius	April and May
(3.)	Sivan	Dæsius	May and June
(4.)	Tamuz	Panemus	June and July
(5.)	Ab	Lous	July and August
(6.)	Elul	Gorpiæus	August and September
(7.)	Tisri	Hyperberetæus	September and October
(8.)	Marchesvan	Dius	October and November
(9.)	Casleu	Apellæus	November and December
(10.)	Tebeth	Audynæus	December and January
(11.)	Shebat	Peritius	January and February
(12.)	Adar	Dystrus	February and March
( )	Veadar, or the *Second Adar*, intercalated.		

N. B. The years I make use of in this version of Josephus under the bare character of anno are those before the Christian era, as those under the character of A. D. are those since. And if the reader desire to know the Annus Mundi, or year of the world corresponding to any such year, according to my Chronological Table, and my Notes on Josephus, he must deduct the year given from 4485, (about the latter end of the next year, to which A. M. 1 I suppose Adam to have been created,) and the remainder will be the Annus Mundi, or year of the world; but in strictness the year from that in which Adam was created inclusive. Thus in order to find the A. M. wherein Moses died, and Joshua entered Canaan, which is there anno 1492, deduct that number out of 4485, the remainder, 2993, is the A. M. by my Chronological Table, and in these Notes. But if any desire the A. M. by the shorter Samaritan Chronology, which I suppose to be the most exact, deduct 249 years from the former A. M., and the remainder will give you the A. M. by that Chronology. Thus from 2993, just now found, deduct 249, the remainder, 2744, is the A. M. sought. And if any desire the Julian period corresponding to any year before the Christian era, they are to deduct the last year out of 4714, which is the first year of the Christian era. The remainder will be the current year of the Julian period. Thus deduct 1492, the year wherein Moses died, and Joshua entered the land of Canaan, from 4714, the remainder is 3222, the year of the Julian period required.

A LIST

OF

ANCIENT TESTIMONIES AND RECORDS CITED BY JOSEPHUS, AND OF COINS REFERRED TO
IN THE NOTES UPON HIM; CONFIRMING OR ILLUSTRATING HIS HISTORY, AND, BY CONSE-
QUENCE, THE HISTORIES OF THE OLD AND NEW TESTAMENT.

IN JOSEPHUS' LIFE

JONATHAN and his partners' letter to Josephus, sect. 44.

Josephus's answer, ib.

Another letter of Jonathan and his partners to Josephus, sect. 45.

Josephus's answer, ib.

One of the 62 letters which Agrippa jun. wrote to Josephus, sect. 65.

Another of those 62 letters, ib.

Photius's account of Justus of Tiberias's chronology, confirmed by coins, ib.

IN THE ANTIQUITIES

BOOK I

A stone pillar extant in the days of Josephus, with inscriptions relating to the oldest discoveries in astronomy, in the land of Seriad, ch. ii. sect. 3.

An Armenian name of the place where the first city was built after the deluge, [Nachidshevan, or] Αποβατήριον, i. e. the *first place of descent* from Mount Ararat, ch. iii. sect. 5.

Berosus's testimony concerning the deluge, sect. 6.

Hieronymus Egyptius's testimony alleged about it, ib.

Mnaseas's testimony alleged about it, with those of many others, ib.

Nicolaus of Damascus's testimony about, ib.

The testimonies of all the Greek ancient writers of antiquities alleged for the long lives of the antediluvians: particularly of Manetho; of Berosus; of Mochus; of Hestiæus; of Hieronymus Egyptius; of Hesiod; of Hecatæus; of Hellanicus; of Acusilaus; of Ephorus; and of Nicolaus of Damascus, sect. 9.

The testimony of the sibyl, concerning the tower of Babel, ch. iv. sect. 3.

The testimony of Hestyæus to the retreat of those that escaped the deluge to the land of Shinar, in Babylonia, ib.

Berosus's testimony concerning Abram, ch. vii. sect. 2.

Hecatæus wrote a book concerning him, ib.

Nicolaus of Damascus's testimony concerning him, ib.

Cleodemus or Malchus's testimony, taken out of Alexander Polyhistor, concerning Abraham's children by Keturah, ch. xv.

BOOK II

The testimonies of all that have written of the acts of Alexander alleged, that the Pamphylian sea did providentially open a passage for him and his army, when God sent him to destroy the Persian empire, ch. xvi. sect. 5.

BOOK III

The Greeks, being not able to deny the truth of the answers by Urim, called the breastplate of the Jewish high priest *the oracle*, ch. viii. sect. 9.

Those that hated the Jews could not deny that it was God who settled their commonwealth, ch. xv. sect. 3.

BOOK VII

Nicolaus of Damascus's testimonies concerning Adad, and his posterity, the Benhadads, kings of Syria, ch. v. sect. 2.

BOOK VIII

An appeal to the Tyrian Archives, concerning Hiram's and Solomon's transactions, relating to the building of the temple, ch. ii. sect. 8.

Menander's testimony concerning Hiram and Solomon, ch. v. sect. 3.

Dius's testimony concerning the same kings, ib.

Herodotus's testimony concerning 330 kings of Egypt, without assigning them particular names, ch. vi. sect. 2. [Of these kings, see Essay on the Old Test. p. 222, and Six Dissertations, p. 190, 191.]

The antiquity of the Jewish nation confessed by all the Greeks; particularly by Demetrius Phalereus, and by Philo senior, and by Eupolemus, as best knowing their history, ib.

Manetho's lies about the Jews, sect. 26, &c., confuted by Josephus at large, sect. 28—31.

Chæremon's lies about the Jews, sect. 32, confuted, sect. 33.

Lysimachus's lies about them, sect. 34, confuted, sect. 35.

BOOK II

Apion's lies about the Jews, sect. 1, &c., where they are also confuted.

The epistles of Alexander the Great, of Ptolemy Lagi, and of the successors of Ptolemy, in behalf of the Jews, appealed to, sect. 4.

A pillar at Alexandria containing the privileges granted the Jews by Cæsar, appealed to, ib. : see sect. 5.

Hecateus's testimony concerning Alexander the Great's kindness to the Jews, ib.

Demetrius Phalereus, and Andreas, and Aristeas appealed to, as concerned in the Septuagint version, ib.

Ptolemy Physcon's concubine Ithaca, or Irene, dissuades him from hurting the Jews, sect. 5.

Posidonius, and Apollonius Molo, and Lysimachus tell lies of the Jews, sect. 7, 14, where they are confuted by Josephus.

Polybius, Strabo, Nicolaus of Damascus, Timagenes, Castor, and Apollodorus appealed to, for the cause of Antiochus's despoiling the temple at Jerusalem, sect. 7.

N. B. I intended, as my proposals show, to have made here, instead of this short list, a complete collection of ancient testimonies and records, confirming or illustrating the history of Josephus, and the books of the Old and New Testament, and had made some progress therein. But when I found that such a work would require time, and would be a large work of itself; and that I had already added three Dissertations more than were promised in my proposals; and that the number of sheets would be already more than my first estimation; I was forced to desist. In the mean time, the reader may easily supply that defect from Eusebius's ancient collection in his Preparatio Evangelica; which well deserves to be translated into English, as well as Josephus; (these two being, by far, the principal authors of antiquity upon this subject;) from the modern collections of Grotius, Of the Truth of the Christian Religion; of Huetius's Demonstratio Evangelica, and Quæstiones Alnetanæ; (although these last be not by any means done with the judicious caution and sagacity of Grotius); of Bishop Stillingfleet's Origines Sacræ, and of many others. To say nothing of my own collections in the Appendix to the Essay to restore the true Text of the Old Testament, and in the Authentic Records; and of the many occasional citations of such ancient testimonies interwoven by commentators in their notes on the Bible, particularly by Grotius and Le Clerc. To say nothing also of Ptolemy's Astronomical Canon, the Chronicle of John Hyrcanus, and many other records of the like nature, not here insisted on.

N. B. Two things may be in this place very pertinently observed, to corroborate the argument from the ancient testimonies for the truth of the Bible, and of Josephus's history derived from it : viz. (1.) That there do not appear, in the genuine records of mankind belonging to ancient times, any testimonies that contradict those produced for them. Take this observation in the words of one that had more thoroughly and judiciously inquired into this matter than almost any other man ever did, I mean the most learned Grotius, who speaks thus: " There remains another way of confuting testimonies, from contrary external testimonies. *But I confidently affirm that there are no such to be found,*" &c.* (2.) That when our Josephus must have been terribly disappointed, as well as the rest of the Jews, that at the time they expected a glorious temporal Messiah, to come to redeem their nation from the Roman yoke, and to set up a kingdom in Judea, another Messiah had come, in a contemptible manner, without any such atttempt for the making that redemption, or setting up that kingdom, whom that nation had crucified; and when our Josephus had himself seen, instead thereof, the utter dissolution of their Jewish commonwealth, and destruction of its capital Jerusalem; when also our Josephus himself was become a captive to idolatrous Romans, and under the greatest temptations to give up Judaism, and desert that religion; when I say all this was certainly his case, that he should still show the firmest adherence to that religion, and his surest belief of its sacred books, and still write the fullest vindications of them against their heathen adversaries, is very surprising. Nor can all this be any other ways accounted for, but because Josephus had so thoroughly studied the books of the Old Testament, and had so thoroughly considered the ancient heathen records that related to them, that he was fully satisfied the evidence for their truth and authority was *plainly unanswerable,* and *perfectly undeniable.* Which I really take to be the true state of those matters, and is the like result of my own long and diligent inquiries about them.

However, the reader may take one specimen of the forementioned work of my own, and that is the testimonies concerning the partition of time by *weeks,* and the memory of the *seventh* or *sabbath day* thereby commemorated, because it is a point of great antiquity, and of great consequence, and be-

* Of the Truth of the Christian Religion, Book III. sect. 13, 14.

cause it is already referred to in my note on the second book against Apion, sect. 40, as standing at the head of such a collection in this place.

Aristobulus, in Eusebius's Præp. Evang. XIII. 12, 13

Homer and Hesiod let us know, what they learned out of our books, that the seventh day was a holy day. Thus says Hesiod:
There is the first day of the month, and the fourth, and the seventh, that holy day.
He says again,
The seventh day is also a day illuminated by the sun.
Homer says thus:
The seventh day came also, which is a holy day.
And again,
It was the seventh day, and thereon were all things perfected.
As also,
On the seventh day we left our floating upon Acheron.
Linus also says thus:
On the seventh day all things were perfected.
And again,
The seventh day is a happy day; the seventh day is the birthday.
The seventh day is among the first, and it is a perfect day.
As also,
All things were made by sevens in the starry heaven; And go round in circles in all the years succeeding one another.
And so far goes Aristobulus.

You may also know what Clement [of Alexandria] says of this argument by what I shall here produce, where the foregoing passages are set down. Only in the room of Linus he has it thus: Nay, indeed, Callimachus the poet writes thus: On the seventh day all things were perfected.

Philo De Mundi Opificio, p. 20

The holy seventh day.] This festival is not peculiar to one city or country, but belongs to all the world, which alone may be properly named the universal festival, and the birthday of the world.

Of the Life of Moses, B. II. p. 657

Who is there that does not honour that holy seventh day? &c.

Josephus against Apion, B. II. sect. 40

There is not any city of the Grecians, nor any of the barbarians, nor any nation whatsoever, whither our custom of resting on the seventh day hath not come; and by which our fasts, and lighting up lamps, and many of our prohibitions as to our food, are not observed.

Theophilus to Autolycus, II. p. 91

As to the seventh day, all men so call it, &c.

Philoponus, De Creatione, VII. 14. See also V. 19

This is agreed to by all mankind, that there are only seven days; which by a continual circulation compose all time, &c.

Archbp. Usher's Letters concerning the Sabbath, and Observation of the Lord's Day

Of the Slavonians themselves (while they yet continued in their ancient paganism) thus writeth Hermoldus, Chronic. Slavor. Lib. I. cap. 84: The people of the land used to come thither on the second day of the week, with their priest and their prince, to have justice done them.——Let us make a prohibition against the lighting of candles on the *sabbath days*, because neither do the gods want light, nor are men themselves delighted with the smoke that proceeds from them, as says Seneca, Epist. 95. As for you who reproach us with the *sun*, and the *sun's day*, consider how near your own practices are to ours. We are not in this remote from your own god Saturn, and his *sabbaths*, Tertull. ad Nationes, cap. 13. I either blamed the birds, or the terrible omens, or that I had religiously observed Saturn's day, Tibul. Eleg. 3. Lib. 1. Lucian also, in his Ψευδολογιϛὴς, speaks of boys getting leave to play on the *seventh days*, Op. Græcolat. p. 893. Edit. Paris. anno 1615. Ælius Lampridius says of Alexander Severus, that he used to go to the temple at the capitol and other temples upon the *seventh day*. Dio Cassius also mentioning Saturn's day, which name yet he owns was not very ancient among the Greeks, adds, that the custom of computing the time by weeks was derived from the Egyptians [among whom the Jews, who ever used it, lived 215 years] to all mankind, Lib. XXXVII. p. 41, 42. And that this was not a new, but a very ancient custom, Herodotus teaches us, in his second book [long before and beyond the designation of the days of the weeks by the seven planets; nay, probably long before the seven planets were distinctly known; from which some groundlessly deduce them]. Josephus also informs us, Antiq. B. XII. ch. v. sect. 5, that the Samaritans, though they were not Jews, yet did they, from ancient times, observe the *sabbath day;* and, as they elsewhere pretend, B. XI. ch. viii. sect. 6, the *sabbatic year* also.

N. B. This *seventh day* from the creation was so very famous, it seems, in old time among the heathen world, that even the very *seventh day* of the month did sometimes derive an honour to itself therefrom. For which otherwise no reason at all appears upon any good evidence whatsoever.

TEXTS OF THE OLD TESTAMENT

PARALLEL TO

JOSEPHUS' HISTORIES

GENESIS		Book.	ANTIQ. Chap.	Sect.
i.	1—31 }			
ii.	1—3 }	I.	i.	1
	4—25	—	—	2, 3
iii.	1—24	—	—	4
iv.	1—15	—	ii.	1
	16—32	—	—	2
	25	—	—	3
iv.	26 }			
v.	1—32 }	—	iii.	1, 2, 4
vi.	1—7 }			
	8—22	—	—	2
vii.	1—24 }			
viii.	1—22 }	—	—	5, 7, 8
ix.	1—17 }			
	28, 29 }	—	—	8
	20—27	—	—	3
x.	1—5	—	vi.	1
	6—20	—	—	3
	21—32	—	—	4
xi.	1—9	—	iv.	1
	10—32	—	vi.	5
xii.	1—9	—	vii.	1
	10—20	—	viii.	1
xiii.	1—12	—	—	3
	13	—	xi.	1
xiv.	1—12	—	ix.	1
	13—16	—	x.	1
	17—24	—	—	2
xv.	1—21	—	—	3
xvi.	1—15	—	—	4
	16— }			
xvii.	1—27 }	—	—	5
xviii.	1—xix. 38	—	xi.	2
	9—15	—	x.	5
	23—33	—	xi.	3
xix.	11, &c.	—	—	4
xx.	1—18	—	xii.	1
xxii.	1—19	—	xiii.	1—4
xxiii.	1—20	—	xiv.	1
xxiv.	1—67	—	xvi.	1—3
xxv.	1—4	—	xv.	1
	7, 8	—	xvii.	1
xxv.	12—18	—	xii.	4
	21—28	—	xviii.	1
	29—34	II.	i.	1
xxvi.	1—31	I.	xviii.	2
xxvii.	1—46	—	—	4—8
xxviii.	1—22	—	xix.	1—3
	6—9	—	xviii.	8

GENESIS		Book.	ANTIQ. Chap.	Sect.
xxix.	1—35	I.	xix.	4, &c.
	31—35	VII.	xi.	5
xxx.	25—43 }			
xxxi.	1—55 }	I.	xix.	9—11
xxxii.	1—32	—	xx.	1, 2
xxxiii.	1—16	—	—	3
xxxiv.	1—31	—	xxi.	1
	25, 26	IV.	vi.	10
xxxv.	1—15	I.	xxi.	2
	16—26	—	—	3
	27—29	—	xxii.	1
xxxvi.	6—8	II.	i.	1
	1—43	—	—	2
xxxvii.	1—16	—	ii.	1
	17—36	—	iii.	1—4
xxxix.	1—23	—	iv.	1—5
xl.	1—23	—	v.	1—3
xli.	1—45	—	—	4—6
	46—57	—	vi.	1
xlii.	1—28	—	—	2—4
	28—38 }			
xliii.	1—14 }	—	—	5
	15—34	—	—	6
xliv.	1—34	—	—	7—9
xlv.	1—28	—	—	10
xlvi.	1—34	—	vii.	1—5
xlvii.	1—31	—	—	6, 7
xlviii.	1—22 }			
xlix.	1—33 }	II.	viii.	1, 2
l.	1—26 }			
EXODUS				
i.	1—22	—	ix.	1, 2
ii.	1—15	—	—	3
	23	—	xiii.	1
ii.	15—25	—	xi.	1
iii.	1—10	—	xii.	1
	14, 15	—	—	4
	11—22	—	—	2
iv.	1—9	—	—	3
	10—31	—	xiii.	1
v.	1—23	—	—	4
vii.	1—13	—	—	3
	14—x. 29	—	xiv.	1
viii.	1—15	—	—	2
	16—19	—	—	3
	20—32	—	—	3
ix.	1—7	—	—	3
	8—12	—	—	4
	13—35	—	—	4

EXODUS		Book.	ANTIQ. Chap.	Sect.
x.	1—20	—	—	4
	21—29	—	—	5
xi.	1—10	—	—	6
xii.	1—51	III.	x.	5
	37—42	—	xv.	1
xiii.	1—22	—	—	1
xiv.	1—31	{ —	—	1
		{ —	xv.	3
	10—12	—	—	4
	13—15	—	xvi.	1
	13—31	—	—	2, 3
xv.	1—21	—	—	4
	22—26	—	i.	1
xvi.	27 } 1—36 }	—	—	3—6
xvii.	1—7	—	—	7
	8—16	—	ii.	1—5
xviii.	1—12	—	iii.	1
	13—27	—	iv.	1, 2
xix.	1—14	—	v.	1
	15—20	—	—	2
	21—25	—	—	3, 4
xx.	1—17	—	—	5
	18—xxiii. 33	—	—	6
xxi. xxii. xxiii.	See under Deuteronomy.			
xxiii.	14—17	—	x.	4
xxiv.	1—18	—	—	8
xxv. xxvi. xxvii. xxxv. } xxxvi. xxxvii. xxxviii. }		—	vi.	1
xxviii. xxix. xxx. xl. and } Levit. &c. passim. }		III.	vi.—x.	
LEVITICUS				
vi.	1—7	IV.	viii.	29
vii.	15—27	III.	xi.	2
viii.	1—35 } 14—22 }	VIII.	viii.	4
ix.	1—24 }	IV.	xi.	1
x.	1—20	—	xii.	2
xi.	1—47	—	—	2
xii.	1—8	—	—	5
xiii. xiv. xv.		—	xi.	3
xvi.	1—34	—	x.	3
xvii.	1—16	—	xi.	2
xviii.	1—30	—	xii.	1
xix.	19	IV.	viii.	11
	13, 14, 19 } 23—25 }	—	—	19,20 31,38
xx.	1—27	III.	xii.	1
xxi.	1—24	IV.	viii.	23
	20	—	—	40
xxii.	1—33	—	—	2
xxiii.	4—14	—	x.	5
	26—32	—	—	3
xxiv.	10—20	—	viii.	6, 33
	19, 20	—	—	35
xxv.	1—55	III.	xii.	3
	35	IV.	viii.	25
xxvii.	30—34	—	—	8
	14	—	—	32

NUMBERS		Book.	ANTIQ. Chap.	Sect.
i.	1—54	III.	xii.	4
ii.	1—34	—	—	4
iii.	1—51	—	—	4
v.	1—31	—	xi.	3
	11—31	—	—	1, 6
vi.	1—27	IV.	iv.	4
ix.	1—14	III.	xii.	6
	15—23	—	—	5
x.	1—10	—	—	6
xi.	11—36 } 1—35 }	—	xiii.	1
xiii.	1—33	{ I. { III.	viii. xiv.	3 1, 2
xiv.	1—5	—	—	3
	6—10	—	—	4
	11—39	—	xv.	1—3
	40—45	IV.	i.	1—3
xv.	1—41	—	{ iv. { viii.	4 13
xvi.	1—40	—	{ ii. { iii.	1—4 1—4
	41—50	—	iv.	1
xvii.	1—13	—	—	2
xviii.	1—32	IV.	iv.	4
xix.	1—22	—	—	6
xx.	1—13	IV.	iv.	6
	14—21	—	—	5
	22—29	—	—	7
xxi.	21—35	—	v.	1—3
xxii.—xxiv.		—	vi.	1—5
xxv.	1—15	—	—	6—13
	16—18	—	vii.	1
xxvii.	12—23	—	—	2
xxviii.	1—31	III.	x.	1
xxix.	12—40	—	—	4
xxxi.	1—54	IV.	vii.	1
xxxii.	1—42	—	—	3
	8—15	III.	xv.	1—3
xxxiii.	37—39	IV.	iv.	7
xxxv.	1—34	{ IV. { —	iv. vii.	3 4
xxxvi.	1—13	{ III. { IV. { —	xii. vii. viii.	3 5 1
DEUTERONOMY				
i.	4	IV.	v.	2
	22—39	III.	xiv.	1, 2
	34—40	—	xv.	1—3
	40—46	IV.	i.	1—3
ii.	1—8	—	iv.	5
	34—37	—	v.	1, 2
iii.	1—17	—	—	2, 3
iv.—xii.		—	viii.	{ 2—5 { 13,44
xiii.	1—18	—	—	45
xiv.	14—29	—	—	8
xv.	12—18 }			
Exod. xxi.	1—11 }	—	—	28

DEUTERONOMY		ANTIQ. Book.	Chap.	Sect.
xvi.	1—17	IV.	viii.	7
xvii.	18—20 } 8—13 }	—	—	14
xix.	6— } 15—21 }	—	—	15
xvii.	14—20	—	—	17
xix. xxvii.	14— } 17— }	—	—	18
xix.	11—13 } 19—21 }	—		33
xx.	1—9	—	—	16
	10—20	—	—	41
xxi.	10—14 } 15—17 }	—	—	23
	18—21	—	—	24
xxii.	1—3	—	—	29
	5, 9	—	—	43
	9, 10	—	—	20
	11	—	—	11
	13—30	—	viii.	23
xxiii.	1, 2, 8, 9	—	— {	23, 40 / 42
	17, 18	—	—	9
	19	—	—	25
	24, 25	—	—	21
xxiv.	1—5	—	—	23
	6, 10—13	—	—	26
	7	—	—	27
	14, 15	—	—	38
	16	—	—	39
	19—25	—	—	21
xxv.	4—	—	—	21
	5—10	—	—	23
	17—19	—	—	44
xxvi.	12—19	—	—	22
	11—26	—	—	44
xxvii.	17	—	—	18
	18	—	—	31
xxxi.	1—30	—	—	44
	9—13	—	—	12
xxxii.	1—52	—	—	44, 47
xxxiii.	1—29	—	—	47
xxxiv.	1—7	—	—	49
	8	—	—	48
	10—12	—	—	49

JOSHUA		Book.	Chap.	Sect.
ii. iii.	1—24 } 1—14 }	V.	i.	1
	15—17	—	—	3
iv.	1—24	—	—	4
v.	8—10	—	—	11
vi.	1—19	—	—	5, 6
	20—27	—	—	7
	26	—	—	8
	17—19	—	—	9
vii.	1, 16—22	—	—	10
	2—5	—	—	12

JOSHUA		ANTIQ. Book.	Chap.	Sect.
vii.	6—9	—	—	13
	10—15 } 23—26 }	—	—	14
viii. xviii.	1—29 } 30—35 } 1— }	—	—	19
ix.	1—19	—	—	16
x.	1, 10 } 11—27 }	—	—	17
	15, 28 } 24 }	—		18, 20
xii. xiii. xxii.	8—32 } 1—9 }	—	—	20
xiii. xviii.	1, 33 } 1—28 }	—	—	21
xiv. xv. xvi. xvii. xix.	} per tot.	V.	i.	22, 23
xx. xxi.	} per tot.	—	—	24
xxii.	1—6	—	—	25
	10—34	—	—	26, 27
xxiii.	1—16	—	—	28
xxiv.	29, 30	—	—	29

JUDGES		Book.	Chap.	Sect.
i.	1—4	—	ii.	1, 7
	5—8	—	—	2
	9—15	—	—	3
ii. iii.	16—36 } 20—26 } 1—7 }	—	—	4, 6
	8—	—	iii.	2
	9—11	—	—	3
	12—14	—	iv.	1
	15—26	—	—	2
iv.	27—31 } 1— }	—	—	3
	1—3	—	v.	1
	21, 22	—	—	4
v.	1, 24 } 1—31 }	—	—	2, 3
vi.	1—6	—	vi.	1
	11—35	—	—	2
vii.	1—8	—	—	3
	9—14	—	—	4
viii.	15—25 } 4—21 }	—	—	5
	1—3	—	—	6
	22—32	—	—	7
ix.	1—6	—	vii.	1
	7—21	—	—	2
	22—33	—	—	3
	34—49	—	—	4
	50—57	—	—	5
x.	3—5	—	—	6
	7—18	—	—	7

JUDGES		Book.	ANTIQ. Chap.	Sect.
xi.	1—11	V.	vii.	8
	12—28	—	—	9
	30, 31, 34, 40	—	—	10
xii.	1—6	—	—	11
	7	—	—	12
	8—10	—	—	13
	11, 12	—	—	14
	13—15	—	—	15
xiii.	1	—	{ —	7
			{ viii.	1
	2—7	—	—	2
	8—23	—	—	3
	24, 25	—	—	4
xiv.	1—6	—	—	5
	7—19	—	—	6
xv.	1—6	—	—	7
	7—17	—	—	8
	18, 19	—	—	9
xvi.	2, 3	—	—	10
	1, 4 }	—	—	4, 11
	4—21 }			
	22—31	—	—	12
xviii.	1—31	—	iii.	1
xix.	1—30	—	ii.	8
xx.	1—14	—	—	9
	17—25	—	—	10
	26—48 }	—	—	11
xxi.	8—14 }			
	13—24	—	—	12
RUTH				
i.	1—18	—	ix.	1
	19—22 }	—	—	2
ii.	1—23 }			
iii.	1—13	—	—	3
	14—18 }	—	—	4
iv.	1—22 }			
1 SAMUEL				
i.	1—17	—	x.	2
	18—28 }	—	—	3
ii.	20, 21 }			
	12—36	—	—	1
iii.	1—21	—	—	4
iv.	1, 2	—	xi.	1
	3—11	—	—	2
	12—18	—	—	3
	19—22	—	—	4
v.	1—12	VI.	i.	1
vi.	1—11	—	—	2
	12—18	—	—	3
	19—21 }	—	—	4
vii.	1, 2 }			
	3—6	—	ii.	1
	7—12	—	—	2
	13, 14	—	—	3
	15—17	—	iii.	1
viii.	1—4	—	—	2
	5, 6	—	—	3
	7—9	—	—	4

1 SAMUEL		Book.	ANTIQ. Chap.	Sect.
viii.	10—18	—	—	5
	19—22	—	—	6
ix.	1—16	—	iv.	1
	17—27 }	—	—	2
x.	1—9 }			
	10—16	—	—	3
	17—19	—	—	4
	19—24	—	—	5
	25—27	—	—	6
xi.	1—3	—	v.	1
	4—9	—	—	2
	7—13	—	—	3
	14, 15	—	—	4
xii.	1—5	—	—	5
	6—25	—	—	6
xiii.	1—7 }	—	vi.	1
	16—23 }			
	8—23 }	—	—	2
xiv.	1—16 }			
	17—31	—	—	3
	32—35	—	—	4
	36—45	—	—	5
	46—52	—	—	6
xv.	1—3	—	vii.	1
	4, 5, 7—9	—	—	2
	6	—	—	3
	10—23	—	—	4
	24—35	—	—	5
xvi.	1—13	—	viii.	1
	13—23	—	—	2
xvii.	1—11	—	ix.	1
	12—32	—	—	2
	33—39	—	—	3
	39—44	—	—	4
	45—54	—	—	5
xviii.	6—16	—	x.	1
	7	—	xii.	2
	17—26	—	x.	2
	27—30	—	—	3
xix.	1—3	—	xi.	1
	4—7	—	—	2
	8—10	—	—	3
	11—17	—	—	4
	18—24	—	—	5
xx.	1—3	—	—	6
	4—8	—	—	7
	9—23	—	—	8
	24—34	—	—	9
	35—42	—	—	10
xxi.	1—9	—	xii.	1
	10—15	—	—	2
xxii.	1—4	—	—	3
	5—10	—	—	4
	11—16	—	—	5
	17—19	—	—	6
	20—23	—	—	8
xxiii.	1—15	—	xiii.	1
	16—25	—	—	2

1 SAMUEL

		Book.	Chap.	Sect.
xxiii.	26—28	VI.	xiii.	3
	29 }			4
xxiv.	1—22 }	—	—	
xxv.	1	—	—	5
	2—13	—	—	6
	14—35	—	—	7
	36—44	—	—	8
xxvi.	1—25	—	—	9
xxvii.	1—12	—	—	10
xxviii.	12	—	xiv.	1
	6—19	—	—	2
	20—25	—	—	3
xxix.	1—11	—	—	1, 5
xxx.	1—31	—	—	6
xxxi.	1—7	—	—	7
	8—13	—	—	8

2 SAMUEL

		Book.	Chap.	Sect.
i.	6—10	—	—	7
	1—27	VII.	i.	1
ii.	1—7	—	—	2
	8—32 }			
iii.	1 }	—	—	3
	2—21	—	—	4
	22—27	—	—	5
	28—39	—	—	6
iv.	1—12	—	ii.	1
v.	1—5	—	—	2
	6—10	—	iii.	1, 2
	14—16	—	—	3
	17—25	—	iv.	1
vi.	1—19	—	—	2
	14, 20—23	—	—	3
vii.	1—29	—	—	4
viii.	1—4	—	v.	1
	5—8	—	—	2, 3
	9—18	—	—	4
ix.	1—13	—	—	5
x.	1—6	—	vi.	1
	7—14	—	—	2
	15—19 }			
xi.	1 }	—	—	3
	1—17	—	vii.	1
	18—27	—	—	2
xii.	1—15	—	—	3
	11	—	ix.	5
	15—25	—	vii.	4
	26—31	—	—	5
xiii.	1—20	—	viii.	1
	21—29	—	—	2
	29—38	—	—	3
	39— xiv. 23	—	—	4
xv.	1—11	—	ix.	1
	12—37	—	—	2
xvi.	1—4	—	—	3
	5—14	—	—	4
	15—23	—	—	5

2 SAMUEL

		Book.	Chap.	Sect.
xvii.	1—14	VII.	ix.	6
	15—22	—	—	7
	23—29	—	—	8
xviii.	1—5	—	x.	1
	6—17	—	—	2
	17, 18	—	—	3
	19—27	—	—	4
	28—33 }			
xix.	1—8 }	—	—	5
	9—15	—	xi.	1
	16—23	—	—	2
	24—30	—	—	3
	31—40	—	—	4
	41—43	—	—	5
xx.	1—6	—	—	6
	7—15	—	—	7
	16—26	—	—	8
xxi.	1—17	—	xii.	1
	18—22	—	—	2
xxii. xxiii.	1—7	—	—	3
	8—39	—	—	4
xxiv.	1—14	—	xiii.	1, 2
	15—17	—	—	3
	18—25	—	—	4

1 KINGS

		Book.	Chap.	Sect.
i.	1—4	—	xiv.	3
	5—21	—	—	4
	22—40	—	—	5
	41—53	—	—	6
ii.	1—9	—	xv.	1
	10, 11	—	—	2, 3
	12	VIII.	i.	1
	13—21	—	—	2
	22—27	—	—	3
	28—35	—	—	4
	36—46	—	—	5
iii.	1 }	—	ii.	1
	4—15 }		vi.	1
iv.	1—19	—	—	3
	20—28	—	—	4
	29—34	—	—	5
v.	1—18	—	—	6, 7, 9
vi.	1—38	—	iii.	1, 2
	8	—	—	1
vii.	1—19	—	v.	1, 2
	13—51	—	iii.	2—9
viii.	1—9	—	iv.	1
	10—21	—	—	2
	22—66	—	—	3—5
ix.	1—9	—	—	6
	11—14	—	v.	3
	15—19	—	vi.	1
	20—22	—	—	3
	26—28	—	—	4
x.	1—13	—	—	5, 6
	14—23	—	vii.	1, 4
	24—26	—	—	3

1 KINGS		Book.	ANTIQ. Chap.	Sect.
xi.	1—13	VIII.	vii	5
	14—25	—	—	6
	26—40	—	—	7
	41—43	—	{ —	8
			{ viii.	1
xii.	1—15	—	—	2
	16—20	—	—	3
	25—33	—	—	4
xiii.	1—10	—	—	5
	1—6	X.	iv.	4
	11—34	VIII.	ix.	1
xiv.	1—20	—	xi.	1, 3, 4
	21—26	—	x.	2
	27—31	—	—	4
xv.	1—9	—	xi.	3
	9—15	—	xii.	1
	16—22	—	—	4
	27—34	—	—	3
xvi.	1—7	—	—	3, 4
	9—24	—	—	5
	29	—	—	6
	30—33	—	xiii.	1
xvii.	1—16	—	—	2
	17—24	—	—	3
xviii.	1—15	—	—	4
	16—46	—	—	5, 6
xix.	1—21	—	—	7
xx.	1—9	—	xiv.	1
	10—21	—	—	2
	22—28	—	—	3
	29—34	—	—	4
	35—43	—	—	5
xxi.	1—29	—	{ xiii.	8
			{ xv.	4
xxii.	1—5	—	—	3
	6—28	—	—	4
	29—40	—	—	5, 6
	40, 51—53	IX.	ii.	1
	41—50	—	{ iii.	2
			{ iv.	1

2 KINGS		Book.	ANTIQ. Chap.	Sect.
i.	1—16	—	ii.	1
	17, 18 }			
ii.	1—15 }	—	—	2
iii.	1—3 }			
	4—27	—	iii.	1, 2
iv.	1—7	—	iv.	2
vi.	8—23	—	—	3
	24—33 }			
vii.	1, 2 }	—	—	4
	3—20	—	—	5
viii.	7—15	—	—	6
	16—29	—	v.	13
ix.	1—37	—	vi.	1—4
x.	1—14	—	—	5
	15—31	—	—	6
	32—36	—	viii.	1

2 KINGS		Book.	ANTIQ. Chap.	Sect.
xi.	1—12	IX.	vii.	1, 2
	13—16	—	—	3
	17—21	—	—	4
xii.	2	—	—	3
	4—16	—	—	2
	17—21	—	—	4
xiii.	1—9	—	—	5
	10—21	—	—	6
	22—25	—	—	7
xiv.	1—7	—	ix.	1
	8—10	—	—	2
	11—20	—	—	3
	23—28	—	x.	1
	29	—	—	3
xv.	1—4	—	—	3
	5—7	—	—	4
	8—29	—	xi.	1
	32—35	—	—	2
	36—38	—	xii.	1
xvi.	1—5	—	—	1, 2
	7—20	—	—	3
xvii.	1, 2	—	xiii.	1
	3—24	—	xiv.	1
	25—41	—	—	3
xviii.	1—7	—	xiii.	1
	8	—	—	3
	13—16	X.	i.	1
	17—37	—	—	2
xix.	1—8	—	—	3
	9—34	—	—	4
	35—37	—	—	5
xx.	1—11	—	ii.	1
	12—19	—	—	2
	20, 21	—	iii.	1
xxi.	1—16	—	—	1
	17, 18	—	—	2
	19—26	—	iv.	1
xxii.	1, 2	—	—	1
	3—20	—	—	2
xxiii.	1—14	—	—	3
	15—20	—	—	4
	21—27	—	—	5
	28—30	X.	v.	1
	31—37	—	—	2
xxiv.	1—4	—	vi.	1
	8—16	—	—	3
	17—20	—	vii.	1
			{ —	3, 4
xxv.	1—26	—	{ viii.	1
			{ ix.	1
	7	—	—	2, 7

1 CHRONICLES		Book.	ANTIQ. Chap.	Sect.
ii.	13 }			
iii.	1—9 }	VII.	viii.	3
vi.	6, 7	VIII.	i.	3
viii.	34	VI.	v.	1
x.	1—7	—	xiv.	7
	8—12	—	—	8

1 CHRONICLES		Book.	Antiq. Chap.	Sect.
x.	13, 14	VI.	xiv.	9
xi.	1—3	{VII.	i.	2
		—	xii.	4
	4—9	—	iii.	1, 2
xiii.	1—14	—	iv.	2
xiv.	3—7	—	iii.	3
	8—17	—	iv.	1
xv.	13	—	—	2
xvii.	1—27	—	—	4
xviii.	1—4	—	v.	1
	5—8	—	—	2, 3
	9—17	—	—	4
xix.	1—7	—	vi.	1
	8—15	—	—	2
	16—19	—	—	3
xx.	1—3	—	—	5
xxi.	1—13	—	xiii.	1
	14—17	—	—	3
	18—30}	—	—	4
xxii.	1}			
	2—5	—	xiv.	1
	6—19	—	—	2
xxiii. xxiv. } xxv. xxvi. }	per tot.	—	—	7
xxvii.	1—34	—	—	8
xxviii.	1—10	—	—	9
	11—21}	—	—	10
xxix.	1—8 }			
	9—25	—	—	11
	23—25	VIII.	i.	1
	26—30	VII.	xv.	3
2 CHRONICLES				
i.	3—10	VIII.	ii.	1
	13—17	—	—	4
ii.	1—10	—	—	6
	11—16	—	—	7
	17, 18	—	—	9
iii.	1, 2	—	iii.	1
	3—17}	—		2—9
iv.	1—22}			
v.	1—12	—	iv.	1
	13, 14}	—	—	2
vi.	1—11}			
	12—42	—	—	3
vii.	1—3	—	—	4
	8—10	—	—	5
	12—22	—	—	6
viii.	1	—	v.	1
	2	—	—	3
	2—6	—	vi.	1
	7—9	—	—	3
	17, 18	—	—	4
ix.	1—12	—	—	5, 6
	13—22	—	vii.	1
	23—25	—	—	3
	27	—	—	4
	29—31	—	—	8

2 CHRONICLES		Book.	Antiq. Chap.	Sect.
	31	—	viii.	1
x.	1—15	—	—	2
	16—19	—	—	3
xi.	5—23	—	x.	1
xii.	1—4	—	—	2
	5—12	—	—	3
	10—16	—	—	4
xiii.	1—12	—	xi.	2
	13—20	—	—	3
xiv.	1, 2	—	—	3
	1—5	—	xii.	1
xv.	12—15}	—	—	2
	1—19}			
xvi.	1—6	—	—	4
xvii.	1—6	—	xv.	1
	7—19	—	—	2
xviii.	1—3	—	—	3
	4—27	—	—	4
	28—34	—	—	5, 6
xix.	1—11	IX.	i.	1
xx.	1—37	—	{—	2, 3
			{iii.	2
xxi.	1—20	—	{iv.	1
			{v.	1
	12—15	—	—	2
	16—19}	—	—	3
xxii.	1}			
	5—9	—	vi.	1—4
	10	—	vii.	1
xxiii.	1—11	—	—	2
	12—15	—	—	3
	16—21	—	—	4
xxiv.	4—14	—	viii.	2
	15—22	—	—	3
	23—27	—	—	4
xxv.	1—13	—	ix.	1
	14—19	—	—	2
	20—28	—	—	3
xxvi.	1—15	—	x.	3
	16—23	—	—	4
xxvii.	1—6	—	xi.	2
	7—9	—	xii.	1
xxviii.	1—8	—	—	1
	9—15	—	—	2
	16—27	—	—	3
xxix.	1—11	—	xiii.	1
	12—36	—	—	2
xxx.	1—12	—	—	2
	13—27	—	—	3
xxxi.	1—21	—	—	3
xxxii.	1—10	X.	i.	1
	11—19	—	—	2
	20	—	—	3
	21—23	—	—	5
	24—30	—	ii.	1
	31	—	—	2
	32, 33	—	iii.	1

2 CHRONICLES		Book.	ANTIQ. Chap.	Sect.
xxxiii.	1—10	X.	iii.	1
	11—20	—	—	2
	21—25 }	—	iv.	1
xxxiv.	1—7 }			
	5—7	—	—	5
	8—28	—	—	2
	29—33	—	—	3
xxxv.	1—21	—	{ — / vii.	5 / 3
	21—27	—	v.	1
xxxvi.	1—8	—	{ — / vi.	2 / 1
	9, 10	—	—	3
	11, 12	—	vii.	1
	21—23	XI.	i.	1
ISAIAH				
xiv.	28—32	IX.	viii.	3
xxxvi.	1	X.	i.	1
	2—22	—	—	2
xxxvii.	1—8	—	—	3
	9—35	—	—	4
	36, 37	—	—	5
xxxviii.	1—22	—	ii.	1
xxxix.	1—8	—	—	2
xliv.	28 }	XI.	i.	2
xlv.	1 }			
JEREMIAH				
i.	2 }	X.	v.	1
xxv.	3 }			
	11 }	XI.	i.	2
xxix.	10 }			
xxvi.	8—24	—	vi.	2
xxxii.	4	—	vii.	2
xxxiv.	3	—	—	2
xxxvii.	11—21	X.	vii.	3
xxxviii.	1—28 }	—	—	4—6
xxxix.	1 }			
	1—10	—	viii.	1
	13	—	—	2
xl.	1—16 }			
xli.	1—18 }	—	ix.	1, 5
xlii.	1—22 }			
xliii.	1—7	—	—	6
	8—13	—	—	7
lii.	1—30	—	viii.	2—7
EZEKIEL				
xii.	13	—	vii.	2
xvii.	20	—	—	2
xviii.	20	IX.	ix.	1
DANIEL				
i.	3—7	X.	x.	1
	8—20	—	—	2
ii.	1—49	—	—	3, 4
iii.	1—30	—	—	5
iv.	1—37	—	—	6
v.	1—31	—	xi.	2—4
vi.	1—3	—	—	4
	4—28	—	—	5, 6

DANIEL		Book.	ANTIQ. Chap.	Sect.
viii.	1—27	—	—	7
ix.	26, 27	—	—	7
JONAH				
i.—iv.		IX.	x.	2
NAHUM				
ii.	8—13	—	xi.	3
EZRA				
i.	1, 2	IX.	i.	1
	3, 4	—	—	2
	5—11	—	—	3
ii.	1—70	—	{ — / iii.	3 / 10
iii.	1—13	—	{ ii. / iv.	1 / 1, 2
iv.	1—5	—	{ i. / iv.	3 / 3
	6—24	—	{ ii. / iv.	1 / 4
	17—24	—	ii.	2
v.	3—5	—	iv.	4
	6—17	—	—	5
vi.	1—5	—	—	6
	6—22	—	—	7—9
vii.	1—26	—	v.	1
	27, 28	XI.	v.	2
viii.	35, 36	—	—	2
ix.	1—15	—	—	3
x.	1—44	—	—	4
3 ESDRAS				
ii.	1—4	—	i.	1
	5—7	—	—	2
	8	—	—	3
	9—24	—	ii.	1
	25—30	—	—	2
iii.	1—12	—	iii.	2
	13—24	—	—	3
iv.	1—12	—	—	4
	13—33	—	—	5
	33—41	—	—	6
	41—46	—	—	7
	47—60	—	—	8
	61—63	—	—	9
v.	1—46	—	—	10
	47—55	—	iv.	1
	56—73	—	—	2, 3
vi.	1—5	—	—	6
	6—22	—	—	5—9
	23—26	—	—	6
	27— vii. 15	—	—	7—9
viii.	1—24	—	v.	1
	25—67	—	—	2
	68—91	—	—	3
	92—ix. 36	—	—	4
ix.	37—55	—	—	5
NEHEMIAH				
ii.	1—8	—	—	6
	9—vii. 73	—	{ — / iii.	7 / 10

		ANTIQ. Book.	Chap.	Sect.
NEHEMIAH				
iv.	1—23 ⎫			
vi.	1—16 ⎬ . . . —	v.	8
xiii.	10—31 ⎭			
ESTHER				
i.	1—22 . . . XI.	vi.	1
ii.	1—20 . . . —	—	2
	21—23 ⎫			
xii.	1—6 ⎬ . . —	—	4
iii.	1—9 . . . —	—	5
	10—15 ⎫			
xiii.	1—7 ⎬ . . —	—	6
iv.	1—16 . . . —	—	7
	17 ⎫			
xiii.	8—18 ⎬ . —	—	8
xiv.	1—19 ⎭			
v.	1—8 ⎫			
xv.	1—16 ⎬ . . —	—	9
v.	9—vi. 14 . . . —	—	10
vii.	1—10 . . . —	—	11
viii.	1—17 ⎫			
xvi.	1—24 ⎬ . . XI.	vi.	12
ix.	1—x. 3 . . . —	—	13
1 MACCABEES				
i.	1—9 . . . XI.	viii.	7
	10—64 . . . XII.	v.	1—3
ii.	1—14 . . . —	vi.	1
	15—48 . . . —	—	2
	49—70 . . . —	—	3
iii.	1—9 . . . —	—	4
	10—26 . . . —	vii.	1
	27—37 . . . —	—	2
	38—60 . . . —	—	3
iv.	1—25 . . . —	—	4
	26—35 . . . —	—	5
	36—55 . . . —	—	6
	56—61 . . . —	—	7
v.	1—15 . . . —	viii.	1
	16—23 . . . —	—	2
	24—36 . . . —	—	3
	37—45 . . . —	—	4
	46—54 . . . —	—	5
	55—68 . . . —	—	6
vi.	1—13 . . . —	ix.	1
	14—17 . . . —	—	2
	18—46 . . . —	—	3
	47—54 . . . —	—	5
	55—59 . . . —	—	6
	60—63 . . . —	—	7
vii.	1—7 . . . —	x.	1
	1—20 . . . —	—	2
	21—25 . . . —	—	3
	26—32 . . . —	—	4
	33—50 . . . —	—	5
viii.	1—32 . . . —	—	6
ix.	1—10 . . . —	xi.	1
	11—22 . . . —	—	2
	23—31 . . . XIII.	i.	1
	32—36 . . . —	—	2
	37—42 . . . —	—	4

		ANTIQ. Book.	Chap.	Sect.
1 MACCABEES				
	42—53 . . . XIII.	i.	3
	54—57 . . . XII.	x.	6
	57—69 . . . XIII.	i.	5
	70—73 . . . —	—	6
x.	1—14 . . . —	ii.	1
	15—20 . . . —	—	2
	21—45 . . . —	—	3
	46—50 . . . —	—	4
	51—58 . . . —	iv.	1
	59—66 . . . —	—	2
x.	67—73 . . . XIII.	iv.	3
	74—89 . . . —	—	4
xi.	1—7 . . . —	—	5
	8—11 . . . —	—	6
	12, 13 . . . —	—	7
	14—18 . . . —	—	8
	19—38 . . . —	—	9
	39, 40 . . . —	v.	1
	41—44 . . . —	—	2
	45—56 . . . —	—	3
	57—59 . . . —	—	4
	60—62 . . . —	—	5
	63—66 . . . —	—	6
	67—74 . . . —	—	7
xii.	1—23 . . . —	—	8
	24—34 . . . —	—	10
	35—38 . . . —	—	11
	39—45 . . . —	vi.	1
	46—51 . . . —	—	2
	52, 53 ⎫			
xiii.	1—6 ⎬ . . —	—	3
	7—11 . . . —	—	3, 4
	12—20 . . . —	—	4, 5
	21—30 . . . —	—	5, 6
	30—33 ⎫			
	41—50 ⎬ . . —	—	6, 7
xiv.	1—3 . . . —	v.	11
	4—24 . . . —	vii.	3
xv.	15—24 . . . —	—	3
	37 . . . —	—	2
xvi.	1—10 . . . —	—	3
	11—24 . . . —	—	4
2 MACCABEES				
iv.	7 . . . XI.	iv.	10
	7—50 . . . XII.	v.	1
v.	1 . . . —	—	2
	11—27 ⎫			
vi.	1—vii. 42 ⎬ . —	—	4
viii.	1—7 . . . —	vi.	4
	8—36 . . . —	vii.	3
ix.	1—29 . . . —	ix.	1
x.	1—8 . . . —	vii.	6
	9—xi. 38 . . . —	ix.	4
xii.	1—45 . . . —	⎧ —	7
			⎩ x.	1
xiii.	1—26 . . . —	ix.	4, 7
xiv.	3—11 . . . —	x.	1, 3
	12—46 . . . —	—	4
xv.	1—37 . . . —	—	5

A HARMONY

OF

THE NUMBERING SYSTEMS IN THE GREEK AND ENGLISH EDITIONS
OF THE WORKS OF FLAVIUS JOSEPHUS

by

Neal Windham

This work is designed for the student who already owns or would like to purchase a copy of the works of Flavius Josephus in English. A very popular translation is William Whiston's *Josephus* (Grand Rapids, Mich.: Kregel, 1960).

The plan of the work is to make usable the various references to the works of Josephus which appear in Greek-English lexicons such as the Bauer-Arndt-Gingrich *Greek-English Lexicon of the New Testament and Other Early Christian Literature* (Chicago: University of Chicago Press, 1957). This is accomplished through parallelling the chapter and paragraph divisions of the English translation with the verse and divisions in the Greek text.

Each page is divided into three columns. The Roman numerals (at the left of each column) indicate the chapter in which the reference will appear. (The chapters are the same in both the Greek and English editions.) The center number shows the paragraph division of the English translation. The final number (to the right of the column) gives the corresponding Greek verse. The book divisions are very obvious.

Not all of the paragraph divisions are included in these listings. However, it is fairly easy to locate the verse without much difficulty in most cases. For instance, if you are looking for a reference in Book XV of the Antiquities, (specifically XV, 102) you would find that verse 96 corresponds with chapter IV, paragraph 2 of the English translation and verse 108 of the Greek corresponds with chapter V, paragraph 1 of the English. Now, there are twelve verse divisions between verses 96 and 108. Since verse 102 lies right in the middle, you would approximate the central point between these two reference points and begin looking for your word. Since the translation may be an old one, you may have difficulty locating the exact reference, but usually there will be no problem.

These listings include Antiquities of the Jews, Wars of the Jews, the Life of Flavius Josephus, and Flavius Josephus Against Apion. These are the works most commonly cited in lexicons. The abbreviations may appear in Latin. Such abbreviations have been given with the various titles as they appear in the text. The order of the works is as follows: Antiquities, pp. 748; Wars, pp. 751; Life of Flavius Josephus pp. 753 and Flavius Josephus Against Apion, p. 753.

THE HARMONY

THE LIFE OF FLAVIUS JOSEPHUS
(Commonly abbreviated Vi)

FLAVIUS JOSEPHUS AGAINST APION
(Commonly abbreviated C. Ap.)

BOOK I

INDEX